Congratulations...

on your purchase of the 2008 edition of the
most complete interstate highway services guide
ever printed!®

the Next EXIT® will save time, money and frustration.
This travel tool will help you find services along the USA
Interstate Highway System like nothing
you have ever used.

PO Box 888
Garden City, UT 84028
www.theNextEXIT.com

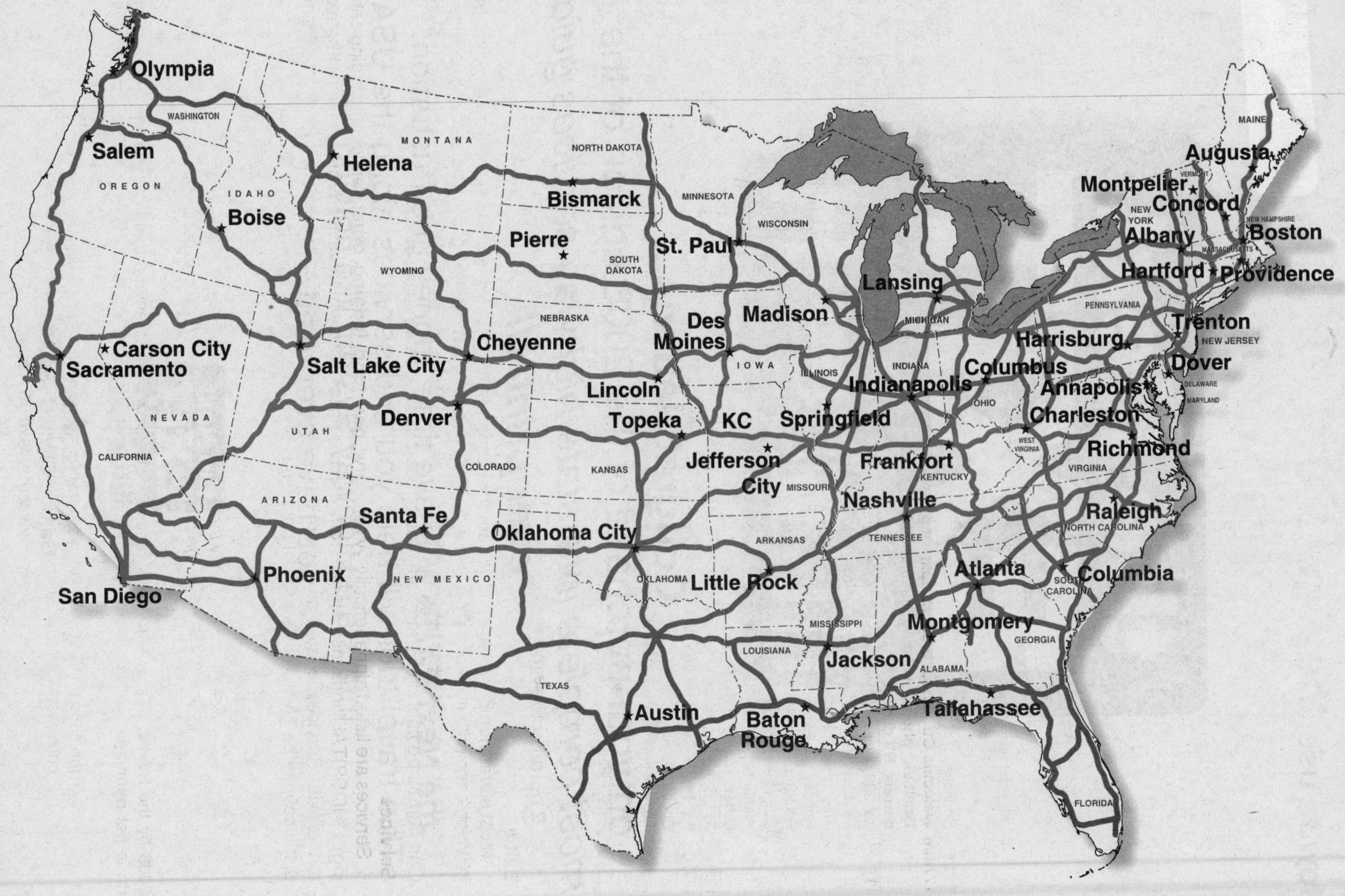

Augusta

Boston

Montpelier Concord

Albany Providence

MAINE

NEW HAMPSHIRE

Hartford Trenton

NEW YORK

Dover

NEW JERSEY

MARYLAND

PENNSYLVANIA

DELAWARE

Harrisburg

Columbus

Annapolis

Charleston

Richmond

VIRGINIA

Raleigh

NORTH CAROLINA

Columbia

SOUTH CAROLINA

FLORIDA

OHIO

WEST VIRGINIA

Indianapolis

Frankfort

KENTUCKY

Nashville

TENNESSEE

Atlanta

GEORGIA

Montgomery

ALABAMA

Tallahassee

Lansing

MICHIGAN

INDIANA

ILLINOIS

Springfield

KC

Jefferson City

MISSOURI

ARKANSAS

Little Rock

MISSISSIPPI

Jackson

LOUISIANA

Baton Rouge

Madison

WISCONSIN

Des Moines

IOWA

St. Paul

MINNESOTA

Topeka

Lincoln

KANSAS

Oklahoma City

OKLAHOMA

Austin

TEXAS

Bismarck

NORTH DAKOTA

Pierre

SOUTH DAKOTA

NEBRASKA

Cheyenne

WYOMING

MONTANA

Helena

Salt Lake City

UTAH

Denver

COLORADO

Santa Fe

NEW MEXICO

ARIZONA

Phoenix

Boise

IDAHO

Carson City

Sacramento

NEVADA

CALIFORNIA

San Diego

Olympia

WASHINGTON

Salem

OREGON

How to use *the Next EXIT*® ① KENTUCKY

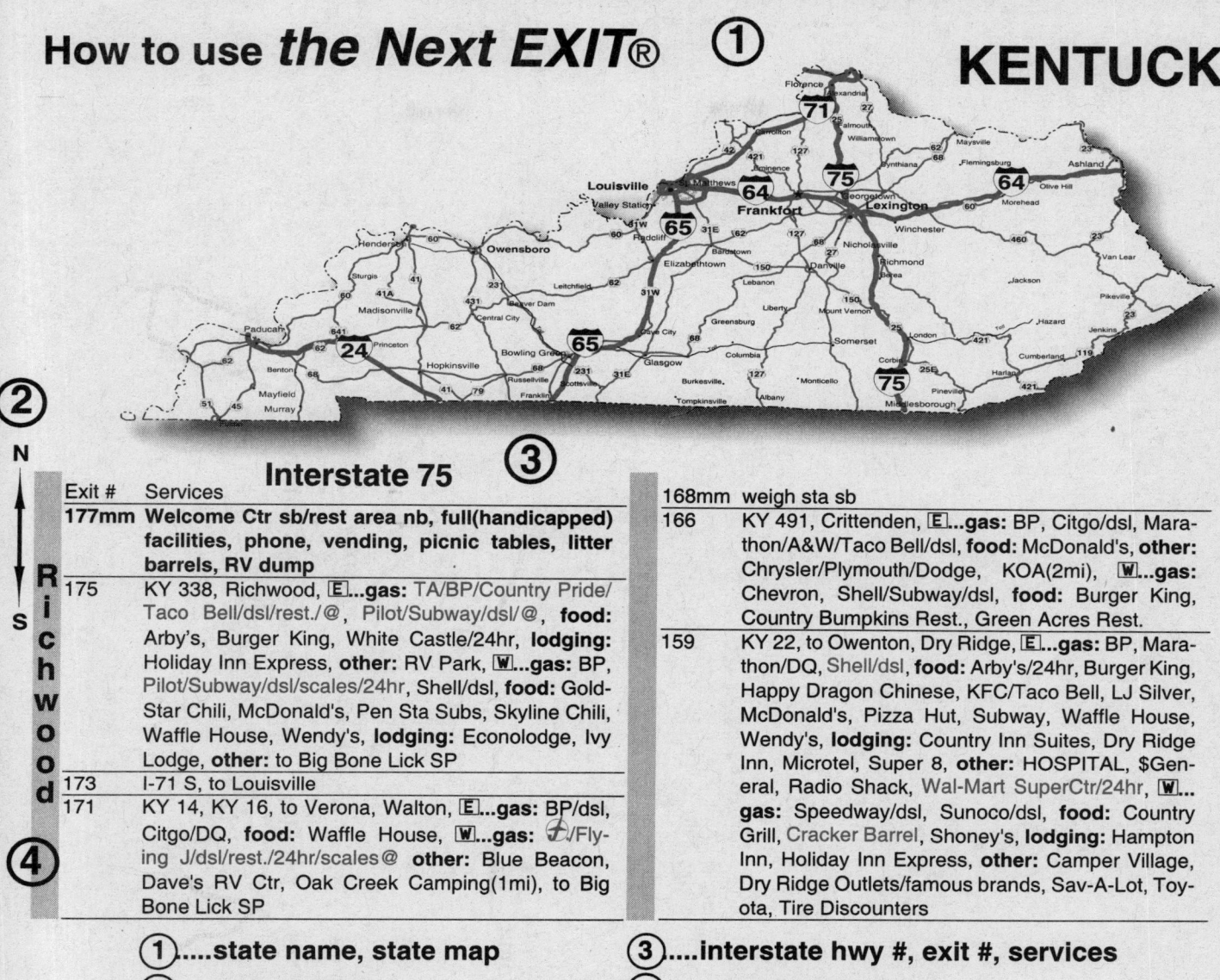

② N / S

④

Interstate 75 ③

Richwood

Exit #	Services
177mm	**Welcome Ctr sb/rest area nb, full(handicapped) facilities, phone, vending, picnic tables, litter barrels, RV dump**
175	KY 338, Richwood, E...gas: TA/BP/Country Pride/Taco Bell/dsl/rest./@, Pilot/Subway/dsl/@, food: Arby's, Burger King, White Castle/24hr, lodging: Holiday Inn Express, other: RV Park, W...gas: BP, Pilot/Subway/dsl/scales/24hr, Shell/dsl, food: Gold-Star Chili, McDonald's, Pen Sta Subs, Skyline Chili, Waffle House, Wendy's, lodging: Econolodge, Ivy Lodge, other: to Big Bone Lick SP
173	I-71 S, to Louisville
171	KY 14, KY 16, to Verona, Walton, E...gas: BP/dsl, Citgo/DQ, food: Waffle House, W...gas: ⬡/Flying J/dsl/rest./24hr/scales@ other: Blue Beacon, Dave's RV Ctr, Oak Creek Camping(1mi), to Big Bone Lick SP

Exit #	Services
168mm	weigh sta sb
166	KY 491, Crittenden, E...gas: BP, Citgo/dsl, Marathon/A&W/Taco Bell/dsl, food: McDonald's, other: Chrysler/Plymouth/Dodge, KOA(2mi), W...gas: Chevron, Shell/Subway/dsl, food: Burger King, Country Bumpkins Rest., Green Acres Rest.
159	KY 22, to Owenton, Dry Ridge, E...gas: BP, Marathon/DQ, Shell/dsl, food: Arby's/24hr, Burger King, Happy Dragon Chinese, KFC/Taco Bell, LJ Silver, McDonald's, Pizza Hut, Subway, Waffle House, Wendy's, lodging: Country Inn Suites, Dry Ridge Inn, Microtel, Super 8, other: HOSPITAL, $General, Radio Shack, Wal-Mart SuperCtr/24hr, W...gas: Speedway/dsl, Sunoco/dsl, food: Country Grill, Cracker Barrel, Shoney's, lodging: Hampton Inn, Holiday Inn Express, other: Camper Village, Dry Ridge Outlets/famous brands, Sav-A-Lot, Toyota, Tire Discounters

① ....**state name, state map** ③ ....**interstate hwy #, exit #, services**

② ....**directional arrow** ④ ....**city locator strip**

Exit

Most states number exits by the nearest mile marker(mm). A few states use consecutive numbers, in which case mile markers are given in ( ). Mile markers are the little green vertical signs beside the interstate at one mile intervals which indicate distance from the southern or western border of a state. Odd numbered interstates run north/south, even numbered run east/west.

Services

Services are listed alphabetically by category...**gas, food, lodging, other** services(including camping). "HOSPITAL" indicates an exit from which a hospital may be accessed, but it may not be close to the exit. Services located away from the exit may be referred to by "access to," or "to...," and a distance may be given. A directional notation is also given, such as N..., S..., E..., or W....

Directional Arrows
Follow exits DOWN the page if traveling from North to South or East to West, UP the page if traveling South to North or West to East.

N E

S W

Table of Contents

Abbreviations used in *the Next EXIT* ®:

AFB	Air Force Base	NP	National Park
B&B	Bed&Breakfast	NRA	Nat Rec Area
Bfd	Battlefield	pk	park
Ctr	Center	pkwy	parkway
Coll	College	rest.	restaurant
Cyn	canyon	nb	northbound
dsl	diesel	sb	southbound
$	Dollar	eb	eastbound
Mem	Memorial	wb	westbound
Mkt	Market	SP	state park
Mtn	Mountain	SF	state forest
mm	mile marker	Sprs	springs
N...	north side of exit	st	street, state
S...	south side of exit	sta	station
E...	east side of exit	TPK	Turnpike
W...	west side of exit	USPO	Post Office
NM	National Monument	vet	veterinarian
NHS	Nat Hist Site	whse	warehouse
NWR	Nat Wildlife Reserve	@	truckstop(full service)
NF	National Forest	red print	RV accessible

For Trans Canada Highway(TCH) information and more,
please visit us on the web at *www.thenextexit.com*

Mad Dog
by

Mark Watson
Winter, 2008

Mexico Insurance, now there is a unique product for you. Anytime I ride the roads near our southern neighbor, I begin to see the solicitations, in both languages. I don't buy because my journey usually ends at the border, but that doesn't stop me from traveling back to a time when peddling insurance paid my bills.

By the fall of 1973 our finances needed rebuilding after a couple of years of college. Answering an ad in the local paper, I was soon hired as an insurance salesman. Debit insurance, I learned when I reported, comprises a very special segment of the health and life insurance market. Even though the overall cost for basic coverage is higher, there are customers willing to pay a weekly premium because it fits their financial circumstances. The "debit" refers to an area in which a group of policyholders live. The debit insurance person is the representative of the company whose job it is to collect the weekly payment from the clients and write new coverage for other people in the neighborhood. It was not the the most exciting work, but I met a lot of interesting folks and I never knew exactly what the next day would bring.

Dogbite Street

One drizzly day after collecting the debit, I began trying to write new policies, working my way down a particular street on foot. I had been sizing up this area for some time, and although other reps had judged this to be unfertile territory, much of my success for new business had come by looking in places overlooked by previous debit men. As I walked into the front yard of the last house on the block, two competing images vied for my attention. The warm fuzzy image had my supervisor beaming with approval when he recognized me as the model salesman once again at the upcoming Friday meeting. The real picture involved a gray female dog under the porch that had ambled out to see if I really intended to climb up those steps.

Most dogs are territorial to a degree in not wanting intruders to violate some predetermined area unknown to anyone except themselves and other dogs. This mother was also nursing a litter of puppies. As she edged toward me, she seemed doubly irritated that I had interrupted feeding time. In order to keep me from detecting her intentions, she sidled in my direction, her head cocked down and away, never looking me in the eye. By the time she had reached the bottom of the steps I was standing safely on the porch, knocking on opportunity's door. The gray-haired man who answered made it instantly clear that he didn't want coverage by us or any other insurance company. After I had exhausted most of my tactics to soften a guy like this, I said goodbye and left. Getting turned down was always difficult, but especially so when it came at the hands of a mongrel's master.

Experience had taught me to handle defeat by leaving an area in a hurry, allowing distance to heal the wound of rejection. The loss of my boss' happy smile weighed on my mind just then as I retreated for the car. In my preoccupation I forgot about the guard dog under the porch. I had taken several steps when out of the corner of my eye I detected gray motion in my direction. Turning my head, I saw her creeping toward me menacingly, still never looking me in the eye. I had heard that dogs knew if you were scared of them by the smell of your ankles. I didn't think I was afraid, but I also didn't see any need to ask for trouble. I thought she would be pleased with my leaving, so I picked up my pace and acted brave in an attempt to bluff her. It didn't work. Just as I reached the street, she decided to remove any doubt about the way her end of the block felt about strangers. In an instant she bit my left leg three inches below the knee. Then, growling, she snapped at me again in the same place for good measure. I swung around with the debit book, a weapon that could have done her some harm had I connected, but having made her point, she backed suspiciously under the porch, peering out at me sideways but never looking me right in the eye.

As far as dog bites go it really wasn't all that bad. It was not a deep, teeth-sinking type bite, but just enough to bring on a blood flow. It seemed prudent to get it dressed properly, so I immediately drove over to the hospital. After experiencing so much trauma all in one day, I thought the emergency room staff would treat me as if I were war wounded, sort of a conquering hero. I entered the hospital announcing to several orderlies that I had been bitten by a dog. Nobody acted concerned, and no one even seemed to pay any attention. I walked down the hall a few steps and said, this time a little louder, "I've been bitten by a dog." I suppose medical personnel accustomed to patients being wheeled in with knife wounds and heart attacks don't rate dog bites very highly. I wasn't sure what it was going to take to get some help, so after a few moments of watching everyone loiter, I took a deep breath and shouted, "I've been bitten by a *mad dog*!"

This spun it differently, and presently I had several professionals looking after me, washing my wounds and making plans to inject me with substances from little rubber topped bottles. All of a sudden, dogbite had become a serious enough malady to warrant some notice. I was beginning to be favorably impressed with the flurry of activity on my behalf, when, by and by, someone asked the question, "Now, how do you know this dog was rabid?"

"Oh, I'm not at all sure it was a rabid dog," I replied, "but she was mad alright. You should have seen the way she went after my calf." The couple working on my leg paused for a moment, looked at me and then glanced at each other. Before long they had finished up and were giving me last minute instructions about how to care for dogbite at home. They gave me a shot of something and told me to go take a look at the dog in a day or so to see if she was foaming.

I never saw her again. I had liked dogs before and I saw no real reason to write off the entire canine species on account of one disgruntled member. After that my heart just wasn't into debit insurance anymore and a college degree began to look even better.

In the time since that fall, I have occasionally found myself in similar circumstances. Once in a while, walking up to an unfamiliar door I'll meet a concerned yard dog trotting out to perform the dogly duties of smelling my ankles. I always speak softly to the animal saying something like "hey puppiee, puppieee," in a soothing voice while reaching out a friendly hand. It's worked every time so far, but just in case, I look right into the dog's eyes, searching the inner beast. That's when I hear a growl and feel the touch of a gray "mad dog's" teeth on my leg and remember debit insurance days.

Interstate 10

E

W

Mobile

Exit #	Services
66.5mm	Alabama/Florida state line
66mm	**Welcome Ctr full(handicapped) facilities, phone, vending, picnic tables, litter barrels, petwalk**
53	rd 64, Wilcox Rd, **N...gas:** BP/Oasis/Stuckeys/dsl/cafe/scales/24hr/@, **other:** HillTop RV Park, fireworks, **S...gas:** Chevron/dsl, Outpost/dsl, **other:** fireworks
44	AL 59, Loxley, **N...gas:** Loves/Arby's/dsl/scales/24hr/@, Shell/dsl/scales, **S...gas:** Chevron/dsl, Exxon/DQ/dsl, RaceWay, **food:** Hardee's, McDonald's, Waffle House, **lodging:** Loxley Motel(3mi), WindChase Inn, **other:** to Gulf SP
38	AL 181, Malbis, **N...food:** Chick-fil-A, Cracker Barrel, FireMtn Grill, McDonald's, Moe's SW Grill, Logans Roadhouse, Olive Garden, Panera Bread, Ruby Tuesday, Stix Asian, Wendy's, **lodging:** Holiday Inn Express, La Quinta, **other:** Barnes&Noble, Belk, Best Buy, Dillards, $Tree, Michael's, Old Navy, PetsMart, Ross, Tuesday Morning, Walgreens, World Mkt, **S...gas:** Chevron/dsl, Shell/LA Subs, **lodging:** Malbis Motel(1mi), **other:** Honda, Lowes Whse, Sam's Club, Toyota
35	US 90, US 98, **N...gas:** BP, Shell, Summit, **other:** Bass Pro Shop, Rite Aid, USPO, **S...gas:** Exxon/dsl, Shell, **food:** Arby's, Burger King, Checker's, Domino's, El Rancho Mexican, Firehouse Subs, Garden Rest., Grand Buffet, Hooters, IHOP, Krystal, Longhorn Steaks, McDonald's, Nautilus Rest., O'Charley's, Pizza Hut, Subway, Taco Bell, Waffle House, Wendy's, Woody's BBQ, Zaxby's, **lodging:** Comfort Suites, Eastern Shore Motel, Hampton Inn, Hilton Garden, Microtel, **other:** HOSPITAL, BooksAMillion, Goody's, Home Depot, Office Depot, Steinmart, TJ Maxx
30	US 90/98, Battleship Pkwy, **S... food:** Felix's Fishcamp
29mm	tunnel begins wb
28mm	tunnel begins eb
27	US 90/98, Battleship Pkwy, Gov't St, **S...food:** Capt's Table Seafood, **lodging:** Best Western, **other:** to USS Alabama
26b	Water St, Mobile, downtown, **N...lodging:** Radisson, Ramada, Renaissance, to Visitors Ctr
26a	Canal St(from eb), same as 26b
25b	Virginia St, Mobile, **N...gas:** Shell/dsl
25a	Texas St(from wb, no return)

24	Broad St, to Duval St, Mobile, **N...gas:** Chevron
23	Michigan Ave, **N...gas:** Exxon, **other:** $General
22b a	AL 163, Dauphin Island Pkwy, **N...gas:** BP, **lodging:** Port City Inn, **other:** Family$, **S...gas:** Exxon/Subway/24hr, FastTime/dsl, Shell/dsl, **food:** Checker's, Gone Fishin Rest., Waffle House, **other:** $General
20	I-65 N, to Montgomery
17	AL 193, Tillmans Corner, to Dauphin Island, **N...gas:** Chevron/24hr, **food:** Burger King, Firehouse Subs, FireMtn Grill, Golden Corral, IHOP, McDonald's, Ruby Tuesday, Sonny's BBQ, Zaxby's, **other:** HOSPITAL, Big Lots, Big 10 Tire, Lowe's Whse, PawPaw's RV Ctr, Radio Shack, Wal-Mart SuperCtr/24hr

1

ALABAMA

Interstate 10

E ↕ W

Theodore

15b a	US 90, Tillmans Corner, to Mobile, **N**...**gas:** BP, Chevron/24hr, RaceWay, Shell, **food:** Arby's, Azteca's Mexican, Barnhill's Buffet, Checker's, CiCi's, Godfather's, KFC, Hooters, McDonald's, Papa John's, Pizza Hut, Pizza Inn, Popeye's, Subway, Taco Bell, Waffle House, **lodging:** Baymont Inn, Comfort Suites, Day's Inn, Econolodge, Hampton Inn, Holiday Inn, InTowne Suites, Knight's Inn, Motel 6, Red Roof Inn, Rodeway Inn, Super 8, **other:** AutoZone, CarQuest, $Tree, Family$, Firestone/auto, FoodWorld/24hr, Goodyear, O'Reilly Parts, Radio Shack, Rite Aid, Sears Essentials, Walgreens, **S**...**gas:** BP/dsl, Chevron/24hr, RaceWay, Shell/dsl/24hr, **food:** Hardee's, Waffle House, **other:** B&R RV Ctr, Jonnys RV Ctr, auto repair, tires, transmissions, USPO
13	to Theodore, **N**...**gas:** BP, Citgo, Liberty, Pilot/Wendy's/dsl/24hr/@, Shell/Subway, Texaco/McDonald's, **food:** Church's, Waffle House, **other:** Advance Parts, Family$, Greyhound Prk, Rite Aid, **S**...**gas:** Chevron/dsl, **other:** I-10 Kamping, Paynes RV Park(4mi), Bellingraf Gardens
10	rd 39, Bayou La Batre, Dawes, no services
4	AL 188 E, to Grand Bay, **N**...**gas:** BP, Citgo/dsl, Energize/Blimpie, Shell/Stuckey's, TA/BP/Buckhorn Rest./dsl/scales/24hr/@, **food:** Waffle House, **S**...**gas:** Chevron/24hr, **food:** Hardee's, **other:** Trav-L-Kamp
1mm	**Welcome Ctr eb, full(handicapped)facilities, info, phone, picnic tables, litter barrels, petwalk, RV dump**
0mm	Alabama/Mississippi state line

Interstate 20

E ↕ W

Exit #	Services
215mm	Alabama/Georgia state line, Central/Eastern time zone
213mm	**Welcome Ctr wb, full(handicapped)facilities, info, phone, vending, picnic tables, litter barrels, petwalk, RV dump, 24hr security**
210	AL 49, Abernathy, **N**...fireworks, **S**...fireworks
209mm	Tallapoosa River
208mm	weigh sta wb
205	AL 46, to Heflin, **N**...**gas:** BP/dsl, **food:** 205 Cafe, **other:** tires, **S**...**gas:** Texaco/dsl/24hr
199	AL 9, Heflin, **N**...**gas:** Texaco/Subway/Taco Bell/dsl/24hr, **food:** Hardee's, Pop's Charburgers, **lodging:** Howard Johnson, **other:** Ford, USPO, **S**...**gas:** BP/dsl, Chevron, **food:** Huddle House
198mm	Talladega Nat Forest eastern boundary
191	US 431, to US 78, no services
188	to US 78, to Anniston, **N**...**gas:** Shell, SuperMart, Texaco/Subway, **food:** Cracker Barrel, DQ, IHOP, KFC, LoneStar Steaks, Sonny's BBQ, Waffle House, Wendy's, Zaxby's, **lodging:** Country Inn& Suites, Hampton Inn, Holiday Inn Express, Jameson Inn, Sleep Inn, Wingate Inn, **other:** Harley-Davidson, Honda, Lowe's Whse, O'Reilly Parts, **S**... **other:** Best Buy, Hobby Lobby, Home Depot, Old Navy, Target, TJ Maxx

Pell City

Leeds

185	AL 21, to Anniston, **N**...**gas:** BP/dsl, Chevron/24hr, Exxon, Shell, **food:** Applebee's, Arby's, Burger King, Capt D's, Domino's, Garfield's Rest., HappyStar Buffet, Hardee's, Jack's Rest., Krystal, Logan's Roadhouse, McAlister's Deli, McDonald's, O'Charley's, Pizza Hut, Red Lobster, Shoney's, Sonic, Starbucks, Taco Bell, Waffle House, Western Sizzlin, **lodging:** Day's Inn, Holiday Inn, Howard Johnson, Liberty Inn, Oxford Inn, Red Carpet Inn, **other:** BooksAMillion, Dillards, $General, Firestone/auto, FoodMax, JC Penney, Rite Aid, Sears/auto, mall, to Ft McClellan, **S**...**gas:** Cowboys/dsl, Express/dsl, Exxon, RaceWay, Shell/Subway/dsl, Texaco, **food:** Chick-fil-A, El Poblano Mexican, Huddle House, Outback Steaks, Waffle House, Wendy's, **lodging:** Comfort Inn, Econolodge, Hampton Inn, Motel 6, Travelodge, **other:** HOSPITAL, Goodyear/auto, Wal-Mart SuperCtr/24hr
179	to Munford, Coldwater, **S**...**gas:** Citgo/dsl, **other:** Anniston Army Depot
173	AL 5, Eastaboga, **S**...**gas:** Shell, **food:** DQ, **other:** to Speedway/Hall of Fame
168	AL 77, to Talladega, **N**...**gas:** Citgo, Phillips 66/dsl, QV/Domino's, **food:** Jack's Rest., KFC/Taco Bell, Waffle House, **S**...**gas:** Chevron/Subway/dsl, Shell/dsl, Texaco/Burger King, **food:** McDonald's, **lodging:** Comfort Inn, Day's Inn, McCaig Motel, **other:** to Speedway, Hall of Fame
165	Embry Cross Roads, **N**...**gas:** Hi-Tech Fuel, **S**...**gas:** Chevron/dsl, Texaco, **food:** Huddle House, **lodging:** McCaig Motel/rest.
164mm	Coosa River
162	US 78, Riverside, **N**...**other:** Safe Harbor Camping, **S**...**gas:** BP/dsl, Chevron, **food:** Lakeview Rest., **lodging:** Riverside Inn
158	US 231, Pell City, **N**...**gas:** Exxon/dsl, **food:** Arby's, Golden Rule BBQ, Krystal, Wendy's, Western Sizzlin, **lodging:** Hampton Inn, Holiday Inn Express, **other:** $Tree, Home Depot, Radio Shack, Wal-Mart SuperCtr/gas/24hr, **S**...**gas:** BP, Chevron, Citgo/dsl, **food:** Burger King, Hardee's, KFC, McDonald's, Pizza Hut, Taco Bell, Waffle House, **lodging:** Ramada Ltd, **other:** HOSPITAL, Chevrolet/Pontiac, Ford/Lincoln/Mercury, Lakeside Camping
156	US 78 E, to Pell City, **S**...**gas:** Chevron/dsl/24hr, Exxon/dsl/24hr, Shell
153	US 78, Chula Vista
152	Cook Springs
147	Brompton, **N**...**gas:** Citgo, **S**...**gas:** Chevron/dsl, **other:** Suncoast RV Ctr/LP
144·	US 411, Leeds, **N**...**gas:** BP/dsl, Raceway, Shell/Subway, **food:** Arby's, Cracker Barrel, Krystal, Milo's Café, Pizza Hut, Ruby Tuesday, Waffle House, Wendy's, **lodging:** Best Western, Comfort Inn, **other:** Food Giant, RV camping, **S**...**gas:** Exxon/24hr, RaceWay, Speedway/dsl, **food:** Capt D's, Guadalajara Jalisco Mexican, Hardee's, KFC, McDonald's, Taco Bell, Waffle House, **lodging:** Day's Inn, **other:** Advance Parts, AutoZone, Lowe's Whse, Radio Shack, Wal-Mart SuperCtr/Subway/24hr
140	US 78, Leeds, **S**...**gas:** Chevron, Exxon, Shell(1mi), **lodging:** Best Value Inn, **other:** Bass Pro Shop

2

Interstate 20

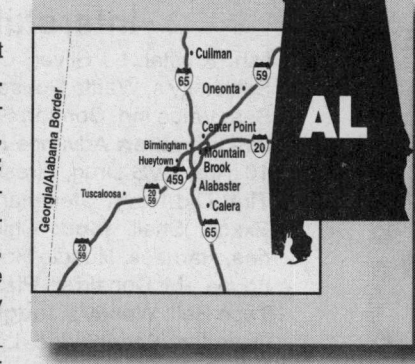

E ↕ W		
139mm	Cahaba River
136	I-459 S, to Montgomery, Tuscaloosa
135	US 78, Old Leeds Rd, **N**...**other:** B'ham Racetrack
133	US 78, to Kilgore Memorial Dr, (wb return at 132), **N**...**gas:** Chevron, Exxon/dsl/24hr, **food:** Golden Rule BBQ, Hamburger Heaven, Jack's Rest., Krystal, Waffle House, **lodging:** Comfort Inn, Eastwood Hotel, Siesta, same as 132, **S**...**gas:** BP, **food:** Arby's, China Buffet, El Mexicano, Gus' Hotdogs, McDonald's, Subway, **lodging:** Best Western, Holiday Inn Express, Quality Inn, **other:** $Tree, Ford, Graham Tire, Sam's Club, Wal-Mart
132b a	US 78, Crestwood Blvd, **N**...**gas:** Exxon, **food:** Barnhill's Buffet, Krystal, Villa Fiesta, Waffle House, **other:** Chevrolet, O'Reilly Parts, Super Petz, **S**...**gas:** BP, Crown/24hr, Shell/24hr, **food:** Arby's, Capt D's, China Garden, Denny's, Emperor House, Hooters, IHOP, KFC, LJ Silver/Taco Bell, Logan's Roadhouse, McDonald's, New China Buffet, Olive Garden, Pizza Hut, Red Lobster, Ryan's, Wendy's, **lodging:** Comfort Inn, Delux Inn, Economy Lodge, Park Inn, USA Lodge, **other:** HOSPITAL, Circuit City, Home Depot, K-Mart, Office Depot, Radio Shack, Sears/auto, TJ Maxx, Waldenbooks, mall
130b	US 11, 1st Ave, **N**...**gas:** BP, Chevron/24hr, Conoco/dsl, Crown, **lodging:** Bama Motel, **other:** AutoZone, Southern Foods, **S**...**food:** McDonald's, Pacific Seafood, **lodging:** Relax Inn, Sky Inn
130a	I-59 N, to Gadsden
I-59 S and I-20 W run together from B'ham to Meridian, MS	
129	Airport Blvd, **N**...**lodging:** Sheraton, **other:** airport, **S**...**gas:** BP, Shell, **food:** Hardee's, Taqueira, **lodging:** Airport Inn, Holiday Inn
128	AL 79, Tallapoosa St, **N**...**gas:** Kangaroo/Subway/dsl, Exxon/dsl
126b	31st St, **N**...**gas:** Citgo, Shell, **food:** McDonald's
126a	US 31, US 280, 26th St, Carraway Blvd, **N**...**gas:** Phillips 66, **food:** Church's, KFC, Rally's
125b	22nd St, **N**...**lodging:** Sheraton
125a	17th St, Civic Ctr
124b a	I-65, S to Montgomery, N to Nashville
123	US 78, Arkadelphia Rd, **N**...**gas:** Chevron/24hr, Jet-Pep, Pilot/Wendy's/dsl/24hr, Shell, **food:** Popeye's, **lodging:** Day's Inn, **S**...**other:** HOSPITAL, to Legion Field
121	Bush Blvd(from wb, no return), Ensley, **N**...**gas:** BP, Exxon, **food:** Wings&Waffles
120	AL 269, 20th St, Ensley Ave, **N**...**food:** KFC, **other:** GMC/Pontiac, Breeze RV, **S**...**gas:** BP, **other:** HOSPITAL, Chevrolet, Chrysler/Plymouth/Jeep, Hyundai, Toyota
119b	Ave I(from wb), no services
119a	Scrushy Pkwy, Gary Ave, **N**...**gas:** BP, Chevron/dsl, **food:** Burger King, Fairfield Seafood, McDonald's, Seafood Express, Subway, Taco Bell, **other:** Family$, Food Fair, **S**...**gas:** Mobil, Texaco, **food:** Omelet Shoppe, **other:** HOSPITAL
118	AL 56, Valley Rd, Fairfield, **N**...**other:** NAPA, **S**...**food:** Papa John's, **lodging:** Inn At Fairfield, **other:** Home Depot, Radio Shack, Sears, Winn-Dixie
115	Allison-Bonnett Memorial Dr, **N**...**gas:** BP/dsl, Phillips 66, RaceWay, Shell/dsl, **food:** Church's, Guadalajara Grill, Hardee's, Subway, **other:** Advance Parts, O'Reilly Parts
113	18th Ave, to Hueytown, **S**...**gas:** Chevron/dsl, **food:** McDonald's
112	18th St, 19th St, Bessemer, **N**...**gas:** Citgo, RaceWay, Shell, **food:** Jack's Rest., **other:** OK Tire/repair, **S**...**gas:** Chevron, **food:** Arby's, Burger King, Krystal, McDonald's, **other:** Lowe's Whse
110	AL Adventure Pkwy, no services
108	US 11, AL 5 N, Academy Dr, **N**...**gas:** Exxon, **food:** Applebee's, Cracker Barrel, Golden Rule BBQ, Santa Fe Steaks, Waffle House, **lodging:** Best Western, Comfort Inn, Country Inn&Suites, Courtyard, Fairfield Inn, Holiday Inn Express, Jameson Inn, **other:** Chevrolet, Chrysler/Jeep/Dodge, **S**...**gas:** BP, Citgo/Church's/dsl, **food:** Burger King, Little Caesar's, McDonald's, Milo's Burgers, Ruby Tuesday, Sonic, Wendy's, Zaxby's, **lodging:** Days Inn, Hampton Inn, Scottish Inn, **other:** HOSPITAL, Big 10 Tire, $Tree, Ford, Goody's, Radio Shack, Wal-Mart SuperCtr/24hr, Winn-Dixie, to civic ctr
106	I-459 N, to Montgomery
104	Rock Mt Lake, **S**...**gas:** Flying J/Conoco/dsl/LP/rest./24hr/@
100	to Abernant, **N**...**gas:** Citgo, **other:** McCalla Camping, **S**...**gas:** BP, Exxon, Petro/Chevron/dsl/rest./24hr/@, **other:** $General, Tannehill SP(3mi)
97	US 11 S, AL 5 S, to W Blocton, **S**...**gas:** BP/KFC/dsl, Exxon/Subway/dsl, Shell/dsl, Texaco, **food:** Jack's Rest.
89	Mercedes Dr, **N**...**lodging:** Wellesley Inn, **S**...**other:** Mercedes Auto Plant
86	Vance, to Brookwood, **N**...**gas:** BP/dsl, Shell/dsl/rest./24hr/@
85mm	**rest area both lanes, full(handicapped)facilities, phone, vending, picnic tables, litter barrels, petwalk, RV dump**
79	US 11, University Blvd, Coaling, **S**...**gas:** Chevron/dsl
77	Cottondale, **N**...**gas:** Chevron/McDonald's, TA/BP/Subway/Taco Bell/dsl/@, Wilco/Wendy's/dsl/24hr, **food:** Pizza Hut, Ruby Tuesday, **lodging:** Hampton Inn, Microtel, **other:** Chevrolet, SpeedCo, USPO, truckwash
76	US 11, E Tuscaloosa, Cottondale, **N**...**gas:** Citgo, Exxon, Shell/dsl, **food:** Burger King, Cracker Barrel, Waffle House, **lodging:** Comfort Inn, Howard Johnson, Super Inn, **other:** transmissions, **S**...**gas:** Pilot/Subway/dsl/24hr/@, Texaco/dsl, **lodging:** Sleep Inn
73	US 82, McFarland Blvd, Tuscaloosa, **N**...**gas:** BP/dsl, Chevron/Subway/dsl, Exxon, RaceWay, Shell/dsl, **food:** Arby's, Burger King, Capt D's, Chuck's Cat-

ALABAMA

Interstate 20

Tuscaloosa

fish, Krystal, LJ Silver, O'Charley's, Red Lobster, Schlotsky's, Waffle House, **lodging:** Best Western, Best Value Inn, Comfort Suites, Guest Lodge, Masters Inn, **other:** Advance Parts, Transmissions, Big 10 Tire, CVS Drug, Firestone, Goodyear/auto, OK Tire, Old Navy, Steinmart, U-Haul, mall, Ⓢ...**gas:** Exxon, Shell, **food:** Chili's, Grand Buffet, Guthries, Hardees, Huddle House, KFC, Logan's Roadhouse, McDonald's, Pizza Hut, Sonic, Subway, Taco Bell, Wendy's, **lodging:** Country Inn& Suites, Days Inn, Econolodge, La Quinta, Motel 6, Quality Inn, Ramada Inn, Super 8, **other:** BooksAMillion, Crysler/Jeep/Dodge, Dillard's, $Tree, FoodWorld, Michael's, Office Depot, Rite Aid, Sam's Club/gas, TJ Maxx, Wal-Mart SuperCtr/24hr,

71b	I-359, Al 69 N, to Tuscaloosa, Ⓝ...**other:** HOSPITAL, U of AL, to Stillman Coll
71a	AL 69 S, to Moundville, Ⓢ...**gas:** Chevron, Exxon/dsl, Parade, Shell/dsl, **food:** Arby's, Golden Rule BBQ, Hooters, IHOP, LoneStar Steaks, OutBack Steaks, Pizza Hut, Ryan's, Waffle House, Wendy's, Zaxby's, **lodging:** Courtyard, Days Inn, Fairfield Inn, Hilton Garden, Jameson Inn, **other:** Advance Parts, K-Mart, Lowe's Whse, Mazda/VW, O'Reilly Parts, to Mound SM
68	Northfort-Tuscaloosa Western Bypass
64mm	Black Warrior River
62	Fosters, Ⓝ...**gas:** BP
52	US 11, US 43, Knoxville, Ⓝ...**gas:** Exxon/dsl, **other:** Knox Hill Camping
45	AL 37, Union, Ⓢ...**gas:** BP/dsl/rest./24hr, Chevron/Subway, **food:** Hardee's, **other:** Greene Co Greyhound Park
40	AL 14, Eutaw, Ⓝ...**other:** to Tom Bevill Lock/Dam, Ⓢ...**gas:** BP, HOSPITAL
39mm	**rest area wb, full(handicapped)facilities, phone, vending, picnic tables, litter barrels, petwalk, RV dump**
38mm	**rest area eb, full(handicapped)facilities, phone, vending, picnic tables, litter barrels, petwalk, RV dump**
32	Boligee, Ⓝ...**gas:** BP/dsl/rest./24hr, Ⓢ...**gas:** Chevron/Subway/24hr
27mm	Tombigbee River, Tenn-Tom Waterway
23	Epes, to Gainesville, no services
17	AL 28, Livingston, Ⓢ...**gas:** BP/dsl/24hr, Chevron/Subway/24hr, Shell/dsl, **food:** Burger King, Diamond Jim's Steaks, Pizza Hut, **lodging:** Comfort Inn, Western Inn(1mi), **other:** repair/24hr
8	AL 17, York, Ⓢ...**gas:** BP/dsl/rest., Parade, **lodging:** Day's Inn/Briar Patch Rest., **food:** York Deli, **other:** HOSPITAL, $General
1	to US 80 E, Cuba, Ⓝ...**gas:** Trkstp/dsl/rest., Ⓢ...**gas:** Chevron, Dixie, **food:** Rocking Chair Diner
.5mm	**Welcome Ctr eb, full(handicapped)facilities, phone, vending, picnic tables, litter barrels, petwalk, RV dump**
	I-20 E and I-59 N run together from Meridian to B'ham
0mm	Alabama/Mississippi state line

Interstate 59

Ft Payne

Gadsden

Exit #	Services
241mm	Alabama/Georgia state line, Central/Eastern time zone
241mm	**Welcome Ctr sb, full(handicapped)facilities, phone, vending, picnic tables, litter barrels, petwalk, RV dump**
239	to US 11, Sulphur Springs Rd, Ⓔ...**other:** Sequoyah Caverns Camping(4mi)
231	AL 40, AL 117, Hammondville, Valley Head, Ⓔ...**other:** Sequoyah Caverns Camping(5mi), Ⓦ...**gas:** Victory Fuel
222	US 11, to Ft Payne, Ⓔ...**gas:** Shell, **other:** Chevrolet, 1 mi Ⓔ...**food:** Arby's, Hardee's, Jack's Rest., KFC, Krystal, Pizza Hut, Subway, **lodging:** Ft Payne Inn, **other:** Foodland/gas, Ⓦ...**gas:** Citgo/dsl, Texaco, **food:** Waffle King
218	AL 35, Ft Payne, Ⓔ...**gas:** Conoco/dsl, **food:** Capt D's, Durango's Mexican, Golden Rule BBQ, McDonald's, New China, Papa John's, Perla Tapatia Mexican, Quizno's, Taco Bell, Wendy's, Zaxby's, **other:** Advance Parts, Big Lots, Buick/Pontiac/GMC, Chrysler/Dodge, $General, O'Reilly Parts, Pamida, Ⓦ...**gas:** Chevron, Kangaroo/Stuckey's/dsl, Victory Fuel, **food:** Burger King, Cracker Barrel, Domino's, Hardee's, Ryan's, Ruby Tuesday, Subway, Waffle House, **lodging:** Day's Inn, Econolodge, Hampton Inn, Holiday Inn Express, **other:** HOSPITAL, $Tree, Ford/Lincoln/Mercury, GNC, Goody's, Kia, K-Mart, Lowes Whse, Radio Shack, Walgreens, Wal-Mart SuperCtr/gas/24hr
205	AL 68, Collinsville, Ⓔ...**gas:** Chevron, **food:** Jack's Rest., Smokin' Joe's Rest., **lodging:** Howard Johnson, **other:** to Little River Canyon, Weiss Lake, Ⓦ...**gas:** Conoco/dsl, Shell
188	AL 211, to US 11, Gadsden, Ⓔ...**gas:** Jet-Pep, **food:** Copper Baratie's Rest., **other:** Noccalula Falls RV Park, Ⓦ...**gas:** Jet-Pep
183	US 431, US 278, Gadsden, Ⓔ...**gas:** Jet-Pep/dsl, Shell, Texaco, **food:** Magic Burger, Waffle House, Wendy's, **lodging:** Best Value Inn, Days Inn, Rodeway Inn, **other:** st police, Ⓦ...**gas:** Chevron/24hr, Exxon, Texaco, **food:** KFC/Taco Bell, Krystal, Lee Super Buffet, McDonald's, Pizza Hut, Subway, **lodging:** Econolodge
182	I-759, to Gadsden
181	AL 77, Rainbow City, to Gadsden, Ⓔ...**gas:** Petro/BP/dsl/scales/24hr/@, **food:** Austin's Rest., **lodging:** Day's Inn, Ⓦ...**gas:** Citgo, Kangaroo/dsl, Pure/dsl, Texaco, **food:** Arby's, Cracker Barrel, DQ, Hardee's, Los Arcos, Ruby Tuesday, Subway, Waffle House, **lodging:** Best Western, Comfort Suites, Holiday Inn Express, **other:** $Tree, O'Reilly Parts, Radio Shack, Wal-Mart SuperCtr/24hr
174	to Steele, Ⓦ...**gas:** Chevron/dsl, JetPep/dsl/@
168mm	**rest area sb, full(handicapped)facilities, phone, vending, picnic tables, litter barrels, petwalk, RV dump**
166	US 231, Whitney, to Ashville, Ⓔ...**gas:** Chevron, Discount/gas, Ⓦ...**gas:** Texaco/dsl, **food:** Jack's Rest., Huddle House, Subway

4

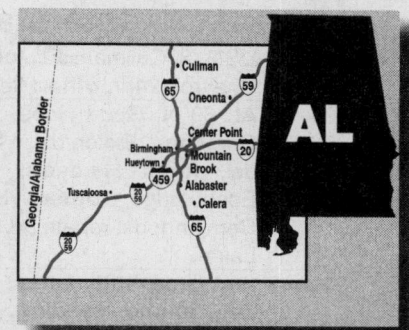

Interstate 59

N → S

165mm	**rest area nb, full(handicapped)facilities, phone, vending, picnic tables, litter barrels, petwalk, RV dump**
156	AL 23, to US 11, Springville, to St Clair Springs, ⬜...**other:** Wal-Mart SuperCtr/Subway
154	AL 174, Springville, to Odenville, ⬜...**gas:** BP/Subway/Dominos, Chevron/24hr, Exxon, Shell/dsl, **food:** Gulf Seafood, Jack's Rest., McDonald's
148	to US 11, Argo, ⬛...**gas:** BP
143	Mt Olive Church Rd, Deerfoot Pkwy, no services
141	to Trussville, Pinson, ⬛...**gas:** BP/dsl, Shell/Subway/dsl, Texaco/dsl, **food:** Applebee's, Arby's, Cracker Barrel, LoneStar Steaks, McDonald's, Papa Johns, Pizza Hut, Taco Bell, Waffle House, Wendy's, **lodging:** Comfort Inn, Holiday Inn Express, Jameson Inn, **other:** Harley-Davidson, ⬜...**gas:** Chevron/24hr, Citgo, Exxon, Shell, **food:** Arby's, Burger King, Chick-fil-A, Costa's BBQ, DQ, East Buffet, Krystal, Milo's Burgers, Moe's SW Grill, Ruby Tuesday, Whataburger, Zaxby's, **other:** VET, CVS Drug, $Tree, GNC, Goody's, K-Mart, Kohl's, Marshall's, Petsmart, Radio Shack, Sam's Club/gas, Walgreens, Wal-Mart SuperCtr/24hr
137	I-459 S, to Montgomery, Tuscaloosa
134	to AL 75, Roebuck Pkwy, ⬜...**food:** Arby's, Barnhill's Buffet, Burger King, Chick-fil-A, Chucke-Cheese, Costa's Cafe, Krystal, McDonald's, Milo's Burgers, Monterrey Mexican, O'Brien's Seafood, O'Charley's, Rally's, Ruby Tuesday, Steak&Ale, Subway, Taco Bell, Waffle House, Wendy's, **lodging:** Best Inn, **other:** HOSPITAL, Chevrolet, CVS Drug, Dodge, $Tree, Firestone/auto, FoodGiant, Ford, Goodyear/auto, Honda, Hyundai, Jo-Ann Fabrics, Lincoln/Mercury, Mr Transmissions, NTB, O'Reilly Parts, USPO, VW, Wal-Mart SuperCtr/24hr
133	4th St, to US 11(from nb), ⬜...**gas:** Exxon, **food:** Arby's, Checker's, Chinese Buffet, Papa John's, Shoney's, Starbucks, Waffle House, **other:** Chrysler/Plymouth, $General, Food World, Goody's, Rite Aid, Suzuki, same as 134
132	US 11 N, 1st Ave, ⬛...same as 131, ⬜...**gas:** Chevron/24hr, Shell, **food:** Krispy Kreme, **other:** Westwood Parts
131	77th Ave(from nb), ⬛...**gas:** Chevron, Exxon, **food:** Burger King, Church's, **other:** CVS Drug, NAPA, U-Haul, accesses same as 132, ⬜...**gas:** Texaco
130	I-20, E to Atlanta, W to Tuscaloosa
	I-59 S and I-20 W run together from B'ham to Mississippi. See Alabama Interstate 20.

Interstate 65

N → S

Exit #	Services
366mm	Alabama/Tennessee state line
365	AL 53, to Ardmore, ⬛...**gas:** William's Service, **lodging:** Budget Inn
364mm	**Welcome Ctr sb, full(handicapped)facilities, info, phone, vending, picnic tables, litter barrels, petwalk, RV dump**

Athens / Decatur / Cullman

361	Elkmont, ⬜...**gas:** Citgo/dsl/rest./@, William's Service/dsl/rest., **food:** Sonny G's BBQ, **other:** antiques, repair
354	US 31 S, to Athens, ⬜...**gas:** Chevron, Texaco/dsl, **food:** McDonald's, Subway, **lodging:** Budget Inn, Mark Hotel, **other:** HOSPITAL, Advance Parts, CVS Drug, K-Mart, Northgate RV Park
351	US 72, to Athens, Huntsville, ⬛...**gas:** Exxon, RaceWay, Shell/Subway, Texaco, **food:** Burger King, Cracker Barrel, Lawler's BBQ, McDonald's, Waffle House, Wendy's, **lodging:** Comfort Inn, Country Hearth Inn, Hampton Inn, **other:** VET, Russell Stover, ⬜...**gas:** Chevron/24hr, Texaco/dsl, **food:** Applebee's, Arby's, Backyard Burger, Bojangles, Hardee's, Krystal, Papa John's, Ruby Tuesday, Shoney's, Sonic, Starbucks, **lodging:** Best Western, Day's Inn, Holiday Inn Express, Sleep Inn, Super 8, **other:** HOSPITAL, Chevrolet, Chrysler/Plymouth/Jeep, $General, Big 10 Tire, Ford/Lincoln/Mercury, Goodyear/auto, Lowes Whse, O'Reilly Parts, Staples, Wal-Mart SuperCtr/gas/24hr, to Joe Wheeler SP
340b	I-565, to Huntsville, to Ala Space & Rocket Ctr
340a	AL 20, to Decatur, ⬜...**gas:** Conoco/dsl, RaceWay, **2 mi** ⬜...**lodging:** Courtyard, Hampton Inn, Holiday Inn
337mm	Tennessee River
334	AL 67, Priceville, to Decatur, ⬛...**gas:** BP/dsl, RaceWay/dsl/24hr, **food:** JW's Steaks, **lodging:** Day's Inn, Super 8, **other:** $General, ⬜...**gas:** Chevron, Pilot/Subway/Wendy's/dsl/scales/24hr, Texaco, **food:** Burger King, DQ, Hardee's, Krystal, Libby's Diner, McDonald's, Smokehouse BBQ, Waffle House, **lodging:** Comfort Inn, **other:** HOSPITAL, Andy's RV Ctr(1mi), Hood RV Ctr
328	AL 36, Hartselle, ⬜...**gas:** BP, Chevron/dsl, Cowboys/dsl, Shell, **food:** Homestyle BBQ, Huddle House, **lodging:** Country Hearth Inn
325	Thompson Rd, to Hartselle, no services
322	AL 55, to US 31, to Falkville, Eva, ⬛...**gas:** BP/dsl/rest., ⬜...**gas:** Chevron
318	US 31, to Lacon, ⬛...**gas:** BP/DQ/Stuckey's, **lodging:** Lacon Motel
310	AL 157, Cullman, West Point, ⬛...**gas:** BP, Chevron, Conoco/Subway/dsl, Shell/dsl/24hr, Texaco/Wendy's/dsl, **food:** Arby's, Backyard Burger, Baxter's Steaks, Burger King, Cracker Barrel, Denny's, KFC, LJ Silver/Taco Bell, McDonald's, Ruby Tuesday, Waffle House, **lodging:** Best Western, Comfort Inn, Hampton Inn, Holiday Inn Express, Sleep Inn, **other:** HOSPITAL, Ford/Lincoln/Mercury, Pontiac/Buick/GMC, ⬜...**gas:** BP, Exxon/dsl, **lodging:** Super 8, **other:** Cullman Camping(2mi)

Interstate 65

N ↑ ↓ S

308	US 278, Cullman, **E...lodging:** Day's Inn, **W...gas:** Chevron/24hr, **other:** flea mkt
304	AL 69 N, Good Hope, to Cullman, **E...gas:** BP, Chevron, Exxon/dsl, Shell/dsl/rest./@, Texaco/dsl, **food:** Hardee's, Waffle House, **lodging:** Econolodge, **other:** HOSPITAL, Good Hope Camping, dsl repair, **W...gas:** JetPep/dsl, to Smith Lake
301mm	**rest area both lanes, full(handicapped) facilities, phone, vending, picnic tables, litter barrels, petwalk, RV dump**
299	AL 69 S, to Jasper, **E...gas:** Citgo, **other:** Millican RV Ctr, **W...gas:** BP/dsl, Chevron/dsl, Dodge City/Conoco/dsl/rest./scales/24hr, Texaco/dsl, Shell/McDonald's/dsl, **food:** Jack's Rest., **other:** CarQuest, $General
291	AL 91, to Arkadelphia, **E...gas:** Conoco/dsl, **other:** Country View RV Park(1mi), **W...gas:** Shell/dsl/rest./24hr/@, **food:** GoodDays Rest.
291mm	Warrior River
289	to Blount Springs, **W...gas:** BP/DQ/Stuckey's, **other:** to Rickwood Caverns SP
287	US 31 N, to Blount Springs, **E...gas:** Citgo/dsl, Conoco/dsl,
284	US 31 S, AL 160 E, Hayden, **E...gas:** Conoco/dsl, Phillips 66, Shell/dsl, **food:** Bryants Seafood
282	AL 140, Warrior, **E...gas:** Chevron/Subway/24hr, Exxon/McDonald's, FuelZ/dsl, **food:** Hardee's, Pizza Hut, Taco Bell, **W...gas:** BP/dsl
281	US 31, to Warrior, **E...other:** Chevrolet
280	to US 31, to Warrior, **E...other:** Chevrolet
279mm	Warrior River
275	to US 31, Morris, no services
272	Mt Olive Rd, **E...gas:** BP(1mi), **W...gas:** Chevron/24hr, Shell, Texaco/dsl, **food:** Jack's Rest.
271	Fieldstown Rd, **E...gas:** BP, Chevron/24hr, RaceWay, Shell, **food:** Arby's, Buffet Garden, Chik-fil-A, DQ, Guthrie's Diner, Fire Mtn Grill, Habenero's Mexican, Jim'n Mic's BBQ, KFC, Little Caesar's, LJ Silver/Taco Bell, McDonald's, Milo's Burgers, Pizza Hut, Ruby Tuesday, Shoney's, Subway, Waffle House, Wendy's, Zaxby's, **other:** Advance Parts, AutoZone, Chevrolet, $Tree, Goody's, Kia/Subaru, Walgreens, Wal-Mart SuperCtr/gas/24hr, **W...gas:** Shell, **food:** Cracker Barrel, **lodging:** Best Western
267	Walkers Chapel Rd, to Fultondale, **E...gas:** Chevron/dsl, Shell/Subway/dsl, **food:** Burger King, Domino's, Hardee's, Jack's Rest., Jalisco Mexican, O'Charley's, Outback Steaks, Taco Bell, Waffle House, Whataburger, **lodging:** Comfort Suites, Fairfield Inn, Hampton Inn, Holiday Inn Express, **other:** CVS Drug, $General, Lowe's Whse, Rite Aid, Target, Winn-Dixie, **W...gas:** Chevron/dsl
266	US 31, Fultondale, **E...gas:** Chevron/24hr, **lodging:** Day's Inn, Super 8
264	41st Ave, **W...gas:** ✈/Flying J/CountryMkt/dsl/scales/24hr/@
263	33rd Ave, **E...gas:** Chevron/dsl, **lodging:** Apex Motel, **W...gas:** Crown, Exxon, **other:** Colonial RV Ctr
262b a	16th St, Finley Ave, **E...gas:** Bama/dsl, BP, Shell/dsl/scales/@, **W...gas:** Chevron/24hr, Citgo/dsl/24hr, Conoco/dsl/@, **food:** Capt D's, McDonald's, Popeye's
261b a	I-20/59, E to Gadsden, W to Tuscaloosa
260b a	3th Ave N, **E...gas:** BP, Shell, Texaco, **food:** Niki's Rest., Mrs Winner's, **lodging:** Tourway Inn, **other:** Buick, Chevrolet, Chrysler/Jeep, Nissan, **W...gas:** Chevron, **food:** Church's, **lodging:** Adams Inn, **other:** to Legion Field
259b a	University Blvd, 4th Ave, 5th Ave, **E...food:** Waffle House, **other:** HOSPITAL, Food Fair, **W...gas:** Chevron, **other:** Goodyear
258	Green Springs Ave, **E...gas:** Chevron, Citgo, **food:** Exotic Wings
256b a	Oxmoor Rd, **E...gas:** Exxon/dsl, Mobil/dsl, Shell, **food:** Burger King, Cuco's Mexican, El Palacio Mexican, KFC, Krystal, McDonald's, Qdoba Mexican, Tuesday Morning, **lodging:** Howard Johnson, **other:** AutoZone, Big Lots, CVS Drug, $Tree, Firestone/auto, Food World, Fred's Drug, Goodyear/auto, Jo-Ann Fabrics, K-Mart, Office Depot, **W...gas:** BP, Chevron/24hr, **food:** Jim & Nick's BBQ, **lodging:** Comfort Inn, Microtel, Oxmoor Inn, Quality Inn, Ramada Inn, Super 8, **other:** VET, Batteries+
255	Lakeshore Dr, **E...gas:** BP, **other:** HOSPITAL, to Samford U, **W...gas:** Chevron, Citgo, **food:** Arby's, Capt D's, Chili's, Chick-fil-A, Dragon Chinese, Hooters, IHOP, McAlister's Deli, Milo's Burger, Landry's Seafood, LoneStar Steaks, O'Charley's, Outback Steaks, Subway, Taco Bell, Taco Casa, Wendy's, Wings Rest., **lodging:** Best Western, Drury Inn, Hampton Inn, Hilton Garden, La Quinta, Residence Inn, Studio+, Sun Suites, TownePlace Suites, **other:** BooksAMillion, Bruno's Foods, Curves, $Tree, Goody's, Lowe's Whse, Old Navy, Radio Shack, Sam's Club/gas, Wal-Mart SuperCtr/24hr, mall
254	Alford Ave, Shades Crest Rd, **E...gas:** Chevron, **W...gas:** BP, Citgo
252	US 31, Montgomery Hwy, **E...gas:** Chevron, Shell, Texaco, **food:** Arby's, Backyard Burger, Brewster's, Capt D's, ChuckeCheese, Hardee's, Pizza Hut, Taco Bell, Waffle House, **lodging:** Baymont Inn, Vestavio Hotel, **other:** HOSPITAL, Aamco, Big 10 Tire, GMC/Saturn/Isuzu, Lincoln/Mercury, NAPA, VW, Volvo, **W...gas:** BP, Chevron, Exxon, Shell, **food:** Burger King, Chick-fil-A, Golden Rule BBQ, Habanero's Mexican, Krispy Kreme, Krystal, Mandarin House, McAlister's Deli, McDonald's, Schlotsky's, Subway, TJ Maxx, Tuesday Morning, Waffle House, **lodging:** Day's Inn, **other:** Advance Parts, BooksAMillion, Bruno's Food, Buick, Chevrolet, Chrysler/Jeep, Circuit City, $Tree, Goodyear/auto, Hancock Fabrics, Honda, Kia, Nissan, Pontiac, Rite Aid, Toyota, transmissions
250	I-459, to US 280
247	Al 17, Valleydale Rd, **E...gas:** BP, **W...gas:** Citgo, Mobil, RaceWay, Shell, **food:** Arby's, IHOP, Milo's Burgers, Papa John's, RagTime Café, Waffle House, Zapata's Mexican, **lodging:** Hampton Inn, InTown Motel, La Quinta, **other:** Rite Aid, Publix, Walgreens

Birmingham

Interstate 65

N ↕ S

C l a n t o n

246	AL 119, Cahaba Valley Rd, Ⓔ...other: to Oak Mtn SP, Ⓦ...gas: BP/dsl, Cowboys/Subway/dsl, RaceWay, Shell, food: Applebee's, Arby's, Capt D's, Chick-fil-A, Cracker Barrel, DQ, Golden Corral, Hooters, KFC, Krystal, McDonald's, O'Charley's, Pier Rest., Pizza Hut, Pollo Volador Mexican, Purple Onion, Ruby Tuesday, Schlotsky's, Shoney's, Sonic, Taco Bell, Texas Roadhouse, Two Pesos Mexican, Waffle House, Wendy's, lodging: Best Western, Comfort Inn, Hampton Inn, Holiday Inn Express, Quality Inn, Ramada Ltd, Sleep Inn, Travelodge, other: HOSPITAL, Firestone/auto, Harley-Davidson, Mazda
242	Pelham, Ⓔ...gas: Chevron/dsl/24hr, Exxon/dsl, Shell, Ⓦ...lodging: Shelby Motel(2mi), other: GS(1mi)
238	US 31, Alabaster, Saginaw, Ⓔ...food: Buffalo Wild Wings, Chick-fil-A, Coldstone Creamery, Full Moon Cafe, Habanero's Mexican, Moe's SW Grill, Ruby Tuesday, Taco Bell, other: Belk, Best Buy, Books-A-Million, Lowes Whse, JC Penney, Ross, Target, TJ Maxx, Wal-Mart SuperCtr/dsl, Ⓦ...gas: Cannon, Chevron/dsl, QuickOut, Shell/dsl, food: Waffle House, 2 mi Ⓦ...food: Arby's, lodging: Shelby Motel, other: HOSPITAL
234	Ⓔ...gas: BP/Subway/dsl, Ⓦ...gas: Chevron/dsl/24hr, Shell/dsl, other: GMC, Cahaba RV Ctr
231	US 31, Saginaw, Ⓔ...gas: BP/dsl, GasBoy, Shell, food: Capt D's, Cracker Barrel, Golden Rule BBQ, Los Potrillos Mexican, McDonald's, Subway, Taco Bell, Yoe Wok Chinese, lodging: Holiday Inn Express, other: Burton RV Ctr, $Tree, Radio Shack, Wal-Mart SuperCtr/gas/24hr, Ⓦ...food: Donna's Café
228	AL 25, to Calera, Ⓔ...gas: Citgo/dsl, Shell/dsl, lodging: Best Value Inn, Day's Inn, Ⓦ...gas: Chevron/dsl, food: Hardee's(1mi), other: $General, to Brierfield Works SP
227mm	Buxahatchie Creek
219	Union Grove, Thorsby, Ⓔ...gas: Chevron/dsl/24hr, Exxon/Subway/dsl, food: Peach Queen Camping, Ⓦ...gas: Shell, food: Jack's Rest., Smokey Hollow Rest.
213mm	**rest area both lanes, full(handicapped)facilities, phone, vending, picnic tables, litter barrels, petwalk, RV dump**
212	AL 145, Clanton, Ⓔ...gas: Chevron/dsl, Ⓦ...gas: BP/Subway, Headco/dsl, other: HOSPITAL, One Big Peach
208	Clanton, Ⓦ...gas: Exxon/dsl/24hr, food: Shoney's, lodging: Guesthouse Inn, other: Heaton Pecans, Dandy RV Ctr
205	US 31, AL 22, to Clanton, Ⓔ...gas: Shell/dsl, Texaco, food: McDonald's, Waffle House, lodging: Best Western, Day's Inn, Holiday Inn Exress, Scottish Inn, other: Peach Park, to Confed Mem Park, Ⓦ...gas: BP/dsl/The Store, Chevron/dsl/24hr, food: Burger King, Capt D's, Hardee's, KFC, Subway, Taco Bell, lodging: Key West Inn, other: Durbin Farms Mkt, Wal-Mart SuperCtr/gas/24hr(2mi)
200	to Verbena, Ⓔ...gas: BP/dsl, Ⓦ...gas: Shell/DQ/Stuckey's/dsl, other: RV camping
195	Worlds Largest Confederate Flag
186	US 31, Pine Level, Ⓔ...other: Confederate Mem Park(13mi), Ⓦ...gas: BP/dsl, Chevron/24hr, Conoco/Subway/dsl, food: Carla's Diner, lodging: Pine Motel, other: HOSPITAL
181	AL 14, to Prattville, Ⓔ...gas: Chevron/dsl/24hr, Entec/dsl, Ⓦ...gas: Exxon, QV, Texaco/DQ/dsl, USA, food: Cracker Barrel, El Torito, Ruby Tuesday, Subway, Waffle House, lodging: Best Western, Comfort Inn, La Quinta, Super 8, other: HOSPITAL
179	US 82 W, Millbrook, Ⓔ...gas: Chevron/dsl, food: Asian Grill, lodging: County Inn&Suites, Key West Inn, Sleep Inn, other: K&K RV Park, Ⓦ...gas: Exxon/Shoneys/24hr, Jet-Pep, Petro, RaceWay, Shell, USA/dsl, food: Burger King, Hardee's, Longhorn Steaks, McDonald's, O'Charley's, Outback Steaks, Steak'n Shake, Waffle House, lodging: Days Inn, Econolodge, Hampton Inn, Holiday Inn, other: Lowe's Whse, 1 mi Ⓦ...food: A&W/KFC, Applebee's, Burger King, Chick-fil-A, Krystal, Ryan's, Sonic, Tequila Grill, lodging: Jameson Inn, other: Bass Pro Shops, Chevrolet, $Tree, Ford, K-Mart, Michael's, Office Depot, Wal-Mart SuperCtr/24hr
176	AL 143 N(from nb, no return), Millbrook, Coosada
173	AL 152, North Blvd, to US 231, no services
172mm	Alabama River
172	Clay St, Herron St, Ⓔ...lodging: Embassy Suites, Ⓦ...gas: Chevron/dsl
171	I-85 N, Day St
170	Fairview Ave, Ⓔ...gas: Citgo/Subway, Gas Depot, food: China King, Church's, McDonald's, other: Advance Parts, AutoZone, CVS Drug, O'Reilly Parts, Rite Aid, Ⓦ...gas: Exxon, other: Calhoun Foods, Family$
169	Edgemont Ave(from sb), Ⓔ...gas: Liberty, other: carwash
168	US 80 E, US 82, South Blvd, Ⓔ...gas: BP/dsl, Entec/dsl, Kangaroo/dsl, TA/dsl/rest./24hr/@, food: Arby's, Capt D's, KFC, McDonald's, Popeye's, Pizza Hut, Taco Bell, Waffle House, lodging: Best Inn, Economy Inn, Travel Inn, other: HOSPITAL, Family$, Ⓦ...gas: Chevron/dsl, Shell/Subway/dsl, Speedy/dsl, food: DQ, Hardee's, Wendy's, lodging: Airport Inn, Comfort Inn, Econolodge, Inn South, Peddler's Inn, Ramada Inn
167	US 80 W, to Selma, no services
164	US 31, Hope Hull, Ⓔ...gas: BP/24hr, Petro+, Saveway/dsl/scales/24hr, lodging: Lakeside Hotel, other: MC RV Park, Ⓦ...gas: BP/Burger King, Chevron/24hr, Liberty/Subway, food: Waffle House, lodging: Best Western, Hampton Inn, Motel 6, other: auto repair
158	to US 31, Ⓔ...gas: BP/DQ/Stuckey's Ⓦ...gas: ⚒/Flying J/CountryMkt/dsl/scales/24hr

7

Interstate 65

N ↑ S

151	AL 97, to Letohatchee, W...**gas:** BP, PaceCar/dsl
142	AL 185, to Ft Deposit, E...**gas:** Shell/dsl/24hr, USA/dsl, **food:** Priester's Pecans, W...**gas:** Chevron/24hr
133mm	**rest areas both lanes, full(handicapped) facilities, phone, vending, picnic tables, litter barrels, petwalk, RV dump**
130	AL10 E, AL 185, to Greenville, E...**gas:** Chevron/dsl/24hr, Citgo, Shell/24hr, USA/dsl, **food:** Arby's, Capt D's, China Town Buffet, Hardee's, KFC, McDonald's, Pizza Hut, Waffle House, Wendy's, **lodging:** Best Value, Day's Inn, **other:** Advance Parts, CVS Drug, $General, Goody's, Russell Stover, Super Foods, to Sherling Lake Park, W...**gas:** Phillips 66/Subway/dsl, QV, Texaco/dsl, **food:** Bates Turkey Rest., Burger King, Cracker Barrel, El Rodeo Mexican, Hook's BBQ, Krystal, Ruby Tuesday, Shoney's, Taco Bell/TCBY, Tomatoes Etc., The Border, **lodging:** Best Western, Comfort Inn, Hampton Inn, Holiday Inn Express, Jameson Inn, **other:** Chevrolet, Chrysler/Dodge/Jeep, Wal-Mart SuperCtr/24hr/gas, Winn-Dixie
128	AL 10, to Greenville, E...**gas:** Shell/Smokehouse/dsl, **other:** HOSPITAL, W...**gas:** BP
114	AL 106, to Georgiana, W...**gas:** BP, Chevron/24hr, **other:** auto repair
107	rd 7, to Garland, no services
101	to Owassa, E...**gas:** BP/dsl, W...**gas:** Exxon/dsl, **other:** Owassa RV Park
96	AL 83, to Evergreen, E...**gas:** Chevron/24hr, Shell, **food:** Burger King, Hardee's, KFC/Taco Bell, McDonald's, **other:** HOSPITAL, W...**gas:** Citgo/Chester's/Subway/dsl, **food:** Black Angus Rest., Pizza Hut, Waffle House, **lodging:** Best Value Inn, Comfort Inn, Day's Inn
93	US 84, to Evergreen, E...**gas:** Shell/dsl, USA/dsl, **other:** PineCrest RV Park, W...**gas:** BP/dsl
89mm	**rest area sb, full(handicapped)facilities, phone, vending, picnic tables, litter barrels, petwalk, RV dump**
85mm	**rest area nb, full(handicapped)facilities, phone, vending, picnic tables, litter barrels, petwalk, RV dump**
83	AL 6, to Lenox, E...**gas:** Exxon/dsl/LP, **other:** Sunshine RV Park(4mi)
77	AL 41, to Range, Brewton, Repton, E...**gas:** BP, W...**gas:** Citgo/dsl, Shell/Stuckey's/dsl, **food:** Old Timer's Cafe, Ranch House Rest.
69	AL 113, to Flomaton, E...**gas:** BP/Subway/dsl, Shell/dsl/scales24hr, **other:** dsl repair, W...**gas:** Minute Stop/dsl/24hr, **food:** Huddle House
57	AL 21, to Atmore, E...**gas:** Exxon/BBQ/dsl, Shell/dsl, **food:** Creek Family Rest., **lodging:** Best Western, **other:** Indian Bingo, W...**gas:** BP/dsl, **other:** to Kelley SP
54	Escambia Cty Rd 1, E...**gas:** BP/Subway/dsl, Citgo/dsl, **other:** to Creek Indian Res
45	to Perdido, W...**gas:** Chevron/dsl
37	AL 287, Gulf Shores Pkwy, to Bay Minette, E...**gas:** BP
34	to AL 59, to Bay Minette, Stockton, E...**other:** HOSPITAL
31	AL 225, to Stockton, E...**other:** to Blakeley SP, Confederate Mem Bfd, W...**gas:** Shell/dsl
29mm	Tensaw River
28mm	Middle River
25mm	Mobile River
22	Creola, E... marine ctr, RV Park, truck repair
19	US 43, to Satsuma, E...**gas:** Chevron/dsl/24hr, Pilot/Arby's/dsl/scales/24hr, **food:** McDonald's, Pintoli's Italian, Waffle House, W...**gas:** BP/dsl, **other:** I-65 RV Park(1.5mi)
15	AL 41, E...**gas:** Chevron, **food:** China Chef, Godfather's Pizza, **other:** Family$, Food World, W...**gas:** Circle K/gas, Shell/Subway/dsl, **other:** $General
13	AL 158, AL 213, to Saraland, E...**gas:** Shell/dsl/24hr, **food:** Ruby Tuesday, Waffle House, Wintzell's Oyster House, **lodging:** Comfort Suites, Day's Inn, Holiday Inn Express, **other:** Wal-Mart SuperCtr/24hr, W...**gas:** Exxon/Subway/Pizza Inn, **lodging:** Hampton Inn, **other:** to Chickasabogue Campground
10	W Lee St, E...**gas:** Minute Stop, Parade/dsl, Shell/Subway, **lodging:** Best Inn
9	I-165 S, to Mobile, to I-10 E
8b a	US 45, to Prichard, E...**gas:** Chevron/24hr, Shell/dsl, **food:** Church's, **other:** Family$, Tiger Foods, W...**gas:** BP/24hr, Conoco/dsl, 1st Stop, Pride Trkstp/dsl/scales, RaceWay, **food:** Burger King, Domino's, Golden Egg Café, McDonald's, **other:** vet
5b	US 98, Moffett Rd, E...**gas:** Exxon/dsl, Texaco, **food:** Burger King, Church's, DQ, McDonald's, Saucy Q BBQ, **other:** Advance Parts, Big 10 Tire, W...**gas:** MinuteStop/dsl, **food:** Hardee's, **lodging:** Super 8
5a	Spring Hill Ave, E...**gas:** Chevron, Shell/dsl, **food:** KFC, McDonald's, **other:** HOSPITAL, AutoZone, Big 10 Tire, CarQuest, Family$, Tiger Foods, W...**gas:** Exxon, Shell/dsl, **food:** Starbucks, Waffle House, Zaxby's, **lodging:** Extended Stay America, Wingate Inn
4	Dauphin St, E...**gas:** BP/dsl, Shell, Summit Gas/dsl, **food:** Checker's, Chick-fil-A, Cracker Barrel, Godfather's, Krystal, McDonald's, Popeye's, Subway, Taco Bell, TCBY, Waffle House, Wendy's, **lodging:** Comfort Inn, Comfort Suites, Red Roof Inn, RodeWay Inn, **other:** Cadillac/Pontiac/GMC, $General, FoodWorld, Hyundai, Lowe's Whse, Mercedes, Mr Transmission, Rite Aid, Subaru, Tuesday Morning, Wal-Mart SuperCtr/24hr, same as 3 & 5a, W...**other:** HOSPITAL
3	Airport Blvd, E...**gas:** BP, **food:** Burger King, Cane's, Golden China, Logan's Roadhouse, Macaroni Grill, Morrison's Cafeteria, Piccadilly's, Wendy's, **lodging:** Marriott, **other:** HOSPITAL, Acura/Jaguar/Infiniti, Barnes&Noble, Belk, Best Buy, BooksAMillion, Dillard's, $Tree, Firestone/auto, Ford, Goodyear/auto, Goody's, Harley-Davidson, Honda, Mitsubishi, Nissan, Old Navy, Saab, Sam's Club/gas, Saturn, Sears/auto, Staples, mall, W...**gas:** Mystik, Shell, **food:** American Café, Arby's, Burger King,

Greenville

Atmore

8

Interstate 65

N ↕ S

Mobile

Carrabba's, China Doll, ChuckeCheese, Denny's, El Chico, Firehouse Subs, Honeybaked Ham, Hooters, IHOP, JR's Smokehouse, LoneStar Steaks, Los Rancheros Mexican, Marble Slab, McDonald's, Moe's SW Grill, O'Charley's, Olive Garden, Panera Bread, Pizza Hut, Popeye's, Quizno's, Red Lobster, Ruby Tuesday, S China Seafood, Starbucks, Subway, Taco Bell, Waffle House, Wanfu, Wings Grill, **lodging:** Airport Inn, Ashberry Suites, Best Inn, Best Value Inn, Courtyard, Day's Inn, Drury Inn, Econolodge, Fairfield Inn, Family Inn, Hampton Inn, Hilton Garden, InTowne Suites, La Quinta, Motel 6, Quality Inn, Ramada Inn Residence Inn, **other:** BooksaMillion, Circuit City, $General, Fresh Mkt Foods, Home Depot, Jo-Ann Fabrics, Michael's, Office Depot, PepBoys, PetsMart, Radio Shack, Ross, SteinMart, TJ Maxx, U-Haul, Walgreens, to USAL

| 1b a | US 90, Government Blvd, **E...gas:** Chevron, Raceway, **food:** McAlister's Deli, Steak'n Shake, **lodging:** Howard Johnson, **other:** Audi/VW, BMW, Buick/Isuzu/Volvo, Chevrolet, Chrysler/Jeep, Dodge, Honda, Isuzu, Kia, Lexus, Lincoln/Mercury, Mazda, Toyota, **W...gas:** Shell/dsl, **food:** Waffle House, **lodging:** Rest Inn |
| 0mm | I-10, E to Pensacola, W to New Orleans, I-65 begins/ends on I-10, exit 20 |

Interstate 85

N ↕ S

Lanett

Opelika

Exit #	Services
80mm	Alabama/Georgia state line, Chattahoochee River
79	US 29, to Lanett, **E...gas:** Big Cat/dsl, BP/dsl, LoBucks/24hr, **food:** Arby's, Burger King, Capt D's, Chuck's BBQ, KFC, Krystal, McDonald's, Pizza Hut, San Marcos Mexican, Subway, Taco Bell, Waffle House/24hr, Wendy's, **other:** HOSPITAL, Advance Parts, $General, $Tree, Wal-Mart SuperCtr/gas/24hr, transmissions, to West Point Lake, **W...gas:** Jetpep, Petro, QV, **food:** Domino's, Ocean Breeze, Sonic, **lodging:** Day's Inn, Econolodge, **other:** AutoZone, CVS Drug, Kroger, O'Reilly Parts, Parts+, vet
78.5mm	**Welcome Ctr sb, full(handicapped)facilities, phone, vending, picnic tables, litter barrels, pet-walk**
77	AL 208, to Huguley, **E...gas:** Spectrum, Jet Pep/dsl, **food:** Waffle House, Waffle King, **lodging:** Holiday Inn Express, **other:** Chevrolet, Chrysler/Dodge/Ford/Lincoln/Mercury, **W...fireworks**
76mm	Eastern/Central time zone
70	AL 388, to Cusseta, **E...gas:** BP, Shell/Country Pride/Subway/dsl/scales/24hr/@ , **W...fireworks**
66	Andrews Rd, to US 29, no services
64	US 29, to Opelika, **E...gas:** BP, **lodging:** Guesthouse Inn, **W...gas:** Tiger/dsl
62	US 280/431, to Opelika, **E...gas:** Chevron, Eagle/dsl, Liberty Gas, Spectrum/Church's/dsl, **food:** Burger King, Durango Mexican, McDonald's, Subway, Wok'n Roll Rest., Yang's Buffet, **lodging:** Day's Inn, Econolodge, GuestHouse Inn, Holiday Inn, Knight's Inn, Motel 6, **other:** Lakeside RV Park(4.5mi), **W...gas:** Jet Pep, Shell, **food:** Capt.

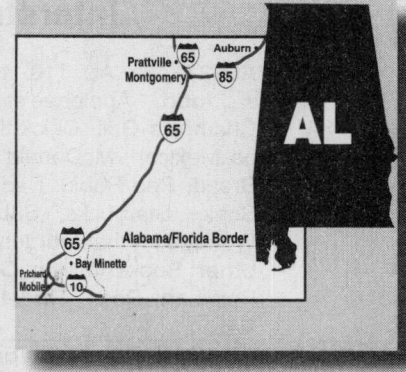

Opelika

D's, Cracker Barrel, Sizzlin Steaks, Thai Rest., Waffle House, **lodging:** Comfort Inn, Travelodge, **other:** Chevrolet, Chrysler/Dodge, Ford, Harley Davidson, Jeep, USA Stores/famous brands

60	AL 51, AL 169, to Opelika, **E...gas:** BP/dsl, Raceway, **food:** Hardee's, **other:** $General, **W...gas:** Shell/dsl, **food:** Wendy's(1.5 mi), **other:** HOSPITAL
58	US 280 W, to Opelika, **E...lodging:** Hampton Inn, **other:** Kohl's, golf, museum, **W...gas:** BP, Chevron/Subway, Liberty Gas, **food:** Arby's, Buffalo Wild Wings, Chick-fil-A, DQ, Golden Corral, Jim Bob's, Moe's SW Grill, Logan's Roadhouse, Longhorn Steaks, O'Charley's, Olive Garden, Outback Steaks, Quizno's, Sonic, Starbucks, Taco Bell, **other:** HOSPITAL, Best Buy, Books-A-Million, Home Depot, Kroger/gas, Lowe's Whse, Office Depot, Ross, Target, TJ Maxx
57	Glenn Ave, **W...gas:** Exxon, QV, **food:** Shakey's Pizza, Waffle House, **lodging:** Hilton Garden, Plaza Hotel, University Motel, **other:** Sam's Club/gas
51	US 29, to Auburn, **E...gas:** BP/dsl/24hr, **lodging:** Hampton Inn, **other:** Leisure Time RV Park, to Chewacla SP, **W...gas:** Chevron/Subway, Raceway, **food:** Arby's, Burger King, Carino's Italian, Firehouse Subs, Golden Rule BBQ, Guthrie's Rest., Hooters, Krystal, Little Caesar's, McDonald's, Panda Chinese, Philly Connection, Pizza Hut, Ruby Tuesday, Santa Fe Steaks, Sonic, Taco Bell, Waffle House, Wendy's, Zaxby's, **lodging:** Best Western, Comfort Inn, Econolodge, Holiday Inn Express, Microtel, Sleep Inn, **other:** Advance Parts, Ford/Lincoln/Mercury, Nissan, Toyota, Wal-Mart SuperCtr/24hr/gas, to Auburn U, tires/repair, vet
44mm	**rest area both lanes, full(handicapped)facilities, phone, vending, picnic tables, litter barrels, pet-walk, RV dump, 24hr security**
42	US 80, AL 186 E, Wire Rd, **E...other:** to Tuskegee NF, dsl repair/tires, **W...gas:** Torch 85/rest./dsl/24hr
38	AL 81, to Tuskegee, **E...**to Tuskegee NHS
32	AL 49 N, to Tuskegee, **E...gas:** BP/dsl
26	AL 229 N, to Tallassee, **E...gas:** Shell/Guthrie's/dsl, **W...**HOSPITAL
22	US 80, to Shorter, **E...gas:** BP/dsl, Chevron/Petro/dsl/rest., Exxon/dsl, **lodging:** Day's Inn, **other:** to Macon Co Greyhound Pk, Windrift RV Park
16	Waugh, to Cecil, **E...gas:** BP/Subway/dsl, **other:** auto repair
11	US 80, to Mt Meigs, **E...gas:** Exxon/Subway/dsl, Liberty/dsl, **food:** Anthony's Rest., Burger King, Cracker Barrel, Jose's Grill, Sommer's Grill, Waffle House, **lodging:** Comfort Inn, Holiday Inn Express, Sleep Inn, **other:** Bruno's Foods, Home Depot, Wal-Mart SuperCtr, **W...gas:** Chevron/dsl/24hr

Opelika / **Auburn**

ALABAMA

Interstate 85

9	AL 271, to AL 110, to Auburn U/Montgomery, E...food: Applebee's, Arby's, BoneFish Grill, Champp's Grill, Chick-fil-A, Chili's, Guthrie's, Ixtapa Mexican, McDonald's, Moe's SW Grill, Panera Bread, Red Robin, Red Star Grill, Ruby Tuesday, Sonic, Starbucks, Subway, Texas Roadhouse, Wendy's, Whataburger, lodging: Hampton Inn, other: BooksAMillion, Costco/gas, Dillard's, Kohl's, Petsmart, Ross, Target, World Mkt, W... HOSPITAL
6	US 80, US 231, AL 21, East Blvd, E...gas: Chevron/24hr, Exxon/dsl/24hr, RaceWay, food: Apple Pie Grill, Arby's, Burger King, Carrabba's, Chick-fil-A, Cuco's Mexican, Golden Corral, Guthrie's, Hooters, Jason's Deli, KFC, McAlister's, McDonald's, Ming's Chinese, O'Charley's, Olive Garden, Piccadilly's, Popeye's, Roadhouse Grill, Schlotsky's, Shogun Japanese, Starbucks, Subway, Taco Bell, Up The Creek Grill, Waffle House, Wendy's, Wings Grill, Zaxby's, lodging: Best Inn, Comfort Inn, Country Inn&Suites, Courtyard, Extended Stay America, Fairfield Inn, Hampton Inn, La Quinta, Quality Inn, Ramada Inn, Residence Inn, SpringHill Suites, Studio+, TownePlace Suites, Wingate Inn, other: Acura, Books-a-Million, $General, Fresh Mkt Foods, Home Depot, Honda, Lowe's Whse, Pontiac/Cadillac, Radio Shack, USPO, other: Barnes& Noble, Marshall's, Michael's, Wal-Mart SuperCtr/24hr, W...gas: BP, Citgo, Liberty Gas/dsl, Shell, Texaco, food: Burger King, Capt D's, Church's, Dreamland BBQ, KFC, Krystal, LoneStar Steaks, McDonald's, Outback Steaks, Red Lobster, Shoney's, Waffle House, lodging: Best Western, Comfort Suites, Drury Inn, Econolodge, Lexington Hotel, Motel 6, other: Audi, BMW, Buick, Cadillac, Chevrolet, Chrysler/Jeep, Ford, Hyundai, Isuzu, Kia, Lexus, Mazda, Mercedes, Mitsubishi, Nissan, Sam's Club/gas, Toyota, VW, to Gunter AFB, 1 mi W...food: Buffet City, Capt D's, Hardee's, IHOP, Ruby Tuesday, other: JC Penney, Sears/auto, mall
4	Perry Hill Rd, E...other: Bruno's Foods, Rite Aid, W...gas: Cannon Gas, Chevron/24hr, food: Hardee's, Subway, lodging: Hilton Garden, Homewood Suites, other: $General, Express Oil Change
3	Ann St, E...gas: BP/dsl, Chevron, food: Arby's, Capt D's, Domino's, Down the St Cafe, Hardee's, KFC, Krystal, McDonald's, Taco Bell, Waffle House, Wendy's, lodging: Day's Inn, other: Big 10 Tire, W...gas: Entec, Exxon, PaceCar, lodging: Stay Lodge, food: Chick-fil-A, Cici's Pizza, Popeye's, other: $Tree, Office Depot, Radio Shack, Ross, Wal-Mart SuperCtr/24hr/gas
2	Forest Ave, E...CVS Drug, W...HOSPITAL
1	Court St, Union St, downtown, E...gas: BP/dsl, Exxon, W...to Ala St U
0mm	I-85 begins/ends on I-65, exit 171 in Montgomery

Interstate 459(Birmingham)

Exit #	Services
33b a	I-59, N to Gadsden, S to Birmingham
32	US 11, Trussville, N...gas: BP/24hr, lodging: Best Inn(3mi), S...gas: Chevron/dsl/24hr, Citgo, RaceWay/24hr, Shell/Wendy's/dsl, food: A&W/KFC, Arby's, BBQ, Chili's, Coldstone Creamery, Jack's Rest., Jim& Nick's BBQ, McDonald's, Quizno's, Starbucks Waffle House, lodging: Hampton Inn, other: Big 10 Tires, BooksAMillion, Harley-Davidson, Home Depot, Lowe's Whse, Mazda, Michael's, Old Navy, Pontiac/GMC/Buick, Staples, Target, TJ Maxx
31	Derby Parkway, W...other: B'ham Race Course
29	I-20, E to Atlanta, W to Birmingham
27	Grants Mill Rd, S...gas: Exxon/dsl, other: BMW/Lexus, Cadillac
23	Liberty Parkway, no services
19	US 280, Mt Brook, Childersburg, N...gas: Chevron, other: Barnes&Noble, PF Chang's, Panera Bread, 1-2 mi S...gas: Exxon, food: Arby's, Burger King, Cracker Barrel, Kobe Japanese, McDonald's, Ralph&Kacoos, Ruby Tuesday, TGIFriday, lodging: Courtyard, Drury Inn, Fairfield Inn, Hampton Inn, Hilton, Holiday Inn Express, Homestead Suites, Marriott, Sheraton, Studio Inn
17	Acton Rd, N...gas: Shell/dsl/24hr, food: Krystal, McDonald's
15b a	I-65, N to Birmingham, S to Montgomery
13	US 31, Hoover, Pelham, N...gas: BP, Chevron, Citgo, Shell, food: BBQ, Chick-fil-A, Fish Mkt Rest., Golden Corral, Habanero's, Krispy Kreme, LoneStar Steaks, McDonald's, Quizno's, Schlotsky's, SteakOut, Subway, lodging: Comfort Inn, Day's Inn, Hampton Inn, Holiday Inn, other: Acura, BooksAMillion, Bruno's Foods, Buick, Cadillac, Chevrolet, Chrysler/Plymouth/Jeep, Circuit City, $Tree, Eckerd, Firestone, Goodyear, Honda, Kia, Mitsubishi, Mr Transmissions, Nissan, Rite Aid, Staples, Toyota, S...gas: Crown Gas, Jet-Pep, Shell/dsl/24hr, food: Alexander's, Burger King, China Buffet, Guthrie's, Jim&Nicks BBQ, McDonald's, Olive Garden, Pizza Hut, Shula's Steaks, StoneFish Grill, Taco Bell, Ted's MT Grill, Top China, Wendy's, lodging: Best Western, Courtyard, Winfrey Hotel, other: Barnes&Noble, Best Buy, Big 10 Tire, Bruno's Foods, Comp USA, Costco/gas, CVS Drug, GNC, Goody's, Hancock Fabrics, Home Depot, Infiniti, JC Penney, K-Mart, Macey's, Marshall's, Mercedes, Michael's, NTB, Office Depot, Sam's Club, Sears, Wal-Mart(1mi), mall
10	AL 150, Waverly, N...gas: Chevron(1mi), Shell(1mi), lodging: Renaissance Motel(6mi), S...gas: BP/dsl/24hr, Exxon, food: Mei China, other: Ford, GNC, Walgreen, Publix/deli
6	AL 52, to Bessemer, N...gas: BP/dsl, S...gas: BP, Crown/Taco Bell, Shell, food: Arby's, McDonald's, Pizza Hut, Subway, Waffle House, Wendy's, lodging: Sleep Inn, other: Cherokee Beach RV Park, $General, CVS Drug, Winn-Dixie
1	AL 18, Bessemer, N...gas: Shell/dsl, S...gas: BP/dsl, food: China King, McDonald's, Subway, other: Advance Parts, CVS Drug, FoodWorld, to Tannehill SP
0mm	I-459 begins/ends on I-20/59, exit 106

10

Interstate 8

Exit #	Services
178b a	I-10, I-8 begins/ends on I-10, exit 199, E to Tucson, W to Phoenix
174	Trekell Rd, to Casa Grande, **2-4 mi** 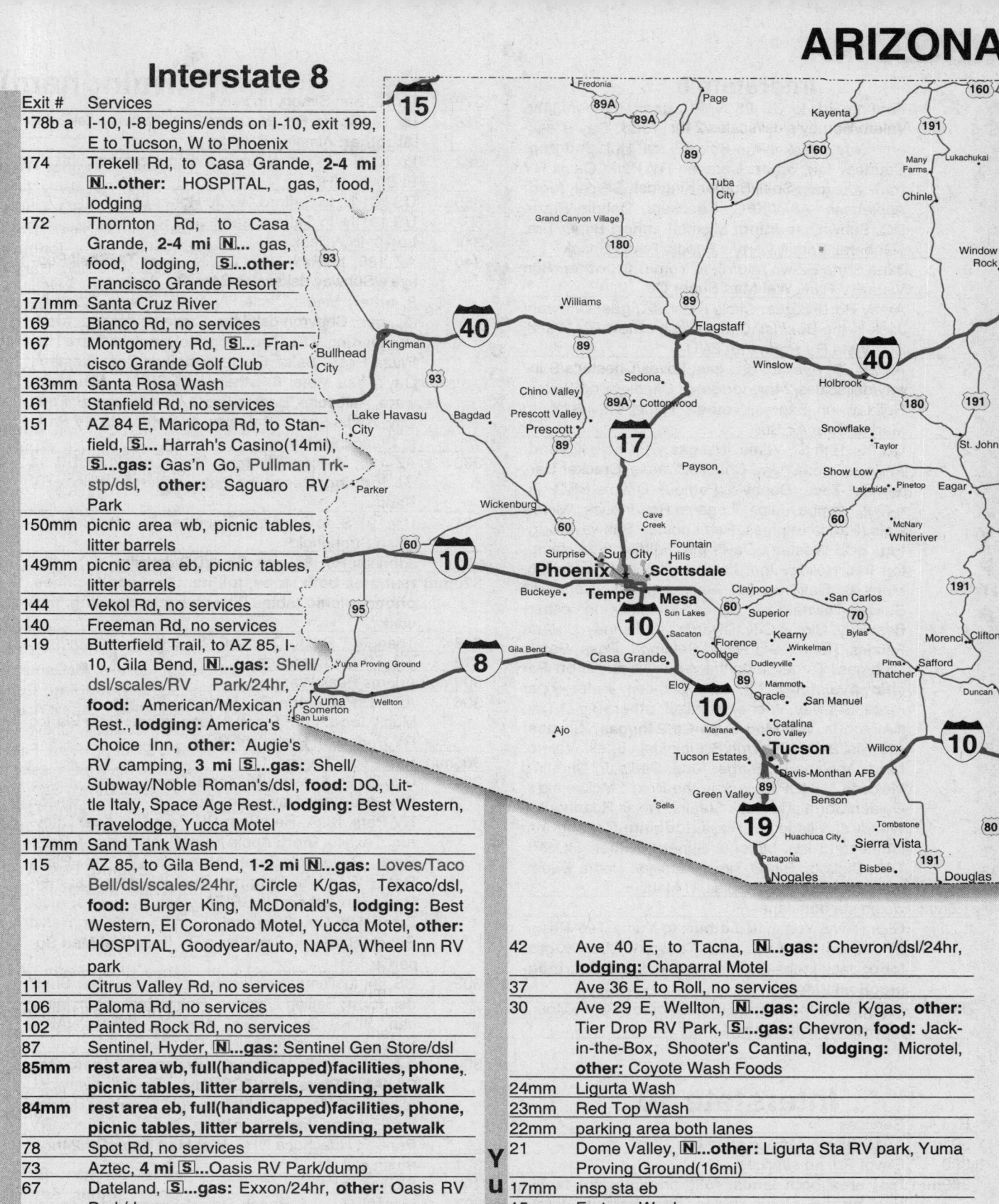**...other:** HOSPITAL, gas, food, lodging
172	Thornton Rd, to Casa Grande, **2-4 mi** 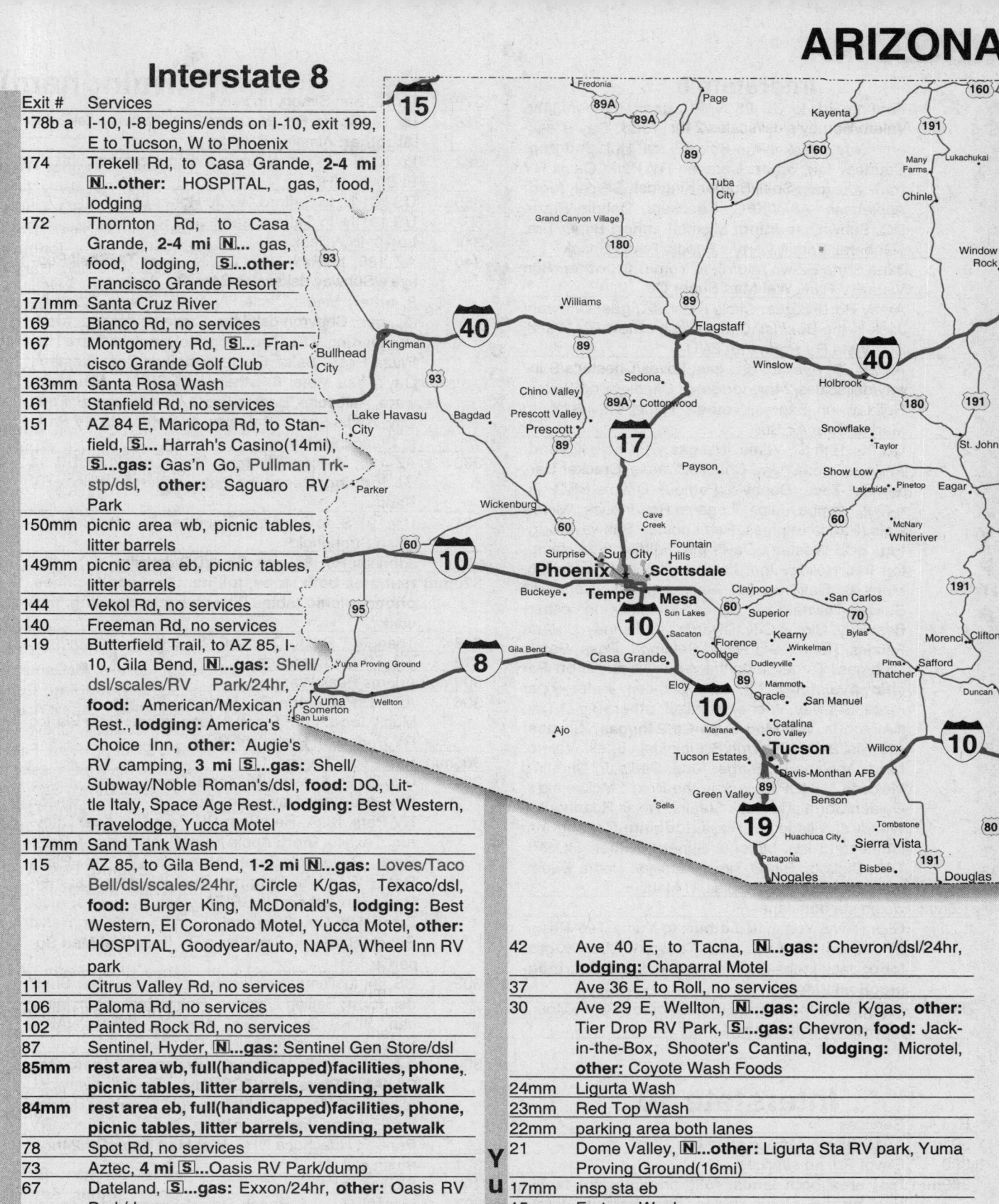**...** gas, food, lodging, 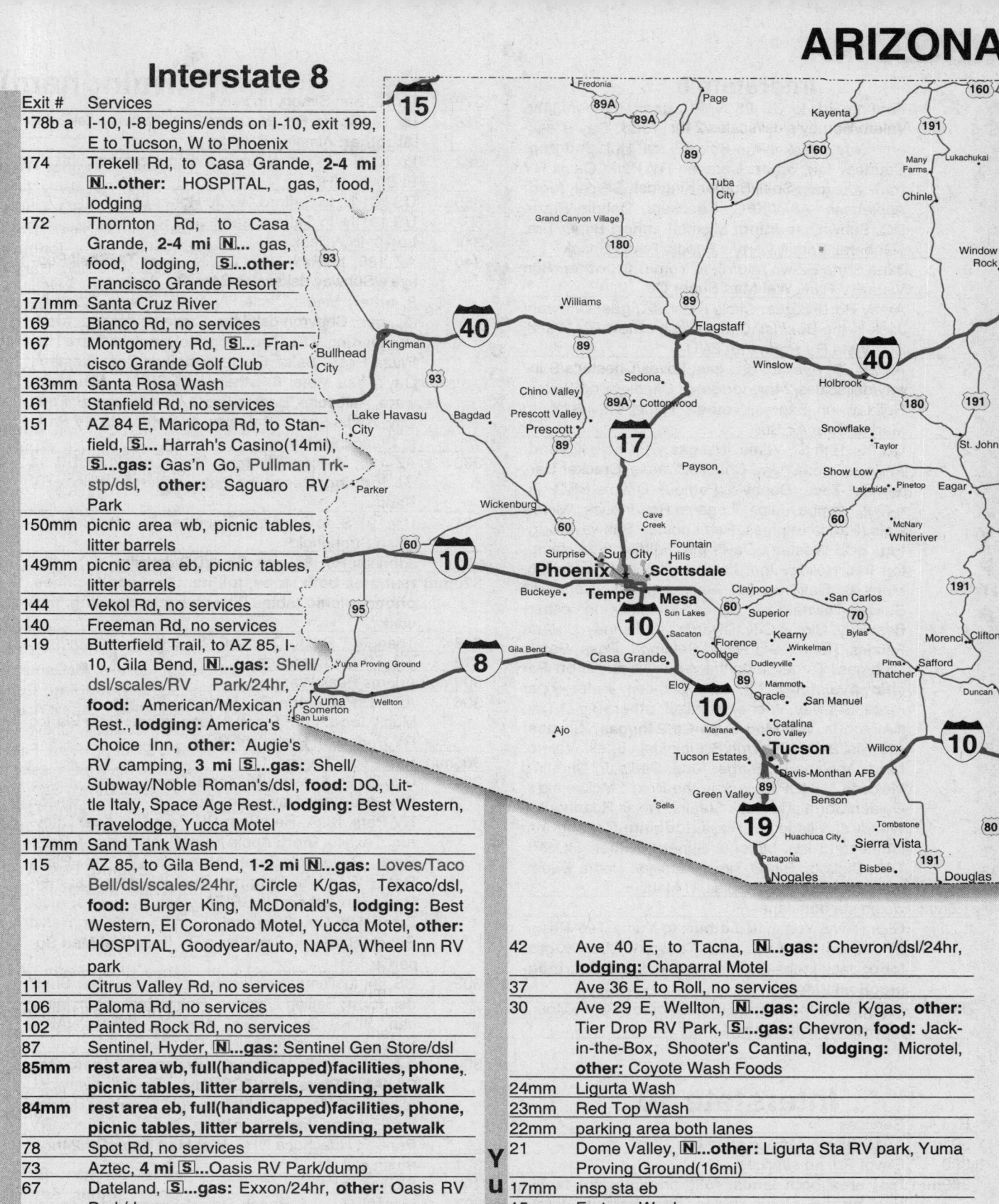**...other:** Francisco Grande Resort
171mm	Santa Cruz River
169	Bianco Rd, no services
167	Montgomery Rd, 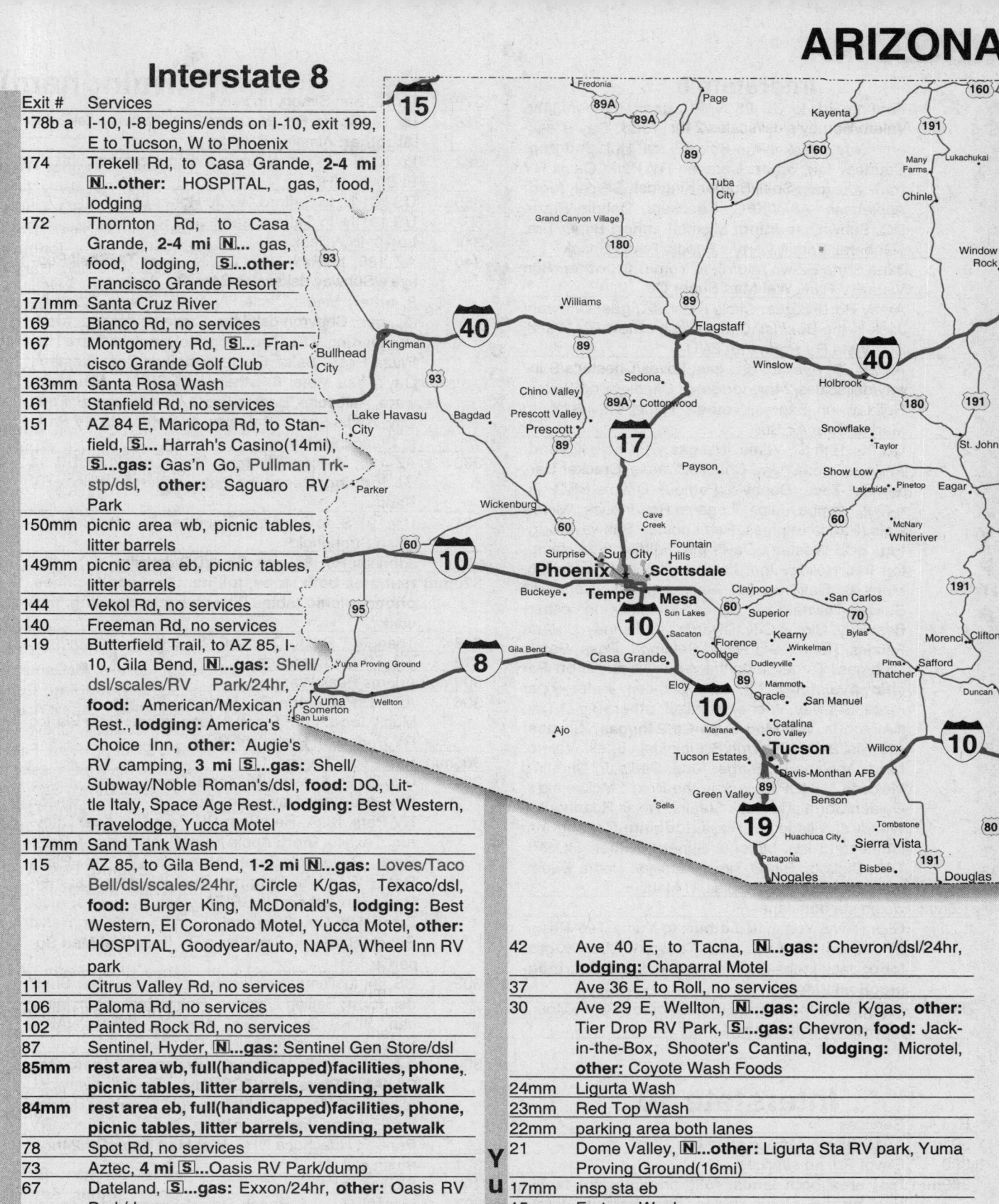**...** Francisco Grande Golf Club
163mm	Santa Rosa Wash
161	Stanfield Rd, no services
151	AZ 84 E, Maricopa Rd, to Stanfield, 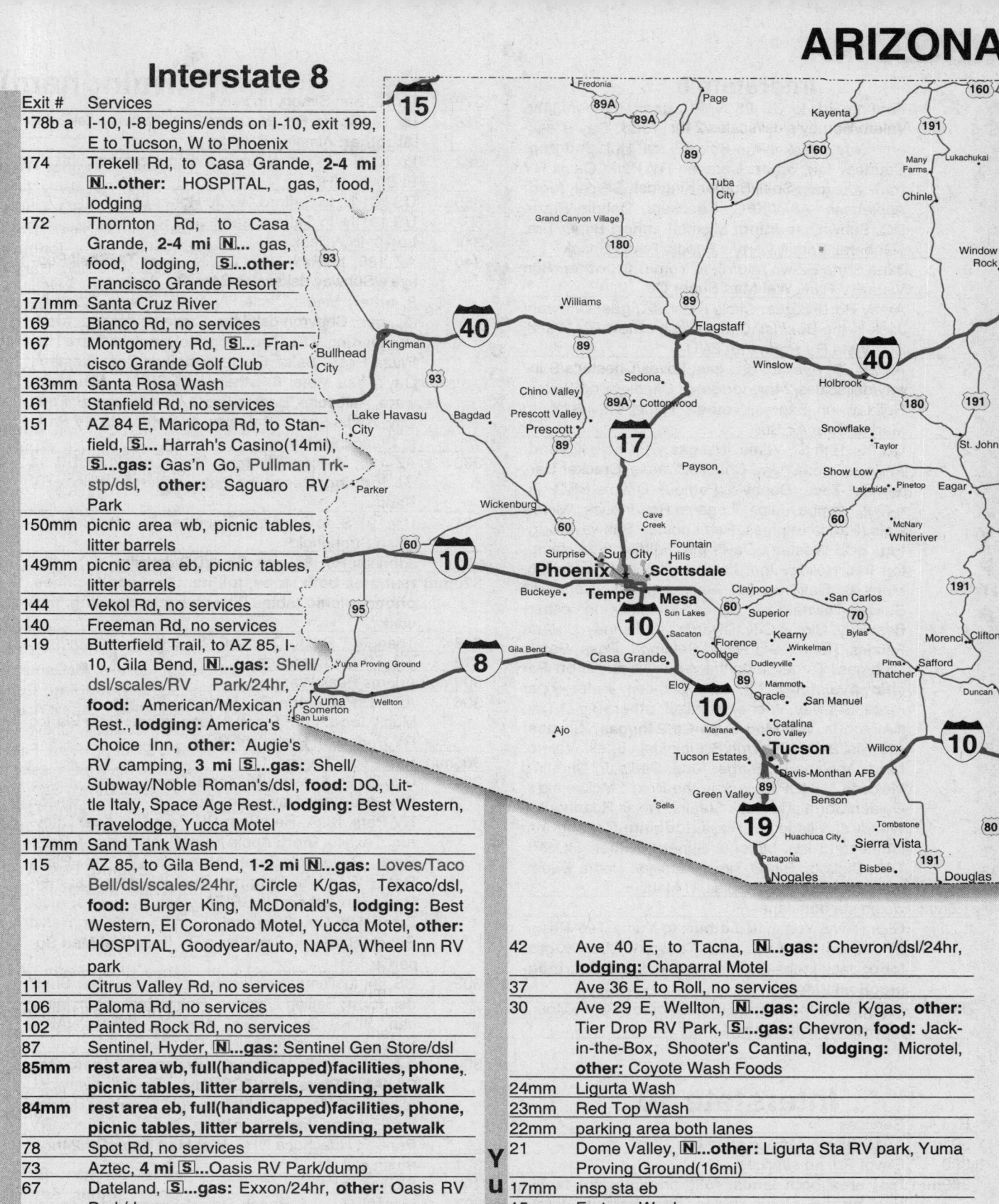**...** Harrah's Casino(14mi), 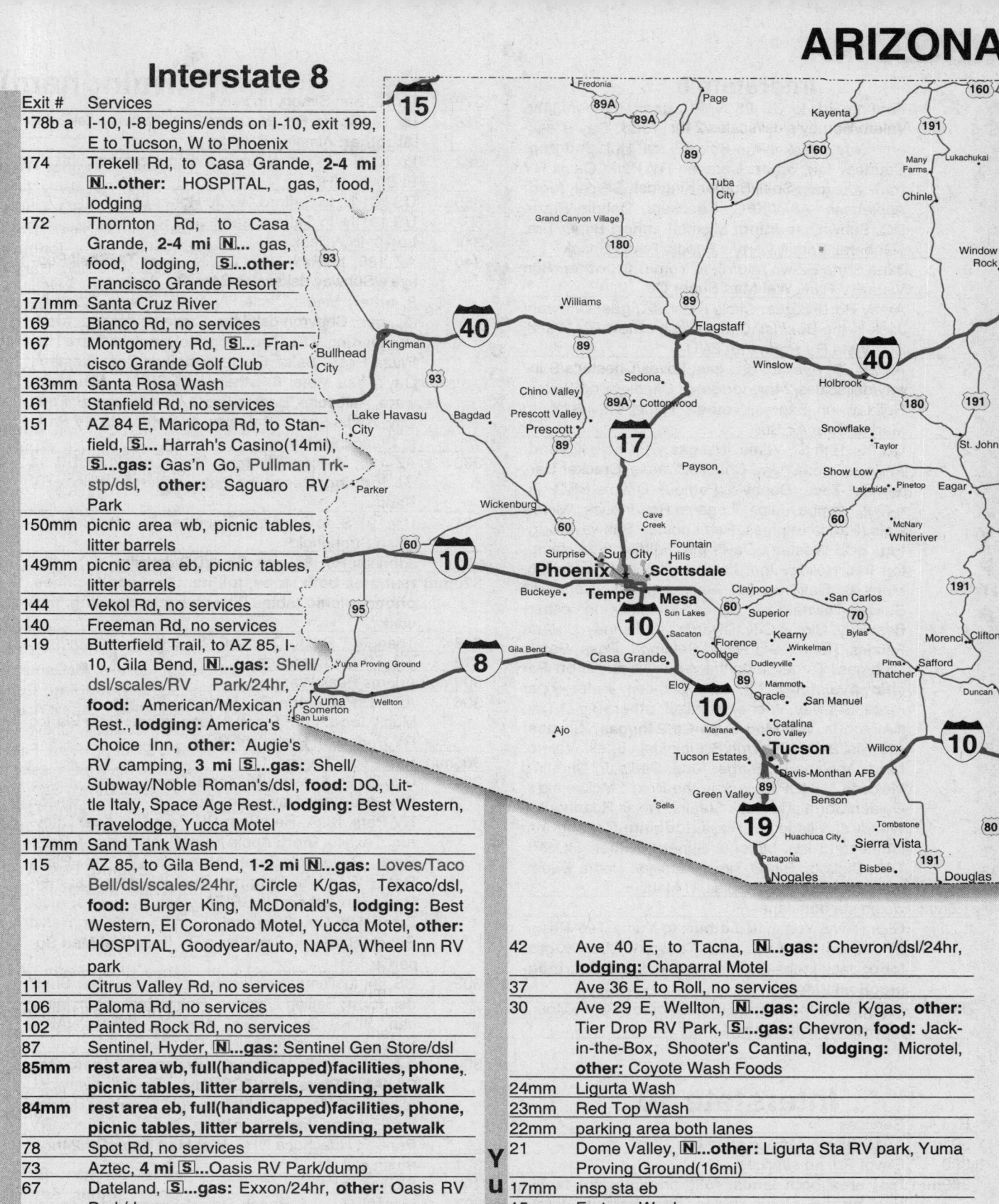**...gas:** Gas'n Go, Pullman Trkstp/dsl, **other:** Saguaro RV Park
150mm	picnic area wb, picnic tables, litter barrels
149mm	picnic area eb, picnic tables, litter barrels
144	Vekol Rd, no services
140	Freeman Rd, no services
119	Butterfield Trail, to AZ 85, I-10, Gila Bend, 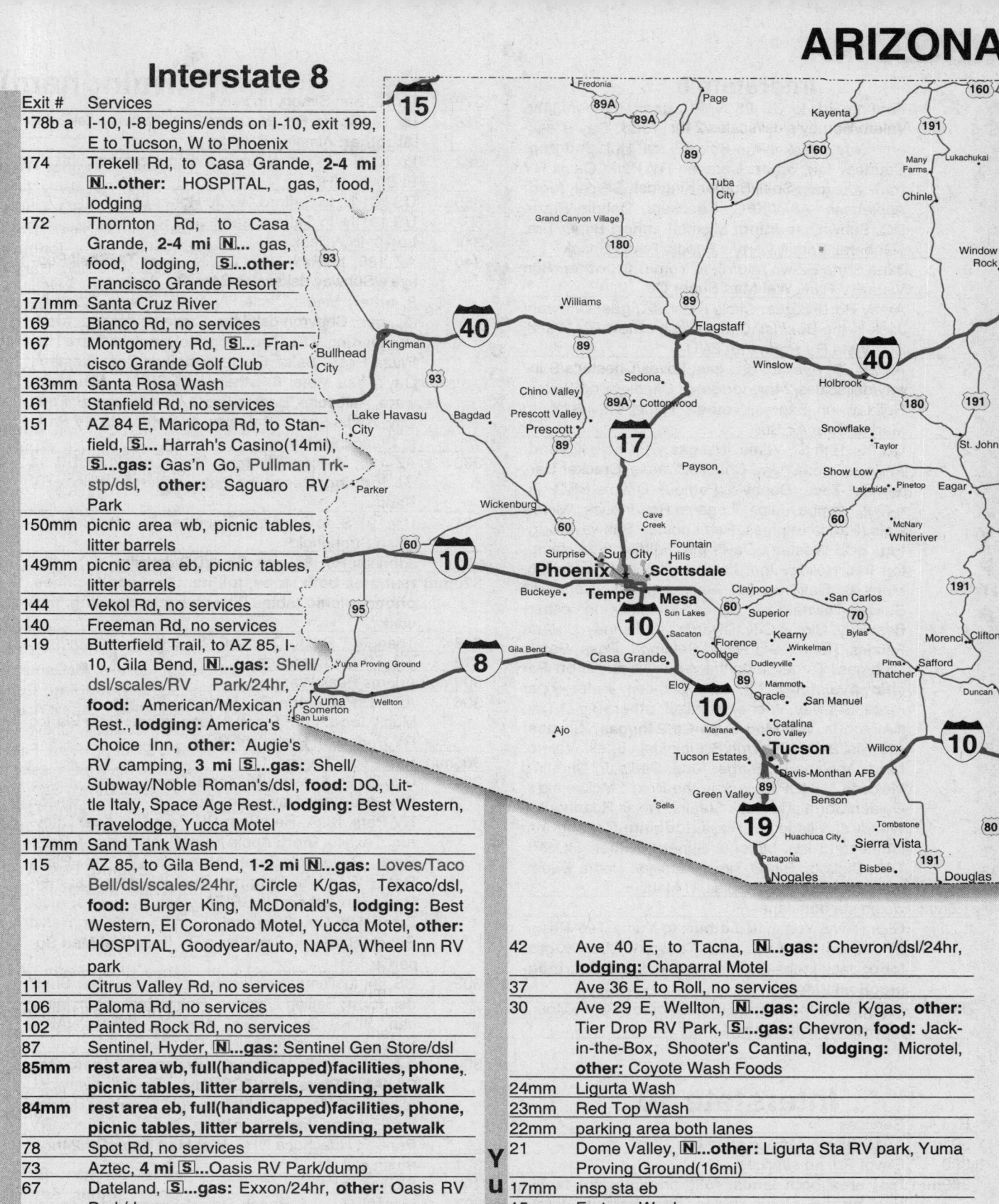**...gas:** Shell/dsl/scales/RV Park/24hr, **food:** American/Mexican Rest., **lodging:** America's Choice Inn, **other:** Augie's RV camping, **3 mi** 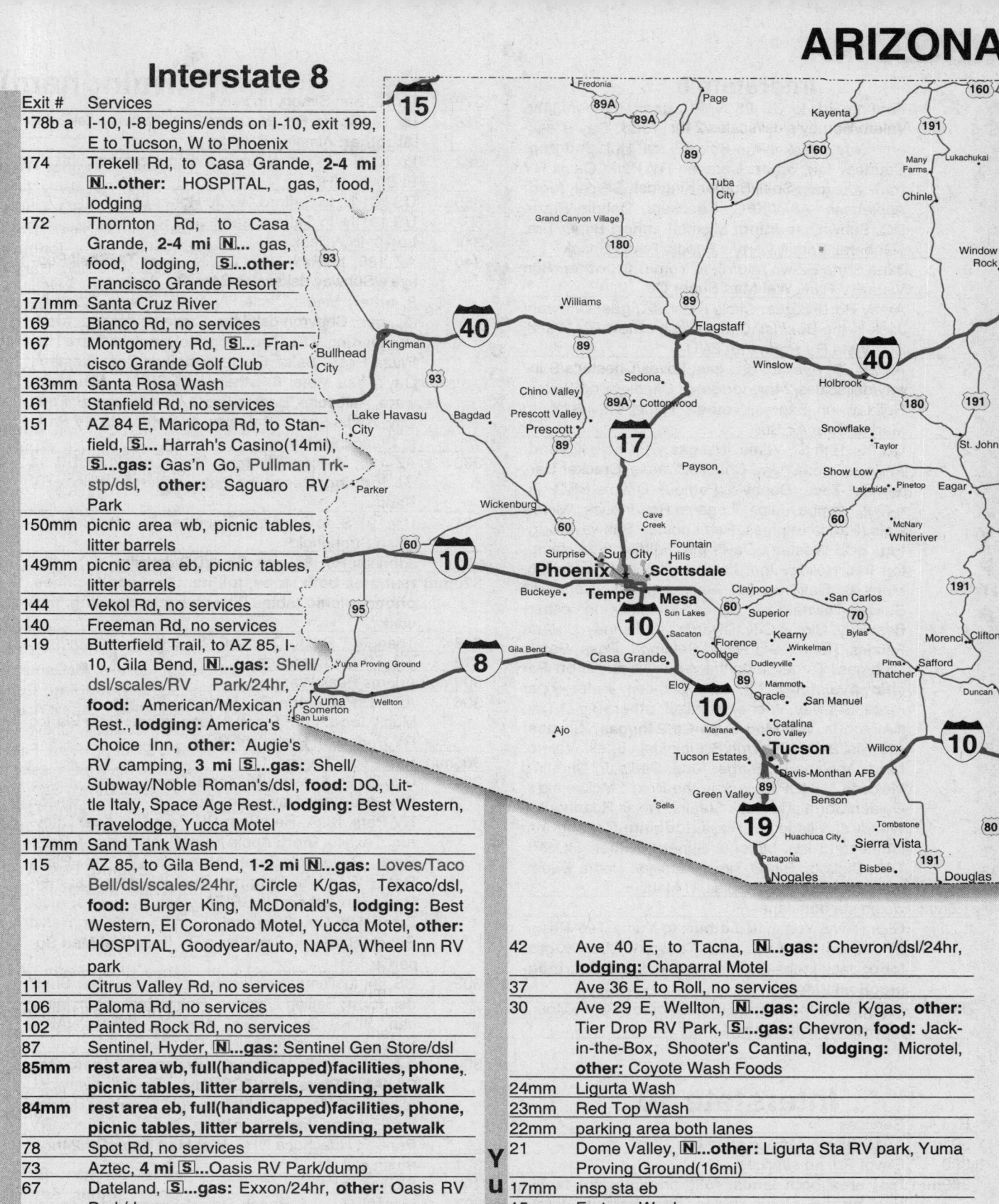**...gas:** Shell/Subway/Noble Roman's/dsl, **food:** DQ, Little Italy, Space Age Rest., **lodging:** Best Western, Travelodge, Yucca Motel
117mm	Sand Tank Wash
115	AZ 85, to Gila Bend, **1-2 mi** 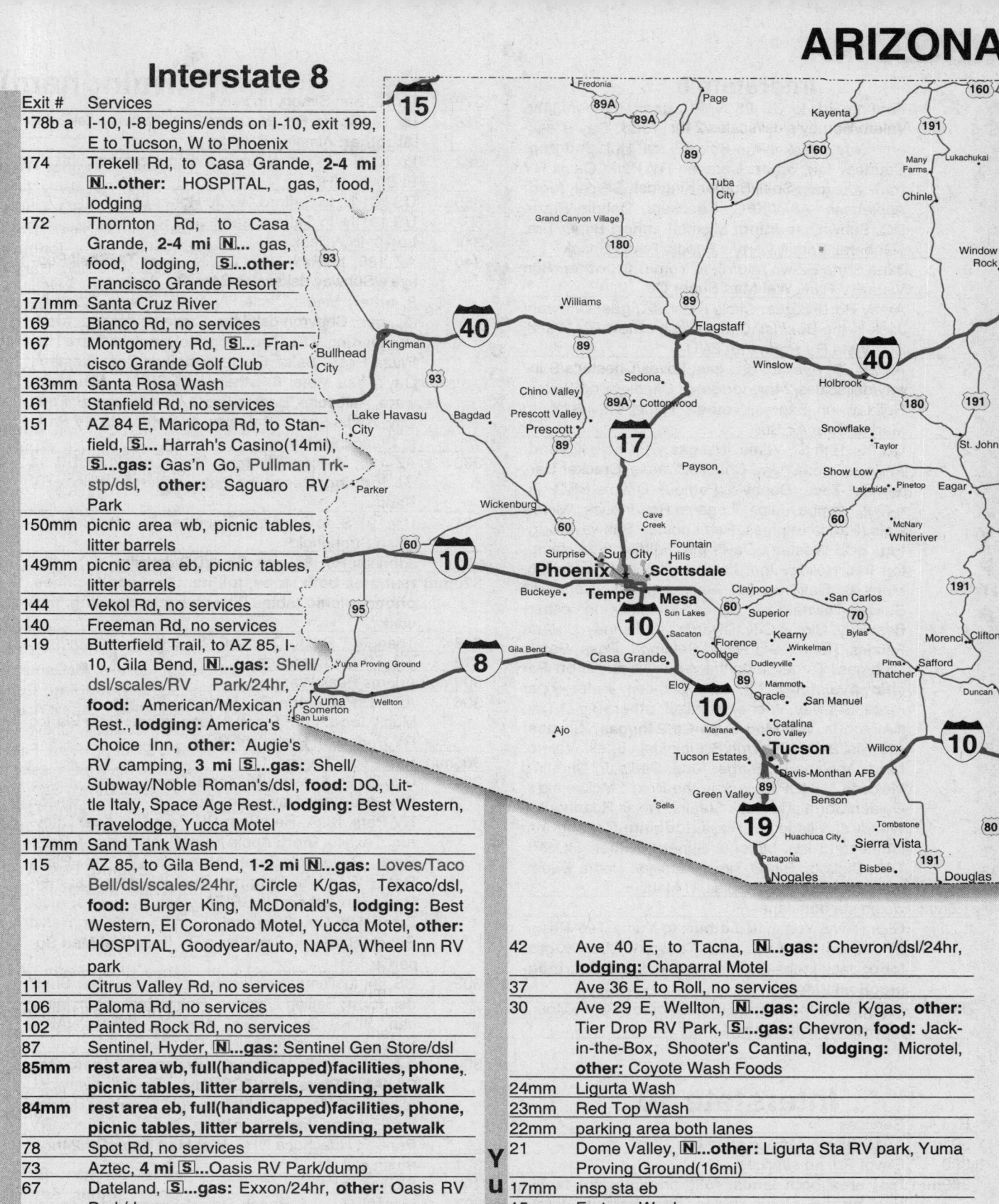**...gas:** Loves/Taco Bell/dsl/scales/24hr, Circle K/gas, Texaco/dsl, **food:** Burger King, McDonald's, **lodging:** Best Western, El Coronado Motel, Yucca Motel, **other:** HOSPITAL, Goodyear/auto, NAPA, Wheel Inn RV park
111	Citrus Valley Rd, no services
106	Paloma Rd, no services
102	Painted Rock Rd, no services
87	Sentinel, Hyder, 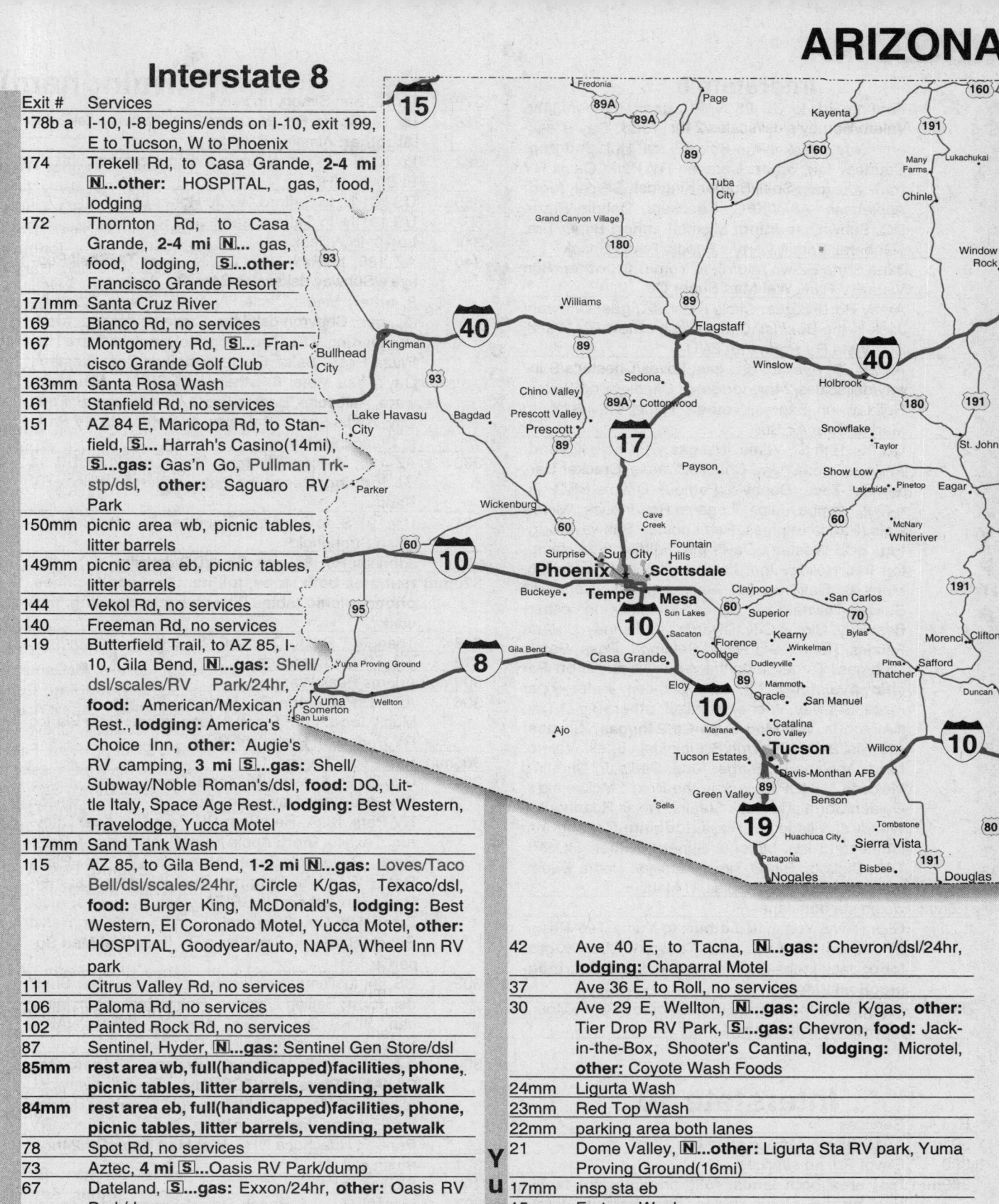**...gas:** Sentinel Gen Store/dsl
85mm	**rest area wb, full(handicapped)facilities, phone, picnic tables, litter barrels, vending, petwalk**
84mm	**rest area eb, full(handicapped)facilities, phone, picnic tables, litter barrels, vending, petwalk**
78	Spot Rd, no services
73	Aztec, **4 mi** 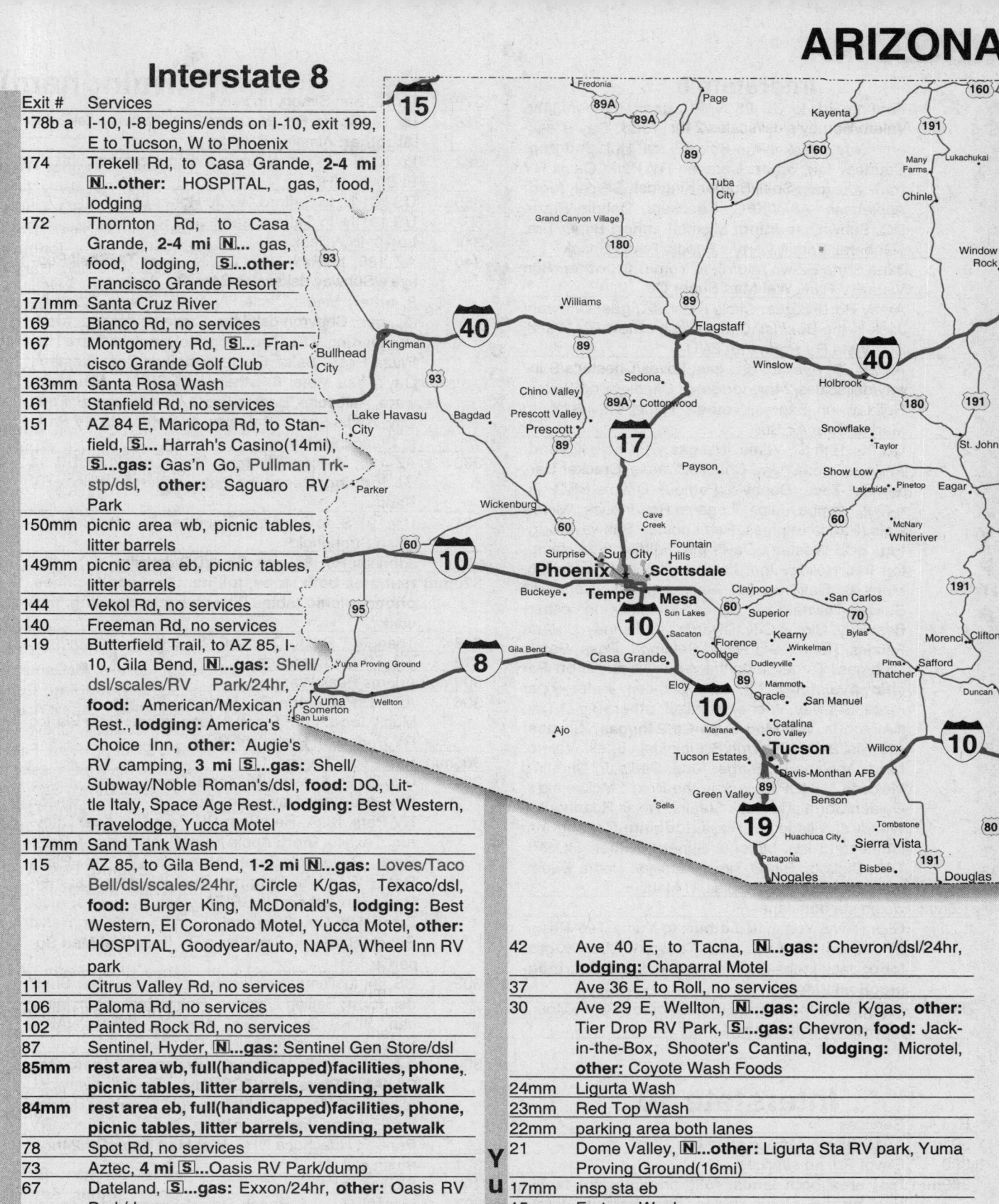**...**Oasis RV Park/dump
67	Dateland, 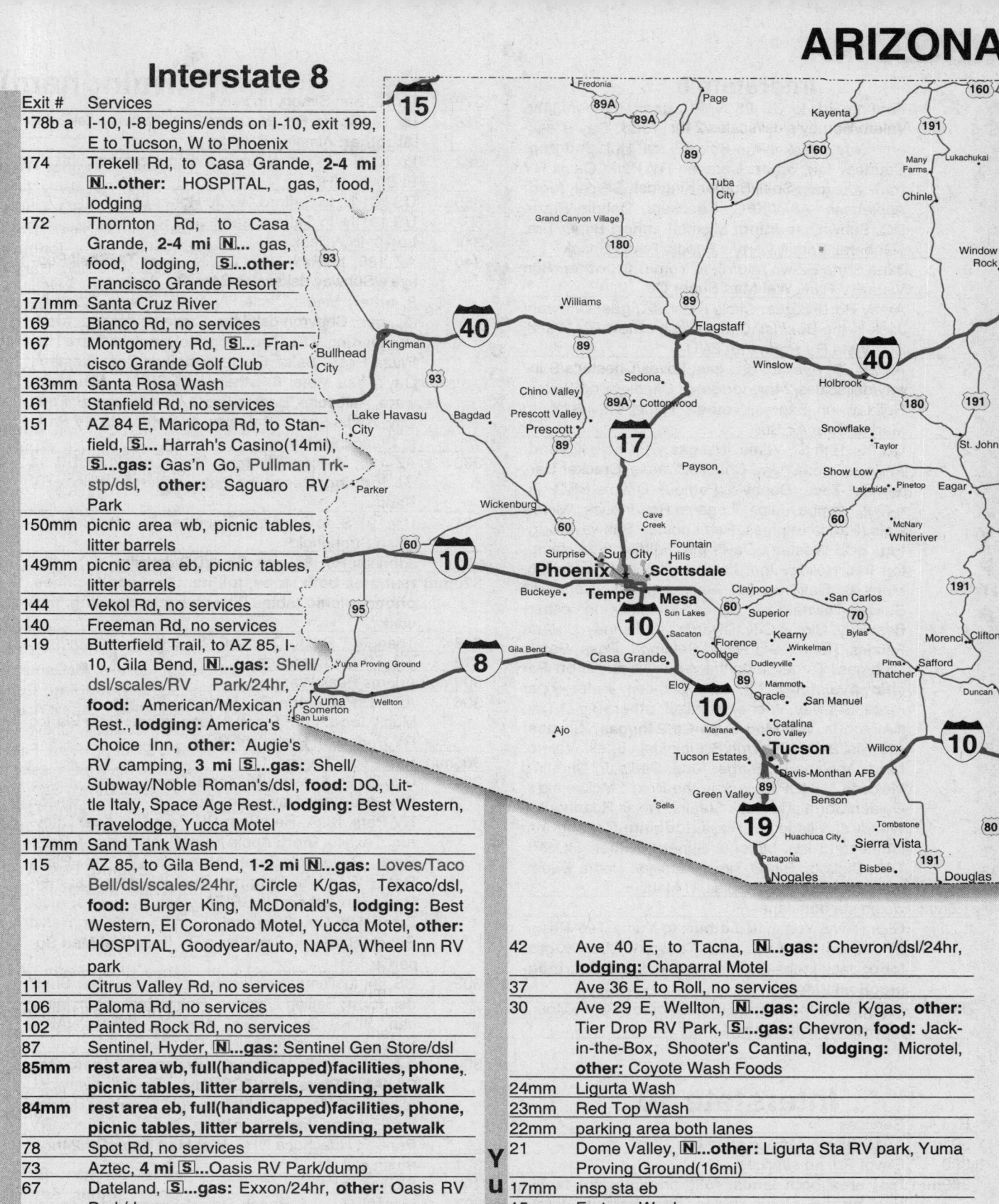**...gas:** Exxon/24hr, **other:** Oasis RV Park/dump
56mm	**rest area both lanes, full (handicapped) facilities, phone, picnic tables, litter barrels, vending, petwalk**
54	Ave 52 E, Mohawk Valley, no services
42	Ave 40 E, to Tacna, 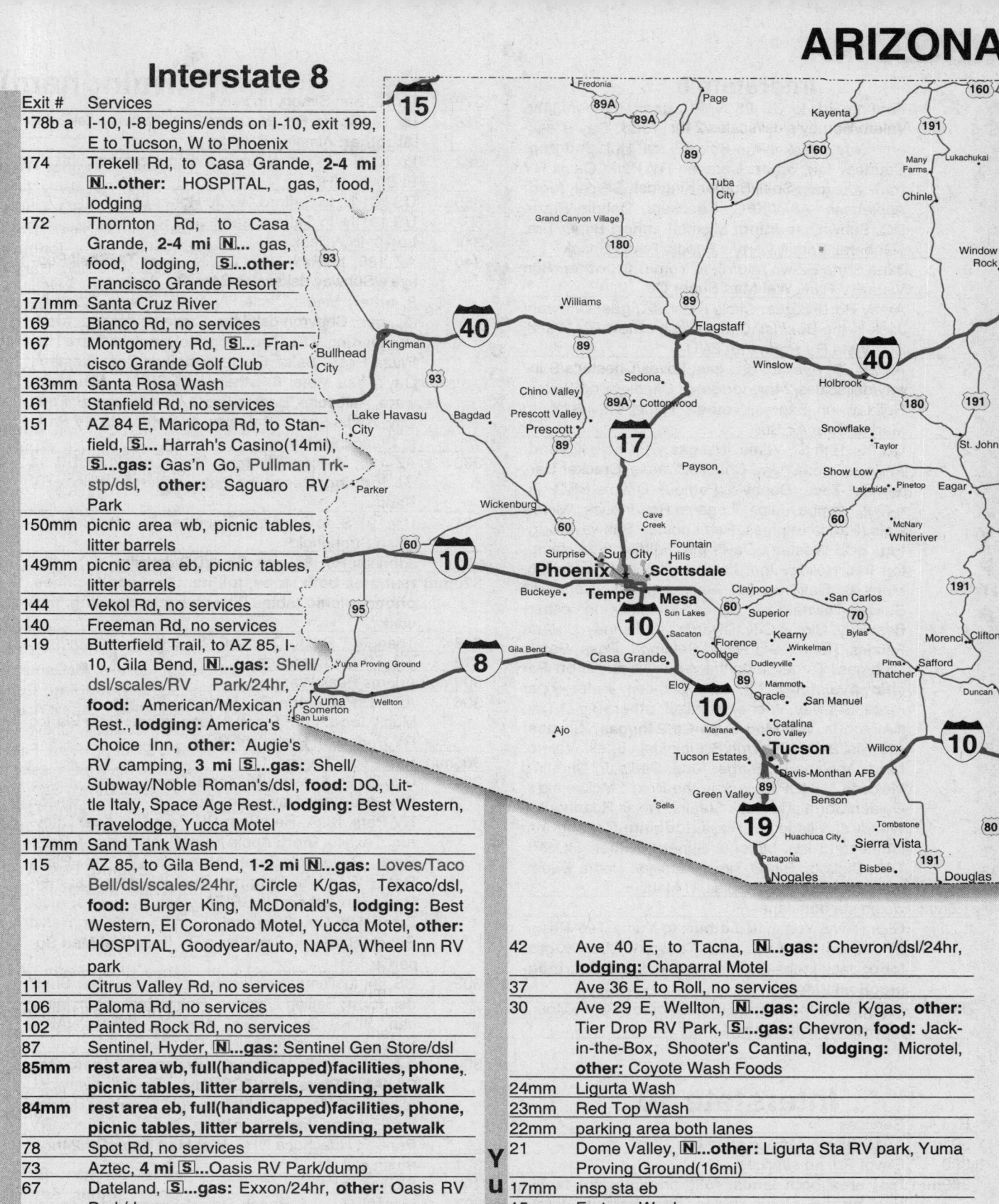**...gas:** Chevron/dsl/24hr, **lodging:** Chaparral Motel
37	Ave 36 E, to Roll, no services
30	Ave 29 E, Wellton, 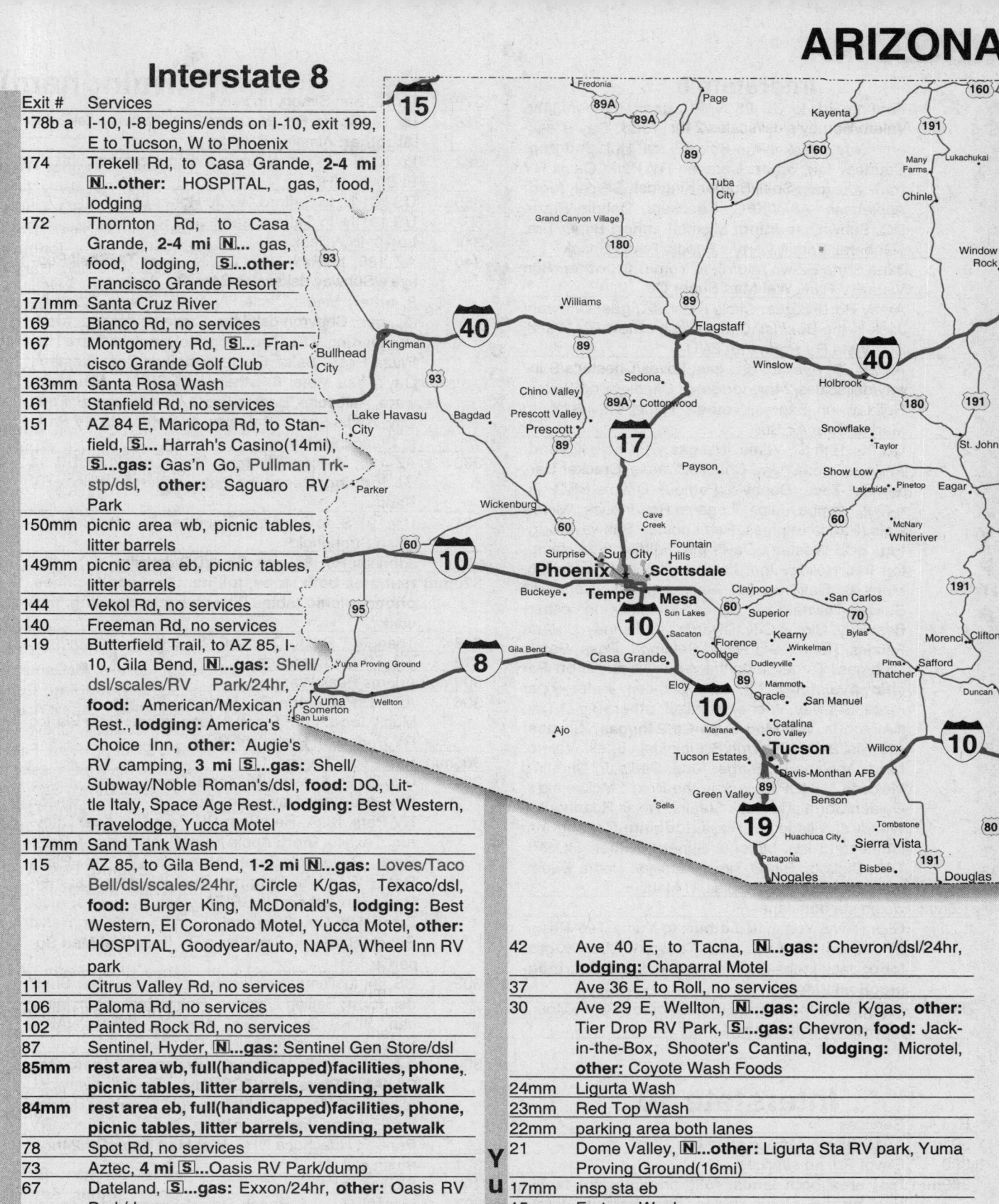**...gas:** Circle K/gas, **other:** Tier Drop RV Park, 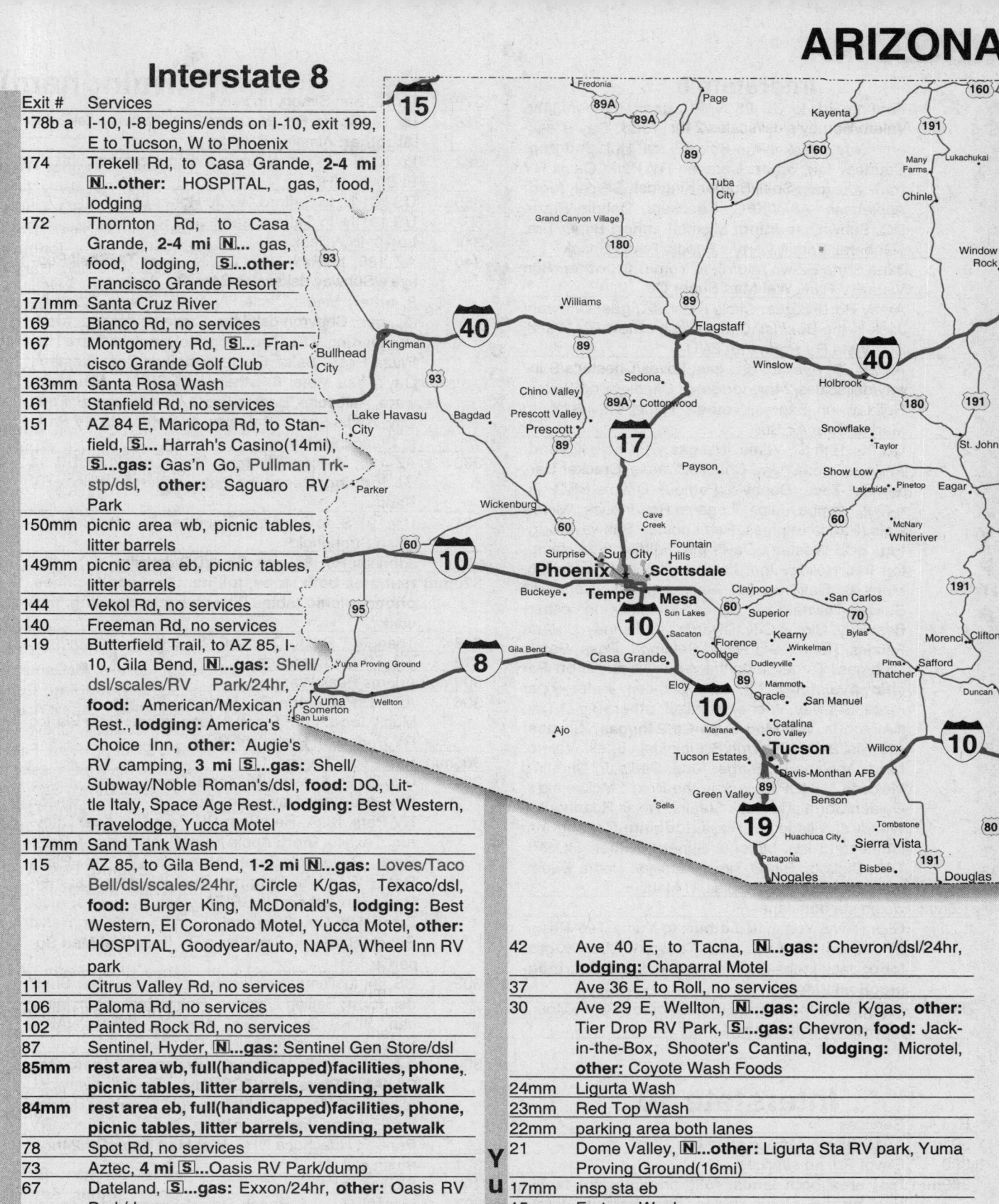**...gas:** Chevron, **food:** Jack-in-the-Box, Shooter's Cantina, **lodging:** Microtel, **other:** Coyote Wash Foods
24mm	Ligurta Wash
23mm	Red Top Wash
22mm	parking area both lanes
21	Dome Valley, 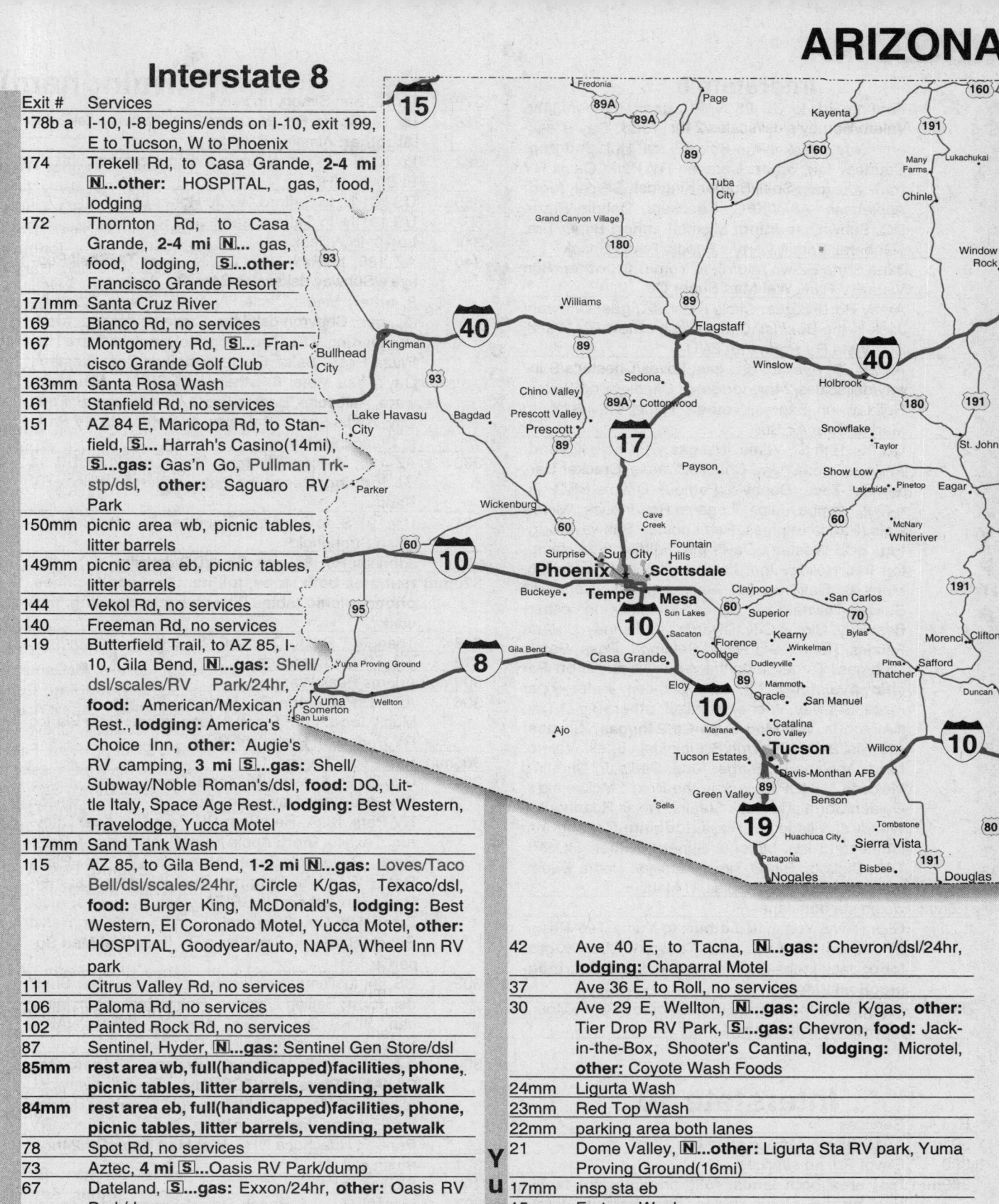**...other:** Ligurta Sta RV park, Yuma Proving Ground(16mi)
17mm	insp sta eb
15mm	Fortuna Wash
14	Foothills Blvd, 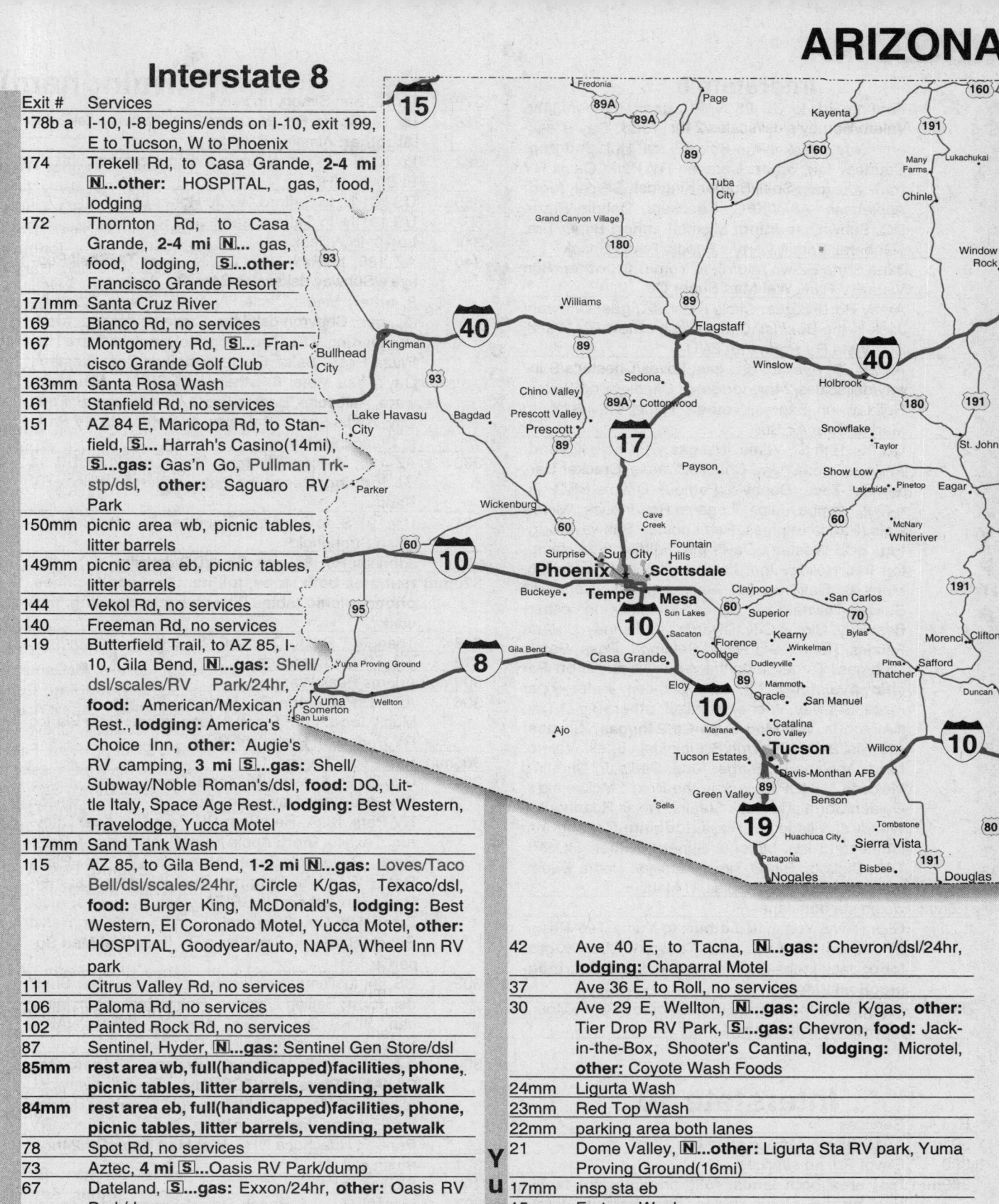**...other:** Sundance RV Park, 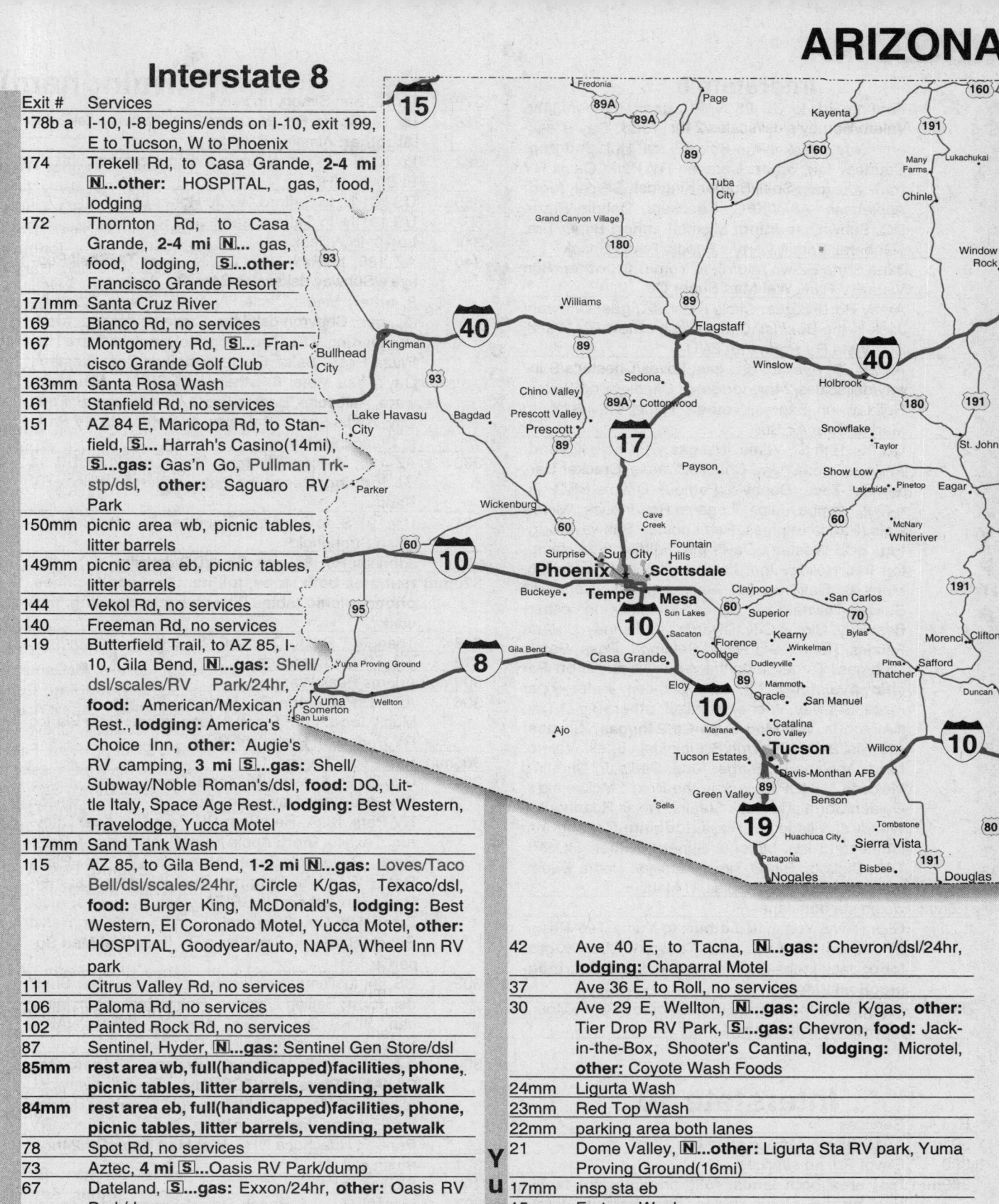**...food:** Domino's, **other:** Ace Hardware, FootHills RV Park, The Grocery Store/gas/dsl, auto/RV care/lube ctr

Yuma

ARIZONA

Interstate 8

<table>
<tr><td>E</td><td>12</td><td>Fortuna Rd, to US 95 N, N...gas: Chevron/24hr, Valero/Barney's/dsl/scales/24hr, food: Day Breakers Cafe, Jack-in-the-Box, Pizza Hut, lodging: Courtesy Inn, other: Caravan RV Park, Oasis RV Park, S...gas: Shell/Burger King/dsl, SP/dsl, food: Applebees, A&W/KFC, Checkers, Debois Pizza, DQ, Subway, lodging: Microtel, other: Big O Tire, $General, Family$, Fry's Foods, Radio Shack</td></tr>
<tr><td>W</td><td>9</td><td>32nd St(no EZ wb return), to Yuma, S...other: Sun Vista RV Park, Wal-Mart Super Ctr</td></tr>
<tr><td></td><td>7</td><td>Araby Rd, S...gas: Circle K/dsl, S...gas: Chevron/ Jack-in-the-Box/dsl, Circle K/dsl, other: RV World, Sun Vista RV Park, to AZWU</td></tr>
<tr><td></td><td>3</td><td>AZ 280 S, Ave 3E, S...gas: Loves/Chester's/Subway/dsl/scales/24hr, lodging: Candlewood Suites, Holiday Inn Express, other: Harley-Davidson, to Marine Corp Air Sta</td></tr>
<tr><td>Yuma</td><td>2</td><td>US 95, 16th St, Yuma, N...gas: 76/Circle K, food: Arnie's Cafe, Chili's, ChuckeCheese, Cracker Barrel, Del Taco, Denny's, Famous Dave's BBQ, In-n-Out, Jamba Juice, Logans Roadhouse, Mimi's Cafe, Panda Express, Red Lobster, Subway, lodging: Best Western, Day's Inn, Fairfield Inn, Hampton Inn, Holiday Inn, La Fuente Inn, Holiday Inn, Motel 6, OakTree Inn, Shilo Inn/rest., SpringHill Suites, TownePlace Suites, Wingate Inn, other: Best Buy, Circuit City, Dillards, JC Penney, Jo-Ann Fabrics, Kohl's, Old Navy, Petsmart, Ross, Sam's Club/gas, Target, auto/tire repair, 2 mi S on Pacific Ave...food: Mr. Lu's Chinese, Peter Piper Pizza, Subway, Wienerschnitzel, other: Big O Tire, NAPA, Kia, Wal-Mart SuperCtr/24hr/gas, S...gas: Arco/dsl/24hr, Chevron/Blimpie/dsl, Shell, Valero, food: Applebee's, Burger King, Carl's Jr, Chretin's Mexican, IHOP, Jack-in-the-Box, McDonald's, Golden Corral, Outback Steaks, Texas Roadhouse, Wendy's, Village Inn Pizza, lodging: Comfort Inn, Interstate 8 Inn, Motel 6, Super 8, other: HOSPITAL, BigLots, Big O Tires, Family$, Home Depot, KIA, Radio Shack, Staples, U-Haul</td></tr>
<tr><td></td><td>1.5mm</td><td>weigh sta both lanes</td></tr>
<tr><td></td><td>1</td><td>Giss Pkwy, Yuma, N...other: to Yuma Terr Prison SP, S on 4th Ave...gas: Chevron, Circle K/gas, food: Jack-in-the-Box, Yuma Landing Rest., lodging: Best Western</td></tr>
<tr><td></td><td>0mm</td><td>Arizona/California state line, Colorado River, Mountain/Pacific time zone</td></tr>
</table>

Interstate 10

<table>
<tr><td>Exit #</td><td>Services</td></tr>
<tr><td>E</td><td>391mm</td><td>Arizona/New Mexico state line</td></tr>
<tr><td></td><td>390</td><td>Cavot Rd, no services</td></tr>
<tr><td></td><td>389mm</td><td>rest area both lanes, full(handicapped) facilities, phone, picnic tables, litter barrels, vending, petwalk</td></tr>
<tr><td></td><td>383mm</td><td>weigh sta eb, weigh/insp sta wb</td></tr>
<tr><td></td><td>382</td><td>Portal Rd, San Simon, no services</td></tr>
<tr><td>W</td><td>381mm</td><td>San Simon River</td></tr>
</table>

<table>
<tr><td>378</td><td>Lp 10, San Simon, no services</td></tr>
<tr><td>366</td><td>Lp 10, Bowie Rd, N...gas: Shell/Subway/dsl/24hr, S...other: Alaskan RV park</td></tr>
<tr><td>362</td><td>Lp 10, Bowie Rd, N...gas, lodging, camping, S...to Ft Bowie NHS</td></tr>
<tr><td>355</td><td>US 191 N, to Safford, N...to Roper Lake SP</td></tr>
<tr><td>352</td><td>US 191 N, to Safford, same as 355</td></tr>
<tr><td>344</td><td>Lp 10, to Willcox</td></tr>
<tr><td>340</td><td>AZ 186, to Rex Allen Dr, N...gas: TA/Shell/Popeye's/Subway/dsl/scales/24hr/@, lodging: Super 8, other: Magic Circle RV Park, Stout's CiderMill, S...gas: Chevron/dsl/24hr, Circle K, Texaco, food: Burger King, KFC/Taco Bell, McDonald's, Pizza Hut, Plaza Rest., Salsa Fiesta, lodging: Best Western, Day's Inn, Motel 6, other: HOSPITAL, Ace Hardware, Autozone, Beall's, Big O Tire, $General, Food City, Radio Shack, Safeway, Grande Vista RV Park, to Chiricahua NM</td></tr>
<tr><td>336</td><td>AZ 186, Willcox, S...gas: Chevron/dsl/LP, 1-3 mi S...lodging: Desert Inn Motel, other: Ft Willcox RV Park</td></tr>
<tr><td>331</td><td>US 191 S, to Sunsites, Douglas, S...other: to Cochise Stronghold</td></tr>
<tr><td>322</td><td>Johnson Rd, S...gas: Shell/DQ/dsl/gifts</td></tr>
<tr><td>320mm</td><td>rest area both lanes, full(handicapped)facilities, phone, picnic tables, litter barrels, vending, petwalk</td></tr>
<tr><td>318</td><td>Triangle T Rd, to Dragoon, S...lodging, camping</td></tr>
<tr><td>312</td><td>Sibyl Rd, no services</td></tr>
<tr><td>309mm</td><td>Adams Peak Wash</td></tr>
<tr><td>306</td><td>AZ 80, Pomerene Rd, Benson, S...gas: Shell/dsl, Mobil, food: G&F Pizza Palace, other: Pato Blanco RV Park, San Pedro RV Park</td></tr>
<tr><td>305mm</td><td>San Pedro River</td></tr>
<tr><td>304</td><td>Ocotillo St, Benson, N...food: Denny's, Jack-in-the-Box, lodging: Day's Inn, Super 8, other: Benson RV Park, KOA, Red Barn RV Park, S...gas: Chevron, Texaco, food: Apple Farm Rest., Country Folks Rest., Galleano's Rest., Magaly's Mexican, Plaza Rest., Wendy's, lodging: Best Western, QuarterHorse Inn, other: HOSPITAL, Ace Hardware, Alco, Dillon RV Ctr, $General, Family$, NAPA, Radio Shack, Safeway, San Pedro RV Park, Wal-Mart SuperCtr</td></tr>
<tr><td>303</td><td>US 80, to Tombstone, Bisbee, 1 mi S...gas: Shell/dsl, food: Beijing Chinese, Reb's Rest., Ruiz Mexican, Shoot Out Steaks, Wendy's, other: NAPA, Safeway, auto/dsl/repair, to Douglas NHL</td></tr>
<tr><td>302</td><td>AZ 90 S, to Ft Huachuca, Benson, S...gas: Gas City/A&W/Pizza Hut/TCBY/dsl, Shell/Subway/dsl, food: KFC/Taco Bell, McDonald's, lodging: Holiday Inn Express, Motel 6, other: Cochise Terrace RV Park, Ft Huachuca NHS, Wal-Mart SuperCtr/24hr</td></tr>
<tr><td>301</td><td>ranch exit eb</td></tr>
<tr><td>299</td><td>Skyline Rd</td></tr>
<tr><td>297</td><td>Mescal Rd, J-6 Ranch Rd, N...gas: QuickPic/dsl/deli/24hr</td></tr>
<tr><td>292</td><td>Empirita Rd</td></tr>
<tr><td>289</td><td>Marsh Station Rd</td></tr>
<tr><td>288mm</td><td>Cienega Creek</td></tr>
</table>

E ↑ | ↓ W

281	AZ 83 S, to Patagonia
279	Vail/Wentworth Rd, **N**...**gas:** QuikMart/gas, **food:** Montgomery's Grill, **other:** to Colossal Caves
275	Houghton Rd, **N**...**other:** to Saguaro NP, camping, **S**...to fairgrounds
273	Rita Rd, **N**...**gas:** Rita Ranch(2mi), **S**...fairgrounds
270	Kolb Rd, **N**...**lodging:** La Quinta(9mi), **S**...**other:** Voyager RV Resort
269	Wilmot Rd, **N**...**gas:** Chevron/A&W/dsl, **lodging:** Travel Inn, **S**...**gas:** Shell/Quizno's
268	Craycroft Rd, **N**...**gas:** TTT/dsl/rest./scales/24hr, Circle K, Spirit/dsl, **other:** Crazy Horse RV Park, **S**...dsl repair
267	Valencia Rd, **N**...**gas:** Arco/Jack-in-the-Box, **other:** Pima Air Museum, **S**...airport
265	Alvernon Way, Davis-Monthan AFB
264b a	Palo Verde Rd, **N**...**gas:** Chevron/Wendy's/dsl, **food:** Brooklyn's Grill, Carl's Jr, Denny's, Waffle House, **lodging:** Crossland Suites, Day's Inn, Fairfield Inn, Holiday Inn, Red Roof Inn, **other:** Freedom RV Ctr, **S**...**gas:** QuikMart/gas, **food:** Arby's, McDonald's, **lodging:** Ramada Inn, Studio 6, **other:** Beaudry RV Ctr/resort, Camping World RV Resort, Holiday Rambler RV Ctr, La Mesa RV Ctr, Factory Outlet/famous brands
263b	Kino Pkwy N
263a	Kino Pkwy S, **S**...**gas:** Shamrock, **food:** Fry's Foods, **other:** AutoZone, Radio Shack, to Tucson Intn'l Airport
262	Benson Hwy, Park Ave, **S**...**gas:** Arco/24hr, Chevron, **food:** Country Folks, KFC, McDonald's, Waffle House, **lodging:** Best Value, Howard Johnson, Motel 6, Quality Inn, Western Inn, **other:** 7-11, Volvo
261	6th/4th Ave, **N**...**gas:** GasCo, **food:** Happy Iguana, Little Caesar's, **lodging:** Econolodge, **other:** Discount Tire, Food City, 99c Store, **S**...**gas:** Shell, **food:** Church's, El Indio, Jack-in-the-Box, LJ Silver, **lodging:** Lazy 8 Motel, **other:** Family$, Spanish Trail
260	I-19 S, to Nogales
259	22nd St, Starr Pass Blvd, **N**...**gas:** Circle K/dsl, **S**... **food:** Kettle, Waffle House, **lodging:** Knight's Inn, La Quinta, Motel 6, Super 8, Travel Inn
258	Congress St, Broadway St, **N**...**gas:** Circle K/gas, **food:** Garcia's Rest., **lodging:** Inn Suites, **S**... **food:** Bennigan's, Carl's Jr, Whataburger, **lodging:** Days Inn, Howard Johnson, Motel 6, Ramada Ltd, River Park Inn, Travelodge
257a	St Mary's Rd, **N**...**gas:** 76, **other:** HOSPITAL, **S**... **gas:** Arco, Shell/24hr, **food:** Burger King, Denny's, Furr's Cafeteria, **lodging:** Ramada Ltd., **other:** Pim Comm Coll
257	Speedway Blvd, **N**...**lodging:** Best Western, **other:** HOSPITAL, Victory Motorcycles, Old Town Tucson, museum, U of AZ, **S**...**gas:** Arco/dsl/24hr

Tucson

256	Grant Rd, **N**... **food:** Sonic, dsl/transmission repair, **S**... **gas:** Circle K, Shamrock, **food:** Del Taco, IHOP, Las Cazuelita's, Subway, Waffle House, **lodging:** Baymont Inn, Comfort Inn, Hampton Inn, Holiday Inn Express, Quality Inn, Super 8, **other:** dsl/transmission repair
255	AZ 77 N, to Miracle Mile
254	Prince Rd, **N**...**other:** U-Haul, tires, **S**...**other:** Prince of Tucson RV Park, golf
252	El Camino del Cerro, Ruthrauff Rd, **N**...**gas:** Arco/24hr, **other:** Ruthrauff RV Ctr, **S**...**gas:** Shell/Jack-in-the-Box
251	Sunset Rd
250	Orange Grove Rd, **N**...**gas:** Arco/24hr, Circle K, **food:** Domino's, Subway, Wendy's, **other:** RV Central, **N on Thornydal**...**food:** El Chalito, Little Caesar's, Quizno's, Weinerschnitzel, **other:** Big O Tire, Costco/gas, Home Depot, Parts+
248	Ina Rd, **N**...**gas:** Chevron/dsl, Circle K, Conoco, QuikMart/dsl, **food:** Arby's, Carl's Jr, DQ, Donut Wheel, Eegee's Cafe, El Pollo Loco, Hooters, Jack-in-the-Box, LJ Silver, McDonald's, Old Father Rest., Peter Piper's Pizza, Pizza Hut, Rubio's Grill, Starbucks, Taco Bell, Waffle House, **lodging:** InTown Suites, Motel 6, Old Father Inn, **other:** BigLots, CarQuest, CVS Drug, Discount Tire, Fry's Foods, Goodyear/auto, JiffyLube, Lowe's Whse, 99c Store, Office Depot, PepBoys, Radio Shack, Target, U-Haul, Walgreens, **S**...**gas:** Circle K, **food:** Denny's, **lodging:** Comfort Inn, Red Roof Inn, Travelodge
246	Cortaro Rd, **N**...**gas:** Circle K/Arby's/dsl, **food:** IHOP, Wendy's, **S**...**gas:** Shell/dsl, **food:** Burger King, Chili's, Cracker Barrel, Eegee's Rest., HotDog Heaven, In-n-Out, KFC, McDonald's, Panda Express, Starbucks, Subway, Taco Bell, Texas Roadhouse, **lodging:** Best Western, Day's Inn, Holiday Inn Express, La Quinta, Super 8, **other:** Ace Hardware, Batteries+, Checker Parts, Kohl's, USPO, Wal-Mart SuperCtr/24hr, access to RV camping
242	Avra Valley Rd, **S**...**other:** Saguaro NP(13mi), RV camping, airport
240	Tangerine Rd, to Rillito, **S**... A-A RV Park, **S**... USPO
236	Marana, **S**...**gas:** Chevron/dsl/LP, Circle K/gas, **other:** Sun RV Park, auto repair
232	Pinal Air Park Rd, **S**...Pinal Air Park
228mm	wb pulloff, to frontage rd
226	Red Rock, **S**...USPO

ARIZONA

Interstate 10

E ↕ W

219 Picacho Peak Rd, N...**gas:** Mobil/DQ/dsl, Shell/dsl, S...**other:** Ostrich Ranch, Pichaco Peak RV Park, to Picacho Peak SP

212 Picacho(from wb), N...**gas:** Premium Gas/tires, **other:** USPO S...Picacho Camping

211b AZ 87 N, AZ 84 W, to Coolidge

211a Picacho(from eb), S...**other:** Picacho RV Park, state prison

208 Sunshine Blvd, to Eloy, N...**gas:** Pilot/Subway/dsl/scales/24hr, dsl repair, S...**gas:** /Flying J/Conoco/Cookery/dsl/scales/24hr, **other:** Blue Beacon

203 Toltec Rd, to Eloy, N...**gas:** Chevron/McDonald's/24hr, Circle K/dsl, **food:** Carl's Jr, El Zarape Mexican, **lodging:** Best Value Inn, Red Roof Inn, **other:** Desert Valley RV Park, dsl/tire repair, S...**gas:** TA/A&W/Taco Bell/dsl/24hr/@, **food:** Pizza Hut, **other:** truckwash

200 Sunland Gin Rd, Arizona City, N...**gas:** Petro/Iron Skillet/dsl/scales/24hr/@, Pride/Subway/dsl/24hr, **food:** Burger King, Eva's Mexican, **lodging:** Day's Inn, **other:** Blue Beacon, Eagle Truckwash, Las Colinas RV Park, S...**gas:** Loves/Arby's/Baskin-Robbins/dsl/24hr, **food:** Golden 9 Rest., Starbucks, **lodging:** Motel 6, **other:** Speedco Lube

Casa Grande

199 I-8 W, to Yuma, San Diego

198 AZ 84, to Eloy, Casa Grande, N...Robson Ranch Rest./Golf, S...**food:** Wendy's, **other:** Casa Grande Outlets/famous brands, Buena Tierra RV Pk

194 AZ 287, Florence Blvd, to Casa Grande, N...**other:** Dillards, JC Penney, Kohl's, Petsmart, Staples, Sunscape RV Park(7mi), Target, **0-2 mi** S...**gas:** Arco/dsl/24hr, Chevron/DQ, **food:** Burger King, Cracker Barrel, Del Taco, Denny's, Golden Corral, IHOP, LJ Silver, Panda Express, Taco Bell, **lodging:** Best Western, Comfort Inn, Mainstay Suites, Super 8, **other:** HOSPITAL, CVS Drug, Palm Creek RV/golf Resort, Wal-Mart SuperCtr/24hr

190 McCartney Rd, N...**other:** to Central AZ Coll

185 AZ 387, to Coolidge, Florence, S...**other:** hwy patrol, RV camping

183mm rest area wb, full(handicapped)facilities, phone, picnic tables, litter barrels, vending, petwalk

181mm rest area eb, full(handicapped)facilities, phone, picnic tables, litter barrels, vending, petwalk

175 AZ 587 N, Casa Blanca Rd, S...**gas:** Shell/dsl

173mm Gila River

167 Riggs Rd, to Sun Lake, N...Akimel Crafts

164 AZ 347 S, Queen Creek Rd, to Maricopa, N...**other:** to Chandler Airport

162b a Wild Horse Pass Rd, Sundust Rd, N...**gas:** Loves/Arby's/diesel/scales/24hr, **other:** Beaudry RV Ctr, S...**other:** Firebird Sports Park, Gila River Casino

Chandler

160 Chandler Blvd, to Chandler, N...**gas:** Chevron, Circle K, Mobil, **food:** Burger King, Denny's, Marie Callender's, Village Inn, Whataburger/24hr, **lodging:** Hampton Inn, Homewood Suites, Motel 6, Radisson, Red Roof Inn, Super 8, **other:** Big O Tire, Harley-Davidson, to Compadre Stadium, to Williams AFB, S...**gas:** Chevron, 7-11, Water&Ice/dsl, **food:** Applebees, Arriba Mexican, Chili's, Cracker Barrel, Del Taco, Hong Kong Buffet, Hooters, Wendy's, **lodging:** Holiday Inn Express, Extended Stay America, InTown Suites, La Quinta, **other:** HOSPITAL, AutoZone, Brakes+, CVS Drug, Discount Tire, Kohl's

159 Ray Rd, N...**gas:** Circle K, Shell/dsl, **food:** Buca Italian, Carrabba's, Charleston's Rest., El Pollo Loco, 5&Diner, Fleming's Steaks, In-n-Out, Jilly's Rest., McDonald's, Outback Steaks, Red Lobster, Roy's Cafe, Rumbi Grill, Tomaso's Italian, TGI Fridays, **lodging:** Courtyard, **other:** Borders Books, CompUSA, Ford, Home Depot, Lexus, Lowe's Whse, Mercedes, Petsmart, Sam's Club, S...**gas:** Circle K/dsl, **food:** Boston Mkt, Cafe Rio, IHOP/24hr, Jack-in-the-Box, Macaroni Grill, Mimi's Café, On-the-Border, Peter Piper Pizza, Pizza Hut, Subway, Sweet Tomatoes, Wendy's, **lodging:** Extended Stay America, **other:** URGENT CARE, Albertson's/Osco/24hr, Barnes&Noble, Best Buy, Jo-Ann Fabrics, Mervyn's, Michael's, Old Navy, Ross, SteinMart, Target

158 Warner Rd, N...**gas:** Circle K, QT, **food:** Port of Subs, S...**gas:** Arco/24hr, Circle K/diesel, **food:** Burger King, ChuckeCheese, DQ, Macayo's, Malaya Mexican, McDonald's, Mello's Pizza, Panda Garden, Quizno's, Ruffino's Italian, **other:** Ace Hardware, Basha's Foods, Big O Tire, Goodyear/auto

157 Elliot Rd, N...**gas:** Chevron, Shell/Circle K, **food:** Applebee's, Arby's, Baja Fresh, Burger King, Chili's, Coco's, Country Harvest Buffet, Fuddrucker's, Gelato BBQ, Guam Cuisine, HoneyBear's BBQ, Kobe Japanese, Kyoto Japanese, Mi Amigos Mexican, Olive Garden, Panda Express, Red Robin Rest., Sooper Salad, Sonic, Subway, Taco Bell, Village Inn Rest., Wendy's, **lodging:** Country Inn&Suites, **other:** Cadillac/GMC, Circuit City, Costco/gas, Discount Tire, Dodge, $Tree, Fiddlesticks Funpark, Ford/Lincoln/Mercury, Honda, Nissan, PetsMart, Saturn, Savers, Staples, Toyota, U-Haul, Wal-Mart, S...**gas:** Mobil/diesel, Shell/Circle K, **food:** Baskin-Robbins, Burrito Co, China Star, KFC, McDonald's, Sub Factory, **lodging:** Clarion, Grace Inn, **other:** Checker Parts, Safeway, Walgreens

Phoenix

155 Baseline Rd, Guadalupe, N...**gas:** Mobil, Shell/Circle K/Popeye's/dsl, **food:** Bennigan's, Carl's Jr, ClaimJumper, El Pollo Loco, 5& Diner, Joe's Crabshack, McDonald's, Rainforest Cafe, Waffle House, Wendy's, **lodging:** Best Western, Candlewood Studios, Holiday Inn Express, InnSuites, Ramada Ltd, Residence Inn, SpringHill Suites, TownePlace Suites, **other:** AutoZone, AZ Mills Factory Shops, CVS Drug, JC Penney Outlet, Marshall's, Pro Auto Parts, Ross, S...**gas:** Arco, QT, 7-11, **food:** Aunt Chilada's Mexican, China Town, Denny's, Sonic, Subway, **lodging:** Homestead Village, Motel 6, **other:** Fry's Electronics, Fry's Foods

154 US 60 E, AZ 360, Superstition Frwy, to Mesa, N...**other:** to Camping World(off Mesa Dr)

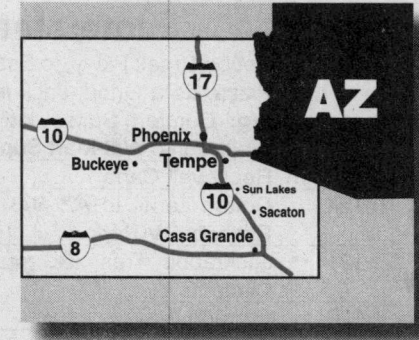

Interstate 10

E

↕

W

P h o e n i x

153b a	AZ 143 N, Broadway Rd E, **on University...** **food:** Denny's, **lodging:** Courtyard, Fairfield Inn, Hilton, Homestead Suites, La Quinta, Sheraton, Sleep Inn, **other:** to Diablo Stadium, **S...gas:** Chevron, Shell/Circle K/Taco Bell/24hr, **food:** Del Taco, George&Dragon, Papa John's, Pizza Hut, Port of Subs, Ranch House Rest., Taco Bell, Whataburger, **lodging:** Hampton Inn, **other:** Staples
152	40th St, **N...gas:** Shell/dsl, **other:** U Phoenix, **S... gas:** Shell/Circle K, **food:** Burger King
151mm	Salt River
151b a	28th St, 32nd St, University Ave, **N...food:** Waffle House, **lodging:** Extended Stay America, Hilton Garden, Holiday Inn Express, Radisson, **other:** AZSU, U Phoenix, **S...gas:** Circle K, **food:** McDonald's
150b	24th St E(from wb), **N...**Air Nat Guard, **lodging:** Motel 6, **S...lodging:** Best Western/rest.
150a	I-17 N, to Flagstaff
149	Buckeye Rd, **N...other:** Sky Harbor Airport
148	Washington St, Jefferson St, **N...gas:** Chevron, Shell, Tiemco/dsl, **food:** Carl's Jr, Mandy's Fish'n Chips, McDonald's, Rally's, **lodging:** Motel 6, Sterling Hotel, **other:** to Sky Harbor Airport, **S...gas:** Circle K, **other:** HOSPITAL
147b a	AZ 51 N, AZ 202 E, to Squaw Peak Pkwy
146	16th St, **N...gas:** Circle K/Shell, **food:** KFC, **S... gas:** Circle K, **food:** Antonio's Rest., Church's, Tradicione's, **other:** Ranch Mkt
145	7th St, **N...food:** McDonald's, **other:** Safeway Foods, Walgreens, **S...gas:** Circle K, Shell, **other:** HOSPITAL, to America West Arena
144	7th Ave, Amtrak, central bus dist
143c	19th Ave, US 60
143b a	I-17, N to Flagstaff, S to Phoenix
142	27th Ave(from eb, no return), **N...lodging:** Comfort Inn
141	35th Ave, **N...food:** Jack-in-the-Box, Rita's Mexican, **S...gas:** Shell/Circle K
140	43rd Ave, **N...gas:** Circle K/dsl, 7-11, Shell, **food:** Filberto's Mexican, Pizza Hut, Salsita's Mexican, Subway, **other:** AutoZone, Fry's Foods, 99c Store, Radio Shack, Walgreens
139	51st Ave, **N...gas:** Chevron/dsl, Circle K, **food:** Burger King, Domino's, El Pollo Loco, McDonald's, Sonic, Waffle House, **lodging:** Budget Inn, CrossLand Suites, Day's Inn, Holiday Inn, InTowne Suites, La Quinta, Motel 6, Red Roof Inn, Travelodge, **other:** Discount Tire, Food City, 7-11, **S...gas:** DZ/dsl, QT/dsl/scales, **food:** Carl's Jr, IHOP, Taco Bell, **lodging:** Hampton Inn, Phoenix West Inn, Super 8, Travelers Inn
138	59th Ave, **N...gas:** Circle K, Shamrock, **food:** Armando's Mexican/24hr, Subway, **other:** AutoZone, Checker Parts, Family$, 7-11, Walgreens, **S...gas:** Liberty/Wendy's/dsl/24hr, **food:** Waffle House, Whataburger/24hr, **other:** Blue Beacon/scales
137	67th Ave, **N...gas:** QT, Circle K/dsl, Shell/dsl, **food:** Church's, **S...gas:** /Flying J/Conoco/CountryMkt/dsl/LP/24hr/@

P h o e n i x

136	75th Ave, **N...** **gas:** Chevron, Circle K/gas, **food:** A&W, Del Taco, Denny's, Starbucks, Whataburger, Taco Bell/Pizza Hut, Taco Del Mar, Texas Roadhouse, Whataburger, **other:** Ford, Home Depot, Lowe's Whse, Petsmart, Staples, Wal-Mart SuperCtr/24hr, **S... gas:** Arco/24hr
135	83rd Ave, **N...gas:** Circle K, QT, **food:** Arby's, Burger King, Jack-in-the-Box, Waffle House, **lodging:** Econolodge, Premier Inn, **other:** Sam's Club
134	91st Ave, Tolleson
133b	Lp 101 N
133a	99th Ave, **N...gas:** Chevron/dsl, **food:** Baja Fresh, Carrabba's, ClaimJumper, Ichiban Rest., Island's Burgers, McDonald's, Subway, Village Inn, **other:** Best Buy, Borders Books, Circuit City, Costco/gas, GNC, Marshall's, Old Navy, PetCo, **S...gas:** Pilot/Wendy's/Subway/dsl/scales/24hr/@, **other:** CarMax
132	107th Ave(from eb), **N...other:** Walgreens, **S... other:** Earnheart RV Ctr, Dodge, Hyundai, Kia, Mazda, Mitsubishi, Nissan, Saturn, Subaru
131	Avondale Blvd., to Cashion, **N...gas:** Mobil, **S... lodging:** Hilton Garden, Homewood Suites, **other:** to Phoenix International Raceway
129	Dysart Rd, to Avondale, **N...gas:** Chevron, Shell/Circle K/dsl, **food:** Big Apple Rest., Carino's Italian, Chick-fil-A, In-n-Out, Jack-in-the-Box/24hr, Mimi's Cafe, NY Pizza, Panda Express, Papa Murphy's, Quizno's, Taco Bell, **lodging:** Wingate Inn, **other:** AutoZone, Discount Tire, $Tree, Jo-Ann Fabrics, Fry's Foods, Kohl's, Lowe's Whse, Petsmart, Wal-Mart SuperCtr/24hr, **S...gas:** QT, **food:** A&W/LJ Silver, Black Bear Diner, Del Taco, Gandolfo's, Golden Corral, KFC, McDonald's, Peter Piper Pizza, Subway, Waffle House, Whataburger, **lodging:** Best Value Inn, Super 8, **other:** Brakemasters, Chevrolet, Chrysler/Dodge/Jeep, Food City, Home Depot, Sam's Club, Suzuki, Walgreens
128	Litchfield Rd, **N...gas:** Mobil/Blimpie/dsl, **food:** Applebee's, Black Angus Steaks, Carl's Jr, Chili's, Chipotle Mexican, Cracker Barrel, Denny's, El Paso BBQ, Fazoli's, Macaroni Grill, Macavo's Mexican, McDonald's, McGrath's Fishouse, On the Border, Starbucks, Subway, TGIFriday, Wendy's, **lodging:** Hampton Inn, Holiday Inn Express, Residence Inn, **other:** HOSPITAL, Barnes&Noble, Best Buy, Michael's, Ross, Target, Wigwam Resort/rest(3mi), to Luke AFB, **S...gas:** Mobil, **food:** Arby's, Burger King, JB's, Schlotsky's, Taco Bell, **lodging:** Best Western, **other:** AutoZone, Fry's Food/drug, Goodyear/auto, 99c Store, Osco Drug, Pontiac/GMC, Radio Shack

ARIZONA

Interstate 10

E	126	PebbleCreek Pkwy, to Estrella Park, **S**...**food:** Bro's Pizza, Its a Grind, Jack-in-the-Box, Subway, **lodging:** Comfort Suites, **other:** Safeway Foods/gas, Walgreens, Wal-Mart SuperCtr/24hr
↕	125mm	Roosevelt Canal
W	124	Cotton Lane, to AZ 303, **N**...st prison, **S**...**other:** Pheonix RV Park
	121	Jackrabbit Trail, **N**...**gas:** Chevron/dsl, **S**...**gas:** Circle K
	120	Verrado Way
	117	Watson Rd, **S**...**food:** Jack-in-the-Box, Palermo's Pizza, Peter Piper Pizza, Subway, Wendy's, **other:** Fry's Foods/gas, Lowes Whse, Petsmart, Walgreens, Wal-Mart SuperCtr, vet
	114	Miller Rd, to Buckeye, **S**...**gas:** Loves/Chester Fried/Subway/dsl/scales/24hr, **food:** Burger King, **lodging:** Day's Inn, **other:** Leaf Verde RV Park
	112	AZ 85, to I-8, Gila Bend, **S**...Subway(3mi)
	109	Sun Valley Pkwy, Palo Verde Rd
	104mm	Hassayampa River
	103	339th Ave, **S**...**gas:** TA/Shell/Subway/dsl/LP/scales/24hr/@, **food:** Country Fair Rest. **other:** truckwash
	98	Wintersburg Rd
	97mm	Coyote Wash
	95.5mm	Old Camp Wash
	94	411th Ave, Tonopah, **S**...**gas:** Chevron/dsl, Mobil/dsl, Shell/Chester's/Noble Roman's/Subway/dsl/LP/24hr, **food:** Tonopah Joe's Rest., **lodging:** Mineral Wells Motel, **other:** USPO, tires/repair, Saddle Mtn RV Park, playground
	86mm	**rest area both lanes, full(handicapped) facilities, phone, picnic tables, litter barrels, petwalk, vending**
	81	Salome Rd, Harquahala Valley Rd
	69	Ave 75E, no services
	53	Hovatter Rd, no services
	52mm	**rest area both lanes, full(handicapped)facilities, phone, vending, picnic tables, litter barrels, petwalk**
	45	Vicksburg Rd, **N**...**gas:** Zip TC/HotStuff/dsl/24hr, **S**...**gas:** Valero/dsl/rest./scales/24hr, **other:** Jobski's dsl Repair/towing, RV Park, tires, wildlife refuge
	31	US 60 E, to Wickenburg, **12 mi N**...**other:** food, camping
	26	Gold Nugget Rd
	19	Quartzsite, to US 95, Yuma, **N**...**gas:** Chevron/dsl, Park Place TC/subs/dsl, Shell/dsl, **food:** Taco Mio, **other:** Beall's, CarQuest, Family$, Radio Shack, Roadrunner Foods, RV camping
	18mm	Tyson Wash
	17	US 95, AZ 95, Quartzsite, **N**...**gas:** Mobil/Burger King/LP, Pilot/DQ/Subway/dsl/scales/24hr, **food:** Best Mexican, Carl's Jr, McDonald's, Quarter Yacht Grill, **other:** RV camping, tires/repair, **S**...**gas:** Loves/Chester's/Subway/dsl/24hr, **lodging:** Super 8, **other:** Desert Gardens RV Park
	11	Dome Rock Rd

5	Tom Wells Rd, **N**...**gas:** Texaco/SunMart/Quizno's/dsl
4.5mm	**rest area both lanes, full(handicapped)facilities, phone, vending, picnic tables, litter barrels, petwalk**
3.5mm	**eb**...AZ Port of Entry, **wb**...weigh sta
1	Ehrenberg, to Parker, **N**...**other:** River Breeze RV Resort, **S**...**gas:** ⚑/Flying J/Wendy's/Cookery/dsl/LP/scales24hr/@, **lodging:** Best Western
0mm	Colorado River, Arizona/California state line, Mountain/Pacific time zone

Interstate 15

Exit #	Services	
29.5mm	Arizona/Utah state line	N
27	Black Rock Rd	↕
21mm	turnout sb	
18	Cedar Pocket, **S**...**other:** Virgin River Canyon RA/camping, parking area	S
16mm	truck parking both lanes	
15mm	truck parking nb	
14mm	truck parking nb	
10mm	truck parking nb	
9	Farm Rd	
8.5mm	Virgin River	
8	Littlefield, Beaver Dam, **E**...**other:** RV park, **1 mi W**...**gas**/dsl, food, lodging, camping	
0mm	Arizona/Nevada state line, Pacific/Mountain time zone	

Interstate 17

Exit #	Services	
341	McConnell Dr, I-17 begins/ends, **N**...**gas:** Chevron, Conoco/dsl, Exxon/Wendy's/dsl, Gasser/dsl, Giant/dsl, Mobil, Circle K, **food:** Arby's, Blimpie, Burger King, Buster's Rest., Carl's Jr, Cilantro's Mexican, Chili's, China Garden, Coco's, DQ, Del Taco, Denny's, Domino's, Fazoli's, IHOP, Jack-in-the-Box, Fuddrucker's, Furr's Café, KFC, McDonald's, Olive Garden, Perkins, Pizza Hut, Quizno's, Red Lobster, Roma Pizza, Sizzler, Souper Salad, Strombolli's, Subway, Taco Bell, TCBY, Village Inn Rest., **lodging:** AZ Motel, AmeriSuites, AutoLodge, Comfort Inn, Crystal Inn, Day's Inn, Econolodge, Embassy Suites, Fairfield Inn, Hampton Inn, Hilton, La Quinta, Motel 6, Quality Inn, Ramada Ltd, Rodeway Inn, Sleep Inn, **other:** Barnes&Noble, Basha's Foods, CarQuest, Checker Parts, Discount Tire, Hastings Books, Jo-Ann Crafts, K-Mart, Michael's, Osco Drug, Safeway, Staples, Target, Walgreen, Wal-Mart	N
340b a	I-40, E to Gallup, W to Kingman	↕
339	Lake Mary Rd(from nb), Mormon Lake, **E**...**gas:** Circle K/dsl, **lodging:** AZ Mtn Inn, access to same as 341	S
337	AZ 89A S, to Sedona, Ft Tuthill RA, Oak Creek Cyn	

Flagstaff

Interstate 17

N ↑ ↓ S

333	Kachina Blvd, Mountainaire Rd, ⒠...**food:** Mountainaire Rest.(2mi), **lodging:** Sled Dog B&B, ⓦ... **gas:** Conoco/Subway/dsl
331	Kelly Canyon Rd
328	Newman Park Rd
326	Willard Springs Rd
322	Pinewood Rd, to Munds Park, ⒠...**gas:** Chevron/dsl, Woody's/dsl, **food:** Lone Pine Rest., **other:** Motel in the Pines/RV camp, USPO, ⓦ...**gas:** Exxon/dsl, **other:** Munds RV Park, auto/RV repair
322mm	Munds Canyon
320	Schnebly Hill Rd
317	Fox Ranch Rd
316mm	Woods Canyon
315	Rocky Park Rd
313mm	scenic view sb, litter barrels
306	Stoneman Lake Rd
300mm	runaway truck ramp sb
298	AZ 179, to Sedona, Oak Creek Canyon, **7-15 mi** ⓦ...**food:** Burger King, Cowboy Club Rest., Joey's Bistro, Taco Bell, **lodging:** Belrock Inn, Hilton Garden, La Quinta, Quality Inn, Radisson/cafe, Wildflower Inn
297mm	**rest area both lanes, full(handicapped)facilities, phone, picnic tables, litter barrels, vending, petwalk**
293mm	Dry Beaver Creek
293	Cornville Rd, McGuireville Rd, to Rimrock, ⒠...**gas:** ExpressFuel, **food:** Tunes Rest, ⓦ...**gas:** 76/dsl, **food:** Crusty's Cafe
289	Middle Verde Rd, Camp Verde, ⒠...**gas:** Mobil/dsl, **food:** Rockets Café, Sonic, **lodging:** Cliff Castle Lodge/casino/rest., **other:** to Montezuma Castle NM, ⓦ...**other:** Distant Drums RV Park
288mm	Verde River
287	AZ 260, to AZ 89A, Cottonwood, Payson, ⒠...**gas:** Arco, Chevron, Shell/Noble Roman's/Subway/dsl/ RVdump/LP/24hr, **food:** A&W/KFC, Burger King, Coldstone Creamery, DQ, Denny's, Los Betos Mexican, McDonald's, Quizno's, Starbucks, Taco Bell, **lodging:** Comfort Inn, Day's Inn, Super 8, **other:** Territorial RV Park(1mi), Trails End RV Park, Zane Grane RV Park, ⓦ...**gas:** Chevron/Wendy's/dsl/ 24hr, **other:** to Jerome SP, RV camping
285	Camp Verde, Gen Crook Tr, **3 mi** ⒠...**food:** Rio Verde Mexican, **lodging:** Territorial Town Inn, **other:** Zane Gray RV Park(9mi), Trail End RV Park, to Ft Verde SP
281mm	safety pullout area nb
278	AZ 169, Cherry Rd, to Prescott
269mm	Ash Creek
268	Dugas Rd, Orme Rd, no services
265.mm	Agua Fria River
262b a	AZ 69 N, Cordes Jct Rd, to Prescott, ⒠...**gas:** Chevron/McDonald's/24hr, Shell/Noble Roman's/ Chester's/dsl/24hr, **food:** CJ's Diner, McDonald's, **lodging:** Cordes Jct Motel/RV Park
262mm	Big Bug Creek
259	Bloody Basin Rd, to Crown King, Horsethief Basin RA
256	Badger Springs Rd
252	**Sunset Point,** ⓦ...**scenic view/ rest area both lanes, full (handicapped) facilities, phone, picnic tables, litter barrels, vending**
248	Bumble Bee, ⓦ... **other:** Horsethief Basin RA
244	Squaw Valley Rd, Black Canyon City, ⒠...**food:** Kid Chileean BBQ/Steaks, **other:** KOA, ⓦ...**gas**
243.5mm	Agua Fria River
242	Rock Springs, Black Canyon City, ⒠...KOA, ⓦ... **gas:** Chevron/dsl/24hr, Shell, **food:** Byler's Kitchen, Rock Springs Café, **lodging:** Bradshaw Mtn RV Resort, Mtn Breeze Motel
239.5mm	Little Squaw Creek
239mm	Moore's Gulch
236	Table Mesa Rd, no services
232	New River, ⒠...**food:** RoadRunner Rest., **other:** Curves, vet
231mm	New River
229	Anthem Way, Desert Hills Rd, ⒠...**gas:** Mobil/dsl, **food:** Auntie Anne's, McDonald's, Native Newyorker Rest., Pizza Hut, Quizno's, Rosati's Pizza, Starbucks, Subway, Taco Del Mar, **other:** Ace Hardware, CVS Drug, Osco Drug, Safeway, ⓦ...**gas:** Chevron/dsl, Mobil/dsl, **food:** Del Taco, Denny's, **lodging:** Hampton Inn, **other:** Anthem Outlets/famous brands/food court, Brake Masters, Discount Tire, U-haul, Wal-Mart SuperCtr/24hr
227	Daisy Mtn Dr, ⒠...**gas:** Circle K, **food:** Jack-in-the-Box, Subway, **other:** CVS Drug, Fry's Foods
227mm	Dead Man Wash
225	Pioneer Rd, ⓦ...**other:** Pioneer RV Park, museum
223	AZ 74, Carefree Hwy, to Wickenburg, ⒠...**gas:** Chevron, **food:** Applebees, AZool Grill, It's-a-Grind, McDonald's, Rays Pizza, Subway, **other:** Albertson's/Osco, Home Depot, Kohl's, ⓦ...**other:** Lake Pleasant Park, camping
219mm	Skunk Creek
218	Happy Valley Rd, ⒠...**gas:** Shell, **food:** Applebees, Bajio, Carl's Jr, Coldstone Creamery, Jack-in-the-Box, Logan's Roadhouse, Panda Express, Quizno's, Rays Pizza, Red Robin, Shane's Ribshack, Starbucks, TGIFriday, Tilly's Grill, **other:** Barnes&Noble, Circuit City, Lowe's Whse, Old Navy, PetCo, Staples, Steinmart, TJ Maxx, Wal-Mart SuperCtr/24hr, World Mkt
217	Pinnacle Peak Rd, ⒠...Phoenix RV Park
215a	Rose Garden Ln, same as 215b
215b	Deer Valley Rd, ⒠...**gas:** Exxon/dsl, Shell/Circle K, **food:** Arby's, Armando's Mexican, Jack-in-the-Box, McDonald's, Sonic, Taco Bell, Wendy's, **other:** RV Ctr, ⓦ...**gas:** Arco, Circle K, **food:** Black Angus, Cracker Barrel, Denny's, El Patron Mexican, Times Square Italian, **lodging:** Best Western, Country Inn&Suites, Extended Stay America, **other:** HOSPITAL, NAPA, Target, U-Haul

ARIZONA
Interstate 17

214c AZ 101 loop, no services

214b Yorkshire Dr, W...**food:** In-n-Out, Jack-in-the-Box, **lodging:** Budget Suites, **other:** HOSPITAL, Costco/gas, W...**gas:** 7-11, **food:** 5&Diner, Jack-in-the-Box, Wendy's, **other:** Michael's, Petsmart, Target

214a Union Hills Dr, E...**gas:** Circle K/dsl, Shamrock, W...**lodging:** Park Plaza Hotel, Sleep Inn, Studio 6

212b a Bell Rd, Scottsdale, to Sun City, E...**gas:** Chevron/dsl, Exxon, Mobil, QT, 76/dsl, **food:** Black Bear Diner, Burger Mania, Caramba Mexican, IHOP/24hr, Jack-in-the-Box, LJ Silver, McDonald's, Papa John's, Quizno's, Waffle House, **lodging:** Best Western, Comfort Inn, Fairfield Inn, Motel 6, **other:** Big O Tire, Checker Parts, Chevrolet, Chrysler/Jeep/Dodge, Ford/Lexus/Isuzu, Kohl's, Lincoln/Mercury, Nissan/Infiniti, Pontiac/Buick/GMC, Sam's Club/gas, Toyota, U-Haul, Wal-Mart SuperCtr, W...**gas:** Chevron, **food:** Applebee's, Denny's, Good Egg Rest., HomeTown Buffet, Hooters, Sizzler, **lodging:** Red Roof Inn, **other:** Fry's Foods

211 Greenway Rd, E...**lodging:** Embassy Suites, La Quinta, **other:** 7-11

210 Thunderbird Rd, E...**gas:** Circle K, **food:** Asian Cafe, Pizza Hut/Taco Bell, Wendy's, **other:** Home Depot, Jiffy Lube, Osco Drug, Walgreen, W...**gas:** QT, **food:** Fazoli's, McDonald's, Quizno's, **other:** Best Buy, Fry's Electronics, Lowe's Whse

209 Cactus Rd, W...**gas:** Chevron/24hr, 7-11, **food:** Cousins Subs, China Harvest, Don Pedro's Mexican, **lodging:** Ramada Inn, **other:** Firestone, Food City

208 Peoria Ave, E...**food:** Fajita's, LoneStar Steaks, Pappadeaux, TGIFriday, **lodging:** AmeriSuites, Candlewood Suites, Comfort Suites, Crowne Plaza, Extended Stay America, Homewood Suites, W...**food:** Bennnigan's, Black Angus, Burger King, China Chan, Chipotle Mexican, El Torito, Fatburger, Island Burger, Lonestar Steaks, Mimi's Cafe, Old Country Buffet, Olive Garden, Pappadeux's, Peter Piper Pizza, Red Lobster, Ruby Tuesday, Samauri Sam's, Sizzler, Souper Salad, Starbucks, Subway, TGI Fridays, Wendy's, Whataburger, **lodging:** Premier Inn, Sheraton, **other:** Barnes&Noble, Brake Master, Circuit City, Dillard's, Firestone/auto, JC Penney, Macy's, Michael's, Old Navy, PetCo, Ross, Sears/auto, Staples, Trader Joe's, mall

208mm Arizona Canal

207 Dunlap Ave, E...**gas:** Shell/dsl, **food:** Blimpie, Fajitas, Fuddrucker's, Lonestar Steaks, Outback Steaks, Sweet Tomato, **lodging:** Budget Lodge, Comfort Suites, Courtyard, Mainstay Suites, Sheraton, Sierra Suites, SpringHill Suites, TownPlace Suites, **other:** Aamco, Firestone, Sun City RV Ctr, mall, W...**gas:** Chevron, **food:** Bobby Q's BBQ, Denny's, Schlotsky's, Subway, **other:** U-Haul, repair

206 Northern Ave, E...**gas:** Circle K, Shell/dsl, **food:** Boston Mkt, Burger King, Del Taco, Denny's/24hr, El Pollo Loco, Los Compadres Mexican, Marie Callender's, McDonald's, Mr. Sushi, Papa John's, Pizza Hut, Starbucks, Subway, **lodging:** Best Western, **other:** Albertson's, Checker Parts, USPO, Walgreens, W...**gas:** Arco, QT, **food:** DQ, Village Inn Rest., **lodging:** Motel 6, Residence Inn, Super 8, **other:** K-Mart, vet

205 Glendale Ave, E...**other:** Ace Hardware, vet, W...**gas:** Circle K/dsl, **food:** Jack-in-the-Box, **other:** Checker Parts, 7-11, Walgreens, to Luke AFB

204 Bethany Home Rd, E...**gas:** Arco/24hr, Shell/Church's/dsl, **food:** McDonald's, Subway, Samauri Sam's, Whataburger, **other:** HOSPITAL, BigLots, Circle K, vet, W...**gas:** Shell, Valero, **food:** Burger King, Great Dragon, Lazy Lou's, **other:** Food City, Jiffy Lube, Savers

203 Camelback Rd, E...**gas:** Arco/24hr, Circle K, **food:** Blimpie, Burger King, Church's, Denny's/24hr, Pepe's Taco Villa, Pizza Hut, **other:** Buick, Checker Parts, Chrysler/Jeep/Dodge, Discount Tire, Firestone/auto, KIA, NAPA, Walgreens, W...**gas:** QT, **food:** DQ, Jack-in-the-Box, McDonald's, Taco Bell, TacoMex, **lodging:** Comfort Inn, **other:** AutoZone, Chevrolet, Circle K, to Grand Canyon U

202 Indian School Rd, E...**gas:** Arco/24hr, **food:** Domino's, Federico's Mexican, Pizza Hut, Subway, **other:** Ace Hardware, CVS Drug, Food City, Skyline RV Ctr, W...**gas:** Circle K, Red Dog/dsl/LP, Shell, Valero, **food:** JB's, Subway, Wendy's, **lodging:** Motel 6, **other:** 7-11, auto repair

201 Thomas Rd, E...**gas:** Chevron/McDonald's, **food:** Arby's, Big Burrito, Denny's, Jack-in-the-Box, Roman's Pizza, Starbucks, **lodging:** Day's Inn, La Quinta, **other:** Circle K, W...**gas:** QT, **food:** Carl's Jr, Subway, **other:** NAPA

200b McDowell Rd, Van Buren, E...**other:** Goodyear, W...**lodging:** Travelodge

200a I-10, W to LA, E to Phoenix

199b Jefferson St(from sb), Adams St(from nb), Van Buren St(from nb), E...**gas:** Circle K/76/24hr, **food:** Jack-in-the-Box, McDonald's, **other:** Suzuki, to st capitol, W...**gas:** Circle K/76, **food:** La Canasta Mexican, Salsita's Mexican, **other:** Penny Pincher Parts, PepBoys

199a Grant St

198 Buckeye Rd(from nb)

197 US 60, 19th Ave, Durango St, E...**food:** Jack-in-the-Box, Whataburger/24hr, to St Capitol

196 7th St, Central Ave, W...**gas:** DZ/dsl

195b 7th St, Central Ave, E...**gas:** Big Tiger/24hr, Circle K, Trailside Gas/dsl/24hr, **food:** McDonald's, Taco Bell, **lodging:** EZ 8 Motel/rest., **other:** HOSPITAL

195a 16th St(no EZ return from sb), E...**food:** Burger King, **other:** Checker Parts, Food City, to Sky Harbor Airport

194 I-10 W to AZ 151, to Sky Harbor Airport

I-17 begins/ends on I-10, exit 150a

Interstate 19

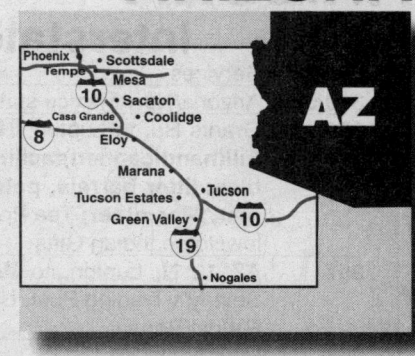

N ← → **S**

Tucson

Exit #	Services
	I-19 uses kilometers (km)
101b a	I-10, E to El Paso, W to Phoenix, I-19 begins/ends on I-10, exit 260
99	AZ 86, Ajo Way, Ⓔ...**gas:** Conoco, 76/Circle K, **food:** Hamburger Stand, Pizza Hut, Subway, Taco Bell, **other:** Fry's Foods, GNC, Goodyear/auto, Mervyn's, U-Haul, Walgreens, auto repair, vet, Ⓦ...**gas:** Chevron/dsl/24hr, Conoco/dsl, Circle K, **food:** Burger King, Domino's, **other:** HOSPITAL, Food City, Jiffy Lube, to Old Tucson, museum
98	Irvington Rd, Ⓔ...**gas:** Arco/24hr, **other:** Fry's Foods, Ⓦ...**gas:** Chevron, **food:** China Olive Buffet, McDonald's, Olive Garden, Panda Express, Starbucks, Subway, **other:** Food City, Home Depot, Marshall's, Petsmart, Ross, Target
95b a	Valencia Rd, Ⓔ...**gas:** Conoco, **food:** Church's, Donut Wheel, Jack-in-the-Box, McDonald's, Peter Piper Pizza, Sonic, Whataburger, Yokohama Rice-Bowl, **other:** Aamco, AutoZone, Brake Masters, Checker Parts, Food City, Jiffy Lube, USPO, Ⓦ...**gas:** Chevron/dsl, 76/Circle K, **food:** Applebee's, Arby's, Burger King, Carl's Jr, Chili's, Chuey's Cafe, Denny's, Dunkin Donuts, Golden Corral, IHOP, Papa John's, Pizza Hut, Taco Bell, Wendy's, **other:** Big O Tire, CVS Drug, Lowe's Whse, 99c Store, Radio Shack, Walgreens, Wal-Mart SuperCtr/24hr, repair, transmissions
92	San Xavier Rd, Ⓦ...**other:** to San Xavier Mission
91.5km	Santa Cruz River
87	Papago Rd, no services, emergency phones sb
80	Pima Mine Rd, Ⓔ...**food:** Agave Rest., Diamond Casino
75	Helmut Peak Rd, to Sahuarita, Ⓔ...**gas:** Shell, **other:** Fry's Foods/drug, USPO
69	US 89 N, Duval Mine Rd., Green Valley, Ⓔ...**food:** Denny's, Pizza Hut, Popeye's, Quizno's, Siagon Flavor, Subway, **other:** Basha's Food, Radio Shack, Walgreens, Wal-Mart SuperCtr/24hr, Ⓦ...**gas:** Circle K/gas, Texaco/DQ/dsl, **food:** Burger King, Domino's, Manuel's Rest., Rigoberto's Mexican, Taco Bell/TCBY, **lodging:** Holiday Inn Express, **other:** Big O Tire, Ford/Lincoln/Mercury/Hyundai, Green Valley RV Resort, Safeway/gas, Titan Missile Museum
65	Esperanza Blvd, to Green Valley, Ⓔ...**gas:** Shell/repair, Ⓦ...**gas:** Texaco/dsl, **food:** AZ Family Rest., China View, Dona's Rest., La Placita Mexican, **lodging:** Baymont Inn, Best Western, **other:** Ace Hardware, Family$, Walgreens
63	Continental Rd, Green Valley, Ⓔ...**food:** Quail Valley Rest., **other:** golf, USPO, **2 mi** Ⓔ...**other:** San Ignacio Golf Club/rest., Ⓦ...**gas:** Chevron, Shell(2mi), **food:** China Vic, HotStuff Pizza, KFC, McDonald's, Starbucks, Trivettie's Rest., **other:** CVS Drug, Parts+, Safeway, TrueValue, Walgreens, to Madera Cyn RA
56	Canoa Rd, Ⓦ... **lodging:** San Ignacio Inn
54km	**rest area both lanes, full (handicapped) facilities, phone, picnic tables, litter barrels, vending, petwalk**
48	Arivaca Rd, Amado, **2-3 mi** Ⓔ...**lodging:** Amado Inn, **other:** Mtn View RV Park, Rex Ranch Resort, Ⓦ...**gas:** Amado Plaza, **food:** Cow Palace Rest., Longhorn Grill, **other:** Amado Mkt
42	Agua Linda Rd, to Amado, Ⓔ...**other:** Mtn View RV Park
40	Chavez Siding Rd, Tubac, **3-5 mi** Ⓔ...**gas:** Tubac Mkt/dsl/deli, **other:** Tubac Golf Resort
34	Tubac, Ⓔ...**gas:** Tubac Mkt/dsl, **food:** Artists Palate, Knob hill Rest., Montura Rest., **other:** Tubac Golf Resort, USPO, to Tubac Presidio SP
29	Carmen, Tumacacori, Ⓔ...gas, food, lodging, **other:** to Tumacacori Nat Hist Park
25	Palo Parado Rd
22	Pec Canyon Rd
17	Rio Rico Dr, Calabasas Rd, Ⓦ...**gas:** Chevron, **food:** La Placita, **other:** IGA Foods, USPO
12	AZ 289, to Ruby Rd, Ⓔ...**gas:** Pilot/Wendy's/dsl/24hr, Ⓦ...**other:** to Pena Blanca Lake RA
8	US 89, AZ 82(exits left from sb, no return), Nogales, **0-3 mi** Ⓔ...**gas:** Circle K/gas **food:** Denny's, **lodging:** Americana Motel, Best Western, Day's Inn, **other:** HOSPITAL, Goodyear/auto, U-Haul, Mi Casa RV Park
4	AZ 189 S, Mariposa Rd, Nogales, Ⓔ...**gas:** Chevron, FasTrip, Jumpin' Jack Gas, 76, **food:** Arby's, Bella Mia Rest., ChinaStar, Denny's, DQ, HomeTown Buffet, Jack-in-the-Box, KFC, McDonald's, Mesquite Grill, Shakey's, Sonic, Taco Bell, Yokohama Rest., **lodging:** Motel 6, Super 8, **other:** Batteries+, BigLots, Chevrolet, $Tree, Ford/Lincoln/Mercury, Home Depot, JC Penney, K-Mart, NAPA, Pontiac/Buick/GMC, Radio Shack, Ross, Safeway, Walgreens, Wal-Mart SuperCtr/24hr(N Grand Ave), Ⓦ...**gas:** Valero/dsl, **food:** Carl's Jr, IHOP, **lodging:** Candlewood Suites, Holiday Inn Express, **other:** Chrysler/Dodge/Jeep
1b	Western Ave, Nogales
1a	International St
0km	I-19 begins/ends in Nogales, Arizona/Mexico Border, **1/2 mi**...**gas:** Circle K/gas, Jumpin'Jack/dsl, **food:** Burger King, Church's, Domino's, Jack-in-the-Box, McDonald's, Noble Roman's, Peter Piper Pizza, Subway, **other:** AutoZone, CarQuest, Checker Parts, Family$, Food City, NAPA, Parts+, PepBoys, Walgreens, museum

Nogales

ARIZONA
Interstate 40

Exit #	Services
359.5mm	Arizona/New Mexico state line
359	Grants Rd, to Lupton, **N**...**rest area both lanes, full(handicapped)facilities, phone, picnic tables, litter barrels, petwalk, gas:** Speedy's/dsl/rest./24hr, **other:** Tee Pee Trading Post/rest., YellowHorse Indian Gifts
357	AZ 12 N, Lupton, to Window Rock, **N**...**other:** Shirley's Trading Post, USPO, **S**...**other:** Scotty's RV/dsl Repair
354	Hawthorne Rd
351	Allentown Rd, **N**...**other:** Chee's Indian Store, Indian City Gifts
348	St Anselm Rd, Houck, **N**...**gas:** Chevron, **other:** Ft Courage Food/gifts
347.5mm	Black Creek
346	Pine Springs Rd
345mm	Box Canyon
344mm	Querino Wash
343	Querino Rd
341	Ortega Rd, Cedar Point, **N**...**gas:** Armco/gas/gifts
340.5mm	insp/weigh sta both lanes
339	US 191 S, to St Johns, **S**...**gas:** Conoco/dsl, **other:** USPO
333	US 191 N, Chambers, **N**...**gas:** Chevron/dsl, **other:** to Hubbell Trading Post NHS, RV camping, **S**...**gas:** Mobil/dsl, **lodging:** Chieftain Inn/rest.
330	McCarrell Rd, no services
325	Navajo, **S**...**gas:** Shell/Subway/Navajo Trading Post/dsl/24hr
323mm	Crazy Creek
320	Pinta Rd
316mm	Dead River
311	Painted Desert, **N**...**gas:** Chevron, **other:** Petrified Forest NP, Painted Desert
303	Adamana Rd, **N**...Stewarts/gifts, **S**...**gas:** Painted Desert Indian Ctr/gas
302.5mm	Big Lithodendron Wash
301mm	Little Lithodendron Wash
300	Goodwater
299mm	Twin Wash
294	Sun Valley Rd, **N**...Root 66 RV camping, **S**...**other:** Knife City
292	AZ 77 N, to Keams Canyon, **N**...**gas:** Conoco/Burger King/dsl/24hr/@, **other:** dsl repair, **S**...**other:** museum
289	Lp 40, Holbrook, **N**...**gas:** Chevron/dsl, Mustang/dsl, **food:** Alberto's Mexican, Denny's, Jerry's Rest., Mesa Rest., **lodging:** Best Inn, Best Western, Comfort Inn, Day's Inn, Econolodge, Motel 6, Ramada Ltd, Sahara Inn, Super 8, Travelodge, **other:** Alley's Tire/Lube, KOA, same as 286
286	Navajo Blvd, Holbrook, **N**...**gas:** Mobil/dsl, Circle K, **food:** Alberto's Mexican, Burger King, Hilltop Cafe, KFC, McDonald's, Pizza Hut, Taco Bell,

lodging: Comfort Inn, Holiday Inn Express, **other:** Checker Parts, $General, KOA, OK RV Park, **S**...**gas:** Chevron/dsl/repair, MiniMart/gas, Mustang/dsl, 76/repair, Super Fuels, Woody's/dsl, **food:** DQ, Rte 66 Cafe, **lodging:** Best Value, El Rancho Motel, **other:** HOSPITAL, Ford/Lincoln/Mercury, Chrysler/Jeep/Dodge, museum, rockshops, transmissions

Exit #	Services
285	US 180 E, AZ 77 S, Holbrook, 1 mi **S**...**gas:** Mustang Gas, Pacific Pride/dsl, **food:** Butterfield Steaks, Wayside Mexican, **lodging:** Best Western, Star Inn, Wigwam Motel, **other:** Safeway, RV repair, rest area/picnic tables/litter barrels, to Petrified Forest NP
284mm	Leroux Wash
283	Perkins Valley Rd, Golf Course Rd, **S**...**gas:** Shell/Country Host Rest./dsl/24hr/@
280	Hunt Rd, Geronimo Rd, **N**...**other:** Geronimo Trading Post
277	Lp 40, Joseph City, **N**...**gas:** Love's/Chester's/Subway/dsl/24hr/@, **S**...**other:** to Cholla Lake CP, RV camping
274	Lp 40, Joseph City, **N**...**gas, food, lodging, RV camping**
269	Jackrabbit Rd
264	Hibbard Rd
257	AZ 87 N, to Second Mesa, **N**...**other:** to Homolovi Ruins SP, camping, **S**...**other:** SW Indian Ctr
256.5mm	Little Colorado River
255	Lp 40, Winslow, **N**...**lodging:** Holiday Inn Express, **S**...**gas:** ⚡/Flying J/CountryMkt/dsl/LP/scales/24hr/@, **food:** Sonic, **lodging:** Comfort Inn(2mi), **other:** Chevrolet, Chrysler/Jeep
253	N Park Dr, Winslow, **N**...**gas:** Chevron, Texaco/SenorD's/dsl/RV dump/scales/24hr/@, **food:** Arby's, Capt Tony's Pizza, Denny's, Pizza Hut, **other:** Checker Parts, $General, Ford, Jiffy Lube, Wal-Mart SuperCtr, **S**...**food:** Alfonso's Mexican, Dominos, KFC, McDonald's, Subway, Taco Bell, **lodging:** Comfort Inn, Econolodge, Motel 6, **other:** HOSPITAL, Basha's Foods, Family$, NAPA, Safeway
252	AZ 87 S, Winslow, **S**...**gas:** Shell/dsl, **food:** Almost Home Buffet, **lodging:** Day's Inn, Rest Inn, Super 8, The lodge, **other:** NAPACare, Old Trails Museum, dsl repair
245	AZ 99, Leupp Corner
239	Meteor City Rd, Red Gap Ranch Rd, **S**...**other:** Meteor City Trading Post, to Meteor Crater
235mm	**rest area both lanes, full(handicapped) facilities, info, phone, picnic tables, litter barrels, petwalk**
233	Meteor Crater Rd, **S**...**gas:** Mobil/Subway/Meteor Crater RV Park, **other:** to Meteor Crater NL
230	Two Guns
229.5mm	Canyon Diablo

Interstate 40

225	Buffalo Range Rd
219	Twin Arrows
218.5mm	Padre Canyon
211	Winona, **N**...**gas:** Shell/dsl/repair
207	Cosnino Rd
204	to Walnut Canyon NM
201	US 89, to Flagstaff, **N**...**gas:** Conoco/dsl, Express/dsl, 76/repair, Shell, **food:** Arby's, Burger King, Del Taco, Jack-in-the-Box, Los Altos Tacos, McDonald's, Pizza Hut, Quizno's, Ruby Tuesday, Sizzler, Taco Bell/LJ Silver, Wendy's, Village Inn Rest., **lodging:** Best Western, Day's Inn, Hampton Inn, Howard Johnson, Luxury Inn, Super 8, Travelodge, **other:** HOSPITAL, Aamco, Big O Tire, Checker's Parts, CVS Drug, Dillard's, Family$, Flagstaff RV Ctr/LP, Goodyear/auto, Honda/Isuzu/Mazda, JC Penney, KOA, PitStop Lube, Safeway, Sears/auto, Toyota, mall, **S**...**gas:** Mobil/dsl, **lodging:** Residence Inn
198	Butler Ave, Flagstaff, **N**...**gas:** Chevron, Conoco/dsl, Shell, Mustang Gas, **food:** Burger King, Country Host Rest., Cracker Barrel, Denny's, Hogs Rest., McDonald's, Outback Steaks, Starbucks, Sonic, Taco Bell, **lodging:** Econolodge, Flagstaff Inn, Holiday Inn Express, Howard Johnson, Motel 6, Quality Inn, Ramada Ltd, Super 8, Travelodge, **other:** NAPA, Sam's Club, **1 mi N on Rte 66**...**gas:** Carter/dsl, **food:** China Star, Dog Haus Cafe, Kachina Mexican, KFC, Salsa Brava Mexican, Subway, **lodging:** Americana Inn, Best Value, Best Western, Red Rose Inn, Relax Inn, Royal Inn, 66 Motel, Travelodge, Timberline Motel, Western Hills Motel, **other:** Albertson's, Auto Value Parts, AutoZone, Buick/Pontiac, Firestone, Fry's Foods/dsl, Nissan/Subaru, PepBoys, U-Haul, **S**...**gas:** Mobil, Sinclair/Little America/dsl/motel/@ , **food:** Black Bart's Steaks/RV Park, vet
197.5mm	Rio de Flag
195b	US 89A N, McConnell Dr, Flagstaff, **N**...**gas:** Chevron/dsl, Conoco/dsl, Gasser/dsl, Giant/dsl, Mobil, Circle K, Shell, Texaco/Wendy's/dsl, **food:** Arby's, August Moon Chinese, Baskin-Robbins, Bella Donna Italian, Blimpie, Buffalo Wild Wings, Burger King, Buster's Rest., Carl's Jr, Casa Bonita, Chili's, China Garden, Coco's, Coldstone, DQ, Del Taco, Denny's, Domino's, Fazoli's, Garcia'a Mexican, IHOP, Jack-in-the-Box, KFC, Mandarin Buffet, McDonald's, Olive Garden, Picazzo's Pizza, Peter Piper Pizza, Pizza Hut, Quizno's, Red Lobster, Roma Pizza, Sizzler, Starbucks, Strombolli's, Subway, Taco Bell, TCBY, Village Inn Rest., **lodging:** AZ Motel, AutoLodge, AmeriSuites, Best Value, Budget Inn, Comfort Inn, Crystal Inn, Day's Inn, Drury Inn, Econolodge, Embassy Suites, Fairfield Inn, Hampton Inn, Hilton Garden, La Quinta, Motel 6, Quality Inn, Ramada Ltd, Rodeway Inn, Sleep Inn, Super 8, **other:** HOSPITAL, Barnes&Noble, Basha's Foods, Hastings Books, Jiffy Lube, Jo-Ann Crafts, Kohl's, Michael's, Staples, Target, Walgreen, Wal-Mart
195a	I-17 S, AZ 89A S, to Phoenix
192	Flagstaff Ranch Rd
191	Lp 40, to Grand Canyon, Flagstaff, **5 mi N**...**gas:** Chevron, **food:** DQ, **lodging:** Best Western, Budget Host, Comfort Inn, Day's Inn, Econolodge, Radisson, Super 8, Travelodge, **S**...**other:** Woody Mtn Camping
190	A-1 Mountain Rd, no services
189.5mm	Arizona Divide, elevation 7335
185	Transwestern Rd, Bellemont, **N**...**gas:** Pilot/McDonald's/Subway/dsl/scales/24hr, **lodging:** Best Value, **S**...**other:** Harley-Davidson/Roadside Grill
183mm	**rest area wb, full (handicapped) facilities, phone, picnic tables, litter barrels, vending, weather info, petwalk**
182mm	**rest area eb, full (handicapped) facilities, phone, picnic tables, litter barrels, vending, weather info, petwalk**
178	Parks Rd, **N**...**food:** Mustang/dsl/24hr, **food:** Rack&Bull Café, **other:** Ponderosa Forest RV Park
171	Pittman Valley Rd, Deer Farm Rd, **S**...**lodging:** Quality Inn/grill
167	Garland Prairie Rd, Circle Pines Rd, **N**...**other:** KOA
165	AZ 64, to Williams, to Grand Canyon, **N**...**gas:** Texaco(8mi), Shell/dsl(4mi), **other:** KOA, **S**...**lodging:** Super 8(4mi), **other:** RV Ctr
163	Williams, **N**...**gas:** Chevron/Subway/dsl, **lodging:** Fairfield Inn, **other:** Cyn Gateway RV Park, to Grand Canyon, **S**...**gas:** Mobil/dsl, Circle K, 76/dsl/repair, **food:** Buckle's Rest., Jack-in-the-Box, McDonald's, Pancho McGillicuddy's Mexican, Pine Country Rest., Pizza Hut, Rod's Steaks, Rosa's Cantina, **lodging:** Budget Host, Downtowner Motel, Econolodge, El Rancho Motel, Gateway Motel, Holiday Inn, Howard Johnson Express, Motel 6, Mountainview Motel, Knight's Inn, Rancho Motel, Rodeway Inn, Rte 66 Inn, Travelodge, **other:** CarQuest, USPO, same as 161
161	Lp 40, Golf Course Dr, Williams, **N**...RV camping, **1-3 mi S**...**gas:** Chevron/dsl, Circle K, Mobil, 76, Shell, **food:** Cruiser's Cafe 66, DQ, Denny's, Jessica's Rest., Old Smokey Rest., Pizza Factory, Ralberto's Mexican, **lodging:** Best Western, Best Value, Budget Host, Canyon Country Inn, Day's Inn, Highlander Motel, Motel 6, Westerner Motel, **other:** HOSPITAL, NAPA, Family$, Safeway, Railside RV Ranch, to Grand Canyon Railway
157	Devil Dog Rd
155.5mm	safety pullout wb, litter barrels
151	Welch Rd
149	Monte Carlo Rd, **N**...**other:** Monte Carlo Truck Repair

E
↕
W

Flagstaff

ARIZONA

Interstate 40

Exit	Description
148	County Line Rd, no services
146	AZ 89, to Prescott, Ash Fork, **N**...**gas:** Mobil/dsl, Mustang, **food:** Ranch House Cafe, **lodging:** Ash Fork Inn
144	Ash Fork, **N**...**lodging:** Ash Fork Inn/rest., **other:** Grand Canyon RV Park, USPO, **S**...**gas:** Chevron/Piccadilly's/dsl, Texaco/dsl/RV Park, **other:** auto repair
139	Crookton Rd, to Rte 66
132mm	weigh sta both lanes
123	Lp 40, to Rte 66, Seligman, **N**...**gas:** Mustang/dsl, Shell/dsl, **lodging:** 66 Motel, **other:** KOA(1mi), to Grand Canyon Caverns, USPO, **S**...**gas:** Chevron/Subway/dsl/24hr
121	Lp 40, to Rte 66, Seligman, **N**...**gas:** Chevron/A&W, **food:** Lilo's Rest.(2mi), 66 Cafe(1mi), **lodging:** Canyon Lodge
109	Anvil Rock Rd
108mm	Markham Wash
103	Jolly Rd, no services
96	Cross Mountain Rd
91	Fort Rock Rd
87	Willows Ranch Rd
86mm	Willow Creek
79	Silver Springs Rd
75.5mm	Big Sandy Wash
73.5mm	Peacock Wash
71	US 93 S, to Wickenburg, Phoenix
66	Blake Ranch Rd, **N**...**gas:** Petro/Mobil/Iron Skillet/Noble Roman's/dsl/rest./scales/24hr/@, **other:** Blake Ranch RV Park, Blue Beacon, SpeedCo Lube
60mm	Frees Wash
59	DW Ranch Rd, Hualapai Mtn Rd, **N**...**gas:** Love's/Chester Fried/Subway/dsl/24hr, **other:** truckwash
57mm	Rattlesnake Wash
53	AZ 66, Andy Devine Ave, to Kingman, **N**...**gas:** Chevron, ♿/Flying J/Conoco/Cookery/dsl/LP/scales/24hr/@, Mobil/dsl, Terrible's/dsl, Texaco, **food:** Arby's, Burger King, Denny's, Jack-in-the-Box, McDonald's, Pizza Hut, Taco Bell, **lodging:** Day's Inn, Econolodge, First Value Inn, Motel 6, Silver Queen Motel, Super 8, Travelodge, **other:** Basha's Foods, Goodyear/auto, Harley-Davidson, K-Mart, KOA(1mi), TireWorld, dsl/tire repair, **S**...**gas:** 76/dsl, Shell/repair, **food:** ABC Rest., JB's, Lo's Chinese, Sonic, **lodging:** Best Value Inn, Best Western, Comfort Inn, Day's Inn, High Desert Inn, Holiday Inn Express, Lido Motel, Relax Inn, Rodeway Inn, Rte 66 Motel, **other:** Chrysler/Jeep/Dodge, NAPA, Sunrise RV Park, Uptown Drug

Exit	Description
51	Stockton Hill Rd, Kingman, **N**...**gas:** Arco/24hr, Chevron, 76/Circle K, **food:** Chili's, Cracker Barrel, Del Taco, Golden Corral, IHOP, In-n-Out, KFC, Papa John's, Sonic, Subway, Taco Bell/24hr, Whataburger, **lodging:** Hampton Inn, **other:** HOSPITAL, AutoZone, Big Lots, Brake Master's, Checker Parts, Chevrolet/Buick/Pontiac/Cadillac, $General, Ford/Lincoln/Mercury, Home Depot, Honda, Hyundai, Nissan, Oil Can Henry's, Smith's Foods/dsl, Staples, Superior Tire, TrueValue, Toyota, Walgreens, Wal-Mart SuperCtr, KOA(2mi), vet, **S**...**gas:** Circle K, **food:** Alfonso's Mexican, DQ, Kingman Co Steaks, Little Caesar's, Pizza Hut, **other:** CarQuest, Family$, Hastings Books, JC Penney, Radio Shack, Safeway
48	US 93 N, Beale St, Kingman, **N**...**gas:** Chevron/dsl, Express Stop, Mobil/dsl/RV dump, 93 Fuel, USA/Subway/dsl/24hr, Shell/dsl/24hr, TA/76/Country Pride/Popeye's/dsl/24hr, Woody's, **food:** Chan Chinese, Lotta Lou's Cafe, Wendy's, **lodging:** Frontier Motel, Knights Inn, **other:** Best Tire, auto/RV repair, truckwash, **S**...**gas:** Chevron/dsl/24hr, **food:** Calico's Rest., Carl's Jr, Quizno's, Roadrunner Cafe, **lodging:** AZ Inn, Motel 6, Quality Inn(1mi), **other:** CarQuest, Ft Beale RV Park, museum
46.5mm	Holy Moses Wash
44	AZ 66, Oatman Hwy, McConnico, to Rte 66, **S**...**gas:** Crazy Fred's Fuel/dsl/café, **other:** truckwash
40.5mm	Griffith Wash
37	Griffith Rd
35mm	Black Rock Wash
32mm	Walnut Creek
28	Old Trails Rd
26	Proving Ground Rd, **S**...**other:** Ford Proving Grounds
25	Alamo Rd, to Yucca, **N**...**gas:** Micromart/dsl/diner, **other:** USPO, **S**...auto repair, towing
23mm	**rest area both lanes, full(handicapped) facilities, phone, picnic tables, litter barrels, vending, petwalk**
21mm	Flat Top Wash
20	Santa Fe Ranch Rd
18.5mm	Illavar Wash
15mm	Buck Mtn Wash
13.5mm	Franconia Wash
13	Franconia Rd
9	AZ 95 S, to Lake Havasu City, Parker, London Br, **S**...**gas:** Chevron/Burger King/dsl, Pilot/Wendy's/dsl/scales, **other:** Prospectors RV Resort
4mm	weigh sta both lanes
2	Needle Mtn Rd
1	Topock Rd, to Bullhead City, Oatman, **N**...**gas:** food, camping, to Havasu NWR ·
0mm	Arizona/California state line, Colorado River, Mountain/Pacific time zone

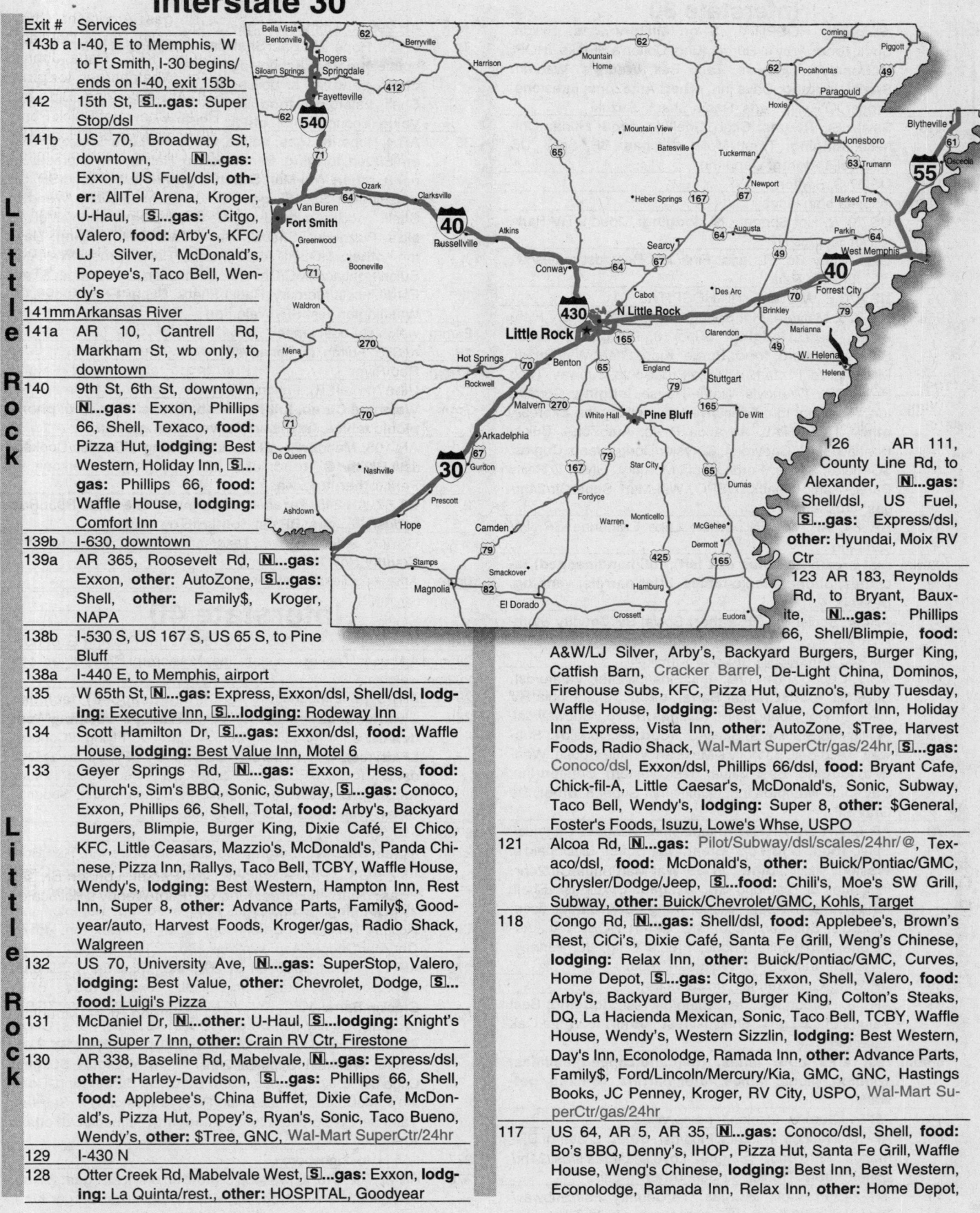

ARKANSAS

Interstate 30

Exit #	Services
143b a	I-40, E to Memphis, W to Ft Smith, I-30 begins/ends on I-40, exit 153b
142	15th St, [S]...**gas:** Super Stop/dsl
141b	US 70, Broadway St, downtown, [N]...**gas:** Exxon, US Fuel/dsl, **other:** AllTel Arena, Kroger, U-Haul, [S]...**gas:** Citgo, Valero, **food:** Arby's, KFC/LJ Silver, McDonald's, Popeye's, Taco Bell, Wendy's
141mm	Arkansas River
141a	AR 10, Cantrell Rd, Markham St, wb only, to downtown
140	9th St, 6th St, downtown, [N]...**gas:** Exxon, Phillips 66, Shell, Texaco, **food:** Pizza Hut, **lodging:** Best Western, Holiday Inn, [S]...**gas:** Phillips 66, **food:** Waffle House, **lodging:** Comfort Inn
139b	I-630, downtown
139a	AR 365, Roosevelt Rd, [N]...**gas:** Exxon, **other:** AutoZone, [S]...**gas:** Shell, **other:** Family$, Kroger, NAPA
138b	I-530 S, US 167 S, US 65 S, to Pine Bluff
138a	I-440 E, to Memphis, airport
135	W 65th St, [N]...**gas:** Express, Exxon/dsl, Shell/dsl, **lodging:** Executive Inn, [S]...**lodging:** Rodeway Inn
134	Scott Hamilton Dr, [S]...**gas:** Exxon/dsl, **food:** Waffle House, **lodging:** Best Value Inn, Motel 6
133	Geyer Springs Rd, [N]...**gas:** Exxon, Hess, **food:** Church's, Sim's BBQ, Sonic, Subway, [S]...**gas:** Conoco, Exxon, Phillips 66, Shell, Total, **food:** Arby's, Backyard Burgers, Blimpie, Burger King, Dixie Café, El Chico, KFC, Little Ceasars, Mazzio's, McDonald's, Panda Chinese, Pizza Inn, Rallys, Taco Bell, TCBY, Waffle House, Wendy's, **lodging:** Best Western, Hampton Inn, Rest Inn, Super 8, **other:** Advance Parts, Family$, Goodyear/auto, Harvest Foods, Kroger/gas, Radio Shack, Walgreen
132	US 70, University Ave, [N]...**gas:** SuperStop, Valero, **lodging:** Best Value, **other:** Chevrolet, Dodge, [S]...**food:** Luigi's Pizza
131	McDaniel Dr, [N]...**other:** U-Haul, [S]...**lodging:** Knight's Inn, Super 7 Inn, **other:** Crain RV Ctr, Firestone
130	AR 338, Baseline Rd, Mabelvale, [N]...**gas:** Express/dsl, **other:** Harley-Davidson, [S]...**gas:** Phillips 66, Shell, **food:** Applebee's, China Buffet, Dixie Cafe, McDonald's, Pizza Hut, Popey's, Ryan's, Sonic, Taco Bueno, Wendy's, **other:** $Tree, GNC, Wal-Mart SuperCtr/24hr
129	I-430 N
128	Otter Creek Rd, Mabelvale West, [S]...**gas:** Exxon, **lodging:** La Quinta/rest., **other:** HOSPITAL, Goodyear

126	AR 111, County Line Rd, to Alexander, [N]...**gas:** Shell/dsl, US Fuel, [S]...**gas:** Express/dsl, **other:** Hyundai, Moix RV Ctr
123	AR 183, Reynolds Rd, to Bryant, Bauxite, [N]...**gas:** Phillips 66, Shell/Blimpie, **food:** A&W/LJ Silver, Arby's, Backyard Burgers, Burger King, Catfish Barn, Cracker Barrel, De-Light China, Dominos, Firehouse Subs, KFC, Pizza Hut, Quizno's, Ruby Tuesday, Waffle House, **lodging:** Best Value, Comfort Inn, Holiday Inn Express, Vista Inn, **other:** AutoZone, $Tree, Harvest Foods, Radio Shack, Wal-Mart SuperCtr/gas/24hr, [S]...**gas:** Conoco/dsl, Exxon/dsl, Phillips 66/dsl, **food:** Bryant Cafe, Chick-fil-A, Little Caesar's, McDonald's, Sonic, Subway, Taco Bell, Wendy's, **lodging:** Super 8, **other:** $General, Foster's Foods, Isuzu, Lowe's Whse, USPO
121	Alcoa Rd, [N]...**gas:** Pilot/Subway/dsl/scales/24hr/@, Texaco/dsl, **food:** McDonald's, **other:** Buick/Pontiac/GMC, Chrysler/Dodge/Jeep, [S]...**food:** Chili's, Moe's SW Grill, Subway, **other:** Buick/Chevrolet/GMC, Kohls, Target
118	Congo Rd, [N]...**gas:** Shell/dsl, **food:** Applebee's, Brown's Rest, CiCi's, Dixie Café, Santa Fe Grill, Weng's Chinese, **lodging:** Relax Inn, **other:** Buick/Pontiac/GMC, Curves, Home Depot, [S]...**gas:** Citgo, Exxon, Shell, Valero, **food:** Arby's, Backyard Burger, Burger King, Colton's Steaks, DQ, La Hacienda Mexican, Sonic, Taco Bell, TCBY, Waffle House, Wendy's, Western Sizzlin, **lodging:** Best Western, Day's Inn, Econolodge, Ramada Inn, **other:** Advance Parts, Family$, Ford/Lincoln/Mercury/Kia, GMC, GNC, Hastings Books, JC Penney, Kroger, RV City, USPO, Wal-Mart SuperCtr/gas/24hr
117	US 64, AR 5, AR 35, [N]...**gas:** Conoco/dsl, Shell, **food:** Bo's BBQ, Denny's, IHOP, Pizza Hut, Santa Fe Grill, Waffle House, Weng's Chinese, **lodging:** Best Inn, Best Western, Econolodge, Ramada Inn, Relax Inn, **other:** Home Depot,

ARKANSAS

Interstate 30

E ↑ W

	S...other: HOSPITAL, **S on Military**...gas: Exxon, Shell, **food:** Arby's, Burger King, Colton's Steaks, IHOP, McDonald's, Quizno's, Taco Bell, Wendy's, Western Sizzlin, **lodging:** Days Inn, **other:** AutoZone, Firestone, Kroger, O'Reilly Parts, Radio Shack, Suzuki
116	Sevier St, **N**...gas: Citgo, Shell/dsl, **food:** Hunan Chinese, **lodging:** Troutt Motel, **S**...gas: BP, Shell, US Fuel/dsl, **lodging:** Capri Inn
114	US 67 S, Benton
113mm	insp sta both lanes
111	US 70 W, Hot Springs, **N**...lodging: Cloud 9 RV Park, to Hot Springs NP
106	Old Military Rd, **N**...gas: Fina/JJ's Rest./dsl/scales/@, **S**...JB'S RV Park
99	US 270 E,, Malvern,, **N**...HOSPITAL
98b a	US 270, Malvern, Hot Springs, **N**...food: Hungry Fisherman Rest., **lodging:** Super 8, **S**...gas: Fina/dsl, Shell/dsl, Valero, **food:** Burger King, Great Wall Buffet, McDonald's, Pizza Hut, Pizza Pro, Sonic, Subway, Taco Bell, TCBY, Wendy's, Waffle House, **lodging:** Comfort Inn, Economy Inn, Executive Inn, Holiday Inn Express, **other:** HOSPITAL, Advance Parts, AutoZone, Buick/Pontiac/GMC, Chevrolet, Chrysler/Dodge/Jeep, Curves, $General, $Tree, Ford/Lincoln/Mercury, GNC, O'Reilly Parts, Radio Shack, USPO, Wal-Mart SuperCtr/24hr/gas, tires/repair
97	AR 84, AR 171, **N**...other: Lake Catherine SP, RV camping
93mm	**rest area(both lanes exit left), full(handicapped) facilities, phone, picnic tables, litter barrels, vending, petwalk**
91	AR 84, Social Hill, **S**...other: Social Hill Country Store/RV Park
83	AR 283, Friendship, **S**...gas: Shell/dsl
78	AR 7, Caddo Valley, **N**...gas: Fina/dsl/24hr, Valero/dsl, Shell/dsl, **food:** Cracker Barrel, **other:** Arkadelphia RV Park, to Hot Springs NP, **S**...gas: Exxon/Subway/dsl, Phillips 66/Stuckey's, Shell/dsl, **food:** McDonald's, Subway, Taco Bell, TaMolly's Mexican, Waffle House, Wendy's, **lodging:** Best Value, Best Western, Comfort Inn, Day's Inn, Hampton Inn, Quality Inn, Super 8, **other:** De Gray SP
73	AR 8, AR 26, AR 51, Arkadelphia, **N**...gas: Citgo/dsl, Shell, **food:** Domino's, Great Wall Buffet, McDonald's, Western Sizzlin, **other:** $Tree, Wal-Mart SuperCtr/24hr, to Crater of Diamond SP, **S**...gas: Exxon/dsl, Shell, **food:** Andy's Rest., Burger King, Cancun Mexican, Mazzio's, Subway, Taco Tico, **other:** HOSPITAL, AutoZone, Brookshire Foods, Fred's Drug, JC Penney, O'Reilly Parts, USPO, Walgreen, repair
69	AR 26 E, Gum Springs, no services
63	AR 53, Gurdon, **N**...gas: Citgo/dsl/rest., **lodging:** Best Value Inn, **S**...gas: Shell/dsl/rest., **other:** to White Oak Lake SP
56mm	**rest area both lanes, full(handicapped)facilities, vending, picnic tables, litter barrels, vending, petwalk**
54	AR 51, Gurdon, Okolona, no services
46	AR 19, Prescott, **N**...gas: Fina/dsl, **other:** Crater of Diamonds SP(31mi), **S**...gas: Love's/Hardee's/dsl/24hr/scales, **food:** Trucker's Rest., **other:** repair
44	AR 24, Prescott, **N**...gas: TA/Country Fair/Subway/Taco Bell/dsl/24hr/@, **S**...gas: Norman's 44 Trkstp/dsl/rest./scales/@, **lodging:** Econolodge, **other:** HOSPITAL, truckwash, to S Ark U

Hope

36	AR 299, to Emmet, **S**...gas: Citgo
31	AR 29, Hope, **N**...gas: Shell/dsl, **food:** Uncle Henry's Smokehouse, **lodging:** Econolodge, Relax Inn, Village Inn/RV park, **other:** carwash, st police, **S**...gas: Exxon/dsl, Shamrock, Shell, Valero/dsl, **food:** Andy's Rest., KFC, **lodging:** Best Value, Economy Inn,. **other:** HOSPITAL
30	AR 4, Hope, **N**...gas: Valero, **food:** Dos Loco Gringos, Western Sizzlin, **lodging:** Best Western, Holiday Inn Express, Super 8, **other:** Wal-Mart SuperCtr/gas/24hr, Millwood SP, Old Washington SP, **S**...gas: Exxon/Baskin-Robbins/Wendy's, Shell, **food:** Amigo Juan Mexican, Burger King, McDonald's, Pizza Hut, Sheba's Rest., Taco Bell, **lodging:** Day's Inn, **other:** HOSPITAL, Advance Parts, Brookshire's/gas, Buick/Pontiac/GMC/Chevrolet, Chrysler/Jeep/Dodge, $Tree, Ford/Lincoln/Mercury, Radio Shack, Super 1 Foods/gas, Old Washington Hist SP, Walgreen
26mm	weigh sta both lanes
18	rd 355, Fulton, no services
17mm	Red River
12	US 67(from EB), Fulton
7mm	**Welcome Ctr eb, full(handicapped)facilities, info, phone, picnic tables, litter barrels, vending, petwalk**
7	AR 108, Mandeville, **N**...gas: ⬧/Flying J/Conoco/Cookery/dsl/LP/24hr/@, **food:** J&R BBQ, **lodging:** Texarkana RV Park, **other:** truckwash
2	US 67, AR 245, Texarkana, **N**...gas: Circle K/dsl, RoadRunner/dsl, **S**...gas: BP/dsl, **food:** T-Town Diner
1	US 71, Jefferson Ave, Texarkana, **N**...KOA, **S**...lodging: Country Host Inn
0mm	Arkansas/Texas state line

Interstate 40

Exit #	Services
285mm	Arkansas/Tennessee state line, Mississippi River
282mm	weigh sta wb
281	AR 131, S to Mound City
280	Club Rd, Southland Dr, **N**...gas: BP/dsl, Pilot/Subway/Wendy's/dsl/@, **other:** Goodyear, **S**...gas: ⬧/Flying J/Conoco/LP/dsl/rest./@, Petro/dsl/rest./24hr/@, Pilot/Subway/DQ/dsl/@, **food:** KFC/Taco Bell, McDonald's, Waffle House, **lodging:** Best Western, Deluxe Inn, Express Inn, Super 8, **other:** Blue Beacon, SpeedCo Lube
279b	I-55 S(from eb)
279a	Ingram Blvd, **N**...lodging: Comfort Inn, Day's Inn, Red Roof Inn, **other:** Ford, Greyhound Park, U-Haul, **S**...gas: Citgo/dsl, **food:** Margarita's, Perkins, Waffle House, Western Sizzlin, **lodging:** Econolodge, Hampshire Inn, Hampton Inn, Holiday Inn, Howard Johnson, Motel 6, Relax Inn, **other:** Chrysler/Dodge/Jeep, same as 280
278	AR 77, 7th St, Missouri St, **N**...gas: Citgo/24hr, **S**...gas: Love's/dsl/24hr, RaceTrac, Shell, Texaco, **food:** BBQ, Cracker Barrel, KFC, Krystal, Mrs Winner's, Pizza Inn, TCBY, **lodging:** Quality Inn, **other:** HOSPITAL, Chief Parts, Goodyear/auto, Hancock Fabrics, Radio Shack, Sawyers RV Park, Sears, Wal-Mart SuperCtr/24hr, **S on Missouri St**...gas: Citgo/dsl, Exxon, Mapco, **food:** Bonanza, Burger King, Domino's, McDonald's, Pizza Hut, Popeye's, Shoney's, Subway, Taco Bell, Walgreen, Wendy's, **lodging:** Ramada Ltd, **other:** Kroger
277	I-55 N, to Jonesboro
276	AR 77, Rich Rd, to Missouri St(from eb only), **S**...gas: Exxon, Phillips 66, Shell, **food:** Applebee's, Bonanza, Burger King, Krystal, Mrs Winners, Popeye's, Shoney's, Wendy's, **lodging:** Ramada Ltd, **other:** Wal-Mart SuperCtr/McDonald's, same as 278

W Memphis

24

Interstate 40

E ↑ ↓ **W**

Forrest City   Brinkley

Exit	Description
275	AR 118, Airport Rd, **S**...**other:** Hog Pen Funpark
275mm	**Welcome Ctr wb, full(handicapped)facilities, info, phone, picnic tables, litter barrels, petwalk**
274mm	weigh sta eb
271	AR 147, to Blue Lake, **S**...**gas:** BP/dsl, Exxon/Chester Fried, **other:** to Horseshoe Lake, RV camping
265	US 79, AR 218, to Hughes, **S**...**food:** Bole's Foods
260	AR 149, to Earle, **N**...**gas:** TA/BP/Country Pride/Burger King/Taco Bell/dsl/scales/24hr/@, Dairy King/Subway/Gas, Valero/dsl, **lodging:** Super 8, **other:** KOA, **S**...**gas:** Shell, **other:** dsl repair
256	AR 75, to Parkin, **N**...**gas:** Express/Stuckey's/dsl/rest., **other:** to Parkin SP(12mi)
247	AR 38 E, to Widener
245mm	St Francis River
243mm	**rest area wb, full(handicapped)facilities, phone, vending, picnic tables, litter barrels, petwalk**
242	AR 284, Crowley's Ridge Rd, **N**...**other:** to Village Creek SP, camping, HOSPITAL
241b a	AR 1, Forrest City, **N**...**gas:** BP/dsl, Phillips 66/Popeye's/dsl, **food:** Denny's, HoHo Chinese, Wendy's, **lodging:** Comfort Inn, Day's Inn, Econolodge, Hampton Inn, Holiday Inn, Super 8, **other:** Chevrolet/Pontiac/Buick, Ford/Lincoln/Mercury, Dodge, st police, **S**...**gas:** Citgo, Exxon, Shell, **food:** Bonanza, Burger King, Dragon China, KFC, McDonald's, Mrs Winners, Old South Pancakes, Pizza Hut, Subway, Taco Bell, Waffle House, **lodging:** Best Western, **other:** Advance Parts, $General, $Tree, Food Giant, SavALot, Wal-Mart SuperCtr/gas/24hr
239	to Wynne, Marianna, no services
235mm	**rest area eb, full(handicapped)facilities, phone, vending, picnic tables, litter barrels, petwalk**
234mm	L'Anguille River
233	AR 261, Palestine, **N**...**gas:** Love's/Chester Fried/Subway/dsl/scales/24hr, **lodging:** Rest Inn, **S**...**gas:** BP/BBQ/dsl, **food:** Head's Cafe
221	AR 78, Wheatley, **N**...**gas:** Phillips 66/dsl/repair, **lodging:** motel, **S**...**gas:** BP/dsl, MapCo/Subway/dsl
216	US 49, AR 17, Brinkley, **N**...**gas:** Exxon/dsl, Flash/dsl, Shell/KFC/dsl, **food:** Western Sizzlin, **lodging:** Baymont Inn, Best Inn, Day's Inn/RV park, Econolodge, **other:** dsl repair, **S**...**gas:** Express/dsl/24hr, Exxon/dsl, Phillips 66, Valero, **food:** Laura's Diner, McDonald's, Pizza Hut, Sonic, Subway, Taco Bell, Waffle House, **lodging:** Best Value, Best Western, Heritage Inn/RV Park, **other:** Chrysler/Dodge/Jeep, $General, Family$, Kroger, MapCo, O'Reilly Parts, Wal-Mart
205mm	Cache River
202	AR 33, to Biscoe
200mm	White River
199mm	**rest areas both lanes, full(handicapped)facilities, vending, picnic tables, litter barrels, no phones**
193	AR 11, to Hazen, **N**...**gas:** Exxon/Chester Fried, **S**...**gas:** Shell/dsl/24hr, T-rix/dsl/RV Park, **food:** Subway, **lodging:** Super 8, Travel Inn
183	AR 13, Carlisle, **S**...**gas:** Conoco/dsl, Exxon/dsl, Phillips 66/dsl, **food:** Nick's BBQ, Pizza 'N More, Sonic, **lodging:** Best Value, Carlisle Motel, **other:** $General
175	AR 31, Lonoke, **N**...**gas:** Phillips 66, Valero/dsl, **food:** McDonald's, **lodging:** Day's Inn, Economy Inn/rest., Holiday Inn Express, Super 8, **S**...**gas:** Shell/Subway, **food:** KFC/Taco Bell, Pizza Hut, Sonic, **lodging:** Perry's Motel/rest., **other:** Chevrolet, Harvest Foods, Wal-Mart
169.5	insp sta both lanes

Little Rock

Exit	Description
169	AR 15, Remington Rd
165	Kerr Rd
161	AR 391, Galloway, **N**...**gas:** Love's/Chester Fried/dsl/24hr, **S**...**gas:** Petro/Mobil/Iron Skillet/dsl/scales/24hr/@, Pilot/Subway/Chester Fried/dsl/scales/24hr/@, IA-80 TruckOMat/dsl/scales, **lodging:** Galloway Inn, **other:** Blue Beacon, Freightliner
159	I-440 W, to airport
157	AR 161, to US 70, **N**...**gas:** Exxon/dsl, **S**...**gas:** Flash/dsl, Hess, Super S Stop, Shell/dsl, **food:** Burger King, KFC/Taco Bell, McDonald's, Sonic, Subway, Waffle House, **lodging:** Best Value, Comfort Inn, Day's Inn, Red Roof Inn, Rest Inn, Super 8
156	Springhill Dr, **N**...**gas:** Phillips 66, **food:** Burger King, Cracker Barrel, Red Lobster, **lodging:** Fairfield Inn, Holiday Inn Express, Residence Inn
155	US 67 N, US 167, to Jacksonville (exits left from eb), Little Rock AFB, 1 mi **N** on US 167/McCain Blvd...**gas:** Phillips 66, Shell, **food:** Applebee's, Arby's, Burger King, Carino's Italian, Chili's, ChuckeCheese, CiCi's Pizza, Denny's, El Porton Mexican, Golden Corral, Hooters, IHOP, Jason's Deli, Kanpai Japanese, McDonald's, Lonestar Steaks, Luby's, Montana Steaks, Outback Steaks, Pizza Hut, Rally's, Red Lobster, Roadhouse Grill, Ryan's, Sonic, Shorty's BBQ, Starbucks, Subway, Taco Bell, TGI Friday, Tia's Mexican, TX Roadhouse, Wendy's, **lodging:** Best Western, Comfort Inn, Hampton Inn, Holiday Inn Express, La Quinta, Super 8, **other:** Aamco, Barnes&Noble, Best Buy, Chrysler/Dodge, Circuit City, Dillard's, Firestone/auto, Ford/Lincoln/Mercury, Gander Mtn, Goody's, Harley-Davidson, Home Depot, JC Penney, Lowe's Whse, Michael's, Office Depot, PepBoys, PetsMart, Saturn, Sears/auto, Target, TJ Maxx, Toyota/Scion, Wal-Mart SuperCtr/gas, mall, vet
154	to Lakewood(from eb)
153b	I-30 W, US 65 S, to Little Rock
153a	AR 107 N, JFK Blvd, **N**...**gas:** Exxon, Express, Shell, **food:** Schlotsky's, **lodging:** Travelodge, **S**...**gas:** Exxon, **food:** Royal Buffet, Waffle House, **lodging:** Country Inn Suites, Hampton Inn, Holiday Inn, Howard Johnson, Motel 6, **other:** HOSPITAL, USPO
152	AR 365, AR 176, Camp Pike Rd, Levy, **N** on Camp Robinson Rd...**gas:** Exxon, EZ Mart, Phillips 66, Shell, **food:** Burger King, EggRoll Express, KFC/Taco Bell, Little Caesars, Mexico Chiquito, McDonald's, Pizza Hut, Rally's, Sonic, Subway, US Pizza, Wendy's, **other:** AutoZone, Fred's Drug, O'Reilly Parts, Wal-Mart/24hr, **S**...**gas:** Phillips 66, Shell, **food:** Cancun Mexican, Chicken King, Church's, **other:** HOSPITAL, Chevrolet, Family$, Kroger, Radio Shack, Sav-A-Lot
150	AR 176, Burns Park, Camp Robinson, **S**...**other:** info, camping
148	AR 100, Crystal Hill Rd, **N**...**gas:** Shell, **S**...KOA
147	I-430 S, to Texarkana
142	AR 365, to Morgan, **N**...**gas:** Phillips 66, Valero/dsl, **lodging:** Day's Inn, **other:** Auto Value Parts, Trails End RV Park, **S**...**gas:** Shell/dsl, **food:** KFC/Taco Bell, McDonald's, Razorback Pizza, Smokeshack BBQ, Subway, Waffle House, **lodging:** Comfort Suites, Quality Inn, **other:** antiques

ARKANSAS
Interstate 40

E ↕ **W**

135	AR 365, AR 89, Mayflower, N...gas: Hess, other: Mayflower RV Ctr(1mi), S...gas: Exxon/dsl, Valero, food: Glory B's Rest., Sonic, other: $General
134mm	insp sta both lanes
129	US 65B, AR 286, Conway, N...gas: Citgo, S...gas: Citgo, Express/dsl, Exxon, Shell, food: Arby's, Joey's Grill, Sonic, Subway, Wendy's, lodging: Budget Inn, Continental Motel, other: HOSPITAL, Chrysler/Dodge/Jeep, Honda, Mapco Express, st police, to Toad Suck SP
127	US 64, Conway, N...gas: BP, Exxon, food: Annie's Rest, Arby's, Chick-fil-a, Chili's, Denny's, Starbucks, Subway, Waffle House, lodging: Best Value, Best Western, Comfort Suites, Day's Inn, Economy Inn, Hampton Inn, Hilton Garden, other: Belk, Best Buy, Chevrolet, Ford/Mercury, GMC/Buick/Pontiac, Goodyear/auto, Home Depot, Honda, Hyundai, Kohl's, Moix RV Ctr, NAPA, Nissan, Old Navy, O'Reilly Parts, PetsMart, Radio Shack, Target, TJ Maxx, Toyota/Scion, repair/transmissions, to Lester Flatt Park, S...gas: RaceWay, Shell/Subway/dsl, Valero/dsl, food: Burger King, Church's, Colton's Steaks, Hardee's, LJ Silver, Mazzio's, McDonald's, Pizza Inn, Popeye's, Quizno's, Rally's, TCBY, Taco Bell, Wendy's, Western Sizzlin, lodging: Kings Inn, other: AutoZone, BigLots, CarQuest, Family$, Fred's Drugs, Goodyear/auto, Hancock Fabrics, Kroger/gas, Radio Shack, Save-a-Lot Foods, Walgreen
125	US 65, Conway, N...gas: Conoco/dsl, Exxon/Subway/dsl, Phillips 66/dsl, Shell/dsl/24hr, food: Acapulco Mexican, China Town, Cracker Barrel, El Chico, La Hacienda Mexican, MktPlace Grill, McDonald's, lodging: Quality Inn, other: JC Penney, Office Depot, Sears, S...gas: Citgo, Fina, Mobil/dsl, food: Backyard Burger, Burger King, CiCi's, Dixie Cafe, Fazoli's, Firehouse Subs, Hart's Seafood, IHOP, McAlister's Deli, New China, Outback Steaks, Ryan's, Salsa'a Grill, Sonic, Starbucks, Subway, Village Inn Rest., Waffle House, Wendy's, lodging: Candlewood Suites, Holiday Inn Express, Howard Johnson, Motel 6, Stacy Motel, Super 8, other: HOSPITAL, Advance Parts, $General, $Tree, Hastings Books, Kelly Tire, Lowe's Whse, Wal-Mart SuperCtr/gas/24hr
124	AR 25 N(from eb), to Conway, S...gas: Hess/dsl, Shell/dsl, food: DQ, KFC, Mazzio's, Popeye's, other: HOSPITAL, U-Haul
120mm	Cadron River
117	to Menifee
112	AR 92, Plumerville, S...other: USPO
108	AR 9, Morrilton, S...gas: Phillips 66/24hr, Murphy USA, Shell/dsl/24hr, food: Bonanza, KFC, Mkt Place Café, McDonald's, Pizza Hut, Pizza Pro, Subway, TCBY, Waffle House, Wendy's, lodging: Super 8, other: HOSPITAL, Chevrolet/Buick/Pontiac, $General, Ford/Lincoln/Mercury, Goodyear, GMC, Kroger, Radio Shack, Wal-Mart SuperCtr/gas/24hr, to Petit Jean SP(21mi), RV camping
107	AR 95, Morrilton, N...gas: Shell/dsl, lodging: Scottish Inn, KOA, S...gas: Love's/Subway/dsl/24hr, Shell, food: Mom&Pop's Waffles, Morrilton Drive Inn, Wendy's(2 mi), lodging: Day's Inn, other: CarQuest
101	Blackwell, N...other: Utility Trailer Sales
94	AR 105, Atkins, N...gas: Exxon/dsl/24hr, Shell/McDonald's/dsl, food: Angelina's Mexican, KFC/Taco Bell, Pizza Meister, Sonic, other: $General, repair, S...Saxton Foods

88	Pottsville, S...food: Pottsville Country Cafe, other: truck repair/wash
84	US 64, AR 331, Russellville, N...gas: ♦/Flying J/Conoco/Country Mkt/dsl/LP/24hr/@, Shell/dsl, other: Ivys Cove RV Retreat, trucklube, S...gas: Phillips 66, Pilot/Subway/Wendy's/dsl/24hr/scales/@, food: CiCi's, Hardee's, Hunan Chinese, McDonald's, Sonic, Waffle House, lodging: Comfort Inn, Ramada Inn, other: HOSPITAL, AutoZone, Belk, Chevrolet, Chrysler/Jeep/Dodge, $Tree, Firestone, JC Penney, K-Mart, Lowe's Whse, Nissan, Staples, Toyota, USPO
83	AK 326, Weir Rd, S...gas: Phillips 66, food: AlDente's Italian, DQ, Popeyes, Ryans, Starbucks, Subway, Taco Bueno, other: Wal-Mart SuperCtr/gas
81	AR 7, Russellville, N...gas: SuperStop/dsl, food: Burger Boy, lodging: Days Inn, Motel 6, other: Outdoor RV Ctr/Park, S...gas: Exxon/dsl/24hr, Phillips 66/dsl/24hr, Shell/24hr, food: Arby's, Burger King, Colton's Steaks, Cracker Barrel, Dixie Café, Dos Rios, La Huerta Mexican, New China, Pizza Inn, Ruby Tuesday, Subway, Waffle House, lodging: Best Value, Best Western, Day's Inn, Fairfield Inn, Hampton Inn, Holiday Inn, Super 8, other: antiques, Russell RV Ctr, to Lake Dardanelle SP, RV camping
80mm	Dardanelle Reservoir
78	US 64, Russellville, S...food: Fat Daddy's BBQ, other: Darrell's Mkt, Mission RV Park, to Lake Dardanelle SP
74	AR 333, London, no services
72mm	**rest area wb, full(handicapped)facilities, phone, picnic tables, litter barrels, vending, petwalk**
70mm	overlook wb lane, litter barrels
68mm	**rest area eb, full(handicapped)facilities, phone, picnic tables, litter barrels, vending, petwalk**
67	AR 315, Knoxville, S...gas: Citgo, Knoxville Mkt, food: JC's Cafe, other: USPO
64	US 64, Clarksville, Lamar, S...gas: Valero/Pizza Pro/dsl, lodging: Dad's Dream RV Park
58	AR 21, AR 103, Clarksville, N...gas: Phillips 66, Shell/dsl, food: Bienvenidos Mexican, Emerald Dragon Chinese, KFC, Mazzio's, McDonald's, Pizza Hut, Sonic, Taco Bell, Waffle House, Wendy's, lodging: Best Western, Comfort Inn, Economy Inn, Super 8, other: HOSPITAL, Chevrolet/Pontiac/GMC, S...gas: Shell/dsl/rest./24hr, food: Arby's, South Park Rest., other: Chrysler/Dodge/Jeep, $Tree, Ford/Lincoln/Mercury, Wal-Mart SuperCtr/dsl/24hr
57	AR 109, Clarksville, N...gas: Conoco/dsl, food: Subway, other: Family$, Harvest Foods/drug, S...gas: Shell/pizza/subsdsl, other: auto repair
55	US 64, AR 109, Clarksville, N...gas: Citgo/dsl, food: Catfish House, Crosswoods Rest, Hardee's, Kountry Kitchen, lodging: Day's Inn, Hampton Inn, S...gas: Exxon/dsl, food: Western Sizzlin, other: st police
47	AR 164, Coal Hill, no services
41	AR 186, Altus, S...food: Wiederkehr Rest., other: Pine Ridge RV Park, winery
37	AR 219, Ozark, N...gas: Love's/Subway/dsl/24hr, Shell/McDonald's/dsl, food: KFC/Taco Bell, lodging: Day's Inn, other: HOSPITAL
36mm	**rest area both lanes, full(handicapped)facilities, phone, picnic tables, litter barrels, petwalk**
35	AR 23, Ozark, 3 mi S...gas: 23 One Stop, food: Hardee's, lodging: Ozark Inn, Oxford Inn, other: HOSPITAL, Aux Arc Park(5mi), to Mt Magazine SP(20 mi)
24	AR 215, Mulberry, S...Vine Prairie Park

Russellville *(vertical label)*

Conway *(vertical label)*

Interstate 40

E ↑↓ **W**	

20 Dyer, **N...gas:** Conoco/dsl, **other:** Freightliner/Western Star, **S...gas:** Phillips 66/dsl, Shell/dsl, **lodging:** Mill Creek Inn

13 US 71 N, to Fayetteville, **N...gas:** Phillips 66, Shell, **food:** Burger King, China Fun, Cracker Barrel, Dairy Queen, KFC, La Fiesta Mexican, Mazzio's, Subway, Taco Bell, **lodging:** Comfort Inn, Meadors Inn, **other:** Crabtree RV Ctr/Park, Curves, $General, KOA(2mi), O'Reilly Parts, to U of AR, Lake Ft Smith SP, **S...gas:** Citgo/dsl, Shamrock, **food:** Braum's, Geno's Pizza, McDonald's, Sonic, **lodging:** Day's Inn, **other:** C&H Tires, Coleman Drug, CV's Foods, Harp's Foods, NAPA/lube/repair, Wal-Mart SuperCtr/gas/auto/24hr

12 I-540 N, to Fayetteville, **N...other:** to Lake Ft Smith SP

9mm weigh sta both lanes

7 I-540 S, US 71 S, to Ft Smith, Van Buren, **S...**HOSPITAL

Ft Smith

5 AR 59, Van Buren, **N...gas:** Phillips 66, **food:** Arby's, Art's BBQ, Burger King, Capt D's, Chili's, China Buffet, Domino's, Firehouse Subs, La Fiesta Mexican, McDonald's, Popeye's, Santa Fe Café, Starbucks, **lodging:** Best Western, Hampton Inn, **other:** Advance Parts, $Tree, Radio Shack, Lowe's Whse, NAPA, Wal-Mart SuperCtr/gas/24hr, USPO, tires, **S...gas:** Shell/dsl/24hr, **food:** Braum's, Big Jake's Steaks, El Torrito Mexican, Gino's Hamburgers, Homerun Pizza, KFC/Taco Bell, Rick's Ribs, Sonic, Subway, Waffle House, Wendy's, **lodging:** Motel 6, Super 8, **other:** CV's Foods, $General, Firestone, Grizzle Tire, Overland RV Park, Outdoor RV Ctr, Walgreen, dsl repair

3 Lee Creek Rd, **N...gas:** Shell, **other:** Park Ridge Camp

2.5mm Welcome Ctr eb, full(handicapped)facilities, info, phone, picnic tables, litter barrels, vending, petwalk

1 to Ft Smith(from wb), Dora, no services

0mm Arkansas/Oklahoma state line

Interstate 55

Exit # Services

72mm Arkansas/Missouri state line

72 State Line Rd, weigh sta sb

71 AR 150, Yarbro, no services

68mm Welcome Ctr sb, full(handicapped)facilities, phone, picnic tables, litter barrels, petwalk

Blytheville

67 AR 18, Blytheville, **E...gas:** Phillips 66/dsl, **food:** Burger King, Capt D's, Skinny's Diner, Zaxby's, **lodging:** Day's Inn, Travelodge, **other:** $Tree, Lowe's Whse, Wal-Mart SuperCtr/24hr, **W...gas:** BP/dsl, Flash Mkt/dsl, Shell, **food:** Cotton Patch Buffet, El Acupulco Mexican, Geatwall Chinese, Grecian Steaks, KFC, La Cabana, Mazzio's, McDonald's, Olympia Steaks, Perkins, Pizza Inn, Sonic, Subway, Taco Bell, Wendy's, **lodging:** Comfort Inn, Hampton Inn, Holiday Inn, Super 8, **other:** HOSPITAL, Advance Parts, Family$, Ford, Fred's Drug, JC Penney

63 US 61, to Blytheville, **E...gas:** BP/dsl, **other:** Shearins RV Park(2mi), **W...gas:** Dodge's Store/dsl, Exxon/Chester Fried/dsl, Shell/McDonald's/dsl/24hr, **lodging:** Best Western, Garden Inn, Relax Inn, Royal Inn(2mi), **other:** Chevrolet, Nissan

57 AR 148, Burdette, **E...other:** NE Ar Coll

53 AR 158, Victoria, Luxora

48 AR 140, to Osceola, **E...gas:** Mobil/dsl, Shell/dsl, **other:** Cotton Inn Rest., Huddle House, **lodging:** Days Inn, Deerfield Inn, Fairview Inn, Plum Point Inn, 3 mi **E...food:** McDonald's, Pizza Inn, Sonic, Subway, **other:** HOSPITAL

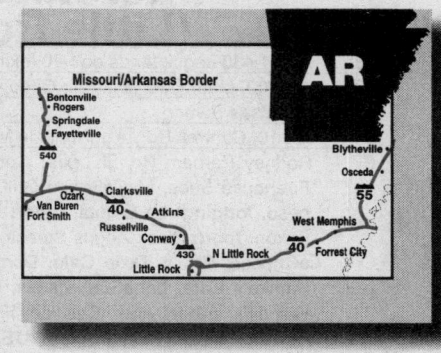

45mm rest area nb, full(handicapped)facilities, picnic tables, litter barrels, petwalk

44 AR 181, Keiser

41 AR 14, Marie, **E...other:** to Hampson SP/museum

36 AR 181, to Wilson, Bassett

35mm rest area sb, full(handicapped)facilities, picnic tables, litter barrels, phones, petwalk

34 AR 118, Joiner

23b a US 63, AR 77, to Marked Tree, Jonesboro, ASU, **E...gas:** Citgo/chicken/pizza

21 AR 42, Turrell, **W...gas:** Exxon/rest./dsl/scales/24hr

17 AR 50, to Jericho

14 rd 4, to Jericho, **E...gas:** Citgo/dsl/24hr, **other:** flea market, **W...gas:** Citgo/Stuckey's, **other:** Chevrolet, RV Park

10 US 64 W, Marion, **E...gas:** Citgo/Subway/FoodCrt/scales, Mapco/dsl, Shell/McDonald's/dsl, **food:** KFC/Taco Bell, Sonic, Tops BBQ, **lodging:** Hallmarc Inn, **other:** $General, Market Place Foods, **W...gas:** BP/dsl, Flash Mkt/Stuckey's, Shell, **food:** Colton's Steaks, Wendy's, Zaxby's, **lodging:** Best Western, Journey Inn, **other:** AutoZone, KOA, to Parkin SP(23mi)

9mm weigh sta both lanes

8 I-40 W, to Little Rock

278 AR 77, Missouri St, 7th St, **E...gas:** Citgo/Blimpie/24hr, **W...gas:** Citgo/dsl, Express, Exxon, Love's/dsl/24hr, Shell/dsl/24hr, Texaco, **food:** Applebee's, Backyard Burger, Bojangles, Bonanza, Burger King, Cracker Barrel, Domino's, Krystal, Mrs Winner's, McDonald's, Pizza Hut, Pizza Inn, Shoney's, Subway, Taco Bell, Wendy's, **lodging:** Ramada Ltd, **other:** Blue Beacon, Chief Parts, Goodyear/auto, Kroger, Sears, USPO, Walgreen, Wal-Mart SuperCtr/24hr

279b I-40 E, to Memphis

279a Ingram Blvd, **E...lodging:** Comfort Inn, Red Roof Inn, **other:** Ford, Greyhound Track, U-Haul, **W...gas:** Citgo/dsl, Shell, **food:** Earl's Rest., Grandy's, Waffle House, Western Sizzlin, **lodging:** American Inn, Best Western, Econolodge, Hampton Inn, Holiday Inn, Howard Johnson, Motel 6, Relax Inn, **other:** Chevrolet, Chrysler/Dodge/Jeep

4 King Dr, Southland Dr, **E...gas:** ⚑/Flying J/Conoco/dsl/LP/rest./24hr/@, Petro/dsl/rest./24hr/@, Pilot/Subway/dsl/@, **food:** KFC/Taco Bell, McDonald's, Waffle House, **lodging:** Best Western, Deluxe Inn, Express Inn, Super 8, **other:** Blue Beacon, SpeedCo, 1/2 mi **E...gas:** BP/dsl, Pilot/Wendy's/dsl/24hr/@, **other:** Goodyear, **W...food:** Pancho's Mexican, **lodging:** Sunset Inn, **other:** Sawyers RV Park

3b a US 70, Broadway Blvd, AR 131, Mound City Rd(exits left from nb), **W...lodging:** Budget Inn

2mm weigh sta nb

1 Bridgeport Rd, no services

0mm Arkansas/Tennessee state line, Mississippi River

ARKANSAS
Interstate 430
(Little Rock)

N ↕ **S**

Little Rock

Exit #	Services
13b a	I-40. I-430 begins/ends on I-40, exit 147.
12	AR 100, Maumelle, W...**gas:** Citgo, **other:** NAPA
10mm	Arkansas River
9	AR 10, Cantrell Rd., W...Pinnacle Mtn SP
8	Rodney Parham Rd., E...**gas:** Conoco, Shell, **food:** El Chico, Firehouse Subs, McCalister's Grill, McDonald's, Mt. Fuji Japanese, **lodging:** La Quinta, **other:** Kroger, USA Drug, W...**gas:** Exxon, **food:** Black Angus Steaks, Burger King, Chili's, Chuck-eCheese, CiCi's, Dixie Café, Dominos, El Acapulco Mexican, Franke's Café, LoneStar Steaks, Olive Garden, Small's Ribs, Wendy's, **other:** Audi, Cadillac, Firestone, Harvest Foods, Jiffy Lube, K-Mart, Radio Shack, USA Drug, Waldenbooks, Wild Oats Mkt
6	I-630, Kanis Rd, Markham St, to downtown, E...**lodging:** Comfort Inn, Motel 6, SpringHill Suites, W...**gas:** Exxon, Texaco, **food:** Denny's, Rega's Grill, Waffle House, Wendy's, **lodging:** AmeriSuites, Courtyard, Embassy Suites, Extended Stay America, Holiday Inn, La Quinta, Ramada Ltd
5	Kanis Rd, Shackleford Rd, E...**food:** Cracker Barrel, **lodging:** Candlewood Suites, Comfort Inn, Motel 6, SpringHill Suites, **other:** JC Penny, W...**gas:** Exxon, Shell, **food:** Denny's, IHOP, Jason's Deli, Julie's Rest., Lenny's Subs, Waffle House, **lodging:** Comfort Inn, Courtyard, Embassy Suites, Hampton Inn, Holiday Inn Select, La Quinta, Residence Inn, Studio+, Wingate Inn, **other:** HOSPITAL, Lexus
4	AR 300, Col Glenn Rd, E...**food:** Subway, Wendy's, **lodging:** Holiday Inn Express, **other:** Toyota/Scion, W...**gas:** Valero/Burger King/dsl, **other:** Jaguar, Kia, Land Rover, Mazda, Nissan
1	AR 5, Stagecoach Rd, E...**food:** Our Place Grill, W...**food:** Jordan's BBQ
0mm	I-30. I-430 begins/ends on I-30, exit 129.

Interstate 440
(Little Rock)

N ↕ **S**

Exit #	Services
11	I-40.
10	US 70, W...**other:** Peterbuilt
8	Faulkner Lake Rd, W...**gas:** BP/mart
7	US 165, to England, S...museum
6mm	Arkansas River
5	Fourche Dam Pike, LR Riverport, N...**gas:** Exxon, Shell, **food:** McDonald's, **lodging:** Travelodge, S...**gas:** Fina/dsl/@, Total/dsl
4	Lindsey Rd, no services
3	Bankhead Dr, N...**lodging:** Comfort Inn, **other:** LR Airport, S...**gas:** Conoco, **food:** Waffle House, **lodging:** Day's Inn, Holiday Inn, Holiday Inn Express
1	AR 365, Confederate Blvd, no services
0mm	I-440 begins/ends on I-30, exit 138.

Interstate 540
(Fayetteville)

N ↕ **S**

Bentonville

Exit #	Services
93	US 71B, Bentonville, I-540 begins/ends on US 71 N.
88	AR 72, Bentonville, Pea Ridge, E...**gas:** Conoco, **food:** River Grille, **lodging:** Courtyard, Simmons Suites, W...**gas:** Shell, **food:** Hot Dog Alley, Smokin' Joe's Ribs
86	US 62, AR 102, Bentonville, Rogers, E...**lodging:** Towne Place Suites, **other:** Harley-Davidson, Sam's Club/gas, Wal-Mart Mkt/gas/24hr, Pea Ridge NMP, W...**gas:** Phillips 66/McDonald's/dsl, Shell/dsl, **food:** Arby's, Sonic, Subway, Taco Bell, **lodging:** Value Place, **other:** GMC/Pontiac/Buick, Wal-Mart Visitor Ctr
85	US 71B, AR 12, Bentonville, Rogers, E...**gas:** BP/dsl, Citgo/dsl, **food:** Abuelo's, Applebee's, Arby's, Atlanta Bread, Carino's Italian, Chick-fil-A, Chili's, CiCi's, Colton's Steaks, Copeland's Rest., Dixie Café, Dixie Cafe, Famous Dave's, IHOP, KFC, King Buffet, McAlister's, O'Charly's, Oscar's Rest., On-the-Border, Outback Steaks, Quizno's, Red Robin, Sonic, Starbucks, **lodging:** AmeriSuites, Candlewood Suites, Country Inn Suites, Fairfield Inn, Hampton Inn, Hartland Lodge, Homewood Suites, Regency Inn, Residence Inn, **other:** Barnes&Noble, Belk, Firestone/auto,

Fayetteville

Honda, Kohl's, Lowe's Whse, Office Depot, Old Navy, PetCo, Staples, Beaver Lake SP, Prairie Creek SP, W...**gas:** Exxon, Phillips 66, **food:** Bojangles, Braum's, Brioso Brazilian, Denny's, Krispy Kreme, Lin's Chinese, Mama Fu's Asian, McCallister's Deli, Moe's Grill, Simon's Pancakes, Shogun Japanese, Taco Bueno, Village Inn, Waffle House, Zaxby's, **lodging:** Amerisuites, Best Western, Clarion, Comfort Inn, Comfort Suites, Day's Inn, Hilton Garden, Holiday Inn Express, La Quinta(1mi), Sleep Inn, SpringHill Suites, Super 8, **other:** HOSPITAL, Buick/Pontiac/GMC, Honda, Hyundai, Nissan, Toyota/Scion

Exit #	Services
83	AR 94 E, Pinnacle Hills Pkway, E...**food:** Hillbilly Smokehouse, Rib House, **lodging:** Best Value(3mi), Ramada Inn(3mi), **other:** HOSPITAL, Best Buy, Dillards, Home Depot, Horse Shoe Bend Park, W...**food:** Plaza Rest., Subway, **lodging:** Embassy Suites
81	Pleasant Grove Rd, E...**food:** Backyard Burger, Chick-fil-A, McDonald's, Starbucks, Subway, Taco Bueno, **lodging:** Super 8, **other:** Curves, Sportsman's Warehouse, Walgreen, Wal-Mart SuperCtr/gas, W...Green Country RV Park
78	AR 264, Lowell, Cave Sprgs, Rogers, E...**gas:** Kum&Go, Phillips 66/dsl, **food:** Arby's, Dominos, DQ, KFC, Mazzio's Pizza, McDonald's, Sonic, Starbucks, Subway, Taco Bell, **other:** Ramada, **other:** New Hope RV Ctr
76	Wagon Wheel Rd, E...to Hickory Creek Park
73	Elm Springs Rd, E...**gas:** Valero/dsl, **lodging:** Magnolia Gardens Inn(3mi), **food:** AQ Chicken House(3mi), Eureka Pizza, Western Sizzlin(2mi), **other:** Chevrolet, Goodyear
72mm	weigh sta nb
72	US 412, Springdale, Siloam Springs, E...**gas:** Citgo, Exxon, Phillips 66/Subway, **food:** Applebee's, Armadillo Grill, Braum's, Chilis, Denny's, Maria's Mexican, McDonald's, Sizzler, Sonic, Taco Bell, Waffle House, Wendy's, **lodging:** Best Western, Comfort Inn, Day's Inn, DoubleTree Hotel, Executive Inn, Extended Stay America, Fairfield Inn, Hampton Inn, Hartland Inn, Holiday Inn, La Quinta, Residence Inn, Sleep Inn, Springdale Motel, Super 8, **other:** Kenworth/Volvo Trucks, Lowe's Whse, Office Depot, W...**gas:** Pilot/Burger King/dsl/24hr/scales/@, **food:** Cracker Barrel, Jose's Mexican, KFC, **other:** Big Lots, Buick/Pontiac/GMC/Jeep, Fred's$, Layman's Harware, Melon RV Ctr
71mm	weigh sta sb
69	Johnson, **1-2 mi** E...**food:** Chick-fil-A, Eureka Pizza, Fire Mtn Grill, Hooter's, Inn at the Mill Rest, James Rest, Shogun Japanese, **lodging:** Inn at the Mill, W...HOSPITAL
67	US 71B, Fayetteville, E...HOSPITAL
66	AR 112, E...**gas:** BP/dsl, **lodging:** Day's Inn(2mi), W...Acura/Chevrolet/Hummer/Honda/Toyota
65	Porter Rd, no services
64	AR 16 W, AR 112 E, Wedington Dr, E...**food:** AQ Chicken House(3mi), Eureka Pizza(2mi), W...**gas:** Citgo/McDonald's/dsl, Phillips 66, **food:** Boar's Nest BBQ, Guido's Pizza, IHOP, Sonic, Subway, Taco Bell, **lodging:** Country Inn Suites, Holiday Inn Express, Quality Inn, **other:** Harp's Food/gas, vet
62	US 62, AR 180, Farmington, E...**gas:** Conoco, Shell, **food:** Arby's, Braum's, Burger King, Charlie's Chicken, Hardee's, JD China, KFC, McDonald's, Mexico Viejo, Sonic, Taco Bell, Taiwan Chinese, Waffle House, Wendy's, **lodging:** Best Western, Red Roof Inn, **other:** USA Drug, W...**food:** Braum's, Denny's, Firehouse Subs, Papa Murphy's, Pavilion Buffet, Ruby Tuesday, **lodging:** Clarion, Comfort Inn, Hampton Inn, Quality Inn, Regency 7 Motel, Super 8, **other:** AutoZone, $Tree, Lowe's Whse, Wal-Mart SuperCtr/gas
61	US 71, to Boston Mtn Scenic Lp, sb only
60	AR 112, AR 265, Razorback Rd, E...to U of AR
58	Greenland, W...**gas:** Phillips 66/McDonalds/dsl/scales, **food:** Sonic
53	AR 170, West Fork, E...**other:** Winn Creek RV Resort(4mi), W...to Devils Den SP
45	AR 74, Winslow, W...to Devils Den SP
41mm	Bobby Hopper Tunnel
34	AR 282, to US 71, Chester, W...Chester Mercantile/gas, USPO
29	AR 282, to US 71, Mountainburg, **1 mi** E...**gas:** BP/dsl/rest/scales, **other:** to Lake Ft Smith SP
24	AR 282, to US 71, Rudy, E...**gas:** Shell/dsl, **other:** KOA, Boston Mtns Scenic Lp
21	Collum Ln, no services
20	to US 71, E...**gas:** Shell, **food:** KFC, Taco Bell, **lodging:** Comfort Inn, Day's Inn
	I-540 N begins/ends on I-40, exit 12.

CALIFORNIA

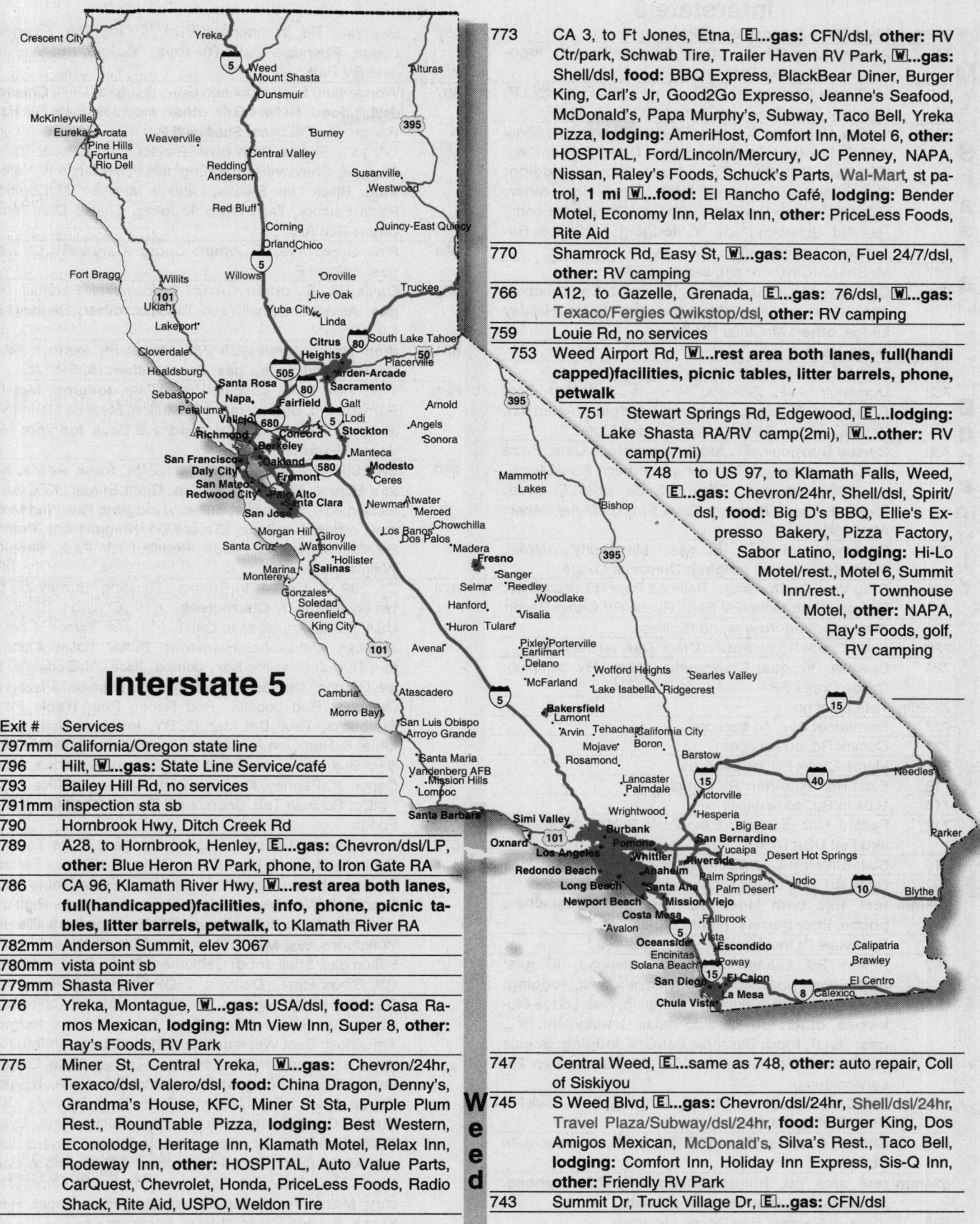

773   CA 3, to Ft Jones, Etna, **E**...**gas:** CFN/dsl, **other:** RV Ctr/park, Schwab Tire, Trailer Haven RV Park, **W**...**gas:** Shell/dsl, **food:** BBQ Express, BlackBear Diner, Burger King, Carl's Jr, Good2Go Expresso, Jeanne's Seafood, McDonald's, Papa Murphy's, Subway, Taco Bell, Yreka Pizza, **lodging:** AmeriHost, Comfort Inn, Motel 6, **other:** HOSPITAL, Ford/Lincoln/Mercury, JC Penney, NAPA, Nissan, Raley's Foods, Schuck's Parts, Wal-Mart, st patrol, **1 mi W**...**food:** El Rancho Café, **lodging:** Bender Motel, Economy Inn, Relax Inn, **other:** PriceLess Foods, Rite Aid

770   Shamrock Rd, Easy St, **W**...**gas:** Beacon, Fuel 24/7/dsl, **other:** RV camping

766   A12, to Gazelle, Grenada, **E**...**gas:** 76/dsl, **W**...**gas:** Texaco/Fergies Qwikstop/dsl, **other:** RV camping

759   Louie Rd, no services

753   Weed Airport Rd, **W**...**rest area both lanes, full(handicapped)facilities, picnic tables, litter barrels, phone, petwalk**

751   Stewart Springs Rd, Edgewood, **E**...**lodging:** Lake Shasta RA/RV camp(2mi), **W**...**other:** RV camp(7mi)

748   to US 97, to Klamath Falls, Weed, **E**...**gas:** Chevron/24hr, Shell/dsl, Spirit/dsl, **food:** Big D's BBQ, Ellie's Expresso Bakery, Pizza Factory, Sabor Latino, **lodging:** Hi-Lo Motel/rest., Motel 6, Summit Inn/rest., Townhouse Motel, **other:** NAPA, Ray's Foods, golf, RV camping

Interstate 5

Exit #	Services
797mm	California/Oregon state line
796	Hilt, **W**...**gas:** State Line Service/café
793	Bailey Hill Rd, no services
791mm	inspection sta sb
790	Hornbrook Hwy, Ditch Creek Rd
789	A28, to Hornbrook, Henley, **E**...**gas:** Chevron/dsl/LP, **other:** Blue Heron RV Park, phone, to Iron Gate RA
786	CA 96, Klamath River Hwy, **W**...**rest area both lanes, full(handicapped)facilities, info, phone, picnic tables, litter barrels, petwalk,** to Klamath River RA
782mm	Anderson Summit, elev 3067
780mm	vista point sb
779mm	Shasta River
776	Yreka, Montague, **W**...**gas:** USA/dsl, **food:** Casa Ramos Mexican, **lodging:** Mtn View Inn, Super 8, **other:** Ray's Foods, RV Park
775	Miner St, Central Yreka, **W**...**gas:** Chevron/24hr, Texaco/dsl, Valero/dsl, **food:** China Dragon, Denny's, Grandma's House, KFC, Miner St Sta, Purple Plum Rest., RoundTable Pizza, **lodging:** Best Western, Econolodge, Heritage Inn, Klamath Motel, Relax Inn, Rodeway Inn, **other:** HOSPITAL, Auto Value Parts, CarQuest, Chevrolet, Honda, PriceLess Foods, Radio Shack, Rite Aid, USPO, Weldon Tire

747   Central Weed, **E**...**same as 748, other:** auto repair, Coll of Siskiyou

745   S Weed Blvd, **E**...**gas:** Chevron/dsl/24hr, Shell/dsl/24hr, Travel Plaza/Subway/dsl/24hr, **food:** Burger King, Dos Amigos Mexican, McDonald's, Silva's Rest., Taco Bell, **lodging:** Comfort Inn, Holiday Inn Express, Sis-Q Inn, **other:** Friendly RV Park

743   Summit Dr, Truck Village Dr, **E**...**gas:** CFN/dsl

29

N ← → S

Mt Shasta

742mm	Black Butte Summit, elev 3912
741	Abrams Lake Rd, E...other: Schwab Tire, W...lodging: Abrams Lake RV Park
740	Mt Shasta City(from sb), E...gas: Pacific Pride/dsl/LP, lodging: Cold Creek Inn, other: KOA
738	Central Mt Shasta, E...gas: 76/dsl, Chevron/dsl, Shell/dsl/LP, Spirit/dsl, food: BlackBear Diner, Burger King, KFC/Taco Bell, RoundTable Pizza, Subway, lodging: Best Western/Treehouse Rest., Travel Inn, other: HOSPITAL, Ace Hardware, KOA, NAPA, Ray's Foods, Rite Aid, Schuck's Parts, W...lodging: Mt Shasta Resort/rest., Lake Siskiyou RV Park
737	Mt Shasta City(from nb), same as 738
736	CA 89, to McCloud, to Reno, E...food: Casa Ramos, Jade Garden, Lilly's Rest., lodging: Swiss Holiday Lodge, other: McCloud RV Park
735mm	weigh sta sb
734	Mott Rd, to Dunsmuir, no services

Dunsmuir

732	Dunsmuir Ave, Siskiyou Ave, E...lodging: Best Choice Inn, W...gas: Chevron/dsl, lodging: Acorn Inn, Bavaria Lodge, Cedar Lodge, Garden Motel
730	Central Dunsmuir, E...food: Cornerstone Cafe, Pizza Factory, lodging: Travelodge, other: Ford/Mercury, USPO, W...gas: Chevron/Subway/dsl/LP, food: Micki's Burgers, lodging: Cave Springs Motel, other: Alpine Mkt
729	Dunsmuir(from nb), E...gas: Manfreddy's/deli/dsl, food: Burger Barn, lodging: Dunsmuir Lodge
728	Crag View Dr, Dunsmuir, Railroad Park Rd, W...other: Railroad Park Motel/RV Park, Rustic RV Camp/Resort
727	(from nb) Crag View dr, no facilites
726	Soda Creek Rd, to Pacific Crest Trail, no services
724	Castella, W...gas: Chevron/dsl, other: RV camping, Castle Crags SP
723mm	vista point nb
723	Sweetbrier Ave, no services
721	Conant Rd, no services
720	Flume Creek Rd, no services
718	Sims Rd, W...other: RV camping
714	Gibson Rd, no services
712	Pollard Flat, E...gas: Exxon/dsl/LP/24hr, food: Pollard Flat USA Rest.
710	Slate Creek Rd, La Moine, no services
707	Delta Rd, Dog Creek Rd, to Vollmers, no services
705mm	**rest area both lanes, full(handicapped)facilities, phone, litter barrels, picnic tables**
704	Riverview Dr, no services
702	Antlers Rd, Lakeshore Dr, to Lakehead, E...gas: Shell/Subway/dsl/24hr, food: Bergie's Rest., lodging: Antlers RV Park, Lakehead Camping, Neu Lodge Motel/café, other: USPO, auto repair, towing/24hr, W...gas: 76/LP, food: Basshole Bar/Grill, lodging: Shasta Lake Motel/RV, Lakeshore Villa RV Park, other: RV service/dump
698	Salt Creek Rd, Gilman Rd, W...lodging: Salt Creek RV Park, Trail In RV Park
695	Shasta Caverns Rd, to O'Brien, W... O'brien Mtn Camping
694mm	**rest area nb, full(handicapped)facilities, phone, picnic tables, litter barrels, petwalk**
693	(from sb)Packers Bay Rd, no services
692	Turntable Bay Rd, no services
690	Bridge Bay Rd, W...food: Tail of a Whale Rest., lodging: Bridge Bay Motel

Redding

689	Fawndale Rd, Wonderland Blvd, E...lodging: Fawndale Lodge, Fawndale Oaks RV Park, W...lodging: Wonderland RV Park
687	Wonderland Blvd, Mountain Gate, E...gas: CFN, Chevron/dsl/LP, food: Nellie's Grill, other: Mountain Gate RV Park, Ranger Sta, W...gas: Shell/dsl/LP
685	CA 151, Shasta Dam Blvd, Project City, Central Valley, W...gas: Chevron/Burger King/dsl/LP, 76/Circle K, Valero, food: Black Oak Steaks, Latino's Mexican, McDonald's, Pizza Factory, Taco Shop, lodging: Shasta Dam Motel, other: Rite Aid
684	Pine Grove Ave, E...other: Cousin Gary's RV Ctr, W...gas: 76/dsl/LP
682	Oasis Rd, E...other: CA RV Ctr/camping, Peterbilt, W...gas: Arco/24hr, Shell/Taco Time/dsl, other: Redding RV Ctr, st patrol
681b	(from sb, no re-entry)CA 273, Market St, Johnson Rd, to Central Redding, W...gas: Exxon, other: HOSPITAL
681a	Twin View Blvd, E...gas: 76/dsl/24hr, lodging: Motel 6, Ramada Ltd, other: Harley-Davidson, Meyer's Marine/RV, W...gas: Pacific Pride/dsl, food: Fat Boys, lodging: Holiday Inn Express
680	CA 299E, **1/2 mi** W...gas: Arco/24hr, food: Arby's, Bartel's Burger, BBQ Pit, Carl's Jr, Giant Burger, KFC/A&W, McDonald's, Starbucks, Subway, lodging: River Inn Motel/rest., other: AutoZone, $Tree, KOA, Kragen Parts, Premier RV Camp, Raley's Foods, Redding RV Park, ShopKO, Walgreens
678	CA 299 W, CA 44, to Eureka,, Redding, Burney, E **between Hilltop & Churncreek...gas:** Chevron, Shell, 76, USA, food: Applebee's, Carl's Jr, Casa Ramos, Chevy's Mexican, Coldstone, Hometown Buffet, Italian Cottage, In-n-Out, Jack-in-the-Box, Jamba Juice, McDonald's, Olive Garden, Outback Steaks, Panda Express, Pizza Hut, Quizno's, Red Lobster, Red Robin, RoundTable Pizza, Starbucks, Taco Del Mar, TCBY, lodging: Holiday Inn, Motel 6, Red Lion Inn, other: Albertson's, Barnes&Noble, Best Buy, Big Lots, Circuit City, Costco, FoodMax, Home Depot, JC Penney, Kragen's Parts, Macey's, Office Depot, PetCo, Schwab Tire, Sears/auto, Target, Wal-Mart, WinCo Foods
677	Cypress Ave, Hilltop Dr, Redding, E...gas: 76/Del Taco/dsl, Spirit, food: Black Bear Diner, Carl's Jr, KFC, La Palomar Mexican, Little Caesar's, McDonald's, RoundTable Pizza, Taco Bell, Wendy's, lodging: Howard Johnson, Park Terrace Inn, other: Buick/Pontiac/GMC, Longs Drug, Rite Aid, Walgreens, Wal-Mart, **1/4 mi E on Hilltop...gas:** Chevron, Hilltop gas, Shell, food: Cattlemens Rest., ChuckeCheese, CR Gibbs Rest., Denny's, IHOP, Jack-in-the-Box, Jade Garden, KFC, Logan's Roadhouse, Marie Callender's, Pizza Hut, Subway, Taco Bell, Tokyo Garden, lodging: Amerihost, Best Western, Comfort Inn, Hampton Inn, Holiday Inn Express, Hilltop Lodge, La Quinta, Motel Orleans, Oxford Suites, W...gas: Beacon/dsl, 76, Shell, USA/dsl, Valero, food: BBQ, California Cattle Rest., Denny's, Giant Burger, Guadalajara Mexican, Lumberjack's Rest., Lyon's Rest., Perko's Rest., Taco Den, lodging: Howard Johnson, Motel 6, Vagabond Inn, other: Aamco, Big A Parts, Big O Tire, Chevrolet, FabricLand, Hyundai, Lincoln/Mercury, Mazda/Toyota/Subaru, Nissan, Office Depot, Radio Shack, Raley's Foods, U-Haul, transmissions
675	Bechelli Lane, Churn Creek Rd, E...gas: Chevron/dsl, Valero, food: Taco Bell, lodging: Super 8, W...gas: Shell/Burger King/dsl, lodging: Hilton Garden

Interstate 5

N ↕ **S**

673 Knighton Rd, E...**gas:** TA/Pizza Hut/Popeye's/dsl/LP/scales/24hr/@, W...**other:** JGW RV Park(3mi), Sacramento River RV Park

670 Riverside Ave, W...**other:** Gamel RV Ctr

668 Balls Ferry Rd, Anderson, E...**gas:** Beacon, 76/dsl, USA, **food:** Big Taco, Burger King, Mariachi Mexican, McDonald's, Papa Murphy's, Peacock Chinese, Perko's Rest., Quizno's, RoundTable Pizza, Subway/gas, Taco Bell, **lodging:** Talley Inn, **other:** MEDICAL CARE, Ace Hardware, $Tree, NAPA, Radio Shack, Rite Aid, Safeway, Schwab Tire, W...**gas:** AFG/food/gas, Chevron, Sarco/dsl, **food:** Giant Burger, KFC, Koffee Korner Rest., **other:** Kragen Parts, Owen's Drugs, RV Ctr

667 CA 273, Factory Outlet Blvd, W...**gas:** Shell/dsl/LP, **food:** Arby's, Baja Burrito, Jack-in-the-Box, LJ Silver, Pizza Pasta Luigi's, Sonic, **lodging:** AmeriHost, **other:** Curves, GNC, Prime Outlets/famous brands, Wal-Mart SuperCtr/24hr, farmers mkt

665 (from sb) Cottonwood, E...**lodging:** Alamo Motel, Travelers Motel

664 Gas Point Rd, to Balls Ferry, E...**gas:** Chevron/Mean-Gene's/dsl/LP, Payless/gas/grocery, **lodging:** Alamo Motel, Travelers Motel, **other:** Alamo RV Park, auto repair, W...**gas:** Holiday/dsl, Sunshine/dsl, **other:** Holiday Foods

662 Bowman Rd, to Cottonwood, E...**gas:** Pacific Pride/dsl, Texaco/dsl

660mm weigh sta both lanes

659 Snively Rd, Auction Yard Rd, (Sunset Hills Dr. from nb)

657 Hooker Creek Rd, Auction Yard Rd, E...**other:** Dill's Tire Repair

656mm rest area both, full(handicapped)facilities, phone, picnic tables, litter barrels, petwalk

653 Jellys Ferry Rd, E...**lodging:** Bend RV Park/LP

652 Wilcox Golf Rd, no services

651 CA 36W(from sb), Red Bluff, W...Exxon/dsl, Ford, same as 650

650 Adobe Rd, W...**gas:** Chevron, **food:** Casa Ramos Mexican, **lodging:** Hampton Inn, **other:** Chevrolet/Cadillac, Home Depot, Hwy Patrol

649 CA 33, CA 99, Red Bluff, E...**gas:** Exxon/dsl, Shell/dsl, **food:** Burger King, Perko's Cafe, KFC, McDonald's, Subway, **lodging:** Best Inn, Best Western, Comfort Inn, Motel 6, W...**gas:** Gas4Less, USA/dsl, **food:** Denny's, Egg Roll King, Java Detour, Los Mariachi, Luigi's Pizza, Marie's Rest., Riverside Dining, RoundTable Pizza, Shari's/24hr, Subway, Wild Bill's Steaks, Winchell's, **lodging:** Best Value, Cinderella Motel, Travelodge, **other:** Foodmaxx, Long's Drug

647a b Diamond Ave, Red Bluff, E...**gas:** Valero, **food:** Las Palmas Mexican, **lodging:** Day's Inn, **other:** HOSPITAL, W...**gas:** Arco/dsl/24hr, Chevron, USA/dsl, **food:** Arby's, Domino's, Jack-in-the-Box, Quizno's, Starbucks, Subway, Taco Bell/24hr, Wendy's, **lodging:** American Inn, Crystal Motel, Lamplighter Lodge, Sky Terrace Motel, Triangle Motel, **other:** $Tree, Ford/Mercury, K-Mart, Kragen Parts, Radio Shack, Raley's Food/drug, Staples, Walgreens, Wal-Mart/auto

642 Flores Ave, to Proberta, Gerber, **1 mi** E...**other:** Wal-Mart Dist Ctr

636 CA 811, Gyle Rd, to Tehama, E...**other:** RV camping(7mi)

(left margin, vertical): Red Bluff

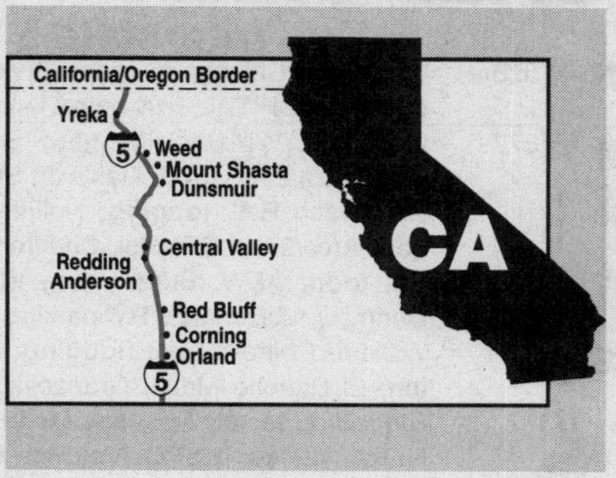

633 Finnell Rd, to Richfield

632mm rest area both lanes, full (handicapped) facilities, phone, picnic tables, litter barrels, petwalk

631 A9, Corning Ave, Corning, E...**gas:** Chevron/24hr, Citgo/7-11, Shell/dsl/LP, 76/dsl, **food:** Burger King, Casa Ramos Mexican, Marco's Pizza, Olive Pit Rest., Papa Murphy's, Quizno's, Rancho Grande Mexican, RoundTable Pizza, Starbucks, Taco Bell, **lodging:** American Inn, Best Western, Comfort Inn, Economy Inn, 7 Inn Motel, **other:** Ace Hardware, Clark Drug, $Tree, Ford/Kia, Heritage RV Park, Kragen Parts, NAPA, Pontiac/Chevrolet/Buick, Rite Aid, Safeway/24hr, Tires+, W...**food:** Giant Burger, **lodging:** Corning RV Park

630 South Ave, Corning, E...**gas:** ⚙/Flying J/Country Mkt Rest./dsl/scales/24hr/@, Petro/Iron Skillet/dsl/rest.//scales/@, TA/Arco/Arby's/Subway/dsl/scales/24hr/@, **food:** Jack-in-the-Box, McDonald's, **lodging:** California Inn, Day's Inn, Holiday Inn Express, **other:** Blue Beacon, Goodyear, Java Truckwash, RV Ctr, RV camping(1-6mi), SpeedCo Lube, Woodson Br SRA/RV Park

628 CA 99W, Liberal Ave, W...**gas:** Chevron/dsl, **lodging:** Ramada Ltd/rest./casino

621 CA 7, no services

619 CA 32, Orland, E...**gas:** 76, **food:** Burger King, Berry Patch Rest., Subway, **lodging:** Amberlight Motel, Orland Inn, **other:** Walgreens, W...**gas:** Sportsman's/dsl, USA/dsl, **food:** Taco Bell, **lodging:** Old Orchard RV Park, Parkway RV Park

618 CA 16, E...**gas:** USA/dsl, **food:** Pizza Factory, **lodging:** Orland Inn, **other:** Longs Drug

614 CA 27, no services

610 Artois, no services

608mm rest area both lanes, full(handicapped)facilities, phone, picnic tables, litter barrels, petwalk, RV dump

607 CA 39, Blue Gum Rd, Bayliss, **2-3 mi** E...**lodging:** Blue Gum Motel

603 CA 162, to Oroville, Willows, E...**gas:** Arco/24hr, Chevron/24hr, Shell/dsl, **food:** BlackBear Diner, Burger King, Casa Ramos, Denny's/24hr, El Dorado Mexican, KFC, McDonald's, RoundTable Pizza, Starbucks, Subway, Taco Bell/24hr, **lodging:** Amerihost, Best Western/rest., Day's Inn, Super 8, Motel 6, **other:** HOSPITAL, CHP, W...**food:** Nancy's Café/24hr, **other:** Wal-Mart, RV Park(8mi), airport

601 CA 57, E...**gas:** 76/CFN/dsl

595 Rd 68, to Princeton, E...to Sacramento NWR

591 Delevan Rd, no services

588 Maxwell(from sb), access to camping

586 Maxwell Rd, E...**other:** Delavan NWR, W...**gas:** CFN, Chevron, **lodging:** Maxwell Inn/rest., **other:** Country Mkt, Maxwell Parts

583 rest area both lanes, full(handicapped)facilities, phone, picnic tables, litter barrels, petwalk

(center margin, vertical): Corning

N ↑↓ S Williams

Exit	Description
578	CA 20 W, Colusa, W...gas: Orv's/dsl/rest., Shell/dsl, other: HOSPITAL, hwy patrol
577	CA 20 E, Williams, E...gas: Shell/Baskin-Robbins/Togo's/dsl/24hr, food: Carl's Jr, Straw Hat Pizza, Subway, Taco Bell, lodging: Holiday Inn Express, W...gas: Arco/24hr, CFN/dsl, Chevron/dsl/24hr, 76, Shell/dsl, food: A&W, Burger King, Casa Lupe Mexican, Denny's, McDonald's/RV parking, Taqueria Mexican, Williams Chinese Rest., lodging: Capri Motel, Comfort Inn, El Rancho Motel, Granzella's Inn/rest., Motel 6, StageStop Motel, Travelers Motel, other: HOSPITAL, NAPA, U-Haul, USPO, ValuRite Drug, camping, hwy patrol
575	Husted Rd, to Williams, no services
569	Hahn Rd, to Grimes, no services
567	frontage rd(from nb), to Arbuckle, E...food: El Jali-science Mexican, W...gas: CFN
566	to College City, Arbuckle, E...gas: Shell/dsl, other: Ace Hardware, W...gas: J&J/grill/dsl
559	Yolo/Colusa County Line Rd, no services
557mm	**rest area both lanes, full(handicapped)facilities, phone, picnic tables, litter barrels, petwalk**
556	E4, Dunnigan, E...gas: Chevron/dsl/24hr, Valero/dsl/LP, food: Bill&Kathy's Rest., Jack-in-the-Box, lodging: Best Value Inn, Best Western, other: USPO, W...gas: 76, lodging: Camper's RV Park/golf
554	rd 8, E...gas: Pilot/Wendy's/dsl/24hr, other: Oasis Grill, lodging: Budget 8 Motel, other: HappyTime RV Park, W...gas: United/dsl
553	I-505(from sb), to San Francisco, callboxes begin sb
548	Zamora, E...gas: Shell/dsl
542	Yolo, 1 mi E...gas
541	CA 16W, Woodland, 3 mi W...other: HOSPITAL
540	West St, W...food: Denny's
538	CA 113 N, E St, Woodland, W...gas: Chevron/dsl, food: Denny's, lodging: Best Western, other: Woodland Opera House(1mi)
537	CA 113 S, Main St, to Davis, W...gas: Valero, food: Denny's, McDonald's, Rafael's Rest., Sonic, Taco Bell, Wendy's, lodging: Comfort Inn, Day's Inn, Motel 6
536	rd 102, E on Main St...gas: Arco, Shell, food: Applebee's, Jack-in-the-Box, RoundTable Pizza, Quizno's, Subway, lodging: Hampton Inn, Holiday Inn Express, other: Home Depot, Staples, Wal-Mart/gas, museum, same as 537, W...gas: Chevron, other: Costco/gas, Target
531	rd 22, W Sacramento, no services
530mm	**Sacramento River**
529mm	**rest area sb, full(handicapped)facilities, phone, picnic tables, litter barrels, petwalk**
528	Airport Rd, E...gas: Arco, other: airport, lodging
525b	CA 99, to CA 70, to Marysville, Yuba City
525a	Del Paso Rd, E...gas: Chevron, food: A&W/KFC, Jack-in-the-box, Jamba Juice, lodging: Hampton Inn, Holiday Inn Express, other: Rite Aid, Safeway/gas
524	Arena Blvd, E...other: Arco Arena, W...food: Starbucks, other: Bel-Air Food&Drug/gas
522	I-80, E to Reno, W to San Francisco
521b a	Garden Hwy, West El Camino, W...gas:Shell/dsl, food: Baja Fresh, Burger King, Carl's Jr, Jack-in-the-Box, Jamba Juice, Togo's, lodging: Courtyard, Hilton Garden, Homestead Village, Residence Inn, Springhill Suites

Sacramento

Exit	Description
520	Richards Blvd, E...gas: Chevron/dsl/24hr, food: Hungry Hunter Rest., Lyon's Rest./24hr, Memphis BBQ, McDonald's, Monterey Rest., Rusty Duck Rest., lodging: Governor's Inn, Hawthorn Suites, Ramada Inn, W...gas: Shell, Valero, food: Coyote Jct Mexican, lodging: Best Western/rest., Comfort Suites, Days Inn, La Quinta, Motel 6, Super 8
519b	J St, Old Sacramento, E...food: Denny's, lodging: Holiday Inn, Vagabond Inn, W...lodging: Embassy Suites, other: Railroad Museum
519a	Q St, downtown, Sacramento, W...lodging: Embassy Suites, to st capitol
518	US 50, CA 99, Broadway, E...services downtown
516	Sutterville Rd, E...gas: Land Park/dsl, other: Wm Land Park, zoo
515	Fruitridge Rd, Seamas Rd, no services
514	43rd Ave, Riverside Blvd(from sb), E...gas: 76/repair
513	Florin Rd, E...gas: Arco/24hr, Chevron/24hr, Shell/repair, food: Rosalinda's Mexican, RoundTable Pizza, Sizzling Wok, other: Bel Air Foods, Kragen Parts, Longs Drug, W...food: Burger King, JimBoy's Tacos, Shari's, Starbucks, Subway, other: Marshall's, Nugget Foods, Radio Shack, Rite Aid
512	CA 160, Pocket Rd, Meadowview Rd, to Freeport, E...gas: Shell/dsl/24hr, food: IHOP, McDonald's, Togo's, Wendy's, other: Home Depot, Staples
508	Laguna Blvd, E...gas: Chevron/McDonald's/dsl, 76/Circle K/dsl/LP, Shell, food: A&W/KFC, Starbucks, Subway, Wendy's, lodging: Extended Stay America, Hampton Inn, other: Big O Tire
506	Elk Grove Blvd, E...gas: Arco/dsl, Chevron/dsl, Shell, food: Carl's Jr, Lyla's Mexican, Pete's Grill, Port City Java, Quizno's, Stone Lake Buffet, lodging: Comfort Suites, other: AAA
504	Hood Franklin Rd, no services
498	Twin Cities Rd, to Walnut Grove, no services
493	Walnut Grove Rd, Thornton, E...gas: CFN/dsl, 76/Subway/dsl
490	Peltier Rd, no services
487	Turner Rd, no services
485	CA 12, Lodi, E...gas: Arco/dsl/24hr, Chevron/Subway/dsl/LP/@, Flying J/Country Mkt Rest./dsl/scales/24hr/@, Shell/Wendy's/dsl, 76/Rocky's Rest./dsl/scales/24hr/@, food: Burger King, Carl's Jr, McDonald's, Starbucks, Taco Bell, lodging: Best Western, Microtel, other: Blue Beacon, Flag City RV Resort, Profleet Trucklube, W...other: Tower Park Marina Camping(5mi)
481	Eight Mile Rd, E...camping, W...gas: Chevron, food: Del Taco, Hawaiian BBQ, Jack-in-the-Box, Jamba Juice, MooMoo's Burgers, Panda Express, Panera Bread, Qdoba Mexican, Sonic, Starbucks, Strings Italian, Subway, Wendy's, other: AAA, Borders Books, Jo-Ann, KOA, Kohl's, Lowes Whse, Office Depot, Petsmart, Ross, Target
478	Hammer Lane, Stockton, E...gas: Arco/24hr, 76/Circle K/dsl, food: Adalberto's Mexican, Carl's Jr, KFC, Little Caesar's, Shirason Japanese, Subway, other: Auto Parts Express, S-mart Foods, W...gas: Quik-Stop, Valero, food: Burger King, Fugi Express, Jack-in-the-Box, Mexico Lindo, Taco Bell, lodging: Vagabond Inn

Stockton

477	Benjamin Holt Dr, Stockton, E...**gas:** Arco, Chevron/dsl/24hr, **food:** Pizza Guys, **lodging:** Motel 6, **other:** Quikstop, W...**food:** McDonald's, Lyon's/24hr, StrawHat Pizza, Subway/TCBY, Wong's Chinese, **other:** Ace Hardware, 7-11
476	March Lane, Stockton, E...**gas:** Citgo/7-11, **food:** Applebee's, Arroyo's Mexican, Black Angus, Carl's Jr, Denny's, El Torito, Jack-in-the-Box, McDonald's, Marie Callender, Red Lobster, StrawHat Pizza, Taco Bell, Wendy's, **lodging:** Comfort Inn, Stockton Brand, **other:** MEDICAL CARE, Longs Drug, Marshall's, Smart Foods, **1/2 mi** E...**food:** Burger King, Outback Steaks, Quizno's, Wienerschnitzel, **other:** $Tree, Mervyn's, Office Depot, Target, W...**gas:** 76/dsl/24hr, 7-11, **food:** Carrow's Rest., In-n-Out, Italian Cuisine, Krispy Kreme, Starbucks, RoundTable Pizza, Old Spaghetti Factory, Wong's Chinese, **lodging:** Extended Stay America, La Quinta, Quality Inn, Super 8, **other:** Home Depot
475	Alpine Ave, Country Club Blvd, same as 474 b
474b	Country Club Blvd(from nb), W...**gas:** Citgo/7-11, USA/Subway/dsl, Safeway/gas, **other:** Big Lots
474a	Monte Diablo Ave, W...**other:** Aamco
473	Pershing Ave(from nb), W...**gas:** Arco, **lodging:** Best-Value
472	CA 4 E, to CA 99, Fresno Ave, downtown, no services
471	CA 4 W, Charter Way, E...**gas:** Arco/dsl, Chevron/24hr, Shell/24hr, **food:** Burger King, Denny's, McDonald's, Quizno's, **lodging:** Best Western, Motel 6, **other:** Checker Parts, Kragen Parts, transmissions, W...**gas:** 76/dsl/rest./scales/24hr, Valero, **food:** Jack-in-the-Box, Taco Bell, **lodging:** Motel 6
470	8th St, Stockton, W...**gas:** CA Stop/dsl, Shell/Subway/dsl, **food:** Boquita Mexican, **lodging:** Econolodge
469	Downing Ave, W...**food:** Jalapeños Mexican, Mtn Mike's Pizza, Subway, **other:** Food4Less/gas
468	French Camp, E...**gas:** 76/Togo's/dsl/@, **other:** Pan Pacific RV Ctr, W...**other:** HOSPITAL
467b	Mathews Rd, E...**gas:** Exxon/CFN/dsl, **other:** RV Ctr, tires/repair, W...**other:** HOSPITAL
467a	El Dorado St(from nb), no services
465	Roth Rd, Sharpe Depot, E...**other:** Freightliner, Kenworth, truck repair
463	Lathrop Rd, E...**gas:** Chevron/24hr, Joe's Trkstp/Subway/dsl, TowerMart/dsl, Valero/dsl, **food:** Country Kitchen, Starbucks, **lodging:** Best Western, Comfort Inn, Day's Inn, **other:** SaveMart Foods, W...**other:** Dos Reis CP, RV camping
462	Louise Ave, E...**gas:** Arco/24hr, 76, **food:** A&W/KFC, Carl's Jr, Denny's, Jack-in-the-Box, McDonald's, Mtn Mikes Pizza, Quizno's, Taco Bell, Valarta Mexican, **lodging:** Hampton Inn, Holiday Inn Express, **other:** Mossdale CP
461	CA 120, to Sonora, Manteca, E...**other:** Oakwood Lake Resort Camping, to Yosemite
460	Mossdale Rd, E...**gas:** Arco/dsl, W...**food:** fruit stand/deli
458b	I-205, to Oakland(from sb, no return)
458a	11th St, to Tracy, Defense Depot, **2 mi** W...**gas:** gas/dsl/food
457	Kasson Rd, to Tracy, W...**gas:** Valley Pacific/dsl
452	CA 33 S, Vernalis, no services
449b a	CA 132, to Modesto, W...**other:** The Orchard Campground

Tracy

446	I-580(from nb, exits left, no return)
445mm	**Westley Rest Area both lanes, full (handicapped) facilities, picnic tables, litter barrels, phone, RV dump, petwalk**
441	Ingram Creek, Howard Rd, Westley, E...**gas:** Beacon, Chevron/dsl/24hr, Joe's Trvl Plaza/Quizno's/dsl/scales/@, Westley TruckStp/dsl, **food:** Carl's Jr, McDonald's, Subway, **lodging:** Best Value Inn, Day's Inn, Econolodge, Holiday Inn Express, Super 8, W...**gas:** Shell/dsl/24hr, **food:** Ingram Creek Rest., fruits, **other:** truck repair
434	Sperry Ave, Del Puerto, Patterson, E...**gas:** Arco/24hr, 76/Subway/dsl, **food:** Denny's, Jack-in-the-Box, KFC/A&W, LJ Silver, Quizno's, Starbucks, Wendy's, **lodging:** Best Western, **other:** Kit Fox RV Park
430mm	vista point nb
428	Fink Rd, Crow's Landing, no services
423	Stuhr Rd, Newman, **5 mi** E...food, lodging, **other:** HOSPITAL, RV camping
422mm	vista point sb
418	CA 140E, Gustine, E...**gas:** 76/dsl, Shell/dsl
409	weigh sta both lanes
407	CA 33, Santa Nella, E...**gas:** Andersen's Gas, Arco/Subway/24hr, Pilot/Del Taco/dsl/24hr/@, TA/76/Popeyes/dsl/rest./24hr/@, **food:** Carl's Jr, Wendy's, **lodging:** Best Western/Andersen's, Holiday Inn Express, W...**gas:** Chevron/24hr, Rotten Robbie/dsl/scales, Shell/Jack-in-the-Box/dsl, Valero/dsl, **food:** Denny's, McDonald's, Quizno's, Starbucks, Taco Bell, **lodging:** Motel 6, Ramada Inn, **other:** Santa Nella RV Park
403b a	CA 152, Los Banos, **6 mi** E...**other:** HOSPITAL, W...**gas:** Petro/dsl/24hr(1mi), **other:** San Luis RV Park
391	CA 165N, Mercy Springs Rd, W...**gas:** Shell
386mm	**rest area both lanes, full(handicapped)facilities, phone, picnic tables, litter barrels, petwalk**
385	Nees Ave, to Firebaugh, W...**gas:** Chevron/CFN/Subway/dsl/scales
379	Shields Ave, to Mendota, no services
372	Russell Ave, no services
368	Panoche Rd, W...**gas:** Chevron/McDonald's, Mobil/Taco Bell/dsl, 76/dsl, Shell/dsl/burgers/@, **food:** Apricot Rest., Foster's Freeze, **lodging:** Best Western/Apricot Inn, **other:** Palms Mkt
365	Manning Ave, to San Joaquin, no services
357	Kamm Ave, no services
349	CA 33 N, Derrick Ave, no services
337	CA 33 S, CA 145 N, to Coalinga, no services
334	CA 198, to Lemoore, Huron, E...**gas:** Shell/Subway/dsl/24hr, **lodging:** Harris Ranch Inn/rest., W...**gas:** Chevron, Mobil/dsl, 76/Circle K, **food:** Burger King, Carl's Jr, Cazuela's Mexican, Denny's, McDonald's, Oriental Express Chinese, Red Robin Rest., Taco Bell, **lodging:** Best Western, Motel 6, Travelodge, **other:** HOSPITAL

N ↑↓ S

325	Jayne Ave, to Coalinga, **W**...**gas:** Arco/24hr, **lodging:** Almond Tree RV Park, **other:** HOSPITAL
320mm	**rest area both lanes, full(handicapped)facilities, phone, picnic tables, litter barrels, petwalk**
319	CA 269, Lassen Ave, to Avenal, **W**...**gas:** Hillcrest TP/Valero/dsl/rest.
309	CA 41, Kettleman City, **E**...**gas:** CFN/dsl, Chevron/McDonald's, Exxon/Subway/dsl, Mobil/dsl/24hr, Kwik-Serv/Quizno's/dsl, Shell/dsl, Valero/dsl, **food:** Carl's Jr, In-n-Out, Jack-in-the-Box, Mike's Roadhouse Café, Pizza Hut/Taco Bell, **lodging:** Best Western, Super 8, **other:** Travelers RV Park
305	Utica Ave, no services
288	Twisselman Rd, no services
278	CA 46, Lost Hills, **E**...**gas:** Texaco/Subway/dsl, **other:** to Kern NWR, **W**...**gas:** Arco/24hr, Beacon/dsl, Chevron/dsl/24hr, Loves/Arby's/dsl, Mobil/McDonald's/, Pilot/Wendy's/dsl/24hr/@, 76/24hr, Shell, **food:** Carl's Jr, Denny's, Jack-in-the-Box, **lodging:** Day's Inn, Motel 6, **other:** KOA
268	Lerdo Hwy, to Shafter, no services
263	7th Standard Rd, Rowlee Rd, to Buttonwillow
259mm	**Buttonwillow Rest Area both lanes, full(handicapped) facilities, phone, picnic tables, litter barrels, petwalk**
257	CA 58, to Bakersfield, Buttonwillow, **E**...**gas:** Arco/24hr, Bruce's/dsl/scales/@, Chevron/dsl/24hr, Mobil/dsl, TA/76/Taco Bell/dsl/24hr/@, Shell/dsl, **food:** Carl's Jr, Denny's, McDonald's, Starbucks, Subway, Taste of India, Tita's Mexican, Willow Ranch Rest., Zippy Freeze, **lodging:** Homeland Inn, Motel 6, Super 8, Willow Inn, **other:** Roger's Produce/gifts, tires/truckwash, **W**...**gas:** Exxon/dsl
253	Stockdale Hwy, **E**...**gas:** Shell/dsl/24hr, 76/24hr, **food:** IHOP, Jack-in-the-Box, **lodging:** Best Inn, Best Western, **W**...**other:** Tule Elk St Reserve
246	CA 43, to Taft, Maricopa, **other:** to Buena Vista RA
244	CA 119, to Pumpkin Center, **E**...**gas:** Mobil/dsl, **W**...**gas:** Chevron/dsl
239	CA 223, Bear Mtn Blvd, to Arvin, **W**...**other:** to Buena Vista RA, RV camping
234	Old River Rd, no services
228	Copus Rd, no services
225	CA 166, to Mettler, **2-3 mi** **E**...gas/dsl, food
221	I-5 and CA 99(from nb, exits left, no return)
219b a	Laval Rd, Wheeler Ridge, **E**...**gas:** Chevron/Subway, TA/dsl/rest./scales/@, **food:** Burger King, Pizza Hut, Taco Bell, **other:** Blue Beacon, repair, **W**...**gas:** Petro/Mobil/Iron Sillet/Subway/dsl/scales/24hr/@, **food:** In-n-Out, McDonald's, Panda Express, Starbucks, Wendy's, **lodging:** Best Western
218	truck weigh sta sb
215	Grapevine, **E**...**gas:** Mobil, **food:** Denny's, Jack-in-the-Box, RanchHouse Rest., **W**...**gas:** 76/dsl, Shell/dsl, **food:** Don Pedro's Mexican, **lodging:** Ramda Ltd.
210	Ft Tejon Rd, **W**...**other:** Ft Tejon Hist SP, tow/repair
209mm	brake check area nb
207	Lebec Rd, **W**...**other:** USPO, CHP, antiques, towing
206mm	**rest areas both lanes, full(handicapped)facilities, phone, vending, picnic tables litter barrels, petwalk**

205	Frazier Mtn Park Rd, **W**...**gas:** Arco, Chevron/Subway/dsl/24hr, ✈/Flying J/dsl/LP/rest./24hr/@, Shell/Quizno's/dsl, **food:** Jack-in-the-Box, Los Pinos Mexican, Noble Roman's, **lodging:** BestRest Inn, **other:** Auto Parts+, towing/repair/radiators/transmissions, to Mt Pinos RA
204	Tejon Pass, elev 4144, truck brake insp sb
202	Gorman Rd, to Hungry Valley, **E**...**gas:** Chevron/dsl/LP, 76, **food:** Carl's Jr, Sizzler, **lodging:** Econolodge, **W**...**gas:** Mobil, **food:** McDonald's, **other:** auto repair
199	CA 138 E(from sb), Lancaster Rd, to Palmdale
198b a	Quail Lake Rd, CA 138 E(from nb), no services
195	Smokey Bear Rd, Pyramid Lake, **W**...**other:** Pyramid Lake RV Park
191	Vista del Lago Rd, **W**...**other:** visitors ctr
186mm	brake inspection area sb, motorist callboxes begin sb
183	Templin Hwy, **W**...**other:** Ranger Sta, RV camping
176b a	Lake Hughes Rd, Parker Rd, Castaic, **E**...**gas:** Citgo/7-11, Castaic Trkstp/dsl/rest./24hr/@, Pilot/Wendy's/dsl/24hr/scales, Shell, **food:** Burger King, Café Mike, Carl's Jr, Del Taco, Denny's, Domino's, El Pollo Loco, Foster Freeze, McDonald's, Starbucks, Subway, Vinny's Pizza, Zorba's Rest., **lodging:** Castaic Inn, Comfort Inn, Day's Inn, Rodeway Inn, **other:** Benny's Tire, Kragen Parts, Ralph's Food, Rite Aid, vet, to Castaic Lake, **W**...**gas:** Mobil, 76/Circle K/Pizza Hut/Taco Bell/repair, **food:** Jack-in-the-Box, Las Rosas, Lollie's Rest., **lodging:** Comfort Suites, **other:** Walgreens, auto repair
173	Hasley Canyon Rd, **W**...**food:** Ameci Pizza/pasta, Coldstone Creamery, Subway, **other:** Ralph's Foods
172	CA 126 W, to Ventura, no services
171mm	weigh sta nb
171	Rye Canyon Rd(from sb), **W**...**gas:** Chevron, Shell, **food:** Del Taco, Jack-in-the-Box, Jimmy Deans, Tommy's Burgers, **other:** funpark
170	CA 126 E, Magic Mtn Pkwy, Saugus, **E**...**food:** Denny's, **lodging:** Best Western/rest., Holiday Inn Express, **W**...**gas:** Chevron, **food:** El Torito, Hamburger Hamlet, Marie Callender's, Red Lobster, Rio Rio Grill, Wendy's, **lodging:** Hilton Garden, **other:** Six Flags of CA
169	Valencia Blvd, **E**...Shell/dsl, **W**...Albertson's
168	McBean Pkwy, **E**...**other:** HOSPITAL, **W**...**food:** Baskin-Robbins, Chili's, ChuckeCheese, ClaimJumper Rest., Indian Cuisine, Jamba Juice, Macaroni Grill, Starbucks, Subway, Wood Ranch BBQ, **other:** Circuit City, Marshall's, Michael's, Old Navy, Staples, Vons Foods, WorldMkt
167	Lyons Ave, Pico Canyon Rd, **E**...**gas:** Chevron/24hr, 76/Circle K, Shell/dsl, **food:** Burger King, Wendy's, **other:** Chevrolet, **W**...**gas:** Arco/24hr, Mobil/Blimpie, Shell, **food:** Carl's Jr, Chuy's Chinese, Coco's, Del Taco, Denny's, Foster's Freeze, El Pollo Loco, Fortune Express Chinese, IHOP, In-n-Out, Jack-in-the-Box, McDonald's, Outback Steaks, Taco Bell, Yamato Japanese, **lodging:** Comfort Inn, Extended Stay America, Fairfield Inn, Hampton Inn, La Quinta, Residence Inn, **other:** Camping World RV Service, GNC, Jiffy Lube, Petsmart, Ralph's Foods, SteinMart, Wal-Mart/auto
166	Calgrove Blvd, no services
162	CA 14 N, to Palmdale, no services
161b	Balboa Blvd (from sb), no services
160a	I-210, to San Fernando, Pasadena

Interstate 5

N ↑↓ **S**

Exit	Description
159	Roxford St, Sylmar, **E**...**gas:** Chevron/dsl, Mobil/dsl, **food:** Denny's/24hr, McDonald's, **lodging:** Good Nite Inn, Motel 6
158	I-405 S(from sb, no return)
157b a	SF Mission Blvd, Brand Blvd, **E**...**gas:** Chevron, Mobil/dsl, 76, **food:** Carl's Jr, Carnita's Mexican, In-n-Out, Pollo Gordo, Popeye's, Winchell's, **other:** HOSPITAL, AutoZone, Rite Aid
156b	CA 118, no services
156a	Paxton St, Brand Ave(from nb), **E**...**gas:** Shell/dsl/24hr
155b	Van Nuys Blvd(no EZ nb return), **E**...**gas:** Vale, **food:** Jack-in-the-Box, KFC/LJ Silver, McDonald's, Pizza Hut, Popeye's, **other:** AutoZone, USPO, **W**...**food:** Domino's, **other:** auto repair
155a	Terra Bella St(from nb), **E**...**gas:** Thrifty
154	Osborne St, to Arleta, **E**...**gas:** Arco/24hr, Chevron/dsl, 76, **food:** El Pollo Loco, Papa's Tacos, Peter Piper Pizza, **other:** BigLots, Food4Less, Target, **W**...**gas:** Mobil/Burger King, **other:** 7-11
153b	CA 170(from sb), to Hollywood, no services
152a	Sheldon St, **E**...**food:** Big Jim's Rest., **other:** Big O Parts, HOSPITAL, auto repair
152	Lankershim Blvd, Tuxford, **E**...**gas:** Superfine/dsl/scales
151	Penrose St, no services
150b	Sunland Blvd, Sun Valley, **E**...**gas:** Mobil, 76, **food:** Acapulco Rest., Carl's Jr, El Pollo Loco, Good Fortune Chinese, Quizno's, Subway, Taco Bell, Town Café, **lodging:** Economy Inn, **other:** Ralph's Foods, 7-11, **W**...**gas:** Exxon, Shell, **food:** Dimion's Rest., McDonald's
150a	GlenOaks Blvd(from nb), **E**...**gas:** Superior/dsl, **lodging:** Willows Motel
149	Hollywood Way, **W**...**gas:** Shell/dsl, **other:** U-Haul, airport
148	Buena Vista St, **W**...**gas:** Exxon/dsl, **food:** Jack-in-the-Box, **lodging:** Quality Inn, Ramada Inn
147	Scott Rd, to Burbank, **E**...**gas:** Sevan/dsl, **W**...**food:** Krispy Kreme, Outback Steaks, Panda Express, Starbucks, Wendy's, **lodging:** Courtyard, Extended Stay America, **other:** Best Buy, Lowe's Whse, Marshall's, Michael's, Staples, Target
146b	Burbank Blvd, **E**...**gas:** 76/repair, **food:** Carl's Jr, ChuckeCheese, El Pollo Loco, Harry's Rest., Hooters, IHOP, In-n-Out, Marie Callender, McDonald's, Popeye's, Pizza Hut, Quizno's, Shakey's Pizza, Starbuck's, Subway, Taco Bell, Tommy's Burgers, Wienerschnitzel, Yoshinoya, **lodging:** Holiday Inn, **other:** Barnes&Noble, Circuit City, CompUSA, CVS Drug, K-Mart, Macy's, Mervyn's, Office Depot, Old Navy, Ralph's Foods, Ross, Sears, Von's Foods, **W**...**gas:** Chevron, **food:** Subway
146a	Olive Ave, Verdugo, **E**...**food:** Black Angus, Brewhouse Rest., **lodging:** Holiday Inn, **other:** Radio Shack, Sears, USPO, **W**...**other:** Chevrolet, 7-11, HOSPITAL
145b	Alameda Ave, **E**...**gas:** Chevron, **food:** Starbucks, Togo's/Baskin-Robbins, **other:** CarMax, CVS Drug, Home Depot, Ralph's Foods, Walgreen, **W**...**gas:** Arco, Shell, **lodging:** Burbank Inn, **other:** U-Haul
145a	Western Ave, **W**...**other:** Gene Autrey Museum
144b a	CA 134, Ventura Fwy, Glendale, Pasadena
142	Colorado St, no services
141a	Los Feliz Blvd, **E**...**other:** HOSPITAL, **W**...**other:** Griffith Park, zoo
140b	Glendale Blvd, **E**...**gas:** GasMart, 76, **food:** Starbucks, Subway, **other:** auto repair, **W**...**gas:** Valero
140a	Fletcher Dr(from sb)
139b a	CA 2, Glendale Fwy
138	Stadium Way, Figueroa St, **E**...**food:** IHOP, McDonald's, **other:** Home Depot, **W**...**other:** to Dodger Stadium
137b a	CA 2, Glendale Fwy, no services
136b	Broadway St(from sb), **W**...**gas:** 76
136a	Main St, **E**...**gas:** Chevron/24hr, 76, **food:** Chinatown Express, Jack-in-the-Box, McDonald's, Mr Pizza, **other:** HOSPITAL, Parts+
135c	I-10 W(from nb), Mission Rd(from sb), **E**...**gas:** 76, **food:** McDonald's, **lodging:** Howard Johnson, **other:** HOSPITAL
135b	Cesar Chavez Ave, **W**...**other:** HOSPITAL
135a	4th St, Soto St, no services
134b	Ca 60 E(from sb), Soto St(from nb), no services
134a	CA 60 W, Santa Monica Fwy, no services
133	Euclid Ave(from sb), Grand Vista(from nb), **E**...**gas:** Arco, USA/dsl, **W**...**gas:** Mobil, Shell, **other:** HOSPITAL
132	Calzona St, Indiana St, **E**...**gas:** Arco/dsl
131b	Indiana St(from nb), **E**...**gas:** Arco/dsl, Valero/dsl
131a	Olympic Blvd, **E**...**food:** McDonald's, **W**...**food:** Jack-in-the-Box, King Taco, **other:** HOSPITAL
130c b	I-710, to Long Beach, Eastern Ave, **E**...**food:** McDonald's
130a	Triggs St(from sb), **E**...**other:** outlet mall, **W**...**food:** Denny's/24hr, **lodging:** Destiny Inn
129	Atlantic Blvd N, Eastern Ave(from sb), **E**...**food:** Carl's Jr, Starbucks, **lodging:** Wyndham Garden, **other:** Hyundai, outlet mall/famous brands, **W**...**food:** Denny's, Steven's Steaks
128b	Washington Blvd, Commerce, **E**...**gas:** Chevron/dsl/repair/24hr, **food:** McDonald's, **lodging:** Crowne Plaza Hotel/casino, Wyndham Hotel, **other:** Firestone, Office Depot, Old Navy, mall, **W**...**gas:** Arco, **food:** Starbucks
128a	Garfield Blvd, **E**...**lodging:** Commerce/Hotel/casino, **other:** Home Depot, Office Depot, **W**...**gas:** 76
126b	Slauson Ave, Montebello, **E**...**gas:** Shell, Valero/dsl, **food:** Burger King, Ozzie's Diner, Quizno's, Starbucks, **lodging:** Best Star Inn, Best Western, Super 8, **W**...**gas:** Arco, **food:** Denny's, **lodging:** Best Value, Ramada Inn
126a	Paramount Blvd, Downey, **E**...**gas:** Shell/Jack-in-the-Box/dsl
125	CA 19 S, Lakewood Blvd, Rosemead Blvd, **E**...**gas:** Mobil, Thrifty, **food:** Foster's Freeze, Sam's Burgers, Starbucks, Taco Bell, **W**...**food:** McDonald's, China Wok, Chris & Pitt's BBQ, Subway, **other:** Ford/Lincoln/Mercury, Ralph's Foods
124	I-605
123	Florence Ave, to Downey, **E**...**gas:** Mobil, **W**...**other:** Chevrolet, Honda, auto repair

Los Angeles Area

CALIFORNIA
Interstate 5

N ↑↓ S

Los Angeles Area

Exit	Description
122	Imperial Hwy, Pioneer Blvd, E...**gas**: Chevron, **food**: Cold Stone Creamery, IHOP, Jack-in-the-Box, King Buffet, McDonald's, Plum Wok Rest, Subway, Togo's, Wendy's, **lodging**: Best Western, **other**: Audi/Porsche, BMW, Firestone/auto, Payless Foods, Rite Aid, Target, W...**gas**: Citgo/7-11, Shell, **food**: Denny's, HongKong Express, Panda King, Rally's, Sizzler, Tacos Mexico, Wienerschnitzel, **lodging**: Comfort Inn, Keystone Motel, Rodeway Inn, Vistaland Motel, **other**: Ford, Wal-Mart
121	San Antonio Dr, to Norwalk Blvd, E...**food**: IHOP, McDonald's, Outback Steaks, Starbucks, **lodging**: Marriott, W...**gas**: 76, **other**: auto repair
120b	Firestone Blvd(exits left from nb), no services
120a	Rosecrans Ave, E...**gas**: Valero/dsl, **food**: Burger King, Casa Adelita Mexican, Jim's Burgers, KFC, Pizza Hut/Taco Bell, Taco Joe, **other**: HOSPITAL, BigSaver Foods, W...**gas**: Arco/24hr, **food**: El Pollo Loco, **lodging**: Saddleback Inn, **other**: El Monte RV Ctr, Nissan, Stier's RV Ctr, Tuneup Masters
119	Carmenita Rd, Buena Park, E...**gas**: 76/dsl, **food**: Jack-in-the-Box, **lodging**: Motel 6, **other**: Ford Trucks, Lowe's Whse, W...**gas**: Arco/24hr, **food**: Carl's Jr, **lodging**: Budget Inn, Dynasty Suites
118	Valley View Blvd, E...**gas**: Arco/dsl/24hr, **food**: Carl's Jr, Elephant Bar Rest, In-n-Out, Northwoods Rest, Red Robin, Subway, **lodging**: Extended Stay America, Holiday Inn Select, Residence Inn, **other**: Staples, W...**gas**: Chevron, **food**: Denny's, El Pollo Loco, Four Seasons Buffet, Starbucks, **other**: Thompson's RV Ctr, to Camping World
117	Artesia Blvd, Knott Ave, E...**gas**: 76/24hr, Shell/Subway/dsl/24hr, **lodging**: Extended Stay America, **other**: Carmax, W...**gas**: Cardlock/dsl, **other**: Chevrolet, Chrysler, Knotts Berry Farm, to Camping World RV Service/supplies
116	CA 39, Beach Blvd, E...**gas**: Chevron, **other**: HOSPITAL, Acura, BMW, Buick/Pontiac/GMC, CarMax, Honda, Hyundai, Nissan, Toyota, VW, W...**gas**: Chevron, Valero, **food**: Arby's, Black Angus, Denny's, Fuddruckers, Karuta Japanese, KFC, Outback Steaks, Pizza Hut, Subway, Wendy's, **lodging**: Hampton Inn, Holiday Inn, Red Roof Inn, **other**: Sater Bro's, Target, to Knotts Berry Farm
115	Manchester(from nb), no services
114b	CA 91 E, Riverside Fwy, W...to airport
114a	Magnolia Ave, Orangethorpe Ave, E...**gas**: Mobil/dsl, **food**: Burger King, Burger Town, Taco Bell, **other**: Harley-Davidson
113c	CA 91 W(from nb)
113b a	Brookhurst St, LaPalma, E...**gas**: Chevron/24hr, **food**: Subway, W...**gas**: Mobil/dsl, **food**: Carl's Jr., Quizno's, **other**: Home Depot, Staples
112	Euclid St, E...**gas**: Mobil, 7-11, **food**: Chris&Pitt's BBQ, Marie Callender's, McDonald's, Subway, **other**: CompUSA, Mervyn's, Kings Drug, Old Navy, Ross, Wal-Mart, W...**gas**: Arco, 76, **food**: Arby's, Burger King, Denny's, **other**: Chevrolet, Radio Shack, SavOn Drug
111	Lincoln Ave, to Anaheim, E...**gas**: Shell/dsl, **food**: El Triunfo Mexican, La Casa Garcia Mexican, Starbuck's, Subway, **other**: vet, W...**other**: Discount Auto Repair, Ford
110b	Ball Rd(from sb), E...**gas**: Arco, Chevron/dsl, Citgo/7-11, Shell, **food**: Big's Pizza, Burger King, El Pollo Loco, McDonald's, Shakey's Pizza, Taco Bell, Subway, **lodging**: Anaheim Motel, Astoria Inn, Best Inn, Courtesy Lodge, Day's Inn, Holiday Inn, Traveler's World RV Park, **other**: laundry, W...**gas**: Arco/24hr, Shell/dsl, **food**: Paris Rest., Spaghetti Sta, **lodging**: Best Western, Budget Inn, Day's Inn, Roadway Inn, Sheraton, Super 8, **other**: Camping World RV Service/supplies
110a	Harbor Blvd, E...**gas**: Shell, **lodging**: Day's Inn, Menage Inn, W...to Disneyland, **food**: Acapulco Mexican, Captain Kidd's, Dennys, IHOP, McDonald's, Millie's Rest., Mimi's Cafe, Tony Roma, **lodging**: Anaheim Resort, Best Inn, Best Western, Camelot Inn, Carousel Inn, Castle Inn Suites, Desert Inn, Fairfield Inn, Howard Johnson, ParkVue Inn, Ramada Inn, Saga Inn, Tropicana Inn, same as 109
109	Katella Ave, Disney Way, E...**gas**: Arco, 76/repair, **food**: CA Country Café, Denny's, El Torito, McDonald's, Ming Delight, Mr Stox Dining, **lodging**: Angel Inn, Ramada Inn, Travelodge, W...**gas**: 7-11, **food**: Del Taco, Flakey Jake's, Subway, Thai&Thai, **lodging**: Arena Inn, Comfort Inn, Desert Palms Suites, Extended Stay America, Hilton, Holiday Inn Express, Marriott, Peacock Suites, Portofino Inn, Radisson, Red Roof Inn, Residence Inn, Staybridge Suites, Super 8, to Disneyland
107c	St Coll Blvd, City Drive, E...**lodging**: Hilton Suites, W...**lodging**: Doubletree Hotel
107b a	CA 57 N, Chapman Ave, E...**gas**: Mobil, **food**: Burger King, Del Taco, Denny's, **lodging**: Hilton Suites, Motel 6, Ramada Inn, **other**: HOSPITAL, to Edison Field, W...**food**: Krispy Kreme, Wendy's, **lodging**: Ayer's Inn, Country Inn/café, DoubleTree, **other**: HOSPITAL, Best Buy
106	CA 22 W(from nb), Garden Grove Fwy, Bristol St
105b	N Broadway, Main St, E...**gas**: 76, **food**: Carl's Jr, FoodCourt, Jamba Juice, Polly's Café, Rubio's Grill, Starbucks, **lodging**: Red Roof Inn, **other**: Barnes&Noble, BMW, Macy's, Nordstrom's, Robinsons-May, SavOn Drug, Bowers Museum, mall, W...**lodging**: Golden West Motel, Travel Inn
105a	17th St, E...**gas**: 76/dsl/24hr, **food**: Hometown Buffet, IHOP, McDonald's, **lodging**: Grand Courtyard Inn, **other**: Chevrolet, CVS Drug, Food4Less, same as 104b, W...**gas**: B&L Gas, Chevron, **food**: Marisco's Seafood, Norm's Rest., YumYum Doughnuts, **other**: 7-11
104b	Santa Ana Blvd, Grand Ave, **E on Grand**...**food**: Denny's, Hawaiian BBQ, Marie Callender, McDonald's, Popeye's, Round-Table Pizza, Starbucks, Subway, Taco Bell/Pizza Hut, Tacos Mexico, **other**: Big O Tire, CVS Drug, $Tree, Food4Less, Goodyear, Target, vet, W...**other**: KIA
104a	(103c from nb), 4th St, 1st St, to CA 55 N, E...**gas**: Chevron, Shell, **food**: Del Taco
103b	CA 55 S, to Newport Beach, no services
103a	CA 55 N(from nb), to Riverside, no services
102	Newport Ave(from sb), W...**gas**: Arco
101b	Red Hill Ave, E...**gas**: Mobil/dsl, Shell/repair, **food**: Del Taco, Denny's, Starbucks, Subway, Wendy's, **lodging**: Key Inn, **other**: Drug Emporium/24hr, U-Haul, W...**gas**: Arco/24hr, Chevron/24hr, Valero/dsl, **food**: Burger King, Pizza Shack, Roderick's, Taco Bell, **other**: Goodyear, 7-11, Stater Bros Foods
101a	Tustin Ranch Rd, E...**food**: McDonald's, **other**: Acura, Buick, Cadillac, Chevrolet, Costco, Dodge, Ford/Lincoln/Mercury, Infiniti, Lexus, Mazda, Nissan, Pontiac, Sears Essentials, Toyota

Interstate 5

N ↕ S

100 Jamboree Rd, **E**...gas: Shell, food: Black Angus, Buca Italian, Burger King, CA Pizza, Chick-fil-A, El Pollo Loco, In-n-Out, Macaroni Grill, On the Border, Panda Express, Pick-up Sticks, Quizno's, Red Robin, Taco Rosa, other: AAA, Barnes&Noble, Best Buy, Circuit City, CompUSA, Costco, Loehmann's, Lowe's Whse, Old Navy, Petsmart, Ralph's Foods, Rite Aid, Ross, Target

99 Culver Dr, **E**...gas: Shell/24hr, other: vet

97 Jeffrey Rd, **E**...gas: Arco, food: Baskin-Robbins, Daphne's Greek, Fatburger, Juice-it-Up, Quizno's, Starbucks, other: Albertson's, Kohl's, **W**...other: Ranch Mkt Foods

96 Sand Canyon Ave, Old Towne, **W**...gas: 76/Circle K, food: Denny's, Jack-in-the-Box, Knollwood Burgers, Tiajuana's Rest., lodging: La Quinta, other: HOSPITAL, Traveland USA RV Park, Irvine RV Ctr

95 CA 133, Laguna Fwy, N to Riverside, S Laguna Beach

94b Alton Pkwy, **E**...gas: Shell/Subway, food: Carl's Jr, Quizno's, Starbucks, Taco Bell, food: Homestead Suites, **W**...food: Cheesecake Factory, Corner Bakery, Dave&Buster's, Ling&Louie's, Panda Express, PF Chang's, Wahoo's, Yardhouse Grill, lodging: DoubleTree, other: Barnes&Noble, Macy's, Nordstroms, Target

94a I-405 N(from nb)

92b Bake Pkwy, same as 92a

92a Lake Forest Dr, Laguna Hills, **E**...gas: Chevron/24hr, Shell/dsl, food: Black Angus, Burger King, Del Taco, Jack-in-the-Box, McDonald's, Mimi's Café, Panera Bread, Pit BBQ, Pizza Hut, RoundTable Pizza, Subway, Taco Bell, The Hat, lodging: Best Western, other: America's Tire, Audi/Jeep, Chevrolet, Ford/Lincoln/Mercury, GMC/Kia, Honda, Isuzu, Jaguar, Mazda, Mercedes/Suzuki, PepBoys, Staples, Subaru, Toyota, VW, **W**...gas: Chevron/24hr, Shell, food: Carl's Jr, Coco's, Del Taco, McDonald's, Quizno's, lodging: Comfort Inn, Courtyard, Quality Suites, Travelodge, other: AZ Leather, Best Buy, BMW/Mini, Books Etc, JC Penney

91 El Toro Rd, **E**...gas: Chevron/dsl, Shell/dsl, USA, food: Arby's, Asia Buffet, Bakers Square, Carino's Italian, Carl's Jr, Coldstone Creamery, Denny's, Flamebroiler, Fuddrucker's, Jack-in-the-Box, Jamba Juice, Johnny Rockets, KFC, McDonald's, MegaBurger, Oeeshi Japanese, Quizno's, Red Lobster, Scarantino's Rest., Sizzler, Starbucks, Subway, Wendy's, other: CVS Drug, Home Depot, House of Fabrics, K-Mart, 99c Store, Office Depot, PetCo, Ralph's Foods, SavOn Drug, Staples, **W**...gas: Chevron/dsl/24hr, Shell/24hr, 76/Circle K, food: BJ's Rest., CA Pizza, Carrows, El Torito, In-n-Out, Island Burgers, Kings FishHouse, KooRooRoo Kitchen, LoneStar Steaks, Nami Seafood Buffet, Pizza Hut, other: HOSPITAL, Dalton's Books, Circuit City, Firestone/auto, JC Penney, Longs Drugs, Macy's, Marshall's, Sears/auto, Trader Joe's, Walgreens, USPO, mall

90 Alicia Pkwy, Mission Viejo, **E**...gas: Chevron/24hr, 76/dsl, food: Carl's Jr, Del Taco, Denny's, Little Caesar's, Subway, Wendy's, Winchell's, other: Albertson's, America's Tire, Buick/Pontiac/Mazda, CVS Drug, Mervyn's, Kragen Parts, Target, **W**...gas: Chevron, 76/dsl, food: Carl's Jr, It's a Grind, Manhattan Grill, Togo's, Wendy's, other: AAA, Big Lots, Buick/Pontiac, Mazda

89 La Paz Rd, Mission Viejo, **E**...gas: Arco/24hr, UltraMar, food: KFC/Pizza Hut, Starbucks, Taco Bell, other: Albertson's, **W**...gas: 76, food: Claim Jumper Rest., DQ, Hot Off the Grill, Jack-in-the-Box, Krispy Kreme, La Salsa, McDonald's, Outback Steaks, Quizno's, Spasso's Italian, Wienerschnitzel, Yamato Japanese, lodging: Holiday Inn, other: Best Buy, Borders Books&Café, CompUSA, Curves, Goodyear/auto, Jo-Ann Fabrics, Just Tires, PetCo, 7-11, to Laguna Niguel Pk

87 Oso Pkwy, Pacific Park Dr, **E**...gas: Chevron/repair, 76/repair, food: Carl's Jr, Starbucks, Subway, lodging: Fairfield Inn

86 Crown Valley Pkwy, **E**...gas: Arco, Chevron, 76, food: Coco's, El Torito, Islands Grill, Versachee Italian, other: HOSPITAL, Macy's, mall, vet, **W**...gas: Chevron/dsl, other: Aamco, Costco

85b Avery Pkwy, **E**...gas: Shell/dsl, food: Carrow's, Del Taco, Jack-in-the-Box, Mongolian BBQ, Quizno's, Starbucks, other: Acura, America's Tire/auto, Infiniti/Audi, Land Rover/Jaguar, Lexus, Parts+, Saab, World Mkt, **W**...gas: Mobil, Shell/dsl/24hr, food: A's Burgers, Carl's Jr, In-n-Out, lodging: Best Value Laguna Inn, other: Costco, Firestone/auto, GMC/Cadillac, Hyundai, Mercedes

85a CA 73 N (toll)

83 Junipero Serra Rd, to San Juan Capistrano, **W**...gas: Shell, Spirit/dsl

82 CA 74, Ortego Hwy, **E**...gas: Chevron/dsl, 76, food: Bravo Burgers, Denny's, lodging: Best Western, other: MEDICAL CARE, **W**...gas: Chevron/24hr, food: Arby's, Carl's Jr, Del Taco, Jack-in-the-Box, Marie Callender's, McDonald's, Sizzler, Subway, Taco Bell, Walnut Grove Rest., lodging: Mission Inn, other: Ralph's Foods, TruValue, San Juan Capistrano

81 Camino Capistrano, **E**...other: Peugeot/VW, **W**...gas: Chevron, food: Baskin-Robbins, Domino's, El Adobe Rest., Eng's Chinese, Harry's Rest., KFC, Pick-up-Stix, Pizza Hut, Ricardo's Mexican, Ruby's Cafe, Starbucks, other: Goodyear, Harley-Davidson, PetCo, Radio Shack, Rite Aid, San Juan Capistrano(1mi), SP

79 CA 1, Pacific Coast Hwy, Capistrano Bch, Capistrano, 1 mi **W**...gas: Arco/24hr, 76, food: A's Burgers, Cario's Mexican, Carl's Jr, Del Taco, Denny's, Jack-in-the-Box, JuiceStop, McDonald's, Subway, lodging: Dana Point Inn, DoubleTree, Harbor Inn, Holiday Inn Express, other: Chevrolet, Chrysler/Jeep, Honda, Nissan, Saturn, Toyota, USPO, vet

78 Camino de Estrella, San Clemente, **E**...gas: 76/dsl, food: Bakers Square, Carl's Jr, China Well, Coldstone Creamery, JuiceStop, Melting Pot, RoundTable Pizza, Rubio's Grill, Subway, Wahoo's Fish Taco, other: HOSPITAL, CVS Drug, Ralph's Foods, Stater Bros Foods, Trader Joe's, **W**...gas: Arco/dsl, food: Las Golondrienas, other: Big Lots, Kragen Parts, Sears Essentials

Mission Viejo — *Capistrano* — *San Juan Capistrano* — *San Clemente*

N ↑ ↓ S

Exit	Description
77	Ave Vista Hermosa, no services
76	Ave Pico, **E**...**gas:** Mobil, **food:** Buono Pizza, Carrow's, Golden Spoon, Juice it Up, McDonald's, **other:** Albertson's, GNC, **W**...**gas:** Chevron, Shell/dsl, **food:** BurgerStop, Del Taco, Denny's/24hr, Pick-up-Stix, Pizza Hut, Subway, Waffle Lady, **lodging:** Country Plaza Inn, **other:** Curves, 99c Store, Staples, Tuesday Morning, USPO, tires/repair
75	Ave Palizada, Ave Presidio, **W**...**gas:** Arco, Valero, **food:** Antoine's Café, Baskin-Robbins, Coffee Bean, KFC, Mr. Pete's Burgers, Ricardo's Mexican, Subway, Starbucks, **lodging:** Holiday Inn, **other:** Albertson's, Ford
74	El Camino Real, **E**...**gas:** Chevron/dsl/24hr, **food:** El Mariachi Rest., **lodging:** San Clemente Inn, Shorehouse Landing, same as 75, **W**...**gas:** Exxon, 76, **food:** FatBurger, KFC, LoveBurger, Pizza Hut/Taco Bell, Taste Of China, Tommy's Rest./24hr, **other:** Kragen Parts, Radio Shack, Ralph's Foods, 7-11
73	Ave Calafia, Ave Magdalena, **E**...**gas:** Chevron, 76, Shell, **food:** El Mariachi Rest., Jack-in-the-Box, Molly Bloom's Cafe, Pipes Cafe, Sugar Shack Cafe, **lodging:** Budget Inn, Calafia Beach Motel, C-Vu Inn, Hampton Inn, LaVista Inn, San Clemente Motel, Travelodge, **other:** San-O Tire, 7-11, **W**...to San Clemente SP
72	Cristianitos Ave, **E**...**food:** Carl's Jr., **lodging:** Comfort Suites, Carmelo Motel, **other:** San Mateo RV Park/dump, **W**...**other:** to San Clemente SP
71	Basilone Rd, **W**...**other:** San Onofre St Beach
67mm	weigh sta both lanes
66mm	viewpoint sb
62	Las Pulgas Rd, no services
59mm	**Aliso Creek rest area both lanes, full (handicapped) facilities, phone, vending, picnic tables, litter barrels, petwalk, RV dump**
54c	Oceanside Harbor Dr, **W**...**gas:** Chevron, Mobil, **food:** Burger King(1mi), Del Taco, Denny's/24hr, **lodging:** Comfort Inn, Sandman Hotel, Travelodge, The Bridge Motel, **other:** to Camp Pendleton
54b	Hill St(from sb), to Oceanside, **W**...**gas:** Mobil, **food:** Carrow's Rest., **lodging:** Comfort Inn
54a	Ca 76 E, Coast Hwy, no services
53	Mission Ave, Oceanside, **E**...**gas:** Arco/24hr, Mobil/dsl, 76/LP, **food:** Arby's, Armando's Tacos, Burger King, China Star, El Charrito Mexican, Jack-in-the-Box, KFC, McDonald's, Mission Donuts, Pizza Hut, **lodging:** Econolodge, Quality Inn, Ramada Ltd, **other:** CarQuest, NAPA, PepBoys, Valu+ Foods, **W**...**food:** Panda Express, Wendy's, **other:** 99c Store, Office Depot
52	Oceanside Blvd, **E**...**gas:** Arco, **food:** Alberto's Mexican, Cosina Italiana, Domino's, IHOP, McDonald's, Papa John's, Pizza Hut, Rosarita's Café, Starbucks, Subway, Taco Bell, Weinerschnitzel, **other:** Boney's Foods, CVS Drug, Longs Drug, Ralph's Food, Von's Food, CHP, **W**...**lodging:** Oceanside Inn
51c	Cassidy St(from sb), **W**...**gas:** Citgo/7-11, Mobil, 76, **other:** HOSPITAL
51b	CA 78, Vista Way, Escondido, **E**...**gas:** Chevron/dsl/24hr, 76, Shell, **food:** Applebee's, Boston Mkt, Burger King, Chili's, ChuckeCheese, Finnigan's Grill, Fuddrucker's, Golden Taipei, Hooters, Macaroni Grill, McDonald's, Mimi's Café, Olive Garden, QuikWok, Rubio's,

Oceanside (side label)

Exit	Description
	Spoon's Grill, Starbucks, Wendy's, West Buffet, **lodging:** Holiday Inn Express, **other:** Best Buy, CVS Drug, $Tree, JC Penney, Macy's, Marshall's, Mervyn's, Michael's, PetCo, Robinsons-May, Saturn, Sears/auto, Staples, Stater Bros Foods, Steinmart, Target, Tuesday Morning, Wal-Mart/auto, World Mkt, **W**...**food:** Hunter Steaks
51a	Las Flores Dr, no services
50	Elm Ave, Carlsbad Village Dr, **E**...**gas:** Shell/24hr, **food:** Lotus Thai Bistro, **W**...**gas:** Carlsbad/LP, Chevron/repair/24hr, 76, Valero, **food:** Al's Cafe, Carl's Jr, Denny's/24hr, Jack-in-the-Box, KFC/Taco Bell, Mikko Japanese, **lodging:** Motel 6, **other:** Albertson's
49	Tamarack Ave, **E**...**gas:** Chevron/24hr, Exxon/dsl, **food:** Village Kitchen, **lodging:** Carlsbad Lodge, Super 8, Travel Inn, **other:** GNC, Rite Aid, Von's Foods, **W**...**gas:** Arco, 76/repair/24hr
48	Cannon Rd, Car Country Carlsbad, **E**...**other:** Acura, Buick, Chevrolet/Cadillac, Ford, Honda, Isuzu, Lexus, Lincoln/Mercury, Mazda, Mercedes, Toyota, VW
47	Carlsbad Blvd, Palomar Airport Rd, **E**...**gas:** Chevron, Mobil/dsl, Citgo/7-11, **food:** Carl's Jr, Islands Burgers, Panda Express, Pat&Oscar's Rest., Subway, Strauss Brewery Rest., Taco Bell, TGIFriday, **lodging:** Holiday Inn, Motel 6, **other:** Costco, Flower Fields/Carlsbad Ranch, Ford, Jiffy Lube, outlet mall, **W**...**gas:** Shell/dsl, **food:** ClaimJumper Rest., In-n-Out, Marie Callender's, McDonald's, Sammy's Pizza, **lodging:** Hilton Garden, **other:** S Carlsbad St Bch
45	Poinsettia Lane, **W**...**gas:** Chevron, **food:** Benihana, El Pollo Loco, Golden Spoon, Jack-in-the-Box, Pick-Up Sticks, Starbucks, Subway, **lodging:** La Quinta, Motel 6, Quality Inn, Ramada, **other:** Ralph's Foods, Rite Aid, Volvo/Porsche
44	La Costa Ave, **E**...vista point, **W**...**gas:** Chevron/dsl
43	Leucadia Blvd, **E**...**lodging:** Howard Johnson, **W**...**gas:** Shell/service
41b	Encinitas Blvd, **E**...**gas:** Chevron, Exxon, O'Brien Sta., **food:** Coco's, Del Taco, Oggi's Pizza, **other:** Albertson's, CVS Drug, NAPA, to Quail Botanical Gardens, vet, **W**...**gas:** Shell, **food:** Denny's, Wendy's, **lodging:** Best Western/rest., Day's Inn, **other:** PetCo
41a	Santa Fe Dr, to Encinitas, **E**...**gas:** Shell, **food:** Carl's Jr, El Nopalito, Papa Tonie's Pizza, **other:** 7-11, **W**...**food:** Today's Pizza, **other:** HOSPITAL, Rite Aid, Von's Foods, vet
40	Birmingham Dr, **E**...**gas:** Chevron, Valero, **food:** Mandarin City, **lodging:** Comfort Inn, **W**...**gas:** Arco/24hr
39mm	viewpoint sb
39	Manchester Ave, **E**...**gas:** 76, **other:** to MiraCosta College
37	Lomas Santa Fe Dr, Solana Bch, **E**...**food:** Baskin-Robbins, Pizza Nova, Samurai Rest., **other:** Ross, Von's Foods, We-R-Fabrics, **W**...**gas:** Arco, Mobil, **food:** Carl's Jr, Denny's, Jamba Juice, Panda Express, Panera Bread, RoundTable Pizza, Starbucks, Togo's, **other:** CVS Drug, Discount Tire, Henry's Foods, Marshall's, Staples
36	Via de La Valle, Del Mar, **E**...**gas:** Chevron, Mobil, **food:** Aliya Bistro, Burger King, Chevy's Mexican, Coffee Bean, McDonald's, Milton's Deli, Paradise Grill, Pasta Pronto, Papachino's Italian, Silver Skillet, Taste of Thai, **other:** Albertson's/SavOn, PetCo, Radio Shack, **W**...**gas:** Arco/24hr, Shell/dsl, **food:** Denny's, FishMkt Rest., Red Tracton's Rest., **lodging:** Hilton, **other:** racetrack

Carlsbad (side label)
Encinitas (side label)

Interstate 5

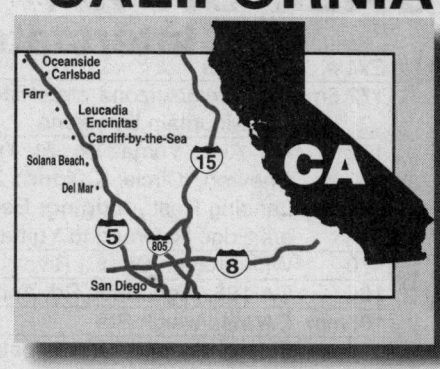

N↕S		
34	Del Mar Heights Rd, **E**...**gas:** Shell/dsl, **W**...**gas:** 7-11, **food:** Elijah's Rest., Jack-in-the-Box, Mexican Grill, **other:** Longs Drug, Von's Foods
33	Carmel Mtn Rd, **E**...**gas:** Arco, Shell/repair, **food:** Taco Bell, Tio Leo's Mexican, **lodging:** DoubleTree Hotel, Hampton Inn, Marriott
32	CA 56 E, Carmel Valley Rd, no services
31	I-805(from sb), no services
29	Genesee Ave, **E**...**other:** HOSPITAL
28b	La Jolla Village Dr, **E**...**food:** Italian Bistro, **lodging:** Embassy Suites, Hyatt, Marriott, **other:** HOSPITAL, to LDS Temple, **W**...**gas:** Mobil/dsl, **food:** BJ's Grill, CA Pizza, Coldstone Creamery, Domino's, Elijah's Deli, El Torito, Flame Broiler, Islands Burgers, RockBottom Café, Rubio's Grill, TGIFriday, Trader Joe's, **lodging:** Sheraton, **other:** HOSPITAL, CVS Drug, Marshall's, Petsmart, Radio Shack, Ralph's Foods, Ross, Whole Foods
28a	Nobel Dr(from nb), **E**...**lodging:** Hyatt, **other:** LDS Temple, **W**...same as 28b
27	Gilman Dr, La Jolla Colony Dr, no services
26b	CA 52 E, Ardath Rd(from nb), no services
26a	Ardath Rd(from nb), no services
23b	CA 274, Balboa Ave, **1 mi E**...**gas:** Shell, **food:** Del Taco, **other:** Albertson's, **W**...**gas:** Mobil, 76/repair, 7-11, **food:** McDonald's, In-n-Out, Rubio's Grill, Wienerschnitzel, **lodging:** Days Inn, Holiday Inn Express, Mission Bay Inn, San Diego Motel, **other:** HOSPITAL, Discount Tire, Express Tire, Ford, Nissan, Toyota, Mission Bay Pk
23a	Grand Ave, Garnet Ave, **W**...**other:** Cadillac
22	Clairemont Dr, Mission Bay Dr, **E**...**gas:** Arco, Shell, **food:** Carl's Jr, HomeTown Buffet, Jack-in-the-Box, KFC, McDonald's, Subway, **lodging:** Best Western, **other:** Chevrolet/VW, Rite Aid, **W**...to Sea World Dr
21	Sea World Dr, Tecolote Dr, **E**...**gas:** Shell, **lodging:** Seaside Motel, **other:** Circle K, Firestone, PetCo, **W**... **lodging:** Hilton, **other:** Old Town SP, Seaworld
20	I-8, W to Nimitz Blvd, E to El Centro, CA 209 S(from sb), to Rosecrans St
19	Old Town Ave, **E**...**gas:** Arco/24hr, Shell, **lodging:** Courtyard, La Quinta
18b	Washington St, **E**...**lodging:** Comfort Inn
18a	Pacific Hwy Viaduct, Kettner St, no services
17b	India St, Front St, Sassafras St, **E**...**gas:** Mobil, Rte 66 Gas, **W**...**other:** airport, civic ctr
17a	Hawthorn St, Front St, **W**...**gas:** Exxon/dsl, **lodging:** Holiday Inn, Motel 6, Radisson, **other:** HOSPITAL
16b	6th Ave, downtown, no services
16a	CA 163 N, 10th St, **E**...**other:** AeroSpace Museum, **W**...**gas:** Shell, **food:** Del Taco, Jack-in-the-Box, Mc-Donald's, **lodging:** Days Inn, Downtown Lodge, El Cortez Motel, Holiday Inn, Marriott, **other:** HOSPITAL
15c b	CA 94 E(from nb), Pershing Dr, B St, civic ctr
15a	CA 94 E, J St, Imperial Ave(from sb),, no services
14b	Cesar Chavez Pkwy, no services
14a	CA 75, to Coronado, **W**...toll rd to Coronado
13b	National Ave SD, 28th St, **E**...**food:** Little Caesar's, Starbucks, Subway, **other:** AutoZone, **W**...**gas:** Shell, **food:** Burger King, Del Taco, El Pollo Loco
13a	CA 15 N, to Riverside
12	Main St, National City, no services
11b	8th St, National City, **E**...**gas:** Arco, Shell/24hr, **food:** Jack-in-the-Box, **lodging:** Holiday Inn, Howard Johnson, Ramada Inn, Super 8, Value Inn, **W**...**gas:** Chevron/dsl
11a	Harbor Dr, Civic Center Dr, no services
10	Bay Marina, 24th St, Mile of Cars Way, **1/2 mi E**...**food:** Denny's, In-n-Out
9	CA 54 E, no services
8b	E St, Chula Vista, **E**...**lodging:** Motel 6, **W**...**food:** Anthony's Fish Grotto, **lodging:** GoodNite Inn
8a	H St, no services
7b	J St(from sb), no services
7a	L St, **E**...**gas:** 7-11, 76, Shell/dsl, **food:** Mandarin Chinese, **lodging:** Best Western, **other:** AutoZone, NAPA, Parts+, Office Depot
6	Palomar St, **E**...**gas:** Arco, **food:** China King, Del Taco, DQ, HomeTown Buffet, KFC, Little Caesar, McDonald's, Subway, **lodging:** Palomar Inn, **other:** Food4Less, Office Depot, 7-11, **E on Broadway**...**food:** Jack-in-the-Box, KFC, Panda Express, Quizno's, Yoshinoya, **other:** Costco/gas, Michael's, Ross, Target, Wal-Mart
5b	Main St, to Imperial Beach, **E**...**gas:** Arco, **food:** AZ Chinese
5a	CA 75(from sb), Palm Ave, to Imperial Beach, **E**...**gas:** Arco, **food:** Armando's Mexican, Papa John's, Wahshing Chinese, **other:** Discount Tire, 7-11, Soto's Transmissions, **W**...**gas:** Arco, 7-11, Shell/repair/24hr, Thrifty, **food:** Boll Weevil Diner, Burger King, Carl's Jr, Carrow's, Coldstone Creamery, El Chile Mexican, Los Pancho's Tacos, McDonald's, Rally's, Red Hawk Steaks, Roberto's Mexican, Subway, Taco Bell, Wienerschnitzel, **lodging:** Super 8, Travelodge, **other:** AutoZone, CVS Drug, Home Depot, Jiffy Lube, Mervyn's, 99c Store, Von's Foods
4	Coronado Ave(from sb), **E**...**gas:** Chevron/service, Shell/service, **food:** Denny's, Taco Bell, **lodging:** EZ 8 Motel, **other:** 7-11, **W**...**gas:** Shell/dsl, **lodging:** Day's Inn, **other:** to Border Field SP
3	CA 905, Tocayo Ave, **W**...**gas:** 7-11
2	Dairy Mart Rd, **E**...**gas:** Arco/24hr, Circle K, **food:** Burger King, Carl's Jr, Coco's, KFC, McDonald's, Roberto's Mexican, **lodging:** Americana Inn, Best Value, Super 8, Valli-Hi Motel, **other:** CarQuest, Radio Shack, Pacifica RV Resort
1b	Via de San Ysidro, **E**...**gas:** Chevron, Exxon, Mobil, 76, **other:** Max's Foods, NAPA, **W**...**gas:** Chevron, **food:** Denny's, KFC, **lodging:** Economy Inn, Knights/RV park, Motel 6
1a	I-805 N(from nb), Camino de la Plaza(from sb), **E**...**food:** Burger King, El Pollo Loco, Jack-in-the-Box, KFC, McDonald's, Subway, **lodging:** Flamingo Motel, Gateway Inn, Holiday Motel, Travelodge, **other:** AutoZone, **W**...**food:** Achiato Mexican, Gingling House Chinese, IHOP, Iron Wok, McDonald's, Pizza Hut/Taco Bell, Sunrise Buffet, **other:** Baja Duty-Free, K-Mart, Ross, Marshall's, factory outlet, border parking
0	US/Mexico Border, California state line, customs, I-5 begins/ends

San Diego Area

CALIFORNIA
Interstate 8

Exit #	Services
172.5mm	California/Arizona state line, Colorado River, Pacific/Mountain time zone
172	4th Ave, Yuma, **N**...Ft Yuma Casino, **S**...gas: Chevron, Circle K, **food**: Jack-in-the-Box, Yuma Landing Rest., **lodging**: Best Western, **other**: Rivers Edge RV Park, to Yuma SP
170	Winterhaven Dr, **S**...Rivers Edge RV Park
166	CA 186, Algodones Rd, Andrade, **S**...to Mexico
165mm	CA Insp/weigh Sta
164	Sidewinder Rd, **N**...st patrol, **S**...gas: Shell/LP, **other**: Pilot Knob RV Park
159	CA 34, Ogilby Rd, to Blythe, no services
156	Grays Well Rd, **N**...Imperial Dunes RA
155mm	**rest area both lanes(exits left), portapotties, picnic tables, litter barrels, petwalk**
151	Gordons Well, no services
146	Brock Research Ctr Rd, no services
143	CA 98, to Calexico, Midway Well, no services
131	CA 115, VanDerLinden Rd, to Holtville, **5 mi N**...gas, food, lodging, RV camping
128	Bonds Corner Rd, no services
125	Orchard Rd, Holtville, **4 mi N**...gas/dsl, food
120	Bowker Rd, no services
118b a	CA 111, to Calexico, **1 mi N**...gas: Shell/dsl/café/scales, **other**: RV park, tires/truckwash
116	Dogwood Rd, **S**...food: Arby's, Carino's, Chili's, ChuckeCheese, Denny's, Famous Dave's BBQ, Jack-in-the-Box, Starbucks, Taco Bell, **lodging**: Fairfield Inn, **other**: Best Buy, Dillard's, JC Penney, Macy's, Marshall's, Old Navy, Ross, Sears/auto, Staples, mall
115	CA 86, 4th St, El Centro, **N**...gas: Arco/24hr, Chevron, Citgo/7-11/dsl, Shell/dsl, **food**: Carl's Jr, China Express, Exotic Thai, Jack-in-the-Box, Mexicali Taco, McDonald's, **lodging**: Holiday Inn Express, Motel 6, **other**: El Sol Foods, Firestone/auto, Goodyear/auto, Ford/Lincoln/Mercury, U-Haul, radiators, **S**...gas: On the Go/Subway, **food**: Dudley's, IHOP, In-n-Out, Millie's Kitchen, Taco Bell, **lodging**: Best Western, Comfort Inn, Rodeway Inn, **other**: AutoZone, Buick/Cadillac/Pontiac, Chevrolet, Chrysler/Dodge/Jeep, Home Depot, Honda, Lucky Foods, Desert Trails RV Park
114	Imperial Ave, El Centro, **N**...gas: Chevron/service, Citgo/7-11/dsl, Shell, USA/dsl, **food**: Del Taco, Denny's, Domino's, KFC, McDonald's, Pizza Hut, Scribble's Rest, TasteeFreez Burgers, **lodging**: Howard Johnson, Laguna Inn, Ramada Inn, Vacation Inn/RV Park, **other**: MEDICAL CARE, Kragen Parts, st patrol, **1-3 mi N**...gas: Arco/24hr, **food**: Applebee's, Burger King, Carl's Jr, Carrow's, Church's, Domino's, El Pollo Loco, Farmer Boys, Golden Corral, Jack-in-the-Box, Little Caesars, Papa John's, Pizza Hut, Popeye's, Quizno's, Rally's, Sizzler, Sonic, Starbucks, Subway, Taco Bell, Wendy's, **lodging**: Day's Inn, Super Star Inn, **other**: Aamco, America's Tire, BigLots, Costco/gas, Food4Less, Goodyear/auto, K-Mart, Kragen Parts, Lowe's Whse, Mervyn's, PepBoys, Rite Aid, Sears/auto, Staples, Target, Toyota, Von's Foods, Walgreens, Wal-Mart SuperCtr Winston Tire

Exit #	Services
111	Forrester Rd, to Westmorland, no services
108mm	**Sunbeam Rest Area both lanes, full(handicapped) facilities, phone, picnic tables, litter barrels, petwalk, RV dump**
107	Drew Rd, Seeley, **N**...Sunbeam RV Park, **S**...Rio Bend RV Park
101	Dunaway Rd, Imperial Valley, elev 0 ft, **N**...st prison
89	Imperial Hwy, CA 98, Ocotillo, **N**...food: Old Hwy Cafe, USPO, **S**...gas: Texaco/dsl, **food**: Desert Kitchen, **other**: auto repair, RV camping, museum
87	CA 98(from eb), to Calexico, no services
81mm	runaway truck ramp, eb
80	Mountain Springs Rd, no services
77	**N**...phone, towing
75mm	brake insp area eb, phone
73	Jacumba, **S**...gas: Shell/Subway/dsl/towing/24hr, Valero/dsl, **other**: RV camping
65	CA 94, Boulevard, to Campo, **S**...gas: MtnTop/dsl, **food**: Salsa Linda, **lodging**: Lux Inn, **other**: auto repair, to McCain Valley RA
63mm	Tecate Divide, elev 4140 ft
62mm	Crestwood Summit, elev 4190 ft
61	Crestwood Rd, Live Oak Springs, **S**...gas: Golden Acorn Trkstp/casino/dsl, **food**: Country Broiler Rest., **lodging**: Live Oak Sprs Country Inn, **other**: Outdoor World RV Camp, info
54	Kitchen Creek Rd, Cameron Station, **S**...food, RV camping
51	rd 1, Buckman Spgs Rd, to Lake Morena, **S**...gas/dsl/LP, food, lodging, RV camping, Lake Morena CP(7mi), Potrero CP(19mi), **rest area both lanes, full(handicapped)facilities, phone, picnic tables, litter barrels, petwalk, RV dump**
48	inp sta, wb
47	rd 1, Sunrise Hwy, Laguna Summit, elev 4055 ft, **N**...to Laguna Mtn RA
45	Pine Valley, Julian, **N**...food: Frosty Burger, Major's Diner, El Rancho Grande Diner, **lodging**: Pine Valley Inn, **other**: Curves, Mtn SuperMkt, to Cuyamaca Rancho SP, vet
44mm	Pine Valley Creek
42mm	elev 4000 ft
40	CA 79, Japatul Rd, Descanso, **N**...food: Descanso Rest., **other**: to Cuyamaca Rancho SP
37mm	vista point eb, elev 3000 ft
36	E Willows, **N**...Alpine Sprs RV Park, Viejas Indian Res, casino
33	W Willows Rd, to Alpine, **N**...Alpine Sprs RV Park, Viejas Outlets/famous brands, casino, same as 36, **S**...ranger sta
31mm	elev 2000 ft
30	Tavern Rd, to Alpine, **N**...gas: Chevron/dsl, Valero, **S**...gas: 76/Circle K, Shell, **food**: Breadbasket Rest., Carl's Jr, China Flavor, La Carreta Mexican, Mediterranean Grill, Subway, **lodging**: Ayer's Inn, **other**: MEDICAL CARE, Alpine Mkt Foods, Radio Shack, Rite Aid, TrueValue, city park
27	Dunbar Lane, Harbison Canyon, **N**...other: RV camping, Flinn Sprgs CP
25mm	elev 1000 ft
24mm	no services, phone

Interstate 8

E ↕ **W**

23	Lake Jennings Pk Rd, Lakeside, **N...gas:** Arco/Jack-in-the-Box/dsl/24hr, to Lake Jennings CP, **other:** RV camping, **S...gas:** 7-11, **food:** Burger King, Karla's Mexican, Marechiaro's Pizza
22	Los Coches Rd, Lakeside, **N...gas:** Eagle/dsl/LP, 7-11, Valero, **food:** Laposta Mexican, Las Cazuela's, Pizza Pan, **other:** RV camping/dump, **S...gas:** Shell/dsl, **food:** Denny's, Giant Pizza, McDonald's, Panda Express, Subway, Taco Bell, **other:** Radio Shack, Von's Foods, Wal-Mart/auto
20b	Greenfield Dr, to Crest, **N...gas:** Chevron/dsl, Exxon/dsl/24hr, **food:** Jack-in-the-Box, Janet's Café, McDonald's, Panchos Taco, **other:** HOSPITAL, Albertson's, Curves, Ford, 99c Store, RV camping, 7-11, auto repair, st patrol, **S...gas:** Mobil/LP
20a	E Main St(from wb, no EZ return), **N...lodging:** Embasadora Motel, Fabulous 7 Motel, HP Inn, **other:** Ford, Vactioner RV Park, **S...gas:** Arco, **other:** Cadillac
19	2nd St, CA 54, El Cajon, **N...gas:** Arco/24hr, Chevron, Exxon/dsl, **food:** Mariachio's Pizza, Rosanna Grilled Panini, **other:** CVS Drug, Parts+, Von's Foods, **S...gas:** 76, Gas Depot, Shell, **food:** A&W/KFC, Arby's, Boll Weevil Rest., Burger King, Carl's Jr, DQ, Estrada's Mexican, IHOP, Jack-in-the-Box, KFC, McDonald's, Pizza Hut, Subway, Taco Bell, Taco Shop/24hr, Tyler's Rest., **other:** Firestone/auto, Jiffy Lube, PetCo, Ralph's Foods, Radio Shack, Rite Aid, Walgreens
18	Mollison Ave, El Cajon, **N...gas:** Chevron, **food:** Denny's, **lodging:** Best Western, Days Inn, **S...gas:** Arco/24hr, KwikTrip/dsl, **food:** Taco Bell, **lodging:** Super 8, Valley Motel
17c	Magnolia Ave, CA 67(from wb), to Santee, **N...food:** Del Taco, Jack-in-the-Box, LJ Silver, Panda Express, **other:** Arco, Food4Less, Target, mall, **S...gas:** Shell/service, **food:** Red Brick Pizza, Wienerschnitzel, **lodging:** Motel 6, Northgate Motel, Rodeway Inn, **other:** Nudo's Drug
17b	CA 67(from eb), same as 17 a&c
17a	Johnson Ave(from eb), **N...food:** Applebee's, Boston Mkt, Burger King, Jamba Juice, KFC, LJ Silver, On the Border, Rubio's, Sizzler, Subway, **other:** Albertson's, Best Buy, Border's Books, Chevrolet, $Tree, Home Depot, Honda, JC Penney, K-Mart, Long Drug, Macy's, Marshall's, Mervyn's, Michael's, Office Depot, Petsmart, Rite Aid, Sears/auto, Wal-Mart, mall, **S...other:** Aamco, Isuzu, Saturn
16	Main St, **N...gas:** Arco/24hr, **food:** Denny's/24hr, 7-11, Sombrero Mexican, **lodging:** Relax Inn, **S...gas:** 76/RV Dump, Chevron, **other:** Nissan, brakes/transmissions
15	El Cajon Blvd(from eb), **N...lodging:** Quality Inn, **S...gas:** Mobil/dsl, Shell, **food:** BBQ, **other:** Chrysler
14c	Severin Dr, Fuerte Dr(from wb), **N...gas:** Arco/24hr, Mobil, **food:** Anthony's Fish Rest., Charcoal House Rest., La Casa Blanca, **lodging:** Holiday Inn Express, **S...food:** Brigantine Seafood Rest.
14b a	CA 125, to CA 94, no services

13b	Jackson Dr, Grossmont Blvd, **N...gas:** Chevron, **food:** Arby's, BJ's Grill, Casa de Pico, Chili's, ClaimJumper, Fuddrucker's, Jamba Juice, McDonald's, Panda Express, Panera Bread, Red Lobster, Rubio's, **other:** Barnes&Noble, Chrysler/Jeep/Dodge, Dodge, Kragen Parts, Long's Drug, Macy's, 7-11, Staples, Target, Wal-Mart, mall, **S...food:** Honeybaked Ham, Jack-in-the-Box, **other:** Circuit City, Discount Tire, Firestone/auto, Ford, Hyundai, Ralph's Foods, Ross, VW
13a	Spring St(from eb), El Cajon Blvd(from wb), **N...other:** Dodge/Kia, Jeep, **S...food:** La Salsa Mexican, **lodging:** La Mesa Lodge, **other:** 99c Store
12	Fletcher Pkwy, to La Mesa, **N...gas:** Shell, **food:** Baker's Square, Carl's Jr., Chipotle Mexican, McDonald's, **lodging:** EZ 8 Motel, Holiday Inn, **other:** Costco, 7-11, **S...food:** La Salsa Mexican, **lodging:** Motel 6, **other:** Chevrolet, San Diego RV Resort
11	70th St, Lake Murray Blvd, **N...gas:** Shell, **food:** Subway, **other:** truck/RV repair, **S...gas:** Shell/dsl/repair, **food:** Aiken's Deli, Denny's, Marie Callender's, **other:** HOSPITAL
10	College Ave, **N...gas:** Chevron/dsl, **other:** Windmill Farms Mkt, **S...other:** HOSPITAL, to San Diego St U
9	Waring Rd, **N...food:** Nicolosi's Italian, **lodging:** Days Inn, Quality Inn
8	Fairmont Ave(7 from eb), to Mission Gorge Rd, **N...gas:** Arco/24hr, Mobil/dsl, Valero/dsl, **food:** Arby's, Burger King, Carl's Jr, Chili's, El Pollo Loco, Jack-in-the-Box, El Pollo Loco, KFC, McDonald's, Rally's, Starbucks, Subway, Szechuan Chinese, **lodging:** Super 8, **other:** HOSPITAL, Aamco, Discount Tire, Home Depot, Honda, Longs Drugs, NAPA, Radio Shack, Rite Aid, Toyota, Tuesday Morning, Von's Foods
7b a	I-15 N, CA 15 S, to 40th St
6b	I-805, N to LA, S to Chula Vista
6a	Texas St, Qualcomm Way, **N...food:** Dave&Buster's, same as 5
5	Mission Ctr Rd, **N...gas:** Chevron, **food:** Bennigan's, Chevy's Mexican, Fuddrucker's, Hooters, In-n-Out, King's Fishouse, Mimi's Cafe, On The Border, Outback Steaks, Pick-Up Sticks, Taco Bell, **lodging:** Marriott, **other:** Best Buy, Borders Books&Café, Chevrolet, Ford, Lincoln/Mercury, Macy's, Marshall's, Michael's, Nordstrom Rack, Old Navy, Macy's, Staples, Target, mall, **S...gas:** Arco/24hr, **food:** Benihana, Denny's, El Torito, Fugi Japanese Steaks, Todai Rest., Wendy's, **lodging:** Comfort Inn, Hilton, La Quinta, Radisson, Ramada Ltd, Red Lion Inn, Sheraton, **other:** Chrysler, Dodge, GMC/Pontiac, Hummer, Mazda, Subaru

CALIFORNIA
Interstate 8

<table>
<tr><td>E</td><td>4c b</td><td>CA 163, Cabrillo Frwy, S...to downtown, zoo</td></tr>
<tr><td></td><td>4a</td><td>Hotel Circle Dr(from eb), CA 163 (from wb)</td></tr>
<tr><td></td><td>3a</td><td>Hotel Circle, Taylor St, N...gas: Chevron, food: DW Ranch Rest., Hunter Steaks, Kelly's Steaks, lodging: Comfort Suites, Crowne Plaza, Handlery Hotel, Motel 6, Town&Country Motel, other: AAA, cinema, golf, S...gas: Chevron, food: Adam's Cafe, Albie's Rest., Ricky's Rest., Tickled Trout, Valley Kitchen, lodging: Best Western, Comfort Inn, Days Inn, DoubleTree Inn, Extended Stay America, Hawthorn Suites, Hilton, Holiday Inn, Howard Johnson, King's Inn/rest., Mission Valley Hotel, Quality Resort, Ramada Inn, Residence Inn, Super 8, Travelodge, Vagabond Inn</td></tr>
<tr><td></td><td>2c</td><td>Morena Blvd(from wb), no services</td></tr>
<tr><td></td><td>2b</td><td>I-5, N to LA, S to San Diego</td></tr>
<tr><td></td><td>2a</td><td>Rosecrans St(from wb), CA 209, S...gas: Chevron, food: Burger King, Del Taco, In-n-Out, McDonald's, Perry's Café, Rally's, lodging: Best Western, Day's Inn, Holiday Inn, Howard Johnson, Quality Inn, Super 8, other: Chrysler/Jeep, Circuit City, Goodyear/auto, House of Fabrics, Staples, SaveOn Drug</td></tr>
<tr><td></td><td>1</td><td>W Mission Bay Blvd, Sports Arena Blvd(from wb), N...to SeaWorld, S...gas: Arco, food: Arby's, Denny's, Jack-in-the-Box, McDonald's, Souplantation, Taco Shop, Wendy's, lodging: Holiday Inn Express, Premier Inn, other: Curves, Home Depot, U-Haul</td></tr>
<tr><td></td><td>0mm</td><td>I-8 begins/ends on Sunset Cliffs Blvd, N...Mission Bay Park, 1/4 mi W...gas: Exxon, Shell, food: Jack-in-the-Box, Kaiserhof Cafe</td></tr>
</table>

E ↕ W — San Diego Area

Interstate 10

<table>
<tr><td>Exit #</td><td>Services</td></tr>
<tr><td>245mm</td><td>California/Arizona state line, Colorado River, Pacific/Mountain time zone</td></tr>
<tr><td>244mm</td><td>inspection sta wb</td></tr>
<tr><td>243</td><td>Riviera Dr, S...other: Riviera RV Camp</td></tr>
<tr><td>241</td><td>US 95, Intake Blvd, Blythe, N...gas: Mobil/dsl, food: Lalo's Mexican, Steaks'n Cakes Rest., Sunset Grille, lodging: Best Western, Days Inn, Desert Winds Motel, Travelers Inn Express, other: Burton's RV Park, auto/RV repair/24hr, to Needles, S...McIntyre Park</td></tr>
<tr><td>240</td><td>7th St, N...gas: Chevron/service, EZ Mart, food: Blimpie, Foster's Freeze, Starbucks, lodging: Astro Motel, Blue Line Motel, Blythe Inn, Budget Inn, Comfort Suites, Dunes Motel, other: Albertson's, AutoZone, Chrysler/Dodge/Jeep, Ford, Rite Aid, RV repair/LP</td></tr>
<tr><td>239</td><td>Lovekin Blvd, Blythe, N...gas: Mobil/Subs/dsl, Shell/Quizno's, food: Carl's Jr, Del Taco, Domino's, El Ranchito Mexican, Jack-in-the-Box, La Casita Dos Mexican, McDonald's, Pizza Hut, Popeye's, Sizzler, Starbucks, lodging: Best Value Inn, Best Western, Budget Host, Hampton Inn, Regency Inn, other: HOSPITAL, Ace Hardware, Big K Mart, CarQuest, Checker Parts, $Tree, Goodyear/auto, Radio Shack, S...gas: Arco/dsl/24hr, Chevron/dsl/24hr, 76/dsl, Shell/DQ/dsl, Valero, food: Burger King, Denny's, KFC, Taco Bell, lodging: Holiday Inn Express, Motel 6, Super 8, other: Chevrolet/Pontiac/Buick/Cadillac, city park/RV dump</td></tr>
</table>

E ↕ W — Blythe

<table>
<tr><td>236</td><td>CA 78, Neighbours Blvd, to Ripley, N...gas: Valero/service, S...to Cibola NWR</td></tr>
<tr><td>232</td><td>Mesa Dr, N...gas: 76/dsl/rest./24hr/@ , Valero/dsl</td></tr>
<tr><td>231</td><td>weigh sta wb</td></tr>
<tr><td>222mm</td><td>Wileys Well Rd, N...rest area both lanes, full (handicapped) facilities, phone, picnic tables, litter barrels, petwalk, S...to st prison</td></tr>
<tr><td>217</td><td>Ford Dry Lake Rd, no services</td></tr>
<tr><td>201</td><td>Corn Springs Rd, no services</td></tr>
<tr><td>192</td><td>CA 177, Rice Rd, to Lake Tamarisk, N...gas: gas/repair/24hr, food: Desert Ctr Cafe, other: camping</td></tr>
<tr><td>189</td><td>Eagle Mtn Rd, no services</td></tr>
<tr><td>182</td><td>Red Cloud Rd, no services</td></tr>
<tr><td>177</td><td>Hayfield Rd, no services</td></tr>
<tr><td>173</td><td>Chiriaco Summit, N...gas: Chevron/Foster's Freez/dsl/24hr, food: Chiriaco Rest., other: Patton Museum, truck/tire repair</td></tr>
<tr><td>168</td><td>to Twentynine Palms, to Mecca, Joshua Tree NM</td></tr>
<tr><td>162</td><td>frontage rd, no services</td></tr>
<tr><td>159mm</td><td>Cactus City Rest Area both lanes, full(handicapped) facilities, picnic tables, litter barrels, petwalk</td></tr>
<tr><td>147mm</td><td>0 ft elevation</td></tr>
<tr><td>146</td><td>Dillon Rd, to CA 86, to CA 111 S, Coachella, N...gas: Chevron/24hr, Loves/Carl's Jr/dsl/24hr/@ , S...gas: TA/Arby's/Arco/Taco Bell/dsl/24hr/@ , Shell/Jack-in-the-Box, other: Spotlight Casino</td></tr>
<tr><td>145</td><td>(from eb), CA 86 S, no services</td></tr>
<tr><td>144</td><td>CA 111 N, CA 86 S, Indio, N...food: Nuevo Paraiso Rest., lodging: Holiday Inn Express, other: Classic RV Park, Fantasy Sprgs Casino/Hotel/Cafe</td></tr>
<tr><td>143</td><td>Jackson St, Indio, N...RV Park, S...Circle K</td></tr>
<tr><td>142</td><td>Monroe St, Central Indio, N...other: RV camping, S...gas: Circle K, 76, Shell/dsl/LP, food: Marisco's Mexican, Mexicali Cafe, lodging: Quality Inn</td></tr>
<tr><td>139</td><td>Jefferson St, Indio Blvd, N...other: Shadow Hills RV Resort, hwy patrol</td></tr>
<tr><td>137</td><td>Washington St, Country Club Dr, to Indian Wells, N...gas: Arco/24hr, Chevron, food: Burger King, Burger Time, Coco's, Del Taco, Mario's Italian, Starbucks, lodging: Comfort Suites, Motel 6, other: Buick/Pontiac/GMC, Ford/Lincoln/Mercury, Giant RV Ctr, Honda, Toyota/Scion, Rite Aid, Stater Bro's, Walgreens, S...gas: Mobil/dsl, 76/Circle K, food: Carl's Jr, China Wok, La Tacita Mexican, Lili's Chinese, Pizza Hut, Quizno's, Subway, Togo's, Wendy's, lodging: Embassy Suites, other: Goodyear/auto</td></tr>
<tr><td>134</td><td>Cook St, to Indian Wells, S...gas: Arco, Mobil, food: Applebees, Jack-in-the-Box, Starbucks, lodging: Courtyard, Hampton Inn, Hilton/Homewood Suites, Residence Inn</td></tr>
<tr><td>131</td><td>Monterey Ave, Thousand Palms, N...gas: Arco/24hr, food: Jack-in-the-Box, S...food: Del Taco, El Pollo Loco, IHOP, McDonald's, Panda Express, Quizno's, Starbucks, Subway, Taco Bell, other: America's Tire, Costco/gas, Home Depot, Petsmart, Sam's Club/gas, Wal-Mart SuperCtr</td></tr>
<tr><td>130</td><td>Ramon Rd, Bob Hope Dr, N...gas: Chevron/24hr, ⚹/Flying J/dsl/LP/rest./24hr, Mobil/dsl, Valero, food: Carl's Jr, Casa de Pasta, Del Taco, Denny's, Guerro Mexican, In-n-Out, McDonald's, lodging: Red Roof</td></tr>
</table>

Indio — Palm Sprgs

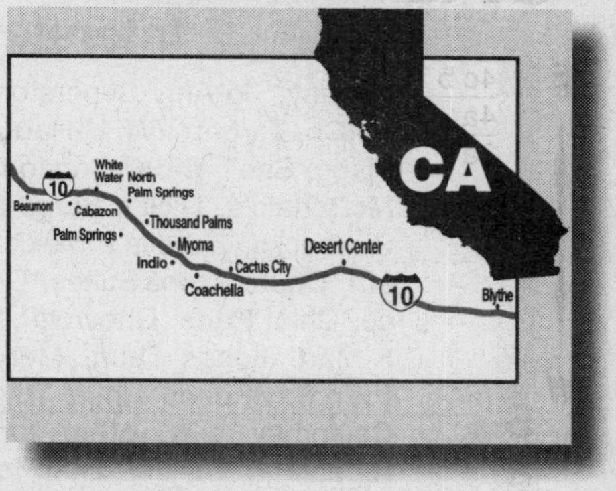

E ↕ W

Inn, **other:** truckwash, [S]...**food:** Sage Grill, Steak House, **other:** HOSPITAL, Agua Caliente Casino/ rest.

126 Date Palm Dr, Rancho Mirage, [S]...**gas:** Arco/24hr, Mobil, Valero, **food:** Domino's

123 Gene Autry Tr, Palm Dr, to Desert Hot Sprgs, [N]...**gas:** Arco, Chevron/Jack-in-the-Box, **other:** Caliente Springs Camping, **3 mi** [S]...to Gene Autry Trail

120 Indian Ave, to N Palm Sprgs, [N]...**gas:** 76/Circle K, Shell, **food:** Denny's, **lodging:** Motel 6, [S]...**gas:** Chevron, Pilot/DQ/Wendy's/dsl/24hr, **food:** Jack-in-the-Box, **other:** HOSPITAL, Bud's Tire

117 CA 62, to Yucca Valley, Twentynine Palms, to Joshua Tree NM, no services

114 Whitewater, many windmills

113mm rest area both lanes, full(handicapped)facilities, phone, picnic tables, litter barrels

112 CA 111(from eb), to Palm Springs

110 Hugeen-Lehmann, no services

106 Main St, to Cabazon, [N]...**gas:** Shell/dsl, **food:** Burger King, Spanky's BBQ, Wheel Inn Rest., [S]...**gas:** Arco/ dsl/24hr

104 Cabazon, same as 103

103 Fields Rd, [N]...**gas:** Chevron, TC/A&W/dsl, **food:** McDonald's, Ruby's Diner, **other:** Hadley Fruit Orchards, Premium Outlets/famous brands, Morongo Reservation/casino

102.5mm Banning weigh sta both lanes

102 Ramsey St(from wb), no services

101 Hargrave St, Banning, [N]...**gas:** 76/Church's, Shell/ dsl/LP, Valero, **lodging:** Country Inn, **other:** tires

100 CA 243, 8th St, Banning, [N]...**gas:** Chevron, **food:** Ahloo Chinese, IHOP, Jack-in-the-Box, **other:** Rite Aid, [S]...**other:** RV camping

99 22nd St, to Ramsey St, [N]...**gas:** Arco/24hr, Shell, **food:** Carl's Jr, Carrow's, Chelo's Tacos, Del Taco, KFC, McDonald's, Pepe's Mexican, Pizza Hut, Sizzler, Starbucks, Subway, Wall Chinese, **lodging:** Day's Inn, Super 8, Travelodge, **other:** Chrysler/ Jeep/Dodge, Ford, Goodyear/auto

Banning

98 Sunset Ave, Banning, [N]...**gas:** Chevron/dsl, **food:** Domino's, Gramma's Kitchen, Gus Jr #7 Burger, **other:** Ace Hardware, AutoZone, BigLots, Chevrolet/ Buick/Pontiac/GMC, Radio Shack, Ray's RV Ctr, Rio Ranch Mkt, Rite Aid, vet

96 Highland Springs Ave, [N]...**gas:** Arco/24hr, Chevron, Valero/dsl, **food:** Applebee's, Burger King, Denny's, Farmhouse Rest., Jack-in-the-Box, Orchid, Papa John's, Pizza Run, Subway, Wendy's, **lodging:** Hampton Inn, **other:** HOSPITAL, Ace Hardware, Food4Less, Kragen Parts, NAPA, Radio Shack, Stater Bros Foods, Walgreens, [S]...**gas:** Mobil, **food:** Baskin-Robbins, Carl's Jr, Chili's, McDonald's, **other:** Albertson's, Best Buy, BK RV Ctr, Home Depot, K-Mart, Kohls, Rite Aid, Ross, Staples, Wal-Mart SuperCtr, hwy patrol

95 Pennsylvania Ave, Beaumont, [N]...**gas:** Circle K, **food:** ABC Rest., Rusty Lantern Rest., **lodging:** Windsor Motel, **other:** Miller RV Ctr, Tom's RV Ctr

Beaumont

94 CA 79, Beaumont, [N]...**gas:** 76, Thrifty Gas, **food:** Baker's DriveThru, McDonald's, El Rancho Steaks, Popeye's, YumYum Donuts/ 24hr, **lodging:** Best Western, Best Value Inn, **other:** Auto Value, NAPA, [S]...**food:** Del Taco, Denny's, **other:** RV camping

93 CA 60 W, to Riverside

92 San Timoteo Canyon Rd, Oak Valley Pkwy, [N]...**lodging:** Holiday Inn Express, **other:** Rite Aid, golf, [S]... golf

91mm rest area wb, full(handicapped)facilities, phone, picnic tables, litter barrels, petwalk

90 Cherry Valley Blvd, truck/tire repair

89 Singleton Rd(from wb), to Calimesa, no services

88 Calimesa Blvd, [N]...**gas:** Arco/24hr, Chevron/dsl, Shell, **food:** Best Wok, Burger King, McDonald's, Subway, Taco Bell, **lodging:** Calimesa Inn, **other:** Stater Bros Foods, bank, [S]...**food:** Big Boy, Jack-in-the-Box

87 County Line Rd, to Yucaipa, [N]...**gas:** FasTrip/gas, Shell/dsl, **food:** Baker's DriveThru, Del Taco, **other:** auto repair/tires

86mm Wildwood Rest Area eb, full(handicapped) facilities, phone, picnic tables, litter barrels, petwalk

85 Live Oak Canyon Rd, Oak Glen, no services

83 Yucaipa Blvd, [N]...**gas:** Arco/dsl/24hr, Chevron, **food:** Baker's DriveThru

82 Wabash Ave(from wb), no services

81 Redlands Blvd, Ford St, [S]...**gas:** 76

80 Cypress Ave, University St, [N]...HOSPITAL, to U of Redlands

79b a CA 38, 6th St, Orange St, Redlands, [N]...**gas:** Chevron, **food:** Redland Rest., **lodging:** Budget Inn, Stardust Motel, **other:** Goodyear, Stater Bros Foods, [S]...**gas:** 76, Shell, **food:** Chipotle Mexican, Denny's, Open Kitchen Chinese, Rubio's, Togo's, Trader Joe's, Starbucks, **other:** Albertson's, Buick/GMC, Kragen Parts, Lincoln/Mercury, NAPA, Office Depot, Von's Foods

77c (77b from wb)Tennessee St, [N]...**food:** Shakey's Pizza, **other:** Home Depot, [S]...**gas:** Shell, **food:** Arby's, Bakers DriveThru, Burger King, Carl's Jr, Coco's, El Pollo Loco, Papa John's, Subway, Taco Bell, **lodging:** Best Western, Comfort Suites, Dynasty Suites, **other:** Ford, Tri-City Mall, USPO

77b (77c from wb)CA 30, to Highlands, [S]...to Tri-City Mall

77a Alabama St, [N]...**food:** Chili's, Chick-fil-A, Denny's, Famous Dave's BBQ, Hawaiian BBQ, Jamba Juice, Macaroni Grill, Mr. Tortilla, Red Robin, Starbucks, **lodging:** Courtyard, Red Lands Motel, Super 8, TownePlace Suites, **other:** Barnes&Noble, Ford, JC

E

↕

W

S a n   B e r n a r d i n o

	Penney, Jo-Ann Superstore, Marshall's, Michael's, PetCo, Target, VW, U-Haul, **S**...**gas:** Arco, Chevron, Flagg, Shell, **food:** Comfort Suites, Del Taco, IHOP, McDonald's, Nick's Burgers, Quizno's, Slim's BBQ, Starbucks, Zabella's Mexican, **lodging:** Best Western, Country Inn&Suites, GoodNite Inn, **other:** Aamco, Chief Parts, Chevrolet, Goodyear/auto, Hyundai, K-Mart, Longs Drug, Mervyn's, Nissan, PepBoys, Pic'n Sav Foods, Ross, Toyota, Tri-City Mall
76	California St, **N**...**other:** funpark, museum, **S**...**gas:** Arco/24hr, Shell/LP/24hr, **food:** Applebee's, Jack-in-the-Box, Jose's Mexican, Panda Express, Subway, Weinerschnitzel, Wendy's, **other:** Food4Less, Just Tires, Radio Shack, Wal-Mart/auto, RV camping
75	Mountain View Ave, Loma Linda, **N**...**gas:** Valero/dsl, **S**...**food:** Domino's, FarmerBoys Burgers, Lupe's Mexican, Subway
74	Tippecanoe Ave, Anderson St, **N**...**gas:** Thrifty Gas, **food:** Chipotle Mexican, Denny's, Elephant Bar Rest., El Pollo Loco, In-n-Out, Jack-in-the-Box, Jamba Juice, Pick-Up Stix, Starbucks, Wendy's, **lodging:** American Inn, Fairfield Inn, Residence Inn, **other:** Costco/gas, Sam's Club, Staples, **S**...**gas:** 76/dsl, **food:** Baker's DriveThru, Del Taco, HomeTown Buffet, KFC, Napoli Italian, Taco Bell, Wienerschnitzel, **other:** Audi, Harley-Davidson, Honda, Jaguar, Porsche, Saab, Saturn, transmissions, to Loma Linda U
73b a	Waterman Ave, **N**...**gas:** 76, Shell/dsl/24hr, **food:** Baja Fresh, Black Angus, Chili's, ChuckeCheese, ClaimJumper, Coco's, Crabby Bob's, El Torito, Guadala-Harry's Diner, IHOP/24hr, King Buffet, Lotus Garden Chinese, Mimi's Café, Olive Garden, Outback Steaks, Panda Express, Pat&Oscar's, Red Lobster, Sizzler, Starbucks, TGIFriday, Togo's, Yamazato Japanese, **lodging:** Best Western, Comfort Inn, Hilton, La Quinta, Quality Inn, Super 8, **other:** Best Buy, Circuit City, Home Depot, Office Depot, Petsmart, **S**...**gas:** Arco/24hr, Beacon/dsl/rest., **food:** Baker's Driv-Thru, Burger King, Gus Jr Burger #8, McDonald's, Popeye's, Starbucks, Taco Bell, **lodging:** Motel 6, **other:** Camping World RV Service/supplies, La Mesa RV Ctr
72	I-215, CA 91
71	Mt Vernon Ave, Sperry Ave, **N**...**gas:** Arco/24hr, **food:** Peppersteak Rest., **lodging:** Colony Inn, **other:** brake/muffler, repair
70b	9th St, **N**...**gas:** Mobil, **food:** Baskin-Robbins, Burger King, Denny's, KFC, McDonald's, P&G's Burgers, Subway, Taco Bell, **lodging:** Hampton Inn, **other:** Parts+, Stater Bros Foods
70a	Rancho Ave, **N**...**food:** Del Taco, Jack-in-the-Box, KFC/Taco Bell, Wienerschnitzel
69	Pepper Dr, **N**...**gas:** Valero, **food:** Baker's DriveThru, **other:** Ford
68	Riverside Ave, to Rialto, **N**...**gas:** Chevron, Thrifty, **food:** Burger King, Coco's, El Pollo Loco, HomeTown Buffet, Jack-in-the-Box, McDonald's, Starbucks, Subway, Taco Joe's, **lodging:** American Inn, Best Western, Rialto Motel, **other:** Wal-Mart, dsl repair, **S**...**gas:** 76/Circle K

66	Cedar Ave, to Bloomington, **N**...**gas:** Arco/24hr, **food:** Baker's DriveThru, Burger King, DQ, FarmerBoys Burgers, Pizza Hut/Taco Bell, **other:** USPO, **S**...**gas:** Citgo/7-11
64	Sierra Ave, to Fontana, **N**...**gas:** Arco/24hr, Mobil, Texaco, **food:** Applebee's, Arby's, Billy J's Rest., Burger King, ChuckeyCheese, DQ, Denny's, Del Taco, El Giro Mexican, In-n-Out, Jack-in-the-Box, KFC, McDonald's, Millie's Kitchen, Papa John's, Pizza Hut/Taco Bell, Popeye's, Sizzler, Subway, 3 Hermanos, Wendy's, Wienerschnitzel, **lodging:** Comfort Inn, Econolodge, Guest House Inn, Motel 6, **other:** HOSPITAL, Aamco, Albertson's, BigLots, Chevrolet, $Tree, Food4Less, Goodyear/auto, Honda/GMC, Kia, KidsRUs, K-Mart, Kragen Parts, Mazda, Nissan, PepBoys, Pic'n Sav Foods, Radio Shack, Rite Aid, SavOn Drug, Stater Bros Foods, Winston Tire, **S**...**food:** China Buffet, Circle K/24hr, Fosters Freeze, Nogales Burgers, **other:** Ross, Target, Mervyn's
63	Citrus Ave, **N**...**gas:** Beacon/gas, 76, **food:** Baker's DriveThru, Taqueria Mexican, **other:** Ford
61	Cherry Ave, **N**...**gas:** Arco/24hr, Chevron/Taco Bell/dsl, Trucktown Trkstp/dsl/24hr/@, **food:** Carl's Jr, **lodging:** Circle Inn Motel, **other:** Ford Trucks, **S**...**gas:** North American Trkstp/dsl, 3 Sisters Trkstp/dsl/@, 76/Circle K, **food:** Farmer Boy's Rest., Mariscos Mexican, **other:** Peterbilt
59	Etiwanda Ave, Valley Blvd, no services
58b a	I-15, N to Barstow, S to San Diego
57	Milliken Ave, **N**...**gas:** Arco, Chevron, Mobil/Subway/dsl, 76/Del Taco/dsl, Shell/dsl, **food:** Baja Fresh, Burger King, Carl's Jr, Coco's, CoffeeBean, Cucina Italian, Dave&Buster's, Del Taco, Denny's, Fazoli's, FoodCourt, In-n-Out, Jack-in-the-Box, McDonald's, NY Grill, Outback Steaks, RainForest Café, Rubio's Rest., Tokyo Wako Japanese, Wendy's, Wienerschnitzel, Wolfgang Puck Café, **lodging:** AmeriSuites, Ayers Suites, Country Suites, Hampton Inn, **other:** America's Tire, Carmax, JC Penney, Jo-Ann Crafts, Sam's Club, mall, **S**...**gas:** TA/76/Subway/Taco Bell/dsl/rest./24hr/@, **other:** RV Ctr
56	Haven Ave, Rancho Cucamonga, **N**...**gas:** Mobil, Benihana, **food:** Black Angus, Crabby Bob's Seafood, El Torito, Quizno's, Tony Roma's, **lodging:** Best Western, Extended Stay America, Hilton, Holiday Inn, La Quinta, **S**...**food:** Panda Chinese, TGIFriday, **lodging:** Fairfield Inn
55b a	Holt Blvd, to Archibald Ave, **N**...**gas:** Arco, Mobil/dsl, **food:** Baker's Drive-thru, Weinerschnitzel
54	Vineyard Ave, **N**...**gas:** 76/Circle K, Shell, **food:** Del Taco, Carl's Jr., One-Dollar Chinese, Pizza Hut/Taco Bell, Popeye's, Quizno's, Rocky's Foods, Sizzler, **other:** AutoZone, Chief Parts, Ralph's Foods, Rite Aid, Stater Bros Foods, **S**...**gas:** Arco/24hr, Mobil, Shell, USA Gas, **food:** Circle K, Cowboy Bugers, Denny's, In-n-Out, Marie Callender, Michael J's Rest., Rosa's Italian, Spires Rest., Yoshinoya Japanese, Wendy's, **lodging:** Ayers Suites, Best Western, Comfort Inn, Country Suites, Countryside Suites, DoubleTree Inn, Express Inn, GoodNite Inn, Ramada Ltd, Red Roof Inn, Residence Inn, Sheraton, Super 8, **other:** Chevrolet/Cadillac

Interstate 10

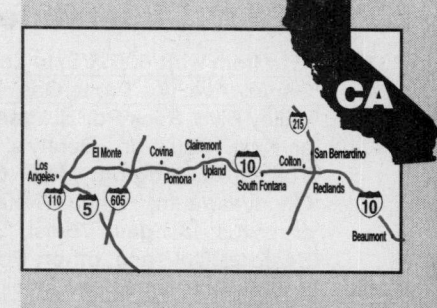

E
↕
W

O n t a r i o

53	San Bernardino Ave, 4th St, to Ontario, ...**gas:** Arco, Chevron, Circle K, Shell, **food:** Baskin-Robbins, Burger King, Carl's Jr, Del Taco, Jack-in-the-Box, Popeye's, Sizzler, Taco Bell/24hr, **lodging:** Motel 6, Quality Inn, **other:** Chief Parts, K-Mart, Radio Shack, Ralph's Foods, Rite Aid, S...**gas:** Arco/24hr, 76, **food:** Alfredo's Mexican, Denny's, KFC, McDonald's, Pizza Hut, YumYum Donuts, **lodging:** CA Inn, Travelodge, West Coast Inn
51	CA 83, Euclid Ave, to Ontario, Upland, N...**food:** Coco's Rest., **other:** HOSPITAL
50	Mountain Ave, to Mt Baldy, N...**gas:** Arco, Chevron, Mobil, Shell/dsl, **food:** BBQ, Carrow's, Denny's, El Burrito, El Torito, Green Burrito, Happy Wok Chinese, Mimi's Café, Mi Taco, Subway, Trader Joe's, Wendy's, **lodging:** Super 8, **other:** Home Depot, Longs Drug, Mervyn's of CA, Staples, S...**gas:** 76/dsl, **food:** Baskin-Robbins, Carl's Jr, Cold Stone Creamery, El Gran Burrito, Mary's Mexican, Quizno's, **other:** Rite Aid, USPO
49	Central Ave, to Montclair, N...**gas:** Chevron, Mobil, Shell/24hr, 7-11, **food:** Burger King, Carl's Jr., El Pollo Loco, Incredible Pizza, Island Burger, KFC, McDonald's, Quizno's, Subway, Tom's Burgers, **other:** MEDICAL CARE, Best Buy, Borders Books, Circuit City, Firestone/auto, Goodyear/auto, Hi-Lo Auto Supply, JC Penney, Just Tires, Macy's, Office Depot, PepBoys, Ross, Sears/auto, mall, same as 48, S...**gas:** 76, **food:** Jack-in-the-Box, LJ Silver, Subway, Wienerschnitzel, **other:** Acura, Costco/gas, Honda, Infiniti, K-Mart, Macy's, Nissan, Target
48	Monte Vista, N...**gas:** Shell, **food:** Acapulco Mexican, Applebee's, Chilis, Black Angus, Elephant Rest., Olive Garden, Red Lobster, Tony Roma's, **other:** HOSPITAL, Lens Crafters, Nordstrom's, Macy's, mall, same as 49
47	Indian Hill Blvd, to Claremont, N...**gas:** Mobil, **food:** Bakers Square, **lodging:** Claremont Lodge, Howard Johnson, S...**gas:** Chevron/McDonald's, 76/dsl, **food:** Burger King, Carl's Jr, Charo Chicken, Denny's, In-n-Out, RoundTable Pizza, 7-11, Starbucks, Wienerschnitzel, **lodging:** Ramada Inn, **other:** MEDICAL CARE, Albertson's, America's Tire, AutoZone, Ford, Kia, Radio Shack, Toyota
46	Towne Ave, N...**gas:** Citgo/7-11, Puma/Subway/dsl, **food:** Jack-in-the-Box, Subway
45b	Garey Ave, to Pomona, N...**gas:** Delta, **other:** HOSPITAL, vet, S...**gas:** Chevron, Shell/dsl, **food:** Del Taco
45	White Ave, Garey Ave, to Pomona, no services
44	(43 from eb)Dudley St, Fairplex Dr, N...**gas:** Arco/dsl, **food:** Coppacabana Rest., Denny's, **lodging:** LemonTree Motel, Sheraton, S...**gas:** Chevron/24hr, **food:** McDonald's
42b	CA 71 S(from eb), to Corona
42a	I-210 W, CA 57 S
41	Kellogg Dr, S...to Cal Poly Inst
40	Via Verde
38b	Holt Ave, to Covina, N...**food:** Blake's Steaks/seafood, **lodging:** Embassy Suites

L o s   A n g e l e s   A r e a

38a	Grand Ave, N...**gas:** Arco/dsl, **food:** Baily's Rest, Denny's, Japanese/Mongolian/Thai Rest., **lodging:** Best Western
37b	Barranca St, Grand Ave, N...**gas:** Shell/repair, **food:** BJ's Rest., Chili's, Dockside Grill, El Torito, Hooters, Marie Callender, Mariposa Mexican, Woodpit BBQ, **lodging:** Best Western, Hampton Inn, Holiday Inn, **other:** Circuit City, Old Navy, Target, S...**food:** In-n-Out, McDonald's, **lodging:** Courtyard, 5 Star Inn
37a	Citrus Ave, to Covina, N...**gas:** Chevron, **food:** Burger King, Carl's Jr, Del Taco, IHOP, Jack-in-the-Box, TGI-Friday, Winchell's, **other:** Acura, Buick, GMC, Honda, Lincoln/Mercury, Longs Drug, Marshall's, Mazda, Mervyn's, Office Depot, Old Navy, Ralph's Foods, Ross, Target, Volvo/VW, S...**gas:** 76/autocare, **food:** Classic Burger, Trader Joe's, **other:** HOSPITAL, Cadillac
36	CA 39, Azusa Ave, to Covina, N...**gas:** Arco/24hr, 76, **food:** Black Angus, Brazillian BBQ, Imperio Rest., McDonald's, Papa John's, Quizno's, Red Lobster, Subway, **lodging:** El Dorado Motel, **other:** Chrysler/Jeep/Dodge, Circuit City, Stater Bro's, S...**gas:** Mobil, Shell, **food:** Carrow's, **other:** Honda, Hummer, Toyota
35	Vincent Ave, Glendora Ave, N...**gas:** Chevron/24hr, **food:** KFC, Pizza Hut, Wienerschnitzel, S...**gas:** 76, **food:** Applebee's, Baja Fresh, Chevy's Mexican, Elephant Rest., Grand Buffet, Pizza Hut, Quizno's, Red Robin, Sakura Japanese, Starbucks, Subway, Wienerschnitzel, **other:** Barnes&Noble, Best Buy, Big O Tire, JC Penney, Macy's, Macy's, Sears/auto, mall
34	Pacific Ave, N...**gas:** 76, S...**gas:** Mobil, Shell, **food:** La Posada Mexican, **other:** HOSPITAL, Discount Tire, K-Mart, Goodyear/auto, JC Penney, Jo-Ann Fabrics, Sears, mall, same as 35
33	Puente Ave, N...**gas:** Chevron, **food:** A&W/LJ Silver, China Palace, Denny's, Farmer Boy's, Guadalajara Grill, McDonald's, Panda Express, Quizno's, Sizzler, Starbucks, **lodging:** Courtyard, Motel 6, **other:** Home Depot, Staples, Wal-Mart, S...**gas:** Valero/dsl, **lodging:** Regency Inn, **food:** Jack-in-the-Box, **other:** Harley-Davidson, Saturn, U-Haul
32b	Francisquito Ave, to La Puente, N...**gas:** V&G, **food:** Papa John's, **other:** hwy patrol, S...**gas:** Chevron, **food:** Carl's Jr, In-n-Out, Wienerschnitzel, **lodging:** Grand Park Inn
32a	Baldwin Pk Blvd, N...**gas:** Arco, Chevron/McDonald's, Shell, USA, **food:** Burger King, IHOP, Jack-in-the-Box, Pizza Hut/Taco Bell, Seven Mares Rest., **other:** HOSPITAL, CVS Drug, Food4Less, Target, S...**food:** In-n-Out, **other:** Altman's RV Ctr
31c	(31b from wb)Frazier St, N...**food:** 7-11, **lodging:** Angel Motel

CALIFORNIA

Interstate 10

Exit	Services
31b a	(31a from wb)I-605 N/S, to Long Beach
30	Garvey Ave, S...Prena Gas
29b	Valley Blvd, Peck Rd, N...gas: Chevron, food: Burger King, Carl's Jr., Denny's, KFC, Shakey's Pizza, Yoshinoya, lodging: Motel 6, other: Ford, Dodge, Goodyear/auto, Honda, K-Mart, Nissan, Toyota/Scion/Lexus, S...gas: 76/dsl, Shell, food: Christina'a Seafood, Del Taco, other: Pontiac/GMC
29a	S Peck Rd(from eb), no services
28	Santa Anita Ave, to El Monte, N...other: Chevrolet, Hyundai, S...gas: 76, food: 7-11
27	Baldwin Avenue, Temple City Blvd, S...gas: Arco/24hr, food: Denny's, Edward's Steaks, same as 27b a
26b	CA 19, Rosemead Blvd, Pasadena, N...food: Denny's, IHOP, Subway, lodging: Ramona Inn, Rosemead Inn, other: Goodyear/auto, Office Depot, Radio Shack, Target, S...food: Jack-in-the-Box, Quizno's, Starbucks
26a	Walnut Grove Ave, no services
25b	San Gabriel Blvd, N...gas: Arco, Mobil, Shell/autocare, food: Carl's Jr, Popeye's, Taco Bell/Pizza Hut, Wienerschnitzel, lodging: Budget Inn, other: AutoZone, San Gabriel Foods, S...gas: Citgo/7-11
25a	Del Mar Ave, to San Gabriel, N...gas: 76, other: auto repair, S...gas: Arco, Chevron/dsl, lodging: Best Value
24	New Ave, to Monterey Park, N...gas: Mobil, to Mission San Gabriel
23b	Garfield Ave, to Alhambra, S...gas: Shell/dsl, SoCal, lodging: Grand Inn, other: HOSPITAL
23a	Atlantic Blvd, Monterey Park, N...gas: Mobil, food: Del Taco, Pizza Hut, Popeye's, other: HOSPITAL, S...lodging: Best Western, other: Ralph's Foods, auto repair
22	Fremont Ave, N...HOSPITAL, tuneup, S...7-11
21	I-710, Long Beach Fwy, Eastern Ave(from wb)
20b a	Eastern Ave, City Terrace Dr, S...gas: Chevron/service, Mobil, food: Burger King, McDonald's
19c	Soto St(from wb), N...gas: Shell, Soto Gas, food: Burger King, other: HOSPITAL, S...gas: Mobil, Pronto
19b	I-5(from wb), US 101 S, N to Burbank, S to San Diego
19a	State St, N...HOSPITAL
17	I-5 N
16b	I-5 S(from eb)
16a	Santa Fe Ave, San Mateo St, S...gas: Shell, other: Hertz Trucks, industrial area
15b	Alameda St, N...food: Jack-in-the-Box, to downtown, S...industrial area
15a	Central Ave, N...gas: Shell/repair
14b	San Pedro Blvd, S...industrial
14a	LA Blvd, N...conv ctr, S...other: Kragen Parts, Radio Shack, Rite Aid
13	I-110, Harbor Fwy
12	Hoover St, Vermont Ave, N...gas: Mobil, Texaco, food: Burger King, King Donuts, McDonald's, other: Honda, PepBoys, Thrifty Drug, Toyota, S...gas: Amin's Oil/dsl Chevron, Valero/dieses, food: Jack-in-the-Box, other: Office Depot, Staples
10	Arlington Ave, N...gas: Chevron, 76, S...Chevron
9	Crenshaw Blvd, S...gas: Chevron, Shell, Thrifty, food: McDonald's, other: U-Haul
8	La Brea Ave, N...gas: Chevron, Shell/dsl/repair, other: Walgreen, transmissions, S...gas: Chevron, other: AutoZone
7b	Washington Blvd, Fairfax Ave, S...gas: Mobil, same as 8
7a	La Cienega Blvd, Venice Ave(from wb), N...gas: Chevron/24h, Mobil, food: Carl's Jr., Del Taco, other: Firestone/auto, S...food: Subway, other: Aamco
6	Robertson Blvd, Culver City, N...gas: Chevron, Mobil, food: Domino's, Taco Bell, other: EZ Lube, Goodyear, museum, S...food: Del Taco, Albertson's, other: Ross, SavOn Drug, Ross
5	National Blvd, N...gas: 76, United Oil, food: Papa John's, Starbucks, Subway, other: Rite Aid, Von's Foods, S...gas: Arco, food: KFC
4	Overland Ave, S...gas: Mobil, food: Winchell's
3b a	I-405, N to Sacramento, S to Long Beach
2c b	Bundy Dr, N...gas: Chevron, Shell/dsl, food: Eddy's Café, Pizza Hut, Taco Bell, other: U-haul
2a	Centinela Ave, to Santa Monica, N...food: Taco Bell, S...food: McDonald's, Trader Joe's, lodging: Santa Monica Hotel
1c	20th St(from wb), Cloverfield Blvd, 26th St(from wb), N...gas: Arco, Shell/repair, other: HOSPITAL
1b	Lincoln Blvd, CA 1 S, N...food: Denny's, food: Norm's Rest., lodging: Holiday Inn, other: Brake Masters, JoAnn Fabrics, Macy's, Sears, Vons Foods, auto repair, transmissions, S...gas: Chevron/24hr, Exxon, food: Jack-in-the-Box, other: EZ Lube, Firestone/auto, U-Haul
1a	4th, 5th,(from wb), N...other: Macy's, Sears, mall
0	Santa Monica Blvd, to beaches, I-10 begins/ends on CA 1.

Interstate 15

Exit #	Services
298	California/Nevada state line, facilities located at state line, Nevada side
291	Yates Well Rd, no services
286	Nipton Rd, E...E Mojave Nat Scenic Area, to Searchlight
281	Bailey Rd, no services
276mm	brake check area for trucks, nb
272	Cima Rd, E...gas, food
270mm	**Valley Wells Rest Area both lanes, full(handicapped) facilities, phone, picnic tables, litter barrels, petwalk**
265	Halloran Summit Rd, E...gas: Hilltop Gas/dsl, other: towing/tires/repair
259	Halloran Springs Rd, no services
248	to Baker(from sb), same as 246
246	CA 127, Kel-Baker Rd, Baker, to Death Valley, W...gas: Arco/24hr, Mobil/dsl, 76/dsl, Shell/Jack-in-the-Box/dsl, Valero/A&W/Pizza Hut/Subway/TCBY, Valero/DQ/dsl, food: Alien Fresh Jerky, Arby's, Big Boy Rest., Burger King, Coco's Rest., Del Taco, Denny's, Mad Greek Café, Starbucks, lodging: BunBoy Motel, Royal Hawaiian Motel, other: Baker Auto Parts, Baker Mkt Foods, Country Store, World's Largest Thermometer, repair

Interstate 15

245	to Baker(from nb), same as 246
239	Zzyzx Rd, no services
233	Rasor Rd, **E**...**gas:** Rasor Rest Sta/gas/dsl/towing/ 24hr
230	Basin Rd, no services
221	Afton Rd, to Dunn, **W**... market
217mm	**rest area both lanes, full(handicapped)facilities, phone, picnic tables, litter barrels, petwalk**
213	Field Rd, no services
206	Harvard Rd, to Newberry Springs, **W**...**other:** Rock-a-Hoola WaterPark/resort(1mi)
198	Minneola Rd, **E**...**gas:** Mobil
197mm	agricultural insp sta sb
196	Yermo Rd, Yermo, no services
194	Calico Rd, no services
191	Ghost Town Rd, **E**...**gas:** Arco/24hr, Mohsen Oil Trkstp/dsl/24hr, **food:** Jack-in-the-Box, Peggy Sue's 50s Diner, **lodging:** OakTree Inn, **W**...**gas:** Clink's #2/ Shell/dsl/24hr, 76, **food:** Jenny Rose' Rest., **other:** Calico GhostTown(3mi), KOA, to USMC Logistics
189	Ft Irwin Rd, no services
186	CA 58 W, to Bakersfield, **W**...**food:** Hacienda Colima, Idle Spur Steaks
184	E Main, Barstow, Montera Rd(from eb), to I-40, **E**... **food:** Doughnut Star Chinese, Imenez's Mexican, Krissy's Café, McDonald's, Panda Express, Pizza Hut, Popeye's, Quizno's, Starbucks, Straw Hat Pizza, Tom's Burgers, **lodging:** Best Western, Travelodge, **other:** Pic'n Sav, mall, **S of I-40...gas:** Arco/24hr, **other:** Wal-Mart/auto/gas, **W**...**gas:** Chevron, Circle K/TCBY, Shell/dsl, Thrifty Gas, Valero, **food:** Arby's, Burger King, Carl's Jr, Carrow's Rest., China Gourmet, Coco's, Del Taco, Gallardo's Mexican, Jack-in-the-Box, KFC, LJ Silver, Ruby's Rest., Sizzler, Taco Bell, Weinerschnitzel, **lodging:** AstroBudget Motel, Best Motel, Budget Inn, California Inn, Day's Inn, Desert Inn, Econolodge, Economy Inn, Quality Inn, Ramada Inn, Rodeway Inn, Super 8, **other:** AutoZone, Food 4 Less, Goodyear, Kragen Parts, Radio Shack, U-Haul/LP, Von's Foods, tires
184a	I-40 E(from nb), I-40 begins/ends
183	CA 247, Barstow Rd, **E**...**gas:** 76, Valero/gas, **food:** Pizza Hut, Jimenez Mexican, **other:** Rite Aid, **W**... **gas:** Chevron/24hr, **other:** HOSPITAL, Food4Less, TrueValue, Mojave River Valley Museum, st patrol,
181	L St, W Main, Barstow, **W**...**gas:** ATC/Mrs. B's Diner/ dsl/rest., Chevron, Thrifty, **food:** BunBoy Rest., Pizza Palace, Robertiroz Mexican, **lodging:** Best Value Inn, Holiday Inn Express, **other:** Home Depot, NAPA, tires/towing
179	CA 58, to Bakersfield, no services
178	Lenwood, to Barstow, **E**...**gas:** Chevron/dsl, ⚑ /Flying J/CountryMkt/dsl/24hr/@, Shell/24hr, 76/dsl, Valero/Circle K, **food:** Arby's, Baja Fresh, Baskin-Robbins, Big Boy, Burger King, Carl's Jr, Del Taco, Denny's, El Pollo Loco, FoodCourt, Hana Grill, In-n-Out, Jack-in-the-Box, KFC, Panda Express, Quigley's, Starbucks, Subway, Taco Bell, Tommy's Burgers, **lodging:** Hampton Inn, Holiday Inn Express, **other:** Blue Beacon, Tanger Outlet/famous brands, **W**...**gas:**

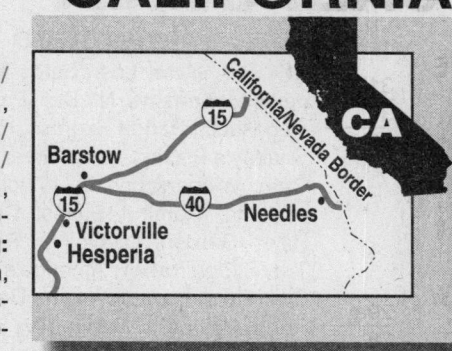

	Pilot/DQ/dsl/ scales/24hr/@, TA/Subway/ dsl/truckwash/ scales/24hr/@, **food:** McDonald's, **lodging:** Red Roof Inn, **other:** Firestone, truck repair
175	Outlet Ctr Dr, Sidewinder Rd, **4 mi E**...**other:** factory outlets
169	Hodge Rd, no services
165	Wild Wash Rd, no services
161	Dale Evans Pkwy, to Apple Valley, no services
157	Stoddard Wells Rd, to Bell Mtn, no services
154	Stoddard Wells Rd, to Bell Mtn, **E**...**food:** Taco Chon, **other:** RV Camping, **W**...**gas:** Mobil, 76, **food:** Denny's, **lodging:** Howard Johnson, Motel 6, Queens Motel
153mm	Mojave River
153b	E St, no services
153a	CA 18 E, D St, to Apple Valley, **E**...**gas:** 76, **other:** HOSPITAL, Cooper Tire, **W**...**gas:** Arco/24hr
151b	Mojave Dr, Victorville, **E**...**gas:** 76/dsl/24hr, **lodging:** Budget Inn, **W**...**gas:** Valero, **lodging:** Sunset Inn, **other:** transmissions
151a	La Paz Dr, Roy Rogers Dr, **E**...**gas:** Chevron, Shell/ A&W/TCBY, USA/dsl, **food:** Bravo Burgers, China Palace, DQ, HomeTown Buffet, IHOP, Jack-in-the-Box, McDonald's, Wendy's, Yum Yum Donuts, **lodging:** New Corral Motel, **other:** Asian Mkt, Costco/gas, Food4Less/24hr, Goodyear/auto, Harley-Davidson, Honda, Jo-Ann Fabrics, 99c Store, Pic'n Sav Foods, Rite Aid, Toyota, Winston Tire, same as 144, **W**...**gas:** Arco/24hr, **food:** Carl's Jr, Dominos, Hawaiian BBQ, Papa Johns, Quizno's, Starbucks, **other:** Home Depot, Honda, Kia, Nissan, Pontiac/GMC, Stater Bros
150	CA 18 W, Palmdale Rd, Victorville, **E**...**food:** All-Star Buffet, Baker's Drive-Thru, Burger King, Carl's Jr, Denny's, Don's Rest., El Pollo Loco, Goody's Rest., Jack-in-the-Box, KFC, Richie's Diner, Starbucks, **lodging:** Green Tree, Red Roof Inn, **other:** Autozone, Cadillac/GMC, Chrysler/Jeep, Dodge, PepBoys, **W**...**gas:** Shell, Thrifty, Valero, **food:** Andrew's Rest., Cask&Cleaver, Coco's, Del Taco, Los Domingos Mexican, LJ Silver, McDonald's, Pina's Mexican, Pizza Hut, Subway, Taco Bell, Tom's #2 Rest., **lodging:** Ambassador Inn, Budget Inn, Days Inn, Ramada Inn, **other:** HOSPITAL, Aamco, AutoZone, Buick/ Pontiac, Chevrolet/Hyundai, Chrysler/Jeep, Ford/Lincoln/Mercury, Honda/Toyota, Kamper's Korner RV, Kia, Nissan, Ralph's Foods, Target, Town&Country Tire, mall
147	Bear Valley Rd, to Lucerne Valley, **E**...**gas:** Arco/ 24hr, Chevron, Citgo/7-11, Mobil, 76/Circle K, Shell, **food:** A&W, Arby's, Baker's Drive-Thru, Burger King, Carl's Jr, Del Taco, Dragon Express, Golden Gate Chinese, Hogi Yogi, Incredible Pizza, John's Pizza,

N ↕ S

Victorville

KFC, LJ Silver, Los Toritos Mexican, Marie Callender's, McDonald's, NY Deli, Panda Express, Quizno's, Red Robin, Panda Express, Pizza Palace, Popeye's, Shakey's Pizza, Stein'n Steer, Straw Hat Pizza, TNT Café, Wienerschnitzel, Winchell's, **lodging:** American Inn, Comfort Suites, Day's Inn, Econolodge, Hilton Garden, La Quinta, Red Roof Inn, Super 8, Travelodge, **other:** America's Tire, AutoZone, Circuit City, Firestone/auto, Home Depot, Jiffy Lube, Kragen Parts, Michael's, Range RV, Staples, Wal-Mart/auto, funpark, **W**...**gas:** Chevron, Valero, **food:** Applebee's, Archibald's Drive-Thru, Baja Fresh Grill, Carinos, Chili's, ChuckeCheese, Cold Stone Creamery, El Pollo Loco, El Tio Pepe Mexican, Farmer Boy's Rest., Greenhouse Café, Jack-in-the-Box, Mimi's Cafe, Olive Garden, On-the-Border, Outback Steaks, Red Lobster, RoadHouse Grill, Starbucks, Subway, Tony Roma, 2 Guys Grill, Wendy's, **lodging:** Hawthorn Suites, **other:** Barnes&Noble, Best Buy, Circuit City, CVS Drug, JC Penney, Kohl's, Lowe's Whse, Mervyn's, Range RV Ctr, Sears/auto, Stater Bro's, Vallarta Foods, mall

143	Main St, to Hesperia, Phelan, **E**...**gas:** Shell/A&W/Popeyes/dsl, Valero/DQ/pizza, **food:** Burger King, Denny's, IHOP, In-n-Out, Jack-in-the-Box, **lodging:** SpringHill Suites, **W**...**gas:** Arco/24hr, 76/Big Boy/dsl, **food:** Baker's Drive-thru, **lodging:** Holiday Inn Express, RV camping
141	US 395, to Adelanto, **W**...**gas:** Pilot/Wendy's/dsl/scales/24hr, **food:** Newt's Outpost Café, **other:** repair
138	Oak Hill Rd, **E**...**gas:** Shell/dsl, **food:** Summit Inn/café, **W**...**other:** RV camping, LP
132	Cajon Summit, elevation 4260, brake check sb
131	CA 138, to Palmdale, Silverwood Lake, **E**...**gas:** Chevron/McDonald's/24hr, **other:** repair, **W**...**gas:** 76/Circle K/Del Taco/LP, Shell/Subway/dsl, **lodging:** Best Western
131mm	weigh sta both lanes, elevation 3000
129	Cleghorn Rd, no services
124	Kenwood Ave, no services
123	I-215 S, to San Bernardino, **E**...**gas:** Arco/24hr, to Glen Helen Park
122	Glen Helen Parkway, no services
119	Sierra Ave, **W**...**gas:** Arco/Jack-in-the-Box/dsl/24hr, Chevron/McDonald's/dsl, Shell/Del Taco/dsl/@, **other:** to Lytle Creek RA
116	Summit Ave, **E**...**gas:** Arco, Chevron, 7-11, Shell/Del Taco, Valero/dsl, **food:** Chili's, Hawaiian BBQ, Jack-in-the-Box, Panera Bread, Quizno's, Roundtable Pizza, Starbucks, Subway, Taco Bell, Wendy's, **other:** CVS Drug, GNC, Kohl's, Marshall's, Michale's, Petsmart, Ross, Staples, Stater Bro's, Target
115b a	CA 210, Highland Ave, **E**...to Lake Arrowhead
113	Base Line Rd, **E**...**gas:** USA, **food:** Denny's, Jack-in-the-Box, Logans Roadhouse, Pizza Hut, Quiznos, Rosa Maria's, Starbucks, **lodging:** Comfort Inn
112	CA 66, Foothill Blvd, **E**...**gas:** Chevron, **food:** Arby's, ClaimJumper Rest., Golden Spoon, In-n-Out, Melting Pot, Panda Buffet, Panda Express, Pizza Hut, Star-

Ontario

bucks, Subway, Taco Bell, Wienerschnitzel, **other:** Costco, Food4Less, Mervyn's, Michael's, Office Depot, Radio Shack, Wal-Mart/auto, **1-2 mi W**...**gas:** Arco, Chevron, Mobil/Subway, **food:** Buffalo Wild Wings, Carino's, Carl's Jr, Carrow's, Chick-fil-A, Del Taco, Denny's, El Torito, Joe's Crab Shack, Old Spagetti Factory, Omaha Jack's Steaks, Red Robin, Starbucks, Wendy's, **other:** AutoZone, Bass Pro Shops, Circuit City, Macy's, Home Depot, Office Depot, Sears Grand

110	4th St, **E**...**gas:** Arco/dsl, **W**...**gas:** Arco/24hr, Mobil/Subway/dsl, 76/dsl, **food:** Applebee's, BJ's Rest., Boston's, Cali Grill, Carl's Jr, Chevy's Mexican, Chipotle, Coco's, Dave&Buster's, Del Taco, El Pollo Loco, Fazoli's, Fuddruckers, Jack-in-the-Box, KFC, Krispy Kreme, McDonald's, Mi Casa Mexican, NY Grill, Olive Garden, Outback Steaks, Quizno's, Rain Forest Cafe, Red Lobster, Rubio's, Starbucks, Subway, TokyoWako, Wendy's, Wienerschnitzel, **lodging:** AmeriSuites, Ayre's Suites, Courtyard, Hampton Inn, Hilton Garden, Homewood Suites, TownePlace Suites, **other:** America's Tire, Big O Tire, Costco/gas, JC Penney, Ontario Mills Mall, Sam's Club, Staples, Target
109b a	I-10, E to San Bernardino, W to LA
108	Jurupa St, **E**...**food:** Starbucks, **other:** Affordable RV, BMW, Buick, Chrysler/Jeep/Dodge, GMC/Pontiac, Honda, Lexus, Mazda, Mitsubishi, Nissan, Saturn, Toyota, Volvo, VW, **W**...**gas:** Arco/24hr, **food:** Carl's Jr, **other:** Ford, Kia, Lincoln/Mercury, Scandia funpark
106	CA 60, E to Riverside, W to LA
104	new exit
103	Limonite Ave, **E**...**other:** Lowes Whse, Michael's, PetCo, Ross, **W**...**gas:** Ralph's, **food:** Applebees, Coldstone Creamery, El Grande Burrito, Quizno's, Red Brick Pizza, Wendy's, **other:** Best Buy, GNC, Home Depot, Kohl's, Petsmart, Staples, Target, TJ Maxx, Von's Foods
100	6th St, Norco Dr, Old Town Norco, **E**...**gas:** Chevron/24hr, Exxon/dsl, **food:** Jack-in-the-Box, McDonald's, **other:** Rite Aid, **W**...**gas:** Arco/24hr, Valero, **food:** Norco's Burgers, Starbucks, Weinerschnitzel, **lodging:** Guesthouse Inn, **other:** Brake Masters, Jiffy Lube, USPO, vet
98	2nd St, **W**...**gas:** 76/dsl, Shell/dsl, Spirit, Texaco, Thrifty, **food:** Burger King, Chipotle Mexican, Del Taco, Denny's, Domino's, Fazoli's, In-n-Out, Little Caesar's, Marie Callender, Miguel's Jr, Pizza Hut, Polly's Cafe, Sizzler, **lodging:** Howard Johnson Express, **other:** America's Tire, AutoZone, Big O Tire, Chrysler, Dodge, Ford, Jeep, Mazda, Mitsubishi, Pontiac, Norco RV, 7-11, Staples, Stater Bro's, Target
97	Yuma Dr, Hidden Valley Pkwy, **E**...**food:** Baja Fresh, Chick-fil-A, **other:** Kohl's, Stater Bro's, **W**...**gas:** Chevron, 76/dsl, Shell/dsl, **food:** Alberto's Mexican, Arby's, Carl's Jr, Jamba Juice, Jack-in-the-Box, McDonald's, Papa John's, Pizza Hut, Quizno's, Rodrigo's Mexican, Rubio's, Starbucks, Wendy's, **lodging:** Hampton Inn, **other:** Albertson's, Big Lots, Kragen Parts, SavOn Drug, Staples, Winston Tire, Walgreens

N ↕ S

L a k e   E l s i n o r e

96b a	CA 91, to Riverside, beaches
95	Magnolia Ave, E...gas: Chevron/dsl, food: Islands Grill, Jack-in-the-Box, other: Lowe's Whse, Office Depot, W...gas: Mobil, Shell, food: A&W/LJ Silver, Burger King, Carl's Jr, Coco's, El Tapatio Mexican, Little Caesar's, Lotus Garden, McDonald's, Pizza Palace, Sizzler, Subway, Zendejas Mexican, lodging: Holiday Inn Express, other: CVS Drug, $Tree, Kragen Parts, Ralph's Foods, Rite Aid, Stater Bros Foods
93	Ontario Ave, to El Cerrito, E...gas: Shell, food: Starbucks, W...gas: Arco/24hr, Chevron/24hr, 76, food: Denny's, In-n-Out, Jack-in-the-Box, McDonald's, Miguel's Mexican, Quizno's, Tommy's Burgers, Wienerschnitzel, other: Albertson's, Home Depot, Long's Drug, Radio Shack, Sam's Club, USPO, Wal-Mart/auto
92	El Cerrito Rd, no services
91	Cajalco Rd, E...food: Chick-fil-A, Chili's, Jamba Juice, King's Fish House, Macaroni Grill, On-the-Border, Panera Bread, Starbucks, Wendy's, other: Barnes&Noble, Best Buy, Kohl's, Marshall's, Michael's, Old Navy, PetCo, Ross, Staples, Target, W...gas: Mobil, food: Golden Spoon, Jack-in-the-Box, NY Pizza, Subway, other: Stater Bros
90	Weirick Rd, E...food: Salsa-Mar, TGI Friday, other: 7 Oaks Gen Store
88	Temescal Cyn Rd, Glen Ivy, E...gas: Shell, W...gas: Arco/dsl/24hr, food: Carl's Jr, Tom's Farms/BBQ
85	Indian Truck Trail, no services
81	Lake St, no services
78	Nichols Rd, W...gas: Arco/24hr, other: VF Outlet/famous brands, auto repair
77	CA 74, Central Ave, Lake Elsinore, E...gas: Arco/24hr, Chevron, Mobil, food: Archibald's, Burger King, Chili's, Coffee Bean, Coldstone Creamery, Del Taco, Douglas Burgers, Panda Express, Taco Del Mar, Wendy's, other: Costco/gas, Lowes Whse, Petsmart, Staples, W...food: El Pollo Loco, Farmer Boys, Golden Chopsticks, Starbucks, other: Home Depot, 99c Store, PetCo, Target, Walgreens
75	Main St, Lake Elsinore, W...gas: 76, lodging: Elsinore Motel, other: Circle K, tires/repair
73	Railroad Cyn Rd, to Lake Elsinore, E...gas: 76/Circle K, food: Denny's, El Pollo Loco, In-n-Out, KFC, Papa John's, Peony Chinese, Quizno's, Starbucks, Wienerschnitzel, other: GNC, Jiffy Lube, Kragen Parts, Von's Foods, Wal-Mart/auto, W...gas: Arco, Chevron, Mobil/dsl, food: Cafe China, Carl's Jr, Coco's, Del Taco, Don Ruben Mexican, McDonald's, Pizza Hut, Sizzler, Subway, Taco Bell, lodging: Lake View Inn, Quality Inn, other: Albertson's, AutoZone, Big O Tire, Buick/Pontiac/GMC, Chevrolet, CVS Drug, Express Tire/auto, Firestone, Ford, NAPA, Radio Shack, Rite Aid, SavOn Drug, 7-11, Stater Bros Foods, vet
71	Bundy Cyn Rd, W...gas: Arco/24hr, food: Jack-in-the-Box
69	Baxter Rd, E...food: Pizza Factory

T e m e c u l a

68	Clinton Keith Rd, E...gas: Chevron, USA, food: McDonald's, Starbucks, Wienerschnitzel, other: HOSPITAL, Albertsons/Sav-on, W...gas: Arco, 7-11, food: Charro Chicken, China Panda, Del Taco, Jack-in-the-Box, Olivera's Rest., Starbucks, other: Stater Bro's
65	California Oaks Rd, Kalmia St, E...gas: Chevron, Mobil/dsl, 76/Circle K, Shell/dsl, food: Burger King, Carl's Jr, Chili's, Craziano's, DQ, KFC, Papa John's, Starbucks, lodging: Comfort Inn, other: Albertson's, AutoZone, Kragen Parts, Radio Shack, Rite Aid, Target, Walgreens, W...gas: Arco/24hr, Chevron, food: Applebee's, Carrow's, Chick-fil-A, Farmer Boys, Jack-in-the-Box, Sizzlin Steer, other: America's Tire, Giant RV Ctr, Kohl's, Lowe's Whse, Office Depot, PetCo, fun ctr
64	Murrieta Hot Springs Rd, to I-215, E...gas: Citgo/7-11, Shell/dsl, food: Carl's Jr, El Pollo Loco, Fazoli's, Richie's Diner, Sizzler, Starbucks, Wendy's, other: Ralph's Foods, Rite Aid, Ross, Sam's Club/gas, Walgreens, W...gas: Citgo, Shell/Popeyes/dsl, food: Arby's, Chuy's, Coldstone Creamery, Denny's, IHOP, McDonald's, MegaToms, Panda Express, Quizno's, Starbucks, Subway, Wienerschnitzel, other: Best Buy, Big Lots, CompUSA, Home Depot, 99c Store, Petsmart, Staples, Wal-Mart/auto
63	I-215 N(from nb), to Riverside
61	CA 79 N, Winchester Rd, E...gas: Chevron, Mobil, food: Alberto's Mexican, Anthony's Ristorante, Baja Fresh, Burger King, Carino's, Carl's Jr, Coldstone Creamery, El Torito, Harry's Grill, Islander Grill, Macaroni Grill, McDonald's, Mimi's Café, On-the-Border, Outback Steaks, Panda Express, Roadhouse Grill, Shogun Chinese, Souplantation, Starbucks, Taco Bell, TGIFriday, Togo's, Yellow Basket Hamburgers, other: America Tire, AutoZone, Barnes&Noble, Big O Tire, Circuit City, Costco/gas, Food4Less, Dodge, Ford, Express Tire, Honda/Acura, Jo-Ann Fabrics, K-Mart, Kragen Parts, Longs Drug, Lowe's Whse, Macy's, Mervyn's, PepBoys, PetCo, Sears/auto, Toyota, TJ Maxx, VW, WinCo Foods, World Mkt, W...gas: Arco/24hr, Chevron/dsl, food: Arby's, Banzai Japanese, Blue Marlin Rest., CA Burgers, ChungKing Chinese, Del Taco, El Pollo Loco, Farmer Boys, Guadalahara Mexican, Hooters, Hungry Hunter, In-n-Out, Jack-in-the-Box, Richie's Diner, Sizzler, Starbucks, Super China, Tony Roma's, Wendy's, lodging: Best Western, Comfort Inn, Extended Stay America, Fairfield Inn, Holiday Inn Express, other: Hyundai, NAPA, VW, st patrol, tires/repair

N↑↓S

59	Rancho California Rd, **E**...**gas:** Arco, Mobil/dsl, Shell/dsl, **food:** Black Angus, Chili's, ClaimJumper, Del Taco, Marie Callender's, Pizza Hut, RoundTable Pizza, Rubio's, Texas Loosey's, Starbucks, **lodging:** Embassy Suites, **other:** Big Lots, CVS Drug, Michael's, Orchard's Foods, Target, Von's Foods, **W**...**gas:** Chevron/repair, 76/Circle K/dsl, **food:** Denny's, Domino's, KFC, McDonald's, Mexico Chiquito's, OldTown Donuts, Penfold's Mexican, Rick's Burgers, Rosa's Café, **lodging:** Hampton Inn, Motel 6, Rancho California Inn, Rodeway Inn, **other:** USPO
58	CA 79 S, to Indio, Temecula, **E**...**gas:** Arco, Mobil, Valero/Circle K/dsl, **food:** Carl's Jr, Del Taco, In-n-Out, Starbucks, Temecula Pizza, **other,** America's Tire, Longs Drug, 7-11, **W**...**gas:** Arco, Shell/dsl/24hr, **food:** Alberto's Mexican, Country Jct Rest., Wienerschnitzel, **lodging:** Ramada Inn, **other:** Express Tire, Firestone, Harley-Davidson, RV service
55mm	check sta nb
54	Rainbow Valley Blvd, **2 mi E**...gas, food, **W**...CA Insp Sta
51	Mission Rd, to Fallbrook, **W**...HOSPITAL
46	CA 76, to Oceanside, Pala, **W**...**gas:** Mobil, **lodging:** Comfort Inn, Pala Mesa Resort, **other:** RV camp
44mm	San Luis Rey River
43	Old Hwy 395, no services
41	Gopher Canyon Rd, Old Castle Rd, **1 mi E**...**lodging:** Welk Resort, **other:** RV camping, gas
37	Deer Springs Rd, Mountain Meadow Rd, **W**...**gas:** Arco/24hr
34	Centre City Pkwy(from sb), no services
33	El Norte Pkwy, **E**...**gas:** Arco/24hr, Shell/dsl, **food:** Arby's, DQ, IHOP, Taco Bell, **lodging:** Best Western, **other:** Goodyear, RV Resort, **W**...**gas:** 76/dsl, Circle K, **food:** Jack-in-the-Box, Wendy's, **other:** Longs Drug, Von's Foods
32	CA 78, to Oceanside, no services
31	Valley Pkwy, **E**...**gas:** Arco/24hr, **food:** Baja Fresh, Chili's, ChuckeCheese, McDonald's, Olive Garden, Panda Express, Subway, Uno Grill, **other:** HOSPITAL, Barnes&Noble, Circuit City, Michael's, PetCo, mall, **W**...**gas:** Express, **food:** Applebee's, Boston Mkt, Burger King, Carl's Jr, Chipotle Mexican, Coco's, Del Taco, Jamba Juice, La Salsa, Panera Bread, Starbucks, Subway, Wendy's, **lodging:** Comfort Inn, Holiday Inn Express, **other:** Home Depot, Mervyn's, 7-11, Staples, Target, TJ Maxx, World Mkt
30	9th Ave, Auto Parkway, **E**...**gas:** AAA, Infiniti, Mercedes, Mervyn's, same as 31
29	Felicita Rd, no services
28	Centre City Pkwy(from nb, no return), **E**...**food:** Center City Café, **lodging:** Palms Inn
27	Via Rancho Pkwy, to Escondido, **E**...**gas:** Chevron/24hr, Shell, **food:** FoodCourt, Macaroni Grill, On-the-Border, Orami Grill, Panera Bread, Red Robin, **other:** JC Penney, Macy's, Nordstrom's, Robinsons-May, Sears/auto, Wild Animal Zoo, mall, **W**...**gas:** Shell/Subway/dsl, **food:** Big Daddy's Steaks, CA Coffee, McDonald's, Starbucks

Escondido

26	W Bernardo Dr, to Highland Valley Rd, Palmerado Rd, no services
24	Rancho Bernardo Rd, to Lake Poway, **E**...**gas:** Arco/24hr, Mobil, **food:** Domino's, **lodging:** Hilton Garden, **other:** Von's Foods, **W**...**gas:** 76/Circle K, Shell/repair, **food:** Elephant Bar Rest., Hooters, **lodging:** Holiday Inn, Rodeway Inn
23	Bernardo Ctr Dr, **E**...**gas:** Chevron, **food:** Burger King, Carl's Jr, Coco's, Denny's, El Torito, Hunan Chinese, Jack-in-the-Box, Quizno's, Rubio's Grill, 7-11, Taco Bell, **other:** CVS Drug, Express Tire, Firestone/auto
22	Camino del Norte, no services
21	Carmel Mtn Rd, **E**...**gas:** Chevron, Shell, Texaco, **food:** Baskin-Robbins, Boston Mkt, Cafe Luna, CA Pizza Kitchen, Carl's Jr, Chevy's Mexican, ClaimJumper, El Pollo Loco, In-n-Out, Islands Burgers, JambaJuice, Marie Callender, McDonald's, Olive Garden, Oscar's Rest., Quizno's, Rubio's Grill, Subway, Taco Bell, TGIFriday's, Wendy's, **lodging:** Residence Inn, **other:** Barnes&Noble, Borders Books, Circuit City, Costco, EZ Lube, GNC, Home Depot, Marshall's, Mervyn's, Michael's, PetCo, Ralph's Foods, Rite Aid, Ross, Sears Essentials, Staples, Trader Joes, USPO, **W**...**gas:** Chevron, **food:** Jack-in-the-Box, Starbucks, **other:** Albertson's, Big O Tire, Office Depot, 7-11
19	CA 56 W, Ted Williams Pkwy, no services
18	Rancho Penasquitos Blvd, Poway Rd, **E**...**gas:** Arco/24hr, **W**...**gas:** Exxon/dsl, Mobil/dsl, 76/dsl, **food:** Burger King, IHOP, McDonald's, Mi Ranchito Mexican, Starbucks, Subway, Taco Bell, **lodging:** La Quinta, **other:** 7-11
17	Mercy Rd, Scripps Poway Pkwy, **E**...**gas:** USA/dsl, **food:** Chili's, Fish Grille, Wendy's, **lodging:** Residence Inn, Springhill Suites, **W**...**gas:** Chevron, **food:** KFC, Starbucks
16	Mira Mesa Blvd, to Lake Miramar, **E**...**food:** ChuckeCheese, Denny's, Filippi's Pizza, Golden Crown Chinese, Lucio's Mexican, Shozen BBQ, Wendy's, **lodging:** Holiday Inn Express, Quality Suites, **other:** Medco Drug, USPO, **W**...**gas:** Arco/24hr, Shell, **food:** Applebee's, Arby's, Buca Italian, Burger King, Café China, In-n-Out, Islands Burgers, Jack-in-the-Box, Jamba Juice, Little Caesar's, McDonald's, Mimi's Café, On the Border, Oscar's Burgers, Panera Bread, Ralph's, Rubio's Grill, Starbucks, Subway, Wendy's, **other:** Albertson's, Barnes&Noble, Best Buy, Home Depot, Longs Drug, Old Navy, Ralph's Foods, Rite Aid, Ross, USPO
15	Carroll Canyon Rd, to Miramar College, **E**...**food:** Carl's Jr
14	Pomerado Rd, Miramar Rd, **W**...**gas:** Arco/dsl, Chevron, Mobil, Shell/24hr, **food:** Carl's Jr, Chin's Rest., Keith's Rest., Pizza Hut, Subway, **lodging:** Best Western, Budget Inn, Holiday Inn Select, **other:** Aamco, Audi/Porsche/VW, Land Rover
13	Miramar Way, US Naval Air Station
12	CA 163 S(from sb), to San Diego

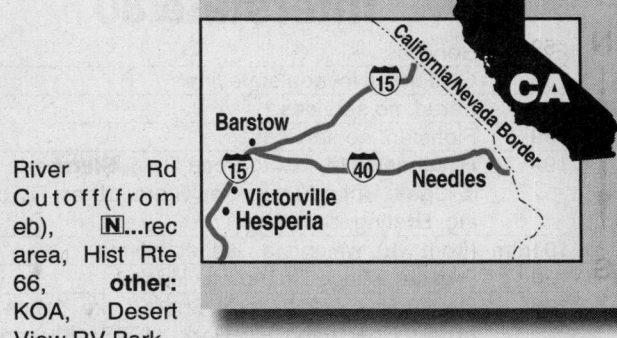

Interstate 15

N ↕ **S**

San Diego Area

11	to CA 52, no services
10	Clairemont Mesa Blvd, ...**food:** Carl's Jr, Giovanni's Pizza, Jack-in-the-Box, La Salsa, McDonald's, Mr Chick Rest., Panda Express, Subway, Sunny Donuts, Taco Bell, Togo's, Wendy's
9	CA 274, Balboa Ave, no services
8	Aero Dr, W...**gas:** Arco/24hr, Shell, **food:** Jack-in-the-Box, McDonald's, Papa John's, Sizzler, Starbucks, Submarina, Taco Bell, **lodging:** Holiday Inn, **other:** $Tree, Fry's Electronics, Radio Shack, Von's Foods, Wal-Mart/auto
7b	Friars Rd W, W...**food:** Dragon Chinese, IHOP, Islands Hamburgers, Little Fish Mkt, McDonald's, Oggi's Pizza, Subway, **other:** Costco, Lowes Whse, San Diego Stadium
7a	Friars Rd E, no services
6b	I-8, E to El Centro, W to beaches
6a	Adams Ave, downtown, no services
5b	El Cajon Blvd, E...**gas:** Chevron/dsl, **other:** KIA, W...**gas:** Mobil
5a	University Ave, E...**gas:** Chevron/dsl
3	I-805, N to I-5, S to San Ysidro, no services
2b	(2c from nb)CA 94 W, downtown
2a	Market St, downtown
1c	National Ave, Ocean View Blvd, no services
1b	(from sb)I-5 S, to Chula Vista, no services
1a	(from sb)I-5 N. I-15 begins/ends on I-5

Interstate 40

E ↕ **W**

Needles

Exit #	Services
155	California/Arizona state line, Colorado River, Pacific/Mountain time zone
153	Park Moabi Rd, to Rte 66, N...boating, camping
149mm	insp both lanes
148	5 Mile Rd, to Topock, Rte 66(from eb)
144	US 95 S, E Broadway, Needles, N...**gas:** Chevron/dsl, Mobil, Shell/dsl, **food:** Domino's, **other:** Basha's Foods, Laundry, Rite Aid, U-Haul, S...**lodging:** Best Value, **other:** tires/repair
142	J St, Needles, N...**gas:** 76/24hr, Valero, **food:** Jack-in-the-Box, McDonald's, **lodging:** Travelers Inn, **other:** NAPA, S...**food:** Denny's, **lodging:** Day's Inn, Motel 6, **other:** HOSPITAL, st patrol
141	W Broadway, River Rd, Needles, N...**food:** KFC, **lodging:** Best Motel, Desert Mirage Inn, River Valley Motel, **other:** Goodyear/auto, KOA(1mi), tire/dsl repair, S...**gas:** Arco/24hr, Chevron/dsl/24hr, Mobil/dsl, Shell/DQ/24hr, **food:** Carl's Jr, China Garden, Taco Bell, Wagon Wheel Rest., **lodging:** Best Western, Budget Inn, Needles Inn, Relax Inn, **other:** Chevrolet/Cadillac/Buick/GMC, auto/RV/tire/repair

Barstow

139	River Rd Cutoff(from eb), N...rec area, Hist Rte 66, **other:** KOA, Desert View RV Park
133	US 95 N, to Searchlight, to Rte 66, no services
120	Water Rd, no services
115	Mountain Springs RdMountain Springs Rd, High Springs Summit, elev 2770
107	Goffs Rd, N...gas/dsl/food, Hist Rte 66
106mm	**rest area both lanes, full(handicapped)facilities, phone, picnic tables, litter barrels, petwalk**
100	Essex Rd, Essex, N...to Providence Mtn SP, Mitchell Caverns
78	Kelbaker Rd, to Amboyto E Mojave Nat Preserve, Kelso, S...Hist Rte 66, **other:** RV camping(14mi)
50	Ludlow, N...**gas:** 76/DQ/24hr, S...**gas:** Chevron/dsl, **food:** Coffee Shop, **lodging:** Ludlow Motel
33	Hector Rd, to Hist Rte 66, no services
28mm	**rest area both lanes, full(handicapped)facilities, phone, picnic tables, litter barrels, petwalk**
23	Ft Cady Rd, N...**gas:** Texaco/dsl/24hr, S...**lodging:** Newberry Mtn RV Park
18	Newberry Springs, N...**other:** Calico/dsl, S...**gas:** Chevron/Kelly's Grill/LP
12	Barstow-Daggett Airport, N...airport
7	Daggett, N...**other:** RV camping(2mi), to Calico Ghost Town
5	Nebo St(from eb), to Hist Rte 66, no services
2	USMC Logistics Base, N...**lodging:** Pennywise Inn
1	E Main St, Montara Rd, Barstow, N...**gas:** Chevron, Barstow Fuel/dsl, Shell/repair, **food:** Burger King, Krissy's Café, Mega Tom's Burger, McDonald's, Panda Express, Quizno's, Starbucks, Straw Hat Pizza, Tom's Burgers, **lodging:** Best Western, Gateway Motel, **other:** Pic'n Sav Foods, 1 mi N...**gas:** Arco/24hr, Chevron, 76/Circle K/Subway/TCBY, Shell, **food:** Arby's, Burger King, Carl's Jr, Carrow's Rest., China Gourmet, Coco's, Del Taco, Denny's, FireHouse Italian, Golden Dragon, IHOP, Jack-in-the-Box, KFC, LJ Silver, Sizzler, Taco Bell, **lodging:** AstroBudget Motel, Best Motel, Budget Inn, Comfort Inn, Day's Inn, Desert Inn, Econolodge, Economy Inn, Executive Inn, Quality Inn, Ramada Inn, Super 8, **other:** AutoZone, Kragen Parts, Radio Shack, U-Haul/LP, Von's Foods, S...**gas:** Arco/24hr, **other:** Wal-Mart/McDonald's/auto/gas
0mm	I-40 begins/ends on I-15 in Barstow

CALIFORNIA
Interstate 80

E

W

Truckee

Exit #	Services
208	California/Nevada state line
201	Farad, no services
199	Floristan, no services
194	Hirschdale Rd, **N**...to Boca Dam, Stampede Dam, **S**...**gas:** United Trails Gen Store, **other:** RV camping, boating, camping
191mm	(from wb), weigh sta., inspection sta.
190	Prosser Village Rd, no services
188	CA 89 N, CA 267, to N Shore Lake Tahoe, **N**...**other:** Coachland RV Park, USFS, **S**...same as 186
186	Central Truckee(no eb return), **S**...**gas:** Beacon, 76, **food:** El Toro Bravo Mexican, Truckee Diner, Wagontrain Café, **lodging:** Hilltop Lodge, Truckee Hotel,
185	CA 89 S, to N Lake Tahoe, **N**...**gas:** Sierra Superstop, **food:** DQ, Panda Express, Pizza Shack, RoundTable Pizza, Sizzler, Zano's Pizza, **other:** Ace Hardware, GNC, New Moon Natural Foods, Rite Aid, Safeway, 7-11, hwy patrol, **S**...**gas:** Shell, **food:** Cheesesteak, China Garden, KFC, McDonald's, Mongolian BBQ, Pizzaria, Subway, Wong's Garden, **other:** Albertson's, Longs Drugs, auto repair, to Squaw Valley, RV camping
184	Donner Pass Rd, Truckee, **N**...**gas:** Shell/dsl, **food:** La bamba Mexican, **lodging:** Sunset Inn, **other:** factory outlet/famous brands, **S**...**gas:** Chevron/dsl/24hr, 76, **food:** Donner House Rest., Donner Lake Pizza, Madigans Pizza, **lodging:** Holiday Inn Express, **other:** chain service, to Donner SP, RV camp/dump
181mm	vista point both lanes
180	Donner Lake(from wb), **S**...**lodging:** Donner Lake Village Resort
177mm	**Donner Summit, elev 7239, rest area both lanes, full(handicapped)facilities, view area, phone, picnic tables, litter barrels, petwalk**
176	Castle Park, Boreal Ridge Rd, **S**...**lodging:** Boreal Inn/rest., **other:** Pacific Crest Trailhead, skiing
174	Soda Springs, Norden, **S**...**gas:** Beacon/LP/dsl, **food:** Summit Rest., **lodging:** Donner Summit Lodge, **other:** chain services
171	Kingvale, **S**...**gas:** Shell
168	Rainbow Rd, to Big Bend, **S**...**lodging:** Rainbow Lodge/rest., **other:** RV camping
166	Big Bend(from eb), no facilites
165	Cisco Grove, **N**...**other:** RV camp/dump, skiing, snowmobiling, **S**...**gas:** Valero/24hr, **other:** chain servICES
164	Eagle Lakes Rd, **N**...**other:** RV camping
161	CA 20 W, to Nevada City, Grass Valley
160	Yuba Gap, **S**...**other:** snowpark, phone, picnic tables, boating, camping, skiing
158	Laing Rd, **S**...**lodging:** Rancho Sierra Inn/café
157mm	vista point wb
158a	Emigrant Gap(from eb), **S**...**gas:** Shell/Burger King/dsl/24hr, **lodging:** Rancho Sierra Inn/café, phone

Colfax

Auburn

Exit #	Services
156	Nyack Rd, Emigrant Gap, **S**...**gas:** Shell/Burger King/dsl, **food:** Nyack Café
155	Blue Canyon, no services
150	Drum Forebay, no services
148b	Baxter, **N**...**other:** RV camping, chainup services, food, phone
148a	Crystal Springs, no services
146	Alta, no services
145	Dutch Flat, **N**...**food:** Monte Vista Rest., **S**...**gas:** Tesoro/dsl, **other:** CHP, RV camping, chainup services, hwy patrol
143	Gold Run(from wb), **N**...gas/dsl, food, phone, chainup
143mm	**rest area both lanes, full(handicapped)facilities, phone, picnic tables, litter barrels, petwalk**
142	Gold Run, **N**...chainup services
140	Magra Rd, Rollins Lake Rd, Secret Town Rd, no services
139	Rollins Lake Road(from wb), RV camping
135	CA 174, to Grass Valley, Colfax, **N**...**gas:** Mel's Gas, 76/dsl, **food:** Little Red Hen, McDonald's, Pizza Factory, Starbucks, Taco Bell, TJ's Roadhouse, **lodging:** Colfax Motel, **other:** Sierra Mkt Foods, NAPA, **S**...**gas:** Chevron/dsl, Tesoro/dsl, **food:** BBQ, Shang Garden Chinese, Subway, Sierra RV Ctr
133	Canyon Way, to Colfax, **S**...**food:** Mom's Kitchen **other:** Chevrolet, Sierra NV Tire/repair
131	Cross Rd, to Weimar, no facilites
130	W Paoli Lane, to Weimar, **S**...**gas:** Weimar Store/dsl
129	Heather Glen, elev 2000 ft, no services
128	Applegate, **N**...**gas:** Applegate Gas/dsl, **other:** chainup services
125	Clipper Gap, Meadow Vista, no facilites
124	Dry Creek Rd, no facilites
123	Bell Rd, **N**...**other:** Aubrun RV Park(3mi), **S**...**food:** HQ House Rest.
122	Foresthill Rd, Ravine Rd, Bowman, **N**...**other:** RV camping/dump, **S**...**gas:** 76, **food:** Burger King, Ikeba's Burgers, Jack-in-the-Box, Sizzler, Starbucks, **lodging:** Best Western, Country Squire Inn/rest. same as 121
121	(from eb)Lincolnway, Auburn, **N**...**gas:** Beacon, Flyers Gas, Thrifty, **food:** Denny's, JimBoy's Tacos, Pizza Hut/Taco Bell/24hr, Wienerschnitzel, Wimpy's Burgers, **lodging:** Best Inn, Comfort Inn, Foothills Motel, Motel 6, Sleep Inn, Super 8, **S**...**gas:** Arco/dsl/24hr, Chevron/dsl/24hr, 76, Shell/dsl, Sierra, **food:** Bakers Square, Baskin-Robbins, Burger King, Burrito Shop, Carl's Jr, Country Waffle, DQ, Ikeba's Burgers, Izzy's BurgerStop, Jack-in-the-Box, KFC, LaBonte's Rest., Lyon's Rest., McDonald's, Sizzler, Subway, Thai Cuisine, TioPepe Mexican, **lodging:** Best Western, Country Squire Inn, Travelodge, **other:** Raley's Foods
120	Russell Ave(from wb), to lincolway from eb, same as 121

Interstate 80

E ↕ W

Citrus Hts

119c	Elm Ave, Auburn, [N]...**gas:** 76, Shell, **food:** Foster's Freeze, **lodging:** Holiday Inn, **other:** Albertson's, Grocery Outlet, Longs Drug, Thrifty Foods, U-Haul, [S]...**gas:** Rowdy Randy's
119b	CA 49, to Grass Valley, Auburn, [N]...**gas:** Shell, **food:** In-n-Out, Marie Callender's, **lodging:** Holiday Inn, **other:** Staples
119a	Maple St, Nevada St, Old Town Auburn, [S]...**gas:** Valero, **food:** Mary Belle's, Tiopete Mexican
118	Ophir Rd (from wb), [N]...**food:** Pizza Lunch, Pop's Place Foods
116	CA 193, to Lincoln, [S]...**other:** truck repair
115	Newcastle, [N]...**other:** transmissions, [S]...**gas:** Arco, Flyers/dsl, **food:** Denny's, CHP
112	Penryn, [N]...**gas:** 76/dsl/LP, Valero/dsl, **food:** CattleBaron's Café
110	Horseshoe Bar Rd, to Loomis, [N]...**food:** Burger King, Quizno's, RoundTable Pizza, Starbucks, Taco Bell, **other:** Raley's Food
109	Sierra College Blvd, [N]...**gas:** Chevron/McDonald's/dsl, Citgo/7-11, **food:** Carl's Jr, **lodging:** Day's Inn, **other:** Camping World RV Service/supplies, Gamel RV Ctr, Harley Davidson, Kia, KOA, antiques
108	Rocklin Rd, [N]...**gas:** Flyers, **food:** A&W/KFC, Arby's, Baskin-Robbins, Burger King, Carl's Jr, Denny's, Jack-in-the-Box, Jamba Juice, Jasper's Giant Burgers, KFC, Outback Steaks, Papa Murphy's, RoundTable Pizza, Starbucks, Subway, Taco Bell, Taco Del Mar, **lodging:** Howard Johnson, Ramada Ltd, **other:** CarQuest, GNC, Kragen Parts, Land Rover, Longs Drug, Mercedes, Radio Shack, Safeway, [S]...**gas:** Arco/24hr, **food:** Casa Bella
106	CA 65, to Lincoln, Marysville, **1 mi N on Stanford Ranch Rd...gas:** 76, Shell, **food:** Applebee's, Carl's Jr, Jack-in-the-Box, **lodging:** Comfort Suites, **other:** Barnes&Noble, FoodSource, Costco, JC Penney, Macy's, Marshall's, Nordstrom's, Old Navy, Wal-Mart
105b	Taylor Rd, to Rocklin(from eb), [N]...**food:** Cattlemen's Rest., **other:** Albertson's(1mi), Pan Pacific RV Ctr, [S]...**gas:** Chevron, 76/Burger King, **lodging:** Courtyard, Fairfield Inn, Hilton Garden, Larkspur Landing Hotel, Residence Inn, **other:** HOSPITAL
105a	Atlantic St, Eureka Rd, [S]...**gas:** 76, Shell, USA, **food:** Brookfield's Rest., Black Angus, Carver's Steaks, In-n-Out, Supermex Rest., Taco Bell, Tahoe Joe's, Wendy's, **lodging:** Marriott, **other:** America'sTire, Buick/GMC, Carmax, Chevrolet, Ford, CompUSA, Home Depot, Nissan, Sam's Club, mall
103b a	Douglas Blvd, [N]...**gas:** Arco/24hr, Beacon, Exxon, 76, **food:** Burger King, Carolina's Mexican, ClaimJumper, McDonald's, San Jose Mexican, Taquiera Mexican, **lodging:** Best Western, Extended Stay America, Heritage Inn, **other:** HOSPITAL, Ace Hardware, Big O Tire, Brakemasters, Chevrolet, $Tree, Firestone/auto, Goodyear, Kragen Parts, Michael's, Old Navy, Price Less Drugs, Radio Shack, Ross, Trader Joe, [S]...**gas:** Arco/24hr, Chevron/24hr, Shell, Carrow's/24hr, **food:** Baja Fresh, Carl's Jr, Carrow's, Del Taco, Denny's, Jack-in-the-Box, Jimboy's Tacos, Outback Steaks, Sizzler, Subway, Togo's, **lodging:** Oxford Suites, Quality Inn, **other:** Albertson's, Lincoln/Mercury, Mervyn's, Office Depot, PetCo, Raley's Foods, Rite Aid, Target, TJ Maxx
102	Riverside Ave, Auburn Blvd, to Roseville, [N]...**gas:** Arco/24hr, Valero/dsl, **food:** Back 40 Rest., Starbucks, Subway, **other:** VET, [S]...**gas:** Flyers/dsl, Shell, Tower, Valero/dsl, **food:** Baskin-Robbins, California Burgers, DQ, Jack-in-the-Box, JimBoy's Tacos, **other:** AutoZone, BMW Motorcycles, Just Tires, K-Mart, Radio Shack, Riebes Parts, Schwab Tire, Village RV Ctr, Winston Tire, transmissions
100	Antelope Rd, to Citrus Heights, [N]...**gas:** 76, **food:** Carl's Jr, Giant Pizza, KFC, McDonald's, Papa Murphy's, Subway, Wendy's, **other:** VET, Albertson's, $Tree, Raley's Foods, Rite Aid, 7-11, USPO
100mm	weigh sta both lanes
98	Greenback Lane, Elkhorn Blvd, Orangevale, Citrus Heights, [N]...**gas:** 76/service, **food:** Baskin Robbins, Carl's Jr, McDonald's, Pizza Hut, Subway, Taco Bell, **other:** Longs Drug, Radio Shack, Safeway
96	Madison Ave, [N]...**gas:** Beacon/24hr, **food:** Brookfield's Rest., Denny's, **lodging:** Madison Inn, Motel 6, **other:** Scandia Funpark, to McClellan AFB, [S]...**gas:** Arco/24hr, 76, Shell/repair, **food:** Boston Mkt, Burger King, El Pollo Loco, IHOP, Jack-in-the-Box, McDonald's, Panda Express, Starbucks, Subway, Taco Bell, **lodging:** Holiday Inn, La Quinta, **other:** Acura, Chevrolet, Ford/Isuzu, Office Depot, Schwab Tire, 7-11, Target, U-Haul
94b	Auburn Blvd, no services
94a	Watt Ave, [N]...**lodging:** Day's Inn, **other:** McClellan AFB, [S]...**gas:** Arco/24hr, Shell, **food:** Carl's Jr, China Taste, DQ, Denny's, KFC, Mtn Mike's Pizza, Quizno's, Starbucks, Subway, Taco Bell, Wendy's
93	Longview Dr, no services
92	Winters St, no services
91	Raley Blvd, Marysville Blvd, to Rio Linda, [N]...**gas:** Arco/24hr, Chevron/dsl/24hr, [S]...**other:** Mkt Basket Foods, Valley Tires, USPO
90	Norwood Ave, [N]...**gas:** Arco/Jack-in-the-Box/24hr, Valero, **food:** Hong Kong Chinese, McDonald's, RoundTable Pizza, Starbucks, Subway, **other:** Rite Aid, Savco Foods
89	Northgate Blvd, Sacramento, [N]...**other:** Fry's Electronics, [S]...**gas:** Circle K, Shell, Texaco/dsl, Valero/dsl, **food:** Burger King, Carl's Jr, IHOP, KFC, LJ Silver, McDonald's, Subway, Taco Bell, Taco Del Mar, **lodging:** Extended Stay America, Quality Inn, **other:** Foodsco Foods, Goodyear/auto, K-Mart, PepBoys, Schwab Tire, transmissions

E
W

Sacramento

Exit	Description
88	Truxel Rd, N...gas: Shell/dsl, food: Applebee's, Carino's Italian, Chili's, Chipotle Mexican, Del Taco, Hooters, In-n-Out, Jamba Juice, On the Border, Quizno's, Starbucks, Steve's Place Pizza, TGI Friday's, other: Arco Arena, Barnes&Noble, Best Buy, Home Depot, Michael's, Old Navy, Petsmart, Raley's Depot, Ross, Staples, Target, Wal-Mart, mall
86	I-5, N to Redding, S to Sacramento, to CA 99 N
85	W El Camino, N...gas: Chevron/Subway/dsl/24hr, 49er Trkstp/Silver Skillet/dsl/scales/24hr/@, food: Burger King, lodging: Fairfield Inn, Super 8
83	Reed Ave, N...gas: 76, food: Jack-in-the-Box, Los Amigo's, Quizno's, Panda Express, Starbucks, Subway, TCBY, lodging: Extended Stay America, other: Ford Trucks, dsl repair, S...gas: Arco/24hr, Shell/McDonald's/dsl, other: Wal-Mart Super Ctr
82	US 50 E, W Sacramento
81	Enterprise Blvd, W Capitol Ave, W Sacramento, N...gas: Chevron/dsl/24hr, Valero/dsl, food: Eppie's Rest/24hr, lodging: Granada Inn, S...gas: 7-11/gas, food: Denny's, Quizno's, Starbucks, Subway, other: KOA
78	Rd 32A, E Chiles Rd, S... Produce Mkt
75	Mace Blvd, N...gas: Arco, S...gas: Chevron/24hr, 76, Spirit/dsl, Valero/dsl, food: Burger King, McDonald's, Mtn Mikes Pizza, Subway, Taco Bell/24hr, Wendy's, lodging: Howard Johnson, Motel 6, other: Chevrolet/Toyota, Chrysler/Jeep, Ford/Mercury/Nissan, Honda, La Mesa RV Ctr, Mazda/VW, Nugget Mkt Foods, Pontiac/Buick/GMC, Schwab Tire, Toyota/Scion, to Mace Ranch
73	Olive Dr(from wb, no EZ return), no services
72b a	Richards Blvd, Davis, N...gas: Shell/24hr, food: Caffe Italia, In-n-Out, Redrum Burger, lodging: University Park Inn, other: NAPA, S...gas: Chevron, food: Applebee's, Del Taco, IHOP, KFC, RoundTable Pizza, Wendy's, lodging: Comfort Suites, Holiday Inn Express, other: Jiffy Lube, Kragen Parts
71	to UC Davis, no services
70	CA 113 N, to Woodland, N...HOSPITAL
69	Kidwell Rd, no services
67	Pedrick Rd, N...gas: Chevron/dsl, 76/LP, other: produce
66b	Milk Farm Rd(from wb), no services
66a	CA 113 S, Currey Rd, to Dixon, S...gas: Arco, CFN/dsl, 76/Popeye's/dsl, Shell/dsl, food: Cattlemen's Rest., Jack-in-the-Box, Taco Del Mar, Wendy's, other: Wal-Mart SuperCtr
64	Pitt School Rd, to Dixon, S...gas: Chevron/24hr, Valero/24hr, food: Arby's, Burger King, Cenario's Pizza, Chevy's Mexican, China Doll, Denny's, Domino's, IHOP/24hr, Mary's Pizza, McDonald's, Pizza Hut, Solano Bakery, Starbucks, Subway, Taco Bell, lodging: Best Western, Microtel, other: Ford, Kragen Parts, Radio Shack, Safeway/dsl
63	Dixon Ave, Midway Rd, N...gas: Truck Stp/dsl, S...gas: Chevron/LP/lube, USA/24hr, food: Carl's Jr, KFC/A&W, Perla Del Mar, lodging: Super 8, other: Dixon Fruit Mkt, $Heaven, Food Market, RV Dump
60	Midway Rd, Lewis Rd, Elmyra, N...RV camping

Vacaville

Exit	Description
59	Meridian Rd, Weber Rd, no services
57	Leisure Town Rd, N... HOSPITAL, S...gas: Kwik-Stop/dsl, Valero, food: Black Oak Rest., Jack-in-the-Box, SplitFire Rest., Vaca Joe's, lodging: Best Value, Extended Stay America, Fairfield Inn, Holiday Inn Express, Motel 6, Residence Inn, Vaca Valley Inn, other: Chevrolet, Chrysler/Dodge/Jeep, Harley-Davidson, Home Depot, Honda, Kohl's, Mazda, Nissan, Toyota, VW
56	I-505 N, to Winters
55	Nut Tree Pkwy, Monte Vista Dr, Allison Dr, N...gas: Citgo/7-11, 76/Circle K, Shell, Valero, food: Arby's, Burger King, Denny's, Hisui Japanese, IHOP, McDonald's, Murillo's Mexican, Nations Burger, Panera Bread, Pelayo's Mexican, Taco Bell, Wendy's, lodging: Best Western, Royal Motel, Super 8, other: HOSPITAL, Best Buy, Big O Tire, Borders, Firestone/auto, Goodyear/auto, Lowes Whse, Nugget Foods, Old Navy, U-Haul, transmissions, S...gas: Arco/24hr, Chevron/24hr, food: Applebee's, Baja Fresh Mexican, BJ's Grill, Black Oak Rest., Carl's Jr, Chevy's Mexican, Chili's, Fresh Choice Cafe, In-n-Out, Jack-in-the-Box, KFC, Mel's Cafe, Popeyes, Quizno's, Starbucks, Tahoe Joe's Rest., TGIFridays, Togo's, lodging: Courtyard, Fairfield Inn, Residence Inn, other: Goodyear, Home Depot, Mervyn's, Michael's, Old Navy, Pontiac/GMC, Ross, Safeway, Sam's Club, Staples, Target, Toyota, Vacaville Stores/famous brands, Wal-Mart/auto
54b	Mason St, Peabody Rd, N...gas: Chevron, Valero, food: A&W/LJ Silver, lodging: Hampton Inn, other: NAPA, Schwab Tire, S...gas: USA Gas, food: Domino's, Solano's Bakery, Wok'n Roll Chinese, other: Costco/gas, Ford/Mercury, Goodyear/auto, 7-11
54a	Davis St, N...gas: Chevron/McDonald's, food: Outback Steaks, lodging: Hampton Inn S...gas: Quik-Stop, other: WinCo Foods, repair
53	Merchant St, Alamo Dr, N...gas: Chevron, Shell/dsl, Valero, food: Baldo's Mexican, Bakers Square, Lyon's/24hr, RoundTable Pizza, Subway, Tin Tin Buffet, lodging: Alamo Inn, other: Big Lots, vet, S...gas: 76, food: Jack-in-the-Box, KFC, McDonald's, Pizza Hut, Port Subs, Starbucks, other: Radio Shack
52	Cherry Glen Rd(from wb), no services
51b	Pena Adobe Rd, S...lodging: Ranch Hotel
51a	Lagoon Valley Rd, Cherry Glen, no services
48	N Texas St, Fairfield, S...gas: Arco/24hr, Chevron, Shell, food: Burger King, RoundTable Pizza, Pollo Loco, lodging: EZ 8 Motel, other: Long's Drugs, Raley's Foods
47	Waterman Blvd, N...food: Dynasty Chinese, Hungry Hunter Rest., RoundTable Pizza, Strings Italian, other: Buick/Pontiac/GMC, Chevrolet/Cadillac, Safeway, to Austin's Place, S...to Travis AFB, museum
45	Travis Blvd, Fairfield, N...gas: Arco/24hr, Chevron/24hr, Shell/dsl, food: Burger King, ChuckeCheese, Denny's, In-n-Out, Peking Rest., Subway, Taco

Interstate 80

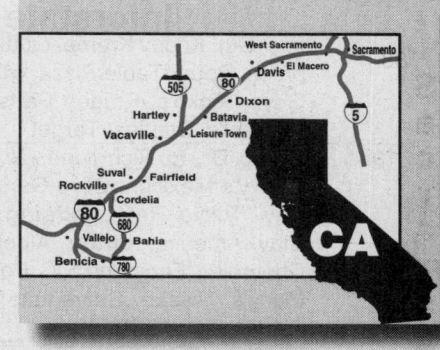

Bell, **lodging:** Courtyard, Holiday Inn, Motel 6, **other:** Raley's Foods, Harley-Davidson, Ford, Hyundai/Daewoo, Nissan, CHP, Ⓢ...**gas:** Shell, **food:** Applebee's, Baja Fresh Mexican, Blue Frog Grill, Carino's Italian, Chevy's Mexican, Coldstone Creamery, FreshChoice Rest., Gordito's Mexican, Great Wall Chinese, Jamba Juice, Marie Callender's, Mimi's Café, Olive Garden, Panda Express, Red Lobster, Starbucks, Subway, **lodging:** Hilton Garden, **other:** HOSPITAL, Barnes&Noble, Best Buy, Circuit City, Firestone/auto, JC Penney, Macy's, Mervyn's, Michael's, Old Navy, Ross, Sears/auto, Trader Joe's, WorldMkt, mall

Exit	Description
44	W Texas St, same as 46, Fairfield, Ⓝ...**gas:** Shell/dsl, **food:** ChuckeCheese, Gordito's Mexican, **lodging:** Extended Stay America, **other:** Mazda/Subaru, Suzuki, Ⓢ...**gas:** Valero, **food:** Baldo's Mexican, McDonald's, Paleyo's Mexican, Scenario's Pizza, **lodging:** Travelodge, **other:** Acura/Honda, Chrysler/Jeep/Dodge, FoodMaxx, Home Depot, Hyundai, Infiniti, Mitsubishi, Nissan, Target, Toyota, Volvo, Walgreens
43	CA 12 E, Abernathy Rd, Suisun City, Ⓢ...**other:** Budweiser Plant, Wal-Mart
42mm	weigh sta both lanes, phone
41	Suisan Valley Rd, Ⓢ...**gas:** Arco/24hr, Chevron, 76/Circle K/dsl/24hr, Shell/dsl, Valero, **food:** Arby's, Bravo's Pizza, Burger King, Carl's Jr, Denny's, Jack-in-the-Box, McDonald's, Starbucks, Subway, Taco Bell, Wendy's, **lodging:** Best Western, Comfort Suites, Days Inn, Fairfield Inn, Holiday Inn Express, **other:** Camping World RV Service, Ray's RV Ctr, Scandia FunCtr
40	I-680(from wb)
39b	Green Valley Rd, I-680(from eb), Ⓝ...**food:** Applebees, Happy Garden Chinese, RoundTable Pizza, Sticky Rice Bistro, Subway, **other:** Costco/gas, Longs Drug, Radio Shack, Safeway, TJ Maxx, Ⓢ...**gas:** Arco, **other:** Saturn
39a	Red Top Rd, Ⓝ...**gas:** 76/Circle K/24hr, **food:** Jack-in-the-Box
36	American Canyon Rd, no services
34mm	**rest area wb, full(handicapped)facilities, info, phone, picnic tables, litter barrels, petwalk, vista parking**
33b a	CA 37, to San Rafael, Columbus Pkwy, Ⓝ...**gas:** Chevron, **food:** Carls Jr., **lodging:** Courtyard, Ⓢ...same as 32
32	Redwood St, to Vallejo, Ⓝ...**gas:** 76, **food:** Denny's, Panda Garden, **lodging:** Best Value Inn, Motel 6, **other:** HOSPITAL, Ⓢ...**gas:** Arco, BonFair, Shell, **food:** Applebee's, Black Angus, Chevy's Mexican, Chinese Cuisine, Coldstone Creamery, IHOP, Jamba Juice, Little Caesar's, Lyon's Rest., McDonald's, Mtn Mike's Pizza, Olive Garden, Panda Express, Quizno's, Red Lobster, Starbucks, Subway, Taco Bell, Wendy's, **lodging:** Comfort Inn, Ramada Inn, **other:** AutoZone, Best Buy, Buick/GMC, Costco/gas, Hancock Fabrics, Home Depot, Honda, Longs Drug, Michael's, PepBoys, Radio Shack, Ross, Safeway, Toyota
31b	Tennessee St, to Vallejo, Ⓢ...**gas:** 76, Valero, **food:** Jack-in-the-Box, Pacifica Pizza, Pizza Guys, **lodging:** Great Western Inn, Quality Inn, **other:** USPO
31a	Solano Ave, Springs Rd, Ⓝ...**food:** Burger King, Church's, El Rey Mexican, Taco Bell, **lodging:** Deluxe Inn, Relax Inn, **other:** Ford, Albertson's, Rite Aid, U-Haul, Ⓢ...**gas:** Chemco, Chevron, Grand Gas, QuikStop, **food:** DQ, India Garden, Pizza Hut, Starbucks, Subway, **lodging:** Islander Motel, **other:** Kragen Parts, Walgreens
30c	Georgia St, Central Vallejo, Ⓝ...**gas:** Safeway, **other:** Ford, Ⓢ...**gas:** Shell/Starbucks/dsl, **food:** Coconut Grove, McDonald's, **lodging:** California Motel
30b	Benicia Rd(from wb), Ⓢ...**gas:** Shell/dsl, **food:** McDonald's, Starbucks
30a	I-780, to Martinez
29b	Magazine St, Vallejo, Ⓝ...**gas:** 76/dsl, **food:** Starbucks, **lodging:** Budget Inn, El Rancho, 7 Motel, **other:** Tradewinds RV Park, Ⓢ...**food:** McDonald's, **lodging:** Travel Inn, **other:** 7-11
29a	CA 29, Maritime Academy Dr, Vallejo, Ⓝ...**gas:** Chevron/24hr, 5 Star Gas, **food:** Subway, **lodging:** Motel 6, Vallejo Inn
28mm	toll plaza, pay toll from eb
27	Pomona Rd, Crockett, Ⓝ...**food:** seafood rest.
26	Cummings Skyway, to CA 4(from wb), to Martinez, no services
24	Willow Ave, to Rodeo, Ⓝ...**food:** Straw Hat Pizza, Subway, **other:** Curves, NAPA, Safeway/24hr, USPO, Ⓢ...**gas:** 76/Circle K/dsl, **food:** Burger King, Mazatlan, Starbucks
23	CA 4, to Stockton, Hercules, Ⓝ...**gas:** Shell, **food:** Jack-in-the-Box, Starbucks, **other:** Radio Shack, Ⓢ on Sycamore...**food:** Burgerama, McDonald's, RoundTable Pizza, Subway, Taco Bell, **other:** Albertson's, Home Depot, Rite Aid, USPO
22	Pinole Valley Rd, Ⓢ...**gas:** Arco/24hr, Chevron/dsl, **food:** China House, Jack-in-the-Box, Papa John's, Red Onion Rest., Subway, **other:** 7-11
21	Appian Way, Ⓝ...**gas:** Beacon, **food:** McDonald's, **other:** Kragen Parts, Longs Drug, Safeway, Ⓢ...**gas:** Valero/dsl, **food:** Burger King, Carl's Jr, HomeTown Buffet, HotDog Sta, KFC, Krispy Kreme, In n' Out, LJ Silver, Panda Express, RoundTable Pizza, Sizzler, Starbucks, Subway, Taco Bell, Wendy's, **lodging:** Day's Inn, Motel 6, **other:** Albertson's, Autozone, Best Buy, Goodyear/auto, K-Mart, Radio Shack
20	Richmond Pkwy, to I-580 W, Ⓝ...**gas:** Chevron, **food:** McDonald's, IHOP, Subway, **other:** Barnes&Noble, Chrysler/Jeep, Circuit City, Ford, Ross, Ⓢ...**gas:** Chevron, Shell/dsl, **food:** Applebee's, Chuck Steak,

CALIFORNIA

Interstate 80

E ↕ W

Richmond

	In-n-Out, Krispy Kreme, Outback Steaks, Panda Express, RoundTable Pizza, **other:** FoodMaxx, GoodGuys, Kinko's, Kragen Parts, Old Navy, Mervyn's, Michael's, Staples, Target
19b	Hilltop Dr, to Richmond, **N**...**gas:** Chevron, **food:** Chevy's Mexican, Olive Garden, Red Lobster, Subway, Tokyo Rest., **lodging:** Courtyard, Extended Stay America, **other:** Albertson's, Buick/Pontiac, Chevrolet, Firestone, JC Penney, Jo-Ann Fabrics, Macy's, Nissan, Sears/auto, mall, **S**...**gas:** Hilltop Fuel/Bobby's BBQ/dsl
19a	El Portal Dr, to San Pablo, **S**...**gas:** Shell, **food:** McDonalds, KFC, **other:** Raley's Foods
18	San Pablo Dam Rd, **N**...**gas:** 76, 7-11, **food:** Burger King, Denny's, Jack-in-the-Box, KFC, Long's Burgers, McDonald's, Nations Burgers, Quizno's, Taco Bell, **lodging:** Holiday Inn Express, **other:** HOSPITAL, Albertson's, K-Mart, Longs Drug, **S**...**other:** CamperLand RV Ctr
17	Macdonald Ave(from eb), McBryde Ave(from wb), Richmond, **N**...**gas:** Arco/24hr, Citgo/7-11, **food:** Burger King, Church's, KFC, Taco Bell, **S**...**gas:** Chevron/24hr, **food:** Bakers Square, Wendy's, **other:** Albertson's, Safeway, auto repair
16	San Pablo Ave, to Richmond, San Pablo, **S**...**gas:** Chevron, 76, **food:** Subway, Wendy's, **other:** Safeway
15	Cutting Blvd, Potrero St, to I-580 Br(from wb), to El Cerrito, **N**...**gas:** Arco, **S**...**gas:** Chevron, 76/dsl, **food:** Carrow's Rest., Church's, Denny's, IHOP, Jack-in-the-Box, McDonald's, **lodging:** Super 8, **other:** $Tree, FoodsCo Foods, Home Depot, Honda, PepBoys, Radio Shack, Staples, Target, Walgreens
14b	Carlson Blvd, El Cerrito, **N**...**gas:** 76, **lodging:** 40 Flags Motel, **S**...**lodging:** Best Value
14a	Central Ave, El Cerrito, **S**...**gas:** 76, Valero, **food:** Burger King, KFC, Nations Burgers, **other:** Branch Mkt Foods, mall
13	to I-580(from eb), Albany
12	Gilman St, to Berkeley, **N**...Golden Gate Fields Racetrack
11	University Ave, to Berkeley, **S**...**gas:** 76, Beacon, **other:** to UC Berkeley
10	CA 13, to Ashby Ave, no services

Berkeley

9	Powell St, Emeryville, **N**...**gas:** Shell, **food:** Chevy's Mexican, **lodging:** Holiday Inn, **S**...**gas:** Beacon, **food:** Burger King, Denny's, Jamba Juice, Lyon's Rest., Starbucks, Trader Joe's, **lodging:** Courtyard, Day's Inn, Sheraton, Wyndham Suites, **other:** Borders Books, Circuit City, Emery Bay Mkt, Good Guys, Jo-Ann Fabrics, Old Navy, Ross
8c b	Oakland, to I-880, I-580, no services
8a	W Grand Ave, Maritime St, no services
7mm	toll plaza wb
5mm	SF Bay
4a	Treasure Island(exits left)
2c b	Fremont St, Harrison St, Embarcadero(from wb)
2a	4th st(from eb), **S**...**gas:** Shell
1	9th st, Civic Ctr, downtown SF
1b a	I-80 begins/ends on US 101 In SF

Interstate 110(LA)

E ↕ W

Los Angeles Area

Exit #	Services
21	I-110 begins/ends on I-10.
20c	Adams Blvd, **E**...**other:** Chevron, Nissan, Office Depot, LA Concention Ctr.
20b	37th St, Exposition Blvd, **E**...repair, **W**...**gas:** Chevron/McDonald's, **lodging:** Radisson
20a	MLK Blvd, Expo Park, **W**...**gas:** Chevron, **food:** McDonald's, Subway
19b	Vernon Ave, **E**...**gas:** Mobil, **W**...**gas:** 76/24hr, Shell, **food:** Burger King, Jack-in-the-Box, **other:** Ralph's Foods
18b	Slauson Ave, **E**...**gas:** Mobil, **W**...**gas:** 76
18a	Gage Blvd, **E**...**gas:** Arco, **food:** Church's
17	Florence Ave, **E**...**gas:** Mobil, **food:** Jack-in-the-Box, **W**...**gas:** Arco, Chevron, Shell/24hr, **food:** Burger King, McDonald's, Pizza Hut
16	Manchester Ave, **E**...**gas:** Arco, **food:** McDonald's, **other:** AutoZone, **W**...**gas:** 76/Circle K, **food:** Church's, Jack-in-the-Box, Tom's Burgers, Popeye's, **other:** Ralph's Foods
15	Century Blvd, **E**...**gas:** Arco, Shell/Subway, **food:** Burger King, **W**...**gas:** 76
14b	Imperial Hwy, **W**...**gas:** Petro Zone, **food:** McDonald's, Jack-in-the-Box
14a	I-105
13	El Segundo Blvd, **E**...**food:** Pizza Hut, Taco Bell, **W**...**food:** Denny's
12	Rosecrans Ave, **E**...**gas:** Arco/24hr, Prena, SC Fuels, **W**...**gas:** Chevron/McDonald's, Mobil, **food:** Jack-in-the-Box, KFC, Popeye's, Subway, **other:** Chief Parts, 7-11
11	Redondo Beach Blvd, **E**...**food:** McDonald's, **W**...**gas:** Mobil, **other:** HOSPITAL
10b a	CA 91, 190th St, **W**...**food:** Carl's Jr, Jack-in-the-Box, Krispy Kreme, McDonald's, Taco Bell/Pizza Hut, **other:** Albertson's, Food4Less, Sam's Club
9	I-405, San Diego Fwy
8	Torrance Blvd, Del Amo, **E**...**food:** Baskin-Robbins, Burger King, Chile Verde, Panda Bowl, **other:** K-mart, **W**...**gas:** Mobil, Shell/dsl
7b	Carson St, **E**...**food:** KFC, **lodging:** Cali Inn, **W**...**gas:** Mobil, Shell, **food:** Bakers Square, Hong Kong Garden, In-n-Out, Jack-in-the-Box, **other:** HOSPITAL, Carson Drug, Kragen Parts, Radio Shack
5	Sepulveda Blvd, **E**...**food:** McDonald's, **other:** Albertson's, Home Depot, Staples, Target, **W**...**gas:** Arco/24hr, Chevron, Mobil, Shell, **food:** Burger King, Carl's Jr, Golden Ox Burger, McDonald's, Pizza Hut/Taco Bell, Popeye's, **lodging:** Motel 6, **other:** $Tree, Food4Less, K-Mart, Rite Aid, Von's Foods
4	CA 1, Pacific Coast Hwy, **E**...**gas:** Shell, **food:** Jack-in-the-Box, **W**...**gas:** Chevron, Mobil/dsl, **food:** Denny's, El Pollo Loco, EZ Burger, **lodging:** Best Western, **other:** HOSPITAL, Discount Parts, Honda, PepBoys
3b	Anaheim St, **E**...**gas:** Shell
3a	C St, **E**...**gas:** Shell/dsl, **other:** radiators, **W**...**gas:** 76 Refinery
1b	Channel St, no services
1a	CA 47, Gaffey Ave, no services
0mm	I-110 begins/ends

Interstate 205(Tracy)

E ↕ W

Tracy

Exit #	Services
12	I-205 begins wb, ends eb, accesses I-5 nb
9	MacArthur Dr, Tracy, Ⓢ...**gas** Chevron/Jack-in-the-Box/Subway/dsl, **other:** Prime Outlet Ctr/famous brands
8	Tracy Blvd, Tracy, Ⓝ...**gas:** Chevron, Shell/dsl, Tracy Trkstp/Mean Gene's Burger/dsl/24hr, **food:** Denny's/24hr, **lodging:** Holiday Inn Express, Motel 6, Ⓢ...**gas:** Arco/24hr, **food:** American Diner, Arby's, Burger King, In-n-Out, McDonald's, Nations Burgers, Subway, Tracy Buffet, Wendy's, **lodging:** Best Western, Microtel, Quality Inn, **other:** HOSPITAL, FoodMaxx, Kragen Parts, Longs Drugs, Walgreens, CHP
6	Grant Line Rd, Antioch, Ⓝ...**gas:** Chevron, **food:** Applebee's, Burger King, Chevy's Mexican, Golden Corral, Gottschalk's, Hometown Buffet, IHOP, Jamba Juice, Olive Garden, Panda Express, Quizno's, Sonic, Starbucks, Strings Italian, Taco Bell, Texas Roadhouse, Wienerschnitzel/TasteeFreeze, **lodging:** Extended Stay America, Fairfield Inn, Hampton Inn, **other:** America's Tire, Barnes&Noble, Chevrolet, Costco/gas, Ford, Home Depot, Hyundai, JC Penney, Michael's, Nissan, Ross, Schwab Tire, Sears/auto, Staples, Target, Toyota, Wal-Mart/McDonald's/auto, World Mkt, mall, Ⓢ...**gas:** Arco/24hr, Citgo/7-11, Shell/dsl, Valero, **food:** Carl's Jr, Chili's, Hawaian BBQ, KFC/A&W, Mtn Mike's Pizza, NYPD Pizza, Orchard Rest., Taco Del Mar, **other:** Cadillac/Pontiac/GMC, Rite Aid, Tracy Marine
4	11th St(from eb), to Tracy, Defense Depot
2	Mtn House Pkwy, to I-580 E, no services
0mm	I-205 begins eb/ends wb, accesses I-580 wb

Interstate 210(Pasadena)

E ↕ W

Exit #	Services
63	I-15 N to Barstow, S to San Diego
62	Day Creek Blvd, Ⓢ...**gas:** Arco/dsl, Shell, **food:** Jack-in-the-Box, Pizza Factory, Starbucks, Wendy's, **other:** Ralph's Foods
60	Mileken Ave, Ⓢ...**gas:** Mobil, **food:** Taco Bell, **other:** Albertsons, CVS Drug, Kragen Parts
59	Haven Ave, Ⓝ...**gas:** 76, 7-11, Mobil, **food:** Del Taco, Dominos, Jack-in-the-Box, **other:** Walgreens
58	Archibald Ave, Ⓢ...**other:** Stater Bros
57	Carnelion St, Ⓢ...**gas:** 76, **food:** El Ranchero Mexican, Papa John's, **other:** Radio Shack, Rite Aid, Vons Foods, Walgreens
56	Campus Ave, Ⓢ...**food:** Carl's Jr, Chick-fil-A, IHOP, Jamba Juice, Quizno's, Starbucks, **other:** Albertsons, Home Depot, Kohl's, Office Depot, Petsmart, Target
54	Mtn Ave, Mount Balde
52	Baseline Rd

San Dimas

Exit #	Services
50	Towne Ave
48	Fruit St, LaVerne, Ⓢ...**gas:** 76, **other:** U of LaVerne
47	Foothill Blvd, LaVerne, Ⓝ...**food:** Denny's, Ⓢ...**gas:** Chevron, Shell
46	San Dimas Ave, , Ⓝ... San Dimas Canyon CP
45	CA 57 S, Lone Hill Ave, Santa Ana, Ⓢ...**gas:** Chevron, **food:** Baja Fresh, Blimpie, Coco's, In-n-Out, Wendy's, **other:** Chevrolet, Dodge, Ford, Home Depot, Hyundai, Kohl's, Sam's Club, Toyota, Wal-Mart/auto
43	Sunflower Ave, no services
42	Grand Ave, to Glendora, Ⓝ...**gas:** 76, Valero, **food:** Denny's, **other:** HOSPITAL
41	Citrus Ave, to Covina, no services
40	Ca 39, Azuza Ave, Ⓝ...**gas:** Arco/24hr, Chevron, Shell/Subway/Del Taco, **food:** Jack-in-the-Box, **lodging:** Super 8, Ⓢ...**gas:** 76, **food:** In-n-Out, **lodging:** Azuza Inn
39	Vernon Ave (from wb), same as 38
38	Irwindale, Ⓝ...**gas:** Arco, **food:** Carl's Jr, Denny's, FarmerBoys Rest., McDonald's, Shanghai Buffet, Taco Bell, **other:** Costco/gas
36b	Mt Olive Dr, no services
36a	I-605 S
35b a	Mountain Ave, Ⓝ...**gas:** Chevron **food:** Old Spaghetti Factory, Tommy's Hamburgers, Weinerschnitzel, **lodging:** Oak Park Motel, **other:** BMW/Mini, Buick, Chevrolet, Ford/Lincoln/Mercury, Honda, Infiniti, Isuzu, Mazda, Mitsubishi, Nissan, Saturn, Staples, Subaru, Target, Walgreens, Ⓢ...**food:** IHOP, Panda Express, **other:** Home Depot, Ross, Wal-Mart
34	Myrtle Ave, Ⓢ...**gas:** Chevron, 76, **food:** Jack-in-the-Box
33	Huntington Dr, Monrovia, Ⓝ...**gas:** Shell, **food:** Acapulco Rest., Applebee's, Black Angus, Burger King, Chili's, ChuckeCheese, Leroy's Rest., McDonald's, Mimi's, Panda Express, Quizno's, RoundTable Pizza, Rubio's, Trader Joe's, **lodging:** Courtyard, **other:** CompUSA, GNC, Marshall's, Office Depot, Rite Aid, tires, Ⓢ...**food:** Baja Fresh, BJ's Grill, ClaimJumper, Daphne's Rest., Derby Rest., Gold Dragon, Macaroni Grill, Olive Garden, Outback Steaks, Red Lobster, Starbucks, Subway, Taisho Rest., Togo's, Tokyo Woko, Tony Roma, **lodging:** Embassy Suites, Extended Stay America, Hampton Inn, Holiday Inn, Homestead Suites, OakTree Inn, Residence Inn
32	Santa Anita Ave, Arcadia, Ⓝ...**gas:** Arco, **food:** McDonald's, **other:** Von's Foods, Ⓢ...**gas:** Chevron, **food:** In-n-Out, **other:** carwash
31	Baldwin Ave, to Sierra Madre, no services

E ↕ W

CALIFORNIA

Interstate 210

E ↑↓ W

Pasadena

Exit	Services
30b a	Rosemead Blvd, **N**...**gas:** Arco, 76, **S**...**gas:** 76, **food:** Coco's, Jack-in-the-Box, **other:** Big-O Tires
29b a	San Gabriel Blvd, Madre St, **N**...**gas:** Arco, 76, **food:** El Torito, **lodging:** Panda Inn, **other:** Ralph's Foods, Ross, **S**...**gas:** 76, **food:** Jack–in-the-Box, **lodging:** Best Western, Holiday Inn Express, Quality Inn, **other:** Buick/Chevrolet/Pontiac/GMC, Cadillac, Circuit City, Hyundai, Jiffy Lube, Staples, Target, Toyota
28	Altadena Dr, Sierra Madre, **S**...**gas:** Chevron, Mobil, **other:** Just Tires, Office Depot
27	Hill Ave, no services
26	Lake Ave, **N**...**gas:** Mobil
25b	CA 134, to Ventura, no services
25a	Del Mar Blvd, CA Blvd, CO Blvd (exits left from eb)
24	Mountain St, no services
23	Lincoln Ave, **S**...**lodging:** Lincoln Motel, **other:** auto repair
22b	Arroyo Blvd, **N**...**food:** Jack-in-the-Box, **S**...to Rose Bowl
22a	Berkshire Ave, Oak Grove Dr, no services
21	Gould Ave, **S**...**gas:** Arco, **food:** Dominos, McDonald's, RoundTable Pizza, Trader Joes, **other:** Firestone, Just Tires, Ralph's Foods
20	CA 2, Angeles Crest Hwy, no services
19	CA 2, Glendale Fwy, **S**...**other:** HOSPITAL
18	Ocean View Blvd, to Montrose, no services
17b a	Pennsylvania Ave, La Crescenta, **N**...**gas:** Mobil, Shell, **food:** Quizno's, Wienerschnitzel, **other:** Nissan, Office Depot, Toyota, Von's Foods, **S**...**other:** Gardenia Mkt/deli
16	Lowell Ave, no services
14	La Tuna Cyn Rd, no services

San Fernando

Exit	Services
11	Sunland Blvd, Tujunga, **N**...**gas:** 76, **food:** Coco's, Sizzler, **other:** Ralph's Foods, Rite Aid, 7-11
9	Wheatland Ave, **N**...**other:** food mkt
8	Osborne St, Lakeview Terrace, **N**...**food:** Ranch Side Cafe, **other:** 7-11
6a	Paxton St, no services
6b	CA 118, no services
5	Maclay St, to San Fernando, **S**...**gas:** Chevron, 76, **food:** El Pollo Loco, KFC, McDonald's, Peter Piper Pizza, Quizno's, Taco Bell, **other:** Home Depot, Office Depot, Radio Shack, Sam's Club
4	Hubbard St, **N**...**gas:** Chevron, **food:** Denny's, **other:** Radio Shack, Rite Aid, **S**...**gas:** Mobil/dsl, Shell, **food:** El Caporal Mexican, Jack-in-the-Box, Shakey's Pizza, Subway, **other:** Vons Foods
3	Polk St, **S**...**gas:** Arco, Chevron/24hr, **food:** KFC, **other:** 7-11
2	Roxford St, **N**...HOSPITAL, **S**...**lodging:** Country Side Inn
1c	Yarnell St, no services
1b a	I-210 begins/ends on I-5, exit 160.

Interstate 215(Riverside)

N ↑↓ S

Exit #	Services
55	I-215 begins/ends on I-15.
54	Devore, **E**...**gas:** Devore Minimart/dsl, Petra
50	Palm Ave, Kendall Dr, **E**...**gas:** 7-11/gas, Mobil/Subway/dsl, **food:** Burger King, Popeye's, Starbucks, **W**...**food:** Denny's
48	University Pkwy, **E**...**gas:** Chevron, 76/Circle K, **food:** Alberto's, Baskin-Robbins/Togo's, Carl's Jr, Del Taco, Dominos, IHOP, KFC, Little Ceasars, McDonald's, Papa John's, Starbucks, Weinerschnitzel, **other:** Ralph's Foods, Staples, **W**...**gas:** Arco/24hr, Shell/dsl/LP, **food:** Jack-in-the-Box, Pizza Hut/Taco Bell, Zendejas Mexican, **lodging:** Day's Inn, Motel 6, **other:** Lowe's Whse, Wal-Mart/Subway
46c b	27th St, **E**...golf, **W**...golf
46a	CA 30 W, Highland Ave, no services
45b	Muscupiade Dr, **E**...**gas:** Shell, Thrifty, **food:** Jack-in-the-Box, **other:** Chevrolet, Home Depot, SavOn Foods, Stater Bros
45a	CA 30 E, Highlands, no services
44b	Baseline Rd, no services
44a	CA 66 W, 5th St, **E**...**lodging:** Econolodge
43	2nd St, Civic Ctr, **E**...**gas:** Arco, Chevron, **food:** China Hut, Del Taco, Denny's, In-n-Out, LJ Silver, Pizza Hut/Taco Bell, **lodging:** Radisson, **other:** Ford, Food4Less, JC Penney, Kelly Tire, Marshall's, mall
42b	Mill St, **E**...**food:** Carl's Jr, Dell Taco, Jack-in-the-Box, McDonald's, **other:** Suzuki/Honda, **W**...**gas:** Shell, **food:** Yum-yum Donuts
42a	Inland Ctr Dr, **E**...**food:** Carl's Jr, Del Taco, Gottschalk's, Jack-in-the-Box, **other:** Macy's, Robinsons-May, Sears/auto, mall, **W**...**food:** Alice's Rest.
41	Orange Show Rd, **E**...**gas:** Arco, Chevron, Exxon, **food:** Denny's, Pancho Villa Mexican, **lodging:** Guest House Inn, Knight's Inn, **other:** BigLots, Chevrolet, Dodge, Firestone, Gottschalk's, Kelly Tire, Macy's, Mazda, Radio Shack, Subaru, 99c Store, Target, **W**...**other:** Cadillac, Giant RV, Isuzu, Jeep, Kia, Mitsubishi, Nissan, Toyota, Volvo, VW
40b a	I-10, E to Palm Springs, W to LA
39	Washington St, Mt Vernon Ave, **E**...**gas:** Arco/24hr, 5 Points, **food:** Arby's, Baker's Drive-Thru, Siquios Mexican, Taco Joe's, Starbucks, **lodging:** Colton Inn, **other:** BigLots, $Tree, Goodyear, Jiffy Lube, **W**...**food:** Burger King, Carl's Jr, Del Taco, Denny's, El Pollo Loco, Jack-in-the-Box, McDonald's, Quizno's, Sassy Steer, Starbucks, Subway, Taco Bell, Zendejas Mexican, **lodging:** Red Tile Inn, **other:** GNC, 99c Store, Radio Shack, Ross, Wal-Mart/auto, multiple RV dealers
38	Barton Rd, **E**...**gas:** Arco, Shell/Circle K, **other:** AutoZone, **W**...**food:** Dorothy's Burgers
37	La Cadena Dr, **E**...**gas:** Shell/dsl/24hr, **food:** Jack-in-the-Box, YumYum Rest., **lodging:** Holiday Inn Express
36	Center St, to Highgrove, **W**...**gas:** Valero
35	Columbia Ave, **E**...**gas:** Arco, **W**...**other:** Circle K
34b a	CA 91, CA 60, Riverside, to beach cities
33	Blaine St, 3rd St, **E**...**gas:** 76, Shell, Valero, **food:** Bakers Drive-Thru, Jack-in-the-Box, Starbucks

San Bernardino

CALIFORNIA

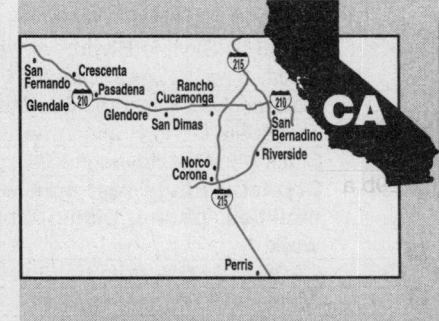

Interstate 215

N ↑↓ S

Riverside

32	University Ave, Riverside, **W**...**gas:** Arco, Mobil, Shell, **food:** Baker's Drive-Thru, BK Subs, Carl's Jr, Coco's, Del Taco, Denny's, Domino's, Green Burrito, Gus Jr, IHOP, Jilberto's Tacos, Papa John's, Quizno's, Santana's Mexican, Shakey's Pizza, Starbucks, Taco Bell, Togo's, Wienerschnitzel, Winchell's, **lodging:** Comfort Inn, Courtyard, Dynasty Suites, Motel 6, Super 8, **other:** Kragen Parts, Rite Aid
31	MLK Blvd, El Cerrito, no services
30b	Central Ave, Watkins Dr, no services
30a	Fair Isle Dr, Box Springs, no services
29	CA 60 E, to Indio, **E** **on Day St**...**gas:** Arco/24hr, Shell/Del Taco/dsl, **food:** Applebees, Baker's Drive-Thru, Café Chinese, Carl's Jr, HomeTown Buffet, McDonald's, Mimi's Cafe, Panda Express, Red Robin, Starbucks, Subway, Wendy's, Wienerschnitzel, **other:** Best Buy, Circuit City, Costco/gas, Home Depot, JC Penney, Jo-Ann Fabrics, Lowes, Macy's, Mervyn's, Old Navy, PetCo, Ralph's Foods, Robinsons-May, Sam's Club/gas, Sears/auto, Staples, Target, Wal-Mart, Win-Co Foods, mall
28	Eucalyptus Ave, Eastridge Ave, **E** **on Day St**...**other:** Sam's Club/gas, Wal-Mart, same as 29
27b	Alessandro Blvd, **E**...**gas:** Arco/24hr, 76/dsl, **other:** Big O Tire, auto repair, **W**...**gas:** Chevron
27a	Cactus Air Blvd, **E**...**gas:** Chevron, Circle K/76/dsl, **food:** Carl's Jr, Richie's Burgers
25	Van Buren Blvd, **E**...**other:** March Field Museum, **W**... **other:** Riverside Nat Cen.
23	Oleander Ave, no services
22	Ramona Expswy, **1 mi E on Perris Blvd**...**gas:** Arco/ 24hr, Mobil, Shell/Subway/dsl, **food:** Taco Bell, **other:** Albertson's, Wal-Mart/auto, **W**...**gas:** 76/Circle K, **food:** Jack-in-the-Box
19	Nuevo Rd, **E**...**gas:** Arco/24hr, Mobil, 76, **food:** Burger King, Carl's Jr, China Buffet, Del Taco, El Pollo Loco, IHOP, Jenny's Rest., McDonald's, Pizza Hut, Sizzler, Starbucks, Taco Bell, **other:** Albertsons, AutoZone, Food4Less, GNC, Kragen Parts, Radio Shack, Rite Aid, Stater Bros Foods, Wal-Mart

Perris

17	CA 74 W, 4th St, to Perris, Lake Elsinore, **E**...**gas:** Shell/24hr, **W**...**gas:** Chevron, **food:** Del Taco, Denny's, Jack-in-the-Box, Jimenez Mexican, Little Caesar's, Nick's Burgers, Popeye's, **lodging:** Day's Inn, **other:** Autozone, CarQuest, Chrysler/Dodge/Jeep, USPO
15	CA 74 E, Hemet, **E**...**other:** motel, Ford/Lincoln/Mercury
14	Ethanac Rd, **E**...**food:** KFC/Taco Bell, **other:** Richardson's RV/Marine, **W**...**gas:** Exxon/dsl
12	McCall Blvd, Sun City, **E**...**gas:** Valero, **food:** Wendy's, **lodging:** Best Value, Super 8, **other:** HOSPITAL, **W**...**gas:** Chevron/dsl, 76, Valero, **food:** Burger King, Coco's, McDonald's, Santana's Mexican, **other:** Stater Bros Foods, Walgreens
10	Newport Rd, Quail Valley, **E**...**gas:** Shell/Del Taco/dsl, **food:** Cathay Chinese, Coldstone Creamery, Jack-in-the-Box, Subway, Taco Bell, **other:** AutoZone, GNC, Ralph's Foods, Ross, Target, **W**...**gas:** Arco/24hr, Mobil, 76/Circle K, **food:** Yellow Basket Cafe
7	Scott Rd, **E**...**gas:** 7-11, **food:** Del Taco, Subway, **other:** Albertson's/SavOn, Curves
4	Clinton Keith Rd

2	Los Alamos, **E**... **gas:** Shell, **food:** CA Grill, Carnita's Mexican, Mama Rosa's Pizza, Peony Chinese, Taco Bell, **W**... **gas:** Mobil/Mc-Donald's, **food:** ChuckeCheese, City Deli/bakery, Jack-in-the-Box, Mongolian BBQ, Subway, **other:** CVS Drug, Radio Shack, Stater Bros Foods
1	Murrieta Hot Springs, **E**...**food:** Carl's Jr, Del Taco, Domino's, Sizzler, **other:** Ralph's Foods, Rite Aid, Ross, Sam's Club/gas, USPO, Weston's Mkt
0mm	I-215 begins/ends on I-15.

Interstate 280(Bay Area)

San Francisco

E ↑↓ W

Exit #	Services
58	4th St, I-280 begins/ends, downtown
57	6th St, to I-80, downtown
56	Mariposa St, downtown
55	Army St, Port of SF
54	US 101 S, Alemany Blvd, Mission St, **E**...**gas:** Shell
52	San Jose Ave, Bosworth St(from nb, no return)
51	Geneva Ave, no services
50	CA 1, 19th Ave, **W**...**gas:** Chevron, **other:** to Bay Bridge, SFSU
49	Daly City, **E**...**gas:** Olympian, 76/dsl/LP, **W**...**gas:** Arco, **food:** Carl's Jr, Domino's, IHOP, In-n-Out, Krispy Kreme, McDonald's, Val's Rest., **lodging:** Hampton Inn
48	Serramonte Blvd, Daly City(from sb), **E**...**other:** Chevrolet, **W**...**gas:** Olympian, 76, **food:** Boston Mkt, Daiso Japanese, Elephant Bar Rest., McDonald's, Starbucks, **other:** Macy's, Mervyn's, Circuit City, Longs Drugs, Office Depot, Petsmart, Ross, Target
47b	CA 1, Mission St, Pacifica, **E**...**gas:** Chevron, Silver/ gas, **food:** Hawaiian BBQ, RoundTable Pizza, Sizzler, **other:** HOSPITAL, Chrysler/Jeep/Dodge, Drug Barn, Ford, Fresh Choice Foods, Home Depot, Infiniti, Isuzu, Jo-Ann Fabrics, Lexus, Mitsubishi, Nissan, Nordstrom's, PetCo, Saturn, Target, mall
46	Hickey Blvd, Colma, **E**...**gas:** Chevron/dsl/24hr, Shell, **W**...**gas:** Shell/dsl/24hr, **food:** Celia's Rest., Moonstar, Outback Steaks, Sizzler, **other:** 7-11
45	Avalon Dr, Westborough, **W**...**gas:** Arco/24hr, Valero/ dsl, **food:** Denny's, McDonald's, **other:** Walgreens/ 24hr, Skyline Coll
43b	I-380 E, to US 101, to SF Airport
43a	San Bruno Ave, Sneath Lane, **E**...**food:** Baskin-Robbins, Carl's Jr, Extreme Pizza, Jamba Juice, Pasta Pomodoro, Taco Bell, **other:** Longs Drugs, Mollie Stones Mkt, **W**...**gas:** Chevron, 76, **food:** Baker's Square, **other:** 7-11
42	Crystal Springs, county park

CALIFORNIA
Interstate 280

E ↑ ↓ W

Exit	Services
41	CA 35 N, Skyline Blvd(from wb, no EZ return), to Pacifica, **1 mi** Ⓦ...**gas:** Chevron
40	Millbrae Ave, Millbrae, Ⓔ...**gas:** Chevron
39	Trousdale Dr, to Burlingame, Ⓔ...HOSPITAL
36	Black Mtn Rd, Hayne Rd, Ⓦ...golf, vista point
36	**Crystal Springs rest area wb, full (handicapped) facilities, phone, picnic table, litter barrels, petwalk**
35	CA 35, CA 92W(from eb), to Half Moon Bay
34	Bunker Hill Dr, no services
33	CA 92, to Half Moon Bay, San Mateo, no services
32mm	vista point both lanes
29	Edgewood Rd, Canada Rd, to San Carlos, Ⓔ...**other:** HOSPITAL
27	Farm Hill Blvd, Ⓔ...**other:** Cañada Coll, phone
25	CA 84, Woodside Rd, Redwood City, **1 mi** Ⓦ...**gas:** Chevron/dsl, **other:** USPO
24	Sand Hill Rd, Menlo Park, **1 mi** Ⓔ...**gas:** Shell, **food:** Starbucks, **other:** Longs Drug, Safeway
22	Alpine Rd, Portola Valley, Ⓔ...**other:** HOSPITAL, Ⓦ...**gas:** Chevron, Shell/autocare, **food:** Red Lotus Cafe, RoundTable Pizza, **other:** Curves
20	Page Mill Rd, Palo Alto, Ⓔ...HOSPITAL, Stanford U
16	El Monte Rd, Moody Rd, no services
15	Magdalena Ave, no services
13	Foothill Expswy, Grant Rd, Ⓔ...**gas:** Chevron/24hr, **food:** Trader Joe's, **other:** Rite Aid, Ⓦ...**other:** to Rancho San Antonio CP
12b a	CA 85, N to Mtn View, S to Gilroy
11	Saratoga, Cupertino, Sunnyvale, Ⓔ...**gas:** Chevron, **food:** Carl's Jr, **lodging:** Cupertino Inn, **other:** Goodyear, Michael's, Rite Aid, repair, Ⓦ...**gas:** Alliance, Chevron, 76, **food:** BJ's Brewhouse, Mandarin Gourmet, Outback Steaks, **lodging:** Cypress Hotel, **other:** Apple Computer Hdqrts, Target
10	Wolfe Rd, Ⓔ...**gas:** Arco/24hr, **food:** Starbucks, **lodging:** Courtyard, Hilton Garden, **other:** Ranch Mkt, Ⓦ...**gas:** 76, **food:** Alexander Steaks, CA Pizza Kitchen, TGIFriday, **other:** FreshChoice Foods, JC Penney, Jiffy Lube, Sears/auto, Vallco Fashion Park, RV Ctr
9	Lawrence Expswy, Stevens Creek Blvd(from eb), Ⓝ...**food:** McDonalds, Mtn Mikes Pizza, Panda Express, Quizno's, Starbucks, **other:** Rite Aid, Safeway, Marshall's, Ⓢ...**gas:** Rotten Robbie gas, 76, **food:** IHOP, Subway, **lodging:** Wellsley Inn, Woodcrest Hotel
7	Saratoga Ave, Ⓝ...**gas:** Arco/24hr, Chevron/24hr, **food:** Black Angus, Burger King, Garden City Rest., Happi House, Harry's Hofbrau, McDonald's, Taco Bell, **lodging:** TownePlace Suites, **other:** Cost+, Goodyear, Jiffy Lube, Lion Foods, PepBoys, 7-11, Toyota, Ⓢ...**gas:** 76, Shell, Valero, **food:** Applebee's, Baskin Robbins, Tony Roma's, **lodging:** MoorPark Hotel
5c	Winchester Blvd, Campbell Ave(from eb)
5b	CA 17 S, to Santa Cruz, I-880 N, to San Jose
5a	Leigh Ave, Bascom Ave, no services
4	Meridian St(from eb), Ⓝ...**other:** Big O Tire, Foodmaxx, Ⓢ...**gas:** Chevron, 76, **food:** KFC, Taco Bell, Wienerschnitzel
3b	Bird Ave, Race St, no services

San Jose

3a	CA 87, Ⓝ...**lodging:** Hilton, Holiday Inn, Hotel Sainte Claire, Marriott
2	7th St, to CA 82, Ⓝ...conv ctr
1	10th St, 11th St, Ⓝ...**other:** 7-11, **other:** to San Jose St U
0mm	I-280 begins/ends on US 101.

Interstate 405(LA)

N ↑ ↓ S

Exit #	Services
73	I-5, N to Sacramento, I-5, N to Sacramento
72	Rinaldi St, Sepulveda, Ⓔ...**gas:** Chevron, 76, **food:** Arby's, Presidente McDonald's, Mexican, Subway, **other:** HOSPITAL, Toyota, Ⓦ...**gas:** Shell, **lodging:** Best Value
71	CA 118 W, Simi Valley
70	Devonshire St, Granada Hills, Ⓔ...**gas:** Arco, Mobil, 76, **food:** Holiday Burger, Millie's Rest., Papa John's, Quizno's, Safari Room Rest, Starbucks, Subway, **other:** Discount Tire, Kwik Serve, Nissan, Ralph's Foods, Rite Aid, Von's Foods, USPO
69	Nordhoff St, Ⓔ...**gas:** Mobil/dsl, **other:** 7-11/24hr, Vallarta Foods, Walgreen, Ⓦ...**gas:** Arco, 76, **food:** Jack-in-the-Box, Pizza Hut
68	Roscoe Blvd, to Panorama City, Ⓔ...**gas:** Exxon, 76, **food:** Burger King, Denny's, Jack-in-the-Box, McDonald's, Panda Express, Quizno's, Taco Bell, Yoshinoya, **lodging:** Holiday Inn Express, **other:** AutoZone, Ford/Lincoln/Mercury/Jaguar/Starbucks, Saturn, Ⓦ...**gas:** Chevron/dsl, Shell/dsl, **food:** Tommy's Burgers, **lodging:** Motel 6
66	Sherman Blvd, Reseda, Ⓔ...**gas:** Chevron, Mobil/LP, **food:** Ameci Pizza, KFC, McDonald's, Starbucks, **other:** BigLots, CVS Drug, Jon's Foods, Ⓦ...**gas:** 76/dsl/24hr, **food:** Taco Bell, **other:** HOSPITAL, USPO
65	Victory Blvd, Van Nuys, Ⓔ **on Sepulveda**...**food:** Carl's Jr, El Pollo Loco, Jack-in-the-Box, Subway, Wendy's, **other:** CVS Drug, El Monte RV Ctr, Costco/gas, Office Depot, PepBoys, Staples, **W on Victory**...**gas:** Arco/24hr, **other:** HOSPITAL
64	Burbank Blvd, Ⓔ...**gas:** Chevron, Shell, **food:** Denny's, **lodging:** Best Western, **other:** Target
63b	US 101, Ventura Fwy
63a	Ventura Blvd(from nb), Ⓔ...**gas:** Mobil, **food:** Denny's, El Pollo Loco, Robinsons-May, **other:** Food Mkt, mall, Ⓦ...**gas:** Chevron, 76, **food:** Corner Bakery Cafe, IHOP, McDonald's, **lodging:** Best West Inn, Courtyard, **other:** Rite Aid
63a	Valley Vista Blvd(from sb), no services
61	Mulholland Dr, no services
59	Sepulveda Blvd, Ⓦ...to Getty Ctr
57	Sunset Blvd, Morega Dr, Ⓔ...**gas:** Chevron/24hr, 76/dsl, **other:** to UCLA, Ⓦ...**lodging:** Luxe Hotel
56	Waterford St, Montana Ave(from nb), no services
55c b	Wilshire Blvd, Ⓔ...downtown, Ⓦ...**gas:** Mobil, **other:** HOSPITAL, 7-11
55a	CA 2, Santa Monica Blvd, Ⓔ...**gas:** Chevron, Mobil, Thrifty, **food:** Chinese Cuisine, Jack-in-the-Box, Jamba Juice, Quizno's, Starbucks, Winchell's, Yoshinoya, Zankau Chicken, **lodging:** Travelodge, **other:** Firestone, 7-11, LDS Temple, Staples, vet, Ⓦ...**gas:** Chevron, 76/24hr, **food:** Subway, **lodging:** Holiday Inn

Los Angeles Area

Interstate 405

CALIFORNIA

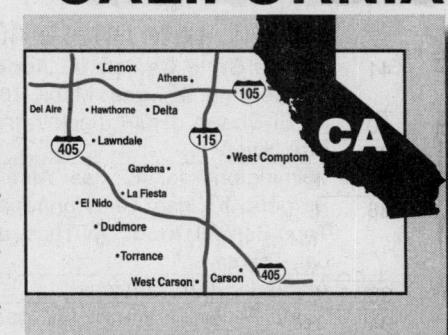

N ↑ S

Hawthorne

54 Olympic Blvd, Peco Blvd(from sb), **E**...**food:** Pazzo Pizzaria, Subway, **other:** 7-11, **W**...**food:** Panda Express, Starbucks, **other:** Best Buy, Marshall's, **other:** USPO

53 I-10, Santa Monica Fwy

52 Venice Blvd, **E**...**gas:** Chevron/service, Shell/dsl, **food:** Carl's Jr, Subway, **lodging:** Ramada, **other:** 7-11, **W**...**gas:** SP/dsl, **food:** FatBurger, **other:** services on Sepulveda

51 Culver Blvd, Washington Blvd, **E**...**food:** Dear John's Café, Taco Bell, **other:** Chevrolet, **W**...**gas:** 76/repair

50b CA 90, Slauson Ave, to Marina del Rey, **E**...**gas:** Arco/24hr, **food:** Del Taco, Shakey's Pizza, **other:** Circuit City, CompUSA, Firestone/auto, Goodyear/auto, JC Penny, Office Depot, Old Navy, Macey's, Pic'n Sav Foods, transmissions, **W**...**gas:** 76, **food:** Denny's, **other:** Albertson's

50a Jefferson Blvd(from sb), **E**...**food:** Coco's, Jack-in-the-Box, **other:** Rite Aid, **W**...to LA Airport

49 Howard Hughes Pkwy, to Centinela Ave, **E**...**gas:** Mobil/dsl, **food:** Sizzler, **lodging:** Ramada Inn, Sheraton, **other:** Ford, JC Penney, Macy's, Robinsons-May, Saturn, mall, **W**...**gas:** Chevron, **food:** Dinah's Rest., Islands Burgers, On the Border, Subway, **lodging:** Extended Stay America, Radisson, **other:** CVS Drug, Howard Hughes Ctr, mall

48 La Tijera Blvd, **E**...**gas:** Mobil, **food:** Burger King, ChuckeCheese, El Pollo Loco, Jamba Juice, KFC, McDonald's, Subway, TGIFriday, **lodging:** Best Western, **other:** CVS Drug, EZ Lube, 99c Store, Ross, Von's Foods, **W**...**gas:** Chevron/dsl/24hr, 76/Circle K, **food:** Buggy Whip Rest., Subway, Wendy's, **other:** USPO

47 CA 42, Manchester Ave, to Inglewood, **E**...**gas:** 76/Circle K/dsl/24hr, **food:** Carl's Jr, Subway, **lodging:** Best Western, Economy Inn, **other:** 7-11, **W**...**gas:** Arco, Mobil, Shell, 76, **food:** Arby's, Burger King, Jack-in-the-Box, Louis Burgers, **lodging:** Day's Inn, **other:** CarMax, Chrysler/Jeep/Dodge, Home Depot, Hyundai

46 Century Blvd, **E**...**gas:** 76, **food:** Burger King, Casa Gamino Mexican, Flower Drum Chinese, Rally's, Subway, **lodging:** Best Western, Comfort Inn, Motel 6, Tiboli Hotel, **other:** AutoZone, **W**...**gas:** Arco/24hr, Chevron/dsl, 76/Circle K, Shell, **food:** Carl's Jr, Denny's, McDonald's, Taco Bell, **lodging:** Hampton Inn, Hilton, Holiday Inn, Marriott, Quality Hotel, Travelodge, Westin Hotel

45 I-105, Imperial Hwy, **E**...**gas:** Arco, Mobil/dsl, Shell, **food:** BBQ, El Pollo Loco, El Tarasco Mexican, Jack-in-the-Box, McDonald's, **other:** J&S Trasmissions, **W**...**food:** Proud Bird Rest.(1mi)

44 El Segundo Blvd, to El Segundo, **E**...**gas:** Chevron/24hr, Thrifty, **food:** Burger King, Christy's Donuts, Jack-in-the-Box, Jase Burgers, Rally's, Subway, **lodging:** El Segundo Inn, **W**...**food:** Denny's, Chappie's Rest, **lodging:** Ramada Inn

43b a Rosecrans Ave, to Manhattan Beach, **E**...**gas:** 76, Mobil/dsl, Shell, **food:** Del Taco, Denny's, El Pollo Loco, Pizza Hut, Starbucks, Subway, **other:** Albertson's, Best Buy, Circuit City, CVS Drug, Food4Less, Ford, Home Depot, Marshall's, Michael's, Office Depot, Ross, **W**...**gas:** Thrifty, **food:** Carl's Jr, China Chef, Chipotle Mexi-

can, Luigi's Rest., McDonald's, Qdoba Mexican, Robeks Juice, Sansai Japanese, Starbucks, **lodging:** Ayres Hotel, **other:** Chevrolet/Pontiac/GMC, Costco/gas, Staples, VW

42b Inglewood Ave, **E**...**gas:** Arco, **food:** Del Taco, Denny's, Domino's, Hong Kong Express, In-n-Out, Quizno's, Wok Wok Chinese, Yoshinoya, **other:** CVS Drug, Marshall's, PetCo, Von's Foods, **W**...**gas:** Arco, 76, Shell/dsl/24hr, **food:** La Salsa Mexican, Leo's Mexican, **other:** Drug Emporium, Goodyear/auto

42a CA 107, Hawthorne Blvd, **E**...**food:** Jack-in-the-Box, Little Caesars, McDonald's, Panda Express, Papa John's, Spires Rest, Taco Bell, Wienerschnitzel, Wendy's, **lodging:** Best Western, Day's Inn, Holiday Inn, **other:** CVS Drug, Kragen Parts, 99c Store, Radio Shack, vet, **W**...**gas:** Arco/24hr, Chevron/dsl, Thrifty, **food:** Boston Mkt, Marie Callendar's, Sizzler, Subway, Taco Bell, Yoshinoya, **other:** AutoZone, CompUSA, Macy's

40b Redondo Beach Blvd (no EZ sb return), Hermosa Beach, **E**...**gas:** Arco/24hr, Prena, Thrifty, **food:** ChuckeCheese, Jack-in-the-Box, **other:** golf, **W**...**food:** Boston Mkt, Pizza Hut, **other:** CVS Drug, Nordstrom's, U-Haul

40a CA 91 E, Artesia Blvd, to Torrance, **W**...**gas:** Chevron, **other:** Carl's Jr., Starbucks, **other:** Winchell's

39 Crenshaw Blvd, to Torrance, **E**...**gas:** Arco/24hr, **food:** Burger King, McDonald's, **other:** , Ralph's Foods, **W**...**gas:** Mobil/dsl, Shell/Subway/dsl, **other:** Jiffy Lube

38b Western Ave, to Torrance, **E**...**gas:** Arco, Chevron, 76/dsl, **food:** Del Taco, Denny's, Papa John's, Starbucks, Wendy's, Yorgo's Burgers, **lodging:** Dynasty Inn, **other:** Albertson's, GNC, Toyota, **W**...**gas:** Mobil, **food:** Mill's Rest., **lodging:** Courtyard, **other:** Lexus

38a Normandie Ave, to Gardena, **E**...**lodging:** Comfort Inn, **W**...**gas:** Shell/dsl, **food:** Carl's Jr, Chile Verde Mexican, Quizno's, Starbucks, Subway, Taco Bell/Pizza Hut, Wienerschnitzel, **lodging:** Extended Stay America, **other:** Goodyear, Office Depot, Wal-Mart

37b Vermont Ave(from sb), **W**...**lodging:** Holiday Inn, **other:** hwy patrol

37a I-110, Harbor Fwy

36 Main St(from nb), no services

36mm weigh sta both lanes

Carson

35 Avalon Blvd, to Carson, **E**...**gas:** Arco/24hr, Chevron, Mobil, Shell, **food:** Chili's, ChuckeCheese, Denny's, FoodCourt, Jack-in-the-Box, McDonald's, Pizza Hut, Quizno's, Shakey's Pizza, Sizzler, Subway, Tony Roma, **lodging:** Quality Inn, **other:** America's Tire, Firestone, Goodyear/auto, Ikea, JC Penney, PepBoys, Sears/auto, mall, **W**...**gas:** Arco/24hr, Mobil, Shell, **food:** Carl's Jr, El Charro, IHOP, **other:** Chrysler/Dodge/Jeep, Ford/Lincoln/Mercury, Isuzu, Kia, Ralph's Foods, USPO

61

CALIFORNIA

Interstate 405

N ↕ S

34	Carson St, to Carson, E...**food:** Del Taco, **lodging:** Comfort Inn, W...**gas:** Mobil, 76/dsl/24hr, **food:** Carl's Jr, El Charro, IHOP, Jack-in-the-Box, Subway, **lodging:** Hilton
33b	Wilmington Ave, E...**gas:** Arco/service, **food:** Carson Burgers, W...**gas:** Chevron/repair/24hr, Shell/Subway/Taco Bell/dsl, **food:** Del Taco, **other:** Chevrolet/Hyundai, Toyota
33a	Alameda St, no services
32d	Santa Fe Ave(from nb), E...**gas:** Arco/24hr, W...**gas:** Chevron/24hr, Shell
32c b	I-710, Long Beach Fwy
32a	Pacific Ave(from sb), no services
30b	Long Beach Blvd, E...**gas:** 76, W...**gas:** Mobil, **other:** HOSPITAL, Toyota
30a	Atlantic Blvd, E...**gas:** Chevron/dsl, Shell/Subway/dsl, **food:** Arby's, Black Angus, Denny's/24hr, El Patio, El Torito, Jack-in-the-Box, **other:** Mercedes, Staples, Target, Walgreen, W...**other:** HOSPITAL, Chrysler/Jeep, Nissan
29c	Orange Ave(from sb), W...**other:** Dodge/Pontiac/GMC
29b a	Cherry Ave, to Signal Hill, E...**gas:** Mobil/dsl, **food:** Fantastic Burgers, **other:** Ford, auto repair, W...**food:** John's Burgers, Charley Brown's Steaks/Lobster, Rib Café, **other:** BMW, Dodge, Firestone, Nissan
27	CA 19, Lakewood Blvd, E...**lodging:** Marriott, W...**gas:** Chevron, Shell/24hr, **food:** Spires Rest., Taco Bell, **lodging:** Holiday Inn, Residence Inn, **other:** HOSPITAL, Ford, Goodyear/auto, Kia
26b	Bellflower Blvd, E...**gas:** Chevron, 76, **food:** Burger King, Carl's Jr, KFC, **other:** Chevrolet, Ford, K-Mart, Lowe's Whse, W...**gas:** Mobil/dsl, 76, **food:** FishTale Rest., Hof's Rest., McDonald's, Quizno's, Wendy's, **other:** HOSPITAL, Borders Books, Circuit City, CompUSA, Goodyear/auto, Rite Aid/24hr, SavOn Drug, Sears, Target
26a	Woodruff Ave(from nb), no services
25	Palo Verde Ave, W...**gas:** 76, **food:** Del Taco, Dr Wi Donuts, Pizza Hut/Taco Bell, Subway
24b	Studebaker Rd, no services
24a	I-605 N
23	CA 22 W, 7th St, to Long Beach, no services
22	Seal Beach Blvd, Los Alamitos Blvd, E...**gas:** Chevron/repair/24hr, Mobil, 76, **food:** Carl's Jr, KFC, Panda Chinese, Spagatini Grill, Winchell's, **other:** Albertson's, Goodyear/auto, Ralph's Foods, Rite Aid, Target, Winston Tire
21	CA 22 E, Garden Grove Fwy, Valley View St, E...**gas:** Mobil, Shell/dsl, **food:** Coco's, DQ, Maxwell's Seafood Rest., Sizzler, **other:** Chevrolet, Ford, Rite Aid, Von's Foods
19	Westminster Ave, to Springdale St, E...**gas:** Arco/24hr, Chevron/dsl, 76/Circle K, Thrifty, 7-11/24hr, **food:** Café Westminster, Carl's Jr, In-n-Out, KFC, La Casa Brita, McDonald's, Taco Bell, Yoshinoya, **lodging:** Motel 6, Travelodge, **other:** Albertson's, America's Tire, Home Depot, Kragen Parts, Radio Shack, Rite Aid, W...**gas:** Chevron/dsl/24hr, Shell/dsl/24hr, **food:** Pizza Hut, Subway, **lodging:** Best Western, Day's Inn
18	Bolsa Ave, Golden West St, E...**food:** Pizza Hut, Popeye's, W...**gas:** Chevron, Mobil, 76, Shell, **food:** Bennigan's, Coco's, El Torito, IHOP, Jack-in-the-Box, **other:** Best Buy, JC Penney, Jo-Ann Fabrics, Jon's Foods, Macy's, Sears/auto, mall
16	CA 39, Beach Blvd, to Huntington Bch, E...**gas:** Shell, **food:** Hof's Rest., Jack-in-the-Box, Mei's Chinese, **lodging:** BeachWest Inn, Princess Inn, Super 8, Westminster Inn, **other:** HOSPITAL, Buick/Pontiac/GMC, K-Mart, PepBoys, Toyota, W...**gas:** Arco, Mobil/service, 76, **food:** Arby's, Burger King, Diedrich's Coffee, El Torito, Jack-in-the-Box, Macaroni Grill, Marie Callender's, Popeye's, Starbucks, **lodging:** Holiday Inn, **other:** Barnes&Noble, Chevrolet, Chrysler/Jeep, Circuit City, Dodge, Ford/Lincoln/Mercury, Just Tires, Marshall's, Mitsubishi, Subaru, Target, VW
15b a	Magnolia St, Warner Ave, E...**gas:** Shell, **food:** Del Taco, Sizzler, **other:** CompUSA, W...**gas:** Chevron, Mobil, **food:** Bullwinkle's Rest., Carrow's, Magnolia Café, Tommy's Burgers, **lodging:** Ramada Inn, **other:** IGA Foods, SavOn Drug
14	Brookhurst Ave, Fountain Valley, E...**gas:** Arco/24hr, Chevron, Thrifty, **food:** Alberto's Mexican, Coco's, Del Taco, **lodging:** Courtyard, Residence Inn, **other:** Thompson's RV Ctr, W...**gas:** Chevron/service/24hr, Shell/dsl, **food:** Black Angus, Stix Chinese, Wendy's, **other:** , Albertson's, Office Depot
12	Euclid Ave, E...**food:** CA Noodle Factory, Cancun Fresh, Carl's Jr, Cofee Bean, George's Burgers, Panda Express, Pita Fresh Grill, Quizno's, Starbuck's, Souplantation, Taco Bell, Z Pizza, **other:** HOSPITAL, Costco/gas, Fry's Electronics, Office Depot, Petsmart, Staples, Tire Whse
11b	Harbor Blvd, to Costa Mesa, E...**food:** Hooters, **lodging:** La Quinta, W...**gas:** Arco, Chevron, Mobil, Shell/dsl, 7-11, **food:** Burger King, Denny's, Domino's, El Pollo Loco, IHOP, Jack-in-the-Box, KFC, LJ Silver, McDonald's, Subway, **lodging:** Costa Mesa Inn, Motel 6, Super 8, Vagabond Inn, **other:** , Albertson's, Big O Tire, Cadillac, Chevrolet, Dodge/Acura, Ford/Lincoln/Mercury, Honda, Infiniti, JustTires, Mazda, Pontiac/Buick, Radio Shack, Rite Aid, Target, Von's Foods, Winchell's
11a	Fairview Rd, E...**other:** Barnes&Noble, Best Buy, Marshall's, Nordstrom's, Old Navy, W...**gas:** Chevron, 76, Shell, **food:** Del Taco, Jack-in-the-Box, Round Table Pizza, Taco Bell, **other:** CVS Drug, Kragen Parts, Stater Bro's
10	CA 73, to CA 55 S(from sb), Corona del Mar, Newport Beach
9b	Bristol St, E...**gas:** Chevron/dsl, Shell/24hr, **food:** Bloomingdale's, Blue Water Grill, Carrow's, Chicago Pizza, Chick-fil-A, China Olive, Chipotle Mexican, Claim Jumper Rest, Clubhouse Cafe, Greek Island Grill, In-n-Out, Jack-in-the-Box, Macaroni Grill, Maggiano's Rest., Magic Wok, McDonald's, Morton's Steaks, Pat & Oscar's, Pizza Hut, Red Robin, Scott Seafood, South Coast Rest, Starbucks, Ztejas Rest, **lodging:** Marriott Suites, Westin Hotel, **other:** , BigLots, CVS Drug, Firestone/auto, Goodyear/auto, Macy's, Michael's, Nordstrom's, Office Depot, PetCo, Radio Shack, Rite Aid, Ross, Target, Sears/auto, Staples, Target, TJ Maxx, Von's Foods, World Mkt, mall, W...**gas:** Chevron, 76/dsl, **food:** Del Taco/24hr, El Pollo Loco, McDonald's, Subway, Wahoo Taco, **lodging:** Hilton, Holiday Inn, **other:** PepBoys, 7-11, vet

Costa Mesa

Interstate 405

N ↕ **S**

Irvine

9a	CA 55, Costa Mesa Fwy, to Newport Bch, Riverside
8	MacArthur Blvd, **E**...**gas:** Chevron, Mobil/Subway, **food:** Agora Rest, Carl's Jr, Juice it Up, McDonald's, Quizno's, Russel's Seafood, Starbucks, Taco Factory, **lodging:** Crowne Plaza Hotel, Holiday Inn, **other:** , **W**...**gas:** Chevron, **food:** El Torito, Gulliver's Ribs, IHOP, **lodging:** Atrium Hotel, Hilton, to airport
7	Jamboree Rd, Irvine, **E**...**lodging:** Courtyard, Hyatt, Residence Inn, **food:** Soup Plantation, **E on Main St**...**gas:** Shell, **food:** Burger King, JambaJuice, **other:** Jiffy Lube, Ralph's Foods, **W**...**food:** California Pizza Kitchen, El Torrito, Daily Grill, FatBurger, Gulliver's, Houston's, IHOP, Inka Grill, Jack Shrimp, Melting Pot Rest, Ruth's Chris Steaks, Subway, Taleo Mexico, Wahoo's Taco, **lodging:** Marriott
5	Culver Dr, **W**...**gas:** Alfie's Gas, Chevron/dsl, **food:** Carl's Jr, Subway, **other:** Ace Hardware, Rite Aid, Wholesome foods Mkt
4	Jeffrey Rd, University Dr, **E**...**gas:** Chevron, Circle K/gas, **food:** Baja Fresh, Cofee Bean, El Cholo Cantina, El Pollo Loco, Golden Spoon, Juice It Up, McDonald's, NY Pizza, Peiwei Asian, Pomodoro Italian, Starbucks, Stix Chinese, Togo's, **other:** Ace Hardware, CVS Drug, Gelson's Mkt, Office Depot, Ralph's Foods, SavOn Drug, HOSPITAL, **W**...**gas:** Mobil/dsl, **food:** IHOP, Korean BBQ, **other:** Ralph's Foods, vet
3	Sand Canyon Ave, **E**...HOSPITAL, **W**...**gas:** Arco/dsl, **lodging:** Juice It Up, Lucca Cafe, Red Brick Pizza, **other:** Albertsons, Starbucks, CVS Drug
2	CA 133, to Laguna Beach, **E**...**other:** DoubleTree Inn
1c	Irvine Center Dr, **E**...**food:** Dave & Buster's, Chang's Chinese Bistro, **other:** Barnes&Noble, **W**...**food:** Burger King
1b	Bake Pkwy, **W**...Toyota
1a	Lake Forest, no services
0mm	I-405 begins/ends on I-5, exit 132.

Interstate 505(Winters)

N ↕ **S**

Winters

Exit #	Services
33	I-5. I-505 begins/ends on I-5., no services
31	CA 12A, no services
28	CA 14, Zamora, no services
24	CA 19, no services
21	CA 16, to Esparto, Woodland, **W**...**gas:** Guy's Food/fuel
17	CA 27, no services
15	CA 29A, no services
11	CA 128 W, Russell Blvd, **W**...**gas:** Chevron/24hr, Interstate/dsl, **food:** RoundTable Pizza, Subway, **other:** Lorenzo Mkt
10	Putah Creek Rd, no crossover...same as 11
6	Allendale Rd, no services
3	Midway Rd, **E**...**other:** RV camping
1c	Vaca Valley Pkwy, no services
1b	I-80 E. I-505 begins/ends on I-80.

Interstate 580(Bay Area)

E ↕ **W**

Exit #	Services
79	I-580 begins/ends, accesses I-5 sb.
76b a	CA 132, Chrisman Rd, to Modesto, **E**...**gas:** 76/dsl, **other:** RV camping(5mi)

Livermore

72	Corral Hollow Rd
67	Patterson Pass Rd, **W**...**gas:** 76/dsl/24hr
65	I-205(from eb), to Tracy
63	Grant Line Rd, to Byron
59	N Flynn Rd, Altamont Pass, elev 1009, no services, **S**...Brake Check Area, many wind-turbines
57	N Greenville Rd, Laughlin Rd, Altamont Pass Rd, to Livermore Lab, **S**...**gas:** Chevron/Subway/dsl, **lodging:** Best Western, La Quinta, **other:** Harley-Davidson
56mm	weigh sta both lanes
55	Vasco Rd, to Brentwood, **N**...**gas:** Arco, Chevron, QuikStop/dsl, 76, Shell/dsl/deli, **food:** A&W/KFC, McDonald's, **S**...**gas:** Citgo/7-11, Valero/dsl, **food:** Blimpie, Jack-in-the-Box, Taco Bell, **lodging:** Quality Inn
54	CA 84, 1st St, Springtown Blvd, Livermore, **N**...**gas:** Chevron, **lodging:** DoubleTree Hotel, Holiday Inn, Motel 6, Springtown Inn, **other:** 7-11, **S**...**gas:** Shell, 76/24hr, Valero/Circle K, **food:** Applebee's, Arby's, Burger King, Chevy's Mexican, Chili's, Crazy Buffet, IHOP, Italian Express, McDonald's, Panda Express, Starbucks, Subway, Taco Bell, Togo's, **other:** America's Tire, Longs Drug, Lowe's Whse, Mervyn's, Office Depot, Radio Shack, Ross, Safeway/gas, Target
52	N Livermore Ave, **S**...**gas:** Chevron/Jack-in-the-Box, Citgo/7-11, **food:** Baja Fresh, Coldstone Creamery, In-n-Out, Popeye's, Quizno's, String's Italian, **lodging:** Hawthorn Suites, **other:** Home Depot, Honda, Schwab Tire, Wal-Mart/auto
51	Portola Ave, Livermore(no EZ eb return)
50	Airway Blvd, Collier Canyon Rd, Livermore, **N**...**gas:** Shell/dsl, **food:** Baskin-Robbins, Wendy's, **lodging:** Courtyard, Hampton Inn, Hilton Garden, Holiday Inn Express, Residence Inn, **other:** Costco Whse/gas, **S**...**food:** Cattlemen's Rest., Chicago Pizza, Starbucks, **lodging:** Extended Stay America, **other:** Chrysler/Jeep, Ford/Lincoln/Mercury, Mazda, 7-11
48	El Charro Rd, O'Fallon Rd, no services
47	Santa Rita Rd, Tassajara Rd, **N**...**other:** Buick/Pontiac/GMC, Saab, Safeway Foods, Saturn, **S**...**gas:** Shell, **food:** Bakers Square, Korea Garden, McDonald's, Quizno's, Subway, Taco Bell, TGI Friday, Thai Quisine, **other:** Acura, BMW, Cadillac, GMC, Hummer, Infiniti, Lexus, Long's Drug, MiniCooper, Mitsubishi, Rose Pavilion, Saab, Saturn, Trader Joe's, Volvo
46	Hacienda Dr, Pleasanton, **N**...**gas:** Shell, **food:** Applebee's, Black Angus, Fuddruckers, Macaroni Grill, Mimi's Cafe, On-the-Border, Papa John's, Woks Up, **lodging:** AmeriSuites, **other:** Barnes&Noble, Best Buy, Ford, Old Navy, TJ Maxx, **S**...**food:** Red Robin, **other:** HOSPITAL, Borders Books, Kohl's, Staples, Wal-Mart/auto
45	Hopyard Rd, Pleasanton, **N**...**gas:** 76/Circle K, Minimart, Shell/dsl, **lodging:** Hilton, Holiday Inn Express, **other:** America's Tire, Dodge, El Monte RV Ctr,

CALIFORNIA

Interstate 580

	Goodyear, Honda, Nissan, Office Depot, Pak'n Sav, RV Ctr, U-Haul, Toyota, S...**gas:** Chevron, Shell/dsl, **food:** Arby's, Burger King, Chef India, Chevy's Mexican, Chili's, Denny's, El Balazo, In-n-Out, Nations Burgers, Pleasant Asian, Starbucks, Taco Bell, **lodging:** Candlewood Suites, Courtyard, Hilton, Larkspur Landing, Marriott, Motel 6, Sheraton, Super 8, **other:** CompUSA, Home Depot, Mercedes
44b	I-680, N to San Ramon, S to San Jose
44a	Foothills Rd, San Ramon Rd, N...**gas:** Chevron, Shell, 76, Valero, **food:** Baskin-Robbins, Burger King, Carl's Jr, Casa Orozzo, China Wall, Hooters, KFC, McDonald's, Outback Steaks, Popeye's, RoundTable Pizza, Starbucks, Subway, Wendy's, **lodging:** Radisson, **other:** Big Lots, Buick, Chevrolet, Chrysler/Jeep, $Tree, Ford, Honda, Isuzu, Jo-Ann Fabrics, Kragen Parts, Long's Drug, Mervyn's, Michael's, PetCo, Rite Aid, Ross, Target, S...**food:** Cheesecake Factory, **lodging:** Crowne Plaza, Residence Inn, Sheraton, **other:** JC Penney, Macy's, Nordstrom's, mall
39	Eden Canyon Rd, Palomares Rd, S...**other:** rodeo park
37	Center St, Crow Canyon Rd, same as 35, S...**gas:** Arco/24hr, Chevron/dsl/, 76, Quikstop, **food:** McDonald's, Starbucks, Subway, **lodging:** Econolodge
35	Redwood Rd(from eb), Castro Valley, N...**gas:** Arco, Chevron, 76/dsl, Shell/dsl, **food:** KFC, McDonald's, Quizno's, RoundTable Pizza, Sizzler, Taco Bell, Wendy's, **other:** Comfort Suites, Holiday Inn Express, **other:** Longs Drug, NAPA, Rite Aid, Safeway
34	I-238 W, to I-880, CA 238, W off I-238...**food:** Jack-in-the Box, **other:** Dodge/Jeep
33	164th Ave, Miramar Ave, E...**gas:** Chevron/dsl, **lodging:** Budget Inn, Fairmont Inn
32b	150th Ave, Fairmont, E...**other:** HOSPITAL, W...**gas:** Shell, 76, Valero, **food:** Denny's, RoundTable Pizza, Tito's Cafe, **other:** Macy's, Pepboys, Target
32a	Grand Ave(from sb), Dutton Ave, W...**gas:** Coast, **other:** Rite Aid
30	106th Ave, Foothill Blvd, MacArthur Blvd, W...**gas:** Arco, **food:** Church's
29	98th Ave, Golf Links Rd, E...**gas:** Shell, W...**gas:** 76
27b	Keller Ave, Mtn Blvd, E...repair
27a	Edwards Ave(from sb, no EZ return), E...US Naval Hospital
26a	CA 13, Warren Fwy, to Berkeley(from eb)
26b	Seminary Rd, E...Observatory/Planetarium, W...**gas:** Arco/24hr
25b a	High St, to MacArthur Blvd, E...**gas:** 76, **food:** Subway, **other:** Albertson's, Kragen Parts, 7-11, W...**gas:** 76, **other:** Walgreens
24	35th Ave(no EZ sb return), E...**gas:** 76, **food:** Taco Bell, W...**gas:** Chevron, QuikStop, 76
23	Coolidge Ave, Fruitvale, E...**gas:** Shell/24hr, **food:** McDonald's, **other:** Longs Drug, Farmer Joe's, W...**gas:** 76
22	Park Blvd, E...Shell, W...Arco, Quikstop, **other:** HOSPITAL
21b	Grand Ave, Lake Shore, E...**gas:** Chevron, 76/24hr, 7-11, **food:** Domino's, KFC, Subway, **other:** Albertson's, Long's Drug, Lucky Foods, W...**gas:** Chevron/dsl/24hr
21a	Harrison St, Oakland Ave, E...**gas:** Quikstop

Left margin (top to bottom): E ↑ W — Pleasanton — Oakland Area

19d c	CA 24 E, I-980 W, to Oakland
19b	West St, San Pablo Ave, E...**lodging:** Extended Stay America, **other:** Best Buy, CompUSA, Home Depot, Jo-Ann Fabrics, Michael's, Office Depot
19a	I-80 W
18c	Market St, to San Pablo Ave, downtown
18b	Powell St, Emeryville, E...**gas:** 76, **food:** Burger King, Denny's, Lyon's Rest., Starbucks, Trader Joe's, **lodging:** Courtyard, Day's Inn, Sheraton, Woodfin Suites, **other:** Barnes&Noble, Borders, Circuit City, Jo-Ann Fabrics, Old Navy, Ross, W...**gas:** Shell, **food:** Chevy's Mexican, **lodging:** Hilton Garden, Holiday Inn
18a	CA 13, Ashby Ave, Bay St, same as 18b
17	University Ave, Berkeley, E...**gas:** 76, University Gas, **food:** Brennan's Cafe, **lodging:** Best Western, **other:** Toyota
16	Gilman St, E...**gas:** Chevron, **other:** Walgreens, Golden Gate Fields
13	Albany St, Buchanan St(from eb), no services
12	Central Ave(from eb), El Cerrito, E...**gas:** Shell, W...Costco/gas
11	Bayview Ave, Carlson Blvd, E...**gas:** 76
10b	Regatta Blvd, E...**gas:** Golden Gate/dsl, W...**food:** Cafe Teatro, Quizno's, **other:** Long's Drug
10a	S 23rd St, Marina Bay Pkwy, E...**gas:** Stop and Save/dsl
9	Harbour Way, Cutting Blvd, E...**gas:** Arco, **food:** El Caballo Mexican, W...Burger King
8	Canal Blvd, Garrard Blvd, W...**gas:** Chevron/dsl, **lodging:** Quality Inn
7b	Castro St, to I-80 E, Point Richmond, downtown industrial
7a	Western Drive(from wb), Point Molate, no services
5mm	Richmond-San Rafael Toll Bridge
2a	Francis Drake Blvd, to US 101 S, E...**lodging:** Extended Stay Deluxe, **other:** BMW, Saab
1b	Francisco Blvd, San Rafael, E...**gas:** Beacon, Circle K, Valero, **food:** Burger King, Picante Cafe, Subway, **lodging:** Days Inn, **other:** Circuit City, Dodge/Isuzu, Ford, Home Depot, Mazda, Tires, W...**food:** Wendy's, **other:** Best Buy, Borders Books, USPO, to San Quentin
1a	US 101 N to San Rafael, I-580 begins/ends on US 101.

Interstate 605(LA)

Exit #	Services
25	Huntington Dr. I-605 begins/ends.
24	I-210
23	Live Oak Ave, Arrow Hwy, E...Santa Fe Dam, W...Irwindale Speedway
22	Lower Azusa Rd, LA St, no services
21	Ramona Blvd, E...**gas:** Mobil, **food:** Del Taco/24hr
20	I-10, E to San Bernardino, W to LA
19	Valley Blvd, to Industry, E...**gas:** Chevron/Subway, 76, **food:** McDonald's, Taco King, **lodging:** Valley Inn
18	CA 60, Pamona Fwy, no services
17	Peck Rd, E...**gas:** Shell, W...**other:** Ford Trucks
16	Beverly Blvd, RoseHills Rd, no services

Right margin: N ↑ ↓ S

Interstate 605

N ← → S

Los Angeles Area

15	Whittier Blvd, E...gas: Arco, 76, food: Carl's Jr, Taco Bell, lodging: GoodNite Inn, other: 7-11, W...gas: Chevron, other: Buick, Chrysler/Dodge, Ford, GMC, Honda, Isuzu, Jeep, Kia, Pontiac, Saturn, Toyota, Volvo
14	Washington Blvd, to Pico Rivera, E...other: Firestone/auto
13	Slauson Ave, E...gas: Arco, Mobil, food: Denny's, lodging: Motel 6, other: Jeep, Kia, Nissan, W...HOSPITAL
12	Telegraph Rd, to Santa Fe Springs, E...gas: Chevron, food: Del Taco, Jack-in-the-Box, KFC, Taco Bell, other: st patrol, W...gas: Arco/dsl
11	I-5
10	Florence Ave, to Downey, E...gas: Mobil, other: Cadillac, Chevrolet, Honda
9	Firestone Blvd, E...gas: 76, food: ChuckeCheese, KFC, McDonald's, Norm's Burgers, Sam's Burgers, lodging: Best Western, other: BMW, Costco, Food4Less, Staples, VW/Audi, W...gas: Arco, Chevron/repair, 76/dsl, food: Starbucks, other: Dodge, Office Depot, Target
8	I-105, Imperial Hwy, E...gas: 76, food: KFC, McDonald's, Pizza Hut/Taco Bell, other: Food4Less, SavOn Drug, W...gas: Arco
7	Rosecrans Ave, to Norwalk, E...gas: Chevron, Mobil, food: Del Taco, McDonald's, W...food: Carrow's Rest, lodging: Motel 6
6	Alondra Blvd, E...gas: Citgo/7-11, Chevron, food: A&W, Alondra's Mexican, KFC, lodging: Spires Rest., other: Home Depot, SavOn Drug, Staples, W...gas: Shell/Subway/24hr
5	CA 91, no services
4	South St, E...other: Macy's, Mervyn's, Nordstrom's, Robinsons-May, Sears/auto, mall, W...gas: Shell/service, UltraMar, other: Buick/GMC/Pontiac, Chrysler/Dodge, Ford, Honda, Hyundai, Infiniti, Isuzu, Saturn, Toyota, Volvo
3	Del Amo Blvd, to Cerritos, E...food: Del Taco, Duke's Burgers, other: Ralph's Foods, W...gas: Mobil
2	Carson St, E...gas: Arco, 76, Shell, food: Jack-in-the-Box, KFC, Little Caesar's, McDonald's, Popeye's, Sky Burgers, Spike's Rest., Taco Bell/Pizza Hut, Wienerschnitzel, lodging: Lakewood Inn, other: Chief Parts, Kragen Parts, W...gas: Chevron/dsl, Mobil/Subway/dsl, food: Denny's, Del Taco, El Pollo Loco, El Torito, FoodCourt, In-n-Out, Jack-in-the-Box, Leucille's BBQ, Roadhouse Grill, Starbucks, TGIFriday, Zen's Buffet, other: America's Tire, Barnes&Noble, GNC, Lowe's Whse, Michael's, Old Navy, Radio Shack, Ross, Staples, Sam's Club/gas, Wal-Mart/auto
1	Katella Ave, Willow St, E...gas: Shell, food: Burger King, McDonald's, other: HOSPITAL
0mm	I-605 begins/ends on I-405.

Interstate 680(Bay Area)

N ← → S

Concord

Exit #	Services
71b a	I-80 E, to Sacramento, W to Oakland, I-680 begins/ends on I-80.
70	Green Valley Rd(from eb), Cordelia, N...other: Costco, Longs Drug, Safeway
69	Gold Hill Rd, W...gas: TowerMart/dsl
65	Marshview Rd
63	Parish Rd
61	Lake Herman Rd, E...gas: Arco/Jack-in-the-Box/dsl, W...gas: Gas City/dsl, Shell/Carl's Jr/dsl/24hr, other: vista point
60	Bayshore Rd, industrial park
58	I-780, to Benicia, toll plaza
56	Marina Vista, to Martinez, no services
55mm	Martinez-Benicia Toll Br
54	Pacheco Blvd, Arthur Rd, Concord, W...gas: 76, Shell/dsl
53	CA 4 E to Pittsburg, W to Richmond
52	CA 4 E, Concord, Pacheco, E...food: Peppermill Coffeeshop, Taco Bell, lodging: Holiday Inn, other: Ford, Hyundai, Infiniti/VW, Toyota, USPO, W...gas: Chevron/24hr, Grand Gas, Shell/24hr, 7-11, food: Burger King, Carrow's, Denny's, KFC, McDonald's, other: Barnes&Noble, Firestone, Goodyear/auto, K-Mart, Kragen Parts, Longs Drug, Marshall's, Mervyn's, Target
51	Willow Pass Rd, Taylor Blvd, E...food: Benihana Rest., Buffet City, Claim Jumper, Denny's, Elephant Bar Rest., El Torito, Fuddruckers, Grissini Italian, JJ North's Buffet, Krispy Kreme, Marie Callender's, Panera Bread, Red Lobster, Sizzler, Tony Roma, lodging: Hilton, other: Circuit City, Cost+, Office Depot, Old Navy, Willows Shopping Ctr, W...food: Baja Fresh, Red Robin, Tahoe Joe's, other: Firestone, JC Penney, Macy's, Sears/auto
50	CA 242(from nb), to Concord
49	Gregory Lane, to Pleasant Hill, E...gas: Valero/dsl, food: Country Waffles, Hawaiian BBQ, Panda Express, Starbucks, lodging: Extended Stay America, other: Jo-Ann Fabrics, Kohl's, Office Depot, W...food: Boston Mkt, Jack-in-the-Box, Lyon's Rest., Nations Burgers, Pizza Hut, lodging: Courtyard, Summerfield Suites, Sun Valley Inn, other: Borders, Rite Aid, Safeway Foods, Staples
48	Oak Park Blvd, Geary Rd, E...gas: Chevron, 7-11, food: Subway, lodging: Embassy Suites, Renaissance Inn, other: Best Buy, W...gas: Chevron, food: Black Angus, Burger King, Curry House, Primavera Pasta, Quizno's, Starbucks, Sweet Tomatos, Wendy's, Yan's China Bistro, lodging: Courtyard, Holiday Inn, other: Mazda/Subaru, Nissan, Staples, Volvo, Walgreens
47	N Main St, to Walnut Creek, E...gas: Chevron/Subway, Shell, USA, food: Black Diamond Brewery/rest., Fuddrucker's, Jack-in-the-Box, Taco Bell, Vino Ristorante, lodging: Marriott, Motel 6, Walnut Cr Motel, other: Cadillac, Chrysler/Jeep, Harley-Davidson, Mercedes, Target, W...gas: 76/dsl/24hr, 7-11, food: Domino's, other: Honda, NAPA
46b	Ygnacio Rd, no services

Interstate 680

N ↕ **San Ramon** / **S San Ramon** / **Fremont**

Exit	Services
46a	CA 24, to Lafayette, Oakland, no services
45	S Main St, Walnut Creek, E...HOSPITAL
43	Livorna Rd, no services
42b a	Stone Valley Rd, Alamo, W...**gas:** Chevron, Shell/dsl, 7-11, **food:** Papa Murphy's, Starbucks, Subway, Taco Bell, **other:** Curves, Longs Drugs, Rite Aid, Safeway
41	El Pintado Rd, Danville, no services
40	El Cerro Blvd, no services
39	Diablo Rd, Danville, E...**gas:** 76/24hr, **food:** Chinese Cuisine, Taco Bell, **other:** Mt Diablo SP(12mi), W... **gas:** 76
38	Sycamore Valley Rd, E...**gas:** Shell, **food:** Denny's, **lodging:** Best Western, W...**gas:** 76/dsl, Valero/dsl
36	Crow Canyon Rd, San Ramon, E...**gas:** Shell, **food:** Burger King, Carl's Jr, Chili's, Max's Diner, O'Zachary's Rest., **lodging:** Extended Stay America, **other:** HOSPITAL, Albertson's, Marshall's, Office Depot, Rite Aid, USPO, W...**gas:** Chevron/repair/24hr, 76, Shell/autocare, Valero, **food:** Boston Mkt, Chipotle Mexican, Giuseppe's Italian, In-n-Out, McDonald's, Quizno's, Taco Bell, TGIFriday, **lodging:** Sierra Suites, **other:** Harley-Davidson, Longs Drug, Safeway, vet
34	Bollinger Canyon Rd, E...**gas:** Valero, **food:** Izzy's Pizza, Subway, **lodging:** Marriott, Residence Inn, **other:** Borders Books, Target, Whole Foods, W... **gas:** Chevron/Foodini's, **food:** Applebee's, Chevy's Mexican, Marie Callender's, **lodging:** Courtyard, Homestead Village
31	Alcosta Blvd, to Dublin, E...**gas:** 76, **other:** 7-11, W... **gas:** Chevron, Shell/dsl, **food:** ChuckeCheese, DQ, Mike's Pizza, McDonalds, Papa Murphy's, Starbucks, Subway, Taco Bell, **other:** Albertson's, Walgreens
30	I-580, W to Oakland, E to Tracy
29	Stoneridge, Dublin, E...**lodging:** Crowne Plaza, Hilton, W...**food:** Black Angus, Taco Bell, **other:** Chrysler/Jeep, Cost+, Honda, Macy's, Nordstrom's, Sears, mall
26	Bernal Ave, Pleasanton, E...**gas:** Shell/Jack-in-the-Box, **food:** Lindo's Mexican
25	Sunol Blvd, Pleasanton, no services
21b a	CA 84, Calvaras Rd, Sunol, W to Dumbarton Bridge
20	Andrade Rd, Sheridan Rd(from sb), E...**gas:** Sunol Super Stp/dsl
19mm	weigh sta nb
19	Sheridan Rd(from nb), no services
18	Vargas Rd, no services
16	CA 238, Mission Blvd, to Hayward, E...**gas:** Shell, **food:** McDonald's, W...HOSPITAL
15	Washington Blvd, Irvington Dist, E...**gas:** QuikStop
14	Durham Rd, to Auto Mall Pkwy, W...**gas:** 76/Circle K/Subway/24hr, Shell/Jack-in-the-Box, **other:** Fry's Electronics, Home Depot, Wal-Mart
12	CA 262, Mission Blvd, to I-880, Warm Springs Dist, W...**gas:** 76, Valero, **food:** Burger King, Carl's Jr, Denny's, KFC, RoundTable Pizza, Starbucks, Subway, Taco Bell, **lodging:** Extended Stay America, **other:** GNC, Longs Drug, Radio Shack, Ross, Safeway, 7-11, Walgreens
10	Scott Creek Rd, no services
9	Jacklin Rd, E...**other:** Bonfare Mkt, W...**gas:** Shell

San Jose

Exit	Services
8	CA 237, Calaveras Blvd, Milpitas, E...**gas:** Shell/repair, 76, **food:** Domino's, Flames CoffeeShop, RoadTable Pizza, Sizzler, Subway, **lodging:** Exectuive Inn, **other:** Oceans SuperMkt, 7-11, W...**gas:** Shell, **food:** El Torito, Giorgio's Italian, It's a Grind, Lyon's Rest., McDonald's, Red Lobster, **lodging:** Embassy Suites, Extended Stay America, **other:** Albertson's, Longs Drug, Mervyn's, Safeway, Staples
6	Landess Ave, Montague Expswy, E...**gas:** Arco, Chevron, 76, **food:** Burger King, Jack-in-the-Box, McDonald's, Taco Bell, Togo's, Wienerschnitzel, **other:** Albertson's, Firestone, Radio Shack, Rite Aid, Target, Walgreens
5	Capitol Ave, Hostetter Ave, E...**gas:** Shell, **food:** Carl's Jr, Popeye's, **other:** SaveMart Foods, W...**gas:** Valero, **other:** Jiffy Lube
4	Berryessa Rd, E...**gas:** Arco/24hr, USA, Valero/repair, **food:** Denny's, Lee's Sandwiches, McDonald's, Taco Bell, **other:** AutoZone, Longs Drug, Safeway
2b	McKee Rd, E...**gas:** 76, Chevron, Shell, **food:** Burger King, HomeTown Buffet, Pizza Hut, Quizno's, Starbucks, Togo's, Wienerschnitzel, **other:** $Tree, Mervyn's, PaknSave Foods, Ross, Target, Walgreens, W...**gas:** World Gas, **food:** Baskin-Robbins, Foster's Freeze, Lee's Sandwiches, McDonald's, RoundTable Pizza, Yum Yum Doughnut, Wendy's, **other:** HOSPITAL, Kohl's
2a	Alum Rock Ave, E...**gas:** Shell/dsl/24hr, **food:** Jack-in-the-Box, Taco Bell, W...**gas:** Chevron, 76/24hr, **food:** Carl's Jr
1d	Capitol Expswy, no services
1c	King Rd, Jackson Ave(from nb), E...**gas:** L&D Gas, Shell, **food:** El Gallo Giro, Jamba Juice, Kings Burger, Panda Express, Starbucks, Super Buffet, Taco Bell, **other:** Target, Walgreens
1b	US 101, to LA, SF
1a	(exits left from sb)I-680 begins/ends on I-280.

Interstate 710(LA)

E ↕ **W**

Exit #	Services
23	I-710 begins/ends on Valley Blvd, E...**gas:** Arco
22b a	I-10
20c	Chavez Ave, no services
20b	CA 60, Pamona Fwy, W...**gas:** Shell, E...**food:** King Taco, Monterrey Hill Rest.
20a	3rd St, no services
19	Whittier Blvd, Olympic Blvd, W...**gas:** Shell, **food:** McDonald's
17b	Washington Blvd, Commerce, W...**gas:** Commerce Trkstp/dsl/rest.
17a	Bandini Blvd, Atlantic Blvd, industrial
15	Florence Ave, E...**food:** IHOP, KFC, McDonald's, Taco Bell, **other:** Food4Less, Ralph's Foods, Rite Aid, Kragen Parts, ToysRUs, W...truck repair
13	CA 42, Firestone Blvd, E...**gas:** Arco, **food:** Burger King, Denny's, Krispy Kreme, McDonald's, Panda Express, Starbucks, Subway, **lodging:** Guesthouse Inn, **other:** El Super Foods, Ford, Jeep, Kia, Nissan, Radio Shack, Sam's Club, Target

Interstate 710

Los Angeles Area

Exit #	Services
12b a	Imperial Hwy, **E**...**gas:** Shell/Subway/dsl, **food:** Carl's Jr., El Pollo Loco, Tacos Mexico, **W**...**gas:** Chevron/dsl, 76, Shell, **food:** Casa Corona, LJ Silver/KFC, Panda Express, Starbucks, Subway, Taco Bell/Pizza Hut, Winchell's, Wienerschnitzel, **other:** AutoZone, Manny's Tires, Radio Shack, Walgreen
11b a	I-105
10	Rosecrans Ave, no services
9b a	Alondra Ave, **E**...Home Depot
8b a	CA 91
7b a	Long Beach Blvd, **E**...**gas:** Mobil/repair, 76, **food:** El Ranchito Mexican, McDonald's, Taco Bell, **W**...**gas:** Arco/24hr, **food:** Chano's Mexican, Jack-in-the-Box, Quizno's, **lodging:** Day's Inn, Luxury Inn
6	Del Amo Blvd, no services
4	I-405, San Diego Freeway
3b a	Willow St, **E**...**gas:** Chevron, **food:** Baskin-Robbins, Chee Chinese, Dominos, Pizza Hut, **other:** Walgreen, **W**...**gas:** Arco, Mobil, 76, **food:** KFC, Popeye's, **other:** AutoZone, Ralph's Foods
2	CA 1, Pacific Coast Hwy, **E**...**gas:** Arco/mart, Chevron, LB Fuel, Valero/dsl, **food:** Burger Express, Hong Kong Empress, **other:** auto repair, **W**...**gas:** 76/service, Shell/Carl's Jr/dsl, PCH Trkstp/dsl, Xpress Minimart, **food:** Golden Star Rest., Jack-in-the-Box, McDonald's, Tom's Burgers, Winchell's, **lodging:** Hyland Motel, SeaBreeze Motel
1d	Anaheim St, **W**...**gas:** Speedy Fuel, **other:** dsl repair
1c	Ahjoreline Dr, Piers B, C, D, E, Pico Ave
1b	Pico Ave, Piers F-J, Queen Mary, no services
1a	Harbor Scenic Dr, Piers S, T, Terminal Island, **E**...**lodging:** Hilton
0mm	I-710 begins/ends in Long Beach

Interstate 780(Vallejo)

Benicia

Exit #	Services
7	I-780 begins/ends on I-680.
6	E 5th St, Benicia, **N**...**gas:** Fast&Easy, **S**...**gas:** Citgo/7-11, Valero/dsl, **food:** China Garden, **other:** Big O Tire, repair, vet
5	E 2nd St, Central Benicia, **N**...**gas:** Valero, **lodging:** Best Western, **S**...**food:** McDonald's, Pappa's Rest.
4	Southampton Rd, Benicia, **N**...**food:** Asian Bistro, Burger King, Coldstone Creamery, Country Waffles, Jamba Juice, Rickshaw Express, RoundTable Pizza, Starbucks, Subway, **other:** Ace Hardware, Radio Shack, Raley's Foods, vet
3b	Military West, no services
3a	Columbus Pkwy, **N**...**gas:** Shell, **food:** Burger King, Napoli Pizza, Subway, **other:** Jiffy Lube, Longs Drugs, **S**...to Benicia RA
1d	Glen Cove Pkwy, **N**...Hwy Patrol, **S**...**food:** Baskin-Robbins, Subway, Taco Bell, **other:** Safeway
1c	Cedar St, no services
1b a	I-780 begins/ends on I-80.

Interstate 805(San Diego)

San Diego Area

Exit #	Services
28mm	I-5(from nb). I-805 begins/ends
27.5	CA 56 E (from nb)
27	Sorrento Valley Rd, Mira Mesa Blvd
26	Vista Sorrento Pkwy, **E**...**gas:** Mobil/dsl, Shell, **food:** Chili's, Jamba Juice, McDonald's, Starbucks, **lodging:** Country Inn, Courtyard, Holiday Inn Express, **other:** Staples
25b a	La Jolla Village Dr, Miramar Rd, 1 mi **E**...**gas:** 76/dsl, **other:** Discount Tire, Firestone, **W**...**food:** Coast Cafe, Cozymel's Cantina, Donovan's Grill, Harry's Grill, Miami Grill, PF Chang's, **lodging:** Embassy Suites, Marriott, **other:** HOSPITAL, Macy's, Nordstom's, Sears, mall
24	Governor Dr, no services
23	CA 52, no services
22	Clairemont Mesa Blvd, **E**...**gas:** Chevron, Mega/Subway/dsl, Shell, **food:** Arby's, Burger King, Carl's Jr, Coco's, Godfather Rest., McDonald's, Players Grill, Quizno's, Rubio's Grill, Souplantation, Starbucks, Tommy's Burgers, **other:** Food4Less, Ford, Jiffy Lube, Ranch Mkt, Sears Essentials, Wal-Mart, **W**...**gas:** Arco/24hr, **food:** Joe's Pizza, Mr. Bon's Rest., VIP Oriental Buffet, **lodging:** Best Western, CA Suites, Motel 6
21	CA 274, Balboa Ave, **E**...**gas:** Arco, Chevron, Exxon/dsl, 76, Shell, **food:** Applebee's, Islands Burger, Jack-in-the-Box, **other:** Albertson's/SavOn, Balboa AutoCare, Chevrolet, Dodge, Saturn
20	CA 163 N, to Escondido, no services
20a	Mesa College Dr, Kearney Villa Rd, **W**...HOSPITAL
18	Murray Ridge Rd, to Phyllis Place, no services
17b	I-8, E to El Centro, W to beaches
16	El Cajon Blvd, **E**...**gas:** Arco/24hr, Ultra, **food: other:** Pancho Villa Mkt, **W**...**gas:** North Park Gas, 76, **food:** Carl's Jr, Jack-in-the-Box, Starbucks, Subway, Wendy's
15	University Ave, **E**...**gas:** Chevron, **food:** Subway, **other:** Radio Shack, **W**...**gas:** Exxon, Thrifty/dsl, **food:** Starbucks, **other:** CVS Drug, Walgreens
14	CA 15 N, 40th St, to I-15
13b	Home Ave, MLK Ave, no services
13a	CA 94, no services
12b	Market St, no services
12a	Imperial Ave, **E**...**gas:** Exxon, Homeland Gas/dsl, **W**...**food:** Domino's, KFC/LJ Silver, Sizzler, Starbucks, **other:** Home Depot, 99c Store
11b	47th St, no services
11a	43rd St, **W**...**food:** Giant Pizza, Jack-in-the-Box, **other:** AutoZone, CVS Drug, Northgate Mkt
10	Plaza Blvd, National City, **E**...**food:** Chow King, DQ, Dragon Garden Chinese, McDonald's, Pizza Hut, Popeye's, Starbucks, Winchell's, **other:** HOSPITAL, AutoZone, Firestone/auto, Ralph's Foods, Walgreens, Well's Drug, vet, **W**...**gas:** Thrifty Gas, **food:** Family House Rest., IHOP, Sizzler, **lodging:** Comfort Inn, Stardust Inn, **other:** Big Lots, CVS Drug, Discount Tire, Jo-Ann Fabrics

CALIFORNIA
Interstate 805

San Diego Area

9	Sweetwater Rd, E...**food:** Applebee's, Outback Steaks, **other:** JC Penney, Mervyn's, Robinsons-May, 7-11, W...**gas:** Chevron/dsl, **food:** Ben's Rest., Carl's Jr, Denny's, Hanaoka Japanese, La Placita Mexican, L&L BBQ, Pizza Hut, Starbucks, Subway, Taco Bell, **other:** Circuit City, Curves, Goodyear, Longs Drug, Staples
8	CA 54, no services
7c	E St, Bonita Rd, E **on Bonita Plaza Rd...food:** Applebee's, **food:** Outback Steaks, Pat&Oscar's Rest., **other:** JC Penney, Macy's, mall, W...**gas:** Chevron, Shell, **food:** Burger King, Denny's, Love's Rest., **lodging:** La Quinta, Ramada Inn, **other:** RV Park
7b a	H St, E...**gas:** Carmalor Gas, **food:** China China, Coldstone Creamery, Jack-in-the-Box, Subway, Taco Bell, **other:** Longs Drug, Marshall's, Vons Foods, mall, RV camping
6	L St, Telegraph Canyon Rd, E...**gas:** Canyon Fuel/dsl, **food:** Mandarin Canyon, McDonald's, Starbucks, Subway, **other:** HOSPITAL, Rite Aid, Olympic Training Ctr, RV camping, W...**gas:** Thrify, **other:** 7-11
4	Orange Ave, E... Olympic Training Ctr
3	Main St, Otay Valley Rd, E...**gas:** Shell, **food:** Panda Express, Souplantation, **other:** Chevrolet, Chrysler/Jeep/Dodge, Ford, Kohl's, Petsmart, Scion, Staples, Toyota, W...**lodging:** Holiday Inn Express
2	Palm Ave, E...**gas:** Arco/24hr, Chevron/24hr, **food:** Carl's Jr, Hometown Buffet, Starbucks, Subway, Taco Bell, **other:** Big O Tires, Home Depot, Radio Shack, USPO, Von's Foods, Wal-Mart, W...**gas:** 76/dsl, **food:** KFC, McDonald's
1b	CA 905, E...Brown Field Airport, Otay Mesa Border Crossing
1a	San Ysidro Blvd, E...**gas:** Arco, Shell, **lodging:** Travelodge, Factory2U, Kragen Parts, Longs Drug, 99c Store, U-Haul, W...**gas:** Chevron, Exxon, Mobil, 76, **food:** Denny's, McDonald's, Si Senor Mexican, **lodging:** Motel 6
	I-805 begins/ends on I-5.

Interstate 880(Bay Area)

Exit #	Services
46b a	I-80 W(exits left). I-80 E/580 W.
44	7th St, Grand Ave, downtown
42b a	Broadway St, E...**food:** KFC, **lodging:** Marriott, W... to Jack London Square
41a	Oak St, Lakeside Dr, downtown, W...**gas:** Shell/dsl
40	5th Ave, Embarcadero, W...**lodging:** Executive Inn, Homewood Suites, Motel 6
39b a	29th Ave, 23rd Ave, to Fruitvale, E...**gas:** Shell, **food:** Boston Mkt, Burger King, DonutStar, Starbucks, **other:** Albertson's, AutoZone, Big Lots, GNC, Office Depot, Radio Shack, W...**gas:** 7-11
38	High St, to Alameda, E...**lodging:** Coliseum Motel, $Inn, **other:** El Monte RV Ctr, W...**gas:** Shell/dsl, **food:** McDonald's, **other:** Home Depot
37	66th Ave, Zhone Way, E...coliseum

Oakland Area

36	Hegenberger Rd, E...**gas:** Arco/24hr, Shell/dsl, **food:** Burger King, Denny's, Jack-in-the-Box/24hr, McDonald's, Sam's Hofbrau, Taco Bell, **lodging:** Comfort Inn, Day's Inn/rest., Fairfield Inn, Motel 6, Quality Inn, **other:** Pak'n Save Foods, GMC/Volvo, Freightliner, AutoParts Club, W...**gas:** Chevron, 76/Circle K/dsl, Super Stop/dsl, **food:** Carrows Rest., Francesco's Rest., Green Garden Buffet, Hegen Burger, In-n-Out, Jamba Juice, Panda Express, Quizno's, Starbucks, Subway, **lodging:** Courtyard, Hilton, Park Plaza Motel, Ramada Inn, **other:** Goodyear, Harley-Davidson, Lexus, Wal-Mart, to Oakland Airport
35	98th Ave, W...airport
34	Davis St, W...**gas:** Shell/Burger King, **food:** Starbucks, Togo's, **other:** Costco/gas, Home Depot, Office Depot, Wal-Mart
33b a	Marina Blvd, E...**gas:** Valero, **food:** Jack-in-the-Box, La Salsa Mexican, Starbucks, **other:** HOSPITAL, Firestone/auto, Ford, Honda, Hyundai, Kia, Marshall's, Nissan, Nordstrom's, Old Navy, KIA, W...**gas:** Flyers/dsl, **food:** A&W/KFC, DairyBelle, Denny's, Mtn Mike's Pizza, **other:** USPO
32	Washington Ave(from nb), Lewelling Blvd(from sb), W...**gas:** Arco, 76, TechCo, **food:** Chili Palace, Hometown Buffet, Jack-in-the-Box, McDonald's, Papa Murphy's, Subway, **other:** Big Lots, Big O Tire, GNC, Longs Drug, 99Cent Store, Radio Shack, Safeway/24hr, SavMax Foods, SP Parts, Walgreens/24hr
31	I-238(from sb), to I-580, Castro Valley
30	Hesperian Blvd, E...**gas:** 76, **food:** Bakers Square, KFC, Mr Pizza, Starbucks, Western Superburger, **other:** House of Fabrics, Kragen Parts, Target, Wheelworks Repair, W...**gas:** Arco, Chevron, 76, **food:** Black Angus, Carrow's Rest., KFC, McDonald's, Taco Bell, **lodging:** Hilton Garden, Vagabond Inn, **other:** Albertson's, Kragen Parts, Radio Shack
29	A St, San Lorenzo, E...**gas:** 76/Circle K, **food:** McDonald's, **lodging:** Best Western, **other:** Costco, tires/repair, W...**gas:** 76/Circle K, **food:** Burger King, Carrow's, Hawaiian BBQ, Jamba Juice, McDonald's, Starbucks, Subway, **lodging:** Day's Inn, Heritage Inn, La Quinta, MainStay Suites, Pheonix Lodge, **other:** $Tree, Target
28	Winton Ave, W...**gas:** Chevron, Valero/dsl, **food:** Applebee's, Coldstone Creamery, Elephant Bar Rest., Marie Calendar's, Panda Express, Panera Bread, **other:** Firestone, JC Penney, Jo-Ann Fabrics, Macy's, Mervyn's, Old Navy, Ross, Sears/auto, mall
27	CA 92, Jackson St, E...**gas:** Valero/24hr, **food:** Asian Wok, Nations Burgers, Popeye's, Subway, Taco Bell, **other:** Albertson's/Sav-On, Grocery Outlet, Longs Drug, Radio Shack, Rite Aid, Safeway, W...San Mateo Br
26	Tennyson Rd, E...**gas:** All American/dsl, 76, Shell, **food:** Jack-in-the-Box, KFC, **other:** Kragen Parts, Walgreens, W...**gas:** 76, **other:** HOSPITAL
25	Industrial Pkwy(from sb), E...**gas:** Valero, W...**lodging:** Pheonix Lodge
24	Whipple Rd, Dyer St, E...**gas:** Chevron/24hr, 76, **food:** Country Waffles, Denny's, Hawaiian BBQ, McDonald's, Panda Express, Quizno's, Starbucks, Taco

Interstate 880

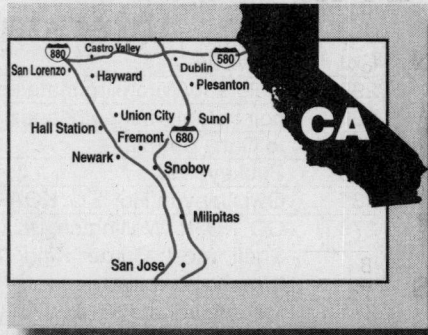

	Bell, Taco Del Mar, **lodging:** Best Value Inn, Motel 6, Super 8, **other:** Circuit City, FoodMaxx, Home Depot, PepBoys, Target, Ⓦ...**gas:** QuikStop/24hr, 76, Shell, **food:** Applebee's, Burger King, Chevy's Mexican, Chili's, FreshChoice, Fuddrucker's, In-n-Out, IHOP, Jamba Juice, Krispy Kreme, La Salsa Mexican, Pasta Pormadora, Texas Roadhouse, TGIFriday, Togo's, Tony Roma's, **lodging:** Extended Stay America, Holiday Inn Express, **other:** Albertson's/SavOn, Best Buy, Borders Books, Lowe's, Michael's, PetCo, RadioShack, Wal-Mart/auto
23	Alvarado-Niles Rd, (same as 24) Ⓔ...**gas:** Shell, **lodging:** Crowne Plaza, **other:** 7-11, Ⓦ...**gas:** Shell, **other:** Wal-Mart/auto
22	Alvarado Blvd, Fremont Blvd, Ⓔ...**food:** Phoenix Garden Chinese, Subway, **lodging:** Motel 6, **other:** Albertson's/SavOn
21	CA 84 W, Decoto Rd to Dumbarton Br, Ⓔ...**gas:** Citgo/7-11, **food:** McDonald's, **other:** Walgreens
19	CA 84 E, Thornton Ave, Newark, Ⓔ...**other:** Chevrolet, U-Haul, Ⓦ...**gas:** Chevron/dsl/24hr, Shell, **food:** Bakers Square, Carl's Jr, KFC, Mtn Mike's Pizza, Taco Bell, **other:** Big Lots, Home Depot, 7-11
17	Mowry Ave, Fremont, Ⓔ...**gas:** Chevron/dsl, QuikStop, 76/Circle K, Valero, **food:** Applebee's, Burger King, Denny's, Hawaiian BBQ, Jerico's Steaks, KFC, Olive Garden, Starbucks, Subway, **lodging:** Best Western, Extended Stay Deluxe, Residence Inn, **other:** HOSPITAL, Albertson's, Cost+, Jo-Ann Fabrics, Ⓦ...**gas:** 76, **food:** Arby's, Bombay Garden, El Burro Mexican, FreshChoice Rest., HomeTown Buffet, Jack-in-the-Box, Lyon's Rest., McDonald's, Red Robin, Sizzler, Subway, Taco Bell, TK Noodles, **lodging:** EZ 8 Motel, Holiday Inn Express, Homewood Suites, Motel 6, Towneplace Suites, Woodfin Suites, **other:** $Tree, Firestone, Ford, Goodyear/auto, Hancock Fabrics, JC Penney, Jiffy Lube, Macy's, Marshall's, Mervyn's, Sears/auto, Staples, Target, mall
16	Stevenson Blvd, Ⓔ...**gas:** Shell, **food:** Jack-in-the-Box, Outback Steaks, **other:** 7-11, Ⓦ...**gas:** Chevron, **food:** Chevy's Mexican, ChuckeCheese, Sizzler, Togo's, **lodging:** Hilton, **other:** Cadillac, FoodMaxx, Ford, Harley-Davidson, Nissan, Pontiac/GMC, PepBoys, Saturn, Tuesday Morning, Wal-Mart
15	Auto Mall Pkwy, Ⓔ...**gas:** Arco, Chevron, **food:** Subway, Ⓦ...**gas:** Shell/dsl, **food:** Chipotle Mexican, Claim Jumper, In-n-Out, Jamba Juice, Panera Bread, PF Chang's, Quizno's, Rubio's, Starbucks, Subway, Wendy's, **lodging:** Hawthorn Suites, **other:** BMW, Circuit City, Costco/gas, Dodge/Isuzu, Honda, Jo-Ann Fabrics, Kia, Kohl's, Lexus, Lowes Whse, Mercedes, Office Depot, Old Navy, Radio Shack, Staples, Toyota
14mm	weigh sta both lanes
13	Fremont Blvd, Irving Dist, Ⓦ...**gas:** Valero, **food:** McDonald's, SmartBrew, **lodging:** GoodNite Inn, Homestead Village, La Quinta, Marriott, **other:** Chrysler, Dodge, Honda, Lexus, Mercedes, Toyota
13b	Warren St(from sb), Ⓦ...**lodging:** Amerisuites, Courtyard, Hampton Inn
13a	Gateway Blvd(from nb), Ⓔ...**lodging:** Holiday Inn Express
12	Mission Blvd, Ⓔ...to I-680, **gas:** 76, Valero, **food:** Carl's Jr, Denny's, Jack-in-the-Box, KFC, Togo's, **lodging:** Holiday Inn Express, Quality Inn, **other:** Longs Drugs, Safeway, 7-11, Walgreens
10	Dixon Landing Rd, Ⓔ...**gas:** Chevron, **food:** Starbucks, **lodging:** Residence Inn, **other:** 7-11
8b	CA 237, Alviso Rd, Calaveras Rd, to McCarthy Rd,, Milpitas, Ⓔ...**gas:** Arco, 76, **food:** Chili's, Denny's, Marie Callender's, RoundTable Pizza, **lodging:** Best Western, Inns of America, Travelodge, **other:** Albertson's, Big Lots, Kragen Parts, SaveMart Foods, 7-11, Walgreens, Ⓦ **on McCarthy Rd...gas:** Chevron, **food:** Applebee's, Black Angus, HomeTown Buffet, In-n-Out, Macaroni Grill, McDonald's, On the Border, Red Robin, Taco Bell, **lodging:** Candlewood Suites, Crowne Plaza, Hampton Inn, Hawthorn Suites, Hilton Garden, Homestead Suites, Staybridge Suites, **other:** Best Buy, Borders Books, Chevrolet, Michael's, Ranch Mkt Foods, Ross, Wal-Mart/auto
8a	Great Mall Parkway, Tasman Dr, Ⓔ...**mall**
7	Montague Expswy, Ⓔ...**gas:** 76, Shell/dsl, Valero, **food:** Jack-in-the-Box, **lodging:** Sleep Inn, **other:** U-Haul, auto repair, Ⓦ...**gas:** Chevron/dsl, **food:** Dave&Buster's, **lodging:** Beverly Heritage Hotel, Sheraton
5	Brokaw Rd, Ⓦ...**other:** Ford Trucks, CHP
4d	Gish Rd (nb only), Ⓦ...**other:** auto/dsl repair/transmissions
4c b	US 101, N to San Francisco, S to LA
4a	1st St, Ⓔ...**gas:** 76, Shell/repair, **food:** Subway, Ⓦ...**gas:** 76, **food:** Cathay Chinese, Denny's/24hr, Gengi Japanese, McDonald's, **lodging:** Clarion, Day's Inn, Executive Inn, EZ 8 Motel, Holiday Inn Express, Homestead Suites, Radisson, Vagabond Inn, Wyndham Garden
3	Coleman St, Ⓔ...**gas:** Valero/dsl, Ⓦ... airport
2	CA 82, The Alameda, Ⓦ...**gas:** Shell/repair, **food:** Cozy Rest., **lodging:** Best Western, Santa Clara Inn, St. Francis Hotel, Valley Inn, **other:** Safeway, Santa Clara U
1d	Bascom Ave, to Santa Clara, Ⓦ...**gas:** Rotten Robbie/dsl, Valero, **food:** Burger King, Normandy House
1c	Stevens Creek Blvd, San Carlos St, Ⓔ...**gas:** Valero/dsl, Valley/dsl, **lodging:** Valley Park Hotel, **other:** HOSPITAL, Ⓦ...**gas:** 76, **food:** Arby's, Burger King, Cheesecake Factory, Jack-in-the-Box, **lodging:** Studio's Inn, **other:** Audi/VW, Best Buy, Chevrolet, Firestone/auto, Goodyear/auto, Isuzu, Lexus, Longs Drugs, Macy's, Mitsubishi, Nordstrom's, Safeway, Subaru, mall
1b	I-280. I-880 begins/ends on I-280
1a	Ca 17 to Santa Cruz.

N ↑↓ S

Ft Collins

Exit #	Services
299	Colorado/Wyoming state line
296	point of interest both lanes
293	to Carr, Norfolk
288	Buckeye Rd
281	Owl Canyon Rd, E... KOA Campground
278	CO 1 S, to Wellington, W...gas: Loaf n'Jug/Blimpie, Shell, food: Burger King/Taco Bell, Subway, lodging: Comfort Inn
271	Mountain Vista Dr, W...Anheiser-Busch Brewery
269b a	CO 14, to US 87, Ft Collins, E...food: Gambler's Steaks, McDonald's, lodging: Mulberry Inn, other: RV service, W...gas: Conoco, Phillips 66/dsl, food: Burger King, Denny's, Waffle House, lodging: Comfort Inn, Day's Inn, Holiday Inn, Motel 6, Plaza Inn, Ramada Inn, Sleep Inn, Super 8, other: to CO St U, stadium
268	Prospect Rd, to Ft Collins, W...other: HOSPITAL, Welcome Ctr, Sunset RV Ctr
267mm	weigh sta both lanes
266mm	**rest area both lanes, full(handicapped)facilities, info, phone, picnic tables, litter barrels, petwalk**
265	CO 68 W, Timnath, W...gas: Texaco, 2-3 mi W... food: Austin's Grill, Carrabba's, Golden Corral, Hunan Chinese, IHOP, Macaroni Grill, Outback Steaks, Papa John's, Quizno's, Subway, Texas Roadhouse, Village Inn Rest., lodging: Courtyard, Hampton Inn, Marriott, Residence Inn, Safeway/gas, Sam's Club
262	CO 392 E, to Windsor, E...gas: Conoco, Loaf n'Jug(3mi), Phillips 66/Subway/dsl, food: Arby's, McDonald's(3mi), lodging: AmericInn, Super 8, W...other: Scott RV Ctr
259	Airport Rd, E...Wal-Mart Depot, W...food: Hooters, other: Harley-Davidson, to airport
257b a	US 34, to Loveland, E...gas: Shamrock/dsl/RV camping, food: Biaggi Italian, Foley's, On-the-Border, PF Changs, Red Robin, Starbucks, lodging: Country Inn&Suites, other: Barnes&Noble, Best Buy, W...gas: Conoco/dsl, food: Arby's(2mi), Blackeyed Pea, Carino's, Chili's, Chipotle Mexican, Cracker Barrel, Hooters, IHOP, KFC/Taco Bell, LoneStar Steaks, McDonald's, Mimi's Cafe, Subway, Waffle House, Wendy's, lodging: Best Western, Comfort Inn, Fairfield Inn, Hampton Inn, Holiday Inn Express, Super 8(2mi), other: HOSPITAL, BMW, Harley-Davidson, JoAnne Fabrics, Loveland Outlets/famous brands, Target, Panera Bread, Ross, RV camping, museum, to Rocky Mtn NP
255	CO 402 W, to Loveland
254	to CO 60 W, to Campion, E...gas: Johnson's Corner/Sinclair/dsl/café/motel/24hr, lodging: Budget Host, other: RV camping/service
252	CO 60 E, to Johnstown, Milliken, W...gas: Loaf'n Jug/Subway
250	CO 56 W, to Berthoud
245	to Mead
243	CO 66, to Longmont, Platteville, E...gas: Conoco/dsl, Shell/Blimpie/dsl, food: Red Rooster Rest., other: Camping World/K&C RV Ctr, Outfitter RV Ctr, W...to Rocky Mtn NP, to Estes Park
241mm	St Vrain River

Thornton

240	CO 119, to Longmont, E...gas: Phillips 66/dsl, food: Carl's Jr, Del Taco, Quizno's, Starbucks, Wendy's, lodging: Best Western, other: Kia, Lexus(2mi)W... gas: Conoco/Subway/dsl/24hr, Shell/dsl, food: Arby's, Burger King, McDonald's, Taco Bell, Waffle House, Wendy's, lodging: Comfort Inn, Day's Inn, Super 8, Travelodge, other: HOSPITAL, Valley Camper RV Ctr, museum, to Barbour Ponds SP
235	CO 52, Dacono, E...Ford, W...gas: Conoco/McDonald's/dsl/LP, food: Pepper Jacks, other: Harley-Davidson, to Eldora Ski Area
232	to Erie, no services
229	CO 7, to Lafayette, Brighton, E...food: GoodTimes Burgers, Heidi's Deli, Village Inn, other: Costco/gas, Circuit City, Home Depot, PetsMart, Sears Grand
228	E-470, tollway, to Limon
226	W...food: Foley's, other: JC Penney, Target
225	136th Ave, W...other: Lowes Whse, Wal-Mart Super Ctr
223	CO 128, 120th Ave, to Broomfield, E...gas: Conoco, Sinclair, Valero/dsl, food: Applebee's, Burger King, Chipotle Mexican, Chick-fil-A, Coldstone, Damon's, Fazoli's, Fuddrucker's, Heidi's Deli, Krispy Kreme, LoneStar Steaks, McDonald's, Panda Express, Olive Garden, OutBack Steaks, Sonic, Souper Salad, TGI Friday, lodging: Hampton Inn, Radisson, Ramada, Sleep Inn, other: Albertson's, Barnes&Noble, Big Lots, Big O Tire, Brakes+, Checker's Parts, Discount Tire, GNC, Michael's, Lens Crafters, Sav-On Foods, Super Target, Tires+, Walgreens, W...gas: Conoco/dsl, Shell/Popeyes/dsl, Valero, food: Chili's, Cracker Barrel, DQ, Hooters, Jade City Chinese, Perkins, Starbucks, Subway, Village Inn Rest., Wendy's, lodging: Comfort Suites, Extended Stay America, Fairfield Inn, La Quinta, Super 8
221	104th Ave, to Northglenn, E...gas: Conoco, Phillips 66, food: Burger King, Denny's, IHOP, Sonic, Subway, Taco Bell/Pizza Hut, Texas Roadhouse, other: HOSPITAL, AutoZone, Home Depot, King's Sooper's, W...gas: Citgo/7-11, Conoco, Shell/dsl, food: Applebee's, Bennigan's, Blackeyed Pea, Cinzinetti's Italian, Chubby's, GoodTimes Burger, Hop's Grill, Le Peep, McDonald's, Quizno's, Taco Bell, Toody's Diner, lodging: Best Value Inn, other: Albertson's, Borders Books, Dodge, Firestone/auto, Ford, Goodyear/auto, Lowe's Whse, Marshall's, Office Depot, Old Navy, Rite Aid, Ross, mall
220	Thornton Pkwy, E...food: DQ, Golden Corral, Starbucks, other: HOSPITAL, GNC, Home Depot, Sam's Club/gas, Tires+, Wal-Mart Super Ctr/24hr, Thornton Civic Ctr, W...gas: Conoco, Valero, Western/gas
219	84th Ave, to Federal Way, E...gas: Conoco, Valero, food: Arby's, Goodtimes Grill, Quizno's, Starbucks, Subway, Taco Bell, Waffle House, lodging: Crossland Suites, other: Walgreen, W...gas: Econogas, Valero/dsl, food: Burger King, DQ, Kings Palace, Pizza Hut, Popeye's, Santiago's Mexican, Village Inn Rest., lodging: Motel 6, other: HOSPITAL, VET, AutoZone, CarQuest, Discount Tire, Sav-A-Lot
217	US 36 W(exits left from nb), to Boulder, W...food: Subway, other: Chevrolet, Toyota

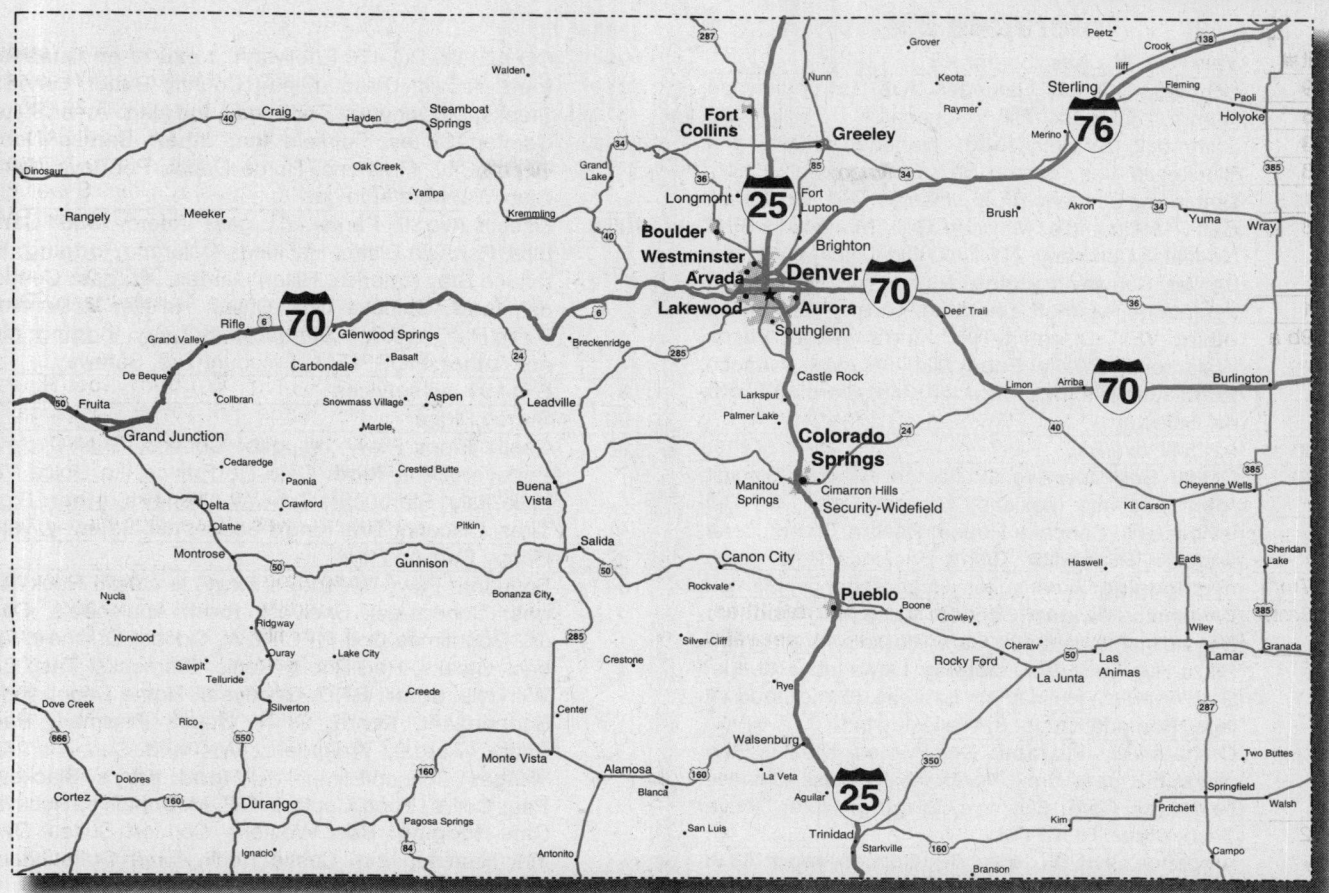

Denver Area

216b a	I-76 E, to I-270 E
215	58th Ave, **E**...**food:** Burger King, McDonald's, Steak Escape, Taco John's, Wendy's, **lodging:** Comfort Inn, **W**...**gas:** Conoco/dsl, Valero/dsl/LP, **lodging:** Super 8, **other:** Checker Parts, Malibu FunPark
214c	48th Ave, **E**...coliseum, airport, **W**...**food:** Village Inn Rest., **lodging:** Best Western, Holiday Inn
214b a	I-70, E to Limon, W to Grand Junction
213	Park Ave, W 38th Ave, 23rd St, downtown, **E**...**gas:** BP/McDonald's, Citgo/7-11, Shell, **food:** Burger King, Denny's, **lodging:** La Quinta, **other:** Goodyear, **W**...**lodging:** Regency Inn, Travelodge
212c	20th St, downtown, Denver, **W**...**food:** Pagliacci's Italian
212b a	Speer Blvd, **E**...downtown, museum, **W**...**gas:** Conoco, Shell, **lodging:** Ramada Inn, Residence Inn, Super 8, Travel Inn
211	23rd Ave, **E**...funpark
210c	CO 33(from nb), no services
210b	US 40 W, Colfax Ave, **W**...**food:** Denny's, KFC, **lodging:** Ramada Inn/rest., Red Lion Inn, **other:** Mile High Stadium
210a	US 40 E, Colfax Ave, **E**...civic center, downtown, U-Haul
209c	8th Ave, **E**...**lodging:** Motel 7, **other:** Bob's Auto Parts
209b	6th Ave W, US 6, **W**...**lodging:** Day's Inn
209a	6th Ave E, downtown, Denver

208	CO 26, Alameda Ave(from sb), **E**...**gas:** BP, Shamrock/dsl, **food:** Burger King, Denny's, **other:** Home Depot, same as 207b **E**...**gas:** Conoco
207b	US 85 S, Santa Fe Dr, **E**...**gas:** BP, Shamrock, **food:** Burger King, Denny's, **other:** Home Depot
207 a	Broadway, Lincoln St, **E**...**food:** Griff's Burgers, **other:** USPO
206b	Washington St, Emerson St, **E**...**other:** WildOats Mkt/café, **W**...**other:** HOSPITAL
206a	Downing St(from nb)
205b a	University Blvd, **W**...to U of Denver
204	CO 2, Colorado Blvd, **E**...**gas:** Conoco, Shamrock, 7-11, Shell, Sinclair, **food:** Arby's, Asian Grill, Bennigan's, Black Eyed Pea, Boston Mkt, GoodTimes Grill, Hooters, KFC, Lazy Dog Café, McDonald's, Noodles&Co, Pizza Hut, Starbucks, Subway, Taco Bell, Village Inn Rest., Wild Oats Cafe, **lodging:** Cherry Creek, Day's Inn, Fairfield Inn, Hampton Inn, Lowes Denver, Ramada, **other:** AAA, Barnes&Noble, Best Buy, Chevrolet/Buick, CompUSA, Circuit City, Mercedes/BMW, Ross, Safeway Foods, VW, Walgreens, **W**...**gas:** Conoco, **food:** A&W/KFC, Dave&Buster's, Denny's, McDonald's, Perkins, **lodging:** La Quinta
203	Evans Ave, **E**...**gas:** Conoco, **food:** Big Papa's BBQ, Breakfast Inn, McDonald's, Palace Chinese, Quiznos, **lodging:** Rockies Inn, **other:** AutoZone, Discount Tire, NAPA, Walgreens, **W**...**lodging:** Cameron Motel, **other:** Ford

N ↕ S — Cherry Hills — Castle Rock

Exit	Description
202	Yale Ave, W...gas: Shamrock
201	US 285, CO 30, Hampden Ave, to Englewood, Aurora, E...gas: BP, Conoco/LP, Phillips 66, Shamrock, Sinclair, food: Applebee's, Benihana, Blackeyed Pea, Boston Mkt, Chicago Grill, Chili's, Domino's, Einstein Bro's, Jason's Deli, Le Peep's Café, McDonald's, Mexican Grill, Mongolian BBQ, Noodles&Company, NY Deli, Old Chicago, On-the-Border, Subway, lodging: Embassy Suites, Hampden Lodge, Marriott, Sheraton, TownePlace Suites, other: VET, Discount Tire, King's Sooper Foods, Walgreens, Whole Food Mkt, W...gas: Conoco, food: Aurelio's Pizza, Burger King, Starbucks, other: Safeway
200	I-225 N, to I-70
199	CO 88, Belleview Ave, to Littleton, E...gas: Sinclair, food: Chipotle Mexican, Harvest Rest., Off Belleview Grill, Pancake House, Panera Bread, Sandwiches+, Starbucks, Tosh's Hacienda Rest., Wendy's, lodging: Amerisuites, Hyatt Regency, Marriott, Wyndham, W...gas: Conoco, Valero/dsl, food: McDonald's, Pappadeaux Café, Paradise Valley Grill, Pizza Hut, Taco Bell, lodging: Day's Inn, Extended Stay America, Holiday Inn Express, HomeStead Village, Ramada, Super 8, Wellesley Inn
198	Orchard Rd, E...food: Del Frisco's Steaks, Shepler's, W...gas: Shell, food: 4Happiness Chinese, Le Peep's Café, Quizno's, lodging: Hotel Denver Tech, other: HOSPITAL,
197	Arapahoe Blvd, E...gas: BP, Conoco, food: A&W, Applebee's, Arby's, Bennigan's, BlackJack Pizza, Burger King, Carrabba's, Country Dinner, Gunther Toody's Rest., IHOP, KFC, Mr. Panda, Outback Steaks, Pizza Hut, Red Lobster, Subway, Susie Wu, Wendy's, lodging: Hampton Inn, Sleep Inn, other: Big A Parts, Buick/Pontiac, Chrysler/Toyota, Discount Tire, Ford, GMC/Cadillac/Subaru, Honda/Mazda, Hyundai, K-Mart, Lowe's Whse, Nissan, Target, USPO, W...gas: Phillips 66/dsl, 7-11, Valero, food: Arby's, Blackeyed Pea, Brooks Steaks, Boston Mkt, Burger King, DQ, Einstein Bro's, Elephant Bar rest., Grady's Grill, KFC, LD Buffet, Macaroni Grill, McDonald's, Papa John's, Quizno's, Red Robin, Ruby Tuesday, Souper Salad, Taco Bell, TCBY, lodging: Residence Inn, Wingate Inn, other: Albertson's, Barnes&Noble, Brakes+, Firestone/auto, GNC, Goodyear/auto, Office Depot
196	Dry Creek Rd, E...food: IHOP, Landry's Seafood, Maggiano's Italian, Trail Dust Steaks, lodging: Best Western, Bradford Suites, Country Inn Suites, Days Inn, Holiday Inn Express, Homestead Suites, La Quinta, Quality Inn, Ramada Ltd, Studio+, W...lodging: Drury Inn
195	County Line Rd, E...lodging: Courtyard, Residence Inn, W...gas: Conoco, food: Buffalo Wild Wings, Burger King, California Pizza Kitchen, Champ's Rest., Chick-fil-A, Fleming's Rest., PF Changs, Red Robin, Rock Bottm Brewery/Cafe, Starbucks, Thai Basil, lodging: AmeriSuites, other: Barnes&Noble, Best Buy, Borders, CompUSA, Costco/gas, Dillard's, Home Depot, JC Penney, JoAnn Fabrics, Nordstrom's
194	CO 470 W, CO 470 E(tollway), 1 exit W on Quebec... food: Arby's, ClaimJumper, Country Buffet, LoneStar Steaks, McDonald's, TGIFriday, lodging: AmeriSuites, Comfort Suites, Fairfield Inn, other: Barnes&Noble, Circuit City, Firestone, Home Depot, PepBoys, Sam's Club, Wal-Mart/auto/gas
193	Lincoln Ave, to Parker, E...gas: Valero, food: Carraba's, PanAsia Bistro, Hacienda Colorado, lodging: Extended Stay America, Hilton Garden, W...gas: Conoco/dsl, food: Chipotle Grill, Chili's, Heidi's, McDonald's, Pizza Hut/Taco Bell, Starbucks, Subway, lodging: Marriott, other: HOSPITAL, Discount Tire, Safeway
191	Exit 191, no services
190	Surrey Ridge
188	Castle Pines Pkwy, W...gas: Conoco, Shell/Circle K/Popeye's/24hr, food: Cafe De France, La Dolce Vita, Little Italy, Starbucks, Subway, Wendy's, other: Big O Tires, Discount Tire, King's Sooper/dsl, Safeway, vet
187	Happy Canyon Rd
184	Founders Pkwy, Meadows Pkwy, to Castle Rock, E...gas: Conoco/dsl, Shell/dsl, food: Applebee's, Carl's Jr., Goodtimes Grill, KFC/A&W, Qdoba, Quizno's, Outback Steaks, Red Robin, Sonic, Starbucks, Taco Bell, Wendy's, other: GNC, Goodyear, Home Depot, King's Sooper/24hr, Kohl's, Office Depot, Petsmart, Radio Shack, Target, Walgreens, Wal-Mart SuperCtr/24hr, W...gas: Conoco/Blimpie/dsl, food: Arby's, Blackeyed Pea, Chili's, Food Court, IHOP, McDonald's, Rockyard Café, lodging: Best Western, Comfort Suites, Day's Inn, Hampton Inn, Castle Rock Prime Outlet/famous brands
183	US 85 N(from nb), Sedalia, Littleton
182	CO 86, Castle Rock, Franktown, E...gas: Conoco, Phillips 66/dsl, Western, food: El Meson Mexican, Little Caesar's, Sapporo Japanese, other: st patrol, W...gas: Shamrock, Shell/dsl, food: Burger King, KFC, Maragrita's Mexican, McDonald's, Shari's/24hr, Taco Bell, Village Inn Rest., Waffle House, Wendy's, lodging: Comfort Inn, Holiday Inn Express, Quality Inn, Super 8, other: Chrysler/Dodge/Jeep, NAPA
181	CO 86, Wilcox St, Plum Creek Pkwy, Castle Rock, E...gas: Citgo/7-11, Conoco, Shamrock/dsl, Western/dsl, food: DQ, El Porral, Pizza Hut, Subway, lodging: Castle Rock Motel, other: Autozone, Big O Tire, Buick/GMC, Chevrolet, Chrysler/Dodge/Jeep, Ford/Lincoln/Mercury, Hummer, Safeway, Walgreens, USPO
174	Tomah Rd, W...other: Castle Rock RV Ctr
173	Larkspur(from sb, no return), 1 mi W...gas: Conoco/dsl/phone
172	South Lake Gulch Rd, Larkspur, 2 mi W...gas: Conoco/dsl/phone, food: Larkspur Pizza Cafe
171mm	rest area both lanes, full(handicapped)facilities, phone, picnic tables, litter barrels, petwalk
167	Greenland, no services
163	County Line Rd, no services
162.5mm	Monument Hill, elev 7352
162mm	weigh sta both lanes
161	CO 105, Woodmoor Dr, E...gas: Conoco, W...gas: Citgo/7-11, Conoco/dsl, food: Arby's, Broiler Room Steaks, Casa Viejo, Domino's, McDonald's, Pizza Hut, Rosie's Diner, Starbucks, Subway, Taco Bell, Village Inn Rest., other: Big O Tire, Curves, Radio Shack, Safeway

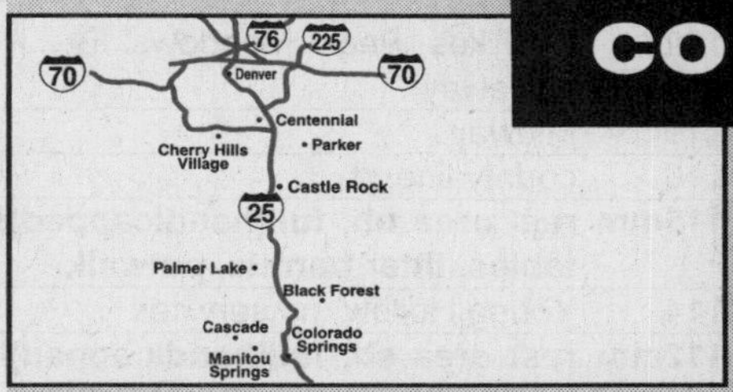

Interstate 25

N ↕ S

Colorado Springs

158	Baptist Rd, E...**gas:** Shell/Circle K/Popeye's/dsl/24hr, **food:** Chili's, Jackson Creek Chinese, Subway, **other:** Home Depot, King's Sooper/24hr, Kohl's, Wal-Mart SuperCtr, W...**gas:** Shamrock/dsl
156b	N Entrance to USAF Academy, W...visitors center
156a	Gleneagle Dr, E...mining museum
153	InterQuest Pkwy, E...**lodging:** Hampton Inn, Residence Inn
151	Briargate Pkwy, E...**food:** Biaggi's, California Pizza Kitchen, Champp's, Colorado Steaks, Panera Bread, PF Changs, Qdoba, Starbucks, Ted's MT Grill, **lodging:** Hilton Garden, Homewood Suites, **other:** Focus on the Family Visitor Ctr, to Black Forest
150b a	CO 83, Academy Blvd, E...**gas:** Conoco, Shamrock/dsl, Shell/dsl, **food:** Applebee's, Blimpie, Boston Mkt, Buca Italian, Buffalo Wild Wings, Burger King, Chipotle Mexican, Country Buffet, Cracker Barrel, Denny's, Egg&I Café, Elephant Bar Rest., Extreme Pizza, Famous Daves, Fat Burger, Fazoli's, IHOP, Jason's Deli, KFC, McDonald's, Mimi's Café, Olive Garden, On-the-Border, Panera Bread, Pizza Hut, Qdoba, Quizno's, Salt Grass Steaks, Schlotsky's Starbucks, Subway, Village Inn Rest., Wendy's, **lodging:** Best Western, Comfort Suites, Day's Inn, Drury Inn, Sleep Inn, Super 8, **other:** Advance Parts, Barnes&Noble, Best Buy, Big O Tire, Borders Books, Checker Parts, Circuit City, CompUSA, Dillard's, $Tree, Firestone/auto, Home Depot, King's Sooper, Marshall's, NAPA, Office Depot, PepBoys, Sam's Club, Sears/auto, Steinmart, USPO, Wal-Mart SuperCtr/24hr, Whole Foods Mkt, mall, to Peterson AFB, W...S Entrance to USAF Academy
149	Woodmen Rd, E...**gas:** Loaf'n Jug/Subway/dsl, **food:** Carl's Jr, Carraba's, **other:** Nissan, W...**gas:** Shell/Circle K, **food:** Old Chicago Pizza, Hooters, Outback Steaks, TGIFriday, Zio's Italian, **lodging:** Comfort Inn, Embassy Suites, Extended Stay America, Fairfield Inn, Hampton Inn, Holiday Inn Express, Microtel, Staybridge Suites
148b a	Corporate Ctr Dr(exits left from sb), Nevada Ave, E...**other:** Harley-Davidson, K&C RV Ctr, W...New South Wales Rest.
147	Rockrimmon Blvd, W...**gas:** Shell, **lodging:** Bradford Suites, Wyndham, to Rodeo Hall of Fame
146	Garden of the Gods Rd, E...**gas:** Conoco, Shell/dsl, **food:** Carl's Jr, Denny's, McDonald's, **lodging:** Econolodge, La Quinta, **other:** Aamco, W...**gas:** Citgo/7-11, Conoco, Phillips 66, Shamrock, **food:** Applebee's, Arby's, Blackeyed Pea, Del Taco, Quizno's, Ranch Steaks, Souper Salad, Sonic, Starbucks, Subway, Taco Bell, Village Inn Rest., Wendy's, **lodging:** AmeriSuites, Day's Inn, Quality Inn, Super 8, **other:** Curves, Discount Tire, to Garden of Gods
145	CO 38 E, Fillmore St, E...**gas:** Citgo/7-11, Shamrock, **food:** Burger King, DQ, **lodging:** Budget Host, **other:** HOSPITAL, Advance Parts, Firestone, W...**gas:** Conoco/dsl, Shell/Circle K/dsl, **food:** Howard's BBQ, Waffle House, **lodging:** Best Western, Central Inn, Motel 6
144	Fontanero St
143	Uintah St, E...**gas:** Citgo/7-11, **other:** Uintah Fine Arts Ctr
142	Bijou St, Bus Dist, E...**other:** Firestone/auto, W...**food:** Denny's, **lodging:** Clarion, **other:** 7-11
141	US 24 W, Cimarron St, to Manitou Springs, W...**gas:** Conoco, Phillips 66, **food:** Arby's, Burger King, Capt D's, La Castia Mexican, McDonald's, Papa John's, Popeye's, Sonic, Subway, Taco John's, Texas Roadhouse, Waffle House, **lodging:** Express Inn, Holiday Inn Express, **other:** Acura, AutoZone, Brakes+, Buick/GMC/Pontiac, Chevrolet, Chrysler, Discount Tire, Dodge, Ford, Gateway RV Ctr, Grease Monkey, Hyundai, Just Brakes, Infiniti, Isuzu, Lexus, Lincoln/Mercury, Mazda, Mercedes, NAPA, Nissan, Office Depot, Porsche, Radio Shack, Saturn, Subaru/Saab/VW, Suzuki, Toyota, Volvo, Wal-Mart SuperCtr/24hr, to Pikes Peak,
140b	US 85 S, Tejon St, E...**other:** Tires 4 Less, W...**gas:** Conoco, **other:** Chrysler/Jeep, access to same as 141
140a	Nevada Ave, E...**lodging:** Chateau Motel, Howard Johnson, Nevada Motel, Samaritan's Inn, **other:** Tire King, W...**gas:** BP, Citgo/7-11, Shamrock, **food:** Burger King, China Kitchen, KFC, McDonald's, Subway, Taco Bell, Taco Express, Wendy's, **lodging:** Chief Motel, Cheyenne Motel, Econolodge, **other:** Big O Tire, Checker Parts, Sears, USPO, Walgreens, access to auto dealers at 141
139	US 24 E, to Lyman, Peterson AFB
138	CO 29, Circle Dr, E...**gas:** Conoco, Shell/Circle K/dsl, **lodging:** Day's Inn, Sheraton, Super 8, **other:** Kohl's, airport, zoo, W...**gas:** Citgo/7-11, **food:** Arby's, Burger King, Carraba's, Carl's Jr, Chili's, Chuck-eCheese, Denny's, Fazoli's, Outback Steaks, Papa John's, Village Inn Rest., Subway, **lodging:** Best Western, Comfort Inn, DoubleTree Hotel, Fairfield Inn, Holiday Inn, La Quinta, Residence Inn, Wingate Inn, **other:** Batteries+, PetCo, Radio Shack, Target
135	CO 83, Academy Blvd, E...to Cheyenne Mtn SP, to airport, W...Ft Carson
132	CO 16, Wide Field Security, E...**other:** Camping Country RV Ctr, Camoing World RV Ctr, KOA, **2 mi E on US 85...gas:** Citgo/7-11, **food:** Domino's, Sonic, **other:** Advance Parts, Curves, Lowes Whse, Safeway Foods/gas
128	to US 85 N, Fountain, Security, E...**gas:** Citgo/7-11, Loaf'n Jug/Subway/dsl, Texaco, **food:** El Rodeo, Grand China, **lodging:** Ute Motel, **other:** USPO, W...**gas:** Tomahawk/Shell/dsl/rest./24hr/@, **lodging:** Fountain Inn, Super 8
125	Ray Nixon Rd
123	no services

N ↕ **S**

Exit	Description
122	to Pikes Peak Meadows, W...Pikes Peak Intn'l Raceway
119	Midway
116	county line rd
115mm	**rest area nb, full(handicapped)facilities, picnic tables, litter barrels, petwalk**
114	Young Hollow, no services
112mm	**rest area sb, full(handicapped)facilities, picnic tables, litter barrels, petwalk**
110	Pinon, W...gas: Sinclair/dsl/repair, lodging: Pinon Tree Inn
108	Bragdon, E...gas: racetrack, W...KOA
106	Porter Draw, no services
104	Eden, W...food: Buffalo Wild Wings, Carino's, Chili's, other: Kohl's, PetCo
102	Eagleridge Blvd, E...gas: Loaf'n Jug, food: Burger King, Texas Roadhouse, other: Big O Tire, Home Depot, Kohl's, Sam's Club/gas, W...gas: Shell/Blimpie/dsl, food: Bellissimo Rest., Cactus Flower Mexican, Cracker Barrel, IHOP, Village Inn Rest., lodging: Comfort Inn, Econolodge, Hampton Inn, La Quinta, Wingate Inn, other: MEDICAL CARE, Tires+, Harley-Davidson, frontage rds access 101

Pueblo

Exit	Description
101	US 50 W, Pueblo, E...gas: Conoco, food: Denny's, Margaritas, Ruby Tuesday, lodging: Sleep Inn, other: Barnes&Noble, Circuit City, Dillards, JC Penney, Ross, Sears/auto, Target, Wal-Mart SuperCtr/24hr, U-Haul, mall, W...gas: Citgo/7-11, Loaf'n Jug, Phillips 66, Shamrock/dsl, food: Angelo's Pizza, Applebee's, Arby's, Blackeyed Pea, Boston Mkt, Burger King, Carl's Jr, Coldstone Creamery, Country Kitchen, DQ, Domino's, Gaetano's Italian, Golden Corral, King's Table Buffet, McDonald's, Olive Garden, Papa Murphy's, Popeye's, Quizno's, Red Lobster, Ruby Tuesday, Starbucks, Subway, SW Grill, Taco Bell, Wendy's, lodging: Days Inn, Motel 6, Pueblo Hotel, Quality Inn, Super 8, other: Aamco, Advance Parts, Albertson's, AutoZone, Batteries+, Checker Parts, Chevrolet, Discount Tire, Dodge, Goodyear/auto, KIA, K-Mart, Lincoln/Mercury, Lowe's Whse, Petsmart, Ross, Staples, Toyota, Walgreens, frontage rds access 102
100b	29th St, Pueblo, E...food: Country Buffet, KFC, Mongolian Grill, Panda Buffet, other: $Tree, King's Sooper Foods, Peerless Tires, mall, W...gas: Phillips 66/dsl, food: Sonic, lodging: USA Motel, other: Safeway foods
100a	US 50 E, to La Junta, E...gas: Loaf'n Jug, Phillips 66, food: KFC, McDonald's, Wendy's, lodging: Value Stay Inn, other: Big R Foods, Goodyear, Walgreens
99b a	Santa Fe Ave, 13th St, downtown, W...food: Taco Bell, Wendy's, lodging: Guesthouse Inn, Travelers Motel, other: HOSPITAL, Chevrolet, Chrysler/Jeep, Ford/Subaru, Honda, Mazda, Nissan, Pontiac, Saturn, VW
98b	CO 96, 1st St, Union Ave Hist Dist, Pueblo, W...gas: Loaf'n Jug, food: Carl's Jr, lodging: Marriott
98a	US 50E bus, to La Junta, W...gas: Phillips 66/dsl, food: Sonic

Exit	Description
97b	Abriendo Ave, W...gas: Texaco
97a	Central Ave, W...gas: Shamrock
96	Indiana Ave, W...other: HOSPITAL, Cobra Automotive
95	Illinois Ave(from sb), W...to dogtrack
94	CO 45 N, Pueblo Blvd, W...gas: Citgo/7-11, Loaf'n Jug, Shamrock/dsl, Western/dsl, food: Pizza Hut/Taco Bell, lodging: Hampton Inn, Microtel, other: RV camping, fairgrounds/racetrack, to Lake Pueblo SP
91	Stem Beach
88	Burnt Mill Rd
87	Verde Rd
83	no services
77	Hatchet Ranch Rd, Cedarwood
74	CO 165 W, Colo City, E...gas: Shamrock/deli/dsl/24hr, other: KOA, W...gas: Shell/Subway/Noble Roman's/dsl, food: Los Cuervo's, Max's Rest., Posie's Place, lodging: Days Inn/rest., **rest area both lanes, full(handicapped)facilities, phone, vending, picnic tables, litter barrels, petwalk**
71	Graneros Rd, access to Columbia House, no services
67	to Apache
64	Lascar Rd
60	Huerfano
59	Butte Rd
56	Redrock Rd
55	Airport Rd

Walsenburg

Exit	Description
52	CO 69 W, to Alamosa, Walsenburg, W...gas: Loaf n' Jug/gas, Phillips 66/dsl/24hr, Western Gas, food: A&W, Alpine Rose Café(2mi), Carl's Jr(2mi), Pizza Hut, Subway(2mi), Tex' Mexican(1mi), lodging: Best Western, Budget Host, to Great Sand Dunes NM, San Luis Valley
50	CO 10 E, to La Junta, W...HOSPITAL, tourist info
49	Lp 25, to US 160 W, Walsenburg, 1 mi W...gas: Loaf'n Jug, food: Carl's Jr. lodging: Knight's Inn(4mi), Lathrop SP, to Cuchara Ski Valley
42	Rouse Rd, to Pryor
41	Rugby Rd, no services
34	Aguilar, E...gas: Cenex/dsl/rest.
30	Aguilar Rd
27	Ludlow, W...point of interest
23	Hoehne Rd
18	El Moro Rd, W...**rest area both lanes, full(handicapped) facilities, picnic tables, litter barrels, petwalk**

Trinidad

Exit	Description
15	US 350 E, Goddard Ave, E...food: Burger King, lodging: Super 8, other: Big R Foods, Family$, W...gas: Shell, food: B Lee's Café, lodging: Frontier Motel/café
14b a	CO 12 W, Trinidad, E...CO Welcome Ctr, gas: Shell, food: McDonald's, Subway, W...gas: Shamrock, food: DQ, lodging: Prospect Plaza Motel, other: Parts+, TrueValue, RV camping, to Trinidad Lake, Monument Lake
13b	Main St, Trinidad, E...gas: Shell, food: McDonald's, Sonic, lodging: Tinidad Hotel, other: CarQuest, Safeway

Interstate 25

13a	Santa Fe Trail, Trinidad, E...lodging: Best Western, other: RV camping
11	Starkville, E...gas: Shell/Wendy's/dsl/24hr, weigh/check sta, food: Bob & Earl's Rest, Taquila's Mexican, lodging: Budget Host, Budget Summit Inn/RV Park, Holiday Inn, other: Bigg's RV Park, to Santa Fe Trail, W...food: Country Kitchen, lodging: La Quinta, Quality Inn, other: Big O Tire, Checker Parts, Chevrolet/Buick, Wal-Mart SuperCtr/gas/24hr
8	Springcreek
6	Gallinas
2	Wootten
1mm	scenic area pulloff nb
0mm	Colorado/New Mexico state line, Raton Pass, elev 7834, weigh sta sb

Interstate 70

Exit #	Services
450mm	Colorado/Kansas state line
438	US 24, Rose Ave, Burlington, N...gas: Conoco, Phillips 66, Sinclair, lodging: Comfort Inn, Hi-Lo Motel, Sloan's Motel, other: HOSPITAL, Buick/Pontiac/GMC, CarQuest, Chevrolet, Family$, Ford/Lincoln/Mercury, Goodyear, Safeway Foods, S...gas: Shell/dsl/24hr, other: RV Camping, truck repair
437.5mm	**Welcome Ctr wb, full(handicapped) facilities, info, phone, picnic tables, litter barrels, petwalk, historical site**
437	US 385, Burlington, N...gas: Conoco/dsl/24hr, On the Go/dsl, food: Arby's, Burger King, McDonald's, Pizza Hut, Route Steaks, Subway, lodging: Best Value, Burlington Inn, Chaparral Motel, Comfort Inn, Western Motel, other: HOSPITAL, Alco, Ford/Lincoln/Mercury, to Bonny St RA, S...RV camping
429	Bethune, no services
419	CO 57, Stratton, N...gas: Cenex/dsl, Conoco/dsl, lodging: Best Western/rest., Claremont Inn/café, other: Marshall Ash Village Camping, auto museum
412	Vona, 1/2 mi N...gas, phone
405	CO 59, Seibert, N...Shady Grove Camping, S...gas: Conoco/dsl, other: tire repair
395	Flagler, N...gas: Loaf&Jug/subs/dsl, lodging: I-70 Diner, lodging: Little England Motel, other: Flagler SWA, RV camping, S...gas: Cenex/dsl other: golf
383	Arriba, N...gas: Phillips 66/dsl/café, motel, S...**rest area both lanes full(handicapped) facilities, picnic tables, litter barrels, point of interest, petwalk,** RV camping
376	Bovina, no services
371	Genoa, N...point of interest, gas, food, phone, S...HOSPITAL
363	US 24, US 40, US 287, to CO 71, to Hugo, Limon, 13 mi S...HOSPITAL
361	CO 71, Limon, N...other: Ace Hardware, Chrysler/Dodge/Jeep, S...gas: Conoco/dsl/24hr, Phillips 66/Wendy's/dsl/24hr, food: Golden China, Pizza Hut, lodging: 1st Inn Gold, Safari Motel, Travel Inn, other: Alco, KOA, st patrol, RV camping

360.5mm	weigh/check sta both lanes
359	to US 24, CO 71, Limon, N...gas: Flying J/dsl/Country Mkt/rest./24hr/scales, other: Country Horizons RV Park, S...gas: Phillips 66, TA/Shell/Subway/Country Fare/dsl/scales/24hr/@, Valero/dsl/24hr, food: Arby's, Denny's, McDonald's, Oscar's Grill, lodging: Best Western, Comfort Inn, Econolodge, Holiday Inn Express, Super 8, Tyme Square Inn, other: camping
354	no services
352	CO 86 W, to Kiowa, no services
348	to Cedar Point, no services
340	Agate, 1/4 mi S...gas/dsl, phone
336	to Lowland, no services
332mm	**rest area wb, full(handicapped)facilities, info, phone, picnic tables, litter barrels, vending, petwalk**
328	to Deer Trail, N...gas: Phillips/dsl, food: Expresso House, S...gas: Shell
325mm	East Bijou Creek
323.5mm	Middle Bijou Creek
322	to Peoria, no services
316	US 36 E, Byers, N...gas: Sinclair, food: Longhorn rest., lodging: Budget Host, other: Thriftway Foods, S...gas: Tri Valley/gas, food: Country Burger Rest., lodging: Lazy 8 Motel(1mi), other: USPO
310	Strasburg, N...gas: Conoco/dsl/24hr, Ray's gas/24hr, food: Pizza Shop, lodging: Strasburg Inn, other: dsl repair, NAPA, KOA, RV camping, USPO
306mm	Kiowa , Bennett, N...**rest area both lanes, full (handicapped)facilities, phone, picnic tables, litter barrels, petwalk**
305	Kiowa(from eb), no services
304	CO 79 N, Bennett, N...Conoco/Hotstuff Pizza/dsl
299	CO 36, Manila Rd, no services
295	Lp 70, Watkins, N...gas: Shell/Tomahawk/dsl/rest./24hr/@, food: Biscuit's Cafe, Lulu's Steakhouse, lodging: Country Manor Motel, other: USPO
292	CO 36, Airpark Rd, no services
289	E-470 Tollway, 120th Ave, CO Springs
288	US 287, US 40, Lp 70, Colfax Ave(exits left from wb), no services
286	CO 32, Tower Rd, N...food: Chili's, Del Taco, Wendy's, other: Wal-Mart Super Ctr/Subway/24hr
285	Airport Blvd, N...Denver Int Airport, S...gas: Flying J/Conoco/dsl/rest./24hr/@, Texaco/McDonald's/dsl, lodging: Comfort Inn, Crystal Inn, other: Harley-Davidson
284	I-225 N(from eb)

COLORADO

Interstate 70

E ↕ W

283	Chambers Rd, **N**...**gas:** Conoco, **food:** A&W/KFC, Applebees, Montana Grill, Outback Steaks, Pizza Hut, Sonic, Subway, Taco Bell/LJ Silver, Uno Pizzaria, Wendy's, **lodging:** AmeriSuites, Country Inn Suites, Hilton Garden, Holiday Inn, Marriott, Sleep Inn, **other:** Tires+, Uhaul, **S**...**gas:** Phillips 66, Valero, **food:** Burger King, **lodging:** Crossland Suites, Extended Stay America, **other:** RV Ctr, Subaru
282	I-225 S, to Colorado Springs
281	Peoria St, **N**...**gas:** BP, Phillips 66, 7-11, **food:** Burger King, Del Taco, GoodTimes Burgers, McDonald's, **lodging:** Best Western/grill, Drury Inn, Timbers Motel, **other:** Big O Tire, **S**...**gas:** BP, Cenex, Conoco, Shamrock/dsl, **food:** Airport Broker Rest., BBQ, Church's, Denny's, IHOP, KFC, Mexican Grill, Old Santa Fe Grill, Pizza Hut/Taco Bell, Quizno's, Subway, Waffle House, Wendy's, **lodging:** Motel 6, Quality Inn, Stay Inn, Traveler's Inn, **other:** ARMY MED CTR, Curves, Goodyear/auto, auto/RV repair
280	Havana St, **N**...**lodging:** Embassy Suites
279	I-270 W, US 36 W(from wb), to Ft Collins, Boulder
278	CO 35, Quebec St, **N**...**gas:** Sapp Bros/Sinclair/Subway/dsl/@, TA/dsl/rest./24hr/@, **lodging:** Comfort Inn, Studio Suites, **other:** Bass Pro Shops, Maceys, Super Target, mall, **S**...**food:** Arby's, Country Buffet, Mariposa Mexican, McDonald's, IHOP, Panda Express, Subway, **lodging:** GNC, Home Depot, Office Depot, Panera Bread, Radio Shack, Ross, Sam's Club, Wal-Mart/gas
277	to Dahlia St, Holly St, Monaco St, frontage rd
276b	US 6 E, US 85 N, CO 2, Colorado Blvd
276a	Vasquez Ave, **N**...**gas:** Pilot/Wendy's/dsl/24hr, **lodging:** Colonial Motel, Western Inn, **other:** Blue Beacon, Ford/Mack Trucks, **S**...**gas:** Citgo/7-11, **food:** Burger King
275c	York St(from eb), **N**...**lodging:** Colonial Motel
275b	CO 265, Brighton Blvd, Coliseum, **N**...**gas:** Citgo/7-11
275a	Washington St, **N**...**food:** Pizza Hut, **S**...**gas:** Conoco, **food:** McDonald's, Muneca Mexican, Quizno's, Subway
274b a	I-25, N to Cheyenne, S to Colorado Springs
273	Pecos St, **N**...**gas:** Safeway, **S**...**gas:** Conoco, Phillips 66/dsl, Circle K, **lodging:** Discount Hotel, **other:** transmissions
272	US 287, Federal Blvd, **N**...**gas:** Sinclair, **food:** Burger King, Goodtimes Burgers, Hamburger Stand, Loco Pollo, McCoy's Rest., McDonald's, Pizza Hut, Subway, Taco Bell, Village Inn Rest., Wendy's, **lodging:** Motel 6, **other:** K-Mart, **S**...**gas:** Amoco, Conoco, 7-11, **food:** Popeye's, **lodging:** Howard Johnson/Las Palmeras Mexican
271b	Lowell Blvd, Tennyson St(from wb), no services
271a	CO 95, **S**...Wild Chipmunk Amusement Park
270	Sheridan Blvd, **S**...**gas:** Shamrock, **food:** Arby's, Oriental Rest., Sunrise Café, **other:** Target, U-Haul, funpark, mall
269b	I-76 E(from wb), to Ft Morgan, Ft Collins
269a	CO 121, Wadsworth Blvd, **N**...**gas:** Citgo/7-11, Conoco, Phillips 66/dsl, **food:** Anthony's Grill, Applebee's, Bennett's BBQ, Bennigan's, Burger

Denver Area

	King, Chipotle Mexican, Coldstone, Einstein Bro.'s, Fazoli's, IHOP, LoneStar Steaks, McDonald's/playplace, Red Robin, Ruby Tuesday, Starbucks, Subway, TX Roadhouse, **other:** Advance Parts, Brakes Plus, Discount tire, Goodyear/auto, Home Depot, Lowe's Whse, Office Depot, PetsMart, Radio Shack, Sam's Club, Tires+, auto repair, mall, **S**...**other:** HOSPITAL, Discount Tire
267	CO 391, Kipling St, Wheat Ridge, **N**...**gas:** Conoco, Shell/Carl's Jr/Circle K/dsl, **food:** Burger King, Denny's, Einstein Bro.'s, Furr's Dining, Qdoba, Quizno's, Subway, **lodging:** American Inn, Motel 6, **other:** Chevrolet/Cadillac, Chrysler/Jeep, GNC, 7-11, Target, **S**...**gas:** Conoco/Circle K, **food:** Pizza Hut/Taco Bell, Village Inn Rest., **lodging:** Comfort Inn, Holiday Inn Express, Interstate Inn, Motel 6, Ramada, **other:** Ketelesen RV Ctr
266	CO 72, W 44th Ave, Ward Rd, Wheat Ridge, **N**...**gas:** Conoco/dsl/transmissions, Phillips 66/dsl, **S**...**gas:** Shamrock/dsl, TA/rest./scales/dsl/24hr/@, **lodging:** Howard Johnson
265	CO 58 W(from wb), to Golden, Central City
264	Youngfield St, W 32nd Ave, **N**...**gas:** Conoco/Circle K, **food:** GoodTimes Burgers, Marie's Country Cafe, **lodging:** La Quinta, **S**...**gas:** Conoco, **food:** Abrusci's Italian, Chili's, DQ, McDonald's, Old Chicago Pizza, Pizza Hut/Taco Bell, Starbucks, Subway, **other:** Camping World RV Ctr/service, Casey's RV Ctr, King's Sooper/24hr, PetsMart, Radio Shack, Walgreens, Wal-Mart
263	Denver West Blvd, **N**...**lodging:** Marriott/rest., **S**...**food:** Keg Steaks, Macaroni Grill, McGrath's Fishouse, Qdoba, **other:** Barnes&Noble, Best Buy, Office Depot, Wild Oats Mkt, same as 262
262	US 40 E, W Colfax, Lakewood, **N**...**gas:** Sinclair, **food:** Arby's, Jack-in-the-Box, **lodging:** Hampton Inn, **other:** CO RV Ctr, Dodge, Home Depot, Honda, Hyundai, Kohl's, NAPA, PetCo, U-Haul, transmissions, **S**...**gas:** Shell/Circle K/dsl/LP, **food:** Cipotle Mexican, Daybreak Rest., Hops Brewery, Keg Steaks, Macaroni Grill, McGrath's Fishouse, Mimi's Cafe, On-the-Border, Outback Steaks, Pei Wei Asian, Qdoba, Quizno's, Wendy's, **lodging:** Courtyard, Day's Inn/rest., Holiday Inn, Residence Inn, **other:** Barnes&Noble, Best Buy, Borders Books, Chevrolet, Lexus, Old Navy, Target, Toyota, Wild Oats Mkt, mall, same as 263
261	US 6 E(from eb), W 6th Ave, to Denver
260	CO 470, to Colo Springs, no services
259	CO 26, Golden, **N**...**gas:** Conoco, **lodging:** Hampton Inn(2mi), **other:** Heritage Sq Funpark, **S**...Music Hall, to Red Rock Park
257mm	runaway truck ramp eb
256	Lookout Mtn, **N**...to Buffalo Bill's Grave
254	Genesee, Lookout Mtn, **N**...to Buffalo Bill's Grave, **S**...**gas:** Conoco/Genesee Store, LP, **food:** Buffalo Moon, Chart House Rest., Christie's Rest., Guido's Pizza, **other:** vet
253	Chief Hosa, **S**...RV Camping, phone
252	(251 from eb), CO 74, Evergreen Pkwy, **S**...**gas:** Conoco, **food:** Burger King, El Rancho Rest., McDonald's, Qdoba, Starbucks, Subway, **lodging:** Quality Suites, **other:** Big O Tire, Home Depot, Jiffy Lube, King's Sooper/deli, Wal-Mart SuperCtr/auto

Interstate 70

E ↑ **W**	

248	(247 from eb), Beaver Brook, Floyd Hill, **S**...antiques
244	US 6, to CO 119, to Golden, Central City, Eldora Ski Area, no services
243	Hidden Valley, no services
242mm	tunnel
241b a	rd 314, Idaho Springs West, **N**...gas: Conoco/McDonald's/dsl, Sinclair, Shell/dsl, Western, **food:** AJ's Cafe, Buffalo Rest., JC Sweet's, King's Derby Rest., Marion's Rest., Starbucks, Subway, Wildfire Motel, **lodging:** H&H Motel, Heritage Inn, Idaho Springs Hotel, JC Motel, Marion's Rest., Peoriana Motel, 6&40 Motel/rest., The Lodge, **other:** CarQuest, Radio Shack, Safeway, USPO
240	CO 103, Mt Evans, **N**...gas: Shell, Sinclair, **food:** 2 Bros Deli, Beaujo's Pizza, Buffalo Restaurant, Paco's, Picci Pizza, Jiggie's Cafe, Subway, Tommy Knocker Grill, West Winds Tavern, same as 241, **S**...to Mt Evans
239	Idaho Springs, **S**...other: camping
238	Fall River Rd, to St Mary's Glacier, no services
235	Dumont(from wb), no services
234	Downeyville, Dumont, **N**...gas: Conoco/Subway/dsl, **food:** Burger King, Starbucks, **other:** ski rentals, weigh sta both lanes
233	Lawson(from eb), no services
232	US 40 W, to Empire, **N**...to Berthoud Pass, Winterpark/Silver Creek ski areas
228	Georgetown, **S**...gas: Conoco/Subway/dsl, Phillips 66/dsl, Shamrock/dsl, **food:** Happy Cooker, Mountaineer's Cafe, New Peking Garden, **lodging:** Georgetown Lodge, Super 8, **other:** visitors ctr
226.5mm	scenic overlook eb
226	Georgetown, Silver Plume Hist Dist, **N**...other: Buckley Bros Mkt, repair
221	Bakerville, no services
220mm	Arapahoe NF eastern boundary
218	no services
216	US 6 W, Loveland Valley, Loveland Basin, ski areas
214mm	Eisenhower/Johnson Tunnel, elev 11013
213mm	parking area eb
205	US 6 E, CO 9 N, Dillon, Silverthorne, **N**...gas: Conoco/dsl, 7-11, Sav-O-Mat, Shell/dsl, **food:** China Gourmet, Mtn Lyon Café, Murphy's Cafe, Old Chicago Grill, Old Dillon Inn Mexican, Quizno's, Village Inn Rest., Wendy's/24hr, **lodging:** Day's Inn, 1st Interstate Inn, La Quinta, Luxury Suites, Quality Inn, Silver Inn, **other:** CarQuest, Chevrolet/Cadillac/Buick, Ford/Mercury, Old Navy, Silverthorn Outlets/famous brands, Target, True Value, **S**...gas: Phillips 66, Shamrock, Tesoro, **food:** Arby's, Bamboo Garden, Blue Moon Deli, Burger King, Coldstone, Dan Brewery Rest., DQ, JJ Chinese, McDonald's, Nick & Willy's Pizza, Pizza Hut, Red Mtn Grill, Ruby Tuesday, SweetPeas, Starbucks, Subway, **lodging:** Comfort Suites, Super 8, **other:** Borders Books, City Mkt Foods, Dillon Stores/famous brands, vet
203.5mm	scenic overlook both lanes, phones

203	CO 9 S, to Breckenridge, Frisco, **S**...gas: Conoco/Wendy's/dsl, 7-11, Shell, Valero/dsl, **food:** A&W, Back Country Brewery/rest., BBQ, KFC, Mexican Bar & Grill, Ore House Steaks, Pizza Hut, Q 4 You BBQ, Starbucks, Subway, Taco Bell, **lodging:** Best Western, Holiday Inn, Ramada Ltd, Summit Inn, **other:** Big O Tire, Discout tire, NAPA, Radio Shack, Safeway, Wal-Mart/Mcdonald's/drugs, vet, to Breckenridge Ski Area, Tiger Run RV Resort(6mi)
201	Main St, Frisco, **S**...gas: Conoco, Loaf N' Jug, **food:** Brewery Rest., Fiesta Mexican, KFC, Pizza Hut, Spruce Inn Steakhouse, **lodging:** Bighorn Reservations, Frisco Lodge, Pearl Head Lodge, Snowshoe Motel, Skyvue Motel, Woodbridge Inn, **other:** RV camping, to Breckenridge Ski Area
198	Officers Gulch, no services, emergency callbox
196mm	scenic area
195	CO 91 S, to Leadville, **1 mi S**...gas: Conoco/dsl, **food:** Quizno's, Starbucks, Tucker's Tavern, **lodging:** Copper Lodging, **other:** to Copper Mtn Ski Resort
190	**S**...rest area both lanes, full(handicapped) facilities, phone, picnic tables, litter barrels
189mm	Vail Pass Summit, elev 10662 ft, parking area both lanes
180	Vail East Entrance, phone, services 3-4 mi S
176	Vail, **S**...other: HOSPITAL, ski info/lodging
173	Vail Ski Area, **N**...gas: Phillips 66, Shell/dsl, **food:** Bagali's Italian, DQ, Domino's, May Palace Chinese, McDonald's, Subway, Taco Bell, Wendy's, **lodging:** Holiday Inn, **other:** City Mkt Foods/deli, Safeway Food/Drug, **S**...gas: Conoco/dsl/LP, **lodging:** Black Bear Inn, Marriott/Streamside Hotel, The Roost Lodge
171	US 6 W, US 24 E, to Minturn, Leadville, **N**...food: Leadville Café, **other:** Ski Cooper ski area, **2.5 mi S**...gas: Phillips 66, **food:** Child Wild Steaks, Minturn Steaks, **lodging:** Minturn Inn
169	Eaglevale, from wb, no return
168	William J. Post Blvd, **S**...food: McDonald's, **other:** Home Depot, Wal-Mart SuperCtr
167	Avon, **N**...gas: Conoco/dsl, Phillips 66, **food:** Pizza Hut, **other:** Goodyear, **S**...food: Burger King, Denny's, Domino's, Fiesta Mexican, Outback Steaks, Quizno's, Starbucks, Subway, **lodging:** Avon Ctr Lodge, Christie Lodge, Comfort Inn, Seasons Hotel, Sheraton, Westin, **other:** City Mkt/drugs, GNC, Office Depot, to Beaver Creek/Arrowhead Ski, Office Depot, ski info/lodging
163	Edwards, **S**...rest area both lanes, full(handicapped) facilities, phone, picnic tables, litter barrel, RV dump, gas: Conoco, Shell/Wendy's/dsl, **food:** Fiesta Cantina, Frides Cafe, Gashaus Rest., Gore Range Brewery, Marble Slab Creamery, Marko's Pizza, Moe's SW Grill, Smiling Moose, Subway, Starbucks, **lodging:** Riverwalk Inn, **other:** to Arrowhead Ski Area, USPO

Interstate 70

E	

162mm	scenic area both lanes
159mm	Eagle River
157	CO 131 N, Wolcott, **N**...to gas, phone, to Steamboat Ski Area
147	Eagle, **N**...**gas:** Shamrock/dsl, **food:** Burger King, Dominos, Mi Pueblo Mexican, **lodging:** AmericInn, Comfort Inn, Holiday Inn Express, **other:** City Mkt Foods, **S**...**gas:** Conoco/pizza, Sinclair/Subway/dsl, **food:** Eagle Diner, Pazzo's Pizzaria, Smiling Moose, Subway, Wendy's, Gourmet China, **lodging:** Best Western, Silverleaf Suites, **other:** Costco/gas(3mi), Curves, **rest area both lanes, full (handicapped)facilities, info**
140	Gypsum, **S**...**gas:** Conoco, Phillips 66/dsl, **food:** Columbine Mkt Deli, Mexican-American Café, **other:** auto/truck repair, airport, **3 mi S**...River Dance Resort camping(3mi)
134mm	Colorado River
133	Dotsero, **N**...**other:** Access to Riverdance RV Camping(3mi)
129	Bair Ranch, **S**...**rest area both lanes, full (handicapped) facilities, picnic tables, litter barrels, petwalk**
128.5mm	parking area eb
127mm	tunnel wb
125mm	tunnel
125	to Hanging Lake(no return eb), no services
123	Shoshone(no return eb), no services
122.5mm	exit to river(no return eb), no services
121	to Hanging Lake, Grizzly Creek, **S**...**rest area both lanes, full(handicapped)facilities, picnic tables, litter barrels,**
119	**No Name, rest area both lanes, full(handicapped) facilities, RV camping, rafting**
118mm	tunnel
116	CO 82 E, to Aspen, Glenwood Springs, **N**...**gas:** Phillip 66/dsl Shell/dsl, **food:** Chomp's Cafe, Fiesta Guadalajara, KFC, Pizza Hut, Qdoba, Subway, Tequila Rest., Village Inn Rest., **lodging:** AmericInn, Best Western, Glenwood Inn, Hampton Inn, Holiday Inn Express, Hotel Colorado, Ramada Inn, Silver Spruce Motel, Starlight Motel, **other:** Land Rover, Mazda, Nissan, Saab, Suzuki, Toyota, Hot Springs Bath, funpark, **0-2 mi S**...**gas:** Conoco, Phillips 66/dsl, Shamrock, Shell, Sinclair, **food:** Arby's, China Town, Domino's, Juicy Lucy Steaks, Mancenelli's Pizza, McDonald's, Pizza Hut, Subway, Taco Bell, Tai Pei Japanese, **lodging:** Caravan Inn, Cedar Lodge, Frontier Lodge, Hotel Denver, **other:** HOSPITAL, Alpine Tire, City Mkt Foods, Harley-Davidson, Honda, NAPA, Office Depot, Rite Aid, Safeway Foods, 7-11, Subaru/Nissan, Wal-Mart, USPO, city park, to Ski Sunlight
115mm	**rest area eb, full(handicapped)facilities, picnic tables, litter barrels**
114	W Glenwood Springs, **N**...**gas:** Phillips 66, 7-11, Shell, **food:** Burger King, CharBurger, Dos Hombres Mexican, Jilberto's Mexican, Oasis Mexican, Ocean Pearl Chinese, **lodging:** Affordable Inn, Best Value Inn, 1st Choice Inn, Ponderosa Motel, Red Mtn Inn, Rodeway Inn, Terra Vista Motel, **other:** Big O Tire, Checker Parts, CarQuest, Chrysler/Dodge, Ford, JC Penney, K-Mart, Radio Shack,

	Staples, Taylor's RV Ctr, mall, **S**...**gas:** Conoco/dsl, **food:** Chili's, DQ, **lodging:** Glenwood Suites, Quality Inn, **other:** Audi/VW, PetCo, Target, Lowe's Whse
111	South Canyon, no services
109	Canyon Creek, no services
108mm	parking area both lanes
105	New Castle, **N**...**gas:** Conoco/dsl, Kum&Go/dsl, **food:** Hong's Garden, New Castle Diner, Subway, **lodging:** Rodeway Inn, **other:** City Mkt Foods/deli, Elk Creek Campground(4mi), KOA(4mi), **S**...**other:** Best Hardware
97	Silt, **N**...**gas:** Conoco/dsl/24hr, Kum&Go, Phillips 66/dsl, Sinclair, **lodging:** Red River Inn(1mi), **other:** auto repair, to Harvey Gap SP, **S**...**lodging:** Heron's Nest RV Park
94	Garfield County Airport Rd, no services
90	CO 13 N, Rifle, **N**...**rest area both lanes, full (handicapped) facilities, phone, picnic tables, litter barrels, RV dump, NF Info,** **gas:** Conoco, Kum&Go/gas, Phillips 66/dsl, Shell, **lodging:** Winchester Motel(1mi), **other:** HOSPITAL, USPO, **S**...**gas:** Kum&Go, Phillips 66/dsl, **food:** Burger King, Dominos, Little Caesar's, McDonald's/playplace, Rib City Grill, Starbucks, Subway, Sonic, Taco Bell, LJ Silver, **lodging:** La Quinta, Red River Inn/rest., Rusty Cannon Motel, **other:** HOSPITAL, Big O Tire, Checker Parts, Radio Shack, Wal-Mart SuperCtr
87	to CO 13, West Rifle
81	Rulison, no services
75	Parachute, **N**...**rest area both lanes, full(handicapped)facilities, info, phone, picnic tables, litter barrels, petwalk,** **gas:** Sinclair/dsl, Shell/dsl/24hr, **food:** El Tapatio Mexican, Hong's Garden Chinese, Hot Stuff Pizza, Outlaws Rest., Subway, Super 8, Westgate Inn/rest., **other:** NAPA, Radio Shack, USPO, vet, **S**...**gas:** Conoco/Wendy's/dsl, **lodging:** Holiday Inn Express, **other:** Family$, Good Sam RV Park(4mi)
63mm	Colorado River
62	De Beque, **N**...**gas:** CFN Fuel, **other:** Canyon Lake Campground, food, lodging, phone, auto repair
50mm	parking area eastbound, Colorado River, tunnel begins eastbound
49mm	Plateau Creek
49	CO 65 S, to CO 330 E, to Grand Mesa, Powderhorn Ski Area
47	Island Acres St RA, **N**...CO River SP, RV camping, **S**...**gas:** Conoco/rest./dsl
46	Cameo, no services
44	Lp 70 W, to Palisade, **3 mi S**...gas, food, lodging
43.5mm	Colorado River
42	US 6, Palisade, **1 mi S**...Fruitstand/store, gas, lodging, **other:** wineries
37	to US 6, to US 50 S, Clifton, Grand Jct, **0-1 mi S**...**gas:** Conoco/dsl, Shamrock/dsl, Sinclair, **food:** Burger King, Dos Hombres Mexican, KFC, Little Caesar's, McDonald's/playplace, Papa Murphy's, Pizza Hut, Qdoba, Sonic, Starbucks, Subway, Taco Bell, Teahouse Chinese, The Diner, Wendy's, **lodging:** Best Western, **other:** Ace Harware, AutoZone, Broomes RV Ctr, Checker Parts, City Mkt Food/gas, Family$, Murdoch's Store, USPO, Walgreens, Wal-Mart SuperCtr(2mi), repair

COLORADO

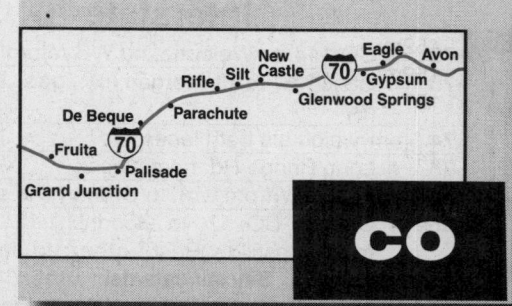

Interstate 70

E ↑
W ↓

Grand Junction

31	Horizon Dr, Grand Jct, **...gas:** Shamrock, Shell/dsl, **food:** Coco's, Diorio's Pizza, Village Inn Rest., Wendy's, **lodging:** Best Value, Comfort Inn, Courtyard, Grand Vista Hotel, Holiday Inn, La Quinta, Motel 6, Ramada Inn, Residence Inn, **other:** Harley-Davidson, USPO, Zarlingo's Repair, **S**...**gas:** Conoco/Subway/dsl, Phillips 66/dsl, **food:** Applebee's, Burger King/playland, Denny's, Nick & Willy's Pizza, Pantuso's Italian, Pizza Hut, Starbucks, Taco Bell, **lodging:** Affordable Inn, Best Western, Country Inn, Doubletree Hotel, Mesa Inn, Quality Inn, Super 8, **other:** HOSPITAL, Safeway Food/drug/gas, golf, visitors ctr, to Mesa St Coll, CO NM
28	Redlands Pkwy, 24 rd, **N**...camping, 0-2 mi **S**...**gas:** Conoco, **food:** Black Bear Diner, Boston's Rest., Burger King, Chili's, McDonald's, Olive Garden, Outback Steaks, Red Lobster, Schlotzky's, Starbucks, Wendy's, **lodging:** Holiday Inn Express, **other:** Barnes & Noble, Best Buy, Circuit City, Home Depot, JC Penny, Kohl's, Office Depot, PetsMart, Sears/auto, Target, recreational park/sports complex
26	US 6, US 50, Grand Jct, 0-4 mi **S**...**gas:** Conoco/A&W/dsl **food:** Bear Rock Cafe, BBQ, Carino's Italian, Carl's JR., Chick-fil-A, Chili's, Chipotle Mexican, ChuckeCheese, Genghis Grill, Golden Corral, IHOP, McDonald's/playplace, Outback Steaks, Panchero's Mexican, Papa Murph's, Red Lobster, Red Robin, Starbucks, Taco Bell, Wendy's **lodging:** Hampton Inn, Hawthorn Suites, Holiday Inn Express, Westgate Inn, **other:** AutoZone, Big O Tire, Borders Books, Cameron's RV Ctr, Centennial RV Ctr, Chrysler/Dodge, Ford/Lincoln/Merury, Gibson RV Ctr, Honda, JC Penney, Lowe's Whse, Michael's, Mobile City RV Park, Nissan, Ross, Sam's Club, Scott RV Ctr, Sears/auto, Subaru, Toyota, Wal-Mart SuperCtr, mall
19	US 6, CO 340, Fruita, **N**...**gas:** Conoco/dsl, **food:** Burger King, Munchie's Burgers/Pizza, **lodging:** Balanced Rock Motel, **other:** HOSPITAL, City Mkt Foods/deli/24hr, USPO, **S**...**Welcome Ctr both lanes, full(handicapped)facilities, phone, picnic tables, litter barrels, RV dump, petwalk, gas:** Conoco/Subway/dsl/24hr, Shell/Wendy's/dsl/24hr, **food:** Chinese-American Rest., McDonald's/playplace, Rib City Grill, Taco Bell, **lodging:** Comfort Inn, La Quinta, Super 8, **other:** CO Mon Trading Co, Peterbilt, camping, dinosaur museum, to CO NM
17mm	Colorado River
15	CO 139 N, to Loma, Rangely, **N**...to Highline Lake SP, gas/dsl, phone
14.5mm	weigh/check sta both lanes, phones
11	Mack, 2-3 mi **N**...gas/dsl, food
2	Rabbit Valley, to Dinosaur Quarry Trail
0mm	Colorado/Utah state line

Interstate 76

Julesburg
Sterling
Ft Morgan

E ↑
W ↓

Exit #	Services
184mm	Colorado/Nebraska state line
180	US 385, Julesburg, **N**...**gas:** Flying J/dsl/rest./24hr, Shell, **food:** Buffalo Cafe, Subway, **lodging:** Budget Host, **other:** HOSPITAL, **Welcome Ctr/rest area both lanes, full(handicapped)facilities, info, RV dump**, **S**...**gas:** Conoco/dsl
172	Ovid, 2 mi **N**...gas, food
165	CO 59, to Haxtun, Sedgwick, **N**...Lucy's Cafe/gas
155	Red Lion Rd, no services
149	CO 55, to Fleming, Crook, **S**...**gas:** Sinclair/dsl/café
141	Proctor, no services
134	Iliff, no services
125	US 6, Sterling, **N**...**gas:** Cenex/dsl, **lodging:** Best Western, 1st Interstate Inn, **other:** HOSPITAL, N Sterling SP, museum, st patrol, **rest area both lanes(full handicapped)facilities, picnic tables, litter barrels, petwalk, vending, RV dump, 1-2 mi N**...**gas:** Sinclair, **food:** Arby's, Burger King, KFC, McDonald's, Pizza Hut, Sonic, Taco John's, Wendy's, **other:** Chrysler/Jeep/Dodge, NAPA, Wal-Mart SuperCtr/24hr, tires **S**...**gas:** Phillips 66/Quizno's/dsl, **food:** Country Kitchen, **lodging:** Comfort Inn, Ramada Inn, Super 8, Travelodge, **other:** Jellystone Camping
115	CO 63, Atwood, **N**...**gas:** Sinclair/dsl, **other:** HOSPITAL, **S**...**food:** Steakhouse, gas/dsl
102	Merino, no services
95	Hillrose, no services
92	to US 6 E, to US 34, CO 71 S
90b a	CO 71 N, to US 34, Brush, **N**...**gas:** Shell/dsl/24hr/@, **food:** China Buffet, Pizza Hut, Wendy's, **lodging:** Best Value, **S**...**gas:** Conoco/dsl, **food:** McDonald's, Subway, **lodging:** Microtel
89	Hospital Rd, **S**...HOSPITAL, golf
86	Dodd Bridge Rd, no services
82	Barlow Rd, **N**...**gas:** Conoco/dsl, **food:** Maverick's Grill, **lodging:** Comfort Inn, Rodeway Inn, **S**...**gas:** Phillips 66/Quizno's/dsl/scales, **food:** Burger King, **other:** $Tree, Wal-Mart SuperCtr/dsl/24hr
80	CO 52, Ft Morgan, **S**...**gas:** Conoco/dsl/24hr, Shell/dsl, Valero/dsl, **food:** Arby's, DQ, KFC, Memories Rest., McDonald's, Sonic, Subway, Taco John's, Wonderful House Chinese, **lodging:** Best Western/rest., Central Motel, Day's Inn, Super 8, **other:** HOSPITAL, AutoZone, Rite Aid

COLORADO

Interstate 76

79	CO 144, to Weldona, no WB return
75	US 34 E, to Ft Morgan, [S]...gas: Loaf'n Jug/A&W/dsl
74.5mm	weigh sta both lanes
73	Long Bridge Rd, no services
66b	US 34 W(from wb), to Greeley, no services
66a	CO 39, CO 52, to Goodrich, [N]...gas: Phillip 66, food: Castillo's Rest., other: to Jackson Lake SP, [S]...gas: Sinclair/cafe/dsl, other: rest area both lanes, full(handicapped)facilities, picnic tables, litter barrels, petwalk, phone, vending
64	Wiggins(from eb), no services
60	to CO 144 E, to Orchard, no services
57	rd 91, no services
49	Painter Rd(from wb), no services
48	to Roggen, N: gas/dsl, [S]...other: USPO
39	Keenesburg, [S]...gas: Phillips 66/dsl, food: Fine Food Rest., gas: Keene Motel
34	Kersey Rd, no services
31	CO 52, Hudson, [S]...gas: Conoco/dsl, Phillips 66/dsl, food: El Faro Mexican, Pepper Pod Rest., other: RV camping, USPO
25	CO 7, Lochbuie, [N]...gas: Shell/dsl
22	Bromley Lane, [N]...gas: Shamrock/dsl, food: Wendy's, other Corner Store, Lowe's Whse, other: HOSPITAL, 2-4 mi [N]...food: Applebee's, Arby's, Kings Sooper/gas, Starbucks, Village Inn, lodging: Brighton Inn, Comfort Inn, [S]...Barr Lake SP
21	144th Ave, [N]...other: Home Depot, Wal-Mart SuperCtr/24hr
20	136th Ave, [N]...Barr Lake RV Park, same as 21
18	E-470 tollway, to Limon (from wb)
16	CO 2 W, Sable Blvd, Commerce City, [N]...gas: Shell/Blimpie/dsl/24hr/@ , to Denver Airport
12	US 85 N, to Brighton, Greeley, no services
11	96th Ave, [S]...other: GMC Trucks, dsl repair
10	88th Ave, [N]...gas: Conoco/Blimpie/dsl, lodging: Holiday Inn Express, Super 8, [S]...flea mkt
9	US 6 W, US 85 S (wb returns st 10), Commerce City, [S]...gas: Shell/dsl, other: GMC/Freightliner, st patrol
8	CO 224, 74th Ave(no EZ eb return), 1 mi [N]...NAPA, [S]...gas: Shamrock/dsl
6b a	I-270 E, to Limon, to airport, to I-25 N, to airport
5	I-25, N to Ft Collins, S to Colo Springs
4	Pecos St, no services
3	US 287, Federal Blvd, [N]...gas: Shamrock/dsl, [S]...food: Taco House
1b	CO 95, Sheridan Blvd, no services
1a	CO 121, Wadsworth Blvd, [N]...gas: Citgo/7-11, Conoco, LuckyMart/dsl, food: Applebee's, Bennigan's, Country Buffet, Fazoli's, Goodberry's Rest., Gunther Toody's Diner, Kokoro Japanese, LoneStar Steaks, McDonald's, Ruby Tuesday, Schlotsky's, Starbucks, Taco Bell, Texas Roadhouse, other: Advance Parts, Costco/gas, Home Depot, Lowe's Whse, Office Depot, Sam's Club, Tires+, Waldenbooks, mall, [S]...other: Discount Tire
0mm	I-76 begins/ends on I-70, exit 269b.

Interstate 225(Denver)

Exit #	Services
12b a	I-70, W to Denver, E to Limon
10	US 40, US 287, Colfax Ave, [E]...gas: Citgo/7-11, Conoco/dsl, food: Arby's, Del Taco, KFC, McDonald's, Pizza Hut/Taco Bell, other: Aamco, Advance Parts, Chevrolet, K-Mart, RV camping, [W]...gas: Conoco, Phillips 66
9	Co 30, 6th Ave, [E]...gas: Conoco, food: Denny's, lodging: Super 8, [W]...gas: Phillips 66/dsl, other: HOSPITAL
8	Alameda Ave, [E]...gas: Conoco, Valero, food: Benny's Cafe, Chili's, Coldstone, Macaroni Grill, Mimi's Cafe, Panda Express, Starbucks, Tgi Friday, other: Atlanta Bread, Barnes&Noble, CompUSA, Foley's, JC Penney, NAPA, Old Navy, Ross, Sears/auto, Target, mall, [W]...gas: Conoco/mart, Shell/repair
7	Mississippi Ave, Alameda Ave, [E]...food: Arby's, Bennigan's, Burger King, Cici's, Chubby's Mexican, ChuckeCheese, Denny's, DQ, Fazoli's, Schlotsky's, Sonic, Subway, lodging: Best Western, Hampton Inn, La Quinta, other: Best Buy, Burlington Coats, Circuit City, Home Depot, JoAnn Fabrics, Sam's Club/gas, Tires +, Wal-Mart, [W]...food: IHOP, McDonald's, Senor Rics, Vietnam House, Waffle House, other: AutoZone, Curves, 7-11, Office Depot
5	Iliff Ave, [E]...gas: Citgo/7-11, food: Applebee's, Boston Mkt, Carrabba's, Fuddrucker's, Japanese Steaks, Joe's Crabshack, Outback Steaks, Rosie's Diner, Ruby Tuesday, Sweet Tomato, Texas Roadhouse, lodging: Comfort Inn, Crestwood Suites, Fairfield Inn, Homestead Suites, Motel 6, [W]...gas: Phillips 66, food: Dragon's Boat, Subway, lodging: DoubleTree
4	CO 83, Parker Rd, [E]...lodging: Radisson, other: Cherry Creek SP, [W]...gas: Phillips 66/dsl, food: DQ, Denny's, Lonestar Steaks, Pizza Hut, Popeyes, Starbucks, Subway, Taco Bell, Wendy's, other: $Tree, Kings Sooper
2b	no services
2	DTC Blvd, Tamarac St, [W]...gas: Conoco, 7-11, food: La Fogata Mexican, Quizno's, Sonic
0mm	I-225 begins/ends on I-25, exit 200.

Interstate 270(Denver)

Exit #	Services
4	I-70, no services
3	[N]...gas: TA/Popeye's/Quizno's/Pizza Hut/dsl24hr/@ , [S]...gas: Sapp Bros/Sinclair/Subway/dsl/@
2b a	US 85, CO 2, Vasquez Ave, [N]...gas: Conoco, food: Arby's, Carls Jr, Chipotle Mexican, GoodTimes Grill, KFC, McDonald's, Pizza Inn, Taco Bell, Taco John's, Wendy's other: Walgreens, Wal-Mart Super Ctr/24hr
1b	York St, no services
1a	I-76 E, to Ft Morgan
1c	I-25 S, to Denver

CONNECTICUT

Interstate 84

Exit #	Services
98mm	Connecticut/Massachusetts state line
74(97)	CT 171, Holland, ...**food:** Traveler's Book Rest., **other:** RV camping
95mm	weigh sta wb
73(95)	CT 190, Stafford Springs, ...**other:** camping(seasonal), motor speedway, st police
72(93)	CT 89, Westford, ...**lodging:** Ashford Motel, camping(seasonal), phone
71(88)	Ruby Rd, ...Citgo, ...**gas:** TA/Shell/Burger King/Country Fried/dsl/scales/24hr/@, **lodging:** Econolodge
70(86)	CT 32, Willington, ...**gas:** HOSPITAL, ...**gas:** Mobil/dsl, Sunoco/dsl, **other:** RV Camping
85mm	**rest area both lanes, full(handicapped) facilities, info, phone, vending, picnic tables, litter barrels, petwalk, campers, RV dump**
69(83)	CT 74, to US 44, Willington, ...gas, food, phone, RV camping, st police
68(81)	CT 195, Tolland, ...**gas:** Gulf/dsl, Mobil, **food:** Papa T's Rest., Subway, **other:** NAPA, RV camping, ...**gas:** Citgo, **other:** Big Y Foods,
67(77)	CT 31, Rockville, ...**gas:** Mobil, Shell, **food:** Burger King, China Taste, McDonald's, Subway, Theo's Rest., Tim Horton, **other:** HOSPITAL, ...Nathan Hale Mon
66(76)	Tunnel Rd, Vernon, no services

Exit #	Services
65(75)	CT 30, Vernon Ctr, ...**gas:** Mobil/24hr, Shell, **food:** ChowderTown, KFC, Vernon Diner, **lodging:** Comfort Inn, Howard Johnson Express, **other:** CarQuest, Vernon Drug
64(74)	Vernon Ctr, Vernon Ctr, ...**gas:** Mobil/24hr, Sunoco, **food:** Acqua Oyster Bar, Angellino's Italian, Anthony's Pizza, D'Angelo's, Denny's, Dunkin Donuts, Friendly's, McDonald's, 99 Rest., Taco Bell, **lodging:** Holiday Inn Express, **other:** Advance Parts, AutoZone, CVS Drug, Firestone, GNC, Goodyear/auto, K-Mart, PriceChopper, Radio Shack, Staples, Stop&Shop, TJ Maxx, TownFair Tire, ...**lodging:** Quality Inn
63(72)	CT 30, CT 83, Manchester, S Windsor, ...**gas:** Shell, **food:** Macaroni Grill, McDonald's, HomeTown Buffet, Outback Steaks, TGIFriday, Uno Pizzaria, **lodging:** Courtyard, **other:** Barnes&Noble, Best Buy, Circuit City, JC Penney, Michael's, Office Depot, Sears/auto, Walgreens, Wal-Mart, same as 62, ...**gas:** Getty, Gulf, Shell/24hr, Xtra, **food:** Century Buffet, Panera Bread, Roy Roger's, **lodging:** Best Value Inn, Extended Stay America, Super 8, **other:** HOSPITAL, Big Y Mkt, Chrysler, Ford/Kia, Kohl's, Lincoln/Mercury/Mazda, Rite Aid, Subaru, Toyota
62(71)	Buckland St, ...**gas:** Exxon/dsl/24hr, **food:** Boston Mkt, Bugaboo Creek Steaks, Chili's, Friendly's, Hooters, John Harvard's Brewhouse, Olive Garden, Taco Bell, **other:** Borders Books, CompUSA, Firestone/auto, Home Depot, Jo-Ann Fabrics, Lowes Whse, Sam's Club, mall, same as 63, ...**gas:** Citgo/dsl, Xtra, **food:** Burger King, Carraba's, ChuckeCheese, Dunkin Donuts, Golden Dragon, McDonald's, Subway, Wendy's, **other:** Buick, Honda, USPO
61(70)	I-291 W, to Windsor
60(69)	US 6, US 44, Burnside Ave(from eb)

CONNECTICUT
Interstate 84

E ↕ **W**

Hartford

59(68)	I-384 E, Manchester
58(67)	Roberts St, Burnside Ave, **N**...**food:** Margarita's Grill, **lodging:** Days Inn, Holiday Inn, **S**...**other:** vet
57(66)	CT 15 S, to I-91 S, Charter Oak Br
56(65)	Governor St, E Hartford, **S**...airport
55(64)	CT 2 E, New London, downtown
54(63)	Old State House, **N**...**other:** Ford/Isuzu, Lincoln/Mercury, **S**...**lodging:** Marriott, Sheraton
53(62)	CT Blvd(from eb), no services
52(61)	W Main St(from eb), downtown
51(60)	I-91 N, to Springfield
50(59.8)	to I-91 S(from wb)
48(59.5)	Asylum St , downtown, **N**...**lodging:** Crowne Plaza, **S**...**lodging:** Hilton, Holiday Inn Express, Residence Inn, **other:** HOSPITAL
47(59)	Sigourney St, downtown, **N**...Hartford Seminary, Mark Twain House
46(58)	Sisson St, downtown, UConn Law School
45(57)	Flatbush Ave(exits left from wb), **N**...Shaw's Foods
44(56.5)	Prospect Ave, **N**...**gas:** Exxon, Shell, **food:** Burger King, D'angelo's, Gold Roc Diner/24hr, HomeTown Buffet, McDonald's, **other:** Shaw's Foods/Osco Drug
43(56)	Park Rd, W Hartford, **N**...to St Joseph Coll
42(55)	Trout Brk Dr(exits left from wb), to Elmwood
41(54)	S Main St, American School for the Deaf
40(53)	CT 71, New Britain Ave, **S**...**gas:** Shell, Sunoco, **food:** California Pizza, Dunkin Donuts, Olive Garden, Red Robin, Starbucks, Wendy's, **lodging:** Courtyard, **other:** Barnes&Noble, Best Buy, Borders, JC Penney, Office Depot, Old Navy, Radio Shack, Sears/auto, Target, mall
39a(52)	CT 9 S, to New Britain, Newington, **S**...HOSPITAL
39(51.5)	CT 4, Farmington, **N**...HOSPITAL
38(51)	US 6 W (from wb), Bristol, **N**...**gas:** Shell
37(50)	Fienemann Rd, to US 6 W, **N**...**gas:** Shell, **food:** Subway, **lodging:** Marriott
36(49)	Slater Rd(exits left from eb), **S**...HOSPITAL
35(48)	CT 72, to CT 9(exits left from wb), New Britain, **S**...HOSPITAL
34(47)	CT 372, Crooked St, **N**...**gas:** Citgo, Sunoco, **food:** Applebee's, Friendly's, Imperial Buffet, LJ Silver/Taco Bell, McDonald's, Starbucks, Wendy's, **lodging:** Plainville Inn, **other:** Big Y Mkt, Ford, Kohl's, Lowe's Whse, Old Navy, VW
33(46)	CT 72 W, to Bristol, no services
32(45)	Ct 10, Queen St, Southington, **N**...**gas:** Cumberland Farms, Exxon, Shell/dsl, **food:** Bertucci's, Burger King, Chili's, D'angelo's, Denny's, Dunkin Donuts, JD's Rest., KFC, McDonald's, Outback Steaks, Puerto Valarta, Randy's Pizza, Ruby Tuesday, Starbucks, Subway, Taco Bell, **lodging:** Motel 6, **other:** HOSPITAL, CVS Drug, $Tree, Shaw's Foods, Staples, TJ Maxx, TownFair Tire, **S**...**gas:** Hess, Mobil, Sunoco, **food:** Blimpie, Brannigan's Ribs, Friendly's, Ponderosa, Subway, Wendy's, Wood'n Tap Grill, **lodging:** Holiday Inn Express, Howard Johnson, Travelers Inn, **other:** Chevrolet, Jaguar, Firestone, PriceChopper Foods, Wal-Mart

Waterbury

31(44)	CT 229, West St, **N**...**gas:** Mobil, Sunoco/dsl/24hr, **S**...**gas:** Citgo, Gulf, **food:** Dunkin Donuts, Giovanni's Pizza, Subway, Valendino's Pizzaria, **lodging:** Residence Inn
30(43)	Marion Ave, W Main, Southington, **N**...ski area, **S**...**gas:** Mobil/repair, **other:** HOSPITAL
29(42)	CT 10, Milldale(exits left from wb), no services
41.5mm	**rest area eb, full(handicapped)facilities, info, phone, picnic tables, litter barrels, petwalk**
28(41)	CT 322, Marion, **S**...**gas:** Sam's Gas, **other:** USPO, **S**...**gas:** Mobil, TA/dsl/scales/24hr/@, **food:** Blimpie, Burger King, DQ, Dunkin Donuts, **lodging:** Day's Inn, Holiday Inn Express, Manor Inn/rest., **other:** Hemlock Hill RV Ctr, Home Depot, radiators
27(40)	I-691 E, to Meriden
26(38)	CT 70, to Cheshire, **N**...**food:** Silver Diner, **lodging:** CT Grand Hotel
25a(37)	Austin Rd(from eb), **N**...**lodging:** CT Grand Hotel, **other:** Costco/gas
25(36)	Scott Rd, E Main St, **N**...**gas:** Exxon, Gulf/dsl, **food:** Dunkin Donuts, **S**...**gas:** Mobil, **food:** Burger King, Friendly's, McDonald's, Nino's Rest., **lodging:** Ramada Inn, Super 8, **other:** BJ's Whse, Cadillac, Chevrolet, CVS Drug, Super Stop&Shop
24	Harper's Ferry (from eb), **S**...**gas:** Gulf, Shell/24hr
24	Harper's Ferry (from eb), Gulf, Shell/24hr
23(33.5)	CT 69, Hamilton Ave, **N**...**gas:** Citgo, **food:** Bertucci's, Chili's, HomeTown Buffet, McDonald's, Ruby Tuedsay, TGIFriday's, **other:** HOSPITAL, Barnes&Noble, JC Penney, Macy's, Sears/auto, Shaw's Foods, Walgreens, mall, **S**...**gas:** Shell, **food:** Dunkin Donuts
22(33)	Baldwin St, Waterbury, **N**...**gas:** McDonald's, **lodging:** Courtyard, **other:** HOSPITAL, same as 23
21(33)	Meadow St, Banks St, **N**...**gas:** Citgo, **other:** 7-11, Shaw's Foods, **S**...**gas:** Sunoco/dsl/24hr, **other:** Home Depot, Petsmart
20(32)	CT 8 N(exits left from eb), to Torrington, **N**...**gas:** Shell, **food:** Burger King, McDonald's
19(32)	CT 8 S(exits left from wb), to Bridgeport
18(32)	W Main, Highland Ave, **N**...**food:** Lena's Deli, **lodging:** Hampton Inn, **other:** HOSPITAL, CVS Drug
17(30)	CT 63, CT 64, to Watertown, Naugatuck, **N**...**food:** Maggie McFly's Rest., **S**...**gas:** Mobil/dsl, **food:** Maples Rest.
16(25)	CT 188, to Middlebury, **N**...**gas:** Mobil, **food:** Patty's Pantry Deli, **lodging:** Crowne Plaza
15(22)	US 6 E, CT 67, Southbury, **N**...**gas:** Shell, **food:** Dunkin Donuts, Friendly's, McDonald's, **lodging:** Heritage Inn, **other:** K-Mart, Stop&Shop, to Kettletown SP, **S**...Mobil
14(20)	CT 172, to S Britain, **N**...**gas:** Mobil/24hr, **food:** Maggie McFly's, Miranda's Pizza, **other:** st police
20mm	motorist callboxes begin eb, end wb
13(19)	River Rd(from eb), to Southbury, no services
11(16)	CT 34, to New Haven, no services
10(15)	US 6 W, Newtown, **S**...**gas:** Mobil/dsl, Shell/24hr, **food:** Blue Colony Diner/24hr, Pizza Palace, **other:** HOSPITAL
9(11)	CT 25, to Hawleyville, **S**...**lodging:** Best Western, Hillside Inn, Microtel

82

Interstate 84

8(8)	Newtown Rd, 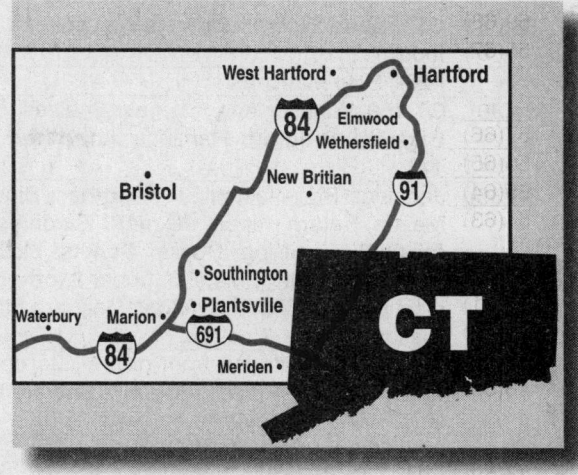**N**...**gas:** Global, Mobil/dsl, **food:** Outback Steaks, **other:** Lowes Whse, **lodging:** Wellesley Inn, **S**...**gas:** BP, Shell, Sunoco, **food:** Bertucci's Italian, Boston Mkt, Burger King, Chili's, Denny's, Dunkin Donuts, Friendly's, Ichiro Steaks, McDonald's, Subway, Taco Bell, Union Buffet, **lodging:** Best Western, Hampton Inn, Holiday Inn/rest., Quality Inn, **other:** Buick/Pontiac, Chrysler/Jeep/Kia, Goodyear/auto, Marshall's, Radio Shack, Staples, Stop&Shop, Target, Wal-Mart
7(7)	US 7N/202E, to Brookfield, (exits left from eb), New Milford, **1 exit N on Federal Rd**...**food:** Applebee's, **lodging:** Best Inn, **other:** Borders Books, Circuit City, Ford, Harley-Davidson, Home Depot, mall
6(6)	CT 37(from wb), New Fairfield, **N**...**gas:** Shell, **food:** McDonald's, **other:** HOSPITAL, to Squantz Pond SP
5(5)	CT 37, CT 39, CT 53, Danbury, **N**...**gas:** Exxon, Shell, **lodging:** Best Value Inn, **S**...**gas:** Mobil, **food:** Dunkin Donuts, Taco Bell, **other:** HOSPITAL, to Putnam SP
4(4)	US 6 W/202 W, Lake Ave, **N**...**gas:** Gulf/dsl, Shell/dsl, Xtra, **food:** Dunkin Donuts, McDonald's, **lodging:** Ethan Allen Hotel, Maron Hotel, Super 8, **other:** CVS Drug, Goodyear/auto, Stop&Shop, **S**...**gas:** Sunoco, **food:** Chuck's Steaks, **lodging:** Residence Inn, to mall
3(3)	US 7 S(exits left from wb), to Norwalk, **S**...**gas:** Exxon, **food:** Coldstone Creamery, Olive Garden, Red Lobster, **other:** Barnes&Noble, JC Penney, Macy's, Sears/auto, mall
2b a(1)	US 6, US 202, Mill Plain Rd, **N**...**gas:** Exxon/dsl, **food:** Desert Moon Café, Starbucks, **lodging:** Comfort Suites, Hilton Garden, **other:** Eckerd, Staples, **S**...**Welcome Ctr/weigh sta, full(handicapped)facilities, info, picnic tables, litter barrels, petwalk, to Old Ridgebury, lodging:** Sheraton
1(0)	Saw Mill Rd, **N**...**lodging:** Comfort Suites(2mi), Danbury Motel, Hilton Garden
0mm	Connecticut/New York state line

Interstate 91

Exit #	Services
58mm	Connecticut/Massachusetts state line
49(57)	US 5, to Longmeadow, MA, **E**...**gas:** Citgo, Mobil, Valero, **food:** Friendly's, McDonald's, Rinaldi's Italian, **lodging:** Radisson, **W**...**food:** Cloverleaf Café
48(56)	CT 220, Elm St, **E**...**gas:** Mobil, **food:** Arby's, Burger King, Denny's, Dunkin Donuts, Figaro Italian, Friendly's, McDonald's, Panera Bread, Ruby Tuesday, TGIFriday, Togo's, Wendy's, **other:** Macy's, Home Depot, Honda, Kohl's, Sears/auto, Target, same as 47
47(55)	CT 190, to Hazardville, **E**...**gas:** Citgo, **food:** Bickford's, D'angelo, Domino's, Dunkin Donuts, Ground Round, Hazard Grille, KFC, McDonald's, Olive Garden, Pizza Hut, Quizno's, Red Lobster, Red Robin, Starbucks, Taco Bell, TCBY, **lodging:** Motel 6, Red Roof Inn, **other:** HOSPITAL, Advance Parts, AutoZone, Barnes&Noble, Bob's Store, CVS Drug, $Tree, Ford, Goodyear, JC Penney, Jo-Ann Fabrics, Michael's, Radio Shack, Shaw's Foods, Staples, Stop&Shop Foods, Walgreen, mall, same as 48
46(53)	US 5, King St, to Enfield, **E**...**gas:** Mobil, **food:** Astro's Rest., **W**...**lodging:** Super 8
45(51)	CT 140, Warehouse Point, **E**...**gas:** Shell/Dunkin Donuts, **food:** Blimpie, Burger King, Cracker Barrel, Friendly's, Kowloon Chinese, Sofia's Pizza, **lodging:** Comfort Inn, **other:** Big Y Foods, Wal-Mart, to Trolley Museum, **W**...**gas:** Sunoco/dsl/24hr, **lodging:** Best Western
44(50)	US 5 S, to E Windsor, **E**...**gas:** Sunoco/dsl, **food:** Dunkin Donuts, E Windsor Rest., Wendy's, **lodging:** Holiday Inn Express
49mm	Connecticut River
42(48)	CT 159, Windsor Locks, **E**...Longview RV Ctr, **W**...**gas:** Gulf, same as 41
41(47)	Center St(exits with 39), **W**...**gas:** Shell/24hr, **food:** Ad Pizzaria, **lodging:** Howard Johnson
40(46.5)	CT 20, **W**...Old New-Gate Prison, airport
39(46)	Kennedy Rd(exits with 41), Community Rd, **W**...**gas:** Shell/dsl/24hr, **other:** K-Mart, Radio Shack, Stop&Shop Foods
38(45)	CT 75, to Poquonock, Windsor Area, **E**...**gas:** Mobil/dsl, **food:** Beanery Rest., China Sea, Domino's, Dunkin Doughnuts, McDonald's, Subway, **other:** to Ellsworth Homestead, **W**...**lodging:** Courtyard, Hilton Garden, Marriott
37(44)	CT 305, Bloomfield Ave, Windsor Ctr, **E**...**gas:** Mobil/dsl, **food:** McDonald's, **W**...**gas:** Gulf, **lodging:** Residence Inn
36(43)	CT 178, Park Ave, to W Hartford

CONNECTICUT
Interstate 91

N ↑ S

Hartford

35b(41)	CT 218, to Bloomfield, to S Windsor, **E**...gas/dsl, food
35a	I-291 E, to Manchester
34(40)	CT 159, Windsor Ave, **E**...gas: Shell/dsl, **W**...gas: Citgo/dsl, **lodging:** Flamingo Inn, **other:** HOSPITAL
33(39)	Jennings Rd, Weston St, **E**...other: Buick/GMC, Mazda, Saturn, repair, **W**...gas: Exxon/dsl, Mobil, **food:** Burger King, Dunkin Donuts, McDonald's, Subway, **lodging:** Motel 6, Super 8, **other:** Champion Auto, Honda, Hyundai, Jaguar, Mitsubishi, Nissan, Toyota
32b(38)	Trumbull St(exits left from nb), **W**...to downtown, **food:** Crowne Plaza, **lodging:** Sheraton, **other:** HOSPITAL, Goodyear
32a	(exit 30 from sb), I-84 W
29b(37)	I-84 E, Hartford
29a(36.5)	US 5 N, CT 15 N(exits left from nb), **W**...downtown, **other:** HOSPITAL, capitol, civic ctr
28(36)	US 5, CT 15 S(from nb), **W**...gas: Citgo, **food:** Burger King, Wendy's
27(35)	Brainerd Rd, Airport Rd, **E**...gas: Shell/dsl, **food:** McDonald's, **lodging:** Day's Inn, **other:** Ford, to Regional Mkt
26(33.5)	Marsh St, **E**...Silas Deane House, Webb House, CT MVD
25(33)	CT 3, Glastonbury, Wethersfield
24(32)	CT 99, Rocky Hill, Wethersfield, **E**...gas: Gulf, Mobil, 7-11, **food:** Bickford's, Blimpie, Dakota Steaks, McDonald's, On-the-Border, Subway, **lodging:** Hampton Inn, Howard Johnson, **W**...gas: Mobil, Shell/dsl, **food:** Bennigan's, China Star Buffet, D'angelo's, Denny's, Dunkin Donuts, Giovanni's Pizza, Ground Round, HomeTown Buffet, KFC, McDonald's, Priya Indian, Red Lobster, Sapporo Japanese, **lodging:** Motel 6, Ramada Inn, **other:** A&P, AutoZone, CVS Drug, Goodyear/auto, Lowe's Whse, Marshalls, Radio Shack, TownFair Tire, Walgreen, Wal-Mart
23(29)	to CT 3, West St, Rocky Hill, Vet Home, **E**...lodging: Marriott, **other:** HOSPITAL, to Dinosaur SP, **W**...gas: Citgo/dsl, Mobil, **food:** Angelo's Pizza, D'angelo's, Subway, **lodging:** SpringHill Suites
22(27)	CT 9, to New Britain, Middletown, no services
21(26)	CT 372, to Berlin, Cromwell, **E**...gas: Sunoco/dsl/repair, Wooster St Pizza, **lodging:** Comfort Inn, Radisson Inn/rest., **other:** Krauszer's Foods, **W**...gas: Citgo/dsl, Mobil/dsl, **food:** Blimpie, Burger King, Cromwell Diner/24hr, Dunkin Doughnuts, Luna Pizza, McDonald's, Oyama Japanese, **lodging:** Courtyard, Holiday Inn, Super 8, **other:** A&P, Fabric Place, Firestone/auto, Wal-Mart/drug
20(23)	Country Club Rd, Middle St, no services
22mm	**rest area/weigh sta nb, full(handicapped) facilities, info, phone, picnic tables, litter barrels, vending, RV dump, petwalk**
19(21)	Baldwin Ave(from sb), no services

Meriden

New Haven

18(20.5)	I-691 W, to Marion, access to same as 16 & 17, ski area
17(20)	CT 15 N(from sb), to I-691, CT 66 E, Meriden, **W**...gas: BP, **food:** Getty, **lodging:** Best Western, Extended Stay America, Residence Inn
16(19)	CT 15, E Main St, **E**...gas: Gulf/dsl, Mobil, Smart Stop, Valero, **food:** American Steaks, Gianni's Rest., Huxley's Café, NY Pizza, Olympos Diner, Subway, **lodging:** Candlewood Suites, Hampton Inn, Ramada Inn, The Inn, **other:** CVS Drug, Ford, Hancock Fabrics, Radio Shack, Volvo, **W**...gas: BP/dsl, Getty/dsl, Gulf/repair, Sunoco/dsl, **food:** Boston Mkt, Burger King, Dunkin Donuts, Friendly's, Great Wall Chinese, KFC, McDonald's, Taco Bell, Wendy's, **lodging:** Executive Suites, Howard Johnson, **other:** HOSPITAL, CarQuest, CVS Drug
15(16)	CT 68, to Durham, **E**...golf, **W**...lodging: Courtyard, Fairfield Inn
15mm	**rest area sb, full(handicapped)facilities, info, phone, picnic tables, litter barrels, petwalk**
14(12)	CT 150(no EZ return), Woodhouse Ave, Wallingford
13(10)	US 5(exits left from nb), Wallingford, **2 mi W** on US 5...to Wharton Brook SP
12(9)	US 5, Washington Ave, **E**...gas: Citgo, Shell, Sunoco, Valero, **food:** Boston Mkt, Burger King, China Buffet, D'angelo, Dunkin Donuts, Friendly's, McDonald's, Quizno's, Rustic Oak Rest., Subway, Wendy's, **other:** CVS Drug, Stop&Shop Food, Walgreen, **W**...gas: Exxon/dsl/24hr, Gulf, **food:** Athena II Diner, Danny's Pizza, Donato's Italian, Roy Rogers, **lodging:** Holiday Inn, **other:** BigY Foods
11(7)	CT 22(from nb), North Haven, **E**...gas: Citgo, Sunoco, **food:** Hunan Chinese, **other:** AutoZone, JC Penney Outlet, Radio Shack, Stop&Shop Foods, TownFair Tire, USPO, same as 12
10(6)	CT 40, to Cheshire, Hamden, no services
9(5)	Montowese Ave, **W**...gas: Sunoco, **food:** McDonald's, Sbarro's, Subway, **other:** Barnes&Noble, BJ's Whse, Circuit City, Home Depot, Target
8(4)	CT 17, CT 80, Middletown Ave, **E**...gas: BP/dsl, Citgo/7-11, Exxon, Shell, Sunoco/24hr, **food:** Burger King, D'angelo, Dunkin Donuts, Exit 8 Diner, KFC, McDonald's, Taco Bell/Pizza Hut, **lodging:** Day's Inn, **other:** Advance Parts, Lowe's Whse, Wal-Mart, **W**...gas: Mobil/dsl
7(3)	Ferry St(from sb), Fair Haven, no services
6(2.5)	Willow St(exits left from nb), Blatchley Ave, **W**...gas: Shell
5(2)	US 5(from nb), State St, Fair Haven, **E**...food: New Star Diner
4(1.5)	State St(from sb), downtown
3(1)	Trumbull St, downtown, **W**...Peabody Museum
2(.5)	Hamilton St, downtown, New Haven, no services
1(.3)	CT 34W(from sb), New Haven, **W**...HOSPITAL, downtown
0mm	I-91 begins/ends on I-95, exit 48.

84

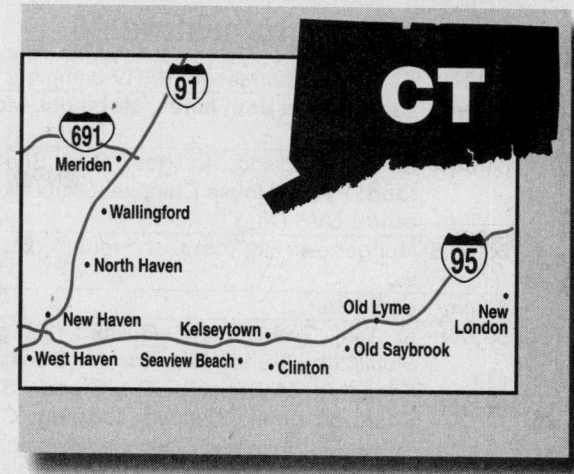

Exit #	Services
112mm	Connecticut/Rhode Island state line
93(111)	CT 216, Clarks Falls, **E**...**gas:** Shell/repair/24hr, to Burlingame SP, **W**...**gas:** Mobil/dsl, Republic/Citgo/dsl/rest./@ , **food:** McDonald's, Tim Horton, **lodging:** Budget Inn, Stardust Motel
92(107)	CT 2, CT 49(no EZ nb return), Pawcatuck, **E**...**gas:** Shell, **other:** HOSPITAL, **W**...**lodging:** Randall's Inn/rest., **other:** FoxWoods(8mi), RV camping
106mm	**Welcome Ctr/rest area sb, full(handicapped) facilities, phone, picnic tables, litter barrels, petwalk, vending**
91(103)	CT 234, N Main St, to Stonington, **E**...HOSPITAL
90(101)	CT 27, Mystic, **E**...**gas:** Mobil, **food:** Bickford's, Domino's, Friendly's, GoFish Rest., Jamm's Seafood, McDonald's, Newport Creamery, Peking Tokyo, Quizno's, Starbucks, Steak Loft, **lodging:** AmeriSuites, Econolodge, Hilton, Howard Johnson, Old Mystic Motel, Seaport Lodge, **other:** Mystic Factory Outlets, aquarium, **W**...**gas:** Mobil, Shell/Subway/Dunkin Donuts/dsl, **food:** Ground Round, Pizza Grille, **lodging:** Best Western, Comfort Inn, Day's Inn, Residence Inn, **other:** Chevrolet, Chrysler/Dodge, Ford, RV camping
100mm	scenic overlook nb
89(99)	CT 215, Allyn St, **W**...camping(seasonal)
88(98)	CT 117, to Noank, **E**...airport, **W**...**food:** Octagon Steaks, Starbucks, **lodging:** Marriott
87(97)	Sharp Hwy(exits left from sb), Groton, **E**...**lodging:** Hampton Inn, to Griswold SP, airport
86(96)	rd 184(exits left from nb), Groton, **E**...**food:** Applebees, 99 Rest., **lodging:** Hampton Inn, Knight's Inn, Quality Inn, **W**...**gas:** Cory's Gas, Hess, Mobil, Shell/dsl, **food:** Chinese Kitchen, Domino's, Flanagan's Diner, KFC, Taco Bell, **lodging:** Best Western, Clarion Inn/rest., Morgan Suites, Super 8, **other:** Honda, Kohl's, Stop'n Shop, to US Sub Base
85(95)	US 1 N, Groton, downtown, **E**...**gas:** Citgo/dsl, **other:** NAPA
94.5mm	Thames River
84(94)	CT 32(from sb), New London, downtown
83(92)	CT 32, New London, **E**...to Long Island Ferry
82a(90.5)	frontage rd, New London, **E**...**food:** Pizza Hut, **other:** AutoZone, Goodyear, Staples, TownFair Tire, TownTown Foods, same as 82, **W**...**food:** Chili's, ChuckeCheese, Outback Steaks, Subway, **lodging:** Holiday Inn, SpringHill Suites, **other:** Marshall's, ShopRite Foods, same as 82
82(90)	New London, **W**...**gas:** Mobil, **food:** Coldstone Creamery, FoodCourt, Olive Garden, Panera Bread, Ruby Tuesday, Subway, Wendy's, **lodging:** Fairfield Suites, Holiday Inn, **other:** Best Buy, Borders Books, Home Depot, JC Penney, Macy's, Marshall's, Michael's, PetCo, Sears, Target, mall
81(89.5)	Cross Road, **W**...**lodging:** Rodeway Inn, **other:** Bob's Store, BJ's Whse/gas, Lowes Whse, Wal-Mart SuperCtr/24hr/McDonald's/drugs
(89mm)	weigh sta both lanes
80(89.3)	Oil Mill Rd(from sb), **W**...**lodging:** Rodeway Inn
76(89)	I-395 N(from nb), to Norwich
75(88)	US 1, to Waterford, no services
74(87)	rd 161, to Flanders, Niantic, **E**...**gas:** Citgo, Mobil, Sunoco/dsl/repair, **food:** Bickford's Rest., Burger King, Dunkin Donuts, KFC, Illiano's Grill, **lodging:** Best Value, Best Western, Day's Inn, Motel 6, Ramada Inn, Sleep Inn, Starlight Motel, **other:** Children's Museum, National Tire, **W**...**gas:** Shell, **food:** Kings Garden Chinese, McDonald's, Shack Rest., Wendy's, **other:** Brooks Drug, IGA Foods, Ford, True Value, RV camping
73(86)	Society Rd, no services
72(84)	to Rocky Neck SP, **2 mi E**...food, lodging, RV camping, to Rocky Neck SP
71(83)	4 Mile Rd, River Rd, to Rocky Neck SP, beaches, **1 mi E**...camping(seasonal)
70(80)	US 1, CT 156, Old Lyme, **W**...**gas:** Shell/dsl, **lodging:** Old Lyme Inn/dining, **other:** A&P, Old Lyme Drug, Griswold Museum
78mm	Connecticut River
69(77)	US 1, CT 9 N, to Hartford, **W**...**food:** Saybrook Fish House, **lodging:** Comfort Inn/rest.
68(76.5)	US 1 S, Old Saybrook, **E**...**gas:** Citgo/dsl, Mobil, **food:** Cloud 9 Deli, Emelio's Italian, Pat's Country Kitchen, Sully's Seafood, **other:** Chrysler/Dodge/Jeep, Daewoo, Isuzu, **W**...**lodging:** Liberty Inn, **other:** Chevrolet/Nissan, Kia, Pontiac/Buick//GMC, Toyota
67(76)	CT 154, Elm St(no EZ sb return), Old Saybrook, **E**...**food:** Pasta Vita Itaian, same as 68
66(75)	to US 1, Spencer Plain Rd, **1 mi E**...**gas:** Citgo/dsl/24hr, **food:** Aleia's Italian, Angus Steaks, Benny's Pizzeria, Cucu's Mexican, Dunkin Donuts/Baskin Robbins, Gateway Indian Cuisine, Luigi's Italian, Thai Cuisine, **lodging:** Day's Inn, Heritage Inn, Sandpiper Motel, Super 8, **other:** ABC Hardware, transmissions
74mm	**rest area sb, full(handicapped) facilities, st police**
65(73)	rd 153, Westbrook, **E**...**gas:** Exxon/Dunkin Donuts, **food:** Denny's, Subway, **lodging:** Sandpiper Hotel, Waters Edge B&B, Westbook Inn B&B, **other:** Honda, Old Navy, Westbrook Factory Stores/famous brands
64(70)	rd 145, Horse Hill Rd, Clinton, no services
63(68)	CT 81, Clinton, **E**...**gas:** Shell, **1 mi E on US 1**...**gas:** Citgo/dsl, Shell/dsl/LP, **food:** Friendly's, McDonald's, **other:** CVS Drug, **W**...**other:** Clinton Crossing Premium Outlets/famous brands

CONNECTICUT
Interstate 95

Exit	Description
62(67)	E...to Hammonasset SP, RV camping, beaches
66mm	**service area both lanes, Mobil/dsl, McDonald's, atm**
61(64)	CT 79, Madison, E...gas: Gulf, Shell, Sunoco, food: Panda House Chinese, Starbucks, Subway, other: CVS Drug
60(63.5)	Mungertown Rd(from sb, no return), E...food, lodging
61mm	East River
59(60)	rd 146, Goose Lane, Guilford, E...gas: Citgo, Mobil/24hr, Shell/dsl, food: Dunkin Donuts, Friendly's, McDonald's, Rio Grande Steakhouse, Shoreline Diner, Wendy's, lodging: Comfort Inn, Tower Motel, other: Chevrolet/Pontiac, W...MEDICAL CTR
58(59)	CT 77, Guilford, on US 1 E...food: Getty, Mobil, other: CVS Drug, to Whitfield Museum, W...st police
57(58)	US 1, Guilford, W...other: Land Rover, Saab
56(55)	rd 146, to Stony Creek, E...lodging: Advanced Motel, W...gas: Berkshire/dsl, Mobil, TA/dsl/rest./24hr/@, food: Dunkin Donuts, Dutchess Rest., Friendly's, USS Chowderpot, lodging: Best Value, Ramada Ltd, other: Stop&Shop Foods
55(54)	US 1, E...gas: Sunoco, Thornton, food: Dunkin Donuts, Marco Pizzaria, McDonald's, Shoreline Rest., Vincent's Drive-In, lodging: Holiday Inn Express, Knight's Inn, Motel 6, other: Dodge, Ford, 7-11/24hr, Walgreen, W...gas: Citgo, Exxon/dsl, Mobil/dsl, food: Margarita's Mexican, Parthenon Diner/24hr, Su Casa Mexican, lodging: Day's Inn
54(53)	Cedar St, Brushy Plain Rd, E...gas: Citgo/repair, Mobil, food: Dragon Chinese, Dunkin Donuts, Townhouse Rest., other: AAA, Chevrolet, Dodge, Mitsubishi, Staples, Subaru, W...Krauszer's Foods
52mm	**service area both lanes, Mobil/dsl/24hr, McDonald's, atm**
52(50)	rd 100, North High St, E...other: to Trolley Museum, W...st police
51(49.5)	US 1, Easthaven, E...gas: Citgo, Hess, Sunoco, food: Boston Mkt, Chili's, Friendly's, McDonald's, lodging: Holiday Inn Express, other: Chevrolet, Hummer, Lexus, TJ Maxx, W...gas: Mobil, Gulf, food: Dunkin Donuts, Wendy's, other: AutoZone, Radio Shack, USPO
50(49)	Woodward Ave(from nb), E...gas: Citgo, other: US Naval/Marine Reserve, Ft Nathan Hale
49(48.5)	Stiles St(from nb), no services
48(48)	I-91 N, to Hartford
47(47.5)	CT 34, New Haven, E...gas: Shell, W...gas: Mobil/dsl, lodging: Fairfield Inn, other: HOSPITAL
46(47)	Long Wharf Dr, Sargent Dr, E...food: Rusty Scupper Rest., W...gas: Mobil/dsl, food: Brick Oven Pizza, lodging: Fairfield Inn
45(46.5)	CT 10(from sb), Blvd, same as 44, W...food: Getty, DQ, Dunkin Donuts, McDonald's

Exit	Description
44(46)	CT 10(from nb), Kimberly Ave, E...lodging: Super 8, W...gas: Getty, food: DQ, Dunkin Donuts, McDonald's, Wendy's, same as 45
43(45)	CT 122, 1st Ave(no EZ return), West Haven, W...gas: BP, other: HOSPITAL, to U of New Haven
42(44)	CT 162, Saw Mill Rd, E...gas: Mobil, food: Pizza Hut, lodging: Econolodge, W...gas: Shell, Mobil, 7-11, food: American Steaks, D'angelo's, Denny's, Dunkin Donuts, Friendly's, Pizza Hut, lodging: Best Western, other: Staples
41(42)	Marsh Hill Rd, to Orange, no services
41mm	**service area both lanes, gas: Mobil/dsl, food: McDonald's**
40(40)	Old Gate Lane, Woodmont Rd, E...gas: Citgo/dsl, Gulf/dsl/24hr, Pilot/Wendy's/dsl/24hr, Shell, food: Bennigan's, Cracker Barrel, D'angelo's, Duchess Rest., Dunkin Doughnuts, Gipper's Rest., lodging: Best Value Inn, Comfort Inn, Mayflower Hotel, Milford Inn
39(39)	US 1, to Milford, E...gas: Gulf/dsl, food: Athenean Diner, Friendly's, Hooters, Imo's Pizza, Pizzaria Uno, lodging: Howard Johnson, Super 8, other: Firestone/auto, Mazda/Volvo, Walgreen, W on US 1...gas: Mobil, food: Baskin-Robbins, Boston Mkt, Burger King, Chili's, Dunkin Donuts, KFC, Little Caesar's, Miami Subs, Mr Sizzzl, McDonald's, Nathan's Famous, Steak&Sword Rest., Subway, Taco Bell, Wendy's, other: Acura, Chrysler/Jeep, Macy's, JC Penney, Michael's, Old Navy, Rite Aid, Sears/auto, Stop&Shop Food, TownFair Tire, USPO, Waldbaum's Foods, mall
38(38)	CT 15, Merritt Pkwy, Cross Pkwy
37(37.5)	High St(from nb, no EZ return), E...gas: Gulf, Shell, lodging: ShoreLine Motel, other: 7-11
35(37)	Bic Dr, School House Rd, E...gas: Citgo, food: Subway, Wendy's, lodging: Fairfield Inn, other: Buick, Chevrolet, Chrysler/Jeep, Dodge, Ford/Lincoln/Mercury, Honda, Kia, K-Mart, Pontiac/Nissan, W...lodging: Red Roof Inn, SpringHill Suites
34(34)	US 1, Milford, E...gas: Gulf, Shell, food: Denny's, Dunkin Donuts, Gourmet Buffet, McDonald's, Taco Bell, lodging: Devon Motel
33(33.5)	US 1(from nb, no EZ return), CT 110, Ferry Blvd, E...gas: Shell/dsl, Sunoco, food: Marina Dock Rest., other: Jo-Ann Fabrics, Shaw's Foods, Staples, Stop&Shop Foods, Walgreen, W...food: Ponderosa, other: Home Depot, Marshalls, Wal-Mart SuperCtr/24hr
32(33)	W Broad St, Stratford, E...gas: BP, food: Getty, other: Ford, repair, W...gas: Gulf, food: Dunkin Donuts
31(32)	South Ave, Honeyspot Rd, E...gas: Gulf/dsl, lodging: Camelot Motel, Honeyspot Motel, W...gas: Citgo/dsl
30(31.5)	Lordship Blvd, Surf Ave, E...gas: Shell/24hr, food: Ramada/rest., other: Harley-Davidson, Ryder, W...gas: Citgo/dsl

Interstate 95

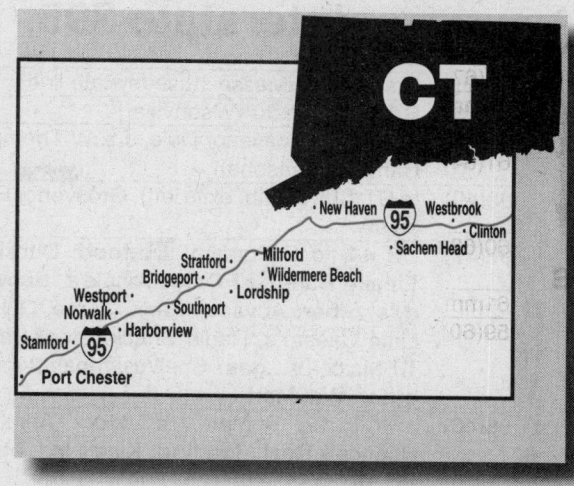

Bridgeport

29(31)	rd 130, Stratford Ave, Seaview Ave, W...HOSPITAL
28(30)	CT 113, E Main St, Pembrook St
27(29.5)	Lafayette Blvd, downtown, W...**lodging:** Day's Inn, **other:** HOSPITAL, Bob's Store, Sears/auto, Barnum Museum
27a(29)	CT 25, CT 8, to Waterbury
26(28)	Wordin Ave, downtown
25(27)	CT 130(from sb, no EZ return), State St, Commerce Dr, Fairfield Ave, E...**food:** Getty, **other:** Mercedes, W...**gas:** Gulf, **food:** McDonald's
24(26.5)	Black Rock Tpk, E...**food:** D'Angelo, **other:** Ford, Lexus, **other:** Staples, W...**other:** Ford/Nissan
23(26)	US 1, Kings Hwy, E...**gas:** Sunoco/dsl, **food:** McDonald's, **other:** Home Depot
22(24)	Round Hill Rd, N Benson Rd, no services
23.5mm	**service area both lanes, gas:** Mobil/dsl, **food:** FoodCourt(sb), **McDonald's/24**
21(23)	Mill Plain Rd, E...**gas:** Mobil, Shell, **food:** DQ, Grotto Rest., McDonald's, Subway, **lodging:** Fairfield Inn, **other:** Brooks Drug, Stop&Shop Food
20(22)	Bronson Rd(from sb), no services
19(21)	US 1, Center St, E...Southport Brewing Co, W...**gas:** Shell/Dunkin Donuts/dsl, **food:** Athena Diner, **lodging:** Tequot Motel, **other:** TownFair Tire
18(20)	to Westport, E...Sherwood Island SP, beaches, W...**gas:** Citgo, Mobil, **food:** Bertucci's Pizza, Burger King, Carver's Ice Cream, Cedar Brook Café, McDonald's, Sherwood Diner, Subway, Woodie's Roadhouse, **other:** Toyota, Radio Shack, st police
17(18)	CT 33, rd 136, Westport, W...**other:** FastStop Mart

Norwalk

16(17)	E Norwalk, E...**gas:** Mobil, Shell/dsl, **food:** Baskin-Robbins/Dunkin Donuts, Eastside Café, Penny's Diner, Subway, **other:** Rite Aid
15(16)	US 7, to Danbury, Norwalk, E...**gas:** Shell, **other:** Chevrolet, W...**gas:** Getty
14(15)	US 1, CT Ave, S Norwalk, E...st police, W...**gas:** BP/dsl, Coastal, **food:** Angela Mia's Café, Pagano's Seafood, Pizza Hut, Post Road Diner, Silver Star Diner, **other:** HOSPITAL, Barnes&Noble, Circuit City, CompUSA, Firestone, GNC, ShopRite Foods, Stop&Shop
13(13)	US 1(no EZ return), Post Rd, Norwalk, W...**gas:** Exxon, Mobil, Shell/24hr, **food:** American Steaks, Burger King, Driftwood Diner, Dunkin Donuts, Friendly's, IHOP, KFC, McDonald's, Pasta Fare Rest., Red Lobster, Wendy's, **lodging:** DoubleTree Hotel, **other:** Costco, Home Depot, Kohl's, LandRover, Old Navy, Radio Shack, ShopRite Foods, Staples, TownFair Tire, same as 14
12.5mm	**service area nb,** Mobil/dsl, McDonald's
12(12)	rd 136, Tokeneke Rd(from nb, no return), W...**food:** deli

Stamford

11(11)	US 1, Darien, E...**gas:** BP, **other:** Chevrolet, Lincoln/Mercury/Jaguar, W...**gas:** Exxon, **lodging:** Howard Johnson/rest., **other:** BMW
10(10)	Noroton, W...**gas:** Citgo, Getty, Shell, **food:** Jake's Place
9.5mm	**service area sb, gas:** Mobil/dsl, **food:** McDonald's
9(9)	US 1, rd 106, Glenbrook, E...**food:** Indian Cuisine, **lodging:** Stamford Motor Inn, W...**gas:** Gulf, **food:** Blimpie, McDonald's, **other:** Aamco
8(8)	Atlantic Ave, Elm St, E...U-Haul, W...**gas:** Exxon, Sunoco, **lodging:** Budget Inn, Marriott, Ramada Inn, **other:** HOSPITAL, Saturn
7(7)	CT 137, Atlantic Ave, E...**lodging:** Westin Hotel, W...**lodging:** Marriott, **other:** JC Penney, mall, same as 8
6(6)	Harvard Ave, West Ave, E...**gas:** Exxon, **food:** City Limits Diner, **lodging:** Fairfield Inn, **other:** Hyundai, USPO, W...**gas:** Getty, Shell/24hr, **food:** Boston Mkt, Corner Deli/pizza, Subway, Taco Bell, **lodging:** Stamford Hotel, Super 8, **other:** HOSPITAL, Firestone
5(5)	US 1, Riverside, Old Greenwich, W...**gas:** Mobil, Shell/24hr, **food:** Italian Ristorante, McDonald's, Taco Bell, **lodging:** Howard Johnson, Hyatt Regency, **other:** A&P, Caldor, Edwards Drug, Staples
4(4)	Indian Field Rd, Cos Cob, W...**lodging:** Howard Johnson, **other:** Bush-Holley House Museum
3(3)	Arch St, Greenwich, E...Bruce Museum, W...**gas:** Shell, **other:** HOSPITAL
2mm	weigh sta nb
2(1)	Delavan Ave, Byram, no services
1mm	Connecticut/New York state line

CONNECTICUT
Interstate 395

Exit #	Services
	55.5mm Connecticut/Massachusetts state line
100(54)	E Thompson, to Wilsonville
99(50)	rd 200, N Grosvenor Dale, **E**...W Thompson Lake Camping(seasonal)
98(49)	to CT 12(from nb, exits left), Grosvenor Dale, same as 99
97(47)	US 44, to E Putnam, **E**...**food:** Dunkin Donuts, Empire Buffet, KFC, McDonald's, Subway, Wendy's, **other:** Advance Parts, $Tree, GNC, K-Mart/Little Caesar's, Radio Shack, Stop&Shop Foods, TJ Maxx, **W**...**gas:** Shell/dsl/repair/24hr, Sunoco, **other:** Wal-Mart
96(46)	to CT 12, Putnam, **W**...**food:** Annie's Buffet, Chance's Rest., **lodging:** King's Inn, **other:** HOSPITAL
95(45)	Kennedy Dr, to Putnam, **E**...Ford/Mercury, **W**...HOSPITAL
94(43)	Ballouville, **W**...**food:** Laurel House Rest., **lodging:** Holiday Inn Express
93(41)	CT 101, to Dayville, **E**...**gas:** Shell/dsl, **food:** Burger King, Bryan's Grill, China Garden, Dunkin Donuts, McDonald's, Subway, Zip's Diner, **other:** Stop&Shop, Wibberley Tire, **W**...**gas:** Mobil/dsl/24hr
92(39)	to S Killingly, **W**...**food:** Giant Pizza, **other:** Bonneville Drug, st police
91(38)	US 6 W, to Danielson, to Quinebaug Valley Coll
90(36)	to US 6 E(from nb), to Providence
35mm	**rest area both lanes, full(handicapped) facilities, gas: Mobil/dsl**
89(32)	CT 14, to Central Village, **E**...**gas:** Gulf, **other:** chevrolet/Jeep, RV camping, **W**...**gas:** Citgo/7-11/dsl/24hr, Sunoco/dsl/LP/repair, **food:** Grandma's Rest., Subway, **lodging:** Plainfield Motel/rest.
88(30)	CT 14A to Plainfield, **E**...RV camping, **1/2 mi** **W**...**gas:** Mobil
87(28)	Lathrop Rd, to Plainfield, **E**...**gas:** Shell/Domino's/dsl, **food:** Dunkin Donuts, HongKong Star Chinese, Subway, Wendy's, **lodging:** Holiday Inn Express, Plainfield Yankee Motel, **other:** Big Y Foods, Ford, Greyhound Park, Mazda, Radio Shack, **W**...**gas:** Citgo, **food:** McDonald's, O'Conner's rest., Pizza Place, **other:** CVS Drug
86(24)	rd 201, Hopeville, **E**...Hopeville Pond SP, RV camping
85(23)	CT 164, CT 138, to Pachaug, Preston, **E**...**other:** $Tree, Hidden Acres RV camping
84(21)	CT 12, Jewett City, **E**...**food:** Ruby Tuesday, **other:** Home Depot, Kohl's, Old Navy, Wal-Mart SuperCtr/24hr, **W**...**gas:** Citgo/7-11, Mobil/Pizza Hut/dsl, Shell/dsl, **food:** McDonald's, **other:** Val-U Foods
83a(20)	CT 169(from nb), Lisbon, **E**...RV camping

Exit #	Services
83(18)	rd 97, Taftville, **E**...**gas:** Getty/dsl, **other:** camping, repair, **W**...**gas:** Citgo/7-11
82(14)	to CT 2 W, CT 32 N, Norwichtown, **E**...**food:** Friendly's, **W**...**gas:** Citgo, Mobil/dsl, Shell/Dunkin Donuts/dsl, **food:** Illiano's Grill, McDonald's, Rena's Pizza, Subway, **lodging:** Comfort Suites, Courtyard, Rosemont Suites, **other:** Ace Hardware
81(14)	CT 2 E, CT 32 S, Norwich, **E**...HOSPITAL, to Mohegan Coll
80(12)	CT 82, Norwich, **E**...**gas:** Mobil, Shell/repair, **food:** Tim Horton, Burger King, Chinese Buffet, Dominic's Pizza, Friendly's, KFC/Taco Bell, McDonald's, Mr Pizza, Papa Gino's, Subway, Wendy's, **other:** Brooks Drug, Jo-Ann Fabrics, ShopRite Foods, Staples, TownFair Tire, **W**...**lodging:** Ramada Inn
79a(10)	CT 2A E, to Ledyard, **E**...to Pequot Res
8.5mm	**nb...st police, phone, sb...Mobil/dsl, rest area, full facilities**
79(6)	rd 163, to Uncasville, Montville, **1 mi** **E**...**gas:** Mobil/McDonald's/dsl, **food:** Dunkin Donuts, Friendly Pizza, Plan B Cafe, Subway, **other:** Beit Bro's Foods, Brooks Drug
78(5)	CT 32(from sb, exits left), to New London, RI Beaches
77(2)	CT 85, to I-95 N, Colchester, **1/2 mi** **E**...**gas:** Shell/dsl, Dunkin Donuts, **lodging:** Oakdell Motel
0mm	I-95. I-395 begins/ends on I-95, exit 76.

Interstate 691

Exit #	Services
	I-691 begins/ends on I-91
12(12)	Preston Ave, no services
11(11)	I-91 N, to Hartford
10(11)	I-91 S, to New Haven, CT 15 S, W Cross Pkwy
8(10)	US 5, Broad St, **N**...**gas:** Cumberland, Mobil/mart, Shell/dsl, **food:** Broad St Pizza, Chinese Gourmet, DQ
7(9)	downtown, Meriden(from wb), **S**...**gas:** Citgo
6(8)	Lewis Ave(from wb, no EZ return), to CT 71, **N**...**food:** Ruby Tuesday, **other:** HOSPITAL, Circuit City, Macy's, JC Penney, Lord&Taylor, Sears/auto, Target, mall, **S**...Citgo/7-11
5(7)	CT 71, to Chamberlain Hill(from eb, no EZ return), **N**...**other:** HOSPITAL, Best Buy, Target, mall, **S**...**gas:** Citgo/7-11
4(4)	CT 322, W Main St(no re-entry from eb), **N**...**gas:** Citgo, **food:** Dunkin Donuts, **other:** HOSPITAL
3mm	Quinnipiac River
3(1)	CT 10, to Cheshire, Southington, **N**...**food:** Tony's Pizza, Whole Donut
2(0)	I-84 E, to Hartford
1(0)	I-84 W, to Waterbury
	I-691 begins/ends on I-84

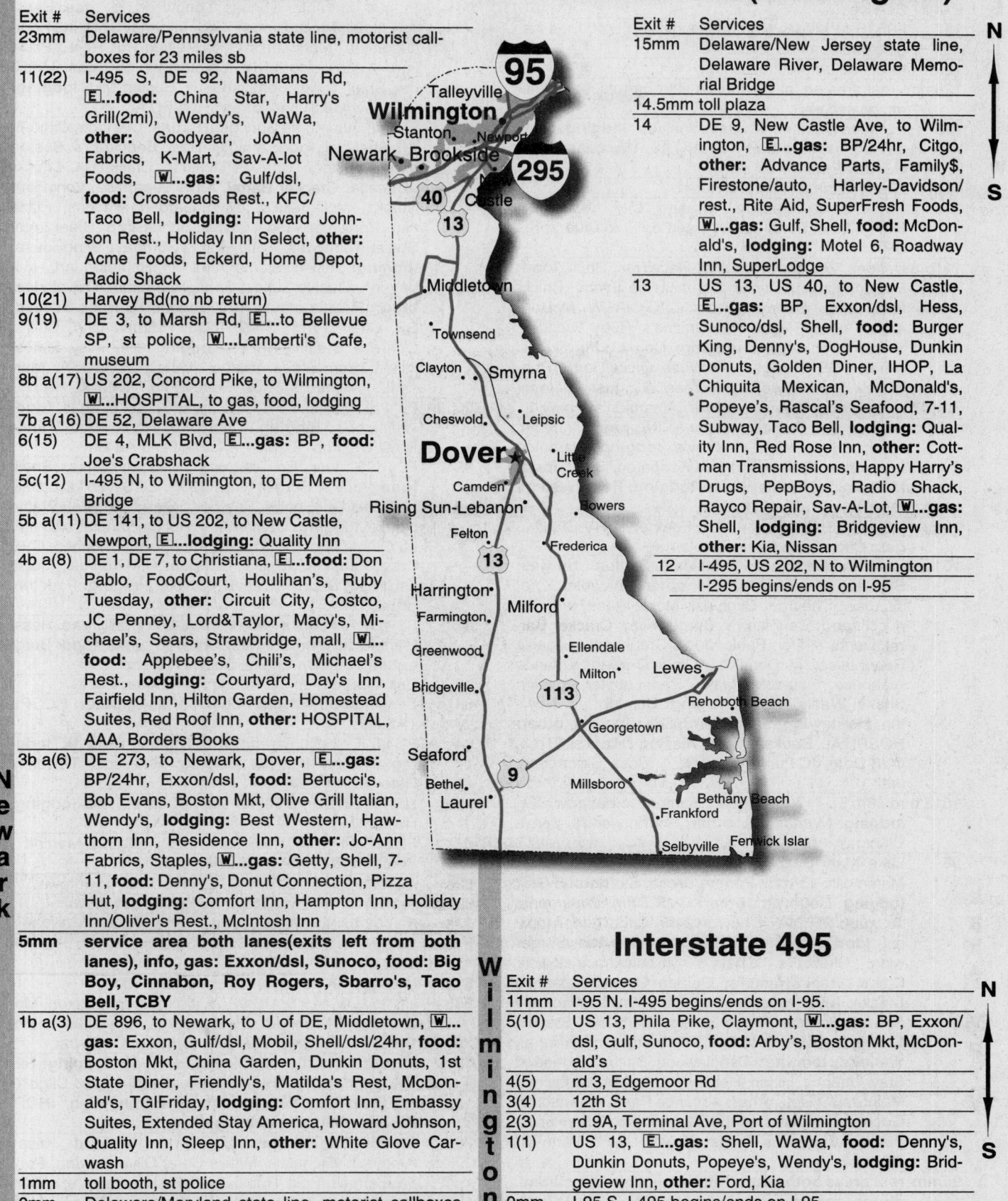

Interstate 95

Exit #	Services
23mm	Delaware/Pennsylvania state line, motorist callboxes for 23 miles sb
11(22)	I-495 S, DE 92, Naamans Rd, **E**...**food:** China Star, Harry's Grill(2mi), Wendy's, WaWa, **other:** Goodyear, JoAnn Fabrics, K-Mart, Sav-A-lot Foods, **W**...**gas:** Gulf/dsl, **food:** Crossroads Rest., KFC/Taco Bell, **lodging:** Howard Johnson Rest., Holiday Inn Select, **other:** Acme Foods, Eckerd, Home Depot, Radio Shack
10(21)	Harvey Rd(no nb return)
9(19)	DE 3, to Marsh Rd, **E**...to Bellevue SP, st police, **W**...Lamberti's Cafe, museum
8b a(17)	US 202, Concord Pike, to Wilmington, **W**...HOSPITAL, to gas, food, lodging
7b a(16)	DE 52, Delaware Ave
6(15)	DE 4, MLK Blvd, **E**...**gas:** BP, **food:** Joe's Crabshack
5c(12)	I-495 N, to Wilmington, to DE Mem Bridge
5b a(11)	DE 141, to US 202, to New Castle, Newport, **E**...**lodging:** Quality Inn
4b a(8)	DE 1, DE 7, to Christiana, **E**...**food:** Don Pablo, FoodCourt, Houlihan's, Ruby Tuesday, **other:** Circuit City, Costco, JC Penney, Lord&Taylor, Macy's, Michael's, Sears, Strawbridge, mall, **W**...**food:** Applebee's, Chili's, Michael's Rest., **lodging:** Courtyard, Day's Inn, Fairfield Inn, Hilton Garden, Homestead Suites, Red Roof Inn, **other:** HOSPITAL, AAA, Borders Books
3b a(6)	DE 273, to Newark, Dover, **E**...**gas:** BP/24hr, Exxon/dsl, **food:** Bertucci's, Bob Evans, Boston Mkt, Olive Grill Italian, Wendy's, **lodging:** Best Western, Hawthorn Inn, Residence Inn, **other:** Jo-Ann Fabrics, Staples, **W**...**gas:** Getty, Shell, 7-11, **food:** Denny's, Donut Connection, Pizza Hut, **lodging:** Comfort Inn, Hampton Inn, Holiday Inn/Oliver's Rest., McIntosh Inn
5mm	**service area both lanes(exits left from both lanes), info, gas: Exxon/dsl, Sunoco, food: Big Boy, Cinnabon, Roy Rogers, Sbarro's, Taco Bell, TCBY**
1b a(3)	DE 896, to Newark, to U of DE, Middletown, **W**...**gas:** Exxon, Gulf/dsl, Mobil, Shell/dsl/24hr, **food:** Boston Mkt, China Garden, Dunkin Donuts, 1st State Diner, Friendly's, Matilda's Rest., McDonald's, TGIFriday, **lodging:** Comfort Inn, Embassy Suites, Extended Stay America, Howard Johnson, Quality Inn, Sleep Inn, **other:** White Glove Carwash
1mm	toll booth, st police
0mm	Delaware/Maryland state line, motorist callbacks

DELAWARE

Interstate 295(Wilmington)

Exit #	Services
15mm	Delaware/New Jersey state line, Delaware River, Delaware Memorial Bridge
14.5mm	toll plaza
14	DE 9, New Castle Ave, to Wilmington, **E**...**gas:** BP/24hr, Citgo, **other:** Advance Parts, Family$, Firestone/auto, Harley-Davidson/rest., Rite Aid, SuperFresh Foods, **W**...**gas:** Gulf, Shell, **food:** McDonald's, **lodging:** Motel 6, Roadway Inn, SuperLodge
13	US 13, US 40, to New Castle, **E**...**gas:** BP, Exxon/dsl, Hess, Sunoco/dsl, Shell, **food:** Burger King, Denny's, DogHouse, Dunkin Donuts, Golden Diner, IHOP, La Chiquita Mexican, McDonald's, Popeye's, Rascal's Seafood, 7-11, Subway, Taco Bell, **lodging:** Quality Inn, Red Rose Inn, **other:** Cottman Transmissions, Happy Harry's Drugs, PepBoys, Radio Shack, Rayco Repair, Sav-A-Lot, **W**...**gas:** Shell, **lodging:** Bridgeview Inn, **other:** Kia, Nissan
12	I-495, US 202, N to Wilmington
	I-295 begins/ends on I-95

Interstate 495

Exit #	Services
11mm	I-95 N. I-495 begins/ends on I-95.
5(10)	US 13, Phila Pike, Claymont, **W**...**gas:** BP, Exxon/dsl, Gulf, Sunoco, **food:** Arby's, Boston Mkt, McDonald's
4(5)	rd 3, Edgemoor Rd
3(4)	12th St
2(3)	rd 9A, Terminal Ave, Port of Wilmington
1(1)	US 13, **E**...**gas:** Shell, WaWa, **food:** Denny's, Dunkin Donuts, Popeye's, Wendy's, **lodging:** Bridgeview Inn, **other:** Ford, Kia
0mm	I-95 S. I-495 begins/ends on I-95

FLORIDA
Interstate 4

E ↑ W

Lake Mary | **Orlando**

Exit #	Services
132	I-95, S to Miami, N to Jacksonville, FL 400. I-4 begins/ends on I-95, exit 260b
129	to US 92(from eb, exits left)
126mm	rest area eb, picnic tables, litter barrels, no services, no security
118	FL 44, to DeLand, **N...gas:** Shell/dsl, **lodging:** Howard Johnson, **other:** HOSPITAL, **S...gas:** Citgo/Subway(2mi)
116	Orange Camp Rd, Lake Helen
114	FL 472, to DeLand, Orange City, **N...other:** KOA(1.5mi), Sunburst RV Park(.5mi), to Blue Sprgs SP
111b a	Deltona, **N...gas:** Hess/dsl, RaceTrac, Shell, **food:** Baskin-Robbins/Dunkin Donuts, Bob Evans, Chick-fil-A, Chili's, Denny's, Fazoli's, KFC/A&W, McDonald's, Perkins, Pizza Hut, Quizno's, Ruby Tuesday, Steak'n Shake/24hr, **lodging:** Country Inn Suites, **other:** HOSPITAL, Lowe's Whse, Office Depot, Publix/deli, Tire Kingdom, Walgreen, **S...gas:** Chevron/repair, **food:** Wendy's, **other:** Albertson's, Family$
108	Dirksen Dr, DeBary, Deltona, **N...gas:** Chevron, **food:** Burger King, Shoney's, **lodging:** Hampton Inn, **other:** Publix, **S...gas:** Kangaroo, Shell, **food:** McDonald's, Waffle House, **lodging:** Best Western/rest.
104	US 17, US 92, Sanford, **N...**Featherlite RV Ctr, **S...gas:** Citgo/Subway
101b c	rd 46, to FL 417 (toll), to Mt Dora, Sanford, **N...gas:** BP/Pizza Hut/dsl, Citgo/7-11, **other:** Chevrolet, Ford, **S...gas:** Chevron, Citgo/dsl, Mobil, RaceTrac, Sunoco, **food:** Bennigan's, Burger King, Cracker Barrel, Denny's, Don Pablo, Joe's Crabshack, Logan's Roadhouse, McDonald's, Olive Garden, Orlando Alehouse, Outback Steaks, Red Lobster, Steak'n Shake, Waffle House, **lodging:** Comfort Inn, Day's Inn, Holiday Inn, SpringHill Suites, Super 8, **other:** HOSPITAL, BooksAMillion, Macy's, Dillard's, $Tree, CVS Drug, JC Penney, Old Navy, Ross, Sears/auto, mall
101a b	rd 46a, FL 417(toll), FL 46, Sanford, Heathrow, **S...lodging:** Marriott, **S...other:** Acura, Honda, Sam's Club/gas
98	Lake Mary Blvd, Heathrow, **N...gas:** Shell, **food:** Mammolito's Pizza, Panera Bread, Stonewood Grill, **lodging:** Courtyard, **other:** CVS Drug, Walgreens, **S...gas:** BP/24hr, Chevron/24hr, Citgo/7-11, Mobil/dsl, **food:** Arby's, Bob Evans, Boston Mkt, Burger King, Checkers, Chevy's Mexican, Chick-fil-A, Chili's, Frank&Naomi's, Golden China, Japanese Steaks, KFC, Krystal, LongHorn Steaks, Macaroni Grill, McDonald's, Papa John's, Starbucks, Steak'n Shake, Subway, Taco Bell, TGIFriday, Uno Pizzaria, Wendy's, **lodging:** Candlewood Suites, Extended Stay America, Hilton, Homewood Suites, La Quinta, MainStay Suites, **other:** Advance Parts, Albertson's, Goodyear, Home Depot, K-Mart, Olson Tire, Publix, Staples, Starbucks, Target, Tires+, USPO, Winn-Dixie, mall
95mm	**rest areas both lanes, full(handicapped)facilities, phone, vending, picnic tables, litter barrels, petwalk, 24hr security**
94	FL 434, to Winter Springs, Longwood, **N...gas:** Hess/dsl, Mobil, **food:** Burger King, Imperial Dynasty, Kobe Japanese, Markham's Grill, Melting Pot Rest., Pizza Hut, Wendy's, **lodging:** Comfort Inn, **S...gas:** Mobil/dsl, Shell, **food:** Bonefish Grill, Boston Mkt, **lodging:** Candlewood Suites, **other:** HOSPITAL, 7-11
92	FL 436, Altamonte Springs, **N...gas:** Chevron, Citgo/7-11, Shell/dsl, **food:** Amigo's Rest, Bennigan's, Boston Mkt, Checker's, Chevy's Mexican, Chick-fil-A, ChuckeCheese, Cracker Barrel, Kobe Japanese, LongHorn Steaks, McDonald's, Olive Garden, Perkins, Pizza Hut, Popeye's, Red Lobster, Schlotsky's, Steak&Ale, Sweet Tomatoes, Taco Bell, TGIFriday, WingHouse, **lodging:** Best Western, Day's Inn, Hampton Inn, Holiday Inn, Quality Suites, SpringHill Suites, Travelodge, **other:** Firestone/auto, Tire Kingdom, U-Haul, **S...gas:** BP, Citgo, Hess, Shell, **food:** Pizzaria Uno, Chili's, Denny's, Steak'n Shake, **lodging:** Embassy Suites, Hilton, Homestead Village, **other:** CompUSA, Marshall's, Michael's, Ross, Sears/auto, TJMaxx,
90b a	FL 414, Maitland Blvd, **N...gas:** Citgo/7-11/gas, **food:** Applebee's, **lodging:** Courtyard, Homewood Suites, Hotel Orlando, Studio+, **S...**Maitland Art Ctr
88	FL 423, Lee Rd, **N...gas:** Citgo/7-11/gas, Shell, **food:** Arby's, Burger King, IHOP, LJ Silver/Taco Bell, McDonald's, Shell's Seafood, Sicilian Pizza, Waffle House, **lodging:** Comfort Inn, Holiday Inn, InTown Inn, La Quinta, Motel 6, Travelers Inn, **other:** Aamco, CVS Drug, Firestone, Infiniti, **S...gas:** Chevron/dsl, Mobil/dsl, **food:** Denny's, Steak'n Shake, **lodging:** Park Inn, **other:** BMW
87	FL 426, Fairbanks Ave(no eb re-entry), **N...gas:** Hess/Blimpie/dsl, **1mi S...gas:** Chevron, Shell, **food:** Burger King, Steak'n Shake, Subway, Wendy's
86	Par Ave(from eb, no re-entry), **S...gas:** Shell
85	Princeton St, **S...gas:** Chevron, Shell, **other:** HOSPITAL
84	FL 50, Colonial Dr(from wb), Ivanhoe Blvd, **N...lodging:** Holiday Inn, **S...lodging:** Radisson, Travelers Hotel
83b	US 17, US 92, FL 50, Amelia St(from eb), **N...lodging:** Holiday Inn
83a	FL 526(from eb), Robinson St, **N...lodging:** Marriott
83	South St(from wb), downtown
82c	Anderson St E, Church St Sta Hist Dist, downtown
82b	Gore Ave(from wb), **S...**HOSPITAL, downtown
82a	FL 408(toll), to FL 526
81b c	Kaley Ave, **S...gas:** Citgo, Sunoco, **other:** HOSPITAL
81a	Michigan St(from wb), **N...gas:** Citgo/dsl
80b a	US 17, US 441 S, US 92 W, **S...gas:** BP, Exxon, Mobil, RaceTrac, **food:** Denny's/24hr, Krystal/24hr, McDonald's, Subway, Wendy's, **lodging:** Day's Inn
79	FL 423, 33rd St, John Young Pkwy, **N...lodging:** Ramada Inn, **other:** Harley-Davidson, **S...gas:** Citgo/7-11, RaceTrac, Shell/dsl, **food:** Burger King, IHOP, KFC, McDonald's, **lodging:** Days Inn/rest.
78	Conroy Rd, **N...gas:** Citgo/7-11, **S...food:** Krispy Kreme, McDonald's, Mimi's Cafe, Olive Garden, Panda Express, Polo Tropical, TGIFriday, Zaxby's, **other:** BJ's Whse/gas, Circuit City, Home Depot, Macy's, Marshall's, Target, mall

90

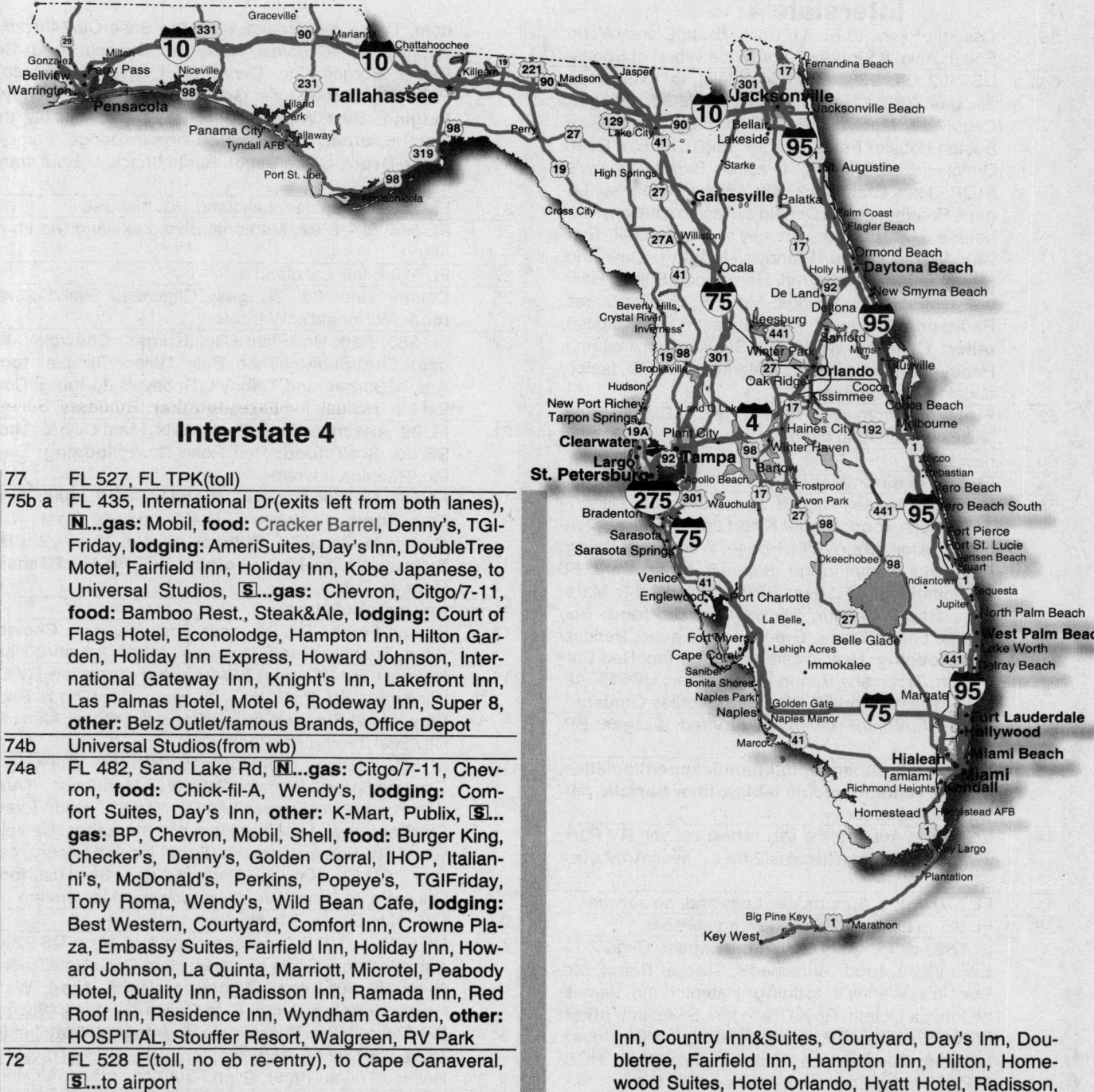

FLORIDA

Interstate 4

E → **W**

Orlando

77	FL 527, FL TPK(toll)
75b a	FL 435, International Dr(exits left from both lanes), 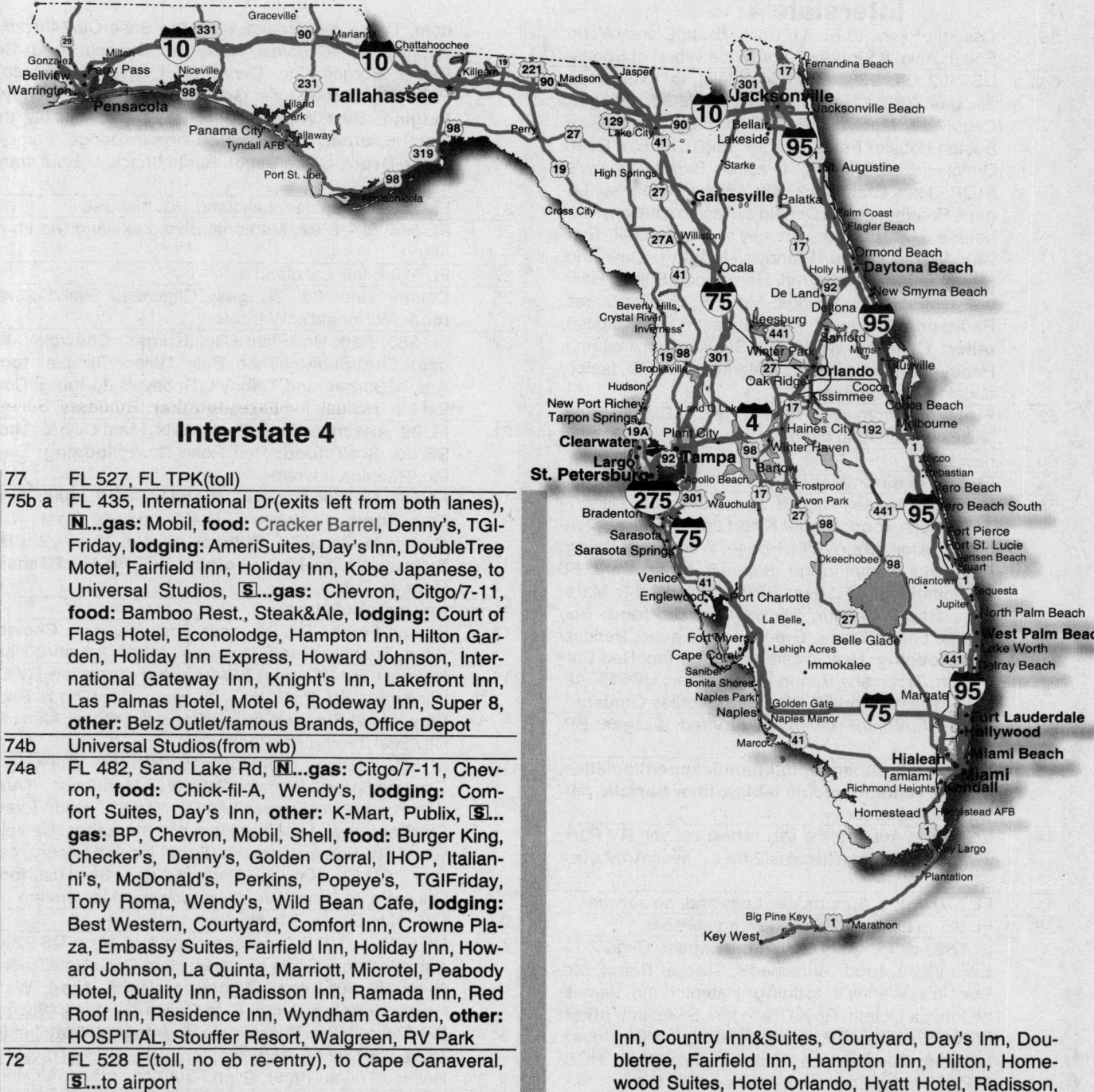...**gas:** Mobil, **food:** Cracker Barrel, Denny's, TGI-Friday, **lodging:** AmeriSuites, Day's Inn, DoubleTree Motel, Fairfield Inn, Holiday Inn, Kobe Japanese, to Universal Studios, S...**gas:** Chevron, Citgo/7-11, **food:** Bamboo Rest., Steak&Ale, **lodging:** Court of Flags Hotel, Econolodge, Hampton Inn, Hilton Garden, Holiday Inn Express, Howard Johnson, International Gateway Inn, Knight's Inn, Lakefront Inn, Las Palmas Hotel, Motel 6, Rodeway Inn, Super 8, **other:** Belz Outlet/famous Brands, Office Depot
74b	Universal Studios(from wb)
74a	FL 482, Sand Lake Rd, N...**gas:** Citgo/7-11, Chevron, **food:** Chick-fil-A, Wendy's, **lodging:** Comfort Suites, Day's Inn, **other:** K-Mart, Publix, S...**gas:** BP, Chevron, Mobil, Shell, **food:** Burger King, Checker's, Denny's, Golden Corral, IHOP, Italianni's, McDonald's, Perkins, Popeye's, TGIFriday, Tony Roma, Wendy's, Wild Bean Cafe, **lodging:** Best Western, Courtyard, Comfort Inn, Crowne Plaza, Embassy Suites, Fairfield Inn, Holiday Inn, Howard Johnson, La Quinta, Marriott, Microtel, Peabody Hotel, Quality Inn, Radisson Inn, Ramada Inn, Red Roof Inn, Residence Inn, Wyndham Garden, **other:** HOSPITAL, Stouffer Resort, Walgreen, RV Park
72	FL 528 E(toll, no eb re-entry), to Cape Canaveral, S...to airport
71	Central FL Pkwy(from eb no reentry), S...**gas:** Chevron, **lodging:** Hilton Garden, Renaissance Resort, **food:** Wendy's, to SeaWorld
68	FL 535, Lake Buena Vista, N...**gas:** Chevron/24hr, Citgo/7-11, Shell/dsl, **food:** AleHouse, Black Angus Steaks, Burger King, Chevy's Mexican, Chili's, China Buffet, Denny's, Dragon Buffet, Hooters, IHOP, Joe's Crabshack, Jungle Jim's, Kobe Japanese, Macaroni Grill, McDonald's, Olive Garden, Pebble's Rest., Perkins, Pizza Hut, Pizzaria Uno, Qdoba Mexican, Red Lobster, Shoney's, Sizzler, Steak'n Shake, Subway, Taco Bell, TGIFriday, Tony Roma, Valerta Mexican, Waffle House, **lodging:** Comfort Inn, Country Inn&Suites, Courtyard, Day's Inn, Doubletree, Fairfield Inn, Hampton Inn, Hilton, Homewood Suites, Hotel Orlando, Hyatt Hotel, Radisson, Residence Inn, SpringHill Suites, StayBridge Suites, Wyndham Hotel, **other:** Eckerd, Gooding's Foods, USPO, Walgreen, S...**gas:** Chevron, Citgo/7-11, Shell, **food:** Bahama Breeze, Bennigan's, Chick-fil-A, Golden Corral, Landry's Seafood, Lobster Feast, LoneStar Steaks, Wendy's, **lodging:** Blue Heron Resort, Courtyard, Embassy Suites, Fairfield Inn, Holiday Inn Resort, Marriott Village, Sheraton, SpringHill Suites, **other:** Premium Outlets, Super Mkt Foods
67	Fl 536, to Epcot, N...DisneyWorld, **1 mi** S...**gas:** Citgo/7-11, **food:** Ponderosa, **lodging:** Buena Vista, Marriott, **other:** CVS Drug, Prime Outlet, to airport, multiple resorts

FLORIDA

Interstate 4

65	Osceola Pkwy, to FL 417(toll), **N**...to DisneyWorld, Epcot, Animal Kingdom, and Wide World of Sports
64b a	US 192, FL 536, to FL 417(toll), to Kissimmee, **N**...**gas:** 76/7-11, to DisneyWorld, MGM, **S**...**gas:** Citgo/7-11, Mobil/dsl, RaceTrac, **food:** Bennigan's, Boston Lobster Feast, Burger King, Charlie's Rest., Checker's, Chick-fil-A, Cracker Barrel, Denny's, IHOP, Joe's Crabshack, KFC, Kobe Japanese, Logans Roadhouse, McDonald's, Pacino's Italian, Ponderosa, Red Lobster, Shoney's, Sizzlin Grill, Subway, Waffle House, Wendy's, **lodging:** Days Inn, Hampton Inn, Holiday Inn, Homewood Suites, Howard Johnson, Hyatt Hotel, Motel 6, Quality Suites, Radisson, Roadway Inn, Super 8, Travelodge, **other:** Camping World RV Service/supplies(3mi), Harley-Davidson, Publix, Walgreens, USPO, factory outlet/famous brands
62	FL 417(toll, from eb), World Dr, **N**...to DisneyWorld, **S**...Celebration, to airport
60	new exit
58	FL 532, to Kissimmee
55	US 27, to Haines City, **N**...**gas:** Chevron, Citgo/7-11, Sunoco, **food:** Burger King, Cracker Barrel, Denny's, McDonald's, Waffle House, Wendy's, **lodging:** Day's Inn, Hampton Inn, Super 8, **other:** Ford, FL CampInn(5mi), **S**...**gas:** BP/dsl, Citgo/7-11, Marathon, RaceWay/24hr, Shell/dsl/service, **food:** Bob Evans, Grand China, GreenLeaf Chinese, Perkins/24hr, **lodging:** Best Western, Quality Inn, Red Carpet Inn, Tropicana Resort Hotel, **other:** HOSPITAL, KOA, Theme World RV Park, to Cypress Gardens
48	rd 557, to Winter Haven, Lake Alfred, **S**...**gas:** BP/dsl
46mm	**rest area both lanes, full(handicapped)facilities, phone, vending, picnic tables, litter barrels, petwalk, 24hr security**
44	FL 559, to Auburndale, **N**...**other:** LeLynn RV Park, **S**...**gas:** Citgo/dsl/scales/24hr, Loves/Arby's/dsl/24hr
41	FL 570 W toll, Auburndale, Lakeland, no services
38	FL 33, to Lakeland, Polk City, no services
33	rd 582, to FL 33, Lakeland, **N**...**gas:** Citgo/7-11, Exxon/24hr, **food:** Applebee's, Cracker Barrel, McDonald's, Wendy's, **lodging:** Hampton Inn, Jameson Inn, La Quinta, Royal Palm Inn, Sleep Inn, **other:** BMW, **S**...**gas:** BP, **food:** Ryan's, Waffle House, **lodging:** Baymont Inn, Hampton Inn, **other:** HOSPITAL, Harley-Davidson, Lakeland RV Camp
32	US 98, Lakeland, **N**...**gas:** BP, Chevron/dsl, Shell/Blimpie, **food:** Beef o'Brady's, Checker's, Chili's, ChuckeCheese, Domino's, Don Pablo, Dragon Buffet, Golden Corral, Hooters, Hungry Howie's, IHOP, KFC, King Buffet, LoneStar Steaks, McDonald's, Olive Garden, Pizza Hut, Red Lobster, Ruby Tuesday, Smokey Bones BBQ, Sonic, Sonny's BBQ, Steak'n Shake/24hr, Subway, Taco Bell, TGIFriday, Zaxby's, **lodging:** Comfort Inn, Comfort Suites, La Quinta, Royalty Inn, **other:** VET, Barnes&Noble, Belk, Best Buy, Circuit City, Dillard's, $General, Goodyear/auto, JoAnn Fabrics, K-Mart, Lowes Whse, PepBoys, RV World, Sam's Club/gas, Staples, Target, Tire King-

	dom, Tires+, Walgreens, Wal-Mart SuperCtr/24hr(2mi), **S**...**gas:** BP, Citgo/dsl, RaceTrac, Sunoco, **food:** Bob Evans, Burger King, Denny's, LJ Silver, McDonald's, Popeye's, Roadhouse Grill, Waffle House, Wendy's, **lodging:** Best Western/rest., Day's Inn, Holiday Inn, Motel 6, **other:** HOSPITAL, Chrysler/Dodge, Family$, Home Depot, Office Depot, Radio Shack, U-Haul, transmissions
31	FL 539, to Kathleen, Lakeland, **S**...hist dist
28	FL 546, to US 92, Memorial Blvd, Lakeland (no eb reentry)
27	FL 570 E toll, Lakeland
25	County Line Rd, **S**...**gas:** Citgo/dsl, Shell/Subway, **food:** McDonald's, Wendy's
22	FL 553, Park Rd, Plant City, **N**...**gas:** Chevrolet, **S**...**gas:** Shell/Subway/Taco Bell, Texaco/Blimpie, **food:** Arby's, Burger King, Denny's, Popeye's, **lodging:** Comfort Inn, Holiday Inn Express, **other:** RV Sales
21	FL 39, Alexander St, to Zephyrhills, Plant City, **S**...**gas:** BP/dsl, Shell, **food:** Red Rose Diner, **lodging:** Day's Inn, Ramada Inn/rest.
19	FL 566, to Thonotosassa, **N**...**gas:** BP, **S**...**gas:** RaceTrac, **food:** Applebee's, BuddyFreddy's Rest., Carraba's, McDonald's, OutBack Steaks, Sonny's BBQ, Subway, Waffle House, **other:** HOSPITAL, $General, Maceys, Publix
19mm	weigh sta both lanes
17	Branch Forbes Rd, **N**...**gas:** Shell, **S**...**gas:** Chevron, Citgo, Sparky's Gas/Subway/dsl, **other:** Advance Parts
14	McIntosh Rd, **N**...**gas:** BP/dsl, **other:** Longview RV Ctr, Windward RV Park(2mi), **S**...**gas:** Citgo/7-11, RaceWay, **food:** Burger King, McDonald's, **other:** Alpha RV Ctr, East Tampa RV Park
10	rd 579, Mango, Thonotosassa, **N**...**gas:** ✈/Flying J/CountryMkt/dsl/LP/scales/24hr/@, Marathon, TA/Arby's/Popeye's/dsl/scales/24hr/@, **food:** Bob Evans, Cracker Barrel, **lodging:** Hampton Inn, **other:** Camping World RV Service/supplies, Ford/Lincoln/Mercury, Lazy Day's RV Ctr, Rally RV Park, **S**...**gas:** Shell/dsl, **food:** Hardee's, Subway, Wendy's, **lodging:** Masters Inn
9	I-75, N to Ocala, S to Naples
7	US 92W, to US 301, Hillsborough Ave, **N on US 92W**...**gas:** Chevron, Circle K, **other:** Hard Rock Hotel/casino, **N on US 301**...**gas:** Citgo/dsl/scales/@, **food:** Waffle House, **lodging:** Motel 6, to Busch Gardens, **S**...**gas:** BP, Citgo, **food:** WingHouse, **lodging:** Holiday Inn Express, La Quinta, Red Roof Inn, **other:** ForeTravel RV, Holiday Travel RV, FL Expo Fair
6	Orient Rd(from eb)
5	FL 574, MLK Blvd, **N**...**food:** McDonald's, **S**...**gas:** BP, Shell/Subway, **food:** Joe's NY Deli(2mi), Wendy's, **lodging:** Masters Inn, **other:** Kenworth
3	US 41, 50th St, Columbus Dr, **N**...**gas:** Shell, **lodging:** Day's Inn, Milner Motel, USA Inn, **S**...**gas:** GK/dsl, Sunoco/dsl, **food:** Checker's, Church's, Eggroll King, McDonald's, Pizza Hut, Subway, Taco Bell, **lodging:** Howard Johnson, **other:** Busch Gardens, Discount Parts
1	FL 585, 22nd, 21st St, Port of Tampa, **S**...**gas:** BP/24hr, **food:** Burger King, McDonald's, Subway, **lodging:** Colombus Hotel, Hilton Garden, **other:** brewery
0mm	I-4 begins/ends on I-275, exit 45b

Interstate 10

E ↕ W

Jacksonville

Exit #	Services
363mm	I-10 begins/ends on I-95, exit 351b.
362	Stockton St, to Riverside, [S]...**gas:** BP, Gate, **other:** HOSPITAL
361	US 17 S(from wb), downtown
360	FL 129, McDuff Ave, [S]...**gas:** BP, Chevron, **food:** Popeye's
359	Lenox Ave, Edgewood Ave(from wb), no services
358	FL 111, Cassat Ave, [N]...**gas:** Chevron, Hess/Blimpie/dsl, Shell/Subway/dsl, **food:** Burger King, McDonald's, Popeye's, **other:** AutoZone, GMC, [S]...**gas:** RaceWay/24hr, **food:** Taco Bell, **other:** Discount Tire, Lowe's Whse, Walgreens, transmissions
357	FL 103, Lane Ave, [N]...**gas:** Fuel Man, Hess/dsl, **food:** Andy's Sandwiches, **lodging:** Day's Inn, Ramada Ltd, [S]...**gas:** BP, Shell/dsl, **food:** Applebee's, Bono's BBQ, Burger King, Cross Creek Steaks, Denny's, Hardee's, KFC, Lee's Drive-In, Linda's Seafood, McDonald's, Piccadilly's, Shoney's, **lodging:** Budget Inn, Diamond Inn, Executive Inn, **other:** Battery Depot, CVS Drug, Eckerd, Firestone, Home Depot, Office Depot, Pep Boys
356	I-295, N to Savannah, S to St Augustine
355	Marietta, [N]...**gas:** Gate/dsl/24hr, Exxon, [S]...**gas:** Shell/dsl
351	FL 115, Chaffee Rd, to Cecil Fields, [N]...**gas:** Kangaroo/dsl/24hr, **other:** Rivers RV Ctr, [S]...**gas:** Chevron, KwikChek/gas, Shell/Subway/dsl/24hr, **food:** Cracker Barrel, Fastboys Wings, King Wok, McDonald's, Quizno's, Wendy's, **lodging:** Hampton Inn, **other:** Winn-Dixie
350mm	**rest area both lanes, full(handicapped) facilities, phone, vending, picnic tables, litter barrels, 24hr security**
343	US 301, to Starke, Baldwin, [N]...**food:** Kenzie's BBQ, [S]...**gas:** BP, Chevron, Pilot/Subway/dsl/24hr/@, TA/Shell/Arby's/dsl/scales/rest./24hr/@, **food:** Burger King, McDonald's, Waffle House, **lodging:** Best Western, **other:** NAPA
336	FL 228, to Maxville, Macclenny, [N]...HOSPITAL, Wal-Mart SuperCtr/24hr, fireworks
335	FL 121, to Lake Butler, Macclenny, [N]...**gas:** BP/dsl, Citgo, **food:** Domino's, Hardee's, KFC, McDonald's, Pizza Hut, Subway, Taco Bell/, Waffle House, Wendy's, Woody's BBQ, **lodging:** American Inn, **other:** HOSPITAL, Advance Parts, $General, Food Lion, Radio Shack, Winn-Dixie, [S]...**gas:** RaceWay, Exxon/dsl, **food:** Burger King, China Buffet, **lodging:** Econolodge, Travelodge
333	rd 125, Glen Saint Mary, [N]...**gas:** Citgo/dsl/24hr
327	rd 229, to Raiford, Sanderson, **1 mi** [N]...gas
324	US 90, to Olustee, Sanderson, [S]...**gas:** Citgo/dsl, to Olustee Bfd
318mm	**rest area both lanes, full(handicapped) facilities, phone, vending, picnic tables, litter barrels, petwalk, 24hr security**

Live Oak

Exit #	Services
303	US 441, to Fargo, Lake City, [N]...**gas:** Chevron/dsl/24hr, **other:** KOA(1mi), Oaks'n Pines RV Park, [S]...**gas:** SuperTest/dsl, Shell/dsl, **lodging:** Day's Inn, **other:** HOSPITAL
301	US 41, to Lake City, [N]...**gas:** Exxon/dsl, **other:** Kelly's RV Park(6mi), to Stephen Foster Ctr, [S]...**gas:** Fastrack, **other:** HOSPITAL
296b a	I-75, N to Valdosta, S to Tampa
294mm	**rest area both lanes, full(handicapped)facilities, phone, vending, picnic tables, litter barrels, petwalk, 24hr security**
292	rd 137, to Wellborn, no services
283	US 129, to Live Oak, [N]...**gas:** Penn/dsl, to Boys Ranch, [S]...**gas:** BP, Chevron, Shell/dsl, Texaco, **food:** China Buffet, Huddle House, Krystal, McDonald's, Subway, Taco Bell/TCBY, Waffle House, Wendy's, **lodging:** Best Western, Econolodge, Holiday Inn Express, Royal Inn, **other:** HOSPITAL, $Tree, Wal-Mart SuperCtr/gas/24hr
275	US 90, Live Oak, [N]...to Suwannee River SP, [S]...**other:** HOSPITAL
271mm	weigh sta both lanes
269mm	Suwannee River
265mm	**rest areas both lanes, full(handicapped) facilities, phone, vending, picnic tables, litter barrels, petwalk, 24hr security**
264mm	weigh sta both lanes
262	rd 255, Lee, [N]...**gas:** Exxon/dsl, **food:** Kountry Kitchen, **other:** to Suwannee River SP, [S]...**gas:** Citgo/rest/dsl/@, Fastrack, **food:** Red Onion Grill
258	FL 53, [N]...**gas:** Citgo/dsl/24hr, Shell/Burger King/dsl/24hr, **food:** Denny's, Waffle House, **lodging:** Day's Inn, Holiday Inn Express, Super 8, **other:** HOSPITAL, [S]...**lodging:** Deerwood Inn, **other:** Jellystone Camping, Madison Camping
251	FL 14, to Madison, [N]...**gas:** Mobil/Arby's/24hr, **other:** HOSPITAL
241	US 221, Greenville, [N]...**gas:** Mobil/DQ
234mm	**rest area both lanes, full(handicapped)facilities, phone, picnic tables, litter barrels, petwalk, 24hr security**
233	rd 257, Aucilla, [N]...**gas:** Citgo, Shell/dsl
225	US 19, to Monticello, [N]...Campers World RV Park, [S]...**gas:** BP, Chevron/McDonald's, Exxon/Wendy's, Mobil/Arby's/dsl, **food:** Huddle House, **lodging:** Day's Inn, Super 8, **other:** KOA, dogtrack
217	FL 59, Lloyd, [S]...**gas:** BP/dsl/rest/scales/24hr/@, Shell/Subway/dsl/@, **lodging:** Capital City Motel
209b a	US 90, Tallahassee, [S]...**gas:** Circle K/dsl, Shell/Subway/dsl, **food:** Creekside Grill, Waffle House, **lodging:** Best Western, **other:** Publix, Tallahassee RV Park

Interstate 10

E ↑ W

Tallahassee

203	FL 61, US 319, Tallahassee, **N**...**gas:** BP/dsl, Chevron, Circle K, Shell, USA Gas, **food:** Applebee's, Bonefish Grill, Firehouse Subs, KFC, Manna Rest., McDonald's, Moe's SW Grill, Pizza Hut, Subway, Taco Bell, TCBY, Waffle House, Wendy's, **lodging:** Motel 6, **other:** Albertson's, BooksAMillion, CVS Drug, Discount Tire, Fresh Mkt Foods, GNC, Publix, Radio Shack, Sav-On, SteinMart, SuperLube, Walgreens, Wal-Mart SuperCtr/24hr(3mi), **S**...**gas:** Citgo, **food:** Boston Mkt, Carraba's, Chick-fil-A, Fazoli's, Osaka Japanese, Outback Steaks, Smokey Bones BBQ, Steak'n Shake, Ted's MT Grill, TGIFriday, Zaxby's, **lodging:** Cabot Lodge, Courtyard, Hampton Inn, Hilton Garden, Residence Inn, Studio+, **other:** HOSPITAL, Advance Parts, Home Depot, Infiniti, Office Depot
199	US 27, Tallahassee, **N**...**gas:** McKenzie/dsl, **food:** Burger King, Taco Bell, Waffle House, **lodging:** Comfort Inn, Fairfield Inn, Hampton Inn, Holiday Inn, Microtel, Quality Inn, **other:** Big Oak RV Park(2mi), Sam's Club, **S**...**gas:** BP/24hr, Chevron/dsl, Circle K, Shell, USA, **food:** Boston Mkt, Chick-fil-A, China Buffet, Cracker Barrel, Crystal River Seafood, DQ, El Chico, Firehouse Subs, Gill's Tavern, Julie's Rest., KFC, Krispy Kreme, Longhorn Steaks, Los Compadres Mexican, McDonald's, Melting Pot Rest., Pizza Hut, Qdoba Mexican, Quizno's, Red Lobster, Roadhouse Grill, Shoney's, Sonny's BBQ, Starbucks, Steak&Ale, Subway, TCBY, Village Inn Rest., Whataburger, Wendy's, Zaxby's, **lodging:** Cabot Lodge, Day's Inn, Econolodge, Howard Johnson, La Quinta, Motel 6, Ramada Inn, Red Roof Inn, Rodeway Inn, Super 8, **other:** AutoZone, Barnes&Noble, Big 10 Tire, CompUSA, Dillard's, $Tree, Firestone/auto, Publix, Ross, Staples, Tire Kingdom, Walgreens, mall
196	FL 263, Tallahassee, **S**...**gas:** Chevron/dsl, Shell/dsl, Stop'n Save Gas, **food:** Waffle House, **lodging:** Sleep Inn, **other:** Harley-Davidson, Home Depot, Lowe's Whse, **2-5 mi S**...**food:** Applebee's, McDonald's, Steak'nShake, Subway, **lodging:** Colony Inn, Day's Inn, Lafayette Motel, Skyline Motel, **other:** RV camping, civic ctr, museum/zoo
194mm	**rest area both lanes, full(handicapped) facilities, phone, vending, picnic tables, litter barrels, petwalk, 24hr security**
192	US 90, to Tallahassee, Quincy, **N**...**gas:** BP, ✈/Flying J/Conoco/dsl/LP/scales/24hr/@, **lodging:** Howard Johnson, **S**...**gas:** Pilot/Subway/dsl/24hr/@, **food:** Waffle House, **lodging:** Best Western, **other:** Lakeside RV Park(4mi)

Chipley

181	FL 267, Quincy, **N**...**other:** HOSPITAL, Wal-Mart Super Ctr/24hr/gas **S**...**gas:** BP/dsl, Pure, **lodging:** Best Value Inn, Hampton Inn, Holiday Inn Express, to Lake Talquin SP
174	FL 12, to Greensboro, **N**...**gas:** BP, Shell/Burger King/dsl, **other:** Beaver Lake Camping
166	rd 270A, Chattahoochee, **N**...to Lake Seminole, to Torreya SP, **S**...**gas:** Shell/dsl, **other:** KOA(1mi)
161mm	**rest area both lanes, full(handicapped)facilities, phone, vending, picnic tables, litter barrels, petwalk, 24hr security**
160mm	Apalachicola River, central/eastern time zone
158	rd 286, Sneads, **N**...Lake Seminole, to Three Rivers SRA
155mm	weigh sta both lanes
152	FL 69, to Grand Ridge, **N**...**gas:** BP, Exxon, GL/gas **lodging:** Durdens Inn
142	FL 71, to Marianna, Oakdale, **N**...**gas:** Exprezit, Pilot/Arby's/dsl/24hr, **food:** Burger King, Firehouse Subs, KFC/LJ Silver, Pizza Hut, PoFolks, Ruby Tuesday, Sonny's BBQ, Waffle House, **lodging:** Comfort Inn, Hampton Inn, Holiday Inn Express, Microtel, Quality Inn, Super 8, **other:** HOSPITAL, Lowe's Whse, Wal-Mart SuperCtr/dsl/24hr, to FL Caverns SP(8mi), **S**...**gas:** Chevron/dsl, Sunoco/dsl, TA/BP/dsl/rest./24hr/@, **food:** McDonald's, **lodging:** Best Western, **other:** camping
136	FL 276, to Marianna, **N**...**gas:** Exprezit/dsl, **lodging:** Day's Inn(3mi), Executive Inn(3mi), **other:** HOSPITAL, to FL Caverns SP(8mi)
133mm	**rest area both lanes, full(handicapped)facilities, phone, picnic tables, litter barrels, petwalk, 24hr security**
130	US 231, Cottondale, **N**...**gas:** BP/dsl, Chevron, **food:** Hardee's, Subway, **S**...**gas:** RaceWay
120	FL 77, to Panama City, Chipley, **N**...**gas:** Exprezit, Exxon/Burger King, **food:** Arby's, JJ's Kitchen, KFC, New Star Chinese, McDonald's, Taco Bell, Waffle House, Wendy's, **lodging:** Day's Inn/rest., Executive Inn, Holiday Inn Express, Super 8, **other:** HOSPITAL, Wal-Mart SuperCtr/gas/24hr, **S**... Falling Water SRA
112	FL 79, Bonifay, **N**...**gas:** Chevron, Exxon/dsl, Tom Thumb/dsl, **food:** Blitch's Rest., Burger King, Hardee's, McDonald's, Pizza Hut, Simbo's Rest., Subway, Waffle House, **lodging:** Economy Inn, Tivoli Inn, **other:** HOSPITAL, Fred's Drug, Hidden Lakes Camping, **S**...FL Springs Camping(8mi)
104	rd 279, Caryville, no services
96	FL 81, Ponce de Leon, **N**...to Ponce de Leon SRA, Vortex Spring Camping, **S**...**gas:** BP/dsl/24hr, Exprezit/Subway/dsl, Exxon/dsl, **other:** Ponce de Leon Motel/RV Park, **rest area both lanes, full(handicapped)facilities, phone, picnic tables, litter barrels, petwalk, 24hr security**

Interstate 10

E ↕ W

85	US 331, De Funiak Springs, N...**gas:** BP, Chevron/24hr, **food:** Arby's, Beef O'Brady's, Burger King, McLain's Steaks, Pizza Hut, Sonic, Subway, Waffle House, **lodging:** Best Value Inn, Day's Inn, Sundown Inn, Super 8, **other:** HOSPITAL, $General, Walgreens, Wal-Mart SuperCtr/gas/24hr, Winn-Dixie, winery, S...**gas:** BP, Emerald Express/dsl, Exprezit Gas, **food:** Hardee's, KFC, McDonald's, Whataburger, **lodging:** Best Western, **other:** HOSPITAL, Long Leash RV Park
70	FL 285, to Ft Walton Bch, Eglin AFB, N...**gas:** RaceWay, S...**gas:** Shell/Subway/dsl/scales/24hr/@, **lodging:** Rodeway Inn, **other:** repair
60mm	**rest area both lanes, full(handicapped) facilities, phone, vending, picnic tables, litter barrels, petwalk, 24hr security**
56	FL 85, Crestview , Eglin AFB, N...**gas:** BP/dsl, Exxon, Mobil, Shell/dsl, **food:** Applebee's, Asian Garden, Backyard Burger, Burger King, Capt D's, McDonald's, Pizza Hut, Popeye's, Ryan's, Sonny's BBQ, Subway, Taco Bell, **lodging:** Budget Host, Econolodge, **other:** HOSPITAL, Advance Parts, AutoZone, Big Lots, Lowe's Whse, Publix, Walgreens, Wal-Mart SuperCtr/24hr, S...**gas:** Citgo/dsl, Exxon/Subway, **food:** Arby's, Cracker Barrel, Hardee's, Hooters, LaBamba Mexican, Nim's Chinese, Shoney's, Waffle House, Wendy's, Whataburger, **lodging:** Comfort Inn, Day's Inn, Hampton Inn, Holiday Inn, Jameson Inn, Regis Inn, Super 8, **other:** Buick/Pontiac/GMC, Chrysler/Dodge/Jeep, Ford/Mercury, museum, RV camping
45	rd 189, to US 90, Holt, N...**gas:** Chevron(1mi), **other:** to Blackwater River SP, Eagle Landing RV Park, S...River's Edge RV Park(1mi)
31	FL 87, to Ft Walton Beach, Milton, N...**gas:** Exxon/Quizno's/dsl/24hr/@, **food:** Waffle House, **lodging:** Holiday Inn Express, **other:** Blackwater River SP, Gulf Pines Camping, KOA, S...**gas:** BP, Shell/dsl, **lodging:** Comfort Inn, Red Carpet Inn
31mm	**rest area both lanes, full(handicapped) facilities, phone, picnic tables, litter barrels, petwalk, 24hr security**
28	rd 89, Milton, N...HOSPITAL, S...Cedar Lakes RV Camping(2mi)
27mm	Blackwater River
26	rd 191, Bagdad, Milton, N...**gas:** Parade/Chester-Fried/dsl, **other:** HOSPITAL, S...**gas:** Chevron/DQ/Stuckey's, Petro/dsl, **other:** Pelican Palms RV Park
22	N FL 281, Avalon Blvd, N...**gas:** BP/dsl, Citgo, **food:** McDonald's, S...**gas:** Shell/Subway/dsl, **food:** Waffle House, **lodging:** Red Roof Inn, **other:** By the Bay RV Park(3mi)
18mm	Escambia Bay
17	US 90, Pensacola, N...**gas:** BP/dsl, S...**gas:** Exxon, **food:** DQ, **lodging:** Ramada Inn/rest.

Crestview

Milton

14mm	truck inspection sta
13	FL 291, to US 90, Pensacola, N...**gas:** BP, Shell/dsl, **food:** Arby's, Barnhill's Buffet, Burger King, Capt D's, Denny's, La Hacienda Mexican, McDonald's, Subway, Taco Bell, Waffle House, **lodging:** Best Value Inn, Comfort Inn, La Quinta, Motel 6, Villager Inn, **other:** AutoZone, CVS Drug, Food World/24hr, Walgreens, S...**food:** Bennigan's, ChuckeCheese, Fazoli's, Los Rancheros Mexican, Piccadilly, Pizza Hut, Popeye's, Steak&Ale, Waffle House, Wendy's, Whataburger, **lodging:** Courtyard, Extended Stay America, Fairfield Inn, Hampton Inn, Holiday Inn Express, Motel 6, Red Roof Inn, Super 8, **other:** HOSPITAL, Belk, Big 10 Tire, Firestone/auto, JC Penney, Mr Transmission, Sears/auto, U-Haul, mall
12	I-110, to Pensacola, Hist Dist, Islands Nat Seashore
10b a	US 29, Pensacola, N...**gas:** BP, Fleet/dsl/scales, **food:** Church's, Hardee's, Waffle House, **other:** Advance Parts, Carpenter's RV Ctr, $Tree, Wal-Mart SuperCtr/gas/24hr, S...**gas:** RaceWay, Shell, **food:** Burger King, Capt D's, Denny's, IHOP, McDonald's, Ruby Tuesday, Smokey's BBQ, Subway, Waffle House, Wendy's, **lodging:** Day's Inn, Econolodge, Executive Inn, Holiday Inn Express, Howard Johnson, Hospitality Inn, Knight's Inn, Luxury Suites, Motel 6, Palm Court, Travelodge, **other:** Buick, Chevrolet, Ford, Harley-Davidson, Isuzu, Jeep, Leisure Tyme RV Ctr, Lincoln/Mercury, Saturn, Suzuki/Toyota
7b a	Fl 297, Pine Forest Rd, N...**lodging:** Best Western, Comfort Inn, Rodeway Inn, **other:** Albertson's/gas, Tall Oaks Camping, S...**gas:** BP, Citgo, Texaco/dsl/café, **food:** Burger King, Carnley's Diner, Cracker Barrel, Hardee's, McDonald's, Ruby Tuesday, Sonny's BBQ, Subway, Waffle House, **lodging:** Holiday Inn Express, Microtel, Ramada Ltd, Sleep Inn, **other:** Food World/24hr, Big Lagoon SRA(12mi), museum
5	US 90 A, N...**gas:** BP, Fleet/Shell/Subway/dsl, **other:** Albertson's/gas, Walgreens, S...Leisure Lakes Camping
4mm	**Welcome Ctr eb, full(handicapped)facilities, info, phone, vending, picnic tables, litter barrels, petwalk, 24hr security**
3mm	weigh sta both lanes
1mm	inspection sta eb
0mm	Florida/Alabama state line, Perdido River

Pensacola

95

FLORIDA

Interstate 75

N ↕ S

Exit #	Services
471mm	Florida/Georgia state line., Motorist callboxes begin sb.
469mm	**Welcome Ctr sb, full(handicapped)facilities, info, phone, vending, picnic tables, litter barrels, petwalk**
467	FL 143, Jennings, [E]...**gas:** Chevron, Texaco, **other:** Budget Lodge, [W]...**gas:** Exxon/dsl, **food:** Jennings House, **lodging:** N Florida Inn, Scottish Inn, **other:** Jennings Camping
460	FL 6, Jasper, [E]...**gas:** BP/Burger King, Indian River Fruit/gas, Penn Oil/Huddle House/dsl, Raceway, **lodging:** Day's Inn, **other:** HOSPITAL, [W]...**gas:** Shell/dsl, Texaco, **food:** Sheffield's Catfish, **lodging:** Scottish Inn, **other:** Suwanee River SP
451	US 129, Jasper, Live Oak, [E]...**gas:** Mobil/DQ/Subway/dsl, **other:** HOSPITAL, [W]...**gas:** BP/Cowboys BBQ/dsl, **other:** Suwanee Music Park(4mi), to FL Boys Ranch
448mm	weigh sta both lanes
446mm	insp sta both lanes
443mm	Historic Suwanee River
439	to FL 136, White Springs, Live Oak, [E]...**gas:** Gate/dsl, Shell/dsl, Texaco, **food:** BB's Country Kitchen, McDonald's, **lodging:** Scottish Inn, **other:** Kelly RV Park(5mi), Lee's Camping(3mi), to S Foster Ctr, [W]...**lodging:** Best Value Inn
435	I-10, E to Jacksonville, W to Tallahassee
427	US 90, to Live Oak, Lake City, [E]...**gas:** BP, B&B/Subway/dsl, Chevron/dsl/24hr, Exxon, Shell, **food:** Applebee's, Arby's, Burger King, Cedar River Seafood, Cracker Barrel, Domino's, Elliano's Coffee, El Potro, Hardee's, IHOP, Japanese Steaks, KFC, Krystal, McDonald's, Moe's SW Grill, Pizza Hut, Red Lobster, Ryan's, Ruby Tuesday, Sonny's BBQ, Steak&Shake, Taco Bell, Texas Roadhouse, Waffle House, Wendy's, Zaxby's, **lodging:** A-1 Inn, Best Inn, Cypress Inn, Day's Inn, Driftwood Inn, Holiday Inn, Jameson Inn, Knight's Inn, Microtel, Ramada Ltd, Rodeway Inn, **other:** HOSPITAL, Advance Parts, AutoZone, Belk, CVS Drug, Food Lion, Ford/Lincoln/Mercury, Goody's, JC Penney, K-Mart, Lowe's Whse, Publix, Radio Shack, Tire Kingdom, Toyota, Wal-Mart SuperCtr/gas/24hr, In&Out RV Park, mall, [W]...**gas:** BP, Chevron, Shell, Texaco/dsl, **food:** Bob Evans, Shoney's, Subway, Waffle House, **lodging:** Best Western, Comfort Inn, Country Inn&Suites, Econolodge, Gateway Inn, Hampton Inn, Motel 6, Quality Inn, Travelodge, White Swan Inn, **other:** Chevrolet/Mazda, Chrysler/Dodge, FL Sports Hall of Fame, Travel Country RV, Wayne's RV Resort
423	FL 47, to Ft White, Lake City, [E]...**gas:** Shell/dsl, [W]...**gas:** BP/dsl, Exxon/dsl, Sean Express, **food:** Little Caesar's, **lodging:** Motel 8, Super 8, **other:** Casey Jones Camping, Freightliner
414	US 41, US 441, to Lake City, High Springs, [E]...**gas:** Chevron/dsl/24hr, EZ Travel Stop, Pitstop/gas, Texaco, **lodging:** Traveler's Inn, Travelodge, [W]...**gas:** BP/dsl, Shell, **food:** Country Sta Rest, Subway, **lodging:** Diplomat Motel, Econolodge, **other:** Turning Wheel RV Ctr, antiques, tires, to O'Leno SP
413mm	**rest areas both lanes, full(handicapped)facilities, phone, vending, picnic tables, litter barrels, petwalk**
409mm	Santa Fe River
404	rd 236, to High Springs, [E]...**gas:** Chevron/fruits/gifts, Shell/dsl, Sunoco, **lodging:** Holiday Inn Express, [W]...High Sprs Camping
399	US 441, to High Sprs, Alachua, [E]...**gas:** BP, **food:** McDonald's, Pizza Hut, Sonny's BBQ, Subway, Waffle House, **lodging:** Comfort Inn, Quality Inn, Travelers Inn/RV Park, [W]...**gas:** Chevron, Citgo/Taco Bell/dsl, Exxon/Wendy's, **food:** Kazbor's Grill, KFC, **lodging:** Day's Inn, Royal Inn
390	FL 222, to Gainesville, [E]...**gas:** Chevron/dsl, Exxon/McDonald's/dsl, Kangaroo/dsl, **food:** Burger King, La Fiesta Mexican, Schlotsky's(3mi), Sonnys BBQ, Wendy's, **other:** Publix, Walgreens, [W]...**gas:** BP/DQ/dsl, **food:** Chutnees Indian Cuisine, **lodging:** Best Western, **other:** Buick, Harley-Davidson, Jeep/Mercedes, auto repair
387	FL 26, to Newberry, Gainesville, [E]...**gas:** BP, Chevron, Citgo, Sunoco, Shell/dsl, **food:** Bono's BBQ, Boston Mkt, Burger King, Don Pablo, FoodCourt, LJ Silver, Macaroni Grill, McAlister's Deli, McDonald's, Perkins, Red Lobster, Ruby Tuesday, Starbucks, Subway, Wendy's, **lodging:** La Quinta, **other:** HOSPITAL, Belk, BooksAMillion, Borders Books, CVS Drug, Dillard's, JC Penney, Macy's, Office Depot, PetCo, Sears/auto, to UFL, mall, [W]...**gas:** BP, Chevron/dsl, Exxon/dsl, Mobil/dsl/LP, **food:** Cracker Barrel, Domino's, GrillMasters Steaks, Hardee's, KFC, Krystal, Napolatanos Rest., Pizza Hut, Shoney's, Taco Bell, Waffle House, Whataburger, **lodging:** Day's Inn, Econolodge, Fairfield Inn, Holiday Inn, Ramada Ltd, **other:** Circuit City, $Tree, Home Depot, JoAnn Fabrics, K-Mart, PepBoys, Publix, Walgreens, Winn-Dixie, tires/repair
384	FL 24, to Archer, Gainesville, [E]...**gas:** BP, Chevron/dsl/24hr, Citgo, Exxon/dsl, Shell, **food:** Atlanta Bread, Bennigan's, Bob Evans, BoneFish Grill, Burger King, Capt D's, Checker's, Chick-fil-A, Chili's, Chipotle Mexican, Coldstone Creamery, DQ, Hops Grill, KFC, McAlister's Deli, McDonald's, Olive Garden, On-the-Border, OutBack Steaks, Panera Bread, Papa John's, Pizza Hut, Rafferty's, Shoney's, Sonny's BBQ, Steak'n Shake, Subway, Taco Bell, Texas Roadhouse, TGIFriday, TJ's Coffee, Waffle House, Wendy's, **lodging:** Cabot Lodge, Comfort Inn, Courtyard, Extended Stay America, Gainseville Inn, Hampton Inn, Motel 6, Red Roof Inn, Super 8, **other:** Albertson's/Savon, Barnes&Noble, Best Buy, CarQuest, CVS Drug, $Tree, Firestone/auto, GNC, Lowe's Whse, Michael's, Old Navy, Publix, Radio Shack, Ross, Target, Wal-Mart, Winn-Dixie, [W]...**gas:** Mobil/dsl, **food:** Cracker Barrel, **lodging:** Country Inn&Suites, Holiday Inn Express, La Quinta, **other:** Sunshine RV Park, to Bear Museum
382	FL 121, to Williston, Gainesville, [E]...**gas:** Citgo/dsl/24hr, Mobil/dsl, **lodging:** Residence Inn(2mi), Travelodge, **other:** Publix, [W]...**gas:** BP/dsl, Chevron/dsl/24hr, Kangaroo/dsl, **food:** 43rd St Deli, **lodging:** Quality Inn, **other:** Fred Bear Museum

Lake City

Gainesville

Interstate 75

N ↑↓ **S**

381mm rest areas both lanes, full(handicapped) facilities, phone, vending, picnic tables, litter barrels, petwalk, 24hr security

374   rd 234, Micanopy, **E**...**gas:** BP, Chevron, **other:** antiques, fruit, to Paynes Prairie SP, **W**...**gas:** Citgo/dsl, Spirit Gas, **lodging:** Knight's Inn

368   rd 318, Orange Lake, **E**...**gas:** Jim's/BBQ, Petro/Mobil/dsl/scales/24hr/@, **food:** Wendy's, **other:** Grand Lake RV Park(3mi), **W**...RV Camping

358   FL 326, **E**...**gas:** BP/dsl, Mobil/McDonald's/dsl, Pilot/Arby's/dsl/scales/24hr/@, Pilot/Wendy's/dsl/24hr/@, **other:** Freightliner, Liberty RV Ctr, auto/truck repair, **W**...**gas:** Chevron/DQ/dsl

354   US 27, to Silver Springs, Ocala, **E**...**gas:** BP/24hr, RaceTrac, SuperTest/dsl, **food:** Burger King, Rascal's BBQ, **lodging:** Golden Palms Inn, **other:** fruits, **W**...**gas:** BP/dsl, Chevron, Texaco, **food:** Penstripe Grill, Waffle House, **lodging:** Budget Host, Comfort Suites, Day's Inn/café, Howard Johnson, Tropical Inn, **other:** $General, Nelson's Trailers, Oaktree Village, Publix, Walgreens, Winn-Dixie

352   FL 40, to Silver Springs, Ocala, **E**...**gas:** BP/dsl, Chevron, RaceTrac/24hr, **food:** McDonald's, Pizza Hut/Taco Bell, Wendy's, Whataburger/24hr, **lodging:** Day's Inn/café, Economy Inn, Motor Inn/RV, Quality Inn, **other:** park, fruits, **W**...**gas:** Shell/dsl, Texaco, **food:** Denny's, Golden Coast Buffet, Waffle House, **lodging:** Comfort Inn, Red Roof Inn, Super 8, **other:** Holiday Trav-L Park, Turning Wheel RV Ctr

O c a l a

350   FL 200 , to Hernando, Ocala, **E**...**gas:** Chevron, Citgo, RaceWay, Shell/dsl, Texaco/dsl, **food:** Applebee's, Arby's, Bella Luna Italian, Bennigans, Bob Evans, Boston Mkt, Burger King, Chick-fil-A, Chili's, ChuckeCheese, Domino's, El Patron Mexican, El Toreo Mexican, Fazoli's, Golden Corral, Grand Buffet, Hooters, Hops Grill, Krystal, Lee's Chicken, LoneStar Steaks, McDonald's, Olive Garden, Outback Steaks, Papa John's, Perkins, Pizza Hut, Red Lobster, Ruby Tuesday, Shell's Rest., Sonic, Sonny's BBQ, Subway, Taco Bell, TGIFriday, Wendy's, **lodging:** Country Inn Suites, Hampton Inn, Hilton, La Quinta, **other:** HOSPITAL, Advance Parts, Barnes&Noble, Belk, Best Buy, Chevrolet/Nissan/Mitsubishi, Circuit City, CVS Drug, $General, Goodyear/auto, Home Depot, JC Penney, JoAnn Fabrics, Kia, K-Mart, Lowe's Whse, Panera Bread, PepBoys, Petsmart, Publix, Sears, Target, Tire Kingdom, TJ Maxx, Walgreens, Wal-Mart SuperCtr/24hr, fruits, mall, **W**...**gas:** BP/24hr, Chevron/24hr, **food:** Burger King, Cracker Barrel, Dunkin Donuts, KFC, Steak'n Shake/24hr, Waffle House, **lodging:** Best Western, Courtyard, Fairfield Inn, Holiday Inn Express, **other:** VET, BMW/porsche, Cadillac, Camper Village RV Park, KOA, Pontiac, Sam's Club/gas, Tires+

346mm rest area both lanes, full(handicapped)facilities, phone, vending, picnic tables, litter barrels, petwalk, 24hr security

341   FL 484, to Belleview, **E**...**gas:** Chevron/fruit/24hr, Citgo, Exxon/dsl, Shell, **food:** Cracker Barrel, Sonny's BBQ, **lodging:** Microtel, Sleep Inn, **other:**

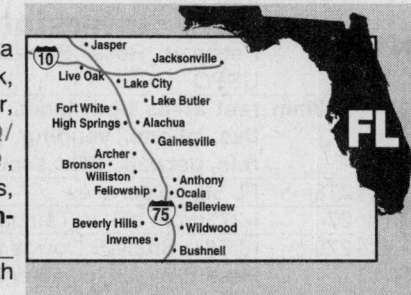

museums, Oscala Ranch RV Park, **W**...**gas:** BP/repair, Pilot/Arby's/DQ/dsl/scales24hr/@, **food:** McDonald's, Waffle House, **other:** auto museum

338mm weigh sta both lanes

W i l d w o o d

329   FL 44, to Inverness, Wildwood, **E**...**gas:** Gate/Steak'n Shake/dsl, Mobil/dsl, Sunoco, **food:** Burger King, Denny's, McDonald's, Waffle House, Wendy's, **other:** Indian River Fruit, KOA, **W**...**gas:** Citgo/dsl/repair/24hr/@, Pilot/dsl/24hr/@, TA/BP/Pizza Hut/Subway/Popeye's/dsl/24hr/@, **food:** IHOP, KFC, **lodging:** Day's Inn/rest., Economy Inn, Super 8, Wildwood Inn

328   FL TPK(from sb), to Orlando, no services

321   rd 470, to Sumterville, Lake Panasoffkee, **E**...**gas:** Spirit/dsl/rest./24hr, **other:** Coleman Correctional, **W**...**gas:** BP/Hardee's/dsl, **other:** Countryside RV Park

314   FL 48, to Bushnell, **E**...**gas:** BP/dsl, Citgo, Mobil/DQ/Stuckey's, Shell/Subway, **food:** Four-Season Chinese, KFC/Taco Bell, McDonald's, Wendy's, **lodging:** GuestHouse Inn, **other:** BlueBerry Hill RV Camp, Red Barn RV Camp, The Oaks Camp(1mi), Wal-Mart SuperCtr/24hr/gas, to Dade Bfd HS, **W**...**gas:** Shell/dsl, Sunoco/dsl, **food:** Sonny's BBQ, Waffle House, **lodging:** Microtel

309   rd 476, to Webster, **E**...Breezy Oaks RV Park(1mi), Sumter Oaks RV Park(1mi)

307mm rest areas both lanes, full(handicapped)facilities, phone, coffee, vending, picnic tables, litter barrels, petwalk, 24hr security

301   US 98, FL 50, to Dade City, **E**...**gas:** BP, RaceTrac, Sunoco, **food:** Cracker Barrel, Denny's, McDonald's, Quinzo's, Waffle House, Wendy's, **lodging:** Day's Inn, Holiday Inn Express, **other:** HOSPITAL(10mi), Curves, Winn-Dixie, USPO, **W**...**gas:** Chevron/Subway/dsl, Hess(3mi), **food:** Burger King, **lodging:** Best Western, Hampton Inn

293   rd 41, to Dade City, **E**...**gas:** Citgo(2mi), **other:** to Sertoma Youth Ranch, **W**...**other:** Travelers Rest Resort RV Park

285   FL 52, to Dade City, New Port Richey, **E**...**gas:** ✈/Flying J/Country Mkt/dsl/LP/scales/24hr/@, **other:** HOSPITAL, Costco, **W**...**gas:** Citgo/dsl/scales/24hr, **food:** Waffle House

279   FL 54, to Land O' Lakes, Zephyrhills, **E**...**gas:** Hess/Blimpie/Godfather's/dsl, RaceTrac, Shell, **food:** Applebee's, Burger King, Carino's Italian, Papa's Pizza, Pizza Hut/Taco Bell, Sonny's BBQ, Subway, Tiki House, Waffle House, Wendy's, **other:** Advance Parts, Ford, Kia, Nissan, Publix, Toyota, Walgreens, Winn-Dixie, Saddlebrook RV Resort(1mi), **W**...**gas:** BP, Circle K/dsl, **food:** Beef o'Brady's, DQ, Cracker Barrel, Denny's, KFC, McDonald's, Outback Steaks, Remington's Steaks, Shanghai Chinese, **lodging:** Best Western, Comfort Inn, Holiday Inn Express, Sleep Inn, **other:** Best Buy, Goodyear, Michael's,

FLORIDA

Interstate 75

Tampa / Brandon (left vertical tab)

Petsmart, Ross, SweetBay Foods, RV camping, USPO

278mm **rest areas both lanes, full(handicapped) facilities, phone, vending, picnic tables, litter barrels, petwalk, 24hr security**

275 FL 56, no services

274 I-275(from sb), to Tampa, St Petersburg

270 rd 581, Bruce B Downs Blvd, E...**gas:** Citgo/7-11, Hess/Blimpie/Godfather's/dsl, Mobil, Shell/Taco Bell/dsl, **food:** Bennigan's, Boston Mkt, Burger King, Chick-fil-A, Chili's, Coldstone Creamery, DQ, Golden China, KFC, Liang's Asian Bistro, Macaroni Grill, McDonald's, Moe's SW Grill, Panera Bread, Papa John's, Quizno's, Ruby Tuesday, Selmon's Cafe, Starbucks, Subway, **lodging:** Holiday Inn Express, Wingate Inn, **other:** Circuit City, Home Depot, Kauffman's Tire, Michael's, Panera Bread, Publix, Walgreens, W...**gas:** Citgo/7-11, **food:** McDonald's, Olive Garden, Red Lobster, Stonewood Grill, **other:** Lowe's Whse

266 rd 582A, Fletcher Ave, W...**gas:** Shell/Subway/dsl, **food:** Baskin Robbins, Bob Evans, Dunkin Donuts, Leeny's Subs, Hooters, Starbucks, Wendy's, **lodging:** Courtyard, Extended Stay America, Fairfield Inn, Hampton Inn, Hilton Garden, Residence Inn, Sleep Inn, **other:** HOSPITAL

265 FL 582, Fowler Ave, Temple Terrace, E...**other:** Happy Traveler RV Park(1mi), flea mkt, W...**food:** IHOP, **lodging:** Ramada Inn, **4 mi** W...**gas:** BP, Chevron, Circle K, **food:** Burger King, Denny's, McDonald's, Perkins, Ryan's, **lodging:** Holiday Inn, La Quinta, Wingate Inn, to Busch Gardens,

261 I-4, W to Tampa, E to Orlando

260b a FL 574, to Mango, Tampa, E...**gas:** Chevron/24hr, Citgo, Shell/Subway/24hr, **food:** McDonald's(2mi), Quizno's, Waffle House, **other:** SweetBay Foods, Walgreens, W...**gas:** BP, Mystik, **lodging:** Crowne Plaza Hotel, Hilton Garden, Residence Inn

257 FL 60, Brandon, E...**gas:** BP, Mobil, Shell, **food:** Bennigan's, Brand&Ale House, Boston Mkt, Chili's, ChuckeCheese, Denny's, Domino's, Don Pablo, Fuego Steaks, Macaroni Grill, Olive Garden, Outback Steaks, Panda Express, Papa John's, Red Lobster, Seltzers Steaks, Smokey Bones BBQ, Steak'n Shake, TGIFriday, Waffle House, **lodging:** Holiday Inn Express, HomeStead Suites, La Quinta, **other:** HOSPITAL, Aamco, Advance Parts, Barnes&Noble, Best Buy, Chrysler/Dodge, CVS Drug, Dillard's, Firestone/auto, JC Penney, Jo-Ann Fabrics, K-Mart, Marshall's, Michael's, PepBoys, Publix, Sam's Club, Sears/auto, Staples, Target, TJ Maxx, mall, W...**gas:** Citgo, GK, Shell, **food:** Bob Evans, Burger King, Cherry's Grill, Hooters, McDonald's, Subway, Sweet Tomatoes, Wendy's, **lodging:** Best Western, Comfort Inn, Courtyard, Day's Inn, Fairfield Inn, Homewood Suites, La Quinta, Red Roof Inn, **other:** Buick, Chevrolet, Circuit City, Dodge, Harley-Davidson, Home Depot, Honda, KIA, Mitsubishi/Hyundai/Suzuki/Yamaha, Nissan, Office Depot, Pontiac/GMC, Toyota, funpark

256 FL 618 W(toll), to Tampa

254 US 301, Riverview, E **on Progress...gas:** RaceTrac, **food:** Steak'n Shake, **other:** CVS Drug, Home Depot, **1mi** W...**gas:** Circle K, 7-11/dsl, Texaco

250 Gibsonton Dr, Riverview, **1 mi** E...**gas:** BP, Hess, Mobil, RaceWay, **food:** Beef O'Brady's, Burger King, Godfather's, McDonald's, Subway, Taco Bell, Wendy's, **other:** Alafia River RV Resort, Hidden River RV Resort(4mi), W...**gas:** BP(1mi)

246 FL 672, Big Bend Rd, Apollo Bch, **1-2 mi** E...**gas:** 7-11, **food:** Blimpie, **3-5 mi** W...**gas:** Chevron, 7-11, **food:**, Cherry Grill

240b a FL 674, Sun City Ctr, Ruskin, E...**Welcome Ctr, gas:** Chevron/24hr, **food:** Beef o' Brady's, Bob Evans, Burger King, Checker's, Denny's, Hungry Howie's, King Buffet, Pizza Hut, Sonny's BBQ, Taco Bell, Wendy's, **lodging:** Comfort Inn, Sun City Ctr Inn/rest., **other:** Home Depot, Radio Shack, SweetBay Foods, Walgreens, Wal-Mart, SunLake RV Resort(1mi), to Little Manatee River SP, W...**gas:** Circle K/dsl, Hess/dsl, RaceTrac, **food:** KFC, McDonald's, Subway, **lodging:** Express Hotel, **other:** Beall's, CVS Drug, D&K Repair, NAPA, Publix

238mm **rest area both lanes, full(handicapped) facilities, phone, vending, picnic tables, litter barrels, petwalk, 24hr security**

229 rd 683, Moccasin Wallow Rd, to Parrish, E...Little Manatee Sprs SRA(10mi), W...**other:** Fiesta Grove RV Park(3mi), Frog Creek RV Park(3mi), Terra Ceia RV Village(2mi), Winterset RV Park(3mi)

228 I-275 N, to St Petersburg

224 US 301, to Bradenton, Ellenton, E...**gas:** BP, Chevron/24hr, RaceWay, Shell/dsl, **food:** Applebee's, Checker's, McDonald's, Ruby Tuesday, Wendy's, **lodging:** Hampton Inn, Holiday Inn Express, Sleep Inn, **other:** Ace Hardware, $Tree, K-Mart, Publix, Walgreens, USPO, Ellenton Garden Camping(1mi), Prime Outlets/famous brands, cleaners, W...**gas:** Pilot/dsl, **food:** Anna Marie's, Crabtrap Seafood, Leverock's Seafood, Waffle House, **lodging:** Best Western, GuestHouse Inn, Ramada Ltd

220b a FL 64, to Zolfo Springs, Bradenton, E...Lake Manatee SRA, W...**gas:** BP/dsl, Circle K/dsl, Citgo/dsl/24hr, RaceTrac, Shell, **food:** Burger King, Cracker Barrel, Denny's, Friendly's, KFC/LJ Silver, McDonald's, Sonny's BBQ, Subway, TCBY, Waffle House, Wendy's, **lodging:** Budget Inn, Comfort Inn, Day's Inn, Econolodge, Holiday Inn Express, Motel 6, **other:** HOSPITAL, Dream RV Ctr, Encore RV Resort(1mi), Harley-Davidson, Wal-Mart SuperCtr/24hr

217b a FL 70, to Arcadia, E...**gas:** Hess/Blimpie/Godfather's/dsl/24hr, **food:** Crisper's Salads, **other:** Sweetbay Foods, W...**gas:** BP/dsl/LP, Circle K, Citgo/7-11, Exxon/dsl, Shell, **food:** Applebee's, Arby's, Bob Evans, Chick-fil-A, Daritino's Pasta, DQ, McDonald's, Hungry Howie's, Subway, **other:** Beall's, CVS Drug, Lowe's Whse, Publix, Tire Kingdom, Tires+, HorseShoe RV Park, Pleasant Lake RV Resort

Interstate 75

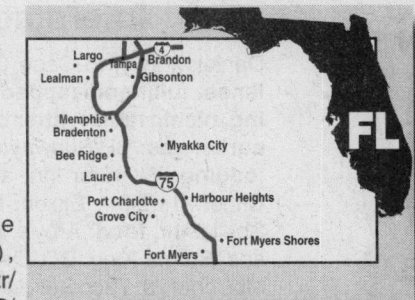

N ↑ ↓ S

Sarasota

213 University Parkway, to Sarasota, **E**...**gas:** Chevron/Subway/dsl, **food:** Chili's, China Coast, Pizza Hut, Ryan's Grill, **lodging:** Fairfield Inn, Holiday Inn, **other:** GNC, Publix, Walgreens, **W**...**food:** Altanta Bread, Bellacino's, BoneFish Grill, Carrabba's, Ruby Tuesday, Stonewood Grill, Wendy's, **lodging:** Comfort Suites, **other:** BJ's Whse, CVS Drug, Staples, Target, **3-6 mi W**...**gas:** Chevron/24hr, Hess, **food:** Applebee's, Burger King, KFC, McDonald's, Ruby Tuesday, Taco Bell, **lodging:** Courtyard, Sleep Inn, SpringHill Suites, **other:** BJ's Whse/gas, Ringling Museum, dogtrack

210 FL 780, Fruitville Rd, Sarasota, **1 mi E**...**other:** Sun'n Fun RV Park(1mi), **W**...**gas:** BP/dsl/LP, Chevron/24hr, Mobil/Blimpie/dsl, RaceTrac, **food:** Applebee's, Bob Evans, Burger King, Checker's, Chick-fil-A, Don Pablo, Gator's, Rest, KFC, Longhorn Steaks, McDonald's, Perkins, Subway, Taco Bell, **lodging:** AmericInn, Homewood Suites(2mi), **other:** Advance Parts, $Tree, CVS Drug, GNC, Publix, Radio Shack, Sam's Club, Target, Winn-Dixie

207 FL 758, Sarasota, **W**...**gas:** BP, Mobil/Subway/dsl/repair, Shell/Blimpie, **food:** Arby's, Checker's, Chili's, Bella Cucina Italian, Grand China Buffet, Italian Buffet, MadFish Grill, McDonald's, Pizza Hut, Steak'n Shake, Sugar&Spice, Taco Bell, Tuesday Morning, Woody's BBQ, **lodging:** Hampton Inn, **other:** HOSPITAL, $Tree, Goodyear/auto, Home Depot, Publix, Radio Shack, Sweet Bay Foods, Walgreens, Wal-Mart

205 FL 72, to Arcadia, Sarasota, **E**...Myakka River SP(9mi), **W**...**gas:** BP/A&W/LJ Silver/dsl, Exxon/dsl, Mobil, 7-11, **food:** Applebee's, Arby's, Burger King, Chick-fil-A, McDonald's, Quizno's, Starbucks, Subway, Waffle House, Wendy's, **lodging:** Comfort Inn, Country Inn&Suites, Days Inn, Holiday Inn Express(5mi), **other:** Beach Club RV Resort(6mi), Beall's, BMW, CVS Drug, Jaguar, Land Rover, Lexus, Publix, Tire Kingdom, Walgreens, Windward Isle RV Park

200 FL 681 S(from sb), to Venice, Osprey, Gulf Bchs

195 Laurel Rd, Nokomis, **E**...**gas:** BP/dsl, Stay'n Play RV Park(1mi), **food:** Fast Food Fast, **W**...**gas:** Citgo/7-11, Hess(3mi), **food:** Blimpie, Godfather's Pizza, **lodging:** Hampton Inn, Holiday Inn, **other:** Encore RV Park(2mi), Scherer SP(6mi)

193 Jaracanda Blvd, Venice, **W**...**gas:** Citgo/Subway/dsl/24hr, Hess/Blimpie/Godfather's/dsl, RaceTrac, **food:** Cracker Barrel, McDonald's, Ping's Chinese, Waffle House, **lodging:** Best Western, La Quinta, **other:** HOSPITAL

191 Englewood Rd, **W**...**other:** Venice Campground(1mi)

182 Sumter Blvd, to North Port, **W**...gas, food, lodging

179 Toledo Blade Blvd, North Port, no services

170 rd 769, to Arcadia, Port Charlotte, **E**...**gas:** Citgo/7-11/dsl, RaceTrac, **lodging:** Hampton Inn, Hotel&Suites, **other:** Lettuce Lake Camping(7mi),

Riverside Camping(5mi), Wal-Mart SuperCtr/24hr, **W**...**gas:** BP/Subway/DQ/dsl, Hess/dsl, Chevron/dsl, 76/Circle K, **food:** Burger King, Cracker Barrel, McDonald's, Taco Bell/Pizza Hut, Waffle House, Wendy's, **other:** HOSPITAL, Ace Hardware, Advance Parts, Curves, CVS Drug, $General, GNC, Publix, USPO, Walgreens, Winn-Dixie

167 rd 776, Port Charlotte

164 US 17, Punta Gorda, Arcadia, **E**...**gas:** Chevron/dsl, RaceWay, Shell/Subway/dsl/24hr, **other:** $General, KOA(2mi), Winn-Dixie, **W**...**gas:** Circle K, **food:** Fisherman's Village Rest., **lodging:** Best Western(2mi), **other:** HOSPITAL, auto/tire repair

161 FL 768, Punta Gorda, **E**...**rest area both lanes, full(handicapped)facilities, phone, vending, picnic tables, litter barrels, petwalk, 24hr security,** Waters Edge RV Park(2mi), **W**...**gas:** BP/DQ/Subway/dsl, Pilot/Arby's/dsl/24hr/@, **food:** Burger King, McDonald's, Pizza Hut, Waffle House, Wendy's, **lodging:** Day's Inn, Motel 6, **other:** Alligator RV Park(2mi), Encore RV Park(2mi)

160mm weigh sta both lanes

158 rd 762, **E**...Babcock-Wells Wildlife Mgt Area, **W**...RV Camping(12mi)

Ft Myers

143 FL 78, to Cape Coral, N Ft Myers, **E**...**gas:** Citgo/Lawhon's Foods/dsl, **other:** Upriver RV Park(1mi), **W**...**gas:** RaceTrac/dsl/24hr, **lodging:** Sunburst RV Resort

141 FL 80, Palm Bch Blvd, Ft Myers, **E**...**gas:** BP/dsl, Citgo, **food:** Cracker Barrel, Waffle House, **lodging:** Comfort Inn, **W**...**gas:** Citgo, Hess/dsl, **food:** DQ, Hardee's, Juicy Lucy's Burgers, Perkins, Pizza Hut, Sonny's BBQ, Subway, Taco Bell, **other:** Big-Lots, CVS Drug, $General, North Trail RV Ctr, Publix, Radio Shack

139 Luckett Rd, Ft Myers, **E**...**other:** Cypress Woods RV Resort, Mark's RV Ctr, **W**...**gas:** Pilot/Subway/dsl/24hr, **other:** Camping World RV Service/supplies, Lazy J's RV Park

138 FL 82, to Lehigh Acres, Ft Myers, **E**...**gas:** Hess/Subway/dsl, **other:** Publix(2mi), **W**...**gas:** Citgo/dsl, Sunoco

136 FL 884, Colonial Blvd, Ft Myers, **E**...**gas:** Home Depot, **W**...**food:** BP, Shell/dsl, **food:** Bob Evans, Chick-fil-A, Steak'n Shake, **other:** Lowe's Whse, Tire Choice, Wal-Mart SuperCtr/24hr/dsl, **1-3 mi W**...**gas** Citgo/7-11, **lodging:** Courtyard, Howard Johnson, La Quinta, Residence Inn, Super 8, **other:** HOSPITAL

FLORIDA

Interstate 75

131	Daniels Pkwy, to Cape Coral, **E**...**rest area both lanes, full(handicapped)facilities, phone, vending, picnic tables, litter barrels, petwalk, 24hr security**, gas: BP/Subway/dsl, **food:** Cracker Barrel, **lodging:** WynStar Inn, airport, **W**...**gas:** Chevron, Citgo/7-11/24hr, Exxon, Hess/dsl, RaceTrac/24hr, Shell/24hr, **food:** Arby's, Bella Rica Italian, Bob Evans, Burger King, DQ, Denny's, Don Honey's BBQ, McDonald's, Taco Bell, Uno Pizzaria, Waffle House, Wendy's, **lodging:** Best Western, Comfort Suites, Country Inn Suites, Econolodge, Hampton Inn, La Quinta, SpringHill Suites, **other:** HOSPITAL, CVS Drug, Publix, Tire Choice
128	Alico Rd, San Carlos Park, **E**...**lodging:** Hilton Garden, Homewood Suites, **other:** Bass Pro Shop, Best Buy, Costco/gas, JC Penney, JoAnn, PetCo, Sears/auto, Staples, Super Target, **W**...**gas:** Hess/dsl, Site/Subway/dsl,
123	rd 850, Corkscrew Rd, Estero, **E**...**gas:** BP/dsl, Chevron/dsl, **food:** McDonald's, Perkins, Rick Johnson Tire, Starbucks, Stoney's Cafe, Subway, **other:** CVS Drug, Germaine Arena, Miramar Outlet/famous brands, Publix, **W**...**gas:** Chevron, Citgo/7-11, Hess/Dunkin Donuts/dsl, **food:** Arizona Pizza, **lodging:** Embassy Suites, Hampton Inn, **other:** Lowe's Whse, Tire Choice, Koreshan St HS, Woodsmoke RV Park(4mi)
116	Bonita Bch Rd, Bonita Springs, **E**...**gas:** Chevron/dsl, Mobil, **other:** Publix, Tire Choice, **W**...**gas:** BP/McDonald's/24hr, Hess/Blimpie/dsl/24hr, **food:** Bob Evans, Waffle House, **other:** Alberstson's/gas, CVS Drug, Home Depot, Walgreens, **1-3 mi W**...**lodging:** AmericInn, Bonita Motel, Comfort Inn, Hampton Inn, Holiday Inn Express, La Quinta, **other:** Imperial Bonita RV Park, to gulf beaches
111	rd 846, Immokalee Rd, Naples Park, **E**...**gas:** Citgo/7-11, Mobil, **food:** Bob Evans, Pizza Hut, **lodging:** Hampton Inn, **W**...**gas:** Shell/dsl, **food:** McDonald's, Pizza Hut, **lodging:** Fairways Motel(2mi), Vanderbilt Inn(5mi), **other:** HOSPITAL, Albertson's/gas, CVS Drug, Publix, Super Target, TrueValue, Wal-Mart SuperCtr, to Wiggins SP
107	rd 896, Pinebridge Rd, Naples, **E**...**gas:** BP/McDonald's/dsl/24hr, **food:** Coldstone Creamery, **other:** HOSPITAL, VET, Publix, Walgreens, **W**...**gas:** Chevron/dsl24hr, RaceTrac, Shell/dsl/24hr, **food:** Applebee's, Burger King, IHOP, Perkins, Roman Oven, Waffle House, **lodging:** Best Western, Hawthorn Suites, Hilton Garden(4mi), Spinnaker Inn, **other:** Harley-Davidson, Johnson Tire
105	no facilites
101	rd 951, to FL 84, to Naples, **W**...**gas:** BP/Edy's Cafe/Subway/dsl, Mobil/dsl/24hr, Shell/dsl/24hr, **food:** Burger King, Checker's, Cracker Barrel, McDonald's, Waffle House, **lodging:** Comfort Inn, Holiday Inn Express, La Quinta, Super 8, **other:** Mazda, Club Naples RV Ctr, Endless Summer RV Park(3mi), KOA
100mm	toll plaza from eb
80	FL 29, to Everglade City, Immokalee

71mm	Big Cypress Nat Preserve, hiking, no security
63mm	**W**...**rest area both lanes, full(handicapped) facilities, phone, vending, picnic tables, litter barrels, petwalk, 24hr security**
49	Gov't Rd, Snake Rd, Big Cypress Indian Reservation, **E**...**gas:** Mobil/dsl, **other:** museum, swamp safari
41mm	rec area eb, picnic tables, litter barrels
38mm	rec area wb, picnic tables, litter barrels
35mm	**W**...**rest area both lanes, full(handicapped) facilities, phone, vending, picnic tables, litter barrels, petwalk, 24hr security**
32mm	rec area both lanes, picnic tables, litter barrels
26mm	toll plaza wb, motorist callboxes begin/end
23	Us 27, FL 25,, Miami, South Bay, no services
22	NW 196th, Glades Pkwy, **W**...**other:** Publix, same as 21
21	FL 84 W(from nb), Indian Trace, **W**...**gas:** Chevron(1mi), Citgo/dsl, **food:** Papa John's
19	I-595 E, FL 869(toll), Sawgrass Expswy, no services
15	Royal Palm Blvd,, Weston, Bonaventure, **W**...**gas:** Exxon, Mobil, **food:** Flanigan's Rest, Max's Grille, Pastability Ristorante, Subway, Wendy's, **lodging:** Amerisuites, Courtyard, Residence Inn, **other:** HOSPITAL, Best Buy, USPO
13b a	Griffin Rd, **E**...**gas:** Shell/dsl, **food:** Burger King, DQ, Outback Steaks, Waffle House/24hr, **other:** Goodyear/auto, Infiniti, Publix, **W**...**gas:** Citgo/7-11, Thumb/gas, **food:** Chili's, McDonald's, Ultimate Burrito, **other:** Home Depot, Honda, Hyundai, Nissan/ Volvo, Publix, Toyota
11b a	Sheridan St, **E**...**gas:** Chevron, **food:** Cracker Barrel, TCBY, **lodging:** Hampton Inn, **other:** HOSPITAL(3mi), BMW, Lincoln/Mercury, **W**...**gas:** Shell, **food:** China One, DQ, McDonald's, Rotelli Cafe, Starbucks, Subway, TGIFriday's, The Original PancakeHouse, **other:** GNC, Lowe's Whse, Publix
9b a	FL 820, Pine Blvd, Hollywood Blvd, **E**...**gas:** Shell, **food:** Arby's, Chili's, Latin-American Grill, LongHorn Steaks, Macaroni Grill, Pines Alehouse, Shell's Seafood, Starbucks, Wendys, **other:** Barnes&Noble, Best Buy, BJ's Whse, Circuit City, Dillard's, Dodge, Home Depot, JC Penney, Macy's, Mercedes, Sears/ auto, Target, Walgreens, **W**...**gas:** BP, Exxon, Shell, **food:** KFC/Taco Bell, McDonald's, Quizno's, Sweet Tomatoes, **other:** Advance Parts, Costco/gas, Lexus, Pontiac/GMC, Publix, Tires+, USPO, Winn-Dixie
7b a	Miramar Pkwy, **E**...**gas:** Chevron, **food:** La Carreta, McDonald's, Polo Tropical, Subway, Wendy's, **lodging:** Hilton Garden, Residence Inn, Wingate Inn, **other:** Publix, USPO, **W**...**gas:** Shell, **food:** Starbucks, **other:** CVS Drug, Home Depot, Marshall's, Panera Bread, Ross, Target, Walgreens
5	to FL 821(from sb), FL TPK(toll)
4	FL 860, NW 186th, Miami Gardens Dr, **E**...**gas:** BP/24hr, Chevron/24hr, **food:** McDonald's, Subway, **other:** CVS Drug, GNC, Publix/deli, Sedenos Foods
2	NW 138th, Graham Dairy Rd, **W**...**gas:** Mobil, Shell, **food:** DQ, McDonald's, Subway, Wendy's, **other:** HOSPITAL, GNC, Publix, Walgreens
1b a	I-75 begins/ends on FL 826, Palmetto Expswy, Multiple services on FL 826

Interstate 95

N ↑↓ S

Exit #	Services
382mm	Florida/Georgia state line, St Marys River, motorist callboxes begin/end.
381mm	inspection sta both lanes
380	US 17, to Yulee, Kingsland, E...Hance's RV Camping/LP, GS Camping/LP, W...gas: BP/24hr, Shell/24hr, lodging: Day's Inn, Econolodge
378mm	**Welcome Ctr sb, full(handicapped)facilities, phone, vending, picnic tables, litter barrels, petwalk, 24hr security**
376mm	weigh sta both lanes
373	FL 200, FL A1A, to Yulee, Callahan, Fernandina Bch, E...gas: Flash/Krystal, Sunoco, food: Burger King, KFC/Pizza Hut, DQ, McDonald's, Wendy's, lodging: Country Inn, Hampton Inn(3mi), Nassau Holiday Motel(3mi), other: Lofton Creek Camping(3mi), to Ft Clinch SP(16mi), W...gas: Citgo/Subway, Exxon, food: Waffle House
366	Pecan Park Rd, E...gas: BP/dsl, Citgo/dsl, W... Flea&Farmer's Mkt, Pecan Park RV Camping
363b a	Duval Rd, E...gas: Mobil, food: Arby's, Cracker Barrel, other: Lowe's Whse, Michael's, Old Navy, Ross, Wal-Mart SuperCtr/24hr, W...gas: BP, Chevron/A&W/Taco Bell, Shell/dsl, Sunoco/Subway, food: Denny's, Longhorn Steaks, Millhouse Steaks, Waffle House, Wendy's, Zaxby's, lodging: Best Western, Comfort Suites, Country Hearth Inn, Courtyard, Day's Inn, Fairfield Inn, Hampton Inn, Hilton Garden, Holiday Inn, Red Roof Inn, Residence Inn, Rodeway Inn, Wingate Inn, other: RV Ctr
362b a	I-295 S , FL 9A, to Blount Island, Jacksonville
360	FL 104, Dunn Ave, Busch Dr, E...gas: Gate/dsl, food: Applebee's, Hardee's, Waffle House, lodging: Executive Inn, other: Sam's Club/gas, USPO, W...gas: BP, Hess, Shell, Texaco, food: Arby's, BBQ, Burger King, Capt D's, Checker's, KFC, Krystal, McDonald's, New China, Pizza Hut, Popeye's, Shoney's, Taco Bell, Wendy's, lodging: Best Value Inn, Best Western, La Quinta, Motel 6, other: Aamco, Advance Parts, BigLots, $Tree, Family$, PepBoys, Publix, Radio Shack, Walgreens, Winn Dixie
358b a	FL 105, Broward Rd, Heckscher Dr, E...zoo, W... lodging: USA Inn
357mm	Trout River
357	FL 111, Edgewood Ave, W...gas: BP/repair, Gas Express, Shell, food: Mardi Gras Grill
356b a	FL 115, Lem Turner Rd, E...food: Hardee's, W... gas: BP/24hr, Hess, Shell/repair, Texaco/dsl, food: Burger King, Checker's, Golden EggRoll, Krystal, Popeye's, Taco Bell, other: Advance Parts, Foods, Tires+, Walgreens, flea mkt
355	Golfair Blvd, E...gas: BP, Shell, W...gas: Chevron/dsl, RaceWay

354b a	US 1, 20th St, to Jacksonville, to AmTrak, MLK Pkwy
353d	FL 114, to 8th St, E...food: McDonald's, other: HOSPITAL
353c	US 23 N, Kings Rd, downtown
353b	US 90A, Union St, Sports Complex, downtown
353a	Church St, Myrtle Ave, Forsythe St, downtown
352c	Monroe St(from nb), downtown
352b a	Myrtle Ave(from nb), downtown
351d	Stockton St, HOSPITAL, downtown
351c	Margaret St, downtown
351b	I-10 W, to Tallahassee
351a	Park St, College St, HOSPITAL, to downtown
351mm	St Johns River
350b	FL 13, San Marco Blvd, E...HOSPITAL
350a	Prudential Dr, Main St, Riverside Ave(from nb), to downtown, E...gas: BP, lodging: Extended Stay America, Hampton Inn, Hilton
349	US 90 E(from sb), to beaches, downtown, W...lodging: Super 8
348	US 1 S(from sb), Philips Hwy, W...lodging: Scottish Inn, Super 8, other: Cadillac, Chevrolet, VW/Volvo
347	US 1A, FL 126, Emerson St, E...gas: Shell, other: Advance Parts, Family$, Food Lion, W...gas: BP/dsl, Gate, food: McDonald's, Taco Bell, lodging: Emerson Inn
346b a	FL 109, University Blvd, E...gas: BP, Hess/dsl, Shell, food: Capt D's, Checker's, DQ, El Potro Mexican, Firehouse Subs, Happy Garden Chinese, KFC, Krystal, Papa John's, Pizza Hut, Ying's Chinese, other: HOSPITAL, CVS Drug, Firestone/auto, Goodyear/auto, NAPA, Winn-Dixie, W...gas: BP/dsl, Chevron, RaceTrac, food: Buckingham Grill, Burger King, Dunkin Donuts/Baskin Robbins, Friendly's, IHOP, Ryan's, Sonny's BBQ, Taco Bell, Waffle House, Wendy's, lodging: Comfort Lodge, Day's Inn, Ramada Inn, Red Carpet Inn, Super 8, other: Chrysler, U-Haul, auto repair
345	FL 109, University Blvd(from nb), E...gas: Gate/dsl, Hess/Blimpie/Godfather's Pizza/dsl
344	FL 202, Butler Blvd, E...food: Dave&Buster's, lodging: Best Western, Econolodge, Holiday Inn Express, Homestead Suites, Howard Johnson, Marriott, Ramada Inn, other: HOSPITAL, USPO, W...gas: BP/dsl, Shell, Texaco/dsl, food: Applebee's, Chick-fil-A, Cracker Barrel, Hardee's, McDonald's, Sonic, Waffle House, Wendy's, Whataburger/24hr, Zaxby's, lodging: Courtyard, Extended Stay America, Jameson Inn, La Quinta, Masters Inn, Microtel, Red Roof Inn, Wingate Inn

Jacksonville

FLORIDA

Interstate 95

341	FL 152, Baymeadows Rd, E...gas: BP/dsl, Chevron, Shell, food: Applebee's, Arby's, Chili's, Domino's, Hardee's, Omaha Steaks, Roadhouse Grill, Subway, Waffle House, lodging: AmeriSuites, Baymeadows Inn, Embassy Suites, Fairfield Inn, Holiday Inn, HomeStead Village, La Quinta, other: Publix, Tires+, W...gas: Exxon/dsl, Shell, Kangaroo, food: Bennigan's, Burger King, Denny's, IHOP, KFC, Larry's Subs, McDonald's, Pagoda Chinese, Pizza Hut, Red Chilies, Red Lobster, Steak&Ale, Taco Bell, Wendy's, lodging: Best Inn, Comfort Inn, Homewood Suites, Residence Inn, Studio 6, other: Goodyear/auto, Harley-Davidson, Office Depot
340	FL 115, Southside Blvd(from nb), E on FL 115...gas: Kangaroo, food: Longhorn Steaks, other: CompUSA, Home Depot, Target, same as 339
339	US 1, Philips Hwy, E...gas: Chevron, RaceTrac, food: Arby's, Buca Italian, Burger King, McDonald's, Mikado Japanese, Olive Garden, Ruby Tuesday, Taco Bell, Waffle House, other: Belk, Best Buy, Chevrolet, Dillard's, Ford, JC Penney, Parisian, Sears/auto, Toyota, mall, W...gas: BP/dsl
337	I-295 N, to rd 9a, Orange Park, Jax Beaches
335	St Augustine Rd
331mm	rest area both lanes, full(handicapped) facilities, phone, vending, picnic tables, litter barrels, petwalk, 24hr security
329	rd 210, E...gas: Citgo/fruit, Pilot/McDonald's/dsl/scales/24hr/@, TA/Shell/Subway/dsl/rest./@, food: Waffle House, W...gas: BP/Subway/dsl, Mobil/dsl, Shell, food: Burger King, Cherry's Grill, China Wok, Tropical Smoothie, other: CVS Drug, Winn-Dixie, fireworks
323	International Golf Pkwy, E...gas: BP/Sbarro's/dsl, Shell/Subway/dsl, lodging: Comfort Suites, W...food: Cino's Pizza, King Wok, NY Subs, lodging: Renaissance, other: Publix, World Golf Village,
318	FL 16, Green Cove Sprgs, St Augustine, E...gas: BP/DQ, Gate/dsl/fruit, Kangaroo, Shell, food: Burger King, McDonald's, Huddle House, Subway, Waffle House, lodging: Country Inn&Suites, Econolodge, Holiday Inn Express, other: Belz Outlet, Camping World, W...gas: Exxon, food: Cracker Barrel, Denny's, KFC, Ruby Tuesday, Shoney's, Sonny's BBQ, Taco Bell, Wendy's, lodging: Best Western, Day's Inn, Hampton Inn, Ramada Ltd, Scottish Inn, Super 8, Wingate Inn, other: Harley-Davidson, St Augustine Outlet Ctr, Premium Outlets/Famous Brands, RV camping
311	FL 207, St Augustine, E...gas: BP/dsl, Chevron/24hr, Hess/Subway/dsl, Indian River Fruit/gas, other: HOSPITAL, Indian Forest RV Park(2mi), KOA(7mi), St Johns RV Park, flea mkt, to Anastasia SP, W...gas: Mobil/dsl, lodging: Comfort Inn
305	FL 206, to Hastings, Crescent Beach, E...gas: Citgo(2mi), ⚑/Flying J/Country Mkt/dsl/24hr/@, other: Gore RV Ctr, to Ft Matanzas NM
302mm	rest areas both lanes, full(handicapped) facilities, phone, vending, picnic tables, litter barrels, petwalk, 24hr security

298	US 1, to St Augustine, E...gas: BP/dsl, Indian River Fruit/gas, Sunoco, other: to Faver-Dykes SP, W...gas: Mobil/dsl, Sunrise/gas, food: Waffle House
289	to FL A1A(toll br), to Palm Coast, E...gas: BP, Exxon/dsl, Kangaroo/dsl, RaceTrac, food: Beef o' Brady's, Cracker Barrel, Denny's, KFC, Marco Polo Chinese, McDonald's, Pizza Hut, Wendy's, lodging: Hampton Inn, Microtel, Sleep Inn, other: CVS Drug, Publix, Staples, Walgreens, W...gas: Shell, Kangaroo, food: Baskin-Robbins/Dunkin Doughnuts, Bob Evan's, Outback Steaks, Perkins, Ruby Tuesday, Sonny's BBQ, Steak'n Shake/24hr, Subway, Taco Bell, TCBY, other: Advance Parts, Beall's, Ford, Home Depot, K-Mart, Radio Shack, Tire Kingdom, Walgreens, Wal-Mart SuperCtr/24hr, Winn-Dixie, USPO
286mm	weigh sta both lanes, phone
284	FL 100, to Bunnell, Flagler Beach, E...gas: BP, Chevron/dsl/24hr, Hess/dsl, Shell, food: Burger King, Domino's, McDonald's, Oriental Garden, Popeye's, Subway, Woody's BBQ, lodging: Caribe Hotel, Holiday Inn Express, other: $General, Winn-Dixie, W...gas: BP/dsl, other: access to HOSPITAL, Chevrolet, Chrysler/Dodge/Jeep
278	Old Dixie Hwy, E...gas: Citgo/7-11, other: Publix, Bulow RV Park(3mi), to Tomoke SP, W...gas: BP/dsl, food: Luigi's Pizza, lodging: Country Hearth Inn, other: Holiday Travel Park
273	US 1, E...gas: Chevron, Mobil/Wendy's/dsl, RaceTrac, Valero/dsl/scales, food: McDonald's, Waffle House, lodging: Comfort Inn, other: RV Ctr, W...gas: Exxon/Burger King, Loves/Arby's/dsl/scales/24hr/@, food: Brusters, DQ, lodging: Best Value, Days Inn, Daytona Hotel, Scottish Inn, Super 8, other: Encore RV Park, Harley-Davidson
268	FL 40, Ormond Beach, E...gas: Chevron, Shell, food: Applebee's, Boston Mkt, Chili's, Chick-fil-A, Denny's/24hr, Papa John's, Quizno's, Schlotsky's, Steak'n Shake, Subway, Taco Bell, Waffle House, Wendy's, lodging: Sleep Inn, other: Beall's, K-Mart, Lowe's Whse, Publix, Ross, USPO, Wal-Mart SuperCtr/24hr, W...gas: BP, Hess, Mobil/dsl, food: Cracker Barrel, McDonald's, lodging: Hampton Inn, Jameson Inn, other: HOSPITAL, Walgreens
265	LPGA Blvd,, Holly Hill, Daytona Beach, E...gas: Citgo/7-11, Shell/dsl, food: Subway(2mi), W...other: Dodge, Ford, Nissan
261b a	US 92, to DeLand, Daytona Bch, E...gas: BP/dsl, Chevron/dsl, Citgo/7-11/dsl, Hess/Blimpie/dsl, Mobil, RaceWay/24hr, Shell/dsl, food: Bob Evans, Buca Italian, Burger King, Cancun Rest., Carrabba's, Checker's, Chick-fil-A, Cracker Barrel, Fazoli's, Friendly's, Hooters, KFC, Krystal, Logan's Roadhouse, Longhorn Steaks, Olive Garden, Pizzaria Uno, Red Lobster, Roadhouse Grill, Ruby Tuesday, Shoney's, Sonny's BBQ, Subway, Taco Bell, Waffle House, Winghouse, lodging: Comfort Suites, Courtyard, Hampton Inn, Hilton Garden, Holiday Inn Express, Homewood Suites, La Quinta, Ramada Inn, Residence Inn, other: HOSPITAL, Barnes&Noble, Best Buy, Circuit City, Dillard's, Dodge/Kia, Firestone/auto, Home Depot, JC Penney, Macy's, Marshall's, Michael's, Old Navy, PepBoys, PetCo, Ross, Sears/auto, Staples, SteinMart, Target,

Interstate 95

TJMaxx, Walgreen, mall, to Daytona Racetrack, **W**...**gas:** BP/dsl, Exxon, Sunoco, **food:** Denny's, IHOP, McDonald's, **lodging:** Day's Inn, Super 8, **other:** RV camping, flea mkt, museum

260b a I-4, to Orlando, FL 400 E, to S Daytona, **E**...**gas:** Chevron/dsl

256 FL 421, to Port Orange, **E**...**gas:** Citgo/dsl, Shell, **food:** Bob Evans, Chick-fil-A, Denny's/24hr, Dustin's BBQ, Papa John's, Quizno's, Tropical Smoothie, **lodging:** Day's Inn, Hampton Inn, Holiday Inn, Palm Plaza Motel, **other:** Lowe's Whse, Panera Bread, Target, Wal-Mart SuperCtr/24hr(1mi), Walgreens, **W**...**gas:** Citgo/7-11, Hess, Texaco, **food:** McDonald's, Subway, Wendy's, **other:** Publix

249b a FL 44, to De Land, New Smyrna Beach, **E**...**gas:** Shell/dsl/fruit, **3 mi E**...**gas:** Circle K, Citgo, **food:** Burger King, Denny's, KFC, McDonald's, **other:** HOSPITAL, Curves, GNC, Harley-Davidson, New Smyrna RV Camp, Publix, Wal-Mart, Winn-Dixie, **W**...**gas:** Chevron/dsl

244 FL 442, to Edgewater, **E**...**gas:** Chevron/dsl/24hr, **3 mi E**...**gas:** Exxon/dsl **food:** Chick-fil-A, Dunkin Doughnuts, Subway

231 rd 5a, Scottsmoor, **E**...**gas:** BP/Stuckey's/dsl, **other:** Crystal Lake RV Park

227mm rest area sb, full(handicapped)facilities, phone, vending, picnic tables, litter barrels, petwalk, 24hr security

225mm rest area nb, full(handicapped)facilities, phone, vending, picnic tables, litter barrels, petwalk, 24hr security

223 FL 46, Mims, **E**...**gas:** Chevron(2mi), **food:** McDonald's, **other:** Willow Lakes Camping, **W**...**gas:** BP, Shell, **other:** KOA/LP, Seasons RV Camp

220 FL 406, Titusville, **E**...**gas:** BP/dsl, Shell/dsl, **food:** 1st Wok, KFC, McDonald's, Quizno's, Subway, Wendy's, **lodging:** Super 8, **other:** HOSPITAL, Advance Parts, Belk, $General, Publix, Tires+, Walgreens, **W**...**gas:** Chevron/dsl

215 FL 50, to Orlando, Titusville, **E**...**gas:** BP/KFC/Pizza Hut/dsl, Circle K/gas, Mobil/dsl, Shell/DQ/dsl, **food:** Burger King, Denny's, Durango Steaks, McDonald's, Peking Buffet, Roadhouse Grill, Sonny's BBQ, Taco Bell, Waffle House, Wendy's, **lodging:** Best Western, Holiday Inn(3mi), Ramada Inn, **other:** Ford/Mercury, Lowe's Whse, Staples, Wal-Mart SuperCtr/gas/24hr, to Kennedy Space Ctr, **W**...**food:** Cracker Barrel, IHOP, **lodging:** Comfort Inn, Day's Inn, Hampton Inn, **other:** Great Outdoors RV Camp

212 FL 407, to FL 528 toll(from sb, no re-entry)

208 Port St John, no services

205 FL 528(wb toll), to Cape Canaveral, City Point

202 FL 524, Cocoa, **E**...**gas:** Shell/dsl, **other:** museum, **W**...**gas:** BP/dsl, **lodging:** Day's Inn, Ramada Inn/rest., Super 8

201 FL 520, to Cocoa Bch, Cocoa, **E**...**gas:** BP/dsl, Chevron, Pilot/Subway/dsl, **food:** IHOP, Olive

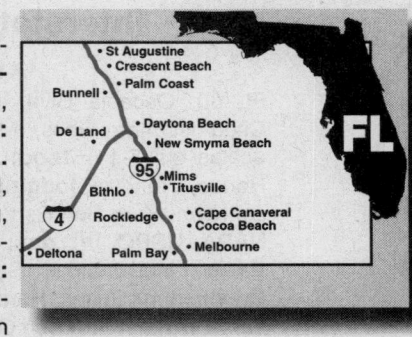

Garden(6mi), Waffle House, **lodging:** Best Western, Budget Inn, **other:** HOSPITAL, **W**...**gas:** Chevron/dsl, Shell/Burger King, Sunoco, **food:** McDonald's, **lodging:** Holiday Inn Express, **other:** Sun Coast RV Ctr

195 FL 519, Fiske Blvd, **E**...**gas:** Citgo/7-11, Shell/dsl(1mi), **lodging:** Swiss Inn, **other:** Lowe's Whse, Space Coast RV Park

191 rd 509, to Satellite Beach, **E**...**gas:** Citgo/7-11, Hess/Blimpie/dsl, **food:** Bob Evans, Denny's, McDonald's, Perkins, Pizzaria Uno, Wendy's, **lodging:** Imperials Hotel, **other:** Eckerd, to Patrick AFB, **W**...**gas:** Chevron/dsl, **food:** Burger King, Chili's, Cracker Barrel, Longhorn Steaks, Mimi's Cafe, Starbucks, Subway, **lodging:** La Quinta, **other:** Belk, Kohl's, PetCo, Ross, Target, Wal-Mart SuperCtr/24hr/gas

183 FL 518, Melbourne, Indian Harbour Beach, **E**...**gas:** BP, Chevron/Baskin Robbins/Dunkin Donuts/dsl, Citgo/7-11, RaceTrac/24hr, **other:** museum, **W**..:Flea Mkt

180 US 192, to Melbourne, **E**...**gas:** BP/dsl, Circle K/gas, Citgo/7-11, Mobil/dsl, Sunoco/dsl, **food:** Denny's, IHOP, Olive Garden(3mi), Steak'n Shake/24hr(3mi), Waffle House, **lodging:** Best Value Inn, Budget Inn, Courtyard, Hampton Inn, Holiday Inn Express, Howard Johnson, York Inn, **other:** HOSPITAL, Sam's Club/gas, Saturn, Target(4mi)

176 rd 516, to Palm Bay, **E**...**gas:** BP/dsl, Citgo/7-11, **food:** Applebee's, Baskin Robbins/Dunkin Donuts, Bob Evans, Chick-fil-A, Cracker Barrel, Denny's, Golden Corral, Starbucks, Taco Bell, Wendy's, **lodging:** Jameson Inn, Ramada Inn, **other:** Albertson's, BJ's Whse/gas, Chevrolet, $Tree, GNC, Harley-Davidson, Wal-Mart SuperCtr/gas/24hr, **W**...**gas:** Citgo/7-11, Shell, **food:** Wendy's, **other:** Publix, Walgreens

173 FL 514, to Palm Bay, **E**...**gas:** Shell/dsl, Sunoco/dsl, **other:** HOSPITAL, Firestone/auto, Ford, Subaru, truck/RV repair, **W**...**gas:** BP/dsl, Hess, Shell, Sunoco/dsl, **food:** Arby's, Baskin-Robbins/Dunkin Donuts, Burger King, IHOP, McDonald's, Sonny's BBQ, Subway, Taco Bell, Texas Roadhouse, Waffle House, Wendy's, Woody's BBQ, **lodging:** Motel 6, **other:** Advance Parts, BigLots, CVS Drug, $General, Goodyear/auto, Home Depot, Publix, Tire Kingdom, USPO, Walgreens, Wal-Mart SuperCtr/24hr

168mm rest areas both lanes, full(handicapped)facilities, phone, vending, picnic tables, litter barrels, petwalk, 24hr security, motorist aid callboxes begin nb/end sb

156 rd 512, to Sebastian, Fellsmere, **E**...**gas:** BP/DQ/dsl, Chevron/McDonald's, Mobil/dsl/LP(2mi), **food:** Subway(2mi), **other:** HOSPITAL, Encore RV Park, Sebastian Inlet SRA, Vero Bch RV Park(8mi)

N↑S

Ft Pierce

147	FL 60, Osceola Blvd, E...gas: Chevron/repair, Citgo/dsl/24hr, Hess, Mobil/dsl, TA/BP/dsl/24hr/scales/@, 7-11, food: Sloane's Rest., Waffle House, Wendy's, lodging: Best Western, Howard Johnson, Vero Bch Rsrt, other: HOSPITAL, VET, NAPA, USPO, W...gas: Shell/dsl, food: Cracker Barrel, McDonald's, Steak'n Shake, lodging: Country Inn&Suites, Hampton Inn, Holiday Inn Express, other: Vero Bch Outlets/famous brands
138	FL 614, Indrio Rd, 3 mi E...gas: BP, food: McDonald's, other: Oceanographic Institute, citrus
133mm	rest areas both lanes, full(handicapped) facilities, phone, vending, picnic tables, litter barrels, petwalk, 24hr security
131b a	FL 68, Orange Ave, E...to Ft Pierce SP, W...gas: ⚡/Flying J/CountryMkt/dsl/LP/scales/24hr/@, other: Blue Beacon
129	FL 70, to Okeechobee, E...gas: Hess/dsl, RaceTrac, Sunoco/dsl, food: Applebee's, Gator's Rest., Golden Corral, Waffle House, other: HOSPITAL, Advance Parts, $Tree, Firestone/auto, Goodyear/auto, Home Depot, Radio Shack, Wal-Mart SuperCtr/gas/24hr, mall, W...gas: Chevron, Citgo/dsl, Exxon, Mobil/Subway, Pilot/Arby's/dsl/24hr/@, Pilot/McDonald's/dsl/scales/24hr/@, Shell/dsl, food: Burger King, Cracker Barrel, Clock Rest., KFC, Red Lobster, Steak'n Shake, Waffle House, Wendy's, lodging: Best Western, Comfort Suites, Day's Inn, Hampton Inn, Holiday Inn Express, Motel 6, Quality Inn, Rodeway Inn, Sleep Inn, Treasure Coast Inn, to FL TPK
126	rd 712, Midway Rd, 3-5 mi E...gas: BP, Mobil, Shell, food: Blimpie, Subway
121	St Lucie West Blvd, E...gas: BP, Chevron/24hr, Citgo/7-11, Shell/Subway/dsl, food: Bob Evans, Burger King, Camille's Cafe, Chili's, Crisper's Rest., Friendly's, Gators Rest., McAlister's Deli, McDonald's, OutBack Steaks, Ruby Tuesday, Wendy's, lodging: Hampton Inn, SpringHill Suites, other: Publix/deli, USPO, Walgreens, Wal-Mart SuperCtr/24hr/gas, W...gas: Mobil/dsl, lodging: MainStay Suites, Sheraton, other: PGA Village
118	Gatlin Blvd, to Port St Lucie, E...gas: BP/dsl/LP, Chevron/Subway/dsl, Shell/Subway/dsl, Sunoco, food: Burger King(2mi), Dunkin Donuts
110	FL 714, to Stuart, Palm City
106mm	rest areas both lanes, full(handicapped) facilities, phone, vending, picnic tables. litter barrels, petwalk, 24hr security
102	FL 713, to Stuart, Palm City, no services
101	FL 76, to Stuart, Indiantown, E...gas: Chevron/24hr, Sunoco/dsl, food: Baskin-Robbins/Dunkin Donuts, Cracker Barrel, McDonald's, Wendy's, other: HOSPITAL, RV camping, W...gas: Shell/deli/dsl, food: DQ, Stuckey's
96	rd 708, to Hobe Sound, E...Dickinson SP(11mi), RV camping

Jupiter / **W Palm Beach**

87b a	FL 706, to Okeechobee, Jupiter, E...gas: Hess, Mobil, Shell, food: Applebee's, Burger King, Duffy's Rest., Dunkin Donuts, Gator's Rest., IHOP, KFC, McDonald's, Subway, Taco Bell, Tomato Pie, lodging: Comfort Inn, Fairfield Inn, other: HOSPITAL, VET, Advance Parts, Books-A-Million, Dodge/Mazda, GNC, Home Depot, PepBoys, Publix, Tire Kingdom, Walgreens, Wal-Mart, Winn-Dixie, to Dickinson SP, hist sites, museum, W...gas: Mobil/dsl, Sunoco, other: info, RV camping, to FL TPK
83	Donald Ross Rd, E...stadium
79c	FL 809 S(from sb), W...to FL TPK, same services as 79b
79a b	FL 786, PGA Blvd, E...food: China Wok, Durango Steaks, lodging: Hampton Inn, Marriott, other: HOSPITAL, Loehmann's Foods, W...gas: Shell/dsl/24hr, food: Beacon St Café, Outback Steaks, lodging: DoubleTree Hotel, Embassy Suites, other: Publix
77	Northlake Blvd, to W Palm Bch, E...gas: Hess, Shell/dsl, food: Applebee's, Arby's, Burger King, Checker's, KFC, McDonald's, Taco Bell, Wendy's, Whataburger, other: HOSPITAL, Buick/Pontiac/GMC, Chevrolet, Chrysler/Jeep/Dodge, Costco, Ford, Home Depot, Kia/Isuzu//Suzuki, K-Mart, Lincoln/Mercury, Panera Bread, PepBoys, Ross, Staples, Subaru, Target, VW/Mitsubishi, W...gas: Chevron, Citgo, Hess, Marathon, Mobil/dsl, Shell, food: Duffy's Grill, Gator's Rest., Pizza Hut, lodging: Inn of America, other: Advance Parts, Albertson's, CVS Drug, Radio Shack, Publix, Winn-Dixie
76	FL 708, Blue Heron Blvd, E...gas: BP/dsl, Shell/dsl, food: Wendy's, other: Honda, KIA, Nissan, W...gas: BP, RaceTrac, Texaco/dsl, food: Burger King, Denny's, McDonald's, Quizno's, lodging: Super 8
74	FL 702, 45th St, E...food: Burger King, IHOP, Subway, lodging: Day's Inn, other: HOSPITAL, Cadillac, Walgreens, W...gas: Mobil, RaceTrac, Sunoco, food: Cracker Barrel, Polo Tropical, Taco Bell, Wendy's, lodging: Courtyard, Extended Stay Deluxe, Red Roof Inn, other: Curves, Harley-Davidson, Studio+, Goodyear/auto
71	Lake Blvd, Palm Beach, E...gas: BP, food: McDonald's, lodging: Best Western, other: HOSPITAL, Best Buy, Dillard's, Firestone/auto, JC Penney, Macy's, Sears/auto, Target, mall, W...gas: Texaco/dsl, food: Carraba's, Chick-fil-A, Hooters, Krispy Kreme, Olive Garden, Picadilly's, Red Lobster, Sweet Tomatoes, lodging: Comfort Inn, La Quinta, other: Walgreens
70b a	FL 704, Okeechobee Blvd, E...gas: Exxon, lodging: Marriott, other: Kravis Ctr, museum, W...gas: Chevron, Texaco, food: Burger King, McDonald's, Shell's Rest., other: Chevrolet, Circuit City, CompUSA, Dodge, Lexus, Lincoln/Mercury, Mitsubishi
69	Belvedere Rd, W...gas: Shell, food: Burger King, Denny's, IHOP, Wendy's, lodging: Courtyard, Hampton Inn, Holiday Inn/rest., Motel 6, Radisson Suites, other: to airport

Interstate 95

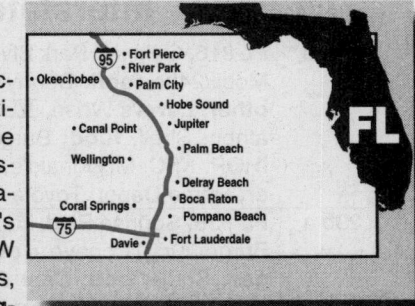

N ↑ S

68	US 98, Southern Blvd, **E**...**food:** Mobil, **other:** Publix/deli, **W**...**lodging:** Hilton
66	Forest Hill Blvd, **E**...**food:** Havana Cafe
64	10th Ave N, **W**...**gas:** Citgo, Shell/dsl/24hr, **food:** China Empire, Flanigans Grill, Wendy's, **other:** $General, Ford, Goodyear, President Foods
63	6th Ave S, **W**...HOSPITAL
61	FL 812, Lantana Rd, **E**...**gas:** Shell, **food:** Dunkin Donuts, KFC, McDonald's, Reggin's Crabhouse, Subway, **lodging:** Motel 6, **other:** Ace Hardware, Beall's, CVS Drug, $General, Publix, 7-11, **W**... **food:** Rosalita's Café, **other:** HOSPITAL, Costco/ gas
60	Hypoluxo Rd, **E**...**gas:** Mobil, Shell/dsl, **food:** Pizza Hut, Popeye's, Subway, Taco Bell, Wendy's, **lodging:** Best Western, Comfort Inn, Super 8, **other:** Sam's Club, Tires+, Tire Kingdom, U-Haul, **W**... **gas:** Chevron, **other:** Advance Parts
59	Gateway Blvd, **E**...**gas:** Shell/dsl, **W**...**gas:** Mobil/ dsl, **food:** Boynton Ale House, Carraba's, Chili's, McDonald's, Original Pancake House, Tuesday Morning, **lodging:** Hampton Inn, **other:** CarMax, CVS Drug, Publix, Target
57	FL 804, Boynton Bch Blvd, **E**...**gas:** Majestic Gas, **lodging:** Holiday Inn Express, **other:** HOSPITAL, USPO, **W**...**gas:** Shell/dsl, Texaco, **food:** Checker's, Krispy Kreme, Lenny's Subs, Subway, TGI-Friday, Waffle House, Wendy's, **other:** BJ's Whse/ gas, Radio Shack, 7-11, **1mi W**...**gas:** Mobil, **food:** Burger King, Golden Corral, Starbucks, Steak'n Shake, **other:** Barnes&Noble, Office Depot, Old Navy, Publix, Wal-Mart SuperCtr/24hr
56	Woolbright Rd, **E**...**gas:** Shell/24hr, **food:** McDonald's, **other:** HOSPITAL, **W**...**gas:** RaceTrac/24hr, **food:** Burger King, Cracker Barrel, Subway, **other:** Home Depot, Lowe's Whse, Staples
52b a	FL 806, Atlantic Ave, **W**...**gas:** Chevron, Shell/dsl, **food:** Burger King, McDonald's, **other:** VET, Aamco, Publix, Tires+, Walgreens
51	rd 782, Linton Blvd, **E**...**gas:** Exxon, **food:** DQ, McDonald's, OutBack Steaks, Polo Tropical, Steak'n Shake, **other:** Chevrolet, Dodge, Ford, Home Depot, Nissan, Ross, Target, **W**...**gas:** Shell, **other:** HOSPITAL, Family$, Winn-Dixie
50	Congress Ave, **W**...**gas:** NeXStore/gas, **lodging:** Hilton Garden, Homestead Motel,
48b a	FL 794, Yamato Rd, **E**...**gas:** Mobil, **other:** CVS Drug, Panera Bread, **W**...**gas:** Chevron/Blimpie/ dsl, **food:** Jamba Juice, McDonald's, Starbucks, Subway, Taco Bell, **lodging:** DoubleTree, Embassy Suites, Hampton Inn, SpringHill Suites, Towne-Place Suites
45	FL 808, Glades Rd, **E on Ftge rd**...**lodging:** Fairfield Inn, **food:** Alexander's Rest, Mon Ami Cafe, Subway, **other:** Barnes&Noble, Circuit City, Jamba Juice, PF Chang's, Whole-Foods Mkt, museum, **W**...**gas:** BP, **food:** Abe&Louie's, Brewzzi Cafe,

Pompano

	Cheesecake Factory, Chipotle Mexican, Coldstone Creamery, Houston Rest., Macaroni Grill, Mario's Italian, Moe's SW Grill, Quizno's, Starbucks, **lodging:** Courtyard, Holiday Inn, Marriott, **other:** Macy's, Sears/auto
44	Palmetto Park Rd, **E**...**gas:** Exxon/24hr, **food:** Denny's, Krispy Kreme, Red's BBQ, Subway, Tomasso's Pizza, **other:** Publix, museums, **W**...**food:** McDonald's(1mi)
42b a	FL 810, Hillsboro Blvd, **E**..:**gas:** BP, Shell/dsl, **food:** McDonald's, Wendy's, **lodging:** Hampton Inn, Hilton, La Quinta, **other:** Advance Parts, **W**...**gas:** Chevron, Mobil/dsl, **food:** Boston Mkt, Checker's, Denny's, **lodging:** Holiday Park, **other:** CVS Drug, Home Depot, Walgreens
41	FL 869(toll), SW 10th, to I-75, **E**...**gas:** Mobil, **food:** Cracker Barrel, **lodging:** Extended Stay America, **W**...**lodging:** Best Western, Comfort Suites,
39	FL 834, Sample Rd, **E**...**gas:** BP, Hess, Mobil, Shell/dsl, **food:** Hops Grill(1mi), **other:** HOSPITAL, 7-11, **W**...**gas:** Chevron, Mobil/dsl, Sunoco/dsl, **food:** Arby's, Checker's, IHOP, McDonald's, Miami Subs, Subway, **other:** CVS Drug, Family$
38b a	Copans Rd, **E**...**gas:** BP, **food:** McDonald's, **other:** Mercedes, PepBoys, Porche/Audi, Wal-Mart, **W**... **gas:** Chevron, **other:** Harley-Davidson, Home Depot, NAPA
36b a	FL 814, Atlantic Blvd, to Pompano Beach, **E**...**gas:** RaceTrac, **food:** KFC/Pizza Hut/Taco Bell, Miami Subs, **1 mi W**...**gas:** BP, Mobil/dsl, Shell/dsl, **food:** Golden Corral, KFC/LJ Silver, McDonald's, Pollo Tropical, Wendy's, **other:** Advance Parts, Chevrolet, CVS Drug, $Tree Radio Shack, Wal-Mart SuperCtr/gas/24hr, USPO, to FL TPK, Power Line Rd has multiple services
33b a	Cypress Creek Rd, **E**...**gas:** BP, Hess, **food:** Duffy's Diner, Jester's Grill, NY Pizza, **lodging:** Extended Stay America, Hampton Inn, Westin Hotel, **W**... **gas:** Hess, Shell/repair, **food:** Arby's, Bennigan's, Burger King, Champp's Grill, Chili's, Hooters, Longhorn Steaks, McDonald's, Moonlite Diner, Quizno's, Steak&Ale, SweetTomatoe's, Wendy's, **lodging:** Courtyard, Extended Stay Deluxe, La Quinta, Marriott, Sheraton Suites, **other:** GNC, Jaguar, Office Depot, Tires+
32	FL 870, Commercial Blvd, Lauderdale by the Sea, Lauderhill, **E**...**food:** Subway, **W**...**gas:** BP, Circle K, Mobil, Shell, Sunoco/dsl, **food:** Burger King, KFC, McDonald's, Miami Subs, Waffle House, **lodging:** El Palacio, Red Roof Inn, **other:** Advance Parts

N ↕ S

Ft Lauderdale

Exit	Description
31b a	FL 816, Oakland Park Blvd, E...gas: BP, Chevron, Mobil/24hr, food: Denny's, Miami Subs, Wendy's, other: Lowe's Whse, W...gas: BP/dsl, Citgo, Marathon, Shell, food: Burger King, Dunkin Donuts, IHOP, KFC, McDonald's, lodging: Day's Inn, other: Home Depot, Toyota, USPO, Walgreens
29b a	FL 838, Sunrise Blvd, E...gas: Citgo, Shell, food: Burger King, Popeye's, other: Advance Parts, W...gas: Shell, food: Capt Crabs, Church's, McDonald's, Subway, lodging: Travelodge
27	FL 842, Broward Blvd, Ft Lauderdale, E...HOSPITAL
26	I-595(from sb), FL 736, Davie Blvd, W...gas: BP, Hess, Mobil, food: Flanigan's Cafe, Subway, Wendy's
25	FL 84, E...gas: Citgo/7-11, Marathon, RaceTrac/24hr, Shell, Sunoco, Texaco, food: Dunkin Donuts, Lil Red's Rest., Little Caesar's, McDonald's, Subway, Wendy's, lodging: Best Western, Candlewood Suites, Hampton Inn, Holiday Inn Express, Motel 6, other: Radio Shack, U-Haul, Winn-Dixie, W...lodging: Ramada Inn, Red Carpet Inn, Rodeway Inn, other: Ford Trucks
24	I-595(from nb), to I-75, E...to airport
23	FL 818, Griffin Rd, E...lodging: Sheraton, Wyndham Inn, W...gas: BP, Citgo/dsl, lodging: Courtyard, other: Bass Pro Shops
22	FL 848, Stirling Rd, Cooper City, E...gas: CF, Mobil, food: AleHouse Grill, Burger King, Dave&Buster's, Quizno's, McDonald's, Moonlite Diner, Sal's Italian, Sweet Tomatoes, Taco Bell, TGIFriday, Wendy's, lodging: Comfort Inn, Hampton Inn, Hilton Garden, La Quinta, Sterling Suites, other: Advance Parts, Barnes&Noble, BigLots, BJ's Whse, GNC, Home Depot, K-Mart/Little Caesar's, Marshall's, Michael's, Old Navy, Ross, to Lloyd SP W...food: Mr M's Sanwiches, Subway, other: Circle K, CVS Drug, PepBoys, Tire Kingdom, Walgreens
21	FL 822, Sheridan St, E...gas: BP, Citgo, Cumberland Farms/gas, same as 22, W...gas: Shell, food: Denny's, lodging: Day's Inn, Holiday Inn
20	FL 820, Hollywood Blvd, E...gas: Shell, lodging: Howard Johnson, Econolodge, W...gas: BP, Chevron, food: Boston Mkt, Coldstone Creamery, McDonald's, Taco Bell, Starbucks, Subway, Wendy's, other: HOSPITAL, Publix, Target, Walgreens
19	FL 824, Pembroke Rd, E...gas: Shell, W...gas: Shell, Sunoco/dsl
18	FL 858, Hallandale Bch Blvd, E...gas: Amerika Gas, Citgo/7-11, Exxon, Shell, food: Burger King, Denny's, IHOP, KFC, Little Caesar's, McDonald's, Polo Tropical, Subway, Wendy's, lodging: Best Western, other: HOSPITAL, Walgreens, Winn-Dixie, W...gas: BP, RaceTrac, other: Advance Parts

Miami

Exit	Description
16	Ives Dairy Rd, E...HOSPITAL, mall, W...gas: BP, food: Subway
14	FL 860, Miami Gardens Dr, N Miami Beach, E...HOSPITAL, Oleta River SRA, W...gas: BP, Chevron, Marathon/dsl, food: Subway, 1 mi W...gas: Raceway, Shell, other: Walgreens
12c	US 441, FL 826, FL TPK, FL 9, E...gas: BP, Chevron, Citgo/7-11, Hess, Valero, lodging: Golden Glades Inn, Holiday Inn, other: HOSPITAL
12b	US 441(from nb), same as 12c
12a	FL 868(from nb), FL TPK N, no services
11	NW 151st (from nb), W...gas: Sunoco, food: McDonald's, other: Advance Parts, Winn-Dixie, services on US 441 N
10b	FL 916, NW 135th, Opa-Locka Blvd, W...gas: BP, Chevron, Libery, Mobil, KwikStop, food: Checker's
10a	NW 125th, N Miami, Bal Harbour, W...gas: Shell, food: Wendy's
9	NW 119th(from nb), W...gas: BP/McDonald's, food: KFC, other: AutoZone, Family$, Walgreens, Winn-Dixie
8b	FL 932, NW 103rd, E...gas: Shell, Texaco, other: 7-11, W...gas: Chevron, Marathon, Sunoco, food: Baskin-Robbins/Dunkin Donuts
8a	NW 95th, E...gas: BP, W...gas: Mobil, Shell, food: McDonald's, other: HOSPITAL, Advance Parts, Walgreens
7	FL 934, NW 81st, NW 79th, E...gas: Chevron/dsl, Citgo/dsl, W...food: Cafe China, Checker's
6b	NW 69th(from sb), no services
6a	FL 944, NW 62nd, NW 54th, W...food: McDonald's, other: Walgreens
4b a	I-195 E, FL 112 W(toll), Miami Beach, E...downtown, W...airport
3b	NW 8th St(from sb), no services
3a	FL 836 W(toll)(exits left from nb), W...HOSPITAL, to Orange Bowl, airport
2d	I-395 E(exits left from sb), to Miami Beach
2c	NW 8th, NW 14th(from sb), Miami Ave, E...Port of Miami, W...to Orange Bowl
2b	NW 2nd(from nb), downtown Miami
2a	US 1(exits left from sb), Biscayne Blvd, downtown Miami
1b	US 41, SW 7th, SW 8th, Brickell Ave, E...lodging: Extended Stay America, Hampton Inn, Holiday Inn Express, food: Burger King, McDonald's, Moe's SW Grill, Subway, Wendy's, other: GNC, Publix, Walgreens, W...gas: Shell, food: Papa John's
1a	SW 25th(from sb), downtown, to Rickenbacker Causeway, E...lodging: Hampton Inn, other: museum, to Baggs SRA
0mm	I-95 begins/ends on US 1. 1 mi S...gas: Citgo, food: Quizno's

Interstate 275(Tampa)

Exit #	Services
59mm	I-275 begins/ends on I-75, exit 274.
53	Bearss Ave, **E...gas:** Citgo/dsl, **other:** Carmax, **W...gas:** BP, CC's/dsl, RaceTrac, Shell, **food:** Burger King, Green Tea Chinese, McDonald's, Perkins, Subway, Wendy's, **lodging:** Quality Inn, **other:** VET, BigLots, CVS Drug, GNC, Publix, Radio Shack
52	Fletcher Ave, **E...gas:** BP, Hess, RaceTrac, Sunoco, Texaco, **food:** Krystal, **lodging:** Day's Inn, **other:** AutoZone, Cadillac, Tire Kingdom, Toyota, **W...gas:** BP, Citgo, **lodging:** Super 8, **other:** Jaguar
51	FL 582, Fowler Ave, **E...gas:** Citgo, GK, Shell, **food:** A&W/LJ Silver, Burger King, Checker's, China Buffet, City Mkt, Denny's, McDonald's, Steak'n Shake, Subway, Waffle House, Woody's BBQ, **lodging:** Howard Johnson, **other:** Family$, Office Depot, Walgreens, **W...lodging:** Economy Inn, Motel 6, Safar Inn, **other:** BMW
50	FL 580, Busch Blvd, **E...gas:** Chevron, Exxon, Marathon, **lodging:** Comfort Inn, **other:** Busch Gardens, **W...food:** Burger King, KFC, **other:** CVS Drug, Firestone/auto, Goodyear, Home Depot, Wal-Mart Mkt/drug
49	Bird Ave(from nb), **W...gas:** Shell, **food:** Checker's, KFC, Wendy's, **other:** K-Mart
48	Sligh Ave, **E...gas:** BP, Sunoco, **W...other:** zoo
47b a	US 92, to US 41 S, Hillsborough Ave, **E...gas:** Citgo, Valero, **food:** Burger King, McDonald's, Wendy's, **other:** Advance Parts, **W...gas:** BP, Circle K, **food:** Starbucks
46b	FL 574, MLK Blvd, **E...gas:** BP, Shell, **other:** Advance Parts, Kash&Karry/drug, Walgreens, **W...gas:** Marathon, **food:** McDonald's, **other:** HOSPITAL
46a	Floribraska Ave
45b	I-4 E, to Orlando, I-75
45a	Jefferson St, downtown E
44	Ashley Dr, Tampa St, downtown W
42	Howard Ave, Armenia Ave, **W...gas:** Texaco/dsl, **food:** Indigo Coffee, Popeye's
41c	Himes Ave(from sb), **W...RJ Stadium**
41b a	US 92, Dale Mabry Blvd, **E...gas:** BP, Mobil/dsl, Shell, **food:** Alexander's Rest., Burger King, Carino's Italian, Carrabba's, Chick-Fil-A, Donatello Italian, Fleming's BBQ, Perkins, Petsmart, Ruby Tuesday, Shells Rest., Starbucks, Village Inn, Wild Oats Mkt, **lodging:** Courtyard, **other:** Borders, CompUSA, CVS Drug, Office Depot, to MacDill AFB, **W...gas:** BP, Exxon/dsl, **food:** Bennigan's, Burger King, Checker's, Chili's, China 1, Crazy Buffet, Denny's, Dunkin Donuts, LongHorn Steaks, Macaroni Grill, McDonald's, Quizno's, Sonic, Sonny's BBQ, Sweet Tomatoes, Taco Bell, Tia's TexMex, Waffle House, Wendy's, **lodging:** Day's Inn, Howard Johnson, **other:** Best Buy, Circuit City, Dodge, Home Depot, K-Mart, Staples, SweetBay Foods, Target, Wal-Mart
40b	Lois Ave, **W...gas:** GK, **food:** Charlies Rest., **lodging:** DoubleTree Hotel, Sheraton
40a	FL 587, Westshore Blvd, **E...gas:** Citgo, Shell, **food:** Chipotle Mexican, Maggiano's Rest., PF Changs, Steak&Ale, Taco Bell, Waffle House, **lodging:** Embassy Suites, Ramada Inn, Wyndam, **other:** JC Penney, Macys, Sears/auto, Walgreens, **W...gas:** Shell/Subway, **food:** Durango Steaks, **lodging:** Best Western, Marriott, Quorum Hotel, SpringHill Suites
39b a	FL 60 W, **W...food:** Outback Steaks, **other:** to airport
32	Fl 687 S, 4th St N, to US 92 (no sb reentry)
31b a	9th St N, MLK St N(exits left from sb), info, airport
30	FL 686, Roosevelt Blvd, no services
28	FL 694 W, Gandy Blvd, Indian Shores, **1-2mi W... food:** Bob Evans, Godfather's Pizza, **lodging:** La Quinta, **other:** Robert's RV Resort
26b a	54th Ave N, **E...gas:** Cracker Barrel, **lodging:** Comfort Inn, Holiday Inn Express, **W...gas:** Citgo, RaceTrac, **food:** Waffle House, **lodging:** Day's Inn, **other:** HOSPITAL, Harley-Davidson, NAPA
25	38th Ave N, to beaches, **E...food:** McDonald's, **W... gas:** Citgo/dsl, **food:** Burger King, Hardee's
24	22nd Ave N, **E...gas:** Mobil, **other:** Sunken Garden, **W...gas:** Citgo/dsl, RaceTrac, **other:** Home Depot, Lowe's Whse
23b	FL 595, 5th Ave N, **E...HOSPITAL**
23a	I-375, **E...The Pier, Waterfront, downtown**
22	I-175 E, Tropicana Fields, **W...HOSPITAL**
21	28th St S, downtown
20	31st Ave(from nb), downtown
19	22nd Ave S, Gulfport, **W...gas:** Chevron, Citgo, Shell, **food:** Church's, **other:** Family$, PriceBuster Foods
18	26th Ave S(from nb), no services
17	FL 682 W, 54th Ave S, Pinellas Bayway, services on US19, **W...gas:** Citgo/7-11, Sunoco, **food:** Bob Evans, Burger King, McDonald's, Papa John's, Popeye's, Taco Bell, **lodging:** Crystal Inn, **other:** CVS Drug, Publix, to Ft DeSoto Pk, St Pete Beach,
16	Pinellas Point Dr, Skyway Lane, to Maximo Park, **E...lodging:** Holiday Inn resort, **W...marina**
16mm	toll plaza sb
13mm	N Skyway Fishing Pier, **W...rest area both lanes, full(handicapped)facilities, phone, vending, picnic tables, litter barrels, petwalk**
10mm	Tampa Bay
7mm	S Skyway Fishing Pier, **E...rest area both lanes, full(handicapped)facilities, phone, vending, picnic tables, litter barrels, petwalk**
6mm	toll plaza nb
5	US 19, Palmetto, Bradenton, no services
2	US 41 last nb exit before toll, Palmetto, Bradenton, **E...gas:** Circle K, **2-4 mi W...gas:** BP/dsl, RaceTrac, 7-11, **lodging:** BayShore Inn
0mm	I-275 begins/ends on I-75, exit 228

FLORIDA

Interstate 295(Jacksonville)

Exit #	Services
35b a	I-95, S to Jacksonville, N to Savannah. I-295 begins/ends on I-95, exit 362b.
33	Duval Rd, W...airport
32	FL 115, Lem Turner Rd, E...food: China Wok, Cross Creek Steak, Larry's Subs, McDonald's(1mi), Subway, Wendy's, other: Home Depot, Radio Shack, Wal-Mart SuperCtr/24hr, W...other: Flamingo Lake Camping
30	FL 104, Dunn Ave, E...gas: Gate/dsl, Shell/24hr(1mi), food: McDonald's
28b a	US 1, US 23, to Callahan, Jacksonville, E...gas: Lil' Champ/gas, W...gas: BP/DQ/dsl, Chevron/dsl, RaceTrac/24hr
25	Pritchard Rd, W...gas: Kangaroo/Subway/dsl/24hr
22	Commonwealth Ave, E...gas: Sprint/dsl, food: Burger King, Hardee's, Waffle House, lodging: Holiday Inn, other: dogtrack, W...food: Wendy's
21b a	I-10, W to Tallahassee, E to Jacksonville
19	FL 228, Normandy Blvd, E...gas: BP/dsl/24hr, food: Burger King, El Potro, Golden Corral, McDonald's, Papa John's, Sonic, Wendy's, other: $Tree, Food Lion, Radio Shack, Walgreens, Wal-Mart SuperCtr/24hr, st patrol, W...gas: RaceTrac, Shell, food: Golden China, Hardee's, McDonald's, Pizza Hut, Popeye's, Subway, Whataburger, other: Advance Parts, CVS Drug, Family$, K-Mart, Publix, Radio Shack, Winn-Dixie
17	FL 208, Wilson Blvd, E...gas: BP/dsl, Hess/dsl, food: Hardee's, McDonald's(1mi), other: Advance Parts, Food Lion, W...gas: Kangaroo
16	FL 134, 103rd St, Cecil Field, E...gas: BP, Gate/dsl, Hess, Shell/24hr, food: Arby's, BarnHill's Buffet, Burger King, Capt D's, Firehouse Subs, Popeye's, Shoney's, Wendy's, Ying's Chinese, lodging: Hospitality Inn, other: Advance Parts, Tires+, Wal-Mart SuperCtr/24hr, W...gas: BP, Chevron, Exxon/dsl, Shell, food: Burger King, DQ, Dragon Garden Chinese, El Potro Mexican, IHOP, KFC, McDonald's, Miami Subs, Mi Toro Mexican, Pizza Hut, Subway, Taco Bell, other: Aamco, AutoZone, Family$, Food Lion, Goodyear/auto, Publix, SavRite Foods, Sun Tires, Walgreens
12	FL 21, Blanding Blvd, E...gas: BP, RaceTrac, Shell, food: Burger King, McDonald's, Pizza Hut, Sunrise Cafe, other: Acura, Best Buy, Cadillac, CVS Drug, $General, Ford, Honda, Office Depot, Petsmart, Saturn, U-Haul, W...gas: BP, Chevron, Kangaroo, Shell, food: Applebee's, Arby's, Bennigan's, Buffalo's, Carino's Italian, Chick-fil-A, Chili's, ChuckeCheese, Denny's, KFC, Longhorn Steaks, Los Toros Mexican, Olive Garden, Outback Steaks, Papa John's, Qdoba Mexican, Quizno's, Red Lobster, Starbucks, Steak&Ale, Taco Bell, Ted's MT Grill, Tony Roma, lodging: Country Inn, Hampton Inn, La Quinta, Motel 6, Red Roof Inn, Super 8, other: HOSPITAL, Belks, Circuit City, Dillard's, Discount Tire, Home Depot, JoAnn Fabrics, Michael's, Panera Bread, Sam's Club/gas, Sears/auto, Publix, Target, TJMaxx, Toyota, Walgreens, mall
10	US 17, FL 15, Roosevelt Blvd, Orange Park, E...lodging: Best Western, W...gas: BP, Chevron/dsl/24hr, RaceWay, Shell, food: Coyote Grill, Cracker Barrel, Dynasty Chinese, Krystal, LJ Silver, McDonald's, Pizza Hut, Sam's Seafood, Subway, Waffle House, Wendy's, lodging: Comfort Inn, Day's Inn, Econolodge, Fairfield Inn, Holiday Inn, Quality Inn, other: Chrysler, Harley-Davidson, Honda, Nissan, VW
7mm	St Johns River, Buckman Br
5b a	FL 13, San Jose Blvd, E...gas: Exxon/dsl/24hr, Lewis/DQ/dsl, Shell, food: Applebee's, Arby's, Bob Evan's, Bono's BBQ, Boston Mkt, Cross Creek Steaks, Famous Amos, Krystal, Popeye's, Steak'n Shake, Subway, TCBY, Village Inn, Wendy's, lodging: La Quinta, Ramada Inn, other: Aamco, Albertson's, Eckerd, Firestone/auto, Goodyear/auto, Office Depot, Publix, Target, Tire Kingdom, Walgreens, W...gas: BP, Gate(3mi), Shell(1mi), food: American Cafe, BoneFish Grill, Chili's, Golden Corral, Kan-Ki Japanese, Krispy Kreme, Moe's SW Grill, Pizza Hut, other: Barnes&Noble, BooksAMillion, Fresh Mkt, Marshall's, Michael's, NAPA, Radio Shack, SteinMart, TJMaxx, U-Haul, Wal-Mart SuperCtr/24hr
3	Old St Augustine Rd, E...gas: BP, Shell, food: Burger King, Larry's Subs, Little Caesars, Little China, Mandarin Chinese, McDonald's, Taco Bell, lodging: Holiday Inn Express, other: $General, Food Lion, Publix/deli, W...gas: Gate/dsl, Kangaroo, food: Firehouse Subs, KFC/Pizza Hut, Subway, other: Lowe's Whse, Walgreens
61 a b	I-295 begins/ends on I-95, exit 337.

GEORGIA

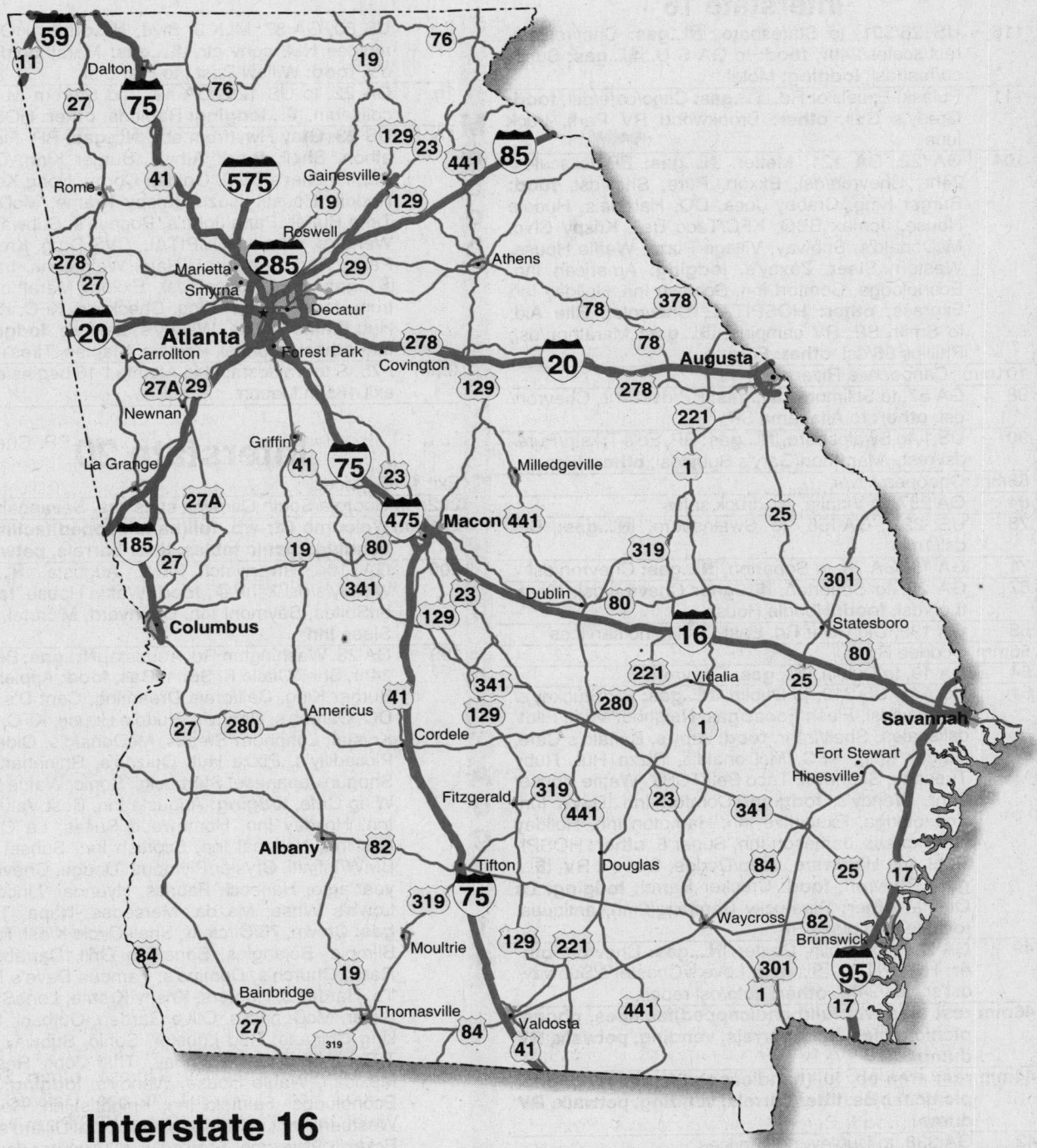

Interstate 16

GEORGIA

Interstate 16

E ⬆ W (direction indicator)

116	US 25/301, to Statesboro, **N**...**gas:** Chevron/dsl/rest/scales/24hr, **food:** to GA S U, **S**...**gas:** Sunoco/rest/dsl, **lodging:** Motel
111	Pulaski-Excelsior Rd, **S**...**gas:** Citgo/cafe/dsl, **food:** Grady's Grill, **other:** Brookwood RV Park, truck lube
104	GA 22, GA 121, Metter, **N**...**gas:** BP/dsl/scales/24hr, Chevron/dsl, Exxon, Pure, Shell/dsl, **food:** Burger King, Crabby Joes, DQ, Hardee's, Huddle House, Jomax BBQ, KFC/Taco Bell, Krispy Chic, McDonald's, Subway, Village Pizza, Waffle House, Western Steer, Zaxby's, **lodging:** American Inn, Econolodge, Comfort Inn, Scottish Inn, Holiday Inn Express, **other:** HOSPITAL, Chevrolet, Rite Aid, to Smith SP, RV camping, **S**...**gas:** Marathon/dsl, Phillips 66/dsl, **other:** Ford
101mm	Canoochee River
98	GA 57, to Stillmore, **S**...**gas:** BP/dsl/24hr, Chevron/dsl, **other:** to Altahama SP
90	US 1, to Swainsboro, **N**...**gas:** BP, Ed's Trkstp/Pure/dsl/rest., Marathon/Gary's Subs/dsl, **other:** tires
88mm	Ohoopee River
84	GA 297, to Vidalia, **N**...truck sales
78	US 221, GA 56, to Swainsboro, **N**...**gas:** BP/dsl(1mi)
71	GA 15, GA 78, to Soperton, **N**...**gas:** Chevron/dsl
67	GA 29, to Soperton, **S**...**gas:** Chevron/dsl, Marathon/dsl, **food:** Huddle House
58	GA 199, Old River Rd, East Dublin, no services
56mm	Oconee River
54	GA 19, to Dublin, **S**...**gas:** Chevron
51	US 441, US 319, to Dublin, **N**...**gas:** BP/Stuckey's/Subway/dsl, Flash Foods/gas, Neighbor's/dsl, Pilot/dsl/scales, Shell/24hr, **food:** Arby's, Buffalo's Café, Burger King, KFC, McDonald's, Pizza Hut, Ruby Tuesday, Shoney's, Taco Bell/TCBY, Waffle House/24hr, Wendy's, **lodging:** Comfort Inn, Day's Inn, Econolodge, Executive Inn, Hampton Inn, Holiday Inn Express, Jameson Inn, Super 8, **other:** HOSPITAL, Ace Hardware, Jeep/Dodge, Steve's RV, **S**...**gas:** Chevron, **food:** Cracker Barrel, **lodging:** La Quinta, **other:** Pinetucky Camping(2mi), antiques, to Little Ocmulgee SP
49	GA 257, to Dublin, Dexter, **N**...**gas:** Chevron, **other:** HOSPITAL, **S**...**gas:** Love's/Chester's/Subway/dsl/scales/24hr, **other:** auto/dsl repair
46mm	**rest area wb, full(handicapped)facilities, phone, picnic tables, litter barrels, vending, petwalk, RV dump**
44mm	**rest area eb, full(handicapped)facilities, phone, picnic tables, litter barrels, vending, petwalk, RV dump**
42	GA 338, to Dudley, no services
39	GA 26, to Cochran, Montrose, no services
32	GA 112, Allentown, **S**...**gas:** Chevron/dsl
27	GA 358, to Danville, no services
24	GA 96, to Jeffersonville, **N**...**gas:** Marathon/dsl, **S**...**gas:** BP/dsl/24hr, **food:** Huddle House/24hr, **lodging:** Best Value, **other:** to Robins AFB, museum
18	Bullard Rd, to Jeffersonville, Bullard, no services
12	Sgoda Rd, Huber, **N**...**gas:** Marathon/dsl
6	US 23, US 129A, East Blvd, Ocmulgee, **N**...**gas:** BP, **food:** DQ, **lodging:** Day's Inn(2mi), **other:** to airport, GA Forestry Ctr, **S**...**gas:** Chevron/Huddle House/dsl, Friendly Gus, **food:** Subway

(Side label: Dublin)

2	US 80, GA 87, MLK Jr Blvd, **N**...**other:** HOSPITAL, Ocmulgee NM, conv ctr, **S**...**gas:** Marathon/dsl, Saf-T-Oil/dsl, **food:** Willow Rest., to Hist Dist
1b	GA 22, to US 129, GA 49, 2nd St(from wb), **N**...**other:** coliseum, **S**...**lodging:** Ramada, **other:** HOSPITAL
1a	US 23, Gray Hwy(from eb), **N**...**gas:** BP, Flash/dsl, Marathon, Shell, **food:** Arby's, Burger King, China Buffet, DQ, Fincher's BBQ, Golden Corral, Hong Kong Express, Huddle House, Isuzu, Krispy Kreme, McDonald's, Old Time Buffet, Papa John's, Popeye's, Subway, Taco Bell, Wendy's, **other:** HOSPITAL, CVS Drug, Kroger, O'Reilly Parts, Radio Shack, U-Haul, Walgreens, transmissions, **S**...**gas:** BP, Conoco/dsl, Exxon, Marathon/dsl, Spectrum, **food:** Burger King, Checker's, KFC, Krystal, Pizza Hut, Waffle House, Wendy's, Zaxby's, **lodging:** Scottish Inn, **other:** Hyundai, Pontiac, Staples, Tires+
0mm	I-75, S to Valdosta, N to Atlanta. I-16 begins/ends on I-75, exit 165 in Macon.

(Side label: Macon)

Interstate 20

Exit #	Services
202mm	Georgia/South Carolina state line, Savannah River
201mm	**Welcome Ctr wb, full(handicapped)facilities, phone, vending, picnic tables, litter barrels, petwalk**
200	GA 104, Riverwatch Pkwy, Augusta, **N**...**gas:** Pilot/Wendy's/dsl/24hr/@, **food:** Waffle House, **lodging:** AmeriSuites, Baymont Inn, Courtyard, Microtel, Quality Inn, Sleep Inn
199	GA 28, Washington Rd, Augusta, **N**...**gas:** BP, Raceway/24hr, Shell/Circle K, Sprint Gas, **food:** Applebee's, A&W, Burger King, California Dreaming, Capt D's, Chick-fil-A, DQ, Damon's, Denny's, Huddle House, KFC, King Buffet, Krystal, Longhorn Steaks, McDonald's, Oldenburg Grill, Piccadilly's, Pizza Hut, Quizno's, Rhinehart's Seafood, Shogun Japanese, Starbucks, Sonic, Waffle House, Wild Wing Cafe, **lodging:** Augusta Inn, Best Value, Hampton Inn, Holiday Inn, Homewood Suites, La Quinta, Masters Inn, National Inn, Scottish Inn, Sunset Inn, **other:** BMW/Infiniti, Crysler/Plymouth/Dodge, Chevrolet, Goodyear/auto, Hancock Fabrics, Hyundai, Lincoln/Mercury, Lowe's Whse, Mazda, Mercedes, Napa, Toyota, **S**...**gas:** Crown, 76/Circle K, Shell/Circle K/dsl, **food:** Arby's, Blimpie, Bojangles, BoneFish Grill, Carrabba's, China Rest., Church's, Domino's, Famous Dave's BBQ, Fazoli's, Hardee's, Hooters, Krispy Kreme, LoneStar Café, LJ Silver, McDonald's, Olive Garden, Outback Steaks, Peking Chinese, Red Lobster, Sonic, Subway, Taco Bell, T-Bonz Steaks, TGIFriday, Thai Jong Rest., Vallarta Mexican, Waffle House, Wendy's, **lodging:** Amerihost, Econolodge, Fairfield Inn, Knight's Inn, Rodeway Inn, Westbank Inn, **other:** BooksAMillion, Dillard's, $General, Eckerd, Firestone, Fred's Drug, Goodyear/auto, Kroger/24hr, PepBoys, SteinMart, Tire Kingdom
196b	GA 232 W, **N**...**gas:** Enmark, Raceway, 76, **food:** Applebee's, Arby's, Bojangles, Burger King, Checker's, China Pearl, Golden Corral, Krispy Kreme, Krystal, Ruby Tuesday, Ryan's, Salsa's Grill, Schlotsky's, Waffle House, Wendy's, **lodging:** Comfort Inn, Howard Johnson, Suburban Lodge, Travelers Inn, **other:** BiLo Foods, $Tree, Home Depot, Lowe's Whse, Sam's Club, Tire Kingdom, Tires+, Walgreen, Wal-Mart/auto/24hr
196a	I-520, Bobby Jones Fwy, **S**...**gas:** BP, **other:** HOSPITAL, Best Buy, Circuit City, Office Depot, Target, to airport

(Side label: Augusta)

110

Interstate 20

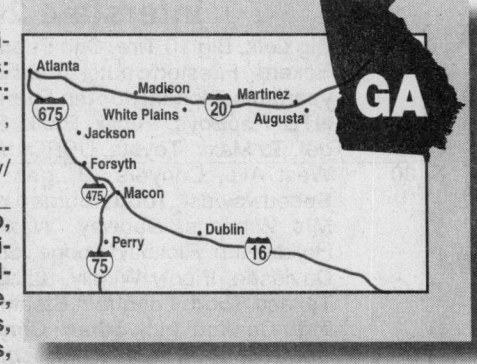

195	Wheeler Rd, ...**gas:** Chevron, ...**gas:** BP/dsl, 76/Circle K/Blimpie, Shell/Circle K/24hr, **food:** Blimpie, O'Charley's(1mi), **lodging:** Augusta Towers, Day's Inn, **other:** HOSPITAL, Harley-Davidson
194	GA 383, Belair Rd, to Evans, ...**gas:** Citgo/Taco Bell, Phillips 66/dsl, 76/Circle K/Blimpie/dsl, Srint Gas, **food:** Burger King, Popeye's, Waffle House, Wendy's, **lodging:** GA Inn, Villager Lodge, **other:** Food Lion, Funsville Park, ...**gas:** BP/DQ/Stuckey's/dsl, Phillips 66, Pilot/Subway/dsl/24hr/@, **food:** A&W/KFC, **Cracker Barrel**, Huddle House, Waffle House, **lodging:** Best Suites, Best Value Inn, Best Western, Econolodge, Hampton Inn, Holiday Inn, Motel 6, Quality Inn, Red Roof Inn, Super 8, Wingate Inn, **other:** Goodyear
190	GA 388, to Grovetown, ...**gas:** BP/dsl, **food:** Waffle House, **2 mi** ...**gas:** 76, **food:** KFC, McDonald's, Subway
189mm	weigh sta both lanes
183	US 221, to Harlem, Appling, ...**gas:** 76, **other:** Ford, Travel Country RV Ctr, ...**gas:** BP/dsl
182mm	**rest area both lanes, full(handicapped) facilities, phone, vending, picnic tables, litter barrels, RV dump, petwalk**
175	GA 150, ...**gas:** BP/USA Trkstp/dsl/rest./24hr/@, **lodging:** Day's Inn, **other:** to Mistletoe SP
172	US 78, GA 17, Thomson, ...**gas:** BP/dsl, Chevron/dsl, **food:** Waffle House, **other:** Chrysler/Dodge/Jeep, Ford/Mercury, Pontiac/GMC, ...**gas:** BP/DQ/dsl/24hr, Raceway/dsl, 76/Blimpie/Circle K, Texaco, **food:** Arby's, Burger King, Checker's, Denny's, Domino's, Hardee's, Krystal, LJ Silver, McDonald's, Mingwah Chinese, Pizza Hut, Taco Bell, Waffle House, Wendy's, Western Sizzlin, Zaxby's, **lodging:** Best Western, Econolodge, Holiday Inn Express, Howard Johnson, Scottish Inn, **other:** HOSPITAL, Advance Parts, AutoZone, BiLo Foods, Buick/Chevrolet/Cadillac, CVS Drug, Family$, Food Lion, K-Mart, Lowe's Whse, **Wal-Mart/MurphyUSA(2mi)**
165	GA 80, Camak
160	E Cadley Rd, Norwood
154	US 278, GA 12, Barnett
148	GA 22, Crawfordville, ...**gas:** BP/dsl, **other:** to Stephens SP, ...**gas:** Pure/dsl/rest./motel/repair/@
138	GA 77, GA 15, Siloam, ...**gas:** BP/dsl, Exxon, **other:** HOSPITAL
130	GA 44, Greensboro, weigh sta, ...**gas:** BP/dsl/24hr, Exxon/Subway, **food:** McDonald's, Pizza Hut, Subway, Waffle House, Wendy's, Zaxby's, **lodging:** Jameson Inn, Microtel, Thrift Court, **other:** HOSPITAL, $General, Motel(3mi), Pontiac/Chevrolet/Buick, ...**gas:** Chevron/dsl/24hr
121	to Lake Oconee, Buckhead, no services
114	US 441, US 129, to Madison, ...**gas:** Chevron/Subway, Citgo, Pilot/dsl/24hr/@, RaceTrac, Shell, **food:** Arby's, Burger King, KFC, Krystal, McDonald's, Pizza Hut, Waffle House, Wendy's, Zaxby's, **lodging:** Comfort Inn, Day's Inn, Hampton Inn, Holiday Inn, **other:** HOSPITAL, Advance Parts, Buick/Chevrolet/Pontiac/GMC, Eckerd, Ingles Foods, Lowe's Whse, **Wal-Mart Super Ctr/24hr**, ...**gas:** TA/BP/Popeye's/Taco Bell/dsl/@, FuelMart/dsl, Shell, **food:** Waffle House, **lodging:** Howard Johnson, Red Roof Inn, Super 8, Wingate Inn, **other:** RV camping
113	GA 83, Madison, ...**gas:** BP, **other:** HOSPITAL, st patrol, ...**gas:** Liberty/gas
108mm	**rest area wb, full (handicapped) facilities, phone, picnic tables, litter barrels, vending, RV dump, petwalk**
105	Rutledge, Newborn, ...**gas:** BP/dsl, **food:** Yesterday Café, **other:** Hard Labor Creek SP
103mm	**rest area eb, full(handicapped)facilities, phone, picnic tables, litter barrels, vending, RV dump, petwalk**
101	US 278, no services
98	GA 11, to Monroe, Monticello, **4 mi** ...**food:** Blue Willow Inn/rest., Log Cabin Rest., Sycamore Grill, ...**gas:** BP, Chevron/dsl
95mm	Alcovy River
93	GA 142, Hazelbrand Rd, ...**gas:** Exxon/dsl, Texaco/24hr, **food:** Little Philly's Hoagies, Waffle House, **lodging:** Comfort Inn, Jameson Inn, **other:** HOSPITAL
92	Alcovy Rd, ...**gas:** Chevron/dsl, Circle K/dsl, Texaco, **food:** BBQ, Chick-fil-A, Dunkin Doughnuts, Krystal, McDonald's, Pizza Hut, Waffle House, Wendy's, **lodging:** Best Western/rest., Cornerstone Lodge, Day's Inn, Econolodge, Super 8, ...HOSPITAL
90	US 278, GA 81, Covington, ...**gas:** BP, Citgo, QT, Raceway, Shell, **food:** Arby's, Bojangles, Burger King, Capt D's, Checker's, Chick-fil-A, DQ, Hardee's, KFC, Longhorn Steaks, Nagano Japanese, Papa John's, Shoney's, Taco Bell/Pizza Hut, Waffle House, Zaxby's, **other:** Advance Parts, Chevrolet, $General, Eckerd, Food Depot, GNC, Ingles Foods, K-Mart, Kroger/Fuel, SaveRite Foods, Tire Depot
88	Almon Rd, to Porterdale, ...**gas:** Chevron/dsl, ...**gas:** BP/Blimpie, Liberty, **food:** McDonald's, Subway(2mi), **other:** Riverside Estates RV Camp, transmissions/repair
84	GA 162, Salem Rd, to Pace, ...**gas:** BJ's Whse/gas, **other:** Saturn, Super 1 RV Ctr, ...**gas:** Chevron/24hr, Phillips 66, QT, RaceWay, **food:** Burger King, Chick-fil-A, Hardee's, Los Bravos Mexican, Subway, Waffle House, **other:** Advance Parts, $General, Eckerd, Food Depot, Ingles/gas, Medicine Shoppe
83mm	parking area wb
82	GA 138, GA 20, Conyers, ...**gas:** BJ's Gas, Citgo, QT, **food:** Blimpie, ChuckeCheese, Cracker Barrel, Don Pablo, Golden Corral, IHOP, O'Charley's, Outback Steaks, Red Lobster, Roadhouse Grill, Sonic, **lodging:** Conyers Inn, Day's Inn, Hampton Inn, Jameson Inn, La Quinta, Ramada Ltd, **other:** Chevrolet, Circuit City, Ford, Goody's, Home Depot, Kohl's, Michael's, NAPA, Office Depot, Old Navy, Staples, Tires+, U-Haul, Wal-Mart SuperCtr/24hr, ...**gas:** Chevron/24hr, Shell/dsl, **food:** Arby's, Applebee's, Burger King, Capt D's, Checker's, Chili's, Chick-fil-A, CiCi's, City Buffet, Donato's Pizza, Hooters, Huddle House, KFC, King Buffet, Krystal/24hr, LJ Silver, McDonald's, Milano Italian, Papa John's, Piccadilly's, Pizza Hut, Popeye's, Ruby Tuesday, Ryan's, Starbucks, Subway, Taco Bell, TCBY, Waffle House, Wendy's, **lodging:** InTown Inn, Suburban Lodge, **other:**

Thomson

Madison

GEORGIA

Interstate 20

	E ↑ ↓ **W** **Conyers**	Big Lots, Big 10 Tire, Cub Foods, Dodge, $General, Eckerd, Firestone/auto, Food Depot, GNC, Goodyear/auto, Honda, Jo-Ann Fabrics, Kroger/gas/24hr, NTB, PepBoys, Publix, Radio Shack, Rite Aid, Target, TJ Maxx, Toyota, USPO, mall
80		West Ave, Conyers, **N**...**gas:** Chevron, Shell/dsl, Speedway/dsl, **food:** Burger King, DQ, Domino's, Mrs Winner's, Subway, Waffle House, **lodging:** Holiday Inn, Richfield Lodge, **other:** Family$, Harley Davidson, Piggly Wiggly, **S**...**gas:** Exxon/dsl/24hr, Texaco, **food:** Longhorn Steaks, McDonald's, **lodging:** Comfort Inn, **other:** Chrysler/Plymouth/Jeep/Dodge, Ford, Hyundai, JustBrakes, Kia, Mitsubishi, Nissan, Suncoast RV Ctr
79mm		parking area eb
78		Sigman Rd, **N**...**gas:** Circle K/gas, **food:** Waffle House, **S**...**other:** Buick/Pontiac/GMC/Mazda, Crown RV Ctr, st police
75	**Lithonia**	US 278, GA 124, Turner Hill Rd, **N**...**gas:** BP/dsl, Citgo/dsl/24hr, RaceTrac, US Discount Gas, **S**... **food:** Applebee's, Atlanta Steaks, Bugaboo Steaks, Chick-fil-A, Firehouse Subs, KFC/Pizza Hut/Taco Bell, McDonald's, Olive Garden, Ruby Tuesday, Smokey Bones BBQ, Steak n' Shake, StoneCrest, Wendy's, Zaxby's, **lodging:** AmeriSuites, Fairfield Inn, Hilton Garden, **other:** Best Buy, Borders Books, Dillard's, Eckerd, JC Penney, Macey's, Marshall's, Panera Bread, Ross, Sam's Club, Sears/auto, Staples, Target, Tires+, mall
74		GA 124, Lithonia, **N**...**gas:** Chevron/24hr, Shell/24, **food:** Capt D's, KFC/Taco Bell, McDonald's, Pizza Hut, SoulFood Rest., Waffle House, Wendy's, **S**... **gas:** Citgo/dsl/24hr, **food:** DQ, Krystal/24hr, Dudley's Rest., Waffle House, **lodging:** Econolodge, Howard Johnson, Microtel, **other:** CVS Drug, $General, Piggly Wiggly, Radio Shack
71		Hillandale Dr, Farrington Rd, Panola Rd, **N**...**gas:** QT/dsl, Shell/dsl, **food:** Burger King, C'est Bon Cajun, Checker's, Cracker Barrel, HotWings/pizza, KFC, McDonald's, Mrs. Winner's, Waffle House, Wendy's, **lodging:** Holiday Inn Express, Motel 6, Super 8, **S**...**gas:** BP/dsl/24hr, Citgo, Shell, **food:** IHOP, New China, Philly Connection, Popeye's, Taco Bell/LJ Silver, Wendy's, **lodging:** Country Hearth, **other:** Lowe's Whse, NAPA AutoCare, Publix, Tires+, Wal-mart SuperCtr/24hr/gas, Walgreen
68		Wesley Chapel Rd, Snapfinger Rd, **N**...**gas:** Shell/dsl, Texaco, **food:** Blimpie, Capt D's, Checker's, Chick-fil-A, China Buffet, Church's, Hardee's, KFC, LJ Silver, Popeye's, Subway, Taco Bell, Waffle House, Wendy's, **lodging:** Day's Inn, Economy Inn, **other:** Ford, Goodyear/auto, Home Depot, Wal-Mart, **S**...**gas:** BP, Chevron/24hr, Mobil, Shell/dsl, **food:** Burger King, DQ, Dragon Chinese, JJ's Fish& Chicken, McDonald's, Pizza Hut, Popeye's, **lodging:** Super Inn
67b a		I-285, S to Macon, N to Greenville
66		Columbia Dr(from eb, no return), **N**...**gas:** Chevron
65		GA 155, Candler Rd, to Decatur, **N**...**gas:** BP/24hr, Citgo, **food:** Blimpie, Dundee's Café, LJ Silver, Pizza Hut, Popeye's, Red Lobster, Supreme Fish Delight, Wendy's, **lodging:** Discover Inn, Econolodge, Howard Johnson, **other:** A-1 Foods, CVS Drug, U-Haul, **S**...**gas:** BP, Chevron/24hr, Circle K, Shell/dsl, Stop&Go, **food:** Arby's, Burger King, Checker's, China Café, Church's, DQ, Dunkin Donuts, KFC/Piz-

	za Hut, McDonald's, Ruby Tuesday, Taco Bell, **lodging:** Best Western, Ramada Ltd, Sunset Lodge, **other:** Advance Parts, Firestone/auto, JC Penney, Kroger, Macy's, PepBoys, Winn-Dixie, mall
63	Gresham Rd, **N**...**gas:** Chevron, **S**...**gas:** BP/24hr/dsl, Phillips 66, Shell, **food:** Church's, **other:** auto repair
62	Flat Shoals Rd(from eb, no return), **N**...**gas:** Exxon
61b	GA 260, Glenwood Ave, **N**...**gas:** BP, Chevron, **food:** KFC, Wild Bean Cafe
61a	Maynard Terrace(from eb, no return), no services
60b a	US 23, Moreland Ave, **N**...**gas:** Exxon, **lodging:** Atlanta Motel, **S**...**gas:** Phillips 66/dsl, Shell, **food:** Checker's, KFC/Taco Bell, Krystal, LJ Silver, Louisiana Fish Gumbo, McDonald's, Mrs Winner's, Wendy's, Zesto, **other:** Checker
59b	Memorial Dr, Glenwood Ave(from eb), no services
59a	Cyclorama, **N**...**gas:** Chevron/Blimpie/dsl, Shell **food:** **other:** Confederate Ave Complex, MLK Site, **S**...**gas:** BP
58b	Hill St(from wb, no return), **N**...**gas:** Shell, **food:** Mrs. Winners
58a	Capitol St(from wb, no return), downtown, **N**...to GA Dome, **S**...Holiday Inn
57	I-75/85
56b	Windsor St(from eb), to Turner Field
56a	US 19, US 29, McDaniel St(eb only), **N**...**gas:** Chevron
55b	Lee St(from wb), Ft McPherson, **S**...**gas:** BP, **food:** Church's, Popeye's, Taco Bell
55a	Ashby St, **S**...**gas:** BP, Exxon, **food:** Church's, Popeye's, Stop 1 Food Court, Taco Bell, **other:** Eckerd, Family$, Sav-a-Lot Foods, Sears, mall
54	Langhorn St(from wb), to Cascade Rd, no services
53	MLK Dr, to GA 139, **N**...**gas:** Chevron/24hr, Shell/dsl/24hr, **S**...**gas:** BP, Right Stuf Gas, **other:** auto repair
52b a	GA 280, Holmes Dr, High Tower Rd, **S**...**gas:** Exxon/dsl, **food:** Church's, McDonald's, **other:** AutoZone
51b a	I-285, S to Montgomery, N to Chattanooga
49	GA 70, Fulton Ind Blvd, **N**...**gas:** Citgo/dsl/24hr, Texaco, **food:** Capt D's, Hardee's, Mrs Winners, Subway, Wendy's, **lodging:** Armada Inn, Fulton Inn, InTown Suites, Ramada Inn, Summit Inn, **S**...**gas:** BP, Chevron, Citgo/dsl, Texaco, **food:** Arby's, Grand Buffet, McDonald's, Temp's Chicken Fingers, Waffle House, **lodging:** Comfort Inn, Super 8, Travelodge, **other:** U-Haul
48mm	Chattahoochee River
47	Six Flags Pkwy(from wb), **N**...**gas:** BP, **food:** Church's, Waffle House, **lodging:** La Quinta, Mark Inn, Royal Inn, Sleep Inn, Wingate Inn, **other:** Arrowhead Camping, **S**...**lodging:** Comfort Inn, Day's Inn, **other:** Sam's Club, Six Flags Funpark
46b a	Riverside Parkway, **N**...**gas:** Citgo, Marathon, QT, **food:** Hong Kong Buffet, Waffle House, **lodging:** La Quinta, **other:** EZ Wash, **S**...**gas:** Pure, **food:** Wendy's, **lodging:** Day's Inn, Sleep Inn, Wingate Inn, **other:** Sam's Club, Six Flags Funpark
44	GA 6, Thornton Rd, to Lithia Springs, **N**...**gas:** BP/24hr, Exxon/dsl, RaceTrac, Shell, **food:** Burger King, Chick-fil-A, Domino's, Hardee's, IHOP, KFC, Krystal, McDonald's, Olive Tree, Ruby Tuesday, Shoney's, Subway, Taco Bell, Waffle House, Wendy's, **lodging:** Budget Inn, Comfort Inn, Hampton Inn, Knight's Inn, Suburban Lodge, **other:** HOSPITAL, Carmax, Chevrolet, Ford, Goodyear/auto, Honda, Kroger, Mazda, Nissan, Saturn, Tires+, VW, **S**...**gas:** Phillips 66,

Interstate 20

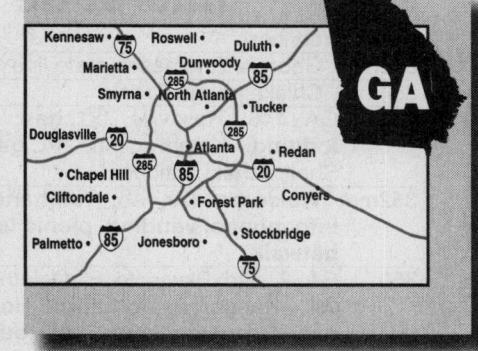

	food: Cracker Barrel, La Fiesta Mexican, **lodging:** Country Inn Suites, Courtyard, Fairfield Inn, Motel 6, SpringHill Suites, **other:** Buick/GMC, Chrysler/Plymouth/Jeep, Dodge, KOA, Mitsubishi, Toyota, Wal-Mart SuperCtr/24hr, to Sweetwater Creek SP
42mm	weigh sta eb
41	Lee Rd, to Lithia Springs, **N**...**gas:** Citgo/dsl, **food:** Hardee's, **other:** transmissions, **S**...**gas:** Chevron/dsl, Shell/Blimpie/dsl, **food:** Waffle House
37	GA 92, to Douglasville, **N**...**gas:** Chevron, Citgo, QT, RaceTrac, Shell/dsl/24hr, **food:** Arby's, BBQ, Burger King, Capt D's, Checker's, Chick-fil-A, Church's, Cracker Barrel, DQ, Kenny's Rest., KFC, Krystal, Longhorn Steaks, McDonald's, Monterrey Mexican, Mrs Winner's, Papa John's, Pizza Hut, Subway, Taco Bell, Waffle House, Wendy's, **lodging:** Bilbo's Motel, Comfort Inn, Country Inn Suites, Day's Inn, Holiday Inn Express, Ramada Ltd, Royal Inn, Super 8, **other:** HOSPITAL, Advance Parts, AutoZone, Big Lots, Checker, Dodge, $General, Kroger/24hr, NAPA, O'Riley Parts, Tires+ **S**...**gas:** QT, Texaco/dsl, **other:** Aamco
36	Chapel Hill Rd, **N**...HOSPITAL, **S**...**gas:** QT/24hr, Shell/dsl **food:** Applebee's, Arby's, Asia Buffet, Blimpie, China Buffet, Joe's Crabshack, McDonald's, Logan's Roadhouse, O'Charley's, Olive Garden, Outback Steaks, TGIFriday, Waffle House, **lodging:** Hampton Inn, InTown Suites, Super 8, **other:** Borders, Circuit City, Dillard's, Eckerd, Firestone/auto, Goody's, Marshall's, Michael's, Old Navy, Ross, Sears/auto, Target, mall
34	GA 5, to Douglasville, **N**...**gas:** RaceTrac, Texaco, **food:** Fire Mtn Grill, Hooters, Waffle House, Zaxby's, **lodging:** Holiday Inn Express, La Quinta, Lee's Motel, Sleep Inn, **other:** $Tree, Honda/Isuzu, Sam's Club, Wal-Mart SuperCtr/24hr, **S**...**gas:** Chevron/24hr, Circle K, Shell, **food:** Applebee's, Buffalo Wild Wings, Burger King, Chili's, Chick-fil-A, China Café, ChuckeCheese, CiCi's, DQ, Dunkin Doughnuts, El Rodeo Mexican, Golden Corral, IHOP, KFC, Krystal, LJ Silver, McDonald's, Papa John's, Pizza Hut, Red Lobster, Ruby Tuesday, Ryan's, Smokey Bones BBQ, Sonny's BBQ, Subway, Taco Bell, Waffle House, Wendy's, **lodging:** InTown Suites, **other:** Advance Parts, Best Buy, Big 10 Tire, Discount Tire, Eckerd, GNC, Goodyear/auto, Home Depot, Jo-Ann Crafts, K-Mart, Kroger, Lowe's Whse, Office Depot, PepBoys, Publix, Radio Shack, Rite Aid, U-Haul, USPO, Walgreen
30	Post Rd, **S**...**gas:** Shell/dsl
26	Liberty Rd, Villa Rica, **N**...**gas:** Shell/dsl, **food:** China Wok, Coffee Town USA, La Fiesta, Mex Grill, Waffle House, **other:** HOSPITAL, Publix, **S**...**gas:** Chevron, Wilco/Hess/Subway/Godfather's Pizza/dsl/24hr/@, **lodging:** American Inn
24	GA 101, GA 61, Villa Rica, **N**...**gas:** BP, Exxon, QT, RaceTrac, Shell/dsl, **food:** Arby's, Hardee's, KFC/Taco Bell, Krystal, McDonald's, Pizza Hut, Subway, Waffle House, Wendy's, **lodging:** Best Western, Days Inn, Hometown Lodge, Super 8, **other:**

	HOSPITAL, CVS Drug, Eckerd, Ingles Foods, Winn-Dixie, **S**...**gas:** QT, Shell/dsl, **food:** Burger King, Capt D's, Domino's, Papa John's, Philly Connection, Waffle House, Zaxby's, **other:** Chevrolet, $Tree, Wal-Mart SuperCtr/Subway/24hr, to W GA Coll
21mm	Little Tallapoosa River
19	GA 113, Temple, **N**...**gas:** Flying J/Conoco/Country Mkt/dsl/24hr/@, Pilot/Subway/Wendy's/dsl/24hr/@, Texaco, **food:** Hardee's, **other:** truckwash,
15mm	weigh sta wb
11	US 27, Bremen, Bowdon, **N**...**gas:** Texaco/dsl, RaceWay, SuperMart/dsl, **food:** Arby's, Chopsticks Chinese, KFC, McDonald's, Papa John's, Pizza Hut, Quizno's, Subway, Wendy's, Zaxby's, **lodging:** Day's Inn, Holiday Inn Express, Hampton Inn, Quality Inn, **other:** HOSPITAL, Advance Parts, $General, Ford, Wal-Mart SuperCtr/24hr/gas(1mi), **S**...**gas:** BP/dsl, Cowboy's, **food:** Waffle House, John Tanner SP
9	Waco Rd, **N**...Love's/Subway/dsl
5	GA 100, Tallapoosa, **N**...**gas:** Citgo/dsl/24hr, Exxon/dsl/24hr, **food:** Waffle House **other:** Big Oak RV park, **S**...**gas:** Citgo/Noble/Janet's Rest./dsl/24hr/@, Pilot/KFC/Taco Bell/dsl/24hr, **food:** DQ, Huddle House, **lodging:** Comfort Inn, **other:** to John Tanner SP
1mm	**Welcome Ctr eb, full(handicapped)facilities, phone, vending, picnic tables, litter barrels, petwalk**
0mm	Georgia/Alabama state line, Eastern/Central time zone

Interstate 59

Exit #	Services
	I-59 begins/ends on I-24, exit 167. For I-24, turn to Tennessee Interstate 24.
20mm	I-24, W to Nashville, E to Chattanooga
17	Slygo Rd, to New England, **W**...**gas:** Citgo/dsl, **other:** KOA(2mi)
11	GA 136, Trenton, **E**...**gas:** Chevron/dsl, Citgo/Kangaroo, Exxon/dsl, **food:** Asian Garden, Hardee's, McDonald's, Pizza Hut, Subway, **lodging:** Days Inn, **other:** Advance Parts, CVS Drug, Family$, Ingles, Plymouth/Dodge, to Cloudland Canyon SP, **W**...**gas:** BP, Citgo, **food:** Huddle House, Krystal, Little Caesar's, Taco Bell, Wendy's, **other:** BiLo, $General, Food Lion
4	Rising Fawn, **E**...**gas:** Citgo/24hr, **W**...**gas:** BP/dsl/24hr, Pilot/Subway/dsl/24hr/@, **other:** camping
0mm	Georgia/Alabama state line, eastern/central time zone

GEORGIA

Interstate 75

N ↕ S

Exit #	Services
355mm	Georgia/Tennessee state line
354mm	Chickamauga Creek
353	GA 146, Rossville, E...**gas:** BP/24hr, Chevron, **lodging:** Knight's Inn, W...**gas:** BP/Subway/dsl, Shell, **other:** antiques
352mm	**Welcome Ctr sb, full(handicapped)facilities, info, phone, vending, picnic tables, litter barrels, petwalk**
350	GA 2, Bfd Pkwy, to Ft Oglethorpe, E...**gas:** BP/dsl, Kangaroo, **lodging:** Hometown Inn, W...**gas:** RaceTrac/24hr, Shell, **other:** HOSPITAL, **1-3 mi** W...**gas:** Conoco/dsl/rest., **food:** BBQ Corral, Fazoli's(3mi), O'Charly's(3mi), Taco Bell(3mi), Zaxby's(3mi), **other:** KOA, Wal-Mart SuperCtr/24hr(3mi), to Chickamauga NP
348	GA 151, Ringgold, E...**gas:** BP/Subway/dsl, Conoco, Shell/dsl, **food:** Cracker Barrel, Hardee's, Krystal/24hr, KFC, Los Reyes Mexican, McDonald's, Pizza Hut, Ruby Tuesday, Taco Bell, Waffle House, **lodging:** Day's Inn, Holiday Inn Express, Red Roof Inn, Super 8, **other:** Advance Parts, CVS Drug, Chevrolet, Chrysler/Plymouth/Jeep, Family$, Ingles, RV camping, North GA RV Ctr, W...**gas:** BP, Kangaroo, Shell, **food:** Domino's, Wendy's, **lodging:** Comfort Inn, **other:** Food Lion, Ford, Northgate RV Ctr, Peterbilt
345	US 41, US 76, Ringgold, E...**gas:** BP, W...**gas:** Chevron, Cochran's/Exxon/dsl/rest./24hr/@, Kangaroo/Subway/dsl, **food:** Waffle House
343mm	weigh sta both lanes
341	GA 201, to Varnell, Tunnel Hill, W...**gas:** Chevron, Shell, **other:** carpet outlets
336	US 41, US 76, Dalton, Rocky Face, E...**gas:** Chevron/Blimpie, RaceTrac, Shell, **food:** Waffle House, **lodging:** Econolodge, Stay Lodge, **other:** HOSPITAL, Checker Parts, Home Depot, Wal-Mart SuperCtr/24hr/gas, W...**gas:** BP/dsl, Exxon, **food:** Denny's, Los Pablos Mexican, Wendy's, **lodging:** Best Western/rest., Motel 6, Royal Inn, Super 8, carpet outlets
333	GA 52, Dalton, E...**gas:** BP/dsl, Chevron/24hr, Kangaroo, RaceTrac/dsl, **food:** Applebee's, A&W/LJ Silver, Burger King, Capt D's, Chick-fil-A, CiCi's, Cracker Barrel, Dairy Queen, Fuddrucker's, IHOP, Jimmy's Rest., KFC, Lizzi's Deli, Longhorn Steaks, McDonald's, O'Charley's, Outback Steaks, Pizza Hut, Schlotsky's, Shoney's, Sonic, Steak'n Shake, Taco Bell, Waffle House, Wendy's, **lodging:** Best Inn, Days Inn, Hampton Inn, Travelodge, **other:** Chevrolet, Chrysler/Jeep, Ford, Harley-Davidson, Isuzu, K-Mart, Kroger, Mr Transmission, Tanger Outlets/famous brands, Walgreen, W...**food:** Chili's, Red Lobster, **lodging:** Comfort Inn, Courtyard, Country Inn Suites, Holiday Inn, Jameson Inn, Quality Inn, Ramada, Wingate Inn, **other:** NW GA Trade/Conv Ctr
328	GA 3, to US 41, E...**gas:** BP/dsl, Pilot/Arby's/dsl/scales/24hr, **food:** Antonio's Mexican, Waffle House, Wendy's, **lodging:** Super 8, W...carpet outlets
326	Carbondale Rd, E...**gas:** Chevron/dsl, Pilot/McDonalds/Subway/dsl/scales, W...**gas:** BP, Exxon
320	GA 136, to Lafayette, Resaca, E...**gas:** /Flying J/Cookery/dsl/LP/rest./24hr/@, **other:** truckwash, truck repair/parts
319mm	**Oostanaula River, rest area sb, full(handicapped) facilities, phone, vending, picnic tables, litter barrels, petwalk**
318	US 41, Resaca, E...**gas:** Hess/Wilco/DQ/Wendy's/dsl/24hr, **food:** Hardee's, **lodging:** Knight's Inn, W...**gas:** Shell/dsl, **lodging:** Best Inn, Budget Inn, Duffy's Motel, Smith Motel, Super 8
317	GA 225, to Chatsworth, E...New Echota HS, Vann House HS, W...**lodging:** Express Inn
315	GA 156, Redbud Rd, to Calhoun, E...**gas:** Citgo/dsl, Kangaroo, **food:** Waffle House, **other:** Food Lion, KOA(2mi), antiques, W...**gas:** BP/dsl, Liberty/Subway, Shell, **food:** Arby's, Shoney's, **lodging:** Ramada Ltd, **other:** HOSPITAL, Eckerd
312	GA 53, to Calhoun, E...**gas:** Shell/dsl, **food:** Cracker Barrel, Longhorn Steaks, **lodging:** Country Inn, Preferred Inn, Quality Inn, **other:** Prime Outlets/famous brands, W...**gas:** BP/Arby's, Chevron/dsl, Kangaroo, RaceWay, **food:** BJ's Rest., Bojangles, Burger King, Capt D's, Checker's, Chick-fil-A, China Cook, DQ, Domino's, Eastern Cafe, Fire Mtn Grill, Gondola Pizza, Huddle House, IHOP, KFC, Krystal/24hr, Little Caesar's, Lizzi's Seafood, LJ Silver/A&W, McDonald's, Papa's Pizza, Pizza Hut, Ruby Tuesday, Subway, Taco Bell, Zaxby's, **lodging:** Comfort Inn, Guest Inn, Hampton Inn, Holiday Inn Express, Jameson Inn, Royal Inn, **other:** Advance Parts, AutoZone, Chrysler/Jeep/Dodge, CVS Drug, $General, GNC, Goodyear/auto, Goody's, Home Depot, Ingles, Kroger/Starbucks/gas, Office Depot, Wal-Mart SuperCtr/gas/24hr
308mm	**rest area nb, full(handicapped)facilities, phone, picnic tables, litter barrels, vending, petwalk**
306	GA 140, Adairsville, E...**gas:** Cowboy's/dsl, Patty's/Citgo/dsl/24hr/@, QT/dsl/scales/24hrs, Shell, **food:** Cracker Barrel, Huddle House, Wendy's, W...**gas:** All American/dsl/scales, BP/dsl, Chevron, Exxon/dsl, **food:** Burger King, Hardee's, McDonald's, Taco Bell, Waffle House, Zaxby's, **lodging:** Best Western, Comfort Inn, Ramada Ltd, **other:** Harvest Moon RV Park
296	Cassville-White Rd, E...**gas:** Food & Fuel, Pilot/McDonald's/Subway/dsl/scales/@, Pure, TA/Burger King/Pizza Hut/Popeye's/Taco Bell/dsl/scales/24hr/@, Texaco/24hr, **lodging:** Sleep Inn, W...**gas:** Chevron, Citgo/dsl, Shell, **food:** Waffle House/24hr, **lodging:** Best Inn, Budget Host/rest., Howard Johnson, Red Carpet Inn, **other:** KOA
293	US 411, to White, E...**gas:** BP/dsl, Texaco, **lodging:** Scottish Inn, W...**gas:** Chevron/dsl, Citgo/dsl/24hr, Horizon/Backyard Burger/Pizza Hut/dsl, **food:** Roman's Steaks, Tom's Place Rest., Waffle House, **lodging:** Courtesy Inn, Holiday Inn/AJ's Cafe, **other:** RV camping, mineral museum, st patrol
290	GA 20, to Rome, E...**gas:** Chevron/Subway/dsl, Exxon/dsl, Kangaroo/dsl, **food:** Arby's, Fruit Jar Cafe, McDonald's, Wendy's, **lodging:** Best Western, Comfort Inn, Country Inn Suites, Econolodge, Motel 6, Ramada Ltd, Super 8, W...**gas:** BP, Shell, **food:** Cracker Barrel, Pappas Pizza House, Pruitt's BBQ, Shoney's, Waffle House, **lodging:** Day's Inn, Hampton Inn, **other:** HOSPITAL, RV camping(7mi), Wal-Mart SuperCtr/gas(1.5mi)
288	GA 113, Cartersville, **2 mi** W...**gas:** BP/dsl, Exxon/dsl, **food:** Applebee's, Burger King, Chick-fil-A, Krystal/24hr, Mrs Winner's, Pizza Hut, Red Lobster, Subway, Waffle House, **lodging:** Knight's Inn, Quality Inn, **other:** Kroger, to Etowah Indian Mounds(6mi)

Ringgold

Dalton

Calhoun

Interstate 75

286mm	Etowah River
285	Emerson, E...**gas**: Texaco/24hr, **lodging**: Red Top Mtn Lodge, **other**: to Allatoona Dam, to Red Top Mtn SP
283	Emerson Allatoona Rd, Allatoona Landing Resort, camping
280mm	Allatoona Lake
278	Glade Rd, to Acworth, E...**gas**: BP/dsl, Shell, **lodging**: Best Value, **other**: McKinney Camping(3mi), to Glade Marina, W...**gas**: Chevron, Petro, Shell, **food**: Bojangles, County Café, Hong Kong Chinese, KFC, Krystal, Papa John's, Pizza Hut, Subway, Taco Bell, Waffle House, **lodging**: Best Inn, **other**: AutoZone, BigLots, Eckerd, Ingles/cafe, K-Mart, NAPA, Radio Shack
277	GA 92, E...**gas**: BP, RaceTrac, **food**: Hardee's, Shoney's, Waffle House, **lodging**: Comfort Suites, Holiday Inn Express, Ramada Ltd, W...**gas**: Chevron/dsl, Shell/DQ/dsl, **food**: Bamboo Garden, Domino's, McDonald's, Ricardo's Mexican, Sonic, Waffle House, Wendy's, Zaxby's, **lodging**: Best Western, Day's Inn, Econolodge, Super 8, **other**: Advance Parts, CVS Drug, Goodyear/auto, Publix, Walgreen
273	Wade Green Rd, E...**gas**: BP, Pure, RaceTrac, **food**: Arby's, Burger King, China King, Dunkin Donuts, Las Palmas Mexican, McDonald's, Mrs Winners, Pizza Hut/Taco Bell, Subway, Waffle House, **lodging**: Travelodge, **other**: BigLots, Eckerd, Goodyear/auto, Publix, W...**gas**: Shell, Texaco/dsl, **food**: BBQ Street, Coldstone, Hunan Chinese, Johnny's Pizza/Subs, Starbucks, Wendy's, **other**: Kroger/gas, Walgreen
271	Chastain Rd, to I-575 N, E...**gas**: Chevron, **food**: Brewsters, Cracker Barrel, Dunkin Donuts, Firehouse Subs, Los Reyes, McCallister's Deli, O'Charley's, Panda Express, Sidelines Grille, ToGo's/Baskin Robbins, Zaxby's, Zucca Pizza, **lodging**: Best Western, Comfort Inn, Extended Stay America, Fairfield Inn, Residence Inn, Suburban Lodge, Super 8, **other**: Circuit City, Goodyear/auto, Outlets Ltd Mall, Wal-Mart/auto, funpark, W...**gas**: Citgo, Swifty Save Gas/Blimpie, Shell/dsl, **food**: Arby's, Mellow Mushroom, Mrs Winners, Quizno's, Waffle House/24hr, Wendy's, **lodging**: Country Inn Suites, SpringHill Suites, Sun Suites, **other**: museum
269	to US 41, to Marietta, E...**gas**: Chevron/24hr, Shell, Texaco/dsl, **food**: Applebee's, Burger King, Fuddrucker's, Longhorn Steaks, McDonald's, New China, Olive Garden, Pizza Hut, Red Lobster, Shogun Japanese, Smokey Bones, Starbucks, Subway, Waffle House, **lodging**: Comfort Inn, Econolodge, Holiday Inn Express, La Quinta, Penang, Provino's, Red Roof Inn, Super 8, **other**: Barnes&Noble, Big 10 Tire, Firestone/auto, Home Depot, Macy's, Marshall's, Publix, Sears/auto, TJ Maxx, mall, W...**gas**: BP, Exxon, **food**: Bahama Breeze, Bailey's Grill, Bugaboo, Carrabbas, Copelands Grill, Creek Steaks, Chick-fil-A, Chili's, ChuckeCheese, Coldstone, Golden Corral, Joe's Crabshack, Macaroni Grill, On-the-Border, Outback Steaks, Rafferty's, Starbucks, Steak'n Shake, Sweet Tomato, TGIFriday, Willy's Mexican, **lodging**: Day's Inn, Hampton Inn, Hilton Garden, Quality Inn, Wingate Inn, **other**: Best Buy, Borders, Buick/Pontiac/GMC, CarMax, Chevrolet, Circuit City,

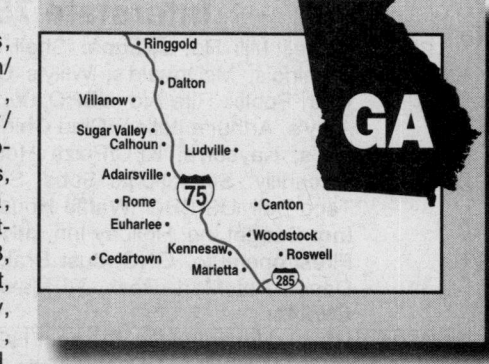

	Costco/gas, Ford/Lincoln/Mercury, Goodyear/auto, Jo-Anne Fabrics, Kia/Toyota, Nissan, Mitsubishi, NTB, Office Depot, Old Navy, PetsMart, Target, mall, to Kennesaw Mtn NP
268	I-575 N, GA 5 N, to Canton
267b a	GA 5 N, to US 41, Marietta
265	GA120, N Marietta Pkwy, W...**gas**: Chevron, Shell/dsl, **food**: Arbys, Bojangles, Chick-fil-A, KFC, **lodging**: Days Inn, Sun Inn, Suburban Lodge, Travelers Motel
263	GA 120, to Roswell, E...**gas**: Chevron/dsl/24hr, QT, Texaco/24hr, **other**: cleaners, W...**gas**: Exxon/dsl, RaceTrac, **food**: Applebee's, Capt D's, China Kitchen, Dairy Queen, Hardee's, Haveli Rest., Piccadilly's, Subway, **lodging**: Best Western, Crowne Plaza, Fairfield Inn, Hampton Inn, Marietta Motel, Ramada Ltd, Regency Inn, Super 8, Wyndham Garden, **other**: DENTIST, U-Haul
261	GA 280, Delk Rd, to Dobbins AFB, E...**gas**: Exxon, RaceTrac, Shell/McDonald's/24hr, **food**: CC Cafeteria, China Wok, Hardee's, KFC/Taco Bell, Murphy's Deli, Ruby Tuesday, Spaghetti Whse, **lodging**: Budget Inn, Courtyard, Drury Inn, Motel 6, Scottish Inn, Sleep Inn, Super 8, Travelers Inn, **other**: Publix, W...**gas**: BP, Chevron/24hr, **food**: Cracker Barrel, D&B Rest., Waffle House, **lodging**: Best Inn, Comfort Inn, Days Inn, Fairfield Inn, Holiday Inn, La Quinta, Quality Inn, Wingate Inn
260	Windy Hill Rd, to Smyrna, E...**gas**: BP, **food**: Boston Mkt, Famous Dave's, Fuddrucker's, Houston's Rest., Jersey Mike's Subs, NY Pizza, Pappasito's Cantina, Pappadeaux Seafood, Philly Cafe, Salgrosso Brazilian, , Schlotsky's, Starbucks, Subway, TGIFriday, **lodging**: Econolodge, Extended Stay Deluxe, Hilton Garden, Hyatt, Marriott, Studio Lodge, **other**: CVS Drug, W...**gas**: Chevron, Citgo, Shell, **food**: Arby's, Chick-fil-A, Fatburger, Halftime Grill, McDonald's, Panda Express, Popeye's, Starbucks, Waffle House, Wendy's, **lodging**: Best Western, Country Inn Suites, Courtyard, Day's Inn, DoubleTree, Hilton, Masters Inn, Red Roof Inn, **other**: HOSPITAL, Target
259b a	I-285, W to Birmingham, E to Greenville, Montgomery
258	Cumberland Pkwy, W...**food**: Doc Green's Rest., Hooters, Moe's SW Grill, Shane's Ribshack, Subway
257mm	Chattahoochee River
256	to US 41, Northside Pkwy
255	US 41, W Paces Ferry Rd, E...**gas**: Chevron, Shell/dsl, **food**: Blue Ridge Grill, Caribou Coffee, Chick-fil-A, Houston's Rest., McDonald's/playplace, OK Café/24hr, Pero's Pizza, Starbucks, Steak'n Shake, Taco Bell, Willy's Rest., **other**: HOSPITAL, Ace Hardware, CVS Drug, Publix, W...**gas**: Exxon/24hr
254	Moores Mill Rd

GEORGIA
Interstate 75

252b Howell Mill Rd, **E**...**gas:** Shell, **food:** Chick-fil-A, Domino's, McDonald's, Willy's Grill, **other:** Goodyear, Publix, Rite Aid, USPO, **W**...**gas:** Shell, **food:** Arby's, Arthur's Italian, Chin Chin Chinese, Einstein Bro's, Kayson's, KFC/Pizza Hut, Mexican, Rest., Piccadilly, Sensational Subs, Starbucks, Subway, Taco Bell, US BBQ, Waffle House, Wendy's, **lodging:** Budget Inn, Holiday Inn, **other:** Ace Hardware, Firestrone/auto, GNC, Just Brakes, Kroger, Office Depot, PetsMart, Ross, TJ Maxx, Wal-Mart Super Ctr/24hr

252a US 41, Northside Dr, **E**...**gas:** HOSPITAL, **W**...**gas:** Shell, **food:** Krystal/24hr, Little Zio's, McDonald's, Waffle House, **lodging:** Day's Inn

251 I-85 N, to Greenville

250 Techwood Dr(from sb), 10th St, 14th St, **E**...**lodging:** Travelodge

249d 10th St, Spring St(from nb), **E**...**gas:** BP, Chevron/24hr, **food:** Checker's, Domino's, Pizza Hut, The Varsity, **lodging:** Fairfield Inn, Regency Suites, Renaissance Hotel, Residence Inn, **W**...**food:** McDonald's, **lodging:** Courtyard, Comfort Inn, **other:** HOSPITAL, to GA Tech

249c Williams St(from sb), downtown, to GA Dome

249b Pine St, Peachtree St(from nb), downtown, **W**... **lodging:** Hilton, Marriott

249a Courtland St(from sb), downtown, **W**...**lodging:** Hilton, Marriott, **other:** GA St U

248d Piedmont Ave, Butler St(from sb), downtown, **W**... **lodging:** Courtyard, Fairfield Inn, Radisson, **other:** HOSPITAL, Ford, MLK NHS

248c GA 10 E, Intn'l Blvd, downtown, **W**...**lodging:** Hilton, Holiday Inn, Marriott Marquis, Radisson

248b Edgewood Ave(from nb), **W**...**other:** HOSPITAL, downtown, hotels

248a MLK Dr(from sb), **W**...st capitol, to Underground Atlanta

247 I-20, E to Augusta, W to Birmingham

246 Georgia Ave, Fulton St, **E**...**lodging:** Comfort Inn, Country Inn& Suites, Holiday Inn, **other:** stadium, **W**...**gas:** BP, **food:** KFC, **other:** to Coliseum, GSU

245 Ormond St, Abernathy Blvd, **E**...**lodging:** Comfort Inn, Country Inn& Suites, **other:** stadium, **W**...st capitol

244 University Ave, **E**...**gas:** Chevron, Exxon, **other:** NAPA, **W**...**food:** Mrs Winner's

243 GA 166, Lakewood Fwy, to East Point

242 I-85 S, to airport

241 Cleveland Ave, **E**...**gas:** BP, Chevron, **food:** Checker's, Church's, McDonald's, Subway, **lodging:** Palace Inn, **other:** Advance Parts, K-Mart, **W**...**gas:** Shell, Marathon, Phillips 66, Texaco, **food:** Blimpie, Burger King, Krystal/24hr, Mrs Winners, **lodging:** American Inn, Day's Inn, **other:** CVS Drug, Kroger

239 US 19, US 41, **E**...**gas:** Chevron/dsl, **food:** Waffle House, **other:** USPO, **W**...**gas:** Texaco, **food:** IHOP, McDonald's, Wendy's, **lodging:** Best Western, to airport

238b a I-285 around Atlanta

237a GA 85 S(from sb), **W**...**food:** Denny's, **lodging:** Burger King, McDonald's, Waffle House, **lodging:** Day's Inn, Day's Lodge

237 GA 331, Forest Parkway, **E**...**gas:** Chevron, Exxon, Happy Store/gas, Shell, **food:** Burger King, McDonald's, Waffle House, **lodging:** Econolodge, Motel 6, Rodeway Inn, **other:** Farmer's Mkt, Chevrolet, **W**... **lodging:** Day's Inn, Ramada Ltd

235 US 19, US 41, GA 3, Jonesboro, **E**...**gas:** Chevron/dsl, Exxon/Subway/dsl, Phillips 66, Shell(1mi), Valero, **food:** Waffle House, **lodging:** Super 8, Travelodge, **other:** Atlanta RV Ctr, **W**...**gas:** FuelMart/dsl, Marathon, RaceTrac/dsl, Shell, Texaco, **food:** Checker's, Dunkin Donuts, Folks Rest., Johnny's Pizza, KFC, Krystal, McDonald's, Red Lobster, Waffle House, **lodging:** Best Value, Comfort Inn, Day's Inn, Econolodge, Holiday Inn Express, **other:** HOSPITAL, $General, Dodge, Office Depot

233 GA 54, Morrow, **E**...**gas:** BP, Chevron, Citgo, Conoco/dsl, Phillips 66/dsl, **food:** Cracker Barrel, Krystal 24hr, Mrs Winner's, Taco Bell, Waffle House, Walter's Cafe, Wendy's, **lodging:** Best Western, Days Inn, Drury Inn, Fairfield Inn, Red Roof Inn, **other:** Wal-Mart SuperCtr/24hr/gas, **W**...**gas:** Exxon/24hr, RaceTrac, Shell/dsl, **food:** Bennigan's, China Café, Indian Cuisine, Japanese Rest., KFC, McDonald's, Pizza Hut, Shoney's, Subway, Waffle House, **lodging:** Hampton Inn, Quality Inn, **other:** Acura/Cadillac, Best Buy, Chevrolet, Harley-Davidson, HobbyLobby, JiffyLube, Kroger, Mazda, Nissan, TJ Maxx, Toyota, mall

231 Mt Zion Blvd, **E**...**gas:** QT, **other:** Chrysler/Dodge/Jeep, Ford, Honda, **W**...**gas:** Chevron, Citgo, Conoco, Exxon/dsl, Texaco/dsl, **food:** Arby's, Blimpie, Brewster's, Chick-fil-A, Chili's, Del Taco, Longhorn Steaks, McDonald's, Mo-Joe's, Mrs Winner's, On-the-Border, Papa John's, Pizza Hut, Steak'n Shake, Subway, TGIFriday, Waffle House, Wendy's, **lodging:** Country Inn&Suites, Extended Stay America, Howard Johnson Express, Sleep Inn, Sun Suites, **other:** Best Buy, Circuit City, Goody's, Home Depot, Michael's, NTB, Old Navy, Publix, Target

228 GA 54, GA 138, Jonesboro, **W**...**gas:** Exxon, Raceway/24hr, **food:** Applebee's, Arby's, Broadway Diner, Burger King, Chick-fil-A, ChinChin Chinese, CiCi's, DQ, Folk's Rest., Frontera Mexican, Golden Corral, Honeybaked Ham, IHOP, KFC, Krystal, LJ Silver, McDonald's, Piccadilly's, Philly Connection, Shoney's, Subway, Taco Bell, Taco Mac, Tokyo Seafood, Waffle House, Wendy's, **lodging:** Best Western, Day's Inn, Comfort Inn, Holiday Inn, La Quinta, Hampton Inn, Motel 6, Red Roof Inn, **other:** HOSPITAL, GNC, Goodyear, K-Mart, Kroger, Lowes Whse, Office Depot, Tires+, **W**...**gas:** BP/24hr, Chevron, PaceCar/dsl, Sunoco/Wendy's, **food:** Ranchero's Mexican, Waffle House, **other:** CarMax, Chrysler/Plymouth/Jeep, CVS Drug, Kohl's

227 I-675 N, to I-285 E(from nb)

224 Hudson Bridge Rd, **E**...**gas:** BP, Citgo/24hr, Phillips 66, Texaco/dsl, **food:** Buckhead Steaks, Chick-fil-A, China Wok, DQ, Dunkin Donuts, McDonald's, Outback Steaks, Subway, Waffle House, Wendy's, **lodging:** AmeriHost Inn, Microtel, **other:** HOSPITAL, **W**... **gas:** Phillips 66, QT, **food:** Domino's, Southern Skillet, Subway, Teddy's Diner/24hr, **lodging:** Super 8, **other:** Kroger, Walgreen, Wal-Mart SuperCtr/24hr

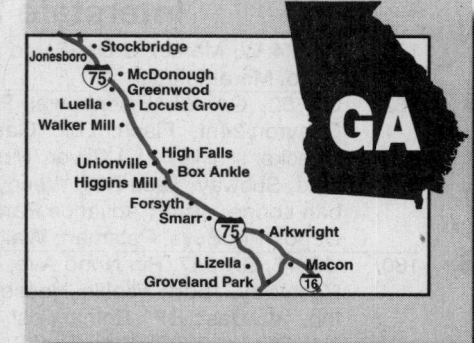

222 Jodeco Rd, E...**gas:** BP, Citgo/24hr, Texaco, **food:** Hardee's, Waffle House, W...**gas:** BP, Chevron/dsl, **food:** Blimpie, **other:** Atlanta So. RV Camping, KOA

221 Jonesboro Rd, E...**gas:** BP, Citgo/dsl, W...**food:** Burger King, Chili's, Cici's Pizza, Golden Corral, Hooter's, Logan's Roadhouse, Longhorn Steaks, McDonald's, O'Charley's, Red Lobster, Subway, Truit's Grill, Wendy's, Woody's BBQ, **other:** Belk, Best Buy, Books-A-Million, BJ's Whse/gas, Home Depot, Marshall's, Radio Shack, Ross, Sam's Club/ gas, Staples, Target, flea market, KOA

218 GA 20, GA 81, McDonough, E...**gas:** BP, Murphy USA, Phillips 66, QT, Texaco, **food:** Applebee's, Arby's, Burger King, China Star, Cracker Barrel, DQ, KFC, IHOP, McDonald's, Mrs Winner's, Pizza Hut, Ruby Tuesday, Ryan's, Taco Bell, Waffle House, Wendy's, Zaxby's, **lodging:** Best Inn, Budget Inn, Economy Inn, Hampton Inn, Super 8, **other:** Lowe's Whse, Wal-Mart SuperCtr/24hr, W...**gas:** Citgo/dsl, Shell/24hr, **food:** DQ, Joey's Grill, Subway, Waffle House, **lodging:** Comfort Inn, Econolodge, Holiday Inn Express, Master's Inn, **other:** Toyota

216 GA 155, McDonough, Blacksville, E...**gas:** Shell, Sunoco/Backyard Burger, Texaco/dsl, **food:** Blimp-ie, **lodging:** Best Value, Budget Inn, Day's Inn, Roadway Inn, **other:** Buick/Pontiac, W...**gas:** BP/ dsl, Chevron, Citgo/dsl/24hr, Mystik/dsl, **food:** Da Vinci's Pizza, El Arriero, Krystal, Milan's Pizza, Sub-way, UMI Steaks, Waffle House, **lodging:** Country Inn&Suites, Quality Inn, Sleep Inn

212 to US 23, Locust Grove, E...**gas:** BP/McDonald's/ dsl, Chevron/Burger King, Citgo/dsl, Exxon/dsl, Lib-erty Gas/Subway, Shell/dsl, **food:** Country Steaks, Denny's, Huddle House, KFC/Pizza Hut/Taco Bell, Sunrise China, Waffle House, Wendy's, Zaxby's, **lodging:** Econolodge, Executive Inn, Ramada Ltd, Red Roof Inn, **other:** Ingles/gas, Napa, Tanger Outlet/famous brands, W...**gas:** Chevron/dsl, Citgo/ DQ/dsl, Exxon/dsl, **lodging:** Scottish Inn, Sundown Lodge, Super 8

205 GA 16, to Griffin, Jackson, E...**gas:** BP, **lodging:** Simmon's BBQ, **other:** Forest Glen RV Park, W... **gas:** BP, Chevron/dsl

201 GA 36, to Jackson, Barnesville, E...**gas:** Love's/ McDonald's/dsl/grill/scales/24hr, TA/Subway/Taco Bell/dsl/scales/24hr/@, Wilco/Hess/DQ/Stuckey's/ Wendy's/dsl/scales/24hr/@, **other:** Blue Beacon, W...**gas:** BP/dsl, ⛵/Flying J/Conoco/Cookery/dsl/ LP/24hr/@, **other:** Sagon RV Ctr, Speedco Lube

198 Highfalls Rd, E...**gas:** Exxon(1mi), **lodging:** High Falls Lodge, **other:** High Falls SP, W... High Falls RV Park

193 Johnstonville Rd, E...**gas:** BP

190mm weigh sta both lanes

188 GA 42, E...**gas:** Shell/24hr, **lodging:** Best Western, Budget Inn, **other:** to Indian Springs SP, RV camp-ing

187 GA 83, Forsyth, E...**lodging:** Econolodge, New Forsyth Inn, Regency Inn, W...**gas:** BP, Citgo/dsl, Marathon, Shell, **food:** Burger King, Capt D's, China Inn, DQ, Hardee's, McDonald's, Pizza Hut, Subway, Taco Bell, Waffle House, Wendy's, **lodging:** Day's Inn, Tradewinds Motel, **other:** Advance Parts, CVS Drug, Family$, Freshway Foods, Wal-Mart

186 Tift College Dr, Juliette Rd, Forsyth, E...Jarrell Plantation HS, KOA, W...**gas:** BP/ dsl, Chevron, Marathon, **food:** Waffle House, **lodg-ing:** Holiday Inn/rest., Hol-iday Inn Express, Super 8, **other:** HOSPITAL, Chrys-ler/Dodge, CVS Drug, Ingles/Deli

185 GA 18, E...Forsyth RV Park, W...**gas:** BP/Stuckeys/ 24hr, Shell/dsl, **food:** Shoney's, **lodging:** Comfort Inn, **other:** Ford, st patrol

181 Rumble Rd, to Smarr, E...**gas:** BP/dsl/24hr, Shell/dsl/ 24hr

179mm rest area sb, full(handicapped)facilities, phone, vending, picnic tables, litter barrels, petwalk

177 I-475 S around Macon(from sb)

175 Pate Rd, Bolingbroke(from nb, no re-entry)

172 Bass Rd, E...**food:** Pig in a Pit BBQ, McDonald's, Quizno's, Starbucks, **other:** Bass Pro Shop, fun-park, W...**gas:** Citgo/dsl/24hr, **other:** to Museum of Arts&Sciences

171 US 23, to GA 87, Riverside Dr, E...**gas:** BP, Marathon/ dsl, Shell, **food:** Jock&Jill's Grill, **other:** Acura, KIA, Lincoln/Mercury, Mercedes, Volvo, W...**food:** Backyard Burger, Cracker Barrel, Hooters, **other:** Lexus, Toyota, same as 169 W

169 to US 23, Arkwright Dr, E...**gas:** Shell/24hr, **food:** Car-rabba's, Logan's Roadhouse, Outback Steaks, Waffle House, Wager's Grill, **lodging:** Comfort Inn, Courtyard, Fairfield Inn, Hampton Inn, Holiday Inn, La Quinta, Red Roof Inn, Residence Inn, Super 8, **other:** Buick/Cadil-lac/GMC/Saturn, W...**gas:** BP/dsl, Chevron/24hr, Mar-athon/dsl, **food:** Arby's, Backyard Burger, Burger King, Chick-fil-A, Chili's, Cheddar's, Cracker Barrel, Dunkin Donuts, El Azteca Mexican, 5 Guys Burgers, Giusep-pi's Italian, Hooters, KFC, Krystal, Longhorn Steaks, Mandarin Chinese, McDonald's, Mikata Japanese, Papa John's, Papoulis' Gyros, Panera Bread, Pizza Hut, Shoki Japanese, Starbucks, Steak'n Shake, Steve B's Pizza, Subway, Taco Bell, Waffle House, **lodging:** Best Inn, Extended Stay Deluxe, Holiday Hotel, Macon Hotel, Quality Inn, Travelodge, Wingate Inn, **other:** HOSPITAL, Ace Hardware, Barnes&Noble, Chrys-ler/Jeep/Dodge, $Tree, GNC, K-Mart, Kroger, Mazda, Pontiac, Publix, Radio Shack, same as 167

167 GA 247, Pierce Ave, E...**lodging:** Days Inn, W...**gas:** BP/dsl, Chevron, Conoco, Exxon, Marathon/Subway/ dsl, Shell, **food:** Applebee's, CJ's Grill, Loco's Deli, Pier 97 Seafood, Pizza Hut, Red Lobster, San Marcos Mexican, S&S Cafeteria, Shogun Japanese, SteakOut Rest., Waffle House, Wendy's, **lodging:** Best Western/ rest., Comfort Inn, Holiday Inn Express, Howard John-son, Motel 6, **other:** Eckerd, ExperTire, Goodyear/ auto

165 I-16 E, to Savannah

164 US 41, GA 19, Forsyth Ave, Macon, E...**food:** Sid's Rest., **other:** hist dist, W...**gas:** BP, **other:** HOSPITAL, museum

GEORGIA

Interstate 75

N ↕ S

163 GA 74 W, Mercer U Dr, E...to Mercer U, W...**gas:** Citgo, Marathon/dsl

162 US 80, GA 22, Eisenhower Pkwy, W...**gas:** BP, Chevron/24hr, Flash, Lolo Gas, **food:** Capt D's, Checker's, IHOP, LJ Silver, McDonald's, Mrs Winners, Subway, Taco Bell, Wendy's, **lodging:** Suburban Lodge, **other:** Advance Parts, Goodyear, Office Depot, PepBoys, Petsmart, Walgreens

160 US 41, GA 247, Pio Nono Ave, E...**gas:** Exxon/dsl, RaceWay, **food:** Waffle House, **lodging:** Masters Inn, W...**gas:** BP, Enmark/dsl, **food:** Arby's, DQ, Hot Wings, KFC, King Buffet, McDonald's, Pizza Hut, Subway, Waffle House, **other:** Advance Parts, $General, O'Reilly Parts, Piggly Wiggly, Roses, USPO, same as 162

156 I-475 N around Macon(from nb)

155 Hartley Br Rd, E...**gas:** BP/KFC/Pizza Hut/dsl/24hr, Marathon/dsl, **food:** Wendy's, **other:** Kroger/gas, W...**gas:** Citgo, **food:** Subway, Waffle House, **lodging:** Ambassador Inn

149 GA 49, Byron, E...**gas:** Chevron/dsl, Shell/24hr, **food:** Burger King, China Buffet, Denny's, Krystal, McDonald's, Pizza Hut, Pizza Pub, Shoney's, Waffle House, Zaxby's, **lodging:** Best Western, Holiday Inn Express, Super 8, **other:** New Castle RV Ctr, Peach Stores/famous brands, antiques, W...**gas:** BP, Citgo/dsl/24hr, Flash/dsl, Marathon, RaceWay, **food:** Capt Jack's Crabshack, DQ, El Ranchito Mexican, Huddle House, Popeye's, Standard BBQ, Subway, Waffle House, **lodging:** Comfort Inn, Day's Inn, Econolodge, Passport Inn, **other:** CarQuest, Chevrolet, Ford, NAPA, Sun Coast RV Ctr

146 GA 247, to Centerville, E...**gas:** Exxon, Flash/dsl, Shell, **food:** Subway, Waffle House, **lodging:** Budget Inn, Econolodge, **other:** HOSPITAL, to Robins AFB, museum, W...**gas:** Pilot/Arby's/dsl/24hr/@, **lodging:** Royal Inn

144 Russel Pkwy, E...museum

142 GA 96, Housers Mill Rd, E...**gas:** Chevron/dsl, **other:** Ponderosa RV Park

138 Thompson Rd, E...**gas:** Texaco/Chester Fried/dsl, **other:** HOSPITAL, W...airport

Perry

136 US 341, Perry, E...**gas:** Amoco, Chevron/24hr, Flash, Shell/dsl, **food:** Arby's, Burger King, Capt D's, Chick-fil-A, Hardee's, Hong Kong Buffet, KFC, Krystal, McDonald's, Pizza Hut, Red Lobster, Sonny's BBQ, Subway, Taco Bell, Waffle House, Wendy's, Zaxby's, **lodging:** Best Inn, Great Inn, Hampton Inn, Howard Johnson, Jameson Inn, Super 8, **other:** HOSPITAL, Advance Parts, $Tree, Fred's Drug, GNC, Kroger, NAPA, Radio Shack, Wal-Mart SuperCtr/24hr, W...**gas:** BP, Chevron, Conoco/dsl, RaceWay/24hr, **food:** Angelina's Café, Applebee's, Green Derby Rest., **lodging:** Comfort Inn, Day's Inn, Econolodge, Guesthouse Inn, Holiday Inn/rest., Knight's Inn, Passport Inn, **other:** Ford, Crossroads Camping

135 US 41, GA 127, Perry, E...**gas:** BP/dsl, Exxon, Flash, Shell, **food:** Cracker Barrel, Subway, Waffle House, **lodging:** Day's Inn, Red Carpet Inn, Relax Inn, Scottish Inn, Travelodge, **other:** Plymouth/Jeep/Dodge, GA Nat Fair, W...**other:** GA Patrol, Fair Harbor RV Park

134 South Perry Pkwy, W...Chevrolet/Buick/Pontiac/GMC, Priester's Pecans

127 GA 26, Henderson, E...Twin Oaks Camping, W...**gas:** Chevron, **lodging:** Henderson Lodge

122 GA 230, Unadilla, E...**gas:** Dixie/dsl, **other:** Chevrolet/Ford, W...**gas:** Pure, **lodging:** Red Carpet Inn

121 US 41, Unadilla, E...**gas:** BP, Shell/DQ/Stuckey's, **food:** Don Ponchos Mexican, Subway, **lodging:** Economy Inn, Scottish Inn, **other:** $General, Piggly Wiggly, Southern Trails RV Resort, auto/tire repair, W...**gas:** Citgo/dsl/rest./24hr/@, **lodging:** Regency Inn

118mm rest area sb, full(handicapped)facilities, phone, vending, picnic tables, litter barrels, petwalk, RV dump

117 to US 41, Pinehurst, W...**gas:** BP/Pinehurst/cafe/dsl/scales/24hr, **lodging:** Budget Inn

112 GA 27, Vienna, W...**gas:** BP/dsl, Marathon

109 GA 215, Vienna, E...**gas:** BP/dsl, W...**gas:** Citgo/dsl, El Cheapo, Shell, **food:** Huddle House/24hr, Popeye's, **lodging:** Knight's Inn, **other:** HOSPITAL

108mm rest area nb, full(handicapped)facilities, phone, vending, picnic tables, litter barrels, petwalk, RV dump

Cordele

104 Farmers Mkt Rd, Cordele, E...**lodging:** Cordele Inn

102 GA 257, Cordele, W...**food:** Pecan House, **other:** HOSPITAL

101 US 280, GA 90, Cordele, E...**gas:** Exxon/dsl, Pilot/Arby's/dsl/scales/24hr/@, Shell, Texaco, **food:** Denny's, Golden Corral, Waffle House, **lodging:** Day's Inn, Fairfield Inn, Ramada Inn, **other:** Ford/Lincoln/Mercury, st patrol, W...**gas:** BP/dsl, Chevron/24hr, Liberty, RaceWay/24hr, **food:** Burger King, Capt D's, Compadres Mexican, Cracker Barrel, Cutter's Steaks, DQ, FarmHouse Buffet, Hardee's, KFC/Pizza Hut/Taco Bell, Krystal/24hr, McDonald's, Shoney's, Subway, Wendy's, Zaxby's, **lodging:** Auburn Inn, Comfort Inn, Deluxe Inn, Econolodge, Hampton Inn, Holiday Inn Express, Premier Inn, Super 8, **other:** CVS Drug, $General, Family$, Harvey's Foods, Radio Shack, Wal-Mart SuperCtr/24hr, to Veterans Mem SP, J Carter HS

99 GA 300, GA/FL Pkwy, W...to Chehaw SP

97 to GA 33, Wenona, E...**lodging:** Royal Inn, **other:** Cornel RV Park, dsl repair, W...**gas:** TA/BP/Popeye's/Pizza Hut/dsl/scales/24hr/@, **other:** KOA

92 Arabi, E...**gas:** Chevron/Plantation House, Pure, **lodging:** Budget Inn, W...**gas:** BP/dsl, **other:** Southern Gates RV Park

85mm rest area nb, full(handicapped)facilities, phone, vending, picnic tables, litter barrels, petwalk

84 GA 159, Ashburn, E...**gas:** Shell/dsl, W...**gas:** Citgo/dsl/24hr, **food:** DQ, Subway, **lodging:** Ashburn Inn/RV Park

82 GA 107, GA 112, Ashburn, W...**gas:** BP, Chevron, Shorty's, **food:** KFC, Huddle House/24hr, Krystal, McDonald's, Pizza Hut, Shoney's, **lodging:** Best Western, Day's Inn, Ramada Ltd, Super 8, **other:** Chevrolet, O'Reilly Parts, Rite Aid, to Chehaw SP

80 Bussey Rd, Sycamore, E...**gas:** Exxon, Shell, **lodging:** Budget Inn, W...**gas:** Chevron/dsl, **other:** tires

78 GA 32, Sycamore, E...to Jefferson Davis Mem Pk(14mi)

76mm rest area sb, full(handicapped)facilities, phone, vending, picnic tables, litter barrels, petwalk

75 Inaha Rd, E...**gas:** Chevron, W...**gas:** BP/Stuckey's

71 Willis Still Rd, Sunsweet, W...**gas:** BP/dsl

69 Chula-Brookfield Rd, E...**gas:** Phillips 66, **lodging:** Red Carpet Inn, **other:** antiques

Interstate 75

Exit	Description
66	Brighton Rd, no services
64	US 41, Tifton, **E**...**gas:** BP/dsl, **other:** HOSPITAL, $General, Harvey's Foods, **W**...**gas:** Petro
63b	8th St, Tifton, **E**...**gas:** Flash, **food:** KFC, Los Compadres, **lodging:** Budget Inn, same as 63a, **W**...**food:** Pit Stop BBQ
63a	2nd St, Tifton, **E**...**gas:** BP, Chevron, **food:** Arby's, Burger King, Checker's, Denny's, Golden Corral, King Buffet, Krystal, LJ Silver, McDonald's, Pizza Hut, Red Lobster, Southern Buffet, Subway, Taco Bell, Waffle House, **lodging:** Econolodge, Super 8, **other:** Advance Parts, Belk, Buick/Pontiac/Cadillac/GMC, $Tree, Jc Penney, **W**...**gas:** Shell/dsl, **lodging:** Quality Inn, Travelodge
62	US 82, to US 319, Tifton, **E**...**gas:** BP, Citgo, Exxon/dsl, **food:** Applebee's, Charles Seafood, Country Buffet, Cracker Barrel, DQ, Red Lobster, Sonic, Waffle House, Western Sizzlin, Zaxby's, **lodging:** Comfort Inn, Courtyard, Fairfield Inn, Hampton Inn, Masters Inn, Microtel, **other:** Advance Parts, Family$, Ford/Lincoln/Mercury, Pecan Outlet, **W**...**gas:** BP/Subway, RaceWay/24hr, Shell/dsl, **food:** BackYard Burger, Burger King, Capt D's, Chick-fil-A, Longhorn Steaks, Shoney's, Sonny's BBQ, Starbucks, Waffle House, Wendy's, **lodging:** Day's Inn, Holiday Inn, Ramada Ltd, Rodeway Inn, **other:** Chevrolet, Chrysler/Jeep, Honda, Lowe's Whse, Mazda, Plymouth/Dodge, Radio Shack, Toyota, Wal-Mart SuperCtr/dsl/24hr
61	Omega Rd, **W**...**gas:** Citgo/Stuckey's/Waffle King/dsl, **lodging:** Motel 6, **other:** Harley-Davidson, Pines RV Park
60	Central Ave, Tifton, **E**...**gas:** Chevron, **food:** Dragon 1 Chinese, **W**...**gas:** Pilot/Subway/Steak'n Shake/dsl/scales/@, **other:** Amy's RV Ctr, Blue Beacon
59	Southwell Blvd, to US 41, Tifton, **E**...**gas:** Loves/Hardees/dsl/24hr/@
55	to Eldorado, Omega, **E**...**gas:** Chevron/Magnolia Plantation, **W**...**gas:** Pure/dsl
49	Kinard Br Rd, Lenox, **E**...**gas:** Dixie/dsl, **lodging:** Knight's Inn, **W**...**gas:** BP/dsl/24hr, Phillips 66/dsl/repair
47mm	**rest area both lanes, full(handicapped)facilities, phone, vending, picnic tables, litter barrels, petwalk**
45	Barneyville Rd, **E**...**lodging:** Relax Inn
41	Rountree Br Rd, **E**...**gas:** Citgo, **W**...to Reed Bingham SP
39	GA 37, Adel, Moultrie, **E**...**gas:** Shell/McDonald's/dsl, Texaco, **food:** DQ, Hardee's, Subway, Waffle House, **lodging:** Budget Lodge, Scottish Inn, Super 8, **other:** Family$, Rite Aid, Winn-Dixie, **W**...**gas:** BP, Citgo/Huddle House/dsl/@, **food:** Burger King, Capt D's, IHOP, Mama's Table, Popeye's, Taco Bell, Wendy's, Western Sizzlin, **lodging:** Day's Inn, Hampton Inn, **other:** Factory Stores/famous brands, to Reed Bingham SP
37	Adel, no services
32	Old Coffee Rd, Cecil, **W**...**gas:** Chevron
29	US 41 N, GA 122, Hahira, Sheriff's Boys Ranch, **E**...**food:** Subway, **W**...**gas:** Big Foot TC/Apple Valley/dsl, BP/Blimpie/TCBY/dsl, **lodging:** Super 8
23mm	weigh sta both lanes
22	US 41 S, to Valdosta, **E**...**gas:** BP, Shell/Subway/dsl, **other:** HOSPITAL, Chevrolet/Mazda, Chrysler/Jeep/Toyota, Ford/Lincoln/Mercury, golf, **W**...**gas:** Citgo/Burger King/DQ/Stuckey's, **lodging:** Day's Inn
18	GA 133, Valdosta, **E**...**gas:** Big Foot/dsl, Chevron, Citgo, Exxon, Phillips 66, Texaco/dsl, **food:** Applebee's, Arby's, Brewsters, Burger King, Chick-fil-A, Cracker Barrel, Denny's, El Potro Mexican, Fazoli's, Hooters, KFC, Krystal, Little Caesar's, Longhorn Steaks, McDonald's, Ole Time Steaks, Outback Steaks, Red Lobster, Ruby Tuesday, Starbucks, Steak'n Shake, Subway, Taco Bell, Texas Roadhouse, Waffle House, Wendy's, **lodging:** Azalea Inn, Country Inn&Suites, Courtyard, Fairfield Inn, Hampton Inn, Holiday Inn Express, Howard Johnson, Jameson Inn, Jolly Inn, La Quinta, Quality Inn, **other:** Belk, Best Buy, Goody's, Home Depot, JC Penney, Old Navy, Publix, Target, Walgreens, mall, **W**...**gas:** BP/dsl, RaceWay, Shell, **lodging:** Best Western, Econolodge, Sleep Inn, **other:** RiverPark Camping
16	US 84, US 221, GA 94, Valdosta, **E**...**gas:** Big Foot/dsl, BP/dsl, Chevron, Citgo/Stuckey's/dsl, Danfair Express, Phillips 66, Shell/dsl, **food:** Aligatou Japanese, Burger King, IHOP, McDonald's, Pizza Hut, Shoney's, Sonic, Waffle House, Wendy's, **lodging:** Day's Inn, Guesthouse Inn, Hampton Inn, Holiday Inn, Motel 6, New Valdosta Inn, Quality Inn, Ramada Ltd, Super 8, **other:** Sam's Club/gas, Wal-Mart Super Ctr/24hr, to Okefenokee SP, **W**...Shell/Huddle House/dsl/24hr, **food:** Austin's Steaks, **lodging:** Comfort Inn, Knight's Inn
13	Old Clyattville Rd, Valdosta, **W**...Wild Adventures Park
11	GA 31, Valdosta, **E**...**gas:** Pilot/Subway/dsl/24hr/@, Wilco/Hess/dsl/scales/24hr/@, **food:** Waffle House, **lodging:** Travelers Inn, **W**...**gas:** BP
5	GA 376, to Lake Park, **E**...**gas:** Chevron, Flash, Phillips 66, RaceWay, Shell, **food:** Chick-fil-A, China Garden, FarmHouse Rest., Hardee's, Lin's Garden Chinese, Shoney's, Sonic, Sonny's BBQ, Subway, Waffle House, **lodging:** Guesthouse Inn, Holiday Inn Express, **other:** Eagles Roost RV Park, Family$, Lake Park Outlets/famous brands, Travel Country RV Ctr, Winn-Dixie, **W**...**gas:** Citgo/dsl, Shell/dsl, **food:** Cracker Barrel, McDonald's, Pizza Hut, Taco Bell, Wendy's, **lodging:** Day's Inn, Hampton Inn, Super 8, Travelodge, **other:** FSA/famous brands, SunCoast RV Ctr
3mm	**Welcome Ctr nb, full(handicapped)facilities, phone, vending, picnic tables, litter barrels, petwalk**
2	Lake Park, Bellville, **E**...**gas:** Mobil/DQ, Shell/dsl, TA/BP/Arby's/dsl/rest./scales/24hr/@, **W**...**gas:** Flying J/Conoco/dsl/LP/rest./scales/24hr/@, **lodging:** Lake Park Inn
0mm	Georgia/Florida state line

N ↕ **S**

Lavonia

Commerce

Suwanee

Exit #	Services
179mm	Georgia/South Carolina state line, Lake Hartwell, Tugaloo River
177	GA 77 S, to Hartwell, E...gas: BP/gifts/dsl, food: Dad's Grill, other: to Hart SP, Tugaloo SP
176mm	Welcome Ctr sb, full(handicapped)facilities, info, phone, picnic tables, litter barrels, vending, petwalk
173	GA 17, to Lavonia, E...gas: RaceTrac/24hr, food: La Cabana Mexican, McDonald's, Subway, Taco Bell, Waffle House, lodging: Best Western, Sleep Inn, other: $General, Lavonia Foods, Rite Aid, W...gas: Chevron/dsl, Exxon/dsl, food: Burger King, Hardee's, Pizza Hut, Wendy's, Shoney's Inn/rest., Zaxby's, lodging: Super 8, other: Chrysler/Dodge/Jeep, Ford, to Tugaloo SP
171mm	weigh sta nb
169mm	weigh sta sb
166	GA 106, to Carnesville, Toccoa, E...gas: Wilco/Hess/DQ/Wendy's/dsl/scales/24hr, W...gas: Echo Trkstp/Chevron/Country Kitchen/dsl/rest./scales/24hr, other: truck repair
164	GA 320, to Carnesville
160mm	**rest area nb, full(handicapped)facilities, phone, vending, picnic tables, litter barrels, petwalk**
160	GA 51, to Homer, E...gas: Shell/Subway/dsl/24hr, other: Sterling RV Ctr, W...gas: ⚡/Flying J/Country Mkt/dsl/24hr, Petro/Pizza Hut/dsl/scales/24hr/@, other: Blue Beacon
154	GA 63, Martin Br Rd
149	US 441, GA 15, to Commerce, Homer, E...gas: Chevron, Shell, TA/76/dsl/rest./24hr/@, food: Capt D's, Chinese Chef, Grand China, Joy's, Longhorn Steaks, Outback Steaks, Papa Jack's, Pizza Hut/Taco Bell, Shoney's, Sonny's BBQ, Waffle House, Zaxby's, lodging: Admiral Benbow Inn, Day's Inn, Hampton Inn, Scottish Inn, other: HOSPITAL, $Tree, Goody's, KOA, Radio Shack, Tanger Outlet/famous brands, Wal-Mart SuperCtr/gas/24hr, W...gas: BP/dsl, Chevron, Citgo, RaceTrac/dsl, Texaco, food: Applebee's, Arby's, Burger King, Checker's, Chick-fil-A, Cracker Barrel, DQ, Denny's, KFC, Krystal, La Fiesta, La Hacienda, McDonald's, Pizza Hut, Ruby Tuesday, Ryan's, Sonic, Starbucks, Subway, Wendy's, lodging: Best Western, Comfort Inn, $Wise Inn, Holiday Inn Express, Howard Johnson, Jameson Inn, Red Roof Inn, Super 8, other: Buick/Pontiac/GMC, Home Depot, Tanger Outlet/famous brands, tires
147	GA 98, to Commerce, E...gas: Citgo/dsl, Flying J/cafe/dsl/24hr/, FuelMart/dsl, other: HOSPITAL W...other: Cody's Fuel
140	GA 82, Dry Pond Rd, W...Freightliner/RV & Truck Repair
137	US 129, GA 11 to Jefferson, E...gas: BP, RaceTrac, Shell, food: Arby's, El Jinete Mexican, McDonald's, Waffle House, Zaxby's, lodging: Comfort Inn, other: museum, W...gas: QT/dsl/24hr, food: Burger King, Waffle House, Wendy's, other: flea mkt
129	GA 53, to Braselton, E...gas: Chevron/dsl, Shell/Golden Pantry/dsl, food: La Hacienda Mexican, Waffle House, lodging: Best Western, W...gas: Pilot/McDonald's/dsl/scales/24hr, food: Cracker Barrel, Dominos, Hickory Wind BBQ, Wendy's, Zaxby's, other: $Store
126	GA 211, to Chestnut Mtn, E...gas: Shell/dsl, food: Subway, Waffle House, W...gas: BP/dsl, food: Blimpie, Chateau Elan Winery/rest., China Garden, Papa John's, lodging: Holiday Inn Express, other: Publix, vet

Exit #	Services
120	to GA 124, Hamilton Mill Rd, E...gas: BP, QT/dsl, food: Arby's, Buffalo's Café, Burger King, Caprese Rest., Dos Copas Mexican, McDonald's, Moe's SW Grill, Rib Shack, Starbucks, Subway, Wendy's, Zaxby's, other: Home Depot, Kohl's, Publix/Deli, auto repair, vet, W...gas: Chevron, Shell/Huddle House/dsl, food: Barbarito's, Beaner's Coffee, Chick-fil-A, Chili's, Log Cabin BBQ, other: CVS Drug, Wal-Mart SuperCtr/gas
115	GA 20, to Buford Dam, E...gas: QT, W...gas:QT/dsl, food: Arby's, Artuzzi's Italian, Bruster's, Buffalo's Cafe, Burger King, Chick-fil-A, Chili's, ChuckeCheese, 5 Guy's Burgers, Kani House, Krispy Kreme, Longhorn Steaks, Liu's Buffet, Macaroni Grill, McDonald's, Mimi's Cafe, Moe's SW Grill, O'Charley's, Olive Garden, On the border, PF Chang's, Quizno's, Red Lobster, Shogun Japanese, Starbucks, Steak n' Shake, Subway, Ted's MT Grill, TGIFriday, Waffle House, Wendy's, lodging: Country Inn/Suites, Hampton Inn, SpringHill Suites, Wingate Inn, other: Belk, Best Buy, Borders Books, Circuit City, Costco/gas, Dillard's, JC Penney, Lowes Whse, Macy's, Mazda, Michael's, Nissan, Nordstrom's, Ross, Sam's Club, Staples, Target, TJ Maxx, Toyota/Scion, Wal-Mart SuperCtr/24hr, Mall of GA, to Lake Lanier Islands
114mm	**rest area sb, full(handicapped)facilities, phone, vending, picnic tables, litter barrels, petwalk**
113	I-985 N(from nb), to Gainesville, no services
111	GA 317, to Suwanee, E...gas: BP, Phillips 66/dsl, Sim's, food: Applebee's, Arby's, Blimpie, Burger King, Checker's, Chick-fil-A, Cracker Barrel, Mrs Winner's, Oriental Garden, Outback Steaks, Philly Connection, Pizza Hut, Subway, Taco Bell/Pizza Hut, Waffle House, Wendy's, lodging: Admiral Benbow Inn, Best Western, Comfort Inn, Courtyard, Days Inn, Fairfield Inn, Holiday Inn, Red Roof Inn, Sun Suites, other: CVS Drug, GNC, Kauffman Tire, W...gas: Chevron/dsl/24hr, RaceTrac, Shell, food: A&W/KFC, Atlanta Bread, CiCi's Pizza, Kacey's Rest., McDonald's, Moe's SW Grill, Shane's Ribshack, Sonic, Wild Wing Cafe, lodging: Motel 6, Super 8, other: $Tree, Office Depot, Radio Shack, Tires +, Wal-Mart SuperCtr/24hr/gas, flea mkt
109	Old Peachtree Rd, E...gas: QT/dsl/24hr, food: McDonald's, lodging: Hampton Inn, other: $World, Publix, W...food: Bistro's Sandwich Cafe, Califonia Dreaming, China Delight, Magnolia Cafe, Sidelines Grille, Subway, Waffle House, lodging: Hilton Garden, Holiday Inn, other: Home Depot
108	Sugarloaf Pkwy, E...lodging: Hampton Inn, W...food: Chick-fil-A, lodging: Hilton Garden, Holiday Inn, other: Gwinnett Civic Ctr
107	GA 120, to GA 316 E, Athens, E...gas: Shell, food: Burger King, Carino's, Jillian's, Zaxby's, other: Bass Pro Shop, Books-a-Million, Burlington Coats, Discount Tire, Eckerd, Food Ct, Mercedes, Nieman-Marcus, Ross, Saks 5th Ave, Sears, Suburban Tire, W...gas: BP, Chevron, food: Carrabba's, China Gate, McDonald's, Roadhouse Grill, Subway, lodging: La Quinta, Suburban Lodge
106	Boggs Rd(from sb, no return), Duluth, W...gas: QT/dsl/24hr
104	Pleasant Hill Rd, E...gas: Chevron/24hr, Circle K, Sim's, food: Bahama Breeze, Blue Marlin, Burger King, Chick-fil-A, East Pearl, GA Diner, Grand Buffet, Ida's Pizza Kitchen, Joe's Crabshack, Krispy Kreme, La Pantera Rosa, Macaroni Grill, McDonald's, Moe's SW Grill, Popeye's, Starbucks, Subway, TGIFriday, Waffle House, Wendy's, lodging: Candlewood Suites, Comfort Suites, Hampton Inn Suites, Holiday Inn Express, Marriott, Residence Inn, Sun Suites, other: Best Buy, $General, Eckerd, Goodyear/auto, Home Depot, Old Time Pottery, Publix,

Interstate 85

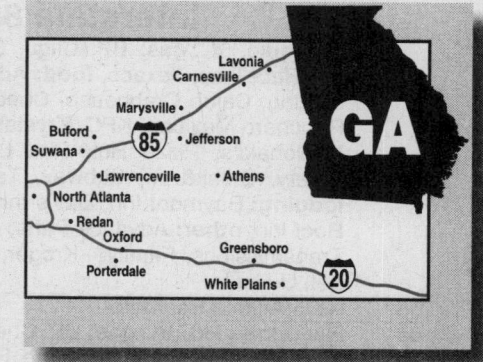

Atlanta Area

Walgreens, **W**...**gas:** BP/dsl, Chevron, Murphy USA/dsl, RaceTrac, **food:** Applebee's, Arby's, Bruster's, Burger King, Checker's, Chili's, Chipotle Mexican, Golden China, Hooters, IHOP, KFC, McDonald's, Olive Garden, On the Border, Panda Express, Pizza Hut, Red Lobster, Ryan's, Starbucks, Steak'n Shake, Subway, Taco Bell, Waffle House, Wendy's, **lodging:** Courtyard, Day's Inn, Extended Stay America, Hyatt Place, InTown Suites, Quality Inn, Wingate Inn, **other:** Barnes&Noble, Batteries+, BMW, Chevrolet, Dodge, Eckerd, Firestone/auto, Ford/Lincoln/Mercury, Fry's Electronics, Goodyear/auto, Honda, Jo-Ann Fabrics, KIA, Macy's, Marshall's, Mazda/Hyundai, Mitsubishi, Nissan, PetCo, Sears/auto, Staples, Target, TJ Maxx, Toyota, Wal-Mart Super Ctr, mall

103 Steve Reynolds Blvd(from nb, no return), **W**...**gas:** QT, Shell, **food:** Dave&Buster's, La Fiesta Mexican, Waffle House, **other:** Circuit City, Costco Whse, Goody's, Kohl's, Sam's Club

102 GA 378, Beaver Ruin Rd, **E**...**gas:** Shell/dsl, QT, **W**...**gas:** Citgo

101 Lilburn Rd, **E**...**gas:** QT/dsl, Shell/dsl/24hr, **food:** Blimpie, Bojangles, Bruster's, Burger King, Hong Kong Buffet, Manhattan Pizza, McDonald's/playplace, Quizno's, Starbucks, Krystal, KFC, Taco Bell, Waffle House, **lodging:** Guesthouse Inn, InTown Suites, **W**...**gas:** Chevron/24hr, QT, **food:** Arby's, El Indo Mexican, El Taco Veloz, Little Caeser's, Mrs Winner's, Papa John's, Pizza Plaza, Waffle House, Wendy's, **lodging:** Knight's Inn, Red Roof Inn, **other:** CarMax, Chrysler/Jeep, CVS Drug, Little Giant Mkt, Lowe's Whse

99 GA 140, Jimmy Carter Blvd, **E**...**gas:** Phillips 66/dsl, Shell, **food:** Checker's, Chick-fil-A, Cracker Barrel, Denny's, Don Taco, KFC, McDonald's, Papa John's, Pizza Hut/Taco Bell, Waffle House, Wendy's, **lodging:** Best Western, Comfort Inn, Courtyard, La Quinta, Motel 6, **other:** Advance Parts, Aldi Foods, CVS Drug, Family$, Goodyear, Office Depot, U-Haul, Walgreens, **W**...**gas:** Chevron/24hr, Citgo, QT/dsl/24hr, **food:** Barnacle's Grill, Five Guys Cafe, Hong Kong Buffet, Hooters, Pappadeaux Steak/seafood, Sonic, Waffle House, Wendy's, **lodging:** Days Inn, Drury Inn, Country Inn Suites, Microtel, **other:** AutoZone, Big 10 Tire, BJ's Whse/gas(3mi), CarQuest, NTB, O'Reilly Parts, PepBoys

96 Pleasantdale Rd, Northcrest Rd, **E**...**food:** Burger King, Pleasantdale Chinese, **lodging:** Peachtree Inn, **W**...**gas:** Exxon/dsl, QT/dsl, **food:** Waffle House, **lodging:** US Economy Lodge

95 I-285

94 Chamblee-Tucker Rd, **E**...**gas:** Shell, Texaco, **lodging:** Masters Inn, **W**...**gas:** QT/dsl, Shell, **food:** DQ, Waffle House, **lodging:** Motel 6, Super 8, **other:** to Mercer U

93 Shallowford Rd, to Doraville, **E**...**gas:** Shell, **food:** Blimpie, Collard Green Cafe, El Salvador, Hop Shing Chinese, **other:** Publix, U-Haul, **W**...**gas:** Circle K, Shell/dsl, **lodging:** Quality Inn

91 US 23, GA 155, Clairmont Rd, **E**...**gas:** Chevron, Shell, **food:** Grand Buffet, IHOP, Mo's Pizza, Popeye's, **other:** Brakes&More/repair, IGA Foods, **W**...**gas:** BP, **food:** Donnie's, McDonald's, Roadhouse Grill, Waffle House, **lodging:** Marriott, Wingate Inn, **other:** NTB, Sam's Club/gas

89 GA 42, N Druid Hills, **E**...**gas:** Chevron/Subway/dsl, QT/dsl/24hr, Shell, **food:** Arby's, Boston Mkt, Burger King, Chick-fil-A, Einstein Bro's, Lettuce Souperise, McDonald's, Moe's SW Grill, Panera Bread, Picadilly's, Starbucks, Taco Bell, TCBY, **lodging:** Courtyard, Homestead Suites, **other:** $Tree, Firestone/auto, Target, **W**...**gas:** Chevron, Exxon, Shell, **food:** Atlanta Diner, Dunkin Doughnuts, Honey Baked Ham, Krystal, Waffle House, **lodging:** DoubleTree, Hampton Inn, Red Roof Inn, **other:** CVS Drug, Just Brakes, vet

88 Lenox Rd, GA 400 N, Cheshire Br Rd(from sb), **E**...**gas:** Shell, **lodging:** La Quinta

87 GA 400 N(from nb), no services

86 GA 13 S, Peachtree St, **E**...**gas:** BP, **food:** Denny's, Wendy's, **lodging:** Intown Inn, La Quinta, **other:** Brake-O

85 I-75 N, to Marietta, Chattanooga

84 Techwood Dr, 14th St, **E**...**gas:** BP, Shell, **food:** CheeseSteaks, La Bamba Mexican, Thai Cuisine, VVV Ristorante Italiano, **lodging:** Best Western, Hampton Inn, Marriott, Sheraton, Travelodge, **other:** Woodruff Arts Ctr, **W**...**food:** Blimpie, **lodging:** Courtyard, Knight's Inn, **other:** CVS Drug, Dillard's, Office Depot, to Georgia Tech

I-85 and I-75 run together 8 mi. See Interstate 75, exits 243-249.

77 I-75 S

76 Cleveland Ave, **E**...**gas:** Citgo/dsl, Marathon, Phillips 66/Blimpie, **food:** Arby's, Burger King, Krystal, Mrs Winner's, McDonald's, **other:** HOSPITAL, BigLots, CVS Drug, $Tree, Kroger, Radio Shack, **W**...**gas:** Shell/dsl, Texaco/dsl, **food:** Chick-fil-A, Church's, KFC, **other:** Chevrolet, CVS Drug, Honda, O'Reilly Parts

75 Sylvan Rd, **E**...**gas:** Citgo, Phillips 66, Shell/dsl, **food:** Chick-fil-A, City Garden Chinese, IHOP, McDonald's, Wendy's, **lodging:** InnCity Suites

74 Loop Rd, Aviation Commercial Center

73b a Virginia Ave, **E**...**gas:** Citgo/dsl, **food:** Hambone's BBQ, Jonny's Pizza, Landmark Diner, Magnolia Grill, Malone's Grill, McDonald's, Pizza Hut, Ruby Tuesday, Schlotsky's, Spondivit's Rest., Waffle House, Wendy's, Willy's Mexican, **lodging:** Courtyard, Drury Inn, Hilton, Renaissance Hotel, Red Roof Inn, Residence Inn, **W**...**gas:** Chevron/Subway/24hr, Shell, **food:** Arby's, Blimpie, Happy Budda Chinese, Harsfield's Grill, KFC/A&W, La Fiesta Mexican, Steak&Ale, Waffle House, **lodging:** Comfort Inn, Crowne Plaza, DoubleTree, Econolodge, Fairfield Inn, Hampton Inn, Holiday Inn, Hyatt Place, Wellesley Inn

72 Camp Creek Pkwy

71 Riverdale Rd, Atlanta Airport, **E**...**food:** Ruby Tuesday, **lodging:** Courtyard, Fairfield Inn, Microtel, Hampton Inn, Holiday Inn, Hyatt Place, La Quinta, Sheraton/grill, Sleep Inn, Springhill Suites, Super 8, **W**...**gas:** Chevron, **food:** Joe's Rest., **lodging:** Day's Inn, Embassy Suites, Hilton Garden, Holiday Inn Express, Marriott, Westin Hotel

69 GA 14, GA 279, **E**...**gas:** Chevron/24hr, **food:** Denny's, Waffle House, **lodging:** Atlanta So. Hotel, La Quinta, Motel 6, Quality Inn, Radisson, **other:** CVS Drug, Good-

Interstate 85

N ↑ S

year/auto, **W**...**gas:** BP, Citgo, Conoco/dsl, Exxon/dsl, RaceTrac, Texaco, **food:** Arby's, Blimpie, Burger King, Cajun Crabhouse, Checker's, Church's, El Ranchero Mexican, KFC, Krystal, Longhorn Steaks, McDonald's, Pizza Hut, Red Lobster, ShowCase Eatery, Steak&Ale, Subway, Taco Bell, Wendy's, **lodging:** Baymont Inn, Day's Inn, Fairfield Inn, Red Roof Inn, **other:** Advance Parts, AutoZone, Cottman Transmissions, Family$, Kroger, Radio Shack, Target, U-Haul

68	I-285 Atlanta Perimeter

66	Flat Shoals Rd, **W**...**gas:** BP, Chevron/dsl, Mobil/dsl, Shell/Blimpie, **food:** Supreme Fish Delight, Waffle House, **lodging:** Motel 6

64	GA 138, to Union City, **E**...**gas:** BP/Blimpie/dsl, RaceTrac, **food:** Waffle House, **lodging:** Econolodge, Super 8, **other:** Buick/Pontiac/GMC, Chevrolet, Chrysler, Dodge, Ford, Honda, Kia/Nissan, Infiniti, Saturn, Toyota, VW, **W**...**gas:** Chevron, QT, Shell, **food:** Arby's, Burger King, Capt D's, Cracker Barrel, IHOP, KFC, Krystal, McDonald's, Papa John's, Pizza Hut, Shoney's, Sonic, Subway, Taco Bell, Wendy's, **lodging:** Best Western, Comfort Inn, Country Hearth Inn, Holiday Inn Express, **other:** Aamco, BigLots, Chevrolet, $Tree, Eckerd, Firestone, Goodyear/auto, Ingles, Kroger, NTB, O'Reilly Parts, PepBoys, Sears/auto, Walgreens, Wal-Mart SuperCtr/24hr, mall

61	GA 74, to Fairburn, **E**...**gas:** BP/dsl/scales, RaceTrac, Shell, **food:** Cafe 74, Chick-fil-A, McDonald's, Waffle House, Wendy's, Zaxby's, **lodging:** Hampton Inn, Holiday Inn Express, Sleep Inn, Wingate Inn, **W**...**gas:** Citgo/dsl, Marathon, Phillips 66/Blimpie/dsl, **lodging:** Efficiency Motel

56	Collinsworth Rd, **W**...**gas:** BP, Marathon/dsl, **food:** Frank's Rest., **other:** South Oaks Camping

51	GA 154, to Sharpsburg, **E**...**gas:** Phillips 66/Blimpie/dsl, Summit/dsl, **food:** Hardee's, Wendy's(mi), **W**...**gas:** Chevron/dsl, Shell/dsl, **food:** Waffle House

47	GA 34, to Newnan, **E**...**gas:** BP, Chevron/dsl, Citgo/Subway, HotSpot/dsl, QT, Shell, **food:** Applebee's, Arby's, Capt. D's, Chinchin Chinese, Dunkin Donuts, Hooters, LongHorn Steaks, Moe's SW Grill, Panda Express, PegLeg Polly's, Red Lobster, Ruby Tuesday, Sprayberry's BBQ, Steak'n Shake, Texas Roadhouse, Waffle House, Wendy's, **lodging:** Hampton Inn, Jameson Inn, Springhill Suites, **other:** Belk, Circuit City, Goodyear, Goody's, Home Depot, Kohl's, Lowe's Whse, Ross, Wal-Mart SuperCtr/24hr, **W**...**gas:** Phillips 66, RaceTrac, **food:** Bugaboo Creek Steaks, Burger King, Chick-fil-A, Chili's, Cracker Barrel, Golden Corral, IHOP, KFC, O'Charley's, Panera Bread, Shane's BBQ, TGI Friday, Waffle House, Zaxby's, **lodging:** Best Western, Comfort Inn, Day's Inn, Holiday Inn Express, La Quinta, Motel 6, **other:** HOSPITAL, BJ's Whse, Chevrolet, Mazda/Jeep/Hyundai, Michael's, Office Depot, Old Navy, Plymouth, Pontiac/Buick/GMC, Publix, Target, Tires+, TJ Maxx, Toyota

41	US 27/29, Newnan, **E**...**gas:** Pilot/Subway/Wendy's/dsl/scales/24hr, **W**...**gas:** BP/dsl/24hr, Chevron, Phillips 66, **food:** Huddle House, McDonald's, Waffle House, **lodging:** Day's Inn, Howard Johnson, Super 8

35	US 29, to Grantville, **W**...**gas:** BP/dsl, Phillips 66/dsl

28	GA 54, GA 100, to Hogansville, **E**...**gas:** Shell/dsl, **W**...**gas:** BP/dsl, Chevron/dsl, SBS, **food:** China

N e w n a n

Cafe, *Dos Compadres, Intnat'l Cafe, McDonald's, Roger's BBQ, Subway, Waffle House, Wendy's, **lodging:** Econolodge, Garden Inn, **other:** Ingles

23mm	Beech Creek
22mm	weigh sta both lanes
21	I-185 S, to Columbus
18	GA 109, to Mountville, **E**...**gas:** Chevron/Domino's/dsl, **lodging:** Quality Inn, **other:** to FDR SP, Little White House HS, **W**...**gas:** BP/dsl, RaceTrac, Shell/Church's/dsl, Spectrum/dsl, Summit/dsl, **food:** Applebee's, Burger King, Conestoga Steaks, Cracker Barrel, Juanito's Mexican, Longhorn Steaks, Los Nopales, Moe's SW Grill, Ryan's, Subway, Waffle House, Wendy's, Zaxby's, **lodging:** Best Western, Comfort Inn, Jameson Inn, Super 8, **other:** Belk, Chrysler/Plymouth/Dodge/Jeep, Ford/Lincoln/Mercury, Home Depot, Honda, Hoofer's RV Park(3mi), JC Penney, mall
14	US 27, to La Grange, **W**...**gas:** BP/24hr, Pure, Shell, **lodging:** Hampton Inn
13	GA 219, to La Grange, **E**...**gas:** Shell/dsl/scales/24hr/@, **food:** Waffle House, **lodging:** Day's Inn, **other:** truckwash, **W**...**gas:** BP/dsl, Pilot/Subway/dsl/scales/24hr, **food:** Arbys, McDonald's, **other:** HOSPITAL
10mm	Long Cane Creek
2	GA 18, to West Point, **E**...**gas:** BP, Shell/dsl/24hr, **lodging:** Travelodge, **W**...**food:** KFC(1.5mi), **other:** to West Point Lake, camping
.5mm	**Welcome Ctr nb, full(handicapped)facilities, phone, picnic tables, litter barrels, vending, petwalk**
0mm	Georgia/Alabama state line, Chattahoochee River

L a G r a n g e

Interstate 95

Exit #	Services
113mm	Georgia/South Carolina state line, Savannah River
111mm	**Welcome Ctr/weigh sta sb, full(handicapped) facilities, info, phone, vending, picnic tables, litter barrels, petwalk**
109	GA 21, to Savannah, Pt Wentworth, Rincon, **E**...**gas:** Enmark/dsl, Pilot/McDonald's/Subway/dsl/scales/24hr, **food:** Waffle House, **lodging:** Hampton Inn, Mulberry Inn, Wingate Inn, **other:** Peterbilt, **W**...**gas:** 76/Circle K/Quizno's/dsl, **food:** Island Grill, Sea Grill, Wendy's, Zaxby's, **lodging:** Comfort Suites, Day's Inn, Holiday Inn Express, Quality Inn, Ramada Ltd, Sleep Inn, Super 8, **other:** CVS Drug, FoodLion, (5mi)Green Piece RV Park, (3mi)Whispering Pines RV Park
107mm	Augustine Creek
106	Jimmy DeLoach Pkwy
104	Savannah Airport, **E**...**gas:** BP, Shell/dsl, **food:** Sneed's Grill, Waffle House, **lodging:** Cambria Suites, Candlewood Suites, Comfort Suites, Country Inn&Suites, Fairfield Inn, Hawthorn Suites, Hilton Garden, Sheraton, Springhill Suites, Staybridge Suites, Towneplace Suites, Wingate Inn, **other:** to airport, **W**...**gas:** Murphy USA, Shell/Subway, **food:** Arby's, Chick-fil-A, Hilliard's Rest., Longhorn Steaks, Ruby Tuesday, Sonic, Zaxby's Café, **lodging:** Red Roof Inn, **other:** Home Depot, Sam's Club/gas, Wal-Mart SuperCtr/McDonald's/gas/24hr
102	US 80, to Garden City, **E**...**gas:** BP, Enmark/dsl, Flash Foods/gas, **food:** Cracker Barrel, Foster's Steaks, Guerrero Mexican, Huddle House, KFC, Krystal, McDonald's, Nagano Japanese, Peking Chinese, Pizza Hut/Taco Bell, Quizno's, Waffle House, **lodging:** Best Western, Jameson Inn, Microtel, Ramada Ltd, Travelodge Suites, **other:**

Interstate 95

	Food Lion, Family$, Wait's RV Ctr/Camping World, to Ft Pulaski NM, museum, **W**...**gas:** BP, Gate/Subway/dsl, Shell, Texaco, **food:** BBQ, Burger King, Domino's, El Potro Mexican, Hardee's, Italian Pizza, Mihn Zing Chinese, Wendy's, Western Sizzlin, **lodging:** Comfort Inn, Econolodge, Holiday Inn, La Quinta, Magnolia Inn, Quality Inn, Sleep Inn, **other:** Napa, auto repair
99b a	I-16, W to Macon, E to Savannah
94	GA 204, to Savannah, Pembroke, **E**...**gas:** BP/dsl, Exxon, Circle K, Shell/dsl, **food:** Cracker Barrel, Denny's, Hardee's, McDonald's, Perkins, Ruby Tuesday, Shoney's, Sonic, **lodging:** Best Value, Best Western, Clarion, Comfort Suites, Country Inn&Suites, Day's Inn, Fairfield Inn, GuestHouse Inn, Hampton Inn, Holiday Inn Express, Howard Johnson, La Quinta, Quality Inn, Red Roof Inn, Roadway Inn, Sancoutique Hotel, Sleep Inn, SpringHill Suites, Wingate Inn, **other:** HOSPITAL, Chevrolet, Factory Stores, Wal-Mart SuperCtr/24hr/gas(2mi), **W**...**gas:** Chevron/dsl/24hr, Shell, **food:** Crabdaddy's Rest, El Potro Mexican, Hooters, Huddle House, Shellhouse Rest, Subway, Waffle House, **lodging:** Clean Stay, Econolodge, Microtel, Travelodge, **other:** Harley-Davidson, Bellaire Woods RV Park(2mi)
91mm	Ogeechee River
90	GA 144, Old Clyde Rd, to Ft Stewart, Richmond Hill SP, **E**...**gas:** Chevron, Exxon, **food:** El Potro Mexican(1mi), Hardee's(1mi), **other:** Kroger/deli, **W**...**gas:** Love's/McDonald's/dsl/scales/24hr/@, Shell/dsl, **other:** Gore's RV Ctr
87	US 17, to Coastal Hwy, Richmond Hill, **E**...**gas:** BP/Subway, Chevron/dsl/24hr, Citgo, RaceWay, **food:** Denny's/24hr, Huddle House, Steamers Rest., Subway, Waffle House, **lodging:** Day's Inn, Motel 6, Royal Inn, Scottish Inn, Travelodge, **W**...**gas:** Exxon/McDonald's/dsl, TA/BP/LJSilver/Pizza Hut/Popeye's/dsl/24hr/@, Shell/dsl, Sunoco, **food:** Arby's, Burger King, KFC/Taco Bell, Waffle House, Wendy's, **lodging:** Best Western, Comfort Suites, Econolodge, Holiday Inn, **other:** KOA
85mm	Elbow Swamp
80mm	Jerico River
76	US 84, GA 38, to Midway, Sunbury, **E**...hist sites, **W**...**gas:** BP/dsl, El Cheapo/dsl, **food:** Holton's Seafood, Huddle House, **other:** HOSPITAL, museum
67	US 17, Coastal Hwy, to S Newport, **E**...**gas:** BP, Chevron/Subway/dsl, Citgo/dsl, Shell/McDonald's, **food:** Jones BBQ, **other:** Newport Camping(2mi), **W**...**gas:** BP
58	GA 99, GA 57, Townsend Rd, Eulonia, **E**...**gas:** BP/dsl, Citgo, **food:** Ms P's Diner **lodging:** Eulonia Lodge, **W**...**gas:** Chevron/dsl/24hr, Shell/dsl, **food:** Huddle House, **lodging:** Day's Inn, Knight's Inn, **other:** McIntosh Lake RV Park, Lake Harmony RV Camp
55mm	weigh sta both lanes, phone
49	GA 251, to Darien, **E**...**gas:** Chevron/dsl/24hr, Citgo, **food:** DQ, McDonald's, Waffle House, **lodging:** Ft King George Motel, **other:** Ford, Inland Harbor RV Park, Tall Pines RV Park, **W**...**gas:** BP, El Cheapo, Mobil/dsl, Shell/dsl, **food:** Burger King, Huddle House, KFC/Pizza Hut/Taco Bell, Larry's Subs, Ruby Tuesday, Smokey Joe's BBQ, TCBY, Wendy's, **lodging:** Comfort Inn, Hampton Inn, Quality Inn, Super 8, **other:** Darien Outlets/famous brands, flea mkt
47mm	Darien River

46.5mm	Butler River
46mm	Champney River
45mm	Altamaha River
42	GA 99, **E**...to Hofwyl Plantation HS
41mm	**rest area sb, full (handicapped) facilities, info, phone, vending, picnic tables, litter barrels, petwalk**

38	GA 25, to US 17, N Golden Isles Pkwy, Brunswick, **E**...**gas:** RaceTrac, **food:** Millhouse Steaks, Ruby Tuesday, **lodging:** Country Inn&Suites, Embassy Suites(2mi), Fairfield Inn, Holiday Inn, Jameson Inn, Microtel, **other:** HOSPITAL, **W**...**gas:** BP, Flash, Shell/dsl, **food:** Huddle House/24hr, La Fuente Mexican, Waffle House, **lodging:** Courtyard, Econolodge, Guest Cottage Motel, Quality Inn, **other:** $General, Harley Davidson, Harvey's Foods
36b a	US 25, US 341, to Jesup, Brunswick, **E**...**gas:** Chevron/dsl/24hr, Exxon/dsl, RaceWay, **food:** Burger King, Cracker Barrel, IHOP, KFC, Krystal/24hr, McDonald's, Pizza Hut, Quizno's, Shoney's, Taco Bell, Waffle House, Wendy's, **lodging:** Day's Inn, Hampton Inn, Knight's Inn, La Quinta, Ramada Inn, Red Roof Inn, **other:** Newcastle RV Ctr, **W**...**gas:** BP, El Cheapo/dsl, Mobil/dsl, Parker's/dsl, Sunoco, **food:** Capt Joe's Seafood, Denny's, Huddle House/24hr, Minh-Shun Chinese, Sonny's BBQ, Subway, Waffle House, **lodging:** Best Western, Comfort Inn, Motel 6, Park Inn, Sleep Inn, Super 8, **other:** Advance Parts, $General, Family$, Fred's Drug, Suncoast RV Ctr, Winn-Dixie
33mm	Turtle River
30mm	S Brunswick River
29	US 17, US 82, GA 520, S GA Pkwy, Brunswick, **E**...**gas:** Citgo/Church's/dsl, El Cheapo, Exxon/Krystal, Mobil, Pilot/Steak'n Shake/Subway/dsl/24hr/@, Shell, **food:** GA BBQ, Huddle House, Krystal, McDonald's, **other:** Blue Beacon, SpeedCo Lube, **W**...**gas:** Shell/dsl, /Flying J/Conoco/Country Mkt/dsl/LP/scales/24hr/@, Mobil, TA/BP/dsl/rest./scales/24hr/@, **food:** Waffle House, **lodging:** GuestHouse Inn, Microtel, Super 8, **other:** $General, Golden Isles Camping
27.5mm	Little Satilla River
26	Dover Bluff Rd, **E**...**gas:** Mobil/dsl, **food:** Choo Choo BBQ
21mm	White Oak Creek
19mm	Canoe Swamp
15mm	Satilla River
14	GA 25, to Woodbine, **W**...**food:** Sunshine/dsl/rest./24hr, **food:** Jack's BBQ, **lodging:** Stardust Motel(3mi)
7	Harrietts Bluff Rd, **E**...**gas:** Exxon/dsl, Shell/Subway, **food:** Huddle House, Jack's BBQ, **W**...**gas:** BP/dsl
6.5mm	Crooked River
6	Laurel Island Pkwy, **E**...**gas:** BP/Arby's/dsl/scales/24hr, Cisco Express/gas, Cone/dsl/24hr, **other:** pecans
3	GA 40, to St Marys, **E**...**gas:** Chevron, Exxon/Krystal, Mobil, Shell/Subway, **food:** Applebee's, Burger King, Chick-fil-A, DQ, KFC, McDonald's, Pablo's Mexican, Pizza Hut, Ponderosa, Shoney's, Sonny's BBQ, Taco Bell, Waffle House, Wendy's, Zaxby's, **lodging:** Best Western, Comfort Inn, Country Inn&Suites, Day's Inn, Hampton Inn, Holiday Inn Express, Magnolia Inn, Sleep Inn, Su-

GEORGIA

Interstate 95

per 8, **other:** HOSPITAL, Chevrolet/Buick, Chrysler/Dodge/Jeep, CVS Drug, $Tree, Ford/Mercury, Kia, K-Mart, Publix, Winn-Dixie, to Submarine Base, **W**...**gas:** Flash/dsl, PetroII/Quizno's/Church's/dsl/scales/24hr/@, RaceWay, **food:** Cracker Barrel, Waffle House, **lodging:** Clean Stay USA, Econolodge, Jameson Inn, Ramada Inn, Scottish Inn

1	St Marys Rd, **E**...**Welcome Ctr nb, full(handicapped)facilities, phone, vending, picnic tables, litter barrels, petwalk, gas:** Cisco/Blimpie/DQ/LJ Silver/Mrs Winners/Pizza Hut/dsl/@, Shell/dsl, **food:** to Cumberland Is Nat Seashore, **W**...**gas:** BP/dsl, Chevron/dsl, Wilco/Hess/Wendy's/dsl/@, **other:** GS RV Park, KOA
0mm	Georgia/Florida state line, St Marys River

Interstate 185(Columbus)

Exit #	Services
48	I-85. I-185 begins/ends on I-85.
46	Big Springs Rd, **E**...BP, **W**...**gas:** Shell
42	US 27, Pine Mountain, **E**...**gas:** BP, Shell/dsl, **food:** Waffle House, **other:** to Callaway Gardens, Little White House HS
34	GA 18, to West Point, **E**...**gas:** Shell/dsl/24hr
30	Hopewell Church Rd, Whitesville, **W**...**gas:** BP/dsl
25	GA 116, to Hamilton, **W**...RV camping
19	GA 315, Mulberry Grove, **W**...**gas:** Chevron/dsl/24hr
14	Smith Rd, no services
12	Williams Rd, **W**...**Welcome Ctr/rest rooms, gas:** BP/dsl/cafe, Shell, **lodging:** Country Inn Suites, Microtel
10	US 80, GA 22, to Phenix City, **W**...Springer Opera House
8	Airport Thruway, **E**...**gas:** Chevron, **food:** Blimpie, Shoney's, **other:** Fred's Drug, Home Depot, Sam's Club, Wal-Mart, **W**...**gas:** BP, Spectrum, **food:** Applebee's, Backyard Burger, Buffet City, Burger King, Capt D's, Hardee's, IHOP, KFC, McDonald's, Outback Steaks, Quepasa Rest., Stevie B's Pizza, Subway, Taco Bell/Pizza Hut, **lodging:** Comfort Suites, Extended Stay America, Hampton Inn, Sheraton, **other:** K-Mart
7	45th St, Manchester Expswy, **E**...**gas:** Chevron, **food:** Applebee's, Burger King, Carino's Italian, Krystal, Ruby Tuesday, WildFish Grill, **lodging:** Courtyard, La Quinta, Super 8, **other:** Best Buy, Chevrolet/Cadillac, Dillard's, K-Mart, Macy's, mall, **W**...**gas:** BP, Chevron, Spectrum, Texaco, **food:** A&W/KFC, Arby's, China Express, Crystal River Seafood, Golden Corral, Logan's Roadhouse, Lucky China, McDonald's, Pizza Hut, Ryan's, Sonic, Subway, Waffle House, Wendy's, **lodging:** Fairfield Inn, Holiday Inn, Shogun Japanese, Sleep Inn, **other:** HOSPITAL, VET, Advance Parts, $General, tires, transmissions
6	GA 22, Macon Rd, **E**...**gas:** Chevron, Spectrum, **food:** Brewster's, Burger King, China Buffet, KFC, Taco Bell, Waffle House, **lodging:** Best Western, Comfort Inn, Day's Inn, **other:** Eckerd, Ford, Kia, Nissan, U-Haul, Walgreens, **W**...**gas:** BP, Chevron, **food:** American Deli, Capt D's, ChuckeCheese, Cici's Pizza, Country BBQ, Denny's, Firehouse Subs, Longhorn Steaks, McDonald's, Schlotzsky's, **lodging:** Efficiency Lodge, La Quinta, **other:** CVS Drug, Firestone/auto, Freds Drug, GNC, Goodyear, Hancock Fabrics, Honda, Publix, Radio Shack

4	Buena Vista Rd, **E**...**gas:** BP, Solo, **food:** Arby's, Burger King, Capt D's, Chef Lee Chinese, Checker's, Church's, Krystal, McDonald's, Pizza Hut, Taco Bell, Waffle House, Zaxby's, **other:** AutoZone, $Tree, Firestone/auto, Goodyear/auto, Rainbow Foods, Wal-Mart/Subway/drugs, Winn-Dixie, repair, **W**...**gas:** Chevron, Spectrum
3	St Marys Rd, **W**...**gas:** BP, FuelTech, **food:** DQ, Hardee's, KFC, **other:** Ace Hardware, $General, Piggly Wiggly
1b a	US 27, US 280, Victory Dr, **1-3 mi W**...**gas:** RaceWay/24hr, **food:** Burger King, Denny's, KFC, McDonald's, Popeye's, Subway, Valarta Mexican, Wendy's, **lodging:** Econolodge, Colony Inn, Day's Inn, Motel 6, **food:** Advance Parts, I-185 begins/ends.

Interstate 285(Atlanta)

Exit #	Services
62	GA 279, S Fulton Hwy, Old Nat Hwy, **N**...**gas:** Chevron, Texaco, **food:** City Cafe, **lodging:** Econolodge, **S**...**gas:** Chevron, Exxon, Shell, **food:** Blimpie, Burger King, Checker's, China Cafeteria, Church's, El Nopal Mexican, KFC/Pizza Hut, Krystal, Longhorn Steaks, McDonald's, Mrs Winner's, Popeye's, Subway, Taco Bell, Waffle House, Wendy's, **lodging:** Clarion, Comfort Inn, Day's Inn, Howard Johnson, Motel 6, Quality Inn, **other:** AutoZone, Cottman Transmissions, Curves, Family$, NAPA, U-Haul
61	I-85, N to Atlanta, S to Montgomery, **Services 1 mi N**... **GA I-85, exit 71. E**...**food:** Ruby Tuesday, **lodging:** Comfort Suites, Courtyard, GA Conv Ctr, Microtel, Hampton Inn, Sheraton/grill, Sleep Inn, Sumner Suites, Super 8, Wingate Inn, **W**...**food:** Bennigan's, **lodging:** Comfort Inn, Day's Inn, Embassy Suites, Marriott, Quality Inn, Ramada, Super 8, Travelodge, Westin Hotel
60	GA 139, Riverdale Rd, **N**...**lodging:** Microtel(2mi), Wingate Inn(2mi), **S**...**gas:** BP, Exxon, QT, Shell/dsl, **food:** Blimpie, Checker's, China Café, Church's, KFC/LJ Silver, McDonald's, Papa John's, Wendy's, **lodging:** Best Western, Country Inn&Suites, Day's Inn, Ramada Inn, **other:** Advance Parts, $General, Family$, U-Haul, Wayfield Foods
59	Clark Howell Hwy, **N**...air cargo
58	I-75, N to Atlanta, S to Macon(from eb), to US 19, US 41, to Hapeville, **S**...**gas:** BP, Chevron/24hr, **food:** Bojangles, Philly Connection, Subway, Waffle House, Wendy's, **lodging:** Home Lodge Motel
55	GA 54, Jonesboro Rd, **N**...**lodging:** Super 8, **S**...**gas:** BP, Citgo/dsl, Phillips 66, Shell/dsl, **food:** Alondra's Mexican/Chinese, Capt D's, Church's, DaiLai Vietnamese, Golden Gate Chinese, LJ Silver, McDonald's, Subway, Taco Bell, **other:** Home Depot, repair
53	US 23, Moreland Ave, to Ft Gillem, **N**...**gas:** BP, Citgo, Conoco/dsl, **S**...**gas:** Citgo, Shell, TA/dsl/24hr/@, **food:** Popeye's, Wendy's, **lodging:** Economy Inn
52	I-675, S to Macon, no services
51	Bouldercrest Rd, **N**...**gas:** BP, Pilot/Wendy's/dsl/24hr, **food:** A&W/LJ Silver, Hardee's, KFC/Pizza Hut, WK Wings, **lodging:** DeKalb Inn, **other:** Family$, Wayfield Foods, **S**...**gas:** Chevron/dsl
48	GA 155, Flat Shoals Rd, Candler Rd, **N**...**gas:** BP, Chevron, Marathon, Shell/dsl, Stop'n Go, **food:** Arby's, Burger King, Checker's, DQ, KFC/Pizza Hut, McDonald's, Subway, Taco Bell, Waffle King, WK Wings, **lodging:** Country Hearth Inn, Gulf American Inn, **other:** BigLots, Macy's, Pep Boys, **S**...**gas:** QT, Phillips 66, **food:** Sonic
46b a	I-20, E to Augusta, W to Atlanta

Interstate 285

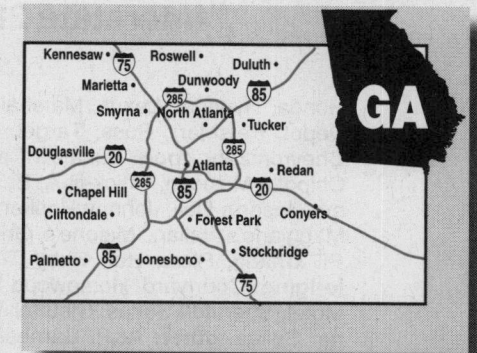

44	GA 260, Glenwood Rd, **E**...**gas:** Marathon, Super 8, **lodging:** Old English Inn, **W**...**gas:** Citgo, Shell, **food:** Church's, Mrs Winner's, **lodging:** Glenwood Inn
43	US 278, Covington Hwy, **E**...**gas:** Chevron/Subway/24hr, Citgo/dsl, **food:** Waffle House, **other:** U-Haul, **W**...**gas:** BP/24hr, QT, Shell/dsl, **food:** Blimpie, Checker's, KFC/Taco Bell, Mrs Winner's, Wendy's, **lodging:** Best Inn, **other:** Advance Parts, Family$, Firestone/auto
42	(from nb), Marta Station
41	GA 10, Memorial Dr, Avondale Estates, **E**...**gas:** Citgo, QT, Shell/dsl, **food:** Applebee's, Arby's, Burger King, Church's, DQ, McDonald's, Pancake House, Pizza Hut, Super China, Waffle House, Wendy's, **lodging:** Savannah Suites, Suburban Lodge, **other:** Advance Parts, AutoZone, Big 10 Tire, $General, Firestone/auto, Office Depot, Radio Shack, U-Haul
40	Church St, to Clarkston, **E**...**gas:** Chevron, Shell/dsl, Texaco, **W**...**gas:other:** HOSPITAL
39b a	US 78, to Athens, Decatur
38	US 29, Lawrenceville Hwy, **E**...**gas:** Phillips 66, Shell, **food:** Waffle House, **lodging:** Knight's Inn, Super 8, **other:** HOSPITAL, **W**...**gas:** BP, USA, **food:** Waffle House, **lodging:** Masters Inn, Motel 6
37	GA 236, to LaVista, Tucker, **E**...**gas:** Chevron, Circle K, **food:** Checker's, Chili's, Folks Rest., IHOP, O'Charley's, Olive Garden, Picadilly's, Schlotsky's, Steak&Ale, Waffle House, **lodging:** Comfort Suites, Country Inn Suites, **other:** Firestone, Target, **W**...**gas:** BP/repair, Citgo/dsl, Shell, **food:** Arby's, Blackeyed Pea, Blue Ribbon Grill, Capt D's, City Cafe, Domino's, DQ, Fuddrucker's, Jason's Deli, McDonald's, Panera Bread, Philly Connection, Pizza Hut, Red Lobster, Taco Bell, Wendy's, **lodging:** Courtyard, Fairfield Inn, Holiday Inn, Magnolia Motel, Quality Inn, Radisson, **other:** Best Buy, $Tree, Goodyear/auto, JC Penney, Kroger, Macy's, Michael's, Office Depot, Publix, TJ Maxx, mall
34	Chamblee-Tucker Rd, **E**...**gas:** Chevron, Citgo, Phillips 66, Shell, **food:** Arby's/Mrs Winner's, China Star, KFC/Taco Bell, Moe's SW Grill, S&S Cafeteria, Taco Bell, **lodging:** Day's Inn, **other:** Ace Hardware, Advance Parts, Eckerd, Goodyear, Kroger, **W**...**gas:** BP, Citgo, **food:** Little Cuba, LoneStar Steaks, McDonald's, Subway, Waffle House, **other:** BigLots, $Tree
33b a	I-85, N to Greenville, S to Atlanta
32	US 23, Buford Hwy, to Doraville, **E**...**gas:** BP/24hr, **food:** Baldino's Subs, Burger King/playland, Checker's, Chick-fil-A, El Pescador, Krystal, Wendy's, **other:** Big 10 Tire, Firestone/auto, Goodyear/auto, K-Mart, 99c Store, **W**...**gas:** Citgo, Shell, **food:** First China, McDonald's, Monterrey Mexican, Waffle House, **lodging:** Holiday Inn
31b a	GA 141, Peachtree Ind, to Chamblee, **W**...**gas:** Citgo, Shell, Texaco, **food:** Arby's, Chick-fil-A, Dunkin Donuts, McDonald's, Piccadilly, Pizza Hut, Waffle House, Wendy's, **other:** Acura, Advance Parts, Audi/VW, Buick/Pontiac/GMC, Chevrolet, Chrysler/Jeep/Dodge, CVS Drug, Dodge, Firestone, Ford, Honda, Hyundai, Kia, Lexus, Mazda, Porsche, Saab, Toyota, VW
30	Chamblee-Dunwoody Rd, N Shallowford Rd, to N Peachtree Rd, **N**...**gas:** BP, Chevron, **food:** Bagel&Co., Burger King, Garcia's Mexican, Guthrie's, Lucky China, Maggie's Creamery, McDonald's, Quizno's, Starbucks, Subway, Waffle House, **other:** Kroger, **S**...**gas:** Exxon/Blimpie/Arby's, Mobil, Phillips 66/dsl, Shell, **food:** Bombay Grill, City Café, La Botana Mexican, Mad Italian Rest., Olde Mill Steaks, Papa John's, Taco Bell, Wendy's, Wild Ginger Thai, **lodging:** Holiday Inn Select, Residence Inn
29	Ashford-Dunwoody Rd, **N**...**gas:** BP, Exxon/Subway, **food:** Applebee's, Brio Tuscan, Bloomingdale's, CA Pizza Kitchen, Denny's, Food Court, Garrison's Broiler, Goldfish, Houlihan's, Jason's Deli, J. Alexander's, Maggiano's Italian, McDonald's, McCormick & Shmick's, PF Chang's, Schlotsky's, **lodging:** Crowne Plaza, Fairfield Inn, **other:** Barnes&Noble, Best Buy, Border's, Dillard's, Firestone/auto, Goodyear/auto, Macey's, Marshall's, Old Navy, Wal-Mart SuperCtr, USPO, mall, **S**...**gas:** Chevron, **food:** Arby's, **lodging:** Hilton Garden
28	Peachtree-Dunwoody Rd(no EZ return wb), **N**...**food:** Arby's, Chequer's Grill, Fuddrucker's, Sweet Tomatos, **lodging:** Comfort Suites, Courtyard, Extended Stay America, Extended Stay Deluxe, Fairfield Inn, Hampton Inn, Hilton Suites, Holiday Inn Express, Homestead Suites, La Quinta, Marriott, Microtel, Residence Inn, Westin, **other:** Costco/gas, Home Depot, PetsMart, Publix, Rite Aid, Ross, Target, TJ Maxx, mall, **S**...HOSPITAL
27	US 19 N, GA 400, **2 mi N**...LDS Temple
26	Glenridge Dr(from eb), Johnson Ferry Rd
25	US 19 S, Roswell Rd, Sandy Springs, **N**...**gas:** BP, Chevron, Exxon, Shell/dsl, **food:** American Pie Rest., Applebee's, Arby's, Boston Mkt, Burger King, Caribbean Cafe, Chicago Pizza, Chick-fil-A, Chipotle Mexican, Domino's, Dunkin Donuts, El Azteca Mexican, El Toro Mexican, IHOP, KFC/Pizza Hut, Landmark Diner, La Rumba Cafe, Longhorn Steaks, Madarin House, McDonald's, Mellow Mushroom Cafe, Noodles Cafe, Panera Bread, Rumi's Kitchen, Ruth's Chris Steaks, Starbucks, Steak'n Shake, Subway, Taco Bell, Waffle House, Wendy's, **lodging:** Comfort Inn, Hampton Inn, Homestead Suites, **other:** HOSPITAL, CVS Drug, DeKalb Tire, $Tree, Hancock Fabrics, Marshall's, NAPA AutoCare, Office Depot, PepBoys, Publix, Target, Toyota, Whole Foods Mkt, **S**...**gas:** Chevron/24hr, Shell, **food:** El Taco Veloz, Frankie's Grill, Kobe Steaks, Mama's Café, **lodging:** Day's Inn/rest., **other:** Kroger/gas(1.5mi)
24	Riverside Dr
22	New Northside Dr, to Powers Ferry Rd, **N**...**gas:** Shell, **S**...**gas:** BP, Chevron/24hr, **food:** McDonald's, Waffle House, Wendy's, **lodging:** Candlewood Suites, Crowne Plaza, Hawthorn Suites, Homestead Suites, **other:** CVS Drug
21	(from wb), **N**...**gas:** Shell, **food:** HillTop Café, Homestead Village, **other:** BMW/Mini
20	I-75, N to Chattanooga, S to Atlanta(from wb), to US 41 N
19	US 41, Cobb Pkwy, to Dobbins AFB, **N**...**gas:** BP, Chevron/24hr, Citgo, Shell, **food:** Arby's, BBQ, Bruster's, Carrabba's, ChuckeCheese, Denny's, Dunkin Donuts, Hardee's, IHOP, Jade Palace, Joe's Crabshack, KFC, McDonald's, Olive Garden, Papa John's, Pizza Hut, Red Lobster, Steak'n Shake, Subway, Sunny's BBQ, The Border Mexican, Waffle House, Wendy's, **lodging:** Hilton, Holiday Inn Express, Wingate Inn, **other:** Best Buy, Cadillac, Buick/Pontiac/Subaru, Chevrolet/Saab, Circuit City, Eckerd,

Atlanta Area

GEORGIA
Interstate 285

<table>
<tr><td colspan="2">Honda, Hyundai, Lexus, Marshall's, Michael's, Office Depot, PetsMart, Ross, Target, Walgreen, S...gas: Chevron/24hr, food: Buffalo's Café, Cheese Factory, Chipotle Mexican, Chick-fil-A, El Toro Mexican, Hooters, Jason's Deli, Johnny Rocket's, Longhorn Steaks, Maggiano's Italian, Malone's Grill, Olde Mill Steaks, PF Chang, Pizza Hut, Ruby Tuesday, Schlotsky's, lodging: Courtyard, Homewood Suites, Renaissance Motel, Sheraton Suites, Stouffer Waverly Hotel, Sumner Suites, other: A&P, Barnes&Noble, Circuit City, Costco/gas, JC Penney, Macy's, Sears/auto, USPO, mall</td></tr>
<tr><td>18</td><td>Paces Ferry Rd, to Vinings, N...food: Panera Bread, lodging: Fairfield Inn, La Quinta, S...gas: QT/24hr, food: Chick-fil-A, Subway, Willy's Grill, lodging: Extended Stay Deluxe, Hampton Inn, Wyndham, other: Eckerd, Goodyear/auto, Home Depot, Publix</td></tr>
<tr><td>16</td><td>S Atlanta Rd, to Smyrna, N...food: Five Guys Burgers, Waffle House, Zio's Italian, lodging: Holiday Inn Express, other: HOSPITAL, S...gas: Pilot/Wendy's/dsl/scales/24hr, Shell/dsl, Texaco, other: Kroger</td></tr>
<tr><td>15</td><td>GA 280, S Cobb Dr, E...lodging: Microtel, other: U-Haul, W...gas: BP/dsl, RaceTrac, Shell, food: Arby's, Mrs Winners, Checker's, Chick-fil-A, China Buffet, IHOP, Krystal/24hr, McDonald's, Subway, Taco Bell, Wendy's, Zaxby's, lodging: AmeriHost, Comfort Inn, Country Inn Suites, Knight's Inn, Sun Suites, other: HOSPITAL</td></tr>
<tr><td>14mm</td><td>Chattahoochee River</td></tr>
<tr><td>13</td><td>Bolton Rd(from nb), no services</td></tr>
<tr><td>12</td><td>US 78, US 278, Bankhead Hwy, E...gas: Citgo/dsl, Petro/Iron Skillet/dsl/rest./scales/24hr/@, Shell/dsl/24hr, food: Mrs Winner's, other: Blue Beacon, W...gas: BP, Marathon</td></tr>
<tr><td>10b a</td><td>I-20, W to Birmingham, E to Atlanta(exits left from nb), W...to Six Flags</td></tr>
<tr><td>9</td><td>GA 139, MLK Dr, to Adamsville, E...gas: Phillips 66, Shell, food: Mrs Winner's, other: Family$, Wayfield Foods, W...gas: Chevron, Shell, food: Checker's, Church's, Golden House Chinese, KFC/Taco Bell, McDonald's</td></tr>
<tr><td>7</td><td>Cascade Rd, E...gas: Marathon, food: Papa John's, other: Kroger, W...gas: BP, Phillips 66, food: Applebee's, China Express, KFC, McDonald's, Moe's SW Grill, Mrs Winner's, Pizza Hut, Quizno's, Starbucks, Subway, Up the Creek, Wendy's, other: HOSPITAL, Eckerd, GNC, Home Depot, Publix, Radio Shack, Tires+</td></tr>
<tr><td>5b a</td><td>GA 166, Lakewood Fwy, E...gas: Chevron, Shell, food: Blimpie, Burger King, Capt D's, Checker's, IHOP, KFC, Taco Bell, Wendy's, other: Goodyear, Firestone, Kroger, Macy's, mall, W...gas: BP, Citgo/dsl, RaceWay, Shell/dsl/24hr, food: Church's, KFC, Mrs Winner's, Wendy's, lodging: Deluxe Inn, other: VET, AutoZone, CVS Drug, Family$</td></tr>
<tr><td>2</td><td>Camp Creek Pkwy, to airport, E...gas: BP, Exxon, Texaco, food: Checker's, McDonald's, Mrs Winner's, lodging: Comfort Suites, W...gas: food: American Deli, Brewster's, Carino's, Chick-fil-A, Jason's Deli, LongHorn Steaks, Panda Express, Red Lobster, Ruby Tuesday, Wendys, other: Barnes&Noble, BJ's Whse/gas, Circuit City, Lowes Whse, Marshall's, Old Navy, Petsmart, Publix, Ross, Staples, Target, Walgreens</td></tr>
<tr><td>1</td><td>Washington Rd, E...gas: Texaco/dsl, W...gas: Chevron, lodging: Regency Inn</td></tr>
</table>

Interstate 475(Macon)

<table>
<tr><td>Exit #</td><td>Services</td></tr>
<tr><td>16mm</td><td>I-475 begins/ends on I-75, exit 177.</td></tr>
<tr><td>15</td><td>US 41, Bolingbroke, 1 mi E...gas: Exxon/dsl/LP, Marathon/dsl</td></tr>
<tr><td>9</td><td>Zebulon Rd, E...gas: Citgo, Shell/Pizza Hut/Taco Bell/24hr, food: Buffalo's Café, Chick-fil-A, Hong Kong Rest., Krystal, Margarita's Mexican, McAlister's Deli, McDonald's, NU Wiener's, Papa John's, Subway, Taki Japanese, Waffle House, Wendy's, lodging: Baymont Inn, Fairfield Inn, Sleep Inn, other: HOSPITAL, GNC, Kohl's, Kroger, Krystal, Lowe's Whse, Radio Shack, Walgreens, Wal-Mart SuperCtr/dsl, USPO, W...gas: Marathon, Polly's Café, other: Advance Parts, CVS Drug</td></tr>
<tr><td>8mm</td><td>rest area nb, full(handicapped)facilities, phone, vending, picnic tables, litter barrels, petwalk</td></tr>
<tr><td>5</td><td>GA 74, Macon, E...gas: RaceWay, food: Waffle House, other: Harley-Davidson/Suzuki, to Mercer U, W...gas: Flash/Subway, Texaco/Church's/dsl, food: Capt D's, Wok&Roll Chinese, lodging: Howard Johnson, other: $General, Food Lion, Tires+, vet, to Lake Tobesofkee</td></tr>
<tr><td>3</td><td>US 80, Macon, E...gas: Marathon/dsl, Raceway, Spectrum/Subway, food: China Buffet, Cracker Barrel, JL's BBQ, McDonald's, Waffle House, lodging: Best Western, Comfort Inn, Day's Inn, Discovery Inn, Economy Inn, Hampton Inn, Holiday Inn, Motel 6, Quality Inn, Red Carpet Inn, Rodeway Inn, Super 8, Travelodge, Villager Inn, other: Wal-Mart SuperCtr/gas/24hr, 1 mi E...gas: Stop n' Shop, food: Applebee's, Chick-fil-A, Cici's, DQ, Golden Corral, KFC, Krystal, Ryan's, Sonny's BBQ, Taco Bell, other: Best Buy, BooksAMillion, Chrysler/Plymouth, CVS Drug, Dillard's, Goody's, Home Depot, Jo-Ann Fabrics, Kroger, Lowe's Whse, Marchall's, Michael's, Nissan, Old Navy, Petsmart, Sam's Club/gas, Target, Toyota, mall, W...gas: Marathon/dsl, Shell, food: Burger King, lodging: Econolodge, Knight's Inn</td></tr>
<tr><td>0mm</td><td>I-475 begins/ends on I-75, exit 156.,</td></tr>
</table>

Interstate 575

<table>
<tr><td>Exit #</td><td>Services</td></tr>
<tr><td>30mm</td><td>I-575 begins/ends on GA 5/515.</td></tr>
<tr><td>27</td><td>GA 5, Howell Br, to Ball Ground</td></tr>
<tr><td>24</td><td>Airport Dr</td></tr>
<tr><td>20</td><td>GA 5, to Canton, E...gas: BP, food: Casey's rest., Chick-fil-A, Hooters, Ryan's, Stevi B's Pizza, Waffle Wouse, Wendy's, lodging: Comfort Inn, Homestead Inn, other: Chevrolet, Toyota, Wal-Mart SuperCtr/24hr, W...gas: Citgo, RaceTrac, food: Applebee's, Arby's, Cracker Barrel, Longhorn Steaks, McDonald's, O'Charley's, Outback Steaks, Panda Express, Red Lobster, Starbucks, Subway, Waffle House, Zaxby's, lodging: Holiday Inn Express, other: Belk, Goody's, Home Depot, Michaels, Publix, Radio Shack, Ross</td></tr>
<tr><td>19</td><td>GA 20 E, Canton, no services</td></tr>
<tr><td>17</td><td>GA 140, to Roswell (from sb), Canton, no services</td></tr>
<tr><td>16</td><td>GA 20, GA 140, E...gas: Pure, W...gas: Citgo, Shell, food: BBQ, Burger King, KFC, Mandarin House, LJ Silver, Papa John's, Taco Bell, Waffle House, other: $General, K-Mart</td></tr>
<tr><td>14</td><td>Holly Springs, E...gas: Citgo/dsl, food: Domino's, Pizza Hut, lodging: Pinecrest Motel, W...gas: BP, Chevron, RaceTrac, Shell, food: Subway, Viva Mexico, Wendy's, Zaxby's, other: Kroger, Publix, Walgreens</td></tr>
<tr><td>11</td><td>Sixes Rd, E...gas: Chevron, QT, W...gas: Citgo</td></tr>
<tr><td>8</td><td>Towne Lake Pkwy, to Woodstock, E...gas: Citgo, Shell, food: McDonald's, Waffle House, Waffle King/24hr, other: Ford, Hyundai, W...gas: Phillips 66</td></tr>
</table>

Interstate 575

7 GA 92, Woodstock, E...**gas:** Chevron, QT, Shell, **food:** Arby's, Burger King, Capt D's, Checker's, Chick-fil-A, DQ, Firehouse Subs, Folk's Kitchen, KFC, McDonald's, Moe's SW Grill, Mrs Winner's, O'Charley's, Resturante Mexico, Ruby Tuesday, Subway, Taco Bell, Waffle House, Wendy's, **lodging:** Comfort Suites, Hampton Inn, Suburban Lodge, **other:** Big 10 Tire, Camping World, CVS Drug, Firestone/auto, Goodyear/auto, Ingles, Just Brakes, W...**gas:** BP, **food:** Carabu Coffee, IHOP, Mi Casa Mexican, Schlotzky's, Steak'n Shake, Taco Mac, **other:** Atlanta Bread, Big Lots, BJ's Whse/gas, Discout Tire, Honda, Home Depot, Kohl's, Lowe's Whse, Office Depot, Old Navy, Target

4 Bells Ferry Rd, W...**gas:** QT/24hr, Shell/dsl, **food:** Arby's, Burger King, Ralph's Grill, Subway, Waffle House, **other:** Eckerd

3 Chastain Rd, to I-75 N, W...**gas:** Chevron, Citgo, Shell, **food:** Arby's, Cracker Barrel, Mrs. Winner's, Los Reyes, O'Charley's, Panda Express, Sidelines Grill, Subway, ToGo's/Baskin Robbins, Waffle House, Wendy's, **lodging:** Best Western, Comfort Inn, Country Inn&Suites, Fairfield Inn, Residence Inn, Springhill Suites, Suburban Inn, **other:** to Kennesaw St Coll

1 Barrett Pkwy, to I-75 N, US 41, E...**gas:** Chevron, Murphy USA/dsl, QT, **food:** Barnacle's Cafe, Buffalo Wild Wings, Burger King, Fuddruckers, KFC, Moe's SW Grill, Quizno's, Starbucks, Texas Roadhouse, Waffle House, Wendy's, Zaxby's, **other:** Atlanta Bread, Barnes&Noble, CVS Drug, $Tree, Firestone, Publix, Ross, SteinMart, Wal-Mart SuperCtr/dsl, W...**gas:** Shell, Texaco, **food:** Applebee's, Fuddrucker's, McDonald's, Olive Garden, Provino's Italian, Red Lobster, Smokey Bones, Starbucks, Waffle House, **lodging:** Comfort Inn, Crestwood Suites, Day's Inn, Holiday Inn Express, La Quinta, Ramada Ltd, Red Roof Inn, **other:** Big 10 Tire, Firestone/auto, Home Depot, Marshall's, Michael's, TJ Maxx, mall

0mm I-575 begins/ends on I-75, exit 268.

Interstate 675

Exit #	Services

10mm I-285 W, to Atlanta Airport, E to Augusta. I-675 begins/ends on I-285, exit 52., no services

7 Anvil Block Rd, Ft Gillem, E...**gas:** BP, **food:** Subway, W...**gas:** Exxon

5 Forest Pkwy, E...**gas:** Texaco/dsl, W...**gas:** QT/dsl/scales, **food:** McDonald's, Waffle House

2 US 23, GA 42, E...**gas:** BP, Texaco, **food:** Horizon/Backyard Burger, Mo-Joe's Café, W...**gas:** Chevron/dsl, Citgo, **food:** Teapot Chinese, Waffle House, **other:** Eckerd, Family$, Food Depot, Goodyear/auto, USPO

1 GA 138, to I-75 N, Stockbridge, E...**gas:** Chevron/24hr, Citgo/dsl, Exxon, Marathon, Shell, **food:** A&W/LJ Silver, Arby's, Blimpie, Burger King, Capt D's, Checker's, DQ, Golden Corral, KFC, King Buffet, McDonald's, Papa John's, Pizza Hut, Popeye's, Ryan's, Taco Bell, Waffle House, Wendy's, Zaxby's, **lodging:** Best Value, Comfort Inn, Holiday Inn Express, Magnolia Inn, Motel 6, Stockbridge Inn, Suburban Lodge, **other:** Advance Parts, Aldi Foods, BigLots, Cub Foods, CVS Drug, $Tree, Eckerd, Goodyear, Ingles Foods, NAPA, Radio Shack, Wal-Mart SuperCtr/24hr/gas, USPO, W...**gas:** Exxon, Raceway/24hr, **food:** Applebee's, Arby's, Broadway Diner, Burger King, Chick-fil-A, ChinChin Chinese, CiCi's, DQ, Folk's Rest., Frontera Mexican, Golden Corral, Honeybaked

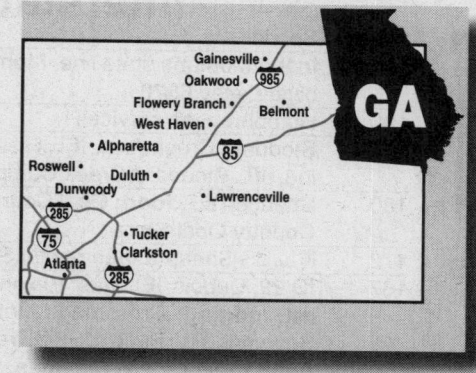

Ham, IHOP, KFC, Krystal, LJ Silver, McDonald's, Piccadilly's, Philly Connection, Shoney's, Subway, Taco Bell, Taco Mac, Tokyo Seafood, Waffle House, Wendy's, **lodging:** Best Western, Day's Inn, Comfort Inn, Holiday Inn, La Quinta, Hampton Inn, Motel 6, Red Roof Inn, **other:** HOSPITAL, GNC, Goodyear, K-Mart, Kroger, Lowes Whse, Office Depot, Tires+

I-675 begins/ends on I-75, exit 227.

Interstate 985 (Gainesville)

Exit #	Services

I-985 begins/ends on US 23, 25mm.

24 to US 129 N, GA 369 W, Gainesville, N...**other:** HOSPITAL, GA Mtn Ctr, S...**gas:** BP/Subway/dsl, Chevron/dsl, Citgo, **food:** Double B Burger, Rabbit Trail Cafe,

22 GA 11, Gainesville, N...**gas:** BP/dsl, Citgo, QT/24hr, **food:** Burger King, McDonald's, **lodging:** Best Western/rest., S...**gas:** Chevron, Shell/dsl, **food:** Waffle House, **lodging:** Motel 6

20 GA 60, GA 53, Gainesville, N...**gas** Citgo/dsl, **food:** El Manarca, McDonald's, Mrs Winners, **lodging:** Best Value Inn, Hampton Inn, S...**gas:** Kangaroo, **food:** Subway, Waffle House

16 GA 53, Oakwood, N...**gas:** BP, Citgo, **food:** Arby's, Baskin-Robbins/Dunkin Donuts, Burger King, DQ, El Sombrero Mexican, Hardee's, KFC, McDonald's, Pizza Hut, Subway, Taco Bell, Waffle House, Zaxby's, **lodging:** Admiral Benbow Inn, Country Inn Suites, Jameson Inn, **other:** Chrysler/Jeep, CVS Drug, Food Lion, RV Ctr, Sam's Club, S...**gas:** Citgo/dsl, QT/dsl, **food:** Checker's, Krystal, Mrs Winners, Sonny's BBQ, Waffle House, Wendy's, **lodging:** Comfort Inn, **other:** AutoZone, Goodyear/auto, Publix, Walgreens

12 Spout Springs Rd, Flowery Branch, N...**gas:** Exxon/dsl, S...**gas:** BP/Subway, Chevron/dsl, **food:** Burger&Shake, China Garden, CrossRoads Grill, Domino's, El Sombrero Mexican, TCBY, Thai Dish, **other:** Eckerd, Publix

8 GA 347, Friendship Rd, Lake Lanier, N...**gas:** BP, Chevron, Shell, Texaco, **food:** Backyard Burger, Blimpie, Burger King, China Garden, Huddle House, McDonald's, Sonia's Mexican, Subway, 3rd Coast, Waffle House, Wendy's, Vinny's NY Grill, Zaxby's, **other:** Advance parts, Publix, S... Harley Davidson, Camper City RV Ctr

4 US 23 S, GA 20, Buford, N...**gas:** QT, Shell, **food:** Arby's, Burger King, Capt D's, Checker's, Golden Buddah, Golden Corral, Huddle House, IHOP, KFC, McDonald's, Saigon Bangkok, Taco Bell, Wendy's, Zaxby's, **lodging:** Days Inn, Holiday Inn Express, **other:** Ace Hardware, Buick/Pontiac/GMC, Dodge/Jeep, Home Depot, KIA, Tuesday Morning, S...**gas:** BP, Chevron, Citgo, Texaco, **food:** Ryan's, Sonny's BBQ, Waffle House, **other:** $Tree, Expert Tire, Honda, Lowe's Whse, Wal-Mart SuperCtr/24hr

0mm I-985 begins/ends on I-85.

IDAHO

Interstate 15

N ↕ S

Idaho Falls

Exit #	Services
196mm	Idaho/Montana state line, Monida Pass, continental divide, elev 6870
190	Humphrey, no services
184	Stoddard Creek Area, E...Historical Site, RV camping, W...Stoddard Creek Camping
180	Spencer, E...**food:** Opal Country Café, **other:** High Country Opal Store
172	E...US Sheep Experimental Sta, no services
167	ID 22, Dubois, E...**gas:** Exxon/dsl/24hr, Phillips 66/dsl, **lodging:** Crossroads Motel, **other:** RV dump, Scoggins RV Park, USPO, **rest area both lanes, full(handicapped) facilities, phone, picnic table, litter barrels, petwalk**, W...to Craters NM, Nez Pearce Tr
150	Hamer, E...**other:** Goodyear, USPO, food, phone
143	ID 33, ID 28, to Mud Lake, Rexburg, W...weigh sta both lanes
142mm	roadside parking, hist site
135	ID 48, Roberts, E...**gas:** Tesoro/dsl/LP, **other:** Roberts Mkt, Western Wings RV Park
128	Osgood Area, E...**gas:** Sinclair/dsl
119	US 20 E, to Rexburg, Idaho Falls, E **on Lindsay... gas:** Sinclair/dsl, **food:** Chili's, Denny's, Outback Steaks, Sandpiper Rest., Smitty's Rest., **lodging:** Best Western, Comfort Inn, Day's Inn, LeRitz Hotel, Motel 6, Quality Inn/rest., Red Lion Hotel, Shilo Inn/rest., Super 8, **other:** KOA, LDS Temple, RV Park
118	US 20, Broadway St, Idaho Falls, E...**gas:** Phillips 66/dsl, **food:** Applebees, Arctic Circle, Cedric's Rest, Chili's, Domino's, Mini's Rest., Quizno's, Wendy's, **lodging:** AmeriTel, Fairfield Inn, **other:** HOSPITAL, American RV, Buick/GMC, Ford, Harley-Davidson, Subaru, LDS Temple, Wal-Mart SuperCtr/24hr, W... **gas:** Chevron/dsl, Exxon, /Flying J/dsl, Maverik, Phillips 66, **food:** Arby's, BBQ, Burger King, DQ, Hong Kong Chinese, Jack-in-the-Box, Little Caesar's, McDonald's, O'Brady's, Papa Murphy's, Pizza Hut, Subway, **lodging:** Comfort Inn, Motel 6, Motel West/rest., **other:** Albertson's, AutoZone, Checker Parts, RiteAid
116	no facilites
113	US 26, to Idaho Falls, Jackson, E...**gas:** Chevron/A&W/dsl, Sinclair/Dad's/dsl/24hr/@, Exxon/dsl, **other:** HOSPITAL, Peterbilt, Sunnyside RV Park, Targhee RV Park
108	Shelley, Firth Area, **1 mi** E...**other:** RV Park/dump
101mm	**rest area both lanes, full(handicapped)facilities, phone, picnic tables, litter barrels, petwalk, geological site**
98	Rose-Firth Area, no services
94.5mm	Snake River
93	US 26, ID 39, Blackfoot, E...**gas:** Chevron/24hr, /Flying J/dsl/LP/24hr, Maverik, **food:** Arctic Circle, Arby's, Domino's, Homestead Rest., KFC, Little Caesar's, McDonald's, Papa Murphy's, Pizza Hut, Sonic, Subway, Taco Bell, Taco Time, Wendy's, Wingers, **lodging:** Best Western, Super 8, **other:** Albertson's, Auto Zone, Checker Parts, Dodge/Ford, Kesler's Foods, Radio Shack, RiteAid, Sav-On, Schwab Tire, Wal-Mart SuperCtr/24hr, W... Phillips 66, Riverside Boot/saddleshop(4mi)
90.5mm	Blackfoot River

Pocatello

Exit #	Services
89	US 91, S Blackfoot, **2 mi** E...**lodging:** Y Motel
80	Ft Hall, W...**gas:** Sinclair/dsl/rest./casino, **other:** Shoshone Bannock Tribal Museum
72	I-86 W, to Twin Falls
71	Pocatello Creek Rd, Pocatello, E...**gas:** Chevron/Burger King, Phillips 66/dsl, Shell/dsl/24hr, **food:** Applebee's, Jack-in-the Box, Perkins, Sandpiper Rest., Subway, **lodging:** AmeriTel, Best Western, Comfort Inn, Holiday Inn, Red Lion Inn, Super 8, **other:** HOSPITAL, KOA(1mi), W...**gas:** Exxon, **food:** Changs Garden Chinese, DQ, Pier 49 Pizza, Senor Iguana's Mexican, SF Pizza, Sizzler, **other:** RiteAid, WinCo Foods, **1 mi** W **on Yellowstone...food:** Arby's, Bamboo Garden, Golden Corral, KFC, McDonald's, Papa Murphy's, Pizza Hut, Schlotsky's, Skipper's, Taco Bell, Taco Time, TCBY, Wendy's, Winger's, **other:** Albertson's, AutoZone, Checker, Ford, Fred Meyer, Harley Davidson, Honda, Jeep, JoAnn Fabrics, Radio Shack, Toyota, Walgreen
69	Clark St, Pocatello, E...**gas:** Maverik/dsl, Shell/Blimpie/dsl, Sinclair/Arctic Circle/dsl, **lodging** Hampton Inn, W...**other:** HOSPITAL, to ID St U, museum
67	US 30/91, 5th St, Pocatello, E...**gas:** Exxon/24hr, **1-2 mi** W...**gas:** Phillips 66/dsl, Shell, Sinclair/dsl, **food:** Elmer's Dining, 5th St Bagels, Goody's Deli, McDonald's, Pizza Hut, Poppa Cafe, Subway, Taco Bell, **lodging:** Best Western, Econolodge, Thunderbird Motel, **other:** HOSPITAL, Albertson's, Cowboy RV Park, Old Fort Hall, info, museum, zoo
63	Portneuf Area, W...**other:** to Mink Creek RA, RV camp/dump
59mm	**rest area/weigh sta both lanes, full(handicapped) facilities, phone, picnic table, litter barrel, vending, petwalk, hist site**
58	Inkom(from sb), **1/2 mi** W...**gas:** Sinclair/dsl/café, **other:** Pebble Creek Ski Area, USPO, repair
57	Inkom(from nb), same as 58
47	US 30, to Lava Hot Springs, McCammon, E...**gas:** /Flying J/dsl/LP/rest./24hr/@, Chevron/A&W/Taco Time/dsl, **food:** Subway, **other:** to Lava Hot Springs RA, McCammon RV Park
44	Lp 15, Jenson Rd, McCammon, E...access to food
40	Arimo, E...**gas:** Sinclair/dsl/deli, **other:** USPO
36	US 91, Virginia, no services
31	ID 40, to Downey, Preston, E...**gas:** Shell/Flags West/dsl/motel/café/24hr/@, **other:** Downata Hot Springs RV camping
25mm	**rest area sb, full(handicapped)facilities, phone, picnic tables, litter barrels, petwalk**
24.5mm	Malad Summit, elev 5574
22	to Devil Creek Reservoir, E...RV camping
17	ID 36, to Weston, to Preston, no services
13	ID 38, Malad City, W...**gas:** Chevron/Burger King, Phillips 66/dsl/café, **food:** Me&Lou's Rest., Subway, **lodging:** Village Inn Motel, **other:** HOSPITAL, Chevrolet/Buick, carwash, **1 mi** W...**gas:** Texaco/dsl, **food:** Chat&Chew Café, **other:** 3R's Tire, True Value, museum, repair, rv dump
7mm	**Welcome Ctr nb, full(handicapped)facilities, info, phone, picnic tables, litter barrels, vending, petwalk**
3	to Samaria, Woodruff, no services
0mm	Idaho/Utah state line

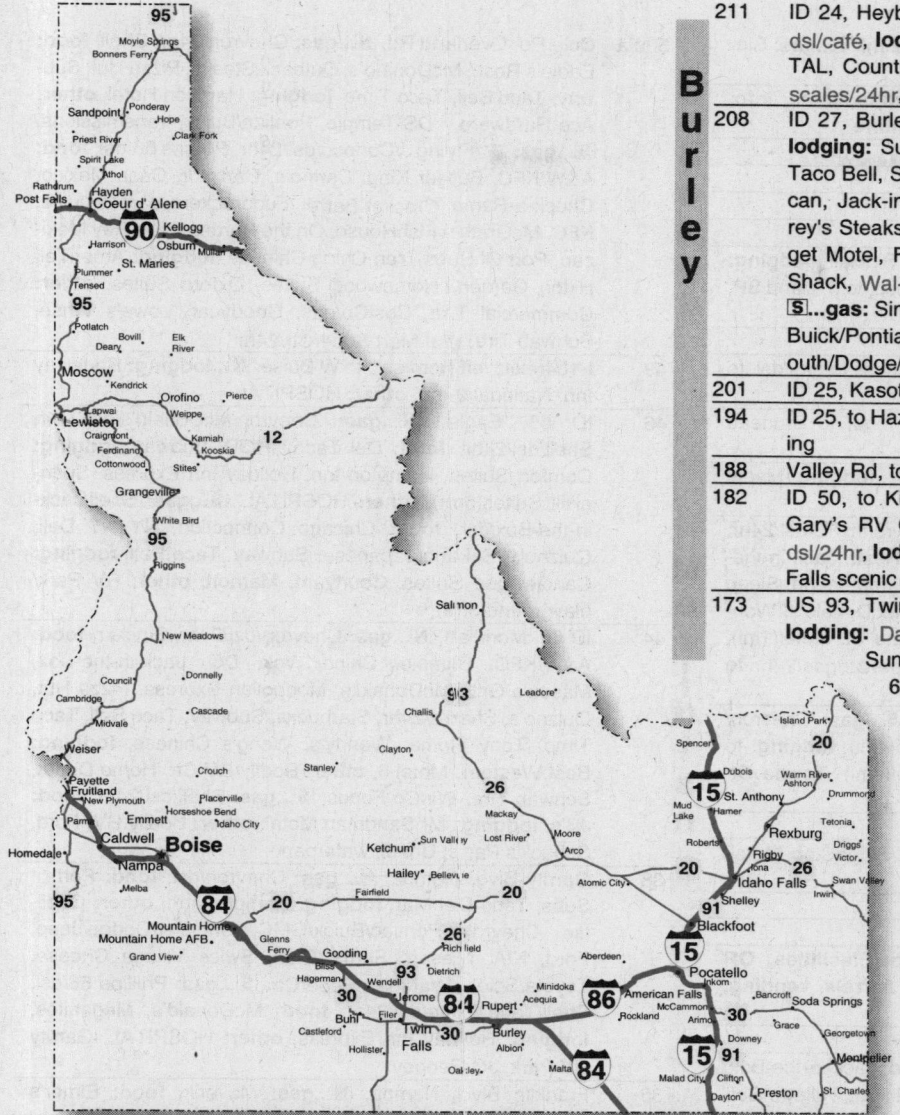

Interstate 84

Burley

Exit #	Services
211	ID 24, Heyburn, Burley, ...gas: Chevron/A&W/dsl, Sinclair/dsl/café, **lodging:** Tops Motel, Wayside Cafe, **other:** HOSPITAL, Country RV Village/park, **S**...gas: Love's/Carl's Jr./dsl/scales/24hr, **other:** Riverside RV Park, truck repair
208	ID 27, Burley, **N**...gas: Phillips 66/dsl, **food:** Conner's Cafe, **lodging:** Super 8, **S**...gas: Chevron/Subway/dsl/24hr, Shell/Taco Bell, Sinclair, **food:** Arby's, Burger King, Garibaldi Mexican, Jack-in-the-Box, JB's, Little Caesar's, McDonald's, Morey's Steaks, Perkins, Wendy's, **lodging:** Best Western, Budget Motel, Fairfield Inn, **other:** HOSPITAL, Cal Store, Radio Shack, Wal-Mart SuperCtr/dsl/24hr, to Snake River RA, **1 mi S**...gas: Sinclair/dsl, **food:** Guadalajara Mexican, KFC, **other:** Buick/Pontiac/GMC, CarQuest, Checker Parts, Chrysler/Plymouth/Dodge/Jeep, Commercial Tire, NAPA, Stoke's Foods
201	ID 25, Kasota Rd, to Paul, no services
194	ID 25, to Hazelton, **S**...gas: Sinclair/dsl/café, **other:** RV camping
188	Valley Rd, to Eden, no services
182	ID 50, to Kimberly, Twin Falls, **N**...gas: Sinclair/dsl, **other:** Gary's RV Ctr/park/dump, **S**...gas: Shell/Blimpie/Taco Bell/dsl/24hr, **lodging:** Amber Inn, **other:** HOSPITAL, to Shoshone Falls scenic attraction
173	US 93, Twin Falls, **N**...gas: ✈/Flying J/Thad's/dsl/24hr/@, **lodging:** Day's Inn, **other:** KOA(1mi), Blue Beacon/24hr, to Sun Valley, **5 mi S**...gas: Chevron/dsl, Exxon, Phillips 66, Sinclair, **food:** Applebee's, Arby's, Arctic Circle, Aztlan Mexican, Blimpie, Burger King, Carino's Italian, Chili's, Coldstone Creamery, DQ, Elmer's, Fiesta, Golden Corral, Hart's Cafe, Idaho Joe's, IHOP, Jack-in-the-Box, Jaker's Rest., JB's, KFC, Mandarin Chinese, McDonald's, Outback Steaks, Perkins, Quizno's, Shari's, Sizzler, Subway, Taco Bell, Taste Of Thai, Tomato's Grill, Wok In Grill, **lodging:** Best American Inn, Best Western, Comfort Inn, Hampton Inn, Holiday Inn Express, Motel 6, Red Lion, Shilo Inn, Super 8, Weston Inn, **other:** HOSPITAL, AutoZone, Barnes&Noble, Buick, Chevrolet/Pontiac/Cadillac, Costco/gas, Dell, $Tree, Ford, Goodyear, Hastings, Home Depot, Honda, JC Penney, Lowe's Whse, Macy's, Michael's, Mitsubishi, Nissan, Old Navy, Petsmart, Schuck's Parts, Schwab Tire, ShopKO, Sportsman's Whse, Target, Tuesday Morning, WinCo Foods, Coll of S ID
171mm	rest area/weigh sta eb, full(handicapped)facilities, phone, vending, picnic tables, litter barrels, petwalk

Jerome

Exit #	Services
168	ID 79, to Jerome, **N**...gas: Chevron/dsl, Shell/Wendy's/dsl, Sinclair/dsl, **food:** Burger King, McDonald's, Pizza Hut, Sonic, **lodging:** Best Western, Crest Motel, **other:** AutoZone, Brockman RV Ctr, Wal-Mart SuperCtr/gas/24hr, **2 mi N**...food: DQ, **lodging:** Holiday Motel, **other:** HOSPITAL, Chevrolet, **S**...food: Subway, **other:** ID RV Ctr/marine
165	ID 25, Jerome, **N**...gas: Sinclair/dsl, **lodging:** Holiday Motel(1mi), **other:** HOSPITAL, RV camping/dump
157	ID 46, Wendell, **N**...food: Subway, **1 mi N**...other: HOSPITAL, Intermountain RV Park, **S**...gas: Sinclair/dsl, **food:** Farmhouse Rest.
155	ID 46, to Wendell, **N**...Intermountain RV Camp/ctr
147	to Tuttle, **S**...other: to Malad Gorge SP, High Adventure RV Park/cafe
146mm	Malad River
141	US 26, to US 30, Gooding, **N**...HOSPITAL, **S**...gas: Phillips 66/dsl/café, Stinker/Sinclair/dsl/24hr, **lodging:** Amber Inn, Hagerman Inn(9mi), Y Inn Motel, **other:** RV camping

Exit #	Services
275mm	Idaho/Utah state line
270mm	**rest area both lanes, full(handicapped) facilities, geological site, phone, picnic tables, litter barrels, petwalk**
263	Juniper Rd, no services
257mm	Sweetzer Summit, elev 5530
254	Sweetzer Rd, no services
245	Sublett Rd, to Malta, **N**...gas: Sinclair/dsl/café, **other:** camping
237	Idahome Rd, no services
234mm	Raft River
229mm	**rest area/weigh sta both lanes, full(handicapped) facilities, phone, picnic tables, litter barrels, petwalk**
228	ID 81, Yale Rd, to Declo, no services
222	I-86, US 30, E to Pocatello
216	ID 77, ID 25, to Declo, **N**...gas: Phillips 66/FoodCourt/dsl, **other:** HOSPITAL, Village of Trees RV Park, to Walcott SP, **S**...gas: Shell/Jake's Café/dsl
215mm	Snake River

IDAHO

Interstate 84

E ↑ ↓ **W**

Exit	Description
137	Lp 84, to US 30, to Pioneer Road, Bliss, **2 mi** S...**gas:** Sinclair/Stinker/dsl/24hr, **other:** camping
133mm	**rest area both lanes, full(handicapped)facilities, info, picnic tables, litter barrels, petwalk, phone**
129	King Hill, no services
128mm	Snake River
125	Paradise Valley, no services
122mm	Snake River
121	Glenns Ferry, **1 mi** S...**gas:** Shell/dsl, Sinclair, **lodging:** Redford Motel, **other:** Carmela Winery/rest., to 3 Island SP, Trails West RV camp/dump
120	Glenns Ferry(from eb), same as 121
114	ID 78(from wb), to Hammett, **1 mi** S...access to gas/dsl, to Bruneau Dunes SP
112	to ID 78, Hammett, **1 mi** S...gas/dsl, food, to Bruneau Dunes SP
99	ID 51, ID 67, to Mountain Home, **2 mi** S...**lodging:** Maple Cove Motel, camping
95	US 20, Mountain Home, N...**gas:** Chevron/KFC/dsl/24hr, Pilot/Arby's/dsl/scales/24hr, **food:** AJ's Rest., Jack-in-the-Box, Subway, **lodging:** Best Western, Hampton Inn, Sleep Inn, S...**food:** Golden Crown Chinese, McDonald's, Wendy's, **lodging:** Hilander Motel(1mi), Towne Ctr Motel(1mi), **other:** HOSPITAL, Curves, Wal-Mart SuperCtr/gas/24hr, to Mtn Home RV Park
90	to ID 51, ID 67, W Mountain Home, S...**gas:** Chevron/Burger King/dsl/24hr, **food:** McDonald's(4mi), **lodging:** to Hilander Motel(4mi), Maple Cove Motel(4mi), Towne Ctr Motel(4mi), **other:** to Mtn Home RV Park
74	Simco Rd, no services
71	Orchard, Mayfield, S...**gas:** Sinclair/dsl/StageStop Motel/rest./24hr, **other:** phone, truckwash
66mm	weigh sta both lanes
64	Blacks Creek, Kuna, historical site
62mm	**rest area both lanes, full(handicapped)facilities, OR Trail info, phone, picnic tables, litter barrels, vending, petwalk**
59b a	S Eisenman Rd, Memory Rd, no services
57	ID 21, Gowen Rd, to Idaho City, N...**food:** Jack-in-the-Box, McDonald's, Perkins, Subway, Taco Del Mar, Tulley's Coffee, **lodging:** Best Western, **other:** Albertson's/gas, GNC, to Micron, S...**gas:** Chevron/24hr, **food:** Burger King, FoodCourt, **other:** Boise Stores/famous brands, ID Ice World
54	US 20/26, Broadway Ave, Boise, N...**gas:** Chevron/dsl/24hr, ✈/Flying J/Conoco/Arby's/dsl/LP/24hr/@, Shell/dsl, **food:** Chili's, Jack-in-the-Box, Port Of Subs, Subway, Wendy's, **lodging:** Courtyard(3mi), **other:** HOSPITAL, Big O Tire, Dowdie's Automotive, Goodyear/auto, Jo-Ann Fabrics, Radio Shack, ShopKO, to Boise St U, S...**gas:** TA/Tesoro/Taco Bell/Subway/dsl/rest./24hr/@, **lodging:** Shilo Inn, **other:** Kenworth, Mtn View RV Park
53	Vista Ave, Boise, N...**gas:** Citgo/7-11, Shell/dsl, Texaco/dsl, **food:** Pizza Hut, **lodging:** Cambria Suites, Comfort Suites, Extended Stay America, Fairfield Inn, Hampton Inn, Holiday Inn/rest., Holiday Inn Express, Super 8, **other:** Parts'n Stuff, museums, st capitol, st police, zoo, S...**gas:** Chevron/McDonald's/24hr, **food:** Denny's, Kopper Kitchen, **lodging:** Best Western, Comfort Inn, InnAmerica, Motel 6, Sleep Inn
52	Orchard St, Boise, N...**gas:** Shell/dsl/24hr, **other:** Mazda/Nissan, GMC, **1-2 mi** N...**food:** Burger King, Jack-in-the-Box, McDonald's, Raedean's Rest., Round Table Pizza, Wendy's, **other:** Albertson's/gas, Walgreens
50b a	Cole Rd, Overland Rd, N...**gas:** Chevron/24hr, Shell, **food:** Eddie's Rest., McDonald's, Outback Steaks, Pizza Hut, Subway, Taco Bell, Taco Time, **lodging:** Harrison Hotel, **other:** Ace Hardware, LDS Temple, Pontiac/Buick, transmissions, S...**gas:** ✈/Flying J/Conoco/dsl/24hr, Phillips 66/dsl, **food:** A&W/KFC, Burger King, Carino's, Carl's Jr, Casa Mexico, Chuck-a-Rama, Cracker Barrel, Fuddruckers, Jamba Juice, KFC, McGrath's FishHouse, On the Border, Pollo Rey Mexican, Port Of Subs, Yen Ching Chinese, **lodging:** AmeriTel, Hilton Garden, Homewood Suites, Oxford Suites, **other:** Commercial Tire, CostCo/gas, Goodyear, Lowe's Whse, Schwab Tire, Wal-Mart SuperCtr/24hr
49	I-184(exits left from eb), to W Boise, N...**lodging:** Rodeway Inn, National 9 Inn, **other:** HOSPITAL
46	ID 55, Eagle, N...**gas:** Chevron/McDonald's/dsl/24hr, Shell/dsl/24hr, **food:** Del Taco, IHOP, Subway, **lodging:** Comfort Suites, Hampton Inn, Holiday Inn Express, SpringHill Suites(5mi), **other:** HOSPITAL, S...**gas:** Shell/Jack-in-the-Box/dsl, **food:** Chicago Connection, NY NY Deli, Quizno's, Sakana Japanese, Subway, Taco Bell, **lodging:** Candlewood Suites, Courtyard, Marriott, **other:** RV Park/playground(3mi),
44	ID 69, Meridian, N...**gas:** Chevron/dsl/24hr, Sinclair, **food:** A&W/KFC, Blimpie, China Wok, DQ, Jack-in-the-Box, Mason's Grill, McDonald's, Mongolian Express, Pizza Hut, Quizno's, Shari's/24hr, Starbucks, Subway, Taco Bell, Taco Time, Tony Roma, Wendy's, Wong's Chinese, **lodging:** Best Western, Motel 6, **other:** Bodily RV Ctr, Home Depot, Schwab Tire, WinCo Foods, S...**gas:** Shell/dsl/24hr, **food:** JB's, **lodging:** Mr Sandman Motel, **other:** Bodily RV, Ford, Schuck's Parts, Uhaul, waterpark
38	Garrity Blvd, Nampa, N...**gas:** Chevron/dsl, **food:** Port of Subs, Taco Del Mar, **lodging:** Hampton Inn, **other:** Cadillac, Chevrolet/Pontiac/Buick/GMC, Chrysler/Dodge/Jeep, Ford, KIA, Nissan, Sam's Club, Swiss Village Cheese, Toyota/Scion, Wal-Mart SuperCtr, S...**gas:** Phillips 66/dsl, Shell/Taco Time/dsl/24hr, **food:** McDonald's, Megabites, **lodging:** Holiday Inn Express, **other:** HOSPITAL, Garrity RV Park, JC Penney
36	Franklin Blvd, Nampa, N...**gas:** Maverik, **food:** Elmer's Rest., Jack-in-the-Box, Noodles Rest., **lodging:** Shilo Inn/rest., **other:** Nelson's RV Ctr, S...**gas:** Chevron/dsl/24hr, Shell/A&W/Taco Bell/dsl/RV dump/24hr, **lodging:** Sleep Inn, **other:** HOSPITAL, Freightliner, Mason Cr RV Park, 7th Heaven RV Ctr
35	ID 55, Nampa, S...**gas:** Shell/dsl, **food:** Denny's/24hr, **lodging:** Days Inn, Shilo Inn, Super 8, **1 mi** S...**food:** Burger King, McDonald's, Pizza Hut, Taco Time, El Tanampa Mexican, **other:** HOSPITAL
33b a	ID 55 S, Midland Blvd, Marcine, S...**food:** Applebees, Arby's, Carl's Jr, Golden Corral, IHOP, Jade Garden, Jalapeno's Mexican, Olive Garden, Outback Steaks, Red Robin, Shari's Rest, Taco Bell, **other:** Best Buy, Big Lots, Big O Tire, Costco/gas, $Tree, Grocery Outlet, Home Depot, JoAnne Fabrics, K-Mart, Kohl's, Lowes Whse, Michael's, Old Navy, PetCo, Ross, ShopKo, Staples, Target, U-Haul, WinCo Foods, World Mkt
29	US 20/26, Franklin Rd, Caldwell, N...**gas:** ✈/Flying J/Conoco/Country Mkt/dsl/LP/rest./scales/24hr/@, **other:** Ambassador RV camping, S...**gas:** Sage/Sinclair/cafe/dsl/24hr, **food:** Perkins/24hr, **lodging:** Best Western, La Quinta
28	10th Ave, Caldwell, N...**gas:** Maverik/gas, **lodging:** I-84 Motel, **other:** Harley-Davidson, S...**gas:** Chevron/24hr, Shell,

Boise

Meridian

Nampa

Boise

Interstate 84

E ↕ W

	food: Carl's Jr, Domino's, Fiesta Mexican, Jack-in-the-Box, KFC, Mr V's Rest., Papa Murphy's, Pizza Hut, Subway, Wendy's, **lodging:** Sundowner Motel, **other:** HOSPITAL, AutoZone, Paul's Food/Drug, Walgreens, tires
27	ID 19, to Wilder, **1 mi** S...**gas:** Tesoro/dsl/24hr
26.5mm	Boise River
26	US 20/26, to Notus, N...**other:** Caldwell Campground, S...**gas:** Sinclair/dsl
25	ID 44, Middleton, N...**gas:** Shell/dsl, **food:** Bud's Burgers/shakes, S...Insp sta eb
17	Sand Hollow, N...**food:** Sand Hollow Café, **other:** Country Corners RV Park
13	Black Canyon Jct, S...**gas:** Sinclair/dsl/motel/rest./scales/24hr, phone
9	US 30, to New Plymouth, no services
3	US 95, Fruitland, N...**gas:** Shell/A&W/dsl, **5 mi** N...**other:** Neat Retreat RV Park, to Hell's Cyn RA
1mm	**Welcome Ctr eb, full(handicapped)facilities, info, phone, picnic tables, litter barrels, petwalk**
0mm	Snake River, Idaho/Oregon state line

Interstate 86

P o c a t e l l o

E ↕ W

Exit #	Services
63b a	I-15, N to Butte, S to SLC. I-86 begins/ends on I-15, exit 72.
61	US 91, Yellowstone Ave, Pocatello, N...**gas:** Exxon, Shell/dsl, Tesoro/dsl, **food:** Arctic Circle, Burger King, Chapala Mexican, Johnny B Goode's Diner, Lei's BBQ, Papa Murphy's, Pizza Hut, Red Lobster, Subway, Wendy's, **lodging:** Motel 6, Ramada Inn, **other:** Budget RV Park, Checker Parts, Family $, Smith's Foods, S...**gas:** ✈/Flying J/dsl/24hr, Phillips 66/dsl, **food:** Del Taco, Denny's, Fazoli's, IHOP, Me&Lou's Rest., McDonald's, Red Lobster, **other:** Dillard's, Ford, Home Depot, JC Penney, K-Mart, Lowe's Whse, Macey's, Michael's, Schwab Tire, Sears, ShopKO, TJ Maxx, Walgreens, Wal-Mart SuperCtr/24hr, dsl repair, mall
58.5mm	Portneuf River
58	US 30, W Pocatello, N...RV dump, S...**gas:** Stinker/dsl
56	N...Pocatello Air Terminal, S...**gas:** Sinclair/dsl/24hr
52	Arbon Valley, S...**gas:** Sinclair/Bannock Peak/dsl, **other:** casino
51mm	Bannock Creek
49	Rainbow Rd, no services
44	no services
40	ID 39, American Falls, N...**gas:** Phillips 66/dsl, Sinclair, **food:** Pizza Hut, Sagebrush Rest., Tres Hermanos Mexican, **lodging:** American Motel, **other:** HOSPITAL, Chevrolet/GMC, NAPA, Schwab Tire, to Am Falls RA, RV Park/dump, S...**lodging:** Hillview Motel
36	ID 37, to Rockland, American Falls, **2 mi** N...**gas:** Shell/dsl/24hr, **lodging:** Falls Motel, **other:** HOSPITAL, **2 mi** S...Indian Springs RV Resort
33	Neeley Area, no services
31mm	**rest area wb, full(handicapped)facilities, phone, picnic table, litter barrel, petwalk, vending, hist site**
28	N...**other:** to Massacre Rock SP, Register Rock Hist Site, RV camping/dump
21	Coldwater Area, no services

19mm	**rest area eb, full (handicapped) facilities, phone, picnic table, litter barrel, petwalk, vending, hist site**
15	Raft River Area, S...**gas:** Sinclair, phone
1	I-84 E, to Ogden. I-86 begins/ends on I-84, exit 222.

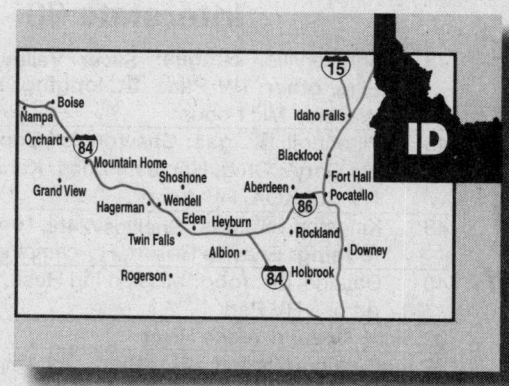

Interstate 90

E ↕ W

K e l l o g g

Exit #	Services
74mm	Idaho/Montana state line,, Pacific/Central time zone Lookout Pass elev 4680
73mm	scenic area/hist site wb
72mm	scenic area/hist site eb
71mm	runaway truck ramp wb
70mm	runaway truck ramp wb
69	Lp 90, Mullan, N...**gas:** Exxon/dsl/24hr, **food:** Mullan Café, **lodging:** Lookout Motel(1mi), **other:** USPO, museum
68	Lp 90(from eb), Mullan, same as 69
67	Morning District, Morning District, no services
66	Gold Creek(from eb), no services
65	Compressor District, no services
64	Golconda District, no services
62	ID 4, Wallace, S...**gas:** Exxon, **food:** Pizza Factory, Smokehouse BBQ, Silver Lantern Drive In, **lodging:** Stardust Motel, **other:** HOSPITAL, Accelerated Parts, Depot RV Park, Harvest Foods, Parts+, TrueValue, museum, repair
61	Lp 90, Wallace, S...**gas:** Conoco/dsl, **food:** Wallace Sta Rest./gifts, **lodging:** Brooks Hotel/rest.,, Molly B-Damm Inn, Wallace Inn, **other:** info ctr, same as 62
60	Lp 90, Silverton, S...**lodging:** Molly B-Damm Inn, **other:** RV camping
57	Lp 90, Osburn, S...**gas:** Shell/dsl/24hr, **other:** Blue Anchor RV Park, auto repair
54	Big Creek, N...**other:** Elk Creek Store/repair, hist site
51	Lp 90, Division St, Kellogg, N...**gas:** Conoco/dsl, **food:** Broken Wheel Rest., Trail Motel, **other:** HOSPITAL, Chevrolet/Pontiac/Buick/Cadillac, Chrysler/Dodge/Jeep, IGA Food, Radio Shack, Schwab Tire, Sunnyside Drug, S...**food:** In Cahoots Cafe, Veranda Rest., **other:** USPO, museum
50	Hill St(from eb), Kellogg, N...**lodging:** Trail Motel, **other:** IGA Foods, NAPA, S...**gas:** Conoco **other:** Pac'n Sav Foods, Silver Mtn Ski/summer resort/rec area, Yokes Foods, museum
49	Bunker Ave, N...**gas:** Conoco/dsl, **food:** McDonald's, Sam's Drive-In, Subway, **lodging:** Silverhorn Motel/rest., **other:** HOSPITAL, S...**food:** Silver Mtn rest., Zany's Café, **lodging:** Baymont Inn, Morning Star Lodge, **other:** museum, RV dump

IDAHO

Interstate 90

E ↑↓ W

48	Smelterville, **N...gas:** Silver Valley Car/trkstp/motel/café, **other:** RV Park, **S...lodging:** motel/café, **other:** Wayside Mkt Foods
45	Pinehurst, **S...gas:** Chevron/dsl, Conoco/dsl/24hr, **other:** Gary's Drug, Harvest Foods, Kohal Drug, Pinehurst RV Ctr, KOA, RV dump
43	Kingston, **N...gas:** Shell/dsl/24hr, **food:** Snakepit Café, **lodging:** Enaville Resort, RV camping, **S...gas:** Exxon
40	Cataldo, **N...food:** Mission Inn Rest., USPO, **S...** Kahnderosa RV Park
39.5mm	Coeur d' Alene River
39	Cataldo Mission, **S...other:** Old Mission SP, Nat Hist Landmark
34	ID 3, to St Maries, Rose Lake, **S...gas:** Conoco/dsl, Rose Lake/dsl, **food:** Rose Lake Cafe, **other:** White Pines Scenic Rte
32mm	chainup area/weigh sta wb
31.5mm	Idaho Panhandle NF, eastern boundary, 4th of July Creek
28	4th of July Pass Rec. Area, elev 3069, Mullan Tree HS, ski area, snowmobile area, turnout both lanes
24mm	chainup eb, removal wb
22	ID 97, to St Maries, L Coeur d' Alene Scenic ByWay, Wolf Lodge District, Harrison, **1 mi N...** Wolf Lodge Campground, **S...other:** KOA, Squaw Bay Resort(7mi)
20.5mm	Lake Coeur d' Alene
17	Mullan Trail Rd, no services
15	Lp 90, Sherman Ave, Coeur d' Alene, **N...other:** forest info, Lake Coeur D' Alene RA/HS, **S...gas:** Cenex/dsl, Shell, Tesoro/dsl, Texaco, **food:** Cricket's Cafe, Eduardo's Rest., Michael D's Eatery, **lodging:** Bates Motel, BudgetSaver Motel, Cedar Motel, City Inn, El Rancho Motel, Flamingo Motel, Holiday Motel, Japan House Suites, La Quinta, Monte Vista, Sandman Motel, Star Motel, State Motel, Sundowner Motel, **other:** Ace Hardware, IGA Foods/24hr, NAPA
14	15th St, Coeur d' Alene, **S...gas:** TAJ Mart, **other:** Jordon's Grocery
13	4th St, Coeur d' Alene, **N...gas:** Citgo/7-11, Conoco/dsl, **food:** Baskin-Robbins, Bruchi's Café, Carl's Jr, DQ, Davis Donuts, Denny's, Godfather's, IHOP, KFC, Little Caesar's, Taco John's, Wendy's, **lodging:** Fairfield Inn, **other:** Hastings Books, Kelly Tire, NAPA, Radio Shack, Schuck's Parts, Schwab Tires, same as 12, **S...gas:** Exxon/dsl, **food:** Phothanh Vietnamese, Subway
12	US 95, to Sandpoint, Moscow, **N...gas:** Chevron, Exxon/dsl, Holiday/dsl, Mobil, Shell/dsl, **food:** Applebee's, Arby's, Burger King, Chili's, Domino's, Elmer's Rest., McDonald's, Perkins, Pizza Hut, Pizza Shoppe, Red Lobster, Taco Bell, **lodging:** Best Inn, Best Western, Budget Host, Comfort Inn, Guesthouse Inn, Holiday Inn, La Quinta, Motel 6, Shilo Inn, Super 8, **other:** Alton's Tires, Buick/Pontiac/GMC, Cadillac/Isuzu, Dodge, $Tree, Ford/Lincoln/Mercury, Fred Meyer, GNC, Grocery Outlet, Home Depot, K-Mart, Office Depot, Safeway/gas, Schwab Tire, Super 1 Foods, Tidyman's Food/24hr, Toyota, U-Haul, Walgreens, radiators, **S...gas:** Shell, **food:** Chopstix Express, Figaro's Italian, Mr Steak, Jack-in-the-Box, Schlotsky's, Shari's, Starbucks, TCBY, **lodging:** AmeriTel, **other:** HOSPITAL, Albertson's/gas, GNC, Rite Aid, ShopKO/drugs, Staples, same as 13

C o e u r d' A l e n e

11	Northwest Blvd, **N...gas:** Texaco/Taco Time/dsl, JiffiStop, **other:** Lowe's Whse, **S...gas:** Exxon, Qwikstop/dsl, Texaco, **food:** Outback Steaks, **lodging:** Day's Inn, Holiday Inn Express, **other:** HOSPITAL, Honda/Kia
8.5mm	**Welcome Ctr/weigh sta eb, rest area both lanes, full (handicapped)facilities, info, phone, picnic tables, litter barrels, petwalk**
7	ID 41, to Rathdrum, Spirit Lake, **N...gas:** Exxon/dsl, **food:** La Cocina Mexican, Papa Murphy's, Starbucks, Subway, Wendy's, **other:** Radio Shack, Subaru, Wal-Mart SuperCtr/gas/24hr, Couer d'Alene RV Park, **S...gas:** Chevron/dsl/24hr, **food:** A&W/KFC, Applebee's, Casey's Rest./brewery, DQ, **lodging:** Comfort Inn, **other:** repair
6	Seltice Way, **N...gas:** Citgo/7-11, Exxon/RV dump, **food:** Dominos, Falls Cafe, La Cabana Mexican, Pizza Hut, **other:** AutoZone, Chevrolet, NAPA, Nissan, Subaru, Super 1 Foods/24hr, Walgreen, **S...gas:** Conoco/dsl/LP, **food:** Arby's/Taco John's, Big Cheese Pizza, Denny's, Hot Rod Café, McDonald's, Moons Mongolian, Old European, Rancho Viejo Mexican, Subway, Taco Bell, Winger's Diner, **other:** VET, Ace Hardware, Alton Tire, Curves, NW Foods, Shuck's Parts, USPO
5	Lp 90, Spokane St, Treaty Rock HS, **N...gas:** 76/dsl, Shell/dsl, **food:** Breakfast Knook, Domino's, Golden Dragon Chinese, Hunter's Steaks, Rob's Seafood/burgers, WhiteHouse Grill, **other:** CarQuest, Mazda, Schwab Tire, Seltice RV Ctr, **S...gas:** Pacific Pride/dsl, **food:** MillTown Grill
2	Pleasant View Rd, **N...gas:** ♨/Flying J/Conoco/dsl/rest./LP/scales/24hr, Shell, **food:** McDonald's, Toro Viejo Mexican, **lodging:** Howard Johnson, **S...gas:** Exxon/Subway/dsl/24hr, **food:** Zip's Rest, **lodging:** Riverbend Inn, Sleep Inn, **other:** GNC, North Idaho Outlets/famous brands, dogtrack
0mm	Idaho/Washington state line

Interstate 184(Boise)

E ↑↓ W

Exit # Services

6mm	I-184 begins/ends on 13th St, downtown, **gas:** Shell, **food:** PF Chang's, **lodging:** Hampton Inn, Safari Inn, **other:** Harley-Davidson, Office Depot, USPO
5	River St(from eb), **W...gas:** Chevron, **food:** McDonald's, **other:** Ford/Mercury
4.5mm	Boise River
3	Fairview Ave, to US 20/26 E, **W...food:** McDonald's, **lodging:** Budget Inn, DoubleTree Inn, Econolodge, **other:** Commercial Tire
2	Curtis Rd, to Garden City, **E...lodging:** Rodeway Inn, **other:** HOSPITAL
1b a	Cole Rd, Franklin Rd, **E...gas:** Chevron/Subway, **lodging:** Harrison Hotel, **other:** Acura/Honda, Buick/Pontiac, Dodge, Jaguar, Land Rover, Volvo, **W...gas:** Maverik, Sinclair, **food:** Burger King, Carl's Jr, Cheesecake Factory, Chili's, Hooters, Jack-in-the-Box, LoneStar Steaks, Old Chicago Pizza, Perkins, Quizno's, Red Robin, Sizzler, Shari's, Starbucks, TGI Friday, Wendy's, Yang Sheng Chinese, **lodging:** Ameritel, Residence Inn, **other:** Best Buy, Borders, Cabela's, Circuit City, Dillard's, JC Penney, Macy's, Mervyn's, Michael's, Office Depot, Old Navy, PetCo, Ross, Saturn, Sears/auto, Target, TJ Maxx, mall, vet
0mm	I-184 begins/ends on I-84, exit 49.

B o i s e

Interstate 24

Exit #	Services
38mm	Illinois/Kentucky state line, Ohio River
37	US 45, Metropolis, **N**...**rest area both lanes, full (handicapped)facilities, info, vending, picnic tables, litter barrels, petwalk**, Citgo/dsl, **S**...**gas:** BP/Quizno's/dsl, Shell/dsl/24hr, **food:** Buggy BBQ, Huddle House, KFC(2mi), McDonald's, Pizza Hut, Ponderosa, Stoner's Steaks, Waffle Hut, **lodging:** Best Inn, Best Western, Comfort Inn, Day Plaza Inn, Day's Inn/rest.(2mi), Holiday Inn Express, Metropolis Inn, Super 8, **other:** HOSPITAL, Buick/Cadillac/Pontiac, Chrysler/Jeep/Dodge, O'Reilly Parts, to Riverboat Casino, Ft Massac SP, camping
27	to New Columbia, Big Bay
16	IL 146, Vienna, **N**...**lodging:** Budget Inn/rest., **S**...**gas:** BP/dsl, Citgo, Gas&Go/dsl, **food:** DQ, Jumbo Grill, McDonald's, Subway, **lodging:** Budget Inn, Limited Inn
14	US 45, Vienna, **S**...**gas:** Casey's, Citgo, **other:** camping
7	to Goreville, Tunnel Hill, **N**...**gas:** Citgo/dsl, **other:** winery, **S**...**other:** to Ferne Clyffe SP, camping
1	I-57, N to Chicago, S to Memphis. I-24 begins/ends on I-57, exit 44.

Interstate 39

Exit #	Services
	I-39 and I-90 run together into Wisconsin. See Illinois Interstate 90.
122b a	US 20 E, Harrison Ave, to Belvidere, **W**...**gas:** Road Ranger/Subway, **food:** Arby's, Bergner's, Burger King, DQ, Franchesco's Rest., Taco Bell, TGIFriday, **other:** Barnes & Noble, Chevrolet, Collier RV Ctr, Harley-Davidson, Hilander Foods/gas, Macey's, Menard's, Sears/auto, Tires+, mall, last nb exit before toll rd
119	US 20 W, Alpine Rd, to Rockford
116.5mm	Kishwaukee River
115	Baxter Rd, **E**...**gas:** Shell/scales/dsl/24hr/@
111	IL 72, to Monroe Center, **E**...**gas:** BP/Sunrise Family Rest./dsl/24hr, Marathon(1mi)
104	IL 64, to Oregon, Sycamore, **W**...Grubsteakers Rest.(2mi)
99	IL 38, to De Kalb, Rochelle, 0-2 mi **W**...**gas:** BP/dsl, Petro/Iron Skillet/scales/dsl/rest./RV Dump/@, Road Ranger/Subway/scales/dsl/24hr, Shell/24hr, **food:** Arby's, China Wok, Culvers, DQ, McDonald's, Pizza Hut, Sunrise Rest., Taco Bell, Wendy's, **lodging:** Colonnade Motel, Comfort Inn, Lincoln Hwy Hotel, US Express, Super 8, **other:** HOSPITAL, Blue Beacon, Curves, $General, Radio Shack, Sullivan's Foods
97a b	I-88 tollway, to Moline, Rock Island, Chicago
93	Steward, no services
87	US 30, to Sterling, Rock Falls, **E**...to Shabbona Lake SP, **W**...Jellystone Camping(16mi)
84.5mm	**rest area both lanes, full(handicapped) facilities, phones, picnic tables, litter barrels, vending, petwalk**
82	Paw Paw, 3 mi **E**...Casey's, **W**...wind turbines
72	US 34, to Mendota, Earlville, **W**...**gas:** BP/Buster's Buffet/scales/dsl/24hr, Road Ranger/dsl/24hr, **food:** McDonald's, Ziggie's Rest., **lodging:** Comfort Inn, Super 8, **other:** HOSPITAL
67.5mm	Little Vermilion River
66	US 52, Troy Grove, **E**...KOA(1mi)
62.5mm	Tomahawk Creek
59b a	I-80, E to Chicago, W to Des Moines
57	US 6, to Peru, La Salle, 1-2 mi **W**...**gas:** Casey's, Shell/24hr, **food:** Hardee's, **lodging:** Daniels Motel
56mm	Illinois River, Abraham Lincoln Mem Bridge

Galena
Lena
Rockford
Freeport
20
Zion
Waukegan
North Chicago
Highland Park
Evanston
94
90
Savanna
52
Polo
De Kalb
Elgin
Skokie
Oak Park
Cicero
Chicago
Sterling
Dixon
88
Aurora
88
Oak Lawn
Rock Falls
Sandwich
34
Joliet
Moline
80
80
55
45
74
6
Mendota
39
La Salle
Ottawa
Bourbonnais
Kewanee
150
Streator
51
Kankakee
34
Galesburg
Knoxville
39
Minonk
Pontiac
57
Monmouth
150
Peoria
Washington
24
Watseka
67
Canton
Pekin
45
Macomb
Bloomington
Le Roy
74
36
Paxton
Lewistown
55
51
150
Rantoul
136
Havana
Clinton
Champaign
Urbana
74
Rushville
Lincoln
Danville
Beardstown
Petersburg
Georgetown
150
Quincy
172
Springfield
Riverton
72
Decatur
45
Tuscola
34
24
Jacksonville
Rochester
Mount Zion
57
Pittsfield
72
Chatham
Charleston
67
Taylorville
Mattoon
70
55
Pana
Casey
51
Effingham
70
Litchfield
Brighton
70
Alton
Vandalia
45
Wood River
40
Lawrenceville
255
57
Flora
Granite City
50
Salem
50
E St. Louis
64
Centralia
64
Mount Vernon
255
51
45
Benton
Carbondale
Harrisburg
Marion
Anna
57
Cairo
24
45

ILLINOIS

Interstate 39

<table>
<tr><td>N
↕
S</td><td>54</td><td>Oglesby, E...gas: BP, Casey's, Phillips 66/dsl, Shell/24hr, food: Delaney's Rest., Burger King, KFC/Taco Bell, McDonald's, Mr. Salsa Mexican, Root Beer Stand, Subway, lodging: Day's Inn, Holiday Inn Express, other: Starved Rock SP</td></tr>
<tr><td></td><td>52</td><td>IL 251, to La Salle, Peru</td></tr>
<tr><td></td><td>51</td><td>IL 71, to Hennepin, Oglesby</td></tr>
<tr><td></td><td>48</td><td>Tonica, E...gas: Casey's, Tonica/dsl</td></tr>
<tr><td></td><td>41</td><td>IL 18, to Streator, Henry</td></tr>
<tr><td></td><td>35</td><td>IL 17, to Wenona, Lacon, E...gas: Casey's(2mi), Shell/Subway/Burger King/dsl/RV dump, food: Pizza Hut, Wright Bro's Grill, lodging: Super 8</td></tr>
<tr><td></td><td>27</td><td>to Minonk, E...gas: Shell/Subway/Woody's Rest./dsl/24hr, lodging: Motel 6, 1 mi E...gas: Casey's</td></tr>
<tr><td></td><td>22</td><td>IL 116, to Peoria, Benson</td></tr>
<tr><td></td><td>14</td><td>US 24, to El Paso, Peoria, E...gas: Freedom/dsl, Shell/Subway/dsl/24hr, food: DQ, Hardee's/24hr, McDonald's/playplace, Oriental Buffet, Woody's Family Rest., lodging: Day's Inn, other: Doc's Drugs, El Paso RV Ctr, Ford, IGA Foods/Chesters, NAPA, Radio Shack, W...food: Monical's Pizza, Olive Branch Rest., lodging: Super 8, other: $General, Hickory Hill Camping(4mi), antiques</td></tr>
<tr><td>N
o
r
m
a
l</td><td>9mm</td><td>Mackinaw River</td></tr>
<tr><td></td><td>8</td><td>IL 251, Lake Bloomington Rd, E...Lake Bloomington, W...other: Evergreen Lake, to Comlara Park, RV camping</td></tr>
<tr><td></td><td>5</td><td>Hudson, 1 mi E...gas: Casey's</td></tr>
<tr><td></td><td>2</td><td>US 51 bus, Bloomington, Normal</td></tr>
<tr><td></td><td>0mm</td><td>I-39 begins/ends on I-55, exit 164. Services N on I-55, exit 165. E...gas: BP/Circle K/24hr, FS/dsl, Mobil/Arby's/dsl, QIK-n-EZ, Shell/24hr, food: Burger King, Denny's, McDonald's, Pizza Hut, Steak'n Shake, Uncle Tom's Pancakes, lodging: Best Western, Holiday Inn, Motel 6, Super 8, other: HOSPITAL, $General, Schnucks Foods, to Ill St U, W...NAPA</td></tr>
</table>

Interstate 55

<table>
<tr><td></td><td>Exit #</td><td>Services</td></tr>
<tr><td>N
↕
S

C
h
i
c
a
g
o

A
r
e
a</td><td>295mm</td><td>I-55 begins/ends on US 41, Lakeshore Dr, in Chicago.</td></tr>
<tr><td></td><td>293a</td><td>to Cermak Rd(from nb)</td></tr>
<tr><td></td><td>292</td><td>I-90/94, W to Chicago, E to Indiana</td></tr>
<tr><td></td><td>290</td><td>Damen Ave, Ashland Ave(no EZ nb return), E...gas: Marathon, food: Burger King, Popeye's, Subway, White Castle, other: $Tree, Dominick's Foods, GNC, Target</td></tr>
<tr><td></td><td>289</td><td>to California Ave (no EZ nb return), E...gas: Citgo, Speedway/Subway/dsl,</td></tr>
<tr><td></td><td>288</td><td>Kedzie Ave, (from sb), E...gas: Citgo</td></tr>
<tr><td></td><td>287</td><td>Pulaski Rd, E...gas: Mobil/dsl, Shell, food: Burger King, Krispy Kreme, Quizno's, Subway, other: Advance Parts, Aldi Foods, Dodge, Pete's Mkt, Target, Walgreens</td></tr>
<tr><td></td><td>286</td><td>IL 50, Cicero Ave, E...gas: Citgo/dsl, Marathon, Phillips 66, food: Dunkin Donuts, McDonald's, Starbucks, Subway, other: Family$</td></tr>
<tr><td></td><td>285</td><td>Central Ave, E...gas: BP/dsl, Citgo, Marathon, food: Burger King, Donald's HotDogs</td></tr>
<tr><td></td><td>283</td><td>IL 43, Harlem Ave, E...gas: Shell, food: Arby's, Subway</td></tr>
</table>

<table>
<tr><td>282b a</td><td>IL 171, 1st Ave, W...other: Brookfield Zoo, Mayfield Park</td></tr>
<tr><td>279b</td><td>US 12, US 20, US 45, La Grange Rd, 1-2 mi W...gas: BP/24hr, Clark, Mobil, Shell, food: Al's Beef, Applebee's, Arby's, Beef'n Brandy, Boston Mkt, Brown's Chicken, Burger King, Dino's Pizza, Dunkin Donuts, Jimmy John's, KFC, Komb's Rest., Ledo's Pizza, LJ Silver, Lone Star Steaks, Main St. Pizza, McDonald's, Nancy's Pizza, NoNo's Pizza, Old Country Buffet, Panda Express, Pizza Hut, Popeye's, Subway, Taco Bell, Taco Taco, Time Out Grill, Wendy's, White Castle, lodging: Holiday Inn, La Grange Motel, other: Aldi Foods, Best Buy, Buick, Cadillac, Chevrolet, Chrysler/Jeep, Circuit City, Discount Tire, $Tree, Firestone/auto, Ford, GNC, Home Depot, Honda, Jo-Ann Fabrics, Kohl's, Lincoln/Mercury, Mazda, Menard's, Mitsubishi, Nissan, PepBoys, Pontiac, Sam's Club/gas, Saturn, Subaru, Target/drugs, Toyota/Scion, VW, Wal-Mart</td></tr>
<tr><td>279a</td><td>La Grange Rd, to I-294 toll, S to Indiana</td></tr>
<tr><td>277b</td><td>I-294 toll(from nb), S to Indiana</td></tr>
<tr><td>277a</td><td>I-294 toll, N to Wisconsin</td></tr>
<tr><td>276c</td><td>Joliet Rd(from nb)</td></tr>
<tr><td>276b a</td><td>County Line Rd, E...food: Bobak's Buffet, Capri Rest., Ciazzi's Cafe, Max&Erma's, Moon Dance Diner, Salerno's Pizza, Subway, lodging: Extended Stay America, Marriott, other: Farmer's Fresh Mkt, Tuesday Morning, W...lodging: SpringHill Suites</td></tr>
<tr><td>274</td><td>IL 83, Kingery Rd, E...gas: Shell/24hr, W...gas: Mobil/dsl, Phillips 66, Shell/24hr, food: Bakers Square, Barnelli's Pasta, Blueberry Hill Pancakes, Burger King, Chicken Basket, Denny's, Dunkin Donuts, Patio Rest., Portillo's HotDogs, Potbelly's Rest., Senor Tequila, Subway, Wendy's, lodging: Holiday Inn, La Quinta, Red Roof Inn, Super 8, other: Firestone, Ford/KIA, K-Mart, Michael's, Staples, Target</td></tr>
<tr><td>273b a</td><td>Cass Ave, W...gas: Shell/24hr, food: Millenium Rest., Rosati's Pizza</td></tr>
<tr><td>271b a</td><td>Lemont Rd, E...Extended Stay America, W...gas: Shell/24hr</td></tr>
<tr><td>269</td><td>I-355 toll N, to W Suburbs</td></tr>
<tr><td>267</td><td>IL 53, Bolingbrook, E...gas: BP, Citgo, Phillips 66/55 Trkstp/dsl/rest./scales/24hr/@, food: Bono's Rest., McDonald's, Pancake House, lodging: La Quinta, Ramada Ltd, Super 8, other: Chevrolet, W...gas: Shell/24hr, Speedway/dsl, food: A&W/LJ Silver, Arby's, Baker's Square, Buco's Mexican, Burger King, Cheddar's, Culver's, Dunkin Donuts, Family Square Rest., Golden Corral, IHOP, KFC, Popeye's, Rancho Santa Fe Mexican, Starbucks, Subway, Wendy's, White Castle, lodging: AmericInn, Hampton Inn, Holiday Inn, SpringHill Suites, other: Aldi Foods, Camping World RV Supplies, CarQuest, $General, Fiesta Mkt, Food-4-Less/gas, Just Tires, Menard's, Murray's Parts, NAPA, U-Haul, Walgreens, Wal-Mart</td></tr>
<tr><td>266mm</td><td>weigh sta both lanes</td></tr>
<tr><td>263</td><td>Weber Rd, E...gas: BP/dsl, GasCity/Dunkin Donuts/dsl, food: Applebee's, A&W/KFC, Burger King, Culver's, Giovanny's Pizza, Little China, McDonald's, Popeye's, Quizno's, Starbucks, Subway, White Castle, lodging: Best Western, other: Ace Hardware, Discount Tire, Dominick's Food/gas, GNC, 7-11, Walgreens, W...gas: Shell/24hr, food: Arby's, Cracker Barrel, Salerno's Pizza, Wendy's, lodging: Comfort Inn, Country&Inn Suites, Extended Stay America</td></tr>
<tr><td>261</td><td>IL 126(from sb), to Plainfield</td></tr>
</table>

Interstate 55

257 US 30, to Joliet, Aurora, E...**gas:** Shell, **food:** Applebee's, Baskin Robbins/DunkinDonuts, Burger King, ChuckeCheese, Diamond's Rest., Hooters, KFC, LoneStar Steaks, McDonald's, Old Country Buffet, Outback Steaks, Pizza Hut, Red Lobster, Steak'n Shake/24hr, Subway, Taco Bell/LJ Silver, Texas Roadhouse, TGIFriday, Wendy's, **lodging:** Comfort Inn, Fairfield Inn, Hampton Inn, Holiday Inn Express, Motel 6, Super 8, **other:** Aldi Foods, Barnes& Noble, Best Buy, Circuit City, Discount Tire, Gander Mtn, Home Depot, Honda, JC Penney, K-Mart, Macy's, NTB, Old Navy, Petsmart, Sears/auto, Target, mall, W...**gas:** BP/dsl/24hr, I-55/Clark/dsl/scales/24hr

253b a US 52, Jefferson St, Joliet, E...**gas:** Citgo/dsl, Phillips 66, Shell/24hr, **food:** KFC/Pizza Hut, McDonald's, **lodging:** Best Budget Inn, Best Western, Elk's Motel, Joliette Inn, Wingate Inn, **other:** HOSPITAL, Ford/Suzuki, Harley-Davidson, Rick's RV Ctr, W...**gas:** BP/dsl/24hr, **food:** Baba's Rest., Burger King, Casa Maya, DQ, Louis Rest., Subway(1mi), **other:** HOSPITAL, Chrysler/Jeep, Goodyear, Jewel-Osco/gas, White Inn

251 IL 59(from nb), to Shorewood, same as 253 W

250b a I-80, W to Iowa, E to Toledo

248 US 6, Joliet, E...**gas:** Citgo/dsl/24hr, Speedway/dsl, **food:** Ivo's Grill, Quizno's, Taco Burrito King, **lodging:** Manor Motel, **other:** Radio Shack, W...**gas:** BP/McDonald's, **food:** Lone Star Rest.(2mi), **other:** to Ill/Mich Tr

247 Bluff Rd, no services

245mm Des Plaines River

245 Arsenal Rd, E...**other:** Exxon/Mobil Refinery

241 to Wilmington, no services

241mm Kankakee River

240 Lorenzo Rd, E...**gas:** Valero/dsl, W...**gas:** Clark/dsl/rest./24hr, Mobil, **food:** R Rest., **lodging:** Motel 55

238 IL 129 S, to Wilmington, Braidwood

236 IL 113, Coal City, E...**food:** Good Table Rest., **other:** Chrysler/Plymouth/Dodge/Jeep, Fossil Rock Camping, W...**gas:** Shell, **3 mi** W...**gas:** BP, Citgo, Mobil/dsl/24hr, **food:** Agizio's, McDonald's, Subway

233 Reed Rd, E...**gas:** Marathon, **food:** Antonia's Italian, **lodging:** Sun Motel, W...**other:** antiques

227 IL 53, Gardner, E...**gas:** Casey's, Gardner Haus Rest., W...**gas:** BP/dsl/24hr

220 IL 47, Dwight, E...**gas:** BP/Burger King/dsl/24hr, Casey's, Marathon/Circle K/dsl/24hr, **food:** Arby's, Dwight Chinese Rest., McDonald's, Pete's Rest., Subway, **lodging:** Classic Motel, Super 8

217 IL 17, Dwight, E...**gas:** Casey's, Shell/50's Rest./Circle K/dsl/24hr, **food:** DQ, Java Drive Thru, Rte 66 Rest., **other:** Chrysler/Dodge/Jeep, Family$, NAPA

213mm Mazon River

209 Odell, E...**gas:** BP, **food:** Wishing Well Café

201 IL 23, Pontiac, **1-3 mi** E...**food:** DQ, **other:** Pontiac RV Ctr, 4H RV Camp(seasonal)

198mm Vermilion River

197 IL 116, Pontiac, E...**gas:** BP/dsl/24hr, Shell, Thornton's/dsl, **food:** Arby's, Baby Bull's Rest., Burger King, Family Table Rest., KFC, McDonald's, Subway, Taco Bell, Wendy's, **lodging:** Comfort Inn, Fiesta Motel(1mi), Holiday Inn Express, Super 8, oth-

er: HOSPITAL, Aldi Foods, AutoZone, Cadillac, Chevrolet/Buick, $Tree, Lincoln/Mercury/Dodge, Wal-Mart SuperCtr, st police, W...**gas:** Citgo

193mm rest area both lanes, full(handicapped)facilities, phone, picnic tables, litter barrels, vending, petwalk

187 US 24, Chenoa, E...**gas:** Casey's, Phillips 66/McDonald's, Shell/Subway/dsl/24hr, **food:** Chenoa Family Rest., Super 8, **other:** Chevrolet

279mm Des Plaines River

178 Lexington, Lexington, E...**gas:** BP/McDonalds/dsl, Freedom/dsl, W...Chevrolet

178mm Mackinaw River

171 Towanda, E...**gas:** FastStop

167 Lp 55 S Veterans Pkwy, to Normal, **0-2 mi** E...**gas:** Marathon/Circle K, **food:** Baker's Square, Bennigan's, Bob Evans, Carlos O'Kelly's, Chili's, Cold Stone, Fazoli's, Logan's Roadhouse, Lonestar Steaks, McDonald's, Monical's Pizza, Hardee's, Outback Steaks, Panera Bread, Pizza Hut, Quizno's, Starbucks, Steak & Shake, Taco Bell, **lodging:** Candlewood Suites, Comfort Suites, Courtyard, Days Inn, Hampton Inn, Holiday Inn Express, Signature Inn, Super8, **other:** HOSPITAL, Aldi Foods, Best Buy, Borders Books, $Tree, Gordman's, Home Depot, Honda, Jewel-Osco, Kroger, Meijer/dsl, Menard's, Mitsubishi, Office Depot, PetCo, Pontiac/Buick, Sam's Club/gas, Saturn, Target, TJ Maxx, Walgreens, Wal-Mart SuperCtr/gas, World Mkt, mall, to airport

165b a US 51B, to Bloomington, E...**gas:** BP/Circle K/24hr, FS/dsl, Mobil/Arby's/dsl, QIK-n-EZ, Shell/24hr, **food:** Burger King, Denny's, McDonald's, Pizza Hut, Steak'n Shake, Uncle Tom's Pancakes, **lodging:** Best Western, Motel 6, Super 8, **other:** HOSPITAL, $General, Schnuks Foods, to Ill St U, W...NAPA

164 I-39, US 51, N to Peru

163 I-74 W, to Peoria

160b a **I-74 and I-55 run together 6 mi.** E...**gas:** BP, Freedom/dsl, Pilot/Wendy's/dsl/24hr/@, Shell, Speedway/dsl, TA/dsl/rest./scales/24hr/@, **food:** Arby's, Burger King, Cracker Barrel, Culver's, KFC, McDonald's, Popeye's, Subway, Taco Bell, Yin Ching Express, **lodging:** Best Inn, Comfort Inn, Days Inn, Econolodge, Hawthorn Suites, Quality Suites, **other:** HOSPITAL, Advance Parts, Aldi Foods, Blue Beacon, Family$, NAPA, W...**gas:** Citgo/dsl, **food:** Bob Evan's, Fiesta Ranchera, Ming's Wok, Steak'n Shake/24hr, **lodging:** Country Inn&Suites, Fairfield Inn, Hampton Inn, Ramada Ltd, Wingate Inn, **other:** $General, Factory Stores/famous brands, F&F, Radio Shack, Wal-Mart SuperCtr/gas/24hr

157b Lp 55 N, Veterans Pkwy, Bloomington, N...**gas:** Clark/24hr, FS, **food:** CJ's Rest., Froggy's Pad Rest., **lodging:** Parkway Inn/rest., Roadway Inn, Sunset Inn, **other:** HOSPITAL, to airport

157a I-74 E, to Indianapolis, US 51 to Decatur

154 Shirley, no services

N ↕ S

Lincoln

Springfield

Exit	Description
149	**W**...rest area both lanes, full(handicapped) facilities, phone, picnic tables, litter barrels, vending, playground, petwalk
145	US 136, **E**...RV Ctr, **W**...gas: Dixie/Stuckey's/scales/dsl/rest./24hr, Shell, **food:** McDonald's, Subway, **lodging:** Super 8
140	Atlanta, **E**...RV camping, **W**...gas: Casey's, FS/dsl, **food:** Country-Aire Rest., **lodging:** Best Value, **other:** NAPA
133	Lp 55, Lincoln, **2 mi E**...gas: Citgo, **lodging:** Budget Inn, **other:** HOSPITAL, Camp-A-While Camp
127	I-155 N, to Peoria
126	IL 10, IL 121 S, Lincoln, **E**...gas: Shell, Thornton/dsl/24hr, **food:** Burger King, Clubhouse Steaks, Cracker Barrel, Culver's, KFC/Taco Bell, LJ Silver, McDonald's, Pizza Hut, Rusty's Grill, Steak'n Shake, Wendy's, **lodging:** Comfort Inn, Crossroads Motel, Holiday Inn Express, Super 8, **other:** HOSPITAL, Aldi Foods, AutoZone, $General, Goody's, Ford/Lincoln/Mercury, Kroger, Radio Shack, Russell Stover, Wal-Mart SuperCtr/auto
123	Lp 55, to Lincoln, **E**...lodging: Lincoln Inn, **other:** HOSPITAL
119	Broadwell, no services
115	Elkhart, no services
109	Williamsville, **E**...gas: Casey's, **food:** Huddle House, **W**...gas: Love's/McDonalds/scales/dsl/24hr, New Salem HS
107mm	weigh sta sb
105	Lp 55, to Sherman, **W**...gas: Casey's, **food:** Cancun Mexican, DQ, Subway, **other:** to Prairie Capitol Conv Ctr, Riverside Park Campground, hist sites, repair
103mm	rest area sb, full(handicapped)facilities, phone, picnic tables, litter barrels, vending, petwalk
102mm	Sangamon River
102mm	rest area nb, full(handicapped)facilities, phone, picnic tables, litter barrels, vending, petwalk
100b	IL 54, Sangamon Ave, Springfield, **W**...gas: BP/Circle K/24hr, Shell/dsl, Speedway/dsl, **food:** Arby's, Burger King, Culver's, Hickory River BBQ, International Buffet, McDonald's, Parkway Cafe, Ryan's, Sonic, Steak'n Shake, Subway, Taco Bell, Wendy's, Wings Etc., Xochimilco Mexican, **lodging:** Northfield Suites, Ramada Ltd, **other:** Harley-Davidson, Lowe's Whse, Menard's, Wal-Mart SuperCtr/gas/24hr, to Vet Mem
100a	Il 54, E to Clinton, **E**...gas: Road Ranger/Stuckey's/dsl, **food:** Star Cafe/24hr **other:** Kenworth/Ryder/Volvo Trucks, truckwash
98b	IL 97, Springfield, **W**...gas: BP/Circle K/24hr, Shell/dsl/24hr, **food:** Arby's, McDonald's, Starbucks, Subway, Wendy's **lodging:** Best Western, **other:** HOSPITAL, Ford, K-Mart, Walgreens, to Capitol Complex
98a	I-72 E, US 36 E, to Decatur
96b a	IL 29 N, S Grand Ave, Springfield, **W**...gas: Road Ranger/dsl/24hr, **food:** Burger King, Godfather's, Mike's Rest., Popeye's, **lodging:** Quest Inn, Red Roof Inn, Super 8, **other:** Advance Parts, AutoZone, Buick, Freightliner, Hyundai, Isuzu, JC Penney, O'Reilly Parts, Pontiac/GMC, Shop'n Save, Volvo museum

Springfield

Exit	Description
94	Stevenson Dr, Springfield, **E**...KOA(7mi), **W**...gas: BP/Circle K/Quizno's, Mobil/Subway/dsl, **food:** Antonio's Pizza, Applebee's, Arby's, Bob Evans, Carlos O'Kelley's, Cheddar's, Cici's Pizza, Denny's, Hardees, Hooters, IHOP, La fiesta Mexican, LJ Silver, Maverick Steaks, McDonald's, Outback Steaks, Panera Bread, Papa John's, Pizza Hut, Quizno's, Red Lobster, Smokey Bones BBQ, Steak'n Shake, Taco Bell, Taipan Chinese, **lodging:** Comfort Suites, Crowne Plaza, Day's Inn/rest., Drury Inn, Hampton Inn, Hilton Garden, Holiday Inn Express, Microtel, PearTree Inn, Signature Inn, Stevenson Inn, **other:** BigLots, CVS Drug, Jo-Ann Fabrics, Radio Shack, ShopKO, USPO, Walgreens
92b a	I-72 W, US 36 W, 6th St, Springfield, **W**...gas: Road Ranger, Thornton's, **food:** Arby's, Bellacino's Rest., Burger King, DQ, Jimmy John's, KFC, McDonald's/playplace, New China, Pizza Hut, Sgt. Pepper's Cafe', Subway, Taco Bell, **lodging:** Route 66, Super 8, Travelodge/rest., **other:** HOSPITAL, AutoZone, Mazda/Lincoln/Mercury, Walgreens, Wal-Mart SuperCtr
90	Toronto Rd, **E**...gas: Quik-n-EZ/dsl, Shell/Circle K, **food:** Antonio's Pizza, Cracker Barrel, HenHouse, China Express, McDonald's, Subway, Taco Bell, Wendy's, **lodging:** Baymont Inn, Motel 6, Ramada Ltd, **other:** HOSPITAL
89mm	Lake Springfield
88	E Lake Dr, Chatham, **E**...other: to Lincoln Mem Garden/Nature Ctr, st police, **W**...KOA
83	Glenarm, **W**...JJ RV Park/LP(4mi)
82	IL 104, to Pawnee, **E**...to Sangchris Lake SP, **W**...gas: Mobil/Auburn Trvl Ctr/Subway/scales/dsl/rest./24hr/@, **other:** antiques/crafts
80	Hist 66, Divernon, **W**...gas: Marathon/Quizno's/dsl, **food:** Bearden's Rest., **other:** antiques
72	Farmersville, **W**...gas: Citgo/dsl/24hr, Shell/24hr, Subway/TCBY, **lodging:** Art's Motel/rest.
65mm	rest area both lanes, full(handicapped)facilities, phone, picnic tables, litter barrels, vending, playground, petwalk
63	IL 48, IL 127, to Raymond, no services
60	IL 108, to Carlinville, **E**...other: Kamper Kampanion RV Park, truck parts, **W**...gas: Shell/dsl/LP/café, **lodging:** Best Western, **other:** antiques, to Blackburn Coll
56mm	weigh sta nb
52	IL 16, Hist 66, Litchfield, **E**...gas: BP/24hr, Casey's, Citgo/Jack-in-the-Box/dsl, Phillips 66/dsl, Shell/24hr, **food:** Arby's, Ariston Café, Burger King, China Town, DQ, Denny's, Domino's, El Rancherito, Jubelt's Rest., KFC, LJ Silver/A&W, Maverick Steaks, McDonald's/playplace, Pizza Hut, Ponderosa, Ruby Tuesday, Subway, Taco Bell, Wendy's, **lodging:** Baymont Inn, Best Value Inn, Comfort Inn, Hampton Inn, Holiday Inn Express, Super 8, **other:** HOSPITAL, Aldi Foods, Chevrolet/Pontiac, Chrysler/Jeep/Dodge, Dodge, $General, $Tree, Firestone/auto, Ford/Mercury, Goodyear/auto, IGA Foods, NAPA, Rainmaker Camping(8mi), Walgreens, Wal-Mart SuperCtr/gas/24hr, **W**...st police
44	IL 138, to Benld, Mt Olive, **E**...gas: Citgo/dsl, **food:** Crossroads Diner, **lodging:** Budget 10 Motel, **other:** Mother Jones Mon.
41	to Staunton, **E**...Country Classic Cars, **W**...gas: Casey's, **food:** DQ, RJ's Rest., Schweppes Rest., Subway, **lodging:** Super 8, **other:** HOSPITAL

Interstate 55

37	Livingston, New Douglas, W...**gas:** BP/dsl/24hr, **food:** Country Inn, Gasperoni's Café
33	IL 4, to Staunton, Worden, W...Gas & Tires
30	IL 140, Hamel, E...Innkeeper Motel, W...**gas:** Shell, **food:** Scotty's Rest., **other:** NAPA
28mm	**rest area both lanes, full(handicapped)facilities, phone, picnic tables, litter barrels, vending, pet-walk**
23	IL 143, Edwardsville, E...**gas:** Phillips 66/dsl, **other:** repair, W...Red Barn Camping(apr-oct)
20b	I-270 W, to Kansas City
20a	I-70 E, to Indianapolis
I-55 S and I-70 W run together 18 mi	
18	IL 162, to Troy, E...**gas:** Phillips 66/dsl, Pilot/Arby's/dsl/scales/24hr, TA/BP/Country Pride/dsl/scales/24hr/@, ZX Gas, **food:** Burger King, China King, DQ, Dominos, Imo's Pizza, Jack-in-the-Box, KFC, Little Caesar's, McDonald's/playplace, Pizza Man, Pizza Hut, Randy's Rest, Subway, **other:** HOSPITAL, Ace Hardware, $General, NAPA Autocare, Speedco, SuperValu Foods, USPO, W...**gas:** Phillips 66/dsl/24hr, **food:** China Garden, Cracker Barrel, Krieger's Grill, Taco Bell, **lodging:** Congress Motel, Holiday Inn Express, Red Roof Inn, Super 8, **other:** Freightliner
17	US 40 E, to Troy, to St Jacob
15b a	IL 159, Maryville, Collinsville, E...**gas:** Phillips 66/dsl, Shell, ZX Gas, **food:** Sharkey's Rest., Steak-Out, Wing Wah Chinese, **other:** Chevrolet, $General, Ford/Lincoln/Mercury, W...**gas:** Fast Stop, **lodging:** Econolodge
14mm	weigh sta sb
11	IL 157, Collinsville, E...**gas:** Casey's, **food:** A&W/LJ Silver, Denny's, Han's Buffet, McDonald's/playplace, Penn Sta Subs, Qdoba Mexican, St Lewis Bread Co, Waffle House, **lodging:** Best Western, **other:** Home Depot, Midas, Radio Shack, Walgreens, Wal-Mart SuperCtr, W...**gas:** Motomart/dsl/24hr, **food:** Applebee's, Arby's, Bandana's BBQ, Bob Evans, Burger King, Culvers, DQ, Pizza Hut, Ponderosa, Ruby Tuesday, Steak'n Shake, White Castle/24hr, Zapata Mexican, **lodging:** Comfort Inn, Days Inn, Drury Inn, Extended Stay Suites, Fairfield Inn, Hampton Inn, Holiday Inn/rest., Super 8, **other:** Buick/Pontiac/GMC, Chrysler/Dodge/Jeep, st police
10	I-255, S to Memphis, N to I-270
9	Black Lane(from nb, no return), E...Fairmount Race-Track
6	IL 111, Great River Rd, Fairmont City, E...**gas:** Phillips 66, **lodging:** Rainbo Motel, Royal Budget Inn, Cahokia Mounds SP, W...Horseshoe SP
5mm	motorist callboxes begin at 1/2 mi intervals nb
4b a	IL 203, Granite City, E...**gas:** Phillips 66/dsl/24hr, **lodging:** Western Inn, W...**gas:** Gateway/Pizza Hut/Taco Bell/dsl/24hr/@, **food:** Burger King, **other:** Gateway Int Raceway
3	Exchange Ave, no services
2	I-64 E, IL 3 N, St Clair Ave
2b	3rd St, no services
2a	M L King Bridge, to downtown E St Louis
1	IL 3, to Sauget(from sb), no services
I-55 N and I-70 E run together 18 mi	
0mm	Illinois/Missouri state line, Mississippi River

S (left margin)

E St Louis Area (left margin)

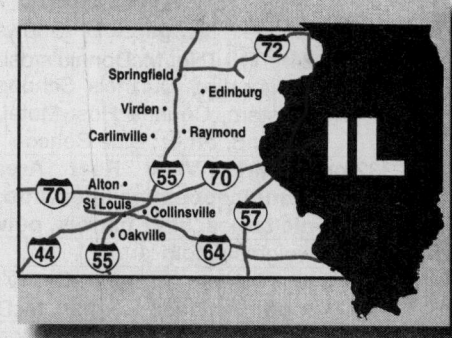

Interstate 57

Exit #	Services
358mm	I-94 E to Indiana, I-57 begins/ends on I-94, exit 63 in Chicago.
357	IL 1, Halsted St, E...**gas:** BP, Mobil, **other:** auto repair, W...**gas:** Clark, Marathon, **food:** McDonald's, **other:** Walgreens
355	111th St, Monterey Ave, W...**gas:** BP, Citgo
354	119th St, W...**gas:** Citgo, **other:** Target
353	127th St, Burr Oak Ave, E...**gas:** Citgo, Shell/Subway, **food:** Burger King, Dillinger's, McDonald's, Wendy's, **lodging:** Holiday Inn Express, Plaza Inn, Heritage Inn, **other:** HOSPITAL, Ace Hardware, Family$, Walgreens, W...**gas:** BP, Phillips 66, **other:** JJ Fish&Chicken
352mm	Calumet Sag Channel
350	IL 83, 147th St, Sibley Blvd, E...**gas:** Citgo, Marathon/dsl, **food:** McDonald's, W...**gas:** Gas Shop, **other:** Curves, USPO
348	US 6, 159th St, E...**gas:** Marathon/dsl, **food:** Burger King, Dunkin Donuts/Baskin-Robbins, McDonald's, Subway, Taco Bell, White Castle, **lodging:** Comfort Inn, **other:** Big Lots, $Tree, Family$, Radio Shack, U-Haul, Walgreens, W...**gas:** Citgo/dsl, Mobil/dsl
346	167th St, Cicero Ave, to IL 50, E...**gas:** BP, Citgo/dsl, **food:** Applebee's, Baskin Robbins/Dunkin Doughnuts, Harold's Chicken, Panda Express, Quizno's, Shark's Fish&Chicken, Starbucks, Subway, Wendy's, **lodging:** Oak Forest, Wal-Mart SuperCtr/24hr, W...**gas:** Shell
345b a	I-80, W to Iowa, E to Indiana, to I-294 N toll to Wisconsin
342a	Vollmer Rd, E...**gas:** Shell/24hr, **other:** HOSPITAL
340b a	US 30, Lincoln Hwy, Matteson, E...**gas:** BP/24hr, Citgo/dsl, Shell, **food:** A&W/LJ Silver, Applebee's, Bakers Square, Burger King, ChuckeCheese, Cracker Barrel, Dominick's, Empire Buffet, Fuddrucker's, IHOP, Jimmy John's, JN Michael's Grill, KFC, Knock Outs Grill, McDonald's, Nino's Pizza, Old Country Buffet, Olive Garden, Panda Express, Panera Bread, Peppy's Mexican, Pizza Hut, Red Lobster, Starbucks, Subway, Taco Bell, Wendy's, White Castle, **lodging:** Country Inn&Suites, Days Inn, Holiday Inn/rest., La Quinta, **other:** Best Buy, Border's, Dodge, Dominick's Foods, Goodyear/auto, Home Depot, Isuzu, JC Penney, K-Mart, Marshall's, Menard's, NTB, Old Navy, Pep Boys, Sam's Club/gas, Sears/auto, Target, Walgreens, Wal-Mart, mall, W... **other:** Buick, Chevrolet, Ford, GMC, Honda, Isuzu, Kia, Mitsubishi, Pontiac, VW
339	Sauk Trail, to Richton Park, E...**gas:** Citgo, **food:** McDonald's, **other:** Walgreens

Chicago (center margin)

N / S (right margin compass)

Interstate 57

N ↕ S

335 Monee, E...**gas:** BP/Subway/dsl, Petro/dsl/rest./24hr/@, Pilot/McDonald's/dsl/scales/24hr/@, **food:** Burger King, Quizno's, Schoops Rest., **lodging:** Best Western, Country Host Motel, Holiday Inn Express, Super 8, **other:** Blue Beacon

332mm Prairie View Rest Area both lanes, full (handicapped)facilities, info, phone, vending, picnic tables, litter barrels, petwalk

330mm weigh sta both lanes

327 to Peotone, E...**gas:** Casey's, Shell/Circle K/24hr, **food:** Bierstede German, McDonald's

322 Manteno, E...**gas:** BP/McDonald's/24hr, Phillips 66/Subway, **food:** Huddle House, KFC/Pizza Hut/Taco Bell, Monical's Pizza, Wendy's, **lodging:** Country Inn&Suites, Howard Johnson, **other:** Curves, Harley-Davidson, W...**gas:** GasCity/dsl

315 IL 50, Bradley, E...**gas:** F&F, Shell/Burger King/Circle K/24hr, **food:** Armenises Rest., Cracker Barrel, LoneStar Steaks, Old Country Buffet, Pizza Hut, Red Lobster, Ruby Tuesday, TGIFriday, White Castle, **lodging:** Fairfield Inn, Hampton Inn, Holiday Inn Express, Lee's Inn, **other:** Barnes&Noble, JC Penney, Marshall's, Michael's, Sears/auto, Staples, Target, mall, W...**gas:** BP/dsl, Speedway/dsl, **food:** Applebee's, Arby's, Bakers Square, Coyote Canyon Steaks, Denny's, El Campesino Mexican, Hong Kong Buffet, IHOP, LJ Silver, McDonald's, Oberweis Ice Cream, Starbucks, Steak'n Shake, Subway, Taco Bell, Tacos Del Norte, VIP Rest., Wendy's, **lodging:** Motel 6, Quality Inn, Super 8, **other:** Aldi Foods, Buick/Nissan, Chevrolet/RV Ctr, $Tree, Honda, Hyundai, Jo-Ann Fabrics, K-Mart, Lowe's Whse, Menard's, Nissan, Wal-Mart/24hr, to Kankakee River SP

312 IL 17, Kankakee, E...**other:** Chrysler/Dodge, Twin River's Camping, W...**gas:** BP, Marathon, Shell/Circle K/24hr, **food:** McDonald's, PoorBoy Rest., Subway, Uncle Johnni's Rest., Wendy's, **lodging:** Best Value Inn, **other:** HOSPITAL, Advance Parts, Walgreens, auto repair

310.5mm Kankakee River

308 US 45, US 52, to Kankakee, E...KOA(3mi), W...**gas:** Gas City/Dunkin Donuts/Subway/dsl, Homestead Italian Steaks, **lodging:** Economy Inn, Fairview Motel, Hilton Garden, **other:** Wal-Mart SuperCtr, airport

302 Chebanse, W... truck repair

297 Clifton, W...**gas:** Phillips 66/DQ/dsl, **food:** CharGrilled Cheeseburgers

293 IL 116, Ashkum, E...**gas:** BP/Noble Roman/dsl, W... **food:** Loft Rest., **other:** st police, tires

283 US 24, IL 54, Gilman, E...**gas:** Apollo/rest./dsl/scales/24hr@, BP/diner/dsl/24hr, K&H Truck Plaza/dsl/scales/24hr/@, Shell, **food:** Burger King, DQ, McDonald's, Monical's Pizza, **lodging:** Budget Host, Super 8, Travel Inn, W...**gas:** BP/Subway/dsl, **other:** R&R RV Ctr

280 IL 54, Onarga, E...**gas:** Casey's(1mi), Phillips 66, **other:** camping, W...**other** Lake Arrowhead RV camping

272 to Roberts, Buckley, no services

268.5mm rest area both lanes, full(handicapped)facilities, vending, phone, picnic tables, litter barrels, petwalk

Kankakee

261 IL 9, Paxton, E...**gas:** Casey's, Phillips 66(1mi), **food:** Hardee's, Monical's Pizza, Pizza Hut, Subway, **other:** Chevrolet/Pontiac/Buick/GMC, W...**gas:** BP, Marathon, **food:** Country Garden Rest., **lodging:** Paxton Inn

250 US 136, Rantoul, E...**gas:** BP/rest./24hr, Phillips 66(1mi), **food:** Arby's, KFC/Taco Bell, LJ Silver, McDonald's, Monical's, Red Wheel Rest., **lodging:** Best Western, Day's Inn/rest., Rantoul Motel, Super 8, **other:** NAPA, Wal-Mart SuperCtr, camping, vet, to Chanute AFB

240 Market St, E...**gas:** Road Ranger/McDonald's/dsl/scales, **other:** D&W Lake Camping, Kenworth, truck/tire repair

238 Olympian Dr, to Champaign, W...**gas:** Mobil/dsl, **food:** DQ, **lodging:** Microtel, **other:** RV/dsl repair

237b a I-74, W to Peoria, E to Urbana

235b I-72 W, to Decatur

235a University Ave, to Champaign, E...HOSPITAL, U of Ill

229 to Savoy, Monticello, E...**gas:** Marathon/dsl/24hr

221.5mm rest area both lanes, full(handicapped)facilities, phones, picnic tables, litter barrels, vending, petwalk

220 US 45, Pesotum, W...**gas:** Citgo, st police

212 US 36, Tuscola, E...**gas:** FuelMart/dsl, W...**gas:** BP/24hr, Citgo/Road Ranger/dsl/scales, Fleet/dsl/24hr, **food:** Burger King, DQ, Denny's, McDonald's, Monical's Pizza, Pizza Hut, Red Bar Buffet, Subway, **lodging:** AmeriHost, Cooper Motel, Holiday Inn Express, Super 8, **other:** Chevrolet/Pontiac/Buick/GMC, Firestone/auto, Ford, IGA Foods, Pamida, Tanger Outlets/Famous Brands, camping

Champaign

203 IL 133, Arcola, E...**gas:** Citgo/dsl, **other:** CampALot, W... **gas:** Shell/Subway/dsl/24hr, Sunrise Gas, **food:** DQ, Hen House, Monical's Pizza, **lodging:** Arcola Inn, Budget Inn, Comfort Inn, Knight's Inn, Country Charm Amish, **other:** $General, NAPA, Rockome Gardens, Arcola Camping

190b a IL 16, to Mattoon, E...**gas:** Citgo, **other:** HOSPITAL, to E IL U, Fox Ridge SP, W...**gas:** Phillips 66/Subway/24hr, **food:** Alamo Steaks, Arby's, Cody's Roadhouse, Cracker Barrel, DQ, El Taquero Mexican, Fazoli's, Jumbo Buffet, McDonald's, Steak'n Shake/24hr, Taco Bell, Wendy's, **lodging:** Comfort Suites, Fairfield Inn, Hampton Inn, Ramada Inn/rest., Super 8, **other:** Aldi Foods, Big Lots, Cross Country RV Ctr, CVS Drug, $General, Home Depot, JC Penney, Sears, Staples, Walgreen, Wal-Mart SuperCtr/gas/24hr, mall

184 US 45, IL 121, to Mattoon, E...**gas:** Citgo/Blimpie/dsl, W...**gas:** Marathon/dsl, Shell, **food:** McDonald's, Subway, **lodging:** Budget Inn, US Grant Motel, **other:** to Lake Shelbyville

Mattoon

177 US 45, Neoga, E...**gas:** BP/Subway/dsl, Citgo, W...**gas:** Phillips 66/dsl/24hr, Casey's(2mi)

166.5mm rest area both lanes, full(handicapped)facilities, vending, phones, picnic tables, litter barrels, petwalk

163 I-70 E, to Indianapolis

I-57 S and I-70 W run together 6 mi

162 US 40, Effingham, E...**gas:** Moto/24hr, **lodging:** Budget Host, **other:** Harley-Davidson, W...**gas:** Citgo/Subway, Phillips 66/Subway, Pilot/McDonald's/Harvest Grill/scales/dsl/24hr, Shell/dsl, **food:** Trailways Rest., **lodging:** Effingham Motel/café, Lincoln Lodge, **other:** truck repair, Camp Lakewood(2mi)

160 IL 33, IL 32, Effingham, E...**gas:** Phillips 66, **food:** KFC, Little Caesar's, LoneStar Steaks, Papa John's, Pizza Hut, **lodging:** Comfort Inn, Fairfield Inn, Hampton Inn,

Effingham

Interstate 57

other: HOSPITAL, Aldi Foods, AutoZone, $General, Family$, K-Mart, Kroger, Midas, Radio Shack, Save-a-Lot Foods, Walgreens, W...**gas:** BP/Quizno's, ✈/Flying J/Country Mkt/dsl/scales/24hr, Phillips 66, TA/Popeye's/Sbarro's/dsl/rest./@, **food:** Arby's, BBQ, Burger King/24hr, Cracker Barrel, Denny's, El Rancherito Mexican, KFC, LJ Silver, McDonald's, Ponderosa, Ryan's, Ruby Tuesday, Starbucks, Steak'n Shake/24hr, Subway, Taco Bell, TGIFriday, Wendy's, **lodging:** Country Inn Suites, Hilton Garden, Holiday Inn Express, Ramada Ltd, Super 8, Travel Inn, Travelodge Suites, **other:** Blue Beacon, $Tree, Ford/Lincoln/Mercury, Kohls, Radio Shack, Speedco Lube, Wal-Mart SuperCtr/gas/dsl/24hr

159	US 45, Effingham, E...**gas:** BP/dsl/24hr, Clark, Dixie Citgo/dsl/rest./24hr, Phillips 66/dsl/24hr, Speedway/dsl, **food:** China Buffet, Culvers, Domino's, Hardee's/24hr, Niemerg's Rest., Papa John's, Subway, **lodging:** Abe Lincoln Motel, Comfort Suites, Day's Inn, Howard Johnson, Paradise Motel, Rodeway Inn, **other:** AutoZone, Family$, Firestone, O'Reilly Parts, SavALot Foods, Walgreens, W...**gas:** Petro/Mobil/Iron Skillet/dsl/rest./24hr/@, **lodging:** Best Western, **other:** Blue Beacon, IA 80 Truck-O-Mat/scales/wash

I-57 N and I-70 E run together 6 mi

157	I-70 W, to St Louis
151	Watson, **5 mi** E...Percival Springs RV Park
150mm	Little Wabash River
145	Edgewood, E...**gas:** Citgo
135	IL 185, Farina, E...**gas:** BP/Subway/dsl, **other:** Ford
127	to Kinmundy, Patoka, no services
116	US 50, Salem, E...**gas:** Clark/dsl, Huck's, Motomart/24hr, Shell, **food:** Austin Fried Chicken, Burger King, Hunan Garden, KFC, La Cabana Mexican, LJ Silver, McDonald's, Pizza Hut, Pizza Man, Subway, Taco Bell, Wendy's, **lodging:** Budget Inn, Continental Motel(2mi), Restwell Motel(1mi), **other:** AutoZone, Chrysler/Dodge/Jeep, MadPricer Foods, Radio Shack, Salem Parts, to Forbes SP, W...**gas:** Phillips 66/dsl, **food:** Applebee's, Arby's, Denny's, **lodging:** Comfort Inn, Salem Inn, Super 8, **other:** Chevrolet/Buick, Ford, Salem Tires, Wal-Mart SuperCtr/24hr/gas

114mm rest area both lanes, full(handicapped)facilities, phones, picnic tables, litter barrels, vending, petwalk, playground

109	IL 161, to Centralia, W...**gas:** Biggie's General Store/cafe/dsl
103	Dix, E...**gas:** Phillips 66/dsl, **lodging:** Red Carpet Inn, **other:** camping
96	I-64 W, to St Louis
95	Mt Vernon, **I-64 and I-57 run together 5 mi.** E...**gas:** BP/dsl/24hr, Mobil, Phillips 66, **food:** Bonanza, Burger King, Fazoli's, Hardee's, Hunan Chinese, KFC, LJ Silver, McDonald's, Papa John's, Pasta House, Pizza Hut, Steak'n Shake/24hr, Subway, Taco Bell, Wendy's, Western Sizzlin, **lodging:** Best Inn, Best Western, Drury Inn, Econolodge, Motel 6, Southgate Inn, Super 8, Thrifty Inn, Villager Lodge, **other:** HOSPITAL, AutoZone, Chevrolet, Country Fair Foods, CVS Drug, $Tree, Ford, Harley-David-

son, JC Penney, Jo-Ann Fabrics, K-Mart, Kroger, Radio Shack, Walgreen, W...**gas:** Hucks/dsl/rest./24hr/@, Shell/7-11/24hr, TA/Popeye's/dsl/24hr/@, **food:** Applebee's, Arby's, Burger King, Chili's, Cracker Barrel, LoneStar Steaks, McDonald's, Ryan's, Sonic, **lodging:** Comfort Inn, Day's Inn, Fairfield Inn, Hampton Inn, Holiday Inn, Ramada Hotel, **other:** Cadillac/Pontiac/Buick/GMC, Fannie Mae Candies, Lowe's Whse, Outlet Mall/famous brands, Quality Times RV Park, Staples, Toyota, Wal-Mart SuperCtr/24hr

92	I-64 E, to Louisville
83	Ina, E...**gas:** Lakeview/dsl/deli/24hr, Love's/McDonald's/scales, **other:** Sherwood Camping(2mi), W...to Rend Lake Coll

79mm rest area sb, full(handicapped)facilities, info, vending, phones, picnic tables, litter barrels, petwalk, playground

77	IL 154, to Whittington, E...**gas:** Shell/24hr, **food:** Giddy's Grill, **other:** Holiday Trav-L Park, W...**lodging:** Seasons at Rend Lake Lodge/rest., **other:** to Rend Lake, golf, Wayne Fitzgerrell SP

74mm rest area nb, full(handicapped)facilities, vending, phones, picnic tables, litter barrels, petwalk, playground

71	IL 14, Benton, E...**gas:** Phillips 66, Shell, **food:** Arby's, Hardee's, KFC/Taco Bell, Pizza Hut, Wendy's, **lodging:** Day's Inn/rest., Gray Plaza Motel, Super 8, **other:** HOSPITAL, AutoZone, KOA(1.5mi), O'Rielly Parts, Plaza Tire, W...**gas:** BP/Burger King/dsl, Shell/dsl/24hr, **food:** Applebee's, Burger King, McDonald's, Subway, **other:** CVS Drug, Wal-Mart SuperCtr/24hr/dsl, to Rend Lake
65	IL 149, W Frankfort, E...**gas:** GasForLess, Shell/dsl, **food:** China Garden, Hardee's, KFC, LJ Silver, Mike's Drive-In, Pancake House/24hr, Sonic, Subway, **lodging:** Gray Plaza Motel, **other:** HOSPITAL, CarQuest, $General, MadPricer Foods, NAPA, W...**gas:** Casey's, **food:** Burger King, EEE Rest, McDonald's, **lodging:** Best Value Inn, **other:** Chevrolet/Pontiac, Chrysler/Dodge, CVS Drug, $Tree, K-Mart, VF Factory Stores
59	to Herrin, Johnston City, E...**gas:** BP/dsl, Shell/dsl/24hr, **food:** DQ, Hardee's, McDonald's, Subway, **other:** NAPA, camping(2mi), W...**other:** HOSPITAL, camping(4mi)
54b a	IL 13, Marion, E...**gas:** Phillips 66/24hr, **food:** Arby's, Fazoli's, Hardee's, KFC, LJ Silver, Papa John's, Pizza Hut, Quizno's, Subway, Tequila's Mexican, Wendy's, **lodging:** Day's Inn, **other:** Aldi Foods, Advance Parts, AutoZone, Chevrolet/Cadillac, Family$, Ford/Lincoln/Mercury/Hyundai, Kroger/gas, Plaza Tire, Radio Shack, SavALot Foods, USPO, W...**gas:** BP/dsl/rest/scales/24hr/@, Phillips 66, **food:** 17th Street Grill, Ap-

Interstate 57

	plebee's, Asian Bistro, Backyard Burger, Bob Evans, Burger King, McDonald's, O'Charley's, Rock'n Roll Buffet, Red Lobster, Ryan's, Sonic, Steak'n Shake, Taco Bell, **lodging:** Best Inn, Drury Inn, Fairfield Inn, Hampton Inn, Motel 6, Super 8, **other:** Buick/GMC/Pontiac/Mercedes, Chrysler/Plymouth/Dodge/Jeep, Dillard's, Harley-Davidson, Home Depot, Kia, Mitsubishi, Sam's Club/gas, Sears, Target, Wal-Mart SuperCtr/24hr, mall
53	Main St, Marion, **E**...**gas:** Shell/dsl, **food:** DQ, **lodging:** Motel Marion/camping, **other:** HOSPITAL, NAPA, **W**...**gas:** Motomart/24hr, **food:** Cracker Barrel, HideOut Steaks, **lodging:** Comfort Inn, Comfort Suites, Holiday Inn Express
47mm	weigh sta both lanes
45	IL 148, **1 mi E**...**gas:** King Tut's Food/dsl/24hr, **lodging:** Lake Tree Inn, **other:** camping, dsl repair
44	I-24 E to Nashville, no services
40	Goreville Rd, **E**...**other:** Ferne Clyffe SP, camping, scenic overlook
36	Lick Creek Rd, **W**...**other:** vineyards
32mm	**Trail of Tears Rest Area both lanes, full(handicapped)facilities, info, phones, picnic tables, litter barrels, vending, petwalk, playground**
30	IL 146, Anna, Vienna, **W**...**gas:** Shell/dsl/rest./24hr, **other:** HOSPITAL, auto/tire repair
25	US 51 N(from nb, exits left), to Carbondale
24	Dongola Rd, **W**...**gas:** BP/dsl
18	Ullin Rd, **W**...**gas:** Citgo/dsl/24hr, **food:** EEE BBQ, **lodging:** Best Western, **other:** st police
8	Mounds Rd, to Mound City, **E**...**other:** K&K AutoTruck/dsl/repair
1	IL 3, to US 51, Cairo, **E**...**lodging:** Belvedere Motel(2mi), Day's Inn, **other:** $General, Mound City Nat Cem(4mi), camping, **W**...camping
0mm	Illinois/Missouri state line, Mississippi River

Interstate 64

Exit #	Services
131.5mm	Illinois/Indiana state line, Wabash River
131mm	**Skeeter Mtn Welcome Ctr wb, full(handicapped) facilities, phone, vending, picnic tables, litter barrels, petwalk**
130	IL 1, to Grayville, **N**...**gas:** Casey's(2mi), Shell/dsl/24hr, **food:** Subway, **lodging:** Best Western/rest., Super 8, **other:** museum, Beall Woods St Park
124mm	Little Wabash River
117	Burnt Prairie, **S**...**gas:** Marathon/dsl, **food:** Chuck-Wagon Charlie's Café, **other:** antiques
110	US 45, Mill Shoals, no services
100	IL 242, to Wayne City, **N**...**gas:** Marathon/dsl
89	to Belle Rive, Bluford, no services
86mm	**rest area wb, full(handicapped)facilities, phone, vending, picnic tables, litter barrels, petwalk**
82.5mm	**rest area eb, full(handicapped)facilities, phone, vending, picnic tables, litter barrels, petwalk**
80	IL 37, to Mt Vernon, **2 mi N**...**gas:** BP/Burger King/dsl/24hr, Marathon/dsl/24hr, **lodging:** Royal Inn, **other:** camping
78	I-57, S to Memphis, N to Chicago

	I-64 and I-57 run together 5 mi. See Interstate 57, exit 95
73	I-57, N to Chicago, S to Memphis
69	Woodlawn
61	US 51, to Centralia, Richview, **S**...access to gas, food
50	IL 127, to Nashville, **N**...to Carlyle Lake, **S**...**gas:** BP/24hr(3mi), Citgo/dsl/24hr, Conoco/dsl/rest., Shell/dsl/24hr, **food:** McDonald's, Subway(3mi), **lodging:** Best Western, Little Nashville Inn/rest., **other:** HOSPITAL
41	IL 177, Okawville, **S**...**gas:** Phillips 66/Burger King/dsl/24hr, **food:** DQ, Hen House/24hr, Golfer's Steakhouse, Subway, **lodging:** Original Springs Motel, Super 8, **other:** truck repair
37mm	Kaskaskia River
34	to Albers, **3 mi N**...**gas:** Casey's
27	IL 161, New Baden, **N**...**gas:** Shell/dsl/24hr, **food:** Good Ol' Days Rest., McDonald's, Outside Inn Rest., Subway, **other:** Chevrolet
25mm	**rest area both lanes, full(handicapped)facilities, info, phone, vending, picnic tables, litter barrels, petwalk**
23	IL 4, to Mascoutah, **3mi N**...**food:** Hardee's, McDonald's, **S**...airport
19b a	US 50, IL 158, **N**...**gas:** Motomart/24hr, **food:** Schiappa's Italian, Subway, **lodging:** Comfort Inn, **S**...**gas:** Citgo/dsl, **other:** HOSPITAL, to Scott AFB
18mm	weigh sta eb
16	to O'Fallon, Shiloh, **N**...**food:** Denny's, **S**...**food:** Applebee's, Arby's, Buffalo Wild Wings, Cafe Avanti, Coldstone Creamery, Cracker Barrel, 54th St. Grille, Golden Corral, Johnny Rocket's, Qdoba Mexican, Quizno's, St. Louis Bread Co., Texas Roadhouse, **lodging:** Drury Inn, Holiday Inn Express, **other:** Dierbergs's Foods, Radio Shack, Target
15mm	motorist callbox every 1/2 mile wb
14	O'Fallon, **N**...**gas:** QT, Shell/24hr, **food:** IHOP, Japanese Garden, Steak'n Shake/24hr, Subway, **lodging:** Baymont Inn, Extended Stay America, Howard Johnson, Sleep Inn, **other:** Chevrolet, Ford, O'Reilly Parts, Saab/Cadillac, **S**...**food:** Chevy's Mexican, Culver's, DQ, Emperor's Wok, Grand Buffet, Hardee's, Jack-in-the-Box, KFC, Lion's Choice, LoneStar Steaks, McDonald's, O'Charley's, Papa Murphy's, Pepper's Rest., Taco Bell, **lodging:** Candlewood Suites, Courtyard, Econolodge, Quality Inn, Ramada Ltd, **other:** BMW, Harley-Davidson, Home Depot, Honda, Hyundai, Kia, Lion's Choice, Mazda, Mitsubishi, Nissan, Sam's Club/gas, Subaru, Suzuki, Toyota/Scion, VW, Wal-Mart SuperCtr
12	IL 159, to Collinsville, **N**...**gas:** Shell, **food:** Applebee's, Bob Evans, Carlos O'Kelly's, Ginger Buffet, Houlihan's, Joe's Crabshack, Lotawalla Creek Grill, Olive Garden, Red Lobster, TGIFriday, **lodging:** Best Western, Comfort Inn, Drury Inn, Fairfield Inn, Hampton Inn, Ramada Inn/rest., Sheraton, Super 8, **other:** Circuit City, Gordman's, Michael's, **S**...**gas:** BP/24hr, Motomart/dsl/24hr, **food:** Boston Mkt, Burger King, Capt D's, Casa Gallardo, Chili's, Denny's, Domino's, Fazoli's, Hardee's, IHOP, Krispy Kreme, Longhorn Steaks, LJ Silver, McDonald's, Old Coun-

Interstate 64

E ↕ W

E St Louis

try Buffet, Outback Steaks, Ponderosa, Popeye's, Quizno's, Rally's, Red Robin, Ruby Tuesday, Russell Stover, Smokey Bones BBQ, Steak'n Shake, St. Louis Bread, Taco Bell, White Castle, **other:** Aamco, Advance Parts, AutoTire, Barnes&Noble, Best Buy, Borders, Dillard's, $Tree, JC Penney, K-Mart, Kohl's, Lowes Whse, Macy's, Marshall's, Office Depot, Old Navy, PetCo, Schnuck's Foods, TJ Maxx, Walgreens, mall

9	IL 157, to Caseyville, **N**...**gas:** BP/24hr, Phillips 66/Subway/repair, **food:** Hardee's, Wendy's, **lodging:** Western Inn, **S**...**gas:** BP/dsl/repair, **food:** Cracker Barrel, DQ, Domino's, McDonald's, Pizza Hut/Taco Bell, **lodging:** Day's Inn, Econolodge, Motel 6, Quality Inn
7	I-255, S to Memphis, N to Chicago
6	IL 111, Kingshighway, **N**...**gas:** BP, Mobil/24hr, Shell, **food:** Church's, Popeye's
5.5mm	motorist callbox every 1/2 mi eb
5	25th St
4	15th St, Baugh
3	I-55 N, I-70 E, IL 3 N, to St Clair Ave, to stockyards
2b a	3rd St, **S**...gas
1	IL 3 S, 13th St, E St Louis, **N**...Casino Queen
0mm	Illinois/Missouri state line, Mississippi River

Interstate 70

E ↕ W

Effingham

Exit #	Services
156mm	Illinois/Indiana state line, no services
154	US 40 W, **S**...South Fork Conv. Mart
151mm	weigh sta wb
149mm	**rest area wb, full(handicapped)facilities, info, phone, picnic tables, vending, litter barrels, petwalk, camping**
147	IL 1, Marshall, **N**...**gas:** Jerry's Rest., **S**...**gas:** Casey's(1mi), Jiffy/dsl/24hr, Marathon/Arby's/dsl, **food:** DQ, McDonald's, Pizza Hut, Sam's Steaks, Subway, Wendy's, **lodging:** Lincoln Motel(2mi), Relax Inn, Super 8, **other:** Lincoln Trail SP, Wal-Mart SuperCtr, antiques, camping
136	to Martinsville, **S**...**gas:** Fast Stop/dsl/24hr
134.5mm	N Fork Embarras River
129	IL 49, Casey, **N**...**other:** RV service, KOA(seasonal), **S**...**gas:** BP/Subway/dsl, Casey's, Speedway, **food:** DQ, Hardee's, Joe's Pizza, KFC, McDonald's, Pizza Hut, **lodging:** Comfort Inn, Casey Motel(1mi)
119	IL 130, Greenup, **S**...**gas:** Citgo/dsl, Phillips 66/Subway, **food:** DQ, Stockyards Rest., Subway, **lodging:** Budget Host, 5 Star Motel, **other:** Chevrolet, $General, antiques, camping, hist sites
105	Montrose, **N**...**other:** Spring Creek Camping(1mi), **S**...**gas:** BP/dsl, Citgo/dsl/24hr, **lodging:** Fairview Inn
98	I-57, N to Chicago
I-70 and I-57 run together 6 mi. See Interstate 57, exits 159-162.	
92	I-57, S to Mt Vernon

Vandalia

91mm	Little Wabash River
87mm	**rest area both lanes, full(handicapped)facilities, info, phone, vending, picnic tables, litter barrels, playground, petwalk, RV dump**
82	IL 128, Altamont, **N**...**gas:** Casey's, Citgo/Stuckey's/Subway/dsl/24hr, Marathon, **food:** Dairy Bar, McDonald's, **lodging:** Altamont Motel/rest., Knight's Inn, **S**...**food:** Longhorn Rest., **lodging:** Super 8
76	US 40, St Elmo, **N**...**gas:** Casey's, Citgo, **lodging:** Waldorf Motel, **other:** Timberline Camping(2mi)
71mm	weigh sta eb
68	US 40, Brownstown, **N**...**other:** Okaw Valley Kamping, Road Angel Camping, **S**...truck repair
63.5mm	Kaskaskia River
63	US 51, Vandalia, **N**...**food:** Chuck Wagon Cafe, LJ Silver, **lodging:** Day's Inn, **S**...**gas:** BP/Burger King/24hr, Marathon, Shell/dsl, **food:** China Buffet, DQ, McDonald's, Pizza Hut, Rancho Nuevo Mexican, Sonic, Subway, Wendy's, **lodging:** Jay's Inn, Travelodge, **other:** HOSPITAL, Aldi Foods, Harmons Foods, hist site
61	US 40, Vandalia, **N**...**gas:** Truckstop/dsl, **S**...**gas:** Fastop/dsl, Murphy USA/dsl, Phillips 66, **food:** China Buffet, KFC/Taco Bell, Los Amigos Mexican, Ponderosa, **lodging:** Holiday Inn Express, Ramada Ltd, **other:** AutoZone, $Box, Wal-Mart SuperCtr/24hr/gas
52	US 40, Mulberry Grove, **N**...**gas:** Citgo/dsl, **other:** Timber Trail Camp-In(2mi), tires, **S**...Cedar Brook Camping(1mi)
45	IL 127, Greenville, **N**...**gas:** Citgo/Domino's/dsl, Shell/dsl/24hr, **food:** Chang's Chinese, KFC/Taco Bell, Lu-Bob's Rest., Red Apple Rest., Mabry's Rest., McDonald's, **lodging:** Budget Host, Econolodge, Super 8, 2 Acre Motel, **other:** HOSPITAL, Ford/Mercury, **S**...to Carlyle Lake, **food:** Circle S Steaks
41	US 40 E, to Greenville, no services
36	US 40 E, Pocahontas, **S**...**gas:** BP/dsl/24hr, Phillips 66/dsl/24hr, **lodging:** Lighthouse Lodge, Powhatan Motel/rest., Tahoe Motel, **other:** truck/tire repair
30	US 40, IL 143, to Highland, **S**...**gas:** Shell/dsl/24hr, **food:** Blue Springs Café, **other:** HOSPITAL, Tomahawk RV Park(7mi)
26.5mm	**Silver Lake rest area both lanes, full(handicapped) facilities, phone, picnic tables, litter barrels, vending, petwalk**
24	IL 143, Marine, 4 mi **S**...**food:** Ponderosa, **lodging:** Holiday Inn Express, **other:** HOSPITAL
21	IL 4, Lebanon, no services
15b a	I-55, N to Chicago, S to St Louis, I-270 W to KC
I-70 and I-55 run together 18 mi. See Interstate 55, exits 1-18.	
0mm	Illinois/Missouri state line, Mississippi River

ILLINOIS
Interstate 72

Exit #	Services
183mm	1 mi E on University...**food:** Arby's, Burger King, Garcia's Pizza, La Bamba's Mexican, McDonald's, Monical's Pizza, Pizza Hut, Sonic, Subway, Taffy's Rest, Texas Roadhouse, Village Inn, **other:** Advance Parts, Aldi Foods, AutoZone, CVS Drug, Firestone/auto, County Mkt Foods, Schnuck's Foods/24hr
182b a	I-57, N to Chicago, S to Memphis, to I-74
176	IL 47, to Mahomet
172	IL 10, Lodge, Seymour
169	White Heath Rd, no services
166	IL 105 W, Market St, N...Ford/Mercury, S...**gas:** Mobil/dsl, **food:** Red Wheel Rest., **lodging:** Best Western, Foster Inn, **other:** vet
165mm	Sangamon River
164	Bridge St, **1 mi** S...**gas:** Mobil, **food:** Best Wok, Hardee's, McDonald's, Monical's Pizza, Subway, **other:** HOSPITAL, $General, Chevrolet/Buick/Pontiac, Chrysler/Dodge/Jeep
156	IL 48, to Weldon, Cisco, S...Friends Creek Camping(may-oct)(3mi)
153mm	**rest area both lanes, full(handicapped) facilities, phone, picnic tables, litter barrels, vending, petwalk**
152mm	Friends Creek
150	Argenta, no services
144	IL 48, Oreana, S...**gas:** Pilot/McDonald's/Subway/dsl/scales/24hr, **lodging:** Sleep Inn, **other:** HOSPITAL, Dodge, Honda, Hyundai, Mitsubishi
141b a	US 51 S, Decatur, N...**gas:** Shell/Circle K, **food:** Applebee's, Cheddar's, Cracker Barrel, HomeTown Buffet, McDonald's, O'Charley's, Pizza Hut, Red Lobster, Steak'n Shake, Subway, Taco Bell, Texas Roadhouse, **lodging:** Baymont Inn, Comfort Inn, Country Inn&Suites, Fairfield Inn, Hampton Inn, Holiday Inn Express, Ramada Ltd; **other:** Advance Parts, Bergner's, Best Buy, Buick/GMC, $Tree, Harley Davidson, JC Penney, Lowe's Whse, Kohl's, Mitsubishi/Hyundai/Honda, Menard's, Petsmart, Sears/auto, Staples, mall, S...**food:** Arby's, Burger King, El Rodeo Mexican, Monical's Pizza, Panera Bread, Quizno's, **other:** Circuit City, Jo-Ann Fabrics, PetCo, Radio Shack, Sam's Club, Walgreens, Wal-Mart SuperCtr/24hr
138	IL 121, Decatur, S...HOSPITAL
133b a	US 36 E, US 51, Decatur, S...**gas:** Phillips 66/Subway/dsl, **lodging:** Day's Inn, Decatur Hotel/rest.
128	Niantic, no services
122	to Mt Auburn, Illiopolis, S...**gas:** Fastop
114	Buffalo, Mechanicsburg, no services
108	Riverton, Dawson, no services
107mm	Sangamon River
104	Camp Butler, **2 mi** N...**lodging:** Best Rest Inn, Best Western, Park View Motel, **food:** Chesapeake Seafood, Starbucks, **other:** golf
103b a	I-55, N to Chicago, S to St Louis, Il 97, to Springfield.
	I-72 and I-55 run together 6 mi. See Interstate 55, exits 92-98
93	IL 4, Springfield, N...**gas:** Hucks, Thorntons, **food:** Applebee's, Arby's, Bakers Square, Buffet King, Burger King, Chili's, China Buffet, Corky's BBQ,

	Denny's, Grand Buffet, Huck's, LoneStar Steaks, Longhorn Steaks, Maverick Rest., McDonald's, Oberweis Ice Cream, Old Country Buffet, Olive Garden, Panera Bread, Pasta House, Perkins, Popeye's, Qdoba Mexican, Sonic, Starbucks, Taco Bell, TGIFriday, **lodging:** Comfort Inn, Courtyard, Fairfield Inn, Sleep Inn, **other:** Barnes&Noble, Best Buy, Circuit City, Curves, Discount Tire, Gordman's, Jo-Ann Crafts, K-Mart, Kohl's, Lowe's Whse, Menard's, Michael's, Office Depot, Old Navy, Petsmart, Sam's Club/gas, Sears/auto, ShopKO, Staples, Target, TJ Maxx, Walgreens, Wal-Mart/auto, vet, S...**gas:** Meijer/dsl, **food:** Bob Evans, O'Charley's, Steak'n Shake, **lodging:** Hampton Inn, Staybridge Suites, **other:** Cadillac, Chevrolet, Chrysler/Dodge/Jeep, Ford, Honda, Saturn, Funpark
91	Wabash Ave, to Springfield, N...**food:** Buffalo Wild Wings, Coz's Pizza, Culver's, **other:** Nissan, S...Colman RV SuperCtr
82	New Berlin, S...**gas:** Phillips 66/The Plaza Rest./dsl
76	IL 123, to Ashland, Alexander, no services
68	to IL 104, to Jacksonville, **2 mi** N...**gas:** BP, **other:** HOSPITAL
64	US 67, to Jacksonville, N...**gas:** Clark/Quizno's/dsl, **lodging:** Comfort Inn, Econolodge, Holiday Inn Express, **other:** Hopper RV Ctr, Walgreens, **2 mi** N...**gas:** BP/dsl, **food:** Classic Diner, DQ, McDonald's, Subway, **lodging:** Super 8, **other:** HOSPITAL, Harpers Food/gas
60	to US 67 N, to Jacksonville, **6 mi** N...HOSPITAL, gas, food, lodging
52	to IL 106, Winchester, N...golf, **2 mi** S...gas, food, lodging
46	IL 100, to Bluffs
42mm	Illinois River
35	US 54, IL 107, to Pittsfield, Griggsville, **4 mi** N...gas, food, lodging, S...**other:** HOSPITAL, Pine Lakes Camping(6mi), st police
31	to Pittsfield, New Salem, **5 mi** S...HOSPITAL, gas, food, lodging, camping
20	IL 106, Barry, S...**gas:** Phillips 66/dsl/24hr, Shell/dsl/24hr, **food:** Ice House, Wendy's, **other:** Truckload Foods, antiques, winery
10	IL 96, to Payson, Hull
4a	I-172, N to Quincy
1	IL 106, to Hull
0mm	**Illinois/Missouri state line, Mississippi River. Exits 157 & 156 are in Missouri.**
157	to Hannibal, MO 179, S...**gas:** Ayerco, BP, Phillips 66, Shell, **food:** Mark Twain Dinette, **lodging:** Hannibal Inn, Hotel Clemens, Super 7 Motel, Travelodge
156	US 61, New London, Palmyra. I-72 begins/ends in Hannibal, MO on US 61., N...**gas:** BP, Conoco/dsl, **food:** Burger King, Country Kitchen, Golden Corral, Hardee's, Hunan Chinese, LJ Silver, McDonalds, Papa Johns, Pizza Hut, Sonic, Taco Bell, **other:** Aldi Foods, Big Lots, $General, Ford, Goody's, Kroger, Radio Shack, TrueValue, Wal-Mart SuperCtr/gas/24hr, **0-2 mi** S...**gas:** Ayerco/Joe's Diner, Shell/dsl, **food:** Cassano's Subs, DQ, Hardee's, KFC, Wendy's, **lodging:** Comfort Inn, Days Inn, Econolodge, Hannibal Inn, Holiday Inn Express, Mark Twain Motel, Super 8, **other:** AutoZone, County Mkt Foods, Injun Joe's RV Camp, Walgreens

Interstate 74

Exit #	Services
221mm	Illinois/Indiana state line, Central/Eastern Time Zone
220	Lynch Rd, Danville, 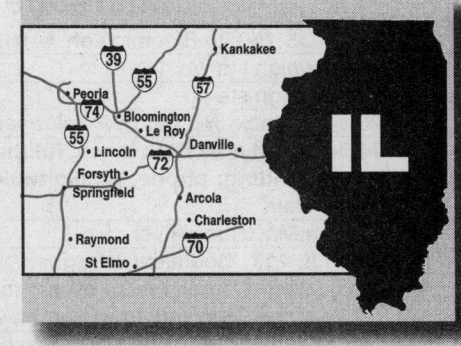**N...gas:** BP/dsl, Marathon(1mi), **food:** Big Boy, **lodging:** Best Western, Comfort Inn, Danville Inn, Fairfield Inn, Holiday Inn Express, Sleep Inn, Super 8
216	Bowman Ave, Danville, **N...gas:** Freedom, Mobil/dsl/24hr, Phillips 66/dsl, **food:** Godfather's, KFC
215b a	US 150, IL 1, Gilbert St, Danville, **N...gas:** BP, Citgo/dsl, Harper, Speedway, Phillips 66, **food:** Arby's, Baskin-Robbins/Dunkin Donuts, Danville Rest., La Potosina, LJ Silver, McDonald's, Pizza Hut, Steak'n Shake, Subway, Taco Bell, **lodging:** Best Western, Day's Inn, **other:** HOSPITAL, Aldi Foods, Ford/Lincoln/Mercury, **S...gas:** Casey's/dsl, Speedway/dsl/24hr, **food:** Burger King, Green Jade Chinese, Monical's Pizza, **other:** AutoZone, Big R, Pontiac/GMC, $General, Family$, Harley-Davidson, Forest Glen Preserve Camping(11mi), NAPA, Toyota
214	G St, Tilton, no services
210	US 150, MLK Dr, **2 mi N...gas:** Marathon, **food:** Little Nugget Steaks, **other:** HOSPITAL, to Kickapoo SP, camping, **S...food:** PossumTrot Rest.
208mm	Welcome Ctr wb, full(handicapped)facilities, info, phones, picnic tables, litter barrels, vending, petwalk
206	Oakwood, **N...gas:** Marathon/dsl/rest./scales/24hr, **S...gas:** Phillips 66/Subway/dsl, Mobil/Oakwood/rest./dsl, Casey's(1mi), **food:** McDonald's, Oaks Grill
200	IL 49 N, to Rankin, **N...camping**
197	IL 49 S, Ogden, **S...gas:** Phillips 66/dsl, **food:** Billy Bud's Steaks, Godfather's Pizza
192	St Joseph, **S...food:** DQ, **other:** antiques
185	IL 130, University Ave
184	US 45, Cunningham Ave, Urbana, **N...food:** A&W, **lodging:** Park Inn, **other:** Farm&Fleet, Toyota, VW, **S...gas:** Freedom/dsl/24hr, Marathon/Circle K/Subway, Speedway/dsl, Shell, **food:** Cracker Barrel, Domino's, Hickory River, Longhorn Steaks, Ned Kelly's Steaks, Steak'n Shake/24hr, **lodging:** Best Value Inn, Best Western, Eastland Suites, Motel 6, Travelers Stay, **other:** Auto Park, $General, Family$, Firestone/auto, NAPA, Sav-A-Lot
183	Lincoln Ave, Urbana, **S...gas:** Marathon/Circle K/Quizno's, Mobil/dsl, Speedway/dsl, **food:** Seasons Rest., Urbana Garden Rest., **lodging:** Holiday Inn/rest., Holiday Inn Express, Ramada Ltd, Sleep Inn, Super 8, **other:** HOSPITAL, Harley-Davidson, to U of IL
182	Neil St, Champaign, **N...food:** Baker's Square, Bob Evans, Chevy's Mexican, Denny's, FoodCourt, McDonald's, Olive Garden, Panera Bread, Smokey Bones, Subway, Taco Bell, **lodging:** Baymont Inn, Comfort Inn, La Quinta, Red Roof Inn, Super 8, **other:** Barnes&Noble, Chevrolet/Cadillac, Chrysler/Dodge/Jeep, JC Penney, Kohl's, Mercedes/Volvo, Office Depot, Osco Drug, Sears/auto, TJ Maxx, mall, same as 181, **S...gas:** Mobil, **other:** JoAnn Fabrics
181	Prospect Ave, Champaign, **N...gas:** Meijer/dsl/24hr, **food:** Applebee's, Bennigan's, Buffalo Wild Wings, Burger King, Cheddar's, Chili's, China Town, Culver's,

Damon's, Fazoli's, HomeTown Buffet, LoneStar Steaks, O'Charley's, Outback Steaks, Pen Sta Subs, Red Lobster, Ruby Tuesday, Ryan's, Steak'n Shake/24hr, Subway, **lodging:** Baymont Inn, Country Inn&Suites, Courtyard, Drury Inn, Extended Stay America, Fairfield Inn, Red Roof Inn, **other:** Aamco, Advance Parts, Best Buy, Borders Books, Circuit City, Ddoge/Jeep, $Tree, Hyundai, Kia, Lowe's Whse, Michael's, Mitsubishi, Petsmart, Sam's Club/gas, Staples, Target, Tires+, Wal-Mart SuperCtr/auto/gas, same as 182, **S...gas:** BP/Circle K, Freedom/dsl, Mobil, **food:** Arby's, Dos Reales Mexican, KFC, Great Wall Chinese, LJ Silver, **lodging:** AmeriInn, Day's Inn, Econolodge, **other:** CarX, $General, Home Depot, NAPA, Tire Barn, RV/dsl repair, Walgreens

Exit #	Services
179b a	I-57, N to Chicago, S to Memphis
174	Lake of the Woods Rd, Prairieview Rd, **N...gas:** BP/dsl, Casey's, Mobil/dsl, **food:** Hideaway Woods Cafe, Subway, **other:** Tin Cup Camping, Lake of the Woods SP, **S...gas:** Citgo, **food:** McDonald's
172	IL 47, Mahomet, **N...other:** R&S RV Sales, **S...gas:** BP, Mobil/dsl, Shell/Domino's/dsl, **food:** Arby's, DQ, Esmerelda's, HenHouse Rest., Los Zarapes, Monical's Pizza, Peking House Chinese, Subway, Taco Loco, The Wok, **lodging:** Heritage Inn, **other:** Ace Hardware, Curves, CVS Drug, IGA Foods, NAPA
166	Mansfield, **S...gas:** BP, **food:** Mansfield Rest.
159	IL 54, Farmer City, **S...gas:** Casey's, Huck's/Quizno's/dsl, **food:** Farmer City Cafe, **lodging:** Budget Motel, Day's Inn, **other:** NAPA, to Clinton Lake RA
156mm	rest area both lanes, full(handicapped)facilities, phone, picnic tables, litter larrels, vending, playground, petwalk
152	US 136, to Heyworth, no services
149	Le Roy, **N...gas:** BP/Hong Kong Express/dsl/24hr, Freedom, Love's/rest./dsl/scales/24hr, **food:** KFC, McDonald's, Roma Ralph's Pizza, Subway, **other:** Doc's Drug, $General, IGA Foods, NAPA, to Moraine View SP, **S...gas:** Shell/Woody's Rest./dsl/scales/24hr, **lodging:** Super 8, **other:** Clinton Lake, camping
142	Downs, **N...gas:** BP/Pizza/Subs/dsl/24hr, **other:** USPO
135	US 51, Bloomington, **N...gas:** Clark/dsl, Huck's, Mobil/dsl, **food:** McDonald's, **other:** HOSPITAL, to IL St U, **S...gas:** Marathon/dsl
134b[157]	Veterans Pkwy, Bloomington, **N...gas:** Clark/24hr, FS, **food:** CJ's Rest., Froggy's Rest., **lodging:** Howard Johnson, **other:** airport
134a	I-55, N to Chicago, S to St Louis, I-74 E
160b a	**I-74 and I-55 run together 6 mi. See Interstate 55, exit 160b a.**
127	I-55, N to Chicago, S to St Louis, I-74 W to Peoria

ILLINOIS

Interstate 74

E — W

125 US 150, to Bloomington, Mitsubishi Motorway

123mm weigh sta wb

122mm weigh sta eb

120 Carlock, [N]...gas: BP/dsl/repair, [S]...camping

114.5mm rest area both lanes, full(handicapped)facilities, vending, phone, picnic tables, litter barrels, petwalk

113.5mm Mackinaw River

112 IL 117, Goodfield, [N]...gas: Shell/Subway/dsl, **food:** Busy Corner Rest., **other:** to Timberline RA, Jellystone Camping(1mi), Eureka Coll, Reagan Home

102b a Morton, [N]...**gas:** BP, Casey's, Citgo/Blimpie/dsl/24hr, Mobil/Arby's/dsl/scales/24hr, **food:** Burger King, Country Kitchen, Cracker Barrel, Culver's, Ruby Tuesday, Steak'n Shake, Taco Bell, Wendy's, **lodging:** Best Western, Comfort Inn, Day's Inn, Holiday Inn Express, Quality Inn, **other:** Freightliner, Wal-Mart SuperCtr/24hr/dsl, [S]...**gas:** Shell/Subway/dsl/24hr, **food:** China Dragon, KFC, Lin's Buffet, McDonald's, Monical's Pizza, Quizno's, **other:** Chrysler/Dodge, CVS Drug, $Tree, Ford, K-Mart, Kroger

101 I-155 S, to Lincoln

99 I-474 W, airport

98 Pinecrest Dr, no services

96 95c(from eb), US 150, IL 8, E Washington St, E Peoria, [N]...**gas:** Fast Stop, **food:** Monical's Pizza, **lodging:** Super 8, **other:** O'Reilly Parts

95b IL 116, to Metamora, [N]...**gas:** Shell, **lodging:** Hampton Inn, **other:** casino

95a N Main St, Peoria, [S]...**gas:** BP/24hr, **food:** A&W/LJ Silver, Applebee's, Bob Evans, China Buffet, Godfather's, Hardee's, Subway, **lodging:** Holiday Inn Express, Motel 6, **other:** Aldi Foods, Advance Parts, Curves, CVS Drug, $General, Goodyear/auto, Kohls, Kroger, ShopKO, Walgreens

94 IL 40, RiverFront Dr, [S]...**gas:** Hucks/Godfather's/24hr, **food:** Applebee's, Arby's, Buffalo Wild Wings, Chili's, Corky's BBQ, Culver's, Ming's Rest., Panera Bread, Papa John's, Quizno's, Shlotzky's, Steak'n Shake, Texas Roadhouse, **lodging:** Embassy Suites, **other:** Lowe's Whse, Radio Shack, Wal-Mart SuperCtr/24hr

93.5mm Illinois River

93b US 24, IL 29, Peoria, [S]...**other:** Sears, civic ctr

93a Jefferson St, Peoria, [S]...**food:** Uno Pizzaria, to civic ctr

92 Glendale Ave, Peoria, [S]...**other:** HOSPITAL, downtown

Peoria

92a IL 40 N, Knoxville Ave, Peoria, [S]...**lodging:** Holiday Inn, **other:** HOSPITAL

91 University St, Peoria, no services

90 Gale Ave, Peoria, **1 mi N on Universtiy...gas:** BP, Phillips 66, **food:** Dynasty Chinese, McDonald's, Steak'n Shake, Wendy's, **other:** AutoZone, Walgreens, Wal-Mart, to Expo Gardens, [S]...to Bradley U, [S]...**gas:** Marathon

89 US 150, War Memorial Dr, Peoria, [N] **on War Memorial...gas:** BP, Shell, **food:** Baskin-Robbins/Dunkin Donuts, Bob Evans, Burger King, Cheddar's, Chevy's Mexican, ChuckeCheese, Denny's, IHOP, Ned Kelly's Steaks, Outback Steaks, Perkins/24hr, Pizza Hut, Red Lobster, Schlotsky's, Steak'n Shake, Subway, Wendy's, **lodging:** AmeriSuites, Baymont Inn, Best Western, Comfort Suites, Courtyard, Extended Stay America, Fairfield Inn, Holiday Inn, Jamison Inn, Red Roof Inn, Residence Inn, Sleep Inn, Super 8, **other:** Best Buy, Chevrolet, Circuit City, Cub Foods, Famous-Barr, Firestone, JC Penney, Lowe's Whse, Macy's, Pontiac/Cadillac, Sears/auto, Target, Tires+, U-Haul, Walgreens, mall

87b a I-474 E, IL 6, N to Chillicothe, [E]...airport

82 Edwards Rd, Kickapoo, [N]...**gas:** Mobil/dsl/service, Shell/Subway/dsl, **food:** Jubilee Café, **other:** craft mall, to Jubilee Coll SP, [S]...**other:** USPO, Wildlife Prairie Park

75 Brimfield, Oak Hill, [N]...**gas:** Casey's

71 to IL 78, to Canton, Elmwood, no services

62mm rest area both lanes, full(handicapped)facilities, phone, picnic tables, litter barrels, vending, petwalk

61.5mm Spoon River

Galesburg

54 IL 97, Lewistown, [N]...**other:** TravL Park Camping(1mi), [S]...**gas:** Mobil/dsl(2mi)

51 Knoxville, [S]...**gas:** Casey's, Phillips 66/Subway/dsl/scales, **food:** Hardee's/24hr, McDonald's, **lodging:** Super 8

48b a E Galesburg, Galesburg, [N]...**lodging:** Best Western, **other:** Harley-Davidson, [S]...**gas:** BP, Mobil/dsl, Phillips 66, **food:** DQ, KFC, Hardee's, Jalisco Mexican, McDonald's, Pizza Hut, Subway, Taco Bell, **lodging:** Holiday Inn Express, **other:** Econo Foods, Family$, Firestone, Goodyear, HyVee Foods/gas, Save-A-Lot Foods, Walgreens, to Sandburg Birthplace, Lincoln-Douglas Debates

46b a US 34, to Monmouth, [N]...**other:** Nichol's dsl Service, [S]...**other:** HOSPITAL

32 IL 17, Woodhull, [N]...**gas:** BP/dsl, Shell/Homestead Rest./dsl/scales, **food:** Subway, [S]...**gas:** Mobil/dsl/rest./scales/24hr, **food:** Woodhull Rest., **other:** Shady Lakes Camping(8mi)

30mm rest area wb, full(handicapped)facilities, vending, picnic tables, litter barrels, phones, playground, petwalk, RV dump

28mm rest area eb, full(handicapped)facilities, vending, picnic tables, litter barrels, phones, playground, petwalk, RV dump

24 IL 81, Andover, [N]...**gas:** Casey's(2mi), camping

14mm I-80, E to Chicago, I-80/I-280 W to Des Moines

8mm weigh sta wb

6mm weigh sta eb

5b US 6, Moline, [S]...**gas:** Citgo, **food:** McDonald's, Montana Jack's, Runway Cafe, Skyline Inn/Rest., **lodging:** Best Western, Country Inn&Suites, Econolodge, Hampton Inn, Holiday Inn, La Quinta, Motel 6, **other:** Airport

Moline

5a I-280 W, US 6 W, to Des Moines

4b a IL 5, John Deere Rd, Moline, [N]...**gas:** BP, Citgo, **food:** Applebee's, Burger King, Carlos O'Kelly's, Culver's, Old Country Buffet, Panera Bread, Ryan's, Starbucks, Steak'n Shake, Subway, Wendy's, **other:** Cadillac, Curves, $Tree, Lowe's Whse, Radio Shack, Staples, Tires+, Volvo, Wal-Mart SuperCtr/24hr, [S]...**gas:** BP, **food:** Arby's, Burger King,'s, Denny's, Garfield's Rest., IHOP, Los Agares Mexican, LJ Silver/A&W, Miss Mamie's, New Mandarin Chinese, Osaka Japanese, Sub-

Interstate 74

way, Taco Bell, Wendy's, **lodging:** Best Western, Comfort Inn, Fairfield Inn, **other:** Best Buy, Chevrolet, Firestone/auto, Ford/Lincoln/Mercury, Goodyear/auto, JC Penney, Pontiac, Sears/auto, Von Maure, Walgeeens, Younkers, mall

3	23rd Ave, Moline
2	7th Ave, Moline, ...**gas:** PetroStop, **lodging:** Stony Creek Inn, **other:**to civic ctr, riverfront
1	3rd Ave(from eb), Moline, ...**gas:** PetroStop, **lodging:** Stony Creek Inn
0mm	Illinois/Iowa state line, Mississippi River. **Exits 4-1 are in Iowa.**
4	US 67, Grant St, State St, Bettendorf, ...**gas:** BP, Clark, Phillips 66/dsl, Shell, **food:** Ross' Rest./24hr, Subway, **lodging:** Traveler Motel, Twin Bridges Motel, **other:** CarQuest, ...**food:** DQ, Village Inn Rest., **lodging:** City Ctr Motel, **other:** $General
3	Middle Rd, Locust St, Bettendorf, ...**gas:** BP, **food:** Bennigan's, China Taste, Grinders Rest., MaidRite Café, McDonald's, Quizno's, Starbucks, Subway, **lodging:** Holiday Inn, **other:** HOSPITAL, Goodyear/auto, Home Depot, Marshall's, Schnuck's Foods, ShopKO, Walgreens
2	US 6 W, Spruce Hills Dr, Bettendorf, ...**gas:** BP/dsl, Phillips 66, **food:** Domino's, Old Chicago Pizza, **lodging:** Courtyard, Heartland Inn, Ramada Inn, The Lodge Hotel/rest., **other:** U-Haul, ...**food:** Applebee's, Burger King, Godfather's, KFC, Panera Bread, Red Lobster, Subway, **lodging:** Day's Inn, Fairfield Inn, La Quinta, **other:** Buick/Pontiac/GMC/Cadillac, Kohl's, Gander Mtn, Gordman's, Lowe's Whse, Sam's Club/gas, st patrol
1	53rd St, Hamilton, ...**gas:** BP, **food:** Biaggi's Italian, Chili's, Red Robin, Ruby Tuesday, Texas Roadhouse, **lodging:** Hampton Inn, Staybridge Suites, **other:** HOSPITAL, Borders Books, Harley-Davidson, HyVee Foods, Michael's, Old Navy, TJ Maxx, Walgreens, ...**gas:** Phillips 66, **food:** Arby's, China Cafe, DQ, Fuddrucker's, Golden Corral, IHOP, Krispy Kreme, QDoba Mexican, Quizno's, Steak'n Shake, Subway, Village Inn Rest., Taco Bell, Wendy's, **lodging:** Sleep Inn, **other:** Best Buy, Staples, Target, Wal-Mart SuperCtr/24hr/gas
0mm	I-74 begins/ends on I-80, exit 298., **Exits 1-4 are in Iowa.**

Interstate 80

Exit #	Services
163mm	Illinois/Indiana state line
161	US 6, IL 83, Torrence Ave, ...**gas:** BP, **food:** Arby's, Burger King, Chili's, Culver's, Dixie Kitchen, Hooters, IHOP, Liang's Garden, New China Buffet, Old Country Buffet, Olive Garden, Rib House, Taco-Burrito's, Wendy's, **lodging:** Comfort Suites, Day's Inn, Extended Stay America, Holiday Inn Express, Howard Johnson Express, Red Roof Inn, Sleep Inn, Super 8, **other:** Best Buy, CarEx, Chrysler/Jeep, $General, Fannie May Candies, Firestone/auto, Home Depot, JustTires, K-Mart, PepBoys, Radio Shack, Ultra Foods, **Wal-Mart Super Ctr**, ...**gas:** Gas for Less, Marathon, Mobil, **food:** China Chef,

Burger King, DQ, Dunkin Donuts, Golden Crown Rest., Jonny's K's Cafe, McDonald's/playplace, Mr. Gyro's, Popolono's Italian, Quizno's, Subway, Tuesday Morning, **other:** Auto Clinic, Chevrolet, PetsMart, Saab, Sam's Club, SunRise Foods, Walgreens, vet

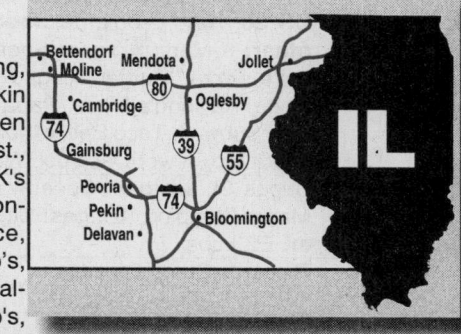

160b	I-94 W, to Chicago, tollway begins wb, ends eb
160a	IL 394 S, to Danville
159mm	Oasis, **gas:** Mobil/dsl, **food:** Auntie Annie's, McDonald's, Panda Express, Starbucks, Subway
157	IL 1, Halsted St, ...**gas:** Citgo/dsl, Marathon/dsl, **food:** Burger King, Maxwell St Grill, **lodging:** Chicago Southland Hotel, Chicago Park Hotel, Comfort Inn, Econolodge, Hilton Garden, Holiday Inn Express, Regency Inn, ...**gas:** Speedway, **food:** Applebee's, Arby's, Boston Mkt, Chili's, Dunkin Donuts, Fannie May Candies, KFC, McDonald's, Panda Express, Popeye's, Quizno's, Starbucks, Subway, Taco Bell, Washington Square Rest., Wendy's, **lodging:** Homewood Hotel, Super 8, **other:** Best Buy, Chevrolet, Discount Tire, $Tree, Firestone/auto, Goodyear/auto, Home Depot, Jewel-Osco, Jo-Ann Fabrics, K-Mart, Menard's, Office Depot, PepBoys, PetCo, Target, TJ Maxx
156	Dixie Hwy(from eb, no return), ...**gas:** Mobil, **food:** Leona's Rest., **other:** golf
155	I-294 N, Tri-State Tollway, toll plaza
154	Kedzie Ave(from eb, no return), ...**gas:** Speedway, ...HOSPITAL
151b a	I-57(exits left from both directions), N to Chicago, S to Memphis
148b a	IL 43, Harlem Ave, ...**gas:** Speedway/dsl, **food:** Al's Beef, Buffalo Wild Wings, Burger King, Chicago Café, **Cracker Barrel**, Culver's, Eggi Grill, Papa John's, Papa Luigi's, Quizno's, Wendy's, **lodging:** Comfort Suites, Fairfield Inn, Hampton Inn, Holiday Inn Select, La Quinta, Sleep Inn, Wingate Inn, ...**food:** Arby's, Taco Bell, TGIFriday, **other:** Best Buy, Carmax, Kohl's, Michael's, PetsMart, SuperTarget, World Music Theatre, Windy City Camping
147.mm	weigh sta wb
145b a	US 45, 96th Ave, ...**food:** Arrenello's Pizza, Arby's, Blackberry's Pancakes, Dunkin Donuts, Quizno's, Silverstar Chinese, Tokyo Steaks, TX Roadhouse, **lodging:** Country Inn Suites, Hilton Garden, **0-3 mi** ...**gas:** BP, Clark, Shell/Circle K/dsl/24hr, **food:** Beggar's Pizza, Burger King, DQ, Denny's, McDonald's, Mindy's Ribs, Morgan's Grill, Rising Sun Chinese, Stoney Pt Grill, Subway, White Castle, Wendy's, **lodging:** Super 8, **other:** Timber View Ctr, Windy City Camping
143mm	weigh sta eb
140	SW Hwy, I 355 N Tollway, US 6 S

Interstate 80

E ↑ **W**

Joliet

137	US 30, New Lenox, **N**...**food:** Williamson's Rest., **other:** K-Mart, **S**...**gas:** Speedway/dsl, **food:** Beggar's Pizza, Burger King, KFC, McDonald's/playplace, Paisono's Pizza, Papa Joe's/LJ Silver, Pizza Hut, Subway, Taco Bell, **other:** Ace Harware, Goodyear/auto, Jewel-Osco/dsl, Walgreens, vet
134	Briggs St, **N**...**gas:** Speedway, **other:** HOSPITAL, Martin Camping, **S**...**gas:** Citgo/dsl, Valero/dsl, **other:** EZ Lube
133	Richards St, no services
132b a	US 52, IL 53, Chicago St
131.5mm	Des Plaines River
131	US 6, Meadow Ave, **N**...to Riverboat Casino
130b a	IL 7, Larkin Ave, **N**...**gas:** Citgo/dsl, Clark, Marathon/24hr, Shell/24hr, Speedway, **food:** A&W/KFC, Bellagio Pizzaria, Bob Evans, Burger King, Dunkin Donuts/Baskin-Robbins, DQ, Quizno's, Steak'n Shake, Subway, Taco Bell, Wendy's, White Castle, Yu's Garden, **lodging:** Budget Inn, Comfort Inn, Motel 6, Holiday Inn, Red Roof Inn, Super 8, **other:** HOSPITAL, Chevrolet/Cadillac, Discount Tire, Ford, Goodyear/auto, K-Mart, Radio Shack, Sam's Club/gas, White Hen, Wal-Mart, to Coll of St Francis, vet, **S**...auto repair
127	Houbolt Rd, to Joliet, **N**...**gas:** BP/deli, 7-11, **food:** Burger King, Cracker Barrel, Arby's, Heros Sports Grill, McDonald's, Split-Second Deli, **lodging:** Fairfield Inn, Hampton Inn, Ramada Ltd, **other:** Riverboat Casino
126b a	I-55, N to Chicago, S to St Louis
125.5mm	Du Page River
122	Minooka, **N**...**gas:** Citgo/dsl/24hr, **S**...**gas:** BP/24hr, Pilot/Arby's/scales/dsl/24hr, **food:** DQ, McDonald's/playplace, Subway, Wendy's, **other:** SuperValu Foods
119mm	**rest area wb, full(handicapped)facilities, vending, phones, picnic tables, litter barrels, playground, petwalk**
117mm	**rest area eb, full(handicapped)facilities, vending, phone, picnic tables, litter barrels, playground, petwalk**
112	IL 47, Morris, **N**...**gas:** BP/Quizno's/scales/dsl/24hr/@, Citgo/dsl, **food:** Bellacino's, Chili's, **lodging:** Comfort Inn, Day's Inn, Holiday Inn Express, **other:** Curves, $General, Menard's, **S**...**gas:** BP, Mobil, Phillips 66, Shell/24hr, **food:** Burger King, Culver's, KFC/LJ Silver, Maria's Ristorante, McDonald's, Morris Diner, Pizza Hut, Subway, Taco Bell, Wendy's, **lodging:** Park Motel, Sherwood Oaks Motel, Super 8, **other:** MEDICAL CARE, Aldi Foods, AutoZone, Big R Store, Chevrolet/Buick/Cadillac, Fisher Parts, Ford, Jewel-Osco, Morris Drug, Pontiac/GMC, Radio Shack, Walgreens, Wal-Mart SuperCtr/24hr, to Stratton SP, transmissions/repair
105	to Seneca, no services
97	to Marseilles, **S**...**gas:** Marathon/Boz Dogs/dsl, **food:** Taco Time, **other:** Four Star Camping, Glenwood Camping(2mi), Prairie Lakes Resort/rest., to Illini SP, RV camping
93	IL 71, Ottawa, **N**...**gas:** Mobil/24hr, Shell/dsl/24hr, **other:** Skydive Chicago RV Park(2mi), **S**...**food:** Hank's Farm Rest., **other:** HOSPITAL
92.5mm	Fox River

Peru

90	IL 23, Ottawa, **N**...**gas:** BP/Subway, **food:** Arby's, Cracker Barrel, Quizno's, Taco Bell, **lodging:** Hampton Inn, Holiday Inn Express, **other:** F&F, Ford/Lincoln/Mercury/Kia, Honda, Toyota, Wal-Mart SuperCtr, **S**...**gas:** BP/dsl/LP, Thornton's/dsl **food:** China Inn, Country Kitchen, Dunkin Donuts, Hardee's, KFC/LJ Silver, Starbucks, **lodging:** Budget Inn, Comfort Inn, Sands Motel(2mi), Super 8, Surrey Motel, **other:** HOSPITAL, Aldi Foods, $Tree, Harley-Davidson, Kroger, Radio Shack, USPO
81	IL 178, Utica, **N**...**gas:** Love's/McDonald's/Subway/scales/dsl/24hr, **other:** Hickory Hollow Camping, KOA(2mi), **S**...**gas:** Shell/Jimmy Johns/dsl, **food:** Duffy's Tavern(2mi), **lodging:** Starved Rock Inn, **other:** to Starved Rock SP
79b a	I-39, US 51, N to Rockford, S to Bloomington
77.5mm	Little Vermilion River
77	IL 351, La Salle, **S**...**gas:** FS/24hr, ✈/Flying J/Country Mkt/dsl/scales/24hr, **food:** UpTown Grill, **lodging:** Daniels Motel, **other:** st police
75	IL 251, Peru, **N**...**gas:** BP, Crazy D's/scales/dsl, Shell/dsl/rest./24hr, **food:** Arby's, McDonald's, Pinecone Rest., Quizno's, Starbucks, Taco Bell/TCBY, **lodging:** Baymont Inn, Econolodge, Kings Inn, Super 8, **other:** Kohl's, Wal-Mart/SuperCtr, **S**...**gas:** BP, **food:** Applebee's, Culver's, DQ, Dunkin Donuts, IHOP, Master Stir Fry, Pizza Hut, Red Lobster, Steak'n Shake, Subway, Wendy's, **lodging:** Fairfield Inn, La Quinta, **other:** HOSPITAL, AutoZone, Big-Lots, Buick/Pontiac/GMC, Chevrolet/Nissan/Mercedes, Chrysler/Jeep, Goodyear/auto, Home Depot, HyVee Food/gas, JC Penney, Jo-Ann Fabrics, K-Mart, Marshall's, Menard's, Mitsubishi, Sears/auto, Staples, Target, Toyota/Scion, Walgreens, mall
73	Plank Rd, **N**...**gas:** Sapp Bros/scales/dsl/@, **food:** Apple Barrel Rest., Burger King/playland, **other:** Kenworth, Volvo Trucks, camping
70	IL 89, to Ladd, **N**...**gas:** Casey's, **S**...**gas:** BP(3mi), **other:** HOSPITAL
61	I-180, to Hennepin
56	IL 26, Princeton, **N**...**gas:** Road Ranger/Stuckey's/scales/dsl/@, **lodging:** Super 8, **S**...**gas:** Phillips 66, Shell/dsl, **food:** Beck's, Big Apple Rest., Burger King, Country Kitchen, Culver's, KFC, McDonald's, Pizza Hut(1mi), Taco Bell, Wendy's, **lodging:** Day's Inn, Econolodge, Princeton Motel, **other:** HOSPITAL, AutoZone, Chevrolet/Pontiac/Buick/Cadillac, $General, O'Reilly Parts, Pennzoil, Sullivan's Food/gas, Wal-Mart SuperCtr, antiques, vet
51.5mm	**rest area both lanes, full(handicapped)facilities, phone, picnic tables, litter barrels, vending, playground, petwalk, RV dump**
45	IL 40, **N**...**lodging:** Day's Inn/Crossroads Rest., **other:** to Ronald Reagan Birthplace(21mi), **S**...**other:** Hennepin Canal SP, camping
44mm	Hennepin Canal
33	IL 78, to Kewanee, Annawan, **N**...**gas:** Shabbona RV Ctr/Camp(3mi), **S**...**gas:** Cenex, Mobil/dsl, **food:** Olympic Flame Rest., Phoenix Grill, **lodging:** US Express, **other:** to Johnson-Sauk Tr SP
27	to US 6, Atkinson, **N**...**gas:** Casey's, Mobil/dsl/rest./24hr

E ↕ **W**	19	IL 82, Geneseo, **N**...gas: BP, Phillips 66/dsl/24hr, Shell, **food:** Culvers, DQ, Hardee's, Happy Joe's Pizza, Genny Dogs, McDonald's, Pizza Hut, Quizno's, Subway, Trapper's Creek, **lodging:** Amerihost, Deck Motel/diner, Super 8(1mi), **other:** HOSPITAL, $General, Ford, Jewel-Osco, Wal-Mart/drugs, vet, **S**...food: KFC
	10	I-74, I-280, W to Moline, E to Peoria, no services
	9	US 6, to Geneseo, **N**...food: Lavender Crest Winery/Cafe, **S**...other: Niabi Zoo
E	7	Colona, **N**...gas: Shell/dsl, **food:** Country Fixins Rest.
M	5mm	Rock River
o	4a	IL 5, IL 92, W to Silvis, **S**...other: to Quad City Downs, Lundeen's Camping
l	4b	I-88, IL 92, E to Rock Falls, no services
i	2mm	weigh sta both lanes
n	1.5mm	**Welcome Ctr eb, full(handicapped)facilities, info, phone, picnic tables, litter barrels, petwalk, scenic overlook**
e	1	IL 84, 20th St, Great River Rd, E Moline, **N**...gas: BP/diesel, Git-Go, **food:** Brothers Rest., **other:** auto repair, camping, The Great River Rd, **3 mi S**...gas: BP, **other:** camping
	0mm	Illinois/Iowa state line, Mississippi River

Interstate 88

	Exit #	Services
	139.5mm	I-88 begins/ends on I-290.
	139	I-294, S to Indiana, N to Milwaukee
	138mm	toll plaza
E ↕ **W**	137	IL 83 N, Cermak Rd, **N**...food: Clubhouse rest., Ditkas Rest., McDonald's, **lodging:** Marriott, Rennaisance Inn, **other:** Macey's, Nieman-Marcus
C	136	IL 83 S, Midwest Rd(from eb), **N**...gas: Shell, **food:** Bennigan's, Burger King, Denny's, Dunkin Donuts, Giordano's rest., Jamba Juice, McDonalds, Noodles & Co, Quizno's, Starbucks, Tin Fish, Vic's Steaks, Subway, **lodging:** Holiday Inn, La Quinta, **other:** Costco/gas, Home Depot, Nordstrom's, Old Navy, TJ Maxx, Walgreens, World Mkt
h	134	Highland Ave(no EZ wb return), **N**...food: Baker's Square, Bennigan's, Bouna Beef, Brio Grille, Buca Italian, Burger King, Capital Grille, Champps Grill, Cheeseburger Paradise, Cici's, Claimjumper Rest., Fuddruckers, Grill Room, Hooters, Joe's Crab Shack, Kyoto, Magnum's, McCormick & Schmick's, Olive Garden, Panera Bread, PF Chang's Chinese, Parker's Grill, Potbelly's, Qdoba, Red Lobster, Rockbottom Brewery, Ruby Tuesday, Starbucks, Taylor Brewing Co, TGIFriday, Tortilo's Hotdogs, **lodging:** Amerisuites, Comfort Inn, Embassy Suites, Holiday Inn Express, Homestead Studios, Hyatt Place, Marriott, Red Roof Inn, Westin Hotel, **other:** HOSPITAL, Best Buy, Circuit City, Firestone/auto, Fry's Electronics, Home Depot, JC Penny, Kohl's, PetsMart, Vonmaur, mall, **S**...food: Parkers Ocean Grill
i c a g o	132	I-355 N(from wb)
A	131	I-355 S(from eb)
r	130	IL 53(from wb), **(1mi)N**...gas: BP, Mobil, **food:** McDonald's, **other:** Wal-Mart
e a	127	Naperville Rd, **N**...food: Mullen's Grill, **lodging:** Hilton, Wyndam, **S**...food: Buona Beef, Maggiano's, McDonald's, Panera Bread, Pizza Hut, TGIFriday, Wendy's,

		lodging: Best Western, Courtyard, Day's Inn, Exel Inn, Fairfield Inn, Hampton Inn, Holiday Inn Select, **other:** Ford, Jeep, Kia, K-Mart, Office Depot, Radio Shack, Subaru
	125	Winfield Rd, **N**...gas: BP, Mobil, **other:** HOSPITAL, Walgreen, **S**...food: Arby's, Al's Italian, Atlanta bread, Buffalo Wild Wings, California Pizza, Chipotle Mexican, Cold Stone Creamery, GoRoma, Max&Erma's, McDonald's, Potbelly's, Red Robin, Rockbottom Brewery, Starbucks, StirCrazy Grill, **lodging:** Springhill Suites, **other:** SuperTarget, Walgreens
	123	IL 59, **N**...food: Riva Steaks/Seafood, **other:** Carmax, **S**...gas: BP, Mobil/dsl, Speedway, **food:** Cracker Barrel, Danny's Grill, Dunkin Donuts/Baskin Robbins, Jimmy John's, Lee's Garden, Starbucks, Steak'n Shake, Subway, TX Roadhouse, Wendy's, **lodging:** Extended Stay America, Fairfield Inn, Red Roof Inn, Sleep Inn, SpringHill Suites, Towneplace Suites, **other:** White Hen Pantry
	119	Farnsworth Ave, **N**...gas: BP, Shell, **food:** Papa Bear Rest., Quizno's, Starbucks, **lodging:** Fox Valley Inn, Motel 6, **other:** Firestone/auto, Premium Outlets/Famous Brands, **S**...gas: Marathon, Phillips 66/dsl, Shell, Speedway, **food:** Dunkin Donuts/Baskin-Robbins, Goody's Drive-Thru, Little Caesars, McDonald's, Mike & Denise's Pizza, Subway, Taco Bell, **other:** AutoZone, Family$, Goodyear, Walgreens, White Hen Pantry
	118mm	toll plaza
	117	IL 31, IL 56, to Aurora, Batavia, **N**...gas: Citgo/dsl, Marathon, **food:** A&W, Tastee Freez, **S**...gas: Mobil, Thornton's, **food:** Culver's, Denny's, KFC, LJ Silver, McDonald's, Popeye's, Quizno's, Taco Bell, Togo's/Baskin-Robbins/Dunkin Donuts, White Castle, **lodging:** Baymont Inn, **other:** HOSPITAL, AutoZone, Cermac Foods, Firestone, GNC, Jewel/Osco, Murray's Parts, Radio Shack, U-Haul, Walgreens
	115	Orchard Rd, **N**...other: Chrysler/Plymouth/Dodge/Jeep, Ford/Lincoln/Mercury, Isuzu, JC Penny, Michaels, NTB, Nissan, PetCo, Pontiac, Saturn, Subaru, Target, **S**...gas: 7-11, **food:** A&W/KFC, Chili's, Coldstone, IHOP, Jimmy John's, Panera Bread, Papa Saverio's, Pizza Hut, Quizno's, Starbucks, Wendy's, **lodging:** Hampton Inn, Holiday Inn, **other:** CVS Drug, Discount Tire, Home Depot, Lowe's Whse
	114	IL 56W, to US 30(from wb, no EZ return), to Sugar Grove, no services
	109	IL 47, Elburn, no services
	94	Peace Rd, to IL 38, **N**...HOSPITAL
D	93mm	**Dekalb Oasis/24hr both lanes, Dekalb Oasis/24hr both lanes, gas: Mobil/dsl, food: McDonald's, Panda Express, Subway**
e	93mm	toll plaza
K a l b	92	IL 38, IL 23, Annie Glidden Rd, to DeKalb, **N**...lodging: Super 8, **2-3 mi N**...gas: BP, Road Ranger/dsl, Marathon, Shell, **food:** Baker's Square, Burger King, Chipotle Mexican, El Burrito Loco, Happy Wok Chinese, Jct Rest., Lukulo's Rest., McDonald's, Papa John's, Potbelly, Pizza Hut, Pizza Villa, Quizno's, Rammy's Subs, Starbucks, Subway, Taco Bell, Tom & Jerry's, Topper's Pizza, Vinny's Pizza, Wendy's, Yen Ching Chinese, **lodging:** Bay-

E ↕ W

mont Inn, Best Western, Travelodge, **other:** $General, Ford, Illini Tire, Schnuck's Food/Drug, to N IL U

91mm	toll plaza
78	I-39, US 51, S to Bloomington, N to Rockford
76	IL 251, Rochelle, **N**...**gas:** BP, Casey's, Shell, **other:** HOSPITAL, Dodge, Ford/Mercury, GMC
55	IL 26, Dixon, **N**...**gas:** BP/Subway/scales/dsl, **food:** Panda Chinese, Pizza Hut, **lodging:** Comfort Inn, Quality Inn, Super 8, **other:** Walmart/Super Ctr/gas/24hr, **1-2 mi N**...**food:** Culver's, Hardee's, **other:** HOSPITAL, to Ronald Reagan Birthplace, to John Deere HS, to St Parks
54mm	toll plaza
44	US 30(last free exit eb), **N**...**gas, food, lodging, camp**
41	IL 40, to Sterling, Rock Falls, **1-2 mi N**...**gas:** Marathon, Mobil/24hr, Shell/deli, **food:** Arby's, Arthur's Deli, Bennigan's, Burger King, Candlelight Rest., Culver's, El Tapatio Mexican, First Wok Chinese, Hardee's, KFC, McDonald's/playplace, Pizza Hut, Red Apple Rest., Subway, **lodging:** All Seasons Motel, Candlelight Inn, Country Inn Suites, Holiday Inn, Super 8, **other:** HOSPITAL, AutoZone, Country Mkt Foods, Curves, $General, Goodyear/auto, Harley-Davidson, O'Reilley Parts, Sav-A-Lot, Walgreens, **Wal-Mart**
36	to US 30, Rock Falls, Sterling
26	IL 78, to Prophetstown, Morrison, **N**...**other:** to Morrison-Rockwood SP, **S**...**gas:** Conoco/dsl(3mi)
18	to Albany, Erie, no services
10	to Port Byron, Hillsdale, **S**...**gas:** Phillips 66/dsl, Shell/**Mama J's Rest./scales/dsl/24hr,**
6	IL 92 E, to Joslin, **N**...**food:** Jammerz Roadhouse(2mi), **S**...**other:** Sunset Lake Camping(1mi)
2	Former IL 2, no services
1b a	I-80, W to Des Moines, E to Chicago
0mm	I-88 begins/ends on I-80, exit 4b. IL 5, IL 92, W to Silvis, to Quad City Downs, Lundeen's Camping

Interstate 90

E ↕ W · Chicago Area

Exit #	Services
0mm	Illinois/Indiana state line, Chicago Skyway Toll Rd begins/ends
1mm	US 12, US 20, 106th St, Indianapolis Blvd, **N**...**gas:** BP/dsl, Mobil, Shell/dsl, **S**...**food:** Burger King, Giappo's Pizza, KFC, McDonald's, **other:** Jewel-Osco, Larry's Repair
2.5mm	**gas:** Skyway Oasis, **food:** McDonald's, **other:** toll plaza
3mm	87th St(from wb)
5mm	79th St, services on 79th St and Stoney Island Ave
5.5mm	73rd St(from wb), no services
6mm	State St(from wb), no services
7mm	I-94 N(mile markers decrease to IN state line), **I-90 E and I-94 E run together. See Interstate 94, exits 43b-59a.**
84	I-94 W...Lawrence Ave, **N**...**gas:** BP
83b a	Foster Ave(from wb), **N**...**gas:** BP, **food:** Checker's, Dunkin Donuts, **other:** Firestone/auto, Goodyear/auto, Walgreen
82c	Austin Ave, to Foster Ave, no services
82b	Byrn-Mawr(from wb), no services
82a	Nagle Ave, no services
81b	Sayre Ave(from wb), no services
81a	IL 43, Harlem Ave, **S**...**gas:** BP, Shell
80	Canfield Rd(from wb), **N**...**other:** Walgreen

79b a	IL 171 S, Cumberland Ave, **N**...**gas:** 7-11, Marathon, **food:** Hooters, McDonald's, Outback Steaks, Starbucks, **lodging:** Holiday Inn, Marriott, SpringHill Suites, Westin Hotel, **other:** Dominick's Foods, **S**...**food:** Bennigan's, **lodging:** Ramada, Rennaisance
0mm	River Road Plaza, **N**...**food:** McDonald's, **lodging:** Marriott, Westin Hotel, **S**...Hyatt(mile markers increase to Rockford)
1mm	I-294, I-190 W, to O'Hare Airport
2mm	IL 72, Lee St(from wb), **N**...**lodging:** Extended Stay America, Quality Inn, Wyndham, **S**...**food:** McDonald's, **lodging:** Best Western, Holiday Inn Express, Holiday Inn Select, Sheraton Gateway, Studio+
5mm	Des Plaines Oasis both lanes, **gas:** Mobil/dsl/24hr, **food:** McDonald's/24hr, Panda Express, Starbucks, Subway
6mm	Elmhurst Rd(from wb), **S**...**gas:** Marathon, McDonald's/playplace, **lodging:** Best Western, Comfort Inn, Day's Inn, La Quinta, Microtel
7.5mm	Arlington Hts Rd, **N on Algonquin**...**gas:** Shell, **food:** Arby's, Baja Fresh, Birch River Grill, Buona Beef, Chicago Pizza, Chili's, Chipotle Mexican, Denny's, Honey Baked Ham, Magnum Steaks, McDonald's, Panda Express, Pappadeaux Rest., Potbelly's, Steak'n Shake, Subway, Yanni's Greek Rest., **lodging:** AmeriSuites, Courtyard, DoubleTree, Motel 6, Radisson, Red Roof Inn, Jameson Suites, Sheraton, **other:** Lowe's Whse, Meijer, NTB, Sam's Club, Staples, Wal-Mart, vet, **S**...**lodging:** Sheraton
11mm	I-290, IL 53, **N**...**lodging:** Embassy Suites, Holiday Inn, Renaissance Inn, **other:** mall, **S**...**lodging:** Amerisuites, Extended Stay America, Residence Inn
13mm	Roselle Rd(from wb), **N**...Medieval Times, **S**...**lodging:** Extended Stay America, **other:** BMW/Mini
16mm	Barrington Rd(from wb), **N**...**lodging:** Hilton Garden, **1 mi S**...**lodging:** Hampton Inn, Hyatt Place, **other:** U-Haul
19mm	IL 59, **N**...**food:** Buffalo Wild Wings, **lodging:** Marriott, **other:** Cabela's, Michael's, PetsMart, Target, to Poplar Creek Music Theatre
21mm	Beverly Rd(from wb), no services
22mm	IL 25, **N**...**food:** Milk Pail Rest., **lodging:** Day's Inn, **S**...**gas:** BP, Citgo, Shell, Speedway/dsl, **food:** Arby's, Baker Hill Pancakes, Subway, Wendy's, **other:** HOSPITAL, NAPA
24mm	IL 31 N, **N**...**gas:** BP, Thornton's/dsl, **food:** Alexander's Rest., Bennigan's, Dunkin Donuts/Baskin-Robbins, **lodging:** Courtyard, Hampton Inn, Holiday Inn, Quality Inn, Super 8, TownePlace Suites
25mm	toll plaza, phone
27mm	Randall Rd, **N**...**food:** Jimmy's Charhouse, **food:** Big Sammy's Hot Dogs, Henessey Rest., Jimmy John's, Panera Bread, Pizza & Pub, Starbucks, **lodging:** Comfort Inn, Country Inn Suites, **S**...HOSPITAL
32mm	IL 47(from wb), to Woodstock, **N**...**other:** Prime Outlets/famous brands, Chevrolet
37mm	US 20, Marengo, **N**...**gas:** Mobil/Arrowhead Rest/Chester's/dsl/scales/24hr/@, Road Ranger/dsl/scales, TA/BP/Burger King/Popeye's/scales/dsl/rest./24hr/@, **food:** McDonald's, Wendy's, **lodging:** Super 8, **other:** Trav-L Park, museums, to Prime Outlets at exit 32(6mi)
41mm	Marengo-Hampshire toll plaza, phone
53mm	Genoa Rd, to Belvidere, **N**...**food:** Applebee's, Arby's, Quizno's, Rosatis, Starbucks, Thai Basil, **other:** Wal-Mart Super-Ctr/gas, camping
55mm	Belvidere Oasis both lanes, **gas:** Mobil/dsl/24hr, **food:** Food Court, McDonald's/24hr, Starbucks, Subway, Taco Bell, phone
56mm	toll plaza
60.5mm	Kishwaukee River
61mm	I-39 S, US 20, US 51, to Rockford, **S**...funpark

Interstate 90

63mm US 20, State St, **N**...**gas:** Mobil, Phillips 66/Subway/dsl, **food:** Cracker Barrel, **lodging:** Baymont Inn, Clocktower Resort, Exel Inn, **S**...**gas:** Road Ranger/dsl, Mobil/dsl, **food:** Applebee's, Atlanta Bread Co, Burger King, Caribou Coffee, Cheddar's, Chili's, Damon's, Denny's, Don Pablo, Dos Reales, Gerry's Pizza, Giovanni's Rest., Hong Kong Buffet, IHOP, KFC, Lino's Pizza, LoneStar Steaks, Machine Shed Rest., McDonald's, Old Chicago Grill, Old Country Buffet, Olive Garden, Outback Steaks, Panda Express, Panino's Drive-Thru, Perkins, PotBelly, Quizno's, Red Lobster, Red Robin, Ruby Tuesday, Starbucks, Steak'n Shake, Subway, Taco Bell, ThunderBay Grille, Tom & Jerry's, Tumbleweed Grill, Tuesday Morning, TX Roadhouse, Uncle Nick's, Wendy's, **lodging:** Candlewood Suites, Comfort Inn, Courtyard, Extended Stay America, Fairfield Inn, Hampton Inn, Hilton Garden, Holiday Inn, Motel 6, Quality Suites, Radisson, Red Roof Inn, Residence Inn, Sleep Inn, Staybridge Suites, Studio+, Super 8, **other:** HOSPITAL, Advance Parts, Aldi Foods, Barnes&Noble, Best Buy, Borders Books, Buick/Pontiac/GMC, Circuit City, CompUSA, Dodge, $Tree, Hancock Fabrics, Home Depot, Jo-Ann Fabrics, K-Mart, Kohl's, Lexus, Lowe's Whse, Marshalls, Michael's, Office Depot, Old Time Pottery, Old Navy, PepBoys, PetsMart, Radio Shack, Sam's Club, Saturn, Target/drug, TJ Maxx, Toyota/Scion, Walgreens, Wal-Mart SuperCtr, World Mkt

66mm E Riverside Blvd, Loves Park, **1-2 mi** **S**...**gas:** BP/24hr, Mobil/dsl, Phillips 66/dsl, Road Ranger/Subway/dsl, Shell, **food:** Arby's, Basil Café, BeefARoo, Burger King, Culver's, DQ, Happy Joe's Pizza, KFC, McDonald's, Sam's Ristorante, Subway, Thai Cuisine, Wendy's, **lodging:** Day's Inn, Holiday Inn Express, **other:** Audi/Honda/Jaguar/Mercedes, Autoworks, Farm&Fleet, Walgreens, to Rock Cut SP, funpark

70mm Il 173, new exit

75.5mm tollbooth, phone(mile markers decrease from W to E to Chicago)

3 Rockton Rd, **S**...**gas:** Love's/Hardee's/dsl/scales/24hr

1.5mm **Welcome Ctr/rest area eb, full(handicapped)facilities, info, picnic tables, litter barrels, phone, petwalk, playground, RV dump**

1 US 51 N, IL 75 W, S Beloit, **S**...**gas:** Road Ranger/McDonald's/dsl, **S**...**gas:** BP/dsl, Road Ranger/Beef a Roo/Subway/scales/dsl/24hr, ⊕/Flying J/Country Mkt/scales/dsl/24hr, **lodging:** Best Western, Knight's Inn, **other:** Ford/Lincoln/Mercury, GMC, Pearl Lake camping(2mi)

0mm Illinois/Wisconsin state line,

Interstate 94

Exit #	Services
77mm	Illinois/Indiana state line
161	US 6, IL 83, Torrence Ave,
	I-94 and I-80 run together 3 mi. See Interstate 80, exit 161.
74[160]b	I-80/I-294 W
74a	IL 394 S to Danville
73b a	US 6,159th St, **N**...**food:** Fuddrucker's, Outback Steaks, **other:** Chevrolet, Honda, Lincoln/Mercury, Nissan/Hyundai, Target, Tire Barn, Toyota, **S**...**gas:** Marathon, **food:** Fannie May Candies, Subway,

lodging: Cherry Lane Motel, **other:** Aldi Foods, Buick/Pontiac, Ford, Stanfa Tire/auto

71b a	Sibley Blvd, **N**...**gas:** Citgo, Mobil/dsl, **food:** McDonald's, Nicky's Gyros, Popeye's, Subway, **lodging:** Baymont Inn, **other:** Dominick's Foods, **S**...**gas:** BP, Shell, **food:** Dusty's Buffet, Wendy's, White Castle
70b a	Dolton
69	Beaubien Woods(from eb), Forest Preserve
68b a	130th St
66b	115th St, **S**...**food:** McDonald's
66a	111th Ave, **S**...**gas:** BP, Shell, **other:** Firestone
65	103rd Ave, Stony Island Ave
63	I-57 S
62	**N**...**gas:** Citgo, Mobil, **food:** Subway
61b	87th St, **N**...**gas:** BP, Shell, **food:** Burger King, McDonald's, **S**...**other:** Best Buy, Home Depot, Jewel-Osco, Marshall's
61a	83rd St(from eb), **N**...**gas:** Shell, **other:** st police
60c	79th St, **N**...**gas:** BP, Mobil, Shell, **other:** Walgreens, **S**...**gas:** Citgo/dsl, **food:** Church's
60b	76th St, **N**...**gas:** BP, Mobil, Shell, **other:** Walgreen/24hr, **S**...**food:** KFC, Popeye's
60a	75th St(from eb), **N**...**gas:** BP, Mobil, Shell, **S**...**food:** KFC, Popeye's
59c	71st St, **N**...**gas:** Citgo, **S**...**food:** McDonald's
59a	I-90 E, to Indiana Toll Rd
58b	63rd St(from eb), **N**...**gas:** Citgo, **S**...**gas:** Mobil
58a	I-94 divides into local and express, 59th St, **S**...**gas:** BP
57b	Garfield Blvd, **N**...**food:** Checker's, Chinese Kitchen, Popeye's, Subway, **other:** Trak Auto, Walgreens, laundry, **S**...**gas:** Mobil, Shell/24hr, **food:** Famous Burritos, Wendy's, **other:** HOSPITAL
57a	51st St, **N**...**food:** McDonald's
56b	47th St(from eb), no services
56a	43rd St, **S**...**gas:** Citgo/dsl, Econo/dsl
55b	Pershing Rd, no services
55a	35th St, **S**...to New Comiskey Park
54	31st St
53c	I-55, Stevenson Pkwy, N to Lakeshore Dr
53b	I-55, Stevenson Pkwy, S to St Louis
52c	18th St, **N**...**other:** Dominick's Foods
52b	Roosevelt Rd, Taylor St(from wb), **N**...**gas:** Citgo
52a	Taylor St, Roosevelt Rd(from eb), **N**...**gas:** Citgo
51h-i	I-290 W, to W Suburbs
51g	E Jackson Blvd, to downtown
51f	W Adams St, to downtown
51e	Monroe St(from eb), downtown, **S**...**lodging:** Quality Inn, **other:** Walgreen
51d	Madison St(from eb), downtown, **S**...**lodging:** Crowne Plaza, **other:** Dominick's Foods, Walgreens
51c	E Washington Blvd, downtown
51b	W Randolph St, downtown
51a	Lake St(from wb), no services
50b	E Ohio St, downtown, **S**...**gas:** Marathon

ILLINOIS
Interstate 94

E	50a	Ogden Ave, no services
	49b a	Augusta Blvd, Division St, N...other: Lexus, Mercedes, S...gas: BP, Shell, food: Pizza Hut
	48b	IL 64, North Ave, N...gas: BP, other: Home Depot, S...gas: Gas Depot, other: Volvo
W	48a	Armitage Ave, S...gas: Citgo, other: Best Buy, Jaguar, Kohl's, Volvo
	47c b	Damen Ave, N...gas: Citgo, car/vanwash
	47a	Western Ave, Fullerton Ave, N...gas: Citgo, food: Burger King, Popeye's, Subway, other: Costco/gas, Cub Foods, Home Depot, Target, S...gas: Marathon, food: KFC
	46b a	Diversey Ave, California Ave, N...gas: Citgo, S...gas: Mobil, food: IHOP/24hr, Popeye's
	45c	Belmont Ave, N...food: Wendy's
	45b	Kimball Ave, N...gas: Marathon/dsl, S...gas: Gas Depot, food: Pizza Hut, Subway, Wendy's, other: Delray Farms Foods, Dominick's Foods, Radio Shack, Walgreen/24hr
	45a	Addison St(from eb), no services
	44b	Pulaski Ave, Irving Park Rd, N...gas: BP, Mobil
	44a	IL 19, Keeler Ave, Irving Park Rd, N...gas: BP, Shell/24hr, other: to Wrigley Field
C h i c a g o A r e a	43c	Montrose Ave
	43b	I-90 W,
	43a	Wilson Ave
	42	W Foster Ave (from wb), S...gas: Citgo, Marathon
	41mm	Chicago River, N Branch
	41c	IL 50 S, to Cicero, to I-90 W
	41b a	US 14, Peterson Ave, no services
	39b a	Touhy Ave, N...gas: BP/dsl, Shell, lodging: Purple Hotel, other: Cassidy Tire, S...gas: BP, Citgo, Shell, food: Burger King, Dunkin Donuts, Jack's Rest./24hr, McDonald's, other: Lee's Auto Parts, PepBoys
	37b a	IL 58, Dempster St, no services
	35	Old Orchard Rd, N...gas: BP, Shell, food: Bloomingdale's, Marshall Fields, other: HOSPITAL, Nissan, mall, S...lodging: Extended Stay America, Hampton Inn
	34c b	E Lake Ave, N...gas: BP, food: Panda Express, Starbucks, other: Borders Books, GNC, Omaha Steaks, S...gas: BP, Shell, food: DQ
	34a	US 41 S, Skokie Rd(from eb)
	33b a	Willow Rd, S...gas: BP, Shell, food: Starbucks, other: Dominick's Foods, Walgreen
	31	E Tower Rd, S...other: VET, BMW, Carmax, Chrysler/Jeep/Dodge, Infiniti, Mercedes, Toyota
	30b a	Dundee Rd(from wb, no EZ return), S...gas: Citgo, Marathon, food: Barnaby's Rest., 41 North Grill, Ruth's Chris Steaks, lodging: Rennaisance
	29	US 41, to Waukegan, to Tri-state tollway
	50mm	IL 43, Waukegan Rd, N...gas: BP, Shell, lodging: Red Roof Inn, Embassy Suites, food: Baja Fresh, Old Country Buffet, other: Best Buy, Borders Books, Home Depot, Jewel-Osco, NTB, Steinmart, TJ Maxx
	53mm	I-294 S, Lake-Cook Rd (from sb), E...lodging: Hyatt
	53.5mm	Deerfield Rd toll plaza, phones
	54mm	Deerfield Rd, W...gas: Mobil, lodging: Marriott Suites
	56mm	IL 22, Half Day Rd, E...lodging: La Quinta
	59mm	IL 60, Town Line Rd, E...HOSPITAL
	60mm	Lake Forest Oasis both lanes, gas: Mobil/dsl, food: Wendy's/24hr, other: info

62mm	IL 176, Rockland Rd(no nb re-entry), E...other: Harley-Davidson, to Lamb's Farm
64mm	IL 137, Buckley Rd(from wb), E...other: to VA HOSPITAL, Chicago Med School
67mm	IL 120 E, Belvidere Rd(no nb re-entry), E...HOSPITAL
68mm	IL 21, Milwaukee Ave(from eb, no sb re-entry), E...other: HOSPITAL, Six Flags
70mm	IL 132, Grand Ave, E...gas: Speedway/dsl, food: Burger King, Cracker Barrel, Culver's, IHOP, Joe's Crabshack, Little Caesar's, McDonald's, Ming's Chinese, Olive Garden, Outback Steaks, Subway, TCBY, lodging: Baymont Inn, Comfort Suites, Country Inn Suites, Grand Hotel, Extended Stay America, Hampton Inn, other: Six Flags Park, W...gas: Mobil, Shell, food: Applebee's, Bakers Square, Boston Mkt, Chili's, Denny's, LoneStar Steaks, Max&Erma's, McDonald's, Pizza Hut, Pizzaria Uno, Red Lobster, Sizzler, Starbucks, Steak'n Shake, Taco Bell, TGIFriday, Wendy's, White Castle, lodging: Comfort Inn, Fairfield Inn, Holiday Inn, other: Circuit City, Dominick's Foods, Gurnee Mills Outlet Mall/famous brands, Home Depot, Honda, Hyundai, JC Penney, Jewel-Osco, Kohl's, Lincoln/Mercury, Michaels, Sam's Club, Sears/auto, Target/drugs, VW, Wal-Mart/drugs
73mm	Waukegan toll plaza, Waukegan toll plaza, phones
76mm	IL 173(from nb, no return), Rosecrans Ave, E...to IL Beach SP
1b	US 41 S, to Waukegan, E...other: Sky Harbor RV Ctr
1a	Russell Rd, W...gas: Citgo/dsl/scales/24hr, TA/Pizza Hut/dsl/24hr/@, other: Peterbilt
0mm	Illinois/Wisconsin state line

Interstate 255(St Louis)

	Exit #	Services
		I-255 begins/ends on I-270, exit 7.
N	30	I-270, W to Kansas City, E to Indianapolis
	29	IL 162, to Glen Carbon, to Pontoon Beach, Granite City
	26	Horseshoe Lake Rd, E...st police
	25b a	I-55/I-70, W to St Louis, E to Chicago, Indianapolis
E a s t S t L o u i s	24	Collinsville Rd, E...gas: BP/24hr, food: Jack-in-the-Box, other: Shop'n Save, W...Fairmount Racetrack
	20	I-64, US 50, W to St Louis, E to Louisville, services 1 mi E off I-64, exit 9.
	19	State St, E St Louis, E...gas: Clark, lodging: Western Inn, other: Holten SP
S	17b a	IL 15, E St Louis, to Belleville, Centreville, E.../Flying J/CountryMkt/dsl/scales/24hr
	15	Mousette Lane, E...HOSPITAL, W...other: GMC/Volvo Trucks
	13	IL 157, to Cahokia, E...gas: Casey's, W...gas: BP/24hr, QT, food: Burger King, Capt D's, China Express, DQ, Domino's, Hardee's, KFC, McDonald's, Pizza Hut, Ponderosa, Popeye's, Rally's, Taco Bell, lodging: Holiday Inn Express, other: Advance Parts, Aldi Foods, AutoZone, CarQuest, $General, GMC/Pontiac, Goodyear/auto, Schnuck's, Walgreen, Wal-Mart/drugs, Cahokia RV Parque(2mi)
	10	IL 3 N, to Cahokia, E St Louis, W...gas: Shell
	9	to Dupo, no services
	6	IL 3 S, to Columbia, E...gas: Citgo, Shell/24hr, other: Chevrolet

Interstate 255

4mm	Missouri/Illinois state line, Mississippi River
3	Koch Rd, no facilities
2	MO 231, Telegraph Rd, **N**...**gas:** Shell, **food:** Hardee's, McDonald's, Pizza Hut/Taco Bell, Steak'n Shake, **other:** Dierberg's Foods, $Tree, Wal-Mart SuperCtr/24hr, Jefferson Barracks Nat Cem, **S**...**gas:** CFM/dsl, **food:** DQ
1d c	US 50, US 61, US 67, Lindbergh Blvd, Lemay Ferry Rd, accesses same as I-55 exit 197, **N**...**food:** Arby's, Hooters, McDonald's, Old Country Buffet, Subway, **other:** Advance Parts, Costco/gas, Dillard's, Discount Tire, Ford, Sears/auto, mall, **S**...**gas:** Citgo, **food:** Jack-in-the-Box, Papa John's, White Castle, **other:** Firestone, Sam's Club
1b a	I-55 S to Memphis, N to St Louis. I-255 begins/ends on I-55, exit 196

Interstate 270(St Louis)
See Missouri Interstate 270(St Louis)

Interstate 294(Chicago)

Exit #	Services
	I-294 begins/ends on I-94, exit 74. Numbering descends from west to east.
	I-294 & I-80 run together 5 mi. See Interstate 80, exits 155-160.
5mm	I-80 W, access to I-57
5.5mm	167th St, toll booth, phones
6mm	US 6, 159th St, **E**...**gas:** BP, Citgo, Mobil, Shell, **other:** Aldi Foods, AutoZone, Walgreen, **W**...**gas:** Clark, Marathon, **food:** Burger King, Dunkin Donuts/Baskin-Robbins, Hung's Garden Chinese, KFC/Pizza Hut, Popeye's, Taco Bell, USA Rest., White Castle, **lodging:** Holiday Inn Express, **other:** Firestone/auto, Radio Shack, U-Haul, Walgreen
11mm	Cal Sag Channel
12mm	IL 50, Cicero Ave, **E**...**gas:** Citgo/7-11, Speedway, **food:** Onion Field Rest., **W**...**gas:** BP, Gas City/Subway/dsl/24hr, **food:** Boston Mkt, IHOP, Pizza Hut, Pizzaria Uno, Popeye's, Portillo's Dogs, Quizno's, Starbucks, **lodging:** Baymont Inn, Hampton Inn, **other:** Best Buy, Dominick's Foods, NTB, PepBoys, Sears/auto
18mm	US 12/20, 95th St, **E**...**gas:** Clark, **food:** Bennigan's, McDonald's, Papa John's, **other:** HOSPITAL, Buick, Honda, Mazda, Sears/auto, mall, **W**...**gas:** Citgo/7-11, Shell, Speedway/dsl, **food:** Arby's, Burger King, Denny's, George's Rest., Quizno's, Schoop's Burgers, Wendy's, **lodging:** Exel Inn, **other:** HOSPITAL, Jewel-Osco, Walgreen
20mm	toll booth, phones
22mm	75th St, Willow Springs Rd, no services
23mm	I-55, Wolf Rd, to Hawthorne Park, no services
25mm	Hinsdale Oasis both lanes, **gas:** Mobil/dsl, **food:** Baskin-Robbins, Wendy's/24hr
28mm	US 34, Ogden Ave, **E**...zoo, **W**...**gas:** BP, Shell/deli, **food:** Dunkin Donuts, McDonald's, Starbucks, **other:** HOSPITAL, Audi/Porsche, Firestone/auto, LandRover, Maserati, Rolls-Royce/Bentley/Ferrari/Lotus, Wild Oats Mkt

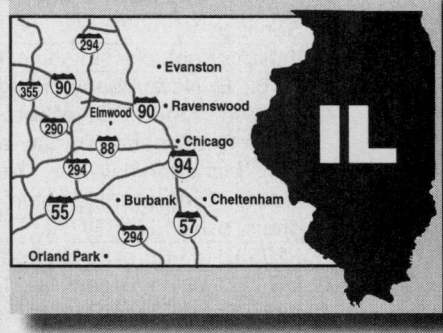

28.5mm	Cermak Rd(from sb, no return)
29mm	I-88 tollway
30mm	toll booth, phones
31mm	IL 38, Roosevelt Rd(no EZ nb return), **E**...**gas:** Citgo/dsl, **lodging:** Hillside Manor Motel
32mm	I-290 W, to Rockford(from nb)
34mm	I-290(from sb), to Rockford
38mm	O'Hare Oasis both lanes, **gas:** Mobil/dsl, **food:** Burger King, TCBY
39mm	IL 19 W(from sb), Irving Park Rd, **E**...**gas:** Clark, Marathon/dsl, **other:** 7-11, Walgreen, **1 mi E**...**gas:** BP/repair, Clark, **food:** DQ, Dunkin Donuts, McDonald's, Subway, Wendy's, **lodging:** Comfort Suites, **other:** Aldi Foods, **W**...**lodging:** Candlewood Suites, Day's Inn, Hampton Inn, Howard Johnson, Sheraton
40mm	I-190 W, **E**...**services from I-90, exit 79**...**gas:** Mobil, **food:** McDonald's, **lodging:** Courtyard, Doubletree, Embassy Suites, Holiday Inn, Hotel Softel, Hyatt, Marriott, Radisson, Rosemont Suites, Westin
41mm	toll booth, phones
42mm	Touhy Ave, **W**...**gas:** Mobil/service, **food:** Tiffany's Rest., **lodging:** Comfort Inn
43mm	Des Plaines River
44mm	Dempster St(from nb, no return), **E**...HOSPITAL, **W**...**food:** Dunkin Donuts, Subway
46mm	IL 58, Golf Rd, **E**...**gas:** Citgo/dsl, Shell, **food:** Omega Rest., Senoya Oriental, **other:** Best Buy, CVS Drug, Golf Mill Mall, Target, auto repair
49mm	Willow Rd, **W**...**food:** TGIFriday, **lodging:** Baymont Inn, Doubletree Suites, Courtyard, Fairfield Inn, Motel 6, **1 mi W on Milwauke E**...**gas:** BP, **food:** Burger King, Denny's, McDonald's, **lodging:** Wingate Inn
53mm	Lake Cook Rd(no nb re-entry), **E**...Hyatt, **lodging:** Embassy Suites
	I-294 begins/ends on I-94.

Interstate 474(Peoria)

Exit #	Services
15	I-74, E to Bloomington, W to Peoria
9	IL 29, E Peoria, to Pekin, **N**...**gas:** Shell/Arby's, Thornton's, **food:** Driftwood Pizza, DQ, Pizza Hut, Taco John's, **lodging:** Ragon Motel, **other:** Riverboat Casino(6mi), **S**...**gas:** Casey's, Shell/Subway/dsl, **food:** Denny's, KFC, McDonald's, **other:** Chrysler/Jeep/Dodge, Toyota
8mm	Illinois River
6b a	US 24, Adams St, Bartonville, **S**...**gas:** BP/dsl, Shell/24hr, **food:** Hardee's, KFC, McDonald's, Tyroni's Café
5	Airport Rd, **S**...**gas:** Phillips 66
3a	to IL 116, Farmington, **S**...Wildlife Prairie Park
0b a	I-74, W to Moline, E to Peoria. I-474 begins/ends on I-74, exit 87.

INDIANA

Interstate 64

E ↕ W — New Albany

Exit #	Services
124mm	Indiana/Kentucky state line, Ohio River
123	IN 62 E, New Albany, N...**gas:** BP/Circle K/24hr, Sunoco, **food:** DQ, **other:** Chevrolet, Firestone/auto, Goodyear/auto, Sav-a-Lot Foods, S...**gas:** BP, Marathon/dsl/24hr, **food:** Subway, Waffle House, **lodging:** Hampton Inn, Holiday Inn Express, **other:** HOSPITAL
121	I-265 E, to I-65(exits left from eb), N...HOSPITAL
119	US 150 W, to Greenville, **1/2 mi** N...**gas:** Marathon, Patriot/Taco Bell, **food:** Beef'o Brady's, China Cafe, Domino's, DQ, Los Indios, Papa John's, Sam's Family Rest., Tumbleweed Grill, **other:** Huber Winery, Rite Aid, Walgreens
118	IN 62, IN 64W, to Georgetown, N...**gas:** Marathon/dsl/24hr, Shell/Circle K, **food:** Korner Kitchen, McDonald's, Pizza King, **lodging:** Motel 6, **other:** Mr. Hardware, Thriftway Foods/drug, S...**gas:** Marathon/dsl
115mm	**Welcome Ctr wb, full(handicapped)facilities, vending, phone, picnic tables, litter barrels**
113	to Lanesville, no services
105	IN 135, to Corydon, N...**gas:** Marathon/dsl, Shell/24hr, **food:** Big Boy, **lodging:** 1st Capitol Hotel, S...**gas:** BP/dsl, Chevron, **food:** Arby's, Burger King, China Best Buffet, Cracker Barrel, Culver's, DQ, Hardee's, LJ Silver, Los Indios, McDonald's, O'Charley's, Papa John's, Pizza Hut, Ryan's, Subway/TCBY, Taco Bell, Waffle Steak/24hr, Wendy's, White Castle, **lodging:** Baymont Inn, Hampton Inn, Holiday Inn Express, Super 8, **other:** MEDICAL CARE, AutoZone, Chevrolet/Pontiac/Buick, CVS Drug, $General, $Tree, Ford/Mercury, Radio Shack, Walgreens, Wal-Mart SuperCtr/24hr, RV camping
100mm	Blue River
97mm	parking area both lanes
92	IN 66, Carefree, N...Veringo Caves, S...**gas:** Country Style Plaza/rest./dsl/scales/24hr, Marathon/dsl/rest./24hr, Sunoco/dsl, **lodging:** Day's Inn, **other:** to Wyandotte Caves, Harrison Crawford SF, auto/truck repair
88mm	Hoosier Nat Forest eastern boundary
86	IN 37, to Sulphur, N...to Patoka Lake, S...gas, food, phone, scenic route
79	IN 37, to Tell City, St Croix, S...to Hoosier NF, rec facilities, phone, to OH River Br
76mm	Anderson River
72	IN 145, to Birdseye, N...to Patoka Lake, S...gas, phone, St Meinrad Coll
63	IN 162, to Ferdinand, N...**gas:** Sunoco/dsl, **food:** Wendy's, **lodging:** Comfort Inn, **other:** Ferdinand SF, S...(8mi)Lake Rudolph RV Camping
58mm	**rest areas both lanes, full(handicapped)facilities, info, vending, picnic tables, litter barrels, phone**
57	US 231, to Dale, Huntingburg, N...HOSPITAL, S...**gas:** Shell/dsl/24hr, **food:** Denny's, **lodging:** Baymont Inn, Motel 6, **other:** Lincoln Boyhood Home, Lincoln SP
54	IN 161, to Holland,Tennyson, no services
39	IN 61, Lynnville, N...**gas:** Country Cupboard
32mm	Wabash & Erie Canal
29b a	I-164 S, IN 57 S, to Evansville, N...**gas:** Sunoco/dsl/24hr
25b a	US 41, to Evansville, N...**gas:** Flying J/CountryMkt/dsl/24hr/@, Pilot/Wendy's/dsl/24hr/@, Pilot/dsl/24hr/@, **lodging:** Quality Inn, **other:** Blue Beacon, S...**gas:** BP/motel, Busler/motel/dsl/scales/24hr, **food:** Arby's, Denny's, McDonald's, Stoll's Rest., Triple Dragon Buffet, **lodging:** Best Western, Comfort Inn, Holiday Inn Express, Super 8, **other:** st police, to U S IN
18	IN 65, to Cynthiana, S...**gas:** Motomart/dsl/24hr
12	IN 165, Poseyville, S...**other:** Chevrolet, New Harmonie Hist Area/SP
7mm	**Black River Welcome Ctr eb, full(handicapped)facilities, phone, picnic tables, litter barrels, petwalk**
5mm	Black River
4	4 IN 69 S, New Harmony, Griffin, **1 mi** N...gas/dsl, food, motel, antiques, USPO, S...Harmony St Park
2mm	Big Bayou River
0mm	Indiana/Illinois state line, Wabash River

Interstate 65

N ↕ S — Merrillville

Exit #	Services
262	I-90, W to Chicago, E to Ohio, I-65 begins/ends on US 12, US 20.
261	15th Ave, to Gary, E...Mack/Volvo Trucks, W...**gas:** Marathon
259b a	I-94/80, US 6W
258	US 6, Ridge Rd, E...**gas:** Marathon/dsl, Speedway/dsl, **food:** Country Lounge Diner, Diner's Choice Rest., W...**gas:** Citgo, Glen Park Gas, Phillips 66
255	61st Ave, Merrillville, E...**gas:** Marathon, Speedway/dsl/24hr, Thornton, **food:** Arby's, Cracker Barrel, McDonald's, Pizza Hut/Taco Bell, Wendy's, **lodging:** Comfort Inn, $Inn, Lee's Inn, **other:** Chevrolet, Menard's, I-65 Repair, **1 mi** W...**gas:** Shell, **food:** Burger King, Subway, **other:** HOSPITAL
253b	US 30 W, Merrillville, W...**gas:** Meijer/dsl/24hr, Mobil/dsl, Shell, Speedway/dsl, **food:** Abuelo's Mexican, Applebee's, Caribou Coffee, Denny's, Dunkin Donuts, Fannie May Candies, Golden Corral, Hooters, House of Kobe, Jonnie's Rest., KFC, LoneStar Steaks, Oriental Buffet, Outback Steaks, Panera Bread, Pepe's Mexican, Pizza Hut, Portillo's Hot Dogs, Starbucks, Steak'n Shake, Subway, Texas Corral Steaks, TJ Maloney's Grill, Wendy's, White Castle, **lodging:** Courtyard, Deluxe Inn, Fairfield Inn, Hampton Inn, Holiday Inn Express, Radisson, Red Roof Inn, Residence Inn, **other:** Aldi Foods, Aamco, CarEx, CarQuest, Celebration Sta, $Tree, Discount Tire, Firestone, Ford, Goodyear/auto, Hyundai/Mitsubishi, Jo-Ann Fabrics, K-Mart, Lincoln/Mercury, Mazda, Midas, NTB, Saturn, Subaru, Toyota, U-Haul, Walgreens, RV Ctr, transmissions

INDIANA

Interstate 65

253a US 30 E, **E**...**gas:** BP/dsl/24hr, Speedway/dsl, **food:** Arby's, Bakers Square, Bennigan's, Bob Evans, Boston Mkt, Chili's, Chipotle Mexican, ChuckeCheese, DQ, Don Pablo, Great China Buffet, Heavenly Ham, Jimmy John's, Joe's Crabshack, KFC/LJ Silver, Longhorn Steaks, McDonald's, Old Country Buffet, Olive Garden, Popeye's, Potbelly, Pizzaria Uno, Popeye's, Quizno's, Red Lobster, Red Robin, Ruby Tuesday, Starbucks, Subway, Taco Bell, TGIFriday, Tuesday Morning, Uno Pizzaria, Wendy's, **lodging:** Day's Inn, Candlewood Suites, Country Inn Suites, Extended Stay America, Holiday Inn, Knight's Inn, La Quinta, Motel 6, Super 8, **other:** Audi, Barnes&Noble, Best Buy, Carmax, Circuit City, Costco/gas, Dodge, Firestone/auto, Home Depot, JC Penney, Kia, Kohl's, Lowe's Whse, Macey's, Michael's, Nissan, Office Depot, Old Navy, PetCo, Sam's Club/gas, Sears/auto, Target, TJ Maxx, Tire Barn, Toyota, VW, Wal-Mart SuperCtr/24hr, mall, vet

247 US 231, Crown Point, **W**...**gas:** Mobil/24hr, **other:** HOSPITAL, Vietnam Vet Mem

241mm weigh sta sb

240 IN 2, Lowell, **E**...**gas:** ✈/Flying J/Cookery/dsl/24hr/@, Mobil/Burger King, Pilot/McDonalds/scales/dsl/24hr, **lodging:** Super 8, **other:** truck wash, **W**...st police

234mm Kankakee River

231mm rest area both lanes, full(handicapped) facilities, phones, info, picnic tables, litter barrels, vending, petwalk

230 IN 10, Roselawn, **E**...**gas:** Gas City/The Diner/scales/dsl/rest./24hr, **W**...**gas:** Family Express, Marathon/Subway, **food:** China Wok, **other:** CarQuest, CVS Drug, $General, Fagen Drug, IGA Foods, TrueValue, Lake Holiday Camping, USPO

220 IN 14 Winamac, **W**...**other:** Fair Oaks Farms Store

215 IN 114, Rensselaer, **E**...**gas:** Family Express/dsl/24hr, **food:** Arby's, KFC, L&G Rest., McDonald's, **lodging:** Holiday Inn Express, Knight's Inn, **other:** HOSPITAL, **W**...**gas:** Grandma's/rest./dsl, Marathon/Trail Tree Rest./dsl/24hr, **food:** Burger King, **lodging:** Economy Inn, **other:** tires/repair/towing/24hr

212mm Iroquois River

205 US 231, Remington, **E**...**gas:** Crazy D's/Pop's Kitchen/scales/rest/dsl, BP/dsl, **food:** Vienna Beef, **other:** HOSPITAL, to St Joseph's Coll

201 US 24/231, Remington, **W**...**gas:** Family Espress/dsl, Petro/Marathon/Iron Skillet/dsl/scales/24hr/@, Pilot/Subway/scales/dsl/24hr, **food:** KFC, McDonald's, **lodging:** Sunset Inn, Super 8 **E**...**other:** Caboose Lake RV

196mm rest area both lanes, full(handicapped)facilities, vending, phone, info, picnic tables, litter barrels, petwalk

Interstate 65

N ↑↓ S

193	US 231, to Chalmers, E...**gas:** BP/Wayfara Rest./DQ/Stuckey's, **food:** DQ
188	IN 18, to Brookston, Fowler, no services
178	IN 43, W Lafayette, E...**gas:** GA/Taco Bell, Phillips 66/Subway/dsl, **food:** McDonald's, **lodging:** Rodeway Inn, **other:** to Tippecanoe Bfd, museum, st police, W...to Purdue U
176mm	Wabash River
175	IN 25, Lafayette, E...**gas:** Family Express/24hr, W...**other:** HOSPITAL, **gas:** Marathon(1mi)
172	IN 26, Lafayette, E...**gas:** Meijer/dsl/24hr, **food:** Cracker Barrel, DQ, Rodeo Rest., Starbucks, Steak'n Shake, White Castle, **lodging:** Baymont Inn, Comfort Inn, Holiday Inn Express, Lee's Inn, Microtel, Motel 6, Quality Inn, TownePlace Suites, **other:** Curves, W...**gas:** BP/dsl/24hr, Shell, Speedway/dsl, **food:** Arby's, Bob Evans, Burger King, Chick-fil-A, Chili's, ChuckeCheese, Cici's Pizza, Country Cafe, Culvers, Denny's, Don Pablo, Fazoli's, Golden Corral, Gordman's, Grindstone Charlie's, Hour Time Rest., Hunan House, IHOP, KFC, Krispy Kreme, Logan's Roadhouse, McDonald's, McCalister', Mt Jack's, Nanking Rest., Olive Garden, Outback Steaks, Pizza Hut, Quizno's, Spageddie's, Steak'n Shake, Subway, Taco Bell, TGIFriday, **lodging:** Best Western, Fairfield Inn, Hampton Inn, Homewood Suites, Knight's Inn, Quality Inn, Ramada Inn, Red Roof Inn, Signature Inn, Super 8, **other:** HOSPITAL, Aamco, Buick/Cadillac/Nissan, CVS Drug, $Tree, Firestone/auto, Home Depot, Jo-Ann Fabrics, Lowe's Whse, Marsh Foods, Sam's Club/gas, Sportsman's Whse, Target, TJ Maxx, Wal-Mart SuperCtr/24hr, vet, USPO, to Purdue U
168	IN 38, IN 25 S, Dayton, E...**gas:** BP/Piccadilly's/24hr, Mobil/dsl
158	IN 28, to Frankfort, E...**gas:** BP/dsl/24hr, Phillips 66, **other:** Harley-Davidson, **2 mi** W...**lodging:** Lincoln Lodge Motel, **other:** HOSPITAL, camping
150mm	**rest area sb, full(handicapped)facilities, info, picnic tables, litter barrels, phone, vending, petwalk**
148mm	**rest area nb, full(handicapped)facilities, info, picnic tables, litter barrels, phone, vending, petwalk**
146	IN 47, Thorntown, W...camping
141	US 52 W(exits left from sb), Lafayette Ave, E...HOSPITAL
140	IN 32, Lebanon, E...**gas:** BP, **food:** Denny's, McDonald's, White Castle, **lodging:** Comfort Inn, **other:** HOSPITAL, AutoZone, Goodyear/auto, W...**gas:** McClure/dsl, **food:** Arby's, Flapjacks Pancakes, KFC, Ponderosa, Steak'n Shake, Subway, **lodging:** Day's Inn, Hoilday Inn Express, Lee's Inn, Super 8, **other:** truckwash
139	IN 39, Lebanon, E...**gas:** GA, **food:** Hardee's, Wendy's, W...**gas:** /Flying J/Country Mkt/dsl/LP/scales/24hr, **lodging:** Quality Inn, **other:** HOSPITAL, Homemade Chocolates
138	to US 52, Lebanon, E...**gas:** Citgo/dsl, **other:** Chevrolet, Ford

Lebanon

133	IN 267, Whitestown, no services
130	IN 334, Zionsville, E...**gas:** CF/Subway/dsl, Citgo, Marathon/Starbucks/Stuckey's/dsl/24hr, **food:** Burger King, **other:** CVS Drug, W...**gas:** TA/BP/Popeye's/scales/dsl/24hr/@
129	I-865 E, to I-465 E, US 52 E(from sb)
126mm	Fishback Creek
124	71st St, **1 mi** E...**gas:** BP, **food:** Bob Evans, Hardee's, Steak'n Shake, **lodging:** Courtyard, Hampton Inn, Residence Inn, Wingate Inn, W...Eagle Creek Park
123	I-465, S to airport
121	Lafayette Rd, E...**gas:** GA, Speedway/dsl, **lodging:** Lee's Inn, W...**gas:** BP, Shell/Circle K/24hr, **food:** Applebee's, Arby's, Church's, Fazoli's, King Wok, Papa John's, Sizzling Wok, Subway, TCBY, Wendy's, **lodging:** Travelodge **other:** HOSPITAL, Batteries+, Chrysler/Jeep, Discount Tire, Family$, Firestone/auto, Kia, NAPA, Nissan, Macey's, PepBoys, Save-a-Lot Foods, Sears/auto, Speedway Parts, Tire Barn, Toyota/Scion, Wal-Mart SuperCtr, mall, transmissions, vet, same as 119
119	38th St(no nb return), W...**gas:** Speedway, **food:** Arby's, ChuckeCheese, Cici's Pizza, KFC/Taco Bell, La Bamba Mexican, McDonald's, New Taste Buffet, Pizza Hut, Popeye's, Red Lobster, Starbucks, Taco Bell, **other:** Aldi Foods, Chevrolet, Dodge/Hyundai, Ford, Honda, K-Mart, NAPA, Office Depot, Tires+, mall, same as 121
117.5mm	White River
117	MLK St(from sb), W...**gas:** Marathon/dsl
116	29th St, 30th St(from nb), Marian Coll, no services
115	21st St, E...**gas:** Shell/Circle K, **other:** HOSPITAL, W...museums, zoo
114	MLK St, West St, downtown
113	US 31, IN 37, Meridian St, to downtown, E...**other:** HOSPITAL
112a	I-70 E, to Columbus
111	Market St, Michigan St, Ohio St, E...**food:** Hardee's, W...**other:** City Market, to Market Square Arena, museum
110b	I-70 W, to St Louis
110a	Prospect St, Morris St, E St
109	Raymond St, E...HOSPITAL, W...**gas:** Speedway, **food:** White Castle, **other:** CVS Drug, Safeway
107	Keystone Ave, E...**gas:** Mystik, **lodging:** Best Value, **other:** HOSPITAL, W...**gas:** Phillips 66/dsl, Speedway, Valero, **food:** Burger King, Denny's, Great Wall Chinese, McDonald's, Starbucks, Subway, Wal-Mart Mkt, Wendy's, **lodging:** Holiday Inn Express, **other:** $General, U of Indianapolis
106	I-465 and I-74
103	Southport Rd, E...**gas:** BP/McDonald's/24hr, Shell/Circle K, **food:** Arby's, Azteca Mexican, Bubbaz Grill, Chick-fil-A, Hardees, El Puerto, Longhorn Steaks, Noble Roman, O'Charley's, Panda Express, Panera Bread, Pen Sta Subs, Pizzaria Uno, Qdoba, Quizno's, Starbucks, Taco Bell, **other:** Aldi Foods, Firestone/auto, Harley-Davidson, Home Depot, Kohl's, Meanard's, Meijer/dsl/24hr, Radio Shack, Staples, Target, W...**gas:** Circle K/gas, 7-11, Speedway/dsl/24hr, **food:**

Indianapolis Area

Interstate 65

Beef & Brew, Bob Evans, Burger King, Carrabba's, Cheeseburger Paradise, Cracker Barrel, Damon's, KFC, McDonald's, Starbucks, Steak'n Shake, TX Roadhouse, Waffle House, Wendy's, **lodging:** Comfort Suites, Best Western, Country Inn Suites, Courtyard, $Inn, Fairfield Inn, Hampton Inn, Jameson Inn, Quality Inn, Super 8, **other:** HOSPITAL

101	CountyLine Rd, Ⓦ...**food:** Buffalo Wild Wings, Quizno's, Subway, **lodging:** Hilton Garden, Holiday Inn Express, **other:** HOSPITAL, Gander Mtn, Kroger, Wal-Mart SuperCtr/gas
99	Greenwood, Ⓔ...**gas:** Road Ranger/Subway/scales/dsl/24hr, Ⓦ...**gas:** Marathon, 7-11/gas, Shell/Circle K, **food:** Arby's, Bob Evans, Byrd's Cafeteria, Denny's, McDonald's, Noble Roman's, Starbucks, Subway, Taco Bell, Waffle House, White Castle, **lodging:** Comfort Inn, InTown Suites, Lee's Inn, Red Carpet Inn, Red Roof Inn, **other:** HOSPITAL, Camping World RV Ctr, Sam's Club
95	Whiteland, Ⓔ...**gas:** ⚑/Flying J/CountryMkt/scales/dsl/24hr/@, Marathon/dsl, **other:** tires, Ⓦ...**gas:** Pilot/Arby's/dsl/24hr/@, Pilot/McDonald's/dsl/scales/24hr/@, **other:** Family RV Ctr
90	IN 44, Franklin, Ⓦ...**gas:** BP/Circle K, **food:** Burger King, Don&Dona's(2mi), McDonald's, Subway, Waffle House, **lodging:** Comfort Inn, Howard Johnson, Quality Inn, Super 7 Inn/rest., Super 8, **other:** HOSPITAL, golf
85mm	Sugar Creek
82mm	Big Blue River
80	IN 252, to Flat Rock, Edinburgh, Ⓦ...**gas:** Marathon/dsl, Shell/dsl
76b a	US 31, Taylorsville, Ⓔ...**gas:** Shell/Circle K/dsl, Speedway/dsl, **food:** A&W/KFC, Burger King, Waffle House, **lodging:** Red Roof Inn, **other:** HOSPITAL, Chevrolet/Buick/Cadillac/GMC, Toyota, Ⓦ...**gas:** Marathon, Thornton/café/dsl, **food:** Arby's, Cracker Barrel, Hardee's, Max&Erma's, McDonald's, Mexico Viejo, Montana Mikes, Ruby Tuesday, Snappy Tomato Pizza, Subway, Taco Bell, **lodging:** Best Western, Hampton Inn, Hilton Garden, Holiday Inn Express, **other:** Goodyear, Harley-Davidson, Premium Outlets/famous brands, antiques, repair
73mm	**rest area both lanes, full(handicapped) facilities, phone, vending, info, picnic tables, litter barrels, petwalk**
68mm	Driftwood River
68	IN 46, Columbus, Ⓔ...**gas:** BP/Circle K/dsl/24hr, Shell, Speedway/dsl, **food:** Burger King, Dimitri's Rest., McDonald's, Snappy Tomato Pizza, Starbucks, Subway, **lodging:** Comfort Inn, Holiday Inn/rest., Sleep Inn, Super 8, **other:** HOSPITAL, Nissan, Sam's Club/gas, Wal-Mart SuperCtr, Ⓦ...**gas:** Marathon, Swifty, **food:** Arby's, Bob Evans, Denny's, KFC, Max's Grill, Noble Roman's, Subway, Taco Bell, Tuesday Morning, Wendy's, **lodging:** Day's Inn, Knight's Inn, Travelodge, **other:** CVS Drug, $General, Jay-C Foods, Tuesday Morning, to Brown Co SP

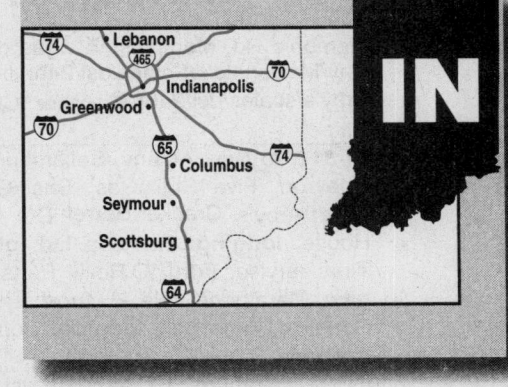

64	IN 58, Walesboro, Ⓦ...**gas:** Marathon/Kathy's Express/dsl, **other:** to RV camping
55	IN 11, to Jonesville, Seymour
54mm	White River
51mm	weigh sta both lanes
50b a	US 50, Seymour, Ⓔ...**gas:** Marathon/Circle K/dsl, Swifty, TA/BP/Country Pride/dsl/24hr/@, **food:** McDonald's, Waffle House, **lodging:** Allstate Inn, Day's Inn, Econolodge, Motel 6, Super 8, **other:** Seymour Shops/famous brands, Ⓦ...**gas:** Shell/Circle K/dsl, Speedway/dsl, Sunoco/dsl, **food:** Applebee's, Arby's, Buffet China, Burger King, Chapala Mexican, Chili's, Cracker Barrel, Dominos, Grand China, Hardee's, KFC, LJ Silver, Max & Erma's, McDonalds, Papa John's, Pizza Hut, Rally's, Ryan's, Santa Fe Mexican, Starbucks, Steak'n Shake, Subway, Taco Bell, Tumbleweed Grill, Wendy's, **lodging:** Hampton Inn, Holiday Inn/rest., Knight's Inn, Lee's Inn, Quality Inn, **other:** HOSPITAL, AutoZone, BigLots, Chevrolet/Buick/Pontiac/GMC, CVS Drug, $General, Ford/Lincoln/Mercury, GNC, Goody's, Home Depot, Jay C Foods, JC Penney, O'Reilly Parts, Radio Shack, Russell Stover Candies, Staples, Wal-Mart SuperCtr/gas, st police
41	IN 250, Uniontown, Ⓔ...**tires,** Ⓦ...**gas:** UnionTown/dsl/rest./24hr, **other:** auto/truck repair
36	US 31, Crothersville, Ⓔ...**gas:** Shell, Ⓦ...**gas:** Marathon
34a b	IN 256, Austin, Ⓔ...**gas:** BP/Circle K, **other:** to Hardy Lake, Clifty Falls SP, Ⓦ...**gas:** Fuelmart/scales/dsl, **food:** A&W
29b a	IN 56, to Salem, Scottsburg, Ⓔ...**gas:** Marathon, MotoMart, Speedway/dsl, Swifty, **food:** Burger King, Cracker Barrel, Oriental Inn, Papa John's, Ponderosa, Sonic, Subway, Taco Bell, **lodging:** Holiday Inn Express, Mariann Motel/rest., **other:** HOSPITAL, Ace Hardware, Advance Parts, AutoZone, CVS Drug, Family$, Ⓦ...**gas:** Marathon, Shell/Circle K, **food:** Arby's, Domino's, LJ Silver, McDonald's, Pizza Hut, Roadhouse USA, Waffle House, Wendy's, **lodging:** Days Inn, Hampton Inn, Super 8, **other:** Big O Tire, Jellystone Camping(4mi), Wal-Mart SuperCtr/gas
22mm	**rest area both lanes, full(handicapped)facilities, info, phone, picnic tables, litter barrels, vending, petwalk**
19	IN 160, Henryville, Ⓔ...**gas:** Shell/Circle K/24hr, Sprint/Subway/dsl, **food:** Schuler's Rest.

INDIANA

Interstate 65

16	Memphis Rd, Memphis, **E**...**gas:** BP, Love's/Subway/McDonald's/Scales/dsl/24hr, **W**...**gas:** Pilot/Arby's/scales/dsl/24hr/@, **other:** Customers 1st RV Ctr
9	IN 311, to New Albany, Sellersburg, **E**...**gas:** BP, Chevron, Five Star Gas, Shell/Circle K, Swifty, **food:** Arby's, Cracker Barrel, DQ, Quizno's, Waffle House, **lodging:** Ramada Ltd, **other:** Carmerica Tires/service, Ford, O'Reilly Parts, st police, **W**...**gas:** Marathon/Circle K, **food:** Burger King, McDonald's, Taco Bell, **lodging:** Comfort Inn, **other:** city park
7	IN 60, Hamburg, **E**...**gas:** BP/dsl/24hr, **W**...**food:** KFC/Pizza Hut, **lodging:** Day's Inn
6b a	I-265 W, to I-64 W, IN 265 E, New Albany
5	Veterans Parkway, **E**...**gas:** HOSPITAL, **W**...**gas:** Speedway/dsl, **food:** Asian Buffet, Cheddars, Chick-fil-A, DQ, Famous Dave's BBQ, IHOP, Kensai Japanese, Longhorn Steaks, McCalisters Deli, Moe's SW Grill, Olive Garden, Panera Bread, Papa Murphy's, Ruben's Mexican, Ruby Tuesday, Sonic, Subway, Taco Bell, **other:** Best Buy, Chevrolet, Lowe's Whse, Old Navy, PetsMart, Sams Club, Staples, Target, Wal-Mart SuperCtr/Subway/gas
4	US 31 N, IN 131 S, Clarksville, New Albany, **E**...**gas:** Thornton/Dunkin Donuts/dsl, **food:** White Castle, **other:** Raben Tire, **W**...**gas:** Speedway/dsl, **food:** Applebee's, Arby's, Big Boy, Bob Evans, Burger King, Capt D's, ChuckeCheese, Denny's, Don Pablo, Fazoli's, Golden Corral, Honey Baked Cafe, Hooters, Iguana Rest., La Frontera Mexican, Logan's Roadhouse, LJ Silver, McDonald's, Mr Gatti's, O'Charley's, Outback Steaks, Papa John's, Pizza Hut, Rally's, Red Lobster, Steak'n Shake/24hr, TX Roadhouse, Tuesday Morning, Wendy's, **lodging:** Best Western, Colonial Motel, Hampton Inn, **other:** AutoZone, Bass Pro Shop, Big K-mart, BigLots, Buick/Pontiac/GMC, Circuit City, Dillard's, $Tree, Firestone/auto, Ford, Goodyear, Hancock Fabrics, Home Depot, Honda, JC Penney, Kia, K-Mart, Kroger/gas, Mazda, Office Depot, O'Reilly Parts, PepBoys, Scion/Toyota, Sears/auto, Suzuki, Toyota, USPO, Walgreens, mall
2	Eastern Blvd, Clarksville, **E**...**lodging:** Best Inn, Comfort Inn, Day's Inn, Motel 6, Super 8, **other:** HOSPITAL, U-Haul, **W**...**gas:** BP, Shell, **lodging:** Best Inn, Holiday Inn, **other:** Camping World/Stinnet RV Ctr
1	US 31 S, IN 62, Stansifer Ave, **E**...**gas:** Thornton, **food:** DQ, **other:** HOSPITAL, Advance Parts, Walgreens, info ctr, **W**...**lodging:** Holiday Inn, **other:** Camping World/Stinnett RV Ctr
0	Jeffersonville, **E**...**gas:** Thornton, **food:** Hardee's, McDonald's, Waffle House, **other:** HOSPITAL, Chrysler/Jeep, Hyundai, Nissan, Walgreens, to Falls of OH SP
0mm	Indiana/Kentucky state line, Ohio River

Interstate 69

Exit #	Services
158mm	Indiana/Michigan state line
157	Lake George Rd, to IN 120, Fremont, Lake James, **E**...**gas:** Petro/Mobil/Baker's St./dsl/24hr/@, **lodging:** Lake George Inn, **other:** Freightliner, **W**...**gas:** Pilot/Wendy's/dsl/scales/24hr/@, Shell/Subway/dsl/24hr/@, **food:** McDonald's, Red Arrow Rest., **other:** Jellystone Camping(5mi), Prime Outlets/famous brands(1mi), fireworks
156	I-80/90 Toll Rd, E to Toledo, W to Chicago
154	IN 127, to IN 120, IN 727, Fremont, Orland, **E**...**food:** Applebee's(2mi), Bennigans(2mi), Ruby Tuesday, **lodging:** Hampton Inn, Ramada Inn(2mi), Super 8, Travelers Inn, **other:** Oak Hill RV camp, golf, **W**...**gas:** Marathon/dsl, **lodging:** Budgeteer Motel, Holiday Inn Express, **other:** Prime Outlets/Famous Brands, to Pokagon SP, Jellystone Camping(4mi)
150	rd 200 W, to Lake James, Crooked Lake, **E**...**gas:** BP/dsl, **W**...**gas:** Marathon, Shell, **other:** Marine Ctr
148	US 20, to Angola, Lagrange, **E**...**gas:** Citgo/Subway/dsl, GA, Speedway/dsl, **food:** McDonald's, Wendy's(1mi), **other:** HOSPITAL, **other:** Circle B RV Prk
145mm	Pigeon Creek
144mm	**rest area sb, full(handicapped)facilities, info, phone, picnic tables, litter barrels, vending, petwalk**
140	IN 4, to Hamilton, Ashley, Hudson, **1 mi** **W**...**gas:** BP/Ashley Deli/dsl
134	US 6, to Waterloo, Kendallville, **W**...**gas:** BP/dsl, Marathon/dsl/24hr, **food:** Morning Star Rest
129	IN 8, to Garrett, Auburn, **E**...**gas:** Citgo, GA, Lassus, Marathon/dsl/24hr, Speedway/dsl, **food:** Applebee's, Arby's/24hr, Ard's Rest., Bob Evans, Burger King, DQ, Fazoli's, KFC, McDonald's, Papa Murphy's, Pizza Hut, Ponderosa, Starbucks, Steak'n Shake, Subway, Taco Bell, TCBY, Wendy's, Zesto Drive-In, **lodging:** Best Western, Comfort Suites, Days Inn, Holiday Inn Express, La Quinta, Super 8, **other:** HOSPITAL, Ace Hardware, Advance Parts, AutoZone, Chevrolet/Pontiac/Buick/RV Ctr, Chrysler/Jeep/Dodge, CVS Drug, Davis RV Ctr, $General, $Tree, Ford, GMC, Kroger, Radio Shack, Staples, Wal-Mart SuperCtr/24hr, museum, **W**...**gas:** Marathon, **food:** Buffalo Wild Wings, Cracker Barrel, FireMtn Grill, Sonic, **other:** Home Depot
126	IN 11-A, to Garrett, Auburn, **E**...Kruse Auction Park, **W**...KOA
116	IN 1 N, Dupont Rd, **E**...**gas:** Citgo/Burger King, **food:** Arby's, Culver's, **lodging:** Comfort Suites, **other:** HOSPITAL, **W**...**gas:** Lassus/Elmo's Pizza, Speedway/dsl, **food:** Bandito's Mexican, Bob Evans, Ground Level Coffee, Laguna Grill, Mancino's Grinders, RolyPoly, Trolley Grill, **lodging:** AmericInn, Sleep Inn, **other:** HOSPITAL
115	I-469, US 30 E

Interstate 69

112b a Coldwater Rd, **E**...**gas:** BP/dsl/24hr, Marathon, Sunoco, **food:** Arby's,'s, Carlos O'Kelly's, Chili's, DeBrand's Chocolate, Hall's Factory Rest., Hunan Chinese, IHOP, LoneStar Steaks, Papa John's, Ponderosa, Quizno's, Rally's, Red Lobster, Red River Steaks, Steak'n Shake, Taco Bell, Wendy's, **lodging:** Hyatt Place, Marriott, **other:** Hyundai, Jo-Ann Fabrics, NAPA, U-Haul, Wal-Mart SuperCtr/24hr, **W**...DQ(1mi)

111b a US 27 S, IN 3 N, **E**...**gas:** Shell, **food:** Arby's, Cap'n Cork, ChuckeCheese, Don Pablo, DQ, Fazoli's, Golden Corral, Hall's Rest., **lodging:** Candlewood Suites, Residence Inn, **other:** Discount Tire, Ford, Honda, Infiniti, Nissan, Pontiac/GMC, Toyota, **W**...**gas:** Lassus/dsl, Marathon, Meijer/dsl/24hr, **food:** Applebee's, Burger King, Cracker Barrel, IHOP, KFC, Logan's Roadhouse, McDonald's, Mega Wraps, O'Charley's, Quizno's, Starbucks, Subway, Taco Bell, Teriyaki Express, Texas Roadhouse, **lodging:** Baymont Inn, Best Value Inn, Courtyard, County Inn&Suites, Day's Inn, Guesthouse Motel, Hampton Inn, Signature Inn, Studio+, **other:** CVS Drug, Gander Mtn, Home Depot, Lowe's Whse, Sam's Club/gas, VW

109b a US 33, Goshen Rd, Ft Wayne, **E**...**gas:** BP, Citgo/Subway/dsl/scales, Marathon, **food:** McDonald's, Pointe Rest., **lodging:** Best Inn, Country Hearth Inn, Knight's Inn, Motel 6, Quality Inn, Red Roof Inn, Travel Inn, **other:** HOSPITAL, Blue Beacon, NAPA, to Children's Zoo

105b a IN 14 W, Ft Wayne, **E**...**gas:** Lassus, Shell/Subway/dsl, Speedway/LP, **food:** Arby's, Bob Evans, Chick-fil-A, El Patron Mexican, Flat Top Grill, Great Wall Buffet, Krispy Kreme, Logan's Roadhouse, O'Charley's, Papa Murphy's, Smokey Bones BBQ, Starbucks, Steak'n Shake, Wendy's, **lodging:** Klopfenstein Suites, **other:** HOSPITAL, Acura, Audi/Porsche, Barnes&Noble, Best Buy, Big Lots, BMW, Cadillac, Chevrolet, Chrysler/Jeep, Dodge, Harley-Davidson, Hummer, KIA, Kohl's, Lexus, Lowe's Whse, Mazda, Meijer/dsl/24hr, NAPA, Old Navy, Petsmart, Pontiac/Buick/GMC, Saab, Saturn, Staples, Subaru, Toyota/Scion, Tuesday Morning, Volvo, Wal-Mart SuperCtr/gas/24hr, to St Francis U, **W**...**food:** Bandito's, **other:** Corvette Museum

102 US 24, to Jefferson Blvd, Ft Wayne, **E**...**food:** Subway(1mi), Taco Bell(1mi), **lodging:** Extended Stay America, Hampton Inn, **other:** HOSPITAL, to In Wesleyan U, **W**...**gas:** Lassus, Marathon, **food:** Antigua Grill, Applebee's, Arby's, Bob Evans, Carlos O'Kelly's, Coventry Tavern Rest., McDonald's, Outback Steaks, Pizza Hut, Sara's Rest., Starbucks, Wendy's, Zesto Drive-In, **lodging:** Comfort Suites, Hilton Garden, Holiday Inn Express, Luxbury Inn, Staybridge Suites, **other:** Kroger, Scott's Foods, Walgreen, st police

99 Lower Huntington Rd, no services

96b a I-469, US 24 E, US 33 S, **E**...to airport

93mm rest area sb, full(handicapped) facilities, info, phone, vending, picnic tables, litter barrels, pet walk

89mm rest area nb, full(handicapped)facilities, info, phone, vending, picnic tables, litter barrels, pet walk

86 US 224, to Huntington, Markle, **E**...**gas:** Marathon/24hr(1mi), Sunoco/Subway, **food:** DQ, Huddle House, Vinatelli's, **lodging:** Guesthouse Inn, Super 8, **other:** HOSPITAL, **W**... repair/tires, to Huntington Reservoir

80mm weigh sta sb/parking area nb

78 IN 5, to Warren, Huntington, **E**...**gas:** Sunoco/dsl, **lodging:** Huggy Bear Motel, **W**...**gas:** Crazy D's/dsl/24hr, Marathon/Subway/dsl/24hr, **food:** McDonald's, Ugalde's Rest., **lodging:** Comfort Inn, Motel 6, **other:** HOSPITAL, RV Camping, fireworks, to Salmonie Reservoir

76mm Salamonie River

73 IN 218, to Warren, no services

64 IN 18, to Marion, Montpelier, **W**...**gas:** BP/Subway/dsl, Marathon/dsl, **food:** Arby's, **lodging:** Days Inn, **other:** HOSPITAL, Harley-Davidson, Jeep/Chrysler, **E**...**gas:** Love's/McDonalds/dsl/scales/24hr

60mm Walnut Creek

59 US 35 N, IN 22, to Upland, **E**...**gas:** Valero/Subway, **food:** Burger King, China 1, Cracker Barrel, Taste of Texas, **lodging:** B&B, Best Western, Super 8, **other:** Mar-Brook Camping, Taylor U, **W**...**gas:** Marathon/dsl/24hr, McClure Trkstp/dsl/24hr, Shell/dsl, **food:** KFC/Taco Bell, Starbucks, **lodging:** Holiday Inn Express, **other:** IN Wesleyan

55 IN 26, to Fairmount, no services

50mm rest area both lanes, full(handicapped)facilities, info, phone, picnic tables, litter barrels, vending, pet walk

45 US 35 S, IN 28, to Alexandria, Albany, **E**...**gas:** Petro/Shell/Iron Skillet/Taco Bell/dsl/scales/24hr/@, **other:** RV Camping

41 IN 332, to Muncie, Frankton, **E**...**gas:** BP/dsl, Citgo/dsl, **other:** HOSPITAL, to Ball St U

34 IN 67, to IN 32, Chesterfield, Daleville, **E**...**gas:** Pilot/Subway/dsl/scales/24hr, Shell, **food:** Arby's, Taco Bell, White Castle, **lodging:** Budget Inn, **other:** HOSPITAL, **W**...**gas:** GA/dsl, Pilot/Cafe/dsl/24hr, **food:** McDonald's, Subway, 3rd Generation Pizza, Wendy's, **lodging:** Best Value Inn, **other:** flea mkt

INDIANA

Interstate 69

Anderson
Indianapolis Area

26	IN 9, IN 109, to Anderson, E...**gas:** Meijer/dsl/24hr, **food:** Culver's, KFC/A&W, Ryan's, **lodging:** Deluxe Inn, Hampton Inn, Quality Inn, **other:** W...**gas:** BP, GA, Marathon, Speedway, **food:** Applebee's, Arby's, Bob Evans, Burger King, China Buffet, Cracker Barrel, Fazoli's, Great Wall Chinese, IHOP, La Charreada Mexican, LoneStar Steaks, McDonald's, Noble Roman's, Panera Bread, Penn Sta Subs, Perkins, Pizza Hut, Olive Garden, Red Lobster, Ritter's, Ruby Tuesday, Starbucks, Steak'n Shake, Subway, Taco Bell, Waffle House, Wendy's, White Castle, Wings Etc., **lodging:** Baymont Inn, Best Inn, Comfort Inn, Days Inn, Fairfield Inn, Garden Inn, Lee's Inn, Motel 6, Rose Carpet Inn, **other:** HOSPITAL, Aldi Foods, Cadillac/GMC, Curves, Freightliner, Kohl's, Old Navy, O'Reilly Parts, Payless Foods, Radio Shack, Target, Tire Barn, Toyota, Wal-Mart SuperCtr, Anderson U, Mounds SP
22	IN 9, IN 67, to Anderson, W...**gas:** GA, **food:** Skyline Chili, **lodging:** Anderson Country Inn(1mi), **other:** HOSPITAL, st police
19	IN 38, Pendleton, E...**gas:** Marathon, **food:** Burger King, McDonald's, Subway
14	IN 13, to Lapel, E...**gas:** BP, W...**gas:** Pilot/Subway/dsl/scales/24hr, **other:** camping
10	IN 238, to Noblesville, Fortville, W...**other:** JC Penney
5	IN 37 N, 116th St, to Noblesville, Fishers, E...**gas:** BP/Wild Bean Cafe, W...**gas:** Shell/autocare, Speedway, **food:** A&W/KFC, Greek Pizzaria, Handel's Ice Cream, Hawg Wild BBQ, McAlister's Deli, McDonald's, O'Charley's, Qdoba Mexican, Quizno's, Starbucks, Station Rest., Steak'n Shake, Subway, Wendy's, **lodging:** Hampton Inn, **other:** Target
3	96th St, E...**gas:** Meijer/dsl/24hr, Shell, VP/dsl, **food:** Applebee's, Bennigan's, Cracker Barrel, Donato's Pizza, Golden Wok Chinese, McDonald's, New China, Noble Roman's, Panera Bread, Pizza Shop, Qdoba Mexican, Ruby Tuesday, Steak'n Shake, **lodging:** Hilton Garden, Holiday Inn, Holiday Inn Express, Hotel Indigo, Studio 6, **other:** Kohl's, Marsh Food/gas, PepBoys, PetCo, Radio Shack, Staples, Tuesday morning, Wal-Mart SuperCtr/gas/24hr, W...**gas:** Marathon, **food:** Arby's, Bob Evans, Burger King, Cheeseburger Paradise, Culver's, Journey Rest., Panda Express, Peterson's Steaks/seafood, Quizno's, Starbucks, Taco Bell, **lodging:** Comfort Suites, Residence Inn, SpringHill Suites, Staybridge Suites, **other:** Aldi Foods, $Tree, Home Depot, NAPA, Sam's Club/gas
1	82nd St, Castleton, E...**food:** Pizza Hut, **lodging:** Country Inn&Suites, Drury Inn, Extended Stay America, Hilton, Super 8, **other:** HOSPITAL, Lowe's Whse, W...**gas:** Speedway, **food:** Applebee's, Arby's, Burger King, Cancun Mexican, Charleston's Rest., Denny's, Fazoli's, Hooters, IHOP, KFC/A&W, Loonlake Lodge Rest., McDonald's, Olive Garden, Penn Sta. Subs, Rally's, Red Lobster, Skyline Chili, Starbucks, Steak'n Shake, Taco Bell, Tuscany Grill, Wendy's, **lodging:** Best Western, Candlewood Suites, Day's Inn, Hampton Inn, Red Roof Inn, **other:** Aamco, Best Buy, Discount Tire, $Tree, Goodyear/auto, Indy Tires, Sears/auto, Tire Barn, mall
0mm	I-465 around Indianapolis. I-69 begins/ends on I-465, exit 37, at Indianapolis

Interstate 70

Richmond

Exit #	Services
156.5mm	Indiana/Ohio state line, weigh sta
156b a	US 40 E, Richmond, N...**gas:** FuelMart/dsl, Petro/Marathon/Pizza Hut/dsl/rest./24hr/@, Swifty, **lodging:** Fairfield Inn, **other:** Blue Beacon, S...**gas:** BP/White Castle, Shell, Speedway, **food:** A&W/LJ Silver, Applebee's, Big Boy, Bob Evans, Buffalo Wings Cafe, Burger King, Chili's, Cici's Pizza, Cracker Barrel, Domino's, Fazoli's, Golden Corral, Hacienda Mexican, Jade House Chinese, KFC, McDonald's, MCL Cafeteria, O'Charley's, Pizza Hut, Red Lobster, Ruby Tuesday, Ryan's, Steak'n Shake, Subway, Super China, Taco Bell, TCBY, Texas Roadhouse, **lodging:** Best Western, Day's Inn, Hampton Inn, Holiday Inn, Lee's Inn, Motel 6, **other:** AAA, Advance Parts, Aldi Foods, BigLots, Chevrolet/Cadillac, Chrysler/Jeep, Curves, Dillards, $General, Expert Tire, Ford/Lincoln/Mercury, Goody's, Goodyear/auto, Hastings Books, JC Penney, Kroger, Lowe's Whse, Midas, SavALot Foods, Sears/auto, Target, Tires+, Toyota/Scion, Tuffy, U-Haul, Walgreens, Wal-Mart SuperCtr/gas/24hr
153	IN 227, to Whitewater, Richmond, **2 mi** N...Grandpa's Farm RV Park(seasonal)
151b a	US 27, to Chester, Richmond, N...**food:** Fricker's Rest., **other:** Best Buy RV Ctr, Dodge, Honda, KOA, S...**gas:** Shell, **food:** Bob Evans, Burger King, Carver's Rest., McDonald's, Pizza Hut, Subway, Taco Bell, Wendy's, **lodging:** Comfort Inn, Super 8, **other:** HOSPITAL, Harley-Davidson, Meijer/dsl/24hr
149b a	US 35, IN 38, to Muncie, N...Love's/Hardee's/dsl/scales/24hr, S...Best Buy RV Ctr, Raper's RV service Ctr
148mm	weigh sta wb
145	Centerville, N...**gas:** BP/DQ/Stuckey's, **lodging:** Super 8, **other:** Goodyear/truck repair, S...Warm Glow Candles
145mm	Nolands Fork Creek
144mm	**rest area both lanes, full(handicapped) facilities, info, vending, phone, picnic tables, litter barrels, petwalk**
141mm	Greens Fork River
137	IN 1, to Hagerstown, Connersville, N...Amish Cheese, S...**gas:** Crazy D's/dsl/rest./24hr, GA/mart/24hr, Shell/mart/24hr, **food:** Burger King, McDonald's
131	Wilbur Wright Rd, New Lisbon, S...**gas:** Marathon/KFC/Taco Bell/dsl/scales/24hr/@, **other:** New Lisbon RV park
126mm	Flatrock River
123	IN 3, to New Castle, Spiceland, N...**lodging:** All American Inn(3mi), Best Western(3mi), Econolodge, Holiday Inn Express(3mi), Super 8, **other:** HOSPITAL, Irwin RV Park(1mi), S...**gas:** Flying J/CountyMkt/dsl/scales/24hr, **food:** Steak'n Shake
117mm	Big Blue River
115	IN 109, to Knightstown, Wilkinson, N...**gas:** GA/Gas Grill/dsl/scales/24hr, **food:** Burger King, **other:** Jellystone Camping

Interstate 70

107mm	**rest area both lanes, full(handicapped) facilities, vending, phone, picnic tables, litter barrels, petwalk**
104	IN 9, Greenfield, Maxwell, **N**...gas: GA/mart, **S**...gas: GA, Shell/Circle K, Sunoco/White Castle, Swifty/mart, **food:** Applebee's, Arby's, Bamboo Garden, Bob Evans, Burger King, Cracker Barrel, Culver's, Domino's, El Rodeo Mexican, Hardee's, KFC, McDonald's, Mi Casa Mexican, MT Mike's Steaks, O'Charley's, Papa Murphy's, Penn Sta. Subs, Pizza Hut, Ponderosa, Quizno's, Ritter's Custard, Starbucks, Steak'n Shake, Subway, Taco Bell, Wendy's, **lodging:** Comfort Inn, $Inn, Hampton Inn, Holiday Inn Express, Quality Inn, Super 8, **other:** Advance Parts, Aldi Foods, Autozone, BigLots, Big O Tire, CVS Drug, $General, $Tree, GNC, Home Depot, Kroger, Marsh Foods, Radio Shack, Wal-Mart SuperCtr/gas/24hr
96	Mt Comfort Rd, **N**...gas: GA/mart, Pilot/Pizza Hut/dsl/scales/24hr, **food:** Burger King, Subway, Wendy's, **other:** Heartland RV Park(2mi), **S**...gas: Shell/mart, **food:** McDonald's, **other:** KOA(seasonal), Mt Comfort RV Ctr
91	Post Rd, to Ft Harrison, **N**...gas: Marathon/7-11, Swifty, **food:** Cracker Barrel, Denny's, Joe's Crabshack, Outback Steaks, Steak'n Shake, Wendy's, **lodging:** InTown Suites, La Quinta, **other:** Lowe's Whse, st police, **S**...gas: Admiral, BP/mart, Shell/mart, Speedway, **food:** Hardee's, KFC/Taco Bell, Little China, Waffle House, **lodging:** Days Inn, Super 8, **other:** CVS Drug, Family$, Home Depot, Marsh Foods
90	I-465(from wb)
89	Shadeland Ave, I-465(from eb), **N**...gas: Marathon, **food:** Bob Evans, **lodging:** Comfort Inn, Comfort Suites, Hampton Inn, Motel 6, **other:** Toyota, U-Haul, **S**...gas: Admiral Gas, Circle K/Quizno's, Marathon, Shell/24hr, Speedway/dsl, **food:** Arby's, Burger King, Blimpie, 4Seasons Diner, Lincoln's Rest., McDonald's, Noble Roman's, Papagalo's Italian, Penn Sta. Subs, Rally's, Red Lobster, Starbucks, Texas Roadhouse, Wendy's, **lodging:** Always Inn, Day's Inn, Fairfield Inn, Holiday Inn/Damon's, Knight's Inn, La Quinta, Marriott, Quality Inn, **other:** Aamco, Buick, CVS Drug, Chevrolet, Dodge, Honda, KIA, Mitsubishi, Nissan
87	Emerson Ave, **N**...gas: BP/McDonald's, Speedway, **S**...gas: Shell, **other:** HOSPITAL
85b a	Rural St, Keystone Ave, **N**...fairgrounds, **S**...gas: Marathon
83b(112)	I-65 N, to Chicago
83a(111)	Michigan St, Market St, downtown, **S**...gas: Citgo, **food:** Hardee's
80(110a)	I-65 S, to Louisville
79b	Illinois St, McCarty St, downtown
79a	West St, **N**...lodging: Comfort Inn, **other:** HOSPITAL, to Union Sta, Govt Ctr, RCA Dome, zoo
78	Harding St, to downtown, **S**...gas: Marathon, **food:** Wendy's
77	Holt Rd, **S**...gas: Shell, **food:** McDonald's, **other:** Ford Trucks
75	Airport Expswy, to Raymond St (no EZ wb return), **N**...gas: Marathon, Speedway/dsl, **food:** Cracker Barrel, Denny's, Indy's Rest., Waffle House, **lodging:** Adam's Mark, Candlewood Suites, Courtyard, Econolodge, Extended Stay Deluxe, Fairfield Inn, Holiday Inn, Hyatt Place, La Quinta, Quality Inn, Ramada, Residence Inn, **other:** NAPA, to airport
73b a	I-465 N/S, I-74 E/W (from wb)
69	(from eb) to I-74 E, to I-465 S
68	Six Points Rd
66	IN 267, to Plainfield, Mooresville, **N**...gas: BP/24hr, Shell/Circle K, Speedway/dsl, Thornton's/dsl, **food:** Arby's, Bob Evans, Burger King, Coachman Rest., Cracker Barrel, Denny's, Golden Corral, Hog Heaven BBQ, McDonald's, Pizza King, Quizno's, Steak'n Shake, Subway, Wendy's, White Castle, **lodging:** Comfort Inn, Day's Inn, Hampton Inn, Homewood Suites, Holiday Inn Express, Homeplace Hotel, Lee's Inn, Motel 6, Ramada Ltd, Staybridge Suites, Super 8, Wingate Inn, **other:** Chateau Thomas Winery, Harley-Davidson
65mm	**rest area both lanes, full(handicapped)facilities, info, vending, phone, picnic tables, litter barrels, petwalk**
59	IN 39, to Belleville, **N**...gas: Marathon/mart, **other:** HOSPITAL, **S**...gas: TA/Country Pride/dsl/rest./24hr/@
51	rd 1100W, **S**...other: Koger's/dsl, repair/towing/24hr
41	US 231, to Greencastle, Cloverdale, **S**...gas: BP/dsl, Marathon/Subway/scales/dsl/24hr, **food:** Arby's, Chicago's Pizza, KFC, McDonald's, Starbucks, Taco Bell, Wendy's, **lodging:** Best Value, Day's Inn, Econolodge, Holiday Inn Express, Motel 6, Super 8, **other:** Clover Tire, Value Mkt Foods, to Lieber SRA
37	IN 243, to Putnamville, **S**...gas: Marathon/dsl/mart, **other:** to Lieber SRA
23	IN 59, to Brazil, **N**...gas: Pilot/McDonald's/Subway/scales/dsl/mart/24hr, **other:** HOSPITAL, **S**...gas: AM Best/Shell/Brazil Grill/dsl/rest./24hr/@, BP/Rally's/dsl/mart, Roadranger/Subway/scales/dsl, **food:** Burger King, Jerry's Rest., **lodging:** Howard Johnson Express
15mm	Honey Creek

INDIANA

Interstate 70

11	IN 46, Terre Haute, **N**...**gas:** Pilot/Arby's/scales/dsl/mart/24hr, Thornton/dsl, **food:** Burger King, McDonald's, **other:** airport, **S**...KOA
7	US 41, US 150, Terre Haute, **N**...**gas:** Marathon/dsl, Thornton's/dsl, **food:** Applebee's, Beef-O-Brady's, Bob Evans, Burger King, Cracker Barrel, 8 China Buffet, Fazoli's, IHOP, LoneStar Steaks, Papa Murphy's, Pizza Hut, Quizno's, Starbucks, Steak'n Shake, TX Roadhouse, Tumbleweed Mesquite Grill, **lodging:** Best Western, Comfort Suites, Econolodge, Drury Inn, Econolodge, PearTree Inn, Ramada Ltd., Signature Inn, Super 8, **other:** AutoZone, Best 1 Tire, Chrysler/Plymouth/Jeep, **S**...**gas:** Speedway/dsl, Thornton's/mart, **food:** Arby's, Boston's Rest, Burger King, Cheeseburger Paradise, DQ, Denny's, Fire Mtn Grill, Garfield's Rest., Golden Corral, Hardee's, KFC, Los Tres Caminos, LJ Silver, McDonald's, Olive Garden, Outback Steaks, Panera Bread, Papa John's, Rally's, Red Lobster, Ruby Tuesday, Ryan's, Starbucks, Subway, Taco Bell, TGIFriday, Wendy's, **lodging:** Hampton Inn, Holiday Inn, Knight's Inn, SpringHill Suites, **other:** HOSPITAL, Aldi Foods, BigLots, BooksAMillion, Buick/Pontiac/Cadillac, Chevrolet/Hyundai/Nissan, Circuit City, Dodge, $Tree, Ford/Kia, Gander Mtn., GMC/Mazda, Goodys, Goodyear/auto, Harley-Davidson, Jo-Ann Crafts, Kia, K-Mart/gas, Kroger/gas, Lowe's Whse, Old Navy, PetCo, Sam's Club/gas, Saturn, Sears/auto, Staples, Toyota, Tire Barn, Walgreens, Wal-Mart SuperCtr/gas, Walgreen
5.5mm	Wabash River
3	Darwin Rd, W Terre Haute, **N**...to St Mary of-the-Woods Coll
1.5mm	**Welcome Ctr eb, full(handicapped)facilities, info, picnic tables, litter barrels, phone, vending, petwalk**
1	US 40 E(from eb, exits left), to Terre Haute, W Terre Haute
.5mm	weigh sta, eb only
0mm	Indiana/Illinois state line

Interstate 74

Exit #	Services
171.5mm	Indiana/Ohio state line
171mm	weigh sta wb
169	US 52 W, to Brookville
168.5mm	Whitewater River
164	IN 1, St Leon, **N**...**gas:** Exxon, Shell/dsl, **S**...**gas:** BP/dsl
156	IN 101, to Sunman, Milan, **S**...**gas:** Exxon/dsl
152mm	**rest area both lanes, full(handicapped) facilities, phone, picnic tables, litter barrels, vending, petwalk**
149	IN 229, to Oldenburg, Batesville, **N**...**gas:** Shell/dsl/24hr, Sunoco, **food:** Acapulco Mexican, China Wok, McDonald's, Starbucks, Subway, Wendy's, **lodging:** Hampton Inn, **other:** $General, Kroger/

	gas, Pamida, **S**...**gas:** BP, **food:** Arby's, DQ, KFC/Taco Bell, La Rosa's Pizza, Skyline Chili, Waffle House, **lodging:** Comfort Inn, **other:** HOSPITAL, CVS Drug
143	to IN 46, New Point, **N**...**gas:** Petro/Marathon/Iron Skillet/dsl/rest./24hr/@, **S**...**gas:** Marathon
134b a	IN 3, to Rushville, Greensburg, **S**...**gas:** BP/dsl, Marathon/DQ/Subway, Shell/24hr, Speedway, **food:** A&W, Arby's, Big Boy, Burger King, Chili's, El Reparo Mexican, El Tapatio Mexican, Great Wall Buffet, KFC, McDonald's, Papa John's, Prime Time Grill, Subway, Taco Bell, Waffle House, Wendy's, **lodging:** Fairfield Inn, Lee's Inn, Holiday Inn Express, **other:** Advance Parts, Aldi Foods, AutoZone, Big O Tire, Chevrolet/Cadillac, Chrysler, CVS Drug, $General, Ford/Mercury, Goody's, Radio Shack, Staples, Wal-Mart SuperCtr/24hr, Walgreens
132	US 421(from eb), to Greensburg
130mm	Clifty Creek
123	Saint Paul, **S**...camping
119	IN 244 E, to Milroy, no services
116	IN 44, to Shelbyville, Rushville, **N**...**gas:** Bigfoot/dsl, **S**...**gas:** BP, Marathon, Shell/24hr, Swifty, **food:** Applebee's, Arby's, Bellacino's, Bob Evans, Burger King, China Buffet, Denny's, Golden Corral(1mi), King's Buffet, LJ Silver, McDonald's, Papa John's, Pizza Hut, Subway, Taco Bell, Wendy's, **lodging:** Lee's Inn, **other:** HOSPITAL, Ace Hardware, Advance Parts, Aldi Foods, Big Lots, Chevrolet, CVS Drug, $General, Ford/Lincoln/Mercury, GNC, Goody's, Kroger/gas, Marsh Foods, NAPA, Radio Shack, Walgreens, Wal-Mart SuperCtr/24hr/gas
115mm	Little Blue River
113mm	Big Blue River
113	IN 9, to Shelbyville, **N**...**gas:** BP, GA, **food:** Cracker Barrel, Wendy's, **S**...**gas:** BP, Shell, **food:** El Emparador Mexican, McDonald's, Santa Fe Steaks, Waffle House, **lodging:** Best Western, Comfort Inn, Day's Inn, Hampton Inn, Super 8, **other:** HOSPITAL, Buick/GMC, Chrysler/Plymouth, Ford/Lincoln/Mercury
109	Fairland Rd, **N**...**gas:** Pilot/McDonald's/dsl/scales/24hr, **other:** Indiana Downs, **S**...**other:** Brownie's Marine
103	London Rd, to Boggstown, no services
102mm	Big Sugar Creek
101	Pleasant View Rd, **N**...**gas:** Marathon
99	Acton Rd, no services
96	Post Rd, **N**...**gas:** Marathon/Subway/dsl/24hr, **food:** McDonald's, **S**...**gas:** Shell/dsl, **food:** Wendy's, **other:** Chevrolet
94b a	I-465/I-74 W, I-465 N, US 421 N,
	I-74 and I-465 run together 21 miles. Exits 2-16, and 52-53.
73b	I-465 N, same services as 16a on I-465
73a	I-465 S, I-74 E
71mm	Eagle Creek
68	new exit

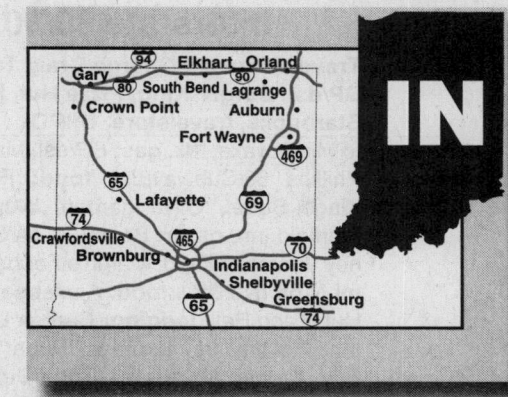

Interstate 74

E ← → **W**

Brownsburg

66	IN 267, Brownsburg, **N...gas:** Citgo/dsl, Shell, **food:** Applebee's, Asia Wok, Hardee's, Ritters Custard, Steak'n Shake, Subway, Trip's Grill, **lodging:** Hampton Inn, Holiday Inn Express, **other:** Big O Tire, **S...gas:** BP/dsl, Speedway/dsl, **food:** Arby's, Blimpie, Bob Evans, Burger King, China's Best, McDonald's, Papa Murphy's, Quizno's, Starbucks, Taco Bell, Wendy's, White Castle, Wing Etc., **lodging:** Comfort Suites, Super 8, **other:** CVS Drug, $Tree, Ford, Kohl's, Kroger/gas, K-Mart, Lowe's Whse, Radio Shack, Wal-Mart SuperCtr/24hr
61	to Pittsboro, **S...gas:** Loves/Godfathers/Subway/dsl/scales/24hr
58	IN 39, to Lebanon, Lizton, **S...** HOSPITAL
57mm	**rest area both lanes, full(handicapped) facilities, phone, picnic tables, litter barrels, vending, petwalk**
52	IN 75, to Advance, Jamestown, **2 mi S...gas,** food, camping
39	IN 32, to Crawfordsville, **S...gas:** Pilot/Subway/dsl/scales/24hr
34	US 231, to Linden, **S...gas:** BP, CTP/dsl/scales/24hr, GA, Marathon/dsl, **food:** Burger King, KFC, McDonald's, Vickery's Cafe(1mi), **lodging:** Comfort Inn, Day's Inn, Holiday Inn, Ramada Ltd., Super 8, **other:** HOSPITAL, KOA(1mi), Sugar Creek Campground(4mi)
25	IN 25, to Wingate, Waynetown, no services
22mm	**rest area both lanes, full(handicapped)facilities, phone, picnic tables, litter barrels, vending, petwalk**
19mm	weigh sta eb/parking area wb
15	US 41, to Attica, Veedersburg, **1/2 mi S...gas:** Marathon/Subway/dsl, **food:** Apple Tree Diner, **other:** to Turkey Run SP, camping
8	Covington, **N...gas:** Shell, **food:** Maple Corner Rest.(1mi), **other:** fireworks
7mm	Wabash River
4	IN 63, to Newport, **N...gas:** BP/Wendy's, Pilot/Arby's/dsl/scales/24hr, **food:** Beefhouse Rest.
1mm	**Welcome Ctr eb, full(handicapped)facilities, info, phone, picnic tables, litter barrels, vending, petwalk**
0mm	Indiana/Illinois state line, Eastern/Central Time Zone

Interstate 80/90

E ← → **W**

Elkhart

Exit #	Services
157mm	Indiana/Ohio state line, no services
153mm	toll plaza, litter barrels
146mm	**service area both lanes, Mobil/dsl, DQ, McDonald's, playground**
144	I-69, US 27, Angola, Ft Wayne, **N...gas:** Petro/Mobil/dsl/LP/24hr/@, Shell/Subway/dsl/24hr/@, Pilot/Wendy's/dsl/24hr/@, **food:** McDonald's, Red Arrow Rest., **lodging:** Redwood Lodge, Lake George Inn, **S...gas:** Marathon/dsl/24hr, **lodging:** Holiday Inn Express, **other:** Prime Outlets/famous brands, **services on IN 120 E...food:** Herb Garden Rest., **lodging:** E&L Motel, Hampton Inn, Super 8, **other:**

	Golf/rest., U-Haul/repair(1mi), **W...**to Pokagon SP, Jellystone Camping(7mi)
131.5mm	Fawn River
126mm	**Travel Plaza eb, Gene S Porter Travel Plaza wb, Mobil/dsl, Fazoli's, Hardee's, ice cream, gifts, RV dump**
121	IN 9, to Lagrange, Howe, **N...gas:** Golden Buddha, **lodging:** Best Value, Hampton Inn, Travel Inn, Walmart, **other:** HOSPITAL(4mi), **2 mi N...food:** Applebee's, Golden Corral, DQ, Wendy's, **lodging:** Comfort Inn, Knight's Inn, Wood Motel, **S...gas:** Clark, **lodging:** Holiday Inn Express, Super 8, **other:** HOSPITAL(8mi)
120mm	Fawn River
108mm	**trucks only rest area both lanes**
107	US 131, IN 13, to Middlebury, Constantine, **N...gas:** Marathon/dsl, **food:** Country Table Rest.(2mi), McDonald's(4mi), **lodging:** PatchWork Quilt Inn(1mi), Plaza Motel, **1 mi S...gas:** BP/Blimpie/dsl, **food:** Yup's DairyLand, **other:** Eby's Pines RV Park, KOA(aprnov), **5 mi S...food:** DQ, Subway, **other:** Coachman RV Factory,
101	IN 15, to Goshen, Bristol, **1 mi S...gas:** Citgo/7-11, Speedway/dsl, **food:** River Inn Rest., **other:** Eby's Pines Camping(3mi)
96	rd 1, E Elkhart, **2 mi S...gas:** BP/dsl, Citgo/7-11, Marathon, **food:** DQ, McDonald's, Subway
92	IN 19, to Elkhart, **N...gas:** Citgo/7-11, Phillips 66/Subway/dsl, **food:** Applebee's, Cracker Barrel, Perkins, Steak'n Shake, **lodging:** Best Western, Candlewood Suites, Comfort Suites, Country Inn Suites, Diplomat Motel, Econolodge, Fairway Inn, Hampton Inn, Hilton Garden, Holiday Inn Express, Knight's Inn, Quality Inn, Sleep Inn, Turnpike Motel, **other:** Aldi Foods, Camping World, CVS Drug, GNC, K-Mart, Martin's Foods, Radio Shack, Tierra RV Ctr, **S...gas:** Marathon/dsl, **food:** Arby's, Bennigan's, Blimpie, Bob Evans, Burger King, Callaghan's Rest., Da Vinci's Pizza, Lazy Bones Rest., McDonald's, Olive Garden, Red Lobster, Ryan's, Taco Bell, Texas Roadhouse, **lodging:** Budget Inn, Day's Inn, Ramada Inn, Red Roof Inn, Signature Inn, Super 8, Weston Plaza, **other:** HOSPITAL, CarQuest, $Tree, Holiday World RV, Wal-Mart SuperCtr/24hr, truck/RV repair, **1 mi S...gas:** Citgo, Shell, Swifty, **food:** DQ, KFC, LJ Silver, Pizza Hut, Matterhorn Rest., Wendy's, **other:** Advance Parts, Ace Hardware, AutoZone, Family$, Walgreen
91mm	Christiana Creek

INDIANA

Interstate 80/90

E ↕ W

90mm	**Travel Plaza eb, George Craig Travel Plaza wb, BP/dsl, Burger King, Pizza Hut, KFC, RV dump, Starbucks, travelstore, USPO**
83	to Mishawaka, **N**...**gas:** BP/dsl, Marathon/Blimpie, Phillips 66/Subway/dsl, **food:** Famous Dave's, Kings Buffet, Olive garden, Wendy's, **lodging:** Fairfield Inn, **other:** Best Buy, CVS Drug, JC Penney, Marshall Field, Martin's Foods, Walgreen, **1-2 mi N on IN 23W**...**food:** Applebee's, Arby's, Pizza Hut, Taco Bell, **lodging:** Carlton Lodge, Hampton Inn, Holiday Inn Express, Super 8, **other:** Best Buy, Kroger, Michael's, Office Depot, Sears, Target, KOA(mar-nov), mall, **2 mi S on Grape Rd & Main St(off IN 23W)**...**gas:** Meijer/dsl/24hr, **food:** Arby's, Burger King, Chili's, LoneStar Steaks, Mancino's Pizza, McDonald's, Old Country Buffet, Outback Steaks, Papa Vino's Italian, Ryan's, Steak'n Shake, Subway, TGIFriday, **lodging:** Best Western, Courtyard, Extended Stay America, SpringHill Suites, **other:** Studio+, Barnes&Noble, Buick/GMC, Chrysler/Plymouth, Circuit City, Discount Tire, Hyundai, Jo-Ann Fabrics, Lowe's Whse, Sam's Club, Wal-Mart SuperCtr/24hr
77	US 33, US 31B, IN 933, South Bend, **N**...**gas:** Admiral, Mobile, **food:** Arby's, Burger King, Damon's, DQ, Eleni's Rest., Family Style Buffet, Fazoli's, KFC, Marco's Pizza, McDonald's, Panorama Rest., Papa John's, Pizza Hut, Steak&Ale, Steak&Shake, Subway, **lodging:** Comfort Suites, Day's Inn, Hampton Inn, Motel 6, Ramada Inn, Super 8, **other:** AutoZone, BMW, Isuzu, Mazda, Napa, Radio Shack, TruValue, Walgreen, **1 mi N on frtge rd**...**gas:** Meijer/dsl/24hr, Phillips 66, **food:** Burger King, McDonald's,**S**...**gas:** Marathon, Phillips 66/dsl, **food:** Bob Evans, Denny's, Great Wall Chinese, King Gyro's, Mikados Japanese, Pancake House, Perkins, Pizza King, Taco Bell, Wendy's, **lodging:** Best Inn, Holiday Inn Express, Howard Johnson, Knight's Inn, Quality Inn, Signature Inn, St Marys Inn, **other:** HOSPITAL, VET, to Notre Dame
76mm	St Joseph River
72	US 31, to Niles, South Bend, **N**...**gas:** Pilot/Subway/scales/dsl/24hr, Speedway/Subway/dsl, **lodging:** Super 8, **2 mi S on US 20**...**food:** 4 Seasons Rest., McDonald's, Ponderosa, Taco Bell, Wendy's, **lodging:** Day's Inn, Quality Inn, **other:** RV Ctr, to Potato Creek SP(20mi), airport, st police
56mm	**Rockne travel plaza both lanes, BP/dsl, DQ, McDonald's, SB Chocolate, phone, RV dump, litter barrel**
49	IN 39, to La Porte, **N**...**lodging:** Hampton Inn, **S**...**lodging:** Best Value Inn, Cassidy Inn & RV, **3mi S**...**gas:** Mobil/dsl, **lodging:** Blue Heron Motel, Holiday Inn Express, Super 8
39	US 421, to Michigan City, Westville, **5 mi N**...**lodging:** Hampton Inn, Holiday Inn, Knight's Inn, **other:** Premium Outlets/famous brands, **S**...Purdue U North Cent
38mm	**trucks only rest area both lanes, litter barrels**

S o u t h B e n d

31	IN 49, to Chesterton, Valparaiso, **N**...**lodging:** Best Western, Hilton Garden, Super 8(3mi), **other:** Sand Creek RV Park(4mi), to IN Dunes Nat Lakeshore, **S**...**lodging:** Hampton Inn(8mi), **other:** Yellow Brick Rd Museum/gifts
24mm	toll plaza
23	Portage, Port of Indiana, **0-2 mi N**...**gas:** Marathon, Shell, **food:** Mark's Grill, **lodging:** Day's Inn, Comfort Inn, Country Inn Suites, Holiday Inn Express, $Inn, Ramada Inn, Super 8, **S**...**gas:** BP, Marathon, **food:** Burger King, Cici's Pizza, Dunkin Donuts, DQ, First Wok Chinese, Jimmy John's, KFC, McDonald's, Starbucks, Subway, Wendy's, **other:** Advance Parts, Ace Hardware, Family$, GNC, Town&Country Mkt/24hr, USPO, Walgreen
22mm	**George Ada TP, both lanes, info, gas: BP/dsl, food: Fazoli's, Hardee's, other: playground, scales both lanes**
21mm	**I-90 and I-80 run together eb, separate wb. I-80 runs with I-94 wb. For I-80 exits 1 through 15, see Indiana Interstate 94.**
21	I-94 E to Detroit, I-80/94 W, US 6, IN 51, Lake Station, **N**...**gas:** BP, ⚡/Flying J/Cookery/scales/dsl/24hr/@, Road Ranger/Subway/dsl/scales/24hr, TA/BP/Subway/Popeye's/dsl/scales/24hr/@, **food:** McDonald's, **other:** Blue Beacon, **S**...**gas:** Mobil/dsl, Road Ranger/Subway/scales/dsl, Shell, **food:** Burger King, DQ, Papa John's, LJ Silver, Reuben's Café, Wendy's, **other:** Ace Hardware, Walgreen
17	I-65 S, US 12, US 20, Dunes Hwy, to Indianapolis
15	IN 53, to Gary, Broadway
14a	Grant St, to Gary, **S**...HOSPITAL
10	IN 912, Cline Ave, to Gary, **N**...casino
5	US 41, Calumet Ave, to Hammond, **S**...**gas:** Marathon, Speedway, **food:** Arby's, Aurelio's Pizza, Dunkin Donuts, Johnel's Rest., KFC, McDonald's, Taco Bell, White Castle, **lodging:** American Inn, Ramada Inn, Super 8, **other:** Aldi Foods, AutoZone, Murray's Parts, Walgreen
3	IN 912, Cline Ave, to Hammond, to Gary Reg Airport, **S**...**gas:** Shell
1mm	toll plaza
1mm	US 12, US 20, 106th St, Indianapolis Blvd, **N**...**gas:** BP/dsl/24hr, Mobil, Shell/dsl, **other:** casino, **S**...**food:** Burger King, Giappo's Pizza, KFC, McDonald's, **other:** Jewel-Osco
0mm	Indiana/Illinois state line

P o r t a g e

G a r y   A r e a

Interstate 94

E ↕ W

Exit #	Services
46mm	Indiana/Michigan state line
43mm	**Welcome Ctr wb, full(handicapped)facilities, info, phone, picnic tables, litter barrels, vending, petwalk**
40b a	US 20, US 35, to Michigan City, **N**...**food:** McDonald's(3mi), **other:** HOSPITAL, **S**...**gas:** Speedway/dsl

162

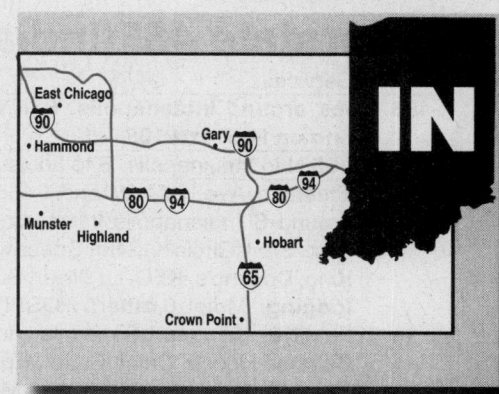

Interstate 94

E ↑ ↓ **W**	
34b a	US 421, to Michigan City, **N**...**gas:** BP/dsl, Citgo/dsl, Meijer/dsl/24hr, Speedway/White Castle/dsl, Xpress/gas, **food:** Applebee's, Arby's, Baker's Square, Bob Evans, Buffalo Wings, Burger King, Chili's, Culver's, Denny's, El Bracero Mexican, IHOP, KFC, LJ Silver, McDonald's, New China, Pizza Hut/Taco Bell, Popeye's, Quizno's, Red Lobster, Ryan's, Schoop's Rest., Starbucks, Steak'n Shake, Subway, Texas Corral, Wendy's, **lodging:** Comfort Inn, Country Inn Suites, Hampton Inn, Holiday Inn, Knight's Inn, Milan Inn, Red Roof Inn, Super 8, **other:** HOSPITAL, Aldi Foods, AutoZone, BigLots, $Tree, Fanny May Candies, Ford/Lincoln/Mercury, JC Penney, Jo-Ann Fabrics, Lowe's Whse, Meijer, Parts+, Radio Shack, Sears/auto, Walgreens, Wal-Mart/auto, **S**...**gas:** Gas City/Subway, **other:** Buick/Pontiac/GMC, Harley-Davidson
29mm	weigh sta both lanes
26b a	IN 49, Chesterton, **N**...to IN Dunes SP, **S**...**gas:** BP/White Castle, Shell/24hr, Speedway/dsl, **food:** Applebee's, A&W/KFC, Arby's, Burger King, China Chef, Cold Stone Creamery, Dunkin Donuts, El Salto Mexican, LJ Silver, McDonald's, Pizza Hut, Quizno's, Schoops Rest., Subway, Sunrise Rest., Taco Bell, Wendy's, **lodging:** Best Western, Econolodge, Hilton Garden(3mi), Super 8, **other:** Advance Parts, Curves, Jewel-Osco, K-Mart, Sand Cr Camping(5mi), Walgreens, to Valparaiso
22b a	US 20, Burns Harbor, **N**...**gas:** Steel City Express/scales/dsl, TA/Subway/Buckhorn Rest./scales/dsl/rest./24hr/@, **other:** Blue Beacon, **S**...**gas:** Mobil, Pilot/McDonald's/Subway/dsl/scales/24hr, **other:** Camp-Land RV Ctr, Chevrolet, Chrysler/Dodge/Jeep, Ford/Mercury, Toyota/Scion, fireworks
19	IN 249, to Port of IN, Portage, **N**...**gas:** Family Express/dsl, **food:** Hooters, Longhorn Steaks, **lodging:** Country Inn Suites, **other:** Bass Pro Shops, **S**...**gas:** Marathon/24hr, Shell, **food:** Denny's, Ryan's Rest., **lodging:** Best Value, Day's Inn, Dollar Inn, Hampton Inn, Super 8, **2 mi S**...**food:** Burger King, Subway, Wendy's
16	access to I-80/90 toll road E, I-90 toll road W, IN 51N, Ripley St, same as 15b&a
I-94/I-80 run together wb	
15b	US 6W, IN 51, **N**...**gas:** BP, Flying J/Cookery/scales/dsl/24hr/@, Road Ranger/Subway/dsl/scales/24hr, TA/BP/Subway/Popeye's/dsl/scales/24hr/@, **food:** McDonald's, **other:** Blue Beacon, **N on US 20**...**gas:** Dunes/scales/dsl repair, Marathon, **food:** Bayside Grill, Ponderosa, **other:** Parts+
15a	US 6E, IN 51S, to US 20, **S**...**gas:** Mobil/dsl, Road Ranger/Subway/scales/dsl, Shell, **food:** Burger King, DQ, Papa John's, LJ Silver, Reuben's Café, Wendy's, **other:** Ace Hardware, Walgreen
13	Central Ave(from eb)
12b	I-65 N, to Gary and toll road
12a	I-65 S(from wb), to Indianapolis

Portage (vertical label)

11	I-65 S(from eb)
10b a	IN 53, Broadway, **N**...**gas:** Citgo, Clark, **food:** JJ Fish, **S**...**gas:** Gas Depot, Mobil, **food:** DQ, Rally's
9	Grant St, **N**...**gas:** Clark, **food:** Chicago Hotdogs, **other:** Country Mkt Foods, Save-a-Lot Foods, Walgreens, **S**...**gas:** Citgo, Flying J/Cookery/scales/dsl/LP/24hr/@, Steel City/dsl/scales/rest./24hr, **food:** A&W/KFC, Burger King, Church's, Dunkin Donuts, J&J Fish, McDonald's, Subway, **other:** Aldi Foods, AutoZone, CarX, $Tree, Fagen Drug, Firestone/auto, Midas
6	Burr St, **N**...**gas:** BP/24hr, Pilot/Subway/dsl/scales/24hr/@, TA/Pizza Hut/Taco Bell/dsl/scales/24hr/@, **food:** J&J Fish & Chicken, Philly's Steaks, Rico's Pizza, **other:** SpeedCo, **S**...**gas:** Citgo/dsl/24hr
5	IN 912, Cline Ave, **S**...**gas:** BP, Clark, Marathon, Shell, Speedway/Subway, **food:** Arby's, DQ, Jedi's Garden Rest., KFC, McDonald's, Pizza Hut, Popeye's, White Castle, **lodging:** Hammond Inn, Motel 6, Super 8, **other:** $Tree, Fannie May Candies, K-Mart, Radio Shack
3	Kennedy Ave, **N**...**gas:** Clark, Mobil/dsl, Speedway, **food:** Burger King, Domino's, McDonald's, **other:** AutoCare, Walgreens, **S**...**gas:** Citgo, **food:** Cholie's Pizza, Cracker Barrel, Doggy Dog Grill, DQ, Firehouse Gyros, Squigi's Pizza, Subway, Wendy's, **lodging:** Courtyard, Fairfield Inn, Residence Inn, **other:** IN Welcome Ctr, Radio Shack, visitors ctr
2	US 41S, IN 152N, Indianapolis Blvd, **N**...**gas:** Gas Stop, Luke, SavAStop, Shell, **food:** Arby's, Dunkin Donuts/Baskin-Robbins, House Of Pizza, Papa John's, Ralley's, Schoop's Burgers, Wheel Rest., Woodmar Rest., **other:** CarEx, Goodyear, Midas, vet, **S**...**gas:** Pilot/scales/dsl/24hr, **lodging:** AmeriHost, **other:** Cabela's
1	US 41N, Calumet Ave, **N**...**gas:** BP/dsl, Gas Mart/dsl, **food:** Barton's Pizza, Dunkin Donuts/Baskin-Robbins, Subway, **other:** Walgreens, **S**...**gas:** BP, Mobil/dsl, Marathon, Shell, **food:** Arby's, Boston Mkt, Burger King, Canton House Chinese, Dunkin Donuts/Baskin-Robbins, Edwardo's Pizza, Fortune House, Munster Gyros, Quizno's, Taco Bell, Wendy's, **other:** CVS Drug, $Jct, Radio Shack, Staples, Target
0mm	Indiana/Illinois state line

Gary Area (vertical label)

INDIANA

Interstate 465(Indianapolis)

Exit #	Services
	I-465 loops around Indianapolis. Exit numbers begin/ end on I-65, exit 108.
53b a	I-65 N to Indianapolis, S to Louisville
52	Emerson Ave, I-74 W and I-465 S run together around S Indianapolis 21 miles., **N...gas:** Marathon, Shell/Circle K, 24hr, Speedway, **food:** Burger King, Domino's, KFC, LJ Silver, Subway, Taco Bell, **lodging:** Motel 6,**other:** HOSPITAL, CVS Drug, Family$, **S...gas:** Speedway/dsl, **food:** Arby's, Bamboo House, China Buffet, Egg Roll, El Puerto, Fazoli's, Fujiyama, Hardee's, McDonald's, Papa John's, Pizza Hut, Ponderosa, Rally's, RibHouse, Steak'n Shake, Subway, White Castle/24hr, Wendy's, **lodging:** Holiday Inn, Red Roof Inn, Super 8, **other:** Advance Parts, AutoZone, Curves, Goodyear/auto, K-Mart, Marsh Foods, NAPA, Radio Shack, Walgreens, Wal-Mart SuperCtr/24hr, vet
	I-74 W and I-465 S run together around S Indianapolis 21 mi
49	I-74 E, US 421 S
48	Shadeland Ave(from nb)
47	US 52 E, Brookville Rd, **E...gas:** Shell, **food:** Burger King
46	US 40, Washington St, **E...gas:** Marathon, **food:** Arby's, China Buffet, Italian Garden, Old Country Buffet, Perkins, Steak'n Shake, Subway, **other:** Ford, Osco Drug, Target, **W...gas:** Thornton's, **food:** Applebee's, Burger King, Bob Evans,'s, Don Pablo, Fazoli's, McDonald's, Pizza Hut, Pi's Chinese, Wendy's, **lodging:** Signature Inn, **other:** K-Mart, PepBoys, Pontiac/GM/Mazda, Suzuki
44b	I-70 E, to Columbus
44a	I-70 W, to Indianapolis
42	US 36, IN 67 N, Pendleton Pike, **E...food:** Bennigan's, Hardee's, Papa's Rest., Popeye's, **lodging:** Knight's Inn, Ramada Inn, **W...gas:** Speedway, Thornton's, **food:** A&W/KFC, Arby's, Denny's, Domino's, LJ Silver, Los Ranchero's, McDonald's, Pizza Hut/Taco Bell, Subway, Waffle House, White Castle, **other:** HOSPITAL, Advance Parts, CVS Drug, Family$, K-Mart/gas, O'Reilly Parts
40	56th St, Shadeland Ave, **E...gas:** Marathon, to Ft Harrison
37b a	I-69, N to Ft Wayne, IN 37, **W...other:** HOSPITAL, services on frontage rds
35	Allisonville Rd, **N...food:** Applebee's, Hardee's, LJ Silver, McDonald's, MCL Cafeteria, Outback Steaks, Smokey Bones BBQ, **lodging:** Courtyard, **other:** Best Buy, Firestone/auto, Kohl's, Marshall's, mall, **S...gas:** Shell, Speedway/dsl, **food:** Bob Evans, ChuckeCheese, Papa John's, Perkins/24hr, White Castle, **lodging:** Jameson Inn, **other:** Circuit City, Kroger, TJ Maxx, **S on 82nd...food:** China Buffet, Panera Bread, **other:** Marsh Foods
33	IN 431, Keystone Ave, **N...gas:** BP/McDonald's, Marathon/dsl, Shell, **food:** Arby's, Bob Evans, Burger King, Subway, **lodging:** Motel 6, **other:** BMW/Mini, Ford, Infiniti, KIA, Toyota/Scion, **S...food:** Champp's, Cooker, Keystone Grill, **lodging:** AmeriSuites, Marriott, Sheraton, Westin Suites, **other:** Kohl's, mall,
31	US 31, Meridian St, **N...lodging:** Courtyard, Signature Inn, Wyndham Garden, **other:** HOSPITAL, Cadillac, **S...gas:** Marathon, Shell/dsl, **food:** Arby's, McDonald's **other:** Kroger
27	US 421 N, Michigan Rd, **N...gas:** Speedway/dsl, **food:** Applebee's, McDonald's, Subway, **lodging:** Country Inn& Suites, Red Roof Inn, **other:** Chevrolet, Marshalls, Pontiac/GMC, Target, **S...gas:** BP, Marathon, Shell, Sunoco, **food:** Arby's, Bob Evans, Boston Mkt, Burger King, Chic-fil-a, China Buffet, Denny's, IHOP, Max&Erma's, O'Charley's, Outback Steaks, Pizza Hut, Qdoba Mexican, Rally's, Ruby Tuesday, Schlosky's, Steak'n Shake, Subway, Taco Bell, Texas Roadhouse, Wendy's, White Castle, Yen Ching Rest., **lodging:** Best Western, Comfort Inn, $Inn, Drury Inn, Embassy Suites, Extended Stay America, Fairfield Inn, Holiday Inn Select, HomeGate Inn, InTown Suites, La Quinta, Microtel, Quality Inn, Residence Inn, Signature Inn, Super 8, Wellesley Inn, **other:** Aamco, Aldi Foods, Costco/gas, Cub Foods, CVS Drug, Discount Tire, $General, $Tree, Firestone, Lowe's Whse, Office Depot, PepBoys, Radio Shack, Staples, Wal-Mart SuperCtr/24hr
25	I-465 W
23	86th St, **E...gas:** Shell/24hr, Speedway, **food:** Atlanta Bread, Arby's, Burger King, Chili's, Macaroni Grill, Longhorn Steaks, Quizno's, Traders Mill Grill, Wendy's, **lodging:** Fairfield Inn, Homestead Suites, Intown Suites, **other:** HOSPITAL, Big O Tires, Marsh Foods, Michaels, Old Navy
21	71st St, **E...gas:** BP, **food:** Bob Evans, Hardee's, LePeep Rest, Max&Erma's, McDonald's, Quizno's, Starbucks, Steak'n Shake, Subway, **lodging:** Clarion Inn, Courtyard, Hampton Inn, Wingate Inn, **W... food:** Bob Evans, Wendy's **lodging:** Residence Inn, Wingate Inn,
20	I-65, N to Chicago, S to Indianapolis
19	56th St(from nb), **E...gas:** Citgo/7-11, Speedway/ dsl
17	38th St, **E...gas:** BP, Marathon, Shell/24hr, **food:** Costa Brava, DQ, Golden Corral, Hooters, LJ Silver, Olive Garden, Ponderosa, Steak&Shake, Subway, White Castle, **lodging:** Day's Inn, Red Carpet Inn, **other:** AutoZone, CVS Drug, $Tree, Family$, Ford, Home Depot, Kroger/gas, O'Reilly Parts, Walgreens, **W...food:** Arby's, Burger King, Chili's, Cracker Barrel, Don Pablo, McDonald's, Pizza Hut/Taco Bell, Ruby Tuesday, TGIFriday, **lodging:** Ramada Ltd, Jameson Inn, **other:** Marsh Foods, Target

Interstate 465

I-74 W and I-465 S run together around S Indianapolis 21 mi

16b	I-74 W, to Peoria
16a	US 136, to Speedway, N...**gas:** Bigfoot, BP, Shell, **food:** Applebee's, Arby's, Blimpie, Buffalo Wild Wings, Burger King, Circle K/gas, Denny's, Hardee's, KFC, LJ Silver, McDonald's, Subway, Taco Bell, Wendy's, White Castle, **lodging:** $Inn, Motel 6, Red Roof, Super 8, **other:** $General, Firestone, Kroger, Marsh Foods, S...**lodging:** Clarion
14b a	10th St, N...**food:** Peking Chinese, Penn Station, Pizza Hut, Wendy's, **other:** HOSPITAL, Lowe's Whse, S...**gas:** GA/Subway, Shell, Speedway/24hr, **food:** Arby's, Fazoli's, Hardee's, McDonald's, Taco Bell, **other:** CVS Drug
13b a	US 36, Rockville Rd, N...**gas:** Marathon/Burger King, **lodging:** Comfort Inn, Sleep Inn, Wingate Inn, **other:** Sam's Club, S...**gas:** Speedway/dsl/24hr, **food:** Bob Evans, **lodging:** Best Western
12b a	US 40 E, Washington St, N...**food:** Burger King, China Buffet, Church's, Fazoli's, McDonald's, Papa John's, Taco Bell, White Castle, **other:** Ace Hardware, Advance Parts, AutoZone, CVS Drug, $Tree, Family$, Kroger/gas, Speedway Parts, U-Haul, Walgreens, transmissions, vet, S...**gas:** Marathon/Circle K, Phillips 66/Noble Roman's/dsl, Thornton/24hr, **food:** Arby's, Hardee's, KFC, LJ Silver, McDonald's, Pizza Hut, Steak'n Shake, **lodging:** $Inn, **other:** Aamco, Goodyear, K-Mart, Sav-A-Lot Foods, TireBarn
11b a	Airport Expressway, E...**gas:** Marathon, **food:** Denny's, Indy's Rest., Waffle House, **lodging:** Adam's Mark Hotel, Amerisuites, Courtyard, Day's Inn, Extended Stay Deluxe, Fairfield Inn, La Quinta, Quality Inn, Ramada Inn, Residence Inn, W...**lodging:** Holiday Inn Select, Radisson
9b a	I-70, E to Indianapolis, W to Terre Haute
8	IN 67 S, Kentucky Ave, E...HOSPITAL, W...**gas:** BP/McDonald's/dsl, Marathon, Swifty, Speedway, Shell, Subway, **food:** Big Boy, Burger King, Culver's, Damon's, Denny's, Hardee's, KFC, **lodging:** Country Inn&Suites
7	Mann Rd(from wb), N...HOSPITAL
4	IN 37 S, Harding St, N...**gas:** Mr Fuel/dsl, Pilot/Subway/dsl/scales/24hr/@, **food:** Omelette Shoppe, **lodging:** Best Inn, Econolodge, **other:** HOSPITAL, Blue Beacon, S...**gas:** ✈/Flying J/Conoco/dsl/LP/rest./scales/24hr/@, Marathon, **food:** Hardee¿½s, McDonald's, Taco Bell, White Castle, **lodging:** Knight's Inn, **other:** Freightliner, SpeedCo, Truck'o Mat/scales
2b a	US 31, IN 37, N...**gas:** BP/24hr, **food:** Arby's, CiCi's, Domino's, DQ, Golden Wok, KFC, King Gyro's, LJ Silver, McDonald's, MCL Cafeteria, Old Country Buffet, Pizza Hut, Steak&Ale, Steak'n Shake, White Castle, **other:** Aldi Foods, AutoTire, AutoWorks, AutoZone, Chrysler/Jeep, Dodge, $General, Family$, Firestone, Ford, Goodyear, Hancock Fabrics, Jo-Ann Fabrics, Jiffy Lube, Kroger/gas, Lincoln/Mercury, Office Depot, Osco Drug, Radio Shack, Save-A-Lot, Target, U-Haul, S...**gas:** Speedway, **food:** Bob Evans, Denny's, 8Lucky Buffet, McDonald's, Red Lobster, Taco Bell, Wendy's, **lodging:** Best Value Inn, Comfort Inn, Day's Inn, Holiday Inn Express, Super 8, Travelodge, **other:** CVS Drug
53b a	I-65 N to Indianapolis, S to Louisville, no services

I-465 loops around Indianapolis. Exit numbers begin/end on I-65, exit 108.

Interstate 469(Ft Wayne)

Exit #	Services
31c b a	I-69, US 27 S., Auburn Road. I-469 begins/ends.
29.15mm	St Joseph River
29b a	Maplecrest Rd, W...**gas:** BP/DQ/Subway/dsl, **food:** Mozzarelli's Pizza, Sonic, **other:** Marsh Foods
25	IN 37, to Ft Wayne, W...**gas:** Meijer/dsl/24hr, **food:** Antonio's Pizza, Applebee's, Bob Evans, Buffalo Wild Wings, Cracker Barrel, Golden Corral, HoneyBee Chinese, McDonald's, Steak'n Shake, Subway, Wendy's, Uno Pizzaria, **other:** Discount Tire, Kohls, Marshall's, Office Depot, Walgreens, Wal-Mart SuperCtr/gas/24hr
21	US 24 E, no services
19b a	US 30 E, to Ft Wayne, E...**gas:** Sunoco/Taco Bell/dsl, **other:** truck/tire repair, W...**gas:** Citgo/dsl/mart, **food:** Garno's Italian, Golden Gate Chinese, Mancino's Grinders, Richard's Rest., Zesto Drive-In, **lodging:** Holiday Inn Express, **other:** Curves, $General
17	Minnich Rd, no services
15	Tillman Rd, no services
13	Marion Center Rd, no services
11	US 27, US 33 S, to Decatur, Ft Wayne, E...**gas:** BP/Subway/dsl
10.5mm	St Marys River
9	Winchester Rd, no services
6	IN 1, to Bluffton, Ft Wayne, W...to airport
2	Indianapolis Rd, W...to airport
1	Lafayette Ctr Rd

N

↑

↓

S

Indianapolis Area

Ft Wayne

IOWA
Interstate 29

Sioux City

Exit #	Services
152mm	Iowa/South Dakota state line, Big Sioux River
151	IA 12 N, Riverside Blvd, **E**...**gas:** Casey's, **other:** $General, Fareway Foods, Riverside Prk, to Stone SP, Pecaut Nature Ctr
149	Hamilton Blvd, **E**...**gas:** Conoco, **food:** Horizon Rest, **lodging:** Quality Inn, **other:** JiffyLube, tires, to Briar Cliff Coll, **W**...**Iowa Welcome Ctr sb, full facilities**, Riverboat Museum
148	US 77 S, to S Sioux City, Nebraska, **W**...**gas:** Conoco/dsl, **food:** DQ, La Fiesta Mexican, McDonald's, Pizza Hut, Taco Bell, **lodging:** Marina Inn, Regency Inn, **other:** Advance Parts, O'Reilly Parts
147b	US 20 bus, Sioux City, **E**...**gas:** Heritage Gas, **food:** Arby's, Burger King, Chili's, Famous Dave's, Hardee's, IHOP, KFC, Perkins/24hr, **lodging:** Best Western, Clarion, Holiday Inn/rest, Marina Inn, **other:** HOSPITAL, Chevrolet, Staples, USPO, Walgreen
147a	Floyd Blvd, **E**...**gas:** Shamrock, **other:** Home Depot, **W**...to Riverboat Casino
146mm	Floyd River
144b	I-129 W, US 20 W, US 75 S
144a	US 20 E, US 75 N, to Ft Dodge, **1 mi E on Lakeport Rd**...**gas:** Casey's, Shell, **food:** Buffalo Wild Wings, Burger King, ChuckeCheese, Coyote Canyon Steaks, Garfield's Rest, Gordman's, Hardee's, HuHot Chinese, Jimmy John's, KFC, LJ Silver/A&W, McDonald's, Olive Garden, Outback Steaks, Pizza Hut, Red Lobster, Red Robin, Starbucks, Tuesday Morning, Village Inn, **lodging:** Comfort Inn, Fairfield Inn, Hampton Inn, Holiday Inn Express, **other:** Barnes&Noble, Best Buy, Buick/Honda/Isuzu, Hy-Vee Foods/gas/24hr, JC Penny, JiffyLube, Jo-Ann Fabrics/crafts, Kohls, Lowe's Whse, Michael's, Old Navy, PetsMart, Sears/auto, Target, Younkers, mall
143	US 75 N, Singing Hills Blvd, **E**...**gas:** Cenex/dsl, Shell/dsl/motel/café/24hr/@, **food:** China Buffet, Culver's, KFC, McDonald's, Pizza Hut, Quizno's, Taco John's, **lodging:** AmericInn, Baymont Inn, Day's Inn, Haven Motel, **other:** Caddilac/Pontiac/GMC, Lincoln/Mercury, Sam's Club/gas, Toyota/Scion, Wal-Mart SuperCtr/gas/24hr, Sgt Floyd Mon, **W**...**gas:** BP/dsl/motel/café/24hr/@, **food:** Wendy's, **lodging:** Super 8, **other:** Kenworth/Peterbilt, truckwash/repair
141	D38, Sioux Gateway Airport, **E**...**gas:** Phillips 66/dsl, Shell/dsl, **food:** Aggies Ranch, China Taste, DQ, Godfather's, Pizza Ranch, Subway, **lodging:** Econolodge, **other:** Curves, mall, **W**...**lodging:** Motel 6, **other:** airport, museum
139mm	**rest area both lanes, full(handicapped) facilities, phone, info, picnic tables, litter barrels, RV dump, wireless internet**
135	Port Neal Landing, no services
134	Salix, **E**...gas, **W**...camping
132mm	weigh sta sb, rest area nb, picnic tables, litter barrels, no services
127	IA 141, Sloan, **E**...**gas:** Shell/dsl, **food:** B&R Pizza, **lodging:** Rip Van Winkle Motel, WinnaVegas Inn, **3 mi W**...**gas:** Heritage Express, **other:** to Winnebago Indian Res/casino

Council Bluffs

Exit #	Services
120	to Whiting, **W**...camping
112	IA 175, Onawa, **E**...gas: Conoco/Subway/dsl/@, Phillips 66/dsl, **food:** DQ, Janz Rest., McDonald's, Michael's Rest., Pizza Hut, **lodging:** Super 8, **other:** HOSPITAL, NAPA, On-Ur-Wa RV Park, Pamida, 2 mi **W**...**other:** KOA, Lewis&Clark SP, Keel Boat Exhibit
110mm	**rest area both lanes, full(handicapped)facilities, phone, info, picnic tables, litter barrels, petwalk, RV dump, wireless internet**
105	E60, Blencoe, no services
96mm	Little Sioux River
95	IA 301, Little Sioux, **E**...gas, **other:** Loess Hills SF(9mi), **W**...Woodland RV Camp
92mm	Soldier River
91.5mm	**rest area both lanes, litter barrels, no services**
89	IA 127, Mondamin, **1 mi E**...**gas:** Jiffy Mart/dsl
82	F50, Modale, **1 mi W**...**gas:** Cenex/dsl
79mm	**rest area both lanes, full(handicapped)facilities, info, phone, picnic tables, litter barrels, RV dump, wireless internet**
75	US 30, Missouri Valley, **E**...**Iowa Welcome Ctr(5mi)**, **gas:** Shell/dsl/24hr, **food:** Arby's, McDonald's, Penny's Diner, Subway, **lodging:** Oaktree Inn, **other:** HOSPITAL(2mi), to Steamboat Exhibit, **W**...**gas:** BP/dsl, Phillips 66/rest/dsl, **food:** Burger King, Taco John's, **lodging:** Day's Inn, Rath Inn, Super 8, **other:** Chevrolet/Pontiac/Buick, Chrysler/Jeep/Dodge
73.5mm	weigh sta both lanes
72.5mm	Boyer River
72	IA 362, Loveland, **E**...**gas:** Conoco/dsl, **W**...to Wilson Island SP(6mi)
71	I-680 E, to Des Moines. **I-29 S & I-680 W run together 10 mi.**
66	Honey Creek, **W**...**gas:** Sinclair/dsl, **food:** Iowa Feed&Grain Co Rest.
61b	I-680 W, to N Omaha, **I-29 N & I-680 E run together 10 mi, W**...Mormon Trail Ctr
61a	IA 988, to Crescent, **E**...**gas:** Phillips 66/dsl, **other:** to ski area
56	IA 192 S(sb only, exits left), Council Bluffs, **E**...**lodging:** Super 7 Inn, **other:** HOSPITAL
55	N 25th, Council Bluffs, **E**...**gas:** Pump'n Munch/dsl, Sinclair/24hr
54b	N 35th St(from nb), Council Bluffs, **E on Broadway**...**gas:** Bucky's Express, Phillips 66/dsl, Sinclair, **food:** Arby's, Burger King, Popeye's, Sonic, Wendy's, **lodging:** Quality Inn
54a	G Ave(from sb), Council Bluffs
53b	I-480 W, US 6, to Omaha
53a	9th Ave, S 37th Ave, Council Bluffs, **E**...**gas:** Shell, Valero, **food:** Red Onion Cafe, **lodging:** Day's Inn, **W**...**other:** Harrah's Casino/hotel, RiverBoat Casino, camping
52	Nebraska Ave, **E**...**gas:** Phillips 66/dsl, **food:** Quaker Steak, Ruby Tuesday, **lodging:** Comfort Suites, SpringHill Suites, **other:** Bass Pro Shop, **W**...**lodging:** AmeriStar Hotel/casino, Hampton Inn, Holiday Inn, **other:** RiverBoat Casino
51	I-80 W, to Omaha
	I-29 and I-80 run together 3 miles. See Iowa Interstate 80, exits 1b-3.
48	I-80 E(from nb), to Des Moines, **E**...HOSPITAL

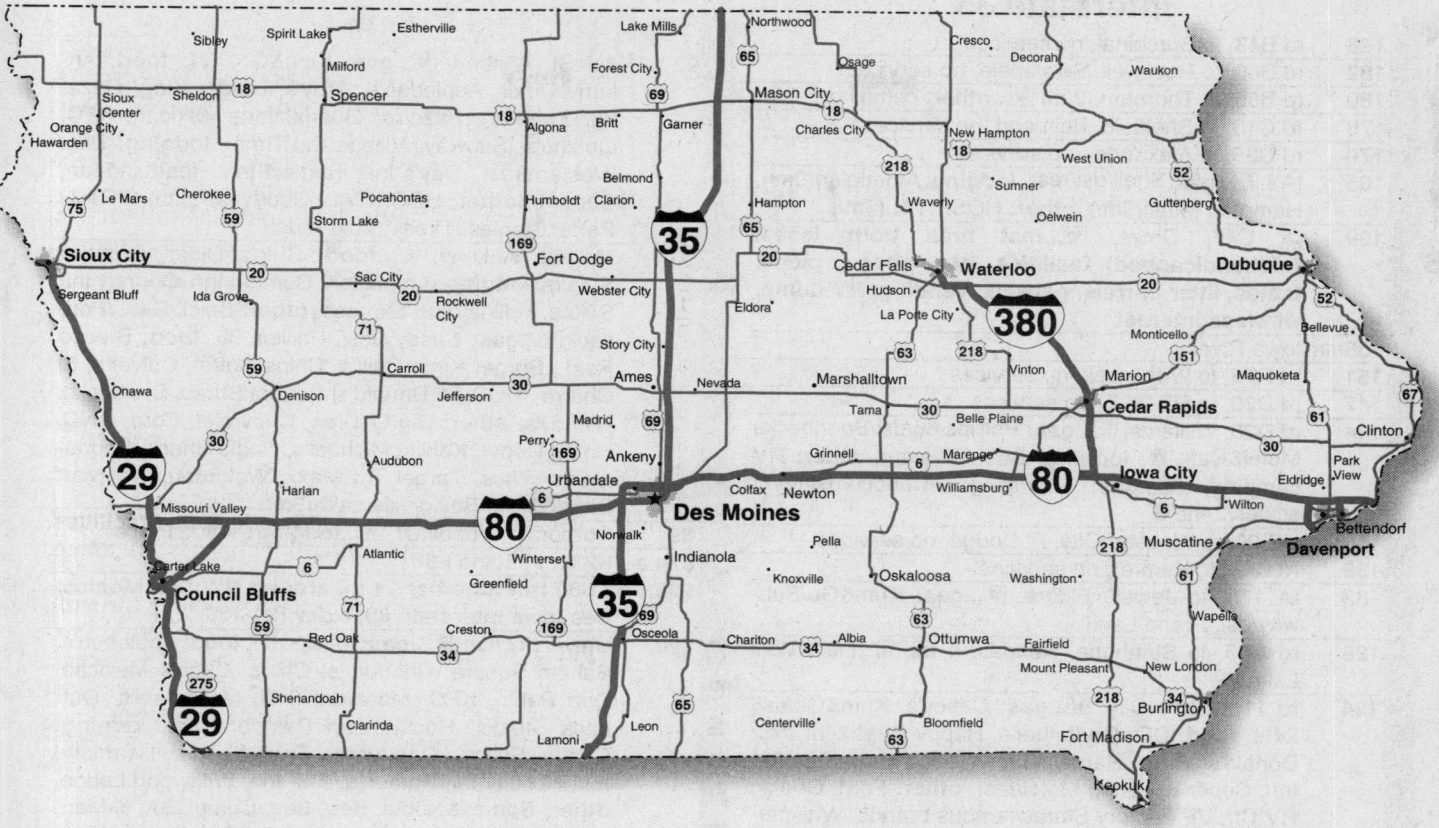

Interstate 29

47	US 275, IA 92, Lake Manawa, **E**...**gas:** Phillips 66, **other:** Iowa School for the Deaf, **W**...**gas:** Ampride
42	IA 370, to Bellevue, **W**...**other:** K&B Saddlery, to Offutt AFB, camping
38mm	**rest area both lanes, full(handicapped) facilities, phone, info, picnic tables, litter barrels, RV dump, petwalk, wireless internet**
35	US 34 E, to Glenwood, **E**...**lodging:** Western Inn(4mi), **other:** RV Park, **W**...**gas:** BP/dsl, **lodging:** Bluff View Motel, **other:** Ford, Harley Davidson
32	US 34 W, Pacific Jct, to Plattsmouth, no services
24	L31, to Tabor, Bartlett, no services
20	IA 145, Thurman, no services
15	J26, Percival, **1-2 mi E**...**gas:** BP/dsl
11.5mm	weigh sta nb
10	IA 2, to Nebraska City, Sidney, **E**...to Waubonsie SP(5mi), **W**...**gas:** BP/Sapp/rest./dsl/scales/24hr, Phillips 66/dsl, Shell/Subway/Crossroads Cafe/dsl/scales/24hr, **food:** Wendy's, **lodging:** Best Value, Super 8, **other:** to Arbor Lodge SP, Victorian Acres Camping(4mi), tire repair
1	IA 333, Hamburg, **1 mi E**...**gas:** Casey's/dsl, **food:** Pizza Hut, **lodging:** Hamburg Motel, **other:** HOSPITAL, Soda Fountain
0mm	Iowa/Missouri state line

Interstate 35

Exit #	Services
219mm	Iowa/Minnesota state line
214	rd 105, to Northwood, Lake Mills, **W**...**Welcome Ctr both lanes, full(handicapped)facilities, picnic tables, litter barrels, vending, petwalk, RV dump, gas:** BP/Burger King/dsl, **lodging:** Country Inn Suites, Royal Motel(7mi), **other:** casino
212mm	weigh sta sb, rest area nb, picnic tables, litter barrels, no services
208	rd A38, to Joice, Kensett, **W**...windmills
203	IA 9, to Manly, Forest City, to Pilot Knob SP
202mm	Winnebago River
197	rd B20, **8 mi E**...Lime Creek Nature Ctr
196mm	**rest area both lanes, picnic tables, litter barrels, no services**
194	US 18, to Mason City, Clear Lake, **E**...**gas:** BP/dsl, **other:** HOSPITAL(8mi), Chevrolet, Freightliner, truck repair, **W**...**gas:** Casey's, Pilot/Subway/dsl/scales, Kum&Go, Shell/Wendy's/dsl, **food:** Arby's, Bennigan's, Burger King, Culver's, Denny's, DQ, KFC/Taco Bell, McDonald's, Perkins/24hr, Pizza Hut, Rice House Chinese, Subway, **lodging:** AmericInn, Best Western/rest., Budget Inn, Microtel
193	rd B35, to Mason City, Emery, **E**...**gas:** Kum&Go/dsl, **lodging:** Super 8, **other:** truckwash, **W**...**other:** Ford, to Clear Lake SP
190	US 18, rd 27 E, to Mason City, no services

Clear Lake

IOWA

Interstate 35

N ↕ S

Exit	Description
188	rd B43, to Burchinal, no services
182	rd B60, to Rockwell, Swaledale, no services
180	rd B65, to Thornton, **2 mi** W...**other:** camping
176	rd C13, to Sheffield, Belmond, no services
170	rd C25, to Alexander, no services
165	IA3, E...**gas:** Shell/dsl/rest., **lodging:** AmericInn(9mi), Hampton Motel(9mi), **other:** HOSPITAL(7mi)
159	rd C47, Dows, W...**rest area both lanes, full(handicapped) facilities info, phone, picnic tables, litter barrels, petwalk, vending, RV dump, wireless internet**
155mm	Iowa River
151	rd R75, to Woolstock, no services
147	rd D20, to US 20 E, no services
144	rd D25, Williams, E...**gas:** Phillips 66/dsl/Boondocks Motel&Cafe/@, **lodging:** Best Western, **other:** RV camping, W...**gas:** ⊕/Flying J/Conoco/dsl/rest./scales/24hr/@
142b a	US 20, to Webster City, Ft Dodge, no services
139	rd D41, to Kamrar, no services
133	IA 175, to Jewell, Eldora, W...**gas:** Kum&Go/Subway/dsl, Prarie Land
128	rd D65, to Stanhope, Randall, **5 mi** W...Little Wall Lake Pk
124	rd 115, Story City, W...**gas:** Casey's, Kum&Go/dsl/24hr, **food:** DQ, Godfather's, Happy Chef/24hr, McDonald's, Pizza Ranch, Subway, **lodging:** Comfort Inn, Super 8, Viking Motel/rest, **other:** Ford, Gookin RV Ctr, VF Factory Stores/famous brands, Whispering Oaks Camping
123	rd E18, to Roland, McCallsburg, no services
120mm	**rest area nb, full(handicapped)facilities, info, phone, picnic tables, litter barrels, vending, wireless internet, RV dump/scenic prairie area sb**
119mm	**rest area sb, full(handicapped)facilities, phone, picnic tables, litter barrels, vending, wireless internet, RV dump**
116	rd E29, to Story, **2 mi** W...Story Co Conservation Ctr
113	13th St, Ames, W...**gas:** BP/Arby's/dsl, Kum&Go/Burger King/dsl, **food:** Buford's Steaks, Starlite Village Rest., **lodging:** Holiday Inn Express, Quality Inn, **other:** HOSPITAL, Harley-Davidson, to USDA Vet Labs, ISU
111b a	US 30, to Nevada, Ames, E...Twin Acres Campground(11mi), W...**gas:** Kum&Go/DQ/Subway/dsl, Shell/dsl/rest./@, **food:** Azteca Mexican, **lodging:** AmericInn, Comfort Inn, Country Inn Suites, Fairfield Inn, Hampton Inn, Heartland Inn, Microtel, Super 8, **other:** to IA St U
109mm	S Skunk River
106mm	weigh sta both lanes
102	IA 210, to Slater, **3 mi** W...**food:** DQ, Subway
96	to Elkhart, W...to Big Creek SP(11mi), Saylorville Lake
94mm	**rest area both lanes, full(handicapped) facilities, info, phone, picnic tables, litter barrels, vending, petwalk, wireless internet**

Ames

Exit	Description
92	1st St, Ankeny, W...**gas:** Kum&Go, QT, **food:** Ankeny Diner, Applebee's, Arby's, Burger King, Cazador Mexican, Fazoli's, Guadalajara Mexican, KFC, Quizno's, Subway, Village Inn Rest., **lodging:** Best Western/rest., Day's Inn, Fairfield Inn, Heartland Inn, Super 8, **other:** HOSPITAL, Goodyear/auto, O'Reilly Parts, Staples, Tires+, auto repair
90	IA 160, Ankeny, E...**food:** Chip's Diner, Outback Steaks, **lodging:** AmericInn, Comfort Inn, Country Inn Suites, Holiday Inn Express, **other:** Buick/GMC/Pontiac, W...**gas:** Casey's/dsl, Phillips 66, **food:** B-bops Rest., Burger King, Chili's, China Buffet, Culver's, El Charro, IHOP, McDonald's, Panera Bread, Starbucks, Wendy's, **other:** Big O Tires, Chevrolet, Ford, GNC, Home Depot, Kohl's, Michael's, Radio Shack, Sportsman's Whse, Target, TJ Maxx, Walgreen, Wal-Mart SuperCtr, to Saylorville Lake(5mi)
89	Corporate Woods Dr, W...**lodging:** Value Place
87b a	I-235, I-35 and I-80
	I-35 and I-80 run together 14 mi around NW Des Moines. See Iowa Interstate 80, exits 124-136.
72c	University Ave, E...**gas:** Phillips 66, **food:** Applebee's, Bakers Square, Cheddar's, Chili's, Cuco's Mexican, Don Pablo, KFC, Macaroni Grill, McDonald's, Outback Steaks, RockBottom Rest./brewery, **lodging:** Chase Suites, Courtyard, Fairfield Inn, Heartland Inn, Holiday Inn/Damon's, The Inn, Wildwood Lodge, **other:** Barnes&Noble, Best Buy, CompUSA, K-Mart, Kohl's, Lowe's Whse, Marshall's, SportMart, World Mkt, W...**gas:** Amoco, Kum&Go/Burger King, QT, **food:** Cracker Barrel, **lodging:** Baymont Inn, Best Western, Country Inn Suites, **other:** HOSPITAL
72b	I-80 W
72a	I-235 E, to Des Moines
70	Civic Pkwy, Mills, E...**gas:** Kum&Go/McDonald's, HyVee/dsl, **food:** Firecreek Grill, Legend's Grill, Quizno's, **other:** HyVee Foods, Walgreen, W...**food:** Applebees, BoneFish Grill, Caribou Coffee, Fuddruckers, Iron Wok, Joseph's Steaks, O'Charly's, Red Robin, **lodging:** Holiday Inn, **other:** Best Buy, Dillards, PetCo, Target, TJ Maxx, Wal-Mart SuperCtr
69b a	Grand Ave, W Des Moines, no services
68.5mm	Racoon River
68	IA 5, **7 mi** E...to airport, to Walnut Woods SP
65	G14, to Norwalk, Cumming, **14 mi** W...John Wayne Birthplace, Madison Co Museum
61mm	North River
56	IA 92, to Indianola, Winterset, W...**gas:** Kum&Go/cafe/dsl, Shamrock/dsl, **food:** Hitchin Post Grill
56mm	Middle River
53mm	**rest area nb, litter barrels, no services**
52	G50, St Charles, St Marys, W...**gas:** Kum&Go, **other, 14 mi:** John Wayne Birthplace, museum
51mm	**rest area sb, litter barrels, no services**
47	rd G64, to Truro, W...**gas:** Kum&Go(1mi)
45.5mm	South River
43	rd 207, New Virginia, E...**gas:** Kum&Go/Subway/dsl

Des Moines

IOWA

Interstate 35

36	rd 152, to US 69, **3 mi** E**...lodging:** Blue Haven Motel, Evergreen Inn, W**...**st patrol
34	Clay St, Osceola, W**...gas:** Kum&Go, **food:** Maid-Rite Cafe, **other:** Lakeside Casino Resort/camping
33	US 34, Osceola, E**...gas:** Casey's/dsl, Shell/rest., **food:** Family Table Rest., McDonald's, Pizza Hut, Subway, **lodging:** Regal Inn, Day's Inn, Super 8, **other:** HOSPITAL, Ford, Chrysler/Dodge/Jeep, Hy-Vee Foods, O'Reilly Parts, Pamida, st patrol, tires, W**...gas:** BP/Arby's/dsl, **food:** KFC/Taco Bell, **lodging:** AmericInn, **other:** Wal-Mart SuperCtr
32mm	**rest area both lanes, full(handicapped)facilities, phone, picnic tables, litter barrels, vending, petwalk, RV dump, wireless internet**
31mm	weigh sta nb, parking area sb
29	rd H45, no services
22	rd J14, Van Wert, no services
18	rd J20, to Grand River, no services
12	rd 2, Decatur City, Leon, E**...gas:** Shell/dsl/rest, **food:** Country Corner Rest., **5 mi** E**...lodging:** Little River Motel, **other:** HOSPITAL
7.5mm	Grand River
7mm	**Welcome Ctr nb/rest area sb, full(handicapped) facilities, info, phone, picnic tables, litter barrels, vending, petwalk, RV dump, wireless internet**
4	US 69, to Davis City, Lamoni, E**...**to 9 Eagles SP(10mi), W**...gas:** Casey's(2mi), **food:** Pizza Hut(2mi), QC Rest, Subway(2mi), **lodging:** Chief Lamoni Motel, Super 8, **other:** CarQuest, auto/truck repair, antiques, IA Welcome Ctr
0mm	Iowa/Missouri state line

Interstate 80

Exit #	Services
307mm	Iowa/Illinois state line, Mississippi River
306	US 67, to Le Claire, N**...Welcome Ctr wb (no trucks), full(handicapped)facilities, picnic tables, litter barrels, phone, petwalk, gas:** Phillips 66/dsl, **food:** Subway, **lodging:** Comfort Inn, Holiday Inn Express, Super 8, **other:** Slagle Foods, **1 mi** N**...gas:** BP, **food:** A&W(2mi), **other:** Buffalo Bill Museum, S**...gas:** BP/dsl
301	Middle Rd, to Bettendorf, no services
300mm	**rest area both lanes, full(handicapped) facilities, phone, picnic tables, litter barrels, vending, petwalk, RV dump**
298	I-74 E, to Peoria, S**...other:** to HOSPITAL, st patrol
295b a	US 61, Brady St, to Davenport, N**...gas:** BP, **other:** Hummer, to Scott CP, S**...gas:** BP, Shell, **food:** Country Kitchen, Cracker Barrel, Hardees, ThunderBay Grille, Village Inn Rest., **lodging:** AmericInn, Best Western/rest., Baymont Inn, Casa Loma Suites, Country Inn&Suites, Day's Inn, Exel Inn, Heartland Inn, Motel 6, Residence Inn, Super 8, **1-2 mi** S**...gas:** Shell, **food:** Burger King, Happy Joe's, LoneStar Steaks, McDonald's, Rudy's Tacos, **lodging:** Clarion, **other:** AutoZone, Acura, $General, Dodge, Sears/auto, Toyota, mall, vet
292	IA 130 W, Northwest Blvd, N**...gas:** ⚡/Flying J/Phillips 66/Cookery/dsl/LP/rest./scales/24hr/@, **lodging:** Comfort Inn, **other:** Interstate RV Park(1mi),

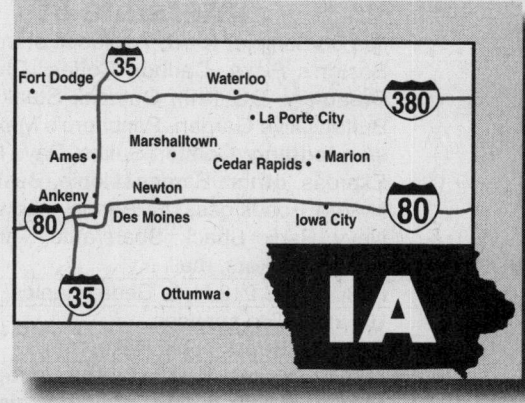

	Farm&Fleet, Peterbilt, truckwash, waterpark, S**...gas:** BP/McDonald's, Sinclair, **food:** Machine Shed Rest., **lodging:** Econolodge
290	I-280 E, to Rock Island
284	Y40, to Walcott, N**...gas:** Pilot/Arby's/dsl/24hr/@, TA/IA 80/BP/DQ/Wendy's/dsl/scales/24hr/@, **food:** Gramma's Kitchen, SpeedCo Lube, **lodging:** Comfort Inn, Super 8, **other:** Blue Beacon, tires, S**...gas:** Pilot/Subway/dsl/24hr/@, **food:** McDonald's, **lodging:** Day's Inn, **other:** Cheyenne RV Ctr
280	Y30, to Stockton, New Liberty, no services
277	Durant, **2 mi** S**...**food
271	US 6 W, IA 38 S, to Wilton, no services
270mm	**rest area both lanes, full(handicapped)facilities, info, phone, picnic tables, litter barrels, vending, petwalk, RV dump, wireless internet**
268mm	weigh sta wb
267	IA 38 N, to Tipton, N**...other:** Cedar River Camping, S**...food:** The Cove Café
266mm	Cedar River
265	to Atalissa, S**...gas:** Phillips 66/dsl/rest./scales/24hr/@
259	to West Liberty, Springdale, S**...gas:** BP/dsl/24hr, **lodging:** Econolodge, **other:** KOA
254	X30, West Branch, N**...gas:** BP/Quizno's/dsl, Casey's, **food:** West Branch Rest., **other:** Jack&Jill Foods, USPO, S**...gas:** Kum&Go, **food:** McDonald's, **lodging:** Best Value Inn, **other:** Chrysler/Dodge/Jeep
249	Herbert Hoover Hwy, N**...** winery(2mi), S**...**golf
246	IA 1, Dodge St, N**...gas:** BP/A&W/Subway/dsl, **lodging:** Quality Inn, S**...gas:** Sinclair, **food:** Bob's Pizza, **lodging:** Travelodge
244	Dubuque St, Iowa City, N**...**Coralville Lake, S**...**HOSPITAL, to Old Capitol, museum
242	to Coralville, N**...food:** River City Grille, **lodging:** Hampton Inn, Holiday Inn, S**...gas:** BP, Conoco **food:** Arby's, Burger King, Cancun Mexican, Edge Rest., Hardee's, KFC, LJ Silver, LoneStar Steaks, McDonald's, Old Chicago Pizza, Papa John's, Peking Buffet, Perkins/24hr, Pizza Hut, Subway, Taco Bell, Taco John's, **lodging:** Baymont Inn, Best Western, Comfort Inn, Day's Inn, Econolodge, Heartland Inn, Marriott, Motel 6, Super 8, **other:** HOSPITAL, Toyota, Walgreens
240	IA 965, to US 6, Coralville, N Liberty, N**...gas:** Conoco, Phillips 66/SS/dsl, **food:** Culver's, McDonald's, Steak'n Shake, Village Inn Rest., Wendy's, **lodging:** AmericInn, Country Inn&Suites, **other:** Colony Country Camping(3mi), Harley-Davidson, Kohl's, **Wal-Mart SuperCtr/Subway/24hr**, S**...gas:** BP, Conoco, Phil-

IOWA

Interstate 80

E ↑ ↓ **W**

Exit	Description
	lips 66/Blimpie, **food:** Applebee's(1mi), Bennigan's, Boston's Pizza, Caribou Coffee, Chili's, Coldstone Creamery, DQ(1mi), Outback Steaks, Old Country Buffet, Olive Garden, Panchero's Mexican, Red Lobster, **lodging:** Comfort Suites, Days Inn, Holiday Inn Express, **other:** Barnes&Noble, Best Buy, Dillard's, HyVee Foods/gas, JC Penney, Lowe's Whse, Old Navy, Radio Shack, Sears/auto, Target, Tires+, U-Haul, Younkers, mall
239b	I-380 N, US 218 N, to Cedar Rapids
239a	US 218 S, no services
237	Tiffin, N...**food:** Jon's Rest.(1mi)
236mm	**rest area both lanes, full(handicapped)facilities, phone, picnic tables, litter barrels, vending, RV dump, petwalk, wireless internet**
230	W38, to Oxford, N...**other:** Sleepy Hollow Camping, Kalona Museum
225	US 151 N, W21 S, N...to Amana Colonies, **lodging:** Heritage Inn, S...**Welcome Ctr**, **gas:** BP, Casey's, **food:** Colony Village Rest., MaidRite Cafe, Little Amana Rest./Winery, 7 Villages Rest., Ox Yoke Rest., **lodging:** Econolodge, Holiday Inn, Super 8
220	IA 149 S, V77 N, to Williamsburg, N...**gas:** BP, Casey's(1mi), Phillips 66/dsl, **food:** Arby's, McDonald's, Pizza Hut, Subway, Taste Of China, **lodging:** Best Western, Crest Motel, Super 8, **other:** GNC, Old Navy, Tanger/famous brands, VF/famous brands, S...**lodging:** Day's Inn
216	to Marengo, N...**gas:** Kum&Go/Subway/dsl, **lodging:** Sudbury Court Motel(7mi), **other:** HOSPITAL
211	to Ladora, Millersburg, no services
208mm	**rest area both lanes, full(handicapped)facilities, phone, vending, picnic tables, litter barrels, petwalk, RV dump**
205	to Victor, no services
201	IA 21, to Deep River, N...**gas:** Phillips 66/SS/dsl/24hr, **food:** Farmer Nick's Rest., **lodging:** Sleep Inn, S...**gas:** KwikStar/dsl/rest./scales/24hr/@, truck repair
197	to Brooklyn, N...**gas:** BP/dsl, **food:** Brooklyn-80 Rest./24hr, **other:** RV camping
191	US 63, to Montezuma, N...**gas:** Sinclair, S...**gas:** Citgo/dsl/rest., FuelMart/dsl/rest., to Fun Valley Ski Area(13mi)
182	IA 146, to Grinnell, N...**gas:** Casey's(1mi), Kum&Go/Subway/dsl, **food:** KFC, Taco Bell, Taco John's, HyVee, **lodging:** Best Western, Comfort Inn, Country Inn, Day's Inn, Super 8, **other:** HOSPITAL(4mi), Chrysler/Plymouth/Dodge/Jeep(1mi), $General, Hyvee Foods, Wal-Mart SuperCtr/gas/24hr(1mi), S...Fun Valley Ski Area(16mi)
180mm	**rest area both lanes, full(handicapped)facilities, phone, vending, weather info, picnic tables, litter barrels, petwalk, playground, RV dump(eb) Wireless Internet**
179	IA 124, to Oakland Acres, Lynnville, no services
175mm	N Skunk River
173	IA 224, Kellogg, N...**gas:** Phillips 66/Best Burger/dsl/rest./24hr, **other:** Kellogg RV Park, Rock Creek SP(9mi), S...Lake Pla-mor Camping, Pella Museum **other:** camping
168	SE Beltline Dr, to Newton, **1 mi** N...**gas:** Casey's/dsl, **food:** Arby's, Taco John's, **lodging:** Mid-Iowa
	Motel, **other:** Plymouth/Jeep, Rolling Acres Camping, Wal-Mart SuperCtr/gas/24hr, S... Iowa Speedway
164	US 6, IA 14, Newton, N...**gas:** Casey's, Phillips 66/Subway/dsl, **food:** Country Kitchen, Culver's, KFC/Taco Bell, Okoboji Grill, Perkins/24hr, Senor Tequila Mexican, **lodging:** Day's Inn, Quality Inn, Ramada Ltd, Super 8, **other:** HOSPITAL, museum, S...**lodging:** Newton Inn/rest., **other:** Ford/Lincoln/Mercury, to Lake Red Rock
159	F48, to Jasper, Baxter, no services
155	IA 117, Colfax, N...**gas:** Colfax Trkstp/BP/McDonald's/dsl/@, **lodging:** Comfort Inn, Microtel, **other:** antiques, truck repair, S...**gas:** Casey's, Kum&Go/Subway/dsl/24hr
153mm	S Skunk River
151	weigh sta wb
149	Mitchellville, no services
148mm	**rest area both lanes, full(handicapped)facilities, phone, picnic tables, litter barrels, petwalk, vending, RV dump, Wireless Internet**
143	Altoona, Bondurant, N...**food:** Quizno's(1mi), S...**gas:** Casey's, **lodging:** Holiday Inn Express, **other:** HyVee Foods(2mi)
142b a	US 65, Hubble Ave, Des Moines, S...**gas:** BP, Bosselman/Pilot/Sinclair/dsl/rest./24hr/@, Git'n Go, **food:** Burger King, Culver's, Godfather's, KFC/Taco Bell, McDonald's, Pizza Hut, Subway, Taco John's, **lodging:** Adventureland Inn, Heartland Inn, Howard Johnson, Motel 6, Settle Inn, **other:** Blue Beacon, Peterbilt, camping, casino
141	US 6 W, US 65 S, Pleasant Hill, Des Moines
137b a	I-35 N, I-235 S, to Des Moines
I-80 W and I-35 S run together 14 mi.	
136	US 69, E 14th St, Camp Sunnyside, N...**gas:** BP/dsl, Phillips 66, **food:** Bonanza, Country Kitchen, **lodging:** Bavarian Inn, Motel 6, Red Roof Inn, Rodeway Inn, **other:** Volvo/GMC, antiques, S...**gas:** Casey's, **lodging:** Amerihost, Travelodge, **1 mi** S...**gas:** Phillips 66, QT/Burger King/dsl/scales, **food:** Arby's, Fazoli's, Happy Joe's Pizza, KFC, McDonald's, Papa Murphy's, Subway, Village Inn Rest., Taco Bell, **other:** Advance Parts, Aldi Foods, CarMax, $General, MidState RV Ctr, O'Reilly Parts, Tires+
135	IA 415, 2nd Ave, Polk City, N...**other:** Harley-Davidson, antiques, flea mkt, S...**gas:** Git'n Go, QT, Shell, **other:** HOSPITAL, Earl's Tire, NAPA, USPO(2mi), st patrol
133mm	Des Moines River
131	IA 28 S, NW 58th St, N...**gas:** Casey's, QT, **food:** North-End Diner, Quizno's, Sonic, Tagliai's Pizza, **lodging:** Best Inn, Best Western, **other:** Acura, Goodyear/auto, HyVee Food, Infiniti, VW/Audi, S...**gas:** BP/dsl/24hr, Phillips 66, QT, Sinclair/dsl, **food:** Arby's, Bennigan's, Burger King, Country Kitchen, Daytona's Grill, Denny's, Famous Dave's BBQ, KFC, McDonald's, Perkins, Pizza Hut, Shangrila Buffet, Village Inn Rest., Wendy's, **lodging:** Comfort Inn, Day's Inn, Holiday Inn, Quality Inn, Red Roof Inn, Sheraton, Super 8, **other:** HOSPITAL, Best Buy, Chevrolet, Chrysler/Plymouth, Daewoo, Firestone/auto, Ford/Mitsubishi, Goodyear/auto, Isuzu, Lincoln/Mercury, Marshall's, NAPA Autocare, Nissan, Office Depot, Sears/auto, Suzuki, Toyota, Younker's, Walgreen, mall

Sidebar labels: Newton, Des Moines

Interstate 80

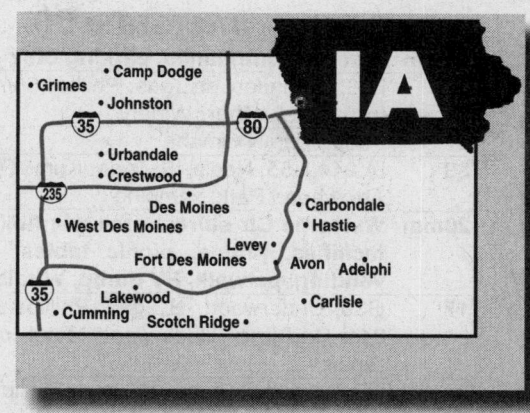

129	NW 86th St, Camp Dodge, **N**...**gas:** Kum&Go, **food:** Burger King, Coldstone Creamery, MaidRite Cafe, McDonald's, Okoboji Grill, Starbucks, Texas Roadhouse, Village Inn Rest., **lodging:** Hilton Garden, Stoney Creek Inn, TownePlace Suites, **other:** Dahl's Foods, **S**...**gas:** BP, Phillips 66, **food:** Arby's, B-Bops Burgers, Culver's, Friedrich's Coffee, Happy Joe's Pizza, Jesse's Steaks, Papa Murphy's, **lodging:** Microtel, **other:** Walgreens
127	IA 141 W, Grimes, **N**...**gas:** BP/dsl/@, Phillips 66/dsl, **food:** MaidRite Cafe, Subway, **lodging:** AmericInn(3mi), to Saylorville Lake, **S**...**food:** Quizno's, **other:** Radio Shack, Target
126	Douglas Ave, Urbandale, **N**...**gas:** Pilot/Grandma Max's/Subway/dsl/24hr/scales/@, **S**...**gas:** Kum&Go/dsl, **food:** Dragon China, **lodging:** Day's Inn, Econolodge, Extended Stay America
125	US 6, Hickman Rd, **N**...**gas:** /Flying J/Conoco/Cookery/dsl/LP/24hr/@, **other:** Dodge, to Living History Farms, **S**...**food:** IA Machine Shed Rest., **lodging:** Clyde Hotel, Comfort Suites, Sleep Inn, **other:** GMC, Goodyear, Honda, Hyundai,
124	(72c from I-35 nb), University Ave, **N**...**gas:** Kum&Go/Burger King, QT, **food:** Biaggi's Rest., Boston's, Caribou Coffee, Cracker Barrel, El Rodeo Mexican, Wendy's, **lodging:** Baymont Inn, Best Western, Country Inn&Suites, La Quinta, **other:** HOSPITAL, Walgreens, **S**...**gas:** BP/MaidRite, **food:** Applebee's, Bakers Square, Cheddar's, Chili's, KFC, Macaroni Grill, McDonald's, Mi Mexico, Outback Steaks, QDoba Mexican, RockBottom Rest./brewery, **lodging:** Chase Suites, Courtyard, Heartland Inn, Ramada Inn, Sheraton, The Inn, Wildwood Lodge, **other:** Barnes&Noble, Best Buy, Borders, CompUSA, K-Mart, Kohl's, Lowe's Whse, Marshall's, Office Depot, Petsmart, SteinMart, Target, World Mkt
I-80 E and I-35 N run together 14 mi	
123b a	I-80/I-35 N, I-35 S to Kansas City, I-235 to Des Moines
122	(from eb)60th St, W Des Moines
121	74th St, W Des Moines, **N**...**food:** Panera Bread, West End Diner, **lodging:** Hampton Inn, StayBridge Suites, **other:** Home Depot, HyVee Food/gas, SteinMart, Target, Walgreens, **S**...**gas:** BP, Culver's, Kum&Go/Subway, **food:** Arby's, Burger King, CK's, McDonald's, Perkins, Quizno's, Taco John's, **lodging:** Candlewood Suites, Fairfield Inn, Quality Inn, Marriott, Motel 6, Wingate Inn
119mm	**rest area both lanes, full(handicapped)facilities, info, vending, phone, picnic tables, petwalk, RV dump, Wireless Internet**
117	R22, Booneville, Waukee, **N**...**food:** Organic Farm Rest., **other:** Timberline Camping(2mi), **S**...**gas:** Kum&Go/24hr, **food:** Rube's Steaks, Waveland Rest.(2mi)
115mm	weigh sta eb
113	R16, Van Meter, 1 mi **S**...**gas:** Casey's
112mm	N Racoon River
111mm	Middle Racoon River
110	US 169, to Adel, DeSoto, **N**... Aircraft Supermkt, John Wayne Birthplace, camping(6mi), **S**...**gas:** Casey's, Kum&Go/dsl, **lodging:** Countryside Inn, Edgetowner Motel
106	F90, P58, **N**...KOA
104	P57, Earlham, **S**...**gas:** Casey's(2mi), **food:** Master Griller(2mi)
100	US 6, to Redfield, Dexter, no services
97	P48, to Dexter, **N**...**gas:** Casey's(2mi), camping
93	P28, Stuart, **N**...**gas:** BP/dsl/24hr, Casey's/dsl/scales, Kum&Go, **food:** Burger King, McDonald's, Subway, **lodging:** AmericInn, Super 8, Stuart Motel, **other:** Chevrolet, $General, Hometown Foods, NAPA, **S**...**gas:** Phillips 66/dsl, **food:** Country Kitchen, **lodging:** motel
88	P20, Menlo, **other:**camping
86	IA 25, to Greenfield, Guthrie Ctr, **S**...**other:** Hospital(13mi), to Preston/Spring Brook SP
85mm	Middle River
83	N77, Casey, 1 mi **N**...**gas:** Kum&Go, **other:** camping
80.5mm	**rest area both lanes, full(handicapped)facilities, phone, picnic tables, litter barrels, vending, petwalk, RV dump, Wireless Internet**
76	IA 925, N54, Adair, **N**...**gas:** Casey's/dsl, Kum&Go/Subway/dsl, **food:** Happy Chef, Smiley's Steaks, **lodging:** Adair Budget Inn, Super 8, **other:** camping
75	G30, to Adair, no services
70	IA 148 S, Anita, **S**...to Lake Anita SP(6mi)
64	N28, to Wiota, no services
61mm	E Nishnabotna River
60	US 6, US 71, to Atlantic, Lorah, **S**...**gas:** Phillips 66/Country Cafe/dsl/24hr, Valero, **lodging:** Day's Inn
57	N16, to Atlantic, **S**...HOSPITAL(7mi)
54	IA 173, to Elk Horn, 6 mi **N**...**Welcome Ctr/Wireless Internet**, **lodging:** AmericInn, **other:** Windmill Museum, gas, food(7mi)
51	M56, to Marne, no services
46	M47, Walnut, **N**...**gas:** BP/McDonald's/24hr, **food:** Villager Buffet, **lodging:** Super 8, to Prairie Rose SP(8mi), **S**...**gas:** Kum&Go/dsl/24hr, **food:** Aunt B's Kitchen, **lodging:** Red Carpet Inn/RV Park, repair
44mm	**rest area/parking only**
40	US 59, to Harlan, Avoca, **N**...**gas:** Conoco/Wings/Taco John's/Maidrite/dsl/24hr/scales/@, **lodging:** Motel 6, **other:** HOSPITAL(12mi), **S**...**gas:** Shell/dsl(1mi), **food:** Embers Rest., **lodging:** Avoca Motel/cafe, Capri Motel(1mi), **other:** Nishna Museum
39.5mm	W Nishnabotna River
34	M16, Shelby, **N**...**gas:** Shell/dsl, **food:** Cornstalk Rest., **lodging:** Shelby Country Inn/RV Park, **S**...**other:** dsl/tire repair

IOWA

Interstate 80

32mm	**rest area both lanes, parking only**
29	L66, to Minden, [S]...**gas:** Phillips 66/A&W/dsl, **lodging:** motel, **other:** Winery
27	I-680 W, to N Omaha
23	IA 244, L55, Neola, [S]...**gas:** Kum&Go/dsl, **other:** to Arrowhead Park, camping
20mm	**Welcome Ctr eb/rest area wb, full(handicapped) facilities, phone, picnic tables, litter barrels, vending, petwalk, RV dump, Wireless Internet**
17	G30, Underwood, [N]...**gas:** Phillips 66/Subway/dsl/24hr, **lodging:** Underwood Motel, **other:** truck/tire repair
8	US 6, Council Bluffs, [N]...**gas:** Phillips 66/dsl(1mi)
5	5 Madison Ave, Council Bluffs, [N]...**gas:** BP, **food:** Burger King, FoodCourt, Great Wall Chinese, KFC, McDonald's, Panera Bread, Pizza Hut, Skeeter Barn's Steaks, Subway, **lodging:** Heartland Inn, **other:** Barnes&Noble, Dillard's, DrugTown, HyVee Food/drug, JC Penney, NTB, Old Navy, Sears/auto, Target, Walgreens, mall, [S]...**gas:** Conoco, Shell/DQ, **food:** Valentino's Rest., Village Inn Rest., **lodging:** Western Inn, **other:** No Frills Foods
4	I-29 S, to Kansas City
3	IA 192 N, Council Bluffs, [N]...to Hist Dodge House, [S]...**gas:** Phillips 66/dsl, Shell/dsl, TA/Pizza Hut/dsl/24hr/@, **food:** Applebee's, Burger King, Cracker Barrel, DQ, Fazoli's, Golden Corral, Hardee's, La Mesa Mexican, LJ Silver, McDonald's, Perkins/24hr, Red Lobster, Subway, Taco Bell, **lodging:** Comfort Inn, Day's Inn, Fairfield Inn, Motel 6, Settle Inn, **other:** Advance Parts, Aldi Foods, Chevrolet/GMC, Best Buy, Buick/Pontiac, Dodge, Ford, Gordman's, Home Depot, Kia, Kohl's, Mazda, Nissan/Cadillac, Plymouth/Jeep/Suzuki, Sam's Club/gas, Subaru, Toyota, TruckOMat, U-Haul, Wal-Mart SuperCtr/24hr, dsl repair
1b	S 24th St, Council Bluffs, [N]...**gas:** Conoco, Pilot/Arby's/dsl/24hr, Sinclair, Sapp Bros/Shell/Burger King/dsl/rest., **food:** Famous Dave's BBQ, Ruby Tuesday, **lodging:** American Inn, Best Western, Country Inn&Suites, SpringHill Suites, Super 8, **other:** Bass Pro Shop, Goodyear, RV camping, Peterbilt, Speed-Co, casino, [S]...**Welcome Ctr, full facilities**
1a	I-29 N, to Sioux City
0mm	Iowa/Nebraska state line, Missouri River

Interstate 235(Des Moines)

Exit #	Services
15	I-80, E to Davenport
13	US 6, E Euclid Ave, [E]...**gas:** Casey's, **food:** Burger King, Dragon House Chinese, Papa John's, Perkins, **other:** $Tree, Hancock Fabrics, HyVee Foods/drug, Walgreen, [W]...**gas:** QT, **other:** Great Outdoor RV Ctr, NAPA
11	Guthrie Ave, [W]...**other:** CarQuest
10a b	IA 163 W, E University Ave, Easton Dr
9	US 65/69, E 14th, E 15th, [N]...**other:** Walgreen, [S]...**food:** McDonald's, Quizno's, **other:** HOSPITAL, st capitol, zoo
8b	E 6th St, Penn Ave(from wb), [N]...HOSPITAL
8a	3rd St, 5th Ave, [N]...**lodging:** Holiday Inn, **other:** HOSPITAL, [S]...**lodging:** Embassy Suites, Marriott, Quality Inn, **other:** Conv Ctr
7	Keo Way, no services
6	MLK Blvd/31st St, Drake U, Governor's Mansion, [S]...airport
5b	42nd St, Science & Art Ctr, [N]...**gas:** Git'n Go, **food:** Papa John's, **other:** Curves
5a	56th St(from wb), [N]...golf
4	IA 28, 63rd St, to Windsor Heights, [S]...Hist Valley Jct, zoo
3	8th St, W Des Moines, [N]...**gas:** Kum&Go, **food:** B-Bop's Café, Burger King, **other:** HyVee Foods, PetCo, Sam's Club/gas, Sears AutoCtr, Wal-Mart SuperCtr/24hr, [S]...**gas:** BP, Kum&Go, **food:** Coach's Corner Grill, Garcia's Mexican, Jimmy's American Café, **lodging:** Best Western
2	22nd St, 24th St, W Des Moines, [N]...**gas:** BP, Phillips 66/dsl, **food:** ChuckeCheese, Culver's, Famous Dave's BBQ, Gordman's, Hardee's, Hooters, LoneStar Steaks, McDonald's, Old Country Buffet, Taco Bell, Village Inn Rest., Zachary's Grill, **lodging:** Studio+, **other:** Firestone/auto, Goodyear/auto, Gordman's, Hancock Fabrics, Michael's, Office Depot, Walgreen
1b	Valley West Dr, W Des Moines, [N]...**gas:** BP/dsl, **food:** Olive Garden, Red Lobster, TGI Friday's, **other:** HyVee Foods, JC Penney, SteinMart, Target, Younker's, mall
0mm	I-235 begins/ends on I-80, exit 123.

Interstate 280(Davenport)

Exit #	Services
18b a	I-74, US 6, Moline, [S]...**gas:** Citgo, **food:** Bender's Rest., Denny's, Harold's Rest., McDonald's, Montana Jack's, Skyline Rest., **lodging:** Best Western, Comfort Inn, Country Inn Suites, Econolodge, Holiday Inn, Holiday Inn Express, La Quinta, Motel 6, Quality Inn, Skyline Inn
15	Airport Rd, Milan, [N]...**food:** (1mi)MaidRite Café, Subway, **other:** Buick/Chevrolet, Firestone
11b a	IL 92, to Andalusia, Rock Island, [S]...KOA Camping
9.5mm	**Iowa/Illinois state line, Mississippi River**
8	rd 22, Rockingham Rd, to Buffalo, no services
6	US 61, W River Dr, to Muscatine, [W]...**gas, camping**
4	Locust St, rd F65, 160th St, [E]...HOSPITAL, to Palmer Coll, St Ambrose U, [W]...**gas:** Citgo/Subway/dsl/@
1	US 6 E, IA 927, Kimberly Rd, to Walcott, [E]...lodging, transmissions
0mm	I-280 begins/ends on I-80, exit 290.

KANSAS

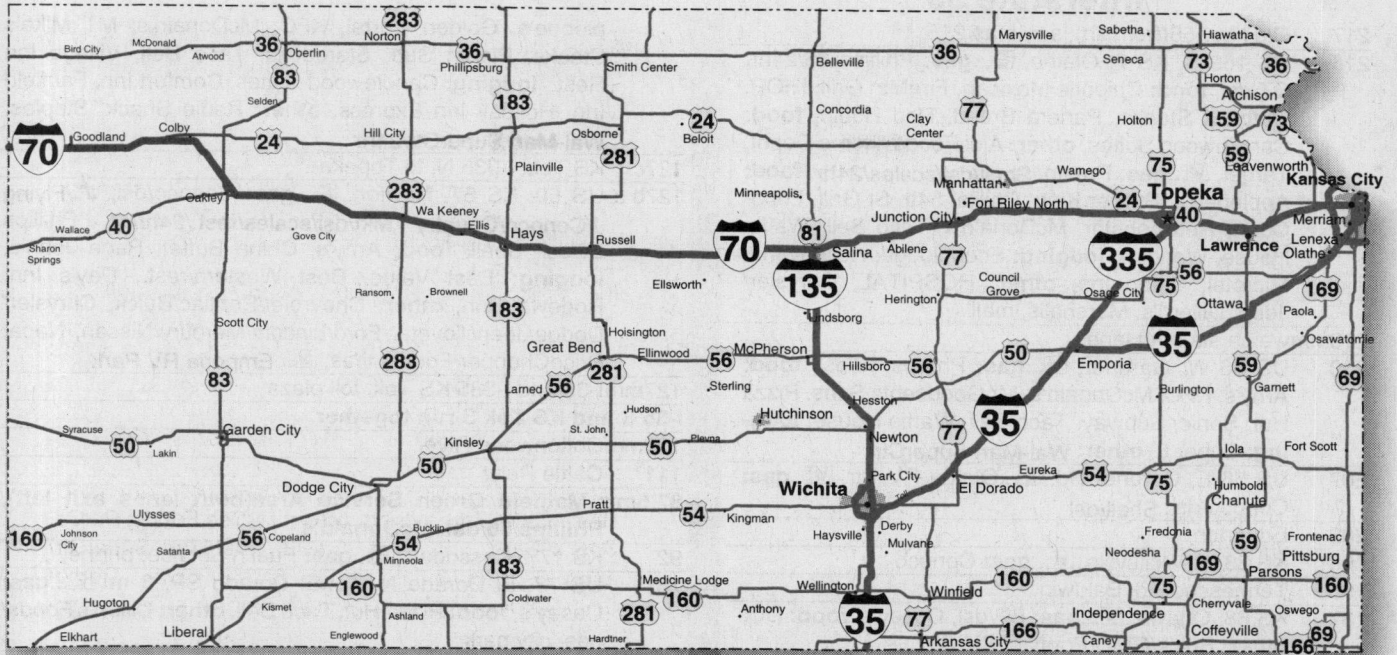

Interstate 35

Exit #	Services
235mm	Kansas/Missouri state line
235	Cambridge Circle
234b a	US 169, Rainbow Blvd, **E**...**gas:** QT, Shell, **food:** Applebee's, Arby's, Burger King, McDonald's, Rosedale BBQ, Sonic, Wendy's, **lodging:** Best Western, Day's Inn, **other:** KU MED CTR, **W**...**food:** KFC, LJ Silver
233a	SW Blvd, Mission Rd
233b	37th Ave(from sb)
232b	US 69 N, **E**...**gas:** QT, Phillips 66, **food:** McDonald's, Taco Bell
232a	Lamar Ave, **E**...**gas:** QT
231b a	I-635(exits left from nb)
230	Antioch Rd(from sb), **E**...**gas:** QT
229	Johnson Dr, **E**...**gas:** Phillips 66, **food:** Arby's, Chili's, Papa John's, **other:** GNC, Home Depot, Marshall's, Old Navy, PetsMart, Walgreen, Walnut Grove RV Park, **W**...**gas:** Phillips 66/dsl
228b	US 56 E, US 69, Shawnee Mission Pkwy, **W**...**food:** Burger King, Denny's, LJ Silver, Perkins, Pizza Hut, Steak'n Shake, Taco Bell, Wendy's
228a	67th St, **E**...**gas:** QT, Shell, **food:** Burger King, Denny's, Winstead's Rest., **lodging:** Comfort Inn, Drury Inn, Fairfield Inn, HomeStead Village, Quality Inn, **other:** BMW, CarMax, K-Mart, VW, **W**...**gas:** Phillips 66, **other:** Jaguar, Land Rover, Mercedes, Porsche
227	75th St, **E**...**gas:** Circle K, Conoco, QT, **food:** KFC, McDonald's, Perkins, **lodging:** Extended Stay America, Wellesley Inn, **other:** HOSPITAL, Acura, JC Penney, Wal-Mart, **W**...**gas:** Citgo/7-11, QT/dsl, Shell, **food:** FireMtn Grill, Ryan's, Sonic, Subway, Taco Bell, Wendy's, **lodging:** Hampton Inn
225b	US 69 S(from sb), Overland Pkwy
225a	87th St, **E**...**food:** Arby's, Green Mill Rest., Tippen's Rest., Wendy's, **lodging:** Holiday Inn, **other:** Gomer's Foods, **W**...**gas:** BP, Shell, **food:** Kahn Chi-

nese, LongBranch Steaks, Mary's Place Gyros, Taco Bell, Zarda BBQ, **other:** NTB, museum

224	95th St, **E**...**gas:** Phillips 66, Shell, **food:** Applebee's, Burger King, China Buffet, Chipotle Mexican, Cielio's Italian, Denny's, Holiday Ham Café, Houlihan's, KFC, McDonald's, Mimi's Café, Ming Palace, Mongolian BBQ, Old Chicago Pizza, On the Border, Outback Steaks, Pizza Hut, Ponderosa, Rainforest Cafe, Ruby Tuesday, Santa Fe Café, Steak&Ale, Taco Bell, TGIFriday, **lodging:** Comfort Inn, Day's Inn, Extended Stay America, Holiday Inn, La Quinta, Motel 6, Radisson, Super 8, **other:** HOSPITAL, Advance Parts, Best Buy, CircuitCity, Dillard's, Firestone, HyVee Foods, JC Penney, Nordstrom's, Sam's Club/gas, SteinMart, mall, **W**...**other:** Costco/gas
222b a	I-435 W & E
220	119th St, **E**...**gas:** Conoco, Phillips 66, Shell, **food:** A&W, Burger King, Carrabba's, Chevy's Mexican, China Café, Cracker Barrel, IHOP, Deli, Jimmy John's, Joe's Crabshack, La Mesa Mexican, LJ Silver, Machine Shed Rest., McDonald's, Rio Bravo Cantina, Ruby Tuesday, Schlotsky's, Souper Salad, Steak'n Shake, Subway, Tres Hombres Mexican, Wendy's, Zio's Italian, **lodging:** Comfort Suites, Fairfield Inn, Hampton Inn, Residence Inn, Value Place Hotel, **other:** Aamco, Best Buy, Barnes&Noble, Borders Books, Dodge, GNC, Goodyear/auto, Home Depot, Honda, Hyundai, Mazda, Old Navy, Radio Shack, Target, U-Haul, transmissions, **W**...Bass Pro Shop
218	135th, Santa Fe St, Olathe, **E**...**gas:** QT, Shell/dsl, **food:** Backyard Burger, Burger King, Corona Garden Mexican, McDonlad's, Perkins, **other:** Ace Hardware, BigLots, Ford, K-Mart, Osco Drug, **W**...**gas:** BP, Phillips 66, QT, **food:** Denny's, McDonald's, Ponderosa, Waffle House, Wendy's, **lodging:** Day's Inn, **other:** Chevrolet, Chrysler/Jeep, Kia, Mazda, Nissan, Pontiac/Buick/GMC; Saturn, Suzuki, Subaru, Toyota

Kansas City Area / Olathe

KANSAS

Interstate 35

217	Old Hwy 56(from sb), same as 215
215	US 169 S, KS 7, Olathe, **E**...**gas:** Phillips 66/24hr, QT/dsl, **food:** Chipotle Mexican, FireMtn Grill, IHOP, Outback Steaks, Panera Bread, Red Robin, **food:** Candlewood Suites, **other:** Aldi Foods, Home Depot, Target, **W**...**gas:** Presto, Shell/dsl/scales/24hr, **food:** Applebee's, Burger King, Chili's, 54th St Grill, FoodCourt, Red Lobster, McDonald's, Taco Bell, Waffle House, Wendy's, **lodging:** Econolodge, Holiday Inn, Microtel, Sleep Inn, **other:** HOSPITAL, Chrysler/Jeep, Dillard's, Marshalls, mall
213mm	weigh sta both lanes
210	US 56 W, Gardner, **W**...**gas:** Phillips 66/dsl, **food:** Arby's, KFC, McDonald's, Mr Goodcents Subs, Pizza Hut, Sonic, Subway, Taco Bell, Waffle House, **lodging:** Super 8, **other:** Wal-Mart SuperCtr
207	US 56 E, Gardner Rd, **E**...Olathe RV Ctr, **W**...**gas:** Conoco/dsl, Shell/dsl
202	Edgerton
198	KS 33, to Wellsville, **W**...**gas:** Conoco
193	Tennessee Rd, Baldwin
187	KS 68, Ottawa, **W**...**gas:** BP/dsl, Casey's, **food:** DQ, **other:** Buick/GMC/Pontiac, RV Ctr
185	15th St, Ottawa
183	US 59, Ottawa, **W**...**gas:** BP, Conoco/dsl, Ottawa Gas, Phillips 66/dsl, **food:** Applebee's, Burger King, DQ, KFC, LJ Silver, McDonald's, Old 56 Rest, Pizza Hut, Sirloin Stockade, Taco Bell, Wendy's, **lodging:** Best Western, Comfort Inn, Econolodge, Super 8, Travelodge, **other:** HOSPITAL, Advance Parts, Chrysler/Dodge/Jeep, CountryMart Foods, $General, $Tree, Wal-Mart SuperCtr/gas
182b a	US 50, Eisenhower Rd, Ottawa
176	Homewood, **W**...RV camping
175mm	**rest area both lanes, full(handicapped)facilities, phone, picnic tables, litter barrels, vending, petwalk, RV dump, wireless internet**
170	KS 273, Williamsburg, **W**...**gas:** Sinclair/café/dsl
162	KS 31 S, Waverly
160	KS 31 N, Melvern
155	US 75, Burlington, Melvern Lake, **E**...**gas:** BP/Subway/dsl, TA/Shell/Wendy's/dsl/scales/24hr/@, **food:** Beto Jct Rest., **lodging:** Wyatt Earp Inn
148	KS 131, Lebo, **E**...**gas:** Casey's, **lodging:** Universal Inn, **W**...to Melvern Lake
141	KS 130, Neosho Rapids, **E**...NWR(8mi)
138	County Rd U, **W**...antiques
135	County Rd R1, **W**...RV camping/phone
133	US 50 W, 6th Ave, Emporia, **1-3 mi E**...**gas:** Casey's, **food:** McDonald's, Pizza Hut, **lodging:** Budget Host
131	KS 57, KS 99, Burlingame Rd, **E**...**gas:** Conoco/dsl, **food:** Hardee's, Mr Goodcents Subs, **other:** Dillon's Food
130	KS 99, Merchant St, **E**...**gas:** Phillips 66/dsl, **food:** Subway, **other:** Emporia St U, Lyon Co Museum
128	Industrial Rd, **E**...**gas:** Conoco, Finish Line, **food:** Bruff's Steaks, Burger King, Gambino's Pizza, Mazzio's, Pizza Hut, Subway, **lodging:** Econolodge, Travelodge, Motel 6, **other:** HOSPITAL, Aldi Foods, CarQuest, Dillon's Food, $General, Family$, Goodyear/auto, Hastings Book, JC Penney, Walgreen, **W**...**gas:** Phillips 66/Wendy's/dsl, Shell, **food:** Ap-

	plebee's, Golden Corral, KFC, McDonald's, MT Mike's Steaks, Planet Sub, Starbucks, Taco Bell, Village Inn Rest., **lodging:** Candlewood Suites, Comfort Inn, Fairfield Inn, Holiday Inn Express, **other:** Radio Shack, Staples, Wal-Mart SuperCtr/24hr
127c	KS Tpk, I-335 N, to Topeka
127b a	US 50, KS 57, Newton, **E**...**gas:** Conoco/dsl, ✈/Flying J/Conoco/Country Mkt/dsl/scales/rest./24hr/@, Phillips 66/dsl, Shell, **food:** Arby's, China Buffet, Papa John's, **lodging:** Best Value, Best Western/rest., Day's Inn, Rodeway Inn, **other:** Chevrolet/Pontiac/Buick, Chrysler/Dodge/Jeep/Toyota, Ford/Lincoln/Mercury/Nissan, Napa, PriceChopper Foods, tires, **W**...Emporia RV Park
127mm	I-35 and I-335 KS Tpk, toll plaza,
	I-35 S and KS Tpk S run together.
125mm	Cottonwood River
111	Cattle Pens
97.5mm	**Matfield Green Service Area(both lanes exit left), Phillips 66/dsl, McDonald's**
92	KS 177, Cassoday, **E**...**gas:** Fuel'n Service, phone
76	US 77, El Dorado N, **E**...El Dorado SP, **3 mi E**...**gas:** Casey's, **food:** Pizza Hut, Taco Bell, **other:** Dillon's Foods/gas, city park
71	KS 254, KS 196, El Dorado, **E**...**gas:** Conoco/dsl, Phillips 66, **food:** Arbys, Cajun Shack, Freddy's Rest., KFC, Kountry Kettle, LJ Silver, McDonald's, Pizza Hut, Sonic, Spangles, Taco Tico, **lodging:** Best Western, Heritage Inn, Holiday Inn Express, Sunset Inn, Super 8, HOSPITAL, **other:** HOSPITAL, Bumper Parts, Deer Grove RV Park, $General, Ford/Lincoln/Mercury, KS Oil Museum, O'Reilly Parts, Pontiac/Buick/Cadillac, Radio Shack, Wal-Mart SuperCtr/Subway
65mm	**Towanda Service Area(both lanes exit left), Phillips 66/dsl, McDonald's**
62mm	Whitewater River
57	21st St, Andover, **W**...golf, phone
53	KS 96, Wichita, **1 mi W** on Kellogg...**gas:** Conoco/Wendy's, **food:** Burger King, McDonald's, Taco Bell, **other:** Acura, Lowe's Whse, Wal-Mart SuperCtr
50	US 54, Kellogg Ave, **E**...McConnell AFB, **W**...**food:** Italian Garden, **lodging:** Comfort Inn, Clubhouse Inn, Day's Inn, Fairfield Inn, Hampton Inn, Marriott, Motel 6, Residence Inn, Studio+, Super 8, **other:** VA HOSPITAL, **E** on Kellogg Ave...**gas:** Conoco/dsl, **food:** Bejing Bistro, Burger King, IHOP, McDonald's, Pizza Hut, Sonic, Subway, Taco Bell, **other:** Acura, Buick/Infiniti, CarMax, Lowe's Whse, Mazda, PepBoys, Porsche/Jaguar, Sears Grand, Sportsman's Whse, VW, Wal-Mart SuperCtr/24hr, **W** on Kellogg Ave...**food:** Arby's, Green Mill Rest., LJ Silver, McDonald's, Old Chicago Pizza, Pizza Hut, Red Lobster, Souper Salad, Steak&Ale, **lodging:** Econolodge, Garden Inn, Wichita Inn, **other:** Advance Parts, Barnes & Noble, Chevrolet/Cadillac, Chrysler/Dodge/Jeep, Dillard's, Firestone/auto, Ford, Hancock Fabrics, Honda, JC Penney, Kia, Lincoln/Mercury, Mitsubishi, Pontiac/GMC/Hyundai, Radio Shack, Sears/auto, Subaru/Isuzu, Target, TJ Maxx, Toyota/Scion, mall
45	KS 15, Wichita, **E**...Boeing Plant
44.5mm	Arkansas River
42	47th St, I-135, to I-235, Wichita, **E**...**gas:** Conoco, **food:** Potbelly's Rest., **lodging:** Comfort Inn, Day's Inn, Holiday Inn Express, Value Place Hotel, **W**...**gas:** Phillips 66, **food:**

Interstate 35

	Applebee's, Braum's, Burger King, Carlos O'Kelly's, Godfather's, KFC, LJ Silver, McDonald's, Panda Rest., Papa John's, Pizza Hut, Quizno's, Spangles Rest., Subway, Taco Bell, Taco Tico, **lodging:** Best Western, Heritage Inn, Red Carpet Inn, **other:** Checker's Foods, Dillon's Foods/gas/dsl, K-Mart, O'Reilly's Parts, Radio Shack
39	US 81, Haysville, 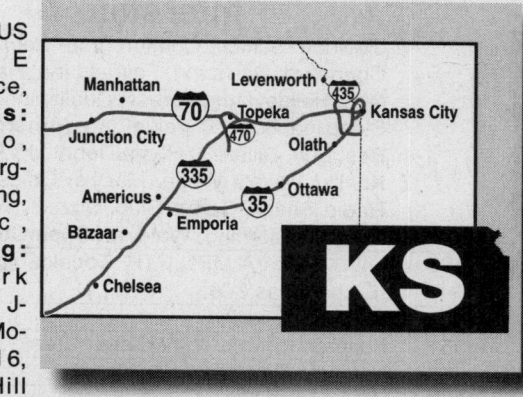**W**...**lodging:** Haysville Inn
33	KS 53, Mulvane, **E**...Mulvane Hist Museum, **W**... Wyldewood Winery
26mm	**Belle Plaine Service Area(both lanes exit left), gas: Phillips 66/dsl, food: McDonald's**
19	US 160, Wellington, **3 mi W**...**lodging:** OakTree Inn, Sunshine Inn, **other:** RV camping
17mm	toll plaza
I-35 N and KS TPK N run together.	
4	US 166, to US 81, South Haven, **E**...**gas:** Cenex/dsl, **lodging:** Economy Inn/rest., **W**...Oasis RV Park
1.5mm	weigh sta nb
0mm	Kansas/Oklahoma state line

Interstate 70

Exit #	Services
423b	3rd St, James St
423a	5th St
422d c	Central Ave, service rd
422b a	US 69 N, US 169 S
421b	I-670
421a	**S**...railroad yard
420b a	US 69 S, 18th St Expswy
419	38th St, Park Dr, access to 10 motels
418b	I-635 N, **N**...**food:** McDonald's, Taco Bell, Wendy's, Dillard's, **other:** JC Penney, mall
418a	I-635 S
417	57th St
415a	KS 32 E(from eb)
415b	to US 40 W, State Ave, Kansas City, **N**...**gas:** Conoco, Phillips 66/dsl, **food:** Arby's, Capt D's, Perkins, McDonald's, Taco Bell, **lodging:** Gables Motel
414mm	weigh sta wb, parking area both lanes, phone
414	78th St, **N**...**gas:** QT, Shell, **food:** Arby's, Burger King, DQ, Hardee's, Lucky Chinese, Sonic, Subway, Wendy's, **lodging:** Microtel, **other:** HOSPITAL, Chevrolet, $Tree, O'Riley Parts, Tires+, Walgreens, **S**...**gas:** BP, **lodging:** American Motel, Comfort Inn
411b	I-435 N, to Woodlands Racetrack, to KCI Airport
411a	I-435 S
410	110th St, **N**...Cabela's, KS Speedway, last free exit wb before KS TPK
225mm	I-70 W and KS TPK run together
224	KS 7, to US 73, Bonner Springs, Leavenworth, **N**... **gas:** Phillips 66/dsl, Shell, **food:** KFC/Taco Bell, Mazzio's, Subway, Waffle House, Wendy's, **lodging:** Holiday Inn Express, Super 8, **other:** museum, **S**...**gas:** Citgo, **food:** Arby's, McDonald's, Mr. Goodcents, **other:** $General, Ford, PriceChopper Foods, Wal-Mart SuperCtr/24hr
217mm	toll booth
209mm	**Lawrence Service Area(both lanes exit left), full facilities, Conoco/dsl, McDonald's**

204	US 24, US 59, to E Lawrence, **S**...**gas:** Conoco, **food:** Burger King, Sonic, **lodging:** Bismark Inn, J-Hawk Motel, Motel 6, SpringHill Suites, **other:** KOA, O'Reilly Parts, outlet
203mm	Kansas River
202	US 59 S, to W Lawrence, **1 mi S**...**gas:** BP, Conoco, Phillips 66, **food:** Burger King, McDonald's, Panda Garden, Taco Bell, **lodging:** Best Value, Best Western, Day's Inn, Econolodge, Hampton Inn, Holiday Inn, Quality Inn, Ramada Inn, Travelodge, Super 8, **other:** HOSPITAL, Advance Parts, Carquest, Firestone/auto, to Clinton Lake SP, to U of KS
197	KS 10, Lecompton, Lawrence, **N**...Perry Lake SP, **S**... Clinton Lake SP,
188mm	**Topeka Service Area, full facilities, Conoco/dsl, Taco Bueno, Hardee's**
183	I-70 W(from wb), to Denver
367mm	toll plaza
366	I-470 W, to Wichita
I-70 E and KS TPK E run together	
365	21st St, Rice Rd, to Shawnee Lake RA
364b	US 40 E, Carnahan Ave, to Lake Shawnee
364a	California Ave, **S**...**gas:** BP/dsl, Phillips 66/dsl, **food:** Arby's, Burger King, Domino's, McDonald's, Pizza Hut, Rosa's Mexican, Subway, **other:** AutoZone, Dillon's Food/gas, $General, Family$, Pricechopper, Walgreens
363	Adams St, downtown
362c	10th Ave(from wb), **N**...**lodging:** Ramada Inn, Red Carpet Inn, **S**...**gas:** BP, **other:** st capitol
362b a	to 8th Ave, downtown, **N**...**lodging:** Capitol Center Inn, Ramada Inn, **other:** to St Capitol, **S**...**gas:** BP
361b	3rd St, Monroe St
361a	1st Ave, **S**...Ryder
359	MacVicar Ave
358b a	Gage Blvd, **S**...**food:** McDonald's, Wendy's, **other:** HOSPITAL
357b a	Fairlawn Rd, 6th Ave, **S**...**gas:** Conoco, Phillips 66, **lodging:** Best Western, Holiday Inn/rest., Motel 6, **other:** NAPA, zoo-rain forest
356b a	Wanamaker Rd, **N**...**food:** Carino's, Red Robin, **lodging:** AmeriSuites, **other:** KS Museum of History, **S**...**gas:** BP, Conoco, Phillips 66/dsl, **food:** Applebee's, Boston Mkt, Burger King, Chili's, Chipotle Mexican, ChuckeCheese, CiCi'S Pizza, Coldstone Creamery, Coyote Canyon Café, Cracker Barrel, Denny's, Golden Corral, Jason's Deli, Hooters, IHOP, Longhorn Steaks, McDonald's, Mike's Subs, Mr. Goodcents, Old Chicago, Olive Garden, On the Border, Panda Buffet, Panera Bread, Papa Johns, Perkins, Pizza Hut, Red Lobster, Ruby Tuesday, Sonic, Spangles, Starbucks, Steak'n Shake, Taco Bell, Texas Roadhouse, Timerline Steaks, Wendy's, **lodging:** Can-

Interstate 70

E ↕ W

dlewood Suites, Comfort Inn, Country Inn&Suites, Courtyard, Day's Inn, Fairfield Inn, Hampton Inn, Motel 6, Holiday Inn Express, Quality Inn, Residence Inn, Sleep Inn, Super 8, ValuePlace, **other:** Barnes&Noble, Best Buy, Dillard's, Home Depot, JC Penney, K-Mart, Kohl's, Lowe's Whse, Macy's, Office Depot, PetCo, Radio Shack, Sam's Club, Suzuki, Target, TJ Maxx, Tuesday Morning, Wal-Mart SuperCtr/24hr, mall

355 I-470 E, to VA MED CTR, Topeka, air museum, **1 mi S**...same as 356

353 KS 4, to Eskridge

351 frontage rd(from eb), Mission Creek

350 Valencia Rd

347 West Union Rd

346 Carlson Rd, to Rossville, Willard

343 frontage rd

342 Eskridge Rd, Keene Rd, to Lake Wabaunsee

341 KS 30, Maple Hill, **S...gas:** BP/dsl/café

338 Vera Rd, no services

336mm rest area(exits left from both lanes), full (handicapped) facilities, phone, picnic tables, litter barrels, RV dump, petwalk

335 Snokomo Rd, Skyline Mill Creek Scenic Drive, Paxico

333 KS 138, Paxico, **N...gas:** Winery/gas

332 Spring Creek Rd

330 KS 185, to McFarland

329mm weigh sta both lanes

328 KS 99, to Alma, **N...** Gas-N-Shop, **S...**Wabaunsee Co Museum

324 Wabaunsee Rd, **N...**Grandma Horners Store& Factory

322 Tallgrass Rd

318 frontage rd

316 Deep Creek Rd

313 KS 177, to Manhattan, **8 mi N...gas:** Phillips 66, **food:** Applebee's, Chili's, McDonald's, Village Inn Rest., **lodging:** Best Western, Comfort Inn, Fairfield Inn, Hampton Inn, Motel 6, Super 8, **other:** Jeep, Nissan, Sears/auto, to KSU

311 Moritz Rd

310mm rest area both lanes, full(handicapped) facilities, phone, picnic tables, litter barrels, petwalk

307 McDowell Creek Rd, scenic river rd to Manhattan

304 Humboldt Creek Rd

303 KS 18 E, to Ogden, Manhattan, **N...other:** to KSU

301 Marshall Field, to Ft Riley, **N...other:** Cavalry Museum, Custer's House, KS Terr Capitol

300 US 40, KS 57, Council Grove, **N...lodging:** Dreamland Motel, **S...**hist church

299 Flinthills Blvd, to Jct City, Ft Riley, **N...gas:** BP/dsl, **food:** Stacy's Rest., **lodging:** Econolodge, Great Western Inn, Red Carpet Inn, Super 8

Jct City

298 Chestnut St, to Jct City, Ft Riley, **N...gas:** Shell/Burger King/dsl/24hr, **food:** Arby's, BBQ, Cracker Barrel, Family Buffet, Mr. Goodcents Subs, Taco Bell, **lodging:** Best Western, Courtyard, Holiday Inn Express, Super 8, Value Place, **other:** Alco, Curves, $General, $Tree, Goody's, Wal-Mart SuperCtr/24hr

296 US 40, Washington St, Junction City, **N...gas:** BP, Casey's, Cenex, Citgo/dsl, Shell/dsl/24hr, **food:** Church's, DQ, Denny's, El Cazador Mexican, KFC, McDonald's, Peking Chinese, Pizza Hut, Sirloin Stockade, Sonic, Subway, **lodging:** Budget Host/RV Park, Comfort Inn, Day's Inn, Ramada Ltd, **other:** Food4Less/24hr, Harley Davidson

295 US 77, KS 18, Marysville, to Milford Lake, **N...gas:** Conoco, Phillips 66/A&W/dsl/24hr, **lodging:** Motel 6, **other:** HOSPITAL

294mm rest area both lanes, full(handicapped)facilities, phone, picnic tables, litter barrels, RV dump, petwalk

290 Milford Lake Rd

286 KS 206, Chapman, **S...gas:** Cenex/dsl, **1 mi S...gas:** Casey's

281 KS 43, to Enterprise, **N...gas:** Shell/dsl, **other:** 4 Seasons RV Ctr/Park

277 Jeep Rd

Abilene

275 KS 15, to Clay Ctr, Abilene, **N...food:** DQ, **lodging:** Brookville Motel, Holiday Inn Express, **S...gas:** BP/dsl, Phillips 66, **food:** Burger King, China Taste, Joe Snuffy's Rest., McDonald's, Pizza Hut, Sonic, Subway, **lodging:** Best Western, Best Value, Super 8, **other:** HOSPITAL, Alco/gas, AutoZone, Chevrolet/Pontiac/Buick, CountryMart Foods, $General, Ford, Chrysler,/Jeep/Dodge, to Eisenhower Museum

272 Fair Rd, to Talmage, **S...**Russell Stover Candy

266 KS 221, Solomon, **S...gas:** Total/dsl/rest./24hr/@

265mm rest area both lanes, full(handicapped)facilities, phone, picnic tables, litter barrels, vending, petwalk

264mm Solomon River

260 Niles Rd, New Cambria

253mm Saline River

253 Ohio St, **S...gas:** ⊕/Flying J/Conoco/Country Mkt/dsl/LP/24hr/@, **other:** HOSPITAL, Harley-Davidson, Kenworth

Salina

252 KS 143, Salina, **N...gas:** Petro/Shell/Wendy's/Pizza Hut/dsl/24hr/@, Valero/Subway/dsl/rest./24hr/@ **food:** Bayard's Café, IHOP, McDonald's, **lodging:** Best Inn, Day's Inn, Holiday Inn Express, Motel 6, Salina Inn, Super 8, **other:** Blue Beacon, KOA, **S...gas:** Bosselman/Sinclair/rest./dsl/24hr/@, Fuel, **lodging:** Best Western, Econolodge

250b a I-135, US 81, N to Concordia, S to Wichita

249 Halstead Rd, to Trenton, no services

244 Hedville, **N...**Sundowner West RV Park, **S...gas:** Cenex/dsl

238 to Brookville, Glendale, Tescott

233 to Beverly, Juniata

225 KS 156, to Ellsworth, **S...** Elkhorn Corner/Pizza/dsl, **other:** Ft Harker Museum, Ft Larned HS

224mm rest area both lanes, full(handicapped)facilities, phone, picnic tables, litter barrels, petwalk, RV dump

221 KS 14 N, to Lincoln

219 KS 14 S, to Ellsworth, **S...gas:** Conoco/dsl

216 to Vesper

209 to Sylvan Grove

206 KS 232, Wilson, **N...gas:** Travel Shoppe/rest., **other:** Wilson Lake(6mi), winery, **N...**RV Parking

199 KS 231, Dorrance, **N...**to Wilson Lake, **S...**gas/food

193 Bunker Hill Rd, **N...gas:** Conoco/dsl/rest/24hr, to Wilson Lake

189 US 40 bus, Pioneer Rd, Russell, no services

187mm rest area both lanes, full(handicapped) facilities, phone, picnic tables, litter barrels, RV dump, petwalk

184 US 281, Russell, **N...gas:** BP/dsl/24hr, Phillips 66/Mesquite Grill/dsl, **food:** A&W, Meridy's Rest., McDonald's,

Interstate 70

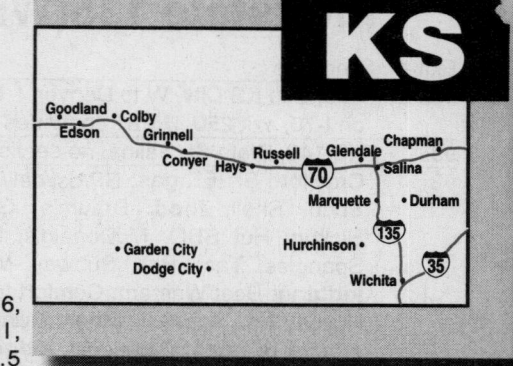

Russell (left margin, with E↕W compass)

Pizza Hut, Sonic, Subway, **lodging:** AmericInn, Day's Inn, Russell's Inn, Super 8, **other:** HOSPITAL, $General, JJJ RV Park, Fossil Creek RV Park, st patrol

180	Balta Rd, to Russell
175	KS 257, Gorham, **1 mi** ...gas, food, phone
172	Walker Ave, no services
168	KS 255, to Victoria, S...**gas:** Ampride/dsl, to Cathedral of the Plains
163	Toulon Ave
161	Commerce Parkway
159	US 183, Hays, N...**gas:** Valero/dsl/24hr, **food:** Applebee's, Carlos O'Kelly's, Golden Corral, IHOP, Red Sun Buffet, Subway, **lodging:** Comfort Inn, Fairfield Inn, Hampton Inn, Sleep Inn, **other:** Chrysler/Jeep/Dodge, Ford/Lincoln/Mercury, Harley-Davidson, Home Depot, Radio Shack, Toyota, Wal-Mart SuperCtr/Subway/gas/24hr, S...**gas:** BP/24hr, Conoco/dsl/24hr, Love's, Phillips 66/dsl, Power Plus Gas, **food:** A&W, Arby's, Burger King, China Garden, Imperial Garden, KFC, LJ Silver, Lucky Buffet, McDonald's, MT Mike's Steaks, Papa John's, Pizza Hut, Sonic, Subway, Taco Bell, Taco Express, Taco Grande, Vagabond Rest., Village Inn Rest., Wendy's, Whiskey Creek Grill, **lodging:** Baymont Inn, Best Western, Comfort Inn, Day's Inn, Econolodge, Holiday Inn, Motel 6, Quality Inn, Super 8, **other:** HOSPITAL, Ace Hardware, Advance Parts, Chevrolet, Chrysler, Curves, Dillon's Foods/gas, Firestone/auto, Hastings Books, JC Penney, NAPA, Tires 4 Less, Walgreens, mall, st patrol
157	US 183 S byp, to Hays, S...**other:** museum, to Ft Hays St U
153	Yocemento Ave
145	KS 247 S, Ellis, S...**gas:** Casey's, Phillips 66/DQ/Subway/dsl/24hr, **lodging:** Ellis House Inn, **other:** to Chrysler Museum, Railroad Museum, RV camping, USPO
140	Riga Rd
135	KS 147, Ogallah, N...**gas:** Schreiner 24hr gas/dsl/café, S...to Cedar Bluff SP(13mi)
132mm	**rest area both lanes, full(handicapped)facilities, picnic tables, litter barrels, petwalk, RV dump**
128	US 283 N, WaKeeney, N...**gas:** Sinclair/dsl/24hr, **lodging:** Budget Host, Super 8, **other:** HOSPITAL
127	US 283 S, WaKeeney, N...**food:** DQ, Frisky Biscuit Cafe, Jade Garden Rest., McDonald's, Pizza Hut, **lodging:** Best Western, KS Kountry Inn, S...**gas:** BP/Real Country Cafe/dsl/rest./24hr, Conoco/Subway/dsl, **lodging:** Econolodge, **other:** KOA, antiques, auto repair
120	Voda Rd
115	KS 198 N, Banner Rd, Collyer
107	KS 212, Castle Rock Rd, Quinter, N...**gas:** Sinclair/dsl, **lodging:** Budget Host/rest., **other:** HOSPITAL, Sunflower RV Park, auto repair, S...**gas:** Shell/dsl/24hr, **food:** DQ
99	KS 211, Park, **1 mi** N...**gas:** Sinclair/dsl
97mm	**rest area both lanes, full(handicapped)facilities, picnic tables, litter barrels, vending, petwalk, RV dump**
95	KS 23 N, to Hoxie
93	KS 23, Grainfield, N...**gas:** Sinclair/dsl

(left margins: **Hays**, **Colby**, **Goodland**)

85	KS 216, Grinnell, N...**gas**(.5 mi)
79	Campus Rd
76	US 40, to Oakley, S...**gas:** TA/Shell/Subway/Buckhorn Rest./scales/dsl/24hr/@, **lodging:** Best Value Inn(1+mi), 1st Interstate Inn, **other:** HOSPITAL, Blue Beacon, Fick Museum
70	US 83, to Oakley, N...**lodging:** Free Breakfast Inn, S...**gas:** Phillips 66/dsl, Sinclair/dsl, **food:** Colonial Steaks, **other:** HOSPITAL, Hi-Plains RV Park, Prairie Dog Town, Fick Museum
62	rd K, Mingo, S...**gas:** gas/dsl/phone
54	Country Club Dr, Colby, **1 mi** N...**lodging:** Country Club Motel, **other:** HOSPITAL, RV camping
53	KS 25, Colby, N...**gas:** Conoco/DQ/dsl, 24-7/dsl, **food:** Arby's, Burger King, China Buffet, DQ, McDonald's, MT Mike's Steaks, Pizza Hut, Sonic, Subway, Taco John's, **lodging:** Day's Inn, Holiday Inn Express, Motel 6, Quality Inn, Super 8, **other:** HOSPITAL, Dillon's Foods/gas, $General, Ford/Lincoln/Mercury, Haas Tire, Prairie Art Museum, Quilt Cabin, Radio Shack, Wal-Mart Super Ctr/24hr, dsl repair, trucklube/wash, S...**gas:** Petro/Phillips 66/scales/dsl, **food:** Baskin-Robbins, Chester Fried, City Limits Steaks, Quizno's, Starbucks, Village Inn Rest., **lodging:** Comfort Inn, Crown Inn, **other:** Chevrolet/Cadillac/Buick/Pontiac, Chrysler/Jeep/Dodge, outlets
48.5mm	**rest area both lanes, full(handicapped)facilities, phone, picnic tables, litter barrels, RV dump, vending, petwalk**
45	US 24 E, Levant
36	KS 184, Brewster, N...**gas:** Fuel Depot/dsl/24hr
35.5mm	**Mountain/Central time zone**
27	KS 253, Edson
19	US 24, Goodland, N...**gas:** Sinclair, **food:** Pizza Hut, **lodging:** Best Value, **other:** KOA, High Plains Museum
17	US 24, KS 27, Goodland, N...**gas:** Conoco, Phillips 66/dsl, **food:** DQ, El Reynaldo's, McDonald's, Steakhouse Diner, Subway, Taco John's, Wendy's, **lodging:** Best Value, Comfort Inn, Economy 9 Motel, Howard Johnson, Super 8, **other:** HOSPITAL, Carquest, Chevrolet/Buick/Pontiac, Firestone/auto, Wal-Mart SuperCtr/24hr, Radio Shack, S...**gas:** Valero/deli/scales/dsl, **lodging:** Holiday Inn Express, **other:** Mid-America Camping
12	rd 14, Caruso, no services
9	rd 11, Ruleton, no services
7.5mm	**Welcome Ctr eb/rest area wb, full(handicapped)facilities, info, phone, picnic tables, litter barrels, petwalk, vending, wireless internet, RV dump**
1	KS 267, Kanorado
.5mm	weigh sta eb
0mm	Kansas/Colorado State Line

KANSAS
Interstate 135(Wichita)

Salina

Exit #	Services
95b a	I-70, E to KS City, W to Denver. I-135 begins/ends on I-70, exit 250. US 81 continues nb.
93	KS 140, State St, Salina, no services
92	Crawford St, E...gas: BP/dsl/deli/@, Citgo, Kwik-Shop, Shell, food: Braum's, Gutierra's Rest., Hickory Hut BBQ, McDonald's, Russell's Rest., Spangles, Taco Bell, Subway, Western Sizzlin, lodging: Best Western, Comfort Inn, Fairfield Inn, Holiday Inn, Super 8, other: Dillan's Foods, Walgreens, W...gas: Cenex/dsl, lodging: Red Coach Inn
90	Magnolia Rd, E...gas: Phillips 66/dsl, Shell/24hr, food: Carlos O'Kelly's, Chili's, China King, Coyote Canyon Café, Domino's, Fazoli's, IHOP, McDonald's, Mr Goodcents Subs, Schlotsky's, Sonic, Subway, Taco Tico, lodging: Candlewood Suites, 1st Inn, other: Advance Parts, AutoZone, Buick/Subaru, Chevrolet/Cadillac, Dillard's, Dillon's Foods/gas, $General, $Tree, Goody's, Honda, JC Penney, JoAnne Fabrics, O'Reilly Parts, Sears/auto, Toyota, mall, W...gas: Conoco
89	Schilling Rd, E...gas: KwikShop/dsl, food: Applebee's, Burger King, Pizza Hut, Red Lobster, Taco Bueno, Tucson's Steaks, Wendy's, lodging: Country Inn&Suites, Courtyard, Hampton Inn, other: Aldi Foods, Cadillac/Chevrolet, Ford, Lowe's Whse, Sam's Club/gas, Target, Wal-Mart SuperCtr/24hr, W...gas: Casey's, lodging: Baymont Inn
88	Waterwell RD, E...other: Ford, Nissan
86	KS 104, Mentor, Smolan
82	KS 4, Falun Rd, Assaria
78	KS 4 W, Lindsborg, E...gas: DQ/Stuckey's/gas
72	US 81, Lindsborg, 4 mi E...other: McPhearson St Fishing Lake, Maxwell WR, W...other: HOSPITAL, gas, food, lodging, phone, camping, museum
68mm	**rest areas(both lanes exit left), full(handicapped) facilities, phone, picnic tables, litter barrels petwalk, RV dump**

McPherson

65	Pawnee Rd, no services
60	US 56, McPherson, Marion, W...gas: BP, Conoco/dsl, food: Applebee's, Arby's, Braum's, KFC, LA Fiesta Mexican, McDonald's, MT Mike's, Perkins, Pizza Hut, Subway, Taco Tico, lodging: Best Value Inn, Best Western, Days Inn, Red Coach Inn, other: HOSPITAL, $General, Wal-Mart SuperCtr/24hr
58	US 81, to Hutchinson, McPherson
54	Elyria
48	KS 260 E, Moundridge, 2 mi W...gas, food, phone
46	KS 260 W, Moundridge, 2 mi W...gas, food, phone
40	Lincoln Blvd, Hesston, E...lodging: AmericInn, W...gas: Cenex/dsl, food: Aggie's Grill, Lincoln Perk Coffee, Pizza Hut, Sonic, Subway, lodging: Hesston Inn
34	N Newton, Avalene, KS 15, E...other: RV camping, W...food: Subway, other: Kaufman Museum

Newton

33	US 50 E, to Peabody (from nb)
31	1st St, Broadway Ave, E...gas: Cenex, Conoco/dsl, Shamrock, food: Applebee's, Charlie's, KFC, lodging: Best Value Inn, Day's Inn, 1st Inn, other: Chevrolet/Cadillac, Chrysler/Dodge/Jeep, Ford/Lincoln/Mercury, W...food: Braum's, MT Mike's, lodging: Best Western
30	US 50 W, KS 15(exits left from nb), to Hutchinson, Newton, W...gas: Cenex, KwikShop/dsl, food: Arby's, Pizza Hut, Sonic, Subway, other: HOSPITAL, AutoZone, Buick/Pontiac/GMC, Dillon's Foods/24hr, $Tree, Wal-Mart SuperCtr/24hr
28	SE 36th St, W...gas: Shell, food: Burger King, other: Newton Outlets/famous brands
25	KS 196, to Whitewater, El Dorado
23mm	**rest areas both lanes, full(handicapped) facilities, phone, picnic tables, litter barrels, vending, petwalk, RV dump**
22	125th St
19	101st St, W...other: RV camping
17	85th St, E...Valley Ctr, KS Coliseum
16	77th St, E...other: Wichita Greyhound Park
14	61st St, E...gas: QT/dsl, Total, food: Applebee's, Cracker Barrel, Pizza Hut, Spangles Rest., Subway, Taco Bell, Wendy's, lodging: Comfort Inn, other: Chevrolet, W...gas: Phillips 66/dsl/@, food: KFC, McDonald's, Sonic, lodging: Super 8, other: Goodyear/auto
13	53rd St, W...gas: Phillips 66, food: Country Kitchen, lodging: Best Western, Day's Inn
11b	I-235 W, KS 96, to Hutchinson
11a	KS 254, to El Dorado
10b	29th St, Hydraulic Ave
10a	KS 96 E
9	21st St, E...gas: BP, other: Wichita St U
8	13th St
7b	8th St, 9th St, Central Ave., E...School of Medicine
6b	1st St, 2nd St, E...AutoZone, W...Chevrolet, Chrysler, Jeep
5b	US 54, US 400, Kellogg Ave, E...gas: QT, food: Chipotle Meixcan, McDonald's, Spangles, Wendy's
5a	Lincoln St, W...gas: QT
4	Harry St, 1 mi E...gas: QT, food: Church's, Denny's, McDonald's, Spangles Rest., Wendy's, W...gas: BP
3	Pawnee Ave, E...gas: QT, W...food: Burger King, Church's, Papa John's, Pizza Hut, Spangles, other: AutoZone, Checker's Foods, $General
2	Hydraulic Ave, E...gas: QT, W...food: McDonald's, Subway
2mm	Arkansas River
1c	I-235 N, 2 mi W...Hilton
1b a	US 81 S, 47th St, E...gas: Conoco, food: Potbelly's Rest., lodging: Comfort Inn, Day's Inn, Holiday Inn Express, W...gas: Phillips 66, food: Applebee's, Braum's, Burger King, Carlos O'Kelly's, Godfather's, KFC, LJ Silver, McDonald's, Panda Rest., Papa John's, Pizza Hut, Quizno's, Spangles Rest., Subway, Taco Bell, Taco Tico, lodging: Best Western, Heritage Inn, Red Carpet Inn, other: Checker's Foods, Dillon's Foods/gas/dsl, K-Mart, O'Reilly's Parts, Radio Shack
0mm	I-135 begins/ends on I-35, exit 42

Wichita

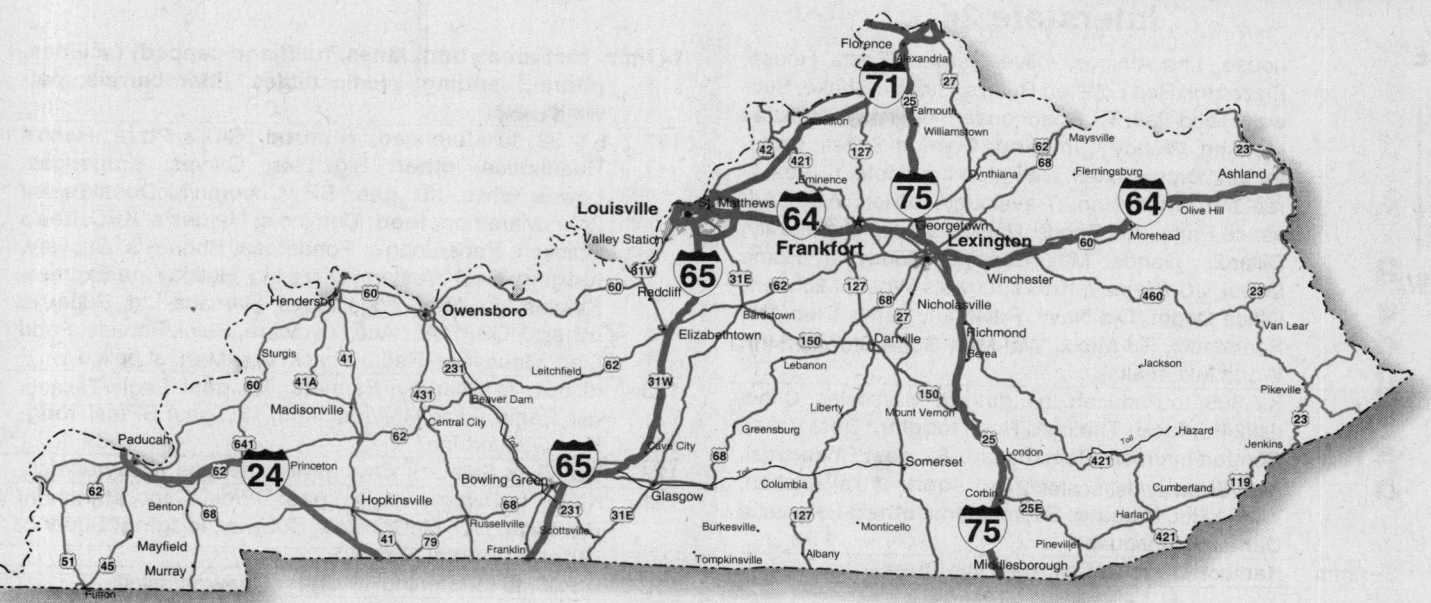

Interstate 24

Exit #	Services
93.5mm	Kentucky/Tennessee state line
93mm	**Welcome Ctr wb, full(handicapped)facilities, phones, picnic tables, litter barrels, vending, pet-walk**
91.5mm	Big West Fork Red River
89	KY 115, to Oak Grove, **N**...to Jeff Davis Mon St HS, **S**...**gas:** Pilot/McDonald's/dsl/scales/24hr/@, Shell/dsl
86	US 41A, to Ft Campbell, Pennyrile Pkwy, Hopkinsville, **N**...**gas:** Chevron/Taco Tico/dsl/24hr, **S**...**gas:** BP/dsl/24hr, ✈/Flying J/Country Mkt/dsl/scales/LP/24hr/@, Pilot/Subway/Wendy's/dsl/scales/24hr, **food:** McDonald's, Waffle House, **lodging:** Comfort Inn, Day's Inn, Holiday Inn Express
79mm	Little River
73	KY 117, to Gracey, Newstead, no services
65	US 68, KY 80, to Cadiz, **S**...**gas:** BP/dsl, Chevron/dsl, Shell/dsl/24hr, **food:** Cracker Barrel, KFC, McDonald's, Taco Bell, Wendy's, **lodging:** Holiday Inn Express, Knight's Inn, 7 Inn, Super 8, **other:** HOSPITAL, Candy's RV Ctr, Chevrolet, antiques, golf, to NRA's
56	KY 139, to Cadiz, Princeton, **S**...**gas:** Chevron/dsl, **other:** Nat Rec Areas
47mm	Lake Barkley
45	KY 293, to Princeton, Saratoga, **N**...**other:** classic car museum, **S**...**gas:** Chevron/dsl, **food:** Farmhouse Rest., **other:** Mineral Mound SP, RV Camping, to KY St Penitentiary
42	to W KY Pkwy eb, no services
40	US 62, US 641, Kuttawa, Eddyville, **N**...**lodging:** Country Hearth Inn, Regency Inn, Relax Inn, **other:** camping, **S**...**gas:** BP/Wendy's/dsl/24hr, Huck's/Quizno's/dsl/scales/24hr/@, Shell, **food:** Huddle House, SW grill, **lodging:** Day's Inn, Hampton Inn, **other:** W KY Factory Outlet, to Lake Barkley, KY Lake Rec Areas, camping
36mm	weigh sta both lanes, phones
34mm	Cumberland River
31	KY 453, to Grand Rivers, Smithland, **N**...**gas:** BP/dsl, **lodging:** Microtel, **S**...**gas:** Cheers/dsl, **food:** Miss Scarlett's, Patti's Rest., **lodging:** Best Western, Grand Rivers Resort(3mi), Lighthouse Landing Resort, **other:** Exit 31 RV Park, NRA's
29mm	Tennessee River
27	US 62, to KY Dam, Calvert City, **N**...**gas:** BP, Shell/dsl, **food:** Cracker Barrel, DQ, McDonald's, Waffle House, Willow Pond Rest., **lodging:** Foxfire Motel, KY Dam Motel, Super 8, **other:** Cypress Lakes Camp, Freightliner, KOA, **S**...**gas:** Love's/Arby's/dsl/scales/rest./24hr
25b a	to Calvert City, Carroll/Purchase Pkwy, services 1 mi N
16	US 68, to Paducah, **S**...**gas:** BP/Southern Pride/Subway/dsl/scales/24hr/@, Roadside, **food:** Subway, **other:** Stuckey's, flea mkt
11	rd 1954, Husband Rd, to Paducah, **N**...**gas:** Exxon/dsl, **lodging:** Best Western, **5 mi N**...**food:** Burger King, Wendy's, Waffle House, **lodging:** Economy Inn, Executive Inn, Hickory House Inn, Travel Inn, **other:** Duck Creek RV Park, **S**...**other:** Harley-Davidson
7	US 45, US 62, to Paducah, **N**...**gas:** BP/dsl, **food:** Burger King, Taco Bell, **other:** HOSPITAL, **S**...**Welcome Ctr both lanes, full(handicapped)facilities, phones, vending, picnic tables, litter barrels, pet-walk, gas:** BP/dsl, Shell/dsl, **food:** Arby's, Backyard Burger, McDonald's, Popeye's, Sonic, Waffle House, **other:** K-Mart
4	US 60, to Paducah, **N**...**gas:** BP, Shell/dsl/24hr, **food:** Applebee's, Bob Evans, Burger King, McDonald's, O'Charley's, Outback Steaks, Rafferty's, **lodging:** Courtyard, Day's Inn/rest., Drury Inn, Hampton Inn, Holiday Inn Express, Residence Inn, Westowne Inn, **other:** Hancock Fabrics, Toyota/Scion, **S**...**gas:** BP, Petro Mart, Shell, **food:** Arby's, Capt D's, Chong's Chinese, ChuckeCheese, Cracker Barrel, Dominos, El Chico's, Fazoli's, Hardee's/24hr, IHOP, Logan's Road-

Paducah

E ↕ **W** **Paducah**

house, Los Amigos, Olive Garden, Pasta House, Pizza Hut, Red Lobster, Ryan's, Steak'n Shake, Subway, Taco Bell, TX Roadhouse, TGIFriday, Tuesday Morning, Wendy's, **lodging:** Comfort Suites, Country Inn, Drury Suites, Hampton Inn, Motel 6, PearTree Inn, Thrifty Inn, Travelodge, **other:** AAA, Advance Parts, Aldi Foods, BooksAMillion, Circuit City, Dillard's, Gander Mtn, Goody's, Goodyear, Home Depot, JC Penney, Kohl's, Lowe's Whse, Michaels, Office Depot, Old Navy, PetsMart, Sam's Club/gas, Sears/auto, TJ Maxx, Wal-Mart SuperCtr/gas/24hr, World Mkt, mall

3 KY 305, to Paducah, **N̄...gas:** BP/dsl/scales, Citgo/dsl/24hr, **food:** Trimble's Rest, **lodging:** Best Value, Comfort Inn/rest., Ramada Ltd, **S̄...gas:** Cheers/dsl, Pilot/Subway/dsl/scales/24hr, **food:** Yu's Kitchen, Waffle Hut, **lodging:** Baymont Inn, **other:** Fern Lake Camping, antiques

0mm Kentucky/Illinois state line, Ohio River

Interstate 64

Exit # Services

192mm Kentucky/West Virginia state line, Big Sandy River

E ↕ **W**

191 US 23, to Ashland, 1-2 mi **N̄...gas:** GoMart, Marathon/dsl, Speedway, **food:** McDonald's, Pizza Inn, Subway, Waffle House, **lodging:** Ashland Inn, Quality Inn, Ramada Ltd, **other:** HOSPITAL

185 KY 180, Cannonsburg, 1-3 mi **N̄...gas:** BP/dsl, Chevron, **food:** Arby's, Burger King, Hardee's, Subway, Taco Bell, Wendy's, **lodging:** Budget Inn, Day's Inn, Fairfield Inn, Hampton Inn, Holiday Inn Express, Knight's Inn, **other:** st police, **S̄...**✈/Flying J/CountryMkt/dsl/scales/24hr/@, Hidden Valley Camping

181 181 US 60, to Princess, **N̄...gas:** BP/dsl, **S̄...gas:** Marathon

179 rd 67, Industrial Parkway, no services

174mm rest area wb, full(handicapped) facilities, phone, vending, picnic tables, litter barrels, petwalk

173mm rest area wb, full(handicapped)facilities, phone, vending, picnic tables, litter barrels, petwalk

Grayson

172 rd 1, rd 7, Grayson, **N̄...gas:** Citgo/dsl, Texaco/dsl/24hr, Superquik/dsl, **food:** A&W/LJ Silver, El Portal Mexican, Huddle House, KFC, LJ Silver, Shoney's, **lodging:** American Inn, Day's Inn, Executive Inn, Holiday Inn Express, Knight's Inn, Quality Inn, Travelodge, **other:** Chrysler/Jeep, Ford, K-Mart, SaveALot Foods, **S̄...gas:** BP, Chevron, Exxon/Hardees, Marathon, Pilot/Wendy's/dsl/scales/24hr/@, Speedway, **food:** Arby's, China House, DQ, Little Caesar's, McDonald's, Pizza Hut, Subway, Taco Bell, **lodging:** Super 8, **other:** Advance Parts, AutoZone, CarQuest, $General, $Tree, Family$, Food Fair, Parts+, Rite Aid

161 US 60, to Olive Hill, **N̄...gas:** BP, **other:** to Carter Caves SP, camping, **S̄...gas:** Marathon/dsl/24hr, **lodging:** Spanish Manor Motel

156 rd 2, to KY 59, to Olive Hill, **S̄...gas:** BP, Sunoco/dsl, **food:** DQ

148mm weigh sta both lanes

141mm rest areas both lanes, full(handicapped) facilities, phone, vending, picnic tables, litter barrels, petwalk

137 KY 32, to Morehead, **N̄...food:** CiCi's Pizza, Reno's Roadhouse, **other:** Big Lots, Curves, Kroger/gas, Lowes Whse, **S̄...gas:** BP, Chevron/McDonald's/dsl/24hr, Marathon, **food:** Domino's, Hardee's, KFC, Lee's Chicken, Papa John's, Ponderosa, Shoney's, Subway, **lodging:** Best Western, Day's Inn, Holiday Inn Express, Knights Inn, Mtn Lodge Motel, Ramada Ltd, Super 8, **other:** HOSPITAL, Ace Hardware, Buick/Pontiac, Food Lion, Goodyear, Radio Shack, Wal-Mart, st police

133 rd 801, to Sharkey, Farmers, **N̄...gas:** Eagle/Texaco/dsl, Eagle Trace Golf/rest.(4mi), **S̄...gas:** BP/dsl, **lodging:** Comfort Inn

123 US 60, to Salt Lick, Owingsville, **N̄...gas:** Chevron/dsl

121 KY 36, to Owingsville, **N̄...gas:** BP/dsl, Citgo, Marathon/dsl, **food:** DQ, McDonald's, Subway, **lodging:** Super 8, **other:** $General, Family$

113 US 60, to Mt Sterling, **N̄...gas:** Chevron/dsl/@

110 US 460, KY 11, Mt Sterling, **N̄...gas:** Chevron/repair/24hr, Shell/Krystal/dsl, **food:** Cracker Barrel, Fairfield Inn, Ramada Ltd, **other:** golf, **S̄...gas:** BP/dsl, Exxon/Subway, Marathon/Huddle House, Speedway/dsl, **food:** Applebee's, Arby's, Burger King, El Camino, Golden Corral, KFC, Lee's Chicken, LJ Silver, McDonald's, Rio Grande Mexican, Wendy's, **lodging:** Budget Inn, Day's Inn/rest., **other:** HOSPITAL, Family$, Ford/Mercury, **S on KY 686...gas:** Fastlane, **food:** Applebees, Hardee's, Little Caesar's, Peking Buffet, Pizza Hut, Taco Bell, **other:** Advance Parts, Chevrolet, Chrysler/Dodge/Jeep, Ford, Wal-Mart SuperCtr/24hr

108mm rest area wb, full(handicapped)facilities, phone, vending, picnic tables, litter barrels, petwalk

101 US 60, no services

98.5mm rest area eb, full(handicapped)facilities, phone, vending, picnic tables, litter barrels, petwalk

98 KY 402(from eb), no services

96b a KY 627, to Winchester, Paris, **N̄...gas:** BP/dsl, Citgo/96 Truck Plza/dsl/rest./scales/, **S̄...gas:** Marathon/dsl, Speedway, **lodging:** Day's Inn, Hampton Inn, Quality Inn, **other:** Chevrolet

Lexington

94 KY 1958, Van Meter Rd, Winchester, **N̄...gas:** Chevron/dsl/24hr, Shell/scales/dsl, **lodging:** Best Value Inn, Holiday Inn Express, **other:** flea mkt, **S̄...gas:** BP/dsl, Speedway/dsl, **food:** Applebee's, Arby's, Burger King, Cantuckee Diner, Capt D's, Domino's, Fazoli's, Golden Corral, Great Wall Chinese, KFC, King Buffet, Little Caesar's, LJ Silver, McDonald's, Papa John's, Pizza Hut, Quizno's, Rally's, Sonic, Subway, Taco Bell, Tacos Too, Taste Of China, Ted's Grill, Waffle House, Wendy's, **lodging:** Best Western, Budget Inn, Travelodge, **other:** HOSPITAL, Advance Parts, AutoZone, Chrysler/Dodge/Jeep, Curves, Family$, Ford/Mercury, Goody's, K-Mart, Kroger, Lowe's Whse, O'Reilly Parts, Radio Shack, Rite Aid, Wal-Mart SuperCtr/24hr, to Ft Boonesborough Camping

87 KY 859, Blue Grass Sta, no services

81 I-75 S, to Knoxville

I-64 and I-75 run together 7 mi. See Kentucky Interstate 75, exits 113-115.

KENTUCKY

75	I-75 N, to Cincinnati, access to KY Horse Park
69	US 62 E, to Georgetown, ...antiques(mi), S... Equus Run Vineyards(2mi)
65	US 421, Midway, S...antiques
60mm	**rest area both lanes, full handicapped facilities, litter barrels, petwalk, vending**
58	US 60, to Frankfort, N...gas: BP, Chevron/dsl, Marathon, Shell food: KFC, Waffle House, lodging: Best Western, Fairfield Inn, other: Cadillac/Pontiac, Chevrolet/Nissan, Chrysler/Jeep, Ford/Lincoln/Mercury, Toyota, to KY St Capitol, KYSU, to Viet Vets Mem, transmissions
55mm	Kentucky River
53b a	US 127, Frankfort, N...gas: BP, Chevron/24hr, Shell/24hr, Speedway, food: A&W/LJ Silver, Applebee's, Arby's, Big Boy, Burger King, Carino's Italian, Chili's, DQ, Fazoli's, Hardee's, KFC, McDonald's, O'Charley's, Panera Bread, Pizza Hut, Qdoba Mexican, Rio Grande Mexican, Shoney's, Starbucks, Steak'n Shake, Subway, Taco Bell, Taco John's, Wendy's, lodging: Best Value Inn, Day's Inn, Hampton Inn, Holiday Inn Express, Super 8(1mi), other: HOSPITAL, Advance Parts, Family$, Goodyear, Goody's, JC Penney, K-Mart, Kroger/24hr, Lowe's Whse, Office Depot, Radio Shack, Rite Aid, Walgreens, Wal-Mart SuperCtr/24hr, Ancient Age Tour, to KY St Capitol, st police
48	KY 151, to US 127 S, S...gas: BP, Chevron/24hr, Shell/Subway/dsl
43	KY 395, Waddy, N...gas: ✈/Flying J/Conoco/Country Mkt/dsl/LP/scales/24hr/@, S...gas: Auto/Truck Plaza/Chester Fried/dsl/scales/24hr
38.5mm	**weigh sta both lanes**
35	KY 53, Shelbyville, N...gas: BP/dsl, Chevron/dsl, food: Cracker Barrel, McDonald's(1mi), Waffle House, other: Chevrolet, Ford/Mercury, Kroger/gas/deli, Lake Shelby Camping(3mi), antiques, S...gas: Chevron/White Castle/dsl, Shell/dsl, lodging: Holiday Inn Express, other: golf
32b a	KY 55, Shelbyville, 1-3 mi N...gas: Shell, food: Arby's, Asian Buffet, DQ, KFC, McDonald's, Subway, Waffle House, Wendy's, lodging: Best Western, Country Hearth Inn, Day's Inn, other: HOSPITAL, AutoZone, Buick/Pontiac/GMC, $Tree, Lowes Whse, Rolling Hills Camping(16mi), Walgreens, Wal-Mart SuperCtr/gas/24hr, S...food: Cattleman's Roadhouse, lodging: Ramada Inn, Taylorsville Lake SP
28mm	**rest area eb, full(handicapped)facilities, info, phone, picnic tables, litter barrels, vending, petwalk**
28	KY 1848, Veechdale Rd, Simpsonville, N...gas: Citgo, Pilot/Wendy's/dsl/scales/24hr, food: DQ, other: golf, S...gas: BP/dsl
19b a	I-265, Gene Snyder Fwy, N...to Tom Sawyer SP
17	S Blankenbaker, N...gas: Circle K, Marathon, lodging: Staybridge Suites, other: Harley-Davidson, S...gas: BP, Chevron, Thornton's/dsl, food: Arby's, BackYard Burger, Burger King, Cracker Barrel, HomeTown Buffet, KFC/A&W, King Buffet, Kingfish Rest., McDonald's, Penn Sta., Ruby Tuesday, Sub-
	way, Taco Bell/LJ Silver, Waffle House, Wendy's, lodging: Candlewood Suites, Comfort Suites, Country Inn&Suites, Hampton Inn, Hilton Garden, Holiday Inn Express, Homestead Suites, Jameson Inn, Microtel, Sleep Inn, Super 8, Wingate Inn, other: Sam's Club/gas
15	Hurstbourne Lane, Louisville, N...gas: BP/Circle K/dsl, Shell/dsl, food: Arby's, Bob Evans, Carraba's, Chili's, Fazoli's, Harper's Rest., Ichiban Chinese, Macaroni Grill, McDonald's, Olive Garden, Panera Bread, Papa John's, Perkins, Picadilly, Sichuan Garden, Skyline Chili, Subway, TGIFriday, Waffle House, lodging: AmeriSuites, Baymont Inn, Courtyard, Days Inn, Drury Inn, Fairfield Inn, Holiday Inn, Hyatt, Red Roof Inn, other: Barnes&Noble, CompUSA, Lowe's Whse, Value Mkt Foods, S...gas: BP/dsl, Shell, Marathon, Meijer/dsl/24hr, food: Applebee's, Blimpie, Buca Rest., Burger King, Camille's Cafe, China Star, ChuckeCheese, Coldstone Creamery, DQ, Damon's, El Toro Mexican, Famous Daves, Jumbo Grill, Lonestar Steaks, McAlister's Deli, Moe's SW Grill, O'Charley's, Old Chicago, Picadilly, Qdoba, Quizno's, Shoney's, Shogun Japanese, Smokey Bones BBQ, Starbucks, Steak'n Shake, Taco Bell, Tumbleweeds Mexican, Wendy's, White Castle, lodging: Clarion, Hampton Inn, Marriott, Red Carpet Inn, other: Autozone, Borders, Cadillac, Carmax, Chevrolet/Subaru, Home Depot, Honda, Hummer, Infiniti, Kroger/gas, Michael's, Office Depot, Pontiac/GMC, Radio Shack, Staples, Target, Wal-Mart/drugs
12b	I-264 E, Watterson Expswy, 1 exit N on US 60...gas: Chevron, food: Alexander's Rest., CA Pizza, Denny's, Hop's Grill, Logan's Roadhouse, McDonald's, Outback Steaks, Rollo Pollo, Ruby Tuesday, Taco Bell, Wendy's, other: Acura, Best Buy, Dillard's, Ford, Galyan's, Goodyear/auto, JC Penney, Kohl's, Sears/auto, SteinMart, Suzuki, Towery's AutoCare, mall
12a	I-264 W, access to HOSPITAL
10	Cannons Lane, no services
8	8 Grinstead Dr, Louisville, S...gas: BP, Chevron, food: Cycler's Cafe, Jim Porter's Rest.
7	US 42, US 62, Mellwood Ave, Story Ave, no services
6	I-71 N(from eb), to Cincinnati, no services
5a	I-65, S to Nashville, N to Indianapolis
5b	3rd St, Louisville, N...food: Hardee's, food: Joe's CrabShack, McDonald's, lodging: Ramada Inn, S... lodging: Galt House Hotel, Marriott, food: Kingfish Rest., other: HOSPITAL
4	9th St, Roy Wilkins Ave, S...KY Art Ctr, science museum, downtown
3	US 150 E, to 22nd St, S...gas: BP/Circle K, Chevron, food: DQ, McDonald's, Subway, other:
1	I-264 E, to Shively, S...airport, zoo
0mm	Kentucky/Indiana state line, Ohio River

N ↕ **S**

Louisville

Exit #	Services
138mm	Kentucky/Indiana state line, Ohio River
137	I-64 W, I-71 N, I-64 E, W...to Galt House, downtown
136c	Jefferson St, Louisville, E...other: HOSPITAL, Walgreens, W...gas: Chevron, Shell, food: McDonald's, Papa John's, lodging: Comfort Inn, Hampton Inn, Marriott, other: Tires+
136b	Broadway St, Chestnut St (from nb), E...other: HOSPITAL, Ford/Lincoln/Mercury, Tires+, W...gas: Speedway, Thornton, food: McDonald's, Taco Bell, lodging: Hampton Inn, Marriott
135	W St Catherine, E...gas: Circle K, Shell,
134b a	KY 61, Jackson St, Woodbine St, W...gas: BP/Circle K, lodging: Day's Inn, Quality Inn, other: Harley-Davidson
133b	US 60A, Eastern Pkwy, Taylor Blvd, E...food: Denny's, Papa John's, Pizza Mia, Snappy Tomato Pizza, Subway, W...gas: BP/dsl, Shell, food: Cracker Barrel, McDonald's, lodging: Country Hearth Inn, other: U of Louisville, Churchill Downs, museum
133a	Crittenden Dr(from sb), W...gas: BP, food: Arby's, Burger King, Cracker Barrel, Hall of Fame Cafe', Hilton Garden, lodging: Country Inn& Suites, Ramada Inn, Super 8 E...food: Denny's, same as 133
131b a	I-264, Watterson Expswy, W...Cardinal Stadium, Expo Center, airport
130	KY 61, Preston Hwy, E on Ky 61...gas: BP/Circle K, Speedway, Thornton, food: Blimpie, Bob Evans, Burger King, Fazoli's, KFC, Little Caesar's, McDonald's, Papa John's, Popeyes, Rally's, Subway, Taco Bell, Waffle House, Wendy's, lodging: Econolodge, Red Roof Inn, Super 8, other: AutoZone, Big O Tire, Chevrolet/KIA, Chrysler, $General, Ford, O'Rielly's Parts, PepBoys, Radio Shack, Staples, Tires+, U-Haul
128	KY 1631, Fern Valley Rd, E...gas: FiveStar, Marathon/Circle K, Thornton/dsl, food: Arby's, Big Boy, Golden Wall Chinese, Hardee's, Indi's Rest., McDonald's, Outback Steaks, Shoney's, Subway, Waffle House, White Castle, Wendy's, lodging: Comfort Suites, Days Inn, Holiday Inn, InTown Suites, Jameson Inn, other: Cottman Transmissions, Lincoln/Mercury, NAPA Care, Sam's Club/gas, Walgreens, W...UPS Depot
127	KY 1065, outer loop, E...Texas Roadhouse, W...food: McDonald's, to Motor Speedway,
125b a	I-265 E, KY 841, Gene Snyder Fwy, no services
121	KY 1526, Brooks Rd, E...gas: BP, Chevron, food: Arby's, Burger King, Cracker Barrel, Tumbleweed Grill, lodging: Fairfield Inn, Hearthstone Inn, other: HOSPITAL, Tinker's RV Ctr, W...gas: BP/Blimpie/dsl, Pilot/Subway/Taco Bell/dsl/24hr/scales/@, Shell/dsl, food: Waffle House, lodging: Comfort Inn, Econolodge, Hampton Inn, Quality Inn
117	KY 44, Shepherdsville, E...gas: BP, Shell/dsl, food: Denny's, Kitchen Rest., lodging: Best Western/rest., Day's Inn, other: KOA(2mi), W...gas: Chevron/dsl/24hr, Speedway/dsl, food: Arby's, Burger King, DQ, Fazoli's, LJ Silver, KFC, McDonald's, Mr Gatti's, Rio's Steaks, Shoney's, Sonic, Subway, Taco Bell, Waffle House, White Castle, lodging:

Elizabethtown

Exit #	Services
	Country Inn&Suites, Motel 6, Super 8, other: $General, Family$, Kroger/gas, NAPA, Rite Aid, Sav-a-Lot
116.5mm	Salt River
116	KY 480, KY 61, E...gas: Love's/Subway/dsl/scales/24hr/@, Shell/dsl, W...gas: Chevron/dsl, other: Grandma's RV Park, Leisure Life RV Ctr
114mm	**rest area sb, full(handicapped)facilities, phone, vending, picnic tables, litter barrels, petwalk**
112	KY 245, Clermont, E...gas: Shell/dsl, other: Jim Beam Outpost, Bernheim Forest, to My Old Kentucky Home SP
105	105 KY 61, Lebanon Jct, W...gas: Pilot/McDonald's/Subway/dsl/scales/24hr/@, 105 QuikStop/dsl
102	KY 313, to KY 434, Radcliff, E...to Patton Museum
94	US 62, Elizabethtown, E...gas: BP/dsl, Marathon/dsl, food: Denny's, Waffle House, White Castle, lodging: Day's Inn, Quality Inn, Super 8, other: KOA(1mi), W...gas: BP/dsl, Chevron/dsl/24hr, Speedway/dsl, food: Burger King, Cracker Barrel, Chalupa's Mexican, Hawk's Grill, KFC/Taco Bell, La Quinta, McDonald's, Ruby Tuesday, Ryan's, Shoney's, Stone Hearth, Subway, TX Outlaw Steaks, Texas Roadhouse, Wendy's, lodging: Best Western, Comfort Inn, Hampton Inn, Holiday Inn Express, Howard Johnson, Fairfield Inn, La Quinta, Motel 6, Ramada Inn, other: HOSPITAL, Advance Parts, CVS Drug, $General, $Tree, Kroger/gas, Skagg's RV Ctr, Walgreens, st police
93	to Bardstown, to BG Pky, E...to My Old KY Home SP, Maker's Mark Distillery
91	US 31 W, KY 61, WK Pkwy, Elizabethtown, E...gas: Chevron/24hr, Shell, food: LJ Silver, lodging: Bluegrass Inn, Budget Motel, Commonwealth Lodge, other: Ryder Trucks, to Lincoln B'Place, W...gas: Chevron, food: Denny's, Jerry's Rest./24hr, Lee's Chicken, lodging: Roadside Inn, other: HOSPITAL
90mm	weigh sta both lanes
86	KY 222, Glendale, E...gas: Pilot/McDiner/dsl/scales/24hr@, other: Glendale Camping, W...gas: Citgo/dsl/rest./24hr, Petro/dsl/rest./scales/24hr/@, lodging: Economy Inn, other: Blue Beacon
83mm	Nolin River
81	KY 84, Sonora, E...gas: BP, Citgo/dsl/rest., Pilot/Subway/dsl/scales/24hr, other: Blue Beacon, to Lincoln B'Place, W...gas: Shell
76	KY 224, Upton, E...gas: Chevron/dsl, W...to Nolin Lake
75mm	eastern/central time zone
71	KY 728, Bonnieville, no services
65	US 31 W, Munfordville, E...gas: BP/Subway/dsl, Citgo/dsl, Marathon/dsl, food: Country Fixen's Rest., DQ, King Buffet, Pizza Hut, Mazatlan Mexican, McDonald's, Sonic, lodging: Super 8, other: $General, Family$, W...gas: Chevron/dsl/24hr, Shell, to Nolin Lake
61mm	**rest area both lanes, full(handicapped)facilities, info, phone, picnic tables, litter barrels, vending, petwalk** Green River
58	KY 218, Horse Cave, E...other: HOSPITAL, W...gas: BP, Chevron/Pizza Hut/dsl/24hr, Marathon/dsl/repair, food: Bee's Rest./24hr, Subway, lodging: Budget Host/rest., Country Hearth Inn, Hampton Inn, other: Jent Factory Outlet, KOA, to Mammoth Cave NP

Interstate 65

53	KY 70, KY 90, Cave City, **E**...**gas:** BP/dsl, Marathon/Burger King/dsl, Citgo/dsl, **food:** Belair Rest., Country Kitchen, Cracker Barrel, DQ, Jerry's Rest., KFC, LJ Silver/A&W, McDonald's, Pizza Hut/Taco Bell, Sahara BBQ/steaks, Wendy's, **lodging:** Best Western, Comfort Inn, Day's Inn/rest., Howard Johnson, Quality Inn, Ramada Ltd, Super 8, **other:** HOSPITAL, Barren River Lake SP(24mi), **W**...**gas:** Shell, **other:** Onyx Cave, Mammoth Cave NP, Jellystone Camping, Singing Hills Camping
48	KY 255, Park City, **E**...**gas:** Shell/dsl/24hr, **lodging:** Parkland Motel, **other:** Park Mammoth Resort(1 1/2mi), tire repair, **W**...to Mammoth Cave NP
43	Nunn Cumberland Pky(toll), to Barren River Lake SP
39mm	**rest area nb, full(handicapped)facilities, phone, vending, picnic tables, litter barrels, petwalk**
38	KY 101, Smiths Grove, **W**...**gas:** BP/dsl, Chevron/Subway/dsl, Shell, **food:** McDonald's, Wendy's, **lodging:** Bryce Motel, **other:** $General, IGA Foods, 7 Springs Park
36	US 68, KY 80, Oakland, no services, no nb return
30mm	**rest area sb, full(handicapped)facilities, phone, vending, picnic tables, litter barrels, petwalk**
28	rd 446, to US 31 W, Bowling Green, **W**...**gas:** BP, Marathon, Shell/Blimpie/24hr, **food:** Hardee's, Jerry's Rest., Wendy's, **lodging:** Continental Inn, Country Hearth Inn, Value Lodge, **other:** HOSPITAL, Corvette Museum, **3 mi W**...Camping World RV Supply, to WKYU
26	rd 234, Bowling Green, no services
22	US 231, Bowling Green, **E**...**gas:** Citgo/dsl, Shell, **food:** Cracker Barrel, Culver's, Denny's, Domino's, Godfather's, Hardee's, Mancino's, Ryan's, Sonic, Waffle House, **lodging:** Best Western, Best Value, Comfort Inn, Day's Inn, Econolodge, Fairfield Inn, Microtel, Quality Inn, Ramada/rest., Super 8, **other:** Harley-Davidson, USPO, **W**...**gas:** BP, Chevron/dsl, RaceWay, Shell/Blimpie/dsl, Speedway, **food:** Applebee's, Arby's, Beijing Chinese, Bob Evans, Buffalo Wild Wings, Burger King, Capt D's, ChuckeCheese, Chick-fil-A, CiCi's, Fazoli's, HomeTown Buffet, KFC, Krystal, Little Caesar's, LoneStar Steaks, Longhorn Steaks, McDonald's, Moe's SW Grill, MT Grille, O'Charley's, Olive Garden, Outback Steaks, Pizza Hut, Ponderosa, Quizno's, Rafferty's, Red Lobster, Ruby Tuesday, Santa Fe Steaks, Shoney's, Smokey Bones BBQ, Sonic, Starbucks, Steak'n Shake, Subway, Taco Bell, TGIFriday, Toots Rest., Tumbleweed Grill, Waffle House, Wendy's, White Castle, **lodging:** Courtyard, Drury Inn, Hampton Inn, Holiday Inn, La Quinta, Motel 6, News Inn, Red Roof Inn, Rodeway Inn, **other:** HOSPITAL, Advance Parts, Best Buy, BMW/Mercedes, Buick/GMC, Cadillac, Chevrolet, Chrysler/Jeep, CVS Drug, Daewoo, Dillard's, $General, Ford/Lincoln/Mercury, Goodyear, Home Depot, Honda, Hyundai/Isuzu/Subaru, JC Penney, K-Mart, KOA, KIA, Kohls, Kroger/gas/24hr, Mazda, Nissan, Office Depot, Old Navy, Pontiac, Sam's Club/gas, Saturn, Scotty's Parts, Sears, Toyota, U-Haul, Wal-Mart SuperCtr/24hr, mall

Franklin

Bowling Green

20	WH Natcher Toll Rd, to Bowling Green, access to W KY U, KY st police
6	KY 100, Franklin, **E**...**gas:** BP/dsl/24hr, Citgo/Blimpie/dsl/24hr/@, **W**...**gas:** Pilot/Subway/dsl/scales/24hr/, Pilot/Wendy's/dsl/scales/24hr/, **lodging:** Day's Inn, Super 8, **other:** HOSPITAL, KOA, SpeedCo/tires/repair
4mm	weigh sta nb
2	US 31 W, to Franklin, **E**...**gas:** Flying J/Conoco/dsl/LP/rest./24hr/@, Keystop/Marathon/Burger King/dsl/24hr/@, **W**...**gas:** BP/Subway/dsl, **food:** Cracker Barrel, McDonald's, Richie's Steaks, Shoney's, Waffle House, **lodging:** Best Western, Comfort Inn, Econolodge, Hampton Inn, Holiday Inn Express, Super 8, **other:** HOSPITAL
1mm	**Welcome Ctr nb, full(handicapped)facilities, phone, vending, picnic tables, litter barrels, petwalk**
0mm	Kentucky/Tennessee state line

Interstate 71

Exit #	Services
	Kentucky/Ohio state line, Ohio River
	I-71 and I-75 run together 19 miles. See Kentucky Interstate 75, exits 175-192.
77[173]	I-75 S, to Lexington
75mm	weigh sta sb
72	KY 14, to Verona, **E**...**gas:** BP/dsl, Chevron/dsl, **other:** Oak Creek Camping(5mi)
62	US 127, to Glencoe, **E**...**gas:** 62 TrkPlaza/rest./dsl, **W**...**gas:** BP/dsl/rest., **lodging:** 127 Motel
57	KY 35, to Sparta, **E**...**gas:** Marathon/dsl, **other:** Sparta RV Park(3mi), **W**...**gas:** BP/dsl, **lodging:** Ramada Ltd, **other:** KY Speedway
55	KY 1039, **W**...KY Speedway
44	KY 227, to Indian Hills, **W**...**gas:** BP/dsl, Chevron/dsl/24hr, Marathon, Shell, **food:** Arby's, Burger King, Hometown Pizza, KFC, LJ Silver, McDonald's, New China, Sonic, Subway, Taco Bell, Waffle House, **lodging:** Best Western, Comfort Inn, Day's Inn, Hampton Inn, Holiday Inn Express, Super 8, **other:** HOSPITAL, AutoZone, Chevrolet, Chrysler/Jeep/Dodge, Ford/Mercury, $General, Kroger/gas, Radio Shack, Rite Aid, Sav-a-Lot Foods, Wal-Mart SuperCtr/gas/24hr, Carroll Butler SP, flea mkt
43.5mm	Kentucky River
43	KY 389, to KY 55, English, no services
34	US 421, Campbellsburg, **W**...**gas:** BP/Subway/dsl, Marathon/dsl, **other:** st police
28	KY 153, KY 146, to US 42, Pendleton, **E**...**gas:** BP, Marathon/dsl, Pilot/Subway/dsl/scales/24hr/@, **W**...**gas:** Pilot/McDonald's/scales/dsl/24hr
22	KY 53, La Grange, **E**...**gas:** BP/dsl, Speedway/Rally's, **food:** Applebees, Burger King, Jumbo Buffet, Papa John's, Ponderosa, Subway, Waffle House, Wendy's, **lodging:** Best Western-Ashbury, Holiday Inn Express,

KENTUCKY

Interstate 71

other: HOSPITAL, Big O Tire, $General, Kroger/gas, Radio Shack, Walgreens, Wal-Mart SuperCtr/24hr, W...**gas:** Chevron/dsl/24hr, Shell/dsl, Swifty, **food:** Arby's, Cracker Barrel, Domino's, DQ, El Torasco, Hometown Pizza, KFC, LJ Silver, McDonald's, Taco Bell, **lodging:** Comfort Suites, Super 8, **other:** Advance Parts, Chevrolet/Pontiac/Buick, Curves, NAPA, Rite Aid, Sav-a-Lot, tires, flea mkt, USPO

18 KY 393, Buckner, W...**gas:** Marathon/dsl, **food:** Subway

17 KY 146, Buckner, E...**other:** Ford, W...**gas:** Shell/dsl, Thornton's/dsl/24hr, **other:** USPO, st police

14 KY 329, Crestwood, Pewee Valley, Brownsboro, E...**gas:** Chevron/24hr, Shell, **2 mi** E...**food:** DQ, Hometown Pizza, Sonic, Starbucks, Subway

13mm rest area both lanes, full(handicapped)facilities, phone, vending, picnic tables, litter barrels, petwalk

9b a I-265, KY 841, Gene Snyder Fwy, E...to Sawyer SP

5 I-264, Watterson Expswy (exits left from sb), E...to Sawyer SP

2 Zorn Ave, E...VA HOSPITAL, W...**gas:** BP, Chevron, **food:** KingFish Rest., **lodging:** Ramada Inn, **other:** Art Museum

1b I-65, S to Nashville, N to Indianapolis

Interstate 75

Exit #   Services

193mm Kentucky/Ohio state line, Ohio River

192 5th St(from nb), Covington, E...**gas:** BP, Shell, Speedway, **food:** Big Boy, Burger King, GoldStar Chili, McDonald's, Skyline Chili, Subway, Taco Bell, Waffle House, White Castle, **lodging:** Courtyard, Extended Stay America, Holiday Inn, Radisson, **other:** Ford/Lincoln/Mercury, Lexus/Toyota, Subaru/VW, Riverboat Casino, W...**lodging:** Hampton Inn

191 12th St, Covington, E...**other:** HOSPITAL, Dodge, museum, same as 192

189 KY 1072(from sb), Kyles Lane, W...**gas:** BP/dsl, Marathon/dsl, Shell/dsl, Speedway, **food:** Big Boy, Reality Coffeehouse, Skyline Chili, Substation II Subs, **lodging:** Day's Inn, Ramada Inn, same as 188

188 US 25, US 42, Dixe Hwy, W...**food:** Pizza Hut, **lodging:** Day's Inn, Ramada, USA Hotel, **other:** $Tree, SteinMart, Walgreens, same as 189, E...**gas:** Sunoco, **food:** Subway, Tuesday Morning, **other:** GNC, Kroger

186 KY 371, Buttermilk Pike, Covington, E...**gas:** BP/dsl, Marathon, Texco/DQ, **food:** Graeter's Ice Cream, Montgomery Inn, Oriental Wok, Papa John's, **lodging:** Drawbridge Inn/rest., Super 8, W...**gas:** BP, Shell, Sunoco/dsl, **food:** Arby's, Bonefish Grill, Burger King, Chipotle Mexican, Domino's, Dunkin Donuts/Baskin-Robbins, Empire Buffet, GoldStar Chili, La Rosa's Pizza, LJ Silver, McDonald's, Outback Steaks, Pizza Hut, Rema's Diner, Skyline Chili, Staples, Subway, **other:** Home Depot, Remke Foods, Walgreens

185 I-275 E and W, W...to airport

184 KY 236, Donaldson Rd, to Erlanger, E...**gas:** BP/deli, Marathon, **food:** Double Dragon Chinese, W...**gas:** Marathon, Speedway/dsl, Sunoco/Subway/dsl, **food:**

Southern Kitchen Rest., Waffle House, **lodging:** Airport Inn, Comfort Inn, Day's Inn, Econolodge, **other:** Goodyear/auto

182 KY 1017, Turfway Rd, E...**gas:** BP, Shell, **food:** Big Boy, Lee's Chicken, McDonald's, New Wok, Ryan's, 3 Amigo's Mexican, **lodging:** Comfort Inn, Courtyard, Ivy Inn, Rodeway Inn, **other:** Big Lots, Office Depot, Remke Foods, funpark, W...**gas:** Meijer/dsl/24hr, **food:** Applebee's, CiCi's Pizza, Cracker Barrel, Dynasty Buffet, Famous Dave's BBQ, Karlo's Italian, Longhorn Steaks, O'Charley's, Rafferty's, Steak'n Shake, Tumbleweeds Grill, Wendy's, **lodging:** Extended Stay America, Hampton Inn, Hilton, Hyatt Place, La Quinta, Red Roof Inn, Studio+, **other:** HOSPITAL, Best Buy, Biggs Foods, Home Depot, Kohl's, Lowe's Whse, Michaels, PetsMart, Sam's Club, Target, Turfway Park Racing

181 KY 18, Florence, E...**gas:** Speedway, TA/Sunoco/Pizza Hut/Popeye's/dsl/rest./24hr/@, **food:** Goodfellow's Dining, Waffle House, **lodging:** Best Value Inn, Best Western, **other:** Chevrolet, W...**gas:** BP/dsl, Chevron, Shell, Speedway, **food:** Cheddars, Hooters, IHOP, Fazoli's, Hooters, La Rosa's, Logan's Roadhouse, LoneStar Steaks, Macaroni Grill, MiYoshi, Panera Bread, Quizno's, **lodging:** Microtel, Stay Lodge, **other:** URGENT CARE, Buick, Chrysler/Jeep, $Tree, Dodge, Ford, Honda, JC Penney, K-Mart, Lincoln/Mercury, Mazda, Nissan, Saturn, Sears/auto, Staples, Tire Discounters, Toyota/Scion, TJ Maxx, Wal-Mart SuperCtr, vet

180a Mall Rd(from sb), W...**food:** Chipotle Mexican, Chuck-eCheese, GoldStar Chili, Hardee's, Olive Garden, Pizza Hut, Skyline Chili, Smokey Bones BBQ, Subway, Taco Bell, **other:** AAA, Barnes&Noble, $General, Jo-Ann Fabrics, Kroger/24hr, Macey's, Michael's, PepBoys, Sears/auto, Staples, mall, same as 180

180 US 42, US 127, Florence, Union, E...**gas:** BP/dsl, Shell, Speedway/dsl, **food:** Big Boy, Bob Evans, Burger King, Camino Real, Capt D's, Dragon Buffet, Dunkin Donuts, Mai Thai, McDonald's, Pen Sta Subs, Pizza Hut, Quality Inn, Rally's, Red Lobster, Subway, Wendy's, **lodging:** Quality Inn, Knight's Inn, Motel 6, Super 8, **other:** Cadillac, Chevron, funpark, W...**gas:** Shell/dsl/24hr, Speedway, **food:** Acapulco Mexican, Arby's, Burger King, DQ, KFC, LJ Silver, Perkins/24hr, Ponderosa, Waffle House, White Castle, Kroger/deli, **lodging:** Travelodge, **other:** Circuit City, PepBoys, Tire Discounters, Walgreens

178 KY 536, Mt Zion Rd, E...**gas:** BP/Rally's/dsl, Mobil, Shell/dsl, Sunoco/dsl, **food:** GoldStar Chili, Hometown Pizza, Jersey Mike's Subs, Margarita's Mexican, Rally's, Steak'n Shake, Subway, **other:** Goodyear/auto, Kroger

177mm Welcome Ctr sb/rest area nb, full(handicapped) facilities, phone, vending, picnic tables, litter barrels, RV dump

175 KY 338, Richwood, E...**gas:** TA/BP/Country Pride/Taco Bell/dsl/rest./@, Pilot/Subway/dsl/@, **food:** Arby's, Burger King, White Castle/24hr, **lodging:** Holiday Inn Express, **other:** RV Park, W...**gas:** BP, Pilot/Subway/dsl/scales/24hr, Shell/dsl, **food:** GoldStar Chili, McDonald's, Pen Sta Subs, Skyline Chili, Waffle House, Wendy's, **lodging:** Econolodge, Ivy Lodge, **other:** Big Bone Lick SP

173 I-71 S, to Louisville

Interstate 75

171	KY 14, KY 16, to Verona, Walton, **E**...**gas:** BP/dsl, Citgo/DQ, **food:** Waffle House, **W**...**gas:** ⊕/Flying J/dsl/rest./24hr/scales@ **other:** Blue Beacon, Dave's RV Ctr, Oak Creek Camping(1mi), to Big Bone Lick SP
168mm	weigh sta sb
166	KY 491, Crittenden, **E**...**gas:** BP, Citgo/dsl, Marathon/A&W/Taco Bell/dsl, **food:** McDonald's, **other:** Chrysler/Dodge, KOA(2mi), **W**...**gas:** Chevron, Shell/Subway/dsl, **food:** Burger King, Country Bumpkins Rest., Green Acres Rest.
159	KY 22, to Owenton, Dry Ridge, **E**...**gas:** BP, Marathon/DQ, Shell/dsl, **food:** Arby's/24hr, Burger King, Happy Dragon Chinese, KFC/Taco Bell, LJ Silver, McDonald's, Pizza Hut, Subway, Waffle House, Wendy's, **lodging:** Country Inn Suites, Dry Ridge Inn, Microtel, Super 8, **other:** HOSPITAL, $General, Radio Shack, Wal-Mart SuperCtr/24hr, **W**...**gas:** Speedway/dsl, Sunoco/dsl, **food:** Country Grill, Cracker Barrel, Shoney's, **lodging:** Hampton Inn, Holiday Inn Express, **other:** Camper Village, Dry Ridge Outlets/famous brands, Sav-A-Lot, Toyota, Tire Discounters
156	Barnes Rd, no facilites
154	KY 36, Williamstown, **E**...**gas:** Citgo/dsl/LP, Shell/dsl, **food:** Red Carpet Rest., **lodging:** Knight's Inn, **other:** HOSPITAL, to Kincaid Lake SP, **W**...**gas:** Marathon/dsl, **food:** El Jalisco Mexican, **lodging:** Best Value, Cedar Valley Resorts, Day's Inn
144	KY 330, to Owenton, Corinth, **E**...**gas:** Marathon/dsl, Noble's Trk Plaza/dsl/rest., **W**...**gas:** BP, **food:** Donna's Diner, **other:** Three Springs Camping
136	KY 32, to Sadieville, **W**...**gas:** Marathon
130.5mm	weigh sta nb
129	KY 620, Delaplain Rd, **E**...**gas:** Pilot/Wendy's/dsl/scales/24hr/@, **food:** Waffle House, **lodging:** Day's Inn, Motel 6, **W**...**gas:** Pilot/McDonald's/dsl/scales/24hr/@, Shell/24hr
127mm	**rest area both lanes, full(handicapped)facilities, phone, vending, picnic tables, litter barrels, petwalk**
126	US 62, to US 460, Georgetown, **E**...**gas:**Standard, **food:** Applebee's, Big Boy, Golden Corral, Gold Star Chili, McDonald's, Mi Mexico, O'Charley's, Papa John's, Starbucks, **other:** Kohl's, Lowe's Whse, Valvoline, Wal-Mart SuperCtr/gas/dsl/24hr, **W**...**gas:** BP, Marathon, Shell/Subway/24hr, Speedway/A&W/dsl, **food:** Cracker Barrel, Fazoli's, KFC, Ruby Tuesday, Waffle House, Wendy's, **lodging:** Best Western, Comfort Suites, Country Inn&Suites, Econolodge, Fairfield Inn, Hampton Inn, Hilton Garden, Microtel, Quality Inn, Super 8, **other:** HOSPITAL, Chevrolet/Pontiac/Buick, Ford, Dodge/Jeep, K-Mart/Little Caesar's, Outlets/famous brands, to Georgetown Coll, same as 125
125	US 460(from nb), Georgetown, **E**...**gas:** BP/dsl, Marathon, Shell, **food:** FatKat Pizza, **lodging:** Econolodge, Super 8, **W**...**gas:** Swifty, **food:** China Buffet, DQ, LJ Silver, Taco Bell, Wendy's, **other:** Outlets/famous brands, Radio Shack, same as 126

Lexington

120	rd 1973, to Ironworks Pike, KY Horse Park, **E**... KY Horse Park Camping, **W**...**gas:** AM Best TruckPlaza, Citgo/Stuckey's/dsl/pizza/24hr, **other:** HOSPITAL
118	I-64 W, to Frankfort, Louisville
115	KY 922, Lexington, **E**...**gas:** Exxon/dsl, Shell/Subway/24hr, **food:** Cracker Barrel, McDonald's, Waffle House, **lodging:** Knight's Inn, La Quinta, Sheraton, **other:** SaddleHorse Museum(4mi), **W**...**gas:** Chevron/dsl, **food:** Denny's, Post Rest., **lodging:** Embassy Suites, Holiday Inn, Marriott/rest., **other:** museum
113	US 27, US 68, to Paris, Lexington, **E**...**gas:** BP/dsl, Marathon, Speedway, **food:** Waffle House, **lodging:** Ramada Inn, **W**...**gas:** Chevron/Subway/dsl/24hr, Shell, **food:** Fazoli's, LJ Silver, Penn Sta., Subway, **lodging:** Day's Inn, Catalina Motel, Red Roof Inn, **1 mi W**...**gas:** Shell, **food:** Burger King, Capt D's, Hardee's/24hr, **other:** Chevrolet, Chrysler/Jeep, Hall's RV Ctr, Kroger/deli, Northside RV Ctr, carwash, to UKY, Rupp Arena
111	I-64 E, to Huntington, WV
110	US 60, Lexington, **W**...**gas:** Shell, Speedway/dsl, Thornton/Subway/24hr, **food:** Arby's, Bob Evans, Cracker Barrel, Hardee's, International Buffet, McDonald's, Waffle House, Wendy's, **lodging:** Baymont Inn, Best Western, BlueGrass Suites, Comfort Inn, Country Inn&Suites, Hampton Inn, HoJo's, Holiday Inn Express, Knight's Inn, Microtel, Motel 6, Quality Inn, Ramada Ltd, Signature Inn, Super 8, Wilson Inn
108	Man O War Blvd, **E**...**gas:** Chevron, **W**...**gas:** BP, Citgo/dsl, Meijer/dsl/24hr, Shell/KFC/Wendy's/24hr, Speedway, **food:** Applebee's, Arby's, Backyard Burger, Burger King, Carrabba's, Chick-fil-A, Chipotle Mexican, Damon's, Don Pablo, Fazoli's, Fire Mtn Grill, GoldStar Chili, Harry's Grill, Logan's Roadhouse, Max&Erma's, McDonald's, Outback Steaks, Pizza Hut, Rafferty's, Ruby Tuesday, Starbucks, Steak'n Shake, Taco Bell, TGIFriday, Waffle House, **lodging:** Courtyard, Hilton Garden, Homewood Suites, Sleep Inn, **other:** HOSPITAL, Audi, Barnes&Noble, Circuit City, Goody's, Kohl's, Old Navy, Radio Shack, Target, Walgreen
104	KY 418, Lexington, **E**...**gas:** Exxon/Arby's/dsl/24hr, Shell/Hardees, **food:** Waffle House, **lodging:** Comfort Suites, Day's Inn, Econolodge, Holiday Inn, Red Roof Inn, **W**...**gas:** BP/dsl, Chevron, Speedway/Subway, **food:** Wendy's, **other:** HOSPITAL, **4 mi W**...**food:** Hooters, KFC, Texas Roadhouse
99	US 25 N, US 421 N, no services
98mm	Kentucky River
97	US 25 S, US 421 S, **E**...**gas:** Marathon/Huddle House/dsl/24hr, flea mkt, **W**...RV camping(2mi)

KENTUCKY
Interstate 75

Exit	Description

Richmond

95 KY 627, to Boonesboro, Winchester, E...gas: BP/dsl, Love's/Arby's/dsl/24hr, food: Hall's Diner(6mi), McDonald's, other: Ft Boonesborough SP, camping, W...gas: Shell/dsl/24hr

90 US 25, US 421, Richmond, E...gas: Shell, food: Cracker Barrel, lodging: Knight's Inn, La Quinta, Motel 6, Red Roof Inn, W...gas: BP, Exxon/Arby's/dsl, Marathon, Shell, food: Big Boy, DQ, Hardee's, Pizza Hut, Subway, Waffle House, Wendy's, lodging: Day's Inn, Super 8, other: $General, NTB, Pennzoil, antiques

87 KY 876, Richmond, E...gas: BP/dsl, Chevron/24hr, Marathon, Shell/dsl/24hr, Speedway/dsl, food: Burger King, Casa Fiesta Mexican, DQ, Fazoli's, Fong's Chinese, Hardee's, Hooters, KFC, King Buffet, Krystal/24hr, Little Caesar's, LJ Silver/A&W, McDonald's, Pizza Hut, Qdoba Mexican, Quizno's, Rally's, Subway, Taco Bell, Waffle House, Wendy's, lodging: Best Western, Econolodge, Quality Qtrs Inn, other: HOSPITAL, BigLots, $General, Goodyear/auto, Suzuki, to EKU, W...gas: BP/dsl, Marathon/Circle K, food: Bob Evans, Ryan's, Starbucks, Steak'n Shake/24hr, lodging: Comfort Suites, Hampton Inn, Holiday Inn Express, Jameson Inn

Berea

77 77 KY 595, Berea, E...food: Artisan Cafe, other: HOSPITAL, Artisan Ctr, to Berea Coll, W...gas: BP/Subway/24hr, Shell, food: Huddle House, La Casa Real, lodging: Country Inn&Suites, Day's Inn, Holiday Inn Express

76 76 KY 21, Berea, E...gas: BP, Marathon/Circle K, Shell/Burger King, Speedway/dsl, food: Arby's, Cracker Barrel, Dinner Bell Rest., Hong Kong Buffet, KFC, Little Caesar's, LJ Silver, Mariachi Mexican, Mario's Pizza, McDonald's, Papa John's, Pizza Hut, Subway, Taco Bell, WanPen Chinese/Thai, Wendy's, lodging: Holiday Motel, Knight's Inn, Super 8, other: HOSPITAL, $General, Ford, Radio Shack, Wal-Mart SuperCtr/24hr, tires, W...gas: BP, Chevron/24hr, Marathon, Shell/dsl, food: Lee's Chicken, Pantry Family Rest., lodging: Comfort Inn, Econolodge, Fairfield Inn, other: Chrysler/Dodge/Jeep, Oh! Kentucky Camping, Walnut Meadow Camping

62 US 25, to KY 461, Renfro Valley, E...gas: Derby City/rest./dsl, Shell/24hr, food: Hardee's, Waffle House, lodging: Heritage Inn, Renfro Valley Inn, other: KOA(2mi), W...gas: BP/Blimpie/24hr, Chevron/Wendy's/24hr, Shell/24hr, Marathon/Taco Tico, food: Arby's, DQ, Denny's, Godfather's/Subway, KFC, McDonald's, The Steakhouse, lodging: Day's Inn, Econolodge, other: HOSPITAL, Rite Aid, to Big South Fork NRA, Lake Cumberland

59 US 25, to Livingston, Mt Vernon, E...gas: BP, Shell/dsl, TravelCtr/dsl, food: Jean's Rest., Pizza Hut, lodging: Kastle Inn/rest., other: Nicely Camping, W...gas: BP, lodging: Super Sleep Inn

51mm Rockcastle River

49 KY 909, to US 25, Livingston, W...gas: 49er/dsl/24hr

London

41 KY 80, to Somerset, London, E...gas: Speedway, food: Arby's, Azteca Mexican, Burger King, China Town, DQ, KFC, McDonald's, Pizza Hut, Sonic, lodging: Carrington Inn, Days Inn, Red Roof Inn, Sleep Inn, Super 8, other: HOSPITAL, Advance Parts, AutoZone, CVS Drug, $General, Kroger/deli, Parsley's Tire/repair, Pontiac/GMC, st police, W...gas: BP/dsl/24hr, Chevron/McDonald's, Clark/dsl, Marathon, Shell/24hr, food: Chris's Buffet, Cracker Barrel, LJ Silver, Shiloh Roadhouse, Taco Bell, Waffle House, lodging: Budget Host, Hampton Inn, other: Westgate RV Camping

38 KY 192, London, E...gas: BP/dsl, Marathon, Shell/Quizno's/dsl, Speedway/dsl, food: Big Boy, Burger King, Capt D's, El Dorado Mexican, Fazoli's, Fiesta Mexican, Golden Corral, Great Wall Chinese, Hardee's, Huddle House, King Buffet, Krystal, McDonald's, O'Malley's, Pizza Hut, Ruby Tuesday, Taco Bell, lodging: Comfort Suites, Hampton Inn, Holiday Inn Express, Ramada Ltd, other: HOSPITAL, Advance Parts, E Kentucky RV Ctr, Goody's, Kroger, Office Depot, Peterbilt, USPO, Wal-Mart SuperCtr/24hr, airport, camping, toll rd to Manchester/Hazard, to Levi Jackson SP, W...to Laurel River Lake RA

34mm weigh sta both lanes, truck haven

30.5mm Laurel River

Corbin

29 US 25, US 25E, Corbin, E...gas: BP, Marathon/dsl/scales/24hr/@, Pilot/McDonald's/Subway/dsl/scales//24hr, food: Burger King, David's Steaks, Huddle House, Shoney's, Waffle King, lodging: Super 8, other: Blue Beacon, Lowes Whse, Wal-Mart SuperCtr/24hr/gas, to Cumberland Gap NP, W...gas: BP/Krystal/dsl, Love's/Hardee's/dsl, Marathon, Shell/dsl/24hr, food: Cracker Barrel, Sonny's BBQ, lodging: Baymont Inn, Comfort Suites, Fairfield Inn, Hampton Inn, Knight's Inn, other: KOA, tires/repair, to Laurel River Lake RA

25 US 25W, Corbin, E...gas: Speedway/dsl, food: Buckner's Grill, Burger King, McDonald's, O'Malley's, Tuscany Garden, Wendy's, lodging: Country Inn&Suites, Day's Inn, Holiday Inn Express, Landmark Inn, other: HOSPITAL, auto repair/tires, W...gas: BP/dsl, Shell/24hr, food: Arby's, China Garden, El Dorado Mexican, Subway, Waffle House, lodging: Best Western, other: to Cumberland Falls SP

15 US 25W, to Williamsburg, Goldbug, W...gas: Shell, Xpress, other: Cumberland Falls SP

14.5mm Cumberland River

11 KY 92, Williamsburg, E...gas: BP/dsl, Exxon/dsl, Shell, food: Arby's, El Dorado Mexican, Hardee's, KFC, McDonald's, Pizza Hut, Quizno's, Sonic, Subway, Taco Bell, TCBY, lodging: Cumberland Inn, Scottish Inn, Super 8, other: AutoZone, Chevrolet, Chrysler/Dodge/Jeep, $General, Firestone, Ford, mufflers/transmissions, museum, W...gas: Shell/dsl, Pilot/Wendy's/dsl/scales, food: Burger King, Huddle House, Krystal, LJ Silver, lodging: Day's Inn, Williamsburg Motel/RV Park, other: Wal-Mart SuperCtr/24hr, to Big South Fork NRA

1.5mm Welcome Ctr nb, full(handicapped)facilities, phone, vending, picnic tables, litter barrels, petwalk

0mm Kentucky/Tennesee state line

Interstate 275(Cincinnati)

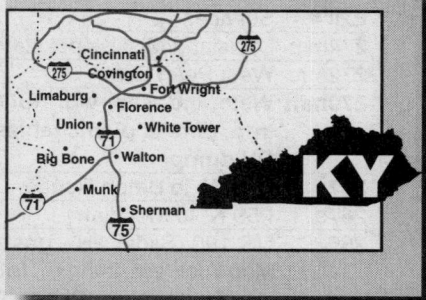

Exit #	Services
84	Louisville, I-75, I-71, N to Cincinnati, S to Lexington
83	US 25, US 42, US 127, **S**...**gas:** Shell, Speedway, **food:** Carrabba's, Max&Erma's, Panera Bread, TGI-Friday, Wendy's, **other:** Dillards
82	rd1303, Turkeyfoot Rd, **S**...HOSPITAL
80	KY 17, Independence, **N**...**gas:** Mobil, Speedway, **food:** Big Boy, Bob Evans, Burger King, Snappy Pizza, Texas Roadhouse, Wendy's, **other:** Tire Discounters, Wal-Mart SuperCtr/24hr
78	KY 16, Taylor Mill Rd, **N**...**gas:** Speedway, **other:** Kroger/gas, **S**...**gas:** BP/dsl, **food:** McDonald's, KFC, Taco Bell
77	KY 9, Maysville, Wilder, **S**...**gas:** Mobil, Shell, **food:** DQ, Waffle House
74a	Alexandria; to US 27, (exits left from sb)
74b	I-471 N, Newport, Cincinnati, **N**...HOSPITAL
73mm	OH/KY state line, OH River
72	Kelogg Ave, **S**...**gas:** Marathon, Airport
71	US 52, no services
69	5 mile rd, **W**...**gas:** BP/dsl, **food:** Big Boy, IHOP, La Rosa Mexican, McDonald's, TGIFriday, Wendy's, **other:** HOSPITAL
65	OH 125, Beechmont Ave, Amelia, **E**...**gas:** Marathon, Shell, Sunoco, **food:** Arby's, China Bistro, Hooters, Red Lobster, Wendy's, **lodging:** Motel 6, **other:** Ford, Lowe's Whse, Walgreen, **W**...**gas:** BP, Speedway, Marathon, **food:** Big Boy, McDonald's, Best Western, Bob Evans, Tony Roma, **lodging:** Best Western, Days Inn, Red Roof Inn, **other:** Home Depot
63b a	OH 32, Betavia, Newtown, **E**...**gas:** BP, Meijer, Shell, Thornton's, **food:** Cheeseburger Paradise, Bob Evans, Burger King, Fazolie's, Max & Erma's, McDonalds, Perkins, Pizza Hut, **lodging:** Comfort Inn, Fairfield Inn, Holiday Inn, **other:** Best Buy, Big's Foods, Circuit City, Dillards, Kohl's, Sears/auto, **W**...**gas:** Speedway, **food:** Big Boy, La Rosa Mexican, Roy Rogers, **lodging:** Comfort Inn, Fairfield Inn, Hampton Inn, Holiday Inn
59	Milford Pkwy, **S**...**gas:** Mobil, **food:** Buffalo Wings, Cracker Barrel, Goldstar Chili, Red Robin, Ruby Tuesday, Texas Roadhouse, Wendy's, **lodging:** Homewood Suites, **other:** Chrysler/Jeep, Office Depot, Target
57	OH 14 W, Forbes Rd, Broadway Ave, **N**...**gas:** Meijer(1mi), **food:** Arby's, Burger King, Dunkin Donuts, IHOP, Taco Bell, White Castle, **other:** K-Mart, Lowe's Whse, **S**...**gas:** BP, Exxon, **food:** Bob Evans, Cazadora Mexican, Charlie Basil's, **lodging:** Holiday Inn Express, Roadhouse Grill, **other:** HOSPITAL, Kroger
54	Wards Corner Rd, **N**...**gas:** BP, Mobil, **food:** Perkins, **lodging:** Hilton Garden, **other:** Lowe's Whse, **S**...**gas:** Mobil, **food:** Big Boy, Dominos, Hilton, Subway
53mm	Little Miami River
52	Loveland, Indian Hill, **1 mi N**...**gas:** Circle K, Marathon, Shell, Speedway, **food:** Arby's, Burger King, Taco Bell, Skyline Chili, Starbucks, Wendy's
50	US 22, OH 3, Montgomery, **N**...**food:** Chili's, DQ, Pizzaria, Starbucks, **S**...**gas:** BP/dsl, Shell, **food:** Goldstar Chili, La Rosa's, McDonald's, Skyline Chili, Wendy's, **other:** HOSPITAL
49	I-71 N to Columbus, S to Cincinnati
47	Reed Hartman Hwy, Blue Ash, **S**...**food:** Goldstar Chili, McDonald's, Starbucks, **lodging:** Amerisuites, Comfort Suites, Doubletree
46	US 42, Mason, **N**... **gas:** BP, **food:** Perkins, McDonald's, Taco Bell, Wendy's, White Castle, **lodging:** Holiday Inn, Motel 6, **other:** CVS Drug, **S**...**gas:** Marathon, Shell, Speedway, **food:** Arby's, Schezwan House, Waffle House, **lodging:** Days Inn, **other:** Goodyear, Tire Discounters
44	Mosteller Rd, **S**...**lodging:** Homewood Suites
43b a	I-75, N to Dayton, S to Cincinnati
42	OH 747, Springdale, Glendale
41	OH 4, Springfield Pk, **N**...**gas:** Shell, Sunoco, **food:** Bahama Breeze, Carlo's Bistro, Pappadeaux, **lodging:** Baymont Inn, Ramda Inn, **S**...**gas:** BP, Shell, **food:** Applebee's, Big Boy, DQ, Penn Station Subs, Perkins, Ponderosa, Rosita's Mexican, White Castle, Wok'n Roll, **lodging:** Extended Stay, Howard Johnson, Super 8, Holiday Inn Express, **other:** Dillard's, Sears
39	Winton Rd, Winton Woods, **N**...**food:** BP, Meijer, **food:** Bob Evans, Chipotle Mexican, Golden Corral, IHOP, McDonald's, Old Spagetti Factory, Panera Bread, Red Lobster, Roadhouse Grill, Ruby Tuesday, Ryan's, Steak'n Shake, **lodging:** Hampton Inn, **other:** Biggs Foods, Home Depot, K-Mart, Kohl's, Outdoor World, **S**...**gas:** Marathon, Mobil, Shell, **food:** Big Boy, Cracker Barrel, Fiesta Brava Mexican, Fuddrucker's, Popeye's, Skyline Chili, Subway, Wendy's, **lodging:** AmeriSuites, Lee's Inn, **other:** Goodyear, Jo-Ann Fabrics, Kroger/gas, Tires+, Wal-Mart SuperCtr/24hr
36	US 127, Hamilton, Mt Healthy, **N**...**gas:** Citgo, Speedway, **food:** Skyline Chili, Wendy's, **S**...**gas:** Sunoco, **food:** Arby's, Big Boy, La Rosa's Pizza, McDonald's, Pizza Hut/Taco Bell, Subway, **other:** Advance Parts, $General
33	US 27, US 126, Colerain Ave, **N**...**gas:** BP, Speedway, **food:** Burger King, Skyline Chili, Steak'n Shake, Wendy's, **other:** Colerain RV Ctr, Wal-Mart, **S**...**gas:** Shell, **food:** Arby's, Big Boy, Bob Evans, Cici's Pizza, KFC, LJ Silver, McDonald's, Olive Garden, Outback Steaks, Pizza Hut, Red Lobster, TGIFriday, White Castle, **lodging:** Red Carpet Inn, **other:** Isuzu, Kia, Macy's, Walgreen
31	Ronald Reagan Hwy, Blue Rock Rd
28	I-74, US 52, E to Cincinnati, W to Indianapolis
21	Kilby Rd, no services
16	US 50, Greendale, Lawrenceburg, **W**...**gas:** Ameristop/dsl, Marathon/dsl, Shell/Circle K/Subway, **food:** Buffalo's, Burger King, McDonald's, **lodging:** Comfort Inn, Holiday Inn Express, Quality Inn, Riverside Inn, **other:** Chevrolet/Pontiac/GMC, Chrysler/Dodge/Jeep, Tire Discounters, Walgreens
14mm	Ohio River, Kentucky/Indiana state line
11	to KY 20, Petersburg, no services
8b a	KY 237, Hebron, **N**...**gas:** BP/DQ/dsl, Mobil/dsl, **food:** Arby's, El Mariachi, Nicky's Pizzaria, Wendy's, **S**...**gas:** Marathon, Mobil/dsl, Shell/Subway, **food:** Burger King, Goldstar Chili, McDonald's, Waffle House
4a b	KY 212, KY 20, **N**...**gas:** ValAir Gas, **lodging:** Country Inn&Suites, Hampton Inn, Marriott, Sheraton, **S**...HOSPITAL, airport
2	Mineola Pike, **N**...**gas:** Mobil/dsl, **food:** Subway, **lodging:** Baymont Inn, Holiday Inn, **S**...**lodging:** Courtyard Inn, Residence Inn

LOUISIANA
Interstate 10

Slidell

Exit #	Services
274mm	Louisiana/Mississippi state line, Pearl River
272mm	West Pearl River
270mm	**Welcome Ctr wb, full(handicapped)facilities, info, phone, picnic tables, litter barrels, petwalk, RV dump**
267b	I-12 W, to Baton Rouge
267a	I-59 N, to Meridian
266	US 190, Slidell, N...gas: Magnolia, Shell/dsl, TA/Mobil/dsl/rest./24hr/@, food: Arby's, Cane's Chicken, China Wok, CiCi's, Denny's, KFC, Los Tres Amigos, McDonald's, Pizza Hut, Quizno's, Shoney's, Taco Bell, Wendy's, lodging: Best Value Inn, Best Western, Day's Inn, Deluxe Motel, Motel 6, other: HOSPITAL, Harley-Davidson, Office Depot, PepBoys, Radio Shack, Rouses Foods, Schwegmann Foods, U-Haul, S...gas: Chevron/Subway/dsl/24hr, RaceTrac, food: Applebee's, Big Easy Diner, Cracker Barrel, Osaka Grill, Outback Steaks, Sonic, Texas Roadhouse, Waffle House, lodging: Best Inn, La Quinta, Ramada Inn, Value Inn, other: HOSPITAL, Lowe's Whse, Wal-Mart SuperCtr/gas, auto repair/transmissions, casino, vet
263	LA 433, Slidell, N...gas: BP, Exxon, Shell, food: China Buffet, Ray's Rest., Waffle House, lodging: Comfort Inn, Hampton Inn, Super 8, other: Chevrolet/Cadillac, Mitsubishi, S...gas: Fleet/Subway/scales/dsl, Texaco/dsl, food: McDonald's, Wendy's, lodging: Holiday Inn, other: Pinecrest RV Park, Chrysler/Dodge/Jeep, Ford/Lincoln/Mercury, Honda, Isuzu, Mazda, Nissan, Pontiac/Buick/GMC, Saturn, Toyota, Slidell Factory Outlet/famous brands, KOA(1mi)
261	Oak Harbor Blvd, Eden Isles, N...gas: Exxon/dsl, food: Marina Cafe, Waffle House, lodging: Sleep Inn, S...gas: Shell/Subway/dsl
255mm	Lake Pontchartrain
254	US 11, to Northshore, Irish Bayou, S...gas: BP
251	Bayou Sauvage NWR, S...swamp tours
248	Michoud Blvd, no services
246b a	I-510 S, LA 47 N, S to Chalmette, N to Little Woods, S...6 Flags of NO
245	Bullard Ave, N...gas: Chevron, Shell, lodging: Comfort Suites, Holiday Inn Express, other: Honda, S...gas: Shell, food: IHOP, McDonald's, lodging: Motel 6, Quarter Hotel, other: HOSPITAL, Chrysler/Jeep, Ford, Home Depot, Nissan, Tire Kingdom, Toyota/Scion, Walgreens
244	Read Blvd, N...food: McDonald's, S...gas: EZ Mart/dsl, food: Popeye's, lodging: Best Western, Best Value Inn, Day's Inn, other: KIA
242	Crowder Blvd, N...gas: Chevron S...gas: Crowder Ctr
241	Morrison Rd, N...gas: EZ Mart
240b a	US 90 E, Chef Hwy, Downman Rd, N...lodging: Super 8, other: Chevrolet, U-Haul, S...gas: Chevron, DZ
239b a	Louisa St, Almonaster Blvd, N...gas: Chevron, Fastpay, food: Burger King, McDonald's, Popeye's, Rally's, other: Goodyear, Home Depot, Walgreens, Winn-Dixie, S...gas: Day&Night/dsl

New Orleans Area

Exit #	Services
238b	I-610 W(from wb)
237	Elysian Fields Ave, N...gas: BP/Marti Gras/Subway/dsl, other: Lowe's Whse
236c	St. Bernard Ave, no services
236b	LA 39, N Claiborne Ave, no services
236a	Esplanade Ave, downtown
235a	Orleans Ave, to Vieux Carre, French Qtr, S...lodging: Days Inn, Holiday Inn, Marriott, Sheraton
235b	Poydras St, N...HOSPITAL, S...to Superdome, downtown
234a	US 90A, Claiborne Ave, to Westbank, Superdome
232	US 61, Airline Hwy, Tulane Ave, N...food: Burger King, S on Carolton...gas: Exxon, Shell, food: KFC, McDonald's, Popeye's, Rallys, other: Family$, Pepboys, USPO, vet, to Xavier U
231b	Florida Blvd, WestEnd, no services
231a	Metairie Rd, no services
230	I-610 E(from eb), to Slidell
229	Bonnabel Blvd, no services
228	Causeway Blvd, N...gas: Exxon, Shell, food: PF Chang's, lodging: Best Western, Hampton Inn, Ramada Ltd, other: Borders Books, Dillard's, Old Navy, S...gas: DZ, Exxon, food: IHOP, lodging: Days Inn, Extended Stay America, La Quinta, Quality Hotel, Residence Inn, Sheraton
226	Clearview Pkwy, Huey Long Br, N...gas: Chevron, Exxon, food: Hooters, Popeye's, Taco Bell, lodging: Sleep Inn, other: Cadillac, Lincoln/Mercury, Sears/auto, Target, Tire Kingdom, S...gas: Chevron, Danny&Clyde, food: Beijing Chinese, Burger King, Piccadilly's, Smoothie King, Subway, lodging: Shoney's Inn/rest., Sun Suites, other: HOSPITAL, Buick/GMC/Pontiac, Firestone
225	Veterans Blvd, N...gas: Chevron, DZ, Shell, food: Burger King, Cuco's Mexican, Denny's, McDonald's, Subway, Taco Bell, lodging: La Quinta, other: Honda, Radio Shack, Rouse's Foods, S...gas: Shell, food: Casa Garcia, Louisiana Purchase, N O Burgers, O'Henry's, Piccadilly's, Popeye's, Tiffin Pancakes, Wendy's, lodging: Sheraton, other: Acura, Best Buy, BigLots, Chevrolet, CompUSA, $General, Home Depot, K-Mart, Lexus, Nissan, Office Depot, PepBoys, PetsMart, TJ Maxx, Toyota, VW, Walgreens, Wal-Mart/auto, vet
224	Power Blvd(from wb), no services
223b a	LA 49, Williams Blvd, N...gas: DZ/dsl, Exxon, Shell, food: Big Daddy's Seafood, Burger King, Cane's Chicken, Fisherman's Cove, Hibachi House, IHOP, Pizza Hut, Popeye's, Rally's, Subway, Taco Bell, Wendy's, lodging: Fairfield Inn, other: AutoZone, Family$, Ford, Office Depot, PetCo, Rite Aid, Tuesday Morning, Wal-Mart Mkt, S...gas: Exxon/dsl, Shell, food: Brick Oven, Denny's, Jazz Seafood/steaks, KFC/LJ Silver, McDonald's, Pizza Connection, Quizno's, Sonic, Subway, Taco Tico, Trough's Seafood, lodging: Airline Inn, Comfort Inn, Contempra Inn, Extended Stay America, La Quinta, New Orleans Hotel, Park Plaza Inn, Radisson, Travelodge, other: Circuit City, CVS Drug, $General, Firestone/auto, Goodyear, NAPA, Radio Shack, Toyota/Scion, U-Haul, mall

LOUISIANA

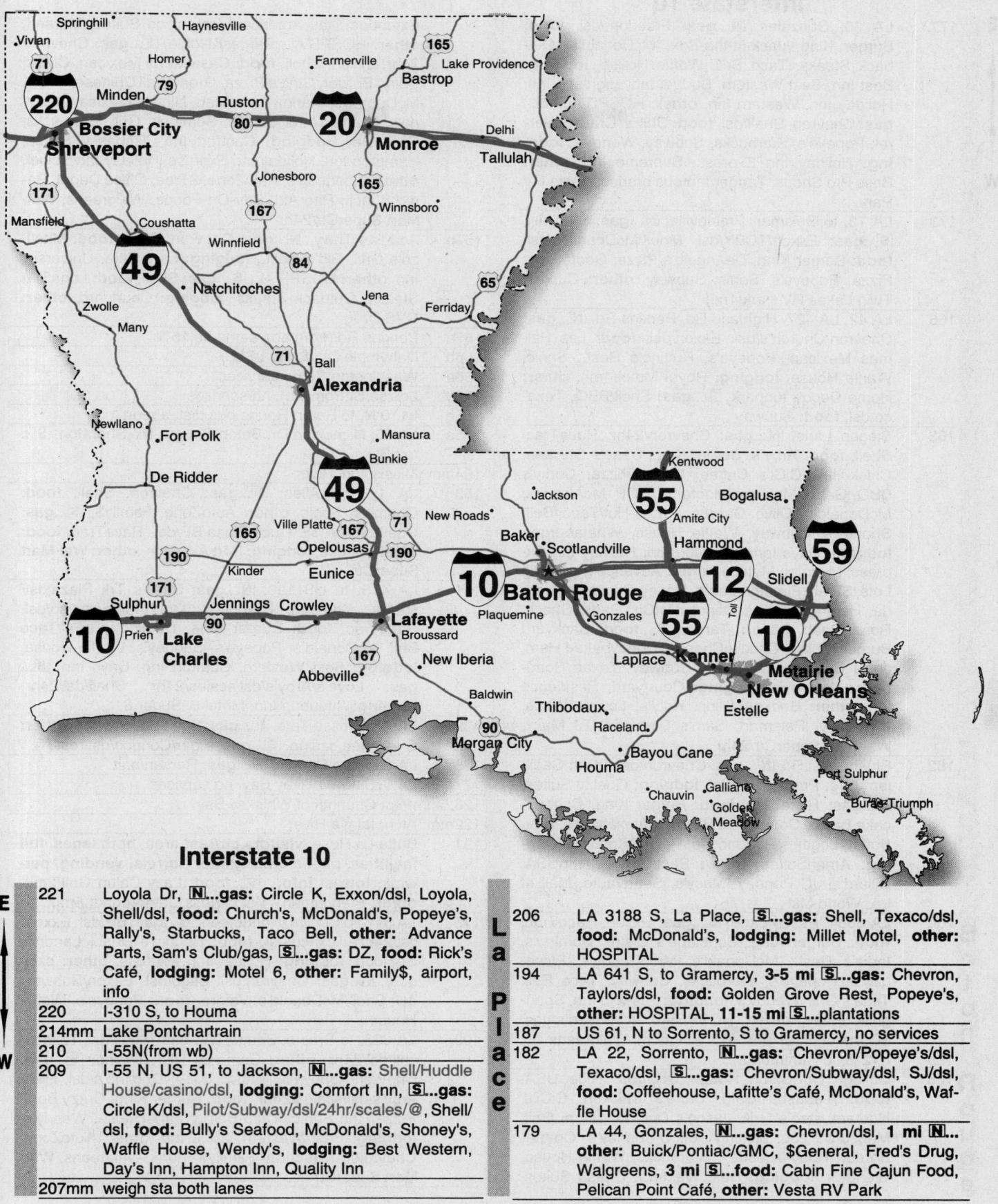

Interstate 10

221	Loyola Dr, ...**gas:** Circle K, Exxon/dsl, Loyola, Shell/dsl, **food:** Church's, McDonald's, Popeye's, Rally's, Starbucks, Taco Bell, **other:** Advance Parts, Sam's Club/gas, **S**...**gas:** DZ, **food:** Rick's Café, **lodging:** Motel 6, **other:** Family$, airport, info
220	I-310 S, to Houma
214mm	Lake Pontchartrain
210	I-55N(from wb)
209	I-55 N, US 51, to Jackson, **N**...**gas:** Shell/Huddle House/casino/dsl, **lodging:** Comfort Inn, **S**...**gas:** Circle K/dsl, Pilot/Subway/dsl/24hr/scales/@, Shell/dsl, **food:** Bully's Seafood, McDonald's, Shoney's, Waffle House, Wendy's, **lodging:** Best Western, Day's Inn, Hampton Inn, Quality Inn
207mm	weigh sta both lanes

La Place

206	LA 3188 S, La Place, **S**...**gas:** Shell, Texaco/dsl, **food:** McDonald's, **lodging:** Millet Motel, **other:** HOSPITAL
194	LA 641 S, to Gramercy, **3-5 mi S**...**gas:** Chevron, Taylors/dsl, **food:** Golden Grove Rest, Popeye's, **other:** HOSPITAL, **11-15 mi S**...plantations
187	US 61, N to Sorrento, S to Gramercy, no services
182	LA 22, Sorrento, **N**...**gas:** Chevron/Popeye's/dsl, Texaco/dsl, **S**...**gas:** Chevron/Subway/dsl, SJ/dsl, **food:** Coffeehouse, Lafitte's Café, McDonald's, Waffle House
179	LA 44, Gonzales, **N**...**gas:** Chevron/dsl, **1 mi N**... **other:** Buick/Pontiac/GMC, $General, Fred's Drug, Walgreens, **3 mi S**...**food:** Cabin Fine Cajun Food, Pelican Point Café, **other:** Vesta RV Park

LOUISIANA
Interstate 10

E ↑ ↓ W

177 LA 30, Gonzales, **N...gas:** Freedom/dsl, **food:** Burger King, Jack-in-the-Box, McDonald's, Outback Steaks, Taco Bell, Waffle House, **lodging:** Best Inn, Best Western, Budget Inn, Highland Inn, Holiday Inn, Western Inn, **other:** HOSPITAL, **S...gas:** Chevron, Shell/dsl, **food:** Chili's, Cracker Barrel, Popeye's, Starbucks, Subway, Wendy's, **lodging:** Holiday Inn Express, Supreme Inn, **other:** Bass Pro Shops, Tanger/famous brands, Vesta RV Park

173 LA 73, to Geismar, Prairieville, **N...gas:** Shell/dsl, **S...gas:** Exxon/TCBY/dsl, Mobil/McDonald's/dsl, **food:** Burger King, DeAngelo's Pizza, Godfather's Pizza, Popeye's, Sonic, Subway, **other:** Curves, Twin Lakes RV Park(1mi)

166 LA 42, LA 427, Highland Rd, Perkins Rd, **N...gas:** Chevron/Church's/dsl, Exxon/dsl, **food:** Las Palmas Mexican, Popeye's, Ruffino's Rest., Sonic, Waffle House, **lodging:** Royal Motel(4mi), **other:** Home Depot, funpark, **S...gas:** Shell/BBQ, Texaco/dsl, **food:** Subway

163 Siegen Lane, **N...gas:** Chevron/24hr, RaceTrac, Shell, **food:** Arby's, Burger King, Cane's Chicken, Chick-fil-A, CiCi's Coffee, CiCi's Pizza, Corky's BBQ, Galo's Mexican, Hooter's, IHOP, McAlister's, McDonald's, Olive Garden, Pizza Hut/Taco Bell, Shoney's, Subway, Waffle House, Whataburger, **lodging:** Days Inn, Hampton Inn, Holiday Inn Express, Microtel, Motel 6, **other:** Advance Parts, Big Lots, $Tree, Firestone/auto, Harley-Davidson, Honda, Hummer, Office Depot, PetCo, Radio Shack, Ross, Saab, Saturn, Target, **S...food:** Backyard Burger, Chili's, ChuckeCheese, Honeybaked Ham, Joe's Crabshack, Sicily's, Subway, Texas Roadhouse, Wendy's, **lodging:** Courtyard, Residence Inn, **other:** BooksAMillion, Kohl's, Lowe's Whse, Old Navy, Petsmart, Sam's Club/gas, TJ Maxx, Wal-Mart SuperCtr/24hr

162 Bluebonnet Rd, **N...gas:** Chevron/dsl, **food:** Cadillac Cafe, Primo's Steaks, **lodging:** Quality Suites, **S...gas:** RaceWay, **food:** Burger King, Cheesecake Bistro, Copeland's Bistro, J Alexander's, King Buffet, Logan's Roadhouse, Ralph&Kacoo's, **lodging:** AmeriSuites, **other:** Best Buy, CompUSA, Dillard's, JC Penney, Macy's, Sears/auto, Mall of LA, World Mkt

160 LA 3064, Essen Lane, **S...gas:** Exxon, RaceTrac, **food:** Burger King, Copeland's Bistro, Domino's, India's Rest., McDonald's, Mr. Gaddy's, Piccadilly's, Popeye's, Starbucks, Subway, Taco Bell, Time's Grill, Wendy's, **lodging:** Fairfield Inn, Springhill Suites, **other:** HOSPITAL, Albertson's/gas, $General, Firestone, Tire Kingdom, Walgreens

159 I-12 E, to Hammond

158 College Dr, Baton Rouge, **N...gas:** Ride USA, **food:** Alabasha Café, Cane's Chicken, CiCi's, Hooters, Izzo's Grill, Jason's Deli, Macaroni Grill, Mansurs Rest., Melting Pot, O'Charley's, On-the-Border, Ruby Tuesday, Starbucks, Waffle House, Wendy's, **lodging:** Best Western, Chase Suites, Extended Stay America, Homewood Suites, Marriott, **other:** HOSPITAL, Barnes&Noble, **S...gas:** Chevron/24hr, Exxon, Shell, **food:** Casa Maria Mexican, Chili's, China Border, Gino's Pizza, Great Wall Chinese, IHOP, McDonald's, Marina's Mexican, Ninfa's Mexican, Quizno's, Ruth's Chris Steaks, Seminola Grill, Starbucks, Taco Bell, **lodging:** Comfort Inn, Embassy Suites, Hampton Inn, Holiday Inn Express, Holiday Inn Select, **other:** Albertson's, AutoZone, $Tree, Office Depot, Radio Shack, Rite Aid, Sav-On Foods, Walgreens, Wal-Mart SuperCtr/24hr

157b Acadian Thwy, **N...gas:** Chevron, Shell, **food:** Mastizo's Grill, Rib's Rest., **lodging:** La Quinta, University Inn, **other:** HOSPITAL, **S...gas:** Shell, **food:** LoneStar Steaks, Outback Steaks, **lodging:** Courtyard, **other:** CVS Drug

157a Perkins Rd (from eb), same as 157b

156b Dalrymple Dr, **S...**to LSU

156a Washington St, no services

155c Louise St(from wb), no services

155b I-110 N, to Baton Rouge bus dist, airport

155a LA 30, Nicholson Dr, Baton Rouge, **N...**Sheraton, **S...**to LSU

154mm Mississippi River

153 LA 1, Port Allen, **N...gas:** Chevron, Shell, **food:** Church's, Sonic, **other:** AutoZone, Family$, **S...gas:** Chevron, LA 1S Truck Plaza/BP/dsl, RaceTrac, **food:** Waffle House, **lodging:** Port Allen Inn, **other:** Wal-Mart SuperCtr

151 LA 415, to US 190, **N...gas:** Cash's Trk Plaza/dsl/scales, Chevron, Exxon/dsl, Gold Mine/casino/dsl, RaceTrac, **food:** Burger King, Domino's, KFC/Taco Bell, McDonald's, Popeye's, Shoney's, Waffle House, **lodging:** Best Western, Comfort Inn, Days Inn, **S...gas:** Love's/Arby's/dsl/scales/24hr, Shell/dsl/24hr, **lodging:** Audubon Inn, Motel 6, Super 8

139 LA 77, Grosse Tete, **N...gas:** Shell/Subway/dsl, **other:** Chevrolet, casino, **S...gas:** Tiger/Conoco/dsl/rest./@

135 LA 3000, to Ramah, **N...gas:** Ramah/bait

127 LA 975, to Whiskey Bay, no services

126.5mm Pilot Channel of Whiskey Bay

122mm Atchafalaya River

121 Butte La Rose **visitors ctr/rest area, both lanes, full facilities, picnic tables, litter barrels, vending, petwalk, tourist info,** , **S...food:** Lazy Cajun Grill(2mi), **other:** Frenchman's Wilderness Camground(.5mi)

115 LA 347, to Cecilia, Henderson, **N...gas:** BP/dsl, Exxon/dsl/24hr, Texaco/dsl, **food:** Boudin's Rest., Landry's Seafood, **lodging:** Holiday Inn Express, **other:** casinos, **S...gas:** Chevron/dsl, Citgo/dsl, Exxon/Subway/dsl, Shell/McDonald's, Valero, **food:** Popeye's, Waffle House

109 LA 328, to Breaux Bridge, **N...gas:** Shell/dsl, Texaco/grill/dsl/24hr, **other:** Campers ULT, casino, **S...gas:** Chevron/Popeye's, Mapco, Mobil/Domino's/dsl, Pilot/Arby's/dsl/scales/24hr, **food:** Burger King, Crazy Bout, Pizza Hut, Sonic, Taco Bell, Waffle House, Wendy's, **lodging:** Best Western, Sona Inn, **other:** AutoZone, Chevrolet, $General, Family$, Ford, Walgreens, Wal-Mart SuperCtr

Interstate 10

Lafayette

108mm	weigh sta both lanes
104	Louisiana Ave, no services
103b	I-49 N, to Opelousas
103a	US 167 S, to Lafayette, **S...gas:** Chevron/dsl/24hr, RaceTrac, Shell, **food:** Checker's, ChopSticks Chinese, KFC, McDonald's, Pizza Hut, Popeye's, Shoney's, Subway, Taco Bell, Waffle House, Wendy's, **lodging:** Baymont Inn, Comfort Suites, Econolodge, Fairfield Inn, Holiday Inn, Howard Johnson, Jameson Inn, La Quinta, Quality Inn, Royal Inn, Super 8, TravelHost Inn, **other:** HOSPITAL, Albertson's/gas, CVS Drug, $General, Firestone/auto, Ford, Home Depot, Super 1 Foods/gas, VW, Wal-Mart SuperCtr/gas/24hr, transmissions
101	LA 182, to Lafayette, **N...gas:** Chevron/McDonald's, TA/Arby's/dsl/scales/24hr/@, Ride USA/dsl, **food:** Burger King, Waffle House, Whataburger, **lodging:** Red Roof Inn, **other:** Honda Motorcycles, **S...gas:** Exxon, RaceTrac, Shell/dsl, **food:** Cracker Barrel, **lodging:** Best Value, Best Western, Day's Inn, Drury Inn, Hilton Garden(2mi), St Francis Motel, **other:** HOSPITAL, Family$, Hyundai, Isuzu/Kia, O'Reilly Parts
100	Ambassador Caffery Pkwy, **N...gas:** Exxon/Subway/dsl/24hr, **other:** Curves, Gauthier's RV Ctr, **S...gas:** Chevron/24hr, RaceTrac/24hr, Shell/dsl, **food:** Burger King, McDonald's, Pizza Hut/Taco Bell, Sonic, Waffle House, Wendy's, **lodging:** Ambassador Inn, Hampton Inn, Sleep Inn, Microtel, **other:** HOSPITAL, Goodyear, Peterbilt
97	LA 93, to Scott, **S...gas:** Chevron/McDonald's, Shell/Church's/dsl/24hr, **food:** Fezzo's Seafood, **lodging:** Holiday Inn Express, Howard Johnson, **other:** Harley-Davidson, KOA
92	LA 95, to Duson, **N...gas:** Texaco/dsl/casino/RV dump/scales/24hr, **S...gas:** BP/Subway/dsl, Chevron/dsl, Exxon/casino/dsl, **lodging:** Super 8, **other:** Frog City RV Park
87	LA 35, to Rayne, **N...gas:** Chevron/dsl, Exxon/Subway/dsl/24hr, **food:** Burger King, McDonald's, **lodging:** Days Inn, **other:** $General, RV camping, **S...gas:** Frog City/Citgo/dsl, Mobil/dsl/24hr, Valero/dsl, **food:** Candyland Ice Cream, DQ, Gabe's Café, Popeye's, **lodging:** The Frog City Inn, **other:** HOSPITAL, Advance Parts, CVS Drug, Family$, O'Reilly Parts, Shop Rite/gas, Walgreens, Winn-Dixie
82	LA 1111, to E Crowley, **S...gas:** Chevron/dsl, Murphy USA/gas, **food:** Chili's, Wendy's, **other:** HOSPITAL, $Tree, GNC, Lowes Whse, Radio Shack, Walgreens, Wal-Mart SuperCtr/24hr/gas

Crowley

80	LA 13, to Crowley, **N...gas:** Conoco/Exit 80/dsl/rest./24hr, **food:** Fezzo's Seafood/steaks, Waffle House, **lodging:** Crowley Inn, Days Inn, La Quinta, **S...gas:** Chevron, Exxon/24hr, RaceWay, Shamrock/dsl, Tobacco+, **food:** Burger King, Cajun Way, China Dragon, DQ, El Dorado Mexican, Golden Seafood, KFC McDonald's, Mr Gatti's, Pizza Hut, PJ's Grill, Popeye's, Sonic, Subway, Taco Bell,

Jennings

	other: AutoZone, Chrysler/Dodge/Jeep, $General, Ford/Mercury/Nissan, Nissan, O'Reilly Parts, Radio Shack, Rite Aid, U-Haul, Winn-Dixie
76	LA 91, to Iota, **S...gas:** Petro/Mobil/Subway/dsl/scales/24hr
72	Egan, **N...food:** Cajun Haven RV Park
67.5mm	**rest areas both lanes full(handicapped) facilities, phone, picnic tables, litter barrels, petwalk, RV dump**
65	LA 97, to Jennings, **N...gas:** Spur/dsl(1.5mi), **S...gas:** Shell/dsl/casino, **lodging:** Day's Inn, **other:** to SW LA St School
64	LA 26, to Jennings, **N...**Boudreaux Inn, Budget Inn, **S...gas:** Chevron, Exxon/dsl, EZ Mart, Jennings Trvl Ctr/dsl, Valero, **food:** Burger King, General Wok Chinese, McDonald's, Mr Gatti's, Pizza Hut, Popeye's, Shoney's, Sonic, Subway, Taco Bell, Waffle House, Walker's Cajun Rest., Wendy's, **lodging:** Comfort Inn, Holiday Inn, **other:** HOSPITAL, AutoZone, Chrysler/Jeep/Dodge, $General, O'Reilly Parts, Rite Aid, Walgreens, Wal-Mart SuperCtr/gas/24hr
59	LA 395, to Roanoke, no services
54	LA 99, Welsh, **S...gas:** Circle R, Conoco/dsl, Exxon/dsl/24hr, **food:** DQ, Perky's Pizza
48	LA 101, Lacassine, **S...gas:** Exxon
44	US 165, to Alexandria, **N...other:** Quiet Oaks RV Park(10mi), **S...** Coushatta Resort/casino, Wood-n Treasures RV Park
43	LA 383, to Iowa, **N...gas:** Exxon/Pit Grill/dsl/24hr, Loves/Hardee's/dsl/24hr, **food:** Burger King, **lodging:** Howard Johnson Express, **other:** United RV Ctr, **S...gas:** Citgo/dsl, Conoco/dsl, Shell, Valero, **food:** Fausto's Chicken, McDonald's, Subway, **other:** $General, I-10 Outlet/famous brands, RV park

Lake Charles

36	LA 397, to Creole, Cameron, **N...**Jean Lafitte RV Park(2mi), Jellystone Camping, **S...gas:** Citgo/dsl, Conoco/dsl/RV dump/24hr, **lodging:** Sunrise Inn(2mi), **other:** casino, RV Camping, truckwash
34	I-210 W, to Lake Charles
33	US 171 N, **N...gas:** Citgo, Exxon/dsl, **food:** Burger King, Church's, Pink Pig BBQ, Subway, Taco Bell, **lodging:** Best Western, Lake Charles Inn, La Quinta, **other:** AutoZone, CVS Drug, Family$, O'Reilly Parts, Walgreens, to Sam Houston Jones SP, **S...lodging:** Holiday Inn Express, Motel 6, Treasure Inn
32	Opelousas St, **N...gas:** Exxon, **S...lodging:** Holiday Inn Express, Motel 6, Treasure Inn
31b	US 90 E, Shattuck St, to LA 14, **N...gas:** Shell/dsl, **S...gas:** PakCo Gas

LOUISIANA

Interstate 10

E ↕ W

31a	US 90 bus, Enterprise Blvd, S...**gas:** BP/dsl/24hr, **food:** Popeye's
30b	downtown
30a	LA 385, N Lakeshore Dr, Ryan St, N...**gas:** Exxon, **food:** Waffle House, **lodging:** Days Inn, LakeView Inn, S...**food:** Montana's Smokehouse, **lodging:** Best Inn, Harrah's Hotel/casino, Lakeview Motel
29	LA 385, (from eb), N...**gas:** Chevron, **food:** Steamboat Bills Rest., Thai Kitchen, Waffle House, **lodging:** Lakeview Motel, Travel Inn/rest., S...**lodging:** Best Suites, **other:** Players Island Casino/hotel
28mm	Calcasieu Bayou, Lake Charles
27	LA 378, to Westlake, N...**gas:** Conoco, Shell, **food:** Burger King, McDonald's, Subway, **other:** Bumper Parts, to Sam Houston Jones SP, S...**lodging:** Inn at the Isle, **other:** Riverboat Casinos
26	US 90 W, Southern Rd, Columbia, N...**gas:** Circle K/gas
25	I-210 E, to Lake Charles
23	LA 108, to Sulphur, N...**gas:** Circle K/gas, Exxon, **food:** Burger King, Chili's, McDonald's, Popeye's, Subway, Taco Bell, Wendy's, **lodging:** Quality Inn, **other:** $General, Lowe's Whse, Radio Shack, Walgreens, Wal-Mart SuperCtr/gas/24hr, S...**gas:** Chevron/Jack-in-the-Box/dsl, Citgo/dsl, **food:** Cracker Barrel, Waffle House, Winner's Choice, **lodging:** Best Western, Days Inn, Crossland Suites, Holiday Inn Express, Super 8, **other:** Goodyear, casino, tires
21	LA 3077, Arizona St, N...**gas:** Conoco/dsl, Exxon, Shell, **food:** Boiling Point Cajun, China Taste, KFC, **other:** CVS Drug, $General, Ford, Kroger/gas, NAPA, Walgreens, vet, S...**gas:** Citgo/dsl, Valero/dsl/casino, **other:** HOSPITAL, Hidden Ponds RV Park
20	LA 27, to Sulphur, N...**gas:** Bayou gas, Chevron, Circle K, Citgo, **food:** Bonanza, Burger King, Casa Ole Mexican, Cajun Charlie's, Checker's, Hollier's Cajun, Hong Kong Chinese, McDonald's, Mr Gatti's, Pitt Grill Cajun, Popeye's, Subway, Taco Bell, Wendy's, **lodging:** Best Value Inn, Econolodge, Hampton Inn, **other:** Brookshire Foods/gas, Family$, Firestone/auto, Goodyear/auto, Jiffy Lube, S...**gas:** Pilot/dsl, Shell/dsl, **food:** Navroskey's Burgers, Pizza Hut, Sonic, Waffle House, **lodging:** Candlewood Suites, Fairfield Inn, La Quinta, Microtel, Wingate Inn, **other:** HOSPITAL, casino, to Creole Nature Trail
8	LA 108, Vinton, N...**gas:** Citgo/dsl, Exxon/dsl, **food:** Cajun Cowboy's Rest., **other:** V RV Park
7	LA 3063, Vinton, N...**gas:** Exxon/dsl/Delta Cafe, **food:** Burger King, Sonic, Subway, N...**gas:** Loves/Arby's/dsl/scales/24hr
4	US 90, LA 109, Toomey, N...**gas:** Chevron/dsl/casino, Spirit/dsl/casino, **other:** casinos, truck repair, S...**gas:** Exxon/dsl, Shell/dsl, **food:** TX Pelican Rest., **other:** RV Park
2.5mm	weigh sta both lanes
1.5mm	**Welcome Ctr eb, full(handicapped) facilities, phone, picnic tables, litter barrels, petwalk**
1	(from wb), Sabine River Turnaround, no services
0mm	Louisiana/Texas state line, Sabine River

Sulphur

Interstate 12

E ↕ W

Exit #	Services
85c	I-10 E, to Biloxi. I-12 begins/ends on I-10, exit 267.
85b	I-59 N, to Hattiesburg
85a	I-10 W, to New Orleans
83	US 11, to Slidell, N...**gas:** Chevron/dsl/24hr, Exxon/dsl, **food:** Burger King, McDonald's, Waffle House, **other:** $General, Lishman's Foods, S...**gas:** Ride USA/Subway/dsl, Shell, **other:** HOSPITAL
80	Airport Dr, North Shore Blvd, N...**food:** IHOP, Quizno's, Sonic, **other:** Circuit City, Petsmart, Ross, Target, S...**gas:** Chevron/24hr, Shell/dsl, **food:** Burger King, Chili's, ChuckeCheese, McDonald's, Olive Garden, Pizza Hut/Taco Bell, Starbucks, Subway, Wendy's, **other:** Best Buy, Dillard's, $Tree, Goodyear/auto, Home Depot, JC Penney, Marshall's, Office Depot, Sam's Club/gas, Sears/auto, Wal-Mart SuperCtr/24hr, mall
74	LA 434, to Lacombe, N...HOSPITAL, S...Big Branch Marsh NWR
65	LA 59, to Mandeville, N...**gas:** Chevron/Subway/dsl, Danny&Clyde's/cafe, Shell, **food:** Sonic, Waffle House, **other:** Abita Brew Pub(4mi), S...**gas:** Kangaroo/Burger King/dsl, Texaco/Domino's/dsl, **other:** VET, Winn-Dixie, to Fontainebleau SP, camping, USPO
63b a	US 190, Covington, Mandeville, N...**gas:** Exxon, RaceTrac, Shell, **food:** Applebee's, Burger King, Cane's, Chick-Fil-A, Copeland's Grill, Ground Pati Rest., IHOP, KFC, McAlister's Deli, Osaka Japanese, Outback Steaks, Piccadilly's, Quizno's, Sonic, Starbucks, Subway, TGIFriday, Waffle House, Wendy's, **lodging:** Best Western, Comfort Inn, Courtyard, Hampton Inn, Holiday Inn, Super 8, **other:** Albertson's, BooksAMillion, Circuit City, GNC, Home Depot, Hyundai, Lowe's Whse, Nissan, Office Depot, Toyota, Wal-Mart SuperCtr/24hr, S...**other:** HOSPITAL, Chrysler/Plymouth, st police, to New Orleans via toll causeway

59 LA 21, to Covington, Madisonville, **N**...**gas:** Kangaroo, Shell, Spur/dsl, **food:** CC's Coffee, Coldstone Creamery, Izabella's Pizza, McDonald's, TJ's Coffee, Subway, **lodging:** La Quinta, **other:** HOSPITAL, Walgreens, **S**...**gas:** Texaco, **food:** Chick-Fil-A, Moe's SW Grill, Quizno's, Wendy's **other:** Belk, Best Buy, JC Penney, Marshall's, Ross, Target, World Mkt, Fairview Riverside SP

57 LA 1077, to Goodbee, Madisonville, **S**...Family RV Park, to Fairview Riverside SP

47 LA 445, to Robert, **1-3 mi N**...**other:** Jellystone Camping, to Global Wildlife Ctr

42 LA 3158, to Airport, **N**...**gas:** Chevron/dsl/24hr, **lodging:** Friendly Inn, **other:** Truckwash, **S**...**other:** HOSPITAL, Berryland RV Ctr

40 US 51, to Hammond, **N**...**gas:** Chevron, Race-Trac, Shell/24hr, **food:** Border Cafe, Burger King, China Garden, Church's, IHOP, McDonald's, Pizza Hut, Quizno's, Ryan's, Taco Bell, Wendy's, **lodging:** Best Western, Supreme Inn, **other:** MEDICAL CARE, Dillard's, Firestone/auto, Harley Davidson, Rite Aid, Sears/auto, U-Haul, Walgreens, mall, **S**...**gas:** Petro/Mobil/Subway/dsl/rest./24hr/@, Pilot/Arby's/dsl/scales/24hr/@, SpeedCo, **food:** Waffle House, **lodging:** Colonial Inn, Days Inn, **other:** HOSPITAL, Blue Beacon, $General, KOA

38b a I-55, N to Jackson, S to New Orleans

37mm weigh sta both lanes

35 Pumpkin Ctr, Baptist, **N**...**gas:** Exxon/dsl, **other:** Camping World RV Service/Supplies, Dixie RV Ctr, Punkin RV Park(2mi), **S**...**gas:** Chevron/24hr

32 LA 43, to Albany, **N**...**gas:** Chevron/Subway, Exxon/dsl, **S**...**gas:** Citgo/dsl, **other:** to Tickfaw SP

29 LA 441, to Holden, **N**...**gas/dsl**, **other:** Dairyland Campers, RV RestStop(1mi), st police

22 LA 63, to Frost, Livingston, **N**...**gas:** Chevron/dsl, Conoco/dsl, Mobil, **food:** Wings BBQ, **S**...**other:** Lakeside RV Park(1mi)

19 to Satsuma, no services

15 LA 447, to Walker, **N**...**gas:** Citgo, Shell/Subway/24hr, **food:** Burger King, Domino's, Jack-in-the-Box, La Fleur's Seafood, McDonald's, Popeye's, Sonic, Waffle House, **other:** AutoZone, $Tree, Wal-Mart SuperCtr/24hr, Winn-Dixie, **S**...**gas:** Chevron/dsl, **other:** Family RV Ctr

12 LA 1036, Juban Rd, no services

10 LA 3002, to Denham Springs, **N**...**gas:** Chevron, Circle K, RaceTrac, Shell/dsl, **food:** Arby's, Burger King, Cactus Café, Chinese Inn, Crawford's Cajun, Don's Rest., Fernando's Mexican, KFC, McDonald's, Pizza Hut, Popeye's, Ryan's, Subway, Waffle House, Wendy's, **lodging:** Best Western, Holiday Inn Express, **other:** Advance Parts, $General, Firestone/auto, Home Depot, Radio Shack, Rite Aid, **S**...**gas:** Pilot/Subway/dsl/scales, Shell, **food:** Piccadilly's, Shoney's, **lodging:** Day's Inn, Highland Inn, **other:** Bass Pro Shop, Dodge/Isuzu, Ford, KOA

8.5mm Amite River

7 O'Neal Lane, **N**...**gas:** Mobil, **lodging:** Comfort Suites, **other:** HOSPITAL, Night's RV Park, Office Depot, Toyota, **S**...**gas:** BP, Chevron/24hr, RaceTrac, **food:** Burger King, Las Palmas Mexican, LoneStar Steaks, McDonald's, Pizza Hut/Taco Bell, Popeye's, Sonic, Subway, Waffle House, Wendy's, **other:** HOSPITAL, $General, $Tree, Radio Shack, Walgreens, Wal-Mart SuperCtr/24hr

6 Millerville Rd, **N**...**gas:** Chevron/dsl/24hr, **food:** Chick-fil-A, **other:** Best Buy, Lowes Whse, Super Target

4 Sherwood Forest Blvd, **N**...**gas:** Exxon, Shell/dsl, **food:** Burger King, ChuckeCheese, Denny's, Jack-in-the-Box, McDonald's, Popeye's, Royal China Buffet, Sonic, Subway, Waffle House, **lodging:** Crossland Suites, Red Roof Inn, Super 8, **other:** Piggly Wiggly, Rite Aid, **S**...**gas:** Shell/24hr, **food:** Bayou Cajun Seafood, Pasta Garden, Pizza Hut, Podnuhs BBQ, Sherwood PoBoys, Taco Bell, **lodging:** Calloway Inn, **other:** Harley-Davidson

2b US 61 N, **N**...**gas:** B-Quik, Chevron, Exxon/dsl, Shell/24hr, Texaco, **food:** Applebee's, Cracker Barrel, McDonald's, Pizza Hut/Taco Bell, Shoney's, Subway, Taste of China, Wendy's, **lodging:** Days Inn, Holiday Inn, Microtel, Motel 6, Ramada Inn, Shoney's Inn, Sleep Inn, **other:** Acura/Infiniti, Albertson's/gas, Dodge, $Tree, Ford/Lincoln/Mercury, Marshall's, Michael's, Nissan/Suzuki, PepBoys, SteinMart, Toyota, Walgreens, transmissions

2a US 61 S, **S**...**gas:** Chevron, Circle K/gas, Exxon/dsl, Jubilee/dsl, **food:** Big Apple Chinese, McDonald's, Waffle House, **lodging:** Deluxe Inn, Plantation Inn, **other:** Cadillac/Volvo, Chevrolet, Home Depot, Mitsubishi, Winn-Dixie

1b LA 1068, to LA 73, Essen Lane, **N**...**gas:** Shell/dsl, **food:** Cane's Rest., Drew Silla Seafood, McDonald's, Voodoo BBQ, **other:** HOSPITAL, Family$, Radio Shack

1a I-10(from wb). I-12 begins/ends on I-10, exit 159 in Baton Rouge

LOUISIANA
Interstate 20

Exit #	Services
189mm	Louisiana/Mississippi state line, Mississippi River
187mm	weigh sta both lanes
186	US 80, Delta, **S**...**gas:** Chevron/Subway/dsl/24hr
184mm	**rest area both lanes, full(handicapped)facilities, phone, picnic tables, litter barrels, petwalk, RV dump**
182	LA 602, Mound, no services
173	LA 602, Richmond, **S**...**other:** Ford
171	US 65, Tallulah, **N**...**gas:** Chevron/dsl, Kangaroo/dsl, Shell/dsl, **food:** KFC, McDonald's, Subway, Wendy's, **lodging:** Day's Inn, Holiday Capri(2mi), Super 8, **other:** HOSPITAL, **S**...**gas:** Conoco/dsl, Love's/Arby's/dsl/24hr/@, TA/dsl/rest./24hr/@, Texaco
164mm	Tensas River
157	LA 577, Waverly, **N**...**gas:** Tiger Trkstp/dsl/rest./24hr/@, **S**...Chevron/Subway/dsl/24hr/@, Shell/dsl, to Tensas River NWR
155mm	Bayou Macon
153	LA 17, Delhi, **N**...**gas:** Chevron/dsl, **food:** Burger King, Boomer's rest., China Garden, DQ, Pizza Hut, Sonic, Subway, **other:** HOSPITAL, Brookshire's Foods, $General, Fred's Drugs, **S**...**gas:** Texaco, **lodging:** Best Western, Executive Inn
150mm	**rest area both lanes, full(handicapped)facilities, phone, picnic tables, litter barrels, petwalk, RV dump**
148	LA 609, Dunn, no services
145	LA 183, rd 202, Holly Ridge, no services
141	LA 583, Bee Bayou Rd, **N**...**gas:** BP/dsl
138	LA 137, Rayville, **N**...**gas:** BP, Pilot/Wendy's/dsl/24hr/@, **food:** McDonald's, **lodging:** Day's Inn, **other:** HOSPITAL, Chevrolet/Pontiac/Buick, $General, Family$, Firestone, Wal-Mart/drug, **S**...**gas:** Citgo/Subway/dsl/24hr, Exxon, RaceWay, **food:** Big John's Rest., Popeye's, Waffle House, **lodging:** Ramada Ltd, **other:** Goodyear
135mm	Beouf River
132	LA 133, Start, **N**...**gas:** Exxon/dsl
128mm	Lafourche Bayou
124	LA 594, Millhaven, **N**...**gas:** EZ Mart/dsl, **other:** st police, to Arsage Wildlife Area
120	Garrett Rd, Pecanland Mall Dr, **N**...**gas:** Citgo/dsl, Shell, **food:** Applebee's, Copeland's Rest., Corky's BBQ, Eastern Empire Chinese, Gator's Rest., IHOP, McAlister's, O'Charleys, Olive Garden, Pizza Hut, Red Lobster, Sonic, **lodging:** Comfort Inn, Courtyard, Holiday Inn, Residence Inn, **other:** Dillard's, Firestone/auto, Home Depot, JC Penney, Ross, Sears/auto, Target, mall, **S**...**gas:** Exxon/dsl, Kangaroo/dsl, **lodging:** Best Western, Day's Inn, **other:** Harley-Davidson, Hope's RV Ctr, Lowe's Whse, Pecanland RV Park, Sam's Club/gas, Shilo RV Camp
118b a	US 165, **N**...**lodging:** Holiday Inn, La Quinta, **other:** Goodyear, KIA, Nissan, Plymouth/Dodge, to NE LA U, **S**...**gas:** Chevron, Citgo, Exxon, Shell, **food:** Burger King, Capt D's, KFC, McDonald's, Podnuah BBQ, Sonic, Subway, Wendy's, **lodging:** Comfort Suites, Hampton Inn, Motel 6, Ramada Ltd
117b	LA 594, Texas Ave, no services
117a	Hall St, Monroe, **N**...HOSPITAL, Civic Ctr, **S**...**food:** Popeye's, **lodging:** Best Value Inn
116b	US 165 bus, LA 15, Jackson St, **N**...HOSPITAL
116a	5th St, Monroe, no services
115	LA 34, Mill St, **N**...**gas:** Citgo **S**...**other:** Clay's RV Service
114	LA 617, Thomas Rd, **N**...**gas:** Raceway, **food:** BBQ, Bennigan's, Burger King, Cane's BBQ, Capt D's, Chick-fil-A, El Chico, El Chili Verde, Grandy's, KFC, McDonald's, Pizza Hut, Popeye's, Shoney's, Subway, Taco Bell, TCBY, Wendy's, **lodging:** Shoney's Inn, Super 8, Wingate Inn, **other:** HOSPITAL, Office Depot, Rite Aid, Walgreen, Wal-Mart SuperCtr/gas/24hr, **S**...**gas:** Citgo/dsl, Exxon/dsl, Texaco, **food:** Chili's, China Garden, Cracker Barrel, Logan's Roadhouse, LoneStar Steaks, Martha's Catfish Buffet, Outback Steaks, Peking Chinese, Pizza Hut, Sonic, Waffle House, **lodging:** Fairfield Inn, Holiday Inn Express, Jameson Inn, Quality Inn, Red Roof Inn, Super 8, **other:** Firestone
112	Well Rd, **N**...**gas:** Shell/dsl/24hr, Texaco/24hr, **food:** DQ, McDonald's, Sonic, Taco Bell, Waffle House, **other:** $General, **S**...**gas:** Pilot/Subway/Wendy's/dsl/24hr/@, **other:** Pavilion RV Park
108	LA 546, to US 80, Cheniere, **N**...**gas:** Exxon/dsl, Shell/dsl
107	Camp Rd, rd 25, Cheniere, **N**... RV Park
103	US 80, Calhoun, **N**...**gas:** Chevron/dsl/rest., Citgo/dsl, **food:** Johnny's Pizza(1mi), **lodging:** Avant Motel
101	LA 151, to Calhoun, **N**...**gas:** Texaco **S**...**gas:** Citgo/Subway/dsl, Exxon, **food:** Buffet Pizza, Huddle House/24hr
97mm	**rest area wb, full(handicapped)facilities, phone, picnic tables, litter barrels, petwalk, RV dump**
95mm	**rest area eb, full(handicapped)facilities, phone, picnic tables, litter barrels, petwalk, RV dump**
93	LA 145, Choudrant, **S**...**gas:** Chevron
86	LA 33, Ruston, **N**...**gas:** Citgo, RaceWay, Shell/Quizno's/dsl, **food:** Cajun Cafe, Cane's Chicken Fingers, Chili's, Hot Rod BBQ, Ryan's, Sonic, Z Buffet, **lodging:** Comfort Inn, Day's Inn, Lincoln Motel, **other:** Buick/GMC, Chevrolet/Pontiac/Cadillac, Chrysler/Plymouth, Firestone, Ford/Lincoln/Mercury, Fred's Drug, Hardware, Toyota, Wal-Mart SuperCtr/gas/24hr, **S**...**gas:** NowSave/dsl, **lodging:** Holiday Inn Express
85	US 167, Ruston, **N**...**gas:** Citgo/Subway, Exxon/A&W, Shell, **food:** Burger King, Capt D's, Huddle House, McDonald's, Peking Chinese, Wendy's, **lodging:** Budget Lodge, Econolodge, Hampton Inn, Ramada Inn, Relax Inn, **other:** $General, Goody's, JC Penney, Office Depot, Radio Shack, Super 1 Foods, **S**...**gas:** BP/dsl, Texaco/dsl, **food:** Pizza Hut, **lodging:** Best Western, **other:** HOSPITAL
84	LA 544, Ruston, **N**...**gas:** Mobil/dsl, **S**...**gas:** Chevron, Citgo/24hr, Exxon, Texaco/dsl, **food:** DQ, Domino's, Johnny's Pizza, Pizza Inn, Quizno's, Subway, TCBY, Waffle House, **lodging:** Super 8, Travel Inn

Tallulah — Monroe — Ruston

81	LA 141, Grambling, S...gas: Chevron/Church's/dsl/24hr, Exxon, other: to Grambling St U
78	LA 563, Industry, S...gas: Texaco/dsl
77	LA 507, Simsboro, no services
69	LA 151, Arcadia, S...gas: BP/dsl, Citgo, Exxon, Texaco, food: El Alazan Mexican, China Dragon, Country Cottage Rest., McDonald's, Sonic, Subway, lodging: Day's Inn, other: Arcadia Tire, Bonnie& Clyde RV Park, Brookshire Foods, Factory Stores/famous brands, Fred's Drugs,
67	LA 9, Arcadia, N...to Lake Claiborne SP, S...gas: Texaco
61	LA 154, Gibsland, N... to Lake Claibourne SP
58mm	**rest area both lanes, full(handicapped) facilities, phone, picnic tables, litter barrels, petwalk, RV dump**
55	US 80, Ada, Taylor, no services
52	LA 532, to US 80, Dubberly, N...Exxon/Mom's Diner/dsl/24hr, Valero/dsl
49	LA 531, Minden, N...gas: Shell/Trucker's Paradise/Subway/dsl/casino/24hr/@, Pizza Hut(3mi), Taco Bell(3mi), Wal-Mart SuperCtr/gas/24hr(3mi)
47	US 371 S, LA 159 N, Minden, N...gas: Chevron/dsl, Citgo/dsl, Mobil/dsl, food: Golden Biscuit, lodging: Best Western, Exacta Inn/rest., Holiday Inn Express, Southern Inn, other: HOSPITAL, Ford/Lincoln/Mercury, S...B&B, to Lake Bistineau SP, camping
44	US 371 N, Cotton Valley, N...gas: Chevron, food: Crawfish Hole #2, Hamburger Happiness, Nicky's Cantina, lodging: Minden Motel(2mi), other: Family$
38	Goodwill Rd, Ammo Plant, S...gas: BP/Rainbow Diner/dsl/24hr, other: Interstate RV Park
33	LA 157, Fillmore, N...gas: Phillips 66, Texaco, other: Hilltop Camping(2mi), Jonny's Rest.,(7mi), S...gas: Exxon, Pilot/Arby's/dsl/24hr/@, food: Waffle House, other: $General, USPO, Lake Bistineau SP
26	I-220, Shreveport, 1 mi N...gas: Raceway, other: Casino
23	Industrial Dr, N...gas: Circle K, Exxon/Subway, Texaco/Popeye's/24hr, food: Barnhill's Buffet, Burger King, Country Kitchen, McDonald's, Popeye's, Taco Bell, Wendy's lodging: Ramada Inn, other: O'Riley Parts, st police, S...gas: Chevron/dsl, Citgo/dsl, lodging: Econolodge, other: Southern RV Ctr
22	Airline Dr, N...gas: Chevron/McDonald's/dsl, Mobil, Valero, food: Applebee's, Arby's, Backyard Burgers, Burger King, Capt D's, Chili's, ChuckeCheese, DQ, IHOP, Little Caesar's, Luby's, Pizza Hut, Popeye's, Red Lobster, Sonic, Starbucks, Taco Bell, Waffle House, lodging: Best Western, Crossland Suites, Super 8, other: Albertson's/gas, BooksAMillion, CVS Drug, Dillard's, Eckerd, Firestone/auto, Goodyear/auto, JC Penney, K-Mart, NAPA, Office Depot, Old Navy, PepBoys, Sears/auto, Walgreens, mall, S...gas: Exxon, Texaco/dsl/24hr, Cir-

	cle K, food: Church's, Darrell's Rest., Outback Steaks, Quizno's, lodging: Microtel, Quality Inn, Red Carpet Inn, other: HOSPITAL, Super1 Food, to Barksdale AFB
21	LA 72, to US 71 S, Old Minden Rd, N...gas: Circle K, Exxon, Valero, food: Burger King, El Chico, McDonald's, Ralph&Kacoo's, RJ's Rest., Subway, Texas Roadhouse, Whataburger, lodging: Hampton Inn, Holiday Inn, La Quinta, Residence Inn, Shoney's Inn/rest., other: Advance Parts, AutoZone, $General, Mazda/Audi, O'Reilly's Parts, VW, S...gas: RaceWay, food: Dragon House Chinese, Waffle House, Wendy's, lodging: Day's Inn, Motel 6
20c	(from wb), to US 71 S, to Barksdale Blvd
20b	LA 3, Benton Rd, same as 21
20a	Hamilton Rd, Isle of Capri Blvd, N...gas: Circle K, Texaco/24hr, food: BBQ, lodging: Comfort Inn, S...gas: Exxon, lodging: Best Value Inn, other: casino
19b	Traffic St, Shreveport, downtown, N...other: Bass Pro Shop, Chevrolet, casino
19a	US 71 N, LA 1 N, Spring St, Shreveport, N...food: Don's Seafood, lodging: Best Western, Holiday Inn
18b-d	Fairfield Ave(from wb), downtown Shreveport, S...HOSPITAL
18a	Line Ave, Common St(from eb), downtown, S...gas: Citgo, other: HOSPITAL
17b	I-49 S, to Alexandria
17a	Lakeshore Dr, Linwood Ave, no services
16b	US 79/80, Greenwood Rd, N...HOSPITAL, S...gas: Citgo, food: El Chico, lodging: Travelodge
16a	US 171, Hearne Ave, N...gas: Citgo/dsl, food: Subway, other: HOSPITAL, S...gas: Raceway, Texaco/dsl, food: KFC, lodging: Howard Johnson
14	Jewella Ave, Shreveport, N...gas: Citgo/dsl, Texaco/dsl/24hr, Valero, food: Burger King, China One, Church's, McDonald's, Popeye's, Subway, Sonic, Whataburger, other: Advance Parts, AutoZone, County Mkt Foods, Eckerd, Family$, O'Riley Parts, Rite Aid, Super 1 Foods, Walgreen
13	Monkhouse Dr, Shreveport, N...food: Denny's, lodging: Best Value Inn, Day's Inn, Guesthouse Inn, Holiday Inn Express, Residence Inn, S...gas: Chevron, Citgo, Exxon/Subway/dsl, food: Waffle House, lodging: Best Western, Hampton Inn, Pelican Inn, Regency Inn, Super 8, other: to airport

LOUISIANA

Interstate 20

E ↕ W

Shreveport

11	I-220 E, LA 3132 E, to I-49 S
10	Pines Rd, **N**...**gas:** BP/dsl, **food:** DQ, Pizza Hut, Popeye's, Subway, **S**...**gas:** Chevron, Exxon/dsl, Shell/Quizno's, **food:** Burger King, Cracker Barrel, Domino's, Dragon Chinese, IHOP, KFC, Nicky's Cantina, Subway, Taco Bell, Waffle House, Wendy's, Whataburger, **lodging:** Courtyard, Fairfield Inn, La Quinta, Holiday Inn, Jameson Inn, **other:** Chrysler/Dodge, CVS, Drug, $General, Family$, GNC, Home Depot, KOA, Kroger, Radio Shack, Rite Aid, USPO, Walgreens, Wal-Mart SuperCtr/gas/24hr
8	US 80, LA 526 E, **N**...**lodging:** Motel 6, **other:** Freightliner, **S**...**gas:** Chevron/dsl, Citgo/dsl, Petro/Mobil/dsl/rest./scales/@, Speedway, **food:** Crescent Landing Catfish Rest.(3mi), Wendy's, **other:** Blue Beacon
5	US 79 N, US 80, to Greenwood, **N**...**gas:** Kelly's/Subway/dsl/rest./24hr/@, Texaco/dsl, **lodging:** Cross Country Inn, Mid Continent Motel,
3	US 79 S, LA 169, Mooringsport, **S**...**gas:** Flying J/Conoco/dsl/LP/rest./24hr/@', Love's/Arby's/dsl/24hr/@, SpeedCo, **food:** Sonic
2mm	**Welcome Ctr eb, full(handicapped)facilities, phone, picnic tables, litter barrels, petwalk, RV dump**
1mm	weigh sta both lanes
0mm	Louisiana/Texas state line

Interstate 49

N ↕ S

Shreveport

Exit #	Services
	I-49 begins/ends in Shreveport on I-20, exit 17.
206	I-20, E to Monroe, W to Dallas
205	King's Hwy, **E**...**food:** Cane's, McDonald's, Piccadilly's, **other:** Dillard's, Sears/auto, mall, **W**...**gas:** Valero/dsl, **food:** Burger King, LJ Silver, Subway, Taco Bell, **other:** HOSPITAL
203	Hollywood Ave, Pierremont Rd, **W**...gas
202	LA 511, E 70th St, **W**...**gas:** Chevron, Circle K, **food:** Sonic, SC Chicken, **E**...**gas:** RaceWay
201	LA 3132, to Dallas, Texarkana, no services
199	LA 526, Bert Kouns Loop, **E**...**gas:** Chevron/Arby's/dsl/24hr, Exxon, **food:** Burger King, KFC, Taco Bell, Wendy's, **lodging:** Comfort Inn, **other:** Home Depot, **W**...**gas:** RaceWay, Shell/dsl, **food:** McDonald's, **other:** Brookshire Foods
196	Southern Loop, new exit
196mm	Bayou Pierre
191	LA 16, LA 3276, to Stonewall, no services
186	LA 175, to Frierson, Kingston, **W**...**gas:** Relay Sta./Exxon/rest./casino/dsl/scales/@
177	LA 509, to Carmel, **E**...**gas:** BP/Eagles Trkstp/dsl/rest.
172	US 84, to Grand Bayou, Mansfield, **W**... New Rockdale RV Prk
169	Asseff Rd, no services

Natchitoches

162	US 371, LA 177, to Evelyn, Pleasant Hill, no services
155	LA 174, to Ajax, Lake End, **W**...**gas:** Spaulding/dsl/@, **other:** Country Livin' RV
148	LA 485, Powhatan, Allen, no services
142	LA 547, Posey Rd, no services
138	LA 6, to Natchitoches, **E**...**gas:** BP/Mkt Express, Exxon/Subway, RaceWay, **food:** Shoney's, Wendy's, **lodging:** Best Western, Holiday Inn Express, Super 8(5mi), Travel Inn Express, **other:** HOSPITAL, Albertson's(3mi), Wal-Mart SuperCtr/24hr(5mi), **W**...**gas:** Chevron/dsl, Citgo, Texaco/dsl, **food:** Burger King, Huddle House, McDonald's, Simpatico's Grille, **lodging:** Comfort Inn, Econolodge, Hampton Inn, **other:** Nakatosh RV Park, to Kisatchie NF
132	LA 478, rd 620, no services
127	LA 120, to Cypress, Flora, **E**...**gas:** Texaco, **other:** to Cane River Plantations
119	LA 119, to Derry, Cloutierville, **E**...to Cane River Plantations
113	LA 490, to Chopin, **E**...**gas:** Phillips 66/dsl
107	to Lena, **E**...USPO
103	LA 8 W, to Flatwoods, **E**...**gas:** Texaco, **other:** to Cotile Lake, RV camping
99	LA 8, LA 1200, to Boyce, Colfax, **6 mi W**...Cotile Lake RV camping
98	LA 1(from nb), to Boyce, no services
94	rd 23, to Rapides Sta Rd, **E**...**gas:** Rapides/dsl, **W**... **LA Welcome Ctr, full handicapped facilites, littler barrels, petwalk, picnic tables, vending, other:** I-49 RV Ctr
90	LA 498, Air Base Rd, **W**...**gas:** Chevron/dsl/24hr, Exxon/dsl, Mobil/dsl, Texaco/BBQ/dsl, **food:** Burger King, Cracker Barrel, McDonald's, **lodging:** La Quinta, Super 8, Travel Express Inn
86	US 71, US 165, MacArthur Dr, **2-3 mi W**...**gas:** BP, Exxon, Mobil, Shell, Texaco, **food:** Fire Mtn Grill, Popeye's, Shoney's, Sonic, Subway, Taco Bell, **lodging:** Clarion, Comfort Inn, GuestHouse Inn, Motel 6, Quality Inn, Ramada Ltd, Super 8, **other:** Advance Parts, $General, Rite Aid, Super 1 Foods
85b	Monroe St, Medical Ctr Dr(from nb), **E**...HOSPITAL
85a	LA 1, 10th St, MLK Dr, downtown
84	US 167 N, LA 28, LA 1, Pineville Expswy(, no ez return nb
83	Broadway Ave, **E**...gas, **1 mi W**...**food:** Wendy's, **other:** BooksAMillion, Harley-Davidson, Lowe's Whse, Target, Wal-Mart SuperCtr/24hr
81	US 71 N, LA 3250, Sugarhouse Rd, MacArthur Dr(from sb), **W**...same as 80 and 83
80	US 71 S, US 167, MacArthur Dr, Alexandria, **1-3 mi W**...**gas:** Chevron/dsl, Exxon, I-49 Trk Plaza/dsl, Mobil, Shell, **food:** Burger King, Cane's Chicken, Capt D's, Carino's Italian, Chili's, Cuco's Mexican, Hacienda Mexican, KFC, Logan's Roadhouse, McDonald's, Outback Steaks, Panda Grill, Pizza Hut, Sonic, Subway, Taco Bell, **lodging:** Best Western, Clarion, Day's Inn, Hampton Inn, Holiday Inn, Ramada Ltd, Super 8, **other:** Albertson's/gas, Dillard's, Dodge, Ford, Hyundai, JC Penney, Petsmart, Sam's Club/gas, U-Haul, mall

Alexandria

Interstate 49

73	LA 3265, rd 22, to Woodworth, **W**...**gas:** Exxon/Blimpie/dsl, **other:** LA Conf Ctr, to Indian Creek RA, RV camping
66	LA 112, to Lecompte, **E**...**gas:** Chevron/Burger King/dsl, **food:** Lea's Lunch, **W**...**gas:** Exxon/dsl, **other:** museum
61	US 167, to Meeker, Turkey Creek, **E**...to Loyd Hall Plantation(3mi)
56	LA 181, Cheneyville, no services •
53	LA 115, to Bunkie, **E**...**gas:** Sammy's/Chevron/dsl/casino/24hr/@
46	LA 106, to St Landry, **W**...to Chicot SP
40	LA 29, to Ville Platte, **E**...**gas:** Exxon/rest./casino/dsl,
35mm	**E**...**rest area/rec area both lanes, full(handicapped)facilities, picnic tables, litter barrels, vending, petwalk, RV dump**
27	LA 10, to Lebeau, no services
25	LA 103, to Washington, Port Barre, **W**...**gas:** Citgo, Mobil, **other:** Family$
23	US 167 N, LA 744, to Ville Platte, **E**...**gas:** Chevron/Subway/dsl, Texaco/dsl, **W**...**gas:** 167/Exxon/dsl/rest./casino/24hr/@, to Chicot SP
19b a	US 190, to Opelousas, **E**...Evangeline Downs Racetrack, **W**...**gas:** Exxon/Blimpie/dsl, Mobil, **other:** HOSPITAL, Lowes Whse, USPO
18	LA 31, to Cresswell Lane, **E**...**lodging:** Holiday Inn, **food:** Casa Ole's, **other:** Chrysler/Dodge/Jeep/Isuzu, Home Depot, Wal-Mart SuperCtr/dsl/24hr, **W**...**gas:** Chevron/dsl/24hr, Shell, Valero, **food:** Burger King, Cresswell Lane, Domino's, Hacienda Mexican, McDonald's, Pizza Hut, Ryan's, Subway, Taco Bell, Wendy's, **lodging:** Best Western, Day's Inn, **other:** CVS Drug, Family$, Firestone, Goody's, Nissan, Pontiac/Buick/Cadillac, Rite Aid, TireWorld, Walgreens
17	Judson Walsh Dr, **E**...**gas:** Texaco/dsl, **W**...**other:** Goodyear/auto
15	LA 3233, Harry Guilbeau Rd, **W**...**lodging:** Best Value Inn, **other:** HOSPITAL, Toyota
11	LA 93, to Grand Coteau, Sunset, **E**...**gas:** Citgo/rest./dsl/24hr, Exxon/Popeye's/dsl, USA TC/dsl, **food:** Beau Chere Rest., **W**...**lodging:** Sunset Inn, **food:** Subway, **other:** $General, Family$, Janice's Foods
7	LA 182, **W**... Primeaux RV Ctr
4	LA 726, Carencro, **E**...Foreman RV Ctr, **W**...**gas:** Chevron/Popeye's/dsl, Texaco/Subway/dsl, **food:** Burger King, McDonald's, **lodging:** Economy Inn, **other:** Kenworth
2	LA 98, Gloria Switch Rd, **E**...**gas:** Chevron/dsl/deli, **food:** Chili's, IHOP, Prejean's Rest., Wendy's, **other:** Stevens RV Ctr, Lowe's Whse, **W**...**gas:** Shell/Church's, **food:** Domino's, Picante Mexican
1b	Pont Des Mouton Rd, **E**...**gas:** Exxon/dsl, Shell/Subway, **food:** Burger King, **lodging:** Motel 6, Plantation Inn, **other:** Gauthier's RV Ctr, st police, **W**...Ford
1a	I-10, W to Lake Charles, E to Baton Rouge, **US 167 S**...**gas:** Chevron/dsl/24hr, RaceTrac, Shell, **food:** Checker's, ChopStix Chinese, Kajun Kitchen, KFC, McDonald's, Pizza Hut, Popeye's, Shoney's, Subway, Taco Bell, Waffle House, Wendy's, Western Sizzlin, **lodging:** Best Western, Comfort Suites, Fairfield Inn, Holiday Inn, Jameson Inn, La Quinta, Quality Inn, Super 8, TravelHost Inn, **other:** HOSPITAL, Albertson's/gas, $General, Firestone/auto, Ford, Home Depot, Rite Aid, Super 1 Foods/gas, VW, Wal-Mart SuperCtr/gas/24hr, transmissions
	I-49 begins/ends on I-10, exit 103.

Opelousas *Lafayette*

Interstate 55

Exit #	Services
66mm	Louisiana/Mississippi state line
65mm	**Welcome Ctr sb, full(handicapped)facilities, tourist info, phone, picnic tables, litter barrels, petwalk**
64mm	weigh sta nb
61	LA 38, Kentwood, **E**...**gas:** BP/dsl, Texaco, **food:** Jam Chicken, Sonic, **other:** HOSPITAL, $General, Family$, Ford/Mercury, IGA Foods, **W**...**gas:** Exxon/Subway/dsl, Kangaroo/dsl, **other:** Chevrolet, Chrysler/Jeep/Dodge
58.5mm	weigh sta sb
57	LA 440, Tangipahoa, **E**...to Camp Moore Confederate Site
53	LA 10, to Greensburg, Fluker, **W**...HOSPITAL
50	LA 1048, Roseland, **E**...**gas:** Chevron/dsl/24hr
47	LA 16, Amite, **E**...**gas:** Exxon/Domino's/dsl, RaceTrac, **food:** Burger King, Church's, Hot Wok, KFC, McDonald's, Popeye's, Sonic, Subway, Wendy's, **lodging:** Comfort Inn, **other:** HOSPITAL, AutoZone, Fred's Drugs, Wal-Mart SuperCtr/dsl, **W**...**gas:** Amite Trkstp/OysterGrill/dsl(2mi), **food:** Ardillo's, **lodging:** Colonial Inn, **other:** Ford, RV Camping
40	LA 40, Independence, **E**...**gas:** Conoco, **other:** HOSPITAL, **W**...Indian Cr Camping(2mi)
36	LA 442, Tickfaw, **E**...**gas:** Chevron/dsl/24hr, **other:** camping, to Global Wildlife Ctr(15mi)
32	LA 3234, Wardline Rd, **E**...**gas:** Chevron, Kangaroo/dsl, Shell, **food:** Burger King, McDonald's, Sonic, Subway, Wendy's, **lodging:** Best Western, **other:** Tony's Tire

LOUISIANA

Interstate 55

H a m m o n d

31	US 190, Hammond, E...**gas:** Chevron/dsl, Exxon/Subway/dsl, Time Saver/dsl/scales/24hr, **food:** Adobe's Mexican, Applebee's, Buffalo Wild Wings, Burger King, Cane's, Chili's, CicC's, Cracker Barrel, KFC, Krystal, McDonald's, PepperTree Grill, Picadilly's, Pizza Hut, Sonic, Taco Bell, Waffle House, Wendy's, **lodging:** Comfort Inn, Executive Inn, Hampton Inn, Super 8, The Inn, **other:** HOSPITAL, Aamco, Advance Parts, Albertson's, AutoZone, Big Lots, BooksAMillion, Chrysler/Jeep/Buick/Dodge, $General, $Tree, Eckerd, Goody's, Lowe's Whse, Office Depot, Radio Shack, Tuesday Morning, Walgreens/24hr, Wal-Mart SuperCtr/gas/24hr, transmissions/repair
29b a	I-12, W to Baton Rouge, E to Slidell
28	US 51 N, Hammond, E...**gas:** RaceTrac, **food:** Catfish Charlie's, CiCi's, Don's Seafood Rest., **lodging:** Econolodge, Holiday Inn/rest., Rockwood Inn, **other:** HOSPITAL, KOA, dsl repair
26	LA 22, to Springfield, Ponchatoula, E...**gas:** Chevron/dsl, Conoco, Exxon/dsl, Shell, **food:** Burger King, China King, KFC, McDonald's, Popeye's, Sonic, Waffle House, Wendy's, **lodging:** Microtel, **other:** AutoZone, CVS Drug, $General, Eckerd, Ford, NAPA, O'Reilly Parts, Walgreens, Winn-Dixie, W...**gas:** Exxon/Domino's/dsl, **other:** Tickfaw SP
23	US 51, Ponchatoula, no services
22	frontage rd(from sb), no services
15	Manchac, E...**food:** Middendorf Café, **other:** phone, swamp tours
7	Ruddock, no services
1	1 US 51, to I-10, Baton Rouge, La Place, S...**gas:** Chevron/24hr, Jet/Citgo/24hr, Shell/dsl, Speedway/Blimpie/Church's/dsl, **food:** Bully's Seafood, Burger King, KFC, McDonald's, Shoney's, Waffle House, Wendy's, **lodging:** Best Western, Holiday Inn Express, **other:** HOSPITAL, La Place RV Camping
	I-55 begins/ends on I-10, exit 209.

L a   P l a c e

Interstate 59

Exit #	Services
11	Pearl River Turnaround. Callboxes begin sb.
5b	Honey Island Swamp, no services
5a	LA 41, Pearl River, E...**gas:** Chevron/gifts
3	US 11 S, LA 1090, Pearl River, W...**gas:** Shell/Subway/dsl, **1 mi** W...Chevron/dsl/24hr, **food:** D&K Rest.
1.5mm	**Welcome Ctr sb, full(handicapped) facilities, info, phone, picnic tables, litter barrels, petwalk, RV dump**
1c b	I-10, E to Bay St Louis, W to New Orleans
1a	I-12 W, to Hammond.
	I-59 begins/ends on I-10/I-12

Interstate 220(Shreveport)

Exit #	Services
	I-220 begins/ends on I-20, exit 26.
17b	I-20, W to Shreveport, E to Monroe
17a	US 79, US 80, N...**gas:** Circle K, RaceWay, **food:** Waffle House, **other:** Curves, LA Downs Racetrack/casino, Hilltop RV Park(7mi), S...**gas:** Chevron/dsl, **food:** Huddle House
15	Shed Rd, no services
13	Swan Lake Rd, no services
12	LA 3105, Airline Dr, N...**food:** McAlister's Deli, **other:** HOSPITAL, Walgreens, S...**gas:** Exxon/dsl, Shell/Subway, Valero/dsl, **food:** Applebee's, Burger King, Capt D's, CiCi's, Fire Mtn Grill, McDonald's, Micky's Cafe, Ruby Tuesday, Sonic, Taco Bell, Trejo's Mexican, Wendy's, **lodging:** Best Western, **other:** $Tree, Home Depot, Lowes Whse, Wal-Mart SuperCtr/gas/24hr
11	LA 3, Bossier City, N...**other:** HOSPITAL, Buick/Pontiac/GMC, Ford, Toyota/Lexus, Maplewood RV Park(3mi), S...**gas:** Chevron/McDonald's/dsl/24hr, **other:** Nissan
7b a	US 71, LA 1, Shreveport, N...**gas:** Citgo, Exxon/dsl, **food:** Domino's, Sonic, Subway, Whataburger/24hr, **other:** Brookshire Foods/gas, NAPA, Walgreens, S...**gas:** Chevron/24hr, RaceWay, Texaco/dsl/24hr, **food:** Burger King, Church's, KFC, McDonald's, Podnuh's BBQ, Sammy's Rest., Taco Bell, **lodging:** Royal Inn, **other:** Advance Parts, AutoZone, CVS Drug, Family$, Kroger, O'Reilly's Parts, Radio Shack, Rite Aid, repair/transmissions
5	LA 173, Blanchard Rd, S...**gas:** Citgo
2	Lakeshore Dr, no services
1a	Jefferson Paige Rd, S...**food:** Denny's, **lodging:** Best Value Inn, Best Western, Day's Inn, Super 8
1b c	I-20, E to Shreveport, W to Dallas.
	I-220 begins/ends on I-20, exit 11.

S h r e v e p o r t

Interstate 610(New Orleans)

Exit #	Services
	I-610 begins/ends on I-10
4	Franklin Ave(from eb), no services
3	Elysian fields, N...HOSPITAL, S...**gas:** Gas4Less, Shell, **food:** Burger King, McDonald's
2b	US 90, N Broad St, New Orleans St (from wb)
2c	Paris Ave(from wb, no return), S...**gas:** Shell/24hr, Spur, **food:** Popeye's
2a	St Bernard Ave(from eb), to LSU School of Dentistry, auto racetrack
1a	Canal Blvd, no services
1b	I-10, to New Orleans
	I-610 begins/ends on I-10

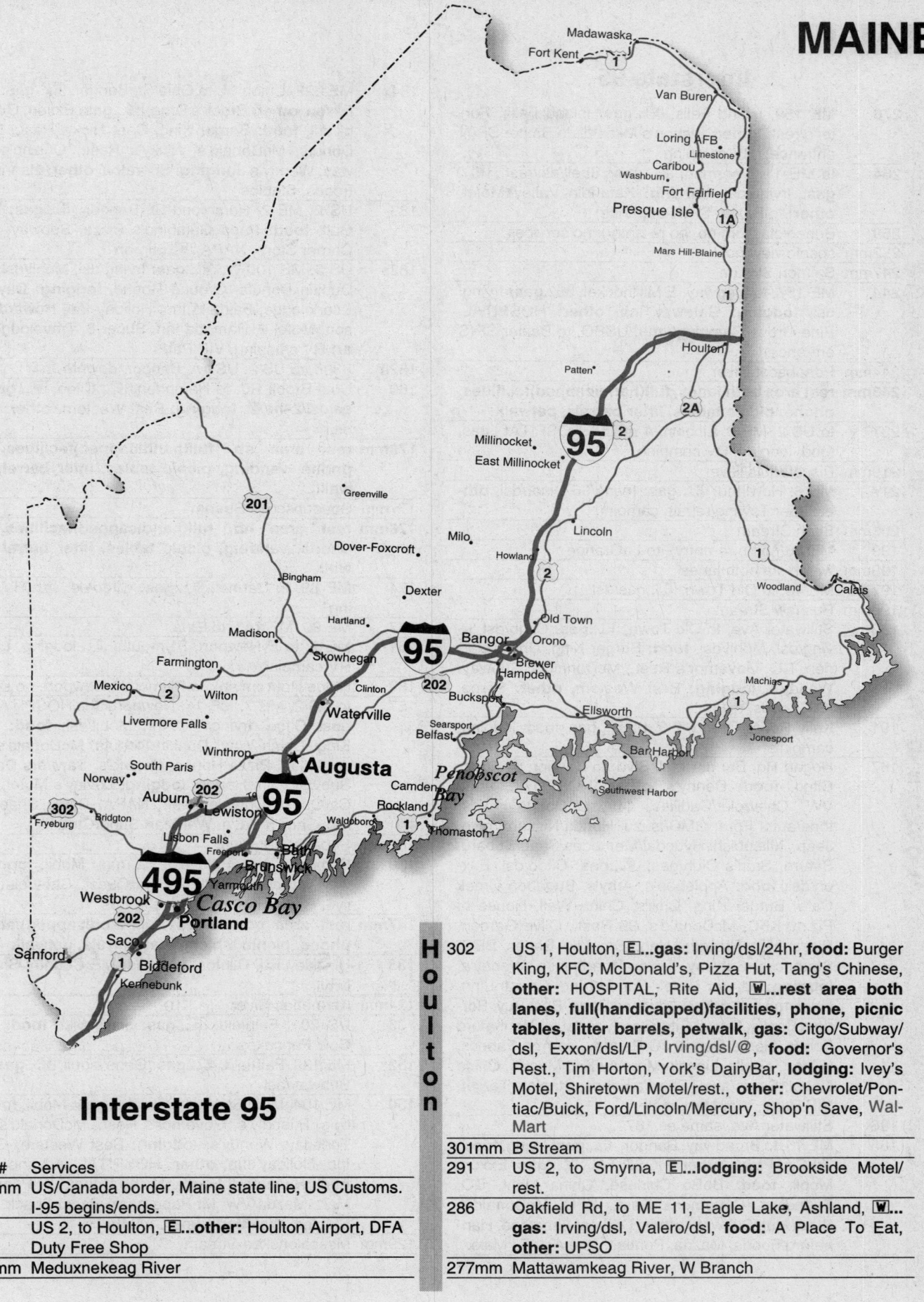

MAINE

Madawaska
Fort Kent
Van Buren
Loring AFB
Limestone
Caribou
Washburn
Fort Fairfield
Presque Isle
Mars Hill-Blaine
Houlton
Patten
Millinocket
East Millinocket
Greenville
Dover-Foxcroft
Milo
Lincoln
Howland
Woodland
Calais
Bingham
Dexter
Old Town
Madison
Hartland
Bangor
Orono
Brewer
Hampden
Machias
Farmington
Skowhegan
Clinton
202
Bucksport
Mexico
Wilton
Waterville
Searsport
Ellsworth
Jonesport
Livermore Falls
Winthrop
Belfast
Bar Harbor
Norway
South Paris
Augusta
Penobscot Bay
Southwest Harbor
Auburn
Lewiston
Camden
Rockland
Waldoboro
Thomaston
Fryeburg
Bridgton
Lisbon Falls
Freeport
Bath
Brunswick
Yarmouth
Westbrook
Casco Bay
202
Portland
Sanford
Saco
Biddeford
Kennebunk

Interstate 95

199

Exit #	Services
305mm	US/Canada border, Maine state line, US Customs. I-95 begins/ends.
305	US 2, to Houlton, **E**...**other:** Houlton Airport, DFA Duty Free Shop
303mm	Meduxnekeag River

Houlton

302	US 1, Houlton, **E**...**gas:** Irving/dsl/24hr, **food:** Burger King, KFC, McDonald's, Pizza Hut, Tang's Chinese, **other:** HOSPITAL; Rite Aid, **W**...**rest area both lanes, full(handicapped)facilities, phone, picnic tables, litter barrels, petwalk, gas:** Citgo/Subway/ dsl, Exxon/dsl/LP, Irving/dsl/@, **food:** Governor's Rest., Tim Horton, York's DairyBar, **lodging:** Ivey's Motel, Shiretown Motel/rest., **other:** Chevrolet/Pontiac/Buick, Ford/Lincoln/Mercury, Shop'n Save, Wal-Mart
301mm	B Stream
291	US 2, to Smyrna, **E**...**lodging:** Brookside Motel/rest.
286	Oakfield Rd, to ME 11, Eagle Lake, Ashland, **W**...**gas:** Irving/dsl, Valero/dsl, **food:** A Place To Eat, **other:** UPSO
277mm	Mattawamkeag River, W Branch

MAINE

N ↕ S

Bangor

276	ME 159, Island Falls, E...**gas:** Island Falls, Porter's/rest., **other:** Bishop's Mkt, W...to Baxter SP(N entrance), RV camping
264	to ME 11, Sherman, E...**gas:** Shell/dsl/rest., W...**gas:** Irving/dsl, **lodging:** Katahdin Valley Motel, **other:** to Baxter SP(N entrance)
259	Benedicta(from nb, no re-entry), no services
252mm	scenic view nb
247mm	Salmon Stream
244	ME 157, to Medway, E Millinocket, W...**gas:** Irving/dsl, **lodging:** Gateway Inn, **other:** HOSPITAL, Pine Grove Camping(4mi), USPO, to Baxter SP(S entrance)
244mm	Penobscot River
243mm	**rest area both lanes, full(handicapped)facilities, phone, picnic tables, litter barrels, petwalk**
227	to US 2, ME 6, Lincoln, **4 mi** E...HOSPITAL, gas, food, lodging, RV camping
219mm	Piscataquis River
217	ME 6, Howland, E...**gas:** Irving/95 Diner/dsl, **other:** 95er Towing/repair, camping
201mm	Birch Stream
199	ME 16(no nb re-entry), to LaGrange
199mm	weigh sta both lanes
197	ME 43, to Old Town, E...**gas:**/dsl
196mm	Pushaw Stream
193	Stillwater Ave, to Old Town, E...**gas:** Citgo/dsl, Irving/dsl, Mobil/dsl, **food:** Burger King, China Garden, DQ, Governor's Rest., McDonald's, Subway, Wendy's, **lodging:** Best Western, **other:** $Tree, IGA Foods, mall
191	Kelly Rd, to Orono, **2-3 mi** E...gas, food, lodging, camping
187	Hogan Rd, Bangor Mall Blvd, to Bangor, E...**gas:** Citgo, **food:** Denny's, **other:** HOSPITAL, Audi/VW, Chevrolet/Cadillac, Chrysler/Dodge, Firestone/auto, Ford, GMC/Isuzu, Honda/Nissan/Volvo, Jeep, Mitsubishi/Hyundai/Mercedes/Saab/Subaru, Saturn, Sam's Club/gas, W...**gas:** Citgo/dsl, Exxon/dsl, **food:** Applebee's, Arby's, Bugaboo Creek Café, Burger King, Chili's, China Wall, House of Pizza, KFC, McDonald's, 99 Rest., Olive Garden, Pizza Hut, Pizzaria Uno, Smokey Bones BBQ, Starbucks, Subway, Texas Roadhouse, Wendy's, **lodging:** Bangor Motel, Comfort Inn, Country Inn, Hampton Inn, **other:** Advance Parts, Best Buy, Borders Books, Circuit City, Goodyear/auto, Hannaford Foods, Home Depot, JC Penney, Jo-Ann Fabrics, K-Mart, Kohl's, Lincoln/Mercury/Kia, Macy's, Office Depot, Sears/auto, Shaw's Foods, Staples, Target, VIP Parts, Wal-Mart, mall
186	Stillwater Ave, same as 187
185	ME 15, to Broadway, Bangor, E...**gas:** Irving, **food:** Tri-City Pizza, **other:** HOSPITAL, W...**gas:** Exxon, Mobil, **food:** BoBo Chinese, China Light, DQ, Friendly's, Governor's Rest., KFC, McDonald's, Pizza Hut, Subway, **other:** Curves, Firestone, Hannaford Foods, Mazda, Pontiac, Rite Aid, TJ Maxx

Waterville

184	ME 222, Union St, to Ohio St, Bangor, E...**gas:** Citgo, Exxon, **other:** Brook's Drug, W...**gas:** Exxon, Gulf, Mobil/dsl, **food:** Burger King, Capt Nick's Rest., Dunkin Donuts, McDonald's, Nicky's Rest., Quizno's, Subway, Wendy's, **lodging:** Sheraton, **other:** Hannaford's Foods, Staples
183	US 2, ME 2, Hammond St, Bangor, E...**gas:** Exxon, Gulf, **food:** Papa Gambino's Pizza, Subway, **other:** Corner Store, NAPA, W...airport
182b	US 2, ME 100 W, W...**gas:** Irving/dsl, Mobil/dsl, **food:** Dunkin Donuts, Ground Round, **lodging:** Day's Inn, Econolodge, Fairfield Inn, Holiday Inn, Howard Johnson, Motel 6, Ramada Inn, Super 8, Travelodge, **other:** RV camping, VIP Parts
182a	I-395, to US 2, US 1A, Bangor, downtown
180	Cold Brook Rd, to Hampden, E...Citgo, W...**gas:** Citgo/dsl/24hr/@, **lodging:** Best Western, **other:** dsl repair
178mm	**rest area sb, full(handicapped)facilities, info, phone, vending, picnic tables, litter barrels, petwalk**
177mm	Soudabscook Stream
176mm	**rest area nb, full(handicapped)facilities, info, phone, vending, picnic tables, litter barrels, petwalk**
174	ME 69, to Carmel, E...**gas:** Citgo/dsl, W...RV camping
167	ME 69, ME 143, to Etna
161	ME 7, to E Newport, Plymouth, E...lodging, LP, W...RV camping
159	Ridge Rd(from sb), to Plymouth, Newport, no services
157	to US 2, ME 7, ME 11, Newport, E...HOSPITAL, W...**gas:** Citgo, Irving/dsl/24hr, Mobil/dsl, **food:** Burger King, China Way, Dunkin Donuts, McDonald's, Pando Italian, Pizza House, Quizno's, Sawyers Dairybar, Subway, Tim Horton, **lodging:** Lovley's Motel, **other:** CarQuest, Chrysler/Jeep, NAPA, Radio Shack, Rite Aid, Shop'n Save, Wal-Mart SuperCtr/24hr
151mm	Sebasticook River
150	Somerset Ave, Pittsfield, E...**gas:** Mobil, **food:** Subway, **other:** HOSPITAL, CarQuest, Chevrolet, Family$, Rite Aid, Shop'n Save Foods
147mm	**rest area both lanes, full(handicapped)facilities, phone, picnic tables, litter barrels, petwalk**
138	Hinckley Rd, Clinton, W...**gas:** ME Country Store/dsl/LP
134mm	Kennebec River
133	US 201, Fairfield, E...**gas:** Jim's Mkt, **food:** Purple Cow Pancakes
132	ME 139, Fairfield, E...**gas:** Gene's/deli, W...**gas:** Pilot/Subway/dsl
130	ME 104, Main St, Waterville, E...**gas:** Mobil, **food:** Arby's, Friendly's, Governor's Rest., McDonald's, Ruby Tuesday, Wendy's, **lodging:** Best Western, Comfort Inn, Holiday Inn, **other:** HOSPITAL, Advance Parts, Audi, Hannaford Foods, Home Depot, JC Penney, K-Mart, Mazda/VW, Mr Paperback, Radio Shack, Sears, Staples, Wal-Mart SuperCtr/24hr
129mm	Messalonskee Stream

Interstate 95

127	ME 11, ME 137, Waterville, Oakland, **E**...**gas:** Citgo/Burger King, Irving/dsl/24hr, Mobil, **food:** Applebee's, DQ, Dunkin Donuts, Grand Asian Buffet, McDonald's, Papa John's, Pizza Hut, Quizno's, Subway, Thai Dish, Weathervane Seafood, **lodging:** Budget Host, Econolodge, Hampton Inn, **other:** HOSPITAL, Chevrolet/Pontiac/Buick, Cadillac/Toyota, Chrysler/Dodge/Jeep, Nissan, Mr Paperback, Rite Aid, Shaw's Food/gas/24hr, **W**...**gas:** Exxon/dsl, Valero, **food:** China Express, **other:** Aubuchon Hardware, CarQuest, Ford/Lincoln/Mercury
120	Lyons Rd, Sidney, no services
117mm	**rest area sb, full(handicapped)facilities, phone, vending, picnic tables, litter barrels, petwalk**
113	rd 3
112	ME 27, ME 8, ME 11, Augusta, **E**...**gas:** Citgo, Getty, **food:** Capt's Seafood, Ground Round, Longhorn Steaks, Olive Garden, Panera Bread, Red Robin, Ruby Tuesday, **lodging:** Holiday Inn, **other:** Barnes&Noble, Circuit City, GNC, Home Depot, Kohl's, Michael's, Old Navy, Sam's Club, Staples, Wal-Mart SuperCtr/24hr, **W**...**gas:** Irving/dsl/24hr, **food:** Great Wall Chinese, KFC/Taco Bell, 99 Rest., Wendy's, **lodging:** Comfort Inn, **other:** Vet
109	US 202, ME 11, ME 17, ME 100, Augusta, **E**...**gas:** Irving/dsl, Shell, **food:** Applebee's, Arby's, Burger King, Capitol Buffet, China King, Damon's, Domino's, DQ, Friendly's, KFC, McDonald's, Pizza Hut, Subway, Wendy's, **lodging:** Best Western, **other:** $Tree, K-Mart, Shaw's Foods, VIP Parts, USPO, vet, **W**...**gas:** Getty, Valero, **food:** Margarita's Mexican, **lodging:** Best Inn, Econolodge, Motel 6, Super 8, **other:** CarQuest, Chrysler/Jeep/Nissan/Subaru, Dodge/Hyundai, HannaFords, KIA, PetCo, Pontiac, Sears/auto, TJ Maxx, Toyota
105mm	Bond Brook
103	to I-295 S, ME 9, ME 126, to Gardiner, (from sb)
102	to I-295 S
98mm	toll plaza
97mm	**service plaza nb, Mobil/dsl, Burger King, atm, gifts**
86	to ME 9, Sabattus
84mm	Sabattus Creek
83mm	**service plaza sb, Mobil/dsl, Burger King, atm, gifts**
80	ME 196, Lewiston, **W** on ME 196...**gas:** Gendron's/dsl, Getty, Shell, Sunoco, **food:** Cathay Hut Chinese, d'Angelo's, Dunkin Donuts, Fanny's Diner, Governor's Rest., KFC/Taco Bell, McDonald's, Wendy's, **lodging:** Chalet Motel, Motel 6, Ramada Inn, Super 8, **other:** HOSPITAL, Aubuchon Hardware, Rite Aid, Shaw's Foods
78mm	Androscoggin River
75	US 202, rd 4, rd 100, to Auburn, **E**...**gas:** Irving/dsl, Mobil/Subway/dsl, **lodging:** Fireside Inn/grill, **other:** Whited RV Ctr, **W**...HOSPITAL
71mm	Royal River
66mm	toll plaza

Vertical label left margin: **N ↕ S** · **Augusta** · **Lewiston**

63	US 202, rd 115, rd 4, to ME 26, Gray, **E**...**gas:** Gulf, Mobil, Shell, Sunoco, **food:** Dunkin Donuts, Subway, McDonald's, **other:** NAPA, TrueValue
59mm	**service plaza both lanes, Mobil/dsl, Burger King, atm, gifts**
55mm	Piscataqua River
53	to ME 26, ME100 W, N Portland, **E**...**gas:** Irving/dsl, **food:** Dunkin Donuts, Patti's Rest., **other:** HOSPITAL, Hannaford Foods
52	to I-295
48	ME 25, to Portland, **E**...**gas:** Citgo, **food:** Applebee's, Quizno's, **lodging:** Rodeway Inn, **other:** BJ's Whse/gas, Chevrolet, Jo-Ann Fabrics, Lowes Whse, **W**...**gas:** Citgo/Subway, Exxon, FuelMart/dsl, **food:** DQ, Denny's, Friendly's, KFC, McDonald's, Panera Bread, Pizza Hut, Ruby Tuesday, Tim Horton, Verillo's, Wendy's, **lodging:** Holiday Inn, Howard Johnson, Motel 6, Super 8, Travelodge, **other:** Chrysler/Dodge/Jeep, DD Auto Parts, Ford/Hyundai, Home Depot, Lexus/Toyota/Scion, NAPA, Shaw's Foods/Osco Drug, Tire Whse, VIP Parts
47mm	Stroudwater River
47	to ME 25, Rand Rd, no services
46	to ME 22, Congress St, same as 45
45	to US 1, Maine Mall Rd, S Portland, **E**...**gas:** Citgo, Mobil, Sunoco, **food:** Burger King, Bugaboo Creek Steaks, Chili's, ChuckeCheese, Friendly's, Great Wall Chinese, IHOP, LoneStar Steaks, Longhorn Steaks, Macaroni Grill, McDonald's, Old Country Buffet, Olive Garden, On the Border, Panera Bread, Pizzaria Uno, Ruby Tuesday, TGIFriday, Tim Horton, Weathervane Seafood, Wendy's, **lodging:** Comfort Inn, Day's Inn, Fairfield Inn, Hampton Inn, Residence Inn, Sheraton, **other:** AAA, Best Buy, Borders Books, Circuit City, $Tree, Macy's, Hannaford Foods, Honda, JC Penney, Lexus/Subaru/Toyota, Macy's, Marshall's, Office Depot, Sears/auto, Shaw's Foods, Shop'n Save, Staples, mall, **W**...**food:** Applebee's, Starbucks, **lodging:** Holiday Inn Express, Marriott, **other:** Old Navy, Target
44	I-295 N(from nb), to S Portland, Scarborough, **1 mi E** on ME 114...**gas:** Citgo/Domino's, **food:** Quizno's, Shogun Japanese, Subway, **lodging:** Residence Inn, TownePlace Suites, **other:** HOSPITAL, Lowes Whse, NAPA, Sam's Club, Shaw's Foods, Wal-Mart
42mm	Nonesuch River
42	to US 1, **E**...Scarborough Downs Racetrack(seasonal)

Vertical label middle: **Portland**

MAINE

Interstate 95

36	I-195 E, to Saco, Old Orchard Beach, **E...lodging:** Hampton Inn, **other:** KOA
35mm	**E...lodging:** Holiday Inn Express/Saco Hotel Conference Ctr
33mm	Saco River
32	ME 111, to Biddeford, **E...gas:** Irving/Subway/dsl, **food:** Amato's Sandwiches, Ruby Tuesday, Wendy's, **lodging:** Best Value Inn, Comfort Suites, **other:** HOSPITAL, AutoZone, Shaw's Foods, VIP Parts, Wal-Mart SuperCtr/24hr, **W...food:** Applebees, Panera Bread, **other:** Best Buy, Home Depot, Kohl's, Lowes Whse, Old Navy, Petsmart, Staples, Target, TJ Maxx
25mm	Kennebunk River
25	ME 35, Kennebunk Beach, **E...lodging:** Turnpike Motel
24mm	**service plaza both lanes, sb...Mobil/dsl, Burger King, Popeye's, Sbarro's, gifts, nb...Mobil/dsl, Burger King, Popeye's, atm, gifts**
19.5mm	Merriland River
19	ME 9, ME 109, to Wells, Sanford, **W...to** Sanford RA
7mm	Maine Tpk begins/ends, toll booth
7	ME 91, to US 1, The Yorks, **E...gas:** Gulf, Irving/dsl, Mobil/dsl, Shell, **food:** Norma's Cafe, Ruby's Grill, Wildcat Pizza, **lodging:** Econolodge, **other:** HOSPITAL, Chrysler/Jeep/Dodge, Curves, Ford, Hannaford's Foods, TrueValue, last exit before toll rd nb
5.5mm	weigh sta nb
5mm	York River
4mm	weigh sta sb
3mm	**Welcome Ctr nb, full(handicapped)facilities, info, phone, vending, picnic tables, litter barrels, petwalk**
2	(2 & 3 from nb), US 1, to Kittery, **E on US 1...gas:** Citgo/dsl, Getty, Irving/dsl/scales, Mobil/dsl, **food:** Burger King, Clam Hut Diner, DQ, McDonald's, Subway, Sunrise Grill, **lodging:** Blue Roof Motel, Rodeway Inn, Super 8, **other:** FSA/Tanger/famous brands, **W...gas:** Mobil
1	ME 103(from nb, no re-entry), to Kittery
0mm	Maine/New Hampshire state line, Piscataqua River

Interstate 295

Exit #	Services
	I-295 begins/ends on I-95, exit 103.
51	ME 9, ME 126, to Gardiner, Litchfield, TOLL PLAZA, **W...gas,** last free nb exit
49	US 201, to Gardiner, **E...gas/dsl, W...gas,** RV camping
43	ME 197, to Richmond, **E...gas:** Citgo/dsl
37	ME 125, Bowdoinham, no services
31	ME 196, to Lisbon, Topsham, **E...gas:** Irving, **food:** Arby's, McDonald's, 99 Rest., Subway, Wendy's, **lodging:** Hannaford Foods, NAPA, Radio Shack, Rite Aid, mall

74.5mm	Androscoggin River
28	US 1, Bath, **1 mi E** on US 1...**gas:** Gulf, Irving/dsl, Mobil/dsl, **food:** Dunkin Donuts, McDonald's, Thai House, **lodging:** Comfort Inn, Econolodge, Maine-Line Motel, Travelers Inn, **other:** HOSPITAL, Chevrolet/Mazda, Ford
71mm	parking area southbound
24	to Freeport(from nb), services 1 mi **E** on US 1
22	ME 125, to Pownal, **E on US 1...gas:** Exxon, **food:** Arby's, Friendly's, McDonald's, Taco Bell, **other:** LL Bean, USPO, outlet mall/famous brands, **W...to** Bradbury Mtn SP
20	Desert Rd, Freeport, **E...gas:** Citgo, **food:** Friendly's, **lodging:** Coastline Inn, Comfort Inn, Hampton Inn, Super 8, **other:** outlet mall/famous brands, RV camping
17	US 1, Yarmouth, **E...rest area both lanes, full (handicapped)facilities, info, food:** Bill's Pizza, Muddy Rudder Rest., **lodging:** Best Western, **other:** Ford, Delorme Mapping, **W...gas:** Citgo/dsl, Shell, **food:** Bill's Pizza, McDonald's, Pat's Pizza, **lodging:** DownEast Village Motel, **other:** Shop&Save
15	US 1, to Cumberland, Yarmouth, **W...gas:** Exxon, Mobil, **food:** 233 Grill, **lodging:** Brookside Motel, **other:** Rite Aid
11	I-295 S, US 1 **S...gas:** Exxon/dsl, Gulf/dsl, Mobil, **food:** Dunkin Donuts, McDonald's, Moose Crossing Rest., **other:** Goodyear, Rite Aid, Shaw's Foods
10	US 1, to Falmouth, **E...gas:** Exxon/dsl, Gulf/dsl, Mobil, **food:** Dunkin Donuts, McDonald's, Moose Crossing Rest., **other:** Goodyear, Rite Aid, Shaw's Foods
9mm	Presumpscot River
9	US 1 S, ME 26, to Baxter Blvd, **W...**The Diner
8	ME 26 S, Washington Ave, **E...other:** U-Haul
7	US 1A, Franklin St, **E...other:** CarQuest, NAPA
6b a	US 1, Forest Ave, **E...gas:** Mobil, **other:** HOSPITAL, AAA, Firestone/auto, Wild Oats Mkt, **W...food:** Arby's, Bleacher's Rest., Burger King, Pizza Hut, **other:** Hannaford Foods
5b a	ME 22, Congress St, **E...food:** Denny's, McDonald's, **lodging:** Fairfield Inn, **other:** HOSPITAL, **W... gas:** Citgo, Getty, Mobil/dsl, **food:** Ananias Italian, **lodging:** DoubleTree Hotel
3mm	Fore River
4	US 1 S, to Main St, to S Portland, services on US 1 away from exit
3	ME 9, to Westbrook St, **W...gas:** Irving/dsl, Mobil/dsl, **food:** Burger King, LoneStar Steaks, Olive Garden, Outback Steaks, TGIFriday, **other:** Chevrolet, Home Depot
2	to US 1 S, to S Portland, services on US 1, **E on US 1...gas:** Citgo/7-11, Exxon, Irving/dsl, Mobil, **food:** Dunkin Donuts, Governor's Rest., Tony Roma's, Yankee Grill, **lodging:** Best Western, Day's Inn, Quality Inn, **other:** Discount Tire
1	to I-95, to US 1, multiple services on US 1, same as 2
	I-295 begins/ends on I-95, exit 44.

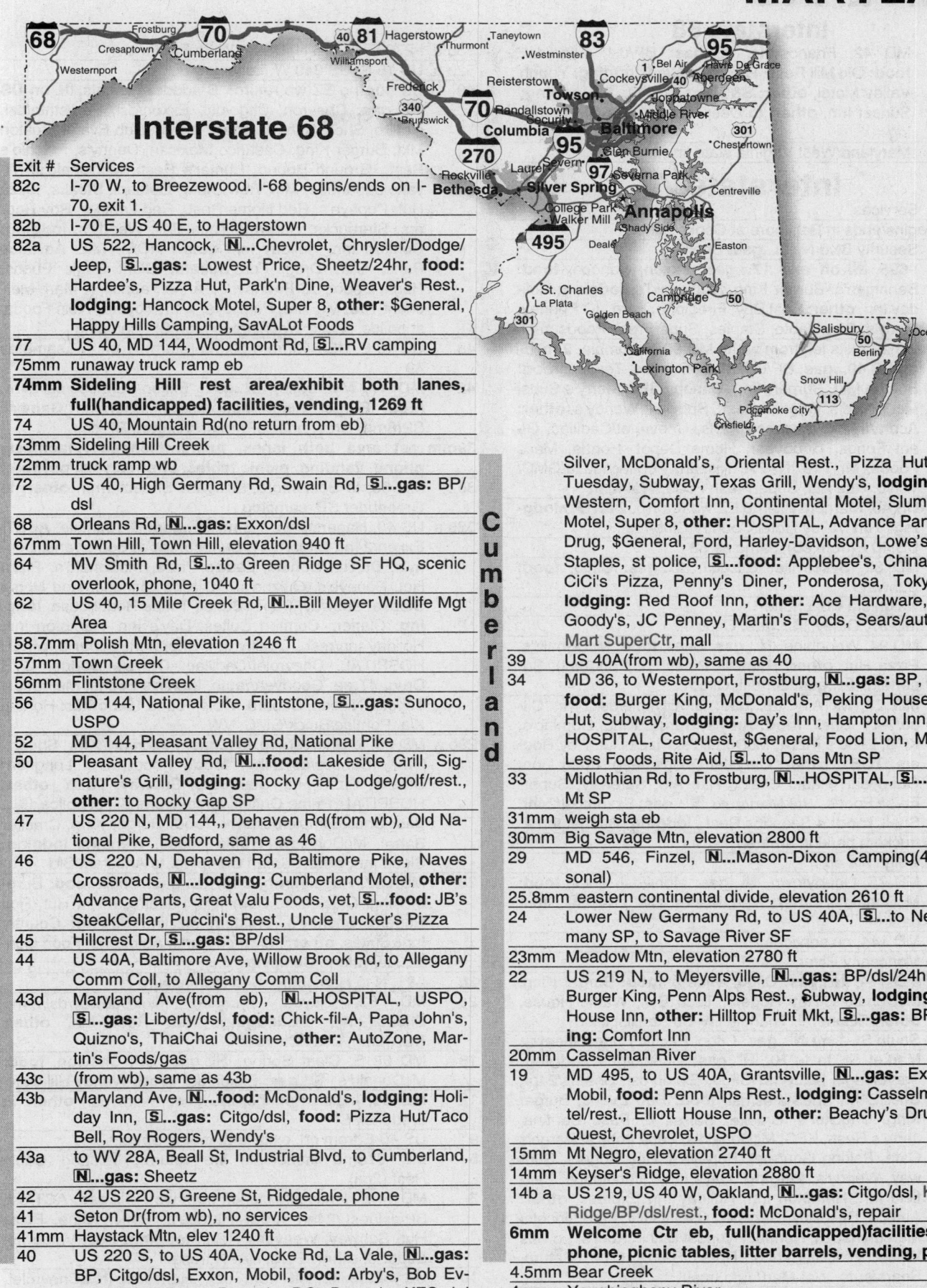

Interstate 68

E ↕ W

Exit #	Services
82c	I-70 W, to Breezewood. I-68 begins/ends on I-70, exit 1.
82b	I-70 E, US 40 E, to Hagerstown
82a	US 522, Hancock, 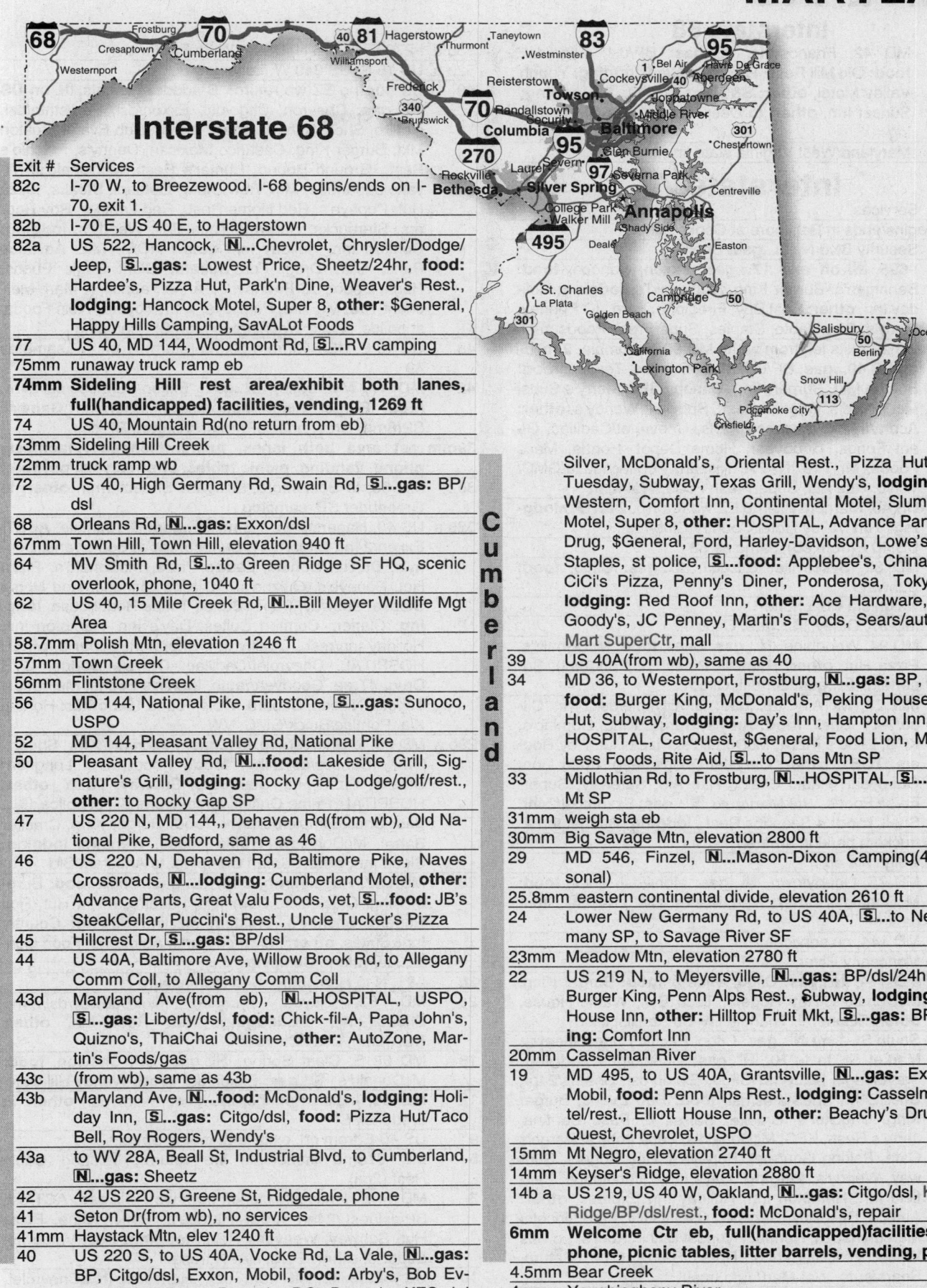...Chevrolet, Chrysler/Dodge/Jeep, Ⓢ...gas: Lowest Price, Sheetz/24hr, **food:** Hardee's, Pizza Hut, Park'n Dine, Weaver's Rest., **lodging:** Hancock Motel, Super 8, **other:** $General, Happy Hills Camping, SavALot Foods
77	US 40, MD 144, Woodmont Rd, Ⓢ...RV camping
75mm	runaway truck ramp eb
74mm	**Sideling Hill rest area/exhibit both lanes, full(handicapped) facilities, vending, 1269 ft**
74	US 40, Mountain Rd(no return from eb)
73mm	Sideling Hill Creek
72mm	truck ramp wb
72	US 40, High Germany Rd, Swain Rd, Ⓢ...gas: BP/dsl
68	Orleans Rd, Ⓝ...gas: Exxon/dsl
67mm	Town Hill, Town Hill, elevation 940 ft
64	MV Smith Rd, Ⓢ...to Green Ridge SF HQ, scenic overlook, phone, 1040 ft
62	US 40, 15 Mile Creek Rd, Ⓝ...Bill Meyer Wildlife Mgt Area
58.7mm	Polish Mtn, elevation 1246 ft
57mm	Town Creek
56mm	Flintstone Creek
56	MD 144, National Pike, Flintstone, Ⓢ...gas: Sunoco, USPO
52	MD 144, Pleasant Valley Rd, National Pike
50	Pleasant Valley Rd, Ⓝ...food: Lakeside Grill, Signature's Grill, **lodging:** Rocky Gap Lodge/golf/rest., **other:** to Rocky Gap SP
47	US 220 N, MD 144,, Dehaven Rd(from wb), Old National Pike, Bedford, same as 46
46	US 220 N, Dehaven Rd, Baltimore Pike, Naves Crossroads, Ⓝ...lodging: Cumberland Motel, **other:** Advance Parts, Great Valu Foods, vet, Ⓢ...food: JB's SteakCellar, Puccini's Rest., Uncle Tucker's Pizza
45	Hillcrest Dr, Ⓢ...gas: BP/dsl
44	US 40A, Baltimore Ave, Willow Brook Rd, to Allegany Comm Coll, to Allegany Comm Coll
43d	Maryland Ave(from eb), Ⓝ...HOSPITAL, USPO, Ⓢ...gas: Liberty/dsl, **food:** Chick-fil-A, Papa John's, Quizno's, ThaiChai Quisine, **other:** AutoZone, Martin's Foods/gas
43c	(from wb), same as 43b
43b	Maryland Ave, Ⓝ...food: McDonald's, **lodging:** Holiday Inn, Ⓢ...gas: Citgo/dsl, **food:** Pizza Hut/Taco Bell, Roy Rogers, Wendy's
43a	to WV 28A, Beall St, Industrial Blvd, to Cumberland, Ⓝ...gas: Sheetz
42	42 US 220 S, Greene St, Ridgedale, phone
41	Seton Dr(from wb), no services
41mm	Haystack Mtn, elev 1240 ft
40	US 220 S, to US 40A, Vocke Rd, La Vale, Ⓝ...gas: BP, Citgo/dsl, Exxon, Mobil, **food:** Arby's, Bob Evans, D'Atri Rest., Denny's, DQ, Denny's, KFC, LJ

Cumberland

Silver, McDonald's, Oriental Rest., Pizza Hut, Ruby Tuesday, Subway, Texas Grill, Wendy's, **lodging:** Best Western, Comfort Inn, Continental Motel, Slumberland Motel, Super 8, **other:** HOSPITAL, Advance Parts, CVS Drug, $General, Ford, Harley-Davidson, Lowe's Whse, Staples, st police, Ⓢ...food: Applebee's, China Buffet, CiCi's Pizza, Penny's Diner, Ponderosa, Tokyo Grill, **lodging:** Red Roof Inn, **other:** Ace Hardware, $Tree, Goody's, JC Penney, Martin's Foods, Sears/auto, Wal-Mart SuperCtr, mall

39	US 40A(from wb), same as 40
34	MD 36, to Westernport, Frostburg, Ⓝ...gas: BP, Sheetz, **food:** Burger King, McDonald's, Peking House, Pizza Hut, Subway, **lodging:** Day's Inn, Hampton Inn, **other:** HOSPITAL, CarQuest, $General, Food Lion, MoreForLess Foods, Rite Aid, Ⓢ...to Dans Mtn SP
33	Midlothian Rd, to Frostburg, Ⓝ...HOSPITAL, Ⓢ...to Dans Mt SP
31mm	weigh sta eb
30mm	Big Savage Mtn, elevation 2800 ft
29	MD 546, Finzel, Ⓝ...Mason-Dixon Camping(4mi/seasonal)
25.8mm	eastern continental divide, elevation 2610 ft
24	Lower New Germany Rd, to US 40A, Ⓢ...to New Germany SP, to Savage River SF
23mm	Meadow Mtn, elevation 2780 ft
22	US 219 N, to Meyersville, Ⓝ...gas: BP/dsl/24hr, **food:** Burger King, Penn Alps Rest., Subway, **lodging:** Elliott House Inn, **other:** Hilltop Fruit Mkt, Ⓢ...gas: BP, **lodging:** Comfort Inn
20mm	Casselman River
19	MD 495, to US 40A, Grantsville, Ⓝ...gas: Exxon/dsl, Mobil, **food:** Penn Alps Rest., **lodging:** Casselman Motel/rest., Elliott House Inn, **other:** Beachy's Drug, CarQuest, Chevrolet, USPO
15mm	Mt Negro, elevation 2740 ft
14mm	Keyser's Ridge, elevation 2880 ft
14b a	US 219, US 40 W, Oakland, Ⓝ...gas: Citgo/dsl, Keyser's Ridge/BP/dsl/rest., **food:** McDonald's, repair
6mm	**Welcome Ctr eb, full(handicapped)facilities, info, phone, picnic tables, litter barrels, vending, petwalk**
4.5mm	Bear Creek
4mm	Youghiogheny River

MARYLAND

Interstate 68

4 MD 42, Friendsville, **N**...**gas:** BP/dsl, Citgo/dsl, **food:** Old Mill Rest., Riverside Cafe, **lodging:** Yough Valley Motel, **other:** S&S Mkt, USPO, **S**...**lodging:** Sunset Inn, **other:** to Deep Creek Lake SP, camping

0mm Maryland/West Virginia state line

Interstate 70

Exit # Services

I-70 begins/ends in Baltimore at Cooks Lane.

94 Security Blvd N, **S**...**gas:** Shell

91b a I-695, **N off exit 17**...**gas:** Exxon, Sunoco, **food:** Bennigan's, Burger King, McDonald's, **lodging:** Holiday Inn, **other:** Best Buy, Firestone, Ford, JC Penney, Macy's, Sears/auto, Staples, SuperFresh Foods, mall

87b a US 29(exits left from wb)to MD 99, Columbia, **2 mi S on US 40**...**gas:** BP/dsl, Shell, Sunoco, Texaco, **food:** Boston Mkt, Burger King, Canopy BBQ, Jerry's Subs, McDonald's, Oriental Rest., Subway, Wendy's, **other:** Acura/Infiniti, Advance Parts, Chevrolet/Cadillac, Giant Foods, Goodyear, Home Depot, Honda, Mar's Foods, Mr Tire, NAPA, Nissan, Pontiac/Isuzu/GMC/Volvo, Rite Aid, SuperFresh Food, Wal-Mart

83 US 40, Marriottsville(no EZ wb return), **2 mi S**...**lodging:** Turf Valley Hotel/Country Club/rest.

82 US 40 E(from eb), same as 83

80 MD 32, Sykesville, **N**...golf, **S**...**gas:** Citgo, **food:** Subway

79mm weigh sta wb, phone

76 MD 97, Olney, **S**...**gas:** Citgo

73 MD 94, Woodbine, **N**...**gas:** Shell, **food:** McDonald's, Pizza Hut, **other:** Ramblin Pines RV Park(6mi), SuperMkt, **S**...**gas:** BP/dsl, Citgo

68 MD 27, Mt Airy, **N**...**gas:** BP/Blimpie/dsl/24hr, Citgo/7-11, Shell, **food:** Arby's, Burger King, Domino's, KFC, Ledo's Pizza, McDonald's, Pizza Hut, Roy Rogers, TCBY, **other:** Chrysler/Dodge/Jeep, Food Lion, Goodyear, Radio Shack, Rite Aid, Safeway, SuperFresh Foods, Wal-Mart/auto, **S**...**gas:** Exxon/dsl/24hr, Shell, **food:** 4 Seasons Rest., **lodging:** Budget Inn

66mm truckers parking area eb

64mm weigh sta eb

62 MD 75, Libertytown, **N**...**gas:** Mobil/dsl, Shell, **food:** McDonald's, **other:** New Market Hist Dist, **S**... funpark

59 MD 144, no services

57mm Monocacy River

56 MD 144, **N**...**gas:** Citgo, Sheetz, **food:** Burger King, McDonald's, Roy Rogers, Taco Bell, Waffle House, **other:** $General, Triangle RV Ctr, to Hist Dist

55 South St, **1 mi N**...**gas:** Citgo, Pacific Pride, Sheetz

54 Market St, to I-270, **N**...**gas:** Costco/gas, **lodging:** Travelodge, **S**...**gas:** Citgo, Exxon/dsl, Sheetz/24hr, Shell/24hr, SouStates/dsl, **food:** Bob Evans, Burger King, Checker's, Cracker Barrel, El Paso Cantina, Jerry's Rest., KFC, McDonald's, Papa John's, Pargo's Café, Peking Gourmet, Popeye's, Roy Rogers, Subway, Wendy's, **lodging:** Days Inn, Econolodge, Fairfield Inn, Hampton Inn, Holiday Inn Express, **other:** Aamco, Best Buy, Chrysler, Circuit City, Ford/Lincoln/Mercury/Isuzu, Honda, Hyundai/Buick, Kohl's, Lowe's Whse, PrecisionTune, Ross, Sam's Club, Saturn, Sears/auto, Wal-Mart/auto, mall

53b a I-270 S, US 15 N, US 40 W, to Frederick

52b a US 15 S, US 340 W, Leesburg

49 US 40A(no EZ wb return), Braddock Heights, **N on US 40**...**gas:** Chevron, Citgo/dsl, Exxon/dsl, Freestate/dsl, GetGo, Shell, Sunoco, **food:** Arby's, Bob Evans, Boston Mkt, Burger King, Casarico Mexican, Denny's, Fritchie's Rest., Ground Round, Hunter's Rest., McDonald's, Miyako Japanese, Mtn View Diner, Outback Steaks, Pizza Hut, Popeye's, Red Horse Rest., Red Lobster, Roy Rogers, Starbucks, Subway, Taco Bell, Wendy's, **lodging:** Comfort Inn, Holiday Inn, **other:** HOSPITAL, Advance Parts, CVS Drug, Ford/Subaru, Giant Eagle Foods, Home Depot, JC Penney, Jo-Anne Fabrics, K-Mart, Merchant Tire, Mr. Tire, PepBoys, 7-11, Toyota, Weis Foods, st police, **S**...to Washington Mon SP, camping

48 US 40 E, US 340(from eb, no return), **1 mi N**...same as 49

42 MD 17, Myersville, **N**...**gas:** Exxon, Sunoco/dsl/24hr, **food:** Burger King, McDonald's, **other:** to Gambrill SP(6mi), Greenbrier SP(4mi), **S**...**gas:** BP/dsl

39mm **rest area both lanes, full(handicapped) facilities, phone, vending, picnic tables, litter barrels, petwalk**

35 MD 66, to Boonsboro, **S**...**gas:** Sheetz(1mi), **other:** to Greenbrier SP, camping

32b a US 40, Hagerstown, **1-3 mi N**...**gas:** BP/Blimpie, AC&T/Exxon/24hr, Citgo/7-11, Sunoco, **food:** Bob Evans, Denny's, Dunkin Donuts, Ledo's Pizza, McDonald's, Pizza Hut, Popeye's, Quizno's, RC King Chinese, Red Horse Steaks, Subway, Super Buffet, Texas Roadhouse, **lodging:** Clarion, Comfort Suites, Day's Inn, Hampton Inn, Holiday Inn/rest., Quality Inn, Sheraton, Super 8, **other:** HOSPITAL, Chevrolet/Cadillac, Chrysler/Dodge, CVS Drug, #Tree, Goodyear/auto, Martin's Foods, Mercedes/Toyota, Nissan, Subaru, Weis Foods, **S**...**other:** Honda, Kia, Pontiac/Buick/GMC, VW

29b a MD 65, to Sharpsburg, **N**...**gas:** Exxon/dsl/24hr, Sheetz/24hr, Sunoco/dsl/24hr, **food:** FoodCourt, Longhorn Steaks, Pizza Hut, Starbucks, Subway, TCBY, **other:** HOSPITAL, Prime Outlets/famous brands, st police, **S**...**gas:** Shell/Blimpie/dsl/24hr, **food:** Burger King, Cracker Barrel, McDonald's, Waffle House, Wendy's, **lodging:** Sleep Inn, **other:** Safari Camping, to Antietam Bfd

28 MD 632, Hagerstown, **2 mi N**...**gas:** Shell, **food:** Burger King, Chick-fil-A, Domino's, Fazoli's, Pizza Hut, Roy Rogers, Shoney's, Western Sizzlin, **lodging:** Country Inn&Suites, **other:** Advance Parts, AutoZone, Food Lion, **S**...Jellystone Camping

26 I-81, N to Harrisburg, S to Martinsburg

24 MD 63, Huyett, **N**...**gas:** Pilot/Subway/dsl/24hr, Sheetz(2mi), **S**...**lodging:** Red Roof Inn, **other:** KOA(2mi), C&O Canal

18 MD 68 E, Clear Spring, **N**...**gas:** BP, Chevron, **food:** McDonald's, **S**...**gas:** Exxon/dsl, **food:** Wendy Hill Café

12 MD 56, Indian Springs, **S**...**gas:** Exxon/dsl, **other:** Ft Frederick SP

9 US 40 E(from eb, exits left), Indian Springs

5 MD 615(no immediate wb return), **N**...Log Cabin Rest.(2mi)

3 MD 144, Hancock(exits left from wb), **S**...**gas:** ACT/dsl, BP/dsl/rest./24hr, **food:** Hardee's, Park'n Dine, Pizza Hut, Subway, Weaver's Rest., **lodging:** Best Value Inn Super 8, **other:** Ford, NAPA, repair

1b US 522(exits left from eb), Hancock, **N**...Chevrolet,

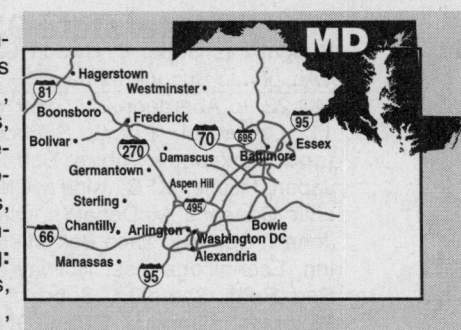

Interstate 70

Chrysler/Dodge/Jeep, **S**...**gas:** Citgo/dsl, Sheetz/dsl, **food:** Hardee's, Lockhouse Rest., Park'n Dine, Pizza Hut, Weaver's Rest., **lodging:** Best Value Inn, Super 8, **other:** $General, Sav-A-Lot Foods, Happy Hills Camp, NAPA

1a	I-68 W, US 40, W to Cumberland
0mm	Maryland/Pennsylvania state line, Mason-Dixon Line

Interstate 81

Exit #	Services
12mm	Maryland/Pennsylvania state line
10b a	Showalter Rd
9	Maugans Ave, **E**...**gas:** Mobil, Sheetz, Shell/Domino's/dsl, **food:** McDonald's, Pizza Hut, Taco Bell, Waffle House, **lodging:** Hampton Inn, **other:** Curves, CVS Drug, $General, **W**...**food:** Burger King, **lodging:** Microtel, **other:** GMC Trucks, Kenworth, U-Haul, Volvo
7b a	MD 58, Hagerstown, same as 6
6b a	US 40, Hagerstown, **E**...**gas:** Exxon/dsl, Liberty, Shell, **food:** Perkin's, Roy Rogers, Wendy's, **lodging:** Clarion, Days Inn, Holiday Motel, Quality Inn, **other:** HOSPITAL, **W**...**food:** Arby's, IHOP, KFC, McDonald's, Panera Bread, Pizzaria Uno, Ryan's, Subway, TGIFriday, Wendy's, **other:** Borders Books, Circuit City, $Tree, Home Depot, Marshall's, Wal-Mart SuperCtr/24hr
5	Halfway Blvd, **E**...**gas:** AC&T/dsl/rest., Sheetz, Shell, **food:** Bonton Rest., Buffalo Wild Wings, Burger King, C&J's Grill, Chick-fil-A, ChuckeCheese, CiCi's Pizza, Fazoli's, Garfield's Rest., Little Caesar's, McDonald's, Olive Garden, Outback Steaks, Pizza Hut, Popeye's, Red Lobster, Roy Rogers, Ruby Tuesday, Sakura Steaks, Shoney's, Taco Bell, Wendy's, **lodging:** Country Inn&Suites, Holiday Inn Express, Motel 6, Plaza Hotel, SpringHill Suites, Travelodge, **other:** CVS Drug, $Tree, Firestone/auto, Ford/Lincoln/Mercury, Hyundai, JC Penney, K-Mart, Lowe's Whse, Martin's Foods/gas, Michael's, Office Depot, PetCo, Sam's Club/gas, Sears/auto, Staples, Target, mall, **W**...**gas:** AC&T, Exxon
4	I-70, E to Frederick, W to Hancock, to I-68
2	US 11, Williamsport, **E**...**gas:** AC&T/dsl, **food:** Burger King, **W**...**gas:** Exxon/dsl, Sheetz, Sunoco/dsl/24hr, **food:** McDonald's, Waffle House, **lodging:** Red Roof Inn, **other:** KOA(4mi)
1	MD 63, MD 68, Williamsport, **E**...**other:** Jellystone, KOA, to Antietam Bfd, **W**...Citgo
0mm	Maryland/West Virginia state line, Potomac River

Interstate 83

Exit #	Services
38mm	Maryland/Pennsylvania state line, Mason-Dixon Line
37	to Freeland(from sb), no services
36	MD 439, Bel Air, **5 mi W**...Morris Meadows Camp
35mm	weigh/insp sta sb
33	MD 45, Parkton, **E**...**gas:** Exxon/dsl
31	Middletown Rd, to Parkton, golf
27	MD 137, Mt Carmel, Hereford, **E**...**gas:** Exxon/dsl, **other:** Graul's Foods, Hereford Drug, NAPA, USPO
24	Belfast Rd, to Butler, Sparks, no services
20	Shawan Rd, Hunt Valley, **E**...**gas:** BP, Exxon/dsl, **food:** Burger King, California Pizza, Caribou Coffee, Carmine's Pizza, Carrabba's, Chipotle Mexican, Da-

mon's, McDonald's, Noodles &Company, Outback Steaks, Quizno's, Panera Bread, Subway, Wendy's, Wong's Kitchen, **lodging:** Chase Suites, Courtyard, Econolodge, Embassy Suites, Hampton Inn, Hunt Valley Marriott, **other:** Giant Foods, Goodyear/auto, Sears/auto, 7-11, Wal-Mart, Wegman's Foods, mall

18	Warren Rd(from nb, no return), Cockeysville, **E**...**gas:** Exxon, **lodging:** Residence Inn, services **E** on York Rd
17	Padonia Rd, Deereco Rd, **E**...**gas:** BP/dsl, Citgo/7-11, Hess, **food:** Applebee's, Bob Evans, Chili's, Macaroni Grill, **lodging:** Day's Hotel, Extended Stay America, **other:** Audi, Chevrolet, Goodyear/auto, Mar's Foods, Mr Tire, Porsche, Rite Aid, Subaru, USPO, services **E** on York Rd
16b a	Timonium Rd, **E**...**gas:** Sunoco/dsl, **food:** Steak&Ale, **lodging:** Holiday Inn, Red Roof Inn, **other:** Eckerd, Infiniti
14	I-695 N
13	I-695 S, Falls Rd, HOSPITAL, st police
12	Ruxton Rd(from nb, no return), no services
10b a	Northern Parkway, **E**...HOSPITAL, Exxon, Shell
9b a	Cold Spring Lane, no services
8	MD 25 N(from nb), Falls Rd, no services
7b a	28th St, **E**...HOSPITAL, **W**...Baltimore Zoo
6	US 1, US 40T, North Ave, downtown
5	MD Ave(from sb), downtown
3	Chase St, Gilford St, downtown
2	Pleasant St(from sb), downtown
1	Fayette St, I-83 begins/ends, downtown Baltimore

Interstate 95

Exit #	Services
110mm	Maryland/Delaware state line
109b a	MD 279, to Elkton, Newark, **E**...**gas:** Citgo/dsl, Petro/Iron Skillet/dsl/rest./24hr/@, Shell/dsl, **food:** Cracker Barrel, KFC/Taco Bell, McDonald's, Waffle House, **lodging:** Econolodge, Elkton Lodge, Hampton Inn, Knight's Inn, Motel 6, **other:** HOSPITAL, Blue Beacon, **W**...**gas:** TA/Mobil/Subway/dsl/24hr/@, 7-11, **other:** to U of DE
100	MD 272, to North East, Rising Sun, **E**...**gas:** /Flying J/dsl/rest./LP/24hr/@, **food:** McDonald's, Schroeder's Deli, Wendy's, **lodging:** Crystal Inn, Holiday Inn Express, **other:** Eckerd, museum, st police, to Elk Neck SP, **W**...**gas:** Citgo, Mobil, **other:** zoo
96mm	**Chesapeake House service area(exits left from both lanes), Exxon/dsl, Sunoco/dsl, Burger King, HotDogs, Pizza Hut, Popeye's, Starbucks, TCBY, gifts**
93	MD 275, to Rising Sun, US 222, to Perryville, **E**...**gas:** Exxon/dsl, Pilot/Subway/dsl/24hr/@, **food:** Denny's, KFC/Taco Bell, **lodging:** Comfort Inn, **other:** HOSPITAL, Prime Outlets/famous brands, Riverview Camping, **W**...**food:** CM Tuggs Diner, Crother's Mkt, **lodging:** Douglass Motel, **other:** st police
92mm	weigh sta/toll booth
91.5mm	Susquehanna River
89	MD 155, to Havre de Grace(last nb exit before toll), **1-3 mi E**...**food:** McDonald's, MacGregor's Rest., **lodging:** Best

Interstate 95

	Budget Inn, Super 8, Swede Suites, **other:** HOSPITAL, **W**...to Susquehanna SP
85	MD 22, to Aberdeen, **E**...**gas:** Amoco/24hr, Citgo/7-11, Crown/dsl, Enroy, Sunoco/dsl, Shell/dsl/24hr, **food:** Applebee's, Arby's, Bob Evans, Family Buffet, Japan House, KFC, King's Chinese, Lee's Hunan, Little Caesar's, McDonald's, Olive Tree Italian, Papa John's, Subway, Taco Bell, Wendy's, **lodging:** Day's Inn, Econolodge/rest., Holiday Inn, Quality Inn/rest., Red Roof, Sheraton, Super 8, Travelodge, **other:** $Express, $General, $Tree, GNC, Klein's Foods, K-Mart, Mars Foods, Pontiac/Cadillac, Radio Shack, Rite Aid, Target, museum
81mm	**MD House service area(exits left from both lanes), Exxon/dsl, Sunoco/dsl, Big Boy, Cinnabon, Hotdog City, Roy Rogers, Sbarro's, TCBY, gifts**
80	MD 543, to Riverside, Churchville, **E**...**gas:** BP/Burger King, Citgo/7-11, Crown/A&W/dsl, Mobil/dsl, **food:** China Moon, Cracker Barrel, Krispy Kreme, McDonald's, Riverside Pizzaria, Ruby Tuesday, Waffle House, **lodging:** Country Inn, Extended Stay America, SpringHill Suites, Wingate Inn, **other:** Eckerd, Klein's Foods, Bar Harbor RV Park(4mi)
77b a	MD 24, to Edgewood, Bel Air, **E**...**gas:** Citgo/dsl, Exxon/Blimpie/dsl, Shell, **food:** Burger King, Denny's/24hr, Giovanni's Rest., Taco Bell, Vitali's Rest., **lodging:** Best Western, Comfort Inn, Day's Inn, Hampton Inn, Holiday Inn Express, Sleep Inn, **W**...**gas:** Exxon/dsl, Wawa, **food:** Chick-fil-A, KFC/Taco Bell, McDonald's, **other:** HOSPITAL, BJ's Whse, Target, Wal-Mart/drugs, Weis Foods
74	MD 152, Joppatowne, **E**...**gas:** BP/dsl, Citgo/High's/dsl, Exxon/dsl, **food:** Friendly's, KFC, IHOP, McDonald's, Venitian Palace, Wendy's, **lodging:** Edgewood Motel, Super 8, **other:** HOSPITAL, RV Ctr, Toyota(1mi)
70mm	Big Gunpowder Falls
67b a	MD 43, to White Marsh Blvd, US 1, US 40, **E on MD 7**...**gas:** BP/dsl, Crown/24hr, Enroy, Shell, Sunoco, **food:** Burger King, WhiteMarsh Diner, **other:** Best Buy, Dodge, Target, to Gunpowder SP, **W on White Marsh Blvd**...**gas:** Citgo/7-11, Exxon/dsl, **food:** Bayou Blues Café, Bertucci's, Chick-fil-A, Chili's, Don Pablo, Fuddrucker's, Lin's Chinese, McDonald's, Olive Garden, Red Brick Sta., Red Lobster, Ruby Tuesday, Taco Bell, TGIFriday, Wendy's, **lodging:** Hampton Inn, Hilton Garden, Residence Inn, **other:** Barnes&Noble, Giant Foods, GNC, Hecht's, IKEA, JC Penney, Lord&Taylor, Macy's, Old Navy, Sears/auto, Staples, USPO, mall, to Gunpowder SP
64b a	I-695(exits left), E to Essex, W to Towson
62	to I-895(from sb)
61	US 40, Pulaski Hwy, **E**...**gas:** BP, Texaco, Shell, **food:** McDonald's
60	Moravia Rd, **E**...**gas:** Citgo/dsl, **other:** Pontiac/GMC, Suzuki
59	Eastern Ave, **W**...**gas:** BP/dsl/24hr, Enroy Gas/dsl, Exxon, **food:** Broadway Diner, Wendy's, **other:** HOSPITAL, Home Depot
58	Dundalk Ave, **E**...**gas:** Citgo, Mobil
57	O'Donnell St, Boston St, **E**...**gas:** TA/Mobil/Subway/dsl/@, **food:** A&W, McDonald's, KFC, Sbarro's, **lodging:** Best Western, Rodeway Inn
56	Keith Ave, no services
56mm	McHenry Tunnel, toll plaza(north side of tunnel)
55	Key Hwy, to Ft McHenry NM, last nb exit before toll
54	MD 2 S, to Hanover St, **W**...downtown, HOSPITAL
53	I-395 N, to MLK, **W**...downtown, Oriole Park
52	Russell St N, **W**...HOSPITAL
51	Washington Blvd, no services
50.5mm	inspection sta nb
50	Caton Ave, **E**...**gas:** Crown Gas, Hess/dsl, Shell/24hr, **food:** McDonald's, McKenzie's Rest., **lodging:** Holiday Inn Express, **other:** Aldi Foods, Toyota, **W**...HOSPITAL
49b a	I-695, E to Key Bridge, Glen Burnie, W to Towson, to I-70, to I-83
47b a	I-195, to MD 166, to BWI Airport, to Baltimore
46	I-895, to Harbor Tunnel Thruway
43	MD 100, to Glen Burnie, **1 mi E on US 1**...**gas:** Citgo/dsl, Exxon/Wendy's, **lodging:** Best Western
41b a	MD 175, to Columbia, **E**...**gas:** Citgo, Exxon/dsl, Shell, **food:** Arby's, Burger King, Frank's Diner, High's Dairy, Jerry's Rest., McDonald's, **lodging:** Best Western, Budget Motel, Fairfield Inn, Holiday Inn, Super 8, **W**...**gas:** Crown Gas, Exxon, **food:** Applebee's, Bob Evans, McDonald's, Olive Garden, TGIFriday, **lodging:** Studio+, **other:** HOSPITAL, to Johns Hopkins U, Loyola U
38b a	MD 32, to Ft Meade, **2 mi E on US 1**...**gas:** BP, Enroy, Exxon, **food:** Burger King, McDonald's, Taco Bell, **lodging:** Comfort Inn, **other:** to BWI Airport
37mm	**Welcome Ctr both lanes, full(handicapped)facilities, info, phone, vending, picnic tables, litter barrels, petwalk, RV Dump**
35b a	MD 216, to Laurel, **E**...**gas:** Crown Gas, Exxon, **food:** McDonald's, **lodging:** Quality Inn, **other:** Weis Food/drug
34mm	Patuxent River
33b a	MD 198, to Laurel, **E**...**gas:** Exxon, **other:** HOSPITAL, **W**...**gas:** Exxon/Blimpie, Shell, **food:** Brass Duck Rest., McDonald's, **lodging:** Best Western
29	MD 212, to Beltsville, **W**...**gas:** Exxon/Blimpie/dsl, Shell, **food:** Magic Cue Rest., McDonald's, Wendy's, **lodging:** Fairfield Inn, Sheraton, **other:** Cherry Hill Park, CVS Drug, Giant Foods
27	I-495 S around Washington
25b a	US 1, Baltimore Ave, to Laurel, College Park, **E**...**gas:** BP, Chevron, Citgo/7-11, Exxon/dsl, Shell/24hr, **food:** Arby's, Burger King, Danny's Burgers, Quizno's, El Mexicano, Jerry's Subs, McDonald's, Moose Creek Steaks, Pizza Hut, Quizno's, Wendy's, **lodging:** Holiday Inn, **other:** Goodyear, Rite Aid, US Agri Library, **W**...**gas:** BP/24hr, Shell, Barnside Diner/24hr, **food:** Baskin-Robbins/Dunkin Donuts, Starbucks, **lodging:** Day's Inn, Econolodge, Hampton Inn, Ramada Ltd, Super 8, **other:** GNC, Home Depot, Honda, Shoppers Foods, VW, to U of MD
23	MD 201, Kenilworth Ave, **E**...**lodging:** Marriott/rest., **1 mi W on Greenbelt**...**gas:** Shell, **food:** Boston Mkt, Checker's, KFC, McDonald's, Popeye's, TGIFriday's, TJ's Roadhouse, **lodging:** Courtyard, Residence Inn, **other:** Cadillac, CVS Drug, Giant Food/drug, Staples, Target
22	Baltimore-Washington Pkwy, **E**...to NASA
20b a	MD 450, Annapolis Rd, Lanham, **E**...**gas:** Mobil, **food:** Burger King, Jerry's Rest., McDonald's, Pizza Hut, Red Lobster, **lodging:** Best Western, Day's Inn/rest., Red Roof Inn, **other:** Ford/Kia, **W**...**gas:** BP, Chevron, Citgo/7-11/24hr, Shell, Sunoco/24hr, **food:** Bojangles, KFC, Popeye's, Wendy's, **lodging:** Ramada Inn, **other:** HOSPITAL, Chrysler/Dodge/Jeep, CVS Drug, Goodyear/auto, JustTires, Lincoln/Mercury, Nissan, Office Depot, Pontiac, Radio Shack, Safeway, Shoppers Foods, Staples

Interstate 95

N ↕ S

Washington DC Area

19b a	US 50, to Annapolis, Washington
17	MD 202, Landover Rd, to Upper Marlboro, E...**food:** Jasper's Rest., Outback Steaks, Ruby Tuesday's, **lodging:** DoubleTree Club Hotel, **other:** FedEx Center, W...**other:** Sam's Club, Sears/auto
16	Arena Dr, W...to Arena
15	MD 214, Central Ave, E...**lodging:** Extended Stay America, Hampton Inn/rest., **food:** ChuckeCheese, **other:** Circuit City, FedEx Center, to Six Flags, W... **gas:** Crown, Exxon/dsl, Shell/autocare, Sunoco/24hr, **food:** DQ, KFC, Jerry's Subs, McDonald's, Pizza Hut, Wendy's, **lodging:** Day's Inn/rest., **other:** Goodyear, Home Depot, NTB, Staples, U-Haul
13	Ritchie-Marlboro Rd, Capitol Hgts
11	MD 4, Pennsylvania Ave, to Upper Marlboro, W... **gas:** Exxon, Shell, Sunoco, **food:** Applebee's, Arby's, IHOP, Pizza Hut, Starbucks, Taco Bell, Wendy's, **other:** CVS Drug, JC Penney, Marshall's, st police
9	MD 337, to Allentown Rd, E...**gas:** Crown, Shell/autocare, **food:** Bojangle's, Checkers, McDonald's, Popeye's, **lodging:** Holiday Inn Express, Motel 6, Ramada Inn, Super 8, **other:** HOSPITAL, Advance Parts, Family$, U-Haul, to Andrews AFB
7	MD 5, Branch Ave, to Silver Hill, E...**gas:** Exxon, Getty, Sunoco, **food:** Wendy's, W...**gas:** Shell/Subway/dsl, **lodging:** Day's Inn, **other:** HOSPITAL, Ford
4b a	MD 414, St Barnabas Rd, Marlow Hgts, E...**gas:** Citgo, Exxon, **food:** Blackeyed Pea, Bojangles, Burger King, KFC, McDonald's, Outback Steaks, Wendy's, **other:** $Tree, Home Depot, Old Navy, Safeway, Staples, W...**gas:** Exxon/dslDQ, Shell/autocare, **food:** McDonald's
3b a	MD 210, Indian Head Hwy, to Forest Hgts, E...**gas:** Mobil, Shell, **food:** Danny's Burgers, Pizza Hut, Ranch House Rest., Taco Bell, **lodging:** Best Western, Oxon Hill Inn, **other:** Advance Parts, USPO, W...**gas:** BP/dsl/24hr, Crown Gas, Shell, 7-11, **food:** Burger King, Cici's Pizza, McDonald's, Wendy's, **other:** Radio Shack, Safeway
2b a	I-295, N to Washingon
0mm	Maryland/Virginia state line, Potomac River, Woodrow Wilson Bridge

Interstate 97

Exit #	Services
17	I-695. I-97 begins/ends on I-695.
16	MD 648, Ferndale, Glen Burnie, E...**gas:** BP, **food:** KFC, McDonald's, Quizno's, Wendy's, **other:** Giant Foods, W...**gas:** Mobil
15b a	MD 176 W, Dorsey Rd, Aviation Blvd, E...**gas:** BP, **food:** KFC, Wendy's, W...to BWI
14b a	MD 100, Ellicott City, Gibson Island
13b a	MD 174, Quarterfield Rd, E...**gas:** Citgo/7-11, Crown Gas, Exxon, **food:** Gary's Grill, WaWa, W... **gas:** Citgo/dsl, Shell/dsl, **other:** Shoppers Foods
12	MD 3, New Cut Rd, Glen Burnie, E **on Veterans Hwy**...**gas:** BP, Crown Gas, Enroy, **food:** KFC/Taco Bell, Wendy's, **other:** CVS Drug, E...**gas:** Exxon/24hr, Mobil, WaWa, **food:** Burger King, Domino's, Friendly's, Pizza Hut, Popeye's, Taco Bell, Wendy's, **other:** HOSPITAL, Giant Foods, Goodyear, Target, Walgreen, Wal-Mart

N ↕ S

10b a	Benfield Blvd, Severna Park, E...**gas:** Exxon/dsl, **lodging:** White Gables Motel, **other:** KOA, access to same as 12
7	MD 3, MD 32, Bowie, Odenton, E...motel
5	MD 178(no EZ sb return), Crownsville
0mm	I-97 begins/ends on US 50/301.

Interstate 270(Rockville)

Frederick

E ↕ W

Exit #	Services
32	I-270 begins/ends on I-70, exit 53.
31b a	MD 85, N...**gas:** Citgo/7-11, Exxon, Sheetz, Shell/dsl, SouStates, **food:** Applebee's, Arby's, Bob Evans, Burger King, Checker's, El Paso, Golden Corral, Jerry's Rest., KFC/Taco Bell, LoneStar Steaks, McDonald's, Pargo's, Popeye's, Roy Rogers, Waffle House, Wendy's, **lodging:** Day's Inn, Econolodge, Holiday Inn, Holiday Inn Express, **other:** Audi/Lincoln/Mercury, Best Buy, Borders Books, Chrysler, Circuit City, CVS Drug, Goodyear/auto, Home Depot, Kohl's, Lowe's Whse, Mr Tire, Sam's Club, Sears, Wal-Mart SuperCtr, S...**gas:** BP/Blimpie, **food:** Chico's Rest, Chipotle Mexican, Cracker Barrel, Macaroni Grill, McDonald's, Panda Express, Starbucks, TGIFriday, **lodging:** Comfort Inn, Courtyard, Extended Stay America, Fairfield Inn, Hampton Inn, Hilton Garden, MainStay Suites, Residence Inn, **other:** Honda, Toyota
30mm	Monocacy River
28mm	viewpoint wb
26	MD 80, Urbana, N...**gas:** Exxon, Citgo/7-11
22	MD 109, to Barnesville, Hyattstown, S...**lodging:** Comus Inn(3mi)
21mm	weigh/insp sta both lanes
18	MD 121, to Clarksburg, Little Bennett Pk, Blackhill Pk, Boyds, N...**gas,** camping(seasonal)
16	MD 27, Father Hurley Blvd, to Damascus, N...**gas:** Chevron/dsl, Exxon, Mobil, **food:** Applebee's, Bob Evans, Burger King, McDonald's, Subway, TCBY, **lodging:** Extended Stay America, **other:** Best Buy, Borders Books, Giant Foods, Home Depot, Kohl's, Michael's, PepBoys, Starbucks, TJMaxx, Target, Wal-Mart, S...**gas:** BP, Citgo/7-11, Exxon, **food:** Burger King, Carrabba's, Chickfil-A, McDonald's, Red Robin, Jasper's Rest., Longhorn Steaks, Ruby Tuesday, Subway, Taco Bell, Wendy's, **lodging:** Fairfield Inn, **other:** Eckerd
15b a	MA 118, to MD 355, N...**gas:** Chevron/dsl, **food:** Burger King, **lodging:** Hampton Inn, S...**gas:** Amoco, Exxon/24hr, Mobil, **food:** Burger King, Pizza Hut, **other:** st police, tire/brake repair
13b a	Middlebrook Rd(from wb)
11b a	MD 124, Quince Orchard Rd, N...**gas:** Exxon, **food:** Boston Mkt, ChuckeCheese, McDonald's, Roy Rogers, Starbucks, Subway, **lodging:** Courtyard, Hilton, Holiday Inn, TownePlace Suites, **other:** Borders Books, CompUSA, CVS Drugs, Ford, JC Penney, Sam's Club, mall, S...**gas:**

MARYLAND

Interstate 270

<table>
<tr><td rowspan="11">R
o
c
k
v
i
l
l
e</td><td></td><td>Shell/dsl, **food:** Chevy's Mexican, Chili's, Denny's, Friendly's, LoneStar Steaks, Starbucks, **lodging:** Motel 6, **other:** Advance Parts, Chevrolet/Hummer, Circuit City, Giant Foods, McGruder's Foods, Staples, Seneca Creek SP</td></tr>
<tr><td>10</td><td>MD 117, Clopper Rd(from wb), same as 11.</td></tr>
<tr><td>9b a</td><td>I-370, to Gaithersburg, Sam Eig Hwy, **S**...**food:** access to Chinese Rest., India Bistro, Pizza Hut, Subway, **other:** Barnes&Noble, Festival Foods, Target, Weis Mkt</td></tr>
<tr><td>8</td><td>Shady Grove Rd, **S**...**lodging:** Marriott, Quality Suites, Residence Inn, Sleep Inn, SpringHill Suites, **other:** HOSPITAL, Barnes&Noble, Target</td></tr>
<tr><td>6b a</td><td>MD 28, W Montgomery Ave, **N**...**lodging:** Woodfin Suites, **S**...**lodging:** Best Western</td></tr>
<tr><td>5b a</td><td>MD 189, Falls Rd, no services</td></tr>
<tr><td>4b a</td><td>Montrose Rd, **N**...**gas**, **S**...st police</td></tr>
<tr><td>2</td><td>I-270/I-270 spur diverges eb, converges wb</td></tr>
<tr><td>1</td><td>MD 187, Old Georgetown Rd, **S**...**gas:** Exxon, **food:** Hamburger Hamlet, **other:** HOSPITAL, CVS Drug, Giant Foods, GNC</td></tr>
<tr><td>1b a</td><td>(I-270 spur)Democracy Blvd, **E**...**lodging:** Marriott, **W**...**gas:** Exxon/Shell/dsl, **other:** Macy's, , Nordstrom's, Sears, mall</td></tr>
<tr><td>0mm</td><td>I-270 begins/ends on I-495, exit 35.</td></tr>
</table>

Interstate 495(DC)
See Virginia Interstate 495(DC)

Interstate 695(Baltimore)

<table>
<tr><td rowspan="28">B
a
l
t
i
m
o
r
e</td><td>Exit #</td><td>Services</td></tr>
<tr><td>48mm</td><td>Patapsco River, Francis Scott Key Br</td></tr>
<tr><td>44</td><td>MD 695(from nb)</td></tr>
<tr><td>43mm</td><td>toll plaza</td></tr>
<tr><td>42</td><td>MD 151 S, Sparrows Point(last exit before toll sb), **E**...**gas:** Citgo/dsl</td></tr>
<tr><td>41</td><td>MD 20, Cove Rd, **W**...**gas:** North Point Fuel</td></tr>
<tr><td>40</td><td>MD 150, MD 151, North Point Blvd</td></tr>
<tr><td>39</td><td>Merritt Blvd, **W**...**gas:** BP, **other:** Ford/Lincoln/Mercury, Hyundai, Mr Tire, Suzuki</td></tr>
<tr><td>38b a</td><td>MD 150, Eastern Blvd, to Baltimore, **E**...**gas:** Enroy Gas, **food:** Super Buffet, **W**...**food:** Applebee's, Checkers, Golden Corral, KFC, **other:** Chevrolet/Nissan, $Tree, Joann Fabrics, Shopper Foods, Staples</td></tr>
<tr><td>36</td><td>MD 702 S(exits left from sb), to Essex</td></tr>
<tr><td>35</td><td>US 40, **N**...**gas:** Citgo, WaWa/gas, **food:** Checkers, DQ, Dunkin Donuts, Hometown Buffet, McDonald's, Panda Express, Wendy's, **other:** Circuit City, $General, Harley-Davidson, Home Depot, NTB, Office Depot, Sam's Club, U-Haul, Wal-Mart/gas, same as 34</td></tr>
<tr><td>34</td><td>34 MD 7, Philadelphia Rd, **N**...**food:** Wendy's, **lodging:** Fairfield Inn, **S**...**gas:** Exxon, **other:** Walgreen, same as 35</td></tr>
<tr><td>33b a</td><td>I-95, N to Philadelphia, S to Baltimore</td></tr>
<tr><td>32b a</td><td>US 1, Bel Air, **N**...**gas:** Exxon, 7-11, **food:** Denny's, Dunkin Donuts, Fisherman's Wharf, IHOP, Krispy Kreme, McDonald's, Taco Bell, **other:** Giant Foods, K-Mart, Merchant Tire/auto, Toyota/Mazda, **S**...**gas:** Crown Gas, Getty, **food:** Carrabba's, McDonald's, Mr Crab, Subway, **other:** Goodyear/auto</td></tr>
<tr><td>31c</td><td>MD 43 E(from eb)</td></tr>
<tr><td>31b a</td><td>MD 147, Harford Rd, **N**...**gas:** BP/24hr, Citgo/7-11, Mobil, Shell/dsl, **other:** CVS Drugs, Chrysler Goodyear, Honda, NAPA</td></tr>
</table>

<table>
<tr><td>30b a</td><td>MD 41, Perring Pkwy, **N**...**food:** Burger King, Denny's, Roy Rogers, **other:** Chevrolet, Ford, Giant Foods, Home Depot Office Depot, Ross, Safeway, **S**...**other:** Dodge, Mazda</td></tr>
<tr><td>29b</td><td>MD 542, Loch Raven Blvd, **S**...**gas:** BP, Crown, Hess, **food** Bel Loc Diner, Hooters, Pizza Hut, Subway, **lodging:** Comfor Inn, Ramada Inn</td></tr>
<tr><td>29a</td><td>Cromwell Bridge Rd, **S**...**lodging:** Holiday Inn</td></tr>
<tr><td>28</td><td>Providence Rd, **S**...Citgo</td></tr>
<tr><td>27b a</td><td>MD 146, Dulaney Valley Rd, **N**...Hampton NHS, **S**...**gas** Mobil/dsl, **food:** Rainforest Cafe, **lodging:** Sheraton, **other** Hecht's, SuperFresh Food, mall</td></tr>
<tr><td>26b a</td><td>MD 45, York Rd, Towson, **N**...**gas:** BP, Exxon/dsl, Friendly's Shell, **S**...**gas:** Crown/dsl, Exxon, **food:** McDonald's, **other** CompUSA, CVS Drug, Ford, Lexus</td></tr>
<tr><td>25</td><td>MD 139, Charles St, **S**...HOSPITAL</td></tr>
<tr><td>24</td><td>I-83 N, to York</td></tr>
<tr><td>23b</td><td>Falls Rd, **N**...**gas:** Exxon/dsl</td></tr>
<tr><td>23a</td><td>I-83 S, MD 25 N, Baltimore</td></tr>
<tr><td>22</td><td>Greenspring Ave, no services</td></tr>
<tr><td>21</td><td>to Stevenson Rd, Park Hghts Rd</td></tr>
<tr><td>20</td><td>MD 140, Reisterstown Rd, Pikesville, **N**...**gas:** Exxon, 7-11 **other:** Barnes&Noble, **S**...**gas:** BP, Mobil/Subway, Shell **food:** McDonald's, Olive Branch Italian, **lodging:** Hilton Garden, Ramada Inn, **other:** Target</td></tr>
<tr><td>19</td><td>I-795, NW Expswy</td></tr>
<tr><td>18b a</td><td>MD 26, Randallstown, Lochearn, **E**...**gas:** Texaco, **other** HOSPITAL, **W**...**gas:** BP, Exxon, 7-11, Shell, **food:** Burger King, Sea Pride Crabhouse, Subway</td></tr>
<tr><td>17</td><td>MD 122, Security Blvd, **E**...**gas:** BP, **food:** Red Lobster Wendy's, **lodging:** Day's Inn, Motel 6, Quality Inn, **other** Chevrolet, Mitsubishi, Nissan, **W**...**gas:** Exxon, Sunoco, **food** Bennigan's, Burger King, McDonald's, **lodging:** Holiday Inn **other:** Best Buy, Firestone, Ford, JC Penney, Macy's, Sears, auto, Staples, SuperFresh Foods, mall</td></tr>
<tr><td>16b a</td><td>I-70, E to Baltimore, W to Frederick</td></tr>
<tr><td>15b a</td><td>US 40, Ellicott City, Baltimore, **E**...**food:** Burger King, ChuckeCheese, KFC, McDonald's, IHOP, **lodging:** Day's Inn Comfort Inn, **other:** Dodge, Firestone, Lowe's Whse, Ross Safeway Foods, Sam's Club/gas, U-Haul, **W**...**gas:** BP/dsl Crown/24hr, Shell, **other:** Circuit City</td></tr>
<tr><td>14</td><td>Edmondson Ave, **E**...**gas:** Exxon, **food:** Royal Farms, **W**... **gas:** Citgo</td></tr>
<tr><td>13</td><td>MD 144, Frederick Rd, Catonsville, **W**...**gas:** BP, Crown, 7-11, **food:** Dunkin Donuts, McDonald's/24hr, Subway</td></tr>
<tr><td>12c b</td><td>MD 372 E, Wilkens, **E**...HOSPITAL</td></tr>
<tr><td>11b a</td><td>I-95, N to Baltimore, S to Washington</td></tr>
<tr><td>10</td><td>US 1, Washington Blvd, **E**...**food:** Wendy's, **lodging:** Beltway Motel/rest., **other:** Home Depot, **W**...**gas:** Exxon, **food:** Burger King</td></tr>
<tr><td>9</td><td>Hollins Ferry Rd, Lansdowne, **E**...**gas:** Mobil, Sunoco/dsl</td></tr>
<tr><td>8</td><td>MD 168, Nursery Rd, **N**...**gas:** Exxon, Shell, **food:** Burger King, KFC, McDonald's, Taco Bell, Wendy's, **lodging:** Motel 6</td></tr>
<tr><td>7b a</td><td>MD 295, **N**...to Baltimore, **S**...BWI Airport</td></tr>
<tr><td>6b a</td><td>Camp Mead Rd(from nb)</td></tr>
<tr><td>5</td><td>MD 648, Ferndale, gas, food, lodging</td></tr>
<tr><td>4b a</td><td>I-97 S, to Annapolis</td></tr>
<tr><td>3b a</td><td>MD 2 N, Brooklyn Park, **S**...**gas:** Exxon, Hess, Shell, **food:** Bennigan's, Bob Evan's, Checker's, Chick-fil-A, ChuckeCheese, Denny's, KFC, Krispy Kreme, McDonald's, Taco Bell, **lodging:** Day's Inn, Hampton Inn, Holiday Inn, **other:** CompUSA, Giant Foods, Just Tires, Lowe's Whse, Target</td></tr>
<tr><td>2</td><td>MD 10, Glen Burnie</td></tr>
<tr><td>1</td><td>MD 174, Hawkins Point Rd, **S**...**gas:** Citgo/deli/dsl</td></tr>
</table>

MASSACHUSETTS

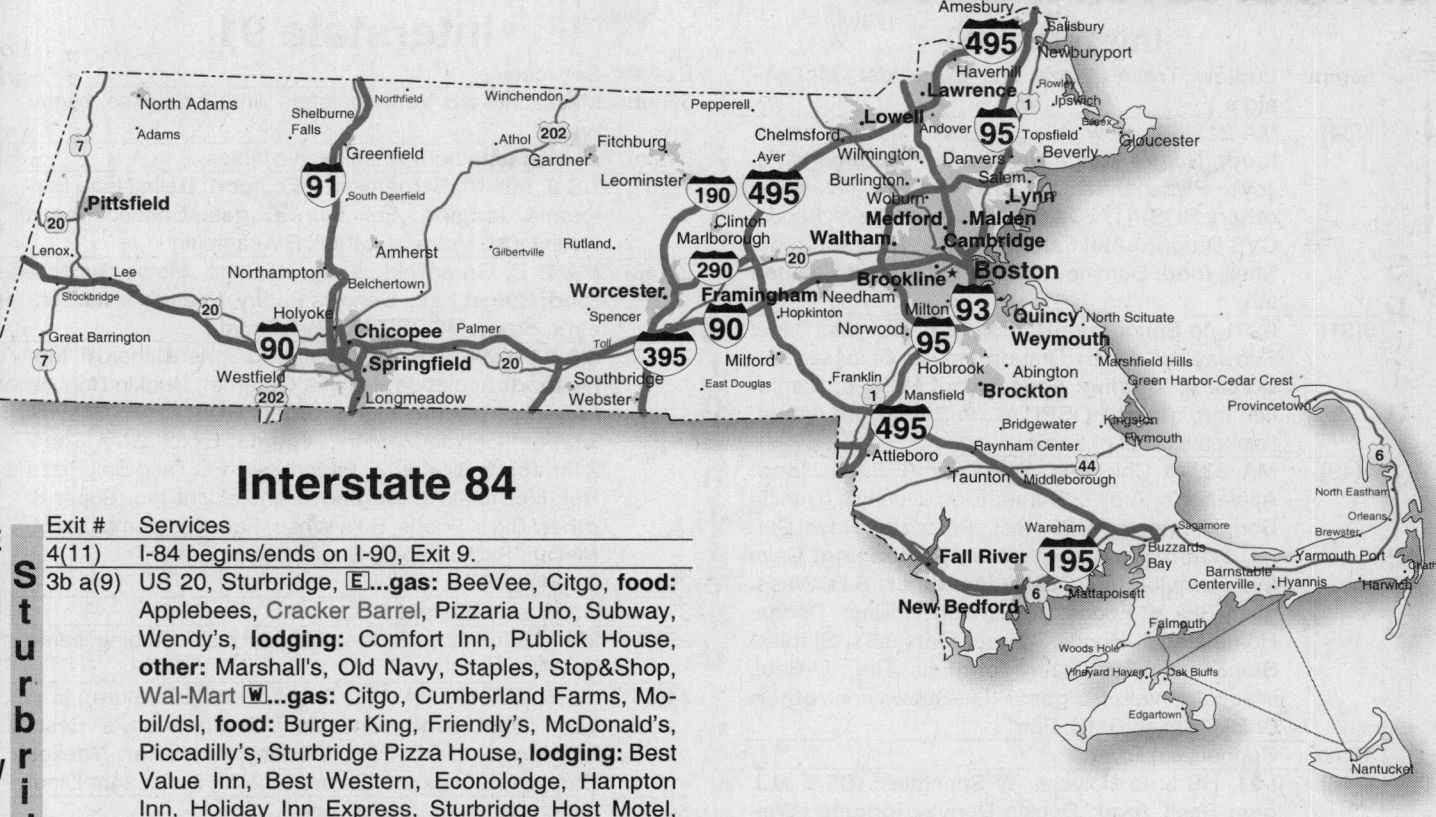

Interstate 84

Exit #	Services
4(11)	I-84 begins/ends on I-90, Exit 9.
3b a(9)	US 20, Sturbridge, **E**...**gas:** BeeVee, Citgo, **food:** Applebees, Cracker Barrel, Pizzaria Uno, Subway, Wendy's, **lodging:** Comfort Inn, Publick House, **other:** Marshall's, Old Navy, Staples, Stop&Shop, Wal-Mart **W**...**gas:** Citgo, Cumberland Farms, Mobil/dsl, **food:** Burger King, Friendly's, McDonald's, Piccadilly's, Sturbridge Pizza House, **lodging:** Best Value Inn, Best Western, Econolodge, Hampton Inn, Holiday Inn Express, Sturbridge Host Motel, Super 8, **other:** HOSPITAL, USPO, st police
2(5)	MA 131, to Old Sturbridge Village, Sturbridge, **S**... Day's Inn, RV camping
4mm	picnic area wb, litter barrels
1(2.5)	Mashapaug Rd, to Southbridge, **E**...**gas:** Mobil/dsl/24hr, Pilot/deli/dsl/rest./scales/24hr/@, Shell/dsl/24hr, **food:** Boston Pizza, Roy Rogers, Sbarro's, **lodging:** Quality Inn
2mm	weigh sta wb
.5mm	picnic area eb
0mm	Massachusetts/Connecticut state line

Interstate 90

Exit #	Services
136mm	I-90 begins/ends on I-93, exit 20 in Boston.
22(134)	Presidential Ctr, downtown
20(132)	MA 28, Alston, Brighton, Cambridge, **N**...HOSPITAL, Guest Quarters
131mm	toll plaza
19(130)	MA Ave(from eb), **N**...**food:** IHOP, McDonald's, **lodging:** Day's Inn
17(128)	Centre St, Newton, **N**...**lodging:** Sheraton, **other:** Cadillac, Chevrolet, Honda, Nissan
16(125)	MA 16, W Newton, **S**...**gas:** Mobil/repair
15(124)	I-95, **N**...**gas:** Marriott
123mm	toll plaza
14(122)	MA 30, Weston, no services
117mm	**Natick Travel Plaza eb, Exxon/dsl, McDonald's, info**
13(116)	MA 30, Natick, **S**...**gas:** Exxon, Getty, Mobil/dsl, **food:** Bickford's, Burger King, McDonald's, Naked Fish Rest., **lodging:** Red Roof Inn, **other:** HOSPITAL, Home Depot, Isuzu, Macy's, Marshalls, Target, mall
114mm	**Framingham Travel Plaza wb, Exxon/dsl, McDonald's, info**
12(111)	MA 9, Framington, **N**...**gas:** Getty, **food:** Subway, Tin Alley Grill, **lodging:** Motel 6, Sheraton, **other:** HOSPITAL, **S**...**food:** Chef Orient, Toyota
11a(106)	I-495, N to NH, S to Cape Cod
105mm	**Westborough Travel Plaza wb, Exxon/dsl, Sbarro's, TCBY, gifts**
11(96)	MA 122, to Millbury, **N**...UMA Med Ctr
10a(95)	MA 146, no services
94mm	Blackstone River
10(90)	I-395 S, to Auburn, I-290 N, Worcester, **N**...**gas:** Shell, **food:** Piccadilly's, **lodging:** Comfort Inn, Ramada Inn, **S**...**gas:** Shell/repair/24hr, **food:** Applebee's, D'angelo's, Friendly's, Wendy's, **other:** HOSPITAL, CVS Drug, Ford/Mercury, Hyundai, Park'n Shop Foods
84mm	**Charlton Travel Plaza wb, Exxon/dsl, McDonald's, info**
80mm	**Charlton Travel Plaza eb, Exxon/dsl, McDonald's, info, st police**
79mm	toll plaza
9(78)mm	I-84, to Hartford, NYC, Sturbridge, access to HOSPITAL
67mm	Quaboag River
8(62)	MA 32, to US 20, Palmer, **S** on MA 32...**gas:** Citgo, Getty, Shell/dsl, **food:** McDonald's, Oriental Express, Subway, **other:** HOSPITAL, Big Y Foods, Brooks Drug, Buick/Chevrolet/Pontiac, repair/transmissions
58mm	Chicopee River
56mm	**Ludlow Travel Plaza wb, Exxon/dsl, Boston Mkt, D'angelo's**

209

MASSACHUSETTS

Interstate 90

55mm	**Ludlow Travel Plaza eb, Exxon/dsl, McDonald's**
7(54)	MA 21, to Ludlow, **N**...**gas:** Gulf, Mobil, Sunoco, **food:** Burger King, Dunkin Donuts, Friendly's, Joy's Pizzaria, McDonald's, Subway, Wendy's, **other:** HOSPITAL, Ace Hardware, Big Y Foods, CVS Drug, Jo-Ann Fabrics, NAPA, **N**...**gas:** Pride, Shell, **food:** Domino's, Wendy's, **lodging:** Comfort Inn
6(51)	I-291, to Springfield, Hartford CT, **N**...**gas:** Pride/Subway/dsl, **food:** Dragon House Chinese, McDonald's, **lodging:** Econolodge, Motel 6, Plantation Inn, **other:** HOSPITAL, to Bradley Int Airport, Basketball Hall of Fame
5(49)	MA 33, to Chicopee, Westover AFB, **N**...**food:** Applebee's, Arby's, Burger King, Denny's, Dunkin Donuts, Friendly's, 99 Rest., Pizza Hut, Royal Buffet, Starbucks, Subway, Wendy's, **lodging:** Days Inn, Hampton Inn, Quality Inn, **other:** BJ's Whse/gas, Big Y Foods, Chevrolet/Cadillac, Dodge, Home Depot, Honda/Subaru, Marshall's, Staples, Stop&Shop Food/gas, TownFair Tire, U-Haul, Wal-Mart, mall, **S**...**gas:** Pride/Subway/dsl, **other:** Buick/Pontiac/GMC, Ford
46mm	Connecticut River
4(46)	I-91, US 5, to Holyoke, W Springfield, **US 5 N**...**gas:** Shell, **food:** Dunkin Donuts, **lodging:** Welcome Inn, **US 5 S**...**food:** Outback Steaks, Piccadilly's, Subway, **lodging:** Corral Motel, Econolodge, Knight's Inn, Springfield Inn, Super 8, **other:** HOSPITAL, BMW, Honda, Lexus, Toyota
41mm	st police wb
3(40)	US 202, to Westfield, **N**...**gas:** Mobil, **food:** Cafe Santorini, NE Pizza, **lodging:** Country Court Motel, **S**...**gas:** Citgo/Subway/dsl, Shell, **food:** Friendly's, Whip City Brewery/rest., Wendy's, **lodging:** Econolodge, **other:** HOSPITAL, repair
36mm	Westfield River
35.5mm	runaway truck ramp eb
29mm	**Blandford Travel Plaza both lane S...Exxon/dsl, McDonalds, gifts, info, vending**
20mm	1724 ft, highest point on MA Tpk
14.5mm	Appalachian Trail
12mm	parking area both lanes, litter barrels
2(11)	US 20, to Lee, Pittsfield, **N**...**gas:** Citgo, Shell/dsl/24hr, Sunoco/repair, **food:** Arizona Pizza, Athena's Rest., Dunkin Donuts, Friendly's, McDonald's, Red Apple Chinese, **lodging:** Pilgrim Inn, Sunset Motel, Super 8, **other:** Brooks Drug, PriceChopper Foods, **S**...**gas:** Lee/dsl, JFS, **food:** Orient Taste, Subway, Villa Pizza, **other:** Prime Outlets/famous brands
10.5mm	Hoosatonic River
8mm	**Lee Travel Plaza both lanes, Exxon/dsl, McDonald's, TCBY, atm, info, vending**
4mm	toll booth, phone
1(2)	MA 41(from wb, no return), to MA 102, W Stockbridge, the Berkshires, **N**...**lodging:** Pleasant Valley Motel, **other:** to Bousquet Ski Area
0mm	Massachusetts/New York state line

Interstate 91

Exit #	Services
55mm	Massachusetts/Vermont state line, callboxes begin/end
54mm	parking area both lanes, picnic tables
28(51)	US 5, MA 10, Bernardston, **E**...**food:** Bella Notte Ristorante, **lodging:** Fox Inn, **W**...**gas:** Sunoco, **food:** Red House Pizzaria, **other:** RV camping
27(45)	MA 2 E, Greenfield, **E**...**gas:** Citgo, Mobil, Sunoco, **food:** Burger King, Denny's Pantry, Friendly's, McDonald's, **other:** HOSPITAL, CVS Drug
26(43)	MA 2 W, MA 2A E, Greenfield, **E**...**gas:** Citgo/dsl, Mobil, **food:** Applebee's, China Gourmet, Dunkin Donuts, **lodging:** GreenField Inn, **other:** HOSPITAL, Chevrolet, Ford/Lincoln/Mercury, **W**...**gas:** Exxon/24hr, Shell/24hr, **food:** Bickford's, Friendly's, KFC/Taco Bell/Pizza Hut, McDonald's, **lodging:** CandleLight Inn, Super 8, **other:** Big Y Foods, BJ's Whse, Family$, Home Depot, Nissan, Radio Shack, Staples, to Mohawk Tr
39mm	Deerfield River
37mm	weigh sta both lanes
25(36)	MA 116(from sb), S Deerfield, hist dist, camping, same as 24
24(35)	US 5, MA 10, MA 116, Deerfield(no EZ return), **E**...**gas:** Mobil, **food:** Chandler's Rest., Wolfy's Rest., **lodging:** Red Roof Inn, Whatley Inn, **other:** Yankee Candle Co, **W**...**gas:** Exxon/dsl/24hr, **food:** 24hr Diner
34.5mm	parking area nb, no services
23(34)	US 5(from sb), no services
22(30)	US 5, MA 10(from nb), N Hatfield, **W**...Diamond RV Ctr
21(28)	US 5, MA 10, Hatfield, **W**...**gas:** Sunoco, **lodging:** Stearns Motel, **other:** Long View RV Ctr, st police
20(26)	US 5, MA 9, MA 10(from sb), Northampton, **W**...**gas:** Citgo, **food:** Bickford's, Burger King, D'angelo's, Friendly's, McDonald's, **other:** HOSPITAL, Big Y Foods, Chevrolet/VW, CVS Drug, Ford, NAPA, Pontiac/GMC/Cadillac, VW
19(25)	MA 9, to Amherst, Northampton, **E**...**gas:** Getty, **food:** Webster's Fishook Rest., **other:** HOSPITAL, to Elwell SP, **W**...**gas:** Citgo
18(22)	US 5, Northampton, **E**...**gas:** Mobil/24hr, **lodging:** Clarion, Inn at Northampton, **W**...**gas:** Shell/24hr, **food:** Burger King, Friendly's, McDonald's, **lodging:** Best Western, Northampton Hotel, **other:** to Smith Coll
18mm	scenic area both lanes
17b a(16)	MA 141, S Hadley, **E**...**gas:** Citgo/dsl, Mobil/dsl, **food:** Dunkin Dounuts, Real China, Subway, **lodging:** Super 8, **other:** Brooks Drug, Walgreen, **W**...to Mt Tom Ski Area
16(14)	US 202, Holyoke, **E**...**food:** Burger King, Denny's, Friendly's, McDonald's, **lodging:** Yankee Pedlar Inn/rest., **other:** HOSPITAL, to Heritage SP, **W**...Soldier's Home
15(12)	to US 5, Ingleside, **E**...**gas:** Shell, **food:** Cracker Barrel, Friendly's, Pizzaria Uno, Ruby Tuesday, **lodging:** Holiday Inn, **other:** HOSPITAL, Barnes&Noble, Best Buy, Circuit City, CompUSA, Macy's, JC Penney, Lord&Taylor, Old Navy, Sears/auto, Target, mall, **W**...**food:** Schermerhorn's Seafood

MASSACHUSETTS

Interstate 91

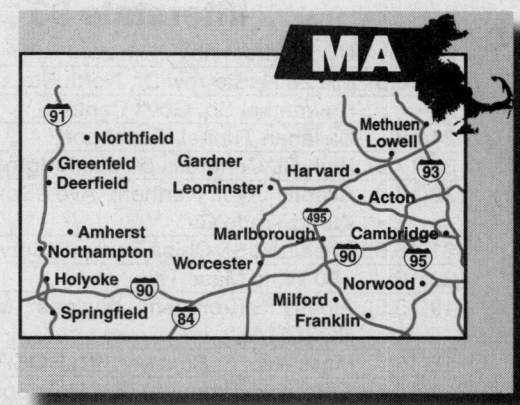

14(11) to US 5, to I-90(Mass Tpk), E to Boston, W to Albany, Ⓔ...HOSPITAL

13b a(9) US 5 N, W Springfield, Ⓔ...**gas:** Pride/dsl, **food:** B'Shara's Rest., Dougnut Dip, On the Border, Outback Steaks, Piccadilly's, Subway, **lodging:** Comfort Inn, Knight's Inn, Red Roof Inn, Residence Inn, Springfield Inn, Super 8, **other:** BMW, Home Depot, Honda/Lexus/Toyota, mall, Ⓦ...**gas:** Citgo/dsl, Mobil, Sunoco/dsl, **food:** Arby's, Boston Mkt, Burger King, Calamari's Grill, Chili's, D'angelo's, Empire Buffet, Friendly's, HomeTown Buffet, KFC, Longhorn Steaks, McDonald's, 99 Rest., Old Country Buffet, Pizza Hut, Wendy's, **lodging:** Best Western, Day's Inn, Econolodge, Hampton Inn, Knoll Motel, Quality Inn, Red Carpet Inn, **other:** Chrysler, Costco, Home Depot, Kohl's, Lincoln/Mercury, Mazda/Mercedes, Michael's, Nissan/Subaru, Stop&Shop Foods, Staples, TownFair Tire

12(8.5) I-391 N, to Chicopee

11(8) Burney Ave(from sb), Ⓔ...**gas:** Mobil, **other:** HOSPITAL

10(7.5) Main St(from nb), Springfield, Ⓔ...**gas:** Mobil

9(7) US 20 W, MA 20A E(from nb), Ⓔ...**food:** McDonald's

8(6.5) I-291, US 20 E, to I-90, Ⓔ...downtown, **lodging:** Holiday Inn, **other:** HOSPITAL

7(6) Columbus Ave(from sb), Ⓔ...**lodging:** Marriott, Sheraton, Ⓦ...**gas:** Pride/dsl/rest., **other:** to Basketball Hall of Fame

6(5.5) Springfield Ctr(from nb), Ⓦ...**gas:** Pride Autotruck/dsl

5(5) Broad St(from sb), same as 4

4(4.5) MA 83, Broad St, Main St, Ⓔ...**gas:** Citgo, Mobil/dsl, Shell/dsl, United, **food:** McDonald's, Wendy's, **other:** Buick/GMC, Hyundai, Saturn, Ⓦ...**gas:** Sunoco/dsl, **lodging:** Hilton Garden

3(4) US 5 N, to MA 57, Columbus Ave, W Springfield, Ⓔ...**gas:** Sunoco, Ⓦ...Chevrolet

2(3.5) MA 83 S(from nb), to E Longmeadow, Ⓔ...**food:** Friendly's

1(3) US 5 S(from sb), no services

0mm Massachusetts/Connecticut state line, callboxes begin/end

Interstate 93

Exit #	Services
47mm	Massachusetts/New Hampshire state line, callboxes begin/end
48(46)	MA 213 E, to Methuen, Ⓔ...HOSPITAL
47(45)	Pelham St, Methuen, Ⓔ...**gas:** Sunoco/24hr, **food:** Dunkin Donuts, McDonald's, Outback Steaks, Ⓦ...**gas:** Getty, **food:** Fireside Rest., **lodging:** Day's Inn/rest., Guesthouse Inn, **other:** Chrysler/Jeep, Pontiac/Nissan
46(44)	MA 110, MA 113, to Lawrence, Ⓔ...**gas:** Getty, **food:** Burger King, Dunkin Donuts, McDonald's/24hr, PapaGino's, Pizza Hut/D'angelo, MktBasket Foods, **other:** HOSPITAL, Ⓦ...**gas:** Citgo, Gulf, **food:** Dunkin Donuts, Jimmy's II Rest., Jackson's Rest., Millhouse Rest.

45(43) Andover St, River Rd, to Lawrence, Ⓔ...**lodging:** Courtyard, Hawthorn Suites, Marriott, SpringHill Suites, Wyndham, Ⓦ...**gas:** Mobil, **food:** Chateu Italian, **lodging:** Residence Inn, Tage Inn

44b a(40) I-495, to Lowell, Lawrence, Ⓔ...HOSPITAL

43(39) MA 133, N Tewksbury, Ⓔ...**gas:** Mobil/Dunkin Donuts/24hr

42(38) Dascomb Rd, East St, Tewksbury, no services

41(35) MA 125, Andover, st police

40(34) MA 62, Wilmington, no services

39(33) Concord St, Ⓔ...Shriners Auditorium

38(31) MA 129, Reading, Ⓦ...**gas:** Mobil, **food:** Burger King, Dunkin Donuts, Michael's Place Rest., 99 Rest.

37c(30) Commerce Way, Atlantic Ave, Ⓦ...**lodging:** Residence Inn, **other:** Target

37b a(29) I-95, S to Waltham, N to Peabody

36(28) Montvale Ave, Ⓔ...**gas:** Mobil, **lodging:** Courtyard, Ⓦ...**gas:** Citgo/dsl, Exxon/24hr, Lukoil, **food:** Bickford's/24hr, Dunkin Donuts, McDonald's, Polcari's Italian, Spud's Rest., Wendy's, **lodging:** Best Western, Comfort Inn, **other:** HOSPITAL

35(27) Winchester Highlands, Melrose, Ⓔ...HOSPITAL(no EZ return to sb)

34(26) MA 28 N(from nb, no EZ return), Stoneham, Ⓔ...**gas:** Mobil, **food:** Friendly's, **other:** HOSPITAL

33(25) MA 28, Fellsway West, Winchester, Ⓔ...HOSPITAL

32(23) MA 60, Salem Ave, Medford Square, Ⓦ...**lodging:** AmeriSuites, **other:** HOSPITAL, to Tufts U

31(22) MA 16 E, to Revere(no EZ return sb), Ⓔ...**gas:** Shell, **food:** Bertucci's, Friendly's, McDonald's, Subway, **lodging:** Howard Johnson Rest., **other:** CVS Drug, Lincoln/Mercury, Marshall's, Kohl's, Shaw's Foods, Stop&Shop Foods, mall, st police, Ⓦ...**gas:** Fred's Gas, Mr. C/dsl, **food:** Avellino's Italian, Burger King, Dunkin Donuts, Pizza Hut, **other:** AutoZone, KIA, Mitsubishi, Staples

30(21) MA 28, MA 38, Mystic Ave, Somerville, Ⓦ...**gas:** Mr. C's Gas, **food:** Burger King, **other:** AutoZone, Lincoln/Mercury

29(20) MA 28(from nb), Somerville, Ⓔ...**food:** Dunkin Donuts, 99 Rest., **lodging:** La Quinta, **other:** Circuit City, Home Depot, K-Mart, Staples, TJ Maxx, mall, Ⓦ...same as 30, **gas:** Gulf, Hess, **lodging:** Holiday Inn, **other:** Radio Shack, Stop&Shop

28(19) Sullivans Square, Charles Town, downtown

Interstate 93

N ↕ S		
B o s t o n A r e a	27	US 1 N(from nb)
	26(18.5)	MA 28 N, Storrow Dr, North Sta, downtown
	25	Haymarket Sq, Gov't Center
	24(18)	Callahan Tunnel, E...airport
	23(17.5)	High St, Congress St, W...**lodging:** Marriott
	22(17)	Atlantic Ave, Northern Ave, South Sta, Boston World Trade Ctr
	21(16.5)	Kneeland St, ChinaTown, no services
	20(16)	I-90 W, to Mass Tpk
	19(15.5)	Albany St(from sb), W...**gas:** Mobil/dsl, **other:** HOSPITAL
	18(15)	Mass Ave, to Roxbury, W...HOSPITAL
	17(14.5)	E Berkeley(from nb), E...New Boston Food Mkt
	16(14)	S Hampton St, Andrew Square, W...**gas:** Shell/24hr, **food:** Bickford's, **lodging:** Holiday Inn Express, **other:** Home Depot, K-Mart/Little Caesar's, Marshall's, Old Navy
	15(13)	Columbia Rd, Everett Square, E...**lodging:** DoubleTree Motel, **other:** JFK Library, to UMA, W...**gas:** Shell
	14(12.5)	Morissey Blvd, E...JFK Library, W...**gas:** Shell, **food:** D'angelo's, **lodging:** Howard Johnson, Ramada Inn, **other:** Stop&Shop Foods
	13(12)	Freeport St, to Dorchester, W...**gas:** Citgo/7-11, **food:** Boston Mkt, **other:** CVS Drug, Dodge, Toyota
	12(11.5)	MA 3A S(from sb, no EZ return), Quincy, E...**gas:** Shell, **food:** Café Pacific, Domino's, **lodging:** Best Western, W...**gas:** Boston Mkt, Citgo/7-11, Exxon, Shell, Sunoco, **food:** Arby's, Bickford's, Ground Round, PapaGino's, Wendy's, **other:** AutoZone, CVS Drug, Ford/Lincoln/Mercury, Pontiac/GMC, Staples, Walgreen
	11b a(11)	to MA 203, Granite Ave, Ashmont, W...**food:** McDonald's
	10(10)	Squantum Ave(from sb), Milton, W...HOSPITAL
	9(9)	Adams St, Bryant Ave, to N Quincy, W...**gas:** Shell/repair
	8(8)	Brook Pkwy, to Quincy, Furnace, E...**gas:** Global, Gulf/dsl, Mobil, **other:** Home Depot, Saturn
	7(7)	MA 3 S, to Cape Cod(exits left from sb), Braintree, E...**lodging:** Marriott
	6(6)	MA 37, to Holbrook, Braintree, E...**gas:** Mobil/24hr, **food:** Boardwalk Café, D'angelo's, Pizzaria Uno, TGIFriday, **lodging:** Sheraton/café, **other:** Circuit City, Firestone/auto, Lord&Taylor, Macy's, Sears/auto, mall, W...**gas:** Sunoco, **food:** Ascari Café, **lodging:** Candlewood Suites, Extended Stay America, Hampton Inn, Holiday Inn Express, **other:** Barnes&Noble, Ford, Nissan, VW
	5b a(4)	MA 28 S, to Randolph, Milton, E...**gas:** Citgo, Mobil/dsl, Shell/repair/24hr, **food:** D'angelo's, Domino's, Dunkin Donuts/Baskin-Robbins/Togo's, Friendly's, IHOP, Lombardo's Rest., Picadilly's Pub, Sal's Calzone Rest., Wong's Chinese, **lodging:** Holiday Inn/rest.
	4(3)	MA 24 S(exits left from sb), to Brockton
	3(2)	MA 138 N, to Ponkapoag Trail, Houghtons Pond

	2b a(1)	MA 138 S, to Stoughton, Milton, E...golf, W...**gas:** Mobil, Shell/dsl, Sunoco, **food:** Baskin-Robbins, Dunkin Donuts
	1(0)	I-95 N, S to Providence. I-93 begins/ends on I-95, exit 12.

Interstate 95

Exit #	Services	N ↕ S
89.5mm	Massachusetts/New Hampshire state line, parking area sb	
60(89)	MA 286, to Salisbury, beaches, E...**gas:** Mobil/dsl, **food:** Dunkin Donuts, Lena's Seafood Rest., Ruby's Kitchen, **other:** camping(seasonal)	
59(88)	I-495 S(from sb)	**A m e s b u r y**
58b a(78)	rd 110, to I-495 S, to Amesbury, Salisbury, E...**gas:** Sunoco/Subway/dsl, **food:** China Buffet, Niko's Place, Simon's, Sylvan St Grille, Winner's Circle Rest., **other:** Chrylser/Jeep/Dodge, U-Haul, radiators, W...**gas:** Best Choice/Domino's/dsl, Gas/Domino's, Irving Gas, Mobil, **food:** Acapulco's Mexican, Burger King, Dunkin Donuts, Friendly's, McDonald's, PapaGino's, Shorty's Diner, **lodging:** Fairfield Inn, **other:** Chevrolet/VW, Stop&Shop Foods	
86mm	Merrimac River	
57(85)	MA 113, to W Newbury, E...**gas:** Mobil/24hr, Shell/repair/24hr, Sunoco, **food:** China One, d'Angelo's, Dunkin Donuts, Giuseppe's Italian, McDonald's, PapaGino's, Wendy's, **other:** HOSPITAL, Brook's Drug, GNC, K-Mart, Marshall's, MktBasket Foods, Radio Shack, Shaw's Foods, Walgreens, White Hen Pantry/deli	
56(78)	Scotland Rd, to Newbury, E...st police	
55(77)	Central St, to Byfield, E...**food:** Gen Store Eatery, Village Diner, W...**gas:** Prime/dsl/repair	
54b a(76)	MA 133, E to Rowley, W to Groveland	
75mm	weigh sta both lanes	
53b a(74)	MA 97, S to Topsfield, N to Georgetown	
52(73)	Topsfield Rd, to Topsfield, Boxford, no services	
51(72)	Endicott Rd, to Topsfield, Middleton, no services	
50(71)	US 1, to MA 62, Topsfield, E...**gas:** Exxon/24hr, Mobil/24hr, **other:** Honda, W...**food:** Quizno's, **lodging:** Sheraton, **other:** CVS Drug, Hyundai, Staples, Stop&Shop, st police	
49(70)	MA 62(from nb), Danvers, Middleton, W...same as 50	
48(69)	Hobart St(from sb), W...**food:** Italian Rest., **lodging:** Comfort Inn, Extended Stay America, Motel 6, **other:** Home Depot, Honda, KIA	
47b a(68)	MA 114, to Middleton, Peabody, E...**gas:** Exxon/dsl/24hr, Sunoco, **food:** Dunkin Donuts, McDonald's, PapaGino's, Quizno's, **other:** Chevrolet/Buick/Pontiac, Dodge, Infiniti, Lexus, Lowe's Whse, Mazda, Mitsubishi, NTB, Petsmart, Subaru, Toyota, Wal-Mart, W...**gas:** Hess, **food:** Chili's, TGIFriday, **lodging:** Motel 6, Residence Inn, TownePlace Suites, **other:** BigLots, Circuit City, Costco, Dodge, Home Depot, LandRover, Mini, NAPA, Pontiac/Hyundai	**P e a b o d y**
46(67)	to US 1, W...**gas:** Best, Gulf/dsl, Shell, Sunoco, **food:** Burger King, **other:** Auto Parts+	

MASSACHUSETTS

Interstate 95

45(66) MA 128 N, to Peabody, no services

44b a(65) US 1 N, MA 129, **E**...**gas:** Shell, **W**...**gas:** Best/gas, Citgo, Gulf, Sunoco, **food:** Bennigan's, Bertucci's, Burger King, Carrabba's, Dunkin Donuts, Wendy's, **lodging:** Carriage House Hotel, Hampton Inn, Homewood Suites, SpringHill Suites, **other:** HOSPITAL

43(63) Walnut St, Lynnfield, **E**...to Saugus Iron Works NHS(3mi), **W**...**lodging:** Sheraton, **other:** golf

42(62) Salem St, Montrose, **E**...**gas:** Prime, Sunoco, **food:** Sub Stop, **W**...**lodging:** Sheraton

41(60) Main St, Lynnfield Ctr, **E**...**gas:** Shell

40(59) MA 129, Wakefield Ctr, N Reading, **E**...**gas:** Exxon, **food:** HoneyDew Donuts, **other:** VET, **W**...**gas:** Gulf, **other:** Chevrolet, dsl repair

39(58) North Ave, Reading, **E**...**gas:** Citgo, **lodging:** Best Western, **other:** Curves, Mazda/Isuzu/Volvo/Saab, **W**...**gas:** Shell/dsl/24hr, **food:** BearRock Cafe, Chili's, Fuddrucker's, Macaroni Grill, Starbucks, **other:** HOSPITAL, Ford, Home Depot, Staples

38b a(57) MA 28, to Reading, **E**...**gas:** Gulf, Hess/dsl, **food:** Baja Fresh, Boston Mkt, Burger King, China Moon, d'Angelo's/PapaGino's, Dunkin Donuts, 99 Rest., Subway, **other:** AutoZone, CVS Drug, Ford, GNC, Marshalls, Radio Shack, Shaw's Foods, Walgreens, **W**...**gas:** Exxon, Mobil, Shell, Sunoco, **food:** Burger King, Domino's, Dunkin Donuts, Harrow's Rest., McDonald's, Starbucks

37b a(56) I-93, N to Manchester, S to Boston

36(55) Washington St, to Winchester, **E**...**gas:** Lukoil, **food:** Dunkin Donuts, FarEast Chinese, The Bistro, **lodging:** Woburn Plaza Motel, **other:** BJ's Whse, Buick/Pontiac/GMC, CompUSA, Jaguar, Mitsubishi, Nissan, Staples, Toyota, **W**...**gas:** Mobil, Sunoco, **food:** China Pearl, d'Angelo's, Joe's Grill, McDonald's, 99 Rest., On the Border, Panera Bread, PapaGino's, Pizza Hut, Pizzaria Uno, TGIFriday, McDonald's, **lodging:** Courtyard, Fairfield Inn, Hampton Inn, Red Roof Inn, **other:** CVS Drug, Hogan Tire, Kohl's, Lowe's Whse, Mkt Basket Foods, NTB, Office Depot, TJ Maxx, USPO, mall

35(54) MA 38, to Woburn, **E**...**lodging:** Holiday Inn, **other:** HOSPITAL, **W**...**gas:** Mobil/dsl, **food:** Applebee's, Dunkin Donuts, **lodging:** Extended Stay Deluxe, **other:** Stop&Shop Foods

34(53) Winn St, Woburn, no services

33b a(52) US 3 S, MA 3A N, to Winchester, **E**...**food:** Bickford's Grille, Café Escadrille, ChuckeCheese, Outback Steaks, Panera Bread, Paparazzi's, **other:** HOSPITAL, CVS Drug, Honda, Marshalls, Michael's, Roach Bro's Foods, **W**...**gas:** Citgo, Hess, **lodging:** Marriott, **other:** HOSPITAL, Audi/Porsche, repair

32b a(51) US 3 N, MA 2A S, to Lowell, **E**...**gas:** Shell, **lodging:** Hilton Garden, **other:** Circuit City, **W**...**food:** Boston Mkt, Burger King, Cheesecake Factory, Chili's, d'Angelo's, Macaroni Grill, McDonald's, Pizzaria Uno, TCBY, **lodging:** Candlewood Suites, Homestead Suites, **other:** Barnes&Noble, Dodge, Kohl's, Macy's, Sears/auto, Staples, mall

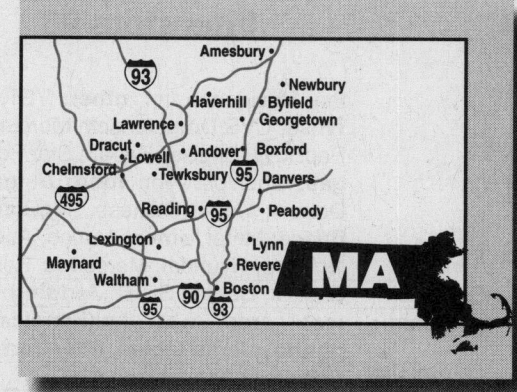

Boston Area

31b a(48) MA 4, MA 225, Lexington, **E**...**gas:** Gulf, Mobil/repair, Shell, **food:** Alexander's Pizza, Starbucks, **other:** Walgreens, **W**...**gas:** Exxon/24hr, Shell/24hr, **food:** d'Angelo's, Friendly's, Lexington Cafe, McDonald's, **lodging:** Bedford Motel, Best Western, Quality Inn, **other:** VET, Curves, Staples

30b a(47) MA 2A, Lexington, **E**...**gas:** Shell, **other:** HOSPITAL, **W**...**lodging:** Sheraton, **other:** to MinuteMan NP, Hanscom AFB

46.5mm travel plaza nb, Mobil/dsl/24hr, HoneyDew Donuts, McDonald's, gifts

29b a(46) MA 2 W, Cambridge

28b a(45) Trapelo Rd, Belmont, **E**...**gas:** Exxon/dsl, Mobil/dsl, Shell, **food:** Boston Mkt, Dunkin Donuts, Friendly's, McDonald's, Panera Bread, PapaGino's, **other:** Osco Drugs, Shaw's Foods

27b a(44) Totten Pond Rd, Waltham, **E**...**gas:** Shell, **food:** Naked Fish Rest., **lodging:** Best Western, Courtyard, Hilton Garden, Holiday Inn Express, Homestead Suites, Westin Hotel, **W**...**food:** Bertucci's Rest., Pizzaria Uno, **lodging:** DoubleTree/rest., **other:** Costco, Home Depot

26(43) US 20, to MA 117, to Waltham, **E**...**gas:** Sunoco/dsl, **W**...**gas:** Mobil

25(42) I-90, MA Tpk

24(41) MA 30, Newton, Wayland, **E**...**gas:** Mobil, **lodging:** Marriott

23(40) Recreation Rd(from nb), to MA Tpk, no services

22b a(39) Grove St, **E**...**lodging:** Holiday Inn Express, **other:** golf

38.5mm travel plaza sb, Mobil/dsl, McDonald's, gifts

21b a(38) MA 16, Newton, Wellesley, **E**...HOSPITAL, **W**...**gas:** Sunoco, **food:** Paparazzi, Starbucks

20b a(36) MA 9, Brookline, Framingham, no services

19(35) Highland Ave, Newton, Needham, **E**...**gas:** Gulf, Hess, **food:** d'Angelo's, Dunkin Donuts, Ground Round, Mandarin Cuisine, McDonald's, Mighty Subs, **lodging:** Sheraton/rest., **other:** PetCo, Staples, **W**...**food:** Bickford's, **other:** Chevrolet, Ford

18(34) Great Plain Ave, W Roxbury, no services

33.5mm parking area sb, phone, litter barrels

17(33) MA 135, Needham, Wellesley, no services

32mm truck turnout sb

16b a(31) MA 109, High St, Dedham, **W**...**gas:** Mobil/dsl

15b a(29) US 1, MA 128, **E**...**gas:** Gulf, **food:** Bickford's, Bugaboo Steaks, Chili's, Joe's Grill, Krispy Kreme, Panera Bread, PapaGino's, TGIFriday, Vinny T's Rest., **lodging:** Comfort Inn, Fairfield Inn, Holiday

213

MASSACHUSETTS

Interstate 95

Boston Area

	Inn, Residence Inn, **other:** VET, Best Buy, BJ's Whse, CVS Drug, Lincoln/Mercury, Nissan, NTB, PepBoys, Speedy Repair, Star Foods, Volvo, W...**gas:** Shell/dsl/24hr, **food:** Burger King, Dunkin Donuts, Jade Chinese, McDonald's, **lodging:** Budget Motel, **other:** Aamco, Audi, Buick, Chrysler/Jeep, Hyundai, Mercedes, Pontiac
14(28)	East St, Canton St, E...**lodging:** Hilton
27mm	**rest area sb, full(handicapped)facilities, phone, picnic tables, litter barrels**
13(26.5)	University Ave, no services
12(26)	I-93 N, to Braintree, Boston, motorist callboxes end nb
11b a(23)	Neponset St, to Canton, E...**gas:** Citgo/repair, Sunoco/repair, **food:** Dunkin Donuts
22.5mm	Neponset River
10(20)	Coney St(from sb, no EZ return), to US 1, Sharon, Walpole, **1 mi** W **on US 1...gas:** Citgo, Mobil, **food:** Caldo's Rest., Dunkin Donuts, Friendly's, IHOP, McDonald's, 99 Rest., Old Country Buffet, Outback Steaks, PapaGino's, Pizza Hut, Starbucks, Taco Bell, TGIFriday, **lodging:** Courtyard, Residence Inn, Sheraton, **other:** Acura, Advance Parts, Barnes&Noble, Brook's Drug, CVS Drug, Home Depot, Kohl's, Lexus, Old Navy, Staples, Stop&Shop Foods, VW, Walgreens, mall
9(19)	US 1, to MA 27, Walpole, W...**gas:** Mobil, **food:** Applebee's, Bickford's, Boston View, Clyde's Roadhouse, Dunkin Donuts, **lodging:** Econolodge, Holiday Inn Express, **other:** BigY Food/drug, **Wal-Mart**, same as 10
8(16)	S Main St, Sharon, E...**food:** Dunkin Donuts, **other:** Brook's Drug, Shaw's Foods, whaling museum
7b a(13)	MA 140, to Mansfield, E...**food:** Domino's, 99 Rest., Piccadilly's, **lodging:** Comfort Inn, Courtyard, Holiday Inn, Red Roof Inn, Residence Inn. W...**gas:** Shell, **food:** PapaGino's, **other:** Radio Shack
6b a(12)	I-495, S to Cape Cod, N to NH
10mm	**Welcome Ctr/rest area nb, full(handicapped) facilities, info, phone, picnic tables, litter barrels, petwalk**
9mm	truck parking area sb
5(7)	MA 152, Attleboro, E...HOSPITAL, W...**gas:** Gulf/dsl, **food:** Bill's Pizza, Piccadilly Rest., Wendy's, **other:** Radio Shack, Shaw's Foods/Osco Drug
4(6)	I-295 S, to Woonsocket, no services
3(4)	MA 123, to Attleboro, E...**gas:** Shell/dsl, **other:** HOSPITAL, zoo
2.5mm	parking area/weigh sta both lanes, no restrooms, litter barrels, motorist callboxes
2b a(1)	US 1A, Newport Ave, Attleboro, E...**gas:** Mobil, Shell, Sunoco, **food:** McDonald's, Olive Garden, **other:** Bob's Store, Home Depot, K-Mart, Mazda, Pontiac, Shaw's Foods
1(.5)	US 1(from sb), E...**lodging:** Day's Inn, **other:** Brooks Drug, Volvo
0mm	Massachusetts/Rhode Island state line

Attleboro

Interstate 195

Exit #	Services
22(41)	I-495 N, MA 25 S, to Cape Cod. I-195 begins/ends on I-495, exit 1.
21(39)	MA 28, to Wareham, N...**gas:** Maxi/dsl/24hr, **food:** Zeadey's Rest., S...**gas:** Mobil/Dunkin Donuts/dsl, Shell/dsl, Valero/dsl, **other:** HOSPITAL, **other:** NAPA, repair
37mm	**rest area eb, info, phone, picnic tables, litter barrels, petwalk, boat ramp**
36mm	Sippican River
20(35)	MA 105, to Marion, S...RV camping(seasonal)
19b a(31)	to Mattapoisett, S...**gas:** Mobil
18(26)	MA 240 S, to Fairhaven, **1 mi** S...**gas:** Citgo/7-11, Gulf, Mutual, Shell, **food:** Applebee's, Blimpie, Burger King, D'angelo's, Dunkin Donuts, Fairhaven Chowder, Great Wall Chinese, McDonald's, 99 Rest., PapaGino's, Pasta House, Pizza Hut, Taco Bell, Uno Pizzaria, Wendy's, **lodging:** Hampton Inn, **other:** AutoZone, Brooks Drug, $Tree, GMC/Buick/Pontiac, GNC, K-Mart, Marshalls, Mazda, Radio Shack, Shaw's Foods, Stop&Shop Foods, Staples, TownFair Tire, Walgreen, Wal-Mart
25.5mm	Acushnet River
17(24)	Coggeshall St, New Bedford, N...**gas:** Citgo/7-11, Sunoco, **food:** Dunkin Donuts, EndZone Café, McDonald's, same as 16
16(23)	Washburn St(from eb), N...**gas:** Shell, Sunoco, **food:** McDonald's
15(22)	MA 18 S, New Bedford, downtown, S...Whaling Museum, hist dist
14(21)	Penniman St(from eb), New Bedford, downtown
13b a(20)	MA 140, N...airport, S...**gas:** Buttonwood/dsl, Sunoco, **food:** Dunkin Donuts, **other:** HOSPITAL, Buttonwood Park/zoo, CVS Drug, Honda, Shaw's Foods, VW
12b a(19)	N Dartmouth, S...**gas:** Gulf, Hess, Mobil/dsl, **food:** Athens Pizzaria, Burger King, D'angelo's, Dunkin Donuts, Friendly's, Jimmy's Pizza, McDonald's, 99 Rest., Old Country Buffet, Panera Bread, PapaGino's, Peking Garden, Quizno's, Taco Bell, Texas Roadhouse, Wendy's, **lodging:** Comfort Inn, Residence Inn, **other:** Best Buy, Chevrolet, Firestone/auto, JC Penney, Lowe's Whse, Saturn, Sears/auto, Stop&Shop Food/gas, TownFair Tire, Toyota, USPO, mall, st police
11b a(17)	Reed Rd, to Dartmouth, **2 mi** S...**gas:** Shell/24hr, **lodging:** Dartmouth Motel
10(16)	MA 88 S, to US 6, Westport, S...**gas:** Mobil/dsl, Rte 6 Gas, **lodging:** Hampton Inn
9(15.5)	MA 24 N(from nb), Stanford Rd, Westport, S...**gas:** Mobil/dsl, Rte 6 Gas, **food:** LePage's Seafood, Priscilla Rest., White's Rest., **lodging:** Hampton Inn
8b a(15)	MA 24 S, Fall River, Westport, N...**gas:** Crosson Gas, **food:** Papa John's, S...**food:** Dunkin Donuts, Subway
7(14)	MA 81 S, Plymouth Ave, Fall River, N...**gas:** Getty, **food:** Burger King, 99 Rest., Wendy's, **other:** CVS Drug, S...**gas:** Shell, **food:** Applebee's, McDonald's, **other:** Goodyear/auto, Walgreen

Fall River

MASSACHUSETTS

Interstate 195

6(13.5)	Pleasant St, Fall River, downtown
5(13)	MA 79, MA 138, to Taunton, [S]...**gas:** Citgo/7-11, Hess, **food:** Denny's, Dunkin Donuts, **lodging:** Day's Inn
12mm	Assonet Bay
4b a(10)	MA 103, to Swansea, Somerset, [N]...**gas:** Getty, **food:** Rogers Rest., **other:** auto repair, [S]...**gas:** Shell/24hr, **food:** TKO Shea's Rest., **lodging:** Quality Inn
3(8)	US 6, to MA 118, Swansea, Rehoboth, [N]...**gas:** Citgo/7-11, Hess, Shell/dsl, **food:** Burger King, D'angelo's, Dunkin Donuts, Friendly's, McDonald's, Ponderosa, Thai Taste, Tim Horton, **other:** BigLots, CarQuest, Firestone/auto, Hi-Lo Foods, Sears/auto, mall, [S]...**gas:** Cumberland/24hr, **food:** Anthony's Seafood, **lodging:** Swansea Motel
6mm	**rest area eb, full(handicapped)facilities, phone, picnic tables, litter barrels, petwalk**
5.5mm	parking area wb
2(5)	MA 136, to Newport, [S]...**gas:** Mobil/24hr, Shell/24hr, **food:** Cathay Pearl Chinese, Domino's, Dunkin Donuts, McDonald's
3mm	weigh sta both lanes
1(1)	MA 114A, to Seekonk, [N]...**gas:** Exxon/dsl, Public, Shell/24hr, **food:** Athens Pizza, Newport Creamery, 99 Rest., **lodging:** Johnson&Wales Inn, Motel 6, [S]...**gas:** Mobil/24hr, Sunoco/dsl, **food:** Applebee's, Bickford's, Bugaboo Creek Steaks, Burger King, Chili's, China Wok, Cisco's Pizza, D'angelo's, Dunkin Donuts, Friendly's, McDonald's, Old Country Buffet, PapaGino's, Subway, Taco Bell, Testa's Italian, TGIFriday, Wendy's, **lodging:** Comfort Inn, Gateway Motel, Hampton Inn, Mary's Motel, Park Inn, Ramada Inn/rest., Town'n Country Motel, **other:** BigLots, Bob's Stores, Circuit City, GNC, Home Depot, JiffyLube, Michael's, PepBoys, Sam's Club, Staples, Stop&Shop Foods, Target, TownFair Tire, Volvo, Wal-Mart/drug
0mm	Massachusetts/Rhode Island state line, **Exits 8-1 are in RI.**
8(5)	US 1A N, Pawtucket, [S]...**gas:** Mobil/dsl, **food:** Subway, **other:** CVS Drug
7(4)	US 6 E, CT 114 S, to Barrington, Seekonk
6(3)	Broadway Ave, [N]...**gas:** Speedy AutoService, [S]...**gas:** Shell, Sunoco/dsl
5(2.5)	RI 103 E, Warren Ave, no services
4(2)	US 44 E, RI 103 E, Taunton Ave, Warren Ave, [N]...**gas:** Exxon
3(1.5)	Gano St, [S]...**lodging:** Radisson
2(1)	US 44 W, Wickenden St, India Pt, downtown, [N]...**gas:** Shell/dsl
1(.5)	Providence, downtown
0mm	I-195 begins/ends on I-95, exit 20 in Providence, RI, **Exits 1-8 are in RI.**

Worcester

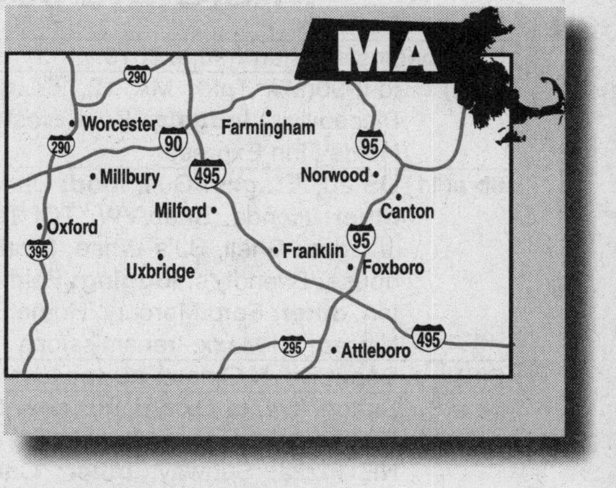

Interstate 290

Exit #	Services
26b a(20)	I-495. I-290 begins/ends on I-495, exit 25.
25b a(17)	Solomon Pond Mall Rd, to Berlin, [N]...**food:** Bertucci's, TGIFriday, **food:** Olive Garden, **lodging:** Comfort Inn, **other:** Best Buy, Borders Books, JC Penney, Sears/auto, Target, mall, [S]...Solomon Pond Grill
24(15)	Church St, Northborough, no services
23b a(13)	MA 140, Boylston, [N]...**gas:** Citgo/dsl, Mobil, **food:** Dunkin Donuts, Other Place Rest.
22(11)	Main St, Worchester, [N]...**gas:** Exxon/24hr, Shell, **food:** Bickford's, Friendly's, McDonald's, Wendy's, **other:** HOSPITAL
21(10)	Plantation St(from eb), [N]...**lodging:** Best Western, **other:** Lowe's Whse, Staples, Stop&Shop, Target
20(8)	MA 70, Lincoln St, Burncoat St, [N]...**gas:** Charter/24hr, Exxon/Subway/24hr, Shell, Sunoco, **food:** Bickford's, Denny's, Dunkin Donuts, Friendly's, McDonald's, Papa Gino's, Taco Bell, Wendy's, **lodging:** Day's Inn, Econolodge, Holiday Inn, **other:** Auto Palace, CVS Drug, Radio Shack, Shaw's Food/24hr, Walgreen
19(7)	I-190 N, MA 12
18	MA 9, Framington, Ware, Worcester Airport, [N]...HOSPITAL
16	Central St, Worcester, [N]...**food:** 99 Rest., **lodging:** Crowne Plaza, Hampton Inn, mall
14	MA 122, Barre, Worcester, downtown
13	MA 122A, Vernon St, Worcester, downtown
12	MA 146 S, to Millbury, no services
11	Southbridge St, College Square, [N]...**gas:** Shell/dsl, **food:** Wendy's, [S]...**gas:** Getty
10	MA 12 N(from wb), Hope Ave, no services
9	Auburn St, to Auburn, [E]...**gas:** Shell, **food:** Arby's, Bickford's, Wendy's, McDonald's, **lodging:** Baymont Inn, Comfort Inn, Holiday Inn Express, **other:** Acura, AutoZone, Firestone, Sears/auto, Shaw's Foods, Staples, mall
8	MA 12 S(from sb), Webster, [W]...**gas:** Shell, **lodging:** Best Western
7	I-90, E to Boston, W to Springfield. I-290 begins/ends on I-90.

E

W

MASSACHUSETTS
Interstate 395

Exit #	Services
	I-395 begins/ends on I-90, exit 10.
7(12)	to I-90(MA Tpk), MA 12, **E**...**gas:** Shell, **food:** Piccadilly's, **lodging:** Best Western, Comfort Inn, Holday Inn Express
6b a(11)	US 20, **E**...**gas:** Gulf, **food:** Dunkin Donuts, KFC, **other:** Honda, Saab/VW, TCI Tires, truck repair, **W**...**gas:** Shell, BJ's Whse, **food:** Chuck's Steakhouse, Friendly's, **lodging:** Fairfield Inn, Hampton Inn, **other:** Ford/Mercury, Home Depot, Mitsubishi, Nissan, TJ Maxx, transmissions
5(8)	Depot Rd, N Oxford, no services
4b a(6)	Sutton Ave, to Oxford, **W**...**gas:** Mobil/24hr, **food:** Cumberland Farms, Dunkin Donuts, McDonald's, NE Pizza, Subway, **other:** Cahill's Tire/Repair, CVS Drug
3(4)	Cudworth Rd, to N Webster, S Oxford, no services
2(3)	MA 16, to Webster, **E**...Subaru, **W**...**gas:** Exxon/24hr, Getty, Mobil, Shell/24hr, **food:** Burger King, D'angelo/Papa Gino's, Empire Wok, Friendly's, Honey Dew Donughts, KFC, McDonald's, **other:** HOSPITAL, Brooks Drug, CVS Drug, Ford, PriceChopper Foods, Walgreen
1(1)	MA 193, to Webster, **E**...HOSPITAL, **W**...**gas:** Citgo/dsl, **food:** Golden Greek Rest., Wind Tiki Chinese, **other:** Goodyear
0mm	Massachusetts/Connecticut state line

Interstate 495

Exit #	Services
	I-495 begins/ends on I-95, exit 59.
55	MA 110(no return nb), to I-95 S, **E**...**gas:** Best Choice/Domino's/dsl, Mobil, Irving, **food:** Acupulco Mexican, Burger King, Dunkin Donuts, Friendly's, McDonald's, **lodging:** Fairfield Inn, **other:** Stop&Shop, Chevrolet/VW, **W**...**gas:** Gulf, **food:** Weiloon Cafe, **other:** Curves, NAPA
54(118)	MA 150, to Amesbury, **W**...RV camping
53(115)	Broad St, Merrimac, **W**...**gas:** Gulf, **food:** Dunkin Donuts
114mm	**parking area sb, phone, restrooms, picnic tables, litter barrels**
52(111)	MA 110, to Haverhill, **E**...HOSPITAL, **W**...**gas:** Getty, Mobil/dsl, **food:** Dunkin Donuts, King's Roast Beef
110mm	parking area nb, phone, picnic tables, litter barrels
51(109)	MA 125, to Haverhill, **E**...**gas:** Citgo, Mobil, **food:** Bros Pizza, **other:** HOSPITAL, **W**...**food:** Burger King, Dunkin Donuts, Friendly's, McDonald's, Taco Bell, Wendy's
50(107)	MA 97, to Haverhill, **E**...HOSPITAL, **W**...Ford
49(106)	MA 110, to Haverhill, **E**...**gas:** Gulf, Sunoco/24hr, **food:** A1 Deli, Chunky's Diner, Dunkin Donuts, McDonald's, 99 Rest., PapaGino's, **lodging:** Best Western, Comfort Inn, **other:** Buick/Pontiac/GMC, Chevrolet, Chrysler, MktBasket Foods
105.8mm	Merrimac River
48(105.5)	MA 125, to Bradford, no services
47(105)	MA 213, to Methuen, **1-2 mi W**...**food:** Bugaboo Steaks, Burger King, ChuckeCheese, Joe's Grill, Macaroni Grill, McDonald's, Starbucks, TGIFriday, Wendy's, **other:** Borders Books, Brooks

Exit #	Services
	Drug, Home Depot, Marshalls, Old Navy, Wal-Mart, Methuen Mall, Stop&Shop Foods
46(104)	MA 110, **E**...**gas:** Gulf, Sunoco/24hr, **other:** HOSPITAL, Ford/Lincoln/Mercury
45(103)	Marston St, to Lawrence, **W**...**other:** Chevrolet, Honda, Isuzu, Kia
44(102)	Merrimac St, to Lawrence, no services
43(101)	Mass Ave, no services
42(100)	MA 114, **E**...**gas:** Exxon, Gulf, Mobil, **food:** Denny's, Friendly's, Lee Chin Cninese, Pizza Hut, **lodging:** Hampton Inn, **W**...**gas:** Shell/dsl, 7-11, **food:** Burger King, Marathon Pizzaria, McDonald's, TCBY, Wendy's, **lodging:** Quality Inn, **other:** HOSPITAL, MktBasket Foods
41(99)	MA 28, to Andover, **E**...**food:** Dunkin Donuts, **other:** Chevrolet
40b a(98)	I-93, N to Methuen, S to Boston
39(94)	MA 133, to N Tewksbury, **E**...**gas:** Mobil/dsl/24hr, **food:** McDonald's, **lodging:** Extended Stay America, **W**...**gas:** Hess, **food:** Cracker Barrel, Wendy's, **lodging:** Fairfield Inn, Holiday Inn/rest., Ramada/rest., Residence Inn
38(93)	MA 38, to Lowell, **E**...**gas:** Shell, **food:** Applebee's, Burger King, Friendly's, IHOP, T-D Waffle, **lodging:** Motel 6, **other:** Home Depot, Honda/VW, Mazda, MktBasket Foods, **W**...**gas:** Shell/dsl, Sunoco, USA/dsl, **food:** Dunkin Donuts, Milan Pizza, McDonald's, Wendy's, **other:** Chevrolet/Pontiac/Buick/GMC, CVS Drug, K-Mart, Saturn, Staples
37(91)	Woburn St, to S Lowell, **W**...**gas:** Exxon
35c(90)	to Lowell SP, Lowell ConX, **1 mi W**...**food:** McDonald's, Outback Steaks, **lodging:** Courtyard, **other:** Shop&Save, Walgreen
35b a(89)	US 3, S to Burlington, N to Nashua, NH
34(88)	MA 4, Chelmsford, **E**...**gas:** Mobil, Sunoco, **food:** Dunkin Donuts, Skip's Rest., 99 Rest., **lodging:** Radisson, **W**...**gas:** Shell, **food:** Ground Round, **lodging:** Best Western
33	MA 4, N Chelmsford(from nb), no services
88mm	motorist aid call boxes begin sb
87mm	**rest area both lanes, full(handicapped)facilities, phone, picnic tables, litter barrels, vending, petwalk**
32(83)	Boston Rd, to MA 225, **E**...**gas:** Exxon/24hr, Gulf/service, Mobil/24hr, **food:** Applebee's, B&B Café, Boston Mkt, Burger King, Chili's, D'angelo's, Dunkin Donuts, McDonald's, **other:** CVS Drug, MktBasket Foods, Osco Drug, to Nashoba Valley Ski Area
31(80)	MA 119, to Groton, **E**...**gas:** Mobil/dsl/24hr, **food:** Dunkin Donuts, Ken's Café, Subway
30(78)	MA 110, to Littleton, **E**...**gas:** Shell, **food:** HOSPITAL, **W**...**gas:** Citgo/dsl, Sunoco/dsl
29b a(77)	MA 2, to Leominster, **E**...to Walden Pond St Reserve
28(75)	MA 111, to Boxborough, Harvard, **E**...**gas:** Exxon/repair, **lodging:** Holiday Inn
27(70)	MA 117, to Bolton, **E**...**gas:** Mobil/dsl, **W**...**gas:** Mobil, **food:** Bolton Pizza, Hebert Ice Cream, **other:** RV camping(seasonal)
26(68)	MA 62, to Berlin, **E**...Best Western, **W**...**gas:** Exxon/24hr, Gulf/24hr, Shell/dsl
66mm	Assabet River
25b(64)	I-290, to Worcester

Interstate 495

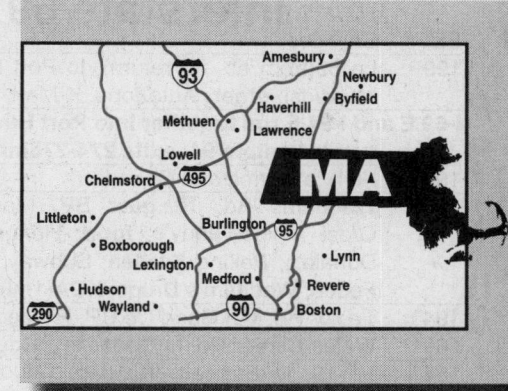

Exit	Services
25a	to MA 85, Marlboro, **E**...**food:** Burger King, Honeydew Donuts, 99 Rest., Piccadilly's
24b a(63)	US 20, to Northboro, Marlboro, **E**...**gas:** Mikey/gas, Mobil, **food:** D'angelo's, Dunkin Donuts, Lakeside Rest., **lodging:** Holiday Inn/rest., **W**...**gas:** Exxon, Shell, **food:** Boston Mkt, China Taste, Longhorn Steaks, McDonald's, Panera Bread, PapaGino's, Starbucks, Subway, Tandoori Grill, Wendy's, **lodging:** Best Western, Embassy Suites, Hornestead Suites, Radisson, **other:** GNC, Victory Foods
23c(60)	Simrano Dr, Marlboro, no services
23b a(59)	MA 9, to Shrewsbury, Framingham, **E**...**gas:** Best Value Gas, Exxon/dsl, **food:** Red Barn Coffee, Wendy's, **lodging:** Red Roof Inn, **other:** Volvo, **W**...**gas:** Mobil/dsl/24hr, **food:** Burger King, Friendly's, McDonald's, Naked Fish Rest., Piccadilly's, **lodging:** Courtyard, Extended Stay America, Residence Inn, Sierra Suites, Studio+, Wyndham Hotel, **other:** HOSPITAL
22(58)	I-90, MA TPK, E to Boston, W to Albany
21b a(54)	MA 135, to Hopkinton, Upton, **E**...**gas:** Gulf, Mobil, **food:** Dino's Pizza, Dynasty Chinese, Golden Spoon Rest.
20(50)	MA 85, to Milford, **W**...**gas:** Gulf/dsl/LP, Mobil, **food:** Cafe 85/deli, Wendy's, **lodging:** Baymont Inn, Day's Inn, Courtyard/rest, Fairfield Inn, Holiday Inn Express, **other:** HOSPITAL
19(48)	MA 109, to Milford, **W**...**gas:** Mobil/Pizza Hut/dsl/24hr, Shell, **food:** Alamo Mexican, Applebee's, Bugaboo Cr Steaks, Burger King, D'angelo, Friendly's, KFC/Pizza Hut, McDonald's, PapaGino's, Richard's Grill, Taco Bell, **lodging:** Radisson/cafe, Tage Inn, **other:** CVS Drug, $Tree, Jo-Ann Fabrics, K-Mart, Radio Shack, Stop&Shop, Victory Foods
18(46)	MA 126, to Bellingham, **E**...**food:** Chili's, McDonald's, **other:** Barnes&Noble, MktBasket Foods, Old Navy, Staples, Wal-Mart, Whole Foods Mkt, **W**...**gas:** Hess/Blimpie, Mobil/24hr, Sunoco/dsl, **food:** DQ, Dunkin Donuts, Outback Steaks, Pizzaria Uno, **other:** Home Depot
17(44)	MA 140, to Franklin, Bellingham, **E**...**gas:** Mobil, Sunoco, **food:** Applebee's, Burger King, D'angelo's, Dunkin Donuts, Friendly's, KFC, Longhorn Steaks, Panera Bread, PapaGino's, Pipinelle's Rest., Pizza Hut, Subway, Taco Bell, Thai Cuisine, Wendy's, **other:** AutoZone, Buick/GMC, Chrysler/Jeep, CVS Drug, GNC, Marshalls, Radio Shack, Stop&Shop, **W**...HOSPITAL, BJ's Whse/gas, **food:** Piccadilly's, **lodging:** Residence Inn
16(42)	King St, to Franklin, **E**...**gas:** Sunoco/24hr, **food:** Dunkin Donuts, Franklin Deli, Gold Fork Rest., Joe's Grill, McDonald's, Goodfella's Rest., McDonald's, **lodging:** Hampton Inn, **other:** Spruce Pond Creamery, **W**...**lodging:** Hawthorn Inn
15(39)	MA 1A, to Plainville, Wrentham, **E**...**gas:** Mobil, **other:** HOSPITAL, **W**...**gas:** Mobil/dsl, **food:** Cracker Barrel, Dunkin Donuts, Ruby Tuesday, Uno Pizzaria, **other:** Premium Outlets/famous brands
14b a(37)	US 1, to N Attleboro, **E**...**gas:** Mobil/D'angelo's/PapaGino's/dsl, **food:** Luciano's Rest., **lodging:** Arbor Inn, **W**...**gas:** Mobil
13(32)	I-95, N to Boston, S to Providence, access to HOSPITAL
12(30)	MA 140, to Mansfield, **E**...**food:** Wendy's, **other:** Home Depot, Shaw's Foods, Staples, 3 mi **E**...**food:** 99 Rest., **lodging:** Comfort Inn, Courtyard, Holiday Inn, Red Roof Inn, Residence Inn, **other:** Stop&Shop Food
11(29)	MA 140 S(from sb, no EZ return), 1 mi **W**...**gas:** Gulf, **food:** Andrea's Pizza, Boston Pizza, Dunkin Donuts, Mandarin Chinese, McDonald's, **other:** $Tree, GNC, Radio Shack
10(26)	MA 123, to Norton, **E**...**food:** Dunkin Doughnuts, **other:** McLaughlin RV Park, QuickStop, **W**...HOSPITAL
9(24)	Bay St, to Taunton, **W**...**food:** Dunkin Donuts, Pizza Hut, Wendy's, **food:** Tedeschi Foods/deli, **lodging:** Extended Stay America, Holiday Inn, **other:** BJ's Whse
8(22)	MA 138, to Raynham, **E**...**gas:** Mobil/dsl, **food:** Spartain's Rest., **W**...**gas:** Exxon/dsl, Mobil/24hr, Shell/dsl/repair, **food:** Bros China Garden, Dunkin Doughnuts, Honeydew Donuts, La Casa Mia Rest., McDonald's, Pepperoni's Pizza, Subway, **other:** HOSPITAL
7b a(19)	MA 24, to Fall River, Boston, 1/2 mi **E**...**food:** Burger King
18mm	weigh sta both lanes
17.5mm	Taunton River
6(15)	US 44, to Middleboro, **E**...**food:** Burger King, Dunkin Donuts, Fireside Grill, Friendly's, PapaGino's, **W**...**gas:** 44 Gas, Mobil/dsl, Shell/dsl, **lodging:** Fairfield Inn, Holiday Inn Express, **other:** Crossroads RV Ctr
5(14)	MA 18, to Lakeville, **E**...**food:** Burger King, Dunkin Donuts, Fireside Grill, Friendly's, PapaGino's, **other:** CVS Drug, Kelly's Tire, Stop&Shop Food, **W**...**other:** Massasoit SP, RV camping(seasonal)
4(12)	MA 105, to Middleboro, **E**...**gas:** Exxon/dsl/24hr, Mobil/dsl, Shell/24hr, Sunoco/24hr, **food:** DQ, Dunkin Donuts, McDonald's, Pappa Timmy's Pizza, Subway, **lodging:** Day's Inn, **other:** AutoZone, Brooks Drug, Chevrolet, Osco Drug
10.5mm	parking area eb, picnic tables
10mm	parking area wb, picnic tables
3(8)	MA 28, to Rock Village, S Middleboro, **E**...**gas:** Citgo/dsl, **other:** Buds RV's, Fred's Repair, **W**...**gas:** Mobil/Dunkin Doughnuts, **food:** Fisher's Rest.
2(3)	MA 58, W Wareham, **E**...**other:** Edaville Family Park, auto repair, to Myles Standish SF, **W**...**gas:** Citgo/7-11, **food:** Dapper Dan's Hotdogs, **other:** RV camping(seasonal)
2mm	Weweantic River
1(0)	I-495 begins/ends on I-195, MA 25 S.

N ↕ **S**

Port Huron

Exit #	Services
199	Lp 69(from eb, no return), to Port Huron, **S**...**gas:** Mobil/dsl, **other:** AutoZone, K-Mart, Sam's Club/gas
	I-69 E and I-94 E run together into Port Huron. See Michigan Interstate 94, exits 274-275mm.
198	I-94, to Detroit and Canada
196	Wadhams Rd, **N**...**gas:** BP, Marathon, Speedy Q/dsl, Shell/Wendy's, **food:** Hungry Howie's, McDonald's, Peking Kitchen, Subway, **other:** Carter's Foods, Wadham's Drugs, KOA(1mi), **S**...golf
194	Taylor Rd, **N**...Good L's CP, RV camping
189	Wales Center Rd, to Goodells, **S**...golf
184	MI 19, to Emmett, **N**...**gas:** Citgo/dsl/scales/rest./24hr, **other:** repair, **S**...**gas:** Marathon/dsl/24hr
180	Riley Center Rd, **N**...KOA
176	Capac Rd, **N**...**gas:** BP/McDonald's/dsl, **food:** Subway(2mi)
174mm	**rest area wb, full(handicapped)facilities, phone, picnic tables, litter barrels, vending, petwalk**
168	MI 53, Imlay City, **N**...**gas:** BP/dsl/24hr, Speedway/dsl, **food:** Big Boy, Big Joe's Pizza, Burger King, DQ, Hungry Howie's, Jet's Pizza, Little Caesar's, Lucky's Steaks, McDonald's, New China, Taco Bell, Wah Wong Chinese, Wendy's/Tim Horton, **lodging:** Day's Inn, M53 Motel, **other:** AutoZone, Chevrolet/Pontiac, Chrysler/Dodge/Jeep, Discount Drug, $Discount, Ford, GNC, IGA Foods, Kroger, NAPA, Pamida, Radio Shack, **S**...camping
163	Lake Pleasant Rd, to Attica, no services
160mm	**rest area eb, full(handicapped)facilities, phone, picnic tables, litter barrels, vending, petwalk**
159	Wilder Rd, no services
158mm	Flint River
155	MI 24, Lapeer, **1 mi N**...**gas:** BP, Clark/dsl, FS, Meijer/dsl/24hr, Speedy Q, **food:** Apple Tree Rest., Arby's, Blind Fish Rest., Brian's Rest., Burger King, Coffee Tree Cafe, DQ, Farmhouse Rest., Hot'n Now, Jet's Pizza, KFC, Little Caesar's, McDonald's, Mr Pita, Nick's Rest., Subway, Taco Bell, Tim Horton, Wah Wong Chinese, Wendy's, **lodging:** Best Western, Fairfield Inn, **other:** HOSPITAL, AutoZone, Curves, $Tree, Home Depot, K-Mart, Kroger, Murray's Parts, Office Depot, Radio Shack, SavALot, st police, vet, **S**...**gas:** Mobil/dsl, **other:** Buick/Pontiac
153	Lake Nepessing Rd, **S**...to Thumb Correctional, camping, golf
149	Elba Rd, **S**...**other:** Country Mkt, Torzwski CP, RV/truck repair
145	MI 15, Davison, **N**...**gas:** Marathon, Shell/dsl, Speedway, **food:** Apollo Rest., Applebee's, Arby's, Big Boy, Big John's Rest., Burger King, Chee Kong Chinese, Country Sun Rest., Hungry Howie's, Italia Gardens, KFC, Little Caesar's, McDonald's, Senor Lucky, Subway, Taco Bell, Tim Horton, **lodging:** Comfort Inn, **other:** AutoValue Parts, GNC, Pontiac/Buick/GMC, Radio Shack, Rite Aid/24hr, Walgreens, repair, **S**...**gas:** Mobil/dsl
143	Irish Rd, **N**...**gas:** Speedway/dsl, **S**...**gas:** Meijer/dsl, Shell/McDonald's/24hr, **other:** Meijer, 7-11
141	Belsay Rd, Flint, **N**...**gas:** 1 stop, Shell/Wendy's/dsl/24hr, **food:** Country Kitchen, Dominos, McDonald's, Taco Bell, **other:** Harley-Davidson, K-Mart, Kroger, Wal-Mart SuperCtr/Subway/auto, **S**...**gas:** Sunoco/A&W/LJ Silver/dsl

Flint

Exit #	Services
139	Center Rd, Flint, **N**...**gas:** Speedway/dsl, **food:** Applebee's, Boston Mkt, Coney Island, Cottage Pizza, Empire Wok, Halo Burger, Moykong Chinese, Old Country Buffet, Ponderosa, Quizno's, Starbucks, Subway, Tim Horton, **lodging:** Best Inn, **other:** Aldi Foods, Discount Tire, Family$, Home Depot, JC Penney, Jo-Ann Fabrics, Lowe's Whse, Old Navy, Staples, VG Foods, mall, **S**...**gas:** Meijer/dsl/24hr, **food:** Bob Evans, Coney Island, DQ, Firkin & Fox Rest., McDonald's, Mancino's/Saloupes, Subway, Walli's Rest., **lodging:** Super 8, **other:** Belle Tire, $Tree, Hungry Howies, Meijer, Office Depot, Saab, Target, TJ Maxx, vet
138	MI 54, Dort Hwy, **N**...**gas:** BP/24hr, Speedway/dsl, Sunoco/dsl, **food:** Big John's Rest., KFC, Little Caesar's, YaYa's Chicken, **other:** HOSPITAL, $General, KanRock Tires, Rite Aid, Walgreens, **S**...**gas:** Marathon, Speedway, Sunoco, **food:** Arby's, Big John's Steaks, Burger King, Carl's BBQ, China Empress, Coney Island, El Potrero, KFC, McDonald's, Subway, Taco Bell, **lodging:** Genessee Inn, Travel Inn, **other:** Aamco, Advance Parts, AutoZone, BigLots, Cadillac/Pontiac, $General, Family$, Goodyear, K-Mart, Rite Aid, 7-11, U-Haul, Walgreen
137	I-475, UAW Fwy, to Detroit, Saginaw
136	Saginaw St, Flint, **N**...**gas:** Sunoco, **other:** HOSPITAL, U MI at Flint, **S**...**other:** ExpertTire, GMC
135	Hammerberg Rd, industrial area
133b a	I-75, S to Detroit, N to Saginaw, US 23 S to Ann Arbor
131	MI 121, to Bristol Rd, **1/2 mi N on Miller Rd**...**gas:** Speedway, **food:** Chili's, ChuckeCheese, Golden Moon Chinese, Halo Burger, LJ Silver, Logan's Roadhouse, Old Country Buffet, Outback Steaks, Ruby Tuesday, Subway, Taco Bell, Valley Diner, **other:** Best Buy, BigLots, Borders Books, Circuit City, Discount Tire, $Tree, Firestone/auto, Gander Mtn, JC Penney, Jo-Ann Fabrics, Macey's, Michael's, Sears/auto, TJ Maxx, mall
129	Miller Rd, **S**...**gas:** Marathon, **food:** Arby's, Burger King, McDonald's, Wendy's, **other:** Kroger/gas
128	Morrish Rd, **S**...**gas:** Admiral/24hr, BP/dsl/24hr, **other:** Sports Creek Horse Racing
126mm	**rest area eb, full(handicapped)facilities, info, phone, picnic tables, litter barrels, petwalk**
123	MI 13, to Saginaw, Lennon, **N**...**gas:** Speedway/dsl
118	MI 71, to Corunna, Durand, **N**...st police, **S**...**gas:** Shell/dsl, Sunoco, **food:** McDonald's, Subway, Wendy's, **lodging:** Quality Inn, Sunset Motel(1.5), **other:** Ace Hardware, Carter's Foods, Chevrolet/Pontiac, Family$, Rite Aid, golf
115mm	Shiawassee River
113	Bancroft, **S**...**gas:** BP/dsl, **other:** RV camping
105	MI 52, to Owosso, Perry, **S**...**gas:** Citgo, Mobil, 7-11/gas, Sunoco/Subway/dsl, **food:** Burger King, Café Sports, McDonald's, Taco Bell, **lodging:** Heb's Inn, **other:** Family$, Ford, IGA Foods, Rite Aid, RV camping, truck repair(1mi)
101mm	**rest area wb, full(handicapped)facilities, phone, picnic tables, litter barrels, petwalk**
98.5mm	Looking Glass River
98	Woodbury Rd, to Laingsburg, Shaftsburg, **S**...RV camping
94	Lp 69, Marsh Rd, to E Lansing, Okemos, **S**...**gas:** Admiral/dsl, Speedway/DQ/dsl, **food:** McDonald's, **other:** Gillett RV Ctr, SavALot
92	Webster Rd, Bath, no services
89	US 127 S, to E Lansing, no services

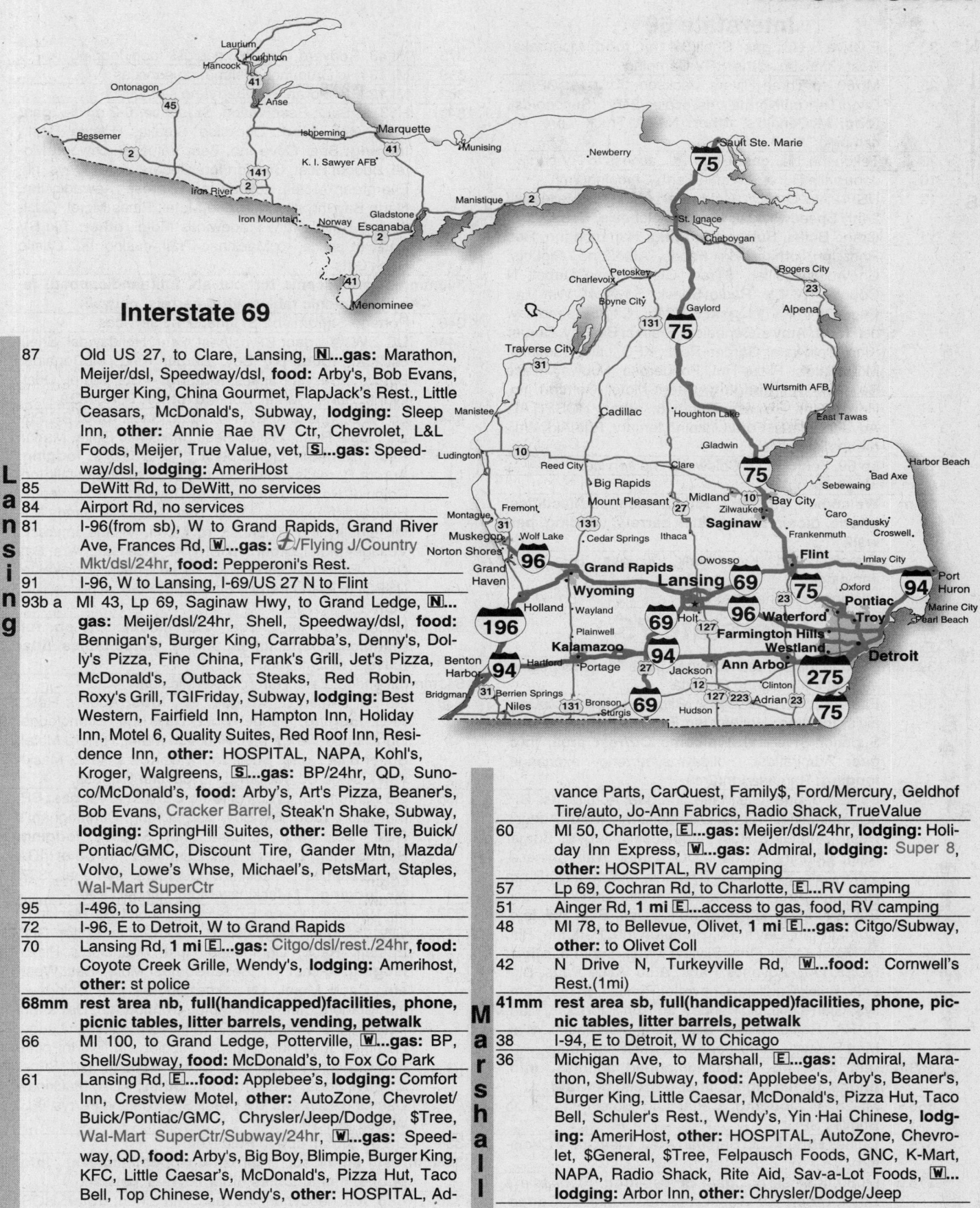

Interstate 69

N ↕ **S**

Lansing

87	Old US 27, to Clare, Lansing, **N**...**gas:** Marathon, Meijer/dsl, Speedway/dsl, **food:** Arby's, Bob Evans, Burger King, China Gourmet, FlapJack's Rest., Little Ceasars, McDonald's, Subway, **lodging:** Sleep Inn, **other:** Annie Rae RV Ctr, Chevrolet, L&L Foods, Meijer, True Value, vet, **S**...**gas:** Speedway/dsl, **lodging:** AmeriHost
85	DeWitt Rd, to DeWitt, no services
84	Airport Rd, no services
81	I-96(from sb), W to Grand Rapids, Grand River Ave, Frances Rd, **W**...**gas:** Flying J/Country Mkt/dsl/24hr, **food:** Pepperoni's Rest.
91	I-96, W to Lansing, I-69/US 27 N to Flint
93b a	MI 43, Lp 69, Saginaw Hwy, to Grand Ledge, **N**...**gas:** Meijer/dsl/24hr, Shell, Speedway/dsl, **food:** Bennigan's, Burger King, Carrabba's, Denny's, Dolly's Pizza, Fine China, Frank's Grill, Jet's Pizza, McDonald's, Outback Steaks, Red Robin, Roxy's Grill, TGIFriday, Subway, **lodging:** Best Western, Fairfield Inn, Hampton Inn, Holiday Inn, Motel 6, Quality Suites, Red Roof Inn, Residence Inn, **other:** HOSPITAL, NAPA, Kohl's, Kroger, Walgreens, **S**...**gas:** BP/24hr, QD, Sunoco/McDonald's, **food:** Arby's, Art's Pizza, Beaner's, Bob Evans, Cracker Barrel, Steak'n Shake, Subway, **lodging:** SpringHill Suites, **other:** Belle Tire, Buick/Pontiac/GMC, Discount Tire, Gander Mtn, Mazda/Volvo, Lowe's Whse, Michael's, PetsMart, Staples, Wal-Mart SuperCtr
95	I-496, to Lansing
72	I-96, E to Detroit, W to Grand Rapids
70	Lansing Rd, **1 mi** **E**...**gas:** Citgo/dsl/rest./24hr, **food:** Coyote Creek Grille, Wendy's, **lodging:** Amerihost, **other:** st police
68mm	**rest area nb, full(handicapped)facilities, phone, picnic tables, litter barrels, vending, petwalk**
66	MI 100, to Grand Ledge, Potterville, **W**...**gas:** BP, Shell/Subway, **food:** McDonald's, to Fox Co Park
61	Lansing Rd, **E**...**food:** Applebee's, **lodging:** Comfort Inn, Crestview Motel, **other:** AutoZone, Chevrolet/Buick/Pontiac/GMC, Chrysler/Jeep/Dodge, $Tree, Wal-Mart SuperCtr/Subway/24hr, **W**...**gas:** Speedway, QD, **food:** Arby's, Big Boy, Blimpie, Burger King, KFC, Little Caesar's, McDonald's, Pizza Hut, Taco Bell, Top Chinese, Wendy's, **other:** HOSPITAL, Advance Parts, CarQuest, Family$, Ford/Mercury, Geldhof Tire/auto, Jo-Ann Fabrics, Radio Shack, TrueValue
60	MI 50, Charlotte, **E**...**gas:** Meijer/dsl/24hr, **lodging:** Holiday Inn Express, **W**...**gas:** Admiral, **lodging:** Super 8, **other:** HOSPITAL, RV camping
57	Lp 69, Cochran Rd, to Charlotte, **E**...RV camping
51	Ainger Rd, **1 mi** **E**...access to gas, food, RV camping
48	MI 78, to Bellevue, Olivet, **1 mi** **E**...**gas:** Citgo/Subway, **other:** to Olivet Coll
42	N Drive N, Turkeyville Rd, **W**...**food:** Cornwell's Rest.(1mi)
41mm	**rest area sb, full(handicapped)facilities, phone, picnic tables, litter barrels, petwalk**
38	I-94, E to Detroit, W to Chicago
36	Michigan Ave, to Marshall, **E**...**gas:** Admiral, Marathon, Shell/Subway, **food:** Applebee's, Arby's, Beaner's, Burger King, Little Caesar, McDonald's, Pizza Hut, Taco Bell, Schuler's Rest., Wendy's, Yin Hai Chinese, **lodging:** AmeriHost, **other:** HOSPITAL, AutoZone, Chevrolet, $General, $Tree, Felpausch Foods, GNC, K-Mart, NAPA, Radio Shack, Rite Aid, Sav-a-Lot Foods, **W**...**lodging:** Arbor Inn, **other:** Chrysler/Dodge/Jeep

Marshall

MICHIGAN

Interstate 69

32	F Drive S, **E...gas:** Shell(3/4 mi), **food:** Moonraker Rest.(3mi), **W...other:** RV Camping
25	MI 60, to Three Rivers, Jackson, **E...gas:** BP/dsl, Citgo/Te-Kon/Norma's/dsl/scales/24hr, Sunoco/dsl, **food:** McDonald's, **other:** NAPA Truck Care, RV camping
23	Tekonsha, **E...gas:** Citgo, **W...**access to RV camp
16	Jonesville Rd, **W...**Waffle Farm Camping(2mi)
13	US 12, to Quincy, Coldwater, **E...gas:** Meijer/dsl/24hr, Speedway/dsl, **food:** Applebee's, Bob Evans, Grand Buffet, Subway, **lodging:** Hampton Inn, Red Roof Inn, **other:** Aldi Foods, AutoZone, BigLots, Chevrolet/Cadillac, $Tree, GNC, Home Depot, N Country RV Ctr, Radio Shack, SavALot, Wal-Mart SuperCtr/24hr, **W...gas:** BP/24hr, Citgo, Speedway/dsl, **food:** Arby's, Benedict's Steaks, Big Boy, Burger King, Coldwater Garden Rest., KFC, Little Caesar's, McDonald's, Pizza Hut, Ponderosa, Subway, Taco Bell, Wendy's, **lodging:** Cadet Motel, Comfort Inn, Holiday Inn Express, Super 8, **other:** HOSPITAL, Advance Parts, Ford/Lincoln/Mercury, Rite Aid, Walgreens, st police
10	Lp 69, Fenn Rd, to Coldwater, no services
8mm	weigh sta nb
6mm	**Welcome Ctr nb, full(handicapped)facilities, phone, picnic tables, litter barrels, vending, petwalk**
3	Copeland Rd, Kinderhook, **W...gas:** BP, **food:** camping
0mm	Michigan/Indiana state line

Interstate 75

S a u l t   S t e   M a r i e

Exit #	Services
395mm	US/Canada Border, Michigan state line, I-75 begins/ends at toll bridge to Canada
394	Easterday Ave, **E...gas:** Citgo/dsl, **food:** McDonald's, **lodging:** Holiday Inn Express, **other:** to Lake Superior St U, **W...Welcome Ctr/rest area, info, gas:** Admiral/dsl, Holiday/dsl/currency exchange, **lodging:** Ramada Inn(2mi)
392	3 Mile Rd, Sault Ste Marie, **E...gas:** Admiral/dsl, BP/dsl, Holiday/dsl, Shell, USA/dsl/24hr, **food:** Abner's Rest., Ang-Gio's Rest., Applebee's, Arby's, Burger King, Country Kitchen, DQ, Great Wall Chinese, Jeff's Café, KFC, Little Caesar's, McDonald's, Pizza Hut, Quizno's, Studebaker's Rest., Subway, Taco Bell, Wendy's, **lodging:** Best Value, Best Western, Comfort Inn, Day's Inn, Hampton Inn, Park Inn, Plaza Motel, Quality Inn, Skyline Motel, Super 8, **other:** HOSPITAL, Advance Parts, Auto Value Parts, BigLots, Buick/Cadillac, Chevrolet/Pontiac, $Tree, Family$, Glen's Mkt, JC Penney, Jo-Ann Fabrics, K-Mart, NAPA, Radio Shack, Sav-A-Lot, Walgreens, Wal-Mart/Subway, st police, Soo Locks Boat Tours
389mm	**rest area nb, full(handicapped)facilities, info, phone, picnic tables, litter barrels, petwalk**
386	MI 28, **E...lodging:** Cedar Log Motel/rest., **W...**to Brimley SP
379	Gaines Hwy, **E...**to Barbeau Area, Clear Lake Camping
378	MI 80, Kinross, **E...gas:** BP/dsl, **food:** Frank&Jim's Diner, **other:** RV West Camping, to Kinross Correctional, airport, golf

373	MI 48, Rudyard, **2 mi W...**gas/dsl, food, lodging
359	MI 134, to Drummond Island, no services
352	MI 123, to Moran, Newberry, no services
348	H63, to Sault Reservation, St Ignace, **0-2 mi E...gas:** Spirit Gas, **food:** Dockside Steaks, Hillside Rest., **lodging:** Bear Cove Inn, Best Value, Birchwood Motel, Budget Host, Comfort Inn, Cedars Motel, Days Inn, Evergreen Motel, Holiday Inn Express, Kewadin Inn, North Bay Inn, NorthernAire Motel, Pines Motel, Quality Inn, Royale Inn, Tradewinds Motel, **other:** Tiki RV Park, st police, to Mackinac Trail, casino, **W...**Castle Rock Gifts
346mm	**rest area/scenic turnout sb, full(handicapped) facilities, picnic tables, litter barrels, petwalk**
345	Portage St(from sb), St Ignace, no services
344b	US 2 W, **W...gas:** BP/dsl/rest./24hr, Holiday/dsl, Shell/dsl/24hr, **food:** Big Boy, Burger King, McDonald's, Subway, Suzy's Pasties, **lodging:** 4 Star Motel, Quality Inn, Sunset Motel, Super 8, **other:** Ford, KOA
344a	Lp 75, St Ignace, **0-2 mi E...gas:** Shell, **food:** BC Pizza, Flame Rest., Galley Rest., Mackinac Grille, Marina Rest., Northern Lights Rest., Pizza Guy's, **lodging:** Aurora Borealis Motel, Bentley's Cafe, Boardwalk Inn, Colonial House, Comfort Inn, Days Inn, Econolodge, Holiday Inn Express, Moran Bay Motel, Normandy Motel, Quality Inn, Thunderbird Motel, Village Inn/rest., Voyager Motel, **other:** HOSPITAL, Ace Hardware, Bay Drug, Family$, Glen's Mkt, Radio Shack, TrueValue, USPO, to Island Ferrys, Straits SP, KOA, st police, **E...**KOA
343mm	toll booth to toll bridge, **E...Welcome Ctr nb, full (handicapped)facilities, phone, picnic tables, litter barrels**, **W...**museum
341mm	toll bridge, Lake Huron, Lake Michigan
339	US 23, Jamet St, **E...gas:** BP, **food:** Audie's Rest., KFC, **lodging:** Budget Host, Days Inn, Econolodge, LightHouse View Motel, Parkside Motel, Riviera Motel, Super 8, **W...gas:** Shell, **food:** Darrow's Rest., Mackinaw Cookie Co, **lodging:** Holiday Inn Express
338	US 23(from sb), **E...Welcome Ctr/rest area, gas:** BP, Marathon, **food:** Big Boy, Burger King, Cunningham's Rest., DQ, KFC, Pancake Chef, Subway, **lodging:** Baymont Inn, Chalet Motel, Courtyard Inn, **other:** IGA Foods/supplies, Mackinaw Outfitters, same as 337, **W...lodging:** Ft Mackinaw Motel, Vindel Motel
337	MI 108(from nb, no EZ return), Nicolet St, Mackinaw City, **E...gas:** Citgo/dsl/LP, **food:** Blue Water Grill, Embers Rest., Lighthouse Rest., Mancino's Pizza, **lodging:** Anchor Inn, BeachComber Motel, Best Western, Capri Motel, Cherokee Shores Inn, Chippewa Inn, Clarion, Clearwater Motel, Comfort Inn, Day's Inn, Econolodge, Grand Mackinaw Resort, Hamilton Lodge, Hampton Inn, Huron Motel, Nicolet Inn, NorthPointe Inn, Quality Inn, Rainbow Motel, Ramada Ltd, Super 8, Travelodge, Waterfront Inn, **other:** KOA, Mackinaw Camping(2mi), Old Mill Creek SP, to Island Ferrys, **W...**Wilderness SP
336	US 31 S(from sb), to Petoskey
328mm	**rest area sb, full(handicapped)facilities, info, phone, picnic tables, litter barrels, petwalk**
326	C66, to Cheboygan, **E...gas:** Marathon, **other:** HOSPITAL, Sea Shell City/gifts, **other:** st police

M a c k i n a w   C i t y

Interstate 75

322	C64, to Cheboygan, **E**...HOSPITAL, LP, airport, st police
317mm	**rest area/scenic turnout nb, full(handicapped) facilities, info, phone, picnic tables, litter barrels, petwalk**
313	MI 27 N, Topinabee, **E**...**lodging:** Johnson Motel, Indian River RV Resort/Camping
311mm	Indian River
310	MI 33, MI 68, **E**...**lodging:** Holiday Inn Express, **other:** Jellystone Park(3mi), **W**...**gas:** BP/dsl, Ken's Gas, Shell/McDonald's/24hr, **food:** Burger King, DQ, Paula's Cafe, Subway, **lodging:** Coach House Motel, **other:** Ken's Mkt, to Indian River Trading Post/RV Resort, to Burt Lake SP
301	C58, Wolverine, **E**...**gas:** Marathon/dsl, **food:** Whistle Stop Rest., **other:** Elkwood Campground(5mi), **W**...**other:** Sturgin River Campground(3mi)
297mm	Sturgeon River
290	Vanderbilt, **E**...**gas:** BP/dsl/LP/RV dump, Spirit Gas, **other:** Village Mkt Foods, auto repair, **W**...**gas:** Mobil/dsl
287mm	**rest area sb, full(handicapped)facilities, info, phone, picnic tables, litter barrels**
282	MI 32, Gaylord, **E**...**gas:** Citgo, Clark, Holiday/24hr, Mobil, Speedway/dsl, **food:** Arby's, Burger King, DQ, KFC, La Senorita Mexican, McDonald's, Quizno's, Subway, TCBY, Wendy's, **lodging:** Baymont Inn, Best Western, Comfort Inn, Quality Inn, Red Roof Inn, **other:** HOSPITAL, Advance Parts, Glen's Foods, Harley-Davidson, Rite Aid, st police, **W**...**gas:** BP, Citgo/dsl, Marathon/dsl, Mobil/dsl, Shell/dsl, **food:** Applebee's, BC Pizza, Big Boy, Bob Evans, China 1, Little Caesar's, Mama Leone's Rest., Mancino's Pizza, Pizza Hut, Ponderosa, Ruby Tuesday, Spicy Bob's Italian, Taco Bell, **lodging:** Day's Inn, Gaylord Travel Inn, Hampton Inn, Holiday Inn Express, **other:** BigLots, Burnside RV Ctr, Chrysler/Dodge/Jeep, Dayton Tire, $Tree, GNC, Home Depot, K-Mart, Lowe's Whse, Radio Shack, Save-A-Lot Foods, Wal-Mart SuperCtr/Subway/24hr, RV camping, transmissions, tires
279mm	45th Parallel...halfway between the equator and north pole
279	Old US 27, Gaylord, **E**...**gas:** Marathon/Subway/dsl, Mobil/dsl, Shell, **food:** Burger King, Mama Leone's, **lodging:** Gaylord Inn, **other:** Chevrolet, Chrysler/Jeep/Nissan, Ford/Lincoln/Mercury, Pontiac/Buick/GMC, RV Ctr, st police, **W**...**lodging:** Bennthums Inn, Marsh Ridge Motel(2mi), KOA(3mi)
277mm	**rest area nb, full(handicapped)facilities, info, phone, picnic tables, litter barrels, petwalk**
270	Waters, **E**...**gas:** BP/dsl, **food:** Hilltop Rest., **W**...**lodging,** Waters Inn, **other:** IGA/gas, RV repair, Waters RV Ctr, USPO, to Otsego Lake SP
264	Lewiston, Frederic, **W**...access to food, lodging
262mm	**rest area sb, full (handicapped) facilities, phone, picnic tables, litter barrels, petwalk**
259	MI 93, **E**...Hartwick Pines SP, **2-4 mi W**...**lodging:** Fay's Motel, North Country Lodge, Pointe North Motel, River Country Motel, Woodland Motel, **other:** Chevrolet/Pontiac/Cadillac, Chrysler/Dodge/Jeep, Curves, Timberly Village RV Park, auto repair
256	(from sb), to MI 72, Grayling, same as 254

254	MI 72(exits left from nb, no return), Grayling, **1 mi W**...**gas:** Admiral Gas/dsl, BP, Citgo/7-11, Clark, Shell, Speedway, Valero, **food:** Big Boy, Burger King, DQ, KFC, McDonald's, Moose Rest., Pizza Hut, Subway, Taco Bell, Wendy's, **lodging:** Day's Inn, Ramada, **other:** HOSPITAL, Ace Hardware, Auto Value Parts, $General, Family$, Ford/Lincoln/Mercury, Glen's Foods/24hr, K-Mart, NAPA, Rite Aid, Save-a-Lot Foods
251mm	**rest area nb, full(handicapped)facilities, info, phone, picnic tables, litter barrels, petwalk, vending**
251	4 Mile Rd, **E**...Jellystone RV Park(5mi), skiing, **W**...**gas:** Marathon/Arby's/dsl/scales/RV Dump/24hr, **lodging:** Super 8
249	US 127 S(from sb), to Clare, no services
244	MI 18, Roscommon, **3.5 mi E**...**gas:** BP, **food:** McDonald's, **W**...**gas:** Valero/dsl, **other:** N Higgins Lake SP, camping, museum
239	MI 18, Roscommon, S Higgins Lake SP, **E**...**other:** gas, food, lodging, camping
235mm	**rest area sb, full(handicapped)facilities, phone, info, picnic tables, litter barrels, petwalk, vending**
227	MI 55 W, rd F97, to Houghton Lake, **5 mi W**...food
222	Old 76, to St Helen, **5 mi E**...food, lodging, camping
215	MI 55 E, West Branch, **E**...**gas:** Citgo/dsl, **food:** Willow Tree Rest.(2mi), **other:** HOSPITAL
212	MI 55, West Branch, **E**...**gas:** Marathon/7-11, Shell/Subway, **food:** Applebee's, Arby's, Big Boy, Burger King, Lumberjack Rest., McDonald's, Ponderosa, Taco Bell, Wendy's, **lodging:** Quality Inn/rest., Super 8, **other:** HOSPITAL, Home Depot, Tanger Outlet/famous brands, Wal-Mart SuperCtr/24hr/Subway/gas, st police, **W**...**gas:** BP/dsl
210mm	**rest area nb, full(handicapped)facilities, info, phone, picnic tables, litter barrels, petwalk, vending**
202	MI 33, to Rose City, Alger, **E**...**gas:** BP/Narski's Mkt/jerky, Mobil/dsl/jerky outlet(1/2mi), Shell/Subway, **other:** camping
201mm	**rest area sb, full(handicapped)facilities, phone, picnic tables, litter barrels, petwalk, vending**
195	Sterling Rd, to Sterling, **6 mi E**...gas, camping
190	MI 61, to Standish, **E**...**other:** HOSPITAL, Standish Correctional, **W**...**gas:** Marathon, Mobil/jerky
188	US 23, to Standish, **2-3 mi E**...gas, food, camping
181	Pinconning Rd, **E**...**gas:** Mobil, Shell/McDonald's/dsl, **food:** Cheesehouse Diner, **lodging:** Pinconning Inn(2mi), **other:** Pinconning Camping, **W**...**gas:** Sunoco/pizza/dsl/24hr
175mm	**rest area nb, full(handicapped)facilities, phone, picnic tables, litter barrels, petwalk, vending**
173	Linwood Rd, to Linwood, **E**...**gas:** BP/Arby's/dsl, Mobil/dsl, **other:** Hoyle's Marina Camping
171mm	Kawkawlin River

Interstate 75

N ↕ **S**	

168 Beaver Rd, to Willard, E...other: to Bay City SP, W...gas: Mobil/jerky

166mm Kawkawlin River

164 to MI 13, Wilder Rd, to Kawkawlin, E...gas: Meijer Food/dsl/24hr, food: Chicago Grill, Cracker Barrel, McDonald's, Ponderosa, Tim Horton, lodging: AmericInn, Fairfield Inn(3mi), other: KanRock Tire

162b a US 10, MI 25, to Midland, E...HOSPITAL

160 MI 84, Delta, E...gas: Mobil/Subway/dsl, Shell, W...gas: Citgo/7-11, Speedway, food: Berger's Rest., Burger King, KFC/Taco Bell, McDonald's, lodging: Econolodge, other: RV World Super Ctr, to Saginaw Valley Coll

158mm rest area sb, full(handicapped)facilities, phone, picnic tables, litter barrels, vending, petwalk

155 I-675 S, to downtown Saginaw, **4 mi** W...food: OutBack Steaks, lodging: Hampton Inn, Super 8

154 to Zilwaukee, no services

153mm Saginaw River

153 MI 13 E Bay City Rd, Saginaw, **2-3 mi** W...lodging

151 MI 81, to Reese, Caro, E...gas: Sunoco/Burger King/dsl, other: GMC/Volvo Trucks, W...gas: ✈/Flying J/Wendy's/dsl/LP/24hr

150 I-675 N, to downtown Saginaw, **6 mi** W...food: OutBack Steaks, lodging: Hampton Inn, Super 8

149b a MI 46, Holland Ave, to Saginaw, W...gas: Admiral, Marathon, Speedway/dsl, Sunoco, food: Arby's, Big John's Steaks, Burger King, McDonald's, Subway, Taco Bell, Texan Rest., lodging: Best Western, Motel 6, Super 7 Inn, other: HOSPITAL, Advance Parts, Save-A-Lot Foods, USPO

144b a Bridgeport, E...gas: Marathon/Subway/dsl, Shell/Blimpie, Speedway/dsl/24hr, food: Bavarian Rest., other: Jellystone Camping(9mi), W...gas: Mobil, TA/Country Pride/dsl/scales/24hr/@, food: Arby's, Big Boy, Cracker Barrel, Little Caesar's, McDonald's, Peking City, Subway, Taco Bell, Wendy's, lodging: Baymont Inn, Knight's Inn, other: Curves, Family$, Kroger, st police

143mm Cass River

136 MI 54, MI 83, Birch Run, E...gas: Mejier, Mobil/dsl/24hr, food: Dixie Rest., Exit Rest., Halo Burger, KFC, Subway, lodging: Best Western, Comfort Inn, Hampton Inn, Holiday Inn Express, Super 8, other: CarQuest, Dixie Speedway, General RV ctr, W...gas: Marathon, 7-11/gas, Sunoco/dsl, food: A&W, Arby's, Applebee's, Big Boy, Bob Evans, Culver's, DQ, Little Caesar's, McDonald's, Quizno's, Starbucks, Taco Bell, Tony's Rest., Uno Pizzaria, Victor & Merek's Pizza, Wendy's, lodging: Country Inn Suites, other: Birch Run Drugs, Chevrolet/Buick/Suzuki, Old Navy, Prime Outlet/famous brands

131 MI 57, to Montrose, E...gas: Mobil/dsl, Shell, Sunoco, food: Arby's, Big John's Steaks, Burger King, DQ, KFC, McDonald's, Subway, Taco Bell, Twins Pizza, Wendy's, other: AutoZone, Chevrolet, Chrysler/Dodge/Jeep, Ford, KanRock Tire, K-Mart, W...gas: BP/dsl, Mobil/dsl, food: Big Boy, other: Wal-Mart SuperCtr/gas

129mm rest area both lanes, full(handicapped)facilities, phone, picnic tables, litter barrels, vending, petwalk

126 to Mt Morris, E...gas: B&B/Burger King/dsl/24hr, W...gas: BP/dsl, carwash

125 I-475 S, UAW Fwy, to Flint

122 Pierson Rd, to Flint, E...gas: BP, Marathon/dsl, food: McDonald's, Papa's Coney's, Subway, lodging: Econolodge, other: Goodyear, Kroger/gas, Murray's Parts, W...gas: Citgo, Meijer/dsl/24hr, Shell/dsl, food: A&W/KFC, Arby's, Big John's Steaks, Bob Evans, Burger King, Cantonese Buffet, Cottage Pizza, Cracker Barrel, Denny's, Halo Burger, LJ Silver, Pizza Hut, Red Lobster, Taco Bell, Tim Horton, Wendy's, YaYa Chicken, lodging: Baymont Inn, Great Western Inn, other: Discount Tire, $Tree, Home Depot

118 MI 21, Corunna Rd, E...gas: Sunoco, food: Badawest Lebanese, Big John's Steaks, Burger King, Halo Burger, Hungry Howie's, Little Caesar's, Starbucks, Taco Bell, Wingfong Chinese, YaYa Chicken, Wing Fong Chinese, other: HOSPITAL, Advance Parts, $General, Kroger/gas, Rite Aid, 7-11, W...gas: BP/dsl, Citgo, Mobil, Shell/Wendy's, Speedway, Valero, food: A&W/KFC, Big Eazy Grill, Burger King, Domino's, Fazoli's, Happy Valley Rest., Krispy Kreme, McDonald's, Subway, White Castle, lodging: Economy Motel, other: Aldi Foods, AutoZone, Buick, CarQuest, $General, GMC, Home Depot, Kroger/gas, Lincoln/Mercury, Lowe's Whse, Rite Aid, Sam's Club/gas, VG's Foods, Walgreens, Wal-Mart SuperCtr/auto, st police

117b Miller Rd, to Flint, E...gas: Speedway/dsl, Sunoco/dsl, food: Applebee's, Arby's, Bennigan's, Cottage Pizza, Don Pablo, Fuddrucker's, KFC, LoneStar Steaks, McDonald's, Papa John's, Qdoba, Subway, West Side Diner, lodging: Comfort Inn, Motel 6, Sleep Inn, other: Belle Tire, K-Mart, W...gas: BP, Marathon, food: BD's BBQ, Bob Evans, Chili's, ChuckeCheese, Coney Island, Famous Dave's, Fire Mtn Grill, Golden Moon, Honey Baked Ham, Hooters, Italia Garden, Logan's Roadhouse, Moe's SW Grill, Old Country Buffet, Olive Garden, Outback Steaks, Pizza Hut, Rib City, Quizno's, Red Robin, Salvatori's Ristorante, Starbucks, Subway, Taco Bell, lodging: Red Roof Inn, Super 8, other: Barnes & Noble, Best Buy, BigLots, Borders Books, Circuit City, Discount Tire, Dodge, Gander Mtn, Goodyear, JC Penney, Jo-Ann Fabrics, Macey's, Office Depot, Old Navy, PetCo, Radio Shack, Ross, Sears/auto, Target, U-Haul, Valley Tire, mall, vet

117a I-69, E to Lansing, W to Port Huron

116 MI 121, Bristol Rd, E...gas: Citgo, Speedway/dsl, food: Coney Island, KFC, McDonald's, lodging: Day's Inn, Rodeway Inn, other: AutoZone, W...gas: Mobil/dsl, other: airport

115 US 23(from sb), W on Hill Rd...gas: Citgo, Meijer/dsl/24hr, Mobil, food: Hill St Grill, Maxie's Rest., McDonald's, Redwood Lodge, Turkey Farm Deli, lodging: AmericInn, Courtyard, Holiday Inn, Residence Inn

111 I-475 N(from nb), UAW Fwy, to Flint

109 MI 54, Dort Hwy(no EZ return to sb), **1-2 mi** E...gas: Marathon/dsl, food: Big Boy, Brick St Grill, Damon's, Starbucks, Wendy's

108 Holly Rd, to Grand Blanc, E...gas: Sunoco/dsl, food: Big Apple Bagels, Da Edoardo Ristorante, Quizno's, lodging: Comfort Inn, Holiday Inn Express, other: BMW/Mercedes/Toyota, W...gas: BP/McDonald's./dsl, food: Arby's, other: HOSPITAL

Interstate 75

N ↑ ↓ **S**

106	Dixie Hwy(exits left from sb, no nb return), Saginaw Rd, to Grand Blanc
101	Grange Hall Rd, Ortonville, **E**...**gas:** Sunoco, **other:** Holly RA, Jellystone Park, st police, **W**...**gas:** Mobil/dsl, **other:** to Seven Lakes/Groveland Oaks SP, RV camping
98	E Holly Rd, **E**...**gas:** Mobil/Subway/dsl/24hr, **other:** Ford, golf
96mm	**rest area both lanes, full(handicapped)facilities, picnic tables, litter barrels, info, phone, vending, petwalk**
95mm	**rest area both lanes, full(handicapped)facilities, picnic tables, litter barrels, info, phone, vending, petwalk**
93	US 24, Dixie Hwy, Waterford, **E**...**gas:** BP/dsl, **other:** Dodge, Kroger/gas(2mi), Saturn, **1-3 mi W**...**gas:** Speedway, **food:** Big Boy, McDonald's, Subway, Taco Bell, Wendy's, **other:** Chrysler/Jeep, Walgreens, to Pontiac Lake RA
91	MI 15, Davison, Clarkston, **E**...**gas:** Sunoco/dsl, **food:** Bullfrog's(5mi), Subway(5mi), **other:** camping, **W**...**gas:** Shell/dsl, **food:** Brioni Grill, Clarkston Grill, DQ, Mesquite Creek Café, **other:** HOSPITAL, Rite Aid(2mi)
89	Sashabaw Rd, **E**...**gas:** Shell/dsl, **food:** Culvers, Ruby Tuesday, **other:** county park, **W**...**gas:** BP/24hr, Citgo, **food:** Caribou Coffee, Chicken Shack, Coney Island, E Ocean Chinese, Guido's Pizza, Hong Kong Chinese, Hungry Howie's, Little Caesars, Marble Slab, McDonald's, Nina's Cafe, Quizno's, Subway, Renderonis Pizza, Rio Wraps, Wendy's, **other:** CVS Drug, GNC, Kroger, vet
86mm	weigh sta sb, parking area nb
84b a	Baldwin Ave, **E**...**gas:** Shell/24hr, Sunoco/dsl, **food:** Arby's, Big Boy, Joe's Crabshack, Longhorn Steaks, Olive Garden, Wendy's, **other:** Best Buy, Costco/gas, Discount Tire, $Castle, Kohl's, Michael's, Old Navy, PetCo, World Mkt, **W**...**gas:** Mobil/24hr, **food:** Chili's, Jimmy John's, Kerry's Coney Island, Max&Emra's, McDonald's, On-the-Border, Oriental Buffet, Quizno's, Rainforest Cafe, Starbucks, Steak'n Shake/24hr, Subway, **other:** Holiday Inn Express, **other:** Bass Pro Shops, Best Buy, Borders Books, Circuit City, Great Lakes Crossing Outlet/famous brands, Marshall's, TJ Maxx, USPO
83b a	Joslyn Rd, **E**...**gas:** Meijer/dsl/24hr, **food:** Applebee's, Montana's Grill, Olive Garden, **other:** Belle Tire, Home Depot, Jo-Ann Fabrics, Sam's Club/gas, Target, **W**...**gas:** Sunoco
81	MI 24, Pontiac(no EZ return), **E**...The Palace Arena, **1 mi E**...**gas:** BP/24hr
79	University Dr, **E**...**gas:** BP, **food:** Coney Island, Jimmy John's, Rio Wraps, Subway, **W**...**gas:** Mobil, Speedway/dsl, **food:** A&W/KFC, Arby's, Burger King, Lelli's Steaks, Mtn Jack's Rest., McDonald's, Taco Bell, Wendy's/Tim Horton, **lodging:** Candlewood Suites, Comfort Suites, Courtyard, Extended Stay America, Extended Stay Deluxe, Fairfield Inn, Hampton Inn, Hilton, Holiday Inn, Hyatt, Motel 6, Staybridge Suites, Wingate Inn, **other:** HOSPITAL, GM

Detroit Area

78	Chrysler Dr, **E**...**other:** Chrysler Museum, Oakland Tech Ctr
77b a	MI 59, to Pontiac, **2 mi on Adams E**...**other:** Wal-Mart/auto, **1 mi W on Opdyke**...**gas:** Fastrack/Tubby's/dsl, Shell
75	Square Lake Rd(exits left from nb), to Pontiac, **W**...HOSPITAL, St Mary's Coll
74	Adams Rd, no services
72	Crooks Rd, to Troy, **W**...**food:** Bangkok Bisrto, Coney Island, Nobana Japanese, Quizno's, Red Robin, Starbucks, **lodging:** Embassy Suites, Hilton
69	Big Beaver Rd, **E**...**food:** Champp's Grill, Shula's Steaks, TGIFriday's, **lodging:** Drury Inn, Marriott, **other:** **W**...**gas:** BP, **food:** Benihana, Maggiano's Italian, Melting Pot Rest., Morton's Steaks, Ruth's Chris Steaks, **other:** mall
67	Rochester Rd, to Stevenson Hwy, **E**...**gas:** Marathon, Shell, **food:** Arby's, Burger King, Caribou Coffee, Coney Island, Hooter's, Hungry Howies, Mr Pita, Orchid Rest., Panera Bread, Pizza Hut/Taco Bell, Qdoba, Ram's Horn Rest., Tubby's Grill, **other:** Discount Tire, Nordstrom's, Office Depot, PetsMart, Radio Shack, transmissions, **W**...**food:** Mtn Jack's Steaks, **lodging:** Holiday Inn, Red Roof Inn, **other:** tires
65b a	14 Mile Rd, Madison Heights, **E**...**gas:** Marathon/dsl, Mobil, Shell, **food:** Azteca Mexican, Blimpie, Bob Evans, Burger King, Chili's, Krispy Kreme, Logan's Roadhouse, McDonald's, Panera Bread, Starbucks, Steak'n Shake, Taco Bell, **lodging:** Motel 6, Red Roof Inn, **other:** Belle Tire, Borders Books, Circuit City, Dodge, Ford, Home Depot, JC Penney, Lowe's Whse, Macey's, NAPA, Office Depot, Radio Shack, Sam's Club, Sears/auto, TJ Maxx, World Mkt, mall, **W**...**gas:** Marathon/Dunkin Donuts, Mobil, Speedway, **food:** Antonis Kitchen, Applebee's, Bennigan's, Big Fish Seafood, Caribou Coffee, Coney Island, McDonald's, Outback Steaks, Quizno's, **lodging:** Best Western, Courtyard, Econolodge, Extended Stay America, Fairfield Inn, Hampton Inn, Residence Inn, **other:** Chevrolet, Costco/gas, Value Ctr Foods
63	12 Mile Rd, **E**...**gas:** Clark, Marathon, **food:** Bellacino's Italian, Blimpie, Green Lantern Rest., Marinelli's Pizza, McDonald's, Red Lobster, Sero's Rest., Starbucks, TX Roadhouse, Tim Horton, **other:** Curves, Home Depot, K-Mart/foods, Lowe's Whse, Radio Shack, auto repair, vet, **W**...**gas:** Marathon/Dunkin Donuts, Speedway, **other:** Chevrolet, Costco/gas
62	11 Mile Rd, **E**...**gas:** Mobil, **food:** Boodles Rest., Cottage Pizza, Jets Pizza, **other:** Advance Parts, CVS Drug, 7-11, Walgreens, repair/tires, vet, **W**...**gas:** BP, Marathon/dsl, Mobil, **food:** KFC, Taco Bell, Tim Horton, Tubby's Subs, **other:** Belle Tire

MICHIGAN

Interstate 75

<table>
<tr><td>N
↕
S</td><td>61</td><td>I-696 E, to Port Huron, W to Lansing, to Hazel Park Raceway</td></tr>
</table>

D **e** **t** **r** **o** **i** **t** **A** **r** **e** **a**	60	9 Mile Rd, John R St, E...**food:** Burger King, Checkers, China 1 Buffet, DQ, Hardee's, McDonald's, Subway, Taco Bell, **lodging:** Days Hotel, **other:** Family$, Kroger, Rite Aid, transmissions, W...**gas:** Mobil, **food:** Tubby's Subs, Wendy's, **other:** Hasting's Parts, repair
	59	MI 102, 8 Mile Rd, **3 mi** W...st fairgrounds
	58	7 Mile Rd, W...**gas:** BP/dsl
	57	McNichols Rd, E...**gas:** Citgo, **food:** Coney Island
	56b a	Davison Fwy, no services
	55	Holbrook Ave, Caniff St, E...**gas:** Mobil/dsl, W...**food:** Coney Island
	54	E Grand Blvd, Clay Ave, W...**gas:** BP/dsl, **food:** Coney Island
	53b	I-94, Ford Fwy, to Port Huron, Chicago
	53a	Warren Ave, E...**gas:** Mobil, Shell, W...**gas:** BP
	52	Mack Ave, E...**gas:** Shell, **food:** McDonald's
	51c	I-375 to civic center, tunnel to Canada, downtown
	51b	MI 3(exits left from nb), Gratiot Ave, downtown
	50	Grand River Ave, downtown
	49b	MI 10, Lodge Fwy, downtown
	49a	Rosa Parks Blvd, E...Tiger Stadium, W...**gas:** Mobil, **other:** Firestone
	48	I-96 begins/ends
	47b	Porter St, E...bridge to Canada, DutyFree/24hr
	47a	MI 3, Clark Ave, E...**gas:** Mobil, W...**gas:** Marathon
	46	Livernois Ave, to Hist Ft Wayne, E...**gas:** Marathon, **food:** KFC/Taco Bell
	45	Fort St, Springwells Ave, E...**gas:** BP/dsl, W...**gas:** Mobil, **food:** McDonald's
	43b a	MI 85, Fort St, to Schaefer Hwy, E...**gas:** BP Sunoco, W...**gas:** Marathon Refinery, **other:** to River Rouge Ford Plant
	42	Outer Dr, W...**gas:** BP/Subway/dsl, Mobil/dsl
	41	MI 39, Southfield Rd, to Lincoln Park, E...**food:** A&W, Bangkok Star Rest., Bill's Place Rest., Tim Horton, **other:** Walgreens, W...**gas:** Marathon, **food:** Dunkin Donuts, **lodging:** Sleep Inn, **other:** Buick, Kroger, Rite Aid
	40	Dix Hwy, E...**gas:** Marathon, Meijer, Welcome, **food:** Coney Island Diner, Ponderosa, **other:** CVS Drug, Farmer Jack's, 7-11, W...**gas:** Mobil, **food:** Big Boy, Burger King, DQ, Dunkin Donuts, LJ Silver, McDonald's, Pizza Hut, Quizno's, Rally's, Taco Bell, **other:** Belle Tire, Family$, Firestone, CVS Drug, Foodland, Sears/auto
	37	37 Allen Rd, North Line Rd, to Wyandotte, E...**gas:** BP, Marathon, Shell, **food:** Anita's Pizza, Chicken Shack, **lodging:** Holiday Inn, **other:** HOSPITAL, Sam's Club/gas, W...**gas:** Mobil, Sunoco, **food:** Arby's, Burger King, K-Bob House, Mallie's Grill, McDonald's, Wendy's, **lodging:** Best Value Inn, Comfort Suites, La Quinta
	36	Eureka Rd, E...**gas:** BP, **food:** Amigo's Mexican, Bob Evans, Denny's, Fire Mtn Grill, Orleans Steaks, **lodging:** Ramada Inn, Super 8, **other:** Vet, W...**gas:** Meijer/dsl/24hr, Mobil/dsl, **food:** Baker's Square, Big Boy, Culver's, Famous Dave's BBQ, Fuddrucker's, Hooters, KFC/Taco Bell, Mongolian BBQ, Mtn Jack's

		Steaks, Ruby Tuesday, Subway, Texas Roadhouse, Wendy's, **lodging:** Red Roof Inn, **other:** MEDICAL CTR, Belle Tire, Best Buy, Borders Books, CVS Drug, Discount Tire, Home Depot, JC Penney, Kohl's, Macy's, Staples, mall
	35	US 24, Telegraph Rd, (from nb, exits left)
	34b	Sibley Rd, Riverview, W...**gas:** Sunoco/Dunkin Donuts/Subway, **other:** RV Ctr
	34a	to US 24(from sb), Telegraph Rd
	32	West Rd, to Trenton, Woodhaven, E...**gas:** Detroiter/Citgo/dsl/rest., Meijer/dsl/24hr, Speedway/dsl, **food:** Applebees, Bob Evans, Burger King, White Castle, Dunkin Donuts, Panera Bread, Pizza Hut, Quizno's, Steak'n Shake, Subway, Taco Bell, **other:** Chevrolet, Discount Tire, Firestone/auto, Ford, Home Depot, K-Mart, Kroger, Michael's, Office Depot, Radio Shack, Target, Wal-Mart/auto, W...**gas:** BP/24hr, Shell, **food:** Andy's Pizza, Domino's, Millie's Rest., McDonald's, **lodging:** Best Western/rest., Knight's Inn, Holiday Inn Express, **other:** SavOn Drug
	29	Gilbralter Rd, to Flat Rock, Lake Erie Metropark, E...**gas:** FasTrack/dsl, **food:** McDonald's, **other:** HOSPITAL, W...**gas:** Marathon, **lodging:** Sleep Inn, **other:** Ford, st police
	28	rd 85(from nb), Fort St, E...HOSPITAL
	27	N Huron River Dr, to Rockwood, E...**gas:** Marathon/Subway/dsl, **food:** Benito's Pizza, Famous Coney Island, Huron River Rest., Ocean Duck Chinese, **other:** Curves, FoodTown Foods, Rite Aid, W...**gas:** Speedway/dsl, **food:** Riverfront Rest.
	26	S Huron River Dr, to S Rockwood, E...**gas:** Sunoco/dsl, **food:** Dixie Café, **other:** USPO
M **o** **n** **r** **o** **e**	21	Newport Rd, to Newport, E...**gas:** BP/Taco Bell/24hr, W...**gas:** Marathon/Burger King/dsl/24hr
	20	I-275 N, to Flint, no services
	18	Nadeau Rd, W...**gas:** Pilot/Arby's/dsl/24hr/@, **other:** HOSPITAL, RV camping
	15	MI 50, Dixie Hwy, to Monroe, E...**gas:** Shell, **food:** Bob Evans, Burger King, Red Lobster, **lodging:** Best Value Inn, Best Western, Hampton Inn, Travel Inn, **other:** Sterling SP, W...**gas:** Pilot/Subway/dsl/24hr/@, TA/BP/Popeye's/Quizno's/Pizza Hut/dsl/24hr/@, **food:** Big Boy, Cracker Barrel, Denny's, McDonald's, Wendy's, **lodging:** Holiday Inn Express, Knight's Inn, **other:** HOSPITAL, to Viet Vet Mem
	14	Elm Ave, to Monroe
	13	Front St, Monroe
	11	La Plaisance Rd, to Bolles Harbor, W...**gas:** Marathon/Taco Bell/dsl, Speedway, **food:** Burger King, McDonald's, Wendy's, **lodging:** AmeriHost, Comfort Inn, Harbor Town RV Resort, **other:** Outlet Mall/famous brands, st police
	10mm	**Welcome Ctr nb, full(handicapped)facilities, phone, info, picnic tables, litter barrels, vending, petwalk**
	9	S Otter Creek Rd, to La Salle, W...antiques
	7mm	weigh sta both lanes
	6	Luna Pier, E...**gas:** Sunoco/dsl, **food:** Ganders Rest., Super 8
	5	to Erie, Temperance, no services
	2	Summit St, no services
	0mm	Michigan/Ohio state line

Interstate 94

Exit #	Services

Port Huron

275mm I-69/I-94 begin/end on MI 25, **Pinegrove Ave in Port Huron...gas:** BP/24hr, Citgo, Speedway, **food:** Chicken Shack, Jet's Pizza, McDonald's, Tim Horton, Wendy's, White Castle, **lodging:** Day's Inn, Holiday Inn Express, **other:** Buick/Pontiac, Can-Am DutyFree, Family$, Ford, Honda, Rite Aid, tollbridge to Canada

274.5mm Black River

274 Water St, Port Huron, N...**Welcome Ctr/rest area, full facilities(only from wb), food:** Cracker Barrel, **lodging:** Best Western, S...**gas:** SpeedyQ/dsl, Speedway/dsl, **food:** Bob Evans, **lodging:** Comfort Inn, Fairfield Inn, Hampton Inn, **other:** Lake Port SP, RV camping

271 I-69 E and I-94 E run together eb, Lp I-69, S...**gas:** Mobil, **food:** Arby's, McDonalds, KFC, Quay St Grill, Wendy's, **other:** Kroger/gas, K-Mart, Sam's Club, to Port Huron

269 Dove St, Range Rd, N...**gas:** Speedway/dsl/24hr, **lodging:** AmeriHost

266 Gratiot Rd, Marysville, S...**gas:** Admiral, BP/dsl/scales/24hr, Marathon/scales/dsl, Meijer, Speedway, **food:** Arby's, Big Boy, Burger King, KFC, 4 Star Rest., Little Caesars Mancino's Pizza, McDonald's, Mr Pita, Pelican Café, Pizza Hut, Taco Bell, Tim Horton, **lodging:** Super 8, **other:** HOSPITAL, AutoZone, Curves, Rite Aid, Wally's Foods

262 Wadhams Rd, N...camping, S...**gas:** Marathon/dsl/showers/24hr, Mobil/dsl

257 St Clair, Richmond, S...**gas:** BP/dsl, **other:** st police

255mm **rest area eb, full(handicapped)facilities, phones, info, picnic tables, litter barrels, petwalk**

251mm **rest area wb, full(handicapped)facilities, phones, info, picnic tables, litter barrels, petwalk**

248 26 Mile Rd, to Marine City, N...**food:** McDonald's(2mi), S...**gas:** Mejier, 7-11/gas, Speedy Q(1mi)

247mm Salt River

247 MI 19(no eb return), New Haven

243 MI 29, MI 3, Utica, New Baltimore, N...**gas:** BP, Marathon/dsl, Meijer/dsl/24hr, Sunoco/dsl, **food:** Applebee's, Arby's, Burger King, Chophouse, Cold Stone, Coney Island, Dimitri's Rest., Empire Buffet, Gus Coney Island, McDonald's, Outback Steaks, Panera Bread, Papa Romano's Pizza, Ruby Tuesday, Subway, Starbucks, TX Roadhouse, Wendy's, White Castle, **lodging:** Chesterfield Motel, **other:** Belle Tire, Best Buy, Discount Tire, GNC, Home Depot, Jo-Ann Fabrics, K-Mart, Kohl's, Lowe's Whse, Michael's, PetCo, Radio Shack, Rite Aid, Staples, Target, TJ Maxx, Walgreen, S...**gas:** Marathon/dsl/24hr, 7-11/gas, Speedway/dsl/24hr, **food:** Big Boy, Buscemis Pizza, Hot'n Now Burgers, Taco Bell, **lodging:** LodgeKeeper, **other:** Chevrolet

241 21 Mile Rd, Selfridge, N...**gas:** Marathon/dsl, Shell, **food:** China King, Hungry Howie's, Quizno's, Subway, **other:** Advance Parts, CVS Drug, same as 240

Detroit Area

240 to MI 59, N...**gas:** 7-11/gas, Marathon, Speedway, **food:** Arby's, Bob Evans, Coney Island, McDonald's, O'Charley's, Taco Bell, Tim Horton, **lodging:** Best Western, **other:** $General, Ford, Wal-Mart SuperCtr

237 N River Rd, Mt Clemens, N...**gas:** BP/dsl, Mobil/Subway/dsl, **food:** McDonald's, **lodging:** Quality Inn, **other:** HOSPITAL, General RV Ctr, Gibralter Trade Ctr

236.5mm Clinton River

236 Metro Parkway, S...**food:** Big Apple Bagels, Little Caesars, McDonald's, Subway, **other:** HOSPITAL, Curves, CVS Drug, GNC, Kroger

235 Shook Rd(from wb), no services

234b a Harper Rd, 15 Mile Rd, N...**gas:** BP/McDonald's, Marathon/dsl, SpeedyQ, Sunoco/dsl/24hr, **food:** Sorrento Pizza, **other:** vet, S...**gas:** FL Gas, **food:** China Moon, Subway, Winners Grill

232 Little Mack Ave(from wb only), N...**gas:** Marathon, 7-11/gas, Sunoco, **food:** Arby's, Burger King, Chili's, Cold Stone, Del Taco, Denny's, Hooters, Longhorn Steaks, McDonald's, Panera Bread, Pizza Hut, Red Robin, Sea Breeze Diner, Tim Horton, Woody's Grill, **lodging:** Days Inn, Eastin Hotel, Holiday Inn Express, Red Roof Inn, Super 8, Victory Inn, **other:** Belle Tire, Firestone, JC Penny, Sam's Club, Sears/Auto, Staples, S...**gas:** Marathon, Meijer/dsl/24hr, Speedway/dsl, **food:** Cracker Barrel, IHOP, **lodging:** Baymont Inn, Gelato Roama Pizza, **other:** Circuit City, Family$, Home Depot, Jo-Ann Fabrics, PetsMart, same as 231

231 (from eb), MI 3, Gratiot Ave, N...**gas:** Shell, Speedway, Sunoco, **food:** Applebee's, Arby's, Big Boy, Bob Evans, ChuckeCheese, Denny's, Famous Dave's, Logan's Raodhouse, McDonald's, Pizza Hut, Starbucks, TX Roadhouse, **lodging:** Best Western, Day's Inn, Econolodge, Extended Stay America, Microtel, **other:** Best Buy, Discount Tire, Firestone/auto, Honda/Acura, Kia, Nissan, Sam's Club/gas, Target, Toyota, U-Haul, mall

230 12 Mile Rd, N...**gas:** American Gas, Mobil/dsl, **food:** BD's Mongolian, Burger King, Jimmy John's, Krispy Kreme, Outback Steaks, **other:** CVS Drug, $Tree, Hyundai/Suzuki, Lincoln/Mercury, Marshall's, Mitsubishi, NAPA, Wal-Mart/Subway, mall, S...**gas:** Marathon

229 I-696 W, Reuther Fwy, to 11 Mile Rd, N...**gas:** BP, S...**gas:** BP/dsl, Speedway, **other:** 7-11

228 10 Mile Rd, N...**gas:** BP/24hr, Mobil, Shell, **food:** Eastwind Chinese, Coney Island, Jet's Pizza, **other:** CVS Drug

MICHIGAN

Interstate 94

E

↕

W

227	9 Mile Rd, **N**...**gas:** Mobil/dsl, Speedway/dsl, Sunoco, **food:** McDonald's, Papa John's, Subway, Taco Bell/Pizza Hut, Wendy's, **other:** Aldi Foods, CVS $Tree, Drug, Fresh Choice Foods, Office Depot, Pete & Franks Mkt, True Value, **S**...**gas:** Mobil/dsl, **lodging:** Shore Pointe·Motel, **other:** BMW, Cadillac, Mercedes
225	MI 102, Vernier Rd, 8 Mile Rd, **S**...**gas:** BP/Subway, Mobil, Sunoco/dsl, **food:** Coney Island, KFC, Taco Bell, Wendy's, **other:** Kroger, Walgreen
224b	Allard Ave, Eastwood Ave, no services
224a	Moross Rd, **S**...**gas:** Shell, **other:** Family Foods, **other:** HOSPITAL
223	Cadieux Rd, **S**...**gas:** BP/Subway, Mobil, Shell, Sunoco, **food:** McDonald's, Taco Bell, Tubby's Subs, Wendy's, White Castle, **other:** Rite Aid
222b	Harper Ave(from eb), **S**...**other:** Family$, Hastings Auto
222a	Chalmers Ave, Outer Dr, **N**...**gas:** BP/Subway/dsl, Marathon, **food:** Coney Island, KFC, Little Caesars, White Castle, **other:** Family$
220b	Conner Ave, **N**...**gas:** BP, Sunoco
220a	French Rd, **S**...**gas:** Marathon
219	MI 3, Gratiot Ave, **N**...**gas:** Marathon/Subway, Speedy, **food:** Coney Island, KFC, McDonald's, **other:** Family$, **S**...**gas:** GasMart, **food:** Burger King
218	MI 53, Van Dyke Ave, **N**...**gas:** BP, Mobil/dsl
217b	Mt Elliott Ave, **S**...**gas:** Marathon, Sunoco/dsl, **food:** Young's BBQ
217a	E Grand Blvd, Chene St, **S**...**gas:** Marathon
216b	Russell St(from eb), to downtown, no services
216a	I-75, Chrysler Fwy, to tunnel to Canada
215c	MI 1, Woodward Ave, John R St, no services
215b	MI 10 N, Lodge Fwy, no services
215a	MI 10 S, tunnel to Canada, downtown
214b	Trumbull Ave, to Ford Hospital
214a	(from wb)Grand River Ave, no services
213b	I-96 W to Lansing, E to Canada, bridge to Canada, to Tiger Stadium
213a	W Grand(exits left from eb), no services
212b	Warren Ave(from eb), no services
212a	Livernois Ave, **S**...**gas:** Marathon/Subway/dsl, Sunoco
211b	Cecil Ave(from wb), Central Ave, no services
211a	Lonyo Rd, **S**...Ford
210	US 12, Michigan Ave, Wyoming Ave, **N**...**gas:** Mobil, **S**...**gas:** BP/dsl, Citgo/dsl, Sunoco/dsl, **food:** YumYum Donuts
209	Rotunda Dr(from wb), no services
208	Greenfield Rd, Schaefer Rd, **N**...**gas:** Mobil, **other:** 7-11, **S**...River Rouge Ford Plant
207mm	Rouge River
206	Oakwood Blvd, Melvindale, **N**...**gas:** Marathon, **food:** Applebee's, Carino's, Coney Island, Chili's, Cold Stone, Little Caesars, Longhorn Steaks, Moe's SW Grill, On-the-Border, Panera Bread, Starbucks, Subway, **other:** Best Buy, Ford Plant, GNC, Home Depot, Jo-Ann Fabrics, Lowe's Whse, Meijer, Michaels, Old Navy, PetCo, Staples, Target, TJ Maxx, UPS, World Mkt, Greenfield Village Museum, **S**...**gas:** BP, **food:** Burger King, Coney Island, McDon-

The letters **D e t r o i t   A r e a** appear vertically along the left margin.

	ald's, O'Henry's, Sabina's, Subway, **lodging:** Best Western, Holiday Inn Express, **other:** Belle Tire, Big A Parts, Curves, CVS Drug, $General, Rite Aid, 7-11
205mm	Largest Uniroyal Tire in the World
204b a	MI 39, Southfield Fwy, Pelham Rd, **N**...**gas:** Marathon, Mobil, Valero/dsl, **food:** Ponderosa Steaks, **other:** 7-11, to Greenfield Village, **S**...**gas:** Marathon, **other:** Walgreen
202b a	US 24, Telegraph Rd, **N**...**gas:** Clark, Shell, Sunoco, **food:** Burger King, Checkers, Dunkin Donuts, Jet's Pizza, KFC, McDonald's, Pizza Hut, Ram's Horn Rest., Subway, Taco Bell, Wendy's, **lodging:** Casa Bianca Motel, **other:** Advance Parts, Aldi Foods, Rite Aid, Walgreen, **S**...**gas:** BP, Citgo, Marathon/dsl, **food:** Burger King, Hungry Howie's, Leon's Rest., Marina's Pizza, Old Country Buffet, Pizza Hut, Popeye's, Quizno's, Subway, Super China, Yum Yum Donuts, **lodging:** Comfort Inn, **other:** AutoZone, Curves, Family$, Radio Shack, Rite Aid, U-Haul, Walgreens, Wal-Mart, st police
200	Ecorse Rd,(no ez eb return), to Taylor, **N**...**gas:** Marathon/scales/dsl, **S**...**gas:** Rich, Speedy/dsl, **food:** Danny's Pizza, Norms Subs
199	Middle Belt Rd, **S**...**gas:** BP/dsl/24hr, **food:** Denny's, McDonald's, Wendy's, **lodging:** Day's Inn, Howard Johnson, Super 8
198	Merriman Rd, **N**...**food:** Bob Evans, **lodging:** Baymont Inn, Best Value, Best Western, Clarion, Comfort Inn, Courtyard, Crowne Plaza Hotel, Doubletree Inn, Econolodge, Extended Stay America, Fairfield Inn, Hampton Inn, Hilton Garden, Holiday Inn, Howard Johnson, Marriott, Metropolitan Motel, Motel 6, PearTree Inn, Ramada Inn, Sheraton, **S**...Wayne Co Airport
197	Vining Rd, no services
196	Wayne Rd, Romulus, **N**...**gas:** Shell, **food:** McDonald's, **S**...**gas:** Mobil/dsl, **food:** Burger King, Subway
194b a	I-275, N to Flint, S to Toledo
192	Haggerty Rd, **N**...**gas:** BP, Mobil/24hr, Travel&Truck Plaza/dsl(2mi), **food:** Burger King(2mi), Subway, **S**...Lower Huron Metro Park
190	Belleville Rd, to Belleville, **N**...**gas:** BP/24hr, Meijer/dsl/24hr, Marathon, **food:** Applebee's, Arby's, Big Boy, Cracker Barrel, McDonald's, O'Charley's, Quizno's, Taco Bell, Tim Horton, Wendy's, **lodging:** Hampton Inn, Holiday Inn Express, Red Roof Inn, **other:** Camping World RV Service/supplies, CVS Drug, $Tree, Firestone/auto, Ford, Meijer, Michal's RV Ctr, U-Haul, Walgreens, Wal-Mart, **S**...**gas:** Shell, **food:** Burger King, China City, Dimitri's Kitchen, Dos Pesos Mexican, Subway, **lodging:** Comfort Inn, Super 8, **other:** USPO
189mm	**rest area wb, full(handicapped)facilities, info, phone, picnic tables, litter barrels, vending, pet-walk**
187	Rawsonville Rd, **S**...**gas:** Mobil/dsl, Speedway/dsl, **food:** Burger King, Denny's, KFC, Little Caesar's, LoneStar Steaks, Maria's Pizza, McDonald's, Pizza Hut, Tim Horton, Wendy's, **other:** $General, $Tree, GNC, K-Mart, KOA(3mi), Radio Shack

Interstate 94

185	US 12, Michigan Ave(from eb, exits left, no return), to frontage rds, airport
184mm	Ford Lake
183	US 12, Huron St, Ypsilanti, **N...gas:** Marathon/dsl, **other:** to E MI U, **S...food:** Baker's Square, McDonald's, Primo Coffee, **lodging:** Marriott, **other:** HOSPITAL, Chevrolet/Pontiac/Buick/GMC, st police
181b a	US 12 W, Michigan Ave, Ypsilanti, **N...gas:** Meijer/dsl/24hr, Rich, Speedway, **food:** Burger King, Taco Bell/Pizza Hut, Tim Horton/Wendy's, **other:** HOSPITAL, Aamco, BigLots, $Tree, 7-11, Sheena's Food/24hr, Radio Shack, Wal-Mart, **S...gas:** Shell, **food:** Domino's, Harvest Moon Rest., McDonald's, Subway
180b a	US 23, to Toledo, Flint
177	State St, **N...gas:** BP/24hr, Mobil, Shell, **food:** Bennigan's, Burger King, CA Pizza, Damon's, Graham's Steaks, Los Tres Mexican, Macaroni Grill, Max&Erma's, Olive Garden, Wendy's, **lodging:** Best Value, Crowne Plaza Hotel, Comfort Inn, Courtyard, Fairfield Inn, Hampton Inn, Hilton, Holiday Inn Express, Motel 6, Red Roof Inn, Sheraton, **other:** Firestone, JC Penney, Mitsubishi, Sears/auto, VW, World Mkt, mall, to UMI, **S...gas:** Citgo/Subway, **food:** Coney Island, McDonald's, Pizza Hut/Taco Bell, **lodging:** Motel 6, **other:** U-Haul
175	Ann Arbor-Saline Rd, **N...gas:** Shell, **food:** Applebee's, Coney Island, Moe's SW Grill, Old Country Buffet, Panera Bread, Subway, **lodging:** Candlewood Suites, **other:** Office Depot, mall, to UMI Stadium, **S...gas:** Meijer/dsl/24hr, **food:** Big Boy, Jet's Pizza, Joe's Crabshack, McDonald's, Outback Steaks, TGIFriday, **other:** Best Buy, Jo-Ann Fabrics, Kohl's, Meijer, Target
172	Jackson Ave, to Ann Arbor, **N...gas:** BP, Marathon, Shell, Sunoco, **food:** Boston Mkt, Burger King, Holiday's Rest., KFC, LJ Silver, Marathon, McDonald's, Quarter Rest., Quizno's, Starbucks, Subway, Taco Bell, Zingerman's Roadhouse, **other:** HOSPITAL, CVS Drug, $Tree, Discount Tire, Goodyear, K-Mart, Kroger, Rite Aid, Staples, TJ Maxx, Walgreens, mall, **S...lodging:** Best Western, Super 8, **other:** Chevrolet/Pontiac/Cadillac, Ford
171	MI 14(from eb, exits left), to Ann Arbor, to Flint by US 23
169	Zeeb Rd, **N...gas:** BP/dsl/24hr, **food:** Grand Pies Co, Metzger's Rest., McDonald's, **S...gas:** Citgo/dsl, Meijer/dsl, **food:** Arby's, Burger King, Panera Bread, Pizza Hut, Subway, Taco Bell, Wendy's, Westside Grill, **other:** Harley-Davidson, Lowe's Whse, Meijer
167	Baker Rd, Dexter, **N...gas:** Pilot/Subway/scales/dsl/24hr, **S...gas:** Pilot/Arby's/dsl/scales/24hr, TA/BP/Popeye's/dsl/rest./scales/24hr/@, **food:** Reddeman Farms Rest.(4mi), McDonald's, **other:** Blue Beacon
162	Jackson Rd, Fletcher Rd, **S...gas:** Clark/dsl/24hr, **food:** Stiver's Rest.
161mm	**rest area eb, full(handicapped)facilities, phone, picnic tables, litter barrels, vending, petwalk**
159	MI 52, Chelsea, **N...gas:** Mobil/dsl, Rich Gas, Sunoco/dsl, **food:** Big Boy, Chelsea Grill, China Gar-
	den, Coney Island, Hungry Howie's, KFC/Taco Bell, Little Caesar's, Main St Coney Island, McDonald's, Subway, Wendy's, **lodging:** Comfort Inn, Holiday Inn Express, **other:** HOSPITAL, Chelsea Drug, Chevrolet/Buick, Chrysler/Dodge/Jeep, Country Mkt Foods/drug, Curves, CVS Drug, Ford, Pamida, Travel Land RV Ctr, vet
157	Jackson Rd, Pierce Rd, **N...**Gerald Eddy Geology Ctr
156	Kalmbach Rd, **N...**to Waterloo RA
153	Clear Lake Rd, **N...gas:** Marathon/dsl
151.5mm	weigh sta both lanes
150	to Grass Lake, **S...gas:** Mobil/Subway, **other:** Apple Creek Campground
150mm	**rest area wb, full(handicapped)facilities, phone, picnic tables, litter barrels, vending, petwalk**
147	Race Rd, **N...**Hideaway RV Camp, to Waterloo RA, camping, **S...**lodging
145	Sargent Rd, **S...gas:** BP/dsl, Mobil/145 Rest/dsl/scales/rest./24hr, **food:** McDonald's, Wendy's, **lodging:** Colonial Inn
144	Lp 94(from wb), to Jackson, no services
142	US 127 S, to Hudson, **3 mi S...gas:** Meijer/dsl/24hr, Speedway, **food:** Domino's, McDonald's, Wendy's, **other:** Advance Parts, Kroger, Parts+, Rite Aid, to MI Speedway
141	Elm Rd, **N...lodging:** Travelodge, **other:** Chevrolet/Dodge/Honda/Hyundai, Ford
139	MI 106, Cooper St, to Jackson, **N...**st police/prison, **S...gas:** Citgo/Subway, **other:** HOSPITAL
138	US 127 N, MI 50, to Lansing, Jackson, **N...food:** Red Lobster, **lodging:** Baymont Inn, Comfort Inn, Fairfield Inn, Hampton Inn, Holiday Inn, Jackson Inn, **other:** vet, **S...gas:** Clark, Marathon, Rich Gas, Shell/24hr, **food:** Arby's, Big Boy, Bob Evans, Dunkin Donuts, Fazoli's, Ground Round, KFC, LJ Silver, Los Tres Amigos, McDonald's, Old Country Buffet, Outback Steaks, Panera Bread, Papa John's, Pizza Hut, Quizno's, Starbucks, Subway, **lodging:** Country Hearth Inn, Motel 6, **other:** Advance Parts, AutoZone, Best Buy, Circuit City, Discount Tire, Home Depot, Kohl's, Kroger, Lowe's Whse, Michael's, Sears/auto, Target, TJ Maxx, Walgreens
137	Airport Rd, **N...gas:** Meijer/dsl/24hr, Shell/Taco Bell/24hr, 7-11, **food:** Burger King, Denny's, Hudson's Rest., McDonald's, Steak'n Shake/24hr, Subway, Wendy's, **other:** Bumper Parts, Meijer, **S...gas:** BP/24hr, **food:** Cracker Barrel, Culvers, Olive Garden, LoneStar Steaks, **lodging:** Country Inn&Suites, **other:** K-Mart, Sam's Club/gas
136	Lp 94, MI 60, to Jackson, no services
135mm	**rest area eb, full(handicapped)facilities, phone, picnic tables, litter barrels, vending, petwalk**
133	Dearing Rd, Spring Arbor, **S...**to Spring Arbor U

MICHIGAN

Interstate 94

E

W

M a r s h a l l

130	Parma, **S**...**gas:** Citgo/dsl/rest./24hr
128	Michigan Ave, **N**...**gas:** BP/Burger King/scales/dsl/24hr, Marathon/dsl/24hr, **other:** RV camping
127	Concord Rd, **N**...St Julian's Winery
124	MI 99, to Eaton Rapids, **S**...lodging
121	28 Mile Rd, to Albion, **N**...**gas:** Mobil, **food:** Arby's, **lodging:** Best Western, **S**...**gas:** FT/dsl/24hr, Marathon, Speedway/dsl/24hr, **food:** Albion Garden, Burger King, Frosty Dan's, Full Moon Rest., KFC, La Casa Mexican, McDonald's, Pizza Hut, **lodging:** Super 9, **other:** HOSPITAL, AutoZone, Chevrolet/Pontiac/Buick, $General, Family$, Felpausch Foods, Ford/Mercury, Pamida, RV camping
119	26 Mile Rd, no services
115	22.5 Mile Rd, **N**...**gas:** Citgo/115 Rest./dsl/24hr
113mm	**rest area wb, full(handicapped)facilities, phone, picnic tables, litter barrels, vending, petwalk**
112	Partello Rd, **S**...**gas:** Loves/Hardee's/scales/dsl/24hr, **food:** Schuler's Rest.
110	Old US 27, Marshall, **N**...**gas:** Shell/Subway/dsl/24hr, **food:** Country Kitchen/24hr, **S**...**gas:** Citgo/KFC/dsl, **food:** Denny's, Pizza Hut(2mi), Schuler's Rest.(2mi), **lodging:** Hampton Inn, Holiday Inn Express, **other:** HOSPITAL, sheriff
108	I-69, US 27, N to Lansing, S to Ft Wayne
104	11 Mile Rd, Michigan Ave, **N**...**gas:** Pilot/scales/dsl/24hr, Sunoco/Te-Khi Trkstp/rest./scales/24hr/@, **S**...**gas:** Citgo/Subway/dsl/24hr, **lodging:** Quality Inn/rest.
103	Lp 94(from wb, no return), to Battle Creek, **N**...HOSPITAL
102mm	Kalamazoo River
100	Beadle Lake Rd, **N**...**food:** Moonraker Rest., **S**...**gas:** Citgo/dsl, **other:** Binder Park Zoo
98b	I-194 N, to Battle Creek
98a	MI 66, to Sturgis, **S**...**gas:** Citgo/Blimpie/dsl, Meijer/dsl/24hr, **food:** Chili's, Don Pablo, McDonald's, Ruby Tuesday, Schlotsky's, Starbucks, Steak'n Shake, **lodging:** Holiday Inn, **other:** Best Buy, Discount Tire, Kohl's, Lowe's Whse, Meijer, Michael's, PetCo, Sam's Club/gas, Staples, TJ Maxx, Walgreens, Wal-Mart SuperCtr/24hr, same as 97
97	Capital Ave, to Battle Creek, **N**...**gas:** BP/24hr, Marathon, **food:** Arby's, LoneStar Steaks, Lux Cafe, McDonald's, Red Lobster, **lodging:** Comfort Inn, Knight's Inn, **S**...**gas:** Citgo, Shell/24hr, Sunoco/Subway/24hr, **food:** Applebee's, Bob Evans, Burger King, Canton Buffet, Cici's Pizza, Cocina Mexicana, Coney Island, Cracker Barrel, Denny's, Don Pablo, Fazoli's, Godfather's Pizza, Old Country Buffet, Pizza Hut, Quizno's, Taco Bell, Tuesday Morning, Wendy's, **lodging:** Baymont Inn, Best Western, Day's Inn, Fairfield Inn, Hampton Inn, Motel 6, Ramada Inn, Super 8, **other:** Apple Valley Foods, Best Buy, Borders Books, $Tree, Firestone/auto, Goodyear/auto, Harley-Davidson, JC Penney, Macey's, Marshall Fields, Sears/auto, Target, mall, vet
96mm	**rest area eb, full(handicapped)facilities, phone, picnic tables, litter barrels, vending, petwalk**

K a l a m a z o o

95	Helmer Rd, **N**...**gas:** Citgo/dsl, **other:** st police, **2 mi** **N**...**gas:** Meijer/dsl/24hr, **food:** Big Boy
92	Lp 94, to Battle Creek, Springfield, **N**...**gas:** Citgo/Arlene's Trkstp/dsl/rest./24hr, Shell/24hr, **other:** RV camping, to Ft Custer RA
88	Climax, **N**...Galesburg Speedway
85	35th St, Galesburg, **N**...**gas:** Shell/Subway/dsl/24hr, **food:** McDonald's, Subway, **other:** Galesburg Speedway, to Ft Custer RA, River Oaks CP, **S**...**other:** Colebrook CP, Scottsville CP, Winery Tours, RV camping
85mm	**rest area wb, full(handicapped)facilities, phone, picnic tables, litter barrels, vending, petwalk**
81	Lp 94(from wb), to Kalamazoo, no services
80	Cork St, Sprinkle Rd, to Kalamazoo, **N**...**gas:** Citgo/dsl, Double Express, Speedway/dsl, **food:** Arby's, Burger King, Chicken Coop, Denny's, Godfather's, Hana East Asian, Perkins, Taco Bell, **lodging:** Best Western, Clarion Hotel, Fairfield Inn, Holiday Inn Express, Red Roof Inn, **other:** vet, **S**...**gas:** BP/dsl/24hr, Speedway/dsl, **food:** Derk's Rest., Hometown Diner, Horizon Inn, McDonald's, Subway/24hr, Wendy's, **lodging:** Comfort Inn, Econolodge, Horizon Inn, Motel 6
78	Portage Rd, Kilgore Rd, **N**...**gas:** BP/Circle K, **food:** China Hut, Cottage Pizza, Uncle Earnie Pancakes, **lodging:** Hampton Inn, **other:** HOSPITAL, **S**...**gas:** Shell/24hr, Speedway, **food:** Angelo's Italian, Bravo Rest., Brewster's, Callahan's Rest., Fat Tony's, McDonald's, Pizza King, Quizno's, Taco Bell, Theo&Stacy's Rest., Subway, **lodging:** Country Inn Suites, Lee's Inn, **other:** AutoValue Parts, museum
76b a	Westnedge Ave, **N**...**gas:** Admiral, Meijer/dsl/24hr, Speedway/dsl, **food:** Arby's, Beaners, Bennigan's, BD BBQ, Hooters, IHOP, Kazoopie's, Lee's Chicken, Mancino's Eatery, Outback Steaks, Papa John's, Pappy's Mexican, Pizza Hut, Root Beer Stand, Steak'n Shake, Stirmax Asian, Subway, Taco Bell, Theo & Stacy's Rest., **other:** BigLots, Discount Tire, Gander Mtn, Goodyear/auto, Lowe's Whse, Meijer, Midas, Office Depot, Rite Aid, **S**...**gas:** Shell/24hr, **food:** Antique Kitchen, Applebee's, Bilbo's Pizza, Bob Evans, Burger King, Carrabba's, Chili's, ChuckeCheese, Cold Stone, Culvers, Empire Chinese, Fazoli's, Heavenly Ham, Jimmy Johns, KFC, Krispy Kreme, Little Caesar's, LJ Silver, Logan's Roadhouse, MacKenzie's Bakery, McDonald's, Noodles & Co, Old Country Buffet, Olive Garden, Panchero's Mexican, Panera Bread, Pizza Hut, Qdoba Mexican, Red Lobster, Red Robin, Schlotsky's, Subway, Taco Bell, TX Roadhouse, Wendy's, **lodging:** Holiday Motel, **other:** AutoZone, Barnes&Noble, Belle Tire, Best Buy, Cadillac/Pontiac/Nissan, Circuit City, $Tree, Fannie Mae Candies, Firestone/auto, Harding's Foods, Home Depot, JC Penney, Jo-Ann Fabrics, K-Mart, Kohl's, MktPlace Foods, Michael's, Old Navy, PepBoys, Pontiac/Cadillac, Radio Shack, Sam's Club, Sears/auto, Target, Walgreens, WorldMkt, mall
75	Oakland Dr, no services

Interstate 94

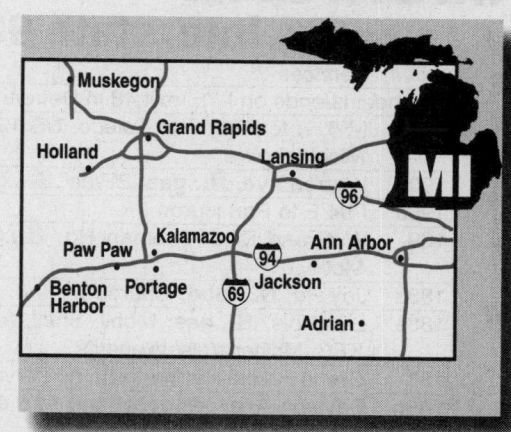

Exit	Description
74b a	US 131, to Kalamazoo, ...to W MI U, Kalamazoo Coll
72	Oshtemo, ...**gas:** Citgo/dsl, Speedway/dsl, **food:** Arby's, Burger King, Culver's, McDonald's, Taco Bell, Wendy's, **lodging:** Hampton Inn, **other:** NAPA, Saturn, S...**food:** Cracker Barrel, **lodging:** Fairfield Inn, Towne Place Suites
66	Mattawan, ...**gas:** Speedway/Subway/dsl/24hr, **food:** Main St Grill, Mancino's Italian, **other:** Freightliner, Rossman Auto/towing, S...**gas:** Shell
60	MI 40, Paw Paw, ...**gas:** BP/24hr, Speedway/dsl/24hr, **food:** Arby's, Big Boy, Burger King, Chicken Coop, Gallagher's Eatery, McDonald's, Pizza Hut, Root Beer Stand, Subway, Taco Bell, Wendy's, **lodging:** Econolodge, Comfort Inn, Super 8, **other:** HOSPITAL, Advance Parts, Chrysler/Dodge/Jeep, Curves, Felpausch Foods, St Julian Winery, Warner Winery
56	MI 51, to Decatur, ...st police, S...**gas:** Citgo/dsl, Marathon/dsl/24hr
52	Lawrence, ...**food:** Waffle House of America
46	Hartford, ...**gas:** Shell/dsl/24hr, **food:** McDonald's, Panel Room Rest.
42mm	**rest area wb, full(handicapped)facilities, phone, picnic tables, litter barrels, vending, petwalk**
41	MI 140, to Niles, Watervliet, ...**gas:** BP/24hr, Citgo, Marathon, Wesco, **food:** Burger King, Chicken Coop, Frosty Boy, Rookies, Subway, Taco Bell, Waffle House, **lodging:** Ramada, **other:** HOSPITAL, Curves, camping
39	Millburg, Coloma, Deer Forest, 0-1 mi ...**gas:** BP/dsl, Marathon, Speedway, Westco/dsl, **food:** Diggins Rest., Friendly Grill, McDonald's, Pizza Hut, Subway, **other:** Ace hardware, Family$, Holiday RV Ctr, Krenek RV Ctr, True Value, S...**gas:** NAPA Auto Care
36mm	**rest area eb, full(handicapped)facilities, phone, picnic tables, litter barrels, vending, petwalk**
34	I-196 N, US 31 N, to Holland, Grand Rapids
33	Lp I-94, to Benton Harbor, 2-4 mi ...airport, sheriff's dept
30	Napier Ave, Benton Harbor, ...**gas:** ⚛/Flying J/Wendy's/dsl/24hr/@ , Shell/dsl/24hr, **lodging:** Super 8, **other:** HOSPITAL, Blue Beacon, S...Chrysler/Dodge/Honda
29	Pipestone Rd, Benton Harbor, ...**gas:** Meijer/dsl/24hr, **food:** Applebee's, Asian Buffet, Burger King, Hacienda Mexican, Hardee's, IHOP, McDonald's, Pizza Hut, Sophia's Pancake House, Steak'n Shake, Super Buffet, Texas Corral, **lodging:** Best Western, Courtyard, Motel 6, Red Roof Inn, **other:** Aldi Foods, Best Buy, $Tree, Home Depot, JC Penney, Lowe's Whse, Meijer, Radio Shack, Sears/auto, Staples, Walgreens, Wal-Mart SuperCtr/Subway/24hr, S...**gas:** Mobil/dsl/24hr, **food:** Bob Evans, **lodging:** Comfort Suites, Holiday Inn Express
28	US 31 S, MI 139 N, Scottdale Rd, to Niles, ...**gas:** Citgo/dsl, Marathon/dsl, **food:** Bejing House, Burger King, Capozio's Pizza, Chicken Coop, Country Kitchen, DQ, Henry's Burgers, KFC, Pizza Hut, Subway, Taco Bell, **lodging:** Economy Inn, Executive Inn/rest., **other:** HOSPITAL, AutoZone, BigLots, Chevrolet, $Tree, Family$, M&W Tire, Midas, NAPA, Office Depot, Old Navy, Rite Aid, Target, TJ Maxx, radiators/repair/transmissions, st police, vet, S...**lodging:** Best Value
27mm	St Joseph River
27	MI 63, Niles Ave, to St Joseph, ...**gas:** BP/24hr, **food:** Nye's Apple Barn, S...**food:** Panera Bread, **other:** Goodyear
23	Red Arrow Hwy, Stevensville, ...**gas:** Admiral, BP, Marathon/dsl, Mobil, Shell/dsl/24hr, **food:** Big Boy, Burger King, Cracker Barrel, Culver's, DQ, Fireside Inn Rest., LJ Silver, McDonald's, Papa John's, Popeye's, Quizno's, Subway, Tony's Rest., **lodging:** Baymont Inn, Candlewood Suites, Comfort Suites, Park Inn, Ray's Motel, **other:** Curves, Walgreen, S...**food:** Five O'Clock Grill, **lodging:** Hampton Inn
22	John Beers Rd, Stevensville, ...to Grand Mere SP, S...**gas:** Marathon/dsl, **food:** Pizza Hut
16	Bridgman, ...**gas:** BP/A&W/dsl/24hr, **other:** to Warren Dunes SP, S...**gas:** JR's Trvl Ctr/dsl/24hr, **food:** McDonald's, **lodging:** Bridgman Inn, 1/2 mi S...**food:** Olympus Rest., Pizza Hut, Roma Pizza, Sammies Rest., Subway, **other:** Chevrolet/Buick, vet
12	Sawyer, ...**gas:** Citgo/scales/dsl/rest./24hr, **food:** Chubby's Diner, S...**gas:** TA/Burger King/Country Pride/Popeye's/Taco Bell/scales/dsl/24hr/@ , **food:** Pizza Hut, **lodging:** Super 8, **other:** USPO
6	Lakeside, Union Pier, ...**other:** St Julian's Winery, antiques, S...RV camping
4b a	US 12, to Three Oaks, New Buffalo, ...**food:** Pizza Hut, st police
2.5mm	weigh sta both lanes
1	MI 239, to Grand Beach, New Buffalo, ...**gas:** Shell/Quizno's, **food:** Hana's Rest.(1mi), McDonald's, Wheel Inn Rest., **lodging:** Best Western, Holiday Inn Express, Rodeway Inn, **other:** $General, S...**gas:** New Buffalo/rest./dsl/24hr, **food:** Wendy's, **lodging:** Obrien's Inn
.5mm	**Welcome Ctr eb, full(handicapped)facilities, info, phone, picnic tables, litter barrels, vending, petwalk**
0mm	Michigan/Indiana state line

MICHIGAN
Interstate 96

Detroit Area

Exit #	Services

I-96 begins/ends on I-75, exit 48 in Detroit.

191 I-75, N to Flint, S to Toledo, US 12, to MLK Blvd, to Michigan Ave

190b Warren Ave, **N**...**gas:** BP/dsl, **S**...**gas:** Marathon

190a I-94 E to Port Huron

189 W Grand Blvd, Tireman Rd, **N**...**gas:** BP/Subway, Mobil

188b Joy Rd, **N**...**food:** Church's

188a Livernois, **N**...**gas:** Mobil, Shell, **food:** Burger King, KFC, McDonald's, Wendy's

187 Grand River Ave(from eb), no services

186b Davison Ave, I-96 local and I-96 express divide, no exits from express

186a Wyoming Ave, no services

185 Schaefer Hwy, to Grand River Ave, **N**...**gas:** BP/24hr, Mobil, **food:** Coney Island, McDonald's, **other:** CVS Drug, **S**...**gas:** Sunoco

184 Greenfield Rd, no services

183 MI 39, Southfield Fwy, exit from expswy and local

182 Evergreen Rd, no services

180 Outer Dr, **N**...**gas:** BP/dsl/lube

180mm I-96 local/express unite/divide

179 US 24, Telegraph Rd, **N**...**gas:** BP, Marathon/dsl, **food:** Arby's, China King, Dunkin Donuts/Baskin-Robbins, McDonald's, Subway, Taco Bell, White Castle, **other:** Chevrolet, Dodge, Family$, Goodyear, Rite Aid, **S**...**gas:** BP, Marathon/dsl

178 Beech Daly Rd, **N**...gas

177 Inkster Rd, **N**...**gas:** BP/Tim Horton, **food:** Panda Chinese, Subway, **lodging:** Super 8, **other:** $General, Hancock Fabrics, 7-11

176 Middlebelt Rd, **N**...**food:** Bob Evans, IHOP, Olive Garden, **lodging:** Comfort Inn, **S**...**food:** Logan's Roadhouse, **lodging:** Crossland Studios, **other:** Costco/gas, Home Depot, Marshall's, Meijer, Michael's, PetCo, Target, Walgreens, Wal-Mart Super-Ctr

175 Merriman Rd, **N**...**gas:** Mobil, Speedway/dsl, **S**...**gas:** Sunoco, **food:** Blimpie

174 Farmington Rd, **N**...**gas:** Mobil/dsl, Sunoco, **food:** Looney Baker, **S**...**gas:** BP, **food:** KFC

173b Levan Rd, **N**...HOSPITAL, to Madonna U

173a Newburgh Rd, no services

171mm I-275 and I-96 run together 9 miles

170 6 Mile Rd, **N**...**food:** Big Boy, CA Pizza Kitchen, Coney Island, Ground Round, Jimmy John's, Louie's Grill, Max&Erma's, Panera Bread, Red Robin, **lodging:** Best Western, Courtyard, Marriott, Radisson, **other:** HOSPITAL, Busch's Fresh Foods, Murray Parts, Rite Aid, Walgreens, mall, **S**...**gas:** BP, Mobil, **food:** Applebee's, Baja Fresh, Brann's Steaks, Buca Italian, Caribou Coffee, Charlie's Grill, Chi Burger, Cold Stone, Claddagh Rest., Flemings, McDonald's, Mitchell's Fishmarket, Noodles & Co, Panchero's, Papa Vino's, PF Chang, Potbelly, **lodging:** Fairfield Inn, Residence Inn, TownePlace Suites, **other:** Barnes&Noble, CVS Drug, Office Depot

169b a 7 Mile Rd, **N**...**food:** Doc's Grill, **lodging:** Embassy Suites, **S**...**food:** Alexander's Rest., Bahama Breeze Rest., Champp's Rest., Gaucho Steaks, Macaroni Grill, **lodging:** AmeriSuites, **other:** Home Depot

167 8 Mile Rd, to Northville, **S**...**gas:** Meijer/dsl/24hr, Speedway/dsl, **food:** Benihana, Big Boy, Chili's, McDonald's, Koney Island, On-the-Border, Quizno's, Starbucks, Taco Bell, Uno Pizzaria, Zoup, **lodging:** Country Inn Suites, Extended Stay America, Hampton Inn, Holiday Inn Express, Sheraton, **other:** Best Buy, Costco/gas, Firestone, Home Depot, Kohl's, Meijer, Target, Trader Joe's, to Maybury SP

165 I-696, I-275, MI 5, Grand River Ave

I-275 and I-96 run together 9 miles.

163 I-696(from eb)

162 Novi Rd, to Walled Lake, Novi, **N**...**gas:** BP, **food:** Buffalo Wild Wings, Carrabba's, ChuckeCheese, Denny's, Oaks Grill, Red Lobster, Subway, **lodging:** Crowne Plaza, Hotel Baronette, Residence Inn, **other:** HOSPITAL, Circuit City, CompUSA, Gander Mtn, JC Penney, Jo-Ann Fabrics, Kohl's, Kroger, Michael's, PetCo, Sears/auto, WorldMkt, mall, **S**...**gas:** Mobil, **food:** Baja Fresh, Big Boy, Bonefish Grill, Boston Mkt, Coney Island, Famous Dave's, Kim's Chinese, Melting Pot Rest., Olive Garden, Red Robin, Steve & Rocky's, TGI-Friday, Wendy's, **lodging:** Courtyard, Wyndham Garden, **other:** Borders Books, CompUSA, Discount Tire, Old Navy, TJ Maxx, auto repair, vet

161mm **rest area eb, full(handicapped) facilities, phone, vending, picnic tables, litter barrels, petwalk**

160 Beck Rd, 12 Mile Rd, **S**...**food:** Coney Island **other:** HOSPITAL, Home Depot, Kroger, Staples, to Maybury SP

159 Wixom Rd, Walled Lake, **N**...**gas:** Marathon/dsl, **food:** Wendy's, **lodging:** Baymont Inn, **other:** to Proud Lake RA, **S**...**gas:** Meijer/dsl/24hr, Mobil, Shell, Valero, **food:** Arby's, Baskin-Robbins/Dunkin Donuts, Burger King, KFC/A&W, McDonald's, Stinger's Grill, Taco Bell, **lodging:** Comfort Suites, **other:** General RV Ctr, Lincoln/Mercury, Meijer

155b a to Milford, New Hudson, **N**...Ford, to RV camping, to Lion Oaks CP, **S**...**gas:** Mobil, Sunoco, **food:** Applebee's, Arby's, Chili's, Cold Stone, Coney Island, Jet's Pizza, McDonald's, Quizno's, Starbucks, Subway, Wendy's, **other:** Chevrolet, Discount Tire, Lowe's Whse, Wal-Mart SuperCtr/24hr

153 Kent Lake Rd, **N**...Kensington Metropark, **S**...**gas:** Mobil

151 Kensington Rd, **N**...Kensington Metropark, **S**...Island Lake RA, food, lodging

150 Pleasant Valley Rd(no return wb), **S**...phone

148b a US 23, N to Flint, S to Ann Arbor

147 Spencer Rd, **N**...**gas:** Mobil, **other:** st police, **S**...to Brighton St RA

145 Grand River Ave, to Brighton, **N**...**gas:** BP, Shell/dsl, **food:** Arby's, Cracker Barrel, Outback Steaks, Pizza Hut, **lodging:** Courtyard, Homewood Suites, **other:** Cadillac/GMC, $General, Ford/Mercury, Honda, **S**...**gas:** Clark/Subway/dsl, **food:** Big Boy, Burger King, Chili's, Coney Island, DQ, KFC, Lil Chef, Little Caesar's, LoneStar Steaks, McDonald's, Panera Bread, Red Robin, Taco Bell, Wendy's, **lodging:** Holiday Inn Express, **other:** AAA, Best Buy, Bob's Tire, Borders Books, Home Depot, Honda, Jo-Ann Etc., Marshall's, Mazda, Meijer/dsl, Michael's, Radio Shack, Rite Aid, PetsMart, Sears, Staples, Target, USPO, mall, to Brighton Ski Area

Interstate 96

141 Lp 96(from wb, no EZ return), to Howell, **N**...**gas:** Shell, Sunoco/dsl, **food:** Applebee's, Bob Evans, Little Caesar's, McDonald's, Mesquite Jct, TW's Italian, **lodging:** Grandview Inn, **other:** Chevrolet, Kohl's, **S**...**gas:** Speedway, **food:** Arby's, Big Boy, Taco Bell, Wendy's

141mm rest area wb, full(handicapped)facilities, phone, vending, picnic tables, litter barrels, petwalk

137 D19, to Pinckney, Howell, **N**...**gas:** Mobil, Shell/dsl, Speedway/dsl, Sunoco/Blimpie/Baskin-Robbins/Dunkin Donuts/dsl, **food:** Coney Island, **lodging:** Kensington Inn, **other:** HOSPITAL, Parts+, Spartan Tire, **S**...**food:** Country Kitchen, **lodging:** Best Western

135mm rest area eb, full(handicapped)facilities, vending, phone, picnic tables, litter barrels, petwalk

133 MI 59, Highland Rd, **N**...**gas:** 7-11, Sunoco/McDonald's/dsl, **food:** Arby's, Castaway Cafe(1mi), HoneyTree Grille, **lodging:** Baymont, **other:** Tanger Outlets/famous brands

129 Fowlerville Rd, Fowlerville, **N**...**gas:** BP/rest./24hr, Shell/dsl, Sunoco/dsl, **food:** A&W/KFC, Big Boy, CO Coffee, Fowlerville Rest., McDonald's, Taco Bell/Pizza Hut, Wendy's, **lodging:** Best Western, **S**...**gas:** Mobil, **food:** Quizno's, Subway, **other:** Chysler/Dodge/Jeep, **other:** Ford

126mm weigh sta both lanes

122 MI 43, MI 52, Webberville, **N**...**gas:** Mobil/dsl/24hr, **food:** Angel's Café, McDonald's, **other:** MI Brewing Co

117 to Dansville, Williamston, **0-3 mi N**...**gas:** Admiral, Marathon/subs/dsl, **food:** Jersey's Giant Subs, Spag's Grill, **S**...**gas:** Sunoco/dsl, **food:** Subway

111mm rest area wb, full(handicapped)facilities, phone, picnic tables, litter barrels, vending, petwalk

110 Okemos, Mason, **N**...**gas:** BP/Dunkin Donuts/24hr, Marathon, Sunoco, **food:** Applebee's, Arby's, Backyard BBQ, Big Boy, Big John's Steaks, Cracker Barrel, Dunkin Donuts, Gilbert&Blake's Seafood, Grand Traverse, Little Caesar's, McDonald's, Panchero's Mexican, Sheshiang Garden, Starbucks, Stillwater Grill, Subway, Taco Bell, **lodging:** Comfort Inn, Fairfield Inn, Hampton Inn, Holiday Inn Express, **other:** 7-11, to stadium

106b a I-496, US 127, to Jackson, Lansing, **N**...St Police

104 Lp 96, Cedar St, to Holt, Lansing, **N**...**gas:** Admiral, Speedway, **food:** Aldaco's Mexican, Applebee's, Barley's Grill, Beaner's, Blimpie, Bob Evans, Boston Mkt, China King, Cici's Pizza, Coney Island, Finley's Rest., Hooters, Jet's Pizza, KFC, Legend's Grill, LJ Silver, Los Tres Amigos, Mr Taco, New China, Pizza Hut, Steak'n Shake, Texas Roadhouse, Wendy's, White Castle/Church's, Zeus Rest., **lodging:** Day's Inn, Econolodge, Governors Inn, Regent Inn, Super 8, **other:** HOSPITAL, Aldi Foods, Belle Tire, Cadillac, Chevrolet, Chrysler/Jeep, Discount Tire, Dodge, Family$, GMC, Harley-Davidson, Hyundai, Kia/Suzuki, Lexus, Lincoln/Mercury, Meijer/dsl/24hr, Mitsubishi, Radio Shack, Saab, Sam's Club/gas, Target, Toyota, Walgreen, **S**...**gas:** Marathon, Speedway/24hr, **food:** Buffalo's SW Café, Burger King, China East Buffet, Dairy Dan, Flapjack's Rest., Hungry Howie, Kang's Buffet, McDonald's, Ponderosa, Sir Pizza,

Subway, **lodging:** Holiday Inn, **other:** AutoZone, Budget Tire, CarQuest, Family$, Kroger, L&L Foods, Lowe's Whse

101 MI 99, MLK Blvd, to Eaton Rapids, **0-3 mi N**...**gas:** Meijer/dsl/24hr, QD, **food:** Arby's, **S**...**gas:** Speedway/Subway/dsl/24hr, Sunoco/dsl, **food:** Coach's Grill, McDonald's, Wendy's

98b a Lansing Rd, to Lansing, **N**...**food:** Arby's, Wendy's, **lodging:** AmeriHost, **S**...**gas:** Citgo/dsl/Windmill Rest./24hr, Don's Trkstp, **food:** Coyote Creek Grill

97 I-69, US 27 S, S to Ft Wayne, N to Lansing

95 I-496, to Lansing

93b a MI 43, Lp 69, Saginaw Hwy, to Grand Ledge, **N**...**gas:** Meijer/dsl/24hr, Shell, Speedway/dsl, **food:** Bennigan's, Burger King, Carrabba's, Denny's, Dolly's Pizza, Fine China, Frank's Grill, Jet's Pizza, McDonald's, Outback Steaks, Red Robin, Roxy's Grill, TGIFriday, Subway, **lodging:** Best Western, Fairfield Inn, Hampton Inn, Holiday Inn, Motel 6, Quality Suites, Red Roof Inn, Residence Inn, **other:** HOSPITAL, NAPA, Kohl's, Kroger, Walgreens, **S**...**gas:** BP/24hr, QD, Sunoco/McDonald's, **food:** Arby's, Art's Pizza, Beaner's, Bob Evans, Cracker Barrel, Steak'n Shake, Subway, **lodging:** SpringHill Suites, **other:** Belle Tire, Buick/Pontiac/GMC, Discount Tire, Gander Mtn, Mazda/Volvo, Lowe's Whse, Michael's, PetsMart, Staples, Wal-Mart SuperCtr

92mm Grand River

91 I-69 N, US 27 N(from wb), to Flint, **S**...**gas:** ♦/Flying J/Country Mkt/dsl/24hr

90 Grand River Ave, to airport, no services

89 I-69 N, US 27 N(from eb), to Flint

87mm rest area eb, full(handicapped)facilities, phone, picnic tables, litter barrels, vending, petwalk

86 MI 100, Wright Rd, to Grand Ledge, **S**...**gas:** Mobil/McDonald's/dsl, Speedway/Subway/24hr

84 to Eagle, Westphalia, no services

79mm rest area wb, full(handicapped)facilities, info, phone, picnic tables, litter barrels, vending, petwalk

77 Lp 96, Grand River Ave, Portland, **N**...**gas:** BP/24hr, Marathon/dsl, Shell/Burger King, Speedway/dsl, **food:** Arby's, China Star, Little Caesar's, Hungry Howie's, McDonald's, Subway, Two Rivers Rest., Wendy's, **lodging:** Best Western, **other:** Family$, Ford, Rite Aid, Tom's Foods, **S**...**food:** Wendy's, **other:** Ford

76 Kent St, Portland, no services

76mm Grand River

73 to Lyons-Muir, Grand River Ave

69mm weigh sta both lanes

67 MI 66, to Ionia, Battle Creek, **N**...**gas:** Meijer/dsl/24hr(4mi), Pilot/Subway/dsl/scales/24hr, **food:** Corner Landing Grill, **lodging:** AmeriHost(6mi), Midway Motel, Super 8, **other:** HOSPITAL, Meijer, Wal-Mart SuperCtr(4mi), RV camping, st police

Lansing

E	64	to Lake Odessa, Saranac, **N**...Ionia St RA, **S**...I-96 Speedway
	63mm	**rest area eb, full(handicapped)facilities, phone, picnic tables, litter barrels, petwalk, vending**
	59	Clarksville, no services
	52	MI 50, to Lowell, **N**...**gas:** Mobil/Subway/dsl, **other:** fairgrounds, **S**...**gas:** Marathon/Noble Roman's/dsl(2mi), **other:** RV camping
W	46	rd 6, to rd 37, no services
	46mm	Thornapple River
	44	36 St, **S**...airport
	43b a	MI 11, 28th St, Cascade, **N**...**gas:** Marathon/dsl, Meijer/dsl/24hr, **food:** Big Boy, Brann's Steaks, Burger King, Culver's, Macaroni Grill, Panera Bread, Pizza Hut, Quizno's, Sundance Grill, Subway, Wendy's, **lodging:** Baymont Inn, Best Western, Country Inn Suites, Crowne Plaza Hotel, Holiday Inn Express, Howard Johnson, **other:** Audi/Subaru/Porsche, Meijer, Mercedes/Volvo/VW, Wal-Mart, **S**...**gas:** BP, Citgo, Shell, Speedway/dsl, **food:** Applebee's, Arby's, Arnie's Rest., Bennigan's, Bob Evans, Burger King, Carabba's, Carlos O'Kelley's, Cantina Mexican, Chili's, ChuckeCheese, Cold Stone, Denny's, Don Pablo, Grand Rapids Brewery, Honey Baked Ham, Hooters, IHOP, Jimmy Johns, Moe's SW Grill, Noodles & Co, Olive Garden, Panera Bread, Perkins, Smokey Bones, Subway, **lodging:** Comfort Inn, Days Inn, Extended Stay America, Fairfield Inn, Hampton Inn, Hilton, Holiday Inn, Homewood Suites, Knight's Inn, Motel 6, Quality Inn, Ramada, Red Roof Inn, Sleep Inn, Springhill Suites, **other:** Acura/Audi/Subaru, Barnes&Noble, Belle Tire, CarQuest, Circuit City, Costco/gas, $Tree, Ford, Fresh Mkt Foods, Gander Mtn, Home Depot, Jo-Ann Fabrics, Lentz Automotive, Lowe's Whse, Nissan, Old Navy, PetsMart, Sam's Club/gas, Staples, Target, TJ Maxx, U-Haul
	40b a	Cascade Rd, **N**...**gas:** Forrest Hills Fuel, Marathon/dsl, **food:** Beaners Rest., Blimpie, China Garden, Forrest Hills Rest, Little Bangkok, Subway, **other:** 7-11/24hr, vet, **S**...**gas:** Shell/Quizno's/dsl, Speedway/dsl, **food:** Jimmy John's, Zoup, **other:** HOSPITAL, Keystone Drug
	39	MI 21(from eb), to Flint
	38	E Beltline Ave, to MI 21, MI 37, MI 44, **N**...**gas:** BP, Meijer/dsl, **food:** O'Charley's, **other:** Meijer, RV camping, **S**...**food:** Uno Pizzaria, **lodging:** Country Inn Suites, **other:** HOSPITAL
	37	I-196(from wb, exits left), Gerald Ford Fwy, to Grand Rapids
	36	Leonard St, **1-2mi S**...**food:** Arby's, McDonald's(24hr), **other:** sheriff's dept
	33	Plainfield Ave, MI 44 Connector, **N**...**gas:** BP, Meijer/dsl/24hr, Speedway, **food:** Arby's, Beaners, Big Apple Bagel, Blimpie, Buddy's Pizza, Cheers Grill, Fred's Pizza, Golden Dragon, KFC, Little Caesar's, Little Caesars, LJ Silver, McDonald's, Oriental Forrest., Papa Ramano's Pizza, Pizza Hut, Russ' Rest., Taco Bell, Wendy's, **lodging:** Grand Inn, Lazy T Motel, **other:** AutoZone, Belle Tire, BigLots, CarQuest, Chevrolet, Chrysler/Jeep, Discount Tire, Dodge, Firestone, Ford, Lincoln/Mercury, Lowe's, Mitsubishi, Goodyear/auto, K-Mart, Meijer, Midas, NAPA, Nissan/VW, NTB, Jeep, Radio Shack, Save-a-Lot

		Foods, Toyota, U-Haul, Walgreens, transmissions, vet, **S** **gas:** BP/24hr, **food:** Breakfast Nook, Denny's
	31mm	Grand River
	31b a	US 131, N to Cadillac, S to Kalamazoo, **1 mi N**...**gas:** **food:** McDonald's
	30b a	Alpine Ave, Grand Rapids, **N**...**gas:** Marathon, 7-11/g **food:** Applebee's, Bennigan's, Buffalo Wild Wings, Che ers, ChuckeCheese, Cold Stone, Culvers, El Burroti Mexic Fire Mtn Grill, First Wok, IHOP, Jimmy John's, Logan's Ro house, McDonald's, Old Country Buffet, Olive Garden, C back Steaks, Panera Bread, Peppino's Pizza, Perkins, Q ba, Quizno's, Russ' Rest., Ryan's, Starbucks, Steak'n Sha Subway, Taco Bell, TGIFriday, Tuesday Morning, Zoup, **lo ing:** Hampton Inn, SpringHill Suites, **other:** Aldi Foods, toZone, Belle Tire, Best Buy, CarQuest, Circuit City, Disco Tire, $Tree, Ford/Kia, Kohl's, Marshall's, Michael's, NA PepBoys, Radio Shack, Sam's Club/gas, Schuler Books, get, TJ Maxx, Walgreens, Wal-Mart SuperCtr/auto, **S**...g Admiral/dsl, Marathon, Meijer/dsl/24hr, Speedway/dsl, **fo** Arby's, Burger King, Casa De Martina, Fazoli's, KFC, LJ ver, McDonald's, Papa John's, Pizza Hut, Ponderosa, W dy's, **lodging:** Motel 6, **other:** Goodyear/auto, Home De Jo-Ann Fabrics, Meijer, Midas, Tuffy Auto, U-Haul
	28	Walker Ave, **S**...**gas:** Meijer/dsl/24hr, **food:** Bob Evans, Donald's, **lodging:** Baymont Inn, Quality In
	26	Fruit Ridge Ave, **N**...**gas:** Citgo/dsl, **S**...**gas:** Citgo/deli/ds
	25mm	**rest area eb, full(handicapped)facilities, phone, pic tables, litter barrels, petwalk**
	25	(24 from eb), 8th Ave, 4Mile Rd(from wb), **S**...**gas:** Marath dsl, **lodging:** Wayside Motel
	23	Marne, **N**...**other:** tires, **S**...**food:** Depot Café, Rinaldi's C **other:** USPO, Ernie's Mkt, fairgrounds/raceway
	19	Lamont, Coopersville, **N**...**food:**, **S**...**food:** Sam's Joint R **other:** LP
	16	B-35, Eastmanville, **N**...**gas:** BP/Subway/dsl, Speedw dsl/24hr, Shell/Burger King/dsl, **food:** Arby's, Little Caes McDonald's, Taco Bell, **lodging:** AmeriHost, Rodeway **other:** Chevrolet/Poniac/Buick, Curves, Family Fare, Fu Sun RV Ctr, Jeep/Dodge, Rite Aid, **S**...**gas:** Pacific Pride **other:** RV camping
	10	B-31(exits left from eb), Nunica, **N**...**food:** Turk's Rest., **gas:** Marathon, **other:** RV camping, golf course/rest.
	9	MI 104(from wb, exits left), to Grand Haven, Spring Lake, **gas:** Marathon, **other:** to Grand Haven SP
	8mm	**rest area wb, full(handicapped)facilities, phone, pie tables, litter barrels, vending, petwalk**
	5	Fruitport(from wb, no return), no services
	4	Airline Rd, **N**...**other:** race track, **S**...**gas:** Speedway Wesco/dsl, **food:** Burger Crest Diner, Dairy Bar, McDona Subway, Village Inn, **other:** Grover Drug, NAPA, Orchard Foods, Pleasure Island Water Park(5mi), USPO, to PJ master SP
	1c	Hile Rd(from eb), **S**...**other:** racetrack
	1b a	US 31, to Ludington, Grand Haven, **N**...**lodging:** Alpine M Bel-aire Motel, Haven Motel, **other:** All Seasons RV C **mi N on Sherman Blvd**...**gas:** Citgo/dsl, Westco/dsl, **fo** Applebee's, Arby's, Fazoli's, McDonald's, Old Country Bu Pizza Ranch, Red Wok, Ruby Tuesday, Subway, Wen **lodging:** Comfort Inn/rest., **other:** HOSPITAL, Circuit Lowe's Whse, PetsMart, Radio Shack, Sam's Club, Sta Target, Wal-Mart SuperCtr/24hr/gas, **S**...**lodging:** AmeriH **other:** airport, racetrack
		I-96 begins/ends on US 31 at Muskegon.

Grand Rapids

Muskegon

Interstate 196(Grand Rapids)

Exit #	Services
81mm	I-196 begins/ends on I-96, 37mm in E Grand Rapids.
79	Fuller Ave, 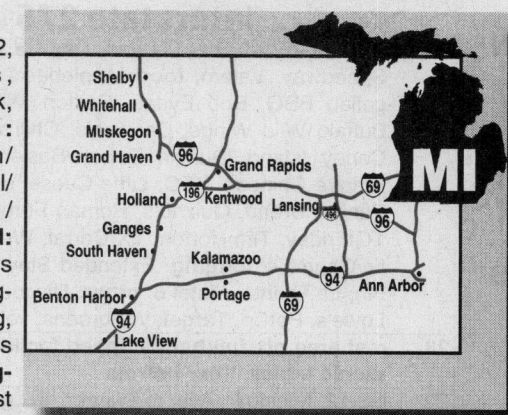**N**...sheriff, **S**...**gas:** Shell/dsl, Speedway/dsl, **food:** Buddy's Pizza/Dogs, Checkers, Elbow Room, KFC, Subway, Taco Bell, Wendy's, **other:** HOSTIPAL, Ace Hardware, Family Foods, Walgreens
78	College Ave, **S**...**gas:** Marathon/Circle K, **food:** McDonald's, **other:** HOSPITAL, Rite Aid, ford museum
77c	Ottawa Ave, downtown, **S**...Gerald R Ford Museum
77b a	US 131, S to Kalamazoo, N to Cadillac
76	MI 45 E, Lane Ave, **S**...**food:** El Ganadero Mexican, **other:** Gerald R Ford Museum, John Ball Park&Zoo, Parts+
75	MI 45 W, Lake Michigan Dr, **N**...to Grand Valley St U
74mm	Grand River
73	Market Ave, **N**...to Vanandel Arena
72	Lp 196, Chicago Dr E(from eb)
70	MI 11(exits left from wb), Grandville, Walker, **S**...**gas:** BP/Subway/dsl, Shell/repair, **lodging:** Day's Inn, **other:** USPO, vet
69b a	Chicago Dr, **N**...**gas:** Meijer/dsl/24hr, **food:** China City, Culver's, KFC, McDonald's, Papa John's, Peppino's Pizza, Perkins, Subway, Taco Bell, **other:** Aldi Foods, AutoZone, BigLots, $General, $Tree, Meijer, Radio Shack, Save-a-Lot Foods, 7-11, Target, **S**...**gas:** Admiral, Speedway/24 hr, **food:** Adobe Mexican, Arby's, Burger King, Dunkin Donuts/Baskin-Robbins, Little Caesar's, Pizza Hut, Russ' Rest., Wendy's, **lodging:** Best Western, Holiday Inn Express, **other:** NAPA
67	44th St, **N**...**gas:** Mobil/dsl, **food:** Burger King, Cracker Barrel, Panera Bread, Steak'n Shake, **lodging:** Comfort Suites, **other:** AAA, Honda, Wal-Mart/auto, **S**...**food:** Famous Dave's, Logan's Roadhouse, Quizno's, Ritter's Custard, Starbucks, Wendy's, **lodging:** Residence Inn(2mi), **other:** Circuit City, Discount Tire, Gander Mtn., Lowe's Whse, PetsMart, World Mkt
64	MI 6 E, to Lansing(exits left from wb)
62	32nd Ave, to Hudsonville, **N**...**gas:** BP/dsl/24hr, Citgo/dsl, **food:** Arby's, Burger King, Maurizio's Pizza, McDonald's, Village Grill, **lodging:** Quality Inn, **other:** Chevrolet, camping, **S**...**gas:** Mobil/Subway/dsl/24hr, **food:** Rainbow Grill, **lodging:** Super 8, **other:** Harley-Davidson, Harvest Foods
58mm	**rest area eb, full(handicapped)facilities, phone, picnic tables, litter barrels, vending, petwalk**
55	Byron Rd, Zeeland, **N**...**gas:** 7-11, **food:** Blimpie, McDonald's, **other:** Curves, 3-5 mi **N**...HOSPITAL, to Holland SP
52	16th St, Adams St, **2 mi N**...**gas:** Meijer/dsl/24hr, **food:** Wendy's, **lodging:** Best Inn, Econolodge, **other:** HOSPITAL, Meijer, **S**...**gas:** Mobil/Subway/dsl, **food:** Burger King
49	MI 40, to Allegan, **N**...**gas:** BP/McDonald's/dsl, **lodging:** Residence Inn, **S**...**gas:** Tulip City/Marathon/dsl/scales/24hr, **food:** Rock Island Rest.
44	US 31 N(from eb), to Holland, **3-5 mi N**...**lodging:** Country Inn, **other:** HOSPITAL, gas, food
43mm	**rest area wb, full(handicapped)facilities, info, phone, picnic tables, litter barrels, vending, petwalk**

41	rd A-2, Douglas, Saugatuck, **N**...**gas:** Marathon/dsl, Shell/Subway/dsl, **food:** Babaloo's Pizza, Burger King, Spectators Grill, **lodging:** Best Western(1mi), Hootin Motel, Timberline Motel(3mi), **other:** $General, NAPA, Saugatuck RV Resort, to Saugatuck SP, **S**...**food:** Ravine's Rest(1mi), **food:** Belvedere Inn, **lodging:** Shangrai-la Motel, **other:** Red Barn Gifts
38mm	Kalamazoo River
36	rd A-2, Ganges, **N**...**gas:** Shell, **lodging:** AmericInn
34	MI 89, to Fennville, **N**...to West Side CP, **S**...**gas:** Shell/24hr, **other:** Cranes Pie Pantry(4mi, seasonal), Lyons Fruits, Winery Tours
30	rd A-2, Glenn, Ganges, **N**...to Westside Cty Park
25mm	**rest area eb, full(handicapped)facilities, phone, picnic tables, litter barrels, vending, petwalk**
26	109th Ave, to Pullman, no services
22	N Shore Dr, **N**...**food:** Tello's Ristorante, **other:** to Kal Haven Trail SP, Cousin's RV Camping/rest.
20	rd A-2, Phoenix Rd, **N**...**gas:** BP/dsl, Marathon/dsl, **food:** Arby's, Checkers, China Buffet, Taco Bell, **lodging:** SouthHaven Motel, **other:** HOSPITAL, AutoZone, Walgreens, st police, **S**...**gas:** Shell, **food:** Big Boy, McDonald's, Sherman's Dairybar, Wendy's, **lodging:** Comfort Suites, Hampton Inn, Holiday Inn Express, Ramada, **other:** $General, Wal-Mart SuperCtr/gas/dsl/24hr
18	MI 140, MI 43, to Watervliet, **0-2 mi N**...**gas:** BP, Shell/dsl/24hr, Xpress/dsl, **food:** Burger King, 50's Drive Inn, McDonald's, Pizza Hut, **lodging:** Great Lakes Inn, LakeBluff Motel, **other:** AutoValue Parts, Buick/Pontiac/Cadillac/GMC, Chevrolet, Chrysler/Dodge/Jeep, Ford, Village Mkt Foods
13	to Covert, **N**...to Van Buren SP, RV camping
7	MI 63, to Benton Harbor, **N**...**food:** DiMaggio's Pizza, Vitale's Mkt/subs, **other:** RV camping
4	to Coloma, Riverside, **S**...**gas:** Marathon/dsl, **other:** KOA
2mm	Paw Paw River
1	Red Arrow Hwy, **N**...Ross Field Airport
0mm	I-94, E to Detroit, W to Chicago

I-196 begins/ends on I-94, exit 34 at Benton Harbor.

Interstate 275(Livonia)

Exit #	Services
	I-275 and I-96 run together 9 miles. See Michigan Interstate 96, exits 165-170.
29	I-96 E, to Detroit, MI 14 W, to Ann Arbor
28	Ann Arbor Rd, Plymouth, **E**...**gas:** BP/Dunkin Donuts/24hr, Shell, **food:** Atlantis Rest., Denny's, Little Caesars, **lodging:** Days Inn, Red Roof Inn, **W**...**food:** Bennigan's, Burger King, McDonald's, Steak&Ale, **lodging:** Comfort Inn, **other:** Cadillac, CVS Drug, Dodge, K-Mart, Lincoln/Mercury, vet

E ↕ **W**

H o l l a n d

B e n t o n   H a r b o r

N ↕ S

MICHIGAN

Interstate 275

Livonia

Exit #	Services
25	MI 153, Ford Rd, Garden City, W...**gas:** BP, Shell, Speedway, Valero, **food:** Applebee's, Arby's, BD Mongolian BBQ, Bob Evans, Boston Mkt., Bowery Grille, Buffalo Wild Wings, Carraba's, Chili's, ChuckeCheese, Coney Island, Dunkin Donuts/Baskin-Robbins, Hunan Empire Chinese, KFC, Little Caesar's, Outback Steaks, Panera Bread, Quizno's, Roman Forum Rest., Subway, TGIFriday, Tim Horton, TX Corral, Wendy's, White Castle/Church's, **lodging:** Extended Stay America, Fairfield Inn, La Quinta, Motel 6, **other:** Discount Tire, Firestone, Lowe's, PetCo, Target, Walgreens, vet
23	**rest area nb, full(handicapped facilities), phone, info, picnic tables, litter barrels**
22	US 12, Michigan Ave, to Wayne, E...**gas:** BP/24hr, Marathon, Shell, Valero/dsl, **food:** Arby's, Jonathan's Rest., McDonald's, Subway, Wendy's, **lodging:** Day's Inn, Fellows Cr Motel, Holiday Inn Express, Super 8, Willo Acres Motel, W...**gas:** Marathon/dsl, 7-11, **food:** Dunkin Donuts, McDonald's
20	Ecorse Rd, to Romulus, E...**gas:** 7-11, W...**gas:** Mobil/Burger King/scales/dsl/24hr
17	I-94 E to Detroit, W to Ann Arbor, E...airport
15	Eureka Rd, E...**gas:** Shell, airport
13	Sibley Rd, New Boston, W...**gas:** Fusion/Subway/dsl, **food:** LC's Chicken, **other:** to Lower Huron Metro Park
11	S Huron Rd, 1 mi W...**gas:** Sunoco/Burger King/dsl, **food:** Jacob's Rest, **other:** RV LP(1mi)
8	Will Carleton Rd, to Flat Rock
5	Carleton, South Rockwood, W...food
4mm	**rest area sb, full(handicapped)facilities, phone, picnic tables, litter barrels**
2	US 24, to Telegraph Rd, W...**gas:** Marathon/dsl, lodging
0mm	I-275 begins/ends on I-75, exit 20.

Interstate 475(Flint)

Flint

Exit #	Services
17.5mm	I-475 begins/ends on I-75, exit 125.
15	Clio Rd, W...**gas:** BP, **other:** Chevrolet
13	Saginaw St, E...**gas:** BP, **food:** McDonald's, Papa John's, Taco Bell, **other:** Advanced Parts, Family$, Kroger/gas, W...**gas:** Marathon, Sunoco, **food:** Burger King, KFC, Little Caesar's
11	Carpenter Rd, no services
10	Pierson Rd, no services
9	rd 54, Dort Hwy, Stewart Ave, E...**gas:** Citgo, **food:** McDonald's
8mm	Flint River
8b	Davison Rd, Hamilton Ave, no services
8a	Longway Blvd, W...**food:** China 1 Buffet, **lodging:** Holiday Inn Express, **other:** HOSPITAL, USPO
7	rd 21, Court St, downtown Flint
6	I-69, W to Lansing, E to Port Huron
5	Atherton Rd(from sb), E...**gas:** Citgo, Marathon, **other:** Curves
4	Hemphill Rd, Bristol Rd, E...**gas:** Sunoco, **food:** Benitos Pizza, McDonald's, New China, **other:** Rite Aid, W...**gas:** Speedway, **food:** Little Caesars, Ole Time Burgers, Tim Horton, Wendy's, **other:** Family$, Kroger/gas
2	Hill Rd, E...**gas:** Speedway, **food:** Applebee's, Bob Evans, **lodging:** Wingate Inn, **other:** Ford, vet, W...**gas:** Sunoco/Tim Horton, **food:** Arby's, Bangkok Peppers, Blimpie, Burger St Grill, Little Caesars, Pizza Hut, Wendy's, **lodging:** Courtyard, Holiday Inn, Residence Inn, **other:** Rite Aid
0mm	I-475 begins/ends on I-75, exit 111

Interstate 696(Detroit)

Detroit Area

Exit #	Services
	I-696 begins/ends on I-94.
28	I-94 E to Port Huron, W to Detroit, 11 Mile Rd, E...**gas:** BP/dsl, Speedway, 7-11
27	MI 3, Gratiot Ave, N...**gas:** BP, **food:** National Coney Island, **other:** Costco/gas, S...**gas:** BP, Mobil/McDonald's, **food:** White Castle, **other:** Goodyear/auto
26	MI 97, Groesbeck Ave, Roseville, N...**gas:** Mobil/dsl, S...**gas:** Marathon, **food:** Wendy's
24	Hoover Rd, Schoenherr Rd, N...**gas:** Sunoco, **food:** Burger King, KFC, S...**gas:** BP, Mobil, **food:**'s, Subway, Taco Bell, Tim Horton, **lodging:** Holiday Inn Express, **other:** CVS Drug, Kroger, Marshall's
23	MI 53, Van Dyke Ave, N...**gas:** BP, **food:** Arby's, Coney Island, Dunkin Donuts, McDonald's, **lodging:** Baymont Inn, **other:** Cadillac/Pontiac/GMC, Dodge, Jo-Ann Fabrics, radiators, S...**gas:** BP/24hr, **food:** Burger King, **other:** Chevrolet, Ford, Toyota, USPO
22	Mound Rd, no services
20	Ryan Rd, Dequindre Rd, N...**gas:** Marathon, **food:** IHOP, **lodging:** Knight's Inn, Red Roof Inn, S...**food:** Bob Evans, McDonald's, **lodging:** Comfort Suites, Ramada Ltd, **other:** Rite Aid, transmissions
19	Couzens St, 10 Mile Rd, S...Hazel Park Racetrack
18	I-75 N to Flint, S to Detroit
17	Campbell Ave, Hilton Ave, Bermuda, Mohawk, S...**gas:** Marathon/dsl
16	MI 1, Woodward Ave, Main St, N...**food:** Burger King, **other:** zoo
14	Coolidge Rd, 10 Mile Rd, S...**gas:** Mobil, Speedway, **food:** Dunkin Donuts, **food:** Jade Palace Chinese, Little Caesar's, LJ Silver, Pizza Hut, Subway, Taco Bell, Wendy's, **other:** CVS Drug, Jo-Ann Fabrics
13	Greenfield Rd, S...**gas:** Mobil, Sunoco, **food:** Dunkin Donuts, **other:** Ford
12	MI 39, Southfield Rd, 11 Mile Rd, S...**gas:** Shell
11	Evergreen Rd, S...**lodging:** Residence Inn
10	US 24, Telegraph Rd, N...**gas:** BP, Marathon, **food:** Denny's, Seoul Garden Korean, **lodging:** Hampton Inn, Embassy Suites, **other:** Belle Tire, Best Buy, Chevrolet, Chrysler/Jeep, Circuit City, Dodge, $General, Farmer Jack's, Ford, Honda/Nissan/Isuzu, Hyundai, Jo-Ann Fabrics, K-Mart, Lexus, Lincoln/Mercury, Office Depot, Pontiac/Buick, USPO, mall, S...**gas:** Mobil, **lodging:** Courtyard, Hilton, Holiday Inn, Marriott
8	MI 10, Lodge Fwy, no services
5	Orchard Lake Rd, Farmington Hills, N...**gas:** Marathon, Mobil, Shell, **food:** Arby's, Hong Hua Chinese, Roberto's Rest., Ruby Tuesday, Starbucks, Steak&Ale, Steamer's Seafood, Subway, Wendy's, **lodging:** Comfort Inn, **other:** Discount Tire, to St Mary's Coll
1	(from wb), I-96 W, I-275 S, to MI 5, Grand River Ave

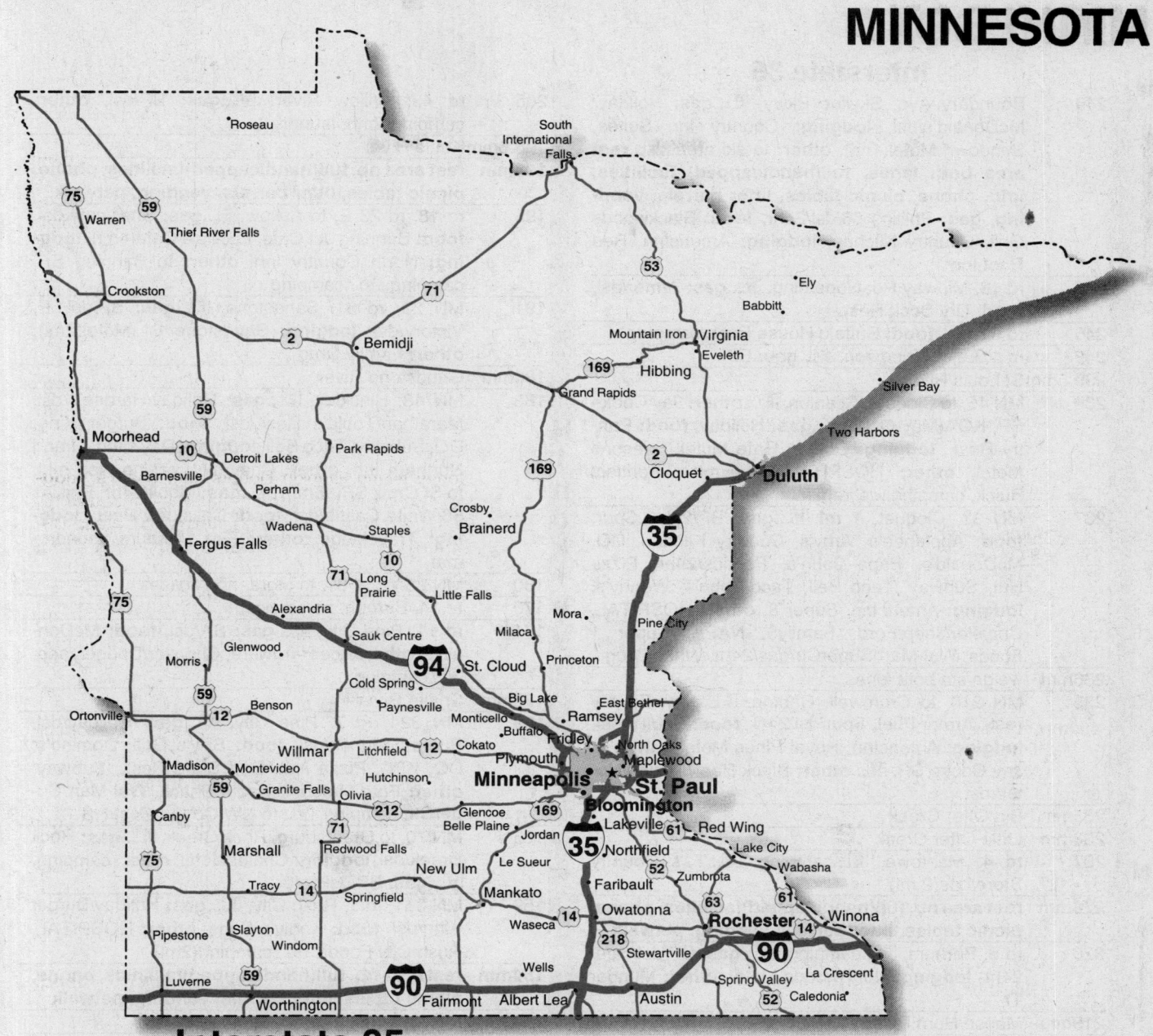

MINNESOTA

Interstate 35

N ↑↓ S Duluth

Exit #	Services
260mm	I-35 begins/ends on MN 61 in Duluth.
259	MN 61, London Rd, to Two Harbors, North Shore, W...gas: Holiday/dsl, ICO/dsl, Spur/dsl, food: Blackwoods Grill, Burger King, KFC, McDonald's, Perkins, Pizza Hut, Subway, Taco John's, Wendy's, lodging: Edgewater Inn, other: vet
258	21st Ave E(from nb), to U of MN at Duluth, same as 259
256b	Mesaba Ave, Superior St, E...gas: ICO/DQ, food: Caribou Coffee, Grandma's Grill, Little Angie's Cantina, Red Lobster, Timberlodge Steaks, Tradewinds Rest., lodging: Canal Park Inn, Comfort Suites, Hampton Inn, Hawthorn Suites, Lake Superior Inn, W...lodging: Holiday Inn, Radisson, Sheraton
256a	Michigan St, E...waterfront, W...HOSPITAL, downtown
255a	US 53 N, downtown, mall, W...other: Kia

Exit #	Services
255b	I-535 spur, to Wisconsin
254	27th Ave W, W...gas: Holiday/Burger King/dsl, Spur/dsl, food: Embers Grill, Quizno's, Subway, lodging: Motel 6
253b	40th Ave W, W...gas: BP/dsl/24hr, food: Perkins/24hr, lodging: Comfort Inn, Super 8
253a	US 2 E, US 53, to Wisconsin
252	Central Ave, W Duluth, W...gas: Conoco/dsl, Holiday/dsl/24hr, food: Coffee Express, Giant Panda, KFC, McDonald's, Pizza Hut, Sammy's Café, Subway, other: Advance Parts, Checker Parts, Falk's Drug, K-Mart, Super 1 Foods, Walgreen, vet
251b	MN 23 S, Grand Ave, E...lodging: Holiday Inn Express
251a	Cody St, E...lodging: Allyndale Motel, other: zoo
250	US 2 W(from sb), to Grand Rapids, 1/2 mi W...gas: Holiday/dsl, Mobil/dsl/LP, food: Blackwoods Grill, Wok-n-Grill, lodging: AmericInn

N
↑
↓
S

Exit	Description
249	Boundary Ave, Skyline Pkwy, E...gas: Holiday/McDonald's/dsl, lodging: Country Inn Suites, Sundown Motel(1mi), other: to ski area, W...rest area both lanes, full(handicapped) facilities, info, phone, picnic tables, litter barrels, vending, gas: Phillips 66/dsl/24hr, food: Blackwoods Grill, Country Kitchen, lodging: AmericInn, Red Roof Inn
246	rd 13, Midway Rd, Nopeming, W...gas: Armor/dsl, food: Dry Dock Rest.
245	rd 61, E...food: Buffalo House Rest./camping
242	rd 1, Esko, Thomson, E...gas: BP
239.5mm	St Louis River
239	MN 45, to Cloquet, Scanlon, E...other: Jay Cooke SP, KOA(May-Oct), W...gas: Holiday, food: Pantry Rest., lodging: Golden Gate Motel, Seasons Motel, other: HOSPITAL, Chevrolet, Pontiac/Buick, camping, dsl repair
237	MN 33, Cloquet, 1 mi W...gas: BP/24hr, Spur, food: Applebee's, Arby's, Country Kitchen, DQ, McDonald's, Papa John's, Perkins/24hr, Pizza Hut, Subway, Taco Bell, Taco John's, Wendy's, lodging: AmericInn, Super 8, other: HOSPITAL, Chrysler/Jeep/Ford, Family$, NAPA, Super 1 Foods, Wal-Mart SuperCtr/gas/24hr, White Drug
236mm	weigh sta both lanes
235	MN 210, to Cromwell, Carlton, E...gas: BP/dsl/rest., Armor Fuel, Spur/dsl/24hr, food: Spirit Rest, lodging: AmericInn, Royal Pines Motel, other: to Jay Cooke SP, W...other: Black Bear Casino/Hotel/rest.
235mm	Big Otter Creek
233mm	Little Otter Creek
227	rd 4, Mahtowa, E...camping, W...TJ's Country Store/gas(2 mi)
226mm	rest area nb, full(handicapped)facilities, phone, picnic tables, litter barrels, vending, petwalk
220	rd 6, Barnum, E...camping, W...gas: BP/dsl/café/24hr, lodging: Northwoods Motel, other: Munger Tr
219mm	Moose Horn River
218mm	Moose Horn River
216	MN 27(from sb, no EZ return), Moose Lake, 1-2 mi W...gas: BP, Cenex, Holiday/dsl, Spur, The Little Store, food: Art's Café, Blue Bear Cafe, DQ, lodging: AmericInn(4mi), Moose Lake Motel, other: HOSPITAL, CarQuest, Chevrolet/Buick/Pontiac, Ford, Super Valu Foods, 1918 Museum, to Munger Trail
214	rd 73(no EZ return from nb), E...other: Alco, Moose Lake SP(2mi), camping, W...gas: Conoco/Subway/dsl, lodging: AmericInn, 2 mi W...lodging: Moose Lake Motel, other: HOSPITAL, Munger Trail, Red Fox Camping
209	rd 46, Sturgeon Lake, Sturgeon Lake E...gas: Phillips 66, W...lodging: Sturgeon Lake Motel, food: Ernie's Rest.(seasonal), other: camping(3mi)
209mm	rest area sb, full(handicapped)facilities, phone, picnic tables, litter barrels, vending, petwalk
206.5mm	Willow River
205	rd 43, Willow River, W...gas: BP/dsl, other: camping(2mi), laundry
198.5mm	Kettle River
198mm	rest area nb, full(handicapped)facilities, phone, picnic tables, litter barrels, vending, petwalk
195	rd 18, rd 23 E, to Askov, E...gas: Shell/cafe/dsl, food: Banning Jct Cafe, Lucille's Cafe(4mi), lodging: North Country Inn, other: to Banning SP, camping, W...camping
191	MN 23, rd 61, Sandstone, E...gas: BP/dsl/LP, Victory/dsl, lodging: Sandstone 61 Motel(2mi), other: Family Drug
184mm	Grindstone River
183	MN 48, Hinckley, E...gas: Holiday/Hardee's/dsl, Marathon/Tobie's Rest./dsl, food: Burger King, DQ, Subway, Taco Bell, lodging: Day's Inn, Grand Northern Inn, other: Chevrolet, casino, flea mkt, to St Croix SP(15mi), W...gas: Mobil/24hr, Phillips 66/White Castle/dsl, food: Cassidy's Rest., lodging: Travelodge, other: Fire Museum, laundromat
180	MN 23 W, rd 61, to Mora, no services
175	rd 14, Beroun, no services
171	rd 11, Pine City, E...gas: SA/dsl, food: McDonald's, other: Ace Hardware, Chrysler/Dodge/Jeep, W...camping
170mm	Snake River
169	MN 324, rd 7, Pine City, E...gas: Holiday/dsl, Pump-n-Munch/dsl, food: Billy's Grill, Domino's, DQ, KFC, Pizza Hut, Red Shed Rest., Subway, other: Ford/Mercury, Radio Shack, Wal-Mart SuperCtr, camping, W...to NW Co Fur Post HS
165	MN 70, to Grantsburg, Rock Creek, E...gas: Rock Creek/dsl, lodging: Chalet Motel, other: camping, W...gas: BP/dsl/café
159	MN 361, rd 1, Rush City, E...gas: Holiday/Burger King/dsl, food: Kooly's Subs, other: HOSPITAL, Rush City Foods, W...camping(2mi)
154mm	rest area nb, full(handicapped)facilities, phone, picnic tables, litter barrels, vending, petwalk
152	rd 10, Harris, 2 mi E...gas/dsl
147	MN 95, to Cambridge, North Branch, E...gas: Casey's, Conoco/dsl, Holiday/dsl, food: DQ, Domino's, KFC/Taco Bell, McDonald's, Oak Inn Rest., Perkins, Pizza Hut, Subway, lodging: AmericInn, Budget Host, other: CarQuest, Fisk Tire, NAPA, Radio Shack, SuperValu Foods, to Wild River SP(14mi), vet, W...food: Applebee's, Burger King, Denny's, other: Chevrolet, Chrysler/Dodge/Jeep, Ford, Tanger Outlet/famous brands
143	rd 17, new exit
139	rd 19, Stacy, E...gas: BP, Phillips 66, food: Pizza Man, Rustic Rest., Stacy Grill, Subway, other: city park, W...gas: Marathon
135	US 61 S, rd 22, Wyoming, E...gas: BP/dsl, Casey's, food: Cornerstone Café, DQ, Joe's Pizza, Subway, Tasty Asia, other: HOSPITAL, Ace Hardware, CarQuest, IGA Foods, W...gas: Shell/dsl, food: McDonald's, Village Inn Rest., other: camping(10mi), golf

Hinckley

Interstate 35

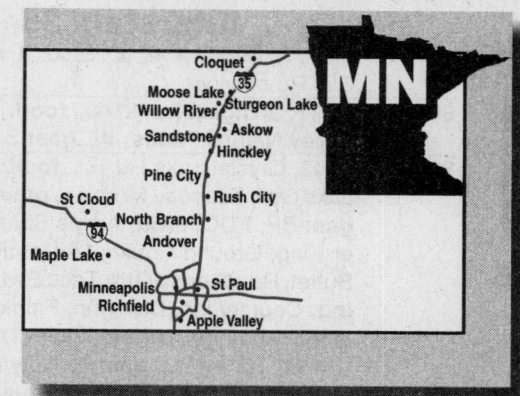

132	US 8(from nb), to Taylors Falls
131	rd 2, Forest Lake, **E**...**gas:** BP/24hr, Holiday/dsl, SA/dsl, **food:** Applebee's, Arby's, Burger King, China Buffet, Cheung Sing Chinese, Culvers, KFC, McDonald's, Papa John's, Perkins, Quack's Cafe, Subway, Sbarro, Taco Bell, White Castle, **lodging:** AmericInn, **other:** HOSPITAL, AutoValue Parts, Champion Auto, Checker Parts, Kennedy Transmissions, Rainbow Foods/24hr, Target, Tires+, Walgreen, Wal-Mart, RV/Auto repair, **W**...**gas:** Holiday/dsl, **food:** Famous Dave's BBQ, Papa Murphy's, Quizno's, Starbucks, Wendy's, **lodging:** Country Inn Suites, **other:** Buick/Pontiac, Chevrolet/Cadillac, Chrysler/Dodge/Jeep, Cub Foods, Ford, GNC, Home Depot, Jiffy Lube
131mm	**rest area sb, full(handicapped)facilities, phone, picnic tables, litter barrels, vending, petwalk**
129	MN 97, rd 23, **E**...camping(6mi), **W**...**gas:** BP/dsl, **other:** Coates RV Ctr, Gander Mtn., camping(1mi)
128mm	weigh sta both lanes
127	I-35W, S to Minneapolis. See I-35W.
123	rd 14, Centerville, **E**...**food:** Dunn Bro.s Coffee, **other:** Otter Lake RV Ctr, **W**...**gas:** Marathon, Mobil/dsl, Shell, **food:** DQ, Embers Rest., Sagers Grill, WiseGuys Pizza, **other:** auto repair
120	rd J(from nb, no return), no services
117	MN 96, **E**...**gas:** Marathon, SA/dsl, **food:** Burger King, Casa Lupita, **lodging:** AmericInn, **other:** Goodyear/auto, NAPA, **W**...**gas:** BP, PDQ, **food:** Applebee's, Arby's/Sbarro's, Caribou Coffee, Culver's, McDonald's, Subway, **other:** Cub Foods, Tires+, USPO, Walgreen
115	rd E, **E**...**gas:** BP, Conoco, SA/dsl, **food:** Jimmy's Rest., Perkins, **lodging:** Country Inn Suites, Holiday Inn Express, **W**...**food:** Dunn Bros Coffee, KFC/Pizza Hut, Major's Cafe, McDonald's, Panera Bread, Papa Murphy's, Wendy's, **other:** Festival Foods, GNC, Radio Shack, Target, Wal-Mart/auto
114	I-694 E(exits left from sb)
113	I-694 W
112	Little Canada Rd, **E**...**gas:** BP, **W**...**gas:** Sinclair, **food:** Porterhouse Rest
111a/b	MN 36 E, to Stillwater/MN 36 W, to Minneapolis
110b	Roselawn Ave, no services
110a	Wheelock Pkwy, **E**...**gas:** BP, Marathon, **food:** Subway, **W**...**gas:** Sinclair/dsl
109	Maryland Ave, **E**...**gas:** Marathon, SA/dsl, **W**... **food:** Wendy's, **other:** K-Mart
108	Pennsylvania Ave, downtown
107c	University Ave, downtown, **E**...**gas:** Conoco, **W**... **other:** HOSPITAL, to st capitol
107b a	I-94, W to Minneapolis, E to St Paul. **I-35 and I-94 run together.**
106c	11th St(from nb), Marion St, downtown
106b	Kellogg Blvd(from nb), downtown, **E**...**food:** Eagle St. Grill, Subway, **lodging:** Holiday Inn, **other:** HOSPITAL
106a	Grand Ave, **E**...HOSPITAL
105	St Clair Ave, no services
104c	Victoria St, Jefferson Ave, no services
104b	Ayd Mill Rd(from nb), no services
104a	Randolph Ave, no services
103b	MN 5, W 7th St, **E**...**food:** Burger King, **W**...**gas:** SA/dsl, **other:** USPO
103a	Shepard Rd(from nb), no services
102mm	Mississippi River
102	MN 13, Sibley Hwy, **W**...**gas:** BP, Holiday/Subway
101b a	MN 110 W, **E**...**food:** Caribou Coffee, Ziggy's Deli, **W**...**gas:** SA
99b a	I-494 W/I-494 E
98	Lone Oak Rd, **E**...**lodging:** Homestead Suites, Microtel, **other:** Sam's Club/gas, USPO, **W**...**gas:** Marathon, **food:** Joe Senser's Grill, Magic Thai Café, **lodging:** Hampton Inn, Residence Inn
97b	Yankee Doodle Rd, **E**...**gas:** Holiday, SA/dsl, **food:** Applebee's, Arby's, Blimpie, Burger King, Cattle Co Rest., Coldstone Creamery, Chili's, Culver's, DQ, Don Pablo, Houlihan's, Jake's Grill, Jimmy John's, KFC, McDonald's, New China Buffet, Noodles & Co, Old Chicago Pizza, Panera Bread, Perkins, Pizza Hut, Pizza Man, Pot Belly, Red Robin, Taco Bell, **lodging:** Residence Inn, Springhill Suites, TownePlace Suites, **other:** Barnes&Noble, Best Buy, Byerly's Foods, Cash Mart, Checker Parts, GNC, Home Depot, Michael's, Office Depot, Old Navy, PetsMart, Rainbow Foods, Tires+, TJ Maxx, Walgreen, **W**...**gas:** BP, SA/dsl, **lodging:** Boston Mkt, Dragon Palace Chinese, Loro Mexican, Starbucks, Steak Bones Grill, **lodging:** Best Western, Extended Stay America, **other:** Italian Pie Shoppe
97a	Pilot Knob Rd, same as 97b, **E**...**gas:** Holiday, **food:** Caribou Coffee, Chilli's, McDonald's, Wendy's, **lodging:** SpringHill Suites, TownePlace Suites, **other:** Firestone, Goodyear, Kennedy Transmissions, Kohl's, Wal-Mart, mall, **W**...**gas:** BP, SA/dsl, **lodging:** Best Western
94	rd 30, Diffley Rd, to Eagan, **E**...**gas:** Shell/dsl, **other:** CVS Drug, **W**...**gas:** Sinclair, **other:** Tires+
93	rd 32, Cliff Rd, **E**...**gas:** Holiday, **food:** Bonfire Grill, Subway, **other:** Ace Hardware, **W**...**gas:** Holiday/dsl, Marathon/dsl, **food:** Baker's Square, Burger King, Boston Mkt, Burger King, DQ, Dolittle's Grill, Greenmill Rest., Hong Wong Chinese, KFC, McDonald's, Quizno's, Starbucks, Taco Bell, Wendy's, **lodging:** Hilton Garden, Holiday Inn Express, Staybridge Suites, **other:** Checker Parts, Cub Foods, Radio Shack, Target, USPO, Walgreen

Interstate 35

N ↑ S

92	MN 77, Cedar Ave, E...Zoo, **1 m** W...access to Cliff Rd services
90	rd 11, E...**gas:** KwikTrip, **food:** Subway, **other:** Valley Natural Foods, W...**gas:** SA/dsl
88b	rd 42, Crystal Lake Rd, E...**food:** Chianti Grill, Ciatti's Grill, Tuesday Morning, **other:** PetsMart, W...**gas:** BP, PDQ, **food:** Arby's/Sbarro's, BBQ, Burger King, Ground Round, McDonald's, Old Country Buffet, Roadhouse Grill, Taco Bell/Pizza Hut, **lodging:** Country Inn, Days Inn, Fairfield Inn, Hampton Inn, Holiday Inn, **other:** HOSPITAL, Home Depot, USPO, **1/2 mi** W...**gas:** Holiday/dsl, SA, Sinclair, **food:** Applebee's, Bakers Square, Buca Italian, Camaranh Bay, Champp's Grill, Chili's, IHOP, KFC, Kings Buffet, Macaroni Grill, Maya Mexican, Olive Garden, Outback Steaks, Panera Bread, Papa John's, Qdoba Mexican, Red Lobster, Starbucks, Wendy's, **lodging:** InTown Suites, **other:** Barnes&Noble, Best Buy, Chevrolet, Circuit City, Cub Foods, Discount Tire, Goodyear/auto, JC Penney, K-Mart, Kohl's, Macy's, Michael's, PetCo, Rainbow Foods, Sears/auto, Target, Tires+, Walgreen, mall
88a	I-35W(from nb), N to Minneapolis. **See I-35W.**
87	Crystal Lake Rd(from nb), W...**gas:** KwikTrip, **other:** Buick, Ford/Lincoln/Mercury, Honda/Nissan, Saturn, Toyota, Beaver Mtn Ski Area
86	rd 46, E...**gas:** KwikTrip, SA/dsl, **food:** KFC, Starbucks, **other:** Harley-Davidson, W...**other:** O'Reilly Parts
85	MN 50, E...**gas:** BP/24hr, F&F/dsl, SA/dsl, **food:** Burger King, Caribou Coffee, DQ, Greenmill Rest., Pizza Hut, Subway, Taco Bell/LJ Silver, Wendy's, **lodging:** Best Value, Comfort Inn, **other:** Family Foods, Goodyear, Walgreen, W...**gas:** Holiday/dsl, **food:** Cracker Barrel, Perkins, **lodging:** AmericInn, **other:** Gander Mtn.
84	185th St W, Orchard Trail, E...**food:** Applebee's, Caribou Coffee, Quizno's, **other:** Marshalls, Target
81	rd 70, Lakeville, E...**gas:** Holiday/dsl, **food:** McDonald's, Subway, Tacoville, **lodging:** Holiday Inn/rest, Motel 6, W...**food:** Harry's Cafe
76	rd 2, Elko, E...**gas:** gas/dsl, E...**other:** Elko Speedway
76mm	**rest area sb, full(handicapped)facilities, phone, picnic tables, litter barrels, vending, petwalk**
69	MN 19, to Northfield, **6-8 mi** E...**gas:** KwikTrip, **food:** Applebee's, Subway, Taco Bell, **lodging:** AmericInn, College City Motel, Country Inn Suites, Super 8, **other:** HOSPITAL, Carleton Coll, St Olaf Coll, W...**gas:** Sunoco/dsl/rest/scales
68mm	**rest area nb, full(handicapped)facilities, phone, picnic tables, litter barrels, vending, petwalk**
66	rd 1, to Dundas, **1 mi** W...**food:** Boonie's Grill
59	MN 21, Faribault, E...**gas:** BP/Pinecone/dsl/rest/scael/24hr., **food:** Hardee's, **lodging:** AmericInn, Best Value Inn, Day's Inn, **2 mi** E...**gas:** Mobil, SA, **food:** Arbys, A&W, Burger King, Cloud 9 Grill, DQ, Hardee's, KFC, Pizza Hut, Taco John's, **lodg-**

Faribault

	ing: Galaxie Inn, Lyndale Motel, **other:** Checker Parts, Ford/Lincoln/Mercury, vet, W...**other:** Harley-Davidson, camping
56	MN 60, Faribault, E...**gas:** BP, Hy-Vee Gas/dsl, KwikTrip, **food:** Arby's, Burger King, Great China Buffet, Hardee's, KFC, Perkins, Pizza Hut, Quizno's, Starbucks, Subway, Taco John's, **other:** HOSPITAL, Auto Value Parts, Buick/Pontiac, Checker Parts, Chevrolet, Chrysler/Jeep, Dodge, Family$, Goodyear/auto, Hy-Vee Foods, JC Penney, Jo-Ann Fabrics, Tires+, Wal-Mart SuperCtr, mall, W...**gas:** Petro/dsl, **food:** DQ, Happy Chef/24hr, **lodging:** Select Inn, **other:** Sakatah Lake SP, camping
55	(from nb, no return), **1 mi** E...**gas:** SA/dsl, KwikTrip, Mobil/dsl, **food:** A&W, Broaster Rest., Burger King, DQ, KFC, Pizza Hut, Quizno's, Southern China Cafe, Subway, Taco John's, **lodging:** AmericInn, Budget Inn, Galaxie Inn, **other:** Ford/Mercury
48	rd 12, rd 23, Medford, W...**food:** McDonald's, **other:** Outlet Mall/famous brands
45	rd 9, Clinton Falls, W...**gas:** KwikTrip/dsl, **food:** Caribou Coffee, Famous Daves BBQ, 43rd St Grill, Sbarros, Sportsman's Grille, Subway, TimberLodge Steaks, Wendy's, **lodging:** Comfort Inn, Holiday Inn, **other:** Cabela's Sporting Goods, Russell-Stover Candies, museum
43	rd 34, 26th St, Airport Rd, Owatonna
42b a	US 14 W, rd 45, to Waseca, Owatonna, E...**food:** Kernel Rest., **lodging:** Budget Host, **other:** AutoZone, CashWise Foods, Chrysler/Dodge/Jeep, Ford/Lincoln/Mercury, W...**gas:** BP/dsl/scales, KwikTrip/dsl, **food:** Culver's, Dunn Bros Coffee, Eastwind Buffet, Happy Chef, McDonald's, Perkins, **lodging:** Best Budget Inn, Owatonna Hotel, Super 8, **other:** $Tree, GNC, Kohls, Lowe's Whse, Radio Shack, Wal-Mart SuperCtr/gas/dsl/24hr
41	Bridge St, Owatonna, E...**gas:** Holiday/dsl, **food:** Applebee's, Arby's, Burger King, DQ, KFC, Papa Murphy's, Quizno's, Starbucks, Subway, Taco Bell, **lodging:** AmericInn, Country Inn Suites, **other:** HOSPITAL, W...**gas:** F&F/dsl, **lodging:** Microtel, **other:** Target
40	US 14 E, US 218, Owatonna, **1 mi** E on rd 6...**gas:** Star/dsl, **food:** El Tequila Mexican, Godfather's, Taco John's, **lodging:** Oakdale Motel, **other:** HOSPITAL, Chevrolet/Pontiac/Buick, Curves, Hy-Vee Foods/24hr, Sterling Drug, TrueValue Hardware, Walgreen, WholesaleTire
38mm	Turtle Creek
35mm	**rest area both lanes, full(handicapped)facilities, phone, picnic tables, litter barrels, vending, petwalk**
34.5mm	Straight River
32	rd 4, Hope, **1/2 mi** E...camping, **1 mi** W...gas, food
26	MN 30, to Blooming Prairie, Ellendale, E...**gas:** Conoco/dsl/rest., W...**gas:** BP/pizza/dsl
22	rd 35, to Hartland, Geneva, **1 mi** E...gas, food
18	MN 251, to Hollandale, Clarks Grove, W...**gas:** BP/dsl/LP, **other:** camping
17mm	weigh sta, both lanes

Owatonna

Interstate 35

13b a	I-90, W to Sioux Falls, E to Austin, W...HOSPITAL
12	US 65 S(from sb), Lp 35, Albert Lea, same as 11
11	rd 46, Albert Lea, E...gas: Luv's/Wendy's/dsl/scales/24hr, TA/Shell/Coldstone/Pizza Hut/dsl/scales/24hr/@, food: Trails Rest., lodging: Comfort Inn, other: KOA(may-oct/6mi), dsl repair, W...gas: KwikTrip, Shell/dsl, food: Burger King, Casa Zamora Mexican, China Buffet, Green Mill Rest, McDonald's, Perkins, Pizza Hut, Starbucks, Subway, Taco John's, Trumble's Rest., Wendy's, lodging: Country Inn Suites, Countryside Inn, Day's Inn, Ramada, Super 8, other: HOSPITAL, AutoZone, Buick/Pontiac/Cadillac/Honda, CarQuest, $Tree, Ford, Home Depot, Honda, Jeep, Mazda, NAPA, Nissan/VW, Radio Shack, Toyota, Volvo, Wal-Mart SuperCtr/gas/dsl, to Myre-Big Island SP
9mm	Albert Lea Lake
8	US 65, Lp 35US 65, Lp 35, Albert Lea, 2 mi W...gas: Freeborn City Co-op/dsl, food: DQ, Hardee's
5	rd 13, to Glenville, Twin Lakes, 3 mi W...camping
2	rd 5, no services
1mm	**Welcome Ctr nb, full(handicapped) facilities, phone, picnic tables, litter barrels, vending, petwalk**
0mm	Minnesota/Iowa state line

Interstate 35W

Exit #	Services
41mm	I-35W begins/ends on I-35, exit 127.
36	rd 23, E...gas: BP/dsl, W...gas: Phillips 66/dsl, food: Caribou Coffee, DQ, McDonald's, Miller's Grill, Subway, Taco Palace, other: Discount Tire, Kohl's, Super Target
33	rd 17, Lexington Ave, E...gas: BP, 1 mi E...food: Burger King, McDonald's, W...food: Applebee's, Arby's, Coldstone's, Green Mill Rest., Joey's Seafood, Quizno's, Taco Bell/LJ Silvers, Wendy's, other: Cub Foods, GNC, Home Depot, Michael's, Radio Shack, Walgreen, Wal-Mart
32	95th Ave NE, to Lexington, Circle Pines, W...Nat Sports Ctr
31b	Lake Dr, E...gas: Shell/dsl
31a	rd J, 85th Ave NE(no EZ return to nb), no services
30	US 10 W, MN 118, to MN 65, no services
29	rd I, no services
28c b	rd 10, rd H, W...gas: BP, food: Best Steaks, Jake's Café, KFC, McDonald's, Mermaid Café, Perkins, Pizza Hut/Taco Bell, RJ Riches Rest., Subway, Saturn, lodging: AmericInn, Day's Inn, other: carwash
28a	MN 96, no services
27b a	I-694 E and W
26	rd E2, W...gas: Phillips 66/dsl
25b	MN 88, to Roseville(no EZ return to sb), E...gas: SA/dsl, lodging: Courtyard, Fairfield Inn, Residence Inn, W...gas: Mobil, PDQ, food: Barley John's, Godfather's, Jake's Café, Main Event Rest., McDonald's, Perkins/24hr, Subway
25a	rd D(from nb), same as 25b

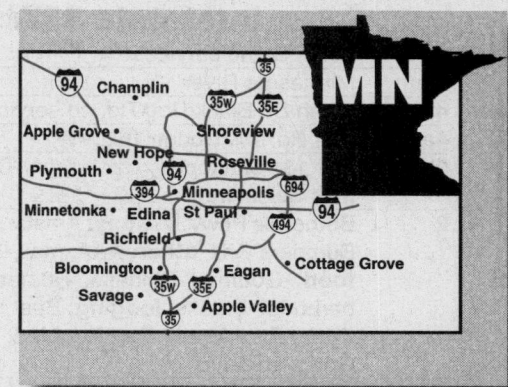

24	rd C, E...food: Burger King, lodging: Holiday Inn, W...lodging: Comfort Inn, other: Chevrolet/Pontiac/GMC, Chrysler/Dodge/Jeep, Volvo
23b	Cleveland Ave, MN 36, E...food: India Palace Rest., Joe Senser's Rest., lodging: Day's Inn, Motel 6, Radisson, Super 8
23a	MN 280, Industrial Blvd(from sb), no services
22	MN 280, Industrial Blvd(from nb), E...lodging: Sheraton
21b a	rd 88, Broadway St, Stinson Blvd, E...Ford Trucks, W...food: Burger King, Country Kitchen, Cousins Subs, McDonald's, Pizza Hut/Taco Bell, other: Home Depot, Old Navy, Rainbow Foods/24hr, Target
19	E Hennepin(from nb), no services
18	US 52, 4th St SE, University Ave, to U of MN, E...gas: BP
17c	11th St, Washington Ave, E...lodging: Holiday Inn, W...gas: Mobil, other: HOSPITAL, Goodyear, to Metrodome
17b	I-94 W(from sb)
17a	MN 55, Hiawatha, no services
16b a	I-94(from nb), E to St Paul, W to St Cloud, to MN 65
15	31st St(from nb), Lake St, E...food: McDonald's, Taco Bell, other: W...HOSPITAL
14	35th St, 36th St, no services
13	46th St, no services
13mm	Minnehaha Creek
12b	Diamond Lake Rd, no services
12a	60th St(from sb), W...gas: Mobil, other: Cub Foods
11b	MN 62 E, to airport, to airport
11a	Lyndale Ave(from sb), E...gas: Shell
10b	MN 62 W, 58th St, no services
10a	rd 53, 66th St, no services
9c	76th St(from sb), no services
9b a	I-494, MN 5, to airport
8	82nd St, E...other: BMW, W...food: Bennigan's, Red Lobster, Wendy's, other: Best Buy, Chevrolet, Infiniti, Kia, Kohl's, Saturn, Suzuki, Toyota
7b	90th St, no services
7a	94th St, E...gas: BP, Goodyear/auto, W...lodging: Holiday Inn
6	rd 1, 98th St, E...gas: Holiday, Sinclair, food: Bakers Square, Burger King, Coldstone, Jimmy John's, New China, Starbucks, Wendy's, other: Bloomington Drug, Coldstone, Checker Parts, Festival Foods, Ford, Radio Shack, Walgreen, W...gas: SA/dsl, food: Denny's

MINNESOTA

Interstate 35W

N ↕ S

5	106th St, no services
5mm	Minnesota River
4b	113th St, Black Dog Rd, no services
4a	Cliff Rd, **E**...Dodge, **W**...VW
3b a	MN 13, Shakopee, Canterbury Downs, **E**...lodging: Select Inn
2	Burnsville Pkwy, **E**...gas: Amstar, Marathon, **food:** Bumpers Grill, **other:** AAA, mall, **W**...gas: Holiday, **food:** Gourmet Chinese, Hooters, Perkins, TimberLodge Steaks, **lodging:** Best Value Inn, LivInn, Prime Rate Motel, Red Roof Inn, **other:** Best Buy, Goodyear/auto, vet
1	rd 42, Crystal Lake Rd. **See Minnesota Interstate 35, exit 88b.**, no services
0mm	I-35W begins/ends on I-35, exit 88a.

Interstate 90

E ↕ W

Exit #	Services
277mm	Minnesota/Wisconsin state line, Mississippi River
275	US 14, US 61, to MN 16, La Crescent, **N**...**Welcome Ctr wb, full(handicapped)facilities, info, phone, picnic tables, litter barrels, vending, petwalk**, **S**...gas: Kwik Trip(1mi)
272b a	Dresbach, no services
270	Dakota, no services
269	US 14, US 61, to Winona(from wb), **N**...to OL Kipp SP/camping
266	rd 12, Nodine, **N**...**other:** Great River Bluff SP, camping, **S**...gas: BP/Subway/dsl/24hr/@
261mm	weigh sta both lanes
257	MN 76, to Houston, Ridgeway, Witoka, **N**...gas, **S**...camping
252	MN 43 N, to Winona, **7 mi** **N**...**food:** Taco Bell, **lodging:** Express Inn, Holiday Inn, Quality Inn, **other:** HOSPITAL
249	MN 43 S, to Rushford, **N**...**other:** Peterbilt Trucks/repair
244mm	**rest area eb, full(handicapped)facilities, phone, picnic tables, litter barrels, vending, petwalk**
242	rd 29, Lewiston, no services
233	MN 74, to Chatfield, St Charles, **N**...gas: Kwik Trip/LP/24hr(2mi), **food:** A&W(2mi), Pizza Factory, Subway(2mi), **other:** Whitewater SP, **S**...gas: BP/dsl, **food:** Amish Ovens Rest./bakery, **other:** RV dump/LP
229	rd 10, Dover, no services
224	MN 42, rd 7, Eyota, **N**...gas: KwikTrip/dsl(3mi)
222mm	**rest area wb, full(handicapped)facilities, phone, picnic tables, litter barrels, vending, petwalk**
218	US 52, to Rochester, **8 mi** **N**...**food:** Old Country Buffet, **lodging:** Hampton Inn, Holiday Inn, Motel 6, Sleep Inn, **other:** Brookside RV Park, **S**...gas: BP/dsl, **other:** KOA(Mar-Oct)(1mi)

209b a	US 63, MN 30, to Rochester, Stewartville, **8-10 mi** **N**...**lodging:** Comfort Inn, Day's Inn, Econolodge, Hampton Inn, Holiday Inn, Super 8, **1 mi** **S**...gas: KwikTrip, **food:** DQ, Subway, **lodging:** AmericInn
205	rd 6, no services
202mm	**rest area eb, full(handicapped)facilities, phone, picnic tables, litter barrels, vending, petwalk**
193	MN 16, Dexter, **S**...gas: BP/Oasis Grill/dsl, Windmill/Phillips 66/Pinecone Rest./dsl/24hr, **food:** Windmill Rest.
189	rd 13, to Elkton, no services
187	rd 20, **S**...Beaver Trails Camping
183	MN 56, to Rose Creek, Brownsdale, **S**...gas: Freeborn City Co-op/dsl/LP
181	28th St NE, no services
180b a	US 218, 21st St NE, to Austin, Oakland Place, **S**...gas: Shell, **lodging:** Austin Motel
179	11th Dr NE, to Austin, **N**...gas: BP/dsl/rest./24hr
178b	6th St NE, to Austin, downtown
178a	4th St NW, **N**...**food:** Culver's, Perkins, Torge's Grill, **lodging:** AmericInn, Day's Inn, Holiday Inn **other:** AutoValue Parts, Chevrolet/Pontiac/GMC, vet, **S**...gas: BP, KwikTrip/Subway, **food:** A&W, Burger King, **other:** HOSPITAL
177	US 218 N, to Owatonna, Austin, Mapleview, **N**...gas: Holiday, **food:** Applebee's, Arby's, KFC/LJ Silver, King Buffet, Quizno's, Wendy's, Yonkers, **other:** Aldi Foods, Cashwise Food/gas/24hr, $Tree, Hy-Vee Foods/gas, JC Penney, K-Mart, O'Reilly Parts, Radio Shack, ShopKO, Staples, Target, Wal-Mart SuperCtr/gas, mall, **S**...gas: Sinclair/McDonald's/dsl, **food:** Hardee's, **lodging:** Super 8
175	MN 105, rd 46, to Oakland Rd, **N**...gas: Mileage/dsl, **food:** Sportts Grill, **lodging:** Countryside Inn, **S**...gas: BP, Shell/dsl, **other:** Chrysler/Dodge/Jeep, Ford/Mercury, camping, vet
171mm	**rest area wb, full(handicapped)facilities, phone, picnic tables, litter barrels, petwalk**
166	rd 46, Oakland Rd, **N**...**other:** KOA/LP, golf(par3)
163	rd 26, Hayward, **S**...gas: Shell(4mi), Freeborn County Co-op, **food:** Pizza Hut(4mi), Trails Rest.(4mi), **other:** Myre-Big Island SP, camping
161.5mm	**rest area eb, full(handicapped)facilities, phone, picnic tables litter barrels, petwalk**
159b a	I-35, N to Twin Cities, S to Des Moines
157	rd 22, Albert Lea, **S**...gas: Hy-Vee Foods/gas/24hr, Shell, **food:** Applebee's, Arby's, DQ, Herberger's, McDonald's, Pizza Ranch, **lodging:** AmericInn, Holiday Inn Express, **other:** HOSPITAL, Ace Hardware, Chevrolet, Famliy$, Harley-Davidson, Radio Shack, ShopKO, mall
154	MN 13, to US 69, to Manchester, Albert Lea, **N**...gas: SA/dsl, **3 mi** **S**...lodging: BelAire Motel
146	MN 109, to Wells, Alden, **S**...gas: BP/dsl/rest., Co-Op Gas, **food:** Tailfins Malt Shop

Austin *(vertical label)*

Albert Lea *(vertical label)*

Interstate 90

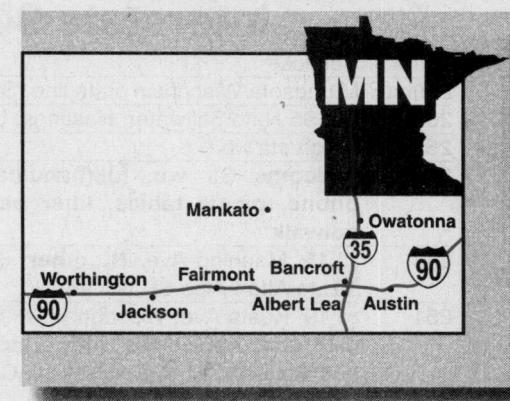

E

W

Fairmont

138	MN 22, to Wells, Keister, ⓢ...camping
134	MN 253, rd 21, to Bricelyn, MN Lake, no services
128	MN 254, rd 17, to Frost, no services
119	US 169, to Winnebago, Blue Earth, ⓢ...gas: Shell/dsl, Sinclair/dsl, **food:** Country Kitchen, DQ, McDonald's, Pizza Hut, Subway, **lodging:** AmericInn, Budget Inn, Super 8, **other:** HOSPITAL, Wal-Mart/drugs, Jolly Green Giant, camping
119mm	**rest area both lanes, full(handicapped) facilities, phone, picnic tables, litter barrels, petwalk, playground**
113	rd 1, Guckeen, no services
107	MN 262, rd 53, to East Chain, Granada, ⓢ...**other:** Flying Goose Camping(May-Oct)(1mi), gas/dsl
102	MN 15, to Madelia, Fairmont, ⓢ...gas: Wal-Mart SuperCtr, **0-2 mi** ⓢ...gas: BP, Cenex/dsl, Phillips 66/dsl, SA/dsl/24hr, **food:** Burger King, China Buffet, Green Mill Rest., KFC, McDonald's, Perkins, Pizza Ranch, Ranch Family Rest., Starbucks, Subway, Taco John's, Wendy's, Wok'n Grill, **lodging:** Budget Inn, Comfort Inn, Holiday Inn, Super 8, **other:** HOSPITAL, Ace Hardware, CarQuest, Chrysler/Dodge/Jeep, Cty Mkt Foods, $Tree, Ford, Freightliner, Goodyear, Hy-Vee Foods, JC Penny, K-Mart, NAPA, Pontiac/Buick/GMC, Radio Shack, Sears, ShopKO, Walgreens, USPO, camping, repair
99	rd 39, Fairmont, ⓢ...**lodging:** Highland Court Motel(2mi)
93	MN 263, rd 27, Welcome, **1/2 mi** ⓢ...gas: Cenex, camping
87	MN 4, Sherburn, **1 mi** ⓢ...gas: Cenex, **other:** camping
80	rd 29, Alpha, no services
73	US 71, Jackson, Ⓝ...gas: SA/dsl, **food:** Burger King/TCBY, **lodging:** Econolodge, Super 8, **other:** KOA, to Kilen Woods SP, ⓢ...gas: BP/DQ, **food:** Embers Rest., Pizza Ranch, Subway, **lodging:** AmericInn, Budget Host, Earth Inn, Prairie Winds Motel, **other:** HOSPITAL, Ace Hardware, Family$, Gordy's Foods, Chevrolet/Buick/Pontiac, Chrysler/Dodge/Jeep, to Spirit Lake
72.5mm	W Fork Des Moines River
72mm	**rest area wb, full(handicapped)facilities, phone, picnic tables, litter barrels, vending, petwalk**
69mm	**rest area eb, full(handicapped)facilities, phone, picnic tables, litter barrels, vending, petwalk**
64	MN 86, Lakefield, Ⓝ...HOSPITAL, gas/dsl, food, camping, to Kilen SP(12mi)
57	rd 9, to Heron Lake, Spafford, no services
50	MN 264, rd 1, to Brewster, Round Lake, ⓢ...camping
47	rd 3(from eb), no return, no services
46mm	weigh sta eb
45	MN 60, Worthington, Ⓝ...gas: BP/Blueline Cafe/dsl/scales, ⓢ...gas: Casey's, Shell/dsl/24hr, **food:** McDonald's, **other:** camping

Worthington

43	US 59, Worthington, Ⓝ...gas: Mobil/dsl, **lodging:** Travelodge, ⓢ...gas: Casey's, Cenex/dsl, Shell, **food:** Arby's, Burger King, Country Kitchen, DQ, Godfather's, Ground Round, Happy Chef, Hardee's, KFC, McDonald's, Perkins/24hr, Pizza Hut, Subway, Taco John's, **lodging:** AmericInn, Budget Inn, Day's Inn, Holiday Inn Express, **other:** HOSPITAL, County Mkt Foods/24hr, Farm and Fleet, Hy-Vee Foods, Chevrolet/Pontiac/Buick/Cadillac, $General, Family$, Ford, JC Penney, O'Reilly Parts, Radio Shack, ShopKO, Walgreens, Wal-Mart SuperCtr/gas/24hr
42	MN 266, rd 25, to Reading, ⓢ...**lodging:** Days Inn, Super 8
33	rd 13, to Wilmont, Rushmore, no services
26	MN 91, Adrian, ⓢ...gas: Cenex/dsl, Kum & Go/Subway/dsl, Minimart/cafe, **food:** Bullpin Grill, Countryside Steaks, **other:** Adrian Camping
25mm	**rest area wb, full(handicapped)facilities, phone, picnic tables, litter barrels, petwalk**
24mm	**rest area eb, full(handicapped)facilities, phone, picnic tables, litter barrels, petwalk**
18	rd 3, Kanaranzi, Magnolia, Ⓝ...camping
12	US 75, Luverne, Ⓝ...gas: Casey's, FuelTime/dsl, Phillips 66/dsl, Shell/dsl, Sinclair, **food:** China Rest., ChitChat's Grill, McDonald's, Subway, Taco John's, Tasty Drive-In, **lodging:** Comfort Inn, Cozy Rest Motel(1mi), Hillcrest Motel(2mi), Sunrise Motel, **other:** HOSPITAL, Ace Hardware, Casey's Store, Chevrolet/Pontiac/Buick/GMC, Chrysler/Dodge/Jeep, $General, Glen's Foods, Macey's, truckwash, to Blue Mounds SP, Pipestone NM, ⓢ...**food:** Magnolia Steaks, **lodging:** Super 8, **other:** Pamida
5	rd 6, Beaver Creek, Ⓝ...gas: Shell/dsl
3	rd 4, Beaver Creek, no services
1	MN 23, rd 17, to Jasper, Ⓝ...**other:** to Pipestone NM, access to gas/dsl
0mm	Minnesota/South Dakota state line, **Welcome Ctr/weigh sta eb, full(handicapped)facilities, info, phone, picnic tables, litter barrels**

MINNESOTA
Interstate 94

E

↕

W

Exit #	Services
259mm	Minnesota/Wisconsin state line, St Croix River
258	MN 95 N, to Stillwater, Hastings, Lakeland
257mm	weigh sta wb
256mm	**Welcome Ctr wb, full(handicapped)facilities, phone, picnic tables, litter barrels, vending, petwalk**
253	rd 15, Manning Ave, **N**...other: StoneRidge Golf, **S**...to Afton Alps SP, ski area
251	rd 19, Keats Ave, Woodbury Dr, **S**...gas: KT, SA/dsl, food: Applebee's, Arby's, Burger King, Caribou Coffee, Chili's, Chin's Asia, Chipotle Mexican, Dino's Rest, DQ, FoodCourt, Outback Steaks, Subway, lodging: Extended Stay America, Holiday Inn Express, other: Gander Mtn, Sam's Club, Wal-Mart/Subway/Auto, outlet mall famous brands
250	rd 13, Radio Dr, Inwood Ave, **N**...food: Buffalo Wild Wings, Caribou Coffee, Machine Shed Rest., Red Lobster, Olive Garden, lodging: Wild Wood Lodge, other: Best Buy, **S**...gas: Hilton Garden, Holiday, food: Blimpie, Champp's, Don Pablo, Quizno's, Starbucks, Sunsets Grill, Taco Bell, TGI-Friday, Wendy's, Zantigo's Mexican, other: VET, Borders Books/Café, Circuit City, CompUSA, Cub Foods, GNC, Hepner's Auto Ctr, Home Depot, Jo-Ann Crafts, LandsEnd Inlet, Old Navy, Tires+
249	I-694 N & I-494 S
247	MN 120, Century Ave, **N**...food: Denny's, Toby's Rest., lodging: AmericInn, Super 8, other: Harley-Davidson, Saturn, **S**...gas: SA, food: Green-Mill Rest., McDonald's, lodging: Country Inn/rest., other: Chevrolet
246c b	McKnight Ave, **N**...3M
246a	Ruth St(from eb, no return), **N**...gas: BP, Sinclair, food: Culver's, HoHo Chinese, Perkins, other: Firestone/auto, Michael's
245	White Bear Ave, **N**...gas: SA/Subway, food: Hardee's, Embers Rest., N China Buffet, lodging: Exel Inn, Ramada Inn, **S**...gas: BP, food: Arby's, Bakers Square, Burger King, Davanni's Pizza/subs, Ground Round, KFC/Pizza Hut, Krispy Kreme, McDonald's, Perkins, Taco Bell, lodging: Holiday Inn, other: Chrysler, Firestone/auto, JC Penney, Target
244	US 10 E, US 61 S, Mounds/Kellogg
243	US 61, Mounds Blvd, **S**...River Centre
242d	US 52 S, MN 3, 6th St, **N**...gas: Holiday, food: Subway
242c	7th St, **S**...gas: SA
242b a	I-35E N, US 10 W, I-35E S(from eb)
241c	I-35E S(from wb)
241b	10th St, 5th St, to downtown
241a	12th St, Marion St, Kellogg Blvd, **N**...lodging: Best Western Kelly Inn, other: Sears, **S**...gas: BP, Holiday, SA, lodging: Savoy Inn, other: HOSPITAL, st capitol
240	Dale Ave, no services
239b a	Lexington Pkwy, Hamline Ave, **N**...gas: BP, food: Chevy's Mexican, Hardee's/24hr, lodging: Sheraton, other: HOSPITAL, Cub Foods, K-Mart, Target

St Paul

238	Snelling Ave, **N**...food: Applebee's, McDonald's, Perkins, lodging: Sheraton, other: Target, **S**...gas: Citgo, other: Tires+, same as 239
235b	Huron Blvd, **N**...gas: Citgo, food: Arnold's Burger Grill, other: HOSPITAL, U of MN
237	Cretin Ave, Vandalia Ave, to downtown
236	MN 280, University Ave, to downtown
235mm	Mississippi River
235a	Riverside Ave, 25th Ave, **N**...gas: Winner, food: Starbucks, **S**...food: Perkins, Taco Bell
234c	Cedar Ave, downtown
234b a	MN 55, Hiawatha Ave, 5th St, **N**...lodging: Holiday Inn, other: to downtown
233b	I-35W N, I-35W S(exits left from wb)
233a	11th St(from wb), **N**...downtown
231b	Hennepin Ave, Lyndale Ave, to downtown
231a	I-394, US 12 W, to downtown
230	US 52, MN 55, 4th St, 7th St, Olson Hwy, **N**...Metrodome, **S**...HOSPITAL, Int Mkt Square
229	W Broadway, Washington Ave, **N**...gas: Holiday, Old Colony/dsl, food: Burger King, **S**...food: Taco Bell, Wendy's, other: Target
228	Dowling Ave N, no services
226	53rd Ave N, 49th Ave N, no services
225	I-694 E, MN 252 N, to Minneapolis
34	to MN 100, Shingle Creek Pkwy, **N**...food: Coyote Grill, Denny's, Olive Garden, TGI Friday, lodging: AmericInn, Comfort Inn, Country Inn&Suites, Crowne Plaza, Days Inn, Extended Stay America, La Quinta, Motel 6, Super 8, **S**...food: Great India, Panera Bread, Perkins, Vallarta's Mexican, other: Best Buy, Kohl's, PepBoys, Target, Tires+
33	rd 152, Brooklyn Blvd, **N**...gas: SA, Shell, food: Culver's, Subway, other: Chevrolet, Dodge, Honda, Mazda, **S**...gas: BP, food: Arby's, Embers Rest., 50's Grill, Taco Bell, other: Cub Foods, Family$, Chrysler/Jeep, Walgreens
31	rd 81, Lakeland Ave, **N**...gas: SA, food: Beach House Grille, Wagner's Drive-In, Wendy's, lodging: Grand Rios, Ramada Inn, **S**...lodging: Best Value Inn, Budget Host
30	Boone Ave, **N**...lodging: Northland Inn/rest., Sleep Inn, **S**...other: Discount Tire, Home Depot
29b a	US 169, to Hopkins, Osseo, no services
28	rd 61, Hemlock Lane, **N** on Elm Creek...gas: Citgo, food: Arby's/Sbarro's, Boston's Grill, Buca Café, Champp's Grill, ChuckeCheese, Don Pablo, Famous Dave's BBQ, Ground Round, Hop's Grill, Houlihan's, Joe's Crabshack, Krispy Kreme, Mongkok Asian, Old Country Buffet, Olive Garden, Panera Bread, Potbelly's, Qdoba, Red Lobster, Starbucks, TimberLodge Steaks, lodging: Courtyard, Hampton Inn, Holiday Inn, Staybridge Suites, other: Best Buy, Border's, Cub Foods, Jo-Ann Fabrics, Kohl's, Old Navy, Tires+, same as 215, **S**...gas: BP, food: Perkins/24hr, lodging: Select Inn
216	I-94 W and I-494

Minneapolis

Interstate 94

E

↑
↓

W

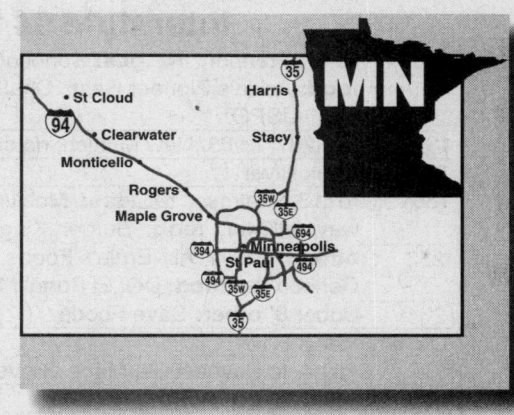

215 rd 109, Weaver Lake Rd, ...**gas:** Citgo, SA/dsl, **food:** Burger King, Bakers Square, Cattle Co Steaks, Champp's, DQ, Don Pablo, Hop's Grill, J Cousineau's Rest., Joe's Crabshack, KFC, Krispy Kreme, McDonald's, Old Country Buffet, Papa John's, Pizza Hut, Starbucks, Subway, Taco Bell, Wendy's, **lodging:** Hampton Inn, Staybridge Suites, **other:** Barnes&Noble, Cub Foods, Gander Mtn, GNC, Goodyear/auto, JC Penney, Kohl's, K-Mart, Michael's, Old Navy, Tires+, USPO, Walgreen, mall, same as 28, Ⓢ...**food:** Applebee's, Fuddrucker's

214mm rest area eb, full(handicapped)facilities, phone, picnic tables, litter barrels

213 rd 30, 95th Ave N, Maple Grove, Ⓝ...**gas:** SA/dsl, Ⓢ...**gas:** Holiday/dsl, **food:** Culver's, McDonald's, Orient Buffet, Quizno's, Ⓢ...**other:** Rainbow Foods, Sam's Club, Target, Wal-Mart SuperCtr/24hr, KOA(2mi)

207 MN 101, to Elk River, Rogers, Ⓝ...**gas:** SA/dsl, TA/Citgo/dsl/scales/24hr/@, **food:** Applebee's, Arby's, Burger King, Culver's, Domino's, DQ, Maynard's, McDonald's, Subway, Taco Bell, Wendy's, **lodging:** Super 8, **other:** Cabela's, Camping World, Kohl's, Target, Tires+, Walgreens, Ⓢ...**gas:** BP, Sinclair/dsl, Holiday, **food:** Anajak Asia, Black Bear Rest., Ember's Rest., Subway, **lodging:** AmericInn, **other:** Ace Hardware, Chevrolet

205.5mm Crow River

205 MN 241, rd 36, St Michael, Ⓢ...**gas:** SA/dsl, **3 mi** Ⓢ...**food:** McDonald's

202 rd 37, Albertville, Ⓝ...**gas:** Conoco/dsl, **food:** Burger King, Subway, Ⓢ...**gas:** BP, Phillips 66, Shell, **other:** Carquest

201 rd 19(from eb), Albertville, St Michael, Ⓝ...**food:** Burger King, Subway, **lodging:** Country Inn&Suites, **other:** Albertville Outlets/famous brands, Ⓢ...**gas:** BP, Mobil, **food:** Casey's, Caribou Coffee, Culver's, Space Aliens Grill, **other:** Ace Hardware, Coburn's Foods

195 rd 75, Monticello, Ⓝ...**gas:** Conoco/dsl, **food:** Hawk's Grill, **other:** HOSPITAL, Home Depot, Target

193 MN 25, to Buffalo, Monticello, Big Lake, Ⓝ...**gas:** Holiday/dsl, **food:** Burger King, Caribou Coffee, DQ, Guadalajara Mexican, KFC, Perkins, Taco Bell, **lodging:** AmericInn, **other:** AutoValue Parts, BMW, Cub Foods, Honda, K-Mart, Monticello RV Ctr, Ⓢ...**gas:** BP, SA/dsl, **food:** Applebee's, Arby's, China Buffet, Culver's, DQ, McDonald's, Subway, **lodging:** Best Western, Comfort Inn, Day's Inn, Select Inn, **other:** Buick/Pontiac/GMC, Checker Parts, Chevrolet, Ford/Mercury, Chrysler/Jeep/Dodge, Goodyear/auto, Suzuki, Wal-Mart SuperCtr/24hr, Lake Maria SP

187mm rest area eb, full(handicapped)facilities, phone, picnic tables, litter barrels, vending, petwalk

183 rd 8, to Silver Creek, Hasty, Maple Lake, Ⓢ...**gas:** Marathon/dsl/rest./scales/24hr/@, **other:** to Lake Maria SP, camping

178 MN 24, to Annandale, Clearwater, Ⓝ...**gas:** Citgo/dsl/rest./scales/24hr, Holiday/24hr, Marathon, **food:** DQ, Burger King, Subway, **lodging:** Best Western, Budget Inn, Day's Inn, **other:** Eagle Trace Golf/grill, KOA(1mi), Coburn's Foods, Ⓢ...**gas:** Shortstop/dsl, **other:** A-J Acres Camping(1mi)

178mm rest area wb, full(handicapped)facilities, phone, picnic tables, litter barrels, petwalk, vending

173 Opportunity dr., Ⓝ...KOA(5mi)

171 rd 7, rd 75, St Augusta, Ⓝ...**gas:** Exxon/dsl, Pilot/McDonald's/dsl/scales/24hr, **food:** Nathan B's Rest., Subway, **lodging:** AmericInn, Holiday Inn Express, Travelodge, **other:** HOSPITAL, tires, Ⓢ...**other:** Pleasureland RV Ctr

167b a MN 15, to St Cloud, to Kimball, **4 mi** Ⓝ...**gas:** SA/dsl, **food:** Applebee's, Arby's, Chipotle Mexican, IHOP, McDonald's, Old Chicago Pizza, Old Country Buffet, Perkins, Pizza Hut, Taco Bell, Starbucks, TimberLodge Steaks, Wendy's, **lodging:** Best Western, Comfort Inn, Country Inn&Suites, Days Inn, Fairfield Inn, Holiday Inn, Quality Inn, Ramada Ltd, Super 8, **other:** HOSPITAL, Barnes&Noble, CashWise Foods, Kohl's, K-Mart, Office Depot, Old Navy, Sam's Club, ShopKO, Ⓢ...**gas:** Shell/dsl(2mi)

164 MN 23, to St Cloud, Rockville, **4-6 mi** Ⓝ...**food:** Culver's, McDonald's, Space Aliens Rest., Taco Bell, **lodging:** Country Inn&Suites, Motel 6, Ramada Ltd, Super 8

162.5mm Sauk River

160 rd 2, to Cold Spring, St Joseph, Ⓝ...**gas:** BP, Holiday, **lodging:** Super 8, **other:** Coll of St Benedict

158 rd 75(from eb exits left), to St Cloud, same as 160, 3 mi N

156 rd 159, St Joseph, Ⓝ...St Johns U, no services

153 rd 9, Avon, Ⓝ...**gas:** Citgo/McDonald's/dsl, Shell/dsl, **food:** Neighbor's Rest., **lodging:** AmericInn, **other:** TrueValue, USPO, Ⓢ...**other:** El Rancho Manana Camping(10mi), auto parts

152mm rest area both lanes, full(handicapped)facilities, phone, picnic tables, litter barrels, vending, petwalk

147 MN 238, rd 10, Albany, Ⓝ...**gas:** Holiday/dsl/24hr, Shell/A&W/Subway/dsl, Tesoro, **food:** DQ, Hillcrest Rest., **lodging:** Country Inn&Suites, **other:** HOSPITAL, Amby's Foods, Ⓢ...**other:** Chrysler/Dodge/Jeep, NAPA

St Cloud

MINNESOTA

Interstate 94

140	rd 11, Freeport, **N**...**gas:** Conoco/dsl, Smiley's/dsl, **food:** Ackie's Pioneer Rest., Charlie's Café, **other:** VET, USPO
137	MN 237, rd 65, New Munich, no services
137mm	Sauk River
135	rd 13, Melrose, **N**...**gas:** Mobil/dsl, Tesoro/Subway/dsl/24hr, **food:** Burger King, Funky's Rest., **other:** HOSPITAL, Ernie's Foods, NAPA, **S**...**gas:** Conoco/dsl, **food:** DQ, El Portal Mexican, **lodging:** Super 8, **other:** Save Foods
132.5mm	Sauk River
131	MN 4, to Paynesville, Meire Grove
128mm	Sauk River
127	US 71, MN 28, Sauk Centre, **N**...**gas:** Casey's, Holiday/dsl, SA/24hr, **food:** DQ, Hardee's, McDonald's, Pizza Hut, Subway, **lodging:** AmericInn, Best Value Inn, Super 8, **other:** HOSPITAL, Coborn's Foods, Ford/Mercury, Louis Ctr/rest area, **S**...**gas:** BP/dsl/café/scales/24hr, **other:** Chevrolet/Pontiac/Buick/Chrysler/Jeep/Dodge, Freightliner
124	Sinclair Lewis Ave(from eb), Sauk Centre
119	rd 46, West Union, no services
114	MN 127, rd 3, to Westport, Osakis, **3 mi** **N**...**gas/**dsl, food, **lodging:** Sportsmans Motel/RV Park
105mm	**rest area wb, full(handicapped)facilities, phone, picnic tables, litter barrels, vending, petwalk**
103	MN 29, to Glenwood, Alexandria, **N**...**gas:** Citgo, F&F/dsl, Holiday, **food:** Burger King, Caribou Coffee, Country Kitchen, Culver's, Dolittle's Café, Hardee's, KFC, McDonald's, Perkins, Pizza Hut, Subway, Taco Bell, Wendy's, **lodging:** AmericInn, Best Inn, Comfort Inn, Day's Inn, Ramada, Super 8, **other:** HOSPITAL, Chevrolet/Cadillac/Mazda, Target, Wal-Mart SuperCtr/24hr, **S**...**gas:** B&H/dsl, Holiday/dsl, **lodging:** Country Inn&Suites, Holiday Inn, **other:** Alexandria RV Ctr, Buick/Pontiac/GMC
100	MN 27, **N**...**lodging:** L Motel, **other:** HOSPITAL, **S**...camping
100mm	Lake Latoka
99mm	**rest area eb, full(handicapped)facilities, phone, picnic tables, litter barrels, vending, petwalk**
97	MN 114, rd 40, to Lowry, Garfield, no services
90	rd 7, Brandon, **2-3 mi** **N**...gas, food, **lodging:** Lake Country Camping(1mi), **S**...camping, ski area
82	MN 79, rd 41, to Erdahl, Evansville, **2 mi** **N**...**gas:** BP/dsl, **S**...**other:** HOSPITAL, camping
77	MN 78, rd 10, to Barrett, Ashby, **N**...gas/dsl, food, camping, **S**...camping
69mm	**rest area wb, full(handicapped)facilities, phone, picnic tables, litter barrels, petwalk, vending**
67	rd 35, Dalton, **N**...camping, **S**...camping
61	US 59 S, rd 82, to Elbow Lake, **N**...**gas:** Citgo/dsl/café/LP/24hr, **other:** HOSPITAL, camping(4mi), **S**...camping
60mm	**rest area eb, full(handicapped)facilities, phone, picnic tables, litter barrels, petwalk, vending**
57	MN 210, rd 25, Fergus Falls, **N**...HOSPITAL
55	rd 1, to Wendell, Fergus Falls, no services
54	MN 210, Lincoln Ave, Fergus Falls, **N**...**gas:** Cenex/dsl, F&F/dsl, Holiday, Tesoro/dsl, **food:** Applebee's, Big Harvest Buffet, Burger King, Burger Time, Debbie's Kitchen, Godfather's, KFC, McDonald's, Papa Murphy's, Perkin's, Pizza Hut, Pizza Ranch, Speedway Grill, Subway, **lodging:** AmericInn, Best Western, Comfort Inn, Day's Inn, Motel 7, Super 8, **other:** HOSPITAL, Advance Parts, Chrysler/Jeep/Dodge, Ford/Lincoln/Mercury, Herbergers, Home Depot, JC Penney, K-Mart, Mazda, NAPA, Parts+, Pontiac/GMC, Radio Shack, SunMart Foods, Target, Tires+, Toyota, mall, **S**...**food:** Mabel Murphy's Rest., **other:** Wal-Mart/drugs/24hr
50	rd 88, rd 52, to US 59, to Fergus Falls, Elizabeth
38	rd 88, Rothsay, **S**...**gas:** Tesoro/dsl/café/24hr, Comfort Zone Inn
32	MN 108, rd 30,to Pelican Rapids, Lawndale
24	MN 24, Barnesville, **N**...**food:** Renee's Drive-in, **1 mi** **S**...**gas:** BP Cenex/dsl, **food:** DQ, **lodging:** motel
22	MN 9, Barnesville, **1 mi** **S**...**gas:** BP, Cenex/dsl, **lodging:** motel, **food:** DQ
15	rd 10, Downer, no services
8mm	Buffalo River
6	MN 336, rd 11, to US 10, Dilworth, no services
5mm	Red River weigh sta eb
2	rd 52, Moorhead, **1-2 mi** **N**...**gas:** Holiday/dsl, **food:** Bennigan's, China Buffet, Perkins, Pizza Ranch, **lodging:** Guesthouse Motel, Travelodge, **other:** HOSPITAL, KOA, Target, **S**...**other:** antiques
2mm	**Welcome Ctr eb, full(handicapped)facilities, info, phone, picnic tables, litter barrels, vending**
1b	20th St, Moorhead(from eb, no return), no services
1a	US 75, Moorhead, **N**...**gas:** Phillips 66, **food:** Blimpie, Burger King, Papa Murphy's, Qdoba, Starbucks, Village Inn, **lodging:** Courtyard, **other:** Curves, SunMart Foods, **S**...**gas:** BP/24hr, Casey's, Citgo, **food:** Subway, **lodging:** Day's Inn, Motel 75, Super 8, **other:** Osco Drug, Pontiac/GMC, TrueValue
0mm	Minnesota/North Dakota state line, Red River

Interstate 494/694

Exit #	Services
	I-494/I-694 loops around Minneapolis/St Paul.
71	rd 31, Pilot Knob Rd, **N**...**lodging:** Courtyard, Fairfield Inn, **S**...**lodging:** Best Western, Crowne Plaza, **food:** LoneOak Café
70	I-35E, N to St Paul, S to Albert Lea
69	MN 149, MN 55, Dodd Rd, **N**...**food:** Ziggy's Deli, **S**...**food:** Caribou Coffee, McDonald's, Subway, **lodging:** Budget Host, Country Inn&Suites,
67	MN 3, Roberts St, **1 mi** **N**...**gas:** BP, Mobil, Holiday, **food:** Acre's Rest., Arby's/Sbarro's, Baker's Square, Buffalo Wings, Burger King, Chipotle Mexican, ChuckeCheese, Culver's, Grand Buffet, KFC, Old Country Buffet, Pizza Hut, Taco Bell, Timber

MINNESOTA

Interstate 494/694

<table>
<tr><td></td><td>Lodge Steaks, White Castle, other: Aamco, Best Buy, Buick/Pontiac, Checker Parts, Chevrolet, Cub Foods, Dodge, Ford, Jo-Ann Fabrics, Kia, K-Mart, Lincoln/Mercury, Mazda, NAPA, Nissan, Rainbow Foods/24hr, Saturn, Target, Tires+, Toyota, VW, Wal-Mart, ...gas: PDQ</td></tr>
</table>

66	US 52, Ⓢ...**gas:** SA, **food:** Old World Pizza, Outback Steaks, **lodging:** Country Inn&Suites, Microtel
65	7th Ave, 5th Ave, no services
64b a	MN 56, Concord St, Ⓝ...**gas:** Conoco/dsl, **lodging:** Best Western Drovers, **other:** Ford Trucks, Goodyear, Peterbilt, Ⓢ...**gas:** EZ Stop, **other:** Chrysler/Jeep/Dodge, Parts+
63mm	Mississippi River
63c	Maxwell Ave, no services
63b a	US 10, US 61, to St Paul, Hastings, Ⓢ...**gas:** BP, SA, **food:** Burger King, Subway, **lodging:** Boyd's Motel, **other:** NAPA
60	Lake rd, Ⓔ...**gas:** SA/dsl, Ⓦ...**lodging:** Country Inn&Suites
59	Valley Creek Rd, Ⓔ...**gas:** BP, SA/dsl/LP, **food:** Chipotle Mexican, DQ, Joey's Seafood Grill, Old Country Buffet, Oriental Rest., Perkins, **lodging:** Red Roof Inn, **other:** Barnes&Noble, Best Buy, Kohl's, Marshall's, Target, Walgreens, Ⓦ...**gas:** PBQ, **food:** Bonfire Rest., Burger King, McDonald's, Pizza Hut, Subway, **lodging:** Hampton Inn, **other:** HOSPITAL, Goodyear
58c	Tamarac Rd, no facilites
58b a	I-94, E to Madison, W to St Paul. **I-494 S begins/ends, I-694 N begins/ends**
57	rd 10, 10th St N, Ⓔ...Wingate Inn, Ⓦ...**gas:** Holiday, **food:** Burger King, KFC, **other:** K-Mart, PetCo, Rainbow Foods/24hr, mall
55	MN 5, Ⓦ...**gas:** Holiday/dsl, **food:** Subway, **other:** st patrol
52b a	MN 36, N St Paul, to Stillwater, Ⓦ...**gas:** F&F/dsl
51	MN 120, Ⓔ...**gas:** BP, Conoco, SA/dsl, **food:** Jethro's, Starbucks, Taco Bell, Zantigo's Cafe, Ⓦ...**gas:** Kelly's Corner/gas
50	White Bear Ave, Ⓔ...**gas:** Gas4Less, SA, **other:** K-Mart, Ⓦ...**gas:** BP, Shell, **food:** Acupulco Chicken, Arby's, Applebee's, Bakers Square, Burger King, Caribou Coffee, Chili's, Denny's, Great Moon Buffet, IHOP, Mama Mia's Pizza, Old Country Buffet, Perkins/24hr, Potbelly's, Red Lobster, Taco Bell, TGI Friday, Vietnam Rest., Wendy's, **lodging:** Best Western, Emerald Inn, **other:** Aamco, Best Buy, Circuit City, Goodyear, JC Penney, Jo-Ann Fabrics, Kennedy Transmission, Michael's, PetCo, Sears/auto, Tires+, mall
48	US 61, Ⓔ...**other:** Acura, Chrysler/Dodge/Jeep, Ford, Honda, Hyundai, Mercury/Lincoln, Saturn, Subaru/Isuzu, Ⓦ...**food:** Chili's, Gulden's Rest., McDonald's, Olive Garden, **lodging:** Best Western, **other:** HOSPITAL, Audi/Porsche, Lexus, Mercedes, Toyota, Venburg Tire, Volvo
47	I-35E, N to Duluth
46	I-35E, US 10, S to St Paul

45	rd 49, Rice St, Ⓝ...**gas:** Marathon, Phillips 66, **food:** Papa John's, Subway, Taco Bell, **other:** Checker Parts, Ⓢ...**gas:** Marathon/dsl, **food:** A&W, Burger King, Caribou Coffee, Taco John's, **other:** Kath Parts
43b	Victoria St, Ⓢ...Bill's Foods
43a	Lexington Ave, Ⓝ...**food:** Greenmill Rest., **lodging:** Hampton Inn, Hilton Garden, Ⓢ...**gas:** BP/dsl, Exxon, Sinclair, **food:** Blue Fox Grill, Burger King, Davanni's Pizza, Papa Murphy's, Perkins, Subway, Wendy's, **lodging:** Holiday Inn, Super 8, **other:** Cub Foods, Goodyear/auto, Kennedy Transmissions, Target
42b	US 10 W(from wb), to Anoka
42a	MN 51, Snelling Ave, **1 mi** Ⓢ...**gas:** Shell, **food:** Flaherty's Grill, Lindey's Steaks, McDonald's, **lodging:** Country Inn&Suites, Holiday Inn
41b a	I-35W, S to Minneapolis, N to Duluth
40	Long Lake Rd, 10th St NW
39	Silver Lake Rd, Ⓝ...**gas:** BP, Sinclair, **food:** Champps, McDonald's, **other:** Ford, Ⓢ...**food:** Culver's, Wendy's,
38b a	MN 65, Central Ave, Ⓝ...**gas:** Holiday/dsl, **food:** Crabhouse, Subway, Ⓢ...**gas:** SA, SuperStop, **food:** A&W/KFC, Applebee's, Arby's, Asia Rest., Buffalo Wild Wings, Cousins Subs, Denny's, Flameburger Rest., La Casita Mexican, McDonald's, Papa John's, Ricky's, Taco Bell, Wendy's, White Castle, **lodging:** Starlite Motel, **other:** Advance Parts, Discount Tire, GNC, Radio Shack, Target, Tires+
37	rd 47, University Ave, Ⓝ...**gas:** Holiday, SA/dsl, **food:** Burger King, McDonald's, Papa Murphy's Pizza, Zantigo's Rest., **other:** Cub Foods, CVS Drug, Goodyear, Home Depot, Petsmart, Walgreens, Ⓢ...**gas:** Bona Bros/repair, Shell
36	E River Rd, no services
35mm	I-494 W begins/ends, I-694 E begins/ends
35c	MN 252, Ⓝ...**gas:** Holiday, SA
35b a	I-94 E to Minneapolis
34	to MN 100, Shingle Creek Pkwy, Ⓝ...**food:** Coyote Grill, Denny's, Olive Garden, TGI Friday, **lodging:** AmericInn, Comfort Inn, Country Inn&Suites, Crowne Plaza, Days Inn, Extended Stay America, La Quinta, Motel 6, Super 8, Ⓢ...**food:** Great India, Panera Bread, Perkins, Vallarta's Mexican, **other:** Best Buy, Kohl's, PepBoys, Target, Tires+

Text running vertically along left: **E ↕ W**, **St Paul**

Text running vertically in center: **Minneapolis**

Interstate 494/694

E ↑ ↓ W

Minneapolis

Exit	Description
33	rd 152, Brooklyn Blvd, **N**...**gas:** SA, Shell, **food:** Culver's, Subway, **other:** Chevrolet, Dodge, Honda, Mazda, **S**...**gas:** BP, **food:** Arby's, Embers Rest., 50's Grill, Taco Bell, **other:** Cub Foods, Family$, Chrysler/Jeep, Walgreens
31	rd 81, Lakeland Ave, **N**...**gas:** SA, **food:** Beach House Grille, Wagner's Drive-In, Wendy's, **lodging:** Grand Rios, Ramada Inn, **S**...**lodging:** Best Value Inn, Budget Host
30	Boone Ave, **N**...**lodging:** Northland Inn/rest., Sleep Inn, **S**...**other:** Discount Tire, Home Depot
29b a	US 169, to Hopkins, Osseo, no services
28	rd 61, Hemlock Lane, **N on Elm Creek**...**gas:** Citgo, **food:** Arby's/Sbarro's, Boston's Grill, Buca Café, Champp's Grill, ChuckeCheese, Don Pablo, Famous Dave's BBQ, Ground Round, Hop's Grill, Houlihan's, Joe's Crabshack, Krispy Kreme, Mongkok Asian, Old Country Buffet, Olive Garden, Panera Bread, Potbelly's, Qdoba, Red Lobster, Starbucks, TimberLodge Steaks, **lodging:** Courtyard, Hampton Inn, Holiday Inn, Staybridge Suites, **other:** Best Buy, Border's, Cub Foods, Jo-Ann Fabrics, Kohl's, Old Navy, Tires+, **S**...**gas:** BP, **food:** Perkins/24hr, **lodging:** Select Inn
27	I-94 W to St Cloud, I-94/694 E to Minneapolis
26	rd 10, Bass Lake Rd, **E**...**gas:** Conoco, **food:** Culver's, McDonald's, **lodging:** Extended Stay America, **other:** mall, **W**...**gas:** BP, Sinclair/LP, **lodging:** Hilton Garden
23	rd 9, Rockford Rd, **E**...**gas:** BP, Holiday, **food:** Chili's, **other:** Checker Parts, Lincoln/Mercury, Old Navy, Radio Shack, Rainbow Foods/24hr, Target, Walgreen, **W**...**gas:** Conoco, PDQ, **food:** Caribou Coffee, Cousins Subs, DQ, LeAnn Chin Chinese, Starbucks, Subway, TGIFriday
22	MN 55, **E**...**gas:** Holiday/dsl, **food:** Denny's, Green Mill Rest., McDonald's, **lodging:** Best Western Kelly, Radisson, Red Roof Inn, **W**...**gas:** Holiday/dsl, **food:** Arby's, Burger King, Davanni's Rest., Grandma's Grill, Mulligan's Grill, New Dynasty Chinese, Perkins, **lodging:** Comfort Inn, Day's Inn, Holiday Inn, **other:** Goodyear/auto, Tires+
21	rd 6, **E**...**gas:** BP/KwikTrip, **other:** Discount Tire, Home Depot
20	Carlson Pkwy, **E**...**gas:** Holiday/dsl, **food:** Subway, **W**...**food:** Italianni's Rest., **lodging:** Country Inn Suites
19b a	I-394 E, US 12 W, to Minneapolis, **1 mi E off of I-394**...**food:** Applebee's, Byerly's Rest., Godfather's, Uno Pizza, Wendy's, **other:** Best Buy, Borders Books, Circuit City, Ford, JC Penney, Jo-Ann Fabrics, Marshall Field, Mazda, Mercedes/BMW, Saab, Sears/auto, Target, Tires+, mall, **1/2 mi W**...**gas:** BP, **food:** Bankok Bowl, BBQ's, Pizza Hut, **other:** Chevrolet, Lexus, Mitsubishi, Nissan
17b a	Minnetonka Blvd, **W**...**gas:** Mobil, **food:** Dunn Bros Coffee
16b a	MN 7, **1 mi W**...**food:** Davanni's Rest., Famous Dave's BBQ, Hopkins House Rest., Lund's Rest., McDonald's, Perkins, Subway, Taco Bell

Minneapolis

Exit	Description
13	MN 62, rd 62, no services
12	Valleyview Rd, rd 39(from sb), no services
11c	MN 5 W, **N**...**lodging:** Extended Stay America, **other:** Land Rover, **S**...**other:** Chevrolet
11b a	US 169 S, US 212 W, **N**...**food:** Don Pablo, **lodging:** AmeriSuites, Courtyard, Fairfield Inn, Hampton Inn, Residence Inn, **S**...**gas:** Phillips 66, **food:** Hop's Grill, **lodging:** Homestead Suites, SpringHill Suites, TownePlace Suites, **other:** Cub Foods, Office Depot
10	US 169 N, to rd 18, no services
8	rd 28(from wb, no return), E Bush Lake Rd
7b a	MN 100, rd 34, Normandale Blvd, **N**...**gas:** Shell/dsl, **food:** Burger King, Chili's, DQ, Embers Rest., Subway, TGIFriday, **lodging:** Days Inn, Radisson, Sheraton, **S**...**lodging:** Country Inn Suites, Crowne Plaza, Hilton Garden, Holiday Inn, La Quinta, Staybridge Inn
6b	rd 17, France Ave, **N**...**gas:** Mobil, **food:** Cattle Co Rest., ChuckeCheese, Fuddrucker's, Hot Wok, Macaroni Grill, McDonald's, Perkins, Quizno's, **lodging:** Best Western, Park Plaza Hotel, **other:** HOSPITAL, Circuit City, CompUSA, Michael's, Office Depot, Old Navy, World Mkt, **S**...**food:** Denny's, Joe Senser's Grill, Olive Garden, **lodging:** Hampton Inn, **other:** Buick/Pontiac/GMC, Ford, Mercedes, Nissan, Toyota/Scion
6a	Penn Ave(no EZ eb return), **N**...**lodging:** Residence Inn, **other:** Best Buy, Buick, Hyundai, Isuzu, **S**...**food:** Applebee's, Atlantic Buffet, Bennigan's, Herburger's, Starbucks, Steak&Ale, Subway, **lodging:** Embassy Suites, **other:** Chevrolet, Chrysler/Pymouth/Jeep, Dodge, Kohl's, Rainbow Foods, Target, TJ Maxx
5b a	I-35W, S to Albert Lea, N to Minneapolis
4b	Lyndale Ave, **N**...**gas:** BP, Conoco, **food:** Boston Mkt, DQ, **lodging:** Candlewood Suites, Hampton Inn, **other:** Best Buy, Borders, Honda, Lands End, Mitsubishi, Radio Shack, Tires+, **S**...**gas:** Phillips 66, **lodging:** Extended Stay America, **other:** Acura, Home Depot, Lincoln/Mercury, Mazda, Subaru
4a	MN 52, Nicollet Ave, **N**...**gas:** SA/dsl, **food:** Burger King, Ember's, Rest, Jumbo Chinese, **lodging:** Candlewood Suites, **other:** Honda, **S**...**gas:** Mobil, Shell, **food:** Kwik Mart, Big Boy, McDonald's, **lodging:** La Quinta, **other:** Home Depot, Sam's Club
3	Portland Ave, 12th Ave, **N**...**gas:** Phillips 66, Sinclair, PDQ Mart, **food:** Arby's, **lodging:** AmericInn, **S**...**gas:** BP, **food:** Denny's, Outback Steaks, Subway, **lodging:** Comfort Inn/rest., Holiday Inn Express, Microtel, Quality Inn, Residence Inn, Travelodge, **other:** Walgreens, Wal-Mart
2c b	MN 77, **N**...**lodging:** Motel 6, **S**...**gas:** BP, SA, **lodging:** AmeriSuites, Best Western, Courtyard, Embassy Suites, Exel Inn, Fairfield Inn, Grand Motel, Marriott, Sheraton, **other:** Nordstrom's, Sears, Mall of America
2a	24th Ave, same as 2c b
1b	34th Ave, Nat Cemetary, **S**...**lodging:** Embassy Suites, Hilton, Holiday Inn
1a	MN 5 E, **N**...airport
0mm	Minnesota River. I-494/I-694 loops around Minneapolis/St Paul.

Interstate 10

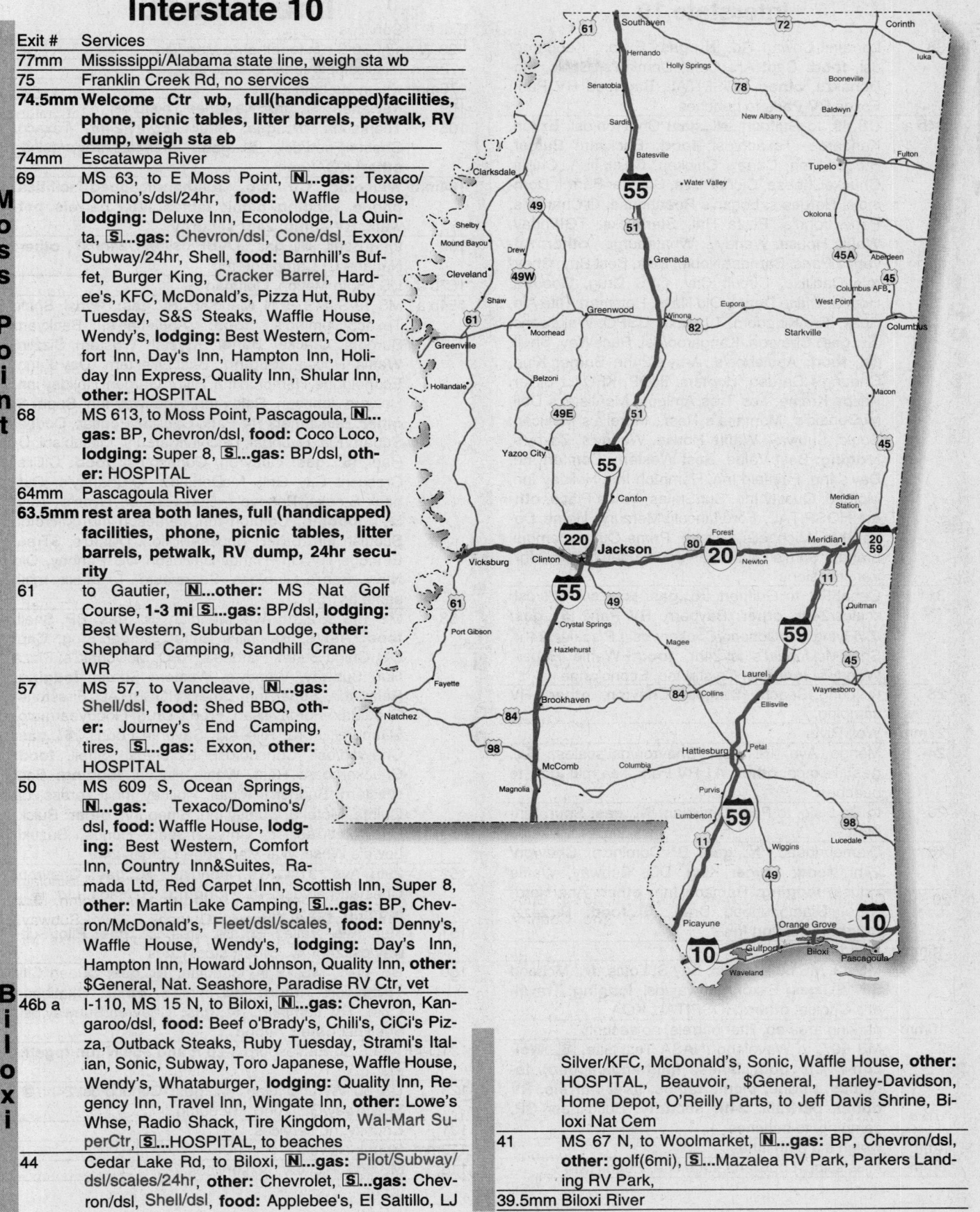

E ↕ **W**

Moss Point

Exit #	Services
77mm	Mississippi/Alabama state line, weigh sta wb
75	Franklin Creek Rd, no services
74.5mm	**Welcome Ctr wb, full(handicapped)facilities, phone, picnic tables, litter barrels, petwalk, RV dump, weigh sta eb**
74mm	Escatawpa River
69	MS 63, to E Moss Point, **N**...**gas:** Texaco/Domino's/dsl/24hr, **food:** Waffle House, **lodging:** Deluxe Inn, Econolodge, La Quinta, **S**...**gas:** Chevron/dsl, Cone/dsl, Exxon/Subway/24hr, Shell, **food:** Barnhill's Buffet, Burger King, Cracker Barrel, Hardee's, KFC, McDonald's, Pizza Hut, Ruby Tuesday, S&S Steaks, Waffle House, Wendy's, **lodging:** Best Western, Comfort Inn, Day's Inn, Hampton Inn, Holiday Inn Express, Quality Inn, Shular Inn, **other:** HOSPITAL
68	MS 613, to Moss Point, Pascagoula, **N**...**gas:** BP, Chevron/dsl, **food:** Coco Loco, **lodging:** Super 8, **S**...**gas:** BP/dsl, **other:** HOSPITAL
64mm	Pascagoula River
63.5mm	**rest area both lanes, full (handicapped) facilities, phone, picnic tables, litter barrels, petwalk, RV dump, 24hr security**
61	to Gautier, **N**...**other:** MS Nat Golf Course, 1-3 mi **S**...**gas:** BP/dsl, **lodging:** Best Western, Suburban Lodge, **other:** Shephard Camping, Sandhill Crane WR
57	MS 57, to Vancleave, **N**...**gas:** Shell/dsl, **food:** Shed BBQ, **other:** Journey's End Camping, tires, **S**...**gas:** Exxon, **other:** HOSPITAL
50	MS 609 S, Ocean Springs, **N**...**gas:** Texaco/Domino's/dsl, **food:** Waffle House, **lodging:** Best Western, Comfort Inn, Country Inn&Suites, Ramada Ltd, Red Carpet Inn, Scottish Inn, Super 8, **other:** Martin Lake Camping, **S**...**gas:** BP, Chevron/McDonald's, Fleet/dsl/scales, **food:** Denny's, Waffle House, Wendy's, **lodging:** Day's Inn, Hampton Inn, Howard Johnson, Quality Inn, **other:** $General, Nat. Seashore, Paradise RV Ctr, vet

Biloxi

46b a	I-110, MS 15 N, to Biloxi, **N**...**gas:** Chevron, Kangaroo/dsl, **food:** Beef o'Brady's, Chili's, CiCi's Pizza, Outback Steaks, Ruby Tuesday, Strami's Italian, Sonic, Subway, Toro Japanese, Waffle House, Wendy's, Whataburger, **lodging:** Quality Inn, Regency Inn, Travel Inn, Wingate Inn, **other:** Lowe's Whse, Radio Shack, Tire Kingdom, Wal-Mart SuperCtr, **S**...HOSPITAL, to beaches
44	Cedar Lake Rd, to Biloxi, **N**...**gas:** Pilot/Subway/dsl/scales/24hr, **other:** Chevrolet, **S**...**gas:** Chevron/dsl, Shell/dsl, **food:** Applebee's, El Saltillo, LJ Silver/KFC, McDonald's, Sonic, Waffle House, **other:** HOSPITAL, Beauvoir, $General, Harley-Davidson, Home Depot, O'Reilly Parts, to Jeff Davis Shrine, Biloxi Nat Cem
41	MS 67 N, to Woolmarket, **N**...**gas:** BP, Chevron/dsl, **other:** golf(6mi), **S**...Mazalea RV Park, Parkers Landing RV Park,
39.5mm	Biloxi River

MISSISSIPPI

Interstate 10

E ↕ W

Gulfport

38	Lorraine-Cowan Rd, **N**...**gas:** Exxon, Kangaroo/dsl, **food:** Capt Al's Cafe, Domino's, Sonic, McDonald's, **other:** HOSPITAL, Baywood RV Park, Foxes RV Park, to beaches
34b a	US 49, to Gulfport, **N**...**gas:** Chevron/dsl, Exxon, Kangaroo, Texaco/dsl, **food:** Backyard Burger, Burger King, Cane's Chicken, Chick-fil-A, Chili's, ChuckeCheese, Cici's Pizza, Cracker Barrel, Domino's, Hardee's, Logan's Roadhouse, O'Charley's, Papa John's, Pizza Hut, Starbucks, TGIFriday, Waffle House, Wendy's, Whataburger, **other:** Advance Parts, Barnes&Noble, Belk, Best Buy, Chevrolet/Cadillac, Circuit City, CVS Drug, Goody's, Honda, Office Depot, Old Navy, Petsmart, Rite Aid, Ross, Tire Kingdom, TJ Maxx, USPO, Walgreens, **S**...**gas:** Chevron, Kangaroo/dsl, RaceWay, Shell/dsl, **food:** Applebee's, Arby's/24hr, Burger King, Choung's Garden, Hooters, IHOP, KFC/LJ Silver, Krispy Kreme, Los Tres Amigos, McAlister's Deli, McDonald's, Montana's Rest., Morelia's Mexican, Sonic, Subway, Waffle House, Wendy's, Zaxby's, **lodging:** Best Value, Best Western, Comfort Inn, Day's Inn, Fairfield Inn, Hampton Inn, Holiday Inn, Motel 6, Quality Inn, SunSuites, Value Place, **other:** HOSPITAL, Ford/Lincoln/Mercury, Home Depot, Kia, Michael's, Nissan, Prime Outlets/famous brands, Sam's Club, Wal-Mart SuperCtr/gas/24hr, transmissions
31	Canal Rd, to Gulfport, **N**...**gas:** Love's/Arby's/dsl/scales/24hr, **other:** Bayberry RV Park, **S**...**gas:** ✈/Flying J/Conoco/Cookery/dsl/LP/scales/24hr, Shell/McDonald's/dsl/24hr, **food:** Waffle House, Wendy's, **lodging:** Crystal Inn, Econolodge
28	to Long Beach, **S**...**gas:** Chevron, **other:** RV camping
27mm	Wolf River
24	Menge Ave, **N**...**gas:** Chevron/dsl/scales, **S**...**gas:** Texaco, **other:** A1 RV Park, flea mkt, golf, to beaches
20	to De Lisle, to Pass Christian, **N**...**gas:** Spur, KinMart
16	Diamondhead, **N**...**gas:** BP/Domino's, Chevron/24hr, **food:** Burger King, DQ, Subway, Waffle House, **lodging:** Ramada Inn, **other:** Ace Hardware, Diamondhead Drug, **S**...**food:** Pizzazz, **lodging:** Comfort Inn
15mm	Jourdan River
13	MS 43, MS 603, to Kiln, Bay St Louis, **N**...McLeod SP, **S**...**gas:** Exxon/Subway/dsl, **lodging:** Traveler's Choice, **other:** HOSPITAL, KOA
10mm	parking area eb, litter barrels, no security
2	MS 607, to Waveland, NASA Test Site, **S**...**Welcome Ctr both lanes, full(handicapped) facilities, phone, picnic tables, litter barrels, RV dump, petwalk, 24hr security,** Buccaneer SP, camping, to beaches
1mm	weigh sta both lanes
0mm	Mississippi/Louisiana state line, Pearl River

Interstate 20

E ↕ W

Meridian

Exit #	Services
	I-20 W and I-59 S run together to Meridian.
172mm	Mississippi/Alabama state line
170mm	weigh sta both lanes
169	Kewanee, **S**...**gas:** Kewanee Trkstp/dsl
165	Toomsuba, **N**...**gas:** Shell/Subway/24hr, Texaco/ChesterFried/dsl, **S**...**gas:** FuelMart/Arby's/dsl/@, **other:** KOA(2mi)
164mm	**Welcome Ctr wb, full(handicapped)facilities, phone, vending, picnic tables, litter barrels, petwalk, RV dump, 24hr security**
160	to Russell, **N**...**gas:** TA/BP/dsl/rest./24hr/@, **other:** Nanabe Cr Camping(1mi)
157b a	US 45, to Macon, Quitman
154b a	MS 19 S, MS 39 N, Meridian, **N**...**gas:** BP/dsl, Shell, Texaco/Domino's, **food:** Applebee's, Backyard Burgers, Cracker Barrel, Krystal, Western Sizzlin, Waffle House, **lodging:** Best Western, Day's Inn, Econolodge, Hampton Inn, Hilton Garden, Holiday Inn, Howard Johnson, Relax Inn, Rodeway Inn, Super 8, **other:** Benchmark RV Park, Cadillac/Pontiac, Dodge/Subaru/Kia, Hyundai, Lincoln/Mercury, Mitsubishi, U-Haul, **S**...**gas:** Chevron, Conoco/dsl, **food:** CiCi's, Crescent City Grill, McDonald's, O'Charley's, Outback Steaks, Popeye's, Red Lobster, Ryan's, Taco Bell, **lodging:** Comfort Inn, Jameson Inn, Microtel, Scottish Inn, **other:** BooksAMillion, Dillard's, $Tree, Ethridge RV Ctr, Harley-Davidson, JC Penney, Old Navy, Sam's Club/gas, Sears/auto, TJ Maxx, mall, same as 153
153	MS 145 S, 22nd Ave, Meridian, **N**...**gas:** BP, Shell, **food:** Arby's, Barnhill's Buffet, Burger King, Capt D's, China Buffet, Hardee's, KFC, McDonald's, Pizza Hut, Subway, Wendy's, Western Sizzlin, **lodging:** Relax Inn, Super Inn, **other:** HOSPITAL, Firestone, FoodMax, Ford/Nissan, Fred's Drug, Goodyear/auto, $General, Ford, Rite Aid, Saverite Foods, **S**...**gas:** Chevron/dsl, Conoco/dsl, Exxon/dsl, Shell, **food:** Checkerboard Rest, Waffle House, **lodging:** Best Western, Budget 8 Motel, Holiday Inn Express, La Quinta, Motel 6, Quality Inn, Sleep Inn, **other:** Buick, Chevrolet/Cadillac, Chrysler/Jeep, Honda, Suzuki, Lowe's Whse, Wal-Mart SuperCtr/gas/24hr
152	29th Ave, 31st Ave, Meridian, **N**...**gas:** Chevron/ChesterFried/dsl/24hr, **lodging:** Ramada Ltd, **S**...**lodging:** Royal Inn
151	49th Ave, Valley Rd, **N**...**tires,** **S**...**gas:** Pilot/Subway/dsl/24hr/@, **other:** stockyards
150	US 11 S, MS 19 N, Meridian, **N**...**gas:** Queen City Trkstp/dsl@, **food:** McDonald's, **other:** Okatibbee Lake, RV camping, **S**...**gas:** Chevron/Subway/dsl, Shell/dsl **other:** Airport
131[149]	I-59 S, to Hattiesburg. **I-20 E and I-59 N run together.**
129	US 80 W, Lost Gap, **S**...**gas:** Conoco/dsl/24hr/@, Spaceway/Grill King, RV dump
121	Chunky, no services
119mm	Chunky River
115	MS 503, Hickory, no services

Interstate 20

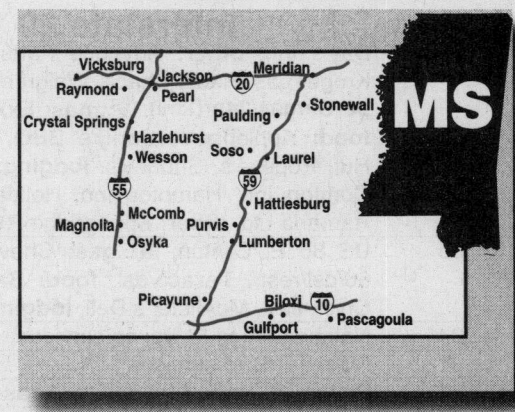

E

↕

W

109	MS 15, Newton, ...**gas:** Texaco/Wendy's/dsl/24hr, **food:** Bo-Ro Rest., **lodging:** Thrifty Inn, **other:** lube, S...**gas:** Chevron/dsl/24hr, Conoco/dsl, Newton Jct/dsl, **food:** Hardee's, KFC/Taco Bell, McDonald's, Pizza Hut, Sonic, Subway, **lodging:** Day's Inn, **other:** HOSPITAL, AutoZone, $General, Piggly Wiggly, Wal-Mart SuperCtr/24hr
100	US 80, Lake, Lawrence, N...**gas:** BP/dsl/rest.
96	Lake, no services
95mm	Bienville Nat Forest, Bienville Nat Forest, eastern boundary
90mm	**rest area eb, full(handicapped)facilities, phone, picnic tables, litter barrels, petwalk, RV dump, 24hr security**
88	MS 35, Forest, N...**gas:** BP/Subway/dsl, Shell, **food:** KFC, McDonald's, Pizza Hut, Wendy's, **lodging:** AppleTree Inn, Comfort Inn, Day's Inn, Holiday Inn Express, Scott Motel, **other:** HOSPITAL, Chevrolet, Honda, Wal-Mart, S...**gas:** Chevron/dsl/24hr, **food:** Santa Fe Steaks
80	MS 481, Morton, no services
77	MS 13, Morton, N...**gas:** Phillips 66/dsl, 77 Truck Ctr/dsl, **other:** HOSPITAL, to Roosevelt SP, RV camping
76mm	Bienville NF, western boundary
75mm	**rest area wb, full(handicapped)facilities, phone, picnic tables, litter barrels, petwalk, RV dump, 24hr security**
68	MS 43, Pelahatchie, N...**gas:** Chevron/Subway/dsl/24hr, Conoco/dsl/rest./RV dump/24hr, **food:** Little Red Smokehouse, **other:** RV camping, S...**gas:** BP/dsl
59	US 80, E Brandon, 2 mi S...**gas:** Conoco,
56	US 80, Brandon, N...**gas:** Texaco, **food:** BBQ, Burger King, CiCi's, Krystal, McDonald's, Popeye's, Taco Bell, **lodging:** Microtel, **other:** AutoZone, S...**gas:** BP, Chevron, Exxon, Mac's Gas, Shell/dsl, Texaco, **food:** DQ, Penn's Rest., Sonic, Subway, Waffle House, Wendy's, **lodging:** Day's Inn, Red Roof Inn, **other:** to Ross Barnett Reservoir
54	Crossgates Blvd, W Brandon, N...**gas:** BP, Exxon, Phillips 66, **food:** Burger King, Domino's, Fernando's Mexican, KFC, Mazzio's, Papa John's, Pizza Hut, Popeye's, Subway, Waffle House, Wendy's, **lodging:** Ridgeland Inn, **other:** HOSPITAL, Big Lots, Buick/GMC, Chevrolet, CVS Drug, $General, Eckerd, Firestone/auto, Ford, Freds Drug, Goodyear/auto, Kroger, Lincoln/Mercury, Wal-Mart SuperCtr/gas/24hr, S...**gas:** Texaco/Domino's, **other:** Home Depot, Honda
52	MS 475, N...**gas:** Chevron, Conoco/dsl, **food:** Krystal(3mi), Subway(3mi), Waffle House, Wendy's(3mi), **lodging:** Quality Inn, Ramada Ltd, Super 8, **other:** Peterbilt, to Jackson Airport
48	MS 468, Pearl, N...**gas:** Conoco, Exxon/dsl, MinuteStop/dsl, Shell/dsl, **food:** Arby's, Bumpers Drive-In, Burger King, Cracker Barrel, Domino's, El Charro's Mexican, Jose's Tamales, KFC, McDonald's, O'Charley's, Pizza Hut, Popeye's, Ruby Tuesday, Ryan's, Shoney's, Sonic, Starbucks, Waffle House, Wendy's, **lodging:** Best Western, Comfort Inn,

Brandon

	Econolodge, Fairfield Inn, Hampton Inn, Holiday Inn Express, Jameson Inn, Motel 6, **other:** transmissions, S...**gas:** Chevron/dsl/24hr, Huff/dsl/24hr, **lodging:** Country Inn Suites, Day's Inn, La Quinta **other:** $General
47b a	US 49 S, Flowood, N...**gas:** Flying J/Conoco/CountryMkt/dsl/LP/24hr/@, Pilot/Krystal/Subway/dsl/24hr/@, **food:** Western Sizzlin, **lodging:** Airport Inn, **other:** Bass Pro Shop, **2-3 mi** S...**food:** DQ, Waffle House, **lodging:** Executive Inn, **other:** Freightliner, Kenworth, Truck-Man RV Center, Tires
46	I-55 N, to Memphis
45b	US 51, State St, to downtown, N...**gas:** Chevron, **other:** ExpressLube, S...**gas:** Speedway/Hardee's/dsl, **other:** Nissan
45a	Gallatin St(from wb), to downtown, N...**gas:** Chevron, Petro/dsl/rest/@, Texaco, **other:** Blue Beacon, Nissan S...**gas:** Pilot/McDonald's/dsl/@, **lodging:** Knight's Inn,
44	I-55 S(exits left from wb), to New Orleans
43b a	Terry Rd, N...**gas:** Shell, **food:** BBQ, Kim's Seafood, Krystal, **lodging:** Tarrymore Motel S...**gas:** Citgo, **lodging:** Express Inn, **other:** Mitsubishi
42b a	Ellis Ave, Belvidere, N...**gas:** BP, Gas+, Shell, **food:** Arby's, Burger King, Capt D's, Church's, Denny's, McDonald's, Pizza Hut, Popeye's, Waffle House, Wendy's, **lodging:** Best Western, Comfort Inn, Day's Inn, Deluxe Inn, Econolodge, Jacksonian Inn, Ramada, Sleep Inn, Super 8, **other:** Advance Auto, AutoZone, Chrysler/Dodge, Family$, Firestone, KIA, O'Riley Parts, Radio Shack, Sav-a-Lot Foods, U-Haul, transmissions, zoo, S...**gas:** Conoco/dsl, Exxon/dsl, **food:** DQ, **other:** Big Lots
41	I-220 N, US 49 N, to Jackson
40b a	MS 18 W, Robinson Rd, N...**gas:** Shell/dsl, Spur, **food:** Arby's, China Buffet, El Chico, Krystal, Mazzio's, McDonald's, Piccadilly's, Pizza Hut, Popeye's, Wendy's, **lodging:** Day's Inn, Sleep Inn, **other:** CarCare, Home Depot, Metro Mall, Office Depot, Sears/auto, USPO, S...**gas:** Mac's, Phillips 66, **food:** IHOP, Waffle House, **lodging:** Comfort Inn, **other:** HOSPITAL, GNC, Wal-Mart SuperCtr/gas/24hr
36	Springridge Rd, Clinton, N...**gas:** Mac's/Burger King, Shell, **food:** Backyard Burger, Capt D's, China Garden, DQ, Jade Buffet, KFC, Little Ceasar's, Mazzio's, McDonald's, Papa John's, Starbucks, Subway, Taco Bell, Waffle House, Wendy's, **lodging:** Clinton Inn,

Jackson

MISSISSIPPI

Interstate 20

Day's Inn, **other:** Advance Parts, Home Depot, Kroger/gas, Radio Shack, Walgreen, Wal-Mart SuperCtr/gas/24hr(2mi), Ⓢ...**gas:** Exxon, Texaco/dsl, **food:** Applebee's, Corky's BBQ, Fazoli's, Pizza Hut, Popeye's, Shoney's, **lodging:** Best Western, Comfort Inn, Hampton Inn, Holiday Inn Express, Ramada Ltd, **other:** Springridge RV Park

35	US 80 E, Clinton, Ⓝ...**gas:** Chevron/dsl, Phillips 66/dsl/rest., Texaco/dsl, **food:** Backyard Burger, Chick-fil-A, McAlister's Deli, **lodging:** Ridgland Inn
34	Natchez Trace Pkwy, no services
31	Norrell Rd, no services
27	Bolton, Ⓝ...**gas:** Chevron, Ⓢ...**gas:** BP/dsl/24hr
19	MS 22, Edwards, Flora, Ⓝ...**other:** Askew Landing RV Camping, Ⓢ...**gas:** BP/dsl, Phillips 66/DQ/Stuckey's, **lodging:** Relax Inn
17mm	Big Black River
15	Flowers, no services
11	Bovina, Ⓝ...**gas:** Texaco/dsl/24hr, **other:** RV camp
10mm	weigh sta wb
8mm	weigh sta eb
6.5mm	parking area eb
5b a	US 61, MS 27 S, Ⓝ...**gas:** Shell/dsl, **food:** Sonic, Ⓢ...**gas:** Texaco/Domino's/dsl, **food:** Bumpers Rest., Rowdy's Rest., **lodging:** Beechwood Inn, Comfort Inn, Jameson Inn, Scottish Inn, **other:** RV camping, same as 4a
4b a	Clay St, Ⓝ...**gas:** Chevron, **lodging:** Battlefield Inn/RV Park, Econolodge, Hampton Inn, Motel 6, Vicksburg Inn, **other:** HOSPITAL, KOA, to Vicksburg NP, Ⓢ...**gas:** Texaco/Domino's/dsl, **food:** China Buffet, Cracker Barrel, Pizza Inn, McAlister's, Scottish Inn, Waffle House, **lodging:** Beechwood Inn/rest., Comfort Inn, Holiday Inn Express, Jameson Inn, Scottish Inn, **other:** Chrysler/Jeep/Toyota, $General, Lincoln/Mercury, Outlet Mall/famous brands/deli, same as 5
3	Indiana Ave, Ⓝ...**gas:** Texaco/Subway/dsl, **food:** Krystal, McDonald's, Waffle House, **lodging:** Best Western, Deluxe Inn, **other:** Chevrolet, Ford/Lincoln/Mercury, Honda, IGA Foods, Mazda, Rite Aid, Ⓢ...**gas:** BP, **food:** KFC, **lodging:** Best Inn, **other:** Buick/GMC/Pontiac/Subaru, Family$,
1c	Halls Ferry Rd, Ⓝ...**gas:** Chevron/24hr, Exxon, **food:** Burger King, Sonic, **lodging:** Travel Inn, **other:** HOSPITAL, Ⓢ...**gas:** Kangaroo/dsl, **food:** Capt D's, DQ, Goldie's BBQ, McRay's, Pizza Hut, Popeye's, Ryan's, Shoney's, Subway, Taco Bell, Taco Casa, TCBY, Wendy's, Whataburger, **lodging:** Day's Inn, Fairfield Inn, Super 8, **other:** Advance Parts, Big Lots, Dillard's, Home Depot, Fred's Drug, JC Penney, Kroger, Walgreen, USPO, mall
1b	US 61 S, Ⓢ...**gas:** BP, Chevron/Domino's, **food:** McDonald's, **other:** Wal-Mart SuperCtr/24hr, same as 1c
1a	Washington St, Vicksburg, Ⓝ...**Welcome Ctr both lanes, full(handicapped)facilities, phone, gas:** Kangaroo/dsl, Shell/Subway/dsl, **food:** Goldie's BBQ, **lodging:** AmeriStar Hotel, **other:** Isle of Capri RV Park, casino, Ⓢ...**food:** Waffle House, **lodging:** La Quinta, Ridgeland Inn
0mm	Mississippi/Louisiana state line, Mississippi River

Interstate 55

Exit #	Services
291.5mm	Mississippi/Tennessee state line
291	State Line Rd, Southaven, Ⓔ...**gas:** Exxon, Horizon, **food:** BBQ, Burger King, Exline's Pizza, McDonald's, Mi Tierra Mexican, Subway, Waffle House, **lodging:** Best Western, Comfort Inn, Holiday Inn Express, Quality Inn, **other:** Firestone/auto, Goodyear/auto, Kroger, Walgreens, Ⓦ...**food:** Capt D's, Checker's, Dales Rest, El Patron Mexican, Mrs Winner's, Sonic, Taco Bell, Wendy's, **other:** Big Lots, Fred's Drug, Rite Aid, Walgreens, tires
289	MS 302, to US 51, Horn Lake, Ⓔ...**gas:** 76/Circle K, Shell, **food:** Backyard Burger, Burger King, Chick-fil-A, Chili's, Coldstone, Danver's, Fazoli's, IHOP, Krystal, La Hacienda, Logan's Roadhouse, LoneStar Steaks, McDonald's, Moe's SW Grill, O'Charley's, Olive Garden, Outback Steaks, Quizno's, Red Lobster, Smokey Bones BBQ, Sonic, Starbucks, Steak'n Shake, TGIFriday, **lodging:** Comfort Suites, Courtyard, Fairfield Inn, Hampton Inn, Residence Inn, **other:** HOSPITAL, Aldi Foods, Chevrolet, Chrysler/Jeep, Circuit City, Dillards, $Tree, Ford, JC Penney, Lowe's Whse, Marshall's, NAPA/repair, Nissan, Office Depot, Old Navy, Pontiac/GMC, Sam's Club/gas, Wal-Mart SuperCtr/24hr, mall, Ⓦ...**gas:** BP, Phillips 66/dsl, Shell/dsl, **food:** Applebee's, Arby's, Bob Evans, Country Home Buffet, ChuckeCheese, Cracker Barrel, Fire Mtn Grill, Grand Buffet, Hooters, KFC, Mrs Winner's, Papa John's, Pizza Hut, Popeye's, Roadhouse Grill, Taco Bell, Texas Roadhouse, Waffle House, Wendy's, Zaxby's, **lodging:** Day's Inn, Drury Inn, Motel 6, Ramada Ltd, Sleep Inn, Super 8, **other:** Family$, Harley Davidson, Home Depot, Kroger, Target, Walgreens
287	Church Rd, Ⓔ...**gas:** Citgo/dsl, Ⓦ...**gas:** Shell/DQ/dsl, **food:** McDonald's, Subway, Waffle House, **lodging:** Country Hearth Inn, Magnolia Inn
285mm	weigh sta both lanes
284	to US 51, Nesbit Rd, Ⓦ...**gas:** BP, **food:** Happy Daze Dairybar, **other:** USPO
282	future I-69 interchange
280	MS 304, US 51, Hernando, Ⓔ...**gas:** Exxon, **food:** Capt D's, Dominos, Guadalahara Mexican, Huddle House, Sonic, **lodging:** Day's Inn, Hernando Inn, Scottish Inn, **other:** Wal-Mart SuperCtr/gas, Ⓦ...**gas:** BP, Citgo/dsl, Shell/dsl, **food:** BBQ, Brick Oven Rest., Church's, McDonald's, Papa John's, Pizza Hut, Quizno's, Sonic, Wendy's, **lodging:** Super 8, **other:** Kroger/gas, NAPA, Piggly Wiggly, Save-a-Lot, Memphis S Camping(2mi), to Arkabutla Lake
279mm	**Welcome Ctr sb, full(handicapped)facilities, phone, picnic tables, litter barrels, petwalk, RV dump, 24hr security**
276mm	**rest area nb, full(handicapped)facilities, phone, picnic tables, litter barrels, petwalk, RV dump, 24hr security**
273mm	Coldwater River
271	MS 306, Coldwater, Ⓦ...**gas:** BP, **food:** Subway, **1-2 mi** Ⓦ...**gas:** Citgo, Exxon/24hr, **other:** Lake Arkabutla, Memphis S RV Park

Interstate 55

N ↕ **S**

265	MS 4, Senatobia, **W**...**gas:** Exxon, FuelMart/dsl, Kangaroo/Huddle House/dsl/scales/24 hr, **food:** Coleman's BBQ, Domino's, KFC, McDonald's, New China Buffet, Pizza Hut, Popeye's, Sonic, Subway, Taco Bell, Waffle House, Wendy's, **lodging:** Days Inn, Motel 6, **other:** HOSPITAL, CarQuest, $General, Fred's Drug, Goodyear/auto, NAPA, Pontiac/Buick/GMC, USPO
257	MS 310, Como, **E**...**gas:** BP/dsl, **food:** Windy City Grille, **other:** N Sardis Lake
252	MS 315, Sardis, **E**...**gas:** Chevron/dsl, Pure/dsl, **food:** BBQ, McDonald's, **lodging:** Lake Inn, Super 8, **other:** to Kyle SP, Sardis Dam, RV camping, **W**...**gas:** Shell/dsl, **food:** Sonic, **lodging:** Knight's Inn, **other:** HOSPITAL, $General, Fred's Drug
246	MS 35, N Batesville, **E**...to Sardis Lake, **W**...**gas:** Mobil, Shell/dsl
243b a	MS 6, to Batesville, **E**...**gas:** BP/dsl, Shell/dsl, **food:** Backyard Burger, **other:** Lowe's Whse, Wal-Mart SuperCtr/dsl/24hr, to Sardis Lake, U of MS, **W**...**gas:** Chevron/dsl, Exxon/dsl, Phillips 66/dsl, Shell/dsl, **food:** Burger King, Capt D's, Cracker Barrel, DQ, Domino's, Hardee's, Huddle House, KFC, McDonald's, Pizza Hut, Popeye's, Sonic, Subway, Taco Bell, Wendy's, Western Sizzlin, **lodging:** AmeriHost, Comfort Inn, Day's Inn, Hampton Inn, Holiday Inn, Ramada Ltd, **other:** HOSPITAL, Advance Parts, AutoZone, $General, Factory Stores/famous brands, Family$, Fred's Drug, Kroger, O'Reilly Parts, Radio Shack
240mm	**rest area both lanes, full(handicapped)facilities, phone, picnic tables, litter barrels, petwalk, RV dump, 24hr security**
237	to US 51, Courtland, **E**...**gas:** Pure/dsl/rest.
233	to Enid Dam, **E**...to Enid Lake, RV camping, **W**...**gas:** Benson's/groceries
227	MS 32, Oakland, **E**...to Cossar SP, Sunrise RV Park, **W**...**gas:** Exxon/dsl, Shell/dsl
220	MS 330, Tillatoba, **E**...**gas:** Conoco/dsl/@
211	MS 7 N, to Coffeeville, **E**...Frog Hollow RV Park, **W**...**gas:** BP/dsl, Shell/dsl
208	Papermill Rd, **E**...Grenada Airport
206	MS 8, MS 7 S, to Grenada, **E**...**gas:** BP, Exxon/dsl, RaceWay, Shell/dsl, **food:** BBQ/Steaks, Burger King, China Buffet, Domino's, Jake&Rip's Café, La Cabana Mexican, McAlister's Deli, McDonald's, Pizza Hut, Pizza Inn, RagTime Grill, Shoney's, Subway, Taco Bell, Wendy's, Western Sizzlin, **lodging:** Best Value Inn, Comfort Inn, Day's Inn, Holiday Inn Express, Jameson Inn, Knights Inn, Super 8, **other:** HOSPITAL, Advance Parts, AutoZone, Chrysler/Dodge, $General, Ford/Lincoln/Mercury, O'Reilly Parts, Toyota, USPO, Wal-Mart SuperCtr/24hr, to Grenada Lake/RV camping, **W**...**gas:** Exxon/HuddleHouse, **lodging:** Country Inn&Suites, Econolodge
204mm	parking area sb, phone, litter barrels
202mm	parking area nb, phone, litter barrels
199	Trout Rd, S Grenada, **E**...to camp McCain
195	MS 404, Duck Hill, **E**...to Camp McCain, **W**...Conoco/dsl

185	US 82, Winona, **E**...**gas:** Exxon, Shell/dsl, **food:** Huddle House, KFC, McDonald's, Pizza Hut, Subway, **lodging:** Budget Inn, Relax Inn, Western Inn, **other:** HOSPITAL, **W**...**gas:** Pilot/Taco Bell/dsl/24hr/scales/@
174	MS 35, MS 430, Vaiden, **E**...**gas:** Chevron/dsl, 35-55/Down Home/motel/dsl/scales/24hr/@, Shell, **other:** NAPA, Vaiden Camping, **W**...**gas:** Exxon/Stuckey's/dsl, **food:** Interstate Grill, **other:** $General
173mm	**rest area sb, full(handicapped)facilities, phone, picnic tables, litter barrels, petwalk, RV dump, 24hr security**
164	to West, **W**...**gas:** West Trkstp/Pure/dsl/@
163mm	**rest area nb, full(handicapped)facilities, phone, picnic tables, litter barrels, petwalk, RV dump, 24hr security**
156	MS 12, Durant, **E**...**gas:** Shell/dsl, **lodging:** Durant Motel/rest., Super 8, **W**...HOSPITAL
150	**E**...Holmes Co SP, RV camping
146	MS 14, Goodman, **W**...to Little Red Schoolhouse
144	MS 17, to Pickens, **E**...**gas:** Texaco/dsl/24hr/@, **food:** HomePlace Rest., J's Deli, **W**...**gas:** BP/dsl/rest./24hr, **other:** to Little Red Schoolhouse
139	MS 432, to Pickens, no services
133	Vaughan, **E**...to Casey Jones Museum
128mm	Big Black River
124	MS 16, to N Canton, **E**... Heritage RV Ctr
119	MS 22, to MS 16 E, Canton, **E**...**gas:** BP/Subway/dsl, Exxon, Nancy's/rest., Shell, **food:** McDonald's, Pizza Hut, Popeye's, Sombrero Mexican, Sonic, Wendy's, Western Sizzlin, **lodging:** Comfort Inn, Econolodge, Hampton Inn, Holiday Inn Express, **other:** HOSPITAL, Ford, to Ross Barnett Reservoir, **W**...**gas:** Chevron/KFC/dsl, Citgo/dsl, Love's/Arby's/dsl/scales/24hr/@, **food:** Bumpers Drive-In, 2 Rivers Steaks
118a b	Nissan Parkway, no services
114a b	Sowell Rd, no facilites
112	US 51, Gluckstadt, **E**...**gas:** Exxon/Krystal/dsl, Kangaroo/Subway/dsl, **lodging:** Super 8, **W**...Camper Corral RV Ctr
108	MS 463, Madison, **E**...**gas:** Shell/dsl, Texaco/Domino's/dsl, **food:** Abner's Rest., Applebees, Backyard Burger, Burger King, Captain's Catch, Chick-Fil-A, Chili's, Coldstone, El Potrillo, Haute Pig Café, **other:** Lowe's Whse, Wal-Mart SuperCtr/24hr **W**...**gas:** Exxon/KFC/dsl, **food:** BoneFish Grill, Papito's Grill, Pizza Inn, Wendy's, **lodging:** Hilton Garden, **other:** HOSPITAL, CVS Drug, Home Depot

Left margin, top to bottom: Batesville, Grenada, Canton

MISSISSIPPI

Interstate 55

105b	Old Agency Rd, **E**...**gas:** Chevron/dsl, **other:** Honda, Pontiac/Buick/GMC
105a	Natchez Trace Pkwy, no services
104	I-220, to W Jackson
103	County Line Rd, **E**...**gas:** BP, Chevron, Exxon/dsl, **food:** Applebee's, Barnhill's, Burger King, Chick-fil-A, Copeland's Rest., Cuco's Mexican, Fuddrucker's, Huntington's Grill, KFC, Krispy Kreme, Mazzio's, McDonald's, Moe's SW Grill, Popeye's, Roadhouse Grill, Ralph&Kacoo's Seafood, Ruby Tuesday, Shoney's, Starbucks, Subway, Taco Bell, Wendy's, Whataburger, **lodging:** Cabot Lodge, Day's Inn, Hilton, Red Roof Inn, **other:** Acura, Barnes&Noble, Best Buy, Cadillac, Circuit City, CompUSA, Dillard's, Goodyear, Isuzu, Marshall's, Mazda, Old Navy, Sam's Club, TJ Maxx, mall, to Barnett Reservoir, **W**...**food:** Olive Garden, Red Lobster, Logan's Roadhouse, Subway, **lodging:** Comfort Suites, Drury Inn, Motel 6, **other:** Fred's Drug, Home Depot, Office Depot, Petsmart, Target
102b	Beasley Rd, Adkins Blvd, **E**...**gas:** Phillips 66, **food:** Cracker Barrel, El Potrillo Mexican, LoneStar Steaks, OutBack Steaks, **lodging:** La Quinta, Super 8, **other:** BMW, Chrysler/Jeep, Ford, Lincoln/Mercury, Nissan, Saturn, Toyota, **W**...**food:** Chili's, McDonald's, **lodging:** Best Western, Fairfield Inn, InTown Suites, Jameson Inn, **other:** Big Lots, K-Mart, Mercedes, frontage rds access 102a
102a	Briarwood, **E**...**gas:** BP, **food:** Burger King, Krystal, Moe's SW Grill, Steam Room Grill, **lodging:** Extended Stay America, **other:** Firestone, Kroger, Office Depot, Saverite Foods, Steinmart, **W**...**food:** Capt D's, Chili's, ChuckeCheese, El Chico's, Hops Grill, Jiquilpan Mexican, Perkins, Popeye's, Red Lobster, Steak&Ale, Su Koon Chinese, **lodging:** Best Inn, Best Value Inn, Comfort Inn, Hampton Inn, **other:** Audi/VW, Chevrolet, Dodge, Jaguar/Saab
100	North Side Dr W, **E**...**gas:** Chevron, Sprint Gas, **food:** Dunkin Donuts, McAlister's Deli, McDonald's, Papa John's, Piccadilly's, Shoney's, SteakOut, Subway, Wendy's, Western Sizzlin, **other:** AutoZone, BooksAMillion, Eckerd, Goodyear/auto, Kroger, Office Depot, **W**...**gas:** BP, Exxon, Shell, **food:** Bennigan's, Broad St Café, Domino's, Hooters, IHOP, Pizza Hut, Waffle House, **lodging:** Holiday Inn, Knight's Inn, Select Hotel, Super 8
99	Meadowbrook Rd, Northside Dr E(from nb)
98c b	MS 25 N, Lakeland Dr, **E**...**gas:** Shell, **food:** Penns Rest.,(2mi), **lodging:** Parkside Inn, **other:** LaFleur's Bluff SP, **W**...HOSPITAL, museum, airport
98a	Woodrow Wilson Dr, downtown
96c	Fortification St, **E**...**lodging:** Residence Inn, **W**...HOSPITAL, Bellhaven College
96b	High St, Jackson, downtown, **E**...**other:** Chevrolet, Infiniti, Lexus, Saturn, **W**...**gas:** Shell/dsl, Texaco/dsl, **food:** Burger King, DQ, Domino's, Popeye's, Shoney's, Taco Bell, Waffle House, Wendy's, Whataburger, **lodging:** Day's Inn, Best Western, Hampton Inn, Holiday Inn Express, Microtel, Quality Inn, Red Roof Inn, Regency Hotel, **other:** HOSPITAL, Honda, museum, st capitol

96a	Pearl St(from nb), Jackson, downtown, **W**...access to same as 96b
94	(46 from nb), I-20 E, to Meridian, US 49 S
45b[I-20]	US 51, State St, to downtown, **N**...**gas:** Chevron, Petro, **other:** Subaru, Pontiac, Volvo **S**...**gas:** Pilot
45a	Gallatin St(from sb), downtown, **S**...**gas:** Pilot/McDonald's/dsl/@, **lodging:** Express Inn, **other:** Daewoo, Hyundai/Mazda, Mitsubishi, Nissan, Toyota
92c	(44 from sb), I-20 W, to Vicksburg, US 49 N
92b	US 51 N, State St, Gallatin St, no services
92a	McDowell Rd, **E**...Petro/dsl/@, Pilot/McDonald's/dsl/@, **lodging:** Knight's Inn, **W**...**gas:** BJ's, Dixie, Shell, Texaco/dsl, **food:** Waffle House, **lodging:** Super S Inn
90b	Daniel Lake Blvd(from sb), **W**...**gas:** Shell, **other:** Harley-Davidson
90a	Savanna St, **E**...**lodging:** Econolodge, Save Inn **W**...**gas:** BP, **other:** Turning Wheel RV Center
88	Elton Rd, **W**...**gas:** Chevron, Exxon/Subway/Chester-Fried/dsl
85	Byram, **E**...**gas:** BP/dsl/24hr, Blue Sky, **food:** Double S Grill, Krystal, Mexican Grill, **other:** Swinging Bridge RV Park, **W**...**gas:** Conoco/dsl, Spur, Texaco/dsl, **food:** Capt'n D's, Dragon Garden Chinese, Mazzio's, McAlister's Deli, McDonald's, Pizza Hut, Popeye's, Sonic, Subway, Taco Bell, Waffle House, Wendy's, **lodging:** Day's Inn, **other:** $General, Market Place Foods, PawPaw's RV Ctr, Super D Drugs
81	Wynndale Rd, **W**...**gas:** Conoco/dsl
78	Terry, **E**...**gas:** Texaco/Subway/dsl/24hr, **other:** USPO, **W**...**gas:** Mac's, **other:** $General, Terry Food's
72	MS 27, Crystal Springs, **E**...**gas:** Exxon/Subway/dsl, Phillips 66/dsl, **food:** McDonald's, Popeye's, **lodging:** Wisteria B&B(2mi), **other:** Ford/Lincoln/Mercury
68	to US 51, S Crystal Springs, gas
65	to US 51, Gallman, **E**...**gas:** Stuckey's/gas
61	MS 28, Hazlehurst, **E**...**gas:** BP, Chevron, Exxon/Subway, Phillips 66, Pump&Save, **food:** Burger King, Country Catfish, KFC, McDonald's, Pizza Hut, Sonic, Stark's Rest., Wendy's, Western Sizzlin, **lodging:** Claridge Inn, Day's Inn, Western Inn, **other:** HOSPITAL, Advance Parts, $General, Family$, Fred's Drugs, Piggly Wiggly, Supervalu Foods, Wal-Mart
59	to S Hazlehurst, no services
56	to Martinsville, no services
54mm	**rest area both lanes, full(handicapped)facilities, phone, picnic tables, litter barrels, petwalk, RV dump, vending, 24hr security**
51	to Wesson, **W**...**gas:** Country Jct trk stp/dsl/rest., **E**...**other:** Lake Lincoln SP
48	Mt Zion Rd, to Wesson, no services
42	to US 51, N Brookhaven, **E**...**gas:** Exxon, Phillips 66/Ernie's Dinner/dsl, Shell/dsl, **other:** HOSPITAL, **W**...**lodging:** Super 8
40	to MS 550, Brookhaven, **E**...**gas:** BP/Domino's, Blue Sky, Exxon/Subway, Fleetway, Shell/dsl/24hr, **food:** Bowie BBQ, Burger King, China Buffet, Cracker Barrel, DQ, El Sombrero Mexican, KFC, Krystal, McDonald's, Mitchell's Steaks, Pizza Hut, Popeye's, Sonic, Taco Bell, Wendy's, Western Sizzlin, **lodging:** Comfort Inn, Day's Inn, Lincoln Inn, Hampton Inn, Spanish

Interstate 55

	Inn, **other:** HOSPITAL, AutoZone, CarQuest, Chevrolet, Chrysler/Dodge/Jeep, Fred's Drugs, Ford/Lincoln/Mercury, Honda, Nissan, Rite Aid, SaveALot Foods, Super D Drugs, Toyota, Walgreens, Wal-Mart SuperCtr/gas/24hr, W...**other:** Home Depot
38	US 84, S Brookhaven, **1 mi** E...**gas:** Exxon/dsl, W...**gas:** Chevron/dsl/24hr
30	Bogue Chitto, Norfield, E...**gas:** Shell/BogueChitto/dsl/@
24	Johnston Station, E...to Lake Dixie Springs
20b a	US 98 W, to Natchez, Summit, E...**gas:** BP/dsl, Shell/dsl, Stop'n Shop/dsl, W...**gas:** Exxon/Subway/dsl, Phillips 66/dsl
18	MS 570, Smithdale Rd, N McComb, E...**gas:** BP, **food:** Burger King, FoodCourt, McDonald's, Piccadilly's, Ruby Tuesday, **other:** HOSPITAL, JC Penney, Lowe's Whse, Sears/auto, Wal-Mart SuperCtr/Subway/24hr, mall, W...**gas:** Chevron/dsl, **food:** Arby's, **lodging:** Deerfield Inn, Hawthorn Inn, **other:** Ford/Lincoln/Mercury
17	Delaware Ave, McComb, E...**gas:** BP/Subway, Blue Sky Gas, Chevron/dsl, Exxon/Krystal, Pure, RaceWay, Shell/dsl, **food:** Burger King, China Gourmet, DQ, Golden Corral, Huddle House, McDonald's, Pizza Hut, Pizza Inn, Popeye's, Sonic, Taco Bell, Wendy's, **lodging:** Comfort Inn, National Inn, Super 8, **other:** HOSPITAL, AutoZone, CVS Drug, $General, Eckerd, Family$, Fred's Drug, Kroger, O'Reilly Parts, W...**lodging:** Day's Inn, **other:** Chrysler/Dodge/Jeep
15b a	US 98 E, MS 48 W, McComb, **1 mi** E...**gas:** Exxon/Subway, Shell, **food:** Church's, Hardee's, KFC, **lodging:** Camellian Motel, Economy Inn, W...**gas:** BP/dsl
13	Fernwood Rd, W...**gas:** Conoco/Fernwood/dsl/rest./scales/24hr/@, **lodging:** Fernwood Motel, **other:** golf, to Percy Quin SP
10	MS 48, Magnolia, **1 mi** E...**gas:** BP, Exxon, **food:** Subway, **other:** RV camping
8	MS 568, Magnolia, E...Pike Co Speedway
4	Chatawa, no services
3.5mm	**Welcome Ctr nb, full(handicapped)facilities, phone, picnic tables, litter barrels, petwalk, RV dump, 24hr security**
1	MS 584, Osyka, Gillsburg, W...RV camping
0mm	Mississippi/Louisiana state line

Interstate 59

Exit #	Services
	I-59 S and I-20 W run together to Meridian.
172mm	Mississippi/Alabama state line
149mm	**I-59 N and I-20 E run together 22 mi. See Mississippi Interstate 20, exits 150-170mm.**
142	to US 11, Savoy, W...to Dunns Falls
137	to N Enterprise, to Stonewall, no services
134	MS 513, S Enterprise, no services
126	MS 18, to Rose Hill, Pachuta, E...**gas:** BP/dsl/24hr

118	to Vossburg, Paulding, no services
113	MS 528, to Heidelberg, E...**gas:** BP/JR's/dsl/24hr, Chevron/Stuckey's/dsl, Exxon/Subway/Pizza Inn/dsl, Shell
109mm	parking area sb, litter barrels, no restrooms
106mm	parking area nb, litter barrels, no restrooms
104	Sandersville, no services
99	US 11, E...**gas:** T&B's/dsl, **lodging:** Magnolia Motel, **other:** KOA(1mi)
97	US 84 E, E...**gas:** Exxon/dsl/scales, Kangaroo/Subway/dsl/24hr, **food:** Hardee's, Ward's Rest., W...**gas:** BP/dsl, Shell/24hr, **food:** KFC, Vic's Biscuits/burgers
96b	MS 15 S, Cook Ave, no services
96a	Masonite Rd, 4th Ave, no services
95d	(from nb), no services
95c	Beacon St, Laurel, W...**gas:** Chevron, PumpSave Gas, **food:** Burger King, Church's, McDonald's, Old Mexico, Popeye's, **lodging:** TownHouse Motel/rest., **other:** Family$, JC Penney, USPO, XpertTire
95b a	US 84 W, MS 15 N, 16th Ave, Laurel, W...**gas:** Exxon/dsl, Shell, Texaco, **food:** DQ, Hardee's, KFC, Shoney's, Subway, Taco Bell, Waffle House, Wendy's, **lodging:** Comfort Suites, Econolodge, Hampton Inn, Holiday Inn Express, Super 8, **other:** HOSPITAL, Advance Parts, $General, Piggly Wiggly, Walgreens, **1 mi** W...**food:** Burger King, Checker's, McDonald's, Pizza Hut, Western Sizzlin, **other:** AutoZone, Ford, KIA, Lowes Whse, Office Depot, Rite Aid, Toyota, Wal-Mart SuperCtr
93	US 11, S Laurel, W...**gas:** Citgo/dsl, Exxon/Subway/dsl, Shell/dsl/24hr, **food:** Hardee's
90	US 11, Ellisville Blvd, E...**gas:** Texaco/dsl, **food:** Huddle House, W...**gas:** Dixie/dsl
88	MS 588, MS 29, Ellisville, E...**gas:** Chevron/dsl, FastTrac, **food:** Domino's, KFC, McDonald's, Pizza Hut, Subway, **other:** Food Tiger, Family$, NAPA, W...**gas:** Exxon/dsl, **food:** Glenda's Diner, **lodging:** Best Western
85	MS 590, to Ellisville, W...auto repair
80	to US 11, Moselle, E...**gas:** BP/dsl
78	Sanford Rd, no services
76	W...Hattiesburg-Laurel Reg Airport
73	Monroe Rd, to Monroe, no services
69	to Glendale, Eatonville Rd, no services
67b a	US 49, Hattiesburg, E...**gas:** BP, Exxon, Kangaroo/Krystal/dsl, Shell, **food:** Arby's, Burger King, Cracker Barrel, DQ, KFC, McDonald's, Pizza Hut, Taco Bell, Waffle House, **lodging:** Budget Inn, Comfort Inn, Econolodge, Howard Johnson, Inn on the Hill,

Interstate 59

N ↕ **S**

Hattiesburg

	La Quinta, Motel 6, Red Carpet Inn, Regency Inn, Scottish Inn, Super 8, **other:** $General, **W**...**gas:** BP/dsl, Chevron, MapleLeaf/dsl, Pure/dsl, Race-Way, Shell/Subway, Stuckey's/dsl, **food:** Sonic, Waffle House, Ward's Burgers, **lodging:** Best Western, Holiday Inn
65b a	US 98 W, Hardy St, Hattiesburg, **E**..**gas:** Exxon, Shell/dsl, Texaco, **food:** Applebee's, Barnhill's Buffet, Bop's Custard, Buffalo Wild Wings, Burger King, Cane's Chicken, CiCi's, Crescent City Grill, Domino's, Front Porch BBQ, Hong Kong Buffet, IHOP, KFC, Krystal, Lenny's Subs, McDonald's, Pizza Hut, Quizno's, Smoothie King, Starbucks, Steak-Out, Subway, Taco Bell, Ward's Burgers, **lodging:** Courtyard, Day's Inn, Fairfield Inn, Western Motel, **other:** VET, CarQuest, CVS Drug, Goodyear/auto, Home Depot, Walgreens, S MS U, **W**...**gas:** BP/dsl, Exxon/Domino's, Kangaroo/Subway, Shell, **food:** Arby's, Backyard Burger, Burger King, Chick-fil-A, Chili's, China Buffet, Coldstone Creamery, Copeland's Rest., FireHouse Subs, Fire Mtn Grill, Hardee's, Krispy Kreme, La Fiesta Brava, Lion's Choice, Logan's Roadhouse, LoneStar Steaks, LongHorn Steaks, Mazzio's, McDonald's, O'Charley's, Olive Garden, Outback Steaks, Pepper's Cafe, Pizza Hut, Popeye's, Red Lobster, Ryan's, Taco Bell, Waffle House, Ward's Burgers, Wendy's, Zaxby's, **lodging:** Comfort Suites, Hampton Inn, Microtel, Sun Suites, **other:** HOSPITAL, Advance Parts, AutoZone, Best Buy, BooksAMillion, Dillard's, $Tree, Firestone/auto, Goodyear/auto, JC Penney, Lincoln/Mercury, Lowe's Whse, Nissan, Office Depot, Old Navy, Radio Shack, Rite Aid, Ross, SaveRite Foods, Sam's Club/gas, Sears/auto, Target, TJ Maxx, Walgreens, Wal-Mart SuperCtr/24hr, mall
60	US 11, S Hattiesburg, **E**...**gas:** Shell/dsl, **W**...**gas:** BP/dsl, Kangaroo/Subway/dsl/24hr
59	US 98 E, to US 49, Lucedale, MS Gulf Coast
56mm	parking area both lanes, litter barrels, no restrooms
51	RD 589, to Purvis, **2 mi W**...**gas:** Shell/dsl, **food:** Pizza Hut, to Little Black Cr Water Park
48mm	Little Black Creek
41	MS 13, to Lumberton, **W**...**gas:** Pure, **other:** $General, to Little Black Cr Water Park
35	Hillsdale Rd, **E**...**gas:** Pure/dsl, **lodging:** to Kings Arrow Ranch, to Lake Hillside Resort
32mm	Wolf River
29	RD 26, to Poplarville, **2 mi W**...**gas:** Kangaroo/dsl, **food:** Burger King, Hardee's
27	MS 53, to Poplarville, **W**...**gas:** Shell/dsl, **other:** Hass-cienda Camping(2mi)
19	to US 11, Millard, no services
15	to McNeill, **W**...**gas:** McNeill Trkstop/dsl/rest.
13mm	parking area sb, litter barrels, no restrooms
10	to US 11, Carriere, **E**...**gas:** I-59 Trk Stp/dsl, **other:** Clearwater RV Camp(5mi)
8mm	parking area nb, litter barrels, no restrooms

Picayune

6	MS 43 N, N Picayune, **E**...**food:** Paul's Pastries, **W**...**gas:** Chevron/dsl, **lodging:** Budget Host(1mi), Picayune Motel, **other:** HOSPITAL, CVS Drug, Winn-Dixie
4	MS 43 S, to Picayune, **E**...**food:** McDonald's, Ryan's, **other:** Chevrolet/Pontiac/Buick/Cadillac, Home Depot, Sun Roamers RV Park, Walgreens, Wal-Mart SuperCtr/gas/24hr, **W**...**gas:** APG/dsl, Chevron, Exxon/dsl, Shell/dsl, Spur, **food:** Arby's, Burger King, Domino's, Hardee's, KFC, McDonald's, Papa John's, Pizza Hut, Popeye's, Shoney's, Subway, Taco Bell, Waffle House, Wendy's, **lodging:** Comfort Inn, Day's Inn, Heritage Inn, **other:** HOSPITAL, Advance Parts, AutoZone, Chrysler/Dodge/Jeep, Curves, $World, Firestone/auto, Ford/Lincoln/Mercury, Fred's Drug, O'Reilly Parts, Pawpaw's RV Ctr, Radio Shack, Rite Aid, Winn-Dixie
3mm	**Welcome Ctr nb, full(handicapped)facilities, phone, vending, picnic tables, litter barrels, petwalk, RV dump**
1.5mm	weigh sta both lanes
1	US 11, MS 607, NASA, **W**...**gas:** Chevron/dsl
0mm	**Mississippi/Louisiana state line, Pearl River. Exits 11-1 are in Louisiana**
11	Pearl River Turnaround. Callboxes begin sb.
5b	Honey Island Swamp, no services
5a	LA 41, Pearl River, **E**...**gas:** Exxon/gifts
3	US 11 S, LA 1090, Pearl River, **W**...**gas:** Shell/Subway/dsl, **1 mi W**...Chevron/dsl/24hr
1.5mm	**Welcome Ctr sb, full(handicapped)facilities, info, phone, picnic tables, litter barrels, petwalk, RV dump**
1c b	I-10, E to Bay St Louis, W to New Orleans
1a	I-12 W, to Hammond. I-59 begins/ends on I-10/I-12. Exits 1-11 are in Louisiana.

Exits 1-11 are in Louisiana.

Interstate 220(Jackson)

Exit #	Services
11mm	I-220 begins/ends on I-55, exit 104.
9	Hanging Moss Rd, County Line Rd, **E**...**gas:** BP
8	Watkins Dr, **E**...**gas:** Shell/Chester Fried, Spur
5b a	US 49 N, Evers Blvd, to Yazoo City, **E**...**food:** KFC, **lodging:** Star Motel, Family$, Food Depot, **W**...**gas:** BP, Exxon/Burger King, Shell/Subway/dsl
3	Industrial Dr, no services
2b a	Clinton Blvd, Capitol St, **E**...to Jackson Zoo, **W**...**gas:** Phillips 66, RaceWay, Shell, **food:** Burger King, McDonald's, Pizza Hut, Popeye's, Sonic, **other:** Family$
1b a	US 80, **E**...**gas: food:** Sonny's BBQ, Capt D's, Denny's, KFC, Taco Bell, Wendy's, Western Sizzlin, **lodging:** Day's Inn, Econolodge, Sleep Inn, Super 8, **W**...**gas:** BP, Exxon/Subway/dsl, **food:** Arby's, El Chico, Krystal, McDonald's, Pizza Hut, Popeye's, Wendy's, **other:** Belk, Dillard's, Ford, Hyundai, McRae's, Sears/auto, mall
0mm	I-220 begins/ends on I-20, exit 41.

Jackson

E ↕ **W**

MISSOURI

Interstate 29

<table>
<tr><td colspan="2">N ↕ S</td><td></td></tr>
<tr><td>Exit #</td><td>Services</td></tr>
<tr><td>124mm</td><td>Missouri/Iowa state line</td></tr>
<tr><td>123mm</td><td>Nishnabotna River</td></tr>
<tr><td>121.5mm</td><td>weigh sta both lanes</td></tr>
<tr><td>116</td><td>rd A, rd B, to Watson, W...fireworks</td></tr>
<tr><td>110</td><td>US 136, Rock Port, Phelps City, E...gas: Shell/dsl, lodging: Rockport Inn, to NW MO St U, W...gas: BP/dsl/24hr, Phillips 66/Subway/dsl/24hr, food: McDonald's, Trails End Rest., lodging: Super 8, other: KOA, fireworks</td></tr>
<tr><td>109.5mm</td><td>Welcome Ctr sb, full(handicapped) facilities, info, phone, picnic tables, litter barrels, petwalk</td></tr>
<tr><td>107</td><td>MO 111, to Rock Port, W...motel/RV Park</td></tr>
<tr><td>106.5mm</td><td>Rock Creek</td></tr>
<tr><td>102mm</td><td>Mill Creek</td></tr>
<tr><td>99</td><td>rd W, Corning, no services</td></tr>
<tr><td>97mm</td><td>Tarkio River</td></tr>
<tr><td>92</td><td>US 59, to Fairfax, Craig, W...gas: Sinclair/dsl</td></tr>
<tr><td>90.5mm</td><td>Little Tarkio Creek</td></tr>
<tr><td>86.5mm</td><td>Squaw Creek</td></tr>
<tr><td>84</td><td>MO 118, Mound City, E...gas: Phillips 66/Subway/dsl, Shamrock/dsl, food: Breadeaux Pizza, McDonald's, Quacker's Steaks, lodging: Audrey's Motel, Super 8, other: Dodge/Jeep, $General, Mound City Foods, W...gas: Shell/dsl/24hr, other: Big Lake SP(12mi)</td></tr>
<tr><td>82mm</td><td>rest area both lanes, full(handicapped)facilities, phone, picnic tables, litter barrels, vending, petwalk</td></tr>
<tr><td>79</td><td>US 159, Rulo, E...gas: Squaw Creek Trkstp/dsl/rest/RV dump/@, W...to Big Lake SP(12mi), to Squaw Creek NWR(3mi)</td></tr>
<tr><td>78mm</td><td>Kimsey Creek</td></tr>
<tr><td>75</td><td>US 59, to Oregon, no services</td></tr>
<tr><td>67</td><td>US 59 N, to Oregon, no services</td></tr>
<tr><td>66.5mm</td><td>Nodaway River</td></tr>
<tr><td>65</td><td>US 59, rd RA, to Fillmore, Savannah, E...gas: Conoco/dsl, other: antiques</td></tr>
<tr><td>60</td><td>rd K, rd CC, Amazonia, W...other: Hunt's Fruit Barn, antiques</td></tr>
<tr><td>58.5mm</td><td>Hopkins Creek</td></tr>
</table>

Interstate 29

N ↑ S

St Joseph

Exit	Description
56b a	I-229 S, US 71 N, US 59 N, to St Joseph, Maryville
55mm	Dillon Creek
53	US 59, US 71 bus, to St Joseph, Savannah, E...AOK Camping, fireworks, W...gas: Phillips 66/dsl
50	US 169, St Joseph, King City, 1-3 mi W on Belt Hwy...gas: Conoco, Phillips 66/Domino's, Shell, food: Bob Evans, Cheddar's, Chili's, Chipotle Mexican, Culver's, Famous Dave's, 54th St Grill, Hardee's, LJ Silver, McDonald's, Panda Express, Ryan's, Sonic, Subway, Taco Bell, Wendy's, other: Advance Parts, Border's Books, Home Depot, Kohl's, Lowe's Whse, Michaels, Sam's Club, Target, Tires+, TJ Maxx, Walgreen, Wal-Mart SuperCtr/24hr
47	MO 6, Frederick Blvd, to Clarksdale, St Joseph, E...gas: Conoco, food: Bandanas BBQ, Country Kitchen, lodging: Day's Inn, Drury Inn, W...gas: Sinclair, Phillips 66/dsl, food: Applebee's, Carlos O'Kelly's, Cracker Barrel, Denny's, Dunkin Donuts, Ground Round, Hazel's Coffee, KFC, McDonald's, Perkins/24hr, Pizza Hut, Red Lobster, Russell Stover, Sonic, Subway, Taco Bell, Whiskey Creek Steaks, Village Steaks, lodging: Budget Inn, Comfort Suites, Hampton Inn, Motel 6, Ramada Inn, Stoney Creek Inn, Super 8, other: HOSPITAL, BigLots, Chevrolet/Mazda, Dillard's, Ford, Firestone/auto, Goodyear/auto, PriceChopper Foods, Sears, RV camp, 1 mi W on US 169...food: Arby's, Blimpie, Burger King, Church's, Fazoli's, Ground Round, LJ Silver, Pizza Hut, Rib Crib BBQ, Schlotsky's, Sonic, Starbucks, Taco Bell, other: Advance Parts, Aldi Foods, AutoZone, Buick/Pontiac/GMC, Cub Foods, CVS Drug, Eckerd, Food-4Less/drugs/24hr, Ford/Lincoln/Mercury, Hastings Books, HyVee Foods, JC Penney, Jo-Ann Fabrics, Office Depot, Radio Shack, U-Haul, Walgreen
46b a	US 36, to Cameron, St Joseph, 1 mi W on US 169...gas: BP/dsl, FL, Shell, food: Burger King, Godfather's, La Mesa Mexican, Pizza Hut, Taco John's, Wendy's, other: $General, Isuzu, Kia, Nissan, QwikLube, Save-a-Lot Foods, Walgreen, Wal-Mart SuperCtr/gas/24hr, to MO W St Coll
44	US 169, to Gower, St Joseph, E...gas: Phillips 66, Loves/Arby's/dsl/scales/24hr, food: Nelly's Mexican, Subway, lodging: Best Western, other: dsl repair, W...gas: Shell/dsl/rest/24hr, food: DQ, McDonald's, San Jose Steaks, Taco Bell, other: Chrysler/Jeep/Dodge, $Tree, Goodyear, Harley-Davidson, Hyundai, Wal-Mart SuperCtr/gas/24hr
43	I-229 N, to St Joseph
39.5mm	Pigeon Creek
35	rd DD, Faucett, W...gas: Farris Trkstp/dsl/motel/rest/24hr/@
33.5mm	Bee Creek
30	rd Z, rd H, Dearborn, New Market, E...gas: Conoco/Subway/dsl/24hr
29.5mm	Bee Creek
27mm	**rest area both lanes, full(handicapped) facilities, phone, picnic tables, litter barrels, vending, petwalk**
25	rd E, rd U, to Camden Point, E...gas: Phillips 66/dsl/rest.

Platte City

Exit	Description
24mm	weigh sta both lanes
20	MO 92, MO 273, to Atchison, Leavenworth, W...gas: Phillips 66, other: to Weston Bend SP
19.5mm	Platte River
19	rd HH, Platte City, E...antiques, W...gas: Casey's, Conoco, Platte City/dsl, food: DQ, Red Dragon Chinese, lodging: Comfort Inn, Travelodge, other: Airport RV Park, Cash Saver Foods, CountryMart Foods, Dodge, CarQuest, USPO, same as 18
18	MO 92, Platte City, E...Basswood RV Park(5mi), W...gas: Casey's, Conoco/KFC, QT/dsl, food: Arby's, Burger King, McDonald's, Mr GoodCents Subs, Pizza Shoppe, Rancho Grande Cantina, Sonic, Subway, Taco Bell/Pizza Hut, Waffle House, lodging: Best Western, Comfort Inn, Super 8, other: Chevrolet/Pontiac/GMC, CVS Drug, Goodyear/auto, Ford, same as 19
17	I-435 S, to Topeka
15	Mexico City Ave, W...lodging: Marriott
14	I-435 E(from sb), to St Louis
13	to I-435 E, E...lodging: Best Western, Clarion, Comfort Suites, Extended Stay America, Fairfield Inn, Holiday Inn, Microtel, Radisson, Sheraton, W...lodging: Marriott, other: KCI Airport
12	NW 112th St, E...gas: BP, Conoco/dsl, lodging: Day's Inn, Extended Stay America, Day's Inn, Hampton Inn, Hilton, Holiday Inn Express, Microtel, W...lodging: Econolodge
10	Tiffany Springs Pkwy, E...gas: Phillips 66, Shell, food: Jade Garden, SmokeBox BBQ, lodging: Embassy Suites, Homewood Suites, W...food: Cracker Barrel, Ruby Tuesday, Waffle House, Wendy's, lodging: AmeriSuites, Chase Suites, Courtyard, Drury Inn, Homeswood Suites, Howard Johnson, MainStay Suites, Ramada Inn, Residence Inn, Sleep Inn, other: Honda, Lexus, Nissan, Saturn, Toyota, Volvo
9b a	MO 152, to Liberty, Topeka

Kansas City

Exit	Description
8	MO 9, rd T, NW Barry Rd, E...gas: Valero/dsl, food: Applebee's, Boston Mkt, Chili's, Chipotle Mexican, 54th St Grill, Hong's Buffet, Hooters, Kato Japanese, LoneStar Steaks, On the Border, Panda Express, Panera Bread, Pizza Hut/Taco Bell, Starbucks, Subway, Wendy's, Winstead's Rest., other: HOSPITAL, HyVee Foods, Lowe's Whse, Old Navy, SteinMart, Wal-Mart SuperCtr/24hr, W...gas: Phillips 66, QT/dsl, Shell, food: Abuelo's Mexican, Hardee's, LJ Silver/A&W, McDonald's, Mimi's Cafe, Minsky's Pizza, Outback Steaks, Rainbow Oriental, Smokehouse BBQ, Sonic, Taco Bueno, lodging: Motel 6, Quality Inn, Super 8, other: Barnes&Noble, CVS Drug, Tires+
6	NW 72nd St, Platte Woods, E...gas: Sinclair/dsl, W...gas: Phillips 66, food: KFC, Papa John's, Tasty Thai, other: Sears Grand
5	MO 45 N, NW 64th St, W...gas: Shell/dsl, food: Goodcents Subs, IHOP, KFC, McDonald's, Nick & Jake's, O'Quigley's Grill, Papa Murphy's, Quizno's, Subway, Thai Place, other: CVS Drug, $General, GNC, Goodyear, Radio Shack
4	NW 56th St(from nb), W...gas: Phillips 66, same as 5
3c	rd A(from sb), Riverside, W...gas: QT, food: Argosy Café, Corner Café, MeanGreen's Cafe, Sonic, lodging: Skyline Inn, Super 8, other: USPO
3b	I-635 S
3a	Waukomis Dr, rd AA(from nb)

Interstate 29

2b	US 169 S(from sb), to KC
2a	US 169 N(from nb), to Smithville
1e	US 69, Vivion Rd, **E**...**gas:** Shell/dsl, **food:** Mc-Doanld's, Steak'n Shake, **other:** Chrysler/Jeep, Chevrolet/Cadillac, Home Depot, Lincoln/Mercury, Mitsubishi, PriceChopper Foods/24hr, **W**...**gas:** Shell, **food:** McDonald's, Subway
1d	MO 283 S, Oak Tfwy(from sb), **W**...**gas:** Phillips 66, **food:** McDonald's
1c	Gladstone(from nb), **E**...**food:** Arby's, 54th St Grill, Perkins, Pizza St Buffet, Ryan's, Smokehouse BBQ, Tippen's Café
1b	I-35 N(from sb), to Des Moines
1a	Davidson Rd
8mm	**I-35 N. I-29 and I-35 run together 6 mi.**
See Missouri Interstate 35, exits 3-8a.	

Interstate 35

Exit #	Services
114mm	Missouri/Iowa state line
114	US 69, to Lamoni, **W**...**gas:** Conoco/dsl/24hr, **other:** RV camping
113.5mm	Zadie Creek
112mm	**MO welcome ctr sb, full(handicapped) facilities, phone, picnic tables, litter barrels, petwalk**
110	weigh sta both lanes
106	rd N, Blythedale, **E**...**gas:** Conoco/fireworks, Phillips 66/dsl/café/motel/24hr/@, **food:** DinnerBell Rest., **lodging:** Painted Lady B&B, Eagle's Landing Motel, **other:** dsl repair, **W**...**gas:** Phillips 66/dsl/24hr, **other:** Eagle Ridge RV Park(2mi)
99	rd A, to Ridgeway, **5 mi W**...Eagle RV Camping
94mm	E Fork Big Creek
93	US 69, Bethany, **W**...**food:** Dos Chiquitas Mexican, **other:** RV Dump
92	US 136, Bethany, **E**...**gas:** Phillips 66/dsl/24hr, **food:** KFC/Taco Bell, McDonald's, **lodging:** Budget Inn, **W**...**gas:** BP/dsl, Casey's, Kum&Go/Wendy's/dsl, **food:** Country Kitchen, DQ, Subway, Taco Bell, TootToot Rest., **lodging:** Best Western, Super 8, **other:** HOSPITAL, Chevrolet/Buick, Russell Stover, Wal-Mart SuperCtr
90mm	Pole Cat Creek
88	MO 13, to Bethany, Gallatin, **3 mi W**...**lodging:** Bethany Motel
84	rds AA, H, to Gilman City, **E**...Crowder SP(24mi)
81mm	**rest area both lanes, full(handicapped) facilities, phone, picnic tables, litter barrels, vending, petwalk**
80	rds B, N, to Coffey, no services
78	rd C, Pattonsburg, **W**...**gas:** Phillips 66/dsl
74.5mm	Grand River
72	rd DD, no services
68	US 69, to Pattonsburg, no services
64	MO 6, to Maysville, Gallatin, no services
61	US 69, Winston, Gallatin, **E**...**gas:** Shell/dsl/rest./24hr
54	US 36, Cameron, **E**...**gas:** BP/rest./dsl/24hr, Cenex/dsl, Shell/Wendy's/dsl/24hr, **food:** McDonald's, Subway, **lodging:** Best Western, Comfort Inn, Crossroads Inn/RV Park, **W**...**gas:** Valero, **food:**

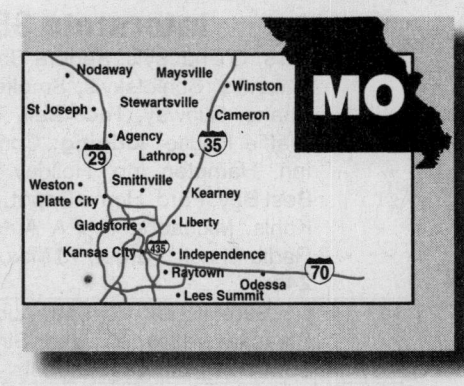

MO

	Burger King, Dominos, DQ, El Maguey Mexican, Kettle Diner, KFC/Taco Bell, Pizza Hut, Sonic, Subway, **lodging:** Day's Inn, Econolodge, Relax Inn, Super 8, **other:** HOSPITAL, Advance Parts, Ford, Chevrolet/Pontiac/Buick, CountryMart Foods, $General, Ford/Mercury, O'Reilley Parts, Radio Shack, Wal-Mart SuperCtr/24hr, W MO Corr Ctr, tires
52	rd BB, Lp 35, to Cameron, **E**...**other:** HOSPITAL, **W**...**gas:** Casey's, Kum&Go, same as 54
49mm	Brushy Creek
48.5mm	Shoal Creek
48	US 69, Cameron, **E**...to Wallace SP(2mi), **W**...**gas:** Shamrock, **other:** fireworks
40	MO 116, Lathrop, **E**...**gas:** Phillips 66/Country Café/dsl, **other:** antiques
34.5mm	**rest area both lanes, full(handicapped) facilities, phone, picnic tables, litter barrels, vending, petwalk**
33	rd PP, Holt, **E**...**food:** Hilltop Grill, **other:** RV Dump, **W**...**gas:** BP/dsl, Conoco/dsl, **lodging:** American Eagle Inn
30mm	Holt Creek
26	MO 92, Kearney, **E**...**gas:** Casey's/gas, Phillips 66/dsl, Shell/dsl, **food:** McDonald's, Sonic, **lodging:** Comfort Inn, Day's Inn, Super 8, **other:** CountryMart Foods, CVS Drug, Kramer Hardware, Red Cross Drug, to Watkins Mill SP, **W**...**gas:** Pilot/Taco Bell/dsl/scales/24hr, Platte Clay Fuels, **food:** Arby's, Burger King, Carlitos Mexican, Hunan Garden Chinese, Subway, **lodging:** Best Western, Econolodge, **other:** Chevrolet, Family$, GoodYear/auto, John's Foods, to Smithville Lake
22mm	weigh sta nb, parking area sb
20	US 69, MO 33, to Excelsior Springs, **E**...HOSPITAL
17	MO 291, rd A, **1 mi E**...**food:** Arby's, CiCi's, LJ Silver, Perkins, Ponderosa, **other:** Chevrolet, CountryMart Foods, Eckerd, Hy-Vee Foods, Liberty RV Ctr, Village Lodge, Walgreen, same as 16, **W**...**gas:** Phillips 66/dsl, QT, **food:** McDonald's, Sonic, Subway, **other:** KCI Airport
16	MO 152, Liberty, **E**...**gas:** BP, **food:** Godfather's, Pizza Hut, Planet Sub, Ponderosa, Red Robin, Starbucks, Subway, Texas Roadhouse, Village Inn Rest., Wendy's, **lodging:** Days Inn, Super 8, **other:** HOSPITAL, Chevrolet, Firestone/auto, Ford, Hy-Vee Foods, Lowe's Whse, Sears Grand, Walgreen, **W**...**gas:** BP, Phillips 66/Circle K, **food:** Applebee's, Backyard Burger, Bob Evans, Buffalo Wild Wings, Burger King, Chili's, Corner Cafe, Cracker Barrel, Golden Corral, KFC, LongHorn Steaks, McDon-

Cameron

Liberty

MISSOURI

Interstate 35

<table>
<tr><td colspan="2" rowspan="1"></td></tr>
<tr><td></td><td>ald's, O'Charley's, Panera Bread, Panda Express, Quizno's, Schlotsky's, SmokeStack BBQ, Steak'n Shake, Subway, Taco Bell, Target, Uno Pizzaria, Waffle House, lodging: Comfort Suites, Fairfield Inn, Hampton Inn, Holiday Inn Express, other: Best Buy, Ford, Home Depot, JC Penny, Jiffy Lube, Kohls, Michael's, NAPA AutoCare, Office Depot, Radio Shack, Target, TJ Maxx, Wal-Mart SuperCtr/24hr</td></tr>
<tr><td>14</td><td>US 69(exits left from sb), Liberty Dr, to Glenaire, Pleasant Valley, E...gas: Sinclair, Shell, other: I-35 RV Ctr, W...gas: QT/dsl</td></tr>
<tr><td>13</td><td>US 69(from nb), to Pleasant Valley, E...gas: Phillips 66/dsl, Shell, Sinclair/24hr, food: KFC, McDonald's, other: auto repair, W...gas: QT/dsl</td></tr>
<tr><td>12b a</td><td>I-435, to St Louis</td></tr>
<tr><td>11</td><td>US 69 N, Vivion Rd, E...gas: BP/dsl, Shell/dsl, food: Church's, McDonald's, W...gas: QT, food: Sonic, Stroud's Rest.</td></tr>
<tr><td>10</td><td>N Brighton Ave(from nb), E...food: Church's, McDonald's</td></tr>
<tr><td>9</td><td>MO 269 S, Chouteau Trfwy, E...gas: Phillips 66, food: IHOP, McDonald's, Ming Garden, Outback Steaks, Papa Murphy's, Popeye's, Subway, Wing Stop, other: Food Festival, Harrah's Casino/rest., Radio Shack, Target, W...food: Wendy's(1mi)</td></tr>
<tr><td>8c</td><td>MO 1, Antioch Rd, E...gas: 7-11/gas, food: Domino's, lodging: Best Western, Econolodge, InnTown Inn, W...gas: Phillips 66, food: Catfish Rest., Waffle House, other: Walgreen</td></tr>
<tr><td>8b</td><td>I-29 N, US 71 N, KCI airport</td></tr>
<tr><td colspan="2">I-35 S and I-29 S run together 6 mi.</td></tr>
<tr><td>8a</td><td>Parvin Rd, E...gas: BP, Shell, lodging: Holiday Inn, other: O'Reilly Parts, W...lodging: Super Inn</td></tr>
<tr><td>6b a</td><td>Armour Rd, E...gas: Phillips 66/dsl, food: Arby's, Burger King, Denny's, McDonald's, lodging: Best Value Inn, La Quinta, other: HOSPITAL, repair, to Riverboat Casino, W...gas: QT, Phillips 66, Shell, food: Pizza Hut, Taco Bell, Wendy's, lodging: American Inn, Quality Inn, other: USPO</td></tr>
<tr><td>5b</td><td>16th Ave, industrial district</td></tr>
<tr><td>5a</td><td>Levee Rd, Bedford St, industrial district</td></tr>
<tr><td>4.5mm</td><td>Missouri River</td></tr>
<tr><td>4b</td><td>Front St, E...Isle of Capri Riverboat Casino/rest.</td></tr>
<tr><td>4a</td><td>US 24 E, Independence Ave</td></tr>
<tr><td>3</td><td>I-70 E, US 71 S, to St Louis</td></tr>
<tr><td>2g</td><td>I-35 N and I-29 N run together 6 mi,</td></tr>
<tr><td>2e</td><td>Oak St, Grand-Walnut St, downtown, E...lodging: Comfort Inn, W...gas: Conoco</td></tr>
<tr><td>2d</td><td>Main-Delaware, Wyandotte St, downtown</td></tr>
<tr><td>2a</td><td>I-70 W, to Topeka, no services</td></tr>
<tr><td>2y</td><td>US 169, Broadway, to downtown</td></tr>
<tr><td>2w</td><td>12th St, Kemper Arena, to downtown</td></tr>
<tr><td>2v</td><td>14th St, to downtown</td></tr>
<tr><td>2u</td><td>I-70 E, to Broadway, E...food: Denny's</td></tr>
<tr><td>1d</td><td>20th St(from sb)</td></tr>
<tr><td>1c b</td><td>27th St, SW Blvd, W Pennway(from nb), E...gas: Phillips 66, other: HOSPITAL</td></tr>
<tr><td>1a</td><td>SW Trafficway(from sb), no services</td></tr>
<tr><td>0mm</td><td>Missouri/Kansas state line</td></tr>
</table>

Interstate 44

<table>
<tr><td>Exit #</td><td>Services</td></tr>
<tr><td>290mm</td><td>I-44 begins/ends on I-55, exit 207 in St Louis.</td></tr>
<tr><td>290a</td><td>I-55 S, to Memphis</td></tr>
<tr><td>290c</td><td>Gravois Ave(from wb), 12th St, N...gas: Citgo/dsl, S...food: McDonald's</td></tr>
<tr><td>290b</td><td>18th St(from eb), downtown</td></tr>
<tr><td>289</td><td>Jefferson Ave, St Louis, N...gas: Phillip's 66, food: Subway, lodging: Holiday Inn Express, S...gas: Conoco, food: Lee's Chicken, McDonald's</td></tr>
<tr><td>288</td><td>Grand Blvd, St Louis, N...gas: BP, lodging: Water Tower Inn other: HOSPITAL, S...food: Jack-in-the-Box, Qdoba Grill</td></tr>
<tr><td>287b a</td><td>Kingshighway, Vandeventer Ave, St Louis, N...gas: BP, other: Jiffy Lube, U-Haul, S...gas: BP, other: Chevrolet, Chrysler/Jeep, Walgreens, to MO Botanical Garden</td></tr>
<tr><td>286</td><td>Hampton Ave, St Louis, N...gas: CFM, Shell, food: Denny's, Jack-in-the-Box, McDonald's, Steak'n Shake, Subway, Taco Bell, S...gas: Shell, food: Burger King, Church's, Hardee's, lodging: Holiday Inn, Red Roof Inn, other: museums, zoo</td></tr>
<tr><td>285</td><td>SW Ave(from wb, no EZ return)</td></tr>
<tr><td>284b a</td><td>Arsenal St, Jamieson St</td></tr>
<tr><td>283</td><td>Shrewsbury(from wb), some services same as 282</td></tr>
<tr><td>282</td><td>Laclede Sta Rd, Murdock Ave(from eb), St Louis, N...food: Imo's Pizza, McDonald's, Starbucks, Subway, other: Subaru, vet</td></tr>
<tr><td>280</td><td>Elm Ave, St Louis, N...gas: BP/repair, other: Schnuck's Food/24hr, S...gas: Shell</td></tr>
<tr><td>279</td><td>(from wb), Berry Rd, no services</td></tr>
<tr><td>278</td><td>Big Bend Rd, St Louis, N...food: Hardee's, Sonic, other: HOSPITAL, Sam's Club/gas, S...gas: Mobil/dsl, QT</td></tr>
<tr><td>277b</td><td>US 67, US 61, US 50, Lindbergh Blvd, N...gas: Shell, food: Arby's, Chilli's, O'Charley's, Steak&Rice Chinese, Texas Roadhouse, Uno Pizzaria, White Castle, lodging: Best Western, other: HOSPITAL, Hancock Fabrics, Harley-Davidson, Lowe's Whse, Office Depot, Target, Wal-Mart SuperCtr/24hr, S...gas: Conoco, Phillips 66, Shell, food: Burger King, Denny's, Fuddrucker's, Lion's Choice, Longhorn Steaks, Ruby Tuesday, Steak'n Shake, St Louis Bread, lodging: Day's Inn/rest., Hampton Inn, Holiday Inn, Quality Inn, other: AutoTire, CompUSA, Home Depot, Marshall's, Old Navy, Petsmart, WorldMkt</td></tr>
<tr><td>277a</td><td>MO 366 E, Watson Rd, access to same as 277b S</td></tr>
<tr><td>276b a</td><td>I-270, N to Chicago, S Memphis</td></tr>
<tr><td>275</td><td>N Highway Dr(from wb), Soccer Pk Rd, N...gas: Road Ranger/dsl/rest.</td></tr>
<tr><td>274a b</td><td>Bowles Ave, N...gas: Road Ranger/dsl, S...gas: BP, Citgo/dsl/24hr, Phillips 66, QT, ZX/dsl, food: Bandana's BBQ, Cracker Barrel, Denny's, Krispy Kreme, McDonald's, Plaza Mexican, Quizno's, Sonic, Souper Salad, White Castle, lodging: Drury Inn, Econolodge, Fairfield Inn, Holiday Inn Express, Motel 6, PearTree Inn, Stratford Inn, TownePlace Inn, other: Goodyear</td></tr>
<tr><td>272</td><td>MO 141, Fenton, Valley Park, N...gas: Motomart, S...gas: Mobil, Phillips 66, QT, food: Bob Evans, Burger King, Culver's, McDonald's, Ruby Tuesday, Steak'n Shake, Subway, Taco Bell, lodging: Drury Inn, Hampton Inn</td></tr>
<tr><td>269</td><td>Antire Rd, Beaumont</td></tr>
<tr><td>266</td><td>Lewis Rd, N...other: Rte 66 SP, golf</td></tr>
</table>

Interstate 44

266mm	Meramec River
265	Williams Rd(from eb)
264	MO 109, rd W, Eureka, [N]...**gas:** Phillips 66, **food:** Burger King, Domino's, DQ, KFC, McDonald's, Pizza Hut, Ponderosa, Smokers BBQ, Subway, Taco Bell, Wendy's, White Castle, **lodging:** Day's Inn, **other:** AutoTire, Firestone, NAPA, Schnuck's Foods, to Babler SP, [S]...**gas:** QT, Shell, **other:** Walgreens
261	Lp 44, to Allenton, [N]...**gas:** Motomart/McDonald's/dsl, **food:** Applebee's, China King, Denny's, KFC, Lion's Choice Rest., Steak'n Shake, **lodging:** Econolodge, Holiday Inn, Super 8, **other:** AutoZone, $Tree, GNC, Radio Shack, Wal-Mart SuperCtr/24hr, to Six Flags, same as 264, [S]...**gas:** Shell/dsl, **other:** Ford, KOA
257	Lp 44, Pacific, [N]...**gas:** Phillips 66, Pilot/dsl/scales/24hr, **food:** Huddle House, lodging: Comfort Inn, [S]...**gas:** Mobil/dsl/24hr, Motomart/24hr, BP/dsl, **food:** Hardee's, KFC, McDonald's, Pizza Hut, Taco Bell, **lodging:** Comfort Inn, Holiday Inn Express, Quality Inn, **other:** Buick/Chevrolet, Chrysler/Jeep/Dodge, $General, IGA Foods, NAPA
253	MO 100 E, to Gray Summit, [S]...**gas:** Phillips 66, **lodging:** Diamond Motel, Gardenway Inn
251	MO 100 W, to Washington, [N]...**gas:** BP/dsl/24hr, FuelMart/Blimpie/Domino's/dsl/24hr, Mr Fuel/Conoco/dsl/scales, Phillips 66/Burger King/dsl
247	US 50 W, rd AT, rd O, to Union, [N]...**other:** Harley-Davidson, **other:** Pin Oak Creek Camping, flea mkt, [S]...to Robertsville SP
247mm	Bourbeuse River
242	rd AH, to Hist Rte 66
240	MO 47, St Clair, [N]...**gas:** Phillips 66/Taco Bell/dsl, **food:** Burger King, El Palenque Mexican, [S]...**gas:** Mobil/dsl, **food:** Hardee's, McDonald's, Subway, **lodging:** Budget Lodge, Super 8, **other:** $General, IGA Foods
239	MO 30, rds AB, WW, St Clair, [N]...repair, [S]...**gas:** BP, Phillips 66
238mm	weigh sta both lanes
235mm	**rest area both lanes(both lanes exit left), full (handicapped)facilities, phone, picnic tables, litter barrels, vending, petwalk**
230	rds W, Stanton, [N]...**lodging:** Stanton Motel, [S]...**other:** KOA, Meramec Caverns Camping(3mi)
226	MO 185 S, Sullivan, [N]...**gas:** /Flying J/Conoco/Country Mkt/dsl/LP/scales/24hr/@, **food:** Domino's, **other:** Chrysler/Jeep/Dodge, Ford, [S]...**gas:** Phillips 66/Burger King, **food:** Applebee's, Bison Grill, DQ, Hardee's, KFC, McDonald's, Pizza Hut, Steak'n Shake, Subway, **other:** $General, O'Reilly Parts, Wal-Mart SuperCtr/24hr, RV Camping, to Meramec SP, same as 225
225	MO 185 N, rd D, Sullivan, [N]...**gas:** Mobil, Phillips 66/dsl, **food:** Domino's, **lodging:** Baymont Inn, Econolodge, Executive Inn, Super 8, **other:** Chrysler/Dodge/Jeep, Ford/Mercury, [S]...**gas:** Fas-Trip/dsl/café, Citgo, **food:** Cracker Barrel, Jack-in-the-Box, Lion's Choice, McDonald's, Pizza Hut, Sonic, Subway, **other:** HOSPITAL, Aldi Foods, Chevrolet/Buick, Goodyear, same as 226
218	rds N, C, J, Bourbon, [N]...**gas:** Citgo/dsl, **lodging:** Budget Inn, [S]...**gas:** Mobil/24hr, **food:** HenHouse Rest., **other:** Suburban RV Ctr, Blue Sprgs Camping(6mi), Riverview Ranch Camping(8mi)
214	rd H, Leasburg, [N]...**gas:** Mobil/dsl, [S]...**other:** Ozark Outdoor RV Park, to Onandaga Cave SP(7mi)
210	rd UU, [S]...**food:** MO Hick BBQ, Mt Peasant Winery
208	MO 19, Cuba, [N]...**gas:** Phillips 66, Voss/dsl/rest./24hr/@, **food:** Country Kitchen, Huddle House, Pizza Hut, **lodging:** Best Western, Super 8, **other:** Blue Beacon, [S]...**gas:** Casey's, Delano/dsl, Mobil/Taco Bell/24hr, **food:** Burger King, Domino's, Hardee's, Jack-in-the-Box, McDonald's, Sonic, Subway, **lodging:** Holiday Inn Express, Wagon Wheel Motel, **other:** Chevrolet/GMC, $General, Mace Foods, O'Reilly Parts, Wal-Mart/drugs, to Ozark Nat Scenic Riverways
203	rds F, ZZ, [N]...Blue Moon RV Park, [S]...Rosati Winery(2mi)
195	MO 8, MO 68, St James, Maramec Sprg Park, [N]...**gas:** Conoco/dsl, Mobil/dsl, Phillips 66/dsl, **food:** John's Café, McDonald's, Pizza Hut, Subway, **lodging:** Econolodge, Economy Inn, **other:** Ford, Goodyear, O'Reilly Parts, St James Winery, [S]...**gas:** Delano/dsl, Phillips 66/dsl, **food:** Burger King, **lodging:** Finn's Motel, **other:** CountryMart Foods, Ford
189	rd V, [S]...**gas:** Loves/McDonald's/Subway/dsl/scales/24hr
186	US 63, MO 72, Rolla, [N]...**gas:** Sinclair, **food:** Steak'n Shake, **lodging:** Drury Inn, Hampton Inn, Sooter Inn, **other:** Lowe's Whse, Plaza Tires, [S]...**gas:** BP, Mobil/dsl, Phillips 66, **food:** Denny's, Donut King, Lee's Chicken, Panera Bread, **lodging:** Budget Motel, **other:** HOSPITAL
185	rd E, to Rolla, [S]...**gas:** Phillips 66, **food:** Applebee's, Arby's, DQ, Hardee's/24hr, Subway, Taco Bell, **other:** HOSPITAL, UMO at Rolla, st patrol
184	US 63 S, to Rolla, [N]...**lodging:** Comfort Suites, Holiday Inn Express, [S]...**gas:** Delano, MotoMart, Rte 66 Gas, **food:** Arby's, Burger King, Domino's, El Rodeo Mexican, Feedlot Rest., Golden Corral, KFC, Kyoto Japanese, Little Caesar's, LJ Silver, Lucky House Chinese, McDonald's, Papa John's, Pizza Hut, Pizza Inn, Shoney's, Sirloin Stockade, Subway, Wendy's, Zeno's Steaks, **lodging:** Best Value, Best Western, Day's Inn, Econolodge, Holiday Inn, Howard Johnson/rest., Western Inn, Wickliffe Inn, **other:** HOSPITAL, Chevrolet, Ford/Lincoln/Mercury, Goodyear/auto, transmissions
179	rds T, C, to Doolittle, Newburg, [S]...**gas:** BP/24hr, **food:** Cookin' From Scratch Rest.
178mm	**rest area both lanes, full(handicapped)facilities, phone, picnic tables, litter barrels, vending, petwalk**

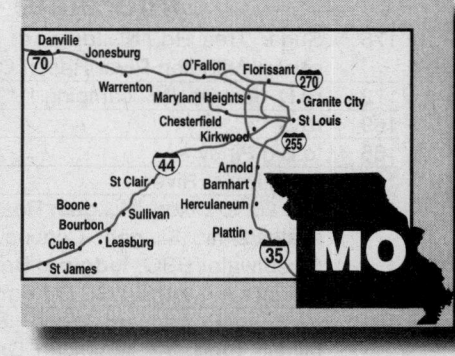

MISSOURI

Interstate 44

E ↕ **W**

176	Sugar Tree Rd, **N**...**lodging:** Vernelle's Motel, **S**... **other:** Arlington River Resort Camping(2mi)
172	rd D, Jerome, **N**...camping
169	rd J
166	to Big Piney
164mm	Big Piney River
163	MO 28, to Dixon, **N**...**gas:** Road Ranger/Subway/dsl/ scales/24hr, **S**...**gas:** Conoco, **food:** Country Café, Sweetwater BBQ, **lodging:** Best Western, Day's Inn, Knight's Inn, **other:** GS RV Park
161b a	rd Y, to Ft Leonard Wood, **N**...**gas:** Conoco, Mobil/dsl, **food:** All American Drive-In, Aussie Jack's, Cracker Barrel, Domino's, Jack's Diner, LJ Silver/ A&W, Pizza Hut, Popeye's, Ruby Tuesday, Ryan's, Subway, Wendy's, **lodging:** Baymont Inn, Candlewood Suites, Comfort Inn, Fairfield Inn, Hampton Inn, Mainstay Suites, Red Roof Inn, **other:** $Tree, Toyota/ Scion, Wal-Mart SuperCtr/24hr, **S**...**gas:** Cenex/dsl, Conoco, **food:** Arby's, Capt D's, Country Kitchen, El Sombrero, KFC, McDonald's, Papa John's, Taco Bell, Waffle House, **lodging:** Budget Inn, Econolodge, Holiday Inn Express, Microtel, Motel 6, Ramada Inn, **other:** AutoZone, Chrysler/Dodge, $General, Family$, Ford/Lincoln/Mercury/Mazda, NAPA, O'Reilly Parts, Radio Shack
159	Lp 44, to Waynesville, St Robert, **N**...**food:** DQ, Sonic, **lodging:** Star Motel, Super 8, **other:** IGA Foods, O'Reilly Parts, Covered Wagon RV Park(2mi), **S**... **gas:** BP/dsl **food:** Pepper's Rest., **lodging:** Microtel, **other:** Cadillac/Pontiac/GMC, Goodyear/auto
158mm	Roubidoux Creek
156	rd H, Waynesville, **N**...**gas:** Casey's, Citgo/dsl, Cody's, **food:** Imperial Rest., McDonald's, Subway, **lodging:** Star Motel(1mi), **other:** Chevrolet/Buick, $General, Price Cutter+, vet
153	MO 17, to Buckhorn, **N**...**gas:** Cenex/dsl, **lodging:** Ft Wood Inn, **S**...**gas:** Shell/dsl, **other:** Glen Oaks RV Park
150	MO 7, rd P to Richland, **S**...**food:** Joe's Place Steaks
145	MO 133, rd AB, to Richland, **N**...**gas:** Conoco/Oasis/ dsl/rest./24hr, **S**...camping
143mm	Gasconade River
140	rd N, to Stoutland, **S**...**gas:** Conoco, **food:** Midway Chinese
139mm	Bear Creek
135	rd F, Sleeper
130	rd MM, **N**...**gas:** Cenex, Phillips 66, **food:** Andy's Rest., **lodging:** Best Western, Budget Inn, Munger Moss Inn, **S**...**gas:** Kum&Go, **other:** HOSPITAL
129	MO 5, MO 32, MO 64, to Hartville, Lebanon, **N**... **gas:** Kum&Go, **food:** Applebee's, Bamboo Garden, BreakTime, Burger King, Country Kitchen, DQ, KFC, LJ Silver, McDonald's, Papa John's, Pizza Hut, Shoney's, Sonic, Subway, Taco Bell, Taco Hut, Wendy's, Western Sizzlin, **other:** Advance Parts, Aldi Foods, AutoZone, Chevrolet, Ford, IGA Foods, NAPA, O'Reilly Parts, Smitty's Foods, Walgreens, to Bennett Sprgs SP, **S**...**gas:** BP, Conoco/dsl, Phillips 66, **food:** Blimpie, Candy's Custard, Capt D's, Domino's, Hardee's, La Mexican Rest., Pizza Hut, **lodging:** Brent-

Lebanon

	wood Motel, **other:** HOSPITAL, $General, FSA/Famous Brands, Goodyear, Lowe's Whse, Wal-Mart SuperCtr/24hr, vet, to Lake of the Ozarks
127	Lp 44, Lebanon, **N**...**gas:** Conoco/dsl/rest./scales/24hr, Phillips 66/dsl, Sinclair/dsl, **food:** Dowd's BBQ, Great Wall Chinese, Waffle House, **lodging:** Day's Inn, Econolodge, Hampton Inn, Holiday Inn Express, Rte 66 Inn, Super 8, Travelers Inn, **other:** Cutlery/Walnut Bowl Outlet, Chrysler/ Dodge/Jeep, Firestone/auto, Ford/Lincoln/Mercury, **S**... **gas:** Phillips 66/dsl, **other:** Buick/Pontiac/GMC/Cadillac, Harley-Davidson, Russell Stover
123	County Rd, **S**...**other:** Happy Trails RV Ctr, KOA
118	rds C, A, Phillipsburg, **N**...**gas:** Conoco/dsl, **S**...**gas:** Citgo, **other:** antiques, tourist info
113	rds J, Y, Conway, **N**...**gas:** Phillips 66, **food:** Rockin Chair Café, **lodging:** Budget Inn, **other:** to Den of Metal Arts, **S**...**gas:** Sinclair/dsl, **other:** Faircountry Foods, USPO
111mm	**rest area both lanes, full(handicapped)facilities, phone, vending, litter barrels, picnic tables, petwalk**
108mm	Bowen Creek
107	County Rd
106mm	Niangua River
100	MO 38, rd W, Marshfield, **N**...**gas:** BP, **food:** Subway, **other:** Chevrolet, Ford, Goodyear/auto, Wal-Mart SuperCtr/gas/24hr, **S**...**gas:** Cenex, Conoco/dsl, Kum&Go/dsl, Mystik, Phillips 66/dsl/24hr, Shell, **food:** Country Kitchen, Dancey's Rest., DQ, El Charro, KFC/Rib Crib, La Hacienda Mexican, McDonald's, Quizno's, Sonic, Subway, Taco Bell, **lodging:** Holiday Inn Express, **other:** $General, O'Reilly Parts, PriceCutter Foods, RV Express RV Park
96	rd B, Northview, **N**...Paradise RV Park
89mm	weigh sta both lanes
88	MO 125, to Fair Grove, Strafford, **N**...**gas:** Phillips 66/ dsl/rest./scales/24hr, TA/BP/Subway/Taco Bell/dsl/ scales/24hr/@, **food:** McDonald's, **other:** Midwest Tire, truckwash, Paradise RV Park(4mi), **S**...**gas:** Conoco/dsl, Kum&Go, **food:** Fox's Pizza, **lodging:** Super 8, **other:** Harter House Foods, Strafford RV Park
84	MO 744, **S**...Peterbilt
82b a	US 65, to Branson, Fedalia, **S**...**gas:** Phillips 66/dsl, **food:** Applebee's(2mi), Ryan's(2mi), Waffle House, **lodging:** American Inn, **other:** st patrol, to Table Rock Lake, Bull Shoals Lake
80b a	rd H to Pleasant Hope, Springfield, **N**...**gas:** Conoco/dsl/ rest./24hr, Phillips 66/dsl, **food:** Waffle House, **lodging:** Budget Lodge, Microtel, Motel 6, Super 8, **other:** to SWSU, **S**...**gas:** Cody's Gas, Conoco/dsl, Phillips 66, QT, **food:** Andy's Rest., Applebee's, Bob Evan's, Braum's, Buckingham Smokehouse, Burger King, Capt D's, Cracker Barrel, Denny's, El Magui Mexican, Fazoli's, Hardee's, Hong Kong Buffet, Jade East Chinese, Krispy Kreme, LJ Silver, McDonald's, Pizza Hut, Pizza Inn, Rib Crib, Ruby Tuesday, Ryan's, Schlotsky's, Shoney's, Sonic, Steak'n Shake, Subway, Taco Bell, Western Sizzlin, Ziggy's Cafe, **lodging:** Best Western, Budget Inn, Candlewood Suites, Comfort Inn, Day's Inn, Drury Inn, Econolodge, Economy Inn, Hampton Inn, Hawthorne Park Inn, Holiday Inn, Krystal Aire Inn, Lamplighter Hotel, La Quinta, Plaza Inn, RainTree Inn, Red Lion Inn, Red Roof Inn, Springfield Inn, **other:** HOSPITAL, Aldi Foods, AutoZone, Cottman Transmissions, K-Mart, O'Reilly Parts, Persell, PriceCutter Foods, U-Haul, Wal-Mart/auto, mall

Springfield

Interstate 44

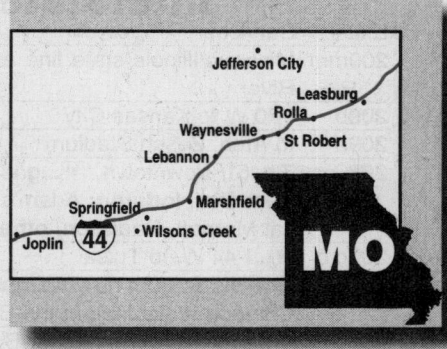

77	MO 13, KS Expswy, **N**...**lodging:** Interstate Inn, **other:** Lowe's Whse, **S**...**gas:** Phillips 66/dsl, QT, **food:** Buffalo Wild Wings, Braum's, CiCi's, Golden Corral, IHOP, Jimmy John's, McAlister's Deli, McDonald's, Panera Bread, Papa John's, Papa Murphys, Pizza Inn, Subway, Taco Bell, Waffle House, Wendy's, **lodging:** Econolodge, **other:** BigLots, Dillon's Foods, $Tree, GNC, Goodyear/auto, O'Reilly Parts, Radio Shack, Staples, Walgreens, Wal-Mart SuperCtr/24hr
75	US 160 W byp, to Willard, Stockton Lake, **S**...**gas:** Cody's Gas, Kum&Go, **lodging:** Baymont Inn, Courtyard
72	MO 266, to Chesnut Expwy, **1-2 mi S**...**gas:** Casey's, Cody's Gas, **food:** Hardee's, McDonald's, Pizza Hut, Taco Bueno, Waffle House, **lodging:** Best Budget Inn, Ramada Ltd
70	rds MM, B, **N**...antiques, fireworks, **S**...**other:** Wilson's Creek Nat Bfd, KOA(1mi)
69	to US 60, Springfield
67	rds N, T, Bois D' Arc, to Republic, **S**...**lodging:** AmericInn(5mi)
66mm	Pond Creek
64.6mm	Dry Branch
64.5mm	Pickerel Creek
61	rds K, PP, **N**...**gas:** BP, Cenex/Hoods/dsl/rest./motel/scales/24hr
58	MO 96, rds O, Z, to Carthage, Halltown, **S**...**gas:** Shell/dsl, **other:** antiques, RV/truck parts
57	to rd PP(from wb)
56.5mm	Turnback Creek
56mm	Goose Creek
52.5mm	**rest area both lanes, full(handicapped)facilities, phone, picnic tables, litter barrels, vending, petwalk**
49	MO 174E, rd CCW, Chesapeake
46	MO 39, MO 265, Mt Vernon, Aurora, **N**...**gas:** Casey's, Phillips 66/dsl, TA/Conoco/Country Pride/dsl/24hr/@, **food:** Bamboo Garden Chinese, KFC/LJ Silver, Mazzio's, McDonald's, Sonic, Subway, Taco Bell, **lodging:** Super 8, USA Inn, **other:** $General, Family$, O'Reilly Parts, Radio Shack, Summer fresh Foods, **S**...**gas:** BP/dsl/rest., **lodging:** Comfort Inn, **other:** to Table Rock Lake, Stockton Lake
44	rd H, to Monett, Mt Vernon, **N**...**other:** Mid-America Dental/Hearing
43.5mm	Spring River
38	MO 97, to Stotts City, Pierce City, **N**...gas/repair, U of MO SW Ctr
33	MO 97 S, to Pierce City, **S**...**gas:** Sinclair/dsl, **food:** Hungry House Cafe, truck/tire repair
29	rd U, to La Russell, Sarcoxie, **N**...Ozark Village Gifts, WAC RV Park, antiques, **S**...**gas:** Citgo/dsl, Kum&Go, **food:** Nansy Rest.
29mm	Center Creek
26	MO 37, to Reeds, Sarcoxie, **N**...truck/tire repair, **S**...gas
22	rd 100 N, **N**...RV parts, **S**...**gas:** Express
21mm	Jones Creek

18b a	US 71 N, MO 59 S, to Carthage, Neosho, **N**...**other:** Coachlight RV Ctr/Camping, **S**...Ballard's Camping
15	MO 66 W, Lp 44(from wb), Joplin, **N**...**lodging:** Tara Motel
15mm	Grove Creek
14mm	Turkey Creek
11b a	US 71 S, MO 249 N, to Neosho, Ft Smith, **S**...**gas:** ⭐/Flying J/Conoco/Country Mkt/dsl/LP/scales/24hr/@, Speedco, **food:** Applebee's(3mi), **other:** Blue Beacon
8b a	US 71, to Neosho, Joplin, **N**...**gas:** Citgo, Conoco, Kum&Go/dsl, Phillips 66, **food:** Applebee's, Arby's, Backyard Burger, Bella Pepper's, Bob Evans, Braum's, Burger King, Candlewood Suites, Capt D's, Casa Montez Mexican, Cheddars, CiCi's, Denny's, Golden Corral, Golden Dragon, Great Wall Chinese, IHOP, Jim Bob's Steaks, KFC, King Palace, LJ Silver, Mazzio's, McDonald's, Noodle&Grill, Olive Garden, Outback Steaks, Pizza Hut, Quizno's, Red Hot&Blue Grill, Red Lobster, Rib Crib, Ruby Tuesday, Ryan's, Schlotzky's, Shoney's, Sonic, Steak'n Shake, Subway, Taco Bell, Taco Hut, Timberline Steaks, Waffle House, Wendy's, **lodging:** Baymont Inn, Best Value, Best Western, Comfort Inn, Day's Inn, Drury Inn, Fairfield Inn, Hampton Inn, Hilton Garden, Holiday Inn, Motel 6, Ramada Inn, Residence Inn, Rodesite Inn, Super 8, **other:** Aldi Foods, Books-A-Million, Chrysler/Dodge, Coachlight RV Ctr, $Tree, Firestone, Food4Less/24hr, Ford/Lincoln/Mercury, Goody's, Hasting's, Home Depot, Hyundai, Jo-Ann Fabrics, Kohl's, Lowe's Whse, Mid-America RV Ctr, Michael's, NAPA, Nissan/Mercedes, Office Depot, O'Reilly Parts, Pennzoil, Petsmart, Sam's Club/gas, Target, Toyota/Scion, VW, Wal-Mart SuperCtr/24hr, **S**...**gas:** Casey's, **food:** Cracker Barrel, Fazoli's, **lodging:** Microtel, TownePlace Suites, **other:** Wheelen RV Ctr
6	MO 86, MO 43 N, to Racine, Joplin, **N**...**gas:** BP, **S**...Harley-Davidson
5.5mm	Shoal Creek
4	MO 43 to Seneca, **N**...**gas:** Loves/Hardee's/dsl/24hr, **other:** Peterbilt, antiques, **S**...**gas:** Conoco/Subway/dsl, Petro/BP/Iron Skillet/dsl/scales/@, Pilot/Wendy's/dsl/scales/24hr, **food:** McDonald's, **lodging:** Sleep Inn, **other:** IA 80 Truckwash, KOA
3mm	weigh sta both lanes
2mm	**Welcome Ctr eb, rest area wb, full(handicapped) facilities, picnic tables, litter barrels, phones, vending**
1	US 400, US 166W, to Baxter Springs, KS, **N**...**other:** Sandstone Gardens
0mm	Missouri/Oklahoma state line

MISSOURI
Interstate 55

N ↕ **S**

St Louis

Exit #	Services
209mm	Missouri/Illinois state line at St. Louis, Mississippi River
209b	I-70 W to Kansas City
209a	to Arch, Busch Stadium
208	7th St, downtown, W...**gas:** BP, **food:** Hardee's, Taco Bell, **lodging:** Adam's Mark Hotel, Drury Plaza, Marriott, Radisson, **other:** Ford Trucks
207c b	W...I-44 W, to Tulsa
207a	Gravois St(from nb), E...**gas:** Citgo, W...**food:** A-1 Chinese Wok, Jack-in-the-Box
206c	Arsenal St, E...Anheuser-Busch Tour Ctr, W...**gas:** Shell
206b	Broadway(from nb), Broadway(from nb)
206a	Potomac St(from nb)
205	Gasconade, W...HOSPITAL
204	Broadway, E...**gas:** Mobil/repair, W...**gas:** Clark, Sinclair, **food:** Crusoe's Rest., Hardee's, McDonald's, Pantera's Pizza, Pizza Hut, Wendy's, **other:** Radio Shack, Walgreen/24hr
203	Bates St, Virginia Ave, W...**gas:** BP, 7-11
202c	Loughborough Ave, W...Schnuck's Foods
202b	Germania(from sb)
202a	Carondelet(from nb), Carondelet(from nb)
201b	Weber Rd
201a	Bayless Ave, E...**gas:** BP, QT, Shell, **food:** McDonald's, W...**gas:** BP, Citgo/7-11, **food:** DQ, Jack-in-the-Box, Subway, Taco Bell, **other:** Goodyear
200	Union Rd(from sb)
199	Reavis Barracks Rd, E...**gas:** BP, Shell, **food:** Steak'n Shake/24hr, **other:** Fabric Whse
197	US 50, US 61, US 67, Lindbergh Blvd, E...**gas:** Phillips 66, **food:** Applebee's, Arby's, Buffalo Wild Wings, ChuckeCheese, KFC, Krispy Kreme, Gingham's Rest., McDonald's, Quizno's, Steak'n Shake, Tucker's Place, **lodging:** Holiday Inn, **other:** Advance Parts, Best Buy, Borders, Circuit City, Chrysler/Dodge, Dillard's, Goodyear, JC Penney, KIA, Marshall's, Sears, Tuesday Morning, mall, W...**food:** Bob Evans, Casa Gallardo's, Culvers, Denny's, O'Charley's, Ponderosa, **lodging:** Motel 6, Oak Grove Inn, **other:** Aldi Foods, Costco/gas, Ford/Lincoln/Mercury, Honda, Hyundai, Mazda, Office Depot, Saturn, Target
196b	I-270 W, to Kansas City
196a	I-255 E, to Chicago
195	Butler Hill Rd, E...**gas:** Phillips 66, **lodging:** Holiday Inn/rest., **other:** Walgreens, W...**gas:** Sinclair, **food:** Burger King, Hardee's, Pizza Hut/Taco Bell, Waffle House, **other:** Schnuck's Foods
193	Meramec Bottom Rd, E...**gas:** Mobil, QT, **food:** Cracker Barrel, **lodging:** 55 South Suites, **other:** Howard RV Ctr
191	MO 141, Arnold, E...**gas:** Citgo, Phillips 66, QT, **food:** Applebee's, BBQ, Burger King, Culpepper's Grill, Denny's, Fazoli's, Hardee's, Jack-in-the-Box, LJ Silver, McDonald's, Papa John's, Steak'n Shake, Taco Bell, **lodging:** Drury Inn, Ramada Ltd, **other:** Eckerd, Kohl's, Lions Choice, Schnuck's Foods, Shop'n Sav Foods, Wal-Mart/auto, mall, W...**gas:** Phillips 66/dsl, **food:** Pasta House
190	Richardson Rd, E...**gas:** QT, Shell/dsl, **food:** Domino's, DQ, Pizza Hut, Ponderosa, Sonic, Subway, Taco Bell, White Castle, **other:** Auto Tire, Firestone, Ford, SavALot Foods, W...**gas:** Citgo/7-11, CFM, Phillips 66/dsl, Shell/Blimpie/dsl, **food:** Burger King, McDonald's, Ruby Tuesday, Waffle House, **lodging:** Comfort Inn, **other:** AutoZone, GNC, Home Depot, Shnuck's Foods/24hr, Target, Walgreen, transmissions
186	Imperial, Kimmswick, E...**gas:** Shell, **food:** Blue Owl(1mi), Southern Kitchen, **other:** auto repair, W...**food:** China Wok, Domino's, La Pachanga, Oasis Grill, to Mastodon SP
185	rd M, Barnhart, Antonia, W...**gas:** Citgo/dsl, **food:** Jenny's Kitchen, **other:** Walgreens, **other:** KOA
184.5mm	weigh sta both lanes
180	rd Z, to Hillsboro, Pevely, E...**gas:** Mobil, **food:** BBQ, Burger King, China House, Domino's, Subway, **other:** $General, IGA Foods, W...**gas:** Mr Fuel, Phillips 66/McDonald's/dsl, **lodging:** Gateway Inn, Super 8, **other:** KOA(2mi)
178	Herculaneum, E...**gas:** QT/Wendy's/dsl, Shell, **food:** Cracker Barrel, Doghouse Diner, DQ, Jack-in-the-Box, W...Chevrolet, Ford, Pontiac/Cadillac/Buick
175	rd A, Festus, E...**gas:** Mobil, Phillips 66/dsl, **food:** Arby's, Bob Evans, Burger King, Capt D's, Fazoli's, McDonald's, Papa John's, Ryan's, Sonic, Steak'n Shake, Subway, Taco Bell, White Castle, **lodging:** Drury Inn, Holiday Inn Express, **other:** Advance Parts, Aldi Foods, $Tree, Home Depot, Radio Shack, Schnuck's Foods, Toyota, Wal-Mart SuperCtr/gas/24hr, W...**gas:** Citgo/7-11/dsl, Phillips 66/Domino's/dsl, **food:** Hardee's, Ruby Tuesday, Waffle House, **lodging:** Baymont Inn, **other:** Dodge, Lowe's Whse
174b a	US 67, Lp 55, Festus, Crystal City, E...**gas:** Phillips 66, 1 mi E...**food:** Arby's, McDonald's, Ryan's, **lodging:** Twin City Motel, **other:** HOSPITAL, Wal-Mart SuperCtr/gas/24hr, same as 175
170	US 61, W...**gas:** BP/dsl/LP
162	rds DD, OO, no services
160mm	**rest areas both lanes, full(handicapped) facilities, picnic tables, litter barrels, phones, vending, petwalk**
157	rd Y, Bloomsdale, E...**gas:** Phillips 66, W...**gas:** Valero/dsl
154	rd O
150	MO 32, rds B, A, to St Genevieve, E...**gas:** BP, **food:** DQ, **lodging:** Microtel(4mi), **other:** HOSPITAL, Hist Site(6mi), W...**gas:** Phillips 66/dsl, **other:** Pontiac/GMC, Hawn SP(11mi)
143	rds N, M, Ozora, W...**gas:** Sinclair, Valero/Subway/dsl, **lodging:** Family Inn/rest.
141	rd Z, St Mary
135	rd M, Brewer, E...propane depot
129	MO 51, to Perryville, E...**gas:** MotoMart/McDonald's/dsl, Phillips 66/dsl, **food:** Burger King, KFC, Ponderosa, Skinny's Diner, Taco Bell, **other:** HOSPITAL, Ford, W...**gas:** Rhodes/dsl, **food:** China Buffet, DQ, **lodging:** Best Western, Comfort Inn, Super 8, **other:** Chevrolet/Pontiac/Buick, Chrysler/Dodge/Jeep, $Tree, KOA(1mi), Wal-Mart SuperCtr/24hr

Perryville

123	rd B, Biehle, **W**...**gas:** Phillips 66, **food:** Country Kettle Rest./gifts
119mm	Apple Creek
117	rd KK, to Appleton, **E**...**food:** Sewing's Rest./repair
111	rd E, Oak Ridge
110mm	**rest area both lanes, full(handicapped) facilities, picnic tables, litter barrels, phones, vending, petwalk**
105	US 61, Fruitland, **E**...**gas:** BP/dsl, Casey's, Rhodes/dsl, **other:** Trail of Tears SP(11mi), **W**...**gas:** D-Mart, **food:** Bavarian Rest., DQ, Pizza Inn, **lodging:** Drury Inn
99	US 61, MO 34, to Jackson, **E**...**food:** Buffalo Wild Wings(4mi), Fazoli's(3mi), **lodging:** Budget Inn, Holiday Lodge, Super 8, **other:** Cape RV Park, **W**...**other:** Wal-Mart SuperCtr/gas/24hr(4mi)
96	96 rd K, to Cape Girardeau, **E**...**gas:** BP, Citgo/dsl, **food:** Blimpie, Bob Evans, Burger King, ChuckeCheese, Cracker Barrel, DQ, El Acapulco, Great Wall Chinese, Logan's Roadhouse, O'Charley's, Olive Garden, Pasta House, Pizza Inn, Red Lobster, Ruby Tuesday, Ryan's, Steak'n Shake, Subway, Taco Bell, Texas Roadhouse, **lodging:** Drury Lodge/rest., Holiday Inn Express, PearTree Inn, Relax Inn(4mi), Victorian Inn, **other:** HOSPITAL, Barnes&Noble, Best Buy, Big Lots, JC Penney, Old Navy, Panera Bread, Schnuck's Foods, mall, to SEMSU, **W**...**gas:** Shell/24hr, **food:** Joeys Grill, McDonald's, Outback Steaks, White Castle, **lodging:** Drury Inn, Hampton Inn, **other:** Circuit City, $Tree, Goody's, Honda, Kohls, Lowe's Whse, Mazda, Sam's Club, Saturn, Staples, Target, Wal-Mart SuperCtr/24hr
95	MO 74 E, same as 96
93a b	MO 74 W, Cape Girardeau
91	rd AB, to Cape Girardeau, **E**...**gas:** Phillips 66/dsl, **food:** Huddle House, **other:** Goodyear, Harley-Davidson, RV America, **W**...Capetown RV Ctr
89	US 61, rds K, M, Scott City, **E**...**gas:** Rhodes, Store 24, **food:** Burger King, Sonic, **other:** $General, NAPA
80	MO 77, Benton, **W**...**gas:** BP/McDonald's/dsl, Express/dsl, **other:** antiques, winery(8mi)
69	rd HH, to Sikeston, Miner, **W**...**gas:** Keller Trkstp/dsl, golf
67	US 60, US 62, Miner, **E**...**gas:** Breaktime/dsl, Express/dsl, **lodging:** Best Western, Holiday Inn Express, **other:** Hinton RV Park, **0-2 mi** **W**...**gas:** Cenex, Citgo, Hucks, Jasper's Gas, QuickChek, Sinclair, **food:** Burger King, Cactus Cantina, China Garden, El Tapatio Mexican, Frankie's Rest., Joseph's Grill, Lambert's Rest., McDonald's, Pizza Hut, Pizza Inn, Ruby Tuesday, Skinny's Diner, Sonic, Subway, Taco Bell, Taco John's, Tammi's BBQ, Wendy's, **lodging:** Comfort Inn, Country Hearth Inn, Drury Inn, PearTree Inn, Super 8, **other:** HOSPITAL, Aldi Foods, AutoZone, Chevrolet/Pontiac/Buick, $General, GMC/Cadillac, Family$, Food Giant,

	Goodyear/auto, Pennzoil, Sikeston Outlets/famous brands, Walgreen
66b	US 60 W, to Poplar Bluff, **3 mi** **W** **on US 61/62**...**gas:** BP, Breaktime, Sinclair, **food:** A&W/LJ Silver, Applebee's, Arby's, China Buffet, DQ, El Bracero Mexican, Hardee's, KFC, McDonald's, Ryan's, Sonic, **lodging:** Day's Inn, **other:** Aldi Foods, Chrysler/Dodge/Jeep, $Tree, Ford/Lincoln/Mercury, GNC, Goody's, JC Penny, Lowe's Whse, O'Reilly Parts, Radio Shack, Wal-Mart SuperCtr/24hr
66a	I-57 E, to Chicago, US 60 W
59mm	St Johns Bayou
58	MO 80, Matthews, **E**...**gas:** TA/Taco Bell/dsl/scales/24hr/@, **other:** truck repair, **W**...**gas:** ♦/Flying J/Conoco/Country Pride/dsl/LP/rest./RV dump/24hr/@, Loves/Chester Fried/Subway/dsl/scales, **other:** truckwash
52	rd P, Kewanee, **E**...**gas:** BP/dsl
49	US 61, US 62, New Madrid
44	US 61, US 62, Lp 55, New Madrid, **E**...**gas:** Cenex/dsl(1mi), **other:** Relax Inn(2mi), **other:** hist site
42mm	**Welcome Ctr nb/rest area both lanes, full(handicapped)facilities, picnic tables, litter barrels, phones, vending, petwalk**
40	rd EE, St Jude Rd, Marston, **E**...**gas:** Pilot/Arby's/scales/dsl/24hr, **lodging:** Super 8, **W**...**gas:** BP/dsl, **lodging:** Budget Inn
32	US 61, MO 162, Portageville, **W**...**gas:** BP/dsl, Casey's, **food:** China King, McDonald's, **lodging:** New Orleans Inn, **other:** dsl repair
27	rds K, A, BB, to Wardell, no services
19	US 412, MO 84, Hayti, **E**...**gas:** Breaktime/dsl, Pilot/scales/dsl, **food:** McDonald's, KFC/Taco Bell, Pizza Hut, **lodging:** Comfort Inn/rest., Econolodge, **other:** HOSPITAL, KOA(6mi), **W**...**gas:** BP/Subway/dsl, Hayti Trvl Ctr/Subway/dsl, R&P, **food:** Apple Barrel, Chubby's BBQ, Los Portales, Patty Ann's, **lodging:** Drury Inn, **other:** HOSPITAL, Carquest, Fred's Foods, Goodyear/auto, repair
17a	I-155 E, to TN, US 412
14	rds J, H, U, to Caruthersville, Braggadocio
10mm	weigh sta nb
8	MO 164, Steele, **W**...**gas:** BP/Subway/Chester Fried/dsl, **lodging:** Deerfield Inn
4	rd E, to Holland, Cooter, no services
3mm	**rest area both lanes, full(handicapped)facilities, picnic tables, litter barrels, phones, vending, petwalk**
1	US 61, rd O, Holland, **W**...**gas:** Shell/dsl/24hr
0mm	Missouri/Arkansas state line

MISSOURI

Interstate 57

Exit #	Services
22mm	Missouri/Illinois state line, Mississippi River
18.5mm	weigh sta both lanes
12	US 62, MO 77, Charleston, **E**...**gas:** Cheers/Quiznos/dsl/scales/24hr, **lodging:** Economy Motel, **W**...**gas:** Casey's(1mi), Phillips 66/dsl, **food:** Cotton Inn Rest., **lodging:** Econolodge, **other:** Chrysler/Dodge/Jeep
10	MO 105, Charleston, **E**...**gas:** BP/Boomland/dsl, Pilot/Subway/dsl/scales/24hr, **food:** Wally's Rest., **other:** Boomland RV Park, **W**...**gas:** Casey's, **food:** China Buffet, DQ, McDonald's, Pizza Hut, **lodging:** Comfort Inn, **other:** Alco, CountryMart Foods, Plaza Tire
4	rd B, Bertrand
1b a	I-55, N to St Louis, S to Memphis. I-57 begins/ends on I-55
I-57 begins/ends on I-55, exit 66.	

Interstate 64

Exit #	Services
41mm	Missouri/Illinois state line, Mississippi River
40b a	Broadway St, to Stadium, to the Arch, **N**...**lodging:** Sheraton, stadium, **S**...**other:** Dobb's Tire
40c	(from wb), I-44 W, I-55 S
39c	11th St(exits left), downtown
39b	14th St, downtown, **N**...**lodging:** Sheraton, **S**...**gas:** BP
39a	21st St, Market St(from wb), **N**...**lodging:** Drury Inn, Hampton Inn
38d	Chestnut at 20th St, **N**...**lodging:** Drury Inn, Hampton Inn
38c	Jefferson Ave, St Louis Union Sta, **N**...**lodging:** Joplin House
38a	Forest Park Blvd(from wb), **N**...**gas:** Shell
37b a	Market St, Bernard St, Grand Blvd, **N**...**gas:** Shell, **food:** Del Taco, **lodging:** Courtyard, Hampton Inn, Hyatt, Drury Inn, Adam's Mark Hotel, Marriott
36d	Vandeventer Ave, Chouteau Ave
36b a	Kingshighway, **N**...**lodging:** Best Western, **other:** HOSPITAL, **S**...**gas:** BP
34d c	Hampton Ave, Forest Park, **N**...museums, zoo, **S**...**gas:** BP, Mobil, **food:** Courtesy Diner, Hardee's, Imo's Pizza, Jack-in-the-Box, Steak'n Shake, Subway
34a	Oakland Ave, **N**...**gas:** BP, Del Taco, HOSPITAL
33d	McCausland Ave, **N**...**gas:** BP, **food:** Del Taco
33c	Bellevue Ave, **N**...HOSPITAL
33b	Big Bend Blvd
32b a	Eager Rd, Hanley Rd, **S**...**gas:** Shell, **other:** Home Depot, Whole Foods Mkt
31b a	I-170 N, **N**...**gas:** Shell, **food:** Burger King, DQ, IHOP, KFC, Steak'n Shake, TGIFriday, Dillard's, Famous Barr, **other:** mall, **S**...**gas:** BP, **food:** Macaroni Grill, Subway, **other:** Borders Books, Circuit City, Dierberg's Foods, Goodyear, Target
30	McKnight Rd
28c	Clayton Rd(from wb)

Exit #	Services
28b a	US 67, US 61, Lindbergh Blvd, **S**...**lodging:** Hilton, **other:** Shnuck's Foods, mall
27	Spoede Rd
26	rd JJ, Ballas Rd, **N**...HOSPITAL, **S**...HOSPITAL
25	I-270, N to Chicago, S to Memphis
23	Mason Rd, **N**...**lodging:** Courtyard, Marriott, **other:** LDS Temple, hwy patrol
22	MO 141, **N**...**food:** Regatta Grille, **lodging:** Courtyard, Marriott, **other:** HOSPITAL, **S**...**food:** Pizza Hut
21	Timberlake Manor Pkwy
20	Chesterfield Pkwy(from wb), same as 19b a
19b a	MO 340, Chesterfield Pkwy, **N**...**gas:** BP, Shell, **food:** Applebee's, Pizzaria Uno, **lodging:** DoubleTree Hotel, Hampton Inn, Residence Inn, **S**...**gas:** Mobil, **food:** Bahama Breeze Rest., Casa Gallardo's, **other:** Dillard's, mall
17	Boones Crossing, Long Rd, Chesterfield Airport Rd, **1 mi S**...**gas:** BP, Mobil, Phillips 66, **food:** Annie Gunn's Rest., Gator Flats Rest., Longhorn Steaks, McDonald's, O'Charley's, Old Country Buffet, Olive Garden, Red Lobster, Red Robin, SmokeHouse Rest., Steak'n Shake, Subway, **lodging:** Hampton Inn, Hilton Garden, **other:** Best Buy, $Tree, Ford, Lowe's Whse, Michael's, Sam's Club, Target, Wal-Mart/auto, WorldMkt
14	Chesterfield Airport Rd(from eb), **S**...**gas:** Phillips 66, **lodging:** Comfort Inn
13mm	I-64 begins/ends, Missouri River

Interstate 70

Exit #	Services
252mm	Missouri/Illinois state line, Mississippi River
251a	I-55 S, to Memphis, to I-44, to downtown/no return
250b	Memorial Dr, downtown, Stadium, **S**...**gas:** Shell, **food:** McDonald's, **lodging:** Day's Inn
250a	Arch, Riverfront, **N**...**lodging:** Econolodge, Embassy Suites, **other:** Conv Center, **S**...**lodging:** Drury Inn, Hampton Inn, Radisson, TWA Dome
249c	6th St(from eb)
249a	Madison St, 10th St, **N**...**gas:** Phillips 66/dsl
248b	St Louis Ave, Branch St
248a	Salisbury St, McKinley Br, **N**...truck repair/24hr, **S**...**gas:** BP, Mobil/dsl
247	Grand Ave, **N**...**gas:** Phillips 66/dsl, **lodging:** Western Inn, **S**...**lodging:** Economy Inn
246b	Adelaide Ave
246a	N Broadway, O'Fallon Park, **N**...**gas:** Mobil/dsl, **other:** Freightliner
245b	W Florissant
245a	Shreve Ave, **N**...Pillsbury Factory, **S**...**gas:** BP
244b	Kingshighway, **3/4 mi S**...**food:** Burger King, McDonald's, Subway
244a	Bircher Blvd, Union Blvd
243b	(243c from eb)Bircher Blvd
243a	Riverview Blvd
243	Goodfellow Blvd, **N**...**gas:** Shell

Interstate 70

St Louis

242b a Jennings Sta Rd, N...**gas:** Shell, S...**food:** McDonald's, **other:** transmission repair

241b Lucas-Hunt Rd, N...**gas:** Shell, **3/4 mi** S...**gas:** Citgo, **food:** Lee's Chicken, McDonald's

241a Bermuda Rd, S...**gas:** Sinclair, **other:** HOSPITAL,

240b a Florissant Rd, N...**gas:** BP/McDonald's, **food:** DQ, Sonic, Taco Bell, **other:** Schnuck's Foods, Walgreen

239 N Hanley Rd, N...**food:** Jack-in-the-Box, S...**gas:** Mobil, **food:** McDonald's

238c b I-170 N, I-170 S, no return

238a N...Lambert-St Louis Airport, S...**lodging:** Renaissance Hotel

237 Natural Bridge Rd(from eb), S...**gas:** BP, Phillips 66, Shell, **food:** Airport Diner, Arby's, Burger King, Denny's, Jack-in-the-Box, KFC, Pizza Hut, Steak'n Shake, Waffle House, Wendy's, DoubleTree, **lodging:** Best Western, Days Inn, Double Tree, Holiday Inn, Renaissance, Travelodge

236 Lambert-St Louis Airport, S...**gas:** BP, **food:** BBQ, Big Boy, Coco's, Grone Cafeteria, Hardee's, Lombardo's Café Rafferty's Rest., Tiffany's Rest., **lodging:** Best Western, Day's Inn, Drury Inn/rest., Hampton Inn, Hilton Garden, Holiday Inn, Marriott, Motel 6

235c Cypress Rd, rd B W, N...to airport

235b a US 67, Lindbergh Blvd, N...**gas:** Shell, **lodging:** Executive Intn'l Inn, Holiday Inn/café, Howard Johnson, S...**gas:** Shell, **food:** Lion's Choice Rest., Steak'n Shake, TGIFriday, **lodging:** Congress Inn, Embassy Suites, Homestead Studios, Radisson, **other:** Chevrolet, Dillard's, Firestone, JC Penney, Sears/auto, mall

234 MO 180, St Charles Rock Rd, N...**gas:** Phillips 66, Shell, **food:** Applebee's, Casa Gallardo's, Fazoli's, Hardee's, Hatfield's/McCoy's Rest., LoneStar Steaks, LJ Silver, McDonald's, Old Country Buffet, Ponderosa, Red Lobster, Shoney's, Steak'n Shake, Taco Bell, Tony Bono's Rest., **lodging:** Knight's Inn, **other:** HOSPITAL, Best Buy, Circuit City, GrandPa's Food/drug, Honda, K-Mart, NTB, Office Depot, Sam's Club, Target, Walgreen/24hr, S...Isuzu

232 I-270, N to Chicago, S to Memphis

231b a Earth City Expwy, N...**gas:** Phillips 66/Jack-in-the-Box/dsl, **other:** McDonald's, **lodging:** Candlewood Suites, Courtyard, Fairfield Inn, Residence Inn, Sheraton, Studio+, S...**gas:** Mobil, **food:** Burger King, Dave&Buster's, **lodging:** Holiday Inn, Doubletree Hotel, Wingate Inn, **other:** Harrah's Casino/Hotel, Riverport Ampitheatre

230mm Missouri River

St Charles

229b a 5th St, St Charles, N...**gas:** BP, Mobil/dsl, MotoMart, **food:** Buffalo Wild Wings, Burger King, Denny's, Jack-in-the-Box, KFC, Lee's Chicken, McDonald's, Subway, Waffle House, **lodging:** Baymont Inn, Best Western, Comfort Suites, Quality Inn, St Charles Inn, **other:** Casino, Bass Pro Shops, Walgreens/24hr, S...**gas:** Phillips 66, QT/dsl, **food:** Cracker Barrel, **lodging:** Best Western Noah's Ark, Day's Inn, Embassy Suites, Fairfield Inn, Howard Johnson, Ramada, Suburban Lodge, Townhouse Inn, **other:** JC Penney, malls, RV park

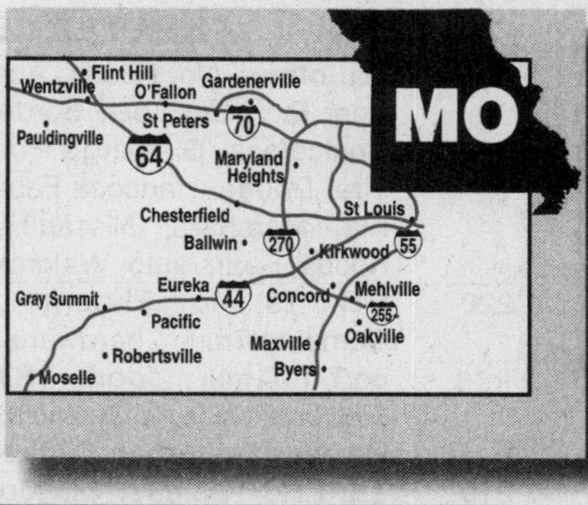

228 MO 94, to Weldon Springs, St Charles, N...**gas:** Citgo, Phillips 66, **food:** Arby's, DQ, Hardee's, Imo's Pizza, LJ Silver, Papa John's, Pizza Hut, Steak'n Shake, Wendy's, **other:** Advance Parts, AutoValue, AutoZone, Chevrolet, Firestone, Radio Shack, Shop'n Save, Walgreen, Valvoline, S...**gas:** QT, **food:** ChuckeCheese, Fazoli's, Gingham's Rest., **lodging:** Best Western, Intown Suites, access to 227

227 Zumbehl Rd, N...**gas:** Citgo, Shell, **food:** Burger King, Culpepper's Grill, **lodging:** Econolodge, Super 8, **other:** Ford, Lowe's Whse, SavALot Foods, S...**gas:** Amoco, BP, Mobil/FoodCourt, **food:** Applebee's, BBQ, Bob Evans, Boston Mkt, Capt D's, Chevy's Mexican, CiCi's Pizza, Golden Corral, Great Wall Chinese, Hardee's, Jack-in-the-Box, Krieger's Grill, LoneStar Steaks, McDonald's, Mr Steak, Old Country Buffet, Popeye's, Quizno's, Subway, Taco Bell, **lodging:** Best Western, Comfort Inn, Red Roof Inn, TownePlace Suites, Travelodge, **other:** BigLots, Dierberg's Foods/24hr, $Tree, GNC, NTB, Sam's Club, Schnuck's Foods/24hr, Wal-Mart/auto, access to 228

225 Truman Rd, to Cave Springs, N...**gas:** BP, Caseys, Citgo, **food:** Taco Bell, Wendy's, **lodging:** Budget Motel, Hampton Inn, Knight's Inn, Motel 6, **other:** Buick/Pontiac, Cadillac, Lincoln/Mercury, Mazda, Saturn, Subaru, Target, Toyota, U-Haul, S...**gas:** Conoco, Culver's, Mobil, QT, **food:** BBQ, Big Boy, Burger King, China Wok, DQ, Denny's, El Mezcal Mexican, Fazoli's, Ground Round, Hooters, IHOP, Jack-in-the-Box, Longhorn Steaks, Lion's Choice Rest., LJ Silver, McDonald's, O'Charley's, Pasta House, Pizza Hut, Ponderosa, Red Lobster, Steak'n Shake, Subway, Super Smokeys BBQ, White Castle, **lodging:** Holiday Inn Select, **other:** HOSPITAL, Chrysler/Jeep, Dodge, Firestone, Home Depot, Kia, K-Mart, Office Depot, Shop'n Save, Target

St Peters

224 MO 370 E

222 Mid-Rivers Mall Dr, rd C, St Peters, N...**gas:** QT/dsl/24hr, **food:** Burger King, **other:** Chevrolet, Honda, Lincoln/Mercury, Mitsubishi, Subaru, S...**gas:** Citgo, Mobil, **food:** Arby's, Bob Evans, Chili's, Domino's, Jack-in-the-Box, Joe's Crabshack, McDonald's, Olive Garden, Pizza Hut/Taco Bell, Red Robin, Ruby Tuesday, Steak'n Shake, Subway, Wendy's, **lodging:** Drury Inn, Extended Stay Amer-

MISSOURI

Interstate 70

E
↑
W

	ica, **other:** Aldi Foods, AutoZone, Barnes&Noble, Best Buy, Big Lots, Borders Books, Circuit City, Costco/gas, Dierberg's Foods, Dillard's, Discount Tire, Dodge, Hancock Fabrics, Isuzu, JC Penney, Kia, Marshalls, Nissan/Hyundai/VW, Schnuck's Foods, Sears/auto, Walgreen
220	MO 79, to Elsberry, **N**...Cherokee Lakes Camping(7mi), hardware, **S**...**gas:** BP, Citgo/7-11(1mi), **food:** Blimpie(1mi), Hardee's, McDonald's(1mi), Quizno's, Sonic, Subway, **other:** Ramada Ltd, **other:** Dierberg's Foods
219	Tru's Rd, **S**...**gas:** Qt, **food:** Smokehouse Rest., **lodging:** Comfort Inn
217	rds K, M, O'Fallon, **N**...**gas:** BP, Conoco, QT, **food:** Blimpie, El Tio's Mexican, Burger King, Hardee's, Jack-in-the-Box, Ponderosa, Rally's, Pizza Hut/Taco Bell, Waffle House, **other:** AutoValue Parts, Firestone, Radio Shack, **S**...**gas:** Citgo/dsl, Dirt-Cheap, Shell, **food:** Arby's, Bob Evans, Fazoli's, IHOP, KFC, Lion's Choice Rest., Longhorn Steaks, McDonald's, Papa John's, Steak'n Shake/24hr, Stefanina's Pizza, **other:** Aldi Foods, AutoZone, K-Mart/drugs, Lowe's Whse, Schnuck's Foods, Shop'n Save Foods, Walgreen, camping
216	Bryan Rd, **N**...**lodging:** Super 8, **other:** Ford, **S**...**gas:** BP, Conoco, Mobil, QT, **food:** DQ, Pantera's Pizza
214	Lake St Louis, **S**...**gas:** Phillips 66/dsl, Shell, **food:** Docside Rest., Denny's, Hardee's, Subway, **lodging:** Day's Inn, **other:** HOSPITAL, IGA Foods
212	rd A, **N**...**lodging:** Econolodge, Knights Inn, **S**...**gas:** Citgo/dsl, **food:** Burger King, Imo's Pizza, **lodging:** Holiday Inn, **other:** Chrysler/Dodge/Jeep, Old Time Pottery
210b a	US 61, US 40, to I-64 E, **S**...**gas:** Phillips 66/dsl, Shell, **other:** HOSPITAL
209	rd Z, Church St, New Melle, **N**...**food:** DQ, **S**...**gas:** Phillips 66/dsl
208	Pearce Blvd, Wentzville Pkwy, Wentzville, **N**...**gas:** Citgo, Culvers, QT/dsl, **food:** Applebees, Blimpie, Bob Evans, Hardee's, Imo's Pizza, Jack-in-the-Box, KFC, McDonald's, Pizza Hut, Queen Buffet, Quizno's, Sonic, Steak'n Shake/24hr, Taco Bell, Waffle House, Wendy's, White Castle, **other:** HOSPITAL, Chevrolet/Buick, Dierberg's Foods, Family$, Home Depot, Kohl's, Radio Shack, Schnuck's Food, St Louis Bread, Walgreens, Wal-Mart/auto/24hr, **S**...**gas:** BP, **food:** China House Buffet, **lodging:** Super 8, **other:** $General, Dodge, Radio Shack, Transmissions
204mm	weigh sta both lanes
203	rds W, T, Foristell, **N**...**gas:** TA/dsl/rest./24hr/@, Mr Fuel/dsl, **lodging:** Best Western, **S**...**gas:** Phillips 66/dsl/café, **other:** dsl repair
200	rds J, H, F, Wright City, **N**...**gas:** Citgo/dsl, Shell/dsl, **food:** McDonald's, Ruiz Castillo's Mexican(1mi), **other:** $General, **S**...**gas:** Phillips 66, **food:** Big Boy, **lodging:** Super 7 Inn, **other:** Volvo
199	(from wb), same as 200
198mm	**rest area both lanes, full(handicapped)facilities, phone, picnic tables, litter barrels, petwalk**
193	MO 47, Warrenton, **N**...**gas:** BP, Citgo, Phillips 66/dsl, **food:** Applebees, Burger King, Jack-in-the-Box, McDonald's, Pizza Hut, Sonic, Subway, Waffle House, **lodging:** Day's Inn, Super 8, **other:** Family$, Ford, Moser's Foods, Wal-Mart SuperCtr/24hr, **S**...**gas:** BP, Phillips 66/dsl, Q-Stop, **food:** Denny's, Hardee's, Imo's Pizza, KFC, Taco Bell, **lodging:** AmeriHost, **other:** AutoZone, CarQuest, Chrysler/Dodge/Jeep, Goodyear/auto, Kelly Tire, Napa, **1/2 mi on frontage rd...other:** Chevrolet/Pontiac, Outlet Ctr/famous brands
188	rds A, B, to Truxton, **S**...**gas:** ✈/Flying J/Conoco/Cookery/dsl/LP/24hr/@, **lodging:** Budget Inn
183	rds E, NN, Y, Jonesburg, **1 mi N**...Jonesburg Gardens Camping, **S**...**gas:** Phillips 66, Shell
179	rd F, High Hill, **S**...**lodging:** Colonial Inn
175	MO 19, New Florence, **N**...**gas:** BP/Hardee's/dsl, Citgo/dsl, Shell/dsl/24hr, **food:** Maggie's Café, McDonald's, **lodging:** Best Inn, Day's Inn, Super 8, **other:** Stone Hill Winery/gifts, U-Haul, auto repair
170	MO 161, rd J, Danville, **N**...**gas:** Citgo, **other:** to Graham Cave SP, Kan-Do RV Park, **S**...Lazy Day RV Park
169.5mm	**rest area wb, full(handicapped)facilities, phone, vending, picnic tables, litter barrels, petwalk**
168mm	Loutre River
167mm	**rest area eb, full(handicapped)facilities, phone, vending, picnic tables, litter barrels, petwalk**
161	rds D, YY, Williamsburg, **S**...**gas:** Conoco/dsl/café/24hr, **food:** Marlene's Rest.
155	rds A, Z, to Calwood, **N**...antiques
148	US 54, Kingdom City, **N**...**gas:** BP, Phillips 66/dsl, **food:** Taco Bell, **other:** to Mark Twain Lake, **S**...**gas:** Conoco/Subway/dsl/@, Shell/Gasper's/dsl/rest./@, Petro/Mobil/Iron Skillet/dsl/rest./24hr/@, Phillips 66/McDonald's/dsl, **food:** Denny's, **lodging:** Comfort Inn, Day's Inn, Red Carpet Inn, Super 8
144	rds M, HH, to Hatton, **S**...**other:** Shoemaker RV Ctr, fireworks
137	rds DD, J, to Millersburg, Stephens, **S**...antiques, to Little Dixie WA
133	rd Z, to Centralia, **N**...**other:** furniture, Loveall's RV
131	Lake of the Woods Rd, **N**...**gas:** BP, Phillips 66/Subway/dsl, **lodging:** Super 8, **other:** Harley Davidson, **S**...**gas:** Shell/dsl/24hr, **food:** Dragon Sea Chinese, Georgia Salad Bar, **other:** RV Park
128a	US 63, to Jefferson City, Columbia, **N**...**gas:** BP, Casey's, QT, **food:** Backyard Burger, Bob Evans, Burger King, China Garden, Cracker Barrel, Golden Corral, Hooters, KFC, McDonald's, Pizza Hut, Steak'n Shake, Taco Bell, Wendy's, **lodging:** Fairfield Inn, Hampton Inn, Residence Inn, Super 8, **other:** Aamco, Bass Pro Shop, Home Depot, KOA, Cottonwood's RV, **S**...**gas:** Breaktime/dsl, **food:** Applebees, Chili's, CiCi's, IHOP, Longhorn Steaks, Quizno's, Sonic, Subway, **lodging:** Best Western, Candlewood Suites, Holiday Inn Express, Hawthorn Suites, La Quinta, Motel 6, Wingate Inn, **other:** HOSPITAL, Lowe's Whse, Nowell's Foods, Patricia's Foods, Sam's Club, Staples, Wal-Mart SuperCtr/24hr(1mi)
128	Lp 70(from wb), Columbia, **N**...**food:** Wendy's, **lodging:** Super 8, **S**...**gas:** Conoco/dsl, **food:** Capt D's, **lodging:** Eastwood Motel, **other:** HOSPITAL, same as 128a

266

Interstate 70

127	MO 763, to Moberly, Columbia, **N**...gas: Breaktime/dsl, **food:** Honest John's Grill, McDonald's, Waffle House, **lodging:** Ramada, Travelodge, **other:** Acura, Chrysler/Dodge, $General, Harley-Davidson, Pontiac/Cadillac, Saturn, Toyota, **S**... **gas:** Phillips 66/dsl, **food:** Burger King, DQ, Everett's Rest., Jack's Rest., Sonic, Taco Bell, **lodging:** Super 7 Motel, **other:** AutoZone
126	MO 163, Providence Rd, Columbia, **N**...gas: BP, **food:** BBQ, Country Kitchen, **lodging:** Best Value Inn, Quality Inn, Red Roof Inn, **other:** Buick/GMC, Ford, Honda, same as 127, **S**...gas: BP, Breaktime/dsl, **food:** Burger King, Church's, DQ, McDonald's, Pizza Hut, Sonic, Subway, Taco Bell, **other:** HOSPITAL, Aldi Foods, AutoZone, Chevrolet/Nissan, Chrysler/Jeep, $General, Lincoln/Mercury, O'Reilly Parts
125	Lp 70, West Blvd, Columbia, **N**...lodging: Comfort Suites, **S**...gas: Breaktime/dsl, Conoco/dsl, Citgo, Phillips 66/dsl, Shell, **food:** Chevy's Mexican, Denny's, Domino's, El Maguey Mexican, Fazoli's, LJ Silver, Olive Garden, Outback Steaks, Perkins, Pizza Hut, Red Lobster, Ryan's, Wendy's, Western Sizzlin, Yen Ching Chinese, **lodging:** Deluxe Inn, Eastwood Inn, Econolodge, Howard Johnson/rest., Scottish Inn, **other:** Advance Parts, Chrysler/Subaru, Firestone/auto, Mitsubishi, Mr Transmissions, PriceChopper Foods, U-Haul, same as 124
124	MO 740, rd E, Stadium Blvd, Columbia, **N**...lodging: Extended Stay America, **S**...gas: BreakTime, Phillips 66, **food:** Applebee's, Burger King, Great Wall, Chinese, Hardee's, KFC, Macaroni Grill, McDonald's, Old Chicago Pizza, Pizza Hut, Red Lobster, Ruby Tuesday, Steak'n Shake, Subway, Taco Bell, Wendy's, **lodging:** Baymont Inn, Day's Inn, Drury Inn, Holiday Inn Select/rest., Motel 6, Regency Inn, Stony Creek Inn, **other:** Best Buy, Circuit City, Dillard's, Ford, Isuzu, JC Penney, K-Mart, Michael's, Old Navy, Radio Shack, Sears/auto, Target, Toyota, Wal-Mart/auto, mall, to U of MO, same as 125
122mm	Perche Creek
121	US 40, rd UU, Midway, **N**...gas: Conoco/dsl/rest., **lodging:** Budget Inn, **other:** Goodyear, Flea Mkt/antiques, **S**...golf
117	rds J, O, to Huntsdale
115	rd BB, Rocheport, **N**...to Katy Tr SP, **S**...antiques
114.5mm	Missouri River
111	MO 98, MO 179, to Wooldridge, Overton, **S**...gas: Phillips 66/dsl/repair
106	MO 87, Bingham Rd, to Boonville, **N**...gas: Conoco/dsl/rest., Phillips 66/dsl, **lodging:** Atlasta Motel/rest.
104mm	**rest area both lanes, full (handicapped) facilities, phone, picnic tables, litter barrels, vending, petwalk**
103	rd B, Main St, Boonville, **N**...gas: Breaktime, Phillips 66/dsl, **food:** Breadeaux Pizza, Domino's, KFC/LJ Silver, La Hacienda Mexican, McDonald's, Pizza Hut, Sonic, Subway, Taco Bell, **lodging:** Day's Inn, Super 8, **other:** HOSPITAL, Daves Mkt, $General,

	Radio Shack, Wal-Mart/café, to Kay Tr SP, **S**...gas: Cenex/dsl, Conoco/Bobber Cafe/dsl/24hr, **food:** Mr. Goodcents Subs, **lodging:** QT Inn, **other:** Bobber Lake Camping
101	US 40, MO 5, to Boonville, **N**...gas: Pilot/Wendy's/dsl/24hr/@, **food:** Arbys, A&W, **lodging:** Comfort Inn, Holiday Inn Express, **other:** Buick, Cadillac, Chevrolet, Ford, Russell Stovers Candy, **S**...other: Chrysler/Dodge/Jeep, to Lake of the Ozarks
98	MO 41, MO 135, Lamine, **N**...to Arrow Rock HS(13mi), tires, **S**...gas: Conoco/Dogwood Rest./dsl, Phillips 66, Shell/dsl/24hr, **other:** antiques, repair
93mm	Lamine River
89	rd K, to Arrow Rock, **N**...to Arrow Rock HS
84	rd J, **N**...gas: BP/DQ/Stuckey's, truck repair
78b a	US 65, to Marshall, **N**...gas: Conoco/dsl, **other:** Lazy Days RV Park, **S**...gas: Breaktime/dsl
77mm	Blackwater River
74	rds YY, **N**...gas: Texaco/dsl/rest./24hr, **S**...gas: BP/dsl/rest.
71	rds EE, K, to Houstonia
66	MO 127, Sweet Springs, **S**...gas: BreakTime/Sonic/dsl, BreakTime, **food:** Brownsville Station Rest, **lodging:** People's Choice Motel, Super 8, **other:** HOSPITAL, NAPA
65.5mm	Davis Creek
62	rds VV, Y, Emma
58	MO 23, Concordia, **N**...gas: Casey's, TA/Subway/dsl/24hr/@, **food:** KFC/Taco Bell, McDonald's, **other:** $General, **S**...gas: Breaktime/dsl, Conoco, Phillips 66 **food:** Biffle's BBQ, Hardee's, Pizza Hut, **lodging:** Best Value, Day's Inn, **other:** NAPA, Patricia's Foods, TrueValue
57.5mm	**rest area both lanes, full(handicapped)facilities, phone, picnic tables, litter barrels, vending, petwalk**
52	rd T, Aullville
49	MO 13, to Higginsville, **N**...gas: BP, Pilot/McDonald's/Subway/dsl/24hr/@, **food:** China Buffet, Pizza Hut, **lodging:** Best Value, Camelot Inn, Classic Motel(4mi); **other:** to Whiteman AFB, to Confederate Mem, **S**...lodging: Super 8/rest., **other:** Interstate RV Park
45	rd H, to Mayview
43mm	weigh sta both lanes
41	rds O, M, to Lexington, Mayview
38	MO 131(from wb), Odessa, **S**...gas: BP/dsl, Shell, **food:** McDonald's, Sonic, Subway, Taco John's, Wendy's, **other:** camping, same as 37
37	MO 131, Odessa, **N**...food: Countryside Diner, **other:** Country Gardens RV Park, **S**...gas: BP/dsl,

Columbia

Concordia

MISSOURI

Interstate 70

E ↑ ↓ W

Exit	Description
	Shell, Sinclair, **food:** McDonald's, Morgan's Rest., Pizza Hut, Sonic, Subway, Taco John's, **lodging:** Parkside Inn, **other:** Chrysler/Dodge/Jeep, Ford, O'Reilly Parts, Prime Outlets/famous brands, Thriftway Foods, RV dump, fireworks, same as 38
35mm	truck parking both lanes
31	rds D, Z, to Bates City, Napoleon, **S**...**gas:** BP/dsl, **other:** fireworks
29.5mm	Horse Shoe Creek
28	rd HF, Oak Grove, **N**...**gas:** TA/Conoco/Popeye's/Pizza Hut/dsl/24hr/@, **lodging:** Day's Inn, **other:** Blue Beacon, KOA, **S**...**gas:** QT/dsl/24hr, Petro/BP/Blimpie/DQ/Wendy's/dsl/@, **food:** BBQ, Hardee's, KFC/Taco Bell, McDonald's, Subway, TJ's Rest., Waffle House, **lodging:** Econolodge, **other:** Speedco Lube, Wal-Mart SuperCtr/24hr
24	US 40, rds AA, BB, to Buckner, **N**...**gas:** McLeroy/dsl, Phillips 66/dsl/rest., **lodging:** Comfort Inn, Travelodge, **other:** Lifestyles RV Ctr, **S**...**gas:** Conoco/Subway/dsl/24hr/@, **food:** Sonic, **lodging:** Kozy Inn, **other:** Trailside RV Park/Ctr
21	Adams Dairy Pkwy, **N**...**lodging:** Days Inn, Rodeway Inn, **other:** Nationwide RV Ctr(1mi), **S**...**gas:** Murphy USA, Phillips 66/Burger King/dsl, **lodging:** Courtyard, Sleep Inn, **other:** Home Depot, Wal-Mart Super Ctr/24hr/gas
20	MO 7, Blue Springs, **N**...**gas:** Phillips 66/dsl, Shamrock, Sinclair, Valero, **food:** Backyard Burger, Bob Evans, Country Hearth, China One, Pizza Hut, Pizza Street, Quizno's, Rancho Grande, Sonic, **lodging:** Days Inn, Econolodge, Motel 6, Ramada Ltd, Rodeway Inn, Super 8, **other:** Ace Hardware, $General, O'Reilly Parts, Osco Drug, PriceChopper Foods, Valvoline, Walgreens, **S**...**gas:** BP/dsl/24hr, QT, Shell, Valero, **food:** Applebee's, Arby's, BBQ, Bua Thai, Burger King, Capt D's, China Buffet, Clancy's, Denny's, Domino's, Einstein Bro's, El Mezcal Mexican, Godfather's, Golden Corral, Jin's Buffet, KFC, LJ Silver, McDonald's, Starbucks, Subway, Wendy's, **lodging:** Hampton Inn, Holiday Inn Express, Quality Inn, **other:** HOSPITAL, Advance Parts, AutoZone, Aldi Foods, Chevrolet, Firestone/auto, Goodyear/auto, Hyundai, NAPA, Office Depot, Radio Shack, Saturn, Winstead's
18	Woods Chapel Rd, **N**...**gas:** BP, **lodging:** American Inn, Best Value Inn, Interstate Inn, **other:** Harley-Davidson, **S**...**gas:** Conoco, Phillips 66/dsl, QT, **food:** China Kitchen, KFC/Taco Bell, McDonald's, Pizza Hut, Subway, Waffle House, **other:** Ford, Hyundai, NAPA, Nissan, same as 20
17	Little Blue Pkwy, 39th St, **N**...**food:** Applebee's, BBQ, Buffalo Wild Wings, Coldstone Creamery, Fazoli's, Hereford House, Indian Bistro, Joe's Crabshack, Macaroni Grill, O'Charley's, On the Border, Starbucks, **lodging:** Hilton Garden, **other:** HOSPITAL, Steinmart, mall entrance, **S**...**gas:** QT, **food:**

Exit	Description
	BD Mongolian, Carrabba's, El Maguay Mexican, Hooters, IHOP, Kobe Steaks, Outback Steaks, Rib Crib, Subway, Wendy's, **lodging:** Comfort Suites, Holiday Inn Express, **other:** Carmax, CompUSA, Costco/gas, Lowe's Whse
16mm	Little Blue River
15b	MO 291 N, Independence, **1 exit N on 39th St**... **gas:** Conoco, QT, Phillips 66, **food:** Applebee's, Arby's, BBQ, Bob Evans, Burger King, Chevy's Mexican, Chili's, Denny's, 54th St Grill, Fazoli's, Fox&Hound Smokehouse, Hops Grill, KFC, LJ Silver, LoneStar Steaks, Longhorn Steaks, Luby's, McDonald's, Mr GoodCents Subs, Souper Salad, Starbucks, TGIFriday, **lodging:** Fairfield Inn, Residence Inn, **other:** HOSPITAL, Albertson's, Barnes&Noble, Best Buy, Circuit City, Dick's Sports, Dillard's, Jo-Ann Fabrics, Kohl's, Marshall's, NTB, Sam's Club/gas, Sears/auto, Target, Wal-Mart SuperCtr/24hr, mall, **S**...**other:** Bass Pro Shops
15a	I-470 S, MO 291 S, to Lee's Summit
14	Lee's Summit Rd, **S**...**food:** Cracker Barrel, Olive Garden, Salty Iguana Mexican, Steak'n Shake, **lodging:** Budget Host, **other:** Home Depot
12	Noland Rd, Independence, **N**...**gas:** Conoco, QT, Shell/dsl, **food:** Denny's, ChuckeCheese, Hardee's, Mr. Goodcents, Sonic, Wally's Steaks, **lodging:** Best Western, Super 8, **other:** Advance Parts, $General, Firestone/auto, Hancock Fabrics, K-Mart, Office Depot, Osco Drug, Walgreens, U-Haul, to Truman Library, **S**...**gas:** Phillips 66, **food:** Arby's, Burger King, Country Kitchen, Fuddrucker's, KFC/Taco Bell, KrispyKreme, McDonald's, Old Country Buffet, Olive Garden, Pizza Hut, Red Lobster, Ruby Tuesday, Steak'n Shake, Wendy's, **lodging:** American Inn, Comfort Inn, Crossland Inn, Quality Inn, Red Roof Inn, **other:** Best Buy, $Tree, HyVee Foods/gas, Old Navy, Old Time Pottery, Pricechopper Foods, Tires+
11	US 40, Blue Ridge Blvd, Independence, **N**...**gas:** Conoco, QT, **food:** A&W/LJ Silver, Burger King, McDonald's, Sonic, Subway, V's Italiano, **lodging:** Deluxe Inn, **other:** Radio Shack, Stadium RV Park, **S**...**gas:** BP, Sinclair, **food:** Applebee's, Big Boy, Hong Kong Buffet, McDonald's, Old Country Buffet, Papa John's, Taco Bell, **lodging:** Sports Stadium Motel, **other:** Cadillac, Family $, JC Penney, O'Riley Parts, 7-11, Wal-Mart Super Ctr, mall
10	Sterling Ave(from eb), same as 11
9	Blue Ridge Cutoff, **N**...**food:** Denny's/24hr, **lodging:** Clarion, Drury Inn, **other:** HOSPITAL, **S**... **gas:** BP/24hr, Conoco/Subway, **food:** Taco Bell, **lodging:** Holiday Inn, **other:** Sports Complex
8b a	I-435, N to Des Moines, S to Wichita
7b	Manchester Trafficway, **N**...**lodging:** Sunset Inn
7mm	Blue River

I n d e p e n d e n c e

Interstate 70

7a	US 40 E, 31st St, 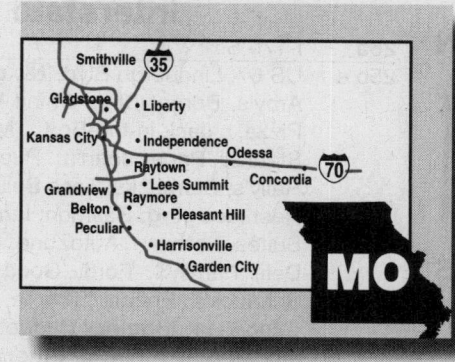**S**...**lodging:** Travelers Inn
6	Van Brunt Blvd, **N**...**gas:** 7-11, **food:** Church's, **S**...**gas:** BP, **food:** McDonald's, Pizza Hut, Taco Bell, **other:** VA HOSPITAL, Family$, Napa
5c	Jackson Ave(from wb)
5b	31st St(from eb)
5a	27th St(from eb)
4c	23rd Ave
4b	18th St, **N**...**gas:** Millenium/Wendy's/dsl
4a	Benton Blvd(from eb), Truman Rd, **N**...**gas:** Phillips 66/Wendy's/dsl, **other:** Advance Parts
3c	Prospect Ave, **N**...**gas:** Innercity gas, **food:** Bryant BBQ, Church's, Gate's BBQ, **S**...**food:** McDonald's
3b	Brooklyn Ave(from eb), **S**...same as 3c
3a	Paseo St, **S**...**gas:** BP, **other:** tires
2m	US 71 S, downtown
2l	I-670, to I-35 S
2j	11th St, downtown
2g	I-29/35 N, US 71 N, to Des Moines
2h	US 24 E, downtown
2e	MO 9 N, Oak St, **N**...**gas:** Valero, **lodging:** Comfort Inn
2d	Main St, downtown
2c	US 169 N, Broadway, downtown
2b	Beardsley Rd
2a	I-35 S, to Wichita
0mm	Missouri/Kansas state line, Kansas River

Interstate 270(St Louis)

Exit #	Services
15b a	I-55 N to Chicago, S to St Louis. I-270 begins/ends in Illinois on I-55/I-70, exit 20.
12	IL 159, to Collinsville, **1 mi N**...**gas:** Conoco, Phillips 66, **food:** Applebee's, China Rest., DQ, Denny's, Hardee's, Jack-in-the-Box, KFC, Papa John's, Ponderosa, Quizno's **other:** Aldi Foods, Buick/Pontiac/GMC, Chrysler/Dodge/Jeep, Home Depot, Lowe's Whse, PetsMart, Radio Shack, Walgreens, Wal-Mart, **S**...HOSPITAL
9	IL 157, to Collinsville, **N**...**food:** Comfort Inn, **S**...**gas:** Phillips 66/24hr
7	I-255, to I-55 S to Memphis
6b a	IL 111, **N**...**gas:** ⚡/Flying J/CountryMkt/dsl/scales/24hr, **food:** Hen House Rest., **lodging:** Best Western, **other:** Speedco Lube, truck/trailer repair, truck wash, **S**...**gas:** Mobil/dsl, **food:** Denny's, McDonald's/playplace, La Mexicana Rest., Taco Bell, **lodging:** Day's Inn, Holiday Inn Express, Super 8, **other:** HOSPITAL, to Pontoon Beach
4	IL 203, Old Alton Rd, to Granite City
3b a	IL 3, **N**...Riverboat Casino, **S**...**gas:** Phillips 66, **food:** Hardee's, Waffle House, **lodging:** Chain of Rocks Motel, Western Inn, **other:** KOA, MGM Camping,
2mm	Chain of Rocks Canal

0mm	**Illinois/Missouri state line, Mississippi River,** motorist callboxes begin eb
34	Riverview Dr, to St Louis, **N**...**Welcome Ctr/rest area both lanes, full(handicapped)facilities, info, picnic tables, litter barrels, phones**
33	Lilac Ave, **N**...USPO, **S**...**gas:** Phillips 66/Jack-in-the-Box/dsl, QT/dsl/24hr, **food:** Hardee's
32	Bellefontaine Rd, **N**...**gas:** Mobil, Shell, **food:** Burger King, Denny's, McDonald's, Pizza Hut, Steak'n Shake, **lodging:** Econolodge, Motel 6, **other:** Advance Parts, Firestone, Schnuck's Foods, bank, **S**...**gas:** BP/24hr, **food:** China Wok, White Castle, **other:** Aldi Foods
31b a	MO 367, **N**...**gas:** QT, **food:** Arby's, Jack-in-the-Box, McDonalds, Subway, **other:** HOSPITAL, Mazda
30b a	Hall's Ferry Rd, rd AC, **N**...**gas:** Citgo, Mobil/dsl, Phillips 66/dsl, QT/24hr, **food:** Applebee's, Capt. D's, Hardee's, Lion's Choice, Popeyes, Red Lobster, Taco Bell, White Castle, Wendy's, **lodging:** Super 8, **other:** Discount Tire, Ford, Lincoln/Mercury, Target, **S**...**gas:** BP/dsl, **food:** Church's, CiCi's Pizza, Cracker Barrel, IHOP, McDonald's, Steak'n Shake, **other:** AutoZone, Buick, Family$ Home Depot, Hyundai, Jo-Ann Fabrics, O'Riley Parts, Saturn, Shop'n Save Foods
29	W Florissant Rd, **N**...**food:** Jack-in-the-Box, Hometown Buffet, Pasta House, **other:** Big Lots, Dierberg's Foods, K-Mart, Firestone, Office Depot, TJ Maxx, **S**...**food:** Arby's, Burger King, Krispy Kreme, Malone's Grill, McDonald's, **other:** Circuit City, $Tree, NTB, Sam's Club/gas, Wal-Mart/auto, Walgreen
28	Elizabeth Ave, Washington St, **N**...**gas:** Sinclair, **food:** Jack-in-the-Box, Mrs O's Café, Pizza Hut/Taco Bell, Subway, **other:** Chevrolet, JC Penney, Schnuck's Foods/24hr, Walgreen, **S**...**gas:** BP/24hr
27	New Florissant Rd, rd N, **N**...**gas:** BP, Shell,
26b	Graham Rd, N Hanley, **N**...**gas:** Citgo/7-11, **food:** Denny's, Fazoli's, Hardee's, LJ Silver, Rosemari's Rest., **lodging:** Hampton Inn, Red Roof Inn, **other:** HOSPITAL, Mitsubishi, **S**...**food:** McDonald's, **lodging:** Day's Inn, **other:** $General, Hancock Fabrics

MISSOURI
Interstate 270

St Louis

Exit	Services
26a	I-170 S
25b a	US 67, Lindbergh Blvd, **N**...**gas:** Phillips 66, **food:** Arby's, Burger King, China Wok, Del Taco, Imo's Pizza, Jack-in-the-Box, McDonald's, Outback Steaks, Papa John's, Pueblo Nuevo Mexican, Rally's, Starbucks, Taco Bell/Pizza Hut, Village Inn Rest., **lodging:** Baymont Inn, Comfort Inn, InTown Suites, **other:** AutoZone, Cadillac, Dierberg's Deli, Family$, Ford, Goodyear, NAPA, Nissan, Schnuck's Foods, Toyota, Walgreen, **S**...**gas:** Citgo/7-11, **lodging:** Budget Inn, Econolodge, Extended Stay America, **other:** USPO, VW/Volvo
23	McDonnell Blvd, **E**...**food:** Denny's, Quizno's, **lodging:** La Quinta, **W**...**gas:** BP, Phillips 66/dsl, QT, **food:** Arby's, Jack-in-the-Box, McDonald's, Steak'n Shake, **other:** Pontiac/GMC
22	MO 370 W, to MO Bottom Rd
20c	MO 180, St Charles Rock Rd, **E**...**gas:** BP, Phillips 66/dsl, Shell, **food:** Casa Gallardo's, Berkshire Grill, Hardee's, Hometown Buffet, McDonald's, Fazoli's, Jack-in-the-Box, LJ Silver/A$W, New China, Ponderosa, Quizno's, Red Lobster, Shoney's, Steak'n Shake, St. Louis Bread, Taco Bell, Tony Bono's Rest., **lodging:** Economy Inn, **other:** HOSPITAL, AutoZone, Best Buy, $Tree, Honda, K-Mart, Kohl's, Office Depot, Target, Walgreen/24hr, **W**...**gas:** QT, **food:** Bob Evans, Olive Garden, Ryan's, Waffle House, **lodging:** Econolodge, Motel 6, Red Roof Inn, Super 8, **other:** Ford
20b a	I-70, E to St Louis, W to Kansas City
17	Dorsett Rd, **E**...**gas:** BP, QT, **food:** BBQ, Syberg's Grill, **lodging:** Best Western, Drury Inn, Hampton Inn, **W**...**gas:** Mobil, Phillips 66, Shell, **food:** Arby's, Denny's, Fuddrucker's, McDonald's, Steak'n Shake, Subway, **lodging:** Baymont Inn
16b a	Page Ave, rd D, MO 364 W, **E**...**gas:** BP, CFM, Citgo/7-11, QT, Sinclair, **food:** Blimpie, Copperfield's Rest., Hardee's, Hooters, Malone's Grill, McDonald's, Stazio's Café, **lodging:** Comfort Inn, Courtyard, DoubleTree, Holiday Inn, Homestead Suites, Red Roof Inn, Residence Inn, Sheraton
14	MO 340, Olive Blvd, **E**...**gas:** BP, Mobil, **food:** Applebee's, Bristol Cafe, Denny's, Domino's, KFC, McDonald's, Lion's Choice Rest., Pasta House, Steakout, **lodging:** Courtyard, Drury Inn, **other:** HOSPITAL, BMW/Land Rover/Cadillac, Borders, Chevrolet, Chrysler/Jeep, Lexus, **W**...**gas:** Schnucks, **food:** Coldstone Creamery, Culpepper's Café, House of Wong, Subway, TGIFriday, **other:** Dierberg's Foods, Kohl's, Walgreens
13	rd AB, Ladue Rd
12b a	I-64, US 40, US 61, E to St Louis, W to Wentzville, **E**...HOSPITAL
9	MO 100, Manchester Rd, **E**...**gas:** BP, **food:** Café America, Houlihan's Rest, IHOP, Lion's Choice Rest., McDonald's, **other:** Famous Barr, Galyan's, Lord&Taylor, Nordstrom's, mall, **W**...**gas:** Phillips 66, Shell, **food:** Applebee's, Casa Gallardo's Mexican, Olive Garden, Red Robin
8	Dougherty Ferry Rd, **S**...**gas:** Citgo/7-11, Mobil, **food:** McDonald's, **other:** HOSPITAL
7	Big Ben Rd, **N**...HOSPITAL
5b a	I-44, US 50, MO 366, E to St Louis, W to Tulsa
3	MO 30, Gravois Rd, **N**...**gas:** BP, Phillips 66, **food:** Bandana BBQ, Outback Steaks, **lodging:** Day's Inn, Holiday Inn, Quality Inn
2	MO 21, Tesson Ferry Rd, **N**...**gas:** BP, **food:** Panda Chinese, Pizza Hut, Red Lobster, **lodging:** Holiday Inn, **other:** Acura, AutoZone, Buick, Toyota, **N on Lindbourgh**...**gas:** Phillips 66, **food:** Burger King, Church's, Olive Garden, Quizno's, Taco Bell, TGIFriday, Waffle House, White Castle, **other:** Buick, Saab, Schnuck's Foods, **S**...**gas:** Shell, **other** Dierberg's Foods
1b a	I-55 N to St Louis, S to Memphis

Interstate 435(Kansas City)

Exit #	Services
83	I-35, N to KS City, S to Wichita
82	Quivira Rd, Overland Park, **N**...**food:** Burger King, Old Chicago Pizza, Pizza Hut, Ponderosa, Taco Bell, **other:** HOSPITAL, CVS Drug, **S**...**food:** McDonald's, Subway, Wendy's, **lodging:** Extended Stay America
81	US 69 S, to Ft Scott
79	US 169, Metcalf Ave., **N**...**gas:** BP, Shell, **food:** Denny's, Dick Clark's Grill, Hooters, Tippin's Café, **lodging:** Clubhouse Inn, Embassy Suites, Hampton Inn, Red Roof Inn, Super 8, Wyndham Garden, **other:** HOSPITAL, Chrysler/Dodge, **S**...**food:** KC BBQ, McDonald's, **lodging:** Courtyard, Drury Inn, Marriott, PearTree Inn
77b a	Nall Ave, Roe Ave, **N**...**gas:** BP, Shell, **food:** DQ, On-the-Border, Panera Bread, Winstead's Grill, **lodging:** Fairfield Inn, **S**...**gas:** BP, **food:** Cactus Grill, McDonald's, Wendy's, **lodging:** AmeriSuites, Courtyard, Hilton Garden, Holiday Inn, Homestead Suites, Sheraton
75b	State Line Rd, **N**...**gas:** BP, Conoco, **food:** Applebee's, McDonald's, Taco Bell, Waid's Rest., Wendy's, **other:** Buick/Cadillac, Ford, Goodyear, Infiniti, Lexus, Volvo, **S**...HOSPITAL, city park
75a	Wornall Rd, **N**...**gas:** QT, Shell, **food:** Applebees, Coach's Rest., Wendy's, **other:** Chevrolet, Toyota, VW

Interstate 435

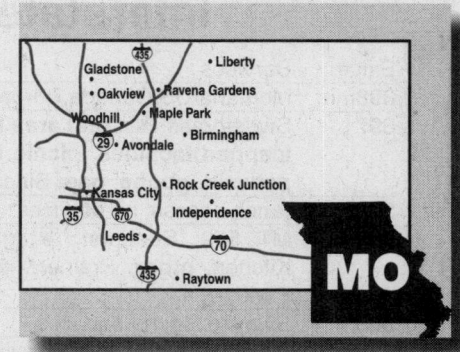

74	Holmes Rd, S...**gas:** Phillips 66, **food:** Burger King, Guacamole Grill, Patrikio's Mexican, Subway, **lodging:** Courtyard, Extended Stay America
73	103rd St(from sb)
71b a	I-470, US 71 S, US 50 E
70	Bannister Rd, E...**gas:** Shell, **food:** China Buffet, McDonalds, Wendy's, **other:** K-Mart, W...**food:** HomeTown Buffet, KFC/Taco Bell, LJ Silver/A&W, Pizza Hut, **other:** Firestone/auto, Home Depot
69	69 87th St., E...**food:** Subway, **lodging:** Day's Inn, Motel 6, Super 8, **other:** Suzuki, W...**gas:** BP/dsl, **lodging:** Baymont Inn
67	Gregory Blvd(same as 66a b), E...**gas:** Shell, **food:** Applebee's, Niece's Rest., Wendy's, **other:** Big Lots, $General, PriceChopper Foods, W...Nature Ctr, IMAX Theatre, zoo
66a b	MO 350 E, 63rd st, E...**gas:** Shell, **food:** Applebee's, Wendy's, **other:** Big Lots, $General, PriceChopper Foods, W...**food:** LC's BBQ, **lodging:** Relax Inn
65	Eastwood Tfwy, W...**gas:** Conoco, **food:** KFC, LC's BBQ, McDonald's, Peachtree Buffet, Pizza Hut, **lodging:** Relax Inn
63c	Raytown Rd, Stadium Dr(nb only), E...**lodging:** Day's Inn, Sports Stadium Motel, Villager Lodge, **other:** Sports Complex
63b a	I-70, W to KC, E to St Louis
61	MO 78, 1 mi E...Church's Chicken
60	MO 12 E, Truman Rd, 12th St, E...**gas:** BP/dsl, Shamrock, W...**gas:** QT
59	US 24, Independence Ave, E...**gas:** QT, **food:** Hardee's, **other:** to Truman Library, W...**other:** CarQuest, Waffle House
57	Front St, E...**gas:** ⚑/Flying J/Conoco/dsl/rest./scales/24hr/@, **other:** Blue Beacon, W...**gas:** Phillips 66, QT, **food:** Denny's, KFC, McDonald's, Pizza Hut, Smugglers Rest, Subway, Taco Bell, Waffle House, Wendy's, **lodging:** La Quinta, Park Place Hotel
56mm	Missouri River
55b a	MO 210, E...**lodging:** Ameristar Hotel/Casino, Red Roof Inn, **other:** Riverboat Casino, Ford/Volvo/GMC/Mercedes Trucks, W...**food:** Arby's, Burger King, Denny's
54	48th St, Parvin Rd, E...RV Park, W...**gas:** QT, **food:** Alamo Mexican, Golden Buffet, KFC, Mama Jo's BBQ, Ponderosa, Waffle House, Wendy's, **lodging:** Comfort Inn, Crossland Suites, Day's Inn, Fairfield Inn, Hampton Inn, Holiday Inn, Super 8
52a	US 69, E...**gas:** Phillips 66, Shell, Sinclair, W...**gas:** Fuel Outlet, **food:** McDonald's, Pizza Hut, Subway, Taco Bell, **other:** CVS Drug, $General, Osco Drug, Sav-A-Lot Foods
52b	I-35, S to KC
51	Shoal Creek Dr
49b a	MO 152 E, to I-35 N, Liberty, E...**food:** Applebee's, Bob Evans, Cracker Barrel, 54th St Grill, Longhorn Steaks, Steak'n Shake, **lodging:** Best Western, Comfort Inn, Fairfield Inn, Hampton Inn, Holiday Inn Express, Super 8

47	NE 96th St
46	NE 108th St
45	MO 291, NE Cookingham Ave, E...to I-35 N
42	N Woodland Ave
41b a	US 169, Smithville, N...**food:** Burger King, McDonald's, Sonic, **lodging:** Super 8
40	NW Cookingham
37	NW Skyview Ave, rd C, N...**gas:** Shamrock(1mi), S...golf(3mi)
36	to I-29 S, to KCI Airport, N...**gas:** Shamrock, S...**gas:** BP, **lodging:** Best Western, Clarion, Comfort Suites, Fairfield Inn, Hampton Inn, Hilton, Holiday Inn Express, Microtel, Radisson, Wyndham Garden
31mm	Prairie Creek
29	rd D, NW 120th St
24	MO 152, rd N, NW Barry Rd
22	MO 45, Weston, Parkville
20mm	**Missouri/Kansas state line, Missouri River**
18	KS 5 N, Wolcott Dr, E...to Wyandotte Co Lake Park
15b a	Leavenworth Rd, E...Woodlands Racetrack
14b a	Parallel Pkwy, E...**gas:** QT, **other:** HOSPITAL
13b a	US 24, US 40, State Ave, E...**food:** Frontier Steaks, W...**other:** Cabela's Sporting Goods, KS Race Track
12b a	I-70, KS Tpk, to Topeka, St Louis
11	Kansas Ave
9	KS 32, KS City, Bonner Springs, W...**gas:** Phillips 66/dsl
8b	Woodend Rd, E...Peterbilt
8.8mm	Kansas River
8a	Holliday Dr, to Lake Quivira
6c	Johnson Dr
6b a	Shawnee Mission Pkwy, E...**gas:** BP/dsl, **food:** Sonic, **other:** museum
5	Midland Dr, Shawnee Mission Park, E...**gas:** Conoco, Shell/Blimpie, **food:** Arizona's Grille, Barley's Brewhaus, Jose Pepper's Grill, Paula&Bill's Ristorante, Wendy's, **lodging:** Hampton Inn
3	87th Ave, E...**gas:** BP, Phillips 66, Shell, **food:** McDonald's, **other:** NY Burrito, Panera Bread, Sonic, Zarda BBQ, K-Mart, museum
2	95th St
1b	KS 10, to Lawrence
1a	Lackman Rd, N...**gas:** QT, Shell
0mm	I-435 begins/ends on I-35.

Kansas City (left side vertical label)

Kansas City (right side vertical label)

MONTANA
Interstate 15

Exit #	Services
398mm	Montana/US/Canada Border
397	Sweetgrass, W...**rest area both lanes, full(hand icapped)facilities, picnic tables, litter barrels, petwalk, phone, gas:** Sinclair, **other:** Duty Free
394	ranch access, no services
389	MT 552, Sunburst, W...gas/dsl, **food:** Kelly's Kitchen, **other:** Prairie Mkt foods, Sunburst RV Park
385	Swayze Rd, no services
379	MT 215, MT 343, to Kevin, Oilmont, W...**food:** Four Corners Café
373	Potter Rd, no services
369	Bronken Rd, no services
366.5mm	weigh sta sb
364	Shelby, E...Lewis&Clark RV Park, W...airport
363	US 2, to Cut Bank, Shelby, E...**gas:** Pilot/Exxon/Subway/dsl/24hr, Sinclair/dsl, **food:** Dash Drive-In, Dixie Inn Steaks, Pizza Hut, South of the Border, The Griddle, **lodging:** Comfort Inn, Crossroads Inn, Dixie Inn, Glacier Motel, O'Haire Motel, **other:** Mark's Tire, 1 mi E...**gas:** Cenex, **other:** HOSPITAL, Albertson's, CarQuest, Ford/Mercury, GMC, Radio Shack, TrueValue, W...**food:** McDonald's, **other:** Pamida/drugs, to Glacier NP
361mm	parking area nb
358	Marias Valley Rd, to Golf Course Rd, E...camping
357mm	Marias River
352	Bullhead Rd, no services
348	rd 44, to Valier, W...Lake Frances RA(15mi)
345	MT 366, Ledger Rd, E...to Tiber Dam(42mi)
339	Conrad, W...**gas:** Cenex/dsl, Exxon/Subway/dsl, MRC/dsl, **food:** A&W/KFC, Conrad's Diner, Home Cafe, House of Pizza, Keg Rest., Main Drive-In, **lodging:** Conrad Motel, Northgate Motel, Super 8, **other:** HOSPITAL, Dan's Tires, IGA Foods, Olson's Drug, Parts+, Radio Shack, Chevrolet/Pontiac/Buick, Ford/Mercury, Pondera RV Park, RV Ctr/LP, TrueValue
335	Midway Rd, Conrad, 4 mi W...HOSPITAL, gas, food, phone, lodging, RV camping
328	MT 365, Brady, 1 mi W...**gas:** Mtn View Co-op/dsl, **other:** USPO, phone
321	Collins Rd, no services
319mm	**Teton River, rest area both lanes, full (handicapped)facilities, phones, picnic tables, litter barrels, petwalk**
313	MT 221, MT 379, Dutton, W...**gas:** Cenex/dsl, **food:** Café Dutton, **other:** USPO
302	MT 431, Power, no services
297	Gordon, no services
290	US 89 N, rd 200 W, to Choteau, W...**gas:** Exxon/dsl, Sinclair/dsl/LP/RV dump, **other:** USPO
288mm	parking area both lanes
286	Manchester, W...livestock auction, same as 290(2mi)
282	US 87 N(from sb), weigh sta, 2-3 mi E...**gas:** Conoco/dsl, Exxon/dsl, **food:** Arby's, Burger King, McDonald's, Pizza Hut, Subway, Taco Bell, Taco John's, **lodging:** Day's Inn, **other:** Albertson's/gas, Checker Parts, $Tree, K-Mart, Sam's Club/gas, ShopKO, Staples, Tire-rama, Wal-Mart Super Ctr/24hr
280	US 87 N, Central Ave W, Great Falls, E...**gas:** Loaf 'N Jug, **food:** A&W/KFC, Arby's, Double Barrel Diner, Ford's Drive-In, Hardee's, Papa John's, **lodging:** Alberta Inn, Central Motel, Day's Inn, La Quinta, **other:** VET, Freightliner, NAPA, U-Haul/LP, Whalen Tire, to Giant Sprgs SP
280mm	Sun River
278	US 89 S, rd 200 E, 10th Ave, Great Falls, E...**food:** China Town, Classic 50's Diner/casino, Golden Corral, Tony Roma's, **lodging:** Airway Motel, Budget Inn, Hampton Inn, Holiday Inn Express, Kanga Inn, **other:** Barnes&Noble, Dick's RV Park, Home Depot, Old Navy, Petco, Smith's Food, 1-3 mi E...**gas:** Cenex/dsl, Conoco, Exxon/Subway, MRC/dsl, Sinclair/dsl, **food:** Applebee's, Arby's, Burger King, Cattin's Rest., China Buffet, Country Kitchen, DQ, Elmer's Rest., 4B's Rest., Fuddrucker's, Godfather's, Hardee's, Jaker's Rib/fish, JB's Rest., KFC, Little Caesar's, McDonald's, Ming's Chinese, Papa John's, Papa Murphy's, Perkin's, Pizza Hut, Prime-Cut Rest., Quizno's, Starbucks, Sting Rest., Taco Bell, Taco John's, Taco Treat, Wendy's, **lodging:** Best Western, Comfort Inn, Extended Stay America, Fairfield Inn, Holiday Inn, La Quinta, Motel 6, Western Motel, **other:** HOSPITAL, Ace Hardware, Albertson's/gas, Checker Parts, Chevrolet/Cadillac/Toyota, County Mkt Food/24hr, Dodge/Hyundai/Suzuki/VW, $Tree, Firestone/auto, Ford, Hancock Fabrics, Harley Davidson, Hastings Books, Herberger's, Honda, JC Penney, Jo-Ann Crafts, K-Mart, KOA(6mi), Lincoln/Mercury, McCollum RVs, NAPA, Nissan, Osco Drug, Parts+, Jeep, Ross, Sears/auto, Target, Tire-Rama, Travel Time RV Ctr, USPO, transmissions, to Malmstrom AFB
277	Airport Rd, E...**gas:** Flying J/Country Mkt./dsl/24/@, Pilot/Conoco/Subway/dsl/café/casino/24hr, **lodging:** Crystal Inn W...airport
275mm	weigh sta nb
270	MT 330, Ulm, E...**gas:** Exxon/dsl/LP, **other:** USPO, W...**food:** Griffin's Rest., to Ulm SP
256	rd 68, Cascade, 1/2 mi E...**gas:** Sinclair, **food:** Billy G's Pizza, **lodging:** Badger Motel/café, **other:** NAPA, Tom's Foods, USPO
254	rd 68, Cascade, 1/2 mi E...same as 256
250	local access, no facilites
247	Hardy Creek, Hardy Creek, W... to Tower Rock SP, food, phone, RV camping
246.5mm	Missouri River
245mm	scenic overlook sb
244	Canyon Access, 2 mi W...camping, food, RV camping, rec area

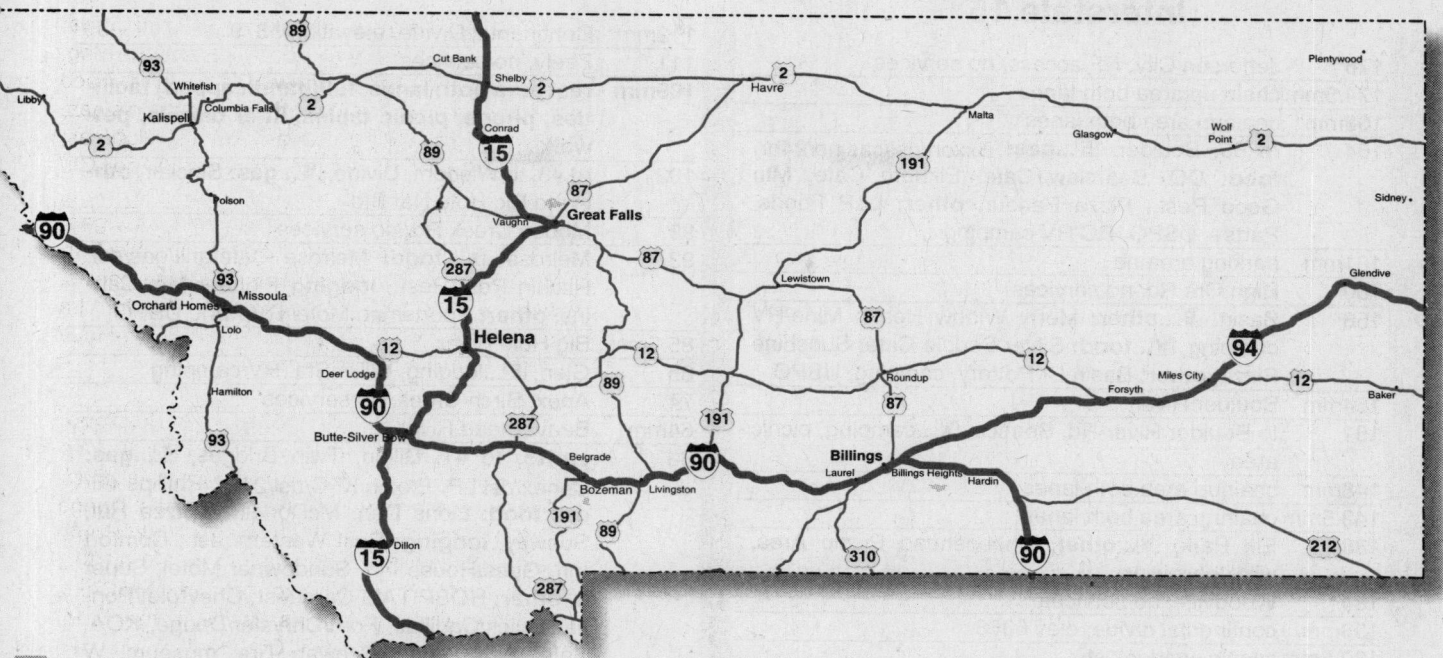

Interstate 15

240	Dearborn, E...RV park, W...food: Dearborn Cafe, lodging: Dearborn Inn, other: auto repair
239mm	**rest area both lanes, full(handicapped) facilities, phone, picnic tables, litter barrels, pet-walk**
238mm	Stickney Creek
236mm	Missouri River
234	Craig, E...food: Izaak's Cafe, Trout Shop Café/lodge, other: rec area, boating, camping
228	US 287 N, to Augusta, no services
226	MT 434, Wolf Creek, Wolf Creek, E...gas: Exxon/dsl, food: Oasis Café, other: MT Outfitters/flyshop/RV/motel, camping, W...food: Frenchman&Me Café, other: USPO
222mm	parking area both lanes
219	Spring Creek, Recreation Rd(from nb), Spring Creek, boating, camping
218mm	Little Prickly Pear Creek
216	Sieben, no services
209	E...to Gates of the Mtns RA, no services
205mm	turnout sb
202mm	weigh sta sb
200	MT 279, MT 453, Lincoln Rd, W...gas: Sinclair/Bob's Mkt/dsl, food: GrubStake Rest., other: Helena Campground(4mi), Lincoln Rd RV Park, to ski area
193	Cedar St, Helena, E...Helena RV Park(5mi), Home Depot, Whalen Tire, W...gas: Conoco/dsl, food: Perkins, Wheat Montana/deli, lodging: Wingate Inn, W on Montana Ave...gas: Cenex/dsl, Exxon/dsl, food: Applebee's, Arby's, Dragon Wall Chinese, DQ, Godfather's, Jade Garden

	Chinese, McDonald's, McKenzie River Pizza, Pizza Hut, Subway, Taco Bell, Taco Del Mar, Taco John's, **lodging:** Quality Inn, **other:** Albertson's/24hr, AutoZone, CarQuest, Checker Parts, Chevrolet, County Mkt Foods, $Tree, Hastings Books, Jo-Ann Fabrics, Kia, K-Mart, Macey's, NAPA, Ross, ShopKO, Target, TireORama, USPO, radiator/transmissions
192b a	US 12, US 287, Helena, Townsend, E...**gas:** Conoco/dsl/24hr, **food:** Burger King, Golden Corral, Pizza Hut, Subway, **lodging:** Hampton Inn, **other:** D&D RV Ctr, Schwab Tire, Staples, Wal-Mart SuperCtr/24hr, st patrol, **other:** Buick/Cadillac/GMC, Chrysler/Jeep/Nissan, D&D RV Ctr, Ford/Lincoln/Mercury, Honda, Montana RV Ctr, Toyota, W...**gas:** Exxon/dsl, Sinclair/24hr, **food:** A&W/KFC, DQ, Frontier Pies, L&D Chinese, McDonald's, Melaque Mexican, Mt Mike's Pizza, Overland Express Rest., Papa John's, Papa Murphy's, Quizno's, Starbucks, Taco Treat, Wendy's, **lodging:** Comfort Inn, Day's Inn, Fairfield Inn, Holiday Inn Express, Jorgenson's Inn, Motel 6, Mtn Valley Inn, Shilo Inn, Super 8, **other:** HOSPITAL, AAA, Albertson's/gas, Dillard's, JC Penney, Osco Drug, Safeway/gas, Tire Factory
187	518, Montana City, Clancy, E...**food:** Hugo's Pizza/casino, W...**gas:** Cenex/dsl, **food:** Jackson Creek Cafe, Montana City Grill, **lodging:** Elkhorn Inn
182	Clancy, E...RV camping, W...**food:** Chubby's Grill, Legal Tender Rest., **other:** USPO, to NF,
178mm	**rest area both lanes, full (handicapped) facilities, phone, picnic tables, litter barrels, pet-walk**

Helena (vertical text in center margin)

MONTANA
Interstate 15

176	Jefferson City, NF access, no services
174.5mm	chain up area both lanes
168mm	chainup area both lanes
164	rd 69, Boulder, E...gas: Exxon/dsl/casino/24hr, food: DQ, Bearclaw Cafe, Elkhorn Cafe, Mtn Good Rest., Pizza Parlour, other: L&P Foods, Parts+, USPO, RC RV camping
161mm	parking area nb
160	High Ore Rd, no services
156	Basin, E...other: Merry Widow Health Mine/RV camping, W...food: Silver Saddle Café, Sunshine Pizza, other: Basin Cr Pottery, camping, USPO
154mm	Boulder River
151	to Boulder River Rd, Bernice, W...camping, picnic area
148mm	chainup area both lanes
143.5mm	chainup area both lanes
138	Elk Park, W...other: Sheepshead Picnic Area, wildlife viewing
134	Woodville, no services
133mm	continental divide, elev 6368
130.5mm	scenic overlook sb
129	I-90 E, to Billings, I-15 S and I-90 W run together 8 mi
127	Harrison Ave, Butte, N...gas: Cenex/dsl, Conoco, food: Arctic Circle, DQ, Denny's, Derby Steaks, Domino's, L&D Chinese, Papa John's, Quizno's, Taco John's, lodging: Day's Inn, Holiday Inn Express, Red Lion Inn, other: Checker Parts, Hastings Books, Toyota, Safeway, S...gas: Conoco/dsl, Exxon/dsl/24hr, Sinclair, food: A&W/KFC, Asia Gardens, Arby's, Burger King, Copper King, 4B's Rest., McDonald's, McKenzie River Pizza, Perkins, Pizza Hut, Silver Bow Pizza, Subway, Taco Bell, Wendy's, lodging: Best Western, Comfort Inn, Hampton Inn, Super 8, other: Bumper-to-Bumper Parts, Chevrolet/GMC/Buick/Cadillac/Pontiac, Chrysler/Dodge/Jeep, $Tree, Ford, Herberger's, Honda, JC Penney, Jo-Ann Crafts, K-Mart, Lincoln/Mercury, Smith Foods, Staples, Subaru, Wal-Mart SuperCtr/Subway/24hr, Whalen Tire
126	Montana St, Butte, N...gas: Cenex/dsl, lodging: Eddy's Motel, other: HOSPITAL, KOA, Safeway, Schwab Tire, S...gas: Conoco, Exxon/dsl
124	I-115(from eb), to Butte, City Ctr
123mm	weigh sta wb
122	Rocker, N...gas: 🍴/Flying J/rest./dsl/LP/24hr, lodging: Rocker Inn Motel, other: weigh sta eb, RV camping, S...gas: Pilot/Conoco/Arby's/Mcdonald's/Subway/dsl/24hr, lodging: Motel 6
I-15 N and I-90 E run together 8 mi	
121	I-90 W, to Missoula, no services
119	Silver Bow, Port of MT Transportation Hub
116	Buxton, no services

112mm	Continental Divide, elevation 5879
111	Feely, no services
109mm	**rest area both lanes, full(handicapped) facilities, phone, picnic tables, litter barrels, petwalk**
102	rd 43, to Wisdom, Divide, W...gas: Sinclair, other: to Big Hole Nat Bfd
99	Moose Creek Rd, no services
93	Melrose, W...food: Melrose Café/grill/gas/dsl, Hitchin Post Rest., lodging Pioneer Mtn Cabins, other: Sportsman Motel/RV Park, USPO
85.5mm	Big Hole River
85	Glen, E...lodging, Willis Sta. RV camping
74	Apex, Birch Creek, no services
64mm	Beaverhead River
63	Lp 15, rd 41, Dillon, Twin Bridges, E...gas: Cenex/dsl/LP, Exxon/KFC/dsl/24hr, Phillips 66/dsl, food: Lions Den, McDonald's, Pizza Hut, Subway, lodging: Best Western/rest., Comfort Inn, GuestHouse Inn, Sundowner Motel, Super 8, other: HOSPITAL, Carquest, Chevrolet/Pontiac/Buick/Cadillac, Ford/Chrysler/Dodge, KOA, Safeway/drug/gas, Schwab Tire, museum, W MT Coll
62	Lp 15, Dillon, E...food: DQ, Sparky's Rest., Taco John's, lodging: Creston Motel, Flyshop Inn, other: HOSPITAL, KOA, Southside RV Park, to WMT
60mm	Beaverhead River
59	MT 278, to Jackson, W...other: Bannack SP, Countryside RV Park
56	Barretts, E...RV camping
52	Grasshopper Creek, no services
51	Dalys(from sb, no return), no services
50mm	Beaverhead River
46mm	Beaverhead River
45mm	Beaverhead River
44	MT 324, E...food: Buffalo Lodge, other: Armstead RV Park, Beaverhead Flyshop, W...other: Clark Cyn Res, rec area, RV camping
38.5mm	Red Rock River
37	Red Rock, no services
34mm	parking area both lanes, litter barrels, restrooms
29	Kidd, no services
23	Dell, E...gas: Cenex/dsl, food: Yesterdays Calfe, lodging: Stockyard Inn, other: USPO
16.5mm	weigh sta both lanes
15	Lima, E...gas: Exxon/dsl, food: Jan's Café, lodging: Mtn Veiw Motel/RV Park, other: Big Sky Service/tires, USPO, ambulance, auto/tire repair
9	Snowline, no services
0	Monida, E...phone, to Red Rock Lakes
0mm	Monida Pass, elevation 6870, Montana/Idaho state line

Interstate 90

MONTANA

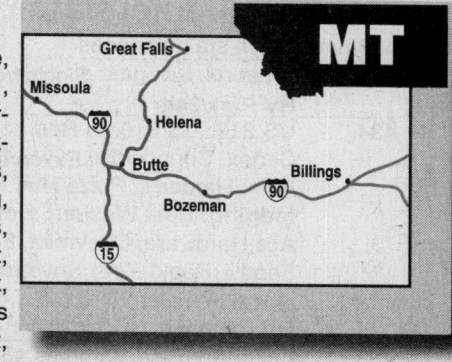

MT

Exit #	Services
559.5mm	weigh sta both lanes
554.5mm	Montana/Wyoming state line
549	Aberdeen, no services
544	Wyola, no services
530	MT 463, Lodge Grass, **1 mi** ...**gas:** gas, dsl, food, lodging, phone
517.5mm	Little Bighorn River
514	Garryowen, **N**...**gas:** Conoco/Subway, **other:** Custer Bfd Museum, **S**...**other:** 7th Ranch RV camp
511.5mm	Little Bighorn River
510	US 212 E, **N**...**gas:** Exxon/KFC/dsl/café/gifts, **food:** Crows Nest Café, **other:** HOSPITAL, to Little Bighorn Bfd, casino, **S**...**other:** Little Bighorn RV Camp/dump
509.5mm	weigh sta, both lanes exit left
509.3mm	Little Bighorn River
509	Crow Agency, **N**...**gas:** Conoco/24hr, **S**...to Bighorn Canyon NRA
503	Dunmore, no services
498mm	Bighorn River
497	MT 384, 3rd St, Hardin, **S**...HOSPITAL, Bighorn Cty Museum, **2 mi** **S**...**lodging:** Western Motel, **other:** Casino Rest./lounge
495	MT 47, City Ctr, Hardin, **N**...**gas:** Shell/dsl, **food:** Purple Cow Rest., **other:** KOA, **S**...**gas:** Cenex/dsl, Conoco/Subway/dsl/LP/24hr, Exxon/dsl, Sinclair/dsl, **food:** DQ, McDonald's, Pizza Hut, Shawna's Steaks, Taco John's, **lodging:** American Inn, Super 8, Western Motel, **other:** HOSPITAL, Grand View Camping/RV Park, Sunset Village RV Park, casinos
484	Toluca, no services
478	Fly Creek Rd, no services
477mm	**rest area both lanes, full (handicapped) facilities, phone, picnic tables, litter barrels, petwalk**
469	Arrow Creek Rd, **N**...**food:** Rock Shop/Cafe
462	Pryor Creek Rd, no services
456	I-94 E, to Bismarck, ND
455	Johnson Lane, **S**...**gas:** Exxon/A&W/Blimpie/dsl/24hr, Flying J/Conoco/Cookery/dsl/LP/rest./24hr/scales/@, **food:** Burger King, DQ, Subway, **lodging:** Holiday Inn Express, **other:** Tour America RV Ctr(1mi)
452	US 87 N, City Ctr, Billings, **N**...**gas:** Conoco/Arby's/dsl/LP, Exxon/dsl, **lodging:** Best Western, **other:** American Spirit RV Ctr, Chevrolet, Metra Rv Ctr, transmissions, **2-4 mi** **N** on US 87...**gas:** Cenex/dsl, Conoco/dsl, Holiday/dsl, **food:** Applebee's, Arby's, Bugz Rest./casino, Burger King, DQ, Fuddrucker's, Godfather's Pizza, Golden Phoenix, Guadalajara Mexican, KFC, Little Caesar's, MacKenzie River Pizza, Main St Grill, McDonald's, Mongolian Grill, Papa John's, Papa Murphy's, Pizza Hut, Subway, Taco Bell, Taco John's, Wendy's, **lodging:** Country Inn&Suites, Foothills Inn, Heights Motel, **other:**

Exit #	Services
	Ace Hardware, Albertson's, Big Lots, CarQuest, Checkers Parts, CVS Drug, O'Reilly Parts, Office Depot, Radio Shack, Schnider's Drug, Target, U-Haul, Walgreens, Wal-Mart SuperCtr/24hr, Western Drug, vet, **S**...**gas:** Cenex/dsl, **other:** RV Camping
451.5mm	Yellowstone River
450	MT 3, 27th St, Billings, **N**...**gas:** Conoco/dsl/24hr, Exxon, Sinclair/repair, **food:** Blondy's, Pizza Hut, **lodging:** Crowne Plaza, War Bonnet Inn/rest. **other:** HOSPITAL, CarQuest, USPO, **S**...KOA, Yellowstone River Camping
447	S Billings Blvd, **N**...**gas:** Conoco/Subway/dsl/24hr, Holiday, **food:** Burger King, DQ, McDonald's, **lodging:** Best Western/Kelly, Day's Inn, Extended Stay America, Hampton Inn, Sleep Inn, Super 8, **S**...**other:** Billings RV Park(2mi), Freightliner, Kenworth, KOA(2mi), Yellowstone River Campground
446	King Ave, Billings, **N**...**gas:** Conoco, Holiday/dsl/LP/RV dump, **food:** Burger King, Del Taco, Denny's, Dos Machos, Fuddrucker's, Gusicks Rest., Jade Palace, Olive Garden, Old Chicago, Outback Steaks, Perkins, Red Lobster, Taco John's, TX Roadhouse, Wheat Montana, **lodging:** Best Western, C'Mon Inn, Comfort Inn, Fairfield Inn, Quality Inn, Residence Inn, Springhill Suites, **other:** Chrysler/Jeep/Kia, Costco/gas, Dodge, Ford, NAPA, Nissan, RV Repair, Subaru/Hyundai, USPO, **N on King Ave**...**gas:** Exxon, Conoco/dsl, Sinclair, **food:** Applebee's, Arbys, Cactus Creek Steaks, Carino's Italian, City Brew Coffee, Famous Dave's, Golden Corral, IHOP, Krispy Kreme, McDonald's, Krispy Kreme, Pizza Hut, Quizno's, Subway, Taco Bell, Wendy's, **lodging:** Hilton Garden, La Quinta, Residence Inn, Western Executive Inn, **other:** Albertson's, Arby's, Barnes&Noble, Best Buy, Borders Books, Chevrolet, Hastings Books, Home Depot, Isuzu, Lowe's Whse, Michael's, Nissan, Office Depot, Old Navy, Petsmart, Ross, ShopKO, Wal-Mart SuperCtr/24hr, World Mkt, mall, **S**...**gas:** Conoco/dsl/24hr, **food:** Cracker Barrel, Emporium Rest., **lodging:** Billings Hotel, ClubHouse Inn, Holiday Inn, Kelly Inn, Motel 6, Ramada Ltd, Red Roof Inn, **other:** Volvo/Mac Trucks, water funpark
443	Zoo Dr, to Shiloh Rd, **N**...**gas:** Holiday/dsl, **food:** MT Rib/Chophouse, Wendy's, **lodging:** Wingate Inn, **other:** Pierce RV Ctr, zoo, **S**...**other:** Harley-Davidson, vet

Hardin

Billings

Billings

275

MONTANA

Interstate 90

E ↕ W

439mm	weigh sta both lanes	
437	E Laurel, **S**...**gas:** Sinclair/dsl/rest./casino/motel/RV Park/24hr	
434	US 212, US 310, to Red Lodge, Laurel, **N**...**gas:** Cenex, Conoco/dsl, Exxon/dsl/24hr, **food:** Burger King, Hardee's, Pizza Hut, Subway, Taco John's, **lodging:** Best Western, Howard Johnson, **other:** Ace Hardware, Chevrolet, Ford, IGA Foods, Jan's Foods, Rapid Tire, Snyders Drug, Wal-Mart SuperCtr, Western Drug, **S**...**other:** Riverside Park/RV Camping, to Yellowstone NP, vet	
433	Lp 90(from eb), same as 434	
426	Park City, **S**...**gas:** Cenex/dsl/café/24hr, **food:** CJ's Motel, **other:** auto/tire repair	
419mm	rest area both lanes, full(handicapped)facilities, phone, picnic tables, litter barrels, petwalk	
408	rd 78, Columbus, **N**...Mtn Range RV Park, **S**...**gas:** Conoco/Big Sky Motel, Pilot/Exxon/dsl/24hr, **food:** Apple Village Café/gifts, McDonald's, Stageline Pizza, **lodging:** Super 8, **other:** HOSPITAL, IGA Foods, JC Tires/repair, casino, museum, to Yellowstone	
400	Springtime Rd, no services	
398mm	Yellowstone River	
396	ranch access, no services	
392	Reed Point, **N**...**gas:** Sinclair/dsl, **lodging:** Hotel Montana/rest., **other:** RV camping, USPO	
384	Bridger Creek Rd, no services	
381mm	rest area both lanes, full(handicapped)facilities, phone, picnic tables, litter barrels, petwalk	
377	Greycliff, **S**...**other:** Prairie Dog Town SP, KOA	
370	US 191, Big Timber, **1 mi N**...**gas:** Conoco/dsl, Exxon, Sinclair/dsl, **lodging:** Grand Hotel, Lazy J Motel, **other:** Spring Creek RV Ranch(4mi), USPO	
369mm	Boulder River	
367	US 191 N, Big Timber, **N**...**gas:** Exxon/dsl, Conoco/dsl, **food:** Country Skillet, Crazy Jane's Eatery/casino, **lodging:** River Valley Inn, Super 8, **other:** CarQuest, Chevrolet, Ford, hist site, visitor ctr, Spring Creek Camping(3mi)	
362	De Hart, no services	
354	MT 563, Springdale, no services	
352	ranch access, no services	
350	East End access, no services	
340	US 89 N, to White Sulphur Sprgs, **S**...airport	
343	Mission Creek Rd, no facilites	
337	Lp 90, to Livingston, **2 mi N**...**gas:** Exxon, **lodging:** motels	
333mm	Yellowstone River	
333	US 89 S, Livingston, **N**...**food:** DQ, Pizza Hut, Taco John's, **lodging:** Best Western, Budget Host, Del Mar Motel, Econolodge, Livingston Inn, Travelodge, **other:** HOSPITAL, Ace Hardware, Chevrolet/Cadillac, Ford/Lincoln/Mercury, Pamida, Radio Shack, RV Park, Western Drug,	

Livingston

	S...**gas:** Cenex/dsl, Conoco/dsl, Exxon/dsl, **food:** Hardee's, McDonald's, Subway, **lodging:** Comfort Inn, Super 8, **other:** Albertson's, KOA(10mi), Olsen's RV Park, to Yellowstone	
330	Lp 90, Livingston, **1 mi N**...**gas:** Yellowstone Trk-stp/dsl/rest./24hr, **lodging:** Del Mar Motel	
326.5mm	chainup/chain removal area both lanes	
324	ranch access, no services	
323mm	chainup/chain removal area wb	
322mm	Bridger Mountain Range	
321mm	turnouts/hist marker both lanes	
319	Jackson Creek Rd, no services	
319mm	chainup area both lanes	
316	Trail Creek Rd, no services	
313	Bear Canyon Rd, **S**...**other:** Bear Canyon Camping	
309	US 191 S, Main St, Bozeman, **N**...**other:** Jeep/Subaru, Sunrise RV Park, **S**...**gas:** Cenex/dsl, Exxon, **food:** MT AleWorks, **lodging:** Alpine Lodge, Best Western, Blue Sky Motel, Continental Motel, Ranch House Motel, Western Heritage Inn, **other:** HOSPITAL, RV service, Goodyear, to Yellowstone	
306	US 191, N 7th, Bozeman, **N**...**gas:** Conoco, Sinclair, **food:** McDonald's, Panda Buffet, **lodging:** Best Value Inn, Fairfield Inn, Microtel, Ramada Ltd, Sleep Inn, Super 8, TLC Inn, **other:** RV supplies, ski area, **S**...**gas:** Conoco/Arby's/dsl, Exxon, Sinclair/dsl, **food:** Applebee's, Bar-3 BBQ, Dominos, DQ, Famous Dave's, KFC, McDonald's, Papa John's, Subway, Taco Bell, Taco John's, The Wok, Wendy's, **lodging:** Best Western, Bozeman/rest., Comfort Inn, Day's Inn, Hampton Inn, Holiday Inn, Royal 7 Inn, **other:** Big O Tire, CarQuest, Firestone/auto, IGA Foods, K-Mart, NAPA, U-Haul, Wal-Mart SuperCtr/24hr, Museum of the Rockies	
305	MT412, N 19th Ave, **N**...**gas:** Exxon, **lodging:** AmericInn, Country Inn&Suites, **S**...**food:** A&W/KFC, Bennigan's, Carino's Italian, Denny's, McKenzie River Pizza, Old Chicago Pizza, Outback Steaks, **other:** Borders Books, Costco, Home Depot, Lowe's Whse, Michaels, Old Navy, Target, Smith's, UPS, USPO, **rest area, full handicapped facilites, picnic tables/litter barrels, petwalk, 2-3 mi S**...**food:** Arby's, Burger King, Perkins, Pizza Hut, Spanish Peaks Brewery/Italian Café, **lodging:** Best Western, C'mon Inn, Hilton Garden, Residence Inn, Wingate Inn, **other:** Ford, museum	
298	MT 291, MT 85, Belgrade, **N**...**gas:** Cenex/dsl, Conoco, Exxon/Subway/dsl, **food:** Burger King, DQ, McDonald's, Pizza Hut, **other:** Albertson's, Osco, IGA Foods, NAPA, Whalen Tire, **S**...**gas:** Flying J/Conoco/dsl/scales/LP, **food:** Country Kitchen, **lodging:** Holiday Inn Express, La Quinta, Super 8, **other:** Harley-Davidson, InterWest Tire, KOA(9mi), truckwash, to Yellowstone NP.	
292.5mm	Gallatin River	

Bozeman Belgrade

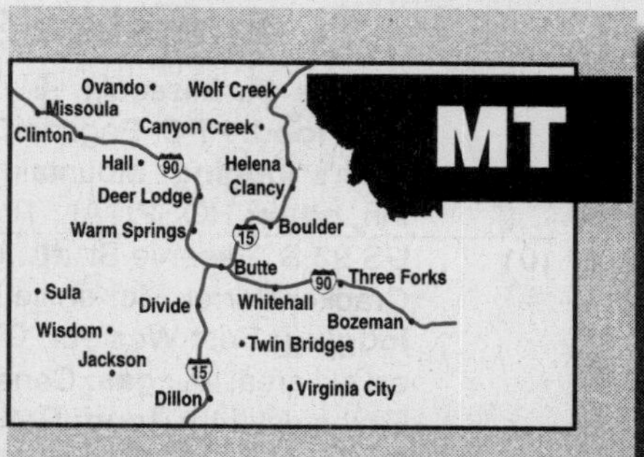

Interstate 90

288	Manhattan, **N**...**gas:** Conoco/dsl, **other:** RV camp
283	Logan, **S**...**other:** Madison Buffalo Jump SP(7mi)
279mm	Madison River
278	MT 205, rd 2, Three Forks, Trident, **N**...Missouri Headwaters SP, **1 mi S**...**lodging:** Broken Spur Motel, Sacajawea Inn, **other:** camping, phone
277.5mm	Jefferson River
274	US 287, to Helena, Ennis, **N**...**gas:** Sinclair/dsl, **food:** Wheat MT Bakery/deli, dsl repair, **other:** to Canyon Ferry SP, Ft 3 Forks, **S**...**gas:** Pilot/Exxon/Subway/dsl/scales/24hr, **other:** Lewis&Clark Caverns SP, KOA(1mi), to Yellowstone NP
267	Milligan Canyon Rd, no services
261.5mm	chain removal area
257mm	Boulder River
256	MT 359, Cardwell, **S**...**gas:** Sinclair/dsl, **other:** to Yellowstone NP, Lewis&Clark Caverns SP, RV camping
249	rd 55, to rd 69, Whitehall, **S**...**gas:** Exxon/Subway/dsl/24hr, **food:** A&W/KFC, **lodging:** Super 8, **other:** camping, casino
241	Pipestone, **S**...**other:** Pipestone Camping(apr-oct), phone
240.5mm	chainup/chain removal area both lanes
238.5mm	runaway ramp eb
237.5mm	pulloff eb
235mm	truck parking both lanes, litter barrels, rest rooms
233	Homestake, Continental Divide, elev 6393
230mm	chain removal area both lanes
228	MT 375, Continental Dr, **S**...**other:** Harley Davidson
227	I-15 N, to Helena, Great Falls
	I-90 and I-15 run together 8 mi. See Montana Interstate 15, exits 122-127.
219	I-15 S, to Dillon, Idaho Falls
216	Ramsay, no services
211	MT 441, Gregson, **3-5 mi S**...food, lodging, Fairmont RV Park(Apr-Oct)
210.5mm	parking area wb, Pintlar Scenic route info
208	rd 1, Pintler Scenic Loop, Georgetown Lake RA, Opportunity, Anaconda, **3-5 mi S**...**other:** HOSPITAL, gas, food, lodging, RV camp/dump, ski area
201	Warm Springs, **S**...gas/dsl, MT ST HOSPITAL
197	MT 273, Galen, **S**...to MT ST HOSPITAL
195	Racetrack, no services
187	Lp 90, Deer Lodge(no wb return), **2 mi S**...**gas:** MRC/dsl/repair, **food:** Monte's Subs, Outlaw Cafe, **lodging:** Downtowner Motel, Scharf's Motel/rest., **other:** HOSPITAL, KOA(seasonal), Radio Shack, Valley Foods, Old MT Prison, Tow Ford Museum, same as 184
184	Deer Lodge, **S**...**gas:** Cenex/dsl, Conoco/dsl/casino, **food:** 4B's Rest., McDonald's, **lodging:** Super 8, **other:** Indian Cr Camping, **1 mi S**...**gas:** Exxon/dsl/casino, **food:** A&W, Pizza Hut, **lodging:** Downtowner Motel, Western Big Sky Inn, **other:** Safeway/deli, Schwab Tire, Grant-Kohrs Ranch NHS
179	Beck Hill Rd
175mm	Little Blackfoot River
175	US 12 E(from wb), Garrison, **N**...phone, hist site, RiverFront RV Park
174	US 12 E(from eb), same as 175
170	Phosphate, no services
168mm	**rest area both lanes, full(handicapped)facilities, phone, picnic tables, litter barrels, petwalk**
166	Gold Creek, **S**...**other:** Camp Mak-A-Dream
162	Jens, no services
154	to MT 1(from wb), Drummond, **S**...**gas:** Cenex/dsl, Conoco/dsl/24hr, Sinclair/dsl/24hr, **food:** Tastee-Freeze, Wagon Wheel Café/Motel, **lodging:** Motel, **other:** Pintler Scenic Lp, Georgetown Lake RA, Goodtime RV Park(3mi)
153	MT 1(from eb), **N**...**other:** Garnet GhostTown, Goodtime RV Park(3mi) **S**...same as 154
150.5mm	weigh sta both lanes
143mm	**rest area both lanes, full(handicapped)facilities, phone, picnic tables, litter barrels, petwalk**
138	Bearmouth Area, **N**...**other:** Chalet Bearmouth Camp/rest., to gas, food, lodging
130	Beavertail Rd, **S**...**other:** to Beavertail Hill SP, rec area, camping(seasonal)
128mm	parking area both lanes, litter barrels/restrooms, no services
126	Rock Creek Rd, **S**...**lodging:** Rock Creek Lodge/gas/casino, **other:** rec area
120	Clinton, **N**...**gas:** Sinclair/dsl, **food:** Clinton Market, Poor Henry's Café(1mi in on frtg rd), **other:** USPO
113	Turah, **S**...Turah RV Park/gas
109.5mm	Clark Fork, Clark Fork
109mm	Blackfoot River
109	MT 200 E, Bonner, **N**...**gas:** Pilot/Exxon/Arby's/Subway/dsl/scales/casino/LP/24hr, Sinclair/dsl **food:** River City Grill, **other:** USPO, hist site
108.5mm	Clark Fork, Clark Fork
107	E Missoula, **N**...**gas:** Ole's Mkt/Diner/Conoco/dsl/24hr, Sinclair/24hr, **food:** Reno Cafe **lodging:** Aspen Motel, RV Park **other:** dsl repair, **2 mi S**...**lodging:** Holiday Inn Express
105	US 12 W, Missoula, **S**...**gas:** Cenex/dsl/24hr, Conoco/dsl/24hr, Pacific Pride/dsl, Sinclair/dsl, **food:** Burger King, Finnegan's, McDonald's, Pizza Hut, Quizno's, Taco Bell, Wow Cafe **lodging:** Best Western, Campus Inn, Creekside Inn, DoubleTree, Downtown Motel, Family Inn, Holiday Inn, Holiday Inn Express, Ponderosa Motel, Thunderbird Motel, **other:** Ace Hardware, Albertson's, Champion Parts, Flyshop, Jim's Casino, O'Reilly's Parts, U of MT, Vietnam Vet's Mem

Left margin labels: **Butte**, **Deer Lodge**

Right margin label: **Missoula**

MONTANA

Interstate 90

104	Orange St, Missoula, Ⓢ...**gas:** Conoco/dsl, Sinclair, **food:** KFC, Pagoda Chinese, Subway, Taco John's **lodging:** Mountain Valley Inn, Orange St Inn, **other:** HOSPITAL, Tire-rama, to City Ctr
101	US 93 S, Reserve St, Ⓝ...**gas:** Conoco/dsl, **food:** Cracker Barrel, McKenzie River Pizza, Starbucks, **lodging:** Best Western, C'Mon Inn, Motel 6, **other:** ski area, Ⓢ...**gas:** Cenex/dsl/LP, Conoco/24hr, Exxon/dsl/24hr, **food:** Carino's, 4B's Rest., IHOP, McDonald's, MT Club rest./casino, Rowdy's Rest., Taco Time/TCBY, **lodging:** Best Inn, Comfort Inn, Courtyard, Hampton Inn, Hilton Garden, Microtel, Ruby's Inn/rest., Super 8, Travelers Inn, **other:** Bretz RV/Marine, Chevrolet, KOA, casinos, dsl repair, 1 mi Ⓢ...**gas:** Conoco, Exxon/dsl, **food:** Arby's, Arctic Circle, Burger King, China Bowl, Famous Dave's, Fuddrucker's, Jack-in-the-Box, Krispy Kreme, Outback Steaks, Perkins, Subway, Taco Bell, Wendy's, **other:** Albertson's/Osco, Barnes&Noble, Best Buy, Chevrolet, Costco/gas, Home Depot, Lowe's Whse, Michael's, Old Navy, Petsmart, Radio Shack, Ross, Staples, Target, TJ Maxx, Walgreens, Wal-Mart SuperCtr/24hr, mall
99	Airway Blvd, Ⓢ...**gas:** Mobil/dsl/24hr, **lodging:** Wingate Inn, **other:** Chrysler/Dodge, Harley Davidson, airport
96	US 93 N, MT 200W, Kalispell, Ⓝ...**gas:** Conoco/dsl/rest./24hr/@, **lodging:** Day's Inn/rest., **other:** Freightliner, Peterbilt, Jellystone RV Park, to Flathead Lake & Glacier NP, Ⓢ...**gas:** Sinclair/4B's/dsl/24hr/@, **lodging:** Redwood Lodge, **other:** Kenworth, RV repair
92.5mm	inspection sta both lanes
89	Frenchtown, Ⓢ...**gas:** Conoco/dsl/café/24hr, Sinclair/rest./laundry, **other:** USPO, to Frenchtown Pond SP
85	Huson, Ⓢ...**gas:** Sinclair/café, **other:** phone
82	Nine Mile Rd, Ⓝ...**other:** Hist Ranger Sta/info, food, phone
81.5mm	Clark Fork
80mm	Clark Fork, Clark Fork
77	MT 507, Petty Creek Rd, Alberton, Ⓢ...access to gas, food, lodging, phone
75	Alberton, Ⓢ...**lodging:** MT Hotel, River Edge Motel/gas, **other:** RV camp, casino
73mm	parking area wb, litter barrels
72mm	parking area eb, litter barrels
70	Cyr, no services
70mm	Clark Fork, Clark Fork
66	Fish Creek Rd, no services
66mm	Clark Fork, Clark Fork
61	Tarkio, no services
59mm	Clark Fork, Clark Fork
58mm	**rest area both lanes, full(handicapped) facilities, phone, picnic tables, litter barrels, petwalk, NF camping(seasonal)**
55	Lozeau, Quartz, no services
53.5mm	Clark Fork, Clark Fork
49mm	Clark Fork, Clark Fork
47	MT 257, Superior, Ⓝ...**gas:** Cenex/24hr, Conoco/dsl, Sinclair/Durango's Rest., **food:** Rosie's Rest., **lodging:** Budget Host, Hilltop Motel, **other:** HOSPITAL, Castle's Foods, Mineral Drug, NAPA, USPO, Ⓢ...**gas:** Pilot/Exxon/dsl/casino/24hr, **other:** Carl's Repair
45mm	Clark Fork, Clark Fork
43	Dry Creek Rd, Ⓝ...NP camping(seasonal)
37	Sloway Area, no services
34mm	Clark Fork, Clark Fork
33	MT 135, St Regis, Ⓝ...**gas:** Conoco/dsl/rest./gifts, Exxon, Sinclair, **food:** Frosty Drive-In, Jasper's Rest., OK Café/casino, **lodging:** Little River Motel, Super 8, **other:** KOA, Nugget Camground, St Regis Campground, USPO, antiques
30	Two Mile Rd, Ⓢ...fishing access
29mm	fishing access, wb
26	Ward Creek Rd(from eb), no services
25	Drexel, no services
22	Camels Hump Rd, Henderson, Ⓝ...**other:** camping(seasonal), antiques(1mi)
18	DeBorgia, Ⓝ...**food:** Billy Big Riggers
16	Haugan, Ⓝ...**gas:** Exxon/dsl/24hr, **lodging:** 10,000 Silver $/motel/rest./casino/RV park
15mm	weigh sta both lanes, exits left from both lanes
10	Saltese, Ⓝ...**food:** MT Grill, **lodging:** Mangold's Motel, **other:** antiques
10mm	St Regis River
5	Taft Area, no services, access to Hiawatha Trail
4.5mm	**rest area both lanes, full(handicapped)picnic tables, litter barrels, petwalk, chainup/removal**
0	Lookout Pass, **other:** access to Lookout Pass ski area/lodge, info
0mm	Montana/Idaho state line, Central/Pacific time zone, Lookout Pass elev 4680

Interstate 94

Exit #	Services
250mm	Montana/North Dakota state line
248	Carlyle Rd, no services
242	MT 7(from wb), Wibaux, Ⓢ...**rest area both lanes, full(handicapped)facilities, phone, picnic tables, litter barrels**, **gas:** Amsler's/dsl, Cenex/dsl, **food:** Tastee Hut, **lodging:** Beaver Creek Inn, **other:** RV camping
241	MT 261(from eb), to MT 7, Wibaux, Ⓢ...same as 242
240mm	weigh sta both lanes
236	ranch access, no services
231	Hodges Rd, no services
224	Griffith Creek, frontage road, no services
222.5mm	Griffith Creek

Interstate 94

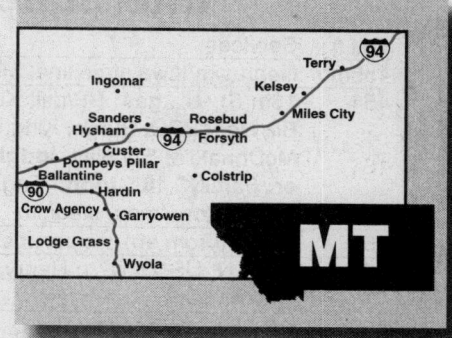

215	MT 335, Glendive, City Ctr, ...**gas:** Conoco, **food:** CC's Café, **lodging:** Comfort Inn, Day's Inn, Super 8, Yellowstone River Inn, **other:** Glendive Camping(apr-oct), museum, S...**gas:** Exxon/dsl, Holiday/gas, Sinclair/dsl/repair, **food:** Taco John's, **lodging:** Best Western, Budget Motel, El Centro Motel, Uptown Motel, **other:** HOSPITAL, to Makoshika SP
215mm	Yellowstone River
213	MT 16, to Sidney, Glendive, N...**gas:** Exxon/dsl, **other:** Green Valley Camping, st patrol, S...**gas:** Conoco/dsl, Sinclair/dsl, **food:** McDonald's, Pizza Hut, Subway, **lodging:** Best Western Downtown, Budget Host, Holiday Lodge, Parkwood Motel, **other:** Albertson's/Osco, Ford, K-Mart
211	MT 200S(from wb, no EZ return), to Circle
210	Lp 94, to MT 200S, W Glendive, S...**gas:** Cenex, **food:** McDonald's, **other:** Bumper Parts, Chevrolet/Pontiac/Buick, Makoshika SP
206	Pleasant View Rd, no services
204	Whoopup Creek Rd, no services
198	Cracker Box Rd, no services
192	Bad Route Rd, S...**rest area/weigh sta both lanes, full(handicapped)facilities, weather info, phone, picnic tables, litter barrels, camping, petwalk**
187mm	Yellowstone River
185	MT 340, Fallon, S...**food:** access to café, **other:** phone
184mm	O'Fallon Creek
176	MT 253, Terry, N...**gas:** Conoco/dsl, **food:** Dizzy Diner, **lodging:** Diamond Motel, Kempton Hotel, **other:** HOSPITAL, Terry RV Oasis
170mm	Powder River
169	Powder River Rd, no services
159	Diamond Ring, no services
148	Valley Access, no services
141	US 12 E, Miles City, N...**other:** RV Camping
138	MT 58, Miles City, N...**gas:** Cenex/dsl/24hr, Conoco, Pilot/Exxon/dsl/24hr, **food:** DQ, 4B's Rest., Gallagher's Rest., KFC, Little Caesar's, McDonald's, Pizza Hut, Subway, Taco John's, Wendy's, **lodging:** Best Western, Budget Inn, Day's Inn, Econolodge, Motel 6, **other:** HOSPITAL, Albertson's/Osco Drug, Chevrolet/Pontiac/Buick, K-Mart, KOA, Wal-Mart SuperCtr/auto/24hr, casinos, S...**food:** Hunan Chinese, **lodging:** Comfort Inn, Guesthouse Inn, Holiday Inn Express, Super 8
137mm	Tongue River
135	Lp 94, Miles City(no EZ eb return), N...**other:** KOA
128	local access, no services
126	Moon Creek Rd, no services
117	Hathaway, no services
114mm	**rest area eb, full(handicapped)facilities, phone, picnic tables, litter barrels, petwalk**
113mm	**rest area wb, full(handicapped)facilities, phone, picnic tables, litter barrels, petwalk, overlook**
106	Butte Creek Rd, to Rosebud, N...food, phone
103	MT 446, MT 447, Rosebud Creek Rd, N...food, phone
98.5mm	weigh sta both lanes
95	Forsyth, N...**gas:** Cenex, Exxon/dsl/24hr, **lodging:** Best Western, Rails Inn Motel(1mi), **other:** Art's Tire, Ford IGA Foods, NAPA, Yellowstone Drug, to Rosebud RA, S...camping
93	US 12 W, Forsyth, N...**gas:** Cenex, Exxon/dsl/24hr, **food:** DQ, **lodging:** Rails Inn, Restwell Inn, WestWind Motel, **other:** HOSPITAL, repair/tires, RV camping
87	MT 39, to Colstrip, no services
82	Reservation Creek Rd, no services
72	MT 384, Sarpy Creek Rd, no services
67	Hysham, **1-2 mi** N...gas, phone, food, lodging
65mm	**rest area both lanes, full(handicapped)facilities, phone, picnic tables, litter barrels, petwalk**
63	ranch access, no services
53	Bighorn, access to phone
52mm	Bighorn River
49	MT 47, to Hardin, Custer, S...**food:** Ft Custer Café, **other:** to Little Bighorn Bfd, camping
47	Custer, S...**gas:** Custer Sta./dsl, **food:** Jct City Saloon/café, **other:** Custer Food Mkt
41.5mm	**rest area wb, full(handicapped)facilities, phone, picnic tables, litter barrels, petwalk**
38mm	**rest area eb, full(handicapped)facilities, phone, picnic tables, litter barrels, petwalk**
36	frontage rd, Waco, no services
23	Pompeys Pillar, N...**other:** Pompeys Pillar Nat Landmark
14	Ballentine, Worden, S...**food:** Long Branch Café/casino
6	MT 522, Huntley, N...gas/phone, **food:** Pryor Creek Café
0mm	I-90, E to Sheridan, W to Billings, I-94 begins/ends on I-90, exit 456.

E ↕ **W**

Omaha

Exit #	Services
455mm	Nebraska/Iowa state line, Missouri River
454	13th St, **N**...**gas**: BP/dsl, Kum&Go, Valero, **food**: Big Horn BBQ, Burger King, Los Portales Mexican, McDonald's, Subway, **lodging**: Comfort Inn, **other**: Family$, **S**...**food**: King Kong Burgers, **other**: Doorly Zoo, Imax, stadium
453	24th St(from eb), no services
452b	I-480 N, US 75 N, to Henry Ford's Birthplace, Eppley Airfield
452a	US 75 S, no services
451	42nd St, **N**...**gas**: BP/dsl, Kwik Shop/gas, **S**...**gas**: Phillips 66, **food**: Burger King, McDonald's, Taco Bell, **other**: HOSPITAL, FastLube
450	60th St, **N**...**gas**: Phillips 66, **other**: NAPA, to U of NE Omaha, **S**...**gas**: Phillips 66/dsl
449	72nd St, to Ralston, **N**...**gas**: BP, **food**: Burger King, Dreamers Grill, Perkins, Spezia Italian, **lodging**: Baymont Inn, Clarion, Comfort Inn, Holiday Inn/rest., Homewood Suites, Howard Johnson, Ramada Inn, Super 8, Travelodge, **other**: HOSPITAL, **S**...**gas**: Cenex/dsl, **food**: Anthony's Steaks
448	84th St, **N**...**gas**: BP, Shell, **food**: Arby's, Denny's, Farmhouse Café, Great Wall Chinese, Husker House, Mangelson's Cafe, McDonald's, Subway, Taco Bell, **lodging**: Econolodge, **other**: EYECARE, Baker's Foods, Goodyear/auto, Hancock Fabrics, Mangelson's Crafts, NAPA AutoCare, ShopKO, **S**...**gas**: QT, Shell/dsl, Sinclair, **food**: Wendy's, **other**: Acura/Isuzu/Kia, Chevrolet, U-Haul
446	I-680 N, to Boystown
445	US 275, NE 92, I thru L St, **N**...**gas**: Cenex, **food**: Austin's Steaks, Wendy's, **lodging**: Clarion, **other**: Buick/Pontiac/GMC, Home Depot, Nelsen's RV Ctr, Sam's Club/gas, Wal-Mart SuperCtr/24hr, **S**...**food**: Village Inn Rest., **lodging**: Baymont Inn, Best Western, Carlisle Hotel, Comfort Inn, Day's Inn, Econolodge, Hawthorn Suites, Holiday Inn Express, Howard Johnson, La Quinta, Motel 6, Super 8, **other**: Goodyear, NE Beef Co, **S on 108th**...**gas**: Conoco/dsl, QT/dsl, **food**: Arby's, Burger King, China 1, Godfather's Pizza, Hong Kong Café, LJ Silver, McDonald's, Perkins, Pizza Hut/Taco Bell, Sonic, Subway, Valentino's, Wendy's, **other**: Albertson's, U-Save Drug
444	Q St, **N**...**gas**: Cenex/dsl
442	126th St, Harrison St, **N**...**other**: Chrysler/Jeep/Dodge, Toyota, **S**...**gas**: Fantasy's, **lodging**: Embassy Suites, Hampton Inn, **other**: Cabela's
440	NE 50, to Springfield, **N**...**gas**: Conoco, Shell/Sapp Bros/Subway/dsl/24hr/@, Woody's/dsl, **food**: Azteca Mexican, Cracker Barrel, Hardee's, McDonald's, **lodging**: Ben Franklin Motel, Budget Inn, Comfort Inn, Countryside Suites, Days Inn, **other**: HOSPITAL, Ford, truckwash, **S**...**gas**: BP/dsl, to Platte River SP
439	439 NE 370, to Gretna, **N**...**gas**: Kum&Go/Quizno's, Phillips 66/dsl, **lodging**: Suburban Inn, **S**... HOSPITAL, Volvo trucks, museum

Lincoln

Exit #	Services
432	US 6, NE 31, to Gretna, **N**...**gas**: Sinclair/dsl/rest./24hr, **food**: McDonald's, **lodging**: Super 8, **other**: Curves, GNC, Nebraska X-ing/famous brands, **S**...**gas**: ⬦/Flying J/Conoco/dsl/LP/rest./24hr/@, **other**: KOA, to Schramm SP
431mm	rest area wb, full(handicapped)facilities, info, phone, picnic tables, litter barrels, petwalk
427mm	Platte River
426	NE 66, to Southbend, **N**...to Mahoney SP, museum
425.5	rest area eb, full(handicapped)facilities, phone, picnic tables, litter barrels, petwalk, vending
420	NE 63, Greenwood, **N**...**gas**: Conoco/cafe/dsl/scales, **other**: RV camping, **S**...**gas**: Shell/dsl, **lodging**: Big Inn, **other**: to Platte River SP
416mm	weigh sta both lanes
409	US 6, to E Lincoln, Waverly, **N**...**food**: McDonald's, **S**...**other**: HOSPITAL
405	US 77 N, 56th St, Lincoln, **S**...**gas**: Phillips 66, **other**: HOSPITAL, Freightliner, **1 mi S**...**food**: Misty's Rest., **lodging**: Howard Johnson, Travelodge, **other**: antiques
404mm	rest area wb, full(handicapped)facilities, info, phone, picnic tables, litter barrels, vending, petwalk
403	27th St, Lincoln, **S**...**gas**: Conoco/Wendy's/dsl, Phillips 66/Subway/dsl, **food**: Arby's, Cracker Barrel, DQ, King Kong Burger, Popeye's/Taco Inn, **lodging**: AmericInn, Best Western, Countryside Suites, Settle Inn, Staybridge Suites, **other**: BMW, Chevrolet/Pontiac/Cadillac/GMC, Dodge, Ford/Lincoln/Mercury/Mazda, Lexus, Toyota, **1-3 mi S**...**gas**: Mobil, Phillips 66, Shell, **food**: Applebee's, Beacon Hill Rest., Burger King, Carlos O'Kelly's, China Buffet, CiCi's Pizza, Culver's, DaVinci's Italian, Godfather's, Golden Corral, IHOP, Little Mexico Rest., McDonald's, Papa John's, Ruby Tuesday, Runza Rest., Schlotsky's, Sonic, Taco Bell, Taco John's, Valentino's, Village Inn, **lodging**: Baymont Inn, Comfort Suites, Country Inn&Suites, Fairfield Inn, Holiday Inn Express, Microtel, Ramada Ltd, Super 8, **other**: AutoZone, Curves, $Tree, GNC, Haas Tire, Home Depot, HyVee Foods, Interstate Battery, Mazda, Michael's, Petsmart, Radio Shack, Sam's Club, ShopKO, Super Saver Foods, Wal-Mart SuperCtr/24hr, to U NE, st fairpark
401b	US 34 W, **S**...RV camping
401a	I-180, US 34 E, to 9th St, Lincoln
399	Lincoln, **N**...**gas**: BP/dsl/24hr, Phillips 66, **food**: Baskin-Robbins, McDonald's, NY Pizza, Perkins/24hr, Quizno's, TacoMaker**lodging**: Airport Inn, Best Value Inn, Day's Inn, Hampton Inn, Holiday Inn Express, Horizon Inn, Motel 6, Ramada Inn, Sleep Inn, Travelodge, to airport, **S**...**gas**: Cenex/dsl, **lodging**: Econolodge, Economy Lodge
397	US 77 S, to Beatrice, **S**...**lodging**: Days Inn
396	US 6, West O St(from eb), **S**...**gas**: Sinclair/dsl, **lodging**: Super 8, Travelodge, **other**: Lincoln/Mercury
395	US 6, NW 48th St, **S**...**gas**: Shoemaker's/Shell/dsl, **food**: Popeye's(2mi), **lodging**: Cobbler Inn, **other**: Harley Davidson, truck repair
388	NE 103, to Crete, Pleasant Dale, no services
382	US 6, Milford, no services

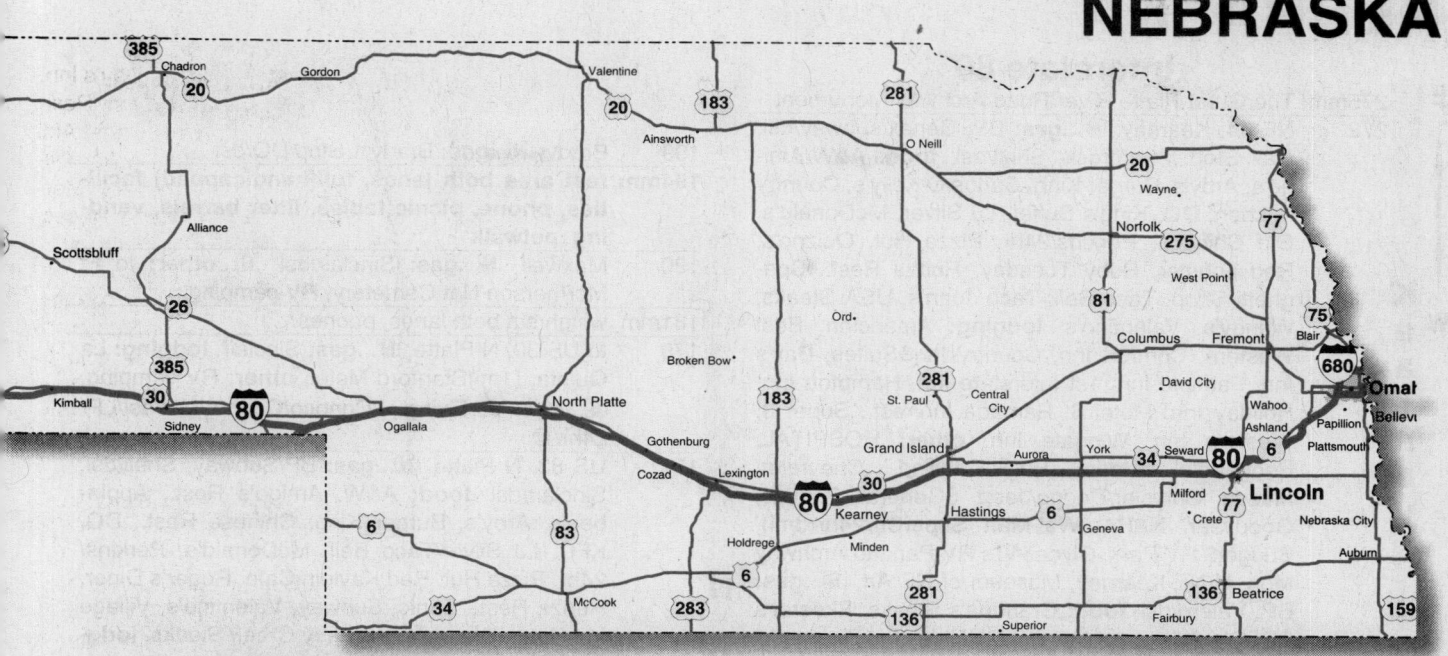

Interstate 80

381mm	**rest area eb, full(handicapped)facilities, phone, picnic tables, litter barrels, petwalk, vending**
379	NE 15, to Seward, **...other:** Ford, 2-3 mi **... food:** McDonald's, **lodging:** Super 8, **other:** HOSPITAL, antiques, **...gas:** Shell/dsl,
375mm	**rest area wb, full(handicapped)facilities, info, phone, picnic tables, litter barrels, petwalk, vending**
373	80G, Goehner, **...gas:** Sinclair
369	80E, Beaver Crossing, 3 mi **...HOSPITAL,** food, RV camping
366	80F, to Utica, no services
360	93B, to Waco, **...gas:** BP/FuelMart/dsl, **food:** Lori's Rest., **...lodging:** Double Nickel Camping
355mm	**rest area wb, full(handicapped)facilities, info, phone, picnic tables, litter barrels, vending, petwalk**
353	US 81, to York, **...gas:** BP/dsl, Byco Fuel, SappBros/Sinclair/Subway/dsl/@, Shell/dsl, **food:** Arby's, Burger King, Country Kitchen, Golden Gate Chinese, KFC/Taco Bell, McDonald's, Taco John's, Wendy's, **lodging:** Best Western, Budget Inn, Comfort Inn, Day's Inn, Quality Inn, Super 8, Yorkshire Motel, **other:** HOSPITAL, Buick/GMC, Chevrolet/Pontiac, Chrysler/Dodge, Wal-Mart SuperCtr/24hr, **...gas:** Petro/Phillips 66/Iron Skillet/Pizza Hut/dsl/24hr/@, Shell/dsl/rest./24hr, **food:** Applebee's, **lodging:** 1st Inn, Holiday Inn, **other:** Blue Beacon
351mm	**rest area eb, full(handicapped)facilities, info, phone, picnic tables, litter barrels, petwalk, vending**
348	93E, to Bradshaw, no services
342	93A, Henderson, **...other:** Good Sam RV park, antiques, **...gas:** FuelMart/dsl, **lodging:** 1st Interstate Inn, **other:** HOSPITAL, RV park
338	41D, to Hampton, no services
332	NE 14, Aurora, **...gas:** Shell/dsl, **food:** McDonald's(3mi), Pizza Hut(3mi), Subway(2.5), **lodging:** Budget Host(3mi), Hamilton Motel/rest., **other:** HOSPITAL, to Plainsman Museum, **...gas:** Love's/Arby's/dsl/scales, Timpte/dsl
324	41B, to Giltner, no services
318	NE 2, to Grand Island, **...other:** KOA
317mm	**rest area wb, full(handicapped)facilities, info, phone, picnic tables, litter barrels, vending, petwalk**
315mm	**rest area eb, full(handicapped)facilities, info, phone, picnic tables, litter barrels, vending, petwalk**
314mm	Platte River
314	Locust Street, to Grand Island, (5-6mi)**...food:** Subway, Tommy's Rest., Wendy's, **lodging:** Budget Host, Holiday Inn, Howard Johnson, Super 8, Travelodge, **other:** Wal-Mart
312	US 34/281, to Grand Island, **...gas:** Bosselman/Pilot/Sinclair/Max's/Subway/dsl/24hr/@, Phillips 66, **food:** 9 Bridge Rest., **lodging:** Motel 6, USA Inn/rest., **other:** HOSPITAL, Mormon Island RA, to Stuhr Pioneer Museum, **...gas:** BP/Arby's, **lodging:** Holiday Inn/rest., Holiday Inn Express, **other:** Peterbilt, Hastings Museum(15mi)
305	40C, to Alda, **...gas:** Sinclair/dsl/scales/24hr, TA/Conoco/Country Pride/dsl/scales/24hr/@, **... other:** Crane Meadows Nature Ctr/rest area
300	NE 11, Wood River, **...gas:** Bosselman/Pilot/Sinclair/Grandma Max's/Subway/dsl/24hr/@, **lodging:** motel/RV park
291	10D, Shelton, **...other:** War Axe SRA
285	10C, Gibbon, **...gas:** Petro Oasis/dsl, **other:** Windmill SP, RV camping, **...lodging:** Country Motel
279	NE 10, to Minden, **...gas:** Shell/dsl, **...other:** Pioneer Village Camping

NEBRASKA

Interstate 80

E ↕ W

Kearney

275mm	The Great Platte River Road Archway Monument
272	NE 44, Kearney, **N...gas:** BP, Cenex/subway/dsl, Gas Stop, Shamrock, Shell/dsl, **food:** A&W/Amigo's, Arby's, Burger King, Carlos O'Kelly's, Country Kitchen, DQ, King's Buffet, LJ Silver, McDonald's, Old Chicago, Perkins/24hr, Pizza Hut, Quizno's, Red Lobster, Ruby Tuesday, Runza Rest., Spaghetti Shop, Taco Bell, Taco John's, USA Steaks, Wendy's, Valentino's, **lodging:** AmericInn, Best Western, Comfort Inn, Country Inn&Suites, Day's Inn, Fairfield Inn, 1st Interstate Inn, Hampton Inn, Holiday Inn, Motel 6, Ramada Inn/rest., Super 8, Western Inn, Wingate Inn, **other:** HOSPITAL, Boogaart's Foods, Buick/Cadillac, Chevrolet/Mazda, Chrysler/Dodge/Jeep, $General, Pontiac, Goodyear, NAPA, Wal-Mart SuperCtr/24hr(3mi), Budget$ RV Park, Clyde&Vi's RV Park, to Archway Mon, U NE Kearney, Museum of NE Art, **S...gas:** BP, Valero/dsl, **food:** Grandpa's Steaks, Skeeter's BBQ, **lodging:** 1st Inn Gold, Holiday Inn Express
271mm	**rest area wb, full(handicapped)facilities, info, phone, picnic tables, litter barrels, petwalk**
269mm	**rest area eb, full(handicapped)facilities, info, phone, picnic tables, litter barrels, petwalk**
263	rd 10 b, Odessa, **N...gas:** Sapp/Shell/dsl/rest./@, **other:** UP Rec Area
257	US 183, Elm Creek, **N...gas:** Bosselman/Pilot/Sinclair/Subway/Little Caesar/dsl/scales/24hr/@, **lodging:** 1st Interstate Inn, **other:** Antique Car Museum, Nebraska Prarie Museum, Nebraska Tire, Sunny Meadows Camping,
248	Overton, no services

Lexington

237	US 283, Lexington, **N...gas:** BP, Casey's, Cenex/dsl, Conoco/KFC/Taco Bell/dsl, **food:** Arby's, Burger King, DQ, Hong Kong Buffet, Little Caesar's, McDonald's, Pizza Hut, Sonic, Taquiera Mexican, Wendy's, **lodging:** Comfort Inn, Day's Inn, 1st Interstate Inn, Gable View Inn, Holiday Inn Express, Minute Man Motel, **other:** HOSPITAL, Advance Parts, Chevrolet/Cadillac/Pontiac/Buick, Goodyear, Plum Creek Foods, Wal-Mart SuperCtr/Subway/24hr/café, museum, **S...gas:** Sinclair/dsl/@, **food:** Kirk's Café, **lodging:** Super 8, to Johnson Lake RA
231	Darr Rd, **S...truckwash/24hr**
227mm	**rest area both lanes, full(handicapped) facilities, info, phone, picnic tables, litter barrels, vending, petwalk**
222	NE 21, Cozad, **N...gas:** BP, Casey's/dsl, **food:** Burger King, DQ, El Paraiso Mexican, Pizza Hut, PJ's Rest., Runza Rest., Subway, **lodging:** Best Value Inn, Circle S Motel/rest, Motel 6, **other:** HOSPITAL, Alco, museum
211	NE 47, Gothenburg, **N...gas:** Shell/dsl/24hr/@, Sinclair/rest./dsl/@, **food:** China Cafe, Lasso Espresso, McDonald's, Mi Ranchito Mexican, Pizza Hut/Taco Bell, Randazzle Cafe, Runza Rest., **lodging:** Pony Express Inn, Super 8, Travel Inn, **other:** HOSPITAL, CarQuest, Pony Express Sta Museum(1mi), Chevrolet/Pontiac/Buick, truck permit sta, **S...KOA/Sinclair**

N Platte

199	Brady, **N...gas:** Brady 1 Stop/DQ/dsl
194mm	**rest area both lanes, full(handicapped) facilities, phone, picnic tables, litter barrels, vending, petwalk**
190	Maxwell, **N...gas:** Sinclair/dsl, **S...other:** to Ft McPherson Nat Cemetary, RV camping
181mm	weigh sta both lanes, phones
179	to US 30, N Platte, **N...gas:** Sinclair, **lodging:** La Quinta, (1mi)Stanford Motel, **other:** RV camping, **S...gas:** 🏷/Flying J/Conoco/CountryMkt/dsl/LP/24hr/@
177	US 83, N Platte, **N...gas:** BP/Subway, Shell/dsl, Sinclair/dsl, **food:** A&W, Amigo's Rest., Applebee's, Arby's, Burger King, Chinese Rest., DQ, KFC, LJ Silver/Taco Bell, McDonald's, Perkins/24hr, Pizza Hut, Red Kayluin Cafe, Roger's Diner, Runza Rest., Sonic, Subway, Valentino's, Village Inn Rest., Wendy's, Whiskey Creek Steaks, **lodging:** Blue Spruce Motel, Hampton Inn, Hospitality Inn, Howard Johnson, Motel 6, Oak Tree Inn, Quality Inn, Royal Colonial Inn, Sands Motel, **other:** Hospital, Advance Parts, $General, Goodyear/auto, Harley-Davidson, Holiday TravL Park, JC Penney, ShopKO, Staples, SunMart Foods, U-Save Drug, Wal-Mart SuperCtr/gas/24hr, mall, museum, to Buffalo Bill's Ranch, **S...gas:** BP, Conoco/Taco Bell/dsl/24hr/@, Phillips 66, Shell/dsl/rest./RV Dump/24hr, **food:** Hunan Chinese, Mi Ranchito, Taco John's, **lodging:** Comfort Inn, Day's Inn, Holiday Inn Express, Ramada Ltd, Super 8, **other:** Cadillac, Chevrolet, Chrysler/Jeep, Dodge, Ford/Lincoln/Mercury, Honda, Toyota/Mazda, truck permit sta, to Lake Maloney RA
164	56C, Hershey, **N...gas:** Western/Jayz Diner/dsl/24hr/@, **other:** Rivers Edge Ranch Store
160mm	**rest area both lanes, full(handicapped) facilities, info, phone, picnic tables, litter barrels, petwalk**
158	NE 25, Sutherland, **N...lodging:** Park Motel(1mi), **S...gas:** Sinclair/dsl/24hr, **other:** RV camping
149mm	Central/Mountain time zone
145	51C, Paxton, **N...gas:** Shell/dsl/24hr, **food:** Ole's Café, **lodging:** Day's Inn, **other** RV camping
133	51B, Roscoe, no services
132mm	**rest area wb, full(handicapped)facilities, info, phone, picnic tables, litter barrels, petwalk**

Ogallala

126	US 26, NE 61, Ogallala, **N...gas:** B&J Gas, BP, Sapp/Shell/dsl/24hr, Sinclair, **food:** Arby's, Burger King, Country Kitchen, McDonald's, Mi Ranchito Mexican, Pizza Hut, Runza Rest., Taco John's, Valentino's, **lodging:** Best Western, Day's Inn, Gray Goose Lodge, Holiday Inn Express, **other:** HOSPITAL, CarQuest, Chevrolet/Buick, NAPA, SunMart Foods, TrueValue, U-Save Drug, to Lake McConaughy, **S...gas:** Conoco/Subway/dsl, TA/dsl/rest./24hr/scales//@, **food:** DQ, KFC/Taco Bell, Wendy's, **lodging:** Comfort Inn, Econolodge, Super 8, **other:** $General, Corral RV Park, Pamida

Interstate 80

124mm	**rest area eb, full(handicapped)facilities, info, phones, picnic tables, litter barrels, petwalk**
117	51A, Brule, **N**...gas: Sinclair/dsl/RV camping
107	25B, Big Springs, **N**...gas: Big Springs/dsl, Bosselman/Pilot/Sinclair/Grandma Max's/Little Caesar's/Subway/dsl/scales/@, **lodging:** Motel 6, **other:** truckwash, **S**...other: McGreer's Camping
102	I-76 S, to Denver
102mm	S Platte River
101	US 138, to Julesburg, no services
99mm	scenic turnout eb
95	NE 27, to Julesburg, no services
88mm	**Lodgepole Creek, rest area wb, full(handicapped) facilities, phone, picnic tables, litter barrels, vending, petwalk**
85	25A, Chappell, **N**...gas: Cenex/dsl, **other:** Creekside Camping, USPO, wayside park
82.5mm	**rest area eb, full(handicapped)facilities, phone, picnic tables, litter barrels, vending, petwalk**
76	17F, Lodgepole, **1 mi N**...gas/dsl, lodging
69	17E, to Sunol, no services
61mm	**rest area wb, full(handicapped)facilities, phone, picnic tables, litter barrels, vending, petwalk**
59	US 385, 17J, Sidney, **N**...gas: Conoco/KFC/Taco Bell/TCBY/dsl, Sapp/Shell/dsl/24hr/@, **food:** Arby's, China 1 Buffet, McDonald's, Mi Ranchito Mexican, Perkins, Quizno's, Runza Rest., Taco John's, **lodging:** AmericInn, Comfort Inn, Day's Inn, Motel 6, **other:** Cabela's SportsGear, Chrysler/Jeep/Dodge, $General, Naddox RV Ctr, Radio Shack, Wal-Mart SuperCtr/24hr, RV camping(2mi), golf, truck permit sta, **3 mi N**...food: KFC, Pizza Hut, **lodging:** Generic Motel, Sidney Motel, Super 8, **other:** HOSPITAL, RV camping, **S**...gas: BP/dsl, **lodging:** Holiday Inn/rest., **other:** truckwash
55	NE 19, to Sterling, Sidney, **2 mi N**...lodging: Best Value
51.5mm	**rest area/hist marker eb, full(handicapped) facilities, phone, picnic tables, litter barrels, vending, petwalk**
48	to Brownson, no services
38	rd 17 b, Potter, **N**...gas: Cenex/dsl/LP, **other:** repair
29	53A, Dix, **1/2 mi N**...gas, food
25mm	**rest area wb, full(handicapped)facilities, phone, picnic tables, litter barrels, vending, petwalk**
22	53E, Kimball, **N**...lodging: (1mi)Day's Inn, **other:** golf
20	NE 71, Kimball, **N**...gas: Sinclair/dsl, **food:** Pizza Hut, Subway, **lodging:** Best Value, (1mi)Day's Inn, 1st Interstate Inn, **other:** HOSPITAL, RV Park, truck permit sta.,
18mm	parking area eb, litter barrel
10mm	**rest area eb, full(handicapped)facilities, info, phone, picnic tables, litter barrels, petwalk**
8	53C, to Bushnell, no services
1	53B, Pine Bluffs, **1 mi N**...RV camping
0mm	Nebraska/Wyoming state line

Sidney *Kimball* (side label)

Interstate 680 (Omaha)

Exit #	Services
29b a	I-80, W to Omaha, E to Des Moines. I-680 begins/ends on I-80, exit 27.
28	IA 191, to Neola, Persia, no services
21	L34, Beebeetown, no services
19mm	**rest area wb, full(handicapped)facilities, info, phone, picnic tables, litter barrels, petwalk**
16mm	**rest area eb, full(handicapped)facilities, info, phone, picnic tables, litter barrels, petwalk**
15mm	**scenic overlook**
71	I-29 N, to Sioux City
66	Honey Creek, **W**...gas: Sinclair/dsl/rest., **food:** Iowa Feed&Grain Co Rest.
3b a (61 b a from wb)	I-29, S to Council Bluffs, IA 988, to Crescent, **E**...gas: Phillips 66, **other:** to ski area
1	County Rd, no services
14mm	Nebraska/Iowa state line, Missouri River, Mormon Bridge
13	US 75 S, 30th St, Florence, **E**...gas: Shell/dsl, **food:** Firehouse Pizza, Zesto Diner, **lodging:** Mormon Trail Motel, **other:** LDS Temple, Mormon Trail Ctr, **W**...gas: Sinclair
12	US 75 N, 48th St, **E**...gas: Phillips 66, **food:** Burger King
9	72nd St, **E**...gas: QuikShop, (1-3 mi) **food:** Famous Dave's BBQ, IHOP, Sonic, Village Inn, **other:** HOSPITAL, **W**...Cunningham Lake RA
6	NE 133, Irvington, **E**...gas: Conoco/dsl, **food:** Burger King, **other:** Wal-Mart/Subway/drugs/24hr
5	Fort St, **W**...gas: KwikShop, Sinclair, **other:** USPO
4	NE 64, Maple St, **E**...gas: BP, **W**... Conoco/dsl, Kum&Go, **food:** Burger King, Godfather's Pizza, KFC, La Mesa Mexican, McDonald's, Perkins, Pizza Hut, Runza, Subway, Taco Bell, **lodging:** Comfort Suites, La Quinta, **other:** Bag'n Save, Champion Parts
3	US 6, Dodge St, **E**...food: Chang's Bistro, Macaroni Grill, Panera Bread, TGIFriday, **lodging:** Hampton Inn, Marriott, **other:** AAA, BMW, Dodge, Ford, Jaguar/Land Rover, JC Penney, Mazda, Von Maur, mall, **W**...gas: BP/Amoco, **food:** Boston Mkt, Burger King, China buffet, DQ, McDonald's, Starbucks, **lodging:** Best Western, Crowne Plaza Motel, **other:** Cadillac, Chevrolet, Hummer, Nissan/Hyundai, Saturn, Toyota
2	Pacific St, **E**...gas: BP, Sinclair, **lodging:** Regency Lodge
1	NE 38, W Center Rd, **E**...gas: Cenex/dsl, **food** Blimpie, Don Carmelo's, Don&Millie's Rest., Garden Cafe, **W**...gas: Phillips 66, **food:** Burger King, Ozark BBQ, Wendy's
0mm	I-680 begins/ends on I-80, exit 446

Omaha (side label)

NEVADA
Interstate 15

Exit #	Services
	Mesquite
123mm	Nevada/Arizona state line, Pacific/Mountain time zone
122	Lp 15, Mesquite, **E**...**NV Welcome Ctr both lanes, full(handicapped)facilities, petwalk, gas:** Chevron/Subway/dsl/24hr, Shell/DQ, Sinclair/Arby's, **food:** Burger King, Canton Chinese, Golden West Rest./casino, Jack-in-the-Box, Jamba Juice, KFC, Mia's Mexican, Pizza Hut, Rio Virgin Grill, Thunderbird Rest., **lodging:** Best Western, Budget Inn, Desert Palms Motel, Up Town Motel, **other:** Ace Hardware, AutoZone, Big O Tire, CarQuest, El Rancho Mkt, GNC, Great Outdoors RV, NAPA, Radio Shack, Rite Aid, Smith's Foods, USPO, dsl repair, museum, **W**...**gas:** Virgin River/76/dsl/LP/RV park, **food:** McDonald's, **lodging:** Eureka Motel/casino, Mesquite Springs Motel, Virgin River Hotel/casino
120	Lp 15, Mesquite, Bunkerville, **E**...**gas:** Arco/24hr, Chevron, Shell/dsl, **food:** Carollo's Rest., Jamba Juice, McDonald's, **lodging:** Casablanca Resort/casino/RV Park, Oasis Resort/casino, Peppermill Resort/casino, Players Island Resort/casino, Valley Inn, **other:** USPO, **W**...**lodging:** Falcon Ridge, **other:** HOSPITAL, Ford, Wal-Mart SuperCtr
112	NV 170, Riverside, Bunkerville, no services
110mm	truck parking both lanes, litter barrels
100	to Carp, Elgin, no services
96mm	truck parking nb, litter barrels
93	NV 169, to Logandale, Overton, **E**...**gas:** Chevron, **lodging:** Best Western(10mi), **other:** Lake Mead NRA, Lost City Museum
91	NV 168, Glendale, **W**...**gas:** Sinclair/dsl/rest.
90.5mm	Muddy River
90	NV 168(from nb), Glendale, Moapa, **W**... gas, **other:** Moapa Indian Reservation, USPO
88	Hidden Valley, no services
87.5mm	parking area both lanes, litter barrels
84	Byron, no services
80	Ute, no services
75	NV 169 E, Valley of Fire SP, Lake Mead NRA, **E**... **gas:** Sinclair/dsl, **other:** casino, fireworks
64	US 93 N, Great Basin Hwy, to Ely, Great Basin NP
60mm	livestock check sta sb
58	NV 604, Las Vegas Blvd, to Apex, Nellis AFB, **E**... **other:** Hitchin' Post RV Park(9mi)
54	Speedway Blvd, Hollywood Blvd, **E**...**gas:** Petro/Mobil/dsl/24hr/@, **other:** Las Vegas Speedway
52	rd 215 W, no services
50	Lamb Ave, **E**... Hitchin Post RV Park
48	Craig Rd, **E**...**gas:** Arco, Pilot/DQ/KFC/Pizza Hut/dsl/scales/24hr, Rebel Gas, Shell, Sinclair/Subway/dsl, **food:** Burger King, Jack-in-the-Box, Zapata's Cantina, **lodging:** Best Western(2mi), Hampton Inn, Super 8, **other:** Firestone, to Nellis AFB, **W**...**gas:** Citgo/7-11, **lodging:** Holiday Inn Express, **other:** Freightliner, dsl repair
	Las Vegas
46	Cheyenne Ave, **E**...**gas:** Arco/24hr, Chevron, **food:** Hamburger Hut, Speedway Grill, Starbucks, **lodging:** Ramada Inn/casino, **other:** vet, **W**...**gas:** Citgo/7-11, Flying J/dsl/LP/rest./24hr/@, Sinclair/Jack-in-the-Box, **food:** Denny's, McDonald's, **lodging:** Comfort Inn, **other:** Blue Beacon, Kenworth, SpeedCo, dsl repair
45	Lake Mead Blvd, **E**...**gas:** Chevron, 76/dsl, **food:** Arby's, Burger King, Carl's Jr., Jack-in-the-Box, McDonald's, Wendy's, **other:** GNC, PepBoys, Rite Aid, 7-11, **W**...**gas:** Arco, **food:** A&W/LJ Silver
44	Washington Ave(from sb), **E**...**lodging:** Best Western, casinos

Exit #	Services
43	D St(from nb), **E**...Best Western, same as 44
42b a	I-515 to LV, US 95 N to Reno, US 93 S to Phoenix
41b a	NV 159, Charleston Blvd, **E**...**gas:** Arco/dsl, **other:** antiques, 7-11, Smith's Foods, tire/repair, **W**...**gas:** 76, Terrible/dsl/casino, **food:** Carl's Jr, Del Taco, McDonald's, Wendy's, **lodging: other:** HOSPITAL, CVS Drug
40	Sahara Ave, **E**...The Strip, **lodging:** Artisan Hotel, Vagabond Inn, **other:** Big O Tire, LV Conv Ctr, multiple casinos/hotels, **W**...**gas:** Chevron, Rebel Gas, 7-11/gas, **food:** Arby's, Blimpie, Burger King, Carl's Jr, Denny's, In-n-Out, Jose Hoggs Rest, KFC, Landry's Seafood, Macaroni Grill, McDonald's, Pizza Hut, Shilla BBQ, TGIFriday's, Wendy's, vet, **lodging:** Palace Station Hotel/casino, **other:** Chevrolet, CompUSA, CVS Drug, Food4Less, Home Depot, Liffy Lube, Lexus, Mazda, Mercedes, Mitsubishi, Office Depot, Rite Aid
39	Spring Mtn Rd(from sb), **E**...**lodging:** Budget Suites, Frontier Hotel, **other:** Mirage, Treasure Island, **W**...**gas:** Arco/24hr, Circle K, United/dsl, **food:** Schlotsky's, **other:** EconoLube/Tune, Discount Tire, Firestone/auto, Goodyear/auto, Lexus, Mercedes, auto/transmission repair
38b a	Dunes Flamingo Rd, **E**...The Strip, **lodging:** Bellagio, Caesar's Palace, Flamingo Hilton, Mirage, Monte Carlo, to UNLV, multiple casinos/hotels, **W**...**gas:** Arco/24hr, Chevron, 76/Del Taco, **food:** Burger King, Outback Steaks, Starbucks, Subway, **lodging:** Gold Coast Hotel, Palms Hotel, Rio Hotel, **other:** Terrible Herbst/wash/lube
37	Tropicana Ave, **E**...**gas:** 76, **food:** Coco's Rest, McDonald's, **lodging:** Bellagio, Excaliber Hotel, Hooters, Mandalay Bay, MGM Grand, Monte Carlo, Motel 6, Tropicana Hotel, **other:** airport, casinos/hotels, **W**...**gas:** Arco/24hr, Chevron/dsl, 76, Shell/Subway, **food:** Burger King, IHOP, In-n-Out, Jack-in-the-Box, KFC, McDonald's, Taco Bell, Taco's Mexico, Wendy's, **lodging:** Best Western, Budget Suites, Golden Palm, Hampton Inn, La Quinta, Motel 6, Orleans Hotel
36	Russell Rd, **E**...**lodging:** Mandalay Bay, **other:** casinos, to airport, **W**...**gas:** Chevron/Herbst/dsl, **lodging:** Courtyard, Fairfield Inn, Holiday Inn Express, Residence Inn
34	to I-215 E, Las Vegas Blvd, to The Strip, McCarran Airport
33	NV 160, to Blue Diamond, Death Valley, **E**...**gas:** Chevron, Citgo/7-11/dsl, **food:** Bootlegger Bistro, Chili's, Canes Rest, Cipotle Mexican, IHOP, La Cosina Mexican, McDonald's, Outback Steaks, Panda Express, Popeyes, Quizno's, Starbucks, Subway, Wienerschnitzel, **lodging:** Budget Suites, Hilton Garden, Microtel, **other:** CVS Drug, Food4Less, Oasis RV Resort, factory outlet/famous brands, **W**...**gas:** Chevron/dsl, TA/Burger King/TacoTime/dsl/LP/scales/24hr/@, Shell, **food:** Bilbo's Grill, Del Taco, Jack-in-the-Box, Subway, **lodging:** Firebird Inn, **other:** Bass ProShops, Kohl's, Office Depot, PetCo, Ross, Silverton Lodge/casino, Target, WorldMkt
31	Silverado Ranch Blvd, **S**...**lodging:** South Point Hotel/Casino
27	NV 146, to Henderson, Lake Mead, Hoover Dam, **E**...**gas:** Arco, Chevron, **food:** Jack-in-the-Box, **2 mi E**...**other:** Camping World, factory outlets
25	NV 161, Sloan, **1 mi E**...Camping World
24mm	bus/truck check sta nb
	Jean
12	NV 161, to Goodsprings, Jean, **E**...**Welcome Ctr nb, gas:** Mobil/dsl, **other:** Gold Strike Casino/hotel/Burger King, USPO, skydiving, **W**...**gas:** Shell/dsl, **other:** Nevada Landing Casino/dsl/24hr, NV Correctional
1	Primm, **E**...**gas:** Chevron, 76/dsl, **food:** Carl's Jr, Food Ct., McDonald's, Starbucks, **other:** Buffalo Bill's Resort/casino, Primm Valley Resort/casino, Prima Donna RV Park, NV Welcome Ctr, factory outlets, **W**...**gas:** Shell/dsl/scales, **lodging:** Whiskey Pete's Hotel/casino/steaks
0mm	Nevada/California state line

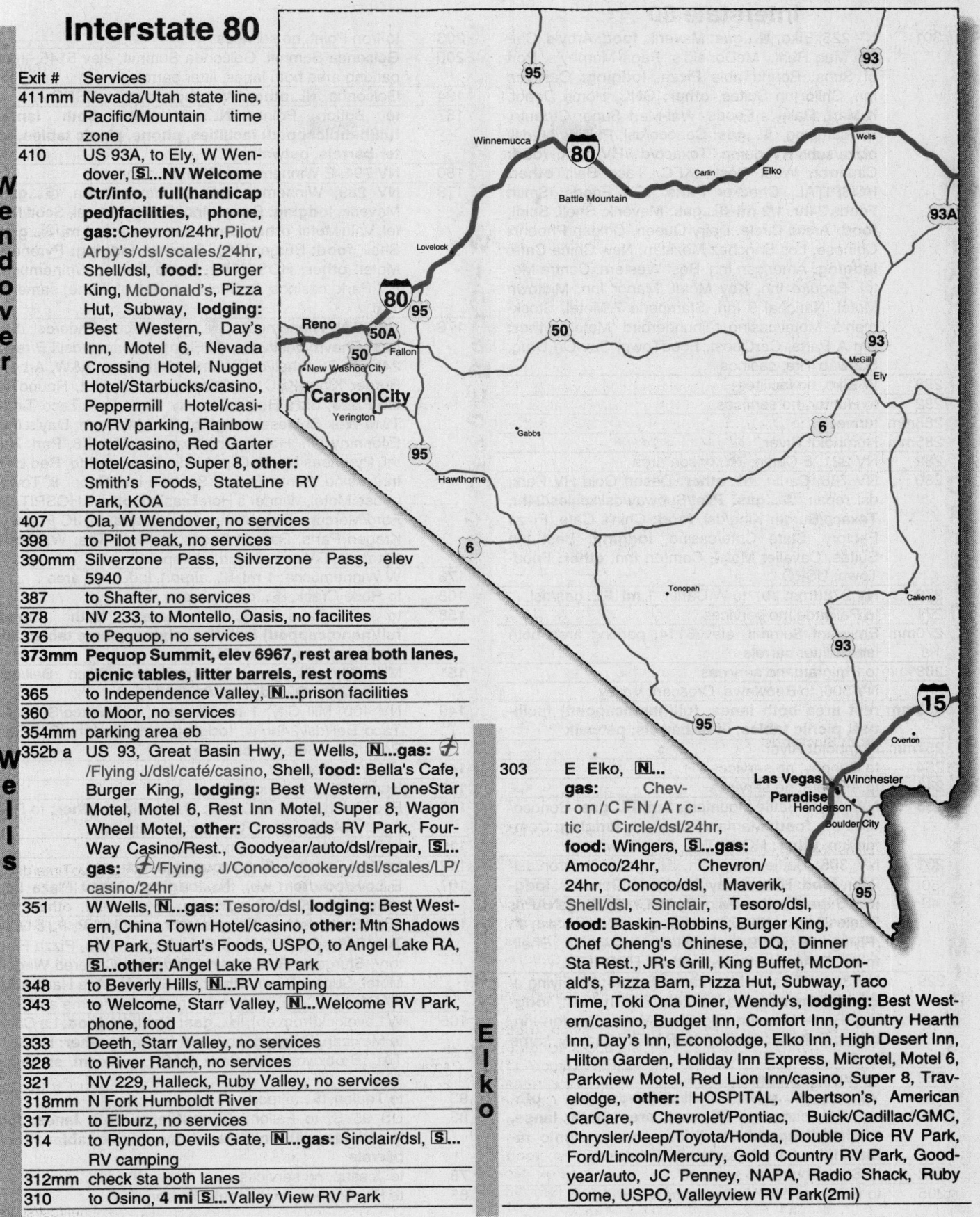

NEVADA

Interstate 80

E ↕ W

Wendover

Wells

Exit #	Services
411mm	Nevada/Utah state line, Pacific/Mountain time zone
410	US 93A, to Ely, W Wendover, **S...NV Welcome Ctr/info, full(handicapped)facilities, phone, gas:** Chevron/24hr, Pilot/Arby's/dsl/scales/24hr, Shell/dsl, **food:** Burger King, McDonald's, Pizza Hut, Subway, **lodging:** Best Western, Day's Inn, Motel 6, Nevada Crossing Hotel, Nugget Hotel/Starbucks/casino, Peppermill Hotel/casino/RV parking, Rainbow Hotel/casino, Red Garter Hotel/casino, Super 8, **other:** Smith's Foods, StateLine RV Park, KOA
407	Ola, W Wendover, no services
398	to Pilot Peak, no services
390mm	Silverzone Pass, Silverzone Pass, elev 5940
387	to Shafter, no services
378	NV 233, to Montello, Oasis, no faciles
376	to Pequop, no services
373mm	**Pequop Summit, elev 6967, rest area both lanes, picnic tables, litter barrels, rest rooms**
365	to Independence Valley, **N...**prison facilities
360	to Moor, no services
354mm	parking area eb
352b a	US 93, Great Basin Hwy, E Wells, **N...gas:** ✈/Flying J/dsl/café/casino, Shell, **food:** Bella's Cafe, Burger King, **lodging:** Best Western, LoneStar Motel, Motel 6, Rest Inn Motel, Super 8, Wagon Wheel Motel, **other:** Crossroads RV Park, Four-Way Casino/Rest., Goodyear/auto/dsl/repair, **S...gas:** ✈/Flying J/Conoco/cookery/dsl/scales/LP/casino/24hr
351	W Wells, **N...gas:** Tesoro/dsl, **lodging:** Best Western, China Town Hotel/casino, **other:** Mtn Shadows RV Park, Stuart's Foods, USPO, to Angel Lake RA, **S...other:** Angel Lake RV Park
348	to Beverly Hills, **N...**RV camping
343	to Welcome, Starr Valley, **N...**Welcome RV Park, phone, food
333	Deeth, Starr Valley, no services
328	to River Ranch, no services
321	NV 229, Halleck, Ruby Valley, no services
318mm	N Fork Humboldt River
317	to Elburz, no services
314	to Ryndon, Devils Gate, **N...gas:** Sinclair/dsl, **S...** RV camping
312mm	check sta both lanes
310	to Osino, **4 mi** **S...**Valley View RV Park
303	E Elko, **N...** **gas:** Chevron/CFN/Arctic Circle/dsl/24hr, **food:** Wingers, **S...gas:** Amoco/24hr, Chevron/24hr, Conoco/dsl, Maverik, Shell/dsl, Sinclair, Tesoro/dsl, **food:** Baskin-Robbins, Burger King, Chef Cheng's Chinese, DQ, Dinner Sta Rest., JR's Grill, King Buffet, McDonald's, Pizza Barn, Pizza Hut, Subway, Taco Time, Toki Ona Diner, Wendy's, **lodging:** Best Western/casino, Budget Inn, Comfort Inn, Country Hearth Inn, Day's Inn, Econolodge, Elko Inn, High Desert Inn, Hilton Garden, Holiday Inn Express, Microtel, Motel 6, Parkview Motel, Red Lion Inn/casino, Super 8, Travelodge, **other:** HOSPITAL, Albertson's, American CarCare, Chevrolet/Pontiac, Buick/Cadillac/GMC, Chrysler/Jeep/Toyota/Honda, Double Dice RV Park, Ford/Lincoln/Mercury, Gold Country RV Park, Goodyear/auto, JC Penney, NAPA, Radio Shack, Ruby Dome, USPO, Valleyview RV Park(2mi)

Wells Elko

NEVADA

Interstate 80

E
↕
W

Elko Carlin Battle Mtn

Exit	Description
301	NV 225, Elko, **N**...gas: Maverik, **food**: Arby's, Coffee Mug Rest., McDonald's, Papa Murphy's, Port of Subs, RoundTable Pizza, **lodging**: OakTree Inn, Shilo Inn Suites, **other**: GNC, Home Depot, K-Mart, Raley's Foods, Wal-Mart Super Ctr/auto, RV camping, **S**...gas: Conoco/dsl, Phillips 66/dsl/pizza/subs/RV dump, Texaco/dsl/RV park, **food**: Cimarron West Rest., KFC, Taco Bell, **other**: HOSPITAL, Checker Parts, IGA Foods, Smith Foods/24hr, **1/2 mi S**...gas: Maverik, Shell, Spirit, **food**: Arctic Circle, Dairy Queen, Golden Phoenix Chinese, Los Sanchez Mexican, New China Café, **lodging**: American Inn, Best Western, Centre Motel, Esquire Inn, Key Motel, Manor Inn, Midtown Motel, National 9 Inn, Stampede 7 Motel, Stockmen's Motel/casino, Thunderbird Motel, **other**: Big A Parts, CarQuest, FoodTown, Sav-On Drug, Schwab Tire, casinos
298	W Elko, no facilites
292	to Hunter, no services
285mm	tunnel
285mm	Humboldt River
282	NV 221, E Carlin, **N**...prison area
280	NV 766, Carlin, **N**...other: Desert Gold RV Park, dsl repair, **S**...gas: Pilot/Subway/dsl/scales/24hr, Texaco/Burger King/dsl, **food**: Chin's Cafe, Pizza Factory, State Café/casino, **lodging**: Best Inn Suites, Cavalier Motel, Comfort Inn, **other**: FoodTown, USPO
279	NV 278(from eb), to W Carlin, **1 mi S**... gas/dsl,
271	to Palisade, no services
270mm	Emigrant Summit, elev 6114, parking area both lanes, litter barrels
268	to Emigrant, no services
261	NV 306, to Beowawe, Crescent Valley
258mm	**rest area both lanes, full(handicapped) facilities, picnic tables, litter barrels, petwalk**
257mm	Humboldt River
254	to Dunphy, no services
244	to Argenta, no services
233	NV 304, to Battle Mountain, **1 mi N**...gas: Conoco/dsl/24hr, **food**: Mama's Pizza/deli, **lodging**: Comfort Inn, **other**: HOSPITAL, FoodTown
231	NV 305, Battle Mountain, **N**...gas: Chevron/dsl/24hr, **food**: Hide-a-way Steaks, McDonald's, **lodging**: Super 8, **other**: Midway Mkt, Mills Drug, NAPA, Radio Shack, USPO, **1 mi N**...gas: Conoco/dsl, ♿/Flying J/Exxon/Blimpie/dsl/casino/24hr/@, Shell, **food**: El Aguila Mexican, **other**: HOSPITAL
229	NV 304, W Battle Mountain, **N**...gas: ♿/Flying J/Exxon/Blimpie/dsl/casino/24hr/@, Shell/dsl, **lodging**: Battle Mtn. Inn, Big Chief Motel, Comfort Inn, **other**: Colt RV camping, NAPA, Tire Factory, same as 231
222	to Mote, no services
216	Valmy, **N**...gas: Shell/USPO/dsl/24hr, **other**: RV camping, **S**...rest area both lanes, full(handicapped) facilities, phone, picnic tables, litter barrels, petwalk, RV dump
212	to Stonehouse, no services
205	to Pumpernickel Valley, no services

Winnemucca Lovelock

Exit	Description
203	to Iron Point, no services
200	Golconda Summit, Golconda Summit, elev 5145, truck parking area both lanes, litter barrels
194	Golconda, **N**...other: Waterhole #1 mkt, USPO,
187	to Button Point, **N**...rest area both lanes, full(handicapped) facilities, phone, picnic tables, litter barrels, petwalk
180	NV 794, E Winnemucca Blvd, no services
178	NV 289, Winnemucca Blvd, Winnemucca, **S**...gas: Maverik, **lodging**: Budget Inn, Frontier Motel, Scott Motel, Valu Motel, **other**: CarQuest, carwash, **1 mi S**...gas: Shell, **food**: Burger King, Subway, **lodging**: Pyrenees Motel, **other**: HOSPITAL, Radio Shack, Winnemucca RV Park, casinos, to Buckeroo Hall of Fame, same as 176
176	US 95 N, Winnemucca, **N**...gas: Pacific Pride/dsl, **S**...gas: Chevron/dsl/24hr, ♿/Flying J/Conoco/dsl/LP/rest./24hr/@, 76, Shell/dsl, Winners/dsl, **food**: A&W, Arby's, Burger King, KFC, McDonald's, Pizza Hut, RoundTable Pizza, Sid's Rest., Subway, Taco Bell, Taco Time, Twin Wok Chinese, **lodging**: Best Western, Day's Inn, Economy Inn, Holiday Inn Express, Motel 6, Park Hotel, Pyrenees Motel, Quality Inn, Ramada Ltd, Red Lion Inn/casino, Santa Fe Inn, Scottish Inn, Super 8, Townhouse Motel, Winner's Hotel/casino, **other**: HOSPITAL, Ford/Mercury, Freightliner, Goodyear/auto, JC Penney, Kragen Parts, Raley's Foods, Schwab Tire, Wal-Mart/auto/gas, RV camping, truck repair
173	W Winnemucca, **1 mi S**...airport, industrial area
168	to Rose Creek, **S**...prison area
158	to Cosgrave, **S**...rest area both lanes, full(handicapped) facilities, phone, picnic tables, litter barrels, petwalk, RV dump
151	Mill City, **N**...gas: TA/Arco/Subway/Taco Bell/dsl/casino/24hr/@, **lodging**: Super 8
149	NV 400, Mill City, **1 mi N**...gas: to TA/Arco/Subway/Taco Bell/dsl/24hr/@, **lodging**: Knights Inn, **S**... Star Point Gen. Sore/RV camping
145	Imlay, no services
138	Humboldt, no services
129	Rye Patch Dam, **N**...food: Oasis Pizza, **other**: to Rye Patch RA, **S**...gas: Rye Patch Trkstp/dsl
119	to Rochester, Oreana, no services
112	to Coal Canyon, **S**...to correctional ctr
107	E Lovelock(from wb), **N**...lodging: Desert Plaza Inn, **other**: Lazy K Camping
106	Main St, Lovelock, **N**...gas: Chevron/dsl/LP, PJ's Gas, Two Stiffs, **food**: Cowpo Cafe, McDonald's, Pizza Factory, Sturgon's Rest./casino, **lodging**: Covered Wagon Motel, Super 10 Inn, **other**: HOSPITAL, Ace Hardware, NAPA AutoCare, playground/restrooms, same as 105
105	W Lovelock(from eb), **N**...gas: Shell/dsl, **food**: La Cacita Mexican, **lodging**: Lovelock Inn/rest., **other**: HOSPITAL, Brookwood RV Park, NAPA, museum, same as 106
93	to Toulon, **S**...airport
83	US 95 S, to Fallon, **S**...rest area both lanes, full(handicapped) facilities, phone, picnic tables, litter barrels
78	to Jessup, no services
65	to Hot Springs, Nightingale, no services

Interstate 80

48	US 50A, US 95A, to Fallon, E Fernley, **N**...gas: **Texaco/dsl, Truck Inn Travel Plaza/dsl/rest/24hr/ casino/@**, **other:** RV camping, tires, **S**...gas: Chevron/dsl/casino, Shell/Taco Bell/dsl/24hr, **food:** Domino's, Jack-in-the-Box, McDonald's, **lodging:** Best Western, Super 8, **other:** American Carcare, Goodyear/auto, Radio Shack, Scolari's Foods, Siverado Rest./casino, to Great Basin NP
46	US 95A, W Fernley, **N**...gas: **Luv's/Arby's/dsl**, **S**... **gas: Pilot/DQ/Wendy's/dsl/24hr, other:** Blue Beacon, SpeedCo, **1 mi S**...gas: Chevron, **lodging:** Best Value Inn
45mm	Truckee River
43	to Pyramid Lake, Wadsworth, **N**...gas: Pyramid Lake gas/dsl/RV camping
42mm	**rest area wb, full(handicapped)facilities, phone, picnic tables, litter barrels, petwalk, check sta eb**
40	Painted Rock, no services
38	Orchard, no services
36	Derby Dam, no services
32	Tracy, Clark Station, no services
28	NV 655, Waltham Way, Patrick, no services
27mm	scenic view, eb
25mm	check sta wb
23	Mustang, **N**...other: RV camping, **S**...Chevron/ dsl
22	Lockwood, no services
21	Vista Blvd, Greg St, Sparks, **N**...gas: Chevron/ McDonald's, QwikStop, **food:** Del Taco, **lodging:** Fairfield Inn, **other:** HOSPITAL, **S**...gas: Petro/ dsl/rest./24hr/@, **lodging:** Super 8
20	Sparks Blvd, Sparks, **N**...gas: Shell/dsl/24hr, **food:** Carl's Jr, Outback Steaks, Subway, **other:** water funpark, **S**...gas: Petro/dsl/rest./24hr/@, **lodging:** Super 8, **other:** Freightliner
19	E McCarran Blvd, Sparks, **N**...gas: Chevron/dsl, GoodCents, **TA/76/dsl/rest./@**, Winners Corner, **food:** Applebee's, Arby's, Black Bear Diner, Burger King, El Pollo Loco, IHOP, Jack-in-the-Box, Jo-Bobs Rest., KFC, Kraig's Rest., McDonald's, Sizzler, Subway, Wendy's, Wienerschnitzel, **lodging:** Aloha Inn, Windsor Inn, **other:** $Tree, Ford/Lincoln/Mercury/Isuzu, GNC, Jo-Ann Fabrics, Longs Drugs, Mervyn's, Radio Shack, Safeway, Sav-On Drug, Suzuki, Victorian RV Park, books, mall, **other:** Albertson's, Goodyear, Kragen Parts, LJ Silver, Longs Drugs, Target, **S**...**food:** Denny's, Super Burrito, **lodging:** Quality Inn, **other:** NAPA
18	NV 445, Pyramid Way(from eb), Sparks, **N**... **gas:** Citgo/7-11, **food:** In-N-Out, **lodging:** Nugget Courtyard, Silver Club Hotel/casino, **S**...**lodging:** Nugget Hotel/casino
17	Rock Blvd, Nugget Ave, Sparks, **N**...gas: Arco/ 24hr, Exxon, Winners, **lodging:** Victorian Inn, Wagon Train Motel, **other:** Kragen Parts, casinos, **S**...**lodging:** Nugget Hotel/casino
16	B St, E 4th St, Victorian Ave, **N**...gas: Arco/24hr, Winners, **lodging:** Motel 6, **other:** Rail City Casino, **S**...gas: Arco/dsl/24hr, Chevron/repair, Pacific Pride/dsl

15	US 395, to Carson City, **1 mi N** on McCarran Blvd... gas: Chevron, Shell/ dsl, **food:** Arby's, Burger King, Del Taco, Szechuan Chinese, Sonic, Subway, Taco Bell, TCBY, Wendy's, **other:** Home Depot, Kragen Parts, Ross, Wal-Mart/auto, WinCo Foods, **S**...**food:** Bally's, **lodging:** Hilton/Casino, Holiday Inn, 6 Gun Motel
14	Wells Ave, Reno, **N**...lodging: Motel 6, **S**...gas: Chevron, Shell, **food:** Carrow's Rest., Denny's, **lodging:** Day's Inn, Econolodge, Holiday Inn, Super 8, **other:** Goodyear
13	US 395, Virginia St, Reno, **N**...food: JimBoy's Taco's, **S**...gas: Shell/dsl, **other:** HOSPITAL, NAPA, Walgreens, to downtown hotels/casinos, to UNVReno
12	Keystone Ave, Reno, **N**...gas: Arco/24hr, 76, **food:** Pizza Hut, **lodging:** Gateway Inn, Motel 6, **other:** Raley's Foods, Sav-On Drug, 7-11, **S**...gas: Chevron, 76/dsl, Winner's Corner, **food:** Baskin-Robbins, Burger King, Jack-in-the-Box, KFC, McDonald's, Port of Subs, Pierino Rest, Taco Bell, Wendy's, **other:** Hilton's, Albertson's, Allied Parts, Olson Tire, Radio Shack, 98 Cents Store, casinos, RV park
10	McCarran Blvd, Reno, **N**...gas: Arco/24hr, Citgo/7-11, **food:** Arby's, Baskin-Robbins, Burger King, Carl's Jr, Chili's, DQ, El Pollo Loco, Hacienda Mexican, IHOP, Jack-in-the-Box, Jamba Juice, KFC, McDonald's, Papa Murphy's, RoundTable Pizza, Starbucks, Taco Bell, **other:** Albertson's, Big O Tire, $Tree, Kragen Parts, QuikLube/gas, Safeway, Sav-On Drug, ShopKO, Tires+, Walgreens, Wal-Mart Super Ctr/McDonald's/24hr, **S**...gas: Citgo/7-11, **other:** VET, Home Depot, K-Mart/Little Caesar's
9	Robb Dr, **N**...gas: Chevron/dsl, **other:** Moxi's Cafe, Papa John's, Port Of Subs, Starbucks, Subway, Tapestries Rest., Zoo Pizza, **other:** AAA, Raley's Foods, Rite Aid, Scolari's Foods
8	W 4th St(from eb), Robb Dr, Reno, **S**...RV camping
7	Mogul, no services
6.5mm	truck parking/hist marker/scenic view both lanes
5	to E Verdi(from wb)
4.5mm	scenic view eb
4	Garson Rd, Boomtown, **N**...gas: Chevron/Boomtown Hotel/dsl/casino, **other:** RV park/dump
3.5mm	check sta eb
3	Verdi(from wb), no services
2.5mm	Truckee River
2	Lp 80, to Verdi, **N**...gas: Arco/dsl/24hr, **food:** Backstop Grill, Jack-in-the-Box, Taco Bell, **lodging:** Gold Ranch Hotel/casino
0mm	Nevada/California state line

NEW HAMPSHIRE
Interstate 89

N

S

Lebanon

Exit #	Services
61mm	New Hampshire/Vermont state line, Connecticut River
20(60)	NH 12A, W Lebanon, E...**gas:** Mobil/24hr, Sunoco/24hr, **food:** Benning St Grill, Board&Basket, Brick Oven Pizza, Chili's, Domino's, Dunkin Donuts, KFC/Taco Bell, 99 Rest., Shorty's Mexican, Subway, **other:** Brooks Drug, GNC, Jo-Ann Fabrics, K-Mart, NE Soap&Herb, PowerHouse Mall/shops, Shaw's Foods, W...**gas:** Citgo/dsl/repair, **food:** Applebee's, Burger King, China Light, D'angelo, Denny's, Friendly's, Koto Japanese, Lantern Buffet, McDonald's, Panera Bread, Pizza Hut, 7 Barrel Brewery, TCBY, Weathervane Seafood, Wendy's, **lodging:** Economy Inn, Fireside Inn, **other:** Ames, AutoZone, Best Buy, BJ' Whse, Borders Books, CVS Drug, Home Depot, JC Penney, PriceChopper Foods, Radio Shack, Shaw's Foods, Staples, Wal-Mart
19(58)	US 4, NH 10, W Lebanon, E...**gas:** Exxon/dsl/24hr, Shell/Blimpie, **food:** China Station, **other:** Family$, Ford, Harley-Davidson, Honda, NAPA, P&C Foods, Radio Shack, W...**gas:** Sunoco
57mm	Welcome Ctr/rest area/weigh sta sb, full(handicapped) facilities, phone, picnic tables, litter barrels, vending, petwalk, weigh sta nb
18(56)	NH 120, Lebanon, E...**gas:** Getty/dsl/rest./24hr/@, **lodging:** Day's Inn, Residence Inn(2mi), **other:** Buick/Pontiac/GMC, Chevrolet/Cadillac/VW, Dodge/Mazda, Nissan/Jeep/Volvo, to Dartmouth Coll, W...**gas:** Citgo/dsl, Shell, **other:** HOSPITAL, U-Haul
17(54)	US 4, to NH 4A, Enfield, E...**food:** Riverside Grill, Shaker Museum, **other:** Tire Kingdom
16(52)	Eastman Hill Rd, E...**gas:** Exxon/Subway/dsl/24hr, W...**gas:** Mobil/dsl/24hr, **other:** Whaleback Ski Area
15(50)	Montcalm, no services
14(47)	NH 10(from sb), no services
13(43)	NH 10, to N Grantham, Grantham, E...**gas:** Gulf/dsl/Gen Store, **food:** Rusty Moose, W...**gas:** Mobil/repair
40mm	rest area nb, full(handicapped)facilities, info, phone, picnic table, litter barrels, vending, petwalk
12A(37)	Georges Mills, W...**other:** to Sunapee SP, food, phone, lodging, RV camping
12(34)	NH 11 W, New London, **2 mi** E...**gas:** Exxon/dsl, **lodging:** Maple Hill Country Inn, **other:** HOSPITAL
11(31)	NH 11 E, King Hill Rd, New London, **2 mi** E...**lodging:** Fairway Motel, food, **2 mi** W...**lodging:** Shaker Mtg House B&B
10(27)	to NH 114, Sutton, E...to Winslow SP, **1 mi** W...lodging, to Wadleigh SB
26mm	rest area sb, full(handicapped)facilities, info, phone, picnic tables, litter barrels, vending, petwalk
9(19)	NH 103, Warner, E...**gas:** Citgo/Subway/Pizza Hut/TCBY, Exxon, Mobil/dsl/24hr, **food:** Dunkin Donuts, Foothills Rest.(1mi), McDonald's, **other:** MktBasket Foods, Rollins SP, W...to Sunapee SP, ski area
8(17)	NH 103(from nb, no EZ return), Warner, **1 mi** E...gas, food, museum, to Rollins SP
15mm	Warner River
7(14)	NH 103, Davisville, W...Pleasant Lake Camping

Concord

12mm	Contoocook River
6(10)	NH 127, Contoocook, **1 mi** E...**gas:** Sunoco, W...**other:** Elm Brook Park, Sandy Beach Camping(3mi)
5(8)	US 202 W, NH 9(exits left from nb), Hopkinton, W...food, RV camping(seasonal)
4(7)	NH 103, Hopkinton(from nb, no EZ return), E...Horse-Shoe Tavern, gas
3(4)	Stickney Hill Rd(from nb), no services
2(2)	NH 13, Clinton St, Concord, E...HOSPITAL, food, W...NH Audubon Ctr
1(1)	Logging Hill Rd, Bow, E...**gas:** Mobil/24hr, **food:** Chen Yang Li Chinese, **lodging:** Hampton Inn
0mm	I-93 N to Concord, S to Manchester, I-89 begins/ends on I-93, 36mm.

Interstate 93

N

S

Littleton

Exit #	Services
2(11)	I-91, N to St Johnsbury, S to White River Jct. I-93 begins/ends on I-91, exit 19.
1(8)	VT 18, to US 2, to St Johnsbury, **2 mi** E...gas, food, lodging, camping
1mm	**Welcome Ctr nb, full(handicapped)facilities, info, phone, picnic tables, litter barrels, vending, petwalk**
131mm	Vermont/New Hampshire state line, Connecticut River. **Exits 1-2 are in VT.**
44(130)	NH 18, NH 135, W...**Welcome Ctr(8am-8pm)/scenic vista both lanes, full(handicapped)facilities, info, phone, picnic tables, litter barrels, petwalk**
43(125)	NH 135(from sb), to NH 18, Littleton, **1-2 mi** W...HOSPITAL, same as 42
42(124)	US 302 E, NH 10 N, Littleton, E...**gas:** Citgo, Cumberland, Gulf, Sunoco/24hr, **food:** Burger King, ClamShell Rest., Deluxe Pizza, Dunkin Donuts, Jing Fong Chinese, McDonald's, Oasis Italian, Pizza Hut, Subway, **other:** Brooks Drug, Medicine Shoppe, Parts+, Rite Aid, W...**gas:** Mobil, **food:** Applebee's, Asian Garden Chinese, **lodging:** Continental Inn, **other:** Aubuchon Hardware, Chevrolet/Buick/Pontiac, Chrysler/Dodge/Jeep, KOA, Shaw's Foods, Staples, Tire Whse, TJ Maxx, VIP Parts/repair, Wal-Mart/drug
41(122)	US 302, NH 18, NH 116, Littleton, E...**gas:** Irving/dsl/24hr, **lodging:** Eastgate Motel/rest., E...**other:** NE Tire
40(121)	US 302, NH 10 E, Bethlehem, E...**gas:** Exxon, **food:** Adair Rest., **lodging:** Angel Mtn B&B, Milborn Inn, **other:** Snowy Mtn Camping, to Mt Washington
39(119)	NH 116, NH 18(from sb), N Franconia, Sugar Hill, W...lodging
38(117)	NH 116, NH 117, NH 142, NH 18, Sugar Hill, E...**lodging:** Franconia Village Hotel, W...**gas:** Mobil, **food:** DutchTreat Rest., Franconia Cafe, Village House Rest., **lodging:** Franconia Inn(2mi), **other:** Frost Museum, Kelley's FoodTown, USPO, camping, gifts, info
37(115)	NH 142, NH 18(from nb), Franconia, Bethlehem, E...**lodging:** Canyonview Motel, Stonybrook Motel
36(114)	NH 141, to US 3, S Franconia, W...golf, food, lodging
35(113)	US 3 N(from nb), to Twin Mtn Lake
112mm	S Franconia, Franconia Notch SP begins sb

Interstate 93

34c(111)	NH 18, Echo Beach Ski Area, view area, info
34b	Cannon Mtn Tramway, 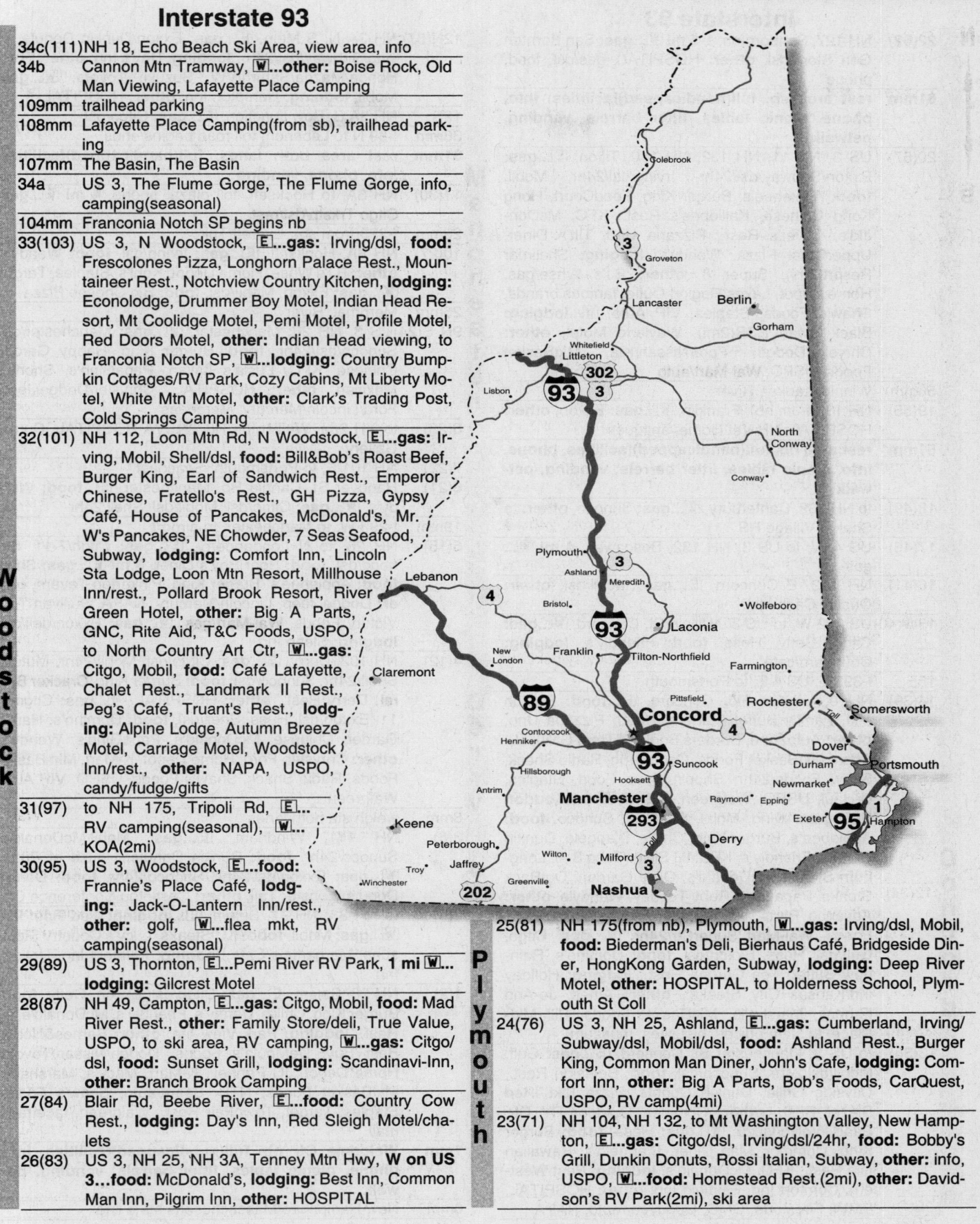...**other:** Boise Rock, Old Man Viewing, Lafayette Place Camping
109mm	trailhead parking
108mm	Lafayette Place Camping(from sb), trailhead parking
107mm	The Basin, The Basin
34a	US 3, The Flume Gorge, The Flume Gorge, info, camping(seasonal)
104mm	Franconia Notch SP begins nb
33(103)	US 3, N Woodstock, **E...gas:** Irving/dsl, **food:** Frescolones Pizza, Longhorn Palace Rest., Mountaineer Rest., Notchview Country Kitchen, **lodging:** Econolodge, Drummer Boy Motel, Indian Head Resort, Mt Coolidge Motel, Pemi Motel, Profile Motel, Red Doors Motel, **other:** Indian Head viewing, to Franconia Notch SP, **W...lodging:** Country Bumpkin Cottages/RV Park, Cozy Cabins, Mt Liberty Motel, White Mtn Motel, **other:** Clark's Trading Post, Cold Springs Camping
32(101)	NH 112, Loon Mtn Rd, N Woodstock, **E...gas:** Irving, Mobil, Shell/dsl, **food:** Bill&Bob's Roast Beef, Burger King, Earl of Sandwich Rest., Emperor Chinese, Fratello's Rest., GH Pizza, Gypsy Café, House of Pancakes, McDonald's, Mr. W's Pancakes, NE Chowder, 7 Seas Seafood, Subway, **lodging:** Comfort Inn, Lincoln Sta Lodge, Loon Mtn Resort, Millhouse Inn/rest., Pollard Brook Resort, River Green Hotel, **other:** Big A Parts, GNC, Rite Aid, T&C Foods, USPO, to North Country Art Ctr, **W...gas:** Citgo, Mobil, **food:** Café Lafayette, Chalet Rest., Landmark II Rest., Peg's Café, Truant's Rest., **lodging:** Alpine Lodge, Autumn Breeze Motel, Carriage Motel, Woodstock Inn/rest., **other:** NAPA, USPO, candy/fudge/gifts
31(97)	to NH 175, Tripoli Rd, **E...** RV camping(seasonal), **W...** KOA(2mi)
30(95)	US 3, Woodstock, **E...food:** Frannie's Place Café, **lodging:** Jack-O-Lantern Inn/rest., **other:** golf, **W...**flea mkt, RV camping(seasonal)
29(89)	US 3, Thornton, **E...**Pemi River RV Park, **1 mi W... lodging:** Gilcrest Motel
28(87)	NH 49, Campton, **E...gas:** Citgo, Mobil, **food:** Mad River Rest., **other:** Family Store/deli, True Value, USPO, to ski area, RV camping, **W...gas:** Citgo/dsl, **food:** Sunset Grill, **lodging:** Scandinavi-Inn, **other:** Branch Brook Camping
27(84)	Blair Rd, Beebe River, **E...food:** Country Cow Rest., **lodging:** Day's Inn, Red Sleigh Motel/chalets
26(83)	US 3, NH 25, NH 3A, Tenney Mtn Hwy, **W on US 3...food:** McDonald's, **lodging:** Best Inn, Common Man Inn, Pilgrim Inn, **other:** HOSPITAL

25(81)	NH 175(from nb), Plymouth, **W...gas:** Irving/dsl, Mobil, **food:** Biederman's Deli, Bierhaus Café, Bridgeside Diner, HongKong Garden, Subway, **lodging:** Deep River Motel, **other:** HOSPITAL, to Holderness School, Plymouth St Coll
24(76)	US 3, NH 25, Ashland, **E...gas:** Cumberland, Irving/Subway/dsl, Mobil/dsl, **food:** Ashland Rest., Burger King, Common Man Diner, John's Cafe, **lodging:** Comfort Inn, **other:** Big A Parts, Bob's Foods, CarQuest, USPO, RV camp(4mi)
23(71)	NH 104, NH 132, to Mt Washington Valley, New Hampton, **E...gas:** Citgo/dsl, Irving/dsl/24hr, **food:** Bobby's Grill, Dunkin Donuts, Rossi Italian, Subway, **other:** info, USPO, **W...food:** Homestead Rest.(2mi), **other:** Davidson's RV Park(2mi), ski area

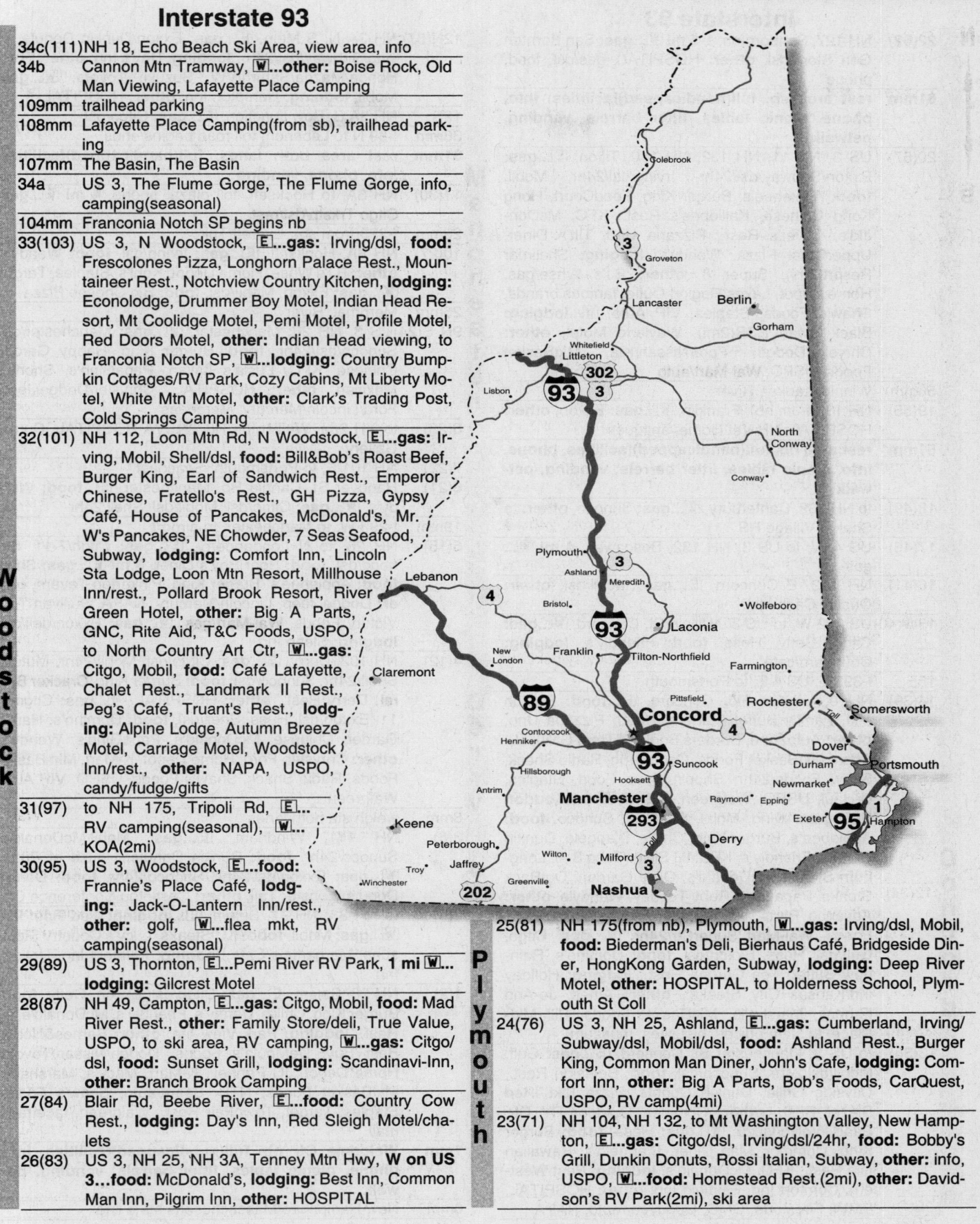

Interstate 93

N ↕ **S**

22(62)	NH 127, Sanbornton, **1-5 mi** W**...gas:** San Bornton Gen Store/dsl, **other:** HOSPITAL, gas/dsl, food, phone
61mm	**rest area sb, full(handicapped)facilities, info, phone, picnic tables, litter barrels, vending, petwalk**
20(57)	US 3, NH 11, NH 132, NH 140, Tilton, E**...gas:** Exxon/Subway/dsl/24hr, Irving/dsl/24hr, Mobil, **food:** Applebee's, Burger King, FoodCourt, Hong Kong Chinese, Kalliopee's Rest., KFC, McDonald's, Oliver's Rest., Pizzaria Uno, Tilt'n Diner, UpperCrust Pizza, Wendy's, **lodging:** Shalimar Resort(3mi), Super 8, **other:** BJ's Whse/gas, Home Depot, Lakes Region Outlet/famous brands, Shaw's Foods, Staples, VIP Auto, W**...lodging:** Black Swan B&B(2mi), Wayland Motel, **other:** Chrysler/Dodge, Ford/Nissan/Kia, MktBasket Foods, USPO, Wal-Mart/auto
56mm	Winnipesaukee River
19(55)	NH 132(from nb), Franklin, W**...gas:** Exxon, **other:** HOSPITAL, NH Vet Home, antiques
51mm	**rest area nb, full(handicapped)facilities, phone, info, picnic tables, litter barrels, vending, petwalk**
18(49)	to NH 132, Canterbury, E**...gas:** Sunoco, **other:** to Shaker Village HS
17(46)	US 4 W, to US 3, NH 132, Boscawen, **4 mi** W**...gas**
16(41)	NH 132, E Concord, E**...gas:** Mobil/dsl, **other:** Quality Cash Mkt
15W(40)	US 202 W, to US 3, N Main St, Concord, W**...gas:** Citgo, Getty, Hess, **food:** Friendly's, **lodging:** Courtyard/café
15E	I-393 E, US 4 E, to Portsmouth
14(39)	NH 9, Loudon Rd, Concord, E**...food:** Boston Mkt, Family Buffet, Panera Bread, Pizzaria Uno, **other:** AutoZone, Borders Books, $Tree, GNC, LL-Bean, MktBasket Foods, Osco Drug, Radio Shack, Shaw Foods/24hr, Shop'n Save Food, Staples, U-Haul, USPO, Walgreen, **1-2 mi** E **on Loudon Rd...gas:** Irving, Mobil, Shell/dsl, Sunoco, **food:** Applebee's, Burger King, Chili's, D'angelo, Dunkin Donuts, Friendly's, KFC, LJ Silver/Taco Bell, Longhorn Steaks, McDonald's, Olive Garden, OutBack Steaks, PapaGino, Ruby Tesday, Wendy's, **other:** Advance Parts, JC Penney, Sears/auto, Shaw's Foods, Wal-Mart SuperCtr/24hr, W**...gas:** Citgo, Gulf/dsl, Hess, Exxon/dsl, **food:** Domino's, Rainbow Buffet, Tea Garden Rest., **lodging:** Holiday Inn/Kansas City Steaks., **other:** Ames, Jo-Ann Fabrics, Marshalls, MktBasket Foods, Pill Mkt-Place, to state offices, hist sites, museum
13(38)	to US 3, Manchester St, Concord, E**...gas:** Gulf, Mobil/dsl/24hr, Sunoco/dsl, **food:** Beefside Rest., Cityside Grille, Dunkin Donuts, Pizza Mkt, Red Blazer Rest., **other:** Chrysler, Outdoor RV Ctr, Saab, Volvo/Isuzu, W**...gas:** Hess, **food:** Burger King, Common Man Diner, D'angelo's, Hawaiian Isle Rest., KFC, McDonald's, **lodging:** Best Western, Comfort Inn, Fairfield Inn, **other:** HOSPITAL, BMW, Firestone, GMC, Goodyear/auto, NAPA
12N(37)	NH 3A N, S Main, E**...gas:** Exxon/Dunkin Donuts, Irving/Subway/dsl/24hr, **lodging:** Day's Inn, **other:** Ford, Honda/Mazda/Saturn/VW, Suzuki, Toyota, W**...gas:** Mobil, **lodging:** Hampton Inn, **other:** HOSPITAL
12S	NH 3A S, Bow Junction, E**...gas:** Citgo/dsl
36mm	I-89 N to Lebanon, toll road begins/ends
31mm	**rest area both lanes, full(handicapped)facilities, info, phone, vending**
11(30)	NH 3A, to Hooksett, toll plaza, phone, **4 mi** E**...gas:** Citgo Trkstp/dsl/rest.
28mm	I-293(from sb), Everett Tpk
10(27)	NH 3A, Hooksett, E**...gas:** Irving/dsl, **food:** Wendy's, **other:** BJ's Whse, Home Depot, Kohl's, Staples, Target, W**...gas:** Exxon, Mobil/dsl, **food:** Big Cheese Pizza
26mm	Merrimac River
9N S(24)	US 3, NH 28, Manchester, W**...gas:** Manchester/dsl, Sunoco/dsl/24hr, **food:** Burger King, Happy Garden Chinese, KFC, Lusia's Italian, PapaGino's, Shorty's Mexican, **other:** HOSPITAL, Chrysler/Dodge/Jeep, Ford/Lincoln/Mercury, Mercedes
8(23)	to NH 28a, Wellington Rd, W**...VA HOSPITAL, Currier Gallery
7(22)	NH 101 E, to Portsmouth, Seacoast
6(21)	Hanover St, Candia Rd, Manchester, E**...food:** Wendy's, W**...gas:** Citgo/dsl, Mobil/dsl, Shell/24hr
19mm	I-293 W, to Manchester, to airport
5(15)	NH 28, to N Londonderry, E**...gas:** Citgo/7-11, Sunoco/dsl, **food:** Poor Boy's Diner, **3 mi** E**...gas:** Shell, **food:** Applebee's, Burger King, Pinkerton Tavern, **other:** Dodge/Jeep, Lincoln/Mercury, NAPA, Sullivan Tire, Victory Foods, Wal-Mart/gas, W**...gas:** Exxon/deli/dsl, **lodging:** Sleep Inn
4(12)	NH 102, Derry, E**...gas:** Citgo/dsl, Mobil/24hr, Mutual, Shell/24hr, Sunoco/dsl, **food:** Burger King, Cracker Barrel, Derry Rest., **other:** HOSPITAL, W**...gas:** Citgo/7-11, Exxon/dsl, Hess, Shell/dsl, **food:** Domino's, Happy Garden Chinese, McDonald's, PapaGino's, Wendy's, **other:** Chrysler, Ford, Home Depot, K-Mart, Mkt Basket Foods, Radio Shack, Shaw's Foods, USPO, VIP Auto, Walgreen
8mm	weigh sta both lanes
3(6)	NH 111, Windham, E**...gas:** Mobil/McDonald's, Sunoco/24hr, **food:** Dunkin Donuts, House of Pizza, W**...gas:** Exxon/dsl/24hr, Sunoco/24hr, **food:** Dunkin Donuts, Lobster Tail, **other:** Castleton Conference Ctr
2(3)	to NH 38, NH 97, Salem, E**...lodging:** Red Roof Inn, W**...gas:** Mobil, **food:** KC Steaks, Lucy's Country Store/subs, Margarita's Cafe, **lodging:** Fairfield Inn, Holiday Inn
1(2)	NH 28, Salem, E**...gas:** Citgo/dsl, Exxon, Getty, **food:** Burger King, Chili's, Denny's, Friendly's, McDonald's, 99 Rest., **lodging:** Park View Inn, **other:** Barnes&Noble, Best Buy, DeMoula's Foods, Dodge/Nissan/Toyota, Home Depot, JC Penney, K-Mart, Macy's, Marshall's, MktBasket Foods, NTB, Sears/auto, Shaw's Foods, Staples, Target, TownFair Rest., Walgreen, racetrack, mall
1mm	**Welcome Ctr nb, full(handicapped)facilities, info, phone, picnic tables, litter barrels, vending, petwalk**
0mm	New Hampshire/Massachusetts state line

Concord · *Manchester* · *Derry*

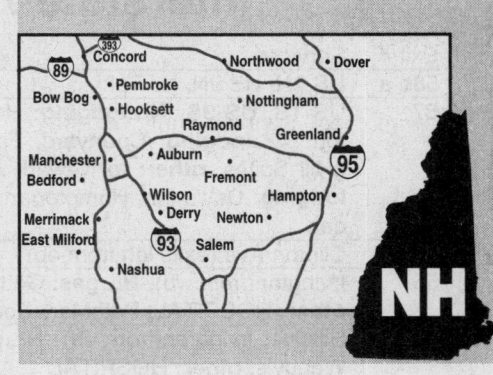

Interstate 95

Exit #	Services
17mm	New Hampshire/Maine state line, Piscataqua River
7(16)	Market St, Portsmouth, Port Authority, waterfront hist sites, E...**lodging:** Sheraton, W...**gas:** Lukoil, Mobil, **food:** Applebee's, Boston Mkt, KFC, Panera Bread, Ruby Tuesday, Wendy's, **lodging:** Courtyard, Hampton Inn, Homewood Suites, **other:** Brook's Drug, Circuit City, Chevrolet, BJ's Whse/gas, K-Mart, Marshall's, MktBasket Foods, Shaw's Foods, TJ Maxx
6(15)	Woodbury Ave(from nb), Portsmouth, E...**lodging:** Anchorage Inn, Best Inn, W...same as 7
5(14)	US 1, US 4, NH 16, The Circle, Portsmouth, E...**gas:** Citgo, Exxon, Shell/dsl, **food:** Bickford's, Momma D's Rest., **lodging:** Anchorage Inn, Best Inn, Best Western, Fairfield Inn, Holiday Inn, Meadow Brook Inn, Port Inn, **other:** HOSPITAL, Buick/Pontiac/GMC/Cadillac, W...**gas:** Mobil, **food:** d'Angelo's, Dunkin Donuts, IHOP, Longhorn Steaks, McDonald's, Pizza Hut, **lodging:** Hampton Inn, Residence Inn, **other:** Barnes&Noble, Best Buy, Ford, Home Depot, Kohl's, Mazda/VW, Nissan, Old Navy, Saturn
4(13.5)	US 4(exits left from nb), to White Mtns, Spaulding TPK, E...HOSPITAL, W...to Pease Int Trade Port
3a(13)	NH 33, Greenland, no services
3b(12)	NH 33, to Portsmouth, E...HOSPITAL, W...**gas:** Sunoco/dsl, TA/dsl/rest./scales/24hr/@, **food:** McDonald's(1mi), **other:** VW
2(6)	NH 101, to Hampton, **1 mi** E on US 1...**food:** McDonald's, **other:** HOSPITAL
5.5mm	toll plaza
4mm	Taylor River
1(1)	NH 107, to Seabrook, toll rd begins/ends, E...**gas:** Getty, Irving/dsl, Mobil, Prime, Sunoco/Subway, Xtra, **food:** Applebee's, Burger King, d'Angelo's, KFC/Taco Bell, McDonald's, 99 rest., Papagino's, Pizza Hut, Wendy's, **lodging:** Hampshire Inn, **other:** Advance Parts, AutoZone, CVS Drug, GNC, Home Depot, Jo-Ann Crafts, Lowes Whse, MktBasket Foods, NAPA, Radio Shack, Shaw's Foods, Staples, Sullivan Tire, TJ Maxx, Wal-Mart, to Seacoast RA, W...**gas:** Citgo, **food:** Capt K's Seafood, McGrath's Dining, **lodging:** Best Western, **other:** Sam's Club, Seabrook Greyhound Pk
.5mm	**Welcome Ctr nb, full(handicapped) facilities, phone, vending, picnic tables, litter barrels, petwalk**
0 mm	**New Hampshire/Massachusetts state line, Welcome Ctr nb, full(handicapped)facilities, phone, vending, picnic tables, litter barrels, petwalk**

Interstate 293 (Manchester)

Exit #	Services
8(9)	I-93, N to Concord, S to Derry. I-293 begins/ends on I-93, 28mm.
7(6.5)	NH 3A N, Dunbarton Rd(from nb), no services
6(6)	Singer Park, Manchester, E...**gas:** Sunoco, **food:** Hooters, **lodging:** Ramada Inn, W...**gas:** Mobil, Shell/dsl, **other:** HOSPITAL
5(5)	Granite St, Manchester(from nb, no EZ return), E...**lodging:** Radisson, W...**gas:** Citgo/7-11, Exxon, **food:** Dunkin Donuts, **other:** HOSPITAL
4(4)	US 3, NH 3A, NH 114A, Queen City Br, E...**gas:** Citgo/7-11, **lodging:** Queen City Inn, Thai Cuisine, W on US 3...**gas:** Hess/dsl, Z1 Gas, **food:** Applebee's, Bickford's, Burger King, Clam King, D'angelo's, DQ, KFC, McDonald's, Papa John's, Subway, Wendy's, **lodging:** Comfort Inn, Econolodge, **other:** Goodyear, Osco Drug, Subaru
3(3)	NH 101, W on US 3...**food:** Carrabba's, China Buffet, Outback Steaks, Qacker's Rest., T-Bones Steaks, **lodging:** Hampton Inn, Wayfarer Inn, **other:** Bob's Store, CVS Drug, Macy's, Marshalls, Radio Shack, Stop'n Shop, Staples, VIP Auto
2.5mm	Merrimac River
2(2)	NH 3A, Brown Ave, S...**gas:** Citgo/Subway/dsl, Citgo/7-11, Mobil/dsl, Shell/repair, **food:** Beijing Chinese, Kwikava, McDonald's, Rick's Café, **lodging:** Super 8, Tage Inn, **other:** Manchester Airport
1(1)	NH 28, S Willow Rd, N...**gas:** Mobil/Pizza Hut/dsl, Sunoco/dsl, **food:** Bickford's, Boston Mkt, Burger King, Cactus Jack's, Chili's, Friendly's, McDonald's, Panera Bread, PapaGino's, Taco Bell, Wendy's, Yee Dynasty Chinese, **lodging:** Fairfield Inn, Holiday Inn Express, Sheraton, **other:** HOSPITAL, AutoZone, Batteries+, Buick/Chevrolet, Circuit City, CVS Drug, $Tree, GMC, Harley-Davidson, Home Depot, Mercedes, Michael's, Nissan/Mitsubishi, Osco Drug, PepBoys, Pontiac/Cadillac/Mazda, Radio Shack, Sam's Club, Stop'n Shop, Tire Whse, Town Fair Tire, U-Haul, VW, S...**gas:** Exxon/dsl, Shell, **food:** Antics Grill, Bertucci's, Bickford's, ChuckeCheese, FoodCourt, Ground Round, Longhorn Steaks, 99 Rest., Olive Garden, Pizzaria Uno, Ruby Tuesday, TGIFriday, **lodging:** Courtyard, TownePlace Suites, **other:** HOSPITAL, Barnes&Noble, Best Buy, Chrysler, Macy's, Ford, Honda, Hyundai, JC Penney, K-Mart, Lexus, NTB, Saturn, Sears/auto, Staples, Toyota, Wal-Mart, mall
0mm	I-93, N to Concord, S to Derry. I-293 begins/ends on I-93

NEW JERSEY
Interstate 78

E ↑ W

N e w a r k

Exit #	Services
58b a	US 1N, US 9N, NJ Tpk
57	US 1S, US 9S, **N**...**lodging:** Holiday Inn, Sheraton, **S**...**lodging:** Courtyard, Fairfield Inn, SpringHill Suites, **other:** to Newark Airport, **3 mi S**...**lodging:** Day's Inn, Hampton Inn, Wyndham Garden
56	Clinton Ave (exits left from eb)
55	Irvington(from wb), **N**...**gas:** Getty, **food:** Wendy's, **other:** HOSPITAL, PathMark Foods
54	Hillside, Irvington(from eb), **N**...**gas:** Getty, **food:** Wendy's, **other:** HOSPITAL
52	Garden State Pkwy
50b a	Millburn(from wb), **N**...**gas:** BP, Exxon, Mobil, **other:** Firestone/auto, Home Depot, Lincoln/Mercury, USPO
49b	(from eb), to Maplewood, same as 50b a
48	to NJ 24, NJ 124, to I-287 N, (from wb), Springfield
48mm	I-78 eb divides into express & local
45	NJ 527(from eb), Glenside Ave, Summit
44	(from eb), to Berkeley Heights, New Providence
43	to New Providence, no services
41	to Berkeley Heights, Scotch Plains, no services
40	NJ 531, The Plainfields, **S**...**gas:** BP/24hr(1mi), **other:** HOSPITAL
36	NJ 651, to Warrenville, Basking Ridge, **N**...**gas:** Exxon/service/24hr, **food:** Dunkin Donuts, **other:** A&P, **S**...**gas:** Exxon
33	NJ 525, to Martinsville, Bernardsville, PGA Golf Museum, **N**...**food:** Ciao Italian, **lodging:** Courtyard, Somerset Hills Inn/rest., **S**...**gas:** Exxon, **other:** KwikPik
32mm	scenic overlook wb
29	I-287, to US 202, US 206, I-80, to Morristown, Somerville, **S**...HOSPITAL
26	NJ 523 spur, to North Branch, Lamington
24	NJ 523, to NJ 517, to Oldwick, Whitehouse, **2-3 mi S**...**gas:** Exxon/dsl/24hr, **food:** McDonald's, Readington Diner
20b a	NJ 639(from wb), to Cokesbury, Lebanon, **S**...**gas:** Exxon/24hr, Shell/24hr, Sunoco, **food:** Bagelsmith Deli, Dunkin Donuts, Spinning Wheel Diner, **lodging:** Courtyard, **other:** to Round Valley RA
18	US 22 E, Annandale, Lebanon, **N**...HOSPITAL, same as 17, **S**...Honda
17	NJ 31 S, Clinton, **N**...**gas:** Exxon, Hess/24hr, Mobil/24hr, **food:** Dunkin Donuts/Baskin Robbins, King Buffet, McDonald's, **lodging:** Courtyard
16	NJ 31 N(from eb), Clinton, **N**...same as 17
15	NJ 173 E, to Pittstown, Clinton, **N**...**gas:** Exxon, Shell/dsl/24hr, **food:** Subway, **lodging:** Holiday Inn Select, **other:** museum, **S**...**food:** Cracker Barrel, Frank's Pizza, Hunan Wok, **lodging:** Hampton Inn, **other:** HOSPITAL, $Tree, ShopRite Foods, TJMaxx, Wal-Mart/grill
13	NJ 173 W(from wb), **N**...**food:** Clinton Sta Diner, same as 12

C l i n t o n

Exit #	Services
12	NJ 173, to Jutland, Norton, **N**...**gas:** Clinton/Citgo/Johnny's Rest./dsl/24hr/@, Exxon/Dunkin Donuts/dsl, **other:** to Spruce Run RA, **S**...**gas:** Shell/dsl, **food:** Bagelsmith Deli
11	NJ 173, West Portal, Pattenburg, **N**...**gas:** Shell/dsl, **food:** Chalet Rest., **other:** Jugtown RV Park, to st police
8mm	**rest area both lanes, picnic tables, litter barrels, no restrooms**
7	7 NJ 173, to Bloomsbury, West Portal, **N**...RV camping, **S**...**gas:** Citgo/dsl/rest./24hr, Pilot/Subway/dsl/scales/24hr/@, TA/Mobil/Buger King/dsl/rest./scales/24hr/@
6mm	weigh sta both lanes
6	Warren Glen, Asbury(from eb), no services
4	Warren Glen, Stewartsville(from wb), no services
3	US 22, NJ 173, to Phillipsburg, **N**...**gas:** Getty, US/dsl/24hr, **other:** HOSPITAL, **1 mi N**...**gas:** Citgo/dsl, **food:** Applebee's, Burger King, McDonald's, Panera Bread, Perkins, Pizza Hut, Ruby Tuesday, Sammy's Diner, **lodging:** Phillipsburg Inn, **other:** Circuit City, $Tree, Home Depot, Honda, Kohl's, Lowe's Whse, Michael's, Old Navy, ShopRite Foods, Staples, Stop'n Shop, Target, Wal-Mart/auto, **S**...**other:** Chevrolet
0mm	New Jersey/Pennsylvania state line, Delaware River

Interstate 80

E ↑ W

Exit #	Services
	I-80 begins/ends at G Washington Bridge in Ft Lee, NJ.
73mm	toll plaza eb
72b	US 1 S, US 9, **N**...**food:** Red Oak Rest., **other:** Staples
72a	US 46, NJ 4, **N**...**gas:** BP, Exxon/Subway, Getty, Gulf, Hess/dsl, Mobil, Sunoco, **food:** Bennigan's, **lodging:** Best Western, Holiday Inn, **S**...**gas:** Mobil, Shell, **lodging:** Courtesy Inn, Hilton
71	Broad Ave, Leonia, Englewood, **N**...**gas:** Gulf, **lodging:** Day's Inn, Executive Inn, **S**...**gas:** Shell
70b a	NJ 93, Leonia, Teaneck, **N**...**gas:** Marriott, **other:** HOSPITAL
68b a	I-95, N to New York, S to Philadelphia, to US 46
67	to Bogota(from eb), no services
66	Hudson St, to Hackensack, **N**...**gas:** Getty
65	Green St, S Hackensack, **S**...**gas:** Exxon, **lodging:** Hilton
64b a	NJ 17 S, to US 46 E, Newark, Paramus, **S**...**gas:** BP/24hr, Exxon, **food:** Baskin-Robbins, **lodging:** Crowne Plaza, **other:** PathMark Foods
63	NJ 17 N, **N**...**gas:** BP/24hr, Citgo, Gulf, Hess/dsl/24hr, **other:** HOSPITAL, CVS Drug, Harley-Davidson, Home Depot
62b a	GS Pkwy, to Saddle Brook, **N**...**gas:** Shell, **lodging:** Howard Johnson, Marriott, **S**...**lodging:** Holiday Inn
61	NJ 507, to Garfield, Elmwood Park, **N**...Marcal Paper Co, **S**...**gas:** Sunoco
60	NJ 20, N to Hawthorne, **N**...**other:** HOSPITAL, Michelin/Cooper Tires

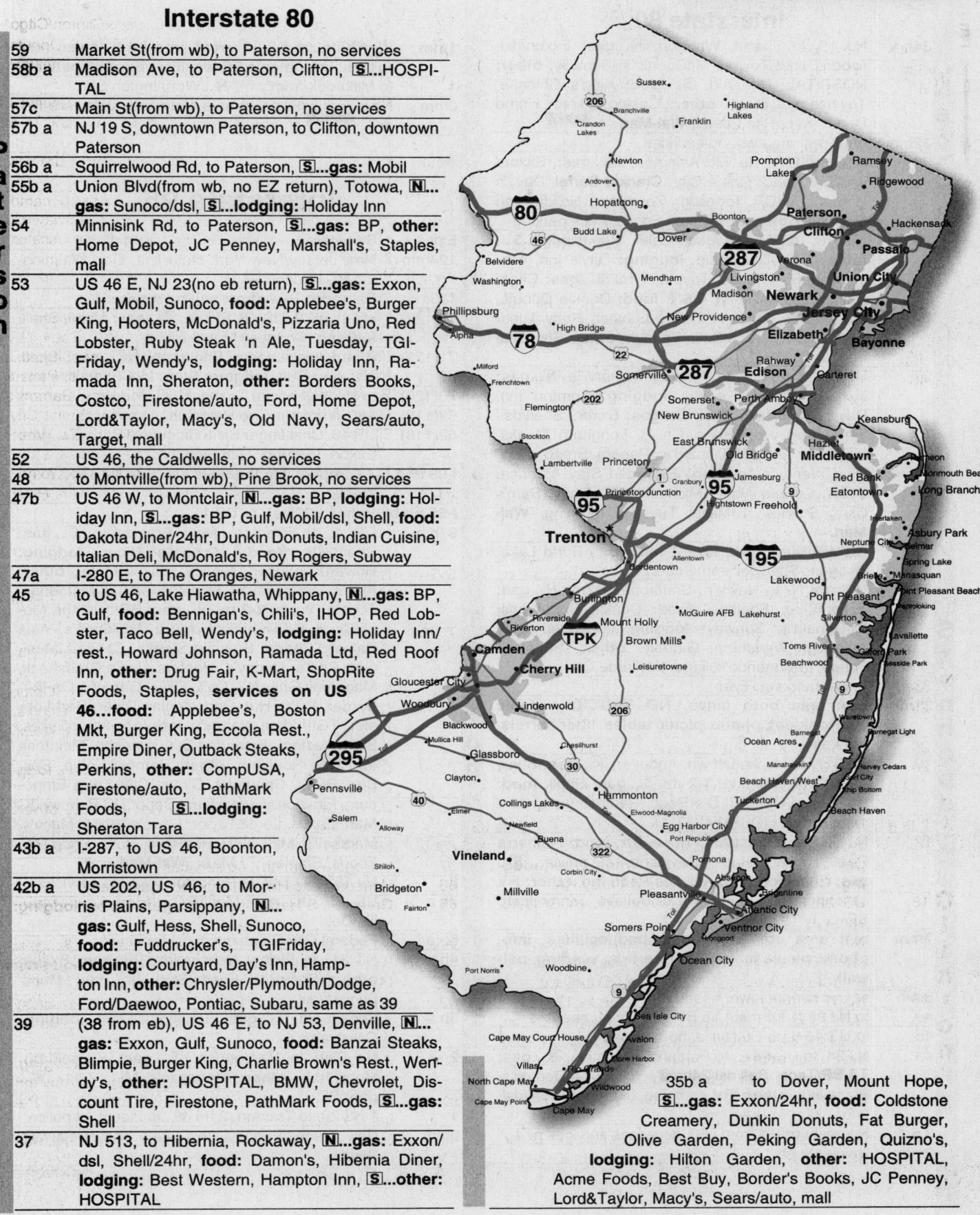

NEW JERSEY

Interstate 80

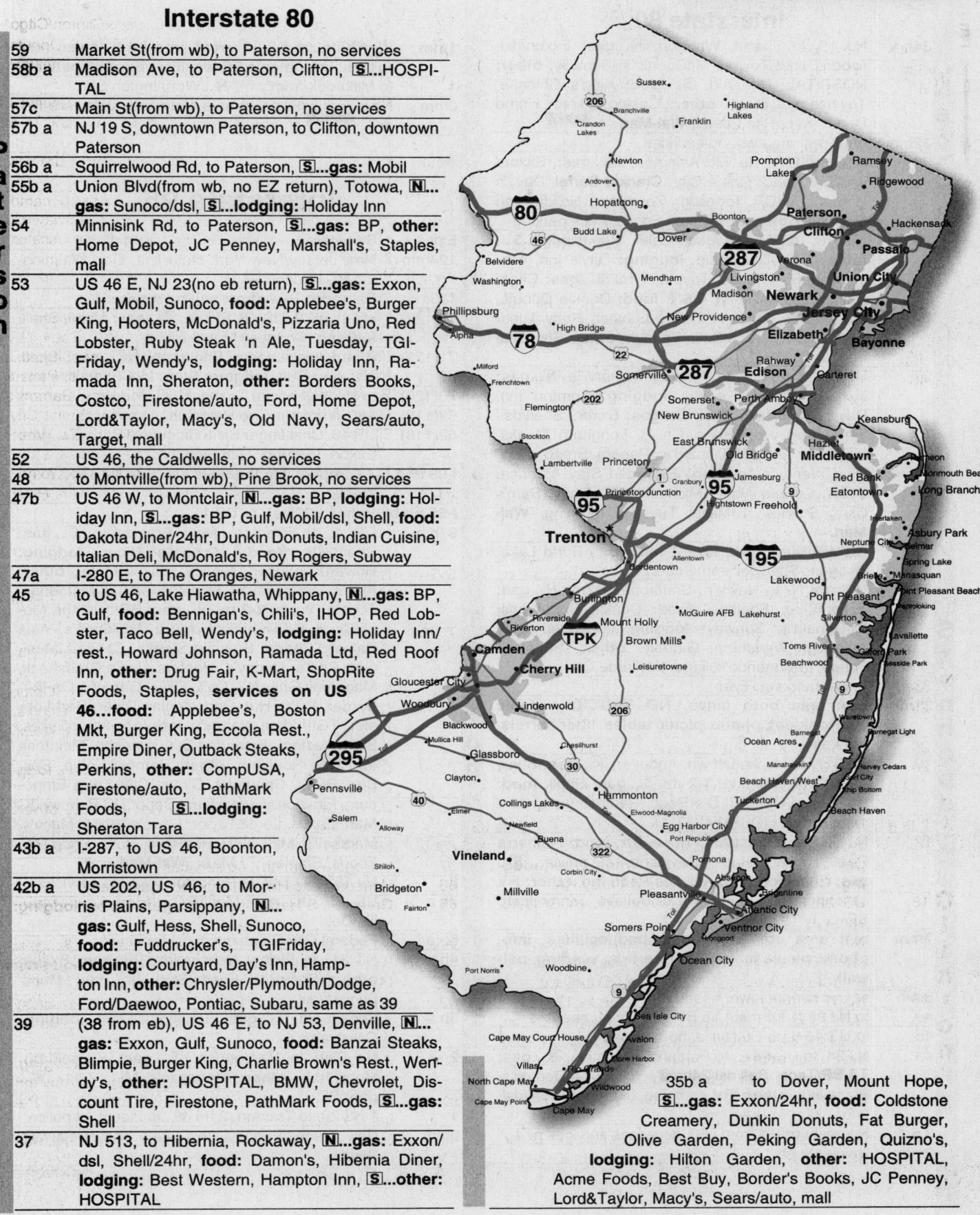

Paterson

59 Market St(from wb), to Paterson, no services

58b a Madison Ave, to Paterson, Clifton, Ⓢ...HOSPITAL

57c Main St(from wb), to Paterson, no services

57b a NJ 19 S, downtown Paterson, to Clifton, downtown Paterson

56b a Squirrelwood Rd, to Paterson, Ⓢ...gas: Mobil

55b a Union Blvd(from wb, no EZ return), Totowa, Ⓝ...gas: Sunoco/dsl, Ⓢ...lodging: Holiday Inn

54 Minnisink Rd, to Paterson, Ⓢ...gas: BP, other: Home Depot, JC Penney, Marshall's, Staples, mall

53 US 46 E, NJ 23(no eb return), Ⓢ...gas: Exxon, Gulf, Mobil, Sunoco, food: Applebee's, Burger King, Hooters, McDonald's, Pizzaria Uno, Red Lobster, Ruby Steak 'n Ale, Tuesday, TGIFriday, Wendy's, lodging: Holiday Inn, Ramada Inn, Sheraton, other: Borders Books, Costco, Firestone/auto, Ford, Home Depot, Lord&Taylor, Macy's, Old Navy, Sears/auto, Target, mall

52 US 46, the Caldwells, no services

48 to Montville(from wb), Pine Brook, no services

47b US 46 W, to Montclair, Ⓝ...gas: BP, lodging: Holiday Inn, Ⓢ...gas: BP, Gulf, Mobil/dsl, Shell, food: Dakota Diner/24hr, Dunkin Donuts, Indian Cuisine, Italian Deli, McDonald's, Roy Rogers, Subway

47a I-280 E, to The Oranges, Newark

45 to US 46, Lake Hiawatha, Whippany, Ⓝ...gas: BP, Gulf, food: Bennigan's, Chili's, IHOP, Red Lobster, Taco Bell, Wendy's, lodging: Holiday Inn/rest., Howard Johnson, Ramada Ltd, Red Roof Inn, other: Drug Fair, K-Mart, ShopRite Foods, Staples, **services on US 46...food:** Applebee's, Boston Mkt, Burger King, Eccola Rest., Empire Diner, Outback Steaks, Perkins, other: CompUSA, Firestone/auto, PathMark Foods, Ⓢ...lodging: Sheraton Tara

43b a I-287, to US 46, Boonton, Morristown

42b a US 202, US 46, to Morris Plains, Parsippany, Ⓝ...gas: Gulf, Hess, Shell, Sunoco, food: Fuddrucker's, TGIFriday, lodging: Courtyard, Day's Inn, Hampton Inn, other: Chrysler/Plymouth/Dodge, Ford/Daewoo, Pontiac, Subaru, same as 39

39 (38 from eb), US 46 E, to NJ 53, Denville, Ⓝ...gas: Exxon, Gulf, Sunoco, food: Banzai Steaks, Blimpie, Burger King, Charlie Brown's Rest., Wendy's, other: HOSPITAL, BMW, Chevrolet, Discount Tire, Firestone, PathMark Foods, Ⓢ...gas: Shell

37 NJ 513, to Hibernia, Rockaway, Ⓝ...gas: Exxon/dsl, Shell/24hr, food: Damon's, Hibernia Diner, lodging: Best Western, Hampton Inn, Ⓢ...other: HOSPITAL

35b a to Dover, Mount Hope, Ⓢ...gas: Exxon/24hr, food: Coldstone Creamery, Dunkin Donuts, Fat Burger, Olive Garden, Peking Garden, Quizno's, lodging: Hilton Garden, other: HOSPITAL, Acme Foods, Best Buy, Border's Books, JC Penney, Lord&Taylor, Macy's, Sears/auto, mall

Interstate 80

E	
↕	
W	

34b a — NJ 15, to Sparta, Wharton, **N**...**gas:** Exxon/dsl, **food:** Donut Towne, McDonald's, Subway, **other:** HOSPITAL, Rite Aid, **S**...**food:** King's Chinese, Townsquare Diner, **other:** Costco, $Tree, Home Depot, ShopRite Foods, Wal-Mart

32mm — truck rest area wb, no services

30 — Howard Blvd, to Mt Arlington, **N**...**gas:** Exxon/dsl/24hr, **food:** China City, Cracker Barrel, Davy's Hotdogs, IHOP, **lodging:** Courtyard, Holiday Inn Express, **other:** QuickChek Foods, truck parking

28 — NJ 10, to Ledgewood, Lake Hopatcong, **S**...**food:** Cliff's Dairymaid, **lodging:** Day's Inn, **other:** ShopRite Foods, Toyota, **1 mi S**...**gas:** Citgo, Delta Gas, Hess/dsl, G&N, **food:** Dunkin Donuts, McDonald's, Pizza Hut, Red Lobster, Ruby Tuesday, Subway, Taco Bell, Wendy's, **other:** ShopRite Foods, Toyota

27 — US 206 S, NJ 182, to Netcong, Somerville, **N**...**gas:** Mobil/dsl, **food:** Perkins, **lodging:** Comfort Inn, Day's Inn, **other:** Ford, **S**...**gas:** Exxon, Shell/dsl/24hr, **food:** Applebees, Chili's, Longhorn Steaks, Macaroni Grill, McDonald's, Panera Bread, Subway, Wendy's, **lodging:** Extended Stay America, **other:** Lowe's Whse, Michael's, Old Navy, Sam's Club, Staples, TJMaxx, Tuesday Morning, Wal-Mart

26 — US 46 W(from wb, no EZ return), to Budd Lake, **S**...**gas:** Shell/dsl, same as 27

25 — US 206 N, to Newton, Stanhope, **1-2mi N**...**gas:** Exxon/24hr, Shell/dsl, **food:** Dunkin Doughnuts, McDonald's, Subway, **lodging:** Extended Stay America, Wyndham Garden, **other:** ShopRite Foods, to Waterloo Village, Int Trade Ctr

23.5mm — Musconetcong River

21mm — **rest area both lanes, NO TRUCKS, scenic overlook(eb), phone, picnic tables, litter barrels, petwalk**

19 — NJ 517, to Hackettstown, Andover, **N**...**gas:** Shell, **other:** RV camping, **1-2 mi S**...**gas:** Shell, **food:** Big Scoop Cafe, BLD's Rest., Panther Valley Inn/rest., **other:** HOSPITAL, 7-11

12 — NJ 521, to Blairstown, Hope, **N**...**food:** Nathan's Rest., **other:** Harley-Davidson, st police, **S**...**gas:** Shell, **lodging:** Millrace Pond Inn, **other:** RV camping(5mi), Land of Make Believe, Jenny Jump SF

7mm — **rest area eb, full(handicapped)facilities, info, phone, picnic tables, litter barrels, vending, petwalk**

6mm — scenic overlook wb, no trailers

4c — to NJ 94 N(from eb), to Blairstown, no services

4b — to US 46 E, to Buttzville, no services

4a — NJ 94, to US 46 E, to Portland, Columbia, **N**...**gas:** TA/BP/Taco Bell/dsl/24hr/@, **food:** McDonald's, Pizza Hut, **other:** RV camping, **S**...**gas:** Shell/dsl/24hr

3.5mm — Hainesburg Rd(from wb), accesses services at 4

2mm — weigh sta eb

1mm — **Worthington SF, S**...**rest area both lanes, restrooms, info, picnic tables, litter barrels, petwalk**

1 — to Millbrook(from wb), **N**...Worthington SF

0mm — New Jersey/Pennsylvania state line, Delaware River

Interstate 95

Exit #	Services
124mm	New Jersey/New York state line, Geo Washington Br, Hudson River
123mm	Palisades Pkwy(from sb), no services
72(122)	US 1, US 9, US 46, Ft Lee, **E**...**gas:** Mobil, Shell, **lodging:** Courtesy Motel, Hilton
71(121)	Broad Ave, Leonia, Englewood, **E**...**gas:** Shell, **W**...**gas:** Gulf, **lodging:** Day's Inn, Executive Inn
70(120)	to NJ 93, Leonia, Teaneck, **W**...**lodging:** Marriott
69(119)	I-80 W(from sb), to Paterson, no services
68(118)	US 46, Challenger Blvd, Ridgefield Park, **E**...**gas:** Exxon, **lodging:** Hampton Inn

I-95 and NJ Turnpike run together sb. See NJ TPK, exits 7a-18.

I-95 nb becomes I-295 sb at US 1.

67b a	US 1, to Trenton, New Brunswick, **E**...**gas:** Shell/24hr, **food:** Michael's Diner, **lodging:** Howard Johnson, Sleepy Hollow Motel, **other:** Acura, Dodge/Isuzu, Lincoln/Mercury, Mercedes, Toyota, Volvo, **1-3 mi W**...**gas:** BP/dsl/24hr, Mobil/Circle K/Blimpie/dsl, **food:** Applebee's, Asia Palace, Charlie Brown's Steaks, Chevy's Mexican, Chili's, Denny's, Hooters, Joe's Crabshack, Macaroni Grill, NY Deli, Olive Garden, On-the-Border, Pizza Hut, Princetonian Diner, Red Lobster, TGIFriday, Wendy's, **lodging:** AmeriSuites, Best Western, Extended Stay America, McIntosh Inn, Red Roof Inn, **other:** Barnes&Noble, Best Buy, BMW, Chevrolet, Circuit City, Drug Emporium, Firestone/auto, Home Depot, JC Penney, K-Mart, Lexus, Lord&Taylor, Lowe's Whse, Macy's, Marshall's, Mini, NTB, PepBoys, Ross, Shop Rite Foods, Staples, TJ Maxx, Wal-Mart, mall
8	NJ 583, NJ 546, to Princeton Pike, no services
7b a	US 206, **W**...**gas:** Mobil/24hr, **food:** Lawrenceville Deli
5b a	Federal City Rd(sb only), no services
4b a	NJ 31, to Ewing, Pennington, **E**...**gas:** Exxon, **other:** ShopRite Foods(3mi), **W**...**gas:** Mobil/Blimpie/dsl
3b a	Scotch Rd, **E**...**gas:** Sunoco/dsl(2mi), **lodging:** Courtyard
2	NJ 579, to Harbourton, **E**...**gas:** Exxon(1mi), Mobil(1mi), **other:** Marrazzo's Mkt, 7-11, **W**...**gas:** BP
1	1 NJ 29, to Trenton, **2 mi W**...museum, st police
0mm	New Jersey/Pennsylvania state line, Delaware River

Stanhope

Trenton

N ↕ S

Turnpike

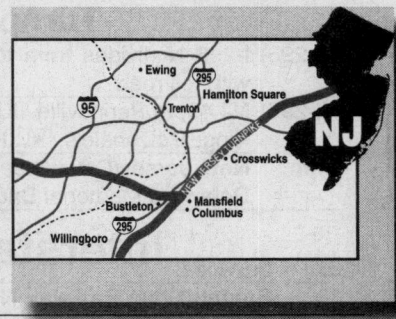

Exit #	Services
18(117)	US 46 E, Ft Lee, Hackensack, last exit before toll sb
17(116)	Lincoln Tunnel
115mm	**Vince Lombardi Service Plaza nb...Sunoco/dsl, Big Boy, Nathan's, Roy Rogers, TCBY, gifts**
114mm	toll plaza, phone
16W(113)	NJ 3, Secaucus, Rutherford, E...gas: Hess, Shell, **lodging:** Hilton, M Plaza Hotel, W...**lodging:** Sheraton, **other:** Meadowlands
112mm	**Alexander Hamilton Service Area sb...Sunoco, Roy Rogers, gifts**
16E(112)	NJ 3, Secaucus, E...Lincoln Tunnel
15W(109)	I-280, Newark, The Oranges
15E(107)	US 1, US 9, Newark, Jersey City, E...Lincoln Tunnel
14c	Holland Tunnel
14b	Jersey City, no services
14a	Bayonne, no services
14(105)	I-78 W, US 1, US 9, **2 mi** W...**lodging:** Fairfield Inn, Holiday Inn, SpringHill Suites, **other:** airport
102mm	**Halsey Service Area, Sunoco, Roy Rogers, other services in Elizabeth**
13a(102)	Elizabeth, E...**lodging:** Courtyard, Extended Stay America, Residence Inn, W...**food:** McDonald's, **lodging:** DoubleTree, Econolodge, Hilton, Sheraton, Wyndham Garden, services on US1/US9
13(100)	I-278, to Verrazano Narrows Bridge
12(96)	Carteret, Rahway, E...**food:** McDonald's, **lodging:** Holiday Inn, W...**food:** Radisson
93mm	**Cleveland Service Area nb...food: Nathans, Roy Roger's, Starbucks, T Edison Service Area sb... gas: Sunoco/dsl, food: Burger King, Dunkin Donuts, Popeye's, Sbarro's, Starbucks**
11(91)	US 9, Garden State Pkwy, to Woodbridge, E... **lodging:** Hampton Inn, Homestead Suites, **other:** Home Depot
10(88)	I-287, NJ 514, to Perth Amboy, E...**lodging:** Courtyard, W...**gas:** Hess/dsl, **lodging:** Holiday Inn,
9(83)	US 1, NJ 18, to New Brunswick, E Brunswick, E... **gas:** Gulf, Hess/dsl, **food:** Grand Buffet, Houlihan's, On-the-Border, **lodging:** Days Inn, Motel 6, **other:** Eckerd, Radio Shack, Sears/auto, W...**gas:** Exxon, **food:** Bennigan's, Fuddrucker's, **lodging:** Hilton, Holiday Inn Express, Howard Johnson
79mm	**Kilmer Service Area, Kilmer Service Area nb... gas: Sunoco/dsl, food: Burger King, Sbarro's, Starbucks, TCBY, other: gifts**
8a(74)	to Jamesburg, Cranbury, E...**lodging:** Holiday Inn/ rest., W...**lodging:** Courtyard, Crowne Plaza
72mm	**Pitcher Service Area sb...gas: Sunoco/dsl, food:** Burger King, Cinnabon, Country Kitchen, Nathan's, Roy Rogers, Sbarro's Mexican, Starbucks, TCBY
8(67)	NJ 33, NJ 571, Hightstown, E...**gas:** Exxon/dsl, Hess/dsl, Mobil, Shell, **food:** 8 Diner, Prestige Diner, **lodging:** Day's Inn, Hampton Inn, Holiday Inn, Quality Inn, **other:** Thriftway Foods, W...**food:** Coach&4 Rest., **lodging:** TownHouse Motel
7a(60)	I-195 W to Trenton, E to Neptune
59mm	**Richard Stockton Service Area sb... gas: Sunoco/dsl, food: Blimpie, Pizza Hut, Starbucks, TCBY, Woodrow Wilson Service Area nb...gas: Sunoco, food: Roy Rogers**
7(54)	US 206, to Bordentown, to Ft Dix, McGuire AFB, to I-295, Trenton, **Services** W **on US 206...gas:** Mobil/dsl, Petro/dsl/rest./24hr/@, Pilot/Wendy's/dsl/@, Sunoco, WaWa, **food:** Burger King, Denny's, **lodging:** Best Western/rest., Comfort Inn, Day's Inn/rest., Hampton Inn, Ramada Inn, **other:** RV Ctr
6(51)	I-276, to Pa Turnpike
5(44)	to Mount Holly, Willingboro, E...**gas:** US gas/dsl, **food:** Applebee's, Cracker Barrel, Karma Rest., McDonald's, **lodging:** Best Western, Hampton Inn, Howard Johnson, W...**gas:** Exxon/dsl, GasWay, Mobil, **food:** Applebee's, Burger King, TGIFriday, **lodging:** Best Western, Econolodge, Holiday Inn Express, **other:** $Tree, Home Depot, Kohl's, Target
39mm	**James Fenimore Cooper Service Area nb...gas: Sunoco/dsl, food: Burger King, Cinabon, Popeye's, Roy Rogers, TCBY, other: gifts**
4(34)	NJ 73, to Philadelphia, Camden, E...**gas:** Exxon, Mobil/Circle K/dsl, 7-11, **food:** Bennigan's, Cracker Barrel, Chili's, Copperfield's Rest., Denny's, Macaroni Grill, McDonald's, Sage Rest., Wendy's, **lodging:** Candlewood Suites, Comfort Inn, Extended Stay America, Hampton Inn, Howard Johnson, McIntosh Inn, Studio+, Wyndham Hotel, **other:** Cadillac, Ford, Saturn, West Marine, **1-2 mi** W...**gas:** Exxon, Gulf/ dsl, Hess, Mobil/dsl, Shell, Texaco, **food:** Bob Evans, Burger King, Dunkin Donuts, KFC, Pizza Hut, **lodging:** Courtyard, Day's Inn, DoubleTree Motel, Econolodge, Fairfield Inn, Laurel Place Inn, Hampton Inn, Motel 6, Radisson, Ramada Inn/rest., Red Roof Inn, Super 8, Track&Turf Motel, **other:** Lincoln/Mercury, Mazda, transmissions, to st aquarium
30mm	Walt Whitman Service Area, **Walt Whitman Service Area sb...gas: Sunoco, food: Cinnabon, Roy Rogers, Nathan's, TCBY, other: gifts**
3(26)	NJ 168, Atlantic City Expwy, Walt Whitman Br, Camden, Woodbury, E...**gas:** WaWa, **lodging:** Blemawr Motel, Comfort Inn, Holiday Inn, **other:** CVS Drug, W...**gas:** BP, Coastal, Valero, Xtra/dsl, **food:** Dunkin Donuts, Papa John's, Pizza Hut, Wendy's, **lodging:** Econolodge
2(13)	US 322, to Swedesboro, W...**gas:** Shell/dsl
5mm	**Barton Service Area sb...gas: Sunoco, Burger King, Nathan's, Pizza Hut, Starbucks, TCBY, Fenwick Service Area nb...gas: Sunoco, food: TCBY**
1(1.2)	Deepwater, W...**gas:** Mobil/dsl, Pilot/Subway/dsl/ 24hr/@, **lodging:** Comfort Suites, Friendship Motor Inn, Holiday Inn, Welsley Inn
1mm	toll road begins/ends

NEW JERSEY

Turnpike

2(I-295)	I-295 N divides from toll road, I-295 S converges with toll road
1(I-295)	NJ 49, to Pennsville, E...gas: Exxon, food: Burger King, McDonald's, W...lodging: Seaview Motel
0mm	New Jersey/Delaware state line, Delaware River, Delaware Memorial Bridge

Interstate 195

Exit # Services

36	Garden State Parkway N. I-195 begins/ends on GS Pkwy, exit 98.
35b a	NJ 34, to Brielle, GS Pkwy S., Pt Pleasant, 2 mi S...gas: Exxon/dsl/24hr, Getty, Lukoil, food: Shogun Japanese
31b a	NJ 547, NJ 524, to Farmingdale, N...food: Mulligans Cafe, other: Chevrolet, to Allaire SP
28b a	US 9, to Freehold, Lakewood, N...gas: Lukoil, food: Ivy League Rest., Stewart's Drive-In, S...gas: Exxon/24hr, Getty, Gulf, WaWa, food: Applebee's, Arby's, Boston Mkt, Burger King, Blimpie, Carino's, Chick-fil-A, China Moon, Coldstone Creamery, Dunkin Donuts, Jersey Mike's, Longhorn Steaks, McDonald's, Panera Bread, Pizza Hut, Starbucks, Taco Bell, lodging: Capri Motel(3mi), other: Barnes&Noble, $Store, Drug Fair, GNC, K-Mart, Kohl's, Lowe's Whse, Office Depot, PathMark Foods, PepBoys, Radio Shack, Staples, Stop&Shop, Target, Walgreens, Wal-Mart
22	to Jackson Mills, Georgia, N...to Turkey Swamp Park, 2 mi S...food: McDonald's, other: ShopRite Foods
21	NJ 526, NJ 527, to Jackson, Siloam
16	NJ 537, to Freehold, N...gas: Remington/dsl/LP, Sunoco, food: FoodCourt, Gianmarco's Pizza, Java Moon Café, other: HOSPITAL, Outlets/famous brands, S...gas: Wawa/dsl/24hr, food: BellaV Pizzaria, Burger King, Chicken Holiday, KFC, McDonald's, Rio Grande Mexican, Tommy's Rest., Vinci's Pizza, other: 6Flags Themepark
11	NJ 524, Imlaystown, S...to Horse Park of NJ
8	NJ 539, Allentown, S...gas: Mobil(1mi), Valero/repair, food: American Hero Deli, other: Crosswicks HP, vet
7	NJ 526(no eb return), Robbinsville, Allentown, 1 mi S...food: La Piazza Ristorante
6	NJ Tpk, N to NY, S to DE Memorial Br
5b a	US 130, N...gas: Delta/dsl, food: Domino's, Dunkin Donuts, Ruster's Deli, ShrimpKing Rest., other: Harley-Davidson, vet, S...gas: GS Fuel/dsl, food: Chick-fil-A, Chili's, China Buffet, Cracker Barrel, Longhorn Steaks, Savoy's Rest., Red Robin, Ruby Tuesday, Wendy's, lodging: Econolodge(4mi), other: Barnes&Noble, BJ's Wholesale, GNC, Harry's Army Navy, Home Depot, Kohl's, Lowe's Whse, Michael's, Ross, ShopRite Foods, USPO, Wal-Mart/auto, mall, to state aquarium
3b a	Hamilton Square, Yardville, N...HOSPITAL
2	US 206 S, S Broad St, Yardville, N...other: 7-11, S...gas: Shell, food: Burger King, McDonald's, Subway, Wendy's, other: Acme Foods, CVS Drug, Eckerd
1b a	US 206, N...food: Fortune House, Taco Bell, S...other: ShopRite Foods
0mm	I-295, I-195 begins/ends.,

Interstate 287

Exit # Services

68mm	New Jersey/New York state line
66	NJ 17 S, Mahwah, 1-3 mi E...gas: Getty, Gulf, Mahwah Fuel/deli, Mobil/Subway/dsl, food: Burger King, Mason Jar Rest., McDonald's, 17 Diner, lodging: Best Western, Comfort Inn, Courtyard, Doubletree, Homewood Suites, Sheraton, Wellesley Inn
59	NJ 208 S, Franklin Lakes, W...food: Blimpie, other: Super Stop'n Shop Foods
58	US 202, Oakland, E...gas: Mobil, W...gas: Exxon/24hr, food: Mike's Doghouse, other: ShopRite Foods
57	Skyline Dr, Ringwood, no services
55	NJ 511, Pompton Lakes, E...other: A&P, W...gas: Getty/dsl, food: Burger King, Dunkin Doughnuts, other: SuperFoodTown
53	NJ 511A, rd 694, Bloomingdale, Pompton Lakes, E...gas: Sunoco, Valero, food: Blimpie
52b a	NJ 23, Riverdale, Wayne, Butler, E...gas: BP, Mobil, Sunoco/dsl, food: Fuddrucker's(3mi), lodging: Welsley Motel(3mi), other: HOSPITAL, A&P, Buick/Pontiac/GMC, W...gas: Mobil, Shell/24hr, food: McDonald's, Ruppert's Rest.
47	US 202, Montville, Lincoln Park, E...gas: Exxon/24hr, food: Harrigan's Rest.
45	Myrtle Ave, Boonton, W...gas: Citgo, Exxon, food: Dunkin Donuts, McDonald's, Subway, other: A&P/24hr, Buick/GMC, Drug Fair, GNCc
43	Intervale Rd, to Mountain Lakes, E...gas: Shell, W...Dodge
42	US 46, US 202(from sb only), W...gas: Exxon, Shell, Sunoco, food: Applebee's, Dunkin Doughnuts, Fuddrucker's, McDonald's, Subway, lodging: Courtyard, Day's Inn, Embassy Suites, Garden Suites, Hampton Inn, other: Chrysler/Jeep/Pontiac/Subaru, Dodge, Ford, GNC
41b a	I-80, E to New York, W to Delaware Water Gap
40	NJ 511, Parsippany Rd, to Whippany, W...gas: Mobil, Shell/dsl, Woroco Gas, food: Frank&Son Pizza, Fuddrucker's(2mi), McDonald's, Wok's Chinese, Subway, lodging: Embassy Suites(1mi)
39b a	NJ 10, Dover, Whippany, E...lodging: Ramada Inn, other: PathMark Foods, W...gas: Mobil, food: Hong Kong Buffet, McDonald's, Wendy's, lodging: Hilton Garden, Marriott, Welsley Motel, other: Barnes&Noble, Buick/GMC/Isuzu, Stop'n Shop Foods
37	NJ 24 E, Springfield, no services
36b a	rd 510, Morris Ave, Lafayette, no services
35	NJ 124, South St, Madison Ave, Morristown, E...food: Friendly's, W...lodging: Best Western, HQ Plaza Hotel, other: HOSPITAL
33	Harter Rd, no services
33mm	rest area nb, full(handicapped)facilities, phone, picnic tables, litter barrels, vending, petwalk
30b a	to US 202, N Maple Ave, Basking Ridge, E...food: Ironwood Rest., lodging: North Maple Inn, W...gas: Gulf, food: Burger King, Friendly's, GrainHouse Rest., Thirsty Turtle Rest., lodging: Olde Mill Inn/rest.
26b a	rd 525 S, Mt Airy Rd, Liberty Corner, 3 mi E...gas: Exxon/24hr, lodging:Courtyard, Summerset Hotel, other: Quick-Pik Foods

Interstate 287

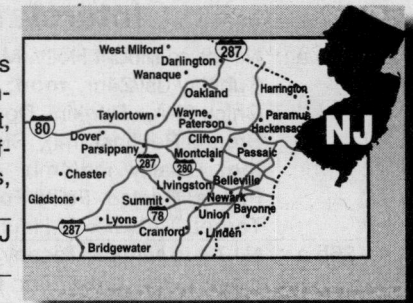

22b a	US 202, US 206, Pluckemin, Bedminster, **E**...**gas:** Exxon, **food:** Burger King, Golden Chinese, **other:** King's Foods, **W**...**gas:** Shell, **food:** Dunkin Donuts
21b a	I-78, E to NY, W to PA
17	US 206(from sb) Bridgewater, **E**...**other:** Buick, **W**...**gas:** Hess, **food:** TGIFriday, **other:** Best Buy, Borders Books, Lord&Taylor, Macy's, mall
14b a	US 22, to US 202/206, **E**...**gas:** Hess/dsl, **other:** Chevrolet/Lexus, **W**...**gas:** BP, **food:** Felix #9 Diner, Fuddrucker's, Red Lobster, **lodging:** Day's Inn, Red Bull Inn, **other:** Acura, Mercedes
13b a	NJ 28, Bound Brook, **E**...**gas:** BP/24hr, Mobil/dsl, **food:** Burger King, Costa del Sol Mexican, Dunkin Doughnuts, Good Time Buffet, Joey's Grill, King Lobster Buffet, Subway, **other:** ShopRite Foods, Walgreen, **W**...**food:** Applebee's, ChuckeCheese, McDonald's, **lodging:** Hilton Garden, **other:** HOSPITAL, Costco, Home Depot, Marshall's, Michael's, Old Navy, PepBoys, Target
12	Weston Canal Rd, Manville, **E**...**gas:** Shell, **W**...**food:** SportsTime Rest., **lodging:** Ramada Inn
10	NJ 527, Easton Ave, New Brunswick, **E**...**lodging:** Marriott, **W**...**gas:** BP, **lodging:** Courtyard, Holiday Inn, Doubletree, Hampton Inn, Staybridge Suites, **other:** HOSPITAL, Garden State Exhibit Ctr
9	NJ 514, River Rd, **W**...**lodging:** Embassy Suites, Sheraton
8.5mm	weigh sta nb
8	Possumtown Rd, Highland Park, no services
7	S Randolphville Rd, Piscataway, **E**...**gas:** Mobil
6	Washington Ave, Piscataway, **W**...**food:** Applebee's, BBQ, TGIFriday, Johnny Careno's, Longhorn Steaks, **other:** ShopRite Foods, same as 5
5	NJ 529, Stelton Rd, Dunellen, **E**...**gas:** Gulf, Mobil, Shell, Texaco/dsl, **food:** KFC, Piancone Ristorante, **lodging:** Ramada Ltd, **other:** Home Depot, NAPA, **W**...**gas:** Exxon, **food:** Burger King, Friendly's, Gianni Pizza, Grand Buffet, McDonald's, Red Lobster, Taco Bell, Uno Pizzaria, Wendy's, **lodging:** Best Western, Day's Inn, Motel 6, Holiday Inn, **other:** K-Mart, Lowe's Whse, PathMark Foods, Pep Boys, Radio Shack, Staples, Stern's, Wal-Mart/auto
4	Durham Ave(no EZ nb return), S Plainfield, **E**...**gas:** Mobil/dsl, **other:** HOSPITAL
3	New Durham Rd(from sb), **E**...**gas:** Shell, **W**...**lodging:** Red Roof Inn, **other:** Walgreen
2b a	NJ 27, Metuchen, New Brunswick, **W**...**gas:** BP, Mobil, **other:** Costco
1b a	US 1, **1-2 mi N** on US 1...**gas:** Exxon/dsl, Getty, RaceWay, **food:** Bennigan's, Blimpie, Boston Mkt, Dunkin Donuts, KFC, Macaroni Grill, McDonald's, Menlo Park Diner, Red Lobster, Ruby Tuesday, Sizzler, Steak&Ale, Uno Pizzaria, Wendy's, White Castle, **lodging:** Lee's Motel, Roosevelt Motel, **other:** Best Buy, Drug Fair, Ford, Goodyear/auto, Macy's, Marshall's, Nordstrom's, Sears/auto, ShopRite Foods, Staples, Stern's, mall, **S**...**gas:** Shell, **food:** Applebee's, Boston Mkt, Burger King, ChuckE-Cheese, Grand Buffet, McDonald's, **lodging:** Welles-

ley Inn, **other:** BJ's Whse, BMW, CompUSA, Home Depot, Infiniti, Mercedes, Office Depot, PepBoys, Stop&Shop Foods

I-287	begins/ends on NJ 440.

Interstate 295

Exit #	Services
67b a	US 1. I-295 nb becomes I-95 sb at US 1. See NJ I-95, exit 67b a.
65b a	Sloan Ave, **E**...**gas:** Exxon, **food:** Burger King, Subway, Taco Bell, Uno Pizzaria, **other:** CVS Drug, Goodyear, ShopRite Foods
64	NJ 535 N(from sb), to NJ 33 E, same as 63
63b a	NJ 33 W, rd 535, Mercerville, Trenton, **E**...**gas:** Mobil, **food:** Aladdin's Cafe, Applebee's, Boston Mkt, Lobster Dock, McDonald's, Pizza Hut, Popeye's, Vincent's Pizza, Wendy's, **other:** Ford/Lincoln/Mercury, auto repair, **W**...**gas:** Exxon/24hr, **food:** Dunkin Donuts, Golden Gate Diner/24hr, **other:** Advance Parts, WaWa
62	Olden Ave N(from sb, no return), **W**...**gas:** Delta
61b a	Arena Dr, White Horse Ave, **W**...**gas:** 7-11
60b a	I-195, to I-95, W to Trenton, E to Neptune
58mm	scenic overlook both lanes
57b a	US 130, US 206, **E**...**gas:** Mobil, Shell/24hr, **food:** Burger King, Denny's, McDonald's, Rosario's Pizza, **lodging:** Best Western, Comfort Inn, Day's Inn, Econolodge, Hampton Inn, **other:** Acme Foods, **W**...st police
56	US 206 S(from nb, no return), to NJ Tpk, Ft Dix, McGuire AFB, **E**...**gas:** Sunoco, **lodging:** Day's Inn, Holiday Inn Express, same as 57
52b a	rd 656, to Columbus, Florence, **E**...**gas:** Petro/dsl/rest./24hr/@, Pilot/Wendy's/dsl/24hr/@
50mm	**rest area both lanes(7am-11pm), full(handicapped)facilities, phone, picnic tables, litter barrels, vending**
47b a	NJ 541, to Mount Holly, NJ Tpk, Burlington, **E**...**gas:** Exxon/dsl/24hr, GasWay, Mobil/dsl, **food:** Applebee's, Burger King, ChuckECheese, Cracker Barrel, FoodCourt, McDonald's, Taco Bell, TGIFriday, **lodging:** Best Western, Econolodge, Hampton Inn, Holiday Inn Express, Howard Johnson, **other:** MEDICAL CARE, $Express, Home Depot, Kohl's, Sears, Target, mall, **W**...**gas:** Exxon, Gulf/repair, Hess/dsl, **food:** Checker's, Friendly's, Subway, Wedgewood Farms Rest., Wendy's, **other:** HOSPITAL, AutoZone, Acme Foods, K-Mart, Marshall's, Wal-Mart/auto
45b a	to Mt Holly, Willingboro, **W**...**gas:** Lukoil, **other:** HOSPITAL, auto repair
43b a	rd 636, to Rancocas Woods, Delran, **W**...**gas:** Exxon/24hr, **food:** Carlucci's Rest.

N ↑ S

Cherry Hill

Exit	Description
40b a	NJ 38, to Mount Holly, Moorestown, **W**...**gas:** Shell/Subway/dsl/24hr, **food:** Baja Fresh, Burger King, Chick-fil-A, Dunkin Donuts, FoodCourt, Panera Bread, Perkins(3mi), Starbucks, TGIFriday, **lodging:** Quality Inn(4mi), **other:** HOSPITAL, Acme Foods, Costco, Fall's Food, GNC, Jo-Ann Fabrics, Target, TJ Maxx, U-Haul, Wegman's
36b a	NJ 73, to NJ Tpk, Tacony Br, Berlin, **E**...**gas:** Exxon, Lukoil/Circle K/dsl/24hr, **food:** Bennigan's, Bob Evans, Denny's, McDonald's, Sage Diner, Tacconelli's Pizza, Wendy's, **lodging:** Comfort Inn, Courtyard, Day's Inn, Econolodge, Fairfield Inn, Hampton Inn, Howard Johnson, Laurel Inn, McIntosh Inn, Radisson, Red Roof Inn, Super 8, Travelodge, Wingate Inn, **W**...**gas:** City Gas, Shell, **food:** Bertucci's, Boston Mkt, Burger King, Chick-fil-A, Don Pablo, Dunkin Donuts, KFC, McDonald's, Friendly's, Old Town Buffet, Panera Bread, Perkins, Pizza Hut, Ponderosa, Taco Bell, Togo's, Wendy's, **lodging:** Bel-Air Motel, Crossland Suites, Motel 6, Quality Inn, Rodeway Inn, Track&Turf Motel, **other:** Acura, Barnes&Noble, Best Buy, Chrysler, Circuit City, CompUSA, $Tree, Drug Emporium, Firestone/auto, Ford, Goodyear/auto, Home Depot, Infiniti, K-Mart, Lexus, Loehmann's, Lord&Taylor, Lowe's Whse, Macy's, Mitsubishi, NTB, Old Navy, PepBoys, Petsmart, Ross, Sears/auto, ShopRite Foods, mall
34b a	NJ 70, to Camden, Cherry Hill, **E**...**gas:** Exxon/24hr, **food:** Big John's Steaks, Burger King, Dunkin Donuts, Friendly's, Korea Garden Rest., McDonald's, Pizzaria Uno, **lodging:** Extended Stay America, Marriott, Residence Inn, **other:** STS Tire/auto, **W**...**gas:** Citgo, Lukoil, WaWa, **food:** Barone's Grill, Denny's, Elephant & Castle, Old Country Buffet, Steak&Ale, Starbucks, Subway, **lodging:** Clarion, Hilton Philadelphia Cherry Hill(3mi), Holiday Inn(3mi), Howard Johnson(4mi), **other:** HOSPITAL, Magaziner's Drug
32	NJ 561, to Haddonfield, Voorhees, **3 mi E**...**gas:** Lukoil/dsl/24hr, **food:** Applebee's, FoodCourt, Fuddruckers, Olive Garden, **lodging:** Hampton Inn, Wingate Inn, **other:** HOSPITAL, USPO, **W**...**gas:** BP, Shell, **food:** Burger King, Quizno's, **other:** Giant Foods, Ford, 7-11, Stop&Shop Foods
31	Woodcrest Station, no services
30	Warwick Rd(from sb), no services
29b a	US 30, to Berlin, Collingswood, **E**...**gas:** BP, Gulf, Exxon, **food:** Church's, KFC, Wendy's, **other:** AutoZone, Drug Emporium, Home Depot, K-Mart, PathMark Foods, transmissions
28	NJ 168, to NJ Tpk, Belmawr, Mt Ephraim, **E**...**gas:** Citgo, Gulf, Jim's Gas, Shell/dsl, Valero/dsl, Xtra/dsl, WaWa, **food:** Burger King, Club Diner, Dunkin Donuts, Wendy's, **lodging:** Bellmar Motel, Comfort Inn, Econolodge, Holiday Inn, Howard Johnson, Red Roof Inn, Super 8, **other:** $Land, CVS Drug, Walgreens, **W**...**gas:** BP, Exxon/LP/24hr, **food:** McDonald's, Subway, Taco Bell, **lodging:** Budget Inn, **other:** AutoZone, CVS Drug
26	I-76, NJ 42, to I-676, Walt Whitman Bridge, Walt Whitman Bridge
25b a	NJ 47, to Westville, Deptford, no services
24b a	NJ 45, NJ 551(no EZ sb return), to Westville, **E**...**gas:** Getty, **other:** HOSPITAL, **W**...Chevrolet
23	US 130 N, to National Park, no services
22	NJ 644, to Red Bank, Woodbury, **E**...**gas:** Mobil, **1 mi W**...**gas:** Crown Point Trkstp/dsl/@, WaWa, **food:** Wendy's
21	NJ 44 S, Paulsboro, Woodbury, **W**...**food:** WaWa, Wendy's, **lodging:** Westwood Motor Lodge
20	NJ 643, to NJ 660, to National Park, Thorofare, **E**...**lodging:** Best Western, **W**...**lodging:** Red Bank Inn
19	NJ 656, to NJ 44, Mantua, no services
18b a	NJ 667, to NJ 678, Clarksboro, Mt Royal, **E**...**gas:** BP/dsl, TA/Exxon/Buckhorn Rest./dsl/rest./@, **food:** Dunkin Donuts, KFC/Taco Bell, McDonald's, Wendy's, **other:** RV camping, **W**...**gas:** Shell/dsl
17	NJ 680, to Mickleton, Gibbstown, **W**...**gas:** Mobil, **food:** Burger King, **lodging:** Ramada Inn/rest, **other:** Advance Parts, Family$, GNC, Rite Aid, ShopRite Foods/FoodCourt
16b	NJ 551, to Gibbstown, Mickleton, no services
16a	NJ 653, to Paulsboro, Swedesboro, no services
15	NJ 607, to Gibbstown, no services
14	NJ 684, to Repaupo, no services
13	US 130 S, US 322 W, to Bridgeport(from sb, no return), no services
11	US 322 E, to Mullica Hill, no services
10	Ctr Square Rd, to Swedesboro, **E**...**gas:** Exxon/dsl, **food:** Applebee's, Dunkin Donuts/Baskin Robbins, McDonald's, Subway, Wendy's, **lodging:** Hampton Inn, Holiday Inn Select, **other:** Acme Foods/drug, Eckerd, WaWa/deli, **W**...**other:** Camping World RV Supplies/service
7	to Auburn, Pedricktown, **E**...**gas:** AutoTruck/dsl/rest./motel
4	NJ 48, Woodstown, Penns Grove, no services
3mm	weigh sta nb
2mm	**rest area nb, full(handicapped)facilities, info, phone, picnic table, litter barrels, vending**
2c	to US 130(from sb), Deepwater, **W**...**gas:** All-American Plaza/Exxon/dsl/24hr/@, /Flying J/CountryMkt/dsl/LP/24hr/@, **other:** HOSPITAL
2b	US 40 E, to NJ Tpk, **E**...**gas:** Mobil/dsl, Pilot/Subway/dsl/24hr/@, **lodging:** Comfort Inn, Econolodge, Friendship Motel, Holiday Inn Express, Quality Inn, Wellesley Inn
2a	US 40 W(from nb), to Delaware Bridge
1c	NJ 551 S, Hook Rd, to Salem, **E**...**lodging:** White Oaks Motel, **W**...HOSPITAL
1b	US 130 N(from nb), Penns Grove, no services
1a	NJ 49 E, to Pennsville, Salem, **E**...**gas:** Exxon/dsl/repair, **food:** Burger King, Cracker Barrel, KFC/Taco Bell, McDonald's, **lodging:** Hampton Inn, **W**...**gas:** Coastal, **lodging:** Seaview Motel
0mm	New Jersey/Delaware state line, Delaware River, Delaware Memorial Bridge

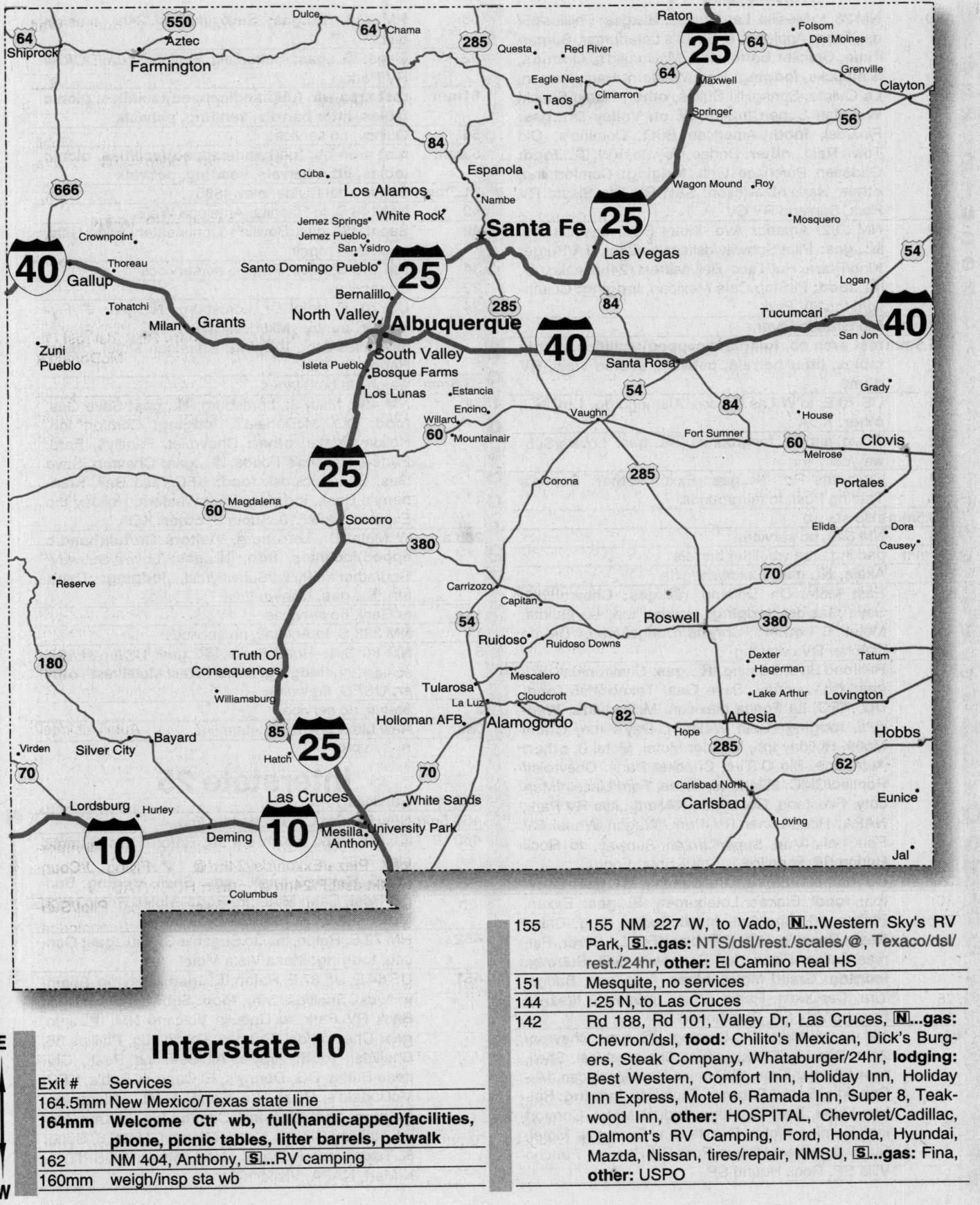

NEW MEXICO

155	155 NM 227 W, to Vado, 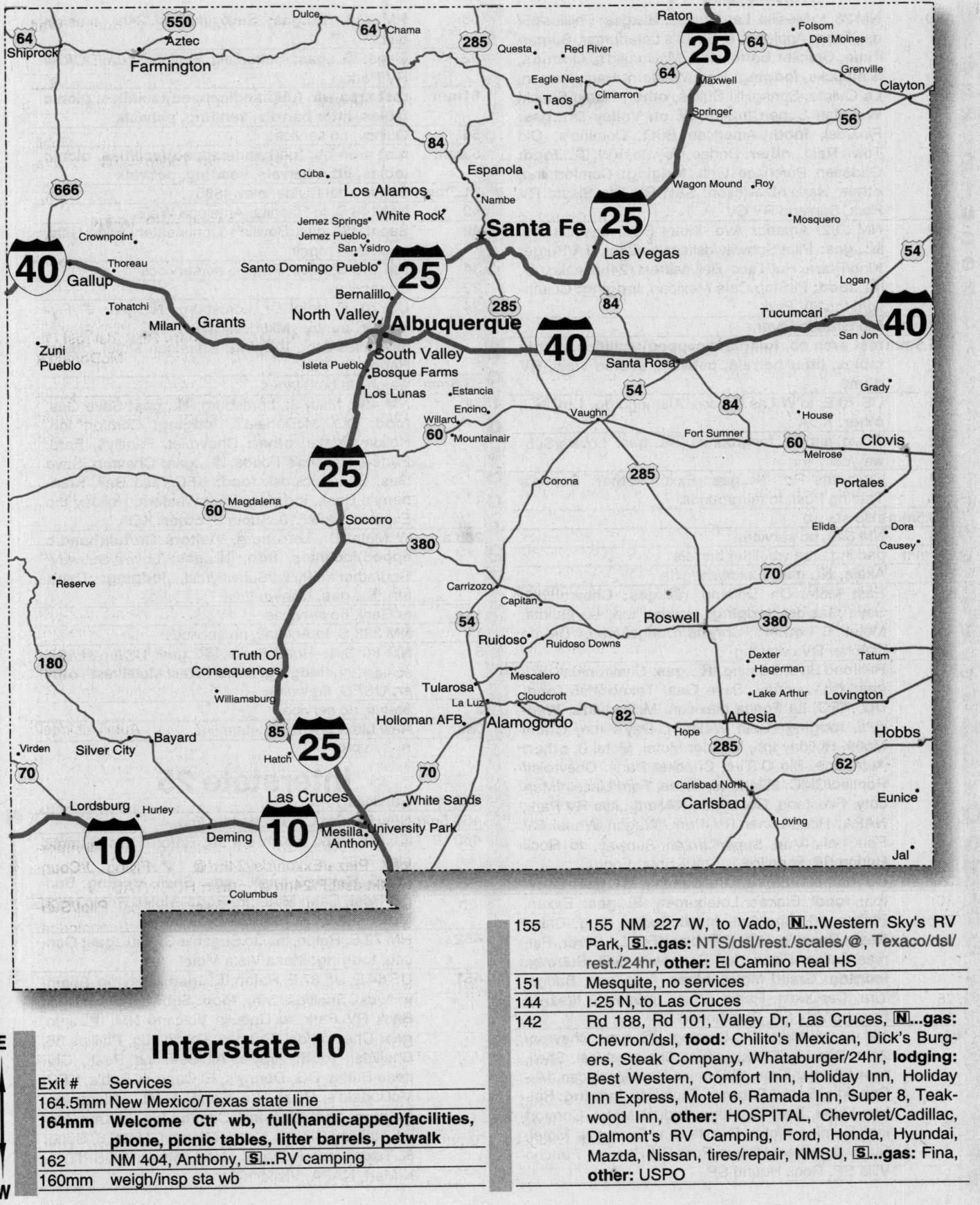...Western Sky's RV Park, S...gas: NTS/dsl/rest./scales/@, Texaco/dsl/ rest./24hr, other: El Camino Real HS
151	Mesquite, no services
144	I-25 N, to Las Cruces
142	Rd 188, Rd 101, Valley Dr, Las Cruces, N...gas: Chevron/dsl, food: Chilito's Mexican, Dick's Burgers, Steak Company, Whataburger/24hr, lodging: Best Western, Comfort Inn, Holiday Inn, Holiday Inn Express, Motel 6, Ramada Inn, Super 8, Teakwood Inn, other: HOSPITAL, Chevrolet/Cadillac, Dalmont's RV Camping, Ford, Honda, Hyundai, Mazda, Nissan, tires/repair, NMSU, S...gas: Fina, other: USPO

E

↕

W

Interstate 10

Exit #	Services
164.5mm	New Mexico/Texas state line
164mm	**Welcome Ctr wb, full(handicapped)facilities, phone, picnic tables, litter barrels, petwalk**
162	NM 404, Anthony, S...RV camping
160mm	weigh/insp sta wb

NEW MEXICO

Interstate 10

140 NM 28, to Mesilla, Las Cruces, **N**...**gas:** Phillips 66/ dsl, **food:** Applebee's, Blake's Lotaburger, Burger-Time, Cracker Barrel, DQ, McDonald's, Quizno's, Starbucks, **lodging:** Best Western, Hampton Inn, La Quinta, SpringHill Suites, **other:** Radio Shack, Wal-Mart SuperCtr/24hr, **N** **on Valley Dr...gas:** Fina/dsl, **food:** American BBQ, Domino's, Old Town Rest., **other:** Dodge, Toyota, VW, **S**...**food:** Gadsden Purchase Grill, **lodging:** Comfort Inn, **other:** Harley-Davidson, S&H RV Ctr, Siesta RV Park, Sunland RV Ctr

139 NM 292, Amador Ave, Motel Blvd, Las Cruces, **N**...**gas:** Pilot/Subway/dsl/scales/24hr, TA/Burger King/Pizza Hut/Taco Bell/dsl/rest./24hr/scales/@, **S**...**food:** PitStop Café Mexican, **lodging:** Coachlight Inn/RV Park

138mm Rio Grande River

135.5mm rest area eb, full(handicapped)facilities, picnic tables, litter barrels, petwalk, scenic view, RV dump

135 US 70 E, to W Las Cruces, Alamogordo, **1 mi N**... **other:** KOA

132 **N**...to airport, fairgrounds, **S**...**gas:** Love's/Subway/dsl/24hr

127 Corralitos Rd, **N**...**gas:** Exxon, **other:** Bowlin's Trading Post, to fairgrounds

120.5mm insp sta wb

116 NM 549, no services

111mm parking area wb, litter barrels

102 Akela, **N**...**gas:** Exxon/dsl/gifts

85 East Motel Dr, Deming, **S**...**gas:** Chevron/dsl, Save Gas/dsl, **lodging:** Holiday Inn, La Quinta, Motel 6, **other:** Chrysler/Dodge/Jeep, Dream Catcher RV camping

82b Railroad Blvd, Deming, **N**...**gas:** Chevron/dsl, **S**... **gas:** Chevron/dsl, Save Gas, Texaco/dsl, **food:** DQ, KFC, La Fonda Mexican, McDonald's, Wendy's, **lodging:** Best Western, Day's Inn, Grand Motel, Holiday Inn, Mirador Motel, Motel 6, **other:** AutoZone, Big O Tire, Checker Parts, Chevrolet/ Pontiac/GMC, $General, $Tree, Ford/Lincoln/Mercury, Firestone, Goodyear, K-Mart, Little RV Park, NAPA, Roadrunner RV Park, Wagon Wheel RV Park, Wal-Mart SuperCtr/24hr/Subway, to Rock Hound SP, st police

82a US 180, NM 26, NM 11, Deming, **N**...**gas:** Chevron, **food:** Blake's Lotaburger, **S**...**gas:** Exxon, Phillips 66, Shell/dsl, **food:** Burger King, China Rest., Denny's, DQ, K-Bob's, KFC, LJ Silver, Palmas Italian, Pizza Hut, Rancher's Grill, Subway, **lodging:** Grand Motel, **other:** AutoZone, Budget Tire, CarQuest, Radio Shack, museum, tires, to Pancho Villa SP, Rockhound SP

81 NM 11, W Motel Dr, Deming, **S**...**gas:** Chevron/ 24hr, Deming TT/dsl/scales, Shamrock/dsl, Shell, **food:** Burger Time, El Camino Real Mexiacan, McDonald's, Sonic, Subway, Taco Bell, **lodging:** Balboa Motel, Best Western, Budget Motel, Comfort Inn, Deming Motel, Deluxe Inn, Executive Motel, Super 8, **other:** Hitchin Post RV Park, to Pancho Villa SP, Rock Hound SP

68 NM 418, **S**...**gas:** Savoy/dsl/rest./24hr, tires/repair

62 Gage, **S**...**gas:** Butterfield Station/Exxon/DQ/dsl/ RV Park

61mm rest area wb, full(handicapped)facilities, picnic tables, litter barrels, vending, petwalk

55 Quincy, no services

53mm rest area eb, full(handicapped)facilities, picnic tables, litter barrels, vending, petwalk

51.5mm Continental Divide, elev 4585

49 NM 146 S, to Hachita, Antelope Wells

42 Separ, **S**...**gas:** Bowlin's Continental Divide Gifts, truck/auto repair

34 NM 113 S,, Muir, Playas, no services

29 no services

24 US 70, E Motel Dr, Lordsburg, **N**...**gas:** ⊕/Flying J/Country Mkt/dsl/scales/24hr,, Pilot/Arby's/ dsl/scales/24hr, **lodging:** American Motel, **other:** Range RV Park

23.5mm weigh sta both lanes

22 NM 494, Main St, Lordsburg, **N**...**gas:** Save Gas, **food:** DQ, McDonald's, **lodging:** Comfort Inn, Holiday Motel, **other:** Chevrolet, Family$, Ford, Parts+, Saucito's Foods, **S**...**gas:** Chevron, Save Gas, Shamrock/dsl, **food:** KFC/Taco Bell, Kranberry's Rest., **lodging:** Best Western, Holiday Inn Express, Motel 10, Super 8, **other:** KOA

20b a W Motel Dr, Lordsburg, **Visitors Ctr/full(handic apped)facilities, info,** **N**...**gas:** Love's/Subway/ Godfather's Pizza/Subway/dsl, **lodging:** Day's Inn, **S**...**gas:** Chevron/dsl

15 to Gary, no services

11 NM 338 S, to Animas, no services

5 NM 80 S, to Road Forks, **S**...**gas:** USA/rest./dsl/ scales/24hr **lodging:** Desert West Motel/rest., **other:** USPO, fireworks

3 Steins, no services

0mm New Mexico/Arizona state line

Interstate 25

Exit #	Services
460.5mm	New Mexico/Colorado state line
460	**E**...RV Park, weigh sta sb, Raton Pass Summit, elev 7834
454	Lp 25, Raton, **2 mi** **W**...**gas:** Shell, **lodging:** Budget Host, Capri Motel, El Portal Motel, Robin Hood Motel, **other:** HOSPITAL
452	NM 72 E, Raton, **E**...to Sugarite SP, **W**...**gas:** Conoco, **lodging:** Mesa Vista Motel
451	US 64 E, US 87 E, Raton, **E**...**gas:** Chevron, Shamrock/dsl, Shell/dsl/24hr, **food:** Subway, **other:** Kick Back RV Park, to Capulin Volcano NM, **W**...info, **gas:** Chevron/dsl, Conoco, Loaf'n Jug, Phillips 66, Shell/dsl, **food:** Arby's, All Seasons Rest., Chinese Buffet, DQ, Denny's, El Capp, K-Bob's, KFC, McDonald's, Pizza Hut, Sands Rest., Village Inn, **lodging:** Best Western/, Comfort Inn, El Kapp Motel, Holiday Classic Motel, Microtel, Motel 6, Super 8, Texan Motel, Travel Motel, **other:** HOSPITAL, K-Mart, NAPA, Visitor's Ctr

NM

Interstate 25

450	Lp 25, Raton, W...gas: Shamrock/dsl, **food:** Sonic, **lodging:** Holiday Inn Express, Oasis Motel, Robin Hood Motel, Westerner Motel, **other:** HOSPITAL, AutoZone, Family$, KOA, SuperSave Foods
446	US 64 W, to Cimarron, Taos, **4 mi** W...NRA Whittington Ctr, camping
440mm	Canadian River
435	Tinaja, no services
434.5mm	rest area both lanes, full(handicapped) facilities, weather info, picnic tables, litter barrels, petwalk
426	NM 505, Maxwell, W...to Maxwell Lakes
419	NM 58, to Cimarron, E...gas: Shell/Russell's/dsl/scales/24hr/@
414	US 56, Springer, E...gas: Conco/dsl, Shell, **lodging:** Oasis Motel
412	US 56 E, US 412 E, NM 21, NM 468, Springer, **1 mi** E...gas: Fina **other:** Ford
404	NM 569, Colmor, Charette Lakes, no services
393	Levy, no services
387	NM 120, to Roy, Wagon Mound, E...gas: Chevron/dsl, Phillips 66/dsl, truck/tire repair
376mm	rest area sb, full(handicapped)facilities, phone, picnic tables, litter barrels, petwalk, RV camp/dump
374mm	rest area nb, full(handicapped)facilities, phone, picnic tables, litter barrels, petwalk, RV camp/dump
366	NM 97, NM 161, Watrous, Valmora, W...Santa Fe Trail, Ft Union NM, no services
364	NM 97, NM 161, Watrous, Valmora, no services
361	no services
360mm	rest area both lanes, litter barrels, no services
356	Onava, no services
352	E...RV camping, W...airport
347	to NM 518, Las Vegas, **1-2 mi** W...gas: Pina/dsl/rest., Phillips 66/Burger King, **food:** Arby's, DQ, Hillcrest Rest., K-Bob's, KFC, McDonald's, Pizza Hut, Taco Bell, **lodging:** Comfort Inn, Day's Inn, Regal Motel, Super 8, **other:** KOA, Storrie Lake SP
345	NM 65, NM 104, University Ave, Las Vegas, E...to Conchas Lake SP, W...gas: Fina/dsl, Shell/dsl, **food:** Arby's, Burger King, Charlie's Cafe, DQ, KFC, Little Moon Chinese, McDonald's, Pizza Hut, Subway, Taco Bell, Wendy's, **lodging:** Budget Inn, Palamino Motel, Sante Fe Trail Inn, Sunshine Motel, Townhouse Motel, **other:** HOSPITAL, Firestone, Hist Old Town Plaza
343	to NM 518 N, Las Vegas, E...other: Garcia Tires, W...lodging: Holiday Inn, **1-4 mi** W...gas: Chevron, Fina, Phillips 66, **food:** McDonald's, Taco Bell, Teresa's Mexican, **lodging:** Plaza Motel, Thunderbird Motel
339	US 84 S, to Santa Rosa, Romeroville, E...KOA, W...gas: Phillips 66/Subway/dsl
335	Tecolote, no services
330	Bernal, no services
325mm	rest area both lanes, picnic tables, litter barrels, no restroom facilities

323	NM 3 S, Villanueva, E...to Villanueva SP, Madison Winery(6mi), RV camping
319	San Juan, San Jose, **3 mi** E...gas/dsl, W...Pecos River RV Camp/phone
307	NM 63, Rowe, Pecos, W...Pecos NM
299	NM 50, Glorieta, Pecos, W...gas: Fina/dsl(4mi), Shell(6mi), **food:** Renate's Rest., **other:** Glorieta Conf Ctr, Pecos NHP
297	Valencia, no services
294	Apache Canyon, W...other: KOA, Rancheros Camping(Mar-Nov)
290	US 285 S, to Lamy, S to Clines Corners, W...other: KOA, Rancheros Camping(Mar-Nov)
284	NM 466, Old Pecos Trail, Santa Fe, W...gas: Chevron/dsl, Sunset Gen Store, **lodging:** to Best Western, Desert Inn, Pecos Trail Inn, The Sands, **other:** HOSPITAL, museums
282	US 84, US 285, St Francis Dr, W...gas: Conoco/Wendy's/dsl, Giant, **food:** Church's
278	NM 14, Cerrillos Rd, Santa Fe, W...lodging: Sleep Inn, **other:** Santa Fe Outlets/famous brands, **1-4 mi** W...gas: Chevron/dsl/24hr, Conoco, Phillips 66/dsl, Shell, **food:** Applebee's, Arby's, Burger King, China Star, CiCi's, Denny's, Kettle, KFC, LJ Silver, Lotaburger, McDonald's, Olive Garden, Outback Steaks, Panda Express, Pizza Hut, Red Lobster, Schlotsky's, Sonic, Taco Bell, Village Inn Rest., **lodging:** Comfort Inn, Day's Inn, Fairfield Inn, Hampton Inn, Holiday Inn Express, Howard Johnson, La Quinta, Luxury Inn, Motel 6, Quality Inn, Ramada, Red Roof Inn, Santa Fe Lodge, Super 8, **other:** Albertson's, Best Buy, Buick/Pontiac, Chevrolet/GMC, Dillard's, Dodge, Firestone/auto, Ford, Honda/Isuzu, JC Penney, Los Campos RV Resort, PepBoys, Sam's Club, Sears/auto, Subaru, Target, VW, Walgreen, Wal-Mart, mall
276b a	NM 599, to NM 14, to Madrid, E...gas: Phillips/dsl/24hr, W...gas: Conoco, Shell, **other:** Santa Fe Skies RV Park
271	CR 50F, La Cienega, W...Pinon RV Park(4mi), racetrack, museum
269mm	rest area nb, full(handicapped)facilities, phone, picnic tables, litter barrels, petwalk
267	Waldo Canyon Rd, no services
263mm	Galisteo River
259	NM 22, to Santo Domingo Pueblo, W...gas: Phillips 66/dsl, **other:** to Cochiti Lake RA
257	Budaghers, W...Mormon Battalion Mon
264	NM 16, Cochiti Pueblo, W...to Cochiti Lake RA
252	San Felipe Pueblo, E...gas: Phillips 66/dsl, **food:** San Felipe Casino/rest.
248	Algodones, no services
242	US 550, NM 44 W, NM 165 E, to Farmington, Aztec, W...gas: Chevron/dsl, Circle K/gas, Conoco/dsl, Shell/Burger King/dsl, **food:** Baskin Robbins, Coro-

Interstate 25 *(Las Vegas / Santa Fe)*

N ↑ ↓ S

Albuquerque (left vertical bar)

	nado Rest., Denny's, Dunkin Donuts, Guang Dong Chinese, KFC, Lotaburger, McDonald's, Pizza Hut, Starbucks, Sonic, Subway, Taco Bell, Wendy's, **lodging:** Day's Inn, Holiday Inn Express, Quality Inn, Super 8, **other:** AutoZone, $ General, Walgreen, to Coronado SP
240	NM 473, to Bernalillo, W...**gas:** Chevron, Conoco/dsl, **food:** Abuelito Mexican, Pueblito Mexican, Range Café, **other:** KOA, Vet, to Coronado SP
234	NM 556, Tramway Rd, E...**gas:** Shamrock/dsl, **other:** casino, W...**gas:** Phillips 66/dsl
233	Alameda Blvd, E...**gas:** Chevron, **food:** Burger King, **lodging:** Comfort Inn, Motel 6, **other:** Audi, Mercedes, Porsche, Toyota, W...**gas:** Phillips 66/dsl, **food:** Carl's Jr, **lodging:** Holiday Inn Express, Ramada Ltd, **other:** Carmax
232	Paseo del Norte, E...**food:** Starbucks, Red Brick Pizza, Subway, **lodging** Country Inn& Suites, Howard Johnson, **other:** Aloha RV Ctr, Lowe's Whse, Target, Walgreen, W...**gas:** Shell, **food:** Arby's, **lodging:** Courtyard, Marriott
231	San Antonio Ave, E...**food:** Cracker Barrel, Kettle, **lodging:** Amberley Suites, Hilton Garden, La Quinta, Quality Suites, Ramada, **other:** HOSPITAL, W...**lodging:** Baymont Inn, Crossland Suites, Hampton Inn, **other:** Mazda, VW
230	San Mateo Blvd, Osuna Rd, Albuquerque, E...**gas:** Circle K, Conoco/dsl, Giant/dsl, Phillips 66, **food:** Applebee's, Arby's, Azuma Grill, Bennigan's, Bob's Burgers, Burger King, Chili's, Furrs Buffet, Hooters, KFC, LJ Silver, McDonald's, Olive Garden, Pizza Hut/Taco Bell, Schlotsky's, Sonic, Starbucks, Subway, SweetTomato, Taco Cabana, Teriyaki Chicken, Texas Roadhouse, Village Inn Rest., Wendy's, Wienerschnitzel, **lodging:** Nativo Lodge, Wyndham, **other:** HOSPITAL, Buick/Pontiac/GMC, Hummer,Cadillac, Just Brakes, Mercedes, Nissan, Subaru/Isuzu, Tires-4-less, Firestone/auto, NAPA, PepBoys, Wild Oats Mkt, W...**gas:** Chevron, Shamrock, **food:** Cajun Kitchen, McDonald's, Quizno's, Wecks Cafe, Whataburger, **lodging:** Motel 6 **other:** Mini/BMW
229	Jefferson St, E...**food:** Carrabba's, Landry's Seafood, OutBack Steaks, **lodging:** Holiday Inn, **other:** HOSPITAL, same as 230, W...**food:** Boston's Pizza, Carino's, Chang's China Bistro, Coldstone Creamery, Dickey's Smokehouse, Food Ct., Fuddrucker's, Jersey Jack's, Mimi's Café, Pappadeaux, Red Robin, Rockfish Café, Subway, Texas Land&Cattle Steaks, **lodging:** Drury Inn, Residence Inn **other:** Lexus
228	Montgomery Blvd, E...**gas:** Chevron/dsl, Conoco/dsl, Fina7/11, **food:** Fiestas Cantina, Lotaburger, **lodging:** Best Western, **other:** HOSPITAL, Discount Tire, W...**gas:** Shell, **food:** Arby's, Carls Jr., IHOP, McDonald's, Panda Express, Starbucks, Wendy's, **lodging:** InTowne Suites, **other:** Acura, Ford, Costco/gas, Home Depot, Sam's Club/gas
227b	Comanche Rd, Griegos Rd, E...UPS Depot

Albuquerque / **Belen** (right vertical bar)

227a	Candelaria Rd, Albuquerque, E...**gas:** Chevron/rest., Circle K, Fina/Subway/dsl, Shell, TA/dsl/24hr/@, **food:** IHOP, Subway, Village Inn Rest., **lodging:** Comfort Inn, Clubhouse Inn, Day's Inn, Fairfield Inn, Hilton, Holiday Inn, Rodeway Inn, Motel 6, Super 8, W...**gas:** Chevron, **food:** Waffle House, **lodging:** Ambassador Inn, Red Roof Inn, **other:** Volvo
226b a	I-40, E to Amarillo, W to Flagstaff
225	Lomas Blvd, E...**gas:** Chevron/7-11, **food:** JB's, Plaza Inn/rest., **other:** Chevrolet, Dodge, Ford, Saturn W...**food:** Burger King, **lodging:** Embassy Suites **other:** HOSPITAL
224	Lead Ave, Coal Ave, Grand Ave, Central Ave, E...**gas:** Texaco, **lodging:** Crossroads Motel, **other:** HOSPITAL W...**gas:** Chevron, **lodging:** Econolodge, Stardust Inn
223	Chavez Ave, E...**lodging:** Motel 6, **other:** sports
222b a	Gibson Blvd, E...**gas:** Phillips 66, **food:** Applebee's, Burger King, Subway, Waffle House, **lodging:** Airport University Inn, Country Inn Suites, Courtyard, Hampton Inn, Hawthorn Suites, Quality Suites, Sleep Inn, **other:** HOSPITAL, Kirtland AFB, museum, W...**gas:** Fina/7-11, **food:** Church's, LotaBurger, **other:** NAPA
221	Sunport(from nb), E...**lodging:** AmeriSuites, Wyndham, **other:** USPO, airport
220	Rio Bravo Blvd, Mountain View, E...golf, **2 mi** W...**gas:** Shamrock, **food:** Burger King, Church's, McDonald's, Pizza Hut, Subway, Taco Bell, **other:** Albertson's, Family$, Walgreen
215	NM 47, E...**gas:** Conoco/dsl, **other:** to Isleta Lakes RA/RV Camping, casino, st police
214mm	Rio Grande
213	NM 314, Isleta Blvd, W...**gas:** Chevron/Subway/dsl/24hr
209	NM 45, to Isleta Pueblo, no services
203	NM 6, to Los Lunas, E...**gas:** Chevron/dsl/24hr, Shamrock, Shell/Wendy's/dsl/24hr, **food:** Benny's #2, China Buffet, McDonald's, Quizno's, Papa John's, Sonic, Starbucks, Village Inn Rest., **lodging:** Comfort Inn, Day's Inn, **other:** AutoZone, Chevrolet, Ford, Home Depot, W...**gas:** Phillips 66/Subway/dsl, **food:** Carino's Italian, Coldstone Creamery, Chili's, KFC, **lodging:** Western Skies Inn, **other:** Wal-Mart SuperCtr/24hr
195	Lp 25, Los Chavez, 1 mi E...**food:** KFC, McDonald's, Pizza Hut/Taco Bell, **lodging:** Hub Motel, **other:** Wal-Mart SuperCtr/gas/24hr
191	NM 548, Belen, 1 mi E...**gas:** Conoco/dsl, **food:** Camino del Llano, KFC, McDonald's, Pizza Hut, Subway, **lodging:** Freeway Inn, W...**food:** Rio Grande Diner, **lodging:** Best Western, Holiday Inn Exress, La Mirada Hotel/RV park, Super 8, OakTree Inn
190	Lp 25, Belen, 1-2 mi E...**gas:** Akins/dsl, Conoco/dsl, Mustang, Phillips 66, **food:** A&W, Arby's, Casa de Pizza, Circle T Burger, KFC, McDonald's, Pizza Hut, TJ's Mexican, **lodging:** Freeway Inn, Hub Motel, Super 8, **other:** AutoZone, Big O Tire

NM

Interstate 25

175	US 60, Bernardo, E...Salinas NM, W...other: Kiva RV Park
174mm	Rio Puerco, no services
169	E...La Joya St Game Refuge, Sevilleta NWR
167mm	**rest area both lanes, full(handicapped) facilities, picnic tables, litter barrels, vending, petwalk**
166mm	Rio Salado, no services
165mm	weigh sta nb/parking area both lanes
163	San Acacia, no services
156	Lemitar, W...Phillis 66/dsl/24hr/@
152	Escondida, W...to st police
150	US 60 W, Socorro, W...gas: Chevron, Exxon/dsl, Phillips 66/dsl, Shamrock, Shell/dsl, food: Burger King, China Best Buffet, Denny's/24hr, Domino's, K-Bob's, KFC, Lotaburger, McDonald's, Pizza Hut, RoadRunner Steaks, Sonic, Subway, Taco Bell, Tina's Rest., lodging: Best Inn, Best Western, Days Inn, Economy Inn, Econolodge, El Camino Motel/rest., Holiday Inn Express, Payless Inn, Rio Grande Motel/rest., Sands Motel, San Miguel Inn, Socorro Inn, Super 8, other: Ace Hardware, Alco, AutoZone, Carquest, Chevrolet/Pontiac/Buick, Chrysler/Dodge/Jeep, Ford/Mercury, NAPA, Family $, Radio Shack, Smith's Foods, to NM Tech, Wal-Mart SuperCtr/24hr
147	US 60 W, Socorro, W...gas: Chevron/dsl/RV dump, Conoco/LP, Shell/dsl, food: Arby's, Armijo's Mexican, lodging: Holiday Inn Express, Motel 6, Sands Motel, other: HOSPITAL, Ace Hardware, Socorro RV Park, to airport
139	US 380 E, to San Antonio, E...gas/food, to Bosque Del Apache NWR
124	to San Marcial, E...other: to Bosque del Apache NWR, Ft Craig
115	NM 107, E...gas: Truck Plaza/dsl/rest./24hr, to Camino Real Heritage Ctr
114mm	**rest areas both lanes, full(handicapped) facilities, picnic tables, litter barrels, petwalk, RV parking, vending**
107mm	Nogal Canyon
100	Red Rock, no services
92	Mitchell Point, no services
90mm	La Canada Alamosa, La Canada Alamosa
89	NM 181, to Cuchillo, to Monticello, 4 mi E: Monticello RV Park
83	NM 52, NM 181, to Cuchillo, 3 mi E...food: Ivory Tusk Inn& Tavern, lodging: Elephant Butte Inn/rest., other: RV Park, Elephant Lake Butte SP
82mm	insp sta nb
79	Lp 25, to Truth or Consequences, E...gas: Chevron/dsl, Circle K, Phillips 66/dsl, food: China Buffet, DQ, Denny's, Hilltop Café, K-Bob's, KFC/Taco Bell, La Cocina Mexican, Los Arcos Steaks, McDonald's, Pizza Hut, Sonic, Subway, lodging: Ace Lodge, Best Western, Comfort Inn, Super 8, other: HOSPITAL, AutoZone, IGA Foods, NAPA, TrueValue, USPO, to Elephant Butte SP
76	(75 from nb)Lp 25, to Williamsburg, E...gas: Chevron/24hr, Conoco/dsl, Phillips 66, Shell/dsl, food: Hacienda Mexican, lodging: Rio Grande Motel, other: Alco, Buick/Chevrolet/GMC/Pon-

	tiac, Cielo Vista RV Park, Shady Corner RV Park, USPO, city park
71	Las Palomas
63	NM 152, to Hillsboro, Caballo, E...Lakeview RV Park/dsl
59	rd 187, Arrey, Derry, E...to Caballo-Percha SPs
58mm	Rio Grande
51	rd 546, to Arrey, Garfield, Derry
41	NM 26 W, Hatch, 1 mi W...gas: Fina/dsl food: DQ, lodging: Village Plaza Motel, other: Franciscan RV Park, USPO
35	NM 140 W, Rincon, no services
32	Upham, no services
27mm	scenic view nb, picnic tables, litter barrels
26mm	insp sta nb
23mm	**rest area both lanes, full(handicapped) facilities, picnic tables, litter barrels, vending, petwalk**
19	Radium Springs, W...Leasburg SP, Fort Selden St Mon, RV camping
9	Dona Ana, W...gas: Chevro/dsl, Citgo, Conoco/dsl, other: Family$, RV camping
6b a	US 70, to Alamogordo, Las Cruces, E...gas: Phillips 66/dsl, Shell, food: Coldstone Creamery, IHOP, New China Buffet, Outback Steaks, Papa Johns, Peter Piper Pizza, Pizzaria Uno, lodging: Century 21 Motel, Fairfield Inn, Motel 6, Staybridge, Super 8, Towneplace Suites, other: HOSPITAL, K-Mart, Sam's Club/gas, Saturn, USPO, W...gas: Chevron, Conoco, Shamrock, Shell, food: BurgerTime, DQ, Domino's, KFC, Little Ceasar's, Lotaburger, McDonald's, Sonic, Subway, Taco Bell, Whataburger/24hr, other: MEDICAL CARE, Albertson's, AutoZone, Checker Parts, Family$, Jiffy Lube, Lowe's Whse, Radio Shack, Walgreen, golf
3	Lohman Ave, Las Cruces, E...gas: Shamrock, Shell, food: Applebee's, Burger King, Cattle Baron Steaks, Carino's Italian, Chili's, ChuckeCheese, Farley's Grill, Garduno's Italian, Golden Corral, Hooters, Jack-in-the-Box, KFC, Lotaburger, Luby's, Pizza Hut, Popeye's, Red Lobster, Sonic, Starbucks, Twisters, Village Inn Rest., lodging: Hilton, other: Albertson's, Barnes&Noble, Dillard's, Discount Tire, Home Depot, JC Penney, Marshalls, Ross, Sears/auto, Target, mall, W...gas: Conoco/dsl, food: Arby's, Carl's Jr, McDonald's, Quizno's, Si Senhor, Subway, Taco Bell, Texas Roadhouse, Wendy's, Wienerschnitzel, other: Best Buy, Hastings Books, Martin Tires, NAPA, Old Navy, Pep-Boys, Rainbow Foods, Staples, Walgreen, Wal-Mart SuperCtr/24hr
1	University Ave, Las Cruces, E...other: HOSPITAL, golf, museum, st police, W...gas: Conoco, food: Bennigan's, DQ, Lorenzo's Italian, McDonald's, lodging: Comfort Suites, Sleep Inn, other: $Tree, Jo-Ann Fabrics, NMSU
0mm	I-25 begins/ends on I-10, exit 144 at Las Cruces.

N
E
S
W

Exit #	Services
373.5mm	New Mexico/Texas state line, Mountain/Central time zone
373mm	**Welcome Ctr wb, full(handicapped)facilities, phone, picnic tables, litter barrels, petwalk**
369	NM 93 S, NM 392 N, to Endee, no services
361	Bard, no services
358mm	weigh sta both lanes
356	NM 469, San Jon, **N**...**gas:** Drivers/cafe/dsl/24hr, to Ute Lake SP, **S**...**gas:** Phillips 66/dsl, Shell, **lodging:** San Jon Motel
343	ranch access, no services
339	NM 278, **N**...airport
335	Lp 40, E Tucumcari Blvd, Tucumcari, **N**...**gas:** Chevron, Conoco, Phillips 66, **food:** Denny's, **lodging:** Comfort Inn, Econolodge, Hampton Inn, Holiday Inn/rest., Howard Johnson, Motel 6, Super 8, **other:** Empty Saddle RV Park, to Conchas Lake SP
333	US 54 E, Tucumcari, **N**...**gas:** ✈/Flying J/Conoco/Country Mkt/dsl/LP/scales/24hr/@, Love's/Chester Fried/Godfather's/dsl, **food:** Deans Rest., Del's Rest., **lodging:** Best Value Inn, **other:** K-Mart, Mtn Rd RV Park, truckwash
332	NM 209, NM 104, 1st St, Tucumcari, **N**...**gas:** Chevron/Subway/dsl/24hr, Phillips 66, Shell/Circle K, Texaco, **food:** A&W/LJ Silver, KFC, K-Bob's, McDonald's, Lotaburger, Pizza Hut, Sonic, **lodging:** Best Western, Day's Inn, Microtel, **other:** HOSPITAL, $General, Family$, Lowe's Foods, st police, to Conchas Lake SP
331	Camino del Coronado, Tucumcari, no services
329	US 54, US 66 E, W Tucumcari Ave, **N**...**food:** Sonic(2mi), **lodging:** Payless Motel, **other:** HOSPITAL, golf
321	Palomas, **S**...**gas:** Shell/DQ/Stuckey's/dsl
311	Montoya, no services
302mm	**rest area both lanes, full(handicapped) facilities, phone, picnic tables, litter barrels, petwalk, RV dump**
300	NM 129, Newkirk, **N**...**gas:** Phillips 66/dsl, **other:** to Conchas Lake SP
291	to Rte 66, Cuervo, **N**...Cuervo Gas/repair
284	no services
277	US 84 S, to Ft Sumner, **N**...**gas:** Chevron/dsl, **food:** DQ, Denny's, Silver Moon Café, **lodging:** Best Western, Budget Inn, Comfort Inn, Hampton Inn, Holiday Inn Express, Motel 6, **other:** Ford, KOA, RV/auto repair, **S**...**gas:** Love's/Carl's Jr/dsl/24hr, TA/Shell/Subway/dsl/24hr/@
275	US 54 W, Santa Rosa, **N**...**gas:** Conoco/Taco Sol, Phillips 66, **food:** KFC/LJ Silver, McDonald's, Rte 66 Rest., **lodging:** Best Western, Day's Inn, La Quinta, Travelodge, **other:** Santa Rosa Camping, **S**...**gas:** Fina, Shell/Circle K/dsl/24hr, **food:** Comet Rest., Joseph's Cantina, Pizza Hut, **lodging:** American Inn, Laloma Motel, Sun'n Sand Motel/rest., Sunset Motel, Super 8, Tower Motel, Western Motel, **other:** HOSPITAL, CarQuest, Goodyear, NAPA, st police, USPO

273.5mm	Pecos River
273	US 54 S, Santa Rosa, **N**...**other:** Santa Rosa Lake SP, **S**...**gas:** Chevron, **food:** Mateo's Rest., **other:** Budget 10 Inn, **other:** NAPA, repair
267	Colonias, **N**...**gas:** Shell/Stuckey's/dsl/rest./@
263	San Ignacio, no services
256	US 84 N, NM 219, to Las Vegas, no services
252	no services
251.5mm	**rest area both lanes, full(handicapped) facilities, phone, picnic tables, litter barrels, petwalk, RV dump**
243	Milagro, **N**...**gas:** Chevron/dsl
239	no services
234	**N**...**gas:** Exxon/Flying C/DQ/dsl/gifts, **other:** repair/24hr
230	NM 3, to Encino, **N**...**other:** to Villanueva SP
226	no services
220mm	parking area both lanes, litter barrels
218b a	US 285, Clines Corners, **N**...**gas:** Phillips 66/Subway/dsl/24hr, Shell/dsl/24hr, **food:** Clines Corners Rest., **S**...**other:** to Carlsbad Caverns NP
208	Wagon Wheel, no services
207mm	**rest area both lanes, full(handicapped) facilities, picnic tables, litter barrels, petwalk**
203	**N**...RV Park
197	to Rte 66, Moriarty, **S**...**gas:** Lisa's/dsl/rest./@, **other:** auto/RV repair, **1-2 mi S**...same as 194, 196
196	NM 41, Howard Cavasos Blvd, **S**...**gas:** Phillips 66/dsl, 76/Circle K/dsl, Shell, **food:** Lotaburger, SuperChina Buffet, **lodging:** Comfort Inn, Sunset Motel, **other:** Family$, USPO, to Salinas NM(35mi), auto repair
194	NM 41, Moriarty, **S**...**gas:** Chevron/24hr, Phillips 66/dsl, TA/Pizza Hut/Subway/dsl/24hr/scales/@, **food:** Arby's, KFC/Taco Bell, McDonald's, **lodging:** Day's Inn, Econolodge, Holiday Inn Express, Ponderosa Motel, Super 8, **other:** Alco, Chevrolet/GMC, $General, IGA Foods, Moriarty Foods, RV Ctr
187	NM 344, Edgewood, **N**...**gas:** Conoco/DQ/dsl, **other:** Wal-Mart SuperCtr, **S**...**gas:** Exxon/dsl, Phillips 66/dsl, **food:** Chili Hills Mexican, China Chef, McDonald's, Pizza Barn, Subway, **other:** AutoZone, $General, Ford, Smith's Foods/gas, Walgreen, USPO, RV Camping
181	NM 217, Sedillo, **S**...**gas:** Phillips 66/dsl
178	Zuzax, **S**...**gas:** Chevron/dsl, **other:** Hidden Valley RV Park
175	NM 337, NM 14, Tijeras, **N**...**food:** Burger Boy(2mi), **other:** to Cibola NF, Turquoise Trail RV Park
170	Carnuel, no services
167	Central Ave, to Tramway Blvd, **S**...**gas:** Chevron/24hr, Fina/7-11, Shell, **food:** Canana's Mexican, Carl's Jr., KFC, Lotaburger, McDonald's, Pizza Hut/Taco Bell, Starbucks, Subway, Waffle House, **lodging:** Budget Host, Comfort Inn, Day's Inn, Deluxe Inn, Econolodge, Rodeway Inn, Sunset Inn, **other:** $Tree, Enchantment RV Ctr, GNC, Goodyear/U-Haul/auto, Meyer's RV, Raley's Foods, Rocky Mtn RV/marine, Smith's/gas, to Kirtland AFB

Santa Rosa

Tucumcari

Interstate 40

166	Juan Tabo Blvd, **N**...**gas:** Chevron/dsl, Phillips 66/Circle K, **food:** China Star, China King, Dominos, Fedrico's Mexican, Lin's Chinese, McDonald's, Olive Garden, Pizza Hut, Taco Bell, Twisters Diner, Village Inn Rest., Wendy's, Winks Rest, **lodging:** Best Value, Super 8, **other:** Albertson's, Big O Tire, Discount Tire, Hastings Books, Sav-On Drug, transmissions, **S**...**food:** Sonic, Wienerschnitzel, **other:** $General, Holiday RV Ctr, Walgreen, repair
165	Eubank Blvd, **N**...**gas:** Chevron, MVD/gas, Phillips 66/Circle K, **food:** Applebee's, JB's, Owl Café, Panda Express, Sonic, **lodging:** Best Buy, Day's Inn, Econolodge, Guesthouse Inn, Holiday Inn Express, Howard Johnson, Quality Inn, **other:** Best Buy, Target, **S**...**food:** Bob's Burgers, Boston Mkt, Chili's, Golden Corral, Pizza Hut, Subway, Taco Bell, Twister's Burritos, Wendy's, **other:** Office Depot, PetsMart, Sam's Club/gas, Toyota, Wal-Mart SuperCtr, auto repair/tires
164	Lomas Blvd, Wyoming Blvd, **N**...**gas:** Circle K, Phillips 66/Subway/dsl, **food:** Dominos, Eloy's Mexican, **other:** HOSPITAL, vet, **S**...**other:** Ford, Dodge, Honda, Hyundai, Mazda/Kia, Subaru, transmissions, Kirtland AFB
162 b a	Louisiana Blvd, **N**...**food:** Bennigan's, Bravo Italian, Buca Italian, Elephant Bar Rest., Fuddrucker's, Garduno's, LePeep, Macaroni Grill, Pei Wei Diner, Japanese Kitchen, Starbucks, Steak&Ale, TGIFriday, **lodging:** AmeriSuites, Homewood Suites, Marriott, **other:** Borders Books, Dillard's, JC Penney, Marshall's, Walgreen, **S**...atomic museum
161 b a	San Mateo Blvd, Albuquerque, **N**...**gas:** Conoco, Giant/dsl, Phillips 66/dsl, Shell/A&W, **food:** Arby's, Bob's Burgers, Boston Mkt, Burger King, Carl's Jr., Denny's, Dos Hermano's, KFC, McDonald's, Pizza Hut, Schlotzsky's, Starbucks, Subway, Taco Bell, Wendy's, **lodging:** La Quinta, **other:** Circuit City, Office Depot, Old Navy, **S**...**gas:** Chevron/dsl
160	Carlisle Blvd, Albuquerque, **N**...**gas:** Chevron, Shell, **food:** Applebee's, China Wok, JB's, Lotaburger, McDonald's, Pizza Hut, Range Cafe, Rudy's BBQ, Sonic, Twisters Grill, Village Inn Rest., Whataburger, **lodging:** AmeriSuites, Candlewood Suites, Comfort Inn, Day's Inn, Econolodge, Elegante Hotel, Hampton Inn, Hilton, Motel 6, Park Plaza Hotel, Quality Inn, Residence Inn, Suburban Motel, Super 8, **other:** BMW, Firestone/auto, Goodyear/auto, JC Penney, Smith's Foods, Walgreen, **S**...**gas:** Phillips 66/Subway/dsl, **food:** Burger King, **other:** HOSPITAL, Wild Oats Mkt
159b c	I-25, S to Las Cruces, N to Santa Fe

159a	2nd St, 4th St, Albuquerque, **N**...**gas:** Chevron/24hr, Love's/Subway/dsl, **food:** Furr's Café, **other:** $Tree, Family$, U-Haul
158	6th St, 8th St, 12th St, Albuquerque, **N**...**gas:** Love's/Subway/dsl, **other:** U-Haul, **S**...**gas:** Chevron, **lodging:** Quality Inn
157b	12th St(from eb), **N**...**gas:** Fina/Arby's/dsl, **other:** Lowe's Whse, Walgreen
157a	Rio Grande Blvd, Albuquerque, **N**...**gas:** Valero, **S**...**gas:** Chevron/24hr, Shell, **food:** Starbucks, **lodging:** Best Western/grill, Hotel Albuquerque, **other:** auto repair
156mm	Rio Grande River
155	Coors Rd, Albuquerque, **N**...**gas:** Chevron/Circle K, Duke City/dsl, Giant Gas/dsl, Valero/dsl/24hr, **food:** Applebee's, Arby's, Chili's, Cracker Barrel, Golden Corral, Great Wall Chinese, IHOP, McDonald's, Panda Express, Papa Murphy's, Quizno's, Royal Buffet, Sonic, Subway, Taco Cabana(1mi), Twisters Burritos, Wendy's, **other:** AutoZone, Brake Masters, Brook's Foods, $Tree, GNC, Goodyear/auto, Home Depot, Jiffy Lube, NAPA, Radio Shack, Staples, Walgreen, Wal-Mart SuperCtr/24hr, vet, **S**...**gas:** Chevron/24hr, Phillips 66/Circle K/dsl, Shell, **food:** Del Taco, Denny's, Furr's Diner, Lotaburger, Marisco's Mexican, McDonald's, New China, Pizza Hut, Popeye's, Subway, Taco Bell, Village Inn Rest., **lodging:** Comfort Inn, Day's Inn, Hampton Inn, La Quinta, Motel 6, Motel 76, **other:** Checker Parts, Discount Tire, U-Haul
154	Unser Blvd, **N**...**gas:** Valero, **other:** to Petroglyph NM
153	98th St, **S**...**gas:** Flying J/Conoco/CountryMkt/dsl/LP/24hr/@, **lodging:** Microtel, **other:** Palasades RV Park
149	Central Ave, Paseo del Volcan, **N**...**other:** American RV Ctr/Camping World, Enchanted Trails RV Camping, Freightliner, to Shooting Range SP, **S**...**gas:** Chevron/dsl/24hr, **other:** American RV Park
140.5mm	Rio Puerco River
140	Rio Puerco, **S**...**gas:** Rte 66 Trvl Ctr/Phillips 66/DQ/Road Runner Cafe/hotel/casino/dsl/rest./@
131	To'Hajiilee, no services
126	NM 6, to Los Lunas, no services
120mm	Rio San Jose, Rio San Jose
117	Mesita, no services
114	NM 124, Laguna, **1/2 mi** **N**...Conoco/dsl
113.5mm	scenic view both lanes, litter barrels

NEW MEXICO

Interstate 40

Exit	Description
108	Casa Blanca, Paraje, S...**gas:** Conoco/Casa Blanca/dsl/24hr, **other:** Casa Blanca Mkt, casino
104	Cubero, Budville, no services
102	Sky City Rd, Acomita, N...**gas:** Sky City/McDonald's/hotel/casino/dsl, **food:** Huwak'a Rest., **other:** RV Park/laundry, casino, S...**rest area both lanes, full(handicapped)facilities, phone, picnic tables, litter barrels, petwalk**, HOSPITAL
100	San Fidel, no services
96	McCartys, no services
89	NM 117, to Quemado, N...**gas:** Skyway/Shell/dsl/gifts, S...El Malpais NM
85	NM 122, NM 547, Grants, N...**gas:** Chevron/dsl/24hr, Conoco/dsl, Fina, Shell/dsl, **food:** Denny's, 4B's Rest./24hr, Grant's Rest., Lotaburger, Pizza Hut, Subway/TCBY, Taco Bell, **lodging:** Best Western, Comfort Inn, Day's Inn, Economy Inn/rest., El Dorado Motel/rest., Holiday Inn Express, Motel 6, Super 8, Travelodge, **other:** HOSPITAL, AutoZone, Checker Parts, Chevrolet/Buick, Chrysler/Jeep/Dodge, $Tree, Wal-Mart SuperCtr/24hr, S...Lavaland RV Park
81b a	NM 53 S, Grants, N...**gas:** Chevron, **food:** Domino's, KFC, McDonald's, **lodging:** Days Inn, Holiday Inn Express, Sands Motel, **other:** Ford/Lincoln/Mercury, NAPA, True Value, USPO, S...**other:** Blue Spruce RV Park, KOA/Cibola Sands RV Park, El Malpais NM
79	NM 122, NM 605, Milan, N...**gas:** Chevron/dsl, Love's/Chester's/Subway/dsl/24hr, **food:** DQ, **lodging:** Crossroads Motel, **other:** Bar-S RV Park, S...**gas:** Petro/Mobil/dsl/scales/24hr/@, **other:** Speedco Lube, st police
72	Bluewater Village, N...**gas:** Exxon/DQ/dsl
63	NM 412, Prewitt, S...to Bluewater SP(7mi)
53	NM 371, NM 612, Thoreau, N...**gas:** Red Mtn Mkt&Deli
47	Continental Divide, 7275 ft, N...**gas:** Chevron, **other:** Continental Divide Trdg Post, towing/repair, S...USPO
44	Coolidge, no services
39	Refinery, N...**gas:** Pilot/Subway/Grandma Max's/dsl/24hr/@
36	Iyanbito, no services
33	NM 400, McGaffey, Ft Wingate, N...**other:** to Red Rock SP, RV camping, museum
26	E 66th Ave, E Gallup, N...**gas:** Chevron/Subway/dsl/24hr, **food:** Denny's/24hr, **lodging:** La Quinta, Sleep Inn, **other:** KOA, to Red Rock SP, museum, st police, S **on Rte 66...gas:** Conoco/dsl, Fina/dsl, Mustang, Shell/Ortega Gifts, **food:** Burger King, KFC, Lotaburger, McDonald's, Sonic, Wendy's, **lodging:** Best Western, Hacienda Motel, Roadrunner Motel, **other:** HOSPITAL
22	Montoya Blvd, Gallup, N...**rest area both lanes, full facilities, info,** S **on Rte 66...gas:** Armco/gas, Chevron, Conoco, Giant Gas, Mustang, Phillips 66, Texaco, **food:** Avalon Rest., Burger King, China Express, Church's, DQ, Earl's Rest., LJ Silver, McDonald's, Papa John's, Pizza Hut, Quizno's, Subway, Taco Bell, Wendy's, **lodging:** El Capitan Motel, El Rancho Motel/rest., Redwood Lodge, **other:** Albertson's, Radio Shack, Walgreen
20	US 666 N, to Shiprock, Gallup, N...**gas:** Giant/dsl, Texaco, **food:** Applebee's, Arby's, Burger King, CA Chinese, Carl's Jr., Church's, Cracker Barrel, DQ, Denny's, Furr's Café, Golden Corral, KFC, King Dragon Chinese, Lotaburger, McDonald's, Pizza Hut, Sizzler, Sonic, Taco Bell, Wendy's, **lodging:** Hampton Inn, Quality Inn, Ramada Ltd, **other:** AutoZone, BigLots, Checker Parts, Chrysler/Dodge/Jeep, Family$, Home Depot, JC Penney, NAPA, Nissan, PepBoys, Radio Shack, Safeway, Wal-Mart SuperCtr/24hr, mall, radiators, S **on Rte 66...gas:** Shell/dsl, **food:** Don Diego's Rest., El Dorado Rest., El Sombrero Mexican, Lotaburger, Shelle's Steaks, Sonic, McDonald's, **lodging:** Best Value Inn, Best Western, Day's Inn, Economy Inn, Super 8, **other:** HOSPITAL, Big O Tire, RV camping
16	NM 118, W Gallup, Mentmore, N...**gas:** Love's/A&W/Baskin-Robbins/Subway/dsl/24hr, Mataya's/Texaco/dsl/24hr/@, Navajo/dsl/24hr, TA/Country Pride/dsl/scales/24hr/@, **lodging:** Howard Johnson, **other:** Blue Beacon, dsl repair, S...**gas:** Best Value/dsl, Chevron/dsl, Conoco, Fina/Allsup's, Shell, **food:** Olympic Kitchen, Ranch Kitchen, Taco Bell, Virgie's Mexican, **lodging:** Best Western, Budget Inn, Comfort Inn, Day's Inn, Econolodge, Gallup Inn, Hampton Inn, Microtel, Motel 6, Red Roof Inn, Travelodge, **other:** USA RV Park
12mm	inspection/weigh sta eb
8	to Manuelito, no services
2mm	**Welcome Ctr eb, full(handicapped)facilities, phone, picnic tables, litter barrels, petwalk**
0mm	New Mexico/Arizona state line

E ↑ W — Grants

Gallup

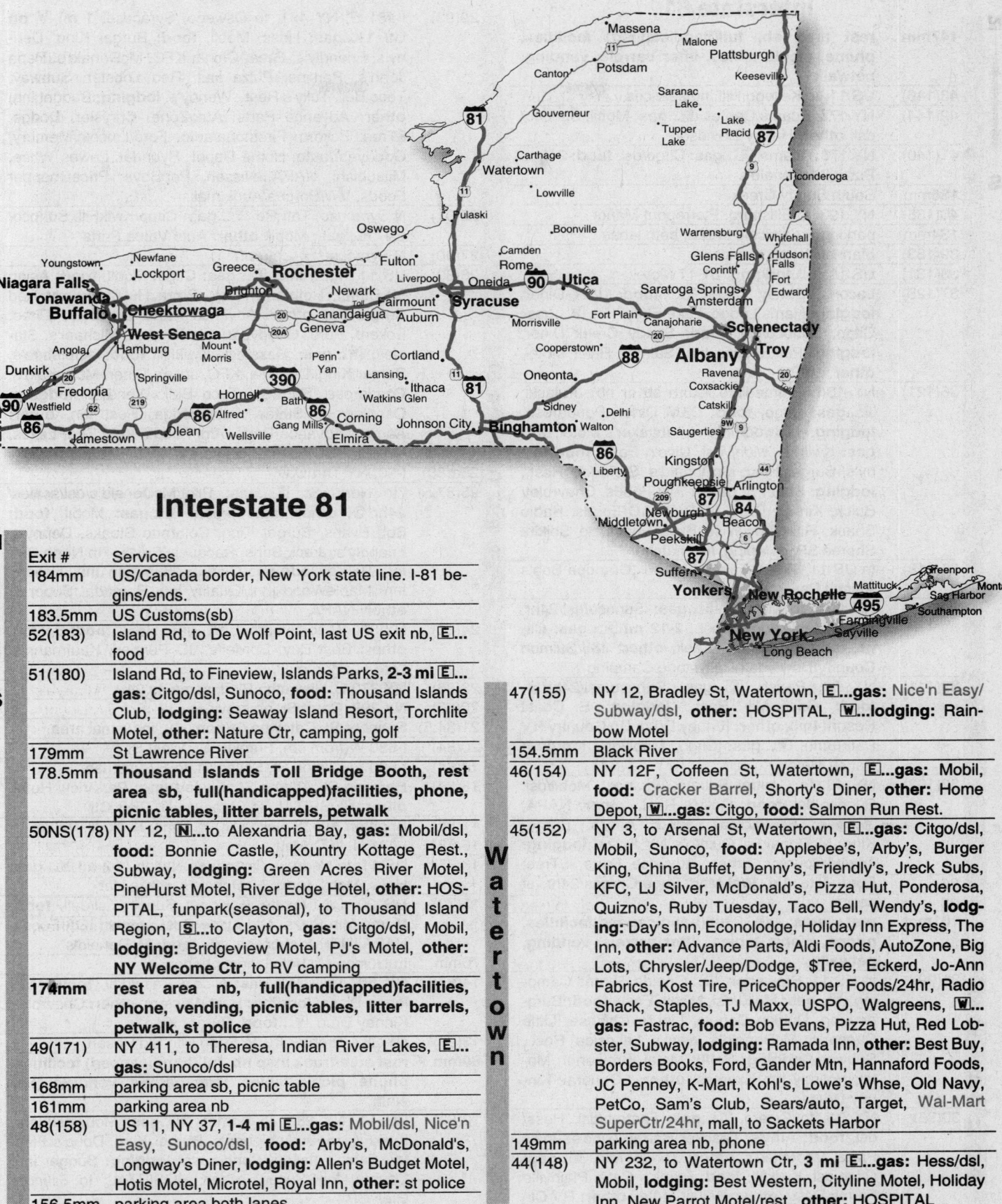

Interstate 81

N ↕ S

Exit #	Services
184mm	US/Canada border, New York state line. I-81 begins/ends.
183.5mm	US Customs(sb)
52(183)	Island Rd, to De Wolf Point, last US exit nb, E...food
51(180)	Island Rd, to Fineview, Islands Parks, **2-3 mi** E...**gas:** Citgo/dsl, Sunoco, **food:** Thousand Islands Club, **lodging:** Seaway Island Resort, Torchlite Motel, **other:** Nature Ctr, camping, golf
179mm	St Lawrence River
178.5mm	**Thousand Islands Toll Bridge Booth, rest area sb, full(handicapped)facilities, phone, picnic tables, litter barrels, petwalk**
50NS(178)	NY 12, N...to Alexandria Bay, **gas:** Mobil/dsl, **food:** Bonnie Castle, Kountry Kottage Rest., Subway, **lodging:** Green Acres River Motel, PineHurst Motel, River Edge Hotel, **other:** HOSPITAL, funpark(seasonal), to Thousand Island Region, S...to Clayton, **gas:** Citgo/dsl, Mobil, **lodging:** Bridgeview Motel, PJ's Motel, **other:** **NY Welcome Ctr**, to RV camping
174mm	**rest area nb, full(handicapped)facilities, phone, vending, picnic tables, litter barrels, petwalk, st police**
49(171)	NY 411, to Theresa, Indian River Lakes, E...**gas:** Sunoco/dsl
168mm	parking area sb, picnic table
161mm	parking area nb
48(158)	US 11, NY 37, **1-4 mi** E...**gas:** Mobil/dsl, Nice'n Easy, Sunoco/dsl, **food:** Arby's, McDonald's, Longway's Diner, **lodging:** Allen's Budget Motel, Hotis Motel, Microtel, Royal Inn, **other:** st police
156.5mm	parking area both lanes

Watertown

Exit #	Services
47(155)	NY 12, Bradley St, Watertown, E...**gas:** Nice'n Easy/Subway/dsl, **other:** HOSPITAL, W...**lodging:** Rainbow Motel
154.5mm	Black River
46(154)	NY 12F, Coffeen St, Watertown, E...**gas:** Mobil, **food:** Cracker Barrel, Shorty's Diner, **other:** Home Depot, W...**gas:** Citgo, **food:** Salmon Run Rest.
45(152)	NY 3, to Arsenal St, Watertown, E...**gas:** Citgo/dsl, Mobil, Sunoco, **food:** Applebee's, Arby's, Burger King, China Buffet, Denny's, Friendly's, Jreck Subs, KFC, LJ Silver, McDonald's, Pizza Hut, Ponderosa, Quizno's, Ruby Tuesday, Taco Bell, Wendy's, **lodging:** Day's Inn, Econolodge, Holiday Inn Express, The Inn, **other:** Advance Parts, Aldi Foods, AutoZone, Big Lots, Chrysler/Jeep/Dodge, $Tree, Eckerd, Jo-Ann Fabrics, Kost Tire, PriceChopper Foods/24hr, Radio Shack, Staples, TJ Maxx, USPO, Walgreens, W...**gas:** Fastrac, **food:** Bob Evans, Pizza Hut, Red Lobster, Subway, **lodging:** Ramada Inn, **other:** Best Buy, Borders Books, Ford, Gander Mtn, Hannaford Foods, JC Penney, K-Mart, Kohl's, Lowe's Whse, Old Navy, PetCo, Sam's Club, Sears/auto, Target, Wal-Mart SuperCtr/24hr, mall, to Sackets Harbor
149mm	parking area nb, phone
44(148)	NY 232, to Watertown Ctr, **3 mi** E...**gas:** Hess/dsl, Mobil, **lodging:** Best Western, Cityline Motel, Holiday Inn, New Parrot Motel/rest., **other:** HOSPITAL

NEW YORK

Interstate 81

N ↑ ↓ S

147mm	**rest area sb, full(handicapped) facilities, phone, picnic tables, litter barrels, vending, petwalk**
43(146)	US 11, to Kellogg Hill, no services
42(144)	NY 177, Adams Center, **E...gas:** Mobil, Sunoco/dsl, **other:** Harley-Davidson
41(140)	NY 178, Adams, **E...gas:** Citgo/dsl, **food:** 2 Bros Pizza, McDonald's
138mm	South Sandy Creek
40(135)	NY 193, to Ellisburg, Pierrepont Manor
134mm	parking area/picnic tables, both lanes
39(133)	Mannsville, no services
38(131)	US 11, **E...lodging:** 81-11 Motel
37(128)	Lacona, Sandy Creek, **E...food:** J&R Diner, **lodging:** Harris Lodge, Lake Effect Inn, **W...gas:** Citgo, Sunoco/dsl, **food:** Sandy Creek Diner, **lodging:** Pink House Inn, Salmon River Motel, **other:** USPO
36(121)	NY 13(no immediate return sb or nb), Pulaski, **E...gas:** Citgo, **food:** C&M Diner, Ponderosa, **lodging:** Redwood Motel, Whitaker's Motel, **W...gas:** KwikFill, Mobil/dsl, Nice'n Easy, **food:** Arby's, Burger King, McDonald's, Stefano's Rest., **lodging:** Super 8, **other:** Aldi Foods, Chevrolet/Buick, Kinney Drug, NAPA, P&C Foods, Radio Shack, Rite Aid, Wise Buys Foods, to Selkirk Shores SP, camping, fish hatchery
35(118)	to US 11, Tinker Tavern Rd, **W...**Grandpa Bob's Animal Park
34(115)	NY 104, to Mexico, **E...gas:** Sunoco/dsl/24hr, **food:** Maple View Rest. **2-12 mi W...gas:** Citgo, **lodging:** Cedar Creek, **other:** J&J/Salmon Country/Dowiedale/Jellystone Camping
33(111)	NY 69, Parish, **E...gas:** Sunoco/dsl/24hr/@, **food:** Grist Mill Rest., **lodging:** E Coast Resort(4mi), **other:** Kinney Drug, Up Country RV Park(8mi), **W...gas:** Citgo, Mobil/dsl, **lodging:** Parish Motel
32(103)	NY 49, to Central Square, **E...gas:** Mobil/dsl, Sunoco/dsl, **food:** Golly's Rest., **other:** NAPA, **W...gas:** Fastrac/gas, **food:** Arby's, Burger King, McDonald's, Quinto's NY Pizza, **lodging:** Town&Country, **other:** Advance Parts, $Tree, Ford, Rite Aid, Wal-Mart SuperCtr/gas/24hr, st police
101mm	**rest area sb, full(handicapped)facilities, phone, picnic tables, litter barrels, vending, petwalk**
31(99)	to US 11, Brewerton, **E...**Oneida Shores Camping, **W...gas:** Mobil/dsl, Nice'n Easy, **food:** Burger King, Dunkin Donuts, LinLi's Chinese, Little Caesar's, McDonald's, Sam's Lakeside Rest., Subway, **lodging:** BelAir Motel, Brewerton Motel, Holiday Inn Express, **other:** $General, Kinney Drugs
30(96)	NY 31, to Cicero, **E...gas:** Fastrac/dsl, Hess/dsl, **food:** Arby's, Cracker Barrel, Gino's&Joe's Pizza, Mcdonald's, **other:** Gander Mtn, **W...gas:** Citgo/dsl, Kwikfill, **food:** Frank's Café, Plainville Farms Rest., **other:** Bellair Motel, **other:** RV Ctr
29(93)	I-481 S, NY 481, to Oswego, Syracuse, **1 mi W on US 11...gas:** Hess, Mobil, **food:** Burger King, Denny's, Friendly's, Great China, KFC, McDonald's, Papa John's, Perkins, Pizza Hut, Red Lobster, Subway, Taco Bell, Tully's Rest., Wendy's, **lodging:** Budget Inn, **other:** Advance Parts, AutoZone, Chrysler, Dodge, $Tree, Eckerd, Firestone/auto, Ford/Lincoln/Mercury, Goodyear/auto, Home Depot, Hyundai, Lowes Whse, Mitsubishi, NAPA, Nissan, PepBoys, PriceChopper Foods, VW/Porche/Audi, mall
28(91)	N Syracuse, Taft Rd, **E...gas:** Citgo/KwikFill, Sunoco/dsl, **W...gas:** Mobil, **other:** Auto Value Parts
27(90)	N Syracuse, **E...**airport
26(89)	US 11, Mattydale, **E...gas:** Citgo, Mobil, **food:** Asian 98 Buffet, Hofmann Rest., Pizza Hut, **lodging:** Red Carpet Inn, **other:** Advance Parts, Big Lots, $Tree, Eckerd, Ford, Goodyear/auto, K-Mart, Michael's, Staples, **W...gas:** Hess/dsl, Kwikfill, **food:** Applebee's, Burger King, Denny's, KFC, Julie's Diner, McDonald's, Ponderosa, Subway, Taco Bell, Wendy's, **lodging:** Candlewood Suites, Econolodge, Rest Inn, **other:** Aamco, Advance Parts, Aldi Foods, Kost Tire, Lexus, Mazda, P&C Foods, Toyota/VW
25a(88)	I-90, NY Thruway
25(87.5)	7th North St, **E...gas:** Pilot/McDonald's/dsl/scales/24hr/@, **other:** auto repair, **W...gas:** Mobil, **food:** Bob Evans, Burger King, Colorado Steaks, Denny's, Friendly's, Jreck Subs, Racquels Pasta, 7th North Buffet, Tully's, **lodging:** Clarion, Hampton Inn, Holiday Inn, MapleWood Inn, Quality Inn, Ramada, Super 8, **other:** NAPA
24(86)	NY 370 W, to Liverpool, **W...gas:** Hess, **food:** Bonton, **other:** Best Buy, Border's, JC Penney, Kaufmann's, Lord&Taylor, mall
23(86)	NY 370 E, Hiawatha Blvd, same as 24
22(85)	NY 298, Court St, no services
21(84.5)	Spencer St, Catawba St(from sb), industrial area
20(84)	I-690 W(from sb), Franklin St, West St
19(84)	I-690 E, Clinton St, Salina St, to E Syracuse
18(84)	Harrison St, Adams St, **E...lodging:** ParkView Hotel, **other:** HOSPITAL, to Syracuse U, Civic Ctr
17(82)	Brighton Ave, S Salina St, **W...gas:** KwikFill, Valero
16a(81)	I-481 N, to DeWitt
16(78)	US 11, to Nedrow, Onondaga Nation, **1-2 mi W...gas:** Hess, Mobil, **food:** McDonald's, Pizza Hut
15(73)	US 20, La Fayette, **E...gas:** Sunoco/dsl/deli, **food:** Mama Mia Pizza, Old Tyme Rest., **other:** IGA Foods, NAPA, USPO, st police, **W...food:** McDonald's
70mm	truck insp sta both lanes, phones
14(67)	NY 80, Tully, **E...gas:** Nice'n Easy/deli, **food:** Marlene's Place, **lodging:** Best Western, **other:** Chevrolet, Kinney Drug, **W...food:** Burger King
13(63)	NY 281, Preble, **E...**to Song Mtn Ski Resort
60mm	**rest area/truck insp nb, full(handicapped) facilities, phone, picnic tables, litter barrels, vending, petwalk**
12(53)	US 11, NY 281, to Homer, **W...gas:** Mobil/dsl/24hr, KwikFill, **food:** Applebee's, Burger King, Doug's Fishfry, Fabio's Italian, Ponderosa, **lodging:** Budget Inn, Country Inn&Suites, **other:** HOSPITAL, to Fillmore Glen SP

Syracuse

Interstate 81

11(52) NY 13, Cortland, E...**food:** Denny's, **lodging:** Comfort Inn, Quality Inn, W...**gas:** Mobil, **food:** Arby's, China Moon, Friendly's, Little Caesar's, McDonald's, Subway, Taco Bell, Wendy's, **lodging:** Hampton Inn, Holiday Inn, **other:** Advance Parts, Eckerd, Family$, Jo-Ann Fabrics, Kost Tire, P&C Foods/24hr, Yellow Lantern Camping, museum

10(50) US 11, NY 41, to Cortland, McGraw, W...**gas:** Citgo/dsl/cafe, Mobil/Subway/dsl/24hr, Sunoco/dsl, **lodging:** Cortland Motel, Day's Inn

9(38) US 11, NY 221, W...**gas:** Citgo, Sunoco/dsl/24hr, XtraMart, **food:** NY Pizzaria, **lodging:** 3 Bear Inn/rest., Greek Peak Lodge, **other:** NAPA, Country Hills Camping

33mm **rest area sb, full(handicapped)facilities, phone, picnic tables, litter barrels, vending, petwalk**

8(30) NY 79, to US 11, NY 26, NY 206(no EZ return), Whitney Pt, E...**gas:** Hess, Kwikfill, Mobil/dsl/24hr, **food:** Aiello's Ristorante, Arby's, McDonald's, Subway, **lodging:** Point Motel, **other:** Chevrolet, NAPA, Parts+, Radio Shack, Strawberry Valley Farms(3mi), to Dorchester Park

7(21) US 11, Castle Creek, W...**gas:** Mobil

6(16) US 11, to NY 12, I-88E, Chenango Bridge, E on US 11...**gas:** Citgo/dsl, Exxon, Hess/dsl, **food:** Arby's, Burger King, China Buffet, Denny's, Dunkin Donuts, Pizza Hut, Ponderosa, Wendy's, **lodging:** Comfort Inn, Day's Inn, **other:** Advance Parts, CVS Drug, Eckerd, Ford/Mazda, Giant Foods, Harley-Davidson, Kost Tire, Lowe's Whse, Radio Shack, Staples, W...**gas:** KwikFill, **food:** Friendly's, McDonald's, Nirchi's Pizza, Spot Diner, Subway, **lodging:** Motel 6, Quality Inn

15mm I-88 begins eb

5(14) US 11, Front St, **1 mi** W...**gas:** Mobil/dsl, Valero, **food:** Applebee's, Coldstone Creamery, Cracker Barrel, Quizno's, Starbucks, **lodging:** Econolodge, Fairfield Inn, Super 8

4(13) NY 17, Binghamton, no services

3(12) Broad Ave, Binghamton, W...**gas:** Valero, **food:** KFC, **other:** CVS Drug, Giant Foods

3(10) Industrial Park, same as 2

2(8) US 11, NY 17, **1-2 mi** W...**gas:** Exxon/dsl, Pilot/Wendy's/dsl/scales/24hr/@, TA/dsl/rest./24hr/@, **food:** Arby's, Burger King, McDonald's, Subway, **lodging:** Del Motel

1(4) US 11, NY 7, Kirkwood, **1-2 mi** W...**gas:** Mobil/dsl/24hr, Xtra, **lodging:** Kirkwood Motel, Wright Motel

2mm **Welcome ctr nb, full(handicapped)facilities, phone, picnic tables, litter barrels, vending, petwalk**

1mm weigh sta nb

0mm New York/Pennsylvania state line

Interstate 84

Exit #	Services
71.5mm	New York/Connecticut state line
21(68)	US 6, US 202, NY 121(from wb), N Salem, same as 20
20N(67.5)	US 6, US 202, NY 22, N...**gas:** Citgo, Mobil/24hr, Valero, **food:** Bob's Diner, Burger King, McDonald's, **other:** Cadillac/Chevrolet, Curves, Ford, Honda, Subaru

20S I-684, to NYC

19(65) NY 312, Carmel, S...**food:** Applebee's, Dunkin Donuts, Friendly's, Gaetano's Deli, McDonald's, Sonoma Cafe, Wendy's, **other:** HOSPITAL, Home Depot, Kohl's, Marshall's, Michael's, st police

18(62) NY 311, Lake Carmel, S...Bob's Towing/dsl

17(59) Ludingtonville Rd, S...**gas:** Hess/Blimpie/dsl/24hr, Sunoco, **food:** Cutiloo's Rest.(2mi), Gappy's Pizza, Lou's Deli

56mm elevation 970 ft

55mm **rest area both lanes, full(handicapped) facilities, phone, vending, picnic tables, litter barrels, petwalk**

16(53) Taconic Parkway, N to Albany, S to New York

15(51) Lime Kiln NY, **3 mi** N...**gas:** Mobil/24hr, **food:** Dunkin Donuts, **lodging:** Royal Inn

13(46) US 9, to Poughkeepsie, N...**gas:** Citgo, Gulf, Mobil/dsl, **food:** A&W/KFC, Boston Mkt, Burger King, Charlie Brown Steaks, Cracker Barrel, Denny's, Hudson Buffet, Panera Bread, Pizza Hut, Ruby Tuesday, Sidewinder's Grill, Stanley's Eatery, Taco Bell, ViaNove Italian, Wendy's, **lodging:** Comfort Inn, Courtyard, Extended Stay America, Hampton Inn, Hilton Garden, Holiday Inn, Homestead Suites, Ramada Inn, Residence Inn, Sierra Suites, **other:** Rite Aid, Sam's Club, ShopRite Foods, Starbucks, Wal-Mart SuperCtr, S...**gas:** Hess/Blimpie/dsl/24hr, **food:** Maya Cafe, McDonald's, **other:** Home Depot

12(45) NY 52 E, Fishkill, N...**gas:** Valero, **food:** Chan's Buffet, Friendly's, **other:** CVS Drug, $King, S...**gas:** Mobil, Sunoco/dsl, **food:** Dunkin Donuts, Hometown Deli, I-84 Diner/24hr, **other:** Lincoln/Mercury

11(42) NY 9D, to Wappingers Falls, **1 mi** N...**gas:** Mobil/dsl, Sunoco

41mm toll booth wb

40mm Hudson River

10(39) US 9W, NY 32, to Newburgh, N...**gas:** Citgo, Mobil, Sunoco, Xtra, **food:** Alexis Diner, Andiamo Pizza, Burger King, China King, McDonald's, Pizza Hut, Subway, **lodging:** Budget Inn, Economy Inn, **other:** Advance Parts, Big Lots, $Tree, Family$, PriceChopper Foods, S...**gas:** Exxon/dsl, Gulf, Sunoco/dsl, **lodging:** Travel Inn, Windsor Inn(4mi), **other:** HOSPITAL, Jo-Ann Fabrics

8(37) NY 52, to Walden, N...**gas:** Citgo/dsl, Sunoco/24hr

7(36) NY 300, to I-87(NY Thruway), Newburgh, N...**gas:** Mobil/24hr, **food:** Driscoll's Rest., Dunkin Donuts, Ground Round, King Buffet, McDonald's, Old Town Buffet, Perkins, Taco Bell, Wendy's, **other:** AutoZone, $Tree, Marshall's, Old Navy, Sears, Stop&Shop, mall, S...**gas:** Hess/Blimpie/dsl, Sunoco, **food:** Applebee's, Burger King, Cosimos Ristorante, Denny's, Gateway Diner, Neptune Diner, Union Sq Rest., Subway, TGIFridays, **lodging:** Hampton Inn, Howard Johnson, Quality Inn, Ramada Inn, Super 8, **other:** Adam's Food Mkt,

NEW YORK

Interstate 84

	Associated Foods, Barnes&Noble, Chevrolet/Cadillac, Chrysler/Plymouth/Dodge/Jeep, Curves, $Tree, Ford/Lincoln/Mercury, Home Depot, Honda, Lowe's Whse, Michael's, Nissan, Kohl's, Radio Shack, Target, Wal-Mart SuperCtr
6(34)	NY 17K, to Newburgh, N...gas: Mobil/24, Gulf, Pilot/Arby's/dsl/scales/24hr, food: Airport Diner, lodging: Comfort Inn, S...gas: Exxon/dsl, lodging: Courtyard, 3 mi S...lodging: Days Inn, Howard Johnson, Quality Inn
33mm	new exit
5(29)	NY 208, Maybrook, N...gas: Exxon/24hr, Mobil, food: Baskin-Robbins/Dunkin Donuts, Burger King, McDonald's, other: Eckerd, ShopRite Foods, S...gas: Hess/Blimpie, TA/Pizza Hut/dsl/rest./@, food: Maybrook Diner, Renee's Deli, Roadside Rest., Subway, lodging: Rodeside Inn, Super 8, other: Blue Beacon, Winding Hills Camping
24mm	**rest area wb, full(handicapped)facilities, phone, vending, picnic tables, litter barrels, petwalk**
4(19)	NY 17, Middletown, N...gas: Mobil/24hr, Sunoco, food: Americana Diner, Applebee's, Baskin-Robbins/Dunkin Donuts, Boston Mkt, Cheeseburger Paradise, Cosimo's Brick Oven, Denny's, Friendly's, KFC, McDonald's, Olive Garden, Perkins, Red Lobster, Ruby Tuesday, Subway, Taco Bell, Wendy's, lodging: Howard Johnson, Middletown Motel, Super 8, other: HOSPITAL, Best Buy, Borders Books, Circuit City, Firestone/auto, Gander Mtn, Hannaford Foods, Home Depot, Honda, JC Penney, Jo-Ann Fabrics, Kohl's, Lowe's Whse, Old Navy, PriceChopper Foods, Rite Aid, Sam's Club, Sears/auto, ShopRite Foods, Staples, Stop&Shop Foods, TJ Maxx, U-Haul, vet, Wal-Mart SuperCtr/24hr, mall, S...gas: Citgo/dsl, Mobil, food: Chili's, El Bandido Mexican, Galleria FoodCourt, Outback Steaks, Red Robin, TGIFriday, lodging: Courtyard, Hampton Inn, Holiday Inn, other: st police
17mm	**rest area eb, full(handicapped)facilities, phone, vending, picnic tables, litter barrels, petwalk**
3(15)	US 6, to Middletown, N...gas: Citgo/dsl/24hr, Mobil, Valero, food: Bradley's Corner Diner, Colonial Diner, Dunkin Donuts, McDonald's, NY Buffet, Perkins, Quinzno's, Subway, Taco Bell, Wendy's, other: HOSPITAL, Acura, Buick/Pontica/GMC, Chevrolet/Isuzu, Mazda, ShopRite Foods, Subaru, S...gas: Citgo, Sunoco/dsl, lodging: Day's Inn, Global Budget Inn, other: Chrysler/Jeep, Nissan, Kia, Suzuki, Toyota, USPO, transmissions
2(5)	Mountain Rd, S...Greenville's Deli
4mm	elevation 1254 ft wb, 1272 ft eb
3	parking area both lanes
1(1)	US 6, NY 23, Port Jervis, N...gas: Sunoco/dsl, food: Arlene&Tom's Diner, Dunkin Donuts/Baskin Robbins, lodging: Deerdale Motel, Painted Aprons Motel, other: HOSPITAL, 84 RV Ctr, Ford/Lincoln/Mercury/Jeep, S...gas: Citgo/dsl, Gulf/dsl, Lukoil, Valero, food: Cumberland Farms, DQ, McDonald's, Village Pizza, lodging: Comfort Inn, other: HOSPITAL, ShopRite Foods, TJ Maxx, mall
0mm	New York/Pennsylvania state line, Delaware River

Interstate 86

Exit #	Services
	I-86 begins/ends on I-87, exit 16, toll booth
131(377)	NY 17, N...other: Outlets/famous brands, S...gas: Exxon/Subway/dsl, Mobil, Sunoco, food: Blimpie, Chili's, McDonald's, TGIFriday's, Uno Pizzaria, lodging: American Budget Inn, other: BJ's Whse, Home Depot, Kohls, TJMaxx, Staples
130a(376)	US 6, Bear Mtn, to West Point(from eb), S...other: BJ's Whse, Home Depot, Wal-Mart SuperCtr/24hr
130(376)	NY 208, Monroe, Washingtonville, N...gas: Sunoco/dsl, lodging: James Motel, Lake Anne Motel, other: Chrysler/Dodge/Jeep, Daewoo, Isuzu, st police, S...gas: Mobil/dsl, food: Burger King, Pizza Hut,
129(375)	Museum Village Rd, S...food: Plum House Rest
128(374)	rd 51(only from wb), Oxford Depot
127(373)	Greycourt Rd(from wb only), Sugar loaf, Warwick, no services
126(372)	NY 94, Chester, Florida, N...gas: Mobil, Shell, Sunoco/dsl, food: Lobster Pier Rest., McDonald's, Sunrise Diner, Wendy's, S...lodging: Holiday Inn Express, other: Radio Shack, Rite Aid, ShopRite Foods, funpark, S...lodging: Chester Inn, other: Black Bear Camping
125(369)	NY 17M E, South St, S...food: Hacienda Mexican, Pizza Deli, other: HOSPITAL
124(368)	NY 17A, NY 207, N...gas: Exxon/Subway/ dsl, Mobil/dsl, Sunoco/dsl, food: Burger King, Country Chicken, Friendly's, Dunkin Donuts, Goshen Diner, Pizza Hut, Plaza Diner, other: CVS Drug, S...lodging: Comfort Inn, other: Chrysler/Plymouth/Dodge/Jeep, Hyundai
122a(367)	Fletcher St, Goshen, no services
122(364)	rd 67, E Main St, Crystal Run Rd, N...gas: Mobil, food: El Bandido Rest., FoodCourt, Outback Steaks, Rusty Nail Rest., TGIFriday's, lodging: Courtyard, Hampton Inn, Holiday Inn, S...gas: Getty/dsl
121(363)	I-84, E to Newburgh, W to Port Jervis
120(363)	NY 211, N...gas: Mobil, Sunoco, food: American Café, Olive Garden, lodging: Howard Johnson, Middletown Motel, Super 8, other: Best Buy, Cosimo's, Macy's, Hannaford's Foods, JC Penney, Sam's Club, Wal-Mart, S...gas: Getty, Mobil, food: Americana Diner, Arby's, Boston Mkt, Burger King, China Buffet, Denny's, Friendly's, Hana Japanese, KFC, Pizza Hut, Red Lobster, Wendy's, Taco Bell, other: AutoZone, Circuit City, Eckerd, Ford, Home Depot, Jo-Ann Fabrics, K-Mart, PriceChopper, ShopRite Foods, Staples, Stop&Shop Foods, U-Haul
119(360)	NY 309, Pine Bush, S...gas: Best Gas/dsl
118a(358)	NY 17M, Fair Oaks, no services
118(358)	Circleville, N...lodging: Economy Inn, Heritage Motel, S...gas: Citgo, Exxon/dsl, Mobil, food: Raffael's Italian, Subway
116(355)	NY 17K, Bloomingburg, S...gas: Citgo, Mobil, food: Gaudio Diner, Q-way Diner, other: Rainbow Valley Camping
113(350)	US 209, Wurtsboro, Ellenville, N...gas: Mobil/dsl, Stewarts/gas, food: Giovanni's Café, lodging: Davidman Motel, Gold Mtn Chalet, Day's Inn, Valley Brook Motel, other: American Family Campground, Spring Glen Camping
112(347)	Masten Lake, Yankee Lake, S...food: Potager Diner, lodging: ValleyBrook Motel, other: WonderWood Camping

(left margin, top to bottom) E ↕ W — Middletown — Port Jervis

(right margin) Middletown

Interstate 86

E ↕ **W**

111(344)	(sb only), Wolf Lake, **S**...**gas:** Billy's/dsl
110(343)	Lake Louise Marie, **N**...**food:** Dodge Inn Rest, **lodging:** Rock Hill Lodge
109(342)	Rock Hill, Woodridge, **N**...**gas:** Exxon/dsl, **food:** Bernie's Diner, LandSea Rest., RockHill Diner, Rock Pizza, **lodging:** Rock Hill Lodge, Rosemond Motel, **other:** Hilltop Farms Camping, Lazy G Camping, **S**...**gas:** Mobil/dsl
108(341)	Bridgeville, same as 109
107(340)	Thompsonville, **S**...**food:** Apollo FoodCourt, Hana Rest., Old Homestead Diner, **lodging:** Affordable Inn, Pines Motel, Raleigh Motel, **other:** Chevrolet, Chrysler/Plymouth/Dodge/Jeep, Toyota
106(339)	(wb only), E. Broadway, **S**...**gas:** Mobil/dsl, **food:** Monitcello Cafe, **lodging:** Travel Inn, Econolodge, **other:** GMC Trucks
105(337)	NY 42, Monticello, **N**...**gas:** Exxon/dsl, Mobil, Valero, **food:** Bro Bruno Diner, Blue Horizon Diner, Giovanni's Café, KFC, Kutshner's Cafe, McDonald's, **other:** Home Depot, ShopRite Foods, **Wal-Mart SuperCtr/24hr**, **S**...**gas:** Stewarts, **food:** Burger King, Monticello Diner, Pizza Hut, Wendy's, **lodging:** Econolodge, Ramada Ltd, **other:** NAPA
104(336)	NY 17B, Raceway, Monticello, **S**...**gas:** Citgo, Exxon/dsl, **food:** Bean Bag Eatery, Kelly's Diner, Taco Maker, **lodging:** Best Western, Raceway Motel, Travel Inn, **other:** Swinging Bridge Camp, Woodstock Camping, airport
102(332)	Harris, **S**...**other:** HOSPITAL, Swan Lake CamP
101(327)	Ferndale, Swan Lake, **S**...**gas:** Exxon/dsl, **food:** McDonald's Burger King, Last Licks Cafe, Wendy's, **lodging:** Day's Inn, Inn by the Falls, Loncoln Motel
100(327)	NY 52 E, Liberty, **N**...**gas:** Sunoco, **food:** Albert's Rest., Burger King, McDonald's, Taco Bell, Wendy's, **lodging:** Best Inn, Day's Inn, Econolodge, **S**...**gas:** Citgo, Exxon/dsl, Gulf, Mobil/24hr, **food:** Dunkin Donuts, Pizza Hut, **lodging:** Liberty Motel, Lincoln Motel, **other:** Eckerd, Ford/Lincoln/Mercury, Pontiac/Buick, Neversink River Camping, Swan Lake Camping, Yogi Bear Camping
99(325)	NY 52 W, to NY 55, Liberty, **S**...**gas:** Exxon, Sunoco, **food:** Dairy Barn, **lodging:** Catskill Motel
98(321)	Cooley, Parksville, **N**...**gas:** Mobil, **food:** Dari-King, W 17 Diner, **lodging:** Best Western, **other:** USPO
97(319)	Morsston, no services
96(316)	Livingston Manor, **N**...**food:** Catskill Rest., Tony's Pizza, **lodging:** Econo Motel, **other:** Covered Bridge Camping, Mongaup Pond Camping, **S**... **lodging:** DeBruce Inn, OZ B&B, Willowemac Motel
313mm	**rest area eb, full(handicapped)facilities, picnic tables, litter barrels, phones, vending, petwalk, truck insp. sta(eb)**
94(311)	NY 206, Roscoe, Lew Beach, **N**...**gas:** Exxon/dsl, Sunoco/dsl, **food:** 1910 Coffeshop, Ramondo's Diner, Roscoe Diner, **lodging:** Reynolds House Motel, Rockland House Motel, Roscoe Motel, Tennanah Lake Motel, **other:** Roscoe Camping, **S**... **gas:** Mobil/dsl, **other:** Beaverkill St Camping(8mi)
93(305)	to Cooks Falls(from wb), no services

M o n t i c e l l o

92(303)	Horton, Cooks Falls, Colchester, **S**...**gas:** Sunoco/dsl, **food:** Riverside Café/lodge, **other:** Russell Brook Camping
90(297)	NY 30, East Branch, Downsville, **N**...**gas:** Sunoco, **other:** Beaver-Del Camping, Catskill Mtn Camping, Oxbow Camping, Peaceful Valley Camping, **S**...**lodging:** E Branch Motel
295mm	**rest area wb, full(handicapped)facilities, picnic tables, litter barrels, phones, vending, petwalk**
89(293)	Fishs Eddy, no services
56(189)	NY 352, Elmira, **S**...**gas:** Citgo, Sunoco/dsl, **food:** Hoss' Rest., McDonald's, Pizza Hut, **lodging:** Coachman Motel, Holiday Inn, Twain Motel, **other:** HOSPITAL
87a(288)	NY 268(from wb), same as 87
87(284)	NY 97, to NY 268, to NY 191, Hancock, Cadosia, **S**... **gas:** Getty, Mobil, Sunoco, **food:** Circle E Diner, Country Bakeshop/rest., Family Rest., Great Wall Chinese, McDonald's, Subway, **lodging:** Colonial Motel, Starlight Lake Inn, **other:** Buick/Chevrolet, NAPA, Parts+
276mm	parking area wb, litter barrels
84(274)	Deposit, **N**...**gas:** Citgo/dsl/24hr, Wheeler's, **food:** Wendy's, **lodging:** Deposit Motel, Laurel Bank Motel, Scott's Motel, **other:** Crystler/Jeep, st police
83(272)	Deposit, Oquaga Lake, no services
82(270)	NY 41, McClure, Sanford, **N**...**gas:** Sun/dsl, **other:** Kellystone Park, **S**...**lodging:** Alexander's B&B/diner, Chestnut Inn/rest., Scott's Family Resort, **other:** Guestward Camping(3mi)*
265mm	parking area eb, picnic tables, litter barrels
81(263)	E Bosket Rd, no services
80(261)	Damascus, **N**...**gas:** Exxon/dsl, **food:** Damascus Diner, **other:** Forest Hill Lake Park Camping
79(259)	NY 79, Windsor, **N**...**gas:** Citgo, Sunoco/dsl, XtraMart, **food:** Subway, **other:** Lakeside Camping, **S**...**food:** Golden Oak Rest., Marian's Pizza
78(256)	Dunbar Rd, Occanum, no services
77(254)	W Windsor, **N**...**gas:** Mobil/dsl, **food:** McDonald's
76(251)	Haskins Rd, to Foley Rd, no services
75(250)	I-81 S, to PA(exits left from wb), **N**...**gas:** Exxon/dsl, **lodging:** Dell Motel
72(244)	I-81 N, US 11, Front St, Clinton St, (no wb re-entry), **S**...**food:** McDonald's, **other:** Advance Parts, K-Mart, antiques
71(242)	Airport Rd, Johnson City, **S**...**gas:** Valero
70(241)	NY 201, Johnson City, **N**...**gas:** Hess, Valero, **food:** Blimpie, China Buffet, Christy's Grill, Dunkin Donuts, Friendly's, McDonald's, Papa John's, Pizza Hut, Ponderosa, Quizno's, Ruby Tuesday, Taco Bell, **lodging:** Best Western, Hampton Inn, La Quinta, Red Roof Inn, **other:** $Tree, Gander Mtn, Giant Foods, JC Penney, Kost Tire, Macy's, Sears/auto, Wegman's Foods, mall, **S**...Home Depot

B i n g h a m t o n

NEW YORK

Interstate 86

E ↑ **W**	

69(239) NY 17C, no services

238mm Susquehanna River

68(237) NY 17C, Old Vestal Rd, (from eb), no services

67(236) NY 26, NY 434, Vestal, Endicott, **2 mi** **S** **on NY 434...gas:** Valero/dsl, **food:** A&W/LJ Silver, Burger King, California Grill, China Wok, McDonald's, Old Country Buffet, Olive Garden, Quizno's, Red Lobster, Stabucks, Subway, Taco Bell, TGIFriday, Uno Pizzaria, **lodging:** Parkway Motel, Vestal Motel, **other:** Advance Parts, Barnes&Noble, Chevrolet, Chrysler/Plymouth/Jeep, $Tree, Ford, Giant Foods, Jo-Ann Fabrics, Kohl's, Kost Tire, Lincoln/Mercury, Lowe's Whse, Michael's, Sam's Club, Subaru, Target, TJ Maxx, Wal-Mart SuperCtr/24hr, vet

66(231) NY 434, Apalachin, **S...gas:** KwikFill, Mobil/dsl, Red Apple, **food:** Blue Dolphin Diner, Dunkin Donuts, McDonald's, Subway, **lodging:** Quality Inn

65(225) NY 17C, NY 434, Owego, **N...gas:** Mobil/dsl, **food:** A&W/KFC, McDonald's, Papa John's, Pizza Hut, Subway, Wendy's, **lodging:** Hampton Inn, Holiday Inn Express, Treadway Motel/rest., **other:** $General, Hickories Park Camping, P&C Foods, Rite Aid, **S...**st police

64(223) NY 96, Owego, **N...lodging:** DeepWell Motel, Sunrise Motel, **S...gas:** Citgo, **food:** Dunkin Donuts

222mm **rest area wb, full(handicapped)facilities, phone, vending, picnic Tables, litter barrels, petwalk**

63(218) Lounsberry, **S...gas:** Valero/rest./dsl

62(214) NY 282, Nichols, **N 2 mi...gas:** Tioga Downs Race Track, **S...gas:** Citgo/Pizza Hut/dsl, **other:** Jim's RV Ctr

212mm **rest area eb, full(handicapped)facilities, picnic tables, litter barrels, phone, vending, petwalk**

208mm Susquehanna River

61(206) NY 34, PA 199, Waverly, Sayre, **S...gas:** Citgo/24hr, KwikFill, **food:** McDonald's, **lodging:** Best Western/rest., **other:** Chevrolet/Buick, Joe's RV Ctr, Nissan

60(204) US 220, to Sayre, Waverly, **N...lodging:** O'brien's Inn, **other:** Clark's Foods, **S...gas:** Citgo, Xtra, **food:** Wendy's, **other:** Aldi Foods, K-Mart, Rite Aid, Top's Foods

59a(202) Wilawana, **S...gas:** Sunoco/Subway/dsl

59(200) NY 427, Chemung, **N...gas:** Dandy/dsl

199mm **rest area wb, full(handicapped)facilities, picnic tables, litter barrels, phone, vending, petwalk**

58(195) rd 2, Lowman, Wellsburg, **N...food:** W Diner, **lodging:** Red Jacket Motel, **S...other:** Gardiner Hill Campsites(4mi), Tillotson Farms Camping(5mi)

56(190) Jerusalem Hill, **S...gas:** Citgo/dsl, KwikFill, Sunoco/Subway, **food:** Hilltop Rest., McDonalds, Pizza Hut, **lodging:** Coachman Motel, Holiday Inn, Mark Twain Motel

54(186) NY 13, to Ithaca, no services

185mm I-86 begins ends., **S...gas:** Mobil, Sunoco, **food:** Dunkin Donuts, LJ Silver, Subway, Wendy's, **lodging:** Motel 6, Red Carpet Inn, **other:** Eckerd, K-Mart

52(184) NY 14, to Watkins Glen, **N...food:** Friendly's, **lodging:** Holiday Inn, Howard Johnson, Knight's Inn, **S...food:** Taste of China, **other:** SavALot Foods

E l m i r a	
C o r n i n g	
B a t h	

52a(183) Commerce Ctr, same as 51

51(182) Chambers Rd, **N...gas:** Mobil/Subway/dsl, Sunoco/dsl, **food:** Chili's, Dunkin Donuts, McDonald's, Olive Garden, Outback Steaks, Red Lobster, Ruby Tuesday, **lodging:** Country Inn&Suites, Hilton Garden, Knights Inn, **other:** BonTon, Firestone, JC Penney, JoAnn Fabrics, Macy's, Sears/auto, mall, **S...food:** Applebee's, New China, Old Country Buffet, Panera Bread, Taco Bell, TGIFriday, Wendy's, **lodging:** Econolodge, Relax Inn, **other:** Barnes&Noble, Best Buy, $Tree, Kost Tire, Lowe's Whse, Michael's, Old Navy, PetCo, Sam's Club, Staples, Subaru, Target, TJ Maxx, Top's Foods, Toyota/Scion, Wal-Mart, museum

50(180) Kahler Rd, **N...**to Airport

49(178) Olcott Rd, Canal St, Big Flats, **N...**airport, antiques, **S...gas:** Sunoco, **food:** Picnic Pizza, **other:** $General

48(171) NY 352, E Corning, **N...gas:** Citgo, **food:** Tag's Rest., **lodging:** Budget Inn, Gatehouse Motel

47(174) NY 352, Gibson, Corning, **N...lodging:** Radisson Inn, to HOSPITAL

46(171) NY 414, to Watkins Glen, Corning, **5mi** **N...other:** Ferenbaugh Camping, KOA, **S...gas:** Citgo/dsl, **lodging:** Comfort Inn, Day's Inn, Staybridge Suites, **other:** HOSPITAL, museums

45(170) NY 352, Corning, **N...gas:** Sunoco, **food:** McDonald's, **S...gas:** Fastrac, **food:** Bob Evans, Burger King, EnEn Chinese, Friendly's, Quizno's, Subway, Wendy's, **lodging:** Fairfield Inn, **other:** AutoZone, CarQuest, Eckerd

44(168) US 15 S, NY 417 W, Gang Mills, **N...lodging:** Best Western, Holiday Inn

43(167) NY 415, Painted Post, **N...gas:** Citgo, **food:** Burger King, Friendly's, McDonald's, Pizza Hut, **other:** AutoValue Parts, CarQuest, $General, Eckerd, Firestone/auto, Jo-Ann Fabrics, **S...gas:** Sunoco, **food:** Denny's, **lodging:** Hampton Inn

167mm parking area wb, litter barrels

42(165) Coopers Plains, **N...**st police

41(161) rd 333, Campbell, **N...other:** Camp Bell Camping(1mi), **S...gas:** Sunoco, **other:** Cardinal Campsites(6mi), antiques

160mm **rest area eb, full(handicapped)facilities, picnic tables, litter barrels, phone, vending, petwalk**

40(156) NY 226, Savona, **N...gas:** Mobil/dsl, **food:** Savona Diner, Subway, **other:** Green Acres Camping

39(153) NY 415, Bath, **N...food:** Chat-a-Whyle Rest.(3mi), **lodging:** Holland American Country Inn, National Hotel, **S...other:** Babcock Hollow Camping(2mi)

38(150) NY 54, to Hammondsport, Bath, **N...gas:** Citgo, KwikFill, Mobil, Sunoco, **food:** Arby's, Burger King, Dunkin Donuts, Ling Chinese, McDonald's, Pizza Hut, Ponderosa, Subway, **lodging:** Budget Inn, Day's Inn, Super 8, Vine-Hurst Inn, **other:** HOSPITAL, Advance Parts, AutoValue Parts, Bath RV Ctr, Chrysler/Plymouth/Dodge/Jeep, Eckerd, Family$, Ford/Lincoln/Mercury, K-Mart, P&C Foods, Rite Aid, Top's Foods, museum, st police, winery, to Keuka Lake

147mm **rest area wb, full(handicapped)facilities, phone, picnic tables, litter barrels, vending, petwalk**

37(146) NY 53, to Prattsburg, Kanona, **S...gas:** Pilot/Subway/dsl/scales/@, Sunoco/Smokey's/dsl/scales, **food:** Tally-Ho Rest., **other:** Wilkin's RV Ctr(1mi), USPO

36(145) I-390 N, NY 15, to Rochester

35(138) Howard, **S...**to Lake Demmon RA, phone

34(130) NY 36, Hornell, Arkport, **other:** Stony Brook SP, Sun Valley Camping, **S...gas:** Sunoco, **food:** Burger King(3mi),

Interstate 86

Hornell	Country Kitchen, Dunkin Donuts, Friendly's(3mi), McDonald's, Ponderosa, Rupert's Rest., Subway, **lodging:** Comfort Inn(3mi), Day's Inn, Econolodge, Sunshine Motel, **other:** Aldi, Chevrolet, Chrysler/Plymouth/Dodge/Jeep, Ford, GNC, NAPA, Wal-Mart/auto, Wegman's Foods
125mm	scenic overlook eb, litter barrels
33(124)	NY 21, to Alfred, Almond, Andover, [S]...**gas:** Mobil, **lodging:** Economy Inn, Saxon Inn Hotel, **other:** Lake Lodge Camping(8mi), Kanakadea Camping
117mm	highest elevation on I-86, elev 2110 ft eb, 2080 ft wb
32(116)	W Almond, no services
31(108)	Angelica, [N]...**gas:** Citgo, **lodging:** Angelica Inn B&B
30(104)	NY 19, Belmont, Wellsville, [N]...6-S Camping(3mi), [S]...**gas:** American Trkstp/Mobil/diner/24hr/@ , **other:** Mothers Piknchikn Camping(6mi)
101mm	**rest area eb, full(handicapped)facilities, phone, picnic tables, litter barrels, vending, petwalk**
29(99)	NY 275, to Bolivar, Friendship, [S]...**gas:** Mobil, Sunoco, Miller&Brandes Gas, **food:** Subway
28(92)	NY 305, Cuba, [N]...**food:** Moonwink's Rest., **lodging:** Econolodge, **other:** $General, Maple Lane RV Park, [S]...**gas:** Exxon, Sunoco/dsl, **food:** McDonald's, **other:** HOSPITAL, Cuba Drug, Giant Foods, Rite Aid
27(84)	NY 16, NY 446, Hinsdale, [N]...**food**, [S]...**gas**
26(79)	NY 16, Olean, [S]...**gas:** Sunoco, **food:** Burger King, Wendy's, **other:** HOSPITAL
Olean 25(77)	Buffalo St, Olean, [S]...**gas:** Citgo/dsl, **other:** HOSPITAL, **2 mi** [S] **on Constitution...gas:** KwikFill, **food:** Applebee's, Burger King, Friendly's, Luigi's Pasta, Pizza Hut, Ponderosa, Quizno's, Tim Horton, **lodging:** Comfort Inn, Country Inn, Microtel, **other:** Advance Parts, Best Western, BJ's Whse/gas, Home Depot, Jo-Ann Fabrics, K-Mart, Radio Shack, Wal-Mart, St Bonaventure U
24(74)	NY 417, Allegany, **1mi** [S]...**gas:** Mobil/dsl, **other:** to St Bonaventure U
73mm	**rest area wb, full(handicapped)facilities, picnic tables, litter barrels, petwalk**
23(68)	US 219 S, [N]...**gas:** M&M/Subway/dsl
66mm	Allegheny River
21(61)	US 219 N, Salamanca, [N]...**lodging:** Holiday Inn Express, [S]...**food:** Red Garter Rest
20(58)	NY 417, NY 353, Salamanca, [N]...**food:** Nafco Quickstop/Burger King, Seneca OneStop/dsl, **food:** McDonald's/24hr, **lodging:** Holiday Inn Express, Mtn View Hotel, **other:** AutoZone, Rail Museum, Seneca-Iroquis Museum, [S]... casino
Salamanca 19(54)	[S]...**other:** Allegany SP, Red House Area
18(51)	NY 280, [S]...**other:** Allegany SP, Quaker Run Area
17(48)	NY 394, Steamburg, [N]...**gas**, **other:** RV camping, [S]...**gas:** M&M/dsl/rest., **other:** camping
16(42)	W Main St, Randolph, [N]...**gas:** Mobil/dsl, **food:** R&M Rest., **lodging**, **other:** RV parking
41mm	**rest area eb, phone, picnic table, litter barrel**
15(40)	School House Rd, no services
39mm	**rest area wb, phone picnic table, litter barrel**
14(36)	US 62, Kennedy, [N]...**gas:** Keystone Gas, **food:** Office Pizza/Subs, [S]...RV camping
32mm	Cassadaga Creek

Jamestown 13(31)	NY 394, Falconer, [S]...**food:** Burger King, McDonald's, Wendy's, **other:** Sugar Creek Stores, **lodging:** Budget Inn, Red Roof Inn
12(28)	NY 60, Jamestown, [N]...**gas:** KwikFill/dsl/deli, **other:** Harley-Davidson, [S]...**gas:** Mobil/McDonald's/dsl, **food:** Bob Evans, Friendly's, **lodging:** Comfort Inn, Hampton Inn, **other:** HOSPITAL, st police
11(25)	to NY 430, Jamestown, [S]...gas, dsl, food, lodging
22mm	**welcome ctr/rest area eb, full(handicapped)facilities, picnic tables, litter barrels, petwalk**
10(21)	NY 430 W, Bemus Point, no services
9(20)	NY 430 E, [N]...**gas:** Mobil, [S]...gas, food, lodging
19mm	Chautauqua Lake
8(18)	NY 394, Mayville, [N]...**gas:** Mobil/dsl, lodging, **other:** RV camping
7(15)	Panama, no services
14mm	Pendergast Creek
10.5mm	French Creek
6(9)	NY 76, Sherman, [N]...**gas:** Keystone Gas, **food:** Village Pizzeria, **other:** Ford, NAPA, USPO
8mm	French Creek
4(1)	NY 430, Findley Lake, [N]...**food:** I-86 Express Rest., **lodging:** Holiday Inn Express, Peek'n Peak Motel, [S]... gas, food, lodging, **other:** RV camping, to Peek'n Peak Ski Area
0mm	New York/Pennsylvania state line. **Exits 3-1 are in PA.**
3	PA 89, North East, Wattsburg, [N]...gas, food
1b a	I-90, W to Erie, E to Buffalo. I-86 begins/ends on I-90,

Interstate 87

Exit #	Services	
176mm	176mm US/Canada Border, NY state line, I-87 begins/ends.	**N**
43(175)	US 9, Champlain, [E]...World Duty Free, [W]...**gas:** Peterbilt Trkstp/dsl/deli/24hr/@ , **other:** repair	
42(174)	US 11 S, to Rouse's Point, Champlain, [E]...**gas:** Mobil, **food:** Chinese Eatery, Pizza+, **other:** Chevrolet/Pontiac(4mi), Kinney Drug, PriceChopper/24hr, Rite Aid, USPO, [W]...**gas:** Exxon/dsl, Mobil/dsl, **food:** McDonald's, Subway	
41(167)	NY 191, Chazy, [E]...st police, [W]...Miner Institute	
162mm	**rest area both lanes, full(handicapped)facilities, info, phone, picnic tables, litter barrels, petwalk**	
40(160)	NY 456, Beekmantown, [E]...**gas:** Mobil/dsl, **lodging:** Pt Auroche Lodge, Stonehelm Motel/café, [W]...Twin Ells Camping	
39(156)	NY 314, Moffitt Rd, Plattsburgh Bay, [E]...**gas:** Stewarts, **food:** Domenic's Rest., Gus' Rest, McDonald's, **lodging:** Pioneer Motel, Rip van Winkle Motel, Super 8, **other:** Plattsburgh RV Park, [W]...**other:** Shady Oaks Camping, to Adirondacks	**S**
38(154)	NY 22, NY 374, to Plattsburgh, [E]...**gas:** Mobil, Sunoco/24hr, **food:** Kinney Drug	

N ↕ S

Plattsburgh

37(153) NY 3, Plattsburgh, Ⓔ...**gas:** Mobil, ShortStop/dsl, Sunoco, **food:** Burger King, Bootlegger Café, DQ, Domino's, IHOP, Jade Buffet, KFC, Little Caesar, Mangia Pizza, McDonald's, Pizza Hut, Subway, Wendy's, **lodging:** Comfort Inn, Holiday Inn, **other:** HOSPITAL, Aldi Foods, BigLots, Buick, Cadillac/Pontiac/GMC, Eckerd, Family$, Firestone/auto, Ford, Honda, Isuzu, Jo-Ann Fabrics, Kinney Drug, Michael's, P&C Foods, Radio Shack, Sam's Club, TJ Maxx, True Value, Wal-Mart SuperCtr/24hr, Ⓦ...**gas:** Exxon, Mobil, Sunoco/Jreck/dsl, **food:** Applebee's, Butcher Block Rest., Friendly's, Lum's, Lindsey Rest., 99 rest., Ponderosa, **lodging:** Best Western, Baymont Inn, Day's Inn, Econolodge, Quality Inn, **other:** Advance Parts, AutoZone, K-Mart, Lowe's Whse, PriceChopper Foods, Sears/auto

151mm Saranac River

36(150) NY 22, Plattsburgh AFB, Ⓔ...**gas:** Citgo, Mobil/dsl/24hr/@, **food:** Burger King(3mi), Ⓦ...**other:** st police

146mm truck insp sta both lanes

35(144) NY 442, to Port Kent, Peru, **2-8 mi** Ⓔ...**other:** Iroquois/Ausable Pines Camping, Ⓦ...**gas:** Citgo/Sugar Creek Diner, Mobil/Subway/Dunkin Doughnuts/dsl, **food:** Cricket's Rest., McDonald's, **other:** Peru Drug, Tops Foods, USPO

143mm emergency phones at 2 mi intervals begin sb/end nb

34(137) NY 9 N, Ausable Forks, Ⓔ...**gas:** Sunoco/dsl, **food:** Pleasant Corner Rest., Mac's Drive-in, Tastee-Freez, Ⓦ...**other:** Prays Mkt, Ausable River RV Camping

136mm Ausable River

33(135) US 9, NY 22, to Willsboro, Ⓔ...gas/dsl, food, lodging, RV camping, to Essex Ferry

125mm N Boquet River

32(124) Lewis, Ⓦ...**gas:** Getty/dsl/24hr/@, Pierce's Gas/dsl, **food:** Trkstp Diner

123mm **rest area both lanes, full(handicapped)facilities, info, phone, picnic tables, petwalk**

120mm Boquet River

31(117) NY 9 N, to Elizabethtown, Westport, Ⓔ...**gas:** Mobil, **lodging:** HillTop Motel, Ⓦ...**other:** HOSPITAL, st police

111mm **rest area nb only, full(handicapped)facilities, phone, picnic tables, litter barrels, vending, petwalk**

30(104) US 9, NY 73, Keene Valley, no services

99mm **rest area both lanes, full(handicapped)facilities, phone, picnic tables, litter barrels, petwalk**

29(94) N Hudson, Ⓔ...**food:** Chuckwagon Rest, **other:** Jellystone Camping, Ⓦ...Blue Ridge Falls Camp

28(88) NY 74 E, to Ticonderoga, Schroon Lake, Ⓔ...**gas:** Sunoco/dsl, **food:** Birches Diner, **lodging:** Schroon Lake B&B, **other:** RV camp/dump, st police, services on US 9 parallel

83mm **rest area both lanes, full(handicapped) facilities, phone, picnic tables, litter barrels, petwalk, vending**

27(81) US 9(from nb, no EZ return), Schroon Lake, to gas/dsl, food, lodging

26(78) US 9(no EZ sb return), Pottersville, Schroon Lake, Ⓔ...**lodging:** Lee's Corner Motel, **other:** Ideal Camping, Wakonda Camping, Ⓦ...**gas:** Mobil, **food:** Black Bear Rest.

25(73) NY 8, Chestertown, Ⓦ...**gas:** Mobil/dsl, **other:** RV camping

24(67) Bolton Landing, Ⓔ...RV camping

66mm parking area sb, picnic tables, no services, Schroon River

64mm parking area nb, picnic tables, no services

23(58) to US 9, Diamond Point, Warrensburg, Ⓦ...**gas:** Citgo/dsl, Mobil, **food:** McDonald's, **lodging:** Super 8, **other:** Ford/Mercury, RV camping, Central Adirondack Tr, ski area

22(54) US 9, NY 9 N, to Diamond Pt, Lake George, Ⓔ...**gas:** Citgo, Mobil, **food:** Boardwalk Rest., Capri Pizzaria, China Wok, Dunkin Donuts, Gino&Tony's Café, Guiseppe's Rest., Jasper's Steaks, JT Kelly's Grill, KFC, Luigi's Italian, Mario's Italian, McDonald's, Pizza Hut, Subway, Taco Bell, Trattoria Siciliano, Trolley Steaks, **lodging:** Admiral Motel, Balmoral Motel, Balsam Motel, Blue Moon Motel, Brookside Motel, Cedarhurst Motel, Choice Inn, Econolodge, Ft Henry Resort, Georgian Lodge, Heritage Motel, Knight's Inn, Lakecrest Motel, Lakehaven Motel, Mohawk Cottages, Motel Montreal, Nordick's Motel/rest., Oasis Motel, O'Sullivan's Motel, Park Lane Motel, Quality Inn, 7 Dwarfs Motel, Sundowner Motel, Surfside Motel, Villager Motel, Windsor Lodge, **other:** Rexall Drug, USPO, Ⓦ...parking area both lanes

21(53) NY 9 N, Lake Geo, Ft Wm Henry, Ⓔ on US 9...**gas:** Mobil, Stewart's Gas, Sunoco, **food:** Adirondack Brewery, A&W, Barnsider Smokehouse, DQ, Mama Riso's Italian, Mountaineer Rest., Prospect Mt Diner, **lodging:** Best Western, Comfort Inn, Holiday Inn, Holly Tree Inn, Howard Johnson/rest., Nomad Motel, Northland Motel, Ramada Inn, Travelodge, Tiki Motel, Super 8, Ⓦ...**gas:** Mobil/dsl/LP, **lodging:** Kathy's Motel

51mm Adirondack Park

20(49) NY 149, to Ft Ann, Ⓔ...**gas:** Mobil/Subway, Sunoco/dsl, **food:** Coach House Diner, Frank's Italian, Logjam Rest., Meeting Place Rest., Montcalm Rest., Trading Post Rest., **lodging:** Day's Inn, French Mtn Motel, Mohican Motel, Rodeway Inn, Samoset Cabins, **other:** Ledgeview RV Park(3mi), Whipporwill/King Phillip/Lake George Camping(2mi), Factory Outlets/famous brands, funpark, st police

Glens Falls

19(47) NY 254, Glens Falls, Ⓔ...**gas:** Citgo, Getty, Hess/Blimpie, **food:** Burger King, China Buffet, Dunkin Donuts, FoodCourt, Friendly's, Ground Round, KFC/A&W, McDonald's, Mrs B's Café, NY Dogs, Old China Buffet, Olive Garden, Pizza Hut, Ponderosa, Queen Diner, Red Lobster, Silo Rest., Taco Bell, Wendy's, **lodging:** Econolodge, Sleep Inn, Welcome Inn, **other:** Advance Parts, AutoZone, BonTon, CVS Drug, Eckerd, Firestone/auto, Goodyear, Home Depot, JC Penney, Jo-Ann Fabrics, Radio Shack, Rite Aid, Sears, Staples, TJ Maxx, Wal-Mart, mall, Ⓦ...**gas:** Mobil, Stewarts Gas, **lodging:** Ramada/rest., st police

18(45) Glens Falls, Ⓔ...**gas:** Citgo, Gulf/24hr, Hess/dsl/24hr, Mobil/24hr, **food:** Carl R's Café, Pizza Hut, Steve's Place Rest., Subway, **lodging:** Best Inn, Queensbury Hotel, **other:** HOSPITAL, CVS Drug, Hannaford Foods, U-Haul, Ⓦ...**gas:** Stewarts, **food:** McDonald's, Super 8

Interstate 87

N ↕ S

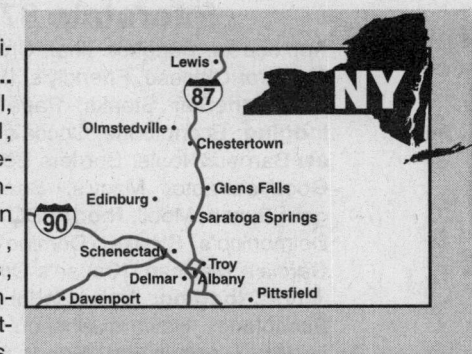

43mm	**rest area both lanes, full(handicapped)facilities, picnic tables, litter barrels, phone, vending, petwalk**
42mm	Hudson River
17(40)	US 9, S Glen Falls, E...**gas:** Citgo, Gulf, Mobil/Subway/dsl/24hr, **food:** Dunkin Donuts, Wishing Well Rest., **lodging:** Budget Inn, Landmark Motel, Sara-Glen Motel, Sunhaven Motel, Swiss American Motel, Town&Country Motel, **other:** American RV Camp, W...Moreau Lake SP
16(36)	Ballard Rd, Wilton, E...**other:** Coldbrook Campsites, golf, W...**gas:** Mobil, Stewarts, Sunoco/Scotty's Rest./dsl/24hr, **lodging:** Mt View Acres Motel, **other:** Alpin Haus RV Ctr, Ernie's Grocery
15(30)	NY 50, NY 29, Saratoga Springs, E...**gas:** Hess/dsl/24hr, Mobil/Blimpie, **food:** Applebee's, Burger King, Denny's, Dunkin Doughnuts, FoodCourt, Friendly's, Gavano's Pizza, Golden Corral, KFC/Taco Bell, McDonald's, 99 Rest., Panera Bread, Ruby Tuesday, TGIFriday, Uno Pizzaria, **lodging:** Super 8, **other:** Barnes&Noble, Best Buy, BJ's Whse, Dodge, Eckerd, Ford/Mercury, Hannaford Foods, Home Depot, JC Penney, Lowe's Whse, Mazda, Old Navy, PriceChopper Foods, Sears/auto, Staples, Subaru, Target, Toyota, Wal-Mart SuperCtr/24hr, mall, W...**lodging:** Birches Motel, Gateway Motel, Residence Inn, Saratoga Motel, **other:** HOSPITAL
14(38)	NY 9P, Schuylerville, **2 mi** E...**gas:** Mobil/Lakeside Mkt/deli, Stewart's Gas, **food:** Bayshore Rest./marina, Tropic Hut Rest., Waterfront Rest., **lodging:** Longfellow Inn/rest., Saratoga Springs Motel, **other:** Lee's RV Park, **2 mi** W...**gas:** Citgo/repair/LP, **lodging:** Holiday Inn, **other:** museum, racetrack
13(25)	US 9, Saratoga Springs, E...**food:** Andy's Pizza, Chez Sophie Rest., DeLucia's Deli, Ripe Public House Rest.(1mi), Tomatoe Rest.(1mi), **lodging:** Maggiore's Motel, Post Road Lodge, **other:** Northway RV, Ballston Spa SP, W...**gas:** Mobil, StewartsMart, **food:** Packhorse Rest., **lodging:** Hilton Garden(1mi), Roosevelt Inn/rest., Thorobred Motel
12(21)	NY 67, Malta, E...**gas:** Mobil/dsl, Sunoco, **food:** Dunkin Donuts, KFC/Taco Bell, Malta Diner, McDonald's, Subway, Tasty Chinese, **lodging:** Cocca's Motel, Fairfield Inn, Riviera Motel, **other:** CVS Drug, GNC, PriceChopper Foods, StewartsMart, st police, W...Saratoga NHP
11(18)	Round Lake Rd, Round Lake, E...**food:** MyWay Cafe, W...**gas:** Citgo/dsl, Sunoco, **food:** CiderMill Rest.(3mi), Good Times Rest., GrandPrix Grill/Inn, **other:** StewartsMart
10(16)	Ushers Rd, E...**gas:** Hess/dsl, Sunoco/dsl, **food:** Ferretti's Rest., **other:** Central Repair, **3 mi** E...**food:** Rusty Nail Rest., W...**other:** StewartsMart
14mm	**rest area nb, full(handicapped)facilities, info, phone, picnic tables, litter barrels, vending, petwalk**
9(13)	NY 146, Clifton Park, E...**gas:** Hess/dsl/24hr, USA/gas, **food:** Burger King, Chili's, Cracker Barrel, Pizza Hut, Red Robin, Sam's Pizzaria, Snyder's Rest., **lodging:** Comfort Suites, **other:** Advance Parts, Aldi Foods, Goodyear/auto, Home Depot, Kohl's, Lowe's Whse, Michael's, W...**gas:** Mobil, Sunoco/dsl, **food:** Applebee's, Denny's, Dunkin Donuts, Friendly's, KFC, McDonald's, Outback Steaks, Quizno's, Ruby Tuesday, Starbucks, Taco Bell, TGIFriday, Wendy's, **lodging:** Best Western, Hampton Inn, **other:** AutoZone, BordersBooks, Chevrolet, CVS Drug, Eckerd, Firestone, Freedom RV Ctr, Hannaford Foods, JC Penney, Jo-Ann Fabrics, K-Mart, Marshall's, PriceChopper Foods, mall, st police
8a(12)	Grooms Rd, to Waterford, **1-2 mi E on US 9...gas:** Getty, Gulf, **food:** 1/2 Moon Diner, Wendy's, **other:** Wal-Mart SuperCtr/24hr
8(10)	Crescent, Vischer Ferry, E...**gas:** Hess/Blimpie/dsl/24hr, **food:** Krause's Rest.(2mi), McDonald's, W...**gas:** Coastal/Mr Subb/dsl/24hr, Sunoco/24hr, **food:** Pancho's Mexican, **other:** CVS Drug, StewartsMart
8mm	Mohawk River
7(7)	NY 7, Troy, **E on US 9N...gas:** Hess/dsl, **lodging:** Hampton Inn, Holiday Inn Express, **other:** Acura, Buick/Pontiac, Dodge, $General, Eckerd, Ford, Prime Outlets/famous brands, Volvo, **E on US 9S...gas:** Mobil, **food:** McDonald's, Subway, **other:** Cottman Transmissions, Infiniti, Marshall's, PriceChopper Foods
6(6)	NY 2, to US 9, Schenectady, E...**gas:** Mobil, **food:** Applebee's, Circle Diner, Dakota Steaks, Ground Round, Krispy Kreme, Uno Pizzaria, Vanilla Bean Café, **lodging:** Cocca's Inn,**other:** Caldor, CVS Drug, Goodyear/auto, JC Penney, Lowe's Whse, Sam's Club, Staples, VW, Wal-Mart, same as 7, W...**gas:** Mobil/24hr, **food:** Bennigan's, Friendly's, Kings Buffet, Sebastian's Rest., Subway, **lodging:** Clarion, Microtel, Super 8, **other:** Target
5(5)	NY 155 E, Latham, E...**food:** DeeDee's Rest., Philly's Grill, Vintage Pizza, **lodging:** Econolodge, **other:** USPO
4(4)	NY 155 W, Wolf Rd, **E on Wolf Rd...gas:** Hess/dsl, Mobil, Sunoco, **food:** Arby's, Ben&Jerry's, Burger King,'s, Denny's, Macaroni Grill, Maxie's Grill, McDonald's, 99 Rest., Olive Garden, Outback Steaks, Pizza Hut, Ponderosa, Real Seafood Co, Red Lobster, Subway, Weathervane Seafood, Wolf Rd Diner, **lodging:** Best Western, Courtyard, Hampton Inn, Holiday Inn, Marriott, Red Roof Inn, **other:** Chevrolet, CVS Drug, Firestone, Ford/Lincoln/Mercury, Hannaford Foods, W...**food:** Calaway Grill, Koto Japanese, **lodging:** Desmond Hotel, Wingate Inn, **other:** Engel's Farmer Mkt, to Heritage Park
2(2)	NY 5, Central Ave, E...**gas:** Mobil, Sunoco, **food:** Wendy's, **lodging:** Scottish Inn, **other:** BJ's Whse, Jo-Ann Fabrics, Marshalls, Staples, Target, **E on Wolf Rd...gas:** Mobil, Sunoco, **food:** American Café,

Saratoga Sprgs

Albany

NEW YORK

Interstate 87

Albany	Applebee's, Bangkok Thai, Chili's, Dunkin Donuts, Emperor Chinese, Friendly's, IHOP, LJ Silver/Taco Bell, LoneStar Steaks, Papa Gino's, Starbucks, **lodging:** Econolodge, Cocca's Inn, Day's Inn, **other:** Barnes&Noble, Borders Books, Firestone/auto, Goodyear/auto, Macy's, Sears/auto, mall, W...**gas:** Exxon, Mobil, **food:** BBQ, Butcher Block Grill, Delmonico's Steaks, Domino's, Empress Diner, Garcia's Mexican, Krause's Diner, Mr Subb, Papa John's, **lodging:** Ambassador Motel, Comfort Inn, Econolodge, Howard Johnson, Northway Inn, Quality Inn, Ramada Ltd, Super 8, **other:** AutoZone, Buick, Goodyear
1W(1)	NY State Thruway(from sb), I-87 S to NYC, I-90 W to Buffalo
1E(1)	I-90 E(from sb), to Albany, Boston
1S(1)	to US 20, Western Ave, **on Western Ave...food:** Burger King, Denny's, TGIFriday, **lodging:** Holiday Inn Express, **other:** JC Penney, mall
1N(1)	I-87 N(from nb), to Plattsburgh
1N	no services
NY State Thruway goes west to Buffalo(I-90), S to NYC(I-87), I-87 N to Montreal	
24(148)	I-90 and I-87 N
23(142)	I-787, to Albany, US 9 W, E...**gas:** Champlain Farms/dsl, **lodging:** Quality Inn, to Knickerbocker Arena, W...**gas:** Stewarts, **lodging:** Econolodge
139mm	parking area sb, phone, picnic tables, litter barrel
22(135)	NY 396, to Selkirk, no services
21a(134)	I-90 E, to MA Tpk, Boston
127mm	**New Baltimore Travel Plaza sb, Mobil/dsl, Big Boy, Mrs Fields, Roy Rogers, Starbucks, TCBY, atm, gifts, info, UPS**
21b(125)	US 9 W, NY 81, to Coxsackie, W...**gas:** Trvl Plaza/dsl/motel/rest./24hr/@, Sunoco/dsl, **food:** McDonald's(5mi), Texarado Steaks, **lodging:** Best Western, Red Carpet Inn, **other:** Boat'n RV Whse
21(114)	NY 23, Catskill, E...**gas:** Mobil, Sunoco/dsl/24hr, **lodging:** Catskill Motel/rest., Quality Inn, **other:** Home Depot, to Rip van Winkle Br, W...**food:** Anthony's Italian, LogSider Café, **lodging:** Astoria Motel, Budget Inn(3mi), Quality Inn, Rip van Winkle Motel, **other:** Indian Ridge Camping, to Hunter Mtn/Windham Ski Areas
103mm	**Malden Service Area nb, Mobil/dsl, Carvel Ice Cream, Hotdogs, McDonald's, atm, gifts, phone, parking area sb**
20(102)	NY 32, to Saugerties, E...**gas:** Getty, Mobil/dsl, Stewarts, **food:** King Buffet, McDonald's, Pizza Star, Starway Café, Subway, **other:** CarQuest, Chrysler/Plymouth/Dodge/Jeep, CVS Drug, Family$, W...**gas:** Hess/Blimpie, dsl, Sunoco/dsl, **food:** Johnny G's Diner, Land&Sea Grill, McDonald's, **lodging:** Catskill Mtn Lodge, Comfort Inn, Howard Johnson/rest., **other:** KOA(2mi), to Catskills
99mm	parking area nb, phone, picnic tables, litter barrels
96mm	**Ulster Travel Plaza sb, Mobil/dsl, Big Apple Bagel, Cinnabon, Nathan's, Roy Rogers, Mrs Fields, TCBY, atm, gifts, phone**
19(91)	NY 28, Kingston, E...**gas:** Citgo/dsl, Mobil, **food:** Friendly's, Gateway Diner, Grand Buffet Rest.,

Newburgh	Picnic Pizza, **lodging:** Holiday Inn, Super 8, **other:** Advance Parts, Hannaford Foods, Radio Shack, Walgreen, W...**food:** Family Diner, International Diner, Roudigan's Steaks, **lodging:** Budget 19 Motel, Ramada Inn/rest., Skytop Motel/steaks, SuperLodge, **other:** Buick, Camper's Barn RV, Ford, Nissan, access to I-587, US 209
18(76)	NY 299, to Poughkeepsie, New Paltz, E...**gas:** Citgo/dsl, Mobil, **food:** China Buffet, College Diner/24hr, **lodging:** Day's Inn, Econolodge, 87 Motel, Rocking Horse Ranch Resort, **other:** Cumberland Farms, to Mid-Hudson Br, W...**gas:** Sunoco/24hr, **food:** Burger King, Dunkin Donuts, Friendly's, McDonald's, Pasquale's Pizza, Pizza Hut, Subway, TCBY, **lodging:** Mohonk Lodge(6mi), Super 8, **other:** Advance Parts, Big A Parts, Eckerd, Radio Shack, Rite Aid, ShopRite Foods, Jellystone(9mi), KOA(10mi)
66mm	**Modena service area sb, gas: Mobil/dsl, food: Arby's, Carvel's Ice Cream/bakery, Uno Pizzaria, McDonald's, other: atm, fax, gifts, UPS**
65mm	**Plattekill Travel Plaza nb, gas: Mobil/dsl, food: Big Boy, Cinnabon, Nathan's, Roy Rogers, other: atm, gifts, info**
17(60)	I-84, NY 17K, to Newburgh, E...**gas:** Getty/dsl, Sunoco/dsl/24hr, **food:** Burger King, Neptune Diner, Pizza Hut, Subway, **lodging:** Day's Inn, Holiday Inn, Howard Johnson/rest., **other:** Adams Foods, Caldor, Buick/Pontiac, Chevrolet/Cadillac, Dodge/Plymouth, Ford, Harley-Davidson, Lincoln/Mercury, NAPA, Nissan, Radio Shack, Rite Aid, ShopRite Foods, W...**gas:** Citgo/dsl, E **on NY 300...gas:** Exxon, Mobil, **food:** Applebee's, Cosimo's Rest., Denny's, Dunkin Donuts, King Buffet, McDonald's, Taco Bell, Wendy's, Yobo Oriental, **lodging:** Hampton Inn, Ramada Inn, Super 8, **other:** AutoZone, Discount Tire, Home Depot, Sears/auto, Wal-Mart/auto, Weis Foods, mall
16(45)	US 6, NY 17, to West Point, Harriman, W...**gas:** Exxon/Subway/dsl, **lodging:** American Budget Inn, **other:** Chevrolet/Buick, Wal-Mart SuperCtr/24hr(1mi), Woodbury Outlet/famous brands, st police
34mm	**Ramapo Service Area sb, gas: Sunoco/dsl/24hr, food: Carvel Ice Cream, Lavazza Coffee, McDonald's, other: atm**
33mm	**Sloatsburg Travel Plaza nb, gas: Sunoco/dsl/24hr, food: Burger King, Dunkin Donuts, Sbarro's, TCBY, other: atm, gifts, info**
15a(31)	NY 17 N, NY 59, Sloatsburg, W...**gas:** Citgo
15(30)	I-287 S, NY 17 S, to NJ. **I-87 S & I-287 E run together.**
14b(27)	Airmont Rd, Montebello, E...**lodging:** Holiday Inn, W...**gas:** Exxon/dsl, **food:** Airmont Diner, Applebee's, Friendly's, Pasta Cucina, Starbucks, Sutter's Mill Rest., Water Wheel Cafe, **lodging:** Wellesley Inn, **other:** HOSPITAL, DrugMart, ShopRite Foods, Walgreen, Wal-Mart
14a(23)	Garden State Pkwy, to NJ, Chestnut Ridge
14(22)	NY 59, Spring Valley, Nanuet, E...**gas:** Gulf, Shell/dsl, **food:** Burger King, Denny's, McDonald's, Subway, **lodging:** Fairfield Inn, **other:** BMW, CarQuest, Pergament, ShopRite Foods, Target, TJ Maxx, mall, W...**gas:** Citgo, **food:** ChuckeCheese, Dunkin Do-

Interstate 87

	nuts, Great China, IHOP, KFC/Taco Bell, Red Lobster, Taco Bell, White Castle/Church's, **lodging:** Day's Inn, Hilton Garden, Nanuet Inn, **other:** Barnes&Noble, Daewoo, Home Depot, Macy's, Marshalls, NAPA, Sears/auto, Staples, Stop'n Shop Foods, mall
13(20)	Palisades Pkwy, N to Bear Mtn, S to NJ
12(19)	NY 303, Palisades Ctr Dr, W Nyack, **E**...Saturn, **W**...**gas:** Mobil, **food:** Grill 303, **lodging:** Nyack Motel, **other:** Barnes&Noble, Best Buy, BJ's Whse, Circuit City, CompUSA, Dave&Buster's, Macy's, Home Depot, JC Penney, Jo-Ann's Etc, Lord&Taylor, Old Navy, Staples, ShopRite Foods, Target, mall
11(18)	US 9W, to Nyack, **E**...**gas:** Mobil, **food:** Hilltop Rest, **lodging:** Best Western, **W**...**gas:** Quality Gas, Shell/dsl, **food:** KFC, McDonald's, **lodging:** Super 8, **other:** HOSPITAL, J&L Repair/tire, Kia, Nissan
10(17)	Nyack(from nb), same as 11
14mm	Tappan Zee Br, Hudson River
13mm	toll plaza
9(12)	to US 9, to Tarrytown, **E**...**gas:** Hess, Shell/repair, **other:** Stop&Shop, **W**...**gas:** Mobil, **food:** El Dorado West Diner, **lodging:** Hilton, **other:** Honda/Subaru, Mavis Tire
8(11)	I-287 E, to Saw Mill Pkwy, White Plains, **E**...**lodging:** Marriott
7a(10)	Saw Mill River Pkwy S, to Saw Mill River SP, Taconic SP
7(8)	NY 9A(from nb), Ardsley, **W**...**lodging:** Ardsley Acres Motel, **other:** HOSPITAL
6mm	**Ardsley Travel Plaza nb, Sunoco/dsl, Burger King, Popeye's, TCBY, vending**
5.5mm	toll plaza, phone
6ba (5)	Stew Leonard Dr, to Ridge Hill, **W**...**other:** Costco, Home Depot, Stew Leonard's Farmfresh Foods
6(4.5)	Tuckahoe Dr, Yonkers, **E**...**gas:** Getty/repair, **food:** Golden Jade Palace, McDonald's, Subway, **lodging:** Tuckahoe Motel, **other:** ShopRite Foods/drug, **W**...**gas:** Gulf, Mobil, **food:** Chinese Food, Domino's, Dunkin Donuts, Totanno's Italian, **lodging:** Holiday Inn, Regency Hotel
5(4.3)	NY 100 N(from nb), Central Park Ave, White Plains, **E**...**gas:** Getty, Shell, Sunoco, **food:** Ground Round
4(4)	Cross Country Pkwy, Mile Sq Rd, **E**...**gas:** Getty, **food:** Burger King, **other:** Ford/Lincoln/Mercury/Subaru, Macey's, Sears/auto, **W**...**gas:** Shell/dsl/24hr, **food:** Burger King, Roy Rogers, **other:** Circuit City, TJ Maxx, to Yonkers Speedway
3(3)	Mile Square Rd, **E**...**gas:** Stop&Shop, Foods, **other:** Circuit City, GNC, Macy's, Thriftway Drug, mall, **W**...**gas:** Getty, Shell/24hr
2(2)	Yonkers Ave(from nb), Westchester Fair, **E**...**gas:** Mobil, **other:** Yonkers Speedway
1(1)	Hall Place, McLean Ave, **E**...**other:** A&P Foods
0mm	New York St Thruway and I-87 N run together to Albany
14(11)	McLean Ave, **E**...**gas:** Shell, **food:** Dunkin Donuts
13(10)	E 233rd , NE Tollway, service plaza both lanes/Mobil
12(9.5)	Hudson Pkwy(from nb), Sawmill Pkwy

(left margin label: N↑S, Nyack)

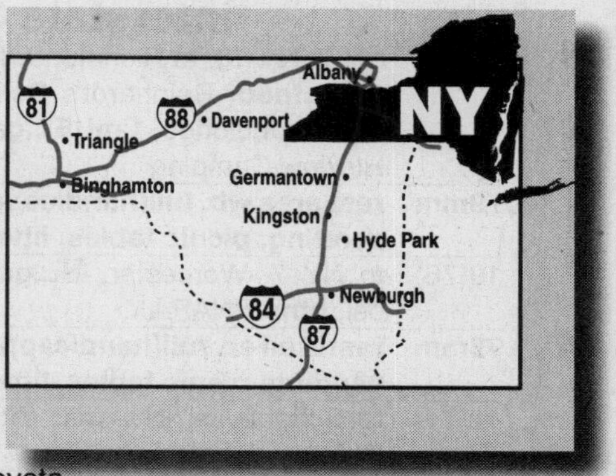

11(9)	Van Cortlandt Pk S, no services
10(8.5)	W 230th St(from sb), W 240th(from nb), **W**...**other:** Target
9(8)	W Fordham Rd, **E**...**gas:** Gaseteria/dsl, **other:** HOSPITAL, Toyota
8(7)	W 179th (from nb), **W**...Roberto Clemente SP
7(6)	I-95, US 1, S to Trenton, NJ, N to New Haven, CT
6(5)	E 153rd t, River Ave, Stadium Rd, **E**...Yankee Stadium
5(5)	E 161st, Macombs Dam Br, **E**...Yankee Stadium
3(3)	E 138th St, Madison Ave Br, **E**...**gas:** Gaseteria/dsl
2(2)	Willis Ave, 3rd Ave Br, **E**...**gas:** Mobil/dsl, **W**...**food:** McDonald's
1(1)	Brook Ave, Hunts Point, **E**...**gas:** BP, Hess
0mm	I-87 begins/ends on I-278.

(right margin label: NYC Area)

Interstate 88

Exit #	Services
25a	I-90/NY Thruway. I-88 begins/ends on I-90, exit 25a.
117mm	toll booth (to enter or exit NY Thruway)
25(116)	NY 7, to Rotterdam, Schenectady, **S**...**gas:** Citgo/Friendly's/Dunkin Donuts/dsl/24hr, **3 mi S**...**gas:** Gulf, **food:** Burger King, McDonald's, Top's Diner, **lodging:** L&M Motel, Rotterdam Motel, **other:** Frosty Acres Camping
24(112)	US 20, NY 7, to Duanesburg, **N**...**gas:** Mobil, **food:** Dunkin Donuts, **other:** st police, **S**...**gas:** Mobil, Stewarts, **food:** Duanesburg Diner
23(101)	NY 30, to Schoharie, Central Bridge, **N**...**gas:** Red Barrel, **other:** Hideaway Camping, Locust Park Camping, **S**...**lodging:** Holiday Inn Express, **2 mi S**...**gas:** Mobil/Subway/dsl, **food:** Dunkin Donuts, **lodging:** Hyland House B&B, Parrott House 1870 Inn, Wedgewood B&B
22(95)	NY 7, NY 145, to Cobleskill, Middleburgh, **2-4 mi N**...**gas:** Hess/dsl, Mobil, **food:** Arby's, Boreali's Diner, Burger King, Dunkin Doughnuts, McDonald's, Subway, Taco Bell, **lodging:** Best Western, Holiday Inn Express(5mi), Gables B&B, Holiday Motel, Howe Caverns Motel/rest., **other:** HOSPITAL, PriceChopper Foods, Twin Oaks Camping, to Howe Caverns, **S**...st police
21(90)	NY 7, NY 10, to Cobleskill, Warnerville, **2 mi N**...**gas:** Hess, Mobil/dsl, **food:** Burger King, Pizza Hut, Sub Express, **other:** HOSPITAL, PriceChopper Foods, **3 mi N**...**food:** Delaney's Rest., **lodging:** Best Western, Gables B&B, **other:** Wal-Mart SuperCtr/24hr

(right margin label: Cobleskill; compass E↑W)

NEW YORK

Interstate 88

E ↕ W

O n e o n t a

20(87) NY 7, NY 10, to Richmondville, [S]...**gas:** Mobil/dsl/24hr, **food:** Reinhardt's Deli, Sub Express, **lodging:** Econolodge, **1 mi** [S]...**gas:** Sunoco/dsl, **other:** Hi-View Camping

79mm rest area wb, full(handicapped)facilities, phone, vending, picnic tables, litter barrels, petwalk

19(76) to NY 7, Worcester, [N]...**gas:** Stewarts, Sunoco/dsl, **other:** NAPA

73mm rest area eb, full(handicapped)facilities, phones, vending, picnic tables, litter barrels, petwalk

18(71) to Schenevus, [N]...**gas:** Citgo, **food:** Schenevus Rest.

17(61) NY 7, to NY 28 N, Colliersville, Cooperstown, **2 mi** [N]...**gas:** Mobil/dsl, **lodging:** Best Western, Knott's Motel, Redwood Motel, **other:** to Baseball Hall of Fame

16(59) NY 7, to Emmons, [N]...**food:** Arby's, Brooks BBQ, Burger King, Farmhouse Rest., Moore's Rest., Perrucci's Pizza, Pizza Hut, **lodging:** Larenzo Motel, Rainbow Inn, **other:** Eckerd, PriceChopper Foods

15 NY 28, NY 23, Oneonta, [N]...**food:** Friendly's, **other:** to Soccer Hall of Fame, [S]...**gas:** Citgo, Hess, Kwikfill, Mobil, **food:** Applebee's, Burger King, Denny's, LJ Silver/Taco Bell, McDonald's, Neptune Diner/24hr, Quizno's, Sabatini's Italian, Subway, Wendy's, **lodging:** Budget Inn, Christopher's Lodge/rest., Clarion, Holiday Inn, Super 8, Townhouse Motel, **other:** HOSPITAL, Aldi Foods, Beaver Spring Camping, BJ's Whse/gas, $Tree, Hannaford's Foods, Home Depot, JC Penney, Kost Tire, NAPA, Wal-Mart SuperCtr/24hr

14(55) Main St(from eb), Oneonta, [N]...**gas:** Citgo, Kwikfill, Stewarts, Sunoco, **food:** Alfresco's Italian, Pepper Joe's Deli, **other:** CVS Drug, cleaners, [S]...**food:** Denny's, McDonald's, Taco Bell, Kountry Livin B&B, **other:** Subaru

13(53) NY 205, **1-2 mi** [N]...**gas:** Citgo, Hess, Mobil, **food:** Burger King, China Buffet King, Duke Diner, Dunkin Donuts, McDonald's, Ponderosa, **lodging:** Celtic Motel, Hampton Inn, Maple Terrace Motel, Oasis Motor Inn, **other:** Chevrolet, Chrysler/Jeep, Honda/Mitsubishi, Nissan, Pontiac/Buick/GMC/Cadillac, Parts+, Rite Aid, to Susquehanna Tr, Gilbert Lake SP(11mi), camping

12(47) NY 7, to Otego, [N]...**other:** KOA, [S]...**gas:** Getty, Red Barrel/dsl/cafe

43mm rest area wb, full(handicapped)facilities, phone, picnic tables, litter barrels, vending, petwalk

11(40) NY 357, to Unadilla, Delhi, [N]...KOA

39mm rest area eb, full(handicapped)facilities, phone, picnic tables, litter barrels, vending, petwalk

10(38) NY 7, to Unadilla, **2 mi** [N]...**gas:** KwikFill, Red Apple, **lodging:** Country Motel(4mi), **other:** Great American Foods, USPO, st police

9(33) NY 8, to Sidney, [N]...**gas:** Citgo/dsl, Hess/dsl, Mobil/dsl, **food:** China Buffet, McDonald's, Pizza Hut, Subway, **lodging:** Algonkin Motel, Country Motel, Super 8, **other:** HOSPITAL, Advance Parts, K-Mart/Little Caesar's, Price Chopper Foods, Quick-Way Foods, Tall Pines Camping, USPO

B i n g h a m t o n

8(29) NY 206, to Bainbridge, [N]...**gas:** Citgo, Sunoco/Taco Xtra/dsl/24hr, **food:** Bob's Family Diner, **lodging:** Algonkin Motel, Susquehanna Motel, **other:** Riverside RV Park, Parts+, to Oquage Creek Park

7(22) NY 41, to Afton, **1-2 mi** [N]...**gas:** Mobil/24hr, Sunoco/dsl, Xtra, **food:** RiverClub Rest., Vincent's Rest., **other:** Afton Golf/rest., Echo Lake Park, Kellystone Park, Smith-Hale HS

6(16) NY 79, to NY 7, Harpursville, Ninevah, [N]...**food:** Gramma's Country Cafe, [S]...**gas:** Red Barrel/dsl, **other:** USPO

5(12) Martin Hill Rd, to Belden, [N]...**gas:** Exxon/Manley/dsl, **other:** Belden Manor Camping

4(8) NY 7, to Sanitaria Springs, [S]...**gas:** Hess/dsl

3(4) NY 369, Port Crane, [N]...to Chenango Valley SP, [S]...**gas:** Fastrac/dsl, KwikFill

2(2) NY 12a W, to Chenango Bridge, [N]...**gas:** Marabito, **other:** NAPA

1(1) NY 7 W(no wb return), to Binghamton, no services

0mm I-81, N to Syracuse, S to Binghamton. I-88 begins/ends on I-81.

Interstate 90

Exit #	Services
B24.5mm	New York/Massachusetts state line
B3(B23)	NY 22, to Austerlitz, New Lebanon, W Stockbridge, [N]...**gas:** Citgo/dsl/scales/24hr, **food:** Lilly's Diner, [S]...**gas:** Sunoco/dsl, **lodging:** Berkshire Spur Motel, **other:** Woodland Hills Camp
B18mm	toll plaza, phone
B2(B15)	NY 295, Taconic Pkwy, **1-2 mi** [S]...gas
B1(B7)	US 9, NY Thruway W, to I-87, toll booth, phone
12(20)	US 9, to Hudson, **1-3 mi** [S]...**gas:** Mobil/dsl/24hr(3mi), Sunoco/dsl(3mi), **food:** McDonald's, **lodging:** Bel Air Motel(1mi), Blue Spruce Motel(4mi), **other:** to Van Buren NHS
18.5mm	**rest area wb, full(handicapped)facilities, phone, picnic tables, litter barrels, vending, petwalk**
11(15)	US 9, US 20, E Greenbush, Nassau, [N]...**gas:** Citgo/dsl, Hess/dsl, **food:** BBQ, Dunkin Donuts, **other:** st police, [S]...**gas:** Mobil(2mi), Stewarts, **food:** Burger King, Goomba's Pizza, Mercato's, My Place Rest., **lodging:** Dewitt Motel, Rodeway Inn, **other:** Chevrolet, Rite Aid, USPO, vet
10(10)	Miller Rd, to E Greenbush, [S]...**gas:** Mobil/dsl, **lodging:** Comfort Inn, **1-3 mi** [S]...**gas:** Stewarts, Sunoco, **food:** Dunkin Donuts, E Greenbush Diner, My Place Rest., Pizza Hut, **lodging:** Dewitt Motel
9(9)	US 4, to Rensselaer, Troy, [N]...**gas:** Mobil, **food:** Applebee's, Ground Round, McDonald's, OffShore Pier Rest., Panera Bread, Starbucks, Subway, **lodging:** Holiday Inn Express, Residence Inn, **other:** $Tree, Grand Union Foods, Home Depot, Petsmart, Radio Shack, Staples, Target, Wal-Mart SuperCtr, [S]...**gas:** Stewart's, **food:** Denny's, Cracker Barrel, **other:** Fairfield Inn, **1-2 mi** [S]...**gas:** Mobil, **food:** Dunkin Donuts, Friendly's, Wendy's, **lodging:** Econolodge
8(8)	NY 43, Defreestville
7(7)	Washington Ave(from eb), Rensselaer

E ↕ W

NEW YORK

Interstate 90

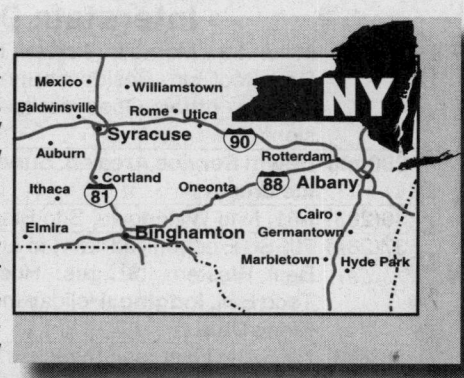

6.5mm	Hudson River
6a	I-787, to Albany
6(4.5)	US 9, Northern Blvd, to Loudonville, ...gas: Stewarts, **food:** Mr Subb, Siena Pizza, Ta-Ke Japanese, **lodging:** Red Carpet Inn, **other:** HOSPITAL

A **Albany**

5a(4)	Corporate Woods Blvd, no services
5(3.5)	Everett Rd, to NY 5, **S**...gas: Hess, **food:** Bob&Ron's Fishfry, Chinese Buffet, Friendly's, Gateway Diner, LJ Silver/Taco Bell, Lucky Garden, McDonald's, Popeye's, Quizno's, Subway, **lodging:** Clarion, **other:** HOSPITAL, Aamco, Advance Parts, AutoZone, Chevrolet, Chrysler/Jeep, CVS Drug, Dodge, $Tree, Eckerd, Ford, Hannaford's Foods/24hr, Home Depot, Honda/Nissan, Mazda, Nissan, PepBoys, Pontiac, PriceChopper Foods, Radio Shack, Suzuki, multiple facilities on NY 5
4(3)	NY 85 S, to Slingerlands
3(2.5)	State Offices, no services
2(2)	Fuller Rd, Washington Ave, **S**...gas: Sunoco, **food:** Dunkin Donuts, **lodging:** Courtyard, CrestHill Suites, Extended Stay America, Fairfield Inn, Red Carpet Inn, TownePlace Inn, same as 1S
1N(1)	I-87 N, to Montreal, to Albany Airport
1S(1)	US 20, Western Ave, **S**...CrossGates Mall Rd, **food:** Bugaboo Creek Steaks, FoodCourt, Hooters, Pizzaria Uno, **other:** Best Buy, Caldor, Macy's, Home Depot, JC Penney, Lord&Taylor, Macy's, Old Navy, Sam's Club, Wal-Mart, mall,
24(149)	I-87 N, I-90 E
153mm	**Guilderland Service Area eb, Sunoco/dsl, McDonald's, Mr Subb**
25(154)	I-890, NY 7, NY 146, to Schenectady, **1 mi** ...exit 8 off I-890, Mobil
25a(159)	I-88 S, NY 7, to Binghamton
26(162)	I-890, NY 5 S, Schenectady
168mm	**Pattersonville Service Area wb, Sunoco/dsl, Big Boy, Cinnabon, Roy Rogers, TCBY, Starbucks, atm, fax, gifts, info, UPS**
172mm	**Mohawk Service Area eb, Sunoco/dsl, Breyer's, McDonald's, fudge**
27(174)	NY 30, Amsterdam, ...gas: Citgo, Mobil, **lodging:** Super 8/diner/24hr, Valleyview Motel, **1 mi** ... **lodging:** Best Western
28(182)	NY 30A, Fonda, ...gas: Citgo/motel/dsl/rest./24hr, Getty/dsl, Gulf/repair, TA/rest/motel/dsl/24hr, **food:** McDonald's, Skip Dog's Grill, **lodging:** Holiday Inn(7mi), Riverside Motel, Super 8, Travelodge, **other:** HOSPITAL
184mm	parking area both lanes, phones, litter barrels
29(194)	NY 10, Canajoharie, ...gas: Gulf, Stewarts, **food:** McDonald's, Pizza Hut, **other:** $General, Rite Aid, **S**...gas: Getty/dsl, Sunoco, **lodging:** Econolodge(1mi), **other:** Chevrolet
210mm	**Indian Castle Service area eb...gas: Sunoco/dsl, food: Big Boy, Mrs Fields, Roy Rogers, other: atm, gifts, UPS. Iroquois Service Area wb...gas: Sunoco/dsl, Burger King, Dunkin Donuts, Freshen's Frozen Treats, TCBY, gifts, UPS**
29a(211)	NY 169, to Little Falls, HOSPITAL, to Herkimer Home

30(220)	NY 28, to Mohawk, Herkimer, ...gas: Fastrac/dsl, Mobil/Subway/dsl, Stewarts, **food:** Applebee's, Burger King, Denny's, Friendly's, KFC/Taco Bell, McDonald's, Pizza Hut, Tony's Pizzaria, Waffle Works, **lodging:** Budget Motel, Herkimer Inn, Inn Towne, **other:** AutoZone, $Tree, Ford/Lincoln/Mercury, Goodyear, K-Mart, Rite Aid, Wal-Mart SuperCtr/24hr, **S**...food: Mohawk Sta Rest., **other:** Factory Depot, to Cooperstown(Baseball Hall of Fame)
227mm	**Schuyler Service Area wb, Sunoco/dsl, Breyer's, Fresh Fudge, McDonald's, atm, st police**

U **Utica**

31(233)	I-790, NY 8, NY 12, to Utica, ...gas: Citgo/dsl, Fastrac, **food:** Burger King, **other:** Big Lots, BJ's Whse, $Tree, Eckerd, Lowe's Whse, PriceChopper Foods, Rite Aid, Wal-Mart SuperCtr/24hr(1mi W on frontage rd), **S**...gas: Hess/dsl, Sunoco/dsl, **food:** Delmonico's Steaks, Denny's, Dunkin Doughnuts, Friendly's, McDonald's, Pizza Hut, Taco Bell, Wendy's, **lodging:** A-1 Motel, Best Western, Happy Journey Motel, Motel 6, Red Roof Inn, Super 8
236mm	I-790(from eb), to Utica
237.5mm	Erie Canal
238mm	Mohawk River
32(243)	NY 232, Westmoreland, **S**...lodging: Carriage House Motel, Quality Inn, **1 mi** **S**...gas/dsl
244mm	**Oneida Service Area eb, Sunoco/dsl, Burger King, Cinnabon, Sbarro's, TCBY, atm, gifts**
250mm	parking area eb, phones, picnic tables, litter barrel
33(253)	NY 365, to Vernon Downs, Verona, ...gas: Citgo, SavOn Gas/dsl, Sunoco, **lodging:** Comfort Suites(6mi), Quality Inn(8mi), Turning Stone Resort/casino, **other:** HOSPITAL, to Griffiss AFB, **S**...gas: SavOn Gas/dsl/repair, **lodging:** Super 8(3mi)
256mm	parking area wb, phones, picnic tables, litter barrel
34(262)	NY 13, to Canastota, **S**...gas: Mobil/dsl, SavOn/dsl/24hr, **food:** Arby's, Canastota Rest., McDonald's, **lodging:** Days Inn, Graziano Motel/rest., Super 8(7mi), **other:** Boxing Hall of Fame, Verona Beach SP Camping
266mm	**Chittenango Service Area wb, Sunoco/dsl, Dunkin Donuts, Freshen's Treats, Sbarro's, TCBY, atm, gifts**
34a(277)	I-481, to Syracuse, Chittenango
35(279)	NY 298, The Circle, Syracuse, **S**...gas: Kwikfill, Mobil/repair, Sunoco/dsl, **food:** Burger King, Denny's, Dunkin Donuts, Joey's Italian, McDonald's, Pronto's Pizza, **lodging:** Candlewood Suites, Carrier Circle Inn, Comfort Inn, Courtyard, Day's Inn, Embassy Suites, Extended Stay America, Fairfield Inn, Hampton Inn, Holiday Inn, Howard Johnson Lodge, John

NEW YORK

Interstate 90

E ↕ W

S y r a c u s e

Milton Inn, Marriott, Microtel, Motel 6, Ramada Ltd, Red Roof Inn, Residence Inn, Super 8, Wyndham Garden, **other:** Goodyear/auto, Speedy Transmissions

280mm **Dewitt Service Area eb, Sunoco/dsl, McDonald's, ice cream**

36(283) I-81, N to Watertown, S to Binghamton

37(284) 7th St, Electronics Pkwy, to Liverpool, N...**lodging:** Best Western, S...**gas:** Hess/Blimpie/24hr, KFC/Taco Bell, **lodging:** Holiday Inn, Knight's Inn, **other:** Kinny Drug

38(286) NY 57, to Liverpool, Syracuse, N...**gas:** Fastrac/dsl, Hess, KwikFill, **food:** Bankok Thai, Hooligan's Grill, Kirby's Rest., Pier 57 Diner, Pizza Hut, Quizno's, Salsaritas Cantina, **lodging:** Super 8, **other:** Aldi Foods, NAPA

39(290) I-690, NY 690, Syracuse, N...**lodging:** Comfort Inn/rest., **other:** Meyers RV Ctr

292mm **Warners Service Area wb, Mobil/dsl/rest., Boston Pizza, Edy's Ice Cream, McDonald's,**

40(304) NY 34, to Owasco Lake, Weedsport, N...Riverforest RV Park, S...**gas:** Fastrac, KwikFill, Sunoco/dsl, **food:** Arby's, Arnold's Rest., DB's Drive-In, Jim's Diner, Old Erie Diner, **lodging:** Best Western, Day's Inn, **other:** Big M Foods, Kinney Drug, NAPA

310mm **Port Byron Service Area eb, Mobil/dsl/rest., Boston Pizza, Edy's ice Cream, McDonald's**

318mm parking area wb, litter barrels, phones

41(320) NY 414, to Cayuga Lake, Waterloo, S...**gas:** Nice'n Easy/dsl, Petro/dsl/rest./scales/24hr/@, **food:** Ma-Gee Country Diner, **lodging:** Holiday Inn(4mi), Microtel(4mi), **other:** Cayuga Lake SP, Waterloo Outlets/famous brands(3mi)

324mm **Junius Ponds Service Area wb, Sunoco/dsl, Dunkin Donuts, Hershey's Ice Cream, Roy Rogers**

42(327) NY 14, to Geneva, Lyons, N...RV camping, S...**gas:** Mobil/dsl/scales, **food:** Gus&Nancy's Diner, **lodging:** Red Carpet Inn, **other:** Waterloo Outlets/famous brands(3mi)

337mm **Clifton Springs Service Area eb, Sunoco/dsl, Roy Rogers, Sbarro's, TCBY, atm, gifts**

43(340) NY 21, to Palmyra, Manchester, N...Hill Cumorah LDS HS(6mi), S...**gas:** Mobil/dsl/24hr, **food:** Lehigh Valley Rest., McDonald's, **lodging:** Roadside Inn

44(347) NY 332, Victor, S...**gas:** Getty's/Subway/dsl, Mobil/dsl, **food:** Di Pacific's Rest., KFC, McDonald's, **lodging:** Best Value Inn, Budget Inn, Econolodge, **other:** CVS Drug, KOA, st police

350mm **Seneca Service Area wb, gas: Mobil/dsl, food: Burger King, Sbarro's, Starbucks, other: atm, info, phone**

45(351) I-490, NY 96, to Rochester, N...**food:** TGIFriday, **lodging:** Hampton Inn, S...**gas:** KwikFill, **food:** Burger King, Charlie's Rest., Chili's, Denny's, Wendy's, **lodging:** Holiday Inn Express, Microtel, Royal Inn, **other:** Ballantyne RV Ctr, Chevrolet

353mm parking area eb, phone, litter barrels

46(362) I-390, to Rochester, N on NY 253W...**gas:** Citgo/dsl, Hess, Sunoco, **food:** McDonald's, Tim Horton,

R o c h e s t e r

Wendy's, **lodging:** Country Inn&Suites, Day's Inn, Fairfield Inn, Microtel, Red Roof Inn, Super 8 **other:** Jeep, Pontiac/GMC

366mm **Scottsville Service Area eb, gas: Mobil/dsl, food: Burger King, Dunkin Donuts, Hershey's Ice Cream, other: atm, info**

376mm **Ontario Service Area wb, gas: Mobil/dsl/deli/pizza, food: Edy's Ice Cream, McDonald's**

47(379) I-490, NY 19, to Rochester, N...Timerline Camping

48(390) NY 98, to Batavia, N...**lodging:** Comfort Inn, Hampton Inn, S...**gas:** Citgo, **food:** Applebee's, Bob Evans, **lodging:** Best Western, Budget Inn, Day's Inn, Holiday Inn, Quality Inn, Ramada Ltd, Super 8, **other:** AutoZone, Home Depot, K-Mart, Wal-Mart SuperCtr/24hr

397mm **Pembroke Service Area eb, gas: Sunoco/dsl, food: Burger King, Popeye's, Starbucks, TCBY, other: atm, gifts, phone, UPS**

48a(402) NY 77, Pembroke, S...**gas:** Flying J/dsl/LP/rest./scales/24hr/@, TA/Citgo/dsl/rest./scales/24hr/@, **food:** Subway, **lodging:** Econolodge, 6 Flags Motel/RV Park(5mi), **other:** Sleepy Hollow Camping(8mi)

412mm **Clarence Service Area wb, full(handicapped)facilities, gas: Sunoco/dsl, food: Burger King, Cinnabon, Pizza Hut, TCBY, other: info, phone**

49(417) NY 78, Depew, 1-3 mi N...**gas:** Mobil, Sunoco, **food:** Applebee's, Arby's, Atlanta Bread, Bennigan's, Bonton, Boston Mkt, Buffalo Wild Wings, Burger King, Cracker Barrel, Dave&Buster's, Denny's, Dibella's Subs, Don Pablo, DQ, Fazoli's, Golden Corral, KFC, McDonald's, Mighty Taco, Moe's SW Grill, Old Country Buffet, Panera Bread, Perkins, Picasso's Pizza, Pizza Hut, Pizza Plant, Ponderosa, Protocol Rest., Red Lobster, Roadhouse Grill, Ruby Tuesday, Spilio's Rest., Starbucks, Subway, Taco Bell, TGI-Friday, Tim Horton, Tulley's Rest., Wendy's, **lodging:** Clarion, Econolodge, Fairfield Inn, Holiday Inn Express, Microtel, Ramada Ltd, **other:** VET, Acura, Barnes&Noble, Big Lots, BJ's Whse, Buick, Chevrolet, Dodge, $General, Dunn Tire, Eckerd/24hr, Firestone/auto, Ford, Home Depot, Honda, JC Penney, Jo-Ann Fabrics, K-Mart, Lowes Whse, Michael's, NTB, Office Depot, Radio Shack, Saturn, Sears/auto, SteinMart, Target, TJ Maxx, Top's Food/deli, Wal-Mart SuperCtr/24hr, Wegman's Foods, mall, S...**gas:** Kwikfill, Mobil, **food:** Bob Evans, John&Mary's Cafe, Salvatore's Italian, **lodging:** Garden Place Hotel, Hospitality Inn, Howard Johnson, Red Roof Inn, **other:** Aamco, CarQuest, Top's Foods

419mm toll booth

50(420) I-290 to Niagara Falls

50a(421) Cleveland Dr(from eb), no services

51(422) NY 33 E, Buffalo, S...airport, st police

52(423) Walden Ave, to Buffalo, N...**food:** Arby's, Bob Evans, McDonald's, Subway, TGIFriday, Tim Horton, Wendy's, **lodging:** Hampton Inn, Residence Inn, **other:** Aldi Foods, Ford, Goodyear/auto, Michael's, Office Depot, Target, Top's Foods, Wal-Mart, S...**gas:** Jim's Trk Plaza/Sunoco/dsl/rest./scales/24hr, **food:** Alton's Rest., Krispy Kreme, McDonald's, Milton's Rest., Olive Garden, Pizza Hut, Smokey Bones

B u f f a l o

NEW YORK

Interstate 90

	BBQ, **lodging:** Millenium Hotel, **other:** Best Buy, Borders Books, Lord&Taylor, JC Penney, K-Mart, Niagara Hobby, Wegman's Foods, mall
52a(424)	William St, no services
53(425)	I-190, to Buffalo, Niagara Falls, **N**...**gas:** KwikFill, **food:** McDonald's, **lodging:** Holiday Inn Express, **other:** Top's Foods
54(428)	NY 400, NY 16, to W Seneca, E Aurora
55(430)	US 219, Ridge Rd, Orchard Park, to Rich Stadium, **S**...**gas:** Citgo, **food:** Wendy's, **lodging:** Hampton Inn, **other:** Aldi, Home Depot, Tops Foods, Wegman's Foods
431mm	toll booth
56(432)	NY 179, Mile Strip Rd, **N**...**gas:** Choice, Citgo, Sunoco, **food:** Blasdelle Pizza, Burger King, Odyssey Rest., **lodging:** Econolodge, **other:** CarQuest, CVS Drug, **S**...**gas:** Citgo, **food:** Applebee's, Bonton, Boston Mkt, ChuckeCheese, McDonald's, Olive Garden, Outback Steaks, Pizza Hut, Red Lobster, Roadhouse Grill, Ruby Tuesday, Starbucks, Subway, TGIFriday, Wendy's, **lodging:** Clarion, Red Carpet Inn, **other:** Aldi Foods, BJ's Whse, Circuit City, Firestone/auto, Home Depot, JC Penney, Jo-Ann Etc, Old Navy, PepBoys, Petsmart, Sears/auto, TJ Maxx, Wegman's Foods, mall
57(436)	NY 75, to Hamburg, **N**...**gas:** Mobil/dsl, **food:** Bob Evans, Denny's, McDonald's, Tim Horton, Wendy's, **lodging:** Comfort Inn, Red Roof Inn, Tallyho Motel, **other:** Chevrolet, Chrysler/Plymouth/Jeep/Mitsubishi, Dodge, Ford, GMC/Pontiac, Kia, **S**...**gas:** Geo, Kwikfill/dsl, Mobil, Stop&Gas, **food:** Arby's, Burger King, Pizza Hut, Subway, **lodging:** Holiday Inn, **other:** VET, Goodyear/auto, Meyer's RV Ctr/Camping World RV Supplies/Service, USPO
442mm	parking area both lanes, phone, litter barrels
57a(445)	to Eden, Angola, **2 mi N**...**gas:** Sunoco/dsl
447mm	**Angola Service Area both lanes, Mobil/dsl, Denny's, McDonald's, phone/fax, gifts**
58(456)	US 20, NY 5, to Silver Creek, Irving, **N**...**gas:** Citgo, Kwikfill, **food:** Burger King, Colony Rest., Millie's Rest., Primo's Rest., Subway, Sunset Grill, Tim Horton, Tom's Rest., **other:** HOSPITAL, to Evangola SP
59(468)	NY 60, Fredonia, Dunkirk, **N**...**lodging:** Dunkirk Motel(4mi), **other:** Lake Erie SP(7mi), **S**...**gas:** Citgo, Kwikfill/dsl, Mobil/dsl, **food:** Applebee's, Arby's, Bob Evans, Burger King, Denny's, KFC/Taco Bell, McDonald's, Pizza Hut, Subway, Tim Horton, Wendy's, Wing City Grill, **lodging:** Best Western, Comfort Inn, Day's Inn, **other:** Aldi, AutoZone, $Tree, Eckerd, Ford/Lincoln/Mercury, GNC, Home Depot, JC Penney, Martin's Foods/gas, NAPA, Radio Shack, Rite Aid, Wal-Mart SuperCtr/24hr/gas
60(485)	NY 394, Westfield, **N**...to Lake Erie SP, camping, **S**...**gas:** Keystone/dsl, **lodging:** Holiday Motel, **other:** HOSPITAL
494mm	toll booth
61(495)	Shortman Rd, to Ripley, **N**...**gas:** Shell/dsl/rest./scales/24hr, **lodging:** Pines Motel, **other:** Lakeshore RV Park
496mm	New York/Pennsylvania state line

(left margin: E↑ W / Dunkirk)

Interstate 95

Exit #	Services
32mm	New York/Connecticut state line
22(30)	Midland Ave(from nb), Port Chester, Rye, **W**...**gas:** BP, Shell, Sunoco, **other:** HOSPITAL, A&P, Home Depot, Staples
21(29)	I-287 W, US 1 N, to White Plains, Port Chester, Tappan Zee
20(28)	US 1 S(from nb), Port Chester, **E**...Subaru
19(27)	Playland Pkwy, Rye, Harrison, no services
18b(25)	Mamaroneck Ave, to White Plains, **E**...**gas:** Shell, **other:** CVS Drug
18a(24)	Fenimore Rd(from nb), Mamaroneck, **E**...**gas:** Citgo
17(20)	Chatsworth Ave(from nb, no return), Larchmont
19.5mm	toll plaza
16(19)	North Ave, Cedar St, New Rochelle, **E**...**food:** McDonald's, Taco Bell, **lodging:** Radisson, Residence Inn, **other:** Stop&Shop Foods, Toyota, **W**...HOSPITAL
15(16)	US 1, New Rochelle, The Pelhams, **E**...**gas:** Getty/dsl, PitStop/24hr, **food:** Thru-Way Diner, **other:** AutoZone, Costco, CVS Drug, Home Depot, NAPA, **W**...repair
14(15)	Hutchinson Pkwy(from sb), to Whitestone Br
13(16)	Conner St, to Mt Vernon, **E**...**gas:** Gulf/dsl, **lodging:** Econolodge, **W**...**gas:** BP, **food:** McDonald's, **lodging:** Andrea Motel, **other:** HOSPITAL
12(15.5)	Baychester Ave(from nb), no services
11(15)	Bartow Ave, Co-op City Blvd, **E**...**gas:** Mobil, **food:** Applebee's, Burger King, Checker's, McDonald's, Red Lobster, **other:** Barnes&Noble, JC Penney, K-Mart, Marshalls, Old Navy, PathMark Foods, Popeye's, Staples, **W**...**gas:** BP, Gulf, Shell/mart, Sunoco/dsl, **food:** Eastern Wok, **other:** A&P Foods, Home Depot, Radio Shack
10(14.5)	Gun Hill Rd(from nb), no services
9(14)	Hutchinson Pkwy, **E**...JC Penney
8c(13.5)	Pelham Pkwy W, no services
8b(13)	Orchard Beach, City Island, no services
8a(12.5)	Westchester Ave(from sb), no services
7c(12)	Pelham Bay Park(from nb), Country Club Rd
7b(11.5)	E Tremont(from sb), **E**...**gas:** Citgo/dsl/24hr, Mobil, **food:** diner
7a(11)	I-695(from sb), to I-295 S, Throgs Neck Br
6b(10.5)	I-278 W(from sb), I-295 S(from nb)
6a(10)	I-678 S, Whitestone Bridge
5b(9)	Castle Hill Ave, **W**...**gas:** Sunoco, **food:** McDonald's
5a(8.5)	Westchester Ave, White Plains Rd, no services
4b(8)	Bronx River Pkwy, Rosedale Ave, **W**...**gas:** Mobil
4a(7)	I-895 S, Sheridan Expsy
3(6)	3rd Ave, HOSPITAL
2b(5)	Webster Ave, **E**...HOSPITAL
2a(4)	Jerome Ave, to I-87, no services
1c(3)	I-87, Deegan Expswy, to Upstate
1b(2)	Harlem River Dr(from sb), no services
1a(1)	US 9, NY 9A, H Hudson Pkwy, 178th St, HOSPITAL
0mm	New York/New Jersey state line, Hudson River, Geo Washington Br

(right margin: NYC Area)

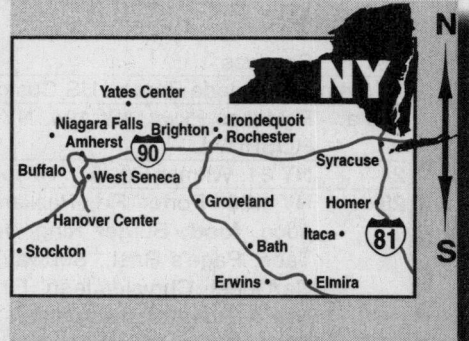

321

NEW YORK
Interstate 190(Buffalo)

E ← → W

Niagara Falls

Exit #	Services
25.5mm	US/Canada Border, US Customs
25b a	R Moses Pkwy, NY 104, NY 265, Lewiston, E... HOSPITAL
24	NY 31, Witmer Rd, E... Hospital, st police
23	NY 182, Porter Rd, Packard Rd, E...gas: Sunoco, **food:** Burger King, JetPort Rest., Mighty Taco, Page's Rest., Subway, Tim Horton, **other:** CarQuest, Chrysler/Jeep, Firestone/auto, K-Mart, NAPA, Prime Outlets/famous brands, U-Haul, W... **food:** Wendy's, **other:** Aldi Foods, Sam's Club, Wal-Mart
22	US 62, Niagara Falls Blvd, E...**food:** Bob Evans, Burger King, Crown Buffet, Dunkin Donuts, Hanna Rest., KFC, Taco Bell, **lodging:** Caravan Motel, Holiday Motel, Hospitality Inn, Howard Johnson, Red Carpet Inn, Swiss Cottage Inn, **other:** Advance Parts, Chevrolet/Buick/Pontiac, $Tree, Ford, Jeep, Radio Shack, Target, Top's Foods/gas, Toyota, W...**lodging:** Econolodge, Scottish Inn, **other:** Home Depot
21a	NY 384, Buffalo Ave, R Moses Pkwy, W...**gas:** Getty, **other:** casino, to NY SP, American Falls
21	La Salle Expswy
20.5mm	Niagara River East, toll booth
20b a	Long Rd, E...**lodging:** Budget Motel, **other:** Country Store
19	Whitehaven Rd, E...**gas:** Getty, **lodging:** Chateu Motel, Holiday Inn, **other:** Top's Foods, KOA(1mi), funpark, W...**other:** VET, Chevrolet, Toyota/Scion
18b a	NY 324 W, Grand Island Blvd, E...**gas:** Mobil, **food:** Burger King, Tim Horton, Wendy's, **lodging:** motel, **other:** NAPA, W...Beaver Island SP
17.5mm	, Niagara River East, toll booth
17	NY 266, last free exit nb
16	I-290 E, to I-90, Albany
15	NY 324, Kenmore Ave, W...U-Haul
14	Ontario St, E...**gas:** Citgo, **food:** McDonald's, Tim Horton, **other:** Advance Parts, W...**food:** Harry's Grille
11	NY 198, Buffalo, downtown
10mm	toll booth
9	Porter Ave, to Peace Bridge, Ft Erie
8	NY 266, Niagara St, downtown, E...**lodging:** Adam's Mark Hotel
7	NY 5 W, Church St, Buffalo, downtown
6	Elm St, E...HOSPITAL, downtown, W...HSBC Arena
5	Louisiana St, Buffalo, downtown
4	Smith St, Fillmore Ave, Buffalo, downtown
3	NY 16, Seneca St, W...**other:** CarQuest
2	US 62, NY 354, Bailey Ave, Clinton St
1	Ogden St, E...**gas:** Sunoco, **food:** Wendy's, **lodging:** Hart Hotel, Holiday Inn Express, **other:** CVS Drug, Volvo/GMC Trucks
.5mm	toll plaza nb
0mm	I-90. I-190 begins/ends on I-90, exit 53.

Interstate 287(NYC)

E ← → W

NYC Area

Exit #	Services
12	I-95, N to New Haven, S to NYC. I-287 begins/ends on I-95, exit 21.
11	US 1, Port Chester, Rye, N...**gas:** Amoco, Mobil, Sunoco, Shell, **food:** Burger King, Maryann 's Mexican, McDonald's, Port Chester Diner, Wendy's, **other:** HOSPITAL, A&P, Goodyear, Kohl's, Medallion Repair, Nissan, Staples
10	Bowman Ave, Webb Ave, no services
9N S	Hutchinson Pkwy, Merritt Pkwy, to Whitestone Br
9a	I-684, Brewster
8	Westchester Ave, to White Plains, S...**other:** Nordstrom's, Westchester Mall Place
7	Taconic Pkwy(from wb), to N White Plains
6	NY 22, White Plains, no services
5	NY 100, Hillside Ave, S...**gas:** Citgo, Getty, Mobil, **food:** Planet Pizza, **other:** Aamco
4	NY 100A, Hartsdale, N...HOSPITAL, S...**gas:** BP, **food:** Burger King, **other:** BMW, Dodge/Hyundai, Jaguar, Nissan/Mazda, Staples, Volvo
3	Sprain Pkwy, to Taconic Pkwy, NYC
2	NY 9A, Elmsford, N...**gas:** Shell, Sunoco, **food:** Red Fox Diner
1	NY 119, Tarrytown, N...**lodging:** Marriott, S...**gas:** Exxon/dsl, Mobil, **lodging:** Extended Stay America, Hampton Inn
I-287 runs with I-87 N.	

Interstate 290(Buffalo)

E ← → W

Buffalo

Exit #	Services
8	I-90, NY Thruway, I-290 begins/ends on I-90, exit 50.
7b a	NY 5, Main St, N...**gas:** Sunoco, **food:** Chico's Pizza/Wings, Subway, Tim Horton, S...**gas:** Valero, **food:** Sonoma Grille, **lodging:** Amherst Motel, **other:** VET
6	NY 324, NY 240, N...**gas:** Getty, **lodging:** Courtyard, S...**other:** Chrysler/Dodge
5b a	NY 263, to Millersport, N...**gas:** Hoolihan's, **lodging:** Comfort Inn, Hampton Inn, Marriott, Red Roof Inn, S...**gas:** Mobil, **lodging:** Homewood Suites, **other:** CarQuest, Hyundai/Subaru, Nissan, Scion/Toyota, VW, Walgreens
4	I-990, to St U
3b a	US 62, to Niagara Falls Blvd, N...**gas:** Exxon, Sunoco, **food:** Bob Evans, Max's Grill, Pancake House, Roadhouse Grill, Ted's Hot Dogs, **lodging:** Blvd Inn, Budget Inn, Extended Stay America, Holiday Inn, Red Carpet Inn, Sleep Inn, **other:** VET, CarQuest, Dodge, Eckerd, Home Depot, Honda, Pontiac/GMC, Wal-Mart, S...**gas:** Mobil, **food:** Applebee's, Arby's, Burger King, Carrabba's, Dibella's Subs, Don Pablo, Krispy Kreme, McDonald's, Ming's Garden, Montana's Grill, Outback Steaks, Panera Bread, Starbucks, Subway, TGIFriday, Tim Horton, Tulley's, **other:** Barnes&Noble, Best Buy, $Tree, Firestone, JC Penney, Jo-Ann Fabrics, K-Mart, Lincoln/Mercury, Lowes Whse, PetCo, Sears/auto, Target, mall

Interstate 290(Buffalo)

2	NY 425, Colvin Blvd, 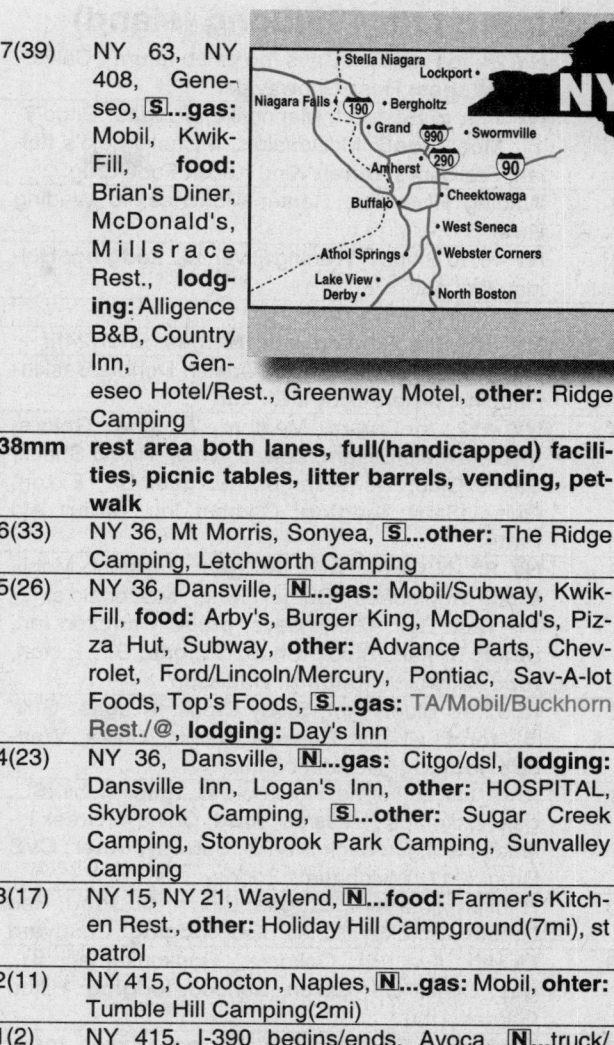**N**...**food:** Athena's Rest., KFC, McDonald's, Subway, Texas Roadhouse, Tim Horton, Wendy's, **other:** Big Lots, BJ's Whse/gas, Family$, Gander Mtn, Goodyear/auto, Top's Foods/gas, **S**...**gas:** Kwikfill
1b a	Elmwood Ave, NY 384, NY 265, **N**...**gas:** Kwikfill, **food:** John's Pizza/Subs, Sam's Cafe, **lodging:** Microtel, **other:** $Tree, Rite Aid, **S**...**gas:** Mobil/dsl, **food:** Arby's, **other:** HOSPITAL
0mm	I-190. I-290 begins/ends on I-190 in Buffalo.

Interstate 390(Rochester)

Exit #	Services
20a b(76)	I-490. I-390 begins/ends on I-490 in Rochester
19(75)	NY 33a, Chili Ave, **N**...**food:** Wishing Well Rest., **S**...**gas:** Sunoco, **food:** Burger King, Subway, **lodging:** Day's Inn
18a b(74)	NY 204, Brooks Ave, **N**...**lodging:** Holiday Inn, **S**...**lodging:** Fairfield Inn, Motel 6, **other:** airport
17(73)	NY 383, Scottsville Rd, **W**...**gas:** Sunoco/Subway/dsl
16(71)	NY 15a, to E Henryetta, **S**...**lodging:** Courtyard, Hampton Inn, HOSPITAL
15(70)	I-590, Rochester,
14(68)	NY 15a, NY 252, **E**...**food:** Outback Steaks, Perkins, Tully's Rest., **other:** Staples, **W**...**gas:** Mobil, **food:** Boston Mkt, Krispy Kreme, Taco Bell, **lodging:** Holiday Inn, **other:** Barnes&Noble, Big Lots, Office Depot, Top's Foods
13(67)	Hylan Dr., **E**...**food:** Cracker Barrel, **lodgin:** Comfort Suites, Homewood Suites, **W**...**gas:** Mobil, **other:** Best Buy, Circuit City, Lowe's Whse, Pep Boys, Sam's Club, Target, Wal-Mart SuperCtr/24hr, mall
12(66)	I-90. NY Thruway, NY 253, **N** on NY 253 **W**...**gas:** Citgo/dsl, Hess, **food:** McDonald's, Peppermints Rest., Tim Horton, Wendy's, **lodging:** Country Inn Suites, Day's Inn, Fairfield Inn, Marriott, Microtel, Red Carpet Inn, Red Roof Inn, Super 8
11(62)	NY 15, NY 251, Rush, Scottsville, **S**...**food:** McDonald's, Wendy's, **lodging:** Cartwright Inn, Days Inn, Fairfield Inn, Red Roof Inn, RIT Inn
10(55)	US 20, NY 5, Avon, Lima, **N**...**food:** Tom Wahls Cafe, **lodging:** Cresthill Motel, Srtatford Motel, **S**...**gas:** Citgo/dsl, Mobil/dsl, **food:** Avon Cafe, Dutch Hollow Cafe, McDonald's, **lodging:** Avon Cedar Lodge, **other:** Chrysler/Dodge/Jeep, Sugar Creek Camping
9(52)	NY 15, **N**...**gas:** Hess/Dunkin Doughnuts/dsl, **food:** Fratelli's Rest., Lakeville Rest., Tee&Gee Cafe, **S**...**other:** Buick/Pontiac/GMC
8(48)	US 20a, Geneseo, **N**...**food:** Arby's, **lodging:** Oak Valley Inn, **other:** Conesus Camping, **S**...**food:** Denny's, Dunkin Donuts, KFC/Taco Bell, McDonald's, Wendy's, **lodging:** Day's Inn

7(39)	NY 63, NY 408, Geneseo, **S**...**gas:** Mobil, Kwik-Fill, **food:** Brian's Diner, McDonald's, Millsrace Rest., **lodging:** Alligence B&B, Country Inn, Geneseo Hotel/Rest., Greenway Motel, **other:** Ridge Camping
38mm	**rest area both lanes, full(handicapped) facilities, picnic tables, litter barrels, vending, petwalk**
6(33)	NY 36, Mt Morris, Sonyea, **S**...**other:** The Ridge Camping, Letchworth Camping
5(26)	NY 36, Dansville, **N**...**gas:** Mobil/Subway, Kwik-Fill, **food:** Arby's, Burger King, McDonald's, Pizza Hut, Subway, **other:** Advance Parts, Chevrolet, Ford/Lincoln/Mercury, Pontiac, Sav-A-lot Foods, Top's Foods, **S**...**gas:** TA/Mobil/Buckhorn Rest./@, **lodging:** Day's Inn
4(23)	NY 36, Dansville, **N**...**gas:** Citgo/dsl, **lodging:** Dansville Inn, Logan's Inn, **other:** HOSPITAL, Skybrook Camping, **S**...**other:** Sugar Creek Camping, Stonybrook Park Camping, Sunvalley Camping
3(17)	NY 15, NY 21, Wayland, **N**...**food:** Farmer's Kitchen Rest., **other:** Holiday Hill Campground(7mi), st patrol
2(11)	NY 415, Cohocton, Naples, **N**...**gas:** Mobil, **ohter:** Tumble Hill Camping(2mi)
1(2)	NY 415, I-390 begins/ends, Avoca, **N**...truck/auto repair, **S**...**gas:** Mobil, **lodging:** Caboose Motel(3mi)

Interstate 495(Long Island)

Exit #	Services
	I-495 begins/ends on NY 25.
73	rd 58, Old Country Road, to Greenport, Orient, **S**...**gas:** Hess/dsl, Exxon, Lukoil, Mobil, **food:** Applebees, Boulder Creek Steaks, Panera Bread, TGI Friday, Taco Bell, Wendy's, **lodging:** Holiday Inn Express, **other:** Best Buy, Borders Books, Chevrolet, CVS Drug, Ford/Lincoln/Mercury, Harley-Davidson, Home Depot, Honda, Michael's, Nissan/Hyundai/Suzuki, PetCo, Tanger/famous brands, Target, Toyota, VW Subaru, Waldbaum's, Walgreens
72	NY 25, (no ez eb return), Riverhead, Calverton, **N**...funpark, **S**...**gas:** Hess, **lodging:** Best Western, **other:** Tanger/famous brands/foodcourt

E

↑

↓

W

NEW YORK

Interstate 495(Long Island)

71	NY 24, to Hampton Bays (no ez eb return), Calverton, **N**...**gas:** Hess/Subway/dsl
70	NY 111, to Eastport, Manorville, **S**...**gas:** Citgo/7-11, Mobil, **food:** McDonald's, Michelangelo's Italian, Starbucks, **other:** King Kullen Food/drug
69	Wading River Rd, Center Moriches, to Wading River
68	NY 46, to Shirley, Wading River, **S**...**lodging:** Holiday Inn, golf
67	Yaphank Ave, no services
66	NY 101, Sills Rd, Yaphank, **N**...**gas:** Shell/24hr
65	Horse Block rd, **N**...**food:** Dunkin Donuts/Baskin-Robbins, **other:** Eddy's RV Ctr
64	NY 112, to Coram, Medford, **N**...**gas:** Getty's, Mobil, **other:** Eckerd, Lowes Whse, Radio Shack, Sam's Club, 7-11, Target, **S**...**gas:** BP, Exxon, Gulf, US/dsl, **lodging:** Comfort Inn, **other:** Aid Parts
63	NY 83, N Ocean Ave, **N**...**gas:** Hess/dsl, Mobil, **food:** Applebees, Burger King, McDonald's, 7-11, Taco Bell, TGI Fridays, **other:** Hampton Inn, **other:** K-Mart, Stop'n Shop, **S**...**gas:** BP, Exxon, **food:** City Grill, **lodging:** Radisson
62	rd 97, to Blue Point, Stony Brook, **N**...**gas:** Gulf, **S**...**food:** Charlie Brown's Steaks, Chili's, Wendy's, **lodging:** Residence Inn
61	rd 19, to Patchogue, Holbrook, **N**...**gas:** Mobil, **S**...**gas:** Exxon/dsl, Hess/dsl, **food:** China 4, Greek Islands Rest, Outback Steaks, Subway, **other:** CVS Drug, 7-11, Waldbaums Foods
60	Ronkonkoma Ave, **N**...**gas:** Exxon, **S**...**food:** Red Lobster, Smokey Bones BBQ, **lodging:** Courtyard
59	Ocean Ave, to Oakdale, Ronkonkoma, **S**...**gas:** Citgo/7-11, Exxon, Sunoco, **lodging:** Hilton Garden(1mi)
58	Old Nichols Rd, Nesconset, **N**...**gas:** Exxon, **food:** Hooters, **lodging:** Marriott, **other:** BJ's Whse, **S**...**gas:** BP
57	NY 454, Vets Hwy, to Hauppauge, **N**...**gas:** Exxon/dsl, **food:** TGIFriday, **S**...**gas:** Citgo/dsl, Getty's, Gulf/dsl/24hr, Shell, Sunoco, **food:** Dave&Buster's, New Horizon Diner, Subway, **lodging:** Hampton Inn, **other:** Eckerd, Stop&Shop Foods, Radio Shack, TJ Maxx, Wal-Mart
56	NY 111, Smithtown, Islip, **N**...**gas:** Exxon/Subway/Domino's/dsl, Mobil, **S**...**gas:** Mobil, **food:** Café La Strada, **lodging:** Holiday Inn Express
55	Central Islip, **N**...**gas:** Mobil, **S**...**gas:** Exxon/dsl
54	Wicks Rd, **N**...**gas:** BP, **other:** Bennigan's, **lodging:** Sheraton, **S**...**gas:** Mobil
53	Sunken Meadow Pkwy, to ocean beaches, Bayshore, no services
52	rd 4, Commack, **N**...**gas:** Mobil/dsl, Shell/repair, **food:** Conca d'Oro Pizza, Ground Round, **lodging:** Hampton Inn, **other:** Costco
51.5mm	parking area both lanes, phone, litter barrels
51	NY 231, to Northport, Babylon, no services
50	Bagatelle Rd, to Wyandanch, no services
49N	NY 110 N, to Huntington, **N**...**lodging:** Marriott

49S	NY 110 S, to Amityville, no services
48	Round Swamp Rd, Old Bethpage, **S**...**gas:** Mobil/dsl, **food:** Old Country Pizza/deli, **lodging:** Homewood Suites, Palace Hotel, Sheraton, **other:** USPO
46	Sunnyside Blvd, Plainview, **N**...**lodging:** Holiday Inn
45	Manetto Hill Rd, Plainview, Woodbury, no services
44	NY 135, to Seaford, Syosset, no services
43	S Oyster Bay Rd, to Syosset, Bethpage, **N**...**gas:** Mobil
42	Northern Pkwy, rd N, Hauppauge, no services
41	NY 106, NY 107, Hicksville, Oyster Bay, **S**...**gas:** BP, Mobil, Sunoco, **food:** Boston Mkt, Boulder Creek Steaks, Broadway Diner, Burger King, Dunkin Donuts, McDonald's, On the Border, **other:** Circuit City, Goodyear/auto, Sears/auto
40	NY 25, Mineola, Syosset, **S**...**gas:** BP, Exxon, Hess/dsl, Shell, **food:** A&W, Burger King, Friendly's, IHOP, McDonald's, Wendy's, **lodging:** Howard Johnson, **other:** Home Depot, Kohl's, 7-11, Staples
39	Glen Cove Rd, **N**...**gas:** Mobil
38	Northern Pkwy E, Meadowbrook Pkwy, to Jones Beach, no services
37	Willis Ave, to Roslyn, Mineola, **N**...**gas:** Exxon, Shell, **other:** repair, **S**...**gas:** Gulf,
36	Searingtown Rd, to Port Washington, **S**...HOSPITAL
35	Shelter Rock Rd, Manhasset, no services
34	New Hyde Park Rd, no services
33	Lakeville Rd, to Great Neck, **N**...HOSPITAL
32	Little Neck Pkwy, **N**...**food:** pizza
31	Douglaston Pkwy, **S**...**gas:** BP, **other:** Macy's, USPO, Waldbaum's Foods, mall
30	E Hampton Blvd, Cross Island Pkwy, no services
29	Springfield Blvd, **S**...**gas:** Exxon, **food:** Dunkin Donuts, McDonald's
27	I-295, Clearview Expswy, Throgs Neck, **N**...**gas:** Gulf, 7-11, **food:** Blue Bay Diner, **other:** Rockbottom Drug
26	Francis Lewis Blvd, no services
25	Utopia Pkwy, 188th St, **N**...**gas:** Citgo, Gulf, Mobil, Sunoco, **S**...**gas:** Citgo, Mobil, Sunoco, **food:** Arby's, Subway, **other:** Radio Shack, USPO
24	Kissena Blvd, **N**...**gas:** Exxon/dsl, **food:** Baskin-Robbins, Dunkin Donuts, **S**...**gas:** Mobil
23	Main St, **N**...**food:** Palace Diner
22	Grand Central Pkwy, to I-678, College Pt Blvd, **N**...**lodging:** Eden Park Hotel, Paris Suites
21	108th St, **N**...**gas:** BP
19	NY 25, Queens Blvd, Woodhaven Blvd, to Rockaways, **N**...**other:** JC Penney, Macy's, mall, **S**...**gas:** BP, **food:** Applebees, **other:** Circuit City, Marshall's, Old Navy, Sears
18.5	69th Ave, Grand Ave(from wb), no services
18	Maurice St, **N**...**gas:** Exxon **S**...**gas:** BP, **food:** McDonald's, **other:** dsl repair
17	48th St, to I-278, **N**...**lodging:** Holiday Inn Express
16	I-495 begins/ends in NYC

Interstate 26

Exit #	Services
71mm	North Carolina/South Carolina state line
69mm	N Pacolet River
67.5mm	**Welcome Ctr wb, full(handicapped)facilities, phone, picnic tables, litter barrels**
67	US 74 E, to NC 108, Columbus, Tryon, **N**...gas: BP/Burger King/dsl, Texaco, **food:** Hardee's, McDonald's, Subway, Waffle House, Wendy's, **lodging:** Day's Inn, **other:** HOSPITAL, CVS Drug, Family$, Food Lion, **S**...gas: Exxon/dsl, Shell, **food:** Dragon Chinese, KFC, **other:** BiLo, $General
59	Saluda, **N**...lodging: Saluda Motel, **other:** camping, **S**...gas: BP/dsl/mart, Texaco/mart, **food:** Apple Mill Rest./gifts, **other:** repair
56mm	Green River
54	US 25, to Greenville, E Flat Rock, access to Carl Sandburg Home
53.5mm	Eastern Continental Divide, 2130 ft
53	Upward Rd, Hendersonville, **N**...gas: Texaco/dsl, **food:** Waffle House, **lodging:** Mtn Inn Suites, **other:** Dish Barn Giftshop, **S**...gas: Exxon/McDonald's/dsl, Shell/Pizza Inn, **food:** Burger King, Cracker Barrel, **lodging:** Holiday Inn Express, **other:** RV camping, to Carl Sandburg Home
49b a	US 64, Hendersonville, **N**...gas: Chevron, Shell/dsl/24hr, Texaco/dsl, **food:** Atlanta Bread Co, Baby Joe's Smokehouse, Chick-fil-A, Fazoli's, Golden Corral, Jack-in-the-Box, O'Charley's, Sonic, Waffle House, **lodging:** Best Western, Hampton Inn, Quality Inn, Ramada Ltd, **other:** HOSPITAL, Advance Parts, CarQuest, $Tree, Ingles, Radio Shack, Staples, Wal-Mart SuperCtr/gas/24hr, World of Clothing, **S**...gas: Chevron/dsl, Exxon/dsl/LP, Shell/dsl, **food:** Applebee's, Arby's, Asaka Japanese, Binion's Roadhouse, Bojangles, Burger King, Checker's, Denny's, Fatz Café, Hardee's, KFC, Krispy Kreme, LJ Silver, McDonald's, Outback Steaks, Pizza Hut, Ryan's, Schlotsky's, Shoney's, Subway/TCBY, Taco Bell, Wendy's, **lodging:** Comfort Inn, Day's Inn, Red Roof Inn, **other:** HOSPITAL, Aldi Foods, Belk, BigLots, BiLo Foods, CVS Drug, Goodyear/auto, Home Depot, JC Penney, K-Mart, Lowe's Whse, Parts+, mall
46mm	weigh sta both lanes, phones
44	US 25, Fletcher, **N**...gas: Exxon/dsl, **food:** Hardee's, Subway, **other:** HOSPITAL, flea mkt, **S**...gas: Citgo/dsl, Shell/Bojangles/Stuckey's/dsl/24hr, United/dsl, **food:** Burger King, Huddle House, **other:** Todd's RV/marine
41mm	**rest area both lanes, full(handicapped)facilities, phone, picnic tables, litter barrels, vending**
40	NC 280, Arden, **N**...gas: Exxon/dsl, Shell/Arby's/dsl, **food:** McDonald's, Pizza Hut, Tijuana Jct Mexican, Waffle House, **lodging:** Budget Motel, Comfort Inn, Day's Inn, Econolodge, Hampton Inn, Holiday Inn/rest., Sun Valley Motel, **other:** Best Buy, Honda/Acura/Kia, Lowe's, Marshall's, Ross, Target, **S**...gas: BP/dsl, **food:** J&S Cafeteria, **lodging:** Fairfield Inn, **other:** Asheville Airport, BMW, Rutledg Lake Camping
37	NC 146, Skyland, **N**...gas: Exxon, Shell/McDonald's/dsl/24hr, **food:** Arby's, Shoney's, Waffle House, **lodging:** Quality Inn, **other:** CVS Drug, **S**...food: La Chiattres Italian
34mm	French Broad River
33	NC 191, Brevard Rd, **N**...other: Saturn/Toyota, **2 mi N**...other: Asheville Farmers Mkt, Bear Creek RV Camp, **S**...gas: Citgo, HotSpot, **food:** China Garden, Garfield's, Harbor Inn Seafood, LJ Silver, Los Volcanes, McDonald's, Ryan's, Stoneridge Grill, Taco Bell, Waffle House, **lodging:** Comfort Suites, Country Inn Suites, Fairfield Inn, Hampton Inn, Holiday Inn Express, Super 8, **other:** Belk, Dillard's, Goody's, K-Mart, Ingles Foods, mall, to Blue Ridge Pkwy
31b a	I-40, E to Statesville, W to Knoxville
27mm	Patton Ave, see I-240(Asheville), exit 3a, 3b
25	rd 251, to UNCA
24	Elk Mtn Rd, Woodfin, no services
23	Merrimon Ave, N Asheville, **N**...gas: Exxon/dsl, **lodging:** Day's Inn, **other:** Food Lion, camping
21	New Stock Rd, **N**...gas: Citgo, **food:** Pizza Hut, **other:** Ingles
19a b	N US 25, W US 70, Marshall, **N**...gas: Shell/dsl, U-fillerup, **food:** Arby's, Bojangles, Burger King, KFC, McDonald's, Waffle House, **other:** Napa, **S**...gas: BP/dsl, Shell/dsl,
18	Weaverville(no EZ return from eb), no services
17	to Flat Creek, no services
15	rd 197, to Jupiter, Barnardsville, no services
13	Forks of Ivy, **N**...gas: BP/dsl, **S**...gas: Exxon/dsl

325

Interstate 26

E	
11	rd 213, to Mars Hill, Marshall, ⓈI...**gas:** Chevron/dsl, Exxon/dsl, Shell/Subway/dsl, **food:** Hardee's, Mountain Harbor Seafood, Pizza Roma, Waffle House, **lodging:** Comfort Inn, **other:** Ford, Napa
9	Burnsville, Spruce Pine, no services
8mm	scenic overlook wb
7mm	runaway truck ramp eb
W	
6mm	**Welcome Ctr. rest area eb, full(handicapped) facilities**
5.5mm	runaway truck ramp eb
5mm	Buckner Gap, elev. 3370
3	to US 23,, Wolf Laurel, no services
2.5mm	runaway truck ramp
0mm	North Carolina/Tennessee state line

Interstate 40

Exit #   Services

E	
420mm	I-40 begins/ends at Wilmington, **Services on US 17, NI...food:** Bob Evans, **other:** Chrysler/Jeep, Lincoln/Mercury/Isuzu, Home Depot, Kia, Nissan, Subaru/Saab/Audi, Toyota, VW, ⓈI...**gas:** Crown/dsl/24hr, Dodge's Store/gas, Exxon/dsl/24hr, Shell, **food:** Buffalo Wings, Burger King, Carrabba's, Chick-fil-A, Cracker Barrel, Hardee's, Hooters, IHOP, KFC, McDonald's, Ruby Tuesday, Sticky Fingers Rest., Taco Bell, Waffle House, Wendy's, **lodging:** Best Western, Day's Inn, Extended Stay America, Fairview Inn, GreenTree Inn, Hampton Inn, Holiday Inn, Howard Johnson, Innkeeper, MainStay Suites, Motel 6, Ramada Inn, Rodeway Inn, Sheraton, Sleep Inn, Super 8, Whitey's Rest, Wingate Inn, **other:** Advance Parts, AutoZone, Batteries+, Buffalo Tire/auto, Buick, Circuit City, Food Lion, Marshall's, Saturn/Suzuki, Target, Wal-Mart SuperCtr/gas/24hr, **Services 2-4 mi Ⓢ on NC 132...gas:** BP, Exxon/dsl, Scotsman, **food:** Applebee's, Bennigan's, Bojangles, Burger King, Checker's, Chili's, Domino's, Golden Corral, Golden Phoenix Chinese, Hardee's, KFC, McAlister's Deli, McDonald's, Outback Steaks, Perkins, Pier 20 Seafood, Rockola Café, Subway, Taco Bell, TCBY, Wendy's, **lodging:** Comfort Inn, Courtyard, Fairfield Inn, Holiday Inn Express, **other:** Barnes&Noble, Best Buy, Chevrolet, Chrysler, CVS Drug, $Tree, Ford, Harris-Teeter/24hr, Honda/Acura, Hyundai, K-Mart, Lowe's Foods, Lowe's Whse, Pontiac/GMC/Mercedes, Sam's Club
420b a	Gordon Rd, NC 132 N, **2 mi NI...gas:** Citgo/dsl, Kangaroo/dsl, **food:** McDonald's, Perkins, Smithfield's Chicken/BBQ, KOA(4mi), ⓈI...**gas:** BP/dsl, Kangaroo/dsl, **food:** Subway
416	new interchange
414	to Brunswick Co beaches, Castle Hayne, ⓈI...**gas:** BP/24hr, Kangaroo, **food:** Hardee's
412	NE Cape Fear River
408	NC 210, ⓈI...**gas:** Exxon/dsl, **food:** Paul's Place Café, **other:** to Moore's Creek Nat Bfd/camping
398	NC 53, Burgaw, **2 mi Ⓢ...food:** Andy's Rest., McDonald's, Pizza Village, Skat's Café, Subway, **lodging:** Burgaw Motel, **other:** HOSPITAL, camping

390	to US 117, Wallace, no services
385	NC 41, Wallace, NI...**gas:** Exxon, **food:** Mad Boar Rest., **lodging:** Holiday Inn Express, River Landing Cottages, **other:** camping, **2-3 mi Ⓢ...to US 117, food:** Andy's Cafe, Hardee's, KFC/Taco Bell, McDonald's, **lodging:** Liberty Inn(4mi)
384	NC 11, Wallace, no services
380	Rose Hill, ⓈI...**gas:** BP/dsl(1mi), Pure/grill, lodging(mi)
373	NC 903, Magnolia, NI...**gas:** BP/dsl/24hr., **lodging:** B&B, **other:** HOSPITAL, Cowan Museum, **2 mi Ⓢ... lodging:** B&B
369	US 117, Warsaw, no services
364	NC 24, to NC 50, Clinton, **rest area both lanes, full(handicapped)facilities, phone, picnic tables, litter barrels, vending, petwalk, 3 mi NI...gas:** Wilco/Hess/Arby's/dsl/24hr/@, **lodging:** Country Squire Inn(7mi), Warsaw Inn, ⓈI...**gas:** Amoco/Bojangles/dsl, BP/dsl, Crown/24hr, Phillips 66/dsl/24hr, Shell/Texaco/dsl, **food:** KFC, McDonald's, Smithfield's BBQ, Subway, Waffle House, Wendy's, **lodging:** Day's Inn, Holiday Inn Express
355	NC 403, to US 117, to Goldsboro, Faison, **3 mi NI... gas:** Exxon, Faison B&B
348	Suttontown Rd, no services
343	US 701, Newton Grove, **1 mi NI...gas:** Exxon/dsl, to Bentonville Bfd
341	NC 50, NC 55, to US 13, Newton Grove, **1.5 mi NI... gas:** Exxon/dsl, **food:** Hardee's, ⓈI...**gas:** BP/McDonald's, Shell, **food:** Smithfield BBQ, Subway
334	NC 96, Meadow, ⓈI...**gas:** BP/dsl(1mi)
328b a	I-95, N to Smithfield, S to Benson, no services
325	NC 242, to US 301, to Benson, ⓈI...**gas:** Citgo/dsl
324mm	**rest area both lanes, full(handicapped)facilities, phone, picnic tables, litter barrels, vending, petwalk, no overnight parking** ▸
319	NC 210, McGee's Crossroads, NI...**gas:** Citgo/DQ/Papa's Subs & Pizza/dsl, Shell/BBQ/dsl/24hr, **food:** McDonald's, **other:** HOSPITAL, ⓈI...**gas:** Mobil/CW's Cafe, **food:** China Star, Italian Pizza/Pasta, KFC/Taco Bell, Subway, Wendy's, **other:** AutoZone, Food Lion, $General
312	NC 42, to Clayton, Fuquay-Varina, NI...**gas:** Wilco/Hess/Wendy's/dsl/24hr, Phillips 66/dsl, **food:** Andy's Rest., China King, Cracker Barrel, Golden Corral, Jersey Mike's Subs, Ruby Tuesday, Papa Subs/Pizza, Pizza Inn, Smithfield BBQ, W 42nd St Grill, White Swan BBQ, **lodging:** Holiday Inn Express, Quality Inn, Super 8, ValuePlace, **other:** CarQuest, Just-Tires, Lowe's Whse, USPO, ⓈI...**gas:** Exxon/Burger King, BP/Subway/dsl/24hr, Citgo/dsl, Shell/dsl, **food:** Bojangles, DQ, Domino's, Jumbo China, KFC/Taco Bell, Marko's Pizza, McDonald's, Waffle House, **lodging:** Hampton Inn, Sleep Inn, **other:** CVS Drug, Food Lion, vet
310	I-540, new exit
306	US 70, to Smithfield, Garner, Goldsboro, **1 mi NI... gas:** Kangaroo/dsl, Shell/dsl, ⓈI...**food:** Buffalo Wild Wings, Chili's, Chick-fil-A, Cold Stone Creamery, McDonald's, Moe's SW Grill, New Japan Express,

Interstate 40

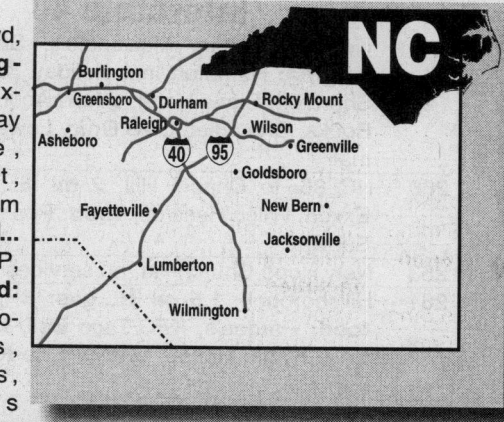

	Logan's Roadhouse, Subway, Wendy's, **other:** Best Buy, BJ's Whse/gas, Kohl's, Michaels, PetsMart, Ross, Staples, Target, TJ Maxx
303	Jones Sausage Rd, Rd, N...**gas:** Hess, Shell/dsl, **food:** Bojangles, Burger King, Smithfield BBQ, Sophie's Deli, S...**gas:** Hess/dsl
301	I-440 E, US 64/70 E, to Wilson
300b a	Rock Quarry Rd, N...**other:** Kroger/gas, S...**gas:** BP/dsl, Exxon, **food:** Burger King, Subway, **other:** Food Lion, Rite Aid
299	Person St, Hammond Rd, Raleigh(no EZ return eb), **1 mi** N...**gas:** Exxon/dsl, **lodging:** King's Motel, **other:** to Shaw U
298b a	US 401 S, US 70 E, NC 50, N...**gas:** Shell, **lodging:** Red Roof Inn, **other:** Parts+, S...**gas:** BP, Crown, Exxon/dsl, Hess/Wilco/dsl, Raceway, **food:** Burger King, El Cerro Mexican, Golden Seafood & Chicken, KFC, **lodging:** Sleep Inn, Super 8, **other:** Sam's Club/gas
297	Lake Wheeler Rd, N...**gas:** Exxon, **food:** Subway, **other:** HOSPITAL, Farmer's Mkt, S...**gas:** Citgo
295	Gorman St, **1 mi** N...**gas:** Exxon/dsl, **food:** Hardee's, McDonald's, Subway, **other:** to NCSU, Reynolds Coliseum, S...**gas:** Kangaroo
293	to I-440, US 1, US 64 W, Raleigh, **.5 mi** S...**gas:** Exxon, Shell, **food:** Chick-fil-A, Cookout, Hardee's, McDonald's, Olive Garden, Pizza Hut, Waffle House, **lodging:** Candlewood Suites, Day's Inn, Red Roof Inn, Motel 6, **other:** Aamco, Borders Books
291	Cary Towne Blvd, Cary, **1 mi** S...**food:** Burger King, Macaroni Grill, McDonald's, Olive Garden, Ragazzi's, Taco Bell, **other:** Belk, JC Penny
290	NC 54, Cary, **1 mi** N...**other:** Comfort Suites, **2 mi** S...**gas:** Citgo, Exxon, Shell, **lodging:** Hampton Inn
289	to I-440, Wade Ave, to Raleigh, N...**other:** HOSPITAL, museum, S...to fairgrounds
287	Harrison Ave, Cary, N...to Wm B Umstead SP, S...**gas:** BP, **food:** Bonefish Grill, Burger King, Carolina Cafe, Chick-fil-A, Maggie's Ice Cream, McDonald's, Moe's SW Grill, NY Pizza, Ruth's Chris Steaks, Starbucks, Wendy's, **lodging:** Embassy Suites, Studio+, TownePlace Suites(3mi), **other:** Colony Tire, Jiffy Lube, Sam's Club
285	Aviation Pkwy, to Morrisville, Raleigh/Durham Airport, N...**lodging:** Hilton Garden
284	Airport Blvd, N...to RDU Airport, S...**gas:** BP/dsl, Mobil, **food:** Bojangles, Cracker Barrel, Hooters, Jersey Mike's Subs, KFC/Taco Bell, Quizno's, Schlotsky's, Texas Steaks, Waffle House, Wendy's, **lodging:** Courtyard, Day's Inn, Extended Stay America, Fairfield Inn, Hampton Inn, Holiday Inn, Holiday Inn Express, Microtel, La Quinta, Residence Inn, Staybridge Suites, **other:** Morrisville Outlets/famous brands/food court
283	I-540, to US 70, Aviation Pkwy
282	Page Rd, S...**food:** Arbys, Bojangles, McDonald's, Starbucks, **lodging:** Comfort Suites, Sheraton/rest., Sleep Inn, Springhill Suites, Wingate Inn, **other:** World Trade Ctr
281	Miami Blvd, N...**lodging:** Extended Stay Deluxe, Marriott, Wyndham Garden, S...**gas:** BP, Shell, **food:** Arby's, Bojangles, Quizno's, Rudino's Grill, Subway, Wendy's, Wok'n Grill, **lodging:** Extended Stay Deluxe, Holiday Inn Express, Homewood Suites, **other:** Atlantic Tire
280	Davis Dr, N...to Research Triangle, S...**lodging:** Radisson
279b a	NC 147, Durham Fwy, to Durham, N...HOSPITAL
278	NC 55, to NC 54, World Trade Ctr, Apex, Foreign Trade Zone 93, N...**gas:** Circle K/dsl, Citgo, **food:** China 1 Rest., Waffle House, **lodging:** Best Value, Comfort Inn, Doubletree Suites, La Quinta, Red Roof Inn, S...**gas:** Crown, Exxon/dsl, Mobil/dsl(1mi), **food:** Arby's, Backyard BBQ, Bojangles, Burger King, Chick-fil-A, Golden Corral, KFC, McDonald's, Mr. Wok, Oh'Brian's, Papa John's, Los Paisano's, Pizza Hut, Starbucks, Subway, Taco Bell, Wendy's, **lodging:** Candlewood Suites, Courtyard, Crestwood Inn, Crossland Suites, Homestead Village, Residence Inn, **other:** Aamco, Alltune/Lube, BigLots, $Tree, Precision Tune, transmissions/tires
276	Fayetteville Rd, N...**gas:** Circle K/dsl, Exxon/dsl, Phillips 66/dsl, **food:** McDonald's, Quizno's, Ruby Tuesday, Rudino's Pizza, Souper Salad, Subs Etc, TCBY, Waffle House, Wendy's, **other:** Eckerd, GNC, Harris-Teeter, Kroger, Walgreens, to NC Central U, S...**food:** Carino's Italian, Chili's, Coldstone Creamery, PF Chang's, Starbucks, Ted's MT Grill, **lodging:** Hilton Garden, **other:** mall, Belks, Best Buy, Hecht's, JC Penney, Macey's, Nordstrom's, Old Navy, Sears/auto
274	NC 751, to Jordan Lake, **1-2 mi** N...**food:** Burger King, McDonald's, Waffle House, Wendy's, S...**gas:** BP, **lodging:** Sheraton
273	NC 54, to Durham, UNC-Chapel Hill, N...**gas:** Shell/dsl, S...**gas:** BP/dsl, Citgo, Shell/dsl, **food:** Hardee's, Nantucket Cafe, **lodging:** Best Western(2mi), Hampton Inn, Holiday Inn Express
270	US 15, US 501, Chapel Hill, Durham, N...**gas:** BP, **food:** Bob Evans, Bojangles, Carrabbas, Hank's Rest., Jason's Deli, Outback Steaks, Philly Steaks, Subway, Tripp's Rest., **lodging:** Comfort Inn, Homewood Suites, **other:** HOSPITALS, Barnes&Noble, Best Buy, Circuit City, $Tree, Home Depot, Kohls, Kroger, Marshall's, Michael's, Old Navy, PetsMart, Saab, Wal-Mart, to Duke U, S...**gas:** BP, Exxon, **food:** Applebee's, Golden Corral, Hardee's, La Ha-

Raleigh / Chapel Hill

E ↑ **W**

	cienda Mexican, McDonald's, Subway, Wendy's, **lodging:** Hampton Inn, Holiday Inn, Red Roof Inn, Sheraton, Siena Hotel, **other:** Acura, BMW, Borders Books, Chevrolet, CVS Drug, Lowe's Whse, Saturn, mall
266	NC 86, to Chapel Hill, **2 mi** [S]...**gas:** BP, Citgo, Exxon, Wilco/Hess/dsl, **food:** Pop's Pizza, Quizno's, Subway
263	New Hope Church Rd, no services
261	Hillsborough, **1.5 mi** [N]...**gas:** BP, Citgo/dsl, Shell, **food:** Hardee's, KFC/Taco Bell, McDonald's, Subway, Waffle House, Wendy's, **lodging:** Holiday Inn Express, Microtel
259	I-85 N, to Durham
	I-40 and I-85 run together 30 mi. See Interstate 85, exits 131-161.
44	to US 70
43	McConnell Rd, [N]...Replacements LTD Outlet [S]... **gas:** Exxon/repair,
41	NC 6, E Lee St, [N]...**gas:** BP/dsl, Phillips 66, **lodging:** Holiday Inn Express, to Coliseum
39	US 29 N, US 70, US 220 N(from eb), to Reidsville, [N]...KOA
38	US 421 S, to Sanford, [S]...**gas:** Pit Stop, **food:** Arby's, Biscuitville, Burger King, Domino's, Gold Express Pizza, McDonald's, Szechuan Chinese, Subway, Taco Bell, Wendy's, **other:** Advance Parts, CVS Drug, $Max, Food Lion, Hall Tire, Key Food Fresh, Tom's Tire
37	S Elm St, Eugene St, [N]...**gas:** Citgo/dsl, Crown, **food:** Bojangles, **lodging:** Homestead Lodge, Landmark Inn, **other:** AutoZone, CarQuest, Family$, Food Lion, O'Reilly Parts, [S]...**gas:** BP, Shell/dsl/24hr, **lodging:** Days Inn, Quality Inn, Super 8, **other:** Home Depot
36b	Randleman Rd, [N]...**gas:** BP, Citgo, Exxon, Solo Gas, **food:** Biscuitville, China Town Express, DQ, KFC, McDonald's, Midori Express, Pizza Hut, Substation II, Subway, **lodging:** Budget Motel, **other:** Advance Parts, Eckerd, Harley-Davidson, Save-a-Lot Foods, [S]...**gas:** BP, Kangaroo/24hr, **food:** Cookout, Mayflower Seafood, Waffle House, Wendy's
36a	US 220, US 29, US 70, to I-85 S, Charlotte
218b a	US 220 S, to I-85 S, Freeman Mill Rd
217b a	High Point Rd, Greensboro, [N]...**gas:** Exxon/dsl, Shell/dsl, **food:** Akashi Japanese, Arby's, Austin's Grill, Bennigan's, Biscuitville, Blue Ribbon, Burger King, Carolina Diner, Chili's, China King, Devereaux Dining, El Paraiso Restorante, Gold India, Ham's Rest., Hooters, La Bamba Mexican, KFC, LoneStar Steaks, Olive Garden, PoFolks, Subway, Taco Bell, **lodging:** Double Tree Inn, Park Lane Hotel, Red Roof Inn, Super 8, Travelodge, **other:** $General, Office Depot, [S]...**gas:** BP, Citgo, Exxon, Texaco, **food:** Bojangles, Burger King, Carrabba's, Chester's Rest., Cookout Café, Darryl's, Krispy Kreme, Kyoto Express, Las Jarochita's, McDonald's, Oh! Brian's, Pizza Inn, Saigon Rest., Smokey Bones, Sonic, Subway, Taco Bell, Tides Seafood, Waffle House,

	Wendy's, **lodging:** Best Western, Comfort Inn, Day's Inn, Drury Inn, Fairfield Inn, Hampton Inn, Ramada Inn, Residence Inn, Sheraton, **other:** Aamco, Advance Parts, Aldi Foods, AutoZone, Belk, Big Lots, Borders Books, Dillard's, City Tire, Family$, Gander Mtn, JC Penney, Merchant Tire/auto, NAPA, PepBoys, Radio Shack, Roses, Sears/auto, TJ Maxx, Walgreens, World Mkt, mall, vet
216	NC 6(from eb, exits left), to Greensboro Coliseum
214b a	Wendover Ave, [N]...**gas:** Exxon/dsl, Shell/dsl, Sheetz, **food:** Bob Evans, Blimpie, Burger King, Cold Stone Creamery, County BBQ, Jake's Diner, K&W Cafeteria, Mario's Pizza, Moe's SW Grill, Panera Bread, Ruby Tuesday, TCBY, Waffle House, **lodging:** Extended Stay America, Hilton Garden, Holiday Inn Express, Microtel, **other:** Acura, BMW, Celebration Station, Chevrolet, Chrysler, Circuit City, Costco/gas, Dodge, Ford/Isuzu, Goodyear, Honda, Mercedes, Mitsubishi, Nissan, PetCo, Saab/Jaguar, Saturn, Staples, Subaru, Volvo, VW, [S]... **food:** Applebee's, Arby's, Biscuitville, Bojangles, Calabash Seafood, Chick-fil-A, Cracker Barrel, Fuddrucker's, Golden Corral, IHOP/24hr, Imperial Gourmet, Kabuto Japanese, La Hacienda Mexican, Logan's Roadhouse, Longhorn Steaks, McDonald's, O'Charley's, Panda Express, Red Lobster, Schlotsky's, Steak'n Shake, Subway, TGIFriday, Taco Bell, Tripp's Rest., Vilarosa Mexican, Wendy's, **lodging:** AmeriSuites, Best Western, Courtyard, La Quinta, Lodge America, SpringHill Suites, Suburban Lodge, Wingate Inn, **other:** Best Buy, Circuit City, Goodyear, Harris-Teeter, Home Depot, Hummer, Kohl's, K-Mart/gas, Lowe's Whse, Sam's Club/gas, Target, Wal-Mart SuperCtr/24hr
213	Guilford College Rd, Jamestown, [N]...**gas:** BP/dsl, **lodging:** Clarion, **other:** to Guilford Coll, [S]...**gas:** Sheetz, **other:** $Tree, Ferrari/Maserati/Porsche, Hummer, Kohl's, Macy's, Old Navy, Pontiac, Saab, Saturn, Target, vet, same as 214
212	new exit
211	Gallimore Dairy Rd, [N]...**other:** Freightliner
210	NC 68, to High Point, Piedmont Triad, [N]...**gas:** Phillips 66/dsl, **food:** Arby's, **lodging:** Comfort Inn, Day's Inn, Embassy Suites, Fairview Inn, Holiday Inn, Homewood Suites, Sleep Inn, **other:** Ford Trucks, to airport, [S]...**gas:** Exxon/dsl, **food:** Bojangles, McDonald's, Pizza Hut/Taco Bell, Ruby Tuesday, Shoney's, Subway, **lodging:** Best Value Inn, Best Western, Comfort Suites, Extended Stay America, Fairfield Inn, Hampton Inn, Motel 6, Red Roof Inn
208	Sandy Ridge Rd, [N]...**gas:** Wilco/Hess/dsl, **other:** Colfax RV Ctr/Camping World, [S]...**gas:** Citgo/dsl, **other:** Farmer's Mkt, Out Of Doors Mart/Airstream
206	Lp 40(from wb), to Kernersville, Winston-Salem, downtown
203	NC 66, to Kernersville, [N]...**gas:** BP, Citgo/McDonald's/dsl, Exxon/Pizza Inn/Subway, **food:** Capt Tom's Seafood, Clark's BBQ, Waffle House, Wendy's, **lodging:** Sleep Inn, **other:** Ford, Merchant Tire/repair, [S]...**gas:** Shell/dsl, **lodging:** Holiday Inn Express
201	Union Cross Rd, [N]...**gas:** Exxon/dsl, QM, **food:** Blue Naples Pizza, Burger King, China Café, **other:** CVS Drug, Food Lion

G r e e n s b o r o

Interstate 40

196	US 311 S, to High Point, no services
195	US 311 N, NC 109, to Thomasville, **S**...**gas:** BP, Wilco/Hess/dsl
193b a	US 52, NC 8, to Lexington, **S**...**gas:** Hess/dsl, Shell, **food:** Hardee's
193c	Silas Creek Pkwy(from eb), same as 192
192	NC 150, to Peters Creek Pkwy, **N**...**gas:** Shell, Wilco/Hess, **food:** Arby's, Bojangles, Burger King, Checker's, China Buffet, Country Roadhouse, Hong Kong Buffet, IHOP, KFC, Little Caesar's, Monterrey Mexican, Old Country Buffet, Perkins, Pizza Hut, Red Lobster, Shoney's, Sonic, Taco Bell, Tokyo Japanese, Wendy's, **lodging:** Comfort Inn(1mi), Innkeeper, Knight's Inn, **other:** Acura/Subaru/Isuzu, Audi, AutoZone, Big Lots, Eckerd, Ford, Hyundai, Kroger, Mazda, NAPA, Office Depot, PharMor Drug, Radio Shack, Suzuki, VW, **S**...**gas:** BP, **food:** Baskin Robbin's, Dunkin Donuts, Libby Hill Seafood, McDonald's, K&W Cafeteria, Wendy's, **lodging:** Holiday Inn Express, **other:** Advance Parts, BiLo, Buick/BMW/Saturn, CVS Drug, Food Lion, Goodyear, Harris Teeter, Honda, K-Mart
190	Hanes Mall Blvd(from wb, no re-entry), **N**...**food:** Chipotle Mexican, Jimmy John's, McDonald's, O'Charley's, Ruby Tuesday, TGIFriday, Tripp's Rest., **lodging:** Day's Inn, Quality Inn, **other:** HOSPITAL, Belk, Dillard's, Firestone, JC Penney, Macy's, Marshall's, Sears/auto, mall, same as 189, **S**...**food:** Baja Fresh Grill, Bojangles, Burger King, ChuckeCheese, Lonestar Steaks, Outback Steaks, Starbucks, Subway, **lodging:** Comfort Suites, Fairfield Inn, Microtel, Sleep Inn
189	US 158, Stratford Rd, Hanes Mall Blvd, **N**...**gas:** BP, Exxon, **food:** Bojangles, Chili's, Golden Corral, Kanpai Japanese, McDonald's, Red Lobster, Sagebrush Steaks, Taco Bell, Texas Roadhouse, **lodging:** Courtyard, Fairfield Inn, **other:** HOSPITAL, Chevrolet, Jo-Ann Fabrics, Macy's, Michael's, NTB, Sears/auto, mall, **S**...**gas:** BP, Shell, **food:** Applebee's, Buffalo Wings, Burger King, Chick-fil-A, Copeland's Grill, Corky's BBQ, Dynasty Buffet, Fuddruckers, Hooters, Jason's Deli, Jimmy's Seafood, KFC/LJ Silver, Little Caesar's, LoneStar Steaks, Longhorn Steaks, Macaroni Grill, Moe's SW Grill, Panera Bread, Qdoba Mexican, Schlotsky's, Subway, **lodging:** Extended Stay America, Hampton Inn, Holiday Inn, La Quinta, Sleep Inn, **other:** Barnes&Noble, Best Buy, Circuit City, Costco/gás, CVS Drug, Discount Tire, Food Lion, Home Depot, Kohl's, Lowe's Whse, Ross, Sam's Club, Target
188	US 421, to Yadkinville, to WFU(no EZ wb return), Winston-Salem, **1/2mi N** off US 421...**gas:** BP/Amoco, Shell, **food:** Boston Mkt, Burger King, McDonald's, Waffle House, Wendy's, **other:** CVS Drug, $Tree, Kroger, Mercedes, Wal-Mart SuperCtr/24hr
184	to US 421, Clemmons, **N**...**gas:** Mobil, Shell, **food:** Applebees, Bambini Italian, El Jinete Mexican, Grecian Corner, KFC, Marble Slab Creamery, Panera Bread, **lodging:** Holiday Inn Express, **S**...**gas:** BP/dsl, Exxon/dsl, Kangaroo, **food:** Arby's, Biscuitville, Brick Oven Pizza, Burger King, Cozumel Mexican,

Winston-Salem

Clemmons

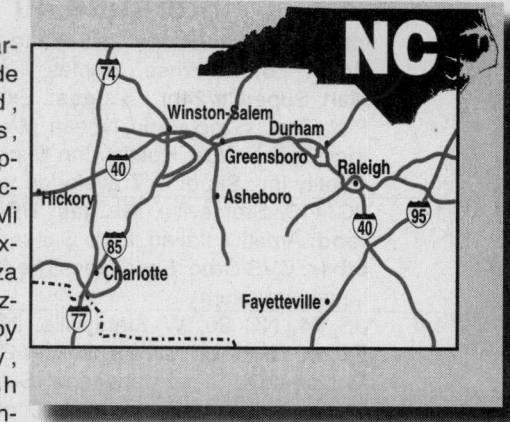

	Cracker Barrel, Dockside Seafood, Domino's, Kimono Japanese, McDonald's, Mi Pueblo Mexican, Pizza Hut, Quizno's, Ruby Tuesday, Sagebrush Steaks, Sonic, Subway, Taco Bell, Waffle House, Wendy's, **lodging:** Holiday Inn, Super 8, Village Inn, **other:** Advance Parts, CarQuest, CVS Drug, $General, Eckerd, K-Mart, Lowe's Foods, Merchant Tire, Parts+, Southern Mkt, Staples, Walgreens, USPO
182	Bermuda Run(from wb, no re-entry), Tanglewood, **S**... **food:** Chang Thai, Lee's Chinese, Papa John's, **other:** Harris-Teeter
182mm	Yadkin River
180	NC 801, Tanglewood, **N**...**food:** Capt's Galley Seafood, Cisson's Rest., Domino's, Subway, **other:** Eckerd, Lowe's Foods, **S**...**gas:** BP/McDonald's/dsl, Deans, Shell, **food:** Bojangles, DQ, Jimmy's Greek, Venezia Italian, Wendy's, **other:** Ace Hardware, CVS Drug, $General, Food Lion, Radio Shack, Walgreens, vet
177mm	**rest areas both lanes, full(handicapped) facilities, phone, vending, picnic tables, litter barrels, petwalk**
174	Farmington Rd, **N**...**gas:** Shell/dsl, **other:** antiques, **S**...**other:** Furniture Gallery, vineyards
170	US 601, Mocksville, **N**...**gas:** Pure/Horn's Rest/DQ/Jersey Mike's/dsl/24hr, **food:** Subway, **other:** RV Superstore, Wal-Mart SuperCtr/24hr, **S**...**gas:** BP/dsl, Exxon, Shell/Taco Bell, **food:** Arby's, Bojangles, Burger King, KFC, McDonald's, Pizza Hut, Wendy's, **lodging:** Comfort Inn, HighWay Inn, Quality Inn, **other:** HOSPITAL, Advance Parts, CVS Drug, $General, Food Lion, Ford/Mercury, Goodyear/auto, Lowe's Whse, USPO, vet
168	US 64, to Mocksville, **N**...**gas:** Exxon/dsl, **other:** Lake Myers RV Resort(3mi), **S**...**gas:** BP
162	US 64, Cool Springs, **N**...**other:** Lake Myers RV Resort(5mi), **S**...**gas:** Shell, **other:** Midway RV Park
161mm	S Yadkin River
154	to US 64, Old Mocksville Rd, **N**...HOSPITAL, **S**...**gas:** Citgo/dsl, Rickie's, **food:** Jaybee's Hotdogs
153	US 64(from eb), 1/2 mi **S**...**gas:** Citgo/dsl, **lodging:** Hallmark Inn, JB's Hotdogs
152b a	I-77, S to Charlotte, N to Elkin
151	US 21, E Statesville, **N**...**gas:** Chevron, Hess/dsl/24hr, PetroExpress, **food:** Applebee's, Bojangles, Burger King, Chick-fil-A, Cracker Barrel, Golden Corral, Hooters, Italian Oven, Jack-in-the-Box, KFC, K&W Cafeteria, Logan's Roadhouse, Lonestar Steaks, McDonald's, Mi Pueblo Café, Pizza Hut/Taco Bell, Pizza Inn, Red Lobster, Ruby Tuesday, Sagebrush Steaks, Schlotsky's, Sorrento Pizza, Wendy's, Zaxby's, **lodging:** Day's Inn, Sleep Inn, **other:** BigLots, Bi-Lo, Chevrolet/Ca-

Statesville

E ↕ W

dillac, Chrysler/Jeep, CVS Drug, Goody's, Home Depot, Lowe's Whse, Staples, Tire Kingdom, Wal-Mart SuperCtr/24hr, [S]...**gas:** Exxon, **food:** Lotus Pier Rest., Szechuan Chinese, Waffle House, **lodging:** Econolodge, Holiday Inn Express, Masters Inn, Quality Inn, Super 8, Travelodge, **other:** st patrol

150	NC 115, Statesville, [N]...**gas:** BP/dsl, Citgo, Shell, **food:** Amalfi's Italian, Little Caesar's, Ol'Bob's BBQ, **other:** CVS Drug, Food Lion, The Family RV Ctr, antiques, museum
148	US 64, NC 90, W Statesville, [N]...**gas:** Citgo/dsl, Exxon, QP, **food:** Arby's, Boxcar Grille, Burger King, McDonald's, Shike Japanese, Subway, Village Inn Pizza, **lodging:** Economy Inn, **other:** CVS Drug, $General, Ingles Foods
146	Stamey Farm Rd, [S]...**gas:** Crown/dsl/rest./24hr
144	Old Mountain Rd, [N]...**gas:** BP, Grand Prix/dsl, **food:** Troy's Rest., [S]...**gas:** BP/dsl, Shell/dsl
143mm	weigh sta both lanes
141	Sharon School Rd, [N]...**gas:** Citgo, **other:** antiques
140mm	Catawba River
138	Oxford School Rd, to Catawba, [N]...**gas:** Exxon/dsl/24hr
136mm	**rest areas both lanes, full(handicapped) facilities, phone, picnic tables, vending, litter barrels, petwalk**
135	Claremont, [S]...**gas:** Shell, **food:** BoxCar Grille, Burger King, Hardee's, Rassie's Subs, **lodging:** Super 8, **other:** $General, Lowe's Foods, RV Ctr
133	Rock Barn Rd, [N]...**gas:** Exxon/dsl, [S]...**gas:** Wilco/Hess/Stuckey's/Subway/Godfather's Pizza/dsl/24hr/
132	to NC 16, Taylorsville, [N]...**gas:** BP, Shell/dsl, **food:** 10th St Rest., **lodging:** Holiday Inn Express
131	NC 16, Conover, [N]...**gas:** BP/dsl, Shell/dsl, **lodging:** Holiday Inn Express, **other:** Wal-Mart SuperCtr
130	Old US 70, [N]...**food:** Domino's, Jack-in-the-Box, Subway, **other:** $General, K-Mart, Lowe's Foods, NAPA, [S]...**gas:** Citgo, Pure, Texaco, **food:** Hardee's(1mi), **other:** USPO
128	US 321, Fairgrove Church Rd, Hickory, [N]...**gas:** BP, Shell, Solo/dsl, **other:** HOSPITAL, McDonald's, Waffle House, to Catawba Valley Coll, [S]...**gas:** Citgo/dsl, Phillips 66, **food:** Bennitt's Smokehouse, Harbor Inn Seafood, Primo's Tacos, Shoney's, Wendy's, **lodging:** Day's Inn, Ramada Inn, **other:** Chrysler/Jeep/Dodge, GMC/Volvo/Ford

H i c k o r y

126	to US 70, NC 155, [S]...**gas:** Citgo, Exxon, Phillips 66, Petro Express, Shell, **food:** Applebee's, Asia Café Buffet, Bob Evans, El Tapatio Mexican, IHOP, Libby Hill Seafood, McDonald's, Melting Pot Rest., O'Charley's, Olive Garden, Taco Bell, Subway, **lodging:** Holiday Inn Express, **other:** Barnes&Noble, Circuit City, $Tree, Goody's, K-Mart, Lowe's Whse, Michael's, Office Depot, Sam's Club, TJ Maxx, Wal-Mart SuperCtr/24hr
125	Hickory, [N]...**gas:** Exxon/Subway/dsl/24hr, Raceway, **food:** Bojangles, Bamboo Garden, Golden Corral, Quizno's, Rockola Café, Texas Roadhouse, Tripp's Rest., **lodging:** Red Roof Inn, **other:** BMW/Mercedes, Chrysler/Jeep, [S]...**gas:** Hess, Servco/

24hr, Shell/dsl, **food:** Arby's, Atlanta Bread, Buffalo Wild Wings, Butch's BBQ, Chick-fil-A, ChuckeCheese, China Garden, CiCi's, Cracker Barrel, Firebonz Rest., Fuddrucker's, Hardee's, Hooters, Jack-in-the-Box, J&S Cafeteria, KFC, Kobe Japanese, Krispy Kreme, Longhorn Steaks, Outback Steaks, Panda Express, Quizno's, Red Lobster, Ruby Tuesday, Sagebrush Steaks, Schlotsky's, Waffle House, Wendy's, Zaxby's, **lodging:** Comfort Suites, Courtyard, Fairfield Inn, Hampton Inn, Holiday Inn Select, Jameson Inn, Sleep Inn, **other:** Aldi Foods, Barnes&Noble, Belk, Best Buy, Circuit City, Dillards, $Tree, Food Lion, Ford, Hancock Fabrics, Home Depot, Honda, JC Penney, Kohl's, Lowe's Whse, Mazda, Mitsubishi, Old Navy, Saturn, Sears/auto, Target, Toyota, Volvo, VW/Porsche, mall

123	US 70/321, to NC 127, Hickory, no services
121	Long View, no services
119b a	Hildebran, [N]...**gas:** Shell/Subway/dsl, **food:** Hardee's, KFC
118	Old NC 10, [N]...**gas:** Pure, Shell/dsl
116	Icard, [S]...**gas:** Southern Star/dsl/24hr, **food:** Burger King, Granny's Kitchen, McDonald's, **lodging:** Icard Inn/rest.
113	Connelly Springs, [N]...**gas:** Citgo, Southern Star/dsl, **other:** HOSPITAL, CVS Drug, Ford, Hyundai, Valdese Weaver
112	Mineral Springs Mtn Rd, Valdese, no services
111	Valdese, no services
107	NC 114, to Drexel, no services
106	Bethel Rd, [S]...**gas:** Exxon/dsl, **lodging:** Economy Inn
105	NC 18, Morganton, [N]...**gas:** BP, **food:** Abele's Rest., Arby's, Capt D's, Coffeehouse, Fatz Café, Harbor Inn Seafood, McDonald's, Sonic, Uptown BBQ, Wendy's, Western Sizzlin, **lodging:** Hampton Inn, Red Carpet Inn, **other:** HOSPITAL, Pontiac/Cadillac/GMC, White Tire, [S]...**gas:** QM/dsl, Texaco, **food:** El Paso Mexican, Sagebrush Steaks, **lodging:** Day's Inn, Holiday Inn/rest., Sleep Inn, to South Mtns SP
104	Enola Rd, [S]...**gas:** Citgo, **food:** Chick-fil-A, Jersey Mike's Subs, **other:** Belk, BigLots, Food Lion, Goody's, Staples, st patrol
103	US 64, Morganton, [N]...**gas:** Citgo, Exxon/dsl/24hr, **food:** Tastee Freez, Village Inn Pizza, **lodging:** Super 8, [S]...**gas:** Citgo, Phillips 66/dsl, RaceWay, **food:** Butch's BBQ, Checker's, Denny's, Dragon Chinese, Hardee's, KFC, Subway, Taco Bell, **lodging:** Comfort Inn, **other:** Clarks Tire, Food Lion, Ingles Foods, Lowe's Whse, Radio Shack, Wal-Mart/drugs
100	Jamestown Rd, [N]...**gas:** BP/dsl/24hr, **food:** Waffle Shop, **other:** Chrysler/Jeep, Ford/Mercury, **2 mi** [N]...**food:** KFC, Taco Bell, **lodging:** Eagle Motel
98	Causby Rd, to Glen Alpine, [S]...B&B/food
96	Kathy Rd, no services
94	Dysartsville Rd, no services
90	Nebo, [N]...**gas:** Citgo/dsl/rest., **other:** to Lake James SP, [S]...**gas:** BP/dsl, **other:** Springs Creek RV Ctr
86	NC 226, to Spruce Pine, Marion, [N]...**gas:** Exxon/dsl, Love's/Subway/Godfather's/dsl/scales, **food:** Hardee's, KFC, **other:** Jellystone RV Park(1mi)

M o r g a n t o n

Interstate 40

85	US 221, Marion, **N**...**lodging:** Hampton Inn, **other:** to Mt Mitchell SP, **S**...**gas:** Shell/dsl/24hr, **food:** Sagebrush Steaks, **lodging:** Day's Inn, Super 8
83	Ashworth Rd, no services
82mm	**rest area both lanes, full(handicapped)facilities, phone, picnic tables, vending, litter barrels, petwalk**
81	81 Sugar Hill Rd, to Marion, **N**...**gas:** BP/dsl, Citgo/dsl, **other:** HOSPITAL, Dodge/Jeep, **S**...**gas:** Exxon/dsl/24hr
76mm	Catawba River
75	Parker Padgett Rd, **S**...**gas:** Stuckey's/DQ/dsl
73	Old Fort, **N**...**gas:** Citgo/dsl, **food:** Hardee's, **lodging:** Bed&Breakfast, **other:** Mtn Gateway Museum, Napa, **S**...**gas:** Super Test/dsl, **food:** McDonald's, **other:** Bumper Parts
72	US 70(from eb), Old Fort, **N**...B&B
71mm	Pisgah Nat Forest, eastern boundary
67.5mm	truck rest area eb
66	Ridgecrest, **N**...**lodging:** B&B
65	(from wb), to Black Mountain, Black Mtn Ctr
64	NC 9, Black Mountain, **N**...**gas:** Exxon, Shell/Subway/24hr, **food:** Pizza Hut, **other:** BiLo/café, Chevrolet, **S**...**gas:** Phillips 66, **food:** Denny's, Huddle House, KFC, McDonald's, Taco Bell, Wendy's, **lodging:** Comfort Inn, **other:** Eckerd, Ingles Foods, Radio Shack
63mm	Swannanoa River
59	Swannanoa, **N**...**gas:** BP/Subway/TCBY, Exxon/dsl, Mystik, **food:** Athens Pizza, Burger King, **other:** Harley-Davidson, Ingles Foods/gas, KOA(2mi), Miles RV Ctr/Park, to Warren Wilson Coll, uspo, **S**...**other:** Mama Gertie's Camping
55	E Asheville, US 70, **N**...**gas:** BP, Citgo/Subway, Conoco, **food:** Arby's, Bojangles, Cocula Mexican, Dj's Diner, Waffle House, Zaxby's, **lodging:** B&B, Day's Inn, Holiday Inn, Motel 6, Quality Inn, Super 8, **other:** VA HOSPITAL, Go Groceries, Top's RV park, to Mt Mitchell SP, Folk Art Ctr
53b a	I-240 W, US 74, to Asheville, Bat Cave, **N**...**food:** KFC, J&S Cafeteria, McDonald's, **lodging:** Comfort Inn, **other:** Advance Parts, BiLo, CVS Drug, Eckerd, Hamrick's, **1-2 mi N on US 74**...**gas:** BP, Exxon/dsl, **food:** Applebee's, Burger King, Carrabba's, Chili's, Chick-fil-A, Damon's, IHOP, O'Charley's, Olive Garden, Red Lobster, Subway, Waffle House, **lodging:** Courtyard, Day's Inn, Econolodge, Extended Stay America, Hampton Inn, Ramada Ltd, **other:** Barnes& Noble, Best Buy, Circuit City, Dillard's, Goody's, Home Depot, Ingles Foods, K-Mart, Lowes Whse, Michael's, Office Depot,, Radio Shack, Ross, Sears/ auto, mall, **S**...**gas:** BP/dsl/LP, Phillips 66, **other:** to Blue Ridge Pkwy
51	US 25A, Sweeten Creek Rd, **1/2 mi S**...**food:** Subway
50	US 25, Asheville, **N**...**gas:** BP, CitiStop, Shell/dsl, **food:** Arby's, Asaka Japanese, Chapala Mexican, Ichiban, Krystal, LJ Silver/A&W, McDonald's, Moe's SW Grill, Subway, Texas Roadhouse, TGIFriday, Wendy's, **lodging:** Baymont Inn, Doubletree Inn, Holiday Inn Express, Howard Johnson, Sleep Inn, **other:**

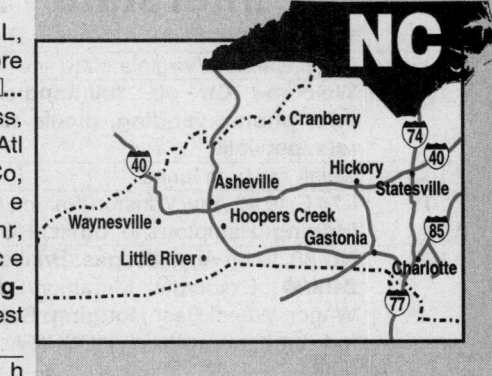

	HOSPITAL, to Biltmore House, **S**...**gas:** Hess, **food:** Atl Bread Co, Huddle House/24hr, Province Rest., **lodging:** Forest Manor Inn
47mm	French Broad River
47	NC 191, W Asheville, **N**...**other:** Asheville Speedway, Bear Creek RV Camping, **S**...**gas:** Phillips 66/dsl, **food:** Moose Cafe, **other:** Farmer's Mkt, **2 mi S**...**lodging:** Comfort Inn, Country Inn&Suites, Fairfield Inn, Hampton Inn, Holiday Inn Express, Super 8
46b a	I-26 & I-240 E, **2 mi N**...multiple services from I-240
44	US 74, W Asheville, **N**...**gas:** BP, Chevron/dsl, Conoco, Exxon, Hess/dsl, Shell/Substation II/24hr, **food:** Applebee's, Asiana Buffet, Burger King, Cracker Barrel, El Chapala Mexican, Fatz Cafe, Hardees, Kountry Kitchen, Krystal, Los Volcanes Mexican, Pizza Hut, Waffle House, Wendy's, **lodging:** Best Western, Comfort Inn, Red Roof Inn, Sleep Inn, Super 8, Whispering Pines Motel, **other:** CarQuest, Chevrolet, Chrysler/Jeep, CVS Drug, Family$, Ingles Foods, Lowe's Whse, Mercedes/Mazda, **S**...**food:** McDonald's, Shoney's, **lodging:** Budget Motel, Ramada Inn, **other:** BiLo Foods, CVS Drug, Home Depot
41mm	weigh sta both lanes
37	E Canton, **N**...**gas:** BP, TA/Buckhorn Rest./dsl/scales/24hr/@, **other:** Goodyear, **S**...**gas:** Exxon/dsl, **lodging:** Day's Inn, Plantation Motel, **other:** KOA
33	Newfound Rd, to US 74, **S**...gas
31	Canton, **N**...**food:** Sagebrush Steaks, **lodging:** Econolodge, **S**...**gas:** BP/dsl, Chevron/DQ, Exxon/ McDonald's/24hr, Shell/Arby's/dsl, **food:** Burger King, Pizza Hut(2mi), Subway(1mi), Taco Bell, Waffle House, **lodging:** Comfort Inn, **other:** Ingles Foods, Chevrolet/ Pontiac/Buick, Ford, RV/truck repair
27	US 19/23, to Waynesville, Great Smokey Mtn Expswy, **3 mi S**...**gas:** Shell/Burger King, **food:** Shoney's, Subway, Taco Bell, **other:** HOSPITAL, Food Lion, GNC, Lowe's Whse, Wal-Mart/drugs, to WCU(25mi)
24	NC 209, to Lake Junaluska, **N**...**gas:** Pilot/Subway/dsl/ scales/24hr/@, **lodging:** Midway Motel, **S**...**gas:** Texaco/cafe/dsl/24hr
20	US 276, to Maggie Valley, Lake Junaluska, **S**...**gas:** BP/ dsl, Citgo, Exxon/dsl/café, **other:** Creekwood Farm RV Park, Pride RV Resort, Winngray RV Park
16mm	Pigeon River
15	Fines Creek, no services
12mm	Pisgah NF eastern boundary
10mm	**rest area both lanes, full(handicapped)facilities, phone, vending, picnic tables, litter barrels, petwalk**
7	Harmon Den, no services
4mm	tunnel both lanes
0mm	North Carolina/Tennessee state line

NORTH CAROLINA
Interstate 77

N ↕ S

Exit #	Services
105mm	North Carolina/Virginia state line
105mm	**Welcome Ctr sb, full(handicapped)facilities, info, phone, vending, picnic tables, litter barrels, petwalk**
103mm	weigh sta both lanes
101	I-74 E, to Mt Airy, Winston-Salem, Greensboro, E...lodging: Hampton Inn, other: HOSPITAL(12mi),
100	NC 89, to Mt Airy, E...gas: Brintle's/Citgo/dsl/rest./24hr/@, Exxon/dsl, Marathon/Subway/dsl, food: Wagon Wheel Rest., lodging: Best Western, Comfort Inn(2mi), other: HOSPITAL(12mi), clothing outlet
93	to Dobson, Surry, E...gas: Citgo/dsl/diner, lodging: Hampton Inn, Surry Inn, other: camping
85	NC 1138, CC Camp Rd, to Elkin, W...gas: Exxon/dsl, Shell/Blimpie/Stuckey's/dsl, 1-3 mi W...gas: Neighbor's, food: Burger King, KFC, McDonald's, lodging: Elk Inn
83	US 21 byp, to Sparta(from nb)
82.5mm	Yadkin River
82	NC 67, Elkin, E...gas: BP/Case Knife Outlet/dsl, Chevron/dsl, food: Arby's, Cracker Barrel, Jordan's Rest., lodging: Holiday Inn Express, other: Holly Ridge Camping(8mi), W...gas: Exxon/Baskin-Robbins/TCBY/dsl, food: Bojangles, Captains Galley, Ham & Eggs Rest., McDonald's, Waffle House, Wendy's, lodging: Comfort Inn, Day's Inn, Hampton Inn, Rose's Motel, other: AutoValue Parts, Buick/Pontiac/GMC, CarQuest, Curves, D-Rex Drug, Family$, Food Lion, vet
79	US 21 S, to Arlington, E...gas: Citgo/Subway/dsl, Shell, lodging: Super 8, W...gas: BP/dsl, food: Glenn's BBQ, lodging: Best Value Inn
73b a	US 421, to Winston-Salem(20mi), E...gas: Shell/Subway/dsl(1mi)
72mm	**rest area nb, full(handicapped)facilities, phone, vending, picnic tables, litter barrels, petwalk**
65	NC 901, to Union Grove, Harmony, E...other: Van Hoy Farms Camping, W...gas: BP/dsl, Shell/Subway/dsl/24hr, food: Burger Barn, lodging: B&B, other: Fiddler's Grove Camping(2mi)
63mm	**rest area sb, full(handicapped)facilities, phone, vending, picnic tables, litter barrels, petwalk**
59	Tomlin Mill Rd, W...gas: Citgo/dsl
56.5mm	S Yadkin River
54	US 21, to Turnersburg, E...gas: Citgo, W...gas: Shell/dsl, food: Arby's, 2mi W...gas: Chick-fil-A, Dunkin Donuts, Golden Corral, Zaxby's
51b a	I-40, E to Winston-Salem, W to Hickory
50	E Broad St, Statesville, E...gas: BP, Citgo/dsl, Kangaroo/dsl, Shell, food: Arby's, Burger King, CiCi's Pizza, Dominos, El Tio's Mexican, IHOP, Jack-in-the-Box, McDonald's, Papa John's, Pizza Hut, Shanghai Buffet, Shoney's, Starbucks, Subway, Wendy's, lodging: Brookwood Inn, Red Roof Inn, other: Belk, Bi-Lo, $General, Eckerd, JC Penney, JR Outlet, K-Mart, Radio Shack, Sears/auto, USPO, mall
49b a	US 70, G Bagnal Blvd, to Statesville, E...gas: BP, Citgo, Circle K, Exxon, food: Brewsters, KFC, Waffle House, lodging: Best Western, Comfort Inn, Hampton Inn, Holiday Inn/rest., Motel 6, Super 8, other: Buick/GMC/Cadillac, Camping World, Dodge, Ford, Harley-Davidson, Holiday Camper, Honda, Lincoln/Mercury, Nissan, Subaru, Toyota/Scion, W...gas: Chevron, Citgo, food: Carolina BBQ, lodging: Best Value Inn, Microtel
45	to Troutman, Barium Springs, E...KOA, RV Repair, W...gas: Chevron/BBQ/dsl
42	US 21, NC 115, to Troutman, Oswalt, E...gas: Hess/Wilco/Subway/dsl/scales/24hr/@, W...gas: Citgo, other: to Lake Norman SP, camping
39mm	**rest area both lanes, full(handicapped)facilities, phone, picnic tables, litter barrels, petwalk, vending**
36	NC 150, Mooresville, E...gas: Accel/dsl, Exxon, Shell/24hr, food: Applebee's, Bob Evans, Cookout Burgers, Denny's, Dominos, FatBoy's Cafe, Jack-in-the-Box, McDonald's, Pizza Hut, Roadhouse Grill, Sonny's BBQ, Taco Bell, Waffle House, Wendy's, lodging: Day's Inn, Fairfield Inn, Holiday Inn Express, Ramada Ltd, other: Belk, Chevrolet, $Tree, Gander Mtn, GNC, Kohl's, Mazda, Staples, Suzuki, Tuesday Morning, Wal-Mart SuperCtr/24hr, W...gas: BJ's Whse/gas, BP/dsl, Citgo/KrispyKreme/BBQ, Servco, Shell/dsl/24hr, food: Arby's, Chick-fil-A, Cracker Barrel, Golden Corral, Hardee's, Hooters, Kyoto Japanese, McDonald's, Monterrey Mexican, Subway, Texas Roadhouse, Velvet Hammer, lodging: Hampton Inn, Sleep Inn, Super 8, Wingate Inn, other: Food Lion, Lowes Whse, Tire Kingdom, Walgreens
33	US 21 N, E...food: Jeffrey's Rest, Legends, McDonald's, Subway, lodging: SpringHill Suites, other: HOSPITAL, W...gas: BP/Arby's/Bojangles, Citgo/dsl, food: Baskin-Robbins/Dunkin Donuts, Sauza's Mexican, other: Food Lion, Woody's Drug, vet
30	Davidson, E...gas: Exxon/dsl, food: North Harbor Rest., other: to Davidson College
28	US 21 S, NC 73, Cornelius, Lake Norman, E...gas: BP, Cashion's/dsl, Citgo/24hr, food: Acropolis Cafe, lodging: Days Inn, Hampton Inn, other: NAPA, W...gas: PetroStop, food: Bojangles, Burger King, KFC, Kobe Japanese, McAlister's Deli, McDonald's, Papa John's, Pizza Hut, PJ Gator's, Quizno's, Starbucks, Subway, Taco Bell, Wendy's, lodging: Best Western, Econolodge, Microtel, other: Chrysler/Jeep, Dodge, Eckerd, Goodyear, Harris-Teeter, SteinMart
25	NC 73, Concord, Lake Norman, E...gas: Shell/dsl, Texaco, food: Atlanta Bread Co, Burger King, Chick-fil-A, Chili's, Fuddrucker's, IHOP, Longhorn Steaks, McDonald's, O'Charley's, Wendy's, lodging: Country Inn&Suites, Hawthorn Suites, Quality Inn, other:Home Depot, Kohl's, Lowe's Whse, Old Navy, Target, W...gas: 76/Circle K/Blimpie/dsl, food: Arby's, Best China, Bob Evans, Bojangles, Carrabba's, Cheeseburger Paradise, DQ, Max&Erma's, Outback Steaks, Quiznos, Subway, lodging: Candlewood Suites, Courtyard, Sleep Inn, other: Food Lion/deli, Walgreens, to Energy Explorium

Left margin labels: **Elkin**, **Statesville**

Interstate 77

23	NC 73, Huntersville, **E**...**gas:** BP, Citgo, Shell/24hr, **food:** Chico's Mexican, Dunkin Donuts-Basin Robbins, Hardee's, Jersey Mike's, Palace of China, Subway, Waffle House, Wendy's, **lodging:** Holiday Inn Express, Red Roof Inn, **other:** $Tree, Eckerd, Food Lion, Ford, Hancock Fabrics, Pontiac/GMC, Radio Shack, Tuesday Morning, USPO, **W**...**gas:** Shell, **food:** CiCi's Pizza, Friendly's, Pizza Hut, Sekisui, Starbucks, **other:** HOSPITAL, Bi-Lo, CVS Drug, GNC, Harris-Teeter
19mm	future I-485
18	Harris Blvd, Reames Rd, **E**...**gas:** BP/Arby's, Shell/dsl, **food:** Bob Evans, Hickory Tavern, Jack-in-the-Box, Lin's Buffet, Quizno's, Waffle House, **lodging:** Comfort Suites, Fairfield Inn, Hilton Garden, Suburban Lodge, **other:** HOSPITAL, to UNCC, Univ Research Park, **W**...**gas:** Chevron, **food:** Chili's, Coldstone Creamery, Firebird Grill, Fox&Hound, Moe's SW Grill, Olive Garden, On-the-Border, Panera bread, Red Robin, TGI Friday, **other:** Belk, Dillard's, Macy's
16b a	US 21, Sunset Rd, **E**...**gas:** 76/Circle K, **food:** Capt D's, Hardee's, KFC, McDonald's, Subway, Taco Bell, Wendy's, **lodging:** Day's Inn, Super 8, **other:** Winn-Dixie, **W**...**gas:** Citgo/dsl, Shell/dsl/scales/24hr, 76/Circle K, **food:** Bojangles, Bubba's BBQ, Cookout Burgers, Denny's, Dominos, Jack-in-the-Box, Waffle House, **lodging:** Microtel, Sleep Inn, **other:** Advance Parts, Aldi Foods, CVS Drug, RV Ctr
13b a	I-85, S to Spartanburg, N to Greensboro
12	La Salle St, **W**...**gas:** Citgo/dsl, Shell/dsl
11b a	I-277, Brookshire Fwy, NC 16
10b	Trade St, 5th St(from nb), **E**...**other:** to Discovery Place, **W**...**gas:** Citgo, **food:** Bojangles
10a	US 21(from sb), Moorhead St, downtown
9	I-277, US 74, to US 29, John Belk Fwy, downtown, **E**...HOSPITAL, stadium
8	Remount Rd(from nb, no re-entry), no services
7	Clanton Rd, **E**...**gas:** PetroExpress/dsl, **food:** McDonald's, Waffle House, Wendy's, **lodging:** Day's Inn, Econolodge, Super 8, **W**...**gas:** BP, Shell/dsl
6b a	US 521, Billy Graham Pkwy, **E**...**gas:** BP, Citgo, Shell/dsl, Sunoco, **food:** Azteca Mexican, Bojangles, Capt D's, Carolina Prime Steaks, IHOP, KFC/Pizza Hut, Krispy Kreme, McDonald's, Murphy's Cafe, Shoney's, **lodging:** Best Western, Day's Inn, Howard Johnson, Ramada Ltd, Sheraton, **other:** Walgreens, to Queens Coll, **W**...**gas:** PetroExpress, Shell, **food:** Omaha Steaks, **lodging:** Embassy Suites, Holiday Inn, InTown Suites, Summerfield Suites, La Quinta, Sleep Inn
5	Tyvola Rd, **E**...**gas:** PetroExpress/dsl, Texaco, **food:** Carolina BBQ, Chili's, China King, Derby Diner, Kiauto Japanese, LoneStar Steaks, McDonald's, Sonny's BBQ, Subway, **lodging:** Candlewood Suites, Comfort Inn, Hilton, Marriott, Quality Inn, Residence Inn, Studio+, **other:** Aldi Foods, Costco/gas, Eckerd, Jaguar, Pontiac/GMC, **W**...**lodging:** Extended Stay America, Wingate Inn, **other:** to Coliseum

4	Nations Ford Rd, **E**...**gas:** Citgo, 76/Circle K/24hr, **food:** Caravel Seafood, **lodging:** Budget Inn, Knights Inn, Motel 6, Ramada Ltd., **W**...**gas:** Shell/Burger King
3	Arrowood Rd, to I-485(from sb), **E**...**gas:** Shell, **food:** Bob Evans, Chick-fil-A, Jack-in-the-Box, Japan Express, LJ Silver, McDonald's, Sonic, Starbucks, Wendy's, **lodging:** AmeriSuites, Courtyard, Fairfield Inn, Holiday Inn Express, Mainstay Suites, Staybridge Suites, TownePlace Suites, **W**...**food:** Ruby Tuesday, **lodging:** Hampton Inn
2	I-485
1.5mm	**Welcome Ctr nb, full(handicapped)facilities, info, phone, vending, picnic tables, litter barrels, petwalk**
1	Westinghouse Blvd, to I-485(from nb), **E**...**gas:** BP/dsl, **food:** Jack-in-the-Box, Subway, Waffle House, **lodging:** Super 8, **W**...**gas:** Shell/dsl, **food:** Burger King
0mm	North Carolina/South Carolina state line

Interstate 85

Exit #	Services
234mm	North Carolina/Virginia state line
233	US 1, to Wise, **E**...**gas:** Citgo/Wise/dsl, **food:** Budget Inn
231mm	**Welcome Ctr sb, full(handicapped)facilities, phone, picnic tables, litter barrels, petwalk**
229	Oine Rd, to Norlina, **E**...**gas:** BP, **W**...**rec area**
226	Ridgeway Rd, **W**...**other:** to Kerr Lake, to St RA
223	Manson Rd, **E**...**gas:** BP/dsl, **other:** camping, **W**... to Kerr Dam
220	US 1, US 158, Fleming Rd, to Middleburg, **E**...**gas:** BP/dsl, **W**...**gas:** Exxon/dsl/scales, **lodging:** Chex Motel/rest.
218	US 1 S(from sb exits left), to Raleigh
217	Nutbush Bridge, **E**...same as 215 on US 158, **W**...**gas:** Exxon/dsl, **other:** Kerr Lake RA
215	US 158 BYP E, Henderson(no EZ return from nb), **E**...**gas:** BP, Hess, Shell, Sunoco, **food:** BBQ, Burger King, Golden China, Subway, Waffle Pancakes, **lodging:** Ambassador Inn, Budget Host, Comfort Inn, Scottish Inn, **other:** $General, Food Lion, Goodyear/auto, Roses, services on US 158
214	NC 39, Henderson, **E**...**gas:** BP, **food:** Andy's Rest., **other:** uspo, **W**...**gas:** BP/dsl, Shell/HotStuff Pizza

Charlotte

Charlotte

Henderson

N ↑ ↓ S

Oxford

213	US 158, Dabney Dr, to Henderson, Ⓔ...**gas:** BP, Parade, Shell, **food:** Bamboo Garden, Bojangles, DQ, Denny's, KFC, McDonald's, Papa John's, Pizza Inn, Subway, Wendy's, **other:** CVS Drug, Family$, Food Lion, Goodyear/auto, Radio Shack, Roses, Ⓦ...**gas:** BP, Shell, **food:** Chick-fil-A, Golden Corral, Smithfields BBQ, Taco Bell, **lodging:** Holiday Inn Express, **other:** Chevrolet/GMC, Chrysler/Dodge, $Tree, Eckerd, Ford/Lincoln/Mercury, K-Mart, Lowe's Whse, Pontiac, Staples, Tires+
212	Ruin Creek Rd, Ⓔ...**gas:** Shell/dsl, **food:** Cracker Barrel, Mazatlan Mexican, SiLo Rest., **lodging:** Day's Inn, Ⓦ...**gas:** BP/Burger King, **food:** Christoper's Grill, Gary's BBQ, Golden Corral, Pizza Hut, Western Sizzlin, **lodging:** Hampton Inn, Jameson Inn, Sleep Inn, **other:** HOSPITAL, Belk, Goody's, JC Penney, Wal-Mart SuperCtr/24hr, mall
209	Poplar Creek Rd, Ⓦ...Vance-Granville Comm Coll
206	US 158, Oxford, Ⓔ...**gas:** Exxon, Ⓦ...**gas:** BP/dsl, **food:** Tony's Rest., **other:** airport
204	NC 96, Oxford, Ⓔ...**gas:** BP/dsl, **lodging:** Best Western, King's Inn, **other:** Honda, Pontiac/Buick/GMC, Ⓦ...**gas:** Exxon/DQ/24hr, Hess, Shell/Pizza Hut/24hr, Texaco, **food:** Burger King, Domino's, KFC, McDonald's, 96 Buffet, Subway, Taco Bell, Wendy's, **lodging:** Econolodge, **other:** HOSPITAL, $Tree, GNC, Lowe's Foods, Wal-Mart
202	US 15, Oxford, **2 mi** Ⓦ...**lodging:** Crown Motel
199mm	**rest area both lanes, full(handicapped)facilities, phone, picnic tables, litter barrels, petwalk**
198mm	Tar River
191	191 NC 56, Butner, Ⓔ...**gas:** BP/dsl, Hess/dsl, **food:** Bob's BBQ, Bojangles, Burger King, El Rio Mexican, KFC/Taco Bell, McDonald's, Pizza Hut, Stone Crab Landing, Subway, Wendy's, **lodging:** Comfort Inn, **other:** Ace Hardware, Advance Parts, Curves, $General, Eckerd, Food Lion, M&H Tires, vet, to Falls Lake RA, Ⓦ...**gas:** Exxon/dsl/24hr, Shell/dsl, **food:** Hardee's, Waffle&Pancake House, **lodging:** Econolodge, Holiday Inn Express, Ramada Ltd, **other:** auto repair
189	Butner, no services
186b a	US 15, to Creedmoor, no services
185mm	Falls Lake
183	Redwood Rd, no services
182	Red Mill Rd, Ⓔ...**gas:** Exxon/repair, **other:** Kenworth/Isuzu Trucks
180	Glenn School Rd, no services
179	E Club Blvd, Ⓔ...**gas:** Exxon
178	US 70 E, to Raleigh, Falls Lake RA, Research Triangle, RDU Airport
177	Avondale Dr, NC 55, Ⓦ...**gas** Shell, **food:** American Hero, Arby's, Hong Kong Buffet, Los Comales, McDonalds, Pizza Village, **other:** Advance Parts, Big Lots, Jiffy Lube
176b a	Gregson St, US 501 N, Ⓔ...**food:** Champps Grill, Tripps Rest., **other:** HOSPITAL, Belk, Macy's, Museum of Life&Science, Office Depot, Sears/auto, mall

Durham

175	Guess Rd, Ⓔ...**gas:** Citgo/dsl, **food:** Hog Heaven BBQ, **lodging:** Best Value Inn, Holiday Inn Express, Super 8, **other:** Eckerd, Ⓦ...**gas:** BP/dsl, Pure, **food:** Bojangles, Honey's Diner/24hr, IHOP, JJ Fish &Chicken, Texas Steaks, Zero's Subs, **lodging:** Red Roof Inn, **other:** CVS Drug, Home Depot, Kroger
174a	Hillandale Rd, Ⓦ...**gas:** BP/dsl, **food:** El Corral, Papa's Grill, Sal's Pizza, **lodging:** Courtyard, Hampton Inn, Howard Johnson, **other:** Kerr Drug
174b	US 15 S, US 501 S(from sb), Ⓔ...**lodging:** Forest Inn
173	173 US 15, US 501, US 70, Colemill Rd, W Durham, Ⓔ...**gas:** BP, Exxon/dsl, Shell/Texaco, **food:** Arby's, BBQ, Bojangles, Burger King, Checker's, Chick-fil-a, KFC/Taco Bell, Cracker Barrel, DogHouse Rest., Domino's, Galley Seafood, Italian Garden Rest., McDonald's, Miami Subs, Subway, Taco Bell, Waffle House, Wendy's, **lodging:** Day's Inn, Fairfield Inn, Holiday Inn, Innkeeper, **other:** HOSPITAL, Autozone, Dodge/Jeep, Eckerd, Kroger, Rite Aid
172	NC 147 S, to US 15 S, US 501 S(from nb), Durham, from nb, no services
170	to NC 751, to Duke U(no EZ return from nb), Ⓔ...**lodging:** Best Western/rest., Scottish Inn, Ⓦ...to Eno River SP
165	NC 86, to Chapel Hill, Ⓔ...**gas:** Pure/dsl, **food:** Papa John's, Subway, **other:** $Hut, Home Depot, Wal-Mart SuperCtr/24hr., Ⓦ...**gas:** BP/dsl
164	Hillsborough, Ⓔ...**gas:** BP, Citgo/dsl, **food:** McDonald's, **lodging:** Holiday Inn Express, Ⓦ...**gas:** Exxon/dsl, Shell, **food:** Bojangles, Casa Ibarra Mexican, Domino's, Hardee's, KFC/Taco Bell, Occoneechee Steaks, Pizza Hut, Subway, Waffle House, Wendy's, **lodging:** Microtel, **other:** AutoZone, CarQuest, Chevrolet/Buick, $Tree, Food Lion, Ford, GNC, Goodyear/auto, Lowe's Foods
163	I-40 E, to Raleigh. **I-85 S and I-40 W run together 30 mi.**
161	to US 70 E, NC 86 N, no services
160	to NC 86 N, Efland, Ⓦ...**gas:** Exxon/dsl
158mm	weigh sta both lanes
157	Buckhorn Rd, Ⓔ...**gas:** BP/dsl, Petro/Mobil/Iron Skillet/dsl/scales/24hr/@, Ⓦ...**gas:** Citgo, Exxon
154	Mebane, Oaks Rd, Ⓔ...**gas:** Shell/dsl/24hr, Sheetz, **other:** Wal-Mart SuperCtr/gas/24hr, Ⓦ...**gas:** BP, Citgo, Shell/dsl/24hr, **food:** Biscuitville, Blue Ribbon Diner, Bojangles, La Fiesta Mexican, McDonald's, Quizno's, Roma Pizza, Waffle House, **lodging:** Budget Inn/rest., **other:** Advance Parts, Autozone, CVS Drug
153	NC 119, Mebane, Ⓔ...**gas:** BP/KFC/Taco Bell/Pizza Hut, **food:** Cracker Barrel, Hibachi Rest., Jersey Mike's, Ruby Tuesday, Smithfield's BBQ, **lodging:** Hampton Inn, Holiday Inn Express, **other:** Lowe's Whse, Ⓦ...**gas:** Phillips 66/Burger King, **food:** Domino's, La Cocina Mexican, Sonic, Subway, YumYum Chinese, **other:** Curves, CVS Drug, Food Lion, vet
152	Trollingwood Rd, Ⓔ...**gas:** Pilot/McDonald's/dsl/scales/24hr, Ⓦ...**gas:** Fuel City/dsl

Interstate 85

N ↑↓ S

Burlington

150 Haw River, to Roxboro, **W...gas:** Hess/Wilco/DQ/Wendy's/dsl/scales/24hr/@, ✈/Flying J/Cookery/dsl/LP/scales/24hr/@, **lodging:** Best Western, **other:** Blue Beacon

148 NC 54, Graham, **E...gas:** BP/dsl/24hr, Exxon/dsl/24hr, QP, **food:** Waffle House, **lodging:** Comfort Suites, **W...food:** MexAm Cafe, **lodging:** Ember's Motel, Travel Inn

147 NC 87, to Pittsboro, Graham, **E...gas:** BP, **food:** Arby's, Bojangles, Burger King, Domino's, Lucky Bamboo, Pizza Hut, Quizno's, Sagebrush Steaks, Sonic, Subway, Wendy's, **other:** Advance Parts, Chevrolet, Curves, Eckerd, Family$, Food Lion, Ford, Jeep, vet, **W...gas:** Citgo/dsl, Exxon/dsl, Shell/dsl, **food:** BBQ&Ribs Rest., Biscuitville, Cookout, McDonald's, Taco Bell, **other:** HOSPITAL, CVS Drug, Lowe's Foods, Walgreen

145 NC 49, Burlington, **E...gas:** BP/dsl, Shell/dsl, **food:** Capt D's, Taco Bell, **lodging:** Econolodge, Microtel, Motel 6, **other:** Harley-Davidson, **W...gas:** BP/dsl, **food:** Biscuitville, Bojangles, Burger King, China Buffet, Hardee's, KFC, Subway, Waffle House, **lodging:** Best Value Inn, Holiday Inn, La Quinta, Scottish Inn, **other:** Dodge, $General, Eckerd, Food Lion, Radio Shack

143 NC 62, Burlington, **E...gas:** E-Z Stop/dsl, **food:** Bob Evans, Hardee's, Waffle House, Wendy's, to Alamance Bfd, **W...gas:** Exxon, 76/Circle K, **food:** Don Pancho's, K&W Cafeteria, Libby Hill Seafood, **lodging:** Ramada Inn, **other:** Cadillac, Chevrolet, $General, Food Lion, Ford, Home Depot, Mitsubishi, auto repair

141 to Burlington, **E...gas:** BP, Kangaroo, **food:** IHOP, Mayflower Seafood, Outback Steaks, **lodging:** Comfort Inn, Hampton Inn, **W...gas:** Phillips 66/dsl, Texaco, **food:** Applebee's, Arby's, Biscuitville, Bojangles, Burger King, Chick-fil-A, Chophouse Grill, Cookout, Cracker Barrel, Crazy Fire Mongolian, Golden Corral, Hooters, KFC, Longhorn Steaks, McDonald's, Namaste Indian Rest., O'Charley's, Panda Express, Panera Bread, Papa John's, Rockola Grill, Ruby Tuesday, Sal's Italian, Starbucks, Steak'n Shake/24hr, Subway, Taco Bell, Wholly Guacamole, **lodging:** Best Western, Country Inn&Suites, Courtyard, Super 8, **other:** HOSPITAL, Belk, Buick/GMC, $Tree, Eckerd, Food Lion, Ford, Honda, K-Mart/gas, Lincoln/Mercury, Lowe's Foods, Mazda, Nissan, JC Penney, Sears/auto, Wal-Mart SuperCtr/24hr, mall, to Elon Coll

140 University Dr, Elon, **W...food:** Chick-fil-A, Chili's, Moe's SW Grill, Olive Garden, Red Robin, Starbucks, **other:** Barnes&Noble, Belk, Best Buy, Dillard's, JC Penny, Michael's, Old Navy, Petsmart, Ross, Target

139mm **rest area both lanes, full(handicapped) facilities, phone, picnic tables,litter barrels, vending**

138 NC 61, Gibsonville, **W...gas:** TA/BP/Burger King/Popeye's/dsl/scales/@, **lodging:** Days Inn

Greensboro

135 RockCreek Dairy Rd, **W...gas:** Citgo, Exxon, **food:** Bojangles, China 1, Domino's, Guacamole Mexican, Jersey Mike's Subs, McDonald's, **other:** Curves, CVS Drug, Food Lion, Midtown Drug

132 Mt Hope Church Rd, **E...gas:** Citgo/Subway/dsl, **W...gas:** Shell/dsl, Wilco/Hess/Wendy's/dsl/24hr, **lodging:** Hampton Inn

131 to US 70, **I-85 N and I-40 E run together 30 mi.**

129 Youngs Mill Rd, **W...lodging:** Holiday Inn Express(3mi)

128 Alamance Church Rd, no services

126b a US 421, to Sanford, **E...gas:** Exxon/dsl, Kangaroo/dsl

124 S Elm, Eugene St, **E...food:** Bojangles, Cracker Barrel, Starbucks, Subway, Wendy's, **other:** Lowe's Whse, Wal-Mart SuperCtr

122a US 220, to Greensboro, Asheboro(from sb), access to I-40

120 N US 29, E US 70, to I-40 W

119 Groometown Rd, **W...gas:** Citgo/dsl

118 US 29 S, US 70 W, to High Point, Jamestown, **W...lodging:** Grandover Resort, **other:** HOSPITAL

115mm Deep River

Thomasville

113 NC 62, Archdale, **E...gas:** Citgo/dsl, **W...gas:** BP/dsl, **lodging:** Best Western

111 US 311, to High Point, Archdale, **E...food:** Amici Pizza, Bamboo Garden, Bojangles, Hardee's, Subway, Wendy's, **lodging:** Innkeeper, **other:** Curves, CVS Drug, $General, $City, Food Lion, Lowe's Foods/24hr, **W...gas:** Circle K/dsl, Exxon/McDonald's, Marathon/dsl, Shell/dsl, **food:** Biscuitville, Libby Hill Seafood, Spiro's Rest., Waffle House, **lodging:** Comfort Inn, Fairfeild Inn, Hampton Inn, Holiday Inn Express, **other:** HOSPITAL, USPO, tires

108 Hopewell Church Rd, no services

106 Finch Farm Rd, **E...gas:** BP/dsl, **W...food:** Subway(1mi)

103 NC 109, to Thomasville, **E...gas:** Petro Express, Shell, **food:** Arby's, Cookout Burgers, Elizabeth's Pizza, Taco Bell, **other:** CVS Drug, $Tree, Ingles Foods, K-Mart, Radio Shack, Wal-Mart SuperCtr/gas, **W...gas:** Exxon/Subway/dsl, Coastal, RaceWay, Hess/Wilco/dsl, Shell, Sunoco, **food:** BBQ Shack, Biscuitville, Bojangles, Burger King, Captain Tom's, China Garden, Hardee's, Hunan Chinese, KFC, Loflin's Rest., Mazatlan Mexican, McDonald's, Mr Gatti's, Papa John's, Peeble's Rest., Ruby Tuesday, Sonic, Sunrise Grille, Waffle House, Wendy's, **lodging:**

NORTH CAROLINA

Interstate 85

Quaility Inn, **other:** Advance Parts, AutoZone, Eckerd, Family$, Food Lion, Mighty$, O'Reilly Parts, Walgreens

102 Lake Rd, W...**gas:** Marathon, Texaco, **lodging:** Day's Inn/rest., Microtel, **other:** HOSPITAL

100mm rest area both lanes, full(handicapped)facilities, phone, vending, picnic tables, litter barrels, petwalk

96 US 64, to Asheboro, Lexington, E...**gas:** Exxon/dsl, W...**gas:** Chevron/dsl, Citgo(1mi), **food:** Randy's Rest., **lodging:** Quality Inn(4mi), **other:** to Davidson Co Coll, NC Zoo

94 Old US 64, E...**gas:** Shell

91 NC 8, to Southmont, E...**gas:** BP/dsl, Citgo, Shell/dsl, **food:** Biscuit King, Burger King, Christo Rest., Jimmy's BBQ, KFC, McDonald's, Ocean View Seafood, Subway, Wendy's, **lodging:** Comfort Suites, Highway 8 Motel, **other:** Food Lion, High Rock Lake Camping(7mi), Kerr Drug, W...**gas:** Exxon/dsl, QM/dsl, **food:** Applebee's, Arby's, Burger King, Cracker Barrel, Golden Corral, Hardee's, King House, Little Caesar's, Pizza Hut(1mi), Stella's Rest., Taco Bell, Zaxby's, **lodging:** Country Hearth Inn, Holiday Inn Express, **other:** HOSPITAL, Belk, $Tree, GNC, Goody's, Lowe's Whse(1mi), Radio Shack, Wal-Mart SuperCtr(1mi)

88 Linwood, W...**gas:** BP/dsl

87 US 29, US 70, US 52(from nb), High Point, W...**other:** HOSPITAL, airport

86 Belmont Rd, W...**gas:** Bill's Trkstp/dsl/scales/24hr/@

85 Clark Rd, to NC 150, no services

83 NC 150(from nb), to Spencer, no services

82 US 29, US 70(from sb), to Spencer, no services

Salisbury

81.5mm Yadkin River

81 Spencer, E...**gas:** Exxon, **other:** camping

79 Spencer Shops SHS, Spencer, E Spencer

76b a US 52, to Albemarle, Salisbury, E...**gas:** BP, Exxon, RaceTrac/24hr, **food:** Applebee's, Gatti's Pizza, IHOP, LoneStar Steaks, Pancho Villa Mexican, Zaxby's, **lodging:** Day's Inn, Economy Inn, Happy Traveler Inn, Super 8, **other:** Aldi Foods, Circuit City, CVS Drug, Dodge, $Tree, Eckerd, Food Lion, GNC, Harley-Davidson, Lowe's Whse, Marshall's, Staples, Tire Kingdom, Walgreens, W...**gas:** 76/Circke K/dsl, Wilco/Hess/dsl, **food:** Blue Bay Seafood, Bojangles, Burger King, C&H Rest., Capt D's, Chick-fil-A, Christo's Rest., Cookout, Cracker Barrel, Hardee's, Honey Baked Ham, KFC, McDonald's, O'Charley's, Outback Steaks, Pizza Hut, Starbucks, Taco Bell, Tokyo Express, Wendy's, **lodging:** Comfort Suites, **other:** HOSPITAL, Advance Parts, AutoZone, Family$, Firestone/auto, Goodyear/auto, K-Mart, Office Depot, USPO, Wal-Mart SuperCtr

75 US 601, Jake Alexander Blvd, E...**food:** Arby's, Farmhouse Rest., **lodging:** Travelodge, **other:** Dan Nicholas Park, NAPA, W...**gas:** BP, Citgo, Exxon/dsl, Shell/dsl, **food:** Casa Grande, Ichiban Japanese, Ryan's, Sagebrush Steaks, Subway, Waffle House, Wendy's, **lodging:** Best Western, Hampton Inn, Holiday Inn, **other:** Chevrolet/Cadillac, Chrysler/Jeep, Ford, Honda/Kia, Magic Mart, Toyota

74 Julian Rd, no services

72 Peach Orchard Rd, W...airport

71 Peeler Rd, E...**gas:** Derrick Trkstp/Shell/CW's Cafe/dsl/24hr/scales, W...**gas:** Hess/Wilco/Bojangles/Subway/dsl/scales/24hr, **other:** auto/dsl repair

70 Webb Rd, E...flea mkt, W...st patrol

68 US 29, US 601, to Rockwell, China Grove, **1 mi** W...**gas:** Gary's BBQ, Hardee's

63 Kannapolis, E...**gas:** Pilot/Subway/dsl/scales, **food:** Waffle House, **lodging:** Best Value

60 Earnhardt Rd, Copperfield Blvd, E...**gas:** Exxon/dsl, BP, **food:** Bob Evans, Bojangles, Cracker Barrel, **lodging:** Hampton Inn, Sleep Inn, **other:** HOSPITAL, Discount Tire, W...**gas:** BP/dsl, **food:** Brewster's, Carino's Italian, Casa Grande Mexican, Dragon Wok, Firehouse Subs, Five Guys Burgers, Logan's Roadhouse, McDonald's, Pizza Pazzo, Ruby Tuesday, Steak & Shake, Subway, Taco Bell, Wendy's, Yamaya Japanese, **lodging:** Holiday Inn Express, **other:** Kohl's, Lowe's Whse, Sam's Club/gas, Wal-Mart SuperCtr/24hr, visitor info

Concord

59mm rest area both lanes, full(handicapped) facilities, phone, vending, picnic tables, litter barrels, petwalk

58 US 29, US 601, Concord, E...**gas:** BP, Citgo, Exxon, Petro Express, Shell/dsl, **food:** Applebee's, Burger King, Capt D's, Chick-fil-A, Chili's, El Vallarta Mexican, Fuji Asian, Golden Corral, KFC, Little Caesar's, Longhorn Steaks, Mayflower Seafood, McDonald's, Moe's SW Grill, Mr C's Rest., O'Charley's, Pizza Hut, Starbucks, Subway, Taco Bell, Waffle House, Wendy's, **lodging:** Holiday Inn Express, Howard Johnson, Mayfair Motel, **other:** HOSPITAL, Belk, Cadillac, Chrysler/Dodge/Jeep, Eckerd, Food Lion, Harris Teeter, JC Penney, Sears/auto, Staples, U-Haul, Walgreen, mall, st patrol, W...**gas:** BP, **food:** CiCi's, Bojangles(2mi), Domino's, IHOP, Ryan's, **lodging:** Comfort Inn, Econolodge, Fairfield Inn, Mainstay Suites, Microtel, **other:** $General, Drug Emporium, Eddie's Pizza/funpark, Fred's Store, Hancock Fabrics, Home Depot, vet

55 NC 73, to Davidson, Concord, E...**gas:** Exxon/dsl, Shell, **food:** McDonald's, Waffle House, W...**gas:** Shell/Huddle House, 76/Circle K/dsl, World Gas, **lodging:** Day's Inn

54 Kannapolis Pkwy, George W. Lyle Pkwy, E...**gas:** Citgo, **food:** Backyard Burger, China Garden, Noodles & Co, Quizno's, **other:** CVS Drug, FoodLion, Harris Teeter, Walgreen, W...**other:** Best Buy, Marshall's, Steinmart, PetsMart, Target

52 Poplar Tent Rd, E...**gas:** Shell/dsl, **food:** R&R BBQ, **other:** to Lowe's Speedway, museum, W...**gas:** Accel/dsl, Exxon/24hr

49 Speedway Blvd, Concord Mills Blvd, E...**gas:** BP/McDonalds, Shell/dsl, Texaco, **food:** Arby's, BBQ, Bob Evans, Bojangles, Carrabbas, ChuckeCheese, Cookout, Cracker Barrel, Five Guys Burgers, Hooters, KFC/Taco Bell, Quizno's, Texas Roadhouse, Jack-in-the-Box, Ruby Tuesday, Sonic, Starbucks, Subway,

Interstate 85

Sunny's BBQ, TX Land & Cattle, TX Roadhouse, Waffle House, Wendy's, Zaxby's, **lodging:** Comfort Suites, Embassy Suites, Hampton Inn, Holiday Inn Express, Sleep Inn, SpringHill Suites, Suburban Lodge, Wingate Inn, **other:** BJ's Whse/gas, Fleetwood RV camping(1.5mi), Harley-Davidson, Honda, Toyota/Scion, to Lowes Motor Speedway, W...**gas:** Citgo, Petro Express, **food:** Applebee's, Charanda Mexican, Chick-fil-A, Foster's Grille, Mayflower Seafood, McCalisters Deli, Olive Garden, On-the-Border, Panera Bread, Razzoo's Cafe, Red Lobster, Roadhouse Grill, Ryan's, Steak'n Shake, Sticky Fingers, TGI Friday, **other:** BassPro Shops, BooksAMillion, Circuit City, Discount Tire, $Tree, Concord Mills Mall, Goodyear, PetCo, Radio Shack, Ross, TJ Maxx

48	I-485, to US 29
46	Mallard Creek Church Rd, E...**gas:** Exxon/24hr, Wilco/dsl(1mi), **other:** Research Park, W...**gas:** Petro Express, **food:** Firehouse Subs, Hickory Tavern
45	Harris Blvd, E...**gas:** BP, **food:** Applebee's, BBQ, Bojangles, Burger King, Cheddar's, Chili's, Chick-fil-A, IHOP, Logan's Roadhouse, Max&Erma's, McDonald's, Shoney's, Smokey Bones, Taco Bell, TGIFriday, TX Land & Cattle, Waffle House, **lodging:** Comfort Suites(1mi), Courtyard, Drury Inn, Hampton Inn, Hilton, Holiday Inn, Homewood Suites, Residence Inn, Sleep Inn, **other:** HOSPITAL, Best Buy, Food Lion, GNC, Kohl's, Lowe's Whse, Michael's, Office Depot, Old Navy, Radio Shack, Sam's Club, Walgreen, Wal-Mart/auto, mall, to UNCC, U Research Park, **0-2 mi** W...**gas:** Citgo, Shell, **food:** Longhorn Steaks, Macaroni Grill, McDonald's, Subway, Wendy's, **other:** Eckerd, Food Lion
43	to City Blvd, no services
42	US 29(nb only), no services
41	Sugar Creek Rd, E...**gas:** BP, RaceWay, Shell/dsl, **food:** Bojangles, McDonald's, Taco Bell, Wendy's, **lodging:** Best Western, Best Value, Brookwood Inn, Continental Inn, Econolodge, Garden Inn, Microtel, W...**gas:** 76/Circle K, **food:** Cookout, Dominic's Cafe, Sugar's Rest., Texas Ranch Steaks, **lodging:** Comfort Inn, Country Hearth Inn, Day's Inn, Ramada Inn, Rodeway Inn, Super 8
40	Graham St, E...**gas:** Exxon/dsl, **lodging:** Budget Inn, **other:** Ford Trucks, UPS, Western Star, W...**gas:** Citgo, **other:** Freightliner
39	Statesville Ave, E...**gas:** Pilot/Subway/dsl/scales/24hr, **other:** CarQuest, W...**gas:** Citgo, Shell/dsl, **food:** Bojangles, **other:** Famliy$
38	I-77, US 21, N to Statesville, S to Columbia
37	Beatties Ford Rd, E...**gas:** Citgo, Phillips 66/dsl, Shell/dsl, **food:** Burger King, KFC/LJ Silver, McDonald's, Subway, Taco Bell, Top's China, **other:** CVS Drug, W...**gas:** BP
36	NC 16, Brookshire Blvd, E...**gas:** BP/dsl, **food:** China City, **lodging:** Brookshire Inn, **other:** HOSPITAL, repair, W...**gas:** Exxon, RaceWay, Sunoco,

food: Bojangles, Burger King, Jack-in-the-Box, Subway

35	Glenwood Dr, E... **lodging:** Knight's Inn, W... **gas:** Shell/dsl
34	NC 27, Freedom Dr, E...**gas:** BP/dsl, 76/Circle K, Shell, Walker/gas, **food:** Beauregard's Rest, Bojangles, Capt D's, Freedom Rest., Gilligan's Rest., KFC, McDonald's, Pizza Hut, Subway, Taco Bell, Tung Hoy Chinese, Wendy's, **other:** Advance Parts, Eckerd, K-mart, Mr. Transmission, Walgreen, U-haul, W...**food:** The Cafe Room, **lodging:** Real Value Inn, **other:** Jiffy Lube
33	US 521, Billy Graham Pkwy, E...**gas:** 76/Circle K/dsl, Shell, **food:** Bojangles, KFC/Taco Bell, Krystal, McDonald's, Wendy's, **lodging:** Comfort Suites, Day's Inn, Sheraton, Springhill Suites, **other:** to Coliseum, airport, W...**gas:** Exxon/dsl, **food:** Cracker Barrel, Prime Sirloin, Waffle House/24hr, **lodging:** Best Value, La Quinta, Quality Inn, Red Roof
32	Little Rock Rd, E...**gas:** Shell, **food:** Hardee's, Waffle House, **lodging:** Airport Inn, Courtyard, Holiday Inn, **other:** Toyota, W...**gas:** Exxon/dsl, **food:** Arby's, Hardee's, Little Rock Deli, Showmar's Rest., Shoney's, Subway, **lodging:** Best Western, Country Inn Suites, Wingate Inn, **other:** Eckerd, Family$, Gerrard Tires
30	I-485, to I-77, Pineville
29	Sam Wilson Rd, E...**gas:** BP(1mi), W...**gas:** Shell/dsl
28mm	weigh sta both lanes
27.5mm	Catawba River
27	NC 273, Mt Holly, E...**gas:** Exxon/dsl, **food:** Arby's, Capt's Seafood, KFC, Niyoshi Japanese, Pizza Hut, Subway, Taco Bell, Waffle House, Wendy's, **other:** Chevrolet, College Park Drug, Eckerd, Family$, Food Lion, Lowe's Whse, NAPA, Radio Shack, Roses, Walgreen, Wal-Mart SuperCtr, W...**gas:** BP/dsl, **lodging:** Holiday Inn Express
26	E...**gas:** BP, Petro Xpress, **food:** Bojangles, Grand Buffet, Hardee's, McDonald's, New China, Papa John's, **lodging:** Hampton Inn, **other:** Advance Parts, Aldi Foods, BiLo, Chrysler/Jeep, Ford, W...Belmont Abbey Coll
24mm	South Fork River
23	NC 7, McAdenville, W...**gas:** Exxon/dsl, **food:** Hardee's, Hillbilly's BBQ/Steaks
22	Cramerton, Lowell, E...**gas:** Hess, Petro Xpress, **food:** Applebee's, Burger King, Chick-fil-A, Dynasty Buffet, Gator's Rest., Hooters, Jack-in-the-Box, Logan's Roadhouse, Moe's SW Grill, Schlotsky's, Shane's Rib Shack, Zaxby's, **other:** Chevrolet/Cadillac, Circuit City, Discount Tire, Honda, Mazda, Kia, Kohl's, Lincoln/Mercury, Misubishi, Nissan, PetsMart, Sam's Club, U-Haul

NORTH CAROLINA

Interstate 85

21	Cox Rd, E...**gas:** Exxon, Petro Xpress, **food:** Arby's, Backyard Burger, Chick-fil-A, Chili's, Chuck-eCheese, Cookout, Golden Corral, Jackson's Cafeteria, Krispy Kreme, Logan's Roadhouse, Longhorn Steaks, McDonald's, Olive Garden, On-the-Border, Panera Bread, Pizza Inn, Ryan's, Ruby Tuesday, Steak&Shake, Subway, **other:** AAA, Best Buy, BooksAMillion, BiLo/24hr, Dodge, Discount Tire, $Tree, Ford/Lincoln/Mercury, Harley-Davidson, Harris-Teeter/24hr, Home Depot, K-mart, Kohl's, Lowe's Whse, Mazda, Michael's, Nissan, Old Navy, PepBoys, Radio Shack, Ross, Tire Kingdom, Walgreen, Wal-Mart SuperCtr, mall, vet, W...**gas:** Citgo, **food:** Arby's, IHOP, **lodging:** Super 8, **other:** HOSPITAL, Eckerd, Harley-Davidson
20	NC 279, New Hope Rd, E...**gas:** Shell, Texaco, **food:** Arby's, Burger King, Capt D's, Checker's, Hong Kong Buffet, McDonald's, Morrison's Cafeteria, O'Charley's, Pizza Hut, Red Lobster, Sake Japanese, Shoney's, Taco Bell, **lodging:** Holiday Inn Express, Ramada Ltd, **other:** Advance Parts, AutoZone, Belk, Dillard's, Firestone/auto, JC Penney, K-Mart, NAPA, Office Depot, Sears/auto, Target, TJ Maxx, mall, W...**food:** Bojangles, Cracker Barrel, KFC, Outback Steaks, Waffle House, **lodging:** Best Western, Comfort Suites, Courtyard, Fairfield Inn, Hampton Inn, **other:** HOSPITAL, Carmax
19	NC 7, E Gastonia, E...**gas:** Shell
17	US 321, Gastonia, E...**gas:** Exxon/dsl/LP, **food:** Los Arcos Mexican, **lodging:** Day's Inn, **other:** Family$, W...**gas:** Citgo/dsl, Perto Xpress/dsl, **food:** Wendy's, Western Sizzlin, **lodging:** Holiday Inn Express, Microtel, Motel 6
14	NC 274, E Bessemer, E...**food:** Burger King(1mi), McDonald's(1mi), W...**gas:** BP/Subway, Citgo/dsl, **food:** Bojangles, Waffle House, **lodging:** Express Inn
13	Edgewood Rd, Bessemer City, E...to Crowders Mtn SP, W...**gas:** Exxon/dsl/24hr, **lodging:** Economy Inn
10b a	US 74 W, US 29, Kings Mtn, no services
8	NC 161, to Kings Mtn, E...**lodging:** Holiday Inn Express, **other:** camping, W...**gas:** BP, **food:** McDonald's, Mi Pueblito Mexican, Taco Bell, Waffle House, Wendy's, **lodging:** Quality Inn, Travelodge, **other:** HOSPITAL
6mm	**rest area sb, full(handicapped)facilities, phone, picnic tables, litter barrels, vending, petwalk**
5	Dixon School Rd, E...**gas:** Citgo/Subway/dsl, **other:** truck/tire repair
4	US 29 S(from sb), no services
2.5mm	**Welcome Ctr nb, full(handicapped)facilities, info, phone, vending, picnic tables, litter barrels, petwalk**
2	NC 216, Kings Mtn, E...to Kings Mtn Nat Military Park
0mm	North Carolina/South Carolina state line

(vertical label: Gastonia)

Interstate 95

Exit #	Services
181mm	North Carolina/Virginia state line, **Welcome Ctr sb, full(handicapped)facilities, phone, picnic tables, litter barrels, vending, petwalk**
180	NC 48, to Gaston, to Lake Gaston, Pleasant Hill, W...**gas:** Pilot/Subway/dsl/scales/24hr
176	NC 46, to Garysburg, W...**gas:** Shell, **food:** Aunt Sarah's, Burger King, **lodging:** Best Western
174mm	Roanoke River
173	US 158, Roanoke Rapids, Weldon, E...**gas:** BP/dsl, Shell/Blimpie, Texaco/dsl, **food:** Ralph's BBQ, Waffle House, **lodging:** Day's Inn, Interstate Inn/RV Park, Orchard Inn, **other:** HOSPITAL, W...**gas:** BP/dsl, Exxon/DQ/Stuckey's, RaceWay, Shell, **food:** Applebee's, Arby's, Burger King, Chick-fil-A, China King, Cracker Barrel, Hardee's, KFC, Little Caesar's, Logans Roadhouse, Mayflower Seafood, McDonald's, New China, Pizza Hut, Ruby Tuesday, Ryan's, Starbucks, Subway, Taco Bell, Texas Steaks, Waffle House, Wendy's, **lodging:** Comfort Suites, Hampton Inn, Jameson Inn, Motel 6, Sleep Inn, **other:** Advance Parts, AutoZone, Belk, $General, $Tree, Eckerd, Firestone/auto, Food Lion, Ford/Lincoln/Mercury/Honda, Goody's, Harley Davidson, Staples, Walgreens, Wal-Mart SuperCtr/gas/24hr
171	NC 125, Roanoke Rapids, W...**gas:** Texaco/dsl, **food:** Chick-fil-A(2mi), Ryan's(2mi), Wendy's(2mi), **lodging:** Hilton Garden, Holiday Inn Express, **other:** Parton Theater, st patrol
168	NC 903, to Halifax, E...**gas:** Citgo/DQ/dsl, Exxon/Subway/dsl, Shell/Burger King/dsl
160	NC 561, to Brinkleyville, E...**gas:** Exxon/24hr, W...**gas:** Citgo/dsl/rest.
154	NC 481, to Enfield, **1mi** W...**other:** KOA
152mm	weigh sta both lanes
150	NC 33, to Whitakers, E...**golf,** W...**gas:** BP/Subway/DQ/Stuckey's/dsl
145	NC 4, to US 301, Battleboro, E...**gas:** BP/dsl, Exxon/DQ, Shell/dsl, Texaco, **food:** BBQ, Denny's, 4Seasons, Hardee's, Shoney's, Waffle House, Wendy's, **lodging:** Best Western/rest., Budget Inn, Comfort Inn, Day's Inn, Deluxe Inn, Guesthouse Inn, Howard Johnson, Red Carpet Inn, Rodeway Inn, Scottish Inn, Super 8
142mm	**rest area both lanes, full(handicapped)facilities, phone, picnic tables, litter barrels, vending, petwalk**
141	NC 43, Red Oak, E...**gas:** BP/dsl, Exxon/dsl/LP, **3mi food:** Chick-fil-A, Ruby Tuesday, Ryan's, W...**lodging:** Econolodge
138	US 64, **1 mi** E **on Winstead...gas:** BP, Exxon, **food:** Cracker Barrel, Outback Steaks, Texas Steaks, **lodging:** Comfort Inn, Courtyard, Hampton Inn, Holiday Inn, Residence Inn, **other:** HOSPITAL, Buick/Pontiac/GMC, Harley-Davidson, Honda, to Cape Hatteras Nat Seashore
132	to NC 58, E...**gas:** Citgo/dsl, **1 mi** W...**gas:** BP/dsl
128mm	Tar River

(vertical label: Roanoke Rapids)

Interstate 95

127 NC 97, to Stanhope, **E**...**gas:** BP/dsl, **other:** airport

121 US 264a, Wilson, **E**...**gas:** Citgo/Subway, Eagle Gas, Kangaroo/dsl/LP, Shell, **food:** KFC/LJ Silver, Waffle House, **lodging:** Prime Inn, **other:** HOSPITAL, Eagle mart, **3-4 mi E**...**gas:** BP, Exxon, Savemore Gas, **food:** Applebee's, Arby's, Burger King, Chick-fil-A, Chili's, CiCi's, Coldstone Creamery, Denny's, El Tapatio, Golden Corral, Hardee's, Ruby Tuesday, Sonic, Subway, Texas Steaks, Wendy's, **other:** HOSPITAL, Belk, BooksAMillion, Chrysler/Jeep/Dodge, Farmfresh Foods, Goody's, Harris-Teeter, Lowe's Whse, Marshall's, Ross, Staples, Target, Toyota/Scion, Wal-Mart SuperCtr/24hr/dsl, **W**...**gas:** BP/dsl, **food:** Bojangles, Burger King, Cracker Barrel, McDonald's, **lodging:** Fairfield Inn, Hampton Inn, Holiday Inn Express, Jameson Inn, Microtel, Sleep Inn, **other:** to Country Doctor Museum

119b a US 264, US 117

116 NC 42, to Clayton, Wilson, **E**...**gas:** Shell/dsl, **other:** HOSPITAL, **W**...**gas:** BP/dsl, **other:** Rock Ridge Camping

107 US 301, Kenly, **E**...**gas:** BP/dsl, Eagle Gas, Exxon/McDonald's/dsl, Fuel Doc, PitStop/Subway, **food:** Moore's BBQ, Nik's Pizza, Patrick's Rest., **lodging:** Budget Inn, Deluxe Inn, Econolodge, **other:** CarQuest, Food Lion, Ford, Family$, Kinley Tires, Tobacco Museum

106 Truck Stop Rd, Kenly, **E**.../Flying J/CountryMkt/dsl/scales/24hr/@, **W**...**gas:** Shell, TA/Wendy's/dsl/24hr/@, Wilco/Hess/dsl/scales/24hr/@, **food:** Waffle House, **lodging:** Day's Inn, Super 8, **other:** Blue Beacon, Speedco Lube, Truck-o-Mat

105.5mm Little River

105 Bagley Rd, Kenly, **E**...**gas:** Big Boy's/Pizza/dsl/24hr

102 Micro, **E**...**gas:** BP/repair, **W**...**gas:** Phillips 66, **other:** USPO

101 Pittman Rd, no services

99mm **rest area both lanes, full(handicapped) facilities, vending, phone, picnic tables, litter barrels, petwalk, hist marker**

98 to Selma, **E**...RVacation

97 US 70 A, to Pine Level, Selma, **E**...**gas:** Citgo/dsl/24hr, Savannah's Gas, **food:** Denny's, Subway, **lodging:** Holiday Inn Express, **other:** J&R Outlet, **W**...**gas:** BP/dsl, Exxon/dsl/24hr, Shell/dsl, **food:** Bojangles, Carolina Rest., Golden China, Golden Corral, Hardee's, KFC, McDonald's, Pizza Hut, Shoney's, Waffle House, **lodging:** Comfort Inn, Day's Inn, Hampton Inn, Luxury Inn, Masters Inn, Regency Inn, Royal Inn, **other:** HOSPITAL

95 US 70, Smithfield, **E**...**lodging:** Log Cabin Motel/rest., Howard Johnson Express, Village Motel, **other:** Ava Gardner Museum, **W**...**gas:** Hess, Shell, Sunoco, **food:** Bob Evans, Burger King, Checker's, CiCi's Pizza, Coldstone Creamery, Cracker Barrel,

El Sombrero Mexican, Outback Steaks, Ruby Tuesday, Smithfield BBQ(2mi), Texas Steaks, Waffle House, Zaxby's, **lodging:** Best Western, Jameson Inn, Sleep Inn, Super 8, **other:** Harley-Davidson, Carolina Premium Outlets/famous brands

93 Brogden Rd, Smithfield, **W**...**gas:** BP/dsl, Citgo

91.5mm Neuse River

90 US 301, US 701, to Newton Grove, **E**...**gas:** BP/dsl, Citgo/dsl, **lodging:** Travelers Inn, **other:** KOA, Ronnie's Tires, to Bentonville Bfd, **W**...**gas:** Exxon/dsl, **lodging:** Four Oaks Motel

87 NC 96, Four Oaks, **W**...**gas:** BP/dsl, **food:** Subway

81b a I-40, E to Wilmington, W to Raleigh

79 NC 50, to NC 27, Benson, Newton Grove, **E**...**gas:** BP/dsl, Citgo, **food:** Waffle House, **lodging:** Dutch Inn, **other:** auto repair, **W**...**gas:** Mobil/McDonald's, Phillips 66/Burger King, Pure, **food:** Charro Mexican, China 8, Domino's, KFC, Pizza Hut, Subway, **lodging:** Day's Inn, **other:** Family$, Food Lion, Kerr Drug

77 Hodges Chapel Rd, **E**...**gas:** Pilot/Subway/dsl/scales/24hr

75 Jonesboro Rd, **W**...**gas:** Sadler's/Shell/DQ/Quizno's/dsl/24hr/@, Texaco/Milestone Diner

73 US 421, NC 55, to Dunn, Clinton, **E**...**food:** Cracker Barrel, Wendy's, **other:** Chrysler/Jeep, Family$, Food Lion, **W**...**gas:** Exxon/dsl, Hess/dsl, Shell, **food:** Bojangles, Burger King, Dairy Freeze, Sagebrush Steaks, Subway, Taco Bell, Triangle Waffle, **lodging:** Econolodge, Hampton Inn, Holiday Inn Express, Jameson Inn, Ramada Inn/rest., **other:** IGA Foods, museum

72 Pope Rd, **E**...**lodging:** Comfort Inn, Red Carpet Inn, Royal Inn, **W**...**gas:** BP, Pure, **food:** Brass Lantern Steaks, Prime Rib, **lodging:** Budget Inn, Express Inn, **other:** Cadillac/GMC

71 Longbranch Rd, **E**...**gas:** Citgo/Hardee's/dsl/scales/24hr, **W**...to Averasboro Bfd

70 SR 1811, **E**...**lodging:** Relax Inn

65 NC 82, Godwin, **W**...Children's Home

61 to Wade, **E**...**gas:** Citgo/dsl, **other:** KOA(1mi), **W**...**gas:** BP/Subway/dsl/24hr

58 US 13, to Newton Grove, I-295 to Fayetteville, **E**...**gas:** Eastgate, Shell, **food:** Quizno's, **lodging:** Day's Inn/rest.

Interstate 95

N

Fayetteville

56	Lp 95, to US 301(from sb), Fayetteville, W...gas: Epco/dsl, Kangaroo/24hr, lodging: Budget Inn, other: HOSPITAL, to Ft Bragg, Pope AFB
55	NC 1832, Murphy Rd, W...gas: Epco/dsl, Kangaroo/24hr, lodging: Scottish Inn
52	NC 24, Fayetteville, W...other: to Ft Bragg, Pope AFB, botanical gardens, museum
49	NC 53, NC 210, Fayetteville, E...gas: Citgo, Exxon, Kangaroo, Mobil, food: Burger King, McDonald's, Pizza Hut, Taco Bell, Waffle House, lodging: Deluxe Inn, Motel 6, Quality Inn, W...gas: BP/Subway/dsl, Exxon/dsl, Shell/dsl, food: Cracker Barrel, Fuller's BBQ, Ruby Tuesday, Shoney's, lodging: Best Western, Comfort Inn, Days Inn, Econolodge, Fairfield Inn, Fayetteville Hotel, Hampton Inn, Holiday Inn, Red Roof Inn, Sleep Inn, Super 8
48mm	rest area both lanes, full(handicapped) facilities, phone, picnic tables, litter barrels, vending, petwalk
47mm	Cape Fear River
46b a	NC 87, to Fayetteville, Elizabethtown, W...other: HOSPITAL, museum, Civic Ctr, to Agr Expo Ctr
44	Claude Lee Rd, W...other: Lazy Acres Camping, to airport
41	NC 59, to Hope Mills, Parkton, E...gas: Kangaroo/24hr, W...gas: BP/dsl, other: Lake Waldo Camping, Spring Valley RV Park
40	Lp 95, to US 301(from nb), to Fayetteville, facilities on US 301(5-7mi)
33	US 301, St Pauls, E...gas: BP/dsl/repair/24hr
31	NC 20, to St Pauls, Raeford, E...gas: BP, Mobil/McDonald's, Pit Row Gas, Shell/Huddle House/dsl/24hr, food: Burger King, lodging: Day's Inn, other: Volvo Trucks, W...gas: Citgo, Exxon/dsl, other: FoodLion
25	US 301, E...gas: BP/dsl
24mm	weigh sta both lanes
22	US 301, E...gas: Exxon, Shell/DQ, food: Burger King, China Wok, Denny's, Hardee's, Huddle House, John's Rest, Outback Steaks, Quizno's, Ruby Tuesday, Ryan's, San Jose Mexican, Smithfield BBQ, Texas Steaks, Waffle House, Wendy's, Zaxby's, lodging: Best Western, Comfort Suites, Hampton Inn, Holiday Inn, Super 8, other: Black's Tire, $Tree, Goody's, Lowe's Foods, Lowe's Whse, Office Depot, Wal-Mart SuperCtr/24hr, st patrol, W...gas: Circle B, Sun-Do/dsl, Pure/dsl, other: Ford/Lincoln/Mercury, Sam's Club/gas
20	NC 211, to NC 41, Lumberton, E...gas: Citgo, Exxon/dsl, Liberty/dsl, food: Arby's, Bojangles, Buger King, Capt D's, Golden City Chinese, Hardee's, KFC, Little Caesar's, McDonald's, River City Grill, Shoney's, Sonic, Subway, Taco Bell, Tokyo Express, Waffle House, lodging: Econolodge, Howard Johnson, Quality Inn, other: HOSPITAL, Advance Parts, Belk, CVS Drug, Food Lion/deli, JC Penney, K-Mart, Walgreens, W...gas: Shell/dsl, Sun-do/dsl, food: Cracker Barrel, Fuller's BBQ Buffet, Lung-Wah Chinese, San Jose Mexican, lodging: Best Value Inn, Comfort Inn, Country Inn&Suites, Day's Inn/rest., Econolodge, Fairfield Inn

S

Lumberton

19	Carthage Rd, Lumberton, E...gas: BP/dsl, lodging: Travelers Inn, W...gas: Circle B, Exxon/dsl, lodging: Knight's Inn, Motel 6
18mm	Lumber River
17	NC 72, E...gas: Atkinson's/dsl, BP/dsl, Dobb's/Stuckey's/Wendy's, Go-Gas/dsl, Mobil/dsl, food: Burger King, Hardee's, Huddle House, McDonald's, Subway, Waffle House, lodging: Budget Inn, Southern Inn, other: Advance Parts, AutoZone, Food Lion
14	US 74, to Laurinburg, Maxton, W...gas: BP/dsl, other: Sleepy Bear's RV Camp
13	US 74, to Wilmington, no services
10	US 301, to Fairmont, no services
7	to McDonald, Raynham, no services
5mm	Welcome Ctr nb, full(handicapped)facilities, phone, picnic tables, litter barrels, vending, petwalk
2	NC 130, to NC 904, Rowland, no services
1b a	US 301, US 501, Dillon, E...gas: Exxon, Shell, food: Hot Tamale Rest., Pedro's Diner, Porky's Truckstp, lodging: Budget Motel, South-of-the-Border Motel, other: Pedro's Campground, W...gas: Shell/dsl, Sun-Do, food: Waffle House, lodging: Day's Inn, Super 8
0mm	North Carolina/South Carolina state line

Interstate 240(Asheville)

Exit #	Services
9mm	I-240 begins/ends on I-40, exit 53b a.
8	Fairview Rd, N...gas: Shell/Blimpie, food: Buddie's Ribs&BBQ, Burger King, J&S Cafeteria, KFC, Little Caesar's, Little Venice, McDonald's, Subway, lodging: Best Western, Ramada Inn, other: Advance Parts, Bilo Foods, CVS Drug, Hamrick's, Kohl's, Petsmart, Subaru, Wal-Mart SuperCtr/24hr S...gas: Citgo, food: Pizza Hut, Rezeals Rest., other: Aldi Foods, Home Depot
7.5mm	Swannanoa River
7	US 70, N...U-Haul, S...gas: BP, Exxon/dsl, food: Applebee's, Bonefish Grill, Burger King, Carraba's, Cheeseburger Paradise, Chili's, China Palace, Chuck-eCheese, Cornerstone Rest., Cracker Barrel, Don Pablo, DQ, East Buffet, Frank's Pizza, Greenery Rest., Guadalahara Mexican, Ham's Rest., Hooters, IHOP, Joe's Crabshack, Lonestar Steaks, Longhorn Steaks, Mikado, Mtn Ear Inn, O'Charley's, Olive Garden, Outback Steaks, Red Lobster, Ruby's BBQ, Subway, Taco Bell, Waffle House, lodging: Best Western, Country Inn&Suites, Courtyard, Day's Inn, Econolodge, Extended Stay America, Hampton Inn, Homewood Suites, InTown Motor Inn, Royal Inn, Spring Hill Suites, other: Belk, Best Buy, Books-a-Million, Circuit City, Dillards, $Tree, Firestone, Goody's, Ingles Foods, K-Mart, Lowe's Whse, Michael's, Office Depot, Radio Shack, Ross, Sears/auto, Target, TJ Maxx, Walgreens
6	Tunnel Rd(from eb), same as 7
5b	US 70 E, US 74A, Charlotte St, N...gas: BP, Pure, food: Fuddruckers, Starbucks, Two Guys Hogi, lodging: B&B, S...food: Tripp's Rest., lodging: Best Western, Renaissance Motel, Civic Ctr

E

W

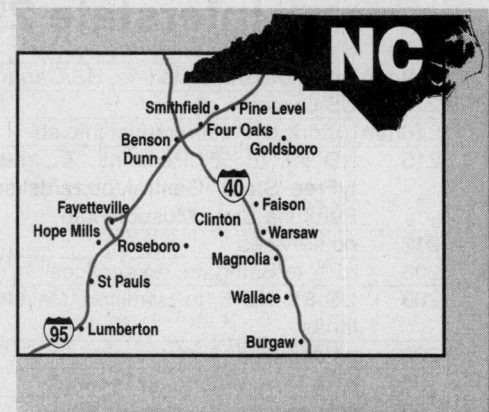

Interstate 240(Asheville)

5a	US 25, Merrymont Ave, **N**...**gas:** Exxon/dsl, Shell, **food:** Bojangles, La Caterina, 3 Pigs BBQ, **other:** Staples
4c	Haywood St(no EZ return to eb), Montford, **S**... **food:** 3 Bros Rest.
4b	Patton Ave(from eb), downtown
4a	US 19 N, US 23 N, US 70 W, to Weaverville
3b	Westgate, **N**...**gas:** Servco, **food:** Jae Thai, Mkt Cafe, **lodging:** Crowne Plaza, **other:** CVS Drug, EarthFare Foods, NTB, Sam's Club/gas
3a	US 19 S, US 23 S, W Asheville, **N**...**gas:** BP, Exxon, **food:** Arby's, Bojangles, Denny's, Green Tea Japanese, KFC, Krispy Kreme, Little Caesar's, LJ Silver/A&W, McDonald's, Mexican Restaurant, Pizza Hut, Ryan's, Subway, Taco Bell, Wendy's, Yoshida Japanese, **other:** Advance Parts, AutoZone, Bilo, Cadillac/Pontiac/GMC, Checker Parts, Curves, Goodyear/auto, Ingles, Kerr Drug, K-Mart, Radio Shack, Sav-Mor Foods, **S**...**food:** Backyard Burger
2	US 19, US 23, W Asheville, **N**...**gas:** Phillips 66, Shell, **S**...**other:** B&B Drug
1c	Amboy Rd(from eb), no services
1b	NC 191, to I-40 E, Brevard Rd, **S**...**gas:** Phillips 66/dsl, **other:** farmers mkt, camping
1a	I-40 W, to Knoxville, no services
0mm	I-240 begins/ends on I-40, exit 46b a

Interstate 440(Raleigh)

Exit #	Services
16	I-40
15	Poole Rd, **W**...**gas:** BP/dsl, Citgo/dsl, **food:** Burger King, McDonald's, Subway KFC/Taco Bell
14	US 64, to Rocky Mount, limited access hwy
13b a	US 64, US 264 E, New Bern Ave, to Wilson, **2-3 mi E**...**gas:** BP, 76/Circle K, Exxon, Phillips 66(1mi), Shell/Texaco, Speedway, Circle K, **food:** Arby's, Burger King, Checker's, Hardee's, K&S Cafeteria, Last Catch Grill, McDonald's, Miami Subs, O'Brian's, Papa John's, Pizza Hut, Subway, Taco Bell, Waffle House, Wendy's, **lodging:** Best Western, Holiday Inn Express, Microtel, Red Roof Inn, Super 8, **other:** Firestone/auto, Ford, Hamrick's, K-Mart, Kroger, Food Lion, Radio Shack, RV Ctr, Winn-Dixie, **W**... HOSPITAL
12	Yonkers Rd, Brentwood Rd, no services
11b a	US 1, US 401, Capital Blvd N, **N**...**gas:** BP, Citgo, Crown Gas, Kangaroo, Shell, **food:** Applebee's(1mi), BBQ, Bojangle's, Buffalo Bro.s, Burger King, Carver's Creek, Don Murray's BBQ, Dunkin Donuts, IHOP, Mayflower Seafood, McDonald's, Outback Steaks, Perkins, Subway, Taco Bell, Vallerta Mexican, Waffle House, Wendy's, **lodging:** Best Western, Comfort Inn, Country Inn, Day's Inn,

Econolodge, Holiday Inn, Homestead Suites, Hotel Europa, Lodge America, Sleep Inn, Travelodge, Wingate Inn, **other:** Eckerd, IGA Foods, USPO

10	Wake Forest Rd, **N**...**food:** Denny's, **food:** Bajama Breze, **lodging:** AmeriSuites, Days Inn, Hilton, **other:** CVS Drug, **S**...**gas:** BP, **food:** A&W/KFC, Applebee's, Bojangles, Jersey Mike's, Melting Pot Rest., Papa John's, Schlotzsky's, Taco Bell, **lodging:** Courtyard, Extended Stay America, Hampton Inn, Residence Inn, **other:** HOSPITAL, Discount Tire, Staples
8b a	6 Forks Rd, North Hills, **N**...**gas:** Exxon, **food:** Bonefish Grill, Panera Bread, Starbucks, **lodging:** Comfort Inn, **other:** Dillard's/JC Penney, GNC, Firestone/auto, Kerr Drug, Target, Winn-Dixie
7b a	US 70, NC 50, Glenwood Ave, Crabtree Valley, **N**... **gas:** BP, Exxon, **food:** McDonald's, PF Chang's, Ruby Tuesday, **lodging:** Candlewood Suites, Courtyard, Crabtree Inn, Fairfield Inn, Holiday Inn, La Quinta, Marriott, Motel 6, Residence Inn, Sheraton, **other:** Barnes&Noble, Belk, Goodyear/auto, Hecht's, Sears/auto, mall
6	Ridge Rd(from nb), same as 7
5	Lake Boone Tr, **W**...**gas:** Phillips 66, **food:** McDonald's, Subway, Wendy's, **other:** HOSPITAL, Eckerd, Food Lion
4b a	to I-40 W, Wade Ave, **W**...to I-40, RD Airport
3	NC 54, Hillsboro St, **E**...**gas:** BP, Citgo, Crowne Gas, Exxon, **food:** Arby's, Bean Sprout Chinese, Quizno's, Snoopy's Hotdogs, Waffle House, **lodging:** Ramada Inn, **other:** to Meredith Coll, to St Mary's
2b a	Western Blvd, **E**...**gas:** Crowne Gas, 76/Circle K, **food:** Domino's, Subway, **other:** to NCSU, Shaw U, **W**...K-Mart
1d	Melbourne Rd(from sb), no services
1c	Jones-Franklin Rd, no services
1b a	I-40. I-440 begins on I-40., **1-2 mi W on Walnut St**...**gas:** Exxon, Shell, **food:** Hardee's, Olive Garden, Pizza Hut, Red Lobster, **lodging:** Best Western, Day's Inn, Motel 6, **other:** Borders Books Michael's, mall

NORTH DAKOTA
Interstate 29

Exit #	Services
218mm	North Dakota state line, US/Canada border
217mm	US Customs sb
216mm	historical site nb, tourist info sb
215	ND 59, rd 55, Pembina, E...gas: Gastrak/dsl/DutyFree Store, Gastrak/pizza/dsl/scales/24hr, other: Pembina State Museum/info
212	no services
208	rd 1, to Bathgate, no services
203	US 81, ND 5, to Hamilton, Cavalier, weigh sta both lanes
200	no services
196	rd 3, Bowesmont, no services
193	no services
191	rd 11, to St Thomas, no services
187	ND 66, to Drayton, E...gas: Cenex/pizza/dsl, Tesoro/dsl, food: Andy's Drive Inn, Rte 66 Café, lodging: Motel 66, Red River Motel, other: USPO, city park
184	to Drayton, 2 mi E...gas: gas/dsl, other: USPO
180	rd 9, no services
179mm	rest area both lanes(both lanes exit left), full(handicapped)facilities, phone, picnic tables, litter barrels, vending, petwalk
176	ND 17, to Grafton, 10 mi W...HOSPITAL, gas, food, lodging: AmericInn
172	no services
168	rd 15, to Minto, Warsaw, no services
164	no services
161	ND 54, rd 19, to Ardoch, Oslo, no services
157	no services
152	US 81, to Gilby, Manvel, W...gas: Manvel/dsl/food
145	US 81 bus, N Washington St, to Grand Forks
141	US 2, Gateway Dr, Grand Forks, E...gas: BP/dsl/24hr, Loaf'N Jug/McDonald's/dsl/@, Stamart, Univ. Sta/dsl, food: Al's Grill, Burger King, Greatwall Buffet, GreenMill Rest., Northside Cafe, Papa Murphy's, lodging: Best Value, Budget Inn, Econolodge, Holiday Inn, Ramada Inn, Select Inn, Super 8, other: Advance Parts, Checker Parts, Chrysler/Dodge/Jeep/Toyota, Ford/Lincoln/Mercury, U-Haul, to U of ND, 1 mi E...food: DQ, Domino's, Taco John's, other: HOSPITAL, Freightliner, U-Haul, auto repair, W...gas: Simonson/dsl/café/24hr/@, Stamart/Tesoro/dsl/RV dump/scales/@, food: Emerald Grill, Perkins, lodging: Settle Inn, other: Budget RV Ctr, port of entry/weigh sta, airport, to AFB
140	DeMers Ave, E...gas: BP, food: Overtime Grill, Red Pepper Cafe, lodging: Hilton Garden, other: HOSPITAL, Alerus Ctr, to U of ND
138	US 81, 32nd Ave S, E...gas: BP, Holiday/Subway/dsl, Tesoro, food: Arby's, Boston's Grill, Buffalo Wild Wings, Burger King, Campbell's Burgers, China Garden, Coldstone's, Culver's, Domino's, DQ, Golden Corral, Grizzly's Steaks, Ground Round, Jimmy John Sandwiches, McDonald's, Papa Murphy's, Pizza Hut, Qdoba Mexican, Quizno's, Red Lobster, Starbucks, Taco Bell, Texas Roadhouse, Village Inn Rest., Wendy's, lodging: AmericInn, C'mon Inn, Comfort Inn, Country Inn Suites, Day's Inn, Fairfield Inn, Holiday Inn Express, Lakeview Inn, Roadking Inn, other: Best Buy, Cadillac, Chevrolet, Chrysler/Toyota, CVS Drug, $Tree, Ford/Lincoln/Mercury, Honda/Nissan,

Hugo's Foods, Hyundai, JC Penney, Jo-Ann Fabrics, Kohl's, Lowe's Whse, Marshall Field, Macy's, Mazda, Michael's, Old Navy, PetCo, Sam's Club/gas, Sears/auto, Super 1 Foods, Target, Tires+, TJ Maxx, Wal-Mart SuperCtr, mall, W...gas: Conoco/Subway/dsl, other: Grand Forks Camping

130	ND 15, rd 81, Thompson, 1 mi W...gas, food
123	to Reynolds, E...to Central Valley School
119mm	insp sta, both lanes
118	to Buxton, no services
111	ND 200 W, to Cummings, Mayville, W...other: Big Top Fireworks, to Mayville St U
104	Hillsboro, E...gas: Cenex/Burger King/dsl/LP/24hr/@, Tesoro/dsl/24hr, food: Country Hearth Rest., lodging: Hillsboro Inn, other: HOSPITAL, Hillsboro Drug, NAPA, RV park, USPO
100	ND 200 E, ND 200A, to Blanchard, Halstad, no services
99mm	rest area both lanes, full(handicapped) facilities, phone, picnic tables, litter barrels, vending, petwalk
92	rd 11, Grandin, E...Co-op/dsl, W...gas: Stop-n-Shop/dsl
86	Gardner, no services
79	Argusville, no services
74.5mm	Sheyenne River
73	rd 17, rd 22, Harwood, E...gas: Cenex/pizza/dsl/LP/café/24hr
69	rd 20, no services
67	US 81 bus, 19th Ave N, E...VA HOSPITAL, Hector Int Airport
66	12th Ave N, E...gas: Stamart/Tesoro/dsl/24hr/scales, Stop'n Go, other: HOSPITAL, to ND St U, W...gas: Cenex/dsl, food: Arby's, lodging: Microtel
65	US 10, Main Ave, W Fargo, E...gas: Tesoro/dsl/24hr, food: Kroll's Diner, other: Checker Parts, NAPA, OK Tire, True Value, transmissions, W...gas: Cenex/Subway/dsl, Simonson/dsl, Stop-n-Go, food: Hardee's, O'Kelly's Rest, Outback Steaks, Quizno's, Season Chinese, lodging: Best Western, other: Aamco, CarQuest, Chevrolet/Buick/Cadillac/Honda, Chrysler/Dodge/Jeep, Cummins dsl, Hyundai, Isuzu/Volvo/GMC, Kenworth, Mac's Hardware, Mercury/Lincoln, Saturn, Subaru, Toyota
64	13th Ave, Fargo, E...gas: BP/24hr, Cenex, Kum&Go/gas, Stamart/dsl, food: Acapulco Mexican, Applebee's, Arby's, Buck's Roadhouse, Burger King, Chuck-eCheese, DQ, Erbert & Gerbert Subs, GreenMill Rest., Ground Round, Hardee's, Juano's Mexican, Mr Steak, Nine Dragons Chinese, Perkins/24hr, Ponderosa, Quizno's, Starbucks, Subway, Taco John's, TCBY, Wendy's, lodging: AmericInn, Best Western, Comfort Inn/Suites, Country Suites, Econolodge, Hampton Inn, Motel 6, Super 8, The Grand Inn, other: Advance Parts, CashWise Foods/drug/24hr, CVS Drug, Family$, Goodyear, JiffyLube, Scheels Hardware, SunMart Food, Tires+/transmissions, W...gas: BP/24hr, Cenex, Tesoro, food: Applebee's, Arby's, Blimpie, Caribou Coffee, Chili's, Culver's, Denny's, DQ, Fuddrucker's, Gordman's, Grandma's Grill, Grizzly's, Godfather's, Happy Joe's Pizza, Herburgers, Hooters, KFC, Krispy Kreme, Kroll's Diner, LoneStar Steaks, McDonald's, Olive Garden, Paradiso Mexican, Pizza Hut, Red Lobster, Royal Fork Buffet, Ruby Tuesday, Schlotsky's, Taco Bell, Taco Time,

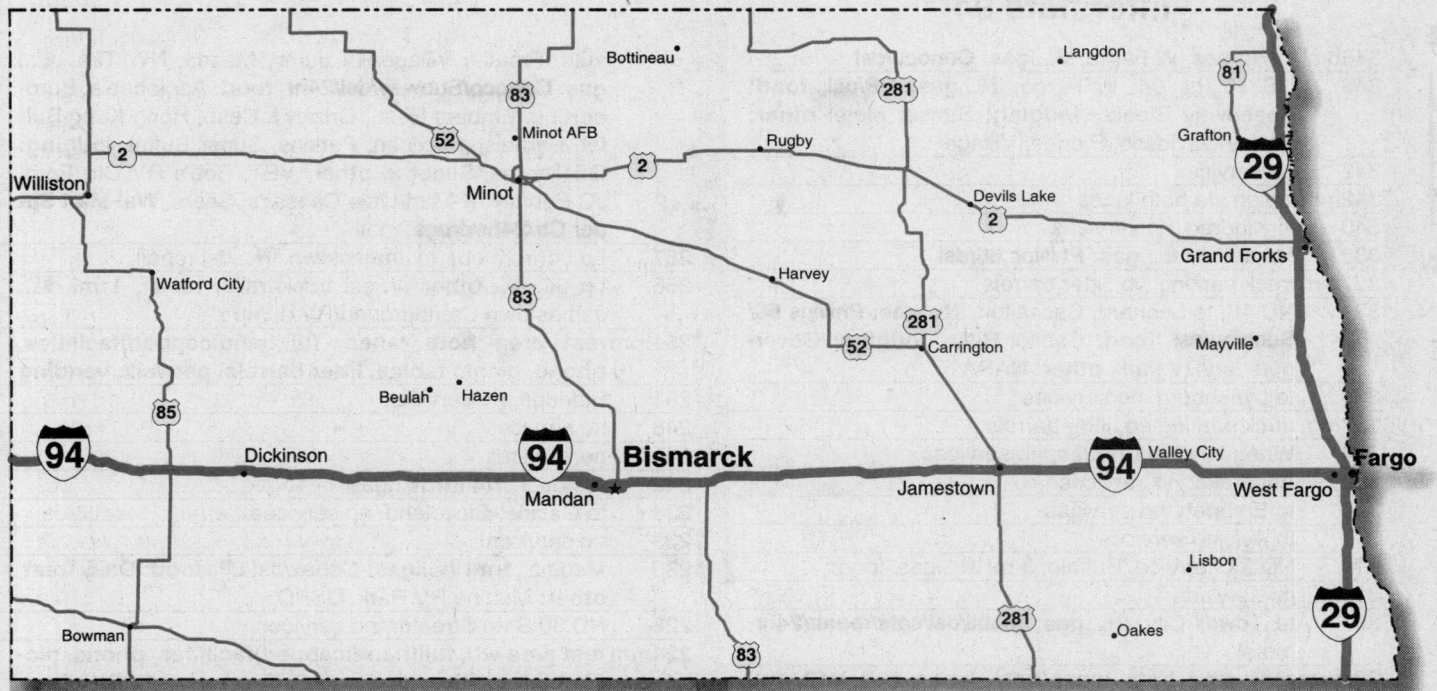

Interstate 29

Texas Roadhouse, TGIFriday, TimberLodge Steaks, **lodging:** Comfort Inn, Day's Inn, Fairfield Inn, Holiday Inn Express, Kelly Inn, Ramada Inn, Red River Lodge, Red Roof Inn, Select Inn, **other:** Advance Parts, Barnes&Noble, Best Buy, BigLots, Chevrolet, $Tree, GNC, Herberger's, Hornbacher's Foods, JC Penney, Jo-Ann Crafts, Kohl's, Lowe's Whse, Michael's, Office Depot, Old Navy, PetCo, Sam's Club, Sears/auto, SunMart Foods, Savers Foods, Target, TJ Maxx, Wal-Mart SuperCtr, Walgreen, USPO, mall

63b a	I-94, W to Bismarck, E to Minneapolis
62	32nd Ave S, Fargo, **E**...**gas:** F&F/dsl, Tesoro, **food:** Arby's, Country Kitchen, Culvers, KFC, Little Caesars, Moe's SW Grill, Papa John's, Quizno's, Starbucks, Subway, Taco John's, Village Inn, **other:** HOSPITAL, Buick/Pontiac/GMC, Ford, Freightliner, JiffyLube, SunMart Foods, **W**...**gas:** /Flying J/Conoco/dsl/LP/motel/24hr/@, **other:** Goodyear/auto, Peterbilt, PleasureLand RV Ctr
60	52nd Ave S, to Fargo, **W**...**other:** Starr Fireworks
56	to Wild Rice, Horace, no services
54	rd 16, to Oxbow, Davenport, no services
50	rd 18, Hickson, no services
48	ND 46, to Kindred, no services
44	to Christine, **1 mi** **E**...gas
42	rd 2, to Walcott, no services
37	rd 4, to Abercrombie, Colfax, **E**...to Ft Abercrombie HS, **3 mi** **W**...gas
31	rd 8, Galchutt, no services
26	to Dwight, no services
24mm	weigh sta both lanes exit left
23b a	ND 13, to Wahpeton, Mooreton, **10 mi** **E**...HOSPITAL, ND St Coll of Science
15	rd 16, to Mantador, Great Bend, no services
8	ND 11, to Hankinson, Fairmount, **E**...**gas:** Tesoro/dsl, **3 mi** **W**...camping

3mm	Welcome Ctr nb, full(handicapped)facilities, phone, picnic tables, litter barrels, petwalk, RV dump
2	rd 22, no services
1	rd 1E, **E**...Dakota Magic Casino/Hotel/rest./gas/dsl
0mm	North Dakota/South Dakota state line

Interstate 94

Exit #	Services
352mm	North Dakota/Minnesota state line, Red River
351	US 81, Fargo, **N**...**gas:** Loaf'n Jug, Stop'n Go, Tesoro, **food:** Cousins Subs, Duane's Grill, Great Harvest Breads, Starbucks, Taco Shop, **other:** HOSPITAL, AutoZone, Hornbacher's Foods, Medicine Shoppe, Scheel's, **S**...**gas:** Phillips 66/dsl, Tesoro, **food:** A&W/LJ Silver, Burger King, Fortune House Chinese, Happy Joe's Pizza, KFC, McDonald's, N American Steaks, Papa Murphy's, Pepper's Café, Randy's Diner, Steak Buffet, Subway, Taco Bell, **lodging:** Expressway Inn, Rodeway Inn, **other:** Hyundai/Nissan, K-Mart, USPO
350	25th St, Fargo, **N**...**gas:** Stop'n Go, **S**...**gas:** BP/dsl, Loaf'n Jug, **food:** Dolittle's Grill, Ruby Tuesday
349b a	I-29, N to Grand Forks, S to Sioux Falls, services 1 mi N, exit 64
348	45th St, **N**...**Visitor Ctr/full facilities, gas:** BP, Petro/dsl/LP/rest./24hr/@, **food:** Bennigan's, Carino's, IHOP, McDonald's, Qdoba Mexican, Space Alien Rest., Subway, Wendy's, **lodging:** C'mon Inn, MainStay Inn, Ramada Inn, Sleep Inn, Staybridge Suites, Wingate Inn, **other:** Home Depot, NAPA, **1-2 mi** **N**...**gas:** Cenex, Stop'n Go, **food:** Applebee's, Culver's, KFC, Olive Garden, Papa Murphy's, Pizza Hut, Quizno's, Schlotsky's, **other:** Sam's Club, Scheel's, Target, Wal-Mart SuperCtr/24hr, **S**...**gas:** Tesoro/DQ/dsl, **food:** Famous Dave's BBQ, Old Chicago Pizza, **other:** Gander Mtn NP, Red River Zoo

Fargo

E ↑ W

NORTH DAKOTA
Interstate 94

E
↕
W

Exit	Services
346b a	to Horace, W Fargo, **S**...**gas**: Conoco/dsl
343	US 10, Lp 94, W Fargo, **N**...**gas**: BP/dsl, **food**: Speedway Steaks, **lodging**: Sunset Motel **other**: Harley-Davidson, Pioneer Village
342	no services
342mm	weigh sta both lanes
340	to Kindred, no services
338	Mapleton, **N**...**gas**: Phillips 66/dsl
337mm	truck parking wb, litter barrels
331	ND 18, to Leonard, Casselton, **N**...**gas**: Phillips 66/ Subway/dsl, **food**: Capitol Rest., **lodging**: Governors Inn/RV park, **other**: NAPA
328	to Lynchburg, no services
327mm	truck parking eb, litter barrels
324	Wheatland, to Chaffee, no services
322	Absaraka, no services
320	to Embden, no services
317	to Ayr, no services
314	ND 38, to Alice, Buffalo, **3 mi N**...gas, food
310	no services
307	to Tower City, **N**...**gas**: Mobil/dsl/café/repair/24hr, motel
304mm	**rest area both lanes(both lanes exit left), full (handicapped)facilities, info, phone, picnic tables, litter barrels, vending, petwalk**
302	ND 32, to Fingal, Oriska, **1 mi N**... Scotty's Grill, gas
298	no services
296	no services
294	Lp 94, to Kathryn, Valley City, **N**...HOSPITAL, camping
292	Valley City, **N**...**gas**: Tesoro/dsl/café/24hr, **food**: Sabir's Rest., **lodging**: AmericInn, Super 8, Wagon Wheel Inn/rest., **other**: HOSPITAL, to Bald Hill Dam, camping, **S**...**other**: Ft Ransom SP(35mi)
291	Sheyenne River
290	Lp 94, Valley City, **N**...**gas**: Tesoro/dsl, **food**: Burger King, Kenny's Rest., Pizza Hut, **lodging**: Bel Air Motel, Valley City Motel, **other**: HOSPITAL, Chrysler/Dodge/Jeep, Ford, Pamida
288	ND 1 S, to Oakes, **S**...Fort Ransom SP (36 mi)
283	ND 1 N, to Rogers, no services
281	to Litchville, Sanborn, **1-2 mi N**...gas, food, lodging
276	Eckelson, **S**...**other**: Prairie Haven Camping/gas/ dsl
275mm	continental divide, elev 1490
272	to Urbana, no services
269	Spiritwood, no services
262	Bloom, **N**...airport
260	Jamestown, **N**...**gas**: BP/dsl/café/@, Stop'n Go, **lodging**: Starlite Motel, **other**: to St HOSPITAL, Chevrolet/Buick/Dodge, Harley-Davidson, camping
259mm	James River
258	US 281, Jamestown, **N**...**gas**: BP/TCBY/24hr, Sinclair/dsl, **food**: Arby's, DQ, Hardee's, McDonald's, Pizza Ranch, Taco Bell, Wagonmaster Rest., **lodging**: Comfort Inn, Day's Inn, Holiday Inn Express, Jamestown Motel, Ranch House Motel, **other**: HOSPITAL, Buffalo Herd/museum, Bumper Parts, Cadillac/Pontiac/GMC, Chrysler/Toyota, Firestone/

J
a
m
e
s
t
o
w
n

Exit	Services
	auto, Frontier Village/RV dump, Mazda, NW Tire, **S**... **gas**: Conoco/Subway/dsl/24hr, **food**: Applebee's, Burger King, Embers Rest., Grizzly's Rest., Hong Kong Buffet, Paradiso Mexican, Perkins, Super Buffet, **lodging**: Quality Inn, Super 8, **other**: VET, Bob's RV Ctr, Ford, JC Penney, K-Mart/Little Caesar's, Sears, **Wal-Mart Super Ctr/24hr/drugs**, mall
257	Lp 94(from eb), to Jamestown, **N**...dsl repair
256	Lp 94, **S**...**other**: Wiest truck/trailer repair, **1 mi S**... Jamestown Campground/RV dump
254mm	**rest area both lanes, full(handicapped)facilities, phone, picnic tables, litter barrels, petwalk, vending**
251	Eldridge, no services
248	no services
245	no services
242	Windsor, **1/4 mi N**...gas
238	to Gackle, Cleveland, no services
233	no services
230	Medina, **1 mi N**...**gas**: Cenex/dsl/LP, **food**: DairyTreat, **other**: Medina RV Park, USPO
228	ND 30 S, to Streeter, no services
224mm	**rest area wb, full(handicapped)facilities, phone, picnic tables, litter barrels, vending, petwalk, RV dump**
221	Crystal Springs, no services
221mm	**rest area eb, full(handicapped)facilities, phone, picnic tables, litter barrels, vending, petwalk, RV dump**
217	Pettibone, no services
214	Tappen, **S**...gas/dsl/food
208	ND 3 S, Dawson, **N**...RV camping, **1/2 mi S**...gas, food, to Camp Grassick, RV camping
205	Robinson, no services
200	ND 3 N, to Tuttle, Steele, **S**...**gas**: Conoco/dsl/24hr, **food**: Lone Steer Motel/café/24hr/RV dump, **lodging**: OK Motel
195	no services
190	Driscoll, **S**...**food**
182	US 83 S, ND 14, to Wing, Sterling, **S**...**gas**: Cenex/dsl/ 24hr, **food**: Darnell's Café, **lodging**: Top's Motel(1mi)
176	McKenzie, no services
170	Menoken, **S**...to McDowell Dam, RV Park
168mm	**rest area both lanes, full(handicapped)facilities, phone, picnic tables, litter barrels, vending, petwalk**
161	Lp 94, Bismarck Expswy, Bismarck, **N**...**gas**: BP/ Quizno's/dsl, **Cenex/dsl/LP/RV Dump/24hr**, **S**...**gas**: **Tesoro/Oasis/dsl/rest./24hr**, **food**: McDonald's, **lodging**: Ramada Ltd, **other**: Capital RV Ctr, Dakota Zoo, Freightliner, Kenworth, OK Tires, Volvo
159	US 83, Bismarck, **N**...**gas**: Best Stop/dsl, BP, Sinclair/ dsl, **food**: Applebee's, Arby's, Burger King, China Star, HongKong Chinese, KFC, Kroll's Diner, McDonald's, Paradiso Mexican, Perkins, Red Lobster, Schlotsky's, Space Alien Grill, Taco Bell, **lodging**: AmericInn, Comfort Inn, Country Inn&Suites, Fairfield Inn, Holiday Inn Express, **other**: Chevrolet, Dan's Foods, Home Depot, K-Mart, NW Tire, Osco Drug, Sears/auto, U-Haul, **Wal-Mart Super Ctr/Subway/24hr**, mall, **S**...**gas**: Conoco/ dsl, Tesoro, **food**: DQ, Hardee's, Intn'l Rest., Minerva's Rest., Pizza Hut, Starbucks, Subway, Taco John's, Woodhouse Rest., **lodging**: Best Western, Day's Inn, Kelly Inn, Select Inn, Super 8, **other**: HOSPITAL

B
i
s
m
a
r
c
k

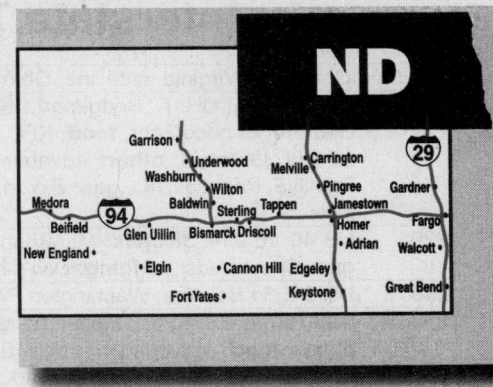

Interstate 94

E

↕

W

Mandan

157	Divide Ave, Bismarck, **N**...**gas:** Conoco/dsl/LP/24hr, **food:** Cracker Barrel, McDonald's, Quizno's, Taco John's/GoodTimes Grill, Texas Roadhouse, Wendy's, **other:** Best Buy, Kohls, Lowe's Whse, **S**...**gas:** Cenex/LP/RV Dump, **other:** Central Mkt Foods
156mm	Missouri River
156	I-194, Bismarck Expswy, Bismarck City Ctr, **1/2 mi** **S**...**lodging:** Colonial Motel, RiverTree Inn
155	to Lp 94(exits left from wb), Mandan, City Ctr, same as 153
153	ND 6, Mandan Dr, Mandan, **1/2 mi** **S**...**gas:** Cenex/24hr, M&H Gas, StaMart/dsl, Tesoro, **food:** Bonanza, Burger King, DQ, Dakota Farms Rest., Domino's, Hardee's, McDonald's, Pizza Hut, Pizza Ranch, Subway, Taco John's, **lodging:** North Country Inn, **other:** Chevrolet, Ford/Mercury, Goodyear/auto, NAPA, NW Tire, Parts+, Subaru, Dacotah Centennial Park, Ft Lincoln SP(5mi)
152	Sunset Dr, Mandan, **N**...**gas:** Conoco, **lodging:** Best Western, Ridge Motel, **S**...**gas:** Tesoro/RV dump, **food:** Fried's Rest., **other:** HOSPITAL
152mm	scenic view eb
147	ND 25, to ND 6, Mandan, **S**...**gas:** Sinclair/Subway/dsl/café/24hr/@
140	to Crown Butte, no services
135mm	scenic view wb, litter barrel
134	to Judson, Sweet Briar Lake, no services
127	ND 31, to New Salem, **N**...Knife River Indian Village(35mi), **S**...**gas:** Cenex/dsl, Tesoro/dsl, **lodging:** Sunset Inn/café, **other:** VET, Food Pride, Gade Drug, World's Largest Cow
123	to Almont, no services
120	no services
119mm	**rest area both lanes, full(handicapped)facilities, phone, picnic tables, litter barrels, petwalk**
117	no services
113	no services
110	ND 49, to Glen Ullin, no services
108	to Glen Ullin, Lake Tschida, **3 mi** **S**...gas, food, lodging, camping
102	Hebron, to Glen Ullin, to Lake Tschida, **3 mi** **S**...gas, food, lodging, camping
97	Hebron, **2 mi** **N**...gas, food, lodging
96.5mm	central/mountain time zone
90	no services
84	ND 8, Richardton, **N**...**gas:** Cenex/dsl, **other:** HOSPITAL, to Assumption Abbey, Schnell RA
78	to Taylor, no services
72	Gladstone, no services
64	Dickinson, **S**...**gas:** Tesoro/Tiger Truckstop/dsl/rest./24hr, **food;** Dakota Diner, **other:** Ford/Lincoln/Mercury, Honda/Toyota, NW Tire, dsl repair

Dickinson

61	ND 22, Dickinson, **N**...**gas:** Cenex/dsl/LP/24hr, Simonson/dsl, **food:** Applebee's, Arby's, Bonanza, Burger King, DQ, El Sombrero Mexican, Papa Murphys Pizza, Ralphy's Pizza, Taco Bell, Taco John's, Wendy's, **lodging:** AmericInn, Comfort Inn, Days Inn, **other:** Albertson's/24hr, Dan's Foods, Goodyear/auto, Herberger's, JC Penney, K-Mart, NAPA, TrueValue, Wal-Mart SuperCtr/Subway/24hr, White Drug, **S**...**gas:** BP/Domino's, Cenex/dsl, Conoco/repair, Holiday/dsl/24hr, **food:** A&W/KFC, Country Kitchen, Domino's, McDonald's, Perkins, Pizza Hut, Subway, **lodging:** Quality Inn, Select Inn, Super 8, Travel Host, **other:** HOSPITAL, Curves, info
59	Lp 94, to Dickinson, **S**...to Patterson Lake RA, camping, **3 mi** **S**...facilities in Dickinson
51	South Heart, no services
42	US 85, to Grassy Butte, Belfield,Williston, **N**...T Roosevelt NP(52mi), **S**...info, **gas:** Conoco/dsl, Tesoro/dsl/24hr, **food:** DQ, **lodging:** Trapper's Inn/rest., **other:** NAPA
36	Fryburg, no services
32	T Roosevelt NP, **Painted Canyon Visitors Ctr, N**...**rest area both lanes, full(handicapped)facilities, phone, picnic tables, litter barrels, petwalk**
27	Lp 94, Historic Medora(from wb), T Roosevelt NP
24.5mm	Little Missouri Scenic River
24	Medora, Historic Medora, Chateau de Mores HS, T Roosevelt NP, **S**...visitors ctr
23	West River Rd (from wb), no services
22mm	scenic view eb
18	Buffalo Gap, **N**...Buffalo Gap Camping(seasonal)
10	Sentinel Butte, Camel Hump Lake, **S**...gas
7	Home on the Range, no services
1	ND 16, Beach, **N**...**lodging:** Outpost Motel, **other:** camping, **S**...**gas:** Cenex/dsl/LP/24hr, ⚛/Flying J/dsl/rest./24hr, **lodging:** Buckboard Inn, **other:** HOSPITAL, **Welcome/Visitor Ctr, full handicapped facilities, litter barrels, petwalk, picnic tables**
1mm	weigh sta both lanes, litter barrel
0mm	North Dakota/Montana state line

Interstate 70

Exit #	Services
225.5mm	Ohio/West Virginia state line, Ohio River
225	US 250 W, OH 7, Bridgeport, **N**...**gas:** Marathon, StarFire, Sunoco/24hr, **food:** KFC, Papa John's, Pizza Hut, Wendy's, **other:** Advance Parts, AutoZone, Family$, Pennzoil, **S**...**gas:** Exxon, Gulf, **food:** Domino's
220	US 40, rd 214, **N**...**gas:** Marathon, Sunoco/dsl, **S**...**gas:** Chevron/dsl, **lodging:** Day's Inn
219	I-470 E, to Bel-Aire, Washington PA
218	Mall Rd, to US 40, to Blaine, **N**...**gas:** BP/dsl, Citgo, Exxon, **food:** Applebee's, Arby's, Buffalo Wild Wings, Burger King, Denny's, Eat'n Park, Outback Steaks, Pizza Hut, Red Lobster, Steak'n Shake, Taco Bell, Wendy's, W Texas Steaks, **lodging:** Best Value Inn, Econolodge, Hampton Inn, Holiday Inn Express, Red Roof, **other:** AutoZone, Chevrolet/Pontiac/Buick/Cadillac, Circuit City, $Tree, Kroger, Lowe's Whse, Sam's Club, Staples, Stewart's RV Ctr, Wal-Mart SuperCtr, **S**...**gas:** USA/dsl, **food:** Bob Evans, Bonanza, Cracker Barrel, Garfield's Rest., LJ Silver, LongHorn Steaks, McDonald's, Rax, Undo's Pizza, **lodging:** Fairfield Inn, **other:** CVS Drug, Jo-Ann Fabrics, JC Penney, K-Mart, Macy's, NTB, Sears/auto, mall
216	OH 9, St Clairsville, **N**...**gas:** BP, **S**...**gas:** Marathon
215	National Rd, **N**...**gas:** Citgo, **food:** Burger King, Subway, WenWu Chinese, **other:** NAPA, Riesbeck's Foods
213	OH 331, Flushing, **S**...**gas:** BP, Marathon/dsl, Sunoco/dsl, **lodging:** Twin Pines Motel
211mm	**rest area both lanes, full(handicapped)facilities, phone, picnic tables, litter barrels, petwalk, vending**
208	OH 149, Morristown, **N**...**gas:** BP/McDonald's/dsl, 208/dsl/rest., **food:** Schlepp's Rest., **lodging:** Arrowhead Motel(1mi), **other:** Ford/Lincoln/Mercury, **S**...**gas:** Chevron/Quizno's/dsl, **other:** Harley-Davidson, Barkcamp SP
204	US 40 E(from eb, no return), National Rd, no services
202	OH 800, to Barnesville, **S**...**other:** HOSPITAL, gas/dsl
198	rd 114, Fairview, no services
193	OH 513, Middlebourne, **N**...**gas:** BP, FuelMart/dsl, Shell, **other:** fireworks
189mm	**rest area eb, full(handicapped)facilities, phone, picnic tables, litter barrels, petwalk, vending**
186	US 40, OH 285, to Old Washington, **N**...**gas:** BP, **S**...**gas:** GoMart/dsl
180b a	I-77 N, to Cleveland, to Salt Fork SP, I-77 S, to Charleston, no services
178	OH 209, Cambridge, 0-1 mi **N**...**gas:** BP/dsl, Sheetz/dsl, Shell, **food:** Bob Evans, China Village, Cracker Barrel, Denny's, DQ, KFC, McDonald's, Papa John's, Pizza Hut, Ruby Tuesday, Subway, Taco Bell, Wendy's, **lodging:** Best Western, Comfort Inn, Day's Inn, Hampton Inn, Holiday Inn, Super 8, **other:** HOSPITAL, Advance Parts, AutoZone, Big Lots, Buick/Pontiac/GMC/Cadillac, $General, Family$, Mor4Less Foods, **S**...**gas:** Pilot/Subway/dsl/scales/24hr, **food:** Arby's, Burger King, Great Chinese, Talaqueta Mexican, **lodging:** AmeriHost, **other:** Aldi Foods, $Tree, $Zone, K-Mart/gas, Radio Shack, Wal-Mart SuperCtr/gas/24hr, Spring Valley RV Park(1mi)
176	US 22, US 40, to Cambridge, **N**...**gas:** Sunoco/dsl, **lodging:** Budget Inn, **other:** Western Shop, RV camping, st patrol
173mm	weigh sta both lanes
169	OH 83, to Cumberland, New Concord, **N**...**gas:** BP, **other:** RV camping, to Muskingum Coll
164	US 22, US 40, Norwich, **N**...**gas:** BP, **lodging:** Baker's Motel, museum
163mm	**rest area wb, full(handicapped)facilities, phone, picnic tables, litter barrels, petwalk, vending**
160	OH 797, Airport, **N**...**gas:** Love's/Arby's/dsl/scales/24hr, **S**...**gas:** BP, Exxon/Subway/dsl, **food:** Denny's, McDonald's, Wendy's, **lodging:** Best Value Inn, Best Western, Holiday Inn, **other:** st patrol
157	OH 93, Zanesville, **N**...**gas:** BP, **S**...**gas:** Marathon, Shell/dsl
155	OH 60, OH 146, Underwood St, Zanesville, **N**...info, **food:** Bob Evans, Olive Garden, Oriental Buffet, Red Lobster, Steak'n Shake, Tumbleweed Grill, **lodging:** Comfort Inn, Fairfield Inn, Hampton Inn, **other:** HOSPITAL, Pick'n Save Foods, **S**...**gas:** Exxon/dsl, **food:** Adornetto Café, Cracker Barrel, Wendy's, **lodging:** Baymont Inn, Econolodge, **other:** Family$, Rite Aid
154	5th St(from eb), no services
153b	Maple Ave(no EZ return from wb), **N**...**gas:** BP, **food:** Big Boy, DQ, Wendy's, **other:** HOSPITAL, CVS Drug, Family$
153a	State St, **N**...**gas:** BP/dsl, **other:** Harley-Davidson, to Dillon SP, **S**...**gas:** BP
153mm	Licking River
152	US 40, National Rd, **N**...**gas:** BP, Exxon/A&W/Blimpie, Starfire, **food:** McDonald's, **lodging:** Super 8
142	US 40(from wb, no EZ return), Gratiot, **N**...RV camping
141	OH 668, US 40(from eb, no return), to Gratiot, same as 142
132	OH 13, to Thornville, Newark, **N**...Dawes Arboretum(3mi), **S**...**gas:** BP, Shell, **other:** RV camping
131mm	**rest area both lanes, full(handicapped)facilities, phone, picnic tables, litter barrels, petwalk, vending**
129b a	OH 79, to Buckeye Lake, Hebron, **N**...**lodging:** Quality Inn, **S**...**gas:** BP/Duke/dsl/@, Valero, **food:** McDonald's, Pizza Hut/Taco Bell, Subway, Wendy's, **lodging:** Super 8, **other:** CarQuest, IGA Foods, KOA(2mi), Blue Goose Marina(2mi)
126	OH 37, to Granville, Lancaster, **N**...**gas:** Marathon/dsl/@, Pilot/Chester's/Subway/dsl/scales/24hr, Starfire Express/dsl, **S**...**gas:** Sunoco/dsl, TA/BP/Sbarro's/Popeye's/dsl/scales/24hr/@, **lodging:** Deluxe Inn, Red Roof Inn, **other:** truckwash, KOA(4mi),
122	OH 158, to Baltimore, Kirkersville, **N**...**lodging:** Regal Inn, **S**...**gas:** ⑦/Flying J/CountryMkt/dsl/scales/24hr/@
118	OH 310, to Pataskala, **N**...**gas:** BP/McDonald's, Speedway/dsl, Sunoco, **food:** DQ, **S**...**gas:** Duke's/dsl
112	OH 256, to Pickerington, Reynoldsburg, **N**...**gas:** BP, Shell/McDonald's, Sunoco/dsl, **food:** Chipotle Mexican, Dynasty Buffet, Logan's Roadhouse, O'Charley's, Panera Bread, Ritter's Custard, Smokey Bones BBQ, TGIFriday's, **lodging:** Country Inn&Suites, Fairfield Inn, **other:** Best Buy, Curves, Gander Mtn, Jo-Ann Fabrics, Marshall's, NTB, Sam's Club/gas, Staples, Tire Discounters, Walgreens, Wal-Mart SuperCtr/gas/24hr, **S**...**gas:** Speedway, **food:** Arby's, Bob Evan's, Cracker Barrel, Dragon Chinese, KFC, La Fozata, LJ Silver, Longhorn Steaks, Quizno's, Steak Shake, Uno Pizzaria, Wendy's, **lodging:** Best Western, Hampton Inn, Holiday Inn Express, **other:** URGENT CARE, Barnes&Noble, Tuesday Morning

Blaine

Cambridge

Zanesville

OHIO

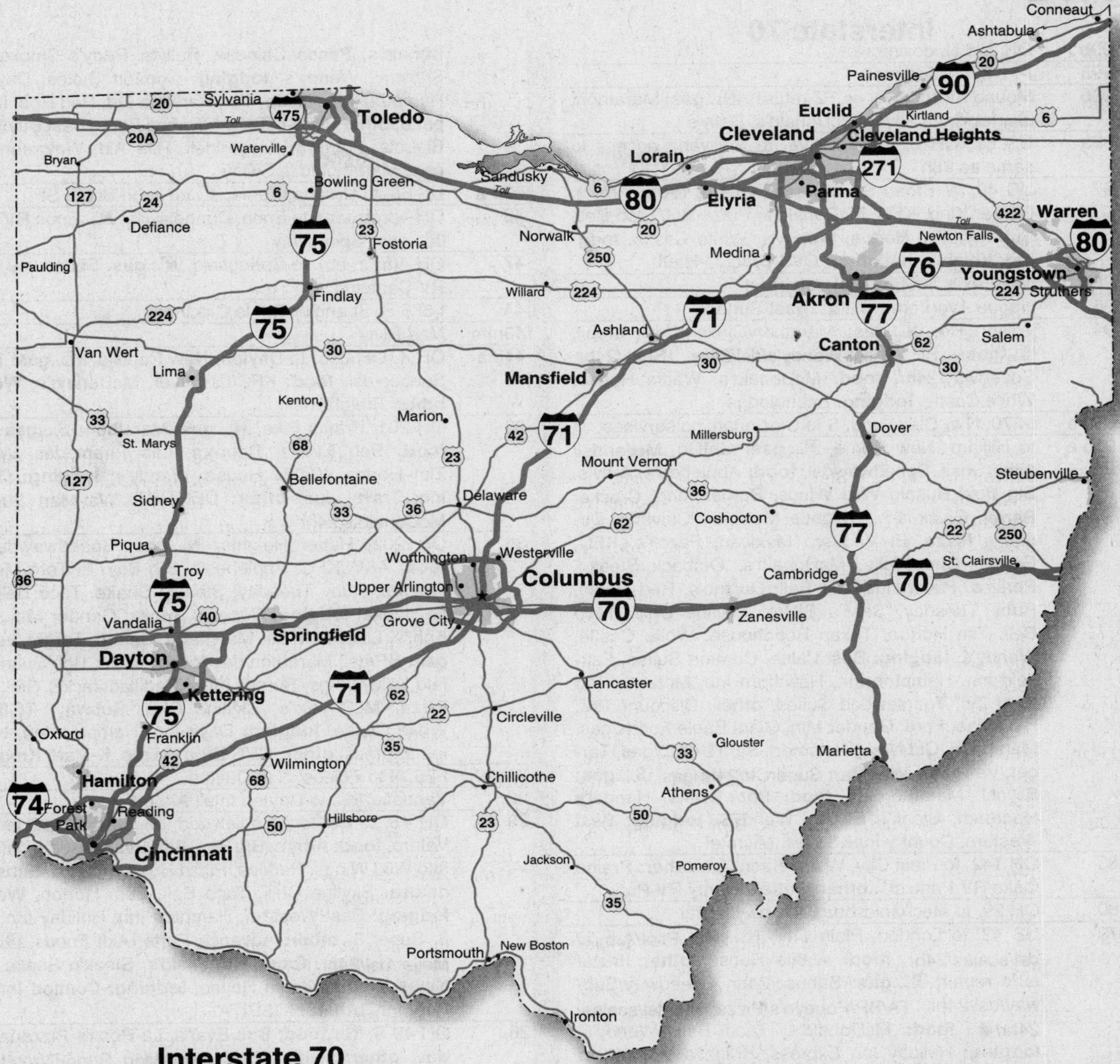

Interstate 70

E
↕
W

110	Brice Rd, to Reynoldsburg, [N]...**gas:** Shell, Speedway, Sunoco, **food:** Burger King, Donato's Pizza, Gengi Japanese, Golden China, Max&Erma's, Popeye's, Subway, TeeJaye's Rest., Tim Horton, Treacher's Seafood, Waffle House, **lodging:** Days Inn, Extended Stay America, La Quinta, Red Roof, Super 8, **other:** Big Lots, Goodyear/auto, Home Depot, Midas, [S]...**gas:** BP, Meijer/dsl/24hr, Speedway, **food:** Applebee's, Arby's, Asian Star, Boston Mkt, Chipotle Mexican, El Chico, KFC/Pizza Hut, McDonald's, Ruby Tuesday, Subway, Starbucks, Steak'n Shake, Taco Bell, Waffle House, **lodging:** Comfort Suites, Econolodge, Motel 6, **other:** Acura, Advance Parts, Aldi, Circuit City, Farber RV Ctr, Firestone/auto, GNC, Honda, Hyundai, JC Penney, Jo-Ann Fabrics, Kroger/deli, Lowe's Whse, Michael's, NTB, Old Navy, PetCo, Sears/auto, Target, Toyota/Scion, Walgreens, mall
108b a	I-270 N to Cleveland, access to HOSPITAL, I-270 S to Cincinnati
107	OH 317, Hamilton Rd, to Whitehall, [S]...**gas:** Sunoco/dsl, Valero, **food:** Arby's, Bob Evans, Buffalo Wild Wings, Burger King, Capt D's, Dragon Buffet, Eastland Buffet, Ichybon Mexican, McDonald's, Olive Garden, Papa John's, Red Lobster, Steak'n Shake, Taco Bell, **lodging:** Hamilton Hotel, Hampton Inn, Holiday Inn, InTown Suites, Knight's Inn, Residence Inn, **other:** $General, Kohl's, Macy's, Pepboys, Staples
105a	to Lancaster, **2 mi** [N]...**food:** Tat Italian, Wendy's
105b	US 33, James Rd, Bexley, [N]...**food:** Tat Italian, Wendy's
103b a	Livingston Ave, to Capital University, [N]...**gas:** BP, Exxon, Speedway/dsl, **food:** Mr Hero Subs, Peking Chinese, Popeye's, Subway, Taco Bell, Wendy's, **other:** Tuffy, [S]...**gas:** Marathon, Shell, **food:** McDonald's, White Castle/24hr
102	Kelton Ave, Miller Ave, [S]...HOSPITAL
101a	I-71 N, to Cleveland, no services
100b	US 23, to 4th St, downtown
99c	Rich St, Town St(exits left from eb), [N]...**gas:** Sunoco, **other:** Ford

OHIO

Interstate 70

E ↑ ↓ W

Exit	Description
Columbus Area	
99b	OH 315 N, downtown
99a	I-71 S, to Cincinnati
98b	Mound St(from wb, no EZ return), **N**...**gas:** Marathon, **S**...**food:** LJ Silver, McDonald's, Rally's
98a	US 62, OH 3, Central Ave, to Sullivant, access to same as 98b
97	US 40, W Broad St, **N**...**gas:** Valero, **food:** Arby's, Burger King, KFC, McDonald's, Pizza Hut/Taco Bell, Subway, Tim Horton, Wendy's, White Castle, **lodging:** Knight's Inn, **other:** CVS Drug, U-Haul
96	I-670(exits left from eb), to airport
95	Hague Ave(from wb), **S**...**gas:** Sunoco
94	Wilson Rd, **N**...**gas:** Marathon/Circle K/dsl, Mobil, **S**...**gas:** BP, Pilot/Wendy's/dsl/24hr, Shell/24hr, Speedway/24hr, **food:** McDonald's, Waffle House, White Castle, **lodging:** Econolodge
93b a	I-270, N to Cleveland, S to Cincinnati, no services
91b a	to Hilliard, New Rome, **N**...**gas:** GetGo, Meijer/dsl/24hr, Shell, Speedway/dsl, **food:** Applebee's, Arby's, Big Boy, Buffalo Wild Wings, Burger King, Cracker Barrel, Chick-fil-A, Chipotle Mexican, Culver's, Donato's Pizza, El Vaquero Mexican, Fazoli's, KFC, Golden Chopsticks, McDonald's, Outback Steaks, Perkins, Pizza Hut/Taco Bell, Quizno's, Red Robin, Ruby Tuesday, Salvi's Bistro, Skyline Chili, Taco Bell, Tim Horton, Texas Roadhouse, White Castle, Wendy's, **lodging:** Best Value, Comfort Suites, Fairfield Inn, Hampton Inn, Hawthorn Inn, Motel 6, Red Roof Inn, Tanglewood Suites, **other:** Discount Tire, Firestone, Ford, Gander Mtn, Giant Eagle Foods/gas, Marshall's, Old Navy, Petsmart, Sam's Club/gas, Target, Valvoline, Wal-Mart SuperCtr/24hr/gas, **S**...**gas:** BP/dsl, Marathon/dsl, **food:** Bob Evans, Handel's Icecream, Steak'n Shake, Wendy's, **lodging:** Best Western, Country Inn&Suites, Microtel
85	OH 142, to Plain City, W Jefferson, **N**...**other:** Prairie Oaks RV Park, **S**...**other:** Pattele Darby RV Park
80	OH 29, to Mechanicsburg, **S**...hwy patrol
79	US 42, to London, Plain City, **N**...**gas:** Pilot/Arby's/dsl/scales/24hr, **food:** Waffle House, **other:** truck/auto repair, **S**...**gas:** Sunoco/24hr, Speedway/Subway/dsl/24hr, TA/BP/Popeye's/Pizza Hut/dsl/scales/24hr/@, **food:** McDonald's, Taco Bell, Wendy's, **lodging:** Holiday Inn Express, Knight's Inn, **other:** HOSPITAL, truckwash
72	OH 56, to London, Summerford, **N**...**gas:** Marathon/24hr, **4 mi S**...HOSPITAL, lodging
71mm	**rest area both lanes, full(handicapped)facilities, phone, picnic tables, litter barrels, vending, petwalk**
Springfield	
66	OH 54, to Catawba, South Vienna, **N**...**gas:** FuelMart/dsl, **S**...**gas:** Speedway/dsl, **other:** Crawford RV Park(1mi), Beaver Valley RV Park(3mi)
62	US 40, Springfield, **N**...**gas:** Rich Gas, **lodging:** Harmony Motel, **other:** antiques, to Buck Creek SP, **S**...Beaver Valley Camping
59	OH 41, to S Charleston, **N**...**other:** HOSPITAL, Harley-Davidson, st patrol, **S**...**gas:** BP/dsl, Prime Fuel/dsl, antiques
54	OH 72, to Cedarville, Springfield, **N**...**gas:** BP/dsl, Shell, Speedway, Sunoco/dsl/24hr, **food:** A&W/LJ Silver, Arby's, Bob Evans, Cassano's Pizza/subs, Church's, Cracker Barrel, Domino's, El Toro Mexican, Hardee's, KFC, Lee's Chicken, Little Caesar's, Mc-
	Donald's, Panda Chinese, Rally's, Rudy's Smokehouse, Subway, Wendy's, **lodging:** Comfort Suites, Day's Inn, Hampton Inn, Holiday Inn, Ramada Ltd, Red Roof Inn, Super 8, **other:** HOSPITAL, Advance Parts, Best Buy RV Ctr, BigLots, Family$, Kroger/deli, Rite Aid, Walgreens, **S**...**gas:** Marathon/dsl, Swifty
52b a	US 68, to Urbana, Xenia, **S**...to John Bryan SP
48	OH 4(from wb) to Enon, Donnelsville, **N**...Enon RV Camp, **S**...**gas:** Speedway
47	OH 4(from eb), to Springfield, **N**...**gas:** Speedway, **other:** RV Camping
44	I-675 S, Spangler Rd, to Cincinnati
43mm	Mad River
41b a	OH 4, OH 235, to Dayton, New Carlisle, **N**...**gas:** BP/dsl, Sunoco/dsl, **food:** KFC/LJ Silver, McDonald's, Wendy's, **other:** Freightliner
38	OH 201, Brandt Pike, **N**...**gas:** Marathon, **S**...**gas:** Shell, **food:** Bob Evans, Denny's, Las Piramedes Mexican, Tim Horton, Waffle House, Wendy's, **lodging:** Comfort Inn, Travelodge, **other:** DENTIST, Wal-Mart SuperCtr/McDonald's/24hr
36	OH 202, Huber Heights, **N**...**gas:** Speedway/dsl/24hr, **food:** A&W/KFC, Applebee's, Big Boy, El Toro Mexican, Fazoli's, Ruby Tuesday, Steak'n Shake, Taco Bell, Waffle House, **lodging:** Super 8, **other:** Gander Mtn, GNC, Kohl's, Lowe's Whse, Marshall's, Saturn, Target, vet, **S**...**gas:** BP/dsl, Marathon/dsl, **food:** Arby's, Bob Evans, Buffalo Wild Wings, Burger King, Cadillac Jack's Grill, CiCi's Pizza, McDonald's, Skyline Chili, Subway, TGIFriday, White Castle, **lodging:** Days Inn, Hampton Inn, Holiday Inn Express, **other:** CVS Drug, $Tree, K-Mart, Kroger/gas
33b a	I-75, N to Toledo, S to Dayton
32	Vandalia, **N**...to Dayton Intn'l Airport
29	OH 48, to Dayton, Englewood, **N**...**gas:** BP, Speedway, Valero, **food:** Arby's, Big Boy, Bob Evans, Bolt's Cafe, Buffalo Wild Wings, Perkins, Pizza Hut, Penn Sta. Subs, Ponderosa, Skyline Chili, Taco Bell, Tom Horton, Wendy's, **lodging:** Best Western, Hampton Inn, Holiday Inn, Motel 6, Super 8, **other:** Advance Parts, Aldi Foods, **S**...**gas:** Meijer/dsl/24hr, **food:** McDonald's, Steak'n Shake, Tumbleweed Grill, Waffle House, **lodging:** Comfort Inn, Red Roof Inn, **other:** HOSPITAL
26	OH 49 S, **N**...**food:** Bob Evans, La Rosa's Pizzaria, Subway, **other:** Radio Shack, Wal-Mart SuperCtr/24hr/gas, **S**...**food:** Wendy's
24	OH 49 N, to Greenville, Clayton, **S**...**gas:** Sunoco/dsl/24hr, **other:** KOA(seasonal)
21	rd 533, Brookville, **N**...**gas:** GA/Subway, **S**...**gas:** Speedway/dsl, Swifty, **food:** Arby's, Brookville Grill, DQ, K's Rest., KFC/Taco Bell, Lee's Chicken, McDonald's, Rob's Rest., Waffle House, Wendy's, **lodging:** Day's Inn, Holiday Inn Express, **other:** AAA, Brookville Parts, Chevrolet, Curves, $General, Family$, IGA Foods, Rite Aid
14	OH 503, to West Alexandria, Lewisburg, **N**...**gas:** Sunoco/Subway/dsl, **food:** Dairy Twist, Grinner's Cafe, **lodging:** Super Inn, **other:** IGA Foods, **S**...**gas:** Valero/dsl
10	US 127, to Eaton, Greenville, **N**...**gas:** TA/BP/Burger King/Subway/dsl/scales/24hr/@, st patrol, **S**...**gas:** Pilot/Subway/dsl/scales/24hr
3mm	**Welcome Ctr eb/rest area both lanes, full(handicapped)facilities, phone, vending, picnic tables, litter barrels, petwalk**
1	US 35 E(from eb), to Eaton, New Hope, no services
0mm	Ohio/Indiana state line, Welcome Arch, weigh sta eb

Interstate 71

Exit #	Services
247b	I-90 W, I-490 E. I-71 begins/ends on I-90, exit 170 in Cleveland.
247a	W 14th, Clark Ave
246	Denison Ave, Jennings Rd(from sb)
245	US 42, Pearl Rd, E...gas: BP, Sunoco, other: HOSPITAL, zoo
244	W 65th, Denison Ave
242b a	W 130th, to Bellaire Rd, W...gas: Sunoco, food: Burger King(1/2mi)
240	W 150th, E...gas: Marathon, Speedway/dsl, food: Denny's, lodging: Marriott, W...gas: BP/Subway/dsl, food: Burger King, MacKenzie's Grill, Somers Rest., Taco Bell, lodging: Holiday Inn, La Quinta
239	OH 237 S(from sb), W...to airport
238	I-480, Toledo, Youngstown, W...airport
237	Snow Rd, Brook Park, E...gas: BP, Citgo, Shell, food: Bob Evans, Goody's Cafe, KFC, McDonald's, Suwaby, lodging: Best Western, Holiday Inn Express, Howard Johnson, other: AutoZone, Top's Foods, W...to airport
235	Bagley Rd, E...food: Bob Evans, W...gas: BP/dsl, Shell, Speedway, food: Burger King, Caribou Coffee, Chipotle Mexican, Damon's, Denny's, Friendly's, McDonald's, Olive Garden, Panera Bread, Perkins, Pizza Hut, Roadhouse Grill, Taco Bell, lodging: Comfort Inn, Courtyard, Motel 6, Plaza Motel, Radisson, Ramada Inn, Red Roof Inn, Studio+, TownePlace Suites, other: HOSPITAL, Aldi Foods, Buick, GMC, K-Mart
234	US 42, Pearl Rd, E...gas: Sunoco/dsl, food: Hunan Chinese, Katherine's Rest., Wendy's, other: Audi/Porsche, Honda, Hyundai, Saturn, W...gas: AP/dsl, food: Buffalo Wild Wings, Jennifer's Rest, Mad Cactus Mexican, lodging: Day's Inn, Kings Inn, La Siesta Motel, Metrick's Motel, Village Motel, other: Circle K, Home Depot, Lowes Whse, Wal-Mart, vet,
233	I-80 and Ohio Tpk, to Toledo, Youngstown
231	OH 82, Strongsville, E...gas: Shell, lodging: Holiday Inn, Motel 6, W...gas: BP/Subway/dsl, Marathon/dsl, Sunoco/dsl, food: Applebee's, Buca Italian, Demetrio's Rest., Longhorn Steaks, Macaroni Grill, Panera Bread, Red Lobster, other: Borders Books, Dillard's, Giant Eagle Foods, JC Penney, Kohl's, NTB, Sears/auto, Target, mall
226	OH 303, Brunswick, E...gas: Shell/dsl/24hr, food: Pizza Hut, other: Camping World RV Supplies/service, Chrysler/Jeep/Toyota, W...gas: BP, GetGo, Marathon/dsl, Sunoco/dsl, food: Arby's, Bob Evans, Burger King, CiCi's Pizza, McDonald's, Starbucks, Steak'n Shake, Subway, Taco Bell, Tony Roma's, Wendy's, lodging: Howard Johnson, Sleep Inn, other: Ford, Giant Eagle Food, K-Mart
225mm	rest area nb, full(handicapped)facilities, phone, picnic tables, litter barrels, petwalk
224mm	rest area sb, full(handicapped)facilities, phone, picnic tables, litter barrels, petwalk
222	OH 3, W...st patrol
220	I-271 N, (from nb) to Erie, Pa
218	OH 18, to Akron, Medina, E...gas: BP/dsl/24hr, Citgo/dsl, Shell/dsl, Sunoco/dsl, food: Alexandri's Rest., Blimpie, Burger King, DQ, lodging: Best Value, Holiday Inn Express, Super 8, Traveler's Choice, other:

	$General, GMC, KIA, Mitsubishi, W...gas: Speedway/dsl, food: Arby's, Bob Evans, Buffalo Wild Wings, Denny's, McDonald's, Pizza Hut, Waffle House, Wendy's, lodging: Hampton Inn, Motel 6, Red Roof Inn, other: HOSPITAL, Aldi Foods, Dodge, Harley-Davidson, Honda, NTB, Pontiac/Buick/Cadillac/GMC
209	I-76 E, to Akron, US 224, W...gas: Pilot/Subway/dsl/scales/24hr, TA/BP/Burger King/Popeye's/dsl/24hr/@, food: Arby's, Country Kitchen, McDonald's, Starbucks, lodging: Super 8, other: Blue Beacon, Chippewa Valley Camping(1mi)
204	OH 83, Burbank, E...gas: BP/dsl, Duke/dsl, Loves/dsl/24hr, W...gas: Pilot/Wendy's/dsl/scales/24hr, food: Bob Evans, Burger King, McDonald's, other: HOSPITAL, Buick/Chevrolet/Pontiac, Chrysler/Jeep/Dodge, Prime Outlets/famous brands
198	OH 539, W Salem
196mm	rest area both lanes, full(handicapped)facilities, phone, vending, picnic tables, litter barrels, petwalk
196	OH 301(from nb, no re-entry), W Salem, no services
191mm	weigh sta sb
186	US 250, Ashland, E...gas: Marathon, food: Perkins, Grandpa's Village/cheese/gifts, other: Hickory Lakes Camping(7mi), W...gas: Citgo, Goasis/Pizza Hut/Popeye's/Starbucks/Taco Bell/dsl/rest./24hr, food: Bob Evans, Denny's, McDonald's, Wendy's, lodging: AmeriHost, Day's Inn, Holiday Inn Express, Super 8, other: HOSPITAL, Home Depot, Wal-Mart SuperCtr/24hr, st patrol, to Ashland U
176	US 30, to Mansfield, E...lodging: Econolodge, other: fireworks
173	OH 39, to Mansfield
169	OH 13, Mansfield, E...gas: Marathon/dsl, food: Cracker Barrel, HillTop Dairy Bar, Steak'n Shake, Wendy's, other: Wal-Mart SuperCtr/Subway/gas/24hr, Mohican SP, lodging: AmeriHost, La Quinta, W...gas: Marathon, food: Arby's, Bob Evans, Burger King, McDonald's, Taco Bell, lodging: Hampton Inn, Super 8, Travelodge, other: HOSPITAL, st patrol
165	OH 97, to Bellville, E...gas: BP, Speedway/dsl, Shell/dsl, food: Burger King, Dutchman Rest., McDonald's, lodging: Day's Inn, Comfort Inn, Knight's Inn, Quality Inn, other: to Mohican SP, W...food: Dinner Barrel Rest., Wendy's, lodging: Mid Ohio Motel
151	OH 95, to Mt Gilead, E...gas: BP, Duke/dsl/rest./24hr, Marathon, food: McDonald's, Wendy's, lodging: Best Western, other: st patrol, W...gas: Sunoco/dsl, Shell/dsl, lodging: Knight's Inn, Leaf Rest., other: HOSPITAL, M Camping, Mt Gilead SP(6mi)
149mm	truck parking both lanes
140	OH 61, Mt Gilead, E...gas: Pilot/Arby's/dsl/Scales/24hr/@, W...gas: BP/Taco Bell, Sunoco/Subway, W...food: Ole Farmstead Rest.

Interstate 71

N ↕ S

Columbus Area

131	US 36, OH 37, to Delaware, E...gas: ⚓/Flying J/Conoco/dsl/LP/rest./scales/24hr/@, Pilot/Subway/dsl/scales/24hr/@, food: Burger King, W...gas: BP/dsl, Shell, food: A&W, Arby's, Bob Evans, Cracker Barrel, KFC/LJ Silver, McDonald's, Subway, Taco Bell, Waffle House, Wendy's, White Castle, lodging: Day's Inn, Hampton Inn, Holiday Inn Express, other: HOSPITAL, Alum Cr SP
129mm	weigh sta nb
128mm	**rest area both lanes, full(handicapped)facilities, phone, vending, picnic tables, litter barrels, petwalk**
121	Polaris Pkwy, to Gemini Pl, E...gas: BP/Blimpie, Shell/24hr, food: Buffalo Wild Wings, McDonald's, Polaris Grill, Quizno's, Skyline Chili, Steak'n Shake, lodging: Best Western, Wingate Inn, other: Polaris Ampitheatre, W...gas: BP, Marathon/Tim Horton, food: Applebee's, Arby's, Bob Evans, Caribou Coffee, Carrabba's, CheeBurger CheeBurger, Cheese Burger Paradise, Chipotle Mexican, Hoggy's Grille, Hooters, Hop's Grill, House of Japan, Krispy Kreme, Magic Mtn Grill, Martini's Italian, Max&Erma's, MiMi's Cafe, O'Charley's, Olive Garden, Panera Bread, Pizza Hut/Taco Bell, Potbelly, Qdoba Mexican, Quaker Steaks, Red Lobster, Red Robin, Smokey Bones BBQ, Starbucks, TGIFriday, Waffle House, Wendy's, lodging: Baymont Inn, Candlewood Suites, Extended Stay Deluxe, Hilton Garden, other: Barnes&Noble, Best Buy, Circuit City, Costco/gas, GNC, JC Penney, Jo-Ann Fabrics, Kroger, Lowe's Whse, Macy's, NTB, Old Navy, Sears/auto, Target, TJ Maxx, Wal-Mart SuperCtr/24hr(3mi), mall
119b a	I-270, to Indianapolis, Wheeling
117	OH 161, to Worthington, E...gas: BP/dsl, Shell, Sunoco, food: Burger King, KFC, LJ Silver, LoneStar Steaks, Max&Erma's, Outback Steaks, Rally's, Red Lobster, Subway, White Castle, lodging: Comfort Inn, Day's Inn, Holiday Inn Express, Knight's Inn, Motel 6, other: Advance Parts, Big Bear Foods, Firestone, Staples, W...gas: GetGo, Shell, Speedway/dsl, food: Bob Evans, McDonald's, Madarin House Chinese, Pizza Hut, Skyline Chili, Subway, Waffle House, Wendy's, lodging: Amerihost, Best Western, Clarion, Country Inn&Suites, Econolodge, Extended Stay America, Hampton Inn, Marriott, Rodeway Inn, Super 8, Travelodge, other: Advance Parts, Chevrolet, Family$, Giant Eagle/gas, Walgreens
116	Morse Rd, Sinclair Rd, E...gas: BP, Speedway, food: McDonald's, Subway, lodging: Howard Johnson, other: Buick, CVS Drug, $General, Ford, GMC, PepBoys, Save-a-Lot Foods, W...gas: Sunoco, food: La Hacienda Mexican, lodging: Best Value Inn, Midwest Hotel/Conv Ctr, Motel 6, other: NTB
115	Cooke Rd, no services
114	N Broadway, W...gas: Sunoco, food: Broadway Mkt Cafe, Subway
113	Weber Rd, W...gas: Speedway/dsl, other: CarQuest, NAPA
112	Hudson St, E...gas: Marathon, Shell, food: Wendy's, lodging: Holiday Inn Express, W...food: Big Boy, other: Aldi Foods, Lowe's Whse, NTB
111	17th Ave, W...food: McDonald's, lodging: Comfort Inn, Day's Inn

Columbus Area

110b	11th Ave, no services
110a	5th Ave, E...gas: Sunoco, food: White Castle, W...gas: Citgo, food: KFC, Popeye's, Rally's, Wendy's, other: AutoZone
109a	I-670
108b	US 40, Broad St, downtown
108a	main st
101a[70]	I-70 E, US 23 N, to Wheeling
100b a[70]	US 23 S, Front St, High St, downtown
106a	I-70 W, to Indianapolis
106b	OH 315 N, Dublin St, Town St
105	Greenlawn, W...gas: Marathon, food: White Castle, other: HOSPITAL
104	OH 104, Frank Rd
101b a	I-270, Wheeling, Indianapolis
100	Stringtown Rd, E...gas: BP, food: Bob Evans, Chipotle Mexican, Church's/White Castle, CiCi's Pizza, Coldstone Creamery, DQ, Longhorn Steaks, O'Charley's, Olive Garden, Panda Express, Red Robin, Smokey Bones BBQ, Steak'n Shake, lodging: Best Western, Drury Inn, Hampton Inn, Holiday Inn Express, Hilton Garden, La Quinta, Microtel, Red Roof Inn, other: Best Buy, Discount Tire, Home Depot, Petsmart, Staples, TJ Maxx, Wal-Mart SuperCtr/24hr, W...gas: Speedway/dsl, Sunoco/Subway, food: Applebee's, Arby's, Burger King, Capt D's, China Bell, Cracker Barrel, Damon's, Fazoli's, Hoggy's Rest., KFC, McDonald's, Perkins/24hr, Pizza Hut, Ponderosa, Rally's, Roadhouse Grill, Ruby Tuesday, Starbucks, Taco Bell, TeeJaye's Rest., Tim Horton, Waffle House, Wendy's, lodging: Comfort Inn, Day's Inn, Motel 6, Saver Motel, Value Inn, other: Aldi Foods, All Tune/lube, Big Bear Food/drug, CVS Drug, GNC, Goodyear/auto, K-Mart, Kroger/24hr, NAPA, Radio Shack, Walgreens
97	OH 665, London-Groveport Rd, E...gas: Marathon, Sunoco/Subway, food: Arby's, McDonald's, Tim Horton/Wendy's, other: Kroger/gas, to Scioto Downs, W...other: Eddie's Repair
94	US 62, OH 3, Orient, W...gas: Sunoco/dsl
84	OH 56, Mt Sterling, E...gas: BP/Subway, Sunoco, lodging: Royal Inn, other: to Deer Creek SP(9mi)
75	OH 38, Bloomingburg, E...fireworks, W...gas: Sunoco/dsl
69	OH 41, OH 734, Jeffersonville, E...gas: ⚓/Flying J/CountryMkt/dsl/scales/LP/24hr/@, other: Walnut Lake Camping, W...gas: BP, Shell/Subway/dsl, food: Arby's, TCBY, Wendy's, lodging: AmeriHost, other: HOSPITAL, Outlets II/famous brands
68mm	**rest area both lanes, full(handicapped)facilities, phone, vending, picnic tables, litter barrels, petwalk**
65	US 35, Washington CH, E...gas: Shell, TA/BP/Pizza Hut/Popeye's/dsl/scales/24hr/@, food: A&W/KFC, Bob Evans, Burger King, McDonald's, Taco Bell/LJ Silver, Waffle House, Wendy's, Werner's BBQ, lodging: AmeriHost, Hampton Inn, other: HOSPITAL, Prime Outlets/famous brands, W...gas: Loves/Hardee's/dsl/scales/24hr, lodging: Budget Motel
58	OH 72, to Sabina
54mm	weigh sta sb
50	US 68, to Wilmington, E...food: Werner's BBQ, other: HOSPITAL, W...gas: BP/DQ/dsl, Pilot/Subway/dsl/scales/24hr, Shell/dsl/24hr, food: Max&Erma's, McDonald's, Wendy's, lodging: Budget Inn, Holiday Inn
49mm	weigh sta nb

Interstate 71

45	OH 73, to Waynesville, Ⓔ...**gas:** BP, Marathon/dsl, **food:** Smarts, **other:** HOSPITAL, RV Park, Ⓦ...Caesar Creek SP(5mi), flea mkt
36	Wilmington Rd, Ⓔ...to Ft Ancient St Mem, RV camping
35mm	Little Miami River
34mm	**rest area both lanes, full(handicapped)facilities, scenic view, phone, vending, picnic tables, litter barrels, petwalk**
32	OH 123, to Lebanon, Morrow, Ⓔ...**gas:** BP, Citgo, **food:** Country Kitchen, **other:** Morgan's RV Park, **3 mi** Ⓦ...**food:** Bob Evans, Skyline Chili, **lodging:** Knight's Inn
28	OH 48, S Lebanon, Ⓔ...**lodging:** Countryside Inn(1mi), Ⓦ...**other:** Lebanon Raceway(6mi), hwy patrol
25	OH 741 N, Kings Mills Rd, Ⓔ...**gas:** Shell/Popeye's, Speedway/dsl, **food:** El Toro Mexican, McDonald's, Ruby Tuesday, Taco Bell, Outback Steaks, **lodging:** Comfort Suites, Great Wolf Lodge, Kings Island Inn, Quality Inn, **other:** Harley-Davidson, Ⓦ...**gas:** BP, Exxon/Subway, **food:** Arby's, Big Boy, Bob Evans, Burger King, DQ, Perkins, Pizza Hut, Skyline Chili, Waffle House, Wendy's, **lodging:** Best Western, Hampton Inn, Microtel, Super 8, **other:** Curves, CVS Drug, GNC, Kroger
24	Western Row, King's Island Dr(from nb), Ⓔ...**gas:** Sunoco, **lodging:** King's Island, **other:** Jellystone Camping, funpark
19	US 22, Mason-Montgomery Rd, Ⓔ...**gas:** Meijer/dsl/24hr, Shell, Sunoco/24hr, **food:** Arby's, Big Boy, Bennigan's, Bob Evans, Boston Mkt, Cracker Barrel, Fazoli's, Fushon Buffet, Golden Corral, KFC, McDonald's, Olive Garden, Pizza Hut, Taco Bell, TGIFriday, Wendy's, **lodging:** Comfort Inn, Quality Inn, Signature Inn, **other:** VET, AutoZone, Barnes&Noble, Best Buy, Circuit City, Chevrolet, CostCo, Firestone/auto, GMC/Buick/Pontiac, Goodyear, Kohl's, Kroger, Lincoln/Mercury, Michael's, Old Navy, Petsmart, Radio Shack, Sam's Club/gas, Target, Tires+, Toyota, Walgreens, Ⓦ...**gas:** BP/dsl, Marathon/dsl/24hr, Shell, **food:** Abuleo's, Amon's Steaks, Applebee's, Burger King, Carrabba's, Chipotle Mexican, China City, Fuddrucker's, LoneStar Steaks, Macaroni Grill, McAlister's Deli, MiMi's Cafe, Noodles, O'Charley's, Palacio Azteca, Polo Grill, Qdoba Mexican, Red Robin, River City Grill, Steak'n Shake, Skyline Chili, Subway, Tumbleweed Grill, Waffle House, Wendy's, Wild Oats Mkt, **lodging:** AmeriSuites, Best Western, Day's Inn, King's Inn, La Quinta, Marriott, Ramada Ltd, Red Roof Inn, **other:** Bigg's Foods, Border's Books, Home Depot, Lowe's Whse, Staples, Subaru, Wal-Mart Super Ctr/24hr
17b a	I-275, to I-75, OH 32
15	Pfeiffer Rd, Ⓔ...HOSPITAL, Ⓦ...**gas:** BP, Shell/dsl, Sunoco/dsl/24hr, **food:** Applebee's, Bob Evans, Buffalo Wild Wings, Subway, Watson Bro's Bistro, **lodging:** Clarion, Courtyard, Embassy Suites, Hampton Inn, Holiday Inn Express, Red Roof Inn, **other:** Office Depot
14	OH 126, Reagan Hwy, Blue Ash
12	US 22, OH 3, Montgomery Rd, Ⓔ...**gas:** BP/dsl, Shell/24hr, **food:** Arby's, Bob Evans, Chipotle Mexican, Ember's, Jalapeno Cafe, KFC, LJ Silver, Outback Steaks, Panera Bread, Red Lobster, Ruby Tuesday, Subway, Taco Bell, TGIFriday, Wendy's, **lodging:** Best Western, **other:** Dodge, Firestone, Goodyear, Hyundai, PepBoys, Staples, Tuesday Morning, Ⓦ...**gas:** Chevron, **food:** Cheesecake Factory, IHOP, KFC, Johnny Rocket's, Macaroni Grill, Max&Erma's, McDonald's, Potbelly's, Starbucks, Wendy's, **other:** HOSPITAL, Barnes&Noble, Dillard's, Firestone/auto, Fresh Mkt Foods, Old Navy, Parisian, Staples, mall
11	Kenwood Rd, (from nb), Ⓦ...HOSPITAL, same as 12
10	Stewart Rd(from nb), to Silverton, Ⓦ...**gas:** Marathon/dsl
9	Redbank Rd, to Fairfax, (no ez sb return), Ⓔ...**gas:** Mobil, Speedway, **other:** BMW
8	Kennedy Ave, Ridge Ave W, Ⓔ...**gas:** Meijer/dsl, **food:** IHOP, **lodging:** Motel 6, **other:** Circuit City, Dodge, Sam's Club/gas, Target, Ⓦ...**gas:** Marathon/dsl, Shell/Subway, Speedway, **food:** Denny's, Golden Corral, Gold Star Chili, KFC, LJ Silver, McDonald's, Old Country Buffet, Pizza Hut, Rally's, Taco Bell, White Castle, Wendy's, **other:** Bigg's Foods, Big Lots, Circuit City, Ford, Goodyear, Home Depot, Lowes Whse, Office Depot, Tire Discounter, Wal-Mart, transmissions
7b a	OH 562, Ridge Ave E, Norwood, Ⓔ...**gas:** BP, **food:** Ponderosa, **other:** AutoZone
6	Edwards Rd, Ⓔ...**gas:** BP, Shell, Speedway, **food:** Boston Mkt, Buca Italian, Chang's China Bistro, Donato's, Don Pablo, Fuddrucker's, GoldStar Chili, J Alexander's Rest., Longhorn Steaks, Max&Erma's, Noodles, Starbucks, **other:** GNC, SteinMart, Ⓦ...**gas:** Shell
5	Dana Ave, Montgomery Rd, Ⓦ...**other:** Xavier Univ, Zoo
3	Taft Rd(from sb), U of Cincinnati
2	US 42, Reading Rd, Gilbert ave(from sb), Ⓦ...**other:** HOSPITAL, art museum, ballpark stadium arena, downtown
1k j	I-471 S
1d	Main St, downtown
1c b	Pete Rose Way, Fine St, stadium, downtown
1a	I-75 N, US 50, to Dayton
I-71 S and I-75 S run together	
0mm	Ohio/Kentucky state line, Ohio River

Cincinnati

OHIO

Interstate 74

Exit #	Services
20	I-75(from eb), N to Dayton, S to Cincinnati, I-74 begins/ends on I-75.
19	Gilmore St, Spring Grove Ave, no services
18	US 27 N, Colerain Ave, no services
17	Montana Ave(from wb), **N**...**gas:** BP
14	North Bend Rd, Cheviot, **N**...**gas:** Citgo, Speedway/dsl, **food:** DQ, Happy Chinese, McDonald's, Perkins, Skyline Chili, Wendy's, **other:** Sam's Club/gas, Tires+, Walgreen, **S**...**gas:** BP, **food:** Bob Evans, **lodging:** TriStar Motel
11	Rybolt Rd, Harrison Pike, **S**...**gas:** BP, Meijer/gas, **food:** Angelo's Pizza, Dante's Rest., **lodging:** Imperial House Motel, **other:** Kohl's
9	I-275 N, to I-75, N to Dayton
8mm	Great Miami River
7	OH 128, to Hamilton, Cleves, **N**...**gas:** BP/dsl, Marathon/dsl, **food:** BierHaus Rest., Wendy's
5	I-275 S, to Kentucky
3	Dry Fork Rd, **N**...**gas:** Citgo, **S**...**gas:** Marathon/dsl, Shell/pizza/dsl
2mm	weigh sta eb
1	New Haven Rd, to Harrison, **N**...**gas:** BP/dsl, **food:** Buffalo Wild Wings, Cracker Barrel, GoldStar Chili, O'Charley's, Subway, **lodging:** Comfort Inn, **other:** Biggs Foods, Ford, Home Depot, Tires+, **S**...**gas:** Marathon/dsl, Shell/24hr, Speedway/dsl, Sunoco, **food:** A&W/KFC, Arby's, Big Boy, Burger King, DQ, McDonald's, Papa John's, Perkins, Pizza Hut, Skyline Chili, Subway, Taco Bell, Waffle House, Wendy's, White Castle, **lodging:** Holiday Inn Express, Quality Inn, **other:** Advance Parts, AutoZone, Big Lots, CVS Drug, Family$, Firestone, GNC, Goodyear/auto, Jo-Ann Fabrics, K-Mart, Kroger, NAPA, Radio Shack, Walgreens
0mm	Ohio/Indiana state line

Interstate 75

Exit #	Services
211mm	Ohio/Michigan state line
210	OH 184, Alexis Rd, to Raceway Park, **W**...**gas:** BP/dsl/24hr, Meijer/dsl/24hr, Pilot/Subway/dsl/scales/24hr/@, **food:** Arby's, Bob Evans, Burger King, Ground Round, McDonald's, Taco Bell, Wendy's, **lodging:** Comfort Inn, Hampton Inn, **other:** Ford Trucks
210mm	Ottawa River
209	Ottawa River Rd(from nb), **E**...**gas:** BP, Citgo, Sunoco, **food:** Little Caesar's, Marco's Pizza, **other:** VETERINARIAN, FoodTown, Rite Aid
208	I-280 S, to I-80/90, to Cleveland, no services
207	Stickney Ave, Lagrange St, **E**...**gas:** BP, Citgo, Sunoco, **food:** McDonald's, Wendy's, **other:** Family$, K-Mart, Sav-a-Lot Foods
206	to US 24, Phillips Ave, **W**...transmissions
205b	Burdan St, **E**...HOSPITAL, **W**... Marathon
205a	to Willys Pkwy, to Jeep Pkwy, no services
204	I-475 W, to US 23, to Maumee, Ann Arbor
203b	US 24, to Detroit Ave, **W**...**gas:** BP/24hr, **food:** KFC, McDonald's, Rally's, **other:** Rite Aid, Sav-A-Lot Foods, U-Haul
203a	Bancroft St, downtown
202	Washington St, Collingwood Ave(from sb, no EZ return), **E**...**gas:** BP, **other:** HOSPITAL, Art Museum, **W**...**food:** McDonald's
201b a	OH 25, Collingwood Ave, **W**...Toledo Zoo

200	South Ave, Kuhlman Dr, no services
200mm	Maumee River
199	OH 65, Miami St, to Rossford, **E**...**lodging:** Day's Inn
198	Wales Rd, Oregon Rd, to Northwood, **E**...**gas:** Shell/Subway/dsl/24hr, **food:** Pizza Hut, **lodging:** Baymont Inn, Comfort Inn
197	Buck Rd, to Rossford, **E**...**gas:** Shell/dsl, **food:** Wendy's, Tim Horton, **W**...**gas:** BP/24hr, Sunoco/dsl, **food:** Denny's, McDonald's, **lodging:** American Inn, Knight's Inn
195	to I-80/90, OH 795, OH Tpk(toll), Perrysburg, **E**...**gas:** Barney's/Subway/dsl, BP/dsl, **lodging:** Courtyard, Hampton Inn, **W**...Bass Pro Shops
193	US 20, US 23 S, Perrysburg, **E**...**gas:** BP/dsl/24hr, Meijer, Sunoco, **food:** Arby's, Bob Evans, Burger King, Chili's, Cracker Barrel, Fricker's, Giant Eagle Foods, McDonald's, Panera Bread, Ralphie's, Shanghai Chinese, Subway, Taco Bell, Wendy's, **lodging:** Best Western, Comfort Inn, Day's Inn, Holiday Inn Express, **other:** Belle Tire, Giant Eagle/gas, GNC, Kohl's, K-Mart, Kroger/gas/24hr, KOA(7mi), Lowe's Whse, Michael's, Petsmart, Target, Walgreens, **W**...**gas:** Speedway/dsl, **lodging:** La Quinta, **other:** AutoZone, Harley-Davidson
192	I-475, US 23 N(exits left from nb), to Maumee, Ann Arbor
187	OH 582, to Luckey, Haskins
181	OH 64, OH 105, to Pemberville, Bowling Green, **E**...**gas:** Meijer/dsl/24hr, **lodging:** Holiday Inn Express, **W**...**gas:** BP/Subway/dsl, Speedway, Sunoco/dsl, **food:** Big Boy, Bob Evans, Burger King, Chipotle Mexican, Domino's, El Zarape Mexican, Fricker's Rest., Hunan Buffet, Jimmy John's, McDonald's, Tim Horton, Waffle House, Wendy's, **lodging:** Best Western, Day's Inn, Hampton Inn, Quality Inn, Victory Inn, **other:** HOSPITAL, Town&Country RV Ctr, to Bowling Green U
179	US 6, to Fremont, Napoleon, **W**...museum
179mm	**rest area both lanes, full(handicapped)facilities, phone, picnic tables, litter barrels, vending, petwalk**
175mm	weigh sta nb
171	OH 25, Cygnet, no services
168	Eagleville Rd, Quarry Rd, **E**...**gas:** FuelMart/dsl
167	OH 18, to Fostoria, North Baltimore, **E**...**gas:** Petro/Mobil/Iron Skillet/dsl/scales/24hr/@, **food:** McDonald's, **other:** Blue Beacon, truck repair, **W**...**gas:** Loves/Arby's/dsl/scales/24hr/@, Sunoco/dsl, **lodging:** Crown Inn, **other:** $General
165mm	Rocky Ford River
164	OH 613, to McComb, Fostoria, **E**...**other:** RV Camping, to Van Buren SP, **W**...**gas:** Pilot/Subway/Taco Bell/dsl/scales/24hr
162mm	weigh sta sb, phones
161	OH 99, **E**...**gas:** Speedway/dsl, Shell/Subway, **lodging:** Comfort Suites, Holiday Inn Express, **other:** Ford, May RV Ctr, hwy patrol **W**... antiques
159	US 224, OH 15, Findlay, **E**...**gas:** BP, Speedway/dsl, Swifty, **food:** Archie's Ice Cream, Burger King, Dakota Grill, Dog House Cafe, KFC/LJ Silver, McDonald's, Ming's Great Wall, Pizza Hut, Ponderosa, Ralphie's, Spaghetti Shop, Steak'n Shake, Subway, Taco Bell, Wendy's, **lodging:** Drury Inn, Red Roof Inn, Rodeway Inn, Super 8, **other:** HOSPITAL, **W**...**gas:** Shell/dsl, **food:** Bob Evans, Coldstone Creamery, Cracker Barrel, Denny's, Margarita's Grill, Max&Erma's, Outback Steaks, Tony's Rest., Wings'n Things, Waffle House, **lodging:** Country Inn&Suites, Hampton Inn, Holiday Inn Express, Quality Inn, **other:** Chrysler/Jeep/Dodge, Peterbilt, Wal-Mart SuperCtr/Subway/gas

158	Blanchard River
157	OH 12, Findlay, E...**gas:** GA/dsl, Marathon/Blimpie/Noble Roman's/dsl, W...**food:** Fricker's Rest., **lodging:** Econolodge
156	US 68, OH 15, to Carey, E...HOSPITAL
153mm	**rest area both lanes, full(handicapped)facilities, phone, picnic tables, litter barrels, vending, petwalk**
145	OH 235, to Ada, Mount Cory, E...TwinLakes Camp
142	OH 103, to Arlington, Bluffton, E...**lodging:** Knight's Inn, W...**gas:** BP, Circle K/dsl **food:** Arby's, Burger King, KFC, McDonald's, Subway, Taco Bell, **lodging:** Comfort Inn, **other:** to Bluffton Coll
140	Bentley Rd, to Bluffton, W...HOSPITAL
135	OH 696, to US 30, to Delphos, Beaverdam, E...**gas:** Speedway/dsl/24hr, W...**gas:** Flying J/Cookery/dsl/scales/LP/24hr, Pilot/McDonald's/Subway/dsl/24hr/@, **other:** Blue Beacon, tires, truck repair
134	Napolean Rd(no nb re-entry), to Beaverdam
130	Blue Lick Rd, E...**lodging:** Best Value
127b a	OH 81, to Ada, Lima, W...**gas:** Marathon/dsl, **food:** Subway, Waffle House, **lodging:** Day's Inn/rest., Econolodge
126mm	Ottawa River
125	OH 309, OH 117, Lima, E...**gas:** BP/dsl, Speedway, **food:** Arby's, Bob Evans, Burger King, Capt D's, China Buffet, Cracker Barrel, Hunan Garden, Little Caesar's, McDonald's, Olive Garden, Pizza Hut, Ponderosa, Ralphie's, Red Lobster, Sedona Grill, Skyline Chili, Subway, Taco Bell, Texas Roadhouse, Tumbleweed Grill, Wendy's, **lodging:** Hampton Inn, Holiday Inn, Motel 6, **other:** Ford, K-Mart, PharmX Drug, Ray's Foods, Sam's Club/gas, Walgreens, Wal-Mart SuperCtr/24hr, W...**gas:** Shell, **food:** Kewbee Hamburger's, Las Cazuelas, **lodging:** Country Inn&Suites, Travelodge, **other:** HOSPITAL, Advance Parts, Curves, $General, Rite Aid, Sav-A-Lot Foods
124	4th St, E...hwy patrol
122	OH 65, Lima, E...**gas:** Speedway/dsl, W...**gas:** Shell/dsl/24hr, **other:** Freightliner, GMC, Mack, Volvo
120	Breese Rd, Ft Shawnee, W...Harley-Davidson
118	to Cridersville, W...**gas:** Fuelmart/Subway/dsl, Speedway/dsl, **food:** Dixie Ley Diner, **other:** $General
114mm	**truck parking both directions/no facilities**
113	OH 67, to Uniopolis, Wapakeneta, no services
111	Bellefontaine St, Wahpakeneta, E...**gas:** TA/Marathon/rest./dsl/scales/@, **lodging:** Knight's Inn, **other:** KOA, W...**gas:** BP/dsl, Shell, **food:** Arby's, Bob Evans, Burger King, Capt D's, Comfort Zone, DQ, El Azteca, Groundhog's Cafe, Lucky Steer Rest., McDonald's, Pizza Hut, Taco Bell, Waffle House, Wendy's, **lodging:** Holiday Inn Express, Super 8, Travelodge, **other:** Advance Parts, Aldi Foods, CVS Drug, Family$, Neil Armstrong Museum, Radio Shack, Wal-Mart SuperCtr/gas/24hr, st patrol
110	US 33, to St Marys, Bellefontaine, E...hwy patrol, KOA
104	OH 219, W...**gas:** Marathon/dsl, Shell/Subway, **lodging:** Budget Host
102	OH 274, to Jackson Ctr, New Breman, E...bicycle museum, W...air stream tours
99	OH 119, to Minster, Anna, E...**gas:** Save a Ton/Apple Valley Café/dsl, W...**gas:** GA, Marathon, **food:** Subway, Wendy's, **other:** lube/wash/repair
94	rd 25A, Sidney

Sidney

Lima

Troy

93	OH 29, to St Marys, Sidney, W...Lake Loramie SP, RV camping
92	OH 47, to Versailles, Sidney, E...**gas:** Shell, Speedway/dsl, **food:** Arby's, China Garden, Subway, Wendy's, Winger's, **other:** HOSPITAL, AutoZone, CVS Drug, $General, DM, NAPA, SavALot Foods, Walgreens, W...**gas:** Sunoco/dsl, Valero, **food:** A&W/LJ Silver, Applebee's, Bob Evans, Burger King, Cazadores Mexican, Culver's, Highmarks Rest., KFC, McDonald's, Perkins, Pizza Hut, Ponderosa, Quizno's, Rally's, Taco Bell, Waffle House, **lodging:** Comfort Inn, Day's Inn, Econolodge, Holiday Inn/rest., Travel Inn, **other:** Aldi Foods, BigLots, Buick/Pontiac/GMC, Chevrolet, Chrysler/Jeep/Dodge, Ford/Lincoln/Mercury, Kelly Tires, Kroger, Lowe's Whse, Menard's, Radio Shack, Staples, Wal-Mart SuperCtr/gas/dsl/24hr
90	Fair Rd, to Sidney, E...**gas:** FuelAmerica, **other:** repair, W...**gas:** Marathon/DQ/dsl, **lodging:** Hampton Inn
88mm	Great Miami River
83	rd 25A, Piqua, W...**gas:** Marathon/MaidRite Cafe/Noble Roman's/dsl, **lodging:** Red Carpet Inn, **other:** Chevrolet, Chrysler/Dodge/Jeep, Sherry RV Ctr, to Piqua Hist Area
82	US 36, to Urbana, Piqua, E...**gas:** Valero, **food:** A&W/LJ Silver, Arby's, China East, China Garden, DQ, KFC, Pizza Hut/Taco Bell, Subway, Waffle House, Wendy's, **other:** BigLots, Home Depot, Goody's, Harley-Davidson, Jo-Ann Fabrics, Wal-Mart SuperCtr, mall, st patrol, W...**gas:** Speedway, **food:** Bob Evans, Cracker Barrel, FoodCourt, McDonald's, Red Lobster, **lodging:** Comfort Inn, Knight's Inn, La Quinta, **other:** Aldi Foods, JC Penney, Sears/auto, mall
81mm	**rest area both lanes, full(handicapped)facilities, phones, picnic tables, litter barrels, vending**
78	rd 25A, E...HOSPITAL
74	OH 41, to Covington, Troy, E...**gas:** BP/dsl, **food:** Al's Pizza, China Garden, McDonald's, Pizza Hut, Subway, **other:** HOSPITAL, Radio Shack, SavALot Foods, to Hobart Arena, W...**gas:** Meijer/dsl/24hr, Shell, Speedway/dsl, **food:** Applebee's, Big Boy, Bob Evans, Burger King, Culver's, Fazoli's, Friendly's, Highmark's Grill, KFC, Outback Steaks, Quizno's, Ruby Tuesday, Skyline Chili, **lodging:** Best Inn, Fairfield Inn, Hampton Inn, Holiday Inn Express, Knight's Inn, Residence Inn, **other:** AutoZone, County Mkt Foods, CVS Drug, Goodyear, Kohl's, Lowe's Whse, Staples, Tire Discounters, Wal-Mart SuperCtr/24hr
73	OH 55, to Ludlow Falls, Troy, E...**gas:** BP, Shell, **food:** Lincoln Sq Rest., Waffle House, Wendy's, **lodging:** Best Western, Econolodge, Super 8, **other:** HOSPITAL, $General, Kroger/gas
69	rd 25A, E...**gas:** BP/Circle K/Subway, Starfire/dsl, **other:** Arbogast RV Ctr, Buick/Pontiac/GMC, Chrysler/Dodge, Ford
68	OH 571, to West Milton, Tipp City, E...**gas:** BP/dsl, Shell, Speedway, **food:** Burger King, Domino's, Fox's Pizza,

N
↑
↓
S

	Ginger Grill, Hickory River Rest., Hong Kong Kitchen, McDonald's, Subway, Taco Bell, **other:** Ace Hardware, CarQuest, CVS Drug, Family$, FoodTown, Goodyear, Honda, **W...gas:** Speedway/dsl, Valero, **food:** Arby's, Big Boy, Bob Evans, Tipp' O the Town Rest., Wendy's, **lodging:** Holiday Inn Express, Travelodge
64	Northwoods Blvd, **E...gas:** $Tree, Kroger/dsl
63	US 40, to Donnelsville, Vandalia, **E...gas:** Speedway/dsl, **food:** Dragon China, Fricker's Rest., **W...gas:** BP/dsl, Shell, Speedway, **food:** Arby's, Burger King, Domino's, KFC/LJ Silver, McDonald's, Pizza Hut, Rib House, Subway, Taco Bell, Waffle House, Wendy's, **lodging:** Super 8, **other:** Goodyear/auto, Rexall Drug, Rite Aid
61b a	I-70, E to Columbus, W to Indianapolis, to airport
59	Wyse Rd, Benchwood Rd, **E...food:** El Rancho Grande Mexican, Little York Pizza, Mr. Lee's, **lodging:** Howard Johnson, Residence Inn, **other:** Discount Tire, Volvo/BMW/VW, **W...food:** Arby's, Bob Evans, Cassano's Pizza, Chipotle Mexican, Coldstone Creamery, Cracker Barrel, Don Pablo, Golden Corral, Hooter's, Joe's Crabshack, LoneStar Steaks, Max&Erma's, McDonald's, New Orleans Bistro, O'Charley's, Olive Garden, Outback Steaks, Panera Bread, Pop's Diner, Red Lobster, Ruby Tuesday, Ryan's, Sake Japanese, Skyline Chili, SmokeyBones BBQ, Steak'n Shake, Tim Horton, **lodging:** Comfort Inn, Country Inn&Suites, Courtyard, Day's Inn, Drury Inn, Extended Stay America, Fairfield Inn, Hampton Inn, Knight's Inn, Motel 6, Ramada Inn, Red Roof Inn, Rodeway Inn, Villager Lodge, **other:** Office Depot, Radio Shack, Sam's Club/gas, Wal-Mart SuperCtr
58	Needmore Rd, to Dayton, **E...gas:** BP/dsl, Shell/McDonald's, **food:** Big Boy, Hardee's, **lodging:** Dayton Executive Hotel, **other:** Goodyear/auto, Tires UnLtd/repair, to AF Museum, **W...gas:** FA, Marathon/dsl, Speedway/dsl, **food:** A&W/LJ Silver, Church's, Domino's, New Peking, Subway, Tim Horton, Waffle House, Wendy's, **other:** Advance Parts, Curves, $General, $Tree, Kroger/gas, O'Reilly Parts, Walgreens, USPO, repair/transmissions
57b	Wagner Ford Rd, Siebenthaler Rd, Dayton, **E...gas:** Sunoco, **lodging:** Holiday Inn
57a	Neva Rd, no services
56	Stanley Ave, Dayton, **E...gas:** Shell, **other:** truck repair, **W...gas:** Clark, **food:** Dragon City Chinese, GoldStar Chili, McDonald's, Rally's, Wendy's, **lodging:** Dayton Motel
55b a	Keowee St, Dayton, downtown
54c	OH 4 N, Webster St, to Springfield, downtown
54mm	Great Miami River
54b	OH 48, Main St, Dayton, **E...gas:** Chevrolet/Cadillac, **W...gas:** BP, **other:** HOSPITAL
54a	Grand Ave(from sb), Dayton, downtown
53b	OH 49, 1st St, Salem Ave, Dayton, downtown
53a	OH 49, 3rd St, downtown
52b a	US 35, E to Dayton, W to Eaton
51	Edwin C Moses Blvd, Nicholas Rd, **E...lodging:** Courtyard, **other:** HOSPITAL, to U of Dayton, **W...gas:** BP/dsl, **food:** McDonald's, Wendy's, **lodging:** Econolodge, **other:** SunWatch Indian Village
50b a	OH 741, Kettering St, Dryden Rd, **E...HOSPITAL, W...gas:** Sunoco/Subway/dsl, **food:** TJ's Rest., **lodging:** Holiday Inn, Super 8, **other:** U-haul

47	Central Ave, W Carrollton, Moraine, **E...gas:** Sunoco, **food:** Big Boy, Fricker's, Waffle House, **other:** auto repair, transmissions, **W...gas:** BP, Speedway, **food:** Drifter's Grill, KFC, McDonald's, Pizza Hut, Taco Bell, Wendy's, **other:** USPO
44	OH 725, to Centerville, Miamisburg, **E...gas:** BP/dsl, Shell, Speedway, **food:** Applebee's, Big Boy, Blimpie, Bone Fish Grill, Bravo Italian, Burger King, Capt D's, Cena Brazilian, Cusina Italian, Dunkin Donuts, Friendly's, Fuddrucker's, Golden Corral, Hardee's, KFC, La Pinata Mexican, Lonestar Steaks, Max&Erma's, McDonald's, O'Charley's, Olive Garden, Panera Bread, PF Chang's, Red Lobster, Rooster's Grill, Rusty Bucket Grill, Sake Japanese, Skyline Chili, Steak'n Shake, Subway, Taco Bell, TGIFriday, Waffle House, Wendy's, **lodging:** Comfort Suites, Courtyard, Doubletree Suites, Holiday Inn, Homewood Suites, Residence Inn, SpringHill Suites, Studio 6, **other:** HOSPITAL, Aldi Foods, Barnes&Noble, Best Buy, Big O Tire, Border's, Circuit City, CompUSA, Cub Foods, Firestone/auto, Goodyear/auto, Home Depot, Honda/Nissan/Mazda, JC Penney, Jo-Ann Fabrics, Kia, Lowe's Whse, Macy's, Michael's, Mitsubishi, Office Depot, PepBoys, Petsmart, Pontiac, Sears/auto, Target, Tire Discounters, TJ Maxx, Toyota, Wal-Mart/SuperCtr, mall, **W...gas:** BP, Marathon, Shell, **food:** Bob Evans, LJ Silver, Perkins, Tim Horton, **lodging:** Day's Inn, Knight's Inn, Red Roof Inn, Super 8, **other:** HOSPITAL, Aamco, Chevrolet, $General, Ford, NAPA
43	I-675 N, to Columbus
38	OH 73, Springboro, Franklin, **E...gas:** Shell, Speedway, **food:** Applebee's, Arby's, Bob Evans, Burger King, China Buffet, KFC/Taco Bell, LJ Silver, McDonald's, Papa John's, Pizza Hut, Royal Wok, Skyline Chili, Subway, Tim Horton, TomKatz Cafe, Wendy's, **lodging:** Hampton Inn, Holiday Inn Express, **other:** K-Mart, Kroger, Radio Shack, Tire Discounters, **W...gas:** Exxon/dsl, Shell, Swifty, **food:** Big Boy, Cazadore's Mexican, Domino's, Gold Star Chili, Lee's Chicken, McDonald's, **lodging:** Econolodge, Knight's Inn, **other:** AutoZone, $General, $Tree, KOI Parts, Marsh Foods, NAPA, Walgreens, Wal-Mart SuperCtr, repair/tires
36	OH 123, to Lebanon, Franklin, **E...gas:** Exxon/Wendy's/dsl/24hr, Pilot/Subway/Pizza Hut/dsl/scales/24hr/@, Shell/scales/dsl, **food:** McDonald's, Waffle House, **lodging:** Quality Inn, **W...gas:** Marathon/White Castle/dsl, Sunoco
32	OH 122, Middletown, **E...gas:** Duke, **food:** McDonald's, Waffle House, **lodging:** Best Value, Super 8, Ramada Inn, Red Carpet Inn, **other:** HOSPITAL, Ford/Mercury/Lincoln, Jeep, **W...gas:** Meijer/dsl/24hr, **food:** Applebee's, Arby's, Big Boy, Bob Evans, Cracker Barrel, El Rancho Grande Mexican, Fazoli's, Fricker's, Golden Corral, Golden Dragon, Goldstar Chili, KFC, La Rosa's, LoneStar Steaks, McDonald's, O'Charley's, Olive Garden, Schlotsky's, Sonic, Steak'n Shake, Wendy's, White Castle, **lodging:** Best Western, Drury Inn, Fairfield Inn, Holiday Inn Express, **other:** Aldi Foods, AutoZone, Buick/GMC/Pontiac, Dillard's, Goodyear/auto, K-Mart, Kohl's, Kroger, Lowe's Whse, SavALot, Sears/auto, Staples, Target, Tire Discounters, Wal-Mart/gas, mall
29	OH 63, to Hamilton, Monroe, **E...gas:** Marathon/WhiteCastle/dsl, Shell/Popeye's/dsl, Stony Ridge Trk Plaza/dsl/scales, **food:** Burger King, GoldStar Chili, Waffle House, Wendy's/Tim Horton, **lodging:** Comfort Inn, **W...gas:** Speedway/dsl, Sunoco/dsl, **food:** Froggy Blue's, McDonald's, Sara Jane's Rest., Subway, **lodging:** Hampton Inn, Howard Johnson, **other:** Curves, flea mkt
	27.5mm rest area both lanes, full(handicapped) facilities, info, phone, picnic tables, litter barrels, vending, petwalk

Dayton

Middletown

Interstate 75

24	OH 129 W, to Hamilton, **W**...Cinncinati Gardens
22	Tylersville Rd, to Mason, Hamilton, **E**...**gas:** Marathon, Thornton's/dsl, Sunoco, **food:** Arby's, Bob Evans, BoneFish Grill, Burger King, Caribou Coffee, Carino's Italian, Chick-fil-A, Chipotle Mexican, Chopsticks, Donato's Pizza, Fazoli's, GoldStar Chili, IHOP, KFC, LJ Silver, Longhorn Steaks, McAlister's Deli, McDonald's, Panera Bread, Perkins, Ruby Tuesday, Skyline Chili, Soho Japanese, Taco Bell, TGIFriday, Twin Dragon, Waffle House, Wendy's, **lodging:** Econolodge, **other:** HOSPITAL, BigLots, Firestone, GNC, Home Depot, Kohl's, Kroger, Office Depot, PetsMart, Radio Shack, Target, Tires+, TJ Maxx, Walgreens, **W**...**gas:** Meijer/dsl/24hr, Shell, Speedway/dsl/24hr, **food:** O'Charley's, Steak'n Shake, **lodging:** Wingate Inn, **other:** Aldi Foods, Lowes Whse, Tire Discounters
21	Cin-Day Rd, **E**...**food:** Big Boy, **lodging:** Holiday Inn Express, **W**...**gas:** Clark, Marathon, Mobil/Subway/dsl, Speedway/dsl, Shell, **food:** Arby's, Casa Tequila Mexican, Domino's, Gunther's Steaks, Papa John's, Waffle House, Wendy's, **lodging:** Knight's Inn, **other:** Ace Hardware, Curves, PetsMart, Walgreens, Wal-Mart SuperCtr/24hr
19	Union Centre Blvd, to Fairfield, **E**...**food:** Bravo Italian, Champps Rest., Mitchell's Fish Mkt, Original Pancakes, Panera Bread, PF Chang's, Red Robin, Smokey Bones BBQ, Steak'n Shake, **other:** Barnes & Noble, **W**...**gas:** BP/Subway/dsl, Circle K/Marathon, Shell, **food:** Applebee's, Bob Evans, Buffalo Wild Wings, Burger King, Chipotle Mexican, Don Pablo, Max&Erma's, McDonald's, Quizno's, Rafferty's, River City Grille, Skyline Chili, Starbucks, Uno Pizzaria, Wendy's, **lodging:** Comfort Inn, Courtyard, Hampton Inn, Marriott, Staybridge Suites, **other:** Mercedes, Volvo
16	I-275 to I-71, to I-74
15	Sharon Rd, to Sharonville, Glendale, **E**...**gas:** Sunoco, Thornton's/dsl, **food:** Big Boy, Bob Evans, Burbank's BBQ, Cracker Barrel, Jim Dandy BBQ, Ruby Tuesday, Skyline Chili, Subway, Waffle House, **lodging:** Baymont Inn, Country Inn & Suites, Drury Inn, Hilton Garden, Holiday Inn Express, La Quinta, Motel 6, Red Roof Inn, Travelodge, **W** on Kimper...**gas:** Sunoco, **food:** Arby's, Burger King, Chili's, ChuckeCheese, Dos Amigos, IHOP, Long John Silver, Macaroni Grill, McDonald's, Pizza Hut, Taco Bell, Subway, Tokyo Japanese, Vincenzo's, Wendy's, **lodging:** Best Buy, Econolodge, Extended Stay Deluxe, Extended Stay America, Hamilton Hotel, LivInn Suites, Residence Inn, Sheraton, **other:** Costco/gas, Nissan, Target, Wal-Mart SuperCtr
14	OH 126, to Woodlawn, Evendale, **E**...GE Plant, **lodging:** Wingate Inn(3mi), **W**...**gas:** Swifty Gas, **lodging:** Travelodge
13	Shepherd Lane, to Lincoln Heights, **E**...GE Plant, **W**...**food:** Taco Bell, Wendy's, **other:** Advance Parts
12	Wyoming Ave, Cooper Ave, to Lockland, **W**...**gas:** Marathon, **food:** DQ, Subway
10a	OH 126, Ronald Reagan Hwy, **E**...Chevrolet
10b	Galbraith Rd(exits left from nb), Arlington Heights
9	OH 4, OH 561, Paddock Rd, Seymour Ave, **E**...to Cincinnati Gardens, **W**...fairgrounds
8	Towne St, Elmwood Pl(from nb)
7	OH 562, to I-71, Norwood, Cincinnati Gardens
6	Mitchell Ave, St Bernard, **E**...**gas:** Marathon, Shell, Sunoco, **food:** White Castle, **lodging:** Holiday Inn Express, **other:** Walgreens, to Cincinnati Zoo, to Xavier U, **W**...**gas:** BP/Subway/dsl, **food:** McDonald's, Rally's, **other:** Advance Parts, Chevrolet, Family$, Ford, Honda, Hyundai, Kroger, Tires+
4	I-74 W, US 52, US 27 N, to Indianapolis
3	to US 27 S, US 127 S, Hopple St, U of Cincinnati, **E**...**gas:** BP/Subway/dsl, **food:** Camp Washington Chili, Isador Italian, White Castle, **other:** HOSPITAL, Family$, **W**...**gas:** Shell, **food:** Wendy's
2b	Harrison Ave, ind dist, **W**...**gas:** BP, **food:** McDonald's
2a	Western Ave, Liberty St(from sb)
1g	Ezzard Charles Dr, **W**...**lodging:** Ramada Inn
1f	US 50W, Freeman Ave, **W**...**gas:** Sunoco, **food:** Big Boy, Pizza Hut/Taco Bell, Wendy's, White Castle, **lodging:** Ramada Inn, **other:** Ford, NAPA, Pontiac/GMC, USPO
1e	7th St(from sb), downtown, **W**...**lodging:** Ramada Inn
1b	5th St, downtown, **E**...**gas:** Crowne Plaza, **lodging:** Sheraton
1a	I-71 N, to Cincinnati, downtown, to stadium
0mm	Ohio/Kentucky state line, Ohio River

Interstate 76

Exit #	Services
	Ohio/Pennsylvania state line
Exits 232-235 are on the Ohio Turnpike. See Ohio Tpk, exits 232-235.	
60mm	I-76 eb joins Ohio TPK(toll)
57	to OH 45, Bailey Rd, to Warren
54	OH 534, to Newton Falls, Lake Milton, **N**...RV camping, **S**...**gas:** BP, **other:** to Berlin Lake, camping
52mm	Lake Milton
48	OH 225, to Alliance, **N**...to W Branch SP, camping, **S**...to Berlin Lake
45.5mm rest area both lanes, full(handicapped)facilities, phone, picnic tables, litter barrels, petwalk	
43	OH 14, to Alliance, Ravenna, **N**...to W Branch SP, **S**...**gas:** Citgo/dsl, **other:** fireworks
38b a	OH 5, OH 44, to Ravenna, **N**...**gas:** BP, Speedway/dsl, **food:** Arby's, McDonald's, Wendy's, **other:** HOSPITAL, **S**...**gas:** Marathon/Circle K/Subway, **food:** Cracker Barrel, David's Rest., **other:** Giant Eagle Foods, auto repair, RV camping
33	OH 43, to Hartville, Kent, **N**...**gas:** BP/dsl, **food:** Bob Evans(2mi), Burger King(2mi), Pizza Hut, Salsita's Mexican, **lodging:** Alden Inn, Day's Inn, Hampton Inn, Holiday Inn, Ramada Inn, Super 8, Tallyho Inn, **other:** to Kent St U, **S**...**gas:** Speedway/dsl, **food:** McDonald's, Subway, Wendy's, **other:** RV camping
31	rd 18, Tallmadge, 1mi **S**...**food:** Brimfield's Steaks, Pizza Serena
29	OH 532, Tallmadge, Mogadore

E

W

OHIO

Interstate 76

27	OH 91, Canton Rd, Gilchrist Rd, N...food: Bob Evans, S...gas: Marathon/Subway/dsl, food: Hardee's, Wendy's, lodging: Best Western
26	OH 18, E Market St, Mogadore Rd, N...gas: Citgo/dsl, Shell, S...food: Arby's, McDonald's, Wendy's, other: $General
25b a	Martha Ave, General St, Brittain, N...gas: Citgo, other: Goodyear World Hdqtrs
24	Arlington St, Kelly Ave, N...Mercedes, Toyota
23b	OH 8, Buchtell Ave, to Cuyahoga, to U of Akron, to U of Akron
23a	I-77 S, to Canton
22b	Wolf Ledges, Akron, downtown, S...gas: BP, food: McDonald's
22a	Main St, Broadway, downtown
21c	OH 59 E, Dart Ave, N...HOSPITAL
21b	Lakeshore St, Bowery St(from eb)
21a	East Ave(from wb)
20	I-77 N(from eb), to Cleveland
19	Battles Ave, Kenmore Blvd
18	I-277, US 224 E, to Canton, Barberton
17b a	OH 619, Wooster Rd, State St, to Barberton, S...gas: Sunoco, other: HOSPITAL, NAPA
16	Barber Rd, S...gas: Sunoco/dsl, food: Tomaso's Italian, lodging: Shamrock Motel, other: Chrysler/Jeep/Nissan/Suzuki
14	Cleve-Mass Rd, to Norton, S...gas: BP, Citgo, Marathon(2mi), food: Charlie's Rest., lodging: Berlin's Motel(2mi)
13b a	OH 21, N to Cleveland, S to Massillon
11	OH 261, Wadsworth, N...gas: Speedway
9	OH 94, to N Royalton, Wadsworth, N...gas: DM, Marathon, food: Applebee's, Arby's, Bob Evans, Burger King, KFC, McDonald's, Pizza Hut, Ponderosa, Subway, Taco Bell, Wendy's, lodging: Holiday Inn Express, Ramada Ltd, other: Buehler's Foods, DrugMart, Goodyear/auto, K-Mart, NTB, Radio Shack, Wal-Mart SuperCtr/24hr, S...gas: BP/dsl, Citgo/DQ, Pennzoil, Sunoco, food: Casa Del Rio Mexican, Country Cafe, Denny's, lodging: Legacy Inn, other: AutoZone, Rite Aid
7	OH 57, to Rittman, Medina, N...gas: Marathon/dsl, other: HOSPITAL, airport
6mm	weigh sta both lanes
2	OH 3, to Medina, Seville, N...food: DQ, Hardee's, Subway, lodging: Comfort Inn, Hawthorn Suites, other: Maple Lakes Camping(seasonal), S...gas: Citgo/dsl, Sunoco, other: RV camping
1	I-76 E, to Akron, US 224, W on US 224...gas: Pilot/Subway/dsl/24hr/@, TA/Burger King/Popeye's/dsl/24hr/@, food: McDonald's, lodging: Super 8, other: Blue Beacon, SpeedCo, Chippewa Valley Camping(1mi)
0mm	I-76 begins/ends on I-71, exit 209.

Interstate 77

Exit #	Services
	I-77 begins/ends on I-90 exit 172, in Cleveland.
163c	I-90, E to Erie, W to Toledo
163b	E 9th St, Tower City
162b	E 22nd St, E 14th St(from nb)
162a	E 30th St, Woodland Ave, Broadway St(from nb), W...USPO
161b	I-490 W, to I-71, E 55th, E...HOSPITAL
161a	OH 14(from nb), Broadway St
160	Pershing Ave(from nb), W...HOSPITAL
159b	Fleet Ave, E...gas: BP/Subway/dsl
159a	Harvard Ave, Newburgh Heights, W...gas: BP/Subway/dsl/24hr, Marathon
158	Grant Ave, Cuyahoga Heights
157	OH 21, OH 17(from sb), Brecksville Rd
156	I-480, to Youngstown, Toledo
155	Rockside Rd, to Independence, E...gas: Shell, Sunoco, food: Bob Evans, Bonefish Grill, Chester's, Chipotle Mexican, Del Monico's Steaks, Denny's, McDonald's, Outback Steaks, Red Robin, Shula's Steaks, Wendy's, Zoup, lodging: Comfort Inn, Doubletree, Embassy Suites, Holiday Inn, La Quinta, Red Roof Inn, other: Lincoln/Mercury, Walgreens, W...gas: BP/dsl, food: Applebee's, Damon's, Longhorn Steaks, lodging: Courtyard, Hampton Inn, Hyatt Place, Residence Inn, Sheraton
153	Pleasant Valley Rd, to Independence, 7 Hills
151	Wallings Rd, no services
149	OH 82, to Broadview Heights, Brecksville, 1 mi E...gas: BP, Shell, food: McDonald's, Panera Bread, Simons Cafe, Starbucks, other: Walgreens, W...gas: BP, food: Coco's, Domino's, Mr. Hero, lodging: Tallyho Motel, other: Curves
147	to OH 21, Miller Rd(from sb)
146	I-80/Ohio Tpk, to Youngstown, Toledo
145	OH 21(from nb), E...gas: Pilot/Wendy's/dsl/scales, food: DQ, lodging: Hampton Inn, Holiday Inn Express, Howard Johnson, Super 8
144	I-271 N, to Erie
143	OH 176, to I-271 S, E...to Coliseum, W...gas: Sunoco, food: Arabica Café, McDonald's, Panda Chinese, Subway, Teresa's Pizza, other: Curves
141mm	rest area both lanes, full(handicapped)facilities, phone, picnic tables, litter barrels, vending, petwalk
138	Ghent Rd, 2 mi E...lodging: Hilton, Sheraton, W...gas: Circle K/dsl, food: Lanning's Rest., Vaccaro's Italian
137b a	OH 18, to Fairlawn, Medina, E...gas: BP, Circle K, GetGo, Shell, Speedway, food: A Wok, Applebee's, Bob Evans, Boston Mkt, Chili's, Chipotle Mexican, Cracker Barrel, Donato's Pizza, Dynasty Chinese, Fleming's Steaks, Friendly's, Honeybaked Ham, Hyde Park Grill, KFC, LoneStar Steaks, Macaroni Grill, Max&Erma's, McDonald's, Olive Garden, Pad Thai, Quizno's, Red Lobster, Ruby Tuesday, Starbucks, Steak'n Shake, Taco Bell, Wendy's, lodging: Courtyard, Hampton Inn, Hilton, Holiday Inn, Quality Inn, Motel 6, Super 8, other: Acme Foods, Barnes&Noble, Best Buy, Borders Books, CompUSA, Ford, Dillard's, $Tree, Giant Eagle Foods, Home Depot, Jo-Ann Fabrics, Lowe's Whse, Macy's, Michael's, Mr. Tire, Old Navy, Petsmart, Sam's Club, Staples, TJ Maxx, Wal-Mart, World Mkt, W...gas: Sunoco/dsl, food: Bennigan's, Burger King, Don Pablo, Longhorn Steaks, Outback Steaks, TGIFriday, Tres Patrilios, Wasabi Grill, lodging: Best Western, Comfort Inn, Extended Stay America, Radisson, Residence Inn, Studio+
136	OH 21S, to Massillon
135	Cleveland-Massillon Rd(from nb)
133	Ridgewood Rd, Miller Rd, E...gas: Circle K/dsl, food: Wendy's
132	White Pond Dr, Mull Ave, E...Rosarita Cantina, golf
131	OH 162, Copley Rd, E...gas: Circle K, other: SavALot Foods, Walgreens, USPO, W...gas: BP/dsl/24hr, food: McDonald's, Pizza Hut

356

Interstate 77

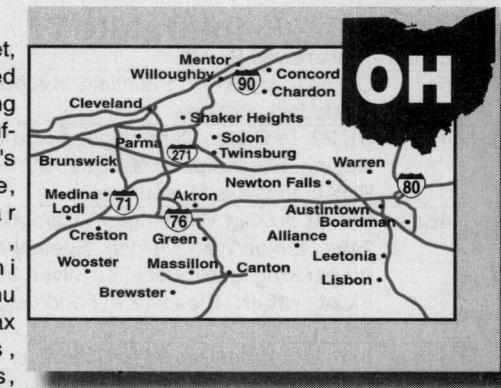

130	OH 261, Wooster Ave, **E**...**gas:** Circle K, Valero, **food:** Ann's Place, Burger King, Church's, New China, Rally's, Subway, White Castle, **other:** Acme Foods, Advance Parts, AutoZone, Family$, **W**...**food:** KFC, **other:** Chevrolet, Toyota/Scion, U-Haul
129	I-76 W, to I-277, to Kenmore Blvd, Barberton
21a	East Ave(from nb). **I-77 S and I-76 E run together**
21b	Lakeshore(from sb), to Bowery St
21c	OH 59 E, Dart Ave, downtown, **E**...HOSPITAL
22a	Main St, Broadway St, downtown, **W**...auto parts
22b	Grant St, Wolf Ledges, **W**...**gas:** BP, **food:** McDonald's, **other:** Family$
125b	I-76 E, to Youngstown, **I-77 and I-76 run together**
125a	OH 8 N, to Cuyahoga Falls, U of Akron
124b	Lover's Lane, Cole Ave
124a	Archwood Ave, Firestone Blvd
123b	OH 764, Wilbeth Rd, **E**...to airport
123a	Waterloo Rd, **W**...**gas:** Marathon, **other:** Acme Foods
122b a	I-277, US 224 E, to Barberton, Mogadore
120	Arlington Rd, to Green, **E**...**gas:** Speedway/dsl, **food:** Applebee's, Church's, Denny's, Friendly's, Golden Corral, IHOP, Pizza Hut, Ryan's, Starbucks, Waffle House, White Castle, **lodging:** Comfort Inn, Quality Inn, Red Roof Inn, **other:** $General, Home Depot, Kohl's, Staples, Wal-Mart/auto, **W**...**gas:** BP, Speedway, **food:** Bob Evans, Burger King, Lion Garden, Mariachi Mexican, McDonald's, Subway, Taco Bell, TGIFriday, Wendy's, **lodging:** Fairfield Inn, Hampton Inn, **other:** Buick/Pontiac/GMC, Chevrolet, Goodyear/auto, Honda/Mazda, Hyundai, Lexus, Lowes Whse, Nissan, Sirpilla RV Ctr/Camping World, Target
118	OH 241, to OH 619, Massillon, **E**...**gas:** Sheetz, Speedway/dsl, **food:** Gionino's Pizza, Subway, **W**...**gas:** BP/Circle K, GetGo, **food:** Arby's, Belgrade Gardens, McDonald's, Menche's Rest., Pancho's Mexican, Quizno's, **lodging:** Cambria Suites, Super 8, **other:** HOSPITAL
113	Akron-Canton Airport, **2 mi** **W**...**lodging:** Hilton Garden, **other:** Clay's RV
112	new exit
111	Portage St, N Canton, **E**...**gas:** Circle K, Marathon, Speedway, Sunoco/dsl, TA/Country Pride/dsl/scales/24hr/@, **food:** Burger King, Cheing's Express, Giesen Haus, KFC, Palambo's Italian, Subway, Sylvester's Italian, **other:** TrueValue, **W**...**gas:** BP/dsl, **food:** Carrabba's, ChuckeCheese, Coldstone Creamery, Cracker Barrel, Donato's Pizza, Don Pablo, Dunkin Donuts/Baskin-Robbins, Hungry Howie's, IHOP, Longhorn Steaks, Lucky Star Chinese, McDonald's, Pizza Hut, Quizno's, Red Robin, Rockne's Cafe, Samantha's, Starbucks, Taco Bell, Wendy's, **lodging:** Best Western, Microtel, Motel 6, **other:** Best Buy, BJ's Whse, Borders Books, Chevrolet, DrugMart, Gander Mtn, Giant Eagle Foods, GNC, Goodyear/auto, Harley-Davidson, Home Depot, Lowe's Whse, Marshall's, Old Navy, Sam's Club/gas, Wal-Mart/Subway/auto
109b a	Everhard Rd, Whipple Ave, **E**...**gas:** Citgo/Subway, Speedway/dsl, **food:** Burger King, Denny's, Fazoli's, McDonald's, Taco Bell, **lodging:** Comfort Inn, Fairfield Inn, Hampton Inn, Residence Inn, **other:** Ford, Saturn, **W**...**gas:** Marathon, **food:** Applebee's, Arby's, Bennigan's, Bob Evans, Bravo Italian, Buffalo Wild Wings, Buffet Dynasty, Chick-fil-A, Chipotle Mexican, Cheeseburger Paradise, CiCi's Pizza, Damon's, Friendly's, Home-

	Town Buffet, HoneyBaked Ham, Hong Kong Buffet, Logan's Roadhouse, LoneStar Steaks, Macaroni Grill, Manchu Café, Max & Erma's, Mulligan's, Olive Garden, Outback Steaks, Panera Bread, Panini's Grill, Papa Bear's, Penn Sta. Subs, Ponderosa, Red Lobster, Ricky Ly's Chinese, Robek's Grill, Ruby Tuesday, Sahara Grill, Starbucks, Steak'n Shake, TGIFriday, Wendy's, **lodging:** Courtyard, Day's Inn, Holiday Inn, Parke Suites, Red Roof Inn, **other:** Advance Parts, Best Buy, Circuit City, Dillard's, $Tree, Firestone/auto, Goodyear/auto, Jo-Ann Crafts, Kohl's, Macy's, Marc's Foods, Michael's, Petsmart, Radio Shack, Sears/auto, Target, TJ Maxx, World Mkt, mall
107b a	US 62, OH 687, Fulton Rd, to Alliance, **E**...City Park, **W**...**gas:** Circle K, **other:** Pro Football Hall of Fame
106	13th St NW, **E**...HOSPITAL
105b	OH 172, Tuscarawas St, downtown
105a	6th St SW(no EZ return from sb), **W**...**food:** Subway, **other:** HOSPITAL, AutoZone
104	US 30, US 62, to E Liverpool, Massillon
103	OH 800 S, **E**...**gas:** Marathon/Subway, Speedway, **food:** Arby's, Taco Bell, Waffle House, **other:** Advance Parts, Firestone
101	OH 627, to Faircrest St, **E**...**gas:** Gulliver's Trvl Plaza/dsl/rest./scales, Speedway/McDonald's, **food:** Wendy's
99	Fohl Rd, to Navarre, **W**...**gas:** Sunoco, KOA(4mi)
93	OH 212, to Zoar, Bolivar, **E**...**gas:** Speedway/Subway, **food:** McDonald's, Pizza Hut, Wendy's, **lodging:** Sleep Inn, **other:** $General, Giant Eagle Foods, NAPA, Zoar Tavern(3mi), vet, to Lake Atwood Region, **W**...**gas:** Marathon/DQ, **other:** KOA
92mm	weigh sta both lanes
87	US 250W, to Strasburg, **3 mi** **E**...**food:** Arby's, **W**...**gas:** Marathon/Quizno's/dsl, **food:** Creekside Cafe, Damon's Pizza, Hardee's, Manor Rest., McDonald's, Subway, **lodging:** Ramada Ltd, Twins Motel
85mm	**rest areas both lanes, full(handicapped)facilities, info, phone, picnic tables, litter barrels, petwalk**
83	OH 39, OH 211, to Sugarcreek, Dover, **E**...**gas:** BP, Speedway/Subway/dsl, **food:** Bob Evans, KFC, McDonald's, Shoney's, Wendy's, **lodging:** Hospitality Inn, **other:** HOSPITAL, Ford/Chrysler/Dodge/Jeep, Lincoln/Mercury/Nissan, tires, **W**...**gas:** Marathon/DQ, **lodging:** Comfort Inn
81	US 250, to Uhrichsville, OH 39, New Philadelphia, **E**...**gas:** Marathon, Sheetz/dsl, Speedway, **food:** Burger King, Denny's, El San Jose Mexican, Hog Heaven, LJ Silver, McDonald's, Pizza Hut, Quizno's, Taco Bell, Texas Roadhouse, **lodging:** Hampton Inn, Holiday Inn, Knight's Inn, Motel 6, Schoenbrunn Inn, Super 8, **other:** Advance Parts, Aldi Foods, Big Lots, $General, Wal-Mart SuperCtr/24hr, **W**...**gas:** Eagle/dsl/rest./24hr, **other:** Harley-Davidson
73	OH 751, to rd 21, Stone Creek, **W**...**gas:** Marathon
65	US 36, Port Washington, Newcomerstown, **W**...**gas:** BP, Duke/dsl/rest., Speedway/Wendy's/24hr, **food:** McDonald's, **lodging:** Hampton Inn, Super 8

Interstate 77

N	64mm	Tuscarawas River
	54	OH 541, rd 831, to Plainfield, Kimbolton, Ⓦ...**gas:** BP, **food:** Jackie's Rest.
	47	US 22, to Cadiz, Cambridge, Ⓔ...to Salt Fork SP(6mi), lodging, RV camping, Ⓦ...**gas:** BP/repair, **other:** HOSPITAL, to Glass Museum, info
C	46b a	US 40, to Old Washington, Cambridge, Ⓦ...**gas:** BP/24hr, Exxon/Wendy's/dsl, Speedway/dsl/24hr, **food:** Burger King, Lee's Rest., LJ Silver, McDonald's, Wally's Pizza, **other:** Riesbeck's Food/deli, SavALot Foods, vet
a	44b a	I-70, E to Wheeling, W to Columbus
m	41	OH 209, OH 821, Byesville, Ⓦ...**gas:** BP/dsl, **food:** McDonald's, **other:** IGA Foods, Family$
b	**39mm**	**rest area nb, full(handicapped)facilities, phone, picnic tables, litter barrels, petwalk, vending**
r	37	OH 313, Buffalo, Ⓔ...**gas:** BP, Duke, **food:** BBQ, Subway, **other:** truck repair, to Senecaville Lak
i	**36mm**	**rest area sb, full(handicapped)facilities, phone, picnic tables, litter barrels, petwalk, vending**
d	28	OH 821, Belle Valley, Ⓔ...**gas:** Sunoco/dsl, **other:** USPO, to Wolf Run SP, RV camping
g	25	OH 78, Caldwel, Ⓔ...**gas:** BP, Pilot/Arby's/dsl/scales/24hr, Sunoco/Subway/dsl, **food:** DQ, Lori's Rest., McDonald's, **lodging:** Best Western, **other:** Chevrolet/Pontiac/Buick
e	16	OH 821, Macksburg, Ⓔ...food, **other:** antiques
	6	OH 821, to Devola, Ⓔ...**gas:** Exxon, Ⓦ...HOSPITAL, BP/dsl/LP, RV camping
	3mm	**rest area nb, full(handicapped)facilities, info, phone, vending, picnic tables, litter barrels, petwalk**
M	1	OH 7, to OH 26, Marietta, Ⓔ...**gas:** GoMart/dsl/24hr, **food:** Cici's, DQ, Ryan's, **lodging:** Comfort Inn, Econolodge, Holiday Inn, **other:** Aldi Foods, Chevrolet/Cadillac, Chrysler/Jeep, Dodge, Ford, Harley-Davidson, Lowe's Whse, NAPA, Pontiac/Buick, Toyota/Scion, Wal-Mart SuperCtr/24hr, Ⓦ...**gas:** BP/dsl, Duke/dsl, GetGo, Marathon/dsl, Speedway/dsl, **food:** Applebee's, Arby's, Brewster's, Bob Evans, Burger King, Capt D's, Chicago Pizza, Empire Buffet, LJ Silver, McDonald's, Napoli's Pizza, Papa John's, Pizza Hut, Quizno's, Shoney's, Subway, Taco Bell, Wendy's, **lodging:** Best Value, Hampton Inn, Super 8, **other:** AutoZone, BigLots, $General, Food4Less, Jo-Ann Crafts, K-Mart, Kroger/24hr, Sav-a-Lot Foods, museum, st patrol
a	0mm	Ohio/West Virginia state line, Ohio River

Interstate 80

	Exit #	Services
	237mm	Ohio/Pennsylvania state line
	237mm	**Welcome Ctr wb, full(handicapped)facilities, info, phone, picnic tables, litter barrels, vending, petwalk**
E	234b a	US 62, OH 7, to Sharon, PA, Hubbard, Ⓝ...**gas:** ✈/Flying J/Country Mkt/Magic Dragon Chinese/dsl/scales/24hr/@, Shell/dsl/rest./motel/24hr/@, **food:** Arby's, Burger King, McDonald's, Waffle House, **lodging:** Best Western, **other:** Blue Beacon, RV camping(2mi), tire repair, Ⓢ...**other** Chevrolet
W	232mm	weigh sta wb
	229	OH 193, Belmont Ave, to Youngstown, Ⓝ...**gas:** Speedway/dsl, **food:** Handel's Ice Cream, Sta Sq Rest., **lodging:** Hampton Inn, Holiday Inn, Super 8, TallyHo-tel, Ⓢ...**gas:** BP, Shell, **food:** Arby's, Asian

Buffet, Armando's Italian, Bob Evans, Cancun Mexican, Denny's, Golden Hunan, Inner Circle Pizza, Jay's Hot Dogs, KFC, LJ Silver, McDonald's, Papa John's, Perkins/24hr, Pizza Hut, Subway, Taco Bell, Wendy's, **lodging:** Days Inn, Quality Inn, **other:** Advance Parts, Aldi Foods, AutoZone, BigLots, Firestone, Goodyear/auto

228	OH 11, to Warren(exits left from eb), Ashtabula
227	US 422, Girard, Youngstown, Ⓝ...**gas:** Shell/dsl/24hr, **food:** Burger King, DQ, JibJab Hotdogs, Subway
226	Salt Springs Rd, to I-680(from wb), Ⓝ...**gas:** BP/Subway/dsl, Sheetz/24hr, **food:** McDonald's, Waffle House, Ⓢ...**gas:** Mr Fuel/dsl/24hr, Petro/dsl/rest./scales/24hr/@, Pilot/Arby's/dsl/24hr/@, **other:** Blue Beacon, SpeedCo, dsl repair
224b	I-680(from eb), to Youngstown
224a	OH 11 S, to Canfield
223	OH 46, to Niles, Ⓝ...**gas:** Citgo/dsl, Pilot/McDonald's/dsl/24hr/@, **food:** Bob Evans, Burger King, IceHouse Rest., Salsita's Mexican, **lodging:** Best Value Inn, Comfort Inn, Ⓢ...**gas:** BP/dsl, FuelMart/dsl, Sunoco/Subway, TA/dsl/rest./scales/24hr/@, **food:** Arby's, Cracker Barrel, DQ, McDonald's, Perkins, Roadhouse Cafe, Starbucks, Taco Bell, Wendy's, **lodging:** Best Western, Country Inn&Suites, Econolodge, Fairfield Inn, Hampton Inn, Knight's Inn, Sleep Inn, Super 8, **other:** Blue Beacon, Freightliner/24hr
221mm	Meander Reservoir
219mm	I-80 wb joins Ohio Tpk(toll)

For I-80 exits 2-218, see Ohio Turnpike.

Interstate 90

	Exit #	Services
	243mm	Ohio/Pennsylvania state line
	242mm	**Welcome Ctr/weigh sta wb, full(handicapped)facilities, info, phone, picnic tables, litter barrels, petwalk**
C	241	OH 7, to Andover, Conneaut, Ⓝ...**food:** Burger King, McDonald's(2mi), **lodging:** Day's Inn, **other:** HOSPITAL, AutoZone, CVS Drug, K-Mart, Evergreen RV Park, Ⓢ...**food:** Beef&Beer Café
o	235	OH 84, OH 193, to Youngstown, N Kingsville, Ⓝ...**gas:** Grab&Go/gas, Marathon/Circle K, **lodging:** Dav-Ed Motel, **other:** Village Green Camping(2mi), Ⓢ...**gas:** Citgo/Subway/dsl, TA/BP/Burger King/dsl/scales/24hr/@, **food:** Kay's Place Diner, **lodging:** Kingsville Motel
n	228	OH 11, to Ashtabula, Youngstown, Ⓝ...HOSPITAL(4mi)
n	223	OH 45, to Ashtabula, Ⓝ...**gas:** ✈/Flying J/dsl/LP/rest./scales/24hr/@, **food:** Mr C's Rest., **lodging:** Best Value Inn, Comfort Inn, Holiday Inn Express, Sleep Inn, **other:** Buccaneer Camping, Ⓢ...**gas:** Pilot/Subway/dsl/scales/24hr, **food:** Burger King, McDonald's, **lodging:** Hampton Inn
e	218	OH 534, Geneva, Ⓝ...**gas:** BP, GetGo, **food:** Best Friends Rest., Chop's Grille, McDonald's, Pizza Hut, Wendy's, **lodging:** Howard Johnson, **other:** HOSPITAL, Goodyear/repair, KOA(8mi), Indian Creek Camping, to Geneva SP, Ⓢ...**gas:** KwikFill/dsl/rest./24hr, **food:** Quizno's, **other:** Kenisse's Camping
a	212	OH 528, to Thompson, Madison, Ⓝ...**food:** JC's Diner, McDonald's, Potbelly's Rest., Ⓢ...**gas:** Marathon/dsl, **other:** Heritage Hills Camping(4mi), radiators
u	205	Vrooman Rd, Ⓢ...**gas:** BP/dsl, **food:** Capps Eatery(1mi)
t	200	OH 44, to Painesville, Chardon, Ⓝ...HOSPITAL, Ⓢ...**gas:** BP/Subway/dsl, Sunoco/dsl, **food:** McDonald's, Palmer's Bistro, Red Hawk Grille, Waffle House, **lodging:** Amerihost, Renaissance, **other:** Reider's Foods, hwy patrol

Interstate 90

198mm **rest area both lanes, full(handicapped)facilities, phone, picnic tables, litter barrels, vending, pet-walk**

195 OH 615, Center St, Kirtland Hills, Mentor, **1-2 mi** 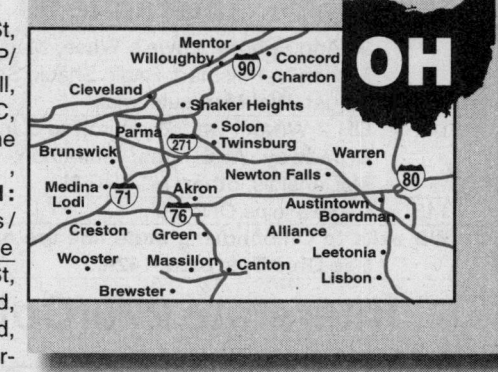... **gas:** BP, **food:** El Rodeo Mexican, Yours Truly Rest., **lodging:** Best Western

193 OH 306, to Mentor, Kirtland, **N**...**gas:** BP/McDonald's/Subway, **lodging:** Motel 6, **S**...**gas:** Marathon, **food:** Burger King, Dino's Rest., GrillSmith, **lodging:** Day's Inn/café, Red Roof Inn, **other:** HOSPITAL

190 Express Lane to I-271(from wb)

189 OH 91, to Willoughby, Willoughby Hills, **N**...**gas:** BP/dsl, Shell/24hr, **food:** Bob Evans, Café Europa, Cracker Barrel, Damon's, Eat 'n Park, Peking Chef, SF Oven, Subway, Texas Roadhouse, Wendy's, **lodging:** Courtyard, Fairfield Inn, Travelodge, **other:** HOSPITAL, CVS Drug, Walgreens

188 I-271 S, to Akron

187 OH 84, Bishop Rd, to Wickliffe, Willoughby, **S**...**gas:** BP/dsl, Shell, **food:** Baker's Square, Burger King, China King, Manhattan Deli, Mazzio's, McDonald's, Quizno's, Subway, **lodging:** Holiday Inn, **other:** HOSPITAL, Curves, CVS Drug, Chevrolet, Giant Eagle Foods, Marc's Foods, Mazda/VW, NTB, Sam's Club, vet

186 US 20, Euclid Ave, **N**...**gas:** Sunoco, **food:** Grand Rodeo Mexican, McDonald's, **lodging:** Comfort Inn, **other:** Dodge/Subaru, Ford, Isuzu, radiators, **S**...**gas:** Shell, **food:** Arby's, KFC, Pizza Hut, Popeye's, R-Ribs, Sidewalk Cafe, Taco Bell, **other:** Advance Parts, $General, Firestone/auto, NAPA, SaveAlot Foods

185 OH 2 E(exits left from eb), to Painesville

184b OH 175, E 260th St, **N**...**gas:** Shell/autocare, **S**...**other:** NTB, Ruff's RV Ctr, transmissions

184a Babbitt Rd, same as 183

183 E 222nd St, **N**...**other:** GMC, **S**...**gas:** Sunoco/dsl/24hr, **food:** Midway Grill, **other:** repair

182b a 185 St, 200 St, **N**...**other:** BP/Subway, **food:** Muldoon's Eatery, **other:** Home Depot, Honda, Hyundai, **S**...**other:** Marathon/diesel, Shell, Speedway

181b a E 156th St, **S**...**gas:** BP/24hr

180b a E 140th St, E 152nd St

179 OH 283 E, to Lake Shore Blvd

178 Eddy Rd, to Bratenahl, no services

177 University Circle, MLK Dr, **N**...**other:** Cleveland Lake SP, **S**...**other:** HOSPITAL, Rockefeller Park

176 E 72nd St

175 E 55th St, Marginal Rds

174b OH 2 W, to Lakewood, downtown, Rock&Roll Hall of Fame, Browns Stadium

174a Lakeside Ave, no services

173c Superior Ave, St Clair Ave, downtown, **N**...**gas:** BP

173b Chester Ave, **S**...**gas:** BP

173a Prospect Ave(from wb), downtown

172d Carnegie Ave, downtown, **S**...**food:** Burger King, **other:** Cadillac

172c b E 9th St, **S**...**other:** HOSPITAL, to Cleveland St U

172a I-77 S, to Akron

171b a US 422, OH 14, Broadway St, Ontario St, **N**...**lodging:** Hilton Garden, **other:** to Browns Stadium

170c b I-71 S, to I-490

170a US 42, W 25th St, **N**...**gas:** Sunoco, **S**...**gas:** Citgo

169 W 44th St, W 41st St, **N**...HOSPITAL

167b a OH 10, West Blvd, 98th St, to Lorain Ave, **N**...HOSPITAL, **S**...**gas:** BP/dsl

Cleveland

166 W 117th St, **N**...**gas:** BP/dsl, Shell, **food:** KFC, **other:** Home Depot, **S**...**food:** Church's/White Castle

165 W 140th St, Bunts Rd, Warren Rd, **N**...**gas:** Circle K, Marathon, **other:** HOSPITAL

164 McKinley Ave, to Lakewood

162 Hilliard Blvd(from wb), to Westway Blvd, Rocky River, **S**...**gas:** BP, Shell

161 OH 2, OH 254(from eb, no EZ return), Detroit Rd, Rocky River

160 Clague Rd(from wb), **S**...**other:** HOSPITAL, same as 159

159 OH 252, Columbia Rd, **N**...**gas:** Speedway, **food:** Carrabba's, Clubhouse Grill, Dave&Buster's, Joe's Crabshack, Outback Steaks, **lodging:** Courtyard, TownePlace Suites, Super 8, **S**...**gas:** BP, **food:** Houlihan's, KFC, McDonald's, Taco Bell, **other:** Chevrolet, CVS Drug, NTB, Tops Foods

156 Crocker Rd, Bassett Rd, Westlake, Bay Village, **N**...**gas:** BP, Shell, **lodging:** Extended Stay Deluxe, Holiday Inn, Red Roof Inn, Residence Inn, **S**...**gas:** Marathon/dsl, **food:** Applebee's, Blake's Seafood, Bob Evans, Cheesecake Factory, Max&Erma's, McDonald's, Subway, TGIFriday, Wendy's, **lodging:** Hampton Inn, **other:** HOSPITAL, Borders Books, CVS Drug, Giant Eagle, GNC, K-Mart, Marc's Foods, Radio Shack, mall

153 OH 83, Avon Lake, **N**...**gas:** GetGo/dsl, Marathon/Circle K, **food:** Bubba's BBQ, Buffalo Wild Wings, Perkins, **other:** Best Buy, Wal-Mart/auto/gas, **S**...**food:** Applebees, Bob Evans, Caribou Coffee, Coldstone Creamery, IHOP, Panera Bread, Quizno's, Red Robin, Subway, Wendy's, **other:** Cosco/gas, Curves, CVS Drug, Home Depot, Kohl's, Marshall's, Michael's, Old Navy, Target, World Mkt

151 OH 611, Avon, **N**...**gas:** BP/dsl, Pilot/Subway/dsl/24hr, **food:** McDonald's, Dianna's Deli, **lodging:** Fairfield Inn, **other:** Avon RV, Goodyear/repair, Harley Davidson, **S**...**gas:** BJ's Whse/gas, **food:** Mulligan's Grille

148 OH 254, Sheffield, Avon, **N**...**food:** Quaker Steak, **other:** Dodge, Ford, KIA, Mazda, Mitsubishi, Nissan, **S**...**gas:** BP, GetGo, Speedway, **food:** Arby's, Burger King, Cracker Barrel, Donato's Pizza, KFC, McDonald's, Pizza Hut, Quizno's, Ruby Tuesday, Steak'n Shake, Subway, Taco Bell, Wendy's, **other:** Aldi Foods, CVS Drug, $General, Drug Mart, Gander Mtn, Giant Eagle, NTB, Sam's Club/gas

147mm Black River

145 OH 57, to Lorain, I-80/Ohio Tpk E, Elyria, **N**...**food:** Burger King, George's Rest., KFC, **other:** HOSPITAL, U-Haul, **S**...**gas:** BP/McDonald's/dsl, Speedway, **food:** Applebee's, Arby's, Bennigan's, Bob Evans, Buffalo Wild Wings, Burger King, Denny's, Eat'n Park, Fazoli's, Golden Corral, Jumbo Buffet, McDonald's, TGIFriday's, Pizza Hut, Qdoba Mexican, Red Lobster, Subway, Tokyo Steaks, Wendy's, **lodging:** Best Western, Comfort Inn, Country Inn&Suites, Econolodge, Holiday Inn, Red Roof Inn, **other:** Best Buy, Curves, Dillard's, $General, $Tree, Family$, Firestone/auto, Home Depot, Honda/Hyundai, JC Penney,

Interstate 90

	Jo-Ann Fabrics, Lowe's Whse, Macy's, Marc's Foods, Michael's, Petsmart, Radio Shack, Sears/auto, Staples, Target, Wal-Mart/auto, mall,
144	OH 2 W(from wb, no return), to Sandusky, **1 mi N on Broadway Av**[E]...**gas:** Marathon, Shell/24hr, **food:** McDonald's, **other:** HOSPITAL
143	I-90 wb joins Ohio Tpk

WB exits to Ohio/Indiana state line are on Ohio Turnpike. See Ohio Tpk, exits 142-0.

Interstate 270(Columbus)

Exit # Services

55	I-71, to Columbus, Cincinnati
52b a	US 23, High St, Circleville, [N]...**gas:** Marathon/Circle K, Speedway/dsl, **food:** A&W/KFC, Arby's, Bob Evans, Burger King, China Town, LJ Silver, Los Campero's, McDonald's, Pizza Hut, Ponderosa, Roadhouse Grill, Skyline Chili, Subway, Taco Bell, Tim Horton, Waffle House, Wendy's, White Castle, **lodging:** Kozy Inn, **other:** AutoZone, Curves, $General, Firestone, Kroger/gas, Lowe's, Walgreens, Wal-Mart, [S]...**gas:** BP/dsl, **lodging:** Budget Inn, **other:** Kioto Downs
49	Alum Creek Dr, [N]...**gas:** Duke/dsl, Sunoco/dsl, **food:** Donato's Pizza, KFC/LJ Silver, Subway, [S]...**gas:** BP/dsl, **food:** Arby's, McDonald's, Taco Bell, Wendy's, **lodging:** Comfort Inn, Sleep Inn
46b a	US 33, Bexley, Lancaster
43b a	I-70, E to Cambridge, W to Columbus
41b a	US 40, [E]...**gas:** BP, Shell, **food:** Bob Evans, Boston Mkt, Hooters, McDonald's, Outback Steaks, Rally's, Steak'n Shake, Texas Roadhouse, **other:** Walgreens, [W]...**gas:** Mobil, Shell, Speedway, **food:** Fuddruckers, Golden Corral, Hunan Chinese, LoneStar Steaks
39	OH 16, Broad St, [E]...**gas:** Meijer/dsl, Speedway/dsl, **food:** Arby's, Chipotle Grill, Church's, Quizno's, Waffle House, White Castle, **lodging:** Country Inn&Suites, **other:** HOSPITAL, [W]...**gas:** Shell, **food:** Applebee's, **lodging:** Ramada Inn
37	OH 317, Hamilton Rd, [E]...**gas:** BP/dsl, Marathon, Speedway/dsl, **food:** Big Boy, Bob Evans, Burger King, Chinese Express, Damon's, Donato's Pizza, Hickory House, KFC, Pizza Hut/Taco Bell, Starbucks, **lodging:** Holiday Inn Express, SpringHill Suites, **other:** Firestone, GNC, Kroger, **2 mi W**[W]...**lodging:** Comfort Suites, Hampton Inn, Hilton Garden
35b a	I-670W, US 62, [E]...**gas:** Speedway/dsl, **food:** City BBQ, Donato's Pizza, McDonald's, Tim Horton, **other:** CVS Drug, [W]...I-670
33	no services
32	Morse Rd, [E]...**gas:** Marathon/DM, Speedway/dsl, **food:** Donato's Pizza, **other:** Mazda, Toyota, [W]...**gas:** BP, Mobil/dsl, Shell/Subway, **food:** Applebee's, Champp's Grill, HomeTown Buffet, Kobe Japanese, Logan's Roadhouse, McDonald's, On-the-Border, Pizza Hut/Taco Bell, Steak'n Shake, Wendy's, **lodging:** Extended Stay America, Hampton Inn, **other:** Best Buy, BMW, Cadillac, Carmax, Circuit City, Discount Tire, Jo-Ann Fabrics, Lexus, Lowe's Whse, Macy's, Mercedes, Nordstrom's, NTB, Sam's Club, Target, Wal-Mart SuperCtr/24hr, mall
30	OH 161 E to New Albany, W to Worthington
29	OH 3, Westerville, [N]...**gas:** BP/dsl, Shell, **food:** Applebee's, Arby's, Chipotle Mexican, McDonald's, Fazoli's, Pizza Hut, Tim Horton, **lodging:** Baymont Inn, Knight's

	Inn, **other:** CarQuest, Firestone/auto, Kroger, [S]...**gas:** Speedway/dsl, Sunoco/dsl, **food:** Carsoni's Italian, China House, Domino's, Subway, **other:** Aldi Foods, Family$, Midas
27	OH 710, Cleveland Ave, [N]...**gas:** Speedway, **food:** Subway, Tim Horton, Wendy's, **lodging:** Quality Inn, Ramada Inn, Signature Inn, **other:** CVS Drug, NAPA, Tuffy, [S]...**food:** Bob Evans, McDonald's, O'Charley's, Steak'n Shake, **lodging:** Embassy Suites, **other:** Home Depot
26	I-71, S to Columbus, N to Cleveland
23	US 23, Worthington, [N]...**food:** Alexander's, Amazon Grill, Bob Evans, Bravo Italian, Buffalo Wild Wings, Champp's Grill, Chipotle Mexican, Columbus Fish Mkt, El Acapulco, Gilbert's Steaks, Lotus Grill, Mitchell's Steaks, Panera Bread, Quizno's, Ruth's Chris Steaks, Starbucks, Sushiko Japanese, Tutt's Italian, **lodging:** AmeriSuites, Courtyard, Days Inn, DoubleTree, Extended Stay America, Motel 6, Homewood Suites, Red Roof Inn, Residence Inn, Sheraton, [S]...**gas:** BP, **food:** Buca Italian, Cosi Grill, Jimmy John's, McDonald's, **lodging:** Econolodge, Holiday Inn
22	OH 315, [N]...**gas:** Marathon/dsl
20	Sawmill Rd, [N]...**gas:** BP, Marathon/dsl, **food:** Burger King, McDonald's, Olive Garden, Subway, Taco Bell, Wendy's, **other:** Buick/Pontiac/GMC, CVS Drug, Ford, Hyundai, Lincoln-Mercury, Mazda, NTB, Subaru, Tire Kingdom, [S]...**gas:** Meijer, Shell, Speedway, **food:** Applebee's, Asian Star, Arby's, BajaFresh, Bob Evans, Boston Mkt, Burger King, Charlie's Subs, Chili's, Chipotle Mexican, Cosi Grill, Don Pablo, Golden Corral, HoneyBaked Cafe, Joe's Crabshack, KFC, Krispy Kreme, McDonald's, Mongolian BBQ, Steak'n Shake, Red Lobster, Ruby Tuesday, Ted's MT Grill, **lodging:** Hampton Inn, Quality Inn, Woodfin Suites, **other:** Barnes&Noble, Big Lots, Borders Books, Cadillac/Honda, Circuit City, Discount Tire, $Tree, Firestone, Jo-Ann Fabrics, Kohl's, Lowe's Whse, PetCo, Sam's Club, Staples, SteinMart, Target, Toyota/Scion, Trader Joe's
17b a	US 33, Dublin-Granville Rd, [E]...**gas:** Marathon, Sunoco, **food:** Bob Evans, Donato's, Max&Erma's, McDonald's, Subway, **lodging:** Best Value Inn, Courtyard, Crowne Plaza, Embassy Suites, Hilton Garden, Red Roof Inn, Residence Inn, **other:** BMW/Mini, CVS Drug, Kroger, Mitsubishi, Mr Tire, USPO
15	Tuttle Crossing Blvd, [E]...**gas:** BP, Mobil, **food:** Bob Evans, Boston Mkt, Chipotle Mexican, Cozymel's, Longhorn Steaks, Macaroni Grill, McDonald's, PF Chang's, Pizza Hut/Taco Bell, River City Grill, TGIFriday, Wendy's, **lodging:** Drury Inn, Homewood Suites, Hyatt Place, La Quinta, Marriott, **other:** JC Penney, Macy's, Sears/auto, mall, [W]...**gas:** Exxon/Subway/dsl, Shell, **food:** Quizno's, Steak'n Shake, Uno Pizzaria, **lodging:** Staybridge Suites, **other:** Best Buy, NTB, Wal-Mart/auto, World Mkt
13	Cemetery Rd, Fishinger Rd, [E]...**gas:** Shell/Subway, Speedway, **food:** Burger King, CheeseBurger Paradise, Chili's, Chiotle Mexican, Damon's, Dave&Buster's, Donato's Pizza, KFC, Panera Bread, Quizno's, Skyline Chili, Spaghetti's, TGIFriday, Tropical Bistro, **lodging:** Comfort Suites, Homewood Suites, **other:** CVS Drug, Home Depot, Lowe's Whse, Radio Shack, Saturn, Staples, Target, Tire Dicounters, [W]...**gas:** BP, Mobil, Speedway, Sunoco, **food:** Bob Evans, Max&Erma's, McDonald's, Tim Horton, Wendy's, **lodging:** Hampton Inn, Motel 6, **other:** Nissan
10	Roberts Rd, [E]...**gas:** Marathon, Thornton's/dsl, **food:** Subway, Tim Horton, Wendy's, [W]...**gas:** Speedway, **food:** Waffle House, **lodging:** Courtyard, Quality Inn, Royal Inn, **other:** Kroger/gas

OHIO

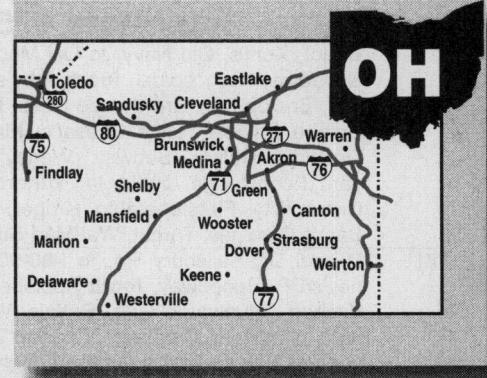

Interstate 270

E ↕ W

8	I-70, E to Columbus, W to Indianapolis
7	US 40, Broad St, E...**gas:** BP, Speedway, **food:** Bob Evans, Boston Mkt, Burger King, McDonald's, Popeye's, TeeJay's, Wendy's, White Castle, **other:** Buick/Pontiac/GMC, Chevrolet, Chrysler/Jeep, Circuit City, Family$, Firestone/auto, Kohl's, NTB, Pepboys, Sears/auto, Staples, Suzuki, Target, Tuffy, W...**gas:** GetGo, Speedway/dsl, Thornton's, **food:** A&W/LJ Silver, Arby's, Big Boy, KFC, Papa John's, Waffle House, **lodging:** Holiday Inn Express, Hometown Inn, **other:** HOSPITAL, CVS Drug, Giant Eagle Foods, Goodyear, Home Depot, Jo-Ann Fabrics
5	Georgesville, E...**gas:** Marathon, Mobil, Sunoco/dsl, **other:** Wal-Mart SuperCtr, W...**food:** Applebee's, Arby's, Bob Evans, Buffalo Wild Wings, Chipotle Mexican, DQ, Fazoli's, Fiesta Mariachi, KFC/LJ Silver, LoneStar Steaks, McDonald's, O'Charley's, Red Lobster, Steak'n Shake, Subway, Wendy's, White Castle, **other:** Advance Parts, GNC, Hyundai/Isuzu/Subaru, KIA, Kroger/gas, Lowe's Whse, NTB, Toyota/Scion, VW
2	US 62, OH 3, Grove City, N...**gas:** BP, S...**gas:** Shell, Speedway, Sunoco, **food:** Big Boy, Brewster's, Burger King, Domino's, Donato's Pizza, McDonald's, Quizno's, Subway, Tim Horton/Wendy's, Waffle House, **lodging:** Knight's Inn
0mm	I-71

Interstate 271(Cleveland)

N ↕ S

Exit #	Services
39mm	I-271 begins/ends on I-90, exit 188
38mm	I-271/I-480, Express Lanes
36	Wilson Mills Rd, Highland Hts, Mayfield, E...**lodging:** Holiday Inn, W...**gas:** BP, Marathon/dsl, **food:** Denny's, Wellington's Rest., **other:** Home Depot, Kohl's, Tuesday Morning
34	US 322, Mayfield Rd, E...**gas:** BP, **food:** TGI Friday, **other:** NTB, Walgreen, W...**gas:** Shell, Speedway, **food:** Bob Evans, Buca Italian, Burger King, Caribou Coffee, Fat Burger, McDonald's, Panini's Grill, Starbucks, **lodging:** Baymont Inn, **other:** HOSPITAL, Best Buy, Costco, CVS Drug, Ford, Giant Eagle Foods, Lincoln/Mercury, Marshall's, Midas, Murray's Parts, Old Navy, Petsmart, World Mkt, Wal-Mart vet
32	Brainerd Rd, Cedar Rd, E...HOSPITAL
29	US 422 W, OH 87, Chagrin Blvd, Harvard Rd, E...**gas:** Marathon, Shell, Sunoco, **food:** Bahama Breeze, Bob Evan's, Corky&Lenny's Rest., McDonald's, Pizza Hut, Uno Café, Wendy's, **lodging:** Extended Stay America, Hampton Inn, Homestead Suites, Super 8, **other:** Saturn, TJ Maxx, Wild Oats Mkt, W...**gas:** BP/Subway, Shell, **food:** PF Chang's, Your's Truly, **lodging:** Clarion, Embassy Suites, Hilton, **other:** Cadillac, Chrysler/Jeep, NTB
28b	Harvard Rd, E...**food:** Red Robin, W...**food:** Abuelo's, Chipotle Mexican, DiBella's Subs, River City Grille, Robek's Cafe, **lodging:** Marriott, **other:** HOSPITAL
28a	OH 175, Richmond Rd, Emery Rd, E...**gas:** BP, GetGo, Marathon/Circle K/Subway, **food:** Baskin Robbins/Dunkin Donuts, Marianne's Bakery, McDonald's, Quizno's, W...**food:** BJ's Whse
27b	I-480 W
26	Rockside Rd, E...**gas:** Sunoco, **food:** City Diner, **lodging:** Red Roof Inn, **other:** Lowe's Whse
23	OH 14 W, Forbes Rd, Broadway Ave, E...**gas:** Sunoco, **food:** Double Dragon Chinese, McDonald's,Subway, Wendy's, **lodging:** Holiday Inn Express, **other:** Sam's Club/gas, W...**gas:** BP, Marathon/Circle K, **other:** HOSPITAL
21	I-480 E, OH 14 E(from sb), to Youngstown
19	OH 82, Macedonia, E...**gas:** Speedway, **food:** Papa John's, W...**gas:** Sunoco, **food:** Applebee's, Arby's, Caribou Coffee, Chili's, Chipotle Mexican, Golden Corral, KFC, Outback Steaks, Panera Bread, Pizza Hut, Qdoba, Steak'n Shake, Taco Bell, Wendy's, **other:** Best Buy, CVS Drug, $Tree, Giant Eagle Foods, GNC, Home Depot, Kohl's, Lowes Whse, NTB, PetCo, Radio Shack, Target, Walgreens, Wal-Mart/auto
18	OH 8, Boston Hts, to Akron, E...**gas:** BP/Subway/dsl, Speedway, **food:** Bob Evans, Denny's, **lodging:** Country Inn&Suites, Days Inn, Knight's Inn, La Quinta, Motel 6, W...same as 19
12	OH 303, Richfield, Peninsula
10	I-77, to I-80, OH Tpk(from nb), to Akron, Cleveland
9	I-77 S, OH 176(from nb), to Richfield
8mm	**rest area both lanes, full(handicapped)facilities, phone, picnic tables, litter barrels, petwalk**
3	OH 94, to I-71 N, Wadsworth, N Royalton, W...**gas:** Marathon
0mm	I-271 begins/ends on I-71, exit 220.

Macedonia

Interstate 275(Cincinnati)

See Kentucky Interstate 275

Interstate 475(Toledo)

N ↕ S

Toledo

Exit #	Services
20	I-75. I-475 begins/ends on I-75, exit 204.
19	Jackman Rd, Central Ave, S...**gas:** Shell, **other:** HOSPITAL
18b	Douglas Rd(from wb)
18a	OH 51 W, Monroe St
17	Secor Rd, N...**gas:** BP, Shell/dsl, **food:** Applebee's, Bob Evans, Boston Mkt, Burger King, China 1 Buffet, Famous Dave's BBQ, Hooters, KFC, Penn Sta. Subs, Red Lobster, Red Robin, Rudy's Hot Dogs, Tim Horton, **other:** Best Buy, Circuit City, Kroger, Murray's Parts, PharmX Drug, Walgreens, S...**gas:** BP, **food:** Big Boy, El Vaquero, McDonald's, Original Pancakes, Pizza Hut, Ponderosa, Popeye's, Taco Bell, Uncle John's Pancakes, **lodging:** Clarion Hotel, Comfort Inn, Red Roof Inn, **other:** Costco/gas, Home Depot, Radio Shack, Sears/auto, Steinmart, U of Toledo
16	Talmadge Rd(from wb, no return), N...**gas:** BP/dsl, Speedway, **food:** Arby's, Panera Bread, **other:** JC Penney, mall
15	Corey Rd(from eb, no return)
14	US 23 N, to Ann Arbor
13	US 20, OH 120, Central Ave, E...**gas:** Speedway, Sunoco, **food:** Big Boy, Bob Evans, Magic Wok, McDonald's, Rally's, Wendy's, **other:** BMW, Cadillac, Chrysler/Jeep, Ford, Honda, Kia, Mitsubishi, Nissan, Saturn, Subaru, Toyota/Scion, W...**gas:** BP, Shell, Speedway, **other:** Lowes Whse
8b a	OH 2, E...**gas:** BP/dsl, **food:** Don Pablo, Texas Roadhouse, **lodging:** Extended Stay America, Knight's Inn, Red Roof Inn, Residence Inn, **other:** HOSPITAL, Home

Interstate 475

N ↑ S

	Depot, Kohl's, Old Navy, to OH Med Coll, **W**...**gas:** BP, Speedway, Sunoco/dsl, **food:** Arby's, Big Boy, Bob Evans, Boston Mkt, Brewhouse Rest., Burger King, Chili's, Empire Chinese, Little Caesar's, Mancino's Pizza, McDonald's, Rally's, Subway, Wendy's, **lodging:** Courtyard, Econolodge, Quality Inn, **other:** Best Buy, Big Lots, Circuit City, Firestone/auto, Kroger, Petsmart, Rite Aid, Sam's Club/gas, Target, Wal-Mart SuperCtr
6	Dussel Dr, Salisbury Rd, to I-80-90/tpk, **E**...**gas:** Barney's/BP, Speedway, **food:** Applebee's, Arby's, Bankok Kitchen, Bluewater Grill, Buffalo Wild Wings, Burger King, Coldstone Creamery, Cracker Barrel, Gino's Pizza, Ground Round, Jimmy John's, Longhorn Steaks, Marie's Diner, Max&Erma's, McDonald's, Panera Bread, Wendy's, Subway, Yoko Japanese, **lodging:** Country Inn&Suites, Courtyard, Fairfield Inn, Homewood Suites, Residence Inn, Studio+, Super 8, **W**...**gas:** BP, **food:** Abuelo's, Bob Evans, Briarfield Café, Carraba's, Fox's Pizza, Ground Round, Mancino's Pizza, **lodging:** Baymont Inn, **other:** Churchill's Foods, vet
4	US 24, to Maumee, Napolean, **N**...**other:** HOSPITAL, Toledo Zoo
3mm	Maumee River
2	OH 25, to Bowling Green, Perrysburg, **N**...**gas:** BP/dsl, Circle K, Shell, **food:** Arby's, Buffalo Wild Wings, Beaner's Coffee, Café Marie, Charlie's Rest., El Vaquero, Gino's Pizza, Hungry Howie, Marco's Pizza, McDonald's, Papa John's, Subway, Wendy's, **other:** Bassett's Mkt Foods, Compounding, Goodyear/auto, Pontiac/GMC, Saab/VW, Toms Tire/repair, Volvo, Young's RV Ctr, **S**...**gas:** Speedway/dsl, **food:** Biaggi's, Bob Evans, Chicago Pizza, Johnny Rockets, Louie's Grill, Maggi's Rest., Max&Erma's, Starbucks, TeaTree Asian, Waffle House, **lodging:** Economy Inn, **other:** Books-a-Million, Tire Man, vet
0mm	I-475 begins/ends on I-75, exit 192.,

Interstate 480(Cleveland)

E ↑ W

Exit #	Services
42	I-80, PA Tpk, I-480 begins/ends, **S**...**gas:** BP, Marathon/Circle K, Shell, Sheetz/24hr, **food:** Applebee's, Arby's, Big Boy, Bob Evans, Burger King, CiCi's Pizza, Denny's, Eat'n Park, KFC, McDonald's, Perkins, Pizza Hut, Rockne's Cafe, Ruby Tuesday, Steak'n Shake, Subway, Taco Bell, Wendy's, **lodging:** Best Western, Econolodge, Fairfield Inn, Hampton Inn, Holiday Inn Express, Microtel, TownePlace Suites, Wingate Inn, **other:** Curves, $Tree, Giant Eagle Foods, Home Depot, Honda, Hyundai, Lowe's Whse, Nissan, Ntb, Staples, Target, Top's Foods, Walgreens, Wal-Mart
41	Frost Rd, Hudson-Aurora
37	OH 91, Solon, Twinsburg, **N**...**food:** Arby's, Pizza Hut, Taco Bell, **other:** Comfort Suites, **other:** Giant Eagle, **S**...**gas:** BP
36	OH 82, Aurora, Twinsburg, **N**...**gas:** BP/dsl, Get'n Go, **food:** Burger King, **lodging:** Super 8, **S**...**gas:** Marathon, Bob Evans, Cracker Barrel, Damon's, Donato's Pizza, McDonald's, Wendy's, **lodging:** Hilton Garden
26	I-271, to Erie, PA
25a b c	OH 8, OH 43, Northfield Rd, Bedford, **N**...**other:** Harley-Davidson, **S**...**food:** McDonald's, Rally's, White Castle
23	OH 14, Broadway Ave, **N**...**gas:** Gulf/dsl, **food:** Burger King, KFC
22	OH 17, Garanger, Maple Hts, Garfield Hts
21	Transportation Blvd, to E 98th St, **S**...**other:** Giant Eagle Foods, JoAnn Fabrics, Wal-Mart
20b a	I-77, Cleveland

Youngstown (vertical)

17	(eb only)OH 176, Cleveland, no services
16	OH 94, to OH 176 S, State Rd, **S**...**gas:** BP, Sunoco/dsl, **other:** Kia
15	US 42, Ridge Rd, **N**...**gas:** BP, **food:** Applebee's, McDonald's, Ponderosa, Starbucks, **other:** Chevrolet, Lowe's Whse, Marc's Foods, TJMaxx, Top's Foods, **S**...**gas:** Speedway, **food:** Arby's, Donato's, **other:** K-Mart, Best Buy
13	Teideman Rd, Brooklyn, **N**...**gas:** Marathon, **S**...**gas:** BP, Speedway, **food:** Carrabba's, Cracker Barrel, Don Pablo's, Max&Erma's, Panera Bread, Schlotsky's, Steak 'n Shake, TGI-Friday's, **lodging:** Extended Stay America, Hampton Inn
12	W 150th, W130th, Brookpark, **S**...**gas:** Marathon, Shell, **food:** Arby's, Big Boy, Bob Evans, Thursday's Grill, **lodging:** Day's Inn, Best Value, **other:** Acura, Dodge, Lexus, Tire Kingdom, Toyota
11	I-71, Cleveland, Columbus
10	S rd 237, Airport Blvd, (wb only)
9	OH 17, Brookpark Rd, **N**...**lodging:** Hilton Garden, **other:** HOSPITAL, **S**...**lodging:** Ramada Inn, airport
7	(wb only)Clague Rd, to WestLake, no services
6	OH 252, to N Olmsted, **N**...**gas:** BP, Shell, **food:** Applebee's, Bennigan's, Chick-fil-A, Chili's, Harry Buffalo, Lonestar Steaks, Macaroni Grill, Red Lobster, Red Robin, **lodging:** Candlewood Suites, Courtyard, Hampton Inn, Homestead Suites, Radisson, Studio+, **other:** Dillard's, Firestone, JC Penney, Michael's, Sears/auto, Wal-Mart, mall
3	Stearns Rd, **2 mi** **S**...**food:** Razzle's Cafe
2	OH 10, Lorain Rd, to OH Tpk, **N**...**gas:** BP, Marathon, Sheetz/24hr, Speedway/dsl, **food:** Gourme Rest., McDonald's, **lodging:** Motel 6, Super 8, **other:** U-Haul
2	OH 10, Lorain Rd, to OH Tpk, **N**...**gas:** BP, Marathon, Sheetz/24hr, Speedway/dsl, **food:** Gourme Rest., McDonald's, **lodging:** Motel 6, Super 8, **other:** U-Haul
0mm	OH 10, to Cleveland, I-480 begins/ends on exit 151, OH Tpk

Ohio Turnpike

Exit #	Services
241mm	Ohio/Pennsylvania state line
239mm	toll plaza, phone
237mm	**Mahoning Valley Travel Plaza eb, Glacier Hills Travel Plaza wb, Valero/dsl/24hr, McDonald's, gifts, phone**
235	I-680(from wb), to Youngstown
232	OH 7, to Boardman, Youngstown, **N**...**gas:** Sheetz/24hr(1mi), **food:** DQ, Smaldino's Family Rest., **lodging:** Budget Inn, Comfort Lodge, Day's Inn, Econolodge, Holiday Inn Express, North Lima Inn, Ramada Ltd, Super 8, **S**...**gas:** Penn Ohio Trksp/dsl/@, Pilot/dsl, Shell/dsl, **food:** Road House Steaks,, **lodging:** Davis Motel, Liberty Inn, **other:** truck repair
218	I-80 E, to Youngstown. OH Tpk runs with I-76 eb, I-80 wb., Niles, **S**... Best Western, Country Inn&Suites, Hampton Inn, Super 8
216	Lordstown(from wb), **N**...GM Plant
215	Lordstown(from eb), **N**...GM Plant
210mm	Mahoning River
209	OH 5, to Warren, **N**...**lodging:** Rodeway Inn, **S**...**lodging:** Econolodge, Holiday Inn Express
197mm	**Portage Service Plaza wb, Bradys Leap Service Plaza eb, Valero/dsl/24hr, FoodCourt, McDonald's, gifts, phone**
193	OH 44, to Ravenna
192mm	Cuyahoga River
187	OH 14 S, I-480, to Streetsboro, **S**...**gas:** Sheetz/24hr, **food:** Ruby Tuedey, **lodging:** Comfort Inn, Fairfield Inn, Hampton Inn, Palms Motel, TownePlace Suites, Wingate Inn, **other:** Defer Tire, Firestone/auto, Home Depot, mall, **1 mi** **S**...**gas:** BP, Clark, DM/24hr, Shell, **food:** Arby's, Big Boy, Bob Evans, Brown Derby Roadhouse, Burger King, Burger Central, DQ, Denny's, Domino's, Golden Flame Steaks, KFC, LJ Silver, McDonald's,

Ohio Turnpike

Mr Hero, New Peking Chinese, Perkins, Pizza Hut, Rally's, Subway, Taco Bell, **lodging:** Best Western, Holiday Inn Express, Microtel, Starlite Motel, Super 8, Wendy's, **other:** CVS Drug, $General, K-Mart, Save-A-Lot Foods, Staples, Wal-Mart, to Kent St U

180	OH 8, to I-90 E, **N**...**gas:** Marathon, **lodging:** Comfort Inn, Holiday Inn, **other:** Harley-Davidson, **S**...**gas:** BP/Subway/dsl, Starfire Express, **other:** to Cuyahoga Valley NRA
177mm	Cuyahoga River
173	OH 21, to I-77, **N**...**gas:** Pilot/Wendy's/dsl/scales, **food:** DQ, **lodging:** Hampton Inn, Holiday Inn Express, Howard Johnson, Super 8, **S**...**gas:** BP/repair, **food:** DQ, Memories Rest., Richfield Rest., Subway, **lodging:** Hampton Inn, Quality Inn, Super 8
170mm	**Towpath Service Plaza eb, Great Lakes Service Plaza wb, gas: Valero/dsl/24hr, food: Burger King, FoodCourt, Panera Bread, Pizza Hut, other: gifts, phone**
161	US 42, to I-71, Strongsville, **N** on US 42...**gas:** AP/dsl, **food:** Buffalo Wild Wings, Jennifer's Rest, Mad Cactus Mexican, **lodging:** Day's Inn, Kings Inn, La Siesta Motel, Metrick's Motel, Village Motel, **other:** Circle K, Home Depot, Lowes Whse, Wal-Mart, vet, **S** on US 42...**food:** Burger King, DQ, J-Bella Rest., KFC, La Volte Grill, Marco's Pizza, Olympia's Cafe, **lodging:** Elmhaven Motel, **other:** Dodge, NAPA, Staples
152	OH 10, to Oberlin, I-480, Cleveland, **N**...**gas:** BP, Marathon, Sheetz/24hr, Speedway/dsl, **food:** Gourme Rest., McDonald's, **lodging:** Motel 6, Super 8, **other:** U-Haul **S**...**other:** Moore's RV Ctr, drive-in theatre(seasonal)
151	I-480 E(from eb), to Cleveland, airport
146mm	Black River
145	OH 57, to Lorain, to I-90, Elyria, **N**...**gas:** BP/McDonald's/dsl, Speedway, **food:** Applebee's, Arby's, Bennigan's, Bob Evans, Buffalo Wild Wings, Burger King, Denny's, Eat'n Park, Fazoli's, Golden Corral, Jumbo Buffet, McDonald's, TGIFriday's, Pizza Hut, Qdoba Mexican, Red Lobster, Subway, Tokyo Steaks, Wendy's, **lodging:** Best Western, Comfort Inn, Country Inn&Suites, Econolodge, Holiday Inn, Red Roof Inn, **other:** Best Buy, Curves, Dillard's, $General, $Tree, Family$, Firestone/auto, Home Depot, Honda/Hyundai, JC Penney, Jo-Ann Fabrics, Lowe's Whse, Macy's, Marc's Foods, Michael's, Petsmart, Radio Shack, Sears/auto, Staples, Target, Wal-Mart/auto, mall, **S**...**gas:** Shell, Speedway **lodging:** Howard Johnson, Super 8
142	I-90(from eb, exits left), OH 2, to W Cleveland, no services
140	OH 58, Amherst, **N**...**gas:** Sunoco/Subway/dsl, **food** DQ, **lodging:** Days Inn, Motel 6, **other:** Chrysler, NAPA, Suzuki, repair, **S**...**other:** Ford
139mm	**Middle Ridge Service Plaza wb, Vermilion Service Plaza eb, Valero/dsl/24hr, Burger King, FoodCourt, Panera Bread, Popeye's, Starbucks, TCBY, gifts, phone, RV parking**
135	rd 51, Baumhart Rd, to Vermilion
132mm	Vermilion River
118	US 250, to Norwalk, Sandusky, **N**...**gas:** BP/Circle K/Dunkin Donuts, Marathon/dsl, **food:** 4Monks Italian, McDonald's, Subway, **lodging:** Comfort Inn, Day's Inn, Hampton Inn, Motel 6, Red Roof Inn, Super 8, **other:** RV Park, to Edison's Birthplace, **S**...**food:** Maw's Place, **lodging:** Colonial Inn, **other:** Chevrolet/Hyundai
110	OH 4
100mm	**Erie Islands Service Plaza wb, Commodore Perry Service Plaza eb, gas: Valero/dsl/24hr, food: Burger King, Cinnabon, Sbarro's, Starbucks, other: phone**
93mm	Sandusky River
91	OH 53, to Fremont, Port Clinton, **N**...**lodging:** Day's Inn/rest., **S**...**gas:** BP/Quizno's/dsl/24hr, **food:** Applebees, **lodging:** Comfort Inn(2mi), Delux Inn, Hampton Inn, Holiday Inn, **other:** HOSPITAL
81	OH 51, Elmore, Woodville, Gibsonburg
80.5mm	Portage River
77mm	**Blue Heron Service Plaza wb, Wyandot Service Plaza eb, Valero/dsl/24hr, Hardee's, Mancino's, phone**
71	I-280, OH 420, to Stony Ridge, Toledo, **N**...**gas:** Petro/Mobil/dsl/rest./scales/24hr/@, Flying J/dsl/rest./scales/24hr/LP/@, **food:** Pizza Hut, **lodging:** Budget Inn, Executive Inn, Howard Johnson, Super 8, **other:** Blue Beacon, **S**...**gas:** FuelMart/Subway/dsl/scales/@, Pilot/dsl/24hr/scales/@, TA/BP/Burger King/Taco Bell/dsl/scales/24hr/@, **food:** McDonald's, **other:** truckwash
64	I-75 N, to Toledo, Perrysburg
63mm	Maumee River
59	US 20, to I-475, Maumee, Toledo, **N**...**gas:** BP/dsl, Shell, Speedway/dsl, **food:** Arby's, Bob Evans, Cottage, McDonald's, Nick's Cafe, Pizza Hut, Steak'n Shake, Subway, Waffle House, **lodging:** Clarion, Motel 6, **other:** Advance Parts, Family$, Goodyear/auto, Jo-Ann Fabrics, K-Mart/Little Caesar's, Murray's Parts, NAPA, Radio Shack, Rite Aid, Savers, Sears/auto, Walgreens, to Toledo Stadium, **S**...**gas:** Speedway, **food:** Big Boy, Brandy's Diner, Chipotle Mexican, Fazoli's, Fricker's, Friendly's, Ralphie's Burgers, Red Lobster, Schlotsky's, Taco Bell, **lodging:** Comfort Inn, Day's Inn, Econolodge, Hampton Inn, Holiday Inn, Red Roof Inn, **other:** Chevrolet, Ford, Honda, Meijer, Toyota
52	OH 2, to Toledo, **S**...**lodging:** Days Inn, Quality Inn, **other:** RV/truck repair
49mm	**service plaza both lanes, Sunoco/dsl/24hr, gifts/ice cream**
39	OH 109, **S**...**gas:** Country Corral/Valero/Winchesters/dsl/24hr/@
34	OH 108, to Wauseon, **S**...**gas:** Shell/Subway/dsl/24hr/@, **lodging:** Arrowhead Motel, Best Western, Holiday Inn Express, Smith's Rest., Super 8, **other:** HOSPITAL, Woods Trucking/repair(1mi), 2 mi **S** on US 20A...**gas:** DM, Mobil, **food:** Burger King, McDonald's, Pizza Hut, Subway, Wendy's, **lodging:** Wauseon Motel, **other:** Wal-Mart/auto
25	OH 66, Burlington, 3 mi **S**...**other:** Sauder Village Museum
24.5mm	Tiffen River
21mm	**service plaza both lanes, info, Sunoco/dsl/24hr, Hardee's/chicken, travel trailer park**
13	OH 15, to Bryan, Montpelier, **S**...**gas:** Marathon/dsl, Pennzoil/dsl, **food:** Country Fair Rest., **lodging:** Econolodge, Holiday Inn Express, Rainbow Motel, Ramada Inn, **other:** Hutch's dsl Repair
11.5mm	St Joseph River
3mm	toll plaza, phone
2	OH 49, to US 20, **N**...**gas:** Mobil/Subway/dsl, **food:** Burger King, **other:** info
0mm	Ohio/Indiana state line

N ↕ **S**

Exit #	Services
236mm	Oklahoma/Kansas state line
231	US 177, Braman, E...gas: Conoco/Grab'n Dash Deli/dsl/motel
230	Braman Rd, no services
229mm	Chikaskia River
225mm	**Welcome Ctr sb, rest area nb, full(handicapped) facilities, phones, picnic tables, litter barrels, vending, petwalk, RV dump**
222	OK 11, to Blackwell, Medford, Alva, Newkirk, E...gas: Conoco/dsl/rest., Shell/dsl, food: Braum's, KFC/Taco Bell, Los Potros Mexican, McDonald's, Plains Man Rest., Subway, lodging: Best Value Inn, Best Western, Comfort Inn, other: HOSPITAL
218	Hubbard Rd, no services
216mm	weigh sta both lanes
214	US 60, to Tonkawa, Lamont, Ponca City, N OK Coll, W...gas: Cenex, lodging: New Western Inn/rest. other: Woodland RV Park
213mm	Salt Fork of Arkansas River
211	Fountain Rd, E...gas: Love's/Chester Fried/Subway/dsl/scales/24hr/RV Dump/@
209mm	parking area both lanes, litter barrels
203	OK 15, to Marland, Billings, E...gas: Conoco/DQ/dsl/scales/24hr
199mm	Red Rock Creek
195mm	parking area both lanes, litter barrels
194b a	US 412, US 64 W, E...Cimarron Tpk(eb), to Tulsa, W...to Enid, Phillips U
193	airport Rd (from nb, no return), no services
191mm	Black Bear Creek
186	US 64 E, to Fir St, Perry, E...gas: Mobil/Subway/dsl, food: Braum's, McDonald's, Pizza Hut, Sonic, Taco Mayo, lodging: Super 8, other: HOSPITAL, museum, W...gas: Exxon/dsl, lodging: Regency Inn
185	US 77, to Covington, Perry, E...lodging: American Inn, W...gas: Conoco/dsl/motel/rest./24hr, other: RV camping
180	Orlando Rd, no services
174	OK 51, to Stillwater, Hennessee, E...gas: Phillips 66/dsl, lodging: Fairfield Inn(12mi), Holiday Inn(13mi), Motel 6(12mi), other: Lake Carl Blackwell RV Park
173mm	parking area sb, no services, litter barrels
171mm	parking area nb, no services, litter barrels
170	Mulhall Rd, no services
166mm	Cimarron River
157	OK 33, to Cushing, Guthrie, W...gas: Love's/Subway/dsl, Shell/dsl, Valero, food: Arby's, Braum's, DQ, El Rodeo Mexican, KFC(2mi), Johnny's Rib-Shack, Mazzio's, McDonald's(3mi), Pizza Hut, lodging: Best Western, Interstate Motel, Sleep Inn, Townhouse Motel(2mi), other: HOSPITAL, OK Terr Museum, Langston U, RV camping
153	US 77 N(exits left from nb), Guthrie, W...food: McDonald's, other: Chrysler/Dodge/Jeep, Ford/Mercury, Pontiac/Buick
151	Seward Rd, E...gas: Shell/cafe/dsl, other: Lazy E Arena(4mi), Pioneer RV park
149mm	weigh sta both lanes
146	Waterloo Rd, E...gas: Shell/dsl, food: Steak&Catfish Diner
143	Covell Rd, no services

(side labels: Blackwell, Guthrie)

Exit #	Services
142	Danforth Rd(from nb), no services
141	US 77 S, OK 66E, to 2nd St, Edmond, Tulsa, W...gas: Conoco, Phillips 66/dsl, food: Coyote Café, Denny's, Fazoli's, IHOP, KFC/Taco Bell, McDonald's, Steak & Shake, Western Sizzlin, lodging: Best Western, Fairfield Inn, Hampton Inn, Holiday Inn Express, Stafford Inn, other: HOSPITAL
140	SE 15th St, Spring Creek, Arcadia Lake, Edmond Park, W...gas: Phillips 66/Circle K/Subway, food: Braum's, other: Wal-Mart SuperCtr/24hr
139	SE 33rd St, W...lodging: Sleep Inn
138d	Memorial Rd, E...gas: Shell/dsl, W...other: Enterprise Square USA
138c	Sooner Rd(from sb), no services
138b	Kilpatrick Tpk
138a	I-44 Tpk E to Tulsa
I-35 S and I-44 W run together 8 mi.	
137	NE 122nd St, to OK City, E...gas: Shell/dsl, Valero/dsl, food: Charly's Rest., IHOP, lodging: Sleep Inn, Travelodge, W...gas: Flying J/Conoco/CountryMkt/dsl/LP/24hr/@, Love's/Subway/Godfathers Pizza/dsl/24hr/@, food: Cracker Barrel, McDonald's, Sonic, Waffle House, lodging: Comfort Inn, Day's Inn, Economy Inn, Motel 6, Quality Inn, Super 8, other: Abe's RV Park, Frontier City Funpark, Oklahoma Visitors Ctr/info/restrooms
136	Hefner Rd, W...gas: Conoco/dsl, same as 137
135	Britton Rd, no services
134	Wilshire Blvd, W...lodging: Executive Inn, other: Blue Beacon
I-35 N and I-44 E run together 8 mi	
133	I-44 W, to Amarillo, W...st capitol, Cowboy Hall of Fame
132b	NE 63rd St(from nb), 1/2 mi E...gas: Conoco/dsl, food: Braum's, lodging: Remington Inn
132a	NE 50th St, Remington Pk, W...other: funpark, info, museum, zoo
131	NE 36th St, W...gas: Phillips 66/dsl/24hr, other: 45th Inf Division Museum
130	US 62 E, NE 23rd St, E...gas/dsl, W...to st capitol
129	NE 10th St, E...gas: Conoco/McDonald's/dsl, W...food: Tom's BBQ
128	I-40 E, to Ft Smith
127	Eastern Ave, OK City, W...gas: Petro/dsl/rest./Blue Beacon/24hr/@, JR's Trvl Ctr/Wendy's/dsl/scales/24hr/@, Shamrock/dsl, food: Waffle House, lodging: Brick-Town Hotel, Best Western, Central Plaza Hotel, Econolodge, Quality Inn, other: Blue Beacon, Lewis RV Ctr
126a	I-40, W to Amarillo, I-235 N, to st capitol
126b	I-35 S to Dallas
125d	SE 15th St, E...gas: Conoco/dsl, food: Kittle's Kitchen, lodging: Green Carpet Inn
125b	SE 22nd St(from nb), no services
125a	SE 25th, E...food: Denny's, McDonald's, Sonic, Taco Bell, Waffle House, lodging: Day's Inn, Guesthouse Suites, Plaza Inn, Royal Inn, Super 8, W...gas: Phillips 66
124b	SE 29th St, E...food: China Queen, Denny's, McDonald's, Sonic, Taco Bell, lodging: Days Inn, Plaza Inn, Royal Inn, Super 8, W...gas: Phillips 66, food: Mama Lou's Rest., same as 125a

(side labels: Oklahoma City)

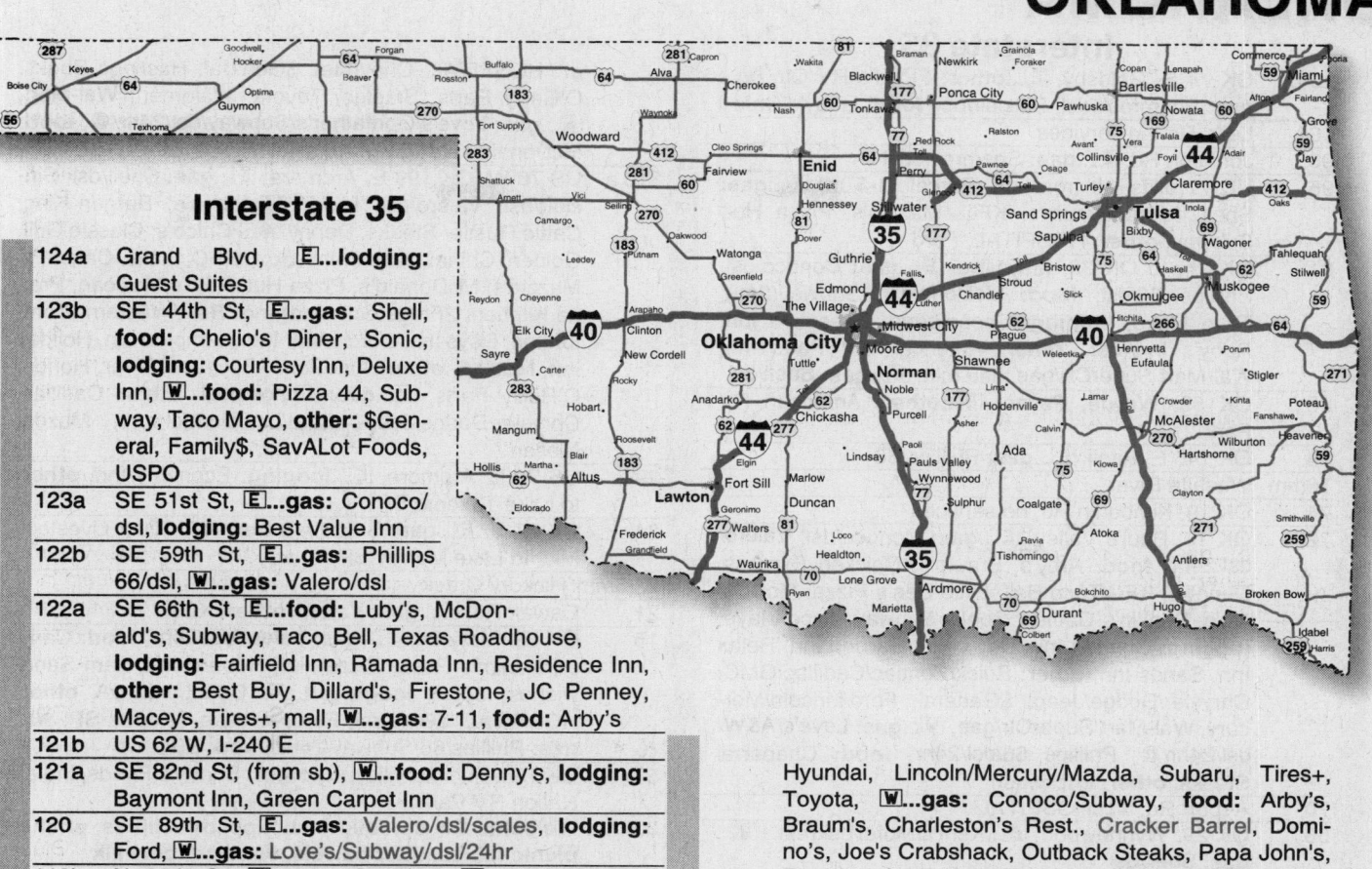

Interstate 35

124a	Grand Blvd, E...**lodging:** Guest Suites
123b	SE 44th St, E...**gas:** Shell, **food:** Chelio's Diner, Sonic, **lodging:** Courtesy Inn, Deluxe Inn, W...**food:** Pizza 44, Subway, Taco Mayo, **other:** $General, Family$, SavALot Foods, USPO
123a	SE 51st St, E...**gas:** Conoco/dsl, **lodging:** Best Value Inn
122b	SE 59th St, E...**gas:** Phillips 66/dsl, W...**gas:** Valero/dsl
122a	SE 66th St, E...**food:** Luby's, McDonald's, Subway, Taco Bell, Texas Roadhouse, **lodging:** Fairfield Inn, Ramada Inn, Residence Inn, **other:** Best Buy, Dillard's, Firestone, JC Penney, Maceys, Tires+, mall, W...**gas:** 7-11, **food:** Arby's
121b	US 62 W, I-240 E
121a	SE 82nd St, (from sb), W...**food:** Denny's, **lodging:** Baymont Inn, Green Carpet Inn
120	SE 89th St, E...**gas:** Valero/dsl/scales, **lodging:** Ford, W...**gas:** Love's/Subway/dsl/24hr
119b	N 27th St, E...**gas:** Shell/dsl, W...**food:** Pickles Rest., **other:** Harley-Davidson, Walker RV Ctr
119a	Shields Blvd(exits left from nb), no services
118	N 12th St, E...**gas:** Sinclair, **food:** Mazzio's, Peking Super Buffet, Sonic, **lodging:** Super 8, W...**gas:** Phillips 66/dsl, 7-11, Shell, **food:** A&W/LJ Silver, Arby's, Braum's, DQ, Grandy's, KFC, Las Fajitas, Mamma Lou's, Mazzio's, McDonald's, Papa John's, Subway, Swadneys Steaks, Taco Bell, Wendy's, Western Sizzlin, **lodging:** Best Western, Candlewood Suites, Comfort Inn, Day's Inn, Motel 6, **other:** Ace Hardware, AutoZone, Family$
117	OK 37, S 4th St, W...**gas:** Valero, **food:** China Wok, Van BBQ
116	S 19th St, E...**gas:** Conoco, Shell, **food:** Braum's, Capt D's, Carl's Jr, DQ, McDonald's, Popeye's, Sara's Rest., Taco Bell, Waffle House, **lodging:** Microtel, **other:** Firestone/auto, Goodyear/auto, Ross, W...**food:** Alfredo's Mexican, Applebees, Buffalo Wild Wings, Burger King, Earl's Ribs, Gordman's, IHOP, McCallister's Deli, Quizno's, Sonic, Subway, **lodging:** La Quinta, **other:** Aldi Foods, $Tree, Home Depot, Kohl's, Lowe's Whse, Radio Shack, Stover Candies, Tires+, Wal-Mart SuperCtr/gas/24hr
114	Indian Hill Rd, E...**food:** Bill's Fishhouse, Indian Hills Rest., **lodging:** Value Place Hotel, **other:** Guy RV Ctr
113	US 77 S(from sb, exits left), Norman
112	Tecumseh Rd, E...**other:** Nissan
110b a	Robinson St, E...**food:** Carl's Jr, Sonic, Taco Bell, **lodging:** Day's Inn, **other:** HOSPITAL, Albertson's/gas, Chrysler/Jeep, Ford, GMC/Pontiac, Honda,

Hyundai, Lincoln/Mercury/Mazda, Subaru, Tires+, Toyota, W...**gas:** Conoco/Subway, **food:** Arby's, Braum's, Charleston's Rest., Cracker Barrel, Domino's, Joe's Crabshack, Outback Steaks, Papa John's, Pizza Hut, Rib Crib, Taste of China, Waffle House, **lodging:** Holiday Inn, **other:** Kia/Isuzu

109	Main St, E...**gas:** Phillips 66, Shell, **food:** Arby's, Braum's, CiCi's, Denny's, Golden Corral, Krispy Kreme, LJ Silver, Panera Bread, Prairie Kitchen, Subway, Taco Cabana, Waffle House, Wendy's, **lodging:** Days Inn, Econolodge, Guest Inn, Quality Inn, Ramada Inn, Super 8, Thunderbird Lodge, Travelodge, **other:** AutoZone, Best Buy, Cadillac, Chevrolet, Dodge/Jeep, Hastings Books, Lowe's Whse, Nissan, Subaru, Target, Tires+, Wal-Mart SuperCtr/gas/24hr, W...**gas:** Conoco/dsl, **food:** Applebee's, BJ's Brewhouse, Burger King, Don Pablo, Charleston's Rest. Chili's, Cracker Barrel, Joe's Crabshack, Marie Callender's, McDonald's, Olive Garden, On the Border, Outback Steaks, Piccadilly's, Red Lobster, Red River Steaks, Rio Cafe, Santa Fe Cattle Co., Village Inn Rest., **lodging:** Fairfield Inn, Hampton Inn, Hilton Garden, Holiday Inn, La Quinta, **other:** Barnes&Noble, Borders Books, Dillard's, IGA Foods, Kia, Michael's, Old Navy, Saab, Sears/auto, SteinMart, mall
108b a	OK 9 E, Norman, E...**gas:** Conoco, Shell, **food:** Arby's, Braum's, Del Rancho Steaks, **lodging:** Residence Inn, Sooner Legends Inn, **other:** to U of OK, W...**food:** Carino's Italian, IHOP, Jasons Deli, Othello's Italian, Red Robin, Souper Salad, **lodging:** Country Inn&Suites, La Quinta, **other:** Home Depot, Michaels, PetsMart, Ross
107mm	Canadian River
106	OK 9 W, to Chickasha, E...**other:** McClain's RV Ctr, W...**gas:** Love's/Subway/dsl/24hr, **food:** Sonic, **other:** casino

OKLAHOMA

N

S

Exit	Services
104	OK 74 S, Goldsby, E...other: Floyd's RV Ctr, W...gas: Shamrock/dsl, Sinclair/dsl, food: Libby's Cafe
101	Ladd Rd, no services
98	Johnson Rd, E...gas: Shamrock/dsl
95	US 77(exits left from sb), Purcell, 1-3 mi E...gas: Shell, food: Braum's, KFC, Mazzio's, Pizza Hut, Subway, other: HOSPITAL, Ford
91	OK 74, to OK 39, Maysville, E...gas: Conoco/dsl, Phillips 66/dsl, food: McDonald's, Subway(2mi), Taco Mayo, lodging: Econolodge, Executive Inn, Ruby's Inn/rest., other: American RV Park(1mi), Wal-Mart SuperCtr/gas, flea mkt, W...gas: Shell/dsl
86	OK 59, Wayne, Payne, E...other: American RV Park
79	OK 145 E, Paoli, E...gas: Phillips 66
76mm	Washita River
74	OK 19, Kimberlin Rd, no services
72	OK 19, Paul's Valley, E...gas: Conoco/dsl, Valero/dsl/24hr, food: Arby's, Braum's, Chicken Express, Denny's, KFC/Taco Bell, Little Ben's Pizza, McDonald's, Punkin's Catfish, Sonic, Subway, Taco Mayo, lodging: Comfort Inn, Day's Inn, Garden Inn, Relax Inn, Sands Inn, other: Buick/Pontiac/Cadillac/GMC, Chrysler/Dodge/Jeep, $General, Ford/Lincoln/Mercury, Wal-Mart SuperCtr/gas, W...gas: Love's/A&W/dsl/24hr/@, Phillips 66/dsl/24hr, food: Chaparral Steaks, other: truckwash
70	Airport Rd, E...HOSPITAL
66	OK 29, Wynnewood, E...Kent's/Motel/dsl/rest., W...gas: Shell/dsl
64	OK 17A E, to Wynnewood, E...GW Exotic Animal Park
60	Ruppe Rd, no services
59mm	rest area both lanes, full(handicapped) facilities, phone, picnic table, litter barrels, petwalk, RV dump
55	OK 7, Davis, E...gas: Conoco, Phillips 66/A&W/dsl/24hr/@, other: Microtel, other: casino, to Chickasaw NRA, W...other: Oak Hill RV Park/gas/deli, to Arbuckle Ski Area
54.5mm	Honey Creek Pass
53mm	weigh sta both lanes
51	US 77, Turner Falls, E...lodging: Arbuckle Mtn Motel, Mtnview Inn(3mi), other: RV camping, W...gas: Sinclair/grill, lodging: Canyon Breeze Motel/RV Park, other: to Arbuckle Wilderness, Botanic Gardens
49mm	scenic turnout both lanes
47	US 77, Turner Falls Area, no services
46mm	scenic turnout both lanes
42	OK 53 W, Springer, Comanche, W...gas: Exxon/dsl
40	OK 53 E, Gene Autry, E...gas: Shell/dsl/café/24hr, food: Broaster Rest, other: Gene Autry Museum(8mi)
33	OK 142, Ardmore, E...gas: Phillips 66/dsl/24hr, food: IHOP, Ponder's Rest., Ryan's, lodging: Guest Inn, La Quinta, Marriott, Regency Inn, Super 8, W...gas: Flying J/Conoco/Country Mkt/dsl/scales/@
32	12th St, Ardmore, E...gas: Valero, other: Lowe's Whse, 1 mi E...gas: Conoco, food: Arby's, Braum's, Burger King, Carl's Jr, Fried Pies, Grandy's, KFC, LJ Silver, Pizza Hut, Taco Bell, Taco Bueno, oth-

Ardmore

Exit	Services
	er: HOSPITAL, Chevrolet, $General, Hastings Books, O'Reilly Parts, Staples, Toyota, Walgreen, Wal-Mart, W...gas: Love's/Godfather's/Subway/dsl/24hr/@, food: McDonald's, lodging: Microtel
31b a	US 70 W, OK 199 E, Ardmore, E...gas: Shell/dsl, Sinclair/dsl, Valero/dsl, food: Applebee's, Burger King, Cattle Rustler Steaks, Denny's, El Chico's, Classic Grill, Golden China, Jack-in-the-Box, KFC, Little Caesar's, Mazzio's, McDonald's, Pizza Hut, Polo's Mexican, Prairie Kitchen, 2Frogs Grill, lodging: Best Western, Comfort Inn, Days Inn, Dorchester Inn, Hampton Inn, Holiday Inn, Motel 6, other: AutoZone, Buy4Less/24hr, Honda, O'Reilly Parts, W...gas: Conoco/dsl, other: Cadillac, Chrysler/Dodge/Jeep, Ford/Lincoln/Mercury, Mazda, Nissan
29	US 70 E, Ardmore, E...lodging: Economy Inn, other: to Lake Texoma SP
24	OK 77 S, E...gas: Sinclair, other: Red River Livestock Mkt, to Lake Murray SP
22.5mm	Hickory Creek
21	Oswalt Rd, W...gas: Valero, other: KOA
15	OK 32, Marietta, E...gas: Valero/dsl/24hr, food: Carl's Jr, Denim's Rest., Pizza Hut, Robertson's Ham Sandwiches, Sonic, lodging: Lake Country Motel, other: HOSPITAL, $General, Ford, to Lake Texoma SP, W...gas: Phillips 66/Subway/24hr, food: BBQ
5	OK 153, Thackerville, W...other: Shorty's Foods, Indian Nation RV Park
3.5mm	Welcome Ctr nb, full(handicapped)facilities, phone, picnic tables, litter barrels, vending, petwalk
1	US 77 N, E...gas: Phillips 66/dsl, lodging: Mictotel, other: Winstar Casino, W...other: Red River RV Resort(3mi)
0mm	Oklahoma/Texas state line, Red River

Interstate 40

E

W

Exit #	Services
331mm	Oklahoma/Arkansas state line
330	OK 64D S(from eb), Ft Smith, no services
325	US 64, Roland, Ft Smith, N...gas: Cherokee Trkstp/Valero/Subway/dsl/scales/24hr, food: Four Star Diner, lodging: Cherokee Inn, Travelodge, other: casino, S...gas: Pilot/Wendy's/dsl/scales/24hr, Shell/dsl/scales, Valero/dsl, food: Arby's, El Celaya Mexican, McDonald's, Mazzio's, Sonic, Subway, lodging: Interstate Inn, other: $General, Marvin's Foods
321	OK 64b N, Muldrow, N...food: Sonic(1mi), S...gas: Shell/dsl, food: Arena Rest, lodging: Best Value, other: auto/dsl repair
316mm	rest area eb, full(handicapped)facilities, info, phone, picnic tables, litter barrels, vending, petwalk, RV dump
313mm	rest area wb, full(handicapped)facilities, info, phone, picnic tables, litter barrels, vending, petwalk, RV dump
311	US 64, Sallisaw, N...gas: Cox's/dsl, ED's Trkstp/Phillips 66/diner/dsl, food: Hardee's, KFC/Taco Bell, Pizza Hut, Sonic, Taco Mayo, lodging: Motel 6, Sallisaw Inn, other: HOSPITAL, AutoZone, $General, Fred's Store, 1 mi N...food: Lessley's Café, other: to Sallisaw RA, Brushy Lake SP(10mi), Sequoyah's Home(12mi)

OKLAHOMA

Interstate 40

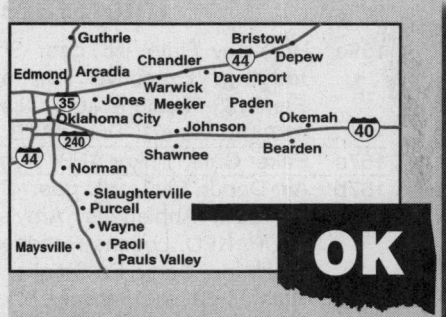

E **S a l l i s a w** **↕** **W**

308	US 59, Sallisaw, ...**gas:** Phillips 66/dsl, **food:** A&W/LJ Silver, Arby's, Braum's, China Panda, KFC, Mazzio's, McDonald's, Subway, Taco Pronto, Western Sizzlin, **lodging:** Best Western, Days Inn, Golden Spur Motel, Super 8, Microtel, **other:** HOSPITAL, $General, Wal-Mart SuperCtr/gas/24hr, casino, to Blue Ribbon Downs, ...**gas:** Shell/dsl, **food:** Ole South Pancakes, **other:** Chevrolet/Buick, Chrysler/Dodge/Jeep, Ford, KOA, to Kerr Lake, truck/tire repair
303	Dwight Mission Rd, **3 mi** ...**other:** Blue Ribbon Downs
297	OK 82 N, Vian, ...**gas:** FL/dsl, **food:** Subway, **lodging:** Siesta Motel, **other:** to Tenkiller Lake RA, USPO, ...**other:** Sequoia NWR
291	OK 10 N, to Gore, ...**other:** Greenleaf SP(10mi), Tenkiller SP(21mi)
290mm	Arkansas River
287	OK 100 N, to Webbers Falls, ...**gas:** Love's/Subway/dsl/24hr, **food:** Charlie's Chicken, Godfather's Pizza, **lodging:** Sleepy Traveler Motel, **other:** parts/tires/repair
286	Muskogee Tpk, to Muskogee, no services
284	Ross Rd, no services
283mm	parking area both lanes, litter barrels
278	US 266, OK 2, Warner, ...**gas:** Phillips 66/dsl, **food:** Subway, **lodging:** Sleepy Traveler Motel, **other:** Auburn RV Park
270	Texanna Rd, to Porum Landing, ...**gas:** Sinclair
265	US 69 bus, Checotah, ...**food:** Pizza Hut, Sonic, ...**gas:** R&D/dsl, Shell/dsl **lodging:** Budget Inn, **other:** Chevrolet/Chrysler/Dodge/Jeep
264b a	US 69, to Eufaula, **1 mi** ...**gas:** Flying J/Conoco/Country Mkt/dsl/LP/24hr/@, Phillips 66/dsl/24hr, **food:** Charlie's Chicken, Simon's Pizza, **lodging:** Best Value Inn, **other:** $General, O'Reilly Parts, Wal-Mart/McDonald's, auto repair
262	to US 266, Lotawatah Rd, ...**gas:** Sinclair
261mm	Lake Eufaula
259	OK 150, to Fountainhead Rd, ...**gas:** Shell/café, **food:** BBQ, **lodging:** Lake Eufaula Inn, **other:** to Lake Eufaula SP
255	Pierce Rd, ...KOA
251mm	rest area both lanes, no services
247	Tiger Mtn Rd, ...**other:** Quilt Barn/antiques
240b a	US 62 E, US 75 N, Henryetta, ...**gas:** Love's/dsl, Phillips 66, Shell, Sinclair, **food:** Arby's, Braum's, KFC, Mazzio's, McDonald's, Sonic, Subway, Taco Mayo, Wilder's Grill, **lodging:** Colonial Motel, Economy Inn, Henryetta Inn/rest., LeBaron Motel, Relax Inn, **other:** Chevrolet, Chrysler/Jeep, Ford, O'Reilly Parts, Wal-Mart, tires, ...Indian Nation Tpk
237	US 62, US 75, Henryetta, ...**gas:** Shell/dsl/24hr, Short Stop, **food:** Pig Out Palace, **lodging:** Green Country Inn, Trail Motel, **other:** HOSPITAL, Henryetta RV Park(2mi), ...**food:** Hungry Traveler Rest., **lodging:** Super 8
231	US 75 S, to Weleetka, ...**gas:** Phillips 66/dsl/café, **food:** Cowpoke's Cafe
227	Clearview Rd, ...casino
221	US 62, OK 27, Okemah, ...**gas:** Conoco/dsl, Valero/Subway/dsl/24hr, **food:** Aspen Rest., Mazzio's,

S h a w n e e

	Sonic, **lodging:** Day's Inn, **other:** HOSPITAL, Chevrolet, Parts+, ...**gas:** Love's/Chester/dsl/24hr, Shell/dsl, **food:** Kellogg's Rest, **other:** truck repair
217	OK 48, to Bristow, Bearden, ...gas
216mm	N Canadian River
212	OK 56, to Cromwell, Wewoka, ...**food:** BBQ, ...**gas:** Shell/dsl/cafe, to Seminole Nation Museum
208mm	Gar Creek
202mm	Turkey Creek
200	US 377, OK 99, to Little, Prague, ...**gas:** Conoco/dsl/24hr, Love's/Subway/dsl/24hr, Sinclair, **food:** Robertson's Ham Sandwiches, Roundup Rest/RV Park, **lodging:** Best Western
197mm	**rest area both lanes, full(handicapped)facilities, phone, picnic tables, litter barrels, petwalk**
192	OK 9A, Earlsboro, ...**gas:** Shell/dsl, **food:** Biscuit Hill Rest.
189mm	N Canadian River
186	OK 18, to Shawnee, ...**gas:** Phillips 66, Sinclair, **food:** Denny's, **lodging:** American Inn, Best Value, Day's Inn, La Quinta, Motel 6, Super 8, ...**food:** Golden Corral, LJ Silver, Sonic, Van's BBQ, **lodging:** Colonial Inn, **other:** Chevrolet/Cadillac, Chrysler/Jeep, Curves, antique auto museum
185	185 OK 3E, Shawnee Mall Dr, to Shawnee, ...**food:** Chili's, Garcia's Mexican, Red Lobster, Santa Fe Steaks, Taco Bueno, Wendy's, **lodging:** Holiday Inn Express, **other:** Dillard's, $Tree, JC Penney, Old Navy, Radio Shack, Sears/auto, Wal-Mart/SuperCtr/24hr/gas, mall, ...**gas:** Phillips 66/Quizno's/dsl, **food:** Applebee's, Braum's, Charlie's Chicken, CiCi's, Cracker Barrel, Delta Café, Garfield's Rest., IHOP, Mazzio's, McDonald's, Schlotsky's(2mi), Sonic, Starbucks, Subway, Taco Bell, **lodging:** Hampton Inn, **other:** CVS Drug, Lowe's Whse, Staples
181	US 177, US 270, to Tecumseh, ...**lodging:** Budget Inn
180mm	N Canadian River
178	OK 102 S, Dale, ...**gas:** Firelake/dsl, **other:** casino
176	OK 102 N, McLoud Rd, ...**gas:** Love's/Subway/dsl/24hr, Sinclair, **food:** Curtis Watson Rest.
172	Newalla Rd, to Harrah, no services
169	Peebly Rd, no services
166	Choctaw Rd, to Woods, ...**gas:** Love's/Subway/dsl/24hr, **other:** KOA, ...**gas:** Phillips 66/dsl, **food:** Sonic, **other:** to Little River SP(11mi)
165	I-240 W(from wb), to Dallas
162	Anderson Rd, ...LP
159b	Douglas Blvd, ...**gas:** Conoco, Shell, **food:** Denny's, LJ Silver, McDonald's, Sonic, Subway, Taco Bell, **other:** Eastland Hills RV Park, ...**other:** Tinker AFB, HOSPITAL

H e n r y e t t a

E ↕ **W**

Okla City

159a Hruskocy Gate, **N**...**gas:** Shell, **food:** China Grill, **lodging:** Executive Inn, **other:** Chrysler/Dodge, Family$, Firestone/auto, Nissan, U-Haul, same as 157, **S**...Gate 7, Tinker AFB

157c Eaker Gate, Tinker AFB, same as 159

157b Air Depot Blvd, **N**...**gas:** Conoco/dsl, Shell/Circle K, **food:** Applebees, Arby's, Chili's, CiCi's pizza, IHOP, KFC, Logans Roadhouse, Old Chicago Grill, Pizza Inn, Santa Fe Steaks, Schlotsky's, Starbucks, Steak & Shake, Subway, Taco Mayo, **lodging:** Best Western, Super 8, **other:** Best Buy, Chevrolet, Cottman Transmissions, Firestone, JC Penney, Kohl's, Lowe's Whse, Marshall's, O'Reilly Parts, Target, U-Haul, Walgreen, **S**...Gate 1, Tinker AFB

157a SE 29th St, Midwest City, **N**...**gas:** Conoco/dsl, Shell, **lodging:** Planet Inn, **other:** O'Reilly Parts, **S**...**other:** Ford, Sam's Club/gas

156b a Sooner Rd, **N**...**gas:** Conoco/Circle K, **food:** Primo's Rest., Waffle House, **lodging:** Comfort Inn, Hampton Inn, Hawthorn Suites, Holiday Inn Express, La Quinta, Sheraton, Studio 6, **other:** Home Depot, Radio Shack, Wal-Mart SuperCtr/Subway, **S**...**lodging:** Motel 6, **other:** Chevrolet/Pontiac/GMC, Tires+, Toyota

155b SE 15th St, Del City, **N**...**gas:** Shell, **other:** Family$, **S**...**food:** Madison's Kitchen, **other:** Mitsubishi

155a Sunny Lane Rd, Del City, **N**...**gas:** Conoco/dsl, **other:** Hyundai, U-Haul, **S**...**gas:** Shell, **food:** Braum's, Pizza Hut, Sonic

154 Reno Ave, Scott St, **N**...**gas:** Sinclair, **lodging:** Value Place Motel, **S**...**gas:** Phillips 66/dsl, 7-11/gas

152 (153 from wb)I-35 N, to Wichita, no services

127 Eastern Ave(from eb), Okla City, **N**...**gas:** Petro/Mobil/dsl/scales/rest./@, JR's Trvl Crt/Corky's Grill/dsl/24hr, Shamrock, **food:** Waffle House, **lodging:** Econolodge, Quality Inn, **other:** Blue Beacon, Lewis RV Ctr

151b c I-35, S to Dallas, I-235 N, to downtown, st capitol

151a Lincoln Blvd, **N**...**gas:** Conoco/Subway/Circle K/dsl, **food:** Earl's Rib Palace, Falcon's Pizza, IHOP, Sonic, **lodging:** Renaissance Inn, **other:** Bass Pro Shop, Bricktown Stadium

150c Robinson Ave(from wb), OK City, **N**...**food:** Spaghetti Whse, Zio's Italian, **lodging:** Courtyard, Residence Inn, Westin Hotel, **other:** U-Haul, Ford

150b Harvey Ave(from eb), downtown, **N**...**lodging:** Courtyard, Renaissance Hotel, Sheraton, Westin Hotel

150a Walker Ave(from eb), **N**...**food:** La Luna Mexican, **other:** Ford/Lincoln/Mercury, **S**...transmissions

149b Classen Blvd(from wb), to downtown, same as 149a

149a Western Ave, Reno Ave, **N**...**gas:** Valero/Subway/dsl, **food:** China Queen, McDonald's, Sonic, Taco Bell, **S**...**gas:** Conoco, Shell, **food:** Sweis Greek Cafe

148c Virginia Ave(from wb), to downtown

148b Penn Ave(from eb), **N**...**gas:** Shamrock, **S**...**other:** Isuzu/Ryder Trucks

148a Agnew Ave, Villa Ave, **N**...**gas:** Phillips 66/dsl

147c May Ave, no services

147b a I-44, E to Tulsa, W to Lawton

146 Portland Ave(from eb, no return), **N**...**gas:** Conoco/Subway/dsl, **other:** water funpark

Okla City

145 Meridian Ave, OK City, **N**...**gas:** Conoco, Shell/dsl, **food:** Denny's, Louie's Grille, McDonald's, Jin wei Aisan, On the Border, Outback Steaks, Shiki, Shorty Small's Rest., Trapper's Rest., **lodging:** Best Western, Builtmore Hotel, Day's Inn, Extended Stay America, Howard Johnson, Motel 6, Red Roof Inn, Residence Inn, Rodeway Inn, Super 8, Travelers Inn, **other:** Chevrolet, **S**...**gas:** Phillips 66/dsl, Sinclair, **food:** Arby's, Bennigan's, Burger King, Charleston Rest., Chili's, Cracker Barrel, Golden Palace Chinese, IHOP, Kona Ranch Steaks, Mazzio's, Panera Bread, Quizno's, Rib Crib, Santa Fe Grill, Sonic, Taco Bueno, Waffle House, Wendy's, Western Sizzlin, Whataburger, Zio's Italian, **lodging:** AmeriSuites, Best Value Inn, Candlewood Suites, Clarion Hotel, Comfort Suites, Courtyard, Embassy Suites, Executive Inn, Governor Suites, Hampton Inn, Hilton Garden, Holiday Inn Express, La Quinta, Meridian Inn, Motel 6, Oak Tree Inn, Ramada Ltd, Regency Inn, Sleep Inn, Wingate Inn

144 MacArthur Blvd, **N**...**gas:** On-Cue, Shell/dsl, **food:** Applebee's, China 1, Coldstone Creamery, Fire Mtn Steaks, Golden Corral, KFC, McDonald's, Sonic, Starbucks, Taco Bueno, Taco Cabana, Texas Roadhouse, **other:** GNC, Office Depot, Petsmart, Radio Shack, Ross, Wal-Mart SuperCtr/24hr, **S**...**lodging:** Green Carpet Inn, Microtel, Super 10 Motel, Travelodge, **other:** Kenworth, Sam's Club/gas

143 Rockwell Ave, **N**...**gas:** Shell, **lodging:** Rodeway Inn, **other:** Home Depot, McClain's RV Ctr, Tires+, **S**...**lodging:** Sands Motel/RV Park/LP, **other:** Rockwell RV Park

142 Council Rd, **N**...**gas:** Shell, Sinclair, **food:** A-1 BBQ, Braum's, McDonald's, Subway, Taco Bell, Wendy's, **lodging:** Best Budget Inn, **other:** Goodyear, **S**...**gas:** TA/Country Pride/dsl/scales/24hr/@, **lodging:** Econolodge, **other:** Council Rd RV Park, IA-80 Truckwash

140 Morgan Rd, **N**...**gas:** Pilot/McDonald's/dsl/24hr/@, TA, Phillips 66/Popeye's/dsl/24hr/@, **other:** Blue Beacon, **S**...**gas:** Flying J/Conoco/cookery/dsl/LP/scales/24hr/@, Love's/Subway/Ricky's Cafe/dsl/scales/24hr/@, **food:** Sonic, **other:** Speedco

139 Kilpatrick Tpk

138 OK 4, to Yukon, Mustang, **N**...**food:** Catcher's Grill, **lodging:** Comfort Inn, Super 7, **other:** Chrysler/Dodge/Jeep, **S**...**gas:** Conoco/dsl, **food:** Burger King, Daylight Doughnuts, Hunan Express, Interurban Grill, KFC, McDonald's, Sonic, Subway, **lodging:** Best Western, **other:** CVS Drug, Homeland Foods, Kottman Transmissions

137 Cornwell Dr, Czech Hall Rd, **N**...Albertson's/Sav-On

136 OK 92, to Yukon, **N**...**gas:** Shell, **food:** A&W/LJ Silver, Braum's, Clint's Cafe, KFC, McDonald's, Primo's Italian, Subway, Taco Mayo, Waffle House, Wendy's, Yukon Buffet, **lodging:** Hampton Inn, **other:** AutoZone, Big Lots, Big O Tire, Chevrolet, $General, &Tree, Hancock Fabrics, Hastings Books, Radio Shack, Tuesday Morning, Wal-Mart SuperCtr/gas/24hr, **S**...**food:** Alfredo's, Carino's Italian, Chili's, Jimmy's Egg Café, Pizza Hut, Quizno's, Rib Crib, Santa Fe Steaks, Starbucks, Taco Bueno, **other:** HOSPITAL, Ford, Kohl's, Kwik Kar, Lowe's Whse, Staples

Interstate 40

132	Cimarron Rd, **N**...Statuary World, **S**...airport
130	Banner Rd, **N**...gas: Shell/dsl/rest.
129mm	weigh st both lanes
125	US 81, to El Reno, **N**...gas: Conoco, Love's/dsl, **food:** China King, Serapio's Mexican, Taco Mayo, **lodging:** Economy Express, Sands Motel, **other:** Chevrolet, Chrysler/Jeep/Dodge, $General, Ford/Lincoln/Mercury, Pontiac/GMC/Buick, **S**...truck repair
123	Country Club Rd, to El Reno, **N**...gas: Conoco, Shell, Valero, **food:** Arby's, Braum's, Carl's Jr, KFC, Little Caesar's, Mazzio's, McDonald's, Pizza Hut, Subway, Taco Bell, **other:** HOSPITAL, Radio Shack, Wal-Mart SuperCtr/dsl/24hr, **S**...gas: Phillips 66/dsl, **food:** Denny's, **lodging:** Best Western/RV Park, Comfort Inn, Day's Inn, Regency Motel
119	Lp 40, to El Reno
115	US 270, to Calumet
111mm	picnic area eb, picnic tables, litter barrels
108	US 281, to Geary, **N**...gas: Shell/Subway/dsl/24hr, **other:** KOA/Indian Trading Post, to Roman Nose SP, **S**...gas: Love's/Chesterfried/Godfather's Pizza/dsl/@
105mm	S Canadian River
104	Methodist Rd, no services
101	US 281, OK 8, to Hinton, **N**...to Roman Nose SP, **S**...gas: Henton Trkstp/Shell/Sonic/dsl, **lodging:** Microtel, **other:** Chevrolet, picnic area, to Red Rock Canyon SP
95	Bethel Rd, no services
94.5mm	picnic area wb, picnic tables, litter barrels
88	OK 58, to Hydro, Carnegie, no services
84	Airport Rd, **N**...gas: Phillips 66/dsl/scales/24hr, Shell/dsl, **food:** Lucille's Roadhouse, **lodging:** Holiday Inn Express, Travel Inn, **other:** HOSPITAL, Buick/Pontiac/GMC, Chevrolet/Cadillac, Chrysler/Dodge/Jeep
82	E Main St, Weatherford, **N**...gas: Conoco/dsl, Phillips 66, Shell/Subway/dsl, Sinclair, Valero, **food:** Alfredo's Mexican, Arby's, Braum's, Carl's Jr, Jerry's Rest., KFC/Taco Bell, Mark Rest., Mazzio's, McDonald's, Nita's, Pizza Hut, Sonic, Taco Mayo, T-Bone Steaks, **lodging:** Best Western, Comfort Inn, Scottish Inn, **other:** HOSPITAL, $General, GNC, O'Reilly Parts, Radio Shack, Walgreens, Wal-Mart, to SW OSU
80	(80a from eb) W Main St, **N**...gas: Shell/dsl, **lodging:** Economy Inn
71	Custer City Rd, **N**...gas: Love's/Subway/dsl/rest., **other:** Cherokee Trading Post
69	Lp 40(from wb), to Clinton, **2 mi N**...food: DQ, **lodging:** Travel Inn
67.5mm	Washita River
66	US 183, Clinton, **S**...gas: Shell/dsl, **other:** Ford/Lincoln/Mercury, Chrysler/Dodge/Jeep
65a	10th St, Neptune Dr, Clinton, **N**...food: Braum's, China King, Lupita's Mexican, Pizza Hut, **lodging:** Day's Inn, Relax Inn, Super 8, **other:** United Foods, Wink's Campground, **S**...gas: Phillips 66/dsl, **lodging:** Clinton Inn
65	Gary Blvd, Clinton, **N**...gas: Conoco, Shell/dsl, **food:** Del Rancho, DQ, Italian Villa, LJ Silver, Mazzio's, McDonald's, Pancake House, Subway, Taco Mayo, **lodging:** Hampton Inn, Ramada Inn, Tradewinds Inn, Travelodge, **other:** HOSPITAL, $General, K-Mart, Rte 66 Museum
62	Parkersburg Rd, **S**...Hargus RV Ctr
61	Haggard Rd, no services
57	Stafford Rd, no services
53	OK 44, Foss, **N**...to Foss RA, **S**...gas/dsl
50	Clinton Lake Rd, **N**...other: KOA/LP/dsl
47	Canute, **S**...gas: Shell, **lodging:** Sunset Inn
41	OK 34(exits left from eb), Elk City, **N**...gas: East Side/dsl, Love's/Subway/dsl, Shell, **food:** Home Cooking Rest., **lodging:** Ambassador Inn, Best Western, Economy Express, Motel 6, Red Carpet Inn, Travel Inn, Travelodge, Super 8, **other:** HOSPITAL, Elk Run RV Park, Rte 66 Museum
40	E 7th St, Elk City, **N**...food: Portobello Grill, same as 41
38	OK 6, Elk City, **N**...gas: Conoco/dsl, Phillips 66/dsl, **food:** Arby's, Denny's, LJ Silver, McDonald's, Quizno's, Starbucks, Western Sizzlin, **lodging:** Bedford Inn, Best Western(3mi), Day's Inn, **other:** Ace Hardware, Elk Creek RV Park, **S**...gas: Phillips 66/dsl, **lodging:** Comfort Inn, Econolodge, Holiday Inn, Ramada Inn, **other:** to Quartz Mtn SP
34	Merritt Rd, no services
32	OK 34 S(exits left from eb), Elk City, no services
26	Cemetery Rd, **S**...gas: TA/Taco Bell/Subway/dsl/scales/24hr/@
25	Lp 40, Sayre, **N**...gas: Shell/dsl, **lodging:** Western Motel(1mi), **other:** HOSPITAL, Ford
23	OK 152, Sayre, **S**...gas: Shell/dsl
22.5mm	N Fork Red River
20	US 283, Sayre, **N**...gas: Flying J/Conoco/CountryMkt/dsl/scales/24hr/@, **lodging:** AmericInn, **other:** to Washita Bfd Site(25mi)
14	Hext Rd, no services
13.5mm	check sta both lanes, litter barrels
11	Lp 40, to Erick,, Hext, no services
10mm	**Welcome Ctr/rest area both lanes, full (handicapped) facilities, phone, picnic tables, litter barrels, petwalk, RV dump**
7	OK 30, Erick, **N**...lodging: Comfort Inn, **S**...gas: Love's/Subway/dsl/scales, **food:** Simple Simon's Pizza, **lodging:** Days Inn
5	Lp 40, Honeyfarm Rd, no services
1	Texola, **S**...gas: gas/dsl/rest., **other:** RV camping
0mm	Oklahoma/Texas state line

E ↕ **W**

Miami

Exit #	Services
329mm	Oklahoma/Missouri state line
321mm	Spring River
314mm	**Oklahoma Welcome Ctr, service plaza wb, Phillips 66/dsl**
313	OK 10, Miami, **N**...**gas:** Citgo/dsl, Conoco, Love's/dsl/24hr, Phillips, **food:** Arby's, McDonald's, Stable's Rest, **lodging:** Best Western/rest., Microtel, Super 8, Townsman Motel/rest., **other:** HOSPITAL, Miami RV Park, to NE OK A&M Coll, vet, **S**...**other:** Chrysler/Plymouth/Dodge/Jeep, casino
312mm	Neosho River
302	US 59, US 69, Afton, **S**...**gas:** Conoco, **3 mi S**...**lodging:** Best Western, OK 66 Motel, **other:** Bears Den Resort Camping
299mm	**rest area eb, rest rooms, picnic table, litter barrel**
289	US 60, Vinita, **N**...**food:** Braum's, McDonald's, Pizza Hut, Simple Simon Pizza, Subway, **lodging:** Holiday Inn Express, **other:** HOSPITAL, Ace Hardware, Chevrolet, Cooper Tires, $General, Wal-Mart SuperCtr/24hr/gas, st patrol
288mm	**service plaza both lanes**, Phillips 66/dsl/24hr, **McDonald's, phone**
286mm	toll plaza
283	US 69, Big Cabin, **N**...**gas:** Shell/Big Cabin/dsl/rest./scales/24hr/@, **lodging:** Super 8, **S**...truck repair
271mm	picnic eb, picnic table, litter barrel
269	OK 28(from eb, no re-entry), to Adair, Chelsea
269mm	**rest area eb, rest rooms, picnic tables, litter barrel**
256mm	**rest area wb, rest rooms, picnic tables, litter barrel, phone**
255	OK 20, to Pryor, Claremore, **N**...**gas:** Kum&Go, **food:** Woody's Cafe, **lodging:** Best Western, Clairmore Inn, Super 8, Travel Inn, **other:** HOSPITAL, Wal-Mart SuperCtr/dsl/24hr, to Rogers U, Will Rogers Memorial, museum
248	to OK 266, Port of Catoosa, **N**...**lodging:** Days Inn
244mm	Kerr-McClellan Navigation System, no services
241mm	Will Rogers Tpk begins eb, ends wb, phones
241	OK 66 E, to Catoosa, no services
240b	US 412 E, Choteau, no services
240a	OK 167 N, 193rd E Ave, **N**...**food:** KFC, McDonald's, Pauline's Buffet, Pizza Hut, Taco Bueno, Taco Mayo, Waffle House, Wendy's, **other:** KOA, O'Reilly Parts, casino, **S**...**gas:** QT, Shell/dsl, **food:** Mazzio's, PortCity Diner, Sonic, Subway, **lodging:** Holiday Inn Express, **other:** Cooper Tires, $General, Family$, Homeland Foods, NAPA, tires/repair
238	161st E Ave, **N**...**gas:** Phillips 66/dsl/scales/rest./24hr, truckwash, **S**...**gas:** QT/dsl/scales/24hr, **food:** Arby's, Burger King, **lodging:** Microtel, **other:** I-44 Auto Auction, **OK Welcome Ctr**
236b	I-244 W, to downtown Tulsa, airport
236a	129th E Ave, **N**...**gas:** ⊘/Flying J/Conoco/dsl/LP/rest./24hr/@, **S**...**food:** McDonald's
235	E 11th St, Tulsa, **N**...**food:** Big Daddy's BBQ, Mazzio's, Rioberto's Mexican, Sonic, Subway, **lodging:** Executive Inn, Garnett Inn, Motel 6, Super 8, **other:** $General, Drug Whse, O'Reilly Parts, **S**...**gas:** QT, **food:** Braum's, Denny's, Taco Bueno, **lodging:** Econolodge, **other:** Whse Foods

Tulsa

Exit #	Services
234b a	US 169, N to Owasso, to airport, S to Broken Arrow
233	E 21st St(from wb), **S**...**food:** El Chico, **lodging:** Comfort Suites, **other:** K-Mart, Dean's RV Ctr
231	(232 from wb) US 64, OK 51, to Muskogee, E 31st St, Memorial Dr, **N**...**gas:** Phillips 66, **food:** CJ's Rest, Country Inn Rest., Whataburger, **lodging:** Best Value, Day's Inn, Delux Inn, Georgetown Plaza Motel, Ramada Inn, Regency Inn, Travelodge, **other:** Homeland Foods, **S**...**gas:** Shell/A&W, **food:** Cracker Barrel, IHOP, McDonald's, Pizza Hut, Village Inn Rest., **lodging:** Best Western, Comfort Inn, Courtyard, Econolodge, Embassy Suites, Extended Stay America, Fairfield Inn, Hampton Inn, Hawthorn Suites, Holiday Inn Express, Park Inn, Quality Inn, Sleep Inn, Studio+, Super 8, **other:** Cavender's Boots, Chevrolet, Chrysler, Nissan
230	E 41st St, Sheridan Rd, **N**...**gas:** Shell, **food:** Carl's Jr, Desi Wok, El Chico, On-the-Border, Panera Bread, Quizno's, Subway, TGIFriday, Whataburger/24hr, **other:** Barnes&Noble, Circuit City, Dillards, JC Penney, Jo-Ann Fabrics, Michael's, Old Navy, Petsmart, Robertson Tire, Ross, **S**...**lodging:** Heritage Inn, La Quinta, **other:** Best Buy, Home Depot
229	Yale Ave, Tulsa, **N**...**gas:** Shell, **food:** McDonald's, **other:** Firestone, Foley's, Mervyn's, Ross, mall, **S**...**gas:** Phillips 66/dsl, QT/24hr, **food:** Applebee's, Arby's, Braum's, Carrabba's, Carino's Italian, Delta Cafe, Denny's, Don Pablo, Outback Steaks, Red Lobster, Steak&Ale, Subway, Taco Bell, Taco Cabana, Village Inn Rest., **lodging:** Baymont Inn, Comfort Inn, Days Inn, Holiday Inn Select, Red Roof Inn, **other:** HOSPITAL, Celebration Sta, Kia, Mazda
228	Harvard Ave, Tulsa, **N**...**gas:** Shell/dsl, **food:** Johnnie's Charcoal Buffet, NYC Pizza, **lodging:** Best Western, Towers Hotel, Tradewinds Motel, **S**...**food:** Blimpie, Chili's, Chimi's Mexican, LoneStar Steaks, LJ Silver/A&W, Lanna Thai, Marie Callender's, McDonald's, Osaka Steaks, Panera Bread, Papa John's, Perry's Rest., Pizza Hut, Rick's Cafe, Sol's Grill, **lodging:** Holiday Inn Express, Howard Johnson, Ramada Inn, **other:** Albertson's, $Tree, Kelly Tire, K-Mart, SteinMart
227	Lewis Ave, Tulsa, **S**...**gas:** Phillips 66, Sinclair, **food:** Domino's, El Chico, Goldie's Patio Grill, SteakStuffers USA, **other:** Tires+, Walgreens
226b	Peoria Ave, Tulsa, **N**...**gas:** QT, **food:** Arby's, Burger St., China Wok, Church's, CiCi's, Mazzio's, KFC, Pizza Hut, Ron's Chili, Taco Bell, Waffle House, **lodging:** Super 8, **other:** Hancock Fabrics, Harley-Davidson, O'Reilly Parts, Radio Shack, Wal-Mart Mkt, **S**...**gas:** Shell, **food:** Braum's, Golden Palace, Kelly's Rest., **other:** AutoZone, $General, Mays Drug
226a	Riverside Dr(from wb), **S**...**lodging:** Victorian Inn
225mm	Arkansas River
225	Elwood Ave, **N**...**other:** Chevrolet, Ford
224b a	US 75, to Okmulgee, Bartlesville, **N**...**gas:** QT/dsl, **food:** Mazzio's, Subway, **other:** $General, Whse Mkt, **S**...**lodging:** Royal Inn, **other:** RV park
223c	33rd W Ave, Tulsa, **N**...**food:** Braum's, Domino's, **S**...**gas:** Citgo, **food:** Rib Crib BBQ
223b	51st St(from wb), no services
223a	I-244 E, to Tulsa, downtown
222c	(from wb), **S**...**lodging:** Value Inn
222b	55th Place, **N**...**lodging:** Capri Motel, Crystal Motel, **S**...**lodging:** Day's Inn, Economy Inn

OKLAHOMA

Interstate 44

222a	49th W Ave, Tulsa, **N**...**food:** Carl's Jr, Mama Lou's Rest., Monterey Café, **lodging:** Gateway Motel, Interstate Inn, Motel 6, **other:** BigLots, $General, May's Drug, Piggly Wiggly, Radio Shack, **S**...**gas:** QT/Wendy's/dsl/scales/24hr, **food:** Arby's, McDonald's, Village Inn Rest., Waffle House, **lodging:** Days Inn, Super 8, **other:** Buick/Pontiac/GMC, Peterbilt, Volvo Trucks
221a	57th W Ave, (from wb), **S**...**food:** Avalon Steaks, **other:** Buick/Pontiac/GMC
221mm	Turner Tkp begins wb, ends eb
218	Creek Tpk E(from eb), no services
215	OK 97, to Sand Sprgs, Sapulpa, **S**...**food:** Freddy's, Subway, **lodging:** Super 8, **other:** HOSPITAL
211	OK 33, to Kellyville, Drumright, Heyburn SP, **S**...**gas:** Shell/dsl
207mm	service plaza wb, **gas:** Phillips 66/dsl
204mm	picnic area eb, litter barrels, picnic tables
197mm	**service plaza eb**, **gas:** Phillips 66/dsl/24hr, **food:** McDonald's
196	OK 48, Bristow, **S**...**lodging:** Carolyn Inn, **other:** HOSPITAL, Wal-Mart SuperCtr
190mm	picnic area eb, litter barrels, picnic tables
182mm	toll plaza
179	OK 99, to Drumright, Stroud, **N**...**lodging:** Best Western/rest., **S**...**gas:** Phillips 66/Subway/dsl, **food:** Mazzio's, McDonald's, Sonic, Steak&Eggs Rest., Taco Mayo, **lodging:** Sooner Motel, **other:** HOSPITAL, auto/tire repair
178mm	**Hoback Plaza both lanes(exits left)**, **gas:** Phillips 66/dsl, **food:** McDonald's
171mm	picnic area eb, litter barrels, picnic tables
167mm	service plaza(from eb), **S**...**gas:** Phillips 66/dsl
166	OK 18, to Cushing, Chandler, **N**...**other:** Chrysler/Jeep/Dodge, **S**...**gas:** Phillips 66, **lodging:** Econolodge, Lincoln Motel, **other:** Chandler Tire
166mm	picnic area wb, phones, litter barrels, picnic tables
158	OK 66, to Wellston, **N**...**gas:** Kum&Go/Subway/dsl/24hr
157	service plaza(from wb), **N**...**gas:** Phillips 66/McDonald's/dsl, **other:** museum info
138d	to Memorial Rd, to Enterprise Square, no services
138a	I-35, I-44 E to Tulsa, Turner Tpk
I-44 and I-35 run together 8 mi. See Interstate 35, exits 134-137.	
130	I-35 S, to Dallas, services on I-35 S
129	MLK Ave, Remington Park, **N**...**food:** County Line BBQ, **lodging:** Garden Inn, **other:** Cowboy Museum, **S**...**food:** McDonald's, **other:** Family$
128b	Kelley Ave, OK City, **N**...**gas:** Conoco, Valero/Subway/dsl, **food:** Sonic
128a	Lincoln Blvd, st capitol, **S**...**lodging:** Oxford Inn, Whitten Inn
127	I-235 S, US 77, City Ctr, Broadway St, **1 exit N**...**gas:** Conoco, Phillips 66/dsl, Shell, **lodging:** Best Western, Holiday Inn
126	Western Ave, **N**...**food:** Camille's Cafe, Deep Fork Rest., Sonic, Flip's Rest.
125c	NW Expswy(exits left from sb)
125	Classen Blvd, (exits left from wb), OK City, **N**...**gas:** Shell, **food:** Cheesecake Factory, Chili's, Elephant Bar Rest., Moe's SW Grill, Olive Garden, **other:**

	Acura, Dillard's, JC Penney, Macy's, Old Navy, Radio Shack, Ross, Wal-Mart SuperCtr/24hr, **S**...**food:** IHOP, McDonald's, **lodging:** AmeriSuites, Courtyard, Hawthorn Suites
125a	OK 3A, Penn Ave, to NW Expswy, **N**...**gas:** Conoco/dsl/24hr, **S**...**gas:** Shell, **food:** Braum's, Coit's Cafe, **lodging:** Habana Inn, **other:** Homeland Foods,
124	N May, **N**...**gas:** Shell/Subway, **food:** San Marco's Mexican, **lodging:** Comfort Inn, Day's Inn, Super 8, **other:** Dodge, O'Reilly Parts, **S**...**other:** Aamco, Ford, Lowes Whse
123b	OK 66 W, NW 39th, to Warr Acres, **N**...**gas:** Valero/McDonald's/dsl, **food:** Asian Palace, Carl's Jr, Chinese Buffet, Jimmy's Egg, Los Mariachi's, Quizno's, **lodging:** Carlyle Motel, Hospitality Inn, **other:** $General
123a	NW 36th St, no services
122	NW 23rd St, **N**...**gas:** Conoco/7-11, **food:** Church's, EggRoll King, Taco Mayo, **other:** Tires+, **S**...**gas:** Conoco, **food:** Arby's, Sonic, **other:** Big O Tire, Family$
121b a	NW 10th St, **N**...**gas:** Shell, **S**...**gas:** 7-11/gas, Sinclair, **other:** $General, Family$, Whittaker's Foods/24hr, antiques, fairgrounds
120b a	I-40, W to Amarillo, E to Ft Smith
119	SW 15th St
118	OK 152 W, SW 29th St, OK City, **E**...**gas:** 7-11/gas, **food:** A&W/LJ Silver, Burger King, KFC/Taco Bell, La Fiesta Mexican, McDonald's, Sonic, Subway, Taco Bueno, **other:** Advance Parts, AutoZone, $General, $Tree, Grider's Foods/gas, O'Reilly Parts, Walgreen, **W**...**gas:** Shell, **other:** U-Haul, transmissions
117	SW 44th St, **W**...auto repair
116b	Airport Rd (exits left from nb), **W**...airport
116a	SW 59th St, **E**...**gas:** Conoco, **W**...Will Rogers Airport
115	I-240 E, US 62 E, to Ft Smith
114	SW 74th St, OK City, **E**...**gas:** TK, Valero, **food:** Braum's, Burger King, Perry's Rest., **lodging:** Cambridge Inn, Ramada Ltd, **other:** $General
113	SW 89th St, **E**...**gas:** Love's/Subway/dsl/24hr, OG, 7-11/gas, Valero/dsl, **food:** McDonald's, Sonic, Taco Mayo, **other:** HOSPITAL, CVS Drug
112	SW 104th St, **E**...**gas:** Valero, **W**...**gas:** Shell/rest./dsl
111	SW 119th St, **E**...**food:** Sonic, **other:** Walker RV Ctr
110	OK 37 E, to Moore, **E**...**gas:** Sinclair/dsl, **food:** Sonic
109	SW 149th St, **E**...**food:** JR's Grill
108mm	S Canadian River
108	OK 37 W, to Tuttle, **W**...**gas:** Conoco/Subway/dsl, Phillips 66, **food:** Braum's, Carlito's Mexican, Carl's Jr, Little Caesar's, Mazzio's, McDonald's, New China, Sonic, **other:** $General, O'Reilly Parts, Wal-Mart SuperCtr/24hr

OKLAHOMA
Interstate 44

107	US 62 S(no wb return), to Newcastle, **E**...casino/gas, **lodging:** Newcastle Motel, **other:** Newcastle RV, Walker RV
99	H E Bailey Spur, rd 4, to Blanchard, Norman
97mm	toll booth, phone
95.5mm	picnic area wb, picnic tables, litter barrels
85.5mm	**service plaza, both lanes exit left, Phillips 66/dsl, McDonald's**
83	US 62, Chickasha, **W**...**gas:** Jay's/dsl, Valero/dsl, **other:** Indian Museum
80	US 81, Chickasha, **E**...**gas:** Conoco/dsl, Phillips 66/dsl, Shell/dsl, **food:** Eduardo's Mexican, Western Sizzlin, **lodging:** Day's Inn, Holiday Inn Express, Royal American Inn, Super 8, **other:** HOSPITAL, Buick/Chevrolet/Pontiac/Cadillac, Chrysler/Plymouth/Dodge/Jeep, $Tree, Goody's, **W**...**gas:** Conoco, Love's, Valero, **food:** Arby's, Braum's, China Moon, Denny's, Domino's, El Rancho Mexican, KFC, LJ Silver, Mazzio's Pizza, McDonald's, Napoli's Rest., New China, Pizza Hut, Quizno's, Sonic, Taco Bell, Taco Mayo, **lodging:** Best Western, Budget Motel, Ranch House Motel, **other:** AutoZone, CVS Drug, Family$, Ford/Lincoln/Mercury, O'Reilly Parts, Radio Shack, Staples, Wal-Mart SuperCtr/Subway/gas
78mm	toll plaza, phone
63mm	picnic area wb, picnic tables, litter barrels
62	to Cyril(from wb), no services
60.5mm	picnic area eb, tables, litter barrels
53	US 277, Elgin, Lake Ellsworth, **E**...**gas:** Shamrock, **food:** Goodcents Subs, Sonic, Taco Tico, **W**...**gas:** Fina/dsl
46	US 62 E, US 277, US 281, to Elgin, Apache, Comanche Tribe, last free exit nb
45	OK 49, to Medicine Park, **W**...**gas:** Love's/Subway/dsl/24hr, **food:** Burger King, Sonic, **other:** Whichita NWR
41	to Ft Sill, Key Gate, **W**...Ft Sill Museum
40c	Gate 2, to Ft Sill, no services
40a	US 62 W, to Cache, **E**...**gas:** Fina/dsl, **W**...**lodging:** Super 8
39b	US 281(from sb), **W**...**lodging:** Ramada Inn
39a	US 281, Cache Rd (exits left from nb), Lawton, **1-3 mi W**...**gas:** Phillips 66, Valero/dsl, **food:** Applebee's, Braum's, Chili's, Chick-fil-A, Fire Mtn Grill, Golden Corral, KFC, Ryan's, Subway, Wendy's, **lodging:** Baymont Inn, Holiday Inn, Super 8, Super 9 Motel, **other:** $General, U-Haul, transmissions
37	Gore Blvd, Lawton, **E**...**gas:** Conoco, **food:** Braum's, Los Tres Amigos, Sonic, Taco Mayo, Woody's Mexican, **lodging:** Best Western, **other:** Curves, casino, **W**...**food:** Arby's(3mi), Cracker Barrel, Mike's Grille, **lodging:** Fairfield Inn, Holiday Inn Express, Ramada Inn(2mi), SpringHill Suites, **other:** Harley-Davidson, Lincoln/Mercury
36a	OK 7, Lee Blvd, Lawton, **E**...**gas:** Phillips 66, **W**...**gas:** Fina/dsl/repair, Shamrock/dsl, Suncountry/dsl, Welch/dsl, **food:** Big Chef Rest., KFC/Taco Bell, Leo&Ken's Rest., Popeye's, Salas Mexican, Sonic, **lodging:** Motel 6, **other:** HOSPITAL, $General, airport, vet
33	US 281, 11th St, Lawton, **W**...**other:** HOSPITAL, gas, food, lodging, airport, to Ft Sill
30	OK 36, Geronimo, no services
20.5mm	**Elmer Graham Plaza, both lanes exit left, Phillips 66/dsl, McDonald's, info**
20	OK 5, to Walters, **E**...**food:** BBQ
19.5mm	toll plaza
5	US 277 N, US 281, Randlett, last free exit nb, **E**...**gas:** Shamrock/dsl
1	OK 36, to Grandfield, no services
0mm	Oklahoma/Texas state line, Red River

Interstate 240(Okla City)

Exit #	Services
16mm	I-240 begins/ends on I-40.
14	Anderson Rd, **S**...**gas:** Conoco
11b a	Douglas Blvd, **N**...Tinker AFB
9	Air Depot Blvd, no services
8	OK 77, Sooner Rd, **N**...**gas:** Shell/dsl, **S**...**gas:** Phillips 66/Popeye's/dsl, Valero/McDonald's/dsl
7	Sunnylane Ave, **S**...**gas:** Valero/Subway/dsl, **lodging:** Value Place Motel
6	Bryant Ave, no services
5	S Eastern Ave, no services
4c	Pole Rd, **N**...**food:** Burger King, Luby's, Taco Bell, TX Roadhouse, **lodging:** Fairfield Inn, Ramada Inn, Residence Inn, **other:** Best Buy, Dillard's, JC Penney, Tires+, Macy's, mall
4b a	I-35, N to OK City, S to Dallas, US 77 S, US 62/77 N
3b	S Shields, **N**...**gas:** Valero/dsl, **other:** Circuit City, Home Depot, **S**...**food:** Chili's, **other:** Ford, Lowe's Whse, Nissan, Saturn, Wal-Mart SuperCtr/gas
3a	S Santa Fe, **S**...**gas:** Shell, **food:** Chili's, IHOP, **other:** Buick, Dodge, Chrysler/Jeep, Staples, Lowe's Whse, Wal-Mart SuperCtr/24hr
2b	S Walker Ave, **N**...**gas:** Shell/7-11, **food:** Rib Crib, **S**...**food:** Carino's, ChuckeCheese, Jimmy's Egg Grill, On-the-Border, Premo's Italian, **other:** Chevrolet, Pep-Boys
2a	S Western Ave, **N**...**gas:** Conoco, **food:** Burger King, House of Szechwan, Nino's Mexican, Taste of China, **other:** Hyundai, Suzuki, Tires+, **S**...**gas:** 7-11/gas, Valero, **food:** A&W/LJ Silver, Arby's, Ashley's Rest./24hr, Grandy's, HomeTown Buffet, KFC, Krispy Kreme, McDonald's, Red Lobster, Steak&Ale, **lodging:** Best Western, Holiday Inn Express, Quality Inn, **other:** Big O Tire, Chevrolet, Honda, Office Depot, Radio Shack
1c	S Penn Ave, **N**...**gas:** Conoco, **food:** Carl's Jr, Denny's, Don Pablo, Golden Corral, Harrigan's Rest., Hooters, Olive Garden, Outback Steaks, Pioneer Pies, Santa Fe Grill, Schlotsky's, **other:** BigLots, Circuit City, GNC, Radio Shack, Michaels, **S**...**gas:** Shell/Circle K, **food:** Hunan Buffet, Joe' s Crabshack, Mazzio's, Pancho's Mexican, Papa John's, Subway, Taco Bueno, Wendy's, Western Sizzlin, **other:** $Tree, Hancock Fabrics
1b	S May Ave, **N**...**gas:** 7-11/gas, **food:** Capt D's, Outlaw's BBQ, Taco Bell, Waffle House, **other:** Albertson's, O'Reilly Parts, **S**...**gas:** Valero, **food:** Braum's, Burger King, Perry's Rest., **lodging:** Cambridge Inn, Ramada Ltd
1a	I-44, US 62, I-240 begins ends on I-44.

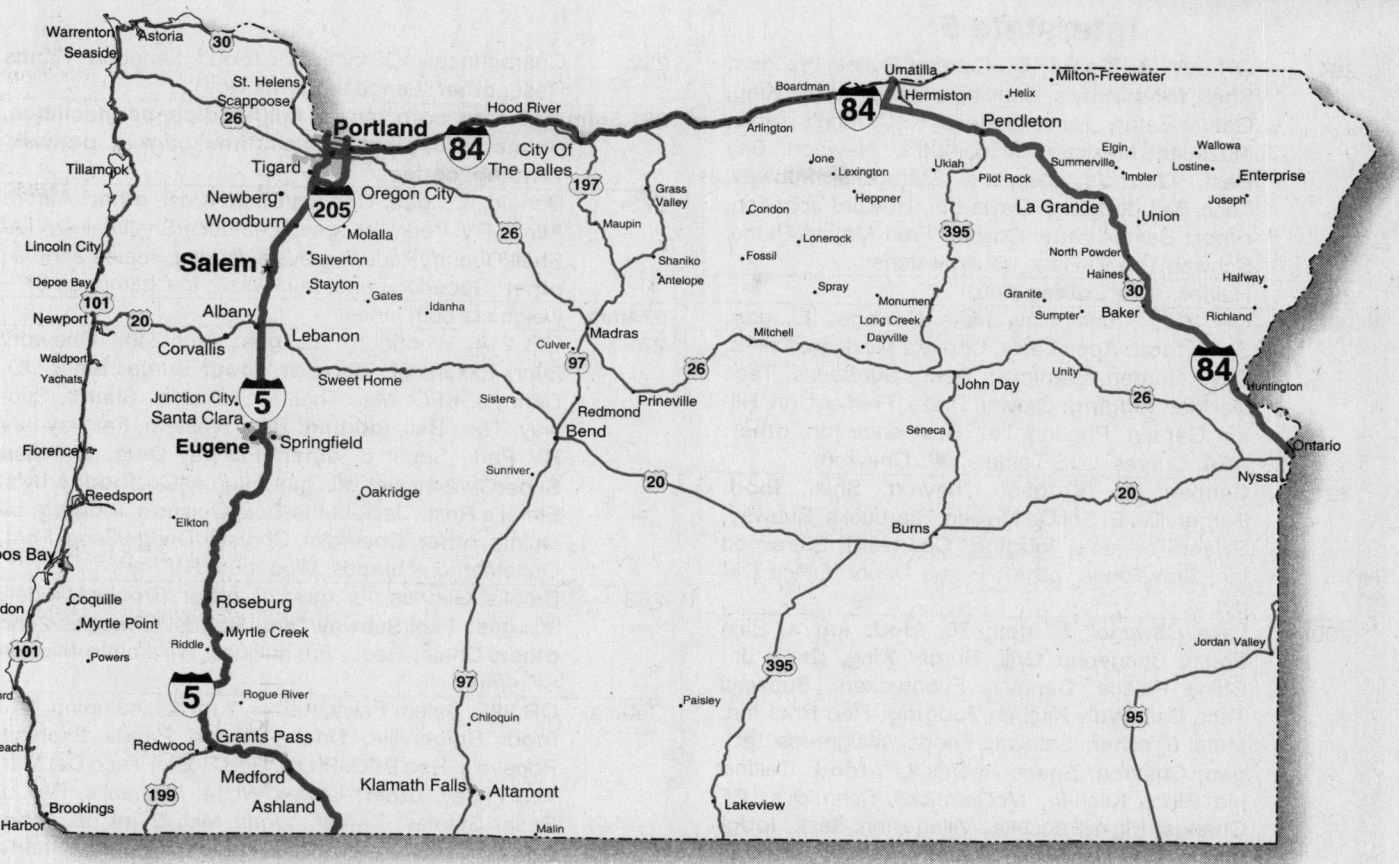

OREGON

Interstate 5

Portland

Exit #	Services
308.5mm	Oregon/Washington state line, Columbia River
308	Jansen Beach Dr, E...**gas:** Chevron/24hr, **food:** Burger King, Starbucks, Taco Bell, **lodging:** Oxford Suites, Red Lion, **other:** Safeway, W...**gas:** Arco, 76/dsl, **food:** BJ's Brewery, Denny's, McDonald's, Newport Bay Rest., Original Joe's, Stanford's Rest., Subway, **lodging:** Thunderbird Hotel, **other:** Barnes&Noble, Circuit City, CompUSA, Firestone, Home Depot, Jansen Beach RV Park, K-Mart, Office Depot, Old Navy, Staples, Target, mall
307	OR 99E S, MLK Blvd, Union Ave, Marine Dr, Expo Ctr, E...**gas:** Jubitz Trvl Ctr/rest/dsl, **food:** El Burrito, Elmer's Rest., Mo's Deli, Portland Cascade Grill, **lodging:** Best Western, Courtyard, Residence Inn, **other:** Blue Beacon
306b	Interstate Ave, Delta Park, E...**gas:** 76, **food:** Burger King, Elmer's Rest., Shari's, **lodging:** Best Western, Day's Inn, Motel 6, **other:** Lowe's Whse, Portland Meadows
306a	Columbia(from nb), same as 306b
305b a	US 30, Lombard St(from nb), W...**other:** Fred Meyer
304	Portland Blvd, U of Portland, W...Arco, 76, **food:** Nite Hawk Cafe, Taco Time, **lodging:** Crown Motel, Super Value
303	Alberta St, Swan Island, W...**lodging:** Palms Motel, Monticello Motel, E...HOSPITAL
302b	I-405, US 30 W, W...to ocean beaches, zoo
302a	Rose Qtr, City Ctr, E...**gas:** 76/Circle K/dsl, Shell/dsl, **food:** Burger King, Chipotle Mexican, McDonald's, Starbucks, Wendy's, **lodging:** Holiday Inn, Red Lion Inn, Shilo Inn, **other:** HOSPITAL, Radio Shack, Ford, 7-11, W...**other:** coliseum
301	I-84 E, US 30 E, services E off I-84 exits
300	US 26 E(from sb), Milwaukie Ave, W...**lodging:** Hilton, Marriott
299b	I-405
299a	US 26 E, OR 43(from nb), City Ctr, to Lake Oswego
297	Terwilliger Blvd, W...**food:** Burger King, KFC, Starbucks, **other:** HOSPITAL, Fred Meyer, to Lewis and Clark Coll.
296b	Multnomah Blvd, no services
296a	Barbur, W...**gas:** Chevron/24hr, Shell, 76/dsl, 7-11, **food:** Old Barn Rest., Szechuan Chinese, Subway, Taco Time, Wendy's, **lodging:** Capitol Hill Motel, Kings Row Motel, **other:** VET, Schwab Tire
295	Capitol Hwy, (from nb), E...**gas:** Shell/dsl, **food:** Juan Colorado Mexican, Koji Japanese, McDonald's, RoundTable Pizza, Starbucks, **lodging:** Hospitality Motel, Ranch Inn

OREGON

Interstate 5

294   OR 99W, to Tigard, **E**...Comfort Suites, **W**...**gas:** Shell, **food:** Arby's, Banning's Rest., Burger King, Gators Eatery, Hihat Chinese, KFC, King's Table, Mazatlan Mexican, Mcdonald's, Newport Bay Rest., Quizno's, Skipper's, Starbucks, Subway, Taco Bell, **lodging:** Day's Inn, Howard Johnson, **other:** Baxter Parts, Costco, Fred Meyer, Petco, Schwab Tire, U-Haul, transmissions

293   Haines St, **W**...**other:** Ford

292   OR 217, Kruse Way, Lake Oswego, **E**...**gas:** Shell, **food:** Applebee's, Chevy's Mexican, Chili's, Olive Garden, Stanford's Rest., Starbucks, Taco Del Mar, **lodging:** Crowne Plaza, Fairfield Inn, Hilton Garden, Phoenix Inn, Residence Inn, **other:** AAA, Curves, LDS Temple, **W**...Chevron

291   Carman Dr, **W**...**gas:** Chevron, Shell, **food:** Burgerville, El Sol De Mexico, Starbucks, Subway, Sweet Tomato's, **lodging:** Courtyard, Sherwood Inn, Travelodge, **other:** Home Depot, Office Depot

290   Lake Oswego, **E**...**gas:** 76, **food:** Arby's, Baja Fresh, Bridgeport Grill, Burger King, Carl's Jr., China Palace, Denny's, Fuddruckers, Subway, Taco Bell, Wu's Kitchen, **lodging:** Red Roof Inn, Motel 6, **other:** Safeway Foods, Walgreens, **W**...**gas:** Chevron, Space Age/dsl/LP, **food:** California Pizza Kitchen, McCormick& Schmick's, PF Changs, Pig'n Pancake, Village Inn Rest., **lodging:** Best Suites, Best Western, Quality Inn, Value Inn, **other:** Borders Books, CarQuest, Whole Foods, Wild Oats Mkt

289   Tualatin, **E**...**gas:** Shell, **food:** McDonald's, **lodging:** Sweetbrier Inn, **W**...**gas:** Chevron, Shell, **food:** Jack-in-the-Box, Lee's Kitchen, Quizno's, Samurai Sam's, Taco Bell, Wendy's, **lodging:** Century Hotel, **other:** HOSPITAL, Fred Meyer, K-Mart, Radio Shack, Safeway, camping

288   I-205, to Oregon City

286   Stafford, **E**...**gas:** 76/dsl/24hr, **food:** Burger King, Coronado Cafe, Moe's SW Grill, Panda Express, PizzaSchmizza, Starbucks, Subway, **lodging:** La Quinta, Super 8, **other:** Costco/gas, Good Sam RV Park, Mercedes, Office Depot, Petsmart, Target, **W**...**gas:** Chevron, **food:** Big Town Gyro, **lodging:** Holiday Inn/rest., **other:** Camping World RV Service/supplies, Chevrolet, Dodge, Nissan, Toyota

283   Wilsonville, **E**...**gas:** 76/dsl, **food:** Applebee's, Arby's, Bellagio's Pizza, Colorado Mexican, DQ, Denny's, Domino's, Izzy's Pizza, Jamba Juice, McDonald's, Papa Murphy's, Quizno's, Red Robin, Shari's/24hr, Subway, Taco Bell, TCBY, Wanker's Café, Wendy's, Wong's Chinese, **lodging:** Best Western, Comfort Inn, SnoozInn, **other:** Fry's Electronics, GNC, Honda, Lamb's Foods, NAPA, Rite Aid, Schwab Tire, USPO; **W**...**gas:** Chevron, **food:** Burger King/24hr, Chili's, Dino's Pizzaria, Domino's, Hunan Kitchen, Starbucks, **lodging:** Phoenix Inn, **other:** Albertson's, 7-11, Walgreens

282.5mm Willamette River

282   Charbonneau District, **E**...**food:** Langdon Farms Rest., **other:** Langdon Farms Golf

281.5mm **rest area both lanes, full(handicapped)facilities, phone, info, picnic tables, litter barrels, petwalk, vending, coffee**

278   Donald, **E**...**gas:** Conoco/Circle K/dsl, **other:** Aurora Acres RV Park, **W**...**gas:** Leather's/Shell/dsl/@, TA/Shell/Country Pride/Popeye's/dsl/rest./scales/24hr/@, **other:** Speedco Lube, truckwash, to Champoeg SP

274mm weigh sta both lanes

271   OR 214, Woodburn, **E**...**gas:** Arco/24hr, Chevron/24hr, Exxon/dsl, 76/repair, **food:** Burger King, DQ, Denny's, KFC, Mae Thai, McDonald's, Shari's, Subway, Taco Bell, **lodging:** Best Western, Fairway Inn/RV Park, Super 8, **other:** Fairway Drug, Wal-Mart SuperCtr/24hr, vet, **W**...**gas:** Stop-N-Go, **food:** Arby's, Elmer's Rest., Jack-in-the-Box, Quizno's, **lodging:** La Quinta, **other:** Chevrolet, Chrysler/Dodge/Jeep, Ford, Outlet/famous brands, Woodburn RV Park

263   Brooks, Gervais, **E**...**gas:** 76, **other:** Brooks Mkt/deli, **W**...**gas:** Pilot/Subway/Taco Bell/dsl/LP/scales/24hr, **other:** Chalet Rest., Freightliner, Willamette Mission SP(4mi)

260b a   OR 99E, Salem Pkwy, Keizer, **2 mi E**...camping, **W**...**food:** Burgerville, On-the-Border, Panda Express, Popeye's, Red Brick Pizza, Red Robin, Taco Del Mar, TGI Friday, **other:** Lowes Whse, Michael's, PetCo, Ross, Staples, Target, World Mkt, **2 mi W**...**food:** Arby's, Carl's Jr., DQ, McDonald's, Porter's, Shari's Rest., Subway, **lodging:** Wittenburg Inn

259mm 45th parallel, halfway between the equator and N Pole

258   N Salem, **E**...**gas:** 76/Circle K, **food:** Figaro's Italian, Guesthouse Rest., McDonald's, Original Pancakes, **lodging:** Best Western, Rodeway Inn, **other:** Cottman Transmissions, Hwy RV Ctr, Roth's Foods, Trailer RV Park, flea mkt, **W**...**gas:** Chevron, 76/Circle K, Pacific Pride/dsl, Shell/dsl, **food:** Don Pedro Mexican, Jack-in-the-Box, **lodging:** Econolodge, Travelers Inn, **other:** Stuart's Parts, to st capitol

256   to OR 213, Market St, Salem, **E**...**gas:** Shell, **food:** Alberto's Mexican, Carl's Jr, Chalet Rest., Denny's, Elmer's, Jack-in-the-Box, Olive Garden, **lodging:** Best Western, Cozzzy Inn, Tiki Lodge, **other:** Best Buy, Bon-Ton, Fred Meyer/gas, Goodyear/auto, Macey's, NAPA, Pic'n Save Foods, Ross, Safeway, Target, mall, **E on Lancaster**...**food:** Blue Willow Rest., China Faith, El Mirador Mexican, Figaro's Italian, Izzy's Pizza, Kyoto Japanese, Outback Steaks, Quizno's, Skipper's, Taco Bell, **other:** Albertson's, American Tire, BigLots, Borders Books, Schwab Tires, Walgreen, **W**...**gas:** Arco/24hr, Chevron, Pacific Pride/dsl, Shell/dsl/24hr, **food:** Almost Home Rest., Baskin-Robbins, Canton Garden, DQ, McDonald's, Newport Bay Seafood, Pietro's Pizza, Roger's 50's Diner, Subway, Tony Roma's, Village Inn, **lodging:** Holiday Lodge, Motel 6, Phoenix Inn, Quality Inn, Red Lion Hotel, Salem Inn, Shilo Inn, Super 8, **other:** Buick/GMC, Heliotrope Natural Foods, InStock Fabrics, Jack's IGA, Kia/Mazda/Isuzu/Suzuki, Nissan

Interstate 5

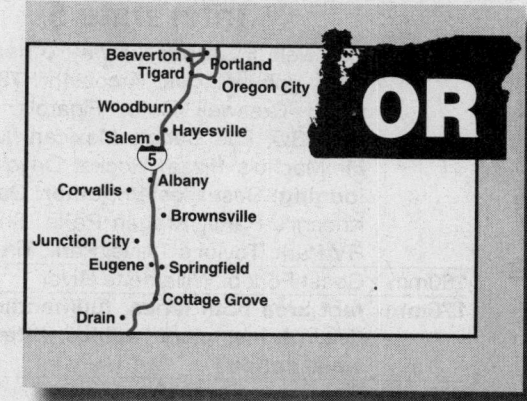

N
S

253 OR 22, Salem, Stayton, **E**...**gas:** Chevron/repair, QuikMart/dsl, Shell/dsl, **food:** Burger King, Carl's Jr, Las Polomas Mexican, McDonald's, Shari's, Subway, **other:** $Tree, Home Depot, ShopKO, WinCo Foods, Salem Camping, to Detroit RA, **W**...**gas:** Pacific Pride, Shell/dsl, **food:** DQ, Denny's, Sybil's Omelette, **lodging:** Best Western, Comfort Suites, Economy Inn, Holiday Inn Express, Motel 6, Residence Inn, Travelodge, **other:** HOSPITAL, AAA, Chevrolet/Cadillac/Subaru, Chrysler, Costco/gas, Jeep/Pontiac, K-Mart/auto, Lowe's Whse, Roberson RV Ctr, Schwab Tire, Toyota, st police

252 Kuebler Blvd, **1-3 mi** **W**...**gas:** Arco/24hr, 76/24hr, **food:** Applebee's, Burger King, Jack-in-the-Box, McDonald's, Quizno's, Shari's/24hr, Subway, **lodging:** Phoenix Inn, **other:** HOSPITAL, Roverson RV Ctr

249 to Salem(from nb), no services

248 Sunnyside, **E**...**other:** Enchanted Forest Themepark, Thrillville funpark, Willamette Valley Vineyards, Forest Glen RV camping, **W**...**gas:** Pacific Pride/dsl

244 to Jefferson, no services

243 Ankeny Hill, no services

242 Talbot Rd, no services

241mm **rest area both lanes, full(handicapped) facilities, info, phone, picnic tables, litter barrels, petwalk**

240.5mm Santiam River

240 Hoefer Rd, no services

239 Dever-Conner, no services

238 S Jefferson, Scio, no services

237 Viewcrest(from sb), no services

235 Millersburg, **E**...Harley-Davidson

234 OR 99E, Albany, **E**...**lodging:** Comfort Suites, Holiday Inn Express, **other:** Harley-Davidson, Knox Butte Camping, **W**...**gas:** Arco/24hr, Chevron, Leather's Fuels, 76/dsl, Shell/dsl, **food:** Arby's, Burger King, Carl's Jr., China Buffet, DQ, Hereford Steer Rest., McDonald's, Lee's Wok, Original Breakfast Diner, Pizza Hut, Red Robin, Skipper's, Subway, Taco Bell, Wendy's, **lodging:** Bamboo Terrace Motel, Best Western/rest., Budget Inn, Day's Inn, Hawthorn Inn, La Quinta, Motel 6, Relax Inn, **other:** HOSPITAL, Big Lots, Costco/gas, K-Mart, Mervyn's, Chrysler/Jeep, Nissan, Lincoln/Mercury, RV camping/repair, to Albany Hist Dist

233 US 20, Albany, **E**...**gas:** Chevron/dsl/24hr, 76/dsl, **food:** LumYuen Chinese, **lodging:** Days Inn, Econolodge, Phoenix Inn, **other:** Chevrolet/Toyota, Home Depot, Honda, Lassen RV Ctr, Mazda, RV camping, st police, **W**...**gas:** 76/dsl, Shell, **food:** Abby's Pizza, Baskin-Robbins, Carl's Jr, Elmer's, Lee's Wok, Los Tequilos Mexican, Original Breakfast Cafe, Sizzler, Skipper's, Starbucks, Sweet Waters Rest., Taco Time, **lodging:** Valu Inn, **other:** HOSPITAL, Albertson's, BigLots, Chrysler/Dodge/Jeep/Subaru/Hyundai, $Tree, Fred Meyer/gas/dsl, Goodyear, Jo-Ann Fabrics, Knecht's Parts, Rite Aid, Schwab Tires, Staples

Albany

228 OR 34, to Lebanon, Corvallis, **E**...**gas:** 76/Pine Cone Cafe/dsl/24hr, **W**...**gas:** Arco/24hr, Chevron/CFN/A&W/dsl, Shell/dsl, Texaco, **other:** to OSU, KOA(5mi)

222mm Butte Creek

216 OR 228, Halsey, Brownsville, **E**...**gas:** Pioneer Villa TrkStp/76/Blimpie/dsl/24hr/@, **lodging:** Travelodge, **other:** parts/repair/towing, **W**...**gas:** Shell/dsl

209 to Jct City, Harrisburg, **W**...**food:** Hungry Farmer Café, **other:** Diamond Hill RV Park

206mm **rest area both lanes, full(handicapped)facilities, info, phone, picnic tables, litter barrels, petwalk**

199 Coburg, **E**...**gas:** Fuel'n Go/dsl, **lodging:** Country Squire Inn, **other:** Ingram RV Ctr, **W**...**gas:** Shell/LP, TA/CFN/Shell/Truck'n'Travel Motel/dsl/rest./24hr/@, **other:** Ford/Freightliner/GMC, Garrity RV Ctr, Paradise RV Ctr, dsl repair, hist dist

197mm McKenzie River

195b a N Springfield, **E**...**gas:** Arco/24hr, Chevron/24hr, 76/Circel K/dsl/24hr, **food:** A&W, Applebee's, Carl's Jr, Denny's, ChinaSun Buffet, Elmer's Rest., FarMan Chinese, Gateway Chinese, HomeTown Buffet, IHOP, Jack-in-the-Box, KFC, McDonald's, Mtn Valley Pizza, Outback Steaks, Roadhouse Grill, Shari's/24hr, Sizzler, Sophia's, Taco Bell, **lodging:** Best Western, Clarion, Comfort Suites, Courtyard, Gateway Inn, Holiday Inn Express, Motel Orleans, Motel 6, Pacific 9 Motel, Quality Inn, Rodeway Inn, Travelodge, Shilo Inn/rest., Super 8, **other:** HOSPITAL, Best Buy, Circuit City, Ross, Sears/auto, Target, USPO, mall, st police, **W**...**other:** Costco/gas, ShopKO, to airport

194b a **E**...HOSPITAL, OR 126 E, Springfield, **W**...I-105 W, Eugene, **2 mi** **W**...**gas:** 76/repair, **food:** Trader Joe's, **lodging:** Red Lion Inn, Residence Inn, **other:** Albertson's, Honda, mall

193mm Willamette River

192 OR 99(from nb), to Eugene, **W**...**food:** Burger King, Wendy's, **lodging:** Best Western, Quality Inn

191 Glenwood, **W**...**gas:** 76/dsl, Shell/dsl/LP/24hr, **food:** Denny's, **lodging:** Motel 6, Phoenix Inn(2mi)

189 30th Ave S, Eugene, **E**...**gas:** Shell/dsl/LP, **other:** Eugene RV Ctr, Harley-Davidson, Shamrock RV Park, marine ctr, mobile village, **W**...**gas:** Astro, 76/dsl

188b rd 99 S(nb only), Goshen, no services

188a OR 58, to Oakridge, OR 99S, **E**...**gas:** 76, **other:** Deerwood RV Camping, **W**...**gas:** Pacific Pride/dsl/rest./24hr, **other:** Big Boy's RV Ctr, tires

186 to Goshen(from nb), no services

Eugene

OREGON

Interstate 5

N ↑ S

182	Creswell, E...**food:** Subway, **other:** Ray's Foods/drug, golf, W...**gas:** Arco/24hr, 76/Taco Bell/dsl, **food:** Creswell Cafe, Figaro's Pizza, Hawaiian BBQ, Los Cabo's Mexican, Mallard's Rest., Mr Macho's Pizza, Rocket Drive-In, TJ's Rest., **lodging:** Best Western, **other:** Dairy Mart, KOA, Knecht's Parts, Kragen Parts, Sherwood Forest RV Park, Taylor's Travel Park, Tire Factory
180mm	. Coast Fork of Willamette River
178mm	**rest area both lanes, full(handicapped) facilities, phone, picnic tables, litter barrels, petwalk, coffee**
176	Saginaw, no services
175mm	Row River
174	174 Cottage Grove, E...**gas:** Chevron/dsl/repair/24hr, Shell, **food:** China Garden, Subway, Taco Bell, **lodging:** Best Western/rest., Village Green Resort, **other:** HOSPITAL, Chevrolet/Pontiac/Buick/GMC, Chrysler/Dodge/Jeep, Ford, Wal-Mart/auto, W...**gas:** Chevron/dsl/LP, 76/dsl, Shell/dsl, **food:** Arby's, Burger King, Carl's Jr, DQ(2mi), Figaro's Pizza, KFC, McDonald's, Subway, Svechuan Chinese, Torero's Mexican, Vintage Inn Rest./24hr, **lodging:** City Ctr Motel, Comfort Inn, Holiday Inn Express, Relax Inn, **other:** HOSPITAL, Chevrolet, $Tree, Ray's Foods, Mazda, Safeway, Village Green Motel/RV Park
172	6th St, Cottage Grove Lake(from sb), **2 mi** E...Cottage Grove RV Park
170	to OR 99, London Rd(nb only), Cottage Grove Lake, **6 mi** E...Cottage Grove RV Park
163	Curtin, Lorane, E...**lodging:** Stardust Motel, **other:** Pass Creek RV Park, USPO, antiques, W...**gas:** 76
162	162 OR 38, OR 99 to Drain, Elkton, no services
161	Anlauf(from nb), no services
160	Salt Springs Rd, no services
159	Elk Creek, Cox Rd, no services
154	Yoncalla, Elkhead, no services
150	OR 99, to OR 38, Yoncalla, Red Hill, W...**other:** Trees of Oregon RV Park
148	Rice Hill, E...**gas:** Chevron/LP/24hr, Pacific Pride/dsl, Pilot/Homestead Rest./Subway/dsl/scales/24hr/@, **food:** Peggy's Rest., **lodging:** Best Western, Ranch Motel/rest., **other:** Rice Hill RV Park, W...**food:** K-R Drive-In
146	Rice Valley, no services
144mm	**rest area sb, full(handicapped)facilities, phone, picnic tables, litter barrels, petwalk**
143mm	**rest area nb, full(handicapped)facilities, phone, picnic tables, litter barrels, petwalk**
142	Metz Hill, no services
140	OR 99(from sb), Oakland, E...**food:** Tolly's Rest., **other:** Oakland Hist Dist
138	OR 99(from nb), Oakland, E...**food:** Tolly's Rest., **other:** Oakland Hist Dist
136	OR 138W, Sutherlin, E...**gas:** Chevron/A&W/dsl/24hr, 76/Subway/dsl, Shell/dsl, **food:** Abbey's Pizza, Apple Peddler Rest., Burger King, Hong Kong Chinese, McDonald's, Papa Murphy's, Pedotti's Italian, **lodging:** Relax Inn, Sutherlin Inn, Town&Country Motel, Umpqua Regency Inn, **other:** CarQuest, I-5 RV Ctr, Schwab Tires, W...**gas:** Mobil/dsl, **food:** Dakota St Pizza, DQ, Taco Bell, **lodging:** Budget Inn, **other:** Hi-Way Haven RV Camp, Oak Hills RV Park, Ray's Foods, dsl repair/towing
135	Wilbur, Sutherlin, E...**gas:** CFN/dsl, Shell, muffler repair
130mm	weigh sta sb, phone
129	OR 99, Winchester, E...**gas,** food, camping, dsl repair, RV Ctr(1mi)
129mm	N Umpqua River
127	Stewart Pkwy, Edenbower Rd, N Roseburg, E...**gas:** Chevron, Shell, **lodging:** Motel 6, Super 8, **other:** Home Depot, Lowe's Whse, Mt Nebo RV Park, W...**gas:** Texaco/Taco Maker/dsl, **food:** Applebee's, Coldstone Creamery, IHOP, Jack-in-the-Box, McDonald's, Red Robin, Subway, Taco Bell, **lodging:** Sleep Inn, **other:** HOSPITAL, Albertson's/gas, Big O Tire, Harley-Davidson, K-Mart, Office Depot, Parkway Drug, Sherm's Foods, Staples, Wal-Mart/auto/drugs, vet
125	Garden Valley Blvd, Roseburg, E...**gas:** Chevron, Shell/dsl/24hr, Texaco, **food:** Brutke's Rest., Elmer's, Jack-in-the-Box, KFC, McDonald's, Taco Bell, WagonWheel Rest., **lodging:** Comfort Inn, Quality Inn, Windmill Inn/rest., **other:** Albertson's, CarQuest, Ford, GMC, NAPA, Rite Aid, transmissions, W...**gas:** Chevron/dsl, 76, Shell/LP/repair, **food:** Arby's, Burger King, Carl's Jr, IHOP, Izzy's Pizza, La Hacienda Mexican, Quizno's, Quicksilver Steaks, Rodeo Steaks, RoundTable Pizza, Sizzler, TomTom Rest., Wendy's, **lodging:** Best Value Inn, Best Western, Econolodge, **other:** Bi-Mart, Fred Meyer, House of Fabrics, JC Penney, Ross, Sears/auto, Schuck's Parts, mall
124	OR 138, Roseburg, City Ctr, E...**gas:** Mobil/dsl, 76/dsl/24hr, Texaco, **food:** Chi's Chinese, Denny's, HiHo Rest., **lodging:** Best Western, Dunes Motel, Holiday Inn Express, Holiday Motel, Travelodge, **other:** Chevrolet/Pontiac/Buick, Honda, Mazda, Rite Aid, Safeway, W...**gas:** Chevron, Shell/Subway, **food:** Charley's BBQ, Gay 90's Deli, KFC, Taco Time, **other:** HOSPITAL, Grocery Outlet
123	Roseburg, E...**other:** to Umpqua Park, camping, museum
121	McLain Ave, no services
120.5mm	S Umpqua River
120	OR 99 N(no EZ nb return), Green District, Roseburg, E...**lodging:** Shady Oaks Motel, **3 mi** E...**food:** HiHo Rest, **lodging:** Best Western, Budget 16, Howard Johnson, W...**other:**T&M RV parts/repair, auto repair
119	OR 99 S, OR 42 W, Winston, W...**gas:** Chevron/Pacific Pride/A&W/dsl/24hr, Love's/Arby's/dsl/scales/@, Shell/dsl, **food:** McDonald's, Papa Murphy's, Scooter's Drive Inn, Subway, Sweet Breeze Inn, **other:** Ray's Foods, Rising River RV, UPS, Western Star RV Park

Roseburg

Interstate 5

N
S

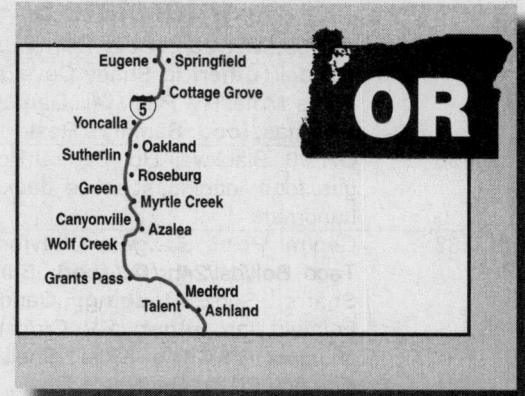

113	Clarks Branch Rd, Round Prairie, W...**lodging:** Quikstop Motel, **other:** On the River RV Park(2mi), Quikstop Mkt, dsl repair
112.5mm	S Umpqua River, S Umpqua River
112	OR 99, OR 42, Dillard, E...**other:** Rivers West RV park, **rest area nb, full(handicapped)facilities, phone, picnic tables, litter barrels, petwalk**
111mm	**rest area sb, full(handicapped)facilities, phone, picnic tables, litter barrels, petwalk,** weigh sta nb
110	Boomer Hill Rd, no services
108	Myrtle Creek, E...**food:** DQ, Golf Course Cafe, Myrtle Creek Cafe, **other:** Myrtle Creek RV Park
106	Weaver Rd, no services
103	Tri City, Myrtle Creek, E...**food:** Broaster House Diner, W...**gas:** Chevron/A&W/dsl/24hr, **food:** McDonald's
102	Gazley Rd, E...Surprise Valley RV Park(1mi)
101.5mm	S Umpqua River, S Umpqua River
101	Riddle, Stanton Park, W...camping
99	Canyonville, E...**food:** Burger King, Cow Creek Café/RV Park/casino, **lodging:** Riverside Motel, 7 Feathers Hotel/RV Park/casino, Valley View Motel, **other:** dsl/RV repair, W...**gas:** 7 Feathers Trkstp/dsl/24/café/@, **lodging:** Best Western
98	OR 99, Canyonville, Days Creek, E...**gas:** 76/dsl, Shell/dsl/24hr, **food:** Country Jct Rest., FeedLot Rest., Sarafino's Italian, **lodging:** Leisure Inn, 7 Feathers Hotel/RV Park/casino, **other:** Gordon's Drug, NAPA, Ray's Foods, W...**other:** Bill's Tire/repair, museum
95	Canyon Creek, no services
90mm	Canyon Creek Pass, Canyon Creek Pass, elev 2020
88	Azalea, no services
86	Barton Rd, Quine's Creek, E...**gas:** Shell/dsl, **other:** Heaven on Earth Rest./bakery/RV camp, Meadow Wood RV Park(3mi)
83	Barton Rd(from nb), E...**other:** Meadow Wood RV Park
82mm	**rest area both lanes, full(handicapped) facilities, phone, picnic tables, litter barrels, petwalk**
80	Glendale, W...**gas:** Country Jct./LP, **food:** Village Inn Rest.
79.5mm	Stage Road Pass, elev 1830
78	Speaker Rd, no services
76	Wolf Creek, W...**gas:** Arco/dsl/24hr, Pacific Pride/dsl, 76/deli/dsl, **food:** Wolf Creek Inn Rest., **other:** Creekside RV park, auto repair
74mm	Smith Hill Summit, elev 1730
71	Sunny Valley, E...**lodging:** Sunny Valley Motel, **other:** Covered Bridge Store/gas, W...**other:** Sunny Valley RV Park
69mm	Sexton Mtn Pass, elev 1960
66	Hugo, W...**other:** Joe Creek Waterfalls RV Camping
63mm	**rest area both lanes, full(handicapped) facilities, phone, info, picnic tables, litter barrels, vending, petwalk**

Grants Pass

61	Merlin, E...**other:** Beaver Creek RV Resort, Twin Pines RV Park, W...**gas:** Shell/dsl, **other:** Rouge Valley RV Ctr, repair
58	OR 99, to US 199, Grants Pass, W...**gas:** Arco, Chevron, 76/dsl/RV dump, Shell/dsl/repair, Texaco/dsl, TownePump Gas, **food:** Angela's Mexican, Baskin-Robbins, Burger King, Carl's Jr, China Hut, DQ, Della's Rest., Denny's, McDonald's, Muchas Gracias Mexican, Papa Murphy's, Pizza Hut, Rouge Rest., Sizzler, Skipper's, Subway, Taco Bell, Wendy's, **lodging:** Budget Inn, Comfort Inn, Hawk's Inn, Hawthorn Suites, La Quinta, Motel 6, Parkway Lodge, Regal Lodge, Riverside Inn, Royal Vue Motel, Shilo Inn, Sunset Inn, Super 8, SweetBreeze Inn, Travelodge, **other:** HOSPITAL, AutoZone, Chevrolet/Nissan/Honda, Chrysler/Dodge/Jeep, Jack's RV Resort, PriceChopper Foods, Radio Shack, Rouge Valley RV Park, Schwab Tire, ToolBox Repair, st police, towing
55	US 199, Redwood Hwy, E Grants Pass, W...**gas:** Arco/24hr, CFN/dsl, Exxon/dsl/LP/24hr, **food:** Applebee's, Abby's Pizza, Arby's, Carl's Jr, Dutch Bro's, Elmer's, JJ North's Buffet, McDonald's, Shari's/24hr, Si Casa Flores Mexican, Subway, Taco Bell, Wild River Brewing Co, **lodging:** Best Western, Discovery Inn, Holiday Inn Express, Knight's Inn, **other:** HOSPITAL, Albertson's/gas, Big Lots, Big O Tire, $Tree, Fred Meyer/gas/dsl, Grocery Outlet, JC Penney, Moon Mnt. RV Park, Rite Aid, RiverPark RV Park, Schuck's Parts, Siskiyou RV Ctr, Staples, Wal-Mart SuperCtr/24hr
48	Rogue River, Rogue River RA, E...**gas:** Chevron/dsl, Shell/dsl, **food:** Abby's Pizza, Betty's Kitchen, Karen's Kitchen, Tarasco Mexican, **other:** Ray's Foods, W...**lodging:** Bella Rosa Inn, Best Western, Rogue River Inn, Motel, Weasku Inn, **other:** Circle W RV Park, Ridgeview RV Park
45b	W...**other: Valley of the Rogue SP/rest area both lanes, full(handicapped) facilities, phone, picnic tables, litter barrels, petwalk, camping**
45mm	Rogue River
45a	OR 99, Savage Rapids Dam, E...**other:** Cypress Grove RV Park
43	OR 99, OR 234, , to Crater Lake, Gold Hill, E...**food:** Red Barn Cafe, **lodging:** B&B, KOA, Lazy Acres Motel/RV Park

OREGON

Interstate 5

40	OR 99, OR 234, Gold Hill, E...food: Gold Hill Mkt/deli, other: to Shady Cove Trail, KOA, Lazy Acres Motel/RV Park, W...Dardanell's RV/Trailer Park/gas, food: Sammy's Rest.
35	OR 99, Blackwell Rd, Central Point, 2-4 mi W... gas, food, lodging, st police, Jacksonville Nat Hist Landmark
33	Central Point, E...gas: Chevron, Pilot/Subway/ Taco Bell/dsl/24hr/@, food: Burger King, KFC, Shari's, Sonic, lodging: Candlewood Suites, Fairfield Inn, other: RV Ctr/camping, funpark, W...gas: 76/Circle K/dsl, Shell/dsl/24hr, food: Abbey's Pizza, BeeGee's Rest., LittleTown Hero Sandwiches, Little Caesar's, Mazatlan Grill, Mc-Donald's, Pappy's Pizza, other: Albertson's
30	OR 62, to Crater Lake, Medford, E...gas: Arco/ dsl, Chevron/dsl, 76, Witham Trkstp/Chevron/ rest./dsl/24hr/@, Gas4Less, Shell/dsl, food: Ab- by's Pizza, Applebee's, Arby's, Asian Grill, Carl's Jr, Chevy's Mexican, DQ, Denny's, Elmer's, IHOP, India Palace, Marie Callender's, McDonald's, Ol- ive Garden, Papa John's, Pizza Hut, Quizno's, Red Robin, Schlotsky's, Si Casa Mexican, Sizzler, Starbucks, Subway, Taco Bell, Taco Delite, Thai Bistro, Wendy's, Williams Bakery, lodging: Best Western, Cedar Lodge, Comfort Inn, Hampton Inn, Motel 6, Reston Inn, Rogue Regency Hotel, Shilo Inn, ValliHai Inn, Windmill Inn, other: AAA RV, Albertson's, Aamco, Barnes&Noble, BiMart Foods, Chevrolet, Circuit City, $Tree, Ford, Fred Meyer, Food4Less, Kohl's, Medford Oaks RV Park, NAPA, OR Tire, Radio Shack, River City RV Ctr, Safeway, Sears, USPO, st police, W...gas: Chevron/dsl, Shell/dsl, food: Burger King, Dom- ino's, Jack-in-the-Box, KFC, King Wah Chinese, Red Lobster, Skipper's, Wendy's, other: HOSPI- TAL, JC Penney, Krecht's Parts, Macy's, Target, Toyota, U-Haul, mall
27	Barnett Rd, Medford, E...gas: Exxon/dsl, Shell/ 24hr, food: DQ, Kopper Kitchen, lodging: Best Western, Day's Inn/rest., Economy Inn, Motel 6, Travelodge, W...gas: Chevron/24hr, Exxon/dsl, Gas4Less, 76/Circle K, Shell/dsl/24hr, food: Abby's Pizza, Apple Annie's, Burger King, Carl's Jr, HomeTown Buffet, Jack-in-the-Box, KFC, Kim's Chinese, McDonald's, McGrath's Fish- House, Pizza Hut, Rooster's Rest., Senor Sam's Mexican, Shari's, Starbucks, Subway, Taco Bell, Wendy's, Zach's Deli, lodging: Best Inn, Comfort Inn, Holiday Inn Express, Fairfield Inn, Red Lion Inn, Residence Inn, Royal Crest Motel, other: Ford/Mercury/Lincoln, Food4Less, Fred Meyer, Harry&David's, Hyundai, K-Mart, Office Depot, Radio Shack, Saturn, Schwab Tires, Staples, Toy- ota, WinCo Foods
24	Phoenix, E...gas: Petro/dsl/rest./RV dump/ 24hr/@, Texaco/dsl, lodging: PearTree Mo- tel/rest./RV park, Super 8, other: Home Depot, Peterbilt/GMC, W...gas: Exxon, 76/Circle K/dsl, food: Angelo's Pizza, Courtyard Café, Luigi's

	Café, McDonald's, Randy's Café, Subway, lodging: Bavarian Inn, Phoenix Motel, other: Ray's Foods, CarQuest, Holiday RV Park, Factory Stores/famous brands
22mm	**rest area sb, full(handicapped)facilities, phone, picnic tables, litter barrels, vending, petwalk**
21	Talent, W...gas: Gas4Less, Shell/dsl, Talent's/dsl/ rest./repair, food: Arbor House Rest., Expresso Café, Figaro's Italian, Senor Sam's Cantina, lodging: GoodNight Inn, other: American RV Resort, Wal- Mart/auto
19	Valley View Rd, Ashland, W...gas: Pacific Pride/dsl, 76/dsl, Shell/dsl/LP, food: Burger King, El Tapatio Mexican, lodging: Best Western, Econolodge, La Quinta, Regency Inn/rest./RV Park, Stratford Inn, other: HOSPITAL, Chevrolet, U-Haul
18mm	weigh sta both lanes
14	OR 66, to Klamath Falls, Ashland, E...gas: Chev- ron, 76/dsl/LP, Shell/dsl, food: A&W/KFC, Denny's, Miguel's, OakTree Rest., lodging: A&W/KFC, Ash- land Hills Inn/rest., Best Western, Holiday Inn Ex- press, Relax Inn, Rodeway Inn, Vista Motel, Windmill Inn, other: Emigrant Lake Camping(3mi), KOA(3mi), Nat Hist Museum, W...gas: Arco/24hr, Texaco, food: Azteca Mexican, DQ, McDonald's, Omar's Rest(1mi), Panda Garden, Quizno's, Taco Bell, Thai Rest., Wendy's, lodging: Knight's Inn/rest., Super 8, other: Albertson's, Radio Shack, Rite Aid, Schwab Tire
11.5mm	chainup area
11	OR 99, Siskiyou Blvd(no nb return), 2-4 mi W...gas: Shell, food: DQ, Figaro's Italian, Goodtimes Café, House of Thai, Little Caesar's, Omar's Rest., Senor Sam's Mexican, Subway, Wendy's, lodging: Best Western, Cedarwood Inn, Hillside Inn, Rodeway Inn, Stratford Inn, other: Radio Shack, Weisinger Brew- ery
6	to Mt Ashland, E...lodging: Callahan's Siskiyou Lodge/rest., other: phone, ski area
4mm	Siskiyou Summit, elev 4310, brake chk both lanes
1	to Siskiyou Summit(from nb), no services
0mm	Oregon/California state line

Interstate 84

Exit #	Services	
378mm	Oregon/Idaho state line, Snake River	
377.5mm	**Welcome Ctr wb, full(handicapped)facilities, info, phone, picnic tables, litter barrels, vending, petwalk**	E
376b a	US 30, to US 20/26, Ontario, Payette, N...gas: Chevron/dsl, food: A&W/KFC, Burger King, Cold- stone Creamery, China Buffet, Country Kitchen, DQ, Denny's, Domino's, McDonald's, Primo's Pizza, Quizno's, Taco Del Mar, Taco Time, Wingers, lodg- ing: Best Western, Colonial Inn, Holiday Inn, Motel 6, Sleep Inn, Super 8, other: Chrysler/Dodge/Jeep, Home Depot, K-Mart, Radio Shack, Staples, Toyota, Wal-Mart SuperCtr/24hr, st police, S...gas: Pilot/Ar- by's/dsl/scales/24hr, Shell/dsl, food: DJ's, Domino's,	W

Interstate 84

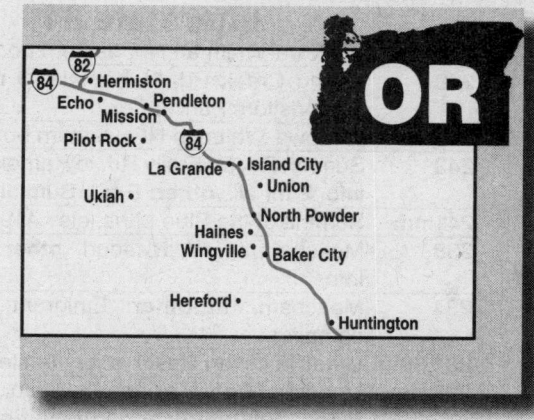

	Far East Chinese, Ogawa's Japanese, Rusty's Steaks, Sizzler, Subway, Taco Bell, Wendy's, **lodging:** Economy Inn, OR Trail Motel, Rodeway Inn, Stockman's Motel, **other:** HOSPITAL, Commercial Tire, NAPA, Schwab Tire, U-Haul, RV repair, 4 Wheeler Museum
374	US 30, OR 201, to Ontario, **N**...to Ontario SP, **S**...**gas:** Shell/dsl, **lodging:** Budget Inn, **other:** HOSPITAL
373.5mm	Malheur River
371	Stanton Blvd, **2 mi S**...to correctional institution
362	Moores Hollow Rd, no services
356	OR 201, to Weiser, ID, **3 mi N**...Catfish Junction RV Park, Oasis RV Park
354.5mm	weigh sta eb
353	US 30, to Huntington, **N**...weigh sta wb, **gas:** Joy Travel Plaza/dsl/rest./motel/@, **other:** to Farewell Bend SP, truck repair, RV camping, info
351mm	Pacific/Mountain time zone
345	US 30, Lime, Huntington, **1 mi N**...gas, food, lodging, to Snake River Area, Van Ornum BFD
342	Lime(from eb), no services
340	Rye Valley, no services
338	Lookout Mountain, **N**...**other:** OR Trail RV Park
337mm	Burnt River
335	to Weatherby, **N**...**rest area both lanes, full (handicapped)facilities, Oregon Trail Info, picnic tables, litter barrels, vending, petwalk**
330	Plano Rd, to Cement Plant Rd, **S**...cement plant
329mm	pulloff eb
327	Durkee, **N**...**gas:** Co-op/dsl/LP/café
325mm	Pritchard Creek
321mm	Alder Creek
317	to Pleasant Valley(from wb), no services
315	to Pleasant Valley(from wb), no services
313	to Pleasant Valley(from eb), no services
306	US 30, Baker, **2-3 mi S**...**gas:** Chevron/dsl, **food:** DQ, **lodging:** Baker City Motel, Bridge Street Hotel, Budget Inn, OR Tr Motel/rest., **other:** HOSPITAL, to st police, same as 304
304	OR 7, Baker, **N**...**gas:** Chevron/dsl, **lodging:** Super 8, Welcome Inn, **S**...**gas:** Shell/Blimpie/dsl/24hr, Sinclair/dsl/rest./scales/24hr, **food:** Arceo's Mexican, DQ, Fong's Chinese, Golden Crown, McDonald's, Papa Murphy's, Pizza Hut, Subway, Sumpter Jct Rest., Taco Time, **lodging:** Best Western, Budget Inn, Eldorado Inn, Rodeway Inn, Western Motel, **other:** HOSPITAL, Albertson's/gas, Bi-Mart Foods, CarQuest, $Tree, Ford/Lincoln/Mercury, Mtn View RV Park(3mi), Rite Aid, Safeway Foods, museum, to hist dist
302	OR 86 E to Richland, **S**...**other:** HOSPITAL, OR Tr RV Park/LP
298	OR 203, to Medical Springs, no services
297mm	Baldock Slough, no services
295mm	**rest area both lanes, full(handicapped) facilities, info, phone, picnic tables, litter barrels, vending, petwalk**
289mm	Powder River

*(left margin: E... W... **Baker**)*

287.5mm	45th parallel...halfway between the equator and north pole
286mm	N Powder River
285	US 30, OR 237, North Powder, **N**...**gas:** Cenex/dsl/café, **lodging:** Powder River Motel, **S**...**other:** to Anthony Lakes, ski area
284mm	Wolf Creek
283	Wolf Creek Lane
278	Clover Creek
273	Frontage Rd
270	Ladd Creek Rd(from eb, no return), no services
269mm	**rest area both lanes, full(handicapped) facilities, info, phone, picnic tables, litter barrels, vending, petwalk**
268	Foothill Rd, no services
265	OR 203, LaGrande, **N**...**other:** Eagles Hot Lake RV Park, airport, **S**...**gas:** Chevron(2mi), ⚛/Flying J/Shell/dsl/rest./scales/24hr, **food:** Smoke-House Rest.(2mi)
261	OR 82, LaGrande, **N**...**gas:** Chevron/dsl, Shell/dsl, **food:** Denny's, Pizza Hut, Quizno's, Starbucks, Taco Bell, **lodging:** LaGrande Inn, **other:** Chrysler/Dodge/Jeep, Ford/Lincoln/Mercury, Grocery Outlet, Thunder RV Ctr, Wal-Mart Super Ctr/24hr, st police, **S**...**gas:** 76/Subway/dsl, Texaco/dsl, **food:** Bear Mtn. Pizza, China Buffet, Cinco de Mayo Mexican, DQ, KFC, La Fiesta Mexican, McDonald's, Moi's Dynasty, Papa Murphy's, Smokehouse Rest., Taco Time, Wendy's, **lodging:** All American Inn, Best Western, Moon Motel, Royal Motel, Sandman Inn, Super 8, Travelodge, **other:** HOSPITAL, Albertson's, $Tree, Kottman Transmissions, Rite Aid, Safeway/gas, Schuck's Parts, Schwab Tire, vet, E OR U, Wallowa Lake
260mm	Grande Ronde River
259	US 30 E(from eb), to La Grande, **1-2 mi S**...**gas:** Chevron, Shell, **food:** Burger King, **lodging:** All-American Motel, Greenwell Motel/rest., Royal Motel, **other:** Safeway/gas, same as 261
257	Perry(from wb), no services
256.5mm	weigh sta eb
256	Perry(from eb), no services
255mm	Grande Ronde River
254mm	scenic wayside
252	OR 244, to Starkey, Lehman Springs, **S**...**other:** Hilgard SP, camping, chainup area

*(right margin: **LaGrande**)*

OREGON

Interstate 84

Pendleton

251mm	Wallowa-Whitman NF, eastern boundary
248	Spring Creek Rd, to Kamela, **3 mi N**...Oregon Trail Visitors Park
246mm	Wallowa-Whitman NF, western boundary
243	Summit Rd, Mt Emily Rd, to Kamela, Oregon Trail info, **2 mi N**...**other:** Emily Summit SP
241mm	Summit of the Blue Mtns, elev 4193
238	Meacham, **1 mi N**...food, **other:** Oregon Trail info
234	Meacham, **S**...**other:** Emigrant Sprs SP, RV camping
231.5mm	Umatilla Indian Reservation, eastern boundary
228mm	Deadman Pass, Oregon Trail info, **rest area both lanes, full(handicapped)facilities, phone(wb), picnic table, litter barrel, petwalk, vending, RV Dump(wb)**
227mm	weigh sta wb, brake check area
224	Poverty Flats Rd, Old Emigrant Hill Rd, to Emigrant Springs SP, no services
223mm	wb viewpoint, no restrooms
221.5mm	eb viewpoint, no restrooms
220mm	wb runaway truck ramp
216	Mission, McKay Creek, **N**...**gas:** Arrowhead Trkstp/Pacific Pride/dsl/24hr, **food:** Cody's Rest., **other:** Wildhorse Casino/RV Park
213	US 30(from wb), Pendleton, **3-5 mi N**...**gas:** Chevron/dsl, Shell, **lodging:** Travelers Inn, **other:** HOSPITAL, Pendleton NHD
212mm	Umatilla Indian Reservation western boundary
210	OR 11, Pendleton, **N**...**other:** HOSPITAL, museum, **S**...**gas:** Chevron/dsl, Shell/dsl/LP, **food:** Shari's/24hr, **lodging:** Best Western, Holiday Inn Express, Motel 6, Red Lion Inn/rest., Super 8, **other:** Mtn View RV Park, st police
209	US 395, Pendleton, **N**...**food:** A&W/Taco Bell, Jack-in-the-Box, KFC, Pizza, **lodging:** B&B, Oxford Suites, Travelodge, Travelers Inn, **other:** Curves, Rite Aid, Safeway/dsl, Wal-Mart SuperCtr/Subway, **S**...**gas:** 76/dsl, **food:** Abby's Pizza, Arby's, Burger King, Denny's, McDonald's, Rooster's Rest., Starbucks, Subway, Wendy's, **lodging:** Econolodge, **other:** Chevrolet/Pontiac/Buick, Honda, Schwab Tire, Thompson RV Ctr
208mm	Umatilla River
207	US 30, W Pendleton, **N**...**gas:** Shell/dsl/LP, **other:** Lookout RV Park
202	Barnhart Rd, to Stage Gulch, **N**...Woodpecker Truck Repair, **S**...**lodging:** Rodeo Inn, **other:** Oregon Trail info
199	Stage Coach Rd, Yoakum Rd, no services
198	Lorenzen Rd, McClintock Rd, **N**...**other:** trailer/reefer repair
193	Echo Rd, to Echo, Oregon Trail Site
188	US 395 N, Hermiston, **N**...**gas:** Chevron/dsl(1mi), Pilot/Subway/McDonald's/dsl/24hr/RV park/@, **5 mi N**...**food:** Denny's/24hr, Jack-in-the-Box, McDonald's, Shari's/24hr, **lodging:** Best Western, Economy Inn, Oak Tree Inn, Oxford Suites, **other:** HOSPITAL, **S**...**other:** Henrietta RV Park(1mi), Echo HS
187mm	**rest area both lanes, full(handicapped) facilities, phone, info, picnic tables, litter barrels, petwalk**
182	OR 207, to Hermiston, **N**...**other:** Space Age/A&W/dsl/24hr, **lodging:** Comfort Inn
180	Westland Rd, to Hermiston, McNary Dam, **N**...trailer repair, **S**...**gas:** Shell/Western Express/dsl/24hr
179	I-82 W, to Umatilla, Kennewick, WA
177	Umatilla Army Depot, no services
171	Paterson Ferry Rd, to Paterson, no services
168	US 730, to Irrigon, **8 mi N**...**other:** Green Acres RV Park, Oregon Trail info
165	Port of Morrow, **S**...**gas:** Pacific Pride/dsl
164	Boardman, **N**...**gas:** Chevron/dsl, Shell/dsl, **food:** C&D Drive-In, Leonard's Cafe, **lodging:** Dodge City Motel, Riverview Motel, **other:** USPO, Boardman RV/Marina Park, **S**...**gas:** Shell/dsl, **lodging:** Econolodge, **lodging:** NAPA Repair/parts, Family Foods, Oregon Trail Library, tires
161mm	**rest area both lanes, full(handicapped) facilities, phone, picnic tables, litter barrels, vending, petwalk**
159	Tower Rd, no services
151	Threemile Canyon, no services
147	OR 74, to Ione, Blue Mtn Scenic Byway, Heppner, Oregon Trail Site, no services
137	OR 19, Arlington, **S**...**gas:** Shell/dsl, **food:** Happy Canyon Cafe, Pheasant Grill, Village Inn, **other:** Ace Hardware, Thrifty Foods, Columbia River RV Park(1mi), city park
136.5mm	view point wb, picnic tables, litter barrels
131	Woelpern Rd(from eb, no return), no services
129	Blalock Canyon, Lewis&Clark Trail, no services
123	Philippi Canyon, Lewis&Clark Trail, no services
114.5mm	John Day River
114	**S**...LePage Park
112	parking area, both lanes, litter barrels, **N**...John Day Dam
109	Rufus, **N**...John Day Visitor Ctr, **S**...**gas:** Pacific Pride/dsl, Shell/dsl, **food:** Bob's T-Bone, Frosty's Café, Hi-Mkt Deli, Larry's Rest., **lodging:** Hillview Hotel, Tyee Motel, **other:** Ed's RV camping
109	Rufus, **N**...John Day Visitor Ctr, **S**...**gas:** Shell/dsl, **food:** Bob's T-Bone, **lodging:** Rufus Inn, Tyee Motel, **other:** RV camping
104	US 97, Biggs, **N**...**other:** Des Chutes Park Bridge, **S**...**gas:** Exxon, 76/Circle K/dsl/24hr, Pilot/McDonald's/dsl/scales/24hr, Linda's/Shell/Subway/rest./dsl, **lodging:** Biggs Motel/café, Dinty's Motel, Travelodge, **other:** Maryhill Museum, dsl repair
100mm	Deschutes River, Columbia River Gorge Scenic Area
97	OR 206, Celilo, **N**...**other:** Celilo SP, restrooms, **S**...**other:** Deschutes SP, Indian Village
92	pullout, eb
88	**N**...to The Dalles Dam

Interstate 84

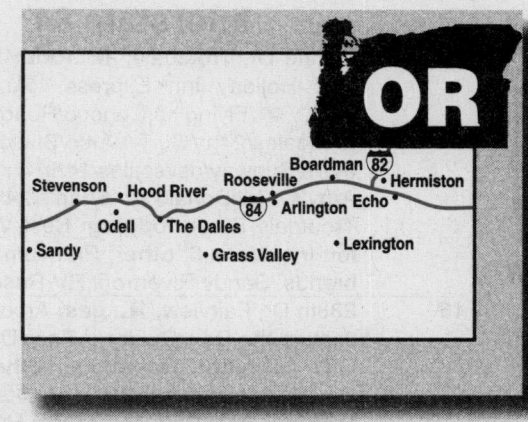

87	US 30, US 197, to Dufur, 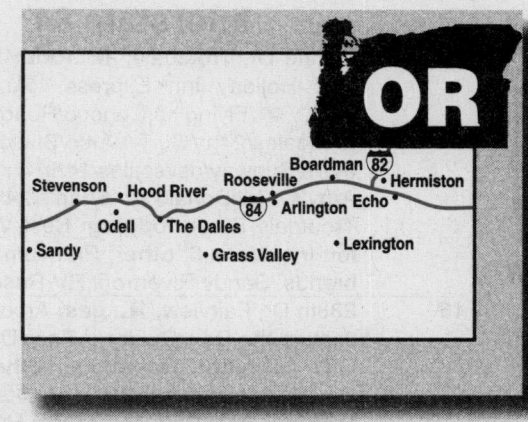...**gas:** Chevron, 76/dsl/24hr, **food:** McDonald's, Portage Grill, **lodging:** Comfort Inn, Shilo Inn/rest., **other:** Columbia Hills RV Park, Lone Pine RV Park, st police, **S**...**food:** Big Jim's Drive-In, **lodging:** Riverview Inn, **other:** Schwab Tire
85	The Dalles, **N...Riverfront Park, restrooms, phone, picnic tables, litter barrels, playground, marina, S...gas:** Chevron, 76/dsl, **food:** BurgervilleUSA, RoadStop Rest., **lodging:** Best Western, Oregon Motel, **other:** HOSPITAL, Fast Auto Repair, Lincoln/Mercury/Toyota, NAPA, camping, USPO, to Nat Hist Dist
83	(84 from wb)W The Dalles, **N**...**food:** Casa El Mirador, Orient Café, Windseeker Rest., **other:** NAPA, Tire Factory, **S**...**gas:** Chevron, Exxon, Shell/dsl, **food:** Arby's, Burger King, Denny's, Ixtapa Mexican, McDonald's, Papa Murphy's, Skipper's, Subway, Taco Bell, Taco Time, **lodging:** Best Western, Cousin's Inn/rest., Motel 6, Shilo Inn, Tillicum Inn, Super 8, **other:** HOSPITAL, Albertson's, Buick/Pontiac/GMC, Chevrolet, Chrysler/Dodge, $Tree, Ford, Fred Meyer, Grocery Outlet, Jo-Ann Fabrics, K-Mart, PetCo, Radio Shack, Rite Aid, Safeway, Schuck's Parts, Staples, Subaru, Walgreens
82	Chenowith Area, **S**...**gas:** Astro/dsl/24hr, **food:** Spooky's Café, **other:** Bi-Mart Foods, Columbia Discovery Ctr, Home Depot, museum, same as 83
76	Rowena, **N**...**other:** Mayer SP, Lewis & Clark info, windsurfing
73mm	**Memaloose SP, rest area both lanes, full (handicapped)facilities, picnic tables, litter barrels, phone, petwalk, RV dump, camping**
69	US 30, Mosier, **S**...**food:** Goodriver Rest. **other:** USPO
66mm	**N...Koberg Beach SP, rest area wb, full facilities, picnic table, litter barrels**
64	US 30, OR 35, to White Salmon, Hood River, **N**...**gas:** Chevron, Shell/24hr, **food:** McDonald's, Riverside Grill, Starbucks, **lodging:** Best Western, **other:** marina, museum, st police
63	Hood River, City Ctr, **N**...**gas:** 76/dsl, **other:** Visitor Ctr, **S**...**food:** Annz Cafe, Gorge Grill, Pietro's Pizza, Sage's Cafe, Taco Del Mar, **lodging:** Hood River Hotel/rest., **other:** HOSPITAL, USPO, same as 64
62	US 30, Westcliff Dr, W Hood River, **N**...**food:** Charburger, **lodging:** Columbia Gorge Hotel, Vagabond Lodge, **S**...**gas:** Chevron/dsl/LP, 76/dsl, **food:** Domino's, DQ, Egg Harbor Cafe, HoHo Rest., McDonald's, Quizno's, Red Carpet Cafe, Starbucks, Subway, Taco Bell, **lodging:** Comfort Suites, Prater's Motel, Riverview Lodge, Stonehedge Inn, **other:** HOSPITAL, Cascade Mkt, Chevrolet/Pontiac/Buick/GMC, Oil Can Henry's, Rite Aid, Safeway, Schwab Tire, Wal-Mart

61mm	pulloff wb
60	service rd wb(no return), no services
58	Mitchell Point Overlook(from eb)
56	**N**...**other:** Viento SP, RV camping, phone
55	Starvation Peak Tr Head(from eb), restrooms
54mm	weigh sta wb
51	Wyeth, **S**...camping
49mm	pulloff eb
47	Forest Lane, Hermon Creek(from wb), camping
45mm	weigh sta eb
44	US 30, to Cascade Locks, **1-4 mi N**...**gas:** CFN, Chevron/LP, Shell/dsl, **food:** Charburger, Salmon Row Cafe, **lodging:** Best Western, Bridge of the Gods Motel, Cascade Motel, Econolodge, **other:** to Bridge of the Gods, Stern Wheeler RV Park
41	Eagle Creek RA(from eb), to fish hatchery
40	**N**...**other:** Bonneville Dam NHS, info, to fish hatchery
37	Warrendale(from wb), no services
35	Historic Hwy, Multnomah Falls, **S**...**other:** Ainsworth SP, scenic loop highway, waterfall area, Fishery RV Park 31 Multnomah Falls(exits left from both lanes), **S**...**lodging:** Multnomah Falls Lodge/Rest.(hist site), camping
31	Multnomah Falls(exits left from both lanes), **S**...Multnomah Falls Lodge/Rest.(hist site), camping
30	**S**...Benson SRA(from eb)
29	Dalton Point(from wb), no services
28	to Bridal Veil(7 mi return from eb), no services
25	**N**...Rooster Rock SP
23mm	viewpoint wb, hist marker
22	Corbett, **2 mi S**...**gas:** Corbett Mkt, **lodging:** Vista House, **other:** Crown Point RV Camping
19mm	Columbia River Gorge scenic area
18	Lewis&Clark SP, to Oxbow SP, lodging, food, RV camping
17.5mm	Sandy River

OREGON

Interstate 84

E ↕ W

Portland

17	Marine Dr, Troutdale, **N**...**food:** Wendy's, **lodging:** Holiday Inn Express, **S**...**gas:** Chevron/24hr, ♨/Flying J/Conoco/Roadside Diner/dsl/LP/scales/24hr/@, TA/Arco/Buckhorn Rest./Popeye's/Subway/dsl/scales/24hr/@, Shell/dsl, **food:** Arby's, McDonald's, Shari's/24hr, Taco Bell, Troutdale Diner, **lodging:** Best Value Inn, Comfort Inn, Motel 6, **other:** Premium Outlets/famous brands, Sandy Riverfront RV Resort
16	238th Dr, Fairview, **N**...**gas:** Arco/dsl/24hr, **food:** Jack-in-the-Box, Quizno's, Taco Del Mar, Yazzie's Grill, **lodging:** Travelodge, **other:** Olinger RV Ctr, Wal-Mart SuperCtr/24hr, **S**...**gas:** Chevron, **lodging:** Best Western, **other:** HOSPITAL
14	207th Ave, Fairview, **N**...**gas:** Shell/dsl, **food:** GinSun Chinese, **other:** American Dream RV Ctr, Portland RV Park, Rolling Hills RV Park, auto repair
13	181st Ave, Gresham, **N**...**gas:** CFN, Chevron, **lodging:** Hampton Inn, **S**...**gas:** 76/Circle K, **food:** Burger King, Jung's Chinese, McDonald's, Shari's/24hr, Wendy's, Xavier's, **lodging:** Comfort Suites, Extended Stay America, Hawthorn Suites, Quality Inn, Sheraton, Sleep Inn, Super 8, **other:** Candy Basket Chocolates, Safeway, 7-11, auto repair, vet
10	122nd Ave(from eb), no services
9	I-205, S to Salem, N to Seattle, to airport, (to 102nd Ave from eb)
8	I-205 N(from eb), **N**...to airport
7	Halsey St(from eb), Gateway Dist
6	I-205 S(from eb)
5	OR 213, to 82nd Ave(eb only), **N**...**lodging:** Capri Motel, Day's Inn, Motel Cabana, **1-3 mi N**...**gas:** 76, Shell, 7-11, **food:** Arby's, Burgerville, Domino's, Pizza Hut, Wendy's, **lodging:** Quality Inn, Shilo Inn, **S**...**food:** Elmer's Rest., Taco Bell, **lodging:** Comfort Inn, Microtel, **other:** NAPA
4	68th Ave(from eb), to Halsey Ave
3	58th Ave(from eb), **S**...**gas:** KC, Shell, **other:** HOSPITAL, Fred Meyer
2	43rd Ave, 39th Ave, Halsey St, **N**...**gas:** Chevron, 76, Shell, **food:** Baja Fresh, Burger King, McDonald's, Subway, Winchell's, **lodging:** Banfield Motel, Rodeway Inn, **other:** Rite Aid, **S**...**other:** HOSPITAL, Buick/Pontiac, Jeep, same as 1
1	33rd Ave, Lloyd Blvd(eb only), **N**...**gas:** 76, Pacific Pride/dsl, Shell/dsl, **food:** Burger King, Domino's, **lodging:** Banfield Motel, Best Western, Holiday Inn, Red Lion Inn, Residence Inn, **other:** JC Penney, Rite Aid, **S**...**food:** Pizza Hut, **other:** Buick
1	to downtown(wb only)
0mm	I-84 begins/ends on I-5, exit 301.

Interstate 205(Portland)

N ↕ S

Portland Area

Exit #	Services
37mm	I-205 begins/ends on I-5. **Exits 36-27 are in Washington.**
36	NE 134th St(from nb), **E**...**gas:** Arco/dsl, **lodging:** Holiday Inn Express, **W**...**gas:** Citgo/7-11, 76, TrailMart/dsl, **food:** Billygan's Roadhouse, Burger King, Burgerville, Figaro's Pizza, Jack-in-the-Box, McDonald's, Round Table Pizza, Taco Bell, **lodging:** Comfort Inn, Holiday Inn Express, Red Lion Inn, Salmon Creek Inn, Shilo Inn, **other:** HOSPITAL, Albertson's/drug/gas, Hi-School Drugs, Long Drug, Safeway/gas, Walgreen, 99 RV Park
32	NE 83rd St, Andreson Rd, Battle Ground, **W**...**gas:** Shell/dsl/24hr, **food:** Krispy Kreme, Meadows Kitchen, Subway, Wendy's, Weinerschnitzel, **other:** Costco/gas, Home Depot
30c b a	WA 500, Orchards, Vancouver, **E**...**gas:** Atco, Gas Towne, 76/Circle K, Shell/24hr, **food:** Applebee's, Burger King, Burgerville, Cisco's Rest., KFC, McDonald's, Subway, **other:** Jo-Ann Crafts, Rite Aid, Toyota, Vanmall RV park, Walgreen, **W**...**gas:** Chevron/24hr, Tesoro/dsl, **food:** Azteca Mexican, Chevy's Mexican, Moshi Japanese, Olive Garden, Outback Steaks, Red Lobster, Red Robin Rest., RoundTable Pizza, Skipper's, Shari's/24hr, Subway, Taco Bell, TCBY, TGIFriday, **lodging:** Best Western, Comfort Suites, Heathman Lodge, Holiday Inn Express, Ramada, Residence Inn, Sleep Inn, Staybridge Inn, **other:** Big Lots, JC Penney, Meijer&Frank, Mervyn's, Nordstrom's, Ross, Sears/auto, Target, mall, RV park
28	Mill Plain Rd, **E**...**gas:** Chevron/24hr, 76/Circle K, Shell/dsl, **food:** Burger King, Burgerville, DQ, Elmer's Rest., Mongolian BBQ, Kings Buffet, McDonald's, McGrath's Fishhouse, Muchas Gracias Mexican, Pizza Hut, Quizno's, Shari's, Starbucks, Taco Bell, **lodging:** Best Western, Extended Stay America, Guesthouse Inn, Phoenix Inn, Quality Inn, **other:** Fred Meyer, Schuck's Parts, Schwab Tire, 7-11, **W**...**gas:** Arco/24hr, 76, **food:** Arby's, Jack-in-the-Box, Old Mill Bread, Subway, **other:** HOSPITAL, Chevrolet, Wal-Mart SuperCtr/24hr, auto/tire repair
27	WA 14, Vancouver, Camas, Columbia River Gorge
25mm	**Oregon/Washington state line. Columbia River. Exits 27-36 are in Washington.**
24	122nd Ave, **E**...**food:** Burger King, China Wok, CoffeeHouse, Jack-in-the-Box, McDonald's, Shari's, Subway, **lodging:** Comfort Suites, Courtyard, Fairfield Inn, Hilton Garden, Holiday Inn Express, La Quinta, Shilo Inn/rest., Silver Cloud Inn, SpringHill Suites, Staybridge Suites, Super 8, **other:** Best Buy, CompUSA, Home Depot, **W**...**lodging:** Hampton Inn, Sheraton/rest.

Interstate 205

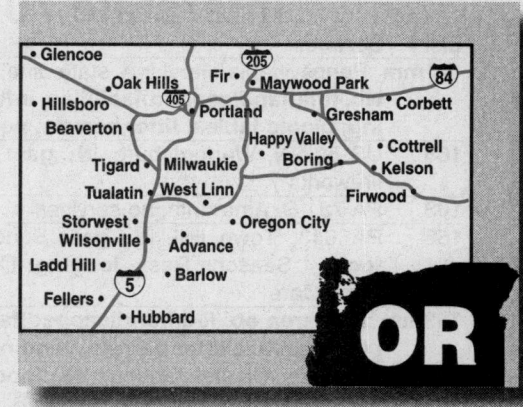

23b a	US 30 byp, Columbia Blvd, E...**gas:** Leather's Fuel/dsl, Shell/dsl, **food:** Bill's Steaks, Elmer's Rest., **lodging:** Best Western, Econolodge, Carolina Motel, Red Lion Hotel, Roadway Inn, **other:** HOSPITAL, W...**gas:** Shell, **lodging:** Holiday Inn, Radisson, Ramada Inn, **other:** camping
22	I-84 E, US 30 E, to The Dalles
21b	I-84 W, US 30 W, to Portland
21a	Glisan St, E...**gas:** 76, **food:** Szechuan Chinese, E **on NE 102nd St**...**gas:** Arco, Applebee's, Carl's Jr, Izzy's Pizza, Quizno's, Circuit City, McDonald's, Rubio's, **other:** Fred Meyer, Mervyn's, Office Depot, Ross, WinCo Foods, mall
20	Stark St, Washington St, E...**food:** Acapulco Mexican, Arby's, Baja Fresh, Burger King, Denny's, Elmer's Rest., Hooters, Izzy's Pizza, Newport Bay Café, Old Chicago Pizza, Old Country Kitchen, Olive Garden, Panda Express, Village Inn, **lodging:** Chesnut Tree Inn, Holiday Inn Express, **other:** Cottman Transmissions, Home Depot, Target, mall, W...**food:** ChuckeCheese, McDonald's, Stark St Pizza, Taco Bell, **lodging:** Rodeway Inn, **other:** 7-11
19	US 26, Division St, E...**gas:** Space Age/dsl, **other:** HOSPITAL, W...**gas:** Chevron/24hr, 76, Shell/dsl, **food:** Carl's Jr, Izzy's Pizza, McDonald's, Sizzler, Subway, Wendy's, **other:** Best Value Inn
17	Foster Rd, **1 mi** W...**gas:** Chevron, 76, Shell, **food:** Arby's, Burger King, IHOP, McDonald's, Wendy's, **lodging:** Econolodge, Home Depot, **other:** U-Haul
16	Johnson Creek Blvd, W...**gas:** 76, **food:** Applebee's, Burger King, Carl's Jr, Denny's, Fuddrucker's, Hometown Buffet, McDonald's, Old Chicago Pizza, Outback Steaks, Papa Joe's, Ron's Café, Starbucks, Subway, Taco Bell, **other:** Best Buy, Fred Meyer/gas, Home Depot, RV Ctrs, Schuck's Parts, Walgreens
14	Sunnyside Rd, E...**food:** A&W/KFC, Baja FreshMex, Burger King, Domino's, Izzy's Pizza, KFC, Quizno's, Starbucks, Subway, Thai House, Wendy's, **lodging:** Best Western, Day's Inn, **other:** HOSPITAL, Office Depot, W...**gas:** 76/LP/24hr, Texaco/dsl/24hr, **food:** Chevy's Mexican, Chili's, Claim Jumper, Macaroni Grill, McDonald's, Old Spaghetti Factory, Olive Garden, Red Robin, Stanford's Rest., Sweet Tomatoes, Taco Time, **lodging:** Courtyard, Monarch Hotel/rest., **other:** America Tire, Barnes&Noble, JC Penney, Macy's, Nordstroms, Old Navy, PetCo, Sears/auto, Target, World Mkt, mall
13	OR 224, to Milwaukie, W...K-Mart, Lowe's Whse
12	OR 213, to Milwaukie, E...**gas:** Chevron/24hr, Pacific Pride, Shell, **food:** Denny's, Elmer's, KFC, McDonald's, Taco Bell/24hr, Wendy's, **lodging:** Clackamas Inn, Hampton Inn, **other:** Fred Meyer, 7-11, W...**lodging:** Comfort Suites
11	82nd Dr, Gladstone, W...**gas:** Arco/24hr, Chevron, **food:** McDonald's, **lodging:** Oxford Suites, **other:** Harley-Davidson, Safeway
10	OR 213, Park Place, E...**gas:** 76/Pacific Pride/dsl, **other:** HOSPITAL, Home Depot, to Oregon Trail Ctr
9	9 OR 99E, Oregon City, E...**gas:** 76, **food:** KFC, **other:** HOSPITAL, Subaru, W...**food:** La Hacienda Mexican, McDonald's, Shari's, Starbucks, Subway, Thai Rest., **lodging:** Rivershore Hotel, **other:** Coastal Ranch Store, $Tree, Firestone/auto, Michael's, Rite Aid
8.5mm	Willamette River
8	OR 43, W Linn, Lake Oswego, E...**gas:** 76, **other:** museum, W...**gas:** Shell/dsl/24hr
7mm	viewpoint nb, hist marker
6	10th St, W Linn St, E...**gas:** Chevron/LP, 76, **food:** Ixtapa Mexican, McDonald's, Shari's/24hr, West Linn Cafe, **other:** Oil Can Henry's, Schwab Tire, vet, W...**food:** Bugatti's Pizza, Jack-in-the-Box, Subway, **other:** Albertson's
4mm	Tualatin River
3	Stafford Rd, Lake Oswego, W...**food:** Corner Saloon, **other:** HOSPITAL
0mm	I-205 begins/ends on I-5, exit 288.

PENNSYLVANIA
Interstate 70

E

W

Breezewood

Exit #	Services
171mm	Pennsylvania/Maryland state line, **Welcome Ctr wb, full(handicapped)facilities, info, phone, vending, picnic tables, litter barrels, petwalk**
168	US 522 N, Warfordsburg, **N...gas:** Exxon/dsl, **S...** fireworks
163	PA 731 S, Amaranth, no services
156	PA 643, Town Hill, **N...gas:** Sunoco/Subway/dsl, **food:** 4 Seasons Rest., **lodging:** Day's Inn, **other:** Napa Care
153mm	**rest area eb, full(handicapped)facilities, phone, picnic tables, litter barrels, vending, petwalk**
151	PA 915, Crystal Spring, **N...food:** CornerStone Family Rest., **other:** auto repair, **S...other:** Country Store/USPO
149	US 30 W, to Everett, S Breezewood(no immediate wb return), **3 mi** **S...food:** Denny's, McDonald's, **lodging:** Penn Aire Motel, Redwood Motel, Wildwood Motel
147	US 30, Breezewood, **Services on US 30...gas:** BP/dsl, Citgo, Exxon/dsl, Mobil/dsl/24hr, Sheetz/24hr, Shell, Sunoco/dsl/café, TA/dsl/rest./24hr/@, Texaco/Subway, **food:** Arby's, Big John's Buffet, Bob Evans, Burger King, DQ, Denny's, Domino's, Family House Rest., Hardee's, KFC, McDonald's, Perkins, Pizza Hut, Taco Bell, Wendy's, **lodging:** Best Western, Breezewood Motel, Comfort Inn/rest., Econolodge, Holiday Inn Express, Penn Aire Motel, Quality Inn, Ramada Inn, Wiltshire Motel, **other:** museum
	I-70 and I-76/PA Turnpike run together. For I-70 and I-76/PA TPK exits 146-75, see Pennsylvania Interstate 76/PA TPK.
58	**PA Tpk. I-70 E/I-76/PA Turnpike E run together.**
57	I-70 W, US 119, PA 66(toll), New Stanton, **N...gas:** Exxon, Sheetz, **food:** Bob Evans, Eat'n Park, KFC, McDonald's, Pagano's Rest., Pizza Hut, Quizno's, Subway, Wendy's, **lodging:** Comfort Inn, Day's Inn, Fairfield Inn, Howard Johnson, Quality Inn, Super 8, **S...gas:** BP/dsl, Sunoco/24hr, **food:** Cracker Barrel, TJ's Rest., **lodging:** New Stanton Motel, **other:** Curves
54	Madison, **N...**KOA
53	Yukon, no services
51b a	PA 31, West Newton
49	Smithton, **N...gas:** Citgo/dsl/rest./scales/@, /Flying J/Country Mkt/dsl/scales/24hr/@
46b a	PA 51, Pittsburgh, **N...gas:** BP/dsl, **food:** Burger King, **lodging:** Sleeper Inn, **other:** Chevrolet/Pontiac/Buick/Cadillac/Kia, Harley-Davidson, **S...gas:** GetGo/dsl/24hr, **lodging:** Holiday Inn, Knotty Pine Motel, Relax Inn
44	Arnold City, no services
43b a	(43 from eb)PA 201, Fayette City, **S...gas:** Exxon/24hr, **food:** A&W/LJ Silver, Burger King, Denny's, Eat'n Park, Hoss' Rest., KFC, Little Bamboo, McDonald's, Pizza Hut, Ponderosa, Sonny's Grille, Starbucks, Subway, Wendy's, **lodging:** Hampton Inn, **other:** Advance Parts, Aldi Foods, Big Lots, Curves, CVS Drug, $General, $Tree, Eckerd, Giant Eagle Foods, GNC, Jo-Ann Fabrics, K-Mart, Lowe's Whse, Radio Shack, Staples, Wal-Mart SuperCtr/24hr
42a	Monessen, no services

Washington

Exit #	Services
42	N Belle Vernon, **S...gas:** BP/McDonald's, Sunoco/dsl, **food:** DQ
41	PA 906, Belle Vernon, no services
40mm	Monongahela River
40	PA 88, Charleroi, **N...gas:** GetGo/dsl, Gulf, Sunoco, **food:** McDonald's, **other:** HOSPITAL
39	Speers, **N...food:** Loraine's Rest., **S...gas:** Exxon
37b a	PA 43, no services
36	Lover(from wb, no re-entry), no services
35	PA 481, Centerville, no services
32b a	PA 917, Bentleyville, **S...gas:** BP/dsl, Pilot/DQ/Subway/dsl/scales/24hr, Sheetz/24hr, **food:** Burger King, CJ's Cafe, McDonald's, **lodging:** Best Western, **other:**Advance Parts, Blue Beacon, $General, Ford, Giant Eagle Foods, Rite Aid
31	to PA 136, Kammerer, **N...lodging:** Carlton Motel, **food:** Carlton Kitchen
27	Dunningsville, **S...lodging:** Avalon Motel
25	PA 519, to Eighty Four, **S...gas:** BP/7-11 Diner/dsl/24hr, Sunoco/dsl
21	I-79 S, to Waynesburg. **I-70 W and I-79 N run together 3.5 mi.**
19b a	US 19, Murtland Ave, **N...gas:** BP, GetGo, **food:** Applebee's, Arby's, Brewster's, Cracker Barrel, Krispy Kreme, McDonald's, Outback Steaks, Panera Bread, Ponderosa, Quizno's, Red Lobster, Red Robin, Starbucks, Subway, Texas Roadhouse, TGIFriday, **lodging:** SpringHill Suites, **other:** Aldi Foods, $Tree, Giant Eagle Foods, GNC, Hyundai, Lowe's Whse, Michael's, Nissan, Petsmart, Radio Shack, Sam's Club, Target, Toyota/Honda, Wal-Mart SuperCtr/24hr, vet, **S...gas:** BP/dsl, Exxon, GetGo, Sunoco, **food:** A&W/LJ Silver, Bob Evans, China Buffet, Eat'n Park/24hr, Evergreen Chinese, KFC, Old Mexico, Papa John's, Pizza Hut, **lodging:** Hampton Inn, Motel 6, **other:** HOSPITAL, Big Lots, Buick/Cadillac/GMC, Firestone/auto, Home Depot, JC Penney, Jo-Ann Fabrics, K-Mart, Staples, Subaru, mall, st police
20	PA 136, Beau St, **S...**to Washington&Jefferson Coll
18	I-79 N, to Pittsburgh. **I-70 E and I-79 S run together 3.5 mi.**
17	PA 18, Jefferson Ave, Washington, **N...gas:** Getgo, **food:** DQ, McDonald's, **other:** Family$, Rite Aid, **S...gas:** CoGo's/dsl, Sunoco, **food:** Burger King, China Buffet, 4Star Pizza, Subway, **other:** Advance Parts
16	Jessop Place, Jessop Place, **N...gas:** Citgo, **S...**auto/truck repair
15	US 40, Chesnut St, Washington, **N...food:** USA Steaks, **other:** Food Fresh, **S...gas:** BP, Starfire, Sunoco/dsl, **food:** Angelo's Rest., Bob Evans, Denny's, Garfield's Rest., JK Chinese, LJ Silver, McDonald's, Pizza Hut, Taco Bell, Wendy's, **lodging:** Comfort Suites, Day's Inn, Econolodge, Ramada Inn, Red Roof Inn, **other:** Eckerd, Gander Mtn, Macy's, Old Navy, Sears/auto, mall
11	PA 221, Taylorstown, **N...gas:** BP/dsl, **other:** truck repair
6	to US 40, PA 231, Claysville, **N...gas:** Exxon, **S...gas:** Petro/Citgo/King's/Sbarro's/Subway/scales/24hr
5mm	**Welcome Ctr eb, full(handicapped)facilities, phone, vending, picnic tables, litter barrels, petwalk**
1	W Alexander, no services
0mm	Pennsylvania/West Virginia state line

Interstate 76

Exit #	Services
354mm	Pennsylvania/New Jersey state line, Delaware River, Walt Whitman Bridge
351	Front St, I-95(from wb), N to Trenton, S to Chester
350	Packer Ave, 7th St, to I-95(fromeb), **S...lodging:** Holiday Inn, **other:** to sports complex
349	to I-95, PA 611, Broad St, no services
348	PA 291, W to Chester, **S...lodging:** Ramada Inn
347a	to I-95 S
347b	Passyunk Ave, Oregon Ave, **S...other:** sports complex
346c	28th St, Vare Ave, Mifflin St(from wb)
346b	Grays Ferry Ave, University Ave, civic center, **N...food:** McDonald's, PathMark Foods, **other:** Radio Shack, **S...gas:** BP/24hr, Hess
346a	South St, no services
345	30th St, Market St, downtown
344	I-676 E, US 30 E, to Philadelphia(no return from eb)
343	Spring Garden St, Haverford, no services
342	US 13, US 30 W, Girard Ave, Philadelphia Zoo, E Fairmount Park
341	Montgomery Dr, W River Dr, W Fairmount Park, W Fairmount Park
340b	US 1 N, Roosevelt Blvd, to Philadelphia
339	US 1 S, **S...lodging:** Adams Mark Hotel, Holiday Inn
340a	Lincoln Dr, Kelly Dr, to Germantown, no services
338	Belmont Ave, Green Lane, **N...other:** CVS Drug, **S...gas:** Sunoco/24hr, **food:** WaWa
337	Hollow Rd(from wb), Gladwyne, no services
332	PA 23(from wb), Conshohocken, **N...lodging:** Marriott
331b a	I-476, PA 28(from eb), to Chester, Conshohocken
330	PA 320, Gulph Mills, **S...to** Villanova U
328	US 202 N, to King of Prussia, **N...gas:** Exxon/dsl, Mobil, WaWa, **food:** Charlie's Place Rest., Dunkin Donuts, Friendly's, Sizzler, TGIFriday, Uno Pizzaria, **lodging:** Econolodge, Holiday Inn, Howard Johnson, McIntosh Inn, **other:** JC Penney, Macy's, Sears/auto, Thrift Drug, mall, **S...**George Washington Lodge
327	US 202 S, Goddard Blvd, to Valley Forge, Valley Forge Park, Valley Forge Park
326	I-76 wb becomes I-76/PA Tpk to Ohio
	For I-76 westbound to Ohio, see I-76/PA Turnpike.

PENNSYLVANIA
Interstate 76/TPK

E
↕
W

Exit #	Services
	PA Tpk runs wb as I-276.
359	Pennsylvania/New Jersey state line, Delaware River Bridge
358	US 13, Delaware Valley, **N**...**gas:** WaWa, **lodging:** Day's Inn, Ramada Inn, **other:** Cadillac, U-Haul, **S**...**gas:** Bristol/dsl, Getty Gas, Mobil, Sunoco, **food:** Burger King, DeGrand Diner, Golden Eagle Diner, Italian Family Rest., McDonald's, Russo's Italian, **lodging:** Comfort Inn, Villager Lodge, **other:** Buick
352mm	**Neshaminy Service Plaza, wb...Welcome Ctr, gas: Sunoco/dsl/24hr, food: Burger King, Nathan's, other: Starbucks, eb...gas: Sunoco/dsl, food: Breyer's, HotDog Co, McDonald's, Nathan's**
351	US 1, to I-95, to Philadelphia, **N**...**food:** Bob Evans, Ruby Tuesday, **lodging:** Courtyard, Hampton Inn, Holiday Inn, McIntosh Inn, **other:** Buick/Pontiac/Saturn/GMC, Home Depot, Sears/auto, Strawbridge's, Target, mall, **S**...**gas:** Amoco/24hr, Exxon/Subway, Sunoco/dsl, Texaco/dsl, **food:** Dunkin Donuts, Papa Yianni's Pizza, **lodging:** Comfort Inn, Howard Johnson, Knight's Inn, Neshaminy Inn, Radisson, Red Roof Inn, Sunrise Inn, **other:** Cadillac/Toyota
343	PA 611, Willow Grove, **N**...**gas:** Mobil, **food:**'s, **lodging:** Candlewood Suites(5mi), Courtyard, **S**...**gas:** Amoco/24hr, Hess/dsl, Mobil, Shell, Sunoco, 7-11, **food:** Bennigan's, China Garden, Domino's, Dunkin Donuts, Friendly's, McDonald's, Nino's Pizza, Ookaa Japanese, Williamson Rest., **lodging:** Hampton Inn, **other:** Best Buy, Firestone, Infiniti, PepBoys, Staples, transmissions
339	PA 309, Ft Washington, **N**...**gas:** Exxon, Mobil/Circle K/dsl, **food:** Friendly's, **lodging:** Best Western, Cherry Tree Hotel, Holiday Inn, **other:** BMW, Mercedes, Volvo
25A	PA Tpk NE Extension, to I-476
333	Germantown Pike, to Norristown, **N**...**gas:** Mobil/Circle K, **lodging:** SpringHill Suites, **other:** HOSPITAL, **S**...**gas:** Mobil/Circle K
328mm	**King of Prussia Service Plaza wb...Sunoco/dsl/24hr, Breyer's, McDonald's**
	PA Tpk runs eb as I-276, wb as I-76.
326	I-76 E, to US 202, I-476, Valley Forge, **N**...**gas:** Shell, **food:** Burger King, Cracker Barrel, Hooters, Hoss' Rest., **lodging:** Comfort Inn, Hampton Inn, MainStay Suites, Radisson, Sleep Inn, **S**...**gas:** Exxon, Mobil, Sunoco, WaWa, **food:** American Grill, CA Pizza, Chili's, Denny's, Houlihan's, McDonald's, **lodging:** Best Western, McIntosh Inn, Motel 6, Sheraton, **other:** Best Buy, Chevrolet, Costco, Crate&Barrel, Home Depot, JC Penney, Sears/auto, mall
325mm	**Valley Forge Service Plaza eb...gas: Sunoco/dsl/24hr, food: Burger King, Mrs Fields, Nathan's, TCBY, gifts**
312	PA 100, to Downingtown, Pottstown, **N**...**other:** CarSense, Harley-Davidson, **S**...**gas:** Gulf/dsl, Sunoco/dsl/24hr, WaWa, **food:** Hoss' Rest., Red Rob-
	in, **lodging:** Best Western, Comfort Inn, Extended Stay America, Fairfield Inn, Hampton Inn, Holiday Inn Express, Residence Inn, Sheraton(6mi), **other:** HOSPITAL
305mm	**Camiel Service Paza wb...Sunoco/dsl/24hr, Mrs Fields, Nathan's, Roy Rogers, Sbarro's, Starbucks, TCBY, gifts**
298	I-176, PA 10, to Reading, Morgantown, **N**...**lodging:** Economy Lodge, Heritage Motel/rest., **other:** HOSPITAL **S**...**food:** McDonald's, **lodging:** Holiday Inn
290mm	**Bowmansville Service Plaza eb...gas: Sunoco/dsl/24hr, food: Big Boy, Mrs Fields, Pizza Hut, Taco Bell, TCBY, other: gifts**
286	US 322, PA 272, to Reading, Ephrata, **N**...**gas:** Citgo/Penn Amish Motel, Exxon/dsl, Shell/dsl, **food:** Zia Maria Italian, Zinn's Diner, **lodging:** Black Horse Lodge/rest., Penna Dutch Motel, **other:** Dutch Cousins Camping, **S**...**gas:** Turkey Hill, **lodging:** Comfort Inn, Holiday Inn, Red Carpet Inn
266	PA 72, to Lebanon, Lancaster, **N**...**gas:** Hess/dsl, Mobil/ChesterFried, **food:** Little Corner of Germany Café, **lodging:** Red Carpet Inn, Rodeway Inn, **S**...**food:** Hitz Mkt/deli, **lodging:** Hampton Inn, Holiday Inn Express, **other:** HOSPITAL, Mt Hope Winery
259mm	**Lawn Service Plaza wb...gas: Sunoco/dsl/24hr, food: Burger King, other: TCBY, RV dump**
250mm	**Highspire Service Plaza eb...gas: Sunoco/dsl/24hr, food: Sbarro's**
247	I-283, PA 283, to Harrisburg, Harrisburg East, Hershey, **N**...**gas:** Sunoco, **food:** Eat'n Park, Taco Bell, Wendy's, **lodging:** Best Western, Day's Inn, Rodeway Inn, **other:** facilities 3-5 mi N
246mm	Susquehannah River
242	I-83, Harrisburg West, **N**...**gas:** BP, Mobil, **food:** Bob Evans, Eat'n Park, McDonald's, Pizza Hut, **lodging:** Comfort Inn, Fairfield Inn, Holiday Inn, Rodeway Inn, **S**...**gas:** Hess, **lodging:** Best Western, Days Inn, Motel 6, Travel Inn, **other:** vet
236	US 15, to Gettysburg, Gettysburg Pike, Harrisburg, **N**...**gas:** Mobil, Shell, **food:** Isaac's Rest., McDonald's, Palumbo Pizza, Subway, **lodging:** Comort Inn, Econolodge, Hampton Inn/rest., Holiday Inn Express, Homewood Suites, **other:** HOSPITAL, U-Haul, **S**...**gas:** Sheetz/24hr, **food:** Burger King, Hoss' Steaks(1mi), McDonald's(1mi), Wendy's, **lodging:** Best Western, Wingate Inn, **other:** Giant Food/24hr
226	226 US 11, to I-81, to Harrisburg, Carlisle, **N**...**gas:** BP, Petro/dsl/24hr/@, Citgo/dsl/24hr, ✈/Flying J/dsl/LP/rest./24hr/@, Pilot/Wendy's/dsl/24hr, Shell/dsl, **food:** Arby's, Bob Evans, Carelli's Subs, Eat'n Park, McDonald's, Middlesex Diner/24hr, Subway, Waffle House, **lodging:** Appalachian Trail Inn, Best Western, Budget Host, Hampton Inn, Holiday Inn, Howard Johnson, Quality Inn, Ramada Ltd, Rodeway Inn, Super 8, **other:** HOSPITAL, Blue Beacon, Giant Foods, **S**...**gas:** Exxon/Taco Bell/24hr, Sheetz/24hr, **food:** Hoss' Rest., **lodging:** Best Western, Motel 6, **other:** HOSPITAL, Chrysler/Jeep, U-Haul

Carlisle

PENNSYLVANIA

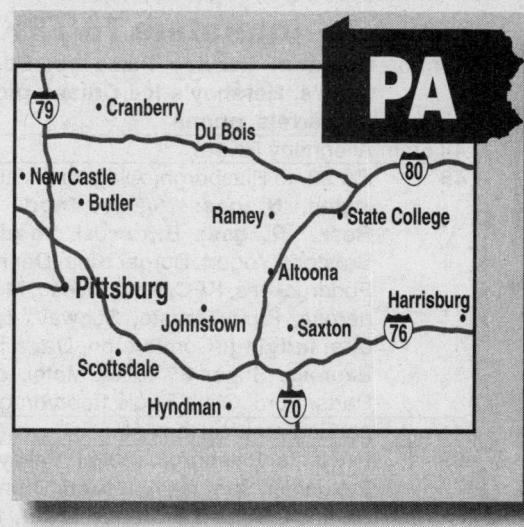

Interstate 76/TPK

219mm **Plainfield Service Plaza eb...gas:** Sunoco/dsl/ 24hr, **food:** Roy Rogers, **other:** TCBY, gifts

203mm **Blue Mtn Service Plaza wb...gas:** Sunoco/dsl/ 24hr, **food:** Nathan's, Hershy's IceCream, Roy Rogers, TCBY

201 PA 997, to Shippensburg, Blue Mountain, Ⓢ...**lodging:** Johnnie's Motel/rest., Kenmar Motel

199mm Blue Mountain Tunnel

197mm Kittatinny Tunnel

189 PA 75, Willow Hill, Ⓢ...**lodging:** Willow Hill Motel/ rest.

187mm Tuscarora Tunnel

180 US 522, Ft Littleton, Ⓝ...**gas:** BP/dsl, Shell/dsl, **food:** The Family Rest., **lodging:** Downes Motel, HOSPITAL

172mm **Sideling Hill Service Plaza both lane**Ⓢ...**gas:** Sunoco/dsl/24hr, **food:** Big Boy, Burger King, TCBY, **other:** gifts

161 US 30, Breezewood, **Services on US 30...gas:** TA/dsl/rest./24hr/@, BP/dsl, Citgo/Dunkin Donuts, Exxon/dsl, Mobil/dsl/24hr, Sheetz/24hr, Shell, Sunoco/dsl/café, Texaco/Subway, **food:** Arby's, Big John's Buffet, Bob Evans, Bonanza, Burger King, DQ, Denny's, Domino's, Family House Rest., Hardee's, KFC, McDonald's, Perkins, Pizza Hut, Taco Bell, Wendy's, **lodging:** Best Western, Breezewood Motel, Comfort Inn/rest., Econolodge, Holiday Inn Express, Penn Aire Motel, Quality Inn, Ramada Inn, Wiltshire Motel, **other:** camping, museum, truck/tire repair

161mm **I-70 W and I-76/PA Turnpike W run together**

150mm roadside park wb

148mm **Midway Service Plaza both lanes, eb...**Sunoco/ dsl/24hr, Cinnabon, Sbarro's, TCBY, gifts, wb... Sunoco/dsl/24hr, KFC, Sbarro's, Starbucks, TCBY, gifts

146 US 220, to I-99, Bedford, Ⓝ...**gas:** Amoco/McDonald's/dsl/24hr, BP/dsl, Sheetz, **food:** Arena Rest., Denny's, Hoss' Rest., Pizza Hut, Wendy's, **lodging:** Best Western, Budget Host, Econolodge, Quality Inn, Super 8, Travelodge, **other:** to Shawnee SP(10mi), Blue Knob SP(15mi), Ⓢ...**lodging:** Hampton Inn

142mm parking area wb

123mm Allegheny Tunnel

112mm **Somerset Service Plaza both lanes, eb...gas:** Sunoco/dsl/24hr, **food:** Big Boy, Roy Rogers, TCBY, **other:** gifts, wb...**gas:** Sunoco/dsl/24hr, **food:** Burger King, TCBY, **other:** gifts

110 PA 601, to US 219, Somerset, Ⓝ...**gas:** KwikFill, Sheetz/24hr, **food:** Hoss' Rest., King's Rest., Pizza Hut, Taco Bell, **lodging:** $ Inn, Economy Inn, **other:** Advance Parts, Chrysler/Jeep, Ford/Lincoln/Mercury, Ⓢ...**gas:** Exxon, Shell/dsl, **food:** Arby's, Bruester's Ice Cream, China Garden, Dunkin Donuts, Eat'n Park, Maggie•Mae's Café, McDonald's, Pine Grill, Summit Diner, Wendy's, **lodging:** Best Western, Budget Host, Day's Inn, Hampton Inn, Holiday Inn, Knight's Inn, Ramada Inn, Super 8, **other:** Dodge, Eckerd, Harley-Davidson

91 PA 711, Donegal, Ⓝ...**food:** Tall Cedars Rest./pizza, Ⓢ...**gas:** BP/Hardee's/Pizza Hut, Exxon/dsl, Sunoco/dsl, **food:** DQ, **lodging:** Day's Inn, Donegal Motel, **other:** golf

78mm **service plaza wb...gas:** Sunoco/dsl/24hr, **food:** McDonald's, **lodging:** Kings Family Rest.

I-70 E runs with I-76/PA Turnpike eb.

75 75 I-70 W, US 119, PA 66(toll), New Stanton, Ⓝ... **gas:** Exxon, Sheetz, **food:** Bob Evans, Eat'n Park, KFC, McDonald's, Pagano's Rest., Pizza Hut, Quizno's, Subway, Wendy's, **lodging:** Comfort Inn, Day's Inn, Fairfield Inn, Howard Johnson, Quality Inn, Super 8, Ⓢ...**gas:** BP/dsl, Sunoco/24hr, **food:** Cracker Barrel, TJ's Rest., **lodging:** New Stanton Motel, **other:** Curves

74.6mm **Hemphill Service Plaza eb...gas:** Sunoco/dsl/ 24hr, **food:** Breyer's, McDonald's, **other:** atm

67 US 30, to Greensburg, Irwin, Ⓝ...**gas:** BP/Blimpie/ dsl, Sheetz/24hr, Shell, **lodging:** Motel 3, **other:** HOSPITAL, Ford, Ⓢ...**gas:** Speedway, Sunoco/ 24hr, **food:** Angelo's Rest., Arby's, Bob Evans, Burger King, DQ, Denny's, Eat'n Park, KFC, LJ Silver, Los Compasinos Mexican, McDonald's, Pizza Hut, Royal China, Subway, Taco Bell, Teddy's Rest., Wendy's, **lodging:** Conley Inn, Holiday Inn Express, Penn Irwin Motel, **other:** Advance Parts, CarQuest, Giant Eagle Foods/24hr, Kohl's, Shop'n Save

61mm parking area eb

57 I-376, US 22, to Pittsburgh, Monroeville, Ⓢ...**gas:** BP, Citgo/dsl, **food:** Arby's, Burger King,'s, China Palace, Cooker Rest., Damon's, Denny's, Dunkin Donuts, Eat'n Park, LJ Silver, LoneStar Steaks, Max&Erma's, McDonald's, Marie's Italian, Outback Steaks, Pizza Hut, Red Lobster, Starbucks, Taco Bell, Wendy's, **lodging:** Day's Inn, Extended Stay America, Hampton Inn, Holiday Inn, King's Motel, Palace Inn, Radisson Inn, Red Roof Inn, SpringHill Suites, SunRise Inn, **other:** HOSPITAL, Buick/ Jeep, Cadillac/Pontiac/GMC/Isuzu, Eckerd, Infiniti, Jo-Ann Fabrics, Marshall's, NTB, Office Depot, Old Navy, Radio Shack, Saturn, to Three Rivers Stadium

PENNSYLVANIA

Interstate 76/TPK

E ← → **W**

Pittsburgh

49mm	**Oakmont Service Plaza eb...Sunoco/dsl/24hr, Arby's, Hershey's Ice Cream, picnic tables, litter barrels, phone**
48.5mm	Allegheny River
48	PA 28, to Pittsburgh, Allegheny Valley, New Kensington, **N**...gas: 76/24hr, **food:** Sam Morgan's Rest., **S**...gas: Exxon/dsl, **food:** Bob Evans, Bruster's Yogurt, Burger King, Denny's, Eat'n Park, Fuddrucker's, KFC, King's Rest., McDonald's, Ponderosa, Ripe Tomato, Subway, Taco Bell, Wendy's, **lodging:** Comfort Inn, Day's Inn, Holiday Inn Express, Super 8, Valley Motel, **other:** Advance Parts, Ford, Giant Eagle Food/drug/24hr
41mm	parking area/call box eb
39	PA 8, to Pittsburgh, Butler Valley, **N**...gas: BP, Exxon/dsl, Sheetz/24hr, **food:** Bruno's Pizza, Eat'n Park, McDonald's, Venus Diner, **lodging:** Comfort Inn, **other:** Advance Parts, Jo-Ann Fabrics, Shop'n Save Foods, Wal-Mart/auto/drugs, mall, **S**...gas: BP, Sunoco/dsl, **food:** Arby's, Baskin-Robbins, Boston Mkt, Burger King, China Bistro, Denny's, Handel's Ice Cream, Hoss' Rest., KFC, McDonald's, Pizza Hut, Pizza Outlet, Quizno's, Subway, Taco Bell, Wendy's, **lodging:** Day's Inn, Econolodge, **other:** HOSPITAL, AutoZone, CVS Drug, Eckerd, Firestone/auto, Ford, Goodyear/auto, Radio Shack, Thrift Drug
31mm	**Butler Service Plaza wb...gas: Sunoco/dsl/24hr, food: Burger King, Mrs Fields, Popeye's, TCBY, other: gifts**
28	to I-79, to Cranberry, Pittsburgh, **N**...gas: BP/dsl, Exxon/dsl/24hr, Gulf, Sheetz/24hr, Sunoco/24hr, **food:** A&W/LJ Silver, Arby's, Bob Evans, Boston Mkt, Bravo Italian, Burger King, Denny's, Dunkin Donuts, Eat'n Park, Hartner's Rest., Hot-Dog Shoppe, Ichiban Steakhouse, Jersey Mike's, King's Rest., Krispy Kreme, LoneStar Steaks, Max&Erma's, McDonald's, Montecello's Grill, Panera Bread, Papa John's, Perkins, Pizzaroma, Primanti Bro's, Subway, TCBY, Wendy's, **lodging:** AmeriSuites, Comfort Inn, Fairfield Inn, Hampton Inn, Holiday Inn Express, Motel 6, Oak Leaf Motel, Red Roof Inn, Residence Inn, Sheraton, **other:** Barnes&Noble, Best Buy, CarQuest, Costco/gas, Curves, GNC, Giant Eagle, Goodyear/auto, Home Depot, Jo-Ann Fabrics, Kuhn's Foods, Michael's, PepBoys, PetCo, Rite Aid, Toyota, USPO, Wal-Mart SuperCtr, mall**S**...gas: BP/dsl, **food:** Gulf, Eat'n Park, Hot Dog Shop, **lodging:** Day's Inn, Residence Inn, **other:** Toyota
23.5mm	pulloff eb
22mm	**Zelienople Service Plaza eb...Welcome Ctr, gas: Sunoco/dsl/24hr, food: Roy Rogers, Mrs Fields, TCBY, other: crafts, gifts**
17mm	parking area eb
13.4mm	parking area eb
13mm	Beaver River
13	PA 8, to Ellwood City, Beaver Valley, **N**...lodging: Alpine Inn, Beaver Valley Motel, Danny's Motel, HillTop Motel, Holiday Inn, Lark Motel, **other:**

Pittsburgh

	HOSPITAL, **S**...food: Giuseppe's Italian, **lodging:** Conley Inn/rest.
10	PA 60(toll), to New Castle, Pittsburgh, **S**...services(6mi), to airport
6mm	pulloff eb
2mm	pulloff eb
2	(from wb), no services

Interstate 78

E ← → **W**

Allentown

Exit #	Services
77	Pennsylvania/New Jersey state line, Delaware River
76mm	**Welcome Ctr wb, full(handicapped)facilities, phone, vending, picnic tables, litter barrels, petwalk, toll booth wb**
75	to PA 611, Easton, **N**...gas: TurkeyHill/gas, **food:** McDonald's(1mi), Perkins(1mi), **other:** Crayola Factory, PEZ Museum, **S**...gas: Exxon
71	PA 33, to Stroudsburg, **1 mi N on Freemansburg Ave...food:** Panera Bread, Ruby Tuesday, Texas Roadhouse, TGIFriday, **other:** Barnes&Noble, Circuit City, Lowes Whse, Michael's, Pet Supplies+, Staples
67	PA 412, Hellertown, **N**...gas: TurkeyHill/gas, **lodging:** Comfort Suites(3mi), **food:** Wendy's, **other:** HOSPITAL, Chevrolet, **S**...gas: Citgo, Mobil/dsl, Sunoco, **food:** McDonald's, Rocco's Pizza, Vassi's Drive-In, Waffle House, **lodging:** Holiday Inn Express, **other:** CVS Drug, 7-11
60b a	PA 309 S, Quakertown, **S**...Center Valley Motel
59	to PA 145(from eb), Summit Lawn, no services
58	Emaus St(from wb), **S**...gas: Gulf
57	Lehigh St, **N**...gas: Hess/dsl, **food:** Arby's, China House, IHOP, Queen City Diner, Ragona's Rest., **lodging:** Day's Inn, **other:** BigLots, CVS Drug, Family$, Home Depot, Dodge/Kia/Isuzu, Lincoln/Mercury, Radio Shack, Redner's Whse, VW, **S**...gas: TurkeyHill/gas, Getty/repair, PipeLine, Sunoco, **food:** Bennigan's, Bob Evans, Domino's, Dunkin Donuts, Friendly's, Japanese Steaks, McDonald's, Papa John's, Perkins, Pizza Hut/Taco Bell, Subway, Wendy's, **other:** Acura, Audi/Mercedes/Porsche, Bon-Ton, Buick/GMC/Jeep/Saturn, Chevrolet/Pontiac/Saab, Chrysler, Food4Less, Ford/Hyundai/Honda, Lehigh Tire, Lexus, Mazda/Volvo, Mitsubishi, PetCo, Staples, SteinMart
55	PA 29, Cedar Crest Blvd, **S**...HOSPITAL
54	US 222, Hamilton Blvd, **N**...gas: Hess, **food:** Baskin-Robbins, Boston Mkt, Burger King, Carrabba's, Friendly's, Ice Cream World, Mango's Rest., McDonald's, Perkins, Subway, Tappan Steaks, TGIFriday, Wendy's, **lodging:** Comfort Inn, Holiday Inn Express, Howard Johnson, **other:** Dorney Funpark, Eckerd, King's Food/drug, Office Depot, **S**...gas: Sunoco, WaWa/gas, **food:** Charcoal Drive-In, Dunkin Donuts, Pizza Hut, **lodging:** Wingate Inn, **other:** Queen City Tire, Subaru
53	PA 309(wb only), no services

Interstate 78

51	to I-476, US 22 E, PA 33 N(eb only), Whitehall
49b a	PA 100, Fogelsville, **N**...**food:** Arby's, Cracker Barrel, Gyros King, LJ Silver, Orient Express, Pasta Connection, Pizza Hut, **lodging:** Comfort Inn, Hawthorn Inn, **other:** Eckerd, STS Tire/repair, bank, cleaners, **S**...**gas:** Shell, Sunoco/24hr, WaWa, **food:** Boston's Grill, Burger King, Damon's, Starlite Diner, Taco Bell, Yocco's Hotdogs, **lodging:** Cloverleaf Inn, Hampton Inn, Hilton Garden, Holiday Inn, Sleep Inn, Staybridge Suites, **other:** Toyota/Scion, Grover Hill Winery, st police
45	PA 863, to Lynnport, **N**...**gas:** Exxon/Subway, Sunoco/dsl, **S**...**lodging:** Super 8
40	PA 737, Krumsville, **N**...**lodging:** Top Motel, **other:** Pine Hill Campground(N to blinker, rgt onto Old Rte 22, 1.5 mi), Robin Hill RV Park(4mi), **S**...**gas:** Shell/dsl, **lodging:** Skyview Rest., **other:** to Kutztown U
35	PA 143, Lenhartsville, **3 mi S**...Robin Hill Park
30	Hamburg, **S**...**gas:** Getty/24hr, **food:** Subway
29b a	PA 61, to Reading, Pottsville, **N**...**gas:** Shell/dsl, **food:** Burger King, Dunkin Donuts/Baskin Robbins, Cracker Barrel, Pizza Hut, Wendy's, **lodging:** Microtel, **other:** Cabela's Outdoor, Harley-Davidson(8mi), st police, **S**...**other:** Schaeffer's RV(4mi)
23	Shartlesville, **N**...**gas:** Sunoco/Stuckey's/DQ, **lodging:** Dutch Motel, **other:** Appalachian Campsites, Martin's RV Ctr, **S**...**food:** Blue Mtn Family Rest., **lodging:** Budget Motel, Haag's Motel/rest., **other:** antiques
19	PA 183, Strausstown, **N**...**gas:** Mobil, **S**...**gas:** Power/dsl, **food:** C&C Pizza
17	PA 419, Rehrersburg, **N**...**gas:** Best/dsl, truck/tire repair
16	Midway, **N**...**gas:** Citgo/dsl, Exxon/dsl, **food:** Midway Diner, **lodging:** Comfort Inn, **S**...auto/truck repair
15	Grimes, no services
13	PA 501, Bethel, **N**...**gas:** Shell/dsl/24hr, **S**...**gas:** Exxon/Subway/dsl
10	PA 645, Frystown, **S**...**gas:** All-American Trkstp/rest./dsl/24hr, Gulf/dsl/24hr
6	(8 from wb, US 22)PA 343, Fredricksburg, **1 mi S**...**gas:** Pacific Pride/dsl, Redner's Whse/mkt, **food:** Esther's Rest., **other:** KOA(3mi)
1	I-81. I-78 begins/ends on I-81, exit 89.

Interstate 79

Exit #	Services
183b a	PA 5, 12th St, Erie, **E**...HOSPITAL, **W**...**gas:** Citgo; Sunoco, **food:** Albacai Japanese, Applebee's, Backyard Burger, Bob Evans, Eat'n Park/24hr, KFC, McDonald's, New China, Panera Bread, Serafini's Italian, Taco Bell, **lodging:** Comfort Inn(2mi), **other:** Advance Parts, Big Lots, CVS Drug, $General, Dunn Tire, Giant Eagle Foods, GNC, NAPA, Rite Aid, Sav-a-Lot Foods, Tuesday Morning, U-HAUL, vet, to Presque Isle SP
182	US 20, 26th St, **E**...**gas:** KwikFill, **food:** Subway, **other:** HOSPITAL, Advance Parts, CVS Drug, Family$, Tops Food/gas/24hr, **W**...**gas:** Citgo, GetGo, **food:** Arby's, Burger King, McDonald's, Pizza Hut, Super Buffet, Tim Horton, Vocelli's Pizza, **other:** Aamco, AutoZone, $General, Ford, Giant Eagle, K-Mart, Radio Shack, TrueValue, vet
180	US 19, to Kearsarge, **E**...**food:** Arby's, Buffalo Wild Wings, Eat'n Park/24hr, KFC, Max&Erma's, McDonald's, Olive Garden, Outback Steaks, Ponderosa, Red Lobster, Roadhouse Grill, Smokey Bones BBQ, Wendy's, **lodging:** Fairfield Inn, Homewood Suites, **other:** HOSPITAL, Barnes&Noble, Borders Books, Cadillac/Audi, Chrysler/Jeep, Gander Mtn, JC Penney, Macy's, Michael's, Office Depot, Old Navy, PetCo, Sears/auto, TJ Maxx, Toyota/Scion, mall, **W**...**gas:** Citgo/dsl, **other:** camping
178b a	I-90, E to Buffalo, W to Cleveland
174	to McKean, **E**...access to gas/dsl, phone, **W**...camping
166	US 6N, to Edinboro, **E**...**gas:** Citgo, Sheetz, **food:** Burger King(2mi), McDonald's(2mi), Perkins(2mi), Subway, Wendy's, **lodging:** Edinboro Inn, **other:** $Tree, Wal-Mart SuperCtr/24hr, vet
163mm	**rest area both lanes, full(handicapped)facilities, phone, vending, picnic tables, litter barrels, petwalk**
154	PA 198, to Saegertown
147b a	US 6, US 322, to Meadville, **E**...**gas:** All American, Citgo/dsl, GetGo, Sheetz/dsl/24hr, Sunoco, **food:** Applebee's, Chovy's Italian, Cracker Barrel, Hoss' Rest., KFC, Perkins, Pizza Hut, Super Buffet, **lodging:** Day's Inn/rest., Holiday Inn Express, Motel 6, **other:** HOSPITAL, Advance Parts, Giant Eagle/24hr, Home Depot, **W**...**gas:** Sheetz, **food:** Burger King, Compadre's Mexican, King's Rest./24hr, McDonald's, Ponderosa, Red Lobster, Subway, **lodging:** Quality Inn, **other:** Aldi Foods, AutoZone, Buick/Pontiac/Cadillac/GMC, Chevrolet, $General, K-Mart, Nissan, Staples, Toyota/Scion, Wal-Mart SuperCtr/24hr, to Pymatuning SP, st police

Erie

Meadville

PENNSYLVANIA
Interstate 79

Exit	Description
141	PA 285, to Geneva, **E**...to Erie NWR(20mi), **W**... **food:** Aunt Bee's Rest./dsl
135mm	rest area/weigh sta both lanes, full(handicapped) facilities, phone, vending, picnic tables, litter barrels, petwalk
130	PA 358, to Sandy Lake, **W**...**other:** HOSPITAL(13mi), to Goddard SP
121	US 62, to Mercer, **E**...**other:** Valley Tire, **W**...**gas:** Sunoco/dsl, **other:** st police
116b a	I-80, E to Clarion, W to Sharon
113	PA 208, PA 258, to Grove City, **E**...**gas:** BP, Citgo/dsl/24hr, **other:** HOSPITAL, **W**...**gas:** Kwik-Fill/Subway, Sheetz/24hr, **food:** Eat'n Park/24hr, Elephant&Castle Rest., Hoss's Rest., King's Rest., McDonald's, Wendy's, **lodging:** Best Western, Comfort Inn, Hampton Inn, Holiday Inn Express, Super 8, **other:** KOA(3mi), Prime Outlets/famous brands
110mm	rest area sb, full(handicapped)facilities, phone, vending, picnic tables, litter barrels, petwalk
107mm	rest area nb, full(handicapped)facilities, phone, vending, picnic tables, litter barrels, petwalk
105	PA 108, to Slippery Rock, **E**...**gas:** QuickStop/dsl, **food:** DQ, **lodging:** Evening Star Motel/rest., **other:** Slippery Rock Camping, to Slippery Rock U
99	US 422, to New Castle, **E**...to Moraine SP, **W**...**other:** Coopers Lake Camping, **other:** to Rose Point Camping
96	PA 488, Portersville, **E**...Bear Run Camping, Moraine SP, **W**...**food:** Brown's Country Kitchen, McConnell's Mill SP(3mi), gas/dsl
88	(87 from nb), to US 19, PA 68, Zelienople, **1-2 mi** **W**...**gas:** Exxon, Unimart/dsl/24hr, **food:** Brewster's, Burger King, DQ, LJ's Rest., Pizza Hut, Subway, Yang's Gourmet, **lodging:** Zelienople Motel, **other:** BiLo, Curves, Dodge, Eckerd, Indian Brave RV Camping
85	(83 from nb), PA 528(no quick return), to Evans City, **W**...**other:** Pontiac/Buick
78	(76 from nb, exits left from nb), US 19, PA 228, to Mars, access to I-76, PA TPK, **E**...**gas:** Citgo/7-11, **food:** Applebee's, Chick-fil-A, DiBella's Subs, Hereford&Hop's, McDonald's, Moe's SW Grill, Olive Garden, On-the-Border, Quizno's, Red Robin, Smokey Bones BBQ, Subway, Taipei Chinese, **lodging:** Marriott, **other:** Kohl's, Lowe's, Petsmart, Staples, Target, TJ Maxx, **W** on US 19...**gas:** BP/dsl, Exxon/dsl/24hr, Gulf, Sheetz/24hr, Sunoco/24hr, **food:** A&W/LJ Silver, Arby's, Bob Evans, Boston Mkt, Bravo Italian, Burger King, Denny's, Dunkin Donuts, Eat'n Park, Hartner's Rest., Hot-Dog Shoppe, Ichiban Steakhouse, Jersey Mike's, King's Rest., Krispy Kreme, LoneStar Steaks, Max&Erma's, McDonald's, Montecello's Grill, Panera Bread, Papa John's, Perkins, Pizzaroma, Primanti Bro's, Subway, TCBY, Wendy's, **lodging:** AmeriSuites, Comfort Inn, Fairfield Inn, Hampton Inn, Holiday Inn Express, Motel 6, Oak Leaf Motel, Red Roof Inn, Residence Inn, Sheraton, **other:** Barnes&Noble, Best Buy, CarQuest, Costco/gas, Curves, GNC, Giant Eagle, Goodyear/auto, Home Depot, Jo-Ann Fabrics, Kuhn's Foods, Michael's, PepBoys, PetCo, Rite Aid, Toyota, USPO, Wal-Mart SuperCtr, mall
77	I-76/Tpk, to Youngstown, **E**...**food:** Quizno's
75	US 19 S(from nb), to Warrendale, services on US 19
73	PA 910, to Wexford, **E**...**gas:** BP/24hr, **food:** Eat'n Park, King's Family Rest./24hr, Starbucks, **lodging:** Best Inn, **other:** **W**...**gas:** Exxon/dsl/24hr, **food:** Carmody's Rest.
72	I-279 S(from sb), to Pittsburgh
68	Mt Nebo Rd, **W**...HOSPITAL, gas
66	to PA 65, Emsworth, no services
65	to PA 51, Coraopolis, Neville Island, **E**...**gas:** Gulf, **other:** Penske/Hertz Trucks
64.5mm	Ohio River
64	PA 51(from nb), to Coraopolis, McKees Rocks
60b a	PA 60, Crafton, **E**...**gas:** Exxon/dsl/24hr, **food:** King's Rest./24hr, **lodging:** Econolodge, Motel 6, Travel Inn, **other:** HOSPITAL, **W**...**gas:** BP/Subway/dsl(1mi), **food:** Juliano's Rest., Primanti Bros
59b	US 22 W, US 30(from nb), **W**...airport
59a	I-279 N, to Pittsburgh
57	to Carnegie, **1-3 mi** **E**...**gas:** BP, Exxon, **food:** LJ Silver, McDonald's, TCBY, **lodging:** Shop'n Save, Ford, mall
55	PA 50, to Heidelberg, **E** on PA 50...**gas:** BP, Exxon, Sunoco, **food:** Arby's, Bob Evans, ChuckeCheese, CiCi's Pizza, Coldstone Creamery, Damon's, DQ, Eat'n Park, KFC, King's Rest., LJ Silver, McDonald's, Mo-Town Pizzaria, NY Deli, Pizza Hut, Starbucks, Subway, Taco Bell, Wendy's, **other:** Big Lots, Curves, Ford, Giant Eagle Foods, Home Depot, Jo-Ann Fabrics, K-Mart/Little Caesar', Shop'n Save Foods, Tuesday Morning, Wal-Mart
54	PA 50, to Bridgeville, **E**...**gas:** BP/dsl, Exxon/dsl, **food:** Burger King, King's Rest./24hr, McDonald's, Wendy's, **lodging:** Holiday Inn Express, **other:** HOSPITAL, Chevrolet, Dodge, $General, **W**...**gas:** Exxon, Sunoco, **lodging:** Knight's Inn
50mm	rest area/weigh sta both lanes, full(handicapped) facilities, phone, vending, picnic tables, litter barrels, petwalk
48	South Pointe, **W**...**food:** Subway, **lodging:** Hilton Garden
45	to PA 980, Canonsburg, **E**...**gas:** Sheetz, **W**...**gas:** BP/24hr, Citgo, **food:** Hoss' Rest., KFC/Taco Bell, LJ Silver, McDonald's, Pizza Hut, Quizno's, Starbucks, Subway, Wendy's, **lodging:** Super 8, **other:** Advance Parts
43	PA 519, Houston, **E**...**gas:** BP/dsl, **W**...**gas:** Sunoco/24hr, **other:** Freightliner
41	Race Track Rd, **E**...**gas:** Exxon, **food:** Buger King, McDonald's, Waffle House, Wendy's, **lodging:** Comfort Inn, Hampton Inn, Holiday Inn, **W**...**gas:** BP/dsl, **other:** Trolley Museum
40	Meadow Lands(from nb, no re-entry), **W**...**other:** Trolley Museum(3mi), golf, racetrack
38	I-70 W, to Wheeling

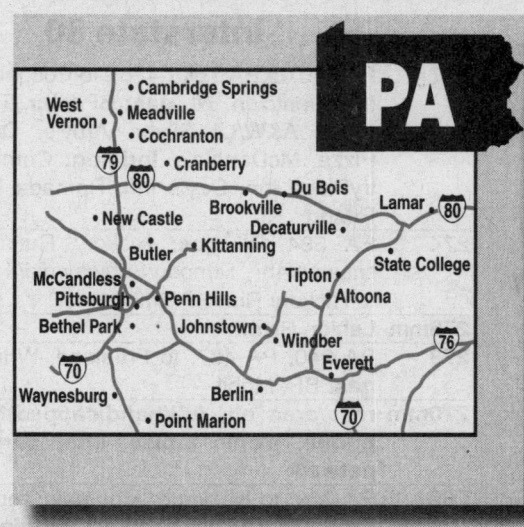

Interstate 79

19b a	US 19, Murtland Ave, **N**...gas: BP, GetGo, **food:** Applebee's, Arby's, Brewster's, Cracker Barrel, Krispy Kreme, McDonald's, Outback Steaks, Panera Bread, Ponderosa, Quizno's, Red Lobster, Red Robin, Starbucks, Subway, Texas Roadhouse, TGIFriday, **lodging:** SpringHill Suites, **other:** Aldi Foods, $Tree, Giant Eagle Foods, GNC, Hyundai, Lowe's Whse, Michael's, Nissan, Petsmart, Radio Shack, Sam's Club, Target, Toyota/Honda, Wal-Mart SuperCtr/24hr, vet, **S**...gas: BP/dsl, Exxon, GetGo, Sunoco, **food:** A&W/LJ Silver, Bob Evans, China Buffet, Eat'n Park/24hr, Evergreen Chinese, KFC, Old Mexico, Papa John's, Pizza Hut, **lodging:** Hampton Inn, Motel 6, **other:** HOSPITAL, Big Lots, Buick/Cadillac/GMC, Firestone/auto, Home Depot, JC Penney, Jo-Ann Fabrics, K-Mart, Staples, Subaru, mall, st police
34	I-70 E, to Greensburg
33	US 40, to Laboratory, **W**...other: KOA
31mm	parking area/weigh sta sb
30	US 19, to Amity, **W**...gas: Exxon/Subway/dsl
23	to Marianna, Prosperity, no services
19	PA 221, to US 19, Ruff Creek, **W**...gas: BP/dsl
20	PA 136, Beau St, **S**...to Washington&Jefferson Coll
14	PA 21, to Waynesburg, **E**...food: Bob Evans, **lodging:** Comfort Inn, **W**...gas: BP/dsl/24hr, Exxon/dsl, GetGo, Sheetz, **food:** Burger King, DQ, Hardee's, KFC, McDonald's, Subway, Wendy's, **lodging:** Econolodge, Super 8, **other:** HOSPITAL, AutoZone, Big Lots, Chevrolet/Cadillac, Chrysler/PLymout/Dodge/Jeep, CVS Drug, Family$, More-4Less Foods, Sav-a-Lot Foods, st police
7	to Kirby, no services
6mm	**Welcome Ctr/weigh sta nb, full(handicapped) facilities, phone, picnic tables, litter barrels, vending, petwalk**
1	Mount Morris, **E**...gas: Citgo/dsl/rest./scales, **other:** Honda/Mazda, **W**...gas: BP/dsl, Marathon, **other:** Mt Morris Campground
0mm	Pennsylvania/West Virginia state line

Interstate 80

Exit #	Services
311mm	Pennsylvania/New Jersey state line, Delaware River
310.5	toll booth wb, phone
310	PA 611, Delaware Water Gap, **S**...**Welcome Ctr/ rest area, full facilities, info, gas:** BP, Gulf/repair, **food:** Doughboys Pizza, Water Gap Diner, **other:** Christmas Factory Gifts
309	US 209 N, PA 447, to Marshalls Creek, **N**...gas: Exxon/dsl/24hr, Gulf, **food:** DQ, Wendy's(2mi), **lodging:** Shannon Motel, **other:** HOSPITAL
308	East Stroudsburg, **N**...gas: Exxon, WaWa, **other:** HOSPITAL, **1 mi N**...food: Arby's, Burger King, China King, Friendly's, JR's rest., McDonald's, **other:** Eckerd, Goodyear/auto, K-Mart, NAPA, Radio Shack, ShopRite Foods, Wal-Mart SuperCtr/24hr, Weis Foods, **S**...lodging: Budget Motel, Super 8
307	PA 191, Broad St, **N**...gas: Gulf, **food:** KFC, McDonald's, **lodging:** Hampton Inn, **other:** HOSPITAL, same as 308 **S**...gas: Sunoco, **lodging:** Budget Host
306	Dreher Ave(from wb, no EZ return), **N**...gas: Wawa
305	US 209, Main St, **N**...gas: Gulf, Mobil, **food:** Perkins/24hr, **lodging:** Clarion, **S**...gas: Exxon/24hr, **lodging:** Alpines Motel
304	US 209, to PA 33, 9th St (from wb), same as 303
303	9th st, (from eb), **N**...gas: BP, **food:** Boston Mkt, Burger King, Dunkin Donuts, Fulay Chinese, McDonald's, Pizza Hut, Ruby Tuesday, **other:** Cadillac, Chevrolet, CVS Drug, $Tree, Nissan
302	PA 611, to Bartonsville, **N**...gas: Exxon/dsl, Citgo/Subway/Pizza Hut/Taco Bell/dsl/scales/24hr, **food:** McDonald's(3mi), Ponderosa(3mi), Red Robin, **lodging:** Comfort Inn, Howard Johnson, Knight's Inn, **other:** Goodyear, Kohl's, Lowes Whse
299	PA 715, Tannersville, **N**...gas: BP, Mobil, **lodging:** Ramada Ltd, **other:** The Crossing Factory Outlet/famous brands, **1-3 mi N**...food: Barley Creek Brewing, Friendly's, **lodging:** Chateau Inn/rest.(5mi), **other:** camping, **S**...gas: Sunoco/24hr, **food:** Tannersville Diner, **lodging:** Day's Inn, Summit Resort, **other:** to Camelback Ski Area, to Big Pocono SP
298	PA 611(from wb), to Scotrun, **N**...gas: Shell, Sunoco/dsl, **food:** Anthony's Steaks, Plaza Deli, **lodging:** Scotrun Diner/motel, **other:** to Mt Pocono
295mm	**rest area eb, full(handicapped)facilities, phone, picnic tables, litter barrels, vending, petwalk**
293	I-380 N, to Scranton, no services
284	PA 115, to Wilkes-Barre, Blakeslee, **N**...gas: WaWa(1mi), **lodging:** Best Western, Blakeslee Inn(2mi), **other:** Fern Ridge Camping, st police, **S**...gas: Exxon/dsl, **other:** to Pocono Raceway

E

W

277	PA 940, to PA Tpk(I-476), to Pocono, Lake Harmony, Allentown, **N**...gas: BP/24hr, Texaco, WaWa, **food:** A&W/LJ Silver, Arby's, Denny's, Gino's Pizza, McDonald's, **lodging:** Comfort Inn, CountryPlace Inn, Day's Inn, Ramada Inn, Split Rock Resort
274	PA 534, **N**...gas: Hickory Run/Exxon/dsl/rest./scales/24hr, Sunoco/Subway/dsl/24hr, **S**...other: to Hickory Run SP(6mi)
273mm	Lehigh River
273	PA 940, PA 437, to Freeland, White Haven, **N**...gas: BP, Mobil
270mm	**rest area eb, full(handicapped)facilities, info, phone, picnic tables, litter barrels, vending, petwalk**
262	PA 309, to Hazleton, Mountain Top, **N**...gas: BP, **food:** Mary's Rest., Wendy's, **lodging:** Econolodge, Holiday Inn Express, **other:** **S**...st police
260b a	I-81, N to Wilkes-Barre, S to Harrisburg
256	PA 93, to Nescopeck, Conyngham, **N**...gas: Pilot/Subway/dsl/scales/24hr/@, Sunoco/repair, **lodging:** Lookout Motel, **S**...gas: Shell/dsl, **food:** Tom's Kitchen(2mi), **lodging:** Best Value Inn, Hampton Inn(4mi), **other:**HOSPITAL
251mm	Nescopeck River
246mm	**rest area/weigh sta both lanes, full (handicapped)facilities, weather info, phone, picnic tables, litter barrels, vending, petwalk**
242	PA 339, to Mainville, Mifflinville, **N**...gas: Loves/Arby's/dsl/24hr, Shell/Blimpie/dsl/scales/24hr, **food:** McDonald's, **lodging:** Super 8/rest., **S**...gas: Citgo/dsl, repair
241mm	Susquehanna River
241b a	US 11, to Berwick, Lime Ridge, Bloomsburg, **N**...lodging: Red Maple Inn(2mi), **other:** HOSPITAL, **S**...gas: Exxon, **food:** Kemler's Rest., Subway, **lodging:** Patriot Inn, **2-5 mi** **S**...gas: Sheetz/dsl/24hr, **food:** Applebee's, Arby's, Burger King, Dunkin Donuts, McDonald's, New China Buffet, Pizza Hut, Taco Bell, Terrapin's Cantina, Wendy's, **other:** Advance Parts, BigLots, Buick/Pontiac/GMC, Chevrolet/Cadillac, CVS Drug, Eckerd, Ford/Honda, Giant Foods/gas, Kost Tire, Radio Shack, Staples, U-Haul, Weis Foods/gas
236	PA 487, to Bloomsburg, Lightstreet, **S**...gas: Sunoco/24hr, **food:** Denny's/24hr, **lodging:** Hampton Inn, Tennytown Motel(2mi), Turkey Hill Inn, **other:** HOSPITAL, to Bloomsburg U
232	PA 42, Buckhorn, **N**...gas: Exxon, Shell/dsl, TA/BP/Subway/dsl/scales/24hr/@, **food:** Burger King, Charlie Brown's Steaks, Cracker Barrel, Gourmet Buffet, KFC, Perkins, Quaker Steak&Lube, Ruby Tuesday, Wendy's, **lodging:** Econolodge, Holiday Inn Express, **other:** Home Depot, JC Penney, Sears, mall, **S**...food: Panera Bread, **other:** $Tree, Indian Head camping(3mi), Lowe's Whse, Office Depot, Wal-Mart SuperCtr/24hr

Bloomsburg

224	PA 54, to Danville, **N**...gas: Mobil/DQ/dsl, Shell/Subway/dsl/24hr, **food:** Country Kitchen, **lodging:** Quality Inn, **S**...food: Friendly's, McDonald's, Mom's Dutch Kitchen, **lodging:** Best Western, Day's Inn, Hampton Inn, Key Motel, Red Roof Inn, **other:** HOSPITAL
219mm	**rest area both lanes, full(handicapped)facilities, info, phone, picnic tables, litter barrels, vending, petwalk**
215	PA 254, Limestonevill, **N**...gas: Milton 32 Trkstp/dsl/rest./24hr, **S**...gas: Petro/Shell/Iron Skillet/Subway/dsl/rest./24hr/@
212b a	I-180 W, PA 147 S, to Muncy, Williamsport, **S**...gas: Sunoco/24hr(1mi)
210.5mm	Susquehanna River
210b a	US 15, to Williamsport, Lewisburg, **S**...gas: Citgo, **food:** Bonanza, **lodging:** Comfort Inn, Holiday Inn Express, **other:** HOSPITAL
199	Mile Run Rd, no services
194mm	**rest area/weigh sta both lanes, full (handicapped)facilities, phone, picnic tables, litter barrels, vending, petwalk**
192	PA 880, to Jersey Shore, **N**...gas: Citgo/dsl/24hr, **food:** Pit-Stop Rest., **S**...gas: Mobil, **other** truck repair
185	PA 477, Loganton, **N**...gas: Mobil, **other:** camping, **S**...food: Twilight Diner, RV Winter SP(12mi)
178	US 220, Lock Haven, **N**...food: Country Barn Rest., **other:** HOSPITAL(7mi), **5 mi** **N**...gas: Sheetz, **other:** Advance Parts, K-Mart, Wal-Mart SuperCtr/24hr, **S**...gas: Citgo/dsl
173	PA 64, Lamar, **N**...gas: Pilot/Subway/dsl/scales/24hr, **food:** Cottage Rest., McDonald's, Perkins, **lodging:** Comfort Inn/rest., Hampton Inn, **S**...gas: Citgo, ⊕/Flying J/Shell/Country Mkt/dsl/LP/scales/@, TA/Mobil/Country Pride/Subway/dsl/rest./scales/24hr/@, **food:** DQ
161	PA 26, US 220 S, to Bellafonte, **S**...other: KOA, to PSU
158	US 220 S, PA 150, to Altoona, Milesburg, **N**...gas: Bestway/dsl/rest./motel/24hr/@, Citgo/dsl, TA/BP/dsl/rest./scales/24hr/@, **food:** Buckhorn Rest., McDonald's, Subway, **lodging:** Holiday Inn, **S**...st police
147	PA 144, to Snow Shoe, **N**...gas: Citgo/dsl/24hr, Exxon/dsl/repair/24hr, **food:** Snow Shoe Sandwich Shop, Subway, **other:** Hall's Foods, repair
146mm	**rest area both lanes, full(handicapped)facilities, phone, picnic tables, litter barrels, vending, petwalk**
138mm	Moshanna River
133	PA 53, to Philipsburg, Kylertown, **N**...gas: Kwik-Fill/motel/dsl/scales, Sunoco/LP, **food:** Roadhouse Rest., **other:** USPO, dsl repair, Black Moshannon SP(9mi), **S**...other: HOSPITAL
123	PA 970, to Shawville, Woodland, **S**...gas: BP/dsl, Pacific Pride/dsl, **food:** Gio's BBQ(2mi)

Interstate 80

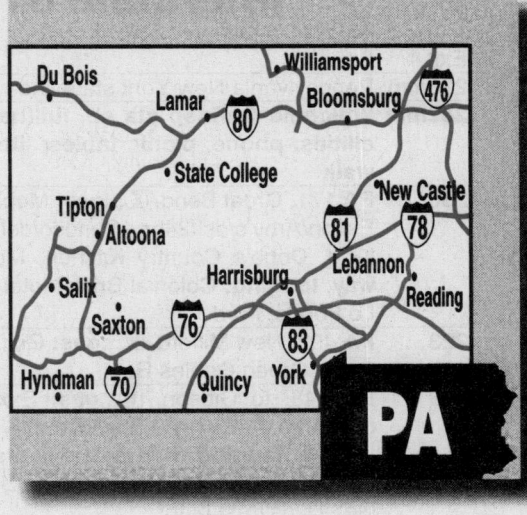

120mm	Susquehanna River, W Branch
120	PA 879, Clearfield, **N...gas:** Sapp Bros/dsl/rest./24hr/2, **lodging:** Econolodge, **S...gas:** BP, Sheetz/24hr, Snappy's Gas, **food:** Arby's, Burger King, Dutch Pantry, KFC/Pizza Hut/Taco Bell, McDonald's, **lodging:** Comfort Inn, Day's Inn, Holiday Inn Express, Super 8, **other:** HOSPITAL, K-Mart, Lowes Whse, Wal-Mart SuperCtr/Subway/gas/24hr
111mm	highest point on I-80 east of Mississippi River, 2250 ft
111	PA 153, to Penfield, **N...**to Parker Dam, to SB Elliot SP, **S...**HOSPITAL
101	PA 255, Du Bois, **N...gas:** BP/24hr, **other:** camping, **S...lodging:** Quality Inn, **other:** HOSPITAL, st police, **1-2 mi S...gas:** Citgo, KwikFill, Sheetz/24hr, **food:** Arby's, Brewster's, Burger King, Eat'n Park/24hr, Hoss' Rest., Italian Oven, LJ Silver/A&W, McDonald's, Perkins/24hr, Ponderosa, Red Lobster, Ruby Tuesday, Subway, Taco Bell, Wendy's, **lodging:** Best Western, DuBois Manor Motel, Hampton Inn, **other:** BigLots, BiLo Foods, $Tree, Eckerd, Goodyear/auto, JC Penney, K-Mart, Lowe's Whse, Old Navy, Ross, Sears, Shop'n Save Foods, Staples, Wal-Mart/drugs, mall
97	US 219, to Brockway, Du Bois, **S...gas:** Pilot/Arby's/dsl/24hr/@, Sheetz/dsl/24hr, **food:** Dutch Pantry Rest., Hoss' Rest.(2mi), **lodging:** Best Western, Clarion, Du Bois Manor Motel(2mi), Holiday Inn Express, **other:** HOSPITAL, Advance Parts, Freightliner, st police
91	new exit
87.5mm	**rest area both lanes, full(handicapped)facilities, phone, picnic tables, litter barrels, vending, pet-walk**
86	PA 830, to Reynoldsville, no services
81	PA 28, to Brookville, to Hazen, **S...**to Brookville, hist dist(2mi)
78	PA 36, to Sigel, Brookville, **N...gas:** Flying J/Country Mkt/dsl/scales/24hr/@, TA/BP/Taco Bell/dsl/scales/24hr/@, **food:** DQ, KFC, McDonald's, Pizza Hut, **lodging:** Howard Johnson, Super 8, **other:** Buick/Pontiac/Cadillac, NAPA, to Cook Forest SP, **S...gas:** Citgo/24hr, Sheetz, **food:** Arby's, Burger King, China Wok, Plyler's Buffet, Subway, **lodging:** Budget Host, Day's Inn, Holiday Inn Express, **other:** Chrysler/Jeep/Dodge, Family$
73	PA 949, Corsica, **N...other:** to Clear Creek SP, **S...**USPO
70	US 322, to Strattanville, **N...gas:** Shell/dsl/rest./24hr/@
64	PA 66 S, to New Bethlehem, Clarion, **N...**to Clarion U
62	PA 68, to Clarion, **N...gas:** BP/24hr, KwikFill/dsl, **food:** Arby's, Eat'n Park, LJ Silver/A&W, McDonald's, Perkins/24hr, Pizza Hut, RRR Roadhouse Rest., Subway, Taco Bell, **lodging:** Comfort Inn, Hampton Inn, Holiday Inn/rest., Microtel, Quality Inn, Super 8, **other:** HOSPITAL, Advance Parts, Aldi Foods, $Tree, JC Penney, K-Mart, Radio Shack, Staples, Wal-Mart SuperCtr/24hr, mall
61mm	Clarion River
60	PA 66 N, to Shippenville, **N...gas:** Citgo, **other:** st police, to Cook Forest SP, camping
56mm	parking area/weigh sta both lanes
53	to PA 338, to Knox, **N...**gas/dsl, **food:** BJ's Eatery, **other:** Wolf's Camping Resort, **S...other:** Good Tire Service
45	PA 478, to St Petersburg, Emlenton, **4 mi S...other:** Golf Hall of Fame
44.5mm	Allegheny River
42	PA 38, to Emlenton, **N...gas:** Citgo/dsl/rest./motel/24hr, Exxon/Subway/dsl/24hr, **other:** Gaslight RV Park, truck/RV repair
35	PA 308, to Clintonville, no services
30.5mm	**rest area both lanes, full(handicapped)facilities, phone, picnic tables, litter barrels, vending, pet-walk**
29	PA 8, to Franklin, Barkeyville, **N...food:** Arby's, Burger King, King's Rest., **lodging:** Comfort Inn, Super 8, **S...gas:** Citgo/dsl/24hr, KwikFill/dsl/rest./24hr/@, TA/BP/Subway/dsl/rest./24hr/@, **other:** to Slippery Rock U
24	PA 173, to Grove City, Sandy Lake, **S...other:** HOSPITAL, Wendell August Forge/gifts(3mi)
19b a	I-79, N to Erie, S to Pittsburgh
15	US 19, to Mercer, **N...gas:** BP, **food:** Burger King, McDonald's, Olde Homestead Rest., **lodging:** Howard Johnson/rest., **other:** KOA, st police, **2 mi S...food:** Iron Bridge Rest.
4b a	PA 18, PA 60, to Sharon-Hermitage, New Castle, **N...gas:** Sunoco/dsl/24hr, **food:** Subway, **lodging:** Comfort Inn, Holiday Inn Express, Quality Inn, Radisson, Super 8, **S on PA 318...gas:** Citgo, **food:** DQ, MiddleSex Diner/24hr, **other:** Auto Value Parts
2.5mm	Shenango River
1mm	**Welcome Ctr eb, full(handicapped)facilities, phone, picnic tables, litter barrels, vending, pet-walk**

PENNSYLVANIA
Interstate 81

Exit #	Services
233mm	Pennsylvania/New York state line
232mm	**Welcome Ctr/insp sta sb, full(handicapped) facilities, phone, picnic tables, litter barrels, petwalk**
230	PA 171, Great Bend, E...gas: Mobil/24hr, W...gas: Exxon/Arby's/dsl/24hr, Sunoco/dsl, **food:** Burger King, Dobb's Country Kitchen, McDonald's, Subway, **lodging:** Colonial Brick Motel/rest., **other:** Bi-Lo Foods, Ford
223	PA 492, New Milford, W...gas: Gulf/dsl, Mobil/24hr, **food:** Green Gables Rest.
219	PA 848, to Gibson, W...gas: Exxon/McDonald's/dsl/24hr, /Flying J/Shell/Country Mkt/dsl/scales/24hr/@, **lodging:** Holiday Inn Express, st police
217	PA 547, Harford, E...gas: Exxon/Subway/dsl/24hr, Getty's/dsl/rest./24hr
211	PA 92, Lenox, E...Elk Mtn Ski Area, Shady Rest Camping(3mi), W...gas: Mobil/dsl/24hr, Shell/dsl, **food:** Bingham's Rest., Lenox Rest., **other:** Lenox Drug
209mm	**Welcome Ctr sb, full(handicapped)facilities, phone, picnic tables, litter barrel, vending, petwalk**
206	PA 374, to Glenwood, Lenoxville, E...to Elk Mountain Ski Resort
203mm	**rest area nb, full(handicapped)facilities, phone, picnic tables, litter barrels, vending, petwalk**
202	PA 107, to Fleetville, Tompkinsville, no services
201	PA 438, East Benton, W...gas: Duchniks/dsl/repair
199	PA 524, Scott, E...gas: BP/dsl, Gulf/dsl/rest/24hr, W...gas: Exxon/Subway, **lodging:** Motel 81, **other:** to Lackawanna SP
197	PA 632, Waverly, E...other: Mr Z's Foods, Rite Aid, W...gas: Sunoco/24hr, Doc's Deli/24hr
194	US 6, US 11, to I-476/PA Tpk, Clarks Summit, W...gas: Shell/dsl, Sheetz/24hr, Sunoco/dsl, **food:** Bennigan's, Burger King, Damon's, Fire Grill, Friendly's, Krispy Kreme, Kyoto, McDonald's, New Century Chinese, Pizza Hut, Quizno's, Subway, Taco Bell, Waffle House, Wendy's, **lodging:** Comfort Inn, Econolodge, Hampton Inn, Nichols Village Inn, Ramada Inn, **other:** Advance Parts, Eckerd, Kost Tire, Radio Shack, Weis Foods
191b a	US 6, US 11, to Carbondale, E...gas: Shell/dsl, Sheetz, **food:** A&W/LJ Silver, Applebee's, Arby's, Burger King, China Wok, ChuckeCheese, Denny's, Don Pablo, 5 Guys Cafe, LoneStar Steaks, McDonald's, Old Country Buffet, Olive Garden, Perkins, Pizza Hut, Pizzaria Uno, Red Lobster, Red Robin, Ruby Tuesday, Smokey Bones BBQ, Subway, TCBY, Texas Roadhouse, TGIFriday, Wendy's, **lodging:** Days Inn, **other:** Aldi Foods, Borders Books, Circuit City, Firestone/auto, Harley-Davidson, Home Depot, Hyundai, JC Penney, Jo-Ann Crafts, K-Mart, Kohl's, Marshall's, Michael's, Pep-Boys, Petsmart, Radio Shack, Sears/auto, Target, TJ Maxx, Wal-Mart SuperCtr/24hr, mall, W...other: to Anthracite Museum

Exit #	Services
190	Main Ave, Dickson City, E...food: Charlie Brown's Steaks, Wendy's, **lodging:** Fairfield Inn, Residence Inn, **other:** Best Buy, Lowe's Whse, Sam's Club/gas, Staples
188	PA 347, Throop, E...gas: Sheetz/24hr, Sunoco/dsl, **food:** Boston Mkt, China World Buffet, McDonald's, Quizno's, Scooters Hot Dogs, Wendy's, **lodging:** Day's Inn, Sleep Inn, Super 8, **other:** Advance Parts, Big Lots, Kost Tire, PriceChopper Foods, Radio Shack, st police, W...gas: Mobil, **food:** Burger King, Friendly's
187	to I-84, I-380, US 6(no return from nb)
186	PA 435, Drinker St, E...gas: Mobil, **lodging:** Holiday Inn, W...gas: Exxon
185	Central Scranton Expwy (exits left from nb), W...HOSPITAL
184	to PA 307, River St, W...gas: Exxon, Mobil, **lodging:** Clarion, **other:** HOSPITAL, CVS Drug, $Tree, Gerrity Foods
182	Davis St, Montage Mtn Rd, E...gas: Exxon, **food:** Rocket's Café, Ruby Tuesday, Stadium Club Rest., **lodging:** Comfort Suites, Courtyard; Hampton Inn, W...gas: BP, Mobil, **food:** LJ Silver, McDonald's, Mugg's Rest., Wendy's, **lodging:** Econolodge, Rodeway Inn, **other:** USPO
180	to US 11, PA 502, to Moosic, (exits left from nb), W...gas: BP/Subway/dsl/24hr
178b a	to US 11, Avoca, E...food: Damon's, **lodging:** Holiday Inn Express, W...gas: Petro/Sunoco/dsl/rest./24hr/@
175b a	PA 315 S, to I-476, Dupont, E...gas: Mobil/dsl, Sunoco/24hr, **food:** Arby's, McDonald's, Perkins, **lodging:** Knight's Inn, Super 8, **other:** Chevrolet, W...gas: Getty, Pilot/Wendy's/dsl/scales/24hr, **lodging:** Victoria Inn, **other:** Wal-Mart
170b a	PA 115, PA 309, Wilkes-Barre, E...gas: Exxon/dsl, Sunoco/dsl, **lodging:** Best Western, **other:** to Pocono Downs, W...gas: Sunoco/24hr, **food:** Denny's, Friendly's, LJ Silver, McDonald's, Perkins, Pizza Hut, TGIFriday, **lodging:** Candlewood Suites, Day's Inn, Hampton Inn, Holiday Inn, Red Roof Inn, **other:** HOSPITAL, Kia, BMW, Subaru, VW, mall
168	Highland Park Blvd, Wilkes-Barre, W...gas: Sheetz/24hr, **food:** Applebee's, Bennigan's, Bob Evans, Boston's Rest., Burger King, Chili's, ChuckeCheese, Cracker Barrel, Grotto, Ground Round, King's Buffet, Logan's Roadhouse, McDonald's, Olive Garden, Outback Steaks, Panera Bread, Pizzaria Uno, Quizno's, Red Robin, Smokey Bones BBQ, Subway, Starbucks, Wendy's, **lodging:** Best Western, Hilton Garden, Ramada Inn, Travelodge, **other:** Barnes&Noble, Best Buy, Circuit City, Kohl's, Lowe's Whse, Office Depot, Old Navy, PetCo, Ross, Sam's Club/gas, Target, TJ Maxx, Wal-Mart SuperCtr/24hr, Wegman's Foods
165b a	PA 309 S, Wilkes-Barre, W...gas: BP/dsl, Gulf, **food:** Mark II Rest., McDonald's, Perkins, Taco Bell, **lodging:** Comfort Inn, Econolodge, **other:** Advance Parts, Eckerd, K-Mart
164	PA 29, to Nanticoke, Ashley, no services
159	Nuangola, W...gas: BP/cafe/24hr
157mm	**rest area/weigh sta sb, full(handicapped) facilities, vending, phone, picnic tables, litter barrels, petwalk**

Scranton

Interstate 81

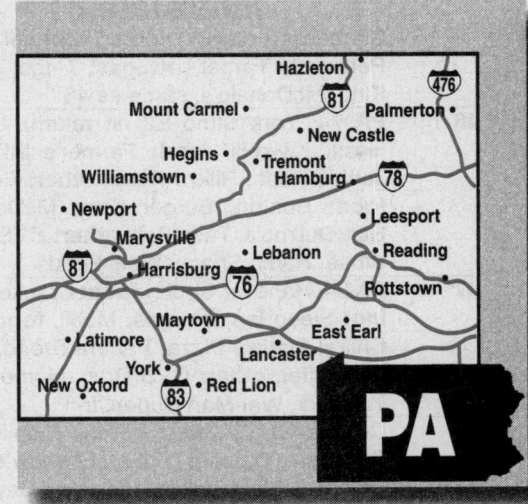

156mm	**rest area/weigh sta nb, full(handicapped) facili-ties, vending, phone, picnic tables, litter barrels, petwalk**
155	to Dorrance, **E**...**gas:** Sunoco/dsl/24hr, **lodging:** Econolodge(2mi), **W**...**gas:** Blue Ridge Plaza/dsl
151b a	I-80, E to Mountaintop, W to Bloomsburg
145	PA 93, W Hazleton, **E**...**gas:** Exxon, Sunoco/dsl/24hr, TurkeyHill, **food:** Bonanza, Damon's, Friend-ly's, Ground Round, McDonald's, Perkins, Pizza Hut, Taco Bell, Wendy's, **lodging:** Best Western(2mi), Comfort Inn, Fairfield Inn, Forest Hill Inn, Ramada Inn, **other:** HOSPITAL, Aldi, Cadillac/Buick/Pon-tiac/GMC, Chrysler/Jeep/Dodge, Mazda, st police, **W**...**gas:** Shell, **lodging:** Hampton Inn
143	PA 924, to Hazleton, **E**...**lodging:** Hazleton Motel, **W**...**gas:** Exxon, Mobil, **food:** Subway
141	PA 424, S Hazleton Beltway, no services
138	PA 309, to McAdoo, **2 mi E**...**lodging:** Pines Mo-tel
134	to Delano, no services
132mm	parking area/weigh sta both lanes
131b a	PA 54, Mahanoy City, **E**...**other:** to Tuscarora/Lo-cust Lake SP, **W**...**gas:** Exxon, Shell/dsl
124b a	PA 61, to Frackville, **E**...**food:** Cracker Barrel, Mc-Donald's, **lodging:** Holiday Inn Express, **other:** Big Lots, K-Mart, Sears/auto, mall, **W**...**gas:** Hess, Mo-bil/Taco Bell/24hr, **food:** Dutch Kitchen, Subway, **lodging:** Econolodge, I-81 Motel, **other:** HOSPI-TAL, Dodge, Goodyear/auto, Rite Aid, st police
119	High Ridge Park Rd, to Gordon, **E**...**lodging:** Coun-try Inn&Suites, **other:** HOSPITAL
116	PA 901, to Minersville, **E**...**food:** 901 Rest.
112	PA 25, to Hegins, **W**...camping
107	US 209, to Tremont, no services
104	PA 125, Ravine, **E**...**gas:** Exxon/Pizza Hut/Quiz-no's/dsl/24hr, **other:** Echo Valley Camping
100	PA 443, to Pine Grove, **E**...**gas:** Exxon/dsl, **food:** Arby's, McDonald's, **lodging:** Comfort Inn, Econolodge, **W**...**gas:** Shell/Subway/dsl/scales/24hr, Sunoco/dsl/24hr, **food:** Gooseberry Farms Rest., **lodging:** Hampton Inn, **other:** KOA(5mi)
90	PA 72, to Lebanon, **E**...**gas:** Exxon/Subway, Hess, **food:** DQ/Sbarro's, Wendy's, **lodging:** Best West-ern, Day's Inn, **other:** KOA(5mi), Lickdale Camp-ing, st police, **W**...**lodging:** Red Carpet Inn
89	I-78 E, to Allentown
85b a	PA 934, to Annville, **2 mi W**...**gas:** Mobil/dsl/24hr, **food:** Funck's Rest., **other:** to IndianTown Gap Nat Cem
80	PA 743, Grantville, **E**...**gas:** Mobil/dsl, **lodging:** Econolodge, Hampton Inn, **W**...**gas:** Exxon, **food:** Mama's Rest., **lodging:** Comfort Suites, Holiday Inn, **other:** racetrack
79mm	**rest area/weigh sta both lanes, full(handicapped)facilities, phone, vending, picnic tables, litter barrels, petwalk**
77	PA 39, to Hershey, **E**...**gas:** Exxon/dsl, Mobil/dsl, Pilot/Pizza Hut/dsl/scales/24hr, **lodging:** Country Hearth Inn, Country Inn&Suites, Howard Johnson, Scottish Inn, **other:** to Hershey Attractions, st po-lice, **W**...**gas:** Citgo/Subway/dsl, TA/dsl/scales/

	24hr/@, Wilco/Hess/Perkins/Stuckey's/dsl/24hr/@, **food:** McDonald's, **lodging:** Comfort Inn, Daystop, **other:** Goodyear
72	to US 22, Linglestown, **E**...**gas:** Citgo/dsl, Hess/dsl, Sunoco/dsl, **food:** Applebee's, Burger King, El Rodeo Mexican, McDonald's, Old Country Buffet, Red Robin, Wendy's, **lodging:** Holiday Inn Express, L&M Motel, Quality Inn, **other:** Advance Parts, Chrysler/Jeep, CVS Drug, Harley-Davidson, Jo-Ann Fabrics, Karn's Foods, Toyota, U-Haul, **W**...**food:** Country Oven Rest., **lodging:** Best Western
70	I-83 S, to York, airport
69	Progress Ave, **E**...**gas:** Citgo/7-11, **food:** Cracker Barrel, Damon's, Macaroni Grill, **other:** st police, **W**...**gas:** Turkey Hill, **food:** Arby's, Western Sizzlin, **lodg-ing:** Best Western/rest., Red Roof Inn
67b a	US 22, US 322 W, PA 230, Cameron St, to Lewis-town
66	Front St, **E**...HOSPITAL, **W**...**gas:** Exxon, Sunoco, **food:** Jade Buffet, McDonald's, Pizza Hut, Taco Bell, Wendy's, **lodging:** Day's Inn, Super 8
65	US 11/15, to Enola, **1 mi E**...**gas:** Mobil/24hr, Suno-co/dsl/24hr, **food:** DQ, Eat'n Park, KFC, McDonald's, Subway, Summerdale Diner, Wendy's, **lodging:** Qual-ity Inn, **other:** Advance Parts, K-Mart, Radio Shack, Rite Aid
61	PA 944, to Wertzville, no services
59	PA 581, to US 11, I-83, Harrisburg, **3 mi E**...**food:** Bob Evans, Burger King, Friendly's, McDonald's, Wendy's, **lodging:** Comfort Inn, Hampton Inn, Holiday Inn
57	PA 114, to Mechanicsburg, **1-2 mi E**...**food:** Arby's, Isaac's Rest., McDonald's, Pizza Hut, Red Robin, Taco Bell, **lodging:** Ramada Ltd
52b a	US 11, to I-76/PA Tpk, Middlesex, **E**...**gas:** Citgo/dsl, ✈/Flying J/Country Mkt/dsl/LP/24hr/scales/@, **food:** Bob Evans, Middlesex Diner/24hr, **lodging:** Appa-lachian Tr Inn, Econolodge, Holiday Inn, Hotel Car-lisle, Super 8, **W**...**gas:** Petro/dsl/rest./24hr/@, Pilot/Wendy's/dsl/24hr/@, Shell/dsl/scales/24hr, Sunoco, **food:** Arby's, Carelli's Subs, Eat'n Park, Hoss' Rest., McDonald's, Subway, Waffle House, **lodging:** Hamp-ton Inn, Howard Johnson/rest., Motel 6, Quality Inn, Ramada Ltd, Rodeway Inn, **other:** Blue Beacon
49	PA 74(no EZ sb return), **E**...**food:** Red Robin,

Interstate 81

	Starbucks, **other:** Kohl's, Michael's, Old Navy, Petsmart, Target, **W**...**gas:** Citgo, **food:** Burger King, McDonald's, same as 48
48	PA 74, York St(no EZ nb return), **W**...**gas:** Gulf, Hess, KwikFill, **food:** Farmer's Mkt Rest., Little John's Rest., Rillo's Rest., **other:** Ford, **1 mi W**... **food:** Bonton, Burger King, McDonald's, Pizza Hut, Quizno's, Taco Bell, **other:** CVS Drug, Lowe's Whse, Radio Shack, Weis Foods
47	PA 34, Hanover St, **E**...**food:** Cracker Barrel, **lodging:** Sleep Inn, **W**...**gas:** Mobil, **food:** Applebee's, Chili's, Mario's Pizza, Panera Bread, Subway, Super Buffet, **other:** CVS Drug, Home Depot, Ross, TJ Maxx, Wal-Mart SuperCtr
45	College St, **E**...**gas:** BP/dsl, Mobil, Shell, **food:** Bonanza, Carelli's Subs, Friendly's, Great Wall Chinese, McDonald's, **lodging:** Day's Inn, Super 8, **other:** Western Village Camping(2mi), **W**... HOSPITAL
44	PA 465, to Plainfield, **E**...st police, **W**...**gas:** Sheetz/24hr, **other:** Subway
38mm	**rest area both lanes, full(handicapped) facilities, phone, picnic tables, litter barrels, petwalk**
37	PA 233, to Newville, **E**...Pine Grove Furnace SP, **W**...Col Denning SP
29	PA 174, King St, **E**...**gas:** Pharoh's/dsl/scales/ 24hr, Sunoco/24hr, **lodging:** Budget Host, **W**... **food:** Burger King(1mi), McDonald's(2mi), Subway, Wendy's, **lodging:** Best Western, **other:** Ford
24	PA 696, Fayette St, **W**...**gas:** Mobil/dsl
20	PA 997, Scotland, **E**...**gas:** Exxon/dsl, **food:** McDonald's, **lodging:** Comfort Inn, Super 8, **other:** Gander Mtn, JC Penney, Sears/auto, mall, **W**... **gas:** BP/dsl, Sunoco/24hr, **lodging:** Sleep Inn
17	Walker Rd, **W**...**gas:** Sheetz/24hr, **food:** Brewster's, **lodging:** Hampton Inn, **other:** Ford, Giant Foods, Kohl's, Target
16	US 30, to Chambersburg, **E**...**gas:** Exxon, Fuel Ctr, Sheetz/24hr, **food:** Arby's, Chris's Country Kitchen, DQ, KFC, Montezuma Mexican, Perkins, Popeye's, Ryan's, Waffle House, **lodging:** Days Inn, **other:** Aldi Foods, Curves, Harley-Davidson, Hoss's, Jo-Ann Fabrics, Lowes Whse, Nissan/Toyota/Scion, Radio Shack, Wal-Mart SuperCtr/Subway, st police, **W**...**gas:** Hess/dsl, **food:** Burger King, Copper Kettle, Hardee's, LJ Silver, McDonald's, Pizza Hut, Ponderosa, Starbucks, Taco Bell, **lodging:** Best Western, Sheraton, **other:** HOSPITAL, Advance Parts, AutoZone, Lincoln/Mercury, Sav-A-Lot Food
14	PA 316, Wayne Ave, **E**...**food:** Bob Evans, Cracker Barrel, **lodging:** Fairfield Inn, Hampton Inn, Red Carpet Inn, **W**...**gas:** KwikFill, Sheetz, **food:** Applebee's, Arby's, Dakota Steaks, Denny's, Montezuma Mexican, Pizza Hut, Red Lobster, Subway, Wendy's, **lodging:** Econolodge, Holiday Inn Express, Quality Inn, **other:** CVS Drug, Giant Foods, K-Mart, Staples, Weis Foods
12mm	weigh sta sb

10	PA 914, Marion, no services
7mm	weigh sta nb
5	PA 16, Greencastle, **E**...**gas:** Green Castle Travel Stop/dsl, TA/BP/dsl/rest./scales/24hr/@, **food:** Arby's, McDonald's, Subway, **lodging:** Econolodge, Rodeway Inn, **other:** Whitetail Ski Resort, **W**...**gas:** Exxon/dsl, **lodging:** Castle Green Motel/rest.
3	US 11, **E**...**gas:** Exxon, **food:** Bro's Pizza, **lodging:** Comfort Inn
2mm	**Welcome Ctr nb, full(handicapped)facilities, phone, picnic tables, litter barrels, vending, petwalk**
1	PA 163, Mason-Dixon Rd, **W**...**lodging:** Best Value Inn, State Line Motel, **other:** Keystone RV Ctr
0mm	Pennsylvania/Maryland state line, Mason-Dixon Line

Interstate 83

Exit #	Services
51b a	I-83 begins/ends on I-81, exit 70.
50b a	US 22, Jonestown Rd, Harrisburg, **E**...**gas:** Shell, Sunoco, **food:** Applebee's, Arby's, Atlanta Bread, Boston Mkt, Colonial Diner, El Rodeo Mexican, Grand Buffet, LJ Silver, McDonald's, Old Country Buffet, Olive Garden, Pizza Hut, Red Lobster, Red Robin, Subway, Taco Bell, Tonino's Pizza, **other:** Aamco, Best Buy, Borders Books, Circuit City, Coscto/gas, CVS Drug, Goodyear/ auto, Home Depot, K-Mart, Kohl's, Michael's, NTB, Old Navy, PepBoys, Sears/auto, Target, Tires+, Weis Foods, mall, **W**...**food:** Dunkin Donuts, Friendly's, Gabriella's Italian, KFC, Roberto's Pizza, **other:** Rite Aid
48	Union Deposit Rd, **E**...**gas:** Sunoco, **food:** Arby's, Burger King, Denny's, Evergreen Chinese, Panera Bread, **lodging:** Hampton Inn, Sheraton, **other:** HOSPITAL, Giant Foods, Rite Aid, Staples, mall, **W**...**gas:** BP, **food:** Charlie Brown Steaks, ChuckeCheese, Hardee's, Great Wall Chinese, JoJo's Pizza, McDonald's, OutBack Steaks, Rita's Drive-Thru, Ruby Tuesday, Starbucks, Subway, Texas Roadhouse, TGIFriday, Waffle House, Wendy's, **lodging:** Comfort Inn, Fairfield Inn, **other:** Hancock Fabrics, Lowe's Whse, PriceRight, Radio Shack, Tuesday Morning, Weis Foods
47	(46b from nb), US 322 E, to Hershey, Derry St, **E**... **gas:** Hess Gas, **food:** Papa John's, **other:** Home Depot, Petsmart
46a b	I-283 S, to I-76/PA Tpk, **facilities E** off I-283 S...**gas:** Exxon/dsl, Sunoco, **food:** Bob Evans, Capitol Diner, Doc Holliday's Steaks, Domino's, Eat'n Park, McDonald's, Waffle House, **lodging:** Courtyard, Econolodge, Holiday Inn, Howard Johnson, La Quinta, Red Roof Inn, Sheraton, Super 8, Travelodge, Wyndham, **other:** Buick, JC Penney, LandRover, Target, VW/Audi, **W**... **gas:** Sunoco, **food:** Taco Bell, Wendy's, **lodging:** Best Western, Day's Inn,
45	Paxton St, **E**...**gas:** Sheetz, **food:** Burger King, Dunkin Donuts, Fuddrucker's, Isaac's Rest., Pizza Hut, Ruby Tuesday, Wendy's, **other:** Bass Pro Shops, Chrysler, JC Penney, Mazda/Subaru/Toyota, Nissan, mall

Interstate 83

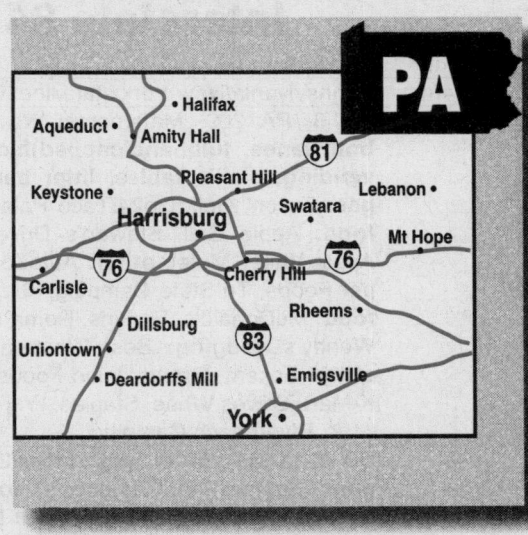

44b	17th St, 19th St, **E**...**gas:** Sunoco, **food:** Bankok Thai Cuisine, Benihana Japanese, Dunkin Donuts, Hardee's, Jumbo Buffet, **other:** Advance Parts, Cadillac/GMC/Pontiac, CarQuest, Dodge, Firestone/auto, Honda, Hyundai/Suzuki/Isuzu, Nissan, Pontiac, Tires+
44a	PA 230, 13th St, Harrisburg, downtown, **W**...**other:** Chevrolet, Saturn
43	2nd St, Harrisburg, downtown, st capitol, **W**...**lodging:** Crowne Plaza, **other:** HOSPITAL
42.5mm	Susquehanna River
42	Lemoyne, **W**...**gas:** BP
41b	Highland Park, **E**...**gas:** Mobil, Turkey Hill, **food:** Ciao Pizzaria, KFC, Royal Subs, **other:** Ace Hardware, Weis Foods
41a	US 15, PA 581 W, to Gettysburg
40b	New Cumberland, **W**...**gas:** BP/dsl, **food:** JoJo's Pizza, McDonald's, New China, Sidoti's Italian, Subway, **other:** CVS Drug, $General
40a	Limekiln Rd, to Lewisberry, **E**...**gas:** BP, Mobil, **food:** Bob Evans, Eat'n Park, McDonald's, Pizza Hut, **lodging:** Comfort Inn, Fairfield Inn, Holiday Inn, Rodeway Inn, **W**...**gas:** Hess, **lodging:** Best Western, Motel 6, Travel Inn, **other:** vet
39b	I-76/PA Tpk
39a	PA 114, Lewisberry Rd, **E**...**lodging:** Day's Inn, Highland Motel, Keystone Inn
38	Reesers Summit, no services
36	PA 262, Fishing Creek, **E**...**gas:** Hess/Blimpie, **food:** Brewster's, Culhane's Steaks, **W**...**gas:** Citgo/dsl
35	PA 177, Lewisberry, **E**...**food:** Hillside Café, **W**...**gas:** Mobil, **food:** Francescos, Summit Rest.
35mm	parking area/weigh sta sb
34	Valley Green(from nb), same as 33
33	PA 392, Yocumtown, **E**...**gas:** Hess/Blimpie/dsl, Henry's Trkstop/dsl, Rutter's, **food:** Alice's Rest., Burger King, Lee's Chinese, Maple Donuts, McDonald's, **lodging:** Super 8, **other:** Eckerd, Family$, Radio Shack, SuperFresh Food
33mm	parking area/weigh sta nb
32	PA 382, Newberrytown, **E**...**gas:** Rutter's/Pizza Hut/dsl/24hr, **W**...**gas:** Exxon/dsl
28	PA 295, Strinestown, **W**...**gas:** Rutter's/24hr, **food:** 83 Diner, Wendy's
24	PA 238, Emigsville, **W**...**gas:** Mobil, **food:** Sibol's Steaks
22	PA 181, N George St, **E**...**gas:** Rutter's, **lodging:** Comfort Inn, Homewood Suites, **W**...same as 21b
21b a	US 30, Arsenal Rd, to York, **E**...**food:** Bob Evans, Round-the-Clock, San Carlo's Rest., **lodging:** Day's Inn, Holiday Inn, Motel 6, Sheraton, **other:** Buick/Pontiac/GMC, **W**...**gas:** BP, Exxon, Rutter's, **food:** Arby's, Burger King, Cheeseburger Paradise, Damon's, Denny's, DQ, El Rodeo Mexican, Friendly's, Hardee's, Hooters, KFC, LoneStar Steaks, LJ Silver, McDonald's, Old Country Buffet, Olive Garden, Pizza Hut, Popeye's, RipTide Seafood, Ruby Tuesday, Smokey Bones BBQ, Starlite Diner, Subway, Taco Bell, TGIFriday, Wendy's, **lodging:** Red Roof Inn, Super 8, **other:** Acura, Advance Parts, AutoZone,

York

	BMW, Chevrolet/Cadillac, Chrysler/Mitsubishi, CVS Drug, Dodge, $General, Harley-Davidson, NTB, Old Navy, PepBoys, Radio Shack, Staples, Wal-Mart SuperCtr, Weis Foods
19	PA 462, Market St, **E**...**gas:** Hess, Mobil, **food:** Applebee's, Arby's, Eat'n Park, Ember's, Outback Steaks, Perkins, Red Lobster, Starbucks, Taco Bell, Wendy's, **lodging:** Quality Inn, **other:** HOSPITAL, Advance Parts, $General, Giant Foods, Lowes Whse, Nissan, NTB, Sam's Club, Saturn, Walgreens, Wal-Mart SuperCtr, Weis Foods
18	PA 124, Mt Rose Ave, Prospect St, **E**...**gas:** Mobil, Rutters, Sunoco, **food:** AlDente Italian, Burger King, Denny's, 5 Guys, Mexitaly, Pizza Hut, Sub Shop, **lodging:** Budget Host, **other:** Curves, CVS Drug, K-Mart, Nello Tire, Weis Foods, **W**...**gas:** Tom's(1mi)
16b a	PA 74, Queen St, **E**...**gas:** Mobil/24hr, **food:** Cracker Barrel, Ruby Tuesday, **lodging:** Country Inn Suites, **other:** Giant Foods, Lincoln/Mercury, **W**...**food:** McDonald's, Pizza Hut/Taco Bell, S York Diner, Subway, **other:** CVS Drug, $General, $Tree, Honda, Jo-Ann Fabrics, Tuesday Morning, Walgreens
15	(from nb)S George St, I-83 spur into York, **W**...HOSPITAL
14	PA 182, Leader Heights, **E**...**food:** Domino's, First Wok, Subway, **W**...**gas:** Rutter's/Pizza Hut, **food:** McDonald's, **lodging:** Holiday Inn Express
10	PA 214, Loganville, **W**...**food:** Mamma's Pizza, Sophie's Rest., **lodging:** Midway Motel, **other:** st police
8	PA 216, Glen Rock, **E**...**lodging:** Rocky Ridge Motel, **other:** Amish Farmers Mkt(2mi)
4	PA 851, Shrewsbury, **E**...**gas:** Crown/dsl, Mobil/dsl/24hr, **food:** Cracker Barrel, Ruby Tuesday, **lodging:** Hampton Inn, **other:** Home Depot, TrueValue, **W**...**gas:** Exxon/dsl/24hr, **food:** Arby's, Chick-fil-A, Emerald Garden Chinese, KFC/Taco Bell, McDonald's, Quizno's, Szechuan Chinese, Subway, Wendy's, **other:** Advance Parts, Curves, $Tree, Giant Foods, GNC, Radio Shack, Wal-Mart SuperCtr/24hr
2mm	**Welcome Ctr nb, full(handicapped)facilities, phone, vending, picnic tables, litter barrels, petwalk**
0mm	Pennsylvania/Maryland state line

PENNSYLVANIA
Interstate 84

E ↕ **W**

Exit #	Services
54mm	Pennsylvania/New York state line, Delaware River
53	US 6, PA 209, Matamoras, **N**...**Welcome Ctr/ both lanes, full(handicapped)facilities, phone, vending, picnic tables, litter barrels, petwalk**, gas: Exxon, Gulf, Go24/Taco Palace, Turkey Hill, food: Apple Grill, Stewart's Drive-Inn, lodging: Apple Valley Motel, other: AutoZone, PriceChopper Foods, Tri-State Camping, **S**...gas: Mobil/dsl, food: McDonald's, Perkins, Roma Pizza, Subway, Wendy's, lodging: Best Western, Scottish Inn, other: Eckerd, Grand Union Foods, Home Depot, K-Mart, Lowes Whse, Staples, Wal-Mart/SuperCtr/ 24hr, Riverbeach Camping
46	US 6, to Milford, **N**...gas: Mobil/24hr, **2 mi S**... gas: Citgo/dsl/24hr, Sunoco/dsl, food: Apple Valley Rest., lodging: Black Walnut B&B, Cliff Park Inn, Sherelyn Motel, Red Carpet Inn
34	PA 739, to Lords Valley, Dingmans Ferry, **S**...gas: Mobil, Sunoco/Taco Xtra/dsl, food: Bruno's Pizza, China Dynasty, McDonald's, other: Curves, Family$, Mr Z's Foods, Rite Aid, USPO
30	PA 402, to Blooming Grove, **N**...st police, to Lake Wallenpaupack
26	PA 390, to Tafton, **N**...Exxon/dsl, to Lake Wallenpaupack, **S**...other: to Promised Land SP
26mm	**rest area/weigh sta both lanes, full(handicapped)facilities, phone, vending, picnic tables, litter barrels, petwalk**
20	PA 507, Greentown, **N**...gas: Exxon/dsl, Mobil/Sbway, food: John's Italian, other: Animal Park(5mi)
17	PA 191, to Newfoundland, Hamlin, **N**...gas: Exxon/ 24hr, Howe's 84/dsl/24hr, food: Twin Rocks Rest., lodging: Comfort Inn/rest.
8	PA 247, PA 348, Mt Cobb, **N**...gas: Gulf/dsl/24hr, other: golf, **S**...gas: Mobil/dsl/24hr
4	I-380 S, to Mount Pocono
2	PA 435 S, to Elmhurst, no services
1	Tigue St, **N**...lodging: Holiday Inn, **S**...gas: Mobil
0mm	I-84 begins/ends on I-81, exit 54

Interstate 90

E ↕ **W**

Exit #	Services
46mm	Pennsylvania/New York state line, **Welcome Ctr/ weigh sta wb, full(handicapped)facilities, phone, vending, picnic tables, litter barrels, petwalk**
45	US 20, to State Line, **N**...gas: KwikFill/dsl/scales/@, NE/Shell/dsl/rest./scales/@, food: McDonald's, **S**...gas: BP/Subway/dsl, lodging: Red Carpet Inn, other: Niagara Falls Info, fireworks

Exit #	Services
41	PA 89, North East, **N**...gas: Shell, lodging: Super 8, Vineyard B&B, **S**...winery
37	I-86 E, to Jamestown
35	PA 531, to Harborcreek, **N**...gas: TA/BP/dsl/rest./ scales/24hr/@, food: Pizza Hut, Subway, lodging: Rodeway Inn, other: Blue Beacon, dsl repair
32	PA 430, PA 290, to Wesleyville, **N**...gas: Citgo, st police, **S**...other: camping
29	PA 8, to Hammett, **N**...gas: Citgo, food: Wendy's, other: HOSPITAL, **S**...lodging: Travelodge, other: Ford/Peterbilt, dsl repair
27	PA 97, State St, Waterford, **N**...gas: Citgo/dsl/ 24hr, Kwikfill, food: Arby's, Barbato's Italian, Doc Holiday's Grill, McDonald's, lodging: Best Western, Day's Inn, Red Roof Inn, Tallyho Inn, other: HOSPITAL, **S**...gas: Pilot/Subway/dsl/scales/ 24hr, Shell/dsl, lodging: Quality Inn, Super 8
24	US 19, Peach St, to Waterford, **N**...gas: Citgo/dsl, Delta Sonic, KwikFill, food: Applebee's, Brewster's, Burger King, China Garden, ChuckeCheese, Cracker Barrel, Damon's, Eat'n Park, Fazoli's, Golden Corral, Longhorn Steaks, McDonald's, Old Country Buffet, Panera Bread, Ponderosa, Safari Grill, Subway, Taco Bell, TGIFriday, Texas Roadhouse, Wendy's, lodging: Courtyard, Motel 6, other: HOSPITAL, Advance Parts, Best Buy, Circuit City, Country Fair/deli, $Tree, Giant Eagle, Home Depot, Jo-Ann Fabrics, K-Mart, Kohl's, Lowe's Whse, Petsmart, Pontiac, Sam's Club, Staples, Target, VW, Wal-Mart/auto, Wegman's Foods, **S**... gas: BP, Citgo, Shell, food: Bob Evans, Boston's Rest., lodging: Comfort Inn, Country Inn&Suites, Econolodge, Hampton Inn, Holiday Inn Express, Microtel, Residence Inn, other: waterpark
22b a	I-79, N to Erie, S to Pittsburgh, **3-5 mi N**...services in Erie
18	PA 832, Sterrettania, **N**...gas: Shell/dsl/24hr, food: Burger King, other: Hill's Family Camping, to Presque Isle SP, **S**...lodging: Best Western, other: KOA
16	PA 98, to Franklin Center, Fairview, **S**...other: Follys Camping(2mi), Mar-Da-Jo-Dy Camping(5mi)
9	PA 18, to Girard, Platea, **N**...gas: Gulf, other: dsl repair, st police, **S**...lodging
6	PA 215, to Albion, E Springfield, **N**...lodging, **S**... gas: Sunoco, lodging
3	US 6N, to Cherry Hill, West Springfield, **N**...lodging on US 20, **S**...gas: BP/dsl/rest./scales/24hr/@
2.5mm	**Welcome Ctr/weigh sta eb, full(handicapped) facilities, info, phone, picnic tables, litter barrels, vending, petwalk**
0mm	Pennsylvania/Ohio state line

Erie

PENNSYLVANIA

Interstate 95

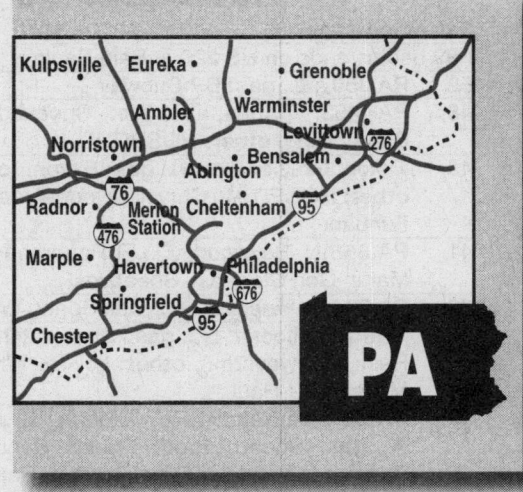

Exit #	Services
51mm	Pennsylvania/New Jersey state line, Delaware River
51	PA 32, to New Hope, W...Washington Crossing Hist Park
49mm	**Welcome Ctr sb, full(handicapped)facilities, vending, phone, picnic tables, litter barrels, petwalk**
49	PA 332, to Yardley, Newtown, W...**lodging:** Hampton Inn, **other:** HOSPITAL, to Tyler SP
46	US 1, Langhorne, Oxford Valley, E...HOSPITAL
44	US 1, PA 413, to Penndel, Levittown, E...**gas:** Shell/dsl/24hr, **food:** ChuckeCheese, Classic Steaks, Dunkin Donuts, Friendly's, Great American Diner, Panera Bread, Quizno's, Ruby Tuesday, Wendy's, **other:** HOSPITAL, Acura, Chevrolet/Buick, China Buffet, China Pearl, Chrysler, Dodge, $Tree, Drug Emporium, Ford, Goodyear/auto, Harley Davidson, Honda, Hyundai/Suzuki, Jeep, K-Mart, Lincoln/Mercury, Lowe's Whse, Marshalls, NTB, Radio Shack, Sam's Club, Subaru, VW/Volvo, Whse Mkt, W...**gas:** Mobil/dsl/24hr, **food:** Denny's, McDonald's, **other:** Toyota, U-Haul
40	PA 413, I-276(from nb), to Bristol Bridge, Burlington, E...**food:** Golden Eagle Diner/24hr, McDonald's, Taco Bell, **other:** HOSPITAL
37	PA 132, to Street Rd, W...**gas:** BP/24hr, Shell, Sunoco/dsl, **food:** Burger King, Denny's, IHOP, KFC, Wendy's, **other:** Firestone, GNC, PepBoys, Radio Shack
35	PA 63, to US 13, Woodhaven Rd, Bristol Park, W...**gas:** Coastal, Mobil, WaWa, **food:** Old Haven Pizza, **lodging:** Hampton Inn, **other:** HOSPITAL, Acme Foods, Hancock Fabrics, Home Depot, **1 mi** W...**gas:** BP, Exxon, Mobil, Sunoco, **food:** Arby's, Boston Mkt, Dynasty Buffet, Don Pablo, Dynasty Rest., Farm Buffet, KFC, McDonald's, Perkins, Pizza Hut, Taco Bell, Wendy's, **other:** CompUSA, JC Penney, Marshall's, Nordstrom's, NTB, SuperFresh Foods, Wal-Mart, mall
32	Academy Rd, W...**other:** HOSPITAL, K-Mart
30	PA 73, Cottman Ave, W...**gas:** Sunoco
27	Bridge St, W...**gas:** Getty Gas, Eckerd, **other:** HOSPITAL
26	to NJ 90, Betsy Ross Brdg, W...**gas:** Sunoco, **food:** Burger King, McDonald's, Wendy's, **lodging:** Hampton Inn, **other:** Home Depot
25	Allegheny Ave, W...**gas:** Sunoco, Wawa, **other:** HOSPITAL
23	Lehigh Ave, Girard Ave, W...**gas:** Exxon, Shell, **food:** Dunkin Donuts, Pizza Hut, Ruby Tuesday, **other:** HOSPITAL, Radio Shack
22	I-676, US 30, to Central Philadelphia, Independence Hall
20	Columbus Blvd, Penns Landing, E...**gas:** BP, Mobil, Sunoco, **food:** Burger King, Boston Mkt, Dave&Buster's, ChartHouse Rest., ChuckeCheese, Enginehouse Rest, Grand King Buffet, Hooters, McDonald's, **lodging:** Hyatt Hotel(1mi), **other:** Hyatt, Home Depot, PepBoys, SavALot Foods, ShopRite Foods, Staples, Target, Wal-Mart
19	I-76 E, to Walt Whitman Bridge, W **on Oregon Ave**...**gas:** Shell, **food:** Burger King, Church's Chicken, McDonald's, Subway, Wendy's, **lodging:** Holiday Inn, **other:** Aldi, K-Mart, to stadium
17	PA 611, to Broad St, Pattison Ave, W...**other:** HOSPITAL, to Naval Shipyard, to stadium
15mm	Schuykill River
14	Enterprise Ave, Island Ave(from sb)
14	Bartram Ave, Essington Ave(from sb)
13	PA 291, to I-76 W(from nb), to Central Philadelphia, E...**gas:** Exxon/dsl, **lodging:** Day's Inn, 4Points Sheraton, Guest Quarters, Hilton, Residence Inn, Sheraton Suites, Westin Suites
12	E... Philadelphia Intl Airport, services same as 10
10	PA 29, Bartrom Ave, (from nb), Cargo City, E...**lodging:** Marriott, Rennaisance Hotel, W...**lodging:** Courtyard, Hampton Inn, Embassy Suites, Extended Stay America, Fairfield Inn, Microtel, Studio+
9b a	PA 420, to Essington, Prospect Park, E...**gas:** Sunoco/dsl, Valero/dsl, **food:** Denny's, Philly Diner, Lehmans Rest., **lodging:** Comfort Inn, Holiday Inn, Motel 6, Ramada Inn, Red Roof Inn, **other:** USPO, WaWa
8	to Chester Waterfront, Ridley Park, W **on US 13**...**food:** Stargate Diner
7	I-476 N, to Plymouth, Meeting
6	PA 352, PA 320, to Edgmont Ave, **1 mi** E **on US 13**...**food:** McDonald's, Popeye's, **other:** Radio Shack, Wal-Mart/Subway
5	Kerlin St(from nb), E...**gas:** BP
4	US 322 E, to NJ, to Barry Bridge, W...**lodging:** Highland Motel
3	(3 from nb, no EZ return)US 322 W, Highland Ave, E...**gas:** Sunoco/dsl/24hr, Ford/Lincoln/Mercury, Goodyear
2	PA 452, to US 322, Market St, E...**gas:** Getty, W...**gas:** Exxon, **food:** McDonald's
1	Chichester Ave, E...**gas:** Sunoco, W...**gas:** BP
0mm	**Pennsylvania/Delaware state line, Welcome Ctr/weigh sta nb, full(handicapped)facilities, phone, picnic tables, litter barrels, petwalk**

PENNSYLVANIA
Interstate 99

Exit #	Services
	I-99 begins/ends on US 220 at Bald Eagle.
52	PA 350, W...**gas:** BP/Subway
48	PA 453, Tyrone, W...**gas:** Sheetz/dsl/24hr, **food:** Burger King, **other:** HOSPITAL
45	Tipton, Grazierville, W...**gas:** Exxon, **food:** Pizza Hut, **other:** HOSPITAL, Chrysler/Dodge/Jeep, DelGrosso's Funpark
41	PA 865 N, Bellwood, E...Ft Roberdeau HS, W...**gas:** Martin Gen Store/dsl, Sheetz/dsl
39	PA 764 S, Pinecroft, W...Oak Spring Winery
33	17th St, Altoona, W...**gas:** Sheetz/24hr, **food:** Hoss' Rest., Subway(2mi), **other:** Lowe's Whse, Railroader Museum, U-Haul
32	PA 36, Frankstown Rd, Altoona, E...Canoe Cr SP, W...**gas:** Sheetz, **food:** Dunkin Donuts, HongKong Buffet, McDonald's, Olive Garden, Papa John's, Perkins, Pizza Hut, Red Lobster, Subway, Wendy's, **lodging:** Day's Inn, Econolodge, Holiday Inn, Super 8, **other:** HOSPITAL, AutoZone, Big A Parts, Cadillac, CVS Drug, Dodge, Eckerd, Lincoln/Mercury, NAPA, Nissan, Radio Shack, Subaru
31	Plank Rd, Altoona, E...**food:** Fazoli's, Friendly's, Jethro's Rest., King's Rest., Outback Steaks, Ruby Tuesday, TGIFriday, **lodging:** Comfort Inn, Ramada Inn, **other:** Circuit City, Firestone/auto, Sam's Club, Target, Wal-Mart, W...**gas:** BP/Subway, **food:** Applebee's, Arby's, Burger King, Cracker Barrel, Denny's, Don Pablo, Eat'n Park, KFC, LJ Silver, Ponderosa, Taco Bell, **lodging:** Hampton Inn, Motel 6, **other:** Advance Parts, BiLo Foods, $General, Giant Eagle Foods, JC Penney, Kaufmann's, K-Mart, PharMor, Sears/auto, Staples, Trak Auto, Weis Foods
28	US 22, to Ebensburg, Holidaysburg, 1 mi E...**food:** McDonald's
23	PA 36, PA 164, Roaring Spring, Portage, E...**gas:** Exxon/LittleCaesar's/24hr, Mobil/Blimpie/dsl, Sheetz/24hr, **food:** Lynn's Rest., **lodging:** Haven Rest Motel, **other:** HOSPITAL, Chrysler/Dodge/Jeep, truck repair
15	Claysburg, King, W...**gas**, **food**
10	to Imler, W...**gas**, **food**, Blue Knob SP(8mi)
7	PA 869, Osterburg, St Clairsville, W...**gas**, **food**
3	PA 56, Johnstown, Cessna, E...**gas:** BP/dsl
1	I-70/76. I-99 begins/ends on US 220. E...**gas:** BP/Mcdonald's, Sheetz, **food:** Arena Rest., Denny's, Hoss' Rest, LJ Silver, Pizza Hut, Wendy's, **lodging:** Budget Host, Best Western, Econolodge, Hampton Inn, Quality Inn, Super 8, Travelodge

Interstate 476

Exit #	Services
131	US 11, US 6. I-476 begins/ends on I-81, same as I-81, exit 194.
122	Keyser Ave, Old Forge, Taylor, no services
121mm	toll plaza
115	I-81, PA 315, Wyoming Valley, Pittston, W...**gas:** Mobil, Pilot/Wendy's/dsl/scales/24hr, Sunoco, **food:** Arby's, McDonald's, Perkins, **lodging:** Knight's Inn, Ramada Inn, **other:** Chevrolet
112mm	toll plaza
105	PA 115, Wilkes-Barre, Bear Creek, E...**gas:** BP, Exxon, PSC
97mm	parking areas both lanes
95	I-80, PA 940, Pocono, Hazleton, W...**gas:** BP/24hr, Texaco, WaWa, **food:** A&W/LJ Silver, Arby's, Denny's, Gino's Pizza, McDonald's, **lodging:** Comfort Inn, CountryPlace Inn, Day's Inn, Ramada Inn, Split Rock Resort
90mm	parking area sb
86mm	Hickory Run Service Plaza both lanes, **gas:** Sunoco/dsl, **food:** Breyer's, McDonald's, hot dogs
74	US 209, Mahoning Valley, Lehighton, Stroudsburg, W...**gas:** Shell/Subway/dsl, **food:** Trainer's Inn Rest., **lodging:** Country Inn&Suites, Hampton Inn
71mm	Lehigh Tunnel
56	I-78, US 22, PA 309, Lehigh Valley, E...**gas:** Gulf, **food:** Dunkin Donuts, Quizno's, Red Robin, Trivet Diner, Wendy's, **lodging:** Comfort Inn, Day's Inn, McIntosh Inn, **other:** BMW, CVS Drug, Infiniti, Jaguar, K-Mart, Land Rover, Staples, W on US 22...**gas:** Mobil, Sunoco, **food:** Chris Rest., Parma Pizza, **lodging:** Best Western, **other:** CVS Drug
56mm	Allentown Service Plaza both lanes, **gas:** Sunoco/dsl, **food:** Big Boy, Hershey's Ice Cream, Pizza Hut, Roy Rogers
44	PA 663, Quakertown, Pottstown, E...**gas:** BP, Mobil/dsl, **food:** Avanti Grill, Faraco's Pizza, **lodging:** Best Western(3mi), Comfort Suites, Hampton Inn, Holiday Inn Express, Rodeway Inn, **other:** HOSPITAL
37mm	parking area sb
31	PA 63, Lansdale, E...**gas:** Exxon, Lukoil, WaWa **food:** Bones Grill, **lodging:** Best Western, Courtyard, Lansdale Motel, Residence Inn, **other:** HOSPITAL
20	Germantown Pike W, to I-276 W, PA Tpk W
19	Germantown Pike E, no services
18b a	(18 from sb), Conshohocken, Norristown, E...**gas:** Lukoil, Sunoco, **food:** Baja Fresh, Burger King, Domino's, LoneStar Steaks, Maria's Pizza, McDonald's, Outback Steaks, Salad Works, Starbucks, **other:** Eckerd, Genuradi's Foods, Marshall's, E on Chemical rd...**food:** Cracker Barrel, Ruby Tuesday, **lodging:** Hampton Inn, **other:** Barnes&Noble, Best Buy, Giant Foods, Lowes Whse, Office Depot, Petsmart, Ross, Target, W...**food:** Papa John's, Uno Pizzaria, Wendy's, **other:** BJ's Whse, Circuit City, Ford, Home Depot, Honda, Michael's, Nissan, Toyota
16b a	(16 from sb), I-76, PA 23, to Philadelpia, Valley Forge
13	US 30, E...**gas:** Shell, **food:** Campus Pizza, Winger's, **other:** HOSPITAL, Fresh Grocer, Radnor Drugs, Staples, USPO, Villanova Hardware, to Villanova U
9	PA 3, Broomall, Upper Darby, E...**food:** Barnaby's Rest, **other:** HOSPITAL, PathMark Foods, carwash
5	US 1, Lima, Springfield, E...**food:** Mesa Mexican, Salad Central, **other:** Circuit City, Jo-Ann Fabrics, Marshall's, Old Navy
3	Baltimore Pike, Media, Swarthmore, E...HOSPITAL, Swarthmore Coll
1	McDade Blvd, E...**gas:** Exxon, **food:** Dunkin Donuts, KFC, McDonald's
0mm	I-476 begins/ends on I-95, exit 7.

Interstate 95

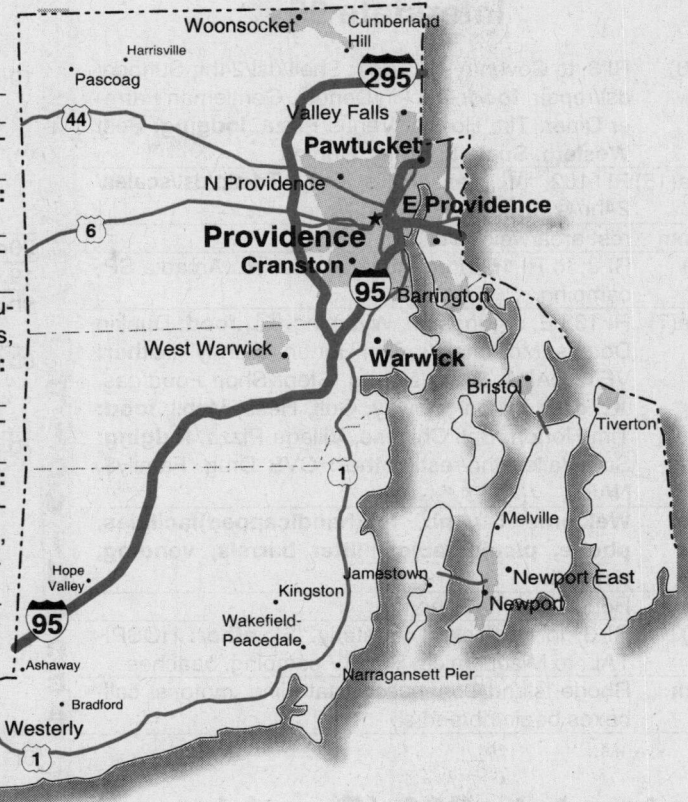

Exit #	Services
43mm	Rhode Island/Massachusetts state line
30(42)	East St, to Central Falls, **E**...**food:** Dunkin Donuts, Subway
29(41)	US 1, Cottage St, **W**...**food:** d'Angelo's, **other:** Firestone
28(40)	RI 114, School St, **E**...**gas:** Sunoco, **other:** HOSPITAL, Hyundai, Tire Pro, to hist dist
27(39)	US 1, RI 15, Pawtucket, **W**...**gas:** Shell/repair, Sunoco/dsl/24hr, **food:** Burger King; Dunkin Donuts, Ground Round, **lodging:** Comfort Inn, **other:** HOSPITAL
26(38)	RI 122, Lonsdale Ave(from nb), **E**...**other:** U-Haul
25(37)	US 1, RI 126, N Main St, Providence, **E**...**gas:** Hess, Shell, **food:** Dunkin Donuts, **other:** HOSPITAL, Brooks Drug/24hr, PepBoys, Shaw's Foods, **W**...**gas:** Gulf/dsl, **food:** Burger King, Chelo's Italian, **other:** AAA, Aamco
24(36.5)	Branch Ave, Providence, downtown, **W**...**gas:** Mobil, **other:** Stop&Shop Foods
23(36)	RI 146, RI 7, Providence, **E**...**gas:** Mobil, **lodging:** Marriott, **other:** HOSPITAL, **W**... USPO
22(35.5)	US 6, RI 10, Providence, **E**...**food:** Cheesecake Factory, Dave&Buster's, **other:** JC Penney, Macy's, Nordstrom's, mall
21(35)	Broadway St, Providence, **W**...**other:** Engle Tire, repair
20(34.5)	I-195, to E Providence, Cape Cod
19(34)	Eddy St, Allens Ave, to US 1(from sb), **W**...**food:** Wendy's, Dunkin Donuts, HOSPITAL
18(33.5)	US 1A, Thurbers Ave, **W**...**gas:** Shell, **food:** Burger King, **other:** HOSPITAL
17(33)	US 1(from sb), Elmwood Ave, **W**...**other:** Cadillac, Tires Whse
16(32.5)	RI 10, Cranston, **W**...Williams Zoo/park
15(32)	Jefferson Blvd, **E**...**gas:** Getty/dsl, Mobil, **food:** Bickford's, Bugaboo Steaks, Dunkin Donuts, **lodging:** Courtyard, Fairfield Inn, Motel 6, **W**...**other:** Colony RV Ctr/Ford Trucks, Ryder
14(31)	RI 37, Post Rd, to US 1, **W**...**gas:** Shell, Sunoco **food:** Burger King, Krispy Kreme, **other:** HOSPITAL, CVS Drug, Lincoln/Mercury
13(30)	**1 mi E**...TF Green Airport, **lodging:** Best Western, Hampton Inn, Hilton Garden, Holiday Inn Express, Homewood Suites, MainStay Suites, Quality Suites, Radisson, Residence Inn
12b(29)	RI 2, I-295 N(from sb)
12a	RI 113 E, to Warwick, **E**...**gas:** Shell/Dunkin Donuts/dsl, **lodging:** Crowne Plaza Hotel, **other:** Lowes Whse, **W**...**gas:** Sunoco, **food:** ChuckeCheese, Wendy's, **other** Kohl's, Sears/auto, WalMart/Subway, mall
11(29)	I-295 N(exits left from nb), to Woonsocket
10b a(28)	RI 117, to Warwick, **W**...HOSPITAL
9(25)	RI 4 S, E Greenwich
8b a(24)	RI 2, E Greenwich, **E**...**gas:** Shell/dsl, **food:** China Buffet, Coldstone Creamery, Dunkin Donuts, McDonald's, Outback Steaks, Panera Bread, Ruby Tuesday, **lodging:** Extended Stay America, **other:** Dave's Mkt, Walgreens, **W**...**gas:** Sunoco/dsl, **food:** Applebee's, Boston Mkt, Denny's, KFC, 99 Rest., PapaGino's, TGI Friday, Wendy's, **lodging:** Comfort Suites, SpringHill Suites, **other:** Acura/BMW, Arlington RV Ctr, Best Buy, GNC, Goodyear/auto, Honda/Volvo, Jo-Ann Fabrics, Lexus/Infiniti, Lowe's Whse, Mazda/Hyundai, Mitsubishi, Nissan, PepBoys, Pontiac/GMC/VW, Sam's Club, Saturn, Shaw's Foods, Stop&Shop Foods, mall
7(21)	to Coventry, **E**...**gas:** Mobil/dsl, **W**...**food:** Applebee's, Cracker Barrel, Denny's, Quizno's, Salad Creations, Wendy's, **lodging:** Hampton Inn, Wingate Inn, **other:** BJ's Whse/gas, Home Depot, WalMart SuperCtr/24hr, auto repair
6a(20)	Hopkins Hill Rd, **W**...park&ride

RHODE ISLAND

Interstate 95

N

↕

S

6(18)	RI 3, to Coventry, **W**...**gas:** Shell/dsl/24hr, Sunoco/dsl/repair, **food:** Dunkin Donuts, Gentleman Farmer Diner, Tim Horton, Venus Pizza, **lodging:** Best Western, Super 8, **other:** Curves
5b a(15)	RI 102, **W**...**gas:** R.I.'s Only Trkstp/dsl/scales/24hr/@, **lodging:** Classic Motel
10mm	rest area/weigh sta sb
4(9)	RI 3, to RI 165(from nb), Arcadia, **W**...Arcadia SP, camping
3b a(7)	RI 138 E, to Kingston, Wyoming, **E**...**food:** Dunkin Donuts, McDonald's, Tim Horton, Wendy's, **other:** VET, NAPA, Brook's Drug, Stop&Shop Food/gas, **W**...**gas:** Exxon/Subway, Gulf, Hess, Mobil, **food:** Tim Horton, Bali Chinese, Village Pizza, **lodging:** Sun Valley Inn/rest., **other:** CVS Drug, Family$, NAPA
6mm	**Welcome Ctr nb, full(handicapped)facilities, phone, picnic tables, litter barrels, vending, petwalk**
2(4)	Hope Valley, no services
1(1)	RI 3, to Hopkinton, Westerly, **E**...**other:** HOSPITAL, to Misquamicut SP, RV camping, beaches
0mm	Rhode Island/Connecticut state line, motorist callboxes begin nb/end sb

Interstate 295 (Providence)

N

↕

S

Exit #	Services
2b a(4)	I-95, N to Boston, S to Providence. I-295 begins/ends on I-95, exit 4 in MA. **Exits 2-1 are in MA.**
1b a(2)	US 1, **E**...**food:** Friendly's, Hearth'n Kettle, Longhorn Steaks, 99 Rest., Panera Bread, TGIFriday, **other:** Best Buy, BJ's Whse, Borders, Circuit City, CompUSA, Macy's, JC Penney, Lord&Taylor, Lowe's Whse, Marshalls, Michael's, Office Depot, Old Navy, Sears/auto, Target, Wal-Mart, mall, **W**...**gas:** Exxon, Shell/Subway, **food:** Applebee's, **lodging:** Holiday Inn Express, Super 8, **other:** Ford, Dodge/Kia, Nissan, Toyota
0mm	Rhode Island/Massachusetts state line. **Exits 1-2 are in MA.**
11(24)	RI 114, to Cumberland, **E**...**gas:** Shell/dsl, **food:** Dunkin Donuts, Honeydew Donuts, **other:** CVS Drug, Dave's Foods, **W**...**food:** J's Deli, Sakis Pizza/subs, **other:** Tedeschi Foods, Diamond Hill Mkt, Diamond Hill SP

Providence

10(21)	RI 122, **E**...**gas:** Gulf, Mutual Gas, **food:** Burger King, Dunkin Donuts, Jacky's Rest., Jim's Deli, McDonald's, Ronzio Pizza, **W**...**food:** Chicken Power, Fortune House Chinese, Subway, **other:** Brooks Drug, CVS Drug, Newport Creamery, Seabra Foods, True Value
20mm	Blackstone River
19.5mm	weigh sta both lanes, phone
9b a(19)	RI 146, Woonsocket, Lincoln, **E**...mall, **2 mi W**...**gas:** Mobil, **other:** Chrysler, Honda, Isuzu
8b a(16)	RI 7, N Smithfield, **W**...**gas:** Citgo/dsl/7-11, **food:** House of Pizza, Roost House Rest., Smith-Appleby House
7b a(13)	US 44, Centerdale, **E**...**gas:** Valero, **food:** Isabella's Deli, **other:** HOSPITAL, NAPA, CarQuest, auto repair, **W**...**gas:** Exxon/Subway/dsl, Mobil, Shell, **food:** A&W, Applebee's, Burger King, Chelo's Grill, Chili's, D'angelo's, Dunkin Donuts, Hoho Chinese, KFC/Taco Bell, McDonald's, Panera Bread, PapaGino's, Pizza Hut, Pizzaria Uno, Subway, TinTsin Chinese, Wendy's, **other:** Brooks Drug, CVS Drug, Home Depot, Kohl's, Old Navy, Radio Shack, Staple's, Stop&Shop Foods, Target, TJ Maxx, to Powder Mill Ledges WR
6(10)	US 6, to Providence, **E**...**gas:** Citgo/7-11, Mobil, Shell/Dunkin Donuts, **food:** Burger King, China Jade, Del's Deli, KFC, Luigi's Italian, McDonald's, Wendy's, **lodging:** Hi-Way Motel, **other:** AutoZone, BJ's Whse, Chevrolet/Buick, CVS Drug, Honda, Pontiac/GMC, Shaw's Foods, USPO, **W**...**lodging:** Bel-Air Motel
6b c(9)	US 6 E Expswy, no services
5(8)	RI Resource Recovery Industrial Park
4(7)	RI 14, Plainfield Pk, **W**...**gas:** Mobil/dsl/24hr
3b a(4)	rd 37, Phenix Ave, **E**...TF Green Airport
2(2)	RI 2 S, to Warwick, **E**...**gas:** Exxon, **food:** Longhorn Steaks, Macaroni Grill, Pizzaria Uno, **other:** JC Penney, Macy's, Marshalls, Radio Shack, mall, **W**...**gas:** Mobil, Shell, Sunoco, **food:** Bickford's, Chili's, ChuckeCheese, Dunkin Donuts, HomeTown Buffet, Kwikava, LoneStar Steaks, McDonald's, PapaGino's, Subway, Taco Bell, Wendy's, **other:** Brooks Drug, CompUSA, Dodge/Subaru, Home Depot, NAPA, Sam's Club, Saturn, Sears/auto, Staples, TownFair Tire, Wal-Mart, mall
1(1)	RI 113 W, to W Warwick, same as 2
0mm	I-295 begins/ends on I-95, exit 11.

SOUTH CAROLINA

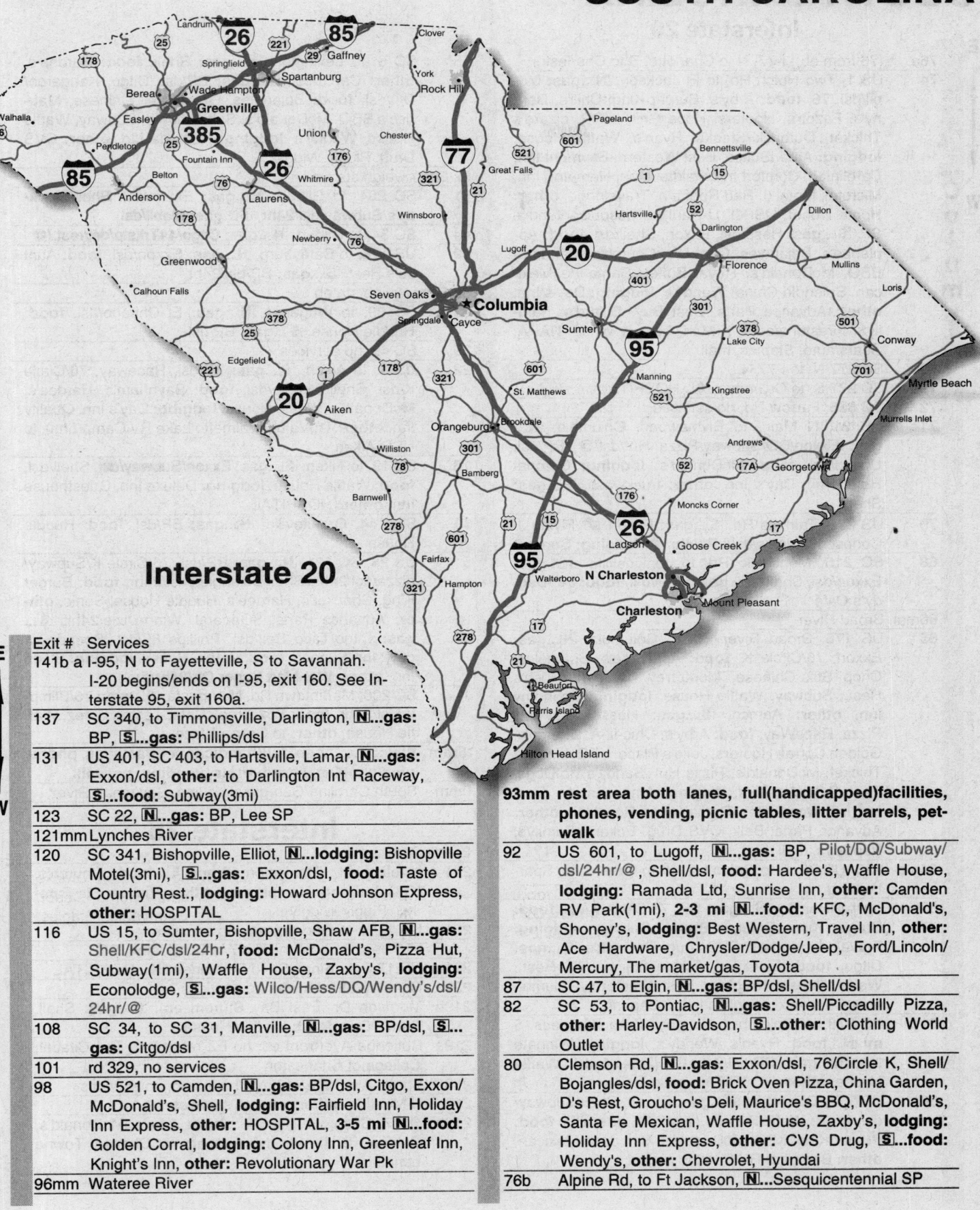

Interstate 20

Exit #	Services
141b a	I-95, N to Fayetteville, S to Savannah. I-20 begins/ends on I-95, exit 160. See Interstate 95, exit 160a.
137	SC 340, to Timmonsville, Darlington, **N**...gas: BP, **S**...gas: Phillips/dsl
131	US 401, SC 403, to Hartsville, Lamar, **N**...gas: Exxon/dsl, other: to Darlington Int Raceway, **S**...food: Subway(3mi)
123	SC 22, **N**...gas: BP, Lee SP
121mm	Lynches River
120	SC 341, Bishopville, Elliot, **N**...lodging: Bishopville Motel(3mi), **S**...gas: Exxon/dsl, food: Taste of Country Rest., lodging: Howard Johnson Express, other: HOSPITAL
116	US 15, to Sumter, Bishopville, Shaw AFB, **N**...gas: Shell/KFC/dsl/24hr, food: McDonald's, Pizza Hut, Subway(1mi), Waffle House, Zaxby's, lodging: Econolodge, **S**...gas: Wilco/Hess/DQ/Wendy's/dsl/24hr/@
108	SC 34, to SC 31, Manville, **N**...gas: BP/dsl, **S**...gas: Citgo/dsl
101	rd 329, no services
98	US 521, to Camden, **N**...gas: BP/dsl, Citgo, Exxon/McDonald's, Shell, lodging: Fairfield Inn, Holiday Inn Express, other: HOSPITAL, 3-5 mi **N**...food: Golden Corral, lodging: Colony Inn, Greenleaf Inn, Knight's Inn, other: Revolutionary War Pk
96mm	Wateree River
93mm	rest area both lanes, full(handicapped)facilities, phones, vending, picnic tables, litter barrels, pet-walk
92	US 601, to Lugoff, **N**...gas: BP, Pilot/DQ/Subway/dsl/24hr/@, Shell/dsl, food: Hardee's, Waffle House, lodging: Ramada Ltd, Sunrise Inn, other: Camden RV Park(1mi), 2-3 mi **N**...food: KFC, McDonald's, Shoney's, lodging: Best Western, Travel Inn, other: Ace Hardware, Chrysler/Dodge/Jeep, Ford/Lincoln/Mercury, The market/gas, Toyota
87	SC 47, to Elgin, **N**...gas: BP/dsl, Shell/dsl
82	SC 53, to Pontiac, **N**...gas: Shell/Piccadilly Pizza, other: Harley-Davidson, **S**...other: Clothing World Outlet
80	Clemson Rd, **N**...gas: Exxon/dsl, 76/Circle K, Shell/Bojangles/dsl, food: Brick Oven Pizza, China Garden, D's Rest, Groucho's Deli, Maurice's BBQ, McDonald's, Santa Fe Mexican, Waffle House, Zaxby's, lodging: Holiday Inn Express, other: CVS Drug, **S**...food: Wendy's, other: Chevrolet, Hyundai
76b	Alpine Rd, to Ft Jackson, **N**...Sesquicentennial SP

403

Interstate 20

76a	(76 from eb), I-77, N to Charlotte, S to Charleston
74	US 1, Two Notch Rd, to Ft Jackson, **N**...**gas:** Mobil/dsl, 76, **food:** Arby's, Burger King, Chili's, Denny's, Fazoli's, Hooters, Hops Grill, IHOP, Lizard's Thicket, Outback Steaks, Ryan's, Waffle House, **lodging:** AmeriSuites, Best Western, Baymont Inn, Carolinian, Comfort Inn, Fairfield Inn, Hampton Inn, Microtel, Motel 6, Red Roof Inn, Travelodge, **other:** Home Depot, USPO, U-Haul, to Sesquicentennial SP, **S**...**gas:** Hess/dsl, Exxon, Shell/dsl, **food:** Applebee's, Bojangles, Capt D's, Church's, Maurice's BBQ, McDonald's, Royal Buffet, Santa Fe Mexican, Splendid China, Wendy's, **lodging:** Day's Inn, **other:** Advance Parts, Best Buy, Dillard's, Family$, Firestone/auto, K-Mart, Lowe's Whse, NAPA, Sears/auto, Staples, mall
73b	SC 277 N, to I-77 N
73a	SC 277 S, to Columbia, **S**...HOSPITAL
72	SC 555, Farrow Rd, no services
71	US 21, N Main, to Blythewood, Columbia, **N**...**gas:** Exxon/DQ/Subway/Pizza Hut/dsl/@, BP/dsl, United/dsl, **food:** McDonald's, **lodging:** Coronet Hotel(1mi), Day's Inn, **other:** truckwash, **S**...**gas:** Shell
70	US 321, Fairfield Rd, **S**...**gas:** Exxon, ✈/Flying J/Conoco/Hardee's/dsl/LP/24hr/@, **lodging:** Super 8
68	SC 215, Monticello Rd, to Jenkinsville, **N**...**gas:** Exxon/dsl, Shell, **S**...**gas:** Shell/dsl, **food:** Big Daddy's Café
66mm	Broad River
65	US 176, Broad River Rd, to Columbia, **N**...**gas:** Exxon, 76/Circle K, **food:** Applebee's, Bojangles, Chop Stix Chinese, Monterrey Mexican, Rush's Rest., Subway, Waffle House, **lodging:** Economy Inn, **other:** Aamco, **S**...**gas:** Hess/Godfather's Pizza, RaceWay, **food:** Arby's, Chic-fil-A, Church's, Golden Corral, Hooters, Julie's Place, KFC, Lizard's Thicket, McDonald's, Pizza Hut, Sandy's HotDogs, Taco Bell, Wendy's, **lodging:** American Inn, Best Inn, InTowne Suites, Ramada Ltd, Royal Inn, **other:** Advance Parts, Belk, CVS Drug, Eckerd, Family$, PepBoys, mall
64b a	I-26, US 76, E to Columbia, W to Greenville, Spartanburg
63	Bush River Rd, **N**...**gas:** BP, 76/Circle K/dsl, **food:** Burger King, Cracker Barrel, Subway, **lodging:** Travelodge, **other:** CVS Drug, Hamrick's, **S**...**gas:** Citgo, **food:** El Chico, Fuddrucker's, Villa Rest., Waffle House, **lodging:** Best Western, Columbiana, Courtyard, Knight's Inn, Sleep Inn
61	US 378, W Colombia, **N**...**gas:** Exxon/Hardees, **5 mi N**...**food:** Ryan's, Wendy's, **lodging:** Wingate Inn, **S**...**gas:** BP/dsl/24hr, 76(2mi), **food:** Waffle House, **other:** HOSPITAL, antiques
58	US 1, W Columbia, **N**...**gas:** Exxon, Shell/Subway/dsl, **food:** Waffle House, **2 mi S**...**gas:** BP, **food:** Burger King, KFC, McDonald's, San Jose Mexican, **other:** Barnyard RV Park, to airport
55	SC 6, to Lexington, **N**...**gas:** Shell, **food:** Hardee's, **other:** CarQuest, **S**...**gas:** BP/dsl, Citgo, Kangaroo/DQ/dsl, **food:** Bojangles, Great Wall Chinese, Maurice's BBQ, McDonald's, Substation II, Subway, Waffle House, Wendy's, **lodging:** Ramada Ltd, **other:** CVS Drug, Piggly Wiggly
52.5mm	weigh sta wb
51	SC 204, to Gilbert, **N**...**gas:** Exxon/dsl, Shell/Stuckey's/Subway/dsl/24hr, **S**...**gas:** Mobil/dsl
44	SC 34, to Gilbert, **N**...**gas:** Citgo/44Trkstp/dsl/rest./@
39	US 178, to Batesburg, **N**...**gas:** Exxon/dsl, **food:** Aunt Jo's Rest. **S**...**gas:** BP/dsl/24hr,
35.5mm	weigh sta eb
33	SC 39, to Wagener, **N**...**gas:** El Cheapo/dsl, **food:** Huddle House, **S**...**gas:** BP/dsl
29	SC 49, no services
22	US 1, to Aiken, **S**...**gas:** BP/dsl, Raceway, 76/Circle K/dsl, Shell/Blimpie/dsl, **food:** Baynham's, Hardee's, McDonald's, Waffle House, **lodging:** Day's Inn, Quality Inn, **other:** TruValue, Palmetto Lake RV Camp(5mi), to USC Aiken
18	SC 19, to Aiken, **S**...**gas:** Exxon/Subway/dsl, Shell/dsl, **food:** Waffle House, **lodging:** Deluxe Inn, Guesthouse Inn, **other:** HOSPITAL
11	SC 144, Graniteville, **N**...**gas:** BP/dsl, **food:** Huddle House
5	US 25, SC 121, **N**...**gas:** BP/dsl, 76/Circle K/Subway/pizza/dsl/24hr, Shell/Bojangles/dsl/24hr, **food:** Burger King, Checker's, Hardee's, Huddle House, Sonic, **other:** Advance Parts, $General, Winn-Dixie/24hr, **S**...**gas:** Citgo/Taco Bell/dsl, Phillips 66/dsl, Speedway/dsl/24hr, Sunoco, **food:** Waffle House, **lodging:** Sleep Inn, **other:** Wal-Mart Super Ctr/24hr(5mi)
1	SC 230, Martintown Rd, N Augusta, **S**...**gas:** 76/Blimpie/dsl/24hr, **food:** Fox Creek Cafe, Tastee Freez, Waffle House, **other:** to Garn's Place
.5mm	**Welcome Ctr eb, full(handicapped)facilities, phone, picnic tables, litter barrels, vending, petwalk**
0mm	South Carolina/Georgia state line, Savannah River

Interstate 26

Exit #	Services
221	Meeting St, Charleston, **2 mi E**...**food:** Church's, KFC, **lodging:** Hampton Inn, **other:** Visitors Ctr, Family$, Piggly Wiggly
221b	US 17 N, to Georgetown, no services
	I-26 begins/ends on US 17 in Charleston, SC.
221a	US 17 S, to Kings St, to Savannah, **N**...HOSPITAL
220	Romney St(from wb), no services
219b	Morrison Dr, East Bay St(from eb), **N**...**gas:** Shell, Sam's Gas, **food:** Huddle House
219a	Rutledge Ave(from eb, no EZ return), to The Citadel, College of Charleston
218	Spruill Ave(from wb), N Charleston, no services
217	N Meeting St(from eb), no services
216b a	SC 7, Cosgrove Ave, **S**...**food:** Arby's, McDonald's, SunFire Grill, Wendy's, **other:** to Charles Towne Landing

SOUTH CAROLINA

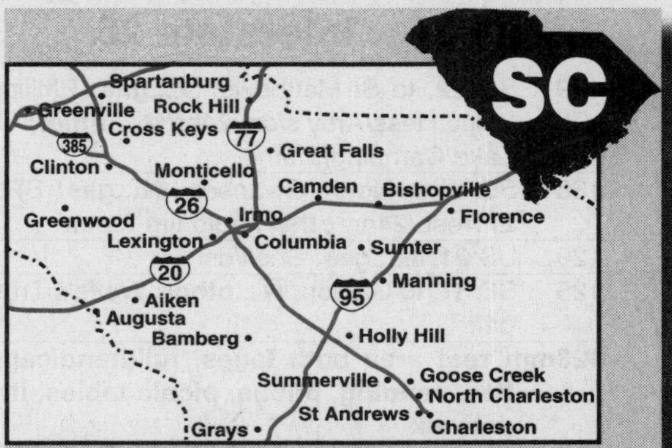

Interstate 26

215 SC 642, Dorchester Rd, N Charleston, [N]...**gas:** Hess/dsl, **lodging:** Howard Johnson, [S]...**gas:** Amoco/dsl, **food:** Alex's Rest./24hr

Charleston

213b a Montague Ave, Mall Dr, [N]...**food:** Piccadilly's, Red Lobster, **lodging:** Courtyard, Sheraton, **other:** Charles Towne Square, Firestone, [S]...**gas:** BP/dsl, Hess/Bojangles/dsl, **food:** Waffle House, **lodging:** Comfort Inn, Day's Inn, Embassy Suites, Extended Stay America, Hampton Inn, Hilton Garden, HomePlace Suites, Homestead Suites, Quality Inn, Ramada Inn, Suite 1, Super 8, Wingate Inn

212c b I-526, E to Mt Pleasant, W to Savannah, airport

212a Remount Rd(from wb, no EZ return), Hanahan, [N] **on US 52/78...gas:** Exxon, Hess/dsl, **food:** Burger King, KFC, McDonald's, Pizza Hut/Taco Bell, **other:** Dodge, Ford, Office Depot

211b a Aviation Pkwy, [N] **on US 52/78...gas:** BP, Exxon, **food:** Arby's, Burger King, Capt D's, China Town, Church's, Grandy's, Huddle House, McDonald's, Old Country Buffet, Pizza Hut, Pizza Inn, Schlotsky's, Shoney's, Sonic, Subway, Tokyo Japanese, Wendy's, **lodging:** Masters Inn, Radisson, **other:** Aamco, Batteries+, $General, $Tree, Goodyear, PepBoys, Radio Shack, Sam's Club, [S]...**gas:** Citgo/dsl, El Cheapo/dsl, **food:** Waffle House, **lodging:** Best Western, Seagrass Inn, Travelodge

N Charleston

209 Ashley Phosphate Rd, to US 52, [N]...**gas:** Exxon, Kangaroo, **food:** Applebee's, Chick-fil-A, China Buffet, ChuckeCheese, Denny's, Don Pablo, Fazoli's, Hardee's, Hooters, Hops Grill, K&W Cafeteria, Krispy Kreme, Noisy Oyster Grill, Olive Garden, Outback Steaks, Perkins, Pizza Hut, Ryan's, Sticky Fingers Rest., Subway, Taco Bell, Waffle House, Wendy's, **lodging:** Clarion, Holiday Inn Express, Red Roof Inn, Residence Inn, Studio+ Hotel, Super 8, **other:** Barnes&Noble, Belk, Best Buy, BooksA-Million, Cicuit City, Dillard's, Firestone/auto, Home Depot, JC Penney, Lexus, Lowe's Whse, Mitsubishi, Nissan, Sears/auto, Target, Toyota, Wal-Mart SuperCtr/24hr, mall, [S]...**gas:** BP, Hess, RaceWay, **food:** Bojangles, Cracker Barrel, Domino's, IHOP, Kobe Japanese, McDonald's, Waffle House, **lodging:** Fairfield Inn, Hampton Inn, Howard Johnson, InTowne Suites, La Quinta, Motel 6, Relax Inn, Sleep Inn

208 to US 52(from wb), to Goose Creek, Moncks Corner

205b a US 78, to Summerville, [N]...**gas:** BP, Hess/dsl, **food:** Arby's, Atl Bread Co, Bruster's, Subway, Waffle House, Wendy's, **lodging:** Fairfield Inn, **other:** HOSPITAL, Charleston Southern U, [S]...**gas:** Speedway/dsl, **other:** KOA

204mm rest area eb, full(handicapped)facilities, vending, phone, picnic tables, litter barrels, petwalk

203 College Park Rd, Ladson, [N]...**gas:** 76, Speedway/dsl, **food:** McDonald's, Waffle House, Wendy's, **lodging:** Best Western, Day's Inn, [S]...**other:** KOA(2mi)

202mm rest area wb, full(handicapped)facilities, vending, phone, picnic tables, litter barrels, petwalk

199b a US 17 A, to Moncks Corner, Summerville, [N]...**gas:** BP, Citgo/dsl, Hess/dsl, Pilot/McDonald's/dsl/24hr, **food:** KFC, Pizza Hut, Subway, **other:** Advance Parts, AutoZone, BiLo, Buick/Pontiac/GMC, CVS Drug, $General, Family$, Food Lion, Ford/Mercury, [S]...**gas:** 76/Circle K, Enmark/dsl, **food:** Applebee's, Bojangles, Burger King, China Town, Fazoli's, Hardee's, Huddle House, IHOP, Papa John's, Perkins/24hr, Ryan's, Shoney's, Waffle House, **lodging:** Comfort Inn, Econolodge, Hampton Inn, Holiday Inn Express, Sleep Inn, **other:** Belk, Chevrolet, Chrysler/Jeep, GNC, Home Depot, Lowe's Whse, Radio Shack, Staples, Target, Wal-Mart SuperCtr/24hr, Winn-Dixie

194 SC 16, to Jedburg, access to Foreign Trade Zone 21

187 SC 27, to Ridgeville, St George, [N]...**gas:** Phillips 66, [S]...**gas:** BP/dsl, **10 mi** [S]...**other:** Francis Beidler Forest

177 SC 453, to Holly Hill, Harleyville, [S]...**gas:** Shell/dsl/LP, **food:** Derrick's Kitchen, **lodging:** Ashley Lodge

174mm weigh sta both lanes

172b a US 15, to Santee, St George, [S]...**gas:** Horizon/Subway/dsl/24hr

169b a I-95, N to Florence, S to Savannah

165 SC 210, to Bowman, [N]...**gas:** Exxon/dsl, [S]...**gas:** BP/dsl/rest., Texaco/Blimpie/dsl/repair

159 SC 36, to Bowman, [N]...**gas:** Pilot/McDonald's/dsl/24hr/repair/@

154b a US 301, to Santee, Orangeburg, [N]...**lodging:** Days Inn, [S]...**gas:** Exxon/Blimpie/dsl, Shell/dsl/24hr, **lodging:** Best Western(7mi), Holiday Inn(8mi), **other:** auto repair

152mm rest area wb, full(handicapped)facilities, vending, phone, picnic tables, litter barrels, petwalk

150mm rest area eb, full(handicapped)facilities, vending, phone, picnic tables, litter barrels, petwalk

149 SC 33, to Cameron, to SC State Coll, Orangeburg, Claflin Coll

145b a US 601, to Orangeburg, St Matthews, [S]...**gas:** Amoco/24hr, Exxon, Shell/Burger King, Speedway/dsl, **food:** Cracker Barrel, Fatz Café, Hardee's, KFC, McDonald's, Ruby Tuesday, Subway, Waffle House, **lodging:** Comfort Inn, Day's Inn, Fairfield Inn, Hampton Inn, Holiday Inn Express, Sleep Inn, Southern Lodge, **other:** HOSPITAL, **other:** Cadillac/Nissan, Chevrolet, Chrysler/Dodge, Nissan

E ↑ | W

139 SC 22, to St Matthews, **S**...**gas:** Phillips 66, Shell, Wilco/Hess/Arby's/dsl/24hr/@, **other:** Sweetwater Lake Camping(2.5mi)

136 SC 6, to North, Swansea, **N**...**gas:** BP, Exxon/dsl/ LP/rest./24hr, **other:** auto/tire repair

129 US 21, **N**...**gas:** Shell/dsl

125 SC 31, to Gaston, **N**...**other:** Wolfe's Truck/trailer repair

123mm rest area both lanes, full(handicapped) facilities, vending, phone, picnic tables, litter barrels, petwalk

119 US 176, US 21, to Dixiana, **S**...**gas:** BP/Subway, Exxon/Stuckey's/dsl, Shell/dsl/@

116 I-77 N, to Charlotte, US 76, US 378, to Ft Jackson

115 US 176, US 21, US 321, to Cayce, **N**...**gas:** Raceway/ 24hr, **food:** Waffle House, **other:** Harley-Davidson, **S**...**gas:** BP, Pilot/DQ/Wendy's/dsl/24hr/@, Shell, **food:** Bojangles, Great China, Hardee's, McDonald's, Subway, **lodging:** Ramada Ltd, **other:** Firestone, Piggly Wiggly

113 SC 302, Cayce, **N**...**gas:** Exxon, Texaco/dsl, **food:** Waffle House, **lodging:** Airport Inn, Cambridge Plaza, Knight's Inn, Masters Inn, **other:** auto repair, **S**...**gas:** Exxon, Raceway, 76/Circle K, **food:** Burger King, Lizard's Thicket, Ryan's, Shoney's, Subway, Waffle House/24hr, **lodging:** Carolina Lodge, Comfort Inn, Country Inn& Suites, Sleep Inn, Travelers Inn, **other:** NAPA, airport

111b aUS 1, to W Columbia, **N**...**gas:** Raceway/dsl, 76/ Circle K, **food:** Domino's, Dragon City Chinese, Hardee's, Maurice's BBQ, Ruby Tuesday, Sonic, Subway, TCBY, Waffle House, Zaxby's, **lodging:** Holiday Inn, **other:** BiLo Foods, $Tree, Harlan Tire, JiffyLube, Kroger, Radio Shack, Walgreen, Wal-Mart SuperCtr/gas/24hr, to USC, **S**...**gas:** Hess, **food:** Applebee's, Popeye's, **other:** Aldi Foods, CVS Drug, Lowe's Whse, U-Haul

Columbia

110 US 378, to W Columbia, Lexington, **N**...**food:** Burger King, Lizard's Thicket, Maurice's BBQ, McDonald's, Rush's Rest., Subway, Waffle House, Western Sizzlin, **lodging:** Day's Inn, Hampton Inn, Ramada/rest., **other:** CVS Drug, Eckerd, Food Lion, U-Haul, **S**...**gas:** 76/Circle K, **food:** Bojangles, Hardee's, Pizza Hut, **lodging:** Executive Inn, **other:** HOSPITAL

108 I-126 to Columbia, Bush River Rd, **N**...**gas:** Shell/dsl, **food:** Blimpie, Capt D's, Chick-fil-A, Hardee's, KFC, Royal China Buffet, Ruby Tuesday, Schlotsky's, Shoney's, Wendy's, **lodging:** Day's Inn, La Quinta, Villager Lodge, Western Inn, **other:** Advance Parts, Firestone/auto, K-Mart, Office Depot, mall, **S**...**gas:** City Gas, RaceWay, Sunoco/dsl, **food:** Cracker Barrel, Royal Tahj Cuisine, **lodging:** Best Western, Courtyard, Day's Inn, Howard Johnson, Quality Inn, **multiple services 1-3 mi N off I-126, Greystone Blvd, N**...**gas:** BP, Shell, **food:** Waffle House, **lodging:** Embassy Suites, Extended Stay America, Residence Inn, Studio+, **other:** Chrysler/Jeep, Dodge, Ford, GMC, Lincoln/Mercury, Honda, Kia, Mitsubishi, **S**...Riverbanks Zoo

107b aI-20, E to Florence, W to Augusta

106b aSt Andrews Rd, **N**...**gas:** Exxon/dsl, **food:** Chic-fil-A, ChuckeCheese, D's Rest., IHOP, Papa John's, Sonic, Top China Buffet, **lodging:** Motel 6, **other:** BiLo Foods, Buick/Pontiac, CVS Drug, $General, Infiniti, Jaguar, Kroger/deli, Nissan, Holiday Kamper RV Park, Walgreen, **S**...**gas:** Hess/dsl, 76/Circle K, Shell, **food:** Domino's, King Buffet, Maurice's BBQ, McDonald's, Pizza Hut, Steak Out, Waffle House, Zaxby's, **lodging:** Red Roof Inn, Super 8, **other:** $General, Food Lion, Tire Kingdom

104 Piney Grove Rd, **N**...**gas:** Sunoco/dsl, **food:** Hardee's, San Jose Mexican, Waffle House, **lodging:** Fairview Inn, **other:** RV/Marine Ctr, **S**...**gas:** Exxon/dsl, Shell, **food:** Roadhouse Grill, **lodging:** Comfort Suites, Microtel, **other:** Carmax, Land Rover, Publix/deli

103 Harbison Blvd, **N**...**food:** Applebee's, Hops Grill, Wendy's, **lodging:** Hampton Inn, **other:** Chevrolet, Home Depot, Hummer, Lowe's Whse, funpark, **S**...**gas:** BP/ 24hr, Exxon/Taco Bell, Hess/dsl, Shell, **food:** Bailey's Grill, Bojangles, Blimpie, Carrabba's, Chili's, Chick-fil-A, Coldstone, D's Rest., Denny's, Fazoli's, LongHorn Steaks, Macaroni Grill, McAlister's, McDonald's, Monterrey Mexican, O'Charley's, Olive Garden, Outback Steaks, Popeye's, Quizno's, Ruby Tuesday, Rush's Rest., Smokey Bones BBQ, Shoney's, Steak& Shake, Sticky Fingers, Sonic, Subway, Super Buffet, Texas Roadhouse, Tokyo Grill, Yamato Japanese, **lodging:** Comfort Suites, Country Inn Suites, Fairfield Inn, Suite 1, Hilton Garden, Holiday Inn Express, TownePlace Suites, Wingate Inn, **other:** Barnes& Noble, Belk, Best Buy, BooksAMillion, Circuit City, Dillard's, Goodyear, Goody's, Marshall's, Michael's, Old Navy, Panera Bread, Publix, Rite Aid, Ross, Sam's Club, Saturn, Sears/auto, Staples, Target, Tire Kingdom, Wal-Mart SuperCtr/24hr, mall

102 SC 60, Ballentine, Irmo, **N**...**lodging:** AmeriSuites, Extended Stay America, **S**...**gas:** Exxon, 76/Circle K, Shell, **food:** Arby's, Bellacino's Pizza, Moe's SW Grill, New China, Papa John's, Quizno's, TCBY, Zaxby's, **other:** CVS Drug, Piggly Wiggly, same as 103

101b aUS 76, US 176, to N Columbia, **1/2 mi N**...**gas:** Exxon/Subway/dsl, **food:** China House, Fatz Café, Food Lion, Hot Dog Heaven, **other:** AutoZone, Eckerd, Publix, Walgreen, **S**...**gas:** BP, Mobil, **food:** Burger King, Oyster House Grill, Waffle House, **other:** Toyota/Scion

97 US 176, to Ballentine, Peak, **N**...**other:** Food Lion, Woodsmoke Camping, **S**...**gas:** Exxon/dsl

94mm weigh sta wb, phones

91 SC 48, to Chapin, **S**...**gas:** BP/dsl, Exxon/Taco Bell/ Blimpie/dsl, Shell/dsl, **food:** Hardee's(3mi), McDonald's, Subway(2mi), Waffle House, **other:** to Dreher Island SP

85 SC 202, Little Mountain, Pomaria, **S**...to Dreher Island SP

82 SC 773, to Prosperity, Pomaria, **N**...**gas:** BP/Subway/ dsl/24hr/@, **other:** Flea Mkt Campground

81mm weigh sta eb

SOUTH CAROLINA

Interstate 26

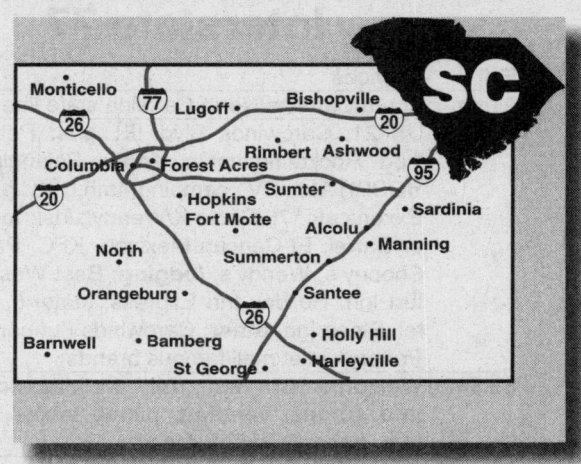

76	SC 219, to Pomaria, Newberry, **2 mi** Ⓢ...**gas:** BP, MurphyUSA, **food:** Burger King, Wendy's, **lodging:** Hampton Inn, Holiday Inn Express, **other:** Wal-Mart SuperCtr/24hr/gas, to Newberry Opera House
74	SC 34, to Newberry, Ⓝ...**gas:** BP, Shell/dsl/24hr, **food:** Bill&Fran's Café, **lodging:** Best Western/rest., Ⓢ...**gas:** Texaco, **food:** Arby's, Capt D's, Hardee's(2mi), McDonald's(2mi), Waffle House, **lodging:** Comfort Inn(2mi), Day's Inn, Economy Inn(2mi), Holiday Inn Express(2mi), **other:** HOSPITAL, to NinetySix HS
72	SC 121, to Newberry, Ⓢ...**gas:** Citgo/dsl/@, **other:** HOSPITAL, to Newberry Coll
66	SC 32, to Jalapa, no services
63.5mm	**rest area both lanes, full(handicapped) facilities, phone, vending, picnic tables, litter barrels, petwalk**
60	SC 66, to Joanna, Ⓢ...**gas:** Chevron, **food:** Carolina Country Kitchen, **other:** Magnolia Camping
54	SC 72, to Clinton, Ⓝ...**gas:** BP, Ⓢ...**gas:** Citgo/dsl/24hr, **food:** Fatz Cafe, **lodging:** Hampton Inn, **other:** HOSPITAL, to Presbyterian Coll, Thornwell Home
52	SC 56, to Clinton, Ⓝ...**gas:** Pilot/Subway/dsl/24hr/@, **food:** Blue Ocean Rest., McDonald's, Waffle House, **lodging:** Comfort Inn, Ⓢ...**gas:** Citgo/dsl, **food:** Hardee's, Waffle House, Wendy's, **lodging:** Clinton Hotel, Day's Inn, Travelers Inn(2mi), **other:** HOSPITAL
51	I-385, to Greenville(from wb)
45.5mm	Enoree River
44	SC 49, to Cross Anchor, Union
41	SC 92, to Enoree, Ⓝ...**gas:** Valero
38	SC 146, to Woodruff, Ⓝ...**gas:** Hot Spot/Shell/Hardee's/dsl/24hr/@, **food:** Big Country Rest./lounge
35	SC 50, to Woodruff, Ⓢ...**gas:** BP/dsl/rest./24hr, **other:** HOSPITAL
33mm	S Tyger River
32mm	N Tyger River
28	US 221, to Spartanburg, Ⓝ...**gas:** Citgo/AuntM's/dsl/24hr, Shell/Subway/dsl/24hr, **food:** Burger King, Hardee's, Waffle House, Walnut Grove Seafood Rest., **other:** HOSPITAL, Pine Ridge Camping(3mi), to Walnut Grove Plantation
22	SC 296, Reidville Rd, to Spartanburg, Ⓝ...**gas:** BP/dsl, Exxon, **food:** Arby's, BBQ, Capri's Italian, Fuddrucker's(1mi), Hong Kong Express, Little Caesar's, McDonald's, Outback Steaks, Ryan's, Waffle House, Zaxby's, **other:** Advance Parts, Rite Aid, to Croft SP, Ⓢ...**gas:** BP/dsl, **food:** Burger King, Denny's, Domino's, Hardee's, Subway, TCBY, Waffle House/24hr, **lodging:** Sleep Inn, Southern Suites, Super 8, **other:** Abbot Farms/fruit, BiLo, BMW, CVS Drug, Eckerd, Harris-Teeter, Saturn, Toyota, Walgreen
21b a	US 29, to Spartanburg, Ⓝ...**gas:** BP, Crown/24hr, Exxon/Subway, Phillips 66, **food:** Aloha Chinese, Burger King, Calzone's Rest., Checker's, Chick-fil-A, CiCi's, DQ, Dunkin Donuts, Firemountain Grill, Fuji's, Golden Corral, Hardee's, Hop's Grill, Jack-in-

(Spartanburg)

	the-Box, Japanese Rest., KFC, LoneStar Steaks, LJ Silver/A&W, Moe's SW Grill, Mr Gatti's, O'Charley's, Old Country Buffet, Papa John's, Pizza Hut, Pizza Inn, Red Lobster, Schlotzsky's, Substation II, Wendy's, **lodging:** Hampton Inn, Hilton Garden, **other:** Barnes&Noble, Belk, Best Buy, Circuit City, Dillard's, $General, Eckerd, Firestone/auto, Home Depot, JC Penney, Lowe's Whse, Michael's, Office Depot, Ross, Sears/auto, Wal-Mart SuperCtr/24hr, mall, Ⓢ...**gas:** Citgo/dsl, Texaco/dsl, **food:** Applebee's, Aunt M's Café, Blimpie, IHOP, McDonald's, Piccadilly's, Prime Sirloin, Shogun Japanese, Taco Bell, Thi Japanese, Waffle House, **other:** Advance Parts, Best Buy, Ingles, Rite Aid, Sam's Club/gas, Target
19b a	Lp I-85, Spartanburg, Ⓝ...**gas:** BP, **food:** Cracker Barrel, **lodging:** Country Hearth Inn, Fairfield Inn, Radisson, Ramada Inn, Residence Inn, Quality Hotel, Ⓢ... **lodging:** Bradford Hotel, Tower Motel
18b a	I-85, N to Charlotte, S to Greenville
17	New Cut Rd, Ⓢ...**gas:** Chevron/dsl, Sunoco/dsl, **food:** Burger King, Fatz Café, McDonald's, Waffle House, **lodging:** Day's Inn, Howard Johnson Express, Quality Inn, Relax Inn
16	John Dodd Rd, to Wellford, Ⓝ...**gas:** Citgo/Aunt M's/dsl, **food:** Arby's, **other:** Camping World/Holiday RV Supply Ctr, Cunningham RV Park(2mi)
15	US 176, to Inman, Ⓝ...**gas:** Racetrac(2mi), FuelStop, 76/Circle K/dsl, **food:** Waffle House, **other:** HOSPITAL Ⓢ...**gas:** Mystik/dsl, **food:** Taco Bell(2mi)
10	SC 292, to Inman, Ⓝ...**gas:** Shell/Subway/dsl/24hr
7.5mm	Lake William C. Bowman, no services
5	SC 11, Foothills Scenic Dr, Chesnee, Campobello, Ⓝ...**gas:** Kangaroo/Aunt M's Café/dsl/@, Ⓢ...**gas:** Phillips 66
3mm	**Welcome Ctr eb, full(handicapped)facilities, info, phones, picnic tables, litter barrels, vending, petwalk**
1	SC 14, to Landrum, Ⓢ...**gas:** BP/Burger King/dsl, HotSpot/gas(2mi), **food:** Denny's, Pizza Hut(1mi), Subway, **other:** BiLo Foods, $General, Ingles/café/gas/24hr
0mm	South Carolina/North Carolina state line

407

SOUTH CAROLINA
Interstate 77

N ↕ S

Rock Hill

Exit #	Services
91mm	South Carolina/North Carolina state line
90	US 21, Carowinds Blvd, E...**gas:** PetroExpress, Red Rocket/fireworks, **food:** Bojangles, **other:** HOSPITAL, RV camping(4mi), W...**gas:** Citgo, Exxon/café, 76/Circle K/Wendy's/dsl, **food:** Cracker Barrel, El Cancun Mexican, KFC, Papa Pino's, Shoney's, Wendy's, **lodging:** Best Western, Comfort Inn, Holiday Inn Express, Motel 6, Plaza Motel, Sleep Inn, **other:** Carowinds Funpark, Carolina Pottery/outlet mall/famous brands
89.5mm	**Welcome Ctr sb, full(handicapped)facilities, info, phone, vending, picnic tables, litter barrels, petwalk/weigh sta nb**
88	Gold Hill Rd, to Pineville, W...**gas:** Exxon/dsl, Gate Gas(2mi), Shell/dsl, **food:** Bojangles(2mi), **other:** Chrysler/Jeep/Dodge, Ford/Hyundai, KOA
85	SC 160, Ft Mill, Tega Cay, E...**gas:** Exxon, **food:** Subway, **other:** Bi-Lo, The Drug Store, W...**gas:** BP/dsl, Circle K, **food:** Backyard Burger, Beef O'Brady's, Bojangles(3mi), Burger King, Papa John's, Pizza Hut, Starbucks, Wendy's, **other:** CVS Drug, Harris-Teeter, Lowes Whse, Walgreens
84.5mm	weigh sta sb
83	SC 49, Sutton Rd, W...**gas:** Loves/Chester/Godfathers/dsl/scales/24hr
82.5mm	Catawba River
82c	US 21, SC 161, Rock Hill, Ft Mill, E...**gas:** Exxon, Phillips 66, **food:** IHOP, Sonny's BBQ, Steak'n Shake, Zaxby's, **other:** Home Depot, Petsmart, museum, W...**gas:** Exxon, Phillips 66, Shell, Valero, **food:** CiCi's Pizza, Hooters, Outback Steaks, Starbucks, **lodging:** Courtyard, Ramada/rest., **other:** HOSPITAL, Aldi Foods, Toyota, U-Haul
82b a	E...**gas:** Exxon, **other:** Conference Ctr, W...**gas:** Citgo, RaceWay, **food:** Arby's, Bojangles, Burger King, Capt's Galley, Chick-fil-A, Denny's, Firebonez, Jack-in-the-Box, Little Caesar's, Marco's Pizza, McDonald's, Penn Sta., Pizza Hut, Sakura Japanese, Shoney's, Subway, Taco Bell, Toyo Grill, Waffle House, Wendy's, **lodging:** Best Value Inn, Country Inn&Suites, Days Inn, Econolodge, Howard Johnson, Microtel, Quality Inn, Regency Inn, Super 8, **other:** Aamco, Advance Parts, Bi-Lo, Chevrolet/Cadillac, $General, Family$, Firestone, NAPA, Nissan, Office Depot, O'Reilly Parts, PepBoys, Winn-Dixie
79	SC 122, Dave Lyle Blvd, to Rock Hill, E...**gas:** BP, **food:** Applebee's, Chick-fil-A, Cracker Barrel, DQ, Hardee's, Longhorn Steaks, Lucky Buffet, O'Charley's, Ryan's, Ruby Tuesday, **lodging:** Hampton Inn, Wingate Inn, **other:** Belk, Discount Tire, Food Lion, Goody's, Honda, JC Penney, Kohl's, Lowe's Whse, Sears/auto, Staples, Tire Kingdom, Wal-Mart SuperCtr 24hr/drugs/gas/24hr, mall, W...**gas:** Citgo, **food:** Bob Evans, Chili's, Dunkin Donuts, Jack-in-the-Box, McCallister's Deli, McDonalds, Midtown Rest., Olive Garden, Panera Bread, Quizno's, Stagebrush Steaks, Subway, Taco Bell, Wendy's, **lodging:** Hillside Inn, Hilton Garden, **other:** Best Buy, Books-a-Million, Ford, Lincoln/Mercury, Michael's, Ross, Target, TJ Maxx, visitor ctr
77	US 21, SC 5, to Rock Hill, E...**gas:** BP/Subway/dsl, Citgo/dsl, Cone/dsl/24hr, **other:** to Andrew Jackson SP(12mi), W...**gas:** Exxon/dsl, Pride/dsl/scales, **food:** KFC, McDonald's, Subway, Waffle House, **other:** to Winthrop Coll
75	Porter Rd, E...**gas:** Citgo, Texaco
73	SC 901, to Rock Hill, York, E...**gas:** Exxon/dsl, /Flying J/CountryMkt/dsl/scales/LP/24hr/@, W... HOSPITAL
66mm	**rest area both lanes, full(handicapped)facilities, phone, picnic tables, litter barrels, vending, petwalk**
65	SC 9, to Chester, Lancaster, E...**gas:** BP/24hr, Liberty/Subway/dsl, Petro Engery/dsl, **food:** Subway, Waffle House, **lodging:** Day's Inn, Econolodge, Relax Inn, **other:** Chevrolet/Ponitac/Buick, Dodge/Jeep, IGA Foods/gas, W...**gas:** Exxon/dsl, **food:** Burger King, Country Omelette/24hr, Front Porch Cafe, KFC, McDonald's, **lodging:** Comfort Inn, Rodeway Inn, Super 8, **other:** HOSPITAL
62	SC 56, to Fort Lawn, Richburg, no services
55	SC 97, to Chester, Great Falls, E...**gas:** Exxon/dsl, W...HOSPITAL
48	SC 200, to Great Falls, E...**gas:** Shell/Grand Central Rest./dsl/@, W...**gas:** Wilco/Hess/DQ/Wendy's
46	SC 20, to White Oak, no services
41	SC 41, to Winnsboro, E...to Lake Wateree SP
34	SC 34, to Winnsboro, Ridgeway, E...**gas:** AM,PM/dsl/24hr, **lodging:** Ridgeway Motel(1mi), **other:** camping(1mi), W...**gas:** Exxon/Blimpie/dsl, **food:** Lois's Cafe, Waffle House, **lodging:** Day's Inn(6mi), Ramada Ltd.
32	Peach Rd, Ridgeway, no services
27	Blythewood Rd, E...**gas:** BP/dsl, Exxon/Bojangles/dsl/24hr, **food:** Hardee's, McDonald's, Pizza Hut/KFC, Southern Pig BBQ, Subway, Waffle House, Wendy's, WG's Wings, **lodging:** Comfort Inn, Holiday Inn Express, **other:** Curves, $General, IGA Foods, W...**other:** Food Lion, Groucho's Deli

Interstate 77

Exit	Services
24	US 21, to Wilson Blvd., **E**...**gas:** BP, Shell/Subway/dsl, **food:** Myer's BBQ
22	Killian Rd, no services
19	SC 555, Farrow Rd, **E**...**gas:** BP, **food:** Bojangles, Cracker Barrel, Wendy's, **lodging:** Courtyard, Residence Inn, **other:** HOSPITAL, Longs Drug, **W**...**gas:** Shell/dsl, **food:** Waffle House, **other:** SC Archives
18	to SC 277, to I-20 W(from sb), Columbia
17	US 1, Two Notch Rd, **E**...**gas:** BP/24hr, Kangaroo, 76/Circle K/dsl, **food:** Arby's, Burger King, Texas Roadhouse, Waffle House, **lodging:** Columbia Plaza hotel, Fairfield Inn, InTown Suites, Quality Inn, Wingate Inn, **other:** U-Haul, USPO, to Sesquicentennial SP, **W**...**food:** Chili's, Fazoli's, Hooters, IHOP, Lizard's Thicket, Outback Steaks, Waffle House, **lodging:** Comfort Inn, Hampton Inn, Jameson Suites, La Quinta, Microtel, Red Roof Inn, Travelodge, **other:** Home Depot, TrueValue
16b a	I-20, W to Augusta, E to Florence, Alpine Rd
15b a	SC 12, to Percival Rd, **W**...**gas:** El Cheapo/gas, Shell, 1/2 mi **W**...**gas:** Exxon
13	Decker Blvd(from nb), **W**...**gas:** El Cheapo
12	Forest Blvd, Thurmond Blvd, **E**...to Ft Jackson, **W**...**gas:** BP/dsl, 76/dsl, Shell/dsl/24hr, **food:** Bojangles, Chick-fil-A, Fatz Café, Golden Corral, Hardee's, McDonald's, RedBone Rest., Steak&Ale, Subway, Wendy's, **lodging:** Extended Stay America, Marlboro Inn, Super 8, **other:** HOSPITAL, $Tree, Sam's Club/gas, Wal-Mart SuperCtr/24hr, museum
10	SC 760, Jackson Blvd, **E**...to Ft Jackson, 2 mi **W**...**gas:** BP, **food:** Applebee's, Bojangles, Burger King, Maurices BBQ, Ruby Tuesday, Subway, **lodging:** Econolodge, Liberty Inn
9b a	US 76, US 378, to Sumter, Columbia, **E**...**gas:** BP, Citgo, Hess/dsl, Sunoco/dsl, **food:** Capt D's, Chick-fil-A, China Chef, Domino's, Fire Mtn. Grill, KFC, McDonald's, Pizza Hut, Popeye's, Rush's Rest., Shoney's, Subway, Vera Cruz Mexican, Waffle House, Zaxby's, **lodging:** Best Western, Comfort Inn, Country Inn Suites, Day's Inn, Hampton Inn, Holiday Inn Express, Sleep Inn, **other:** Advance Parts, $Tree, Family$, Firestone/auto, Food Lion, Goodyear/auto, Interstate Batteries, Lowe's Whse, NAPA, Piggly Wiggly, Pontiac/GMC, Radio Shack, Sears, Tire Kingdom, U-Haul, USPO, Walgreen, Wal-Mart SuperCtr/gas/24hr/auto, **W**...**gas:** Corner Pantry/gas, 76/Circle K(1mi), Shell, **food:** CiCi's, Hardee's, Sonic, Substation II, Wendy's, **lodging:** Economy Inn, **other:** HOSPITAL, $General, Eckerd, Jo-Ann Fabrics, Precision Tune, Sava-Lot Foods, Target
6b a	Shop Rd, **W**...to USC Coliseum, fairgrounds
5	SC 48, Bluff Rd, 1 mi **E**...**gas:** 76, **W**...**gas:** Shell/Burger King/dsl, **food:** Bojangles(2mi)
3mm	Congaree River
2	Saxe Gotha Rd, no services
1	US 21, US 176, US 321(from sb), Cayce, **W**...accesses same as SC I-26, exit 115.
0mm	I-77 begins/ends on I-26, exit 116.

Columbia (vertical label)

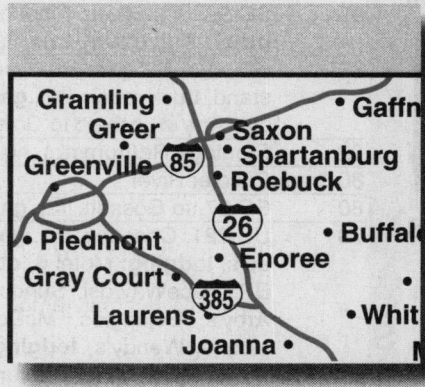

Interstate 85

Exit #	Services
106.5mm	South Carolina/North Carolina state line
106	US 29, to Grover, **E**...**gas:** BP/dsl, **W**...**gas:** Exxon/dsl, Hickory Point/gas, Wilco/Hess/DQ/Wendy's/dsl/scales/24hr
104	SC 99, **E**...**gas:** Mr. Waffle/dsl/rest./scales/24hr/@
103mm	**Welcome Ctr sb, full(handicapped)facilities, info, phone, picnic tables, litter barrels, vending, petwalk**
102	SC 198, to Earl, **E**...**gas:** BP/dsl, Shell/gas, **food:** Hardee's, **W**...**gas:** Citgo/dsl, Flying J/Cookery/dsl/scales/LP/rest./24hr/@, **food:** McDonald's, Waffle House
100mm	Buffalo Creek
100	SC 5, to Blacksburg, Shelby, **W**...**gas:** Sunoco/Subway/dsl/scales/24hr, Texaco/dsl
98	Frontage Rd(from nb), **E**...**food:** Broad River Café
97mm	Broad River
96	SC 18, **W**...**gas:** Kangaroo/Krystal/dsl, Sunoco/dsl
95	SC 18, to Gaffney, **E**...**gas:** Kangaroo/Aunt M's Rest/dsl, Mr Petro/dsl, **food:** Mr Waffle, **other:** HOSPITAL, Suzuki, to Limestone Coll
92	SC 11, to Gaffney, **E**...**gas:** Citgo, Fastpoint, **food:** Applebee's, Blue Bay Seafood, Bojangles, Bruster's, Burger King, Chinese Buffet, Daddy Joe's BBQ, Domino's, KFC, McDonald's, Pizza Hut, Ruby Tuesday, Ryan's, Sagebrush Steaks, Sonic, Subway, Super China, Taco Bell, Waffle House, Wendy's, Zaxby's, **lodging:** Jameson Inn, Super 8, **other:** Advance Parts, Belk, BigLots, BiLo, $Tree, Eckerd, Ingles Foods, Lowe's Whse, Radio Shack, Walgreen, Wal-Mart SuperCtr/gas, USPO, to Limestone Coll, **W**...**gas:** Texaco/dsl, **lodging:** Homestead Lodge, Quality Inn, **other:** to The Peach, Foothills Scenic Hwy
90	SC 105, SC 42, to Gaffney, **E**...**gas:** BP/DQ/dsl, Pilot/Arby's/dsl/scales/24hr, **food:** Bronco Mexican, Clock Rest., Starbucks, Subway, Waffle House, **lodging:** Holiday Inn Express, Roof Inn, **W**...**gas:** Citgo/Burger King, Texaco, **food:** Cracker Barrel, FoodCourt, La Fogata Mexican, Outback Steaks, **lodging:** Hampton Inn, **other:** Hamrick's, Prime Outlets/famous brands, fruit stand
89mm	**rest area both lanes, full(handicapped) facilities, phone, picnic tables, litter barrels, vending, petwalk**

Gaffney (vertical label)

SOUTH CAROLINA
Interstate 85

87	SC 39, **E**...**other:** Pinecone Camping(1.5mi), **W**...**other:** Rug Outlet, fruit stand/peaches/fireworks
83	SC 110, **E**...**gas:** Hot Spot/dsl, **other:** NAPA, fruit stand, truck repair, **W**...**gas:** Auto Trkstp/Mr Waffle/dsl/24hr/@, **other:** to Cowpens Bfd, fruitstand
82	Frontage Rd(from nb), no services
80.5mm	Pacolet River
80	SC 57, to Gossett, **E**...**gas:** Hot Spot/dsl
78	US 221, Chesnee, **E**...**gas:** Citgo/dsl, **food:** Hardee's, **lodging:** Motel 6, **other:** fruit stand, **W**...**gas:** BP, RaceWay/dsl, Sunoco/Burger King/dsl, **food:** Arby's, Bojangles, McDonald's, Subway, Waffle House, Wendy's, **lodging:** Hampton Inn, Holiday Inn Express, **other:** Advance Parts, $General, Harley-Davidson, Ingles Foods
77	Lp 85, Spartanburg, services along Lp 85 exits E
75	SC 9, Spartanburg, **E**...**food:** Denny's, **lodging:** Fairfield Inn, **1-3 mi E on Lp 85**...**gas:** Exxon, **lodging:** Best Western, Comfort Inn, **W**...**gas:** BP/Burger King/dsl, Pure, RaceWay, **food:** Bruster's Ice Cream, Capri's Italian, Copper River Grill, Fatz Café, LJ Silver, McDonald's, Pizza Hut, Pizza Inn, Ron's BBQ, Waffle House, Zaxby's, **lodging:** Days Inn, Comfort Inn, **other:** CVS Drug, Ingles/gas, USPO
72	US 176, to I-585, **E**...**food:** Steak&Ale, **other:** to USC-S, Wofford/Converse Coll, **W**...**gas:** BP, RaceWay, **food:** Waffle House, **other:** Masters RV Ctr
70b a	I-26, E to Columbia, W to Asheville
69	Lp 85, SC 41(from nb), to Fairforest, no services
68	SC 129, to Greer, no services
67mm	N Tyger River
66	US 29, to Lyman, Wellford, no services
63	SC 290, to Duncan, **E**...**gas:** Citgo/dsl, 76/Circle K, Spinx/DQ/dsl, **food:** A&W/KFC, Burger King, Clock Rest., Denny's, Jack-in-the-Box, Paisanos Italian, Pizza Inn, Taco Bell, Thai Cuisine, Waffle House, Zaxby's, **lodging:** Hampton Inn, Jameson Inn, Microtel, **other:** Curves, **W**...**gas:** Phillips 66, Pilot/Wendy's/dsl/scales/24hr, TA/BP/DQ/rest./dsl/scales/24hr/@, **food:** Arby's, BBQ, Bojangles, Hardee's, McDonald's, Waffle House, **lodging:** Comfort Inn, Day's Inn, Holiday Inn Express, Quality Inn, Travelodge, **other:** Sonny's RV Ctr, Speedco Lube
62.5mm	S Tyger River
60	SC 101, to Greer, **E**...**gas:** Grand/dsl, Lil' Cricket/gas, Sunoco, **food:** Senor Garcia's Mexican, Subway, Theo's Rest., **W**...**gas:** Exxon/Burger King, **food:** Waffle House, **lodging:** Super 8
58	Brockman-McClimon Rd, no services
57	**W**...**other:** Greenville-Spartanburg Airport
56	SC 14, to Greer, **E**...**gas:** Citgo/dsl, **W**...**gas:** Spinx/DQ/dsl, **other:** HOSPITAL, Goodyear, Outdoor World RV Ctr
55mm	Enoree River
54	Pelham Rd, **E**...**gas:** BP/dsl, **food:** Burger King, Corona Mexican, Waffle House, **lodging:** Best Western, **W**...**gas:** BP/dsl, Spinx, **food:** Atlanta Bread Co, Bojangles, Burtollos Pizza, California Dreaming Rest., Chick-fil-A, China Wok, Chop-

house 47, Chops Cajun, Happy China, Hardee's, Jack-in-the-Box, Joe's Crabshack, Logan's Roadhouse, Macaroni Grill, Mayflower Seafood, McDonald's, On the Border, Ruby Tuesday, Schlotsky's, Starbucks, Stax Omega Buffet, Subway, Wendy's, **lodging:** Best Western, Courtyard, Extended Stay America, Fairfield Inn, Hampton Inn, Holiday Inn Express, Marriott, Microtel, Residence Inn, Wingate Inn, **other:** BiLo/24hr, CVS Drug, Goodyear/auto, Ingles, Radio Shack, Walgreen

52mm	weigh sta nb
51	I-385, SC 146, Woodruff Rd, **E**...**gas:** Blue Jay/dsl, **food:** Bluefire Grill, Bob Evan's, Burger King, Cracker Barrel, Fatz Café, Fuddrucker's, IHOP, Lieus Bistro, Midori's Rest., Mimi's Cafe, Monterrey Mexican, Panera Bread, PF Chang, Quizno's, Red Robin, Sticky Fingers, TCBY, Waffle House, **lodging:** Drury Inn, Hampton Inn, **other:** Barnes&Noble, Best Buy, BiLo, Circuit City, Goodyear/auto, Hamrick's Outlet, Lowe's Whse, PetsMart, Ross, Sams Club, Whole Foods Mkt, funpark, vet, **W**...**gas:** BP, RaceWay/24hr, **food:** Blimpie, Capri's Italian, Carraba's, Flatrock Grille, Jack-in-the-Box, McDonald's, Ruby Tuesday, TGIFriday, Waffle House, **lodging:** Crowne Plaza, Comfort Inn, Day's Inn, Embassy Suites, Fairfield Inn, Holiday Inn Express, La Quinta, Marriott(3mi), Microtel, **other:** BJ's Whse/gas, Costco/gas, Firestone/auto, Goody's, Home Depot, Lowe's Whse, Old Navy, Target, mall
48b a	US 276, Greenville, **E**...**food:** Waffle House, **lodging:** Red Roof Inn, **other:** CarMax, **W**...**gas:** BP, Exxon/dsl, Murphy USA, Sunoco, **food:** Arby's, Bailey's Grille, Bojangles, Burger King, Hooters, Jack-in-the-Box, KFC, McDonalds, Olive Garden, Ryan's, Subway, Taco Bell/Pizza Hut, Zaxby's, **lodging:** Best Inn, Day's Inn, Embassy Suites, **other:** Acura/Honda, Advance Parts, AutoZone, Bi-Lo, BMW/Mini, BooksAMillion, Buick, Chrysler/Jeep, Dodge, $General, Ford, Kia, Lexus, Lincoln/Mercury, Marshall's, Mazda, Mercedes, Michael's, Nissan, Office Depot, Pepboys, PetsMart, Pontiac/GMC, Saab, SteinMart, Suzuki, Toyota, Volvo, VW/Audi/Porsche
46c	rd 291, Pleasantburg Rd, Mauldin Rd, **W**...**gas:** BP, Citgo/dsl, Spinx, **food:** Jack-in-the-Box, Subway, **lodging:** Quality Inn, Value Place, **other:** Aamco, Advance Parts, BiLo/gas, CVS Drug, Home Depot, Tire Kingdom
46b a	US 25 bus, Augusta Rd, **E**...**gas:** Mike&Jack, Spinx, Sunoco, **food:** Burger King, Waffle House, **lodging:** Camelot Inn, Holiday Inn, Motel 6, Southern Suites, **W**...**food:** Big Papa's Grill, **lodging:** Economy Inn, Traveler's Inn, **other:** Home Depot
44	US 25, White Horse Rd, **E**...**gas:** Spinx/Subway/dsl, **W**...**gas:** Citgo/McDonald's, RaceWay, **food:** Waffle House, **other:** HOSPITAL, Freightliner
44a	SC 20(from sb), to Piedmont, no services
42	I-185 toll, US 29, to Greenville, **W**...HOSPITAL
40	SC 153, to Easley, **E**...**gas:** Breakers/dsl, **food:** Waffle House, **W**...**gas:** BP, Citgo/dsl, RaceWay, **food:** Arby's, Bojangles, Burger King, Cracker Barrel, El Soreno Mexican, Hardee's, Huddle House, KFC, McDonald's, Pizza Hut/Taco Bell, Sonny BBQ, Sonic, Subway, Zaxby's, **lodging:** Executive Inn, Super 8, **other:** Advance Parts, BiLo, Eckerd

SOUTH CAROLINA

Interstate 85

N ↕ S

Anderson

Exit	Services
39	SC 143, to Piedmont, W...**gas:** Shell/dsl, **other:** Ace Hardware, antiques
35	SC 86, to Easley, Piedmont, E...**gas:** Pilot/McDonald's/dsl/scales/24hr, **food:** Hardee's(1.5mi), Las Margaritas, Subway(1.5mi), W...**gas:** BP/grill/dsl
34	US 29(from sb), to Williamston, no services
32	SC 8, to Pelzer, Easley, E...**gas:** Shell/dsl
27	SC 81, to Anderson, E...**gas:** BP/dsl, Exxon, Pumper's Gas/dsl, **food:** Arby's, KFC/Pizza Hut, McDonald's, Waffle House, **lodging:** Holiday Inn Express, **other:** HOSPITAL, W...**gas:** Travel Ctr/DQ/dsl/scales/24hr, **food:** Charlie's Wings
23mm	**rest area sb, full(handicapped)facilities, phone, vending, picnic tables, litter barrels, petwalk**
21	US 178, to Anderson, E...**gas:** Shell/dsl, **2 mi** E...**food:** Applebee's, Chick-fil-a, Fazoli's, O'Charley's, Ruby Tuesday, **lodging:** La Quinta, Mainstay Suites, Quality Inn, Super 8, **other:** Publix/deli
19b a	US 76, SC 28, to Anderson, E...**gas:** Exxon/dsl, **food:** Charlie T's Wings, Fuddruckers, Hardee's, **lodging:** Day's Inn, Hilton Garden, Royal American Motel, **other:** Aldi Food, Buick/GMC, Chrysler, Publix, Russell Stover, **1 mi** E...**gas:** BP/dsl, Shell, **food:** Chick-fil-A, Chili's, Grand China, Jack-in-the-Box, Longhorn Steaks, O'Charley's, Olive Garden, Panera Bread, Sonny BBQ, TX Roadhouse, Zaxby's, **lodging:** Best Value Inn, **other:** Aldi Foods, Best Buy, Curves, Ford, GNC, Harley-Davidson, Honda, KIA, K-Mart, Mazda, Old Navy, O'Reilly Parts, Ross, Sam's Club, Target, Wal-Mart SuperCtr, vet, W...**gas:** HotSpot/McDonald's, RaceWay/dsl/24hr, **food:** Buffalo's Café, Cracker Barrel, Fats Cafe, Hooters, Outback Steaks, Subway, Waffle House, Wendy's, Wild Wing Cafe, **lodging:** Comfort Suites, Country Inn Suites, Fairfield Inn, Hampton Inn, Holiday Inn Express, Jameson Inn, **other:** to Clemson U
18mm	**rest area nb, full(handicapped)facilities, phone, vending, picnic tables, litter barrels, petwalk**
15mm	Lake Hartwell
14	SC 187, to Clemson, Anderson, E...**gas:** Fuel-Club/dsl/24hr/@, **food:** Huddle House/24hr, **other:** KOA(1mi), W...**gas:** BP/dsl, **food:** Famous Pizza Grill, **lodging:** Budget Inn, **other:** to Clem Research Pk
12mm	Seneca River, Lake Hartwell
11	SC 24, SC 243, to Townville, E...**gas:** Exxon/dsl, Sunoco/dsl/24hr, **food:** Subway, **other:** Savannah River Scenic Hwy, W...**gas:** Shell/dsl, **food:** Circle's Cafe, TCBY, **other:** GS RV Park(3mi)
9mm	weigh sta nb
4	SC 243, to SC 24, E...**gas:** Exxon, Mobil/dsl/LP/rest./scales/24hr, W...**gas:** Marathon/Russell's Gen. Store
2	SC 59, to Fair Play, W...fireworks
1	SC 11, to Walhalla, W...**food:** Gazebo Rest., **other:** fireworks, to Lake Hartwell SP
.5mm	**Welcome Ctr nb, full(handicapped)facilities, info, phone, picnic tables, litter barrels, vending, petwalk**
0mm	South Carolina/Georgia state line, Lake Hartwell, Tagaloo River

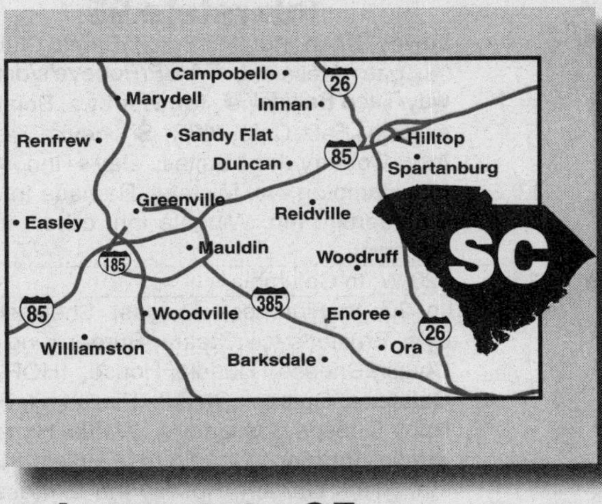

Interstate 95

N ↕ S

Dillon

Florence

Exit #	Services
198mm	South Carolina/North Carolina state line
196mm	**Welcome Ctr sb, full(handicapped)facilities, info, phone, vending, picnic tables, litter barrels, petwalk**
195mm	Little Pee Dee River
193	SC 9, SC 57, to N Myrtle Beach, Dillon, E...**gas:** BP/24hr, Exxon, Mobil, Sunoco/dsl, **food:** Bojangles, Burger King, Fiesta Tapatia, Huddle House, Shoney's, Subway, Waffle House, Wendy's, Zaxby's, **lodging:** Best Value Inn, Comfort Inn, Deluxe Inn, Hampton Inn, Holiday Inn Express, Knights Inn, Ramada Ltd, **other:** HOSPITAL, Bi-Lo Foods, CVS Drug, $General, Food Lion, Wal-Mart, W...**gas:** BP/dsl, **lodging:** Econolodge, Super 8
190	SC 34, to Dillon, E...**gas:** BP/Stuckey's/DQ, **other:** repair
181	SC 38, Oak Grove, E...**gas:** BP/Subway/dsl/24hr, /Flying J/Cookery/dsl/LP/scales/24hr/@, Shell/McDonald's/dsl/24hr, W...**gas:** Wilco/Hess/DQ/Wendy's/dsl/scales/24hr, **lodging:** Best Western, **other:** auto/truck repair
175mm	Pee Dee River
172mm	**rest area both lanes, full(handicapped)facilities, phone, picnic tables, vending, litter barrels, petwalk**
170	SC 327, E...**gas:** BP, Pilot/Wendy's/dsl/scales/24hr, **food:** McDonald's, **lodging:** Holiday Inn Express, **other:** to Myrtle Beach, Missile Museum, W...**gas:** Citgo/dsl
169	TV Rd, to Florence, E...**other:** KOA(1mi), Peterbilt, dsl repair, W...**gas:** BP, Petro/Shell/Pizza Hut/dsl/rest./24hr/@, **lodging:** Best Value Inn, **other:** Blue Beacon
164	US 52, to Darlington, Florence, E...**gas:** Citgo/dsl, Exxon/Pizza Hut/dsl, RaceWay/24hr, Shell, **food:** Arby's, Cracker Barrel, Denny's, Hardee's, Huddle House, Longhorn Steaks, McDonald's, Olive Garden, Quincy's, Quizno's, Red Lobster, Ruby Tuesday, Waffle House, Wendy's, Western Sizzlin, **lodging:** Best Western, Comfort Inn, Courtyard, Econolodge, Hampton Inn, Holiday Inn, Knight's Inn, Motel 6, Red Roof Inn, Suburban Lodge, Super 8, **other:** HOSPITAL, Best Buy, Chrysler/Jeep, $Tree, Home Depot, Kohl's,

N

S

	Lowes Whse, Pontiac/Buick, Sam's Club, Wal-Mart, W...**gas:** Hess/dsl, TA/BP/Popeye's/dsl, Pilot/Subway/Taco Bell/dsl/@, **food:** Arby's, Bojangles, Burger King, Fatz Café, KFC, Shoney's, Zaxby's, **lodging:** Country Inn&Suites, Day's Inn, Guesthouse Inn, Hampton Inn, Microtel, Ramada Inn, Sleep Inn, Thunderbird Inn, Wingate Inn, **other:** to Darlington Raceway
160b	I-20 W, to Columbia
160a	Lp 20, to Florence, E...**gas:** Shell/dsl, **food:** Arby's, Bruster's Ice Cream, Burger King, Chick-fil-A, ChuckeCheese, Huddle House, IHOP, Morrison's Cafeteria, Outback Steaks, Pizza Hut, Red Lobster, Ruby Tuesday, Shoney's, Waffle House, Western Sizzlin, **lodging:** Courtyard, Fairfield Inn, Hampton Inn, Hilton Garden, Holiday Inn Express, Red Roof Inn, SpringHill Suites, **other:** Advance Parts, Belk, Best Buy, Chevrolet, $Tree, Goody's, JC Penney, Lowe's Whse, Sam's Club, Sears/auto, Target, Wal-Mart/drugs, mall
157	US 76, Timmonsville, Florence, E...**gas:** BP/dsl, Exxon/McDonald's/dsl, Kangaroo/dsl, Phillips 66, **food:** Shooky's Diner, Swamp Fox Diner, Waffle House, **lodging:** Day's Inn, Howard Johnson Express, W...**gas:** Sunoco, **lodging:** Ramada, Tree Room Inn/rest., Swamp Fox Camping(1mi)
153	Honda Way, W...Honda Plant
150	SC 403, to Sardis, E...**gas:** BP/dsl, **lodging:** Budget Inn, W...**gas:** Exxon/dsl
147mm	Lynches River
146	SC 341, to Lynchburg, Olanta, E...**lodging:** Relax Inn
141	SC 53, SC 58, to Shiloh, E...**gas:** Exxon/dsl, **other:** DonMar RV Ctr, to Woods Bay SP, W...**gas:** Shell
139mm	**rest area both lanes, full(handicapped) facilities, phone, vending, picnic tables, litter barrels, petwalk**
135	US 378, to Sumter, Turbeville, E...**gas:** BP, Citgo/dsl/24hr, **food:** Compass Rest., **lodging:** Day's Inn, Knight's Inn, W...**gas:** Exxon/dsl, **other:** Pineland Golf Course
132	SC 527, to Sardinia, Kingstree, no services
130mm	Black River
122	US 521, to Alcolu, Manning, W...**gas:** Exxon/dsl, **food:** MD Fried Chicken(2mi)
119	SC 261, to Paxville, Manning, E...**gas:** Mobil, Shell/24hr, TA/BP/Popeye's/Pizza Hut/dsl/scales/24hr/@, **food:** Arby's, Huddle House, Jose's Mexican, Mariachi's, Shoney's, Waffle House, Wendy's, Zaxby's, **lodging:** Best Western, Comfort Inn, Hampton Inn, Holiday Inn Express, Ramada, **other:** HOSPITAL, AutoZone, Chrysler/Jeep/Dodge, Ford, **1 mi** E...**food:** Burger King, KFC, Sonic, **other:** Campers Paradise RV Park, CVS Drug, $General, Goodyear/auto, Radio Shack, Southern holiday RV Ctr, Wal-Mart SuperCtr/Subway/gas/drugs, W...**gas:** Horizon/dsl, Paxville/24hr, **lodging:** Super 8, **other:** auto repair
115	US 301, to Summerton, Manning, W...**gas:** Shell/dsl/24hr, **food:** Georgio's Greek, **lodging:** Econolodge

Santee

108	SC 102, Summerton, E...**gas:** BP/DQ/Stuckey's, **other:** TawCaw RV Park(6m), W...**lodging:** Best Inn, Day's Inn, Deluxe Inn, Knight's Inn
102	US 15, US 301 N, to Santee, E...**gas:** BP/dsl, **food:** Bigwater Country Rest., **lodging:** Bigwater Camping, Lenora's Inn, Santee Resort/Motel, **other:** RV camping, W...**gas:** Shell/dsl, **other:** to Santee NWR
100mm	Lake Marion
99mm	**rest area both lanes, full(handicapped)facilities, phone, info, vending, picnic tables, litter barrels, petwalk**
98	SC 6, to Eutawville, Santee, E...**gas:** BP/Bojangles, Chevron/LP, Citgo, Mobil, **food:** Captain's Quarters, Coaster's Seafood, Fio's Italian, Huddle House, KFC, Pizza Hut, Shoney's, Subway, Theo's Rest., **lodging:** Best Western, Day's Inn, Hampton Inn, Howard Johnson, Ramada, Super 8, Travelodge, **other:** $General, Piggly Wiggly, Russell Stover Candy, Santee Outlets/famous brands, W...**gas:** Citgo, Exxon, Hess/dsl, Horizon/Noble Roman's/dsl/24hr, Shell/dsl, **food:** Burger King, Cracker Barrel, Maurice's BBQ, McDonald's, Peking Chinese, Waffle House, Wendy's, **lodging:** Baymont Inn, Budget Motel, Clark Inn/rest., Comfort Inn, Country Inn Suites, Holiday Inn, Lake Marion Inn, Quality Inn, **other:** CarQuest, CVS Drug, Family$, Food Lion, USPO, to Santee SP(3mi)
97	US 301 S(from sb, no return), to Orangeburg
93	US 15, to Santee, Holly Hill
90	US 176, to Cameron, Holly Hill, W...**gas:** Exxon/dsl
86b a	I-26, W to Columbia, E to Charleston
82	US 178, to Bowman, Harleyville, E...**gas:** BP/Blimpie/Chester Fried/Pizza Inn, Wilco/Hess/Wendy's/DQ/dsl/scales/24hr, **lodging:** Peachtree Inn, **other:** antiques, W...**gas:** Shell/dsl, **other:** tires/truck repair
77	US 78, to Bamberg, St George, E...**gas:** Exxon/KFC, Monoco, Shell/Subway/TCBY, **food:** Georgio's Rest., Grady's Cafe, Hardee's, McDonald's, Pizza Hut, Skynyrd's Grill, Waffle House, Western Sizzlin, **lodging:** Best Value, Comfort Inn/RV park, Econolodge, Quality Inn, **other:** Chevrolet/Pontiac/GMC, CVS Drug, $General, Family$, Firestone/auto, Ford, Jolly Acres RV Park, Radio Shack, Ried's Foods, USPO, W...**gas:** BP, Shell/Taco Bell/dsl, **food:** Huddle House, **lodging:** Country Hearth Inn, Day's Inn, Southern Inn, Super 8
68	SC 61, Canadys, E...**gas:** BP, El Cheapo Fuel/scales, Shell/Subway/dsl, **other:** truck lube/repair, to Colleton SP(3mi)
62	SC 34, no services
57	SC 64, Walterboro, E...**gas:** BP/Subway/TCBY/dsl/24hr, Horizon, Shell/DQ/Stuckey's, Mobil, Sunoco/dsl, **food:** Arby's, Burger King, Capt D's, Checker's, Huddle House, KFC, McDonald's, Olde House Café, Subway, Taco Bell, Waffle House, Wendy's, **lodging:** Best Value, Carolina Lodge, Sleep Inn, Southern Inn, **other:** HOSPITAL, Advance Parts, AutoZone, Belk, BiLo, $General, Ford/Mercury, Parks Parts, Piggly Wiggly, Radio Shack, Reid's Foods, W...**gas:** BP/dsl, **lodging:** Super 8, **other:** $Tree, PetCo, Wal-Mart SuperCtr/gas/dsl

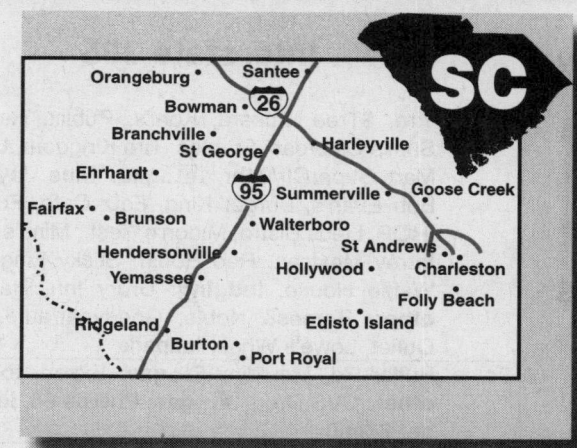

Interstate 95

53 SC 63, to Varnville, Walterboro, Hampton, E...**gas:** BP/McDonald's, Citgo, El Cheapo, Exxon, Shell/DQ, **food:** Glasshouse Rest., KFC, Longhorn Steaks, Ruby Tuesday, Shoney's, Waffle House, **lodging:** Best Western, Comfort Inn/rest., Econolodge, Motel 6, Quality Inn, Ramada Inn, Royal Inn, Rice Planter's Inn, **other:** fireworks, W...**gas:** BP/dsl, **food:** Cracker Barrel, **lodging:** Day's Inn, Deluxe Inn, Hampton Inn, Holiday Inn Express, Microtel, Royal Inn, **other:** Green Acres Camping

47mm **rest area both lanes, full(handicapped)facilities, phone, vending, picnic tables, litter barrels, pet-walk**

42 US 21, to Yemassee, Beaufort

40mm Combahee River

38 SC 68, to Hampton, Yemassee, E...**gas:** Chevron, **other:** Family$, W...**gas:** BP/Subway/TCBY, Exxon/dsl, Shell/dsl, **food:** J's Rest., **lodging:** Palmetto Lodge/rest., Super 8

33 US 17 N, to Beaufort, E...**gas:** BP/dsl, Exxon, Shell, Texaco/TCBY/Subway, **food:** Confederate Railroad, Denny's, McDonald's, Waffle House, Wendy's, **lodging:** Best Western, Budget Inn, Hampton Inn, Holiday Inn Express, Knight's Inn, **other:** KOA, Oaks RV Camping

30.5mm Tullifinny River

29mm Coosawhatchie River

28 SC 462, to Coosawhatchie, Hilton Head, Bluffton, W...**gas:** Chevron/dsl, Citgo, Exxon/Chester Fried/dsl/rest.

22 US 17, Ridgeland, W...**gas:** Sunoco, **lodging:** Plantation Inn, **other:** HOSPITAL

21 SC 336, to Hilton Head, Ridgeland, E...**other:** Boat RV Ctr, W...**gas:** BP/dsl, Chevron/dsl/24hr, Citgo, Exxon, **food:** Bella Pizza, Burger King, Cabrito's Mexican, Hong Kong Chinese, Huddle House, Jasper's porch Rest., KFC, Subway, Waffle House, **lodging:** America's Inn, Best Value, Carolina Lodge, Comfort Inn/rest., **other:** HOSPITAL, Curves, $General, Food Lion, Harvey's Foods, Rite Aid

18 SC 13, to US 17, US 278, to Switzerland, Granville, Ridgeland, no services

8 US 278, to Bluffton, Hardeeville, E...**gas:** BP/Huddle House/Wendy's/dsl/scales, Exxon, Kangaroo/McDonald's, **other:** HOSPITAL, W...**gas:** Chevron/Noble Roman/TCBY/Subway/dsl, Exxon, Mobil/Kangaroo/dsl, **food:** KrispyKreme, **lodging:** Motel 6

5 US 17, US 321, to Savannah, Hardeeville, E...**gas:** Chevron/dsl, El Cheapo, Exxon/Blimpie, Shell/24hr, **food:** American Diner, KFC, Mi Tierrita Mexican, Waffle House, **lodging:** Day's Inn, Economy Inn, Sleep Inn, **other:** fireworks, to Savannah NWR, W...**gas:** BP/dsl, Citgo, Exxon, Sunoco/dsl, **food:** Burger King, Mi Tierrita Mexican, New China Rest., Shoney's, Squat'n Gobble Grill, Wendy's, **lodging:** Comfort Inn, Deluxe Inn, Econolodge, Howard Johnson Express, Knight's Inn, Quality Inn, Super 8, **other:** $General, NAPA, antiques

4.5mm **Welcome Ctr nb, full(handicapped)facilities, info, phone, picnic tables, litter barrels, vending, pet-walk**

4mm weigh sta both lanes

0mm South Carolina/Georgia state line, Savannah River

Interstate 385(Greenville)

Exit #   Services

42 US 276, Stone Ave, to Travelers Rest., to Greenville Zoo, E...**other:** CarQuest, W...**gas:** Spinx, **1-2 mi** W...service on US 276, I-385 begins/ends on US 276.

40b a SC 291, Pleasantburg Dr, E...**gas:** Sunoco, **food:** Jack-in-the-Box, Little Caesar's, Olive Tree, Pizza Hut, S&S Cafeteria, Sonic, Steak&Ale, Subway, Taco Casa, Wendy's, **other:** CVS Drug, Walgreens, to BJU, Furman U, W...**gas:** Citg/dsl, **food:** Domino's, Krispy Kreme, **lodging:** Quality Inn, Sleep Inn, **other:** transmissions

39 39 Haywood Rd, E...**gas:** BP, Exxon/dsl, **food:** Domino's, LongHorn Steaks, Outback Steaks, Tony's Pizzaria, **lodging:** AmeriSuites, Courtyard, GuestHouse Suites, Hawthorn Inn, Hilton, La Quinta, Quality Inn, Residence Inn, **other:** Firestone, TJ Maxx, W...**gas:** Crown, Shell, Texaco, **food:** Arby's, Applebee's, Bennigan's, Blackeyed Pea, Buffalo's Café, Burger King, Chili's, ChuckeCheese, CityRange Steaks, Don Pablo, Hardee's, Italian Mkt/grill, Jack-in-the-Box, Jason's Deli, Kanpai Tokyo, O'Charley's, Ruby Tuesday, Senor Wrap's, Starbucks, Steak'n Shake, Waffle House, Wendy's, **lodging:** Hampton Inn, Studio+, **other:** Barnes&Noble, Belk, Circuit City, Dillard's, Discount Tire, Goodyear, Harley-Davidson, JC Penney, LensCrafters, Macey's, NTB, Sears/auto, mall

37 Roper Mtn Rd, E...**other:** BiLo Foods, W...**gas:** Amoco, BP/dsl, Exxon/Pantry, RaceTrac, **food:** Atl Bread Co, Backyard Burger, Burger King, Capri's Italian, Cracker Barrel, Fazoli's, LoneStar Steaks, McDonald's, Miyabi Japanese, Rafferty's, Remington's Rest., Waffle House, **lodging:** Day's Inn, Crowne Plaza, Embassy Suites, Fairfield Inn, Holiday Inn Select, La Quinta, Travelodge, **other:** BJ's Whse, CompUSA, Goody's, Home Depot, Lowe's Whse, Old Navy, Target, mall

36b a I-85, N to Charlotte, S to Atlanta

35 SC 146, Woodruff Rd, E...**gas:** Spinx, **food:** Applebee's, AZ Steaks, Bojangles, Bone Fish Grill, Boston Pizzaria, Brewster's, Burger King, Chick-fil-A, Chili's, Fazoli's, Grand Buffet, Hardee's, Jersey Mike's Subs, KFC, King Buffet, McAlister's Deli, Moe's SW Grill, Perkins, Ryan's, Sonic, Starbucks, Subway, Taco Bell, Topper's Rest., Waffle House, Wendy's, Zaxby's, **other:** Ace Hardware, Aldi Foods, BiLo Foods, Discount

SOUTH CAROLINA

Interstate 385

Tire, $Tree, Eckerd, Kohl's, Publix, Radio Shack, Sam's Club/gas, Staples, Tire Kingdom, USPO, **Wal-Mart SuperCtr/24hr**, **W**...**gas:** Blue Jay/dsl, **food:** Bob Evan's, Burger King, Fatz Café, Fuddrucker's, IHOP, Lieus Bistro, Midori's Rest., Mimi's Cafe, Monterrey Mexican, Red Robin, Sticky Fingers, TCBY, Waffle House, **lodging:** Drury Inn, Hampton Inn, **other:** Barnes& Noble, Goodyear/auto, Hamrick's Outlet, Lowe's Whse, funpark

34	Butler Rd, Mauldin, **E**...**gas:** Exxon, **food:** Arby's, **other:** CVS Drug, **W**...**gas:** Phillips 66, **lodging:** Super 8(3mi)
33	Bridges Rd, Mauldin
31	I-185 toll, SC 417, to Laurens Rd, **E**...**gas:** BP, **food:** Hardee's, Jack in the Box, **other:** HOSPITAL, **S**...**food:** A&W, LJSilver, **lodging:** Masters Inn
30	I-185 toll, US 276, Standing Springs Rd
29	Georgia Rd, to Simpsonville, no services
27	Fairview Rd, to Simpsonville, **E**...**gas:** Pumper's, **food:** Carolina Rest., CoachHouse rest., Hardee's, Little Caesar's, McDonald's, Milano Pizzaria, New China Buffet, Subway, **lodging:** Palmetto Inn, **other:** HOSPITAL, Advance Parts, AutoZone, Chevrolet, $General, Rite Aid, **W**...**gas:** BP, Exxon, **food:** Applebee's, Arby's, AZ Steaks, Beef o'Brady's, Brewster's, Burger King, Chic-fil-A, Cracker Barrel, Dragon Den Chinese, Hungry Howie's, Jack in the Box, Jersey Mike's, KFC, McDonalds, O'Charley's, Panera Bread, Pizza Hut, Quizno's, Ruby Tuesday, Ryan's, Starbucks, Taco Bell, Tequila's Mexican, Waffle House, Wendy's, **lodging:** Comfort Inn, Day's Inn, Hampton Inn, Holiday Inn Express, **other:** Belk, BiLo, CVS Drug, $Tree, GNC, Ingles, Goodyear/auto, Home Depot, Kohl's, Lowe's Whse, Publix, Ross, Target, Tire Kingdom, TJ Maxx, Walgreen, **Wal-Mart SuperCtr/gas/24hr**, USPO
26	Harrison Bridge Rd(from sb), no services
24	Fairview St, **E**...**gas:** Phillips 66, **food:** Hardee's, Waffle House, **other:** carwash
23	SC 418, to Fountain Inn, Fork Shoals, **E**...**gas:** Exxon/Subway/dsl/24hr
22	SC 14 W, Old Laurens Rd, to Fountain Inn
19	SC 14 E, to Gray Court, Owings, no services
16	SC 101, to Woodruff, Gray Court, no services
10	SC 23, to Ora, no services
9	US 221, to Laurens, Enoree, **E**...**gas:** Exxon/Sub Express/dsl/24hr, **food:** Hunts Bros. Pizza, Waffle House, **lodging:** Budget Lodge, **W**...**Wal-Mart Dist Ctr, lodging:** Travel Inn(2mi)
6mm	**rest area both lanes(both lanes exit left), full (handicapped)facilities, phone, vending, picnic tables, litter barrels, petwalk**
5	SC 49, to Laurens, Union, no services
2	SC 308, to Clinton, Ora, **W**...**other:** HOSPITAL, to Presbyterian Coll in Clinton
0mm	I-26 S to Columbia, I-385 begins/ends on I-26 at 52mm.

Interstate 526(Charleston)

Exit #	Services
33mm	I-526 begins/ends.
32	US 17, **N**...**gas:** Exxon, Hess, **food:** Subway, **lodging:** Day's Inn, Red Roof Inn, **other:** Advance Parts, CVS Drug, 1 mi **N**...**gas:** Shell, **food:** Burger King, Chili's, IHOP, LongHorn Steaks, On The Border, TGIFriday, **other:** Barnes&Noble, Belk, Eckerd, Lowe's Whse, Old Navy, **S**...**gas:** Amoco, Speedway, **food:** Applebee's, Arby's, Chick-fil-A, China Buffet, Domino's, KFC, La Hacienda Mexicana, McDonald's, Papa John's, **other:** $General, Office Depot, Publix, USPO, VW, Wal-Mart, 1 mi **S**...**gas:** Hess, 76, Shell, **food:** Hardee's, Huddle House, Outback Steaks, Shoney's, Wendy's, **lodging:** Comfort Inn, Day's Inn, Extended Stay America, Holiday Inn, Masters Inn, **other:** Cadillac/Chevrolet, Ford, Firestone/auto, Radio Shack, Staples
30	Long Point Rd, **N**...**gas:** Exxon, **food:** Bamboo Garden, Mo's Café, Sonic, Starbucks, Subway, Waffle House, **other:** Food Lion, Harris Teeter Foods, Charles Pinckney NHS
26mm	Wando River
24	Daniel Island, **S**...Queen Anne's Steaks/seafood, Hampton Inn
23b a	Clements Ferry Rd, no services
21mm	Cooper River
20	Virginia Ave(from eb), **S**...**gas:** Hess Depot, **other:** Marathon Refinery
19	N Rhett Ave, **N**...**gas:** Hess, **food:** Hardee's, **other:** Eckerd, Food Lion, **S**...**gas:** BP
18b a	US 52, US 78, Rivers Ave, **N**...**gas:** Amoco/dsl, Shell, **food:** McDonald's, **other:** Family$, Merchant Auto, NAPA, Piggly Wiggly, **S**...**lodging:** Catalina Inn
17b a	I-26, E to Charleston, W to Columbia
16	Montague Ave, Airport Rd, **S**...**food:** Wendy's, **lodging:** Embassy Suites, Hilton Garden
15	SC 642, Dorchester Rd, Paramount Dr, **N**...**gas:** BP, 76, **food:** Wendy's, **S**...**gas:** Amoco, Exxon, **food:** Burger King, Checker's, Huddle House, **lodging:** Super 8, **other:** Buick/Pontiac/GMC
14	Leeds Ave, **S**...**other:** HOSPITAL, boat marina
13mm	Ashley River
12	SC 61, Ashley River Rd, **N**...**food:** Chick-fil-A, McDonald's, O'Charley's, Quizno's, Sonic, **other:** HOSPITAL, Home Depot
11	Sam Rittenburg Blvd, **S**...**other:** Belk, Dillard's, JC Penney, Sears/auto, mall
10	US 17, SC 7, **services from US 17**, **E**...**gas:** BP, Shell, Speedway, **food:** Capt D's, Checker's, China Gourmet, CiCi's, McDonald's, Red Lobster, Ruby Tuesday, Taco Bell, **lodging:** Holiday Inn Express, Motel 6, **other:** Mazda, Mitsubishi, Piggly Wiggly, **W**...**gas:** Exxon, Hess, 76/Circle K, **food:** Waffle House, **lodging:** Econolodge, Hampton Inn, In-Town Suites, **other:** Acura, Advance Parts, Chrysler/Jeep, Costco/gas, CVS Drug, Food Lion, Toyota
	I-526 begins/ends on US 17.

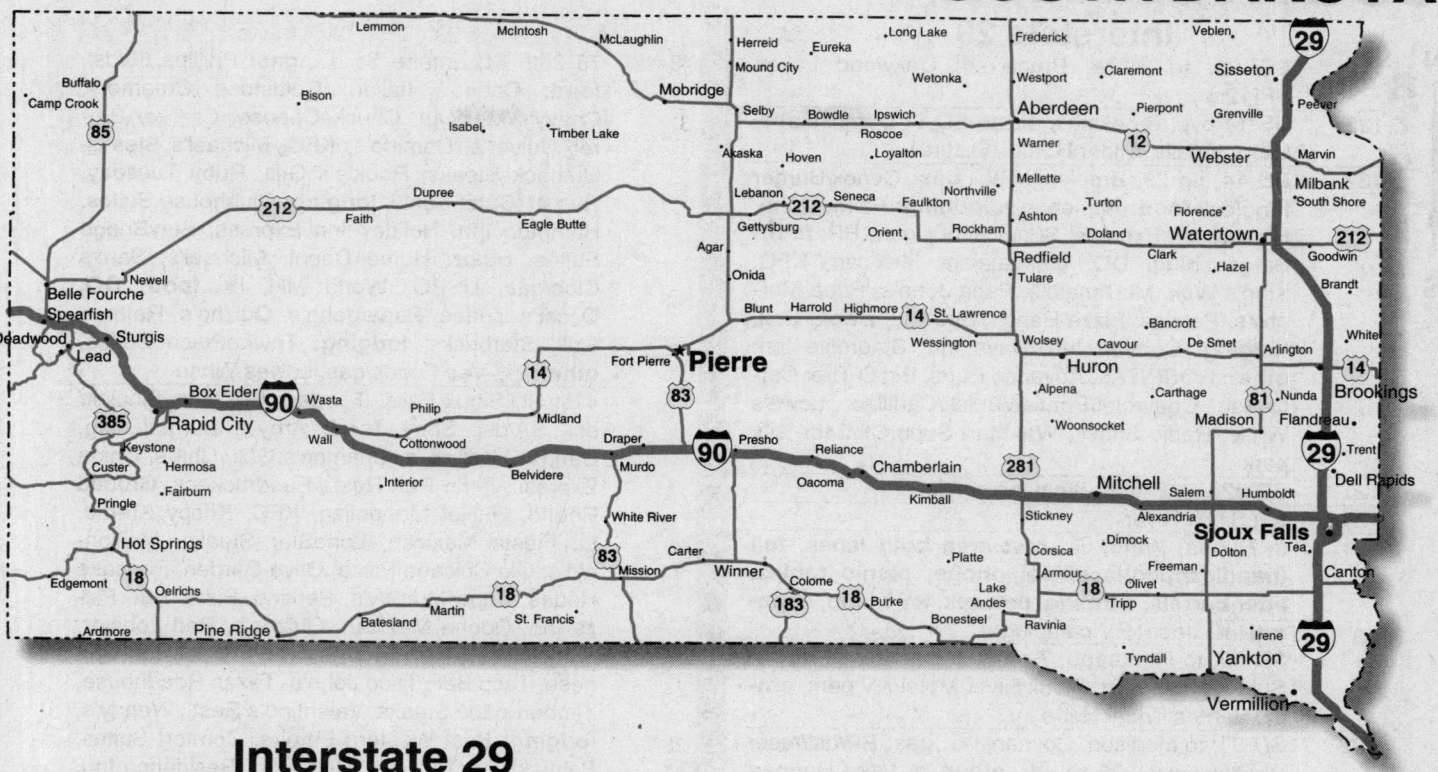

Interstate 29

Exit #	Services
253mm	South Dakota/North Dakota state line
251mm	**Welcome Ctr sb, full(handicapped) facilities, info, phone, picnic tables, litter barrels, pet-walk**
246	SD 127, to Rosholt, New Effington, 3 mi Ⓦ...gas, food, RV camping, Sica Hollow SP(24mi)
242	no services
235mm	weigh sta sb
232	SD 10, Sisseton, Ⓔ...gas: Dakota Connection/dsl/casino/24hr, **food:** Crossroads Cafe, 1-3 mi Ⓦ...gas: Alco, BP/dsl, Cenex/dsl, Sinclair/dsl, **food:** Cottage Rest., DQ, Pizza Hut, Subway, Taco John's, **lodging:** Holiday Motel, I-29 Motel, Super 8, Viking Motel, **other:** Camp Dakotah, Chevrolet, Family$, NAPA Parts, SuperValu Foods/gas, to Roy Lake SP(25mi), Ft Sisseton SP(35mi)
224	Peever, Sioux Tribal Hqtrs, Ⓔ...gas: Cenex/dsl, Ⓦ...Pickerel Lake(16mi)
213	**SD 15, to Wilmot, rest area both lanes, full (handicapped)facilities, phone, picnic tables, litter barrels, petwalk, RV dump, st patrol, 7 mi** Ⓔ...gas, food, to Hartford Beach SP(17mi)
207	US 12, Summit, Ⓔ...gas: Conoco/dsl/24hr, Ⓦ...Blue Dog Fish Hatchery(15mi), Waubay NWR(19mi)
201	to Twin Brooks, no services
193	SD 20, to South Shore, Stockholm, no services
185	to Waverly, 4 mi Ⓦ...other: Dakota Sioux Casino/rest.
180	US 81 S, to Watertown, 5 mi Ⓦ...gas: Conoco, **other:** HOSPITAL, Bramble Park Zoo, airport

Watertown

Exit #	Services
177	US 212, Watertown, Ⓔ...gas: BP/Subway/Grainery Cafe/dsl/24hr, **lodging:** Holiday Inn Express, **other:** Truckers QuikLube, tires, Ⓦ...gas: Shell/dsl, **food:** Applebees, Culvers, Hunter's Rest., McDonald's, Starbucks, **lodging:** Comfort Inn, Country Inn Suites, Day's Inn, **other:** HOSPITAL, $Tree, Redlin Art Ctr, Wal-Mart SuperCtr/24hr, 1-2 mi Ⓦ...gas: BP/dsl, Cenex/dsl, Conoco/dsl, **food:** Arby's, Burger King, China Buffet, Domino's Pizza, DQ, Dragon Wall Chinese, Godfather's, Herberger's, Little Caesar's, Papa John's, Papa Murphy's, Perkins, Pizza Hut, Quizno's, Senor Max's Mexican, Subway/TCBY, Taco John's, **lodging:** Drake Hotel, Travelers Inn, **other:** Advance Parts, Buick/Nissan, Chrysler/Dodge/Jeep, EconoFoods, Firestone/auto, Ford/Lincoln/Mercury, Goodyear/auto, Herberger's, Hy-Vee Foods, JC Penney, Jo-Ann Fabrics, K-Mart, NAPA Parts, Nissan, Osco Drug, Pronto Parts, ShopKO, Target, Tires+, Walgreen, mall, to Sandy Shore RA(10mi)
164	SD 22, to Castlewood, Clear Lake, 9 mi Ⓔ...gas: Cenex/dsl, **other:** HOSPITAL
161mm	**rest area both lanes, full(handicapped)facilities, phone, picnic tables, litter barrels, vending, petwalk, RV dump**
157	to Brandt, no services
150	SD 28, SD 15 N, to Toronto, 7 mi Ⓦ...gas, food, lodging, 24 mi Ⓦ...Lake Poinsett RA, SD Amateur Baseball Hall of Fame

N ↕ S

Brookings

Exit	Description
140	SD 30, to White, Bruce, **W**...Oakwood Lakes SP(12mi)
133	US 14 byp, Brookings, **W**...to SD St U, museums, Laura Ingalls Wilder Home, **E**...tires
132	US 14, Lp 29, Brookings, **E**...**gas:** Cenex/Burger King/dsl, **food:** Applebee's, **lodging:** Fairfield Inn, Holiday Inn Express, Super 8, **W**...**gas:** BP, **food:** Burger King, DQ, Guadalajara Mexican, KFC, King's Wok, McDonald's, Papa John's, Papa Murphy's, Perkins, Pizza Ranch, Subway, Z'Kota Grill, **lodging:** Comfort Inn, Days Inn, Staurolite Inn, **other:** HOSPITAL, Advance Parts, Big O Tire, CarQuest, Chevrolet/Pontiac/Buick/Cadillac, Lowe's Whse, Radio Shack, Wal-Mart SuperCtr/24hr, city park
127	SD 324, to Elkton, Sinai, no services
124mm	Big Sioux River
121	to Nunda, Ward, **E**...**rest area both lanes, full (handicapped)facilities, phone, picnic tables, litter barrels, vending, petwalk, RV dump, st patrol, W**...food, RV camping
114	SD 32, to Flandreau, **7 mi E**...**gas:** Cenex, **food:** Subway, **lodging:** Sioux River Motel/RV park, **other:** Santee Tribal Hqtrs
109	SD 34, to Madison, Colman, **W**...**gas:** BP/dsl/rest., Shell/dsl/rest., **20 mi W**...**other:** to Lake Herman SP, Dakota St U, museum
104	to Trent, Chester, no services
103mm	parking area both lanes
98	SD 115 S, Dell Rapids, **E**...Chevrolet/Pontiac, **3 mi E**...**gas:** Kum&Go, Shell, **food:** Pizza Ranch, **lodging:** Bilmar Inn, **other:** HOSPITAL
94	SD 114, to Baltic, **E**...**gas:** flea mkt **10 mi E**...**other:** to EROS Data Ctr, US Geological Survey
86	to Renner, Crooks, no services
84b a	I-90, W to Rapid City, E to Albert Lea
83	SD 38 W, 60th St, **E**...**gas:** ⛽/Flying J/Country Mkt/dsl/24hr/scales/@, **lodging:** Quality Suites, **other:** Freightliner Trucks, Harley-Davidson, Northview Campers, repair, **W**...**other:** fireworks
82	Benson Rd, no services
81	SD 38 E, Russell St, Sioux Falls, **E**...**gas:** BP/24hr, Citgo, Food'n Fuel, **food:** Burger King, Country Kitchen, Roll'n Pin Rest., **lodging:** Arena Motel, Best Western, Brimark Inn, Kelly Inn, Motel 6, Oaks Hotel, Ramada Inn, Ramkota/rest., Sheraton, Sleep Inn, Super 8, **other:** Schaap's RV Ctr, auto repair, st patrol
80	Madison St, **E**...fairgrounds
79	SD 42, 12th St, **E**...**gas:** BP/24hr, Cenex, F&F, **food:** Burger King, Burger Time, Godfather's, Golden Harvest Chinese, KFC, McDonald's, Pizza Hut, Subway, Taco Bell, Taco John's, Tomacelli's Pizza, Wendy's, **lodging:** Nite's Inn(1mi), Ramada Ltd, **other:** HOSPITAL, Ace Hardware, BMW/Toyota, Chevrolet, $General, Jack's Campers, JiffyLube, K-Mart, Lewis Drug, Saturn, Toyota/Scion, Walgreen, city park, to Great Plains Zoo/museum, **W**...**gas:** Cenex/dsl, Citgo, Phillips 66/dsl, **food:** Z'Kota Grille, **lodging:** Westwick Motel, **other:** Tower RV Park, to USS SD Battleship Mem

Sioux Falls

Exit	Description
78	78 26th St, Empire St, **E**...**gas:** Phillips 66/dsl, **food:** Carino's Italian, Coldstone Creamery, Chevy's Mexican, ChuckeCheese, Cracker Barrel, Culver's, Domino's, KFC, Michael's Steaks, Outback Steaks, Rookie's Grill, Ruby Tuesday, Rue 41 Cafe, Sonic, **lodging:** Clubhouse Suites, Hampton Inn, Holiday Inn Express, StayBridge Suites, **other:** Home Depot, Michael's, Sam's Club/gas, USPO, World Mkt, **W**...**food:** DQ, Oscar's Coffee, Papa John's, Quizno's, Referee Grill, Starbucks, **lodging:** TownePlace Suites, **other:** Hy-Vee Foods/gas, Lowes Whse
77	41st St, Sioux Falls, **E**...**gas:** BP/24hr, Sinclair/dsl, SA/dsl, Shell, **food:** Arby's, Burger King, Carlos O'Kelly's,'s, Champp's Grill, Chili's, China Express, Fry'n Pan Rest., Fuddrucker's, Ground Round, HuHot Mongolian, KFC, Krispy Kreme, La Fiesta Mexican, LoneStar Steaks, McDonald's, Old Chicago Pizza, Olive Garden, Pancake House, Papa Murphy's, Perkins, Pizza Hut, Pizza Inn, Qdoba Mexican, Quizno's, Red Lobster, Schlotsky's, Starbucks, Subway, Szechwan Chinese, Taco Bell, Taco John's, Texas Roadhouse, TimberLodge Steaks, Valentino's Rest., Wendy's, **lodging:** Best Western Empire, Comfort Suites, Fairfield Inn, Microtel, Radisson, Residence Inn, Rodeway Inn, Super 8, **other:** Advance Parts, Barnes&Noble, Batteries+, Best Buy, Big O Tire, Checker Parts, Chrysler/Jeep/Mazda, Curves, Ford/Lincoln/Mercury, Goodyear/auto, Hancock Fabrics, Hyundai/Nissan, JC Penney, JiffyLube, Macy's, Old Navy, PetCo, Radio Shack, Sears/auto, ShopKO, Target, Tires+, Toyota, Village Automotive, Walgreen, Wal-Mart SuperCtr, VW, Younkers, mall, **W**...**gas:** Citgo, Shell/dsl, **food:** Burger King, Denucci's Pizza, Godfather's, IHOP, Little Caesars, Peking Chinese, Perkins/24hr, Subway, **lodging:** AmericInn, Baymont Inn, Day's Inn, Red Roof Inn, **other:** Lewis Drug, USPO
75	I-229 E, to I-90 E
73	Tea, **E**...**gas:** Larry's Trkstp/dsl/café, **1.5mi W**...Red Barn Camping
71	to Harrisburg, Lennox, **W**...RV camping
68	to Lennox, Parker, no services
64	SD 44, Worthing, **W**...**other:** Chevrolet/Pontiac/Buick, Great Plains RV Ctr
62	US 18 E, to Canton, **E**...**gas:** Shell/pizza/dsl, **lodging:** motel/RV park, **W**...repair
59	US 18 W, to Davis, Hurley, no services
56	to Fairview, **E**...to Newton Hills SP(12mi)
53	to Viborg, no services
50	to Centerville, Hudson, no services
47	SD 46, to Irene, Beresford, **E**...**gas:** Casey's, Conoco/Burger King/dsl, Sinclair/dsl, **food:** Emily's Café, Stone Hearth Cafe, Subway, **lodging:** Crossroads Motel, Super 8, **other:** Chevrolet, Fiesta Foods, Windmill Camping, repair, **W**...**gas:** Cenex/cafe/dsl/24hr, **other:** Radio Shack
42	to Alcester, Wakonda, no services
41mm	truck check(from sb)
38	to Volin, **E**...to Union Grove SP(3mi)

Interstate 29

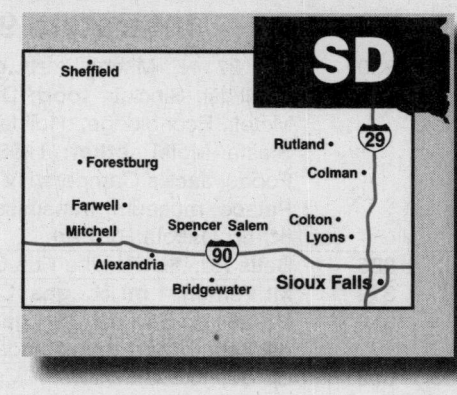

31	SD 48, to Akron, Spink, no services
26	SD 50, to Vermillion, **E...Welcome Ctr/rest area both lanes, full(handicapped)facilities, info, phone, picnic tables, litter barrels, petwalk, RV dump, W...gas:** Conoco/dsl/cafe/24hr, **6-7 mi W...gas:** Casey's/gas, Phillips 66, **food:** Burger King, Pizza Hut, Subway, Taco John's, **lodging:** Comfort Inn, Holiday Inn, Prairie Inn, Super 8, Westside Inn, **other:** HOSPITAL, Hy-Vee Foods, to U of SD, to Lewis & Clark RA
18	Lp 29, to Burbank, Elk Point, **E...gas:** BP/dsl, Casey's, **food:** Cody's Rest., **lodging:** HomeTowne Inn
15	to Elk Point, **1 mi E...gas,** food, lodging, **W...fire-works**
13mm	weigh sta nb, parking area sb
9	SD 105, Jefferson, **E...gas:** BP/Choice Cut Rest./dsl
4	McCook, **1 mi W...other:** KOA(seasonal), Adams Homestead/nature preserve
2	N Sioux City, **E...gas:** Cenex, Goode/dsl/rest/casino, **food:** Glass Palace Rest.(1mi), McDonald's, Taco John's, **other:** USPO, fireworks, **W...gas:** Casey's/gas, Freeway Express/Chester Fried, **lodging:** Comfort Inn, Hampton Inn, Red Carpet Inn, Super 8, **other:** KOA, to Sodrac Dogtrack
1	**E...other:** Dakota Dunes Golf Resort, **W...gas:** Phillips 66/dsl, **food:** Graham's Grill, **lodging:** Country Inn Suites
0mm	South Dakota/Iowa state line, Big Sioux River

Interstate 90

Exit #	Services
412.5mm	South Dakota/Minnesota state line
412mm	**Welcome Ctr wb/rest area eb, full(handicapped) facilities, info, phone, picnic tables, litter barrels, petwalk, RV dump(wb), weigh sta both lanes**
410	Valley Springs, **N...**Palisades SP(7mi), **S...**Beaver Creek Nature Area, gas, food
406	SD 11, Brandon, Corson, **S...**Palisades SP(10mi), **S...gas:** BP/dsl, Shell, Sinclair/McDonald's/dsl, **food:** Brandon Steaks, Dominos, DQ, Pizza Ranch, Subway, Taco John's, Tailgater's Grill, **lodging:** Comfort Inn, Holiday Inn Express, **other:** Lewis Drug, Sunshine Foods, True Value, to Big Sioux RA(2mi)
402	EROS Data Ctr, **N...other:** fireworks, Jellystone RV Park, tires
400	I-229 S
399	SD 115, Cliff Ave, Sioux Falls, **N...gas:** TC's Minimart/dsl, **other:** Spader RV Ctr, KOA, **S...gas:** BP, Holiday/dsl, Pilot/Grandma Max's Rest./Subway/dsl/24hr/@, Shell, **food:** Arby's, Burger King, McDonald's, Perkins, Rocco's Italian, Taco Bell, Taco John's, **lodging:** Cloud Nine Motel, Comfort Inn, Day's Inn, Super 8, **other:** HOSPITAL, Blue Beacon, Graham Tire, Kenworth, Peterbilt, Volvo
398mm	Big Sioux River
396b a	I-29, N to Brookings, S to Sioux City
390	SD 38, Hartford, **N...other:** Camp Dakota RV Park, Goos RV Ctr, **S...gas:** Cowboy Town/dsl
387	rd 17, Hartford, **N...gas:** Phillips 66/dsl, **food:** Pizza Ranch
379	SD 19, Humboldt, **N...gas:** Mobil/dsl, Shell/Town&Country Store/dsl(1mi), **food:** Main Cafe(1mi), **other:** USPO
375mm	E Vermillion River
374	to SD 38, Montrose, **5 mi S...other:** Battle Creek Res., Lake Vermillion RA, RV camping
368	Canistota, **4 mi S...lodging:** Best Western
364	US 81, to Yankton, Salem, **4 mi N...gas:** Cenex, Sinclair, **lodging:** Home Motel, **other:** Camp America
363.5mm	W Vermillion River
363mm	**rest area both lanes, full(handicapped) facilities, phone, picnic tables, litter barrels, vending, petwalk, RV dump, st patrol**
357	to Bridgewater, Canova, no services
353	Spencer, Emery, **S...gas:** FuelMart/Subway/dsl/casino/24hr
352mm	Wolf Creek
350	SD 25, Emery, Farmer, **N...**to DeSmet, Home of Laura Ingalls Wilder
344	SD 262, to Fulton, Alexandria, **S...gas:** Shell/dsl, **food:** Joe's Cafe
337mm	parking area both lanes
335	Riverside Rd, **N...**KOA(1mi)
334.5mm	James River
332	SD 37 S, to Parkston, Mitchell, **N...gas:** BP/24hr, Cenex/dsl, Conoco, Phillips 66, Pilot/Shell/Subway/dsl/scales/24hr, **food:** Arby's, Bonanza, Burger King, Country Kitchen, DQ, Kinder's Cafe, McDonald's, Perkins, Pizza Hut, Pizza Ranch, Twin Dragon Chinese, **lodging:** AmericInn, Best Western, Quality Inn, Day's Inn, Super 8, Thunderbird Motel, **other:** HOSPITAL, Advance Parts, Big K-Mart, R&R RV Park, Rondee's Campground, Walgreens, transmissions, **1-2 mi N...other:** to Corn Palace, Museum of Pioneer Life, **S...gas:** Shell/Godfather's/Taco Bell/dsl/24hr, **food:** Culver's, KFC, Quizno's, Ruby Tuesday, **lodging:** Comfort Inn, Hampton Inn, Kelly Inn, **other:** Cabela's, $Tree, Radio Shack, Wal-Mart SuperCtr/gas/24hr

SOUTH DAKOTA

Interstate 90

E ↕ W

330	SD 37 N, Mitchell, N...**gas:** Cenex/dsl/24hr, Shell/dsl, Sinclair, **food:** DQ, **lodging:** Anthony Motel, Econolodge, Holiday Inn/rest., Motel 6, Siesta Motel, **other:** HOSPITAL, County Fair Foods, Jack's Campers/RV ctr., Mr. Tire, to Corn Palace, museum, transmissions, weigh sta, S...**other:** Dakota RV Park
325	Betts Rd, S...Famil-e-Fun Camping
319	Mt Vernon, **1 mi** N...**gas:** Cenex, Sinclair/dsl
310	US 281, to Stickney, S...**gas:** Sinclair/Deli Depot/dsl/24hr, **other:** to Ft Randall Dam
308	Lp 90, to Plankinton, N...**gas:** Cenex, Sinclair/Al's Cafe/dsl, **food:** Golden Pheasant, **lodging:** Cabin Fever Motel/RV Park, Smart Choice Inn, **other:** Gordy's Camping, USPO, repair
301.5mm	**rest area both lanes, full(handicapped) facilities, phones, picnic tables, litter barrels, RV dump**
296	White Lake, **1 mi** N...**gas:** A-Z Gas, Cenex/dsl, **lodging:** A-Z Motel, **other:** USPO
294mm	Platte Creek
293mm	parking area both lanes
289	SD 45 S, to Platte, S...**other:** to Snake Cr/Platte Cr RA(25mi)
284	SD 45 N, Kimball, N...**gas:** BP/tires, Phillips 66/dsl/24hr, **food:** Ditty's Diner, Frosty King Drive-In, **lodging:** Dakota Winds Motel, Super 8, **other:** Parkway Campground, repair/tires, S...**other:** tractor museum
272	SD 50, Pukwana, **2 mi** N...gas, food, lodging, S...**other:** Snake/Platte Creek Rec Areas(25mi)
265	SD 50, Chamberlain, N...**gas:** BP/DQ/dsl, **lodging:** AmericInn, S...**gas:** SA/dsl, **other:** Happy Camper Campground
264mm	**rest area both lanes, full(handicapped) facilities, scenic view, info, phones, picnic tables, litter barrels**
263	Chamberlain, N...**gas:** Sinclair/dsl, **food:** Casey's Café, McDonald's, Pizza Hut, Subway(1mi), Taco John's, **lodging:** Best Western(1mi), Bel Aire Motel(1mi), Riverview Inn, Super 8, **other:** Crow Creek Sioux Tribal Hqtrs
262mm	Missouri River
260	SD 50, Oacoma, N...**gas:** BP/Arby's/dsl, Conoco/dsl, Shell/dsl, **lodging:** Al's Oasis/Motel/Campgroung/cafe/mkt, Cedar Shore Motel(3mi), Comfort Inn, Day's Inn, Holiday Inn Express, **other:** Chevrolet/Buick/Pontiac, Hi&Dri Camping, Old West Museum
251	SD 47, to Winner, Gregory, no services
248	SD 47, Reliance, N...**gas:** BP/dsl(1mi), Cenex(1mi), **other:** Sioux Tribal Hqtrs, to Big Bend RA
241	to Lyman, no services
235	SD 273, Kennebec, N...**gas:** Conoco/dsl, **food:** Pony Express Café, **lodging:** Budget Host, Kings Inn, **other:** KOA

Chamberlain

226	US 183 S, Presho, N...**gas:** Conoco/dsl, Sinclair/dsl, **lodging:** Coachlight Inn, Hutch's Motel/café/RV Park, Sweeney's B&B, **other:** New Frontier RV park, museum, repair
225	lp 90, Presho, same as 226
221mm	**rest area wb, full(handicapped)facilities, info, phone, picnic tables, litter barrels, RV dump, petwalk**
220	no services
218mm	**rest area eb, full(handicapped)facilities, info, phone, picnic tables, litter barrels, RV dump, petwalk**
214	Vivian, no services
212	US 83 N, SD 53, to Pierre, N...**gas:** Sinclair/dsl, **food:** Vivian Jct Rest., **other:** HOSPITAL(34mi)
208	no services
201	Draper, N...**gas:** Farmer's Oil/Cafe
194mm	parking area both lanes
192	US 83 S, Murdo, N...**gas:** BP/dsl, HHH/Shell/dsl, Kwikmart/dsl, Sinclair/dsl, **food:** Murdo Drive-In, Star Rest., The Diner, **lodging:** American Inn, Anchor Inn, Best Western, Day's Inn, Iversen Inn, Landmark Country Inn, Sioux Motel, Super 8, **other:** American RV Park/camping, Murdo Foods, Super Value Foods, auto museum, USPO, S...**lodging:** Country Inn, **other:** to Rosebud
191	Murdo, N...access to same as 192
188mm	parking area both lanes, litter barrels
183	Okaton, S...gas, Ghost Town
177	no services
175mm	central/mountain timezone
172	to Cedar Butte, no services
170	SD 63 N, to Midland, N...**gas:** Shell, **other:** 1880's Town, KOA
167mm	**rest area wb, full (handicapped)facilities, phones, picnic tables, litter barrels, RV dump, petwalk**
165mm	**rest area eb, full (handicapped)facilities, phones, picnic tables, litter barrels, RV dump, petwalk**
163	SD 63, Belvidere, S...**gas:** BP/dsl/café, Sinclair/dsl
152	Lp 90, Kadoka, N...**gas:** Conoco/dsl/rest./24hr, S...**other:** Badlands Petrified Gardens, camping
150	SD 73 S, Kadoka, N...**lodging:** Dakota Inn/rest., S...**gas:** BP, Conoco/dsl, **food:** H&H Rest., Happy Chef, **lodging:** Best Value, Best Western, Budget Host, Ponderosa Motel/RV park, Wagon Wheel Motel, **other:** Kadoka Kampground, to Buffalo Nat Grasslands, repair
143	SD 73 N, to Philip, **15 mi** N...HOSPITAL
138mm	scenic overlook wb
131	SD 240, S...**gas:** BP, **lodging:** Badlands Inn/Best Value(9mi), Cedar Pass Lodge/rest.(9mi), **other:** Circle 10 Camping, Prairie Home NHS, KOA(11mi), to Badlands NP
129.5mm	scenic overlook eb

Murdo

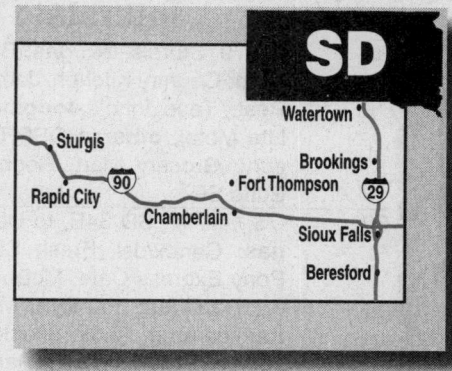

Interstate 90

127	no services
121	Bigfoot Rd, no services
116	239th St, no services
112	US 14 E, to Philip, no services
110	SD 240, Wall, ...gas: BP/dsl, Exxon, Philllips 66/ Subway, food: Cactus Café, DQ, Elkton House Rest., Red Rock Rest., Subway, Wall Drug Rest., lodging: Anne's Motel, Best Value Inn, Best Western, Day's Inn, Econolodge, Fountain Hotel, Motel 6, Sunshine Inn, Super 8, The Wall Motel, Welsh Motel, other: NAPA, Ace Hardware, NAPA, Wall Drug/gifts/rest., The Arrow Campground, Wounded Knee Museum, S...to Badlands NP, RV camping
109	W 4th Ave, Wall, 1-2 mi N...access to same as 110
107	Cedar Butte Rd, no services
101	rd T-504, Jensen Rd, to Schell Ranch
100mm	**rest area both lanes, full(handicapped) facilities, info, phone, picnic tables, litter barrels, RV dump, vending, petwalk**
99.5mm	Cheyenne River
98	Wasta, N...gas: BP/dsl, lodging: Redwood Motel, other: Sunrise Campgrnd
90	173rd Ave, to Owanka, no services
88	171st Ave(from eb, no re-entry), no services
84	167th Ave, rd 497, N...Olde Glory Fireworks
78	161st Ave, New Underwood, 1/2 mi S...gas: Sinclair, lodging: Jake's Motel, other: Boondocks Camping, Steve's General Store/gas/motel/rest
69mm	parking area both lanes
67	to Box Elder, Ellsworth AFB, N...gas: Loaf'n Jug, other: museum
63	(eb only), to Box Elder, Ellsworth AFB
61	Elk Vale Rd, N...gas: /Flying J/Conoco/CountryMkt/dsl/LP/RV dump/24hr/scales/@, S...gas: BP, Mobil/dsl, food: Ardy's, McDonalds, lodging: Fairfield Inn, La Quinta, other: I-90 RV Ctr, KOA(seasonal)(3mi), transmissions
60	Lp 90, to Mt Rushmore, Rapid City, 1-3 mi S... food: KFC, LJ Silver, lodging: Holiday Inn Express, Stardust Motel, other: HOSPITAL, Nat Coll of Mines/Geology
59	La Crosse St,, Rapid City, N...gas: BP/24hr, Phillips 66, food: Boston's Rest, Burger King/TCBY, Denny's, Fuddrucker's, Minerva's Rest., Outback Steaks, TGIFriday, lodging: Best Value, Best Western, Country Inn Suites, Econolodge, Grand Stay Hotel, Holiday Inn Express, Super 8, other: Sears/auto, Old Navy, PetsMart, mall, st patrol, S...gas: Cenex/dsl, Exxon/24hr, food: ChuckeCheese, Golden Corral, McDonald's, Mongolian Grill, MillStone Rest., Perkins/24hr, Schlotsky's, Subway, lodging: AmericInn, Comfort Inn, Dakota Pines Motel, Day's Inn, Fair Value Inn, Foothills Inn, Grand Gateway Hotel, Hampton Inn, Microtel, Motel 6, Quality Inn, Thrifty Motel, other: Sam's Club/gas, Walgreens, Wal-Mart SuperCtr/gas
58	Haines Ave, Rapid City, N...gas: Conoco, food: Applebee's, Chili's, Hardee's, Herburger's, IHOP, Olive Garden, Red Lobster, lodging: Best Value, Grand Stay Motel, other: $Discount, Best Buy, Borders, Hancock Fabrics, Herbergers, JC Penney, Kohl's, Lowe's Whse, Target, Tires+, to Rushmore Mall, S...gas: Loaf'n Jug, food: ChuckeCheese, Taco John's, Wendy's, other: HOSPITAL, ShopKO, same as 59
57	I-190, US 16, to Rapid City, to Mt Rushmore, 1 mi S on North St...gas: Conoco, Exxon, lodging: Holiday Inn, Howard Johnson, Radisson, Starbucks, other: Ace Hardware, Albertson's/Osco Drug
55	Deadwood Ave, N...other: Dakota RV Ctr, Harley-Davidson/cafe, Lazy JD Camp(6mi), S...gas: Pilot/Sinclair/Subway/dsl/scale/24hr/@, food: A&W(2mi), Culver's(3mi), Wendy's(3mi), Windmill Rest., lodging: Best Western, Sun Inn(3mi), other: Black Hills Dogtrack, Chevrolet, dsl repair
51	Black Hawk Rd, N...other: Three Flags Camping(1mi), S...food: Cenex, Culver's, lodging: Family Inn, other: USPO
48	Stagebarn Canyon Rd, N...other: RV camping, S...gas: C-Store/gas, Sinclair/Haggar's Mkt/food, food: Rookies Rest., lodging: Ramada, other: Mid-States RV Ctr, auto repair
46	Piedmont Rd, Elk Creek Rd, N...Elk Creek Resort/ Camping, other: to Petrified Forest, lodging: Elk Creek Resort, other: to Petrified Forest, camping, S...gas: Conoco/dsl, other: Sacora Camping/Grill
44	Bethlehem Rd, S...other: Bethlehem RV Park(2mi), Jack's RV Ctr(2mi), Historic Food
42mm	**rest area both lanes, full(handicapped)facilities, info, phones, picnic tables, litter barrels, RV dump, petwalk, vending**
40	Tilford, S...Behtlehem Rd RV Park(2mi), Clifford Gulch RV Park
39mm	weigh sta eb
37	Pleasant Valley Rd, N...other: Elkview Camp, S... other: Bulldog Camping, Rush-No-More Camping
34	S...other: Black Hills Nat Cemetary, Katmandu Camping, No Name RV Park, Suzie's RV Camping

SOUTH DAKOTA
Interstate 90

E ↑ / **W** ↓

Sturgis

32   SD 79, Sturgis, Ⓝ...**gas:** BP, Conoco, Exxon/dsl, **food:** Country Kitchen, Jambonz Rest., Phil-Town Rest., Taco John's, **lodging:** Best Western, Star-Lite Motel, **other:** HOSPITAL, Ford/Lincoln/Mercury, Grocery Mart, Rodney RV Park, to Bear Butte SP

30   US 14A W, SD 34E, to Deadwood, Sturgis, Ⓝ...**gas:** Cenex/dsl, Fresh Start, **food:** Pizza Hut, Pony Express Cafe, McDonald's, Pizza Hut, **other:** CarQuest, Famliy$, Mr Tire, O'Reilly Parts, Pamida/drug, Radio Shack, Day's End Camping, Ⓢ...**gas:** Conoco/dsl, RanchMart, **food:** Burger King, DQ, Pizza Ranch, Subway, **lodging:** AmericInn(11mi), Holiday Inn(11mi), Day's Inn, Super 8/rest., **other:** Chevrolet

23   SD 34 W, to Belle Fourche, Whitewood, Ⓝ...**other:** Northern Hills RV Ctr, Ⓢ...**gas:** Arpil's/dsl, BP, **food:** Shea's Diner, **lodging:** Iron Horse Inn, Tony's Motel, Whitewood Rest., **other:** USPO

17   US 85 S, to Deadwood, **9-12 mi Ⓢ in Deadwood...food:** Cadillac Jack's Diner, 4Aces Buffet, Pizza Hut, Silverado Café, **lodging:** AmericInn, Elkridge Motel, Franklin Motel, Holiday Inn Express, Mineral Dance Motel, Super 8, Deadwood Gulch Resort, **other:** KOA, Whistler Gultch Camping, Winner's Casino

Spearfish

14   US 14A, Spearfish Canyon, Ⓝ...**food:** Applebee's, **lodging:** Comfort Suites, Fairfield Inn, Holiday Inn/rest., Quality Inn, **other:** Wal-Mart SuperCtr/24hr, Ⓢ...**gas:** BP/dsl, **food:** KFC/LJ Silver, Perkins, Pizza Ranch, **lodging:** All American Inn, Howard Johnson, Super 8, **other:** Ace Hardware, Ford/Lincoln/Mercury, K-Mart, auto museum

12   Jackson Blvd, Spearfish, Ⓢ...**gas:** BP, Conoco/dsl, Loaf'n Jug, **food:** Arby's, Domino's, Millstone Rest., Papa Murphy's, Pizza Hut, Quizno's, Subway, **lodging:** Best Western, Travelodge, **other:** HOSPITAL, CarQuest, Black Hills St U, fish hatchery, same as 10

10   US 85 N, to Belle Fourche, Ⓢ...**food:** Burger King, Cedar House Rest., DQ, Golden Dragon Chinese, McDonald's, Subway, Taco Bell, **lodging:** Best Western, Day's Inn, Travelodge, **other:** HOSPITAL, Bob's Drug, Cadillac/GMC, Chevrolet/Buick/Cadillac, Jeep, Jo's Camping, KOA, Safeway/drug/gas, USPO, Valley Corner Store, same as 12

8   McGuigan rd, W Spearfish, Ⓢ...KOA(1mi)

2   1 mi Ⓝ...McNenny St Fish Hatchery

1mm   **Welcome Ctr eb, full(handicapped)facilities, info, phone, picnic tables, litter barrels, RV dump, petwalk**

0mm   South Dakota/Wyoming state line

Interstate 229(Sioux Falls)

N ↑ / **S** ↓

Sioux Falls

Exit #	Services
10b a	I-90 E and W. I-229 begins/ends on I-90, exit 400.
9	Benson Rd, Ⓦ...**gas:** BP/pizza, **gas:** Marlin's Rest., **other:** Ford Trucks, Western Star
7.5mm	Big Sioux River
7	Rice St, Ⓔ...winter sports, Ⓦ...to stockyards
6	SD 38, 10th St, Ⓔ...**gas:** Mobil, Sinclair, **food:** A&W, Applebee's, Arby's, Boston's Rest., Denny's, DQ, Domino's, Fryn' Pan Rest., KFC, Pizza Hut, Quizno's, Ruby Tuesday, Taco Bell, Tomacelli's Italian, **lodging:** Super 8, **other:** AutoZone, Family$, Hy-Vee Foods, K-Mart, Pronto Parts, ShopKO, Sunshine Foods, Valvoline, USPO, Ⓦ...**gas:** Cone's Gas, Get'n Go/dsl, Phillips 66/dsl/mart, Shell, **food:** Burger King/TCBY, BurgerTime, Godfather's, Little Caesar's, McDonald's, Pizza Inn, Puerto Vallarta, Stake-Out, Subway, Taco John's, Z'Kota Grille, **lodging:** Rushmore Motel, **other:** Jiffy Lube, Lewis Drug, vet
5.5mm	Big Sioux River
5	26th St, Ⓔ...**gas:** Shell/dsl, **food:** Cherry Creek Grill, Dario's Pizza, McDonald's, SaiGon Panda, **other:** city park, Ⓦ...**other:** HOSPITAL
4	Cliff Ave, Ⓔ...**gas:** Get'n Go, **food:** China Star, **other:** Curves, Lewis Drug, Sunshine Foods, Walgreens, city park
3	SD 115, Lp 229, Minnesota Ave, Ⓔ...city park, **1 mi** Ⓦ...**gas:** BP, Sinclair, **food:** Burger King, Camilles Cafe, Culver's, Famous Dave's BBQ, Golden Bowl Chinese, Little Caesar's, McDonald's, Subway, Z'kota Grille, **other:** Ace hardware, Dodge, $Tree, GMC/Buick, Hy-Vee Foods/gas, Kia, Lewis Drug, Mitsubishi/Toyota, Staples, vet
2	Western Ave, Ⓔ...**gas:** Shell/dsl, **food:** Bracco Cafe, DQ, Izzy's Cafe, Nucci, Scooters Coffee, Ⓦ...**gas:** Cenex/dsl, Gas Stop, **food:** Burger King, Champp's Café, China Buffet, Huhot Mongolian, La Fiesta Mexican, Lonestar Steaks, Papa Murphy's, Pizza Hut, Qdoba Mexican, Quizno's, Redrossa Pizza, Valentino's Italian, **other:** Checker Parts, Curves, Goodyear/auto, Hancock Fabrics, Radio Shack
1.5mm	Big Sioux River
1c	Louise Ave, Ⓔ...**lodging:** Homewood Suites, **other:** HOSPITAL, Ⓦ...**gas:** BP, Phillips 66/dsl, **food:** Applebee's, Burger King, Culvers, McDonald's, Wendy's, **lodging:** Honda/Mercedes, mall
1b a	I-29 N and S. I-229 begins/ends on I-29, exit 75.

420

Interstate 24

Exit # Services

185b a	I-75, N to Knoxville, S to Atlanta. I-24 begins/ends on I-75, exit 2 in Chattanooga.
184	Moore Rd, 🅂...**food:** Chef Lin Buffet, Provino's Italian, **other:** $Tree, Radio Shack, Sears Essentials/auto
183	(183a from wb), Belvoir Ave, Germantown Rd
181a	US 41 S, to East Ridge(from eb), 🅂...**food:** Westside Grill, King's Lodge, **other:** Ford Trucks
181	Fourth Ave, to TN Temple U, Chattanooga, N... **gas:** Camboi, Citgo/dsl, Conoco, Exxon/Blimpie/dsl, High Tech Fuel, **food:** Bojangles, Burger King, Capt D's, Central Park, Hardee's, Krystal/24hr, Subway, Waffle House, **lodging:** Villager Lodge, **other:** BiLo, $General, Goodyear, Mr Transmission, Stop n' Save Foods, repair, 🅂...**gas:** Citgo
180b a	US 27 S, TN 8, Rossville Blvd, N...**other:** U-Haul, to Chickamauga, UT Chatt, 🅂...**gas:** Exxon, RaceWay/ dsl/24hr, **lodging:** Hamilton Inn, **other:** NTB
178	US 27 N, Market St, to Lookout Mtn, Chattanooga, N...**gas:** BP/dsl, Citgo, **lodging:** Best Value, Day's Inn, Marriott, Ramada Inn, Staybridge Suites, **other:** Ford, Nissan, U-Haul, to Chattanooga ChooChoo, 🅂...**food:** KFC, **lodging:** Comfort Suites, Hampton Inn, Motel 6
175	Browns Ferry Rd, to Lookout Mtn, N...**gas:** BP, Exxon/dsl, **food:** China Gourmet, **lodging:** Best Value Inn, **other:** CVS Drug, $General, Food Lion, 🅂...**gas:** Conoco/dsl, Shell/dsl, **food:** Hardee's, McDonald's, Subway, **lodging:** Comfort Inn, Econolodge, Quality Inn, Sleep Inn
174	US 11, US 41, US 64, Lookout Valley, N...**food:** Waffle House, **lodging:** Day's Inn, **other:** Racoon Mtn Camping(2mi), 🅂...**gas:** BP/dsl/24hr, Kangaroo, **food:** Circle C Catfish, Cracker Barrel, Taco Bell, Wendy's, **lodging:** Baymont Inn, Best Western, Budget Motel, Comfort Inn, Country Inn&Suites, Hampton Inn, Holiday Inn Express, Knight's Inn, Ramada Ltd, Super 8, **other:** Ace Hardware, Lookout Valley Camping, Wal-Mart SuperCtr, st patrol
172mm	**rest area eb, full(handicapped)facilities, phone, picnic tables, litter barrels, vending, petwalk**
171mm	Tennessee/Georgia state line
169	GA 299, to US 11, N...**gas:** Exxon/dsl/24hr, 🅂...**gas**, BP/Momma's Chicken/dsl/24hr/@, Pilot/Subway/dsl/ scales/24hr/@, RaceWay/24hr
167	I-59 S, to Birmingham
167mm	Tennessee/Georgia state line, Central/Eastern time zone

161	TN 156, to Haletown, New Hope, N...**gas:** BP/dsl(1mi), **other:** Hales RV Park, 🅂...**gas:** Chevron/fireworks, **other:** On The Lake Camping
160mm	Tennessee River/Nickajack Lake
159mm	**Welcome Ctr wb/rest area eb, full(handicapped) facilities, phone, vending, picnic tables, litter barrels, petwalk**
158	US 41, TN 27, Nickajack Dam, N...**gas:** Texaco, 🅂... **gas:** BP/dsl/fireworks, **other:** Shellmound Camping
155	TN 28, Jasper, N...**gas:** BP/dsl(1mi), Exxon/dsl, **food:** Dairy Queen(1mi), Hardee's, Western Sizzlin, **lodging:** Acuff Country Inn, 🅂...**gas:** BP/Quizno's/ dsl, **other:** HOSPITAL
152	US 41, US 64, US 72, Kimball, S Pittsburg, N...**gas:** BP/fireworks, Scot/dsl, Phillips 66/fireworks, Race-Way, **food:** A&W/LJ Silver, Arby's, Cracker Barrel, Domino's, KFC, Krystal, McDonald's, Pizza Hut, Shoney's, Subway, Taco Bell, Waffle House, Wendy's, **lodging:** Budget Host, Comfort Inn, Country Hearth Inn, Day's Inn, Holiday Inn Express, **other:** HOSPITAL, Chevrolet/Pontiac/Buick, $Tree, Goody's, Lowe's Whse, Radio Shack, Wal-Mart SuperCtr/24hr, to Russell Cave NM, **3 mi** 🅂...**other:** Lodge Cast Iron
143	Martin Springs Rd, N...**gas:** Chevron/dsl/fireworks
135	US 41 N, Monteagle, N...**gas:** Citgo/dsl/rest./24hr, Mystik/dsl, **food:** BBQ, **other:** AutoSure Parts, S Cumberland RV Park, 🅂...**Day's Inn**
134	US 64, US 41A, to Sewanee, Monteagle, N...**gas:** BP/McDonald's, **lodging:** American Eagle Inn, **oth-er:** to S Cumberland SP, 🅂...**gas:** Citgo, Shell/dsl, **food:** Bluewater Lodge Rest., Hardee's, Monteagle Diner, Pizza Hut, Smokehouse BBQ, Subway, Waffle House, **lodging:** Best Western, Regency Inn, **other:** $General, Firestone/U-Haul/auto, Fred's Drugs, Mon-teagle Winery, Piggly Wiggly, to U of The South
133mm	**rest area both lanes, full(handicapped)facilities, phone, picnic tables, litter barrels, vending, pet-walk**
128mm	Elk River
127	US 64, TN 50, to Winchester, Pelham, N...**gas:** BP, Phillips 66, Shell/Texaco/Stuckey's, 🅂...**gas:** Exxon/ dsl, **other:** to Tims Ford SP/RV camping
119mm	trucks only parking area both lanes
117	to Tullahoma, USAF Arnold Ctr, UT Space Institute
116mm	weigh sta both lanes

TENNESSEE
Interstate 24

114 US 41, Manchester, **N...gas:** BP/24 Truckers/dsl/@, Marathon, Shell, **food:** Huddle House, O'Charley's, **lodging:** Comfort Inn, Holiday Inn Express, Ramada Ltd, Scottish Inn, Super 8, Trucker's Inn, **other:** Country Cabin Camping, Chrysler/Dodge/Toyota, KOA, Nissan, Toyota, museum, **S...gas:** Citgo, Kangaroo, RaceWay, **food:** Arby's, Burger King, Capt D's, KFC, Krystal, McDonald's, Pizza Hut, Shoney's, Subway, Taco Bell, Waffle House, Wendy's, **lodging:** Best Value, Country Inn Suites, Day's Inn, Royal Inn, **other:** Advance Parts, AutoZone, BiLo Foods, Chevrolet, Curves, Family$, Ford/Lincoln/Mercury, Fred's Drug, Goodyear, Napa, Russell Stover, carwash

111 TN 55, Manchester, **N...gas:** BP/dsl, Citgo/dsl/24hr, Co-op gas, **other:** to Rock Island SP, **S...gas:** BP, **food:** Hardee's, J&G Pizza/Steaks, Sonic, **other:** HOSPITAL, Gateway Tires, to Jack Daniels Dist HS, Old Stone Fort

110 TN 53, Manchester, **N...gas:** BP, Kangaroo, Shell/dsl, **food:** Cracker Barrel, D Crockett's Roadhouse, Emma's Rest., Oak Rest., **lodging:** Ambassador Inn, Economy Inn, Hampton Inn, **S...gas:** Shell/dsl/24hr, **food:** Los 3 Amigos Mexican, Waffle House, **lodging:** Econolodge, **other:** HOSPITAL, repair

110mm Duck River

105 US 41, **N...gas:** BP/dsl/24hr/@, Shell/dsl, **food:** RanchHouse Rest., **S...to** Normandy Dam, Dickle HS

97 TN 64, to Shelbyville, Beechgrove, **N...other:** auto parts/repair, **S...gas:** Citgo

89 Buchanan Rd, **N...gas:** Love's/McDonald's/dsl/@, Texaco/Outpost Rest/dsl, **S...gas:** Citgo/dsl/rest./24hr, **food:** Huddle House

84 Joe B. Jackson Pkwy, no services

81 US 231, Murfreesboro, **N...gas:** BP/dsl/24hr, Exxon, RaceWay/24hr, Shell, **food:** Arby's, Burger King, Cracker Barrel, King's Table Rest., Krystal, Panda Buffet, Parthenon Steaks, Shanghai Chinese, Shoney's, Waffle House/24hr, Wendy's, **lodging:** Best Value, Knight's Inn, Quality Inn, Ramada Ltd, Regal Inn, Scottish Inn, **other:** HOSPITAL, Dodge, Honda, Mazda, **S...gas:** Citgo/24hr, Express/dsl/24hr, Phillips 66/dsl/24hr/@, **food:** La Siesta Mexican, McDonald's, Pizza Hut/Taco Bell, Sonic, Subway, Waffle House, **lodging:** Howard Johnson, Quality Inn, **other:** Eckerd, Gateway Tire, Toyota/Scion

78 TN 96, to Franklin, Murfreesboro, **N...gas:** BP, Phillips 66/Church's/White Castle/dsl, Shell/Jack-in-the-Box, Texaco/Burger King/24hr, **food:** Arby's, Applebee's, Bellacino's Pizza, Chick-fil-A, Cracker Barrel, Don Pablo, Fazoli's, IHOP, KFC, McDonald's, OutBack Steaks, Red Lobster, Ryan's, Santa Fe Steaks, Starbucks, Steak'n Shake, Subway, Waffle House, Wendy's, **lodging:** Best Western, Comfort Inn, Country Inn Suites, Day's Inn, DoubleTree, Fairfield Inn, Hampton Inn, Holiday Inn, Microtel, Motel 6, Red Roof Inn, Sleep Inn, Super 8, Wingate Inn, **other:** BooksAMillion, Dillard's, HobbyLobby, Home Depot, JC Penney, Lowe's Whse, Old Navy, Sears, Staples, Target, TJ Maxx, Wal-Mart SuperCtr/gas/24hr, mall, to Stones River Bfd, **S...gas:** BP/dsl/24hr, Chevron/24hr, Exxon/24hr, Kangaroo/dsl, **food:** Corky's BBQ,

China Garden, Hardee's, Las Palmas, O'Charley's, Sonic, Subway, Taco Bell, Waffle House, Whit's BBQ, **other:** $General, Kohl's, Kroger, Old Time POttery, Sam's Club/gas, Walgreen

76 Manson Pike, Medical Center Pkwy, to Stones River Nat. Bfd

74b a TN 840, to Lebanon, Franklin

70 TN 102, Lee Victory Pkwy, Almaville Rd, to Smyrna, **S...gas:** BP, Kangaroo/Quizno's/dsl, Mapco Mart, **food:** McDonald's, Legends Steaks, Ringalino's, **lodging:** Deerfield Inn, **other:** Tennessee Expo

66 TN 266, Sam Ridley Pkwy, to Smyrna, **N...gas:** Citgo/dsl/24hr, Shell/dsl, **food:** Arby's, A&W/LJ Silver, Blue Coast Burrito, Catfish House, Chili's, Famous Dave's, Hickory Hills Cafe, Jim'n Nick's BBQ, Logan's Roadhouse, Papa John's, Sonic, Starbucks, Subway, Wendy's, **lodging:** Day's Inn, **other:** CVS Drug, Kroger/gas, Publix, Nashville I-24 Camping(3mi), **S...food:** Cracker Barrel, O'Charley's, Ruby Tuesday, **lodging:** Fairfield Inn, Hampton Inn, Sleep Inn, **other:** I-24 Expo

64 Waldron Rd, to La Vergne, **N...gas:** Exxon/24hr, Marathon/24hr, Kangaroo, Pilot/Subway/dsl/24hr/@, **food:** Arby's, Hardee's, Krystal/24hr, McDonald's, Waffle House, **lodging:** Comfort Inn, Holiday Inn Express, Super 8, **other:** Music City Camping(3mi), RV service, **S...gas:** Mapco/dsl/24hr, **lodging:** Sleep n' Go

62 TN 171, Old Hickory Blvd, **N...gas:** BP, Chevron, Citgo, Shell/dsl/24hr, TA/BP/Burger King/Popeye's/dsl/24hr/@, **food:** El Arroyo Mexican, Waffle House, **lodging:** Best Western

60 Hickory Hollow Pkwy, **N...gas:** BP, Citgo/24hr, Express, Shell, **food:** Applebee's, Arby's, Bailey's Grill, Burger King, ChuckeCheese, Courtyard Café, Cracker Barrel, KFC, Logan's Roadhouse, McDonald's, O'Charley's, Outback Steaks, Pizza Hut, Red Lobster, Subway, TGI-Friday, Wendy's, **lodging:** Country Inn Suites, Day's Inn, Fairfield Inn, Hampton Inn, Holiday Inn, Ramada Inn, **other:** Best Buy, Chevrolet, Circuit City, Dillard's, Dodge, Eckerd, Firestone/auto, Kroger, Mazda, NTB, Office Depot, Sears, mall, transmissions, **S...gas:** BP/dsl, Shell, **food:** Evergreen Chinese, IHOP, Olive Garden, Shoney's, Steak'n Shake, Waffle House/24hr, **lodging:** Knight's Inn, Quality Inn, Quarters Inn, **other:** Acura, Goodyear, Home Depot, KIA, Target

59 TN 254, Bell Rd, same as 60

57 Haywood Lane, **N...gas:** Marathon, **food:** Hardee's, Pizza Hut, **other:** $General, Food Lion, Walgreen, **S...gas:** Phillips 66/dsl/24hr

56 TN 255, Harding Place, **N...gas:** Chevron/dsl, Exxon, Shell/dsl/24hr, **food:** Applebee's, Arby's, KFC, McDonald's, Pizza Hut/Taco Bell, Subway, Waffle House, Wendy's, **lodging:** Capstone Inn, Drury Inn, Executive Inn, Motel 6, PearTree Inn, Suburban Lodge, Super 8, **other:** Sam's Club/gas, **S...gas:** Express, Shell, **food:** Burger King, Hooters, Jalapenos, Jack-in-the-Box, Waffle House, **lodging:** Best Value Inn, Economy Inn, Motel 6, **other:** HOSPITAL

54b a TN 155, Briley Pkwy

53 I-440 W, to Memphis

52 US 41, Murfreesboro Rd, **N...gas:** BP, Shell, Texaco, **food:** Bennigan's, Denny's, Dunkin Donuts, Golden Corral, Krystal, Los Reyes Mexican, Piccadilly's, Pizza Hut, Red Lobster, Taco Bell, Waffle House, **lodging:**

Interstate 24

Budget Lodge, Day's Inn, Economy Inn, Econolodge, Holiday Inn Express, Howard Johnson, Quality Inn, Ramada Inn, Scottish Inn, **other:** CarQuest, Office Depot, bank, **S**...**food:** Jack-in-the-Box, **other:** Chevrolet, Dodge

52b a	I-40, E to Knoxville, W to Memphis
	I-24 and I-40 run together 2 mi. See Interstate 40, exits 212-213.
50b	I-40 W
48	James Robertson Pkwy, **N**...**gas:** Citgo, Shell, **S**...**gas:** Exxon, TA/Subway/dsl/24hr/@, **food:** Shoney's, **lodging:** Ramada Ltd, Stadium Inn, **other:** Titan Stadium, st capitol
47a	US 31E
47	N 1st St, Jefferson St, **N**...**gas:** Express/dsl, **S**...**gas:** Mystic Gas, **lodging:** Day's Inn, Knight's Inn, **other:** U-Haul
	I-24 and I-65 run together. See Interstate 65, exit 87ba.
44b a	I-65, N to Louisville, S to Nashville
43	TN 155, Briley Pkwy, Brick Church Pike
40	TN 45, Old Hickory Blvd, **N**...**gas:** Citgo/dsl, Shell/Subway/dsl, Phillips 66/dsl/24hr, **food:** Country Kitchen, Jack-in-the-Box(3mi), Hot Wings, **lodging:** Super 8
35	US 431, to Joelton, Springfield, **S**...**gas:** BP/Subway/dsl/24hr, Shell, **food:** Family Rest., Mazatlan Mexican, McDonald's, Subway, **lodging:** Day's Inn, **other:** Curves, Family$, OK Camping
31	TN 249, New Hope Rd, **N**...**gas:** Shell/Taco Tico, **S**...**gas:** BP/dsl, Citgo/dsl/24hr, **food:** Sullivan's Rest.
24	TN 49, to Springfield, Ashland City, **N**...**gas:** BP, Express/dsl/24hr, Phillips 66/dsl/24hr, **other:** HOSPITAL, **S**...**gas:** Horizon/Wendy's, Shell/dsl, **food:** Sonic, Subway, **other:** $General, Hill Foods
19	TN 256, Maxey Rd, to Adams, **N**...**gas:** BP/dsl, **S**...**gas:** Shell/deli/dsl/24hr
11	TN 76, to Adams, Clarksville, **N**...**gas:** Shell/dsl/24hr, **S**...**gas:** BP/dsl/24hr, Marathon, **food:** Don Poncho Mexican, Homeplace Rest., McDonald's, Waffle House, **lodging:** Comfort Inn, Day's Inn, Holiday Inn Express, Quality Inn, Super 8, **other:** HOSPITAL
9mm	Red River
8	TN 237, Rossview Rd, **S**...Dunbar Cave SP
4	US 79, to Clarksville, Ft Campbell, **N**...**gas:** BP/dsl/24hr, **food:** Cracker Barrel, **other:** Sam's Club/gas, Spring Creek Camping(2mi), Clarksville RV Ctr, **S**...**gas:** BP/dsl/24hr, Citgo/dsl, Shell/dsl, **food:** Applebee's, Arby's, Burger King, Capt D's,'s, Chuck-eCheese, Church's/White Castle, DQ, Golden Bowl Buffet, Golden Corral, Golden Rule BBQ, IHOP, KFC, Krystal, Logan's Roadhouse, LJ Silver, Longhorn Steaks, McDonald's, O'Charley's, Old Chicago Pizza, Olive Garden, Outback Steaks, Ponderosa, Quizno's, Rafferty's, Red Lobster, Ryan's, Shogun Japanese, Shoney's, Starbucks, Steak'n Shake, Taco Bell, Waffle House, Wendy's, **lodging:** Best Value, Best Western, Candlewood Suites, Comfort Inn, Country Inn Suites, Day's Inn, Econolodge, Guesthouse Inn, Hampton Inn, Holiday Inn, Microtel, Ramada Ltd, Red Roof Inn, Royal Inn, Super 8, Wingate Inn, **other:** HOSPITAL, Advance Parts, Belk, Best Buy, BooksAMillion, Borders Books, Goodyear/auto, Hancock Fab-

rics, JC Penny, Kohl's, K-Mart, Lowe's Whse, Office Depot, PetsMart, Sears/auto, Target, TJ Maxx, U-Haul, WalMart SuperCtr/gas/24hr, mall, winery, to Austin Peay St U, to Land Between the Lakes

1	TN 48, to Clarksville, Trenton, **N**...**gas:** Shell/dsl, **other:** Clarksville RV Camping, antiques, **S**...**gas:** BP, Mystic, **food:** Rib Dr. BBQ, Sonic, **other:** $General
.5mm	**Welcome Ctr eb, full(handicapped)facilities, phones, vending, picnic tables, litter barrels, petwalk**
0mm	Tennessee/Kentucky state line

Interstate 26

Exit #	Services	
46	to I-81	E
45	Eastern Star Rd, no services	
42	rd 75, to Bobby Hicks Pkwy, **N**...**gas:** Exxon/dsl, BP/dsl, **food:** Burger King, DQ, Papa John's, Pizza Hut, Taco Express, TCBY, McDonalds, Wendy's, other: Rite aid, $General, White's foods, **S**...**gas:** BP/dsl	
38	rd 354, to Boons Creek Rd, **N**...**food:** Bob Evans, **S**...**gas:** BP/24hr, Shell/dsl, food: Burger King, Cracker Barrel, El Matador Mexican, Kemosabee's Roadhouse, Wendy's, Waffle House, **lodging:** Jameson Inn	W
36	TN 381, to St of Franklin Rd, to Bristol, **N**...**gas:** BP/McDonald's, **food:** El Chico Mexican, Golden Corral, Logan's Roadhouse, Outback Steaks, Subway, **lodging:** Comfort Suites, **other:**, Radio Shack, WalMart Super Ctr/gas, **S**...**gas:** Exxon(2mi), **food:** Atlanta Bread Co., Carrabba's, Chick-fil-a, Chili's, China Chef, Fuddruckers, IHOP, Wendy's, **lodging:** Hampton Inn(2mi), Sleep Inn, **other:** Barnes&Noble, Best Buy, Circuit City, Home Depot, K-Mart, Lowe's Whse, Old Navy, Ross	
35	US 11 E, US 19 N, to Roan St, **N**...**gas:** Citgo, **food:** Harbor House Seafood, Hardee's, Perkins, Sonic, **lodging:** Best Western, Holiday Inn, Ramada Ltd, Super 8, **other:** Ford, **S**...**gas:** Sunoco, **food:** Hooters, McDonald's, Ryan's, Shoney's, Subway, TCBY, **lodging:** Day's Inn, Fairfield Inn, Red Roof Inn, **other:** Walgreen	
33	rd 400, Unaka Ave, Watauga Ave	
32	32 rd 91, Market St, **N**...**food:** DQ, McDonald's, **S**...**gas:** BP, **other:** museum	
31	31 US 321, TN 67, Elizabethton, **N**...**gas:** Shell/dsl, **food:** Schlotsky's, **S**...**gas:** BP/dsl, **food:** Arby's, Burger King, Jerry's Café, LJ Silver, **lodging:** Comfort Inn, Carnegie Hotel, **other:** Advance Parts, Food City, Kroger/24hr, E TN St Univ., Roan Mtn. SP	
28	rd 359 N, Okolona Rd, **N**...**gas:** BP, Exxon/dsl, lodging: Budget Inn	

TENNESSEE

Interstate 26

23	rd 173, Unicoi Rd, **N**...**gas:** Phillips 66, **food:** Maple Grove Café, **lodging:** Budget Inn(3mi), **other:** Grandview Camping(7mi), **S**...Woodsmoke Camping
21	Tinker Rd, no services
19	Tinker Rd, no services
19	Main St, Erwin, **N**...**gas:** BP/24hr, Exxon/dsl, **food:** Amigo Mexican, Backwoods BBQ, Hardee's, KFC, Pizza Hut, Wendy's
18	TN 81, rd 107, Erwin, Jonesboro, **N**...**gas:** Shell/dsl/24hr, **food:** Huddle House/24hr, McDonald's, Sonic, **other:** HOSPITAL, **S**...**food:** River's Edge Pizza, **lodging:** Super 8
15	Jackson-Love Hwy, Erwin, Jonesboro, **N**...**gas:** Appco Gas/A&W/LJ Silver, **lodging:** Best Southern Motel(1mi), Holiday Inn Express, **other:** Nolichucky Gorge Camping(2mi)
13mm	S Indian Creek
12	US 19 W, rd 352, Temple Hill Rd, **N**...**gas:** Exxon(2mi)
10mm	S Indian Creek
9	Clear Brach Rd, **N**...Acorn Ridge RV Park
7.5mm	Scenic Overlook wb (no trucks)
5	Flagpond Rd, no services
1mm	Scenic Overlook eb (no trucks)
.5mm	brake check area
0mm	Tennessee/North Carolina state line

Interstate 40

Exit #	Services
451mm	Tennessee/North Carolina state line
451	Waterville Rd, no services
226mm	truck sta
447	Hartford Rd, **N**...**gas:** Citgo/dsl, **S**...**gas:** BP/towing, **food:** Bean Trees Cafe, **other:** whitewater rafting
446mm	**Welcome Ctr wb, full(handicapped)facilities, phones, vending, picnic tables, litter barrels, petwalk, NO TRUCKS**
443	Foothills Pkwy, to Gatlinburg, Great Smoky Mtns NP, **S**...camping
443mm	Pigeon River
440	US 321, to Wilton Spgs Rd, Gatlinburg, **N**...**gas:** Sunoco/dsl/rest./repair, **S**...**gas:** BP, **other:** Arrow Creek Camping(14mi), CrazyHorse Camping(12mi), Jellystone Camping(12mi)
439mm	Pigeon River
435	US 321, to Gatlinburg, Newport, **N**...**gas:** Exxon/dsl/24hr, Shell, **food:** Arby's, Burger King, Hardee's, KFC, La Carreta Mexican, McDonald's, Pizza Hut, Pizza+, SageBrush Steaks, Shoney's, Subway, Taco Bell, **lodging:** Motel 6, Parkway Inn, **other:** HOSPITAL, Town&Country Drug, **S**...**gas:** BP/TCBY, **food:** Cracker Barrel, Papa John's, Quizno's, Ryan's, Ruby Tuesday, Waffle House/24hr, Wendy's, **lodging:** Best Western, Family Inn, Holiday Inn, **other:** $General, Goody's, Lowe's, Save-A-Lot, Wal-Mart SuperCtr/gas/24hr

432b a	US 70, US 411, US 25W, to Newport, **N**...**gas:** BP, Exxon/dsl/24hr, TimeOut Travel Ctr/Huddle House/dsl, Phillips 66, **food:** Lois' Country Kitchen, Sonic, **lodging:** Budget Motel, Comfort Inn, Relax Inn, **other:** Chevrolet/Pontiac/Buick, Chrysler/Jeep/Dodge, Ford/Mercury, KOA, TMC Camping, **S**...**gas:** BP, Citgo/24hr, Texaco/dsl, Shell, **lodging:** Family Inn/rest.
426mm	**rest area wb, full(handicapped)facilities, phone, vending, picnic tables, litter barrels, petwalk**
425mm	French Broad River
424	TN 113, Dandridge, **N**...**gas:** BP/dsl
421	I-81 N, to Bristol
420mm	**rest area eb, full(handicapped)facilities, phone, vending, picnic tables, litter barrels, petwalk**
417	TN 92, Dandridge, **N**...**gas:** BP, Pilot/Subway/dsl/scales/24hr/@, **food:** Capt's Galley, Hardee's, McDonald's, Perkins, Ruby Tuesday, **lodging:** Econolodge, **S**...**gas:** Shell/Wendy's/dsl, Texaco/KFC/dsl, **food:** Shoney's, Waffle House, **lodging:** Comfort Inn, Holiday Inn Express, Jefferson Inn, Super 8, **other:** Advance Parts
415	US 25W, US 70, to Dandridge, **S**...**gas**, **food:** Sonic(3mi)
412	Deep Sprgs Rd, to Douglas Dam, **N**...**gas:** Love's/Chester Fried/Subway/dsl, **S**...**gas:** TR Trkstp/Chevron/dsl/rest/scales/24hr
407	TN 66, to Sevierville, Pigeon Forge, Gatlinburg, **N**...**gas:** Citgo/Huddle House/dsl, **food:** Chophouse, Cracker Barrel, McDonald's, **lodging:** Motel 6, **other:** Bass Pro Shops, KOA, **S**...**gas:** BP/DQ, Exxon/Subway/dsl, Shell/Krystal/dsl, **food:** FlapJack's, Wendy's, **lodging:** Best Western, Comfort Inn, Day's Inn, Ramada Ltd, **other:** Russel Stover, RV Camping, TN RV Ctr, USPO, flea mkt, **3-10 mi S**...multiple services/outlets
402	Midway Rd, no services
398	Strawberry Plains Pk, , **N**...**gas:** BP/dsl, Exxon/Pizza Hut/dsl, Shell, **food:** McDonald's, Outback Steaks, Ruby Tuesday, Waffle House, Wendy's, **lodging:** Comfort Inn, Country Inn&Suites, Econolodge, Hampton Inn, Holiday Inn Express, Ramada Ltd, Super 8, **other:** TN RV Camping World, **S**...**gas:** Pilot/Subway/dsl/scales/24hr/@, Weigel's, **food:** Arby's, Burger King, Cracker Barrel, Golden Wok Chinese, KFC, Krystal, Puleo's Grille, Taco Bell, **lodging:** Best Western, Fairfield Inn, La Quinta, Motel 6
395mm	Holston River
394	US 70, US 11E, US 25W, Asheville Hwy, **N**...**gas:** Mobil/dsl, RaceWay, **food:** Subway, Wendy's, **lodging:** Gateway(1mi), Sunbeam Motel(2mi), **other:** Advance Parts, $General, Food Lion, city park, **S**...**gas:** Exxon, Shell/dsl, **food:** Waffle House/24hr, **lodging:** Day's Inn, **other:** Kroger/gas
393	I-640 W, to I-75 N
392	US 11W, Rutledge Pike, **N**...**gas:** Shell/dsl, **other:** $General, U-Haul, repair, **S**...**gas:** BP, **food:** Buddy's BBQ, Hardee's, Shoney's, **lodging:** Family Inn, **other:** NAPA, Sav-a-Lot Foods, transmissions, to Knoxville Zoo
390	Cherry St, Knoxville, **N**...**gas:** Marathon/dsl, Weigel's, Subway, **food:** Happy Garden Chinese, **lodging:** Red Carpet Inn, **other:** Goodyear, **1 mi S**...**gas:** Exxon, **food:** Arby's, KFC, McDonald's, Subway, Taco bell, Wendy's, WishBone's Wings, **lodging:** Regency Inn, **other:** Advance Parts, Family$, O'Reilly Parts, Walgreens

Interstate 40

389 US 441 N, Broadway, 5th Ave, **1/2 mi** N...**gas:** BP, Conoco, Star, **food:** Burger King, Capt D's, KFC, Krystal, SteakOut, Subway, Taco Bell, Wendy's, **other:** CVS Drug, $General, Family$, Firestone, Kroger/deli/24hr, Radio Shack, Tires+, USPO, Walgreens/24hr, transmissions

388 US 441 S(exits left from wb), downtown, S...**lodging:** Hilton, Holiday Inn, Krowne Plaza, **other:** to Smokey Mtns, to U of TN

387b TN 62, 17th St, N...**gas:** Pilot/dsl, **lodging:** Best Inn, **other:** $General

387a I-275 N, to Lexington

386b a US 129, University Ave, to UT, airport

385 I-75 N, I-640 E

I-40 W and I-75 S run together 17 mi.

383 Peppermill Rd, N...**lodging:** Holiday Inn/rest., S...**gas:** BP, Pilot/dsl, **food:** Burger King, Longhorn Steaks, McDonald's, Mexicali Rose, Pizza Hut, Red Lobster, Ruby Tuesday, Sonic, Taco Bell, Taco Rancho Mexican, TGI Friday, Waffle House, Wendy's, **lodging:** Econolodge, Howard Johnson, Super 8, **other:** Buick/GMC, Firestone, same as 380

380 US 11, US 70, West Hills, S...**gas:** BP, Shell, Weigel's, **food:** Arby's, Applebee's, Backyard Burger, Blackeyed Pea, Cancun Mexican, Checker's, Chick-fil-A, Chili's, Cozymel's Grill, Hardee's, KFC, Macaroni Grill, Michael's Prime Rib, Mr Gatti's, O'Charley's, Olive Garden, Papa John's, PF Chang's, Sawyer's Cafe, Subway, Taco Bell, Texas Roadhouse, **lodging:** Comfort Hotel, Howard Johnson, Quality Inn, **other:** Belk, BiLo Foods, Borders Books, Dillard's, $General, Food City, Goody's, JC Penney, K-Mart, Kohl's, NTB, Office Depot, Old Navy, O'Reilly Parts, Sears, Staples, U-Haul, Walgreens, mall, st patrol

379 Bridgewater Rd, N...**gas:** Exxon/Subway, Pilot/McDonald's/dsl, **food:** Pizza Hut/Taco Bell, **lodging:** Red Carpet Inn, Sleep Inn, **other:** Sam's Club, Wal-Mart SuperCtr/24hr, S...**gas:** BP/dsl, Pilot/dsl, Texaco/dsl, **food:** Burger King, ChuckeCheese, Don Pablo, Logan's Roadhouse, Mrs Winners, Old Country Buffet, Omelet House, Ryan's, Shoney's, Tony Roma, Wendy's, **lodging:** Family Inn, Holiday Inn, Scottish Inn, **other:** AutoZone, BooksAMillion, Buy4Less Foods, Cadillac, Firestone/auto, Ford, Dodge, GMC, Goodyear, Isuzu, Mitsubishi, Nissan, SuperX Drug

378 Cedar Bluff Rd, N...**gas:** Pilot/Taco Bell, Shell, Weigel's, **food:** Arby's, Burger King, Cracker Barrel, KFC, McDonald's, Papa John's, Quizno's, Starbucks, Subway, Waffle House, Wendy's, **lodging:** Budget Inn, Econolodge, Hampton Inn, Holiday Inn, Ramada Inn, Sleep Inn, **other:** HOSPITAL, $General, Food City, Walgreens, S...**gas:** Exxon, **food:** Applebee's, Cancun Mexican, Carrabba's, Corky's Ribs/BBQ, Denny's, Famous Dave's, Fazoli's, Hops Grill, IHOP, Outback Steaks, Peerless Rest., Puleo's Cafe, Sonny's BBQ, **lodging:** Best Western, Clubhouse Inn, Comfort Inn, Courtyard, Extended Stay America, Guesthouse Suites, La Quinta, Microtel, Red Roof Inn, Residence Inn, **other:** Best Buy, Celebration Sta, Chevrolet, Chrysler, Circuit City,

Ford, Jo-Ann Fabrics, Kia, Lowe's Whse, Michael's, Saturn, Staples, Volvo, Walgreens

376 I-140 E, TN 162 N, to Maryville, N...to Oak Ridge Museum

374 RD 131, Lovell Rd, N...**gas:** Texaco/dsl, TA/dsl/rest./24hr/scales/@, **food:** McDonald's, Taco Bell, Waffle House, **lodging:** Best Western, Travelodge, Vista Inn, **other:** Harley-Davidson, Passport RV Ctr, S...**gas:** Citgo, Pilot/Wendy's/dsl/scales/24hr, **food:** Arby's, Carino's Italian, Chili's, Connor's Rest., Krystal, McDonald's, Mimi's Cafe, Ruby Tuesday, Shoney's, Wasabi Japanese, **lodging:** Candlewood Suites, Day's Inn/rest., Homewood Suites, Motel 6, SpringHill Suites, **other:** Belk, BMW, CarMax, Goody's, Honda, Land Rover, Lexus, Mercedes, Super Target, Toyota, Wal-Mart SuperCtr/24hr

373 Campbell Sta Rd, N...**gas:** Marathon/dsl, Shell/dsl, **lodging:** Comfort Suites, Country Inn&Suites, Super 8, **other:** Buddy Gregg RV Ctr, S...**gas:** BP, Pilot/dsl, Weigel's, **food:** Cracker Barrel, Hardee's, Silver Spoon Grill, Wendy's, Yellow Mushroom, **lodging:** Baymont Inn, Holiday Inn Express, **other:** Gander Mtn, Walgreens

372mm weigh sta both lanes

369 Watt Rd, N...**gas:** Flying J/Conoco/dsl/LP/24hr/@, Speedco, **other:** Freightliner, S...**gas:** Petro/Exxon/dsl/24hr/@, TA/BP/Burger King/Perkins/Pizza Hut/dsl/24hr/@, **other:** Blue Beacon

I-40 E and I-75 N run together 17 mi.

368 I-75 and I-40

364 US 321, TN 95, Lenoir City, Oak Ridge, N...**gas:** Melton Hill Mkt/gas, **other:** Crosseyed Cricket Camping(2mi), **4-5 mi** S...**food:** KFC, Krystal, Ruby Tuesday, **lodging:** Comfort Inn, Days Inn, Econolodge, Ramada Ltd

363mm parking area wb, phone, litter barrel

361mm new exit

360 Buttermilk Rd, N...Soaring Eagle RV Park

356 TN 58 N, Gallaher Rd, to Oak Ridge, N...**gas:** BP/dsl, Weigels/dsl, **food:** Huddle House, **lodging:** Day's Inn, Kingston Inn, **other:** 4 Seasons Camping, S...**gas:** Citgo/dsl(1mi)

355 Lawnville Rd, N...**gas:** Pilot/dsl

352 TN 58 S, Kingston, N...**lodging:** Knight's Inn, **other:** NAPA, S...**gas:** Exxon/dsl, RaceWay, Shell, **food:** Hardee's, McDonald's, Pizza Hut, Sonic, Subway, Taco Bell, **lodging:** Comfort Inn, **other:** Family$, Marina RV Park, to Watts Bar Lake, Piggly Wiggly, USPO

351mm Clinch River

350 US 70, Midtown, S...**other:** Kroger/Starbucks, Lowe's Whse, Patterson RV Supplies, Walgreen

Interstate 40

E ↑ ↓ W

Harriman

347	US 27, Harriman, **N...gas:** Phillips 66/Subway/dsl, Shell, **food:** Hardee's, KFC, Los Primos Mexican, LJ Silver, McDonald's, Pizza Hut, Ruby Tuesday, Taco Bell, Wendy's, **lodging:** Best Western, **other:** to Frozen Head SP, Big S Fork NRA, **S...gas:** BP, Exxon, Shell/Krystal/dsl/24hr, **food:** Cancun Mexican, Cracker Barrel, Shoney's, **lodging:** Caney Creek Inn, Holiday Inn Express, Super 8, **2-3 mi S...food:** Capt D's, Domino's, Sonic, **other:** HOSPITAL, Goody's, Radio Shack, Wal-Mart SuperCtr/gas/24hr
340	TN 299 N, Airport Rd
339.5mm	eastern/central time zone line
338	TN 299 S, Westel Rd, **N...gas:** BP/dsl, **S...gas:** Shell/dsl, **other:** Lighthouse RV Park
336mm	parking area/weigh sta eb, litter barrel
329	US 70, Crab Orchard, **N...gas:** BP/dsl, Liberty/dsl, **other:** KOA(4mi), **S...other:** Cumberland Trails SP, Wilson SP
327mm	**rest area wb, full(handicapped)facilities, phone, picnic tables, litter barrels, petwalk, vending**
324mm	**rest area eb, full(handicapped)facilities, phone, picnic tables, litter barrels, petwalk, vending**
322	TN 101, Peavine Rd, Crossville, **N...gas:** BP/Bean Pot Rest., Exxon/dsl, Phillips 66, **food:** Hardee's, McDonald's, **lodging:** Holiday Inn Express, **other:** Deer Run Resort, KOA Camping, Roam-Roost RV Campground, to Fairfield Glade Resort, **S...gas:** Texaco/dsl, **food:** Cancun Mexican, Taco Bell, **lodging:** Comfort Suites, Super 8, **other:** HOSPITAL, Tennessee RV Ctr, Cumberland Mtn SP

Crossville

320	TN 298, Crossville, **N...**antiques, golf, winery, **S...gas:** BP/DQ/Pizza Hut/dsl, Shell/24hr, **food:** Big Boy's BBQ, Genesis Grill, Krystal(2mi), Wendy's(2mi), **other:** HOSPITAL, Factory Outlet/famous brands, Save-A-Lot Foods, antiques, auto repair
318mm	Obed River
317	US 127, Crossville, **N...gas:** BP/dsl, Exxon/Subway/dsl/24hr, Horizon, Shell/dsl, **food:** Huddle House, Shoneys, **lodging:** Best Western, La Quinta, Ramada Inn, **0-2 mi S...gas:** BP, Chevron, Citgo, Jiffy Gas, Phillips 66/dsl, Sunoco, **food:** Arby's, Burger King, Cancun Mexican, Cracker Barrel, Dickie's BBQ, La Costa Mexican, McDonalds, Papa Johns, Ruby Tuesday, Ryan's, Sonic, Taco Bell, TCBY, Vegas Steaks, Waffle House, Zaxby's, **lodging:** Best Value, Days Inn, Heritage Inn, **other:** HOSPITAL, Chevrolet/Cadillac/Buick/Pontiac/GMC, Chrysler/Dodge/Jeep, $Tree, GNC, Goodys, Lowe's Whse, Staples, Wal-Mart SuperCtr/gas, Walgreen, tires, to Cumberland SP
311	Plateau Rd, **N...gas:** Citgo/dsl, **food:** Papa Lorenzo's Pizza, **S...gas:** BP/dsl, Exxon
306mm	parking area/weigh sta wb, litter barrels
301	US 70 N, TN 84, Monterey, **N...gas:** Phillips 66, Shell, **food:** Burger King, Cup N' Saucer Rest., DQ, Subway
300	US 70, Monterey, **N...gas:** Citgo/dsl, **food:** Hardee's
291mm	Falling Water River

Cookeville

290	US 70, Cookeville, **N...gas:** BP(1mi), **S...gas:** Citgo, **lodging:** Alpine Suites
288	TN 111, to Livingston, Cookeville, Sparta, **N...**Cordell SP, **S...gas:** Citgo/dsl, Mid Tenn Trkstp/Phillips 66/Subway/dsl/24hr/@, **food:** Huddle House, **lodging:** Knight's Inn
287	TN 136, Cookeville, **N...gas:** BP/TCBY, Chevron/dsl, Citgo, Exxon, Shell/dsl, **food:** Applebee's, Arby's, Burger King, Capt D's, Cheddars, Chick-fil-A, Chili's, China Star, Cracker Barrel, DQ, Fazoli's, Golden Corral, IHOP, Jack-in-the-Box, King Buffet, Krystal, LJ Silver, Logan's Roadhouse, Longhorn Steaks, McDonald's, Mr Gatti's, New China, Nick's Rest., O'Charley's, Outback Steaks, Pizza Hut, Puleo's Grill, Quizno's, Red Lobster, Ryan's, Shoney's, Sonic, Steak'n Shake, Subway, Taco Bell, Waffle House, Wendy's, **lodging:** Best Value, Best Western, Comfort Inn, Comfort Suites, Day's Inn, Garden Hotel, Hampton Inn, Super 8, **other:** Auto Value Parts, BigLots, Cadillac/Honda, CVS Drug, $Tree, Firestone/auto, Goody's, Harley-Davidson, JC Penney, Kroger/gas, Lowe's Whse, Radio Shack, Toyota, U-haul, Wal-Mart SuperCtr/gas, mall, st patrol, transmissions, **S...gas:** Exxon/dsl, Marathon/dsl, Pilot/dsl, **food:** CJ's Wings, KFC, Waffle House, **lodging:** Baymont Inn, Country Hearth Inn, Country Inn Suites, Holiday Inn Express, **other:** Dodge, Sam's Club/gas
286	TN 135, Burgess Falls Rd, **N...gas:** BP, Exxon, RaceWay/dsl, Shell/dsl, **food:** Applebee's, Arby's, Chick-fil-A, El Palenque Mexican, Hardee's, Steak'n Shake, Thai Cuisine, Toot's, Waffle House, **lodging:** Key-West Inn, **other:** HOSPITAL, Chrysler/Jeep, GMC, Goodyear, Kia/Mitsubishi, Mazda, Middle TN RV Ctr, Nissan, Toyota, U-Haul, to TTU, **S...gas:** Citgo/dsl, **lodging:** Star Motor Inn/rest.
280	TN 56 N, Baxter, **N...gas:** Loves/McDonalds/Subway/dsl/24hr, Shell/dsl(1mi), **food:** Wagonwheel Rest.(1mi), **other:** Camp Discovery(2mi), Twin Lakes RV Park(2mi)
276	Old Baxter Rd, **S...gas:** Citgo/dsl, **other:** fireworks
273	TN 56 S, to Smithville, **S...gas:** BP/dsl, Phillips 66, **food:** Rose Garden Rest., **lodging:** Lakeside Inn, Timber Ridge Inn
268	TN 96, Buffalo Valley Rd, **S...**to Edgar Evins SP
267mm	Caney Fork River
267mm	**rest area both lanes, full(handicapped)facilities, info, phone, picnic tables, litter barrels, petwalk, vending**
266mm	Caney Fork River
263mm	Caney Fork River
258	TN 53, Gordonsville, **N...gas:** Exxon/KFC/Taco Bell, Shell/dsl, **food:** McDonald's, Timberloft Café, Waffle House, **lodging:** Comfort Inn, **other:** to Cordell Hull Dam, **S...gas:** KeyStop/dsl, **food:** Cornerstone Cafe, **other:** $General
254	TN 141, to Alexandria, no services
252mm	parking area/weigh sta both lanes, picnic tables, litter barrels
245	Linwood Rd, **N...gas:** BP/dsl
239	US 70, Lebanon, **N...gas:** Citgo/dsl, RaceWay, **S...gas:** Phillips 66/Uncle Pete's/dsl/rest/scales

Interstate 40

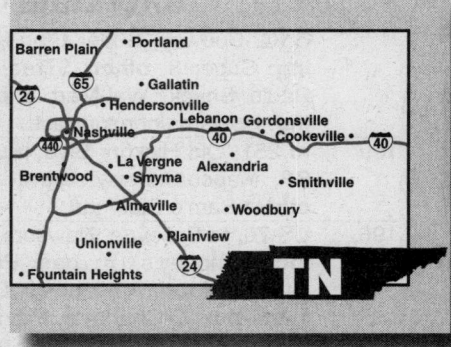

238	US 231, Lebanon, ...**gas:** Exxon, Mapco, Shell, **food:** Applebee's, Arby's, Cici's Pizza, Cracker Barrel, Demo's Steaks, Hardee's, Jack-in-the-Box, KFC, King Buffet, McDonald's, Mrs Winner's, Pizza Hut, Ponderosa, Ryan's, Shoney's, Subway, Taco Bell, Waffle House, Wendy's, White Castle, Zaxby's **lodging:** Best Value, Best Western, Comfort Inn, Executive Inn, Hampton Inn, Holiday Inn Express, **other:** HOSPITAL, Aldi Foods, $Tree, Goody's, Lowe's Whse, Wal-Mart SuperCtr/24hr, ...**gas:** Citgo/dsl, Pilot/Subway/dsl/24hr/scales, **food:** O'Charley's, Sonic, **lodging:** Comfort Suites, Country Inn Suites, Day's Inn, Knight's Inn, Super 8, **other:** Prime Outlets/famous brands, flea mkt, to Cedars of Lebanon SP, RV camping
236	S Hartmann Dr, ...**gas:** Mapco, Shell, **food:** Chili's, Outback Steaks, **other:** HOSPITAL, Home Depot, **2mi** ...**food:** Ruby Tuesday
235	TN 840 W, to Murfreesboro, no services
232	TN 109, to Gallatin, ...**gas:** Citgo, Mapco, Shell/McDonald's/dsl/24hr, **food:** Bellacino's Pizza, Brewster's Grille, Sonic, Subway, Waffle House, Wendy's, **lodging:** Sleep Inn, Value Place Inn, **2 mi** ...**other:** Countryside Resort Camping
229	new exit
226mm	truck sta, eb only
226	TN 171, Mt Juliet Rd, ...**gas:** BP/McDonald's/dsl, Citgo, Exxon/dsl, Mapco/dsl, Shell/dsl/24hr, **food:** Arby's, Capt D's, ...**gas:** Mapco/dsl, **food:** Chick-fil-A, Cracker Barrel, Logan's Roadhouse, O'Charly's, Olive Garden, Panera Bread, Red Robin, Ruby Tuesday, Steak&Shake, Taco Bell, Waffle House, **lodging:** Hampton Inn, Microtel, Quality Inn, **other:** Belk, Best Buy, BooksAMillion, Curves, JC Penny, JoAnne Fabrics, Kroger, Old Navy, PetsMart, Ross, Target, TJ Maxx, to Long Hunter SP
221	TN 45 N, Old Hickory Blvd, to The Hermitage, ...**gas:** Express/dsl, RaceWay, Shell/24hr, **food:** Applebee's, DQ, IHOP, Jack-in-the-Box, O'Charley's, Outback, Subway, Taki Japanese, Waffle House, **lodging:** Best Inn, Comfort Inn, Motel 6, Suburban Lodge, Super 8, Vista Hotel, **other:** HOSPITAL, CVS Drug, Kroger, Walgreen, ...**gas:** Phillips 66/White Castle, Shell/McDonald's, Texaco
219	Stewart's Ferry Pike, ...**gas:** Mapco, ...**gas:** Mapco, Shell/dsl, **food:** China King, Cracker Barrel, Hacienda Mexican, Sal's Pizza, Waffle House, **lodging:** Best Value Inn, Best Western, Country Inn Suites, Day's Inn, Family Inn, Sleep Inn, **other:** $General, FoodLion, vet
216	(216 c from eb)TN 255, Donaldson Pk, ...**gas:** BP/dsl, Citgo, Mapco, RaceWay, Shell/Subway/dsl/24hr, **food:** Arby's, Backyard Burger, BBQ, Burger King, Darfon's, Domino's, Don Chile's, KFC, McDonald's, New China, Papa John's, Pizza Hut/Taco Bell, Ruby Tuesday, Shoney's, Subway, Waffle House, Wendy's, **lodging:** Country Inn Suites, Drury Inn, Fairfield Inn, Hampton Inn, Holiday Inn Express, La Quinta, Radisson, Springhill Suites, Super 8, Wingate Inn, **other:** Advance Parts, K-Mart, Walgreens
216b a	(from eb), ...Nashville Intn'l Airport
215b a	TN 155, Briley Pkwy, to Opryland, **on Elm Hill...gas:** Citgo, Mapco, **food:** Jack-in-the-Box, Waffle House, **lodging:** Alexis Inn, Comfort Suites, Courtyard, Embassy Suites, Extended Stay, Hampton Inn, Hilton Garden, Holiday Inn Select, Homestead Suites, Hotel Preston, La Quinta, Marriott, Residence Inn, Studio+, **2 mi** **on Lebanon Pike...food:** Capt D's, **other:** to Camping World RV Service, KOA, ...**gas:** Phillips 66, **food:** Mazatlan Mexican, Panda House, Subway, **lodging:** Hotel Preston
213b	I-24 W
213a	I-24 E/I-440, E to Chattanooga
213	US 41(from wb no return), to Spence Lane, ...**other:** Kenworth, ...**gas:** Shell, Texaco, **food:** Denny's, Waffle House, **lodging:** Day's Inn, Holiday Inn Express, Rodeway Inn, Sunrise Inn, Super 8, same as 212
212	Fessler's Lane(from eb, no return), ...**other:** Freightliner, Harley-Davidson, ...**gas:** Express/dsl, Shell/dsl, **food:** Burger King, Krystal, McDonald's, Mrs Winners, Sonic, Wendy's, **lodging:** Best Value, same as 213
211mm	Cumberland River
211b	I-24 W
211a	I-24E, I-40 W
210c	US 31 S, US 41A, 2nd Ave, 4th Ave, ...**lodging:** Stouffer Hotel, ...museum
210b a	I-65 S, to Birmingham
209b a	US 70 S, Charlotte Ave, Nashville, ...**gas:** Exxon, **food:** McDonald's, **lodging:** Sheraton, **other:** Chrysler, Nissan, Country Music Hall of Fame, Conv Ctr, transmissions, ...**gas:** Exxon, **food:** Burger King, Subway, White Castle, **lodging:** Comfort Inn, Guesthouse Inn, **other:** Chevrolet, Lincoln/Mercury, Pontiac/GMC, Subaru, Toyota
208b a	I-65, N to Louisville, S to Birmingham
207	28th Ave, Jefferson St, Nashville, TN St U, ...**gas:** Citgo, Phillips 66, **food:** Subway, Wendy's, **other:** Family$, ...HOSPITAL
206	I-440 E, to Knoxville
205	46th Ave, W Nashville, ...Harley-Davidson, ...**gas:** Mapco, Shell, **food:** McDonald's
204	TN 155, Briley Pkwy, ...**gas:** Exxon, Shell/dsl, ...**food:** Burger King, Church's/White Castle, 5 De Maio, Domino's, Jack-in-the-Box, KFC, Krystal, New China, Papa John's, Shoney's, Uncle Bud's Catfish, Waffle House, Wendy's, **lodging:** Baymont Inn, Best Western, Comfort Inn, Days Inn, **other:** AutoZone, CVS Drug, Ford, Goodyear/auto, Kroger, NTB, Pep-Boys, Walgreen
201b a	US 70, Charlotte Pike, ...**gas:** Exxon, Shell/dsl/24hr, **food:** Bojangles, Cracker Barrel, Krystal, Nick's

Lebanon

Nashville

Nashville

TENNESSEE
Interstate 40

E
↑
↓
W

D i c k s o n

	BBQ, Subway, Super China, Waffle House, **lodging:** Super 8, **other:** $Tree, GNC, Lowe's Whse, Radio Shack, Wal-Mart SuperCtr/24hr, **S...lodging:** Howard Johnson/rest.
199	rd 251, Old Hickory Blvd, **N...gas:** Shell, **S...gas:** BP, Mapco/Subway, **food:** Sonic, Waffle House, **other:** Sam's Club/gas
196	US 70, to Bellevue, Newsom Sta, **N...gas:** Mapco, **food:** Shoney's, **S...gas:** BP, Express/dsl, Shell/dsl/24hr, **food:** Applebee's, Champions Grill, Jack-in-the-Box, O'Charley's, Pizza Hut, Quizno's, Ruby Tuesday, Sir Pizza, Sonic, Subway, Taco Bell, Waffle House, Wendy's, **lodging:** Hampton Inn, Microtel, **other:** Circuit City, Dillard's, $Tree, Firestone/auto, Home Depot, Michael's, Old Navy, Piggly Wiggly, Publix, Staples, USPO, Walgreen/24hr, mall
195mm	Harpeth River
192	McCrory Lane, to Pegram, **N...gas:** Eddie's Mkt, **4 mi S...** Loveless Cafe, Natchez Trace Pkwy
190mm	Harpeth River
188mm	Harpeth River
188	rd 249, Kingston Springs, **N...gas:** BP, Mapco/Blimpie/dsl, Shell/Arby's, **food:** McDonald's, Sonic, **lodging:** Best Western, Econolodge, Relax Inn, Scottish Inn, **other:** Curves, USPO, **S...gas:** Petro/Chevron/Pizza Hut/Quick Skillet/dsl/showers/24hr/@
182	TN 96, to Dickson, Fairview, **N...gas:** BP, Express, **lodging:** Deerfield Inn, Fairview Inn, **other:** M Bell SP(16mi), **S...gas:** /Flying J/Conoco/Country Mkt/dsl/LP/24hr/@, Horizon/Backyard Burger/dsl
175	TN 840, no services
172	TN 46, to Dickson, **N...gas:** BP/dsl/24hr, Citgo, Pilot/Wendy's/dsl/24hr/@, Shell, **food:** Arby's, Burger King, Cracker Barrel, McDonald's, Ruby Tuesday, Subway, Waffle House/24hr, Wang's China, **lodging:** Baymont Inn, Best Value, Comfort Inn, Econolodge, Hampton Inn, Knight's Inn, Motel 6, Ramada Ltd, Super 8, **other:** HOSPITAL, Chevrolet, Dickson RV Park, to M Bell SP, **S...gas:** Phillips 66, Shell, O'Charley's, **lodging:** Day's Inn, Holiday Inn
170	**rest area both lanes, full(handicapped)facilities, phone, picnic tables, litter barrels, vending, pet-walk**
166mm	Piney River
163	rd 48, to Dickson, **N...gas:** Phillips 66/Reed's/dsl, **S...gas:** Shell, **other:** Tanbark Camping
152	rd 230, Bucksnort, **N...gas:** Citgo, **food:** Rudy's Rest., **lodging:** Travel Inn
149mm	Duck River
148	rd 50, Barren Hollow Rd, to Turney Center
143	TN 13, to Linden, Waverly, **N...gas:** Pilot/Arby's/dsl/24hr/@, Phillips 66, Shell, **food:** Log Cabin Rest., Loretta's Kitchen, McDonald's, **lodging:** Best Western, Day's Inn, Holiday Inn Express, Super 8, **other:** KOA, **S...gas:** Exxon/dsl, Texaco, **lodging:** Southside Motel/rest.
141mm	Buffalo River
137	Cuba Landing, **N...other:** TN River RV Park, **S...food:** Cuba Landing Rest./gas

J a c k s o n

133mm	Tennessee River
133	rd 191, Birdsong Rd, **N...lodging:** Lakeside RV Resort/marina(9mi), **S...**Good Sam RV Park
131mm	**rest area both lanes, full(handicapped)facilities, phone, vending, picnic tables, litter barrels, pet-walk**
126	US 641, TN 69, to Camden, **N...gas:** Exxon/Subway/TCBY/dsl, Phillips 66/North 40/dsl/rest./@, Shell/dsl, **other:** tire/truck repair, to NB Forrest SP, **S...gas:** BP/dsl, Shell/dsl, **lodging:** Day's Inn/rest., **other:** HOSPITAL
116	rd 114, **S...other:** to Natchez Trace SP, RV camping
110mm	Big Sandy River
108	TN 22, to Lexington, Parkers Crossroads, **N...gas:** BP/McDonald's/24hr, Citgo/dsl/24hr, Phillips 66/dsl, **food:** Bailey's Rest., Dairy Queen, Subway, **lodging:** Knight's Inn, **other:** USPO, city park, **S...gas:** Exxon, **food:** Cotton Patch Rest., **lodging:** Best Western, **other:** HOSPITAL, RV camping, to Shiloh Nat Bfd(51mi)
103mm	parking area/weigh sta eb, litter barrels, phone
102mm	parking area/weigh sta wb, litter barrels
101	rd 104, **N...gas:** Exxon, Conoco/101 TP/rest/24hr/@, **other:** golf(3mi)
93	rd 152, Law Rd, **N...gas:** Phillips 66/dsl/deli/24hr, **S...gas:** BP/dsl
87	US 70, US 412, Jackson, **N...gas:** Coastal/dsl, **S...gas:** BP/dsl, Love's/Hardee's/dsl/24hr/@
85	Christmasville Rd, to Jackson, **N...gas:** BP/Subs-n-More/dsl, Exxon/dsl/24hr, **lodging:** Howard Johnson Express, **other:** $General, **S...gas:** Shell(1mi)
83	Campbell st, **N...gas:** Exxon/dsl **S...lodging:** Hampton Inn
82b a	US 45, Jackson, **N...gas:** BP, Exxon, **food:** Cracker Barrel, **lodging:** Knight's Inn, Microtel, **other:** Batteries+, Smallwoods RV Ctr(4mi) **S...gas:** BP, Citgo, Exxon, RaceWay, **food:** Backyard Burger, Barley's Cafe, Burger King, Capt D's, China Palace, DQ, Folks Rest., KFC, Krystal, LJ Silver, McDonald's, Pizza Hut, Pizza Inn, Popeye's, Shoney's, Sonic, Subway, Suede's Rest., Taco Bell, Waffle House, Wendy's, **lodging:** Baymont Inn, Executive Inn, Old English Inn, Ramada Ltd, Sheraton/rest., Super 8, Traveler's Mtl, **other:** Advance Parts, AutoZone, Belk, CarQuest, Firestone/auto, Goodyear/auto, Fred's Drug, JC Penney, Kroger/24hr, Macy's, Office Depot, Radio Shack, Sears/auto, WaldenBooks, mall
80b a	US 45 Byp, Jackson, **N...gas:** BP/dsl, Exxon, **food:** Backyard Burger, Baskin-Robbins, Buffalo Wings, Chili's, Chick-fil-A, China Pan, Corky's BBQ, Domino's, Fazoli's, IHOP, Jason's Deli, KFC, Lenny's Subs, Moe's SW Grill, LoneStar Steaks, Longhorn Steaks, Olive Garden, Peking Chinese, Perkins, Picasso Pizza, Schlotsky's, Starbucks, Steak'n Shake, TGI Friday, Wendy's, **lodging:** AmeriHost, Comfort Inn, Country Inn Suites, Jameson Inn, Red Roof Inn, **other:** Best Buy, Home Depot, Kohl's, Lowe's Whse, Marshalls, Nissan, Ross, Sam's Club/gas, Saturn, Wal-Mart SuperCtr/gas/24hr, **1 mi N on 45 BP...gas:** Exxon, **food:** Arby's, Burger King, LJ Silver, McDon-

Interstate 40

ald's, Outback, **other** Steinmart, **S**...**gas:** BP/Circle K, Citgo, Coastal/dsl, Phillips 66/dsl, 76, **food:** Arby's, Barnhill's Buffet, Burger King, Dunkin Donuts, El Chico's, Logan's Roadhouse, McDonald's, Mrs Winner's, O'Charley's, Pizza Hut, Sonic, Subway, Tuesday Morning, Village Pizza, Waffle House, **lodging:** Best Western, Comfort Inn, Day's Inn, DoubleTree, Econolodge, Fairfield Inn, Holiday Inn, Motel 6, Old Hickory Inn, **other:** HOSPITAL, Cadillac/Pontiac/Buick/Toyota, $General, Hancock Fabrics, Harley-Davidson, King Tires, K-Mart, to Pinson Mounds SP, Chickasaw SP

79	US 412, Jackson, **S**...**gas:** Citgo/dsl, Exxon, Horizon TP, **food:** CG's Rest., **lodging:** Day's Inn, **other:** Jackson RV Park
78mm	Forked Deer River
76	rd 223 S, **S**...**other:** McKellar-Sites Airport, Whispering Pines RV Park
74	Lower Brownsville Rd, no services
73mm	**rest area both lanes, full(handicapped)facilities, info, phone, picnic tables, litter barrels, vending, petwalk**
68	rd 138, Providence Rd, **N**...**gas:** BP/dsl, **lodging:** Scottish Inn, **S**...**gas:** TA/Citgo/Subway/dsl/rest./24hr/@, **other:** Joy-O RV Park, truck repair
66	US 70, to Brownsville, **S**...**gas:** FuelMart/dsl/24hr, **lodging:** Motel 6
60	rd 19, Mercer Rd, no services
56	TN 76, to Brownsville, **N**...**gas:** BP, Citgo/Subway/dsl/24hr, **food:** DQ, KFC, McDonald's, Pizza Hut/Taco Bell, **lodging:** Best Western, Comfort Inn, Day's Inn, Hotel O'Bannon, **S**...**gas:** BP/dsl, Exxon/Huddle House/dsl/24hr
55mm	Hatchie River
52	TN 76, rd 179, Koko Rd, to Whiteville
50mm	weigh sta both lanes, phone
47	TN 179, to Stanton, Dancyville, **S**...**gas:** Exit 47 Trkstp/dsl/rest./24hr/@
42	TN 222, to Stanton, **N**...**lodging:** Countryside Inn, **S**...**gas:** Exxon/dsl, Pilot/Chester's/Subway/dsl/@, **lodging:** Deerfield Inn
35	TN 59, to Somerville, **S**...**gas:** BP/dsl, **food:** Longtown Rest.
29.5mm	Loosahatchie River
25	TN 205, Airline Rd, to Arlington, **N**...**gas:** Exxon/Subway/dsl, Shell/Chester's/dsl, **S**...**gas:** Horizon/Backyard Burger/dsl, **other:** vistor ctr
24	TN 385, rd 204, to Arlington, Millington, Collierville
20	Canada Rd, Lakeland, **N**...**gas:** BP/McDonald's, Shell, **food:** Cracker Barrel, Waffle House, **lodging:** Day's Inn/rest., Relax Inn, Super 8, **S**...**gas:** Exxon/Subway/dsl, **other:** Factory Outlet/famous brands/food court, KOA, Old Time Pottery
18	US 64, to Bartlett, **N**...**gas:** Shell, **food:** Abuelo's, Bob Evans, Buffalo Wings, Burger King, Don Pablo, El Portoi, Firebird's Grill, Hooters, Luby's, Memphis Pizza, Olive Garden, Schlotsky's, Smokey Bones, Steak'n Shake, Texas Roadhouse, Waffle House, **lodging:** Best Western, Fairfield Inn, Holiday Inn Express, SpringHill Suites, **other:** Firestone, Goodyear/auto, Hummer, Lowe's Whse, Macey's, Pontiac/GMC, Sam's Club/gas, Sears/auto, Wal-Mart

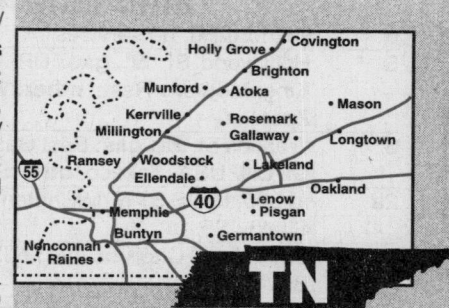

SuperCtr/24hr, same as 16, **S**...**gas:** BP, Citgo/dsl, Schnuck's, 76/Circle K, **food:** Backyard Burger, KFC, **other:** Kroger, Walgreen

16b a	TN 177, to Germantown, **N**...**gas:** 76/Circle K, Shell, **food:** Alexander's Rest., Bahama Breeze, Burger King, Chili's, Chick-fil-A, Colton's Steaks, Hunon Chinese, IHOP, Joe's Crabshack, Logan's Roadhouse, Macaroni Grill, McDonald's, Melting Pot, On-the-Border, Red Lobster, Red Sun Buffet, Taco Bell, Wendy's, **lodging:** AmeriSuites, Extended Stay Deluxe, Hampton Suites, Wellesley Inn, **other:** Barnes&Noble, Best Buy, Chevrolet, Chrysler/Dodge, Circuit City, Dillard's, Ford, Home Depot, Honda, JC Penney, Michael's, Office Depot, Old Navy, Sears/auto, Target, TJ Maxx, Walgreen, mall, **S**...**gas:** Shell, **food:** Shogun Japanese, Howard's Doughnut's, Waffle House, Wendy's, **lodging:** Best Inn, Comfort Suites, Microtel, Quality Suites, Wingate Inn, **other:** Costco/gas, Kohl's, Toyota
15b a	Appling Rd, **N**...**gas:** BP, Horizon, **1 mi N**...**gas:** Shell, **food:** Coletta's Italian, Suburban Lodge, **S**...**gas:** BP
14	Whitten Rd, **N**...**gas:** Citgo, Mapco, Shell/Burger King, **food:** Sidecar Café, **other:** Harley-Davidson, **S**...**gas:** BP, Shell/Backyard Burger/dsl, **other:** Walgreens
12	Sycamore View Rd, **N**...**gas:** Citgo/dsl, Texaco, **food:** Cajun Catfish Co., Capt D's, Church's, Cracker Barrel, IHOP, KFC, Krystal, McDonald's, Mrs Winner's, Perkins, Ruby Tuesday, Shoney's, Sonic, Taco Bell, Waffle House, **lodging:** Baymont Inn, Drury Inn, Econolodge, Extended Stay America, Memphis Plaza, Ramada Ltd, Red Roof Inn, **other:** Walgreens, **S**...**gas:** Citgo, Exxon, Mapco, 76/Circle K/dsl, **food:** Burger King, China Buffet, Playita Mexican, Subway, Wendy's, **lodging:** Best Value Inn, Best Western, Day's Inn, Fairfield Inn, La Quinta, Memphis Inn, Motel 6, Quality Inn, Super 8, **other:** Parts+
10.5mm	Wolf River
10b a	(from wb)I-240 W around Memphis, I-40 E to Nashville
12c	(from eb)I-240 W, to Jackson, I-40 E to Nashville
12b	Sam Cooper Blvd(from eb)
12a	US 64/70/79, Summer Ave, **N**...**gas:** Mapco/dsl, Shell, **food:** Waffle House, **lodging:** Guest Inn, **other:** Ford, U-Haul, mall, **S**...**gas:** Exxon, **food:** Arby's, Great China, McDonald's, NamKing Chinese, Wendy's, **other:** Curves, Firestone/auto, Fred's Drug, Goodyear/auto, Piggly Wiggly
10	TN 204, Covington Pike, **N**...**gas:** BP, Shell, **food:** McDonald's, Wendy's, **other:** Audi/VW, Buick, Cadillac, Chevrolet, Crysler/Jeep/Dodge, Honda, Hyundai, Isuzu/Mazda, Kia, Mitsubishi, Nissan, Pontiac/GMC, Sam's Club, SuperLo Food/gas, Volvo
8b a	TN 14, Jackson Ave, **N**...**gas:** Citgo/dsl, Shell, **lodging:** Day's Inn, Sleep Inn, **other:** Raleigh Tire, transmissions, **S**...**gas:** Citgo/dsl, Mapco, **other:** AutoZone, Kelly Tire, O'Reilly Parts

TENNESSEE

Interstate 40

Exit #	Services
6	Warford Rd, no services
5	Hollywood St, N...gas: BP, Mapco, food: Burger King, Mother's Rest., other: Walgreens, S...other: Zoo
3	Watkins St, N...gas: Best Gas, BP, Jubilie Express, Oil City USA, Texaco, other: Family $, U-Haul
2a	rd 300, to US 51 N, Millington, N...other: Meeman-Shelby SP
2	Smith Ave, Chelsea Ave, N...gas: Citgo, S...gas: BP
1g f	TN 14, Jackson Ave, N...lodging: Rainbow Inn, S...gas: Mapco
1e	I-240 E
1d c b	US 51, Danny Thomas Blvd, N...gas: Exxon, food: KFC, Ronald McDonald House, Wendy's, other: St Jude Research Ctr
1a	2nd St(from wb), downtown, S...lodging: Holiday Inn, Marriott, Sheraton, Wyndham Garden, other: Conv Ctr
1	Riverside Dr, Front St(from eb), Memphis, S...lodging: Comfort Inn, other: Conv Ctr, Riverfront
0mm	Tennessee/Arkansas state line, Mississippi River

Interstate 55

Exit #	Services
13mm	Tennessee/Arkansas state line, Mississippi River
12c	Delaware St, Memphis, W...lodging: Super 8
12b	Riverside Dr, downtown Memphis, E...TN Welcome Ctr
12a	E Crump Blvd(from nb), E...museum
11	McLemore Ave, Presidents Island, industrial area
10	S Parkway, 1/2 mi E...gas: BP/dsl
9	Mallory Ave, industrial area
8	Horn Lake Rd(from sb), no services
7	US 61, 3rd St, E...gas: BP, Exxon/mart, food: BBQ, Capt D's, Church's Chicken, LotABurger, Taco Bell, other: Walgreens, W...gas: Express, PitStop, food: KFC, McDonald's, Subway, lodging: Rest Inn, other: CarQuest, Fuller SP, Indian Museum
6b a	I-240
5b	US 51 S, Elvis Presley Blvd, to Graceland, W...gas: Citgo/dsl, Exxon, Phillips 66, food: Capt D's, China Buffet, KFC, Taco Bell, lodging: American Inn, Day's Inn, Graceland Inn, Heartbreak Hotel, Motel 6, Scottish Inn, other: HOSPITAL, Advance Parts, Davis RV Ctr, Dodge, KOA, Walgreens, transmissions, to Graceland
5a	Brooks Rd, E...gas: BP, Express/dsl, Exxon, food: Popeye's, lodging: Airport Inn, Brooks Inn, Clarion, Quality Inn, Travelodge, other: Freightliner, Peterbilt, Toyota
3mm	**Welcome Ctr nb, full(handicapped)facilities, phone, vending, picnic tables, litter barrels, petwalk**
2b a	TN 175, Shelby Dr, Whitehaven, E...gas: BP/dsl, Citgo/Subway, Conoco, Exxon, lodging: Colonial Inn, W...gas: BP, Citgo, Shell, food: Burger King, CK's Coffee, IHOP, Picadilly, other: Family$, Goodyear/auto, Schnuck's Foods, U-Haul
0mm	Tennessee/Mississippi state line

Interstate 65

Exit #	Services
121.5mm	Tennessee/Kentucky state line
121mm	**Welcome Ctr sb, full(handicapped)facilities, phone, picnic tables, litter barrels, vending, petwalk**
119mm	weigh sta both lanes
117	TN 52, Portland, E...gas: Shell/dsl/fireworks, lodging: Deerfield Inn, other: HOSPITAL, W...gas: BP/dsl, lodging: Budget Host, other: fireworks
116mm	Red River
113mm	Red River
112	TN 25, Cross Plains, E...gas: BP, food: Sad Sam's Deli, Diggs Chicken other: antiques, fireworks W...gas: Express/dsl, Shell/dsl
108	TN 76, White House, E...gas: Keystop, Nervous Charlie's/dsl, Shell, food: A&W/KFC, Cracker Barrel, DQ, Hardee's, Lighthouse Rest., McDonald's, Sonic(1mi), Subway, Taco Bell, Waffle House, Wendy's, lodging: Comfort Inn, Holiday Inn Express, other: Eckerd, Kroger/gas, USPO, park/playground, W...gas: BP, food: Stop 30 BBQ, lodging: Day's Inn
104	rd 257, Bethel Rd, E...gas: Phillip 66/dsl/rest./24hr, W...gas: Shell, other: Owl's Roost Camping
98	US 31 W, Millersville, E...gas: Citgo/dsl, RaceWay, Shell/dsl, food: Subway, Waffle House, lodging: Holiday Rest Motel/RV park(2mi), W...gas: BP/dsl, lodging: Economy Inn, other: Nashville Country Camping
97	rd 174, Long Hollow Pike, E...gas: BP/dsl, Exxon, Mapco, food: Arby's, Capt D's, Cracker Barrel, Domino's, Kabuto Japanese, KFC, McDonald's, Quizno's, Shoney's, Subway, Waffle House, Wendy's, lodging: Comfort Inn, Best Western, Days Inn, Executive Inn, Hampton Inn, Quality Inn, Red Roof Inn, other: K-Mart, Kroger, W...gas: Shell/dsl, food: Hardee's, Jack-in-the-Box, Krystal/24hr, Poncho Villa Grill, Sonic, lodging: Holiday Inn Express, Motel 6, other: Eckerd, Walgreens
96	Rivergate Pky, E...gas: Citgo/dsl, Shell, food: Coach's Grill, Cracker Barrel, El Chico, Hooters, Jakes Grill, Las Palmas Mexican, McDonald's, Mrs Winner's, O'Charley's, Papa John's, Subway, Waffle House, Wendy's, lodging: Best Value Inn, Comfort Suites, Rivergate Lodge, Rodeway Inn, other: HOSPITAL, Cadillac, CVS, Dillard's, Firestone, Goodyear, Hecht's, Home Depot, JC Penney, Nissan, NTB, Sears/auto, Tuesday Morning, mall, E on Gallatin...food: Arby's, Burger King, Calhoun's Cafe, Checker's, Chick-fil-A, Chili's, ChuckeCheese, Fafari's Rest., Fazoli's, IHOP, Krispy Kreme, LJ Silver/A&W, Logan's Roadhouse, Longhorn Steaks, Hometown Buffet, Olive Garden, Outback Steaks, Panera Bread, Pargo's Café, Pizza Hut, Rafferty's, Red Lobster, Santa Fe Steaks, Starbucks, Steak'n Shake, TGI Friday, Taco Bell, other: Best Buy, BooksAMillion, CarMax, Chevrolet, Chrysler/Jeep, Circuit City, Dillards, Goody's, Harley-Davidson, Home Depot, Honda, Isuzu, Jo-Ann's Etc., Lincoln/Mercury, Marshall's, Michael's, Office Depot, Old Navy, PepBoys, Petsmart, SteinMart, Sam's Club/gas, Target, TJ Maxx, Walgreens, Wal-Mart/drugs, W...gas: Chevron, Volunteer
95	TN 386, Vietnam Veterans Blvd(from nb)

E
W
N
S

Memphis

Nashville

Interstate 65

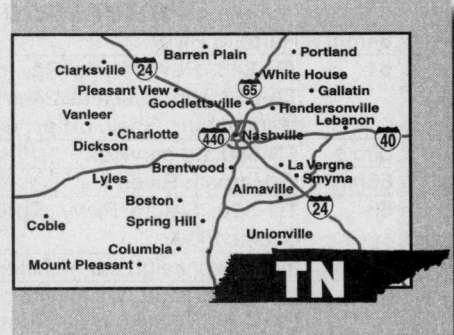

92	rd 45, Old Hickory Blvd, **E**...**other:** HOSPITAL, to Old Hickory Dam
90b	TN 155 E, Briley Pkwy, **E**...to Opreyland
90a	US 31W, US 41, Dickerson Pike, **E**...**gas:** Exxon, Express/dsl, Shell, **food:** Arby's, Burger King, Capt D's, China King, Domino's, Gyros, Jay's Rest., KFC, Lee's Chicken, McDonald's, Mrs Winner's, Pizza Hut, Subway, Taco Bell, Waffle House, Wendy's, **lodging:** Day's Inn, Econolodge, Sleep Inn, Super 8, **other:** Advance Parts, AutoZone, Camping World RV Supply, CVS Drug, Family$, KOA, Kroger, Walgreens
88b a	I-24, W to Clarksville, E to Nashville
87b a	US 431, Trinity Lane, **E**...**gas:** Citgo, Pilot/Subway/dsl, **food:** Krystal, White Castle, **lodging:** Cumberland Inn, Delux Inn, **W**...**gas:** Chevron, Exxon, **food:** Jack-in-the-Box, Jack's BBQ, McDonald's, Ponderosa, Subway, Taco Bell, Waffle House, **lodging:** Best Value Inn, Comfort Inn, Country Hearth Inn, Country Music Inn, Day's Inn, Quality Inn, Regency Inn, Super 8, Travelodge, **other:** Family$, to American Bapt Coll
86	I-24 E, to I-40 E, to Memphis
86mm	Cumberland River
85	US 41A, 8th Ave, **E**...to st capitol, **gas:** Citgo/tires, **W**...**gas:** Exxon, Arby's, **food:** Krystal, McDonald's, Pizza Hut, Subway, Taco Bell, Wendy's, **lodging:** Springhill Suites, **other:** Cadillac/Honda
84b a	I-40, E to Knoxville, W to Memphis
209[I-40]	US 70, Charlotte Ave, Church St, **E**...**food:** McDonald's, **other:** Nissan, **W**...**gas:** Exxon, **food:** Burger King, White Castle, **lodging:** Best Western, Comfort Inn, **other:** Chevrolet/Pontiac/GMC, Chrysler/Jeep, Firestone, Isuzu/Subaru
82b a	I-40, W to Memphis, E to Nashville
81	Wedgewood Ave, **W**...**gas:** BP, Exxon, Citgo, **food:** Burger King, Krystal, McDonald's, Mrs Winner's, **other:** $General, $Tree, Kroger, U-Haul, Walgreens
80	I-440, to Memphis, Knoxville
79	Armory Dr, **E** on Powell...**gas:** Citgo, Shell, **food:** Applebee's, Rafferty's, Subway, Wendy's, **other:** BMW/Mini, CarMax, CompUSA, Home Depot, Michael's, Ross, Staples, mall
78b a	rd 255, Harding Place, **E**...**gas:** Express, Marathon, Shell, **food:** Cracker Barrel, Mama Mia's Italian, Santa Fe Grill, Waffle House, **lodging:** La Quinta, Red Roof Inn, Traveler's Rest Hist Home
74	TN 254, Old Hickory Blvd, to Brentwood, **E**...**food:** Capt D's, Cold Stone Creamery, LongHorn Steaks, Panera Bread, Qdoba Mexican, Shoney's, Waffle House, **lodging:** AmeriSuites, Holiday Inn, Steeplechase Inn, **other:** GNC, Target, **W**...**gas:** BP, Citgo, Exxon, Shell/dsl, **food:** Brentwood Grill, Chick-fil-A, Corky's BBQ, Mazatlan Mexican, McAlister's Deli, Mrs Winner's, O'Charley's, Papa John's, Ruby Tuesday, Starbucks, Vittles Rest., Wendy's, **lodging:** Brentwood Suites, Courtyard, Extended Stay America, Hampton Inn, Hilton Suites, Main-

stay Suites, Studio+, **other:** Cadillac, CVS Drug, Eckerd, Fresh Mkt Foods, Harris-Teeter, Office Depot, SteinMart, TJ Maxx, USPO, Walgreens

71	TN 253, Concord Rd, to Brentwood
69	rd 441, Moores Lane, Galleria Blvd, **E**...**gas:** MapCo/dsl, Shell, **food:** Amerigo's Grill, Applebee's, Beef o'Brady's, Butcher Block, Cozymel's, Green Hills Grill, Joe's Crabshack, Outback Steaks, Shogun Japanese, Sonic, Starbucks, **lodging:** AmeriSuites, Homestead Suites, Red Roof Inn, Studio Suites, Wingate Inn, **other:** Acura/Lexus, CVS Drug, Home Depot/gas, Mercedes, Michael's, Petsmart, Publix, VW, Walgreens, **W**...**gas:** BP, Shell/dsl, **food:** J Alexander's Rest., Backyard Burger, Buca Italian, Chili's, Macaroni Grill, McDonald's, Pizza Hut/Taco Bell, Red Lobster, Schlotsky's, Smokey Bones BBQ, Stoney River Steaks, Subway, **lodging:** Sleep Inn, **other:** Barnes&Noble, Best Buy, CompUSA, Dillard's, Infiniti, JC Penney, Old Navy, Ross, Sears/auto, Target, Wild Oats Mkt, mall
68b a	Cool Springs Blvd, **E**...**food:** Mexicani Grill, **lodging:** Embassy Suites, Marriott, **W**...**gas:** Exxon, Shell, **food:** Atl Bread, Baja Fresh, BoneFish Grill, Carrabba's, Golden Corral, Jack-in-the-Box, McAlister's Deli, McDonald's, Ming Chinese, Moe's SW Grill, Omikoshi Japanese, PF Chang's, Ruby Tuesday, Starbucks, TGIFriday, Wendy's, **lodging:** Country Inn&Suites, Hampton Inn, **other:** Borders Books, Circuit City, Harley-Davidson, Harris-Teeter, Home Depot, Jo-Ann Fabrics, Kohl's, Kroger, Lowe's Whse, Marshall's, Sam's Club, Saturn, Staples, Walgreens, Wal-Mart SuperCtr/24hr, to Galleria Mall
66	new exit
65	TN 96, to Murfreesboro, Franklin, **E**...**gas:** Exxon, Mapco, Shell, **food:** Cracker Barrel, Sonic, Steak'n Shake, **lodging:** Best Value Inn, Comfort Inn, Day's Inn, Holiday Inn Express, La Quinta, Ramada Ltd, **other:** Buick/Pontiac/GMC/Kia, Chevrolet, Food Lion, Honda/Volvo, Hyundai, Walgreens, **W**...**gas:** BP/dsl, Mapco/dsl, Shell/dsl, **food:** Arby's, ChopHouse Chinese, CiCi's, Hardee's, Jack-in-the-Box, KFC, La Hacienda Mexican, McDonald's, O'Charley's, Papa John's, Pizza Hut, Shoney's, Starbucks, Subway, Taco Bell, Waffle House, Wendy's, **lodging:** Best Western, Quality Inn, **other:** VET, Big Lots, Chrysler/Dodge, CVS Drug, $General, Eckerd, Ford/Mercury, Goody's, Hancock Fabrics, Home Depot, Kroger, Mazda, Nissan, SteinMart, Toyota, USPO, to Confederate Cem at Franklin

TENNESSEE
Interstate 65

64mm	Harpeth River
61	TN 248, Peytonsville Rd, to Spring Hill, **E**...**gas:** TA/BP/dsl/rest./scales/24hr/@, **W**...**gas:** Citgo, Mapco/24hr, Shell, **other:** Goose Creek Inn/rest.
59b a	TN 840, no services
58mm	W Harpeth River
53	TN 396, Saturn Pkwy, Spring Hill, Columbia, TN Scenic Pkwy
48mm	truck insp/weigh sta nb, litter barrels
46	US 412, TN 99, to Columbia, Chapel Hill, **E**...**gas:** Chevron, Loves/Arbys/dsl/scales/24hr, **W**...**gas:** BP, Citgo/dsl, Horizon/Wendy's/dsl, TJ's/Burger King, **food:** Cracker Barrel, Waffle House, **lodging:** Best Value Inn, Comfort Inn, Hampton Inn, Holiday Inn Express, Relax Inn, **other:** HOSPITAL
40.5mm	Duck River
37	TN 50, to Columbia, Lewisburg, **E**...**other:** HOSPITAL, TN Walking Horse HQ, **W**...**gas:** Shell/dsl, **other:** to Polk Home
32	rd 373, to Lewisburg, Mooresville, **E**...**gas:** Exxon/dsl
27	rd 129, to Lynnville, Cornersville, **E**...**other:** Texas T Camping
25mm	parking area sb, litter barrels
24mm	parking area nb, litter barrels
22	US 31A, to Pulaski, **E**...**gas:** BP/dsl/rest./scales/24hr/@, **food:** McDonald's, Subway, **lodging:** Vista Motel, **W**...**gas:** Pilot/dsl/scales, Shell/dsl/24hr
14	US 64, to Pulaski, **E**...**gas:** BP/dsl, Citgo, Shell/dsl, **food:** Sarge's Shack Rest., **lodging:** Super 8, **other:** TN Valley RV Park, to Jack Daniels Distillery, **W**...HOSPTIAL, to David Crockett SP
6	rd 273, Bryson, **E**...**gas:** Phillips 66/dsl/rest./@, **lodging:** Best Value Inn, **W**...**gas:** Marathon(2mi)
4mm	Elk River
3mm	**Welcome Ctr nb, full(handicapped) facilities, info, phone, picnic tables, litter barrels, pet-walk**
1	US 31, rd 7, Ardmore, **E**...**gas:** Chevron/dsl/24hr, Exxon/Church's/dsl, **1-2 mi E**...**gas:** Shell/repair, **food:** DQ, Hardee's, McDonald's, Subway
0mm	Tennessee/Alabama state line

Interstate 75

Exit #	Services
161.5mm	Tennessee/Kentucky state line
161mm	**Welcome Ctr sb, full(handicapped)facilities, phone, vending, picnic tables, litter barrels, pet-walk**
160	US 25W, Jellico, **E**...**gas:** BP, Exxon/dsl, **food:** El Charito, KFC, **lodging:** Jellico Motel, **W**...**gas:** BP/Wendy's, Shell/Arby's/dsl, **food:** Hardee's, Subway, **lodging:** Best Value Inn, Day's Inn/rest., **other:** HOSPITAL, camping, fireworks, to Indian Mtn SP
156	Rarity Mtn rd, no services
144	Stinking Creek Rd, no services
141	TN 63, to Royal Blue, **E**...**gas:** Shell/Stuckey's/24hr, **food:** Perkins, **W**...**gas:** Shell/Stuckey's/dsl, Pilot/Subway/dsl/24hr, **lodging:** Comfort Inn, **other:** fireworks, to Big South Fork NRA

134	US 25W, TN 63, Caryville, **E**...**gas:** Shell/24hr, **food:** Loui's Rest., Waffle House/24hr, **lodging:** Econolodge, Family Inn, Hampton Inn, Super 8, Thacker Christmas Inn, **other:** HOSPITAL, to Cove Lake SP, **W**...**gas:** BP, **food:** Shoney's, Scotty's Hamburgers, **lodging:** Budget Host
130mm	weigh sta both lanes, phones
129	US 25W S, Lake City, **W**...**gas:** BP/Sonic, Citgo, Exxon/Subway/dsl/24hr, Shell, **food:** Cracker Barrel, KFC/Taco Bell, McDonald's, **lodging:** Day's Inn, Blue Haven Motel, Lake City Motel, Lamb's Inn/rest., **other:** $General, same as 128
128	US 441, to Lake City, **E**...**gas:** BP, Sunoco, **other:** Mountain Lake Marina(4mi), **W**...**gas:** Exxon/dsl/24hr, Mystik, Shell, **food:** Cottage Rest., La Fiesta, Subway, **lodging:** Blue Haven Motel, Lake City Motel, Lamb's Inn, **other:** Advance Parts, $General, antique cars, to Norris Dam SP, same as 129
126mm	Clinch River
122	TN 61, Bethel, Norris, **E**...**gas:** Shell, **food:** Shoney's, **other:** Fox Inn Camping, antiques, museum, **W**...**gas:** BP, Exxon/Burger King/Subway/dsl/24hr, Get'n Go, Phillips 66, **food:** Arby's, Golden Girls Rest., Hardee's, Harrison's Grill, Krystal/24hr, McDonald's, Waffle House, Wendy's, Zaxby's, **lodging:** Best Western, Country Inn&Suites, Holiday Inn Express, Norris Inn, Super 8, **other:** Ford, Big Pine Ridge SP
117	TN 170, Racoon Valley Rd, **E**...**gas:** BP/dsl, Pilot/dsl/scales/24hr, **W**...**lodging:** Valley Inn/camping, **other:** Escapee's RV Park
112	TN 131, Emory Rd, to Powell, **E**...**gas:** BP/Buddy's BBQ/dsl, Chevron, Pilot/DQ/Taco Bell/dsl/24hr/@, **food:** Aubrey's Rest., McDonald's, KFC, Krystal, Ruby Tuesday, Steak'n Shake, Subway, Wendy's, Zaxby's, **lodging:** Country Inn&Suites, Holiday Inn Express, **other:** CVS Drug, Family$, Ingles, Toyota, **W**...**gas:** Exxon/24hr, Shell/dsl/24hr, Weigel's, **food:** Hardee's, Shoney's, Waffle House/24hr, **lodging:** Comfort Inn
110	Callahan Dr, **E**...**gas:** Weigel's, **lodging:** Knight's Inn, Quality Inn/rest., **other:** Honda, **W**...**gas:** BP, **food:** Burger King(2mi), Chick-fil-A, Chili's(2mi), Golden Corral(2mi), McDonald's, Ruby Tuesday(2mi), Wendy's(2mi), **lodging:** Scottish Inn, **other:** GMC/Volvo, Mac Trucks
108	Merchant Dr, **E**...**gas:** BP/dsl, Citgo/dsl, Pilot/dsl, Shell/dsl, **food:** Applebee's, Cracker Barrel, El Chico's, Highway Host, Hooter's, Logan's Roadhouse, O'Charley's, Pizza Hut, Starbucks, Sonic, Puelo's Grill, Ramsey's Rest., Ryan's, Waffle House, **lodging:** Best Western, Comfort Inn, Day's Inn, Econolodge, Hampton Inn, Sleep Inn, **other:** Ingles, Valvoline, **W**...**gas:** Citgo, Exxon/Godfather's, Pilot/Conoco, Shell, **food:** Arby's, Burger King, Cancun Mexican, Capt D's, Darryl's Rest., Great American Steaks, IHOP, Mandarin House, McDonald's, Outback Steaks, Pizza Inn, Quaker Steak, Red Lobster, Subway, Waffle House/24hr, **lodging:** Best Value, Clarion Inn, Econolodge, Motel 6, Super 8, **other:** Food Lion, Walgreens

Interstate 75

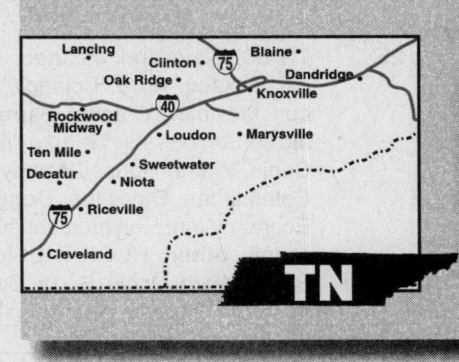

107	I-640 & I-75,
3b{I-640}	US 25W, Clinton Hwy, **N** on US 25...other: Chevrolet, Dodge, Ford, Nissan, services on frontage rds
1{I-640}	TN 62, Western Ave, **N**...gas: Exxon/dsl, RaceTrac, Texaco/dsl, food: Central Park, KFC, LJ Silver, McDonald's, Ruby Tuesday, Shoney's, Sonic, Subway, Taco Bell, Wendy's, other: CVS Drug, Kroger, Walgreen, **S**...gas: BP, food: Hardee's, Krystal, other: Advance Parts, O'Reilly Parts, USPO

I-75 and I-40 run together 17 mi. See Interstate 40, exits 369-385.

84 b a[368]	I-40, W to Nashville, E to Knoxville
81	US 321, TN 95, to Lenoir City, **E**...gas: BP/Buddy's BBQ/TCBY/dsl, Exxon/Subway/dsl, Mobil, Shell/dsl, Texaco/dsl, food: Aubrey's Rest., Burger King(1mi), Capt D's, Chili's, China Buffet, Cracker Barrel, Dinner Bell Rest., KFC, McDonald's, Monterrey Mexican, Quizno's, Shoney's, Tokyo Express, Waffle House, Zaxby's, lodging: Days Inn, Hampton Inn, Holiday Inn Express, King's Inn/rest., other: $Tree, Goody's, Home Depot, Radio Shack, Wal-Mart SuperCtr/gas/24hr, Great Smokies NP, Ft Loudon Dam, **W**...gas: Citgo/dsl, Shell/dsl, food: Krystal, Ruby Tuesday, lodging: Comfort Inn, Econolodge, Ramada Ltd, other: Chevrolet, Pontiac/Buick/GMC
76	Rd 324, Sugar Limb Rd, **W**...to TN Valley Winery
74mm	Tennessee River
72	TN 72, to Loudon, **E**...gas: BP/McDonald's, Shell/Wendy's, food: Log Cabin BBQ, lodging: Country Inn&Suites, Super 8, other: to Ft Loudon SP, **W**...gas: Citgo, food: Over the Hill Grill, lodging: Best Value Inn, other: Express Camping
68	Rd 323, to Philadelphia, **E**...gas: BP/dsl, food: cheese factory/store(2mi)
62	Rd 322, Oakland Rd, to Sweetwater, **E**...food: Dinner Bell Rest., **W**...other: KOA
60	TN 68, Sweetwater, **E**...gas: BP, RaceWay, Shell/dsl, food: Bradley's BBQ, Burger King, Country Star Rest., KFC, McDonald's, Sonic, Wendy's, lodging: Best Value Inn, Comfort Inn, Day's Inn, Knights Inn, other: HOSPITAL, to Lost Sea Underground Lake, **W**...gas: BP/dsl, Conoco, Kangaroo/dsl, food: Cracker Barrel, lodging: Best Western, Quality Inn, other: flea mkt, to Watts Bar Dam, tires/repair
56	Rd 309, Niota, **E**...gas: BP/dsl/rest./scales/24hr/@, other: TN Country Camping, **W**...tires
52	Rd 305, Mt Verd Rd, to Athens, **E**...gas: BP(1mi), Citgo, food: Subway, other: Overniter RV Park, **W**...gas: BP, lodging: Amada Inn

49	TN 30, to Athens, **E**...gas: BP, Exxon, Kangaroo, RaceWay, Shell/DQ/dsl/24hr, food: Applebee's, Burger King, Hardee's, KFC, Krystal, McDonald's, MexiWing, Monterrey Mexican, Ruby Tuesday, Shoney's, Subway, Waffle House, Wendy's, lodging: Day's Inn, Econolodge, Hampton Inn, Holiday Inn Express, Homestead Inn, Knight's Inn, Motel 6, Super 8, other: HOSPITAL, Athens I-75 Camping, Russell Stover, to TN Wesleyan Coll, **W**...gas: Shell, food: Cracker Barrel, lodging: Homestead Inn, other: Chrysler/Jeep, Pontiac/Buick/Cadillac/GMC
45.5mm	**rest area both lanes, full(handicapped)facilities, phone, vending, picnic tables, litter barrels, petwalk**
42	TN 39, Riceville RD, **E**...gas: Citgo/dsl, lodging: Relax Inn, Rice Inn(2mi)
36	TN 163, to Calhoun, **E**...food: Hardee's(3mi), other: Hiwassee/Ocoee River SP
35mm	Hiwassee River
33	Rd 308, to Charleston, **E**...gas: Citgo, other: 33 Camping, **W**...gas: Shell/dsl/rest./24hr
27	Paul Huff Pkwy, **1 mi E**...gas: Phillips 66, food: Applebee's, Capt D's, Chili's, CiCi's, DQ, Fazoli's, Golden Corral, IHOP, McDonald's, O'Charley's, Outback Steaks, Panera Bread, Ryan's, Sonic, Steak'n Shake/24hr, Taco Bell, lodging: Jameson Inn, other: AutoZone, Belk, BooksAMillion, Buick/Pontiac, CVS Drug, $Tree, Eckerd, Food Lion, Goodyear/auto, Home Depot, JC Penney, K-Mart, Lowe's Whse, PetCo, Sears, Staples, TJ Maxx, Wal-Mart SuperCtr/gas/24hr, mall, **W**...gas: Exxon, Shell/Subway, Texaco, food: Denny's/24hr, Hardee's, Waffle House, Wendy's, lodging: Classic Suites, Comfort Inn, EQ Motel, Hampton Inn, Ramada Ltd, Super 8, other: Kohls, Target

TENNESSEE

Interstate 75

N ↑↓ S

25	TN 60, Cleveland, E...**gas:** BP, RaceWay, Shell/dsl, Texaco, **food:** Bojangle's, Burger King, Cancun Mexican, Cracker Barrel, Hardee's, McDonald's, Schlotsky's, Sharkey's Seafood, Shoney's, Sonic, Waffle House, Wendy's, Zaxby's, **lodging:** Colonial Inn, Day's Inn, Douglas Inn, Econolodge, Economy Inn, Howard Johnson, Knight's Inn, Travel Inn, **other:** HOSPITAL, to Lee Coll, W...**gas:** Shell, **food:** Uncle Bud's Catfish, **lodging:** Baymont Inn, Holiday Inn, Wingate Inn
23mm	truck/weigh sta nb
20	US 64 byp, to Cleveland, **1-4 mi** E...**gas:** Exxon, FuelMart, Shell, **food:** Hardee's, McDonald's, Subway, Taco Bell, **lodging:** Whitewater Lodge, **other:** Chrysler/Jeep/Dodge, Honda, Toyota, W...**gas:** Exxon/dsl/24hr, Horizon/DQ/dsl/24hr, **other:** KOA(1mi)
16mm	scenic view sb
13mm	truck/weigh sta, litter barrels sb
11	US 11 N, US 64 E, Ooltewah, E...**gas:** BP, RaceWay, Shell, **food:** Arby's, Bojangles, Burger King, Cracker Barrel, Capt D's, Hardee's, McDonald's, Subway, Taco Bell, Wendy's, **other:** BiLo, Wal-Mart SuperCtr/24hr, W...**gas:** BP/Quizno's/dsl, **food:** Krystal, Waffle House, **lodging:** Super 8, **other:** to Harrison Bay SP
8	no services
7b a	US 11, US 64, Lee Hwy, E...**gas:** Exxon, W...**gas:** Chevron, Shell, **food:** City Cafe, Waffle House, **lodging:** Best Inn, Best Western/rest., Comfort Inn, Econolodge, Motel 6, Park Inn, Wellesley Inn, **other:** Harley-Davidson, Jaguar/Land Rover/Porsche
5	Shallowford Rd, E...**food:** Alexander's, Arby's, Central Park, CiCi's, Country Place Rest., Famous Dave's, Krystal, Logan's Roadhouse, Macaroni Grill, McAlister's Deli, McDonald's, Mi Aroma, Smokey Bones BBQ, Starbucks, Steak'n Shake/24hr, Souper Salad, Taco Bell, **lodging:** Quality Inn, Wingate Inn, **other:** Barnes&Noble, Best Buy, BooksAMillion, Circuit City, Firestone/auto, Ford, FreshMkt Foods, Home Depot, Lowe's Whse, Office Depot, Old Navy, Petsmart, SteinMart, Walgreens, Wal-Mart SuperCtr/24hr, W...**gas:** BP, Citgo, Shell, **food:** Applebee's, Asia Buffet, Blimpie, Cancun Mexican, Cracker Barrel, Domino's, Fazoli's, GlenGene Deli, Godfather's, KFC, McDonald's, O'Ace's Grill, O'Charley's, Papa John's, Pizza Hut, Sonic, Shoney's, Subway, Texas Roadhouse, Waffle House, Wendy's, **lodging:** Comfort Inn, Country Inn&Suites, Day's Inn, Fairfield Inn, Guesthouse Inn, Hampton Inn, Hilton Garden, Holiday Inn, Holiday Inn Express, Homewood Suites, Knights Inn, La Quinta, MainStay Suites, Ramada Ltd, Red Roof Inn, Sleep Inn, **other:** HOSPITAL, BiLo, CVS Drug, Goodyear, U of TN/Chatt

Chattanooga

4a	(from nb)Hamilton Place Blvd, E...**food:** Acropolis, Big River Grill, BoneFish Grill, Carraba's, DQ, El Mason, Fox&Hound Grill, Olive Garden, Outback Steaks, PF Chang's, Piccadilly's, Red Lobster, Ruby Tuesday, Sticky Fingers BBQ, Kampai Of Tokyo, **lodging:** Courtyard, **other:** Belk, Dillard's, Firestone, Goody's, JC Penney, Marshall's, Michael's, Ross, Sears/auto, Staples, TJ Maxx, World Mkt, mall
4	TN 153, Chickamauga Dam Rd
3b a	TN 320, Brainerd Rd, E...**gas:** BP, **food:** Subway, **other:** BMW
2	I-24 W, to I-59, to Chattanooga, Lookout Mtn
1.5mm	**Welcome Ctr nb, full(handicapped)facilities, phone, vending, picnic tables, litter barrels, petwalk**
1b a	US 41, Ringgold Rd, to Chattanooga, E...**gas:** BP, Texaco, **lodging:** Best Value Inn, Comfort Inn, Crown Inn, Econolodge, Howard Johnson, Ramada Ltd, **other:** BiLo Foods, Camping World RV Ctr/Shipp's RV Ctr/park, Family$, W...**gas:** Conoco/dsl, Shell/dsl, **food:** A&W/LJ Silver, Arby's, Burger King, Central Park Burger, Cracker Barrel, Hardee's, Krystal, McDonald's, PortoFino Italian, Shoney's, Taco Bell, Teriyaki House, Uncle Bud's Catfish, Waffle House, Wally's Rest., **lodging:** Best Inn, Day's Inn, Holiday Inn Express, Super 8, Superior Creek Lodge, Waverly Motel, **other:** Holiday Travel Park, U-Haul
0mm	Tennessee/Georgia state line

Interstate 81

N ↑↓ S

Exit #	Services
75mm	Tennessee/Virginia state line, **Welcome Ctr sb, full (handicapped)facilities, info, phone, vending, picnic tables, litter barrels, petwalk**
74b a	US 11W, to Bristol, Kingsport, E...**lodging:** Day's Inn, Hampton Inn, **other:** HOSPITAL, **1-2 mi** E...**gas:** Shell, **food:** Burger King, KFC, LJ Silver, McDonald's, Pizza Hut, Shoney's, Taco Bell, Wendy's, W...**gas:** Exxon, **food:** Truby's Diner, **lodging:** Best Western, Bristol Inn
69	TN 394, to Blountville, E...**gas:** BP/Subway/dsl, **food:** Arby's, Burger King(1mi), **other:** Advance Parts, Bristol Int Speedway
66	TN 126, to Kingsport, Blountville, E...**gas:** Exxon/dsl, W...**gas:** Chevron/24hr, **food:** McDonald's, **other:** FSA/famous brands
63	Rd 357, Tri-City Airport, E...**gas:** Exxon/Taco Bell/Krystal/dsl, Shell/Subway/dsl/24hr, **food:** Cracker Barrel, Wendy's, **lodging:** La Quinta, Sleep Inn, **other:** Hamrick's Clothing Outlet, W...**gas:** Citgo/dsl, **lodging:** Red Carpet Inn, **other:** $General, KOA, Rocky Top Camping, Sam's Club

Bristol

Interstate 81

60mm	Holston River
59	RD 36, to Johnson City, Kingsport, **E...gas:** Citgo/dsl, **lodging:** Super 8, **W...gas:** BP/LP, Exxon, Shell/dsl, Sunoco, **food:** Arby's, Burger King, Edo's Grill, Hardee's, HotDog Hut, La Carreta Mexican, Little Caesar's, McDonald's, Motz's Italian, Perkins/24hr, Pizza Hut, Sonic, Subway, Wendy's, **lodging:** Best Western, Comfort Inn, **other:** Advance Parts, CVS Drug, $General, Firestone/auto, Fred's Drug, Ingles/cafe, USPO, to Warrior's Path SP
57b a	I-26 to Johnson City, ETSU, I-181 to Kingsport
56	Tri-Cities Crossing, no services
50	TN 93, Fall Branch, **W...other:** auto auction, st patrol
44	Jearoldstown Rd, **E...gas:** Marathon
41mm	**rest area sb, full(handicapped)facilities, phone, vending, picnic tables, litter barrels, petwalk**
38mm	**rest area nb, full(handicapped)facilities, phone, vending, picnic tables, litter barrels, petwalk**
36	RD 172, to Baileyton, **E...gas:** Pilot/Subway/dsl/scales/@, **W...gas:** BP/dsl/24hr, Marathon/dsl/24hr/@, Shell/Subway/dsl/24hr, **food:** Pizza+, **lodging:** 36 Motel, **other:** Baileyton Camp(2mi), Family$
30	TN 70, to Greeneville, **E...gas:** Exxon/DQ/Stuckey's/dsl
23	US 11E, to Greeneville, **E...gas:** BP/Wendy's, Mobil/Subway, **other:** to Andrew Johnson HS, **W...gas:** Exxon/dsl, Phillips 66/dsl/rest./scales, **food:** McDonald's, Taco Bell, **lodging:** Best Western, Super 8
21mm	weigh sta sb
15	Rd 340, Fish Hatchery Rd, no services
12	TN 160, to Morristown, **E...gas:** Phillips 66, **W...gas:** Shell/dsl, **lodging:** Days Inn(6mi), Hampton Inn(12mi), Motel 6(6mi), **other:** to Crockett Tavern HS
8	US 25E, to Morristown, **E...gas:** Shell/dsl/repair, **food:** Sonic(2mi), **lodging:** Twin Pines Motel(3mi), **W...gas:** BP/dsl, **food:** Cracker Barrel, Hardee's, **lodging:** Holiday Inn/rest., Parkway Inn, Super 8, **other:** to Cumberland Gap NHP
4	rd 341, White Pine, **E...gas:** Pilot/McDonald's/dsl/scales/24hr/@, **lodging:** Crown Inn, **W...gas:** Wilco/Hess/Wendy's/dsl/scales/24hr/@, **food:** Huddle House/24hr, **lodging:** Day's Inn, **other:** to Panther Cr SP
2.5mm	**rest area sb, full(handicapped)facilities, phone, picnic tables, litter barrels, vending, petwalk**
1b a	I-40, E to Asheville, W to Knoxville. I-81 begins/ends on I-40, exit 421.

Interstate 640(Knoxville)

Exit #	Services
9mm	I-640 begins/ends on I-40, exit 393.
8	Millertown Pike, Mall Rd N, **N...gas:** Exxon/DQ/24hr, Shell, **food:** Applebee's, Burger King, Don Pablos, KFC, Krystal, McDonald's, Piccadilly's, Pizza Inn, Proffit's, Ruby Tuesday, Taco Bell, Texas Roadhouse, Wendy's, **other:** Circuit City, Dillard's, JC Penney, Kohl's, Sam's Club, Sears/auto, Target, Wal-Mart SuperCtr/gas, mall, **S...gas:** Shell, **food:** Cracker Barrel, Little Caesars, O'Charley's, Subway, **other:** Food Lion, Home Depot, Lowe's Whse, PepBoys
6	US 441, to Broadway, **N...gas:** BP, Chevron, Citgo, Conoco, Phillips 66, Pilot/dsl, **food:** Arby's, Austin's Steaks, Cancun Mexican, Chop House, CiCi's, Fazoli's, Hardee's, Krispy Kreme, Larry's Subs, LJ Silver, McDonald's, Papa John's, Ruby Tuesday, Sonic, Subway, Taco Bell, **lodging:** Best Western, **other:** Advance Parts, AutoZone, Batteries+, BigLots, CVS Drug, $General, Firestone, Food City/gas, Goodyear, Kroger/24hr, NAPA, Target, Walgreen, **S...gas:** Conoco, **food:** Buddy's BBQ, Sam's Rest., Shoney's, **other:** BiLo Foods, CVS Drug, Food Lion, Home Depot, K-Mart, NAPA, Office Depot, transmissions
3a	I-75 N to Lexington, I-275 S to Knoxville
3b	US 25W, Clinton Hwy, **N** on US 25...**other:** Chevrolet, Dodge, Ford, Nissan, services on frontage rds
1	TN 62, Western Ave, **N...gas:** Exxon/dsl, RaceTrac, Texaco/dsl, **food:** Central Park, KFC, LJ Silver, McDonald's, Ruby Tuesday, Shoney's, Sonic, Subway, Taco Bell, Wendy's, **other:** CVS Drug, Kroger, Walgreen, **S...gas:** BP, **food:** Hardee's, Krystal, **other:** Advance Parts, O'Reilly Parts, USPO
0mm	I-640 begins/ends on I-40, exit 385.

E ↕ **W**

Orange | **Beaumont**

Exit #	Services
880.5mm	Texas/Louisiana state line, Sabine River
880	Sabine River Turnaround, RV camping
879mm	**Welcome Ctr wb, full(handicapped)facilities, phone, picnic tables, litter barrels, vending, petwalk**
878	US 90, Orange, **N**...**gas:** Mobil/dsl, **other:** airboat rides, **S**...**other:** Western Store
877	TX 87, 16th St, Orange, **N**...**gas:** Chevron, Shamrock, **food:** Pizza Hut, Subway, **other:** Ace Hardware, Buick/Pontiac/Toyota, $General, Eckerd, MktBasket/deli, Radio Shack, **S**...**gas:** Exxon, Shell/dsl, Valero, **food:** Burger King, Casa Ole, Church's, DQ, Jack-in-the-Box, McDonald's, Popeye's, Sonic, Taco Bell, **other:** Buick/Pontiac, Cadillac/GMC, CVS Drug, HEB Foods, Kroger, Modica Tires, O'Reilly Parts, Toyota, Walgreens
876	Adams Bayou, frontage rd, Adams Bayou, **N**... **food:** Gary's Café, Waffle House, **lodging:** Best Western, Best Value Inn, Executive Inn, Motel 6, Ramada Inn, Quality Inn, Super 8, **other:** Pontiac/Buik/GMC, Toyota, **S**...**gas:** Chevron/dsl, **lodging:** Holiday Inn Express, same as 877
875	FM 3247, MLK Dr, **N**...**food:** Richard's Grill, **S**... **other:** HOSPITAL, Chrysler/Dodge/Jeep
874	US 90, Womack Rd, to Orange, **S**...HOSPITAL
873	TX 62, TX 73, to Bridge City, **N**...**gas:** Exxon/dsl/24hr, Flying J/Conoco/Cookery/dsl/LP/scales/24hr, **other:** Oakleaf Park RV Park, tires/repair, **S**...**gas:** Pilot/Subway/Wendy's/dsl/scales/24hr, Shell/Church's/dsl, Valero, **food:** Jack-in-the-Box, McDonald's, Sonic, Waffle House, Whataburger
870	FM 1136, no services
869	FM 1442(from wb), to Bridge City, **S**...Lloyd's RV Ctr
868.5mm	**rest areas both lanes, full(handicapped) facilities, vending, picnic tables, litter barrels**
867	frontage rd(from eb), no services
865	Doty Rd(from wb), frontage rd, no services
864	FM 1132, FM 1135, **N**...**food:** Burr's BBQ, **lodging:** Budget Inn
862c	Timberlane Dr(from eb), no services
862b	Old Hwy(from wb), no services
862a	Railroad Ave, no services
861d	TX 12, Deweyville, no services
861c	Denver St, **N**...**gas:** Conoco/dsl
861b	Lamar St(from wb), **N**...**gas:** Conoco/dsl
861a	FM 105, Vidor, **N**...**gas:** Chevron/dsl, Shell, Valero, **food:** Casa Ole, Church's, DQ, Domino's, Jack-in-the-Box, McDonald's, Ming's Buffet, Navrosky's, Popeye's, Senor Toro, Waffle House, **other:** Ace Hardware, AutoZone, Curves, CVS Drug, Mktbasket Foods, O'Reilly Parts, Radio Shack, Walgreens, Wal-Mart, **S**...**gas:** Exxon/dsl, Texaco, **food:** Burger King, Great Wall Chinese, KFC, Pizza Hut, Sonic, Subway, Taco Bell, Whataburger, **lodging:** La Quinta, **other:** $General, Family$, auto repair, tires
860b a	Dewitt Rd, frontage rd, W Vidor, no services
859	Bonner Turnaround(from eb), Asher Turnaround(from wb), **N**...**other:** Boomtown RV Park, **S**...**gas:** Chevron/dsl/24hr

Exit #	Services
858	Rose City, no services
856	Old Hwy 90 (from eb), Rose City, no services
855b	Magnolia St (from wb), no services
855a	US 90 bus, to downtown, Port of Beaumont
854	ML King Pkwy, Beaumont, **N**...**gas:** Conoco, **food:** Texas Brotha, **S**...**gas:** Exxon, Shamrock/dsl, **food:** McDonald's
853b	11th St, **N**...**food:** Cafe Del Rio, Red Lobster, Rocky's Roadhouse, Waffle House, **lodging:** Best Value Inn, Days Inn, Holiday Inn, Red Carpet Inn, Sleep Inn, Super 8, Travel Inn, **other:** MktBasket, **S**...**gas:** Texaco/dsl, Fina, **food:** Checker's, Chula Vista Mexican, Luby's, **lodging:** Howard Johnson, Interstate Inn, **other:** HOSPITAL
853a	US 69 N, to Lufkin
852	Harrison Ave, Calder Ave, Beaumont, **N**...**gas:** Shell/dsl, Valero, **food:** Casa Ole Mexican, Chili's, Olive Garden, Willie Ray's BBQ, **S**...**gas:** Chevron, **food:** Church's, McDonald's, **lodging:** Econolodge, La Quinta, **other:** HOSPITAL, Chevrolet, transmissions
851	US 90, College St, **N**...**gas:** Exxon/dsl, RaceWay, **food:** Acapulco Mexican, Carrabba's, China Border, Floyd's Cajun Cafe, Golden Corral, Hooters, Outback Steaks, Tokyo Japanese, Waffle House, **lodging:** Best Western, Comfort Inn, Travelodge, **other:** Advance Parts, AutoZone, Harley-Davidson, O'Reilly Parts, Pennzoil, **S**...**gas:** Exxon, Mobil, Shell, Texaco, **food:** Baytown Seafood, China Hut, DQ, IHOP, Jack-in-the-Box, KFC, Pizza Hut, Quizno's, Sonic, Taco Bell, Taste Of China, Wendy's, Whataburger, **lodging:** Courtyard, Econolodge, Economy Inn, Elegante Motel, Fairfield Inn, Motel 6, **other:** HOSPITAL, CVS Drug, Discount Tire, Dodge, Firestone/auto, Ford/Lincoln/Mercury, GMC/Cadillac, Honda, Jeep, MktBasket Foods, Mazda, Mercedes, Mitsubishi, Nissan, NTB, Office Depot, Sam's Club/gas, U-Haul, Volvo, Walgreens
850	850, wb only, same as 851
849	US 69 S, Washington Blvd, to Port Arthur, airport
848	Walden Rd, **N**...**gas:** Shell, **food:** Pappadeaux Seafood, Sonic, **lodging:** Holiday Inn/rest., La Quinta, **other:** USPO, **S**...**gas:** Petro/Mobil/dsl/scales/24hr/@, Shell, **food:** Carino's Italian, Cheddar's, Cracker Barrel, Jack-in-the-Box, Joe's Crabshack, Waffle House, **lodging:** Candlewood Suites, Hilton Garden, Knight's Inn, Super 8, **other:** Blue Beacon
847	Brooks Rd(from wb), **S**...**other:** Gulf Coast RV Resort
845	FM 364, Major Dr(from eb), same as 847
843	Smith Rd, no services
838	FM 365, Fannett, **N**...**gas:** Bar-H Store/gas/BBQ
837.5mm	picnic areas both lanes, tables, litter barrels, handicapped accessible
833	Hamshire Rd, no services
829	FM 1663, Winnie, **N**...**gas:** Exxon/dsl, Shell/dsl/24hr, Texaco/Burger King/dsl, **food:** McDonald's, Taco Bell, Whataburger/24hr, **lodging:** Holiday Inn Express, **other:** RV Park, **S**...**gas:** Chevron/dsl, Mobil/Subway/dsl/scales/24hr, **food:** Al-T Seafood, Hunan Chinese, Jack-in-the-Box, Pizza Inn, Waffle House, **lodging:** Best Western, Motel 6, Quality Inn,

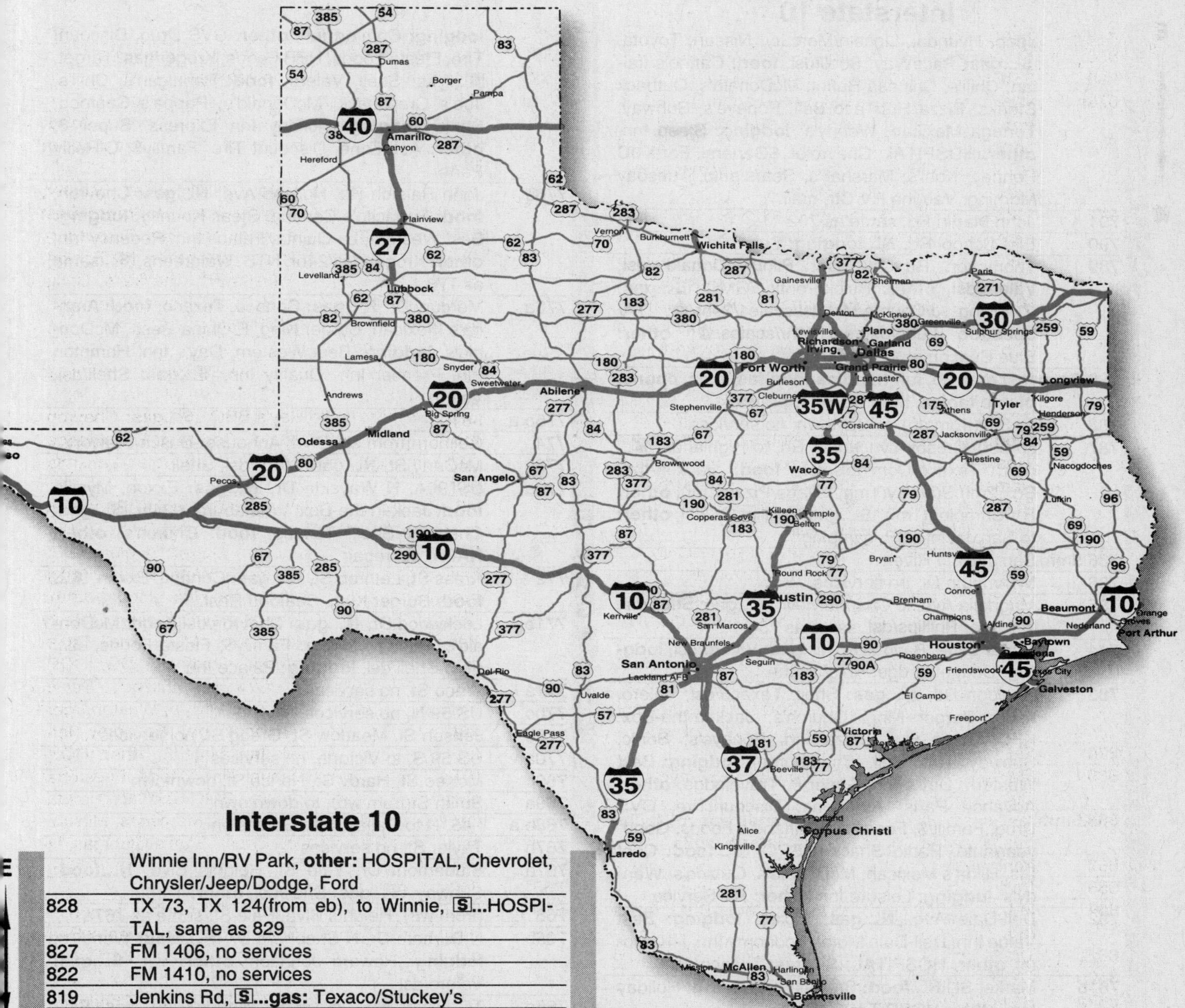

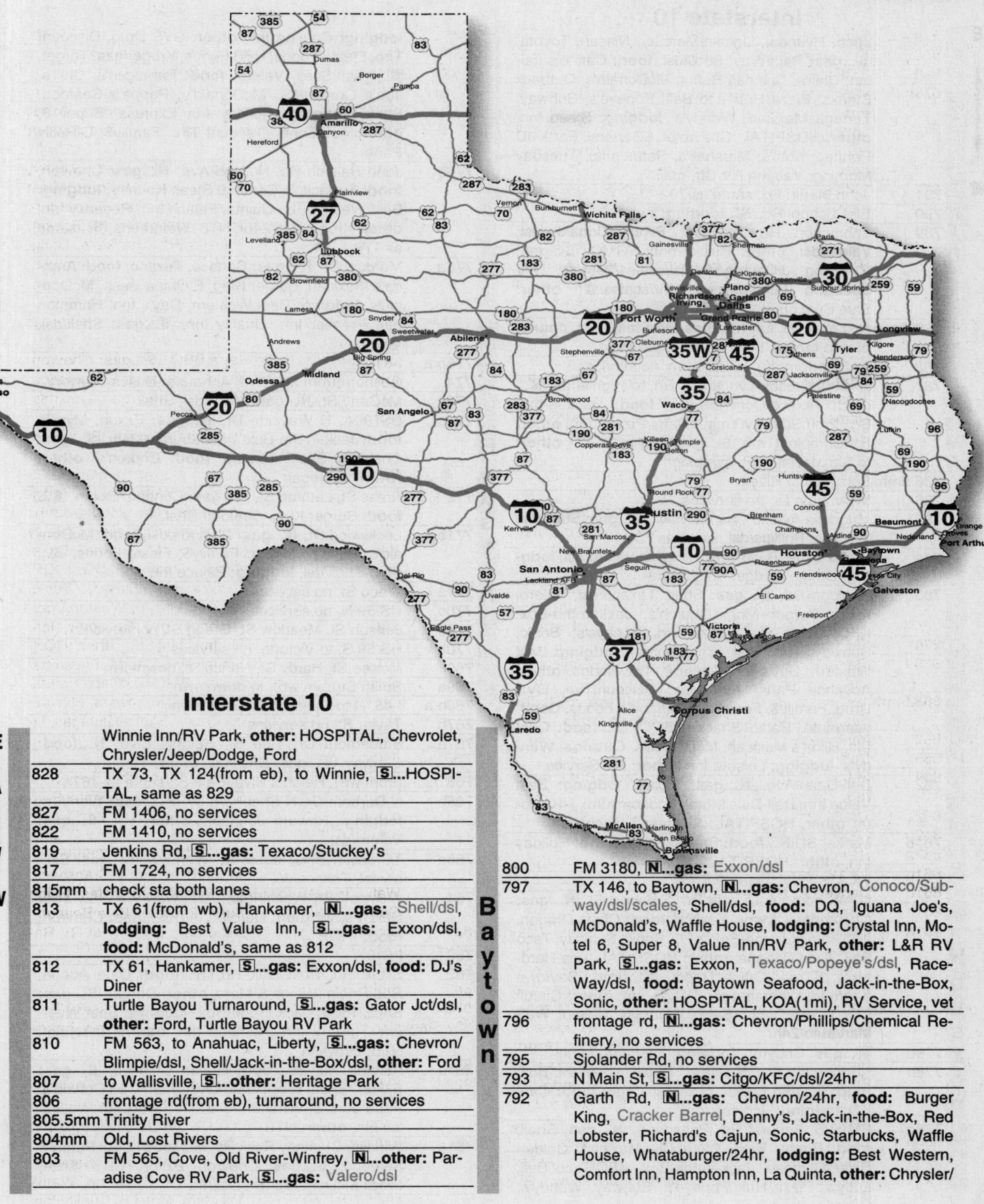

Interstate 10

	Winnie Inn/RV Park, **other:** HOSPITAL, Chevrolet, Chrysler/Jeep/Dodge, Ford
828	TX 73, TX 124(from eb), to Winnie, [S]...HOSPITAL, same as 829
827	FM 1406, no services
822	FM 1410, no services
819	Jenkins Rd, [S]...**gas:** Texaco/Stuckey's
817	FM 1724, no services
815mm	check sta both lanes
813	TX 61(from wb), Hankamer, [N]...**gas:** Shell/dsl, **lodging:** Best Value Inn, [S]...**gas:** Exxon/dsl, **food:** McDonald's, same as 812
812	TX 61, Hankamer, [S]...**gas:** Exxon/dsl, **food:** DJ's Diner
811	Turtle Bayou Turnaround, [S]...**gas:** Gator Jct/dsl, **other:** Ford, Turtle Bayou RV Park
810	FM 563, to Anahuac, Liberty, [S]...**gas:** Chevron/Blimpie/dsl, Shell/Jack-in-the-Box/dsl, **other:** Ford
807	to Wallisville, [S]...**other:** Heritage Park
806	frontage rd(from eb), turnaround, no services
805.5mm	Trinity River
804mm	Old, Lost Rivers
803	FM 565, Cove, Old River-Winfrey, [N]...**other:** Paradise Cove RV Park, [S]...**gas:** Valero/dsl

Baytown

800	FM 3180, [N]...**gas:** Exxon/dsl
797	TX 146, to Baytown, [N]...**gas:** Chevron, Conoco/Subway/dsl/scales, Shell/dsl, **food:** DQ, Iguana Joe's, McDonald's, Waffle House, **lodging:** Crystal Inn, Motel 6, Super 8, Value Inn/RV Park, **other:** L&R RV Park, [S]...**gas:** Exxon, Texaco/Popeye's/dsl, RaceWay/dsl, **food:** Baytown Seafood, Jack-in-the-Box, Sonic, **other:** HOSPITAL, KOA(1mi), RV Service, vet
796	frontage rd, [N]...**gas:** Chevron/Phillips/Chemical Refinery, no services
795	Sjolander Rd, no services
793	N Main St, [S]...**gas:** Citgo/KFC/dsl/24hr
792	Garth Rd, [N]...**gas:** Chevron/24hr, **food:** Burger King, Cracker Barrel, Denny's, Jack-in-the-Box, Red Lobster, Richard's Cajun, Sonic, Starbucks, Waffle House, Whataburger/24hr, **lodging:** Best Western, Comfort Inn, Hampton Inn, La Quinta, **other:** Chrysler/

TEXAS

Interstate 10

	Jeep, Hyundai, Lincoln/Mercury, Nissan, Toyota, **S...gas:** RaceWay, Shell/dsl, **food:** Carino's Italian, Chili's, Chinese Buffet, McDonald's, Outback Steaks, Pizza Hut/Taco Bell, Popeye's, Subway, Tortuga Mexican, Wendy's, **lodging:** Sleep Inn, **other:** HOSPITAL, Chevrolet, $General, Ford, JC Penney, Kohl's, Marshall's, Sears/auto, Tuesday Morning, Vaughn RV Ctr, mall
791	John Martin Rd, same as 792
790	Ellis School Rd, **N...lodging:** Super 8
789	Thompson Rd, **N...gas:** Pilot/McDonald's/dsl, Valero/dsl, **other:** Buick/Pontiac/GMC, **S...gas:** ⬡/Flying J/CountryMkt/dsl/scales/24hr/@, TA/SpeedCo Lube/dsl/rest./24hr/scales/@, **other:** Blue Beacon, truck repair
788.5mm	**rest area eb, full(handicapped)facilities, phone, picnic tables, litter barrels, petwalk**
788	sp 330(from eb), to Baytown, no services
787	sp 330, Crosby-Lynchburg Rd, to Highlands, **N...gas:** Texaco/Domino's/dsl, **food:** Jack-in-the-Box(2mi) Subway(1mi), Village Pizza(1mi), **other:** RV Camping(1mi), **S...gas:** Phillips 66/dsl, **other:** to San Jacinto SP, camping
786.5mm	San Jacinto River
786	Monmouth Dr, no services
785	Magnolia Ave, to Channelview, **N...gas:** Shell/dsl, **S...gas:** Phillips/dsl, same as 784
784	Cedar Lane, Bayou Dr, **N...gas:** Valero/dsl, **lodging:** Budget Lodge, Knight's Inn
783	Sheldon Rd, **N...gas:** Shell, Texaco/dsl, Valero, **food:** Burger King, Church's, Jack-in-the-Box, KFC, Pizza Hut, Pizza Inn, Popeye's, Sonic, Subway, Taco Bell, Whataburger, **lodging:** Best Western, Day's Inn, Super 8, Travelodge, **other:** Advance Parts, AutoZone, DiscountTire, CVS Drug, Family$, FoodFair, Garland's Foods, Goodyear/auto, Radio Shack, USPO, **S...food:** Capt D's, Hilda's Mexican, McDonald's, Quizno's, Wendy's, **lodging:** Leisure Inn, **other:** RV Service
782	Dell-Dale Ave, **N...gas:** Exxon, **lodging:** Best Value Inn, Dell-Dale Motel, Economy Inn, I-10 Motel, **other:** HOSPITAL, **S...gas:** Texaco/dsl
781b	Market St, **N...food:** Brewsky's, **lodging:** Holiday Inn, **other:** HOSPITAL
781a	TX 8, Sam Houston Pkwy
780	(779a from wb)Uvalde Rd, Freeport St, **N...gas:** Chevron/dsl, Mobil, Texaco, **food:** China Dragon, IHOP, Jack-in-the-Box, KFC, Sonic, Subway, Taco Bell, Taco Cabana, **other:** HOSPITAL, Ace Hardware, $Tree, Office Depot, **S...food:** Baytown Seafood, Whataburger, Wing's Inn, **other:** Circuit City, Home Depot, Sam's Club/gas, U-Haul, Wal-Mart/auto/24hr
779b	**N...gas:** Chevron, **lodging:** Interstate Motel
778b	Normandy St, **N...gas:** Shell/Jack-in-the-Box, **food:** Golden Corral, **S...gas:** Citgo, **food:** Cafe KO, **lodging:** Scottish Inn
778a	FM 526, Federal Rd, Pasadena, **N...gas:** Shell, **food:** Burger King, Casa Ole Mexican, Golden River Chinese, Jack-in-the-Box, KFC/Taco Bell, Luby's, Pizza Hut, Popeye's, Subway, Wendy's,

	lodging: Comfort Inn, **other:** CVS Drug, Discount Tire, Fiesta Foods, HEB Foods, Kroger/gas, Target, **S...gas:** Shell, Valero, **food:** Bennigan's, Chili's, Joe's Crabshack, McDonald's, Pappa's Seafood, Sonic, **lodging:** Holiday Inn Express, Super 8, **other:** AutoZone, Discount Tire, Family$, O'Reilly Parts
776b	John Ralston Rd, Holland Ave, **N...gas:** Chevron, **food:** Papacito's Cantina, Steak Kountry, **lodging:** Best Western, La Quinta, Palace Inn, Regency Inn, **other:** Kroger/deli/24hr, NTB, Walgreens, **S...same as 778**
776a	Mercury Dr, **N...gas:** Conoco, Texaco, **food:** Aranda's Mexican, Burger King, E China Rest., McDonald's, **lodging:** Best Western, Day's Inn, Hampton Inn, Premier Inn, Quality Inn, **S...gas:** Shell/dsl, Valero
775b a	I-610
774	Gellhorn(from eb) Blvd, Anheuser-Busch Brewery
773b	McCarty St, **N...gas:** Mobil/dsl, Shell
773a	US 90A, N Wayside Dr, **N...gas:** Exxon, Mystik, **food:** Jack-in-the-Box, Whataburger/24hr, **S...gas:** Chevron, Shell, Texaco, **food:** Church's, **other:** NAPA, dsl repair
772	Kress St, Lathrop St, **N...gas:** Conoco, Exxon, **S... food:** Burger King, Seafood Rest.
771b	Lockwood Dr, **N...gas:** Chevron/dsl, **food:** McDonald's, Subway, **other:** Family$, Fiesta Foods, **S...gas:** Shell/dsl, **lodging:** Palace Inn
771a	Waco St, no services
770c	US 59 N, no services
770b	Jenson St, Meadow St, Gregg St, no services
770a	US 59 S, to Victoria, no services
769c	McKee St, Hardy St, Nance St, downtown
769a	Smith St(from wb), to downtown
768b a	I-45, N to Dallas, S to Galveston
767b	Taylor St, no services
767a	Studemont Dr, Yale St, Heights Blvd, **N...food:** Subway, **S...gas:** Shell/dsl, **other:** Target
766	(from wb), Heights Blvd, Yale St, same as 767a
765b	N Durham Dr, N Shepherd Dr, **N...food:** Wendy's, **lodging:** Howard Johnson, **other:** vet, **S...gas:** Valero/dsl
765a	TC Jester Blvd, **N...food:** Wendy's, **S...gas:** Exxon/dsl, Texaco/dsl
764	Westcott St, Washington Ave, Katy Rd, **N...food:** Denny's, **lodging:** Comfort Inn, **S...gas:** Chevron, **food:** IHOP
763	I-610
762	Silber Rd, Post Oak Rd, **N...food:** Cafe Adobe, Red Robin, Wings & More, **other:** Dodge, **S...gas:** Shell, **food:** Jack-in-the-Box, **lodging:** Best Western, Holiday Inn, Ramada Inn, **other:** Chevrolet, NTB, carwash
761b	Antoine Rd, **N...food:** Hunan Chinese, **S...gas:** Exxon, Shell, **food:** Blue Oyster Grill, McDonald's, Papa John's, Whataburger/24hr, **lodging:** Wellesley Inn, **other:** NTB
761a	Wirt Rd, Chimney Rock Rd, **N...food:** Capt Penny's Seafood, **S...gas:** Chevron, Exxon/TCBY, Shell, **food:** McDonald's, Steak&Ale

Interstate 10

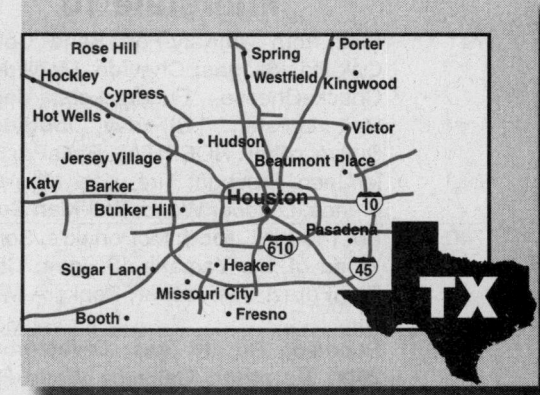

760 Bingle Rd, Voss Rd, ...Home Depot, S...gas: Citgo, Mobil, Shell, **food:** Goode Co BBQ, Marie Callender, Mason Jar Rest., Pappy's Café, Redwood Grill, SaltGrass Steaks, Sweet Tomatos, TX BBQ, **other:** HOSPITAL

759 Campbell Rd(from wb), same as 758b

758b Blalock Rd, Campbell Rd, N...**food:** Ciro's Italian, Sonic, **other:** Adam's Automotive, Fiesta Foods, LubeStop, Mail It, cleaners, S...gas: Chevron/McDonald's/dsl, Exxon, Texaco, **other:** HOSPITAL, Kroger, Walgreen

758a Bunker Hill Rd, N...gas: Exxon, **food:** CiCi's, **other:** Best Buy, Costco/gas, Lowe's Whse, Michael's, PepBoys, Radio Shack, S...gas: Texaco/dsl, Circle K, **food:** Charlie's Burgers, Guadalajara Mexican, Quizno's, Subway, **lodging:** Day's Inn, Howard Johnson, Super 8, **other:** Ford, Goodyear/auto, Marshall's, Nissan, Ross, Target

757 Gessner Rd, N...gas: Exxon, **food:** BBQ, Bennigan's, Chili's, Cici's, DQ, McDonald's, Murphy's Deli, Schlotsky's, Taco Bell, Wendy's, Whataburger/24hr, **other:** BrakeCheck, Eckerd, Home Depot, Honda, Kroger, NAPA, Radio Shack, Sam's Club/gas, Tuesday Morning, U-Haul, Wal-Mart, S...gas: Shell, **food:** Fuddrucker's, Jack-in-the-Box, Jason's Deli, Macaroni Grill, Olive Garden, Pappasito's, Papadeaux Seafood, Taste of TX Rest., **lodging:** Radisson, Sheraton, **other:** HOSPITAL, Circuit City, Cost+, Dillards, Foley's, Ford, Goodyear, Macys, Mervyn's, Office Depot, Sears/auto, Target, World Mkt, mall

756 TX 8, Sam Houston Tollway

755 Willcrest Rd, N...other: Discount Tire, Kia, Mazda, NTB, S...gas: Citgo/dsl, Exxon/McDonald's/24hr, Texaco, **food:** Carabbas, China View, Denny's, IHOP, Steak&Ale, Taco Cabana, **lodging:** Extended Stay America, Hampton Inn, La Quinta, Radisson

754 Kirkwood Rd, N...other: Lexus, Lincoln/Mercury, Saturn, Toyota, same as 753b, S...gas: Chevron/dsl, Shell/24hr, **food:** Carrabba's, IHOP/24hr, Kingfish Mkt, Mesa Grill, Original Pasta Co, Subway, Taco Cabana, **lodging:** Extended Stay America, Hampton Inn, **other:** Chevrolet, Discount Tire, Subaru

753b Dairy-Ashford Rd, N...other: Buick, Chrysler/Dodge, Infiniti, Lexus, Nissan, Toyota, Volvo, S...gas: Exxon/TCBY/dsl, Shamrock, **food:** Beck's Prime Rest., Subway, TX Cattle Steaks, Whataburger, **lodging:** Courtyard, Guesthouse Inn, Holiday Inn Express, **other:** Audi/Porsche, Cadillac, Mitsubishi, Pontiac/GMC/Suzuki

753a Eldridge Pkwy, N...gas: Conoco/dsl, **lodging:** Omni Hotel, S...gas: Valero

751 TX 6, to Addicks, N...gas: Shell, **food:** Cattlegard Rest., Waffle House, **lodging:** Crowne Plaza, Drury Inn, Red Roof Inn, Studio 6, **other:** Sam's Club/gas, S...gas: Exxon, Chevron, Conoco/dsl, Texaco/dsl, **food:** Blimpie, DQ, Denny's/24hr, El Yucatan Mexican, Jack-in-the-Box, Wendy's, **lodging:** Baymont

Inn, Bradford HomeSuites, Fairfield Inn, La Quinta, Motel 6, Super 8, Townplace Suites, **other:** Acura, BMW, USPO, carwash

748 Barker-Cypress Rd, N...gas: Texaco, **food:** Subway, S...food: Cracker Barrel, Lulu's Buffet, **lodging:** Fairfield Inn, TownePlace Inn, **other:** Chrysler/Jeep, Dodge, Hoover RV Ctr, Hyundai, Subaru, VW

747 Fry Rd, N...gas: Chevron, Phillips 66, Shamrock/dsl, Shell/24hr, **food:** Applebee's, Bennigans, Burger King, Church's, DQ, Denny's, Godfather's, McDonald's, Panda Express, Pizza Hut, Sonic, Souper Salad, Subway, Taco Bell, Victor's Mexican, Waffle House, Whataburger, **other:** Best Buy, Goodyear, HEB Food/gas, Home Depot, Kohl's, Ross, Sam's Club/gas, Walgreen, Wal-Mart Super Ctr/24hr/gas, S...gas: Chevron, Citgo, Shell, **food:** Baskin-Robbins, Boston Mkt, Capt Tom's Seafood, El Chico, Fazoli's, IHOP, Jack-in-the-Box, Ninfa's Café, Omar's Mexican, Orient Express, Outback Steaks, Quizno's, Wendy's, **other:** Albertson's, Ford, Lowe's Whse, NTB, PetsMart, Radio Shack, Target, Uhaul

745 Mason Rd, S...gas: Chevron/24hr, Exxon/24hr, Shamrock, Shell/24hr, **food:** Babin's Seafood, BBQ, Blackeyed Pea, Burger King, Carino's Italian, Carrabba's, Chick-fil-A, Chili's, CiCi's, DQ, Fuzzy's Pizza, Hartz Chicken, Jack-in-the-Box, Jason's Deli, KFC, Landry's Seafood, Little Caesar's, LJ Silver, Luby's, McDonald's, Monterey Mexican, Papa John's, Pizza Hut, Popeye's, SaltGrass Steaks, Schlotsky's, SpagEddie's, Subway, Taco Bell, Taco Cabana, Taquiera Mexican, TCBY, Whataburger/24hr, **lodging:** Comfort Inn, Hampton Inn, Holiday Inn, Sleep Inn, Super 8, **other:** CarQuest, Discount Tire, Dodge, Eckerd, Firestone/auto, Goodyear/auto, HEB Food/gas, K-Mart, Kroger, Randall's Food, Walgreen, transmissions

743 TX 99, Grand Pkwy, Peek Rd, N...other: JC Penny, S...gas: Shell/dsl, **food:** A&W, Popeye's, Taquirea Arrandas, **lodging:** Best Western, Comfort Inn, Holiday Inn Express, La Quinta, Super 8, **other:** Chevrolet, Isuzu, Kia, Kroger

TEXAS

Interstate 10

E ↕ **W**

Sealy

Exit	Description
741	(742 from wb)Katy-Fort Bend County Rd, Pin Oak Rd, **S**...**gas:** Chevron, Mobil/dsl/24hr, **food:** ChuckeCheese, Fuddruckers, Jack-in-the-Box, Red Lobster, TGIFriday, **lodging:** SpringHill Suites, **other:** HOSPITAL, BassPro Shops, Chrysler/Jeep, Discount Tire, Katy Mills Outlet/famous brands, Outdoor World, Wal-Mart SuperCtr/24hr
740	FM 1463, **N**...**food:** McDonald's, Sonic, **other:** RV World of TX, Yamaha, **S**...**gas:** Chevron, **food:** RainForest Café, **other:** Books-A-Million, Pyle RV Ctr
737	Pederson Rd, **N**...**gas:** Loves/Arby's/dsl/scales/24hr, **S**...**other:** Camping World RV Super Ctr, Holiday World RV Ctr
732	FM 359, to Brookshire, **N**...**gas:** Exxon/dsl, /Flying J/CountryMkt/dsl/scales/24hr/@, Shell, **food:** Orlando's Pizza, **lodging:** Executive Inn, **other:** KOA, **S**...**gas:** Chevron/dsl, Citgo/dsl, Exxon/Burger King/dsl/24hr, **food:** Jack-in-the-Box, **lodging:** La Quinta, **other:** Ford Trucks, truckwash
731	FM 1489, to Koomey Rd, **N**...**gas:** Exxon/dsl, **food:** Ernesto's Mexican, **lodging:** Carefree Inn, **other:** RV Park
730mm	picnic areas(both lanes exit left), tables, litter barrels
729	Peach Ridge Rd, Donigan Rd, no services (730 from wb)
726	Chew Rd(from eb), **S**...golf
725	Mlcak Rd(from wb), no services
724mm	check sta wb
723	FM 1458, to San Felipe, **N**...**gas:** Exxon/Subway/dsl/scales/24hr, **other:** to Stephen F Austin SP(3mi), **S**...**other:** Goodyear/auto
721	(from wb) US 90, **N**...**gas:** Shell/dsl, **other:** Ford, **S**...**other:** Sealy Mall
720a	Outlet Ctr Dr, **N**...**gas:** Shell/dsl, **S**...to Sealy Mall
720	TX 36, to Sealy, **N**...**gas:** Shell/dsl, **food:** DQ, Hartz Chicken, McDonald's, Sonic, Tony's Rest., **other:** Chevrolet/Pontiac/Buick/GMC, Jones RV Ctr, Walgreen, **S**...**gas:** Chevron/dsl/24hr, Mobil/dsl, Shell/dsl/24hr, **food:** Hinze's BBQ, Hunan Chinese, Jack-in-the-Box, KFC/Taco Bell, Omar's Mexican, Pizza Hut, Subway, Whataburger/24hr, **lodging:** Best Western, Holiday Inn Express, Rodeway Inn, **other:** Chrysler/Dodge/Jeep, Radio Shack, Wal-Mart SuperCtr/gas
718	US 90(from eb), to Sealy, no services
716	Pyka Rd, **N**...**gas:** Exxon/dsl/rest./showers/24hr/@
713	Beckendorff Rd, no services
709	FM 2761, Bernardo Rd, no services
704	FM 949, **N**...Happy Oaks RV Park(3mi)
701mm	no services
699	FM 102, to Eagle Lake, **N**...**other:** Happy Oaks RV Park, antiques, **S**...**other:** Eagle Lake SP(14mi)
698	Alleyton Rd, **N**...**food:** Mikeska's BBQ, **S**...**gas:** Shell/Taco Bell/BBQ/dsl, **other:** Chrysler/Jeep/Dodge, Ford

Columbus

Exit	Description
697mm	Little Colorado River
696	TX 71, Columbus, **N**...**gas:** Chevron/dsl/24hr, Shell/dsl, **food:** DQ, Denny's, Guadalajara Mexican, Jack-in-the-Box, Pizza Hut, Schobel's Rest., Whataburger, **lodging:** Columbus Inn, Holiday Inn Express, **other:** HOSPITAL, AutoZone, Buick/Chevrolet, HEB Foods, Radio Shack, Wal-Mart/drugs, **S**...**gas:** Citgo/Church's/dsl, Valero/dsl, **food:** McDonald's, Nancy's Steaks, Sonic, Subway, **lodging:** Country Hearth Inn
695	TX 71(from wb), to La Grange, no services
693	FM 2434, to Glidden, no services
692mm	**rest areas both lanes, full(handicapped) facilities, vending, phone, picnic tables, litter barrels, RV dump, petwalk**
689	US 90, to Hattermann Lane, **N**...Motorcoach RV Park
682	FM 155, to Wiemar, **N**...**gas:** Exxon/dsl, Shell/BBQ/dsl, Texaco, **food:** DQ, Subway/Texas Burger, **lodging:** Czech Inn, **other:** HOSPITAL, $General, Tire Pro, **S**...**other:** Buick/Chevrolet
678mm	E Navidad River
677	US 90, **N**...**food:** Casa deCortez Mexican
674	US 77, Schulenburg, **N**...**gas:** Chevron/dsl, Exxon/dsl, **food:** McDonald's, **lodging:** Executive Inn, Oak Ridge Motel/rest., **other:** Ford, **S**...**gas:** Exxon, Shell/dsl, Valero/Subway, **food:** DQ, Frank's Rest., Guadalajara Mexican, Oak Ridge Smokehouse, Whataburger, **lodging:** Holiday Inn Express, **other:** $General, Schulenberg RV Park
672mm	W Navidad River
668	FM 2238, to Engle, no services
661	TX 95, FM 609, to Flatonia, **N**...**food:** Joel's, BBQ, San Jose Mexican, **S**...**gas:** Exxon/24hr, Shell/McDonald's/Grumpy's Rest./motel, Valero, **food:** DQ, Robert's Steaks, **lodging:** Carefree Inn, **other:** NAPA
658mm	picnic areas both lanes, tables, litter barrels
653	US 90, Waelder, **N**...**gas:** Shell/dsl/cafe
649	TX 97, to Waelder, no services
642	TX 304, to Gonzales, no services
637	FM 794, to Harwood, no services
632	US 90/183, to Gonzales, **N**...**gas:** Love's/Subway/dsl/scales/24hr, **lodging:** Coachway Inn(2mi), **S**...**gas:** Shell/Buc-ee's/dsl, **other:** to Palmetto SP, camping
630mm	San Marcos River
628	TX 80, to Luling, **N**...**gas:** Exxon(2mi), Valero/Church's/dsl/24hr, **food:** DQ(2mi), **other:** HOSPITAL, Riverbend RV Park
625	Darst Field Rd, no services
624.5mm	Smith Creek
620	FM 1104, no services
619mm	**rest area both lanes, full(handicapped) facilities, phone, picnic tables, petwalk**
617	FM 2438, to Kingsbury, no services
616mm	truck weigh sta both lanes
614.5mm	Mill Creek
612	US 90, no services

Interstate 10

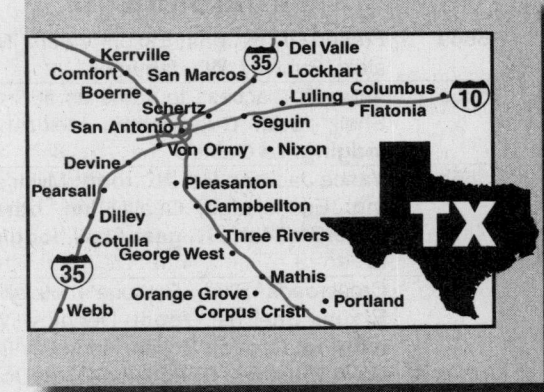

611mm	Geronimo Creek
610	TX 123, to San Marcos, ...gas: Exxon/dsl, Chevron/Subway/dsl, Shamrock/dsl, food: Chili's, IHOP, Los Cucos Mexican, R&B Steaks, lodging: Comfort Inn, Hampton Inn, Holiday Inn, other: tires, S...gas: Valero/dsl, food: Taco Cabana, other: HOSPITAL, River Shade RV
609	TX 123, Austin St, S...gas: Mobil/dsl, other: Chevrolet, Home Depot
607	TX 46, FM 78, to New Braunfels, N...gas: Texaco/Jack-in-the-Box/dsl, lodging: Alamo Inn, S...gas: Chevron/dsl, Exxon/DQ/dsl, food: Dixie Grill, Hong Kong Chinese, Kettle, McDonald's, Soilitas Mexican, Whataburger/24hr, lodging: Best Western, La Quinta, Super 8, other: Chrysler/Dodge/Jeep
605	FM 464, N...other: Twin Palms RV Park
605mm	Guadalupe River
604	FM 725, to Lake McQueeney, N...other: America RV Ctr, D&A RV Resort, Explore USA RV Ctr
603	US 90 E, US 90A, to Seguin, N...other: Explorer USA RV Sales
601	FM 775, to New Berlin, N...gas: Mobil/Subway/dsl/scales/24hr
600	Schwab Rd, no services
599	FM 465, to Marion, no services
599mm	Santa Clara Creek
597	Santa Clara Rd, N...auto racetrack
595	Zuehl Rd, no services
594mm	Cibolo Creek
593	FM 2538, Trainer Hale Rd, S...gas: Exxon/dsl/rest./24hr, Texaco/dsl
593mm	Woman Hollering Creek
591	FM 1518, to Schertz, N...gas/dsl/repair
589	Pfeil Rd, Graytown Rd, no services
589mm	Salatrillo Creek
587	LP 1604, Randolph AFB, to Universal City
585.5mm	Escondido Creek
585	FM 1516, to Converse, N...gas: Shell/Church's/dsl/motel/scales, S...other: Peterbilt/GMC/Freightliner
585mm	Martinez Creek
583	Foster Rd, N...gas: ⛽/Flying J/Conoco/Cookery/dsl/LP/scales/24hr/@, Valero/Subway/dsl/24hr, food: Jack-in-the-Box/24hr, lodging: La Quinta, other: Speedco Lube, Charlie's, Truckwash, S...gas: TA/Chevron/Burger King/Pizza Hut/Popeye's/dsl/24hr/@
582.5mm	Rosillo Creek
582	Ackerman Rd, Kirby, N...gas: Pilot/Subway/dsl/scales/24hr, other: Blue Beacon, S...gas: Petro/Mobil/dsl/scales/24hr/@, KFC/Taco Bell, Pizza Hut, food: Wendy's, lodging: Relay Station Motel, other: Petrolube, truckwash
581	I-410
580	LP 13, WW White Rd, N...gas: Chevron, Fina/dsl, food: Frijoles Rest., Wendy's, lodging: Motel 6, Red Roof Inn, Rodeway Inn, other: Ford/Volvo Trucks, RV camping, tires, S...gas: Exxon/A&W/dsl, food: Bill Miller BBQ, McDonald's, Mexican Rest., Popeye's, Pizza Hut, Sandrita's Mexican,

	Sonic, Subway, lodging: Econolodge, Quality Inn, Rosepark Inn, Super 8, other: Ford/Freightliner, Volvo Trucks, tires
579	Houston St, N...gas: Valero/dsl, lodging: Best Value Inn, S...gas: Chevron, lodging: Day's Inn, Passport Inn
578	Pecan Valley Dr, ML King Dr, N...gas
577	US 87 S, to Roland Ave, S...food: Whataburger/24hr, lodging: Super 8
576	New Braunfels Ave, Gevers St, S...gas: Fina, Valero, food: McDonald's
575	Pine St, Hackberry St, S...food: Little Red Barn Steaks
574	I-37, US 281
573	Probandt St, N...food: Jack-in-the-Box, Miller's BBQ, S...gas: Valero, other: to SA Missions HS, tires
572	**I-10 and I-35 run together 3 miles**
155b	Durango Blvd, downtown, downtown, E...lodging: Best Western, Comfort Suites, Courtyard, Fairfield Inn, Holiday Inn, La Quinta, Ramada Ltd, Residence Inn, Woodfield Suites, other: HOSPITAL, W...food: McDonald's, lodging: Microtel, Motel 6, Radisson
155a	South Alamo St, E...gas: Exxon, Shell, food: Church's, Eddie's Drive Thru, McDonald's, Piedra's Negras, Pizza Hut, Wendy's, lodging: Comfort Inn, Day's Inn, Ramada Ltd, other: USPO, W...gas: Conoco, lodging: Microtel
154b	S Laredo St, Ceballos St, same as 155b
154a	Nogalitos St, no services
153	I-10 E, US 90 W, US 87, to Kelly AFB, Lackland AFB, to Kelly AFB, Lackland AFB
570	**I-10 and I-35 run together 3 miles**
569c	Santa Rosa St, downtown, to Our Lady of the Lake U
568	spur 421, Culebra Ave, Bandera Ave, S...to St Marys U
567	Lp 345, Fredericksburg Rd(from eb upper level accesses I-35 S, I-10 E, US 87 S, lower level accesses I-35 N)
566b	Hildebrand Ave, Fulton Ave, S...gas: Exxon, 7-11, lodging: Galaxy Motel

San Antonio

TEXAS

Interstate 10

E ↑ | **W** ↓

Exit	Description
566a	Fresno Dr, **N**...**gas:** Exxon, Valero, **food:** McDonald's, Subway, Whataburger
565c	(from wb), access to same as 565 a b, **S**...**gas:** Shell, **food:** Guadalahara Mexican, Starbucks, **lodging:** La Quinta
565b	Vance Jackson Rd, **N**...**food:** Miller's BBQ, **lodging:** Econolodge, Quality Inn, **other:** Wal-Mart SuperCtr/24hr, **S**...**gas:** Shell, **lodging:** La Quinta
565a	Crossroads Blvd, Balcone's Heights, **N**...**gas:** Exxon, Shell/dsl, **food:** Denny's, Whataburger, **lodging:** Comfort Suites, Rodeway Inn, **S**...**food:** Dave&Buster's, El Pollo Loco, McDonald's, **lodging:** Sumner Suites, Super 8, **other:** Firestone/auto, Mazda, RV Ctr, Target, Toyota, mall, transmissions
564b a	I-410, facilities off of I-410 W, Fredericksburg Rd
563	Callaghan Rd, **N**...**gas:** Mobil, Valero, **food:** Las Palapas Mexican, Subway, **lodging:** Embassy Suites, Marriott, **other:** $General, Ford, Lexus, Mazda, Sun Harvest Foods, Toyota, **S**...**gas:** Exxon, **food:** Mamacita's Rest., **other:** Lowe's Whse
561	Wurzbach Rd, **N**...**gas:** Mobil/dsl, **food:** Bennigan's, Bolo's Grille, County Line BBQ, Fuddrucker's, Golden Corral, Honeybaked Ham, Jason's Deli, Pappasito's Cantina, Popeye's, Quizno's, Sea Island Shrimphouse, Starbucks, Taste Of China, TX Land&Cattle, Wasabi Grill, **lodging:** AmeriSuites, Homewood Suites, Knight's Inn, Omni Hotel, Staybridge Suites, Studio+, **other:** BigLots, Ford, HEB Food/gas, Eckerd/24hr, Toyota, **S**...**gas:** Shell/dsl, **food:** Alamo Café, Arby's, Benihana, Chester's Burgers, China Sea, Church's, Denny's, El Taco Tote, IHOP, Jack-in-the-Box, Jim's Rest., Luby's, McDonald's, Pizza Hut, Sombrero Rosa Café, Taco Bell, Taco Cabana, Tony Roma, Village Inn, Wendy's, **lodging:** Baymont Inn, Best Western, Candlewood Suites, Drury Inn, Hawthorn Suites, Holiday Inn Express, Motel 6, Residence Inn, Sleep Inn, **other:** CarMax
560b	frontage rd(from eb), **N**...**food:** Water St Seafood, **other:** Chrysler/Jeep, Kia, Nissan
560a	Huebner Rd, **N**...**food:** Champp's, La Madeline, Macaroni Grill, On the Border, SaltGrass Steaks, **other:** Borders, Old Navy, Ross, **S**...**gas:** Chevron, Exxon, **food:** Burger King, Cracker Barrel, Jim's Rest., **lodging:** AmeriSuites, Day's Inn, Hampton Inn, Homestead Village, **other:** Cadillac/Hummer
559	Lp 335, US 87, Fredericksburg Rd, **N**...**food:** Outback Steaks, Pearl Inn, **other:** Buick/GMC, Land Rover, **S**...**gas:** Texaco, **food:** Krispy Kreme, **lodging:** Days Inn, Studio 6
558	De Zavala Rd, **N**...**gas:** Chevron, Exxon/dsl, Shell/Subway, **food:** Burger King, Carrabba's, Chili's, Joe's Crabshack, KFC/Taco Bell, Logan's Roadhouse, McDonald's, Sonic, Taco Cabana, **lodging:** Best Western, Econolodge, Super 8, **other:** Barnes&Noble, Chevrolet, HEB Food/gas, Home Depot, Hyundai, Marshall's, Petsmart, Target, **S**...**food:** A&W, CiCi's, IHOP, LJ Silver, Matamros, Quizno's, Schlotsky's, TGIFriday, Whataburger, Zio's Italian, **other:** Buick, Discount Tire, Sam's Club, Wal-Mart SuperCtr/24hr
557	Spur 53, Univ of TX at San Antonio, **N**...**other:** Jaguar/Mazerati/Ferrari, **lodging:** Howard Johnson, **S**...**lodging:** La Quinta, **other:** Costco/gas, Honda
556b	frontage rd, no services
556a	to Anderson Lp, **S**...**lodging:** Comfort Inn, **other:** to Seaworld
555	La Quintera Pkwy, **S**...**food:** Olive Garden, **lodging:** Motel 6, **other:** to La Cantera Pkwy
554	Camp Bullis Rd, **N**...**gas:** Citgo, **food:** Chick-fil-A, Mimi's Cafe, TGI Friday, **other:** Bass Pro Shop, Best Buy, JC Penney, Lowe's Whse, Old Navy, Ross, Russell Park, Target, WorldMkt, **S**...**gas:** Shell, **lodging:** Rodeway Inn, Motel 6(2mi)
551	Boerne Stage Rd(from wb), to Leon Springs, **N**...**gas:** Shamrock/dsl, **food:** Leon Springs Grill, McDonald's, Sonic, **S**...**food:** Las Palapas Mexican, Longhorns Rest., Pappa Nacho's, Quizno's, Starbucks, **other:** GNC, HEB Foods/gas
550	FM 3351, Ralph Fair Rd, **N**...**gas:** Exxon/dsl, Valero/dsl, **S**...**gas:** Shell/Domino's/dsl
546	Fair Oaks Pkwy, Tarpon Dr, **S**...**other:** American Dream RV Ctr, Harley-Davidson, **S**...**gas:** Chevron/dsl/café, Exxon/dsl/café, **other:** Chrysler/Jeep, Explore USA RV Ctr(1mi), Harley-Davidson, Hoover RV Ctr
543	Boerne Stage Rd, to Scenic LP Rd, **N**...**gas:** Citgo/dsl/24hr, **food:** Alamo Café, Copeland's Seafood/steaks, Caverns Inn/rest., **other:** Alamo Fiesta RV Park, Ancira RV Ctr, Chevrolet, Ford, Mercedes, NAPA, Pontiac/Buick/GMC, Toyota/Scion, to Cascade Caverns
542	(from wb), same as 540 **N**...**gas:** Shamrock, **food:** Burger King, El Matador, Wendy's, **other:** AutoZone, $Tree, Jiffy Lube, Wal-Mart SuperCtr/gas
540	TX 46, to New Braunfels, **N**...**gas:** Exxon/Taco Bell/dsl, Shell/dsl/24hr, Valero, **food:** Burger King, Church's, DQ, Denny's, Little Caesar's, Margarita's Café, Pizza Hut, Quizno's, Shanghai Chinese, Sonic, Taco Cabana, Wendy's, **lodging:** Best Western, Holiday Inn Express, Key to the Hills Motel, **other:** HEB Food/gas, Radio Shack, Walgreens, **S**...**food:** Chili's, Starbucks, Whataburger, **other:** Home Depot

Interstate 10

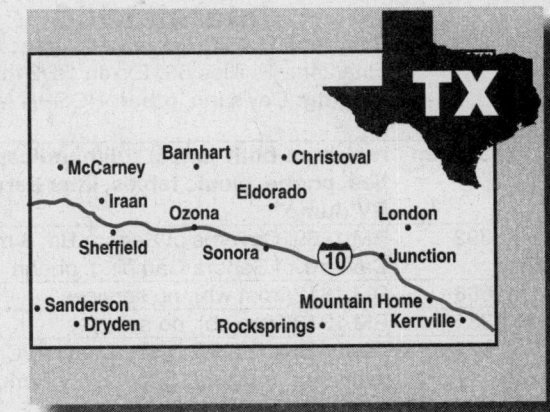

Exit	Description
539	Johns Rd, **N**...**lodging:** La Quinta, **S**...**gas:** Valero/dsl/LP
538mm	Cibolo Creek
538	Ranger Creek Rd, no services
537	US 87, to Boerne, no services
533	FM 289, Welfare, **N**...**food:** Po-Po Family Rest., **other:** Top of the Hill RV Park(1mi)
532mm	Little Joshua Creek
531mm	picnic area wb, tables, litter barrels
530mm	Big Joshua Creek
529.5mm	picnic area eb, tables, litter barrels
527	FM 1621(from wb), to Waring, no services
526.5mm	Holiday Creek
524	TX 27, FM 1621, to Waring, **N**...**vet**, **S**...**gas:** Chevron/dsl, Shell/24hr
523.5mm	Guadalupe River
523	US 87 N, to Comfort, **N**...**gas:** Chevron/McDonald's/dsl, **S**...**gas:** Exxon/dsl/24hr, **food:** DQ, **lodging:** Executive Inn, **other:** $General, USA RV Park
521.5mm	Comfort Creek
520	FM 1341, to Cypress Creek Rd, no services
515mm	Cypress Creek
514mm	**rest areas both lanes, full(handicapped) facilities, vending, phone, picnic tables, litter barrels, petwalk, playground, wireless internet**
508	TX 16, Kerrville, **N**...**gas:** Exxon/dsl, **other:** Chevrolet/Pontiac/Buick/Cadillac, RV camping, **0-2 mi** **S**...**gas:** Chevron/Subway/dsl, Exxon, Shell/McDonald's/dsl/24hr, T&C, Valero/dsl, **food:** Acapulco Mexican, Bamboo Asian, Cracker Barrel, DQ, Denny's, IHOP, KFC, Jack-in-the-Box, Luby's, McDonald's, Roma's Italian, Santo Coyote, Schlotsky's, Sonic, Tabas Mexican, Taco Bell, Taco Casa, Valentino's Italian, **lodging:** Best Value Inn, Budget Inn, Comfort Inn, Day's Inn, Econolodge, Hampton Inn, Holiday Inn Express, La Quinta, Motel 6, Whitten Inn, Yo Ranch Hotel, **other:** HOSPITAL, Advance Parts, Big Lots, $Tree, Hastings Books, Home Depot, Kerrville RV Ctr, Lowe's Whse, O'Reilly Parts, Walgreens, vet
505	FM 783, to Kerrville, **S**...**gas:** Exxon/dsl, **3 mi** **S** **on TX 27**...**gas:** Shell, **lodging:** Inn of the Hills, **food:** Billy Gene's, Cafe Riverstone, Chili's, CiCi's Pizza, Culver's, DQ, La Four Seafood, Lakehouse Rest., Mamcita's, McDonald's, Pizza Hut, Quizno's, Starbucks, Sonic, Subway, Taco Casa, Wendy's, Whataburger, **other:** AutoZone, CVS Drug, Discount Tire, HEB Foods, Wal-Mart SuperCtr/24hr
503.5mm	scenic views both lanes, litter barrels
501	FM 1338, **N**...**other:** Buckhorn RV Resort, **S**... **other:** KOA(2mi)
497mm	picnic area both lanes, tables, litter barrels
492	FM 479, **S**...Lone Oak Store
490	TX 41, no services
488	TX 27, to Ingram, Mountain Home, no services
484	Midway Rd, no services
477	US 290, to Fredericksburg, no services
476.5mm	service rd eb
472	Old Segovia Rd, no services
465	FM 2169, to Segovia, **S**...**gas:** Phillips 66/dsl/rest., **lodging:** Econolodge/RV park
464.5mm	Johnson Fork Creek
462	US 83 S, to Uvalde, no services
461mm	picnic area eb, tables, litter barrels
460	(from wb), to Junction, no services
459mm	picnic area wb, tables, litter barrels
457	FM 2169, to Junction, **N**...**gas:** Shell/dsl, **S**...**lodging:** Day's Inn/rest., **other:** RV camping, S. Llano River SP
456.5mm	Llano River
456	US 83/377, Junction, **N**...**gas:** Chevron/dsl, Conoco/dsl, Valero/McDonald's/dsl/24hr, **food:** Cooper's BBQ, JR's Rest., Tia Nina Mexican, **lodging:** Best Value Inn, **S**...**gas:** Exxon, Fina/dsl, Shell/dsl, **food:** DQ, Issac Rest., La Familia Mexican, Lum's BBQ, Sonic, **lodging:** Best Western, Hills Motel, Lazy T, Legends Inn, Rodeway Inn, **other:** HOSPITAL, KOA(.5mi), Food Basket Foods, TrueValue, to S Llano River SP
452.5mm	Bear Creek
451	RM 2291, to Cleo Rd, no services
448mm	North Creek
445	RM 1674, **S**...camping
444.5mm	Stark Creek
442mm	Copperas Creek
442	RM 1674, to Ft McKavett, **N**...to Ft McKavett SHC
439mm	N Llano River
438	Lp 291(from wb), to Roosevelt, same as 437
437	Lp 291(from eb, no EZ return), to Roosevelt, **1 mi** **N**...**gas:** Simon Bros Mercantile/dsl, **other:** USPO
429	RM 3130, to Harrell, no services
423mm	parking area both lanes, litter barrels
420	RM 3130, to Baker Rd, no services
412	Allison Rd, RM 3130, no services
404	RM 3130, RM 864, **N**...to Ft McKavett St HS, **3 mi** **S**...**gas:** TC/dsl, **lodging:** Best Value Inn, Holiday Host Motel, **other:** HOSPITAL
400	US 277, Sonora, **N**...**gas:** Shell/dsl, **food:** Sutton Co Steaks, **lodging:** Day's Inn, **other:** vet, **S**... **gas:** Chevron/dsl, Exxon/dsl/24hr, Fina/dsl, T&C/dsl, **food:** Country Cookin Café, DQ, La Mexicana Rest., Pizza Hut, Sonic, **lodging:** Best Value Inn, Best Western, Comfort Inn, **other:** Alco, Family$, Parts+

Interstate 10

E ↕ W

Ozona

399	(from eb)LP 467, Sonora, [S]...**gas:** Chevron/dsl, Fina/24hr, Phillips 66, Exxon/dsl/24hr, **food:** DQ, **lodging:** Day's Inn, **other:** HOSPITAL, RV camping
394mm	**rest area both lanes, full(handicapped) facilities, phone, picnic tables, litter barrel, petwalk, RV dump**
392	RM 1989, Caverns of Sonora Rd, **8 mi** [S]...**other:** Caverns of Sonora Camping, phone
388	RM 1312(from wb), no services
381	RM 1312(from eb), no services
372	Taylor Box Rd, [N]...**gas:** Chevron/Circle Bar/dsl/rest./24hr, **lodging:** Super 8/RV Park, **other:** auto museum
368	LP 466, [N]...same as 365 & 363
365	TX 163, Ozona, [N]...**gas:** Chevron/dsl, Exxon, Texaco/dsl/café, T&C/Country Cookin Cafe/Godfather's/dsl, **food:** Café NextDoor, DQ, Sonic, Subway, **lodging:** Best Value, Best Western, Economy Inn/RV Park, **other:** HOSPITAL, $General, NAPA, to David Crockett Mon, [S]...**gas:** Chevron, **food:** El Chato
363	Lp 466, to Ozona, no services
361	RM 2083, Pandale Rd, no services
357mm	Eureka Draw
351mm	Howard Draw
350	FM 2398, to Howard Draw, no services
349mm	parking area wb, litter barrels
346mm	parking area eb, litter barrels
343	TX 290 W, [S]...Ft. Lancaster Historic Site
337	Live Oak Rd, no services
336.5mm	Live Oak Creek
328	River Rd, Sheffield, [S]...**gas:** Fina/dsl
327.5mm	Pecos River
325	TX 290, TX 349, to Iraan, Sheffield, [N]...HOSPITAL
320	frontage rd, no services
314	frontage rd, no services
309mm	**rest area both lanes, full(handicapped) facilities, phone, picnic tables, litter barrels, petwalk, wireless internet**
307	US 190, FM 305, to Iraan, [N]...HOSPITAL
298	RM 2886, no services
294	FM 11, Bakersfield, [N]...**gas:** Exxon, [S]...**gas:** Chevron/dsl/café, **other:** phone
288	Ligon Rd, [N]...many windmills
285	McKenzie Rd, [S]...**other:** Domaine Cordier Ste Genevieve Winery
279mm	picnic area eb, tables, litter barrels
277	FM 2023, no services
273	US 67/385, to McCamey, [N]...**other:** picnic area wb, tables, litter barrels
272	University Rd, no services
264	Warnock Rd, [N]...**other:** KOA/BBQ/cafe
261	US 290 W, US 385 S, [N]...**gas:** Exxon/TCBY/dsl, [S]...**gas:** T&C, **lodging:** Econolodge, **food:** DQ, Pizza Hut, Sonic, Subway, **other:** HOSPITAL, RV camping
259b a	(259 from eb)TX 18, FM 1053, Ft Stockton, [N]...**gas:** Apache Fuel Ctr/dsl, Exxon, Fina/dsl, Shell/Burger King/dsl, **other:** I-10 RV Park

Ft Stockton

257	US 285, to Pecos, Ft Stockton, [N]...**other:** Comanche Land RV Park, golf, [S]...**gas:** Chevron/T&C/dsl, Exxon/dsl/rest., Shell, Valero/dsl, **food:** IHOP, KFC/Taco Bell, McDonald's, Pizza Hut, Pizza Pro, Sonic, Steak House, Subway, **lodging:** Day's Inn, Hampton Inn, Holiday Inn Express, Knight's Inn/Atrium West, La Quinta, Motel 6, Town&Country Motel, **other:** Ace Hardware, AutoZone, Chevrolet/Pontiac/Buick, $General, Ford/Lincoln/Mercury, Goodyear/auto, Mktbasket Foods, Wal-Mart, tires/repair
256	to US 385 S, Ft Stockton, **1 mi** [S]...**gas:** Shell/dsl, Valero/dsl, **food:** Alpine Rest., DQ, K-Bob's Steaks, KFC, Sonic, Subway, **lodging:** Best Western, Comfort Inn, Econolodge, Motel 6, Sleep Inn, Super 8, **other:** HOSPITAL, Ford, to Ft Stockton Hist Dist, Big Bend NP
253	FM 2037, to Belding, no services
248	US 67, FM 1776, to Alpine, [S]...to Big Bend NP
246	Firestone, no services
241	Kennedy Rd, no services
235	Mendel Rd, no services
233mm	**rest area both lanes, full(handicapped) facilities, phone, picnic tables, litter barrels, petwalk**
229	Hovey Rd, no services
222	Hoefs Rd, no services
214	(from wb), FM 2448, no services
212	TX 17, FM 2448, to Pecos, [N]...picnic area, litter barrels, [S]...**gas:** Fina/dsl/café, RV Camping
209	TX 17, [S]...**other:** to Davis Mtn SP, Ft Davis NHS
206	FM 2903, to Balmorhea, [S]...**other:** to Balmorhea SP
192	FM 3078, to Toyahvale, [S]...**other:** to Balmorhea SP
188	Giffin Rd, no services
187	I-20, to Ft Worth, Dallas
186	I-10, E to San Antonio (from wb)
185mm	picnic area both lanes, tables, litter barrels
184	Springhills, no services
181	Cherry Creek Rd, [S]...**gas:** Chevron/24hr
176	TX 118, FM 2424, to Kent, [N]...**gas:** Chevron/dsl, [S]...**other:** to McDonald Observatory, Davis Mtn SP, Ft Davis
173	Hurd's Draw Rd, no services
166	Boracho Sta, no services
159	Plateau, [N]...**gas:** Exxon/dsl/rest./24hr
153	Michigan Flat, no services
146	Wild Horse Rd, no services
146mm	weigh sta wb

Van Horn

145mm	**rest area both lanes, full(handicapped) facilities, picnic tables, litter barrels, petwalk**
140b	Ross Dr, Van Horn, [N]...**gas:** Chevron, Exxon/dsl, Love's/Subway/dsl/24hr, **lodging:** Comfort Inn, Day's Inn/rest., Desert Inn, Sands Motel/rest., **other:** El Campo RV Park, [S]...**other:** Mountain View RV Park/dump
140a	US 90, TX 54, Van Horn Dr, [N]...**gas:** Shell/dsl, **food:** Village Inn, **other:** HOSPITAL, $General, NAPA, Radio Shack, USPO, [S]...**gas:** Exxon, Pilot/Wendy's/dsl/24hr, **food:** Papa's Café, **other:** KOA, RV Dump

Interstate 10

E ↕ W

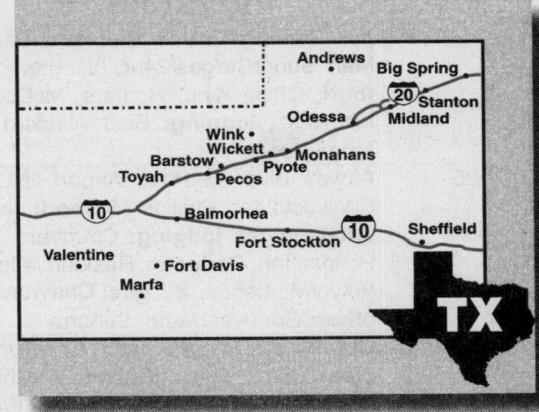

138 Lp 10, to Van Horn, **N**...**food:** Chuey's Rest., DQ, Pizza Hut, **lodging:** Best Western, Budget Inn, Econolodge, Economy Inn, Knights Inn, Motel 6, Ramada Ltd, **other:** Eagles Nest RV Park, Goodyear, IGA Foods, Pueblo Foods, USPO, auto/dsl repair, **S**...**gas:** Chevron/dsl/24hr, **food:** McDonald's, **lodging:** Holiday Inn Express, Super 8, **other:** tires/repair

137mm truck weigh sta eb

136mm scenic overlook wb, picnic tables, litter barrels

135mm Mountain/Central time zone line, Mountain/Central time zone line

133 (from wb)frontage rd, no services

129 to Hot Wells, Allamore, no services

108 to Sierra Blanca(from wb), same as 107

107 FM 1111, Sierra Blanca Ave, **N**...**gas:** Exxon/dsl/24hr, **food:** Michael's Rest., **other:** Sierra Blanca RV Park, truck/tire repair, USPO, to Hueco Tanks SP, **S**...**gas:** Chevron, **food:** La Familia, **other:** Stagecoach Trading Post

105 (106 from wb)Lp 10, Sierra Blanca, same as 107

102.5mm inspection sta eb

99 Lasca Rd, **N**...**other:** picnic area both lanes, picnic tables, litter barrels, no restrooms

98mm picnic area eb, tables, litter barrels, no restrooms

95 frontage rd(from eb), no services

87 FM 34, **S**...**gas:** Driver's Travel Mart/dsl/rest./24hr

85 Esperanza Rd, no services

81 FM 2217, no services

78 TX 20 W, to McNary, no services

77mm truck parking area wb

72 spur 148, to Ft Hancock, **S**...**gas:** Shell/dsl, **food:** Angie's Rest., **other:** Ford Hancock Motel

68 Acala Rd, no services

55 Tornillo, no services

51mm **rest area both lanes, full(handicapped) facilities, picnic tables, litter tables, petwalk**

49 FM 793, Fabens, **S**...**gas:** Exxon, **lodging:** Fabens Inn/Cafe, **other:** S&S Foods, **1 mi S**...**food:** Church's, McDonald's, Subway, **food:** Charlie Bigg's, **other:** Family$

42 FM 1110, to Clint, **S**...**gas:** Exxon/dsl, **lodging:** Cotton Valley Motel/RV Park/rest./dump

37 FM 1281, Horizon Blvd, **N**...**gas:** Flying J/Bonito's Rest./scales/@, Love's/Chester Fried/Subway/dsl/scales/24hr/@, **lodging:** Americana Inn, **other:** Freightliner **S**...**gas:** Petro/Mobil/Blimpie/dsl/scales/24hr/@, **food:** McDonald's, **lodging:** Deluxe Inn, **other:** Blue Beacon

35 Eastlake Blvd., no services

34 TX 375, Americas Ave, **N**...**gas:** Chevron/dsl/24hr, Exxon, Shamrock/dsl, **lodging:** Microtel, Value Place, **other:** GMC, Mission RV Camping, Peterbilt, **S**...**other:** RV camping, El Paso Mus of Hist

32 FM 659, Zaragosa Rd, **N**...**gas:** Chevron/dsl, **food:** Arby's, Barrigos, BJ's Grill, Cheddar's, Furr's Buffet, Great American Steaks, IHOP, Krispy Kreme, LJ Silver/Taco Bell, Logan's Roadhouse, Macaroni Grill, Outback Steaks, Peiwei Asian, Peter Piper Pizza, San Francisco Oven, Starbucks, Whataburger/24hr, **lodging:** Holiday Inn Express,

El Paso

Red Roof Inn, **other:** Chevrolet, Circuit City, Discount Tire, Kohl's, Lowe's Whse, Michael's, Nissan, Office Depot, World Mkt, **S**...**gas:** Fina/7-11, Shamrock/dsl, **food:** Howah Chinese

30 Lee Trevino Dr, **N**...**gas:** Exxon, **food:** Chili's, Jack-in-the-Box, Taco Cabana, Whataburger, **lodging:** La Quinta, Red Roof Inn, Studio 6, **other:** Discount Tire, Firestone, Ford, Isuzu, Home Depot, Lexus, NTB, Sears/auto, Toyota, mall, **S**...**gas:** Valero/24hr, **lodging:** Ramada, **other:** Chrysler/Jeep/Dodge, Nissan, Harley-Davidson, Hyundai

29 Lomaland Dr, **N**...**food:** Denny's, Edelweiss Rest., **lodging:** AmeriSuites, **S**...**gas:** Fina/7-11, **food:** Julio's Café, Lin's Buffet, Rudy's BBQ, Shangri-La Rest., **lodging:** HomeGate Studios, Ramada, Westar Suites, **other:** Harley-Davidson

28b Yarbrough Dr, El Paso, **N**...**gas:** Chevron/24hr, Shell, **food:** Beijing Chinese, Bennigan's, Burger King, Grandy's, Hong Kong Buffet, LJ Silver, McDonald's, Quizno's, Sonic, Subway, Texas Roadhouse, Wendy's, Whataburger, Wienerschnitzel, Wyatt's Cafeteria, **lodging:** Day's Inn, **other:** Marshall's, Mervyn's, PepBoys, Radio Shack, Ross, Wal-Mart SuperCtr/gas/24hr, **S**...**gas:** Valero/24hr, **food:** Applebee's, Fuddrucker's, LaMalenche Café, Pizza Hut, Tony Roma, **lodging:** Baymont Inn, Comfort Inn, InTown Suites, La Quinta, Suburban Lodge

28a FM 2316, McRae Blvd, **N**...**gas:** Chevron/24hr, **food:** ChuckeCheese, Jack-in-the-Box, KFC, Pizza Hut, Red Barrel Grill, Taco Bell, **lodging:** La Quinta, **other:** HOSPITAL, Barnes&Noble, Best Buy, BigLots, Firestone/auto, Goodyear/auto, Jo-Ann Fabrics, K-Mart, Michael's, Office Depot, Walgreens, **S**...**gas:** Chevron, Circle K, Exxon, Fina/7-11, Phillips 66/dsl, **food:** Whataburger, **other:** Hyundai/Saturn

27 Hunter Dr, Viscount Blvd, **N**...**gas:** Fina/7-11, Valero, **food:** Carrow's Rest., Grand China Buffet, K-Bob's, Red Lobster, Taco Bell, **lodging:** La Quinta, **other:** Barnes&Noble, Best Buy, CompUSA, Firestone, **S**...**gas:** Exxon/Subway/dsl, Shell, **food:** Whataburger/24hr, **other:** Family$, Food City

26 Hawkins Blvd, El Paso, **N**...**gas:** Chevron, Shamrock, Shell, **food:** Arby's, Burger King, Country Kitchen, DQ, Golden Corral, IHOP, Landry's Seafood, Luby's, Olive Garden, Red Lobster, Taco Cabana, Wyatt's Cafeteria, **lodging:** Howard Johnson, **other:** Circuit City, Dillard's, JC Penney, Office De-

Interstate 10

E

W

El Paso

pot, Pennzoil, Sam's Club/gas, Sears/auto, Wal-Mart SuperCtr/gas/24hr, [S]...**gas:** Shamrock/dsl, **food:** China King, Hooters, McDonald's, Village Inn Rest., **lodging:** Best Western, **other:** Tony Lama Boots

25	Airway Blvd, El Paso Airport, [N]...**gas:** Valero, Shell/dsl/24hr, Phillips 66, **food:** Jack-in-the-Box, Whataburger, **lodging:** Courtyard, Hampton Inn, Holiday Inn, Radisson, Residence Inn, **other:** VW/Volvo/Mercedes, [S]...**gas:** Chevron/dsl/rest./24hr, **other:** Goodyear/auto, Subaru
24b	Geronimo Dr, [N]...**gas:** Chevron/24hr, **food:** Steak&Ale, Taco Cabana, **other:** Dillard's, Mervyn's, Office Depot, Target, Walgreen, mall, [S]...**gas:** Circel K/gas, Fina/7-11, Phillips 66, **food:** Senses De Brazil, Bombay Bicycle Club, Denny's, **lodging:** AmeriSuites, Embassy Suites, La Quinta
24a	Trowbridge Dr, [N]...**gas:** Fina, Thunderbird Gas, **food:** Alexandrio's Mexican, Luby's, McDonald's, Steak&Ale, Whataburger, **lodging:** Budget Inn, **other:** Ford, Nissan, Toyota
23b	US 62/180, to Paisano Dr, [N]...**food:** Jack-in-the-Box, McDonald's, **other:** Ford, U-Haul, to Carlsbad
23a	Raynolds St, [S]...**food:** Arby's, **lodging:** Motel 6, Super 8, **other:** HOSPITAL
22b	US 54, Patriot Fwy
22a	Copia St, El Paso, [N]...**gas:** Valero, **food:** KFC
21	Piedras St, El Paso, [N]...**gas:** Exxon, **food:** Burger King, McDonald's, **other:** Family$
20	Dallas St, Cotton St, [N]...**gas:** Valero, **food:** Church's, Subway
19	TX 20, El Paso, downtown, [N]...**gas:** Chevron, [S]...**gas:** Texaco, **food:** Burger King, **lodging:** Holiday Inn Express, Travelodge
18b	Franklin Ave, Porfirio Diaz St, no services
18a	Schuster Ave, [N]...Sun Bowl, [S]...to UTEP
16	Executive Ctr Blvd, [N]...**gas:** Valero/24hr, **food:** Burger King, **lodging:** Howard Johnson, **other:** Ford
13b a	US 85, Paisano Dr, to Sunland Park Dr, [N]...**gas:** Valero/24hr, **food:** Barriga's Café, Carino's Italian, ChuckeCheese, Grand China, Great American Steaks, IHOP, Olive Garden, PF Chang's, Red Lobster, Sonic, Whataburger/24hr, **other:** Barnes&Noble, Best Buy, Circuit City, Dillard's, JC Penney, Office Depot, PetsMart, Sears/auto, Target, mall, [S]...**gas:** Shamrock/dsl/24hr, Shell, **food:** La Malinche Mexican, McDonald's, Sonic, Subway, **lodging:** Best Western, Comfort Suites, Holiday Inn, Sleep Inn, Studio+, **other:** GMC/Pontiac/Buick, Sunland Park RaceTrack
12	Resler Dr(from wb), no services
11	TX 20, to Mesa St, Sunland Park, [N]...**gas:** Chevron/dsl/24hr, Circle K/gas, Phillips 66, Valero/dsl/24hr, **food:** Carrow's/24hr, Chili's, CiCi's, Cracker Barrel, Denny's, Famous Dave's, Golden Corral, Jaxon's Rest/brewery, K-Bob's, LJ Silver/A&W, Papa John's, Popeye's, Rancher's Grill, Red Lobster, Souper Salad, Subway, Taco Bell,

Taco Tote, Tony Roma, Wienerschnitzel, Wendy's, Whataburger, **lodging:** Baymont Inn, Comfort Inn, La Quinta, Red Roof Inn, **other:** Albertson's, Big-Lots, Checker Parts, Fabric Whse, Firestone/auto, Goodyear/auto, Home Depot, PepBoys, SteinMart, Wal-Mart SuperCtr/24hr, [S]...**gas:** Chevron/dsl/24hr, Valero/dsl/24hr, **food:** Ay Caramba Mexican, Burger King, Church's, Golden China, Hudson's Grill, Jack-in-the-Box, KFC, Leo's Mexican, Luby's, McDonald's, Peter Piper Pizza, Pizza Hut, Subway, Taco Cabana, Village Inn Rest., **lodging:** Best Value Inn, Day's Inn, Extended Stay America, Motel 6, Travelodge, **other:** AutoZone, Big 8 Foods, Furr's Foods, Hobby Lobby, Martin Tires, Radio Shack, Sam's Club/gas, Walgreen

9	Redd Rd, [N]...**food:** Applebee's, Burger King, Double Dave's Pizza, Pizza Hut, Starbucks, **other:** Albertson's/gas, Checker Parts, Ford, Kohl's, Lowe's Whse, [S]...**gas:** Phillips 66/dsl, Circle K/gas, **other:** Chevrolet, Honda
8	Artcraft Rd, [S]...**gas:** Shell/dsl, **lodging:** Microtel
6	Lp 375, to Canutillo, [N]...**gas:** Shell/Taco Bell/dsl, **other:** to Trans Mountain Rd, Franklin Mtns SP, [S]...**gas:** Shorty's/Subway/dsl, **other:** RV camping
5mm	truck check sta eb
2	Westway, Vinton, [N]...**gas:** Petro/Mobil/Blimpie/dsl/scales/24hr/@, **other:** American RV Center, Camping World(1mi), PetroLube/tires, [S]...**gas:** gas/24hr, **other:** Volvo/Mac, truck repair
1mm	**Welcome Ctr eb, full(handicapped)facilities, info, phone, picnic tables, litter barrels, petwalk, weigh sta wb**
0	FM 1905, Anthony, [N]...**gas:** ⚡/Flying J/Conoco/dsl/LP/24hr/@, **lodging:** Super 8, **rest area wb, full(handicapped) facilities, picnic tables, litter barrels**, [S]...**gas:** Fina/7-11/dsl, Piggy Bank/Burger King/dsl/24hr, Pilot/Subway/Wendy's/dsl/24hr/@, **food:** Great American Steaks, **lodging:** Best Western, **other:** Big 8 Foods, $General, truckwash
0mm	Texas/New Mexico state line

Interstate 20

E

W

Exit #	Services
636mm	Texas/Louisiana state line
635.5mm	**Welcome Ctr wb/parking area eb, full(handicapped)facilities, phone, picnic tables, litter barrels, petwalk**
635	TX 9, TX 156, to Waskom, [N]...**gas:** Chevron/Burger King/dsl, Exxon/dsl, **food:** DQ, Hunt Bro's Pizza, Jim's BBQ, **other:** Family$, USPO
633	US 80, FM 9, FM 134, to Waskom, [N]...**gas:** Texaco, **food:** Catfish Village Rest. **lodging:** Daynight Inn, [S]...**other:** Miss Ellie's RV Park
628	to US 80(from wb), to frontage rd(from eb)
624	FM 2199, to Scottsville, no services
620	FM 31, to Elysian Fields, no services
617	US 59, Marshall, [N]...**gas:** Exxon/24hr, Texaco/24hr, **food:** Applebee's, Catfish Exress, Golden Corral, Gucci's Pizza, IHOP, McDonald's, Subway,

Interstate 20

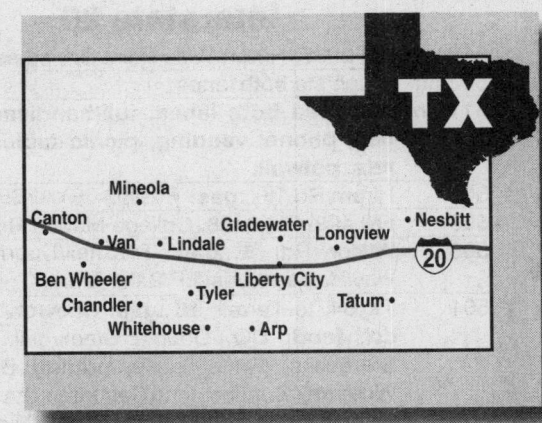

<table>
<tr><td rowspan="2" style="writing-mode:vertical">E ↕ W</td></tr>
</table>

E ↕ W

Marshall

Waffle House, Wendy's, Whataburger, **lodging:** Best Western, Comfort Suites, Express Inn, Fairfield Inn, Hampton Inn, Holiday Inn Express, La Quinta, **other:** Chevrolet/Cadillac, Chrysler/Dodge/Jeep, Ford/Lincoln/Mercury, Toyota, Country Pines RV Park(8mi), S...**gas:** Chevron/dsl, Conoco/rest./dsl/24hr, Shamrock/dsl, **food:** Hungri Maverick Rest., **lodging:** Best Value Inn, Econolodge, Motel 6, Super 8

614	TX 43, to Marshall, S...to Martin Creek Lake SP
610	FM 3251, no services
608mm	**rest area both lanes, full(handicapped)facilities, phone, vending, picnic tables, litter barrels**
604	FM 450, Hallsville, N...**gas:** Shamrock/dsl, **other:** 450 Hitchin' Post RV Park, to Lake O' the Pines
600mm	Mason Creek
599	FM 968, Longview, N...**lodging:** Fairfield Inn(8mi), Wingate Inn(8mi), **other:** Kenworth Trucks, S...**gas:** Chevron/Natl TrkStp/Justin's Cafe, Exxon/dsl, **other:** Goodyear, truck repair
596	US 259 N, TX 149, to Lake O' Pines, N...**gas:** Exxon/Grandy's/dsl, Texaco/dsl, **food:** Burger King, Whataburger, **lodging:** Comfort Suites, Microtel, Super 8, **other:** HOSPITAL, S...**gas:** Valero/dsl, **lodging:** Holiday Inn Express, **other:** to Martin Lake SP
595b a	TX 322, Estes Pkwy, N...**gas:** Chevron/Subway/dsl, Shamrock, Texaco/dsl/24hr, **food:** DQ, Jack-in-the-Box, McDonald's, Pizza Hut, Waffle House, **lodging:** Day's Inn, ElmBrook Inn, Express Inn, Guest Inn, La Quinta, Longview Inn, Stratford Inn, S...**gas:** Fina/dsl, **food:** KFC/Taco Bell, **lodging:** Hampton Inn, Motel 6
593mm	Sabine River
591	FM 2087, FM 2011, no services
589b a	US 259, TX 31, Kilgore(exits left from both lanes), **1-3 mi** S...**food:** Kilgore Café, **lodging:** Budget Inn, Comfort Inn, Day's Inn, Holiday Inn Express, Homewood Suites, Ramada Inn, S...**other:** E Texas Oil Museum
587	TX 42, Kilgore, N...**gas:** Shamrock, **food:** Bodacious BBQ, S...**gas:** Exxon/dsl, **other:** E TX Oil Museum, **3mi** S...**other:** Wal-Mart SuperCtr
583	TX 135, to Kilgore, Overton, N...**gas:** Exxon/dsl, **other:** Shallow Creek RV Resort
582	FM 3053, Liberty City, N...**gas:** Chevron/Whataburger/dsl, Exxon/Subway/dsl, Fina, **food:** Bob's BBQ, DQ, Java House, Sonic
579	Joy-Wright Mtn Rd, no services
575	Barber Rd, no services
574mm	picnic area both lanes, picnic tables, litter barrels, handicapped accessible
571b	FM 757, Omen Rd, to Starrville, no services
571a	US 271, to Gladewater, Tyler, no services
567	TX 155, N...**gas:** Citgo/dsl/24hr, S...**lodging:** Day's Inn
565	FM 2015, to Driskill-Lake Rd, no services
562	FM 14, N...**food:** Bodacious BBQ, **other:** Northgate RV Park, to Tyler SP, S...**other:** CB Shop
560	Lavender Rd, no services

Canton

557	Jim Hogg Rd, N...**gas:** Shell/dsl
556	US 69, to Tyler, N...**gas:** RaceWay, Shamrock/dsl, **food:** Amigo's Mexican, Burger King, Domino's, Eastern Buffet, Juanita's Mexican, LoneStar Steaks, McDonald's, Pizza Inn, Sonic, Subway, Taco Bell, Tosado's Cafe, **lodging:** Comfort Inn, Day's Inn, Express Inn, Hampton Inn, **other:** Lowe's Whse, Wal-Mart SuperCtr/gas, S...**gas:** Chevron, Exxon, **food:** Cracker Barrel, DQ, Wendy's, **lodging:** Best Value Inn
554	Harvey Rd, S...**other:** Yellow Rose RV Park
552	FM 849, N...**gas:** Chevron/24hr
548	TX 110, to Grand Saline, N...**gas:** Exxon/dsl, S...**gas:** Shamrock/dsl
546mm	check sta eb
544	Willow Branch Rd, N...**gas:** Conoco/dsl/rest., **other:** Willow Branch RV Park
540	FM 314, to Van, N...**gas:** Love's/Carl's Jr/dsl/24hr/@, **food:** DQ, **lodging:** Van Inn
538mm	**rest area both lanes, full(handicapped)facilities, phone, vending, picnic tables, litter barrels, petwalk**
537	FM 773, FM 16, no services
536	Tank Farm Rd, no services
533	Oakland Rd, to Colfax, N...**gas:** Shamrock/dsl
530	FM 1255, N...**other:** Fish & Jog RV Park
528	FM 17, to Grand Saline, no services
527	TX 19, N...**gas:** Exxon/Burger King, Texaco/dsl/24hr, **food:** Jewl's Rest., Ranchero Rest., Whataburger/24hr, **lodging:** Comfort Inn, Luxury Suites, Super 8, S...**gas:** Chevron/dsl/24hr, Phillips 66/dsl/24hr, Shell/dsl, **food:** DQ, Dairy Palace, Jerry's Pizza, Juanita's Mexican, KFC/Taco Bell, McDonald's, Senorita's Mexican, **lodging:** Best Western, Day's Inn, **other:** Chrysler/Dodge/Jeep, Ford/Mercury, to First Monday SP, RV camping, LP
526	FM 859, to Edgewood, N...**other:** Edgewood Heritage Park, S...**other:** to First Monday SP
523	TX 64, to Canton, no services
521	Myrtle Springs Rd, N...trailer sales, S...**other:** Marshall's RV Ctr, RV camp/dump, U-Haul
519	Turner-Hayden Rd, no services
516	FM 47, to Wills Point, N...to Lake Tawakoni, S...**gas:** Shamrock/24hr, **food:** Robertson's Café/gas, Interstate Motel/café

TEXAS

Interstate 20

512	FM 2965, Hiram-Wills Point Rd, no services
512mm	weigh sta both lanes
511mm	**rest area both lanes, full(handicapped) facilities, phone, vending, picnic tables, litter barrels, petwalk**
509	Hiram Rd, **S...gas:** Phillips 66/dsl/BBQ/Café
506	FM 429, FM 2728, College Mound Rd
503	Wilson Rd, **S...gas:** TA/Shell/Country Fair/Subway/Pizza Hut/dsl/LP/24hr/@
501	TX 34, to Terrell, **N...gas:** Chevron/24hr, Exxon/dsl, **food:** DQ, Double Steak/grill, Schlotsky's, Starbucks, Waffle House, **lodging:** Best Inn, Best Western, Comfort Inn, Day's Inn, La Quinta, Motel 6, **other:** HOSPITAL, Home Depot, **S...gas:** Citgo/dsl, Phillips 66, Shamrock/dsl/24hr, **food:** Applebee's, Carmona's Cantina, McDonald's, Wendy's, **lodging:** Super 8, **other:** Tanger Outlet/famous brands
499b	Rose Hill Rd, to Terrell, no services
499a	to US 80, W to Dallas, **N...gas:** Exxon/dsl, Shell, **food:** Dennys, Grandy's, Subway
498	FM 148, to Terrell, **N...gas:** Exxon/Denny's/dsl, Shell/dsl, **food:** Grandy's, Philly Connection
493	FM 1641, **S...gas:** Exxon/Pizza Inn/dsl
491	FM 2932, Helms Tr, to Forney, **N...gas:** Shell/Subway/dsl
490	FM 741, to Forney, no services
487	FM 740, to Forney, **S...**Forney RV park
483	Lawson Rd, Lasater Rd, no services
482	Belt Line Rd, to Lasater, **S...gas:** Shell/KFC/Pizza Hut/Subway, **other:** RV park
481	Seagoville Rd, **N...gas:** Fina, Valero, **lodging:** Best Value Inn, **S...food:** Lindy's Rest.
480	I-635, N to Mesquite
479b a	US 175, **S...gas:** Shell
477	St Augustine Rd, **S...gas:** Shell/dsl, **food:** Sonic
476	Dowdy Ferry Rd, no services
474	TX 310 N, Central Expsy
473b a	JJ Lemmon Rd, I-45 N to Dallas, S to Houston
472	Bonnie View Rd, **N...gas:** /Flying J/Conoco/dsl/LP/rest./24hr/@, Shell, **food:** Jack-in-the-Box, **lodging:** Ramada Ltd, **other:** Blue Beacon, Speedco Lube, **S...gas:** TA/Exxon/Burger King/Taco Bell/Pizza Hut/dsl/scales/24hr/@
470	TX 342, Lancaster Rd, **N...gas:** Chevron/24hr, USA/Texaco/Subway/dsl/rest./scales/24hr/@, **food:** BBQ, **S...gas:** Citgo/Subway, Pilot/Wendy's/dsl/24hr/2, **food:** McDonald's, Sonic, Taco Bell, LJ Silver, Whataburger, William's Chicken, **lodging:** Day's Inn, Quest Inn
468	Houston School Rd, **S...gas:** Exxon/dsl, **food:** Whataburger
467b a	I-35E, N to Dallas, S to Waco, **1 mi** **N...**off of I-35E, **gas:** Shell, **food:** McDonald's
466	S Polk St, **N...gas:** Citgo, Conoco/dsl, Exxon, **food:** Sonic, Subway, **S...gas:** Love's/Carl's Jr/dsl/24hr
465	Wheatland/S Hampton Rds, **N...gas:** Shell/dsl, **S...gas:** Chevron/McDonald's, RaceWay, **food:** Arby's, Cheddar's, Jack-in-the-Box, Popeye's,

	Sonic, Spring Creek BBQ, Taco Bell, Wendy's, **lodging:** Comfort Inn, Super 8, **other:** HOSPITAL, Home Depot, Buick/GMC/Pontiac, Home Depot, Honda, Lincoln/Mercury, Lowe's Whse, Mazda, Petsmart, Sam's Club/gas, Saturn, Wal-Mart SuperCtr/24hr
464b a	US 67, Love Fwy
463	Camp Wisdom Rd, **N...gas:** Chevron/McDonald's, Exxon, TA, **food:** Catfish King Rest., Denny's, Taco Bell/LJ Silver, Tuesday Morning, **lodging:** Best Value Inn, Holiday Inn, Lexington Suites, Motel 6, Ramada Inn, Royal Inn, **other:** Chief Parts, Chrysler/Jeep, Ford, Nissan, **S...gas:** Citgo, **food:** Bennigan's, Blimpie, Burger King, Jack-in-the-Box, McDonald's, Olive Garden, Owens Rest., Red Lobster, Subway, Wendy's, **other:** Advance Parts, Best Buy, K-Mart, NTB, PepBoys, Pontiac, Target, Toyota
462b a	Duncanville Rd(no EZ wb return), **S...gas:** Exxon, Shell/dsl, **food:** Arby's, KFC, Mr Gatti's, Whataburger, **lodging:** Hilton Garden, Motel 6, **other:** Goodyear, Kroger, Radio Shack
461	Cedar Ridge Rd
460	TX 408, no services
458	Mt Creek Pkwy, no services
457	FM 1382, to Grand Prairie, **N...gas:** Shell/dsl, Valero/dsl, **food:** Waffle House, **S...gas:** RaceTrac, **food:** Jack-in-the-Box, **other:** to Joe Pool Lake
456	Carrier Pkwy, to Corn Valley Rd, **N...food:** Chick-fil-A, Don Pablo, Starbucks, Taco Cabana, Whataburger, **other:** Home Depot, Kohl's, Target, **S...gas:** Fina, Shell, **food:** BBQ, Boston Mkt, Cheddar's, Chili's, Denny's, IHOP, Little Caesar's, McDonald's, Subway, TCBY, **lodging:** Holiday Inn Express, **other:** Albertson's, CVS Drug, Pep Boys, Walgreen
454	Great Southwest Pkwy, **N...gas:** Chevron/24hr, Conoco/dsl, **food:** Beto's, Carino's Italian, Chucke-Cheese, KFC, McDonald's, Taco Bell, Taco Bueno, Texas Roadhouse, Waffle House, Wendy's, Wienerschnitzel, **lodging:** Day's Inn, Quality Inn, **other:** HOSPITAL, Harley-Davidson, **S...gas:** Exxon, Shamrock/Burger King, Shell/Subway/dsl, **food:** Applebee's, Arby's, Burger King, Schlotsky's, Sonic, **lodging:** Comfort Inn, **other:** Discount Tire, Dodge, $Tree, Kroger, Office Depot, Sam's Club, Wal-Mart SuperCtr/24hr, to Joe Pool Lake
453b a	TX 360, no services
452	Frontage Rd, no services
451	Collins St, New York Ave, **N...gas:** Mobil, RaceTrac, **food:** Jack-in-the-Box, Pizza Hut, **other:** Acura, Crysler, Mazda/VW/Kia, Saturn, **S...gas:** QT, Shamrock, Shell, **food:** McDonald's, Sonic, Taco Bueno, **other:** Lincoln/Mercury, Nissan, Ponitac/GMC/ Buick
450	Matlock Rd, **N...gas:** Citgo/7-11, Fina/dsl, **food:** Abuelo's Mexican, BBQ, IHOP, Mercado Juarez Café, SaltGrass Steaks, Spaghetti Whse, Tony Roma's, Wendy's, **lodging:** Comfort Inn, Hampton Inn, La Quinta, **other:** HOSPITAL, CompUSA, Lowe's Whse, Michael's, Old Navy, **S...gas:** Citgo/7-11, Shamrock, Shell, **food:** Joe's Pizza, **other:** Fry's Electronics, NTB

Interstate 20

449 FM 157, Cooper St, 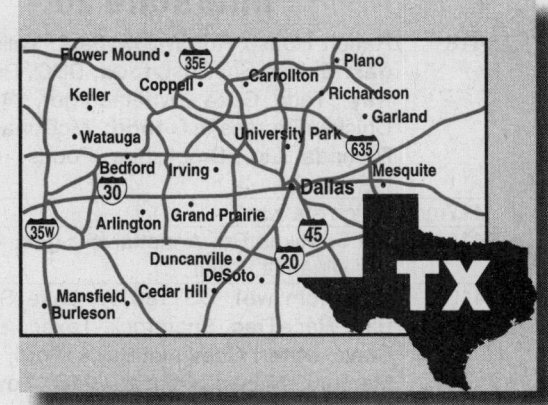**N...gas:** Fina, Mobil, Shell, 7-11, **food:** BBQ, Bennigan's, Blackeyed Pea, Chili's, China Café, CiCi's, Don Pablo, Golden Corral, Grandy's, Jack-in-the-Box, Jason's Deli, KFC, McDonald's, On the Border, Outback Steaks, Owens Rest., Razzoo's Cajun Café, Red Lobster, Salt Grass Steaks, Schlotsky's, Souper Salad, Spaghetti Whse, Starbucks, Texana Grill, Thai Cuisine, Wendy's, Whataburger, **lodging:** Days Inn, Holiday Inn Express, Homestead Village, La Quinta, Studio 6, **other:** Barnes&Noble, Best Buy, Dillard's, Discount Tire, Hancock Fabrics, Hyundai, JC Penney, Mervyn's, Office Depot, Sears/auto, Subaru, Target, TJ Maxx, mall, **S...gas:** Chevron, Citgo/7-11, Conoco, Mobil, **food:** Applebee's, Arby's, Boston Mkt, Burger King, Burger St, Chick-fil-A, Denny's, Dos Gringo's Mexican, El Fenix Mexican, HomeTown Buffet, LJ Silver, Luby's, Macaroni Grill, McDonald's, Old Country Buffet, Olive Garden, Popeye's, Shoney's, Sonic, Taco Bueno, TGIFriday, **other:** Circuit City, Ford, GMC, Home Depot, Isuzu, K-Mart, Kroger, Pontiac, Ross, Wal-Mart SuperCtr/24hr

448 Bowen Rd, **N...gas:** Conoco/dsl, Shell/24hr, **food:** Bobby V, Cracker Barrel, **S...gas:** Shell

447 Kelly-Elliott Rd, Park Springs Blvd, **N...gas:** Citgo, 7-11, **S...gas:** Exxon, Fina/Blimpie, **other:** camp

445 Green Oaks Blvd, **N...gas:** Conoco, Minyard, Shell, **food:** Arby's, BBQ, Boston Mkt, Burger King, Grandy's, Hooters, Jack-in-the-Box, KFC, Koltr's BBQ, Mac's Grill, Pizza Hut, Pizza Inn, Taco Bell, Taipan Chinese, Whataburger, **other:** Albertson's, Eckerd/24hr, Office Depot, **S...gas:** Chevron/24hr, Citgo/7-11, Shamrock, **food:** Cheddar's, IHOP, Fazoli's, Khaki's, McDonald's, O'Riley's, Pancho's Mexican, Schlotsky's, Sonic, Steak&Ale, Taco Bueno, Waffle House, **other:** AutoZone, Discount Tire, $General, Winn-Dixie

444 US 287 S, to Waxahatchie

443 Bowman Springs Rd(from wb)

442b a I-820 to Ft Worth, US 287 bus, **N...gas:** Citgo, **lodging:** Great Western Inn, **S...gas:** Chevron, **food:** DQ

441 Anglin Dr, Hartman Lane, **N...gas:** Conoco/dsl, **lodging:** Super 8, **S...gas:** Conoco/dsl

440b Forest Hill Dr, **S...gas:** Chevron/24hr, Conoco, Shell/dsl, **food:** Braum's, Capt D's, CiCi's, DQ, Denny's, Domino's, Jack-in-the-Box, Luby's, McDonald's, Sonic, Starbucks, Subway, **lodging:** Comfort Inn, **other:** Brookshire Foods, Discount Tire, $Tree, Eckerd, Walgreen

440a Wichita St, **N...gas:** Chevron, **food:** Taco Casa, Wendy's, **S...gas:** Conoco, Fina, Texaco, **food:** Chicken Express, McDonald's, Pizza Hut, Schlotsky's, Taco Bueno, Whataburger

439 Campus Dr, **N...other:** Ford, Chrysler/Jeep, **S... other:** Sam's Club/gas

438 Oak Grove Rd, **1 mi N...gas:** Shell, **food:** Burger King, Denny's, Jack-in-the Box, McDonald's, Whataburger, **lodging:** Day's Inn, **S...gas:** Shamrock

437 I-35W, N to Ft Worth, S to Waco

436b Hemphill St, **N...gas:** Shell/dsl **S...other:** Chevrolet

436a FM 731(from eb), to Crowley Ave, **N...other:** $General, SavALot Food, **S...gas:** Chevron, Conoco/dsl, DQ, Pizza Hut/Taco Bell

435 McCart St, **N...gas:** Conoco/dsl, Fina, Shell, Valero, **S...gas:** Shell/24hr

434b Trail Lakes Dr, **S...gas:** Shell, **food:** Pancho's Mexican, Starbucks, Wendy's, **other:** CVS Drug

434a Granbury rd, **N...gas:** Phillips 66, **S...food:** Super Buffet, **other:** JoAnne Fabrics

433 Hulen St, **N...gas:** Shell/dsl, **food:** ChuckeCheese, Grady's Grill, Hooters, Olive Garden, Souper Salad, Subway, TGIFriday, **lodging:** TownePlace Suites, **other:** Albertson's, Circuit City, Home Depot, Office Depot, Savon foods, TJ Maxx, **S...gas:** Valero, **food:** BBQ, Bennigan's, Denny's, Jack-in-the-Box, McDonald's, Red Lobster, **lodging:** Hampton Inn, **other:** Borders, Ross, mall

431 (432 from wb), TX 183, Bryant-Irvin Rd, **N...food:** Mimi's Café, **other:** Best Buy, CompUSA, Kohls, Lowe's Whse, Michael's, Sam's Club, **S...gas:** Chevron/24hr, Exxon, QT, Shell, Texaco, **food:** Blackeyed Pea, Chic-Fil-A, Cousin's BBQ, Fuddruckers, IHOP, Joe's Crabshack, Outback Steaks, Quizno's, Razzoo's Cajun, Rio Mambo, SaltGrass Steaks, Sam's Rest., Schlotzsky's, Starbucks, Subway, Yogi's Deli, **lodging:** AmeriSuites, Holiday Inn Express, Hyatt, La Quinta, **other:** HOSPITAL, Buick, Costco/gas, Ford, Goodyear/auto, Mazda, Saturn, Suzuki, Staples, Target, Walgreen

430mm Clear Fork Trinity River

429b Winscott Rd, no services

429a US 377, to Granbury, **N...gas:** Phillips 66/dsl **food:** Cracker Barrel, **lodging:** Best Western, **S...gas:** Chevron, Exxon, RaceTrac/24hr, Shell, **food:** DQ, McDonald's, Waffle House, Whataburger/24hr, **other:** Albertson's

428 I-820, N around Ft Worth

426 RM 2871, Chapin School Rd, no services

425 Markum Ranch Rd, no services

421 I-30 E(from eb), to Ft Worth

420 FM 1187Aledo, Farmer, parking, **S...other:** Cowtown RV Camping

419mm weigh sta eb

TEXAS

Interstate 20

E

↑
↓

W

Weatherford

418	Ranch House Rd, Willow Park, Willow Park, **N**...**gas:** Exxon, Shell/dsl, **food:** BBQ, Pizza Hut, Subway, Taco Casa, Whataburger, **S**...**gas:** Shell/ChickenExpress/dsl, **food:** McDonald's, **lodging:** Ramada Ltd, Brookshire Foods, Cowtown RV Park(1mi)
417mm	weigh sta wb
415	FM 5, Mikus Rd, Annetta, **S**...**gas:** Citgo/dsl/Driver's Diner/@, Shell
413	(414 from wb), US 180 W, Lake Shore Dr, **N**...**gas:** RaceTrac, Shamrock, Texaco/dsl, **food:** DQ, Sonic, **other:** Chevrolet/Buick, Ford, Jeep, Lincoln/Mercury, Nissan, Pontiac/GMC, Toyota, Walmart SuperCtr/Subway/gas/24hr, **S**...**gas:** Chevron/dsl, Valero
410	Bankhead Hwy, **S**...**gas:** Love's/Subway/dsl/24hr/@
409	FM 2552 N, Clear Lake Rd, **N**...**gas:** Petro/Mobil/dsl/rest./24hr/@, **food:** Catfish O'Harlis, Jack-in-the-Box, **lodging:** Best Western, Sleepgo, **other:** HOSPITAL, Blue Beacon, **S**...**gas:** Chevron/dsl
408	TX 171, FM 1884, FM 51, Tin Top Rd, Weatherford, **N**...**gas:** Exxon/Popeye's/24hr, Mobil, **food:** Applebee's, BBQ, Baja Sun, Braum's, China Garden, Cotton Patch Cafe, Dickey's BBQ, Golden Corral, IHOP, Kroger, LJ Silver, McDonald's, Montana Rest., Schlotsky's, Starbucks, Subway, Taco Bell, Taco Bueno, Wendy's, Whataburger/24hr, **lodging:** La Quinta, Super 8, **other:** AutoZone, $Tree, Discount Tire, Home Depot, Wal-Mart SuperCtr/gas/24hr, **S**...**gas:** Exxon/Subway/dsl, Shell/Burger King/dsl/24hr, **food:** Chic-Fil-A, Chili's, Coldstone Creamery, On The Border, Waffle House, **lodging:** Best Value Inn, Comfort Suites, Hampton Inn, Holiday Inn Express, Motel 6, **other:** Best Buy, GNC, Kohl's, Lowe's Whse, NTB,, Ross, Target
407	Tin Top Rd(from eb), same as 408
406	Old Dennis Rd, **N**...**gas:** Conoco/dsl/24hr/@, **lodging:** Day's Inn, **S**...**gas:** Pilot/Wendy's/dsl/24hr/@
402	(403 from wb), TX 312, to Weatherford, **S**...**other:** RV camping
397	FM 1189, to Brock, **N**...**gas:** Shamrock/dsl, **S**...tires
394	FM 113, to Millsap, **N**...**gas:** gas/dsl/RV camping
393mm	Brazos River
391	Gilbert Pit Rd, no services
390mm	**rest area both lanes, full(handicapped)facilities, phone, vending, picnic tables, litter barrels, petwalk**
386	US 281, to Mineral Wells, **N**...**gas:** Fina, Shell/Subway/dsl
380	FM 4, Santo, **S**...**food:** Sunday Creek BBQ, **other:** Windmill Acres RV Park
376	Blue Flat Rd, Panama Rd, no services
373	TX 193, Gordon, no services
370	TX 108 S, FM 919, Gordon, **N**...**gas:** Citgo/Bar-B/dsl/rest., **S**...**gas:** Exxon/dsl, **other:** Longhorn Inn/Country Store
367	TX 108 N, Mingus, **N**...**gas:** Thurber Sta/gas, **food:** Smoke Stack Café, **S**...**food:** NY Hill Rest.

364mm	Palo Pinto Creek
363	Tudor Rd, picnic area, tables, litter barrels
362mm	Bear Creek, picnic area both lanes, tables, litter barrels
361	TX 16, to Strawn, no services
358	(from wb), frontage rd, no services
356mm	Russell Creek
354	Lp 254, Ranger, no services
351	(352 from wb), College Blvd, no services
349	FM 2461, Ranger, **N**...**gas:** Love's/Subway/Godfather's/dsl/24hr/@, **food:** DQ, **lodging:** Best Value Inn, Relax Inn(2mi), **S**...**gas:** Chevron/dsl
347	FM 3363(from wb), Olden, **S**...**food:** TX Cattle Exchange Steaks
345	FM 3363(from eb), Olden, **S**...**food:** TX Steaks
343	TX 112, FM 570, Eastland, Lake Leon, **N**...**gas:** Fina/Subway, Shell, **food:** Asia rest., BBQ, Chicken Express, DQ, McDonald's, Pizza Inn, Sonic, Starbucks, Taco Bell, **lodging:** Super 8/RV park, **other:** AutoZone, Buick/Chevrolet/Cadillac, GMC/Pontiac $General, Ford/Mercury, Wal-Mart/Super Ctr/gas/dsl/24 hr, **S**...**gas:** Exxon/dsl/24hr, **food:** Pulido's Mexican, **lodging:** Budget Host, Ramada Inn,
340	TX 6, Eastland, **N**...**gas:** Chevron/dsl, **other:** HOSPITAL, **S**...**gas:** Shell/dsl
337	spur 490, **N**...**other:** The Wild Country RV Park
332	US 183, Cisco, **N**...**gas:** Chevron, Citgo/dsl, **food:** BBQ, Cisco Café, DQ, Pizza Heaven, Sonic, Subway, **lodging:** Oak Motel, **S**...**gas:** Fina/dsl, **other:** Ford
330	TX 206, Cisco, **N**...**lodging:** Best Western, **other:** HOSPITAL
329mm	picnic area wb, tables, litter barrels, handicapped accessible
327mm	picnic area eb, tables, litter barrels, handicapped accessible
324	Scranton Rd, no services
322	Cooper Creek Rd, no services
320	FM 880 N, FM 2945 N, to Moran, no services
319	FM 880 S, Putnam, **N**...**gas:** gas/dsl/café, **other:** USPO
316	Brushy Creek Rd, no services
313	FM 2228, no services
310	Finley Rd, no services
308	Lp 20, Baird, **1 mi S**...antiques
307	US 283, Clyde, **N**...**food:** DQ, **S**...**gas:** Conoco/dsl, **food:** Allsup's, Robertson's Café, **lodging:** Baird Motel/RV park
306	FM 2047, Baird, **N**...**other:** Chevrolet/Pontiac/GMC, Chrysler/Dodge/Jeep
303	Union Hill Rd, no services
301	FM 604, Cherry Lane, **N**...**gas:** Chevron/dsl/24hr, **food:** Subway, Whataburger/24hr, **S**...**gas:** Fina/dsl/café, Shell/dsl/24hr, **food:** DQ/24hr, **other:** Franklin RV Ctr, IGA Foods
300	FM 604 N, Clyde, **N**...**other:** Dodge, **S**...**gas:** Conoco, **other:** White's RV Park
299	FM 1707, Hays Rd, no services
297	FM 603, Eula Rd, no services
296.5mm	**rest area both lanes, full(handicapped) facilities, phone, picnic tables, litter barrels, petwalk**

Interstate 20

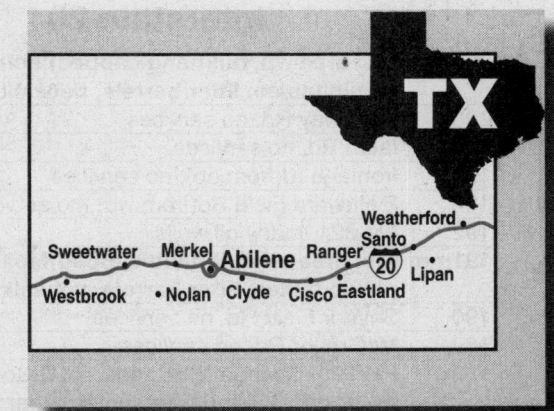

294	Buck Creek Rd, no services
292b	Elmdale Rd, no services
292a	Lp 20(exits left from wb), **S**...**lodging:** Travelodge
290	TX 36, Lp 322, **S**...airport, zoo
288	TX 351, **N**...**gas:** Allsup's/dsl, Chevron, Fina/Subway/dsl, **food:** Cracker Barrel, DQ, Skillet's Café, **lodging:** Comfort Inn, Day's Inn, Executive Inn, Holiday Inn Express, Whitten Inn, **other:** Wal-Mart SuperCtr/gas/24hr, **S**...**lodging:** Super 8, **other:** HOSPITAL
286c	FM 600, Abilene, **N**...**gas:** Exxon/dsl, Fina/dsl, **food:** Denny's/24hr, **lodging:** Best Western, La Quinta, **S**...**gas:** Chevron/dsl, **other:** Stover's Candies
286	US 83, Pine St, Abilene, **N**...Firestone, **S**...**gas:** Fina, **lodging:** Budget Host, **other:** HOSPITAL
285	Old Anson Rd, **N**...**gas:** Texaco/dsl, **lodging:** Travel Inn, **S**...**gas:** Texaco/dsl, **lodging:** Econolodge, Quality Inn(2mi)
283a	US 277 S, US 83(exits left from wb), **S**...**gas:** Fina
282	FM 3438, Shirley Rd, **S**...**lodging:** Motel 6, **other:** KOA
280	Fulwiler Rd, to dyess air force base
279	US 84 E, to Abilene, **1-3 mi S**...services
278	Lp 20, **N**...**gas:** Conoco/dsl/rest./24hr, **other:** dsl repair, **S**...**gas:** Conoco/dsl/@
277	FM 707, Tye, **N**...**gas:** ✈/Flying J/Country Mkt/dsl/LP/24hr/@, **S**...**gas:** Fina, Shell/dsl
274	Wells Lane, no services
272	Wimberly Rd, no services
270	FM 1235, Merkel, **N**...**gas:** Fina/dsl, Shell/dsl/café/24hr
269	FM 126, **N**...**food:** Subway, **lodging:** Scottish Inn, **S**...**gas:** Fina/dsl/rest./24hr, Shell, **food:** DQ, **lodging:** Merkel Motel/rest.
267	Lp 20, Merkel, **1mi S**...access to gas, food, lodging
266	Derstine Rd, no services
264	Noodle Dome Rd, no services
263	Lp 20, Trent, no services
262	FM 1085, **S**...**gas:** Fina/dsl/24hr
261	Lp 20, Trent, no services
259	Sylvester Rd, no services
258	White Flat Rd, oil wells
257mm	**rest area both lanes, full(handicapped) facilities, phone, vending, picnic tables, litter barrels, petwalk**
256	Stink Creek Rd, no services
255	Adrian Rd, no services
251	Eskota Rd, no services
249	FM 1856, no services
247	TX 70 N, Sweetwater, **N**...**food:** Whataburger
246	Alabama Ave, Sweetwater, no services
245	Arizona Ave(from wb), same as 244
244	TX 70 S, Sweetwater, **N**...**gas:** Chevron/dsl, Fina/dsl/24hr, **food:** Big Rail Rest., DQ, McDonald's, Subway, Wendy's, **lodging:** Holiday Inn, Motel 6, **other:** HOSPITAL, AutoZone, Ford/Mercury, Wal-Mart SuperCtr/gas/24hr, **S**...**gas:** Chevron, Shell, **food:** Buck's BBQ, Golden Chick, Schlotsky's,

	Taco Bell, **lodging:** Comfort Inn, Days Inn, Ranch House Motel, **other:** Chevrolet/Pontiac/Buick/Cadillac, $General, K-Mart,
243	Hillsdale Rd, Robert Lee St, **N**...**other:** Bewley's Service
242	Hopkins Rd, **S**...**gas:** TA/Conoco/Pizza Hut/dsl/24hr/@, **other:** Goodyear, Rolling Plains RV Park
241	Lp 20, Sweetwater, **N**...gas, food, lodging, **S**...RV camping
240	Lp 170, **N**...airport, camping
239	May Rd, no services
238b a	US 84 W, Blackland Rd, no services
237	Cemetery Rd, no services
236	FM 608, Roscoe, **N**...**gas:** Shell, T&C/dsl, **S**...**food:** DQ
235	to US 84, Roscoe, **S**...**other:** travel stop/rest./truck repair/dsl
230	FM 1230, no facilites
229mm	picnic area wb, tables, litter barrels, handicapped accessible
228mm	picnic area eb, tables, litter barrels, handicapped accessible
227	Narrell Rd, no services
226b	Lp 20(from wb), Loraine, no services
226a	FM 644 N, Wimberly Rd, no services
225	FM 644 S, **1 mi S**...access to gas, food
224	Lp 20, to Loraine, **1 mi S**...gas, food
223	Lucas Rd, **S**...**other:** 223 RV Park
221	Lasky Rd, no services
220	FM 1899, no services
219	Lp 20, Country Club Rd, Colorado City, no services
217	TX 208 S, **S**...**food:** Skeet's Texas Grill
216	TX 208 N, **N**...**gas:** Chevron/dsl, **food:** DQ, Subway, **lodging:** Day's Inn, **S**...**gas:** Phillips 66/dsl, **food:** Pizza Hut, Sonic, **lodging:** Best Value Inn, **other:** HOSPITAL, Alco
215	FM 3525, Rogers Rd, **2 mi S**...access to gas, food
214.5mm	Colorado River
213	Lp 20, Enderly Rd, Colorado City, no services
212	FM 1229, no services
211mm	FM 1229, Morgan Creek
210	FM 2836, **S**...**gas:** Fina/dsl, **other:** to Lake Colorado City SP, picnic area, camping
209	Dorn Rd, no services
207	Lp 20, Westbrook, no services
206	FM 670, to Westbrook, no services

TEXAS

Interstate 20

<table>
<tr><td>204mm</td><td>rest area wb, full(handicapped)facilities, phone, picnic tables, litter barrels, petwalk</td></tr>
<tr><td>200</td><td>Conaway Rd, no services</td></tr>
<tr><td>199</td><td>Iatan Rd, no services</td></tr>
<tr><td>195</td><td>frontage rd(from eb), no services</td></tr>
<tr><td>194</td><td>E Howard Field Rd(from wb), no services</td></tr>
<tr><td>192</td><td>FM 821, many oil wells</td></tr>
<tr><td>191mm</td><td>rest area eb, full(handicapped)facilities, phone, picnic tables, litter barrels, petwalk</td></tr>
<tr><td>190</td><td>Snyder Field Rd, no services</td></tr>
<tr><td>189</td><td>McGregor Rd, no services</td></tr>
<tr><td>188</td><td>FM 820, Coahoma, N...gas: T&C/Country Cookin/dsl, food: DQ, lodging: motel, other: USPO</td></tr>
<tr><td>186</td><td>Salem Rd, Sand Springs, no services</td></tr>
<tr><td>184</td><td>Moss Lake Rd, Sand Springs, N...gas: Fina/dsl, S...RV camping</td></tr>
<tr><td>182</td><td>Midway Rd, no services</td></tr>
<tr><td>181b</td><td>Refinery Rd, N...gas: Fina Refinery</td></tr>
<tr><td>181a</td><td>FM 700, , N...airport, RV camping, 2 mi S...HOSPITAL</td></tr>
<tr><td>179</td><td>US 80, Big Spring, S...gas: Fina/7-11, food: Denny's, lodging: Camlot Inn, Comfort Inn, Best Western Inn, other: $General, Chevrolet/Pontiac/Buick</td></tr>
<tr><td>178</td><td>TX 350, Big Spring, N...gas: Shell/dsl, S...other: truck repair</td></tr>
<tr><td>177</td><td>US 87, Big Spring, N...gas: Exxon/dsl, TA/Popeye's/Subway/dsl/24hr/@, lodging: Advantage Inn, Motel 6, Super 8, S...gas: Chevron/dsl, Fina/dsl, food: DQ, lodging: Holiday Inn Express</td></tr>
<tr><td>176</td><td>TX 176, Andrews, no services</td></tr>
<tr><td>174</td><td>Lp 20 E, Big Springs, S...gas: Shell/dsl, other: HOSPITAL, airport</td></tr>
<tr><td>172</td><td>Cauble Rd, no services</td></tr>
<tr><td>171</td><td>Moore Field Rd, no services</td></tr>
<tr><td>169</td><td>FM 2599, no services</td></tr>
<tr><td>168mm</td><td>picnic area both lanes, tables, littter barrels</td></tr>
<tr><td>165</td><td>FM 818, no services</td></tr>
<tr><td>158</td><td>Lp 20 W, to Stanton, N...RV camping</td></tr>
<tr><td>156</td><td>TX 137, Lamesa, S...gas: Phillips 66/Country Cookin Rest./Subway/dsl/24hr, food: Sonic</td></tr>
<tr><td>154</td><td>US 80, Stanton, 2 mi S...access to gas, food, lodging</td></tr>
<tr><td>151</td><td>FM 829(from wb), no services</td></tr>
<tr><td>144</td><td>Loop 250, 2-3 mi N...facilities in Midland</td></tr>
<tr><td>143mm</td><td>frontage rd(from eb), no services</td></tr>
<tr><td>142mm</td><td>picnic area both lanes, tables, litter barrels, hist marker</td></tr>
<tr><td>140</td><td>FM 307(from eb), no services</td></tr>
<tr><td>138</td><td>TX 158, FM 715, Greenwood, N...gas: Shell/dsl, food: KD's BBQ, Whataburger/24hr, S...gas: T&C/Subway/dsl</td></tr>
<tr><td>137</td><td>Old Lamesa Rd, no services</td></tr>
<tr><td>136</td><td>TX 349, Midland, N...gas: Fina/dsl, Phillips 66/dsl, food: Sonic, Starbucks, lodging: Comfort Inn, Howard Johnson, West Texas Inn, other: $Tree, IGA/gas, Family$, McAllister's Deli, Petroleum Museum, Wal-Mart SuperCtr/gas/24hr, S...gas: Exxon/Burger King/dsl, T&C/Country Cookin, Texaco/dsl</td></tr>
</table>

<table>
<tr><td>134</td><td>Midkiff Rd, N...gas: Chevron, T&C/Subway/dsl, 1 mi N on Wall St...Fina/7-11, Exxon, food: Denny's, lodging: Best Western, Day's Inn, Executive Inn, La Quinta, Sleep Inn, other: HOSPITAL, Chevrolet, Chrysler/Jeep, Honda, Kia, Lincoln/Mercury, Mercedes/Volvo, Nissan</td></tr>
<tr><td>131</td><td>TX 158, Midland, N...lodging: Travelodge, S...other: RV camping</td></tr>
<tr><td>126</td><td>FM 1788, N...gas: Chevron/dsl, Pilot/McDonald's/dsl, Warfield/Mobil/Subway/dsl/@, other: Western Auto, museum, airport</td></tr>
<tr><td>121</td><td>Lp 338, Odessa, N...food: Denny's, McDonald's, lodging: Day's Inn, Grand Hotel, La Quinta, Motel 6, other: U of TX Permian Basin, 1 mi N...gas: Fina/7-11, lodging: Elegante Hotel, 3 mi N on TX 191 W..food: Chili's, Fazoli's, Logan's Roadhouse, McDonald's, On-the-Border, Quizno's, Whataburger, lodging: Fairfield Inn, Hampton Inn, other: Albertson's, Circuit City, Home Depot, Sears/auto, Sam's Club/gas, Wal-Mart SuperCtr/24hr</td></tr>
<tr><td>118</td><td>FM 3503, Grandview Ave, N...gas: Fina/dsl, other: Freightliner/Peterbilt,</td></tr>
<tr><td>116</td><td>US 385, Craine, Andrews, N...gas: Chevron, food: DQ, lodging: Best Western, Delux Inn, Villa West Inn, other: HOSPITAL, S...gas: Fina/dsl, Shell/dsl, lodging: Motel 6, other: city park</td></tr>
<tr><td>115</td><td>FM 1882, N...gas: T&C/Country Cookin S...gas: Love's/McDonald's/Subway/dsl/24hr</td></tr>
<tr><td>113</td><td>TX 302, Odessa, no services</td></tr>
<tr><td>112</td><td>FM 1936, Odessa, N...gas: Citgo/dsl</td></tr>
<tr><td>108</td><td>Moss Ave, Meteor Crater, no services</td></tr>
<tr><td>104</td><td>FM 866, Meteor Crater Rd, no services</td></tr>
<tr><td>103.5mm</td><td>weigh sta both lanes/parking area eb, litter barrels</td></tr>
<tr><td>101</td><td>FM 1601, Penwell, no services</td></tr>
<tr><td>93</td><td>FM 1053, no services</td></tr>
<tr><td>86</td><td>TX 41, N...Monahans Sandhills SP, camping</td></tr>
<tr><td>83</td><td>US 80, Monahans, 2 mi N...gas: Citgo, other: HOSPITAL, RV camping</td></tr>
<tr><td>80</td><td>TX 18, Monahans, N...gas: Chevron/dsl/24hr, food: Bar-H Steaks, Big Burger, DQ, McDonald's, Pappy's BBQ, Sonic, other: HOSPITAL, Alco Discount, CarQuest, $General, Family$, Kwik Lube, Lowe's Foods, Country Club RV Park(2mi), S...gas: Fina/dsl/24hr, Kent Gas, TC/Subway/dsl, lodging: Colonial Inn, Texan Inn, other: Chevrolet/Pontiac/Buick/GMC, Chrysler/Dodge/Jeep</td></tr>
<tr><td>79</td><td>Lp 464, Monahans, no services</td></tr>
<tr><td>76</td><td>US 80, Monahans, 2 mi N...other: to Million Barrel Museum, RV camping</td></tr>
<tr><td>73</td><td>FM 1219, Wickett, N...gas: Shell/Allsup's, S...gas: Mobil/Subway/dsl/24hr</td></tr>
<tr><td>70</td><td>TX 65, no services</td></tr>
<tr><td>69.5mm</td><td>rest area both lanes, full(handicapped) facilities, phone, picnic tables, litter barrels, petwalk</td></tr>
<tr><td>66</td><td>FM 1927, to Pyote, no services</td></tr>
<tr><td>58</td><td>frontage rd, multiple oil wells</td></tr>
<tr><td>52</td><td>Lp 20 W, to Barstow, no services</td></tr>
<tr><td>49</td><td>FM 516, to Barstow, no services</td></tr>
<tr><td>48mm</td><td>Pecos River</td></tr>
</table>

Left margin: E ↑ W, Big Spring, Midland

Right margin: Odessa, Monahans

Interstate 20

44	Collie Rd, no services
42	US 285, Pecos, N...gas: Chevron/24hr, Exxon, ✈/Flying J/Conoco/dsl/24hr/@, Shell/dsl, food: DQ, Pizza Hut, lodging: Motel 6, Quality Inn, OakTree Inn, other: AutoZone, Wal-Mart/24hr, museum
40	Country Club Dr, N...st patrol, S...gas: Chevron/Subway, lodging: Best Western/rest., other: Chevrolet, RV camping, municipal park
39	TX 17, Pecos, N...other: Goodyear, st patrol, S...food: DQ, lodging: Best Western, other: Chevrolet/Buick
37	Lp 20 E, 2 mi N...food: KFC, Sonic, lodging: Town&Country Motel
33	FM 869, no services
29	Shaw Rd, S...to TX AM Ag Sta
25mm	picnic area both lanes, tables, litter barrels, handicapped accessible
22	FM 2903, to Toyah, no services
13	McAlpine Rd, no services
7	Johnson Rd, no services
3	Stocks Rd, no services
0mm	I-20 begins/ends on I-10, 187mm.

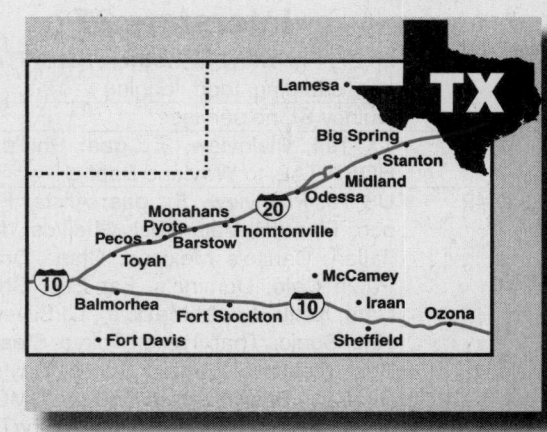

Interstate 27

Exit #	Services
	I-27 begins/ends on I-40, exit 70 in Amarillo.
123b	I-40, W to Albuquerque, E to OK City
123a	26th Ave, E...gas: Fina, W...food: DJ Burgers, La Campana Mexican
122c	from sb only
122b	34th Ave, Tyler St, E...gas: Conoco, Shell, Valero, food: Sonic
122a	FM 1541, Washington St, Parker St, Moss Lane, W...food: Hungry Howie's
121b	Hawthorne Dr, Austin St, E...lodging: Amarillo Motel, other: Honda Motorcycles, W...other: Scottie's Transmissions
121a	Georgia St, E...gas: Phillips 66/dsl, food: BBQ, Waffle House, other: Buick/Pontiac/GMC, Honda, Mazda, Nissan, Sizemore RV, Subaru, Toyota, Wal-Mart SuperCtr/24hr/gas
120b	45th Ave, E...gas: Fina, food: Waffle House, other: repair, W...gas: Exxon, Valero, food: Abuelo's Mexican, Burger King(.5mi), Gatti's Pizza, Grand Burger, McDonald's, Whataburger, other: Advance Parts, BMW, Dodge, $General, Drug Emporium
120a	Republic Ave, no services
119b	Western St, 58th Ave, E...gas: Phillips 66, food: Sonic, other: $General, W...gas: Shell/dsl, Valero, food: Arby's, Braum's, LJ Silver, Ming Palace Chinese, Pizza Hut, Wendy's, other: Aamco, Stout RV Ctr, U-Haul, USPO
119a	W Hillside, no services
117	Bell St, Arden Rd, E...other: transmissions, W...gas: Shell/24hr, food: Burger Palace, LJ Silver, Popeye's, Sonic, other: $General

116	Lp 335, Hollywood Rd, E...gas: Love's/Subway/dsl/24hr, Phillips 66/dsl, food: McDonald's, Waffle House, Whataburger, lodging: Comfort Suites, Day's Inn, W...other: HOSPITAL(8mi)
115	Sundown Lane, no services
113	McCormick Rd, E...other: Ford, W...other: Family Camping Ctr
112	FM 2219, E...other: Stater's RV Ctr
111	Rockwell Rd, E...other: Chevrolet, W...other: Buick/GMC/Pontiac
110(from sb)	US 87 S, US 60 W, Canyon
109	Buffalo Stadium Rd, W...stadium
108	FM 3331, Hunsley Rd, no services
106	TX 217, to Palo Duro Cyn SP, Canyon, E...other: Palo Duro RV Park, RV camping, W...lodging: Holiday Inn Express(2mi), other: Plains Museum, to WTA&M
103	FM 1541 N, Cemetery Rd, no services
99	Hungate Rd, no services
98mm	parking area both lanes, litter barrels
96	Dowlen Rd, no services
94	FM 285, to Wayside, no services
92	Haley Rd, no services
90	FM 1075, Happy, W...gas/dsl
88b a	US 87 N, FM 1881, Happy, same as 90
83	FM 2698, no services
82	FM 214, no services
77	US 87, Tulia, 1-2 mi E...gas: Phillips 66, food: Pizza Hut, Sonic, lodging: Lasso Inn, other: HOSPITAL, Ford, airport
75	NW 6th St, Tulia, 1 mi E...gas: Phillips 66, Shell, food: DQ, Pizza Hut, Sonic, lodging: Lasso Motel, W...same as 74
74	TX 86, Tulia, E...lodging: Lasso Motel, other: HOSPITAL, W...gas: Rip Griffin/Phillips 66/Subway/Chester's/dsl/scales/24hr/@, lodging: Select Inn
70mm	parking area both lanes, litter barrels
68	FM 928, no services
63	FM 145, Kress, 1 mi E...gas/dsl, food, phone
61	US 87, County Rd, no services
56	FM 788, no services
54	FM 3183, to Plainview, W...truck service

TEXAS

Interstate 27

Plainview

53	Lp 27, Plainview, E...other: HOSPITAL, access to gas, camping, food, lodging
51	Quincy St, no services
50	TX 194, Plainview, E...gas: Phillips 66, other: HOSPITAL, to Wayland Bapt U
49	US 70, Plainview, E...gas: Allstar Fuel/dsl, Conoco, Fina/dsl, Valero/dsl, Shell/dsl, food: Alfredo Italian, Carlito's Mexican, China Dragon, Cotton Patch Café, Domino's, Far East Chinese, Furr's Café, Kettle, Leal's Mexican, LJ Silver/A&W, Pizza Hut, Sonic, Thai Taste, Tokyo Steaks, lodging: Best Western, Comfort Suites, Day's Inn, other: Beall's, Buick/Pontiac/Cadillac/GMC, Chrysler/Jeep, $Tree, Ford/Lincoln/Mercury/Toyota, GNC, Hastings Books, NAPA, O'Reilly Parts, Pinnell Drug, Radio Shack, United Foods, W...gas: Chevron, Phillips 66/dsl, 76, food: Burger King, Chicken Express, Chili's, IHOP, Little Mexico, McDonald's, New China, Quizno's, Sonic, Starbucks, Subway, Taco Bell, Wendy's, lodging: Best Value, Holiday Inn Express, other: JC Penney, Wal-Mart SuperCtr/24hr/gas
45	Lp 27, to Plainview, no services
43	FM 2337, no services
41	County Rd, no services
38	Main St, no services
37	FM 1914, Cleveland St, E...gas: Co-op, food: Sylvia's Cafe, W...HOSPITAL
36	FM 1424, Hale Center, no services
32	FM 37 W, no services
31	FM 37 E, no services
29mm	**rest area both lanes, full(handicapped) facilities, phone, picnic tables, litter barrels, petwalk, tornado shelter**
27	County Rd, no services
24	FM 54, W...RV park/dump
22	Lp 369, Abernathy, W...Filling Sta Cafe/dsl
21	FM 597, Main St, Abernathy, W...gas: Conoco/dsl, food: DQ, Shady's BBQ, other: $General, USPO
20	Abernathy(from nb), no services
17	County Rd 53, no services
15	Lp 461, to New Deal, same as 14
14	FM 1729, E...gas: Fina/rest./dsl/scales/24hr
13	Lp 461, to New Deal, no services
12	access rd(from nb), no services
11	FM 1294, Shallowater, no services
10	Keuka St, E...other: DHL, Fed Ex
9	Airport Rd, E...airport, W...other: Lubbock RV Park/LP/dump
8	FM 2641, Regis St, no services
7	Yucca Lane, E...Pharr RV Ctr
6 b a	Lp 289, Ave Q, Lubbock, E...other: Pharr RV
5	B. Holly Ave, Municipal Dr, E...other: Mackenzie Park
4	US 82, US 87, 4th St, to Crosbyton, W...gas: ⊕/Flying J/CountryMkt/dsl/24hr/@, other: to TTU
3	US 62, TX 114, 19th St, no services

Lubbock

2	34th St, E...gas: Phillips 66, food: Pete's Drive Inn, W...food: Simple Simon's Pizza, other: AutoZone, Hall Drug, I-27 RV Ctr
1c	50th St, E...gas: Fina, food: El Jalapeno Café, Prince Castle, W...gas: Bolton Fuel, Conoco, Valero, food: Bryan's Steaks, Burger King, China Star, Church's, DQ, Domino's, Grand Buffet, KFC, LJ Silver/A&W, McDonald's, Pinocchio's Pizza, Pizza Hut/Taco Bell, Subway, Taco Villa, Whataburger, Wienerschnitzel, lodging: Howard Johnson, other: Chrysler/Jeep, $General, O'Reilly Parts, United Food/drug/gas, USPO, Walgreen, Woody Tire
1b	US 84, E...lodging: Circus Inn, Day's Inn, W...lodging: Best Western, Comfort Inn, Holiday Inn Express, Motel 6, Quality Inn, Ramada, Super 8, Value Place
1a	Lp 289, no services
1	82nd St, W...gas: Phillips 66
	I-27 begins/ends on US 87 at 82nd St in S Lubbock.

Interstate 30

Exit #	Services
223mm	Texas/Arkansas state line
223b a	US 59, US 71, State Line Ave, Texarkana, N...gas: Citgo/dsl, EZ Mart, Mobil, Shell, Speedway, food: Cajun Harbor, Denny's, IHOP, Pizza Inn, Red Lobster, Waffle House, lodging: Best Western, Budget Host, Clarion, Comfort Suites, Holiday Inn, Hampton Inn, Holiday Inn Express, La Quinta, Quality Inn, Sheraton, Super 8, other: Firestone/Auto, KOA, tires, S...gas: Exxon, RaceWay, Shell, State Line Gas, food: Arby's, Backyard Burger, Baskin-Robbins, Bennigan's, Burger King, Cattleman's Steaks, China King, Colima's Mexican, El Chico, KFC, La Carreta Mexican, Little Caesars, LJ Silver, Mandarin House, McDonald's, Papa John's, Pizza Hut, Pizza Inn, Popeye's, Quizno's, Schlotsky's, Subway, Taco Bell, Taco Tico, Wendy's, Whataburger/24hr, lodging: Ambassador Inn, Best Value, Best Western, Comfort Inn, Day's Inn, Econolodge, Economy Inn, Executive Inn, Express Inn, Knight's Inn, La Quinta, Motel 6, other: Albertson's, AutoZone, Chevrolet/Buick, Jeep, Radio Shack, Suzuki, Wal-Mart SuperCtr/24hr, Walgreen
223mm	**Welcome Ctr wb, full(handicapped) facilities, info, phone, picnic tables, litter barrels, vending, petwalk**

Texarkana

E
↑
W

Interstate 30

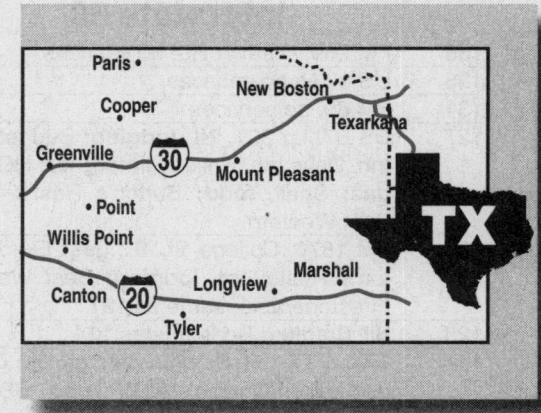

222 TX 93, FM 1397, Summerhill Rd, ...**gas:** Shell, Valero/Subway/dsl, **food:** Amigo Juan's, Applebee's, McDonald's, Shogun Japanese, Waffle House, **lodging:** Motel 6, **other:** Ford/Freightliner, Goodyear/auto, Honda, S...**gas:** Shell/24hr, **food:** Bryce's Rest., **other:** Buick/Pontiac/GMC, Curves, Ford, Mazda/Nissan/GMC, Mercedes

220b FM 559, Richmond Rd, N...**gas:** Chevron, Exxon, Shell, **food:** Buffalo Wild Wings, Burger King, Carino's Italian, Cracker Barrel, Chick-fil-a, Cici's Pizza, DQ, Domino's, Jumbo Chinese, Little Caesars, McAlister's Deli, On-the-Border, Pizza Hut, Popeye's, Randy's BBQ, Red Lobster, Ruby Tuesday, Sonic, Starbucks, Taco Bell, TaMolly's Mexican, Texas Roadhouse, Wendy's, **lodging:** Comfort Suites, Courtyard, TownePlace Suites, **other:** Best Buy, Chevrolet, Discount Tire, $Tree, Gander Mtn, Home Depot, Hyundai, Kohls, Old Navy, PetsMart, Sam's Club/gas, Staples, Super 1 Food/gas, Target, TJ Maxx, S...**gas:** Valero/dsl, **food:** Arby's, Chili's, ChuckeCheese, El Chico, Golden Corral, Grandy's, Lee's Chinese, Luby's, McDonald's, Olive Garden, Outback Steaks, Quizno's, Subway/Baskin-Robbins, **lodging:** Hampton Inn, **other:** AutoZone, Albertson's, Books-A-Million, Buick/Pontiac/GMC, Cavender's Boots, Dillard's, JC Penney, Jeep, Mazda, Michael's, Office Depot, Ross, Saturn, Sears/auto, Walgreen, mall

220a US 59 S, Texarkana, S...**gas:** Exxon/Wendy's, **food:** DQ, Subway, **other:** Lowe's Whse, Radio Shack, Wal-Mart SuperCtr/gas/24hr, mall

218 FM 989, Nash, N...**gas:** Road Runner/dsl, **food:** Dixie Diner, **other:** McKinnon RV Ctr, S...**gas:** Exxon/Burger King/dsl, **other:** Peterbilt/GMC, to Lake Patman

213 FM 2253, Leary, N...**other:** Palma RV Ctr

212 spur 74, Lone Star Army Ammo Plant, S...**gas:** Shell

208 FM 560, Hooks, N...**gas:** Texaco/dsl/24hr, **food:** Old Farm Mkt/BBQ, **other:** Hooks Camper Ctr., S...**gas:** Texaco/Subway/dsl/scales/24hr, **food:** DQ, Sonic, TasteeHouse Rest., **other:** Family$, tires

206 TX 86, S...**other:** Red River Army Depot

201 TX 8, New Boston, N...**gas:** Shell/dsl, Valero, **food:** Pitt Grill, **lodging:** Tex Inn, **other:** Chevrolet, Chrysler/Jeep/Dodge, S...**gas:** Shell, **food:** Catfish King, Church's, DQ, KFC/Taco Bell, McDonald's, Nana's Diner, Pizza Hut, Randy's BBQ, Sonic, **lodging:** Best Western, Bostonian Inn, Holiday Inn Express, **other:** HOSPITAL, Brookshire's Foods/gas, Curves, CVS Drug, Ford/Mercury, Wal-Mart SuperCtr/24hr/gas, RV park

199 US 82, DeKalb, 1/2 mi N...**gas:** Shell

198 TX 98, 1/2 mi N...**gas:** Shell

193mm	Anderson Creek
192	FM 990, N...**gas:** FuelStop/Culpeppers Rest/dsl
191mm	**rest area both lanes, full(handicapped) facilities, phone, picnic tables, litter barrels, vending, petwalk**
186	FM 561, no services
181mm	Sulphur River
178	US 259, to DeKalb, Omaha, no services
174mm	White Oak Creek
170	FM 1993, no services
165	FM 1001, S...**gas:** Exxon/dsl
162b a	US 271, FM 1402, FM 2152, Mt Pleasant, N...**gas:** Exxon/dsl/24hr, **food:** Applebee's, Blalock BBQ, Pitt Grill, **lodging:** Holiday Inn Express, Super 8, **other:** KOA, S...**gas:** Shell/dsl, Valero/Subway/dsl, **food:** Burger King, DQ, Luigi's Italian, McDonald's, **lodging:** Best Western/rest., **other:** HOSPITAL, Chevrolet/Cadillac, Family$, vet
160	US 271, FM 1734, Mt Pleasant, N...**gas:** BP/dsl, **food:** Senorita's Mexican, **other:** Buick/Pontiac/GMC(1mi), Lowe's Whse, Toyota, S...**gas:** Exxon/dsl, Shell/dsl, **food:** El Chico, Western Sizzlin, **lodging:** Comfort Inn, Day's Inn, Executive Inn
158mm	weigh sta both lanes
156	frontage rd, no services
153	spur 185, to Winfield, Millers Cove, N...**gas:** BP/dsl, Chevron, Winfield Trkstp/dsl/café, **other:** dsl repair, S...**gas:** Shamrock/dsl
150	Ripley Rd, N...**other:** Lowe's Distribution
147	spur 423, N...**gas:** Love's/Subway/dsl/scales/24hr, **lodging:** American Inn, Economy Inn
146	TX 37, Mt Vernon, N...**gas:** Shell/dsl, **other:** HOSPITAL, S...**gas:** Exxon/dsl, Fina/dsl/24hr, **food:** Burger King, DQ, Mt Vernon Cafe, **lodging:** Super 8, **other:** to Lake Bob Sandlin SP, auto repair
143	**rest area both lanes, full(handicapped)facilities, phone, picnic tables, litter barrels, vending, petwalk**
142	County Line Rd(from eb), no services
141	FM 900, Saltillo Rd, no services

TEXAS

Interstate 30

E ↑↓ W

136	FM 269, Weaver Rd, no services
135	US 67 N, no services
131	FM 69, no services
127	US 67, Lp 301, **N**...**lodging:** Budget Inn, Comfort Inn, Days Inn, Holiday Inn, **other:** HOSPITAL, **S**...**gas:** Shell, **food:** Burton's Rest./24hr, **lodging:** Best Western
126	FM 1870, College St, **S**...**gas:** Exxon, **food:** Burton's Rest./24hr, **lodging:** Best Western, **other:** Firestone/auto, same as 127
125	Bill Bradford Rd, same as 124
124	TX 11, TX 154, Sulphur Springs, **N**...**gas:** Chevron/dsl, Exxon/Quizno's/A&W, **food:** BBQ, Broadway Buffet, Chicken Express, Domino's, John's Diner, KFC, La Familia Mexican, Peddlar's Pizza, Pitt Grill, Pizza Hut, Popeye's, San Rimo Italian, Sonic, Subway, TaMolly's Mexican, **lodging:** Holiday Inn Express, Royal Inn, **other:** HOSPITAL, AutoZone, Brookshire's Food/gas, Cadillac, Chevrolet/Buick/GMC, Chrysler/Jeep, Curves, CVS Drug, $General, Family$, Ford, FSA Outlet/famous brands, Nissan, O'Reilly Parts, USPO, **S**...**gas:** Exxon/dsl, Shell, **food:** Braum's, Burger King, Chili's, Dominos, Furr's Rest., Jack-in-the-Box, K-Bob's Steaks, McDonald's, Pizza Inn, Taco Bell/LJ Silver, Whataburger, **lodging:** Holiday King Motel, **other:** Discount Tire, Eckerd, Fred's Drug, Lowe's Whse, Radio Shack, Wal-Mart SuperCtr/gas/24hr(1mi), factory outlet
123	FM 2297, League St, **N**...**gas:** Chevron/dsl, Shell
122	TX 19, to Emory, **N**...**gas:** Chevron, **other:** HOSPITAL, **S**...**gas:** Phillips 66/dsl/rest./24hr, Pilot/Arby's/dsl/scales/24hr/@, **other:** Shady Lake RV Park(2mi), to Cooper Lake
120	US 67 bus, no services
116	FM 2653, Brashear Rd, no services
112	FM 499(from wb), no services
110	FM 275, Cumby, **N**...**gas:** Phillips 66, **S**...**gas:** Shell/24hr
104	FM 513, FM 2649, Campbell, **S**...to Lake Tawakoni
101	TX 24, TX 50, FM 1737, to Commerce, **N**...**gas:** Valero/dsl, **other:** to E TX St U
97	Lamar St, **N**...**gas:** Exxon/dsl, **lodging:** Budget Inn, Dream Lodge Motel
96	Lp 302, no services
95	Division St, **S**...**other:** HOSPITAL, Puddin Hill Fruit Cakes
94b	US 69, US 380, Greenville, **N**...**gas:** Valero/dsl, **food:** Ninja's Grill, Senorita's Mexican, **lodging:** American Inn, Best Western, Royal Inn, **other:** Hyundai, **S**...**gas:** Exxon, Fina/dsl, **food:** Arby's, Burger King, Catfish Cove Rest., McDonald's, **lodging:** Econolodge, Economy Inn, Motel 6, Quality Inn, Super 8
94a	US 69, US 380, Greenville, **N**...**food:** Old Whiskers Buffet, **S**...**gas:** Valero, **other:** Chrysler/Dodge/Jeep, Nissan
93b a	US 67, TX 34 N, **N**...**gas:** Chevron, Exxon, **food:** Applebee's, Chick-fil-A, Chicken Express, CiCi's,

Greenville

	Grandy's, IHOP, Jack-in-the-Box, KFC, LJ Silver/A&W, Pizza Hut, Popeye's, Royal Drive-In, Ryan's, Schlotsky's, Sonic, Soulman's Texmex, Starbucks, Steak Angus, Subway, Taco Bell, Taco Bueno, TCBY, Tony's Italian, Wendy's, Whataburger/24hr, **lodging:** Hampton Inn, **other:** HOSPITAL, Ace Hardware, Belk, BigLots, Brookshire's Foods, Buick/Pontiac, Cadillac, Goody's, JC Penney, Lowes Whse, O'Reilly Parts, Staples, USPO, Walgreen, mall, **S**...**gas:** Exxon/dsl/24hr, Valero/dsl, **food:** Chili's, Cracker Barrel, Dickey's BBQ, Eastrock Buffet, Paesano Italian, Red Lobster, Tamolly's Mexican, **lodging:** Holiday Inn Express, La Quinta, **other:** $Tree, Ford/Lincoln/Mercury, Home Depot, Mitsubishi, Radio Shack, RV Ctr, Wal-Mart SuperCtr/24hr/gas
90mm	Farber Creek
89	FM 1570, **S**...**lodging:** Luxury Inn
89mm	E Caddo Creek
87	FM 1903, **N**...**gas:** Chevron/Pizza Inn/dsl, **other:** fireworks, **S**...**gas:** Exxon/Pancake House/dsl, Pilot/McDonald's/dsl/scales/24hr, **other:** tire repair
87mm	Elm Creek
85	FM 36, Caddo Mills, **N**...KOA
85mm	W Caddo Creek
83	FM 1565 N, **N**...**gas:** Exxon/dsl
79	FM 2642, **N**...Budget RV Ctr
77b	FM 35, Royse City, **N**...**gas:** Exxon/dsl, Texaco/Subway/dsl/scales/24hr/@, **food:** Soulman's BBQ, **other:** Family$
77a	TX 548, Royse City, **N**...**gas:** Shell/dsl, **food:** Jack-in-the-Box, McDonald's, **lodging:** Sun Royse Inn, **other:** tires, **S**...**gas:** Exxon/KFC/Quizno's, **food:** Sonic, **other:** Royce City Hardware, auto repair
73	FM 551, Fate, no services
70	FM 549, **S**...**gas:** Love's/Carl's Jr./dsl/scales/24hr
69	(from wb), frontage rd, **N**...Super 8
68	TX 205, to Rock Wall, **N**...**gas:** RaceWay, Shell, **food:** Braum's, DQ, Jowilly's Grill, KFC, Luigi's Italian, Pizza Hut, Pizza Inn, Subway, Whataburger, **lodging:** Holiday Inn Express, Super 8, Value Place, **other:** Chevrolet, Dodge, Ford/Mercury, **S**...**gas:** TA/Burger King/Starbucks/dsl/rest./24hr/scales/@, Valero/dsl
67	FM 740, Ridge Rd, **N**...**gas:** Chevron, Mobil, Shell, **food:** Arby's, Burger King, Carrabba's, Culver's, Dominos, Grandy's, IHOP, McDonald's, Schlotsky's, Steak&Shake, Waffle House, Wendy's, **other:** Goodyear/auto, Kwik Kar Lube, Wal-Mart SuperCtr/24hr, cleaners, **S**...**gas:** Chevron, Exxon/Pizza Inn, Shamrock/dsl, Shell, **food:** Applebee's, Bahama Buck's Ice Cream, Blackeyed Pea, Buffalo Wild Wings, Carino's Italian, Chick-fil-A, Chili's, ChuckeCheese, CiCi's Pizza, El Chico, Jack-in-the-Box, McDonald's, On-the-Border, Sonic, Starbucks, Subway, Taco Bell/Pizza Hut, TCBY, TGIFriday's, **lodging:** Country Inn Suites, **other:** Albertson's, BestBuy, Circuit City, Discount Tire, $Tree, Eckerd, GNC, Home Depot, Kohl's, Lowe's Whse, Michael's, Old Navy, PetCo, Radio Shack, Ross, Staples, SteinMart, Target, Walgreen, to Lake Tawakoni, vet

Interstate 30

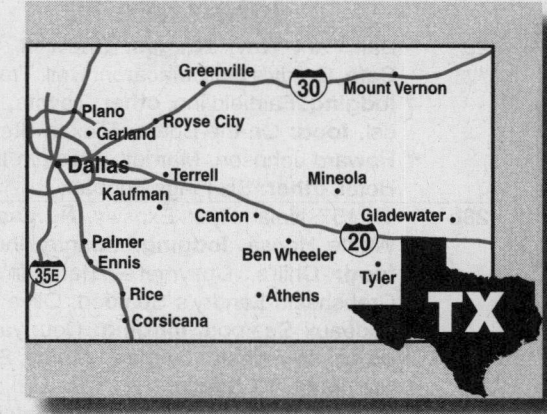

Exit	Description
67a	Horizon Rd, Village Dr, ...**gas:** Shamrock, **food:** Café Express, RanchHouse Rest., Saltgrass Steaks, Culpeper Cattle Steaks, **lodging:** Hilton Garden
66mm	Ray Hubbard Reservoir
64	Dalrock Rd, Rowlett, ...**gas:** Exxon, Valero/dsl, **lodging:** Comfort Suites, **other:** HOSPITAL, Express Drug
63mm	Ray Hubbard Reservoir
62	Bass Pro Rd, ...**lodging:** Best Western, **other:** to Hubbard RA, ...**gas:** Shell, **other:** Bass Pro Shop
61	Zion Rd(from wb), ...**gas:** Conoco/dsl, Texaco, **lodging:** Jack-in-the-Box, **lodging:** Discovery Inn
60b	Bobtown Rd(eb only), ...**gas:** Shell **food:** Jack-in-the-Box
60a	Rose Hill Dr, no services
59	Beltline Rd, Garland, ...**gas:** Conoco, QT, 7-11/gas, **food:** Chili's, Denny's, India Morning, KFC, LJ Silver, McDonald's, QT, Starbucks, Subway, Taco Bell/Pizza Hut, Taco Casa, Taco Cabana, Whataburger, Wendy's, **other:** Albertson's, $General, GNC, Radio Shack, Tuesday Morning, Walgreens, Wal-Mart SuperCtr/24hr, ...**gas:** Shell/dsl, **food:** Baker's Ribs, Buffet King, Burger King, DQ, Grandy's, Sonic, Waffle House, Williams Chicken, **lodging:** Day's Inn, I-30 Inn, Motel 6, **other:** Kroger
58	Northwest Dr, ...**gas:** Shell, Valero/dsl, **other:** Nissan, ...**gas:** Fina, **food:** Jack-in-the-Box, **other:** Lowe's Whse
56c b	I-635 S-N, no services
56a	Galloway Ave, Gus Thomasson Dr(from eb), ...**food:** KFC, ...**food:** Celebration Sta, Checker's, Circuit City, Grandy's, Hooters, Kroger, Olive Garden, Outback Steaks, Posades Cafe, Red Lobster, Steak&Ale, TGIFriday, Luby's, On-the-Border, Subway, Wendy's, **lodging:** Courtyard, Crossland Suites, Delux Inn, Fairfield Inn, **other:** HOSPITAL, BigLots, Nichols RV Ctr, other multiple facilities, Bigtown Mall
55	Motley Dr, ...**gas:** Shell/dsl, **food:** Castillo Mexican, **lodging:** Astro Inn, Executive Inn, ...**gas:** Chevron, **food:** Mesquite Grill, **lodging:** Microtel, **other:** HOSPITAL, Dodge, to Eastfield Coll
54	Big Town Blvd, ...**gas:** Valero/dsl, **lodging:** Mesquite Inn, ...**other:** Affordable RV Ctr
53b	US 80 E(from eb), to Terrell, ...Toyota
53a	Lp 12, ...**lodging:** Lamplighter Motel, Super 8, **other:** Chevrolet, ...**food:** CiCi's, Taco Cabana, Whataburger, **lodging:** Holiday Inn Express, **other:** $Tree, Ford, Sam's Club, Staples, Wal-Mart SuperCtr/gas/24hr
51	(52 a from wb), Highland Rd, ...**gas:** Exxon, **food:** Country China, Denny's, Kettle, Luby's, McDonald's, Owen's Rest., **lodging:** La Quinta, ...**gas:** RaceWay, Shell/dsl, **food:** Burger King, Capt D's, Furr's Dining, Grandy's, KFC, Pizza Hut, Popeye's, Taco Bell, Wendy's, **lodging:** Exel Inn, Howard Johnson, Motel 6, Super 7 Inn, **other:** AutoZone, CVS Drug
50b a	Ferguson Rd, ...**gas:** Texaco, ...**other:** Brake-O, U-Haul
49b	Dolphin Rd, Lawnview Ave, Samuell Ave, ...**lodging:** Best Value Inn
49a	Winslow St, ...**gas:** Circle K/gas, Shell/dsl/repair, **food:** McDonald's, ...**gas:** Shell/24hr
48b	TX 78, E Grand, ...fairpark, arboretum
48a	Carroll Ave, Central Ave, Peak St, Haskell Ave, ...**gas:** Valero, **other:** HOSPITAL, tires, ...**gas:** Fina, **food:** Joe's Burgers
47	2nd Ave, ...**food:** McDonald's, **other:** Cotton Bowl, fairpark
46b	I-45, US 75, to Houston
46a	Central Expswy, downtown
45	I-35E, N to Denton, to Commerce St, Lamar St, Griffin St, ...**gas:** Fina, **food:** McDonald's, **lodging:** Ramada Inn
44b	I-35E S, Industrial Blvd
44a	I-35E N, Beckley Ave(from eb)
43b a	Sylvan Ave(from wb), ...**gas:** Shell/Quizno's/dsl, **other:** HOSPITAL, Family$, USPO/24hr
42	Hampton Rd N, **1 mi** ...**food:** Burger King, KFC/Taco Bell
41	Hampton Rd S(no EZ eb return), ...**gas:** Mobil, ...**gas:** Exxon, Shell, **food:** Jack-in-the-Box, DQ, Luby's, Wendy's, **other:** AutoZone, Goodyear/auto, O'Reilly Parts
39	Cockrell Hill Rd, no services
38	Lp 12, ...**gas:** Exxon, **food:** Burger King
36	MacArthur Blvd, ...**other:** U-Haul
34	Belt Line Rd, ...**gas:** Chevron, **lodging:** Day's Inn, Motel 6, Ramada Ltd, **other:** Ford, Ripley's Museum, ...**gas:** Shell/Subway, Valero, **food:** DQ, McDonald's
32	NW 19th, ...**gas:** Valero, ...**gas:** Mobil, **food:** Denny's, McDonald's, Pizza Hut, Taco Bell, Whataburger, **lodging:** La Quinta
30	TX 360, Six Flags Dr, Arlington Stadium, ...**gas:** Shell, **food:** Grand Buffet, Ninfa's Café, Saltgrass Steaks, TrailDust Steaks, Candlewood Suites, **lodging:** Day's Inn, Fairfield Inn, Flagship Inn, Hilton, Park Inn, Radisson Suites, **other:** Studio+, Super 8, Wingate Inn, ...**gas:** Shell/dsl, Valero, **food:** Bennigan's, Denny's, Jack-in-the-Box, Luby's, McDonald's, Owen's Rest., Steak&Ale, **lodging:** Baymont Inn, La Quinta, **other:** Dillard's, JC Penney, K-Mart, Sears/auto, Six Flags Funpark, mall

D a l l a s

TEXAS

Interstate 30

29 Ball Park Way, **N**...**gas:** Chevron, **food:** Frijoles Café, Grady's Grill, Macaroni Grill, TrailDust Steaks, **lodging:** Fairfield Inn, **other:** Toyota, **S**...**gas:** Fina/dsl, **food:** On-the-Border, Texas Steaks, **lodging:** Howard Johnson, Marriott, Stadium Inn, Wyndham Hotel, **other:** Six Flags Funpark

28b TX 157, Nolan Ryan Expswy, **N**...**gas:** Mobil, **food:** Waffle House, **lodging:** Country Inn Suites, **S**...**food:** Chili's, Cozymel's, Harrigan's Grill, Joe's Crabshack, Landry's Seafood, Olive Garden, Pappadeaux Seafood, **lodging:** Courtyard, Day's Inn, **other:** Wyndham Garden, **other:** Barnes&Noble, SteinMart, TX Stadium

28a FM 157, Collins St, **N**...**food:** Whataburger, **other:** HOSPITAL, Dodge, **S**...**food:** Pappasito's Cantina, **other:** Home Depot

27 Lamar Blvd, Cooper St, **N**...**gas:** Mobil, **food:** Jack-in-the-Box, **other:** CVS Drug, Kroger, **S**...**gas:** 7-11, Shell, **food:** Burger King, Denny's

26 Fielder Rd, **S**...**other:** to Six Flags(from eb)

25mm Village Creek

24 Eastchase Pkwy, **N**...**food:** Jack-in-the-Box, **other:** CarMax, Sam's Club/gas, Wal-Mart SuperCtr/24hr, **S**...**gas:** Chevron, Shell/dsl, **food:** IHOP, McDonald's, Whataburger, **other:** Office Depot, Old Navy, Ross, Target

23 Cooks Lane, **S**...**gas:** Mobil

21c Bridgewood Dr, **N**...**gas:** Mobil, Shell, **food:** Bennigan's, Luby's, Wendy's, **other:** Discount Tire, Home Depot, Kroger, U-Haul, **S**...**gas:** Shell/dsl/24hr, Valero, **food:** Burger King, McDonald's, Pizza Hut, Taco Bueno, Whataburger/24hr

21b a I-820

19 Brentwood Stair Rd(from eb), **N**...**gas:** Chevron, Shell/dsl, **food:** Chuy's Mexican, Steak&Ale, **other:** Kroger, **S**...**gas:** Shell

18 Oakland Blvd, **N**...**gas:** Phillips 66, Shell/dsl, **food:** Burger King, Taco Bell, Waffle House, **lodging:** Motel 6

16c Beach St, **S**...**gas:** 7-11, **lodging:** Ambassador Hotel, Best Western

16b a Riverside Dr(from wb), **S**...**lodging:** Great Western Inn

15b a I-35W N to Denton, S to Waco

14b Jones St, Commerce St, Ft Worth, downtown

14a TX 199, Henderson St, Ft Worth, downtown

13b Summit Ave, downtown

13a 8thth Ave, downtown

12d Forest Park Blvd, **N**...**food:** Pappadeaux Café, Pappasito's, **S**...**other:** HOSPITAL

12b Rosedale St, no services

12a University Dr, City Parks, **S**...**lodging:** SpringHill Suites

11 Montgomery St, **S**...**gas:** Shell/dsl, **food:** Whataburger, **other:** visitor info

10 Hulen St, Ft Worth, **S**...**food:** Chick-fil-A, Coldstone, Micocina, **other:** Borders Books, WorldMkt

9b US 377, Camp Bowie Blvd, Horne St, **N**...**food:** Uncle Julio's Mexican, **S**...**gas:** Exxon, Fina, 7-11/gas, Shell, Texaco/dsl, **food:** Jack-in-the-Box, Mexican

Inn, Pizza Hut/Taco Bell, Szechuan Chinese, Subway, Taco Bueno, Wendy's

9a Bryant-Irvin Rd, **S**...**gas:** Shell, same as 9b

8b Ridgmar, Ridglea, **N**...**gas:** Valero/dsl

8a TX 183, Green Oaks Rd, **N**...**food:** Applebee's, Chili's, Don Pablo, Grand Buffet, Jack-in-the-Box, Olive Garden, Quizno's, Starbucks, Taco Bueno, **lodging:** Courtyard, **other:** Albertson's, Best Buy, $Tree, Dillard's, Firestone/auto, Foley's, JC Penney, Mervyn's, Macey's, Neiman Marcus, NTB, Office Depot, Old Navy, PetsMart, Ross, Sam's Club/gas, Sears/auto, U-Haul, Wal-Mart SuperCtr, **S**...**food:** Tommy's Burgers, **lodging:** Comfort Suites, Green Oaks Hotel, Hampton Inn

7b a Cherry Lane, TX 183, spur 341, to Green Oaks Rd, **N**...**gas:** Conoco, Shell, Valero, **food:** ChuckeCheese, IHOP/24hr, Luby's, Popeye's, Ryan's, Subway, Taco Bell, Wendy's, **lodging:** Days Inn, La Quinta, Super 8, **other:** Big Lots, Ford, Home Depot, O'Reilly Parts, U-Haul, Wal-Mart/auto, **S**...**lodging:** Hampton Inn, Holiday Inn Express, Quality Inn, **other:** Dodge, Mitsubishi, Nissan, Target

6 Las Vegas Trail, **N**...**gas:** Chevron/24hr, **food:** McDonald's, Waffle House, **lodging:** Day's Inn, **other:** Acura, Lincoln/Mercury, vet, **S**...**gas:** Shell/dsl, Texaco, Valero/dsl, **food:** Pancake House, **lodging:** Best Budget Suites, Comfort Inn, Courtesy Inn, Motel 6, **other:** AutoZone, Kia

5b c I-820 S and N, no services

5a Alemeda St(from eb, no EZ return), no services

3 RM 2871, Chapel Creek Blvd, no services

2 spur 580 E, no services

1b Linkcrest Dr, **S**...**gas:** Chevron/dsl, Mobil/dsl

0mm I-20 W. I-30 begins/ends on I-20, exit 421.

Interstate 35

Exit #	Services
504mm	Texas/Oklahoma state line, Red River
504	frontage rd, access to Texas Welcome Ctr
503mm	parking area both lanes, no services
502	**Welcome Ctr sb, full(handicapped)facilities, TX Tourist Bureau/info, phone, picnic tables, litter barrels**
501	FM 1202, Prime Outlets Blvd, **E**...**other:** Chrysler/Dodge/Jeep, Ford/Mercury, **W**...**gas:** Hilltop/Conoco/dsl/café/@, **food:** Applebee's, Cracker Barrel, **lodging:** Hampton Inn, La Quinta, **other:** Prime Outlets/famous brands, Western Outfitter, Harper's Steaks, RV camping
500	FM 372, Gainesville, **E**...**gas:** Gainesville Trkstp/dsl/rest., **W**...**gas:** Hitchin' Post/Shell/cafe/dsl/scales/24hr/@
498b a	US 82, to Wichita Falls, Gainesville, Sherman, **E**...**gas:** Conoco/dsl, Exxon, Phillips 66/dsl, Shell, Valero/dsl, **food:** Denny's, Whatburger/24hr, **lodging:** Bed&Bath Inn, Budget Host, Comfort Inn, Delux Inn, Super 8, 12 Oaks Inn, **other:** HOSPITAL, **W**...**gas:** Exxon/dsl, **food:** Luigi's Italian, **lodging:** Comfort Suites, Day's Inn, Holiday Inn
497	frontage rd, no services

Interstate 35

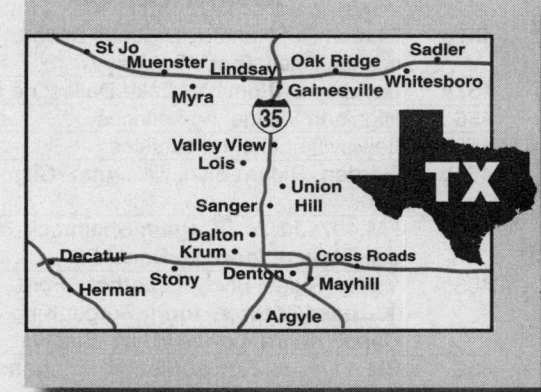

496b	TX 51, FM 51, California St, Gainesville, **E**...**gas:** Chevron, Conoco/dsl, **food:** Arby's, Braum's, Burger King, Grandy's, IHOP, McDonald's, Starbucks, Taco Bell, Taco Casa, Sonic, Wendy's, **lodging:** Holiday Inn Express, Quality Inn, **other:** Cadillac, Dodge, Goodyear/auto, N Central TX Coll, Scivally's Foods, **W**...**gas:** Valero/dsl, **food:** Chili's
496a	to Weaver St, no services
496mm	Elm Fork of the Trinity River
495	frontage rd, no services
494	FM 1306, no services
492mm	picnic area sb, tables, litter barrels
491	Spring Creek Rd, no services
490mm	picnic area nb, picnic tables, litter barrels
489(488 from nb)	FM 1307, to Hockley Creek Rd
487	FM 922, Valley View, **W**...**gas:** Chevron/dsl/24hr, **food:** DQ, **other:** USPO
486	Fm 1307, no services
485	frontage rd(from sb), no services
483	FM 3002, Lone Oak Rd, **E**...gas/dsl
482	Chisam Rd, no services
481	View Rd, **W**...**other:** Sundown Ranch RV Park
480	Lois Rd, **E**...**other:** Wal-Mart Dist Ctr
479	Belz Rd, Sanger, same as 478
478	FM 455, to Pilot Pt, Bolivar, **E**...**gas:** QuikTrack, Shell, **food:** DQ, Migualito's Mexican, Sonic, Subway, **lodging:** Sanger Inn, **other:** USPO, cleaners/laundry, **W**...**gas:** Chevron/Subway/24hr, Fuel 4 TX, **food:** Chicken Express, Jack-in-the-Box, McDonald's, **other:** Chevrolet, Family$, IGA Foods, QuickCar Lube, RV Park, Ray Roberts Lake and SP
477	Keaton Rd, **E**...**food:** Mr Gatti's, No Frills Grill, **W**...**gas:** Shamrock/dsl, **other:** RV Ctr
475b	Rector Rd, no services
475a	FM 156, to Krum, no services
474	Cowling rd(from nb), no services
473	FM 3163, Milam Rd, **E**...**gas:** Love's/Subway/dsl/24hr
472	Ganzer Rd, no services
471	US 77, FM 1173, Lp 282, to Denton, Krum, **E**...**gas:** TA/Pizza Hut/Taco Bell/dsl/scales/24hr/@, **food:** Good Eats Café, **other:** HOSPITAL, Denton Stores/famous brands, **W**...**gas:** Fina/dsl/café/scales/24hr, **other:** Foster's Western Shop, to Camping World RV Supply, Fun Time RV Ctr
470	Lp 288, same services as 469 from sb
469	US 380, University Dr, to Decatur, McKinney, **E**...**gas:** Chevron, RaceTrac, **food:** Braum's, ChinaTown Café, Cracker Barrel, Luigi's Pizza, McDonald's, **lodging:** Best Western, Fairfield Inn, **other:** Albertson's/drugs, Dodge, K-Mart, Toyota, **W**...**gas:** Conoco/dsl, Shell/dsl, Valero, **food:** DQ, Denny's, Sonic, Waffle House, **lodging:** Exel Inn, Howard Johnson, Motel 6, **other:** HOSPITAL, Ancira RV Ctr, Camping World RV Supply, to TX Woman's U
468	FM 1515, Airport Rd, W Oak St, no services
467	I-35W, S to Ft Worth
	I-35 divides into E and W sb, converges into I-35 nb. See Texas I-35 W.
466b	Ave D, **E**...**gas:** Citgo, Exxon/dsl, **food:** Burger King, IHOP/24hr, McDonald's, Pancho's Mexican, Taco Cabana, **lodging:** Comfort Suites, **other:** $General, Sack'n Save Foods, to NTSU, **W**...**lodging:** Radisson
466a	McCormick St, **E**...**gas:** Phillips 66, Shell/dsl, **lodging:** Comfort Suites, Royal Hotel, **W**...**gas:** Citgo, Fina/dsl/U-Haul
465b	US 377, Ft Worth Dr, **E**...**gas:** Citgo, RaceTrac, Shamrock, **food:** Carino's Italian, ChuckeCheese, Kettle, Taco Bueno, Whataburger/24hr, **lodging:** La Quinta, **other:** Home Depot, U-Haul, **W**...**gas:** Citgo, Conoco, Total/dsl, **food:** Outback Steaks, **lodging:** Day's Inn
465a	FM 2181, Teasley Ln, **E**...**gas:** Citgo/7-11, **food:** Applebee's, Braum's, Carino's, KFC/Pizza Hut, **lodging:** Holiday Inn, **other:** Brookshires Foods, bank, **W**...**gas:** Exxon, Fina, Shell, **food:** Little Caesar's, OutBack Steaks, Pizza Hut, Rudy's Rest., **lodging:** Ramada Inn, Super 8
464	US 77, Pennsylvania Dr, Denton, **E**...**food:** Burger King, Wendy's, **lodging:** Denton Inn, **other:** Dillard's, JC Penney, Kroger, Mervyn's, Office Depot, PepBoys, Ross, Sears/auto, Wal-Mart, transmissions, mall, same as 463
463	Lp 288, to McKinney, **E**...**food:** BBQ, Burger King, El Chico, Grandy's, On the Border, Texas Roadhouse, Wendy's, Wienerschnitzel, **other:** Discount Tire, Kroger, Mervyn's, Old Navy, Sears/auto, **W**...**gas:** Chevron, **food:** Blackeyed Pea, Chili's, Jack-in-the-Box, Luby's, Red Lobster, Red Pepper's Rest., Schlotsky's, Tia's Mexican, **other:** Albertson's, same as 464
462	State School Rd, Mayhill Rd, **E**...**gas:** Shell/dsl, **food:** Olive Garden, **other:** HOSPITAL, Hyundai, **W**...**gas:** Chevron, Exxon/café, **other:** Albertsons, Cadillac, Chevrolet, Dodge/Toyota, FunTime RV Ctr, Lincoln/Mercury/Mazda/Isuzu, Pontiac/Buick/GMC
461	Sandy Shores Rd, Post Oak Dr, **E**...**other:** Ford, McClain RV Ctr, **W**...**other:** Chrysler/Jeep/Kia, Lincoln/Mercury/Mazda, Nissan
460	Corinth Pkwy, **E**...**gas:** Chevron/dsl/repair, **other:** McClain RV Ctr, camping, **W**...**other:** Harley-Davidson
459	frontage rd, **W**...**other:** Destiny RV Resort
458	FM 2181, Swisher Rd, **E**...**gas:** Phillips 66, **W**...**gas:** Chevron/McDonald's, Exxon/Wendy's, **food:** Burger King, Chick-fil-A, Chili's, Jack-in-the-Box, KFC/Pizza Hut/Taco Bell, Mr Gatti, Starbucks, Whataburger, **other:** Albertson's, Discount Tire, GNC, Radio Shack, Wal-Mart SuperCtr/gas/24hr

Denton (vertical label on left margin)

TEXAS

Interstate 35

457b Denton Rd, Hundley Dr, Lake Dallas, E...**gas:** Phillips 66, Shell, **food:** Subway

457a Hundley Dr(from nb), Lake Dallas, no services

456 Highland Village, no services

456mm Lewisville Lake, no services

454b Garden Ridge Blvd, W...**gas:** Citgo, **other:** city park

454a FM 407, Justin, E...**gas:** Shamrock, W...**gas:** Fina/dsl, Texaco, **food:** McDonald's

453 Valley Ridge Blvd, E...**other:** Ford, May RV Ctr, W...**gas:** Chevron, **food:** Burger King, **other:** Home Depot, Kohl's, Lowes Whse, Staples

452 FM 1171, to Flower Mound, E...**gas:** Mobil, **food:** IHOP, Taco Bueno, **lodging:** Days Inn, Howard Johnson, **other:** HOSPITAL, W...**gas:** Chevron, Exxon/dsl, **food:** Burger King, Golden Corral, Grandy's, Whataburger/24hr, **other:** Home Depot, Kohl's, Lowe's Whse, Staples, U-Haul, same as 451

451 Fox Ave, E...**gas:** Shell/dsl, **food:** Braum's, W...**gas:** Chevron/24hr, Conoco/Quizno's/dsl, QuickTrack Gas, Shamrock, **food:** Blackeyed Pea, Cracker Barrel, El Chico, **lodging:** Budget Inn, Hampton Inn, Microtel, **other:** Atlas Transmissions, VW

450 TX 121, Lewisville, E...**gas:** Citgo/7-11, RaceTrac, **food:** BBQ, Owens Rest., Pancho's Mexican, **lodging:** Pines Motel, Ramada Ltd, **other:** Chevrolet/Subaru, Dodge, W...**gas:** Chevron, Citgo/7-11, Conoco, Fina, Shamrock, Texaco/dsl, **food:** Burger King, Chili's, Church's, IHOP, Ming Garden Chinese, KFC, LJ Silver, McDonald's, Subway, Taco Bell, Waffle House, Whataburger/24hr, **lodging:** Budget Inn, Day's Inn, Spanish Trails Inn, Super 8, **other:** Chief Parts, Eckerd, Firestone/auto, Food Lion, Kroger, Nissan/Saturn, transmissions

449 Corporate Drive, E...**gas:** Conoco, **food:** China Dragon, Fox&Hound Grill, Hartford Grill, Hooters, On the Border, **lodging:** Extended Stay America, Hearthside Inn, Motel 6, **other:** Aamco/Just Brakes, Cavender's Boots, W...**gas:** Exxon/Quizno's/Pizza Inn/TCBY, Fina/dsl, **food:** Chili's, El Fenix Mexican, Jack-in-the-Box, Kettle, **lodging:** Best Western, La Quinta, Sun Suites, **other:** Honda, Kia, NTB, Saturn

448b a FM 3040, Round Grove Rd, E...**food:** Abuelo's Mexican, Bennigan's, ChuckeCheese, Hooters, Jack-in-the-Box, Mimi's Cafe, Olive Garden, SaltGrass Steaks, Subway, **lodging:** Homewood Suites, **other:** Best Buy, Circuit City, Honda, Ross, Target, W...**gas:** Chevron, Exxon, RaceTrac, Texaco, **food:** Applebee's, Cantina Laredo, Carino's Italian, Chick-fil-A, Chipotle Mexican, Christina's Mexican, Cotton Patch Café, Don Pablo, Famous Dave's BBQ, Good Eats Grill, IHOP, Logan's Roadhouse, Luby's, Macaroni Grill, McDonald's, Outback Steaks, Red Lobster, Schlotsky's, Sonic, SpagEddie's Italian, Taco Cabana, TGIFriday, Tony Roma, Water Garden Chinese, Wendy's, **lodging:** Comfort Inn, Country Inn Suites, **other:** Barnes&Noble, BigLots, Borders Books, Circuit City, CompUSA, Dillard's, Discount Tire, Foley's, JC Penney, Marshall's, Michael's, Office Depot, Old Navy, Sears/auto, Target, mall

446 Frankford Rd, E...**food:** La Hacienda Ranch Grill, **other:** Volvo

445b Pres Geo Bush Tpk, no services

445 Trinity Mills Rd, E...**other:** HOSPITAL, Buick/GMC/Pontiac, Home Depot, PepBoys, RV Ctr

444 Whitlock Lane, Sandy Lake Rd, E...**gas:** Shell, **food:** Pizza Bro's, **lodging:** Rodeway Inn, **other:** RV camping, W...**gas:** Chevron, **food:** McDonald's, **lodging:** Delux Inn

443 Belt Line Rd, Crosby Rd, E...**gas:** Conoco, **other:** Ford, NTB

442 Valwood Pkwy, E...**gas:** Chevron/Subway, Texaco, **food:** DQ, Denny's, El Chico, Grandy's, Jack-in-the-Box, Redline Burgers, Rosita's Mexican, Taco Bueno, Taquiera Arrandas, Waffle House, **lodging:** Comfort Inn, Guest Inn, Red Roof, Royal Inn, W...**gas:** Fina/dsl, **lodging:** Day's Inn, **other:** Chevrolet, U-Haul, transmissions

441 Valley View Lane, W...**gas:** Mobil, Shell, **food:** Michael's Rest., **lodging:** Best Western, Day's Inn, Econolodge, La Quinta

440b I-635 E

440c I-635 W, to DFW Airport

439 Royal Lane, E...**gas:** Fina, Shell, **food:** McDonald's, Wendy's, Whataburger/24hr, W...**gas:** Chevron, **food:** Jack-in-the-Box

438 Walnut Hill Lane, E...**gas:** Chevron, Shell, Texaco/Quizno's/dsl, **food:** Bennigan's, Burger King, Chili's, Denny's, Old San Francisco Steaks, Red Lobster, Steak&Ale, Taco Bell, TGIFriday, Tony Roma's, Trail Dust Steaks, Wild Turkey Grill, **lodging:** Country Inn Suites, Drury Inn, Hampton Inn, W...**gas:** Chevron, Texaco/dsl, **other:** RV Ctr

437 Manana Rd(from nb), same as 438

436 TX 348, to DFW, Irving, E...**gas:** Exxon/dsl, **food:** Cabo Cantina, IHOP, Luby's, Schlotsky's, Waffle House, **lodging:** Clarion Suites, Comfort Suites, Courtyard, Hearthside Inn, Homestead Suites, La Quinta, Radisson, Springhill Suites, Studio 6, W...**gas:** Exxon, **food:** Bennigan's, Blackeyed Pea, Chili's, Don Pablo, Humperdinck's Grill, Jack-in-the-Box, Jason's Deli, Joe's Crabshack, McDonald's, Olive Garden, Outback Steaks, Papadeaux Seafood, Pappasito's Mexican, Red Lobster, Taco Bell/Pizza Hut, Tony Roma's, Wendy's, **lodging:** Red Roof Inn

435 Harry Hines Blvd(from nb), E...**gas:** RaceTrac, **food:** Arby's, **other:** U-Haul, same as 436

434b Regal Row, E...**gas:** Texaco/Grandy's, **food:** Denny's, Whataburger/24hr, **lodging:** La Quinta, Red Roof Inn, W...**lodging:** Fairfield Inn

434a Empire, Central, E...**gas:** Chevron/McDonald's, **food:** Sonic, Wendy's, **lodging:** Budget Suites, Candlewood Suites, InTowne Suites, Wingate Inn, **other:** Office Depot, W...**gas:** Exxon, **food:** Burger King, Schlotsky's, Taco Bell/Pizza Hut

433b Mockingbird Lane, Love Field Airport, E...**gas:** Mobil, Shell, **food:** Jack-in-the-Box, **lodging:** Budget Suites, Clarion Hotel, Comfort Inn, Crowne Plaza, InTown Suites, Residence Inn, **other:** Sheraton, W...**gas:** Chevron, Exxon, **food:** McDonald's, Wendy's, **other:** Goodyear

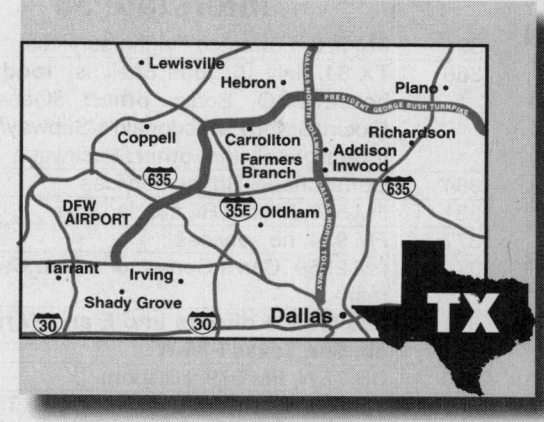

433a (432b from sb)TX 356, Commonwealth Dr, E...**gas:** Texaco/dsl, **lodging:** Marriott, **other:** W...**lodging:** Delux Inn

432a Inwood Rd, E...**gas:** Exxon, **other:** HOSPITAL, Chevrolet, W...**gas:** Fina, Texaco, **food:** Whataburger/24hr, **lodging:** Homewood Suites

431 Motor St, E...**gas:** Chevron, **food:** Denny's, W...**gas:** Shell, **food:** Ninfa's Grill, Wok Chinese, **lodging:** Embassy Suites, Marriott Suites

430c Wycliff Ave, E...**food:** JoJo's Rest., **lodging:** Renaissance Hotel, **other:** Intn'l Apparel Mart

430b Mkt Ctr Blvd, E...**other:** World Trade Ctr, W...**gas:** Shell, **food:** Denny's, **lodging:** Courtyard, Fairfield Inn, Hilton Garden, Ramada Inn, Sheraton, Wilson World Hotel, Wyndham Garden

430a Oak Lawn Ave, W...**gas:** Texaco/dsl, **food:** Denny's, Medieval Times Rest., **lodging:** Holiday Inn, **other:** to Merchandise Mart

429c HiLine Ave(from nb), no services

429b Continental Ave, Commerce St W, downtown, E...**food:** Hooters, W...**gas:** Exxon, **food:** McDonald's

429a to I-45, US 75, to Houston

428e Commerce St E, Reunion Blvd, Dallas, downtown

428d I-30 W, to Ft Worth

428a I-30 E, to I-45 S

428b Industrial Blvd, E...**gas:** Chevron, W...**gas:** Fina/dsl, Shamrock

427b I-30 E

427a Colorado Blvd, E...HOSPITAL

426c Jefferson Ave, E...**gas:** Texaco, W...**gas:** Shell

426b TX 180 W, 8th St, E...**gas:** Shell/dsl

426a Ewing Ave, E...**food:** McDonald's, W...**other:** Chrysler/Jeep, Pontiac/GMC, Honda, Hyundai

425c Marsalis Ave, E...**lodging:** Dallas Inn, W...**gas:** Citgo, Mobil

425b Beckley Ave, 12th St, sb only, W...**gas:** Exxon, Shamrock, **food:** Wendy's

425a Zang Blvd, W...**gas:** Exxon, Shamrock, **food:** Wendy's

424 Illinois Ave, E...**gas:** Chevron, **food:** William's Chicken, Bud&Ben Brakes, **other:** HOSPITAL, W...**gas:** Exxon, **food:** IHOP, Jack-in-the-Box, Sonic, Taco Bell, **other:** OakTree Inn, **other:** Kroger

423b Saner Ave, no services

423a (422b from nb)US 67 S, Kiest Blvd, W...**gas:** Shell/repair, **food:** McDonald's, **lodging:** Dallas Inn, **other:** Subaru/VW, Suzuki

421b Ann Arbor St, no services

421a Lp 12E W, E...**gas:** RaceWay, **lodging:** Delux Inn

420 Laureland, E...**lodging:** Master Suite Motel, W...**gas:** Conoco, Mobil, **lodging:** Embassy Motel, Linfield Inn

419 Camp Wisdom Rd, E...**gas:** Exxon, **lodging:** Oak Cliff Inn, W...**gas:** Shell/24hr, **food:** McDonald's, **lodging:** Suncrest Inn, **other:** U-Haul

418c Danieldale Rd(from sb), no services

418b I-635/I-20 E, to Shreveport

418a I-20 W, to Ft Worth

417 Wheatland Rd(from nb), no services

416 Wintergreen Rd, E...**other:** repair, W...**gas:** Citgo/7-11, **food:** Cracker Barrel, Golden Corral, Waffle House, **lodging:** Holiday Inn Express, Red Roof Inn

415 Pleasant Run Rd, E...**gas:** Chevron/24hr, RaceTrac, Shell/Blimpie/dsl, **food:** Bienvenidos Mexican, Evergreen Buffet, Subway, Waffle House, **lodging:** Great Western Inn, Royal Inn, Spanish Trails Motel, Super 8, **other:** Chrysler/Jeep, PepBoys, transmissions, W...**gas:** Chevron, Exxon, **food:** Burger King, El Chico, Golden Corral, KFC, LJ Silver, Luby's, McDonald's, On the Border, Outback Steaks, Pizza Inn, Taco Bueno, Wendy's, **lodging:** Best Western, **other:** HOSPITAL, Chevrolet, Discount Tire, Ford, Kroger, K-Mart, Office Depot, Ross

414 FM 1382, Desoto Rd, Belt Line Rd, E...**food:** Chili's, Whataburger, **other:** Wal-Mart SuperCtr/gas/24hr

413 Parkerville Rd, W...**gas:** Exxon/Subway, **other:** U-Haul

412 Bear Creek Rd, W...**gas:** Shell/dsl, **food:** Bubba's BBQ, Jack-in-the-Box, Whataburger, **other:** HiHo RV Park, transmissions

411 FM 664, Ovilla Rd, E...**gas:** Exxon/TCBY/24hr, RaceTrac/24hr, **food:** LJ Silver/Taco Bell, McDonald's, Whataburger, **lodging:** Comfort Inn, **other:** Brookshire's Foods, CVS Drug, W...**gas:** Exxon/Subway, Shamrock

410 Red Oak Rd, E...**gas:** Citgo/dsl, Nock's/Shell/Pizza Inn/Subway/dsl, **food:** Denny's, Merryland Chinese, **lodging:** Day's Inn, W...**other:** Hilltop Travel Trailers

408 US 77, TX 342, to Red Oak, E...golf

406 Sterrett Rd, E...fireworks

405 FM 387, E...**gas:** Phillips 66/dsl

404 Lofland Rd, industrial area, no services

403 US 287, to Ft Worth, E...**food:** Jack-in-the-Box, McDonald's, Taco Bell, Waffle House, **lodging:** Hampton Inn, **other:** Chevrolet/Cadillac, Jeep, W...**other:** Buick/Pontiac/GMC, Chrysler/Dodge, Ford/Mercury

401b US 287 bus, Waxahatchie, E...**lodging:** Best Western, Super 8

401a Brookside Rd, E...**lodging:** Best Value Inn, Days Inn

399b FM 1446, no services

399a FM 66, FM 876, Maypearl, E...**lodging:** Texas Inn, W...**gas:** Chevron/dsl, StarMart/dsl/24hr

397 to US 77, to Waxahachie, no services

393mm rest area both lanes, full(handicapped)facilities, phone, picnic tables, litter barrels, vending, petwalk

Interstate 35

N ↕ S

Hillsboro

391	FM 329, Forreston Rd, no services
386	TX 34, Italy, E...gas Shell/dsl, food: DQ, Smokehouse BBQ, Sonic, other: $General, W...gas: Exxon/Grandy's/Mcdonald's/Subway/Pizza Inn/dsl, lodging: Italy Inn, other: truckwash
384	Derrs Chapel Rd, no services
381	FM 566, Milford Rd, no services
377	FM 934, no services
374	FM 2959, Carl's Corner, W...gas: Carl's Trkstp/dsl/rest.
371	**I-35 W. I-35 divides into E and W nb, converges sb, See Texas I-35 W.**
370	US 77 N, FM 579, Hillsboro
368b	FM 286, E...food: LoneStar Café, Taco Bell, Wendy's, lodging: Hampton Inn, Super 8, other: Prime Outlets/famous brands, W...gas: Exxon, Valero/dsl, food: Braum's, Domino's, DQ, El Conquistador Mexican, El Taco Jalisco, McDonald's, Pizza Hut, lodging: Best Western, Comfort Inn, other: HOSPITAL
368a	TX 22, TX 171, to Whitney, E...gas: 7-11, Love's/Subway/Pizza Hut/dsl/scales/24hr/@, food: Arby's, Blackeyed Pea, Burger King, IHOP, Merryland Chinese, McDonald's, Starbucks, Taco Bell, lodging: Day's Inn, Holiday Inn Express, Motel 6, Super 8, W...gas: Chevron, Exxon, Mobil, Shell/dsl, food: Chicken Express, Jack-in-the-Box, KFC, Schlotsky's, Whataburger/24hr, lodging: Thunderbird Motel/rest., other: Buick/Pontiac/GMC, Chevrolet/Cadillac, Chrysler/Dodge/Jeep, Ford/Mercury, Wal-Mart SuperCtr/gas/24hr
367	Old Bynum Rd(from nb), no services
364b	TX 81 N, to Hillsboro(exits left from nb)
364a	FM 310, E...gas: Exxon/dsl, W...gas: Fina/diese/24hr, food: Up In Smoke BBQ
362	Chatt Rd, no services
359	FM 1304, W...gas: Mobil/Subway/dsl/24hr, other: antiques
358	FM 1242 E, Abbott, E...gas: Exxon, food: Smokin' Cafe
356	Co Rd 3102, no services
355	County Line Rd, E...food: Yianni's Rest, other: KOA
354	Marable St, E...other: KOA
353	FM 2114, West, E...gas: Chevron, Fina/dsl, Shell/Czech Bakery, food: Bush's Chicken, Subway, DQ, other: Ford, W...gas: Exxon, Texaco, lodging: Czech Inn, other: Chevrolet
351	FM 1858, no services
349	Wiggins Rd, no services
347	FM 3149, Tours Rd, no services
346	Ross Rd, E...gas: Shell/dsl/24hr, W...gas: Exxon/dsl/24hr, other: I-35 RV Park, antiques
345	Old Dallas Rd, E...antiques, W...other: I-35 RV Park
343	FM 308, Elm Mott, E...gas: Exxon/DQ, Fina/dsl, Shell/Jct Cafe/dsl/scales/24hr, W...gas: Chevron/dsl/24hr, food: BBQ, Heitmiller Steaks
342b	US 77 bus, W...RV Park
342a	FM 2417, Crest Dr, W...gas: Valero/dsl, food: Bush's Chicken, DQ, lodging: Everyday Inn, other: Family$, auto repair

Waco

341	Craven Ave, Lacy Lakeview, E...gas: Chevron, W...gas: BP/dsl, Shell/pizza
340	Myers Lane(from nb), no services
339	to TX 6 S, FM 3051, Lake Waco, E...gas: Valero/dsl, food: Beall's Rest, Casa Ole,'s, Domino's, El Conquistador, Jack-in-the-Box, Luby's, Little Caesars, Pizza Hut, Popeye's, Sonic, Subway, Wendy's, Whataburger/24hr, lodging: Country Inn Suites, other: Advance Parts, $General, HEB/gas, Home Depot, Radio Shack, Sam's Club, Wal-Mart SuperCtr/24hr/gas, W...gas: Chevron, Citgo, Shell, food: Burger King, Cracker Barrel, KFC, McDonald's, Papa John's, Starbucks, lodging: Fairfield Inn, Hampton Inn, Hawthorn Inn, Knight's Inn, other: to airport
338b	Behrens Circle(from nb), E...food: Jack-in-the-Box, Sonic, same as 339, W...food: Cracker Barrel, gas: Shell/dsl/LP, lodging: Comfort Inn, Country Inn, Day's Inn, Delta Inn, Hawthorn Inn, Hampton Inn, Knight's Inn, Motel 6, other: Eckerd
337	(338a from nb)US 84, to TX 31, Waco Dr, E...food: ChopStix, lodging: Value Place Suites, other: AutoZone, Family$, HEB Food/gas, Sam's Club/gas, W...gas: Texaco, other: HOSPITAL
335c	Lake Brazos Dr, MLK Blvd, E...food: Summer Palace Chinese, lodging: Holiday Inn, RiverPlace Inn/café, W...food: Doc's Riverfront Rest., lodging: Travel Inn, Victorian Inn, other: HOSPITAL
335mm	Brazos River
335b	FM 434, University Parks Dr, E...food: China Grill, IHOP, Jim's Rest., Quizno's, Thai Cuisine, lodging: Best Western, other: Baylor U, W...food: Arby's, Jack-in-the-Box, lodging: Clarion, Lexington Inn, Residence Inn
335a	4th St, 5th St, E...gas: Exxon/Subway/TCBY/dsl, Shell/dsl, food: China Grill, Denny's, IHOP, Lupito's Mexican, Pizza Hut, lodging: Best Western, La Quinta, other: Baylor U, W...gas: BP, Shamrock, food: Fazoli's, LJ Silver, McDonald's, Taco Bell, Taco Cabana, Wendy's, Whataburger/24hr, lodging: Clarion, other: to Baylor U
334b	US 77 S, 17th St, 18th St, E...gas: BP, Chevron, Shell/dsl, food: Burger King, Fazolies, Popeye's, Schlotsky's, Vitek's BBQ, Wendy's, Whataburger, lodging: Budget Inn, Comfort Inn, Econolodge, Super 8, other: Harley-Davidson, W...gas: Phillips 66/dsl, Shell, food: Mexico Lindo, Renee's Rest., Taquiera Mexican, other: HOSPITAL
333a	Lp 396, Valley Mills Dr, E...gas: Chevron, food: Denny's, El Chico, Elite Café, Rudy's BBQ, TX Roadhouse, Trujillo's Mexican, lodging: Astro Motel, Comfort Suites, La Quinta, Motel 6, other: Isuzu/Mazda, Suzuki, W...gas: Valero, food: Bush's Chicken, Church's Chicken, DQ, Jack-in-the-Box, Papa John's, Sonic, Taco Bueno, lodging: Comfort Inn, other: Eckerd, Jeep, Lincoln/Mercury, Volvo/Freightliner
331	New Rd, E...gas: Chevron/dsl, lodging: New Road Inn, Relax Inn, Rodeway Inn, W...gas: 🦅/Flying J/CountryMkt/dsl/scales/24hr/@, food: Hooters, IHOP, lodging: Quality Inn, other: Harley Davidson
330	Lp 340, TX 6, W...food: Camille's Cafe, Logan's Roadhouse, Smokey Bones BBQ, other: Belk, Best Buy, Books-A-Million, Kohl's, Ross, Old Navy, **2 mi** W...food:

Interstate 35

TEXAS

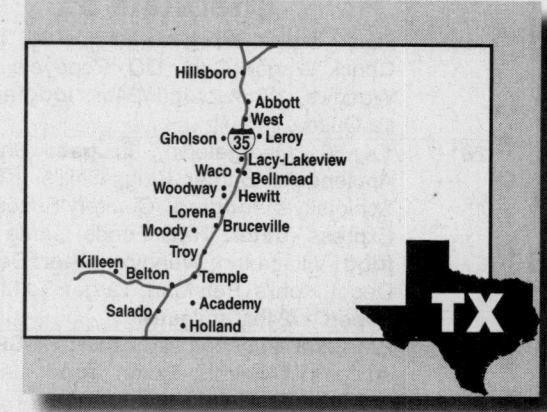

Chick-fil-A, Luby's, McDonald's, Outback Steaks, TGIFriday, Wienerschnitzel, **lodging:** Extended Stay America, Fairfield Inn, **other:** CompUSA, Ford, Honda, Lowe's Whse, Toyota, Wal-Mart SuperCtr/24hr

328	FM 2063, FM 2113, Moody, E...**gas:** Pilot/Subway/Wendy's/dsl/scales/24hr/@, **food:** McDonald's, W...**gas:** Shell/24hr, Valero/dsl, **lodging** Sleep Inn
325	FM 3148, Moonlight Dr, W...**gas:** Conoco/dsl, **other:** Walkabout RV Ctr
323	FM 2837(from sb), Lorena, W...**gas:** Brookshire Bros/gas, **food:** Pizza House
322	Lorena, E...**gas:** Phillips 66/dsl, **food:** Baytown Seafood, W...**gas:** Chevron/dsl, **food:** Bush's Chicken, Ruthy's Mexican, **other:** $General
319	Woodlawn Rd, no services
318b a	Bruceville, E...**gas:** Conoco/dsl, **other:** picnic area both lanes, litter barrels, picnic tables
315	TX 7, FM 107, Eddy, **1 mi** E...RV Park, W...**gas:** BP, Shell/Subway/dsl/24hr, **other:** Family$, to Mother Neff SP
314	Old Blevins Rd, no services
311	Big Elm Rd, E...fireworks
308	FM 935, Troy, E...**gas:** Shell, **other:** Troy Foods, W...**gas:** Exxon, **other:** All-American RV Ctr
306	FM 1237, Pendleton, W...**gas:** Love's/Subway/dsl/24hr, **other:** Temple RV Park
305	Berger Rd, W...**gas:** Exxon/dsl/scales/24hr, **lodging:** Sharon Jean's Rest, **other:** Lucky's RV Park, Temple RV Park, repair
304	Lp 363, Dodgen Loop, W...**gas:** Shell/Wendy's/dsl, Valero/dsl/24hr
303	spur 290, N 3rd St, Temple, E...**gas:** S-2 Gas, **lodging:** Texas Inn, W...**lodging:** Continental Inn
302	Nugent Ave, E...**gas:** Exxon/dsl, **lodging:** Comfort Suites, Econolodge, Holiday Inn Express, Red Roof Inn, W...**gas:** BP/dsl, Chevron, **food:** Denny's, **lodging:** Best Western, Day's Inn, Motel 6, Stratford House Inn, Travelodge, **other:** Ford/Lincoln/Mercury, Harley Davidson
301	TX 53, FM 2305, Adams Ave, E...**gas:** Valero, **food:** Arby's, Chick-fil-A, Gatti's Rest., Jim's Rest., KFC, LJ Silver, McDonald's, Pizza Hut, Starbucks, Subway, Taco Bell, Wendy's, Whataburger, **lodging:** La Quinta, **other:** HOSPITAL, Advance Parts, Ford, W...**food:** Catfish Shack, **lodging:** Best Western, **other:** Chrysler/Jeep, $General, Lincoln/Mercury, Harley-Davidson, Jeep
300	Ave H, 49th –57th Sts, E...**gas:** Shell, **food:** Las Casas Mexican, W...**gas:** Shell
299	US 190 E, TX 36, E...**gas:** Shell, Texaco/dsl, **food:** Golden Corral, Jack-in-the-Box, Luby's, Phillip's Steakhouse, **lodging:** Best Value, Budget Inn, Regency Inn, **other:** HOSPITAL, Ancira RV Ctr, Chevrolet/Toyota, Dodge, K-Mart, Saturn, Subaru, W...**food:** Chili's, Best Buy, Burger King, Chili's, Home Depot, IHOP, McDonald's, Target
298	nb only, to frontage rd, E...**lodging:** Residence Inn, **other:** Subaru
297	FM 817, Midway Dr, E...**gas:** Phillips 66, **food:** Taquiera Mexican, **lodging:** Holiday Inn, Super 8/rest., **other:** BMW, Nissan, Saab, Volvo, W...**gas:** Valero, **other:** Buick/Pontiac/GMC, Fed Ex, Suzuki, VW

294b	FM 93, 6th Ave, E...**gas:** Shell/dsl, **food:** McDonald's, **other:** Chevrolet, Toyota, W...**food:** Buger King, Great SW Rest., Pizza Hut, Subway, Whataburger, **lodging:** Ramada Ltd, River Forest Inn, **other:** U of Mary Hardin Baylor
294a	Central Ave, W...**gas:** Shell/dsl, **food:** BBQ, Burger King, Bobby's Burgers, Great SW Rest., Jalisco's Mexican, Pizza Hut, Sonic, Whataburger, **lodging:** Ramada Ltd, **other:** AutoZone, Goodyear
293b	TX 317, FM 436, Main St, no services
293a	US 190 W, to Killeen, Ft Hood, no services
292	Lp 121(same as 293a), E...**gas:** Valero/dsl/rest./24hr, **lodging:** Budget Host, W...**gas:** Mobil/dsl/24hr, **lodging:** La Quinta, **other:** Ford, auto/tire repair
290	Shanklin Rd, no services
289	Tahuaya Rd, E...**other:** Hi-Way Parts
287	Amity Rd, no services
286	FM 2484, E...**lodging:** Holiday Inn Express, W...to Stillhouse Hollow Lake
285	FM 2268, Salado, E...**gas:** Conoco/Brookshire Foods, **food:** Subway, **lodging:** Holiday Inn Express, W...**gas:** Chevron, **food:** Cowboys BBQ, Robertson's Rest., Sonic
284	Stagecoach Rd, E...**gas:** Exxon/Burger King, **food:** Arbys, DQ, Roy T's Subway, Subway, W...**gas:** Texaco/dsl, **food:** DQ, **lodging:** Super 8
283	FM 2268, FM 2843, to Holland, Salado, E...**lodging:** Stagecoach Inn
282	FM 2115, E...**gas:** Valero/dsl, **other:** RV camping
281mm	**rest area both lanes, full(handicapped)facilities, phone, picnic table, litter barrels, vending, pet-walk, RV dump**
280	Prairie Dell, no services
279	Hill Rd, W...**other:** RV Park
277	Yankee Rd, no services
275	FM 487, to Florence, Jarrell, E...**gas:** Exxon/dsl, Shamrock/dsl/scales, Shell, **food:** Burger King, Denny's, W...**gas:** Shell, **other:** USPO
271	Theon Rd, E...**gas:** Explore USA RV Ctr, W...**gas:** Shell/Subway/dsl/24hr
268	fm 972(fom nb), Walburg, E...**other:** Crestview RV Ctr
266	TX 195, E...**gas:** Mobil/dsl
265	toll 130, to Austin, new exit
264	Lp 35, Georgetown, no services
262	RM 2338, Lake Georgetown, E...**food:** KFC, Luby's, McDonald's, Quizno's, Sonic, Subway, **lodging:** Holiday Inn Express, **other:** Albertson's, Eckerd, Parts+,

Temple

TEXAS

Interstate 35

Georgetown

	Radio Shack, **W**...**gas:** Phillips 66, Texaco, **food:** Chuck Wagon Café, DQ, Popeye's, Taco Bueno, Wendy's, Whataburger/24hr, **lodging:** Day's Inn, La Quinta
261	TX 69, Georgetown, **E**...**gas:** Shell/dsl, **food:** Applebee's, Burger King, Chili's, KFC/Taco Bell, Schlotsky's, **lodging:** Comfort Suites, Holiday Inn Express, **other:** HEB Foods, same as 262, **W**...**food:** Village Inn, Wendy's, **other:** Best Buy, Home Depot, Kohl's, PetsMart, Target, TJ Maxx, Wal-Mart SuperCtr/24hr, antiques
260	RM 2243, Leander, **E**...**other:** HOSPITAL, USPO, **W**...**gas:** Chevron, Exxon, **food:** Jack-in-the-Box, **lodging:** Quality Inn
259	Lp 35, **W**...**other:** RV Outlet Ctr, to Interspace Caverns
257	Westinghouse Rd, **E**...**other:** Chevrolet/Buick, Chrysler/Dodge/Jeep, Ford, Kia, Mazda, Mitsubishi, VW
256	RM 1431, Chandler Rd, **E**...**other:** Round Rock Outlet, Hummer, Mazda, JC Penny, Volvo

Round Rock

254	FM 3406, Round Rock, **E**...**gas:** Chevron, Citgo/7-11, Texaco, **food:** Arby's, Castaways Seafood, Fuddruckers, Gatti's Pizza, Giovanni's Italian, McDonald's, Schlotsky's, Sonic, **other:** Firestone, GMC/Pontiac, Honda, Pennzoil, Toyota, **W**...**gas:** Phillips 66/24hr, **food:** Carino's Italian, China One, Chuy's Mexican, Cracker Barrel, Bennigan's, Denny's, Golden Corral, Mesa Rosa Mexican, Rudy's BBQ, SaltGrass Steaks, **lodging:** AmeriSuites, Courtyard, Hilton Garden, Holiday Inn, La Quinta, Red Roof Inn, SpringHill Suites, Super 8, **other:** Nissan
253b	US 79, to Taylor, **E**...**gas:** Chevron, **food:** Arby's, Baskin-Robbins, DQ, Famous Sam's Café, Fuddrucker's, KFC, LoneStar Café, LJ Silver, Sirloin Stockade, **other:** HOSPITAL, AutoZone, HEB/deli, **W**...**gas:** Exxon/dsl, Shell/dsl/24hr, **food:** BBQ, IHOP, K-Bob's Rest., Taco Bell, Thundercloud Subs, **lodging:** Country Inn Suites, La Quinta, Red Roof Inn, Sleep Inn, Value Place Motel, **other:** Eckerd, USPO
253a	Frontage Rd, **E**...**gas:** Shell, **food:** Arby's, Beal's Cafe, Castaway's Seafood/steaks, DQ, Damon's, KFC, Taco Bell, **lodging:** Best Western, Wingate Inn, **W**...**food:** La Marguarita, Mr Gatti, Popeye's, Taco Bell, **lodging:** Ramada Ltd, **other:** CVS Drug, USPO
252b a	RM 620, **E**...**gas:** Shell/dsl/24hr, **lodging:** Candlewood Suites, Crossland Suites, Extended Stay America, **other:** bank, **W**...**gas:** BP, Phillips 66, **food:** Grandy's, Little Caesar's, McDonald's, Starbucks, **lodging:** Comfort Suites, Staybridge Suites, **other:** mall
251	Lp 35, Round Rock, **E**...**food:** Cici's Pizza, Outback Steaks, Whataburger, **lodging:** Residence Inn, **other:** Aamco, Advance Parts, BigLots, Brake Check, Diahatsu, $General, transmissions, **W**...**gas:** Exxon, Shell, **food:** Burger King, Jack-in-the-Box, Luby's, Peter Piper Pizza, Taco Cabana, **lodging:** Day's Inn, **other:** Albertson's, Hastings Books, NTB, Walgreen

250	FM 1325, **E**...**gas:** Chevron, Mobil/dsl, **food:** Applebee's, Chick-fil-A, Chili's, El Chico, Jason's Deli, Joe's Crabshack, Macaroni Grill, McDonald's, Subway, **lodging:** Hampton Inn, **other:** Best Buy, Discount Tire, Goodyear/auto, Home Depot, Michael's, PetsMart, Ross, Steinmart, Target, Wal-Mart SuperCtr/24hr, **W**...**gas:** Shell, **food:** Antonio's Cantina, Fast Eddie's Rest, Hooters, Krispy Kreme, Olive Garden, Starbucks, **lodging:** Baymont Inn, Extended Stay America, **other:** Barnes&Noble, Circuit City, Kohl's, Lowe's Whse, Marshall's, Office Depot, Old Navy, PetCo, Sam's Club/gas
248	Grand Ave Pkwy, **E**...**gas:** Texaco/Subway/dsl, **food:** Cheddar's, Fish Daddy's Grill, Jack-in-the-Box, Posado's Mexican, Taco Cabana, TX Roadhouse, **other:** Firestone, **W**...**gas:** Chevron/McDonald's, **other:** Goodyear/auto
247	FM 1825, Pflugerville, **E**...**gas:** RaceTrac, **food:** Jack-in-the-Box, Sonic, Taco Cabana, Wendy's, **other:** Firestone/auto, HEB Foods, cinema, **W**...**gas:** Exxon, Shell/Church's, **food:** BBQ, IHOP, KFC, Miller's BBQ, Whataburger, **lodging:** Holiday Inn Express, Quality Suites, **other:** Goodyear/auto
246	Howard Lane, **E**...**gas:** Citgo, Shell/dsl, **food:** Arby's, Baby Acapulco, McDonald's, Subway, Wings'n More, **other:** Home Depot, Kohl's, NTB, **W**...**gas:** Valero/dsl
245	FM 734, Parmer Lane, to Yager Lane (244 from nb), **E**...**food:** Bennigan's, Carino's, Chick-fil-A, Chili's, Golden Wok, Schlotzsky's, Subway, **other:** HEB Food/gas, JC Penny, Kohl's, PetsMart, Radio Shack, Ross, Sears Grand, Target, **W**...**gas:** Citgo/7-11, Exxon, **food:** Red Robin, Starbucks, Village Inn, **lodging:** Residence Inn, SpringHill Suites, **other:** CarMax, Lowe's Whse, Wal-Mart SuperCtr/24hr/gas
243	Braker Lane, **E**...**gas:** Valero, **food:** Jack-in-the-Box, Whataburger/24hr, **other:** Harley-Davidson, U-Haul, **W**...**gas:** Shell/dsl, **lodging:** Austin Motel, **other:** vet
241	Rundberg Lane, **E**...**gas:** Exxon, **food:** Golden Corral, Jack-in-the-Box, Mr Gatti's, Old San Francisco Steaks, **lodging:** Extended Stay America, Ramada Inn, **other:** Albertson's, Chevrolet, $General, U-Haul, Wal-Mart SuperCtr/24hr, **W**...**gas:** Chevron, Conoco, Shell, **food:** Sonic, **lodging:** Austin Suites, Budget Inn, Holiday Inn Express, Home-Style Inn, Motel 6, Red Roof Inn, Super 8, Travelodge, Wingate Inn
240a	US 183, Lockhart, **E**...**gas:** Exxon, **food:** DQ, Jack-in-the-Box, Old San Francisco Steaks, **lodging:** Day's Inn, Ramada Inn, Wellesley Inn, **other:** Chevrolet, **W**...**gas:** Chevron/dsl/24hr, Texaco/dsl, **lodging:** Motel 6, Red Roof Inn, Super 8, Travelodge Suites, Wingate Inn
239	St John's Ave, **E**...**gas:** Shell, **food:** Chili's, Fuddruckers, Japon Japanese, Jim's Rest., Owen's Rest, Pappadeaux, Pappasito's Mexican, Steak&Egg, Sushi Japan, **lodging:** Crowne Plaza, Budget Host, Day's Inn, DoubleTree, Drury Inn, Hampton Inn, Red Lion Hotel, Studio 6, **other:** Dodge, Home Depot, Volvo, Wal-Mart SuperCtr/24hr, **W**...**gas:** Conoco/dsl, Exxon, **food:** Antonio's TexMex, Applebee's, Bennigan's, Carrabba's, Denny's, Quizno's, **lodging:** AmeriSuites, Comfort Inn, Country Inn Suites, Baymont Inn, Holiday Inn Express, La Quinta, Sheraton, Sumner Suites, **other:** Office Depot

Interstate 35

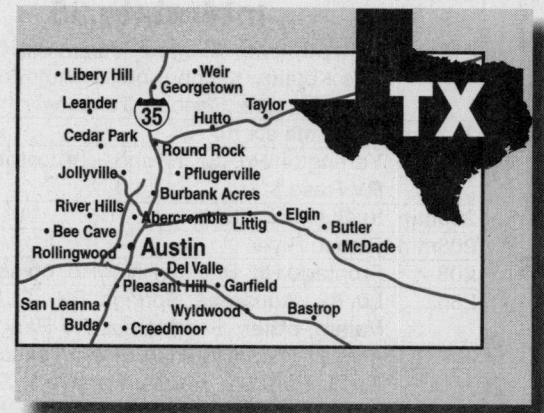

238b	US 290 E, RM 222, same as 238a, frontage rds connect several exits
238a	51st St, E...**gas:** Exxon, Chevron, Phillips 66, Shell, **food:** Burger King, Chili's, Dixie's Roadhouse, El Torito, Fuddrucker's, Grandy's, LJ Silver, McDonald's, Pappasito's, Sonic, Subway, Texas Steaks, Whataburger, **lodging:** Doubletree Hotel, Drury Inn, Econolodge, Embassy Suites, Holiday Inn, Homestead Village, Red Lion Hotel, Studio 6 Suites, **other:** Advance Parts, $Tree, Firestone, FoodLand, Jo-Ann Crafts, Ross, Target, Volvo, Walgreen, W...**gas:** Shell, **food:** Baby Acapulco, Bombay Bicycle Club, Capt's Seafood, Carrabba's, IHOP, India Cuisine, Outback Steaks, Quizno's, **lodging:** Courtyard, Drury Inn, Fairfield Inn, Hilton, La Quinta, Motel 6, Quality Inn, Ramada Ltd, Rodeway Inn, Super 8, **other:** Dillard's, Ford, Office Depot
237b	51st St, same as 238a
237a	Airport Blvd, E...**food:** BBQ, W...**food:** Jack-in-the-Box, Wendy's, GNC, Goodyear, **other:** Best Buy, HEB Foods, Marshall's, Old Navy, PetCo, Sears/auto
	upper level is I-35 thru, lower level accesses downtown
236b	39th St, E...**gas:** Chevron, **food:** Subway, **other:** Fiesta Foods, HiLo Parts, O'Reilly Parts, U-Haul, W...**gas:** Shell/dsl, **other:** Tune&Lube, tires, to U of TX
236a	26th-32nd Sts, E...**food:** Subway, **lodging:** Day's Inn, W...**lodging:** Rodeway Inn, **other:** HOSPITAL
235b	Manor Rd, same as 236a, E...**food:** Denny's, **lodging:** Double Tree, W...**lodging:** Rodeway Inn, **other:** U of TX, st capitol
235a	MLK, 15th St, W...HOSPITAL
	upper level is I-35 thru, lower level accesses downtown
234c	11th St, 12th St, downtown, E...**gas:** Chevron, Shell, **food:** Wendy's, **lodging:** DoubleTree Hotel, Super 8, **other:** CVS Drug, Eckerd, W...**gas:** Exxon, Mobil, Shell, **food:** Wendy's, **lodging:** Crowne Plaza, Marriott, Hilton Garden Inn, Hilton Garden Inn, Omni Motel, Radisson, Sheraton, **other:** HOSPITAL, museum, st capitol
234b	8th-3rd St, W...**food:** IHOP
234a	Cesar Chavez St, Holly St, downtown
233	Riverside Dr, Town Lake, E...**gas:** Citgo, **lodging:** Extended Stay America, W...**gas:** Chevron/dsl, **lodging:** Holiday Inn
232mm	Little Colorado River
232b	Woodland Ave, no services
232a	Oltorf St, E...**gas:** Shell/dsl, **food:** Kettle, La Taraza Grill, Luby's, **lodging:** Best Value Inn, Country Garden Inn, Exel Inn, La Quinta, Motel 6, Suburban Lodge, W...**gas:** Chevron, Exxon, **food:** Denny's, Starbucks, **lodging:** Clarion, Quality Inn
231	Woodward St, E...**gas:** Shell/dsl, **food:** Country Kitchen, **lodging:** Wyndham Garden, same as 232, W...**other:** Home Depot
230b a	US 290 W, TX 71, Ben White Blvd, St Elmo Rd, E...**gas:** Shell, **food:** Domino's, Jim's Rest., McDonald's, Sigon Kitchen, Subway, Western Choice Steaks, **lodging:** Best Western, Comfort Suites, Courtyard,
	Fairfield Inn, Hampton Inn, Marriott, Omni Hotel, Red Roof Inn, Residence Inn, SpringHill Suites, **other:** Acura, Sam's Club/gas, W...**food:** Burger King, Furr's Cafeteria, IHOP, Pizza Hut, Taco Cabana, **lodging:** Candlewood Suites, Day's Inn, Hawthorn Suites, La Quinta, **other:** HOSPITAL, BMW, Dodge/Jeep, Ford, GMC, Honda, Hyundai, Kia, Lincoln/Mercury, Mazda, NTB, Nissan, Pontiac/Cadillac/Mazda, Suzuki/Kia, Toyota
229	Stassney Lane, W...**food:** Chili's, Logan's Roadhouse, Macaroni Grill, Rockfish Grill, Texas Cattle Co Steaks, **other:** Albertson's/gas, Fiesta Foods, Lowe's Whse
228	Wm Cannon Drive, E...**gas:** Exxon, **food:** Applebee's, McDonald's, Taco Bell, **other:** Brake Check, Chrysler, Discount Tire, HEB Foods, Hyundai/Subaru, Mitsubishi, Nissan, Radio Shack, Target, W...**gas:** Shell/dsl, **food:** Burger King, Gatti's Pizza, KFC, LJ Silver, Peter Piper Pizza, Taco Cabana, Whataburger/24hr, Wendy's, **other:** Advance Parts, BigLots, Chevrolet, CVS Drug, $General, Firestone
227	Slaughter Lane, Lp 275, S Congress, E...**gas:** Shell/dsl, **food:** IHOP, **other:** Home Depot, Lone Star RV Resort, U-Haul, W...**gas:** Texaco, Valero/dsl, **food:** Chili's, Miller BBQ, Sonic, Starbucks, Steak&Shake, Subway, Jack-in-the-Box, TGIFriday's, TX Roadhouse, Whataburger, **other:** PetsMart, Wal-Mart SuperCtr/24hr/gas
226	Slaughter Creek Overpass, no services
225	FM 1626, Onion Creek Pkwy, E...**gas:** Shell, Texaco, **other:** Harley-Davidson
224	frontage rd(from nb), no services
223	FM 1327, no services
221	Lp 4, Buda, E...**gas:** Chevron/McDonald's, Shell/dsl, **lodging:** Best Value, Interstate Inn, **other:** Allstar RV Ctr, Ford, Marshall's RV Ctr, W...**gas:** Chevron/24hr, Shell, **food:** Chili's, Cracker Barrel, Jack-in-the-Box, Sonic, Subway, **other:** Cabela's, HEB Food/gas, Radio Shack, Wal-Mart SuperCtr
220	FM 2001, Niederwald, E...**gas:** Texaco, **other:** Camper Clinic RV Ctr, W...**other:** Crestview RV Ctr/Park
217	Lp 4, Buda, E...**gas:** Conoco/dsl/24hr, W...**gas:** Exxon/dsl, Valero/Pizza Hut/dsl, **food:** Burger King, **lodging:** Best Western, **other:** Home Depot
215	Bunton Overpass, E...**gas:** Exxon/KFC/LJ Silver, W...HEB Foods/gas

Austin

Interstate 35

N

↕

S

San Marcos

213	FM 150, Kyle, **E**...gas: Valero/dsl, **food:** DQ, Karen's Kountry Kitchen, **other:** AutoZone, Goodyear/auto, **W**...gas: Conoco, Texaco
211mm	weigh sta sta nb
210	Yarrington Rd, **E**...Hyundai, **W**...other: Plum Creek RV Resort
209mm	truck check sta sb
208mm	Blanco River
208	Frontage Rd, Blanco River Rd, no services
206	Lp 82, Aquarena Springs Rd, **E**...gas: Conoco, Valero, **other:** San Marcos RV Park, **W**...gas: Exxon/dsl, Phillips 66/dsl, Shell, Texaco, **food:** Jim's Rest., Pancake House, Popeye's, Sonic, **lodging:** Best Value, Comfort Inn, La Quinta, Motel 6, Quality Inn, Ramada Ltd, Rodeway Inn, Stratford Inn, Super 8, University Inn, **other:** to SW TX U, RV camping
205	TX 80, TX 142, Bastrop, **E**...gas: Chevron, Conoco, Exxon, RaceWay, Shell/dsl, Valero, **food:** Arby's, DQ, Fazolies, Jason's Deli, Subway, Taste of China, **lodging:** Executive Inn, **other:** AutoZone, CVS Drug, $General, Eckerd, Hastings Books, Wal-Mart SuperCtr/24hr, **W**...gas: Chevron, Circle K/gas/24hr, Valero, **food:** A&W/LJ Silver, Applebee's, Burger King, Church's, CiCi's, IHOP, KFC, Logan's Roadhouse, LJ Silver, Logan's Roadhouse, McDonald's, MT Mike's, Pizza Hut, Taco Cabana, Wendy's, **lodging:** Best Western, Budget Inn, Day's Inn, Gateway Inn, Microtel, ParkSide Inn, Red Roof Inn, Rodeway Inn, **other:** Best Buy, Brake Check, HEB Foods/gas, JC Penney, Office Depot, Target, Walgreen
204mm	San Marcos River
204b	CM Allen Pkwy, **W**...gas: Chevron, Conoco/dsl, Shell/dsl, **food:** Chinese Buffet, DQ, Red Robin, Sonic, **lodging:** Best Western, Econolodge
204a	Lp 82, TX 123, to Seguin, **E**...gas: Conoco, Valero, **food:** Burger King, Carino's, Chili's, FasTaco, Golden Corral, Luby's, McDonald's, Red Lobster, Whataburger/24hr, **lodging:** Comfort Suites, Holiday Inn Express, **other:** HOSPITAL, Chevrolet/Buick, Ford/Mercury, Jeep/Chrysler, transmissions
202	FM 3407, Wonder World Dr, **E**...gas: Exxon, Shell/Church's, **food:** Jack-in-the-Box, Pitt BBQ, Taco Bueno, Wienerschnitzel, **other:** HOSPITAL, Discount Tire, Lowe's Whse, Marshalls, PetsMart, Ross, Sams Club/gas, **W**...gas: Valero/dsl, **food:** BBQ, **other:** Chrysler/Dodge, transmissions
201	McCarty Lane, **E**...other: Discount Tire, **W**...other: Chrysler/Dodge, Nissan
200	Centerpoint Rd, **E**...food: Bennigan's, Cracker Barrel, Food Court, LoneStar Café, Outback Steaks, Subway, Taco Bell, Wendy's, **other:** Cavender's Boots, Old Navy, Prime Outlets/famous brands, Tanger Outlet/famous brands, **W**...gas: Valero/dsl, **food:** McDonald's, Quizno's, Starbucks, Whataburger/24hr, **lodging:** AmeriHost, **other:** Honda
199	Posey Rd, **E**...other: Tanger Outlets/famous brands, Toyota/Scion, same as 200
196	FM 1106, York Creek Rd, no services
195	Watson Lane, Old Bastrop Rd, **E**...fireworks

New Braunfels

193	Conrads Rd, Kohlenberg Rd, **E**...Roman Holiday RV Ctr, **W**...gas: TA/Country Fare Rest/Popeye's/Subway/dsl/scales/24hr/@, **food:** Coconut's Rest.
191	FM 306, FM 483, Canyon Lake, **E**...gas: Conoco/Quizno's/dsl, Texaco, **other:** I-35 RV Camping, Wal-Mart Dist Ctr, **W**...gas: Chevron, Exxon/dsl, **food:** Burger King, GristMill Rest., **other:** Camping World RV Supply/SW RV Ctr, transmissions
190c	Post Rd, no services
190b	Lp 35 S, New Braunfels, **W**...gas/dsl, **food:** Capparelli's Italian, **lodging:** Hawthorn Inn
190a	frontage rd, **E**...gas: Shell, **other:** Discount Tire, Home Depot, **W**...gas: McDonald's, **food:** Wendy's, **lodging:** Best Western, Comfort Suites, Motel 6, Quality Inn
189	TX 46, Seguin, **E**...gas: Conoco/dsl, Exxon, Shell/dsl, **food:** Chili's, Luby's, Olive Garden, Oma's Haus Rest., Village Inn, **lodging:** Best Value, La Quinta, Oakwood Inn, Stratford House, Super 8, **other:** Circuit City, Discount Tire, Home Depot, K-Mart, Kohl's, Office Depot, **W**...gas: Chevron/24hr, Texaco, **food:** Applebee's, IHOP, McDonald's, New Braunfels Smokehouse, Pizza Hut, Skillet's Rest., Taco Bell, Taco Cabana, Wendy's, **lodging:** Best Western, Comfort Suites, Day's Inn, Hampton Inn, Holiday Inn, Motel 6, Rodeway Inn, Quality Inn, Sleep Inn, **other:** HOSPITAL, Walgreen
188	Frontage Rd, **W**...food: Mamacita's Rest., Ryan's, **other:** Hastings Books
188mm	Guadalupe River
187	FM 725, Lake McQueeny Rd, **E**...gas: Chevron/24hr, **food:** Arby's, Burger King, China Kitchen, CiCi's, Guadalajara Mexican, LJ Silver/A&W, Subway, Whataburger/24hr, **other:** Aamco, BigLots, Family$, Ford/Lincoln/Mercury, Jeep, Radio Shack, **W**...gas: Exxon/dsl, Shell/dsl, **food:** Adobe Café, DQ, Jack-in-the-Box, Rally's, Steaks to Go, **lodging:** Budget Host, Budget Inn, Faust Hotel, **other:** HOSPITAL, CVS Drug, NAPA AutoCare, River Ranch RV Resort, transmissions
186	Walnut Ave, **E**...gas: Exxon/Subway, Valero, **food:** Chick-fil-A, McDonald's, Popeye's, Schlotsky's, Taco Bell, **lodging:** Red Roof Inn, **other:** Chevrolet, Lowes Whse, Wal-Mart SuperCtr/gas/auto, **W**...gas: Shell/dsl, **food:** KFC, Mr Gatti's, Papa John's, Shanghai Chinese, Starbucks, **other:** AutoZone, Brake Check, $Tree, GNC, HEB Foods/deli/gas, Radio Shack, Ross, Target, U-Haul, Walgreen
185	FM 1044, no services
184	FM 482, Lp 337, Ruekle Rd, **E**...gas: Shell/Blimpie/dsl, **other:** Buick/Pontiac/GMC, Kia, Mazda, **W**...Suzuki
183	Solms Rd, **W**...gas: Exxon
182	Engel Rd, **E**...other: Stamann RV Ctr
180	Schwab Rd, no services
179mm	**rest area both lanes, full(handicapped) facilities, phone, picnic tables, litter barrels, vending, petwalk, RV Dump**
178	FM 1103, Cibolo Rd, Hubertus Rd, **E**...gas: Shell/dsl
177	FM 482, FM 2252, **E**...Stone Creek RV Park
176	Weiderstein Rd, same as 175

TEXAS

Interstate 35

175 FM 3009, Natural Bridge, E...**gas:** Valero, **food:** Chili's, La Pasadita Mexican, McDonald's, Miller's BBQ, Schlotsky's, Sonic, Taco Cabana, **lodging:** Hampton Inn, **other:** HEB Food/gas, Radio Shack, W...**gas:** Valero/Subway/dsl, Shell/dsl, **food:** Arby's, Denny's, Jack-in-the-Box, KFC/Taco Bell/Pizza Hut, Starbucks, Wendy's, **lodging:** Atrium Inn, Country Inn, **other:** Factory Shoestore, Wal-Mart SuperCtr/24hr/gas

174b Schertz Pkwy, E...**gas:** Shell

174a FM 1518, Selma, E...**gas:** Phillips 66/dsl, **food:** Ruddy's BBQ, **other:** Honda/Mitsubishi, Saturn, W...**other:** Crestview RV Ctr

173 Old Austin Rd, Olympia Pkwy, E...**food:** Chick-fil-A, Chili's, Freddy's Custard, Hooters, Macaroni Grill, Red Robin, Sea Island Srimp, Subway, TGI-Friday's, **lodging:** Holiday Inn Express, **other:** Best Buy, Borders Books, Costco/gas, Home Depot, Old Navy, Ross, Target, WorldMkt, W...**other:** Retama Park RaceTrack

172 TX 218, Anderson Lp, P Booker Rd, E...**food:** Buffalo Wild Wings, Coldstone Creamery, IHOP, Outback Steaks, Texas Roadhouse, Village Inn, **lodging:** Comfort Inn, Value Place, **other:** Ford, Nissan, Home Depot, Hyundai, Kohls, Target, to Randolph AFB, W...**food:** Camino Ranch Steak, **other:** to SeaWorld

171 Topperwein Rd, same as 170

170 Judson Rd, to Converse, E...**food:** Denny's, India Cuisine, Kettle, Subway, Whataburger/24hr, **lodging:** Best Value, La Quinta, **other:** HOSPITAL, Chevrolet, Chrysler, Ford, Hyundai, Nissan, Pontiac/GMC, Toyota, W...**gas:** Exxon, **lodging:** Best Western, **other:** Kia, Mazda, Sam's Club/gas, Subaru

169 O'Conner Rd, Wurzbach Pkwy, E...**gas:** Exxon/dsl, **food:** McDonald's, Quizno's, Subway, Taco Cabana, **other:** Chrysler/Jeep, Lowe's Whse, Walgreen, W...**gas:** Shell/dsl, Valero, **food:** Jack-in-the-Box, Jim's Rest., Mi Casa Mexican, Sonic, **lodging:** Holiday Inn Express, **other:** Mazda

168 Weidner Rd, E...**gas:** Citgo/dsl, **lodging:** Day's Inn, Comfort Suites, W...**gas:** Chevron, **lodging:** Budget Host, Quality Inn, Park Inn, Super 8, **other:** Harley-Davidson, Volvo

167b Thousand Oaks Dr, Starlight Terrace, E...**gas:** Valero/dsl, **other:** Suzuki, W...**lodging:** Park Inn

167a Randolph Blvd, E...**other:** TravelTown TX RV Ctr, W...**lodging:** Best Western, Comfort Inn, Continental Inn, Day's Inn, Howard Johnson, Motel 6, Road-Way Inn, Ruby Inn, **other:** Suzuki

166 I-410 W, Lp 368 S, W...**other:** to Sea World

165 FM 1976, Walzem Rd, E...**gas:** Chevron, Shell, Valero/dsl, **food:** Applebee's, ChuckeCheese, Church's, IHOP, Jack-in-the-Box, Las Palapas Mexican, LJ Silver, Luby's, McDonald's, Marie Callendar's, Olive Garden, Pizza Hut, Red Lobster, Shoneys, Starbucks, Subway, Taco Bell, Taco Cabana, Wendy's, Whataburger, **lodging:** Hampton Inn, Peartree Inn, **other:** AutoZone, CarQuest, Cavender's Boots, Circuit City, Dillard's, Discount Tire, Firestone/auto, Home Depot, Michael's, PepBoys, Radio Shack, Target, Wal-Mart SuperCtr/24hr, W...**gas:** Mobil, **food:** Sonic, **other:** NTB

164b Eisenhauer Rd, E...**gas:** Exxon/dsl, **lodging:** Hawthorn Suites, Value Place Hotel, **other:** $General, Hancock Fabrics

164a Rittiman Rd, E...**gas:** Exxon, Shell/dsl, Valero/dsl, **food:** Burger King, Church's, Cracker Barrel, Denny's, Guadalajara Mexican, Jack-in-the-Box, McDonald's, Rally's, Taco Cabana, Whataburger/24hr, **lodging:** Best Value, Best Western, Comfort Suites, Halmark Inn, La Quinta, Motel 6, Rittiman Inn, Super 8, **other:** Cummins dsl Repair, W...**gas:** Chevron/dsl, Valero, **food:** Miller's BBQ, Popeye's, Sonic, Wendy's

163 I-410 S(162 from nb, exits left from sb)

161 Binz-Engleman Rd(from nb), same as 160

160 Splashtown Dr, E...**gas:** Valero/Subway/dsl/24hr, **lodging:** Delux Inn, W...**food:** Grady's BBQ, **lodging:** Best Value, Day's Inn, Holiday Inn/rest., Microtel, Super 8, Travelodge

159b Walters St, E...**food:** McDonald's, W...**lodging:** Econolodge, **other:** to Ft Sam Houston

159a New Braunfels Ave, E...**gas:** Shell/dsl, Texaco/Burger King, W...**gas:** Chevron, Valero/dsl/24hr, **food:** Sonic, **lodging:** Antonian Suites, Ramada Suites, **other:** to Ft Sam Houston

158c N Alamo St, Broadway, no services

158b I-37 S, US 281 S, to Corpus Christi

158a US 281 N(from sb), to Johnson City

157b a Brooklyn Ave, Lexington Ave, N Flores, downtown, E...**lodging:** Super 8, **other:** HOSPITAL, W...**food:** Luby's

156 I-10 W, US 87, to El Paso

155b Durango Blvd, downtown, E...**lodging:** Best Western, Courtyard, Fairfield Inn, Holiday Inn, La Quinta, Residence Inn, Woodfield Suites, **other:** HOSPITAL, W...**food:** McDonald's, **lodging:** Motel 6, Radisson

155a South Alamo St, E...**gas:** Exxon, Shell, **food:** Church's, Denny's, McDonald's, Piedras Negras Mexican, Pizza Hut, Wendy's, **lodging:** Best Western, Comfort Inn, Day's Inn, Holiday Inn, La Quinta, Ramada Ltd, Residence Inn, **other:** USPO, W...**gas:** Conoco, **lodging:** Microtel

154b S Laredo St, Ceballos St, same as 155b

154a Nogalitos St, no services

153 I-10 E, US 90 W, US 87, to Kelly AFB, Lackland AFB

TEXAS

Interstate 35

Exit	Description
152b	Malone Ave, Theo Ave, **E**...**food:** Taco Cabana/24hr, **W**...**gas:** Shamrock, Shell
152a	Division Ave, **E**...**gas:** Chevron, **food:** Miller's BBQ, Whataburger/24hr, **lodging:** Quality Inn, **W**...**food:** Sonic, **other:** transmissions
151	Southcross Blvd, **E**...**gas:** Exxon, Shell, **W**...**gas:** Shell/dsl, **food:** Taquiera Mexican
150b	Lp 13, Military Dr, **E**...**gas:** Chevron, Texaco, **food:** Applebees, Denny's, KFC, Pizza Hut, Taco Cabana, **lodging:** La Quinta, **other:** AutoZone, Brake Check, Discount Tire, U-Haul, **W**...**gas:** Exxon, Mobil, **food:** Chili's, China Buffet, Hungry Farmer Rest, Jack-in-the-Box, KFC, LJ Silver, Luby's, McDonald's, Mr Gatti, Panda Express, Pizza Hut, Wendy's, Whataburger, **other:** Best Buy, $Tree, Firestone/auto, HEB Foods, Home Depot, JC Penney, Mervyn's, Office Depot, Old Navy, Sears/auto, Target, Walgreen, mall,
150a	Zarzamora St(149 fom sb), same as 150b
149	Hutchins Blvd(from sb), **E**...**gas:** Valero/dsl, **lodging:** Motel 6, **other:** HOSPITAL, **W**...**other:** Chevrolet, Ford, Kia
148b	Palo Alto Rd, **W**...**gas:** Valero
148a	TX 16 S, spur 422(exits left from sb), Poteet, **E**...**gas:** Chevron, **W**...**gas:** Phillips 66, **other:** $General, NAPA
147	Somerset Rd, **E**...**gas:** Shell/dsl, **W**...**other:** Dodge, Ford Trucks
146	Cassin Rd(from nb), no services
145b	Lp 353 N
145a	I-410, TX 16
144	Fischer Rd, **E**...**gas:** Valero/Subway/dsl/24hr, **lodging:** D&D Motel, **other:** Speedlube, RV camping, **W**...**gas:** Love's/Carl's Jr/dsl/24hr
142	Medina River Turnaround(from nb), no services
141	Benton City Rd, Von Ormy, **W**...**gas:** Shell/dsl/Parador Café
140	Anderson Lp, 1604, **E**...**gas:** Exxon/Burger King/dsl/24hr, **W**...**gas:** Valero/Church's/Pizza Hut/dsl/scales/24hr, **other:** Alamo River RV Resort, to Sea World
139	Kinney Rd, no services
137	Shepherd Rd, **E**...truck repair, **W**...gas/dsl, dsl repair
135	Luckey Rd, no services
133	TX 132 S(from sb), Lytle, same as 131
131	FM 3175, FM 2790, Benton City Rd, **E**...**other:** NAPA, **W**...**gas:** Conoco/dsl/24hr, **food:** DQ, McDonald's, Miller's BBQ, Sonic, Topis Mexican, Willie's Cafe, **lodging:** Day's Inn, **other:** $General, HEB Food/gas
129mm	**rest area both lanes, full(handicapped)facilities, phone, picnic tables, litter barrels, vending, petwalk**
127	FM 471, Natalia, no services
124	FM 463, Bigfoot Rd, **E**...Ford
122	TX 173, Devine, **E**...**gas:** Exxon/dsl, **food:** Panco Villa Mexican, **other:** Chevrolet, Chrysler/Jeep/Dodge, **W**...**gas:** Chevron/McDonald's/Subway/dsl, **food:** CCC Steaks, DQ(2mi), Pizza Inn, Sonic, **lodging:** Country Corner Inn, Curves
121	TX 132 N, Devine, **E**...**other:** Gusville RV Park
118.5mm	weigh sta both lanes
114	FM 462, Bigfoot, no services
111	US 57, to Eagle Pass, **W**...**gas:** Valero/dsl
104	Lp 35, **3 mi E**...**gas:** Valero, **food:** McDonald's, Sonic, **lodging:** Executive Inn, **other:** HOSPITAL
101	FM 140, Pearsall, **E**...**gas:** Chevron/dsl, **food:** Cowpokes BBQ, **lodging:** Best Western, Rio Frio Motel, Royal Inn, **other:** HOSPITAL, GMC, **W**...**gas:** Exxon/Subway/dsl/24hr
99	FM 1581, to Divot, Pearsall, no services
93mm	parking/picnic area both lanes, litter barrels, handicapped accessible
91	FM 1583, Derby, no services
90mm	Frio River
86	Lp 35, Dilley, no services
85	FM 117, **E**...**food:** Garcia Café/motel, **lodging:** Relax Inn, **W**...**gas:** Exxon, **food:** DQ, **lodging:** Safari Motel, Sona Inn, **other:** RV Park
84	TX 85, Dilley, **E**...**food:** Millie's Mexican, **other:** HOSPITAL, Chevrolet/Pontiac, Super S Foods/dsl, **W**...**gas:** Shell/Church's/dsl/24hr, Valero/dsl/24hr, **lodging:** Executive Inn
82	County Line Rd, to Dilley, no services
77	FM 469, Millett, no services
74	Gardendale, no services
69	68 from nb, Lp 35, Cotulla, **E**...Super S Food/gas
67	FM 468, to Big Wells, **E**...**gas:** Exxon/Wendy's/dsl/24hr, Conoco/Country Store/rest., Valero/Pollo Grande/dsl/24hr, **food:** DQ, **lodging:** Executive Inn, Village Inn, **other:** tire repair, **W**...**gas:** Chevron/McDonald's/dsl/scales/24hr
65	Lp 35, Cotulla, no services
63	Elm Creek Interchange, no services
59mm	parking/picnic area both lanes, litter barrels, handicapped accessible
56	FM 133, Artesia Wells, no services
48	Caiman Creek Interchange, no services
39	TX 44, Encinal, **E**...**gas:** Love's/Subway/Chester Fried/dsl/scales/24hr
38	TX 44(from nb), Encinal, no services
32	San Roman Interchange, no services
29mm	inspection sta nb
27	Callaghan Interchange, no services
24	255 toll, Camino Colombia toll rd, to Monterrey
22	Webb Interchange, no services
18	US 83 N, to Carrizo Springs, **E**...**TX Travel Info Ctr(8am-5pm)/rest area, full facilities, picnic tables, litter barrels, petwalk, wireless internet, W**...RV Camping
14mm	parking area, sb

TEXAS

Interstate 35

13	Uniroyal Interchange, **E**...gas: Pilot/McDonald's/Subway/dsl/scales/24hr/@, **other:** Blue Beacon, **W**...gas: ♨/Flying J/CountryMkt/dsl/scales/24hr/@, TA/Burger King/dsl/scales/24hr/@
10	Port Laredo Carriers Dr(from nb), no services
9	Industrial Blvd, to Bob Bullock Lp(from sb only)
8b	Lp 20 W, to Solidarity Bridge
8a	Lp 20 W, to to World Trade Bridge, Milo
7	Shilo Dr, Las Cruces Dr, sb only, no services
4	FM 1472, Del Mar Blvd, **E**...gas: Chevron/repair, Exxon/dsl, **food:** Applebee's, Bennigan's, Burger King, Carino's Italian, CiCi's, DQ, IHOP, Jack-in-the-Box, Las Asadas Mexican, Lin's Chinese, McDonald's, Quizno's, Whataburger, **lodging:** Extended Stay America, Hampton Inn, Residence Inn, **other:** Albertson's, Best Buy, HEB Foods, Honda, Lowe's Whse, Marshall's, Old Navy, Radio Shack, Target, **W**...gas: Shell/dsl, **food:** Golden Corral, **lodging:** Day's Inn, Executive House Motel, Motel 6, **other:** Harley Davidson
3b	Mann Rd, **E**...food: Krispy Kreme, Lin's Chinese, Logan's Roadhouse, Luby's, Olive Garden, Sirloin Stockade, **lodging:** Residence Inn, **other:** Buick, Dillard's, Foley's, Ford/Lincoln/Mercury, Honda, Lowes Whse, Mazda, Mervyn's, Pontiac/Cadillac/GMC, Sears/auto, Toyota, mall, **W**...food: Chili's, Golden Corral, Outback Steaks, Pancake House, Subway, Taco Palenque, **lodging:** Days Inn, Family Garden Inn, Fiesta Inn, La Hacienda Motel, Motel 6, Springhill Suites, **other:** $General, Home Depot, Michael's, Office Depot, Ross, Wal-Mart/auto/24hr
3a	San Bernardo Ave, **E**...gas: Shell/dsl, **food:** Chick-fil-A, Emperor Chinese, Fuddrucker's, LJ Silver, Logan's Roadhouse, Luby's, Peter Piper Pizza, Red Lobster, **lodging:** Fairfield Inn, **other:** HEB Foods, K-Mart, Mervyn's, NAPA, PepBoys, Sears/auto, SteinMart, mall, **W**...gas: Chevron, **food:** Burger King, Coyote Creek Rest., DQ, Dunkin Donuts, Hacienda Mexican, Kettle, McDonald's, Pizza Hut, Popeye's, Taco Bell, Taco Palenque, Tori Cafe, Wendy's, Whataburger, **lodging:** Best Western, Fiesta Inn, Gateway Inn, Monterey Inn, Motel 6, Red Roof Inn, **other:** Gonzales Auto Parts, Goodyear/auto, Radio Shack, Sam's Club
2	US 59, Saunders Rd, **E**...gas: Conoco, Gas USA, Shell, **food:** Jack-in-the-Box, **other:** HOSPITAL, **W**...gas: Chevron/dsl/24hr, Conoco, Exxon/Burger King/dsl, Shell, Valero, **food:** Church's, Denny's, Popeye's, Pizza Hut, **lodging:** Civic Ctr Inn, Courtyard, El Cortez Motel, Executive Inn, Holiday Inn, La Quinta, Mayan Inn, **other:** Advance Parts, AutoZone, Mexico Insurance, Ramirez Tire
1b	Park St, to Sanchez St, **W**...gas: Conoco/dsl, **food:** KFC, La Mexicana Rest., Pizza Hut, Popeye's
1a	Victoria St, Scott St, Washington St, **E**...gas: Exxon, Shell, Valero, **W**...gas: Chevron, Exxon/24hr, **food:** KFC, Mariachi Express, McDonald's, Wendy's, **other:** Firestone/auto, Goodyear/auto, transmissions
	I-35 begins/ends in Laredo at Victoria St...access to multiple services

Laredo

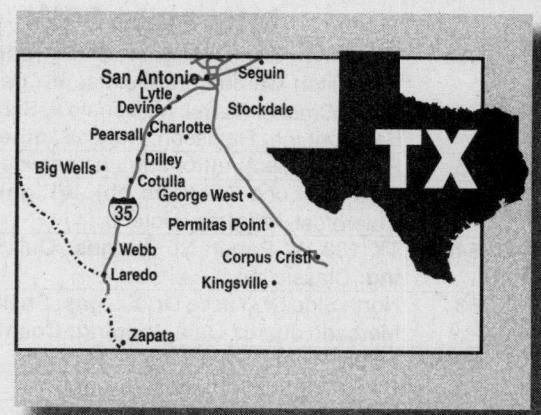

Interstate 35W

Exit #	Services
	I-35W begins/ends on I-35, exit 467.
85b	W Oak St, **E**...HOSPITAL
85a	I-35E S
84	FM 1515, Bonnie Brae St, **E**...HOSPITAL
82	FM 2449, to Ponder, no services
79	Crawford Rd, no services
76	FM 407, to Justin, Argyle, **W**...gas: Phillips 66/dsl/24hr, **other:** Corral City RV Park, Paradise Foods
76mm	picnic area both lanes, litter barrels, picnic tables
74	FM 1171, to Lewisville, no services
72	Dale Earnhardt Way, **E**...same as 70, **W**...TX Motor Speedway
70	TX 114, to Dallas, Bridgeport, **E**...gas: 7-11, Shell/A&W/LJ Silver/dsl, **food:** Waffle House/24hr, **lodging:** Comfort Suites, Sleep Inn, **other:** to DFW Airport, **W**...lodging: Doral Hotel, **other:** TX Motor Speedway
68	Eagle Pkwy, **W**...airport
67	Alliance Blvd, **W**...other: to Alliance Airport, FedEx
66	to Westport Pkwy, Keller-Haslet Rd, **E**...lodging: Hampton Inn, Residence Inn, **W**...gas: Mobil/Wendy's/dsl, **food:** Bryan's BBQ, Schlotsky's, Snooty Pig, Subway, Taco Bueno, **other:** USPO
65	TX 170 E, **E**...gas: Pilot/McDonald's/dsl/24hr/@, **food:** IHOP, **other:** Cabela's/cafe
64	Golden Triangle Blvd, to Keller-Hicks Blvd, **E**...other: Chrysler/Jeep/Dodge
63	Heritage Trace, **E**...food: Cheddar's, **other:** JC Penney
61	North Tarrant Pkwy
60	US 287 N, US 81 N, to Decatur
59	Basswood(sb only), **E**...gas: Chevron/Jack-in-the-Box/dsl, **food:** Sonic, **other:** Home Depot
58	Western Ctr Blvd, **E**...gas: 7-11, Shell, **food:** Black-eyed Pea, Braum's, Chili's, Denny's, Domino's, Dublin Square Rest., Macaroni Grill, On-the-Border, Posados Cafe, Quizno's, SaltGrass Steaks, Shady Oak BBQ, Wendy's, Zio's Italian, **lodging:** Best Western, Residence Inn, **other:** Kauffman Tire, **W**...food: Boston's, Joe's Crabshack, Starbucks, Waffle House, Whataburger, **lodging:** Holiday Inn Express
57b a	I-820 E&W
56b	Melody Hills, no services

Interstate 35W

N ↑ S

56a	Meacham Blvd, **E**...**gas:** Shell, **lodging:** Comfort Inn, Hilton Garden, La Quinta, **W**...**gas:** Texaco/dsl, **food:** Cracker Barrel, McDonald's, Subway, **lodging:** Baymont Inn, Radisson, Super 8, **other:** USPO
55	Pleasantdale Ave(from nb), no services
54c	33rd St, Long Ave(from nb), **W**...**gas:** Conoco/dsl, Valero/dsl, **lodging:** Motel 6
54b a	TX 183 W, Papurt St, **W**...**gas:** QuikStop/dsl, **lodging:** Classic Inn
53	North Side Dr, Yucca Dr, **E**...**gas:** Shell/dsl, **W**...**food:** Mercado Juarez Café, **lodging:** Country Inn&Suites
53mm	Trinity River
52e	Carver St(from nb), no services
52d	Pharr St, no services
52b	US 377N, Belknap
52a	US 377 N, TX 121, to DFW
51a	I-31 E, to Avalene(from nb), downtown Ft Worth
50c a	I-30 W, E to Dallas
50b	TX 180 E(from nb), no services
49b	Rosedale St, **W**...HOSPITAL
49a	Allen Ave, **E**...**gas:** Chevron, **W**...HOSPITAL
48b	Morningside Ave(from sb), same as 48a
48a	Berry St, **E**...**gas:** Chevron/McDonald's, **food:** Texas Style Rest., **other:** Autozone, Sack'n Save Foods, **W**...**gas:** RaceTrac, **other:** U-Haul
47	Ripy St, **E**...**other:** transmissions, **W**...**lodging:** Astro Inn
46b	Seminary Dr, **E**...**gas:** RaceWay, **food:** Empress Cafe, Grandy's, Golden Corral, Jack-in-the-Box, Sonic, Subway, Taco Cabana, Whataburger, **lodging:** Day's Inn, Delux Inn, Regency Inn, Super 7 Inn, **other:** NAPA, **W**...**gas:** Shell, **food:** Denny's, **other:** Dillard's, Dodge, $General, Firestone/auto, JC Penney, Sears
46a	Felix St(from nb), **E**...**gas:** Fina, **food:** Los Cantaritos Mexican **lodging:** Best Value Inn, **W**...**food:** McDonald's, **other:** Carnival Foods, Family$
45b a	I-20, E to Dallas, W to Abilene
44	Altamesa, **E**...**lodging:** Radisson, **W**...**food:** Rig Steaks, Waffle House, **lodging:** Baymont Inn, Best Western, Comfort Suites, La Quinta, Motel 6, South Lp Inn
43	Sycamore School Rd, **W**...**gas** Exxon, QT/dsl, Shell, **food:** Chicken Express, Jack-in-the-Box, Whataburger, **other:** $General, Home Depot, Radio Shack, RV Ctr
41	Risinger Rd, **W**...**other:** Camping World RV Service/Supplies, McClain's RV Ctr
40	Garden Acres Dr, **E**...**gas:** Love's/Subway/dsl/scales/24hr, **lodging:** Microtel, **other:** HOSPITAL, Happy Camper RV Ctr, **W**...**other:** Sun Time RV Ctr
39	FM 1187, McAlister Rd, **E**...HOSPITAL, **W**...**gas:** Citgo/dsl, Shamrock/dsl/24hr, **food:** Taco Bell, Waffle House, **lodging:** Howard Johnson
38	Alsbury Blvd, **E**...**gas:** Chevron/24hr, Mobil/dsl, **food:** Chili's, Country Steaks, Cracker Barrel, IHOP, McDonald's, Mexican Inn Cafe, On the Border, Outback Steaks, Spring Creek BBQ, Tai-Pan Chinese, **lodging:** Holiday Inn Express, Super 8, **other:** Discount Tire, Ford, Lowe's Whse, **W**...**gas:** Shell/24hr, **food:** Applebees, Arby's, Buffalo Wild Wings, Burger King, Chick-fil-A, Coldstone Creamery, Logan's Roadhouse, Olive Garden, Quizno's, Red Lobster, Sonic, Taco Cabana, Wendy's, **other:** Albertson's, Best Buy, Borders Books, Chevrolet, JC Penney, Kohl's, K-Mart, Michael's, Old Navy, PetsMart, Ross, Staples
37	TX 174, Wilshire Blvd, to Cleburne, **W**...Wal-Mart Super Ctr/24hr(2mi), from sb, same as 36
36	FM 3391, TX 174S, Burleson, **E**...**gas:** Citgo/dsl, Mobil, **food:** Miranda's Cantina, Sonic, Waffle House, **lodging:** Comfort Suites, Day's Inn, **W**...**gas:** Chevron, **other:** $General
34	Briaroaks Rd(from sb), **W**...RV camping
33mm	**rest area sb, full(handicapped)facilities, phone, picnic tables, litter barrels**
32	Bethesda Rd, **E**...**gas:** Valero, **food:** Milana's Rest., **lodging:** 5 Star Inn, **other:** RV Ranch Park, **W**...**other:** Buffalo Ridge RV Park, Mockingbird Hill RV Park
31mm	**rest area nb, full(handicapped)facilities, phone, picnic tables, litter barrels**
30	FM 917, Mansfield, **E**...**gas:** Shell/Sonic/dsl, **W**...**gas:** Shell/dsl, **food:** RanchHouse Rest., **other:** Smith's RV Ctr
27	Rd 604, Rd 707, **E**...**other:** Ancira RV Ctr
26b a	US 67, Cleburne, **E**...**gas:** Chevron, Exxon/Subway/24hr, Shell, **food:** Chicken Express, KFC, McDonald's, Pizza Hut, Sonic, Waffle House, Whataburger, **lodging:** Super 8, **other:** Brookshire Foods, Doc's RV Camping, Family$, Motor Home Specialist, Parts+, Wal-Mart SuperCtr
24	FM 3136, FM 1706, Alvarado, **E**...**gas:** Conoco/dsl, Shell/Grandy's/dsl/24hr, **food:** Alvarado House Rest.
21	Rd 107, to Greenfield, no services
17	FM 2258, no services
16	TX 81 S, Rd 201, Grandview, no services
15	FM 916, Maypearl, **W**...**gas:** Chevron/dsl, Mobil/Subway
12	FM 67, no services
8	FM 66, Itasca, **E**...**gas:** Valero/dsl/café/24hr, **W**...**gas:** gas/dsl, **food:** DQ, **other:** Ford, picnic tables, litter barrels
7	FM 934, **E**...picnic tables, litter barrels, **W**...**gas:** Exxon, **food:** Golden Chick Cafe
3	FM 2959, **E**...to Hillsboro Airport
	I-35W begins/ends on I-35, 371mm.

Interstate 37

San Antonio

Exit #	Services
142b a	I-35 S to Laredo, N to Austin. I-37 begins/ends on I-35 in San Antonio.
141c	Brooklyn Ave, Nolan St(from sb), downtown
141b	Houston St, **E**...**lodging:** Red Roof Inn, **other:** tires, **W**...**food:** Denny's, **lodging:** Crockett Hotel, Day's Inn, Hampton Inn, Holiday Inn, Hyatt Hotel, Marriott, La Quinta, Residence Inn, **other:** to The Alamo
141a	Commerce St, downtown, **W**...**food:** Dennys, **lodging:** La Quinta, Marriott, **other:** Macy's
140b	Durango Blvd, downtown, **E**...**food:** Bill Miller BBQ, **other:** to Alamo Dome
140a	Carolina St, Florida St, **E**...**gas:** Citgo
139	I-10 W, US 87, US 90, to Houston, **W**...**other:** to Sea World

Interstate 37

138c	Fair Ave, Hackberry St, **E**...**food:** Jack-in-the-Box, KFC, Popeye's, Taco Bell, Tapatia Mexian, Whataburger/24hr, **other:** Brake Check, Family$, Home Depot, **W**...**gas:** Exxon, Shell
138b	E New Braunfels Ave(from sb), **E**...**food:** Chick-fil-A, Hong Kong Buffet, Jim's Rest., Luby's, McDonald's, Taco Cabana, Pizza Hut, Wendy's, **other:** mall, **W**...**gas:** Exxon
138a	Southcross Blvd, W New Braunfels Ave, **E**...**gas:** McDonald's, Taco Cabana, Wendy's, **W**...**gas:** Exxon, **food:** Burger King, Sonic
137	Hot Wells Blvd, **W**...**food:** IHOP, **lodging:** Motel 6, Super 8
136	Pecan Valley Dr, **E**...**gas:** Citgo/dsl, **food:** KFC/Taco Bell, Pizza Hut, **lodging:** La Quinta, Pecan Valley Inn, **other:** AutoZone, O'Reilly Parts, **W**...HOSPITAL
135	Military Dr, Lp 13, **E**...**gas:** Shell, Valero, **food:** Jack-in-the-Box, **lodging:** Best Western, **other:** Mission Trail RV park, **W**...**gas:** Valero/Subway/dsl, **food:** Buffalo Wild Wings, Burger King, Carino's Italian, Chick-fil-A, Chili's, El Taco Tote, Little Caesars, LJ Silver/A&W, Panda Express, Peter Piper Pizza, Starbucks, Subway, Village Inn Rest, Whataburger/24hr, **lodging:** La Quinta, **other:** Advance Parts, Best Buy, BigLots, Discount Tire, $Tree, Hancock Fabrics, HEB Food/gas, Home Depot, Office Depot, PetCo, Radio Shack, Ross, Target, Walgreen, Wal-Mart SuperCtr, to Brooks AFB
133	I-410, US 281 S
132	US 181 S, to Floresville, **E**...**gas:** Fina/dsl, Shell
130	Donop Rd, Southton Rd, **E**...**gas:** Valero/dsl/RV dump, **food:** Braunig Lake Café, Tom's Burgers, **lodging:** Comfort Inn, **other:** Braunig Lake RV Resort, **W**...**gas:** Shell/dsl, **other:** car/truckwash
127	San Antonio River Turnaround(from nb), Braunig Lake, no services
127mm	San Antonio River
125	FM 1604, Anderson Lp, **E**...**gas:** Conoco/dsl/24hr, **food:** Burger King, **W**...**gas:** Citgo/dsl, Exxon/dsl, **food:** Bill Miller BBQ, Whataburger
122	Priest Rd, Mathis Rd, no services
120	Hardy Rd, no services
117	FM 536, no services
113	FM 3006, no services
112mm	picnic area both lanes, handicapped accessible, picnic tables, litter barrels
109	TX 97, to Floresville, **E**...**gas:** Chevron/dsl/rest., **other:** Chrysler/Dodge/Jeep
106	Coughran Rd, no services
104	spur 199, Leal Rd, to Pleasanton(no immediate sb return), same as 103
103	US 281 N, Leal Rd, to Pleasanton, **E**...**gas:** Valero/dsl, **food:** DQ, K&K Cafe, **lodging:** Kuntry Inn
98	TX 541, McCoy, no services
92	US 281A, Campbellton, 2 mi **W**...**gas:** Kuntry Korner gas, **food:** Stetson's Cafe
88	FM 1099, to FM 791, Campbellton, no services
83	FM 99, Whitsett, Peggy, **E**...**gas:** Shell/dsl, **food:** cafe, **W**...**gas:** Chevron/dsl
82mm	**rest area sb, full(handicapped)facilities, phone, picnic tables, litter barrels**
78mm	**rest area nb, full(handicapped)facilities, phone, picnic tables, litter barrels**

76	US 281A, FM 2049, Whitsett, no services
75mm	truck weigh sta sb
74mm	truck weigh sta nb
72	US 281 S, Three Rivers, 4 mi **W**...**gas:** Valero, **food:** DQ, Subway, **lodging:** Best Western, Econolodge, **other:** to Rio Grande Valley
69	TX 72, Three Rivers, **W**...**gas:** Valero/dsl/café/24hr, **other:** tires, to Choke Canyon SP
65	FM 1358, Oakville, **E**...**food:** Van's BBQ, **W**...**gas:** Oakville Mercantile/gas
59	FM 799, no services
56	US 59, George West, **E**...**gas:** Valero/dsl/24hr, **W**...**gas:** Shell/Subway/24hr, Valero/Burger King/dsl/24hr, **other:** Rockin'N RV Park
51	Hailey Ranch Rd, no services
47	FM 3024, FM 534, Swinney Switch Rd, **W**...**other:** Mikes Mkt/gas(1mi), to KOA(4mi)
44mm	parking area sb
42mm	parking area nb
40	FM 888, no services
36	TX 359, to Skidmore, Mathis, **W**...**gas:** Valero/dsl(1mi), Shell/McDonald's/dsl, Texaco/Subway/dsl, **food:** Pizza Hut, **lodging:** Best Western, **other:** Lake Corpus Christi SRA
34	TX 359 W, **E**...**other:** Adventure TX RV Ctr, **W**...**gas:** Valero/dsl, **lodging:** Pizza Hut, **other:** Ford, to Lake Corpus Christi SP
31	TX 188, to Sinton, Rockport, no services
22	TX 234, FM 796, to Odem, Edroy, no services
20b	Cooper Rd, no services
19.5mm	picnic area both lanes, handicapped accessible, tables, litter barrels
17	US 77 N, to Victoria, no services
16	LaBonte Park, **W**...info, picnic tables, litter barrels
15	Sharpsburg Rd(from sb), Redbird Ln, no services
14	US 77 S, Redbird Ln, to Kingsville, Robstown, 1 mi **W** on **FM 624**...**gas:** Valero/Burger King/dsl, Shell, **food:** BBQ, Chili's, CiCi's, Denny's, Good'n Crisp Chicken, K-Bob's, Miller's BBQ, Pizza Hut, Popeye's, Quizno's, Sonic, Subway, Whataburger/24hr, Wienerschnitzel, **lodging:** Comfort Inn, **other:** HOSPITAL, Beall's, CVS Drug, Firestone/auto, Home Depot, Radio Shack, Wal-Mart SuperCtr/24hr
13b	Sharpsburg Rd(from nb), no services
13a	FM 1694, Callicoatte Rd, Leopard St, no services
11b	FM 24, Violet Rd, Hart Rd, **E**...**food:** Chicken Shack, Roadhouse Cafe, **lodging:** La Quinta, **W**...**gas:** Exxon/Circle K/dsl, Valero/dsl, **food:** DQ, Domino's, KFC/LJ Silver, McDonald's, Schlotsky's, Sonic, Subway, Taco Bell,

Interstate 37

N ↕ **S**

Corpus Christi

	Whataburger/24hr, **lodging:** Hampton Inn, **other:** AutoZone, Family$, HEB Food/gas, O'Reilly Parts, Walgreen
11a	McKinzie Rd, E...**gas:** Shell, **lodging:** La Quinta, W... **gas:** Valero/dsl
10	Carbon Plant Rd, no services
9	FM 2292, Up River Rd, Rand Morgan Rd, W...**gas:** Valero/dsl, **food:** Whataburger/24hr
7	Suntide Rd, Tuloso Rd, Clarkwood Rd, W...**other:** Freightliner Trucks
6	Southern Minerals Rd, E...**gas:** refinery
5	Corn Products Rd, Valero Way, E...**other:** Kenworth, W...**gas:** PetroFleet, **food:** Jalisco Rest., **lodging:** Best Value, Red Carpet Inn, Super 8, Travelodge
4b	Lantana St, McBride Lane(from sb), W...**lodging:** Airport Inn, Motel 6
4a	TX 358, to Padre Island, W...**gas:** Shell/dsl, **lodging:** Drury Inn, Holiday Inn, Quality Inn, **other:** Wal-Mart Super Ctr/24hr(6mi)
3b	McBride Lane(from nb), W...**lodging:** Ramada Ltd, **other:** Greyhound Raceway
3a	Navigation Blvd, E...**gas:** Valero/dsl, **lodging:** Rodeway Inn, W...**gas:** Exxon/dsl, **food:** Denny's, **lodging:** Best Western, Day's Inn, Hampton Inn, La Quinta, **other:** CarQuest
2	Up River Rd, E...refinery
1e	Lawrence Dr, Nueces Bay Blvd, W...**gas:** Valero, **food:** Church's, **lodging:** Red Roof Inn, **other:** Aamco, HEB Foods, Firestone, USPO
1d	Port Ave(from sb), W...**gas:** Coastal, Shell, **food:** Vick's Burgers, **lodging:** Comfort Inn, **other:** Radio Shack, Port of Corpus Christi
1c	US 181, TX 286, Shoreline Blvd, Corpus Christi, W... HOSPITAL
1b	Brownlee St(from nb), no services
1a	Buffalo St(from sb), **1 mi W on Shoreline** E...**gas:** Valero/dsl, **food:** Burger King, Joes Crabshack, Landry's Seafood, Subway, Whataburger, **lodging:** Bayfront Inn, Best Western, Super 8, **other:** USPO,
	I-37 begins/ends on US 181 in Corpus Christi.

Interstate 40

E ↕ **W**

Shamrock

Exit #	Services
177mm	Texas/Oklahoma state line
176	spur 30(from eb), to Texola
175mm	picnic area wb, picnic tables, litter barrels
173mm	picnic area eb, picnic tables, litter barrels
169	FM 1802, Carbon Black Rd, no services
167	FM 2168, Daberry Rd, N...**gas:** Valero/dsl, **other:** RV Park
165mm	check sta wb
164	Lp 40(from wb), to Shamrock, **1 mi** S...**lodging:** Budget Inn, **other:** HOSPITAL, museum
163	US 83, to Wheeler, Shamrock, N...**gas:** Chevron/ Pizza Hut/Taco Bell/dsl, Conoco/dsl, **food:** Mitchell's Rest., **lodging:** Best Western, Irish Inn/rest., **other:** Ace Hardware, mall, S...**gas:** Phillips 66/Subway/ 24hr, Valero/dsl, **food:** DQ, McDonald's, **lodging:** Budget Host, Econolodge, Sleep Inn, Western Motel
161	Lp 40, Rte 66(from eb), to Shamrock, S...**gas:** Chevron
157	FM 1547, Lela, **1 mi** S...**other:** RV Camping

152	FM 453, Pakan Rd, no services
150mm	picnic area wb, tables, litter barrels
149mm	picnic area eb, tables, litter barrels
148	FM 1443, Kellerville Rd, no services
146	County Line Rd, no services
143	Lp 40(from wb), to McLean, to gas, no services
142	TX 273, FM 3143, to McLean, N...**gas:** Shell, **food:** Red River Steaks, **lodging:** Cactus Inn, **other:** RV Camping
141	Rte 66(from eb), McLean, same as 142
135	FM 291, Rte 66, Alanreed, S...**gas:** Conoco/motel/café/ RV park, **other:** USPO
132	Johnson Ranch Rd, ranch access, no services
131mm	**rest area wb, full(handicapped)facilities, phone, picnic tables, litter barrels, petwalk**
129mm	**rest area eb, full(handicapped)facilities, phone, picnic tables, littler barrels, petwalk**
128	FM 2477, to Lake McClellan, N...**other:** Lake McClellan RA/RV dump
124	TX 70 S, to Clarendon, S...camping
121	TX 70 N, to Pampa, no services
114	Lp 40, Groom, no services
113	FM 2300, Groom, S...**gas:** Texaco/dsl, **food:** DQ, **lodging:** Chalet Inn
112	FM 295, Groom, S...**other:** Biggest Cross, **1 mi** S... gas
110	Lp 40, Rte 66, no services
109	FM 294, no services
108mm	parking area wb, litter barrels
106mm	parking area eb, picnic tables, litter barrels
105	FM 2880, grain silo, no services
98	TX 207 S(from wb), to Claude, no services
96	TX 207 N, to Panhandle, N...**gas:** Love's/Subway/dsl/ 24hr, S...**lodging:** Budget Host, Conway Inn/cafe
89	FM 2161, to Rte 66, no services
87	FM 2373, no services
87mm	picnic areas both lanes, litter barrels
85	Amarillo Blvd, Durrett Rd, access to camping
81	FM 1912, N...**gas:** Phillips 66/dsl, S...**gas:** Valero/Am Best/dsl/rest./scales/24hr/@, Country Fresh Rest.
80	FM 228, N...**other:** AOK RV Park
78	US 287 S(from eb), FM 1258, Pullman Rd, same as 77
77	FM 1258, Pullman Rd, N...**gas:** USA Travel Plaza/Arby's/dsl/scales/24hr, S...**other:** Custom RV Ctr
76	spur 468, N...**gas:** Flying J/Conoco/dsl/LP/rest./ scales/24hr/@, Shell/dsl, **lodging:** Holiday Inn, **other:** GMC/Volvo/Mac Trucks, tourist info, S...**gas:** Speedco
75	Lp 335, Lakeside Rd, N...**gas:** Pilot/McDonald's/dsl/ rest./24hr/@, **food:** Waffle House, **lodging:** Airport Plaza Hotel, Best Value Inn, Quality Inn, Super 8, **other:** UPS, Peterbilt Trucks, KOA(2mi), S...**gas:** Petro/Mobil/ dsl/rest./@, **other:** Blue Beacon
74	Whitaker Rd, N...**lodging:** Big Texan Inn/café, **other:** RV camping, S...**gas:** Love's/Subway/dsl/@, TA/Exxon/FoodCourt/dsl/24hr/@, **lodging:** Budget Inn, **other:** Blue Beacon
73	Eastern St, Bolton Ave, Amarillo, N...**gas:** Shell/dsl, Valero/dsl, **food:** Stockman's Rest., **lodging:** Motel 6, Red Roof Inn, Value Place, S...**gas:** Chevron/dsl, **lodging:** Best Western, Motel 6, **other:** Ford Trucks
72b	Grand St, Amarillo, N...**gas:** Shell, **food:** Henk's BBQ, KFC, **lodging:** Motel 6, Travelodge, Value Inn, **other:** Family$, O'Reilly Parts, U-Haul, S...**gas:** Exxon, Phillips

Interstate 40

66, food: Braum's, Chicken Express, McDonald's, Pizza Hut, Sonic, Subway, Taco Cabana, Taco Villa, Whataburger, **lodging:** Motel 6, **other:** Advance Parts, AutoZone, Big Lots, $General, Wal-Mart SuperCtr/gas/24hr, same as 73

72a Nelson St, N...**food:** Cracker Barrel, KFC, **lodging:** Ashmore Inn, Budget Host, Econolodge, La Kiva Hotel, Ramada Inn, Sleep Inn, Super 8, Travelodge, **other:** Qtrhorse Museum, S...**gas:** Chevron, Shell/dsl, **lodging:** Camelot Inn, **other:** Chevrolet

71 Ross St, Osage St, Amarillo, N...**gas:** Conoco/dsl, Shell/dsl, **food:** Burger King, El Tapatio's Mexican, IHOP, Longhorn Diner, LJ Silver, McDonald's, Popeye's, Schlotsky's, Subway, **lodging:** Coachlight Inn, Comfort Inn, Day's Inn, Holiday Inn, Microtel, S...**gas:** Valero, **food:** Arby's, Denny's, Fiesta Grande Mexican, Sonic, Taco Bell, Wendy's, **lodging:** Hampton Inn, Howard Johnson, La Quinta, Ramada Ltd, **other:** Chevrolet, Ford, Hyundai, Sam's Club/gas, USPO

70 I-27 S, US 60 W, US 87, US 287, to Canyon, Lubbock, N...**other:** Goodyear/auto

69b Washington St, Amarillo, N...**other:** S...**gas:** Phillips 66, Shell, **food:** DQ, Subway, **other:** CVS Drug

69a Crockett St, access to same as 68b

68b Georgia St, N...**gas:** Shell/Subway, **food:** Schlotzky's, TGIFriday, **lodging:** Ambassador Hotel, S...**gas:** Phillips 66, **food:** Bennigan's, Burger King, Denny's, Furr's Café, LJ Silver, Moe's SW Grille, Red Lobster, Taco Villa, TX Roadhouse, Western Sizzlin, Whataburger, **lodging:** Baymont Inn, Comfort Suites, Econolodge, Holiday Inn Express, Motel 6, Quality Inn, Travelodge, **other:** HOSPITAL, Cadillac, Chrysler/Dodge, Discount Tire, Hastings Books, Home Depot, K-Mart, Mitsubishi, Office Depot, Radio Shack, Saturn

68a Julian Blvd, Paramount Blvd, N...**gas:** Chevron, Shell, **food:** Arby's, Chili's, Macaroni Joe's, Nick's Rest., Pancho's Mexican, Pizza Hut, Schlotzsky's, Wendy's, **lodging:** Harley Hotel, same as 67, S...**gas:** Valero, **food:** Caboose Diner, Cactus Grill, Cajun Magic, Calico Country Café, El Chico, Godfather's, Kabuki's Japanese Steaks, LJ Silver, New China, Orient Express, Peking Rest., Pizza Planet, Popeye's, Ruby Tequila's Mexican, Steak&Ale, **other:** Pennzoil

67 Western St, Amarillo, N...**gas:** Phillips 66, Shell, **food:** Beef Rigger Rest., Bourbon St. Cafe, Braum's, Burger King, Chili's, Cty Line BBQ, Legends Grill, Marie Callender's, McDonald's, Pancho's Mexican, Rosa's Cafe, Sonic, Subway, Taco Bell, S...**gas:** Phillips 66, **food:** Bennigan's, Blue Sky Rest., Catfish Shack, DQ, IHOP, Furr's Café, Gary's BBQ, IHOP, Olive Garden, Taco Cabana, Vince's Pizza, Waffle House, Wienerschnitzel, **lodging:** Baymont Inn, Holiday Inn Express, **other:** Discount Tire, NAPA, O'Reilly Parts, Radio Shack, same 68

66 Bell St, Amarillo, N...**gas:** Taylor, Valero, **lodging:** AmeriSuites, Fairfield Inn, HomeGate Suites, Motel 6, Quality Inn, Residence Inn, **other:** Big A Parts, Harley-Davidson, S...**gas:** Chevron, Shell, **food:** Donut Stop, King & I Chinese, Popeye's, Starbucks, Taco Bueno, **other:** Albertson's

65 Coulter Dr, Amarillo, N...**gas:** Phillips 66/dsl, **food:** Arby's, Golden Corral, Luby's, My Thai Café, Subway, Taco Bell, Waffle House, **lodging:** Best Western, Comfort Inn, Courtyard, Day's Inn, Executive Inn, La Quinta, Quality Inn, **other:** HOSPITAL, Chevrolet, Discount Tire, Dodge, Firestone/auto, Nissan, S...**gas:** Chevron/KFC, Shell, **food:** BBQ, Braum's, ChinaStar, ChuckeCheese, CiCi's, Hoffbrau Steaks, Jason's Deli, McDonald's, Outback Steaks, Pizza Hut, Santa Fe Rest., Sonic, Subway, Taco Villa, TCBY, Wendy's, Whataburger, Wienerschnitzel, **lodging:** Hampton Inn, 5th Season Inn, **other:** Best Buy, Goodyear/auto, IGA Foods, Lowe's Whse, Sears/auto

64 Soncy Rd, to Pal Duro Cyn, N...**food:** Carino's Italian, Furr's Buffet, Joe's Crabshack, Red Robin, Lin's Chinese, Logan's Roadhouse, **lodging:** Comfort Inn, Country Inn&Suites, Drury Inn, Extended Stay America, Homewood Suites, **other:** Discount Tire, S...**gas:** Valero/dsl/24hr, **food:** Applebee's, DQ, Fazoli's, Hooters, Legends Steaks, McDonald's, On-the-Border, Ruby Tuesday, Starbucks, Subway, Zoo-kini's Grill, **other:** Barnes&Noble, Best Buy, Circuit City, Dillard's, Ford, Home Depot, K-Mart, Kohl's, Mazda, Mervyn's, Old Navy, Ross, Sears, Target, World Mkt, mall

62b Lp 40, Amarillo Blvd, N...Gander Mtn.

62a Hope Rd, Helium Rd, S...**other:** RV camping, antiques

60 Arnot Rd, S...**gas:** Love's/A&W/Subway/dsl/@, Texas Trading Co/gifts, **other:** Oasis RV Resort/dump

57 RM 2381, to Bushland, N...grain silos, S...**gas:** Shell/dsl, **other:** USPO, RV camping/dump(1mi)

55mm parking area wb, litter barrels

54 Adkisson Rd, no services

53.5mm parking area eb, litter barrels

49 (50 from wb)FM 809, to Wildorado, S...**gas:** Phillips 66/dsl, **lodging:** Royal Inn

42 Everett Rd, no services

37 Lp 40 W, to Vega, **1 mi** N...**lodging:** Bonanza Motel, **other:** Walnut RV Park, same as 36

36 US 385, Vega, N...**gas:** Conoco/dsl/24hr, Fina, Phillips 66, Shamrock, **food:** DQ, **lodging:** Best Western/café, Comfort Inn, **other:** CarQuest, S...gas/dsl

35 to Rte 66, to Vega, N...**lodging:** Best Western/café, **lodging:** Bonanza Motel(1mi), **other:** Walnut RV Park(1mi), same as 36

32mm picnic area both lanes, litter barrels

28 to Rte 66, Landergin, no services

22 TX 214, to Adrian, N...**lodging:** Fabulous 40's Motel, S...**gas:** Phillips 66/dsl/café, **other:** Tommy's Foods

18 FM 2858, Gruhlkey Rd, S...**gas:** Shell/Stuckey's/rest./dsl

473

TEXAS

Interstate 40

15	Ivy Rd, no services
13mm	picnic area both lanes, picnic tables, litter barrels
5.5mm	turnout
0	Lp 40, to Glenrio, no services
0mm	Texas/New Mexico state line, Central/Mountain time zone

Interstate 44

Exit #	Services
15mm	Texas/Oklahoma state line, Red River
14	Lp 267, E 3rd St, **W...other:** Burk RV Park
13	Glendale St, **W...food:** Subway, **other:** Beall's, Family$, Sav-A-Lot Foods, Wal-Mart
12	Burkburnett, **E...lodging:** Hampton Inn, **W...gas:** Fina/7-11, **food:** Braum's, Feedlot Rest., Lite Pan Asian, Mazzio's, McDonald's, Whataburger/24hr, **other:** CarQuest, Chevrolet/Pontiac, Ford
11	FM 3429, Daniels Rd, no services
9mm	picnic area both lanes, picnic table, litter barrels, petwalk
7	East Rd, no services
6	Bacon Switch Rd, no services
5a	FM 3492, Missile Rd, **E...food:** El Mejicano Rest., Hunan Chinese, Pizza Hut, **other:** st patrol, **W... gas:** Exxon/dsl
5	Access Rd, no services
4	City Loop St, no services
3c	FM 890, **W...food:** Cracker Barrel, KFC/Taco Bell, Subway, **other:** Wal-Mart SuperCtr/gas/24hr, vet
3b	sp 325, Sheppard AFB, no services
3a	US 287 N, to Amarillo, **W...gas:** Shell, **food:** Carl's Jr, **lodging:** Ramada Ltd
2	Maurine St, **E...gas:** Fina/7-11/dsl, Shell/dsl, **lodging:** Best Value Inn, Comfort Inn, Motel 6, Quality Inn, **other:** Chevrolet, Mazda, **W...gas:** Fina/7-11, **food:** China Star, Denny's, El Chico, LJ Silver, Whataburger/24hr, **lodging:** Best Western, Candlewood Suites, La Quinta, Super 8, Travelers Inn
1d	US 287 bus, Lp 370, **W...gas:** Conoco/dsl, **lodging:** Travelodge
1c	Texas Tourist Bureau, **E...gas:** $Saver, **W...lodging:** The Inn
1b	Scotland Park(from nb), no services
1a	US 277 S, to Abilene, no services
0mm	I-44 begins/ends in Witchita Falls, **1-2 mi** Ⓢ **in Wichita Falls...gas:** Valero, **food:** Arby's, Burger King, Carl's Jr, IHOP, McDonald's, Popeye's, Subway, **lodging:** Econolodge, Holiday Inn, Howard Johnson, Knights Inn, **other:** HOSPITAL

Interstate 45

Exit #	Services
286	to I-35 E, to Denton. I-45 begins/ends in Dallas.
285	Bryan St E, US 75 N
284b a	I-30, W to Ft Worth, E to Texarkana, access to HOSPITAL
283b	Pennsylvania Ave, to MLK Blvd, **E...gas:** Shamrock, **W...food:** KFC/Taco Bell
283a	Lamar St, no services
281	Overton St(from sb), **W...gas:** Chevron
280	Illinois Ave, Linfield St, **E...lodging:** Star Motel, **W... gas:** Shell/dsl

Exit #	Services
279b a	Lp 12, no services
277	Simpson Stuart Rd, **W...other:** to Paul Quinn Coll
276b a	I-20, W to Ft Worth, E to Shreveport, no services
275	TX 310 N(from nb, no re-entry)
274	Dowdy Ferry Rd, Hutchins, **E...gas:** Exxon/Subway, Shell/dsl, **lodging:** Gold Inn, **W...food:** DQ, Jack-in-the-Box
273	Wintergreen Rd, no services
272	Fulghum Rd, **E...gas:** Love's/Carl's Jr/dsl/scales/24hr, **W...**weigh sta, both lanes
271	Pleasant Run Rd, no services
270	Belt Line Rd, to Wilmer, **E...gas:** Shell/dsl, Texaco/Pizza Inn/dsl, **W...gas:** Exxon/Sonic/dsl, Shell/Church's/Subway/dsl, **other:** $General
269	Mars Rd, no services
268	Malloy Bridge Rd, no services
267	Frontage Rd, no services
266	FM 660, **W...gas:** Shamrock/dsl, **food:** DQ
265	Lp 45, Ferris, nb only, no services
263a b	Lp 561, no services
262	frontage rd, no services
260	Lp 45, no services
259	FM 813, FM 878, Jefferson St, **W...other:** Goodyear
258	Lp 45, Palmer, **E...gas:** Exxon/Subway/dsl/scales/24hr, **other:** golf, **W...gas:** Mobil/dsl/Quizno's/24hr, **lodging:** Palmer Motel
255	FM 879, Garrett, **E...gas:** Exxon/dsl, **W...gas:** Chevron/dsl
253	Lp 45, **W...gas:** Shell/Subway/dsl, **lodging:** Geneva Inn(2mi)
251b	TX 34, Ennis, **E...gas:** Fina/dsl, Shell/dsl, **food:** Bubba's BBQ, McDonald's, **lodging:** Best Western, Day's Inn, Holiday Inn Express, **other:** Ford, **W...gas:** Chevron/dsl, Exxon/dsl/24hr, **food:** Arby's, Braum's, Burger King, Chili's, Corral Buffet, Denny's, DQ, Domino's, Golden Corral, IHOP, Jack-in-the-Box, KFC, Sonic, Starbucks, Subway, Taco Bell/Pizza Hut, Taco Cabana, Waffle House, Wall Chinese Café, Wendy's, Whataburger/24hr, **lodging:** Ennis Inn, Quality Inn, **other:** HOSPITAL, AutoZone, Chevrolet/Pontiac, Chrysler/Dodge, $Tree, Ford/Mercury, Pennzoil, Pontiac/Buick, Radio Shack, Wal-Mart SuperCtr/gas/24hr, RV camping
251a	Creechville Rd, FM 1181, , **W...**HOSPITAL
249	FM 85, Ennis, **E...lodging:** Budget Inn, **W...gas:** Exxon/Subway, **other:** Blue Beacon, **other:** repair
247	US 287 N, to Waxahatchie, no services
246	FM 1183, Alma, **W...gas:** Chevron
244	FM 1182, no services
243	Frontage Rd, no services
242	Rice, no services
239	FM 1126, **W...gas:** Phillips 66
238	FM 1603, **E...gas:** Fina/dsl/24hr, **other:** Casita RV Trailers
237	Frontage Rd, no services
235b	Lp I-45(from sb), to Corsicana
235a	Frontage Rd, no services
232	Roane Rd, E 5th Ave, no services
231	TX 31, Corsicana,, **E...gas:** gas/dsl, **food:** Jack-in-the-Box, **lodging:** Best Western, Colonial Inn, **other:** Chevrolet/Cadillac/Pontiac/Buick, **W...gas:** Chevron, Exxon/Subway/dsl, **food:** Bill's Fried Chicken, DQ, McDonald's, **lodging:** Comfort Inn, **other:** HOSPITAL, Chrysler/Dodge/Jeep, Ford/Lincoln/Mercury, to Navarro Coll

(Side markers: I-40: E / W; I-44: E, Wichita Falls, W; I-45: N / S; Dallas; Ennis)

Interstate 45

N

S

229	US 287, Palestine, E...**gas:** Exxon/Wendy's/dsl, Shell/dsl/24hr, **food:** Chili's, Sonic, **lodging:** Hampton Inn, Holiday Inn, **other:** Gander Mtn, Home Depot, Russell Stover Candies, VF Outlet/famous brands, W...**food:** Cancun Mexican, Waffle House, **lodging:** Corsicana Inn, Motel 6, Royal Inn, Travelers Inn
228b	Lp 45(exits left from nb), Corsicana, **2 mi** W...services in Corsicana
228a	15th St, Corsicana, no services
225	FM 739, Angus, E...**gas:** Conoco/dsl, Exxon/dsl, **other:** to Chambers Reservoir, RV park, W...**gas:** Citgo/dsl, **other:** Camper Depot
221	Frontage Rd, no services
220	Frontage Rd, no services
219b	Frontage Rd, no services
219a	TX 14(from sb), to Mexia, Richland, W...**gas:** Shell
218	FM 1394(from nb), Richland, W...**gas:** Shell
217mm	**rest area both lanes, full(handicapped) facilities, phone, picnic tables, litter barrels, vending, petwalk**
213	TX 75 S, FM 246, to Wortham, W...**gas:** Texaco/dsl
211	FM 80, to Streetman, Kirvin
206	FM 833, no services
198	FM 27, to Wortham, E...**gas:** Shell/BBQ, **food:** Gilberto's Mexican, **lodging:** La Quinta, **other:** HOSPITAL, Cedar Grove RV Park(3mi), W...**gas:** Exxon, Love's/Burger King/dsl/24hr/scales, **lodging:** Budget Inn, **other:** Deer Crossing RV Park(1mi)
197	US 84, Fairfield, E...**gas:** Chevron, Exxon, Shell/dsl, **food:** DQ, Jack-in-the-Box, McDonald's, Ponte's Diner, Sam's Rest., Sonic, Subway/Texas Burger, **lodging:** Day's Inn, Holiday Inn Express, Super 8, **other:** Brookshire Foods/gas, Chevrolet, Chrysler/Jeep/Dodge, Fred's Store, W...**gas:** Shell/dsl, Texaco/dsl, **food:** Dalia's Mexican, I-45 Rest., KFC/Taco Bell, Pizza Hut, Sammy's Rest., **lodging:** Best Value, Regency Inn, **other:** Ace Hardware, Ford/Mercury
189	TX 179, to Teague, E...**gas:** Exxon/dsl/cafe, Citgo/dsl/cafe
187mm	picnic area both lanes, tables, litter barrels
180	TX 164, to Groesbeck, no services
178	US 79, Buffalo, E...**gas:** Conoco, Gilliam's/dsl, Shell/dsl, **food:** Subway/Texas Burger, **other:** Brookshire Foods/gas, Family$, W...**gas:** Exxon/Church's/Pizza Inn/dsl/scales, Mobil/dsl, Shamrock/dsl/24hr, **food:** Dickey's BBQ, DQ, Longhorn BBQ, Pitt Grill/24hr, Rainbow Rest., Rancho Mexican, Sonic, **lodging:** Best Western, Comfort Inn, Economy Inn
175mm	Bliss Creek
166mm	weigh sta sb
164	TX 7, Centerville, E...**gas:** Chevron, Shell/Woody's BBQ/dsl, **food:** Country Cousins Café, Texas Burger/Subway, **lodging:** Day's Inn, W...**gas:** Exxon/24hr, Shell/Woody's BBQ/dsl, **food:** DQ, Jack-in-the-Box, Roble's Mexican
160mm	picnic area sb, tables, litter barrels, hist marker, handicapped accessible
159mm	Boggy Creek
156	FM 977, to Leona, W...**gas:** Exxon/dsl
155mm	picnic area nb, picnic tables, litter barrels, handicapped accessible
152	TX OSR, to Normangee, W...**gas:** Chevron/dsl, **other:** Yellow Rose RV Park/café
146	TX 75, no services

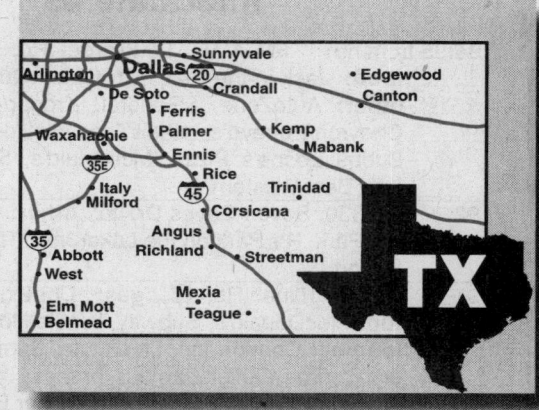

Huntsville

142	US 190, TX 21, Madisonville, E...**gas:** Exxon/BBQ/dsl, **food:** Robel's Mexican, **lodging:** Best Western, Carefree Inn, W...**gas:** Chevron/Church's, Exxon, Shell/Subway/24hr, **food:** China Café, Jack-in-the-Box, Lakeside Rest., McDonald's, Pizza Hut, Sonic, Texas Burger, **lodging:** Budget Motel, Western Lodge, **other:** HOSPITAL, Toyota
136	spur 67, E...Home on the Range RV camping/LP(3mi)
132	FM 2989, no services
124mm	**rest area both lanes, full(handicapped)facilities, phone, picnic tables, litter barrels, vending, petwalk**
123	FM 1696, no services
118	TX 75, E...**gas:** Shell/Hitchin Post/dsl/24hr/@, **other:** Texas Prison Museum, truckwash, W...**gas:** Pilot/Wendy's/dsl/scales/24hr/@, **food:** Rodeo Mexican
116	US 190, TX 30, E...**gas:** Valero/dsl, **food:** Bandera Grill, Church's, El Chico, Mr Gatti's, Golden Corral, Imperial Garden Chinese, Jct Steaks, McDonald's, Popeye's, Sonic, The Jct Rest., Whataburger/24hr, **lodging:** Comfort Inn, Econolodge, La Quinta, Motel 6, **other:** HOSPITAL, AutoZone, Brookshire Foods/gas, CVS Drug, &General, Firestone/auto, Hastings Books, Jeep/Dodge, Nissan, O'Reilly Parts, Pontiac/Buick/GMC, Walgreen, vet, W...**gas:** Exxon/dsl, Chevron/24hr, Shell/24hr, **food:** Bob Luby's Seafood, Burger King, Chili's, CiCi's, Denny's, Grand Buffet, IHOP, Jack-in-the-Box, KFC, Pizza Hut, Schlotzsky's, Starbucks, Subway, Taco Bell, **lodging:** Holiday Inn Express, **other:** Chrysler/Jeep/Dodge, Discount Tire, $Tree, GNC, Home Depot, JC Penny, Kroger, Office Depot, Radio Shack, Wal-Mart SuperCtr/gas/24hr
114	FM 1374, E...**gas:** Exxon/dsl, Shell, **food:** DQ, Margaritas Rest., **lodging:** Gateway Inn, Super 8, **other:** Ford/Lincoln/Mercury, W...**gas:** Chevron, Citgo/dsl, Shamrock/dsl, **food:** Country Inn Steaks, **lodging:** Quality Inn, Sam Houston Inn, **other:** HOSPITAL
113	TX 19(from nb), Huntsville, E...**food:** Catfish Palace Rest.(2mi)
112	TX 75, E...**gas:** Citgo,**food:** Jack-in-the-Box, Wendy's, **lodging:** Baker Motel, **other:** Houston Statue, to Sam Houston St U, museum
109	Park 40, W...**other:** to Huntsville SP
105mm	picnic area both lanes, tables, litter barrels
103	FM 1374/1375(from sb), to New Waverly, W...**gas:** Mystick Gas(1mi)
102	FM 1374/1375, TX 150(from nb), to New Waverly, E...**gas:** Shell/Subway/dsl(1mi), W...**food:** Waverly Rest.
101mm	weigh sta nb
98	TX 75, Danville Rd, Shepard Hill Rd, E...**other:** Convenience RV Park/repair

TEXAS

Interstate 45

94(95 from nb) FM 1097, Longstreet Rd, to Willis, E...**food:** Jack-in-the-Box, Mr Gatti, Quizno's, Sonic, **other:** AutoZone, $General, Kroger/gas, W...**gas:** Chevron/Popeye's, Shell/Taco Bell/dsl/24hr, **food:** Bubba Leone's Pizza, McDonald's, Subway, **lodging:** Best Western

92 FM 830, Seven Coves Dr, W...**other:** Omega Farms RV Park, RV Park on the Lake(3mi), Thousand Trails Resort

91 League Line Rd, E...**gas:** Chevron/McDonald's, **food:** McDonald's, Subway, Waffle House, Wendy's, **lodging:** Comfort Inn, La Quinta, Supreme Inn, **other:** Conroe Outlets/famous brands, W...**gas:** Citgo, Shell/Jack-in-the-Box, **food:** Cracker Barrel

90 FM 3083, Teas Nursery Rd, Montgomery Co Park, E...**gas:** Exxon/dsl, **food:** Applebees, Buffalo Wild Wings, **other:** Kohls, Old Navy, PetsMart, Ross, TJ Maxx, convention center(4mi)

88 Lp 336, to Cleveland, Navasota, E...**gas:** Mobil/dsl, Shell/24hr, Valero/dsl, **food:** Arby's, Burger King, Chili's, China Delight, Denny's, Domino's, Los Cucos Mexican, LJ Silver/A&W, Margarita's Mexican, McDonald's, Papa John's, Pizza Hut, Quizno's, Sonic, Subway, TX Roadhouse, Whataburger, **lodging:** Holiday Inn Express, **other:** Buick/Pontiac, CVS Drug, Discount Tire, $Tree, GNC, Goodyear/auto, HEB Foods/gas, Just Brakes, Kroger/gas, Michael's, Walgreen, W...**gas:** Chevron/24hr, **food:** Casa Ole Mexican, El Bosque Mexican, Ryan's, Tuesday Morning, KFC, **other:** Goody's, GNC, Hancock Fabrics, JC Penney, Lowe's Whse, 99Cent Store, PetCo, Radio Shack, PetCo, Sam's Club/gas, Wal-Mart SuperCtr/24hr

87 TX 105, Conroe, E...**gas:** Shamrock, **food:** Burger King, CiCi's, Imperial Garden Chinese, Jack-in-the-Box, Kettle, Luther's BBQ, McDonald's, Outback Steaks, Steak&Ale, Taco Bell, Tast of China, **other:** HOSPITAL, BigLots, CVS Drug, Eckerd/24hr, Firestone/auto, Hyundai, Kia, Kroger, NTB, Suzuki, W...**gas:** Exxon/TCBY, **food:** Bennigan's, Chick-fil-A, Golden Corral, Luby's, Panera Bread, Starbucks, Subway, **other:** Best Buy, Buick/GMC/Isuzu, Hastings Books, Home Depot, Office Depot, Radio Shack, Target

85 FM 2854, Gladstell St, E...**gas:** Citgo/dsl, **lodging:** Motel 6, **other:** HOSPITAL, Ford/Mercury, Honda, Mitsubishi, Nissan, W...**gas:** Shamrock, Shell/dsl, **food:** IHOP, **lodging:** Baymont Inn, Day's Inn, **other:** Cadillac, Chrysler/Jeep/Dodge, Dodge, Ford/Mercury, Fun Country RV Ctr, Mazda, Toyota/Scion

84 TX 75 N, Frazier St, E...**gas:** Chevron, Conoco/dsl, **lodging:** Corporate Inn, Holiday Inn, Ramada Ltd, **other:** U-Haul, W...**gas:** Shell, **food:** China Buffet, IHOP, Pizza Hut, Taco Cabana, Waffle House, **lodging:** Baymont Inn, **other:** HOSPITAL, Albertson's, Discount Tire, K-Mart, Kroger

83 Crighton Rd, Camp Strake Rd, no services

82 River Plantation Dr, no services

82mm San Jacinto River

81 FM 1488, to Hempstead, Magnolia, E...**gas:** Citgo/dsl, W...**gas:** Shamrock, **other:** CamperLand RV Ctr

80 Needham Rd(from sb), no services

79 TX 242, Needham, E...**gas:** Shell, **food:** Mama Juanita's Mexican, McDonald's, Quizno's, **other:** Woodland Lakes RV Resort(2mi), W...**gas:** Chevron, **food:** Burger King, Chucke-Cheese, Dominos, Fazoli's, Popeye's, Sonic, Subway, Taco Cabana, Wendy's, Whataburger/24hr, Willie's Grill, Wings & More, **lodging:** Country Inn Suites, Fairfield Inn, **other:** HOSPITAL, BMW/Mini, Firestone/auto, Kohl's, Lowe's, Walgreen, Wal-Mart SuperCtr/gas/24hr

78 Needham Rd(from sb), Tamina Rd, same as 77

77 Woodlands Pkwy, Robinson, Chateau Woods, E...**gas:** Conoco/dsl, **food:** Babin's Steaks, Buca italian, Chuy's, Hooters, Lupe Tortilla, Pancho's Mexican, Pappadeaux Rest., Pizza Hut, Red Lobster, Red Robin, Saltgrass Steaks, Tom's Steaks, **lodging:** Budget Inn, **other:** Discount Tire, Home Depot, Jo-Ann Fabrics, Michael's, NTB, Office Depot, Old Navy, Sam's Club, SteinMart, Walgreen, W...**gas:** Mobil, Shamrock, Shell, Texaco, Valero, **food:** Blackeyed Pea, Chili's, Denny's, Guadalajara Mexican, Kirby's Steakhouse, Landry's Seafood, Luby's, Macaroni Grill, Outback Steaks, Pancho's Mexican, Red Lobster, **lodging:** Best Value, Comfort Inn, Day's Inn, Drury Inn, Hampton Inn, Homewood Suites, La Quinta, Marriott, Spring Inn, **other:** HOSPITAL, Best Buy, Dillard's, Marshall's, Mervyn's, Ross, Target, World Mkt, mall

76 Research Forest Dr, Tamina Rd, E...**gas:** Chevron/dsl, Coastal/lube, Shamrock, Stop'n Go, Texaco, **food:** Casa Elena Mexican, LJ Silver, Pappa's BBQ, **other:** Food Basket, Firestone, W...**gas:** Shell, **food:** Carrabba's, Denny's, El Chico, IHOP, Jack-in-the-Box, Kyoto Japanese, Macaroni Grill, Olive Garden, TGIFriday's, Tortuga Mexican, **lodging:** Crossland Suites, Courtyard, Residence Inn, **other:** Circuit City, Goodyear/auto, JC Penny, Sears/auto, Woodlands Mall

73 Rayford Rd, Sawdust Rd, E...**gas:** Conoco, Shell, Valero, **food:** Dry Dock Rest, Jack-in-the-Box, LJ Silver, McDonald's, Popeye's, Sonic, Taqueria Arandas, Thomas BBQ, **lodging:** Hawthorn Suites, Holiday Inn Express, **other:** AutoZone, Firestone, Just Brakes, O'Reilly Parts, W...**gas:** Mobil/dsl, Shell, Texaco, **food:** Carrabba's, Grandy's, IHOP, India Cuisine, Kyoto Japanese, Sam's Rest., Subway, Taipei Chinese, Tortuga, Woodland Chinese, **lodging:** Extended Stay America, Red Roof Inn, Super 8, **other:** Discount Tire, Eckerd, Goodyear/auto, Harley-Davidson, HEB Foods, Kroger

72a Spring Crossing Dr, W...**gas:** Texaco/dsl

72b to Hardy Toll Rd from sb, no services

70b Spring-Stuebner Rd, E...Vaughn RV Ctr

70a FM 2920, to Tomball, E...**gas:** Exxon, **food:** El Palenque Mexican, McDonald's, Pizza Hut, Wendy's, **other:** BigLots, $General, Kroger, Radio Shack, Vaughn's RV Ctr, Walgreen transmissions, W...**gas:** Chevron, RaceWay, Texaco, **food:** Burger King, Taco Bell, Whataburger/24hr, **lodging:** Travelodge, **other:** Ford, U-Haul

68 Holzwarth Rd, Cypress Wood Dr, E...**gas:** Shell, Texaco/dsl, **food:** Arby's, Burger King, Chick-fil-A, Gander Mtn., Hartz Chicken, Pizza Hut/Taco Bell, Quizno's, Sonic, Taco Cabana, Wendy's, Whataburger, **other:** Albertson's, $Tree, Gander Mtn, GNC, Kohl's, Kroger, Lincoln/Mercury, Michael's, Radio Shack, Ross, Toyota/Scion, Wal-Mart SuperCtr/24hr, W...**gas:** Chevron/24hr, **food:** Denny's, Jack-in-the-Box, Pizza Hut, Starbucks, Popeye's, **lodging:** Day's Inn, Motel 6, **other:** Best Buy, Ford, Home Depot, Lowe's Whse, Office Depot, Target, Texan RV Ctr, Walgreen

Interstate 45

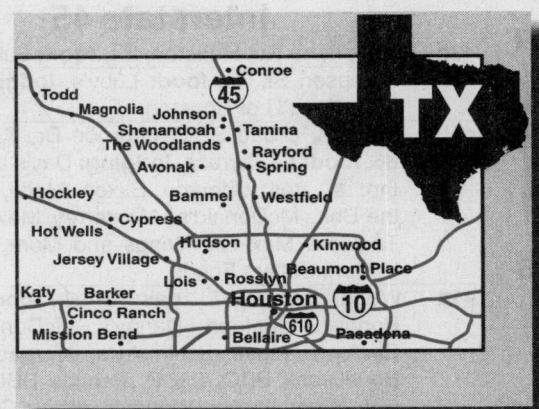

N ↑↓ S

66 FM 1960, to Addicks, **E...gas:** Chevron, RaceTrac, Shell, **food:** Jack-in-the-Box, Sonic, TX Roadhouse, Waffle House, **lodging:** Best Value, Day's Inn, Holiday Inn, Ramada Inn, **other:** Acura, BMW, Chevrolet, Honda, Mercedes, Mistubishi, PetsMart, Radio Shack, **W...gas:** Exxon, Shell/dsl/24hr, Texaco/dsl, **food:** Bennigan's, Cici's Pizza, Coney Island, Grandy's, Hooters, Ixtapa Mexican, Jack-in-the-Box, Jojo's Rest., Luby's, McDonald's, Outback Steaks, Pizza Hut, Popeye's, Red Lobster, Steak&Ale, Subway, Taco Bell, **lodging:** Baymont Inn, Comfort Suites, Fairfield Inn, Hampton Inn, Motel 6, **other:** GolfSmith, Infiniti, Jaguar/LandRover, Lexus, NTB, Saturn, mall

64 Richey Rd, **E...gas:** Texaco/Church's, **food:** Atchafalaya River Café, China Bear, Pappasito's Cantina, **lodging:** Holiday Inn, Lexington Suites, **other:** Cadillac, Carmax, Discount Tire, Nissan, Sam's Club, **W...gas:** ♻/Flying J/Conoco/Country Mkt/dsl/24hr/scales/@, **food:** Cracker Barrel, House of Creole, Jack-in-the-Box, Joe's Crabshack, Lupe Tortilla, SaltGrass Steaks, Whataburger, Zio's Italian, **other:** Jones RV Ctr, U-Haul

63 Airtex Dr, **E...gas:** Texaco, Valero, **other:** Acura, Cadillac, LoneStar RV Ctr, Nissan, **W...food:** Cracker Barrel, Jack-in-the-Box, McDonald's, Whataburger, **lodging:** Best Western, Guesthouse Suites, SunSuites, **other:** Celebration Sta

62 Rankin Rd, Kuykendahl, **W...gas:** Chevron/McDonald's, Shell, **food:** Luby's, **lodging:** Studio+, SunSuites, **other:** BMW, Buick/Subaru, Hummer, Hyundai, Kia/GMC/Pontiac, Mercedes, Mitsubishi, Saab, Suzuki, Volvo, VW

61 Greens Rd, **E...food:** Whataburger, **lodging:** Day's Inn, Marriott, Wyndham Hotel, **other:** Circuit City, Dillard's, Foley's, JC Penney, Mervyn's, mall, **W...food:** Burger King, Luby's, **lodging:** Baymont Inn, Comfort Inn, **other:** Kroger, Office Depot, Target

60c Beltway E, no services

60b TX 8, **E...lodging:** La Quinta, Marriott, **other:** Dillard's, Sears/auto, mall, **W...food:** Marco's Mexican

60a TX 525, **E...gas:** Exxon, Shamrock, Shell, Texaco, **food:** Burger King, Champ's Rest., China Border, Denny's/24hr, Furr's Cafeteria, LJ Silver/A&W, Mambo Seafood, Moon Palace Chinese, Mucho Mexico, Pizza Hut, Pizza Inn, Steak&Ale, **other:** Firestone/auto, Honda, Randall's Foods, Walgreen, **W...food:** Gordito's Mexican, Pappa's Rest., Quizno's, Wendy's, **lodging:** Best Value Inn, **other:** Best Buy, Discount Tire, Dodge, GNC, Home Depot, Pontiac/GMC, Radio Shack, NTB, Wal-Mart SuperCtr/24hr

59 FM 525, West Rd, **E...gas:** Exxon, Shell, **food:** McDonald's, Pizza Hut, Wendy's, Wings & More, **other:** Fiesta Foods, **W...gas:** Exxon, Shell, **food:** Panda Express, Pizza Inn, Sonic, Subway, Taco Bell, Taco Cabana, Taquiera Arrandas, **lodging:** Best Western, GreenChase Inn, Holiday Inn Express, La Quinta, Ramada Ltd, **other:** CVS Drug, Family$, Fry's Electronics, K-Mart, Lincoln/Mercury, PepBoys

57 TX 249, Gulf Bank Rd, Tomball, **E...gas:** Conoco, Exxon/dsl, Mobil/dsl, **other:** Discount Tire, Kroger, **W...gas:** Shell, **food:** KFC, Pizza Inn, Sonic, **lodging:** American Inn, La Quinta, **other:** Chevrolet, Chrysler/Jeep, CVS Drug, Eckerd, Family$, Ford, Mazda, Saturn

56 Canino Rd, **E...lodging:** Taj Inn, **W...gas:** Shell, **food:** Denny's, Luby's, **lodging:** Gulfwind Motel, Passport Inn, **other:** Ford, Isuzu, Nissan, Toyota, Walgreen

55b a Little York Rd, Parker Rd, **E...gas:** Chevron, Exxon, Shell, Texaco, **food:** Schlotsky's, Whataburger, **lodging:** Olympic Motel, **other:** HOSPITAL, FoodTown, Goodyear, **W...gas:** Chevron/24hr, Shell, **food:** Capt D's, Denny's, Hartz Chicken, Jack-in-the-Box, KFC, LJ Silver, McDonald's, Popeye's, **lodging:** Best Value Inn, Econolodge, Symphony Inn, Town Inn, **other:** Family$, Walgreen

54 Tidwell Rd, **E...gas:** Exxon, **food:** Pancho's Mexican, Pizza Inn, Subway, Taco Cabana, Thomas BBQ, **other:** BigLots, CVS Drug, Eckerd, Jo-Ann Fabrics, Radio Shack, **W...lodging:** Guest Motel, Southwind Motel, **other:** U-Haul

53 Airline Dr, **E...gas:** Chevron, Conoco, **other:** Discount Tire, Fiesta Foods/drug, **W...food:** Little Mexico, Whataburger, same as 52

52 Crosstimbers Rd, **E...gas:** Shell, Texaco/dsl, **food:** Burger King, CiCi's, IHOP, James Coney Island, McDonald's, Pancho's Mexican, Pappas BBQ, Taco Bell, Taco Cabana, Wendy's, **other:** Discount Tire, Fiesta Foods, Firestone, mall, **W...gas:** Chevron/dsl, Citgo, **food:** Little Mexico Rest., Wendy's, Whataburger/24hr, **lodging:** Howard Johnson, Luxury Inn, Palace Inn, Super 8, Texan Inn, **other:** Coach USA RV Ctr, U-Haul

51 I-610

50b Calvacade St, Link Rd, **E...gas:** Exxon, Shell, **W...lodging:** Astro Inn

50a Patton St, **E...gas:** Chevron/24hr, **lodging:** Classic Inn, Luxury Inn, **W...gas:** Shell/dsl/24hr

49b N Main St, Houston Ave, **E...gas:** Citgo, **food:** Casa Grande Mexican, **lodging:** Best Value, Luxury Inn, **W...gas:** Exxon/dsl, **food:** KFC, McDonald's, Whataburger/24hr, **other:** Auto Supply

48b a I-10, E to Beaumont, W to San Antonio

47d Dallas St, Pierce St(from sb), **E...other:** HOSPITAL

47c McKinney St(from sb, exits left), no services

47b Houston Ave, Memorial Dr, downtown, **W...lodging:** Double Tree Hotel

47a Allen Pkwy(exits left from sb)

46b a US 59, N to Cleveland, S to Victoria, **E...gas:** Chevron, **food:** BBQ, **W...gas:** Texaco, **food:** McDonald's, Taco Bell, **other:** BMW

45b a South St, Scott St, Houston, **E...gas:** Shell, **other:** Firestone, to TSU

44 Cullen Blvd, Houston, **E...gas:** Valero/dsl, to U of Houston

Houston

Interstate 45

N ↑ ↓ S

43b	Telephone Rd, Houston, Ⓔ...**food:** Luby's
43a	Tellepsen St, Ⓔ...**food:** Luby's, **lodging:** Day's Inn, Ⓦ...**other:** U of Houston
41b	US 90A, Broad St, S Wayside Dr, Ⓔ...**gas:** Phillips 66, **food:** La Terraza, **lodging:** Day's Inn, Red Carpet Inn, Ⓦ...**gas:** Chevron, Exxon, Mobil, **food:** Jack-in-the-Box, McDonald's, Monterrey Mexican, Subway, Taquiera Mexican, Wings and More, **other:** $Tree, K-Mart, Sellars Foods
41a	Woodridge Dr, Ⓔ...**gas:** Shell, **food:** Bennigan's, Bonnie's Seafood, Denny's, McDonald's, Pappa's Seafood House, Schlotsky's, Ⓦ...**gas:** Citgo, **food:** BoneBreak BBQ, IHOP, Pappas BBQ, Sonic, Subway, Whataburger, Wendy's, **other:** Chevrolet/Buick, Dillard's, HEB Food/gas, Home Depot, Lowe's Whse, Marshall's, Office Depot, Old Navy, Radio Shack, Ross, mall
40c	I-610 W
40b	I-610 E, to Pasadena, Ⓔ...**food:** Bennigan's
40a	Frontage Rd(from nb)
39	Park Place Blvd, Broadway Blvd, Ⓔ...**gas:** Shell, Ⓦ...**food:** Kelley's Rest., Los Campos, **other:** Chevrolet, Dodge, Family$
38b	Howard Dr, Bellfort Dr(from sb), Ⓔ...**gas:** Shell, **food:** Jack-in-the-Box, Wendy's, Ⓦ...**gas:** Citgo, **food:** Chilo's Seafood, **lodging:** Camelot Inn, Mustang Inn, Palace Inn, Passport Inn, **other:** HEB Food/gas, Pep-Boys
38	TX 3, Monroe Rd, Ⓔ...**gas:** Chevron, Shell, Valero, **food:** DQ, Jack-in-the-Box, Luther's BBQ, Ninfa, Wendy's, **other:** Firestone, NTB, U-Haul, Ⓦ...**gas:** Chevron/dsl, Texaco/dsl, **food:** Luby's, Manny's Seafood, Pappa's BBQ, **lodging:** Best Western, Holiday Inn Express, Quality Inn, Smile Inn, **other:** Firestone, Kottman Transmissions, Radio Shack, Suzuki, U-Haul
36	College Ave, Airport Blvd, Ⓔ...**gas:** Shamrock, Shell, **food:** DQ, Waffle House, **lodging:** Best Value, Day's Inn, Fairfield Inn, Rodeway Inn, **other:** RV Ctr, Ⓦ...**gas:** Exxon, Mobil, Shell, Valero, **food:** Church's Chicken, Denny's, Taco Cabana, **lodging:** AmeriSuites, Baymont Inn, Comfort Inn, Country Inn, Courtyard, Drury Inn, Hampton Inn, Holiday Inn Express, La Quinta, Marriott/Damon's, Motel 6, Red Roof Inn, Regency Inn, SpringHill Suites, Super 8, Travel Inn, **other:** Discount Tire
35	Edgebrook Dr, Ⓔ...**gas:** Chevron, Exxon, RaceTrac, **food:** Burger King, Aranda's Bakery, Jack-in-the-Box, KFC, Popeye's, Subway, Taco Bell, Taquiera Arrandas, Waffle House, **lodging:** Airport Inn, **other:** Eckerd, Family$, Fiesta Foods, Firestone, Office Depot, Terry Vaugn's RV Ctr, Walgreens, Ⓦ...**gas:** Exxon, Shell, Circle K, **food:** James Coney Island, KFC, LJ Silver, McDonald's, Pizza Hut, Whataburger, **other:** Academy Sports, Honda, NTB
34	S Shaver Rd, Ⓔ...**gas:** Conoco, RaceWay, **food:** McDonald's, **lodging:** Island Suites, **other:** Acura, Honda, Kia, Pontiac/GMC, Saturn, Toyota, Vaughn's RV Ctr, Ⓦ...**gas:** Chevron/24hr, Exxon, Mobil, **food:** Arby's, Burger King, Pancho's Mexican, Wendy's, **lodging:** Scottish Inn, **other:** Best Buy, Circuit City, Discount Tire, $Tree, Honda, Jo-Ann Fabrics, Macy's, Nissan, NTB, Target, Wal-Mart SuperCtr/gas

33	Fuqua St, Ⓔ...**gas:** Shamrock, **food:** Chili's, Fuddrucker's, Las Haciendas, Luby's, Olive Garden, Schlotzsky's, TGIFriday, **lodging:** Studio 6, Sun Suites, **other:** Chrysler/Jeep, Dodge, Ford, Honda, Hyundai, Isuzu, Lincoln/Mercury, Ⓦ...**food:** Bennigan's, Black-eyed Pea, Boston Mkt, Bouderaux's Cajun Kitchen, Casa Mexican, Casa Ole, CiCi's Pizza, Fox&Hound, Golden Corral, Gringo's Mexican, IHOP, Joe's Crabshack, Outback Steaks, Steak&Ale, Subway, Taco Cabana, Taco Bell, TX Cattle Steaks, Whataburger, **other:** BigLots, CarMax, Chevrolet, Firestone, JC Penney, Kroger, Macy's, Old Navy, Radio Shack, Ross, Sam's Club, Subaru, Tire Station, mall
32	Sam Houston Tollway, no services
31	FM 2553, Scarsdale Blvd, Ⓦ...**gas:** Shell, **other:** Chevrolet, Mitsubishi
30	FM 1959, Dixie Farm Rd, Ellington Field, Ⓔ...**gas:** Shell/dsl, **food:** Subway, **lodging:** Howard Johnson, **other:** HOSPITAL, Dodge, Infiniti, Ⓦ...**gas:** RaceWay, Shell/dsl, **food:** McDonald's, Popeye's, **lodging:** Palace Inn, **other:** Lonestar RV, VW
29	FM 2351, Clear Lake City Blvd, to Clear Lake RA, Friendswood, no services
27	El Dorado Blvd, Ⓔ...**gas:** Shell, **food:** DQ, Ⓦ...**food:** Sonic, Texas Roadhouse, Whataburger, **other:** Cadillac, Hummer, Kohl's, Lexus, Radio Shack, Sam's Club/gas, Wal-Mart SuperCtr/24hr
26	Bay Area Blvd, Ⓔ...**food:** Red Lobster, TGI Friday's, **other:** HOSPITAL, Barnes&Noble, CompUSA, Lowe's Whse, Michael's, Old Navy, Oshman's Sports, Steinmart, to Houston Space Ctr, Ⓦ...**gas:** Shell, **food:** Chick-fil-A, Denny's/24hr, McDonald's, Olive Garden, **lodging:** Best Western, **other:** Circuit City, Dillard's, Macy's, Office Depot, Sears/auto, Target, U of Houston, mall
25	FM 528, NASA rd 1, Ⓔ...**gas:** Conoco, Shamrock, Texaco, **food:** Cheddar's, Chili's, Hooters, IHOP, Las Haciendas Mexican, Pappasito's Cantina, Saltgrass Steaks, Waffle House, Vito's, **lodging:** Best Western, Comfort Suites, La Quinta, Motel 6, **other:** HOSPITAL, Audi, Best Buy, Big Lots, Fry's Electronics, Home Depot, Honda, Mazda, Volvo, Ⓦ...**food:** Hot Wok Chinese, Pappa's, Subway, **other:** Fiesta Foods, Radio Shack, Tuesday Morning
23	FM 518, League City, Ⓔ...**gas:** RaceWay, Shell/dsl, **food:** Applebee's, Burger King, Jack-in-the-Box, KFC, Little Caesar's, Pepper's Beef, Sonic, Subway, Sudie's Seafood, **other:** Academy Sports, BMW, Eckerd, Just Brakes, Kroger, Mercedes, Walgreens, Ⓦ...**gas:** Chevron, Exxon/24hr, Mobil, **food:** Cracker Barrel, Hartz Chicken, McDonald's, Taco Bell, Waffle House, Wendy's, **lodging:** Super 8, **other:** Discount Tire, Space Ctr RV Park, U-Haul
22	Calder Dr, Brittany Bay Blvd, Ⓔ...**other:** Nissan, Toyota, camping, Ⓦ...**other:** Holiday World RV Ctr
20	FM 646, Santa Fe, Bacliff, Ⓔ...**food:** Denny's, Panda Express, Whataburger, **other:** Best Buy, Home Depot, JC Penney, Lowes Whse, Radio Shack, Wal-Mart Super Ctr, Ⓦ...**gas:** Valero/dsl, **food:** Chili's, Subway, Taco Cabana, **other:** HEB Foods/gas, Kohl's, PetCo
19	FM 517, Dickinson Rd, Hughes Rd, Ⓔ...**food:** Jack-in-the-Box, Monterey Mexico, Pizza Inn, **other:** Adventure Out RV Park, Buick/Pontiac/GMC/Subaru, CVS

(Side label: League City)

Interstate 45

N ← → S

Drug, Family$, Food King, Radio Shack, 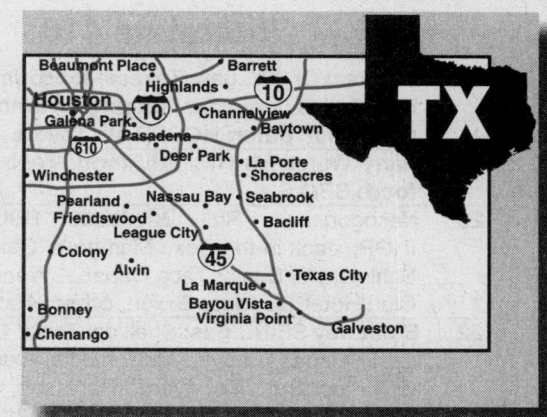**W**...**gas:** Mobil, Shell/dsl, **food:** Burger King, Dickenson's Seafood, Heartbreak Grill, KFC, McDonald's, Pizza Hut, Sonic, Subway, Taco Bell, Wendy's, Whataburger/24hr, **lodging:** Day's Inn, El Rancho Motel, **other:** Ford, Kroger, Subaru, Target, Walgreens

17	Holland Rd, **W**...to Gulf Greyhound Park
16	FM 1764 E(from sb), Texas City, same as 15
15	FM 2004, FM 1764, Hitchcock, **E**...**gas:** Shell, **food:** Gringo's Cafe, Jack-in-the-Box, Olive Garden, Popeye's, Ryan's, Uncle Chan's, **lodging:** Best Western, Fairfield Inn, Hampton Inn, Holiday Inn Express, **other:** HOSPITAL, Chevrolet/Toyota/RV Ctr, Dillard's, JC Penney, Lowe's Whse, Macy's, Sam's Club/gas, Sears/auto, mall, **W**...**gas:** Mobil/Subway, Shell, **food:** IHOP, Sonic, Waffle House, Wendy's, Whataburger, **lodging:** Super 8, **other:** Chevrolet/RV Ctr, Gulf Greyhound Park, Radio Shack, Toyota/Scion, Wal-Mart SuperCtr/24hr/gas
13	Century Blvd, Delany Rd, **E**...**gas:** Valero, **W**...**food:** Acupulco Mexican, **lodging:** Super 8, Travelodge, **other:** VF Factory Outlet/famous brands
12	FM 1765, La Marque, **E**...**gas:** Chevron/24hr, **food:** Domino's, Jack-in-the-Box, Kelley's Rest., Sonic
11	Vauthier Rd, no services
10	**E**...**gas:** Valero, **food:** McDonald's, **W**...**gas:** Shell/dsl, **other:** Oasis RV Park
9	Frontage Rd(from sb), no services
8	Frontage Rd(from nb), no services
7c	Frontage Rd, no services
7b	TX 146, TX 6(exits left from nb), Texas City, **W**...**gas:** EZ Mart
7a	TX 146, TX 3, no services
6	Frontage Rd(from sb), no services
5	Frontage Rd, no services
4	Frontage Rd, Village of Tiki Island, **W**...**gas:** Valero **other:** public boat ramp
4mm	West Galveston Bay
1c	TX 275, FM 188(from nb), Port Ind Blvd, Teichman Rd, Port of Galveston, **E**...**gas:** Exxon, Mobil/dsl, Valero, **lodging:** Howard Johnson, Motel 6, **other:** Chevrolet, Chrysler/Dodge/Jeep, Ford, Honda, Mazda, Mitsubishi, Nissan, Toyota/Scion
1b	71st St(from sb), **E**...**gas:** EZ Mart/gas, same as 1c
1a	TX 342, 61st St, to W Beach, **E**...**gas:** Chevron, **other:** GNC, Home Depot, NTB, Target, **W**...**gas:** RaceWay, **food:** Church's, McDonald's, Taco Bell, **lodging:** Day's Inn, **other:** Big Lots, Chevrolet/Pontiac/Buick/Cadillac, Chrysler/Jeep, Family$, Honda, O'Reilly Parts, U-Haul, USPO, **1-2 mi W**...**gas:** Chevron/dsl, Exxon/dsl, Valero, **food:** China Island, CiCi's Pizza, Happy Buddah, Jack-in-the-Box, KFC, Little Caesar's, Luby's, Mario's Italian, McDonald's, Papa John's, Pizza Hut, Popeye's, Quizno's, Starbucks, Subway, Taco Cabana, Waffle House, Whataburger, **lodging:** Baymont Inn, Beachcomber Inn, Best Value Inn, Quality Inn, Super 8, **other:** Curves, CVS Drug, Firestone/auto, Hastings Books, HEB Foods, Office Depot, Randall's Food/gas, Ross, Walgreens

I-45 begins/ends on TX 87 in Galveston.

Galveston (vertical label, left margin)

Interstate 410(San Antonio)

Exit #	Services
53	I-35, S to Laredo, N to San Antonio
51	FM 2790, Somerset Rd
49	TX 16 S, spur 422, **N**...**gas:** Chevron, **food:** Church's Chicken, Subway, **other:** HOSPITAL, to Palo Alto Coll, **S**...**gas:** Shamrock
48	Zarzamora St, no services
46	Moursund Blvd, no services
44	US 281 S, spur 536, Roosevelt Ave, **N**...**gas:** Shell/dsl, **other:** dsl repair, RV camping
43	Espada Rd(from eb), no services
42	spur 122, S Presa Rd, to San Antonio Missions Hist Park, **S**...**gas:** Whiteside/dsl
41	I-37, US 281 N
39	spur 117, WW White Rd, no services
37	Southcross Blvd, Sinclair Rd, Sulphur Sprs Rd, **N**...HOSPITAL
35	US 87, Rigsby Ave, **E**...**gas:** Exxon/TacoMaker, Shamrock/dsl, **food:** Denny's, Jack-in-the-Box, McDonald's, Taco Bell, **other:** Radio Shack, Wal-Mart SuperCtr/gas/24hr, **W**...**gas:** Chevron, **food:** Barnacle Bill's Seafood, BBQ, Pizza Hut, Sonic, Subway, Taco Cabana, Whataburger, **lodging:** Day's Inn, **other:** Aamco, Advance Parts
34	FM 1346, E Houston St, **W**...**gas:** Chevron, Shamrock, **food:** McDonald's, Wendy's, **lodging:** Comfort Inn, Motel 6
33	I-10 E, US 90 E, to Houston, I-10 W, US 90 W, to San Antonio
32	Dietrich Rd(from sb), FM 78(from nb), to Kirby
31b	Lp 13, WW White Rd, no services
31a	FM 78, Kirby, no services
30	Binz-Engleman, Space Center Dr(from nb)
I-410 and I-35 run together 7 mi, See Interstate 35, exits 164 thru 165.	
27	I-35, N to Austin, S to San Antonio
26	Lp 368 S, Alamo Heights
25b	FM 2252, Perrin-Beitel Rd, **N**...**gas:** Chevron/dsl, Mobil, Shamrock, **food:** Denny's, KFC/Taco Bell, Quizno's, Schlotsky's, Taco Bell, Taco Cabana, Wendy's, Wienerschnitzel, **lodging:** Comfort Inn, Econolodge, Welsley Inn, **S**...**food:** Jim's Rest.

TEXAS

Interstate 410

25a Starcrest Dr, N...gas: Texaco, food: Jack-in-the-Box, Los Patios Mexican, lodging: Hawthorn Inn, Hill-Coutry Inn, other: HOSPITAL, Toyota

24 Harry Wurzbach Hwy, N...food: Taco Cabana, S...food: BBQ Sta.

23 Nacogdoches Rd, N...food: BBQ, Church's, IHOP, Jack-in-the-Box, Mamma's Cafe, Pizza Hut, Schlotsky's, Sonic, Taco Cabana, Wendy's, lodging: Club Hotel, S...gas: Exxon, other: Audi/VW, Volvo

22 Broadway St, N...gas: Shell/dsl, food: Crystal Steaks, Las Palapas, Luby's, McDonald's, Oceans Seafood Grill, lodging: Courtyard, Radisson, Ramada Inn, other: Firestone, S...gas: Citgo, Shamrock, food: Chesters Hamburgers, Jim's Rest., Quizno's, Whataburger, lodging: Residence Inn, TownHouse Motel, other: Infiniti, Jiffy Lube

21 US 281 S, Airport Rd, Jones Maltsberger Rd, N...food: Applebee's, Smokey Onion, lodging: Drury Suites, Hampton Inn, Holiday Inn Select, PearTree Inn, S...gas: Texaco/dsl, food: Pappadeaux, Red Lobster, Texas Land&Cattle, lodging: Courtyard, Day's Inn, Fairfield Inn, La Quinta, Renaissance Hotel, Staybridge Suites, other: Hyundai/Kia, Mitsubishi, Subaru, Target, Wal-Mart/24hr

20 TX 537, N...food: Arby's, Jason's Deli, Subway, TGI-Friday, lodging: DoubleTree Hotel, Hilton, other: Barnes&Noble, Best Buy, Chevrolet, Circuit City, Honda, Lincoln/Mercury, Marshall's, Mazda, Ross, S...food: Arby's, Bennigan's, El Pollo Loco, Luby's, McDonald's, Taco Cabana, Texas Cattle Co., other: Dillard's, Dodge, Foley's, Macy's, Mervyn's, Saks 5th, Sears/auto, mall

19b FM 1535, FM 2696, Military Hwy, N...food: Crown Buffet, Guajillos Mexican, Souper Salad, S...food: Denny's, Jim's Rest.

19a Honeysuckle Lane, Castle Hills, no services

17b (from wb), S...gas: Shell, food: DQ, Dunkin Donuts, Subway, other: Firestone, HEB Foods/gas

17 Vance Jackson Rd, N...gas: Mobil, Phillips 66, Shamrock, food: Burger King, Jack-in-the-Box, KFC, McDonald's, Steak&Ale, Sonic, Taco Cabana, Tom's Ribs, Whataburger, lodging: Embassy Suites, Marriott, other: Aamco, CarQuest, Discount Tire, Target, Tire Sta, transmissions, S...gas: Exxon, food: Subway, other: U-Haul

16b a I-10 E, US 87 S, to San Antonio, I-10 W, to El Paso, US 87 N

15 Lp 345, Fredericksburg Rd, E...gas: Shell, food: Church's, Dave&Buster's, Jack-in-the-Box, Jim's Rest., Kettle, Luby's, N China Rest., Taquiera Mexican, lodging: AmeriSuites, Best Value Inn, Comfort Suites, SpringHill Suites, other: BMW, Target, W...gas: Mobil, lodging: Holiday Inn, other: K-Mart

14 Callaghan Rd, Babcock Ln, E...gas: Chevron, Exxon, Shamrock, food: Marie Callender's, Popeye's, lodging: Comfort Inn, Hampton Inn, Super 8, Travelodge Suites, other: GMC/Pontiac, W...gas: Conoco, food: Burger King, Chili's, ChopSticks Chinese, Cook's Steaks, DingHow Chinese, El Chico, Golden Corral, HomeTown Buffet, Joe's Crabshack, Landry's Seafood, Paulo Italian, Pizza Hut, Quizno's, Red Lobster, Wendy's, Whataburger, other: HOSPITAL, Cavander's Boots, Home Depot, Sam's Club, Wal-Mart SuperCtr/24hr

13b Rolling Ridge Dr, W...food: Jack-in-the Box, KFC, Las Palapas Mexican, same as 14

13a TX 16 N, Bandera Rd, Evers Rd, Leon Valley, E...food: Outback Steaks, other: Albertson's, Audi, HEB Foods, Office Depot, Old Navy, Saturn, Toyota, U-Haul, W...gas: Exxon, Shamrock, Shell, food: Applebee's, BBQ, IHOP, Jack-in-the-Box, Jason's Deli, Jim's Rest., KFC, Luby's, McDonald's, Olive Garden, Schlotsky's, Taco Cabana, lodging: Super 8, other: Aamco, Best Buy, BigLots, Chevrolet, Circuit City, Dillard's, Eckerd, Honda, Marshall's, NTB

11 Ingram Rd, E...gas: Shell/dsl, food: Bennigan's, Calloway's Rest., Fazoli's, KFC/Taco Bell, Krispy Kreme, Pepe's, Texas Roadhouse, lodging: Day's Inn, Econolodge, Holiday Inn Express, Red Roof Inn, other: Aamco, BrakeCheck, W...food: Applebee's, Burger King, ChuckeCheese, Denny's, Jack-in-the-Box, Jason's Deli, Olive Garden, Subway, Whataburger, lodging: Best Western, Super 8, other: Barnes&Noble, Best Buy, Dillard's, Best Buy, $Tree, Firestone, Foley's, JC Penney, Mervyn's, Michael's, Ross, Sears/auto, mall

10 FM 3487, Culebra Rd, E...food: Barnacle Bill's Seafood, BBQ, Denny's, McDonald's, Wendy's, lodging: La Quinta, Ramada Ltd, other: Chrysler/Dodge/Jeep, Mazda/Nissan/Daewoo, to St Mary's U, W...gas: Phillips 66, RaceTrac, Shamrock, food: Blimpie, Fuddrucker's, lodging: InTown Inn, other: Firestone/auto, Ford, Mitsubishi

9b a TX 151, W...gas: Chili's, food: Carino's Italian, Cracker Barrel, lodging: Quality Inn, other: Home Depot, Lowe's Whse, Wal-Mart SuperCtr/gas/24hr, to Sea World

7 (8 from sb)Marbach Dr, E...gas: Exxon, food: IHOP, McDonald's, other: PepBoys, W...gas: Chevron/dsl, Texaco/dieel, food: Acadiena Café, Burger King, Golden Wok, Jack-in-the-Box, Jim's Rest., KFC, LJ Silver, Luby's, McDonald's, Mr Gatti's, Pancho's Mexican, Peter Piper Pizza, Pizza Hut, Red Lobster, Sonic, Subway, Taco Bell, Taco Cabana, Whataburger/24hr, other: Advance Parts, BigLots, Discount Tire, $General, $Tree, Eckerd, Firestone/auto, HEB Food, Target

6 US 90, to Lackland AFB, E...lodging: Country Inn Motel, other: Explore USA RV Ctr, W...gas: Shamrock, Shell/dsl, food: Andrea's Mexican, lodging: Motel 6, Super 8

4 Valley Hi Dr, to Del Rio, San Antonio, E...gas: Mobil, Phillips 66/dsl, Shamrock, food: Church's Chicken, McDonald's, Pizza Hut, Sonic, other: AutoZone, HEB Food/gas, Radio Shack, W...to Lackland AFB

3b a Ray Ellison Dr, Medina Base, W...gas: Shamrock/Subway

2 FM 2536, Old Pearsall Rd, E...gas: Shamrock/dsl, Shell/dsl, food: BBQ, Mexico Taqueria, McDonald's, Sonic

1 Frontage Rd, no services

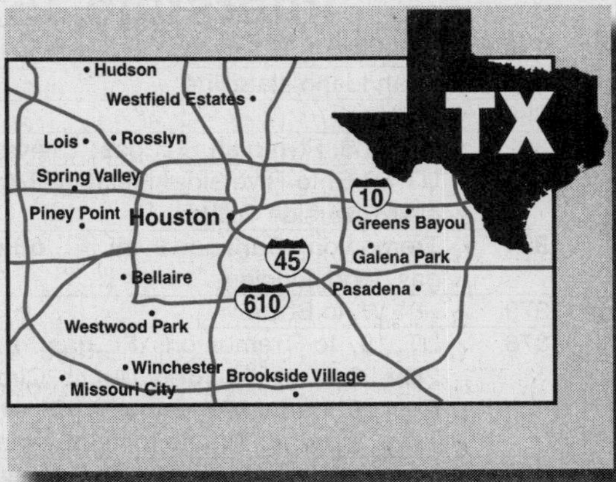

Interstate 610(Houston)

Exit #	Services
38c a	TX 288 N, downtown, access to zoo
37	Scott St, [N]...**gas:** Citgo, Valero
36	FM 865, Cullen Blvd, [N]...**lodging:** Crystal Inn, [S]...**gas:** Chevron/McDonald's, Mobil, Shamrock, Shell, **food:** Timmy Chan, **lodging:** Crown Inn, Cullen Inn
35	Calais Rd, Crestmont St, MLK Blvd, [N]...**gas:** Exxon, Shamrock, **food:** Burger King
34	S Wayside Dr, Long Dr, [N]...**gas:** Chevron, Phillips 66, Shell, **food:** Church's, Wendy's, **other:** Fiesta Foods, [S]...**gas:** Valero, Shell
33	Woodridge Dr, Telephone Rd, [N]...**gas:** Shell/dsl, **food:** IHOP, KFC/Taco Bell, McDonald's, Papa John's, Wendy's, **lodging:** South Lp Inn, **other:** Lowe's Whse, Old Navy, [S]...**gas:** Texaco, **food:** BBQ, Burger King, KFC, Piccadilly's Cafeteria, Spanky's Pizza, Whataburger, **other:** Dodge, Ford, mall
32b a	I-45, S to Galveston, N to Houston, to airport
31	Broadway Blvd, [S]...**gas:** Shamrock/dsl, Texaco/dsl
30c b	TX 225, to Pasadena, San Jacinto Mon
29	Port of Houston Main Entrance
28	Clinton Dr, to Galina Park, no services
27	Turning Basin Dr, industrial area
26b	Market St, no services
26a	I-10 E, to Beaumont, I-10 W, to downtown
24b	Wallisville Rd, [E]...**gas:** Mobil/dsl, Phillips 66, **food:** McDonald's
24	US 90 E, [E]...**gas:** Chevron, Luv's/Arby's/dsl, Phillips 66, **food:** Luby's, Wendy's, [W]...**gas:** Citgo
23b	N Wayside, [E]...**gas:** Shamrock
23a	Kirkpatrick Blvd, no services
22	Homestead Rd, Kelley St, [N]...**gas:** Shell/dsl, **food:** Whataburger, **lodging:** Super 8
21	Lockwood Dr, [N]...**gas:** Chevron/McDonald's, Shell, **food:** Chan Chinese, Church's, Popeye's, **other:** Popeye's, Family$, [S]...HOSPITAL
20a b	US 59, to downtown
19b	Hardy Toll Rd, no services
18	Irvington Blvd, Fulton St, [N]...**gas:** Chevron, [S]...**gas:** Shell/dsl
17b c	I-45, N to Dallas, S to Houston
17a	(eb only) Airline Dr, [S]...**gas:** Shell, **food:** Jack-in-the-Box, **lodging:** Western Inn
16	Yale St, N Main St, Shamrock, [N]...**gas:** Exxon, **other:** Harley Davidson, [S]...**gas:** Mobil, Shell, **food:** Burger King, Church's Chicken, KFC/Pizza Hut/Taco Bell, **lodging:** Western Inn
15	TX 261, N Shepherd Dr, [N]...**food:** Sonic, Taco Cabana, [S]...**gas:** Chevron, Shell, Texaco/dsl, **food:** Wendy's, Whataburger, **other:** Home Depot, PepBoys
14	Ella Blvd, [N]...**gas:** Exxon, Shell/24hr, Texaco, **food:** A&W, Blimpie, Burger King, Jack-in-the-Box, KFC, LJ Silver, McDonald's, Popeye's, Taco Bell, [S]...**gas:** Shell, **food:** BBQ, **other:** HOSPITAL, Lowe's Whse
13c	TC Jester Blvd, [N]...**gas:** Chevron, Mobil, Shell, **food:** Atchafalaya Kitchen, Denny's, Golden Gate Chinese, Juanita's Mexican, Luisitos Mexican, Po' Boys Sandwiches, **lodging:** Courtyard, SpringHill Suites, [S]...**gas:** Phillips 66
13b a	US 290, no services
12	W 18th St, [N]...**food:** CiCi's, **lodging:** Sheraton, **other:** Foley's, JC Penney, mall, [S]...**food:** Whataburger
11	I-10, W to San Antonio, E to downtown Houston
10	Woodway Dr, Memorial Dr, [E]...**gas:** Shamrock, **food:** Steak'n Egg, [W]...**gas:** Exxon, Shell, **food:** Shug's Rest.
9b	Post Oak Blvd, [E]...**lodging:** Drury Inn, La Quinta, [W]...**food:** Champp's Rest., McCormick&Schmick's Café
9a	San Felipe Rd, Westheimer Rd, FM 1093, [E]...**gas:** Mobil, Shell, **lodging:** Courtyard, Hampton Inn, La Quinta, **other:** Circuit City, CVS Drug, NTB, Target, [W]...**gas:** Shell, **food:** Champp's Rest., Luke's Burgers, **lodging:** Crowne Plaza Hotel, HomeStead Suites, Marriott, Sheraton, **other:** Best Buy, Dillard's, Nieman-Marcus
8a	US 59, Richmond Ave, [E]...**lodging:** Holiday Inn, Extended Stay America, **other:** CVS Drug, [W]...**gas:** Shell, **other:** Dillards
7	Bissonet St, West Park Dr, Fournace Place, [E]...**food:** Beudreax's Kitchen, **lodging:** Candlewood Suites, **other:** Home Depot, [W]...**gas:** Shell/dsl/repair
6	Bellaire Blvd, no services
5b	Evergreen St, no services
5a	Beechnut St, [E]...**gas:** Chevron, **food:** Boston Mkt, IHOP, Lowe's Whse, McDonald's, Outback Steaks, **other:** bank, [W]...**gas:** Citgo, Shell, **food:** Escalante Mexican Grill, James Coney Island, Saltgrass Steaks, Smoothie King, **other:** Borders Books, GNC, Marshall's, mall
4a	S Post Oak Rd, Brasswood, [E]...**gas:** Citgo, **food:** Outback Steaks, **lodging:** Day's Inn, [W]...**other:** Target, Wal-Mart
3	Stella Link Rd, [N]...**gas:** Chevron, **food:** Jack-in-the-Box, **other:** Discount Tire, Food City, Radio Shack, [S]...**gas:** Exxon, Phillips 66/dsl, Shell
2	US 90A, [N]...**gas:** Chevron, Conoco, Shamrock, **food:** Arby's, Bennigan's, Burger King, Church's, Denny's/24hr, KFC, McDonald's, Shoney's, Taco Bell, Wendy's, **lodging:** Grand Plaza Hotel, Howard Johnson, Villa Motel, **other:** CVS Drug, Discount Tire, Ford, Honda, Walgreen, [S]...**gas:** Chevron, Shell, **food:** Golden Corral, Pizza Hut/Taco Bell, Whataburger/24hr, **lodging:** CareFree Inn, La Quinta, Motel 6, Super 8, **other:** Chevrolet, Firestone, Mazda, Nissan, Toyota, U-Haul, to Buffalo Speedway
1c	Kirby Dr(from eb), [N]...**food:** Shell, **food:** Burger King, **lodging:** Radisson, [S]...**food:** Joe's Crabshack, Pappadeaux Seafood, Pappasito's Cantina, **other:** Cavender's Boots, NTB, Pontiac/GMC, Sam's Club, Toyota
1b a	FM 521, Almeda St, Fannin St, [N]...**gas:** Chevron, Shell, **food:** Burger King, **lodging:** Scottish Inn, **other:** Astro Arena, [S]...**gas:** Shell, **food:** McDonald's, **other:** Aamco, to Six Flags

Interstate 15

Exit #	Services
400.5mm	Utah/Idaho state line
398	Portage,
392	UT 13 S, Plymouth, E...gas: Chevron/Subway/dsl
385	UT 30 E, to Riverside, Fielding, 1 mi E...gas: Sinclair/Riverside Grill/dsl
381	Tremonton, Garland, 2 mi E...other: HOSPITAL, gas, food, lodging
379	I-84 W, to Boise
376	UT 13, to Tremonton, E...gas: Exxon/Arby's/dsl/24hr, 2-3 mi E...food: Arctic Circle, Crossroads Rest., El Parral Mexican, JC'S Diner, Subway, Taco Time, lodging: Marble Motel, Sandman Motel
372	UT 240, to UT 13, to rec area, Honeyville, E...other: Crystal Hot Springs Camping
370mm	rest area sb, full(handicapped)facilities, info, phone, picnic tables, litter barrels, vending, petwalk
365	UT 13, Brigham City, W...other: to Golden Spike NHS
363	Forest St, Brigham City, W...other: Bear River Bird Refuge
362	US 91, to US 89, Brigham City, Logan, E...gas: Chevron/Blimpie/24hr, Citgo/7-11, ⚡/Flying J/dsl/rest./24hr, Sinclair, food: Arby's, Aspen Grill, Beto's Mexican, Burger King, Hunan Chinese, J&D's Rest., KFC/Taco Bell, Little Caesar's, McDonald's, Pizza Hut, Pizza Press, Sonic, Subway, Taco Time, Wendy's, Wingers, lodging: Bushnell Motel, Crystal Inn, Galaxie Motel, Howard Johnson Express, other: HOSPITAL, AutoZone, Checker Parts, Chevrolet/Pontiac/Buick/Cadillac, Chrysler/Dodge/Jeep, Radio Shack, ShopKO, Wal-Mart SuperCtr/gas/24hr, RV camping, to Yellowstone NP via US 89, W...gas: ⚡/Flying J/Crt St Grill/dsl/scales/rest., lodging: Comfort Inn
361mm	rest area nb, full(handicapped)facilities, phone, picnic tables, litter barrels, vending, petwalk
359	Port of Entry both lanes
357	UT 315, to Willard, Perry, E...gas: ⚡/Flying J/Country Mkt/Pepperoni's/dsl/LP, other: KOA(2mi)
351	UT 126, to US 89, to Utah's Fruit Way, Willard Bay, W...other: Smith & Edwards Hardware
349	UT 134, N Ogden, Farr West, E...gas: Exxon/Wendy's, Maverik, 7-11, food: Arby's, Domino's, Jumbo Burger, McDonald's, Melina's Mexican, Subway, other: Kwik Lube W...gas: Conoco/dsl
346	to Harrisville, Defense Depot, W...gas: Chevron/dsl, dsl repair
344	UT 39, 12th St, Ogden, E...gas: Chevron, Phillips 66, Shell/dsl, lodging: Best Western/rest., 1-2 mi E...gas: Chevron, food: Denny's, KFC, McDonald's, Sizzler, Village Inn Rest., lodging: Motel 6, other: to Ogden Canyon RA, W...gas: Pilot/DQ/Subway/Taco Bell/dsl/24hr/@, food: Iron Pan Bistro, lodging: Sleep Inn, Western Inn
343	UT 104, 21st St, Ogden, E...gas: Chevron/Arby's/dsl, ⚡/Flying J/Conoco/dsl/LP/24hr, Phillips 66/dsl, food: Cactus Red's Rest., McDonalds, Outlaw Rest., lodging: Big Z Motel/rest., Best Rest, Best Western, Comfort Suites, Holiday Inn Express, Marriott, other: Justus RV Ctr, RV Repair, W...food: CJ's Rest., lodging: Sleep Inn, other: Century RV Park
342	(from nb), UT 53, 24th St, Ogden, E...gas: Sinclair/dsl
341b a	UT 79 W, 31st St, Ogden, 1-2 mi E on Wall St...gas: Citgo/7-11, food: Arby's, Golden Corral, JJ North's Buffet, Sizzler, lodging: Day's Inn, Hampton Inn, Marriott, other: HOSPITAL, Dillard's, Chevrolet, Ford/Lincoln/Mercury, RV Ctr, mall, to Weber St U, W...airport
340	I-84 E(from sb), to Cheyenne, Wyo
339	UT 26(from nb), to I-84 E, Riverdale Rd, E...gas: Conoco/dsl, Sinclair, food: Applebee's, Boston Mkt, Carl's Jr, Chili's, La Salsa Mexican, McDonald's, lodging: Red Roof Inn, other: Chrysler/Jeep, Circuit City, Harley-Davidson, Home Depot, Honda/Nissan, Isuzu, Lincoln/Mercury/Toyota/Kia, Mazda, Mitsubishi, Pontiac/Buick/GMC, Saturn, Target, Toyota, Wal-Mart SuperCtr/24hr, Wilderness RV
338	UT 97, Roy, Sunset, E...other: Air Force Museum, W...gas: Exxon/dsl, Phillips 66, 7-11, Sinclair, food: Arby's, Arctic Circle, Blimpie, Burger King, Central Park, DQ, Denny's, KFC, McDonald's, Panda Express, Pizza Hut, Ponderosa, Sonic, Subway, Taco Bell, Village Inn Rest., Wendy's, lodging: Quality Inn, Motel 6, other: Albertson's, AutoZone, BrakeWorks, Checker Parts, Citte RV Ctr, Early Tires, Goodyear, Discount Tire, Radio Shack, RiteAid, Smith's/gas, Walgeen, transmissions
335	UT 103, Clearfield, E...Hill AFB, W...gas: Chevron, Conoco, PetroMart, 7-11, Texaco, Circle K, food: Arby's, Carl's Jr, KFC, McDonald's, Skipper's, Subway, Taco Bell, Winger's, lodging: Clarin Inn, Days Inn, The Cottage Inn, other: Big O Tire, Sierra RV
334	UT 193, Clearfield, to Hill AFB, E...gas: Chevron, Maverik, W...food: Chevron, Wendy's,
332	UT 108, Syracuse, E...gas: Chevron, Phillips 66/dsl, Circle K, food: Applebee's, Carl's Jr., Cracker Barrel, Famous Dave's, Golden Corral, JB's, Marie Calender's, Outback Steaks, Quizno's, Red Robin, SF Pizza, TimberLodge Steaks, Tony Roma's, lodging: Courtyard, Fairfield Inn, Hampton Inn, Hilton Garden, Holiday Inn Express, La Quinta, TownePlace Suites, other: Barnes&Noble, Lowe's Whse, Office Depot, Old Navy, Target, W...gas: Citgo/7-11, Conoco, food: Arby's, McDonald's, other: HOSPITAL, RV Ctr
331	UT 232, UT 126, Layton, E...gas: Mobil, Phillips 66, Texaco, food: Denny's, Garcia's, McDonald's, Olive Garden, Red Lobster, Sizzler, Tony Roma, Training Table Rest., Wendy's, lodging: Comfort Inn, other: JC Penney, Mervyn's, mall, to Hill AFB S Gate, W...gas: ⚡/Flying J, food: Blimpie, Burger King, China Buffet, Fuddrucker's, IHOP, KFC, Krispy Kreme, LoneStar Steaks, McGrath's FishHouse, Taco Bell, other: Batteries+, Bed Bath and Beyond, Chevrolet, Discount Tire co., Dodge, Home Depot, NTB, Jeep, Pontiac/Cadillac/GMC, Ream's Foods, Sam's Club, ShopKO, Staples, Wal-Mart SuperCtr/24hr
330	to UT 126(from nb), Layton, E...food: Little Orient Chinese, other: repair, W...gas: Texaco, other: Jensen's RV
328	UT 273, Kaysville, E...gas: Chevron/McDonald's, Citgo/7-11, Phillips 66/dsl, Sinclair, food: Arby's, Cutler's Sandwiches, DQ, Joanie's Rest., Gandolfo's, KFC, Subway, Taco Maker, Taco Time, Wendy's, Winger's, lodging: West Motel, other: Albertson's, Checker Parts, Schwab Tire, Walgreens, W...other: Camping World/Jensen RV Ctr, 1st Choice Cars, Kia
325mm	parking area both lanes

Side labels: N, S, Brigham City, Ogden, Roy, Layton

Interstate 15

325 UT 225, Lagoon Dr, Farmington(from sb), ▣..**food:** Subway, **other:** amusement park, camping

324 US 89 N, UT 225(from nb), **1 mi** ▣..**gas:** Conoco/Smith's Foods/dsl, Maverik/gas, **food:** Arby's, Aunt Pam's, Burger King, Little Caesar's, Subway, **other:** Goodyear/auto, RV Park, to I-84

322 UT 227(from nb), Lagoon Dr, to Farmington, ▣..**food:** Subway, **other:** Lagoon Funpark/RV Park

319 Centerville, ▣..**gas:** Chevron, Phillips 66/dsl, **food:** Arby's, Arctic Circle, Burger King, Carl's Jr, DQ, Del Taco, IHOP, Jake's Shakes, LoneStar Steaks, McDonald's, Subway, Taco Bell, TacoMaker, Wendy's, **other:** Albertson's, Home Depot, LandRover, Radio Shack, Schwab Tire, Target/foods, ▣..**other:** RV Ctr

317 US 89 S(exits left from sb), UT 131, 500W,, S Bountiful, ▣..**gas:** Chevron/24hr, Exxon/dsl, Phillips 66/dsl, Sinclair/dsl, **food:** Alicia's Rest., Starbucks, **lodging:** Country Inn Suites, **other:** Office Depot, Parts+, PetCo, Goodyear, Jiffy Lube, tires

316 UT 68, 500 S, W Bountiful, Woods Cross, ▣..**gas:** Exxon, Texaco, **food:** Applebee's, Blimpie, Burger King, Carl's Jr, Christopher's Steaks, ChuckaRama, Coldstone, Del Taco, HogiYogi, KFC, La Frontera Mexican, McDonald's, Panda Express, Pizza Hut, Rinny's Rest., Sizzler, Subway, SuCasa Mexican, Taco Bell, Winger's, **other:** HOSPITAL, Albertson's, AutoZone, Barnes&Noble, Big O Tire, Checker Parts, Costco, Firestone/auto, Michael's, Radio Shack, Ross, ShopKO, TJ Maxx, Walgreens, ▣..**gas:** Phillips 66/A&W/dsl, **lodging:** InTowne Suites

315 26th S, N Salt Lake, ▣..**gas:** Chevron/dsl/mart, Sinclair, Tesoro, **food:** Apollo Burger, Arby's, Atlantis Burger, Empire Chinese, McDonald's, Subway, Taco Time, Village Inn, Wendy's, **lodging:** Best Western, Comfort Inn, **other:** Ace Hardware, Chevrolet/Pontiac/Buick/Kia, Discount Tire, Dodge, Ford/Lincoln/Mercury, Honda, K-Mart, Mazda, Mitsubishi, Nissan, Schwab Tire, Smith's Foods, Toyota, Tunex, U-Haul, ▣..**gas:** Conoco, **food:** Denny's, Lorena's Mexican, **lodging:** Hampton Inn, Motel 6, **other:** Goodyear

314 Center St, Cudahy Lane(from sb), N Salt Lake, ▣..gas

313 I-215 W(from sb), to airport

312 US 89 S, to Beck St, N Salt Lake

311 2300 N

310 900 W, ▣..**food:** Tia Maria's Mexican, **lodging:** Regal Inn, Salt City Motel, **other:** 7-11, Self's conv/rest.

Salt Lake

309 600 N, ▣..**other:** HOSPITAL, LDS Temple, downtown, to UT State FairPark

308 I-80 W, to Reno, airport

307 400 S, Downtown

306 600 S, SLC City Ctr, **1 mi** ▣..**gas:** Chevron, Phillips 66/dsl, Circle K, **food:** Burger King, DQ, Denny's, McDonald's, Wendy's, **lodging:** Embassy Suites, Hampton Inn, Little America, Motel 6, Quality Inn, Ramada Inn, Residence Inn, Super 8, **other:** Ford, Toyota, to Temple Square, LDS Church Offices

305c-a 1300 S, 2100 S UT 201 W, West Valley, ▣..**gas:** Phillips 66, Texaco, **food:** Atlantis Burgers, Carl's Jr, McDonald's, Wienerschnitzel, **other:** CompUSA, Costco/gas, Home Depot, Petsmart, U-Haul, Wal-Mart SuperCtr/24hr, ▣..**gas:** ⚑/Flying J/Conoco/dsl/LP/rest./24hr, **food:** Wendy's, **other:** Best Buy, Blue Beacon, Cadillac, Chevrolet, $Tree, Ford, Goodyear, Hummer, Mitsubishi, NAPA, Office Depot,

304 I-80 E, to Denver, Cheyenne

303 UT 171, 3300 S, S Salt Lake, ▣..**gas:** Citgo/7-11, Phillips 66, **food:** Apollo Diner, Burger King, McDonald's, Taco Bell, **lodging:** Bonneville Inn, Day's Inn, Roadrunner Motel, ▣..**gas:** Maverik/gas, **other:** Sam's Club/gas, GMC

Interstate 15

N

↑
|
↓

S

Sandy

301 UT 266, 4500 S, Murray, Kearns, **E...food:** McDonald's, **other:** UpTown Tire, **W...gas:** Chevron, Conoco, Shell/dsl, Sinclair/Burger King/dsl, Texaco, **food:** Burger King, Denny's, Wendy's, **lodging:** Fairfield Inn, Hampton Inn, Holiday Inn Express, Quality Inn, **other:** InterMtn RV Ctr, Lowe's Whse

300 UT 173, 5300 S, Murray, Kearns, **E...HOSPITAL,** **W...gas:** Chevron, Conoco, Sinclair, 7-11, **food:** KFC, Schlotsky's, **lodging:** Reston Hotel, **other:** Smith's Foods, FunDome, Jenson's RV Ctr

298 I-215 E and W

297 UT 48, 7200 S, Midvale, **E...gas:** Chevron, Conoco, Phillips 66, Sinclair, Texaco/LP, **food:** Chili's, Denny's, John's Place, KFC, McDonald's, Midvale Mining Café, Sizzler, South Seas Café, Taco Bell, Village Inn Rest., **lodging:** Best Western, Day's Inn, Discovery Inn/café, Executive Inn, La Quinta, Motel 6, Rodeway Inn, Sandman Inn, Super 8, **other:** Cadillac/Buick, carwash, to Brighton, Solitude Ski Areas, Walgreen, **W...gas:** Sinclair/Subway/dsl

295 UT 209, 9000 S, Sandy, **E...gas:** Chevron, Sinclair, **food:** Arby's, Burger King, Fuddrucker's, Hardee's, Johanna's Kitchen, Sconecutter's Rest., Sweet Tomato, **lodging:** Comfort Inn, Majestic Rockies Motel, **other:** Early Tires, Firestone, Ford, Lowe's Whse, to Snowbird, Alta Ski Areas, **W...gas:** Maverik, Tesoro, **food:** KFC, Village Inn **other:** HOSPITAL, Aamco

293 106th S, Sandy, S Jordan, **E...gas:** Conoco, Phillips 66, Tesoro, **food:** Bennett's BBQ, Bennigan's, Carver's Prime Rib, Chili's, Eat a Burger, HomeTown Buffet, Jim's Rest., Johanna's Rest., Subway, TGIFriday, Village Inn, Wendy's, **lodging:** Best Western, Courtyard, Extended Stay America, Hampton Inn, Marriott, Residence Inn, TownePlace Suites, **other:** DENTIST, Best Buy, Chevrolet, Chrysler/Jeep, Costco/gas, Dillard's, Goodyear, Honda, JC Penney, Mervyn's, Nissan, Target, Toyota, mall, **W...food:** Denny's, **lodging:** Country Inn Suites, Sleep Inn, Super 8, **other:** Buick/GMC/Pontiac, CarMax, VW, Wal-Mart SuperCtr

Draper

291 UT 71, 12300 S, Draper, Riverton, **E...gas:** Chevron, /Flying J/dsl, **food:** Arby's, Arctic Circle, Café Rio Mexican, Carl's Jr, Del Taco, Fazoli's, Guadalahonky's Mexican, Jamba Juice, KFC, McDonald's, Panda Express, Pizza Hut, Quizno's, Ruby Tuesday, Sonic, Teriyaki Express, Wendy's, Wienerschnitzel, Wingers Diner, **lodging:** Comfort Inn, Fairfield Inn, Ramada Ltd, **other:** Brown RV, Camping World RV Supplies(1mi), Discount Tire, Goodyear/auto, Greenbax, Kohl's, Mountain Shadows Camping, Smith's Foods, FSA Outlets/famous brands **W...gas** Phillips 66, **other:** Wal-Mart SuperCtr

289 Bangerter Hwy, **W...gas** Exxon, 7-11, **food:** Quizno's

288 UT 140, Bluffdale, **E...gas:** Chevron/dsl, **other:** Kohl's, Camping World RV Supplies(2mi), Quality RV Ctr, **W...gas:** Common Sense/gas, 7-11, **other:** st prison

284 UT 92, to Alpine, Highland, **E...other:** Cabela's, **W...gas:** Chevron/Iceberg Café/dsl, Maverik/dsl, **lodging:** Hampton Inn, **other:** Lone Peak RV Ctr, Thanksgiving Point/café , to Timpanogas Cave

282 US 89 S, 12th W, to UT 73, Lehi, **W...gas:** Chevron

279 UT 73, to Lehi, **E...gas:** Texaco/dsl, **food:** Applebee's, 1 Man Band Diner, **lodging:** Motel 6, **other:** Lowe's Whse, **W...gas:** Chevron/dsl/24hr, Phillips 66/Wendy's/24hr, **food:** Arctic Circle, Dutch Oven Rest., KFC/Pizza Hut, McDonald's, Papa Murphy's, Subway, Tepenyki Japanese, Wingers, **lodging:** Best Western, Comfort Inn, Day's Inn, Super 8, **other:** Albertson's, Big O Tire, Checker Parts, GNC, Dave's Chiropractic, USPO, museum

278 Main St, American Fork, **E...gas:** Phillips 66/dsl/24hr, Texaco, **food:** Chili's, Cobblestone Pizza, Del Taco, Ottavio's Italian, Pier 49, Sonic, Wendy's, **other:** HOSPITAL, Chevrolet, Chrysler/Dodge/Jeep, $Tree, Home Depot, K-Mart, Kohl's, Old Navy, Smith's Foods, Subaru/Suzuki, Target, Wal-Mart SuperCtr/24hr

276 5th E, Pleasant Grove, **E...gas:** Conoco/Blimpie, **food:** Carl's Jr, Denny's, McDonald's, Taco Bell, **lodging:** Quality Inn, **other:** Stewart's RV Ctr, **1-2 mi E...gas:** Circle K, Phillips 66, Texaco, **food:** Arby's, Del Taco, Golden Corral, Hardee's, KFC, Subway, Wendy's, **other:** HOSPITAL, American Camping, Chevrolet, **W...other:** Buick/GMC/Pontiac, Ford, Land Rover

275 Pleasant Grove, **E...food:** Bajio Grill, Panda Express, Sonic, Wienerschnitzel, **other:** BMW, Macey's foods

273 Orem, Lindon, **E...gas:** Exxon/dsl, Holiday, **food:** Costa Vida Mexican, Del Taco, **other:** Discount Tire, Home Depot, Lexus, Mercedes, Schwab Tire, **W...gas:** Sinclair/dsl

272 UT 52, to US 189, 8th N, Orem, **E...gas:** Phillips 66, **lodging:** La Quinta, **1 mi E...food:** Arby's, DQ, Denny's, Sonic, **other:** to Sundance RA

Orem

271 Center St, Orem, **E...gas:** Conoco, 7-11, **other:** HOSPITAL, funpark, **1-2 mi E...food:** Burger King, Hardee's, KFC, Panda Express, Taco Bell, Wendy's, **W... gas:** Tesoro, **food:** La Casita Blanca Mexican, **lodging:** Econolodge, **other:** LP

269 272 UT 265, 12th St S, University Pkwy, , **E...gas:** Texaco/Wendy's/dsl/24hr, Sinclair, **food:** IHOP, Krispy Kreme, McDonald's, McGrath's FishHouse, Subway, **lodging:** Comfort Inn, Hampton Inn, La Quinta, **other:** Ford, JiffyLube, Mazda, Saturn, Wal-Mart SuperCtr, **1-3 mi E...gas:** Chevron, **food:** Applebee's, Arby's, Carrabba's, Chili's, Fuddrucker's, Golden Corral, Noodles & Co., Outback Steaks, Pizza Hut, Sizzler, Village Inn, **lodging:** Best Western, Courtyard, **other:** Barnes&Noble, Circuit City, Honda, JC Penney, Jo-Ann Fabrics, Lowe's Whse, Mervyn's, Mitsubishi, Nissan, Office Depot, Old Navy, Ross, Subaru, TJ Maxx, mall, to BYU, many services on US 89, **W...gas:** Chevron

Provo

265b a UT 114, Center St, Provo, **E...gas:** Conoco, Phillips 66, Shell, Sinclair/dsl, 7-11, **other:** HOSPITAL, Firestone/auto, auto repair, **1 mi E...lodging:** Marriott, Travelers Inn, Travelodge, **other:** Albertson's, Checker Parts, Firestone, **W...gas:** Chevron, Shell, **lodging:** Econolodge, **other:** KOA, Lakeside RV, to Utah Lake SP

263 US 189 N, University Ave, Provo, **E...gas:** Chevron/24hr, Conoco/dsl, Maverik, Sinclair, **food:** A&W/KFC, Arby's, Burger King, ChuckaRama, Fazoli's, Hogi Yogi, McDonald's, Papa Murphy's, Ruby River Steaks, Sizzler, Taco Bell, Taco Time, Village Inn Rest., Wendy's, **lodging:** Best Western, Colony Inn, Fairfield Inn, Hampton Inn, La Quinta, Motel 6, National 9 Inn, Sleep Inn, Super 8, **oth-**

Interstate 15

Exit	Services
	er: Curves, Dillard's, GoodEarth Foods, Home Depot, JC Penney, K-Mart, Les Schwab, NAPA, Sam's Club/gas, Sears/auto, Staples, Silver Fox RV Camping, mall, to BYU, **1 mi** E...**food:** Los Three Amigos Mexican, **lodging:** Best Western, Hotel Roberts, Safari Motel, Western Inn, **other:** CarQuest, VW/Audi, auto repair
261	UT 75, Springville, E...**gas:** /Flying J/dsl/rest./scales/24hr/scales, Maverik, **food:** McDonald's(1mi), **lodging:** Best Western, **other:** E Bay RV Park, **RestStop**
260	UT 77, Springville, Mapleton, E...**gas:** Phillips 66/Quizno's/dsl, **food:** Del Taco, DQ, IHOP, Mongolian Grill, Pizza Hut, Quizno's, Wendy's, **other:** Big O Tire, JiffyLube, Wal-Mart SuperCtr/gas, W...**gas:** Sinclair/Arby's/dsl, **food:** Cracker Barrel, **lodging:** Day's Inn, **other:** Quality RV Ctr
258	US 89 S, US 6 E(from sb), to Price, E...**gas:** Chevron/dsl, Phillips 66, Texaco, **food:** Arby's, Burger King, Carl's Jr, JB's, KFC, McDonald's, Papa Murphy's, Subway, Taco Bell, Taco Maker, Wendy's, Winger's, **lodging:** Holiday Inn Express, Western Inn, **other:** Albertson's/gas, Checker Parts, Fakler's Tire, K-Mart, Radio Shack, RV Ctr
257	US 6 E, UT 156, Spanish Fork, E...**gas:** Chevron, Conoco/dsl, Phillips 66, Texaco/dsl/LP, **food:** Amber Rest., Arby's, Bajio Grill, Burger King, Hogi Yogi, JB's, KFC, Little Caesar's, McDonald's, North's Buffet, Sonic, Subway, Taco Bell, Taco Time, Wendy's, **lodging:** Escalante B&B, **other:** Albertsons, Dollar Tree, K-Mart, Macey's Foods, ShopKO, W...**gas:** Conoco/dsl, **other:** Chevrolet, Chrysler/Jeep, Ford, RV Ctr
253	UT 164, to Spanish Fork, no services
250	UT 115, Payson, E...**gas:** Chevron/dsl, /Flying J/Cookery/dsl/LP/rest./scales/24hr/@, Sinclair, **food:** McDonald's, Subway, **lodging:** Comfort Inn, **other:** HOSPITAL, Checker Parts, Payson Foods, RiteAid, dsl repair, Mt Nebo Loop
248	Payson, Salem, E...**gas:** Chevron, Sinclair/Arby's/dsl, **food:** Hogi Yogi, **other:** Wal-Mart SuperCtr, W...**gas:** Phillips 66/Wendy's/dsl
244	248 US 6 W, Santaquin, E...**other:** TrueValue, W...**gas:** Chevron/dsl, Conoco/dsl, Sinclair, **food:** Main St Pizza, Main St Mkt, SantaQueen Burgers, Subway, Sorenson's Apple Farm, **other:** Nat Hist Area, Tintic Mining Dist, auto/tire care
242	to S Santaquin
233	UT 54, Mona
228	UT 28, to Nephi, **2-4 mi** W...services
225	UT 132, Nephi, E...**gas:** Tesoro/dsl/LP, **food:** Taco Time, One Man Band Rest., **other:** Burn's Bros RV Park(5mi), W...**gas:** Chevron/Arby's/dsl, Phillips 66/Wendy's/dsl, Sinclair, **lodging:** Economy Inn, **other:** HOSPITAL, Big O Tire, Hi-Country RV Park
222	UT 28, to I-70, Nephi, E...**gas:** Chevron/dsl, Sinclair/dsl/24hr, Texaco/dsl/24hr, **food:** Burger King, Family Tree, Mickelson's Rest., Subway, **lodging:** Motel 6, Roberta's Cove Motel, Super 8, W...**gas:** /Flying J/Pepperoni's/dsl/LP/scales/24hr/@, **lodging:** Best Western, Safari Motel, **other:** HOSPITAL, Ford/Mercury, Big A Parts, dsl repair

Nephi

Exit	Services
207	to US 89, Mills
202	Yuba Lake, phone, boating, camping, rec facilities
188	US 50 E, to I-70, Scipio, E...**gas:** Sinclair/dsl, Texaco, **lodging:** Super 8, W...**gas:** Chevron/DQ/dsl/rest stop
184	ranch exit
178	US 50, to Delta, W...gas, phone, to Great Basin NP
174	to US 50, Holden
167	Lp 15, Fillmore, **1-3 mi** E...**gas:** Chevron/dsl, Sinclair/dsl, **food:** 5 Buck Pizza, Old Frontier Steaks, **lodging:** Apple Creek Inn, Best Western/rest., **other:** HOSPITAL, CarQuest, WagonsWest RV Park, antiques, W...**gas:** Chevron/Subway/rest stop, Texaco
163	Lp 15, to UT 100, Fillmore, E...**gas:** Chevron/Arby's/dsl/24hr, Maverik, **lodging:** Apple Creek Inn, **other:** HOSPITAL, KOA, W...**gas:** Texaco/Burger King, **lodging:** motel
158	UT 133, Meadow, E...**gas:** Chevron/dsl, Shell/dsl
153mm	view area sb
151mm	view area nb
146	Kanosh, **2 mi** E...gas, chainup area
138	ranch exit, no services
135	Cove Fort, Hist Site, Hist Site, E...**gas:** Chevron/Subway, **other:...rest stop**
132	I-70 E, to Denver, Capitol Reef NP, Fremont Indian SP
129	Sulphurdale, chainup area
125	ranch exit
120	Manderfield, chainup area nb
112	to UT 21, Beaver, Manderfield, E...**gas:** Chevron/dsl, Conoco/dsl, Shell, **food:** Arby's, Arshel's Café, El Bambi Café, Garden of Eden, Hunan Chinese, McDonald's, Subway, **lodging:** Best Western/rest., Country Inn, Day's Inn, Rodeway Inn, **other:** HOSPITAL, KOA(1mi), W...**gas:** Texaco/Wendy's/dsl, **lodging:** Super 8, **other:** to Great Basin NP
109	to UT 21, Beaver, E...**gas:** Phillips 66, Shell/Burger King/dsl/24hr, **lodging:** Comfort Inn, **other:** HOSPITAL, Cache Valley Cheese, Mike's Foodtown, NAPA, RV Parts/repair/dump, W...**gas:** Chevron/DQ/dsl/24hr, **food:** KanKun Mexican, Timberline Rest., **lodging:** Quality Inn, RV park, **other:** truckwash, to Great Basin NP
100	ranch exit, no services
95	UT 20, to US 89, to Panguitch, Bryce Canyon NP
88mm	**rest area both lanes, full(handicapped) facilities, phone, picnic table, litter barrel, petwalk, hist site**
82	UT 271, Paragonah
78	UT 141, E...**lodging:** Day's Inn, **other:** ski areas, W...**gas:** TA/Subway/Taco Bell/LP/dsl/scales/24hr
75	UT 143, **2 mi** E...**lodging:** Jedadiah's Inn/rest., Day's Inn, **other:** to Brian Head/Cedar Breaks Ski Resorts
71	Summit, W...**gas:** Sunshine Travel Plaza/dsl/rest./@

Beaver

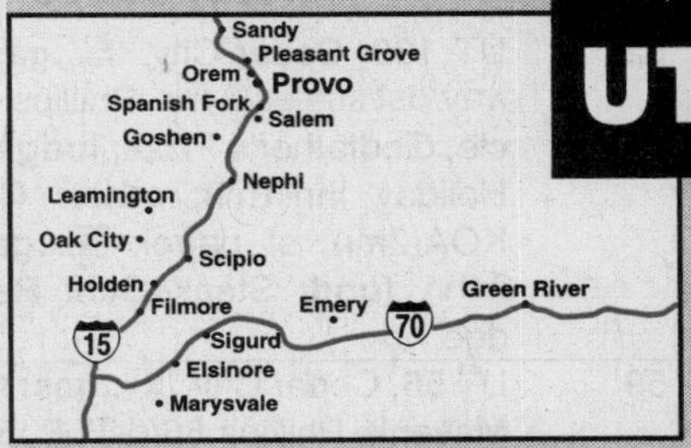

UTAH

Interstate 15

N ↕ S

Cedar City

62	UT 130, Cedar City, E...**gas:** Loves/Carl's Jr/Subway/dsl/scales/24hr, Phillips 66/dsl, **food:** Arctic Circle, Godfather's Pizza, **lodging:** Best Western(3mi), Holiday Inn(1mi), **other:** Country Aire RV Park, KOA(2mi), st patrol, W...**gas:** Maverik, Shell/dsl/24hr, **food:** Steak&Stuff Rest., **lodging:** Travelodge
59	UT 56, Cedar City, E...**gas:** Chevron, FoodMart/dsl, Maverik, Phillips 66/dsl/LP, Shell, Tesoro, Shell/dsl, **food:** Arby's, Burger King, Denny's, KFC, IHOP, McDonald's, Shoney's, Sonic, Taco Bell, Wendy's, **lodging:** Abbey Inn, Comfort Inn, Econolodge, **other:** Chevrolet/Buick, L&S Tire, NAPA, **1 mi** E...**gas:** Texaco/service, **food:** China Garden, Godfather's, Papa Murphy's, Pizza Factory, Sizzler, Sullivan's Café, **lodging:** Best Western, Rodeway Inn, Valu Inn, Zion Motel, **other:** Dodge/Chrysler/Jeep, Goodyear, GMC, Lin's Mkt, USPO, W...**gas:** Sinclair/dsl, **food:** Gondola Italian, Subway, **lodging:** Crystal Inn, Motel 6, Super 8
57	Lp 15, to UT 14, Cedar City, **1 mi** E...**gas:** Chevron/repair/24hr, Conoco/dsl, Phillips 66/dsl, Shell, Sinclair/dsl, **food:** DQ, Domino's, Hogi Yogi, Hunan Chinese, Pizza Hut, Subway, Taco Time, **lodging:** Best Value Inn, Days Inn, Holiday Inn Express, Ramada Ltd, Rodeway Inn, SpringHill Suites, **other:** HOSPITAL, Albertson's, Allied Tire, AutoZone, Big O Tire, Checker Parts, GNC, Radio Shack, Smith's Food/gas/24hr, to Cedar Breaks, Navajo Lake, Bryce Cyn, Duck Crk, W...**gas:** Chevron/dsl, **food:** Applebee's, Baker House B&B, Chili's, Costa Vida, Del Taco, Panda Express, Pizza Hut, Quizno's, Starbucks, Subway, Winger's, **lodging:** Hampton Inn, **other:** GNC, Home Depot, Jiffy Lube, Tunex, Wal-Mart SuperCtr/gas/24hr
51	Kanarraville, Hamilton Ft, no services
44mm	**rest area both lanes, full(handicapped)facilities, phone, picnic tables, litter barrels, petwalk, hist site**
42	New Harmony, Kanarraville, W...**gas:** Texaco/dsl
40	to Kolob Canyon, Zion's NP, E...**other:** tourist info/phone, scenic drive
36	ranch exit
33	ranch exit
31	Pintura
30	Browse
27	UT 17, Toquerville, **9 mi** E...**food:** Hunan Chinese, Subway, **lodging:** Motel 6, Travelodge, **other:** to Zion NP, Grand Cyn, Lake Powell
23	Leeds, Silver Reef(from sb), **3 mi** E...**other:** Leed's RV Park/gas, hist site, museum
22	Leeds, Silver Reef(from nb), same as 23
16	UT 9, to Hurricane, E...**gas:** Shell/Arby's/dsl, **lodging:** Holiday Inn Express, **other:** Harley-Davidson, Wal-Mart Dist Ctr, **10 mi** E...**gas:** Chevron, Shell, **food:** Calydascope Cafe, Coral Canyon Grille, **lodging:** Comfort Inn, Motel 6, Travelodge, **other:** to Zion NP, Grand Canyon, Lake Powell, RV Camping

St George

13	Washington Pkwy
10	Middleton Dr, Washington, E...**gas:** Phillips 66/dsl, Sinclair, **food:** Arby's, Arctic Circle, Bajio Cafe, Burger King, Del Taco, Gandolfo's, IHOP, Jack-in-the-Box, Little Caesars, Ruby Tuesday, Sonic, SteakOut, Texas Roadhouse, Toro Moro Mexican, Wendy's, **lodging:** Country Inn&Suites, Red Cliffs Inn, **other:** Albertson's, AutoZone, Best Buy, Big Lots, Costco/gas, Dillard's, Discount Tire, Home Depot, Kohl's, JC Penney, Jiffy Lube, PetCo, Sears/auto, Sportsman's Whse, Tunex, Wal-Mart SuperCtr/gas, mall, W...**gas:** Chevron/dsl/LP, Texaco/24hr, **other:** auto repair
8	St George Blvd, St George, E...**gas:** Chevron/Subway/dsl, Texaco, **food:** Applebee's, Arby's, Carl's Jr, Chili's, ChuckaRama, Don Jose Mexican, Famous Dave's BBQ, Fazoli's, Golden Corral, Mongolian BBQ, Outback Steaks, Panda Express, Papa John's, Red Lobster, Ruby River Steaks, Sharky's Mexican, Starbucks, Village Inn Rest., Winger's, **lodging:** Best Inn, Courtyard, Hampton Inn, Ramada Inn, Shoney's Inn/rest., Tuesday Morning, **other:** HOSPITAL, Harmon's Foods, Lowe's Whse, Michael's, Old Navy, Ross, Settler's RV Park, Staples, Sunrise Tire, Target, TJ Maxx, Zion Factory Stores/famous brands, same as 10, W...**gas:** Chevron, Maverik/gas, Sinclair/Domino's/LP/dsl, Shell, Texaco/dsl, **food:** A&W/KFC, Burger King, Cafe Rio, China King, Denny's, Ernesto's Mexican, McDonald's, Panda Garden, Pizza Hut, Taco Bell, Taco Time, Wendy's, Wienerschnitzel, **lodging:** Best Western, Comfort Inn, Coronada Inn, Day's Inn, Econolodge, GuestHouse Inn, Howard Johnson, Motel 6, Rodeway Inn, Sands Motel, SunTime Inn, Travelodge, **other:** Big O Tire, Checker Parts, Desert Coach RV Ctr, Honda Motorcycles, Kauffman Transmissions, NAPA, Rite Aid, St Geo RV, to LDS Temple
6	UT 18, Bluff St, St George, E...**gas:** Chevron/dsl/24hr, Texaco/dsl/24hr, **food:** Cracker Barrel, Jack-in-the-Box, Subway, **lodging:** Ambassador Inn, Comfort Inn, Fairfield Inn, Hilton Garden, **other:** Buick/Pontiac/GMC, Firestone/auto, Hyundai, Saturn, U-Haul, W...**gas:** Shell, Texaco, **food:** Arby's, Bluffs Rest., Burger King, Claimjumper Steaks, DQ, Denny's, JB's, McDonald's, Palms Rest., Pancho&Lefty's Mexican, Pier 49, Pizza Hut, San Francisco Pizza, Tony Roma, **lodging:** Best Western, Budget Inn, Claridge Inn, Comfort Suites, Holiday Inn, Howard Johnson, Quality Inn, Ridgeview Inn, South Lodge Inn, Super 8, **other:** HOSPITAL, Albertson's, AutoZone, Big O Tire, Chevrolet/Cadillac, Ford/Lincoln/Mercury, Goodyear, Honda, Jo-Ann Fabrics, Mazda, Mitsubishi, NAPA, Nissan, Painter's RV Ctr, Chrysler/Dodge/Jeep, Radio Shack, Subaru, TempleView RV Park, Toyota, funpark
4	Bloomington, E...**gas:** /Flying J/Burger King/dsl/scales/24hr, W...**gas:** Chevron/Subway/Taco Bell, **food:** Arby's, Hunan Chinese, Wendy's, **lodging:** La Quinta, Wingate Inn, **other:** Wal-Mart SuperCtr/dsl
2	**Welcome Ctr nb, full(handicapped)facilities, picnic tables, litter barrels, phone, petwalk**
1	Port of Entry/weigh sta both lanes
0mm	Utah/Arizona state line

Interstate 70

Exit #	Services
232mm	Utah/Colorado state line
228mm	**view area wb, litter barrels**
227	Westwater
221	ranch exit
214	to Cisco
204	UT 128, to Cisco
193	Yellowcat Ranch Exit
190mm	**Welcome Ctr wb, full(handicapped)facilities, vending, info, picnic tables, litter barrels**
187	Thompson Springs, N...gas: Shell/dsl, other: café, camping, lodging
182	US 191 S, Crescent Jct, to Moab, S...to Arches/Canyonlands NP
181mm	**rest area eb, full(handicapped)facilities, scenic view, picnic tables, litter barrels**
175	ranch exit, no services
164	UT 19, Green River, **1-3 mi** N...gas: Phillis 66/Burger King/dsl, Silver Eagle/Blimpie, Westwinds Trkstp/Sinclair/rest, food: Bookcliff Rest., Tamarisk Rest., lodging: Best Western, Comfort Inn, Holiday Inn Express, Motel 6, Super 8, Ramada Ltd, Rodeway Inn, other: KOA, Powell River Museum, tires/repair, same as 160
160	UT 19, Green River, **0-2 mi** N...gas: Chevron/Subway/dsl, Conoco/Arby's/dsl, food: Ben's Cafe, Chowhound, Sleepy Hollow Motel, lodging: Budget Inn, Robbers Roost, other: Foodland Foods, Green River SP, NAPA, Shady Acres RV Park, USPO, city park, same as 164
157	US 6 W, US 191 N, to Price, Salt Lake
147	UT 24 W, to Hanksville, to Capitol Reef, Lake Powell
144mm	**rest area wb, restrooms(handicapped), litter barrels**
141.5mm	runaway truck ramp eb
140mm	**rest area both lanes, view area, restrooms (handicapped), litter barrels**
139mm	runaway truck ramp eb
136mm	brake test area eb
129	ranch exit, no services
120mm	**rest area both lanes, restrooms(handicapped), litter barrels**
114	to Moore, **N...rest area both lanes, restrooms (handicapped), litter barrels**
105	ranch exit
102mm	**rest area both lanes, restrooms(handicapped), litter barrels**
91	ranch exit, no services
89	UT 10 N, UT 72, to Emery, Price, **12 mi** N...gas, S...to Capitol Reef NP
84mm	**S...rest area both lanes, full(handicapped)facilities, litter barrels, petwalk**
72	ranch exit
61	Gooseberry Rd
56	US 89 N, to Salina, US 50 W, to Delta, **0-1 mi** N...gas: Conoco/dsl, Phillips 66/dsl, Sinclair/Burger King/dsl, food: Denny's, El Mexicano Mexican, Mom's Cafe, Subway, lodging: Best Western, Rodeway Inn, Super 8, other: Barrett Foods, Butch Cassidy RV Camp, NAPA, auto repair, radiators, NEXT SERVICES 108 MI EB

E ↕ **W**

Green River

Salina

Exit #	Services
48	UT 24, to US 50, Sigurd, Aurora, **1-2 mi** S...gas, food, to Fishlake NF, Capitol Reef NP

Exit #	Services
40	Lp 70, Richfield, **0-2 mi** S...gas: Chevron, ⛽/Flying J/Pepperoni's/dsl/LP/rest./24hr, Maverik, Shell, Sinclair, Texaco/dsl, food: Arby's, Chuckwagon Steaks, JB's Rest., McDonald's, South China Rest., Subway, Taco Time, lodging: Appletree Inn, Best Western, Budget Host, Day's Inn/rest., Quality Inn, Super 8, Travelodge, other: HOSPITAL, Albertson's/drug, Big O Tire, Chevrolet, Buick/Pontiac/Cadillac/GMC, Family$, Ideal Dairy, KOA, Lin's Mkt, NAPA, USPO, RV/truck repair
37	Lp 70, Richfield, S...gas: Phillips 66/Wendy's/dsl, food: KFC/Taco Bell, Papa Murphy's, Wingers, lodging: Comfort Inn, Fairfield Inn, Hampton Inn, other: Home Depot, **1-2 mi** S...gas: Conoco/dsl/Munchie's RV Park, Texaco/Burger King/dsl, food: Lotsa Motsa Pizza, McDonald's, Pizza Hut, Subway, lodging: Days Inn, Quality Inn, Romanico Inn, other: Ace Hardware, Albertson's, Big Kmart, Checker Parts, Chevrolet, $Tree, Ford/Mercury, Home Depot, K-Mart, KOA, Wal-Mart SuperCtr/24hr, to Fish Lake/Capitol Reef Parks, st patrol
31	Elsinore, Monroe, S...gas: Silver Eagle/gas
25	UT 118, Joseph, Monroe, S...gas: Flying U Country Store/dsl, other: RV park
23	US 89 S, to Panguitch, Bryce Canyon
17	N...other: Fremont Indian Museum, info, phone, camping
13mm	brake test area eb
8	Ranch Exit
3mm	Western Boundary Fishlake NF
1	Historic Cove Fort, N...gas: Chevron(2mi)
0mm	I-15, N to SLC, S to St George. I-70 begins/ends on I-15, exit 132.,

Richfield

Interstate 80

Exit #	Services
197mm	Utah/Wyoming state line
193	Wahsatch
189	ranch exit
185	Castle Rock
182mm	Port of Entry/weigh sta wb
180	Emery(from wb)
170	**Welcome Ctr wb/rest area eb, full(handicapped)facilities, phone, vending, picnic tables, litter barrels, petwalk, RV dump**
169	Echo, **1 mi** N...gas/dsl, food, lodging
168	I-84 W, to Ogden, I-80 E, to Cheyenne
166	view area both lanes, litter barrels
164	Coalville, N...gas: Phillips 66/dsl/mart, lodging: Best Western, other: Holiday Hills RV Camp/LP, Camper-World RV Park, S...gas: Chevron/dsl, Sinclair, other: Griffith's Foods, NAPA, USPO, to Echo Res RA

E ↕ **W**

Interstate 80

Exit	Services
155	UT 32 S, Wanship, **N**...**food:** Spring Chicken Café, **S**...**gas:** Sinclair/dsl, **other:** to Rockport SP
150	toll gate promontory
146b a	US 40 E, to Heber, Provo, **N**...**gas:** Sinclair/Blimpie/dsl, **S**...**other:** Home Depot
145	UT 224, Kimball Jct, to Park City, **N**...**other:** Chevrolet, Ford/Mercury, RV camping, **S**...**gas:** Chevron, **food:** Arby's, Bajio Grill, Coldstone Creamery, Gandalfo's Deli, Ghidottis Italian, Loco Lizard Cantina, McDonald's, Panda Express, Quizno's, Starbucks, Subway, Ruby Tuesday, Taco Bell, Wendy's, Wild Oats Cafe, Wingers, **lodging:** Best Western, Hampton Inn, Holiday Inn Express, **other:** GNC, Smith's Foods, USPO, Wal-Mart, Outlet Mall/famous brands, RV camping, to ski areas
144mm	view area eb
141	ranch exit, **N**...**gas:** Phillips 66/Blimpie, **food:** Pizza Hut, **other:** to Jeremy Ranch, **S**...**food:** Booster Juice, Cafe Sabor, Oh Shucks Grill, **other:** Albertson's, camping, ski area
140	Parley's Summit, , **S**...**gas:** Sinclair/dsl, **food:** No Worries Café
137	Lamb's Canyon
134	UT 65, Emigration Canyon, East Canyon, Mountaindale RA
133	utility exit(from eb)
132	ranch exit
131	(from eb) Quarry
130	I-215 S(from wb)
129	UT 186 W, Foothill Dr, Parley's Way, **N**...HOSPITAL
128	I-215 S(from eb)
127	UT 195, 23rd E St, to Holladay
126	UT 181, 13th E St, to Sugar House, **N**...**gas:** Chevron, Texaco, **food:** Olive Garden, Red Lobster, Sizzler, Training Table Rest., Wendy's, **other:** ShopKO
125	UT 71, 7th E St, gas: Texaco, **other:** Firestone, **N**...**food:** McDonald's
124	US 89, S State St, **N**...**gas:** Citgo/7-11, Chevron, Texaco/dsl, **food:** Burger King, Skipper's, Taco Bell, Uncle Sid's Rest., Wendy's, Woody's Drive-In, **other:** Buick, Chrysler/Jeep, Discount Tire, Dodge, Honda, Jeep, Suzuki, transmissions, **S**...**food:** KFC, Pizza Hut, **lodging:** Ramada Inn
123mm	I-15, N to Ogden, S to Provo
	I-80 and I-15 run together approx 4 mi. See Interstate 15, exits 305-307.
121	600 S, to City Ctr
120	I-15 N, to Ogden
118	UT 68, Redwood Rd, to N Temple, **1 mi N on N Temple E**...**gas:** Chevron/Subway/dsl, Maverik, Pilot/Arby's/dsl/scales/24hr, Tesoro, **food:** A&W/KFC, Burger King, Carls Jr, Denny's, Taco Bell, Wendy's, **lodging:** Airport Inn, Candlewood Suites, Comfort Suites, Day's Inn, Holiday Inn Express, Motel 6, Quality Inn, Radisson, Utah St Fairpark, **S**...HOSPITAL
117	I-215, N to Ogden, S to Provo
115b a	40th W, W Valley Fwy, **N**...to Salt Lake Airport
114	Wright Bros Dr(from wb), **N**...same as 113
113	5600 W(from eb), **N**...**gas:** Phillips 66/mart, **food:** Perkins, Pizza Hut, Subway, **lodging:** Best Western, Comfort Inn, Courtyard, Fairfield Inn, Hilton, Holiday Inn, Holiday Inn Express, La Quinta, Microtel, Residence Inn, Super 8
111	7200 W, **N**...visitor ctr
104	UT 202, Saltair Dr, to Magna, **N**...**other:** Great Salt Lake SP, beaches
102	UT 201(from eb), to Magna
101mm	view area wb
99	UT 36, to Tooele, **S**...**gas:** Chevron/Subway, ⚡/Flying J/Conoco/Country Mkt/dsl/LP/24hr/@, TA/Amoco/Burger King/Taco Bell/dsl/rest./scales/24hr/@, Shell/dsl, KFC(10mi), **food:** McDonald's, **lodging:** Oquirrh Motel/RV Park, **other:** HOSPITAL, Blue Beacon
88	to Grantsville
84	UT 138, to Grantsville, Tooele
77	UT 196, to Rowley, Dugway
70	to Delle, **S**...**gas:** Delle/Sinclair/dsl/café/24hr, phone
62	to Lakeside, Eagle Range, military area
56	to Aragonite
54mm	**rest area both lanes, full(handicapped)facilities, phone, picnic tables, litter barrels, petwalk, vending**
49	to Clive
41	Knolls
26mm	architectural point of interest
10mm	**rest area both lanes, full(handicapped)facilities, phone, picnic tables, litter barrels, vending, petwalk, observation area**
4	Bonneville Speedway, **N**...**gas:** Sinclair/dsl/café/24hr
3mm	Port of Entry, weigh sta both lanes
2	UT 58(no EZ wb return), Wendover, **S**...**gas:** Sinclair/dsl, Shell/dsl, Texaco/dsl, **food:** McDonald's, Subway, Taco Mexican, **lodging:** Best Western, Day's Inn, Econolodge, Motel 6, Super 8, Western Ridge Motel, **other:** Family$, Fred's Foods, Bonneville Speedway Museum, Silversmith Casino, Stateline Inn/casino, RV park, USPO, auto repair
0mm	Utah/Nevada state line, Mountain/Pacific time zone

Interstate 84

Exit #	Services
120	I-84 begins/ends on I-80, exit 168 near Echo, Utah.
115	to Henefer, Echo, 1/2 mi S...**other:** USPO, to E Canyon RA, 1/2 mi **S**...**other:** USPO, to E Canyon RA
112	Henefer, **S**...gas, food, lodging
111	Croydon
111mm	Devil's Slide Scenic View
108	Taggart, **N**...gas, food, phone
106	ranch exit
103	UT 66, Morgan, E Canyon RA, **N**...Ford, **S**...**gas:** Chevron, Phillips 66, Shell, **food:** Chicken Hut, Spring Chicken Café, Steph's Drive-In, **other:** Jubilee Foods, USPO, city park
96	Peterson, **N**...**gas:** Sinclair(3mi), **other:** to Snow Basin, Powder Mtn, Nordic Valley Ski Areas, **S**...**gas:** Phillips 66/dsl
94mm	**rest area wb, full(handicapped)facilities, picnic tables, litter barrels, petwalk**

Interstate 84

92	UT 167(from eb), to Huntsville, **N**...gas: Sinclair/dsl(2mi), other: trout farm(1mi), to ski areas
91mm	rest area eb, full(handicapped)facilities, picnic tables, litter barrels, petwalk
87b a	US 89, to Layton, Ogden, Hill AFB, **N**...food: McDonald's(2mi), 1/2 mi **S**...gas: Shell
85	S Weber, Uintah, no services
81	to I-15 S, UT 26, Riverdale Rd, **N**...gas: Conoco/dsl, Sinclair, food: Applebee's, Boston Mkt, Carl's Jr, Chili's, La Salsa Mexican, McDonald's, other: Chrysler/Jeep, Circuit City, Harley-Davidson, Home Depot, Honda/Nissan, Isuzu, Lincoln/Mercury/Toyota/Kia, Lowe's Whse, Mazda, Mitsubishi, PepBoys, Pontiac/Buick/GMC, Sam's Club/gas, Target, Wal-Mart SuperCtr/24hr, Wilderness RV, **S**...food: McDonald's, lodging: Motel 6
	I-84 and I-15 run together. See Interstate 15, exits 341-376.
41	I-15 N to Pocatello
40	UT 102, Tremonton, Bothwell, **N**...gas: Chevron/Quizno's/dsl/wash/24hr, Sinclair/Burger King/dsl/scales/@, food: Denny's/24hr, McDonald's, Wendy's, lodging: Hampton Inn, Western Inn, other: HOSPITAL(4mi), Jack's RV, truck/tire repair, 1 mi **N**...gas: Maverik, Phillips 66/dsl, Tesoro, lodging: Marble Motel, other: Alco, **S**...other: to Golden Spike NM
39	to Garland, Bothwell, **N**...HOSPITAL
32	ranch exit
26	UT 83 S, to Howell
24	to Valley
20	to Blue Creek
17	ranch exit
16	to Hansel Valley
12	ranch exit
7	Snowville, **N**...gas: Chevron/Subway/dsl, ⚒/Flying J/Pepperoni's/dsl/LP/24hr, food: Mollie's Café, Ranch House Diner, lodging: Outsiders Inn, other: Lotti Dell RV camping
5	UT 30, to Park Valley
0mm	Utah/Idaho state line

Interstate 215 (Salt Lake)

Exit #	Services
29	I-215 begins/ends on I-15.
28	UT 68, Redwood Rd, **W**...gas: ⚒/Flying J/dsl/rest./mart/24hr/@, Maverik/24hr, food: Subway, other: BMW(motorcycles)
25	22nd N, no services
23	7th N, **E**...gas: Exxon, Maverik, Pilot/Arbys/dsl/scales/24hr(1.5 mi), food: Arby's, KFC, McDonald's, Taco Bell, Wendy's, lodging: Motel 6, **W**...lodging: Airport Inn, Baymont Inn, Candlewood Suites, Comfort Suites, Holiday Inn Express, Radisson
22b a	I-80, W to Wendover, E to Cheyenne
21	California Ave, **E**...gas: Chevron/dsl, Sapp Bros/Sinclair/Burger King/dsl/@, food: Great American Diner, Subway, other: Goodyear

20b a	UT 201, W to Magna, 21st S, **W**...other: Goodyear, Kenworth
18	UT 171, 3500 S, W Valley, **E**...gas: Sinclair, food: Applebee's, Chili's, Costa Vida Mexican, Cowloon Moon, Cracker Barrel, Denny's, IHOP, Training Table, lodging: Baymont Inn, Country Inn Suites, Crystal Inn, Extended Stay America, La Quinta, Ruby Tuesday, Sleep Inn, other: HOSPITAL, PepBoys, **W**...food: Apollo Burger, other: Big O Tire, Firestone, JC Penney, Macy's, Mervyn's, Staples
15	UT 266, 47th S, **E**...gas: Conoco/dsl, food: Dee's Rest., KFC, Pizza Hut, Taco Time, Taco Bell, Village Inn, Wendy's, other: Albertson's, Goodyear/auto, Marie Callender's, Rite Aid, Walgreens, **W**...gas: Chevron, food: Arby's
13	UT 68, Redwood Rd, **E**...gas: Chevron, Tesoro, food: Applebee's, Apollo Burger, Arby's, Bajio Grill, Burger King, Carl's Jr, Golden China, Great Harvest Bread, HoneyBaked Ham, McDonald's/playplace, Old Spaghetti Factory, Panda Express, Papa John's, Souper Salad, Starbucks, Subway, TX Roadhouse, lodging: Homestead Suites, other: $Tree, Harmon's, Jo-Ann Fabrics, PetsMart, Radio Shack, Ross, ShopKO, Tuesday Morning, Wal-Mart SuperCtr/auto
12	I-15, N to SLC, S to Provo
11	same as 10(from eb), same as 10(from eb)
10	UT 280 E, **E**...other: Sam's Club, **W**...food: Applebee's, Arby's, Hooters, Jason's Deli, La Salsa Mexican, Macaroni Grill, Olive Garden, Red Lobster, Taco Bell, Wendy's, Village Inn, other: HOSPITAL
9	Union Park Ave, **E**...food: Black Angus, Carl's Jr, Chili's, Denny's, Famous Dave's BBQ, LaSalsa Mexican, Marie Callender's, Outback Steaks, Sweet Tomato, Tony Roma's, lodging: Best Western, Crystal Inn, Extended Stay America, Homewood Suites, other: Albertson's, Barnes&Noble, Circuit City, Home Depot, Old Navy, Ross, Smith's Foods, Target, Wal-Mart/auto, **W**...gas: Tesoro, lodging: Crystal Inn, Motel 6, Super 8
8	UT 152, 2000 E, **E**...gas: Chevron, food: KFC, Panda Express, Taco Bell, **W**...food: Wendy's
6	6200 S, **E**...food: Loco Lizards Café, Mikado Café, Quizno's, other: Alta, Brighton, Snowbird, Solitude/ski areas
5	UT 266, 45th S, Holladay, **W**...gas: Tesoro
4	39th S, **E**...gas: Chevron, Sinclair, food: Barbacoa Grill, Rocky Mtn Pizza, other: Ace Hardware, Dan's Foods, **W**...HOSPITAL
3	33rd S, Wasatch, **W**...gas: Tesoro, food: Burger King, KFC, McDonald's, Taco Bell, Wendy's
2	I-80 W

VERMONT
Interstate 89

N ↑ ↓ S

Exit #	Services
130mm	I-89 Begins/Ends, US/Canada Border, Vermont state line
129.5mm	**rest area sb, full facilities, phone, picnic tables, litter barrels, petwalk**
22(129)	US 7 S, Highgate Springs, E...other: Ammex DutyFree, 3 mi E...gas: Mobil/dsl
129mm	Latitude 45 N, midway between N Pole and Equator
128mm	Rock River
21(123)	US 7, VT 78, Swanton, E...gas: Exxon/dsl/24hr, W...gas: Mobil/dsl, Shell, Sunoco/dsl, food: Big Wok Chinese, Dunkin Donuts, McDonald's, other: Grand Union Foods, NAPA
20(118)	US 7, VT 207, St Albans, W...gas: Mobil, Shell/dsl, food: Burger King, Dunkin Donuts, KFC/Taco Bell, McDonald's, Pizza Hut, other: Chevrolet, Ford, Hannaford Foods, Indian Motorcycles, Kinney Drug, Radio Shack, Sears, Staples
19(114)	US 7, VT 36, VT 104, St Albans, W...gas: Exxon, Mobil, Shell/dsl, lodging: Econolodge, other: HOSPITAL, Lincoln/Mercury, USPO, st police
111mm	**rest area both lanes, full(handicapped) facilities, info, phone, picnic tables, litter barrels, vending, petwalk**
18(107)	US 7, VT 104A, Georgia Ctr, E...gas: Citgo, Mobil/dsl, Shell, food: Potbelly Café, other: GA Auto Parts, Homestead RV Park, Interstate Auto Service
17(98)	US 2, US 7, Lake Champlain Islands, E...gas: Mobil, Shell/dsl, other: camping(4mi), W...other: to NY Ferry, camping(6mi)
96mm	weigh sta both lanes
16(92)	US 7, US 2, Winooski, E...gas: Mobil, food: Friendly's, lodging: Hampton Inn, other: Shaw's Foods, W...gas: Citgo, GoGo Gas, Shell/dsl, food: Burger King, Libby's Diner, McDonald's, Rathskellar Rest., lodging: Fairfield Inn, Motel 6
15(91)	VT 15(no EZ nb return), Winooski, E...lodging: Day's Inn, Handys Extended Stay Suites, W...gas: Exxon, Mobil, other: USPO
90mm	Winooski River
14(89)	US 2, Burlington, E...gas: Citgo/repair, Exxon, Mobil, Shell/dsl, Sunoco, food: Al's Cafe, Applebee's, Burger King, CheeseTraders, Dunkin Donuts, Friendly's, KFC, McDonald's, Outback Steaks, Quizno's, Zachary's Pizza, lodging: Anchorage Inn, Best Western, Clarion, Comfort Inn, Day's Inn, Holiday Inn, SwissHost Motel, University Inn, other: Barnes&Noble, BonTon, Brooks Drug, Grand Union Foods, Hannaford's Foods, JC Penney, Jo-Ann Fabrics, Natural Foods Mkt, Sears/auto, mall, W...gas: Exxon, Mobil, lodging: Sheraton, other: HOSPITAL, Advance Parts, Michael's, Staples

13(87)	I-189, to US 7, Burlington, **2 mi** W on US7 N ...gas: Citgo, Shell, food: Blimpe, China Express, KFC, TGIFriday, lodging: Liberty Inn, Town&Country Motel, other: Bond Parts, Radio Shack, Hyundai/Subaru, Radio Shack, **2 mi** W on US 7 S...gas: Exxon, Gulf, Mobil, Sunoco, Shell, food: Burger King, Cactus Pete's Rest., Denny's, Friendly's, Koto Japanese, McCarty's Steaks, McDonald's, Olive Garden, Perry's Rest., Pizza Hut, lodging: Super 8, other: Advance Parts, Audi/VW, Chrysler/Saturn, Hannaford's Foods, K-Mart, Pontiac/Cadillac, Tire Whse
12(84)	VT 2A, to US 2, to Essex Jct, Williston, E...gas: Citgo, Mobil/24hr, Sunoco/dsl/subs/24hr, food: Chili's, Friendly's, Longhorn Steaks, 99 Rest., Ponderosa, lodging: Fairfield, other: Best Buy, Circuit City, City Drug, Hannaford's Foods, Home Depot, Marshall's, Shaw's Foods, Staples, WalMart, st police, W...lodging: Courtyard, Residence Inn
82mm	**rest area both lanes(7am-11pm), full(handicapped)facilities, phone, picnic tables, litter barrels, vending, petwalk**
11(79)	US 2, to VT 117, Richmond, E...lodging: Checkered House Motel, W...gas: Mobil/dsl/24hr
67mm	rest area sb, no services
66mm	rest area nb, no services
10(64)	VT 100, to US 2, Waterbury, E...gas: Exxon/dsl/24hr, Mobil/dsl/24hr, food: Lydia's Grill, lodging: Best Western/rest, Thatcher Brook Inn/rest., W...gas: Citgo, food: Zachary's Pizza, other: USPO
9(59)	US 2, to VT 100B, Middlesex, W...gas: Getty, lodging: Camp Meade Motel/rest., other: museum, st police
8(53)	US 2, Montpelier, **1 mi** E...gas: CF/gas, Citgo, Exxon/dsl, Gulf/dsl, Mobil, Sunoco/repair, food: La Pizzaria, Sarducci's Rest., Subway, lodging: Capitol Plaza Hotel, Montpelier Inn, other: Bond Parts, Shaw's Foods, camping(6mi), to VT Coll
7(50)	VT 62, to US 302, Barre, E...gas: Mobil/dsl/24hr, food: Applebee's, lodging: Comfort Suites, other: Honda, Shaw's Foods, Staples, **1 mi** E...lodging: Hilltop Inn, other: HOSPITAL, Cadillac/GMC/Toyota, JC Penney, Jo-Ann Fabrics, camping(7mi)
6(47)	VT 63, to VT 14, S Barre, **4 mi** E...gas, food, lodging, camping, info
5(43)	VT 64, to VT 12, VT 14, Williamstown, **6 mi** E...gas/dsl, food, lodging, camping, W...to Norwich U
41mm	highest elevation on I-89, 1752 ft
34.5mm	**rest area/weigh sta both lanes(7am-9pm), full(handicapped)facilities, info, phone, litter barrels, petwalk**
4(31)	VT 66, Randolph, E...other: RV camping(1mi), W...gas: Mobil, food: McDonald's, lodging(3mi), other: HOSPITAL, RV camping(5mi)

Interstate 89

N ↕ S

3(22)	VT 107, Bethel, **E**...**gas:** Shell/dsl, **food:** Eaton Rest., Village Pizza, **other:** to Jos Smith Mon(8mi), **1 mi W**...**gas:** Citgo/dsl/LP, **other:** Books Drug, NAPA, USPO, st police
14mm	White River
2(13)	VT 14, VT 132, Sharon, **E**...**lodging:** 1/2 Acre Motel, **W**...**gas:** Citgo/dsl, Gulf/dsl, Mobil, **food:** Dixie's Kitchen, Sandy's Drive Inn, **lodging:** Columns Motel, **other:** Sharon Trading Post, USPO, Jos Smith Mon(6mi)
9mm	**rest area/weigh sta both lanes(7am-11pm), full facilities, phone, info, picnic tables, litter barrels, vending, NO HANDICAPPED FACILITIES**
7mm	White River
1(4)	US 4, to Woodstock, Quechee, **3 mi E**...**gas:** Shell/dsl/24hr, **lodging:** Hampton Inn, Super 8
1mm	I-91, N to St Johnsbury, S to Brattleboro
0mm	Vermont/New Hampshire state line, Connecticut River

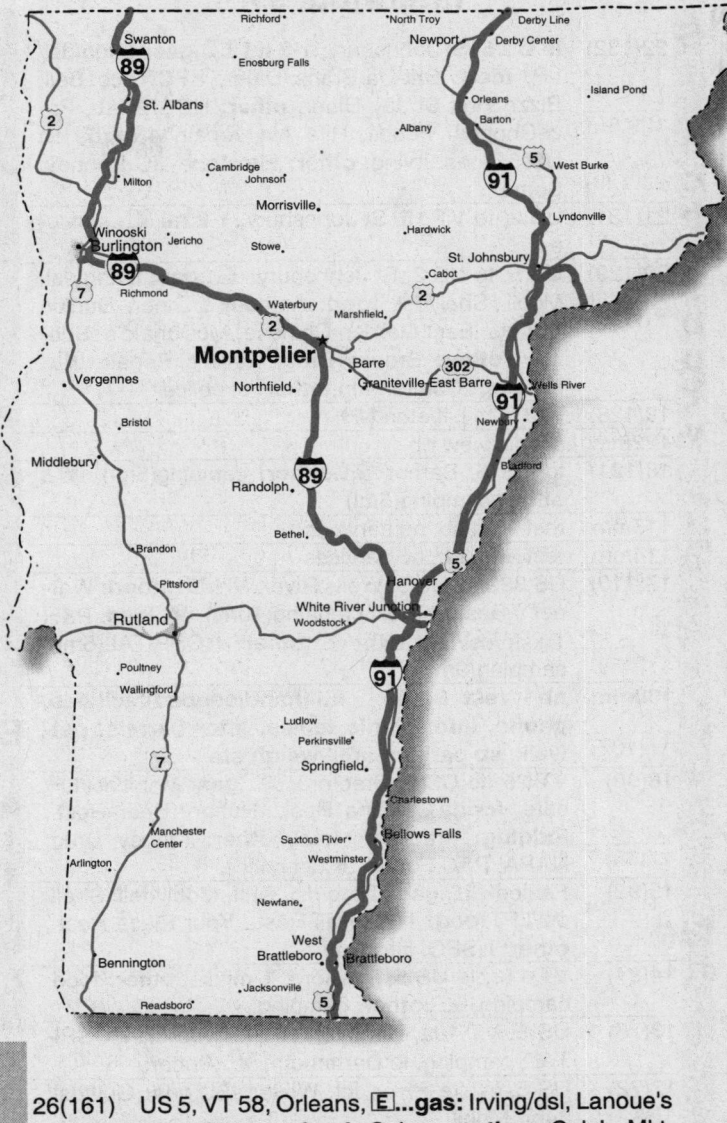

Interstate 91

N ↕ S

Derby Ctr

Exit #	Services
178mm	I-91 begins/ends., US/Canada Border, Vermont state line, US Customs
29(177)	US 5, Derby Line, **E**...Ammex Dutyfree, **1 mi W**...**gas:** Irving/dsl
176.5mm	**Welcome Ctr sb, full(handicapped)facilities, info, picnic tables, litter barrels, phone, pet-walk, Midpoint between the Equator and N Pole**
28(172)	US 5, VT 105, Derby Ctr, **E**...**gas:** Citgo, Exxon/dsl/24hr, Gulf, Mobil/dsl, **food:** Palace Rest., **other:** Bernie's Repair/tires, Cow Fireside Camping, st police, **W**...**gas:** Gulf/Dunkin Donuts/dsl, Mobil, Shell/dsl/24hr, **food:** McDonald's, Roaster's Cafe, Village Pizza, **lodging:** Inn at The Hill, Pepin's Motel, Super 8, **other:** HOSPITAL, Kinney Drug, Parts+, Jeep, Rite Aid, Shop&Save Foods, RV camping
27(170)	VT 191, to US 5, VT 105, Newport, **3 mi W**...**other:** HOSPITAL, Border Patrol, camping, info
167mm	parking area nb, rest area/weigh sta sb
26(161)	US 5, VT 58, Orleans, **E**...**gas:** Irving/dsl, Lanoue's Gas, Sunoco, **food:** Subway, **other:** Cole's Mkt, Orleans Gen Store, camping(8mi)
156.5mm	Barton River
25(156)	VT 16, Barton, **1 mi E**...**gas:** Gulf, Irving/dsl, Mobil/dsl/repair, **food:** Ming's Chinese, Richie's Rest., Village Coffeehouse, **lodging:** PineCrest Motel, **other:** C&C Foods, Ford, USPO, camping(2mi)
154mm	parking area nb
150.5mm	highest elevation on I-91, 1856 ft
143mm	scenic overlook nb
141mm	**rest area sb, full(handicapped)facilities, info, picnic tables, litter barrels, phone**
24(140)	VT 122, Wheelock, **2 mi E**...gas, food, lodging
23(137)	US 5, to VT 114, Lyndonville, **E**...**gas:** Gulf/dsl, Mobil/Dunkin Donuts, **food:** McDonald's, **lodging:** Colonnade Inn, Hoagie's Pizza, **other:** Ace Hardware, NAPA, Rite Aid, White Foods, **W**...**lodging:** Lyndon Motel

VERMONT

Interstate 91

N ↕ S

St Johnsbury

22(132)	to US 5, St Johnsbury, **1-2 mi** E...**gas:** Citgo/dsl/LP, **food:** Brit-Da-Brans Diner, KFC/Taco Bell, Pizza Hut, St Jay Diner, **other:** HOSPITAL, PriceChopper Foods, Rite Aid, repair, 4 mi E on US 5...**gas:** Irving, **other:** Firestone, JC Penney, Sears
21(131)	US 2, to VT 15, St Johnsbury, **1-2 mi** E...services
20(129)	US 5, to US 2, St Johnsbury, E...**gas:** Irving/dsl, Mobil, Shell/dsl, **food:** Anthony's Diner, Dunkin Donuts, East Garden Chinese, McDonald's, Subway, **other:** Brooks Drug, Kevin's Repair, W... **lodging:** Comfort Inn, **other:** st police
19(128)	I-93 S to Littleton NH
122mm	scenic view nb
18(121)	to US 5, Barnet, E...**other:** camping(5mi), W... **other:** camping(5mi)
115mm	rest area sb, no services
114mm	rest area nb, no services
17(110)	US 302, to US 5, Wells River, NH, E...**food:** Warner's Rest., **other:** camping(10mi), W...**gas:** P&H Trkstp/dsl/rest./24hr/@, **other:** HOSPITAL(5mi), camping(9mi)
100mm	**nb rest area, full(handicapped)facilities, phone, info, picnic tables, litter barrels, petwalk, sb parking area/weigh sta**
16(98)	VT 25, to US 5, Bradford, E...**gas:** Mobil/dsl/LP/café, **food:** Colatina Rest., Hungry Bear Rest., **lodging:** Bradford Motel, **other:** Kinney Drug, NAPA, P&C Foods, W...st police
15(92)	Fairlee, E...**gas:** Citgo/dsl, Gulf, Mobil/deli, Shell/dsl/LP, **food:** Third Rail Rest., Your Place Rest., **other:** USPO, camping
14(84)	VT 113, to US 5, Thetford, **1 mi** E...**other:** food, camping, W...**other:** camping
13(75)	US 5, VT 10a, Hanover, NH, E...**other:** HOSPITAL, camping, to Dartmouth, W...Subaru
12(72)	US 5, White River Jct, Wilder, E...**gas:** Gulf/dsl/24hr, Mobil
11(71)	US 5, White River Jct, E...**gas:** Exxon/Subway/dsl, Gulf/dsl, Mobil, Sunoco/repair, **food:** AJ's Steaks, Canton House Rest., China Moon Cafe, Crossroads Café, Gillam's Rest., McDonald's, **lodging:** Coach an' Four Motel, Comfort Inn, Pines Motel, Ramada Inn, **other:** Ford/Lincoln/Mercury/Hyundai, Jct Mktplace, Toyota, USPO, W...**gas:** Citgo, Shell, **lodging:** Best Western, Comfort Suites, Hampton Inn, Holiday Inn Express, Super 8, **other:** HOSPITAL, Saab
10N(70)	I-89 N, to Montpelier, no services
10S	I-89 S, to NH, airport

White River Jct

68mm	**rest area/weigh sta both lanes(7am-11pm), full(handicapped)facilities, picnic tables, litter barrels, phone, vending, petwalk**
9(60)	US 5, VT 12, Hartland, E...HOSPITAL, W...**gas:** Mobil(1mi), info
8(51)	US 5, VT 12, VT 131, Ascutney, E...**gas:** Citgo/dsl, Gulf/dsl, Mobil, Sunoco/dsl, **food:** RedBarn Cafe, Roadside Cafe, **lodging:** Yankee Village Motel, **other:** HOSPITAL, Max' Country Store, USPO
7(42)	US 5, VT 106, VT 11, Springfield, W...**gas:** Mobil/dsl/24hr, **food:** Howard Johnson Rest., **lodging:** Holiday Inn Express, **other:** HOSPITAL, camping
39mm	rest area both lanes, no services
6(34)	US 5, VT 103, to Bellows Falls, Rockingham, E... **gas:** Shell, **lodging:** Every Day Inn, W...**gas:** Sunoco/dsl/24hr, **other:** st police(6mi)
5(29)	VT 121, to US 5, to Bellows Falls, Westminster, **3 mi** E...gas, food, phone, lodging
24mm	rest area both lanes, no services
22mm	weigh sta sb
20mm	parking area nb
4(18)	US 5, Putney, E...**lodging:** Putney Inn/rest., W... **gas:** Sunoco/dsl/LP/24hr, **other:** camping(3mi)
3(11)	US 5, VT 9 E, Brattleboro, E...**gas:** Agway, Citgo/dsl/24hr, Mobil, Sunoco, **food:** Bickford's, Dunkin Donuts, Friendly's, KFC, McDonald's, Pizza Hut, Steak-out Rest., Village Pizza, **lodging:** Best Inn, Colonial Motel, Hampton Inn, Holiday Inn Express, Motel 6, Quality Inn, Super 8, **other:** Ford/Mercury, GNC, Hannaford Foods, Home Depot, NAPA, Pontiac/Buick/GMC, Radio Shack, Rite Aid, Staples, Subaru, U-Haul, USPO
2(9)	VT 9 W, to rd 30, Brattleboro, E...**gas:** Sunoco, W...**gas:** Shell, **food:** Country Deli, **other:** to Marlboro Coll, st police
1(7)	US 5, Brattleboro, E...**gas:** Gulf/dsl, Mobil/Dunkin Donuts, Shell/Subway/dsl, **food:** Burger King, Millenium Pizzaria, VT Inn Pizza, **lodging:** Econolodge, **other:** HOSPITAL, Brooks Drug, CarQuest, Chevrolet/Cadillac, Chrysler/Jeep, PriceChopper Foods, Walgreen, to Ft Dummer SP
6mm	**Welcome Ctr nb, full(handicapped)facilities, info, phone, picnic tables, litter barrels, vending, petwalk, playground**
0mm	Vermont/Massachusetts state line

Brattleboro

Interstate 93
See New Hampshire Interstate 93

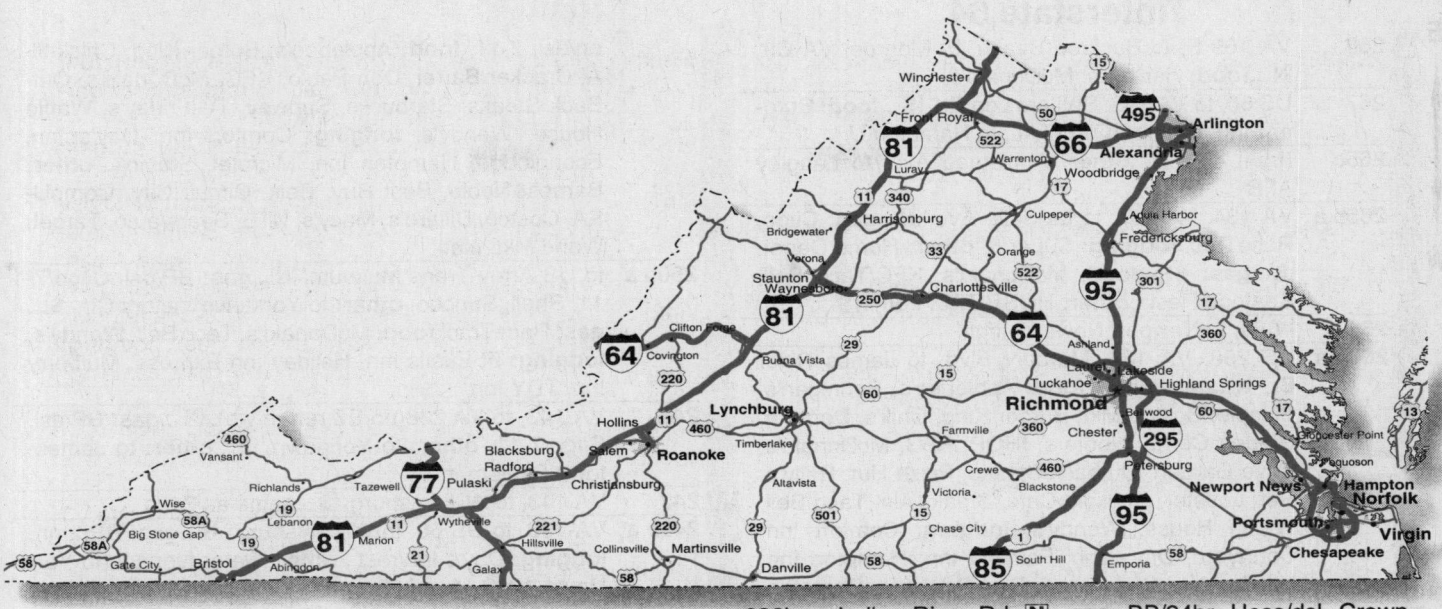

Interstate 64

<table>
<tr><td>E ↑ ↓ W</td><td>Exit #</td><td>Services</td></tr>
<tr><td></td><td>299b a</td><td>I-264 E, to Portsmouth. I-64 begins/ends on I-264.</td></tr>
<tr><td></td><td>297</td><td>US 13, US 460, Military Hwy, N...gas: Exxon</td></tr>
<tr><td></td><td>296b a</td><td>US 17, to Portsmouth, 4 mi S...camping</td></tr>
<tr><td></td><td>294mm</td><td>S Br Elizabeth River</td></tr>
<tr><td></td><td>292</td><td>VA 190, to VA 104(from eb, no EZ return), Dominion Blvd, S...gas: BP, Shell, food: Burger King, Hardee's, other: Family$, Food Lion, Rite Aid</td></tr>
<tr><td></td><td>291b a</td><td>I-464 N, VA 104 S, to Elizabeth City, Outer Banks, same services as 292</td></tr>
<tr><td rowspan="2">N o r f o l k</td><td>290b a</td><td>VA 168, Battlefield Blvd, to Nag's Head, Manteo, N...other: Merchant's Auto Ctr, S...gas: BP/dsl/24hr, Shell/Blimpie, food: Applebee's, Burger King, Chik-fil-A, ChuckeCheese, Dunkin Donuts, Golden Corral, Grand China Buffet, Hardee's, Ryan's, Taco Bell, TGIFriday's, Waffle House, Wendy's, lodging: Day's Inn, Super 8, other: $Tree, Home Depot, K-mart, Lowe's Whse, Sam's Club, Walgreen, Wal-Mart SuperCtr/24hr</td></tr>
<tr><td>289b a</td><td>Greenbrier Pkwy, N...gas: Citgo, food: Burger King, Taco Bell, Wendy's, lodging: Hampton Inn, Holiday Inn, Motel 6, Wellesley Inn, other: Acura, BMW, Chevrolet, Cloth World, Dodge, Food Lion, Ford, Honda, Hyundai, Isuzu, Mitsubishi, Pontiac, Subaru, Volvo, U-Haul, transmissions, S...food: Atlas Grill, Blimpie, Boston Mkt, Cheers Grill, Cooker, Don Pablo, Fazoli's, Fuddruckers, Joe's Crabshack, LoneStar Café, McDonald's, Old Country Buffet, Olive Garden, Panera Bread, Pargo's, Ruby Tuesday, Starbucks, TCBY, Winston's Café, Food Lion, Harris-Teeter/24hr, lodging: Comfort Suites, Courtyard, Extended Stay America, Fairfield Inn, Sun Suites, other: Barnes&Noble, Best Buy, Circuit City, Dillard's, $General, Drug Emporium, Macy's, Marshall's, Michael's, Office Depot, Old Navy, Sears/auto, Target, TJ Maxx, ViVo Italian, mall</td></tr>
</table>

<table>
<tr><td>286b a</td><td>Indian River Rd, N...gas: BP/24hr, Hess/dsl, Crown, Shell, food: Hardee's, S...gas: Sunoco/dsl, food: Capt D's, 7-11, Waffle House, lodging: Founder's Inn</td></tr>
<tr><td>285</td><td>E Branch Elizabeth River</td></tr>
<tr><td>284b a</td><td>I-264, to Norfolk, VA 44, to VA Beach(exits left from eb), 1/2 mi E off 1 exit N, Newtown Rd...gas: BP, Chevron, Exxon, Shell, 7-11, food: Adam's Rest., Denny's/24hr, Golden Corral, Texas Steaks, Wendy's, lodging: Hampton Inn, Holiday Inn, La Quinta, Ramada Inn</td></tr>
<tr><td>282</td><td>US 13, Northampton Blvd, N...lodging: Quality Inn, Sleep Inn, other: to Chesapeake Bay Br Tunnel</td></tr>
<tr><td>281</td><td>VA 165, Military Hwy(no EZ eb return), N...gas: BP/dsl, Shell/dsl/24hr, food: Andy's Pizza, Golden Corral, Pizza Hut, Wendy's, lodging: Econolodge, other: Aamco, Chevrolet/Kia, Chrysler, Food Lion, K-Mart, Mazda/Suzuki, S...gas: Citgo, Exxon, Shell, food: DQ, lodging: Econolodge, Hampton Inn, Hilton, Holiday Inn Select, other: Firestone, Target</td></tr>
<tr><td>279</td><td>Norview Ave, N...gas: Shell, food: Golden Corral, Wendy's, other: K-Mart/gas, to airport & botanical garden</td></tr>
<tr><td>278</td><td>VA 194 S(no EZ return), no services</td></tr>
<tr><td>277b a</td><td>VA 168, to Tidewater Dr, N...gas: Citgo/7-11, food: Hardee's</td></tr>
<tr><td>276c</td><td>to US 460 W, VA 165, Little Creek Rd, N...gas: Shell, S...gas: BP, Exxon, food: McDonald's, Mr Jim's Submarines, KFC, Taco Bell, Wendy's, other: AutoZone, Eckerd, Farm Fresh, Hannaford Foods, Kroger</td></tr>
<tr><td>276b a</td><td>I-564 to Naval Base</td></tr>
<tr><td>274</td><td>Bay Ave(from wb), to Naval Air Sta</td></tr>
<tr><td>273</td><td>US 60, 4th View St, Oceanview, N...gas: BP/dsl/24hr, lodging: Econolodge, Super 8(1mi), other: Harrison Boathouse/Pier, S...other: to Norfolk Visitors Ctr, info</td></tr>
<tr><td>272</td><td>W Ocean View Ave, N...food: Willoughby's Seafood, S...food: Fisherman's Wharf Rest., lodging: Day's Inn</td></tr>
<tr><td>270mm</td><td>Chesapeake Bay Tunnel</td></tr>
<tr><td>269mm</td><td>weigh sta eb</td></tr>
</table>

Interstate 64

268	VA 169 E, to Buckroe Beach, Ft Monroe, VA Ctr, N...food: Hardee's, McDonald's
267	US 60, to VA 143, Settlers Ldg Rd, S...food: Burger King, other: HOSPITAL, to Hampton U
265c	(from eb), N...other: Armistead Ave, to Langley AFB
265b a	VA 134, VA 167, to La Salle Ave, N...gas: Citgo, RaceTrac, lodging: Super 8, other: Home Depot, S...gas: BP, food: McDonald's, KFC/Taco Bell, Seafood Rest., other: HOSPITAL, Family$
264	I-664, to Newport News, Suffolk
263b a	US 258, VA 134, Mercury Blvd, to James River Br, N...gas: Shell, food: Applebee's, Bennigan's, Blimpie, Boston Mkt, Burger King, Chili's, Denny's, Golden Corral, Hooters, IHOP, KFC, McDonald's, Olive Garden, Outback Steaks, Pizza Hut, Rally's, Red Lobster, Rockola Café, Steak&Ale, Taco Bell, Waffle House, Wendy's, lodging: Comfort Inn, Courtyard, Day's Inn, Fairfield Inn, Hampton Inn, Holiday Inn, Quality Inn, Red Roof Inn, Sheraton, other: Chevrolet/Mazda, Chrysler/Jeep, Ford, JC Penney, NAPA, Office Depot, Target, Wal-Mart SuperCtr/24hr, S...gas: Citgo/7-11, Miller's Gas, food: Crabber's, Cracker Barrel, Lone Star Steaks, Old Country Buffet, Pizza Hut, Sonic, Texas Steaks, Waffle House, lodging: Best Western, Econolodge, Interstate Inn, La Quinta, Savannah Suites, other: Advance Parts, Auto Express, BassPro Shop, BigLots, CarQuest, Circuit City, $General, Lowe's Whse, Nissan, PepBoys, Radio Shack, Toyota, Volvo
262	VA 134, Magruder Blvd(from wb, no EZ return), N...gas: Citgo/7-11, Exxon, other: Dodge/Acura
261b a	Center Pkwy, to Hampton Roads, S...gas: Citgo, food: ChuckeCheese, Cujo's Grill, McDonald's, Peking Chinese, Ruby Tuesday, Subway, Taco Bell, Topeka's Steaks, other: BooksAMillion, $Tree, Eckerd, FarmFresh Foods, FoodLion, TJMaxx
258	US 17, J Clyde Morris Blvd, N...gas: BP, Shell/dsl, Sunoco, food: Chatfield's Grill, Domino's, Hardee's, New China, Waffle House, lodging: BudgetLodge, Holiday Inn, Host Inn, PointPlaza Hotel, Super 8, other: Advance Parts, $General, Food Lion, Rite Aid, 7-11/24hr, S...gas: Citgo/dsl/24hr, Exxon, Kangaroo, WaWa, food: Angelo's Steaks, BBQ, Burger King, Hong Kong Chinese, Papa John's, Pizza Hut, Subway, Taco Bell/KFC, lodging: Motel 6, Omni Hotel/rest., other: HOSPITAL, BMW/Honda, $Tree, Eckerd, Radio Shack, museum
256b a	Victory Blvd, Oyster Point Rd, N...gas: BP, Citgo/dsl, Shell, food: Arby's, Burger King, Chick-fil-A, FarmFresh Deli, Fuddrucker's, Hardee's, Starbucks, lodging: CandleWood Suites, Courtyard, Hampton Inn, Hilton Garden, TownePlace
255b a	VA 143, to Jefferson Ave, N...gas: BP, Shell/dsl, food: Castle Italian, Golden Corral, lodging: Travelodge(2mi), other: HOSPITAL, Aamco, Acura, Cadillac/GMC, FarmFresh Foods/deli, Home Depot, Lowe's Whse, Sam's Club/gas, Wal-Mart SuperCtr/24hr, Saturn, airport, S...gas: Citgo, Exx-

	on/dsl, 7-11, food: Applebee's, Burger King, Chick-fil-A, Cracker Barrel, Don Pablo, KFC, McDonald's, Out-Back Steaks, Starbucks, Subway, TGIFriday's, Waffle House, Wendy's, lodging: Comfort Inn, Day's Inn, Econolodge, Hampton Inn, Microtel, Studio+, other: Barnes&Noble, Best Buy, Belk, Circuit City, CompUSA, Costco, Dillard's, Macy's, NTB, Sears/auto, Target, World Mkt, mall
250b a	to US Army Trans Museum, N...gas: BP/dsl, Citgo/7-11, Shell, Sunoco, other: to Yorktown Victory Ctr, S...gas: RaceTrac, food: McDonald's, Taco Bell, Wendy's, lodging: Ft Eustis Inn, Holiday Inn Express, Mulberry Inn, TDY Inn
247	VA 143, to VA 238(no EZ return wb), N...gas: BP/dsl, Citgo/7-11, other: to Yorktown, S...other: to Jamestown Settlement
243	VA 143, to Williamsburg, S...same as 242a
242b a	VA 199, to US 60, to Williamsburg, N...gas: BP(2mi), lodging: Day's Inn/rest., other: water funpark, to Yorktown NHS, 1 mi S...gas: Citgo/7-11, Crown Gas, Shell, Starbucks, Subway, Wendy's, food: Burger King, LJ Silver, McDonald's, Wendy's, lodging: Courtyard, Howard Johnson, Marriott/rest., Quality Inn, Rodeway Inn, other: 1st Settlers Camping, to William&Mary Coll, Busch Gardens, to Jamestown NHS
238	VA 143, to Colonial Williamsburg, Camp Peary, 2-3 mi S...gas: Citgo/7-11, Shell, food: Cracker Barrel, Golden Corral, Hardee's, Ledo's Pizza, McDonald's, Pizzaria Uno, lodging: Best Western/rest., Comfort Inn, Country Hearth Inn, Day's Inn, Econolodge, Hampton Inn, Holiday Inn/rest., Homewood Suites, Howard Johnson/rest., King William Inn, Quality Inn/rest., Red Roof Inn, other: HOSPITAL, Anvil Camping
234	VA 646, to Lightfoot, 1-2 mi N...other: KOA, 2-3 mi S...gas: Exxon/dsl, Mobil/dsl, Shell/dsl, food: BBQ, Burger King, Hardee's, KFC, Lightfoot Rest., McDonald's, Sonic, Subway, lodging: Colonial Hotel, Day's Inn, Quality Inn, Super 8, other: Ford/Lincoln/Mercury, Home Depot, Lowe's Whse, Pottery Camping(3mi), Wal-Mart SuperCtr/24hr
231b a	VA 607, to Norge, Croaker, N...gas: Citgo/7-11, other: American Heritage RV Park, to York River SP, 1-2 mi S...gas: Shell/dsl, food: FarmFresh Deli, KFC, Candle Factory Rest., Wendy's, lodging: Econolodge, Quality Inn, Red Roof Inn
227	VA 30, to US 60, to West Point, Toano, N...food: StoneHouse Cafe, S...gas: Exxon/dsl/LP, Shell/Stuckey's/dsl, food: McDonald's
220	VA 33 E, to West Point, N...gas: Exxon/dsl
214	VA 155, to New Kent, Providence Forge, S...gas: Exxon/dsl, food: DQ, Pepito's Mexican, other: Colonial Downs Racetrack, Rockahock Camping(8mi)
213mm	rest area both lanes, full(handicapped)facilities, phone, vending, picnic tables, litter barrels, pet-walk
211	VA 106, to Talleysville, to James River Plantations
205	VA 33, VA 249, to US 60, Bottoms Bridge, Quinton, N...gas: BP/dsl, Exxon/dsl, food: New Peking Chinese, Subway, other: Eckerd, Food Lion, USPO, S...gas: Shell/dsl, food: McDonald's, MarketPlace Foods

Hampton

Williamsburg

VIRGINIA

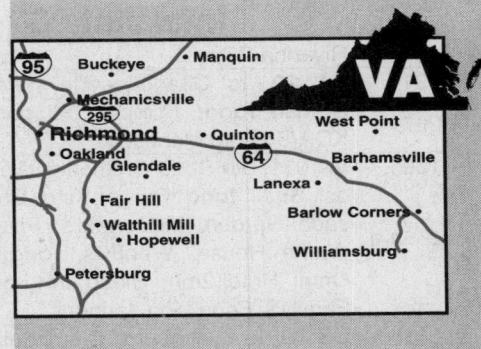

Interstate 64

204mm	Chickahominy River
203mm	weigh sta both lanes
200	I-295, N to Washington, S to Rocky Mount, to US 60
197b a	VA 156, Airport Dr, to Highland Springs, ...gas: BP/dsl, Citgo/7-11, Shell/dsl, food: Bojangles, Domino's, Hardee's, Pizza Hut, Subway, other: Advance Parts, CVS Drug, Winn-Dixie, S...gas: BP, EC/dsl, Shell/dsl, food: Arby's, Aunt Sarah's, Burger King, Waffle House, lodging: Comfort Inn, Courtyard, Day's Inn, DoubleTree, Econolodge, Hampton Inn, Hilton/rest., Microtel, Motel 6, Super 8, Wingate Inn, other: to airport
195	Laburnum Ave, N...gas: Chevron/repair, Shell, S...gas: Applebee's, food: Subway, Taco Bell, other: Ukrop's Foods, 3/4 mi S...gas: BP/24hr, Exxon, 7-11, food: Aunt Sarah's, Bojangles, Burger King, Capt D's, China King, DQ, Hardee's, KFC, McDonald's, Papa John's, Wendy's, Western Sizzlin, lodging: Airport Inn, Hampton Inn, Holiday Inn, Sheraton/rest., Super 8, Wyndham Garden, other: CVS Drug, $General, $Tree, Firestone/auto, Ford, Hannaford Foods, Radio Shack, Rite Aid, Trak Auto
193b a	VA 33, Nine Mile Rd, N...gas: BP, Exxon/Subway, food: Burger King, McDonald's, S...HOSPITAL
192	US 360, to Mechanicsville, N...gas: Chevron, Citgo/dsl, food: McDonald's, S...gas: BP, Citgo, food: Church's, Hook's Rest.
190	I-95 S, to Petersburg, 5th St, N...other: Richmond Nat Bfd Park, S...lodging: Marriott, other: st capitol, coliseum.
	I-64 W and I-95 N run together. See Virginia Interstate 95, exits 76-78.
187	I-95 N(exits left from eb), to Washington
186	I-195, to Powhite Pkwy, Richmond
185b a	US 33, Staples Mill Rd, Dickens Rd
183	US 250, Broad St, Glenside Dr, N...gas: Chevron/DQ, food: Bob Evans, lodging: Best Western, Comfort Inn, Embassy Suites, other: K-Mart, same as 181, S...other: HOSPITAL, to U of Richmond
181	Parham Rd, N on Broad...gas: BP/24hr, Citgo, Crown/dsl, Exxon, Shell, food: Aunt Sarah's, Bennigan's, Blue Marlin Seafood, Bojangles, Burger King, Casa Grande Mexican, Famous Dave's BBQ, Friendly's, Fuddruckers, Hardee's, Hooters, KFC, LoneStar Steaks, LJ Silver, Olive Garden, OutBack Steaks, Piccadilly's, Red Lobster, Shoney's, Steak&Ale, Taco Bell, TGIFriday, Waffle House, Wendy's, lodging: Fairfield Inn, Quality Inn, Suburban Lodge, Super 8, other: HOSPITAL, BooksA-Million, CVS Drug, Ford/Lincoln/Mercury, Honda/ Mitsubishi, Hyundai/Subaru, Infiniti, Mazda/BMW, Mercedes, Nissan, PepBoys, Staples, Toyota, Ukrop's Foods, transmissions, 1 mi S...gas: BP, Exxon, food: McDonald's, Topeka Steaks, lodging: Ramada Inn
180	Gaskins Rd, N...gas: BP/24hr, Shell/dsl, food: O'Charley's, lodging: Courtyard, Holiday Inn Express, Residence Inn, Studio+, N on Broad...food:

	Applebee's, Arby's, Blackeyed Pea, Boston Mkt, Burger King, Golden Corral, IHOP, KFC, McDonald's, Peking Chinese, Rockola Café, Ruby Tuesday's, Ryan's, Subway, Taco Bell, Tripp's Rest., Wendy's, Zorba's Greek/ Italian, other: Borders Books, Cadillac, Chrysler/Jeep, Circuit City, Costco, Drug Emporium, Evans Foods, Food Lion, Fresh Fields Foods, Goodyear/auto, Hannaford Foods, Lowe's Whse, Sam's Club, VW, mall
178b a	US 250, Short Pump, N...gas: BP/dsl, Citgo, Exxon/ dsl, Shell/dsl, food: Leonardo's Pizza, Starbucks, Thai Garden Rest., lodging: AmeriSuites, Comfort Suites, Hampton Inn, Hilton Garden, Homestead Village, Homewood Suites, other: CompUSA, Firestone/auto, 1 mi S...gas: BP, Citgo/7-11, Crown, food: Burger King, Capt D's, Domino's, McDonald's, Taco Bell, TGI-Friday, Wendy's, lodging: Candlewood Suites, other: Barnes&Noble, Best Buy, CarQuest, Goodyear/auto, Home Depot, Kohl's, Lowe's Whse, Target, Ukrop's Foods, Wal-Mart SuperCtr/24hr
177	I-295, to I-95 N to Washington, to Norfolk, VA Beach, Williamsburg
175	VA 288, no services
173	VA 623, to Rockville, Manakin, N...gas: Citgo(2mi), S...gas: BP/DQ/dsl, Exxon/dsl(1mi), Shell/dsl, food: BBQ, lodging: Alley's Motel(1mi), other: $General, Food Lion
169mm	**rest area both lanes, full(handicapped)facilities, vending, phone, picnic tables, litter barrels, petwalk**
167	VA 617, to Goochland, Oilville, N...gas: Exxon, S... gas: BP/Bullets/dsl/24hr
159	US 522, to Goochland, Gum Spring, N...gas: Exxon/ dsl/mart, S...gas: BP(2mi), Citgo, food: DQ
152	VA 629, Hadensville, S...other: Royal VA Golf/rest.
148	VA 605, Shannon Hill, no services
143	VA 208, to Louisa, Ferncliff, 7 mi N...other: Small Country Camping, S...gas: Citgo/dsl, Exxon/dsl
136	US 15, to Gordonsville, Zion Crossroads, S...gas: BP/ McDonald's/dsl/24hr, Citgo/Blimpie/dsl, Exxon/Burger King/dsl, Shell/dsl, lodging: Crescent Inn/rest., Zion Roads Motel
129	VA 616, Keswick, Boyd Tavern, N...lodging: Keswick Hotel, S...gas: BP(1mi)
124	US 250, to Shadwell, 2 mi N...gas: BP, Liberty, Shell, food: Aunt Sarah's, Burger King, McDonald's, Ponderosa, Taco Bell, Wendy's, lodging: Town&Country Motel, White House Motel, other: HOSPITAL, S... lodging: Ramada Inn

VIRGINIA

Interstate 64

E ↑ W

C h a r l o t t e s v i l l e

123mm	Rivanna River
121	VA 20, to Charlottesville, Scottsville, **N**...gas: BP/dsl, **food:** Blimpie, **S**...**gas:** Exxon, **other:** KOA(9mi), to Monticello
120	VA 631, 5th St, to Charlottesville, **N**...gas: Exxon/dsl, Shell, **food:** Burger King, Domino's, Hardee's, Jade Garden, McDonald's, Pizza Hut/Taco Bell, Waffle House, Wendy's, **lodging:** Holiday Inn, Omni Hotel(2mi), Sleep Inn, **other:** CVS Drug, Family$, Food Lion, laundry
118b a	US 29, to Lynchburg, Charlottesville, **1-4 mi N**... **gas:** BP, Citgo/dsl, Exxon, Shell, **food:** Blimpie, Hardee's, Shoney's, Subway, **lodging:** Best Western, Boar's Head Inn, Budget Inn, English Inn, Econolodge, **other:** HOSPITAL, UVA, **S**...gas: Exxon/dsl
114	VA 637, to Ivy, no services
113mm	**rest area wb, full(handicapped)facilities, phone, vending, picnic tables, litter barrels, petwalk**
111mm	Mechum River
108mm	Stockton Creek
107	US 250, Crozet, **1 mi N**...**gas:** Exxon, **1 mi S**... **other:** Misty Mtn Camping
105mm	**rest area eb, full(handicapped)facilities, phone, vending, picnic tables, litter barrels, petwalk**
104mm	scenic area eb, litter barrels, no truck or buses
100mm	scenic area eb, litter barrels, hist marker, no trucks or buses
99	US 250, to Waynesboro, Afton, **N**...**lodging:** Colony Motel, **other:** to Shenandoah NP, Skyline Drive, ski area, to Blue Ridge Pkwy, **S**...**lodging:** Afton Inn
96	VA 622, to Lyndhurst, Waynesboro, **3 mi N**...**gas:** Shell, Quality Inn
95mm	South River
94	US 340, to Stuarts Draft, Waynesboro, **N**...**gas:** Citgo/7-11/dsl, Exxon/dsl, **food:** Arby's, Burger King, KFC, Shoney's, S River Grill, Taco Bell(1mi), Wendy's, Western Sizzlin, **lodging:** Best Western, Day's Inn, Deluxe Motel(2mi), Holiday Inn Express, Skyline Motel(2mi), Super 8, **other:** HOSPITAL, Waynesboro N 340 Camping(9mi), **S**...gas: Shell/dsl, **other:** Waynesboro Outlet Village, museum

L e x i n g t o n

91	Va 608, to Stuarts Draft, Fishersville, **N**...**gas:** Shell/dsl, **lodging:** Hampton Inn, **other:** HOSPITAL, **S**... **gas:** Exxon/McDonald's, **other:** Shenadoah Acres Camping(8mi), **other:** Walnut Hills Camping(9mi)
89mm	Christians Creek
87	I-81, N to Harrisonburg, S to Roanoke
	I-64 and I-81 run together 20 miles. See Interstate 81, exits 195-220.
56	I-81, S to Roanoke, N to Harrisonburg
50	US 60, VA 623, to Lexington, **3 mi S**...**lodging:** Day's Inn
43	VA 780, to Goshen, no services
35	VA 269, VA 850, Longdale Furnace, **S**...**lodging:** Longdale Inn, **2 mi S**...**lodging:** North Mtn Motel
33mm	truck rest area eb

C o v i n g t o n

29	VA 269, VA 850, **S**...**gas:** Exxon/dsl/rest.
27	US 60 W, US 220 S, VA 629, Clifton Forge, **N**... **other:** to Douthat SP, Alleghany Highlands Arts/crafts, Buckhorne Camping(2mi), **S**...**gas:** Citgo/dsl, Exxon, **lodging:** The Park Motel
24	US 60, US 220, Clifton Forge, **1 mi S**...**gas:** Shell/dsl, **food:** DQ, Hardee's, Taco Bell
21	to VA 696, Low Moor, **S**...HOSPITAL
16	US 60 W, US 220 N, to Hot Springs, Covington, **N**...**gas:** BPEtna, Exxon/Burger King/24hr, Shell, **food:** Western Sizzlin, **lodging:** Best Value Inn, Best Western, Holiday Inn Express, **other:** Buick/Pontiac/GMC, to ski area, **S**...**food:** McDonald's, **lodging:** Comfort Inn, **other:** $General, K-Mart, Radio Shack
14	VA 154, to Hot Springs, Covington, **N**...**gas:** Exxon/Arby's, Sunoco, **food:** Great Wall Chinese, Hardee's, KFC, Little Caesar's, Subway, Wendy's, **lodging:** Budget Motel, Highland Motel, Townhouse Motel, **other:** Advance Parts, AutoZone, CVS Drug, Family$, Food Lion, Kroger, **S**...**food:** China House, Mama Pizza, **other:** $Tree, GNC, Wal-Mart SuperCtr/24hr
10	US 60 E, VA 159 S, Callaghan, **S**...**gas:** Marathon/dsl/LP
7	VA 661, no services
2.5mm	**Welcome Ctr eb, full(handicapped)facilities, phone, picnic tables, litter barrels, petwalk**
1	Jerry's Run Trail, **N**...to Allegheny Trail
0mm	Virginia/West Virginia state line

Interstate 66

E ↑ W

D C   A r e a

Exit #	Services
77mm	Independence Ave, to Lincoln Mem. I-66 begins/ends in Washington, DC.
76mm	Potomac River, T Roosevelt Memorial Bridge
75	US 50 W(from eb), to Arlington Blvd, G Wash Pkwy, I-395, US 1, **S**...Iwo Jima Mon
73	US 29, Lee Hwy, Key Bridge, to Rosslyn, **N**...**lodging:** Marriott, **S**...**lodging:** Best Western, Holiday Inn
72	to US 29, Lee Hwy, Spout Run Pkwy(from eb, no EZ return), **N**...**gas:** Shell, **lodging:** Virginia Inn, **S**... **food:** Chick's Cafe, **other:** CVS Drug, Eckerd/24hr, Starbucks, Giant Foods
71	VA 120, Glebe Rd(no EZ return from wb), **N**...HOSPITAL, **S**...**gas:** Circle K, Mobil, **food:** Blackeyed Pea, **lodging:** Comfort Inn, Holiday Inn
69	US 29, Sycamore St, Falls Church, **N**...**gas:** Exxon, **S**...**lodging:** Econolodge
68	Westmoreland St(from eb), same as 69
67	to I-495 N(from wb), to Baltimore, Dulles Airport
66	VA 7, Leesburg Pike, to Tysons Corner, Falls Church, **N**...**gas:** Exxon, **food:** China King, Jerry's Subs/Pizza, Starbucks, TCBY, **other:** Whole Foods Mkt, **S**... **gas:** Citgo, **food:** LJ Silver, McDonald's
64b a	I-495 S, to Richmond

Interstate 66

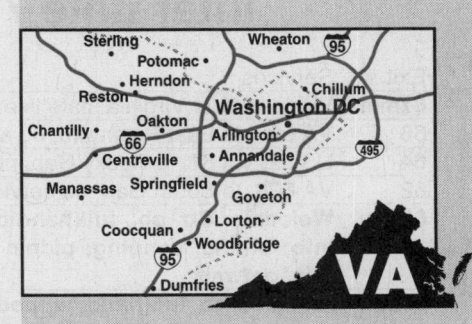

62	VA 243, Nutley St, to Vienna, **S...gas:** Exxon, **other:** CVS Drug, **1 mi S on Lee Hwy...gas:** Chevron, Citgo, Shell, Sunoco/dsl, **food:** Applebee's, IHOP/24hr, LoneStar Steaks, McDonald's, Subway, TCBY, **lodging:** Econolodge, **other:** Harley-Davidson, Jeep, Radio Shack, Safeway, Saturn, Kia
60	VA 123, to Fairfax, **S...gas:** Exxon, Shell/24hr, Sunoco, **food:** Denny's, Fuddrucker's, Hooters, Indian Cuisine, KFC, Outback Steaks, Red Lobster, 29 Diner, **lodging:** Best Western, Welsley, **other:** Buick/Isuzu, Chevrolet, Chrysler/Dodge, Ford/Lincoln/Mercury, Honda, Hyundai, Mazda, Rite Aid, Toyota, to George Mason U
57a b	US 50, to Dulles Airport, **N...food:** Bennigans, Subway, **lodging:** Extended Stay America, Holiday Inn, **other:** JC Penney, Lord&Taylor, Macy's, Sears/auto, mall, **S...gas:** BP, Shell/dsl, **food:** Burger King, Ruby Tuesday, Wendy's, **lodging:** Candlewood Suites, Comfort Inn/rest., Courtyard, Hampton Inn, **other:** Borders Books, Circuit City, Ford, Giant Foods, Honda, VW
56mm	weigh sta both lanes
55	Fairfax Co Pkwy, to US 29, **N...4 Lakes Mall, gas:** Exxon, Mobil, **food:** Applebee's, Blue Iguana Café, Burger King, Cooker Rest., Don Pablo, Eatery Rest., FoodCourt, Fresh Fare Rest., Olive Garden, Pizza Hut, Red Robin, TCBY, TGIFriday, Tony's Pizza, Wendy's, **lodging:** Hyatt Hotel, **other:** HOSPITAL, Barnes&Noble, Best Buy, BJ's Whse, CompUSA, Food Lion, Galyan's, Kohl's, Michael's, Radio Shack, Target, Wal-Mart
53b a	VA 28, to Centreville, Dulles Airport, Manassas Museum, **S...gas:** Mobil/dsl, **food:** Chesapeake Bay Seafood, Jake's Rest., LoneStar Steaks, McDonald's, **lodging:** SpringHill Suites, **other:** Drug Emporium, Giant Foods, Jo-Ann Fabrics, Peoples Drug, same as 52
52	US 29, to Bull Run Park, Centreville, **N...gas:** Mobil, **other:** Goodyear/auto, **S...gas:** Exxon, Mobil/dsl, 7-11, **food:** BBQ, Carrabba's, Copeland's Café, Domino's, Hunter Mill Deli, LoneStar Steaks, McDonald's, Quizno's, Ruby Tuesday, Wendy's, **other:** SpringHill Suites, **other:** CVS Drug, Jo-Ann Fabrics, Radio Shack, Shoppers Foods, Tire Express, same as 53
49mm	**rest area both lanes, full(facilities)facilities, phone, picnic tables, litter barrels, petwalk**
47b a	VA 234, to Manassas, **N...gas:** Shell/dsl, **food:** Chicago Pizza, Cracker Barrel, Golden Corral, Uno Pizzaria, Wendy's, **lodging:** Country Inn Suites, Courtyard, Fairfield Inn, Holiday Inn, **other:** Borders, Kohl's, Old Navy, Manassas Nat Bfd, **S...gas:** BP, Citgo/7-11, Exxon, RaceTrac/dsl/24hr, Shell/repair, Sunoco/24hr, **food:** American Steak/buffet, Anita's Mexican, Arby's, Bertucci's Pizza, Blimpie, Bob Evans, Boston Mkt, Burger King, Checker's, Chelsea's Rest., Chili's, Chipotle Mexican, Damon's, Denny's, Domino's, Don Pablo's, Hooters, KFC, Little Caesar's, Logan's Roadhouse, McDonald's, Old Country Buffet, Olive Garden, Pizza Hut, Red Lobster, Ruby Tuesday, Schlotsky's, Shoney's, Starbucks, Subway, Taco Bell, TGIFriday, Wendy's, Wok'n Roll, Zipani

Manassas

	Bread Café, **lodging:** Best Western, Comfort Suites, Day's Inn, Hampton Inn, Red Roof Inn, Super 8, **other:** Aamco, Barnes&Noble, Best Buy, Camping World RV Service/supples, Circuit City, Costco/gas, CVS Drug, Chevrolet, Food Lion, Giant Foods, GMC/Pontiac, Home Depot, Honda, JC Penney, K-Mart, Lowe's Whse, Macy's, Marshall's, Merchant Auto Ctr, NTB, Office Depot, PepBoys, Reines RV Ctr, Saturn, Sears/auto, Shoppers Club, Staples, Super Fresh Foods, U-Haul, Upton's, Wal-Mart
44	VA 234, Manassas, airport
43b a	US 29, to Warrenton, Gainesville, **S...gas:** Citgo/7-11, Mobil, RaceTrac, Shell/dsl/24hr, **food:** Burger King, Joe's Italian/pizza, KFC/Pizza Hut/Taco Bell, McDonald's, Steakmaster's Grill, Subway, Wendy's, **other:** Giant Foods/drug, Hillwood Camping, Lowe's Whse, Target/foods
40	US 15, Haymarket, **N...other:** Greenville Farm Camping, **S...gas:** Mobil/dsl/24hr, Sheetz/dsl/24hr, **food:** McDonald's, Subway
31	VA 245, to Old Tavern, **1 mi N...gas:** BP/dsl
28	US 17 S, Marshall, **N...gas:** BP/McDonald's/dsl, **food:** Foster's Grille, Great Wall Chinese, Subway, **other:** HOSPITAL, FoodLion, Radio Shack
27	VA 55 E, VA 647, Marshall, **1 mi N...gas:** Chevron/dsl/LP, Exxon/dsl, **food:** Marshall Diner
23	US 17 N, VA 55, Delaplane(no eb re-entry)
20mm	Goose Creek
18	VA 688, Markham, no services
13	VA 79, to VA 55, Linden, Front Royal, **S...gas:** Exxon/dsl/24hr, Mobil/24hr, **food:** Applehouse Rest., **4-5 mi S...food:** Burger King, KFC, **lodging:** Center City Motel, Hampton Inn, Quality Inn, Pioneer Motel, Super 8, **other:** Goonie Creek Camping(10mi), KOA(seasonal), to Shenandoah NP, Skyline Drive, ski area
11mm	Manassas Run
7mm	Shenandoah River
6	US 340, US 522, to Winchester, Front Royal, **N...gas:** Quarle's/Bullet's/dsl, **other:** Ford, **S...gas:** Exxon/Dunkin Doughnuts, Shell, **food:** McDonald's, **lodging:** Hampton Inn, **other:** HOSPITAL, **1-3 mi S...gas:** East Coast, Shell, **food:** Arby's, Hardee's, Pizza Hut, Tastee Freez Rest., Wendy's, **lodging:** Bluemont Motel, Blue Ridge Motel, Budget Inn, Cool Harbor, Front Royal Motel, Relax Inn, Shenandoah Motel, Super 8, Twin Rivers Motel, **other:** Gooney Creek Camping(7mi), KOA(6mi), Southfork Camping(2mi)
1b a	I-81, N to Winchester, S to Roanoke
0mm	I-66 begins/ends on I-81, exit 300.

VIRGINIA

Interstate 77

N ↕ S

Wytheville

Exit #	Services
67mm	Virginia/West Virginia state line, East River Mtn
66	VA 598, to East River Mtn, no services
64	US 52, VA 61, to Rocky Gap, no services
62	VA 606, to South Gap, no services
62mm	**Welcome Ctr sb, full(handicapped) facilities, info, phone, vending, picnic tables, litter barrels, petwalk**
60mm	**rest area nb, full(handicapped)facilities, phone, vending, picnic tables, litter barrels, petwalk**
58	US 52, to Bastian, E...gas: BP/dsl, food: Front Porch Cafe, W...gas: Citgo/dsl, Exxon/dsl
56mm	runaway ramp nb
52	US 52, VA 42, Bland, E...gas: Citgo, food: Subway, other: $General, W...gas: Shell/DQ/dsl, food: Log Cabin Rest., lodging: Big Walker Motel
51.5mm	weigh sta both lanes
48mm	Big Walker Mtn
47	VA 717, 6 mi W...other: to Deer Trail Park/NF Camping
41	VA 610, Peppers Ferry, Wytheville, E...food: Sagebrush Steaks, lodging: Best Western, Sleep Inn, Super 8, W...gas: Kangaroo/dsl/scales/24hr, TA/BP/Subway/Taco Bell/dsl/scales/24hr/@, food: Country Kitchen, lodging: Comfort Suites, Hampton Inn, Ramada/rest., Travelite
40	I-81 S, to Bristol, US 52 N
	I-77 and I-81 run together 9 mi. See Interstate 81, exits 73-80.
32	I-81 N, to Roanoke
26mm	New River
24	VA 69, to Poplar Camp, E...gas: Pure/gas, other: to Shot Tower SP, New River Trail Info Ctr, W...gas: Citgo/dsl
19	VA 620, airport
14	US 58, US 221, to Hillsville, Galax, E...gas: Citgo/Subway, food: Peking Palace, lodging: Red Carpet Inn, other: HOSPITAL, W...gas: BP/24hr, Cockerham's Trkstp/dsl/24hr, Exxon/DQ/dsl, Marathon, Shell, food: Countryside Rest., McDonald's, Pizza Inn/TCBY, Shoney's, Wendy's, lodging: Best Western, Comfort Inn, Hampton Inn, Holiday Inn Express, Super 8, other: Carrollwood Camping(1mi)
8	VA 148, VA 775, to Fancy Gap, E...gas: Chevron(2mi), Citgo/dsl, lodging: Lakeview Motel/rest., Mountaintop Motel/rest., other: Fox Trail Camping, Utt's Camping, to Blue Ridge Pkwy, W...gas: BP, Kangaroo/dsl, lodging: Countryview Inn, Day's Inn
6.5mm	runaway truck ramp sb
4.5mm	runaway truck ramp sb
3mm	runaway truck ramp sb
1	VA 620, no services
.5mm	**Welcome Ctr nb, full(handicapped) facilities, info, phone, picnic tables, litter barrels, petwalk**
0mm	Virginia/North Carolina state line

Interstate 81

Winchester

Exit #	Services
324mm	Virginia/West Virginia state line
323	RD 669, to US 11, Whitehall, E...gas: Exxon, W...gas: ✈/Flying J/Country Mkt/dsl/LP/scales/24hr/@
321	RD 672, Clearbrook, E...gas: Citgo/dsl, food: Olde Stone Rest.
320mm	**Welcome Ctr sb, full(handicapped)facilities, phone, vending, picnic tables, litter barrels, petwalk**
317	US 11, Stephenson, W...gas: Citgo, Exxon/dsl, Liberty/Blimpie/dsl, Sheetz/dsl/24hr, food: Burger King, Denny's, McDonald's, Pizza Hut/Taco Bell, Tastee Freez, Venice Italian, lodging: Comfort Inn, Econolodge, Holiday Inn Express(3mi), other: HOSPITAL
315	VA 7, Winchester, E...gas: Exxon, Sheetz/24hr, food: Quizno's, Starbucks, other: Dodge, Martin's Foods, PetCo, W...gas: Chevron/dsl, Exxon/Subway, Liberty/dsl, Shell/dsl, food: Arby's, Camino Real Mexican, KFC, LJ Silver, McDonald's, Pizza Hut, Sam's Hot Dogs, Wendy's, lodging: Hampton Inn, Shoney's Inn/rest., other: AutoZone, CVS Drug, Food Lion,
314mm	Abrams Creek
313	US 17/50/522, Winchester, E...gas: BP/dsl, Exxon, Shell/dsl, food: Asian Garden, Cracker Barrel, Golden Corral, Hoss' Steaks, IHOP, Los Tolteco's Mexican, Perkin's, Texas Steaks, Waffle House, lodging: Comfort Inn, Holiday Inn, Fairfield Inn, Red Roof Inn, Sleep Inn, Super 8, Travelodge, other: Big Lots, Costco/gas, Food Lion, Harley-Davidson, Jo-Ann Fabrics, Nissan, W...gas: Sheetz/24hr, food: Bob Evans, Chick-fil-A, Chili's, China Jade, CiCi's, KFC, McDonald's, Olive Garden, Panda Express, Pargo's, Perkins, Pizza Hut/Taco Bell, Rancho Mexican, Red Lobster, Ruby Tuesday, Sam's Hotdogs, Subway, Wendy's, lodging: Best Western, Hampton Inn, Wingate Inn, other: BooksAMillion, Border's, $Tree, Home Depot, Food Lion, JC Penney, K-Mart, Kohl's, Kroger, Lowes Whse, Martin's Foods, PepBoys, Ross, Sears/auto, Staples, Target, Wal-Mart SuperCtr/24hr, mall, to Shenandoah U
310	VA 37, to US 50W, W...food: McDonald's, Outback Steaks, lodging: Country Inn&Suites, other: Honda, VW, 1 mi W...lodging: Best Value Inn, Day's Inn, Echo Village Motel, Relax Inn, Royal Inn, other: HOSPITAL, Candy Hill Camping(6mi), CarQuest
307	VA 277, Stephens City, E...gas: Chevron, Citgo/7-11, Shell/dsl, food: Arby's, Burger King, KFC/Taco Bell, McDonald's, Seafood Buffet, Subway, Waffle House, Wendy's, lodging: Comfort Inn, Holiday Inn Express, other: Curves, Food Lion, Martin's Foods/gas, Rite Aid, W...gas: Exxon, Sheetz/24hr
304mm	weigh sta both lanes
302	RD 627, Middletown, E...gas: Exxon/dsl, W...gas: Citgo/7-11, Liberty/dsl, lodging: Super 8, Wayside Inn/rest., other: to Wayside Theatre
300	I-66 E, to Washington, Shenandoah NP, Skyline Dr

Interstate 81

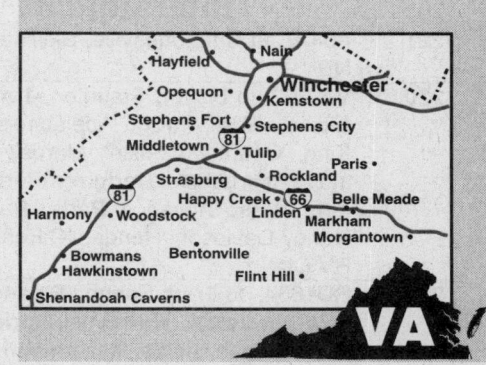

298	US 11, Strasburg, Ⓔ...**gas:** BP/dsl, Exxon/dsl/LP, **food:** Arby's, Battleview Rest., Burger King, McDonald's, **lodging:** Hotel Strasburg/rest., Ramada Inn, **other:** Family$, Food Lion, Rite Aid, Ⓦ...**other:** Battle of Cedar Creek Camping, to Belle Grove Plantation
296	US 48, VA 55, Strasburg, Ⓔ...**other:** to Hupp's Hill Bfd Museum
291	RD 651, Toms Brook, Ⓔ...**lodging:** Budget Inn, Ⓦ...**gas:** Love's/Arby's/dsl/scales/24hr/@, Wilco/Hess/DQ/dsl/scales/24hr/@, **food:** Milestone Rest., **other:** truckwash
283	VA 42, Woodstock, Ⓔ...**gas:** Liberty/7-11, Sheetz, Shell, **food:** Arby's, Hardee's, KFC, McDonald's, Pizza Hut, Ponderosa, Taco Bell, Wendy's, **lodging:** Budget Host, Comfort Inn, Holiday Inn Express, **other:** HOSPITAL, Rite Aid, to Massanutten Military Academy, Ⓦ...**gas:** Exxon/dsl/24hr, Sunoco, **food:** China Wok, Cracker Barrel, Domino's, 5 Guys Cafe, Subway, **other:** $Tree, Lowes Whse, Wal-Mart SuperCtr/24hr
279	VA 185, RD 675, Edinburg, Ⓔ...**gas:** BP/dsl, Exxon/dsl, Shell/dsl/24hr, **food:** Subway, **other:** Creekside Camping(2mi)
277	VA 614, Bowmans Crossing, no services
273	VA 292, RD 703, Mt Jackson, Ⓔ...**gas:** Citgo/7-11, Exxon/dsl, Liberty/Blimpie/dsl/scales/24hr, Sheetz/Wendy's/dsl/24hr, **food:** Burger King, Denny's, Godfather's, **lodging:** Best Western/rest., **other:** $General, Food Lion/24hr, USPO, to Mt Jackson Hist Dist
269	RD 730, to Shenandoah Caverns, Ⓔ...**gas:** Chevron/dsl
269mm	N Fork Shenandoah River
264	US 211, New Market, Ⓔ...**gas:** BP/Blimpie/dsl, Chevron/dsl, Exxon/dsl, Shell/dsl, Texaco, **food:** Appleseed's Rest., Burger King, Godfather's, McDonald's, Pizza Hut, Southern Kitchen, **lodging:** Budget Inn, Quality Inn, Shenvalee Motel/rest., **other:** Rancho Camping, to Shenandoah NP, Skyline Dr, Ⓦ...**gas:** Citgo/7-11, **lodging:** Day's Inn, **other:** to New Market Bfd
262mm	**rest area both lanes, full(handicapped) facilities, phone, vending, picnic tables, litter barrels, petwalk**
257	US 11, VA 259, to Broadway, Ⓔ...**gas:** Liberty/Burger King/Blimpie/Godfather's/dsl, **3-5 mi** Ⓔ...**other:** KOA, Endless Caverns Camping
251	US 11, Harrisonburg, Ⓦ...**gas:** Exxon/dsl, **lodging:** Economy Inn
247b a	US 33, Harrisonburg, Ⓔ...**gas:** BP/Blimpie/dsl, Citgo/dsl, Royal, **food:** Applebee's, Bob Evans, Bravo's Italian, Chili's, China Jade, Domino's, El Charro Mexican, Golden Corral, Great Wok, IHOP, Jess' Lunch, LJ Silver, O'Charley's, Outback Steaks, Panera Bread, Quizno's, Red Lobster, Ruby Tuesday, Shoney's, Taco Bell, Texas Steaks, Waffle House, Wendy's, **lodging:** Best Western, Comfort Inn, Courtyard, Econolodge, Guesthouse Inn, Hampton Inn, Holiday Inn, Jameson Inn, Mo-

	tel 6, Sleep Inn, **other:** Barnes&Noble, BooksAMillion, Circuit City, Home Depot, K-Mart, Kohl's, Kroger, Lowe's Whse, Michael's, Nissan, Office Depot, Old Navy, PepBoys, Petsmart, Saturn, Staples, Target, TJ Maxx, Wal-Mart SuperCtr/gas/24hr, to Shenandoah NP, Skyline Dr, mall, Ⓦ...**gas:** Chevron/dsl, Exxon/dsl, Royal, Sheetz, **food:** Arby's, China Inn, Golden China, Hardee's, KFC, Kyoto, McDonald's, Mr Gatti's, Pizza Hut, Sam's Hotdogs, Subway, **other:** HOSPITAL, Advance Parts, Big Lots, CVS Drug, Food Lion
245	VA 659, Port Republic Rd, Ⓔ...**gas:** Exxon/Subway/dsl, Liberty/Blimpie/dsl, Texaco, **food:** DQ, **lodging:** Day's Inn, Ⓦ...**other:** HOSPITAL, to James Madison U
243	US 11, to Harrisonburg, Ⓦ...**gas:** BP/dsl, Citgo/7-11, Exxon/dsl, Harrisonburg Trkstp/diner/dsl/scales, Liberty, **food:** Burger King, Cracker Barrel, McDonald's, Taco Bell, Waffle House, **lodging:** Country Inn&Suites, Holiday Inn Express, Ramada Inn, Red Carpet Inn, Rockingham Motel, Super 8, **other:** Advance Parts, AutoZone, BMW, Buick/Pontiac/GMC, Chrysler, Ford/Lincoln/Mercury, Hyundai, Kia, Subaru, Toyota
240	VA 257, RD 682, Mount Crawford, **1-3 mi** Ⓦ...**gas:** Exxon/dsl, **food:** Burger King, Ever's Buffet, **lodging:** Village Inn
235	VA 256, Weyers Cave, Ⓔ...**gas:** Texaco/dsl, Ⓦ...**gas:** BP/Subway/dsl, Exxon/dsl, **lodging:** Augusta Motel(4mi), **other:** Freightliner, to Grand Caverns
232mm	**rest area both lanes, full(handicapped)facilities, phone, vending, picnic tables, litter barrels, petwalk**
227	RD 612, Verona, Ⓔ...**gas:** BP/Subway/dsl, **food:** Waffle Inn, Ⓦ...**gas:** Augusta Fuel/dsl, Citgo/Wendy's/dsl, Exxon, **food:** Arby's, Burger King, Hardee's, McDonald's, **lodging:** Ramada Ltd, **other:** Food Lion, KOA(3mi), antiques
225	VA 275, Woodrow Wilson Pkwy, Ⓔ...**lodging:** Quality Inn/rest., Ⓦ...**lodging:** Day's Inn, Holiday Inn/rest.
222	US 250, Staunton, Ⓔ...**gas:** Exxon/McDonald's/24hr, Texaco/dsl, **food:** Cracker Barrel, Mrs Rowe's Rest., Shoney's, Texas Steaks, Wendy's, **lodging:** Best Western, Guesthouse Inn, Sleep Inn, Ⓦ...**gas:** Sheetz, **food:** Burger King, Chili's, 5 Guys Diner, Quizno's, Ryan's, Waffle House, **lodging:** Comfort Inn, Econolodge, Super 8, **other:** AutoZone, Lowe's Whse, Martin's Foods/gas, TireMart, Toyota, Wal-Mart SuperCtr/24hr, American Frontier Culture Museum

H a r r i s o n b u r g

Interstate 81

221	I-64 E, to Charlottesville, Skyline Dr, Shenandoah NP
220	VA 262, to US 11, Staunton, **1 mi** W...**gas:** Citgo, Exxon, Shell, **food:** Applebee's, Arby's, Burger King, Country Cookin', Hardee's, KFC, McDonald's, Red Lobster, **lodging:** Budget Inn, Hampton Inn, **other:** Advance Parts, Buick/Pontiac/GMC, Harley-Davidson, Honda, JC Penney, Nissan, Rule RV Ctr
217	RD 654, to Mint Spring, Stuarts Draft, E...**gas:** BP/Subway/dsl, Exxon/dsl, **lodging:** Day's Inn, Shenandoah Acres Resort(8mi), W...**gas:** Citgo/Stuckey's/dsl/24hr, **lodging:** Relax Inn, Walnut Hill Camping(4mi)
213b a	US 11, US 340, Greenville, E...**gas:** BP/Subway, Pilot/Arby's/dsl/24hr/@, Shell, **food:** Edelweiss Rest., **lodging:** Budget Host
205	RD 606, Raphine, E...**gas:** Exxon/Burger King, Fuel City/dsl, Sunoco/dsl, Whites/dsl/24hr/motel/@, W...**gas:** Wilco/Hess/Wendy's/dsl/scales/24hr/@, **lodging:** Day's Inn/rest. **other:** Koogler RV Ctr
200	RD 710, Fairfield, E...**gas:** BP/McDonald's/dsl/24hr, Texaco, **food:** Whistle Stop Cafe, W...**gas:** Exxon/Subway/dsl, Shell/dsl
199mm	**rest area sb, full(handicapped)facilities, phone, vending, picnic tables, litter barrels, petwalk**
195	US 11, Lee Hwy, E...**lodging:** Maple Hall Lodging/dining, W...**gas:** Citgo/dsl/24hr, Shell/dsl, **food:** Aunt Sarah's, **lodging:** Days Inn, Howard Johnson/rest., Ramada Inn, **other:** Lee-Hi Camping
191	I-64 W(exits left from nb), US 60, to Charleston
188b a	US 60, to Lexington, Buena Vista, **3-5 mi** E...**gas:** BP, Exxon, **food:** Hardee's, KFC, LJ Silver, McDonald's, Pizza Hut, Taco Bell, Wendy's, **lodging:** Budget Inn, Buena Vista Inn, **other:** HOSPITAL, to Glen Maury Park, to Stonewall Jackson Home, Marshall Museum, to Blue Ridge Pkwy, W...**gas:** Exxon/dsl/24hr, **lodging:** Day's Inn, Hampton Inn, **other:** to Washington&Lee U, VMI
180	US 11, Natural Bridge, E...**gas:** Shell/dsl, **food:** Fancy Hill Diner, **lodging:** Relax Inn, W...**gas:** Shell/dsl, **food:** Pink Cadillac Diner, **lodging:** Budget Inn, **other:** KOA
175	US 11 N, to Glasgow, Natural Bridge, E...**gas:** Exxon, **lodging:** Natural Bridge Hotel/rest., **other:** to James River RA, Jellystone Camping
168	VA 614, US 11, Arcadia, E...**gas:** Shell, **food:** Mtn View Rest., **lodging:** Wattstull Inn, **other:** Middle Creek Camping(6mi), **2 mi** W...**food:** Burger King, Ransone's Grill
167	US 11(from sb), Buchanan, no services
162	US 11, Buchanan, E...**gas:** Exxon/dsl, **other:** to BR Pkwy, W...**gas:** Texaco/Subway/24hr
158mm	**rest area sb, full(handicapped)facilities, phone, vending, picnic tables, litter barrels, petwalk**
156	RD 640, to US 11, E...**gas:** Exxon/Brugh's Mill/dsl, **food:** Greenwood Rest.
150	US 11/220, to Fincastle, E...**gas:** Citgo/dsl/24hr, Dodge's/dsl, Pilot/Subway/dsl/24hr, TA/BP/dsl/@, **food:** Country Cookin', Cracker Barrel, Hardee's,

	McDonald's, Shoney's, Taco Bell, Waffle House, Wendy's, **lodging:** Comfort Inn, Day's Inn, Holiday Inn Express, Red Roof Inn, Travelodge, **other:** Berglun RV Ctr, CVS Drug, Winn-Dixie, W...**gas:** BP/dsl, Exxon/dsl/24hr, **food:** Bojangles, Pizza Hut, **lodging:** Econolodge, Howard Johnson
149mm	weigh sta both lanes
146	VA 115, Cloverdale, E...**gas:** Exxon, Shell/dsl, **food:** Anthony's Rest., Burger King, El Rodeo Mexican, Hardee's, McDonald's, Subway, **lodging:** Country Inn&Suites, Day's Inn/rest., Fairfield Inn, Hampton Inn, Knight's Inn, **other:** CVS Drug
143	I-581, US 220, to Roanoke, Blue Ridge Pkwy(exits left from sb), **1 mi** E...**food:** El Toreo, Waffle House, **lodging:** Hampton Inn, Knights Inn, Quality Inn, Super 8, **2-3 mi** E on Hershberger...**gas:** BP, Exxon, Shell, **food:** Abuelo's, Applebee's, Buffalo Wild Wings, Chick-fil-A, Hardee's, IHOP, Logan's Roadhouse, O'Charley's, Olive Garden, Red Robin, Ruby Tuesday, Smokey Bones BBQ, Subway, Texas Steaks, TGIFriday, **lodging:** AmeriSuites, Best Western, Comfort Inn, Courtyard, Extended Stay America, Holiday Inn, Howard Johnson, MainStay Suites, Wyndham, **other:** Belk, Circuit City, JC Penney, Old Navy, Sears/auto, Staples, Target, U-Haul, Wal-Mart SuperCtr/gas/24hr, mall
141	VA 419, Salem, **1-2 mi** E...**gas:** BP, Liberty/Burger King, **food:** Hardee's, Country Cookin' Rest., Fuddrucker's, McDonald's, **lodging:** Baymont Inn, Econolodge, Holiday Inn Express, Quality Inn, **other:** HOSPITAL, Chevrolet, Kroger/gas, W...**gas:** BP/dsl, Citgo
140	VA 311, Salem, **1 mi** E...**food:** Mac&Bob's Cafe, **1 mi** W...**food:** Hanging Rock Grill/golf
137	VA 112, VA 619, Salem, E...**gas:** BP, Chevron, Exxon, Go-Mart, Sheetz/24hr, Shell/dsl, **food:** Anthony's Cafe, Applebee's, Arby's, Bojangles, Burger King, Denny's, Dynasty Buffet, El Rodeo Mexican, Hardee's, KFC, LJ Silver, Mamma Maria Italian, McDonald's, Omelet Shoppe, Pizza Hut, Quizno's, Shoney's, Sonic, Subway, Taco Bell, Wendy's, **lodging:** Comfort Inn, Econolodge, Super 8, **other:** Advance Parts, AutoZone, Big Lots, $Tree, Food Lion, Goodyear, K-Mart, Kroger, Mitsubishi, Snyder's RV, Walgreens, Wal-Mart SuperCtr/24hr, W...**lodging:** Best Value Inn, Holiday Inn
132	VA 647, to Dixie Caverns, E...**gas:** Citgo, Shell, **lodging:** Budget Host, **other:** Dixie Caverns Camping, st police
129mm	**rest area nb, full(handicapped)facilities, phone, vending, picnic tables, litter barrels, petwalk**
128	US 11, VA 603, Ironto, E...**gas:** Citgo/24hr, W...**gas:** Citgo/Dixie's/Subway/dsl/24hr
118c b a	US 11/460, Christiansburg, E...**gas:** Shell/dsl, **food:** Denny's, Cracker Barrel, **lodging:** Day's Inn, Fairfield Inn, Holiday Inn Express, Quality Inn, Super 8, **other:** Interstate RV Camping, W...**gas:** BP, Exxon/Subway, Pure/dsl, RaceWay, **food:**

Interstate 81

	Hardee's, McDonald's, Pizza Hut, Ruby Tuesday, Shoney's, Waffle House, Wendy's, **lodging:** Econolodge, Howard Johnson, **other:** HOSPITAL, Advance Parts, Chevrolet/Subaru, Chrysler/Dodge, Ford/Toyota, Honda, Toyota, to VA Tech
114	VA 8, Christiansburg, W...**gas:** Citgo, **1 mi food:** Anthony's Cafe, Burger King, Domino's, Hardee's, **1 mi lodging:** Budget Inn, **other:** $General, repair
109	VA 177, VA 600, W...**gas:** BP/dsl, Marathon, **lodging:** Best Western(4mi), Comfort Inn(4mi), Super 8(4mi), E...**other:** HOSPITAL
107mm	**rest area both lanes, full(handicapped) facilities, phone, vending, picnic tables, litter barrels, petwalk**
105	VA 232, RD 605, to Radford, W...**lodging:** Executive Motel(4mi), **other:** museum
101	RD 660, to Claytor Lake SP, E...**lodging:** Claytor Lake Inn, Sleep Inn, W...**gas:** Citgo/DQ/dsl, Shell/Omelet Shoppe/Taco Bell/dsl
98	VA 100 N, to Dublin, E...**gas:** BP, Exxon/Subway/dsl, **food:** Shoney's, **lodging:** Comfort Inn/rest., Hampton Inn, Holiday Inn Express, W...**gas:** Liberty/Blimpie/dsl, Marathon, **food:** Bojangles, Burger King, McDonald's, Waffle House, Wendy's, **lodging:** Super 8, Travel Inn, **other:** HOSPITAL, Wal-Mart SuperCtr, to Wilderness Rd Museum
94b a	VA 99 N, to Pulaski, E...**lodging:** Day's Inn, W...**gas:** Exxon, **food:** KFC, **other:** HOSPITAL
92	RD 658, to Draper, E...**gas:** BP, **other:** to New River Trail SP
89b a	US 11 N, VA 100, to Pulaski, no services
86	RD 618, Service Rd, W...**gas:** I-81/Citgo/dsl/rest., **lodging:** Gateway Motel
84	RD 619, to Grahams Forge, W...**gas:** Kangaroo/DQ/dsl/24hr, Love's/Subway/dsl/scales/24hr/@, **food:** Patty's Kitchen, **lodging:** Fox Mtn Inn/rest., Trail Motel
81	I-77 S, to Charlotte, to Blue Ridge Pkwy. I-81 S and I-77 N run together 9 mi., Galax
80	US 52 S, VA 121 N, to Ft Chiswell, E...**gas:** BP/Burger King/dsl, ⌖/Flying J/Cookery/dsl/scales/24hr/@, **food:** Wendy's, **lodging:** Hampton Inn, Super 8, **other:** Blue Beacon, Ft Chiswell Outlets/famous brands, GS Camping, NAPA, W...**gas:** BP, Citgo/dsl, **food:** McDonald's, **lodging:** Comfort Inn, **other:** Speedco, Little Valley RV Ctr
77	Service Rd, E...**gas:** Citgo/Subway/dsl/24hr, ⌖/Flying J/Cookery/dsl/LP/24hr/@, Hess/dsl, **food:** Burger King, **other:** KOA, W...**gas:** Exxon/dsl, Wilco/Hess/Arby's/DQ/dsl/scales/24hr/@, **other:** Truck o' Mat, st police
73	US 11 S, Wytheville, E...**gas:** BP, Citgo/Quizno's, Kangaroo, **food:** Applebee's, Cracker Barrel, DQ, El Puerto, Hardee's, KFC, Ocean Bay Seafood, Peking Rest., Pizza Hut, Shoney's, Sonic, Waffle House, Wendy's, **lodging:** Budget Host, Day's Inn, Deluxe Inn, Econolodge, Motel 6, Quality Inn, Red Carpet Inn, Travelodge, **other:** HOSPITAL, CVS Drug, Food Lion, Ford, Harley-Davidson, K-Mart, Nissan

(side label) **Wytheville**

	I-81 N and I-77 S run together 9 mi
72	I-77 N, to Bluefield, **1 mi N, I-77 exit 41** E...**food:** Sagebrush Steaks, **lodging:** Best Western, Sleep Inn, Super 8, W...**gas:** Kangaroo/dsl/24hr, TA/BP/Subway/Taco Bell/dsl/24hr/@, **food:** Country Kitchen, **lodging:** Comfort Suites, Hampton Inn, Ramada/rest.
70	US 21/52, Wytheville, E...**gas:** BP/dsl, Exxon, **food:** Arby's, China Wok, KFC/Taco Bell, Little Caesar's, McDonald's, Ocean Bay Seafood, Quizno's, Ruby Tuesday, Sonic, Subway, Wendy's, **other:** HOSPITAL, CVS Drug, $Tree, Food Lion, Goody's, Lowe's Whse, Old Navy, Radio Shack, Wal-Mart SuperCtr/24hr, W...**gas:** Kangaroo, **lodging:** Comfort Inn
67	US 11(from nb, no re-entry), to Wytheville
61mm	**rest area nb, full(handicapped)facilities, phone, vending, picnic tables, litter barrels, petwalk, NO TRUCKS**
60	VA 90, Rural Retreat, E...**gas:** Chevron/dsl, Sunoco/dsl, **food:** McDonald's, Subway, Tuscan Grill, **other:** to Rural Retreat Lake, camping
54	rd 683, to Groseclose, E...**gas:** Shell/dsl, **food:** The Barn Rest., **lodging:** Relax Inn
53.5mm	**rest area sb, full(handicapped)facilities, phone, vending, picnic tables, litter barrels, petwalk**
50	US 11, Atkins, W...**gas:** Citgo/Subway/dsl/24hr, Exxon/Pizza+, **lodging:** Comfort Inn
47	US 11, to Marion, W...**gas:** BP/Subway, Chevron/dsl/24hr, Exxon/dsl, **food:** Arby's, Burger King, McDonald's, Pizza Hut, Puerto Mexican, Sonic, **lodging:** Best Western/rest., Econolodge, Rodeway Inn, **other:** HOSPITAL, Advance Parts, Chrysler/Jeep/Dodge, Ford, Ingles, O'Reilly Parts, Radio Shack, Rite Aid, to Hungry Mother SP(4mi), Wal-Mart, **1 mi** W...**food:** KFC/Taco Bell, LJ Silver, McDonald's, Wendy's, **other:** AutoZone, Chevrolet/Ponitac/Buick/GMC, CVS Drug, $General, Family$, Food City, Food Lion, Rite Aid
45	VA 16, Marion, E...**gas:** Exxon/dsl, **food:** AppleTree Rest., **other:** to Grayson Highlands SP, Mt Rogers NRA, **1 mi** W...**gas:** BP, Chevron, **food:** Hardee's, KFC, LJ Silver, Wendy's, **lodging:** Royal Inn, **other:** USPO
44	US 11, Marion, W...**gas:** Marathon
39	US 11, RD 645, Seven Mile Ford, E...**lodging:** Budget Inn/rest., W...**other:** Interstate Camping/food
35	RD 107, Chilhowie, E...**gas:** Citgo, **lodging:** Knight's Inn, W...**gas:** Chevron, Citgo, Exxon/dsl, Rouse Fuel, **food:** McDonald's, Subway, TasteeFreez, **lodging:** Budget Inn(1mi), **other:** Curves, $General, Food City/gas

(side label) **Marion**

Interstate 81

N ↕ S		
Abingdon	32	US 11, to Chilhowie, E...other: RV Park
	29	VA 91, to Damascus, Glade Spring, E...gas: Petro/dsl/rest./24hr/@ , Shell/Subway/dsl, **food:** Giardino's Italian, Pizza+, Wendy's, **lodging:** Swiss Inn/rest., Travelodge, **other:** $General, W... **gas:** Chevron/dsl/24hr, Coastal, Exxon, **other:** CarQuest
	26	VA 737, Emory, W...**food:** Emory Crossing Deli, **other:** to Emory&Henry Coll
	24	VA 80, Meadowview Rd, W...auto repair
	22	VA 704, Enterprise Rd, no services
	19	US 11/58, to Abingdon, E...**gas:** Shell/Subway/ dsl, **food:** Pizza+, **lodging:** Holiday Lodge, **other:** to Mt Rogers NRA, W...**gas:** Chevron/dsl/24hr, Citgo, Exxon/dsl, **food:** Burger King, Cracker Barrel, DaVinci's Cafe, Harbor House Seafood, Huddle House, Wendy's, **lodging:** Alpine Motel, Holiday Inn Express, Quality Inn
	17	US 58A, VA 75, Abingdon, E...**gas:** Valero, **food:** Domino's, LJ Silver, **lodging:** Hampton Inn, **other:** Mr Transmission, W...**gas:** Chevron, Citgo/dsl, Exxon, **food:** Arby's, China Wok, Hardee's, KFC, McDonald's, Papa John's, Pizza Hut, Shoney's, Taco Bell, Wendy's, **lodging:** Martha Washington Inn, Super 8, **other:** HOSPITAL, Advance Parts, CVS Drug, $General, Food City, Kroger, K-Mart, Radio Shack
	14	US 19, VA 140, Abingdon, W...**gas:** Chevron/dsl/ 24hr, Exxon, Shell/dsl, **food:** DQ(1mi), McDonald's, Subway, **lodging:** Budget Inn(3mi), Comfort Inn, **other:** CarQuest, Ford, Riverside Camping(10mi)
	13.5mm	**TRUCKERS ONLY rest area nb, full(handicapped) facilities, phone, vending, picnic tables, litter barrels**
	13	VA 611, to Lee Hwy, W...**gas:** Shell/dsl
	10	US 11/19, Lee Hwy, W...**gas:** BP/dsl, Chevron, **lodging:** Beacon Inn, Deluxe Inn, Evergreen Inn, Skyland Inn
	7	Old Airport Rd, E...**gas:** Citgo/Bojangles, Shell/dsl, **food:** Bob Evans, Sonic, **lodging:** La Quinta, W... **gas:** BP/dsl, Citgo/Wendy's, Conoco/dsl, **food:** Chili's, Chop's Rest., Damon's, El Patio Mexican, Fazoli's, Golden Corral, IHOP, Kobe Japanese, Logan's Roadhouse, Los Arco's, O'Charley's, Outback Steaks, Perkins, Pizza Hut, Red Lobster, Ruby Tuesday, Subway, Taco Bell, **lodging:** Courtyard, Holiday Inn, Microtel, Motel 6, **other:** Advance Parts, Curves, $General, Lowe's Whse, Office Depot, Wal-Mart SuperCtr/24hr, Sugar Hollow Camping
	5	US 11/19, Lee Hwy, E...**gas:** Citgo, Shell, **food:** Arby's, Burger King, Hardee's, KFC, LJ Silver, McDonald's, Shoney's, Wendy's, **lodging:** Budget Inn, Super 8, **other:** CVS Drug, Family$, Parts+, USPO, W...**gas:** Exxon, **lodging:** Comfort Inn, **other:** Blevins Tire, Buick/Pontiac, Lee Hwy Camping
	3	I-381 S, to Bristol, **1 mi** E...**gas:** Chevron, Citgo/ dsl, **food:** Applebee's, Ryan's, **lodging:** Days Inn, Econolodge

Bristol	1	US 58/421, Bristol, **1 mi** E...**gas:** Chevron, Citgo, **food:** Burger King, Capt D's, Chick-fil-A, KFC, Krispy Kreme, LJ Silver, Maggie's Diner, McDonald's, Shoney's, Sonic, Taco Bell, Wendy's, **lodging:** Howard Johnson, Knight's Inn, **other:** HOSPITAL, Belk, Chrysler/Jeep, Dodge, $General, Family$, Goody's, K-Mart, Kroger, Lincoln/Mercury, Sears/auto, Walgreens, mall
	0mm	**Virginia/Tennessee state line, Welcome Ctr nb, full(handicapped)facilities, info, phone, vending, picnic tables, litter barrels, petwalk, NO TRUCKS**

Interstate 85

	Exit #	Services
	69mm	I-85 begins/ends on I-95.
Petersburg	69	US 301, Wythe St, Washington St, Petersburg, W... **lodging:** Regency Inn
	68	I-95 S, US 460 E, to Norfolk, Crater Rd, E...HOSPITAL, **3/4 mi** E...**gas:** Exxon/dsl, RaceTrac/dsl, Shell, **food:** Hardee's, **lodging:** California Inn, **other:** to Petersburg Nat Bfd
	65	Squirrel Level Rd, E...**other:** to Richard Bland Coll, W...**gas:** BP
	63b a	US 1, to Petersburg, E...**gas:** Chubby's, Exxon/ dsl/24hr, Shell/Burger King, **food:** Hardee's, Waffle House, **lodging:** Holiday Inn Express, W...**gas:** BP, **food:** McDonald's
	61	US 460, to Blackstone, E...**gas:** EastCoast/Subway/ dsl/LP, **food:** Huddle House, **lodging:** Day's Inn(3mi), W...**gas:** Shell/dsl, Valero(1mi), **other:** airport
	55mm	**rest area both lanes, full(handicapped) facilities, phone, picnic tables, litter barrels, vending, petwalk**
	53	VA 703, Dinwiddie, W...**gas:** Exxon/dsl, **food:** HomePlace Rest.(3mi), Rumorz Cafe, **other:** to 5 Forks Nat Bfd
	52mm	Stony Creek
	48	VA 650, DeWitt, no services
	42	VA 40, McKenney, W...**gas:** Citgo, Exxon, **other:** auto repair, **1.5 mi** W...**lodging:** Economy Inn
	40mm	Nottoway River
	39	VA 712, to Rawlings, E...**other:** VA Battlerama, W... **gas:** Chevron/Davis/dsl/24hr, Citgo/dsl, **lodging:** Nottoway Motel/rest.
	34	VA 630, Warfield, W...**gas:** Exxon/dsl
	32mm	**rest area both lanes, full(handicapped) facilities, phone, picnic tables, litter barrels, vending, petwalk**
	28	US 1, Alberta, W...**gas:** Exxon
	27	VA 46, to Lawrenceville, E...**other:** to St Paul's Coll
	24	VA 644, to Meredithville, no services
	22mm	weigh sta both lanes
	20mm	Meherrin River
	15	US 1, to South Hill, E...**gas:** Citgo/deli, W...**gas:** Valero, **food:** Kahill's Diner, Rumorz

Interstate 85

12	US 58, VA 47, to South Hill, E...**gas:** RaceWay, Shell/dsl, **food:** Applebee's, Arby's, Bojangles, Domino's, Taste of Italy, **lodging:** Hampton Inn, Holiday Inn Express, Super 8, **other:** $Tree, Wal-Mart Superctr/24hr, W...**gas:** Citgo, Exxon/dsl, Kangaroo/dsl, Petrol, **food:** Brian's Steaks, Burger King, Cracker Barrel, Denny's, Down Home Buffet, Hardee's, KFC/Taco Bell, McDonald's, New China, Pizza Hut, Subway, Wendy's, **lodging:** Best Value Inn, Comfort Inn, Crossroads Inn, **other:** HOSPITAL, CVS Drug, $General, Food Lion, Goodyear/auto, Home Depot, Roses
4	VA 903, to Bracey, Lake Gaston, E...**gas:** BP/DQ/Subway/dsl, Exxon/Simmon's/dsl/rest./scales/24hr/@, **other:** Americamps Camping(5mi), W...**gas:** Shell/Pizza Hut/Quizno's, **food:** Memphis Grill, **lodging:** Lake Gaston Inn
3mm	Lake Gaston
1mm	**Welcome Ctr nb, full(handicapped)facilities, phone, picnic tables, phones, litter barrels, vending, petwalk**
0mm	Virginia/North Carolina state line

Interstate 95

Exit #	Services
178mm	Virginia/Maryland state line, Potomac River, W Wilson Mem Br
177c b a	US 1, to Alexandria, Ft Belvoir, E...**food:** Alexandria Diner, Great American Steak Buffet, **lodging:** Day's Inn, Relax Inn, Red Roof Inn, **other:** Chevrolet, Chrysler/Jeep, Dodge, W...**gas:** Exxon/24hr, Hess
176b a	VA 241, Telegraph Rd, E...**gas:** Hess/dsl, W...**lodging:** Courtyard, Holiday Inn
174	Eisenhower Ave Connector, to Alexandria
173	rd 613, Van Dorn St, to Franconia, E...**lodging:** Comfort Inn, **1 mi** W...**gas:** Exxon, Shell, **food:** Dunkin Donuts, Jerry's Subs, McDonald's, Papa John's, Red Lobster, **other:** Aamco, Giant Foods, NTB, Radio Shack
170a	I-495 N, I-495 & I-95 N run together to MD, to Rockville
170b	I-395 N, to Washington
169b a	rd 644, Springfield, Franconia, E...**gas:** Mobil, 7-11, **food:** Bennigan's, **lodging:** Best Western, Comfort Inn, Courtyard, Day's Inn, Hampton Inn, Hilton, Holiday Inn, **other:** HOSPITAL, Barnes&Noble, Circuit City, CVS Drug, Firestone/auto, Ford, Isuzu/Kia, JC Penney, Macy's, mall, W...**gas:** BP, Mobil, Shell, **food:** Bob Evans, Dragon Sea Buffet, KFC, McDonald's, Outback Steaks, Peking Garden, Popeye's, Subway, **lodging:** Holiday Inn Express, Red Roof Inn, TownePlace Suites, **other:** CVS Drug, Dodge, Giant Foods, Goodyear/auto, K-Mart, Radio Shack, Subaru/VW, Toyota
167	VA 617, Backlick Rd(from sb), W...**gas:** InterFuel/dsl, **other:** Chevrolet, Nissan
166b a	VA 7100, Newington, to Ft Belvoir, E...**gas:** Exxon/dsl, W...**gas:** Exxon, **food:** McDonald's

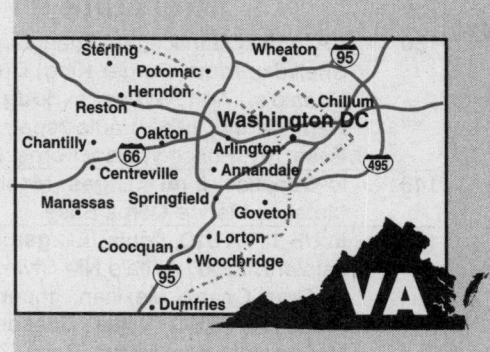

163	VA 642, Lorton, E...**gas:** Shell/24hr, W...**gas:** Shell, **food:** Burger King, Café Platters, Gunston Wok, **lodging:** Comfort Inn
161	US 1 S(no nb re-entry, exits left from sb), to Ft Belvoir, Mt Vernon, Woodlawn Plantation, Gunston Hall, **1 mi** E...**gas:** BP, Crown, Exxon, Shell, **food:** Denny's, DixieBones BBQ, Capotil Grill, Dunkin Donuts, McDonald's, Taco Bell, **lodging:** Econolodge, Hampton Inn, Quality Inn, Roadway Inn, Virginia Inn
160.5mm	Occoquan River
160b a	VA 123 N, Woodbridge, Occoquan, E...**gas:** Mobil, **food:** Lum's, Subway, Taco Bell, **lodging:** Comfort Inn, Econolodge, Hampton Inn, Quality, **other:** Aldi Foods, Ford, Food Lion, GNC, Radio Shack, Trak Auto, W...**gas:** BP, Exxon/dsl, Mobil, Shell, **food:** KFC, McDonald's, VA Grill, Wendy's, **other:** 7-11
158b a	VA 3000, Prince William Pkwy, Woodbridge, W...**gas:** Citgo, Exxon, Mobil, Shell, Sunoco, WaWa, **food:** Boston Mkt, Chick-fil-A, IHOP, Macaroni Grill, Old Country Buffet, Taco Bell, Wendy's, **lodging:** Fairfield Inn, Holiday Inn Express, Sleep Inn
156	VA 784, Potomac Mills, E...**gas:** Exxon, Wawa/gas, **food:** Checkers, McDonald's, Taco Bell, **other:** HOSPITAL, Hyundai, Kia, Lincoln/Mercury, Mazda, Mitsubishi, Nissan, Radio Shack, Safeway, Trak Auto, to Leesylvania SP, W...**gas:** Exxon, Mobil, Shell, **food:** Blackeyed Pea, Bob Evans, Burger King, Chesapeake Bay Seafood, Chili's, Domino's, El Charro Mexican, Jazz St Grill, Jerry's Subs, McDonald's, Olive Garden, Outback Steaks, Pizza Hut, Popeye's, Silver Diner, Wendy's, **lodging:** Day's Inn, Wytestone Suites, **other:** Circuit City, Firestone/auto, K-Mart, Marshall's, Michael's, NTB, Staples, U-Haul
155mm	**rest area both lanes, full(handicapped)facilities, phone, vending, picnic tables, litter barrels, petwalk, NO TRUCKS**
154mm	truck rest area/weigh sta both lanes
152	VA 234, Dumfries, to Manassas, E...**gas:** BP/dsl/24hr, Chevron/service, Shell/dsl, **food:** Golden Corral, KFC, McDonald's, Subway, Taco Bell, **lodging:** Sleep Inn, Super 8, **other:** NAPA Autocare, Weems-Botts Museum, W...**gas:** Citgo/7-11, Exxon/Blimpie, Shell, **food:** Cracker Barrel, MontClair Rest., Tiziano Italian, Waffle House, **lodging:** Day's Inn, Econolodge, Hampton Inn, Holiday Inn Express

N ↕ S

Exit	Description
150	VA 619, Quantico, to Triangle, **E**...**gas:** Exxon, Shell/dsl, **food:** Burger King, Dunkin Donuts, McDonald's, 7-11, Wendy's, **lodging:** Best Value, Ramada Inn, **other:** auto repair, to Marine Corps Base, **W**...Prince William Forest Park
148	to Quantico, **2 mi** **E**...**gas:** Mobil/dsl, Spring Lake Motel, to Marine Corps Base
143b a	to US 1, VA 610, Aquia, **E**...**gas:** BP, Exxon, Shell/dsl/24hr, **food:** Anita's NM Style, Carlos O'Kelly's, El Gran Charro Mexican, Imperial Garden, KFC, Kingstreet BBQ, Little Caesar's, Mad Moose, McDonald's, Pizza Hut, Ruby Tuesday, Subway, VA BBQ, Wendy's, **lodging:** Day's Inn, Hampton Inn, **other:** BigLots, GNC, Radio Shack, Rite Aid, Tires+, **W**...**gas:** BP/dsl, Citgo/7-11/dsl, WaWa, **food:** Applebee's, Bob Evans, Burger King, Chick-fil-A, Chili's, CiCi's, Dunkin Donuts, 5Guys Burgers, Hardee's, IHOP, Kobe Japanese, McDonald's, Moe's SW Grill, Outback Steaks, Pancho Villa Mexican, Panera Bread, Popeye's, Ruby Tuesday, Starbucks, Taco Bell, Tops China, Wendy's, **lodging:** Comfort Inn, Country Inn, Holiday Inn Express, Super 8, Wingate Inn, **other:** AutoZone, CVS Drug, $General, Giant Foods, Home Depot, Kohl's, Lowe's Whse, Merchants Tire, Michael's, Staples, Target, Toyota, Wal-Mart/auto, Aquia Pines Camping
140	VA 630, Stafford, **E**...**gas:** BP, Mobil, Shell/dsl, **food:** McDonald's, **lodging:** Bradshaw Motel(3mi), **W**...**gas:** BP/dsl, Shell/dsl
137mm	Potomac Creek
136	new exit
133b a	US 17 N, to Warrenton, **E**...**gas:** Exxon/dsl, Mobil/dsl, RaceWay, **food:** Arby's, Illiano Pizzaria, Paradise Diner, **lodging:** Howard Johnson Express, Motel 6, **other:** CarQuest, **W**...**gas:** BP/dsl, Chevron, Citgo/7-11, EastCoast/Subway/dsl, Shell/dsl, **food:** Burger King, Emerald's Grill, Hardee's, Johnny Appleseed Rest., McDonald's, Pizza Hut, Ponderosa, ServiceTown Rest., Taco Bell, Waffle House, Wendy's, **lodging:** Best Inn, Comfort Inn, Day's Inn, Holiday Inn, Quality Inn, Ramada Ltd, Sleep Inn, Super 8, Travelodge, Wingate Inn, **other:** Advance Parts, Blue Beacon, CVS Drug, Food Lion
132.5mm	Rappahannock River
132mm	**rest area sb, full(handicapped)facilities, phone, picnic tables, litter barrels, petwalk, vending**
130b a	VA 3, to Fredericksburg, **E**...**gas:** BP/dsl/24hr, Liberty Gas, Mobil/dsl, RaceWay, Shell, 7-11, Wawa/24hr, **food:** Arby's, Bob Evans, Café daVanzo, Carlos O'Kelly's, Chesapeake Bay Seafood, CiCi's, Dunkin Donuts, Friendly's, KFC, Kings Buffet, LoneStar Steaks, LJSilver, McDonald's, Popeye's, Shoney's, Subway, TCBY, Top's Chinese, Wendy's, **lodging:** Best Western, Hampton Inn, **other:** HOSPITAL, Batteries+, $King, Hancock Fabrics, Home Depot, PepBoys, Radio Shack, Staples, **W**...**gas:** BP, Citgo/7-11, Crown Gas, Exxon/dsl/24hr, Shell, Sheetz, Wawa/24hr, **food:** A&W/LJ Silver, Applebee's, Aunt Sarah's, Bonefish Grill, Boston Mkt, Burger King, Carrabba's, Cracker Bar-

Exit	Description
	rel, Denny's, Fuddrucker's, IHOP, Joe's Crabshack, Ledo Pizza, Little Caesar's, Logan's Roadhouse, McDonald's, O'Charley's, Old Country Buffet, Olive Garden, Outback Steaks, Panera Bread, Popeye's, Red Lobster, Red White&Blue BBQ, Ruby Tuesday, Starbucks, Taco Bell, TGIFriday, Waffle House, **lodging:** Econolodge, Holiday Inn Select, Ramada Inn, Ryan's, Sheraton, Super 8, **other:** Belk, Best Buy, BJ's Whse, Borders Books, Circuit City, Giant Foods, GNC, JC Penney, Kohl's, K-Mart, Lowe's Whse, Macy's, Merchants Tire, Michaels, NTB, Office Depot, Old Navy, Sears/auto, Shoppers Foods, Target, Wal-Mart SuperCtr/gas/24hr, mall
126	US 1, US 17 S, to Fredericksburg, **E**...**gas:** BP, Citgo/7-11, Exxon/Subway, Mobil, Shell/dsl, **food:** Arby's, Denny's, El Charro Mexican, Friendly's, Golden Corral, Hooters, McDonald's, Pancho Villa Mexican, Pizza Hut, Ruby Tuesday, Shoney's, Taco Bell, Waffle House, Wendy's, Western Sizzlin, **lodging:** Day's Inn/rest., Econolodge, Fairfield Inn, Holiday Inn, Howard Johnson, Ramada Inn, Super 8, TownePlace Inn, **other:** Buick/Pontiac/GMC, Cadillac, CarQuest, CVS Drug, Goodyear/auto, Honda/Nissan/Mazda/VW, Merchants Tire, Rite Aid, **W**...**gas:** Exxon/Blimpie, RaceTrac/dsl/24hr, **food:** Aunt Sarah's, Burger King, Cracker Barrel, Damon's, Durango's Steaks, Golden China, KFC, McDonald's, Subway, **lodging:** Comfort Inn, Sleep Inn, WyteStone Suites, **other:** Massaponax Outlet Ctr/famous brands, KOA(6mi), Wal-Mart SuperCtr/gas/24hr
118	VA 606, to Thornburg, **E**...**gas:** BP, Shell/dsl, **other:** to Stonewall Jackson Shrine, **W**...**gas:** Citgo/dsl, Exxon, Valero, **food:** Angela's Rest., Burger King, McDonald's, Subway, **lodging:** Holiday Inn Express, Lamplighter Motel, **other:** KOA(7mi), to Lake Anna SP
110	VA 639, to Ladysmith, **E**...**gas:** Shell/dsl, **W**...**gas:** Citgo/dsl, Exxon/dsl, **food:** Guiseppe's Rest., Perky's Pizza, Subway, **other:** Express Tire/repair, Food Lion
108mm	**rest area both lanes, full(handicapped)facilities, vending, phone, picnic tables, litter barrels, petwalk**
104	VA 207, to US 301, Bowling Green, **E**...**gas:** BP/dsl, Chevron, Exxon/dsl, Mr Fuel/dsl, Petro/dsl/rest./24hr/@, Pilot/Subway/DQ/dsl/24hr/@, Shell/dsl, Speedco, **food:** McDonald's, Wendy's, **lodging:** Holiday Inn Express, Howard Johnson, **other:** Blue Beacon, Russell Stover Candies, to Ft AP Hill, **W**...**gas:** Exxon/dsl, Flying J/Country Mkt/dsl/24hr/@, **food:** Aunt Sarah's, Waffle House, **lodging:** Comfort Inn, Day's Inn/rest., Red Roof Inn, Travelodge, **other:** CarQuest, USPO
98	VA 30, Doswell, **E**...to King's Dominion Funpark, **gas:** Citgo/7-11, Shell/dsl, **food:** All American Rest., Burger King, Denny's, **lodging:** Best Western, Econolodge, **other:** All American Camping, King's Dominion Camping, truckwash
92	VA 54, Ashland, **E**...**gas:** Mobil, **W**...**gas:** BP, TA/dsl/rest./@, Citgo/dsl, EastCoast/Blimpie/dsl, Exxon/Subway, Shell/dsl, **food:** Arby's, Burger King,

F r e d e r i c k s b u r g

Interstate 95

Capt D's, Cracker Barrel, DQ, Azteca Mexican, Hardee's, Jersey Mike's Subs, KFC, McDonald's, PapaLou Pizza, Pizza Hut, Ponderosa, Popeye's, Ruby Tuesday, Shoney's, Taco Bell, Waffle House, Wendy's, **lodging:** Ashland Inn, Budget Inn, Comfort Inn, Day's Inn, Econolodge, Hampton Inn, Holiday Inn Express, Microtel, Quality Inn, Ramada Inn, Sleep Inn, Super 8, Travelodge, **other:** AutoZone, BigLots, Buick/Pontiac, CarQuest, Family$, Food Lion, Radio Shack, Rite Aid, U-Haul, Ukrop's Foods

89	VA 802, to Lewistown Rd, E...**gas:** Shell, TA/Mobil/ Pizza Hut/dsl/café/24hr/@, **other:** Americamps RV Camp, W...**lodging:** Cadillac Motel, **other:** Kosmo Village Camping, Rolling Hills RV Ctr
86b a	VA 656, Elmont, to Atlee, E...**gas:** BP, Sheetz(1mi), **food:** Burger King, McDonald's(1mi), W **on US 1... gas:** Citgo/7-11, Mobil, Shell/Subway/dsl, **food:** Applebee's, Burger King, Chick-fil-A, Chili's, Food-Court, Gino's Ristorante, McDonald's, O'Charley's, Panera Bread, Papa John's, Quizno's, Red Robin, Ruby Tuesday, Sbarro's, Shoney's, Subway, Wendy's, **lodging:** Best Western/rest., SpringHill Suites, VA Crossings Resort, **other:** Circuit City, Dillard's, Firestone/auto, Goodyear/auto, JCPenney, Macy's, Michael's, Sears/auto, Target, Ukrop's Foods, Walgreen, mall
84b a	I-295 W, to I-64, to Norfolk
83b a	VA 73, Parham Rd, W...**gas:** Citgo/7-11, EC/dsl, Exxon/DQ, Shell/dsl, **food:** Aunt Sarah's, Burger King, Denny's, El Paso Mexican, Hardee's, KFC, Little Caesar's, McDonald's, Papa Lou's Pizza, Subway, Taco Bell, Waffle House, Wendy's, **lodging:** Econolodge, Holiday Inn, Knight's Inn, Quality Inn, Shoney's Inn, Sleep Inn, **other:** CVS Drug, Food Lion, Kroger, Lowe's Whse, Wal-Mart SuperCtr/24hr
82	US 301, Chamberlayne Ave, E...**gas:** Mobil/dsl, **food:** McDonald's, **lodging:** Quality Inn, Ramada Ltd, Super 8
81	US 1, Chamberlayne Ave(from nb), same as 82
80	Hermitage Rd, Lakeside Ave(from nb, no return), W...**gas:** BP, EC/Subway, **other:** Goodyear/auto, Ginter Botanical Gardens
79	I-64 W, to Charlottesville, I-195 S, to U of Richmond
78	Boulevard(no EZ nb return), E...**lodging:** Holiday Inn, W...**gas:** Citgo/dsl, **food:** BBQ, **lodging:** Day's Inn, **other:** HOSPITAL, to VA HS, stadium
76	Chamberlayne Ave, Belvidere, E...**other:** HOSPITAL, VA Union U
75	I-64 E, VA Beach, to Norfolk, airport
74c	US 33, US 250 W, to Broad St, W...**other:** HOSPITAL, st capitol, Museum of the Confederacy
74b	Franklin St, E...**other:** Richmond Nat Bfd Park
74a	I-195 N, to Powhite Expswy, downtown
73.5mm	James River
73	Maury St, to US 60, US 360, industrial area
69	VA 161, Bells Rd, E...Port of Richmond, W...**gas:** Exxon/dsl/24hr, Shell/dsl, **food:** Hardee's, McDonald's, **lodging:** Candlewood Suites, Ramada Inn, Red Roof Inn

67b a	VA 895 (toll E), VA 150, to Chippenham Pkwy, Falling Creek, W...**gas:** BP, Chevron/dsl, RaceTrac, Shell/dsl, **food:** Blimpie, Burger King, Hardee's, Wendy's
64	VA 613, to Willis Rd, E...**gas:** Exxon, Shell, **food:** Arby's, Aunt Sarah's, Waffle House, **lodging:** Econolodge, Ramada, **other:** Drewy's Bluff Bfd, Hayden's RV Ctr, W...**gas:** Chevron, Citgo/7-11, Mobil/dsl, Shell/dsl, **food:** Bridgette's Rest., Burger King, DQ, McDonald's, **lodging:** Country Inn Suites, Sleep Inn, Super 8, VIP Inn, **other:** flea mkt
62	VA 288 N, to Chesterfield, Powhite Pkwy, to airport
61b a	VA 10, Chester, E...**gas:** RaceTrac/24hr, **food:** Hardee's, Imperial Seafood, **lodging:** Comfort Inn, Courtyard, Hampton Inn, Holiday Inn Express, Homewood Suites, Quality Inn, **other:** HOSPITAL, to James River Plantations, City Point NHS, Petersburg NBF, W...**gas:** BP, Citgo/7-11/dsl, Crown/dsl, EC/dsl, Exxon/dsl, Shell, **food:** Applebee's, Burger King, Capt D's, Cracker Barrel, Denny's, Friendly's, Hooter's, KFC, McDonald's, Pizza Hut, Shoney's, Subway, Taco Bell, Waffle House, Wendy's, Western Sizzlin, **lodging:** Clarion, Day's Inn, Fairfield Inn, Howard Johnson, Super 8, **other:** Aamco, Chevrolet, CVS Drug, K-Mart, Lowe's Whse, Rite Aid, Target, Trak Auto, Ukrops Foods, Winn-Dixie, Roadrunner Camping(2mi), to Pocahontas SP
58	VA 746, to Ruffinmill Rd, E...**gas:** Exxon/dsl(2mi), Shell/dsl, WaWa(2mi), **lodging:** Chester Inn, W...**gas:** Chevron/dsl, **food:** McDonald's, Subway, **lodging:** Day's Inn, Interstate Inn/rest.
54	VA 144, Temple Ave, Hopewell, to Ft Lee, E...**gas:** BP/24hr, Chevron/dsl, Citgo, Crown, Exxon/Subway, Shell/Burger King, **food:** Applebee's, Arby's, Burger King, Golden Corral, La Carreta Mexican, LoneStar Steaks, McDonald's, Old Country Buffet, Outback Steaks, Red Lobster, Ruby Tuesday, Sagebrush Steaks, Taco Bell, Wendy's, **lodging:** Comfort Inn, Hampton Inn, Hilton Garden, Holiday Inn Express(5mi), Innkeeper, **other:** Belk, BooksA-Million, Chevrolet/Cadillac/Buick/Nissan, Circuit City, Dillard's, $Tree, Home Depot, JC Penney, Jo-Ann Fabrics, K-Mart, Macy's, Marshall's, Michael's, Sam's Club, Sears/auto, Staples, Target, U-Haul, Wal-Mart SuperCtr/24hr, mall, W...**gas:** Shell, **food:** Hardee's, **other:** U-Haul, to VSU

(Richmond) *(Chester)*

505

VIRGINIA

Interstate 95

N ↕ S

Petersburg

53	S Park Blvd(from nb), E...same as 54
52.5mm	Appomattox River
52	Washington St, Wythe St, E...**gas:** BP, Citgo, Crown, Shell/dsl, **food:** DQ, Steak&Ale, **lodging:** Best Value, Econolodge, Holiday Inn, King Motel, Ramada, Royal Inn, Star Motel, Super 8, **other:** Petersburg Nat Bfd, W...**gas:** Shell, **food:** Aunt Sarah's, **lodging:** Best Inn, Quality Inn, Radisson, Ramada Inn, HOSPITAL
51	I-85 S, to South Hill, US 460 W
50d	Wythe st, E...**gas:** Exxxon/dsl, Valero/dsl, **lodging:** Best Value Inn, Jade Garden, King Motel, Red Carpet Inn, Royal Inn, Super 8, Travelodge, W... **lodging:** Quality Inn, Ramada Inn,
50b c	E...**gas:** Citgo/7-11, **lodging:** Flagship Inn
50a	US 301, US 460 E, to Crater Rd, County Dr, E... **gas:** BP, Citgo, RaceWay, **food:** Hardee's, McDonald's, **lodging:** Armada Inn, California Inn, Knight's Inn, Quality Inn, **other:** HOSPITAL
48b a	Wagner Rd, W **on Crater Rd...gas: food:** Capt D's, KFC, Pizza Hut, Taste of China, Taco Bell, **other:** Curves, CVS Drug, $Tree, $General, Lincoln/Mercury, Pepboys, Radio Shack, Ukrops Foods, Walgreens, Wal-Mart SuperCtr/24hr, vet
47	VA 629, to Rives Rd, W...**gas:** Citgo, Texaco/dsl, **lodging:** Heritage Motel, **1-2 mi** W...**food:** Arby's, Burger King, Mad Italian, McDonald's, Pizza Hut, Subway, Taco Bell, **lodging:** Crater Inn, LaSalle Motel, **other:** Softball Hall of Fame Museum, same as 48 on US 301
46	I-295 N(exits left from sb), to Washington
45	US 301, E...**gas:** Shell/dsl, W...**gas:** Exxon, **food:** Lighthouse Rest., Nanny's BBQ, Steven-Kent Rest., **lodging:** Best Western, Comfort Inn, Day's Inn/rest., Hampton Inn, Holiday Inn Express, Quality Inn
41	US 301, VA 35, VA 156, E...**gas:** Chevron/dsl, **lodging:** Econolodge, **other:** South 40 camp resort, W...**lodging:** Knight's Inn, Traveler's Inn
40mm	weigh sta both lanes
37	US 301, Carson, W...**gas:** BP/dsl, Shell/dsl
36mm	**rest area nb, full(handicapped)facilities, phone, vending, picnic tables, litter barrel, petwalk**
33	VA 602, W...**gas:** Chevron/dsl, Davis/Exxon/Subway/Starbucks/dsl/scales/24hr, **food:** Burger King, Denny's/24hr, **lodging:** Hampton Inn, Sleep Inn
31	VA 40, Stony Creek, to Waverly, W...**gas:** Shell/dsl/24hr, Sunoco, **food:** Tastee Hut
24	VA 645, no services
20	VA 631, Jarratt, W...**gas:** Exxon/Blimpie/Pizza Hut/dsl/24hr, Race-in/dsl, **other:** Ford
17	US 301, **1 mi** E...**lodging:** Knight's Inn, Reste Motel, **other:** Jellystone Park Camping
13	VA 614, to Emporia, E...**gas:** Shell/dsl
12	US 301(from nb), no services

Emporia

11b a	US 58, Emporia, to South Hill, E...**gas:** BP/DQ/Subway/dsl, Citgo/Burger King, Exxon/LJ Silver/Stuckey's, Shell, Texaco, **food:** Applebee's Arby's, Cracker Barrel, DQ, Hardee's, KFC, McDonald's, Pizza Hut, Wendy's, **lodging:** Fairfield Inn, Holiday Inn, US Inn, **other:** HOSPITAL, Advance Parts, CVS Drug, $Tree, Eckerd, Food Lion, NAPA, Radio Shack, Wal-Mart SuperCtr/24hr, W...**gas:** Exxon, Petrol, Shell/Sadler/dsl/rest./scales/24hr, **food:** Bojangles, Pueblo Viejo, Shoney's, **lodging:** Best Western, Day's Inn, Hampton Inn, Holiday Inn Express, Quality Inn, Sleep Inn
8	US 301, E...**gas:** BP/Simmon's/dsl/rest./scales/24hr, Exxon, **lodging:** Comfort Inn, Red Carpet Inn/rest., **other:** truck repair
4	VA 629, to Skippers, E...**gas:** Loves/McDonald's/dsl/scales/24hr, W...**gas:** Shell/dsl, **lodging:** Best Value Inn, **other:** Cattail Creek Camping(2mi)
3.5mm	Fountain's Creek
.5mm	**Welcome Ctr nb, full(handicapped)facilities, phone, vending, picnic tables, litter barrels, petwalk**
0mm	Virginia/North Carolina state line

Interstate 264(Norfolk)

E ↕ W

Exit #	Services
22	Birdneck Rd, I-264 begins/ends., S...**gas:** Citgo/dsl, Shell, **food:** McDonald's, **lodging:** DoubleTree Hotel, Howard Johnson, Quality Inn, **other:** museum
21	Va Beach Blvd, First Colonial Rd, N...**gas:** Shell, **food:** Applebee's, Burger King, McDonald's, Taco Bell, Wendy's, **other:** K-Mart, S...**other:** 7-11, NAPA
20	US 58 E, to VA Beach Blvd(eb only), N...**gas:** Citgo/7-11, **food:** Hardee's, Tuesday Morning, **other:** Food Lion, TJMaxx
19	Linhaven Pkwy, N...**gas:** Citgo/7-11, **other:** Audi, Ford, Jaguar, Porsche, S...**food:** McDonald's
18	Rosemont, N...**gas:** Citgo, **food:** Wendy's, **lodging:** Econolodge, **other:** Eckerd, S...**gas:** Hess, Shell, WaWa, **food:** Burger King, Denny's, Four Seasons Chinese, KFC, Mi Casita Mexican, Wendy's, **other:** Dodge, Eckerd, Home Depot, Harris Teeter, Honda, Sam's Club/gas, Walgreen
17a b	Independance Blvd, S...**gas:** BP, Citgo/7-11, Crowne Plaza, Shell, **food:** Golden Corral, McDonald's, Pizza Hut, Starbucks, Trip's Rest, Wendy's, **lodging:** Day's Inn, Extended Stay America, Fairfield Inn, InTown Suites, **other:** Best Buy, Circuit City, Sears/auto
16	Witchduck, no services

506

VIRGINIA

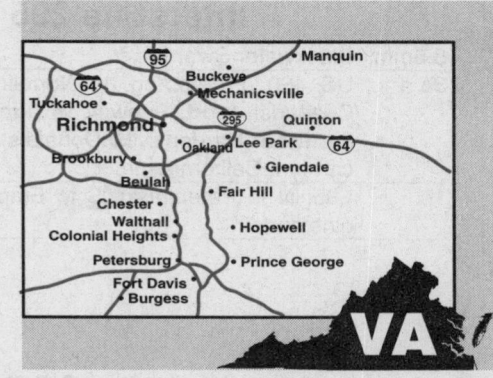

Interstate 264

15a b	Newtown Rd, **N**...**gas:** Citgo, Crown Royal, **food:** Wendy's, **lodging:** TownePlace Suites, **S**...**gas:** BP, Shell, **food:** Denny's, 7-11, **lodging:** Courtyard, Hampton Inn, Holiday Inn, La Quinta, Red Roof Inn, SpringHill Suites **other:** Rite Aid
14b a	I-64. US 13, to Military Hwy
13	US 13, Military Hwy, **N**...**food:** Wendy's, **lodging:** Best Western, Day's Inn
12	Ballentine Blvd, **N**...**other:** HOSPITAL, Norfolk SU
11b a	US 460, VA 166/168, Brambleton Ave, Campostello Rd, **N**...**gas:** 7-11
10	Tidewater Dr, City Hall Ave, **N**...**food:** Hooters, Jillian's Rest, Joe's Crabshack, King's Chinese, Outback Steaks, **lodging:** Omni Hotel, Sheraton
9	St Paul's Blvd, Waterside Dr, to Harbor Park Stadium
8	I-464 S, to Chesapeake
7.5mm	tunnel
7b a	VA 141, Effingham St, Crawford St, **N**...**other:** Naval HOSPITAL, **S**...**other:** Shipyard
6.5mm	weigh sta eb
6	Des Moines Ave(from eb), no services
5	US 17, Frederick Blvd, Midtown Tunnel, **S**...**gas:** BP
4	VA 337, Portsmouth Blvd, no services
3	Victory Blvd, **N**...**gas:** Exxon, **food:** DQ, Pizza Hut, Ruby Tuesday, Wendy's, **other:** AutoZone, $Tree, FarmFresh Food/drug, Ford, Lowe's Whse, Radio Shack
2b a	Greenwood Dr, no services
0mm	I-264 begins/ends on I-64, exit 299.

Interstate 295(Richmond)

Exit #	Services
53b a	I-64, W to Charlottesville, E to Richmond, to US 250, I-295 begins/ends.
51b a	Nuckols Rd, **1 mi N**...**gas:** BP, Miller's Gas/dsl, **food:** Chen's Chinese, Subway, **other:** CVS Drug, FoodLion, Walgreen, **S**...**gas:** Exxon, **food:** Capital Alehouse, Mkt Cafe
49b a	US 33, Richmond, **1mi S**...**other:** Ukrop's Foods
45b a	Woodman Rd, **1mi S**...**gas:** BP, Citgo, **other:** CVS Drug, Meadow Farm Museum
43	I-95, US 1, N to Washington, S to Richmond(exits left from nb), **services on US 1, N**...**gas:** BP/dsl, Mobil, Shell, **food:** Burger King, Chick-fil-A, Chili's, FoodCourt, **lodging:** Best Western, SpringHill Suites, **other:** AmeriCamps, Kosmo Village, mall, **1-2 mi S**...**gas:** Exxon, EastCoast/dsl, Shell, WaWa/dsl, **food:** Aunt Sarah's, El Paso Mexican, Hardee's, McDonald's, Subway, Taco Bell, Waffle House, Wendy's, **lodging:** Broadway Motel, Cavalier Motel, Econolodge, GuestHouse Inn, Howard Johnson, Knight's Inn, Quality Inn, Shoney's Inn, **other:** Food Lion, Eckerd, Firestone, Lowe's Whse, Wal-Mart SuperCtr/24hr

41b a	US 301, VA 2, **E**...**gas:** BP/dsl, Shell/dsl, **food:** Burger King, McDonald's, Subway, **W**...**gas:** Exxon/dsl, **food:** Friendly's
38b a	VA 627, Pole Green Rd, **E**...**gas:** Citgo, **food:** Subway, **W**...**gas:** BP/café, Citgo, **other:** Strawberry Hill Funpark, fairgrounds
37b a	US 360, **1 mi E**...**gas:** Crown, Shell/dsl, **food:** Applebee's, Arby's, Cracker Barrel, IHOP, McDonald's, Mexico Rest., Outback Steaks, Ruby Tuesday, Taco Bell, Waffle House, Wendy's, **lodging:** Hampton Inn, Holiday Inn Express, **other:** BJ's/Gas, $Tree, Home Depot, Kohl's, Target, Ukrops Foods, Wal-Mart SuperCtr/24hr, **W**...**gas:** BP, Citgo/7-11, Mobil/dsl, **food:** Colonial Rest., **other:** NAPA, to Mechanicsville
34b a	VA 615, Creighton Rd, **E**...**gas:** BP/dsl, **5 mi W**...**gas:** Citgo, **food:** McDonald's
31b a	VA 156, **E**...**gas:** Citgo/dsl, **other:** to Cold Harbor, **4 mi W**...**gas:** BP/dsl, Citgo, Shell/dsl, **food:** Antonio's Pizza, Hardee's, Popeye's, **lodging:** Courtyard, Day's Inn, Econolodge, Hampton Inn, Hilton, Holiday Inn, Microtel, Motel 6, Wingate Inn
28	I-64, to US 60, **W**...**other:** museum
25	Rd 895 W(toll), to Richmand, no services
22b a	VA 5, Charles City, **E**...**gas:** BP, Exxon/dsl, **food:** DQ, **other:** Shirley Plantation, **W**...**gas:** BP, **other:** Richmond Nat Bfd
18mm	James River
15b a	VA 10, Hopewell, **E**...**gas:** BP/dsl, Citgo, **food:** Burger King, **lodging:** Evergreen Motel, **other:** HOSPITAL, James River Plantations, **W**...**gas:** EastCoast/Subway/dsl, Exxon/dsl, WaWa, **food:** Burger King, Chen's Rest., Cracker Barrel, Denny's, Friendly's, Jalapeño's, McDonald's, River's Bend Cafe, Waffle House, Wendy's, **lodging:** AmeriSuites, Clarion, Comfort Inn, Hampton Inn, Holiday Inn Express
13mm	Appomattox River
9b a	VA 36, Hopewell, **E**...**gas:** Chevron, Petrol, **food:** El Nopal Mexican, Hong Kong's Rest., Rosa'a Italian, **lodging:** Econolodge, Innkeeper, **other:** Advance Parts, AutoZone, **W**...**gas:** BP/dsl/24hr, Exxon/Bullets, Pilot/dsl/24hr, Shell, **food:** Burger King, Denny's, DQ, Japanese Steaks, Kanpai Japanese, McDonald's, Papa John's, Pizza Hut, Shoney's, Subway, Taco Bell, Waffle House, Wendy's, Western Sizzlin, Willie's Diner, **lodging:** Candlewood Suites, Comfort Inn, Hampton Inn, Holiday Inn Express, **other:** Chevrolet, Family$, Food Lion, Rite Aid, U-Haul, US Army Museum, Winn-Dixie/deli, to Petersburg NBF

507

VIRGINIA

Interstate 295

N ↕ S

5.5mm	Blackwater Swamp
3b a	US 460, Petersburg, to Norfolk, E...**gas:** East-Coast/dsl, **food:** Subway, W...**gas:** BP(3mi), Exxon, **food:** Hardee's, McDonald's, **lodging:** American Inn, California Inn
1	I-95, N to Petersburg, S to Emporium, I-295 begins/ends

Interstate 495(DC)

N ↕ S

Exit #	Services
27	I-95, N to Baltimore, S to Richmond. I-495 & I-95 S run together., no services
28b a	MD 650, New Hampshire Ave, N...**gas:** Amoco/24hr, Exxon/dsl, Shell/autocare/24hr, 7-11, **food:** KFC, Shoney's, **other:** CVS Drug, Radio Shack, Safeway
29b a	MD 193, University Blvd, no services
30b a	US 29, Colesville, N...**gas:** BP, Shell, 7-11/Jerry's Subs, **food:** McDonald's, **other:** Safeway
31b a	MD 97, Georgia Ave, Silver Springs, S...**gas:** BP/dsl, Exxon/dsl, Shell, Texaco/dsl, **food:** Hunan Chinese, **other:** CVS Drug, Merchants Tire, Snider's Foods, Staples
33	MD 185, Connecticut Ave, N...**other:** LDS Temple, S...**gas:** BP, Citgo, Sunoco, **food:** Chevy Chase Foods
34	MD 355, Wisconsin Ave, Bethesda, no services
35	(from wb), I-270
36	MD 187, Old Georgetown Rd, S...**other:** HOSPITAL
38	I-270, to Frederick
39	MD 190, River Rd, Washington, Potomac
40	Cabin John Pkwy, Glen Echo(from sb), no trucks
41	Clara Barton Pkwy, Carderock, Great Falls, no trucks
42mm	**Potomac River, Virginia/Maryland state line. Exits 41-27 are in Maryland.**
43	G Washington Mem Pkwy, no trucks
44	VA 193, Langley, no services
45b a	VA 267 W(toll), to I-66 E, to Dulles Airport
46b a	VA 123, Chain Bridge Rd, W...**lodging:** Hilton
47b a	VA 7, Leesburg Pike, Tysons Corner, Falls Church, E...Doubletree, W...**gas:** BP/dsl, Crown Gas, Exxon, Mobil, Shell, **food:** Chili's, McDonald's, NY Deli, Olive Garden, On-the-Border, Pizza Hut, **lodging:** Marriott, **other:** Best Buy, Borders Books, Ford, Nordstrom's, 7-11, mall
49c b a	I-66(exits left from both lanes), to Manassas, Front Royal

DC Area

50b a	US 50, Arlington Blvd, Fairfax, Arlington, N...**lodging:** Marriott, S...**gas:** Shell, **food:** Uno Pizzaria, **lodging:** Residence Inn, **other:** HOSPITAL, CVS Drug, Giant Foods
51	VA 657, Gallows Rd, S...**gas:** Exxon, 7-11, **other:** HOSPITAL
52b a	VA 236, Little River Tpk, Fairfax, N...**gas:** Citgo, Mobil/repair, 7-11, **food:** McDonald's, Wendy's
54b a	VA 620, Braddock Rd, Ctr for the Arts, Geo Mason U, S...**gas:** Mobil/dsl, 7-11, **other:** Rite Aid, Safeway
56c b a	I-95 S, I-395 N, I-95 N. I-495 & I-95 N run together.

Interstate 664(Portsmouth)

N ↕ S

Exit #	Services
14	I-664 begins/ends on I-64, exit 299.
13b a	US 13, US 58, US 460, Military Hwy, **1-2mi** N...**gas:** Citgo/7-11, Shell, **food:** Arby's, Boston Mkt, Burger King, Chick-fil-A, Hooters, KFC, Wendy's, Home Depot, IHOP, Schlotzsky's, Sonic, Taco Bell, Uno Pizzaria, Uptown Buffet, **lodging:** Best Western, Day's Inn, Econolodge, Motel 6, Ramada Ltd, **other:** FarmFresh Foods/gas, FoodLion, Lowe's Whse, Nissan, PepBoys, Target, Walgreens, Wal-Mart SuperCtr/24hr
12	VA 663, Dock Landing Rd, no services
11b a	VA 337, Portsmouth Blvd, E...**lodging:** Holiday Inn Express, gas, food
10	10 VA 659, Pughsville Rd, E...**gas:** Citgo, Shell
9b a	US 17, US 164, E...**gas:** Citgo/7-11, **other:** AutoValue Parts, Honda, Chevrolet, W...**gas:** food, lodging, to James River Br, museum
8b a	VA 135, College Dr, E...**gas:** Citgo/7-11, Shell/Burger King, **food:** McDonald's, Ruby Tuesday, Subway, Wendy's, **other:** FoodLion, Radio Shack, Wal-Mart SuperCtr/24hr
11.5mm	insp sta nb
9mm	James River
8mm	tunnel
7	Terminal Ave, no services
6	25th St, 26th St, E...**gas:** Citgo/7-11, **food:** McDonald's
5	US 60 W, 35th St, Jefferson Ave, E...**gas:** Citgo, **food:** Burger King, Church's, KFC
4	Chesnut Ave, Roanoke Ave, no services
3	Aberdeen Rd, E...**gas:** Citgo/dsl, W...**food:** Hardee's, McDonald's, Wendy's
2	Powhatan Pkwy, no services
1b a	I-64, W to Richmond, E to Norfolk. I-664 begins/ends on I-64

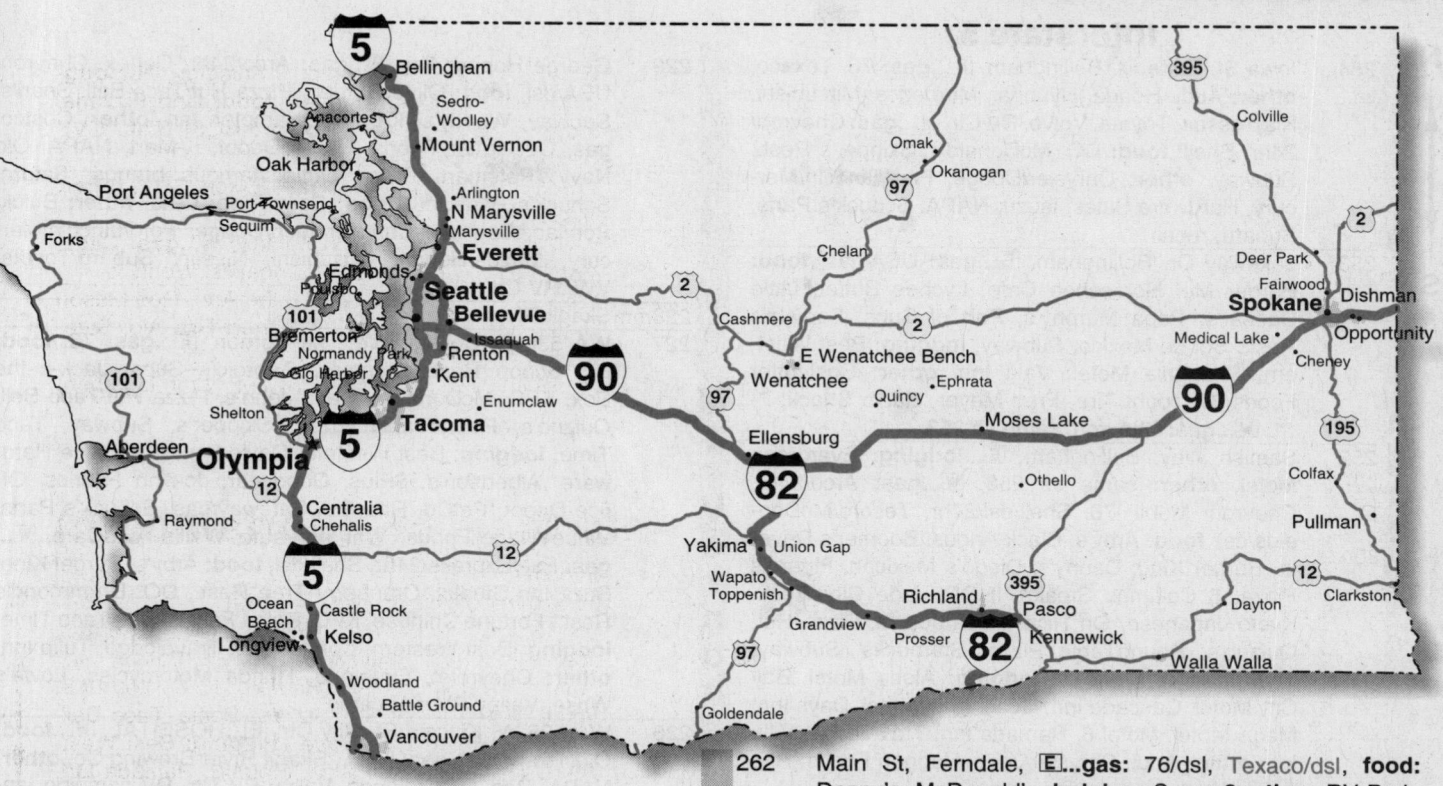

WASHINGTON

Interstate 5

Exit #	Services
277mm	USA/Canada Border, Washington state line, customs
276	WA 548 S, Blaine, E...gas: MP/dsl, 76/dsl, Shell/dsl, USA/dsl/24hr, food: Big Al's Diner, Pasa del Norte Mexican, other: Ammex Duty Free, to Peace Arch SP, W...gas: Chevron/repair, food: Bella Marina Rest., Great Northern Cafe, Ocean Bay Rest., Pizza Factory, Seaside Bakery, Subway, Truffle's Seafood Rest., lodging: Anchor Inn, Bayside Motel, Cottage by the Bay B&B, International Motel/cafe, other: Coast to Coast Hardware, NAPA
275	WA 543 N(from nb, no return), truck customs, E...gas: Chevron/dsl, Exxon/dsl, Shell/dsl, food: Burger King, Little Caesars, other: VET, CostCutters, Rite Aid
274	Peace Portal Drive(from nb, no return), Blaine, W...gas: Shell, other: Semi-ah-moo Resort, camping
270	Birch Bay, Lynden, W...gas: Shell/Subway/dsl/24hr, lodging: Semi-ah-moo Resort, other: Birch Bay Outlet/famous brands, SeaBreeze RV Park(5mi)
269mm	Welcome Ctr sb, full(handicapped)facilities, info, phone, picnic tables, litter barrels, petwalk, vending
267mm	rest area nb, full(handicapped)facilities, info, phone, picnic tables, litter barrels, petwalk, vending
266	WA 548 N, Grandview Rd, Custer, W...gas: Arco/24hr, Birch Bay SP
263	Portal Way, E...gas: Shell/dsl, food: Madison's rest., other: Cedars RV Park
263mm	Nooksack River

Exit #	Services
262	Main St, Ferndale, E...gas: 76/dsl, Texaco/dsl, food: Denny's, McDonald's, lodging: Super 8, other: RV Park, U-Haul, W...gas: Exxon/dsl/LP, 76, Shell/Domino's/dsl, food: Bob's Burgers, DQ, Mounts Cafe, Quizno's, lodging: Scottish Lodge, other: VET, Costcutter Foods, Haggen's Foods, NAPA, Schwab Tire, Walgreens
260	Slater Rd, Lummi Island, E...gas: Arco/24hr, other: El Monte RV, antiques, 5 mi W...gas: 76, Shell/dsl, other: Eagle Haven RV Park(8mi), Silver Reef Casino/Red River café(10mi), Lummi Ind Res
258	Bakerview Rd, E...gas: Fred Meyer/gas, W...gas: Arco/24hr, Exxon/dsl/24hr, 76, food: Mykono's Greek Rest., lodging: Hampton Inn, Shamrock Motel, other: airport, RV Park, st patrol
257	Northwest Ave, E...other: Chevrolet/Cadillac
256b	Bellis Fair Mall Pkwy, E...other: Sears, Target, mall
256a	WA 539 N, Meridian St, E...gas: Exxon/dsl, Shell/dsl, food: Arby's, Boston's Pizza, Burger King, China Buffet, Coldstone, DQ, Denny's, Godfather's, Izzy's Pizza, Kowloon Garden, McDonald's, McHale's Rest., Olive Garden, Pizza Hut, Quizno's, Red Robin, Shari's/24hr, Starbucks, Taco Bell, Taco Time, Tad Thai, Wendy's, lodging: Best Western, Comfort Inn, Day's Inn, Holiday Inn Express, Quality Inn, other: AAA, Barnes&Noble, Best Buy, Bon-Marche, Circuit City, Costco/gas, Costcutter Foods, Home Depot, JC Penney, Mervyn's, Nordstrom's, Office Depot, Petco, Rite Aid, Ross, Safeway, Schuck's Parts, Schwab Tire, Sears, Target, U-haul, Walgreens, Wal-Mart/auto, mall, st patrol, to Nooksack Ind Res, W...food: Eleni's Rest., lodging: Rodeway Inn, Travel House Inn
255	WA 542 E, Sunset Dr, Bellingham, E...gas: Chevron/dsl/24hr, Exxon, Shell/Subway/Domino's/dsl, food: A&W/KFC, Applebee's, Hawaii BBQ, Jack-in-the-Box, Panda Express, RoundTable Pizza, Taco Bell, other: Costcutter Foods, Farmers Outlet, Jo-Ann Fabrics, K-Mart, Lowe's Whse, Rite Aid, Tuesday Morning, Walgreens, USPO, to Mt Baker, W...other: HOSPITAL

N ↕ S

Bellingham

254	Iowa St, State St, Bellingham, **E**...**gas:** 76, Texaco, **other:** Audi, Honda, Hyundai, Mercedes, Mitsubishi, Kia, Nissan, Toyota, Volvo, RV Ctr, **W**...**gas:** Chevron/24hr, Shell, **food:** DQ, McDonald's, Skipper's Rest., Subway, **other:** Chrysler/Dodge, Ford/Lincoln/Mercury, Hardware Sales, Isuzu, NAPA, Schuck's Parts, Subaru, repair
253	Lakeway Dr, Bellingham, **E**...**gas:** USA/gas, **food:** Burger Me, Horseshoe Cafe, Lychee Buffet, Little Caesar's, Papa Murphy's, Port of Subs, Sadighi's Rest., Sol de Mexico, Subway, **lodging:** Best Western, Shangrila Motel, Valu Inn, **other:** Costcutter Foods, Discount Tire, Fred Meyer, Radio Shack, 7-11, **W**...**gas:** Chevron, same as 252
252	Samish Way, Bellingham, **E**...**lodging:** Evergreen Motel, **other:** same as 253, **W**...**gas:** Arco/24hr, Chevron, Mobil, 76, Shell/dsl/24hr, Tesoro/McDonalds/dsl, **food:** Arby's, Black Angus, Boomer's Drive-In, Burger King, Denny's, Diego's Mexican, Figaro's Pizza, 5 Columns Steaks, IHOP, Jade City Rest., Kyoto Japanese, On Rice, Papa John's, Pizza Hut, Quizno's, RoundTable Pizza, Starbucks, Subway, Thai Cuisine, Wendy's, **lodging:** Aloha Motel, Bay City Motel, Cascade Inn, Coachman Motel, Days Inn, Mac's Motel, Motel 6, Ramada Inn, Travelodge, Villa Inn, **other:** Audi, Chrysler/Jeep, Haggen Foods, Rite Aid, VW
250	WA 11 S, Chuckanut Dr, Bellingham, Fairhaven Hist Dist, **W**...**gas:** Arco, Chevron/repair, **food:** Dos Padres Mexican, SkyLark Café, Tony's Café, Win's Drive-In, **other:** Food Pavilion, Larrabee SP, to Alaska Ferry
246	N Lake Samish, **W**...**gas:** Shell/dsl, **other:** Lake Padden RA, RV camping
242	Nulle Rd, S Lake Samish, no services
240	Alger, **E**...**gas:** Shell/dsl/LP/RV dump, **food:** Alger Grille, **lodging:** Whispering Firs Motel/RV Parking
238mm	**rest area both lanes, full(handicapped)facilities, phone, picnic tables, litter barrels, vending, petwalk**
236	Bow Hill Rd, **E**...Chevron/dsl, Skagit Hotel Casino/rest.
235mm	weigh sta sb
234mm	Samish River
232	Cook Rd, Sedro-Woolley, **E**...**gas:** 76/dsl, Shell/dsl, **food:** Avalon, Bob's Burgers, Buzz Inn Steaks, Iron Skillet Rest.(4mi), **lodging:** 3 Rivers Inn(5mi), **other:** HOSPITAL, KOA
231	WA 11 N, Chuckanut Dr, **E**...**other:** Camping World, Foley's RV/marine, Kia, st patrol, to Larrabee SP
230	WA 20, Burlington, **E**...**gas:** Shell/dsl, Tesoro, **food:** Beary Patch Rest., Burger King, China Wok, El Cavador, 5-20 Grill, Jack-in-the-Box, Krispy Kreme, Outback Steaks, Pizza Factory, Red Robin, Subway, **lodging:** Cocusa Motel, **other:** HOSPITAL, Bon-Marche, Fred Meyer, Haggen Foods, JC Penney, Macy's, Schwab Tire, Sears/auto, Target, mall, to N Cascades NP, **W**...**gas:** Arco/dsl/24hr, Chevron/dsl, **food:** McDonald's, **lodging:** Holiday Inn Express, Mark II Motel, **other:** Harley-Davidson, to San Juan Ferry

Mt Vernon

229	George Hopper Rd, **E**...**gas:** Arco/24hr, Cenex, Chevron, USA/dsl, **food:** Olive Garden, Pizza Hut/Taco Bell, Shari's, Subway, Wendy's, **lodging:** Hampton Inn, **other:** Costco/gas, Costcutter Foods, Home Depot, K-Mart, NAPA, Old Navy, Petsmart, Prime Outlets/famous brands, Saturn, Schuck's Parts, **W**...**food:** Easy Rider Cafe, **other:** Buick/Pontiac, Cadillac, Chrysler/Jeep/Dodge, Ford/Lincoln/Mercury, Mazda/Honda, Mitsubishi, Nissan, Subaru/Toyota, VW, RV Ctr
228mm	Skagit River
227	WA 538 E, College Way, Mt Vernon, **E**...**gas:** 76, **food:** Big Scoop Rest., Denny's, Georgio's Subs, Jack-in-the-Box, KFC, McDonald's, Papa John's, Pizza Hut/Taco Bell, Quizno's, RoundTable Pizza, Skipper's, Subway, Taco Time, **lodging:** Best Western, Day's Inn, **other:** Ace Hardware, Albertson's, $Plus, Goodyear, Jo-Ann Fabrics, Office Depot, PetCo, Rite Aid, Safeway/gas, Schuck's Parts, ValueVillage Foods, Wal-Mart/auto, Walt's AutoCare, **W**...**gas:** FuelExpress/24hr, Shell/dsl, **food:** Arby's, Burger King, Buzz Inn Steaks, Cranberry Tree Rest., DQ, Drummond's Rest., Fortune Chinese, KFC, Royal Fork Buffet, Taco Time, **lodging:** Best Western, Comfort Inn, Travelodge, Tulip Inn, **other:** Chevrolet, Firestone, Honda Motorcycles, Lowe's Whse, Valley RV, RV camp
226	WA 536 W, Kincaid St, City Ctr, **E**...HOSPITAL, **W**...**food:** Old Towne Grainery Rest., Skagit River Brewing Co, **other:** NAPA, Red Apple Foods, Valley RV Ctr, RV camping, antiques
225	Anderson Rd, **E**...**gas:** Fuel Express, 76/dsl, **other:** Lifestyles RV Ctr, **W**...**gas:** Chevron, Gasco Trkstp/dsl, **other:** Freightliner, Pulsbo RV Ctr
224	WA 99 S(from nb, no return), S Mt Vernon, **E**...**gas:**/dsl, food
221	WA 534 E, Conway, Lake McMurray, **E**...**gas:** Shell/dsl/24hr, **W**...**gas:** 76/dsl, Shell/dsl, **food:** Conway Deli, **lodging:** Channel Lodge/Rest.(11mi), **other:** Blake's RV Park/marina
218	Starbird Rd, **W**...**lodging:** Hillside Motel
215	300th NW, no services
214mm	weigh sta nb
212	WA 532 W, Stanwood, Bryant, **W**...**gas:** 76/dsl, Shell/dsl, 4 mi **W**...**food:** Burger King, DQ, Mkt St Café, McDonald's, **other:** Haggen Foods/cafe/24hr, Camano Island SP(19mi)
210	236th NE, no services
209mm	Stillaguamish River
208	WA 530, Silvana, Arlington, **E**...**gas:** Chevron/24hr, 76/Circle K, Shell, Tesoro, **food:** Denny's, O'Brien Turkeyhouse, **lodging:** Arlington Motel, **other:** HOSPITAL, to N Cascades Hwy, **W**...**gas:** 76/dsl
207mm	**rest area both lanes, full(handicapped)facilities, phone, picnic tables, litter barrels, coffee, vending, RV dump, petwalk**
206	WA 531, Lakewood, **E**...**gas:** Arco/24hr, Mobil, 76/dsl/LP, RV dump, Shell/24hr, 7-11/Citgo, **food:** Alfy's Pizza, Buzz Inn Steaks, Dominos, Food Pavillion, Jack-in-the-Box, KFC, McDonald's, Starbucks, Taco Time, **lodging:** Crossroads Inn, Hawthorn Suites, Smokey Point Motel, **other:** Chrysler/Jeep, Harley Davidson, Lowe's Whse, Pontiac/Buick/GMC, Rite Aid, Safeway/gas/24hr, Schuck's Parts, Schwab Tire, **W**...**gas:** Chevron/24hr, **food:** Village Rest., **other:** Costco/gas, to Wenburg SP

Interstate 5

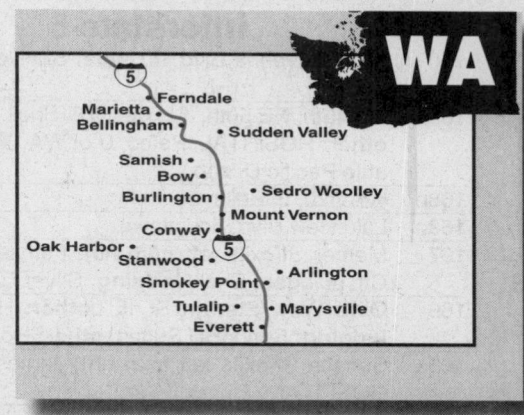

202	116th NE, **E...gas:** Shell/dsl, Texaco, **W...gas:** Donna's Trkstp/Gull/dsl/24hr/@, **food:** McDonald's, Starbucks, **other:** Albertsons/Savon, Kohls, Ross, Seattle Premium Outlets/famous brands, WinCo, st patrol
200	88th St NE, Quil Ceda Way, **E...gas:** Citgo/7-11, 76, Shell/dsl/LP, **food:** Applebees, Quizno's, Starbucks, **other:** Haggen's Foods/24hr, **W...food:** Port of Subs, Taco Del Mar, **other:** Home Depot, Wal-Mart/SuperCtr/24hr/auto/gas, casino
199	WA 528 E, Marysville, Tulalip, **E...gas:** Arco/24hr, Chevron/24hr, 76, Shell/Subway/dsl, **food:** Burger King, Don's Rest./24hr, DQ, Jack-in-the-Box, Las Margaritas Mexican, **lodging:** Village Motel/Rest., **other:** Albertson's, JC Penney, Rite Aid, Schwab Tire, Staples, **W...gas:** 76, **food:** Arby's, Las Margaritas, McDonald's, Taco Time, Wendy's, **lodging:** Best Western/rest., Comfort Inn, **other:** Chevrolet/Subaru, RV SuperMall, to Tulalip Indian Res
198	Port of Everett(from sb), Steamboat Slough, st patrol
195mm	Snohomish River
195	Port of Everett(from nb), Marine View Dr
194	US 2 E, Everett Ave, City Ctr, **W...gas:** Shell/dsl, Schwab Tire
193	WA 529, Pacific Ave(from nb), **W...gas:** Chevron, 76, **food:** Denny's, Roaster Rest., **lodging:** Best Western, Gardner Bay Inn, Holiday Inn, Howard Johnson, Inn at the Center, Marina Village Inn(3mi), **other:** HOSPITAL
192	Broadway, to Evergreen Way, City Ctr, **W...gas:** Arco/24hr, Chevron, Exxon, 76, Shell, **food:** Alfy's Pizza, Buzz Inn Steaks, Iver's Seafood, Jack-in-the-Box, King's Table, McDonald's, O'Donnell's Café, Petosa's On Broadway, Taco Bell, **lodging:** Day's Inn, Royal Motor Inn, Travelodge, **other:** Ford
189	WA 526 W, WA 527, Everett Mall Way, Everett, **E...gas:** Arco/24hr, Exxon, Shell/dsl, **food:** Alfy's Pizza, Burger King, Buzz Inn Steaks, McDonald's, Wendy's, **lodging:** Extended Stay Deluxe, Travelodge, **other:** VET, **1 mi W on Evergreen Way...gas:** Chevron, Shell, 7-11, **food:** Denny's, Godfather's, Taco Bell, Taco Time, Village Inn Rest., **lodging:** Comfort Inn, Days Inn, Extended Stay America, Motel 6, Sunrise Inn, **other:** Bon-Marche, Buick/Pontiac, Discount Tire, Dodge/Jeep, Firestone/auto, Fred Meyer, K-Mart, mall
188mm	**rest area/weigh sta sb, full(handicapped) facilities, info, phone, picnic tables, litter barrels, coffee, RV dump**
186	WA 96, 128th SW, **E...gas:** 76, Shell/dsl/24hr, **food:** O'Donnells Rest., **lodging:** Comfort Inn, Holiday Inn, Quality Inn, **other:** Lakeside RV Park, Silver Lake RV Park, **W...gas:** Arco/24hr, Chevron/24hr, Citgo/7-11, Shell, Texaco, **food:** A&W/KFC, DQ, Denny's, McDonald's, Mitzel's Kitchen, Mongolian Grill, Pizza Hut, Skipper's, Starbucks, Subway, Taco Bell/24hr, **lodging:** Best Western, Cypress Inn, Everett Inn, Holiday Inn Express, Motel 6, **other:** Albertson's/Savon, $Tree, Goodyear/auto, Maple RV Park, transmissions
183	164th SW, **E...gas:** Arco, Shell/dsl/24hr, **food:** Capri Ristorante, Jack-in-the-Box/24hr, Panda Express, Starbucks, Subway, Taco Del Mar, Taco Time, **other:** Curves, Radio Shack, Walgreens, Wal-Mart, **W...gas:** Shell/Quizno's/dsl, **other:** Alderwood Mall Blvd
182	**E...I-405 S, to Bellevue, W...WA 525, Alderwood Mall Blvd, to Alderwood Mall, gas:** Arco/24hr, **food:** Keg Steaks/seafood, TCBY, **lodging:** Residence Inn, **other:** Marshall's, Michael's, Nordstrom's, Sears/auto, Target, Evans Tire
181	44th Ave W, to WA 524, Lynnwood, **E...gas:** Arco, 76, Shell, Texaco, **food:** McDonald's, **lodging:** Embassy Suites, Extended Stay America, Hampton Inn, **other:** Albertson's, Barnes&Noble, Best Buy, Circuit City, Lowe's Whse, Old Navy, Petco, Staples, **W...gas:** Arco, Chevron/24hr, 76/dsl, 7-11, Shell/repair, **food:** Applebee's, Azteca Mexican, Black Angus, Buca Italian, Burger King, Cafe India, Chipotle Mexican, Country Harvest Rest., Denny's, IHOP, Jack-in-the-Box, KFC, McDonald's, Olive Garden, Panda Express, Red Lobster, Rock Grill, Small World Cuisine, Starbucks, Subway, Taco Del Mar, Tony Roma's, Wendy's, **lodging:** Best Western, Comfort Inn, Courtyard, Holiday Inn Express, La Quinta, **other:** AAA, CompUSA, Firestone/auto, Fred Meyer, Goodyear/auto, Hancock Fabrics, Marshall's, Michael's, Radio Shack, Target, mall, USPO
179	220th SW, Mountlake Terrace, Mountlake Terrace, **W...gas:** Shell/dsl, 7-11, **food:** Azteca Mexican, Port of Subs, Starbucks, Subway, **other:** HOSPITAL
178	236th St SW(from nb), Mountlake Terrace
177	WA 104, Edmonds, **E...gas:** Chevron/24hr, Shell/dsl, **food:** Canyons Rest., McDonald's, Starbucks, Subway, **lodging:** Studio 6, **other:** CompUSA, Office Depot, RiteAid, Schuck's Parts, **1-2 mi W on WA 99...gas:** 76/dsl, **food:** Arby's, Barlee's Rest., China Clipper Rest., Denny's, Godfather's, KFC, Scott's Grill, Starbucks, Todo Mexico, **lodging:** Day's Inn, **other:** Costco, GNC, Home Depot, Nissan, Petco, Radio Shack, VW
176	NE 175th St, Aurora Ave N, to Shoreline
175	WA 523, NE 145th, 5th Ave NE, **1 mi W on WA 99...food:** Las Margaritas Mexican, Shari's, Taco Time, Wendy's, **other:** $Store, Schuck's Parts
174	NE 130th, Roosevelt Way, **nb only, 1 mi W on WA 99...food:** Burger King, KFC, **lodging:** Best Western, **other:** Albertson's, Buick/GMC, Firestone, K-Mart, Office Depot, Rite Aid, Sam's Club
173	1st Ave NE, Northgate Way, **E...food:** Azteca Mexican, Baskin-Robbins, California Pizza Kitchen, Jaithai, Marie Callender's, Quizno's, Red Robin, Starbucks, Subway, Tony Roma's, **other:** Best Buy, Curves, Discount Tire, JC Penney, Macys, Nordstrom's, Ross, Target, TJ Maxx, mall, **W...gas:** Chevron, 76, Shell/dsl, **food:** Arby's, Birkshire Grill., McDonald's, **lodging:** Hotel Nexus, **other:** 7-11
172	N 85th, Aurora Ave
171	WA 522, Lake City Way, Bothell

Interstate 5

N

↕

S

Seattle

170	(nb only)Ravenna Blvd, 🅔...**gas:** Shell/dsl, **other:** QFC Foods
169	NE 45th, NE 50th, 🅔...**gas:** 76, Shell, **food:** Subway, **other:** HOSPITAL, Petco, U of WA, 🅦...**other:** to Seattle Pacific U, zoo
168b	WA 520, to Bellevue
168a	Lakeview Blvd, downtown
167	Mercer St(exits left from nb), Fairview Ave, Seattle Ctr, 🅦...**gas:** Shell, **lodging:** Silver Cloud Inn
166	Olive Way, Stewart St, 🅔...**other:** HOSPITAL, 🅦...**lodging:** SpringHill Suites, **other:** Honda
165a	Seneca St(exits left from nb), James St, 🅔...**other:** HOSPITAL
165b	Union St, 🅔...Summerfield Suites, 🅦...**food:** Ruth's Chris Steak, **lodging:** Renaissance Inn
164b	4th Ave S, to Kingdome, 1 mi 🅦...same as 163
164a	I-90 E, to Spokane
163	6th Ave, S Spokane St, W Seattle Br, Columbian Way, 1 mi 🅦 **on 4th Ave**...**gas:** Arco, **food:** Arby's, Burger King/24hr, Denny's, McDonald's, Subway, Taco Bell, **other:** Sears, auto repair, transmissions
162	Corson Ave, Michigan St(exits left from nb), same as 161
161	Swift Ave, Albro Place, 🅦...**gas:** Shell, **food:** Thai Rest., **lodging:** Georgetown Inn
158	Pacific Hwy S, E Marginal Way, 🅦...**gas:** Chevron, **food:** Randy's Rest., **lodging:** Econolodge, Red Lion Inn, Travelodge, **other:** HOSPITAL
157	ML King Way, no services
156	WA 539 N, Interurban Ave(no EZ return to sb), Tukwila, 🅔...**gas:** Pacific Pride/dsl, **food:** Gordy's Rest., 🅦...**gas:** 76/dsl, Shell/dsl, **food:** Emerald Green, Jack-in-the-Box, Quizno's, **lodging:** Day's Inn, **other:** Harley-Davidson
154b	WA 518, Burien, 🅦...**lodging:** Extended Stay America
154a	I-405, N to Bellevue
153	S Center Pkwy, (from nb), 🅔...**gas:** Chevron/dsl, **food:** Applebees, Azteca Mexican, Claim Jumper, Denny's, Jack-in-the-Box, Mizu Steaks, Newport Bay Rest., Olive Garden, Outback Steaks, Quizno's, Red Robin, Sizzler, Starbucks, Subway, Stanford's Rest, Taco Bell, Tony Roma, Zoopa, **lodging:** DoubleTree Inn, **other:** Best Buy, Borders, CompUSA, Jo-Ann Fabrics, Macy's, Old Navy, Petsmart, Sears/auto, Ross, Target, mall
152	S 188th, Orillia Rd, 🅔...**other:** KOA, 🅦...**gas:** 76/dsl, **food:** Dennys, Daves Diner, Jack in the Box, Taco Bell, **lodging:** Airport Plaza Hotel, Clarion, Comfort Inn, Day's Inn, DoubleTree, Econolodge, Hampton Inn, La Quinta, Motel 6, Quality Inn, Super 8, **other:** NAPA, 7-11
151	S 200th, Military Rd, 🅔...**gas:** Shell/dsl, **lodging:** Motel 6, 🅦...**gas:** Chevron, Citgo/7-11, 76, **lodging:** Best Western, Fairfield Inn, Hampton Inn, MiniRate Motel, Skyway Inn, Sleep Inn
149	WA 516, to Kent, Des Moines, 🅔...**other:** Poulsbo RV Ctr, 🅦...**gas:** Arco/24hr, Shell/dsl/24hr, **food:** Burger King, McDonald's, Pizza Hut, Red Robin, Subway, Taco Bell/24hr, Wendy's, **lodging:** Best Western, Century Motel, Day's Inn, Kings Arms Motel, New Best Inn, **other:** $Tree, Radio Shack, 7-11, Walgreens, repair, to Saltwater SP

Seattle

Tacoma

147	S 272nd, 🅦 **on Pacific Hwy**...**gas:** Arco/24hr, Shell/dsl **food:** Fox Hollow Coffee, Jack-in-the-Box, McDonald's Quizno's, Redondo Grill, Sally's Grill, Subway, Taco Bell Thai 3, **other:** Ace Hardware, Albertson's, Bartell Drug, Firestone/auto, Rite Aid, Safeway/24hr, Schuck's Parts
143	S 320th, Federal Way, 🅦...**gas:** Arco/24hr, 76/Circle K Shell/dsl/24hr, **food:** Applebee's, Arby's, Azteca Mexican Black Angus, Blimpie, Burger King, Cafe Arizona, Chipotle Mexican, Coco's, CucinaCucina, Coldstone, Denny's Dunkin Donuts, Filling Sta., Godfather's, Grand Buffet Ivar's Seafood, KFC, L&L Hawaiian BBQ, Marie Callender McDonald's, McHale's Rest., Mongolian Grill, Old Country Buffet, Outback Steaks, Pizza Hut, Qdoba Mexican, Quizno's, Red Lobster, Red Robin, Subway, Taco Bell, Taco Del Mar, Taco Time, TCBY, 3 Amigos, Tokyo Japanese Steaks Tony Roma, Torero's Mexican, Tulley's Coffee, Wendy's, **lodging:** Best Western, Comfort Inn, Courtyard, Extended Stay America, La Quinta, **other:** Best Buy, Big Lots, Borders Books, Firestone/auto, Goodyear/auto, Jo-Ann Fabrics, K Mart, Mervyn's, Michaels, Old Navy, Petsmart, Radio Shack Rite Aid, Ross, Safeway/24hr, Sears/auto, Target, TJ Maxx Top Foods, Wal-Mart/auto, mall, to Dash Point SP
142b a	WA 18 E, S 348th, Enchanted Pkwy, 🅔...**other:** funpark 🅦...**gas:** Ernie's/dsl, Shell/dsl, **food:** Burger King, DQ, Denny's, Jack-in-the-Box, McDonald's, Olive Garden, Popeye's Shari's, Taco Bell, Time Out grill, **lodging:** Holiday Inn Express, Quality Inn, Super 8, **other:** HOSPITAL, Chevrolet Circuit City, Costco/gas, Ford, Home Depot, Lowe's Whse NAPA, Office Depot, Schwab Tire, Wal-Mart Super Ctr/24hr
141mm	weigh sta sb
137	WA 99, Fife, Milton, 🅔...**gas:** Arco/24hr, Chevron/dsl/24hr 76/dsl, Shell/24hr, **food:** DQ, Johnny's Rest., **lodging:** Motel 6, **other:** Acura, Baybo's RV Ctr, Cadillac, Hummer, Infiniti Tacoma RV Ctr, Volvo, 🅦...**gas:** Arco, 76/Circle K, **food:** Arby's, Baskin-Robbins, Burger King, Denny's, Happy Sushi, KFC/A&W, McDonald's, Mitzel's Kitchen, Pizza Experience, Pizza Hut/Taco Bell, Poodle Dog, Quizno's, Subway Taco Del Mar, Taco Time, Wendy's, **lodging:** Best Value Best Western, Comfort Inn, EQC Motel/casino, Kings Motel, Quality Inn, **other:** Camping World/RV Service/supplies Curves, Fife Drug, Great American RV Ctr, NAPA, Schwab Tire
136b a	Port of Tacoma, 🅔...**other:** BMW, Honda, Mercedes, Peterbilt, Sam's Club, RV Sales, 🅦...**gas:** CFN/Goodyear Chevron, Flying J/dsl/LP/rest./24hr, Shell/dsl, **food:** Fife City Grill, Jack-in-the-Box, **lodging:** Best Inn, Day's Inn Econolodge, Extended Stay America, Howard Johnson Sunshine Motel, Travelodge, **other:** Goodyear/dsl, Harley Davidson, Land Rover/Jaguar/Lexus, Nissan
135	Bay St, Puyallup, 🅔...**gas:** Shell, **other:** Majestic RV Park(4mi), 🅦...**gas:** Arco/24hr, **lodging:** La Quinta, **other:** to Tacoma Dome
133	WA 7, I-705, City Ctr, 🅦...**other:** Tacoma Dome, **lodging:** Best Western, Courtyard, Sheraton **other:** museum
132	WA 16 W, S 38th, Gig Harbor, to Bremerton, 🅦...**gas:** Tesoro, **food:** Arby's, Azteca Mexican, Burger King, Chevy's Mexican, Krispy Kreme, McDonald's, Mervyn's, Quizno's, Red Robin, Subway, TGIFriday, Wendy's, **lodging:** Extended Stay America, **other:** Best Buy, Borders, Circuit City, CompUSA, Costco/gas, $Tree, Ford, Hancock Fabrics, Hyundai, JC Penney, Jo-Ann Fabrics, Michael's, PetCo, Ross, Sears/auto, Tire Sta, Toyota, mall, to Pt Defiance Pk/Zoo, mall
130	S 56th, Tacoma Mall Blvd, 🅦...**gas:** Shell, **food:** Chucke Cheese, Subway, Tony Roma

Interstate 5

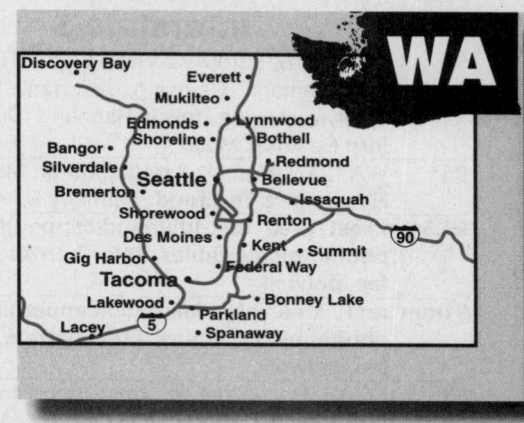

129 S 72nd, S 84th, E...**gas:** Chevron/24hr, Exxon, **food:** Applebee's, Burger King, DQ, Elmer's Rest., Famous Dave's, IHOP, Mongolian Grill, Olive Garden, Popeye's, Red Lobster, RoundTable Pizza, Shari's, Starbucks, Taco Bell, Zoopa Café, **lodging:** Best Western, Howard Johnson, Motel 6, Shilo Inn, Travelodge, **other:** MegaFoods, W...**gas:** Arco/24hr, **food:** Calzone's Italian, Hooters, Jack-in-the-Box, Quizno's, Yankee Diner, **lodging:** Day's Inn, **other:** Home Depot, to Steilacoom Lake

128 (from nb)same as 129, E...**gas:** 76, Shell/dsl, **food:** Copperfield's Rest., Denny's, Subway, **lodging:** Best Western, Comfort Inn, Econolodge, Holiday Inn Express, King Oscar Motel, Red Lion Inn, Sherwood Motel, Tacoma Inn, W...**gas:** Tesoro, **food:** Ruby Tuesday, **other:** Discount Tire, cinema

127 WA 512, S Tacoma Way, Puyallup, Mt Ranier, W...**gas:** Arco/24hr, Chevron, Citgo/7-11, 76/Circle K, Shell/dsl, **food:** Burger King, DQ, Denny's, IHOP, Ivar's Seafood, Mazatlan Mexican, McDonald's, Sizzler, Starbucks, Subway, Taco Guaynas, Wendy's, **lodging:** Best Value, Budget Inn, Knights Inn, Quality Inn, Western Inn, **other:** Schuck's Parts, transmissions

125 to McChord AFB, Lakewood, E...**gas:** Texaco, W...**gas:** 76/dsl, Shell/dsl, **food:** A&W/KFC, Black Angus, Denny's, Happy Days Diner, Pizza Hut, Wendy's, **lodging:** Best Western, La Quinta, Madigan Motel, **other:** HOSPITAL, VET, Aamco, BMW, 7-11, U-Haul, mall

124 Gravelly Lake Dr, W...**gas:** Arco/repair, 76/24hr, **food:** El Toro Mexican, **other:** same as 125

123 Thorne Lane, Tillicum Lane, no services

122 Camp Murray, E...**other:** HOSPITAL, W...**gas:** Chevron/repair, **food:** Baskin-Robbins, Domino's, Gertie's Grill, KFC, McDonald's, Papa John's, Pizza Hut, Subway, Taco Bell, Teriyaki House, **other:** AutoZone, 7-11

120 Ft Lewis, E...**other:** Ft Lewis Military Museum

119 Du Pont Rd, Steilacoom, W...**gas:** 76, **food:** Starbucks, Subway, Steilacoom Deli

118 Center Dr, W...**food:** Bruceski's Pizza, Farrelli's, Harbor Rock Grill, Koko's Wok, Pegasus Cafe, Quizno's, Subway, **lodging:** GuestHouse Inn, Liberty Inn

117mm weigh sta nb

116 Mounts Rd, Old Nisqually, W...**other:** Riverbend Camping(seasonal)

115mm Nisqually River

114 Nisqually, E...**gas:** Chevron/repair, Exxon/dsl(1mi), Shell/dsl/LP, **food:** Nisqually Grill, Normo's Burgers, Shipwreck Café, **other:** Lost Lake RV Resort, Nisqually RV Park

111 WA 510 E, Marvin Rd, to Yelm, E...**gas:** Chevron/24hr, 76/Circle K, Shell/dsl, Tesoro, **food:** Blimpie, Burger King, Coldstone, DQ, Godfather's, Hawk's Prairie Rest., Jack-in-the-Box, McDonald's, Panda Express, Panera Bread, Papa Murphy's, RoundTable Pizza, Ruby Tuesday, Taco Del Mar, Taco Time, **lodging:** King Oscar Motel, **other:** Best Buy, Big Lots, Costco/gas, Harley Davidson, Home Depot, MegaFoods/24hr, Radio Shack, Rite Aid, Safeway/24hr, Schuck's Parts, Schwab Tire, Walgreens, Wal-Mart Super Ctr/

Subway/24hr, W...**gas:** Pacific Pride/dsl, **food:** Mayan Mexican, **other:** Tolmie SP(5mi), RV camping

109 Martin Way, Sleator-Kenny Rd, E...**food:** Main Chinese Buffet, Pizza Hut/Taco Bell, **other:** Discount Tire, ShopKO, Top Food/24hr, W...**gas:** Arco/24hr, Exxon/dsl, 76/Circle K, Shell/dsl/24hr, **food:** Bailey's Rest., Burger King, Casa Mia Rest., Denny's, El Serape Mexican, IHOP, Mandarin House, Red Lobster, Shari's Rest./24hr, Subway, **lodging:** AmeriTel, Bailey Motel, Comfort Inn, Day's Inn, Holiday Inn Express, Holly Motel, Super 8, **other:** HOSPITAL, Firestone/auto, Gary's Tire, NAPA

108 Sleator-Kenny Rd, E...**gas:** Shell/dsl, **food:** Applebee's, Arby's, McDonald's Wendy's, Winchell's/24hr, **other:** $Tree, Firestone/auto, Fred Meyer, Marshall's, Mervyn's, Michael's, Office Depot, Radio Shack, Rite Aid, Sear/auto, Target, W...**food:** Jack-in-the-Box, Panda Express, **other:** HOSPITAL, K-Mart, Lowes Whse, Safeway/gas, same as 109

107 Pacific Ave, E...**gas:** Chevron, Shell/dsl, **food:** DQ, Shari's, Sizzler, Taco Time, **other:** Albertson's/Savon, Home Depot, Ross, mall, W...**other:** Columbus RV Ctr, Ford

105 St Capitol, W...**gas:** Chevron/24hr, Shell/Subway/dsl/24hr, **food:** Casa Mia Rest., Chinese Buffet, DQ, Jack-in-the-Box, McDonald's, Oriental Chinese, Saigon Rest., Starbucks, **lodging:** Clarion, Econolodge, Olympia Inn, Phoenix Inn, Ramada Inn, **other:** Pontiac/Cadillac/Saturn

104 US 101 N, W Olympia, to Aberdeen, W...**gas:** Arco, Chevron, Citgo/7-11, Shell/dsl, **food:** Jack-in-the-Box, **lodging:** Extended Stay America, Red Lion Motel, **other:** HOSPITAL, Honda, to Capitol Mall

103 2nd Ave, no services

102 Trosper Rd, Black Lake, E...**gas:** Shell/dsl/24hr, **food:** Arby's, Brewery City Pizza, Burger King, Cattin's Rest./24hr, El Sarape Mexican, Happy Teriyaki, Jack-in-the-Box, KFC, McDonald's, Pizza Hut, Subway, Taco Bell, **lodging:** Best Western, Motel 6, **other:** Ace Hardware, Goodyear, Schuck's Parts, W...**gas:** Chevron/24hr, 76/Circle K, **food:** Best Buffet, Blimpie, Nickelby's Rest., Panda Express, Papa Murphy's, Quizno's, **other:** Albertson's/gas, AutoZone, Costco/gas, Fred Meyer, Home Depot, MegaFoods/24hr

101 Airdustrial Way, E...**gas:** Chevron, Shell, **food:** DQ(1mi), Quizno's, **lodging:** Comfort Inn, GuestHouse Inn, Olympia Camping

WASHINGTON
Interstate 5

N ↑ ↓ S

Exit	Description
99	WA 121 S, 93rd Ave, Scott Lake, **E**...**other:** American Heritage Camping, **W**...**gas:** Exxon/dsl(1mi), Shell/rest/dsl/LP, **food:** Hannah's Diner/24hr, **lodging:** Restover Motel
95	WA 121, Littlerock, **3 mi E**...**other:** Millersylvania SP, RV camping, **W**...**food:** Farmboy Drive-In
93.5mm	**rest area sb, full(handicapped)facilities, info, phone, picnic tables, litter barréls, vending, coffee, petwalk**
91mm	**rest area nb, full(handicapped)facilities, info, phone, picnic tables, litter barrels, vending, coffee, petwalk**
88	US 12, Rochester, **W**...**gas:** Arco/24hr, 76/dsl, Shell/dsl/LP/repair, **food:** DQ, Grand Mound Pizza/deli, Little Red Barn Rest./24hr, Lucky Eagle Casino/café, Royal India Rest., **other:** Outback RV Park(2mi), Harrison RV Park(3mi)
82	Harrison Ave, Factory Outlet Way, Centralia, **E**...**gas:** Arco/24hr, Shell/dsl, **food:** Burger King, Burgerville, Casa Ramos Mexican, DQ, Godfather's, Panda Chinese, Pizza Hut, Quizno's, Shari's/24hr, TCBY, Thai Dish, Wendy's, **lodging:** Econolodge, Ferryman's Inn, King Oscar Motel **other:** HOSPITAL, VF/famous brands, **W**...**gas:** Chevron, Shell, Texaco/Circle K, **food:** Arby's, Country Cousin Rest., Denny's, Dominos, Jack-in-the-Box, McDonald's, Papa Murphy's, Starbucks, Subway, Taco Bell, **lodging:** Motel 6, **other:** GNC, Midway RV Park, Outlet Mall/famous brands, Rite Aid, Safeway/gas, Schuck's Parts, Schwab Tire
82mm	Skookumchuck River
81	WA 507, Mellen St, **E**...**gas:** Chevron, Shell, **food:** Coconut Grill, Subway, **lodging:** Holiday Inn Express, Pepper Tree Motel/RV Park, Travel Inn, **other:** RV Dump, **W**...HOSPITAL
79	Chamber Way, **E**...**gas:** Shell/dsl/24hr, **food:** McDonald's, Jalisco Mexican, Subway, **other:** VET, Ford/Lincoln/Mercury/Toyota, Goodyear/auto, RV Ctr, museum, vistor info, **W**...**gas:** Texaco/Burger King/dsl/LP, **food:** Applebees, Buckaroo's Pizza, Starbucks, Taco Del Mar, Wendy's, **other:** $Tree, GNC, Grocery Outlet, Home Depot, K-Mart/Little Caesar's, Michael's, Radio Shack, Scion/Toyota, Wal-Mart/Super Ctr/24hr/auto, st patrol
77	WA 6 W, Chehalis, **E**...**gas:** Cenex/dsl, Time Gas, **food:** Dairy Bar, **other:** NAPA, Schwab Tire, **W**...**food:** Sowerby's Rest., **other:** Rainbow Falls SP(16mi), museum, truck parts
76	13th St, **E**...**gas:** Arco/24hr, Chevron, **food:** Denny's, Jack-in-the-Box, Kit Carson Rest., Subway, **lodging:** Best Western, Chalice Inn, Relax Inn, **other:** Baybo's RV Ctr, **W**...RV park/dump
72	Rush Rd, Napavine, **E**...**gas:** Shell/dsl/@, **food:** Burger King, McDonald's, RibEye Rest./24hr, Subway, **other:** Dave's RV Ctr, RV park, **W**...**gas:** Chevron/FoodCourt/dsl/24hr, Shell/dsl, **food:** Uhlmann RV Ctr
72mm	Newaukum River
71	WA 508 E, Onalaska, Napavine, **E**...**gas:** 76/dsl/KC Truck Parts
68	US 12 E, Morton, **E**...**gas:** Arco/24hr, Shell/dsl, **food:** Spiffy's Rest./24hr, **other:** KOA, to Lewis&Clark SP, Mt Ranier NP, **W**...**gas:** Texaco/dsl/rest./24hr, **food:** The Mustard Seed Rest.
63	WA 505, Winlock, **E**...**other:** RV park(3mi), **W**...**gas:** Shell/dsl/LP
60	Vader Rd, Toledo, no services
59	WA 506 W, Vader, **E**...**gas:** Shell/dsl, **food:** Beesley's Cafe, **W**...**gas:** Chevron/Subway/dsl/24hr, **food:** Country House Rest., Rick's Rest.
59mm	Cowlitz River
57	Barnes Dr, Jackson Hwy, **W**...**gas:** GeeCee's/dsl/café/24hr/@, **other:** repair, RV camping
55mm	**rest area both lanes, full(handicapped)facilities, phone, picnic tables, litter barrels, vending, petwalk**
52	Toutle Park Rd, **E**...**other:** Paradise Cove RV Park/general store
50mm	Toutle River
49	WA 504 E, Castle Rock, **E**...**gas:** Chevron, Shell/dsl, Texaco/dsl, **food:** Burger King, C&L Burgers, El Compadre Mexican, Peper's 49er Diner, Papa Pete's Pizza, Pizza Parlor, RoseTree Rest., Subway, **lodging:** Mt St Helens Motel, 7 West Motel, Silver Lake Motel/resort, Timberland Inn, **other:** Seaquest SP(5mi)
48	Huntington Ave, no services
46	Pleasant Hill Rd, **E**...**other:** Cedars RV Park
44mm	weigh sta sb, phone
42	Ostrander Rd, no services
40	to WA 4, Kelso-Longview, **1 mi W**...**gas:** Texaco, **lodging:** Best Western, Budget Inn, Townhouse Motel, **other:** HOSPITAL, Parts+, transmissions
39	WA 4, Kelso, to Longview, **E**...**gas:** Arco/24hr, Shell, **food:** Denny's, Highlander Rest., McDonald's, Shari's/24hr, Subway, **other:** RV Park, **lodging:** Motel 6, Red Lion Motel, Super 8, **other:** Rite Aid, **W**...**gas:** Chevron/repair, **food:** Azteca Mexican, Burger King, ChuckeCheese, DQ, Izzy's Pizza, North's Buffet, Red Lobster, Starbucks, Taco Bell, **lodging:** Best Western, Comfort Inn, GuestHouse Inn, **other:** JC Penney, Macys, Safeway/drug, Sears/auto, Target, mall, museum
36	WA 432 W, to WA 433, US 30, Kelso, **E**...**other:** U-Neek RV Ctr, **1-3 mi W**...**gas:** Arco, Chevron/dsl, 76/dsl, Shell, **lodging:** Best Western, Ramada Ltd., **other:** HOSPITAL, Ford/Lincoln/Mercury, Home Depot, Longview RV Ctr, Peterbilt, Toyota, st patrol
32	Kalama River Rd, **E**...**food:** Fireside Café, **other:** Camp Kalama RV Park/gifts
31mm	Kalama River
30	Kalama, **E**...**gas:** Texaco, **food:** Burger Bar, Columbia Inn/rest., Playa Azul Mexican, Subway, **lodging:** Kalama River Inn, **other:** Big A Parts, USPO, antiques, **W**...**gas:** Spirit/gas, **other:** RV camping
27	Todd Rd, Port of Kalama, **E**...**gas:** Shell/dsl/café/24hr
22	Dike Access Rd, **W**...**gas:** CFN/dsl/24hr, **other:** Columbia Riverfront/Lewis River/Woodland Shores RV Parks
21	WA 503 E, Woodland, **E**...**gas:** Arco/24hr, Chevron, Shell/dsl, **food:** Burgerville, Casa Tatatia, DQ, Oak-Tree Rest., Rosie's Rest., South China Rest., Subway, **lodging:** Best Western, Econolodge, Lewis River Inn, **other:** CarQuest, Hi-School Drug, Letterbox, Radio Shack, Sav-On Foods, U-Haul, Woodland Shores RV Park, **W**...**gas:** Shell, **food:** Guadalahara Mexican, McDonald's, Terrelli's Pizza, Whimpy's Rest., **lodging:** Hansen's Motel, Lakeside Motel, Scandia Motel, **other:** Chevrolet, NAPA, Safeway/gas, repair
20mm	N Fork Lewis River
18mm	E Fork Lewis River

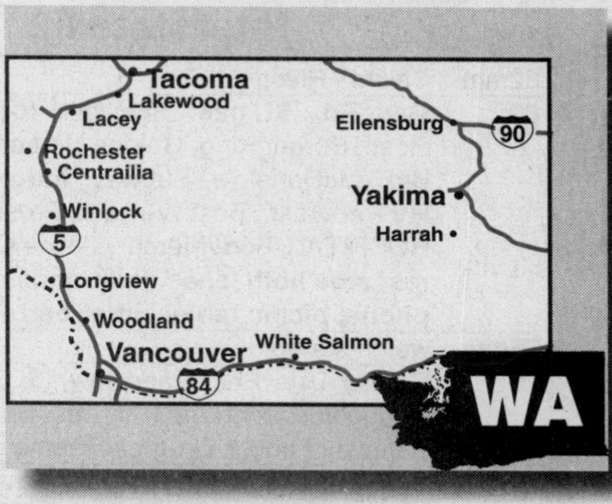

Interstate 5

16	NW 319th St, La Center, **E**...**gas:** Shell/dsl/24hr, **food:** Twin Dragons Rest., **other:** Paradise Point SP, Tri-Mountain Golf/rest.
15mm	weigh sta nb
14	WA 501 W, NW 269th St, **E**...**gas:** Arco/24hr, 76/Circle K/dsl, **food:** Country Café, Papa Pete's Pizza, Subway, **other:** to Battleground Lake SP(14mi), Big Fir RV Park(4mi), Ridgefield WR, Tri-Mountain RV Park, **W**...**gas:** Chevron/dsl
13mm	**rest area sb, full(handicapped)facilities, info, phone, picnic tables, litter barrels, vending, petwalk, RV dump**
11mm	**rest area nb, full(handicapped)facilities, info, phone, picnic tables, litter barrels, vending, petwalk, RV dump**
9	NE 179th St, **E**...**food:** Jollie's Rest./24hr, **other:** Poulsbo RV, **W**...**gas:** Chevron/dsl, **other:** RV Park
7	I-205 S(from sb), to I-84, WA 14, NE 134th St, Portland Airport, **E**...**gas:** Arco, Citgo/7-11, 76, TrailMart/dsl, **food:** Billygan's Roadhouse, Burger King, Burgerville, Jack-in-the-Box, McDonald's, Round Table Pizza, Taco Bell, **lodging:** Comfort Inn, Holiday Inn Express, Olympia Motel, Red Lion, Salmon Creek Inn, Shilo Inn, **other:** HOSPITAL, Albertson's/gas, Long's Drugs, Zupan's Mkt, 99 RV Park, **W**...**gas:** Mobil/dsl, **lodging:** University Inn, **other:** VET, Fred Meyer
5	NE 99th St, **E**...**gas:** Arco/24hr, Citgo/7-11, Time Gas, **food:** Burgerville, Carl's Jr, Del Taco, Domino's, Fat Dave's Rest., Quizno's, **other:** Harley-Davidson, Nissan/Kia, Walgreen, Wal-Mart/auto/gas, Winco Foods/gas/24hr, **W**...**gas:** Arco/24hr, Chevron/24hr, **food:** Applebee's, Bortolemi's Pizza, McDonald's, Papa John's, Primo's Subs, Subway, **other:** Albertson's, $Tree, Office Depot, PetCo, Target
4	NE 78th St, Hazel Dell, **E**...**gas:** Citgo/7-11, Exxon, Texaco/dsl, **food:** Baja Fresh, Burger King, Dragon King Chinese, Izzy's Rest., KFC, McDonald's, Pizza Hut, PeachTree Rest., Skipper's, Smokey's Pizza, Starbucks, Steakburger, Subway, Taco Bell, **lodging:** Quality Inn, **other:** America's Tire, CarQuest, Cottman Transmissions, Firestone, Fred Meyer, Dodge, Ford, Goodyear, Mazda, Nissan, Radio Shack, Schuck's Parts, U-Haul, **W**...**gas:** Shell/dsl/LP, **food:** Figaro's Pizza, Wendy's, **other:** Rite Aid, Ross, RV Pro, Safeway
3	NE Hwy 99, Main St, Hazel Dell, **E**...**other:** HOSPITAL, **W**...**gas:** Arco, **other:** Safeway, transmissions
2	WA 500 E, 39th St, to Orchards, no services
1d	E 4th, Plain Blvd W, to WA 501, Port of Vancouver, no services
1c	Mill Plain Blvd, City Ctr, **W**...**gas:** Chevron, **food:** Black Angus, Cattle Co Rest., Burgerville, Denny's, **lodging:** Hilton, Shilo Inn, **other:** Ford, Lincoln/Mercury, Pontiac/Cadillac/GMC, Jeep, Mitsubishi, Suzuki, Clark Coll, st patrol
1b	6th St, downtown, **W**...**lodging:** Hilton, Red Lion
1a	WA 14 E, to Camas, **E**...HOSPITAL
0mm	Washington/Oregon state line, Columbia River

(left margin: N, S, Vancouver)

Interstate 82

Exit #	Services
11mm	I-82 Oregon begins/ends on I-84, exit 179.
10	Westland Rd, **E**...**other:** to Umatilla Army Depot, **other:** HOSPITAL
5	Power Line Rd, no services
1.5mm	Umatilla River
1	US 395/730, Umatilla, **E**...**food:** Jack-in-the-Box(5mi), **lodging:** Best Western(8mi), Desert Inn/rest.(2mi), **other:** Hatrock Camping(8mi), to McNary Dam, **W**...**gas:** Shell/Crossroads Trkstp/dsl/rest./24hr, Tesoro/Subway/dsl, **lodging:** Tillicum Motel, Umatilla Inn, **other:** Red Apple Mkt, USPO, st police, Welcome Ctr, weigh sta
132mm	Washington/Oregon state line, Columbia River
131	WA 14 W, Plymouth, **N**...**other:** RV camping, to McNary Dam
130mm	weigh sta wb
122	Coffin Rd, no services
114	Locust Grove Rd, no services
113	US 395 N, to I-182, Kennewick, Pasco, **2-5 mi N**...**gas:** Chevron, Exxon, Tesoro, **food:** A&W/KFC, Carl's Jr, Denny's, DQ, Jack-in-the-Box, McDonald's, KFC/Taco Bell, Papa Murphy's, Starbucks, Subway, **lodging:** Best Western, Day's Inn, Econolodge, Holiday Inn Express, La Quinta, Travelodge, **other:** GNC, Harley-Davidson, Hastings Books, Home Depot, Radio Shack, Rite Aid, Safeway/food/drug, Walgreens, Wal-Mart SuperCtr/24hr/gas
109	Badger Rd, W Kennewick, **N**...**gas:** Shell/Subway/dsl/24hr, **3 mi N**...**lodging:** Guesthouse Suites, Red Lion, Super 8
104	Dallas Rd, **3 mi N**...**gas:** Conoco/dsl/24hr, **food:** Hotstuff Pizza/subs
102	I-182, US 12 E, to US 395, Spokane, HOSPITAL, services in Richland, Pasco
96	WA 224, Benton City, **N**...**gas:** Conoco/cafe/dsl/24hr, **other:** Beach RV Park
93	Yakitat Rd, no services
88	Gibbon Rd, no services
82	WA 22, WA 221, Mabton, **S**...**gas:** Conoco, **2 mi S**...**food:** Blue Goose Rest., **lodging:** Prosser Motel, **other:** HOSPITAL, to WA St U Research, to Wine Tasting Facilities, museum

(right margin: E ↕ W)

(left margin of I-82: Kennewick)

82mm	Yakima River
80	Gap Rd, Ⓢ...gas: Shell/dsl, food: Blue Goose Rest., Burger King, Golden Horse Rest., KFC/Taco Bell, McDonald's, Subway, lodging: Barn Motel/RV Park/rest., Best Western, Prosser Motel, other: HOSPITAL, Ford/Mercury, Wine Country RV Park, rest area both lanes, full(handicapped)facilities, phone, picnic tables, litter barrels
76mm	weigh sta eb
75	County Line Rd, Grandview, Ⓢ...gas: Cenex/dsl, Conoco/dsl/24hr(1mi), 1 mi Ⓢ...lodging:other: Safeway Food & Drug/gas, same as 73
73	Stover Rd, Wine Country Rd, Grandview, Ⓢ...gas: Chevron/Subway/dsl, Conoco/dsl/24hr, food: DQ, Eli&Kathy's Breakfast, Garcios Drive-thru, New Hong Kong, 10-4 Café, Subway, lodging: Apple Valley Motel, Grandview Motel, other: Chrysler/Jeep/Dodge, Grandview Market, RV Ctr/park/dump, Safeway, Schwab Tire, auto repair
69	WA 241, to Sunnyside, Ⓝ...gas: Arco/dsl/24hr, Shell/TacoMaker/dsl/24hr, Texaco/dsl, food: Arby's, Burger King, King China Buffet, DQ, KFC, McDonald's, Papa Murphy's, Pizza Hut, Skipper's, Subway, Taco Bell, lodging: Best Western, Rodeway Inn, other: Buick/Chevrolet/Nissan, $Tree, GNC, JC Penney, Staples, Wal-Mart SuperCtr/24hr/auto/gas
67	Sunnyside, Port of Sunnyside, Ⓝ...gas: Chevron/CFN/dsl, food: Jack-in-the-Box, other: HOSPITAL, BiMart Foods, Ⓢ...other: DariGold Cheese
63	Outlook, Sunnyside, 3 mi Ⓝ...food: Burger Ranch, Snipe's Rest., lodging: Country Inn, Sunnyside B&B, other: RV camping
58	WA 223 S, to Granger, Ⓢ...gas: Conoco/dsl
54	Division Rd, Yakima Valley Hwy, to Zillah, Ⓢ...other: Teapot Dome NHS
52	Zillah, Toppenish, Ⓝ...gas: Chevron/dsl, Shell/dsl/24hr, food: El Porton Mexican, McDonald's, Subway, lodging: Comfort Inn
50	WA 22 E, to US 97 S, Toppenish, Ⓝ...food: Gold Nugget Café/casino, 3-4 mi Ⓢ...food: Legends Buffet/casino, McDonald's, lodging: Best Western Toppenish other: HOSPITAL, Murals Museum, RV Park, to Yakima Nation Cultural Ctr
44	Wapato, Ⓝ...gas: Shell/dsl
40	Thorp Rd, Parker Rd, Yakima Valley Hwy, Ⓝ...other: Sagelands Vineyard/Winery
39mm	Yakima River
38	Union Gap(from wb), 1 mi Ⓢ...food: Peppermint Stick Drive-In, other: gas, lodging, museum
37	US 97(from eb), 1 mi Ⓢ...gas: Exxon, Shell, other: Canopy RV Ctr, NAPA
36	Valley Mall Blvd, Yakima, Ⓢ...gas: Arco/dsl/24hr, Cenex/dsl, Shell/Gearjammer/dsl/Subway/24hr/@, food: Burger King, Denny's/24hr, Godfather's, IHOP, Jack-in-the-Box, A&W/KFC, McDonald's, Miner's Drive-In, Old Country Buffet, Outback Steaks, SeaGalley Rest., Shari's, Shangrila Chinese, Skipper's, Taco Bell, lodging: Best Western, Cobblestone Inn, Quality Inn, Super 8, other: Big A

Parts, Borders, Franks Tire, Gap Autoparts, Goodyear, Lowe's Whse, Office Depot, Old Navy, Rite Aid, Sears/auto, ShopKO, dsl/repair, mall, st patrol, TJ Maxx

34	WA 24 E, Nob Hill Blvd, Yakima, Ⓝ...other: K-Mart, Sportsman SP, KOA, dsl/repair, International, Ⓢ...gas: Arco/24hr, Chevron/dsl/24hr, CFN/dsl, Citgo/7-11, Time/dsl, food: Arby's, McDonald's, other: HOSPITAL, 19th Hole RV Park, Freightliner, Peterbuilt, Shuck's Parts, Volvo, museum
33	Yakima Ave, Yakima, Ⓝ...gas: Chevron, Shell/Chester's/dsl, food: Burger King, lodging: Oxford Inn, Oxford Suites, other: Chevrolet, GMC/Honda, Mazda, Wal-Mart SuperCtr/McDonald's/24hr, Ⓢ...gas: Arco/24hr, Citgo/7-11, food: Asian Express, DQ, Food Pavillion, Pizza Hut, Taco Bell, lodging: Fairfield Inn, Holiday Inn Express, Red Lion Motel, other: Howard Johnson, JC Penney, Mervyn's, Schwab Tire, Target, mall
31b a	US 12 W, N 1st St, to Naches, Ⓢ...gas: Arco/dsl/24hr, Exxon, Shell/repair, food: Arctic Circle, China Sun Buffet, Espinoza's Mexican, Golden Moon Chinese, Jack-in-the-Box, Peking Palace, Pepper's, Pizza Hut, Red Apple Rest., Red Lobster, Subway, Wendy's, Zenezina Italian, lodging: Best Western, Clarion Hotel, Day's Inn, Economy Inn, Motel 6, Nendels Inn, Ramada Inn, Sun Country Inn, Tourist Motel, Yakima Inn, other: Harley Davidson, Nendel's, Trailer Inn RV park
30	WA 823 N, Rest Haven Rd, to Selah, no services
29	E Selah Rd, Ⓝ...other: fruits/antiques
26	WA 821 N, to WA 823, Canyon Rd, Ⓝ...gas: Chevron/dsl/Noble Romans
24mm	rest area eb, full(handicapped)facilities, phone, picnic tables, litter barrels, RV dump
23mm	Selah Creek
22mm	rest area wb, full(handicapped)facilities, phone, picnic tables, litter barrels, RV dump
21mm	S Umptanum Ridge, 2265 elev
19mm	Burbank Creek
17mm	N Umptanum Ridge, 2315 elev
15mm	Lmuma Creek
11	Military Area, Military Area, no services
8mm	view point both lanes, Manastash Ridge, 2672 elev
3	WA 821 S, Thrall Rd, no services
0mm	I-90, E to Spokane, W to Seattle. I-82 begins/ends on I-90, exit 110.

Interstate 90

Exit #	Services
300mm	Washington/Idaho state line, Spokane River
299	State Line, Port of Entry, Ⓝ...Welcome Ctr/rest area both lanes, weigh sta, full(handicapped) facilities, phone, picnic tables, litter barrels, petwalk, Ⓢ...gas: Gas n' Go, Shell
296	Otis Orchards, Liberty Lakes, Ⓝ...gas: Shell/dsl, food: HomePlate Grill, lodging: Best Western, other: Buick/GMC/Hummer/Pontiac, Porsche, Ⓢ...gas: Chevron/LP, 76, food: Burger King, Carl's Jr, Domino's, McDonald's, Palenque Mexican, Papa Murphy's, Pizza Hut, Quizno's, Taco Bell, Taco Time, Subway, lodging: Comfort Inn, other: Albertson's, Alton Tire, Curves, GNC, Home depot, RNR RV Ctr, Land Rover, Safeway/gas, Sav-on

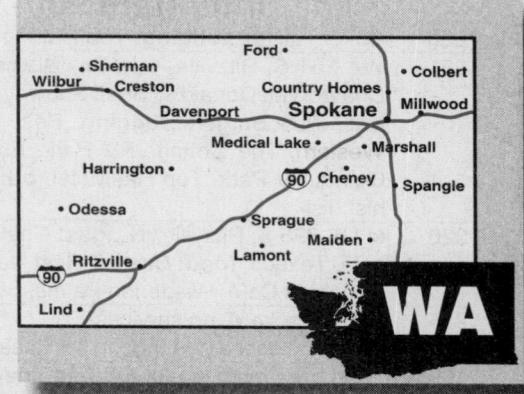

294 Sprague Ave(from wb, no EZ return), Ⓢ...**other:** North Country RV/marine, Nut Factory, auto repair

293 Barker Rd, Greenacres, Ⓝ...**gas:** Conoco/dsl, **food:** Roadside grill, Wendy's, **other:** Alpine Motel/RV Park, KOA, Ⓢ...**gas:** Exxon/Subway/dsl/24hr, Shell/dsl/24hr, **other:** NW RV Ctr, repair

291b Sullivan Rd, Veradale, Ⓝ...**gas:** Chevron/Blimpie/TCBY, Shell, **food:** Arby's, Krispy Kreme, McDonald's, Outback Steaks, Tony Roma, Red Robin, **lodging:** Comfort Inn, La Quinta, Oxford Suites, Residence Inn, **other:** Barnes&Noble, Best Buy, Circuit City, Staples, TJ Maxx, mall, Ⓢ...**gas:** Chevron, 76, Shell/dsl, Tesoro, **food:** A&W, Bruchi's Rest., DQ, Godfather's, Jack-in-the-Box, KFC, McDonald's, Mongolian BBQ, Noodle Express, Panda Express, Pizza Hut, Quizno's, Schlotsky's, Shari's/24hr, Starbucks, Subway, Taco Bell, Wendy's, **lodging:** Comfort Inn, Mirabeau Park Hotel, **other:** Ace Hardware, $Tree, Fred Meyer, Hancock Fabrics, Hastings Books, Michael's, Petsmart, Ross, Walgreens, WalMart SuperCtr/24hr/auto, Yokes Foods

291a Evergreen Rd, Ⓝ...**food:** Black Angus, Boston's Rest, IHOP, TGI Friday, **other:** JC Penney, Old Navy, Sears/auto, TJ Maxx, mall, Ⓢ...**gas:** Shell

289 WA 27 S, Pines Rd, Opportunity, Ⓝ...**gas:** Citgo/7-11, **food:** Old Matthews Rest., Ⓢ...**gas:** Holiday, Shell/dsl, 76, **food:** Applebee's, Denny's, DQ, Jack-in-the-Box, Old Country Buffet, Quizno's, **lodging:** Best Western, **other:** HOSPITAL, Standard Battery, Walgreens

287 Argonne Rd, Millwood, Ⓝ...**gas:** Holiday/dsl, **food:** Burger King, Denny's, Domino's, DQ, Jack-in-the-Box, Longhorn BBQ, Marie Callender's, McDonald's, Papa Murphy's, Subway, Wendy's, **lodging:** Motel 6, Super 8, **other:** Albertson's/gas, Yoke's Foods, Savon, Schuck's Parts, Walgreens, $ Tree Ⓢ...**gas:** 76/dsl, Shell, Exxon, **food:** Casa de Oro Mexican, Godfather's, Outback Stake House, Perkins, Starbucks, **lodging:** Holiday Inn Express, Quality Inn, **other:** Curves, Rite Aid/24hr, Safeway

286 Broadway Ave, Ⓝ...**gas:** ✈/Flying J/Conoco/Rest./dsl/LP/24hr/@/international, **food:** Zip's Burgers, Goodyear, **lodging:** Broadway Inn, **Other:** Schwab Tire, White/Volvo/GMC, Kenworth, Peterbuilt Ⓢ...**other:** 7-11

285 Sprague Ave, Ⓝ...**food:** Dragon Garden Rest, IHOP, Jack-in-the-Box, McDonald's, Subway, Wendy's, **lodging:** ParkLane Motel, **other:** Costco/gas, Grocery Outlet, Freightliner, Home Depot, K-Mart, Lowe's Whse, Radio Shack, Shuck's Parts, Ⓢ...**gas:** Exxon, **food:** Puerta Vallarta Mexican, Starbucks, Taco Time, Zip's Burger, **other:** Alton's Tire, Chrysler, Dodge, Ford, Hyundai, Nissan/Saab, RV camping, transmissions

284 Havana St(from eb, no EZ return), Ⓝ...**food:** Jack-in-the-Box, McDonald's

283b Freya St, Thor St, Ⓝ...**gas:** Chevron, Tesoro/dsl, **food:** Wolf Lodge Steaks, Ⓢ...**gas:** Citgo/7-11, Conoco/dsl, **other:** Fred Meyer

283a Altamont St, Ⓢ...**gas:** 76

282b 2nd Ave, Ⓝ...**lodging:** Shilo Inn, **other:** Office Depot

282a WA 290 E, Trent Ave, Hamilton St, Ⓝ...**gas:** Shell/dsl, **lodging:** Shilo Inn, **other:** Office Depot

281 US 2, US 395, to Colville, Ⓝ...**gas:** Citgo/7-11, Shell/repair, Tesoro/dsl, **food:** Arby's, Dick's Hamburgers, Franky Doodles Rest., Jack-in-the-Box, McDonald's, Pizza Hut, Starbucks, Subway, Taco Time, Top China, **lodging:** Best Value, Econolodge, Howard Johnson, **other:** Firestone, Ford, Schwab Tire, U-Haul, Ⓢ...**lodging:** Quality Inn, **other:** HOSPITAL

280b Lincoln St, Ⓝ...**gas:** Chevron, Conoco/dsl, Shell, **food:** Burger King, Carl's Jr, Godfather's, IHOP, Jack-in-the-Box, Molly's Fine Dining, Taco Bell, Taste of Asia, Wendy's, Wild Sage Bistro, Zip's Burgers, **lodging:** Ramada Inn, Rodeway Inn, **other:** Cadillac, Honda, Lexus, Lincoln/Mercury, Mazda, Mercedes, Saturn, Tire Factory, Toyota, Ⓢ...HOSPITAL

280a downtown, Ⓝ...**gas:** Chevron/McDonald's, Conoco/dsl, Shell, Texaco, **food:** Arctic Circle, Frank's Diner, Subway, **lodging:** Select Inn, **other:** AAA, Chevrolet, Land Rover, NAPA, Safeway

279 US 195 S, Pullman, to Colfax

277b a US 2 W (no ez wb return), to Grand Coulee Dam, Fairchild AFB, Ⓝ...**lodging:** Day's Inn, Hampton Inn, Motel 6, Ramada Inn, Travelodge, West Winn Motel

276 Geiger Blvd, Ⓝ...**gas:** ✈/Flying J/Exxon/Subway/dsl/LP/24hr, **food:** Denny's, Subway, **lodging:** Airway Express Inn, Best Western, **other:** USPO, st patrol, Ⓢ...**gas:** Shell/dsl/LP, Hideaway RV Park

272 WA 902, Medical Lake, Ⓝ...**gas:** Shell/dsl, **other:** Overland Sta/RV Park, Ⓢ...**gas:** Petro/dsl/rest./24hr, **lodging:** Super 8, **other:** Freightliner, Yogi Bear Camping

270 WA 904, Cheney, Four Lakes, Ⓢ...**gas:** Exxon, **lodging:** Willow Springs Motel(6mi), **other:** Peaceful Pines RV Park, Ford, E WA U

264 WA 902, Salnave Rd, to Cheney, Medical Lake, **2 mi** Ⓝ...camping

257 WA 904, Tyler, to Cheney, no services

254 Fishtrap, Ⓢ...**other:** Fishtrap RV camping/tents

245 WA 23, Sprague, Ⓢ...**gas:** Chevron/dsl, **food:** Viking Drive-In, **lodging:**, Sprague Motel, **other:** 4 Seasons RV Park, Sprague Lake Resort/RV Park

242mm rest area both lanes, full(handicapped)facilities, phone, picnic tables, litter barrels, tourist/weather info, petwalk, free coffee

231 Tokio, Ⓢ...weigh sta both lanes, **gas:** Exxon/Templin's Café/dsl, **other:** RV Park

Spokane

WASHINGTON

Interstate 90

E ↕ W

Moses Lake

226	Coker Rd, S...**lodging:** Top Hat Motel
221	WA 261 S, Ritzville, City Ctr, N...**gas:** Conoco/dsl, Chevron/McDonald's, Shell/Subway/dsl, **food:** Perkins, Zip's Burgers, **lodging:** Best Value Inn, Best Western, The Cottage/RV Park, Empire Motel, La Quinta/RV Park, Top Hat Motel, **other:** HOSPITAL, hist dist
220	to US 395 S, Ritzville, N...**gas:** Chevron, Exxon/dsl/café, Texaco, **food:** Circle T Rest, Jake's Café, Texas John's Café, Wispering Palms, **other:** st patrol
215	Paha, Packard, no services
206	WA 21, Odessa, to Lind, no services
199mm	**rest area both lanes, full(handicapped)facilities, phone, picnic tables, litter barrels, vending, RV dump, petwalk**
196	Deal Rd, to Schrag, no services
188	U Rd, to Warden, Ruff, no services
184	Q Rd, no services
182	O Rd, to Wheeler, no services
179	WA 17, Moses Lake, N...**gas:** Cenex, Conoco/dsl, Ernie's Trkstp/Chevron/dsl/café/24hr/@, Exxon, 76/dsl, Shell/dsl, **food:** Arby's, Bob's Cafe, Burger King, DQ, Denny's, McDonald's, Shari's Rest./24hr, Starbucks, **lodging:** Holiday Inn Express, Shilo Inn/rest./24hr, **other:** HOSPITAL, **1 mi** N...**food:** DQ, Subway, **lodging:** El Rancho Motel, **other:** $tree, Ford, Honda, Nissan, Sun Country RV Park, USPO, **2 mi** N...**food:** A&W/KFC, Arctic Circle, Domino's, Godfather's, Jack-in-the-Box, KFC, Pizza Hut, Sporty's Steaks, Taco Time, **lodging:** Travelodge, **other:** Buick/Chevrolet/Pontiac, CarQuest, Chrysler/Jeep/Dodge, Ford, Rite Aid, Safeway, Schwab Tire, S...**other:** I-90 RV, Mardon RV Park(15), Willows RV Park(2mi), Potholes SP(15mi)
177mm	Moses Lake
176	WA 171, Moses Lake, **1 mi** N...**gas:** Cenex/24hr, Exxon/dsl, 76/dsl, Shell/dsl, **food:** Ann's Diner, El Rodeo Mexican, Kiyoji's Rest., Perkins/24hr, **lodging:** Best Western/rest., Interstate Inn, Motel 6, Oasis Budget Inn, Super 8, **other:** HOSPITAL, VET, OK Tires, Big Sun Resort/RV Hookups, Lake Front RV Park, S...**lodging:** Lakeshore Motel
175	Westshore Dr(from wb), N...**other:** Moses Lake SP, to Mae Valley, S...**other:** st patrol
174	Mae Valley, N...**other:** Suncrest Resort/RV, S...**gas:** Conoco/dsl, **other:** Pier RV Park, st patrol
169	Hiawatha Rd, no services
164	Dodson Rd, no services
162mm	**rest area wb, full(handicapped)facilities, phone, picnic tables, litter barrels, petwalk, RV dump**
161mm	**rest area eb, full(handicapped)facilities, phone, picnic tables, litter barrels, petwalk, RV dump**
154	Adams Rd, no services
151	WA 281 N, to Quincy, N...**gas:** Shell/dsl/pizza/subs, **other:** HOSPITAL(12mi)
149	WA 281 S, George, N...HOSPITAL(12mi), S...**gas:** Exxon/dsl/24hr, 76/Subway/dsl, **food:** Martha Inn Café, **other:** RV camp
143	Silica Rd, to The Gorge Ampitheatre
139mm	Wild Horses Mon, scenic view both lanes
137	WA 26 E, to WA 243, Othello, Richland

Ellensburg

Cle Elum

137mm	Columbia River
136	Huntzinger Rd, Vantage, N...**gas:** Shell, Texaco/dsl, **food:** Blustry's Rest, Harvest Room Rest., **lodging:** Motel Vantage, **other:** KOA, Vantage Gen. Store, to Ginkgo/Wanapum SP(3mi), auto repair, **4 mi** S...**other:** Gettys Cove RV Park
126mm	**Ryegrass, elev 2535, rest area both lanes, full(handicapped)facilities, phone, picnic tables, litter barrels, petwalk**
115	Kittitas, N...**gas:** Shell/dsl/LP/24hr, **other:** Olmstead Place SP
110	I-82 E, US 97 S, to Yakima
109	Canyon Rd, Ellensburg, N...**gas:** Astro/dsl, Chevron/24hr, Eagle Trkstp/dsl, 76, Shell/24hr, **food:** Arby's, Baskin-Robbins, Burger King, Fiesta Mexican, Golden Dragon Chinese, KFC, Los Cabos Mexican, McDonald's, Matterhorn Rest., Papa Murphy's, Pizza Hut, Quizno's, RanchHouse Rest., Skipper's, Subway, Taco Bell, Taco Del Mar, **lodging:** Best Western, Comfort Inn, Ellensburg Inn, Holiday Inn Express, Nites Inn, Super 8, **other:** HOSPITAL, VET, CarQuest, Chevrolet, $Store, NAPA, Radio Shack, Rite Aid, Schwab Tire, Super 1 Food/24hr, TrueValue, S...**gas:** /Flying J/Exxon/Sak's/dsl/scales/LP/24hr/@, **food:** Buzz Inn Steaks, **lodging:** Days Inn/RV park
106	US 97 N, to Wenatchie, N...**gas:** Chevron, Conoco/dsl/RV dump, Pilot/Subway/dsl/24hr, 76/dsl, **food:** Copper Kettle(2mi), DQ, Jack-in-the-Box(3mi), Perkins, **lodging:** Harold's Motel(2mi), I-90 Inn, Regal Lodge(2mi), **other:** Buick/Pontiac/GMC, Canopy Country RV Ctr, Chrystler/Jeep, Ford, Truck/RV Wash, S...**other:** KOA, st patrol
101	Thorp Hwy, N...**other:** antiques/fruits/vegetables
93	Elk Heights Rd, Taneum Creek, no services
92.5mm	Elk Heights, elev 2359
89mm	**Indian John Hill, elev 2141, rest area both lanes, full (handicapped)facilities, phone, picnic tables, litter barrels, RV dump, petwalk, vending**
85	WA 970, WA 903, to Wenatchie, N...**gas:** Conoco/repair, Gas Save, 76/dsl, Shell/dsl/24hr, **food:** Cottage Café/24hr, DQ, Giant Burger, McKean's Drive-In, Sunset Cafe, **lodging:** Aster Inn, Cascade Mtn Inn, Chalet Motel, **other:** VET, CarQuest, PriceChopper Foods, Trailer Corral RV Park
84	Cle Elum(from eb, return at 85), N...**gas:** Chevron/dsl, Conoco, Shell/Subway/dsl, **food:** Burger King, DQ, El Caporal Mexican, Los Cabos Mexican, Mama Vallones, Sunset Café, YumYang Chinese, **lodging:** Cle Elum Motel, Timber Lodge Motel, Traveler's Inn, Snowcap Lodge, Stewarts Lodge, **other:** HOSPITAL, Cle Elum Hardware, NAPA, Safeway/gas, Trailer Corral RV Park, museum
81mm	Cle Elum River
80	Roslyn, Salmon la Sac, no facilites
80mm	weigh sta both lanes, phone
78	Golf Course Rd, S...**other:** Sun Country Golf/RV Park
74	W Nelson Siding Rd, no services
71	Easton, S...**gas:** CB's Store/dsl/LP, **other:** USPO, John Wayne Tr, Iron Horse SP
71mm	Yakima River

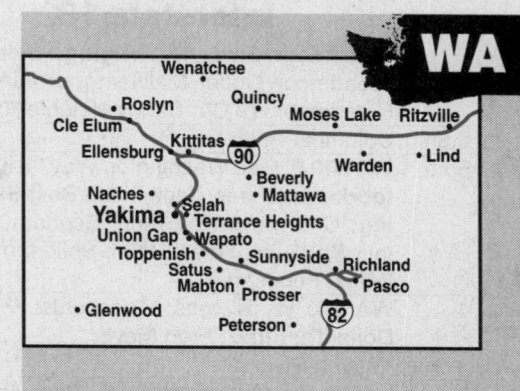

Interstate 90

70	Lake Easton SP, **N**...**gas:** Shell/RV Town/dsl/café, **food:** Mtn High Burger, **other:** Silver Ridge Ranch RV Park, repair, **S**...**other:** Lake Easton SP
63	Cabin Creek Rd, no services
62	Stampede Pass, elev 3750, to Lake Kachess, camping both lanes
56mm	parking area, eb(.5mi)
54	Hyak, Gold Creek, **S**... Ski Area
53	Snoqualmie Pass, elev 3022, info, **S**...**gas:** Chevron, **food:** Family Pancake House, **lodging:** Summit Lodge, **other:** to rec areas
52	W Summit(from eb), same as 53
47	Tinkham Rd, Denny Creek, Asahel Curtis, **N**...**other:** chain area, **S**...**other:** RV camping/dump
45	USFS Rd 9030, **N**...**other:** to Lookout Point Rd
42	Tinkham Rd, **S**...RV camping
38	**N**...**other:** fire training ctr
35mm	S Fork Snoqualmie River
34	468th Ave SE, Edgewick Rd, **N**...**gas:** 76/BBQ/dsl, Shell/Subway/dsl/24hr, TA/dsl/rest./@, **lodging:** Edgewick Inn, NW Motel/RV Park
32	436th Ave SE, North Bend Ranger Sta, **1 mi N**...gas, food, lodging, **S**...Gordy's BBQ
31	WA 202 W, North Bend, Snoqualmie, **N**...**gas:** Chevron/dsl, 76/dsl, Shell/dsl, **food:** Arby's, Blimpie, Burger King, McDonald's, Subway, Taco Time, **lodging:** North Bend Motel, Sallish Lodge, Sunset Motel, **other:** HOSPITAL, NorthBend Stores/famous brands, Safeway/deli/24hr, Shuck's Parts, museum, st patrol
27	North Bend, Snoqualmie(from eb), no services
25	WA 18 W, Snoqualmie Pkwy, Tacoma, to Auburn, **N**...weigh sta
22	Preston, **N**...**gas:** Shell/dsl/24hr, **food:** Espresso Café, Savannah's Burgers, **other:** USPO, LP, NAPA, Snoqualmie River RV Park(4mi), **S**...**other:** Blue Sky RV Park
20	High Point Way, no services
18	E Sunset Way, Issaquah, **S**...**gas:** Shell(1mi), **food:** Domino's, Flying Pie Pizza, Front St Mkt, Issaquah Brewhouse, Korean Grill, Las Margaritas, Mandarin Garden, Shagrila Garden Chinese, Stan's BBQ
17	E Sammamish Rd, Front St, Issaquah, **N**...**gas:** 76, **food:** Cojo Café, Coldstone, Fatburger, Jamba Juice, Krispy Kreme, McDonald's, Qdoba Mexican, Quizno's, Starbucks, **other:** Albertson's, Fred Meyer, Home Depot, Walgreens, **S**...**gas:** Arco/repair, Chevron/24hr, Shell, **food:** Boehms Chocolates, Extreme Pizza, Skipper's, **other:** U-Haul
15	WA 900, Issaquah, Renton, **N**...**gas:** Arco/24hr, **food:** IHOP, Red Robin, Tully's Coffee, **lodging:** Holiday Inn, Motel 6, **other:** Barnes&Noble, Costco/gas, Lowe's Whse, Office Depot, Petsmart, Trader Joe's, to Lk Sammamish SP, **S**...**gas:** Shell, **food:** Baskin-Robbins, Burger King, Denny's, Georgio's Subs, Jack-in-the-Box, Jet City Pizza, KFC/Taco Bell, Lombardi's Italian, McDonald's, O'Char Bistro, Schlotsky's, Starbucks, Subway, Taco Del Mar, Taco Time, Thai Cuisine, **other:** Chevrolet, Firestone/auto, Ford, Harley-Davidson, Panera Bread, PetCo, QFC Foods, Rite Aid, Ross, Safeway Foods, Schuck's Parts, Target, USPO

Bellevue (side label)

Issaquah (side label)

13	SE Newport Way, W Lake Sammamish
11	SE 150th, 156th, 161st, Bellevue, **N**...LDS Temple, **gas:** Shell, **food:** DQ, Greenwood Mandarin Chinese, India Quisine, Lil' Jon's Rest., McDonald's, Starbucks, Tulley's Coffee, **lodging:** Day's Inn, Embassy Suites, Silver Cloud Inn, **other:** Ford, 7-11, Subaru/VW, Safeway, Toyota, **S**...**gas:** 76, Standard/24hr, Shell/dsl/24hr, **food:** Baskin-Robbins, Domino's, Outback Steaks, Pizza Hut, **lodging:** Homestead Suites, **other:** Albertson's, Honda, Rite Aid, Schuck's Parts
10	I-405, N to Bellevue, S to Renton, services off I-405 S, exit 10
9	Bellevue Way
8	E Mercer Way, Mercer Island
7c	80th Ave SE(exits left from wb)
7b a	SE 76th Ave, 77th Ave, Island Crest Way, Mercer Island, **S**...**gas:** Chevron, 76/repair, Shell/dsl/repair, **food:** McDonald's, Starbucks, Subway, Thai Rest., Tully's Coffee, **lodging:** Travelodge, **other:** Island Foods, TrueValue, Walgreens
6	W Mercer Way(from eb), same as 7
5mm	Lake Washington
3b a	Ranier Ave, Seattle, downtown, **N**...**gas:** Shell/dsl, **other:** VET
2c b	I-5, N to Vancouver, S to Tacoma
2a	4th Ave S, to King Dome
	I-90 begins/ends on I-5 at exit 164.

Interstate 182(Richland)

Exit #	Services
14b a	US 395 N, WA 397 S, OR Ave, **N**...**gas:** Flying J/dsl/scales/rest., Shell, **food:** Burger King, Subway, **lodging:** King City, **other:** Goodyear, Peterbilt, **S**...**lodging:** Budget Inn, **I-182 begins/ends on US 395 N.**
13	N 4th Ave, Cty Ctr, **N**...**gas:** CFN/dsl, **lodging:** Airport Motel, Starlite Motel, **S**...**other:** HOSPITAL, RV park, museum
12b	N 20th Ave, **N**...**lodging:** Best Western, Red Lion Inn
12a	US 395 S, Court St, **S**...**on Court St. gas:** Arco/24hr, Conoco, Exxon/Jack-in-the-Box, Shell, Tesoro, **food:** A&W/KFC, Arby's, Burger King, McDonald's, Pizza Hut, Quizno's, Round Table Pizza, Subway, Taco Bell, Wendy's, **other:** Albertson's, Chief RV Ctr, Chevrolet, Ford, K-Mart, Rite Aid, Toyota, U-Haul, Walgreens
9	rd 68, Trac, **N**...**gas:** Shell, Tesoro, **food:** IHOP, King China Buffet, McDonalds, Subway, Taco Bell, **lodging:** Amerisuites, **other:** Wal-Mart Super Ctr/24hr, Yogi Yokes Mkt

E

W

Interstate 182

E
Richland
W

7	Broadmoor Blvd, **N**...**lodging:** Sleep Inn, **other:** Broadmoor Outlet Mall/famous brands, **S**...**other:** Broadmoor RV Ctr, Sandy Heights RV Park
6.5mm	Columbia River
5b a	WA 240 E, Geo Washington Way, to Kennewick, **N**...**food:** Applebees, Jack In the Box, Starbucks, **lodging:** Courtyard, Day's Inn, Economy Inn, Hampton Inn, Red Lion, Royal Hotel, Shilo Inn, **other:** $Tree, Winco Foods/gas
4	WA 240 W, **N**...**gas:** Conoco/dsl, 7-11, **food:** McDonald's, **other:** Fred Meyer
3.5mm	Yakima River
3	Keene Rd, Queensgate, **N**...**gas:** Arco/mart, Shell, **food:** Burger King, **other:** Wal-Mart Super Ctr/auto/gas, **S**...**other:** RV Park(3mi)
0mm	I-182 begins/ends on I-82, exit 102.

Interstate 405(Seattle)

N ↕ **S**

Seattle Area

Exit #	Services
30	I-5, N to Canada, S to Seattle, I-405 begins/ends on I-5, exit 182.
26	WA 527, Bothell, Mill Creek, **E**...**food:** Canyon's Rest., McDonald's, Thai-Rama, **lodging:** Extended Stay Deluxe, **other:** Lake Pleasant RV Park, **W**...**gas:** Arco, Chevron, Shell/dsl, **food:** Applebee's, Arby's, Baskin-Robbins, Bonefish Grill, Denny's, Grazi Ristorante, Guaymas Mexican, Jack-in-the-Box, Outback Steaks, Qdoba Mexican, Quizno's, Starbucks, Taco Bell, Taco Time, Tully's Coffee, **lodging:** Comfort Inn, **other:** VET, Albertson's, Bartell Drug, QFC Foods, Rite Aid, 7-11
24	NE 195th St, Beardslee Blvd, **E**...**gas:** Shell/Quizno's/dsl, **food:** Teryaki Etc, **lodging:** Country Inn&Suites, Residence Inn
23b	WA 522 W, Bothell, no services
23a	WA 522 E, to WA 202, Woodinville, Monroe
22	NE 160th St, **E**...**gas:** Chevron, Shell/dsl/24hr, **food:** Denice's Cafe
20	NE 124th St, **E**...**gas:** Arco/24hr, 76/dsl, Chevron/24hr, Shell/dsl/24hr, 7-11, **food:** Denny's, Georgio's Subs, Old Country Buffet, Pizza Hut, Subway, Taco Bell, **lodging:** Baymont Inn, Comfort Inn, Motel 6, The Inn, **other:** HOSPITAL, CompUSA, Discount Tire, Firestone, Infiniti, Larry's Mkt, Rite Aid, Ross, Schucks Parts, mall, **W**...**gas:** Arco/24hr, 76, **food:** Azteca Mexican, Burger King, Cocorino, Domino's, McDonald's, Olive Garden, Starbucks, Subway, Taco Time, Wendy's, **lodging:** Courtyard, **other:** Buick/Pontiac/GMC, Fred Meyer, GNC, QFC Food/24hr
18	WA 908, Kirkland, Redmond, **E**...**gas:** Arco/dsl, Chevron/24hr, 76/Circle K, Shell/dsl, Texaco/dsl, **food:** Domino's, Garlic Jim's, McDonald's, Outback Steaks, Pegasus Rest., Starbucks, Subway, Tres Hermanos Mexican, **other:** Chevrolet, Costco, Honda, Mazda, Nissan, Petco, Safeway, Schuck's Parts, 7-11, Tuesday Morning, U-Haul, Walgreens, **W**...**gas:** Chevron, Shell, **food:** Acropolis Pizza, Cafe Creek, Papa John's, Subway, TGIFriday, Wendy's, **other:** VET, Goodyear
17	NE 70th Pl, no services
14b a	WA 520, Seattle, Redmond
13b	NE 8th St, **E**...**gas:** Arco/24hr, Chevron/dsl, Shell/dsl, **food:** Burger King, Denny's, **lodging:** Coast Hotel, Extended Stay America, **other:** HOSPITAL, Best Buy, Buick/Pontiac, Ford, Home Depot, Larry's Mkt, Lincoln/Mercury, Whole Foods Mkt, **W**...**food:** Starbucks, **lodging:** Courtyard, Paragon
13a	NE 4th St, **E**...**other:** Ford, **W**...**lodging:** Best Western, Doubletree Hotel, Hilton, Hyatt, Ramada Ltd., Red Lion/Bellevue Inn, Sheraton
12	SE 8th St, no services
11	I-90, E to Spokane, W to Seattle
10	Cold Creek Pkwy, Factoria, **E** on **Factoria Blvd**...**gas:** 76/Circle K, **food:** Applebee's, Burger King, Jamba Juice, KFC, Keg Steaks, McDonald's, Old Country Buffet, Peking Wok, Quizno's, Red Robin, Starbucks, Subway, Taco Bell, Taco Time, Thaiginger Rest., **other:** VET, Mervyn's, Nordstrom's, Old Navy, Oriental Foods, Petco, QFC Foods, Rite Aid, Safeway, Schuck's Parts, 7-11, Target, mall
9	112th Ave SE, Newcastle, phone
7	NE 44th St, **E**...**food:** Denny's/24hr, McDonald's, Subway, **lodging:** Econolodge
6	NE 30th St, **E**...**gas:** Arco/24hr, **W**...**gas:** Chevron/24hr, Shell, **other:** 7-11
5	WA 900 E, Park Ave N, Sunset Blvd NE, **W**...**other:** Fry's Electronics
4	WA 169 S, Wa 900 W, Renton, **E**...**food:** Shari's, **lodging:** Quality Inn, **other:** Aqua Barn Ranch Camping, **W**...**food:** Burger King, Stir Rest., **lodging:** Renton Inn, **other:** 7-11,
2	WA 167, Rainier Ave, to Auburn, **E**...HOSPITAL, **W**...**gas:** Arco/24hr, Chevron, 76/Subway/dsl, Shell, USA Minimart, **food:** A&W/KFC, Applebees, Arby's, Burger King, Denny's, Georgio's Subs, IHOP, Jack-in-the-Box, King Buffet, Mazatlan Mexican, McDonald's, McHales Rest., PanAsia, Panda Express, Pizza Hut, Popeye's, Qdoba Mexican, Quizno's, Taco Bell, Taco Time, Torero's Mexican, Wendy's, Yankee Grill, **lodging:** Holiday Inn, **other:** Cadillac, Chevrolet, Chrysler/Jeep, Dodge/Toyota, Ford, Fred Meyer, Firestone, Honda/Mazda/Hyundai/Suzuki/Kia, Isuzu, Lincoln/Mercury, Mitsubishi, Pontiac/Buick/GMC, Radio Shack, Safeway/gas, Sam's Club/gas, Schuck's Parts, Schwab Tire, Scion, Subaru/Peugeot, Walgreen, Wal-Mart/auto
1	WA 181 S, Tukwila, **E**...**gas:** Chevron/dsl, 76/dsl, Shell/dsl, **food:** Barnaby's Rest., Burger King, Jack-in-the-Box, McDonald's, Quizno's, Sizzler, Starbucks, Taco Bell, Teriyaki Wok, Wendy's, Zoopa Café, **lodging:** Best Western, Courtyard, DoubleTree Suites, Embassy Suites, Hampton Inn, Homestead Suites, Red Lion Hotel, Residence Inn, **other:** Acura, Barnes&Noble, Circuit City, Curves, Firestone, JC Penney, Lowe's Whse, Macys, Mervyn's, Nordstrom's, Office Depot, Sears/auto, 7-11, Target, mall, **W**...**gas:** 76, **lodging:** Comfort Suites, Homewood Suites
0mm	I-5, N to Seattle, S to Tacoma, WA 518 W. I-405 begins/ends on I-5, exit 154.

Weirton

70

Wheeling

250

Moundsville

Morgantown

68

Kingwood

Fairmont

Sisterville

Shinnston

Grafton

Martinsburg

81

Vienna

Parkersburg

50

Clarksburg

Romney

50

Philippi

119 250

Thomas

220

Moorefield

Weston

Buckhannon

Middleport

79

Glenville

33

Harman

19

Elkins

219

Durbin

Franklin

33

Ripley

Spencer

119

Sutton

Mill Creek

64

60

St. Albans

Charleston

Marlinton

Huntington

Chesapeake

Montgomery

Richwood

Madison

Fayetteville

60

Oak Hill

Falling Spring

119

Beckley

64 Lewisburg

Holden

Macarthur

Hinton

Williamson

19

Union

52

77

219

Welch

Princeton

War

Bluefield

Interstate 64

Exit #	Services
184mm	West Virginia/Virginia state line
183	VA 311, Crows(from eb), no services
181	US 60, WV 92(no ez wb return), White Sulphur Springs, **N**...**gas:** BP/Godfather's, Shell, **food:** Hardee's, Legends Rest., McDonald's(5mi), Pizza Hut, Taco Bell, Wendy's(4mi), **lodging:** Budget Inn, Greenbrier Motel, Old White Motel, **other:** Family$, Food Lion, NAPA, Rite Aid, to Midland Trail, ski area, **S**...**lodging:** Allstate Motel, **other:** Twilite Camping
179mm	**Welcome Ctr wb, info, full(handicapped) facilities, phone, picnic tables, litter barrels, petwalk**
175	US 60, WV 92, Caldwell, **N**...**gas:** Chevron/dsl/24hr, Shell/Subway/dsl, StopIn/gas, **food:** Granny's House Rest., Greenbrier's Mountainaire Rest., McDonald's, Taco Bell, Wendy's, **lodging:** Budget Inn, Dixon Hotel, Village Motel, **S**...**other:** Greenbrier SF, camping
173mm	Greenbrier River
169	US 219, Lewisburg, Hist Dist, **N**...**lodging:** Day's Inn, **S**...**gas:** Exxon/dsl, Shell, **food:** Applebee's, Arby's, Bob Evans, Hardee's, Shoney's, Subway, Western Sizzlin, **lodging:** Brier Inn, Econolodge, Hampton Inn, Rodeway Inn, Super 8, **other:** HOSPITAL, Wal-Mart SuperCtr/gas/24hr
161	WV 12, Alta, **S**...**gas:** Chevron(1mi), **food:** Grandpa's Rest., **other:** Greenbrier River Camping(14mi)
156	US 60, Midland Trail, Sam Black Church, **N**...**gas:** Citgo, Exxon/dsl, Shell/dsl
150	Dawson, **S**...**lodging:** Dawson Inn/RV camping
147mm	runaway truck ramp wb
143	WV 20, Green Sulphur Springs, **N**...**gas:** Chevron/dsl
139	WV 20, Sandstone, Hinton, **S**...**gas:** Citgo/dsl, **other:** to Pipestem Resort Park
138mm	New River
133	WV 27, Bragg Rd, mandatory truck stop eb
129	WV 9, Shady Spring, **N**...**other:** to Grandview SP, **S**...**gas:** Exxon/dsl, Shell/dsl, **other:** Little Beaver SP
125	WV 307, Airport Rd, Beaver, **N**...**gas:** Shell/dsl, **lodging:** Sleep Inn, **S**...**gas:** Amoco/dsl, Chevron, Exxon, GoMart/gas, **food:** Hardee's, LJ Silver, McDonald's, Pizza Hut, **lodging:** Glade Spgs Resort, Patriot Motel
124	US 19, E Beckley, **N**...**gas:** Exxon, GoMart/gas, Speedway, **food:** Capt D's, **lodging:** Greenbank Motel, Honey Rock Motel, PineCrest Motel, **other:** last exit before toll rd wb
121	I-77 S, to Bluefield
I-64 and I-77 run together 61 mi. See Interstate 77, exits 42 through 100.	
59	I-77 N(from eb), to I-79

E

W

WEST VIRGINIA
Interstate 64

E ↓ W

58c	US 60, Washington St, **N**...**gas:** Exxon, GoMart/gas, **food:** Arby's, **other:** Lincoln/Mercury, **S**...**food:** LJ Silver, Shoney's, **lodging:** Embassy Suites, Hampton Inn, Holiday Inn Express, Marriott, **other:** HOSPITAL, civic ctr, mall	
58b	US 119 N(from eb), Charleston, downtown	
58a	US 119 S, WV 61, MacCorkle Ave, **S**...**food:** Steak&Ale	
56	Montrose Dr, **N**...**gas:** Chevron/Blimpie, Exxon/dsl, Speedway, **food:** Hardee's, **lodging:** Microtel, Ramada Inn, Wingate Inn, **other:** Advance Parts, Chevrolet, Chrysler, Dodge, Hyundai, Kia, Rite Aid, Toyota, VW	
55	Kanawha Tpk, no services	
54	US 60, MacCorkle Ave, **S**...**gas:** Chevron, **food:** Bob Evans, KFC, LJ Silver, McDonald's, Pizza Hut, Schlotsky's, Taco Bell, Wendy's, **other:** HOSPITAL, Aamco, Firestone, Harley-Davidson, Honda, Mitsubishi, Save-A-Lot Foods	
53	Roxalana Rd, to Dunbar, **S**...**gas:** GoMart/gas, **food:** BiscuitWorld, Capt D's, Gino's Pizza, McDonald's, Shoney's, Subway, Wendy's, **lodging:** Super 8, Travelodge, **other:** Advance Parts, Aldi, CarQuest, CVS Drug, Family$, Jo-Ann Fabrics, Kroger, NTB, Radio Shack	
50	VW 25, Institute, **S**...**gas:** GoMart/gas	
47b a	WV 622, Goff Mtn Rd, **N**...**gas:** Chevron/24hr, Exxon, GoMart, Speedway, **food:** A&W, Biscuit-World, Bob Evans, Capt D's, Domino's, Gino's Pizza, McDonald's, Papa John's, Pizza Hut, Rice Bowl, Subway, Taco Bell, Wendy's, **lodging:** Motel 6, **other:** Advance Parts, Kroger/gas, NAPA, Rite Aid, **S**...**food:** Arby's, Burger King, Coco's Chinese, Cracker Barrel, DQ, Fazoli's, Golden Corral, TGIFriday, **lodging:** Comfort Inn, Sleep Inn, **other:** $Tree, Goody's, Lowe's Whse, Radio Shack, Staples, Wal-Mart SuperCtr/24hr	
45	WV 25, Nitro, **N**...**gas:** Pilot/Arby's/dsl/scales/24hr/@, **other:** Chevrolet Trucks, **S**...**gas:** Chevron, Exxon, Speedway, **food:** BiscuitWorld, Checker's, DQ, Gino's Pizza, McDonald's, Subway, Wendy's, **lodging:** Econolodge, **other:** Chevrolet	
44.3mm	Kanawha River	
44	US 35, St Albans, **S**...**gas:** Chevron/dsl, 7-11	
41	new exit	
39	WV 34t, Winfield, **N**...**gas:** BP/Arby's, GoMart/dsl, **food:** Applebee's, Bob Evans, Hardee's, Taste of Asia, **lodging:** Day's Inn, Holiday Inn Express, Red Roof Inn, **other:** Advance Parts, Big Lots, $General, Tuesday Morning, USPO, **S**...**gas:** Exxon/dsl, GoMart/gas, TA/dsl/rest./scales/24hr/@, **food:** Burger King, Capt D's, China Chef, Gino's Pizza, KFC, McDonald's, Monty's Pizza, Papa John's, Shoney's, Subway, Taco Bell, TCBY, Wendy's, **lodging:** Hampton Inn, **other:** AutoZone, K-Mart, Kroger, Rite Aid	
38mm	weigh sta both lanes	

35mm	**rest area both lanes, full(handicapped)facilities, phone, vending, picnic tables, litter barrels, petwalk**
34	WV 19, Hurricane, **N**...**other:** Chevrolet, Ford, Saturn, **S**...**gas:** Chevron/dsl, Exxon, Go-Mart, **food:** BiscuitWorld/Gino's Pizza, McDonald's, Mi Pueblito, Pizza Hut, Subway, **lodging:** Super 8, **other:** Rite Aid, vet
28	US 60, Milton, **1-3 mi S**...**gas:** Chevron/dsl, Exxon, Go-Mart, Marathon, Rich Gas, **food:** Biscuit World, Gino's Pizza, McDonald's, Wendy's, **other:** Advance Parts, Foxfire RV Park, Jim's Camping, Sav-A-Lot foods, vet
20	20 US 60, Mall Rd, Barboursville, **N**...**gas:** Chevron, Exxon/dsl, **food:** Applebee's, Arby's, Bob Evans, Burger King, Chick-fil-A, Chili's, Fuddrucker's, IHOP, Logan's Roadhouse, McDonald's, Olive Garden, Panera Bread, Ruby Tuesday, Wendy's, **lodging:** Comfort Inn, Holiday Inn, **other:** Best Buy, Borders Books, Chrysler/Jeep, Circuit City, Firestone/auto, JC Penney, Jo-Ann Fabrics, Kohl's, Lowe's Whse, Macy's, Michael's, NTB, Sears/auto, mall, Wal-Mart SuperCtr/24hr, **S**...**gas:** BP, Exxon, **food:** Cracker Barrel, Famous Dave's BBQ, Gino's Pizza, Outback Steaks, Sonic, Subway, Taco Bell, TCBY, **lodging:** Best Western, Hampton Inn, **other:** Cadillac, Lincoln/Mercury, Mazda, Toyota, to Foxfire Camping Resort
18	US 60, to WV 2, Barboursville, **N**...**food:** Bellacino's, O'Charley's, **other:** $Tree, Home Depot, Marshall's, Office Depot, Target, **S**...**gas:** Chevron, **food:** Hooters, Hardee's, Pizza Hut, **other:** Kroger/gas, Rite Aid
15	US 60, 29th St E, **N**...**gas:** GoMart/dsl, Sunoco, **food:** Arby's, Penn Sta., Subway, Wendy's, **lodging:** Holiday Inn, Stone Lodge Inn, **other:** HOSPITAL, Curves, **S**...**gas:** Exxon, **food:** Fazoli's, Golden Corral, McDonald's, Shoney's, Taco Bell, **lodging:** Day's Inn, Red Roof Inn, **other:** Chrysler/Dodge/Jeep, CVS Drug, Nissan/Mitsubishi/VW, Office Depot, Pontiac/GMC/Buick/Isuzu, Subaru
11	WV 10, Hal Greer Blvd, **1-3 mi N**...**gas:** BP, Chevron, Go-Mart, **food:** Arby's, Marshall Café, McDonald's, Wendy's, **lodging:** Holiday Inn, Radisson, Ramada Ltd, Super 8, **other:** HOSPITAL, **S**...**other:** Beech Fork SP(8mi)
10mm	**Welcome Ctr eb, full(handicapped)facilities, phone, vending, picnic tables, litter barrels, petwalk**
8	WV 152 S, WV 527 N, **S**...**gas:** Speedway, **food:** DQ, Laredo Steaks
6	US 52 N, W Huntington, Chesapeake, **N**...**gas:** Go-mart, Marathon, Speedway/24hr, **food:** Pizza Hut, Shoney's, **lodging:** Coach's Inn, **other:** HOSPITAL, Family$
1	US 52 S, Kenova, **1-3 mi N**...**gas:** Chevron, Exxon, **food:** Burger King, McDonald's, Pizza Hut, **lodging:** Hollywood Motel
0mm	West Virginia/Kentucky state line, Big Sandy River

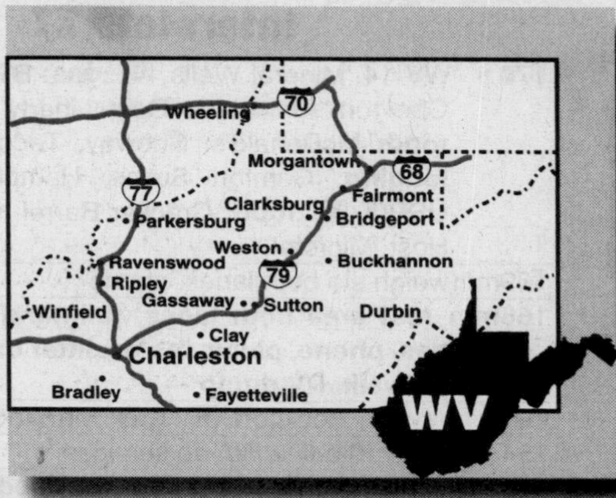

Interstate 68

E ↔ W

Morgantown

Exit #	Services
32mm	West Virginia/Maryland state line
31mm	**Welcome Ctr wb, full(handicapped)facilities, picnic tables, litter barrels, phone, vending, petwalk**
29	rd 5, Hazelton Rd, N...**gas:** Mobil/dsl, S...**other:** Big Bear Camping(3mi), Pine Hill RV Camp(4mi)
23	WV 26, Bruceton Mills, N...**gas:** BP/Subway/dsl/24hr, Sandy's/Mobil/dsl/24hr, **food:** Mill Place Rest., Subway, Twila's Rest., **lodging:** Maple Leaf Motel, **other:** Hostetler's Store, USPO, 15 mi S...**lodging:** Heldreth Motel
18mm	Laurel Run
17mm	runaway truck ramp eb
16mm	weigh sta wb
15	WV 73, WV 12, Coopers Rock, N...**other:** Chestnut Ridge SF, GS Camping(2mi)
12mm	runaway truck ramp wb
10	WV 857, Fairchance Rd, Cheat Lake, N...**gas:** BP/dsl/24hr, Exxon/dsl, **food:** China Kitchen, Pizza'n Pasta, Subway, **lodging:** Lakeview Resort, S...**food:** Burger King, Dimitri's Steaks
9mm	Cheat Lake
7	rd 705, Pierpont Rd, N...**gas:** BP/Subway/TCBY, Exxon/Taco Bell/dsl, **food:** Bob Evans, IHOP, Outback Steaks, Ruby Tuesday, Wendy's, **lodging:** Holiday Inn Express, Super 8, **other:** HOSPITAL, BooksAMillion, GNC, Harley-Davidson, Lowe's Whse, Michael's, Shop'n Save Foods, to WVU Stadium, S...**gas:** Crestpoint, **food:** Tiberio's
4	rd 7, to Sabraton, N...**gas:** BP, Exxon/24hr, Sheetz/24hr, **food:** Arby's, Burger King, Hardee's, Hero Hut, KFC, LJ Silver, McDonald's, Pizza Hut, Rio Grande Mexican, Subway, Wendy's, **lodging:** SpringHill Suites, **other:** Advance Parts, CVS Drug, $General, Family$, Food Lion, Ford, Kroger/dsl, Sav-a-Lot Foods, USPO, S...**gas:** Allstar/dsl
3mm	Decker's Creek
1	US 119, Morgantown, N...**gas:** Exxon/dsl, **lodging:** Comfort Inn, Ramada Inn/rest., S...**food:** Subway, **other:** Wal-Mart SuperCtr/24hr, to Tygart L SP
0mm	I-79, N to Pittsburgh, S to Clarksburg. I-68 begins/ends on I-79, exit 148.

Interstate 70

E ↔ W

Wheeling

Exit #	Services
14mm	West Virginia/Pennsylvania state line
13mm	**Welcome Ctr wb, full (handicapped) facilities, phone, vending, picnic tables, litter barrels, petwalk**
11	WV 41, Dallas Pike, N...**gas:** TA/dsl/rest./@, **lodging:** Comfort Inn, S...**gas:** Citgo/Country Kitchen/Taco Joe/Ck Burger/dsl/scales/24hr, Exxon, Mobil/DQ/dsl, **lodging:** Holiday Inn Express, **other:** RV camping
10	rd 65, to Cabela Dr, N...**food:** Applebee's, Bob Evans, Cracker Barrel, Eat'n Park, McDonald's, Wendy's, **other:** Cabela's, Target, Wal-Mart SuperCtr
5	US 40, WV 88 S, Tridelphia, N...**gas:** Marathon, **food:** Christopher's Café, Hoss' Rest., Pizza Hut, Subway, Wendy's, **lodging:** Super 8, **other:** Family$, Riesbeck's Foods, S...**gas:** BP, Exxon/dsl, Mobil, **food:** Arby's, DQ, Ernie's Rest., McDonald's, Silver Chopsticks, **other:** Advance Parts, NAPA, Rite Aid, museum
5a	I-470 W, to Columbus
4	WV 88 N(from eb), Elm Grove, same as 5
3.5mm	weigh sta wb
2b	Washington Ave, N...**gas:** Exxon, **food:** Greco's Rest., Subway, **other:** Kroger/gas S...**food:** Figaretti's Italian, **other:** HOSPITAL
2a	rd 88 N, to Oglebay Park, N...**gas:** Exxon, Sheetz, **food:** Bob Evans, Hardee's, LJ Silver, Perkins, Super Buffet, TJ's Rest, **lodging:** Hampton Inn, **other:** Advance Parts, CVS Drug, Kroger/gas, NTB, Radio Shack
1b	US 250 S, WV 2 S, S Wheeling
1a	US 40 E, WV 2 N, Main St, downtown, S...**lodging:** Best Western
1mm	tunnel
0	US 40 W, Zane St, Wheeling Island, N...**gas:** Exxon/dsl, **food:** Conv Mart, DQ , FoodCourt, KFC
0mm	West Virginia/Ohio state line, Ohio River

Interstate 77

N ↔ S

Parkersburg

Exit #	Services
186mm	West Virginia/Ohio state line, Ohio River
185	WV 14, WV 31, Williamstown, W...**gas:** GoMart, 7-11/gas(1mi), **food:** Dutch Pantry, Subway(1mi), **lodging:** Day's Inn, **other:** Glass Factory Tours, **WV Welcome Ctr/rest area, full facilities, info, picnic tables, litter barrels**
179	WV 2 N, WV 68 S, to Waverly, E...**gas:** Exxon, **other:** airport, W...**gas:** BP, Chevron(3mi), **food:** Hardee's(3mi), Pepper's Mexican, **lodging:** Red Carpet Inn, **other:** HOSPITAL
176	US 50, 7th St, Parkersburg, E...**lodging:** Parkersburg Inn, **other:** to North Bend SP, W...**gas:** GoMart, 7-11, **food:** Bob Evans, Burger King, Colombo's Rest., DQ, LJ Silver, McDonald's, Mountaineer Rest./24hr, Omelet Shoppe, **lodging:** Econolodge, Holiday Inn, Knight's Inn, Red Roof Inn, Travelodge, **other:** Kroger/dsl, Toyota, Family$, to Blennerhassett Hist Park, vet
174	WV 47, Staunton Ave, **1 mi** E...**gas:** Exxon/dsl, Finish-Line Gas, **food:** Subway, W...**gas:** Citgo/dsl
174mm	Little Kanawha River
173	WV 95, Camden Ave, E...**gas:** Marathon/dsl, **1-4 mi** W...**gas:** BP, **food:** Hardee's, **lodging:** Blennerhassett Hotel, **other:** HOSPITAL, Grandad's Mkt/dsl

N ↑ ↓ S

170 WV 14, Mineral Wells, E...**gas:** BP/dsl/repair/24hr, Chevron, FinishLine Gas, Liberty Trkstp/dsl/24hr, **food:** McDonald's, Subway, Taco Bell, Wendy's, **lodging:** Comfort Suites, Hampton Inn, **other:** USPO, W...**food:** Cracker Barrel, **lodging:** Ameri-Host, Microtel

169mm weigh sta both lanes, phone

166mm rest area both lanes, full(handicapped) facilities, phone, picnic tables, litter barrels, vending, petwalk, RV dump

161 WV 21, Rockport, W...**gas:** Marathon

154 WV 1, Medina Rd, no services

146 WV 2 S, Silverton, Ravenswood, W...**gas:** BP/dsl, Exxon/24hr, Marathon/dsl/24hr, **food:** DQ, Gino's Pizza, McDonald's(3mi), Wendy's(3mi), Subway(4mi), **lodging:** Scottish Inn, **other:** Ruby Lake Camping,

138 US 33, Ripley, E...**gas:** BP/dsl/24hr, Exxon/24hr, Marathon/dsl, **food:** KFC, LJ Silver, McDonald's, Pizza Hut, Taco Bell, Wendy's, **lodging:** Best Western/rest., Super 8, **other:** Kroger, NAPA, Rite Aid, Sav-A-Lot, Wal-Mart, vet, W...**gas:** Exxon/dsl/24hr, **food:** Bob Evan's, Ponderosa, Shoney's, Subway, **lodging:** Holiday Inn Express, **other:** HOSPITAL

132 WV 21, Fairplain, E...**gas:** BP/7-11/dsl, GoMart/dsl, Marathon, **food:** Biscuit World, Burger King, DQ, Fratello's Italian, **other:** Ford, Statts Mills RV Park(6mi), W...**lodging:** 77 Motel

124 WV 34, Kenna, E...**gas:** Exxon

119 WV 21, Goldtown, no services

116 WV 21, Haines Branch Rd, Sissonville, **4 mi** E...**other:** Rippling Waters Campground

114 WV 622, Pocatalico Rd, E...**gas:** MtnMart/gas, **other:** FasChek Foods/drug

111 WV 29, Tuppers Creek Rd, W...**gas:** BP/Subway/dsl, **food:** Gino's(2mi), Tudor's Biscuit World, Wendy's(2mi)

106 WV 27, Edens Fork Rd, W...**gas:** Chevron/dsl/country store, **lodging:** Sunset Motel(3mi)

104 I-79 N, to Clarksburg, no services

102 US 119 N, Westmoreland Rd, E...**gas:** BP/7-11/24hr, GoMart/24hr, **food:** Hardee's/24hr, **lodging:** Parsley Motel

101 I-64, E to Beckley, W to Huntington

100 Broad St, Capitol St, W...**food:** Charleston House Rest., **lodging:** Fairfield Inn, Holiday Inn, Marriott, Super 8, **other:** HOSPITAL, CVS Drug, Family$, GMC, Honda Motorcycles, JC Penney, Kroger

99 WV 114, Capitol St, E...**airport,** W...**gas:** Exxon, Domino's, **food:** KFC/Taco Bell, McDonald's, Wendy's, **other:** to museum, st capitol

98 35th St Bridge(from sb), W...**gas:** Sunoco, **food:** KFC/Taco Bell, McDonald's, Steak Escape, Shoney's, Subway, Wendy's, **other:** HOSPITAL, to U of Charleston

97 US 60 W(from nb), Kanawha Blvd

96 US 60 E, Midland Trail, Belle, W...**food:** Gino's, **lodging:** Budget Host

96mm W Va Turnpike begins/ends

95.5mm Kanawha River

95 WV 61, to MacCorkle Ave, E...**gas:** BP/Subway/dsl, GoMart/dsl/24hr, **food:** Bob Evans, IHOP, McDonald's, Texas Steaks, Wendy's, **lodging:** Comfort Suites, Country Inn&Suites, Day's Inn, Knight's Inn, Motel 6, Red Roof Inn, **other:** Advance Parts, K-Mart, W...**gas:** Ashland/Blimpie/24hr, Chevron/7-11, Exxon/dsl/24hr, Marathon, GoMart/24hr, **food:** Applebee's, Arby's, Azteca Mexican, Capt D's, China Buffet, Cracker Barrel, Hooters, La Carreta Mexican, Pizza Hut/Taco Bell, Ponderosa, Shoney's, Southern Kitchen/24hr, Shoney's, **other:** Foodland, Kroger/gas, Lowe's Whse, NAPA, Subaru, Suzuki, mall, vet

89 WV 61, WV 94, to Marmet, E...**gas:** Exxon/Subway/dsl/24hr, GoMart, Sunoco, **food:** BiscuitWorld, Gino's Pizza, Hardee's, KFC, LJ Silver, Sam's Hotdogs, Wendy's, **other:** Family$, Kroger/deli, Rite Aid, W...**other:** Ford(1mi)

85 US 60, WV 61, East Bank, E...**gas:** GoMart/dsl/24hr, **food:** Gino's Pizza, McDonald's, Shoney's, **other:** Chevrolet, Gilmer Foods, Kroger, tire repair

82.5mm toll booth

79 Cabin Creek Rd, Sharon, no services

74 WV 83, Paint Creek Rd, no services

72mm Morton Service Area nb, gas: Exxon/dsl, **food: Burger King, Pizza Hut, Starbucks, TCBY, atm**

69mm rest area sb, full(handicapped)facilities, phone, picnic tables, litter barrels

66 WV 15, to Mahan, 1/2 mi W...**gas:** Sunoco/dsl/24hr

60 WV 612, to Mossy, Oak Hill, 1/2 mi E...**gas:** Exxon/dsl/repair/24hr, **other:** RV camping

56.5mm toll plaza, phone

54 rd 2, rd 23, Pax, E...**gas:** BP

48 US 19, N Beckley, **1 mi** E...**gas:** BP/Subway/dsl, **food:** Garfield's Rest., **lodging:** Best Value Inn, **other:** JC Penney, Sears/auto, **4 mi E on US 19/WV 16** S...**gas:** Exxon, **food:** Bob Evans, Burger King, Checker's, Fazoli's, Hardee's, LoneStar Steaks, LJ Silver, McDonald's, Rio Grande Mexican, Ryan's, Wendy's, **other:** Acura, AutoZone, Buick, Chevrolet/Cadillac, Chrysler, CVS Drug, Dodge, Honda, Hyundai, Staples, Subaru/Kia, U-Haul, Wal-Mart SuperCtr/24hr

45mm Tamarack Service Area both lanes, W...gas: Exxon/dsl, **food: Burger King, Sbarro's, Starbucks, TCBY, other: gifts**

44 WV 3, Beckley, E...**gas:** Chevron/dsl, Exxon, Marathon, Shell/Hardee's/24hr, **food:** Applebee's, Burger King, DQ, Hibachi Japanese, McDonald's, Omelette Shop, Outback Steaks, Pancake House, Pizza Hut, **lodging:** Best Western, Comfort Inn, Courtyard, Fairfield Inn, Quality Inn, Super 8, **other:** CVS Drug, Kroger/gas, W...**gas:** BP/Subway, GoMart/dsl, **food:** Bob Evans, Cracker Barrel, Ruby Tuesday, Texas Roadhouse, Wendy's, **lodging:** Country Inn&Suites, Day's Inn, Hampton Inn, Holiday Inn, Microtel, Park Inn

42 WV 16, WV 97, to Mabscott, **2 mi** E...**food:** Biscuit-World, **lodging:** Budget Inn, **other:** HOSPITAL, W...**gas:** BP/dsl, GoMart, **food:** Godfather's, Subway, **other:** Wal-Mart/SuperCtr/24hr, USPO

Charleston

Beckley

Interstate 77

40	I-64 E, to Lewisburg
30mm	toll booth, phone
28	WV 48, to Ghent, **E**...**gas:** BP, Exxon/dsl, Marathon/dsl, **food:** Subway, **lodging:** Glade Springs Resort(1mi), Appalachian Resort Inn(12mi), **other:** to ski area, **W**...**lodging:** Econolodge
26.5mm	Flat Top Mtn, elevation 3252
20	US 19, to Camp Creek, **E**...**gas:** Exxon/dsl, **W**...**other:** Camp Creek SP/RV camping
18.5mm	scenic overlook/parking area/weigh sta sb, Bluestone River, no services
17mm	**Bluestone Service Area/weigh sta nb, full (handicapped) facilities, scenic view, picnic area, Exxon/dsl, Blimpie, Starbucks, TCBY, atm/fax**
14	WV 20, Athens Rd, **E**...**gas:** Citgo, **other:** Pipestem Resort SP
9mm	WV Turnpike begins/ends
9	US 460, Princeton, Pearisburg, **E**...**Welcome Ctr**, **food:** Outback Steaks, Ryan's, **other:** $Tree, Radio Shack, Wal-Mart SuperCtr/24hr, **W**...**gas:** BP/dsl, Chevron/dsl/24hr, Exxon/dsl/24hr, Marathon/Subway/dsl, **food:** Applebee's, Bob Evans, Burger King, Capt D's, Chili's, Cracker Barrel, DQ, Hardee's, McDonald's, Omelette Spot, Shoney's, Taco Bell, Texas Roadhouse, Wendy's, **lodging:** Budget Inn, Comfort Inn, Day's Inn, Hampton Inn, Holiday Inn Express, Ramada Ltd, Sleep Inn, Super 8, Turnpike Motel, **other:** HOSPITAL, Hyundai, K-Mart, Lowes Whse
7	WV 27, Ingleside Rd(from nb, no re-entry)
5	WV 112(from sb, no re-entry), to Ingleside
3mm	East River
1	US 52 N, to Bluefield, **4 mi** **W**...**food:** LJ Silver, Wendy's, **lodging:** Brier Motel, Econolodge, Highlander Motel, Holiday Inn/rest., Knight's Inn, Ramada Inn, **other:** HOSPITAL
.5mm	West Virginia/Virginia state line, East River Mtn
0mm	West Virginia/Virginia state line

Interstate 79

Exit #	Services
160mm	West Virginia/Pennsylvania state line
159	**Welcome Ctr sb, full(handicapped)facilities, info, picnic tables, litter barrels, phone, vending, pet-walk**
155	US 19, WV 7, **E**...**gas:** Sheetz, **3 mi** **E**...**gas:** Get-Go, Sheetz, **food:** Burger King, Cheddars, Chili's, Eat'n Park, EverGreen Buffet, Golden Corral, LJ Silver, Longhorn Steaks, McDonald's, Olive Garden, Shoney's, Wendy's, **lodging:** Best Western, Day's Inn, Econolodge, Euro Suites, Friends Inn, Hampton Inn, Holiday Inn, **other:** HOSPITAL, Barnes&Noble, Best Buy, CVS Drug, Giant Eagle Foods, Goody's, Old Navy, PetCo, Sam's Club, Target, TJ Maxx, Wal-Mart SuperCtr, to WVU
152	US 19, to Morgantown, **E**...**gas:** BP/dsl, Exxon, Getty, **food:** Arby's, Maggie's, McDonald's, Pizza Hut, Subway, Taco Bell, **lodging:** Clarion, Econolodge, **other:** Advance Parts, Big Lots, **W**...**food:** Bob Evans, Burger King, Garfield's Rest., **other:** Belk, JC Penney, K-Mart, Lowe's Whse, Sears/auto, mall

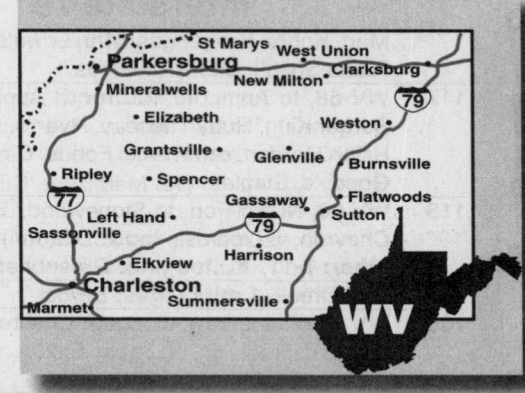

150mm	Monongahela River
148	I-68 E, to Cumberland, MD, **1 mi** **E**...**gas:** Exxon/dsl/24hr, **lodging:** Regatta Grill, **lodging:** Comfort Inn, Morgantown Motel, Ramada Inn/rest.
146	WV 77, to Goshen Rd, no services
141mm	weigh sta both lanes
139	WV 33, E Fairmont, **E**...**gas:** Chevron, **W**...**gas:** Exxon/24hr, K&T/BP/dsl, **other:** RV camping, tires, vet
137	WV 310, to Fairmont, **E**...**gas:** BP, Exxon/dsl/24hr, **food:** Simmering Pot Rest., Subway, **lodging:** Holiday Inn, **other:** to Valley Falls SP, vet, **W**...**gas:** Chevron, **food:** KFC, McDonald's, Wendy's, **other:** HOSPITAL
136	new exit
135	WV 64, Pleasant Valley Rd, no services
133	Kingmont Rd, **E**...**gas:** BP/Subway/dsl, **food:** Cracker Barrel, **lodging:** Super 8, **W**...**gas:** Chevron/dsl/24hr, King/dsl, **food:** DJ's Diner, **lodging:** Comfort Inn
132	US 250, S Fairmont, **E**...**food:** Arby's, Bob Evans, Dragon Buffet, Hardee's, McDonald's, Subway, Taco Bell, TJ's Rest., **lodging:** Day's Inn, Fairfield Inn, Red Roof Inn, **other:** Ace Hardware, Advance Parts, Chrysler/Dodge, $General, GNC, Harley-Davidson, JC Penney, Jo-Ann Fabrics, Sam's Club, Sav-a-Lot Foods, Shop'n Save, Wal-Mart/drugs, mall, to Tygart Lake SP, **W**...**gas:** Exxon/dsl/24hr, GoMart/dsl/24hr, Sunoco, **lodging:** Country Club Motel(4mi), **other:** HOSPITAL, Buick/Pontiac/GMC, Ford/Lincoln/Mercury, Toyota, Trailer City RV Ctr
125	WV 131, Saltwell Rd, to Shinnston, **E**...**food:** Oliverio's Rest.(4mi), **W**...**gas:** Exxon/Subway/dsl/24hr
124	rd 279, Jerry Dove Dr, **E**...**lodging:** Microtel, Wingate Inn
123mm	**rest area both lanes, full(handicapped)facilities, info, phone, picnic tables, litter barrels, vending, pet-walk, RV dump**
121	WV 24, Meadowbrook Rd, **E**...**gas:** GoMart/Blimpie/24hr, Sheetz, **food:** Bob Evans, **lodging:** Hampton Inn, **W**...**gas:** Exxon/dsl, **food:** Arby's, Burger King, Garfield's Rest., **other:** Jo-Ann Fabrics, **food:** Outback Steaks, **lodging:** Super 8, **other:** Honda, JC Penney, Jo-Ann Fabrics, NTB, Old Navy, Sears/auto, Target, mall
119	US 50, to Clarksburg, **E**...**gas:** Chevron/dsl/24hr, Exxon/dsl, GoMart/gas, Speedway, **food:** Damon's, Denny's Grand China, KFC, Little Caesar's, LJ Silver, Maxey's Rest., McDonald's, Panera Bread, Taco Bell, Texas Roadhouse, USA Steaks, Wendy's, **lodging:** Comfort Inn, Day's Inn, Holiday Inn, Knight's Inn, Sleep Inn, **other:** HOSPITAL, Big Lots, Chevrolet, Home Depot, K-

WEST VIRGINIA
Interstate 79

N ↑ S

	Mart, Kohl's, Kroger/gas/24hr, Lowe's Whse, Nissan, Radio Shack, Sam's Club/gas
117	WV 58, to Anmoore, **E**...**food:** Applebee's, Arby's, Burger King, Ruby Tuesday, Ryan's, Subway, **other:** Hilton Garden, **other:** Aldi Foods, Circuit City, $Tree, Goody's, Staples, Wal-Mart SuperCtr/24hr
115	WV 20, Nutter Fort, to Stonewood, **E**...**gas:** BP/dsl, Chevron, Exxon/dsl, **food:** DQ(3mi), Subway(3mi), **other:** 7-11, **W**...**lodging:** Greenbrier Motel
110	Lost Creek, **1 mi E**...**gas:** BP/dsl
105	WV 7, to Jane Lew, **E**...**gas:** Chevron/dsl/rest., I-79 Trkstp/dsl/rest./@, **W**...**gas:** Exxon, Gomart, **other:** glass factory tours
99	US 33, US 119, to Weston, **E**...**gas:** Sheetz/24hr, **food:** Gino's Pizza, McDonald's, Pizza, Hut, Steer Steakhouse, Subway, **lodging:** Budget Host(3mi), Comfort Inn/rest., Hampton Inn(9mi), Super 8, **other:** Advance Parts, Family$, GNC, Kroger, Radio Shack, Wal-Mart, **W**...**gas:** BP, **food:** Hardee's, KFC, LJ Silver, Pizza Hut, Wendy's, **other:** HOSPITAL, $General, Ford, NAPA, SavALot, Twin Lakes Camper Sales, to Canaan Valley Resort, Blackwater Falls
96	WV 30, to S Weston, **E**...**other:** to S Jackson Lake SP, Broken Wheel Camping
91	US 19, to Roanoke, **E**...**gas:** Marathon, **other:** Whisper Mtn Camping, to S Jackson Lake SP
85mm	**rest area both lanes, full(handicapped)facilities, info, picnic tables, litter barrels, phone, vending, petwalk, RV dump**
79.5mm	Little Kanawha River
79	WV 5, Burnsville, **E**...**gas:** Exxon/24hr, **lodging:** 79 Motel/rest., **other:** NAPA, **W**...**gas:** Gomart, **food:** Gino's Pizza, **other:** Cedar Cr SP
78mm	Saltlick Creek
67	WV 4, to Flatwoods, **E**...**gas:** Ashland/dsl, Chevron/dsl, Exxon/dsl, Go-Mart/dsl, **food:** DQ, KFC/Taco Bell, McDonald's, Shoney's, **lodging:** Day's Inn, Sutton Lake Motel, **other:** Ace Hardware, Chevrolet/Buick, to Sutton Lake RA, camping, **W**...**gas:** Ashland/motel/dsl, **food:** China Buffet, Shoney's, Wendy's, **other:** Flatwood Stores/famous brands
62	WV 4, Gassaway, to Sutton, **E**...**lodging:** Century Inn(2mi), Elk Motel, **W**...**gas:** GoMart, **food:** LJ Silver, Pizza Hut, **other:** HOSPITAL, CVS Drug, Ford/Mercury, Jeep/Dodge, Kroger/deli, Super$
57	US 19 S, to Beckley
52mm	Elk River
51	WV 4, to Frametown, **E**...antiques
49mm	**rest area both lanes, full(handicapped)facilities, picnic tables, phone, litter barrels, vending, petwalk, RV dump**
46	WV 11, Servia Rd, no services
40	WV 16, to Big Otter, **E**...**gas:** GoMart/dsl, **W**...**gas:** Exxon/dsl
34	WV 36, to Wallback, **10 mi E**...**food:** Gino's Diner, BiscuitWorld
25	WV 29, to Amma, **E**...**gas:** Exxon/dsl
19	US 119, VW 53, to Clendenin, **E**...**gas:** BP/dsl/24hr, **food:** BiscuitWorld, Gino's Diner, **other:** Shafer's Superstop

Charleston

9	WV 43, to Elkview, **E**...**gas:** GoMart/dsl, **W**...**gas:** Exxon/Arby's/dsl, Speedway/dsl/24hr, **food:** Bob Evans, McDonald's, Pizza Hut, Ponderosa, Subway, **lodging:** Country Inn&Suites, **other:** Advance Parts, CVS Drug, $Tree, GNC, K-Mart, Kroger, Radio Shack
5	WV 114, to Big Chimney, **1 mi E**...**gas:** Exxon, **food:** Hardee's/24hr, **other:** Rite Aid, Smith's Foods
1	US 119, Mink Shoals, **E**...**food:** Harding's Family Rest., **lodging:** Sleep Inn
0	I-77, S to Charleston, N to Parkersburg. I-79 begins/ends on I-77, exit 104.

Interstate 81

Exit #	Services
26mm	West Virginia/Maryland state line, Potomac River
25mm	**Welcome Ctr sb, full(handicapped)facilities, info, phone, picnic tables, litter barrels, petwalk**
23	US 11, Marlowe, Falling Waters, **1 mi E**...**other:** Falling Waters Camping, **W**...**gas:** BP/dsl, Citgo/7-11, **other:** Outdoor Express RV Ctr
20	WV 901, Spring Mills Rd, **E**...**food:** Barney's Rest., **lodging:** Econolodge, **W**...**gas:** Shell/dsl, **food:** Domino's, **lodging:** Holiday Inn Express
16	WV 9, N Queen St, Berkeley Springs, **E**...**gas:** Citgo, Exxon/Subway/dsl, Sheetz/24hr, **food:** Denny's, Golden China, Hoss's, KFC, LJ Silver, McDonald's, Waffle House, **lodging:** Comfort Inn, Knight's Inn, Super 8, Travelodge, **other:** Advance Parts, **W**...**gas:** Citgo, Shell/dsl
14	RD 13, Dry Run Rd, **E**...**food:** Hot Dog Hut, **other:** HOSPITAL
13	RD 15, Kings St, Martinsburg, **E**...**gas:** BP/dsl, Sheetz/24hr, **food:** Applebee's, Arkena's Cafe, Asian Garden, Burger King, Cracker Barrel, El Ranchero Mexican, Kobe Japanese, Outback Steaks, Pizza Hut, Shoney's, Wendy's, **lodging:** Day's Inn, Holiday Inn/rest., **other:** HOSPITAL, Chevrolet/Toyota, Tanger/famous brands, Wal-Mart SuperCtr/24hr, same as 12
12	WV 45, Winchester Ave, **E**...**gas:** Citgo/dsl, Sheetz/24hr, Shell/dsl, **food:** Arby's, Bob Evans, Chick-fil-A, China City Buffet, McDonald's, Papa John's, Quizno's, Ryan's, Ruby Tuesday, Taco Bell, Texas Steaks, Waffle House, Wendy's, **lodging:** Comfort Suites, Economy Inn, Hampton Inn, Heritage Motel, Kristalite Inn, Relax Inn, Scottish Inn, **other:** Advance Parts, AutoZone, Food Lion, JC Penney, K-mart, Lowe's Whse, Martin's Foods/gas, Sears/auto, mall, Nahkeeta RV Camping(3mi), same as 13
8	RD 32, Tablers Sta Rd, **2 mi E**...**lodging:** Pikeside Motel
5	WV 51, Inwood, to Charles Town, **E**...**gas:** Citgo/7-11, Exxon, Liberty, Sheetz, Shell/dsl, **food:** Burger King, DQ, KFC, McDonald's, Pizza Hut, Pizza Oven, Subway, Viva Mexican, Waffle House, **lodging:** Hampton Inn, **other:** Family$, Food Lion, **W**...**other:** Lazy-A Camping(9mi)
2mm	**Welcome Ctr/weigh sta nb, full(handicapped) facilities, info, phone, vending, picnic tables, litter barrels, petwalk**
0mm	West Virginia/Virginia state line

Martinsburg

N ↑ S

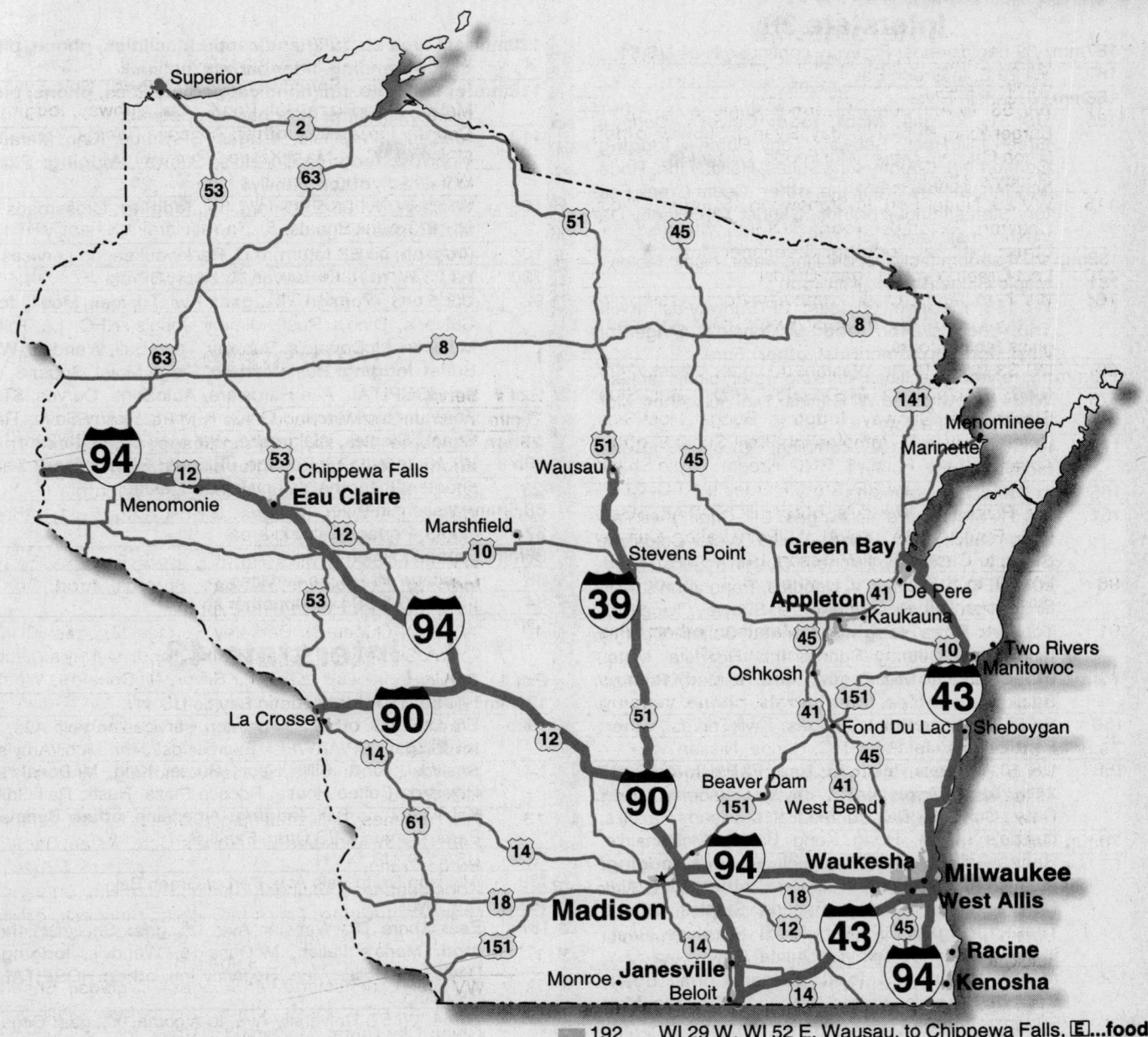

WISCONSIN

Interstate 39

Wausau

Exit #	Services
211	US 51, rd K, Merrill, **E**...antiques
210mm	Prairie River
208	WI 64, WI 70, Merrill, **W**...**gas:** BP/dsl/24hr, Kwik-Trip/dsl, Mobil/dsl, **food:** Burger King, Diamond Dave's Tacos, Hardee's, McDonald's, Pine Ridge Rest., Taco Bell, Three's Company Dining, **lodging:** Best Western, Super 8, **other:** Piggly Wiggly, Radio Shack, Wal-Mart, to Council Grounds SP
206mm	Wisconsin River
205	US 51, rd Q, Merrill, **E**...**gas:** Citgo/dsl/rest./24hr, **other:** antiques
197	rd WW, to Brokaw, **W**...**gas:** Citgo/dsl
194	US 51, rd U, rd K, Wausau, **E**...**gas:** F&F/gas, Kwik-Trip/gas, Mobil, **food:** A&W, McDonald's, Taco Bell, **other:** Chrysler/Jeep, Toyota/Isuzu/Mercedes
193	Bridge St, **W**...HOSPITAL
192	WI 29 W, WI 52 E, Wausau, to Chippewa Falls, **E**...**food:** Annie's Rest., King Buffet, Little Caesar's, **lodging:** Baymont Inn, Exel Inn, Ramada, Subway, Country Inn Suites, **other:** County Mkt Foods, same as 191
191	Sherman St, **E**...**gas:** BP, **food:** Applebee's, Cousins Subs, Hudson's Grill, McDonald's, Schlotzky's, **lodging:** Courtyard, Hampton Inn, Super 8, **other:** HOSPITAL, **W**...**food:** Burger King, Hardee's, Schlotsky's, 2510 Deli, **other:** Audi/Nissan/VW, Home Depot
190mm	Rib River
190	rd NN, **E**...**gas:** Mobil, **food:** Krumbee's Bakery, **lodging:** Wausau Inn, **W**...**gas:** Citgo/dsl/24hr, Mobil/dsl, **food:** El Mezcal, Hoffman House Rest., Shakey's Pizza, Subway, **lodging:** Best Western, **other:** Rib Mtn Ski Area, st patrol
188	rd N, **E**...**gas:** BP/24hr, Phillips 66/dsl, **food:** Country Kitchen/24hr, El Tapatio, Fazoli's, HongKong Buffet, McDonald's, Rococo's Pizza, Wendy's, **lodging:** Country Inn&Suites(1mi), Day's Inn, **other:** Aldi, Best Buy, Chevrolet, King's RV Ctr, Mazda, Nissan, Petco, Peterbilt, Sam's Club, Saturn, TJ Maxx, Volvo, Wal-Mart SuperCtr

527

WISCONSIN

Interstate 39

N ↕ S

187mm	I-39 begins/ends. Freeway continues N as US 51.
187	WI 29 E, to Green Bay
186mm	Wisconsin River
185	US 51, **E**...**gas:** Mobil, **food:** Culver's, Denny's, Green Mill Rest., Subway, Tony Roma's, **lodging:** Comfort Inn, Country Inn&Suites, Holiday Inn, Rodeway Inn, Stoney Creek Inn, **other:** Cedar Creek Factory Stores/famous brands, Gander Mtn, Harley Davidson, mall, visitor ctr
183mm	sb, restroom facilities, drinking water, picnic tables
181	Maple Ridge Rd, **W**...Kenworth
179	WI 153, Mosinee, **W**...**gas:** BP/Subway/dsl, Kwik-Trip, Shell/dsl/24hr, **food:** McDonald's, StageStop Rest., **lodging:** AmeriHost, **other:** Ford
178mm	nb, restroom facilities, drinking water, picnic tables
175	WI 34, Knowlton, to WI Rapids, **1 mi W**...**other:** Mullins Cheese Factory
171	rd DB, Knowlton, **E**...camping, **W**...**other:** to gas, food, lodging
165	rd X, **E**...food, camping
161	US 51, Stevens Point, **W**...**gas:** BP, Citgo, KwikTrip/24hr, Quick Mart, **food:** China Wok, Coldstone Creamery, Country Kitchen, Cousin's Subs, Hardee's, KFC, McDonald's, Noodles, Papa John's, Perkins, Pizza Hut, Rococo's Pizza, Subway, Taco Bell, Topper's Pizza, **lodging:** Comfort Suites, Country Inn&Suites, Country Springs Inn, Roadstar Motel, **other:** County Mkt Foods, Jeep, K-Mart, Pontiac/Buick
159	WI 66, Stevens Point, **W**...**gas:** KwikTrip/dsl, **other:** Ford/Lincoln/Mercury/GMC, Honda, Nissan
158	US 10, Stevens Point, **E**...**gas:** F&F/dsl, Mobil/dsl/24hr, **food:** Applebee's, Arby's, Cranberry Creek Cafe, Culver's, DQ, El Mezcal Mexican, Fazoli's, Grazie's Italian, Hong Kong Buffet, McDonald's, Rudy's Grill, Subway, Taco Bell, Wendy's, **lodging:** Fairfield Inn, Holiday Inn Express, **other:** VET, Aldi, Copp's Foods, Hancock Fabrics, Staples, Target, Tires+, **W**...**gas:** BP/24hr, **food:** Sunshine Rest., **lodging:** Best Western, La Quinta, Royale Inn
156	rd HH, Whiting, **E**...**food:** Golden Corral, **other:** Best Buy, Kohl's, Lowes Whse, PetCo, Wal-Mart SuperCtr/24hr
153	rd B, Plover, **W**...**gas:** BP/Burger King, Mobil/Maidrite/dsl, **food:** Bamboo House, Big Apple Bagels, Cousins Subs, El Tapatio Mexican, IHOP, McDonald's, Subway, **lodging:** AmericInn, Hampton Inn, **other:** VET, Copp's Foods, $Tree, ShopKO, Toyota
151	WI 54, to Waupaca, **E**...**gas:** Shell/Arby's/dsl/scales/24hr, **food:** 4Star Family Rest., Shooter's Rest., **lodging:** Elizabeth Inn/Conv Ctr, **other:** Craft's RV Ctr, tire repair
143	rd W, Bancroft, to WI Rapids, **E**...**gas:** Citgo/dsl, **food:** Lakeshore II
139	rd D, Almond, no services
136	WI 73, Plainfield, to WI Rapids, **E**...**gas:** BP, Mobil/dsl/scales, **food:** Hooligan's Grill, **lodging:** R&R Motel, **W**...**gas:** Phillips 66/Subway/dsl
131	rd V, Hancock, **E**...**gas:** Citgo, **food:** Country Kettle, **other:** camping
127mm	weigh sta both lanes(exits left)
124	WI 21, Coloma, **E**...**gas:** Mobil/A&W/dsl, **lodging:** Mecan Inn, **other:** camping, **W**...**gas:** BP/dsl

Portage

120mm	rest area sb, full(handicapped)facilities, phone, picnic tables, vending, litter barrels, petwalk
118mm	rest area nb, full(handicapped)facilities, phone, picnic tables, vending, litter barrels, petwalk
113	rd E, rd J, Westfield, **W**...**gas:** BP/Burger King, Marathon, Mobil/dsl, **food:** McDonald's, Subway, **lodging:** Pioneer Motel/rest., **other:** Family$
106	WI 82 W, WI 23 E, Oxford, **E**...**lodging:** Crossroads Motel, **W**...**gas:** Citgo/dsl
104	(from nb, no EZ return)rd D, Packwaukee, no services
100	WI 23 W, rd P, Endeavor, **E**...**gas:** BP/dsl
92	US 51 S, Portage, **E**...**gas:** KwikTrip/dsl, Mobil, **food:** Culver's, Dino's Rest., Jimmy John's, KFC, La Tolteca Mexican, McDonald's, Subway, Taco Bell, Wendy's, World Buffet, **lodging:** Best Western, Ridge Motel, Super 8, **other:** HOSPITAL, Ace Hardware, AutoZone, Curves, $Tree, Ford/Lincoln/Mercury, GNC, K-Mart, Pick'n Save, Radio Shack, Staples, Walgreens, Wal-Mart SuperCtr/24hr
89b a	WI 16, to WI 127, Portage, **E**...**gas:** BP/dsl, **food:** Sharpshooter Grill, **other:** Chrysler/Dodge/Jeep
88.5mm	Wisconsin River
87	WI 33, Portage, **W**...ski area
86mm	Baraboo River
85	Cascade Mt Rd, no services
84	I-39, I-90 & I-94 run together sb

Interstate 43

Green Bay

Exit #	Services
192mm	I-43 begins/ends at Green Bay on US 41.
192b	US 41 S, US 141 S, to Appleton, services on Velp Ave, **1 mi S**...**gas:** BP/A&W/dsl, Express/dsl/24hr, Mobil/Arby's, Shell/dsl, **food:** Bill's Rest., Burger King, McDonald's, Riverside Coffee House, Rococo Pizza, Rustic Rail Grill, Subway, Taco Bell, **lodging:** AmericInn, **other:** Bumper Parts, Curves, CVS Drug, Family$
192a	US 41 N, US 141 N
189	Atkinson Dr, to Velp Ave, Port of Green Bay
188mm	Fox River
187	East Shore Dr, Webster Ave, **W**...**gas:** Shell/dsl/24hr, **food:** Maria's Italian, McDonald's, Wendy's, **lodging:** Day's Inn, Holiday Inn, Regency Inn, **other:** HOSPITAL, RV dump
185	WI 54, WI 57, University Ave, to Algoma, **W**...**gas:** Citgo, Marathon, Mobil, Shell/A&W, **food:** Cousins Subs, Guanjitos Mexican, Harvest Cafe, Kahn's Mongolian, Lee's Cantonese Chinese, Pizza Hut, Ponderosa, Rococo's Pizza, Subway, Taco Bell, **other:** NAPA, SuperValu Foods, Walgreens, U of WI GB
183	Mason St, rd V, **E**...**gas:** Shell/dsl, **food:** Culver's, Ground Round, Makinaw's Grill, **lodging:** AmeriHost, Country Inn Suites, **other:** HOSPITAL, **1 mi W**...**gas:** BP, Citgo, Mobil/dsl, Shell, **food:** Applebee's, Arby's, Burger King, China Buffet, China Kitchen, Country Kitchen, DQ, Fazoli's, KFC, Little Caesars, McDonald's, Papa John's, Papa Murphy's, Perkins, Pizza Hut, Starbucks, Taco Bell, **other:** Advance Parts, Aldi Foods, AutoZone, Cadillac, Chevrolet, Copps Foods, Cub Foods, Dodge, $General, Goodyear/auto, Hyundai, K-Mart, Kohl's, Mazda, PetCo, ShopKO, Tires+, Walgreen, Wal-Mart/Subway
181	Eaton Rd, rd JJ, **E**...**gas:** BP/McDonald's/dsl, **food:** Blimpie, Hardee's, Jimmy John's, Taco John's, Tumbleweed's Grill, **other:** Harley-Davidson, Ford, Home Depot, Kia, **W**...**gas:** Express/Subway/dsl, Gasmart, **food:** Ravine Grill, **other:** Farm & Fleet/gas, Festival Foods

Interstate 43

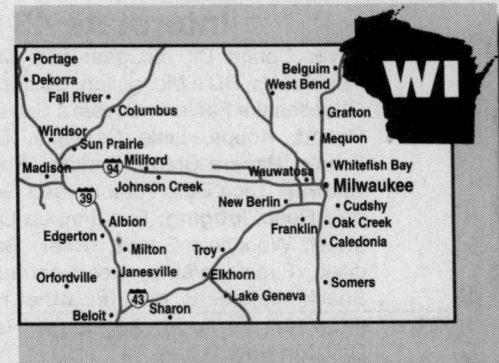

N ↑
S ↓

Milwaukee (vertical)

180	WI 172 W, to US 41, **1 exit** W...**gas:** BP/Taco Bell/24hr, Citgo/Country Express/dsl/rest./scales/24hr, Kwik Trip, Shell, **food:** Burger King, McDonald's, Subway, Tuscon's Rest., **other:** HOSPITAL, Target, to stadium, **5 mi** W...multiple services
178	US 141, to WI 29, rd MM, Bellevue, E...**gas:** Shell/ Arby's/dsl, W...repair
171	WI 96, rd KB, Denmark, E...**gas:** BP/dsl, **food:** Lorrie's Café, McDonald's, Steve's Cheese, Subway, **other:** Shady Acres Camping
168mm	**rest area both lanes, full(handicapped)facilities, phone, vending, picnic tables, litter barrels, petwalk**
166mm	Devils River
164	WI 147, rd Z, Maribel, W...**gas:** Citgo/dsl, **other:** Devils River Camp
160	rd K, Kellnersville, W...**gas:** BP, food(2-3 mi)
157	rd V, Hillcrest Rd, Francis Creek, E...**gas:** Citgo/Subway/dsl, Marathon/diner/dsl
154	US 10 W, WI 310, Two Rivers, to Appleton, E...**gas:** Mobil, **other:** HOSPITAL, W...**gas:** Cenex
153mm	Manitowoc River
152	US 10 E, WI 42 N, rd JJ, Manitowoc, E...**food:** Time-Out Grill, **other:** HOSPITAL, antiques, maritime museum
149	US 151, WI 42 S, Manitowoc, E...**gas:** Mobil/dsl/24hr, Shell/dsl/24hr, **food:** Applebee's, Arby's, Burger King, Charcoal Grill, Cold Stone, Country Kitchen, Culver's, DQ, Fazoli's, 4 Seasons Rest., McDonald's, Penguin Drive-In, Perkins, Ponderosa, Starbucks, Wendy's, **lodging:** Birch Creek Inn, Comfort Inn, Heritage Inn, Holiday Inn, Super 8, **other:** HOSPITAL, Buick/Pontiac/GMC/Cadillac, Chrysler/Dodge/Jeep, Lowe's Whse, PetCo, Tires+, Wal-Mart SuperCtr/24hr, museum, vet, W...**gas:** BP/McDonald's/24hr, **food:** Subway, **lodging:** AmericInn
144	rd C, Newton, E...**gas:** Mobil/dsl, **other:** antiques
142mm	weigh sta sb, phone
137	rd XX, Cleveland, E...**gas:** Citgo/Burger King/dsl, **food:** Cleveland Family Rest., **other:** Wagner's RV Ctr
128	WI 42, Howards Grove, E...**gas:** BP/dsl/24hr, **food:** Hardee's, Harry's Diner, Shuff's Rest., **lodging:** Comfort Inn, **other:** Gander Mtn, Jo-Ann Fabrics, W...**gas:** Citgo/Cousins Subs/dsl
126	WI 23, Sheboygan, E...**gas:** BP, **food:** Applebee's, China Buffet, Cousin's Subs, Culver's, Hardee's, IHOP, Kiko of Tokyo, McDonald's, Pizza Hut/Taco Bell, Ponderosa, Quizno's, **lodging:** La Quintas, Ramada Inn, Super 8, **other:** HOSPITAL, Aldi Foods, BigLots, Chrysler/Jeep/Subaru, Firestone/auto, Ford/Lincoln/ Mercury, Honda/Mazda/Toyota, Hyundai, JC Penney, Kohl's, Piggly Wiggly, Sears/auto, ShopKO, Walgreen, mall, W...**lodging:** Pinehurst Inn
123	WI 28, rd A, Sheboygan, E...**gas:** Citgo/dsl/24hr, Mobil/McDonald's/dsl, **food:** Cold Stone, Jimmy John's, Perkins, Starbucks, Taco Bell, Wendy's, **lodging:** AmericInn, Holiday Inn Express, **other:** Harley-Davidson/Cruisers Burgers, Wal-Mart SuperCtr, W...**food:** Arby's, Century Buffet, Chili's, **other:** Best Buy, $Tree, Elder-Berman, Home Depot, Michael's, PetsMart, Radio Shack, Target, TJ Maxx
120	rds OK, V, Sheboygan, E...**gas:** Citgo/dsl, **food:** Handlebar Rest., Judi's Rest., **lodging:** Sleep Inn, **other:** Nissan, to Kohler-Andrae SP, camping, **1 mi** W...**other:** Horn's RV Ctr
116	rd AA, Foster Rd, Oostburg, W...**food:** Pizza Ranch, Subway
113	WI 32 N, rd LL, Cedar Grove, W...**gas:** Citgo/dsl/repair, **food:** Country Grove Rest., **lodging:** Lakeview Motel
107	rd D, Belgium, E...**lodging:** Lake Church Inn, **other:** Harrington Beach SP, W...**gas:** BP/DQ/dsl/24hr, How-Dea Trkstp/dsl/scales, Mobil/McDonald's/dsl/24hr, **food:** Bic's Place, Curly's Rest., Hobo's Korner Kitchen, Subway, **lodging:** AmericInn, **other:** NAPA
100	WI 32 S, WI 84 W, Port Washington, E...**gas:** Citgo/dsl, Mobil, **food:** Arby's, Luigi's Italian, McDonald's, Pizza Hut, Subway, **lodging:** Country Inn Suites, Holiday Inn, **other:** Allen-Edmonds Shoes, Goodyear/auto, Sentry Foods, True Value, W...**lodging:** Nisleit's Country Rest.
97	(from nb, exits left), WI 57, Fredonia
96	WI 33, to Saukville, E...**gas:** Mobil/dsl/24hr, **food:** Beanie's, Culver's, LJ Silver/KFC, **lodging:** Best Western, **other:** Buick/Pontiac/Cadillac, Dodge, Ford/Lincoln, Pick'n Save Foods, Piggly Wiggly, Walgreens, Wal-Mart/drug, W...**gas:** Exxon/McDonald's, **food:** Bubblet's Rest., DQ, Foster St Rest., Lam's Chinese, Papa Murphy's, Quizno's, Subway, Taco Bell, **lodging:** Super 8
93	WI 32 N, WI 57 S, Grafton, **1-2 mi** E...**gas:** Citgo, **food:** Dairy House Rest., Mamma Mia's Cafe, Pied Piper Rest., Smith Bros Fish(4mi), **lodging:** Best Western, Holiday Inn, W...**food:** Flannery's Cafe
92	WI 60, rd Q, Grafton, E...**food:** GhostTown Rest., W... **gas:** Citgo/DQ/dsl, **food:** Charcoal Grill, Quizno's, Starbucks, Subway, **lodging:** Baymont Inn, **other:** Costco/ gas, Home Depot, Target
89	rd C, Cedarburg, W...**gas:** Mobil/dsl, **food:** Cedar Crk Settlement Café(6mi), **lodging:** StageCoach Inn, Washington House Inn, **other:** HOSPITAL
85	WI 57 S, WI 167 W, Mequon Rd, W...**gas:** Citgo/dsl, Mobil/24hr, Sendik's, Shell, **food:** Casa Grande Mexican, Caribou Coffee, Chancery Rest., Cousins Subs, Culver's, DQ, Hong Palace Chinese, Jimmy John's, McDonald's, Panera Bread, Starbucks, Subway, **lodging:** Best Western, Chalet Motel, **other:** Ace Harware, Kohl's, Office Depot, Pick'n Save Foods, Sendik's Foods, Walgreen, vet
83	rd W, Port Washington Rd(from nb only)
82b a	WI 32 S, WI 100, Brown Deer Rd, E...**gas:** BP/24hr, Sendik's/dsl, **food:** Benji's Deli, Coldstone Creamery, Cousins Subs, La Paisa Mexican, McDonald's, Noodles & Company, Outback Steaks, Pizza Hut, Qdoba Mexican, Spring Garden Chinese, Subway, **other:** Best Buy, Borders Books, CVS Drug, Kohl's Foods, Land's Inlet, Osco Drug, Walgreens, W...**lodging:** Courtyard, Sheraton
80	Good Hope Rd, E...**gas:** BP, **food:** Jimmy John's, Samurai Japanese, Stonecreek Coffee, King's Wok, Willy's Pizza, **lodging:** Manchester East Hotel, Radisson, Residence Inn, **other:** Pick'n Save Foods, to Cardinal Stritch U

N ↑↓ S

Milwaukee

Exit	Description
78	Silver Spring Dr, **E...gas:** BP, Citgo, Mobil, **food:** Applebee's, BD's Mongolian, Boston Mkt, Burger King, Cheesecake Factory, Cousin's Subs, Denny's, Ground Round, Kopps, Little Caesar's, McDonald's, Papa John's, Panera Bread, Perkins, Pizza Hut, Quizno's, Subway, Taco Bell, Tumbleweed Grill, Wendy's, Zappa's Rest., **lodging:** Exel Inn, La Quinta, NorthShore Motel, Woodfield Suites, **other:** Barnes&Noble, Cadillac, Firestone/auto, Goodyear/auto, Kohl's, Radio Shack, Walgreens, mall, **W...other** HOSPITAL
77b a	(from nb), **E...food:** Anchorage Rest., **food:** Solly's Grill, **lodging:** Hilton
76b a	WI 57, WI 190, Green Bay Ave, **E...food:** Anchorage Rest., **other:** Home Depot, **W...gas:** Citgo, **food:** Burger King, **other:** Buick, Jaguar/Volvo
75	Atkinson Ave, Keefe Ave, **E...gas:** Mobil, **W...gas:** BP, Citgo/dsl
74	Locust St, no services
73c	North Ave(rom sb), **E...food:** Wendy's, **W...food:** McDonald's
73a	WI 145 E, 4th St(exits left from sb), Broadway
72c	Wells St, **E...lodging:** Hilton, **other:** HOSPITAL, Civic Ctr, museum
72b	(from sb), I-94 W, to madison
72a	(310c from nb, exits left from sb), I-794 E, I-94 W to Madison, to Lakefront, downtown
311	WI 59, National Ave, 6th St, downtown
312a	Lapham Blvd, Mitchell St, **W...gas:** Citgo
312b	(from nb), Becher St, Lincoln Ave, no services
314a	Holt Ave, **E...gas:** Andy's/dsl, **food:** Applebee's, Arby's, Little Caesars, Quizno's, Starbucks, Wendy's, **other:** $General, Home Depot, Pick'n Save Food, Sentry Foods, Target, vet, **W...other:** HOSPITAL, to Alverno Coll
314b	Howard Ave, no services
10b	(316 from sb), I-94 S to Chicago, airport
9b a	US 41, 27th St, **E...gas:** BP, Citgo, Mobil, **food:** Arby's, Baskin-Robbins/Dunkin Donuts, Burger King, Chancery Rest., Famous Dave's, JanBo Chinese, Pizza Hut, Rusty Skillet Rest., Subway, **lodging:** Suburban Motel, **other:** AutoZone, Dodge, K-Mart, Target, USPO, Walgreens, **W...food:** Boston Mkt, Denny's, Los Burritos Tapatios, McDonald's, Taco Bell, **lodging:** Hospitality Suites, **other:** HOSPITAL, AAA, Advance Parts, Chevrolet, Chrysler/Jeep, Ford, Goodyear, GMC/Hyundai, Kohl's
8a	WI 36, Loomis Rd, **E...gas:** Citgo, **food:** Los Mariachi's, **other:** Walgreens, **W...food:** George Webb, **other:** to Alverno Coll
7	60th St, **E...gas:** Speedway/dsl, **food:** Wendy's Grille, **other:** Harley-Davidson, **W...gas:** Speedway
5b	76th St(from sb, no EZ return), **E...food:** Applebee's, Boston Mkt, Burger King, George Webb, Ground Round, Hooters, KFC, Kopp's Burgers, McDonald's, Olive Garden, Outback Steaks, Pizza Hut, Red Lobster, TGIFriday, Top's Burgers, Wendy's, **other:** Barnes&Noble, Best Buy, Borders Books, BreadSmith, Circuit City, Cub Foods, Firestone/auto, Goodyear/auto, Isuzu, Office Depot, SteinMart, Valvoline, **W...other:** Trak Auto
5a	WI 24 W, Forest Home Ave, **E...gas:** Citgo, **other:** Boerner Botanical Gardens
61	(4 from sb), I-894/US 45 N, I-43/US 45 S

Exit	Description
60	US 45 S, WI 100, 108th St(exits left from sb), **E...gas:** BP, Citgo, Mobil, **food:** A&W, Amore Italian, Balisteri Italian, Chili Pepper Rest., Open Flame Rest., Pizza Hut, Taco Bell, Tuesday Morning, Wendy's, **other:** AutoZone, Curves, vet, **W...gas:** Phillips 66, **food:** Forum Rest., McDonald's, Omega Custard, Organ Piper Pizza, **other:** Aldi Foods, Badger Transmissions, Goodyear, Mr P Tire, Walgreens, Wal-Mart/drug, vet
59	WI 100, Layton Ave(from nb, exits left), Hales Corner, same as 60
57	Moorland Rd, **E...gas:** Mobil/dsl, **food:** Applebee's, TX Roadhouse, **lodging:** La Quinta, **W...gas:** Mobil/24hr, Speedway/dsl/24hr, **food:** Buffalo Wild Wings, Micocina Mexican, Quizno's, Taco Bell, Tumbleweed Grill, **lodging:** Baymont Inn, Best Western, Country Inn Suites, **other:** Michael's, Sportsman's Whse, Target
54	rd Y, Racine Ave, **1-2 mi E...gas:** Citgo/dsl, KwikTrip, **other:** Culver's, Cousins Subs, McDonald's
50	WI 164, Big Bend, **W...gas:** Citgo/dsl, **food:** Coach House Grill, Long Neck's Rest, McDonald's
44mm	Fox River
43	WI 83, Mukwonago, **E...gas:** BP/dsl, **other:** Home Depot, Wal-Mart SuperCtr/24 hr, **W...gas:** Citgo, Shell, **food:** Antigua Real Cafe, Boneyard Grill, Dominos, DQ, Mario's, Taco Bell, **lodging:** Sleep Inn
38	WI 20, East Troy, **W...gas:** BP, Road Ranger/Subway/dsl/24hr, Shell/McDonald's, **food:** Burger King, **other:** CarQuest, Chrysler/Dodge
36	WI 120, East Troy, **E...lodging:** Alpine Valley Resort, **W... lodging:** Country Inn Suites
33	Bowers Rd, **E...to** Alpine Valley Music Theatre
32mm	**rest area both lanes, full(handicapped)facilities, phone, picnic tables, litter barrels, vending, petwalk**
29	WI 11, Elkhorn, fairgrounds, no services
27b a	US 12, to Lake Geneva, **E...HOSPITAL**
25	WI 67, Elkhorn, **E...gas:** BP/dsl, **lodging:** AmericInn, **other:** Chevrolet/Buick/GMC, Chrysler/Dodge/Jeep, **W...gas:** Speedway/dsl/24hr, **food:** Burger King, **lodging:** Thomas Inn, **other:** Dehaan Auto/RV Ctr
21	WI 50, Delavan, **E...gas:** Shell/dsl/24hr, **food:** Chili's, China One, Culvers, Domino's, Panera Bread, Papa Murphy's, Quizno's, Starbucks, Subway, Yoshi Japanese, **other:** Aldi Foods, Greyhound DogTrack, Kohl's, Lowe's Whse, Radio Shack, Staples, Wal-Mart SuperCtr/24hr, **W...gas:** Mobil/24hr, **food:** Cousins Subs, KFC, McDonald's, Perkins, Pizza Hut, Subway, Taco Bell, Wendy's, **lodging:** Comfort Suites, Econolodge, Super 8, **other:** Chevrolet/Cadillac, $Tree, Ford/Lincoln/Mercury, GNC, Pick'n Save, Piggly Wiggly, ShopKO, Walgreens
17	rd X, Delavan, Darien, **W...gas:** BP
15	US 14, Darien, **E...gas:** Citgo/dsl, **food:** West Wind Diner
6	WI 140, Clinton, **E...gas:** BP, Citgo, **food:** Subway, **other:** Ford
2	rd X, Hart Rd, **E...food:** Butterfly Fine Dining
1b a	I-90, E to Chicago, W to Madison, **W...gas:** BP, Exxon/Subway/dsl, Shell, Pilot/DQ/Taco Bell/dsl/24hr/@, Speedway/dsl, **food:** Applebee's, Arby's, Asia Buffet, Burger King, Cousins Subs, Country Kitchen, Culver's, DQ, Fazoli's, McDonald's, Papa Murphy's, Perkins, Wendy's, **lodging:** Beloit Inn, Comfort Inn, Econolodge, Fairfield Inn, Holiday Inn Express, Super 8, **other:** Buick/Pontiac, Chevrolet/Cadillac/Nissan, Radio Shack, Staples, Tires +, Wal-Mart SuperCtr/24hr

Delavan

I-43 begins/ends on I-90, exit 185 in Beloit.

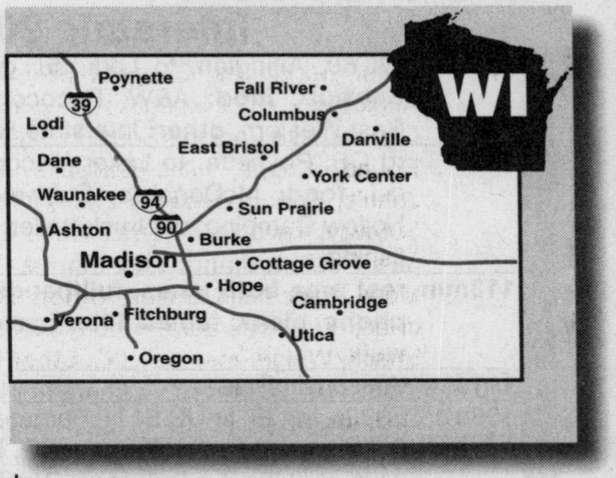

Interstate 90

E ↕ W

Beloit / Janesville / Madison

Exit #	Services
187mm	Wisconsin/Illinois state line. **I-90 & I-39 run together nb.**
187mm	**Welcome Ctr wb, full(handicapped)facilities, info, phones, picnic tables, litter barrels, vending, petwalk**
185b	I-43 N, to Milwaukee
185a	WI 81, Beloit, [S]...**gas:** BP, Exxon/Subway/dsl, Mobil/McDonald's/dsl, Pilot/Taco Bell/dsl/scales/24hr, Shell, Speedway/dsl, **food:** Applebee's, Arby's, Asia Buffet, Atl Bread, Burger King, Cousins Subs, Country Kitchen, Culver's, Papa Murphy's, Wendy's, **lodging:** Best Value, Comfort Inn, Econolodge, Fairfield Inn, Holiday Inn Express, **other:** Aldi Foods, Buick/Pontiac, Chevrolet/Cadillac, Radio Shack, Staples, Tires+, Wal-Mart SuperCtr/24hr
183	Shopiere Rd, rd S, to Shopiere, [S]...**gas:** Rollette/dsl/24hr, **other:** HOSPITAL, camping
181mm	weigh sta, wb
177	WI 351, Janesville, [S]...**gas:** BP, KwikTrip, **food:** El Jardin Mexican, Cursing Stone Grill, **other:** to Blackhawk Tec Coll, Rock Co Airport
175b a	WI 11, Janesville, to Delavan, [N]...**gas:** BP/Subway/dsl/24hr, **food:** Denny's, **lodging:** Baymont Inn, [S]...**gas:** BP, **food:** DQ, Hardee's, **lodging:** Lannon Stone Motel
171c b	US 14, WI 26, Janesville, [N]...**gas:** TA/Mobil/Wendy's/dsl/scales, **food:** Damon's, Fuddruckers, IHOP, Old Country Buffet, Starbucks, Subway, TX Roadhouse, **lodging:** Holiday Inn Express, Microtel, **other:** Best Buy, Gander Mtn, GNC, Home Depot, Michael's, Old Navy, PetCo, Staples, Tires+, TJ Maxx, [S]...**gas:** Kwik Trip/dsl/24hr, **food:** Applebee's, Arby's, Asia Buffet, Big Boy, Burger King, CK Grill, Cousins Subs, Culver's, El Chipala Mexican, Famous Dave's, Fazoli's, Ground Round, Hardee's, Hooters, KFC, Little Caesars, Milio's Cafe, McDonald's, Noodle's & Co, Olive Garden, Papa Murphy's, Peking Chinese, Perkins, Pizza Hut, Prime Quarter Steaks, Red Robin, Shakey's Pizza, Taco Bell, World Buffet, **lodging:** Select Inn, **other:** HOSPITAL, Aldi Foods, F&F, Ford/Lincoln/Mercury, Harley-Davidson, Hyundai, JC Penney, Kohl's, K-Mart, Mazda, Mercedes, Sears/auto, ShopKO, Target, VW, Woodman Foods/gas, mall
171a	[N]...**gas:** Phillips 66/dsl, **food:** Cracker Barrel, Best Western/rest., Hampton Inn, Motel 6, Hampton Inn, **other:** Chrysler/Jeep/Dodge, Sam's Club, Wal-Mart SuperCtr, [S]...same as 171c b
168mm	**rest area eb, full(handicapped)facilities, phone, picnic tables, litter barrels, vending, petwalk**
163.5mm	Rock River
163	WI 59, Edgerton, to Milton, [N]...**gas:** Mobil/Subway/dsl, Shell/Taco John's, **food:** Cousins Subs, Culver's, McDonald's, Red Apple Rest., WI Cheese Store, **lodging:** Comfort Inn, **other:** marina, [S]...**gas:** BP
160	US 51S, WI 73, WI 106, Oaklawn Academy, to Deerfield, [N]...**other:** Hickory Hills Camping, [S]...**gas:** BP/dsl/scales/24hr/@, KwikTrip, **food:** Ray's Rest., Subway, Winchester Rest., **lodging:** Towne Edge Motel, **other:** HOSPITAL, Janesville RV Ctr
156	US 51N, to Stoughton, [S]...**lodging:** Coachman's Inn/rest., HOSPITAL
148mm	weigh sta wb
147	rd N, Cottage Grove, to Stoughton, [S]...**gas:** BP/Arby's/24hr, Road Ranger/Subway/dsl, **other:** Lake Kegonsa SP, fireworks
146mm	weigh sta eb
142b a	(142a exits left from wb)US 12, US 18, Madison, to Cambridge, [N]...**gas:** Mobil/dsl, **food:** Subway, **lodging:** Best Value, Wingate Inn, **other:** Harley-Davidson, [S]...**gas:** Cenex/dsl, Mobil/dsl, Phillips 66/Arby's/dsl, Shell/dsl, **food:** Denny's, Quizno's, Wendy's, **lodging:** Day's Inn, Rodeway Inn, **other:** HOSPITAL, UWI
138a	I-94, E to Milwaukee, W to La Crosse, **I-90 W and I-94 W run together for 93 miles,** (exits left from EB)
138b	WI 30, Madison, [S]...airport
135c b	US 151, Madison, [N]...**gas:** BP, **food:** Cheesehaus, Happy Wok, Subway, **lodging:** Courtyard, Staybridge Suites, Woodfield Suites, **other:** Buick, Chevrolet, Chrysler/Dodge, Ford, Isuzu, Kia, Nissan, Toyota
135a	US 151, Madison, [N]...**gas:** BP, **food:** Chicago Grill, **lodging:** Courtyard, Holiday Inn Express, Grand Stay Suites, La Quinta, Staybridge Suites, **other:** Buick, Chevrolet, Crysler, Ford/Lincoln/Mercury, Toyota, [S]...**gas:** BP/24hr, Shell, **food:** Applebee's, Arby's, Carlos O'Kelly's, Chili's, Country Kitchen, Cracker Barrel, Denny's, Hardee's, IHOP, KFC, McDonald's, Noodles & Co., Old Country Buffet, Olive Garden, Outback Steaks, Panera Bread, Perkins, Potbelly's Rest, Pizza Hut, Red Lobster, Red Robin, Rocky's Pizza, Subway, Takumi Japanese, TGIFriday, Tumbleweed Grill, TX Roadhouse, Wendy's, **lodging:** Best Western, Comfort Inn, Crowne Plaza Hotel/rest., Econolodge, Excel Inn, Hampton Inn, Microtel, Motel 6, Red Roof Inn, Residence Inn, Select Inn, Super 8, **other:** Barnes & Noble, Best Buy, Circuit City, $Tree, Firestone/auto, Gander Mtn, Home Depot, JC Penney, Jo-Ann Fabrics, Kohl's, Marshall's, Office Depot, Old Navy, PetsMart, Sears, ShopKO, Tuesday Morning, mall, st patrol, vet
132	US 51, Madison, De Forest, [N]...**gas:** BP/dsl/scales, Shell/Pinecone Rest/dsl/24hr, **food:** Cousin's Subs, [S]...**gas:** TA/Mobil/Subway/Taco Bell/dsl/rest./scales/24hr/@, **lodging:** Economy Motel, **other:** Goodyear, Peterbilt, Volvo/White/GMC/Freightliner, WI RV World, camping
131	WI 19, Waunakee, [N]...**gas:** Kwik Trip, Mobil, Speedway/dsl, **food:** A&W, McDonald's, Rodeside Grill, **lodging:** Day's Inn, Super 8, **other:** Mousehouse Cheesehaus, Kenworth Trucks, Truckwash, Western Star, [S]...**lodging:** Country Inn Suites(4mi)
126	rd V, De Forest, to Dane, [N]...**gas:** BP, Phillips 66/Arby's/dsl, **food:** Burger King, Culver's, DeForest Rest., McDonald's, Subway, **lodging:** Holiday Inn Express, **other:** Cheese Chalet, KOA, [S]...**gas:** Exxon/dsl, **lodging:** Comfort Inn

WISCONSIN

Interstate 90

E ↕ W

119 WI 60, Arlington, to Lodi, [S]...**gas:** Mobil/Cousins Subs/dsl, **food:** A&W, Rococo's Pizza, **lodging:** Best Western, **other:** Interstate RV Ctr

115 rd CS, Poynette, to Lake Wisconsin, [N]...**gas:** BP/dsl, **food:** McDonald's, Subway, **other:** Smokey Hollow Camping, dsl truck/trailer repair, motel, trout fishing

113mm rest area both lanes, full(handicapped)facilities, phone, picnic tables, litter barrels, vending, petwalk

111mm Wisconsin River

108b a I-39 N, WI 78, to US 51 N, Portage, [N]...**other:** HOSPITAL, to WI Dells, [S]...**gas:** BP, Petro/DQ/Subway/dsl/rest./24hr/@, **lodging:** Comfort Suites, Day's Inn, Devil's Head Resort/Conv Ctr, **other:** Blue Beacon

106mm Baraboo River

106 WI 33, Portage, [N]...**other:** HOSPITAL, [S]...**gas:** BP, **other:** Kamp Dakota, SkyHigh Camping, to Cascade Mtn Ski Area, Devil's Lake SP, Circus World Museum, Wayside Park

92 US 12, to Baraboo, [N]...**gas:** BP/dsl, Exxon, Mobil/dsl/24hr, Sinclair/Subway/dsl, **food:** Buffalo Phil's Grille, Burger King, Cracker Barrel, Culver's, Damon's, Danny's Diner, Denny's, Dominos, Field's Steaks, McDonald's, Monk's Grill, Ponderosa, Sarento's Rest., Wintergreen Grill, Uno Pizzaria, **lodging:** Alakai Hotel, Great Wolf Lodge, Country Squire Motel, Grand Marquis Inn, Holiday Inn Express, Kalahari Resort, Lake Delton Hotel, Ramada Ltd., Wilderness Hotel, Wintergreen Hotel/grill, **other:** Broadway Theater, Kalahari Conv Ctr, Mkt Sq Cheese, Sundara Resort, Tanger Outlets Famous Brands, WI Cheese, museum, [S]...**lodging:** Motel 6, **other:** HOSPITAL, Scenic Traveler RV Ctr, Jellystone Camping, Red Oak Camping, Mirror Lake SP

89 WI 23, Lake Delton, [N]...**gas:** Phillips 66, Shell/dsl, **food:** Brathouse Grill, Denny's Diner, Howie's Rest., KFC, Los Primos, Moosejaw Pizza, **lodging:** Econolodge, Hilton Garden, Kings Inn, Malibu Inn, Olympia Motel, **other:** Crystal Grand Music Theatre, Springbrook Camping, Jellystone Camping, USPO, [S]...**food:** McDonald's, Northwoods Grill, **other:** Home Depot, Kohls, Wal-Mart SuperCtr/Subway/gas/24hr, Country Roads RV Park, Wannabee Campground

87 WI 13, Wisconsin Dells, [N]...**gas:** BP/dsl, Mobil/Arby's/dsl, Shell, **food:** Applebee's, Bunyan's Rest., Burger King, Cold Stone, Country Kitchen, Denny's, Green Mill Rest., IHOP, McDonald's, Mexican Rose Rest., Outlaw Steakhouse, Perkins, Quizno's, Starbucks, Taco Bell, Wendy's, **lodging:** AmericInn, Best Western, Comfort Inn, Day's Inn, Howard Johnson, Polynesian Hotel, Super 8, **other:** KOA, Sherwood Forest Camping, Tepee Park Camping, Walgreens, golf, waterpark, info

85 US 12, WI 16, Wisconsin Dells, **0-3 mi [N]...food:** Crabby's Seafood, Starbucks, **lodging:** Days Inn, Mayflower Motel, **other:** to Rocky Arbor SP, American World RV Park/Hotel, KOA, Rocky Arbor SP, Sherwood Forest Camping, Standing Rock Camping, [S]...**gas:** BP, **food:** Piccadilly's, **lodging:** Arrowhead Camping, Edge-O-the-Dell RV Camping, Summer Breeze Resort

79 rd HH, Lyndon Sta, [S]...**gas:** BP/Subway/dsl/24hr

76mm rest area wb, full(handicapped)facilities, phone, picnic tables, litter barrels, vending, petwalk

74mm rest area eb, full(handicapped)facilities, phone, picnic tables, litter barrels, vending, petwalk

69 WI 82, Mauston, [N]...**gas:** Mauston TP/Taco Bell/24hr, Pilot/Wendy's/dsl/scales/24hr, Shell/24hr, **food:** Country Kitchen, **lodging:** Best Western Oasis, Country Inn, Super 8, **other:** to Buckhorn SP, [S]...**gas:** KwikTrip/BP/scales/dsl, Marathon, Mobil, **food:** CJ's Italian, Culver's, Garden Valley Rest., McDonald's, Pizza Hut, Roman Castle Rest., Subway, **lodging:** Best Value Inn, **other:** HOSPITAL, Buckhorn SP, Family$, K-Mart, Pick'n Save, Walgreens

61 WI 80, New Lisbon, to Necedah, [N]...**gas:** Mobil/A&W/Subway/dsl/@, New Lisbon Trkstp/dsl/24hr/@, **lodging:** Edge O' the Wood Motel, Travelers Inn, **other:** Buckhorn SP, Chrysler/Jeep, Ford, fireworks, [S]...**gas:** KwikTrip/24hr, **other:** Barnes Foods, True Value, Elroy-Sparta ST Tr

55 rd C, Camp Douglas, [N]...**other:** wayside, to Camp Williams, Volk Field, [S]...**gas:** BP/dsl, Mobil/Subway/dsl, **food:** German Haus Rest., **lodging:** German Haus Rest., K&K Motel, **other:** to Mill Bluff SP

51mm weigh sta eb

48 rd PP, Oakdale, [N]...**gas:** Road Ranger/Subway/dsl/scales/24hr, **other:** Granger's Camping, KOA, Mill Bluff SP, truck/car wash, antiques, [S]...**gas:** Love's/Hardee's/dsl/scales/24hr, **other:** Mill Bluff SP

47.5mm weigh sta wb

45 I-94 W, to St Paul, **I-90 E and I-94 E run together for 93 miles**

Tomah

43 US 12, WI 16, Tomah, [N]...**gas:** BP, KwikTrip/dsl/24hr, **food:** Burnstadt's Café, DQ, Embers Rest., European Café, **lodging:** Daybreak Inn, **other:** HOSPITAL, vet

41 WI 131, Tomah, to Wilton, [N]...**gas:** Mobil/dsl, KwikTrip/dsl(24hr), **food:** Burnstadts Cafe, **lodging:** Brentwood Motel, Daybreak Inn, **other:** VA MED CTR, [S]...st patrol

28 WI 16, Sparta, Ft McCoy, [N]...**gas:** BP, Kwiktrip/dsl, **lodging:** Best Western, **other:** HOSPITAL

25 WI 27, Sparta, to Melvina, [N]...**gas:** Cenex/dsl, KwikTrip, Phillips 66/Taco Bell, Shell/dsl, **food:** Burger King, Country Kitchen, Culver's, DQ, KFC, McDonald's, Pizza Hut, Subway, **lodging:** Best Nights Inn, Country Inn, Super 8, **other:** HOSPITAL, Ace Hardware, Chevrolet/Buick/Pontiac, Family$, Ford/Mercury, Piggly Wiggly, Walgreen, Wal-Mart SuperCtr/24hr(2mi, WI 16), [S]...camping

22mm rest area wb, full(handicapped)facilities, phone, picnic tables, litter barrels, vending, petwalk

20mm rest area eb, full(handicapped)facilities, phone, picnic tables, litter barrels, vending, petwalk

La Crosse

15 WI 162, Bangor, to Coon Valley, [N]...gas, [S]...**other:** Chevrolet

12 rd C, W Salem, [N]...**gas:** Cenex/cafe/dsl/24hr, **other:** Coulee Region RV Ctr, NAPA, Neshonoc Camping, [S]...**gas:** BP/Quizno's/dsl, **lodging:** AmericInn

10mm weigh sta eb

5 WI 16, La Crosse, [N]...**food:** Cold Stone Creamery, Manny's Mexican, Outback Steaks, Quizno's, **lodging:** Baymont Inn, Hampton Inn, Microtel, **other:** $Tree, Freightliner, Gander Mtn, Wal-Mart SuperCtr/Subway, Woodman's Foods/gas/lube, Aldi Foods, Home Depot, [S]...**gas:** Kwik Trip/dsl/24hr, **food:** Carlos O'Kelly's,'s, ChuckeCheese, Culver's, Fazoli's, Jimmy John's, McDonald's, Hong Kong Buffet, Old Country Buffet, Olive Garden, Perkins, Starbucks, TGIFriday, **lodging:** Holiday Inn Express, Stony Creek Inn, **other:** HOSPITAL, Barnes&Noble, Best Buy, Goodyear/auto, F&F, JC Penny, Kohl's, Macy's, Marshall

Interstate 90

Field, Michael's, Sears/auto, ShopKO, Target, mall

4	US 53 N, WI 16, to WI 157, La Crosse, **N**...other: Harley-Davidson, **S**...**gas**: Kwik Trip/gas, TO, **food**: Applebee's, Bakers Square, Burger King,'s, Famous Dave's BBQ, Panera Bread, Papa Murphy's, Red Lobster, Rococo's Pizza, Subway, Taco Bell, Wendy's, **lodging**: Comfort Inn, Day's Inn, **other**: HOSPITAL, Barnes & Noble, Curves, Festival Food/24hr, GNC, Goodyear/auto, K-Mart, Macey's, Office Depot, PetCo, Sam's Club, Tires+, TJ Maxx, SuperLube, La Crosse River St Trail
3	US 53 S, WI 35, to La Crosse, **S**...**gas**: Kwik Trip, **food**: Burger King, Coney Island, Edwardo's Pizza, Hardee's, KFC, La Crosse Rest., McDonald's, North Country Steaks, Perkins, Pizza Hut, Subway, **lodging**: Best Value, Best Western, Brookstone Inn, Econolodge, Exel Inn, Settle Inn, Super 8, **other**: Curves, ShopKO/drug, U-Haul, Walgreens, to Great River St Trail, Viterbo Coll
2.5mm	Black River
2	rd B, French Island, **N**...other: airport, **S**...**gas**: BP/dsl, Kwik Trip, **lodging**: Day's Inn/rest.
1mm	**Welcome Ctr eb, full(handicapped)facilities, info, phone, picnic tables, litter barrels, vending, pet-walk**
0mm	Wisconsin/Minnesota state line, Mississippi River

Interstate 94

Exit #	Services
349mm	Wisconsin/Illinois state line, (from nb), weigh sta nb
347	WI 165, rd Q, Lakeview Pkwy, **E**...**gas**: BP/dsl, **food**: Culver's, McDonald's, Radisson/rest., **other**: Prime Outlets/famous brands, **Welcome Ctr, full facilities**, **W**...other: GolfShack Whse
345	rd C, **E**...**gas**: Phillips 66/dsl, **food**: Chester Fried
345mm	Des Plaines River
344	WI 50, Lake Geneva, to Kenosha, **E**...**food**: Citgo/dsl, Shell, Woodman's/gas, **food**: Buffalo Wild Wings, Noodles Cafe, Perkins, Quizno's, Starbucks, Texas Roadhouse, White Castle, **lodging**: La Quinta, Super 8, **other**: HOSPITAL, Gander Mtn, **W**...**gas**: BP, Speedway/Subway/dsl, **food**: Arby's, Cracker Barrel, Jennifer's Rest., KFC, McDonald's, Taco Bell, Wendy's, **lodging**: Best Western, Country Inn&Suites, Day's Inn, Quality Suites, Value Inn, **other**: BMW, Cadillac, Carmax, Chevrolet, Ford, GM, Jeep, Mitsubishi, Toyota,
342	WI 158, to Kenosha, **E**...Harley-Davidson, **W**...antiques
340	WI 142, rd S, to Kenosha, **E**...**gas**: Citgo/dsl, Mobil/dsl, **other**: HOSPITAL, **W**...**food**: Mars Cheese Castle Rest., StarBar Rest., **lodging**: Oasis Inn, **other**: to Bong RA
339	rd E, **E**...**gas**: Marathon/dsl/24hr
337	County Line Rd, rd KR, **E**...other: to Great Lakes Dragaway, **W**...**food**: Apple Holler Rest.
335	WI 11, Burlington, to Racine, no services
333	US 20, Waterford, to Racine, **E**...**gas**: KwikTrip/dsl/24hr, Shell/Cousins Subs/dsl, **food**: Burger King, McDonald's, **lodging**: Holiday Inn Express, Ramada Ltd, **other**: HOSPITAL, **W**...**gas**: Citgo/5th Wheel Grill/Wendy's/dsl/24hr/@, Petro/Mobil/Iron Skillet/dsl/scales, **food**: Culver's, Spokes Rest., Subway, **lodging**: Grandview Inn, **other**: Burlington RV Ctr

329	rd K, Thompsonville, to Racine, **E**...**gas**: Pilot/Arby's/dsl/24hr/@, **W**...**gas**: Mobil/A&W
328mm	weigh sta eb
327	rd G, **W**...**other**: Black Jack's Fireworks
326	7 Mile Rd, **E**...**gas**: BP/24hr, **other**: Jellystone Park, RV repair, **W**...**gas**: Mobil/24hr, antiques
325	US 41 N(from wb), to 27th St
322	WI 100, to Ryan Rd, **E**...**food**: McDonald's, Wendy's, **other**: Goodyear/Cummins dsl, **W**...**gas**: Flying J/Country Mkt/dsl/24hr/@, Mobil, Pilot/Subway/dsl/LP/24hr/@, Shell/A&W/KFC/dsl, **food**: Arby's, Cousins Subs, Perkins, Starbucks, **other**: Blue Beacon, Freightliner/repair, Pick'n Save, Walgreens
320	rd BB, Rawson Ave, **E**...**gas**: BP/24hr, Mobil, **food**: Applebee's, Burger King, **lodging**: La Quinta
319	rd ZZ, College Ave, **E**...**gas**: Shell/Subway, Speedway/dsl, **food**: Branded Steer Rest., McDonald's, **lodging**: Comfort Suites, Country Inn&Suites, Exel Inn, Hampton Inn, MainStay Suites, Radisson, Ramada/rest., Red Roof, **W**...**gas**: BP/24hr, Citgo/dsl, **other**: VIP Foodmart, Boy Blue DairyMart
318	WI 119, no services
317	Layton Ave, **E**...**gas**: Andy's/dsl, Clark, **food**: Martino's Rest., Porterhouse Rest., Prime Qtr Steaks, **other**: Checkers Parts, Radio Shack, **W**...**food**: Spring Garden Rest., **lodging**: Howard Johnson
316	I-43 S, I-894 W(I-94 exits left from eb), to Beloit
314b	Howard Ave, to Milwaukee, **W**...to Alverno Coll
314a	Holt Ave, **E**...**gas**: Andy's/dsl, **food**: Applebee's, DQ, Quizno's, Starbucks, Subway, **other**: $General, Home Depot, Pick'n Save Foods, **E on Chase**...**gas**: Citgo/Jewel-Osco, **food**: Arby's, ChuckeCheese, Wendy's, **other**: Target, **W**...HOSPITAL
312b a	Becher St, Mitchell St, Lapham Blvd, **W**...**gas**: BP, Citgo
311	WI 59, National Ave, 6th St, downtown
310a	13th St(from eb), **E**...HOSPITAL
310b	I-43 N, to Green Bay
310c	I-794 E, **E**...**lodging**: Hilton, Holiday Inn, **other**: to downtown and Lake Michigan Port of Entry
309b	26th St, 22nd St, Clybourn St, St Paul Ave, **N**...**other**: HOSPITAL, to Marquette U
309a	35th St, **N**...**gas**: BP, Speedway, **other**: HOSPITAL
308c b	US 41, no services
308a	VA Ctr, **N**...other: Miller Brewing, **S**...other: County Stadium
307b	68th-70th St, Hawley Rd, no services
307a	68th St, **N**...other: Valvoline
306	WI 181, to 84th St, **N**...HOSPITAL, **S**...other: Olympic Training Facility

Vertical margin labels: E / W Kenosha, Milwaukee

E ↕ **W**

Exit	Description
305b	US 45 N, to Fond du Lac, **N**...HOSPITAL
305a	I-894 S, US 45 S, to Chicago, to airport
304b a	WI 100, **N**...**gas:** Citgo, Mobil, Shell/dsl, **food:** Cousins Subs, Edwardo's Pizza, Giuseppi's Pizza, Pizza Hut, Qdoba, Starbucks, Taco Bell, **lodging:** Exel Inn, **other:** zoo, **S**...**gas:** MiniMart/dsl, Speedway/dsl, **food:** DQ, Fazoli's, McDonald's, Wendy's, **other:** Checker Parts, U-Haul, Walgreens
301b a	Moorland Rd, **N**...**gas:** Mobil, **food:** Bakers Square, Bravo Grill, Fuddrucker's, Houlihan's, McDonald's, Pizzaria Uno, **lodging:** Sheraton, **other:** VET, Barnes&Noble, Circuit City, Firestone/auto, Goodyear/auto, JC Penney, Office Depot, PetCo, Sears/auto, Walgreen, mall, **S**...**gas:** Mobil, **food:** Maxwell's Rest., **lodging:** Best Western, Brookfield Suites, Country Inn&Suites, Midway Motel, Residence Inn, **other:** Walgreen, golf
297	US 18, rd JJ, Blue Mound Rd, Barker Rd, **1-2 mi** **N**...**gas:** BP/24hr, Mobil, **food:** Applebee's, Boston Mkt, Burger King, Charhouse, ChuckeCheese, Heineman's Rest., KFC, Kopp's Cafe, Krispy Kreme, La Quinta, McDonald's, Melting Pot, Olive Garden, Pedro's Mexican, Perkins, Starbucks, Subway, TGI Friday, Tony Roma's, Wendy's, Zorba's Grill, **lodging:** Courtyard, DoubleTree, Fairfield Inn, Hampton Inn, Motel 6, Quality Inn, **other:** Acura, Advance Parts, Best Buy, CompUSA, GNC, Jo-Ann Fabrics, K-Mart, Mazda/Lexus, NTB, Pick'n Save, VW, **S**...**gas:** PDQ Gas, **food:** Arby's, Cousin's Subs, Famous Daves, McDonald's, Oscar's Cafe, Schlotsky's, Taco Bell, Wendy's, **lodging:** Extended Stay America, Holiday Inn, Select Inn, Super 8, **other:** Chrysler, Firestone, Ford/Lincoln/Mercury, Home Depot, Sam's Club, Target, Tires+, Walgreen, st patrol
295	WI 164, Waukesha, **N**...**gas:** KwikTrip/gas, **lodging:** Marriott, **S**...**other:** HOSPITAL, to Carroll Coll
294	rd J, to Waukesha, **N**...**gas:** Mobil, **food:** Machine Shed Rest., Thunder Bay Grille, **lodging:** Comfort Suites, Radisson, **S**...**other:** Expo Ctr, Peterbilt,
293c	WI 16 W, Pewaukee(from wb), **N**...**other:** GE Plant
293b a	rd T, Wausheka, Pewaukee, **S**...**gas:** Mobil, **food:** Brisco Co Grill, Canyon City Cafe, Caribou Coffee, Cousins Subs, Culver's, Denny's, Fazoli's, McDonald's, Peking House, Qdoba Mexican, Rococo's Pizza, Subway, Weissgerber's Gasthaus Rest., Wendy's, **lodging:** Best Western, **other:** Firestone/auto, Jo-Ann Fabrics, Office Depot, Osco Drug, Pick'n Save Foods, Radio Shack, Walgreens
291	rd G, **N**...**lodging:** Country Springs Inn
290	rd SS, no services
287	WI 83, Hartland, to Wales, **N**...**food:** Applebees, Hardee's, McDonald's, Panera Bread, Perkins, Starbucks, **lodging:** Country Pride Inn, Holiday Inn Express, **other:** Amish Barn Gifts, Best Buy, GNC, Kohl's, Marshall's, Sentry Foods, Walgreen, **S**...**gas:** BP/dsl/24hr, PDQ/dsl/24hr, **food:** Breadworks Café, Burger King, DQ, Marty's Pizza, Quizno's, Rococo's Pizza, Subway, **lodging:** La Quinta, **other:** Ace Hardware, Home Depot, PetCo, Target, Tires+, Wal-Mart/drugs
285	rd C, Delafield, **N**...**gas:** Mobil/deli, **other:** to St John's Military Academy, **S**...**other:** to Kettle Moraine SF
283	rd P, to Sawyer Rd(from wb), no services
282	WI 67, Dousman, to Oconomowoc, **N**...**gas:** BP, KwikTrip, **food:** Culver's, Pizza Hut, Rococo's Pizza, Schlotsky's, Subway, K-Mart, **lodging:** Olympia Resort, **other:** HOSPITAL, VET, Pick'n Save, Sentry Foods, **S**...**other:** to Kettle Morraine SF(8mi), Old World WI Hist Sites(13mi)
277	Willow Glen Rd(from eb, no return), no services
275	rd F, Ixonia, to Sullivan, **N**...**gas:** BP/dsl, **other:** Concord Gen Store, **S**...camping
267	WI 26, Johnson Creek, to Watertown, **N**...**gas:** BP/McDonald's/dsl, Shell/dsl/rest./24hr/@, **food:** Arby's, **lodging:** Comfort Suites, Day's Inn, **other:** Goodyear/auto, Johnson Creek Outlet Ctr/famous brands, **S**...**gas:** Citgo/A&W/KFC/dsl/24hr, **food:** Culver's, Subway, **other:** HOSPITAL, Kohl's, to Aztalan SP
266mm	Rock River
264mm	**rest area wb, full(handicapped)facilities, phone, picnic tables, litter barrels, vending, petwalk**
263mm	Crawfish River
261mm	**rest area eb, full(handicapped)facilities, phone, picnic tables, litter barrels, vending, petwalk**
259	WI 89, Lake Mills, to Waterloo, **N**...**gas:** Citgo/dsl/24hr, **lodging:** Rodeway Inn, **S**...**gas:** BP/dsl/24hr, KwikTrip/dsl/24hr, **food:** McDonald's, Pizza Pit, Subway, **lodging:** Pyramid Motel/RV park, **other:** Buick/Chevrolet/Cadillac, Country Campers RV Ctr, to Aztalan SP
250	WI 73, Deerfield, to Marshall, no services
244	rd n, Sun Prairie, Cottage Grove, **N**...**gas:** BP/dsl, Citgo/dsl, **S**...**food:** McDonald's
240	I-90 E
	I-94 and I-90 run together 93 miles. See Interstate 90, exits 48-138.
147	I-90 W, to La Crosse
143	US 12, WI 21, Tomah, **N**...**gas:** Mobil/dsl, **food:** A&W/LJ Silver, Four Star Rest., Perkins, **lodging:** AmericInn, Holiday Inn, Microtel, Super 8, **other:** Humbird Cheese/gifts, **S**...**gas:** BP/KwikTrip/dsl/rest./24hr, Citgo, Mobil, Shell/dsl/cheese, **food:** Burnstad's Amish Café, China Buffet, Culver's, Ground Round, Hardy Platter, KFC, McDonald's, Perkins, Pizza Hut, Quizno's, Subway, Taco Bell, **lodging:** Comfort Inn, Cranberry Suites, Econolodge, **other:** HOSPITAL, Advance Parts, $Tree, Ford/Lincoln/Mercury, U-Haul, Wal-Mart SuperCtr/gas/dsl/24hr, to Ft McCoy(9mi), **S** on US 12...**food:** Burger King, **other:** Ace Hardware, Chevrolet/Buick, Chrysler/Dodge/Jeep, Firestone/auto, Ford/Lincoln/Mercury, Radio Shack
135	rd EW, Warrens, **N**...**gas:** BP, **other:** Jellystone Resort, **S**...**food:** Bog Rest.
128	rd O, Millston, **N**...**other:** Black River SF, camping, **S**...**gas:** Hartland/dsl, Phillips 66, **other:** USPO
123mm	**rest area/scenic view both lanes, full(handicapped) facilities, phone, picnic tables, litter barrels, vending, petwalk**
116	WI 54, **N**...**gas:** BP/Subway/Taco Johns/dsl/LP, **food:** Perkins, **lodging:** Best Western Arrowhead/rest., Holiday Inn Express, Super 8, **other:** Black River RA, Parkland Camp, casino, **S**...**gas:** Flying J/Cookery/dsl/24hr/@, KwikTrip/dsl, **food:** Burger King, DQ, Hardee's, Hardy Platter, McDonald's, Oriental Kitchen, Pizza Hut, **lodging:** Day's Inn, **other:** $Tree, Wal-Mart SuperCtr/24hr

Madison Tomah

Interstate 94

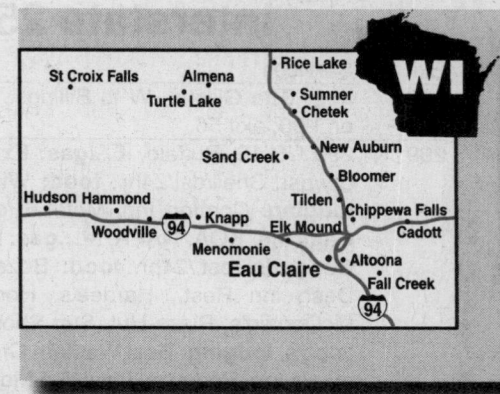

115mm Black River

115 US 12, Black River Falls, to Merrillan, ...**lodging:** Pines Motel, **S**...**gas:** BP, Holiday/dsl, Mobil/dsl, **food:** Hardee's, KFC, Subway, Sunrise Rest., **other:** HOSPITAL, Ace Hardware, Harley-Davidson, IGA Foods, NAPA, Pontiac/Buick/GMC

105 to WI 95, Hixton, to Alma Center, **N**...**lodging:** Motel 95, **other:** KOA(3mi), **S**...**gas:** Cenex/dsl, Hixton Trvl/dsl/rest./24hr

98 WI 121, Northfield, Pigeon Falls, to Alma Center, **S**...**gas:** Cenex/dsl, **food:** BeeBee's Diner, Jackie's Café

88 US 10, Osseo, to Fairchild, **N**...**gas:** BP/DQ, Mobil/dsl, Shell/Elderberry's/dsl, **food:** Hardee's, Moe's Diner, **lodging:** 10-7 Inn, Super 8, **other:** Chevrolet, Ford, Stony Cr RV Park, **S**...**gas:** Citgo, Speedway/dsl, **food:** McDonald's, Subway, **lodging:** Red Carpet Inn, **other:** HOSPITAL

81 rd HH, rd KK, Foster, **S**...**gas:** BP/dsl/LP, **food:** Foster Cheesehaus

70 US 53, Eau Claire, **N** off Golf Rd...**gas:** Conoco/dsl, **food:** A&W, Applebee's, Bakers Square, Buffalo Wild Wings, Coldstone Creamery, Fazoli's, Jade Garden, McDonald's, Noodles, Olive Garden, Panera Bread, TGIFriday, TimberLodge Steaks, Younker's, **lodging:** Country Inn Suites, Grandstay, Heartland Inn, **other:** Aldi Foods, Best Buy, Borders Books, Gander Mtn, Kohl's, Michael's, Office Depot, PetCo, Sam's Club, Sears/auto, Target, TJ Maxx, Wal-Mart SuperCtr/24hr, mall, **S**...**other:** st police

68 WI 93, to Eleva, **N**...**gas:** Holiday, KwikTrip, **food:** Burger King, DQ, **lodging:** Econolodge, **other:** Chrysler, Firestone/auto, Goodyear/auto, Jeep, Lincoln/Mercury, Nissan, Saturn, Subaru, VW/Audi, same as 70, **S**...**gas:** BP, **other:** Buick/Pontiac/Cadillac/GMC/Hyundai, Ford

65 WI 37, WI 85, Eau Claire, to Mondovi, **N**...**gas:** BP, Citgo/dsl, **food:** Arby's, China Buffet, Godfather's, GreenMill Rest., Hardee's, Heckel's Rest., McDonald's, Randy's Rest., Red Lobster, Subway, Taco Bell, TCBY, Wendy's, YenKing Chinese, **lodging:** Best Western, Comfort Inn, Day's Inn/rest., Exel Inn, Hampton Inn, Holiday Inn/rest., Park Inn, Plaza Hotel, Quality Inn, Roadstar Inn, **other:** HOSPITAL, Castle Foods, Mazda/Toyota, Radio Shack, ShopKO

64mm Chippewa River

59 to US 12, rd EE, to Eau Claire, **N**...**gas:** BP/Burger King/dsl/24hr, Holiday/Subway/dsl/24hr, **food:** Anderson's Grill, Embers Rest., McDonald's, **lodging:** AmericInn, Day's Inn, Super 8, **other:** HOSPITAL, Freightliner, Mack/Volvo Trucks, Peterbilt, auto repair/towing, **S**...US RV Ctr, trailer repair

52 US 12, WI 29, WI 40, Elk Mound, to Chippewa Falls, **S**...**gas:** U-Fuel, **food:** LaCheese Rest.,

49mm weigh sta wb

45 rd B, Menomonie, **N**...**gas:** Cenex/dsl/rest./scales, **S**...**gas:** KwikTrip/BP/Subway/dsl/scales/24hr, **food:** Country Kitchen, Culver's, **lodging:** Comfort Inn, **other:** HOSPITAL, AOK RV Ctr, Kenworth, Wal-Mart Dist Ctr

44mm Red Cedar River

43mm **rest areas both lanes, full(handicapped)facilities, phone, picnic tables, litter barrels, vending, petwalk, weather info**

41 WI 25, Menomonie, **N**...**gas:** Cenex, **food:** Applebee's, China Buffet, Subway, **other:** HOSPITAL, Aldi Foods, $Tree, Radio Shack, Wal-Mart SuperCtr/24hr, Edgewater Camping, GS Camping, **S**...**gas:** Citgo, F&F/dsl, Holiday, SA/dsl, **food:** Arby's, DQ, Green Mill Rest., Kernel Rest., KFC, McDonald's, Perkins, Pizza Hut, Taco Bell, Taco John's, Wendy's, **lodging:** AmericInn, Best Western, Country Inn&Suites, Motel 6, Super 8, **other:** Advance Parts, Chevrolet, Chrysler, K-Mart, Mkt Place Foods, O'Reilly Parts, Walgreens, to Red Cedar St Tr

32 rd Q, to Knapp, no services

28 WI 128, Wilson, Elmwood, to Glenwood City, **N**...**gas:** KwikTrip/BP/dsl/24hr, **food:** Hearty Platter Rest., **S**...**other:** Eau Galle RA, camping, truck repair

24 rd B, to Baldwin, **N**...**lodging:** Woodville Motel, **S**...**other:** Eau Galle RA, camping

19 US 63, Baldwin, to Ellsworth, **N**...**gas:** Freedom/dsl, KwikTrip/BP/Subway/dsl, **food:** A&W, DQ, Hardee's, McDonald's, **lodging:** AmericInn, **other:** HOSPITAL, **S**...**gas:** Citgo/dsl/LP/24hr, **lodging:** Super 8

16 rd T, Hammond

10 WI 65, Roberts, to New Richmond

8mm weigh sta eb

4 US 12, rd U, Somerset, **N**...**gas:** Citgo/dsl/24hr, TA/Mobil/dsl/rest./24hr/@, **lodging:** Best Value, **other:** JR Steaks, to Willow River SP, **S**...**other:** Curves

3 WI 35, to River Falls, U of WI River Falls, no services

2 rd F, Carmichael Rd, Hudson, **N**...**gas:** BP, Freedom/dsl, Holiday, **food:** Applebee's, Cousins Subs, Culver's, KFC, Papa Murphy's, Taco John's, **lodging:** Royal Inn, **other:** Econo Foods, GNC, Pontiac/GMC, Target, **S**...**Welcome Ctr both lanes, full(handicapped)facilities, phone, picnic table, litter barrel, info, petwalk, gas:** F&F/dsl, Holiday/Subway, KwikTrip/dsl, **food:** Arby's, Burger King, Country Kitchen, Denny's, McDonald's, Perkins/24hr, Pizza Hut, Subway, Taco Bell, Wendy's, **lodging:** Best Western, Comfort Inn, Fairfield Inn, Holiday Inn Express, Super 8, **other:** HOSPITAL, Checker Parts, Chevrolet/RV Ctr, Chrysler/Dodge/Jeep, County Mkt Foods, Ford/Mercury, Home Depot, NAPA, Tires+, Wal-Mart, to Kinnickinnic SP

1 WI 35 N, Hudson, **1 mi** **N**...**gas:** Freedom/dsl, Holiday, **food:** DQ, Subway, **other:** City Mkt Foods

0mm Wisconsin/Minnesota state line, St Croix River

N / S — Buffalo / Casper (left margin direction indicator)

Exit #	Services
300	I-90, E to Gillette, W to Billings. I-25 begins/ends on I-90, exit 56.
299	299 US 16, Buffalo, **E...gas:** Exxon/dsl, Johnson Cty/dsl, Shell/dsl/24hr, **food:** Winchester Steaks, **lodging:** Comfort Inn, Motel 6, **other:** Deer Park Camping, KOA, NAPA, **W...gas:** Bighorn/dsl/24hr, Cenex/dsl/rest./24hr, **food:** Bozeman Tr Steaks, Dash Inn Rest., Hardee's, Hoot'n Howl Rest., McDonald's, Pizza Hut, Sub Shop, Subway, Taco John's, **lodging:** Best Western Crossroads, Horsemen's Inn, Rodeway Inn, Wyo Motel, Super 8, **other:** HOSPITAL, Ace Hardware, Family$, Indian RV Camp
298	US 87, Buffalo, **W...gas:** Kum-N-Go, Sinclair/dsl/pizza, **other:** Nat Hist Dist Info
291	Trabing Rd, no services
280	Middle Fork Rd, no services
274mm	parking area both lanes, litter barrels
265	Reno Rd, no services
254	Kaycee, **E...gas:** Exxon/dsl, Shell/dsl, **food:** Country Inn Diner, **lodging:** Cassidy Inn, Siesta Motel, **other:** Kaycee Foods, NAPA Repair, Powder River RV Park, USPO, museum, **W...rest area both lanes, full(handicapped)facilities, phone, picnic tables, litter barrels, petwalk, gas:** Sinclair/dsl/LP/motel, **other:** KC RV Park
249	TTT Rd, no services
246	Powder River Rd, no services
235	Tisdale Mtn Rd, no services
227	WY 387 N, Midwest, Edgerton, no services
223	no services
219mm	parking area both lanes, litter barrels
216	Ranch Rd, no services
210	Horse Ranch Creek Rd, Midwest, Edgerton
197	Ormsby Rd, no services
191	Wardwell Rd, to Bar Nunn, **W...gas:** Minimart/dsl, **other:** KOA
189	US 20, US 26 W, to Shoshone, Port of Entry, airport
188b	WY 220, Poplar St, **E...food:** El Jarro Mexican, JB's, **lodging:** Best Western, Hampton Inn, Holiday Inn, Motel 6, Quality Inn, **W...gas:** Exxon, **food:** Burger King, Casper's Rest., DQ, **other:** Harley-Davidson, to Ft Casper HS
188a	Center St, Casper, **E...gas:** Conoco/dsl, Shell/dsl, **food:** PoorBoys Steaks, Taco John's, **lodging:** Holiday Inn, National 9 Inn, **W...gas:** Cenex, **food:** Platte River Rest., **lodging:** Day's Inn, Parkway Plaza Motel
187	McKinley St, Casper, **E...gas:** Loaf'n Jug/dsl, **lodging:** Ranch House Motel, **other:** repair/transmissons
186	US 20, US 26, US 87, Yellowstone St, **E...other:** Audi/VW, dsl repair, **W...gas:** Shell, **other:** HOSPITAL, Checker Parts, Chevrolet/Subaru

Casper (left margin)

Exit #	Services
185	WY 258, Wyoming Blvd, E Casper, **E...gas:** Kum&Go/dsl, Loaf'n Jug/dsl, **food:** Applebee's, IHOP, Outback Steaks, **lodging:** C'mon Inn, Comfort Inn, Shilo Inn, Super 8, **other:** KOA(1mi), Smith RV Ctr, **W...gas:** Cenex, Exxon/dsl, ⚡/Flying J/Conoco/Cookery/dsl/LP/24hr/@, **food:** Arby's, Burger King, DQ, Hardee's, HomeTowne Buffet, KFC/LJ Silver, McDonald's, Perkins, Pizza Hut, Red Lobster, Taco Bell, Taco John's, Village Inn Rest., Wendy's, **lodging:** Coutyard, Holiday Inn Express, **other:** AutoZone, Buick/Cadillac/Pontiac/GMC, Ford/Mercury, Home Depot, Hyundai, JC Penney, K-Mart, Nissan, Old Navy, Safeway Foods, Sam's Club/gas, Sears/auto, Target, Volvo, Walgreens, Wal-Mart SuperCtr/24hr, to Oregon Tr, mall
182	WY 253, Brooks Rd, Hat Six Rd, **E...gas:** Sinclair/dsl/@, **food:** Lou's Rest., **lodging:** Sleep Inn, **other:** to Wilkins SP
171mm	parking area both lanes, litter barrels
165	Glenrock, **2 mi E...gas:** Phillips 66, **other:** Deer Creek Village RV Camping(apr-nov)
160	US 87, US 20, US 26, E Glenrock, **E...gas:** Phillips 66, **food:** Paisley Shaul Cafe, **food:** Subway/TCBY, **lodging:** Hotel Higgins B&B, **other:** Deer Creek RV Camping, to Johnston Power Plant
156	Bixby Rd, no services
154	Barber Rd, no services
153mm	parking area both lanes, litter barrels
151	Natural Bridge, no services
150	Inez Rd, no services
146	La Prele Rd, no services
140	WY 59, Douglas, **E...gas:** Conoco/Subway/dsl, Maverik/dsl, **food:** Arby's, La Costa Mexican, McDonald's, **lodging:** Best Western, Holiday Inn Express, Super 8, **other:** HOSPITAL, Buick/Chevrolet/GMC/Pontiac, Chevrolet, KOA, Lone Tree RV Park, Pioneer Museum, WY St Fair,
135	US 20, US 26, US 87, Douglas, **E...gas:** Broken Wheel/Sinclair/dsl/rest./@, **food:** Country Inn Rest., **lodging:** Alpine Inn, 1st Interstate Inn, **other:** HOSPITAL, auto repair, **1-2 mi E...food:** KFC/Taco Bell, Pizza Hut, Taco John's, Village Inn Rest., **lodging:** PLains Motel, **other:** Ace Hardware, Chrysler/Dodge/Jeep, Ford/Mercury, Pamida, Safeway
129mm	parking area both lanes
126	US 18, US 20 E, Orin, **E...Orin Jct Rest Area both lanes, full(handicapped)facilities, phones, picnic tables, litter barrels, petwalk, RV dump, gas:** Orin Jct Trkstp/dsl/café
125mm	N Platte River
111	Glendo, **E...gas:** Sinclair/dsl, **food:** Glendo Marina Café, **lodging:** Howard's Motel, **other:** to Glendo SP, RV camping
104	to Middle Bear, no services
100	Cassa Rd, no services

Douglas (right margin)

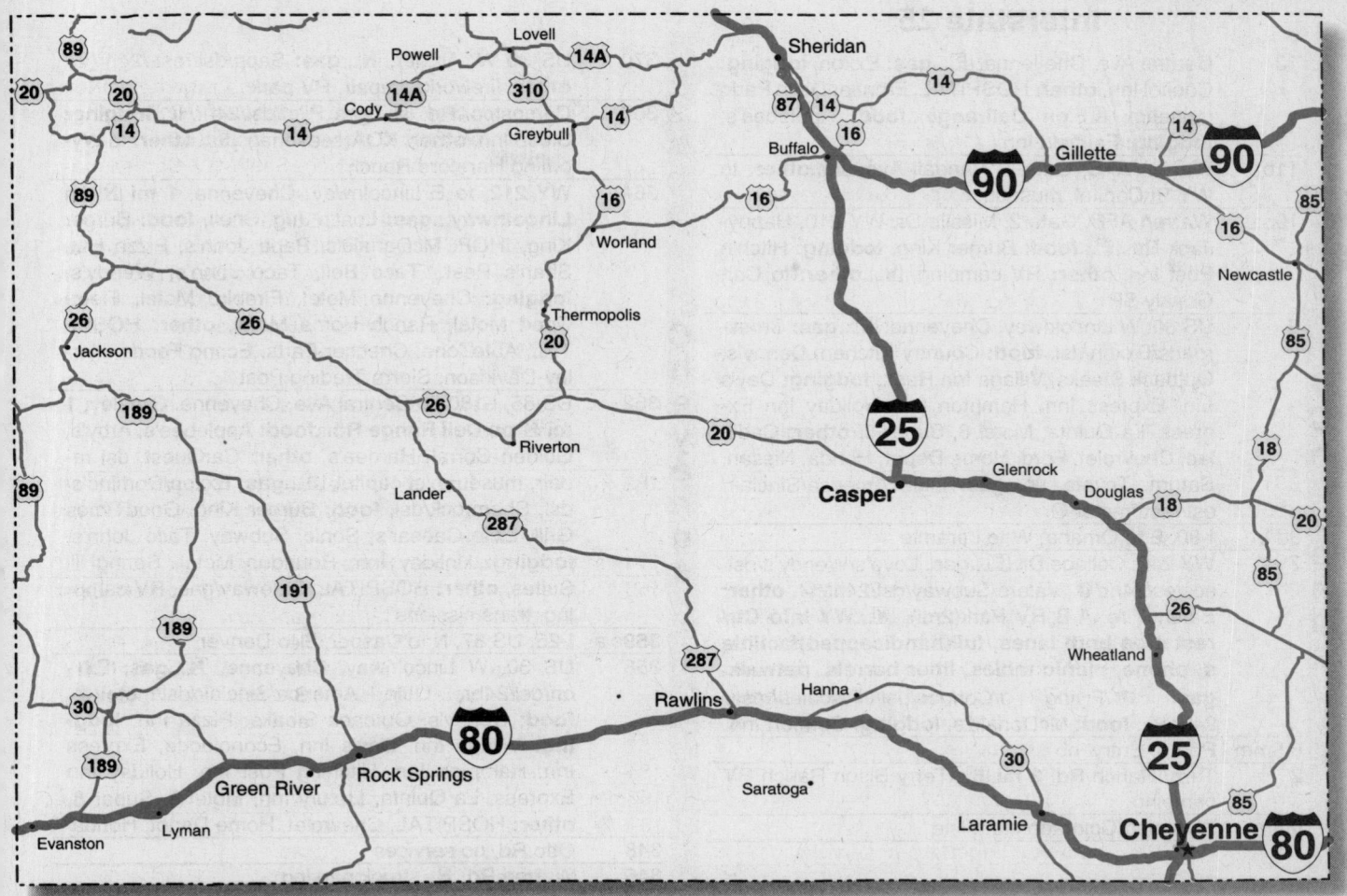

Interstate 25

<table>
<tr><td>N
↕
S

W
h
e
a
t
l
a
n
d</td><td>

94	El Rancho Rd, no services
92	US 26 E, Dwyer, Ⓔ...**rest area both lanes, full (handicapped)facilities, picnic tables, litter barrel, petwalk, RV dump** to Guernsey SP, Ft Laramie NHS
87	Johnson Rd, no services
84	Laramie River Rd, no services
84mm	Laramie River
80	US 87, Laramie Power Sta, Wheatland, Laramie Power Sta, Ⓔ...**gas:** Sinclair/A&W/dsl/24hr, **food:** TimberHaus Rest., **lodging:** Best Western, Super 8, **other:** Chevrolet/Pontiac/Buick/Cadillac, Chrysler/Dodge/Jeep, Family$, Ford/Mercury, Pamida/drug, Safeway, same as 78
78	US 87, Wheatland, Ⓔ...**gas:** Cenex/dsl, Conoco/dsl, Shell/dsl, **food:** Arby's, Burger King, Pizza Hut, Subway, Taco John's, Wheatland Rest., **lodging:** Motel 6, Vimbo's Motel/rest., Wyo Motel, **other:** HOSPITAL, Ⓦ...**gas:** Exxon/dsl, Conoco/dsl, **other:** Radio Shack, RV park
73	WY 34 W, to Laramie, no services
70	Bordeaux Rd, no services
68	Antelope Rd, no services

</td><td>

66	Hunton Rd, no services
65.5mm	parking area both lanes, litter barrels
65	Slater Rd, no services
64mm	Richeau Creek
57	TY Basin Rd, Chugwater, no services
54	Lp 25, Chugwater, Ⓔ...**gas:** Sinclair/dsl, **food:** Buffalo Grill, **lodging:** Super 8, **other:** GS RV Park, **rest area both lanes, full(handicapped) facilities, phone, picnic tables, litter barrels, petwalk, RV dump**
47	Bear Creek Rd, no services
39	Little Bear Community, no services
36mm	Little Bear Creek
34	Nimmo Rd, no services
33mm	Horse Creek
29	Whitaker Rd, no services
25	ranch exit, no services
21	Ridley Rd, no services
17	US 85 N, to Torrington, no services
16	WY 211, Horse Creek Rd, Ⓦ...**food:** Little Bear Rest.(2mi)
13	Vandehei Ave, Ⓔ...**gas:** Loaf'n Jug/Subway, Ⓦ...**gas:** Shamrock/dsl

</td></tr>
</table>

WYOMING

Interstate 25

12	Central Ave, Cheyenne, **E**...**gas:** Exxon, **lodging:** Capitol Inn, **other:** HOSPITAL, Frontier Days Park, museum, **E on Dellrange...food:** Applebee's, **lodging:** Fairfield Inn
11b	Warren AFB, Gate 1, Randall Ave, **E**...**other:** to WY St Capitol, museum
10b d	Warren AFB, Gate 2, Missile Dr, WY 210, Happy-Jack Rd, **E**...**food:** Burger King, **lodging:** Hitchin Post Inn, **other:** RV camping, **W**...**other:** to Curt Gowdy SP
9	US 30, W Lincolnway, Cheyenne, **E**...**gas:** Cross-roads/Exxon/dsl, **food:** Country Kitchen, Denny's, Outback Steaks, Village Inn Rest., **lodging:** Day's Inn, Express Inn, Hampton Inn, Holiday Inn Express, La Quinta, Motel 6, Super 8, **other:** Cadillac, Chevrolet, Ford, Home Depot, Honda, Nissan, Saturn, Toyota, **W**...**gas:** Little America/Sinclair/dsl/rest./motel/@
8d b	I-80, E to Omaha, W to Laramie
7	WY 212, College Dr, **E**...**gas:** Love's/Wendy's/dsl/scales/24hr/@, Valero/Subway/dsl/24hr/@, **other:** Bailey Tire, A-B RV Park(2mi), **W**...**WY Info Ctr/rest area both lanes, full(handicapped)facilities, phone, picnic tables, litter barrels, petwalk, gas:** Flying J/Conoco/dsl/LP/scales/rest./24hr/@, **food:** McDonald's, **lodging:** Comfort Inn
6.5mm	Port of Entry, nb
2	Terry Ranch Rd, **2 mi E**...Terry Bison Ranch RV camping
0mm	Wyoming/Colorado state line

Interstate 80

Exit #	Services
402mm	Wyoming/Nebraska State line
401	WY 215, Pine Bluffs, **N**...**gas:** Cenex/A&W/dsl/24hr/@, Conoco/Subway/dsl, Race Track/dsl, Sinclair/dsl, **food:** Uncle Fred's Rest., **lodging:** Gator's Motel, **other:** NAPA, USPO, Pine Bluff RV Park, **S**...**Welcome Ctr/rest area both lanes, full(handicapped)facilities, info, phone, playground, nature trail, picnic tables, litter barrels, petwalk**
391	Egbert, no services
386	WY 213, WY 214, Burns, **N**...Antelope Trkstp/dsl/cafe/@
377	WY 217, Hillsdale, **N**...**gas:** TA/BP/Burger King/Taco Bell/dsl/motel/24hr/@, **other:** Wyo RV Camping
372mm	Port of Entry wb, truck insp

370	US 30 W, Archer, **N**...**gas:** Sapp/dsl/rest./24hr/@, **other:** fireworks, repair, RV park
367	Campstool Rd, **N**...**gas** Pilot/dsl/24hr/@, **lodging:** Sleep Inn, **other:** KOA(seasonal), **S**...**other:** to Wyoming Hereford Ranch
364	WY 212, to E Lincolnway, Cheyenne, **1 mi N on Lincolnway...gas:** Loaf'n Jug, Shell, **food:** Burger King, IHOP, McDonald's, Papa John's, Pizza Hut, Shari's Rest., Taco Bell, Taco John's, Wendy's, **lodging:** Cheyenne Motel, Firebird Motel, Fleetwood Motel, Ranch Home Motel, **other:** HOSPITAL, AutoZone, Checker Parts, Econo Foods, Harley-Davidson, Sierra Trading Post
362	US 85, I-180, to Central Ave, Cheyenne, Greeley, **1 mi N on Dell Range Rd...food:** Applebee's, Arby's, Golden Corral, Hardee's, **other:** CarQuest, dsl repair, museum, st capitol, **S**...**gas:** Exxon/Domino's/dsl, Shamrock/dsl, **food:** Burger King, GoodTimes Grill, Little Caesar's, Sonic, Subway, Taco John's, **lodging:** Holiday Inn, Roundup Motel, SpringHill Suites, **other:** HOSPITAL, Safeway/gas, RV camping, transmissions
359c a	I-25, US 87, N to Casper, S to Denver
358	US 30, W Lincolnway, Cheyenne, **N**...**gas:** Exxon/dsl/24hr, Little America/Sinclair/dsl/motel/@, **food:** Denny's, Outback Steaks, Pizza Inn, **lodging:** Village Inn, Day's Inn, Econolodge, Express Inn, Hampton Inn, Hitching Post Inn, Holiday Inn Express, La Quinta, Luxury Inn, Motel 6, Super 8, **other:** HOSPITAL, Chevrolet, Home Depot, Honda
348	Otto Rd, no services
345	Warren Rd, **N**... truck parking
344mm	no services
343.5mm	no services
342	Harriman Rd, no services
341mm	parking area both lanes
339	Remount Rd, no services
335	Buford, **N**...fireworks, **S**...**gas:** Buford Trading Post/dsl/24hr
333mm	point of interest, parking area both lanes
329	Vedeauwoo Rd, **S**...to Ames Monument, Nat Forest RA
323	WY 210, Happy Jack Rd, **N**...**rest area both lanes, full(handicapped)facilities, phone, picnic tables, litter barrels, petwalk, Lincoln Monument, elev. 8640, to Curt Gowdy SP**
322mm	chain up area both lanes
316	US 30 W, Grand Ave, Laramie, **1-2 mi N**...**gas:** Conoco/dsl, Loaf'N Jug, **food:** Applebee's, Arby's, Bailey's Rest., Burger King, Godfather's Pizza, Hong Kong Buffet, McDonald's, Papa Murphy's, Sonic, Subway, Taco Bell, Taco John's, Village Inn, Wendy's, Winger's, **lodging:** Comfort Inn, Hampton Inn, **other:** HOSPITAL, Albertson's/gas, Chevrolet/Cadillac/Buick/Pontiac, Ford/Lincoln/Mercury, Goodyear, Staples, Toyota, Wal-Mart SuperCtr/24hr, conf. ctr

Interstate 80

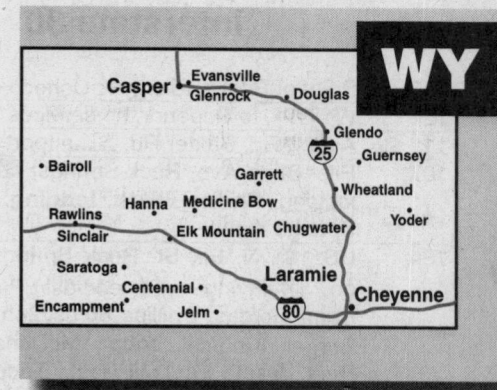

313 US 287, to 3rd St, Laramie, Port of Entry, N...**gas:** Loaf 'N Jug, Conoco/dsl, Exxon, Phillips 66/dsl, Shell/dsl, **food:** Burger King, Chuck Wagon Rest., Great Wall Chinese, **lodging:** 1st Inn Gold, Laramie Inn/rest., Motel 8, Sunset Inn, **other:** HOSPITAL, Honda/Nissan/Isuzu, Laramie Plains Museum, NAPA, S...**lodging:** Motel 6, Ramada Inn

312mm Laramie River

311 WY 130, WY 230, Snowy Range Rd, Laramie, S... **gas:** Conoco/dsl, Phillips 66/dsl, Sinclair/dsl/LP, **food:** McDonald's, Subway, **lodging:** Best Value Inn, Howard Johnson, to Snowy Range Ski Area, WY Terr Park

310 Curtis St, Laramie, N...**gas:** Pilot/Wendy's/dsl/24hr/@, Valero/café/dsl, **lodging:** Best Western, Day's Inn, Econolodge, Holiday Inn Express, Quality Inn, Super 8, **other:** HOSPITAL, Goodyear/service/towing, KOA, **1 mi** N **on 3rd...food:** Pizza Hut, Shari's Rest., **other:** Checker Parts, Family$, Hastings, Jeep/Subaru, K-Mart, Safeway Foods, S...**gas:** Petro/Iron Skillet/dsl/scales/24hr/@, Blue Beacon, **lodging:** Baymont Inn

307mm parking area both lanes, litter barrels

297 WY 12, Herrick Lane, no services

290 Quealy Dome Rd, S...**gas:** Sinclair/dsl/24hr

279 Cooper Cove Rd, no services

272mm Rock Creek

272 WY 13, to Arlington, N...gas, RV camping

267 **Wagonhound Rd,** S**...rest area both lanes, full (handicapped)facilities, phone, picnic tables, litter barrels, petwalk**

262mm parking area both lanes

260 CR 402, no services

259mm Medicine Bow River, E Fork

257mm Medicine Bow River

255 WY 72, Elk Mtn, to Hanna, N...**gas:** Conoco/dsl,

238 Peterson Rd, no services

235 US 30/87, WY 130, N...**gas:** Shell/dsl/café

229mm N Platte River

228 **Ft Steele HS,** N**...rest area both lanes, full(handicapped)facilities, phone, picnic tables, litter barrels, petwalk**

221 E Sinclair, N...**gas:** Phillips 66/dsl/rest./24hr, **other:** to Seminoe SP, camping

219 W Sinclair, N...**other:** to Seminoe SP, camping

215 Cedar St, Rawlins, N...**gas:** City Mkt, Conoco/dsl, Phillips 66/dsl, Shell/KFC/Taco Bell, Sinclair, **food:** McDonald's, Pizza Hut, Subway, Taco John's, **lodging:** Comfort Inn, Day's Inn, 1st Choice Inn, Holiday Inn Express, Quality Inn, OakTree Inn, The Key Motel, **other:** Alco, Buick/Chevrolet/Pontiac/GMC, CarQuest, Checker Parts, Chrysler/Dodge/Jeep, City Mkt Food/gas, Pamida, TDS Tire, museum, Frontier Prison NHS, to Yellowstone/Teton NP

214 Higley Blvd, Rawlins, N... KOA, S...**gas:** TA/Shell/Subway/dsl/24hr/@, **lodging:** Best Value Inn

211 WY 789, to US 287 N, Spruce St, Rawlins, N...**gas:** Conoco/dsl, Exxon/dsl, Phillips 66, Sinclair/dsl, **food:** Cappy's Rest., Golden 8 Chinese, **lodging:** Best Western, Budget Inn, Econolodge, Express Inn, Ideal Motel, La Bella, Super 8, Sunset Motel, Travelodge, **other:** HOSPITAL, Family$, RV World, V1/LP, Western Hills Camping, **1 mi** N...**lodging:** Economy Inn, **other:** Ford/Lincoln/Mercury

209 Johnson Rd, N...**gas:** ✈/Flying J/dsl/LP/rest./scales/24hr/@

206 Hadsell Rd(no return), no services

205.5mm continental divide, elev 7000

204 Knobs Rd, no services

201 Daley Rd, no services

196 Riner Rd, no services

190mm parking area wb, litter barrels

189mm parking area eb, picnic tables, litter barrels

187 WY 789, Creston, Baggs Rd, no facilites

184 Continental Divide Rd, no services

173 Wamsutter, N...**gas:** Loves/Chester Fried/Subway/dsl/24hr/@, Sinclair/dsl/LP/@, S...**gas:** Conoco/dsl/repair/café/24hr, Phillips 66/dsl/@, **food:** Broadway Café, **lodging:** Wamsutter Motel

170 Rasmussen Rd, no services

168 Frewen Rd, no services

166 Booster Rd, no services

165 Red Desert, no services

158 Tipton Rd, continental divide, elev 6930

156 GL Rd, no services

154 BLM Rd, no services

152 Bar X Rd, no services

150 Table Rock Rd, no services

146 Patrick Draw Rd, no services

144mm **rest area both lanes, full(handicapped)facilities, phone, picnic tables, litter barrels, petwalk**

143mm parking area both lanes, litter barrels

142 Bitter Creek Rd, no services

139 Red Hill Rd, no services

136 Black Butte Rd, no services

135mm parking area both lanes

WYOMING

Interstate 80

130	Point of Rocks, **N**...**gas:** Conoco/dsl
122	WY 371, to Superior, no services
111	Airport Rd, Baxter Rd, **S**...airport
107	Pilot Butte Ave, Rock Springs, **S**...**gas:** Mobil/dsl/lodging, Phillips 66/dsl, **lodging:** Sands Inn/cafe, Springs Motel
104	US 191 N, Elk St, Rock Springs, **N**...**gas:** Exxon, ✈/Flying J/Conoco/dsl/LP/rest./scales/24hr, Kum&Go/gas, Phillips 66/dsl/24hr, Shell, Texaco/Burger King/dsl, **food:** McDonald's, Renegade Rest., Santa Fe Trail Rest., Taco Time, **lodging:** Best Western, Econolodge/rest.,**other:** Buick/Pontiac/GMC, Chrysler/Jeep, to Teton, Yellowstone Nat Parks via US 191, **S**...**gas:** Exxon/dsl, **lodging:** Day's Inn
103	College Dr, Rock Springs, **S**...**gas:** Loaf'N Jug/dsl/24hr, **food:** Domino's **other:** HOSPITAL, W WY Coll
102	WY 430, Dewar Dr, Rock Springs, **N**...**gas:** Exxon, Loaf'N Jug, Sinclair/dsl, **food:** Applebee's, China King, KFC/LJ Silver, Pam's BBQ, Taco Time, **lodging:** Best Value Inn, Motel 6, La Quinta, The Inn, **other:** Chevrolet/Cadillac, Chrysler/Dodge/Subaru, $Tree, Don's RV Ctr, Harley-Davidson, Home Depot, K-Mart, JC Penney, NAPA, Smith's Food, **S**...**gas:** Kum&Go, Mobil/dsl, **food:** Arby's, Bonsai Chinese, Burger King, Golden Corral, IHOP, JB's, McDonald's, Pizza Hut, Popeye's, Quizno's, Sonic, Subway, Taco Bell, Village Inn Rest., Wendy's, Wingers, Wonderful House Chinese, **lodging:** Hampton Inn, Holiday Inn, Motel 8, Quality Inn, Super 8, Wingate Inn, **other:** HOSPITAL, Albertson's, AutoZone, Big O Tire, Checker Parts, Curves, Hastings Books, NAPA, Walgreens, Wal-Mart SuperCtr/gas/24hr
99	US 191 S, E Flaming Gorge Rd, **N**...**other:** KOA(1mi), **S**...**gas:** Conoco/dsl/café/24hr/@, **food:** Big Wheeler Rest., Log Inn Steaks, **other:** fireworks, transmissions
94mm	Kissing Rock
91	US 30, to WY 530, Green River, **(2mi)S**...**gas:** Loaf'N Jug/gas **food:** Arctic Circle, China Garden, Don Pedro's Mexican, McDonald's, Pizza Hut, Subway, Taco John's, Taco Time, **lodging:** (1mi)Super 8, (1mi)Western Motel, **other:** Expedition NHS, to Flaming Gorge NRA, same as 89
89	US 30, Green River, **S**...**gas:** Exxon, Sinclair/dsl, **food:** Green River Rest., McDonald's, Penny's Diner, Pizza Hut, Taco Time, **lodging:** OakTree Inn, Super 8, Western Inn, **other:** Adam's RV Service, NAPA, Tex's RV Camp, to Flaming Gorge NRA
87.5mm	Green River
85	Covered Wagon Rd, **S**...**other:** Adams RV parts/service, Tex's Travel Camp
83	WY 372, La Barge Rd, **N**...to Fontenelle Dam
78	(from wb), no services
77mm	Blacks Fork River
72	Westvaco Rd, no services
71mm	parking area both lanes
68	Little America, **N**...**gas:** Sinclair/Little America Hotel/rest./dsl/24hr@, **other:** RV camping
66	US 30 W, to Teton, Yellowstone, Fossil Butte NM, Kemmerer, no services
61	Cedar Mt Rd, to Granger, no services
60mm	parking area both lanes, litter barrels
54mm	parking area eb, litter barrels
53	Church Butte Rd, no services
49mm	parking area wb, litter barrels
48	Lp 80, Lyman, Ft Bridger, Hist Ft Bridger
45mm	Blacks Fork River
41	WY 413, Lyman, **N**...**gas:** Gas'n Go/dsl/cafe/@, **S**...**rest area both lanes, full(handicapped)facilities, phone, picnic tables, litter barrels, petwalk, food:** Taco Time, **other:** Gateway Inn(2mi), KOA(1mi)
39	WY 412, WY 414, to Carter, Mountain View
34	Lp 80, to Ft Bridger, **S**...**gas:** Phillips 66, **lodging:** Wagon Wheel Motel, **other:** Ft Bridger RV Camp, Ft Bridger NHS, to Flaming Gorge NRA
33.5mm	parking area eb, litter barrels
33	Union Rd, no services
30	Bigelow Rd, **N**...**gas:** TA/Tesoro/Burger King/Taco Bell/Fork In the Road/dsl/scales/24hr/@, **S**...fireworks
28	French Rd, no services
28mm	French Rd, parking area both lanes
24	Leroy Rd, no services
23	Bar Hat Rd, no services
21	Coal Rd, no services
18	US 189 N, to Kemmerer, to Nat Parks, Fossil Butte NM
15	Guild Rd(from eb), no services
14mm	parking area both lanes
13	Divide Rd, no services
10	Painter Rd, to Eagle Rock Ski Area, to Eagle Rock Ski Area
6	US 189, Bear River Dr, Evanston, **N**...**gas:** Sinclair/dsl, Pilot/Subway/dsl/scales/24hr/@, **food:** Bear Town Rest., Don Pedro Mexican, **lodging:** Best Value Inn, Holiday Inn Express, Motel 6, Prairie Inn, Vagabond Motel, **other:** Bear River RV Park, CarQuest, Ford/Mercury, Goodyear, Phillip's RV Park, Wyo Downs Racetrack, tires, **S**...**Welcome Ctr both lanes, full (handicapped)facilities, phone, picnic tables, litter barrels, petwalk, RV dump(seasonal), playground,** Bear River SP

Interstate 80

5	WY 89, Evanston, **N**...**gas:** Chevron/Domino's/dsl, Maverik, Sinclair, **food:** Arby's, DragonWall Chinese, McDonald's, Papa Murphy's, Shakey's Pizza, Sonic, Starbucks, Subway, Wendy's, **lodging:** Best Value Inn, **other:** HOSPITAL, AutoZone, Chevrolet/Buick, Jubilee/gas, Murdock's, NAPA, Radio Shack, Wal-Mart Super Ctr, **S**...WY St Hospital
3	US 189, Harrison Dr, Evanston, **N**...**gas:** Chevron/dsl, ⊕/Flying J/dsl/rest./scales/24hr/@, Gasamart, Sinclair, **food:** JB's, Legal Tender, Lotty's Rest., Taco Time, TC's Steaks, **lodging:** Best Western/rest., Comfort Inn, Day's Inn, DX Motel, Economy Inn, HighCountry Inn, Holiday Inn Express, Howard Johnson, The Lodge, Weston Inn, **other:** HOSPITAL, Automotive+, Chrysler/Jeep, GMC/Pontiac/Cadillac, USPO, **S**...**other:** HOSPITAL, fireworks
.5mm	Port of Entry eb, weigh sta wb
0mm	Wyoming/Utah state line

Interstate 90

Exit #	Services
207mm	Wyoming/South Dakota state line
205	Beulah, **N**...**gas:** Conoco/Buffalo Jump/dsl/LP, **lodging:** The Mill, **other:** Sand Creek Camping, USPO, Ranch A NHP(5mi)
204.5mm	Sand Creek
199	WY 111, to Aladdin, to Vore Buffalo Jump NHP
191	Moskee Rd, no services
189	US 14 W, Sundance, **N**...**gas:** BP/dsl/24hr, **food:** Aro Rest.(2mi), Subway(2mi), **lodging:** Bear Lodge, Best Western, Budget Host Arrowhead, **other:** HOSPITAL, Mt View Camping, to Devil's Tower NM, museum, **S**...**rest area both lanes, full(handicapped)facilities, info, phone, picnic tables, litter barrels, playground, petwalk, RV dump,** port of entry/weigh sta
187	WY 585, Sundance, **N**...**gas:** BP/dsl, Fresh Start/dsl, **food:** Subway, **lodging:** Best Western, Decker's Motel, Pineview Motel, Rodeway Inn, Sundance Mtn Inn, **other:** Decker's Foods
185	to WY 116, to Sundance, **S**...**gas:** Conoco/dsl/service, **food:** ARO Rest., Subway, **lodging:** Bear Lodge, Best Western, Budget Host, **other:** Mt View Camping, to Devil's Tower
178	Coal Divide Rd, no services
177mm	parking area both lanes, litter barrels
172	Inyan Kara Rd, no services
171mm	parking area both lanes, litter barrels
165	Pine Ridge Rd, to Pine Haven, **N**...to Keyhole SP
163mm	parking area both lanes, litter barrels
160	Wind Creek Rd, no services
154	US 14, US 16, **S**...**gas:** Conoco/dsl, **food:** Donna's Diner, Subway, Taco Time, **lodging:** Cozy Motel, Moorcourt Motel, Wyo Motel, **other:** Dihl's Foods, USPO, museum, city park

153	US 16 E, US 14, W Moorcroft, **N**...**rest area both lanes, full(handicapped)facilities, phone, picnic tables, litter barrels, petwalk**
152mm	Belle Fourche River
141	Rozet, no services
138mm	parking area both lanes
132	Wyodak Rd, no services
129	Garner Lake Rd, **S**...**other:** Harley-Davidson, High Plains Camping, WY Marine/RV ctr, auto repair
128	US 14, US 16, Gillette, Port of Entry, **N**...**gas:** Cenex, Conoco, Maverik/dsl, **food:** Mona's American/Mexican, Taco John's, Village Inn Rest., **lodging:** Howard Johnson, National 9 Inn, Smart Choice Inn, **other:** Crazy Woman Camping(2mi), East Side RV Ctr., **S**...**other:** High Plains Camping
126	WY 59, Gillette, **N**...**gas:** Cenex/dsl, Conoco, **food:** Hardee's, Maria's Mexican, McDonald's, Papa John's, Pokey's BBQ, Prime Rib Rest., Starbucks, Subway, **lodging:** Best Value, Rolling Hills Motel, **other:** Radio Shack, Smith's Foods, Tire Factory, city park, **S**...**gas:** Exxon, ⊕/Flying J/dsl/rest./24hr, Loaf'n Jug, **food:** A&W/LJ Silver, Applebee's, Arby's, Burger King, DQ, Goodtimes Grill/Taco John's, Golden Corral, KFC, Papa Murphy's, Perkins/24hr, Pizza Hut, Popeye's, Quizno's, Taco Bell, Wendy's, **lodging:** Clarion, Comfort Inn, Day's Inn, Fairfield Inn, Holiday Inn Express, Wingate Inn, **other:** Ace Hardware, Albertson's, Checker Parts, Chrysler/Dodge/Jeep, GNC, Goodyear/auto, Home Depot, K-Mart, Office Depot, O'Reilly Parts, Osco Drug, Tire-O-Rama, Walgreens, Wal-Mart SuperCtr, city park, RV dump

WYOMING

Interstate 90

124	WY 50, Gillette, **N**...**gas:** Conoco/dsl/24hr, Shell/Burger King/dsl, **food:** Granny's Kitchen, Hong Kong Rest., Pizza Hut, Subway, **lodging:** Best Western/rest., Budget Inn, Comfort Inn, Hampton Inn, Motel 6, Super 8, **other:** HOSPITAL, Don's Foods, **S**...**gas:** Cenex/dsl, **other:** Bighorn Tire, Chevrolet/Cadillac/Buick
116	Force Rd, no services
113	Wild Horse Creek Rd, no services
110mm	parking area both lanes
106	Kingsbury Rd, no services
102	Barber Creek Rd, no services
91	Dead Horse Creek Rd, no services
89mm	Powder River
88	Powder River Rd, **N**...**gas:** Exit 88 Fuel/dsl, Powder River Trvl Plaza/dsl/camping, **rest area both lanes, full(handicapped)facilities, phone, picnic tables, litter barrels, petwalk**
82	Indian Creek Rd, no services
77	Schoonover Rd, no services
73.5mm	Crazy Woman Creek
73	Crazy Woman Creek Rd, no services
69	Dry Creek Rd, no services
68.5mm	parking area both lanes, litter barrels
65	Red Hills Rd, Tipperary Rd, no services
60mm	parking area both lanes, litter barrels
58	US 16, to Ucross, Buffalo, **S**...**gas:** Cenex/dsl/rest./24hr, Exxon/dsl, **other:** Bighorn Tire, **1-3 mi S**...**gas:** Johnson Cty/dsl, Shell/dsl/24hr, **food:** Bozeman Tr Steaks, Dash Inn Rest., Hardee's, Hoot'n Howl Rest., McDonald's, Pizza Hut, Sub Shop, Subway, Taco John's, Winchester Steaks, **lodging:** Best Western Crossroads, Comfort Inn, Horsemen's Inn, Motel 6, Rodeway Inn, Super 8, Wyo Motel, **other:** HOSPITAL, Ace Hardware, Deer Park Camping, Family$, Indian RV Camp, KOA, NAPA, Nat Hist Dist
56b	I-25 S, US 87 S, to Buffalo, no services
56a	25 Bus, 90 Bus, to Buffalo, services 2mi south
53	Rock Creek Rd, no services
51	Lake DeSmet, **1 mi N**...Lake Stop gas, Lake Stop Motel, Lake Desmet RV park
47	Shell Creek Rd, no services

44	US 87 N, Piney Creek Rd, to Story, Banner, **N**...**other:** Ft Phil Kearney, museum, **5 mi S**...Wagon Box Rest., Wagon Box Cabins
39mm	scenic turnout wb, litter barrel
37	Prairie Dog Creek Rd, to Story, no services
33	Meade Creek Rd, to Big Horn, no services
31mm	parking area eb, litter barrel
25	US 14 E, Sheridan, **N**...**lodging:** Comfort Inn, **other:** Big Sky RV Ctr, **S**...**gas:** Exxon/dsl, Holiday, Loaf'n Jug/dsl, Maverik, **food:** Arby's, Burger King, Golden China, JB's, Los Agaves, Ole's Pizza, Perkins/24hr, Starbucks, Subway, Taco Bell, Taco John's, Wendy's, **lodging:** Day's Inn, Holiday Inn, Mill Inn, Parkway Motel, **other:** Ace hardware, Albertson's/Osco Drug, Checker Parts, $Tree, Firestone, Ford/Lincoln/Mercury, Goodyear, Home Depot, NAPA, O'Reilly Parts, Pontiac/Cadillac, Safeway Foods, Toyota, Walgreens, **Wal-Mart SuperCtr/24hr,** Whse Mkt Foods, mall, to Hist Dist, Sheridan Coll
23	WY 336, 5th St, Sheridan, **N**...**gas:** Rock Stop/Subway/dsl, **lodging:** Wingate Inn, **rest area both lanes, full(handicapped)facilities, info, phone, picnic tables, litter barrels, petwalk, RV dump, 1-2 mi S**...**gas:** Cenex, Holiday/dsl, **food:** DQ, Pablo's Mexican, Quizno's, Rid & Chophouse, **lodging:** Alamo Motel, Best Value, Best Western, Hampton Inn, Motel 6, Sheridan Inn, **other:** HOSPITAL, Honda, Main St Drub, Peter D's RV Sheradon Cty Museum, park, radiators
20	Main St, Sheridan, **S**...**gas:** Conoco, Exxon/dsl/scales/24hr, Shell/dsl, **food:** Country Kitchen, McDonald's, Pizza Hut, **lodging:** Aspen Inn, Budget Host, Super Save Motel, Trails End Motel, Stage Stop Motel, Sundown Motel, Super 8, **other:** Hospital, K-Mart, KOA
16	to Decker, Montana, port of entry
15mm	Tongue River
14	Acme Rd, no services
9	US 14 W, Ranchester, **1mi S**...**gas:** Big Country Oil/dsl, **other:** Western Motel, **other:** Foothills Campground, Lazy R campground, to Yellowstone, Teton NPs, Conner Bfd NHS, Ski Area
1	Parkman, no services
0mm	Wyoming/Montana state line

Help a friend with

Published annually, *the Next EXIT*® provides the best USA Interstate Highway information available. Use this form to order another copy of *the Next EXIT*® for yourself or someone special. Thank you!

Please send_____copies of *the Next EXIT*® to the address below. I enclose my check or money order for $20.95 per copy.
(Canadian orders = $22.95US)

name...

street...

city...

state.................. zip...good through 12/31/2008

4 ways to order:

1) mail to: the Next EXIT, inc.
PO Box 888
Garden City, UT 84028

2) order on the Web at
www.thenextexit.com

3) call: 1-800-NEX-EXIT(639-3948),
and use your charge card.

4) fax: 1-435-946-8808,
and use your charge card.

the Next EXIT® is available online at www.thenextexit.com.